Oxford Dictionary of National Biography

Volume 22

Oxford Dictionary of National Biography

IN ASSOCIATION WITH

The British Academy

From the earliest times to the year 2000

Edited by

H. C. G. Matthew

and

Brian Harrison

Volume 22

Gibbes–Gospatric

OXFORD
UNIVERSITY PRESS

OXFORD
UNIVERSITY PRESS

Great Clarendon Street, Oxford OX2 6DP

Oxford University Press is a department of the University of Oxford.
It furthers the University's objective of excellence in research, scholarship,
and education by publishing worldwide in

Oxford New York

Auckland Bangkok Buenos Aires Cape Town
Chennai Dar es Salaam Delhi Hong Kong Istanbul Karachi
Kolkata Kuala Lumpur Madrid Melbourne Mexico City Mumbai Nairobi
São Paulo Shanghai Taipei Tokyo Toronto

Oxford is a registered trade mark of Oxford University Press
in the UK and in certain other countries

Published in the United States
by Oxford University Press Inc., New York

First published 2004

British Library Cataloguing in Publication Data
Data available

Library of Congress Cataloging in Publication Data
Data available: for details see volume 1, p. iv

ISBN 0-19-861372-5 (this volume)
ISBN 0-19-861411-X (set of sixty volumes)

Text captured by Alliance Phototypesetters, Pondicherry
Illustrations reproduced and archived by
Alliance Graphics Ltd, UK
Typeset in OUP Swift by Interactive Sciences Limited, Gloucester
Printed in Great Britain on acid-free paper by
Butler and Tanner Ltd,
Frome, Somerset

LIST OF ABBREVIATIONS

1 *General abbreviations*

AB	bachelor of arts
ABC	Australian Broadcasting Corporation
ABC TV	ABC Television
act.	active
A$	Australian dollar
AD	*anno domini*
AFC	Air Force Cross
AIDS	acquired immune deficiency syndrome
AK	Alaska
AL	Alabama
A level	advanced level [examination]
ALS	associate of the Linnean Society
AM	master of arts
AMICE	associate member of the Institution of Civil Engineers
ANZAC	Australian and New Zealand Army Corps
appx *pl.* appxs	appendix(es)
AR	Arkansas
ARA	associate of the Royal Academy
ARCA	associate of the Royal College of Art
ARCM	associate of the Royal College of Music
ARCO	associate of the Royal College of Organists
ARIBA	associate of the Royal Institute of British Architects
ARP	air-raid precautions
ARRC	associate of the Royal Red Cross
ARSA	associate of the Royal Scottish Academy
art.	article / item
ASC	Army Service Corps
Asch	Austrian Schilling
ASDIC	Antisubmarine Detection Investigation Committee
ATS	Auxiliary Territorial Service
ATV	Associated Television
Aug	August
AZ	Arizona
b.	born
BA	bachelor of arts
BA (Admin.)	bachelor of arts (administration)
BAFTA	British Academy of Film and Television Arts
BAO	bachelor of arts in obstetrics
bap.	baptized
BBC	British Broadcasting Corporation / Company
BC	before Christ
BCE	before the common (*or* Christian) era
BCE	bachelor of civil engineering
BCG	bacillus of Calmette and Guérin [inoculation against tuberculosis]
BCh	bachelor of surgery
BChir	bachelor of surgery
BCL	bachelor of civil law
BCnL	bachelor of canon law
BCom	bachelor of commerce
BD	bachelor of divinity
BEd	bachelor of education
BEng	bachelor of engineering
bk *pl.* bks	book(s)
BL	bachelor of law / letters / literature
BLitt	bachelor of letters
BM	bachelor of medicine
BMus	bachelor of music
BP	before present
BP	British Petroleum
Bros.	Brothers
BS	(1) bachelor of science; (2) bachelor of surgery; (3) British standard
BSc	bachelor of science
BSc (Econ.)	bachelor of science (economics)
BSc (Eng.)	bachelor of science (engineering)
bt	baronet
BTh	bachelor of theology
bur.	buried
C.	command [identifier for published parliamentary papers]
c.	*circa*
c.	*capitulum pl. capitula*: chapter(s)
CA	California
Cantab.	Cantabrigiensis
cap.	*capitulum pl. capitula*: chapter(s)
CB	companion of the Bath
CBE	commander of the Order of the British Empire
CBS	Columbia Broadcasting System
cc	cubic centimetres
C$	Canadian dollar
CD	compact disc
Cd	command [identifier for published parliamentary papers]
CE	Common (*or* Christian) Era
cent.	century
cf.	compare
CH	Companion of Honour
chap.	chapter
ChB	bachelor of surgery
CI	Imperial Order of the Crown of India
CIA	Central Intelligence Agency
CID	Criminal Investigation Department
CIE	companion of the Order of the Indian Empire
Cie	Compagnie
CLit	companion of literature
CM	master of surgery
cm	centimetre(s)

Cmd	command [identifier for published parliamentary papers]
CMG	companion of the Order of St Michael and St George
Cmnd	command [identifier for published parliamentary papers]
CO	Colorado
Co.	company
co.	county
col. *pl.* cols.	column(s)
Corp.	corporation
CSE	certificate of secondary education
CSI	companion of the Order of the Star of India
CT	Connecticut
CVO	commander of the Royal Victorian Order
cwt	hundredweight
$	(American) dollar
d.	(1) penny (pence); (2) died
DBE	dame commander of the Order of the British Empire
DCH	diploma in child health
DCh	doctor of surgery
DCL	doctor of civil law
DCnL	doctor of canon law
DCVO	dame commander of the Royal Victorian Order
DD	doctor of divinity
DE	Delaware
Dec	December
dem.	demolished
DEng	doctor of engineering
des.	destroyed
DFC	Distinguished Flying Cross
DipEd	diploma in education
DipPsych	diploma in psychiatry
diss.	dissertation
DL	deputy lieutenant
DLitt	doctor of letters
DLittCelt	doctor of Celtic letters
DM	(1) Deutschmark; (2) doctor of medicine; (3) doctor of musical arts
DMus	doctor of music
DNA	dioxyribonucleic acid
doc.	document
DOL	doctor of oriental learning
DPH	diploma in public health
DPhil	doctor of philosophy
DPM	diploma in psychological medicine
DSC	Distinguished Service Cross
DSc	doctor of science
DSc (Econ.)	doctor of science (economics)
DSc (Eng.)	doctor of science (engineering)
DSM	Distinguished Service Medal
DSO	companion of the Distinguished Service Order
DSocSc	doctor of social science
DTech	doctor of technology
DTh	doctor of theology
DTM	diploma in tropical medicine
DTMH	diploma in tropical medicine and hygiene
DU	doctor of the university
DUniv	doctor of the university
dwt	pennyweight
EC	European Community
ed. *pl.* eds.	edited / edited by / editor(s)
Edin.	Edinburgh
edn	edition
EEC	European Economic Community
EFTA	European Free Trade Association
EICS	East India Company Service
EMI	Electrical and Musical Industries (Ltd)
Eng.	English
enl.	enlarged
ENSA	Entertainments National Service Association
ep. *pl.* epp.	*epistola(e)*
ESP	extra-sensory perception
esp.	especially
esq.	esquire
est.	estimate / estimated
EU	European Union
ex	sold by (*lit.* out of)
excl.	excludes / excluding
exh.	exhibited
exh. cat.	exhibition catalogue
f. *pl.* ff.	following [pages]
FA	Football Association
FACP	fellow of the American College of Physicians
facs.	facsimile
FANY	First Aid Nursing Yeomanry
FBA	fellow of the British Academy
FBI	Federation of British Industries
FCS	fellow of the Chemical Society
Feb	February
FEng	fellow of the Fellowship of Engineering
FFCM	fellow of the Faculty of Community Medicine
FGS	fellow of the Geological Society
fig.	figure
FIMechE	fellow of the Institution of Mechanical Engineers
FL	Florida
fl.	*floruit*
FLS	fellow of the Linnean Society
FM	frequency modulation
fol. *pl.* fols.	folio(s)
Fr	French francs
Fr.	French
FRAeS	fellow of the Royal Aeronautical Society
FRAI	fellow of the Royal Anthropological Institute
FRAM	fellow of the Royal Academy of Music
FRAS	(1) fellow of the Royal Asiatic Society; (2) fellow of the Royal Astronomical Society
FRCM	fellow of the Royal College of Music
FRCO	fellow of the Royal College of Organists
FRCOG	fellow of the Royal College of Obstetricians and Gynaecologists
FRCP(C)	fellow of the Royal College of Physicians of Canada
FRCP (Edin.)	fellow of the Royal College of Physicians of Edinburgh
FRCP (Lond.)	fellow of the Royal College of Physicians of London
FRCPath	fellow of the Royal College of Pathologists
FRCPsych	fellow of the Royal College of Psychiatrists
FRCS	fellow of the Royal College of Surgeons
FRGS	fellow of the Royal Geographical Society
FRIBA	fellow of the Royal Institute of British Architects
FRICS	fellow of the Royal Institute of Chartered Surveyors
FRS	fellow of the Royal Society
FRSA	fellow of the Royal Society of Arts

FRSCM	fellow of the Royal School of Church Music
FRSE	fellow of the Royal Society of Edinburgh
FRSL	fellow of the Royal Society of Literature
FSA	fellow of the Society of Antiquaries
ft	foot *pl.* feet
FTCL	fellow of Trinity College of Music, London
ft-lb per min.	foot-pounds per minute [unit of horsepower]
FZS	fellow of the Zoological Society
GA	Georgia
GBE	knight or dame grand cross of the Order of the British Empire
GCB	knight grand cross of the Order of the Bath
GCE	general certificate of education
GCH	knight grand cross of the Royal Guelphic Order
GCHQ	government communications headquarters
GCIE	knight grand commander of the Order of the Indian Empire
GCMG	knight or dame grand cross of the Order of St Michael and St George
GCSE	general certificate of secondary education
GCSI	knight grand commander of the Order of the Star of India
GCStJ	bailiff or dame grand cross of the order of St John of Jerusalem
GCVO	knight or dame grand cross of the Royal Victorian Order
GEC	General Electric Company
Ger.	German
GI	government (*or* general) issue
GMT	Greenwich mean time
GP	general practitioner
GPU	[Soviet special police unit]
GSO	general staff officer
Heb.	Hebrew
HEICS	Honourable East India Company Service
HI	Hawaii
HIV	human immunodeficiency virus
HK$	Hong Kong dollar
HM	his / her majesty('s)
HMAS	his / her majesty's Australian ship
HMNZS	his / her majesty's New Zealand ship
HMS	his / her majesty's ship
HMSO	His / Her Majesty's Stationery Office
HMV	His Master's Voice
Hon.	Honourable
hp	horsepower
hr	hour(s)
HRH	his / her royal highness
HTV	Harlech Television
IA	Iowa
ibid.	*ibidem*: in the same place
ICI	Imperial Chemical Industries (Ltd)
ID	Idaho
IL	Illinois
illus.	illustration
illustr.	illustrated
IN	Indiana
in.	inch(es)
Inc.	Incorporated
incl.	includes / including
IOU	I owe you
IQ	intelligence quotient
Ir£	Irish pound
IRA	Irish Republican Army
ISO	companion of the Imperial Service Order
It.	Italian
ITA	Independent Television Authority
ITV	Independent Television
Jan	January
JP	justice of the peace
jun.	junior
KB	knight of the Order of the Bath
KBE	knight commander of the Order of the British Empire
KC	king's counsel
kcal	kilocalorie
KCB	knight commander of the Order of the Bath
KCH	knight commander of the Royal Guelphic Order
KCIE	knight commander of the Order of the Indian Empire
KCMG	knight commander of the Order of St Michael and St George
KCSI	knight commander of the Order of the Star of India
KCVO	knight commander of the Royal Victorian Order
keV	kilo-electron-volt
KG	knight of the Order of the Garter
KGB	[Soviet committee of state security]
KH	knight of the Royal Guelphic Order
KLM	Koninklijke Luchtvaart Maatschappij (Royal Dutch Air Lines)
km	kilometre(s)
KP	knight of the Order of St Patrick
KS	Kansas
KT	knight of the Order of the Thistle
kt	knight
KY	Kentucky
£	pound(s) sterling
£E	Egyptian pound
L	lira *pl.* lire
l. *pl.* ll.	line(s)
LA	Lousiana
LAA	light anti-aircraft
LAH	licentiate of the Apothecaries' Hall, Dublin
Lat.	Latin
lb	pound(s), unit of weight
LDS	licence in dental surgery
lit.	literally
LittB	bachelor of letters
LittD	doctor of letters
LKQCPI	licentiate of the King and Queen's College of Physicians, Ireland
LLA	lady literate in arts
LLB	bachelor of laws
LLD	doctor of laws
LLM	master of laws
LM	licentiate in midwifery
LP	long-playing record
LRAM	licentiate of the Royal Academy of Music
LRCP	licentiate of the Royal College of Physicians
LRCPS (Glasgow)	licentiate of the Royal College of Physicians and Surgeons of Glasgow
LRCS	licentiate of the Royal College of Surgeons
LSA	licentiate of the Society of Apothecaries
LSD	lysergic acid diethylamide
LVO	lieutenant of the Royal Victorian Order
M. *pl.* MM.	Monsieur *pl.* Messieurs
m	metre(s)

m. *pl.* mm.	membrane(s)
MA	(1) Massachusetts; (2) master of arts
MAI	master of engineering
MB	bachelor of medicine
MBA	master of business administration
MBE	member of the Order of the British Empire
MC	Military Cross
MCC	Marylebone Cricket Club
MCh	master of surgery
MChir	master of surgery
MCom	master of commerce
MD	(1) doctor of medicine; (2) Maryland
MDMA	methylenedioxymethamphetamine
ME	Maine
MEd	master of education
MEng	master of engineering
MEP	member of the European parliament
MG	Morris Garages
MGM	Metro-Goldwyn-Mayer
Mgr	Monsignor
MI	(1) Michigan; (2) military intelligence
MI1c	[secret intelligence department]
MI5	[military intelligence department]
MI6	[secret intelligence department]
MI9	[secret escape service]
MICE	member of the Institution of Civil Engineers
MIEE	member of the Institution of Electrical Engineers
min.	minute(s)
Mk	mark
ML	(1) licentiate of medicine; (2) master of laws
MLitt	master of letters
Mlle	Mademoiselle
mm	millimetre(s)
Mme	Madame
MN	Minnesota
MO	Missouri
MOH	medical officer of health
MP	member of parliament
m.p.h.	miles per hour
MPhil	master of philosophy
MRCP	member of the Royal College of Physicians
MRCS	member of the Royal College of Surgeons
MRCVS	member of the Royal College of Veterinary Surgeons
MRIA	member of the Royal Irish Academy
MS	(1) master of science; (2) Mississippi
MS *pl.* MSS	manuscript(s)
MSc	master of science
MSc (Econ.)	master of science (economics)
MT	Montana
MusB	bachelor of music
MusBac	bachelor of music
MusD	doctor of music
MV	motor vessel
MVO	member of the Royal Victorian Order
n. *pl.* nn.	note(s)
NAAFI	Navy, Army, and Air Force Institutes
NASA	National Aeronautics and Space Administration
NATO	North Atlantic Treaty Organization
NBC	National Broadcasting Corporation
NC	North Carolina
NCO	non-commissioned officer
ND	North Dakota
n.d.	no date
NE	Nebraska
nem. con.	*nemine contradicente*: unanimously
new ser.	new series
NH	New Hampshire
NHS	National Health Service
NJ	New Jersey
NKVD	[Soviet people's commissariat for internal affairs]
NM	New Mexico
nm	nanometre(s)
no. *pl.* nos.	number(s)
Nov	November
n.p.	no place [of publication]
NS	new style
NV	Nevada
NY	New York
NZBS	New Zealand Broadcasting Service
OBE	officer of the Order of the British Empire
obit.	obituary
Oct	October
OCTU	officer cadets training unit
OECD	Organization for Economic Co-operation and Development
OEEC	Organization for European Economic Co-operation
OFM	order of Friars Minor [Franciscans]
OFMCap	Ordine Frati Minori Cappucini: member of the Capuchin order
OH	Ohio
OK	Oklahoma
O level	ordinary level [examination]
OM	Order of Merit
OP	order of Preachers [Dominicans]
op. *pl.* opp.	opus *pl.* opera
OPEC	Organization of Petroleum Exporting Countries
OR	Oregon
orig.	original
OS	old style
OSB	Order of St Benedict
OTC	Officers' Training Corps
OWS	Old Watercolour Society
Oxon.	Oxoniensis
p. *pl.* pp.	page(s)
PA	Pennsylvania
p.a.	per annum
para.	paragraph
PAYE	pay as you earn
pbk *pl.* pbks	paperback(s)
per.	[during the] period
PhD	doctor of philosophy
pl.	(1) plate(s); (2) plural
priv. coll.	private collection
pt *pl.* pts	part(s)
pubd	published
PVC	polyvinyl chloride
q. *pl.* qq.	(1) question(s); (2) quire(s)
QC	queen's counsel
R	rand
R.	Rex / Regina
r	recto
r.	reigned / ruled
RA	Royal Academy / Royal Academician

RAC	Royal Automobile Club
RAF	Royal Air Force
RAFVR	Royal Air Force Volunteer Reserve
RAM	[member of the] Royal Academy of Music
RAMC	Royal Army Medical Corps
RCA	Royal College of Art
RCNC	Royal Corps of Naval Constructors
RCOG	Royal College of Obstetricians and Gynaecologists
RDI	royal designer for industry
RE	Royal Engineers
repr. *pl.* reprs.	reprint(s) / reprinted
repro.	reproduced
rev.	revised / revised by / reviser / revision
Revd	Reverend
RHA	Royal Hibernian Academy
RI	(1) Rhode Island; (2) Royal Institute of Painters in Water-Colours
RIBA	Royal Institute of British Architects
RIN	Royal Indian Navy
RM	Reichsmark
RMS	Royal Mail steamer
RN	Royal Navy
RNA	ribonucleic acid
RNAS	Royal Naval Air Service
RNR	Royal Naval Reserve
RNVR	Royal Naval Volunteer Reserve
RO	Record Office
r.p.m.	revolutions per minute
RRS	royal research ship
Rs	rupees
RSA	(1) Royal Scottish Academician; (2) Royal Society of Arts
RSPCA	Royal Society for the Prevention of Cruelty to Animals
Rt Hon.	Right Honourable
Rt Revd	Right Reverend
RUC	Royal Ulster Constabulary
Russ.	Russian
RWS	Royal Watercolour Society
S4C	Sianel Pedwar Cymru
s.	shilling(s)
s.a.	*sub anno*: under the year
SABC	South African Broadcasting Corporation
SAS	Special Air Service
SC	South Carolina
ScD	doctor of science
S$	Singapore dollar
SD	South Dakota
sec.	second(s)
sel.	selected
sen.	senior
Sept	September
ser.	series
SHAPE	supreme headquarters allied powers, Europe
SIDRO	Société Internationale d'Énergie Hydro-Électrique
sig. *pl.* sigs.	signature(s)
sing.	singular
SIS	Secret Intelligence Service
SJ	Society of Jesus
Skr	Swedish krona
Span.	Spanish
SPCK	Society for Promoting Christian Knowledge
SS	(1) Santissimi; (2) Schutzstaffel; (3) steam ship
STB	bachelor of theology
STD	doctor of theology
STM	master of theology
STP	doctor of theology
supp.	supposedly
suppl. *pl.* suppls.	supplement(s)
s.v.	*sub verbo* / *sub voce*: under the word / heading
SY	steam yacht
TA	Territorial Army
TASS	[Soviet news agency]
TB	tuberculosis (*lit.* tubercle bacillus)
TD	(1) *teachtaí dála* (member of the Dáil); (2) territorial decoration
TN	Tennessee
TNT	trinitrotoluene
trans.	translated / translated by / translation / translator
TT	tourist trophy
TUC	Trades Union Congress
TX	Texas
U-boat	*Unterseeboot*: submarine
Ufa	Universum-Film AG
UMIST	University of Manchester Institute of Science and Technology
UN	United Nations
UNESCO	United Nations Educational, Scientific, and Cultural Organization
UNICEF	United Nations International Children's Emergency Fund
unpubd	unpublished
USS	United States ship
UT	Utah
v	verso
v.	versus
VA	Virginia
VAD	Voluntary Aid Detachment
VC	Victoria Cross
VE-day	victory in Europe day
Ven.	Venerable
VJ-day	victory over Japan day
vol. *pl.* vols.	volume(s)
VT	Vermont
WA	Washington [state]
WAAC	Women's Auxiliary Army Corps
WAAF	Women's Auxiliary Air Force
WEA	Workers' Educational Association
WHO	World Health Organization
WI	Wisconsin
WRAF	Women's Royal Air Force
WRNS	Women's Royal Naval Service
WV	West Virginia
WVS	Women's Voluntary Service
WY	Wyoming
¥	yen
YMCA	Young Men's Christian Association
YWCA	Young Women's Christian Association

2 *Institution abbreviations*

All Souls Oxf.	All Souls College, Oxford
AM Oxf.	Ashmolean Museum, Oxford
Balliol Oxf.	Balliol College, Oxford
BBC WAC	BBC Written Archives Centre, Reading
Beds. & Luton ARS	Bedfordshire and Luton Archives and Record Service, Bedford
Berks. RO	Berkshire Record Office, Reading
BFI	British Film Institute, London
BFI NFTVA	British Film Institute, London, National Film and Television Archive
BGS	British Geological Survey, Keyworth, Nottingham
Birm. CA	Birmingham Central Library, Birmingham City Archives
Birm. CL	Birmingham Central Library
BL	British Library, London
BL NSA	British Library, London, National Sound Archive
BL OIOC	British Library, London, Oriental and India Office Collections
BLPES	London School of Economics and Political Science, British Library of Political and Economic Science
BM	British Museum, London
Bodl. Oxf.	Bodleian Library, Oxford
Bodl. RH	Bodleian Library of Commonwealth and African Studies at Rhodes House, Oxford
Borth. Inst.	Borthwick Institute of Historical Research, University of York
Boston PL	Boston Public Library, Massachusetts
Bristol RO	Bristol Record Office
Bucks. RLSS	Buckinghamshire Records and Local Studies Service, Aylesbury
CAC Cam.	Churchill College, Cambridge, Churchill Archives Centre
Cambs. AS	Cambridgeshire Archive Service
CCC Cam.	Corpus Christi College, Cambridge
CCC Oxf.	Corpus Christi College, Oxford
Ches. & Chester ALSS	Cheshire and Chester Archives and Local Studies Service
Christ Church Oxf.	Christ Church, Oxford
Christies	Christies, London
City Westm. AC	City of Westminster Archives Centre, London
CKS	Centre for Kentish Studies, Maidstone
CLRO	Corporation of London Records Office
Coll. Arms	College of Arms, London
Col. U.	Columbia University, New York
Cornwall RO	Cornwall Record Office, Truro
Courtauld Inst.	Courtauld Institute of Art, London
CUL	Cambridge University Library
Cumbria AS	Cumbria Archive Service
Derbys. RO	Derbyshire Record Office, Matlock
Devon RO	Devon Record Office, Exeter
Dorset RO	Dorset Record Office, Dorchester
Duke U.	Duke University, Durham, North Carolina
Duke U., Perkins L.	Duke University, Durham, North Carolina, William R. Perkins Library
Durham Cath. CL	Durham Cathedral, chapter library
Durham RO	Durham Record Office
DWL	Dr Williams's Library, London
Essex RO	Essex Record Office
E. Sussex RO	East Sussex Record Office, Lewes
Eton	Eton College, Berkshire
FM Cam.	Fitzwilliam Museum, Cambridge
Folger	Folger Shakespeare Library, Washington, DC
Garr. Club	Garrick Club, London
Girton Cam.	Girton College, Cambridge
GL	Guildhall Library, London
Glos. RO	Gloucestershire Record Office, Gloucester
Gon. & Caius Cam.	Gonville and Caius College, Cambridge
Gov. Art Coll.	Government Art Collection
GS Lond.	Geological Society of London
Hants. RO	Hampshire Record Office, Winchester
Harris Man. Oxf.	Harris Manchester College, Oxford
Harvard TC	Harvard Theatre Collection, Harvard University, Cambridge, Massachusetts, Nathan Marsh Pusey Library
Harvard U.	Harvard University, Cambridge, Massachusetts
Harvard U., Houghton L.	Harvard University, Cambridge, Massachusetts, Houghton Library
Herefs. RO	Herefordshire Record Office, Hereford
Herts. ALS	Hertfordshire Archives and Local Studies, Hertford
Hist. Soc. Penn.	Historical Society of Pennsylvania, Philadelphia
HLRO	House of Lords Record Office, London
Hult. Arch.	Hulton Archive, London and New York
Hunt. L.	Huntington Library, San Marino, California
ICL	Imperial College, London
Inst. CE	Institution of Civil Engineers, London
Inst. EE	Institution of Electrical Engineers, London
IWM	Imperial War Museum, London
IWM FVA	Imperial War Museum, London, Film and Video Archive
IWM SA	Imperial War Museum, London, Sound Archive
JRL	John Rylands University Library of Manchester
King's AC Cam.	King's College Archives Centre, Cambridge
King's Cam.	King's College, Cambridge
King's Lond.	King's College, London
King's Lond., Liddell Hart C.	King's College, London, Liddell Hart Centre for Military Archives
Lancs. RO	Lancashire Record Office, Preston
L. Cong.	Library of Congress, Washington, DC
Leics. RO	Leicestershire, Leicester, and Rutland Record Office, Leicester
Lincs. Arch.	Lincolnshire Archives, Lincoln
Linn. Soc.	Linnean Society of London
LMA	London Metropolitan Archives
LPL	Lambeth Palace, London
Lpool RO	Liverpool Record Office and Local Studies Service
LUL	London University Library
Magd. Cam.	Magdalene College, Cambridge
Magd. Oxf.	Magdalen College, Oxford
Man. City Gall.	Manchester City Galleries
Man. CL	Manchester Central Library
Mass. Hist. Soc.	Massachusetts Historical Society, Boston
Merton Oxf.	Merton College, Oxford
MHS Oxf.	Museum of the History of Science, Oxford
Mitchell L., Glas.	Mitchell Library, Glasgow
Mitchell L., NSW	State Library of New South Wales, Sydney, Mitchell Library
Morgan L.	Pierpont Morgan Library, New York
NA Canada	National Archives of Canada, Ottawa
NA Ire.	National Archives of Ireland, Dublin
NAM	National Army Museum, London
NA Scot.	National Archives of Scotland, Edinburgh
News Int. RO	News International Record Office, London
NG Ire.	National Gallery of Ireland, Dublin

NG Scot.	National Gallery of Scotland, Edinburgh
NHM	Natural History Museum, London
NL Aus.	National Library of Australia, Canberra
NL Ire.	National Library of Ireland, Dublin
NL NZ	National Library of New Zealand, Wellington
NL NZ, Turnbull L.	National Library of New Zealand, Wellington, Alexander Turnbull Library
NL Scot.	National Library of Scotland, Edinburgh
NL Wales	National Library of Wales, Aberystwyth
NMG Wales	National Museum and Gallery of Wales, Cardiff
NMM	National Maritime Museum, London
Norfolk RO	Norfolk Record Office, Norwich
Northants. RO	Northamptonshire Record Office, Northampton
Northumbd RO	Northumberland Record Office
Notts. Arch.	Nottinghamshire Archives, Nottingham
NPG	National Portrait Gallery, London
NRA	National Archives, London, Historical Manuscripts Commission, National Register of Archives
Nuffield Oxf.	Nuffield College, Oxford
N. Yorks. CRO	North Yorkshire County Record Office, Northallerton
NYPL	New York Public Library
Oxf. UA	Oxford University Archives
Oxf. U. Mus. NH	Oxford University Museum of Natural History
Oxon. RO	Oxfordshire Record Office, Oxford
Pembroke Cam.	Pembroke College, Cambridge
PRO	National Archives, London, Public Record Office
PRO NIre.	Public Record Office for Northern Ireland, Belfast
Pusey Oxf.	Pusey House, Oxford
RA	Royal Academy of Arts, London
Ransom HRC	Harry Ransom Humanities Research Center, University of Texas, Austin
RAS	Royal Astronomical Society, London
RBG Kew	Royal Botanic Gardens, Kew, London
RCP Lond.	Royal College of Physicians of London
RCS Eng.	Royal College of Surgeons of England, London
RGS	Royal Geographical Society, London
RIBA	Royal Institute of British Architects, London
RIBA BAL	Royal Institute of British Architects, London, British Architectural Library
Royal Arch.	Royal Archives, Windsor Castle, Berkshire [by gracious permission of her majesty the queen]
Royal Irish Acad.	Royal Irish Academy, Dublin
Royal Scot. Acad.	Royal Scottish Academy, Edinburgh
RS	Royal Society, London
RSA	Royal Society of Arts, London
RS Friends, Lond.	Religious Society of Friends, London
St Ant. Oxf.	St Antony's College, Oxford
St John Cam.	St John's College, Cambridge
S. Antiquaries, Lond.	Society of Antiquaries of London
Sci. Mus.	Science Museum, London
Scot. NPG	Scottish National Portrait Gallery, Edinburgh
Scott Polar RI	University of Cambridge, Scott Polar Research Institute
Sheff. Arch.	Sheffield Archives
Shrops. RRC	Shropshire Records and Research Centre, Shrewsbury
SOAS	School of Oriental and African Studies, London
Som. ARS	Somerset Archive and Record Service, Taunton
Staffs. RO	Staffordshire Record Office, Stafford
Suffolk RO	Suffolk Record Office
Surrey HC	Surrey History Centre, Woking
TCD	Trinity College, Dublin
Trinity Cam.	Trinity College, Cambridge
U. Aberdeen	University of Aberdeen
U. Birm.	University of Birmingham
U. Birm. L.	University of Birmingham Library
U. Cal.	University of California
U. Cam.	University of Cambridge
UCL	University College, London
U. Durham	University of Durham
U. Durham L.	University of Durham Library
U. Edin.	University of Edinburgh
U. Edin., New Coll.	University of Edinburgh, New College
U. Edin., New Coll. L.	University of Edinburgh, New College Library
U. Edin. L.	University of Edinburgh Library
U. Glas.	University of Glasgow
U. Glas. L.	University of Glasgow Library
U. Hull	University of Hull
U. Hull, Brynmor Jones L.	University of Hull, Brynmor Jones Library
U. Leeds	University of Leeds
U. Leeds, Brotherton L.	University of Leeds, Brotherton Library
U. Lond.	University of London
U. Lpool	University of Liverpool
U. Lpool L.	University of Liverpool Library
U. Mich.	University of Michigan, Ann Arbor
U. Mich., Clements L.	University of Michigan, Ann Arbor, William L. Clements Library
U. Newcastle	University of Newcastle upon Tyne
U. Newcastle, Robinson L.	University of Newcastle upon Tyne, Robinson Library
U. Nott.	University of Nottingham
U. Nott. L.	University of Nottingham Library
U. Oxf.	University of Oxford
U. Reading	University of Reading
U. Reading L.	University of Reading Library
U. St Andr.	University of St Andrews
U. St Andr. L.	University of St Andrews Library
U. Southampton	University of Southampton
U. Southampton L.	University of Southampton Library
U. Sussex	University of Sussex, Brighton
U. Texas	University of Texas, Austin
U. Wales	University of Wales
U. Warwick Mod. RC	University of Warwick, Coventry, Modern Records Centre
V&A	Victoria and Albert Museum, London
V&A NAL	Victoria and Albert Museum, London, National Art Library
Warks. CRO	Warwickshire County Record Office, Warwick
Wellcome L.	Wellcome Library for the History and Understanding of Medicine, London
Westm. DA	Westminster Diocesan Archives, London
Wilts. & Swindon RO	Wiltshire and Swindon Record Office, Trowbridge
Worcs. RO	Worcestershire Record Office, Worcester
W. Sussex RO	West Sussex Record Office, Chichester
W. Yorks. AS	West Yorkshire Archive Service
Yale U.	Yale University, New Haven, Connecticut
Yale U., Beinecke L.	Yale University, New Haven, Connecticut, Beinecke Rare Book and Manuscript Library
Yale U. CBA	Yale University, New Haven, Connecticut, Yale Center for British Art

3 *Bibliographic abbreviations*

Adams, *Drama*	W. D. Adams, *A dictionary of the drama*, 1: *A–G* (1904); 2: *H–Z* (1956) [vol. 2 microfilm only]
AFM	J O'Donovan, ed. and trans., *Annala rioghachta Eireann / Annals of the kingdom of Ireland by the four masters*, 7 vols. (1848–51); 2nd edn (1856); 3rd edn (1990)
Allibone, *Dict.*	S. A. Allibone, *A critical dictionary of English literature and British and American authors*, 3 vols. (1859–71); suppl. by J. F. Kirk, 2 vols. (1891)
ANB	J. A. Garraty and M. C. Carnes, eds., *American national biography*, 24 vols. (1999)
Anderson, *Scot. nat.*	W. Anderson, *The Scottish nation, or, The surnames, families, literature, honours, and biographical history of the people of Scotland*, 3 vols. (1859–63)
Ann. mon.	H. R. Luard, ed., *Annales monastici*, 5 vols., Rolls Series, 36 (1864–9)
Ann. Ulster	S. Mac Airt and G. Mac Niocaill, eds., *Annals of Ulster (to AD 1131)* (1983)
APC	*Acts of the privy council of England*, new ser., 46 vols. (1890–1964)
APS	*The acts of the parliaments of Scotland*, 12 vols. in 13 (1814–75)
Arber, *Regs. Stationers*	F. Arber, ed., *A transcript of the registers of the Company of Stationers of London, 1554–1640 AD*, 5 vols. (1875–94)
ArchR	*Architectural Review*
ASC	D. Whitelock, D. C. Douglas, and S. I. Tucker, ed. and trans., *The Anglo-Saxon Chronicle: a revised translation* (1961)
AS chart.	P. H. Sawyer, *Anglo-Saxon charters: an annotated list and bibliography*, Royal Historical Society Guides and Handbooks (1968)
AusDB	D. Pike and others, eds., *Australian dictionary of biography*, 16 vols. (1966–2002)
Baker, *Serjeants*	J. H. Baker, *The order of serjeants at law*, SeldS, suppl. ser., 5 (1984)
Bale, *Cat.*	J. Bale, *Scriptorum illustrium Maioris Brytannie, quam nunc Angliam et Scotiam vocant: catalogus*, 2 vols. in 1 (Basel, 1557–9); facs. edn (1971)
Bale, *Index*	J. Bale, *Index Britanniae scriptorum*, ed. R. L. Poole and M. Bateson (1902); facs. edn (1990)
BBCS	*Bulletin of the Board of Celtic Studies*
BDMBR	J. O. Baylen and N. J. Gossman, eds., *Biographical dictionary of modern British radicals*, 3 vols. in 4 (1979–88)
Bede, *Hist. eccl.*	*Bede's Ecclesiastical history of the English people*, ed. and trans. B. Colgrave and R. A. B. Mynors, OMT (1969); repr. (1991)
Bénézit, *Dict.*	E. Bénézit, *Dictionnaire critique et documentaire des peintres, sculpteurs, dessinateurs et graveurs*, 3 vols. (Paris, 1911–23); new edn, 8 vols. (1948–66), repr. (1966); 3rd edn, rev. and enl., 10 vols. (1976); 4th edn, 14 vols. (1999)
BIHR	*Bulletin of the Institute of Historical Research*
Birch, *Seals*	W. de Birch, *Catalogue of seals in the department of manuscripts in the British Museum*, 6 vols. (1887–1900)
Bishop Burnet's History	*Bishop Burnet's History of his own time*, ed. M. J. Routh, 2nd edn, 6 vols. (1833)
Blackwood	*Blackwood's* [Edinburgh] *Magazine*, 328 vols. (1817–1980)
Blain, Clements & Grundy, *Feminist comp.*	V. Blain, P. Clements, and I. Grundy, eds., *The feminist companion to literature in English* (1990)
BL cat.	*The British Library general catalogue of printed books* [in 360 vols. with suppls., also CD-ROM and online]
BMJ	*British Medical Journal*
Boase & Courtney, *Bibl. Corn.*	G. C. Boase and W. P. Courtney, *Bibliotheca Cornubiensis: a catalogue of the writings … of Cornishmen*, 3 vols. (1874–82)
Boase, *Mod. Eng. biog.*	F. Boase, *Modern English biography: containing many thousand concise memoirs of persons who have died since the year 1850*, 6 vols. (privately printed, Truro, 1892–1921); repr. (1965)
Boswell, *Life*	*Boswell's Life of Johnson: together with Journal of a tour to the Hebrides and Johnson's Diary of a journey into north Wales*, ed. G. B. Hill, enl. edn, rev. L. F. Powell, 6 vols. (1934–50); 2nd edn (1964); repr. (1971)
Brown & Stratton, *Brit. mus.*	J. D. Brown and S. S. Stratton, *British musical biography* (1897)
Bryan, *Painters*	M. Bryan, *A biographical and critical dictionary of painters and engravers*, 2 vols. (1816); new edn, ed. G. Stanley (1849); new edn, ed. R. E. Graves and W. Armstrong, 2 vols. (1886–9); [4th edn], ed. G. C. Williamson, 5 vols. (1903–5) [various reprs.]
Burke, *Gen. GB*	J. Burke, *A genealogical and heraldic history of the commoners of Great Britain and Ireland*, 4 vols. (1833–8); new edn as *A genealogical and heraldic dictionary of the landed gentry of Great Britain and Ireland*, 3 vols. [1843–9] [many later edns]
Burke, *Gen. Ire.*	J. B. Burke, *A genealogical and heraldic history of the landed gentry of Ireland* (1899); 2nd edn (1904); 3rd edn (1912); 4th edn (1958); 5th edn as *Burke's Irish family records* (1976)
Burke, *Peerage*	J. Burke, *A general* [later edns *A genealogical*] *and heraldic dictionary of the peerage and baronetage of the United Kingdom* [later edns *the British empire*] (1829–)
Burney, *Hist. mus.*	C. Burney, *A general history of music, from the earliest ages to the present period*, 4 vols. (1776–89)
Burtchaell & Sadleir, *Alum. Dubl.*	G. D. Burtchaell and T. U. Sadleir, *Alumni Dublinenses: a register of the students, graduates, and provosts of Trinity College* (1924); [2nd edn], with suppl., in 2 pts (1935)
Calamy rev.	A. G. Matthews, *Calamy revised* (1934); repr. (1988)
CCI	*Calendar of confirmations and inventories granted and given up in the several commissariots of Scotland* (1876–)
CClR	*Calendar of the close rolls preserved in the Public Record Office*, 47 vols. (1892–1963)
CDS	J. Bain, ed., *Calendar of documents relating to Scotland*, 4 vols., PRO (1881–8); suppl. vol. 5, ed. G. G. Simpson and J. D. Galbraith [1986]
CEPR letters	W. H. Bliss, C. Johnson, and J. Twemlow, eds., *Calendar of entries in the papal registers relating to Great Britain and Ireland: papal letters* (1893–)
CGPLA	*Calendars of the grants of probate and letters of administration* [in 4 ser.: *England & Wales, Northern Ireland, Ireland*, and *Éire*]
Chambers, *Scots.*	R. Chambers, ed., *A biographical dictionary of eminent Scotsmen*, 4 vols. (1832–5)
Chancery records	chancery records pubd by the PRO
Chancery records (RC)	chancery records pubd by the Record Commissions

CIPM	*Calendar of inquisitions post mortem*, [20 vols.], PRO (1904–); also *Henry VII*, 3 vols. (1898–1955)
Clarendon, *Hist. rebellion*	E. Hyde, earl of Clarendon, *The history of the rebellion and civil wars in England*, 6 vols. (1888); repr. (1958) and (1992)
Cobbett, *Parl. hist.*	W. Cobbett and J. Wright, eds., *Cobbett's Parliamentary history of England*, 36 vols. (1806–1820)
Colvin, *Archs.*	H. Colvin, *A biographical dictionary of British architects, 1600–1840*, 3rd edn (1995)
Cooper, *Ath. Cantab.*	C. H. Cooper and T. Cooper, *Athenae Cantabrigienses*, 3 vols. (1858–1913); repr. (1967)
CPR	*Calendar of the patent rolls preserved in the Public Record Office* (1891–)
Crockford	*Crockford's Clerical Directory*
CS	Camden Society
CSP	*Calendar of state papers* [in 11 ser.: *domestic*, *Scotland*, *Scottish series*, *Ireland*, *colonial*, *Commonwealth*, *foreign*, *Spain* [at Simancas], *Rome*, *Milan*, and *Venice*]
CYS	Canterbury and York Society
DAB	*Dictionary of American biography*, 21 vols. (1928–36), repr. in 11 vols. (1964); 10 suppls. (1944–96)
DBB	D. J. Jeremy, ed., *Dictionary of business biography*, 5 vols. (1984–6)
DCB	G. W. Brown and others, *Dictionary of Canadian biography*, [14 vols.] (1966–)
Debrett's Peerage	*Debrett's Peerage* (1803–) [sometimes *Debrett's Illustrated peerage*]
Desmond, *Botanists*	R. Desmond, *Dictionary of British and Irish botanists and horticulturists* (1977); rev. edn (1994)
Dir. Brit. archs.	A. Felstead, J. Franklin, and L. Pinfield, eds., *Directory of British architects, 1834–1900* (1993); 2nd edn, ed. A. Brodie and others, 2 vols. (2001)
DLB	J. M. Bellamy and J. Saville, eds., *Dictionary of labour biography*, [10 vols.] (1972–)
DLitB	Dictionary of Literary Biography
DNB	*Dictionary of national biography*, 63 vols. (1885–1900), suppl., 3 vols. (1901); repr. in 22 vols. (1908–9); 10 further suppls. (1912–96); *Missing persons* (1993)
DNZB	W. H. Oliver and C. Orange, eds., *The dictionary of New Zealand biography*, 5 vols. (1990–2000)
DSAB	W. J. de Kock and others, eds., *Dictionary of South African biography*, 5 vols. (1968–87)
DSB	C. C. Gillispie and F. L. Holmes, eds., *Dictionary of scientific biography*, 16 vols. (1970–80); repr. in 8 vols. (1981); 2 vol. suppl. (1990)
DSBB	A. Slaven and S. Checkland, eds., *Dictionary of Scottish business biography, 1860–1960*, 2 vols. (1986–90)
DSCHT	N. M. de S. Cameron and others, eds., *Dictionary of Scottish church history and theology* (1993)
Dugdale, *Monasticon*	W. Dugdale, *Monasticon Anglicanum*, 3 vols. (1655–72); 2nd edn, 3 vols. (1661–82); new edn, ed. J. Caley, J. Ellis, and B. Bandinel, 6 vols. in 8 pts (1817–30); repr. (1846) and (1970)
DWB	J. E. Lloyd and others, eds., *Dictionary of Welsh biography down to 1940* (1959) [Eng. trans. of *Y bywgraffiadur Cymreig hyd 1940*, 2nd edn (1954)]
EdinR	*Edinburgh Review, or, Critical Journal*
EETS	Early English Text Society
Emden, *Cam.*	A. B. Emden, *A biographical register of the University of Cambridge to 1500* (1963)
Emden, *Oxf.*	A. B. Emden, *A biographical register of the University of Oxford to* AD *1500*, 3 vols. (1957–9); also *A biographical register of the University of Oxford,* AD *1501 to 1540* (1974)
EngHR	*English Historical Review*
Engraved Brit. ports.	F. M. O'Donoghue and H. M. Hake, *Catalogue of engraved British portraits preserved in the department of prints and drawings in the British Museum*, 6 vols. (1908–25)
ER	The English Reports, 178 vols. (1900–32)
ESTC	*English short title catalogue, 1475–1800* [CD-ROM and online]
Evelyn, *Diary*	*The diary of John Evelyn*, ed. E. S. De Beer, 6 vols. (1955); repr. (2000)
Farington, *Diary*	*The diary of Joseph Farington*, ed. K. Garlick and others, 17 vols. (1978–98)
Fasti Angl. (Hardy)	J. Le Neve, *Fasti ecclesiae Anglicanae*, ed. T. D. Hardy, 3 vols. (1854)
Fasti Angl., 1066–1300	[J. Le Neve], *Fasti ecclesiae Anglicanae, 1066–1300*, ed. D. E. Greenway and J. S. Barrow, [8 vols.] (1968–)
Fasti Angl., 1300–1541	[J. Le Neve], *Fasti ecclesiae Anglicanae, 1300–1541*, 12 vols. (1962–7)
Fasti Angl., 1541–1857	[J. Le Neve], *Fasti ecclesiae Anglicanae, 1541–1857*, ed. J. M. Horn, D. M. Smith, and D. S. Bailey, [9 vols.] (1969–)
Fasti Scot.	H. Scott, *Fasti ecclesiae Scoticanae*, 3 vols. in 6 (1871); new edn, [11 vols.] (1915–)
FO List	*Foreign Office List*
Fortescue, *Brit. army*	J. W. Fortescue, *A history of the British army*, 13 vols. (1899–1930)
Foss, *Judges*	E. Foss, *The judges of England*, 9 vols. (1848–64); repr. (1966)
Foster, *Alum. Oxon.*	J. Foster, ed., *Alumni Oxonienses: the members of the University of Oxford, 1715–1886*, 4 vols. (1887–8); later edn (1891); also *Alumni Oxonienses … 1500–1714*, 4 vols. (1891–2); 8 vol. repr. (1968) and (2000)
Fuller, *Worthies*	T. Fuller, *The history of the worthies of England*, 4 pts (1662); new edn, 2 vols., ed. J. Nichols (1811); new edn, 3 vols., ed. P. A. Nuttall (1840); repr. (1965)
GEC, *Baronetage*	G. E. Cokayne, *Complete baronetage*, 6 vols. (1900–09); repr. (1983) [microprint]
GEC, *Peerage*	G. E. C. [G. E. Cokayne], *The complete peerage of England, Scotland, Ireland, Great Britain, and the United Kingdom*, 8 vols. (1887–98); new edn, ed. V. Gibbs and others, 14 vols. in 15 (1910–98); microprint repr. (1982) and (1987)
Genest, *Eng. stage*	J. Genest, *Some account of the English stage from the Restoration in 1660 to 1830*, 10 vols. (1832); repr. [New York, 1965]
Gillow, *Lit. biog. hist.*	J. Gillow, *A literary and biographical history or bibliographical dictionary of the English Catholics, from the breach with Rome, in 1534, to the present time*, 5 vols. [1885–1902]; repr. (1961); repr. with preface by C. Gillow (1999)
Gir. Camb. opera	*Giraldi Cambrensis opera*, ed. J. S. Brewer, J. F. Dimock, and G. F. Warner, 8 vols., Rolls Series, 21 (1861–91)
GJ	*Geographical Journal*

Gladstone, *Diaries*	*The Gladstone diaries: with cabinet minutes and prime-ministerial correspondence*, ed. M. R. D. Foot and H. C. G. Matthew, 14 vols. (1968–94)
GM	*Gentleman's Magazine*
Graves, *Artists*	A. Graves, ed., *A dictionary of artists who have exhibited works in the principal London exhibitions of oil paintings from 1760 to 1880* (1884); new edn (1895); 3rd edn (1901); facs. edn (1969); repr. [1970], (1973), and (1984)
Graves, *Brit. Inst.*	A. Graves, *The British Institution, 1806–1867: a complete dictionary of contributors and their work from the foundation of the institution* (1875); facs. edn (1908); repr. (1969)
Graves, *RA exhibitors*	A. Graves, *The Royal Academy of Arts: a complete dictionary of contributors and their work from its foundation in 1769 to 1904*, 8 vols. (1905–6); repr. in 4 vols. (1970) and (1972)
Graves, *Soc. Artists*	A. Graves, *The Society of Artists of Great Britain, 1760–1791, the Free Society of Artists, 1761–1783: a complete dictionary* (1907); facs. edn (1969)
Greaves & Zaller, *BDBR*	R. L. Greaves and R. Zaller, eds., *Biographical dictionary of British radicals in the seventeenth century*, 3 vols. (1982–4)
Grove, *Dict. mus.*	G. Grove, ed., *A dictionary of music and musicians*, 5 vols. (1878–90); 2nd edn, ed. J. A. Fuller Maitland (1904–10); 3rd edn, ed. H. C. Colles (1927); 4th edn with suppl. (1940); 5th edn, ed. E. Blom, 9 vols. (1954); suppl. (1961) [see also *New Grove*]
Hall, *Dramatic ports.*	L. A. Hall, *Catalogue of dramatic portraits in the theatre collection of the Harvard College library*, 4 vols. (1930–34)
Hansard	*Hansard's parliamentary debates*, ser. 1–5 (1803–)
Highfill, Burnim & Langhans, *BDA*	P. H. Highfill, K. A. Burnim, and E. A. Langhans, *A biographical dictionary of actors, actresses, musicians, dancers, managers, and other stage personnel in London, 1660–1800*, 16 vols. (1973–93)
Hist. U. Oxf.	T. H. Aston, ed., *The history of the University of Oxford*, 8 vols. (1984–2000) [1: *The early Oxford schools*, ed. J. I. Catto (1984); 2: *Late medieval Oxford*, ed. J. I. Catto and R. Evans (1992); 3: *The collegiate university*, ed. J. McConica (1986); 4: *Seventeenth-century Oxford*, ed. N. Tyacke (1997); 5: *The eighteenth century*, ed. L. S. Sutherland and L. G. Mitchell (1986); 6–7: *Nineteenth-century Oxford*, ed. M. G. Brock and M. C. Curthoys (1997–2000); 8: *The twentieth century*, ed. B. Harrison (2000)]
HJ	*Historical Journal*
HMC	Historical Manuscripts Commission
Holdsworth, *Eng. law*	W. S. Holdsworth, *A history of English law*, ed. A. L. Goodhart and H. L. Hanbury, 17 vols. (1903–72)
HoP, *Commons*	*The history of parliament: the House of Commons* [*1386–1421*, ed. J. S. Roskell, L. Clark, and C. Rawcliffe, 4 vols. (1992); *1509–1558*, ed. S. T. Bindoff, 3 vols. (1982); *1558–1603*, ed. P. W. Hasler, 3 vols. (1981); *1660–1690*, ed. B. D. Henning, 3 vols. (1983); *1690–1715*, ed. D. W. Hayton, E. Cruickshanks, and S. Handley, 5 vols. (2002); *1715–1754*, ed. R. Sedgwick, 2 vols. (1970); *1754–1790*, ed. L. Namier and J. Brooke, 3 vols. (1964), repr. (1985); *1790–1820*, ed. R. G. Thorne, 5 vols. (1986); in draft (used with permission): *1422–1504*, *1604–1629*, *1640–1660*, and *1820–1832*]
IGI	*International Genealogical Index*, Church of Jesus Christ of the Latterday Saints
ILN	*Illustrated London News*
IMC	Irish Manuscripts Commission
Irving, *Scots.*	J. Irving, ed., *The book of Scotsmen eminent for achievements in arms and arts, church and state, law, legislation and literature, commerce, science, travel and philanthropy* (1881)
JCS	*Journal of the Chemical Society*
JHC	*Journals of the House of Commons*
JHL	*Journals of the House of Lords*
John of Worcester, *Chron.*	*The chronicle of John of Worcester*, ed. R. R. Darlington and P. McGurk, trans. J. Bray and P. McGurk, 3 vols., OMT (1995–) [vol. 1 forthcoming]
Keeler, *Long Parliament*	M. F. Keeler, *The Long Parliament, 1640–1641: a biographical study of its members* (1954)
Kelly, *Handbk*	*The upper ten thousand: an alphabetical list of all members of noble families*, 3 vols. (1875–7); continued as *Kelly's handbook of the upper ten thousand for 1878* [1879], 2 vols. (1878–9); continued as *Kelly's handbook to the titled, landed and official classes*, 94 vols. (1880–1973)
LondG	*London Gazette*
LP Henry VIII	J. S. Brewer, J. Gairdner, and R. H. Brodie, eds., *Letters and papers, foreign and domestic, of the reign of Henry VIII*, 23 vols. in 38 (1862–1932); repr. (1965)
Mallalieu, *Watercolour artists*	H. L. Mallalieu, *The dictionary of British watercolour artists up to 1820*, 3 vols. (1976–90); vol. 1, 2nd edn (1986)
Memoirs FRS	*Biographical Memoirs of Fellows of the Royal Society*
MGH	Monumenta Germaniae Historica
MT	*Musical Times*
Munk, *Roll*	W. Munk, *The roll of the Royal College of Physicians of London*, 2 vols. (1861); 2nd edn, 3 vols. (1878)
N&Q	*Notes and Queries*
New Grove	S. Sadie, ed., *The new Grove dictionary of music and musicians*, 20 vols. (1980); 2nd edn, 29 vols. (2001) [also online edn; see also Grove, *Dict. mus.*]
Nichols, *Illustrations*	J. Nichols and J. B. Nichols, *Illustrations of the literary history of the eighteenth century*, 8 vols. (1817–58)
Nichols, *Lit. anecdotes*	J. Nichols, *Literary anecdotes of the eighteenth century*, 9 vols. (1812–16); facs. edn (1966)
Obits. FRS	*Obituary Notices of Fellows of the Royal Society*
O'Byrne, *Naval biog. dict.*	W. R. O'Byrne, *A naval biographical dictionary* (1849); repr. (1990); [2nd edn], 2 vols. (1861)
OHS	Oxford Historical Society
Old Westminsters	*The record of Old Westminsters*, 1–2, ed. G. F. R. Barker and A. H. Stenning (1928); suppl. 1, ed. J. B. Whitmore and G. R. Y. Radcliffe [1938]; 3, ed. J. B. Whitmore, G. R. Y. Radcliffe, and D. C. Simpson (1963); suppl. 2, ed. F. E. Pagan (1978); 4, ed. F. E. Pagan and H. E. Pagan (1992)
OMT	Oxford Medieval Texts
Ordericus Vitalis, *Eccl. hist.*	*The ecclesiastical history of Orderic Vitalis*, ed. and trans. M. Chibnall, 6 vols., OMT (1969–80); repr. (1990)
Paris, *Chron.*	*Matthaei Parisiensis, monachi sancti Albani, chronica majora*, ed. H. R. Luard, Rolls Series, 7 vols. (1872–83)
Parl. papers	*Parliamentary papers* (1801–)
PBA	*Proceedings of the British Academy*

Pepys, *Diary*	*The diary of Samuel Pepys*, ed. R. Latham and W. Matthews, 11 vols. (1970–83); repr. (1995) and (2000)
Pevsner	N. Pevsner and others, Buildings of England series
PICE	*Proceedings of the Institution of Civil Engineers*
Pipe rolls	*The great roll of the pipe for . . .*, PRSoc. (1884–)
PRO	Public Record Office
PRS	*Proceedings of the Royal Society of London*
PRSoc.	Pipe Roll Society
PTRS	*Philosophical Transactions of the Royal Society*
QR	*Quarterly Review*
RC	Record Commissions
Redgrave, *Artists*	S. Redgrave, *A dictionary of artists of the English school* (1874); rev. edn (1878); repr. (1970)
Reg. Oxf.	C. W. Boase and A. Clark, eds., *Register of the University of Oxford*, 5 vols., OHS, 1, 10–12, 14 (1885–9)
Reg. PCS	J. H. Burton and others, eds., *The register of the privy council of Scotland*, 1st ser., 14 vols. (1877–98); 2nd ser., 8 vols. (1899–1908); 3rd ser., [16 vols.] (1908–70)
Reg. RAN	H. W. C. Davis and others, eds., *Regesta regum Anglo-Normannorum, 1066–1154*, 4 vols. (1913–69)
RIBA Journal	*Journal of the Royal Institute of British Architects* [later *RIBA Journal*]
RotP	J. Strachey, ed., *Rotuli parliamentorum ut et petitiones, et placita in parliamento*, 6 vols. (1767–77)
RotS	D. Macpherson, J. Caley, and W. Illingworth, eds., *Rotuli Scotiae in Turri Londinensi et in domo capitulari Westmonasteriensi asservati*, 2 vols., RC, 14 (1814–19)
RS	Record(s) Society
Rymer, *Foedera*	T. Rymer and R. Sanderson, eds., *Foedera, conventiones, literae et cuiuscunque generis acta publica inter reges Angliae et alios quosvis imperatores, reges, pontifices, principes, vel communitates*, 20 vols. (1704–35); 2nd edn, 20 vols. (1726–35); 3rd edn, 10 vols. (1739–45), facs. edn (1967); new edn, ed. A. Clarke, J. Caley, and F. Holbrooke, 4 vols., RC, 50 (1816–30)
Sainty, *Judges*	J. Sainty, ed., *The judges of England, 1272–1990*, SeldS, suppl. ser., 10 (1993)
Sainty, *King's counsel*	J. Sainty, ed., *A list of English law officers and king's counsel*, SeldS, suppl. ser., 7 (1987)
SCH	Studies in Church History
Scots peerage	J. B. Paul, ed. *The Scots peerage, founded on Wood's edition of Sir Robert Douglas's Peerage of Scotland, containing an historical and genealogical account of the nobility of that kingdom*, 9 vols. (1904–14)
SeldS	Selden Society
SHR	*Scottish Historical Review*
State trials	T. B. Howell and T. J. Howell, eds., *Cobbett's Complete collection of state trials*, 34 vols. (1809–28)
STC, 1475–1640	A. W. Pollard, G. R. Redgrave, and others, eds., *A short-title catalogue of . . . English books . . . 1475–1640* (1926); 2nd edn, ed. W. A. Jackson, F. S. Ferguson, and K. F. Pantzer, 3 vols. (1976–91) [see also Wing, *STC*]
STS	Scottish Text Society
SurtS	Surtees Society
Symeon of Durham, *Opera*	*Symeonis monachi opera omnia*, ed. T. Arnold, 2 vols., Rolls Series, 75 (1882–5); repr. (1965)
Tanner, *Bibl. Brit.-Hib.*	T. Tanner, *Bibliotheca Britannico-Hibernica*, ed. D. Wilkins (1748); repr. (1963)
Thieme & Becker, *Allgemeines Lexikon*	U. Thieme, F. Becker, and H. Vollmer, eds., *Allgemeines Lexikon der bildenden Künstler von der Antike bis zur Gegenwart*, 37 vols. (Leipzig, 1907–50); repr. (1961–5), (1983), and (1992)
Thurloe, *State papers*	*A collection of the state papers of John Thurloe*, ed. T. Birch, 7 vols. (1742)
TLS	*Times Literary Supplement*
Tout, *Admin. hist.*	T. F. Tout, *Chapters in the administrative history of mediaeval England: the wardrobe, the chamber, and the small seals*, 6 vols. (1920–33); repr. (1967)
TRHS	*Transactions of the Royal Historical Society*
VCH	H. A. Doubleday and others, eds., *The Victoria history of the counties of England*, [88 vols.] (1900–)
Venn, *Alum. Cant.*	J. Venn and J. A. Venn, *Alumni Cantabrigienses: a biographical list of all known students, graduates, and holders of office at the University of Cambridge, from the earliest times to 1900*, 10 vols. (1922–54); repr. in 2 vols. (1974–8)
Vertue, *Note books*	[G. Vertue], *Note books*, ed. K. Esdaile, earl of Ilchester, and H. M. Hake, 6 vols., Walpole Society, 18, 20, 22, 24, 26, 30 (1930–55)
VF	*Vanity Fair*
Walford, *County families*	E. Walford, *The county families of the United Kingdom, or, Royal manual of the titled and untitled aristocracy of Great Britain and Ireland* (1860)
Walker rev.	A. G. Matthews, *Walker revised: being a revision of John Walker's Sufferings of the clergy during the grand rebellion, 1642–60* (1948); repr. (1988)
Walpole, *Corr.*	*The Yale edition of Horace Walpole's correspondence*, ed. W. S. Lewis, 48 vols. (1937–83)
Ward, *Men of the reign*	T. H. Ward, ed., *Men of the reign: a biographical dictionary of eminent persons of British and colonial birth who have died during the reign of Queen Victoria* (1885); repr. (Graz, 1968)
Waterhouse, *18c painters*	E. Waterhouse, *The dictionary of 18th century painters in oils and crayons* (1981); repr. as *British 18th century painters in oils and crayons* (1991), vol. 2 of *Dictionary of British art*
Watt, *Bibl. Brit.*	R. Watt, *Bibliotheca Britannica, or, A general index to British and foreign literature*, 4 vols. (1824) [many reprs.]
Wellesley index	W. E. Houghton, ed., *The Wellesley index to Victorian periodicals, 1824–1900*, 5 vols. (1966–89); new edn (1999) [CD-ROM]
Wing, *STC*	D. Wing, ed., *Short-title catalogue of . . . English books . . . 1641–1700*, 3 vols. (1945–51); 2nd edn (1972–88); rev. and enl. edn, ed. J. J. Morrison, C. W. Nelson, and M. Seccombe, 4 vols. (1994–8) [see also *STC, 1475–1640*]
Wisden	*John Wisden's Cricketer's Almanack*
Wood, *Ath. Oxon.*	A. Wood, *Athenae Oxonienses . . . to which are added the Fasti*, 2 vols. (1691–2); 2nd edn (1721); new edn, 4 vols., ed. P. Bliss (1813–20); repr. (1967) and (1969)
Wood, *Vic. painters*	C. Wood, *Dictionary of Victorian painters* (1971); 2nd edn (1978); 3rd edn as *Victorian painters*, 2 vols. (1995), vol. 4 of *Dictionary of British art*
WW	*Who's who* (1849–)
WWBMP	M. Stenton and S. Lees, eds., *Who's who of British members of parliament*, 4 vols. (1976–81)
WWW	*Who was who* (1929–)

Gibbes, Charles (1603?–1681), Church of England clergyman, was born at Honington, Warwickshire, where he was baptized on 4 November 1603, the sixth son of Sir Ralph Gibbes and his wife, Gertrude, daughter of Sir Thomas Wroughton of Broadhenton, Wiltshire. On 26 June 1621 (when he was said to be aged sixteen) he matriculated from Magdalen College, Oxford, graduating BA on 20 February 1623. The following year he was admitted to a fellowship at Merton College, and proceeded MA on 25 June 1628. At university, Wood relates, Gibbes became 'a noted disputant, orator and quaint preacher' (Wood, *Ath. Oxon.*, 4.12). Nothing is known of his wife, Anne, other than the fact that she survived Gibbes and inherited his property. In 1637, on presentation of the warden and fellows of Merton, he was instituted to the rectory of Gamlingay, Cambridgeshire, but on 3 September 1646 the House of Lords passed an ordinance granting the living to one Matthew Elliston. In 1643, in the period of royalist advance in the west, Gibbes had been collated (20 March) and installed (9 September) to the prebend of Combe Octava, in the cathedral of Wells, where his brother-in-law Walter *Ralegh (1586–1646), was dean. However, Ralegh was imprisoned following his capture while with royalist forces in the summer of 1645, and Gibbes, as he claimed in a petition of 1660, was at some point forced to withdraw to Canterbury, and for many years was reduced to teaching at a private school there. In this petition Gibbes applied for a prebend of Canterbury Cathedral, but it was not granted. On 30 April 1661, on the resignation of John Meredith, Gibbes was admitted to the rectory of Stanford Rivers, Essex. On 20 May 1662 he was presented by the king to a canonry of St Peter's, Westminster, on the death of Peter Heylin, and was installed on 21 May; he was also awarded a DD. *XXI Sermons … upon Several Subjects and Occasions*, preached to the parishioners at Stanford Rivers, was published in 1677. Gibbes died on 16 September 1681 and was buried in his church.

J. M. Rigg, *rev.* Stephen Wright

Sources *Walker rev.* • Foster, *Alum. Oxon.* • Wood, *Ath. Oxon.*, new edn • W. Camden, *The visitation of the county of Warwick in the year 1619*, ed. J. Fetherston, Harleian Society, 12 (1877), 213 • J. Walker, *An attempt towards recovering an account of the numbers and sufferings of the clergy of the Church of England*, 2 pts in 1 (1714) • I. M. Green, *The re-establishment of the Church of England, 1660–63* (1978) • *Fasti Angl., 1541–1857*, [Bath and Wells] • *Fasti Angl., 1541–1857*, [Ely] • R. Newcourt, *Repertorium ecclesiasticum parochiale Londinense*, 1 (1708) • A. Hughes, *Politics, society and civil war in Warwickshire, 1620–1660* (1987) • *IGI* • *ESTC*

Gibbes, Sir George Smith (1771–1851), physician, was the son of the Revd George Gibbes DD (1740–1812), rector of Woodborough in Wiltshire, and his wife, Mary. He was educated at Dr Mant's school in Southampton and matriculated at Exeter College, Oxford, on 9 April 1788; he graduated BA in 1792. After election to a fellowship at Magdalen College, Oxford, in 1795, he was awarded the degree of BM in 1796 and became DM in 1799. He was admitted a candidate of the Royal College of Physicians in 1803, became a fellow in the following year, and delivered the Harveian oration in 1817. He was also a fellow of the Royal Medical Society of Edinburgh. Smith Gibbes practised in Bath, where he had an extensive practice. He spent a period as honorary physician to the Bath City Dispensary, and he served the Bath General or Mineral Water Hospital in the same capacity between 1804 and 1818, though his presence at administrative meetings was infrequent despite being a member of the management committee. In 1819 he was appointed physician-extraordinary to Queen Charlotte, and he received a knighthood from George IV a year later.

Sir George Smith Gibbes (1771–1851), by John Keenan, 1798

Smith Gibbes's reputation suffered at the hands of satirists when his first essay on the conversion of muscle into a substance resembling spermaceti, printed in the *Philosophical Transactions* of 1794, was ridiculed as a way of solving the problem of congested graveyards by turning corpses into candle wax. However, his two volumes on the Bath waters (*A Treatise on the Bath Waters*, 1800; and *A Second Treatise on the Bath Waters*, 1803), together with a semi-popular but philosophical exposition of the principles of medicine, published for private circulation in 1818, challenged the assertion that he was a 'more alarming kind of quack' (Schnorrenberg, 194). Moreover, Smith Gibbes—a fellow of the Royal Society from 1796—had scientific interests beyond medicine, and he prepared a number of papers on aspects of natural philosophy, as well as an account of the contents of a bone cave in the Mendip hills for which he was admitted to the Linnean Society. These concerns were reflected in his involvement with the second of four philosophical societies in Bath and in his selection as the inaugural speaker when the Literary and Scientific Institution opened in 1825.

Smith Gibbes was also more generally active in the local community. He was a magistrate for Somerset; he became secretary of an abortive scheme to found a public library in Bath in 1801; and, having been elected a free citizen of the city in 1810, he was a member of the corporation until 1834. He was a man of many parts: 'a universal genius', talented in 'music, painting, philosophy, chemistry, mechanism'. However, such catholic tastes led George Monkland to allege in his *Literature and Literati of Bath* (1854) that 'like too many of the genius tribe he was as fickle as he was versatile in his pursuits' (p. 58). Yet even this critic conceded that he was 'kind-hearted, liberal in his medical profession, social in his habits and a very agreeable companion'.

Smith Gibbes was married twice. On 27 March 1799 he married Frances Sealey (*d.* 1822), daughter of Edward Sealey of Bridgwater; they had five children. On 1 May 1826 he married Mary Chapman (*d.* 1865), daughter of Captain T. Chapman of the 23rd regiment; there were no children from his second marriage. On retiring from medicine in 1835, he moved to Cheltenham. He died at the age of eighty on 23 June 1851 in Sidmouth, Devon, and was buried in the family vault at Woodborough. He was commemorated by a mural tablet in All Saints' Church, Sidmouth, where his son, the Revd Heneage Gibbes (1802–1887), was the incumbent. Another son, George Smith Gibbes (1809–1833), died in Madras after falling from his horse. ANNE BORSAY

Sources J. Murch, *Biographical sketches of Bath celebrities, ancient and modern* (1893), 135–7 • B. B. Schnorrenberg, 'Medical men of Bath', *Studies in Eighteenth-Century Culture*, 13 (1984), 194 • H. Torrens, 'The four Bath philosophical societies, 1779–1959', *A pox on the provinces: Proceedings of the 12th Congress of the British Society for the History of Medicine*, ed. R. Rolls, J. Guy, and J. R. Guy (1990), 185 • W. J. Williams and D. M. Stoddart, *Bath: some encounters with science* (1978), 72 • Munk, *Roll* • Foster, *Alum. Oxon.* • G. Monkland, *The literature and literati of Bath: an essay* (1854) • Venn, *Alum. Cant.* • *The record of the Royal Society of London*, 4th edn (1940) • *DNB*

Archives Bath Central Library, Bath General Hospital and Bath Corporation archives

Likenesses J. Keenan, oils, 1798, RCP Lond. [*see illus.*] • T. West, etching, 1803, Wellcome L.

Gibbes, James Alban (1611?–1677), Latin poet, was probably born at Valognes in France, the son of William Gibbes of Bristol, and his wife, Mary Stonor. His father had been educated at Brasenose College, Oxford; his mother was from an Oxfordshire Catholic family, and his father converted to Roman Catholicism as a result of their marriage. They initially lived in London, but moved to France in 1609 to exercise their religion more freely. James Alban Gibbes spent his early years with his parents in France, and returned to England in his ninth year; his parents had chosen to return shortly before. His father enjoyed a successful medical practice, eventually acting as physician to Queen Henrietta Maria (no doubt recommended in part by his Catholicism and long residence in France).

Gibbes was sent abroad again to receive a Roman Catholic education, at the English College at St Omer. He subsequently acted as tutor to Philip, son of Endymion Porter, in the late 1630s, and travelled in the Low Countries, Spain, Germany, and Italy. Like many other youthful travellers, Gibbes took advantage of the opportunity to study

James Alban Gibbes (1611?–1677), by Albert Clouet (after Pietro da Cortona)

at some of the universities along his route, notably in Padua (from November 1641), which had a distinguished medical faculty. He was a pupil there of the eminent anatomist Johann Vesling (1598–1649). Vesling's anatomy lectures were attended, a few years later, by John Evelyn and Edmund Waller; Vesling was himself also an accomplished Latin poet. There was a thriving international student community in Padua, including religious and political exiles from the British Isles.

In 1644 Gibbes moved to Rome; for two years he acted as tutor to Almerico, son of Francis, duke of Modena. This employment did not, however, prevent him from taking additional patrons, including Cardinal Luigi Capponi, and medical positions. On 5 November 1644 (a potentially delicate date for meetings between protestant travellers and English Catholics) John Evelyn was introduced to two English physicians, 'Dr Bacon and Dr Gibbs', the latter being 'an excellent poet'; in January 1645 Evelyn was shown the Ospedale di Santo Spirito by 'Dr Gibbs, a famous poet, and countryman of ours' (*Diary of John Evelyn*, 1.154, 215). Gibbes flattered in Latin verse each of the various popes under whom he lived, receiving favours from them in return; in 1647 Alexander VII made him professor of rhetoric at the Sapienza College (worth the equivalent of £60 per annum). Gibbes himself was a patron and friend of the artists Pietro da Cortona and Salvator Rosa.

Gibbes continued to act as resident physician to Cardinal Spada, whose favour his poetic talents helped to secure, and later to Prince Guistiniani. Isaac Basire, travelling with his pupils, consulted Gibbes in 1649: he was told to eat meat in Lent. Gibbes was a friend of the Jesuit Athanasius Kircher, whose regards he sent to Abraham Hill FRS. In February 1659 Gibbes travelled to Naples with William Cavendish (later duke of Devonshire) and Wentworth Dillon, Lord Roscommon; although he liked Naples, and stayed for some years, he found Messina 'very nasty, smells intolerably bad, and looks as if it was but a half-built town, fit only for the inhabitants' (letter, 1661, quoted in Chaney, 18–19). On 1 December 1664 Gibbes wrote from Naples to Abraham Hill, for whom he had collected coins and curiosities: 'I have settled my affairs in such a manner as to set out next week for England. The pleasure I feel at the hopes of seeing my friends and yourself in particular is inexpressible' (Chaney, 229).

Gibbes had begun to publish his Latin poems and orations in the 1650s. His *Astraea regnans* (1655) contains alcaic odes, a prose celebration of papal virtues, and sixty-four unusual lines of hendecasyllables, entitled 'Clementia': composed in 1653, the poem is a (perhaps ironic) complaint that he had been turned down for the post of keeper at the Vatican Library:

> Quid Romae facerem, tot albus annis
> Fortunae scopus et petitor atrae?
> ('What am I to do at Rome, a white man [punning perhaps on his name, Alban, 'white'] for so many years an applicant, a target of black fortune?' Money, 43)

For so assiduous a collector of patronage, in several fields, this is somewhat melodramatic.

Gibbes's poetic fame spread outside Rome. Few British authors enjoyed such a continental reputation: one might compare him with George Buchanan, John Barclay, John Owen, Elizabeth Jane Weston, or Thomas Dempster. These all, like Gibbes, used Latin to gain a wide and admiring audience. Emperor Leopold awarded Gibbes the title of 'poet laureate', by diploma dated 2 May 1667. Although Gibbes wrote some long hexameter poems, his most important work imitated Horace's odes: first issued in 1665, his lyric collection received a second, better known, edition (1668), the title boasting of his recent laurels, and closeness to Horace himself: *Carminum Jacobi Albani Ghibbesii, poetae laureati caesarii, pars lyrica: ad exemplum Q. Horati Flacci quamproxime concinnata* ('the lyrical part of the poems of James Alban Gibbes, imperial poet laureate: as near as possible to the model of Horace'). The structure is rather artificial: Gibbes is determined to have four books of odes, one of epodes, and a 'Carmen saeculare', just like Horace. He wants to outdo Horace, in fact, by having a few more poems in each book than Horace had, while keeping their relative proportions the same. Although he tries a little too hard to impress, his lyric works are indeed a fine achievement.

After some cogitation and advice, Gibbes decided that the most effective form of self-advertisement would be to present the emperor's gold medal and chain, the outward signs of his laureate dignity, to Oxford. He announced the gift to the vice-chancellor in a letter of 5 April 1670, mentioning his father's studies at Oxford, and his own long absence from England. Though a self-imposed exile for most of his life, he cherished his English origin and friends. His reward from Oxford, in February 1671, was the degree of MD: he was delighted with an honour never before awarded to an English Catholic, but was distressed at the slowness with which the diploma was sent (not until August 1673). Ralph Bathurst MD, president of Trinity College, Oxford, wrote a Latin poem in his honour (Money, 44). Gibbes was adept at the Renaissance art of giving and receiving extravagant praise; the last publication of his lifetime is a volume celebrating Philip Thomas Howard's promotion to cardinal, *Carmina marmoribus Arundelianis fortasse perenniora* (1676). The title deliberately alludes to Horace, *Odes*, iii.30: the poems may last longer than the marbles of Howard's grandfather, and, by implication, Gibbes is another immortal bard.

Wood called Gibbes the 'Horace of this age', adapting a phrase of Richard Lassels (*Voyage of Italy*, 1670; quoted in Chaney, 226); Gibbes himself printed a critic's sycophantic suggestion that Horace had been the Gibbes of his own age, Gibbes the Horace of ours (Money, 44). Wood also calls him 'a very conceited man, a most compact body of vanity' (Wood, *Ath. Oxon.*: *Fasti*, 2.342). Gibbes died on 26 June 1677. His vanity appears in his will, which showed great concern for his physical and literary monuments; unlike Horace, he (wisely) declined to rely on his poems alone for immortality. An Italian protégé, Benedetto Hercolani, whom he had trained as a physician, was his chief heir, instructed to take and preserve the name of Ghibbesio.

Several British poets of the seventeenth and eighteenth centuries have been compared to Horace. Ben Jonson (especially in *Poetaster*) could link himself to Horace; Alexander Pope was a brilliant imitator of Horace's satires and epistles (but not lyrics) in the vernacular. Neither of those great writers came as close to Horace's most characteristic poetic form, the Latin ode, as did Gibbes. His odes do not match the brilliance of his ancient model; they may surpass in quantity, but certainly not in quality, the work of other British Latin lyricists, the best and wittiest of whom is probably Anthony Alsop. Nevertheless, in the view of many contemporaries, and indeed in his own estimation, Gibbes was a poet of considerable substance, worthy of the European reputation that he enjoyed.

D. K. Money

Sources *DNB* • D. K. Money, *The English Horace: Anthony Alsop and the tradition of British Latin verse* (1998) • E. Chaney, *The evolution of the grand tour* (1998) • L. Bradner, 'Musae Anglicanae: a supplemental list', *The Library*, 5th ser., 22 (1967), 93–101 • A. Lytton Sells, *The paradise of travellers* (1964) • D. K. Money and H. T. Swan, 'Doctors as poets: laudatory verses addressed to Antonio Molinetti by British medical students at Padua, 1650–4', *Journal of Medical Biography*, 3 (1995), 139–47 • J. P. Tomasinus, *Gymnasium Patavinum* (1654) • *Diary of John Evelyn*, ed. A. Dobson (1906); repr. (1996) • Wood, *Ath. Oxon.*:

Fasti (1820), 338–42 · C. Dodd [H. Tootell], *The church history of England, from the year 1500, to the year 1688*, 1 (1737) · H. R. F. Brown, *Inglesi e scozzesi all'università di Padova dall'anno 1618 sino al 1765* (Venice, 1922) · A. Bertolotti, 'Un professore alla Sapienza di Roma nel secolo XVII poco conosciuto', *Il Buonarroti* (1886), 249–58 · *Familiar letters … between Abraham Hill and several eminent … persons* (1767)
Likenesses A. Clouet, engraving (after P. da Cortona), NPG [*see illus.*] · P. da Cortona, engraving, repro. in J. A. Gibbes, *Carminum*

Gibbings, Robert John (1889–1958), wood-engraver and book designer, was born at 5 Clarence Terrace, Cork, on 23 March 1889, the second son of Revd Edward Gibbings (1859–1924), later canon of Cork Cathedral, and his wife, Caroline Rouvière (1860–1907), the daughter of Robert Day, a businessman and notable antiquarian of Cork. He was educated at local schools and, as he himself claimed, 'in the snipe bogs and trout streams of Munster' (*The Grammarian*, 1, May 1958, 11). At the age of eighteen he matriculated at University College, Cork, where for two years, at the wishes of his parents, he studied medicine. In 1911, following his own ambition, he went to London and became a student at the Slade School of Art. The following year he attended the Central School of Arts and Crafts, where he was taught the technique of wood-engraving by Noel Rooke. Gibbings married twice: first, on 30 April 1919, Mary, known as Moira (*b*. 1894), the daughter of Colonel Edward G. Pennefather, with whom he had three sons and a daughter; and second, on 18 May 1937, Elisabeth (1909–1989), the daughter of Arthur Herbert Empson, with whom he had one son and two daughters. Patience Empson, Elisabeth's sister, was his assistant and companion for many years and contributed support and help with his work.

In August 1914 Gibbings was commissioned in the 4th Royal Munster Fusiliers. In 1915 he served in Gallipoli, where he was shot through the throat. He was sent to Malta to convalesce, and the effects of sunlight and shade on the buildings there were to have a strong influence on his early wood-engraving. In March 1918 he was invalided out of the army with the rank of captain. He then helped to form the Society of Wood Engravers, of which he was the first honorary secretary. He remained an active member for many years and a regular exhibitor in the society's annual exhibitions. To its first exhibition, in 1920, he contributed twelve prints. As a result he was commissioned to engrave a number of designs for advertisements and other commercial work. In 1921 he produced the first book of his own work, *Twelve Wood Engravings*. In 1923 he was commissioned to illustrate Samuel Butler's *Erewhon*, and the next year, by Harold Taylor, the founder of the Golden Cockerel Press, to illustrate *The Lives of Gallant Ladies*, by Pierre de Bourdeilles, seigneur de Brantôme. While Gibbings was working on these blocks Taylor fell ill, and the Golden Cockerel Press would have closed down had Gibbings not been enabled to buy it with financial support from a friend.

The press was at Waltham St Lawrence, in Berkshire. With Gibbings as its director and book designer it produced seventy-two books between 1924 and 1933, of which nineteen were illustrated by Gibbings himself. Forty-eight of its productions were illustrated with wood-

Robert John Gibbings (1889–1958), by Howard Coster, 1938

engravings. Among the engravers whom Gibbings employed—several of whom were given their first commissions by him—were John Nash, David Jones, Eric Ravilious, Blair Hughes-Stanton, John Farleigh, and, most notably, Eric Gill, whose editions of *The Canterbury Tales* (1929–31) and *The Four Gospels* (1931) were probably the most significant achievements of the press. For several years it enjoyed commercial success, but it was severely hit by the international slump and in 1933 Gibbings sold his financial interest. During the period of his collaboration with Gill, Gibbings took up sculpture and produced at least four finished works in stone, one of which, *Tahitian Woman*, is in the Victoria and Albert Museum. Following a trip to Germany in 1928 he became an influential and enthusiastic member of the naturist movement.

In the previous years, Gibbings had undertaken a few commissions for other publishers, including illustrations for *The Charm of Birds* (1927) by Edward Grey, Lord Grey of Fallodon. In 1929 he had spent four months in Tahiti, having been commissioned to illustrate a book that James Norman Hall was to write. Instead of this, his visit resulted in two books, *The Seventh Man* (1930) and *Iorana* (1932), both written and illustrated by himself. Also in 1932 he printed a volume of his own wood-engravings for the Orient Line, *Fourteen Wood Engravings*, based on drawings he had made on a number of their cruises. He then illustrated books for several British publishers. For the Limited Editions Club of New York he illustrated *Le Morte d'Arthur* (1936). This was followed by two further volumes written and illustrated by Gibbings himself, a children's adventure book, *Coconut Island* (1936), and a historical narrative, *John Graham (Convict) 1824* (1937). In 1936 Gibbings was appointed lecturer in book production at the University of Reading, a post which he held until 1942. He visited the West Indies and the Red Sea to make underwater drawings of fish and coral for his book *Blue Angels and Whales* (1938). This was the first title published in the Pelican Special series, and Gibbings also became art director of the Penguin Illustrated Classics. In 1938 the National University of Ireland made him an honorary MA.

In 1939 Gibbings undertook a book about his exploration of the River Thames in a punt, and this enjoyed a great success when published as *Sweet Thames Run Softly* (1940). It was the first of a series combining topographical impressions, personal anecdote, and observations of nature, illustrated with the author's engravings. For many months in 1941 he lived in a remote cottage at Llangurig, Montgomeryshire, close to Plynlimmon, writing and illustrating *Coming Down the Wye* (1942). He then returned to Ireland to produce *Lovely is the Lee* (1945), which became a 'book-of-the-month' choice in the United States. *Over the Reefs* (1948) was the fruit of a long visit to the south seas, and *Sweet Cork of thee* (1951) celebrated another return to Ireland. *Coming Down the Seine* (1953) and *Trumpets from Montparnasse* (1955) recorded visits to France and Italy, during the second of which Gibbings resumed painting in oils, which he had abandoned after his student days. The popularity of these books made him well known and led to engagements as a public speaker, many radio broadcasts, particularly for the overseas service of the BBC, and appearances on television. On his return to England Gibbings bought a cottage at Long Wittenham in Berkshire. Prophetically entitled *Till I End my Song*, his last book, again about the Thames, was completed there despite increasing ill health. He died of cancer at the Churchill Hospital, in Oxford, on 19 January 1958, three months after its publication, and was buried on 22 January in St Mary's churchyard, Long Wittenham.

A tall, massively built man, with twinkling eyes, aquiline features, and a beard, Gibbings had great natural charm, a fund of Irish humour, and an exceptional store of miscellaneous knowledge of birds, fishes, plants, geology, and archaeology. His work as a book designer at the Golden Cockerel Press was rivalled only by that of Francis Meynell at the Nonesuch Press. As a wood-engraver he was one of the leaders of the revival of this art. His own work was at first characterized by bold contrasts and organization of masses, with a skilful use of the 'vanishing line'. Later his technique became more subtle, with greater emphasis on gradation of texture. Gibbings occasionally incorporated his initials, R. G., in the engraved image itself; more commonly, he signed his prints with his full name, Robert Gibbings, or his initials in pencil. The eight 'river books', containing altogether nearly 500 engravings, all closely integrated with his own text, represent a remarkable combination of the talents of author, illustrator, and book designer. Gibbings reached a huge audience with his books, and perhaps did more than anyone in the twentieth century to popularize the art of wood-engraving. Examples of his wood-engravings are in the Victoria and Albert Museum, London, and the Robert Gibbings collection, Reading University.

J. C. H. HADFIELD, *rev.* M. J. ANDREWS

Sources T. Balston, *The wood-engravings of Robert Gibbings* (1949) • P. Empson, ed., *The wood engravings of Robert Gibbings, with some recollections by the artist* (1959) • A. M. Kirkus, P. Empson, and J. Harris, *Robert Gibbings: a bibliography* (1962) • M. Andrews, '*Sweet Cork of thee*, and the popular books of Robert Gibbings', *Matrix: a review for printers and bibliophiles*, 15 (1995), 81–102 • J. Dreyfus, *A typographical masterpiece* (1991) • T. Balston, 'The river books of Robert Gibbings', *Alphabet and Image*, 8 (1948), 39–49 • F. MacCarthy, 'Gibbings and Gill: arcady in Berkshire', *Matrix: a review for printers and bibliophiles*, 9 (1989), 27–36 • M. Bott and M. Andrews, 'Robert Gibbings and the University of Reading', *Matrix: a review for printers and bibliophiles*, 9 (1989), 63–8 • M. C. Salaman, 'The woodcuts and colour-prints of Captain Robert Gibbings', *The Studio*, 76 (1919), 3–8 • T. Balston, *English wood-engraving, 1900–1950* (1951) • U. Reading, Robert Gibbings collection • U. Cal., Los Angeles, William Andrews Clark Memorial Library, Gibbings material • private information (2004) • *CGPLA Eng. & Wales* (1958) • b. cert. • R. J. Hodges, *Cork and county Cork in the twentieth century: contemporary biographies*, ed. W. T. Pike (1911) • d. cert.

Archives Ransom HRC, letters • U. Cal., Los Angeles, William Andrews Clark Memorial Library, letters, MSS, typescripts, drawings, wood-engravings, photographs, and printed books • U. Cal., Los Angeles, corresp. and literary papers • U. Reading | LUL, corresp. with Duckworth and Co. | FILM British Pathé News, Pinewood Studios, Buckinghamshire, short films

Likenesses H. Coster, photographs, 1938, NPG [*see illus.*] • M. Hutson, bronze bust, exh. RA 1948 • M. Gerson, photograph, 1954, NPG

Wealth at death £5356 18*s*. 9*d*.: probate, 17 July 1958, *CGPLA Eng. & Wales*

Gibbins family (*per. c.*1770–1919), manufacturers and bankers, came to prominence with **Joseph Gibbins senior** (1756–1811), who became a button maker in Birmingham. As businessmen, Quakers were required to act with scrupulous honesty in all their business dealings and Joseph Gibbins was said to have given up his business in the 1790s when competition in the trade began to involve the selling of inferior shoddy goods to the public, a practice strictly forbidden within the Society of Friends. In 1797, reputedly with the financial help of Matthew Boulton, he went into business at the Rose Copper Works at Swansea, where he was a supplier to Boulton's Birmingham minting business. Gibbins appears to have first been manager and then treasurer of the company and, at his death in 1811, he owned 150 shares in the firm as well as shares in other metallurgical concerns.

The Rose Copper Works had offices at both Swansea and Birmingham and from here Gibbins expanded his business interests to the banking sector. In 1804, in partnership with Samuel Galton and his son Samuel Tertius Galton, he set up a bank in Birmingham and in 1809 invested in the Swansea bank of Gibbins and Eaton. Joseph Gibbins and his wife, Martha (1758–1827), had numerous children. Among this large family were Joseph; Thomas, an industrialist who had visited Brazil in the early 1820s; Brueton, partner of Joseph Gibbins junior in the Birmingham Banking Company, founded in 1829; George; William; Martha; Margaret; and Mary. Of those members of the family possessing commercial interests, it is **Joseph Gibbins junior** (1787–1870) who is best-known as a Quaker banker in the west midlands.

In 1811 Joseph Gibbins succeeded to his father's share in the Swansea bank of Gibbins and Eaton, and by 1818 he had also acquired Joseph senior's share in the Birmingham bank of Gibbins, Smith, and Goode. In 1836 the House of Commons established the secret committee on joint stock banks and Joseph Gibbins junior was called by the committee as a witness. From his evidence it is clear that Gibbins had been active in bank promotion in the

1820s and early 1830s. In the course of his evidence he stated that he was the originator of the Birmingham Banking Company, founded in 1829; the Gloucester Banking Company, founded in 1831; and, in part, of the Hampshire Banking Company, founded in 1834. He also held a small interest in several other companies.

Evidence of the direct financing of industry by banks in the early phases of Britain's industrialization is difficult to establish. However, the business activities of the younger Joseph Gibbins offer an example of the practice, commonly adopted by entrepreneurs, of borrowing from banks in which they held a partnership in order to finance their manufacturing interests. In 1813 Joseph purchased a chemical works at Melin Crythan in south Wales, a firm in which he was actively involved for the next five years. By 1826 the Melin Crythan works was in receipt of finance from the Banbury bank of Gillett and Tawney. In an age when the ability to raise borrowed capital relied heavily upon local credit networks the granting of direct finance to a firm at such a geographical distance appears unusual at first sight. However, a closer examination reveals the business connection between south Wales and Banbury to have been yet another link in the impressive religious and kinship network which was so much a part of the Quaker business world.

In August 1821 Martha [**Martha Gillett** (1798–1882)], a sister of the younger Joseph Gibbins, married **Joseph Ashby Gillett** (1795–1853), Quaker shag and shalloon manufacturer of Neithrop, Banbury. Her husband, born on 4 September 1795, was the eldest son of William Gillett (1767–1849), Quaker farmer, textile manufacturer, and semi-banker, of Upper Brailes, near Shipston-on-Stour. The couple had a daughter and four sons, including Charles Gillett (1830–1895). On her marriage Martha received a settlement which allowed Joseph Ashby Gillett to purchase a partnership in Whiteheads Bank at Shipston-on-Stour. The settlement allowed him to borrow £5000 without interest. A part of this sum represented money to which his bride would become entitled on her mother's death. The trustees of this settlement were two of Martha's brothers, Joseph and Brueton Gibbins, and their cousin, Jeffery Bevington Lowe of Eatington, who had married Margaret Whitehead and was a partner in Whiteheads Bank.

By 1822 Gillett's brother-in-law, Joseph Gibbins, had provided £6000 of capital towards the purchase of the Banbury New Bank (established 1784) from R. and C. Tawney. Although the brothers-in-law were co-partners in the bank, Joseph Gibbins continued to concentrate on his other banking interests, leaving Gillett to manage the Banbury bank. From this point, until its amalgamation with Barclays Bank Ltd in 1919, the Banbury bank always retained at least one Gillett as a partner and became known colloquially as Gilletts Bank. Joseph Ashby Gillett died in 1853, but his wife, Martha, survived him, and died on 27 May 1882 at 2 West Street, Banbury.

The story of the Banbury bank might have been different, since the bank was forced to close its doors for several weeks during the financial crisis of 1825–6. Joseph Gibbins was, at least in part, responsible for the bank's vulnerability at this time. Gibbins had adopted the practice of discounting Birmingham and Swansea bills using the funds of the Banbury bank to do so. This practice was risky, since it was tantamount to rediscounting, and indeed brought down both the Birmingham and the Swansea banks in 1825 and also caused temporary suspension at Banbury. As a result of his actions Joseph Gibbins was compelled to retire as a partner in the Banbury bank when the firm underwent reconstruction after the crisis. Indeed, from the records of the Birmingham bank of Gibbins, Smith, and Goode, it appears that Gibbins was perhaps less cautious in his business activities than his Quaker religion advised. The bank is said to have had a note circulation which was in excess of its five rival banks put together and, according to the balance sheet at bankruptcy, even after the run on the bank in 1825 which led to its closure, over £52,000 remained in outstanding notes.

The financial fortunes of Joseph Gibbins had revived sufficiently by the late 1840s to allow him to recompense the Banbury bank for his earlier failing. The bank again faced serious financial difficulties during the crisis of 1847–8. On this occasion, however, it was Joseph Gibbins who came to the rescue by depositing a special loan of £4285 with the bank. In 1866 Joseph again gave financial assistance to the Banbury branch of the family when he lent his nephew Charles Gillett £4000 to increase his capital in the Banbury bank where Charles was now a partner. Two years later Charles received a further £2000 as a gift from his uncle plus a legacy of nearly £1000 on Joseph's death on 24 March 1870 at Houndshill, near Stratford upon Avon.

The religious and kinship links by marriage between the Gillett and Gibbins families were further reinforced by the early joint business activities of the younger Joseph Gibbins and Joseph Ashby Gillett. This banking partnership between the brothers-in-law is illustrative of the close kinship network which typified the Quaker business world of the day. From this beginning Joseph Ashby Gillett went on to forge a successful career in the banking sector and he is undoubtedly an outstanding figure in the history of Gilletts Bank. While Joseph Gibbins held interests in manufacturing, he was most notable for his involvement in banking and in particular bank promotion. Indeed, Joseph Gibbins played a significant role in the establishment and growth of banking not only in Birmingham but also in south Wales. ANN PRIOR

Sources W. F. Crick and J. E. Wadsworth, *A hundred years of joint stock banking* (1936) • E. Gibbins, ed., *Records of the Gibbins family* (1911) • P. W. Matthews, *History of Barclays Bank Limited*, ed. A. W. Tuke (1926) • L. S. Pressnell, *Country banking in the industrial revolution* (1956) • A. M. Taylor, *Gilletts bankers at Banbury and Oxford* (1964) • bankruptcy of Messrs. Gibbins, Smith, and Goode of Birmingham (stopped payment 17 Dec 1825, declared bankrupt 19 Dec 1825, High Court of Justice in Bankruptcy, G/39/48 • *Aris's Birmingham Gazette* (6 Feb 1826) • 'Secret committee to inquire into the state of joint stock banks', *Parl. papers* (1836), 9.411, no. 591 • will, PRO, PROB 11/1524, sig. 332 [Joseph Gibbins senior] • *CGPLA Eng. & Wales*

(1870) [Joseph Gibbins jun.] • *CGPLA Eng. & Wales* (1882) [Martha Gillett] • d. cert. [Joseph Ashby Gillett] • d. cert. [Joseph Gibbins junior] • d. cert. [Martha Gillett]

Wealth at death under £300,000—Joseph Gibbins junior: probate, 26 April 1870, *CGPLA Eng. & Wales* • £2614 9s. 11d.—Martha Gillett: probate, 18 July 1882, *CGPLA Eng. & Wales*

Gibbins, Henry de Beltgens (1865–1907), economic historian, born at Port Elizabeth, Cape Colony, on 23 May 1865, was the eldest son of Joseph Henry Gibbins of Port Elizabeth, Cape Colony, and his wife, Eleanor, daughter of the Hon. J. de Beltgens of Stanford, Dominica. Educated at Bradford grammar school, he won a scholarship at Wadham College, Oxford, in 1883, and obtained a second class in classical moderations in 1885, and a second class also in the final classical schools in 1887. He graduated BA in the following year. In 1890 he won the Cobden prize for an economic essay in the University of Oxford, and in 1896 received the degree of DLitt at Dublin. He married Emily, third daughter of Dr J. H. Bell of Bradford, with whom he had one daughter.

From 1889 to 1895 Gibbins was assistant master at the Nottingham high school. He was ordained deacon in 1891 and priest in 1892, being curate of St Matthew's, Nottingham, from 1891 to 1893. From 1895 to 1899 he was vice-principal of Liverpool College; from 1899 to 1906 headmaster of King Charles I School at Kidderminster; in 1906 he was made principal of Lennoxville University in Canada. Ill health obliged him to leave Canada after a short stay. On 13 August 1907 he was killed by a fall from a train in the Thackley Tunnel between Leeds and Bradford.

Gibbins published a number of works on economic history, including *Industrial History of England* (1890), *English Social Reformers* (1892), *British Commerce and Colonies* (1893), and *The English People in the Nineteenth Century* (1898). He was a contributor to Palgrave's *Dictionary of Political Economy* and edited for Messrs Methuen their Social Questions of the Day series (1891) and also their Commercial series (1893). His *Economic and Industrial Progress of the Century* (1903) remains a useful source. His writings popularly illustrated the historical methods of economic study.

M. Epstein, *rev.* H. C. G. Matthew

Sources *The Times* (14 Aug 1907) • Foster, *Alum. Oxon.* • private information (1912) • *CGPLA Eng. & Wales* (1907)

Wealth at death £4329 4s. 8d.: probate, 27 Nov 1907, *CGPLA Eng. & Wales*

Gibbins, Joseph, senior (1756–1811). *See under* Gibbins family (*per. c.*1770–1919).

Gibbins, Joseph, junior (1787–1870). *See under* Gibbins family (*per. c.*1770–1919).

Gibbon, Benjamin Phelps (1802–1851), engraver, was the son of Benjamin Gibbon, vicar of Penally, Pembrokeshire, and his wife, Jane. He was educated at the Clergy Orphan School, and afterwards apprenticed to the stipple engraver Edward Scriven. Although in his youth he exhibited an inclination for the stage, on completing his articles (*c.*1824) he placed himself under the line engraver John Henry Robinson, and soon attained great proficiency. His plates, some of which are engraved in line and others in a mixed style, are distinguished by a delicacy of touch and an economy of line. The majority of Gibbon's animal and portrait engravings were done for print publishers such as F. G. Moon and M'Lean, and were chiefly after contemporaneous artists, most frequently Sir Edwin Landseer. It was after Landseer that Gibbon engraved *The Twa Dogs* (1827) and *The Travelled Monkey* (1828). Samuel Redgrave identified Gibbon as the engraver of William Mulready's *The Wolf and the Lamb*, which was sold in 1828 in aid of the Artists' Annuity Fund; others have, however, questioned this attribution.

Gibbon took more interest in portraits than in subject pictures, although he did not engrave many. Some of his portraits appear in the 1827 edition of Horace Walpole's *Anecdotes on Painting*, and he also produced a half-length portrait of Queen Victoria, after William Fowler (1840), and a head of his master, Edward Scriven, after Andrew Morton, engraved for John Pye's *Patronage of British Art* (1845). Although he was unmarried, Gibbon looked after several orphans. He was of a delicate constitution, and he died at his home in Albany Street, Regent's Park, London, on 28 July 1851, having suffered an attack of English cholera.

R. E. Graves, *rev.* Asia Haut

Sources B. Hunnisett, *An illustrated dictionary of British steel engravers*, new edn (1989) • R. K. Engen, *Dictionary of Victorian engravers, print publishers and their works* (1979) • M. H. Grant, *A dictionary of British etchers* (1952) • Redgrave, *Artists* • T. M. Rees, *Welsh painters, engravers, sculptors (1527–1911)* (1912) • J. H. Slater, *Engravings and their value*, rev. F. W. Maxwell-Barbour, 6th edn (1929) • *Art Journal*, 13 (1851), 238 • *The Athenaeum* (6 Sept 1851), 956 • A. Graves, *Catalogue of the works of Sir Edwin Landseer* (1875)

Gibbon, Charles (*fl.* 1589–1604), writer, was a member of Cambridge University, although there is no record of his college affiliation, or of his having graduated. He was probably in holy orders and he appears to have resided at Bury St Edmunds, London, and King's Lynn. Between 1589 and 1604 he published at least six, or possibly seven, books, mostly addressing questions of theology, good conduct, and the Christian life.

Gibbon's 1594 work, *The praise of a good name; the reproach of an ill name … with certain pithy apothegues very profitable for this age*, is dedicated to 'some of the best and most civil sort of the inhabitants of St. Edmond's Bury', and it appears to have been written in answer to some calumny under which the author was smarting. Two years later a C. G., possibly Gibbon, dedicated his *Watch-Worde for Warre* to the mayor and aldermen of King's Lynn. Gibbon's last known work, *The Order of Equalitie* (1604), is perhaps the most important; it is an appeal for proportional equalization of the incidence of taxation.

Alsager Vian, *rev.* Elizabeth Goldring

Sources Cooper, *Ath. Cantab.*, vol. 2 • *ESTC*

Gibbon, Charles (1843–1890), novelist, was born of humble parentage on the Isle of Man and moved with his parents to Glasgow at an early age. After receiving an elementary education there he became a clerk but switched to journalism before he was seventeen. One of his reviews in 1860 attracted favourable attention from the actor

Charles Kean, then on tour. A year or so later Gibbon moved to London, and in 1864 he published his first three-volume novel, *Dangerous Connexions*, which reached a second edition eleven years later. *The Dead Heart* appeared in 1865, and before his death at the age of forty-seven he had published nearly forty novels, many of which were serialized in *All the Year Round* and *Once a Week*. They included his best, *Robin Gray*, in 1869, the story of Jeanie Lindsay, a young Scottish girl who falls in love with a fisherman wrongly thought to be lost at sea. Other Scottish novels followed, including *The Braes of Yarrow* (1881), *The Golden Shaft* (1882), *By Mead and Stream* (1884), and *A Princess of Jutedom* (1886), 'Jutedom' being Dundee.

Gibbon was always at his best with stories of a regional flavour, and his Scottish novels have been compared with those of William Black. Michael Sadleir, who gives a comprehensive list of Gibbon's works, describes him as 'a sentimental counterpart of the sensational (Benjamin) Farjeon'. In later life, however, he tried to break away from this distinction, with little success, and his novels lapsed into the predictable and unimaginative. His non-fiction works were *The Life of George Combe* (1878), about the Scottish phrenologist, and *The Casquet of Literature* (1873–4), a six-volume anthology which included extracts from Queen Victoria's highland journals at the wish of the queen. But ill health compelled him to cease writing and move to the Norfolk coast, where he lived in a beach house bought with a recent legacy (East View House, North Denes). He died there on 15 August 1890; he was survived by his wife and children.

A. F. Pollard, *rev.* Katharine Chubbuck

Sources *The Athenaeum* (23 Aug 1890), 255 • J. Sutherland, 'Gibbon, Charles', *The Longman companion to Victorian fiction* (1988), 244 • C. Gibbon, introduction, *The life of George Combe: author of 'The constitution of man'*, 2 vols. (1878) • C. Gibbon, 'Introduction', in C. Gibbon, *Storm-beaten* (1862) • *East Anglian handbook* (1891), 191, 202 • M. Sadleir, *XIX century fiction: a bibliographical record based on his own collection*, 1 (1951) • d. cert. • *CGPLA Eng. & Wales* (1890)

Wealth at death £1954 1s. in UK: administration with will, 16 Dec 1890, *CGPLA Eng. & Wales*

Gibbon, Edward (1737–1794), historian, was born at Lime Grove, Putney, on 27 April 1737, the son of Edward Gibbon (1707–1770), MP and farmer, and his first wife, Judith (1709/10–1747), the daughter of James Porten. His life reveals much about literary relations between England and Europe, about the changing fortunes of the Enlightenment in England, and about conditions of authorship during the second half of the eighteenth century.

Ancestry and early life The Gibbons were a well-established Kentish family, a branch of which had in the seventeenth century moved to London and become involved in commerce. Gibbon's great-grandfather had been a linen draper, and his grandfather, the first Edward Gibbon (1666–1736), was a successful man of business. Happily his 'opinions were subordinate to his interest' (*Autobiographies*, 10) and accordingly, notwithstanding his Jacobite inclinations, as an army contractor the continental campaigns of William III had made him a wealthy man. In 1716 he became a director of the South Sea Company, and inevitably 'his fortune was overwhelmed in the shipwreck of the year twenty, and the labours of thirty years were blasted in a single day' (ibid., 11). A fortune of over £100,000 was reduced to £10,000. Yet he was unconquered by adversity, and had perhaps managed to protect some of his assets by means of prudent transferrals of property to close relations in his wife's family. He rebuilt his fortune, and at his death in 1736 he was once more a man of substance.

Edward Gibbon (1737–1794), by Sir Joshua Reynolds, 1779

In 1707 had been born his only son, Edward Gibbon, the father of the historian. The grandfather was a Jacobite of great financial acumen; the son inherited the Jacobitism, but not the shrewdness; and in the grandson all trace of the grandfather's abilities and opinions was extinguished. Edward Gibbon senior had been educated initially by the nonjuror William Law (1686–1761), who according to a family tradition portrayed his pupil as Flatus in *A Serious Call to a Devout and Holy Life* (1732); Flatus, whose 'sanguine temper and strong passions promise him so much happiness in everything, that he is always cheated, and satisfied with nothing'. Thereafter Edward Gibbon senior attended Westminster School and Emmanuel College, Cambridge; he entered the House of Commons in 1734 as member for Petersfield, in which neighbourhood the Gibbons owned a considerable estate. He moved in Jacobite circles in Hampshire, and was in at the kill when Walpole was forced from office. On 3 June 1736 he married Judith, daughter of James Porten, a neighbour of the Gibbons in Putney, and it was from this union, 'a marriage of inclination and esteem' (*Autobiographies*, 19), that Edward Gibbon the historian was born, some five months after the death of his grandfather, on 27 April 1737. There were six further children, none of whom lived for more than a year, and Mrs Gibbon herself died on 26 December 1747. Gibbon had been largely neglected by his mother, and his father—cast into depression by the death of his wife—was beginning to advance down the path of undramatic yet unremitting dissipation (entertainment, gambling, neglect of business) which was to erode the family wealth and prevent Gibbon's circumstances from ever being truly easy. The sickly child was cared for by his aunt, Catherine Porten, who instilled in him that love of reading which on her death in 1786 Gibbon cited as 'still the pleasure and glory of my life' (*Letters*, 3.46). His early education was entrusted initially to a private tutor, the clergyman, minor author, and grammarian John Kirkby, and then to the grammar school at Kingston. In January 1748 he entered Westminster School. The shock of arrival at this public school, which Gibbon later recalled as 'a cavern of fear and sorrow' (*Autobiographies*, 60), was mitigated by the fact that his aunt Porten undertook at the same time to run a boarding-house for the school, and it was with her that Gibbon lodged during his two years at Westminster. In 1750 a mysterious nervous illness obliged him to leave off formal schooling and take the waters in Bath. During the next two years the uncertain state of his health inhibited any regular schemes of education. However, Gibbon's constitution suddenly recovered at the end of 1751, and his father then made two serious errors of judgement which were full of implication for the future life of his son. In the first place, and on the recommendation of his close friends David and Lucy Mallet, he decided to entrust Gibbon's education to the feckless and neglectful Revd Philip Francis. It was clear within two months that the experiment had been a failure, and in response to this disappointment Edward Gibbon senior thereupon embraced 'a singular and desperate measure' (ibid., 56). He resolved to send his son without further ado to Oxford; and thereby committed his second blunder.

Residence in Oxford and conversion to Catholicism Gibbon emerged from childhood with an uneven education, but a great and unblunted appetite for reading. Edward Gibbon senior had arranged for his son to proceed to Magdalen College, Oxford, as a gentleman commoner, and in April 1752 Gibbon arrived in Oxford 'with a stock of erudition which might have puzzled a Doctor, and a degree of ignorance of which a schoolboy would have been ashamed' (*Autobiographies*, 394). In his *Memoirs* Gibbon drew a damning picture of Oxford, as a university sunk in port and prejudice, and almost completely indifferent to its educational mission. It is a picture which seems now to have been overdrawn. But that the university failed him, there can be no doubt. His first tutor, Dr Waldegrave, was a learned and pious man who seems to have taken his duties seriously, but who was out of his depth when it came to directing the studies of this unusual student. When Waldegrave departed for a college living in Sussex, Gibbon was transferred 'with the rest of his live stock' to Dr Winchester, who, according to Gibbon, 'well remembered that he had a salary to receive, and only forgot that he had a duty to perform' (ibid., 81). Deprived of any regular course of instruction, Gibbon soon fell into habits of indolence and absenteeism, interspersed with bouts of intense but miscellaneous reading—what at the end of his life he was to call the 'blind activity of idleness' (ibid., 84).

In the vacancy left by study, Gibbon pursued a course of reading which insensibly disposed him to Roman Catholicism. In one draft of the *Memoirs* (and one only), he attributed his apostasy to a brilliant but perverse reading of Conyers Middleton on miracles: he alleges that he construed the ironic inexplicitness of Middleton's exposé of the groundlessness of the Catholic church's claim to miraculous powers as in fact an assertion of its continuing validity. Gibbon claimed that his inference was not 'absurd' (*Autobiographies*, 85). But in the 1790s Gibbon had strong reasons for wishing to distance himself from Middleton, and casting the earlier writer as a causal agent in one of the great catastrophes of his life may have seemed a tempting strategy. A further awkward consideration is that, if we wish to adhere to the theory of Middleton's agency, we have to postulate a Gibbon who was unable to read irony—surely a great improbability. Furthermore, John Baker Holroyd, later Lord Sheffield, seems to have been sceptical about the story of Middleton's agency in Gibbon's conversion. At this point in his edited version of the *Memoirs* he inserts a footnote reporting that Gibbon spoke to him about his conversion to Catholicism only once, and on that occasion he attributed his decision to a reading of the polemical writings of the Elizabethan Jesuit Robert Parsons (E. Gibbon, *Miscellaneous Works*, 1796, 1.45 n.*).

Whatever the origin of the impulse, the fact is not in doubt. On 8 June 1753 Gibbon 'abjured the errors of heresy' and was received into the Romish faith by Baker, one of the chaplains of the Sardinian ambassador. If the 'humanity of the age' (*Autobiographies*, 88) was averse to persecution, there were still in 1753 numerous penal statutes in force against Roman Catholics, and the affair made sufficient stir for Lewis, a Roman Catholic bookseller of Covent Garden who had acted as go-between, to be summoned before the privy council and questioned. The crisis elicited from Gibbon's father a characteristic response of contradictory extremity. His first thought was that scepticism was the best antidote to credulity, and so Gibbon was sent to the poet and sceptic David Mallet, by 'whose philosophy [he] was rather scandalized than reclaimed' (ibid., 130). He next sought the advice of his relative Edward Eliot, who recommended a period of residence in Switzerland. Accordingly Gibbon was entrusted to the care of Mr Pavilliard, a Reformed minister of Lausanne. After leaving London on 19 June 1753, he arrived at Pavilliard's dwelling, 16 rue Cité-derrière, on 30 June.

Exile in Lausanne Gibbon's first period of residence in Lausanne (1753–8) was one of remarkable development on several fronts. In his *Memoirs* he fully recognized the significance of this episode in his life; 'whatever have been the fruits of my education, they must be ascribed to the fortunate shipwreck which cast me on the shores of the

Leman lake' (*Autobiographies*, 239). If it was indeed at Lausanne that, as he was to put it in another draft, 'the statue was discovered in the block of marble' (ibid., 152), then substantial credit for releasing Gibbon's true identity must rest with Pavilliard, whom his charge would later praise as 'the first father of my mind' (ibid., 297). His wisdom, tact, and kindness were evident immediately in the steps he took to humanize the severe regime which Edward Gibbon senior wished to impose on the son who had displeased him. In recognizing so quickly how to handle the latter and negotiate with the former, the Swiss pastor must have formed swift and accurate judgements of the characters of both father and son. The first priority was the need to rectify Gibbon's religious opinions. Here Pavilliard found that he was engaged in an intellectual war of attrition, having to dispatch each separate error individually. The seriousness of mind Gibbon demonstrated in demanding to be conquered, rather than merely capitulating, is surely admirable. It was only when he chanced upon what he took to be a decisive argument against transubstantiation (which may have been a confused recollection of John Tillotson's celebrated argument against that doctrine) that 'the various articles of the Romish creed disappeared like a dream' (ibid., 137). On Christmas day 1754, he took communion, returned to protestantism, and 'suspended [his] Religious enquiries' (ibid., 137): a form of words compatible with many different shades of both belief and unbelief.

This indiscretion now behind him (and some spectacular losses at faro with a Mr Gee atoned for), under Pavilliard's guidance Gibbon began a programme of serious and methodical reading in classical and modern literature. In the first place, he began to repair the shortcomings in his reading facility in Latin. Thereafter he studied mathematics, and the logic of De Crousaz. Although he left off these subjects before his mind was 'hardened by the habit of rigid demonstration, so destructive of the finer feelings of moral evidence' (*Autobiographies*, 142), they nevertheless must have reinforced the ability for analysis which gradually began to assert itself in the notes Gibbon kept of his reading. Gibbon followed the advice of Locke, and 'digested' his reading into a 'large Commonplace-book', although this was a practice concerning which he later had misgivings, agreeing with Johnson that 'what is twice read is commonly better remembered than what is transcribed' (ibid., 143–4). It was at this time, too, when the possibilities of the life of the mind were becoming vivid to him, and when he may have first suspected the extent of his own abilities, that Gibbon first encountered some of the writers who would most influence his mature work: Blaise Pascal, Jean-Philippe de la Bléterie, and Pietro Giannone. In due course he became sufficiently emboldened to enter into correspondence on points of classical philology with established scholars such as Jean-Baptiste Crevier, Johann Breitinger, and Johann Gesner. It is worth bearing in mind that Gibbon received his most effectual education in an environment of European classicism, and that his earliest scholarly writings suggest aspirations to a similar career for himself. Moreover, at this stage in his life French was for him the natural language of composition.

In the autumn of 1755 Gibbon's father gave permission for his son, accompanied by Pavilliard, to undertake a tour of Switzerland. The purpose of the tour was not to imbibe 'the sublime beauties of Nature' (*Autobiographies*, 144), but rather to view at first hand the different constitutions of the various cantons, to visit the most substantial towns and cities, and to make the acquaintance of the most eminent persons. In what may be a foretaste of his mature historical interests, he recalls being particularly struck by the abbey of Einsidlen, a palace 'erected by the potent magic of Religion' (ibid., 145).

Early in his residence at Lausanne Gibbon had begun the first of the two important friendships of his life. Georges Deyverdun, a young Swiss of good family but only moderate abilities, became the companion of his studies. Later, in 1757, Gibbon met Suzanne Curchod (who was subsequently to become Mme Necker, and the mother of Mme de Staël): here he formed a romantic, but ultimately fruitless, attachment which was to founder on the rocks of implacable paternal opposition. Two further connections Gibbon made while at Lausanne throw suggestive light over his intellectual, rather than emotional, life. He became the friend of a local protestant minister, François-Louis Allamand, with whom he debated Locke's metaphysics: by engaging with Allamand's dissimulated scepticism, Gibbon 'acquired some dexterity in the use of … philosophic weapons' (*Autobiographies*, 147). Second, when Voltaire took up residence in Lausanne, Gibbon (who was now moving in polite Vaudois society) was occasionally invited to the theatrical performances and the supper parties which followed them. Gibbon later said that as a young man he had 'rated [Voltaire] above his real magnitude' (ibid., 148). Certainly in the later volumes of the *Decline and Fall* he permits himself some sharp asides at Voltaire's expense. Nevertheless, the Frenchman's influence is palpable in the first volume of the history, and it is not difficult to imagine the young Englishman being inspired, not by Voltaire's scandalous philosophy, to be sure, but rather by the way in which Voltaire embodied literary celebrity. Perhaps uncoincidentally, it was during his last few months at Lausanne that Gibbon began to sketch the outline and collect the materials for his own first literary work, the *Essai sur l'étude de la littérature*.

Return to England: militia service and the *Essai sur l'étude de la littérature* On 8 May 1755 (his son's birthday, according to the new calendar) Edward Gibbon senior had married Dorothea Patton (*d.* 1796), introducing her to his son by letter as the 'Lady that saved your life at Westminster by recommending Dr. Ward when you was given over by the regular Physicians' (*Private Letters*, 1.9). Gibbon approached his stepmother with understandable, although happily unnecessary, apprehension. He would soon be able to entrust his journal with the sentiment that 'I love her as a companion, a friend and a mother' (*Gibbon's Journal*, 72). On Gibbon's return to England his father, whose financial difficulties had become pressing, persuaded him to permit the cancelling of the entail on the family estate; much-needed money might then be raised by a mortgage on the property. In return, Gibbon was to receive an annuity of £300. He thus achieved a measure of independence, but was still in fact very much under his father's control. When Gibbon informed his father that while in Lausanne he had fallen in love with the pretty, but penniless, Suzanne Curchod, his father's opposition to the match was unyielding. This intransigence placed Gibbon in a dilemma between marriage and scholarship, since his annuity was insufficient for him to study and be a husband. In his *Memoirs* Gibbon recorded his capitulation to his father's insistence in a phrase which has done him lasting harm among the sentimental; 'I sighed as a lover, I obeyed as a son' (*Autobiographies*, 239). The literariness of the expression (it alludes to a phrase in Corneille's *Polyeucte*) has been construed as coldness. Yet in its allusiveness it might equally hint at the central place already occupied by literature in Gibbon's emotional, as well as intellectual, existence.

Between 1758 and 1763 Gibbon's life was divided between the family estate at Buriton and his London lodgings in New Bond Street. In London he had never enough money to cut the figure he desired. Nevertheless he frequented the cosmopolitan and philosophic salon of the francophile Lady Hervey, sought relaxation in regular theatregoing, and was often to be found in the company of David Mallet. In Hampshire his life was less fashionable but more profitable. For country pursuits he had little relish, although his letters record that he occasionally went hunting and accompanied his father to the local races. It was also out of filial duty that Gibbon became involved in Hampshire politics, where his father continued to be active. Edward Gibbon senior's scheme to buy his son a seat in the House of Commons for £1500 eventually dwindled into Gibbon's contesting the seat of Petersfield in the election of 1761, and emerging as an honourable loser at little expense. But even amid these distractions he was able to pursue a literary life of sorts. The library at Buriton was acknowledged to be his 'peculiar domain' (*Autobiographies*, 248). It was a mixed collection of books, including 'much trash of the last age … much High Church divinity and politics', but also 'some valuable Editions of the Classics and Fathers' (ibid., 248). On the advice of Mallet he began to re-acquaint himself with 'the purity, the grace, the idiom, of the English style' (ibid., 251) by studying Swift and Addison, and some of the qualities of his mature prose might be traced to the contrasting but complementary influences of these writers. At this stage of his life Gibbon attended church for morning and evening service. He records that the reflections prompted by the lessons (but not the sermons) drove him to Grotius's *De veritate religionis Christianae*, and thence—he implies for the first time—to a 'regular tryal of the evidence of Christianity' (ibid., 249); a telling although silent judgement on the circumstances of his conversion to Roman Catholicism. It was also at this time that he purchased the twenty volumes of the *Mémoires de l'Académie des Inscriptions*, a work which eventually would be of major importance for the *Decline and Fall*.

The main claim on Gibbon's time during these years, however, was the South Hampshire militia, in which he served as captain and his father as major. Their commissions were dated 12 June 1759; the regiment was embodied in May 1760; and it was disembodied on 23 December 1762. At the end of his life Gibbon was willing to credit the militia with bestowing on him a 'larger introduction into the English World' (*Autobiographies*, 401); it was, for instance, through the militia that Gibbon met John Wilkes. Yet, despite leading him into such lively company, even at the time this 'mimic Bellona' was more resented than enjoyed (ibid., 299).

It was during his militia service that Gibbon published his first book, and thereby lost (as he put it) his literary maidenhead. In France, *philosophes* such as D'Alembert had disparaged as minute and arid the work of the *érudits*, or scholars, especially those associated with the Académie des Inscriptions. The *Essai sur l'étude de la littérature* (1761), which Gibbon had begun in Lausanne, and which he had completed at Buriton, sought to reconcile the *érudits* and the *philosophes* by arguing that 'all the faculties of the mind may be exercised and displayed by [the] study of ancient litterature' (*Autobiographies*, 167). The argument of the *Essai* was a temperate reproach to what Gibbon saw as the intellectual arrogance of the *philosophes*. But, as Gibbon would later acknowledge, stylistically the *Essai* was an act of prolonged homage to Montesquieu.

In 1762 Gibbon began also to revolve subjects for a work of biographical or historical narrative, entertaining the possibility of writing on Ralegh, on the history of the liberty of the Swiss, and on the history of Florence under the Medicis. On closer inspection, he decided to reject all these possibilities, but the very fact of their being weighed is a sign of growing literary ambition. The form which that ambition was to take was determined by the next major event in Gibbon's life. 'According to the law of custom, and perhaps of reason, foreign travel completes the education of an English Gentleman' (*Autobiographies*, 198); Gibbon's father had agreed, after some travailing, to pay for a European tour. Within seven days of the demobilization of the South Hampshire militia Gibbon was making preparations. He left Dover on 25 January 1763, and arrived in Paris three days later.

Grand tour Gibbon found Paris thronged with English, but the *Essai* distinguished him to some extent among the crowd, and procured for him the reception of a man of letters. He was received by Mme Geoffrin, engaged in one or two inconsequential flirtations, and mingled (albeit warily) with *philosophes* such as Helvétius and D'Holbach. In May he travelled, by way of Dijon and Besançon, to Lausanne, where he was to remain until the spring of 1764. He resumed his acquaintance with Voltaire and with Suzanne Curchod, and it was apparently at Ferney that the final rupture with Suzanne occurred. Gibbon has been reproached for coldness in the way he ended this attachment; if so, it was more probably the result of inexperience than calculated brutality.

Gibbon's early months in Lausanne were marked by some mildly riotous episodes in which he and some other young Englishmen lodging in the town, too much enlivened by burgundy, created nocturnal disturbances. One of these companions was William Guise, with whom Gibbon would the following year make the tour of Italy. Later they were joined by John Baker Holroyd. A cavalryman in the regular army, Holroyd initially teased Gibbon over his militia career, and their friendship began slowly, although it was to become the most important relationship of Gibbon's adult life. He now began to prepare himself for what promised to be the most valuable portion of his tour with some hard study of Italian antiquity, and composed a 'Recueil géographique' of ancient Italy. The intervals of study were filled with largely innocent recreation among the various *sociétés* in which the youth of Lausanne were allowed to meet.

The extension of Gibbon's tour to Italy was imperilled at almost the last moment by his father's financial difficulties, but these were for the moment resolved. Gibbon and Guise left Lausanne on 18 April 1764, crossed the Alps, and spent the first summer in Florence. Here Gibbon occupied himself in learning Italian. In the autumn they moved on to Rome, and (at least as Gibbon chose later to present it) the conception of his life's work:

> It was at Rome, on the fifteenth of October, 1764, as I sat musing amidst the ruins of the Capitol, while the barefooted fryars were singing Vespers in the temple of Jupiter, that the idea of writing the decline and fall of the City first started to my mind. (*Autobiographies*, 302)

There are good reasons for believing that it did not happen quite like that. But there seems no reason to doubt that the experience of this tour enriched Gibbon's mind 'with a new stock of ideas and images' (ibid., 302), and influenced the direction and nature of the *Decline and Fall*. From Rome they moved to Naples and Venice, which was not to Gibbon's taste: 'a fine bridge spoilt by two Rows of houses upon it, and a large square decorated with the worst Architecture I ever yet saw' (*Letters*, 1.193). These final months of Gibbon's tour were marred by the embarrassment of his credit being stopped. It was apparently a misunderstanding, although one symptomatic of the complicated state of the family's finances, which required Gibbon to forget the idea of prolonging his travels in the south of France. He was back in England by late June 1765, but not before he had paused for ten days in Paris to visit Suzanne Curchod, now transformed from a young Swiss woman on the verge of destitution and spinsterhood into the wife of the wealthy financier Jacques Necker.

The search for direction, 1765–1770 On his return from the continent Gibbon resumed the pattern of life he had formed before his tour. He retained his commission in the militia, rising to the ranks of major and, in 1768, lieutenant-colonel. This involved him in only a month of drilling each year, but he gradually found this connection more irksome and less diverting, and consequently he resigned his commission in 1770. When in London he frequented clubs such as the Cocoa Tree (still in the 1760s the haunt of tories), the excitingly named, although actually respectable, School of Vice, and the Romans, a weekly gathering of those who had made the tour of Italy. However, Gibbon's ability to enjoy London society was diminished by the worsening state of the family finances, and by the deteriorating state of his father's health. Gibbon devoted much time and energy to attempts at remedying the former, but his father, made petulant and suspicious by illness, frustrated his son's schemes for improvement. Only after Edward Gibbon senior's death could decisive action be taken.

Relief from these difficulties came in the form of friendship, study, and writing. In 1765 Georges Deyverdun had come to London, and was to spend the next four summers at Buriton. In due course he obtained a post as clerk in the northern department of the office of the secretary of state, and he and Gibbon began to collaborate on various literary projects. He helped Gibbon by translating for him the German sources for a projected 'History of the Swiss republics', which Gibbon began to compose in French. David Hume (who was then under-secretary in the office where Deyverdun worked) encouraged Gibbon to persevere with this history, advising him only that if he were writing for posterity English was preferable to French. But when in 1767 the work in progress was read to a London literary circle, and was coolly received, Gibbon decided to abandon it. Their next project was a literary periodical, the *Mémoires littéraires de la Grande Bretagne* (1768–9), which was designed to inform continental readers of developments in English literature. But since it was published in London and not distributed abroad among its intended readership, it unsurprisingly failed to achieve its goal. Other works, if not immediately more fruitful, can nevertheless be judged more positively when viewed in the long perspective of Gibbon's literary career, either because they indicate approaches (albeit hesitant) towards the subject matter of the *Decline and Fall*, or because they display the gradual forging of the technical and stylistic resources on which the great history would rely. Gibbon later regretted the *Critical Observations on the Sixth Book of Vergil's 'Aeneid'* (1770), his anonymous attack on Warburton's theory of Virgil as an initiate in the Eleusinian mysteries. But it shows Gibbon beginning to deploy irony for polemical purposes, and refining his understanding of the handling of historical evidence. The unpublished essay on oriental history, 'Sur la monarchie des Mèdes' (dated 1758–63 by Sheffield, but which mentions the death of J. P. Bougainville and which must therefore postdate 1763), shows Gibbon reflecting with productive criticism on the principles and practice of philosophic history. Other tantalizing hints about Gibbon's scholarly projects in the later 1760s point forward to the *Decline and Fall*, in particular 'an ample dissertation on the miraculous darkness of the passion', which has not survived, but in which Gibbon tells us that he 'privately drew [his] conclusions from the silence of an unbelieving age' (*Autobiographies*, 285).

Independence and publication of the *Decline and Fall*, volume 1, 1770–1776 Gibbon's father died on 12 November 1770, his constitution undermined by financial anxiety. In one draft of the *Memoirs* Gibbon acknowledged that 'the tears of a son are seldom lasting', adding that his 'father's death, not unhappy for himself, was the only event that could save me from an hopeless life of obscurity and indigence' (*Autobiographies*, 288). Sheffield cautiously omitted these phrases from his conflated text of the various manuscripts. Yet it is the case that the death of his father did usher in a period of Gibbon's life when he was able to reside in London and cut a more prominent and prosperous figure there. Gibbon's friendship with Holroyd had steadily strengthened, to the point where he often stayed at Holroyd's Sussex estate, Sheffield Place. Guided by Holroyd, who was an efficient and practical man of business, the Gibbon family finances were reorganized and simplified (although it would be years before the Buckinghamshire property of Lenborough was disposed of, and even then not satisfactorily). But by the end of 1772 Buriton had been let, Mrs Gibbon had retired to Bath, and Gibbon was elegantly housed in 7 Bentinck Street, Cavendish Square—a fashionable part of London. He began to entertain, and socialized at Boodle's Club. For the first time he could arrange his life entirely in accordance with his own wishes; and only now did he enjoy 'the first of earthly blessings, independence' (ibid., 307). In 1774 multiple honours descended upon him: he became a member of Johnson's Club, 'a large and luminous constellation of British stars' (ibid., 307 n. 27); he was admitted as a mason; and in October 1774 he was returned as the member of parliament for Liskeard, thanks to the influence of his kinsman Edward Eliot. At almost the same time as he was returned to parliament Gibbon had been negotiating the contract for the *Decline and Fall* with the eminent firm of Strahan and Cadell. For during the previous years, Gibbon had 'gradually advanced from the wish to the hope, from the hope to the design, from the design to the execution, of my historical work, of whose nature and limits I had yet a very inadequate notion' (ibid., 411). The press was set to work in June 1775, and on 17 February 1776 volume 1 of the *Decline and Fall* appeared at a price of 1 guinea, unbound.

The book sold with great rapidity. The first edition of volume 1—which almost at the last minute Strahan had ordered to be doubled in size from 500 to 1000 copies—was exhausted 'in a few days' (*Autobiographies*, 311). A second followed in June 1776, a third in 1777, and the fourth in 1781. Nor does Gibbon seem to have exaggerated when at the end of his life he recalled that 'my book was on every table, and almost on every toilette' (ibid., 311). From the chorus of praise, the admiration of Adam Ferguson, Joseph Warton, and Horace Walpole must have been deeply gratifying. It was, however, David Hume's letter of congratulation which according to Gibbon 'overpaid the labour of ten years' (ibid., 311–12). But its praise was laced with the warning tones of bitter experience:

> When I heard of your undertaking (which was some time ago) I own that I was a little curious to see how you would extricate yourself from the subject of your two last chapters [that is, chapters 15 and 16, on the early Christian church]. I think you have observed a very prudent temperament; but it was impossible to treat the subject so as not to give grounds of suspicion against you, and you may expect that a clamour will arise. (ibid., 312 n. 30)

Hume, we know, would have shunned the character of a prophet, yet so it came to pass.

In an unpublished note to Gibbon's *Miscellaneous Works* Sheffield threw a complex light over the vexed question of Gibbon's treatment of Christianity. On the one hand, he endorsed what Gibbon said in his *Memoirs*, that the clerical attack on the *Decline and Fall* had surprised him. But on the other, he recollected that when Gibbon was composing the first volume he had confided in Sheffield that 'there would be much difficulty and Delicacy in respect to that part which gives the History of the Christian Religion' (Yale University, Beinecke MS 10.3.b.11). He also noted that Gibbon considered withdrawing the offensive chapters from the second edition, 'then at the press' (ibid.). The sequence of stances Sheffield sketches in this note—initial wariness, subsequent surprise when Gibbon discovered that (despite what he had imagined was a prudent demeanour) he had not managed to avoid antagonizing the orthodox, and finally a willingness to defer to his critics by deleting the cause of offence—is confirmed by collation of the text of chapters 15 and 16 in the first two editions. The second edition was published before any attack on the *Decline and Fall* had seen print; nevertheless, the revisions Gibbon made for that edition show, in the first place, that he knew very well what his clerical opponents had found offensive, and in the second, that he was willing to mute or otherwise disguise those damaging elements. Gibbon's ideas on the origin and progress of Christianity were at many points identical to, or derivable from, the work of the most orthodox toilers in the vineyard of the protestant Enlightenment, such as Johann Lorenz von Mosheim. What shocked many of Gibbon's readers was the way chapters 15 and 16 demonstrated how easily that same work could support irreligious beliefs. It was his very proximity to the orthodox which made Gibbon's book both so offensive and so difficult to demolish. Yet its implication, that the governing oligarchy of Hanoverian England, to which the *Decline and Fall* was addressed and from within which it was composed, was a cadre of tolerant but unbelieving magistrates, and its rule a government of the credulous by the indifferent, could not pass unchallenged.

Reception of the *Decline and Fall*, volume 1, and publication of volumes 2–3, 1776–1781 The published attacks on the *Decline and Fall* began with James Chelsum's *Remarks* (1776; 2nd, significantly enlarged, edn, 1778), and continued with—to mention only the most significant—Richard Watson's *Apology for Christianity* (1776), Henry Davis's *Examination* (1778), Joseph Milner's *Gibbon's Account of Christianity Considered* (1781), Joseph Priestley's *History of the Corruptions of Christianity* (1782), and Joseph White's Bampton lectures (1784); Gibbon had therefore managed to displease all stripes of religious opinion, from high-church dogmatists to dissenters. Their lines of attack resolved into two main charges: first, that Gibbon had merely restated in a fashionable form the familiar arguments levelled by infidels against Christianity since late antiquity; and second that, in order to make his opinions seem less scandalous, he had manipulated the historical record, quoting selectively and even with deliberate inaccuracy. Gibbon waited until 1779 to reply to his critics in a pamphlet which was immediately recognized as a classic of literary polemic: his *Vindication of some Passages in the Fifteenth and Sixteenth Chapters*.

In the *Vindication* Gibbon said that he had been stung to reply to his critics only when, with the publication of Henry Davis's attack on him in 1778, the ground of contention was shifted from his religious to his literary and even moral character. But he seems first to have discussed the possibility of writing a vindication with William Robertson over dinner when Davis's *Examination* was not yet published, and when he had been enraged by the publication of the second edition of Chelsum's *Remarks*. The decision to direct the *Vindication* at Davis must therefore be construed as a tactical choice. Davis had given Gibbon an opportunity to scatter his enemies by engaging them on the terrain of scholarly accuracy and fair-dealing. This was more to his liking than the boggy and equivocal ground of the irreligious tendencies of chapters 15 and 16: for as we have seen, the revisions to these chapters made for the second edition show that Gibbon knew very well why and where these chapters might give offence. Indignation, therefore, came to him more easily in the character of a historian than in that of a believer. More attacks appeared, to which Gibbon did not deign to reply, although in volume 2 of the *Decline and Fall* some notes vented his irritation at attacks on his scholarly accuracy. The *Vindication* was Gibbon's only public engagement with his detractors and, in the opinion of all but the detractors themselves, his victory was complete. Horace Walpole warmed to its lethal ironies when he praised it as 'the feathered arrow of Cupid, that is more formidable than the club of Hercules' (E. Gibbon, *Miscellaneous Works*, 1814 edn, 2.159).

The success of the *Decline and Fall* smoothed Gibbon's path into fresh areas of society. We find him joining new clubs, such as Almack's, and amusing himself by attending lectures in chemistry and anatomy. In May 1777 he left London to spend six months in Paris, where he found the tribute of flattery much more ample and to his taste than had been the case during his earlier visit in 1763. His political career continued. In a footnote to chapter 22 of the *Decline and Fall*, Gibbon corrected Montesquieu's misapprehension that Jacobite toasts were illegal in England. It was important for him to believe that the political climate of the time was such that party divisions and animosities were obsolete, for only then would politeness be secure. It had therefore pleased him that both supporters of the royal prerogative and whigs of radical temper had perceived a reflection of their own, widely divergent, political beliefs in the first volume of the *Decline and Fall*. But the war with the American colonists, now in its third year, threatened once more to infect English political life with the curse of party. For the duration of the conflict Gibbon stayed, in respect at least of his actions, if not his sentiments, loyal to Lord North. He even composed a state paper, the *Mémoire justificatif* (1779), criticizing the French for their involvement in the dispute with the colonists. But he was never an enthusiast for the armed struggle, in which he found the issues of right and wrong obscure, the practical consequences appalling. It may be that here we can trace the influence of Charles James Fox, whom Gibbon met from time to time at Almack's, and with whose circle he socialized.

Gibbon had reasons of the most persuasive kind for standing by Lord North. His financial situation was pressing. Because of an amiable tendency to regard luxuries as necessities, his expenditure comfortably exceeded his income. Attempts to sell the Lenborough estate had still come to nothing, and the price of land was now falling because of the war. The alternatives were to abandon his expensive and fashionable life in London, or to acquire a fresh source of income. Gibbon's preferred solution was to receive one of the lucrative sinecures in the gift of government, but these were unlikely to be bestowed on those who had deserted to Fox in the lobbies of the house. In July 1779 he received the reward of his silent loyalty, and was appointed to the Board of Trade and Plantations at a salary of £750. For the time being, his situation was eased. And throughout all these distractions he had been writing and studying: 'shall I add that I never found my mind more vigorous or my composition more happy than in the winter hurry of society and Parliament?' (*Autobiographies*, 316). In September 1780 Gibbon lost his seat in parliament when Edward Eliot transferred his loyalty to the opposition, 'and the Electors of Leskeard are commonly of the same opinion as Mr. Eliot' (ibid., 322). In this interval of Gibbon's senatorial life, volumes 2 and 3 of the *Decline and Fall* were published on 1 March 1781.

Retirement to Lausanne and publication of the *Decline and Fall*, volumes 4–6, 1781–1788 The public received the second and third volumes of the *Decline and Fall* politely, but (as was only to be expected) without the excitement which Gibbon had found so flattering in 1776. He wisely gave himself a year's holiday after the publication of his second instalment, spending time in Brighton and at Hampton Court, and reading Greek literature. In June 1781 through the influence of Lord North he was returned to parliament as the member for Lymington. In May 1782 the Board of Trade was suppressed on grounds of economy, and Gibbon consequently found himself without the salary which could alone make viable a metropolitan existence, at least in the style he considered appropriate. For a while he hung on in the hope of something else (a post in the customs and a secretaryship at the embassy in Paris were apparently discussed). Against the background of the astonishing political manoeuvres of 1782–3, and the gymnastics of Charles James Fox, which he observed with amazement but also growing detachment, Gibbon resumed work on the *Decline and Fall*, and by 1783 volume 4 was virtually complete. When it was clear that his political masters were going to do nothing for him, he set about extricating himself from the financial embarrassments which could only become more tightly constricting were he to remain in England.

In May 1783 Gibbon wrote to his friend Georges Deyverdun, to explore the possibility of living with him in Lausanne. It was a project they had apparently discussed with enthusiasm on many occasions. Now that Deyverdun had inherited La Grotte, a house of sufficient size (and one which had formerly been the property of a Franciscan convent), there were no practical obstacles to prevent the realization of this favourite scheme. Despite the misgivings of both Sheffield and his stepmother, Gibbon left Bentinck Street for Lausanne on 1 September 1783. Although all was not quite prepared for his reception, Gibbon soon professed great satisfaction with his new life, which was by some margin less fashionable than that he had led in London, but in the main more wholesome, and more genially sociable.

The pace of composition now slackened, but by June 1787 Gibbon had completed the manuscript of the final three volumes of his history, and he embalmed the complex emotion of the moment in a celebrated passage of the *Memoirs*:

> It was on the day, or rather the night, of the 27th of June, 1787, between the hours of eleven and twelve, that I wrote the last lines of the last page in a summer-house in my garden. After laying down my pen I took several turns in a *berceau*, or covered walk of Acacias, which commands a prospect of the country, the lake, and the mountains. The air was temperate, the sky was serene, the silver orb of the moon was reflected from the waters, and all Nature was silent. I will not dissemble the first emotions of joy on the recovery of my freedom, and perhaps the establishment of my fame. But my pride was soon humbled, and a sober melancholy was spread over my mind by the idea that I had taken my everlasting leave of an old and agreeable companion, and that, whatsoever might be the future fate of my history, the life of the historian must be short and precarious. (*Autobiographies*, 333–4)

In August he travelled to London with the manuscript, for which he received £4000 from Strahan and Cadell: for its day, a good price. In November he was proposed by Reynolds for the chair of ancient history at the Royal Academy, the death of Dr Thomas Francklin having occasioned a vacancy. Social visits to Sheffield Place, to Mrs Gibbon in Bath, and to friends in London, together with the chaperoning of Wilhelm de Sévery, the son of Swiss friends, occupied Gibbon until, on 8 May 1788, the double festival of his fifty-first birthday and the publication of the third instalment of the *Decline and Fall* could be celebrated with a literary dinner given by Cadell. By the end of July he was back in Lausanne, but not before, at the trial of Warren Hastings in Westminster Hall, he had heard Sheridan turn aside for a moment from the arraignment of successful crimes to praise his 'luminous page' (ibid., 336 and n.*); a caricature of Gibbon published by William Holland later that same year bears the legend 'The Luminous Historian'.

The History of the Decline and Fall of the Roman Empire In October 1775 William Strahan, Gibbon's publisher, conveyed to its author his opinion of the first volume of the *Decline and Fall*, then in press:

> though I will not take upon me absolutely to pronounce in what manner it will be received at first by a capricious and giddy public, I will venture to say, it will ere long make a distinguished figure among the many valuable works that do honour to the present age; will be translated into most of the modern languages, and will remain a lasting monument of the genius and ability of the writer. (E. Gibbon, *Miscellaneous Works*, 1814 edn, 2.139)

In December 1788 Adam Smith congratulated Gibbon on the completion of the great work: 'by the universal assent of every man of taste and learning … it sets you at the very head of the whole literary tribe at present existing in Europe' (ibid., 429). What were the characteristics of Gibbon's history which led the majority of the reading public promptly to concur with Strahan and Smith, and acknowledge it to be a work of extraordinary distinction?

In the first place, the *Decline and Fall* fused technical advances which originated in widely separated—even opposed—fields of study, and developed their historiographic potential with a remarkable sureness of touch. The critical geography associated with J. B. B. d'Anville; the broadening of the range of evidence useful to the historian arising from the publications of the Académie des Inscriptions; the protocols for the analysis and evaluation of conflicting testimony generated by the pyrrhonists of the seventeenth century, and given elegant literary expression in the work of the French *philosophe* historians: Gibbon drew upon them all, but allowed himself to be confined by none.

A similar independence is to be found in the substantive vision of the history. It is often assumed that the *Decline and Fall* is a straightforward lament for departed glory, and that the dominant emotional colouring of the work is that of an elegy. But Gibbon was the enemy of empire as a political form, and a friend to the freedom of nations, for 'there is nothing perhaps more adverse to nature and reason than to hold in obedience remote countries and foreign nations, in opposition to their inclination and interest' (*Decline and Fall*, 3.142). However much Gibbon may have admired the artistic and cultural achievement of Rome, he was no admirer of empire as a political system. This disenchantment with empire influenced Gibbon's assessment of the barbarians who overran the western provinces of the empire in the fifth century. Gibbon's admiration for the barbarians had its limits. He remained convinced that the pastoral state of nations was a condition of intellectual, ethical, and material impoverishment. Recounting the atrocities perpetrated by the Thuringian allies of Attila, he distanced himself emphatically from the modish cult of the noble savage, promulgated by contemporaries such as Rousseau: 'Such were those savage ancestors, whose imaginary virtues have sometimes excited the praise and envy of civilized ages!' (ibid., 2.343). But barbarians such as the Huns, despite themselves, had created a hinge linking the Roman empire to the civilized republic of commercial states in which the history of that transformation was now itself being written. And if Gibbon's view of the barbarians was unexpectedly positive, the same could in the end be said for his attitude towards religion. Although Gibbon seems not to have enjoyed any lively Christian faith himself (at least after his brush with

Catholicism), he nevertheless saw as a historian that the Christian church had played an important role in keeping civil society alive during the collapse of the Roman empire, and had thereby permitted the transferral of precious elements of culture from the ancient world to the modern.

Gibbon's prose, the vehicle for this subtle historical vision, has been found by some to be decorous and mannered to a fault. Perhaps this estimation relies on no very close reading, since Gibbon's writing arguably does exhibit change and development within an overall continuity of manner. But if it were truly so, then this would enforce the judgement that the *Decline and Fall* is a very different book when viewed in the perspective of literary aesthetics, rather than as a contribution to a series of intellectual debates. For in the latter, the *Decline and Fall* is remarkable for the way Gibbon pushed at the edges of received opinions, and found fresh and fruitful ways of linking approaches and subjects which elsewhere lay unconnected. It is for this reason that the *Decline and Fall* occupies the summit of European Enlightenment historiography. It engages with, carries forward, and extends what is most vital in that body of writing.

The French Revolution and death of Deyverdun, 1789–1793 Shortly after Gibbon's return to Lausanne, Deyverdun died, carried away in July 1789 by a series of apoplectic strokes. Deyverdun's will gave Gibbon a life interest in La Grotte, and his financial situation was now more healthy thanks to sales of property in England, so his material circumstances were if anything improved. But Gibbon was profoundly shaken by the death of his friend, and lapsed into a depression from which he only gradually emerged, to resume once more the mild pleasures of society.

Deyverdun expired almost as the French Revolution was born. Gibbon was at first moderately encouraged by the turn of events in France. The *ancien régime* had needed urgent reform, as he acknowledged. But his sanguine hopes were soon abandoned as the violent character of the revolution asserted itself. When Sheffield and his family journeyed to Lausanne to visit Gibbon in 1791, they came by way of Paris, and reported gloomily on what they had seen there; this sombre news was confirmed by the September massacres of 1792 and the execution of Louis XVI in 1793. The closeness of the historian of decline to the epochal events which began the dismantling of the culture from within which and, to some degree, on behalf of which he had written make these closing years one of the most fascinating periods of Gibbon's life.

Although Gibbon had not abandoned literary pursuits, the projects to which he now turned his hand—the *Memoirs*, revisions of the *Decline and Fall* and the collection of materials for a seventh volume, historical excursions from the research done for the later volumes of the *Decline and Fall*, such as the *Antiquities of the House of Brunswick*—exist only as drafts, fragments, or marginal jottings. Nevertheless, a common thread runs through many of them. Burke's analysis of the French Revolution, which allotted a causal and villainous role to the French *philosophes*, had imparted new energy and new direction to the drama of Gibbon's reputation. Gibbon had sent for Burke's *Reflections* as soon as it was published, and on reading it he had been immediately converted to Burke's point of view. It was, however, a poignant conversion, since Gibbon cannot have been unaware that Burke's diagnosis of the toxins which had created the revolutionary infection was full of implication for himself, as the most prominent—perhaps the only—embodiment of Enlightenment in England. Suddenly the number of publications attacking him, which had gradually subsided during the 1780s, increased. In the final five years of Gibbon's life we see him obliged to re-enter the lists he thought he had quitted for good in 1779 with the publication of the *Vindication*, and contend once again over his reputation, albeit silently. In particular the various drafts of the *Memoirs* show Gibbon experimenting with different strategies for implicitly repudiating the hostile accounts of the tendency of his life and work which had been given new currency by the revolution. Even his agreement to collaborate with the faintly absurd John Pinkerton in the project of publishing the materials of English medieval history, along the lines of the great Benedictine venture which under the supervision of Bouquet had published the sources of French history up to 1060, can plausibly be viewed as in part a tactical move calculated to dilute his perceived affinity with the now invidious attitudes typical of French philosophy.

Return to England and death, 1793–1794 The French Revolution claimed an unexpected victim when Lady Sheffield died in April 1793; she had fallen sick while caring for émigrés at Guy's Hospital. Gibbon set out at once on the potentially dangerous journey across Europe to be with his newly widowed friend. He found Sheffield already reconciled to his loss, and spent a pleasant summer with him in the Sussex countryside. It was soon clear, however, that Gibbon's own health was not sound. For many years he had neglected a swelling in his groin; a hernia sustained while serving in the militia had formed a sac in which collected fluid from the peritoneal cavity, the fluid itself being produced by a cirrhotic condition of the liver. Its size was now so great—'almost as big as a small child' was the disconcerting simile on which Gibbon's pen settled (*Letters*, 3.359)—that even Gibbon, who had ignored the problem for as long as possible, and who engagingly believed that it had escaped the notice of others, was driven to seek the assistance of the surgeons. It is said that even under the knife he did not lose his good humour, but amused his doctors with a riddle which intriguingly linked his present complaint to his parliamentary career: 'Why is a fat man like a Cornish Borough? Because he never sees his member' (letter from Timothée Francillon to David Levade, De Beer, *Gibbon*, 120). He was tapped three times during the winter of 1793–4, and prodigious quantities of fluid were drawn off. On the third occasion the knife was dirty. Peritonitis set in, and developed swiftly. Three days after his last operation, and only one day after he had pronounced that he was good for a further 'ten, twelve, or perhaps twenty years' (E. Gibbon, *Miscellaneous*

Works, 1796, 1.298), at 12.45 p.m. on 16 January 1794, in London, Gibbon died. He was buried in the north transept of the parish church at Fletching, Sussex (an area reserved for the tombs of the Sheffield family), and an epitaph by Dr Parr was engraved on his monument. By his will he left the bulk of his property (thought by Edmond Malone to be in the region of £26,000) to his cousins, Charlotte and Stanier James Porten; Wilhelm de Sévery received £3000 and Gibbon's household effects in Lausanne. Sheffield had encouraged Gibbon to allow his books to be preserved as a collection at Sheffield Place 'where they would … be handed down seris nepotibus as the Gibbonian Library'. But Gibbon, as a 'friend to the circulation of property of every kind', decided instead that a public sale would be the most 'laudable' method of disposal (*Letters*, 3.263 and n. 15). They were bought for £950 by William Beckford, and neglected. On 20 December 1934 several hundred items from Gibbon's library were auctioned by Sothebys.

Publication of the *Miscellaneous Works* and subsequent reputation On Gibbon's death his papers came into the possession of his friend and literary executor, Lord Sheffield, who set about preparing them for publication. The *Miscellaneous Works* were published in two quarto volumes in 1796, a third volume of supplementary material being published in 1815 after a second edition, of five octavo volumes, had been published in 1814. The centre piece of this collection is Sheffield's edited version of Gibbon's *Memoirs of my Life*. At the historian's death this work had been left as six manuscript drafts, often differing quite sharply from each other in matters of emphasis and even at times of fact, and only one of which had been completed. With equal judgement, freedom, and shrewdness, Sheffield conflated, suppressed, and selected from this mass of material. He thereby created the image of Gibbon's life and personality which was known to the nineteenth century, and which was literally unquestionable until Sheffield's grandson, the third earl, sold the Gibbon manuscripts in his possession to the British Museum in 1895.

Gibbon's reputation in the century following his death was marked by an ambivalence expressed in Thomas Durham Whitaker's review of the 1814 *Miscellaneous Works*. While he admired his technical accomplishment as a historian, Whitaker deplored Gibbon's irreligion, which he thought made him 'an English classic who now begins to sleep upon the shelf' (*Quarterly Review*, 12, January 1815, 390). In a similar dividedness of response John Henry Newman lamented the fact that 'the only English writer who has any claim to be considered an ecclesiastical historian, is the unbeliever Gibbon' (J. H. Newman, *An Essay on the Development of Christian Doctrine*, 1845, 5). Nevertheless, the *Decline and Fall* remained in print, with notable editions by H. H. Milman, William Smith, and finally J. B. Bury, in whom this nineteenth-century tradition of editing reached its pinnacle. In France there was an impressive edition by Guizot, while in Germany Niebuhr, Mommsen, and Ranke all acknowledged in Gibbon a historian whom, on his subject, it was impossible to surpass. It was only with the commemoration of the centenary of Gibbon's death by the Royal Historical Society in 1894 that educated opinion in England began to find Gibbon's reputation for irreligion less of an impediment to an appreciation of his merits. Roughly the first half of the twentieth century was notable for advances in the editing of Gibbon's personal writings and lesser works: here the names of J. E. Norton and G. A. Bonnard are pre-eminent. Biographies by D. M. Low, and more recently Patricia Craddock, have rescued Gibbon from both the malicious simplifications of his detractors and the cosmetic art of his own *Memoirs*. Arnaldo Momigliano's address of 1953, 'Gibbon's contributions to historical method', initiated a revival of interest in Gibbon among intellectual historians, and set the scholarly agenda for the second half of the century. The bicentenary of the publication of the first volume of the *Decline and Fall* in 1976 was marked by two collections of essays by various hands, as was also the bicentenary of Gibbon's death in 1994. The tendency of scholarship on Gibbon at the end of the twentieth century has been disaggregative, in respect of both text and context. In 1994 the first edition of the *Decline and Fall* to be based on thorough bibliographical scrutiny of the earliest editions was published, displaying with new clarity the evolution of Gibbon's work as it moved from edition to edition and instalment to instalment. At the same time the historiography of the Enlightenment has begun to discriminate different phases and kinds within the broad phenomenon. In this enriched perspective, Gibbon emerges with new centrality and fresh interest as a figure who managed to hold together tendencies and perspectives which elsewhere were more commonly found in conflict.

Iconography There is a miniature of Edward Gibbon senior by Lewis dating from approximately 1757. A sketch in red chalk by Thomas Patch may represent Gibbon during his tour of Italy. However, the earliest certain image we possess of Gibbon himself is the small portrait by Henry Walton, executed in 1773 as one of a group of four (the others being of Gibbon's friends George Wilbraham, Godfrey Bagnall Clarke, and Booth Grey); one of the four extant versions of the portrait is now in the National Portrait Gallery, London. Sheffield praised it as 'by far the best likeness of him [Gibbon] that exists' (E. Gibbon, *Miscellaneous Works*, 1814 edn, 1.xi). The Joshua Reynolds portrait, an engraved version of which served as frontispiece for later editions of the *Decline and Fall*, was painted in 1779. It makes an interesting contrast with that painted in 1781 by George Romney as a commission from William Hayley, where Gibbon, less formally posed, directs the viewer's attention towards the quarto volumes of the *Decline and Fall*. The 1796 edition of the *Miscellaneous Works* incorporated a silhouette of Gibbon by Mrs Brown showing the historian at the very end of his life, and in which his corpulency is very evident (E. Gibbon, *Miscellaneous Works*, 1796, 1.435 n.*); the originals are in the British Museum. The British Museum also contains a pen and ink profile of Gibbon by Lady Diana Beauclerk, and some sketches of him by Lavinia, Countess Spencer, which date from 1785, and which emphasize, albeit with an engaging crudity of technique, a piercingness in Gibbon's gaze. The earl of Ilchester's collection contains a pen and ink sketch by

William Wallace showing Gibbon in conversation, and dating from 1791. A Wedgwood plaque was made in 1787, and a reproduction of the image it displayed was printed in the *European Magazine* in 1788. A sketch by Brandoin showing Gibbon seated in the garden at La Grotte and in which the genital swelling eventually to cause his death is plainly visible was lithographed by C. Constans.

DAVID WOMERSLEY

Sources *The autobiographies of Edward Gibbon*, ed. J. Murray (1896) · *The letters of Edward Gibbon*, ed. J. E. Norton, 3 vols. (1956) · *Gibbon's journal to January 28th. 1763*, ed. D. M. Low (1929) · *Le journal de Gibbon à Lausanne, 17 août 1763 – 19 avril 1764*, ed. G. Bonnard (Lausanne, 1945) · *Gibbon's journey from Geneva to Rome*, ed. G. A. Bonnard (1961) · E. Gibbon, *The history of the decline and fall of the Roman empire*, ed. D. J. Womersley, 3 vols. (1994) · J. E. Norton, *A bibliography of the works of Edward Gibbon* (1940) · *The private letters of Edward Gibbon*, ed. R. E. Prothero, 2 vols. (1896) · D. M. Low, *Edward Gibbon, 1737–1794* (1937) · P. B. Craddock, *Young Edward Gibbon: gentleman of letters* (1982) · P. B. Craddock, *Edward Gibbon: luminous historian, 1772–1794* (1989) · G. R. De Beer, 'The malady of Edward Gibbon', *Notes and Records of the Royal Society*, 7 (1949–50), 71–80 · A. Momigliano, 'Gibbon's contributions to historical method', *Studies in Historiography* (1966), 40–55 · G. Giarrizzo, *Edward Gibbon e la cultura europea del Settecento* (1954) · J. G. A. Pocock, 'Between Machiavelli and Hume: Gibbon as civic humanist and philosophical historian', *Daedalus*, 105 (1976), 153–69 · J. G. A. Pocock, 'Gibbon's *Decline and fall* and the world view of the late Enlightenment', *Eighteenth-Century Studies*, 10 (1976–7), 287–303 · J. G. A. Pocock, 'Gibbon and the shepherds: the stages of society in the *Decline and fall*', *History of European Ideas*, 2 (1981), 193–202 · J. G. A. Pocock, 'Superstition and enthusiasm in Gibbon's history of religion', *Eighteenth-Century Life*, 8 (1982–3), 83–94 · D. J. Womersley, *The transformation of 'The decline and fall of the Roman empire'* (1988) · G. W. Bowersock, J. Clive, and S. R. Graubard, eds., *Edward Gibbon and the 'Decline and fall of the Roman empire'* (1977) · D. J. Womersley, ed., *Edward Gibbon: bicentenary essays* (1997) · R. McKitterick and R. Quinault, eds., *Edward Gibbon and empire* (1997) · P. B. Craddock, *Edward Gibbon: a reference guide* (1987) · G. R. de Beer, *Gibbon and his world* (1968)

Archives BL, autobiography, journals, corresp., etc., Add. MSS 34715–34716, 34874–34877, 37532, 37722 · BL, library catalogue, Add. MS 46141 · Magd. Oxf., corresp. and accounts · MHS Oxf., papers · University of Chicago · Yale U. | NL Scot., letters to William Robertson · Yale U., Beinecke L., Osborn MSS, letters

Likenesses H. Walton, oils, 1773, NPG · J. Reynolds, oils, 1779, priv. coll. [*see illus.*] · G. Romney, oils, 1781, priv. coll. · Lavinia, Countess Spencer, pencil sketches, 1785, BM · Wedgwood medallion, 1787 (after J. Reynolds, 1779?), V&A · caricature, coloured etching, 1788, NPG · W. Wallace, pen-and-ink drawing, 1791, priv. coll. · Mrs Brown, silhouette, 1794, BM; repro. in J. B. Holroyd, ed., *Miscellaneous works of Edward Gibbon* (1796), frontispiece · D. Beauclerk, pen-and-ink drawing, BM · C. Constans, lithograph (after C. Brandoin), BM, NPG · J. Hall, line engraving (after J. Reynolds), BM; repro. in E. Gibbon, *The history of the decline and fall of the Roman empire*, 6 vols. (1776–88) · J. Romney, line engraving (after G. M. Brighty), NPG · J. Walpole or T. Walpole, pencil drawing, BM · chalk drawing, NPG · watercolour caricature, NPG; posthumous

Wealth at death approx. £26,000

Gibbon, Sir (Ioan) Gwilym (1874–1948), civil servant, was born at Ystradyfodwg, Glamorgan, on 26 November 1874, the son of David Gibbon, colliery overman, and his wife, Ann Williams. He was educated at Oswestry high school and entered public service with the Post Office in 1894. Studying externally he achieved a first-class degree in mental and moral science at the London School of Economics in 1898, and won a merit in the civil service exams in 1902. He entered the Local Government Board as a first-class clerk in 1903, rising to the position of assistant private secretary to Herbert Lewis in 1912. At the same time he studied the European experience of unemployment insurance and attained a DSc (Econ) in 1911.

During the First World War, Gibbon was seconded as an acting principal to the Ministry of National Service. He was given charge of the intelligence and military service departments, whose job it was to produce men for the army and navy. He also acted as secretary of the central tribunal under the Military Services Acts, which involved the supervision of more than 2000 local tribunals. For this arduous work he was appointed a CBE in 1918. In 1926 the French government attempted to make him a member of the Légion d'honneur, but as a full-time British civil servant he was unable to accept.

In 1919 Gibbon joined the Local Government Board's successor, the Ministry of Health, where he stayed first as assistant secretary (1919) and then as principal assistant secretary (1925) until his retirement in 1936. He never married, and lived alone at the Hotel Stuart, Richmond, Surrey, devoting himself to the work of the ministry. He played a major role in general policy and was director of the intelligence and statistics department (1919–21), the town and country planning divisions (1921–34), and the local government division (1934–6). In recognition of his work he was made CB in 1931 and knighted in 1936.

Gibbon was an admirer of the empiricist philosophy of Hume, and believed passionately in the rigorous accumulation of facts and examination of policy options. On this basis he was both a controversial and an influential figure. Fellow senior officials found him obsessive and argumentative but ultimately innovative. Junior officials found him a harsh and conscientious critic of flabby thinking, but equally admired him as a role model. He was an expert drafter of ministerial briefs, notably for the complex local government reform of 1929.

Gibbon's biggest influence came in the planning field, which was trying to come to terms with extensive unregulated urban development. He helped to develop a ministry view on the need for comprehensive planning powers, correlating developments across both built and unbuilt areas. This informed the 1932 Town and Country Planning Act. He also attempted to develop a framework of financial good practice for local government. In particular he introduced systems for evaluating local authority performance in loan-financed capital expenditure, and used the ministry's power of loan sanction to discipline errant authorities. Critics often suggested that this promoted central control, but Gibbon insisted that financial self-discipline was essential to a healthy local democracy.

Gibbon devoted much of his spare time to the Institute of Public Administration, where he was director of research and later vice-president. Among other works he published *Problems of Town and Country Planning* (1937) and (with R. W. Bell) *A History of the London County Council, 1889–1939* (1939) as well as many articles in the institute's journal and the journal of the Royal Statistical Society. He believed strongly in marrying administrative experience with academic scholarship, simultaneously both inspiring other officials and encouraging further research in universities. Throughout his career he believed in a role for public administration tempered by the assumption of limited government. Sustaining his interests into retirement he grew pessimistic about the move towards a welfare state, and tended 'to see the approach of economic disaster' (Ross, 24). He died at the Nightingale Nursing Home, Twickenham, Middlesex, on 4 February 1948, leaving approximately £50,000 to Nuffield College, Oxford, to fund an annual fellowship for public officials to take time off to study problems of government.

JONATHAN BRADBURY

Sources PRO, MH 107/34 [ministry of health personal file] • A. J. Waldegrave, T. H. Sheepshanks, and D. N. Chester, *Public Administration*, 26 (1948), 122–6 • W. A. Ross, 'Local government board and after: retrospect', *Public Administration*, 34 (1956), 17–25 • 'Royal commission on the local government of Greater London', *Parl. papers* (1923), 12/1.567, Cmd 1830 [incl. memorandum and oral evidence by G. Gibbon] • S. V. Ward, 'List Q: a missing link in inter-war public investment', *Public Administration*, 62 (1984), 348–57 • *CGPLA Eng. & Wales* (1948) • *DNB*

Archives BL, corresp. with W. J. Ashley, Add. MS 42242 • BLPES, Sir Arnold Plant collection, transcript of a BBC radio broadcast on growth of towns • Welwyn Garden City Central Library, corresp. with Frederic Osborn

Wealth at death £57,864 0s. 5d.: probate, 17 April 1948, *CGPLA Eng. & Wales*

Gibbon, John (1629–1718), herald, was born in London on 3 November 1629, the eldest surviving son of Robert Gibbon (1594–1643), citizen and draper of Watling Street, London, and his wife, Mary, daughter of Lionel Edgar (or Ettghar) of Framsden, Suffolk. Gibbon's grandfather Robert had gone to London from Rolvenden, Kent. The historian Edward Gibbon was his brother's great-grandson.

Gibbon attended Merchant Taylors' School for two years after being admitted on 11 December 1639. According to his more famous relation, he attended Jesus College, Cambridge, but did not take a degree (Gibbon, 10). His first employment was as domestic tutor to Thomas, Lord Coventry, at Allesborough, Worcestershire. In the 1650s he travelled widely, probably owing to his royalist sympathies. He saw military service in Europe, where he learned Spanish and French, and lived for a time in Jersey.

In 1657 Gibbon sailed to Virginia where he lived for three years, working as estate manager for Colonel Richard Lee, the secretary of state, with whom he returned to London shortly after the Restoration. He recalled his life there fondly, despite its hardships, stating in 1676 that 'I love Virginia, being a most goodly country' (*CSP dom.*, *1676–7*, 403). In 1682 he wrote of how he had watched a group of Native Americans engage in a war dance. Their shields and bodies were colourfully painted in personal emblems, leading him to observe 'that Heraldry was ingrafted naturally into the sense of humane race' and therefore deserved 'a greater esteem than now-a-days is put upon it' (*Introductio*, 1682, 156).

Soon after his return to London, Gibbon married his wife, Susannah (*d.* 1704), about whom nothing else is known. On 9 February 1665 he settled in a house in the parish of St Katharine by the Tower, where the family lived until 1701; the house passed to Gibbon's nephew after his death. His long-standing interest in heraldry and the influence of William Dugdale led to Gibbon's appointment as Bluemantle pursuivant-at-arms. The patent was dated 10 February 1668, though he was not actually created Bluemantle until 16 April 1671. He was well known to other, more prominent heralds, yet never received any preferment after his initial appointment. According to Mark Noble he behaved arrogantly towards his colleagues, convinced that his destiny, foreseen in endless astrological calculations, was unaffected by his behaviour (Noble, 363). Nevertheless, as Gibbon himself related, he was appointed to the college at a time when 'the ceremony of funerals (as accompanied with officers of arms) began to be in the wane' (*Introductio*, 161). His chief achievement was not the compilation of genealogies or county collections but his writings on the practice and history of heraldry. His most significant publication was the *Introductio ad Latinam blasoniam* (1682). In the style of earlier antiquarian essays, this collected together heraldic theory and, through the presentation of the arms of several European magnates, attempted to establish a new method of blazon. Like much of his writing, Gibbon's *magnum opus* combined Latin and English, prose and verse, in an enthusiastic if disconcerting manner.

Gibbon was a fervent supporter of James, duke of York, publishing several tracts. The first of these was *Day-Fatality, or, Some Observation of Days Lucky and Unlucky* (1679; reissued 1686), published in honour of York's birthday and prophesying a great future for him. Several exchanges with Henry Care followed, Gibbon's defences of James being published as *Touch of the Times* (1679), and *Flagellum Mercurii anti-ducalis* (1679). The exclusion of the duke of Monmouth from the succession in favour of the duke of York saw Gibbon produce another tract, *Unio dissidentium: Heir Apparent and Presumptive Made One* (1680), reprinted in part as *A Panegyrick to His Royal Highness upon His Majesties Late Declaration* (1680). Next came *Prince-Protecting Providences* (1682; reissued with *Day-Fatality* in 1686), relating tales of miraculous royal escapes from danger. His final political publication, *Edovardus Confessor redivivus: the piety and vertues of holy Edward the Confessor, reviv'd in the sacred Majesty of King James the II* (1688), was in hindsight particularly misguided, as it offered the discovery of the Confessor's crucifix at Westminster Abbey among other signs as irrefutable evidence of the king's blessed future.

The advent of William and Mary curtailed Gibbon's opportunities as a writer and herald, though like most of the other heralds he eventually took the oath of allegiance. He continued to work at the College of Arms, and corresponded with several notable authors such as John Strype. Gibbon wrote an account of the role of heralds in European history entitled 'Heraldo-Memoriale' which was published in abridged form (J. Stow, *Survey of London*, ed. J. Strype, 1720, 1.143–5).

Writing in 1709, Thomas Hearne recorded that Gibbon

had a 'great Character' as a herald and Latinist, but 'notwithstanding this, I take him to be a whimsical and craz'd Person' due to his political writings (*Remarks and Collections of Thomas Hearne*, ed. C. Doble, 1886, 2.194). Hearne was not alone in his opinion, for Gibbon's publications were curious if not fanatical manipulation of astrological prognostications in support of James II that went beyond conventional notions of providence. Gibbon died on 2 August 1718 in the parish of St Faith, London, and was buried near his wife on 6 August at St Mary Aldermary, the church of his baptism. PETER SHERLOCK

Sources A. Wagner, *Heralds of England: a history of the office and College of Arms* (1967) • E. Gibbon, *Memoirs of my life*, ed. G. A. Bonnard (1966) • M. Noble, *A history of the College of Arms* (1804) • *The visitation of London, anno Domini 1633, 1634, and 1635, made by Sir Henry St George*, 1, ed. J. J. Howard and J. L. Chester, Harleian Society, 15 (1880), 310 • Mrs E. P. Hart, ed., *Merchant Taylors' School register, 1561–1934*, 2 vols. (1936) • parish register, St Mary Aldermary, 15 Nov 1629 [baptism] • parish register, St Mary Aldermary, 6 Aug 1718 [burial] • will, PRO, PROB 11/565, sig. 160
Archives NRA, priv. coll., antiquarian notebook | BL, Lansdowne MS 778 • BL, Stowe MS 670 • CUL, Strype corresp., Add. MSS 1–10

Gibbon, Lewis Grassic. *See* Mitchell, (James) Leslie (1901–1935).

Gibbon, Nicholas, the elder. *See* Gibbens, Nicholas (*fl.* 1601–1602).

Gibbon, Nicholas (1605–1697), Church of England clergyman, was born at Poole, Dorset, the son of Nicholas Gibbon (*fl.* 1592–1605), clergyman, of Heckford, Dorset. He was admitted to Queen's College, Oxford, in 1622, but soon afterwards migrated to St Edmund Hall. He graduated BA in 1626 and proceeded MA in 1629. He became rector of Sevenoaks, Kent, in 1631 and proceeded BD and DD in 1639. Ejected from Sevenoaks in 1643, Gibbon was replaced in February 1645 by Thomas Kentish, formerly vicar of Haddenham, Buckinghamshire. Kentish was discharged by the committee for plundered ministers in July 1645 for not paying Gibbon's wife, Mary, the required fifth of the revenues of the benefice to support herself and her children. Meanwhile Gibbon had had to work as a farm labourer in order to support his wife and eleven children. Summoned before the Kent county committee and asked how he spent his time he answered that he studied during part of the night, and performed manual labour by day, and showed his hardened hands, remarking to some who scoffed, 'Mallem callum in manu quam in conscientia' ('I should prefer a callous on the hand than on the conscience'; Walker, 251). He was then offered possession of his living if he would take the covenant, but he refused to do so.

Nevertheless, Gibbon was an advocate of reconciliation between rival religious parties. In *The Tender of Doctor Gibbon unto the Christian Church for the Reconciliation of Differences* (1645?), he offered to provide a basis for resolving theological disputes. In *The reconciler: earnestly endevouring to unite in sincere affection the presbyters and their dissenting brethren* (1646), he urged the presbyterians and Independents to cease their partisan attacks on each other and to engage in free and open discussions. On Gibbon's request a committee of the House of Lords considered the question of his being restored to the living of Sevenoaks, and on 22 March 1647 the house voted in Gibbon's favour, citing *The Tender* and the possibility of his being 'useful unto this Church and State' (*JHL*, 1646–7, 94). The motion was forwarded to the Commons but no subsequent action was taken. In 1648 Gibbon was called upon by Charles I on the Isle of Wight to discuss with him and his council the contested issue of church government. Gibbon also spoke to a commission of ministers sent by parliament to confer with the king. He supported the practice of the apostles who, he said, were sent out by Christ with the power to send out or ordain others to perform pastoral duties. Gibbon's *A Summe or Body of Divinity Real* (1651) illustrated on a single large broadsheet his model of Christian doctrine, focusing on the Trinity and on the covenant of grace. It was reissued in 1653.

At the Restoration Gibbon regained the rectory of Sevenoaks, and was also put in possession of the rectory of Corfe Castle, Dorset, to which he had been presented more than ten years before. A further proposal by Gibbon for an agreement between rival religious parties appeared as *Theology Real and Truly Scientificall in Overture for the Conciliation of All Christians* (1663?) with a commendatory letter by Robert Sanderson, bishop of Lincoln, dated 1 August 1661. Other versions of his epitome of doctrine were published as *A proscheme: (that is) the scheme or diagram divested of its mathematical habitude and digested into chapters* (1680?), *The scheme or diagramme adjusted for future use in a larger prodromus* (1680?), and *Theology real and truly scientifical, in overture for the conciliation of all Christians: (and after them) the theist, atheist, and all mankind* (1687?). Richard Baxter wrote that he had discussed with Gibbon the latter's 'Scheme of Theology', then still in manuscript, in the 1650s. Rather than finding Gibbon's work a means of uniting all Christians, Baxter found it 'secretly and cunningly fitted to usher in a Socinian Popery', by undermining belief in Christ's divinity (*Reliquiae Baxterianae*, 1/2.205). Judging by the repeated publications of Gibbon's writings, they seem to have appealed to many who wanted to find a way to resolve religious differences peacefully. Gibbon died and was buried at Corfe Castle on 12 February 1697.

W. B. PATTERSON

Sources J. Walker, *An attempt towards recovering an account of the numbers and sufferings of the clergy of the Church of England*, 2 pts in 1 (1714), 251–2 • *Walker rev.*, 216 • Wood, *Ath. Oxon.*, 1st edn, 1.850, 865, 897–8 • *Reliquiae Baxterianae, or, Mr Richard Baxter's narrative of the most memorable passages of his life and times*, ed. M. Sylvester, 1 vol. in 3 pts (1696), pt 1, p. 78; pt 2, pp. 205–6; pt 3, p. 69 • *CSP dom.*, 1638–9, 120, 493; 1639, 358, 372, 436–7 • *JHL*, 8 (1645–6), 496 • *JHL*, 9 (1646–7), 93 • *JHC*, 4 (1644–6), 721 • L. B. Larking, ed., *Proceedings principally in the county of Kent in connection with the parliaments called in 1640, and especially with the committee of religion appointed in that year*, CS, old ser., 80 (1862), 184–5 • E. Hasted, *The history and topographical survey of the county of Kent*, 2nd edn, 3 (1797), 105 • J. Hutchins, *The history and antiquities of the county of Dorset*, 3rd edn, ed. W. Shipp and J. W.

Hodson, 1 (1861), 541–2 • *Calamy rev.*, 306 • theses in sacred theology, Oxford University, 6 July 1639, PRO, SP 16/425/29

Gibbons family (*per. c.*1735–1863), ironmasters, colliery proprietors, and bankers came to prominence with **John Gibbons** (1703–1778), who was active as an ironmonger by the mid-1730s. By origin the family were yeoman farmers who steadily acquired modest amounts of land in the parish of Sedgeley in the sixteenth and seventeenth centuries. Landownership led them into mineral exploitation, and the Gibbonses were engaged in the coal trade from at least the 1620s. Their entry into the burgeoning metalware manufacturing sector in the west midlands was at the initiative of John Gibbons. The son of William Gibbons (1673–1744), farmer and coal proprietor, and his wife, Elizabeth Hawksford, Gibbons evidently flourished as a putting-out nailer, since from the 1750s he moved into primary iron processing, leasing first Pitchford forge in Shropshire, then a succession of forges in the Stour valley on the border of Staffordshire and Worcestershire.

John Gibbons and his wife, Grace Austin (1708–1785), had three sons, who carried on their father's business after his death in 1778: **Thomas Gibbons** (1730–1813), **William Gibbons** (1732–1807), and **Benjamin Gibbons** (1735–1832) were ironmasters as well as ironmongers. Benjamin Gibbons was entrusted with management of the iron business around Kingswinford, which in the 1780s comprised forges at Hyde and Lye and warehouses at Stourport, Lower Gornal, and Hyde. Thomas Gibbons took charge of the merchant house at Wolverhampton which was subsequently developed as a bank; and in 1775 he married Mary Moseley (*d.* 1833). At the same time William Gibbons ran the family's merchant house at Bristol, buying pig iron for the midland forges and overseeing the export of metalwares to the American market. In 1778 William married Phyllis Watkins (1760–1791).

The brothers took full advantage of the boom in the iron industry which followed the end of the American War of Independence. They extended their interests rapidly, taking in kinsmen as junior partners and mortgaging land to supply investment funds when circulating capital could not be spared from the ironware business. Thus, Benjamin Gibbons built a blast furnace at Bilston in 1787, taking his cousins William and Benjamin Bickley as partners; and in 1788 he joined his two brothers in leasing a furnace at the Level, as well as a forge and slitting mill at Cradley. In this way the Gibbonses emerged as major figures in the iron industry of their native region, operating seven blast furnaces with associated forge capacity by 1812. William Gibbons achieved eminence as a citizen of Bristol as well, becoming mayor of the city in 1800–01. Indeed, William Gibbons also became an industrial lobbyist of national reputation. He was a spokesman for the iron trade during the debates on Britain's commercial future in the wake of the American débâcle, giving voice to ironmasters' anxieties concerning the 'Irish propositions' in 1785, in which William Pitt the younger sought to establish free trade with Ireland; and he also took issue with the commercial treaty negotiated in the same year with France by William Eden. Later, he twice led campaigns to avert the taxation of pig iron during the Napoleonic wars, in 1797–8 and in 1806, on each occasion with success.

The single partnership which had governed the family's affairs in the late eighteenth century was divided up after the death at Bristol of William Gibbons in 1807. The Bristol house was signed over to his only son, William (1782–1848), who was married to Anne Every (1784–1855). At the same time the midland property was divided between his surviving brothers. After the death of Thomas Gibbons in 1813 at Teignmouth his share in the midland banking and ironmaking businesses passed to his three sons: John (1777–1851) [*see below*], Benjamin (1783–1873) and Thomas (1787–1829). The control of this new generation was consolidated a year later with the retirement of the elder Benjamin Gibbons, who made over the Level furnaces and other industrial plant to his nephews in return for an annuity, a capital sum of £24,000, and the Corbyns Hall estate which the family had purchased in 1779. The separating off of Benjamin Gibbons's interests was providential, for it was to allow the family to recover from the bankruptcy which overwhelmed it in the post-war slump. The three brothers were gazetted bankrupt as bankers in March 1816, pulling the iron business down with them. Something was saved from the wreck when the eighty-year-old Benjamin Gibbons, in the guise of a preferential creditor, compelled the assignees to transfer the Level works and collieries to him. Benjamin senior lived until 1832.

From this foundation the family was able to rebuild its fortune. The three sons of Thomas Gibbons (1730–1813) were involved in a set of interlocking partnerships, centred on the Level works but extending to Corbyns Hall, where three new furnaces were built in the mid-1820s, and to the Ketley works near Dudley. **John Gibbons** (1777–1851), ironmaster, proved the most technically adept of the brothers, publishing two short works on industrial practice: *Practical Remarks on the Construction of the Staffordshire Blast Furnace* (1839) and *Practical remarks on the use of the cinder pig in the puddling furnaces, and on the management of the forge and mill* (1844). He was married to Elizabeth Steen (*d.* 1889), who survived his death in 1851.

As a whole, the family was innovative, being one of the earliest south Staffordshire iron partnerships to adopt J. B. Neilson's patent hot-blast technology when it became widely available in the mid-1830s. However, there was little they could do to overcome the declining competitiveness of south Staffordshire as a pig iron-producing region, eclipsed as it was by Scotland and Cleveland in the middle decades of the nineteenth century. The family's problems in the iron trade were for a long time compensated for by the resilience of their coal interests. The long-established Gibbons habit of buying land stood them in good stead, for it furnished them with a good deal of mineral-rich real estate in south Staffordshire. The Corbyns Hall estate proved a consistent source of wealth in this respect. Yet the family's difficulties were compounded by entrepreneurial (and demographic) failure. A new generation of ironmasters did not emerge, leaving the elder Benjamin

Gibbons, a childless bachelor, to preside over a slow running down of the business. The Level works were relinquished in the mid-1840s and the Ketley furnaces were never worked after 1858. The Corbyns Hall furnaces were the last to go, being blown out in 1869.

The last burst of entrepreneurial dynamism in the iron trade came from the Bristol branch of the family, not the west midland. **Benjamin Gibbons** (1815–1863), ironmaster, the youngest son of William Gibbons (1782–1848), entered the iron industry via firebrick manufacture. He leased the Hallfields furnace in the Black Country in 1846 and the Tipton Green ironworks in 1847. In the mid-1850s he took over the Millfield works, only a short distance from the now derelict Bilston furnace which his family had built in 1788, but by the end of the decade he had begun a partial withdrawal from the west midland iron trade. Hallfields and Tipton Green were both given up in 1859. Millfield remained in his hands, but Benjamin Gibbons's attention was now directed to the Forest of Dean, where he had purchased the Soudley ironworks in 1856. His premature death on 3 September 1863 at Athol House, Edgbaston, Birmingham, ended any chance of a renewal of the family's involvement in the iron industry. He was survived by his wife, Emily. In the later nineteenth century the surviving branches of the family lived as *rentier* gentry. CHRIS EVANS

Sources W. A. Smith, 'The Gibbons family: coal and ironmasters, 1750–1873', PhD diss., U. Lond., 1978 • M. Le Guillou, 'William Gibbons and the proposed taxes on the iron trade', *Journal of West Midlands Regional Studies*, 2 (1968), 1–5 • pedigree of the Gibbons family, Bristol RO, Acc. 32688/192/13 and 7 • *CGPLA Eng. & Wales* (1863) [Benjamin Gibbons (1815–1863)]

Archives priv. coll., business and family papers • priv. coll., papers [William Gibbons] • Staffs. RO, business and estate papers, D 695/1/12 | Dudley Archives and Local History Service, Coseley, Staffordshire, Cradley Forge accounts, Acc. 8440

Wealth at death under £30,000—Benjamin Gibbons: probate, 4 Dec 1863, *CGPLA Eng. & Wales*

Gibbons, Benjamin (1735–1832). *See under* Gibbons family (*per.* c.1735–1863).

Gibbons, Benjamin (1815–1863). *See under* Gibbons family (*per.* c.1735–1863).

Gibbons, Carroll Richard (1903–1954), band leader and pianist, was born in Clinton, Massachusetts, USA, on 4 January 1903. Details of his family background are not available. He played the piano from his childhood days and studied music in Boston at the New England Conservatory of Music, but had decided early in life that he would like to make a career in the dance-band world. He went to London in 1924 with the Boston Orchestra (actually a mere quintet of violin, saxophone, banjo, piano, and drums), which played at the Berkeley Hotel and as a relief band to the famous Orpheans and the Havana Band at the Savoy Hotel. His main aim in going to London had been to undertake further piano studies at the Royal Academy of Music, but he was soon totally involved in the world of dance music and relinquished any more serious intentions. Occasionally in 1923 and 1924 he played with the Savoy Havana Band under Debroy Somers. By 1926 he had

Carroll Richard Gibbons (1903–1954), by Sasha, 1932 [left, with his band]

become principal pianist with the Sylvians, a similar sort of unit to the Boston Orchestra but one which made many recordings augmented by brass from the Savoy Orpheans. By the beginning of 1927 he had taken over from Somers as director of the Savoy Orpheans. The contract between the manager of the band and the Savoy Hotel expired at the end of that year, so in 1928 Carroll Gibbons took the band on a tour of Germany. When they returned in March the group was disbanded but was soon reformed without Carroll Gibbons in their ranks.

By then Gibbons had taken up an appointment as director of music to His Master's Voice records (1928–9), and he worked for British and Dominion Films in 1929 while continuing his own recording career with the New Mayfair Dance Orchestra, which could call on a very mixed bag of leading musicians who were available to him through his now influential position. Small groups from the orchestra were used to accompany recordings by such varied artists as the Romanian musical comedy star George Metaxa, the great black singer Paul Robeson, Noël Coward, Gracie Fields, and George Baker, to mention but a few. Carroll also composed, and he recorded his own song 'Garden in the Rain' with Metaxa in 1928. He left His Master's Voice in 1929, Ray Noble taking over the job, and was back in the USA in 1930 and 1931 to work in Hollywood as staff composer to MGM.

On his return to London in the late summer of 1931 Gibbons became joint director with a fellow American, Howard Jacobs, of the New Savoy Hotel Orpheans, he took over sole leadership when Jacobs left to go to the Berkeley Hotel. He retained the post until just before he died in 1954, and he was appointed director of entertainments of the Savoy Hotel in 1950. During the 1930s he made frequent broadcasts with his band the Boy Friends, using his own composition 'On the Air' as signature tune. He made only two further visits to the USA, one in 1933, when he made a few recordings with Ben Selvin's orchestra, and the second in 1939 for a holiday after which, because of wartime restrictions, he was nearly unable to get back. On his return he briefly led a sixteen-piece touring band before coming firmly back into the fold at the Savoy in 1940. The Orpheans recorded very regularly for Columbia Records, the more popular song recordings being made under the name Carroll Gibbons and his Boy Friends. The band was never strongly influenced by jazz, although Gibbons made use of many good jazz soloists, but maintained a light saloon style, as might be expected in a band which had the violinists Paul Fenoulhet, George Melachrino, and Reg Leopold in its ranks. Gibbons himself played in a quietly romantic manner that took him into the world of impressionism, a style typified by his own 'Midnight in Mayfair'. He recorded some duets with the visiting American band leader, pianist, and composer Johnny Green, the writer of 'Body and Soul', and a few sides with Ronnie Munro's orchestra. The vocalists he used at the Savoy were in the same somewhat straight mould, including ladies like Anne Lenner and Rita Williams who were especially favoured for their light and intelligent touch. His own best-known composition remained 'On the Air', which became his regular signature tune. Typically he recorded it with a clear-cut vocal by Dorothy Stedeford and a violin obbligato by Matty Malneck. The touches that he added to other people's tunes were always subtle and sensitive, as can be heard in his solo recording of 'When Day is Done'. He wrote and part-wrote several stage works, including *Up with the Lark* (1927), *Sylvia* (1927), *Open your Eyes* (1929), *Gaieties* (1945), and *Big Boy* (1945); and he published a number of songs in London, including 'I'm so Jealous' (1927), 'Misunderstood' (1927), 'Garden in the Rain' (1928), 'I'll be Getting Along' (1929), 'I Think of You' (1945), and 'It was Swell while it Lasted' (1945).

Gibbons was a small soft-spoken man, in keeping with his music, and was remembered for his quiet announcements and his drawling 'Goodnight, everybody' at the end of his broadcasts. He died of a coronary thrombosis at 20 Devonshire Place, St Marylebone, London, on 10 May 1954, survived by his wife, Joan. PETER GAMMOND

Sources A. McCarthy, *The dance band era* (1971) • B. Rust, disc notes, *The Carroll Gibbons story*, WRC SH 167/8 • d. cert. • S. Jackson, *The Savoy: the romance of a great hotel* (1964) • A. Shipton, 'Gibbons, (Richard) Carroll', *New Grove*, 2nd edn

Likenesses Sasha, photograph, 1932, Hult. Arch. [*see illus.*]

Gibbons, Christopher (*bap.* **1615**, *d.* **1676**), organist and composer, was baptized on 22 August 1615 at St Margaret's, Westminster, the third of the seven children of the composer Orlando *Gibbons (*bap.* 1583, *d.* 1625) and his wife, Elizabeth (1590–1626), daughter of John Patten, keeper of the king's closet; he may have been named after Sir Christopher Hatton (*d.* 1619), a patron of his father. In the mid-1620s he was probably a choirboy of the Chapel Royal. In January 1627 he was nominated through the signet office for admission as a scholar of Charterhouse School; the governors approved his election on 21 June. Following the death of his mother he was entrusted in 1628 to the custody of his uncle, Edward Gibbons, master of the choristers and formerly succentor of Exeter Cathedral. Christopher probably spent much of the next decade in Exeter.

Christopher Gibbons (*bap.* **1615**, *d.* **1676**), by unknown artist, *c.*1664

On 25 June 1638, at the lord chamberlain's request, Gibbons was appointed 'organist and singing man' of Winchester Cathedral in succession to Thomas Holmes, with an annual salary of £30. On 14 December 1642 parliamentarian troops under Sir William Waller raided the cathedral and seized organ pipes as trophies. Gibbons then joined the royalist army, yet despite the fact that Winchester fell to parliamentary forces in October 1645, he nominally remained organist of Winchester until 1661, and on 2 June 1648 the committee for sequestrations directed that arrears of salary due to him should be paid.

Gibbons married Mary, daughter of Robert Kercher (*d.* 1644), one of the prebendaries of Winchester Cathedral, on 23 September 1646 at St Bartholomew-the-Less, West Smithfield. Following his marriage he settled in London, where he was active as a music teacher during the Commonwealth. In John Playford's *A Musicall Banquet* (1651) he was listed as one of the city's 'excellent and able Masters … For the Organ or Virginall'. According to John Aubrey, he became organist to Sir John Danvers, whose house in Chelsea contained a fine chamber organ. Sir Constantijn Huygens's son Lodewijck heard him play there on 10 March 1652, and also in consort music at the house of the violinist Davis Mell a fortnight later. On 12 July 1654, during a visit to Oxford, John Evelyn was taken to hear him play the organ in Magdalen College chapel.

It appears that Gibbons's first wife had died by 1655, so she cannot have been the Mary Gibbons who was buried at Westminster Abbey in April 1662, as has often been stated. On 22 April 1655 a Christopher Gibbons of St Giles Cripplegate, who was almost certainly the musician, was married at St Clement Danes to a widow, Elizabeth Filbridge, whose maiden name seems to have been Ball. Five children of this marriage were baptized at St Clement Danes between February 1656 and June 1660, of whom the first, named Orlando after his grandfather, died in infancy. A grant of £5 was made to Gibbons in 1655 by the trustees for the maintenance of ministers.

Gibbons was involved in at least two of the private operatic entertainments that took place in London during the Commonwealth. In William Davenant's *The Siege of Rhodes*, performed in autumn 1656 at Rutland House, he was one of the small band of instrumentalists. Matthew Locke's autograph score for the 1659 presentation of Shirley's masque *Cupid and Death* at the Military Company's house in Leicester Fields includes settings by Gibbons of three songs, each preceded by a suite of airs and ending with a chorus; perhaps the composition was undertaken collaboratively—Gibbons must have known Locke since the 1630s, when the latter was a chorister at Exeter—though it has been conjectured that Gibbons's portions of the music could have been taken over from an earlier version of the masque given in March 1653 in honour of the Portuguese ambassador.

At the Restoration, Gibbons was appointed to the places in the Chapel Royal and the king's private musick once held by his father, which had become vacant through Thomas Warwick's death in 1652. On 19 June 1660 at Baynard's Castle 'Mr Gybbons [was] approved of by the King', who probably heard him play while being entertained to supper there by the earl of Pembroke. Instructions were given for 'an organ to be made for him', and six days later he was sworn in as virginalist in the private musick at a fee of £86 a year (Ashbee, *Records*, 1.3). With William Child and Edward Lowe he became one of the three organists of the Chapel Royal; by September 1660 he had also been appointed organist of Westminster Abbey at a stipend of £10 a year. He played at the funeral of Mary, princess of Orange, on 29 December 1660 and at the king's coronation on 23 April 1661. He was still organist of Winchester Cathedral on 28 February 1661, when he petitioned the king to intercede with the dean and chapter of Winchester over property at Freefolk, near Whitchurch in Hampshire, to which he claimed right of tenancy through his marriage to Mary Kercher; his petition, which was supported by the archbishop of York, the dean of Westminster, and four bishops, was clearly successful, for the property was bequeathed by his widow, Elizabeth, to their eldest daughter. He had resigned his Winchester post by June 1661, however. On 28 October 1662 Gibbons was named as one of the eleven assistants of the corporation for regulating 'the Art and Science of Musique' in Westminster. Pepys was on friendly terms with him, and heard him take part in chamber music several times during the 1660s, usually at the earl of Sandwich's house.

Gibbons received the DMus degree from the University of Oxford in 1664; Anthony Wood noted that he was 'licensed to proceed' on 7 July 'by vertue of his Majesties Letters', and that his exercises, which included the anthem 'Not unto us, o Lord' (Bodl. Oxf., MS mus. sch. C.139), were performed four days later at an Act ceremony in the university church of St Mary 'with very great honour to himself and his faculty' (Wood, *Ath. Oxon.: Fasti*, 2.833). From Westminster Abbey he received a special grant of £5 to defray the expenses incurred by taking his degree. Wood characterized him as 'a person most excellent in his faculty, but a grand debauchee' who would 'sleep at Morning Prayer when he was to play on the organ' (Clark, 2.5), and an autograph annotation on the manuscript of one of his organ verses—'drunke from the Cather[i]ne Wheele' (Christ Church, Oxford, Mus. 1142A)—also suggests a bibulous disposition. Between 1663 and 1665 he became enmeshed in controversy over plans for a new organ at Worcester Cathedral, and was accused by the dean, Thomas Warmestry, of corruptly trying to procure the contract for the organ builder William Hathaway. Gibbons was appointed master of the choristers at Westminster Abbey in 1664, following the death of the elder Henry Purcell, but he relinquished this post, together with that of organist of the abbey, with effect from 25 March 1666. By 1664 the Gibbons family occupied a house in New Street, between Great Almonry and Orchard Street, Westminster, where Gibbons was still living in July 1671. On 16 December 1674 he was appointed organist of St Martin-in-the-Fields at a salary of £20 (out of which he was expected 'to pay the bellowes blower').

Gibbons died in the parish of St Margaret's, Westminster, on 20 October 1676 and was buried in Westminster Abbey cloisters on 24 October. His place as organist of the Chapel Royal went to his pupil John Blow, and that as virginalist in the private musick to Christopher Preston. At the time of his death he was owed £280 in court wages. His second wife, Elizabeth, died in 1682.

As a keyboard player Gibbons was an important figure in Commonwealth and Restoration music. Two Oxford antiquaries, Anthony Wood and Thomas Ford, noted that Henry Purcell was his pupil. His three voluntaries for 'double' (two-manual) organ are a valuable legacy of the 'skill & Talent' that Evelyn admired. Roger North characterized his compositions as 've[ry] bold, solid, and strong, but desultory and not without a lit[t]le of the *barbaresque*', and called him 'a great master in the ecclesiasticall stile, and also in consort musick' (*Roger North on Music*, 299). His 'ecclesiasticall' works are represented most typically by his verse anthems with organ, and his 'consort musick' by the fantasia-suites for one or two violins, bass viol, and organ, mid-century examples of a genre that owed its origins and popularity largely to Charles I's patronage.

CHRISTOPHER D. S. FIELD

Sources A. Ashbee and D. Lasocki, eds., *A biographical dictionary of English court musicians, 1485–1714*, 2 vols. (1998) • C. D. S. Field, 'Gibbons, Christopher', *New Grove*, 2nd edn • C. G. Rayner and S. F. Rayner, 'Christopher Gibbons: "that famous musitian"', *Musica Disciplina*, 24 (1970), 151–71 • H. W. Shaw, *The succession of organists of the Chapel Royal and the cathedrals of England and Wales from c.1538* (1991) • A. Ashbee, ed., *Records of English court music*, 1 (1986) • A. Ashbee, ed., *Records of English court music*, 3 (1988) • A. Ashbee, ed., *Records of English court music*, 5 (1991) • A. Ashbee, ed., *Records of English court music*, 8 (1995) • J. Harley, *Orlando Gibbons and the Gibbons family of musicians* (1999) • *Brief lives, chiefly of contemporaries, set down by John Aubrey, between the years 1669 and 1696*, ed. A. Clark, 2 vols.

(1898) • L. Huygens, *The English journal, 1651–1652*, ed. and trans. A. G. H. Bacharach and R. G. Collmer (1982) • Evelyn, *Diary* • Pepys, *Diary* • *Roger North on music*, ed. J. Wilson (1959) • Wood, *Ath. Oxon.: Fasti*, 1st edn • *The life and times of Anthony Wood*, ed. A. Clark, 5 vols., OHS, 19, 21, 26, 30, 40 (1891–1900) • B. Marsh and F. A. Crisp, eds., *Alumni Carthusiani: a record of the foundation scholars of Charterhouse, 1614–1872* (1913) • *The diary of John Young STP, dean of Winchester, 1616 to the Commonwealth*, ed. F. R. Goodman (1928) • A. Freeman, 'The organs and organists of St. Martin-in-the-Fields, London', *The Organ*, 1 (1921), 1–19 • M. Tilmouth, 'A calendar of references to music in newspapers published in London and the provinces (1660–1719)', *Royal Musical Association Research Chronicle*, 1 (1961) • *CSP dom.*, *1660–61*; *1663–4* • E. F. Rimbault, ed., *The old cheque-book, or book of remembrance, of the Chapel Royal, from 1561 to 1744*, CS, new ser., 3 (1872) • parish register, Westminster, St Margaret's, 22 Aug 1615 [baptism]

Likenesses oils, *c.*1664, U. Oxf., faculty of music [*see illus.*] • J. Caldwall, engraving (after A. Van Dyck), repro. in J. Hawkins, *A general history of the science and practice of music*, 5 vols. (1776)

Wealth at death left all estate to widow: will, PRO, PROB 11/352, sig. 140 • arrears of £279 10s. in salary still owing to widow on her death; property to daughter: will, PRO, PROB 11/372, sig. 4 [Elizabeth Gibbons]

Gibbons, Edward (*bap.* **1568**, *d.* in or before **1650**), musician, was baptized at St Mary the Great, Cambridge, on 21 March 1568, son of William Gibbons (*c.*1540–1595), innkeeper and member of the waits, and his wife, Mary (*d.* 1603), and elder brother of Orlando *Gibbons (*bap.* 1583, *d.* 1625). Details of his early education are unknown, but it was as 'Mus. Bac from Cambridge' that he was incorporated at Oxford on 7 July 1592. From 1592 to 1598 he was a lay clerk at King's College, Cambridge, and instructor of the choristers, who for a time included Orlando Gibbons.

Another brother, **Ellis Gibbons** (*bap.* 1573, *d.* 1603), was baptized at Holy Trinity, Cambridge, on 30 November 1573. He published two uninspired madrigals in *The Triumphes of Oriana* (1601), and married Joan Dyer, before dying in the parish of St Benet Paul's Wharf, London, in May 1603. His will, drawn up that year, describes Edward as 'of Acton', perhaps correctly 'Exon' (that is, Exeter).

By 1607 Edward Gibbons was in Exeter; there is no authority for Anthony Wood's references to his employment elsewhere. In 1608 he became instructor of the choristers at Exeter Cathedral, a task he often deputed to others. A dispensation gave him a vicar's place in 1609, but he was twice accused of negligence in his duties. His few compositions, vocal and instrumental, were probably written before this; competent, and occasionally moving, they survive in a number of libraries (BL, Harleian MS 7340; Christ Church, Oxford, MS Mus 43, 1220–1224; Bodl. Oxf., MSS mus. sch. d.212–216; Durham Cath. CL, MS Hunter 33). He was custos of the college of priest-vicars by 1614, and succentor from 1615 to 1627.

When Orlando Gibbons's widow died in 1626 Edward Gibbons assumed responsibility for her children, including Christopher *Gibbons (*bap.* 1615, *d.* 1676). Edward's wife, Jane, whom he had married by 1596 and with whom he had six children, was buried on 7 April 1628; he afterwards married Mary Bluet. His wives brought him money, and he owned an estate at Dunsford. It is said that during the civil war he and his family were turned out of their home. He last signed the cathedral accounts in 1645, and died before July 1650, when administration of his estate was granted in the prerogative court of Canterbury. He was survived by his wife, Mary, who was buried on 9 January 1664.

John Harley

Sources registers, St Mary the Great and Holy Trinity, Cambridge, Cambs. AS • will register, Ely archdeaconry court, Cambs. AS, Cambridge, vol. 5, fol. 183; vol. 6, fols. 152*v*–153*v* [William Gibbons; Mary Gibbons] • register of convocation, 1582–95, Oxf. UA, NEP/Supra/Reg L • commons books, 1591/2–1597/8, King's Cam. • mundum books, King's Cam., 19.5–20.5 • will of Ellis Gibbons, PRO, PROB 10/216 [copy at PROB 11/101, fol. 252*r*] • grant of administration for Orlando Gibbons, PRO, PROB 6/13, fol. 52*r* • grant of administration, PRO, PROB 6/25, fol. 119*r* • certificate of residence, PRO, E115/172/99 • assessment for ship money, PRO, SP 16/344/102 • registers, Exeter Cathedral, dean and chapter archives, D&C 3553, 3557, 3801, 3802 • Laud visitations, HLRO, Main MS 1634 • J. Walker, *An attempt towards recovering an account of the numbers and sufferings of the clergy of the Church of England*, 2 pts in 1 (1714) • Venn, *Alum. Cant.* • Wood, *Ath. Oxon.*, 1st edn • J. Harley, *Orlando Gibbons and the Gibbons family of musicians* (1999)

Gibbons, Ellis (*bap.* **1573**, *d.* **1603**). *See under* Gibbons, Edward (*bap.* 1568, *d.* in or before 1650).

Gibbons, Grinling (1648–1721), woodcarver and sculptor, was born on 14 April 1648 in Rotterdam, the Netherlands, one of four known children of James Gibbons (*fl.* 1637–1659), draper, and Elizabeth Grinling (*fl.* 1637–1659). Both his parents were English. James Gibbons had been admitted to the freedom of the Drapers' Company in London in 1638, and Elizabeth Grinling was the daughter of an English tobacco merchant in Rotterdam. The name Grinling, so often mispronounced and misspelt even in Gibbons's own day (Grinlin, Grinlen, Grinilin, Greenlin, Grindlin, Grinsted, Gringling, Gringlin, Grialin, Griblin, Grymlin, Grimling, Grimblin, and Grumblin do not exhaust the list of examples) is a metronymic, memorializing his mother's maiden name. Elizabeth Grinling's great-grandfather was Sir Simon Hansacre of Worcestershire. James Gibbons's father was a freeman of the Merchant Taylors' Company, and his grandfather a husbandman in Northamptonshire. Although it is likely that English was Grinling Gibbons's first language, the phonetic spellings in his six surviving letters show that he spoke English with a Dutch accent, and the Dutch-inspired diacritical marks he introduces into his English writing suggest that he was also literate in Dutch.

Early training and the *King David* relief Gibbons did not emigrate to England until he was past his apprenticeship years, 'about 19 years of Age', according to his contemporary Thomas Murray, in a memoir transcribed by George Vertue (Vertue, *Note books*, 1.125–6); he may have been drawn by the prospect of a construction boom after the great fire of London (1666). The spectacular high-relief foliage carving by which Gibbons is remembered has its roots in an early training in European wood sculpture techniques, but where these were inculcated is unknown. Gibbons is traditionally assumed to have been apprenticed to Artus Quellinus (1609–1668), sculptor of the town hall of Amsterdam, or to his cousin Artus Quellinus (1625–1700), who worked mainly in Antwerp. The marble relief

Grinling Gibbons (1648–1721), by Sir Godfrey Kneller, *c.*1690

sculpture of the Amsterdam town hall undoubtedly influenced Gibbons when he turned his attention fully to decorative carving, and the broad scope of most Netherlandish workshops meant that Gibbons's apprenticeship probably included an introduction to marble and stone and the full-scale human figure. But Gibbons did not arrive in England with the same focus on the marble medium and the large human figure seen in other émigré sculptors from the Quellinus and similar workshops. Instead Gibbons's first documented work takes the form of small-scale wood statuettes and figural reliefs, in a tradition leading back to the great limewood carvers of the German Renaissance. Such sculpture was part of the production of the Quellinus and many other north European workshops, making it difficult in the absence of documentation to place Gibbons's apprenticeship. One or two fugitive hints that an early *wanderjahr* may have taken Gibbons as far as Italy remain uncorroborated.

Upon his arrival in England (*c.*1667) the young carver went first to York, where he worked in a journeyman capacity under the architect and builder John Etty (*c.*1634–1708). Gibbons's own training and agenda is revealed by his earliest surviving work, the small boxwood *King David* relief (*c.*1667–70; priv. coll.) after Johannes Sadeler I (1550–*c.*1600), whose engraving is after Peter Candid (1548–1628; born Peter de Witte). In this composition David plays the harp and St Cecilia the organ, amid a heavenly consort of musicians singing a motet by Orlando di Lasso (1532–1594); Gibbons's choice of this subject is the first suggestion of the strong musical interest that would emerge in his later carving. At York Gibbons is also known to have produced a 6 inch by 4 inch wood sculpture depicting Elijah with a juniper tree and an angel. This is now lost, as is a boxwood portrait of Charles II that he may also have produced during these years.

These early carvings suggest that Gibbons arrived in England with a finer set of tools than those possessed by native-born carvers, a familiarity with exotic European media such as boxwood and limewood (rather than oak, the traditional material of English carvers), and ambitions to produce figural reliefs and statuettes in the style of European wood sculptors.

The Tintoretto *Crucifixion* relief; discoveries of Gibbons by John Evelyn and Sir Peter Lely By 1670 Gibbons had moved to the royal dockyard town of Deptford, where according to Murray he supported himself by ship carving. It was here, near the beginning of 1671, in 'a poore solitary thatched house in a field', that his famous discovery by the diarist John Evelyn occurred (Evelyn, *Diary*, 3.567, 21 Jan 1671). Happening to glance in the cottage window as he walked past one day, Evelyn perceived the young carver at work on a limewood relief after Tintoretto's *Crucifixion* (1565; Scuola di San Rocco, Venice); Gibbons had before him the engraving by Agostino Carracci. Evelyn asked to be admitted, and upon entering found himself astonished at 'the curiosity of handling, drawing & studious exactnesse' of Gibbons's sculpture, and charmed by the young man's reserved and pleasing manner (ibid.). He describes Gibbons as 'likewise *Musical*, & very Civil, sober & discreete in his discourse' (ibid., 568). Evelyn seems to have felt socially at ease with Gibbons, who in later years wrote in familiar (if less than perfectly literate) terms to at least one of his patrons. That Gibbons was unusually handsome is suggested by the earliest surviving portrait of him, a chalk drawing by Sir John Medina (*c.*1686; BM).

Although its authenticity has been questioned by those unfamiliar with the trajectory of Gibbons's early career, the limewood *Crucifixion* relief now at Dunham Massey, Cheshire, assuredly is Gibbons's Deptford carving. The posing of Gibbons's figures is sometimes awkward, but more startling are the hard, flat, conventionalized (though finely detailed) blossoms that make up the frame of the relief, evidence that Gibbons had yet to develop the fluent naturalism of his later foliage carving.

Within a month Evelyn brought Christopher Wren and Samuel Pepys to visit Gibbons in his obscure cottage. Wren's reaction to the *Crucifixion* relief is unrecorded by Evelyn, but the fact that Gibbons played no part in Wren's early rebuilding of London after the great fire suggests that he did not fully share Evelyn's response to the sculpture. More than a decade was to pass before Gibbons was hired for any Wren project, by which time the carver had established his reputation by other means.

On 1 March that year Evelyn presented Gibbons and his Tintoretto relief to Charles II at Whitehall Palace. Although the king seemed to react favourably, he did not purchase the sculpture, and when one of Queen Catherine's dressing-ladies 'began to find faults with several things in the worke, which she understood no more than an Asse or Monky' (Evelyn, *Diary*, 1 March 1671, 3.572), the indignant Evelyn immediately had the carving taken away. Gibbons had originally set its price at £100 but later sold the carving to Sir George Viner for £80.

Gibbons seems to have retained his interest in figural relief sculpture even as the tides of his career carried him towards decorative carving; at his death he was reported to have amassed 'a fine collection of picture Models & other Curiosities' (Vertue, *Note books* 1.126). His most impressive sculpture of this kind, *The Stoning of St Stephen* (uncertain date; V&A), seems to have been done for his own pleasure, and according to Horace Walpole was 'long preserved in the Sculptor's own house' (Walpole, vol. 2, p. 169). No direct pictorial source has been found for this relief, with its finely executed backdrop of architectural façades. The influence of paintings of scenes of martyrdom is evident, however, especially Giorgio Vasari's altarpiece for the church of Santo Stefano dei Cavalieri, Pisa (1571). No print after this painting has been found, suggesting the possibility that Gibbons (who is known to have collected and dealt in pictures) had acquired a drawing.

After his rejection at Whitehall Gibbons may have concluded that virtuoso wood sculptures on religious themes did not make for a promising career in Restoration England. When he emerges into the light again, later in 1671, it is not as a figural sculptor but as a carver of decoration, commissioned by Thomas Betterton (1635–1710) to produce the carved ornament for his new Dorset Garden Theatre (dem.). Here Gibbons was discovered again, this time by a figure no less influential than Evelyn and rather more useful to Gibbons's career: the court artist Sir Peter Lely (1618–1680), who admired 'particularly the Capitals cornishes & Eagles' (Vertue, *Note books*, 1.125) in the theatre and made enquiries after the carver. Lely was a close friend of Hugh May (1621–1684), who was to become the architect for the most important royal project of the time, Charles II's rebuilding of Windsor Castle.

The advocacy of Lely and May, rather than Evelyn and Wren, produced the commissions that allowed Gibbons to invent his new decorative style. Almost certainly it was Hugh May who secured Gibbons's employment at Holme Lacy, Herefordshire, and Cassiobury Park, Hertfordshire, in the mid-1670s, his first major country-house commissions. And it was May together with Lely who arranged a second presentation to the king, this time at Windsor Castle at the outset of May's rebuilding (*c.*1675). Now Gibbons displayed to the monarch not a European relief sculpture but 'one great Chimney peice of carving in wood … representing a feston of many fishes shells & other ornaments' (Vertue, *Note books*, 1.126). This time the king immediately hired Gibbons, whose subsequent decorative work at Windsor Castle (*c.*1676–82) set the seal of royal approval on his new high-relief foliage style, and established his fame.

Family, residences, and royal appointments The surname of Gibbons's wife, Elizabeth (buried 30 November 1719), is unknown, as is the date and place of their marriage. But their first child, James, was baptized in St Botolph, Aldgate, London, on 23 May 1672, a date that is consistent with the surmise that Gibbons's stay in Deptford ended in the middle of 1671 with his marriage and move to London. Elizabeth Gibbons gave birth to at least twelve children; neither Grinling (*b.* 1675) nor any other son survived to maturity. At least five daughters lived into adulthood, but Gibbons's direct line is believed to have become extinct shortly after his own death.

By 1672 Gibbons's address is recorded as La Belle Sauvage, an inn on Ludgate Hill just below St Paul's Cathedral. Here he carved a pot of flowers 'of light wood so thin & fine that the coaches passing by made them shake surprizingly' (Vertue, *Note books*, 4.11). Gibbons retained these premises as a workshop at least into the 1680s. In January 1672 Gibbons was admitted by patrimony to the Drapers' Company. He became a livery man in 1685, was elected renter warden in 1705, second master warden in 1712, and master warden in 1714, and in 1718, 1719, and 1720 stood unsuccessfully for the mastership of the company. Gibbons was also a member of the exclusive St Luke's Club, a small fraternity of distinguished artists and virtuosi; he served as the club's steward in 1691 and 1709. In 1672 Gibbons registered the first of his nine apprentices appearing in the Drapers' records; his large workshop drew others into its orbit, both journeymen and skilled independent carvers and sculptors.

By 1678 Gibbons and his growing family had moved to Bow Street, Covent Garden, a fashionable London neighbourhood popular with well-to-do artists such as Lely. A double portrait by John Closterman, which survives only in the engraving by John Smith (*c.*1691), shows Gibbons and his wife surrounded by conventional trappings of success: rich fabric and noble classical architecture fill the scene; Elizabeth Gibbons fingers a string of pearls while Gibbons himself adopts a complacent pose. Gibbons's house in Bow Street was 'furnish'd like a Cabinet, not onely with his own work, but divers excellent Paintings of the best hands' (Evelyn, *Diary*, 8 Aug 1679, 4.179). The house collapsed in January 1702 and was rebuilt as a substantial brick structure, which Gibbons then insured for the sizable sum of £700. A 'summer house' stood at the rear of the property.

Gibbons's long-delayed appointment as master sculptor and carver in wood was eventually made by William III on 2 December 1693 upon the death of the incumbent, the obscure Henry Phillips; in practice Gibbons had held that position for many years. Gibbons also received a late, somewhat odd appointment as master carpenter to the crown on 11 November 1719. Gibbons died intestate at his home in Bow Street on 3 August 1721, and on 10 August was buried in London at St Paul's, Covent Garden, where his wife had been buried two years before. An unmarried daughter, Elizabeth, administered her father's estate. On 15 November 1722 (probably Vertue's error for 1721) a sale of his collection was held. Vertue reports that Gibbons's paintings, books, and drawings sold for 'about 840 pounds (besides moddels)' (Vertue, *Note books*, 3.10), and that two 'chimney peices carv'd in Wood by himself of festoons fruit & flowers. fish & fowl' were offered for 100 guineas and 120 guineas, '& for no less' (ibid., p. 9).

Early overmantels; reredos carvings Gibbons's training in European wood sculpture provided him with the tools, the medium, and the technical skills that made it possible for him to develop a new kind of carved decoration. Rather than using oak, Gibbons retained his European sculptural medium, limewood (linden wood), with its remarkable working properties and striking pale tone. And instead of the conventionalizing treatment of foliage prevalent in Britain, Gibbons's more sculptural approach to botanical subjects gave them an unprecedented realism. His carved flowers, fruit, and foliage took inspiration from the Dutch still-life painting of his day, and like the wave of European flower painters who emigrated to London during these years, Gibbons catered to the growing British taste for naturalism. The firmness, crispness, and strength of limewood allowed a new fineness of detail and radically thin undercutting, and the appliqué character of Gibbons's carvings allowed them to be completely pierced in many places. Gibbons left his wood without finish except on very rare occasions when it was gilded, or whitened to match marble. The paleness of natural limewood, contrasting with the oak panelling to which it was nailed, suddenly brought carving to the fore of any decorative scheme.

In his work for Windsor Castle, and for Cassiobury Park and Holme Lacy before it, Gibbons adopted as his principal vehicle the three-sided carved surround, consisting of a cresting (called by Gibbons the 'top pees') and two side drops. This was an established decorative form in England by the time of Gibbons's arrival, most notably in the work of Edward Pierce (*c.*1635–1695) and Cornelius Austin (*fl.* *c.*1665–*c.*1700). At Windsor Castle, where Gibbons's first bills began appearing in 1676–7, Gibbons's surrounds tend to impress by opulence and scale rather than any delicate orchestration of forms. There is often a pattern of slight asymmetry between the side drops, which at other times turn into cascades of foliage unrelieved by groupings of material.

Sir Jeffry Wyatville's remodelling of the interior of the Chapel Royal in 1827, with the attendant loss of almost all Gibbons's carving, has deprived later generations of the work at Windsor that most impressed his contemporaries. In his diary entry for 16 June 1683 Evelyn's enthusiasm was unbounded, and in 1698 Celia Fiennes called the Chapel Royal woodcarving 'the pattern and masterpiece of all such work … so thinn the wood and all white natural wood without varnish' (*Illustrated Journeys*, 218). One consequence of this triumph was the granting to Gibbons of a pension of £100 per annum 'for repairing cleansing and preserving the carved work in Windsor Castle' (Colvin, 328), an award that attests to the value attached by his contemporaries to the whiteness of Gibbons's carving.

Gibbons's most forward-looking work at Windsor Castle is his carving for the alcoves in the King's dining room (*c.*1676–8), where the incorporation of large game creatures has the effect of encouraging decisive groupings and a rhythmic formal order in the design. In his country-house work of the 1670s and early 1680s Gibbons developed the game overmantel, in which a foliage design similarly is interlarded with the dramatic shapes of birds, fish, and crustaceans. Examples can be found at Sudbury Hall, Derbyshire (1678), and at Badminton House, Gloucestershire (1683). Gibbons's fashionable new limewood style was quickly taken up by native English carvers, and the game overmantel became the chief vehicle for the dispersal of his style across Britain.

Gibbons's first work for a Wren building was his large reredos carving for St James's, Piccadilly (1684). The cresting of this massive surround is crowned by pierced acanthus whorls. This device, which introduces an airy vortex motion into a design, was one of Gibbons's distinctive innovations and subjected by him to continuous experimentation. Gibbons's only other altar carving for a Wren interior was at St Mary Abchurch (1686), in the City of London. His letter of 12 May 1686 to a churchwarden there suggests that on matters of design and payment Gibbons dealt not with Wren but directly with church officials (Guildhall Library, London, MS 3925). Since it was one of Gibbons's patrons, Sir Robert Gayer, who paid for the altar at St James's Piccadilly, it is likely that in both churches Gibbons was operating as an independent contractor rather than an employee of Wren. Gibbons's third reredos, for the chapel at Trinity College, Oxford (*c.*1693), is the most elegant of his altar carvings. With its small cresting area and its narrow drops, the form of this subtly drawn, finely cut surround resembles that of a princely overmantel.

The 'Cosimo' and 'Modena' panels Though it dates from relatively early in Gibbons's career, the 'Cosimo' panel (so named by David Green in 1964) is widely regarded as his supreme masterpiece. Gibbons was paid £150 for the carving, which was commissioned in 1682 by Charles II and sent as a gift to Cosimo III de' Medici, the duke of Tuscany; it remains in the Palazzo Pitti, Florence. Offered the prospect of his work being displayed in a sophisticated European court, Gibbons rose to the occasion by inventing an extravagant version of a 'trophy' carving here celebrating not the triumphs of war or the hunt, but the benefits of good governance and the arts of peace. Gibbons's design takes the form of a broad four-sided foliage border enclosing an assemblage of objects symbolizing political authority, love, sculpture, painting, music, and human ingenuity generally, among other things including a portrait medallion of Pietro da Cortona (1596–1669) and a carved facsimile of a page of music from a guitar instruction book published in London in 1682.

Gibbons's second Italian presentation panel was almost certainly occasioned by the death of Charles II in 1685. It was probably commissioned by the king's brother and successor James II, or by James's wife Mary, and sent as a gift to her father Alfonso IV, duke of Modena. Whereas the 'Cosimo' panel celebrates princely friendship, the 'Modena' panel (*c.*1686; Galleria Estense, Modena) laments 'Death the Leveller', and especially the death of princes. Among its *vanitas* imagery it includes a sheet of music with a famous lyric by the playwright James Shirley (*bap.*

1596, *d.* 1666). Gibbons, not surprisingly given his musical interests, uses a musician's version of the text:

> The Glories of our birth and State,
> are shadows not substantial things.

This panel has sustained damage at almost every point, making it difficult to gauge the richness of the original composition. The 'Cosimo' and 'Modena' panels are the only two woodcarvings to bear Gibbons's signature, and in each case he adds the word 'Inventor' after his name to assert that he is the designer of the composition as well as its maker.

Gibbons also is likely to have carved the 'Cullen' panel (date uncertain; priv. coll.), which now in large part is made up of replacement work by the Victorian restorer W. G. Rogers. In the 'Kirtlington' panel (*c.*1690–1700; priv. coll.) Gibbons took up once again the fish, fowl, and crustaceans of his earlier years, here modelled with unmatched realism and arranged in an exquisitely balanced still-life tableau.

Woodcarving of the 1690s The Whitehall Palace fire of 1698 has deprived us of what were probably Gibbons's most impressive and innovative chimney-pieces, for the apartments of James II (*c.*1687) and William and Mary (*c.*1689). At least two of these were floor-to-ceiling 'continued' chimney-pieces, made up of marble mantelpieces with human figures, limewood overmantels (for which Gibbons was paid £55 and £60, his highest prices for overmantel carving), and in one case a marble relief with Goliath as its subject. That these chimney-pieces were of Gibbons's own design is demonstrated by his accomplished drawings with similar combinations of materials and figures collected in the 'Hampton Court album' (Sir John Soane's Museum, London). These thirty-nine sheets were probably unspecific proposals intended to elicit commissions similar to those at Whitehall Palace, but now for the 1689–94 phase of Wren's construction at Hampton Court. Queen Mary's death in 1694 halted royal projects before any of these inventive designs could be executed.

Something of the flavour of the more ambitious, trophy-filled Soane designs comes over in Gibbons's greatest work in England, in the Carved Room (*c.*1692) at Petworth House, Sussex. Here Gibbons adopted a unique double surround form which generated added space for trophy groupings in a middle drop, and in a huge cresting area above. Among the best-known details are a pair of Grecian vases especially admired by Horace Walpole, and a grouping of exceptionally accurate musical instruments with notated sheets of music from Henry Purcell's *The Fairy Queen*.

Gibbons's delight in illusionism is also revealed by the *trompe-l'œil* point lace cravat incorporated into this music trophy. A more sumptuous example is the famous cravat owned by Horace Walpole in the eighteenth century (V&A) and once worn by him at a reception for foreign visitors to Strawberry Hill. Another is included among finely executed small carvings collected together in a panel at Chatsworth House, Derbyshire. Some of Gibbons's most exquisite swags and garlands of flowers (1691–5) embellish Wren's Library at Trinity College, Cambridge. To commemorate the library's benefactors, Gibbons provided small armorial carvings, forming a series of variations revealing his great felicity as a designer.

By far the most costly of Gibbons's woodcarving projects was his work for the choir of St Paul's Cathedral, where he was paid a total of £2992 11*s.* 4 ½*d.* for carving in lime and oak. The unusually highly modelled oak setting into which his decoration at St Paul's is incorporated, left somewhat confining spaces for Gibbons's limewood embellishments. Gibbons was probably responsible for the design of this oak decoration. His workshop had long provided enrichment of oak moulding features at royal palaces, generating income that often matched receipts from his more showy limewood work.

Gibbons's majestic carvings at Hampton Court Palace (*c.*1699–1701) embody his last surviving experiments with the overmantel form. The growth of symmetry apparent in his work since the early 1680s here reaches its climax, while at the same time Gibbons pares back his vocabulary to his quintessential language of flowers, fruits and foliage. His later designs allow for the carving to be subdivided into separate tasks assigned to individual carvers in his large and busy workshop. The quest for ease of production also impelled changes in Gibbons's construction methods. His early foliage work was carved from a thickness of several boards glued together before the work began; in his mature compositions the layers were carved first and then nailed together.

With the death of William III in 1702 and the accession of Queen Anne, fashion moved away from Gibbons's limewood carving style. Although other commissions are recorded, the only work to survive is a large reredos carving (*c.*1711) for the refitted chapel at Hampton Court. In the eighteenth century Gibbons's workshop was occupied almost entirely with work in marble and stone.

Sculpture in bronze and marble; decorative carving in stone Although Gibbons is remembered principally for his limewood carving, he also pursued a parallel and probably far more lucrative career as the master of a workshop providing statues, tomb monuments, and decorative stonework. He is first associated with a bronze equestrian statue of Charles II (1679–80) *all'antica* at Windsor Castle; the king himself chose its innovative 'accurate' Roman dress. Evelyn described the statue as the work of 'Gibbons &c.', and a payment of £400 was made to Gibbons for the elaborate marble relief carving on the pedestal (though this was probably carried out by John Nost). In the 1680s Gibbons's workshop also produced a stylistically coherent group of royal statues of the Roman victor type, including among others a large and much-praised *Charles II* (marble, 1684; now lost) for the Royal Exchange; *Charles II* (bronze, *c.*1686) which remains at the Royal Hospital, Chelsea, and the exceptionally accomplished *James II* (bronze, 1688), now outside the National Gallery in Trafalgar Square. The attribution of these works is complicated by the presence of the highly trained Flemish sculptors whom Gibbons had gathered into his workshop by the end of the 1670s.

These included Arnold Quellin (the nephew of Artus Quellinus I), John Nost, and Anthony Verhuke, joined in the next decade by, among others, Laurens Van der Meulen and Pierre Van Dievoet. Their experience and skill as makers of statues may have exceeded his own. There is no record that Gibbons himself had produced full-scale human figures, or any work at all in marble or bronze, in the decade and more since he had arrived in England. (As late as 1683 and 1684 Evelyn and Wren implied Gibbons had only recently turned to statuary work and had yet to establish his reputation in this field.) Some of these statues may have been cast from full-scale wooden models carved by Gibbons, but there is evidence that his assistants acted as designers and executants of much of the sculptural work from the Gibbons workshop.

George Vertue, for example, transcribes a poisonous story related by Gibbons's assistant Nadauld about the statue of *Charles II* in the Royal Exchange. One day when the king came to inspect the work Gibbons took up a hammer and chisel to demonstrate his skill, but 'strikeing somewhat too hard, broke off a piece that should not have been' (Vertue, *Note books*, 5.58–9). Vertue adds that 'tho he was a most excellent Carver in wood he was neither well skilld or practized. in Marble or in Brass. for which works he imployd the best Artists he coud procure' (ibid.). According to Vertue the statue of *Charles II* was actually the work of Arnold Quellin; this has been questioned, however, since the figure was produced during a turbulent period when Gibbons had brought a law suit against Quellin, his erstwhile 'servant' and then full partner (1681–3). Gibbons and Quellin patched up their relationship and co-operated to make the elaborate altar for James II's Whitehall Chapel in 1686.

That his assistants could play a central role in the design of a major commission is suggested by the finest statue from Gibbons's workshop, the bronze *James II*. Drawings that appear to be preliminary studies for this figure have survived (BM), and are not in Gibbons's hand. Vertue attributes the statue to Van der Meulen, Van Dievoet, and the wax modeller Thomas Beniere. Recent research has sought to reinstate Gibbons as the presiding creative genius of his marble and bronze workshop during the 1680s, but attributional problems surrounding Gibbons's sculptural production are unlikely ever to be fully resolved. His aspirations, at least, are clear: in Sir Godfrey Kneller's solemn portrait (late 1680s; Hermitage Museum, St Petersburg) Gibbons is portrayed as a marble figure sculptor in the European tradition, measuring a cast from Bernini's *Pluto and Proserpine*.

In the 1680s, meanwhile, Gibbons's rapidly growing business in funerary monuments soon made his the dominant stone and marble workshop of the day. His first known monument, to Sir Roger Burgoyne (*c.*1679, Sutton, Bedfordshire) has an air of clumsiness and inexperience, but the hand of Quellin can be discerned in the lively kneeling figures of John and Sir Henry Ferrers on their double monument (*c.*1681; Tamworth, Staffordshire). Other monuments with full-length figures during these years include those to Archbishop Richard Sterne (1684; York Minster); the seventh earl of Rutland and the eighth earl of Rutland (both 1684–6; Bottesford, Leicestershire); and the third Viscount Campden (1684).

Quellin died in 1686, and Van der Meulen and Van Dievoet returned to the continent in 1689. Gibbons's workshop now produced what has been described as 'a cold, but misunderstood classicism' in the human figure (Whinney, 126), mixed with baroque decorative elements. None the less his workshop continued to thrive into the eighteenth century. Among his principal monuments are those to the first duke of Beaufort with two standing figures of Justice and Truth (1701; Badminton, Gloucestershire); to Sir Cloudesley Shovell (1708; Westminster Abbey), in which the foppish presentation of 'the brave rough English admiral' drew the immediate censure of Joseph Addison; and to the first duke of Chandos (1717; Whitchurch, Middlesex), who when he saw the monument demanded a reduction in his bill, and failing in this castigated Gibbons. Gibbons's prices suggest high profits (as well as expensive materials): for the Campden and the Beaufort monuments Gibbons charged £1000.

Among over thirty monuments known to be from Gibbons's workshop are many smaller wall tablets, some like the monument to the young Robert Cotton (*d.* 1697) (Conington, Cambridgeshire) with finely carved foliage. A marble font at St James's, Piccadilly, London, depicting Adam and Eve (*c.*1685) may be from Gibbons's workshop; well documented is his somewhat cumbersome marble relief showing the meeting of Neptune and Galatea (1701; Dalkeith House, Midlothian, Scotland).

In high-relief foliage work in stone, such as the exterior decoration he provided for St Paul's Cathedral (1694–8) and Hampton Court Palace (1690s), Gibbons succeeds in transferring to the harder medium something of the fluent naturalism of his limewood carving. Martial imagery predominates in his stone work (1708–12) at Blenheim Palace, for which Gibbons's bill exceeded £4000. It is a measure of the change in his practice by then that his charges for woodcarving at Blenheim came to only £36 10*s.* 2*d.*

Achievement and reputation Gibbons invented a style of foliage woodcarving that was unprecedented in its finely modelled naturalism and subtlety of design, its startling projection and flamboyant pale tone. Long celebrated as the greatest British woodcarver, Gibbons might be said to rank among the greatest of all decorative woodcarvers, except that his intensely sculptural approach often lifts traditionally 'decorative' forms and subjects above their usual station, making his work difficult to classify. Gibbons rejected the conception of swags and drops as marginal texture for the eye, and modelled his botanical subject matter with the attentiveness that a sculptor might bestow on the human form. In the 'Cosimo' panel (and later in the 'Modena' and 'Kirtlington' panels) Gibbons went further, moving woodcarving from decorative margin to the centre of attention, to create what was described by its recipient Cosimo (III) de' Medici as a 'quadro d'Intaglio in Legno' ('carved picture in wood'; PRO, SP 101/80): a still-life painting turned into a three dimensional tableau. The great illusionistic trophy groupings in Gibbons's later surrounds similarly establish a middle ground between sculpture, ornament, and still-life composition.

Made fashionable by Charles II's commissions at Windsor Castle in the mid-1670s, Gibbons's huge overmantels of flowers, fruits, leaves, and game were immediately imitated by native-born carvers. High-relief foliage ornament became a distinctive feature of grand English baroque interiors during the last quarter of the seventeenth century and well into the eighteenth century in provincial contexts. The skills of many of the carvers who flourished during these years—especially Edmund Carpenter, John Selden, Samuel Watson, Jonathan Maine, Thomas Young, and John Le Sage—sometimes approached Gibbons's own, causing many later misattributions. Gibbons's style remained a uniquely British phenomenon, save for isolated instances (his assistant Laurens Van der Meulen, for example, carved foliage frames somewhat in the manner of Gibbons upon his return to the continent).

Gibbons's achievement as a sculptor in marble and bronze is more equivocal. In an important series of royal statues his workshop introduced the 'Roman emperor' figure to Britain. Gibbons's sculpture practice 'bridges the gap between the Berninesque art of Bushnell and the mature classical-baroque of Michael Rysback' (Whinney, 129). In the period between 1679 and 1686 the more supple work of his Flemish assistants often conceals Gibbons's own stiffly solid classicism. Examples of his sculpture from later years, when his workshop was staffed by less able carvers, make it clear that the fluency that permeates Gibbons's woodcarving is absent from his treatment of the human figure. Absent, too, is the humanity and psychological insight that animate portrait busts by Gibbons's near-contemporary, Edward Pierce.

In the early 1680s Evelyn and others predicted that Gibbons would rise to pre-eminence as a sculptor of the human figure in marble. In the event, Gibbons's sculptural career was carried out against a background of workshop quarrels, complaints by unhappy clients, and often the selection of rival sculptors for important public commissions. But it was a story of commercial success. In an age otherwise distinguished mainly by the work of Caius Gabriel Cibber (1630–1700), John Nost (*fl.* 1678–1729), and William Stanton (1639–1705), Gibbons's tomb and monument workshop was able to win the lion's share of important commissions, at least until his erstwhile assistant Francis Bird (1667–1731) set up a competitive practice early in the eighteenth century.

It was as a woodcarver that Gibbons's fame was established, however, and it is as a woodcarver that his fame has persisted. His influence on practitioners of the craft reached beyond that of his particular style; carvers have admired the technical prowess that in his hands makes wood seem a flexible substance, modelled like clay rather than carved. Among the general public Gibbons is one of a few genuinely popular British artists; in 1914 Avray Tipping observed that his name was 'a household word' (Tipping, xi). Gibbons's carving usually is without symbolic references, requiring no special knowledge for its enjoyment. Its cunning execution, together with its sculptural presence, has preserved the appeal of Gibbons's work through times when carved decoration was out of fashion.

In the nineteenth century foliage carving in Gibbons's manner was revived by craftsmen such as Edward Wyatt (1757–1833) and William Gibbs Rogers (1792–1872), and, by the end of the century, by émigré carvers in North America. Meanwhile, insensitive restorations of Gibbons's own carvings were often carried out, giving decidedly inferior replacement work pride of place in many Gibbons compositions; the already-darkened carvings were often varnished, effacing the pale tone essential to their effect. Wholesale misattributions further muddied his achievement, and at the same time Gibbons's name, like Thomas Chippendale's, diffused to become synonymous with the style he invented.

Soon after his death the life of Gibbons became encrusted with legend and lore. In the eighteenth century George Vertue even-handedly transcribed into his notebooks contradictory reports about the carver. Many of the errors transcribed by Vertue and a few of his own making appear in Horace Walpole's *Anecdotes of Painting in England* (1762–71). Walpole confirmed Gibbons's place in the canon of English artists, however, and his evident affection for his work produced the finest eulogy to Gibbons's essential achievement: 'There is no instance of a man before Gibbons who gave to wood the loose and airy lightness of flowers, and chained together the various productions of the elements with a free disorder natural to each species' (Walpole, vol. 2, p. 168). The publication of John Evelyn's diary in 1818 brought to light the dramatic details of Gibbons's discovery in Deptford, an account that greatly appealed to the Victorian reader. Gibbons became the subject of a fanciful historical painting by Edward Matthew Ward, *Grinling Gibbons' First Introduction to the Royal Court* (1869; priv. coll.), and a sentimental novel by Austin Clare, *The Carved Cartoon* (1874); in the twentieth century a melodramatic children's play was adapted from the latter.

In the popular imagination Gibbons was imbued with an unusually vivid life, and a number of stories about the carver were transmitted orally down the generations. The most famous of these is the apparently undying myth that Gibbons included a peapod in his carvings as a form of signature, open, it is sometimes said, if he had received his payment for the commission. Until recently Gibbons's formidable carving technique was widely regarded as a lost secret, but conservation work after the fire at Hampton Court Palace in 1986 caused several of his methods to be rediscovered. An exhibition of Gibbons's work at the Victoria and Albert Museum, 'Grinling Gibbons and the Art of Carving' (1998), on the 350th anniversary of his birth also broadened understanding of the carver; it drew large crowds, suggesting that Grinling Gibbons's distinctive name has remained lodged in the nation's collective memory.

DAVID ESTERLY

Sources Vertue, *Note books* • Evelyn, *Diary* • H. Walpole, *Anecdotes of painting in England*, ed. R. Wornum, new edn, 3 vols. (1849); repr. (1876) • *The illustrated journeys of Celia Fiennes, c.1682–1712* (1984) • *The diary of Ralph Thoresby … now published from the original manuscript*, 2 vols. (1830) • A. Cunningham, *The lives of the most eminent British painters, sculptors, and architects*, 6 vols. (1829–33) • administration, PRO, PROB 6/97, fol. 188*r* • D. Green, *Grinling Gibbons: his work as carver and statuary* (1964) • H. A. Tipping, *Grinling Gibbons and the woodwork of his age* (1914) • G. Beard, *The works of Grinling Gibbons* (1989) [incl. survey of Gibbons's monumental work] • D. Esterly, *Grinling Gibbons and the art of carving* (1998) • H. M. Colvin and others, eds., *The history of the king's works*, 5 (1976) • M. Whinney, *Sculpture in Britain, 1530 to 1830*, rev. J. Physick, 2nd edn (1988) • K. Gibson, 'The emergence of Grinling Gibbons as a "statuary"', *Apollo*, 150 (Sept 1999), 21–9 • L. E. Lock, lecture delivered at the V&A, 27 Jan 1999 • L. Sayce and D. Esterly, '"He was likewise *Musical* …": an unexplored aspect of Grinling Gibbons', *Apollo*, 460 (June 2000), 11–21

Archives BM, department of prints and drawings, drawings, proposal for a monument to William and Mary • GL, drawings, proposals for organ cases for St Paul's Cathedral | All Souls Oxf., drawings, proposal for two overmantels at Hampton Court Palace, proposal for a monument to Queen Mary, proposal for figures in a mausoleum for Charles I, sometimes attributed to Gibbons • BL, Evelyn MSS, diary of John Evelyn • Bodl. Oxf., drawings, proposal for the saloon, Blenheim Palace • Bodl. Oxf., receipts for work done in York Minster • GL, St Paul's Cathedral building accounts • PRO, AO 1/2478/270 (E351/3450), AO 1/2479/272, works 5/42, C9/415/250

Likenesses J. Medina, chalk drawing, *c*.1686, BM • G. Kneller, oils, *c*.1690, Hermitage Museum, St Petersburg [*see illus.*] • J. Smith, mezzotint, 1690 (after G. Kneller), NPG • J. Smith, double portrait, mezzotint, *c*.1691 (with his wife; after J. Closterman, now lost), BM, NPG • G. Gibbons(?), self-portrait(?), medallion, Chatsworth House, Derbyshire • G. Kneller, oils, copy, NPG • double portrait, chalk drawing (with his wife; after J. Closterman), Scot. NPG • mezzotint, NPG

Wealth at death paintings, books, and drawings sold for 'about 840 pounds (besides moddels)': Green, *Grinling Gibbons*, 175; Vertue, *Note books*, 3.10

Gibbons, John (1544–1589), Jesuit, was born in the diocese of Bath and Wells, possibly at Bridgwater, Somerset. He was educated at Wells grammar school and in 1561 matriculated at Lincoln College, Oxford. He left Oxford without a degree and in 1569 entered the German College, Rome. There he graduated DPhil and DTh in 1576. Pope Gregory XIII presented him to a canonry in Bonn, which he resigned in 1578 in order to enter the Society of Jesus, which he did at Trier on 8 October of that year. His younger brother Richard *Gibbons (1547/1553–1632) also became a Jesuit.

In 1583 Gibbons was asked to go on the English mission, but declined on the grounds that he lacked the necessary courage, promising instead to do all he could with his pen. Accordingly he set about compiling a volume of important letters and papers relating to the persecution of Catholics in England. The complete work was published at Trier as *Concertatio ecclesiae catholicae in Anglia* (1583), containing copies of many original documents, especially relating to Edmund Campion, and Latin editions of works on the persecution by Robert Parsons and William Allen. The purpose of this important collection was presumably to influence educated opinion on the continent in favour of the English Catholics. A much expanded second edition appeared in 1588.

By 1584 Gibbons was rector of the Jesuit college in Trier. In 1583 and 1584 he presided at academic disputations in the university, respectively on communion in both kinds and on the cult of the saints, subsequently published as *De sacrosancte eucharistiae* (1583) and *Disputatio theologica de sanctis* (1584). Under the pseudonym Joannes Aquapontanus he wrote *Confutatio virulentae disputationis Georgii Sohn* (1589). In August or September 1589 he died while on a visit to the monastery of Himmelrode, near Trier.

PAUL ARBLASTER

Sources D. M. Rogers, introduction, in [J. Gibbons and J. Fenn], *Concertatio ecclesiae catholicae in Anglia adversus Calvinopapistas et puritanos* (1970) • T. M. McCoog, *The Society of Jesus in Ireland, Scotland, and England, 1541–1588* (1996) • T. M. McCoog, *English and Welsh Jesuits, 1555–1650*, 2, Catholic RS, 75 (1995), 190, 343 • A. de Backer and others, *Bibliothèque de la Compagnie de Jésus*, new edn, 3, ed. C. Sommervogel (Brussels, 1892), 1402–3 • M. E. Williams, 'Campion and the English continental seminaries', *The reckoned expense: Edmund Campion and the early English Jesuits*, ed. T. M. McCoog (1996), 285–9 • Gillow, *Lit. biog. hist.*, 2.437

Gibbons, John (1703–1778). *See under* Gibbons family (*per. c*.1735–1863).

Gibbons, John (1777–1851). *See under* Gibbons family (*per. c*.1735–1863).

Gibbons, Orlando (*bap.* 1583, *d.* 1625), composer and keyboard player, was born in Oxford and baptized there at St Martin's, Carfax, on 25 December 1583, the youngest son of William Gibbons (*d.* 1595) and his wife, Mary (*d.* 1603), later landlady of an inn. William was a 'wait', a town musician, in Cambridge from 1567, held a similar post in Oxford from 1580 to 1588, and then moved back to Cambridge. William's eldest surviving son, Edward *Gibbons, was master of the choristers at King's College, Cambridge (1592–8), and later lay vicar and (by dispensation) succentor of Exeter Cathedral, being appointed 'teacher of the choristers' in 1608, a post he held until the interregnum. His third son, Ellis *Gibbons [*see under* Gibbons, Edward] was also a composer, contributing one madrigal, or perhaps two, to Morley's *The Triumphes of Oriana* (1601).

From February 1596 until autumn 1598 Orlando Gibbons was a chorister at King's College, Cambridge, under his brother Edward. He entered the university, and was a sizar of King's College. He was in Cambridge to witness his mother's will in March 1603. Payments to a person named Gibbons in King's College accounts between 1595/6 and 1601/2 'pro musica in festo Dominae Reginae' and 'pro musica in festo purificationis' may relate to services by the town waits whom his father previously led (Harley, 13).

Early career and marriage From 1603 until his death Gibbons was a musician in the Chapel Royal. His name first appears in the Chapel Royal cheque book in a list of forty-one signatories to an agreement on conditions of service under James I, dated 19 May 1603. According to a summary of appointments in the cheque book compiled about 1627, he was formally sworn in as gentleman of the Chapel Royal on 21 March 1605, succeeding Arthur Cock who, as organist of Exeter Cathedral (1598–1602), knew Edward Gibbons. Between 1603 and 1605 Gibbons may have served as gentleman-extraordinary (that is, unsalaried substitute). Although he was renowned as a keyboard player, not until 1615 is there a record in the cheque book naming him (with Edmund Hooper) as one of the two organists of the Chapel Royal.

On 17 February 1606 Gibbons married Elizabeth (*bap.* 1590, *d.* 1626), daughter of John Patten (*d.* 1623), yeoman of the vestry of the Chapel Royal, at St Mary Woolchurch in the City of London. By 1609 Gibbons was living in the Woolstaple (now Bridge Street) in the parish of St Margaret, Westminster, where many court musicians and servants resided. The couple's seven children were baptized at St Margaret's, among them the eldest surviving son, the composer Christopher *Gibbons, named after his patron, Sir Christopher Hatton (*d.* 1619). Hatton was second cousin and heir of Sir Christopher Hatton (1540–1591), Queen Elizabeth's lord chancellor. It was to him that Gibbons dedicated *The First Set of Madrigals and Mottets* (1612), claiming to have composed the works in Hatton's house. This may have been his house in Faringdon near St Bartholomew-the-Great, rather than Clayhall, Barking, or Kirby Hall, Northamptonshire, or the house in Westminster (close to that of Gibbons) that he occupied from 1612. Hatton was only a minor figure of the gentry, but his wife was sister to Sir Henry Fanshawe, patron of music and an officer in the household of Henry, prince of Wales.

Career in court music Apart from his association with Hatton, Gibbons's career was centred on the court. His endeavours and compositions suggest that he hoped for significant preferment there. In 1611 he petitioned the queen as 'an humble suitor' for her help to gain a lease worth 40 marks (£26 14*s.* 2*d.*), a matter referred to Lord Salisbury. He was the junior of the three contributors to *Parthenia* (the others being John Bull and William Byrd), the keyboard collection published to celebrate the marriage of the king's daughter, Princess Elizabeth, to Frederick, elector palatine, in 1613: the prominence of the notes E and F in *The Queen's Command* suggests a specific wedding tribute. The pavan and galliard 'Lord Salisbury', the wedding anthem 'Blessed are all they' (1613) for the earl of Somerset, and anthems associated with senior clergy who held royal chaplaincies (Godfrey Goodman, William Laud, and Anthony Maxey) imply that he was well connected in court circles. On 26 June 1614 a payment to him of 60*s.* was authorized by royal warrant for the annual feast of the gentlemen of the Chapel Royal. On 19 July 1615 he was rewarded by two grants totalling £150 from James I 'for and in consideration of the good and faithful service heretofore done unto ourself by Orlando Gibbons our organist' (PRO, SP 39/5 m. 38; Ashbee, 8.73). He composed an anthem, 'Great king of gods', and a court song, 'Do not repine, fair sun', for the king's visit to Scotland in 1617, attended by the Chapel Royal. In 1613 someone named Gibbons accompanied Princess Elizabeth after her marriage on the journey to Heidelberg as an attendant of the earl of Arundel (John Coprario and the harpist Daniel Callinder attended the duke of Lennox). By this time Gibbons was the most talented keyboard player and keyboard composer available to the court. His eminent predecessors Byrd and Bull had acknowledged his prowess by including his music in *Parthenia*; but Byrd was long retired to Essex, and Bull, who had worked in the households of both Prince Henry and Princess Elizabeth, had fled abroad.

The king's eldest surviving son, Charles, became prince of Wales at the age of sixteen in 1616, and Gibbons is listed in the first payments of 1617 as one of seventeen musicians who formed the nucleus of the prince's musical establishment. A number of them had previously served Prince Henry. Charles's regular musicians also included the younger Alfonso Ferrabosco, Thomas Ford, Robert Johnson, the elder Thomas Lupo, and Angelo Notari. Each received an annual salary of £40. Among other musicians associated with Charles's musical establishment, John Coprario seems to have been particularly important: what was later to become 'the lutes and voices' in the Caroline court was formed in the prince's household at this time, and both Coprario and Gibbons composed for the ensemble.

Gibbons added a third post associated with the court, as virginalist, in September 1619. The accounts of the king's treasurer of the chamber record: 'Orlando Gibbons to attend in His Highnesses Privy Chamber which was heretofore supplied by Walter Earle deceased at £46 per annum from Michaelmas 1619'. The dedication of the first printing of Gibbons's *Fantasies of Three Parts* to Edmund Wray, groom of the privy chamber, may be significant: Wray was a protégé of George Villiers, then a favourite of Prince Charles and a rising court star, before his disgrace and banishment from court in 1622. A fourth post was added in 1623, when Gibbons and Thomas Day, a fellow member of both the Chapel Royal and the prince's household, jointly succeeded John Parsons at Westminster Abbey as organist and master of the choristers. At this time almost half of the singing men at Westminster Abbey were also gentlemen of the Chapel Royal. An account of the visit of the French ambassador and his retinue to the abbey on 15 December 1624 on the betrothal of Henrietta Maria to Charles records that 'at their entrance, the organ was touched by the best finger of that age, Mr. Orlando Gibbons' (Hacket, 210). One royal favour seems not to have borne fruit: a monopoly to make strings for instruments granted to Gibbons and four others, recorded at the signet office in May 1622, was withdrawn at the last minute, probably because of general parliamentary opposition to monopolies. At the funeral of James I in March 1625 Orlando Gibbons was listed among the Chapel Royal as senior organist in the cheque book and as privy organist in the lord chamberlain's accounts; he was also listed as organist of Westminster Abbey in the lord chamberlain's accounts.

Gibbons had taken the degree of MusB at Cambridge in 1606. There is now some doubt as to whether he was admitted to the degree of DMus at Oxford (Harley, 64–6). William Heather, also a gentleman of the Chapel Royal, received the degree on 17 May 1622, and both Anthony

Wood and William Gostling assert that Gibbons's 'O clap your hands' was used as Heather's 'commencement song'. The version of a letter dated 18 May 1622 and printed by William Camden, which he received from the vice-chancellor, William Piers, states that Gibbons received the degree, but there is no record of it in the university registers. Unlike Heather and Nathaniel Giles (who received the degree that same day) he was never styled 'Dr'.

Musical compositions The extant compositions are the best source of information on Gibbons as musician. They represent the output of perhaps fewer than twenty years, by comparison with over fifty years' worth of works from his older contemporary Byrd. Gibbons has been presented as a master of serious polyphonic music. However, the seriousness and contrapuntal dexterity of the 'full' anthems and the madrigals and motets are complemented by vitality in his verse anthems and wit in his consort music, and by the full range of expressiveness in the keyboard music. The sacred music in the full style ranges from music for four voices in the largely syllabic, 'short' style (the anthem 'Almighty and everlasting God' and the first or short service) to more extended polyphonic psalms and anthems for five and six voices ('Hosanna to the son of David' and 'O Lord, in thy wrath'). Gibbons's attention to word-setting is apparent even in the simpler works, as is his instinctive contrapuntal facility. The setting for eight voices of Psalm 47, 'O clap your hands', has features typical of an Italian *canzona* or polychoral motet. The second service is an outstanding example of an early seventeenth-century 'verse' style service, with accompaniment perhaps originally intended for instrumental ensemble. His verse anthems are among the finest of the genre, from the simple alternation of solo voice and five-part chorus in 'This is the record of John' to the more complex scoring patterns of 'See, the word is incarnate'. Gibbons shows little interest in overt word-painting, but the expressive declamation, the rhythmic treatment of the chorus writing, and the short passages of vocal bravura are hallmarks of his musical modernity. Little sacred music by Gibbons was published in his lifetime. He contributed to two collections: William Leighton's *The Teares or Lamentacions of a Sorrowful Soule* (1614) includes two fine small-scale pieces for four voices, and fifteen 'songs' appeared in George Wither's *The Hymns and Songs of the Church* (1623), a publication bound in with editions of the metrical psalms.

Most of Gibbons's secular vocal music is found in *The First Set of Madrigals and Mottets* (1612), completed before he was thirty. It is a collection which has affinity with Byrd and the traditions of English partsong (for example the famous 'The Silver Swan') and consort song; 'Nay let me weep' may have been written to mark the death of Prince Henry. The seriousness of the whole collection may have been influenced by the prince's death as much as by the pervasive spirit of Jacobean melancholy typified by Walter Ralegh's 'What is our life'. Two vocal works are found outside the 1612 publication. 'Do not repine, fair sun' is in the consort song tradition, though on a larger scale. *The Cryes of London* sets vendors' common street cries sung by solo voices against the high polyphonic tradition of the instrumental In nomine played by viols. This is a piece made perhaps for court amusement.

Much of Gibbons's ensemble music may have been written for the court, and for some of the new instrumental groups. The fantasias for 'great dooble basse' and five of the three-part printed fantasias are particularly suited to violins; a small number, by their lines, phrasing, and texture, suggest performance by wind instruments. There remains a substantial body of music probably intended for viols, including the unusual two-part fantasias, the varied group of In nomines, the six-part fantasias, pavan, and galliard, and the finely wrought variations on 'Go from my window'. The music for 'great dooble basse' quotes from popular melodies and idioms, and was perhaps written specifically for the burgeoning string band entertaining Charles I during his years as prince of Wales. John Woodington was instructed to copy some of this music in 1634, an indication of its continuing popularity at court. John Lilly and Stephen Bing copied other ensemble works into Christopher Hatton's 'great set' of partbooks in the 1630s. The printed fantasias (*c.*1620) were reissued in Amsterdam in 1648; Henry Purcell used a manuscript which contained some of Gibbons's ensemble music; and other works appear in sources used by viol consorts in Oxford in the later seventeenth century, including those owned by Narcissus Marsh, later archbishop of Dublin.

Gibbons's corpus of keyboard music is not so extensive as those of Byrd and Bull, but ranks with them in quality. In the keyboard fantasias Gibbons uses small rhythmic and melodic motifs, sometimes worked closely in dense counterpoint, framed within larger periods, with a particular penchant for a final climax, as may be observed in the fantasia 'for double organ'. Lord Salisbury's pavan and galliard from *Parthenia* are the best known but are untypical: most of the other pavans and galliards are unpaired and have written-out reprises. Most include polyphonic detail and keyboard bravura. These features are less evident in the almans and corantos and in the masque dances, which provide the only evidence of Gibbons's possible association with Jacobean masque, but are probably settings made after the event. Among the grounds and variations, *The Italian Ground* and *The Queen's Command* are relatively short; *The Woods so Wild* and *The Hunt's up* (or *Peascod Time*) are more extended sets of variations in the tradition of Byrd, Bull, and Farnaby. Gibbons is relatively uninterested in the obsessive application of figurative and rhythmic patterns (an English characteristic dating back to the mid-sixteenth century), but there is ample evidence of virtuoso keyboard writing, tempered by contrapuntal ingenuity and innate musical judgement.

Death and posthumous reputation In May 1625 preparations were made to receive the new queen, Henrietta Maria, whom Charles I had married by proxy in Paris at the beginning of the month. On 31 May the court set out for Canterbury, with the Chapel Royal in attendance. Gibbons was taken ill suddenly, and the royal physicians were summoned: there was fear that he had plague. He died on

Whitsunday, 5 June 1625, at Canterbury, and was buried in Canterbury Cathedral on the following day. The doctors described precisely his coma and final seizure, attributed at the post-mortem to a brain haemorrhage, and their report is preserved in domestic state papers. (Perhaps the origin of this haemorrhage went back to the unprovoked and violent attack on Gibbons by Henry Eveseed, the disturbed yeoman of the vestry, on 29 June 1620.) The attention Gibbons's death attracted in court circles, in particular its formal observation, investigation, and reporting, perhaps suggests how close he may have been to the new king.

Gibbons died intestate. After some thirteen months, letters of administration were granted on 13 July 1626 to his widow by the dean and chapter of Westminster, but she was already dead. Elizabeth was buried at St Margaret's, Westminster, on 2 July 1626. Her will, noted by Fuller Maitland in the *Dictionary of National Biography*, has not been traced by subsequent scholars. A letter from the royal signet office (20 January 1627) directed that their eldest son, Christopher, be granted a scholarship at Charterhouse School, and his election was confirmed by the governors (21 June 1627). There are no surviving records to confirm that he attended, however. A statement by Anthony Wood suggests that he may have moved to Exeter to his uncle, Edward, who was guardian to the surviving children.

Gibbons's widow erected a plaque in Canterbury Cathedral in 1626, with a fine bust of the composer by Nicholas Stone, which is the most reliable likeness. It omits his age and may therefore have been completed after Elizabeth's death. A copy by A. G. Walker was placed in Westminster Abbey (1907). Later engravings, one (perhaps by James Cole) published in John Dart's history of Canterbury Cathedral (1726), and another by Charles Grignion in Sir John Hawkins's *A General History of the Science and Practice of Music* (1776), are probably based upon it. A portrait hanging in the faculty of music, Oxford, is thought to be an eighteenth-century copy of an original dating from about 1620, perhaps that bequeathed to the Oxford music school by Gibbons's 'scholar' John Hingston in 1683.

Gibbons's ensemble music was well represented in the repertory of viol consorts meeting in Oxford in the years after the Restoration, and Anthony Wood ranked him as 'one of the rarest musicians and organists of his time'. In spite of his fame as a keyboard player and his standing in court music, little is known of Orlando Gibbons as a person. It is by his music that succeeding generations have known him. His reputation as a composer has traditionally rested on his church music, some of which circulated very widely in the seventeenth century and has continued to remain in the cathedral repertory, notably the short service. By their inclusion in printed collections (such as those by John Barnard, 1641, and William Boyce, 1760–73) some anthems have remained in the repertory of English cathedral choirs since the Restoration. Late nineteenth- and early twentieth-century publications have also emphasized his church music: Ouseley's anthology (1873), *Tudor Church Music*, volume 4 (1925), selections in the Tudor church music octavo series, and the use of eleven of his 'hymn' tunes in *The English Hymnal* (1906). The volume of madrigals and motets appeared in Fellowes's series English Madrigalists in 1915. His instrumental music has fared less well: although some items were edited and printed, notably in E. F. Rimbault's pioneering edition of the *Fantasies of Three Parts* (1843), the collected keyboard music appeared only in 1962, and the ensemble music in 1982.

Edmund Fellowes styled Gibbons 'the last of the Tudor school of composers'. In fact his career was almost entirely Jacobean, and he worked with a progressive group of musicians who held particular favour with Charles I before and after he came to the throne. Overemphasis of the serious and polyphonic qualities of his music can obscure the lightness and modernity also evident in Gibbons's music. JOHN HARPER

Sources J. Harley, *Orlando Gibbons and the Gibbons family of musicians* (1999) [with list of works] · J. Harper, 'Gibbons, Orlando', *New Grove*, 2nd edn [with list of works] · A. Ashbee, ed., *Records of English court music*, 3 (1988); 4 (1991); 8 (1995); 9 (1996) · E. F. Rimbault, ed., *The old cheque-book, or book of remembrance, of the Chapel Royal, from 1561 to 1744*, CS, new ser., 3 (1872) · J. Hacket, *Scrinia reserata: a memorial offer'd to the great deservings of John Williams*, 2 pts (1693) · H. W. Shaw, *The succession of organists of the Chapel Royal and the cathedrals of England and Wales from c.1538* (1991) · P. Holman, *Four and twenty fiddlers: the violin at the English court, 1540–1690* (1993) · D. Pinto, 'Gibbons in the bedchamber', *John Jenkins and his time: studies in English consort music*, ed. A. Ashbee and P. Holman (1996) · P. Brett, 'English music for the Scottish progress of 1617', *Source materials in the interpretation of music*, ed. I. Bent (1981), 209–26 · C. Monson, *Voices and viols in England, 1600–1650* (1982) · J. Harper, 'The distribution of the consort music of Orlando Gibbons in seventeenth-century sources', *Chelys*, 12 (1983), 3–18 · J. Harper, 'Orlando Gibbons: the domestic context of his music and Christ Church Mus. 21', *MT*, 124 (1983), 767–70 · P. Vining, 'Orlando Gibbons: the portraits', *Music and Letters*, 58 (1977), 415–29 · E. H. Fellowes, *Orlando Gibbons: a short account of his life and work* (1925) [2nd edn as *Orlando Gibbons and his family* (1951)] · P. Vining, 'Gibbons and his patrons', *MT*, 124 (1983), 707–9 · J. P. Wainwright, *Musical patronage in seventeenth-century England: Christopher, first Baron Hatton (1605–70)* (1997) · parish register, Westminster, St Margaret's [baptism, burial: Elizabeth Patten, wife]

Likenesses N. Stone, relief medallion on monument, 1626, Canterbury Cathedral; copies by N. Stone and A. G. Walker, Westminster Abbey · oils, 18th cent. (after unknown portrait, *c.*1620), U. Oxf., faculty of music · J. Cole?, engravings (after bust by N. Stone?), repro. in J. Dart, *The history and antiquities of the Cathedral Church of Canterbury* (1726) · C. Grignion, engravings (after bust by N. Stone?), repro. in J. Hawkins, *A general history of the science and practice of music*, 5 vols. (1776)

Gibbons, Richard (1547/1553–1632), Jesuit, younger brother of John *Gibbons, was born either on 25 March 1547, at an unknown place, or in Wells, Somerset on 1 March 1553. After making his lower studies in England he went through a two years' course of philosophy at Louvain and in the German College at Rome. He entered the Society of Jesus on 1 September 1572. He again studied philosophy for three years, and was professor of mathematics and philosophy for thirteen years, partly in Rome and partly in France. He was also a professor of canon law and Hebrew for some time in Italy, Spain, and Portugal, besides holding a like office at Tournai, Toulouse, Douai, and Louvain, where he was also prefect of studies. He was ordained at Bordeaux on 17 December 1583.

For a while Gibbons was preacher in the Jesuit college at St Omer. He was professed of the four vows in the college of Coimbra in Portugal in 1591. During most of his life he was restless. He did not make friends easily and was fond of reminding his fellow Jesuits of their faults. He passed his latter years in Douai, Louvain, and St Omer, where he devoted himself to translating into English pious works about mental prayer by Luis de Granada, Luis de la Puente, Vincenzo Bruno, and Luca Pinelli. He also translated a work by Robert Bellarmine as *Short Catechism*. Towards the end of his life he spent more of his time editing quarto tomes of Latin works. He died in Douai on 25 June 1632.

THOMPSON COOPER, *rev.* THOMAS H. CLANCY

Sources H. Foley, ed., *Records of the English province of the Society of Jesus*, 6 (1880), 725; 7 (1882–3), 299 · T. M. McCoog, ed., *Monumenta Angliae*, 1: *English and Welsh Jesuits, catalogues, 1555–1629* (1992), 328–9 · A. F. Allison and D. M. Rogers, eds., *The contemporary printed literature of the English Counter-Reformation between 1558 and 1640*, 2 vols. (1989–94) · T. M. McCoog, *English and Welsh Jesuits, 1555–1650*, 2, Catholic RS, 75 (1995), 190

Gibbons, Sarah (1634/5–1659), Quaker preacher in America, was probably born in Bristol, though nothing is known of her parentage. She is remembered for her resilience in puritan New England. According to one pithy epithet, she was 'twice imprisoned, once her Clothes sold, once whipt, and three times banished' (Norton, 105).

Sarah Gibbons was, apparently, twenty-one years old when she first crossed to New England in the *Speedwell* in late summer 1656. No account in her own hand exists, so not only is her literacy unverifiable but also her response to these dramatic experiences. Gibbons travelled to Boston alongside her fellow Quakers Christopher Holder, Thomas Thrifton, William Brend, John Copeland, Mary Prince, Mary Weatherhead, and Dorothy Waugh. On their arrival in August 1656, they were interrogated, imprisoned (for eleven weeks), and sentenced to banishment. The authorities feared their facility 'to trouble the Magistrates and infect the people' (Norton, 11).

Many of these original Quakers nevertheless returned to New England the following June (1657), this time on the *Woodhouse*. Using Rhode Island as a base from 1657 to her death in 1659, Gibbons moved between New Amsterdam (New York), Barbados, Salem, and Boston. Record of her experiences is fragmentary. In either April or August 1658 she and Dorothy Waugh travelled 60 miles from Newport to Salem, braving 'storms and tempests … great of frost and snow' (Norton, 69; Jones, 73). Just as this expedition was 'moved by the measure of God', so, on their return to Boston, they believed themselves 'required' to visit people 'puffed up in pride, and high-mindedness' (Norton, 69). Gibbons and Waugh interrupted rival preacher John Norton's church service; one report has them smashing bottles as a sign of the preacher's spiritual emptiness, but this is probably apocryphal (Jones, 108). Arrested, imprisoned, and whipped at the instigation of Governor John Endecott, the women (Quaker hagiography records) praised God even as the cords striped and tore the flesh. Commenting on the conditions of imprisonment, Sarah Gibbons 'demanded of him [Endecott] if it were justice or equity we should be kept and not suffered to have food for our money' (Norton, 71).

Account of Gibbons's death survives in its most complete form in contemporary manuscripts. Gibbons drowned while trying to land at Providence, Rhode Island. William Robinson records, in a letter written on 12 July 1659, that the Quaker had died because the leaking canoe into which she climbed filled quickly with water. He notes that other passengers were saved. She was buried in Richard Scot's orchard one day after the accident.

CATIE GILL

Sources H. Norton, *New Englands ensigne* (1659) · R. M. Jones, *The Quakers in the American colonies* (1911) · William Robinson to George Fox, 12 July 1659, RS Friends, Lond., MS vol. 366 · 'Dictionary of Quaker biography', RS Friends, Lond. [card index] · J. Besse, *A collection of the sufferings of the people called Quakers*, 2 vols. (1753) · G. A. Selleck, *Quakers in Boston, 1654–1964: three centuries of Friends* (1976) · J. Bowden, *The history of the Society of Friends in America*, 2 vols. (1850)

Archives RS Friends, Lond., Swarthmore MSS

Gibbons, (Edward) Stanley (1840–1913), postage stamp dealer, was born on 21 June 1840 in Plymouth, the youngest child in the family of three sons and two daughters of William Gibbons (*d.* 1867), pharmaceutical chemist, and his wife, Elizabeth Langridge, of Portsea, Hampshire. He left Hallorans' Collegiate Establishment, Plymouth, at the age of fifteen to become a junior clerk in the Naval Bank. On the death of his eldest brother only a few weeks later, he was apprenticed to his father as a chemist.

(Edward) Stanley Gibbons (1840–1913), by unknown photographer

Already interested in the new hobby of stamp collecting, he started to trade in stamps in 1856 from a desk in his father's shop. He began trading as E. S. Gibbons, then as E. Stanley Gibbons, and later as Stanley Gibbons & Co. A lucky deal in 1863 caused his business to take off: he bought two sacks of Cape of Good Hope triangular stamps for £5 from two sailors who had won them in a raffle in Cape Town. He later claimed to have made £500 on the deal. In November 1865 he issued a sixteen-page price list and catalogue, the forerunner of Gibbons's catalogues.

On his father's death in 1867 Gibbons took over the chemist's business, and in the 1871 census he was described as 'chemist and dealer in foreign stamps'. He sold the chemist's business in 1872 and moved to new premises at Plymouth Hoe. Here he published his first Gibbons 'V.R.' stamp album, followed by the 'Improved' and illustrated 'Imperial' albums.

In 1874 Gibbons moved to London, first to Clapham Common, and then in 1876 to 8 Gower Street. He started a monthly magazine, the *Philatelic Record*, which was superseded by the *Monthly Journal* in 1890.

At the age of fifty, in 1890, Gibbons retired and sold his business to Charles J. Phillips of Birmingham for £25,000. It became a private limited company, continuing as Stanley Gibbons Ltd, and he remained chairman until his death. The firm first moved to the Strand in 1891. In his retirement Gibbons travelled all over the world, visiting San Francisco, Egypt, Japan, Cochin, and the Hanoi exhibition, witnessing the crash of the Orient Express at Tirnova in Bulgaria in 1894.

Gibbons was married five times. His first wife, whom he married in 1872, was Matilda Woon, daughter of a Congregational minister. She died in 1877. He married his second wife, Maggie A. Casey, daughter of a Twickenham publican, in 1887. She died in 1899 and he then married a woman called Georgina, who appears to have died in 1905. His fourth wife, whom he married in 1905, was a widow, Mrs Bertha Barth of Chelsea, daughter of Edwin Boswith, a railway clerk. She died during a visit to Ceylon in 1908. His final marriage, in 1909, was to a widow, Mrs Sophia Crofts, of Kensington, daughter of a wine merchant. Stanley Gibbons died at his home, 4L Portman Mansions, Marylebone, London, on 17 February 1913. He had no children.

G. E. DIXON, *rev.*

Sources C. V. Phillips, 'Fifty years of philately: the history of Stanley Gibbons Ltd', *Gibbons Stamp Weekly* (Jan–April 1906) • J. Holman, *Gibbons Stamp Monthly* (July–Aug 1990) • *Catalogue of Gibbons catalogue centenary exhibition* (1965) • private information (1993)

Likenesses photograph, Stanley Gibbons, London [*see illus.*]

Wealth at death £13,172 11*s.* 4*d.*: resworn probate, 1 May 1913, *CGPLA Eng. & Wales*

Gibbons, Stella Dorothea (1902–1989), novelist, was born on 5 January 1902 in Malden Crescent, London, the only daughter and eldest of three children of (Charles James Preston) Telford Gibbons, medical doctor, and his wife, Maude Phoebe Standish Williams. She grew up in the dismal environment of Kentish Town where her father had his medical practice in Malden Crescent. Her childhood

Stella Dorothea Gibbons (1902–1989), by Mark Gerson, 1955

was unhappy and turbulent. She withdrew into stories and solitary games in her attic room to avoid the constant family rows which revolved around her preposterous father. He was unfaithful with a succession of governesses, against a noisy background of self-dramatizing uncles and aunts. Fortunately her mother was quiet and sensible, so she had some emotional refuge from the storms.

Gibbons was educated at home and then sent to the North London Collegiate School for Girls. At University College, London, she did a two-year course on journalism (set up for soldiers who had returned from the First World War). Her first job, in 1923, was as a cable decoder for British United Press. For the next decade she worked as a London journalist for various publications, including the *Evening Standard* and *The Lady*. Her first published book was a slim volume of poems (*The Mountain Beast*, 1930). No one could have guessed that the author of this neo-Georgian verse was about to spring a comic classic upon the world. *Cold Comfort Farm* (1932) was written as a parody of the novels of D. H. Lawrence and Mary Webb, with asterisks marking all the purple passages for the reader's delectation and mirth. Her characters soon became household names and her heroine Flora Poste a synonym for common sense. Flora goes to stay with her cousins, the Starkadders, on their decrepit farm in Sussex. From dawn to dusk the Starkadders live in a ferment of unruly passion but she manages them with cunning and dispatch, including the seething matriarch in the attic, Aunt Ada Doom.

Even minor characters like Mr Mybug, who is unable to

look at a hill without thinking of women's breasts, are a comic delight, as are the cows, Feckless, Graceless, Pointless, and Aimless, who tend to lose their legs. All over the English-speaking world her fans quoted chunks of the novel to each other, rocking with laughter, and the expression 'something nasty in the woodshed' gained a permanent place in the language.

After such a towering success so young the rest of Stella Gibbons's professional life was an anticlimax, despite her excessive industry and talent. Her second novel, *Bassett* (1934), was fuelled by an unhappy affair with a German businessman. In 1933 she met and married Allan Bourne Webb, an actor and singer, the son of the Revd Charles Johnston Bourne Webb. They had one daughter and lived happily ever after (not always grist to a writer's mill). Her subsequent writing (including poetry and short stories) was published at the rate of almost one book a year, until 1970. There were almost thirty of them. Some of the novels, like *Miss Linsey and Pa* (1936), *My American* (1939), and *Here be Dragons* (1956), were reasonably well received. The novel she preferred was *Ticky* (1943), a satire on army life, which flopped. In 1940 she tried to revive the magic formula with *Christmas at Cold Comfort Farm*, but it lacked the panache of the original, as did *Conference at Cold Comfort Farm* (short stories, 1949).

Stella Gibbons took her poetry more seriously than her prose and some of it, about nature and the pollution of the seas, was prophetic. Her *Collected Poems* was published in 1950. Longman was her main publisher until 1955, when she moved to Hodder and Stoughton. She was a member of the Royal Society of Literature (fellow, 1950) and was awarded the Femina Vie Heureuse prize in 1933 for *Cold Comfort Farm*.

After her marriage, Stella Gibbons had moved to 19 Oakeshott Avenue, London, a mock-Tudor house in a Hampstead backwater. She remained there after her husband's death in 1959. During their long marriage the only suffering he caused her was his absence in the army during the Second World War. In the last part of her life she held an 'at home' once a month. She was known to expel guests from these tea parties if they were shrill, dramatic, or wrote tragic novels. The irony of her creative life is that the thing she hated most, overheated emotions, had given her the most inspiration. Ordinary life and personal goodness, which she enjoyed writing about, yielded a more pallid harvest. Many of her other novels have been dismissed unfairly, but some have dated. Her great joys were nature, music, and reading. She was an intensely private person, not easy to interview. Her appearance was of the blue-eyed, refined English variety and her beauty endured, as did her upright carriage, typical of Edwardian ladies who were forced as girls to walk around with a book balanced on their heads. She died on 19 December 1989 at home in Oakeshott Avenue, London. JILL NEVILLE, *rev.*

Sources *Publishers' Weekly* (19 May 1934) · S. J. Kunitz and H. Haycraft, eds., *Twentieth century authors: a biographical dictionary of modern literature* (1942) · *The Independent* (20 Dec 1989) · *The Times* (20 Dec 1989) · private information (1996) · personal knowledge (1996)

Likenesses M. Gerson, photograph, 1955, NPG [*see illus.*] · photograph, 1977, Hult. Arch.

Gibbons, Thomas (1720–1785), Independent minister and diarist, was born at Reach, Swaffham Prior, near Newmarket, on 31 May 1720, the son of Thomas Gibbons (*c.*1700–1757), sometime Independent minister at Olney, Buckinghamshire, and Royston, Hertfordshire, and his wife, Grace (1698/9–1764). After grammar school he was sent to the dissenting academy at Deptford under Abraham Taylor, and later studied under John Eames at Moorfields. Isaac Watts was among those who examined him for the ministry. Gibbons was ordained on 27 October 1743 as minister of the Independent church at Haberdashers' Hall, and in 1754 was elected jointly by the Congregational Fund and the King's Head Society tutor in logic, metaphysics, and rhetoric at the Mile End dissenting academy, which moved to Homerton in 1769. He held both these positions for the rest of his life. He was Sunday evening lecturer at the meeting-house in Monkwell (commonly Mugwell) Street from 1759 to 1781, and was both a merchants' lecturer at Pinners' Hall from 1761 to 1777 and a Coward lecturer at Little St Helen's from 1761 to 1774. He raised funds for New Jersey College, the forerunner of Princeton, which awarded him an MA in 1760. In 1764 he received the degree of DD from Aberdeen University.

Gibbons married Hannah Shuttlewood at St Nicholas Cole Abbey, London, on 3 July 1744. She was the younger daughter of John Shuttlewood, Independent minister at Mill Yard, Goodman's Field, London, and granddaughter of an ejected minister of the same name in Leicestershire. Gossip made Hannah twice as old as Gibbons on marriage, but they had four children, all sons, of whom two survived to manhood, and she outlived him.

Though since neglected, Gibbons was a highly influential figure in eighteenth-century evangelical dissent. He was a close friend of Isaac Watts and wrote his first biography, using Watts's own papers and correspondence, an invaluable source for later biographers. A leader of the London Independent ministers after Watts's day, he was well regarded by Philip Doddridge and found favour equally with the countess of Huntingdon and George Whitefield. Even Dr Johnson took to him, surprised perhaps to encounter a dissenting minister who could entertain him. It was Gibbons's charm of manner and ease of conversation, as well as his talent for business and avoidance of party, which gave him standing. Unsurprisingly he proved an effective lobbyist in the political campaign to release dissenting ministers from the obligation to subscribe to the Thirty-Nine Articles. As tutor for thirty years at a leading academy, a Calvinist but an admirer of Richard Baxter, his influence on generations of dissenting ministers was considerable.

Many of Gibbons's forty-five publications are sermons for funerals or patriotic occasions. Of the rest, apart from *The Memoirs of the Rev Isaac Watts DD* (1780), the chief are *Hymns Adapted to Divine Worship* (1769); a textbook entitled *Rhetoric* (1767), much used in dissenting academies; and two works dedicated to the countess of Huntingdon—

Juvenilia (1750), a collection of religious verse with Whitefield, Doddridge, and Arthur Onslow, speaker of the Commons, among the subscribers, and *Female Worthies, or, The Lives and Memoirs of Eminently Pious Women* (1777). A collection entitled *Sermons on Evangelical and Practical Subjects* was published posthumously in 1787. Gibbons's hymns showed Watts's influence if not his art, and like the poetry attracted a measure of satirical criticism from outside his circle.

Gibbons's diary, however, is an invaluable account of the life of a busy eighteenth-century London minister with wide interests and acquaintance. It was kept from 29 November 1749 to 17 February 1785, the day he had a fatal stroke. The entries are mainly factual and unreflective, except when illness or the anticipation of death intrude, but this adds to their immediacy. They convey a sense that until he aged he rarely ate a meal alone or without transacting business of some kind. The diary, which is in the Congregational Library, now at Dr Williams's Library, is partly edited. Some extracts have been published.

From 1750 Gibbons lived in Hoxton Square, London. He suffered his stroke in the coffee house there and died at his home five days later, on 22 February 1785, without recovering his speech. He was buried in Bunhill Fields on 3 March. John Handby Thompson

Sources W. Wilson, *The history and antiquities of the dissenting churches and meeting houses in London, Westminster and Southwark*, 4 vols. (1808–14), vol. 3, pp. 178–83 • *Protestant Dissenter's Magazine*, 2 (1795), 489–93 • B. Davies, *Israel's testament* (1785) • *The tears of friendship: sacred to the memory of Dr. Gibbons by a member of his church* (1785) • A. P. Davis, *Isaac Watts: his life and works* (1948), 58, 173, 226 • *Calendar of the correspondence of Philip Doddridge*, ed. G. F. Nuttall, HMC, JP 26 (1979), 990, 1434, 1440, 1455 • Boswell, *Life*, 4.126, 278, 494 • [A. C. H. Seymour], *The life and times of Selina, countess of Huntingdon*, 1 (1839), 111–12, 126, 200, 206 • J. Julian, ed., *A dictionary of hymnology*, rev. edn (1907), 420 • T. H. Sims, *Homerton College, 1695–1978* (1979), 9, 10 • H. McLachlan, *English education under the Test Acts: being the history of the nonconformist academies, 1662–1820* (1931), 119, 176–8, 287, 305, 315 • T. Gibbons, diary, 1749–85, DWL, Congregational Library • *DNB* • *IGI*

Archives DWL, diary | DWL, John Horsey's student notes on Gibbons's lectures

Likenesses J. Boden, coloured engraving, 1785, DWL • J. Spilsbury, mezzotint (after J. S. Webster), BM, NPG • portrait, repro. in *Protestant Dissenter's Magazine*, facing p. 489

Gibbons, Thomas (1730–1813). *See under* Gibbons family (*per.* c.1735–1863).

Gibbons, William (1649–1728), physician, born at Wolverhampton, Staffordshire, on 25 September 1649, was the son of John Gibbons (*d.* 1693), of that town, and Elizabeth, daughter of Roland Frith, of Thorns. From Merchant Taylors' School, London, he went to St John's College, Oxford, in 1668, graduating BA in 1672, MA in 1675, and DM in 1683. He practised as a physician in London and joined the Royal College of Physicians in 1691, becoming fellow in 1692 and censor in 1716. In 1697 he attended the lord chancellor.

Gibbons is not remembered by any writings, but chiefly as Mirmillo in *The Dispensary* of Sir Samuel Garth. He was one of the college fellows who opposed the project of dispensaries for the poor in the 1690s, and so incurred the satire of Garth, a leading supporter of the scheme, who makes him say:

> While others meanly asked whole months to slay,
> I oft despatched the patient in a day.

Gibbons was a staunch critic of the college's attempts to strengthen its authority in London medicine. He freely admitted to telling the Society of Apothecaries, London, who opposed the dispensary, all of the college's plans. He also supported a bill put forward by the apothecaries in 1694 to increase their civic privileges. Gibbons spoke against the college at the important trial of Joannes Groenevelt for unauthorized practice. He is described by contemporaries as 'pretty old Dr. Gibbons', and 'nurse Gibbons', and as taking his fees with alacrity. However, the Harveian oration of the year following his death took a more generous line, ascribing to him erudition, honesty, candour, love of letters, piety, benevolence, and other Christian virtues.

According to Wadd, the credit of making mahogany fashionable belongs to Gibbons. His brother, a West Indies shipmaster, brought home some of that wood as ballast, and gave it to the doctor, who was building a house in Covent Garden. The carpenters, finding it too hard for their tools, threw it aside; but some of it was afterwards used to make a candle-box, which looked so well that a bureau of the same wood was built. When finished and polished the bureau was so pleasing that it became an object of admiration to visitors, among others the duchess of Buckingham, who had one like it made, and so brought the wood into fashion. There is some doubt about this story, for it is known that the Society of Apothecaries were in possession of mahogany chairs by the 1670s.

Gibbons died on 25 March 1728. He was a liberal benefactor to Wolverhampton, his native place, and left St John's College £1000.

Charles Creighton, *rev.* Patrick Wallis

Sources Munk, *Roll* • Foster, *Alum. Oxon.* • W. Wadd, *Mems., maxims, and memoirs* (1827), 148 • H. J. Cook, *Trials of an ordinary doctor: Joannes Groenevelt in 17th-century London* (1994) • G. Clark and A. M. Cooke, *A history of the Royal College of Physicians of London*, 3 vols. (1964–72) • C. Wall, *A history of the Worshipful Society of Apothecaries of London*, ed. H. C. Cameron and E. A. Underwood (1963) • J. Gloag, *John Gloag's dictionary of furniture* (1969) • Nichols, *Illustrations*, 2.801

Archives RCP Lond., account of death of duke of Gloucester • Surrey HC, report on the death of duke of Gloucester

Likenesses oils, before 1729, St John's College, Oxford

Wealth at death over £1000: Munk, *Roll*

Gibbons, William (1732–1807). *See under* Gibbons family (*per.* c.1735–1863).

Gibbs, Antony (1756–1815), merchant, was born at the family home in the cathedral close in Exeter and baptized on 3 March 1756 at Mint Presbyterian Meeting-House, Exeter, the sixth in the family of five sons and six daughters of George Abraham Gibbs, surgeon at the Royal Devon and Exeter Hospital, and his wife, Anne Vicary; an elder son, Sir Vicary *Gibbs, became chief justice of common pleas.

Gibbs went to Exeter grammar school. He was then apprenticed for five years to a Mr Brook of Exeter, a merchant in the Spanish trade. His first trading venture was in

1788 as a woollen exporter, principally to Spain and Italy; he was also briefly involved with a woollen-cloth factory near Exeter. On 3 October 1784 he married Dorothea Barnetta (*d.* 1820), the youngest daughter of William Hucks, a Yorkshire wine merchant; they had seven children, two of whom died in infancy. In 1787–9, in circumstances that are unclear, he got into financial difficulties, losing not only his own money but some of his family's: it became a matter of pride to make good those losses.

The first step in Gibbs's financial recovery involved setting up an agency business in Madrid to serve English and other textile manufacturers. In August 1789 he took ship with his wife and children to Corunna, thence overland to Madrid. His family found the hot summers unbearable and in 1792 they returned, in poor health. Early in 1793 Gibbs suffered a terrible accident when the carriage he was travelling in from Madrid to Seville went out of control—he fell from it, and was run over by one of the wheels. Later, he joined a partnership in Malaga to sell Spanish produce in England. When Spain declared war in 1796, Gibbs faced another financial crisis; but he was eventually able to use Lisbon as an illicit (and profitable) means of entry to the Spanish market for English woollens. When peace came in 1801, he was able to set up a profitable business in Cadiz. However, the outbreak of war again in 1805 forced him to close in Cadiz, and once more he had to struggle to survive. A key to the realization of his assets in Spain was a perilous shipment to Peru; the success of at least the outward journey meant financial relief, but it was not until the war with Spain ended in 1808 that Gibbs's difficulties really began to abate. The reopening of the Cadiz house, and the opening of a London house in partnership with his eldest son under the style Antony Gibbs & Son, marked the beginning of a period of real prosperity. Debts were paid and a profitable trade to and from the south of Spain energetically fostered. He moved his family from Great Russell Street to Denmark Hill in 1809, to Dulwich Common in 1810, and in 1812 brought them back to a house in Powis Place, where they remained until his death.

The siege of Cadiz by the French between 1810 and 1812 led to the closure of the Cadiz house; but when the siege was abandoned trade and profits rapidly regained their former levels. In 1813 a second son was taken into partnership, and the London house became Antony Gibbs & Sons.

By 1814 Gibbs was suffering not only from his earlier carriage accident but also from severe loss of memory. Shortly after returning from a visit to Redland, he suffered a stroke on 5 December 1815; he died five days later at his house, 2 Powis Place, Great Ormond Street, London. In his will he left everything to his wife, so that her income and assets depended on the firm's prosperity. It was the trading contacts that he had established in Spain which enabled his firm, after his death, to exploit so efficiently the opportunities afforded in South America after its liberation from Spanish control.

IAN DOOLITTLE, *rev.* ANITA MCCONNELL

Sources J. A. Gibbs, *The history of Antony and Dorothea Gibbs* (1922) • will, PRO, PROB 11/1578, sig. 138 • J. A. Gibbs, *Pedigree of the family of Gibbs*, 3rd edn (1932)
Archives GL

Gibbs, Cecil Armstrong (1889–1960), composer, was born at The Vineyards, Great Baddow, near Chelmsford, Essex, on 10 August 1889, the first child of the London businessman David Cecil Gibbs (1850–1912) and his first wife, Ida (1865–1891), daughter of the Revd James Thornely Whitehead, a Unitarian minister. Gibbs's mother died in 1891 after bearing a stillborn second son, and Gibbs was subsequently cared for by his five maiden aunts. He very early showed musical talent but was steered away from a career in music by his father, who inflicted substantial psychological damage on his sensitive son. Gibbs attended the Wick School, Hove (1899–1902), Winchester College (classical scholarship 1902–8), won an exhibition and sizarship for history at Trinity College, Cambridge (BA, 1911), and, his father having died in 1912, gained a MusB in 1913.

After a year teaching at Copthorne School, East Grinstead, and finding himself unable to join the army (he was refused on medical grounds) Gibbs taught classics, history, and English at his old school, the Wick. Adrian Boult funded a year's study at the Royal College of Music (1919–20) where Gibbs studied theory with Charles Wood, score reading and conducting with Boult, and composition with Vaughan Williams, for which he won the Arthur Sullivan prize.

Gibbs taught at the Royal College of Music from 1921 to 1939; he was awarded a doctorate of music (composition) at Cambridge in 1931, and the Cobbett gold medal for chamber music in 1934; and he was vice-chairman of the British Federation of Music Festivals from 1937 to 1952. Gibbs married Honor Mary Mitchell (1892–1958); they had a son, David (1919–1943), and a daughter, Elizabeth (*b.* 1922). His spiritual home was in Danbury, Essex, where he founded the Danbury Choral Society and conducted it from 1921 to 1960. During the Second World War he temporarily moved his household to Cumberland, where he involved himself thoroughly in the county's musical affairs. In 1951 he chaired the selection committee for the British Federation of Music Societies' national competition festival and he continued to compose, conduct, adjudicate, and find willing publishers for his work until his death of pneumonia on 12 May 1960 in the Chelmsford and Essex Hospital. Gibbs was buried in Danbury churchyard on 16 May.

A large man with considerable public presence, booming voice, red hair, and a temper to match, inside Gibbs was insecure, agoraphobic, and frightened by the increasing speed of the world around him and what he saw as the destructive progress of 'science'. A man of contradictions, consumed by fears and mighty joys, his ambition was to produce a top-rate light opera or a magnificent string quartet. He composed many grand works such as the choral symphony *Odysseus* (1937–8) and wrote for film and stage, but few of these undertakings exhibit the quality of craftsmanship that is so evident in his some 160 songs. As

Cecil Armstrong Gibbs (1889–1960), by Herbert Lambert, *c.*1922

a miniaturist he excelled; a constant source of inspiration was the poetry of his friend Walter de la Mare, and Gibbs's settings of 'Five Eyes' (1917) and 'Silver' (1920) have an enduring appeal. Gibbs found especial satisfaction in his music festival work and wrote generously for amateur performers, of whom he was a self-proclaimed champion. RO HANCOCK-CHILD

Sources R. Hancock-Child, *A ballad-maker: the life and songs of C. Armstrong Gibbs* (1993) • C. A. Gibbs, 'Common time', unpubd autobiography, 1958, priv. coll. • private information (2004) [family] • *The Times* (13 May 1960)
Archives CUL, letters to Edward Dent
Likenesses photographs, 1893–1959, priv. coll.; repro. in Hancock-Child, *Ballad-maker* • H. Lambert, photograph, *c.*1922, NPG [*see illus.*] • Dowie, pastel drawing, priv. coll.
Wealth at death £60,421 13*s*.: probate, 28 June 1960, *CGPLA Eng. & Wales*

Gibbs, Henry Hucks, first Baron Aldenham (1819–1907), merchant and merchant banker, was born at Powis Place, Queen Square, Bloomsbury, London on 31 August 1819, the eldest son of the fourteen children of George Henry Gibbs (1785–1842) of Aldenham, Hertfordshire, and Clifton Hampden, Oxfordshire, and his wife, Caroline (1794–1850), sixth daughter of Charles Crawley, rector of Stowe-nine-Churches, Northamptonshire. The family business was started by his grandfather Antony *Gibbs (1756–1815), the son of an Exeter surgeon who owned a small property at Clyst St George (in the possession of the family since 1560). Antony's elder brother Vicary (1751–1820) became a judge, and his brother George (1753–1818) became a merchant in Bristol. The family came from a modest landed, professional, and mercantile background, and Antony's status within gentry society was confirmed when he married Dorothea Barnetta Hucks, who came from a minor landed family.

Joins family firm Gibbs was educated at Redland near Bristol and at Rugby School, before entering Exeter College, Oxford, where he graduated with third-class honours in classics in 1841. His initial intention was to read for the bar, but he joined the firm. When his father died in 1842, he inherited a good landed estate worth £6000 a year. George Henry Gibbs had inherited the Hucks estates at Clifton Hampden in Oxfordshire, and in 1842 he unexpectedly inherited a further 1500 acres of land as a result of a complex search for heirs in the Hucks lineage (Stone and Stone, 114–6). George Henry felt he should give away part of his windfall to other members of the family, for it 'is not mine but one which Dame Fortune has been pleased to shower upon our family'. He stressed that the Gibbs were a united family in which the fortunes of one were the property of all. (G. H. Gibbs to W. Gibbs, 14 June 1842, Guildhall MS 11021/17). His brother William held up their brotherly affection as a model to be followed by the next generation, 'convinced as I am that strong family affection when chastened and cemented by religion is one of the best preservatives against the temptation of the world and a happy means of confirming us in our hopes of a better' (W. Gibbs to G. H. Gibbs, 29 June 1842, Guildhall MS 11021/17). Such sentiments were, indeed, to characterize the Gibbs family in the future. In 1909 the family estate amounted to 3035 acres in Hertfordshire, 1309 acres in Oxfordshire, and a further 128 acres in Middlesex and Berkshire; in all the 4472 acres were worth £9438 a year (Gibbs, vol. 1, 1910, 103–4).

Gibbs therefore had the option of retreating into the life of a landed gentleman but in 1843 he joined the family business of Antony Gibbs & Sons, merchants and merchant bankers, of which his uncle William Gibbs (1790–1875) had become the senior partner (or 'prior' as the head of the firm was known) on the death of George Henry. It took some time for him to settle to a career in the City, and his mind repeatedly turned to the life of a cultured country gentleman, with interests in scholarship and high-churchmanship. In 1846 his uncle William expressed concern that he was neglecting business, warning that

> great exertion will be necessary on your part for this purpose … I don't mean to say that I should ever wish you … to make those great sacrifices to business which necessity imposed on your dear father and myself in our early days but that your attention to compting house matters should be more *continuous* than it has hitherto been and that during the hours devoted to business your mind and attention should be entirely and *continuously* occupied with it to the exclusion of private letter writing, reading the newspaper, conversation, or anything else *which should take your mind off from the grand object in view.* (W. Gibbs to H. H. Gibbs, 2 March 1846, Guildhall MS 11021/18)

William recommended his nephew to retire to his estate if he found the business oppressive but Gibbs felt that he should stay in the business, for retiring to the country 'would have too much tendency to make my life an idle one' (H. H. Gibbs to W. Gibbs, 25 March 1846, Guildhall MS 11021/21). Although he became 'as complete a merchant as a young man beginning with something like £100,000 in his pocket can be expected to be' (G. Gibbs to W. Gibbs, no date, Guildhall MS 11021/18), he was inclined—at least in his uncle's opinion—to use his facility in writing and

Henry Hucks Gibbs, first Baron Aldenham (1819–1907), by James Faed (after George Frederic Watts, 1876–7)

understanding in order to undertake business too quickly and superficially, and to neglect the 'very dry' work of accounts.

> Unfortunately you now feel that whether you are at the compting house or not the business of the House will not in the least be prejudiced and will go on just the same and you are therefore I think too often tempted to break in on that regular systematic and continuous attention to business during compting house hours which it would be so desirable for you on every count to observe. (W. Gibbs to H. H. Gibbs, 5 April 1852, Guildhall MS 11021/18)

Gibbs eventually became prior in 1875, but had in reality been the dominant influence on the firm since 1858 when his uncle retired from active involvement in the business. William did, however, leave £1 million of capital in the firm at 5 per cent, which was lent to Gibbs after his death in 1875 for a further 20 years—an amount of capital that Gibbs thought led the firm into problems after 1864 in finding adequate outlets.

Expansion of firm Gibbs—like so many other members of the family—was obsessed by the history of the family and a need to restore and enhance its status. His motivation was not simply to reorganize and consolidate its status as a landed family but also to restore its mercantile dignity. Antony Gibbs's business as a wool merchant in Exeter failed in 1789, and he was obliged to sell the family's land at Clyst St George. Subsequently he moved to Spain as an importer of English cloth and exporter of wine and fruit until the French invasion forced him to leave. In 1808 he and his son George Henry formed the firm of Antony Gibbs & Sons in London, trading with Spain and its colonies in Latin America. William joined the partnership in 1813. Antony's failure was a formative influence on the sons who regretted that they had been forced into business at a young age without attending university. They were devoted to restoring the dignity of the family. 'They both equally laboured to repair their father's misfortune', Gibbs remarked in 1857 (H. H. Gibbs to G. Gibbs, 23 January 1857, Guildhall MS 11036/1), paying off his debts and dreaming of regaining the ancestral acres. The pursuit of mercantile success and the purchase of landed property were not alternatives in the mind of Gibbs, but part of a single project of re-establishing the dignity of the family. He admitted to having 'an absurd amount of family feeling', and he vied with his uncle William over who should have the honour of purchasing the 'lost inheritance' of land in Clyst St George. 'I shall have Clyst St George engraven on my heart, as Q. Mary had her lost Calais' (H. H. Gibbs to G. Gibbs, 23 January 1857, Guildhall MS 11036/1).

Until 1842 Antony Gibbs & Sons was a relatively modest and unadventurous concern but it was transformed by what William considered an 'act of insanity' (cited in Mathew, *DBB*): making loans to the government of Peru on the security of a concession to sell guano. The government retained ownership of the deposits, but Gibbs obtained the monopoly for most of Europe for this valuable fertilizer. Gibbs exulted in his new empire of bird droppings. 'As Louis XIV said, for us now "il n'y a plus de Pyrénées, ni d'Alpes non plus." France, Spain, Italy and Belgium are united in a vast monarchy of Guano!' (ibid.). A more ribald rhyme emphasized 'The house of Gibbs that made their dibs by selling turds of foreign birds' (private information). The firm was transformed, and the net profits mounted from £17,156 in 1848 to £125,562 in 1858. Subsequently, the guano monopoly was threatened by the growth of economic nationalism and Gibbs turned to more speculative lending and investment, encouraged by the large sums left in the firm by his uncle. His policy was initially not successful, and results fell from an average annual net profit of £137,244 in 1860–64 to an average net loss of £15,276 in 1865–9. However, the firm did make a successful transition into a merchant bank, dealing in foreign exchange, acceptances and commercial credit, with occasional flotations of government loans.

In Latin America the firm successfully replaced Peruvian guano with nitrates, initially in Peru and subsequently in Chile when territory was transferred as a result of the War of the Pacific of 1879–83. Unlike guano, where the government retained ownership, the firm was responsible for both the production and the marketing of nitrates, and negotiated combinations to control the industry. In 1881 the declining merchant house of Antony's elder brother George (1753–1818)—Gibbs, Bright & Co. of Liverpool and Bristol—was acquired, along with Bright Brothers in Melbourne, Sydney, Brisbane, and Dunedin. Gibbs, Bright & Co. traded to the West Indies which was not profitable, and the Bristol house was closed in 1887. There was no major shift to Australia, where profits from shipping and trade were often offset by losses from mining investments. The main interest of the firm continued to be in fertilizers from Latin America.

Bimetallism In 1853 Gibbs became a director of the Bank of England and remained on the court until 1901, serving as governor from 1875 to 1877. He was a member of the royal commission on the stock exchange between 1877 and 1878, and of that on the depression of trade and industry in 1885–6. He became notorious in the City as an advocate of bimetallism, providing leadership as president of the Bimetallic League. Sir William Harcourt, his neighbour at Nuneham Courtney, was made into one of the participants in a dramatic, but sadly unstaged, conversation of 114 pages on the merits and flaws of monetarizing silver. The expansion of the production of silver caused a depreciation against gold-based currencies, leading to problems in silver-based economies such as Mexico, Peru, Chile, and India. Gibbs's involvement in trade with silver-based countries made him aware of the problems caused by disruption of currency, and he argued that merchants were more aware of the difficulties than bankers who simply played with the exchanges. Bimetallism would, he argued, allow 'the restoration of the Par of Exchange between Gold and Silver using Countries, the establishment of One Money in the World of Commerce in place of two disjointed monies' (H. H. Gibbs to W. Harcourt, 17 May 1889, Guildhall MSS 11021/25).

Gibbs's case rested not only on the international problems of unbalanced exchanges, but on the consequences for British society. Despite the apparent benefits of falling prices he believed that workers would soon suffer when the erosion of industrial profits led to the closure of concerns and a loss of employment. Further, falling prices benefited creditors and the banks against productive interests. He dismissed the claim of bankers that England was the financial centre of the world and that the gold standard should not be disturbed: their position in fact rested on commerce, about which bankers knew nothing. 'Oh Lord, Lord! as Pepys would say; to think of a man of your intelligence', he wrote to Harcourt in 1892:

> echoing that newspaper rubbish about the prosperity of England resting upon its being a place where you could *always get Gold!*. … The Money Market! There is your error! You take the Money Market to comprise the whole of the Commerce of England. … You have elected to march with the Drones, and against the Working bees. I take the other side … it is the industrious class, the Farmer, the Merchant, and the Manufacturer, who are the great employers of labour, and … the Banker and the Annuitant do comparatively little for them. (H. H. Gibbs to W. Harcourt, 14 November 1892, Guildhall MS 11021/25)

His attempt to create an alliance of workers, manufacturers, and merchants was doomed to failure.

Other interests Although bimetallism was Gibbs's main interest in political life, he was a significant figure in City Conservatism. In 1854 he complained that the Conservatives in the City were opposing the government and backing Disraeli and Derby. He was inclined to support the government, 'who profess to be Liberal Conservatives; and that is what every good politician should be' (H. H. Gibbs to W. Gibbs, 16 May 1854, Guildhall MS 11021/18). Subsequently he supported Salisbury as the leader of the party on the grounds that he was the most capable Conservative statesman with the 'most Liberal grasp of mind' who offered 'a truly liberal Conservatism and conservative Liberalism' (H. H. Gibbs to Greenwood, 4 May 1881, Guildhall MS 11021/21). He was active in the transformation of the City from Liberalism to Conservatism, attracting men such as George Goschen to the party and opposing the old guard of the corporation. In 1887 his close friend and member for the City, John Gellibrand Hubbard, remarked that 'I accept your voice as the voice of the City' (J. G. Hubbard to H. H. Gibbs, 25 June 1887, Guildhall MS 11021/24). He was involved with other members of the family in establishing the *St James Gazette* in 1880, a loss-making paper which they owned until 1888. Although he was invited to stand for parliament for Bristol in 1862, he declined this and other offers and only succumbed in April 1891 when he won a by-election in the City. He stood down at the general election of July 1892. When he was raised to the peerage as Baron Aldenham on 31 January 1896, he commented that 'my chief claim arose from my standing in the gap when the government wanted a safe candidate for the City, and my serving 15 months in Parliament against my will—no great achievements!' (note by H. H. Gibbs, Guildhall MS 11021/27).

Gibbs had wide interests outside his business, as his uncle was well aware, but of which he was unrepentant. He was a landowner whose passion for country pursuits survived the mishap of shooting off his right hand in 1864. He was a JP in both Middlesex and Hertfordshire, and served as the high sheriff of Hertfordshire in 1884. He was appointed a trustee of the National Portrait Gallery by W. H. Smith in 1890, and was president of Guy's Hospital from 1880 to 1896. He was a noted bibliophile with a celebrated library. He edited texts for the Early English Text Society and the Roxburghe Club, wrote a study of the Spanish card game of *ombre*, and was an active member of the Philological Society from 1859, for which he sub-edited the letters C and K for the *New English Dictionary*, a venture he considered 'rather as a child of my own' (note by H. H. Gibbs, Guildhall MS 11021/20). His main interest, however, was religion.

Gibbs's uncle William Gibbs was a supporter of the Tractarians, and both he and his sons were leading benefactors of Keble College, Oxford. William was involved in building a number of churches and in the restoration of Exeter and Bristol cathedrals. His country house at Tyntesfield near Bristol was lavishly rebuilt in the style of the old town hall in Prague and the cathedral of San Marco, with a large chapel designed by Arthur Blomfield in the style of the Sainte-Chapelle, which was served by high-church clergymen who lived in celibacy in a cottage in the rose garden. This was the world of high Anglicanism in which Gibbs was at home. He was a member of council of Keble College; supported the Anglican sisterhood at Christ Church, Albany; restored the churches at Clifton Hampden and Aldenham; served as a member of the house of laymen of the province of Canterbury and as treasurer of

Church House; and was involved in the London Church Building Society. In 1862 he joined the English Church Union, becoming a trustee in 1876, serving as president, and sitting on the council until his death. He devoted time and money to the new diocese of St Albans, and was actively involved—in acrimonious dispute with Sir Edmund Beckett, Lord Grimthorpe—in the restoration of the abbey. He was a leading member of the Club of Nobody's Friends, a body started by William Stevens, a wholesale hosier who was devoted to the church and often entertained like-minded people. In 1806 it was agreed to form a club which would dine three times a year. It continued after Stevens's death, with thirty clerical and thirty lay members who included J. G. Hubbard, W. H. Smith, and William Butterfield. Gibbs became president. Not surprisingly the firm was permeated with high Anglicanism: not only was the head known as the prior but the branches were referred to as 'Septuagint', 'Pharisees', and 'Sadducees'.

Family life Gibbs married on 6 May 1845 Louisa Anne (*b.* 1818), third daughter of William *Adams, doctor of laws and fellow of the College of Advocates. She died on 17 April 1897. They had six sons and a daughter. The eldest son, Alban George Henry, succeeded his father as MP for the City between 1892 and 1906, with a hiatus in 1904 when he resigned as a result of the sale of Chilean ships to the British government. Vicary *Gibbs, the third son, was MP for St Albans between 1892 and 1904, and produced a new edition of the *Complete Peerage* which had been compiled by his mother's brother George Edward Cokayne (who married Gibbs's sister in 1856). The fifth son, Kenneth, was vicar of Aldenham and archdeacon of St Albans; the sixth and youngest son, Henry Lloyd, died the day after his father. The business heir was the fourth son, Herbert Cokayne *Gibbs, first Lord Hunsdon (1854–1935), who became a partner in 1882. Henry Hucks Gibbs died at his home, Aldenham House, Hertfordshire, on 13 September 1907 of bladder and prostate disease, and exhaustion; he was buried in Aldenham churchyard.

MARTIN DAUNTON

Sources W. M. Mathew, 'Gibbs, Henry Hucks', *DBB* • W. M. Mathew, *The house of Gibbs and the Peruvian guano monopoly* (1981) • H. Blakemore, *British nitrates and Chilean politics, 1886–1896: Balmaceda and north* (1974) • R. Greenhill and R. Miller, 'The Peruvian government and the nitrate trade, 1873–9', *Journal of Latin American Studies*, 5 (1973) • R. G. Greenhill, 'Merchants and the Latin American trades', *Business imperialism, 1840–1930: an inquiry based on British experience in Latin America*, ed. D. C. M. Platt (1977), 159–97 • R. G. Greenhill, 'The nitrate and iodine trades, 1880–1914', *Business imperialism, 1840–1930: an inquiry based on British experience in Latin America*, ed. D. C. M. Platt (1977), 231–83 • W. Maude, *Merchants and bankers: a brief record of Antony Gibbs and Sons … 1808–1958* (privately printed, London, 1958) • M. J. Daunton, 'Inheritance and succession in the City of London in the nineteenth century', *Business History*, 30 (1988), 269-86 • M. Girouard, *The Victorian country house*, rev. edn (1979), 243–51 • GEC, *Peerage*, new edn, vol. 1 • L. Stone and J. F. Stone, *An open elite? England, 1540–1880* (1984) • E. H. H. Green, 'Rentiers versus producers? The political economy of the bimetallic controversy, *c.*1880–1898', *EngHR*, 103 (1988), 588–612 • GL, Guildhall MSS 11021/17, 11021/18, 11021/20, 11021/21, 11021/24, 11021/25, 11021/27, 11036/1 • private information (2004) [Christopher Gibbs and J. Mordaunt Crook]

Archives BLPES, corresp. and papers relating to bimetallism • GL, corresp. • Herts. ALS, D/EAM | Balliol Oxf., letters to Sir Louis Mallet • BL, corresp. with Arthur James Balfour, Add. MS 49791, *passim* • Bodl. Oxf., corresp. with Sir William Harcourt • GL, records of Antony Gibbs & Sons • U. Edin. L., corresp. with J. O. Halliwell-Phillipps

Likenesses G. F. Watts, portrait, 1878, priv. coll.; formerly in possession of Lord Aldenham, 1912 • G. F. Watts, portrait, 1896, priv. coll.; formerly in possession of Herbert Gibbs, 1912 • V. Blanchard, carte-de-visite, NPG • J. Faed, mezzotint (after G. F. Watts, 1876–7), NPG [*see illus.*] • Maull & Polyblank, cabinet photograph, NPG • Pet, chromolithograph, NPG

Wealth at death £703,729 6*s.* 2*d.*: probate, 20 Dec 1907, *CGPLA Eng. & Wales* • £668,211: Mathew, 'Gibbs, Henry Hucks' • £703,700: *DNB*; GEC, *Peerage*

Gibbs, Herbert Cokayne, first Baron Hunsdon of Hunsdon (1854–1935), merchant banker, was born on 14 May 1854 at Frognal, Hampstead, Middlesex, the fourth son of merchant banker Henry Hucks *Gibbs, first Baron Aldenham (1819–1907), and Louisa Anne (1818–1897), daughter of William Adams. After schooling at Winchester College (1868–71), he attended Trinity College, Cambridge (BA, 1877). Following a course of training (1877–9), in 1879 he joined Antony Gibbs & Sons, the family firm, at 22 Bishopsgate, London. He married Anna Maria (1862–1938), daughter of Richard Durant, of High Canons, Hertfordshire, in 1885. The couple had three sons and three daughters.

Founded in 1808 the Gibbs firm originally had connections with Spain, and by 1820 it had adopted the west coast of South America as a field for its activities. Guano became its main interest from 1842, transforming the house from a small mercantile establishment to a prominent City merchant bank. When Gibbs joined, output of guano was declining, successfully substituted by the new nitrate fertilizers. The firm became a major participant in the financing, production, and trade of Chilean nitrate when Chile annexed the rich Peruvian province of Tarapacá during the Pacific War at the end of 1880. Gibbs was sent to Valparaiso (March 1880 to 1881) to supervise the closure of the Peruvian branches and the investment in nitrate *oficinas*. After 1881 the house also had widespread interests in Australasian businesses, mainly in shipping, import trading, and mining; and it later became involved in other mining ventures elsewhere, through participation in the Exploration Company.

During the second half of the nineteenth century Antony Gibbs & Sons underwent substantial transformation. In the 1860s it had carried on an enormously profitable commission business, with annual profits of up to £137,000. Later it was forced by a decline in this trade into enterprises in which it had no experience. Its main staple remained nitrate but this was extraordinarily speculative and unprofitable, especially in the last two decades of the century when annual profits dropped as low as £15,000. Over the same period there was also a sharp decline in the capital base of the firm (due to heavy withdrawals by partners). 'Could any depositor who was not a relation leave his money with us if he knew the position?' argued Gibbs in 1902 (Gibbs MS 11044/2, fol. 284). His father had entered parliament in 1891, representing the City of London; and other Gibbs partners were similarly distracted by parliamentary commitments. This dangerous lack of active leadership was to be ended by Herbert Gibbs: a full partner and director from 1882, he was to be the key figure in the company from 1900 to 1933. He was responsible for the nitrate side of the business, which became the supplier of thousands of tons of nitrate required by the Ministry of Munitions during the First World War. When the Nitrate and Soda Executive was formed to co-ordinate purchases among the allies in 1917, Gibbs was appointed director of purchases for Europe, and the firm kept its complicated accounts without charge. In recognition of his war services the French government conferred on him the Légion d'honneur in 1918. He was created Baron Hunsdon of Hunsdon in 1923.

Under Gibbs's firm leadership, the fortunes of the firm recovered. By the early 1920s the capital of Antony Gibbs & Sons stood at over £2 million. However, in 1920, when wartime demand had ceased, the nitrate industry was suffering a severe crisis. While supply increased rapidly, consumption stagnated. To counter the threat of German synthetic nitrate, to stabilize prices, and to improve consumption, Gibbs organized a pool of European nitrate-holders in February 1921. He was elected chairman and his firm appointed as agents. Of the million tons held by the pool only 100,000 tons were sold in the first half of 1921. After unsuccessful negotiations with the Chilean Association of Nitrate Producers concerning prices, in the face of a deteriorating social and financial situation in Chile President Alessandri invited Gibbs to an emergency meeting. Gibbs sailed on 25 August 1921 and in October an agreement was reached: the association would reduce prices to 14*s.* to stimulate sales, but it would compensate the pool by reimbursing £1.5 million.

These and related events constituted a major difficulty for Antony Gibbs & Sons. The firm suffered a severe loss of working capital, and new developments were sharply restricted. In 1930, under a special act of the Chilean government, the Compañía de Salitre de Chile (Cosach) was organized; this became the sole producer of nitrate and iodine. Nationalization put an end to what was still the main business of the house, the management of *oficinas* and supply stores. Exports of nitrate were also monopolized and the firm ceased to have any interests in nitrate business, except as credit managers for the group of London banks who helped to finance Cosach's activities and as agents for the sale of iodine.

In addition to his role in the family firm, Gibbs was chairman of the Alianza Nitrate Company from 1895 to 1928, and of the Pan de Azúcar Nitrate Company from 1901 to 1926. He was a director of the Rio de Janeiro City Improvement Company from 1884, and its chairman from 1905 to 1935. From 1908 he also sat on the board of the Australian Mutual Provident Society.

A dynamic member of the business community, Gibbs was described as 'shrewd and capable, but above all transparently honest' (*The Times*, 27 May 1935). Active on behalf of the Conservative Party, Gibbs was also chairman of the City of London Conservative Association from 1912 to 1932. He shared his political interests with his wife, who was president of the women's branch of the association. From 1924 to 1932 he was president of the 1912 Club, his brainchild, created to combat socialism and radicalism in the East End constituencies. Under his leadership, in 1924 the association protested against the formation of a Labour government; and it denounced the depressing effect of the December 1923 general election on the real value of the British government's long-dated securities, as a warning to the Liberals over collaboration with MacDonald.

In 1914 Gibbs had opposed Irish home rule: 'No compromise is possible in this question. The Home Rule Bill must go; for the only alternatives are national dishonour or civil war' (*The Times*, 8 April 1914); and he raised funds for the Ulster Union Defence League. He combated modern social legislation which 'relieved individuals from responsibility and weakened the character of the nation' (*The Times*, 3 April 1924). The changes introduced since 1907 by successive governments in taxation methods were also regrettable, according to Gibbs. He condemned the heavy consequences of death taxes and of super-tax for British industry and trade, and favoured a constitutional review that would put an end to the Commons' sole control over finance.

Gibbs took part in the parliamentary delegation sent to Russia in 1912, returning the visit of the Duma. In 1919 he was member of the Indemnity Committee, concerned with war debts, and the war cabinet agreed he should be one of the delegates to the Paris peace conference; he was replaced at the last moment by Lord Sumner. He then delivered a speech on German indemnity, and a copy of this was taken to Paris by the delegates. In 1926 Gibbs helped to create and was first chairman of the Empires Industries Association, to increase trade within the empire after the dissolution of the British Commonwealth Union. A commissioner of the Public Works Loan Board from 1884, he served as deputy chairman in 1908, and chairman from 1921. Some sixty-five Labour MPs voted in 1930—unsuccessfully—against the continuance of Gibbs in this office, remembering that during the 1926 strike he had said that the miners were the enemies and that starvation was a proper weapon to be used against them.

Gibbs published a number of works dealing with genealogy, currency, and taxation. In 1908 he had bought a country house, Briggens, in the manor of Hunsdon, near Ware, Hertfordshire. This fueled his interest in local history, and led to his publication of *The Parish Register of Hunsdon* (1915) and the *History of Gibbs of Fenton, in Dartington* (1925). Although more concerned about the practice of business than about economic theory, Gibbs was a convinced bimetallist, writing *A Bimetallic Primer* (1894), *Address on Bimetallism* (1895), and several letters and articles. He shared his views with his father, a fervent advocate of bimetallism, and founder, along with Henry Riversdale Grenfell, of the Bimetallic League in the early 1880s, and later its president.

Appointed an income tax commissioner in 1886, Gibbs

became increasingly interested in fiscal matters, publishing on the subject several pamphlets, articles, and letters in the press. In *The Incidence of Income Tax and Wasting Securities* (1904), he exposed the anomalies of the law over assets which became exhausted after a period of time, such as quarries or mines, and campaigned to bring up the question of these depreciating funds. In 1920 he gave evidence on 'wasting assets abroad' before the royal commission on income tax. In these questions and many other public topics he was a valued correspondent of *The Times*.

Like his brother Vicary *Gibbs, Herbert Gibbs was an accomplished gardener and an excellent shot. A lifelong fly-fisher he later took up painting watercolours and sketching. He was a Hertfordshire magistrate and also served as high sheriff of the county in 1913. Gibbs died after a short illness on 22 May 1935 at his home, Briggens, Hertfordshire. He was buried at St Dunstan's Church, Hunsdon, on 25 May. INÉS ROLDÁN

Sources J. A. Gibbs, *The history of Antony and Dorothea Gibbs* (1922) • H. Blakemore, *British nitrates and Chilean politics, 1886–1896: Balmaceda and north* (1974) • R. Gibbs, *Pedigree of the family of Gibbs of Pytte in the parish church of Clyst St George*, 4th edn (1981) • W. Maude, *Merchants and bankers: a brief record of Antony Gibbs and Sons … 1808–1958* (privately printed, London, 1958) • M. Monteón, *Chile in the nitrate era: the evolution of economic dependence, 1880–1930* (1982) • R. G. Greenhill, *Antony Gibbs and Sons and the organization of the iodine trade, 1870–1914* (1970) • R. G. Greenhill, 'Merchants and the Latin American trades', *Business imperialism, 1840–1930: an inquiry based on British experience in Latin America*, ed. D. C. M. Platt (1977), 159–97 • R. P. T. Davenport-Hines, 'Gibbs, Herbert Cokayne', *DBB* • W. M. Mathew, *The house of Gibbs and the Peruvian guano monopoly* (1981) • *Hansard 5L* (1923–35) • *The Times* (24 May 1935) • *The Times* (27 May 1935) • *The Times* (3 April 1924) • *Bankers' Magazine*, 140 (1935), 33 • d. cert. • *CGPLA Eng. & Wales* (1935) • private information (2004) • GEC, *Peerage* • GL, Gibbs MS 11044/2

Archives GL • ING Barings, London | PRO, FO 16, 371 • University of Sheffield, corresp. with W. A. S. Hewins

Likenesses E. U. Eddis, group portrait, drawing, 1860, priv. coll. • W. E. Miller, drawing, 1882, priv. coll. • J. Hay, crayon, 1932, priv. coll. • W. Ouless, oils, Briggens, Hunsdon, Hertfordshire • photograph, repro. in *The Times* (15 Feb 1933)

Wealth at death £116,285 18*s*. 4*d*.: probate, 16 Aug 1935, *CGPLA Eng. & Wales*

Gibbs, Sir Humphrey Vicary (1902–1990), farmer and colonial administrator, was born on 22 November 1902 at 9 Portman Square, London, the third son and sixth and youngest child of Herbert Cokayne *Gibbs, first Baron Hunsdon of Hunsdon (1854–1935), merchant banker, and his wife, Anna Maria (1862–1938), fourth daughter of Richard Durant, of High Canons, Hertfordshire. The Gibbs family was wealthy and well connected in the City of London, which at various times his grandfather Henry Hucks *Gibbs, first Baron Aldenham, and his uncle Alban George Henry Gibbs, second Baron Aldenham, represented in parliament. His brothers Walter Durant Gibbs, fourth Baron Aldenham, and Sir Geoffrey Cokayne Gibbs were notable bankers in the City.

Gibbs was educated at Ludgrove preparatory school, Eton College (where he was head of Pop), and Trinity College, Cambridge, which he left after a year to pursue training courses in various branches of agriculture. In 1928 he emigrated to Southern Rhodesia, where he purchased a 6000 acre farm near Bulawayo. He gained a reputation for progressive farming and formed the Rhodesia National Farmers' Union. Regarding soil and wildlife conservation as a matter of great urgency, he successfully campaigned for a national resources board. On 17 January 1934 he married Molly Peel Nelson (1912–1997), second daughter of John Peel Nelson, businessman, of Bulawayo. They had five sons.

In 1947 Gibbs was invited to stand for parliament as a member of Sir Godfrey Huggins's ruling United Party and was elected as member for Wankie. He was not a natural parliamentarian: Huggins remarked that he was 'far too honest' (*DNB*). Although he later quipped that his only parliamentary contributions had been to say 'Hear, hear', he spoke significantly on the creation of national parks and a maize levy on European farmers to assist in developing African agriculture. He retired from parliament in 1953, but retained the chairmanship of the United Party until 1959. He refused to become involved in a plot to make him leader of the Liberal Party, choosing farming and several directorships in leading Rhodesian firms over party politics. Strongly involved in supporting the development of the Anglican church in Central Africa, and of European and African education, he helped in 1939 to found the Cyrene mission near Bulawayo, which became famous as a centre for African arts and crafts. He played a leading role in founding Peterhouse and Mizeki College, and developed an enthusiastic interest in multiracial schooling. For many years he chaired the Beit Trust, which provided funds to causes throughout the federation.

In 1959 Gibbs accepted the post of governor of Southern Rhodesia, the first 'Rhodesian' so appointed. Tall, charming, strikingly handsome, and regarded as 'above party', he was thought of as ideal for the post. The governorship of Southern Rhodesia, a self-governing colony, was largely ceremonial, resembling the role of a dominion governor-general, rather than the governorship of a dependency, even if its prerogatives were theoretically extensive. Invariably the governor acted on the advice of his prime minister. Gibbs felt constitutionally bound, for example, to authorize Sir Edgar Whitehead's controversial Law and Order Maintenance Act (1960). Following the Rhodesian Front's electoral victory in 1962, his speeches from the throne reflected the growing cabinet hostility towards what it regarded as British duplicity in withholding independence. In May 1963 he also became acting governor-general of the Federation of Rhodesia and Nyasaland, overseeing the final details of its dissolution. He exercised his constitutional right to warn when he attempted unsuccessfully to persuade his prime minister, Winston Field, to face down his extremist critics within the Rhodesian Front. Ian Smith, who succeeded as prime minister, however, pledged to gain independence under white minority rule, if necessary through an illegal unilateral declaration of independence (UDI).

From the outset Gibbs seemed somewhat unassertive in his dealings with Smith. In April 1965, on the qualified advice of the chief justice, he granted Smith a dissolution even though parliament had two years to run. This was one area where he had more authority than a dominion governor-general. The British government, moreover, reaffirmed its policy of non-intervention in the colony, so that he had no alternative advice on which to rely. Unconventionally, when he met the opposition leader, David Butler, to ascertain whether he could form a government in the event of Smith resigning, both the chief justice and Smith were present at the interview. The Rhodesian Front went on to a crushing election victory. UDI now seemed certain, a crisis for which Gibbs was politically ill equipped. While legality lasted, he felt constitutionally obliged to follow Smith's advice by authorizing a state of emergency on 5 November 1965, even though it presaged UDI, which followed on 11 November. The British government immediately reaffirmed Gibbs's position as the only lawful authority in the rebel colony, although he himself would have preferred to retire to his farm. He dismissed the cabinet, which cut off his salary, household utilities, telephone, official car, and police escort. He refused a salary from Britain, used a public telephone box to contact Whitehall, and continued to hold court at Government House in defiance of Smith. The regime denounced him as a fellow traveller of the British Labour Party, because his loyalty to the sovereign was now effectively routed through the Commonwealth relations secretary and Wilson. Gibbs's influence was minimal, since civil servants and the security forces were encouraged to remain at their posts. The regime installed a rival officer administering the government, claiming to continue to govern in the name of the queen of Rhodesia, whom it distinguished from Wilson's constitutional instrument. Gibbs's peculiar position was encapsulated in his advice to Sam Putterill, the army commander, in 1966: 'Sam, you had better open Parliament, for not to do so would be a confrontation. But don't appear as if you are enjoying it!' (Flower, 82).

Gibbs accompanied Smith to the abortive negotiations on board *Tiger* in 1966 and *Fearless* in 1968, and in 1969, following Smith's decision to declare a republic, he was allowed to retire to his farm. Having been appointed OBE in 1959, KCMG in 1960, and KCVO in 1965, he was promoted GCVO and sworn a privy counsellor on retirement. Parliament later awarded him £66,000 compensation for some of the costs incurred following UDI. He received honorary degrees from the universities of Birmingham and East Anglia, both in 1969. As a founder of the multiracial organization People against Racial Discrimination he campaigned unsuccessfully for accepting the Anglo-Rhodesian settlement proposals of 1971. Although vindicated by the lawful independence of Zimbabwe in 1980, as a traditional monarchist he had no natural enthusiasm for a republic which now denied the queen the allegiance he had championed. In 1983, following a gun attack on his wife's car by a deranged employee, and with widening government repression in Matabeleland, he decided to retire to Borrowdale, Harare, where he died on 5 November 1990, after a short illness. He was survived by his wife, Molly, who had been made DBE in 1969 in recognition of her charitable work, and by their five sons. A memorial service was held in the chapel of the Order of the British Empire, St Paul's Cathedral, on 15 January 1991.

DONAL LOWRY

Sources *DNB* · *The Times* (6 Nov 1990) · *The Times* (7 Nov 1990) · *The Times* (20 Nov 1990) · *The Independent* (9 Nov 1990) · *WWW* · Burke, *Peerage* · *Rhodesia Herald* · *Bulawayo Chronicle* · Debates of the Southern Rhodesian legislative assembly, 1948–53 · Lord Alport, *Sudden assignment* (1965) · J. Barber, *Rhodesia: the road to rebellion* (1967) · R. Blake, *A history of Rhodesia* (1978) · F. Clements, *Rhodesia: the course to collision* (1969) · C. Dupont, *The reluctant president* (1978) · K. Flower, *Serving secretly: an intelligence chief on record Rhodesia into Zimbabwe 1964 to 1981* (1987) · I. Hancock, *White liberals, moderates and radicals in Rhodesia, 1953–1980* (1984) · R. Hodder-Williams, *White farmers in Rhodesia, 1890–1965: a history of the Marandellas district* (1983) · P. Joyce, *Anatomy of a rebel. Smith of Rhodesia: a biography* (1974) · L. J. McFarlane, 'Justifying rebellion: black and white nationalism in Rhodesia', *Journal of Commonwealth Political Studies*, 6 (1968), 54–79 · A. Megahey, *Humphrey Gibbs, beleaguered governor: Southern Rhodesia, 1959–69* (1998) · P. Murphy, *Party politics and decolonization: the conservative party and British colonial policy in tropical Africa, 1951–1964* (1995) · I. Smith, *The great betrayal* (1997) · A. R. W. Stumbles, *Some recollections of a Rhodesian speaker* (1980) · H. Wilson, *The labour government, 1964–1970* (1974) · J. R. T. Wood, *The Welensky papers: a history of the Federation of Rhodesia and Nyasaland* (1983) · K. Young, *Rhodesia and independence: a study in British colonial policy* (1967)

Archives Peterhouse, Marondera, Zimbabwe, Peterhouse School Archives, Gibbs Building, Gibbs MSS, corresp., press cuttings, autobiographical sketch | Bodl. RH, Sir Robert Tredgold MSS · Bodl. RH, Sir Roy Welensky MSS · Bodl. RH, Sir Edgar Whitehead MSS | FILM BBC

Likenesses photograph, repro. in *The Times* (7 Nov 1990) · photograph, repro. in *The Independent* · portrait; in Rhodesian parliament until March 1966

Gibbs, James (*bap.* **1673**, *d.* **1724**), physician and poet, son of James Gibbs, vicar of Gorran in Cornwall, and his wife, Mary, was baptized at Gorran on 16 June 1673. He was a student of Exeter College, Oxford. In a letter to Archbishop Tenison, preserved among the manuscripts in Lambeth Palace Library, he solicits Tenison's 'favour and assistance' in promoting 'a new metrical version of the Psalms'. The letter is undated, but in 1701 his translation of the first fifteen of the psalms of David was published in London, and a second edition followed in 1712. A copy of the latter was discovered in Swift's library, containing some severe marginal criticism by the dean, including the verse:

Thy heavy hand restrain;
Have mercy, Dr. Gibbs:
Do not, I pray thee, paper stain
With rhymes retail'd in dribbs.
(*Works*, 2.370)

As well as poetry, Gibbs published *Observations of various eminent cures of scrophulous distempers, commonly call'd the king's evil* (1712). It contains an essay written in his defence after a trial at Launceston in 1710 which concerned his cure of a lad from Plymouth. He attacks the idea that unlearned and untrained persons could cure the disease. The methods he describes employ a variety of medicines and require a knowledge of physic that can only be acquired after 'Long Labour and expensive studies'. Some of the cases relate to persons living at Tregony, Gorran, and other places in Cornwall, where he practised. Gibbs died at Tregony on 4 April 1724.

W. F. Wentworth-Shields, *rev.* Patrick Wallis

Sources Boase & Courtney, *Bibl. Corn.*, 1.171–2, 3.1193 • *The works of Jonathan Swift … with a memoir of the author*, ed. [T. Roscoe], 2 (1841), 369–72 • Nichols, *Lit. anecdotes*, 1.286 • *IGI* • P. J. Wallis and R. V. Wallis, *Eighteenth century medics*, 2nd edn (1988) • A. M. Roos, 'Luminaries in medicine: Richard Mead, James Gibbs, and solar and lunar effects on the human body in early modern England', *Bulletin of the History of Medicine*, 74 (2000)
Archives LPL, Lambeth MS 937, art. 24, 25

Gibbs [Gibb], **James** (**1682–1754**), architect, was born on 23 December 1682 at Fittysmire, Aberdeen, the son of Patrick Gibb, a prosperous merchant, and his second wife, Ann Gordon. A son, William (*d.* 1708–9), from Patrick's first marriage, was the only surviving sibling of Gibbs. Both his parents were Scottish Roman Catholics.

Early years and education Gibbs was educated at the grammar school and at Marischal College, Aberdeen. According to 'A manuscri[pt] by Mr. Gibbs memorandums, &c.', which is semi-autobiographical, following his parents' death about 1700, he went to the Netherlands, perhaps to live with relatives, Peter and Elspeth Morison; this residence was followed by travels through France, Germany, Austria, and Italy, during which he examined a wide range of historical and modern buildings. On 12 October 1703 he registered at the Scots College in Rome to train as a priest. By August 1704, having been terrified by the rector's rudeness, he left without taking his vows.

According to a fellow student, James Gordon, Gibbs remained in Rome to 'apply himself to painting, seemingly to have a great genious for that employment' (Friedman, *James Gibbs*, 5–6). He may already have considered an architectural career, since a letter of 1713 from John Erskine, earl of Mar, to Robert Harley claims that he 'studied architecture at Rome and elsewhere sixteen years' (*Portland MSS*, 10.301). In a letter of 11 August 1717 he refers to 'my old masters' Carlo Fontana, then the most influential architect in Rome, and Ambramo Paris (*Stuart Papers*, 2.568), and he may also have been taught by Pietro Francesco Garroli, professor of perspective at the Accademia di San Luca. Gibbs was the first Briton to receive a professional architectural training abroad. In 1706 he was living in the strada Paolina, near the piazza di Spagna. He remained in Rome until late 1708, a period which had the most profound impact on his early career and on the formation of a personal style that combined late baroque and antique classical architectural vocabularies, which was rivalled in England only by that of his contemporary Nicholas Hawksmoor.

Early work, 1709–1719 Gibbs had arrived in London by November 1708. As early as February 1709 he could write of having 'a great many very good friends here … of the first rank and quality … but their promises are not a present relief for my circumstances' (*Egmont MSS*, 2.234–5). He soon received a sinecure commission at the garrison at Stirling Castle from the earl of Mar, for whom he designed

James Gibbs (1682–1754), by John Michael Rysbrack, 1726

a lodge (*c*.1710; dem.) at nearby Alloa in Clackmannanshire. His first known architectural design, it derives from Bernini's Palazzo Chigi, Rome. He remodelled a house (1710; dem.) in the privy gardens at Whitehall, London, for Mar and Hugh Campbell, third earl of Loudoun, joint secretaries of state for Scotland. Gibbs quickly established his presence in the capital. In 1711 he became a founder member of Sir Godfrey Kneller's cosmopolitan academy of painting in Great Queen Street. He designed the dedication engraving to Prince George of Denmark in John Flamsteed's *Historia coelestis* (1712), purloining a plate from Andrea Pozzo's *Perspectiva pictorum et architectorum* (1702).

On 18 November 1713, with the help of Mar, Robert Harley, and Christopher Wren, Gibbs secured the coveted co-surveyorship, with Hawksmoor, to the commissioners for the building of fifty new churches. He had already submitted in 1713 two remarkable wooden models for avant-garde churches in the form of antique classical temples. He then proposed one based on the temple of Fortuna Virilis, Rome, and another of a more baroque flavour, both for St Mary-le-Strand (1714), together with a scheme for a 250 foot high column in the Strand dedicated to Queen Anne, based on Trajan's column, Rome; this was abandoned at the queen's death on 1 August 1714.

Gibbs's final design for St Mary's, approved on 4 November 1714, for which he made a wooden model, was erected at a cost of £20,106; the building accounts are preserved at Lambeth Palace. The church was his first public building. Its lavish, exquisite detailing relies on Francesco Borromini and Fontana, blatantly Roman associations which were condemned by a later critic, Batty Langley, as 'a mere groupe of absurdities' (*Grub-Street Journal*, 254, 7 Nov 1734, 1). In December 1715 Gibbs was deprived of his surveyorship, which he blamed on 'a false report … that misrepresented me as a papest and a disaffected person, which … is intirly false and scandalous' (Friedman, *James Gibbs*, 10), but was permitted to oversee the completion of St Mary's, which was consecrated on 1 January 1724. A mezzotint of about 1723 by Peter Pelham, after a lost portrait by Hans Hysing, shows the architect well dressed and confident, holding a plan of his church, but losing the surveyorship was a mighty blow. He toyed with the idea of joining Mar—then exiled for his leading part in the unsuccessful Jacobite rising—at Paris in 1716–17—but 'Necessity requires to prefer a little profit to pleasure' (*Stuart Papers*, 2.568).

Gibbs now set about re-establishing his public career. On 18 December 1716 he was admitted to the St Luke's Club, which his friend George Vertue described as one of 'the Tip top Clubbs of all, for men of the highest Character in Arts' (Friedman, *James Gibbs*, 21), and aligned himself with the gardener Charles Bridgeman, the sculptor John Michael Rysbrack, and the painter Sir James Thornhill, with whom he subsequently collaborated. Gibbs served as club steward in 1719. During these wilderness years he was employed mainly by tories and Jacobites on private, domestic commissions. For James Johnson, former secretary of state for Scotland, he built a beautiful octagonal pavilion (1716–21) at Twickenham, Middlesex (now the Orleans House Museum), with its rich, proto-rococo decoration executed by Gibbs's favourite plasterers, Carlo Giuseppe Artari and Giovanni Bagutti. For Sir William Wyndham he radically remodelled the Tudor fabric of Witham Park, Somerset, by inserting a double temple portico entrance (*c*.1717; dem.), anticipating Robert Adam's later and more famous example at Osterley Park, Middlesex. The remodelling of the Elizabethan mansion at Cannons, near Edgware, Middlesex (1716–20; dem. 1747), for James Brydges, first duke of Chandos, created spectacular baroque façades and opulently furnished apartments, including a chapel where George Frideric Handel served as kapellmeister, which led Daniel Defoe to proclaim it the 'most magnificent palace … in England' (D. Defoe, *A Tour through the Whole Island of Great Britain*, 1962, 1.6). Gibbs produced a number of alternative schemes for remodelling Lowther Hall, Westmorland (*c*.1717–28), the great country house of Henry Lowther, third Viscount Lonsdale, but failed to realize any of them. He created a famous library and chapel at Wimpole Hall, Cambridgeshire (1713–32), for Edward Harley, second earl of Oxford; Thornhill celebrated this work in a poem entitled 'A Hue and Cry' (1721), in which he praised 'Gibbesius … a man of great Fame' (*Wren Society*, 17, 1940, 12). For Harley's poet, Matthew Prior, Gibbs planned a Palladian villa in Essex (1720), which was unrealized owing to Prior's death in 1721. Gibbs attended his funeral in Westminster Abbey and was a beneficiary of his will. In 1719–20 Gibbs remodelled Alexander Pope's villa at Twickenham (dem.).

However, Gibbs also attracted patronage from a few prominent whigs. Richard Boyle, third earl of Burlington, commissioned a pair of quadrant Doric colonnades and service blocks for his town house in Piccadilly, London (1715–16; dem. 1868), and John Campbell, second duke of Argyll and Greenwich, a pioneer Palladian villa at Sudbrook, near Petersham, Surrey (1715–19). In 1719 Gibbs added the upper stages of the steeple of St Clement Danes, London, a church designed by Wren, who was then still alive. In the same year he was among a group of architects who signed a report condemning the inadequate repairs to the House of Lords made by the surveyor-general of the king's works, William Benson, and his deputy, Colen Campbell. In 1720 Gibbs subscribed to John Gay's *Poems on Several Occasions*.

Public reputation, 1720–1730 In 1720 Gibbs became, in the words of Horace Walpole, 'the architect most in vogue' (Walpole, 44). He was among 'the ablest architects' considered by the Radcliffe trustees on 27 July capable of designing the new library proposed for Oxford (Gillam, 99). On 3 October he was invited to design St George's, Hanover Square, London, though the job was given to John James. On 24 November Gibbs was appointed architect for rebuilding the royal parish church of St Martin-in-the-Fields, London, the voluminous building accounts for which are held in the City of Westminster Archives Centre. These and a large number of preparatory drawings reveal that he had already, on 29 July 1720, presented an ambitious scheme for a large, domed rotunda church, but owing to site difficulties he was forced to revise this by May–June 1721 into a rectangular, pseudoperipteral temple form in which the Corinthian hexastyle portico and the lofty, multitiered steeple soaring out of its roof are tied together by paired *in antis* columns placed in the side bays directly below the steeple, one of Gibbs's most fertile inventions. The scheme was presented as a fine wooden model (now in the Royal Institute of British Architects' drawings collection). Further major changes were made to the design, the first stone was laid on 19 March 1722, and the completed building was consecrated on 20 October 1726; the cost totalled £33,661, with the architect's fee at £632 4*s*. 6*d*. In *A Critical Review of the Publick Buildings, Statues and Ornaments in, and about London and Westminster* (1734) James Ralph praised the portico as 'at once elegant and august, and the steeple … one of the most tolerable in town' (p. 31), while according to André Rouquet, in *The Present State of the Arts in England* (1755), 'the architect has shew the elegance of his taste, and the solidity of his judgment' (pp. 95–6).

Gibbs's daring and innovative masterpiece, St Martin's became the most influential church in the English-speaking world of the eighteenth century. Alexander Gordon, in the preface to *Itinerarium septentrionale* (1726), claimed that if 'such Buildings as the great Artist Mr. Gibbs has adorn'd London with, continues to be carried on, very few Cities in Europe … will contend with it for Magnificence'. Other important ecclesiastical work followed. In 1721 he designed the Marylebone Chapel in Vere Street, London, for Edward Harley (completed 1724; now offices), and in 1723 All Saints' (now the cathedral), Derby (completed 1726), his most important church in the provinces. He was described as one of 'the greatest architects in the kingdom' in connection with repairs to Lincoln Minster in 1726 (Friedman, *James Gibbs*, 16).

Gibbs was the first major British architect to specialize in designing church monuments. The most important examples, made between 1723 and 1731, are in Westminster Abbey, particularly those to John Holles, first duke of Newcastle, James Craggs, John Dryden, Ben Jonson, and Matthew Prior; a design for Shakespeare's monument was not realized. His splendid monument to the philanthropist Edward Colston (1728–9; All Saints', Bristol), should be noted. Rysbrack was his favourite carver:

> While Gibbs displays his elegant Design
> And Rysbracks Art does in the Sculpture shine …
> Each Artist here, perpetuates his Name,
> And shares … an Immortal Fame.
> (Vertue, *Note Books*, 3.21)

In 1723 he sat to Rysbrack for a portrait bust in terracotta (lost), which in 1726 was carved in white marble (Victoria and Albert Museum, London). This portrays Gibbs in a noble, pensive pose intentionally reminiscent of Edward Pierce's celebrated bust of Wren (G. Balderston, 'Rysbrack's Busts of James Gibbs and Alexander Pope from Henrietta Street', *The Georgian Group Journal*, 11, 2001, 1–28).

In April 1723 Gibbs was elected a governor of St Bartholomew's Hospital, Smithfield, London, and he opened an account at Drummond's Bank, with a balance of £1055 11*s.* 4*d.* In 1725 he took long leases of several terrace houses in Marylebone, which he had designed (the interior of 11 Henrietta Street, demolished in 1956, survives in the Victoria and Albert Museum), and by 1726 he was living in a house at the corner of Henrietta Street and Wimpole Street, which contained his office, library, and art collection. As a Marylebone resident he undertook various parochial duties. He was elected a member of the Society of Antiquaries in London in March 1726, and a fellow of the Royal Society in 1729. In 1727 he was appointed architect of the ordnance through the patronage of the duke of Argyll, a post which paid an annual salary of £120 for life but which was apparently a sinecure.

Although some of Gibbs's domestic work of the 1720s remained conservative, such as Ditchley House, Oxfordshire (1720–27), his attempts to pioneer the new taste for Palladian architecture now made that the dominant feature of his domestic style, as at Kelmarsh Hall, Northampton (1728–32), though baroque features continued to assert themselves, as in the corner domes added to Sir Robert Walpole's Houghton Hall, Norfolk (*c.*1727–35). In September 1726 Gibbs replaced the recently deceased Sir John Vanbrugh as Viscount Cobham's architect at Stowe, Buckinghamshire, the greatest landscape garden of the age, and during the next twenty-three years he designed and erected a series of exceptional buildings, most of which survive, including the originally obelisk-crowned Boycott Pavilions (1728–9), the Temple of Friendship (1739–41), and Palladian Bridge (1738–42). In the Temple of Liberty (1741–7) he used a Gothic vocabulary to express an eighteenth-century concept of liberty in which British early medieval history was associated with a renewed nationalism based on whig precepts of constitutional democracy. Walpole confessed that 'in the heretical corner of my heart I adore the Gothic building, which by some unusual inspiration Gibbs has made pure and beautiful and venerable' (Friedman, *James Gibbs*, 197). A letter dated 4 August 1765 confirms that Gibbs also designed the 114 foot high Cobham column (1746–9), though apparently he did not authorize the fluting (PRO 30/8/62 Part 1, fol. 101). He worked in other gardens, sometimes collaborating with Bridgeman; these survive only in fragments, notably at Hartwell, Buckinghamshire (1723–40), and Tring Park, Hertfordshire (1724–39). During the 1720s he became the leading architect at Cambridge, though his schemes proved too ambitious to have been fully realized. Of the quadrangular design for a new public building (1721) consisting of a library, consistory, and Senate House, only the latter wing, containing a long richly decorated room, enclosed by engaged temple-fronted façades, was built (1722–30). Likewise only one of the austere fellows' buildings of his Palladian ensemble for King's College (1724–42) was erected.

Many of these collegiate and garden buildings, houses, monuments and churches, especially St Martin-in-the-Fields, were illustrated in the 150 engraved plates in *A Book of Architecture*, which Gibbs published in 1728, having attracted 481 subscribers, each of whom paid 4 guineas. In the introduction he recommended the book to 'Gentlemen as might be concerned in Building, especially in the remote parts of the Country, where little or no assistance for Designs can be procured … which may be executed by any Workman who understands Lines' (p. 1). It is arguably the most influential pattern book in the history of British architecture, and was used throughout Britain and its colonies abroad; a second edition was published in 1739. Some of the designs reappeared in 1731 in *Thirty three shields & compartments for monumental inscriptions, coats of arms, &c. of great use to artists & others, neatly engrav'd from the designs of that curious architect, Mr. Jam: Gibbs*, published by John Clark, an engraver and bookseller. In 1732 Gibbs issued *Rules for drawing the several parts of architecture in a more exact and easy manner than has been heretofore practiced, by which fractions, in dividing the principal members and their parts, are avoided*. This also proved a success and appeared in editions in 1736, 1738, and 1753.

The middle years, 1730–1750 This period began optimistically. At St Bartholomew's Hospital Gibbs succeeded in erecting three of the four buildings proposed in 1728: the administration block (1728–38) containing the court room and a staircase decorated by William Hogarth, and two ward blocks (1735–53), while the final component was erected posthumously (1758–68) to his design. These were the first London buildings to use Bath stone. Gibbs gave his designs and time free of charge. He was responsible for the chapels at Witley Court, Worcestershire (1733–5), and Sir William Turner's Hospital, Kirkleatham, Yorkshire (1741–*c.*1750), both of which he filled with sumptuous furnishings rescued from his demolished chapel at Cannons;

an impressive town house for Maria Shireburn, dowager duchess of Norfolk, at 16 Arlington Street, Westminster (1734–40; now Over-Seas House), the Thomlinson Library (1736) attached to St Nicholas, Newcastle upon Tyne, and additional bookshelves in the Codrington Library, Oxford (1740–50). His design (1741) for rebuilding St Nicholas West Church, Aberdeen, was executed in 1751–5 by James Wylie. Gibbs advised on new improvements to Magdalen College, Oxford (1728), and adjudicated in building disputes connected with the Grosvenor Estate, Mayfair (1720–28), Kingsland Hospital, Hackney, London (1726), the new exchange, Bristol (1741), and Tetbury church, Gloucestershire (1742–4). In appreciation for the library room created at 49 Great Ormond Street, London (dem. 1876), Dr Richard Mead presented him in 1734 with a silver cup inscribed 'Jacomo Gibbs … eximio architecto' ('outstanding architect'). Such was his reputation that his name was sought to endorse Francis Price's *The British Carpenter* (1733) and *The Builder's Dictionary* (1734). A glimpse of Gibbs, in company with Bridgeman, Rysbrack, Vertue, and other artists may be caught in Gawen Hamilton's oil painting *A Conversation of Virtuosi* (1735; National Portrait Gallery, London). Robert Morris promoted him in 'The Art of Architecture: a Poem' (1742):

> Gibbs may be said, most Times in Dress to please
> And few can decorate with greater Ease.
> (p. 4)

However, these years were not free of troubles for Gibbs. In 1731 he lost the job of designing St Giles-in-the-Fields, London, to the younger Henry Flitcroft; in 1734 Batty Langley attacked the block-rusticated window motif, known as a Gibbs-surround, popularized at St Martin's Church, as 'a most terrible absurdity', and St Clement Danes's steeple as 'a most intolerable clumsy performance' (*Grub-Street Journal*, 249, 3 Oct 1734, 2; and 253, 31 Oct 1734, 1); in 1737 Gibbs lost the important London Mansion House competition to George Dance senior; he was described as 'a Person wholly unskilled' (pp. 6–7) in the business of building arbitration in an unsavoury political pamphlet entitled *City Corruption and Maladministration Display'd* (1738). Designs for new houses at Hampstead Marshall, Berkshire (1739), and Catton Hall, Derbyshire (1741), and garden buildings for Kiveton Park, Yorkshire (1741), never got beyond the drawing board.

Final years Hawksmoor's death in 1736 brought Gibbs the prestigious post of new architect to the Radcliffe trustees, with an annual salary of £100. His first proposals for a library at Oxford, issued in bound sets of engravings entitled *Bibliotheca Radcliffiana* (1737 and 1740), reveal his debt to Hawksmoor's unrealized designs, but developed into a more compact, domed rotunda, containing a majestic circular reading room reminiscent of an ancient mausoleum—a form which revealed the library's additional function as a memorial to Dr John Radcliffe. Gibbs is shown, dressed in a velvet coat and brocaded silk waistcoat, measuring one of the library plans in John Michael Williams's oil portrait (*c.*1737–40; National Portrait Gallery, London). The foundation-stone was laid on 11 June 1737. Gibbs published his final designs in *Bibliotheca Radcliviana, or, A Short Description of the Radcliffe Library, at Oxford* (1747). Containing twenty-three finely engraved plates showing all aspects of the design and construction of the building and praising the chief craftsmen by name, the volume was in a format then unprecedented in British architectural publications. Bernard Baron's lavishly engraved portrait of the eminently confident architect, after a drawing (lost) by Hogarth, forms the frontispiece. The new library, costing £43,226 6*s.* 3*d.*, opened on 13 April 1749. This was the occasion of festive public celebrations, during which Gibbs received a master of arts degree from the university on 12 April.

Although the library occupied his attention for more than ten years, Gibbs was concerned with other important work. In 1740 he designed an octagonal mausoleum in memory of Marwood William Turner attached to the church at Kirkleatham, Yorkshire, inspired by a reconstruction of the famous ancient mausoleum at Halicarnassus, Asia Minor, in J. B. Fischer von Erlach's *Entwurff einer historischen Architectur* (1721), a copy of which was in Gibbs's library. This majestic late work proves that he never entirely abandoned the extravagant baroque of his formative years. More sedate is the house and church built for Sir John Astley at Patshull, Staffordshire (1742). Vertue reported in 1746 that he 'has fortund [*sic*] very well … by his industry and great business of publick & private works' (Vertue, *Note Books*, 3.133). Between 1747 and 1752 Gibbs supplied alternative designs for Newbridge, co. Dublin, for Archbishop Charles Cobbe, one of which was carried out as the present house, the architect's only known executed Irish commission (T. Friedman and A. Cobbe, 'James Gibbs and the design of Newbridge House', in A. Lang, ed., *Clerics and Connoisseurs*, 2001, 27–36).

Andrea Soldi's oil portrait of Gibbs (*c.*1746; National Galleries of Scotland, Edinburgh) reveals the gaunt, strained features of a man long suffering from a painful kidney disease. In June 1749 he sought relief in the medicinal waters at Aix-la-Chapelle in Germany, before returning to London in September of that year. Though now virtually retired from practice, he continued to attend the Radcliffe trustees' meetings and to advise on finishing details for the library until as late as 1753. In a final spurt of creativity he designed and built Bank Hall (now the town hall) at Warrington (1749–50), for Thomas Patten, a local ironmaster, which demonstrates that he had lost nothing of his powers as a great Palladian architect: it was reported at the time that he considered this 'the masterpiece of all his Designs in this way' (Friedman, *James Gibbs*, 149). He also remodelled Ragley Hall, Warwickshire (begun 1751), for Francis Seymour Conway, first earl of Hertford, creating a leviathan and sumptuously stuccoed entrance hall (completed by 1768) unmatched in grandeur by any other English room of the age.

Death and assessment Gibbs was a bachelor and despite public denials and fear of exposure remained a Roman Catholic: he received the last rites from his director, Bishop Petre, vicar apostolic of the London district. He was a wealthy man, possessing seven London properties bringing an annual rent of £525 and some £4000 in the bank. He made his will on 9 May 1754, leaving small amounts to various friends and charities, including £400 to his draughtsman, John Borlack, his own house and art collection to the Scottish painter Cosmo Alexander, which Alexander later sold (*A catalogue of the genuine and curious collection of pictures … of that ingenious architect James Gibbs*, Langford's, London, 25–6 March 1756), and the bulk of his fortune, including plate and three properties in Marylebone, to Lord Erskine, the son of his early patron Lord Mar. Oxford University received Rysbrack's truthful but unflattering marble bust of Gibbs (1726), with its wigless, egg-shaped skull and naked shoulders (Bodl. Oxf., Radcliffe Camera), eight volumes of office drawings, together with drawings by other architects (Ashmolean Museum), and an extensive library of architectural and other books still held in the Bodleian Library, each carrying an engraved bookplate by Baron, dated 1736, with Gibbs's head in profile.

Gibbs died on 5 August 1754 at his house in Henrietta Street and was buried four days later in St Marylebone parish church, commemorated by a simple wall tablet. The obituaries praised him as 'an eminent architect' (*GM*, 387), 'well known for his great Abilities in Architecture' (*Daily Advertiser*).

Interest in Gibbs and his buildings has never flagged: Horace Walpole devoted three pages to him in volume 4 of his *Anecdotes of Painting in England* (1771), and he received his due in every significant nineteenth-century dictionary of art and architecture. His achievement was best understood, however, by Sir John Summerson, the foremost twentieth-century scholar of English classicism. Devoting a whole chapter to Gibbs in his *Architecture in Britain, 1530–1830* (1953), Summerson described him as 'one of the most individual of English architects. Not a profound innovator [he] possessed an ability to select and combine the characteristics of other architects and fuse them into a style of his own' (Summerson, 357). TERRY FRIEDMAN

Sources T. Friedman, *James Gibbs* (1984) [fully documented life, catalogue of works, list of drawings, collections, and fine art library] • Colvin, *Archs.* • T. Friedman, 'Gibbs's library at St Nicholas, Newcastle-upon-Tyne', *Architectural History*, 41 (1998), 261–5 • J. Ingamells, ed., *A dictionary of British and Irish travellers in Italy, 1701–1800* (1997), 398–9 • H. Walpole, *Anecdotes of painting in England … collected by the late George Vertue, and now digested and published*, 2nd edn, 4 vols. (1765–71), vol. 4, pp. 44–7 • J. Dallaway, *Observations on English architecture* (1806), 153–6, 192 • E. Cresy, *The lives of celebrated architects* (1826), 296–7 • A. Cunningham, *The lives of the most eminent British painters, sculptors, and architects*, 4 (1831), 284–99 • J. Gwilt, *An encyclopedia of architecture* (1842), 219–20 • [W. Papworth], ed., *The dictionary of architecture*, 11 vols. (1853–92) • E. B. Chancellor, *The lives of British architects* (1909), 233–45 • *GM*, 1st ser., 24 (1754), 387 • *Daily Advertiser* [London] (9 Aug 1754) • register of students, Scots College, Rome • E. G. W. Bill, ed., *The Queen Anne churches: a catalogue of the papers in Lambeth Palace Library of the Commission for Building Fifty New Churches* (1979) • L. Arbace, 'Artari family', in J. Banham, *Encyclopedia of interior design*, 1 (1997), 55–8 • R. Wilson-North and S. Porter, 'Witham, Somerset: from Carthusian monastery to country house to Gothic folly', *Architectural History*, 40 (1997), 81–98 • T. Friedman, 'The palace of the princely Chandos', in M. Airs, *The eighteenth century great house* (1996), 101–20 • S. G. Gillam, *The building accounts of the Radcliffe Camera*, OHS, new ser., 13 (1958) • E. Harris and N. Savage, *British architectural books and writers, 1556–1785* (1990), 208–13 • T. Friedman, 'Baroque into Palladian: the designing of St. Giles-in-the-Fields', *Architectural History*, 40 (1997), 115–43 • M. Whiffen, 'The progeny of St Martin-in-the-Fields', *ArchR*, 100 (1946), 3–6 • J. Summerson, *Architecture in Britain, 1530–1830* (1969), chap. 21 • S. Lang, 'Gibbs: a bicentenary review of his architectural sources', *ArchR*, 116 (1954), 20–26 • B. Little, *The life and works of James Gibbs* (1955) • *The manuscripts of his grace the duke of Portland*, 10 vols., HMC, 29 (1891–1931), vol. 10 • *Report on the manuscripts of the earl of Egmont*, 2 vols. in 3, HMC, 63 (1905–9), vol. 2 • *Calendar of the Stuart papers belonging to his majesty the king, preserved at Windsor Castle*, 7 vols., HMC, 56 (1902–23), vol. 2

Archives LPL, corresp. and papers • Sir John Soane's Museum, London, 'A manuscript by Mr. Gibbs, memorandums, &c.' containing 'A few short cursory remarks on some of the finest antient and modern buildings in Rome, and other parts of Italy' (pp. 1–70) and 'A short accompt of Mr James Gibbs…after his returne from Italy' (pp. 83–102) | King's AC Cam., corresp. and papers relating to King's College, Cambridge

Likenesses J. M. Rysbrack, marble bust, 1726, V&A [*see illus.*] • G. Hamilton, group portrait, oils, 1735 (*A conversation of virtuosi … at the King's Armes*), NPG • B. Baron, bookplate line engraving, 1736, BM; repro. in Friedman, *James Gibbs*, pl. 4 • A. Soldi, oils, 1737, St Martin-in-the-Fields, London • J. M. Williams, oils, *c*.1737–1740, NPG • A. Soldi, oils, *c*.1746, NG Scot. • attrib. A. Soldi, oils, *c*.1746, St Martin-in-the-Fields, London • oils, 1749, Oriel College, Oxford • J. M. Williams, oils, 1752, Bodl. Oxf.; version, NPG • B. Baron, line engraving (after W. Hogarth, *c*.1747), BM, NPG; repro. in Friedman, *James Gibbs*, pl. 6 • P. Pelham, mezzotint (after H. Hysing, 1723), BM, NPG; repro. in Friedman, *James Gibbs*, pl. 3 • J. M. Rysbrack, marble bust, second version, Bodl. Oxf.

Wealth at death £4000 in seven London properties (annual rent £525), furniture, art collection, library, and architectural drawings: will, 1754, PRO

Gibbs, Joseph (1699–1788), organist and composer, was born on 23 December 1699. He was prominent in the musical life of East Anglia, and was organist of St Nicholas's, Harwich (*c*.1734), of Dedham, in Essex (*c*.1744), and, from 1748, of St Mary-le-Tower, Ipswich. He gave benefit concerts in Dedham for nearly forty years, and was probably a member of the Ipswich Musical Society. It was probably through this society that he met Thomas Gainsborough, who painted his portrait.

About 1746 Gibbs published *Eight Solos for a Violin with a Thorough Bass for the Harpsichord*, with a dedication to Sir Joseph Hankey. They are complex, technically demanding pieces, displaying a 'vigour and urgency rare in English music of the time as well as a melodic gift of some charm' (*New Grove*). He also published *Six Quartettos for Two Violins, Tenor and Violoncello or Harpsichord* (1777), which are of less interest.

Gibbs, who was married with a son and two daughters, died in Ipswich on 12 December 1788 and was buried in a civic funeral in front of the organ in St Mary-le-Tower. One of his daughters became an organist.

L. M. MIDDLETON, *rev.* K. D. REYNOLDS

Sources C. Cudworth, 'Gibbs, Joseph', *New Grove* • *GM*, 1st ser., 58 (1788), 1130

Likenesses T. Gainsborough, oils, *c*.1755, NPG [*see illus.*]

Gibbs [*née* Logan; *other married name* Colman], **Maria** [Mary] (1770–1850), actress, was one of the three daughters of an

Joseph Gibbs (**1699–1788**), by Thomas Gainsborough, *c.*1755

Irishman named Logan connected with the provincial theatre. Her two sisters were also actresses. Her godfather, the actor John Palmer, brought her on to the stage at the Haymarket, where on 18 June 1783 she made her first appearance, as Sally in *Man and Wife* by George Colman the elder. After one season at the Haymarket she accompanied Palmer in his unsuccessful venture at the Royalty Theatre in Wellclose Square (Goodman's Field), where her performances were popular. At the opening of the house on 20 June 1787, as Mrs Gibbs, she played Biddy in Garrick's *Miss in her Teens*, and she continued there during Palmer's management. Nothing is known of her first husband, Gibbs. The Royalty closed for a few days owing to a challenge to Palmer by Colman and others about the theatre's licence, but it was open again on 3 July with 'a variety of musical, scenic and pantomimic exhibitions'. Mrs Gibbs became involved with Palmer in the vexed question of the privileges of the patent houses, and spoke a prologue at her benefit on the injustice of the patent monopoly, but her support of Palmer offended other managers, by whom she was practically boycotted. At the Whitechapel she boxed on the stage, copying Dorothy Jordan in *The Romp*. On 15 June 1793, at the Haymarket, she was Bridget in *The Chapter of Accidents* by Sophia Lee. She played the full winter season at Drury Lane in 1794, and continued there in the winters of 1795 to 1798 at a salary of £6 a week. A poem to her was written and published by Thomas Bellamy in 1795. It was then stated that her voice was more suited to the smaller Haymarket than to Drury Lane. In August 1796 a critical article appeared in the *Monthly Mirror* attributing her success to the close intimacy which had grown up between her and the younger George *Colman. It was said that she and Colman were secretly married after his first wife had died, but contemporary publications speculated that they did not in fact marry. Colman created various roles especially for her which she played between 1797 and 1803 at Covent Garden and at the Haymarket; the latter remained her home. In duenna parts she succeeded Isabella Mattocks and obtained a reputation as the second Mrs Jordan. A son, Edmund Craven Colman, was born in June 1802. She was temporarily at Covent Garden in 1804–5 earning £10 a week. In 1817 she was at the Haymarket and played Jane 'inimitably' in John O'Keefe's *Wild Oats*, and by 12 September of that same year she was at Covent Garden in *The Belle's Stratagem* and as Audrey in *As You Like It*.

After Colman's death in 1836 she left the stage and moved to Brighton on a secure and independent income which she had established for her retirement. Her forte was pert, bustling, vulgar chambermaids and agreeable ladies such as the termagent Miss Stirling. She was known as 'the best laugher' on the stage at the time. She was fair and plump, with blue eyes and a sweet singing voice. She had good looks, good taste, and a good temper, and was cheerful, honest, affectionate, and liberal in her charitable acts. She died at Burlington Cottage, Brighton, on 6 June 1850. JOSEPH KNIGHT, *rev.* J. GILLILAND

Sources Mrs C. Baron-Wilson, *Our actresses*, 2 vols. (1844) • Highfill, Burnim & Langhans, *BDA* • *Theatrical Inquisitor, and Monthly Mirror*, 11 (1817), 139, 225–6, 229 • T. Gilliland, *The dramatic mirror, containing the history of the stage from the earliest period, to the present time*, 2 vols. (1808) • Genest, *Eng. stage* • R. B. Peake, *Memoirs of the Colman family*, 2 vols. (1841) • *The biography of the British stage, being correct narratives of the lives of all the principal actors and actresses* (1824) • P. Hartnoll, ed., *The Oxford companion to the theatre*, 3rd edn (1967) • *The thespian dictionary, or, Dramatic biography of the present age*, 2nd edn (1805) • Adams, *Drama* • W. C. Lane and N. E. Browne, eds., *A. L. A. portrait index* (1906) • Hall, *Dramatic ports.* • d. cert.

Likenesses S. De Wilde, watercolour drawing, 1809, Garr. Club • Cooper, engraving (after De Wilde), repro. in *La belle assemblée* (1812) • S. De Wilde, oils (as Blanch in *The iron chest*), Garr. Club • S. De Wilde, oils (as Selina in *The tale of mystery*), Garr. Club • engraving, repro. in *Authentic memoirs of green-room* (1814) • engraving, repro. in Gilliland, *Dramatic mirror* • engraving (after De Wilde), repro. in *Oxberry's Dramatic Biography* • engravings, repro. in Highfill, Burnim & Langhans, *BDA* • nine portraits, Harvard TC • prints, BM, NPG

Gibbs [*née* Cox], **Olive Frances** (**1918–1995**), local politician and political campaigner, was born on 17 February 1918 at 1–3 Christ Church Old Buildings, St Thomas's, Oxford, the daughter of Lazarus Cox, then a private in the Army Service Corps but in peacetime a letterpress printer, and his wife, Mary Ann, formerly Quarn. Her aunt delivered her. She was baptized in 1918 at St Thomas's Church and the Oxford high-church tradition was an important influence on her life. Hers was a comfortably off working-class family, with good housing and a steady income. She was frightened of her spasmodically violent father and learned from his dictatorial behaviour a lifelong considerateness and concern for the position of those like her browbeaten mother, whose family was partly of Portuguese extraction. She attended St Thomas's School, won a scholarship to Oxford high school, but preferred to hold it at Milham Ford School, where in due course she passed the school certificate in seven subjects but also set a record of thirty-seven detentions. In 1934 Mother Anna Verena, Olive's godmother, arranged a post for her in Juan-les-Pins, France, as a companion to a French girl in the hope that the change of climate would end Olive's pleurisy. Having learned good French, and in better health, she returned to Oxford in March 1936. Frustrated in her ambition to be a newspaper reporter, she then worked until October 1944 as a librarian at Oxford Central Library. She regularly attended mass at St Thomas's and was from time to time a Sunday school teacher. On 14 September 1940 she married Edmund Reginald Gibbs, son of R. W. M. Gibbs (a prominent left-wing councillor in Oxford) and his wife, Rose. Edmund Gibbs was later, after an unhappy time as a local government civil servant, company secretary to Headington (later Oxford) United, a successful chartered accountant in Oxford, and, like his wife, a prominent figure in the life of the city. The Gibbses moved in left-wing circles and causes in Oxford but without joining a political party. The births of their two sons, in 1944 and 1951, were separated by Edmund Gibbs's service in the Royal Artillery. Olive recalled that she 'hated pregnancy' (Gibbs, 110). Olive joined the Oxford City Labour Party not on the question of nuclear weapons or capital punishment, both of which she passionately opposed, but on an issue of school closures in 1952. She represented with considerable, though not total, success a group of mothers whose nursery schools were being closed by the tory council. In May 1953 she was elected councillor for West ward, which comprised a miscellany of political and class interests, and Oxford University Press and the area of Victorian artisan housing known as Jericho, in which Thomas Hardy set parts of *Jude the Obscure*. The frosty reception which her gender and her left-wing views provoked from her fellow Labour councillors made her ever welcoming to new political figures. Worried about her children's illnesses and unnerved by the challenges of public work in Oxford, and also, she believed, suffering a delayed reaction to her father's treatment of her, she suffered a nervous breakdown in 1954. She recovered from this, partly through working politically for M. R. D. Foot in a council by-election and partly through psychiatric treatment from Dr Sam Davidson.

Olive Gibbs's long career in local government was distinguished by two campaigns, in both of which she was successful. She and her husband led a revolt of six Labour councillors on the majority Labour group on the question of the building of a road through Christ Church meadows, one of the earliest proposals to raise the question of conservation priorities as against motor convenience in urban areas. The road was not built, and Olive was temporarily expelled from the Labour group in 1959. In the 1960s she successfully prevented the Jericho area from being demolished—the fate that befell the similar Oxford area of St Ebbe's. Olive Gibbs was not a theoretical conservationist, but represented what became a much more general hostility to needless 'progress'; in such campaigns she was prepared to work with whatever allies she could find, regardless of the party line. She retired from the city council in 1983 and from Oxfordshire county council in 1985, having sat on the latter for twelve years and been its first Labour chair (1984–5). She was lord mayor of Oxford in 1974–5 and 1982, and in 1985–6 was lady mayoress, supporting her friend Roger Dudman, a widower. She was an energetic chair of the college of further education and a governor of Oxford Polytechnic.

Though for family reasons she declined to stand for parliament, Olive Gibbs played some part in national politics. In 1955 she was 'upset by Nye Bevan, horribly upset' when he changed his position on the nuclear bomb (Taylor, 282). She was one of the founders of the Campaign for Nuclear Disarmament (CND) in 1958 and was a very active national chairwoman in 1964–5, 'popular, hardworking, enthusiastic and committed' (Taylor and Pritchard, 14). She disapproved of direct action and, when students painted CND graffiti on college walls, she personally scrubbed it out. She became a firm friend of Michael Foot, of whom she remarked that 'we shared just about everything, except a sleeping bag.' Her period in the chair coincided with the start of Wilson's Labour government; its failure to respond adequately to the demands of CND was a disappointment but not a surprise. On reflection, she concluded: 'after 1961, it was impossible to be committed both to the labour party and to CND and yet many of us attempted to do just that' (unpublished typescript).

Despite this wider involvement, Olive Gibbs's political skills were essentially local: she astutely understood the complex class and status issues of a university and manufacturing city such as Oxford, and she knew how to get her way. In 1989 she published her autobiography up to the 1950s, a lively and candid account. A cheery but not a boisterous personality in the Labour mould, she was short and in her latter years ample, with frizzy brown hair and green-brown eyes. A heavy smoker from the 1950s, she suffered from cancer and died of carcinoma of the lung caused by tobacco, on 28 September 1995 at 95 Iffley Road, Oxford, the Gibbs's home since 1953. Her husband and their two sons, Andrew and Simon, survived her.

H. C. G. MATTHEW

Sources *The Times* (29 Sept 1995) · [O. Gibbs], *'Our Olive': the autobiography of Olive Gibbs* (1989) · b. cert. · d. cert. · R. Newman, *The road and Christ Church meadow, 1923–74* (1988) · P. Duff, *Left, left, left* (1971) · R. Taylor, *Against the bomb* (1988) · R. Taylor and C. Pritchard, *The protest makers* (1980) · personal knowledge (2004) · private information (2004)

Likenesses photographs, repro. in Gibbs, *'Our Olive'*

Wealth at death under £145,000: probate, 14 Nov 1995, *CGPLA Eng. & Wales*

Gibbs, Philip (1696–1752), Presbyterian minister and historian of shorthand, was born at Trowbridge, Wiltshire, on 15 February 1696, the son of James Gibbs, a clothier, and his wife, Anne Bailey. His family were prominent presbyterians and lived in Duke Street. Nothing is known of his education except that he began the study of divinity under 'Calvinistical Tutors'.

In 1715 Gibbs was appointed assistant to Revd Robert Bragge at the Independent chapel in Paved Alley, Lime

Street, London. He was later chosen as one of the first of William Coward's Friday evening lecturers at the meeting-house in Little St Helen's, Bishopsgate. In 1729 he moved to Hackney, where he became joint pastor with John Barker at a presbyterian meeting-house.

Gibbs's importance rests on two works published in successive years. In 1736 there appeared *An Historical Account of Compendious and Swift Writing*. It was the first history of shorthand to be published, and was a survey which covered systems used in the classical era to that of his contemporary James Weston. Published in the same volume was his own system of shorthand which was complex and cumbersome. Gibbs was a better historian than a stenographer, but his system appears to have been the first to distinguish between long and short vowels.

Gibbs's religious testament, published in 1737, entitled *A Letter to the Congregation of Protestant Dissenters at Hackney, with a Postscript*, was a theological bombshell from a hitherto orthodox dissenter. He put forward a form of unitarian thought which was far in advance of his time. The work went to numerous editions, producing a flurry of responses and ensuring dismissal from his post.

Gibbs's writings are clear and erudite, qualities accepted even by his critics. His theological view was seen as so extreme that future employment as a dissenting minister was unlikely. Gibbs became a cloth factor, and went into partnership with Michael Deane at the woollen mart at Blackwell Hall, City of London. He died in 1752, probably in February, and in his will made generous bequests to various dissenting ministers, the poor of their congregations, and to his brother James and family in Trowbridge. He gave 733 books to Dr Williams's Library; their titles show the range and catholicity of his interests. There is no evidence to suggest that he ever married or had children. ALAN RUSTON

Sources will, PRO, PROB 11/793, fol. 64 · J. H. Lewis, *An historical account of the rise and progress of shorthand* (privately printed, London, 1825?), 109 · W. Wilson, *The history and antiquities of the dissenting churches and meeting houses in London, Westminster and Southwark*, 4 vols. (1808–14), vol. 1, pp. 213, 249; vol. 2, p. 42 · 'A view of the dissenting interest in London of the Presbyterian and Independent denominations, from the year 1695 to the 25 of December 1731, with a postscript of the present state of the Baptists', DWL, MS 38.18, 1731, fol. 21 · book of benefactors, DWL, MS Mod., Fol. 66, 32–65 · E. H. Butler, *The story of British shorthand* (1951), 67 · J. Westby-Gibson, *The bibliography of shorthand* (1887), 72 · M. Levy, *A history of shorthand writing* (1862), 11, 80–81 · *London a complete guide* (1749) · *London a complete guide* (1752) · W. D. Jeremy, *The Presbyterian Fund and Dr Daniel Williams's Trust* (1885), 3, 127, 145 · parish registers, Wilts. & Swindon RO [dissenters' births] · lease on presbyterian meeting-house, Trowbridge, 24 June 1734, Wilts. & Swindon RO

Wealth at death approx. £1500: will, PRO, PROB 11/793, fol. 64

Gibbs, Sir Philip Armand Hamilton (1877–1962), writer and journalist, was born at 33 Redcliffe Road, Kensington, London, on 1 May 1877, the fifth of the seven children of Henry James Gibbs, a civil servant at the Board of Education, and his wife, Helen Hamilton. His names were registered at birth as Philip Amande Thomas. The children were educated at home, their instruction supervised by their father. Henry Gibbs frequently contributed essays to *The Globe* newspaper and also published several novels. This literary knack he passed to his daughter, Helen, and three of his sons, Cosmo, Arthur, and Philip.

Philip Gibbs's particular aptitude and ambitions directed him to a career in journalism. His first appointment was with Cassell, supervising the publication of their school textbooks. In 1898 he married Agnes Mary (*d.* 1939), daughter of the Revd William John Rowland, with whom he had one son, Anthony, who also became a novelist. In the following year he published his first book, *Founders of the Empire* (1899), which was popular with schools for many years. He then joined Tillotsons, an old-fashioned literary agency which was an offshoot of a Lancashire family printing firm. His job was to buy works that were suitable for serialization. One of his early successes was Arnold Bennett's *The Grand Babylon Hotel*. Once serialized, the rights were sold on to provincial and overseas newspapers. It was Gibbs's involvement and knowledge of this very profitable business that attracted the attention of Alfred Harmsworth. In 1902 he appointed Gibbs literary editor of the *Daily Mail*. The association was short-lived, and Gibbs followed the familiar path of those dismissed from Carmelite House, to Pearson's *Daily Express*. He was employed as a special correspondent, but this appointment also proved short-lived. Rather than agree to write a series of articles that were contrary to his convictions, he chose to resign.

Gibbs next supposed that he might earn his living writing history books. But though he earned some literary credit for his *Men and Women of the French Revolution*, and a biography, *George Villiers, Duke of Buckingham*, he was soon persuaded he would not make his fortune writing history. Thus he joined the *Daily Chronicle*, to edit its magazine page, and he also became literary editor of the short-lived Liberal daily, *Tribune*. It was his brief stay with the *Tribune* that provided him with the material for *The Street of Adventure* (1909). He wrote this, the first successful Fleet Street novel, in a month. 'It was not fiction but reporting' (Fyfe, 133). Though it was a huge popular success, he sadly made no money from his enterprise because his royalties were swallowed up by legal costs for a threatened libel action by his colleague Randall Charlton. His next novel, *Intellectual Mansions, S. W.* (1910), was also a financial disaster, sabotaged by the suffragettes. Despite these vicissitudes, his career as a journalist with the *Daily Chronicle* flourished. He was an exceptionally gifted reporter and his eyewitness accounts, which included the siege of Sidney Street, earned him respect and distinction in Fleet Street. In 1909 he exposed the claim of Dr Cook, the American explorer, to be the first man to reach the north pole.

In 1912 Gibbs had his first experience of war reporting. He was attached, as correspondent and artist for the *Daily Graphic*, to the Bulgarian army. It was a tough assignment made even more difficult by severe censorship restrictions. Subsequently, with Bernard Grant, who had served as a correspondent with the Turkish army, they published a highly successful joint account of the 1912 Balkan war, *Adventures of War with Cross and Crescent* (1913). He travelled in Germany for the *Daily Chronicle* in 1913, hoping that he might find evidence to counter 'the harm created by the jingoes'. He was 'not at all convinced that war was inevitable' (Gibbs, 134). A short if lively period in Ireland describing gun running served as prologue to the First World War. In August 1914 Gibbs made his way to France and, despite the great difficulties placed in the way of reporters by the military, sent home a series of dispatches that were 'a triumph of enterprise and insight' (*The Times*, 12 March 1962).

In 1915 Gibbs was one of the five official correspondents accredited to the British expeditionary force. Despite a frail physique and nervous temperament, he displayed stamina, courage, and resource while reporting some of the stiffest fighting of the war. His dispatches were published jointly by the *Daily Chronicle* and *Daily Telegraph*, and were given worldwide circulation, for which he received no payment, when syndicated by the *New York Times*. He subsequently collected his war dispatches, publishing them as *The Soul of the War* (1915), *The Battles of the Somme* (1917), and *From Bapaume to Passchendaele* (1918). In *Realities of War* (1920), no longer hindered by the censor, he was able to sum up an experience he described as having 'changed him utterly'. The book went through several editions in the inter-war years. The various prefaces he wrote reflected his changing perception of the First World War. Increasingly the dread grew of 'another war, even more efficient in machine-made slaughter' (Preface to *Realities of War*, 1936 edn, xiii). His vivid writing on the campaigns of the First World War confirmed him as the best-known British war correspondent, in recognition of which, in 1920, he was appointed KBE and made a chevalier of the Légion d'honneur. Between 1919 and 1921 Gibbs made three successful lecture tours of the United States of America. An effective public speaker, he was a persuasive advocate of Anglo-American solidarity. This, he passionately believed, was the best guarantee of world peace.

In 1920, angered by the support the *Daily Chronicle* gave to Lloyd George's Irish policy, he resigned, but not before he had achieved the notable journalistic coup of being the first to obtain an interview for publication with the pope, Benedict XV (Gibbs was himself a Roman Catholic). The next year, from 1921 to 1922, he edited the *Review of Reviews*. Thereafter he was always a freelance, earning his livelihood primarily from his fiction writing. Altogether he was the author of some fifty novels. They were always eagerly and widely read but rarely warranted critical attention. As a novelist he was an excellent journalist. He was observant, quick-witted, sympathetic; he possessed an unerring eye for the human essentials in any incident and a gift for discovering the significant in the commonplace. A visit to Russia in 1921, on behalf of the Imperial Famine Relief Fund, provided the material and inspiration for his novel *The Middle of the Road* (1922). Its characterization and local colour are owed entirely to his newspaper-conditioned response to the passing show. Very few of his novels are, like *The Age of Reason* (1928), true exercises in imagination and story-telling.

Gibbs was an enthusiastic proponent of the belief that, 'in spite of all the delays and disappointments, critics and intriguers, hypocrites and saboteurs' (Gibbs, 358), the League of Nations was the best available mechanism for maintaining world peace. His frequent visits to Geneva provided him with abundant material for a study of Europe in the 1920s, *Since then* (1930). There followed at regular intervals throughout the 1930s a series of studies that were intended to reflect the fears and uncertainties of contemporaries for the future. *European Journey* (1934), *England Speaks* (1935), *Ordeal in England* (1937), and *Across the Frontiers* (1938) all demonstrate what an outstanding reporter of the contemporary political scene he was.

Between 1935 and 1936 Gibbs was a member of the royal commission on the private manufacture of and trading in arms. He counted the experience 'interesting … though very time wasting' (Gibbs, 429). A visit to Germany left him with grave fears for the worst, yet he was most reluctant to admit that war was inevitable. He was never a pacifist. His experiences in the First World War, however, gave him a passionate aversion to the wastefulness of war. The year 1939 found him once more a war correspondent, this time representing the *Daily Sketch*. Shortage of newsprint caused him to be recalled from France before the conclusion of the phoney war. He returned to the life of a novelist, save in 1941, when he revisited the United States of America to lecture on behalf of the Ministry of Information.

Failing eyesight was an increasingly serious handicap for Gibbs in his later years. His writing was now confined almost exclusively to volumes of reminiscence. His first exercise in this genre had appeared in 1923, *Adventures in Journalism*. In the post-war years he published three more volumes: *The Pageant of the Years* (1946), *Crowded Company* (1949), and *Life's Adventure* (1957). He was a fluent and prolific writer, and few contemporary reporters approached his mastery of his craft. 'Nothing Gibbs ever wrote was uninteresting', a literary critic of the *Manchester Guardian*, reviewing one of his books, observed. 'He could not be unreadable if he tried'. Gibbs died at the Milton Chest Hospital, Godalming, Surrey, on 10 March 1962.

REGINALD POUND, *rev.* A. J. A. MORRIS

Sources *The Times* (12 March 1962) · P. Gibbs, *The pageant of the years* (1946) · H. H. Fyfe, *Sixty years of Fleet Street* (1949) · H. M. Tomlinson, *All our yesterdays* (1915) · b. cert. · *WWW* · F. C. Burnand, ed., *The Catholic who's who and yearbook* (1910) · *CGPLA Eng. & Wales* (1962)

Archives King's Lond., Liddell Hart C., corresp. with Sir B. H. Liddell Hart · U. Newcastle, Robinson L., letters to Frederic Whyte | SOUND BL NSA, documentary recording

Likenesses W. Stoneman, three photographs, 1920–45, NPG · M. Bone, drawing, repro. in Gibbs, *Pageant* · H. Coster, photographs, NPG · A. Priest, portrait, priv. coll. · Sava, drawing, repro. in P. Gibbs, *Life's adventure* (1957)

Wealth at death £14,544 0s. 6d.: probate, 4 May 1962, *CGPLA Eng. & Wales*

Gibbs, Sir Samuel (1770–1815), army officer, was born on 21 February 1770, the son of Colonel Samuel Gibbs of Horsley Park, Surrey, and his wife Arabella, daughter of Sir William *Rowley, admiral of the fleet, and widow of William Martin (*d.* 1766), naval officer. Sir George *Martin, admiral of the fleet, was Gibbs's half-brother. Gibbs was commissioned an ensign in the 102nd foot in October

1783. His regiment being disbanded soon after, he travelled to the continent to receive a military education. He remained abroad and on half pay until 1788, when he was appointed to the 60th foot, with which he served in Upper Canada. In 1792 he was promoted lieutenant in the 11th foot and joined his regiment in Gibraltar, before returning to England in February 1793. Having been appointed aide-de-camp to Lieutenant-General James Grant, he then served with the 11th, who were acting as marines in the Mediterranean Fleet, at the capture of Corsica in 1794. At the end of 1795 he obtained a company and acted as captain and adjutant in Gibraltar until his return to England in April 1796. There he resumed his duties as Grant's aide-de-camp. In May 1798 he joined the expedition to cut the sluices at Ostend and was taken prisoner. Major-General Sir Eyre Coote, his commander, described Gibbs as having 'eminently distinguished himself' (Cannon, 50). He was sent back to England when an exchange of prisoners took place that Christmas. After being promoted major, in 1800 he took command of the 11th during successful operations against the Swedish and Danish West Indian islands.

In 1802 Gibbs was promoted lieutenant-colonel and given command of the 10th West India regiment of foot. Following his return to England his command was disbanded, and he was appointed to the 12th battalion of reserve before being given the 59th regiment, which he led in the expedition to the Cape of Good Hope in 1805–6. In April 1806 Gibbs and the 59th arrived at Madras, and in 1808–9 he led a brigade in the Travancore War; he also played a leading role in the suppression of a serious mutiny at Seringapatam (August 1809). On 28 July 1810 he received the brevet rank of colonel, in December that year he participated in the capture of Mauritius, and in March 1811 he joined the expedition to capture Java. Given command of the right brigade, consisting of British and East India Company troops, he distinguished himself during the attack on Fort Cornelis on 26 August. On 16 September Gibbs led his brigade in the final attack which persuaded the Dutch General Janssens to surrender the island.

Following his return to England Gibbs was promoted major-general on 4 June 1813 and appointed to command the British garrison at Stralsund in 1813 and in the Netherlands the following year. In the autumn of 1814 he was appointed second in command of an expedition to America led by Sir Edward Pakenham. The assault against New Orleans on 8 January 1815, however, was bloodily repulsed and Gibbs, in command of one of the main columns, was mortally wounded. He died on 9 January, and his body was shipped to England. Gibbs, who had been appointed KCB on 2 January 1815, left his estate to his brother and two sisters. A monument by Richard Westmacott to both him and Pakenham was later erected in St Paul's Cathedral.

E. J. Rapson, *rev.* Alan Harfield

Sources service record, PRO, WO 25/745, fol. 13 • J. Philippart, ed., *The royal military calendar*, 2 (1815) • W. Thorn, *Memoir of the conquest of Java* (1815) • R. Reilly, *The British at the gates: the New Orleans campaign in the war of 1812* (1974) • R. Cannon, ed., *Historical record of the eleventh, or north Devon regiment of foot* (1845) • W. J. Wilson, ed., *History of the Madras army*, 3 (1883) • *LondG* (21 Jan 1812) • R. G. Burton, 'The conquest of Java', *Journal of the United Service Institution of India*, 31 (Jan 1902) • PRO, PROB 11/1567 (187) • *Army List* (1784–1815) • J. Corfield and C. Skinner, *The British invasion of Java in 1811* (1999)

Likenesses R. Westmacott, effigy, St Paul's Cathedral

Gibbs, Sir Vicary (1751–1820), judge and politician, was born at Exeter on 27 October 1751, the second-born and first surviving son of George Abraham Gibbs (*c.*1724–1794) and his wife, Anne Vicary. George Gibbs was a surgeon and apothecary at the Exeter Hospital, and the Vicarys also hailed from that city.

Vicary Gibbs attended Eton College between 1764 and 1771, and then matriculated at King's College, Cambridge. At both institutions he was a notable classicist; at Eton he was a king's scholar, and he was named Craven scholar while at university. In 1774 he was elected to a college fellowship, a year before he graduated BA. He continued a senior member of King's until his marriage to Frances Cerjat (*d.* 1843), the daughter of Major William Mackenzie, on 8 July 1784. Although this change in status necessitated the surrender of his fellowship, his was not an academic career cut short by marriage. He had enrolled as a student at Lincoln's Inn in 1769, before coming up to university, and he seems to have been committed to the law from an early stage. He nevertheless retained a love of classical literature and of English drama, and could quote extensively from the works of Shakespeare, Jonson, and Farquhar (Townsend, 242–3).

Apart from his undoubted intelligence, Gibbs commenced his career with few of the attributes that usually presaged success. He lacked both fortune and an impressive family pedigree. His personal appearance did not recommend him, as he was short, thin, and harsh-faced, while his voice was 'shrill, sharp, and unmusical' (Townsend, 279). Nor was his temperament conducive to a more favourable impression. He had 'an undergrowth of kindly feelings' (ibid.), but his public demeanour was hard and ungracious. His incivility, condescension, and sarcasm earned him the nickname Vinegar Gibbs. This disagreeableness probably circumscribed his society at school and university. He was far from friendless, but he failed to establish the useful connections among the up-and-coming which might have stood him in good stead from either a professional or a political point of view.

Rather than risk the uncertainties of life at the bar straight away, Gibbs worked first as a special pleader, a member of an inn who drew up pleadings and attended judges in chambers but did not appear as an advocate in court. Having built up a strong professional reputation in this capacity, he was then called to the bar in 1783. The transition to advocacy was a successful one, and he proved himself both on the western circuit and in Westminster Hall. If he showed disdain for solicitors, harangued juries like an 'angry scold', and made it clear to fellow counsel that he had little faith in any opinion but his own, he also demonstrated an ability to marshal evidence, to apply legal principles, and to respond to an opponent's argument (Townsend, 279, 276–8). His professional abilities, all

Sir Vicary Gibbs (1751–1820), by Samuel William Reynolds senior and Thomas Goff Lupton, pubd 1815 (after William Owen, exh. RA 1814)

the more impressive given the unattractive manner of their presentation, were recognized in December 1794 when he was named a king's counsel.

Gibbs's career also assumed a political dimension during the 1790s, though whether he would attach himself to the government or the opposition was not immediately clear. In July 1793 he defended the Baptist preacher William Winterbotham in two trials for seditious words (*State trials*, 22.823–907). His performance, albeit in a losing cause, so impressed John Horne Tooke that he recommended Gibbs as junior counsel to assist Thomas Erskine, when Tooke and Thomas Hardy were indicted for treason in the autumn of 1794 (ibid., 24.199–1408; 25.1–745). Professional observers considered that the acquittals of both men resulted from the happy combination of Erskine's eloquence and Gibbs's summation of the evidence (Brougham, 130–31). Gibbs had already come to the notice of the government, and had been appointed recorder of Bristol in February. The losing prosecutor in the treason trials, Attorney-General Sir John Scott, became more forcefully aware of Gibbs's abilities, and complimented him on his skilful, principled efforts on behalf of his clients. Shortly thereafter Gibbs received his silk gown—a mark of professional achievement but also a gift of the government. Nor were further marks of esteem lacking from the opposition, in the form of the junior and then senior legal appointments to the prince of Wales in 1795 and 1800. Nevertheless, the king was convinced that Gibbs could be recruited to the government side, and secured his appointment as chief justice of Chester in 1804 (HoP, *Commons, 1790–1820*, 17). An appointment to the Welsh bench was an attractive post for the aspiring politician, as it could be held along with a seat in parliament. No impediment existed, therefore, when William Pitt arranged for Gibbs's return in December of that year as member for Totnes, a seat controlled by the duke of Bolton. In February 1805 he became solicitor-general and was knighted. He was in post less than a year, and resigned with his colleagues following Pitt's death in January 1806.

In the spring of 1806 Gibbs's political future looked bleak. Unwilling to support the Grenvilles, then contributing to the 'ministry of all the talents', he was not returned for Totnes. Upon restoration of a Pittite government in the following year, however, his fortunes changed quickly. He accepted the post of attorney-general, and Lord Ailesbury's seat of Great Bedwin, in Wiltshire. At the general election in May 1807 he was returned as a member for Cambridge University, unseating Lord Henry Petty. Gibbs continued to represent his university for the remainder of his parliamentary career.

Gibbs held the office of attorney-general for just over five years, in the Portland and Perceval governments. During this period he gained notoriety by the enthusiasm with which he filed *ex officio* informations against the alleged publishers of seditious libels. Between 1808 and 1810 he commenced forty-two such actions, by which a defendant could be tried without a grand jury indictment, in contrast to the fourteen filed by his predecessors between 1800 and 1807. He also introduced legislation authorizing the bailable arrest of persons against whom informations had been filed (48 Geo. III c. 58). This measure was never applied, and indeed many of those accused of seditious libel during Gibbs's tenure were never brought to trial. His most significant House of Commons work occurred during the inquiry into military corruption in 1809. In this context he strongly supported the duke of York, whose mistress had used her influence to sell officers' commissions. The ability of that lady to fend off the attorney-general's questions, however, provoked considerable delight among the press, many of whose members had suffered from his professional attention. Gibbs was not a frequent parliamentary performer, and generally confined his remarks to subjects related to his official situation. Many lawyers failed to charm the house, but Gibbs may have suffered more than most. On the occasions when he did speak, he revealed a very conservative outlook, as indicated by his hostility to reform of parliament, the criminal law, and public administration, as well as by his opposition to Catholic emancipation.

In May 1812 Gibbs resigned his post to become a puisne judge in the court of common pleas. This decision has been ascribed to poor health (Foss, *Judges*, 297), and, indeed, poor health seems to have dogged Gibbs from middle age onwards. Henry Brougham regarded the move as an expression of personal anxiety (1.133). The assassination of Spencer Perceval, claimed Brougham, had caused the aggressive prosecutor to lose his nerve, and to seek a less turbulent appointment. Certainly it was less lucrative. In moving to the bench Gibbs would have lost a fee-based income of approximately £10,000 p.a., in exchange for a judge's salary of £2500 and insignificant patronage. In November 1813 he improved his situation somewhat, when he was named chief baron in the court of exchequer, and sworn of the privy council. Shortly thereafter, in February 1814, he achieved a more significant promotion when he returned to the common pleas as chief justice. He presided in that court for four and a half years, during which time he demonstrated a thorough mastery of the law. Commentators disagree about whether promotion effected an improvement in his public manners. While providing anecdotes to the contrary, Townsend opined that Gibbs 'smoothed down the asperities of temper', and ascribed such outbursts as occurred to the twin irritants of declining health and advancing years (Townsend, 290–93). The former led to his resignation in November 1818, and he spent his last years in a retirement largely consumed by professional reminiscence and the perusal of favourite works of literature.

Gibbs died on 8 February 1820 at his home in Russell Square, London, and was buried in the family vault at St Mary the Virgin, Hayes, in Kent. An inscription was provided by his friend Lord Stowell. Gibbs left an estate sworn at less than £80,000 in personal property, a figure said to have been reduced by significant provisions for family members during his life. He was survived by his wife and daughter, Maria Elizabeth, and they were his principal beneficiaries. R. A. Melikan

Sources W. C. Townsend, *The lives of twelve eminent judges*, 1 (1846) · Foss, *Judges* · HoP, *Commons*, *1790–1820* · H. Brougham, *Historical sketches of statesmen who flourished in the time of George III* (1839) · R. A. Austen-Leigh, ed., *The Eton College register, 1753–1790* (1921) · *GM*, 1st ser., 90/1 (1820), 640 · will, PRO, PROB 11/1626, sig. 143 · Canon Thompson, *A history of Hayes* (1935) · *State trials* · *IGI*

Archives HLRO, MS opinions · Middle Temple, London, MSS | BL, corresp. with second earl of Liverpool, Add. MSS 38242–38243, 38260, 38320–38323, 38378, 38571–38574, *passim* · E. Sussex RO, letters to third earl of Ashburnham · King's Cam., letters to Prince Hoare relating to King's College, Cambridge · NRA, priv. coll., corresp. with Spencer Perceval · Sandon Hall, Staffordshire, Harrowby Manuscript Trust, corresp. with Richard Ryder

Likenesses S. W. Reynolds senior and T. G. Lupton, mezzotint, pubd 1815 (after W. Owen), BM, NPG [*see illus.*] · T. Rowlandson, caricature, *c*.1815, Laing Art Gallery, Newcastle · P. Hoare, portrait; formerly in possession of Mr H. Hucks Gibbs of Aldenham House, near Elstree, 1889 · Mrs Hoare of Bath, portrait; formerly in possession of Mrs Burrell Hayley of Catsfield, 1889 · W. Owen, portrait; formerly in possession of Mrs Burrell Hayley of Catsfield, 1889 · S. W. Reynolds senior and T. G. Lupton, mezzotint, replica, Eton College

Wealth at death under £80,000 in personal property: *GM*, 110, 640; will, PRO, PROB 11/1626, sig. 143

Gibbs, Vicary (1853–1932), genealogist and gardener, was born at Hampstead, Middlesex, on 12 May 1853, the second surviving son of the prominent banker Henry Hucks *Gibbs (1819–1907) and his wife, Louisa Anne (*d*. 1897), third daughter of Dr William Adams. He was great-great-nephew of the judge Sir Vicary Gibbs (1751–1820), whose dry humour he was supposed to have inherited. George Edward *Cokayne (1825–1911), the original compiler of *The Complete Peerage*, who in 1873 changed his name from Adams, was his mother's brother, and married his father's sister. Gibbs was educated at Eton College and (from 1873) at Christ Church, Oxford, where he was awarded a third class in classical moderations in 1874. In 1880 he was called to the bar by Lincoln's Inn. He became, however, a partner in the family business of Antony Gibbs & Sons, merchants and bankers, from 1882 to 1932, and a director of many other business concerns. In 1892 he was elected Conservative member of parliament for the St Albans division. In 1904 the Contractors Act (1782) was invoked against Gibbs and his brother Alan, also an MP, as their business had accepted an Admiralty contract; both

Vicary Gibbs (1853–1932), by Lafayette, 1927

brothers resigned their seats and stood at by-elections, Vicary Gibbs being defeated and Alan returned unopposed. Vicary Gibbs stood unsuccessfully for Bradford Central in 1906.

By a family arrangement Gibbs continued to live at Aldenham House, near Elstree, where he developed gardens of worldwide renown. He gradually built up a magnificent collection of the rarer trees and flowering shrubs, especially of American thorns, exhibiting a keen eye for variations of foliage and habit. Opposed to the formal garden associated with Reginald Blomfield, he was possibly influenced by the work of prominent contemporaries William Robinson and Gertrude Jekyll. Gibbs regularly issued catalogues of his surplus plants at moderate prices. He also published many pamphlets on aspects of gardening, and was vice-president of the Royal Horticultural Society and holder of the Victoria medal of honour in horticulture.

Gibbs was also an accomplished genealogist and published articles in the journal *The Genealogist*. He contributed information to the first edition of *The Complete Peerage*, and had the insight to take it over and plan a second edition on a new scale. He spent many years collecting material and the first volume was published in 1910, dedicated to his uncle. After the original issue of volume 5 in 1921 ill health forced him to relinquish the editorship to Herbert Arthur Doubleday, whose name had been associated with that of Gibbs on the title-page since volume 3, published in 1913. With the publication of the fifth volume Gibbs also ceased to be responsible for the cost of the enterprise, for which he had paid in full until 1919. Until his death he continued to give valued advice to the editor, and notes contributed by him appeared in all subsequent volumes, even after his death, up to the last volume in 1998.

Gibbs's revised edition of *The Complete Peerage* dealt with medieval peerages with a far higher degree of scholarship than did Cokayne's original work, which relied too much on printed sources, such as William Dugdale's *The Baronage of England* (1675–6); it also bears witness in its less austere footnotes to the remarkable range of Gibbs's reading and information. He delighted in apt quotations which give a thumbnail portrait or a vignette of contemporary manners and often reflect his characteristic sardonic humour. The Gibbs and Doubleday edition still remains a standard work.

Gibbs died of encephalitis, unmarried, at his London house, 12 Upper Belgrave Street, on 13 January 1932. He was buried in Aldenham church. P. W. Hammond

Sources *The Times* (14 Jan 1932) • *The Times* (22 Jan 1932) • *DNB* • GEC, *Peerage*, new edn • private information (1995) • J. Foster, *Men-at-the-bar: a biographical hand-list of the members of the various inns of court*, 2nd edn (1885) • Foster, *Alum. Oxon.* • d. cert. • G. R. Searle, *Corruption in British politics, 1895–1930* (1987)
Archives GL, business and family papers • RBG Kew, corresp. | LUL, letters to J. H. Round • W. Sussex RO, corresp. with Oswald Barron
Likenesses R. G. Eves, oils, exh. 1925, National Provident Institution office, London • Lafayette, photograph, 1927, NPG [*see illus.*] • J. D. Miller, print (after G. Richmond), BM • J. B. Wirgman, portrait, priv. coll.
Wealth at death £146,972 9*s.* 11*d.*: probate, 15 June 1932, *CGPLA Eng. & Wales*

Giberne, Agnes (1845–1939), writer, was born on 19 November 1845 in Belgaum, India, the daughter of Major Charles Giberne (formerly de Giberne, of Huguenot descent) and Lydia Mary Wilson. After her father's retirement the family left India when she was an infant and lived in various European locations before settling in England. Educated at home, Giberne started writing stories as a young girl with her sisters. Her first known published work is a sentimental tale, *A Visit to Aunt Agnes: for Very Little Children* (1864). Many of her earlier publications appeared under her initials 'A G', and are typical works of Victorian evangelical fiction emphasizing childish faults and the need for salvation. With *The Curate's Home* (1869) Giberne started publishing under her own name. This was one of many historical and contemporary works for older girls, some of which were published by the Religious Tract Society; she also contributed two long serials to the *Girl's Own Paper* (1882, 1899).

Alongside her evangelistic and didactic fiction, and some devotional works, Giberne also wrote several highly regarded, often reprinted scientific textbooks for children on astronomy and geology. *Sun, Moon and Stars* (1879) included a foreword by Charles Pritchard, Oxford professor of astronomy. Giberne's other main work was *A Lady of England* (1895), a standard biography of Charlotte Maria Tucker, another Victorian children's writer. Most of Giberne's work appeared between 1870 and 1910, though she continued to publish new fiction into the late 1920s.

Giberne remained unmarried, staying in her father's household until into her fifties, and in later life lived in Eastbourne. She was of independent means, and her writing arose from her religious, historical, and scientific interests rather than the necessity of earning a living. Giberne was a minor but prolific and versatile author whose variety of writing interests resulted in over a hundred books, and a sometimes surprising juxtaposition of titles. She died at 16 Motcombe Road, Eastbourne, on 20 August 1939. Belinda Copson

Sources L. Sage, ed., *Cambridge guide to women's writing in English* (1999) • J. Rowbotham, *Good girls make good wives: guidance for girls in Victorian fiction* (1989) • *WWW* • G. Avery, *Nineteenth century children* (1965) • Blain, Clements & Grundy, *Feminist comp.* • d. cert.
Likenesses photograph, repro. in *Girl's Own Paper*, issue 1000 (25 Feb 1899)
Wealth at death £539 18*s.* 11*d.*: probate, 1939, *CGPLA Eng. & Wales*

Giberne, Maria Rosina (1802–1885), artist and convert to Roman Catholicism, was born on 13 August 1802 at Clapton, London, the seventh child of Mark Giberne (*d.* 1846), a wine merchant, and his wife, Rebecca Sharp (*d.* 1847). Her father came from French stock: the Huguenot de Gibernes had arrived in England in the seventeenth century. Maria Rosina was baptized in London in September 1802. With her sisters she was educated at home and sent to Paris in youth to become fluent in French.

An elder sister married an Anglican clergyman, Walter Mayers, the schoolmaster who had converted John Henry

Newman to a living faith in 1816. Maria Giberne, visiting her sister at Worton in Oxfordshire, met Newman there about 1827. His sisters stayed with the Gibernes at their home in Wanstead and the second brother, Francis Newman (1805–1897), courted Maria ardently. Attractive and vivacious, she had many suitors but never married; her fiancé, Robert Murcott, died young.

At about the age of twenty Maria Giberne had embraced the evangelical tenets of the low-church party, and thenceforth religion ruled her life. Her theological opinions changed, however, in 1828. She was visiting the Newman family when the youngest, Mary, fell ill and died, and in that year she adopted high-church views, influenced by admiration of the family, especially of John Henry Newman. Later she became an enthusiastic Tractarian, publishing two pious storybooks for children, *Little Mary* (1840) and *Henry Vernon* (1843). On leaving home to live with a female friend in Cheltenham, she corresponded regularly with Newman, her spiritual director. She was disturbed by his doubts and hesitations, then by his conversion to Rome, but followed him, being received into the Roman Catholic church on 19 December 1845. After a period in Birmingham she moved to Rome in 1846, staying with the Colonna family and making a living as an artist, working in chalks and then in oils. Thomas Mozley, in his published reminiscences of the Oxford Movement, spoke of her as the movement's 'Prima Donna' and described her in Rome, praising her dark, imperious looks and her portraiture. Her paintings betray the amateur, but she could catch a likeness and, from her girlhood, did many portraits, including those of Newman, William Wilberforce, and Pope Pius IX. Later she copied religious paintings for English churches.

Back in England in 1850 Maria Giberne helped in the Oratory parish in Birmingham and went to Italy in 1851 to bring back witnesses for Newman's defence, two women seduced by a former Dominican priest, Giacinto Achilli: Newman was to stand trial for allegedly defaming the Italian who was touring England to denounce the Roman Catholic church. After this hard task, gladly undertaken, she returned to Rome and her painting, living with the Borghese family. Back in England in 1859 she announced her determination to become a nun. Her age and her difficult, over-emotional temperament caused her friends to doubt whether she would be accepted, but after an unsuccessful stay at the Visitation convents at Westbury and at Paray-le-Monial she was finally professed in this order at the convent in Autun in 1863, taking the religious name of Sister Maria Pia in honour of Pius IX who had encouraged her. Her friendship and her correspondence with Newman continued: he admired her persistence and her cheerful acceptance of exile in France. Her courage failed just once, when Garibaldi's troops overran Autun in 1870: she was sent to Switzerland to recover from a breakdown. Newman's cardinalate delighted her and she sent illustrations of the life of St Francis of Sales for his cardinal's chapel. She died suddenly of a stroke on 2 December 1885 at the convent in Autun. Although seen primarily as the follower of a great religious leader, Giberne's sincere personal faith and determined character make her a striking individual among nineteenth-century Roman Catholic converts.

JOYCE SUGG

Sources *The letters and diaries of John Henry Newman*, ed. C. S. Dessain and others, [31 vols.] (1961–) • T. Mozley, *Reminiscences, chiefly of Oriel College and the Oxford Movement*, 2 (1882) • I. G. Sieveking, *Memoir and letters of Francis W. Newman* (1909) • M. Trevor, *Newman*, 1: *The pillar of the cloud* (1962) • M. Trevor, *Newman*, 2: *Light in winter* (1962) • S. O'Faolain, *Newman's way* (1952) • L. Sieveking, *The eye of the beholder* (1957) • M. R. Giberne, autobiographical memoirs, Birmingham Oratory, Newman MSS

Archives Birmingham Oratory, Newman MSS

Likenesses M. R. Giberne, self-portrait, watercolour, after 1863, Birmingham Oratory • De la Cour, miniature (after M. R. Giberne, 1822), repro. in Trevor, *Newman: the pillar of the cloud* • M. R. Giberne, self-portrait, drawing (in youth), Birmingham Oratory

Gibson, Alexander, Lord Durie (*d.* 1644), judge, was the eldest son of George Gibson of Goldingstones (*d. c.*1590), a clerk of session, and Elizabeth Airth of that ilk in Stirlingshire. He married Margaret, the eldest daughter of eminent lawyer Thomas *Craig of Riccarton (1538–1608), on 14 January 1596. The couple had three sons: Sir Alexander *Gibson of Durie (*d.* 1656), Sir John of Pentland, and George of Balhousie, and a daughter, Margaret, who married Thomas Fotheringham of Powrie.

Gibson graduated MA at the University of Edinburgh in August 1588, and was admitted clerk of session, in the presence of James VI, on 14 December 1594. Having resided for some years at Wester Granton, near Edinburgh, he obtained the lands of Nether Liberton, near Biggar, in 1612. In 1614 he purchased the lands of Durie, near Leven, Fife, and was thereafter styled Alexander Gibson of Durie, although he continued to maintain all three properties during his lifetime. He was clerk to the parliaments of 1612 and 1617, and was appointed a lord of session on 10 July 1621, taking the title Lord Durie. On the recommendation of Thomas Hamilton, earl of Melrose, he served on the privy council from 1622 to 1625, during which period he was 'one of the most active in attendance' (*Reg. PCS*, 1.xxvii).

Having found much favour under James VI and I, Gibson's rise to prominence was brought to an abrupt halt at the accession of Charles I. In 1625 the new king ruled that the office of judge of session was incompatible with membership of the privy council. Gibson, along with several other members, was called upon to resign from the council, or relinquish his paid judgeship. From November 1625 his name ceases to appear on the sederunt. In 1628, at the instigation of the king, he was created a baronet of Nova Scotia. He seems to have refused the dignity however, presumably because he remained aggrieved over the circumstances of his removal from the council. To make matters worse, Charles made no such distinction concerning his bishops, who served on both the privy council and the court of high commission. As a commissioner for reviewing the laws of the country in 1633, Gibson compiled a tract attacking the constitution of the latter court as unlawful (University of Edinburgh, Laing MS 1.291). He passed the work on to his nephew and godson Archibald

Alexander Gibson, Lord Durie (*d.* 1644), by Robert White, pubd 1690 (after David Paton)

Johnston of Wariston, who later revised this 'litle treatise written excellently weal be my L. Durie' (*Diary of Sir Archibald Johnston*, 293). It was used to great effect by Wariston in 1638, in his capacity as architect of the covenanting revolution.

Gibson's religious sympathies lay with the presbyterian party, and he showed a keen interest in the affairs of the kirk. As early as 1599 James had 'threttin[ed] him with hanging' (Calderwood, 5.770), because of his support for the nonconformist minister Robert Bruce. Gibson was an elder to the kirk at his parish of Scoonie, in the presbytery of Kirkcaldy, in 1627. In that year he and William Rigg of Athernie, an avowed presbyterian activist, successfully opposed the appointment of Walter Lamont to the latter benefice, probably because of the expectant minister's episcopalian leanings. Gibson actively supported the covenanting rebellion after the riot of 1637, and hosted meetings at Granton where plans for continued opposition to royal policy were discussed. His election as a member of the committee of estates, in 1640, was a mark of the esteem in which he was held by the new regime.

A man 'of penetrating wit and clear judgement, polished and improved by much study and exercise', Gibson was a keen student of the civil law (Forbes, 28). He kept an assiduous record of the more important decisions of the session from 11 July 1621 to 16 July 1642. The digest, commonly referred to as 'Lord Durie's practicks', was published by his grandson Sir Alexander *Gibson (*d.* 1693) at Edinburgh in 1690. By all accounts, Gibson's influence at the law courts of the capital was considerable. He was, so it is said, twice kidnapped in the course of his duties—in 1604 and at some time between 1625 and 1630. On the latter occasion his opinion was known to be unfavourable in the matter of a lawsuit brought by the earl of Traquair. As a consequence, the unfortunate judge was carried off, to be imprisoned in a 'blind and obscure room in the country … though otherways civilly and well entertained' (Forbes, 28). He was returned unharmed after the court had ruled in favour of the earl. The story was later immortalized, and considerably embellished, by Sir Walter Scott in his ballad 'Christie's will'. Scott's liberal use of literary licence aside, the account was widely held to be based on fact.

Whatever the veracity of such tales, Gibson was a highly respected lawyer and judge, being vice-president of the college of justice on many occasions. Tellingly, however, it was under the covenanting regime that he reached the pinnacle of his profession. He served as lord president of the court of session in 1642 and 1643. Gibson died at his house in Durie on 10 June 1644, and was buried at Scoonie kirk. VAUGHAN T. WELLS

Sources *Diary of Sir Archibald Johnston of Wariston*, 1, ed. G. M. Paul, Scottish History Society, 61 (1911) • *Reg. PCS*, 2nd ser., vol. 1 • D. Calderwood, *The history of the Kirk of Scotland*, ed. T. Thomson and D. Laing, 8 vols., Wodrow Society, 7 (1842–9), vol. 6 • *Fasti Scot.*, new edn, vol. 5 • J. M. Thomson and others, eds., *Registrum magni sigilli regum Scotorum / The register of the great seal of Scotland*, 11 vols. (1882–1914), vol. 7 • *Scots peerage* • *State papers and miscellaneous correspondence of Thomas, earl of Melros*, ed. J. Maidment, 2 vols., Abbotsford Club, 9 (1837) • G. Brunton and D. Haig, *An historical account of the senators of the college of justice, from its institution in MDXXXII* (1832) • W. Forbes, *A journal of the session* (1714) • W. Scott, *The minstrelsy of the Scottish border*, ed. T. Henderson, 4 vols. (1849) • P. F. Tytler, *An account of the life and writings of Sir Thomas Craig of Riccarton* (1823) • *Jus feudale … with the books of the feus: a translation*, trans. J. A. Clyde (1934) • Anderson, *Scot. nat.* • H. Paton, ed., *The register of marriages for the parish of Edinburgh, 1595–1700*, Scottish RS, old ser., 27 (1905) • *DNB* • Burke, *Peerage* • U. Edin. L., Laing MSS

Archives U. Edin., Laing MSS, 1.291

Likenesses R. White, line engraving, 1690 (after D. Paton), BM, NPG; repro. in A. Gibson, *The decisions of the lords of council*, ed. W. A. F. C. (1690) [*see illus.*] • pen and ink, and wash drawing (after D. Paton), NPG • portrait, Advocates' Library, Edinburgh; repro. in 'Lord Durie's practicks'

Gibson, Alexander, Lord Durie (*d.* **1656**), judge, was the eldest son of Alexander *Gibson, Lord Durie (*d.* 1644), lord of session, and Margaret, eldest daughter of the eminent lawyer Sir Thomas Craig of Riccarton. He married, first, Marjorie Hamilton, with whom he had a daughter; and second, in 1625, Cecilia, daughter of Thomas Fotheringham of Powrie. With Cecilia he had four sons, the eldest being Sir Alexander Gibson of Durie (*d.* 1661), who was elected to Richard Cromwell's parliament in 1659. Gibson was educated at Edinburgh University, probably under James Fairlie, a regent of the university and later bishop of Argyll. He was clerk of session conjointly with his father upon the latter's promotion to the bench in 1621. In 1628, as 'ane of the clerks of secret counsell', he was admitted burgess and guild-brother of Edinburgh (Watson, 202).

Gibson was an adherent of the presbyterian party within the Church of Scotland. He was the cousin and confidant of Archibald Johnston of Wariston, the leading covenanting lawyer, and was a witness at the baptism of Wariston's eldest son in 1638. He opposed the imposition of the service book, protested against the royal proclamations of 1638, and petitioned the presbytery of Edinburgh against the bishops in November of the same year. He was, along with Wariston, one of those nominated as clerk to the general assembly at Glasgow in 1638, but lost the election to his cousin. He was commissary-general of the forces raised to resist Charles I in 1640, but was afterwards knighted (15 March 1641) and appointed lord clerk register (13 November 1641). Subsequently, the close relationship between Gibson and Wariston deteriorated sharply. In 1645 Gibson appeared before the committee of estates to answer 'some unwarrantable … misconstructions of [his] complyance … with James Grahame and the unnaturall rebels' (Stevenson, 55). He was exonerated, but Wariston remained convinced that 'Duree had colluded' with Montrose's campaign against the covenanters (*Diary of Sir Archibald Johnston*, ed. Fleming, 50). Nevertheless, Gibson was made a commissioner of the exchequer on 1 February 1645, and sat on the committee of estates from 1645 to 1648. He became lord of session in 1646, taking the title Lord Durie. He joined with the engagers in 1649, an act which further alienated Wariston from the company of his cousin. Thereafter, according to a contemporary, 'Durie and his lady [were] debarred from the table because of their malignancie' (*Diary of Mr John Lamont*). In the same year, under the Act of Classes, he was deprived of his offices. Despite this loss, he was one of those appointed to confer 'with the commission of the church' in 1651, and served on the committee for 'managing the affairs of the army' (Stevenson, 161, 170). In 1652 and 1654 he was a commissioner to attend the English parliament, which had determined on an incorporative union with Scotland. In that year, or so it was reported, he travelled to London 'to be preferrit', but returned 'disappointed' (Nicoll, 121). He died at Durie in June 1656, and was buried at his parish kirk of Scoonie, in Fife.

RICHARD HOOPER, *rev.* VAUGHAN T. WELLS

Sources *Diary of Sir Archibald Johnston of Wariston*, 1, ed. G. M. Paul, Scottish History Society, 61 (1911) • *Diary of Sir Archibald Johnston of Wariston*, 2, ed. D. H. Fleming, Scottish History Society, 2nd ser., 18 (1919) • D. Stevenson, ed., *The government of Scotland under the covenanters*, Scottish History Society, 4th ser., 18 (1982) • *The diary of Alexander Brodie of Brodie … and of his son James Brodie*, ed. D. Laing, Spalding Club, 33 (1863) • *The letters and journals of Robert Baillie*, ed. D. Laing, 3 vols. (1841–2) • J. Nicoll, *A diary of public transactions and other occurrences, chiefly in Scotland, from January 1650 to June 1667*, ed. D. Laing, Bannatyne Club, 52 (1836) • G. Brunton and D. Haig, *An historical account of the senators of the college of justice, from its institution in MDXXXII* (1832) • *Scots peerage* • C. B. B. Watson, ed., *Roll of Edinburgh burgesses and guild-brethren, 1406–1700*, Scottish RS, 59 (1929) • *Fasti Scot.*, new edn, vols. 5, 7 • *The diary of Mr John Lamont of Newton, 1649–1671*, ed. G. R. Kinloch, Maitland Club, 7 (1830) • *Diary of Sir Archibald Johnston of Wariston*, 3, ed. J. D. Ogilvie, Scottish History Society, 3rd ser., 34 (1940) • J. M. Thomson and others, eds., *Registrum magni sigilli regum Scotorum / The register of the great seal of Scotland*, 11 vols. (1882–1914), vol. 7 • M. D. Young, ed., *The parliaments of Scotland: burgh and shire commissioners*, 1 (1992) • F. J. Grant, ed., *The commissariot record of St Andrews: register of testaments*, Scottish RS, old ser., 8 (1902), pt 15

Gibson, Sir Alexander (*b.* before **1637**, *d.* **1693**), legal official, was the eldest son of Sir John Gibson of Pentland and Addiston, Edinburgh, and Jean, daughter and heir of Alexander Hay of Kennet, Clackmannanshire. He was brother of Colonel Sir John *Gibson (1637–1717). His father was the second son of Alexander *Gibson, Lord Durie (*d.* 1644), and has been described as a distinguished royalist who accompanied Charles II to the battle of Worcester in 1651, where he lost a leg and was knighted for his gallant behaviour. Gibson was appointed a justice of the peace for the shire of Edinburgh in March 1667 and a clerk to the Scottish privy council in June 1668 in place of Peter Wedderburn, and is listed as one of the three principal clerks of session in June 1676. He demitted the office of clerk to the privy council in October 1680 'due to the great charge he had in the Session as one of the Clerks thereof'. He had fulfilled his role with 'great integrity, faithfulness and diligence' and was replaced by Patrick Menzies (*Reg. PCS*, 7.89). He took the test, the oath of loyalty to royal supremacy in church and state, in September 1681 as clerk of the college of justice, but failed to do so as heritor of either Ratho or Pencuil parishes. He received a knighthood in 1682. He is listed as a commissioner of supply for the shire of Edinburgh in 1689 and 1690.

Gibson edited the influential collection of legal decisions compiled by his grandfather Lord Durie, *Decisions of the lords of council and session in most cases of importance, debated and brought before them: from July 1621 to July 1642*, published in 1690 and commonly known as 'Lord Durie's practicks'. He married Helen, daughter of Sir James Fleming of Rathobyers, Edinburghshire. Their four sons and five daughters included Sir John Gibson (*d.* 1704), his heir, Thomas Gibson of Cliftonhall, and James, a lieutenant-general in the service of the queen of Hungary. Gibson died in 1693.

RICHARD HOOPER, *rev.* DEREK JOHN PATRICK

Sources Anderson, *Scot. nat.* • *Reg. PCS*, 3rd ser., vol. 2 • *Reg. PCS*, 3rd ser., vol. 6 • *Reg. PCS*, 3rd ser., vol. 7 • *APS*, *1670–86*; *1689–95* • *Journals of Sir John Lauder*, ed. D. Crawford, Scottish History Society, 36 (1900) • D. M. Walker, *The Scottish jurists* (1985)

Archives Buckminster Park, Grantham, corresp. with duke of Lauderdale

Gibson, Alexander (**1800–1867**), botanist, was born at Laurencekirk, Kincardineshire, on 24 October 1800, the son of William Gibson, farmer, and his wife, Rachel (*née* Bruce). After taking his degree of doctor of medicine at Edinburgh, in January 1825 he became an assistant surgeon with the East India Company. In the same year he went out to India, and served some years in the Indian navy. There he studied the native languages, and passed examinations in Hindustani, Mahrati, and Gujarati.

In 1836 Gibson was appointed vaccinator for the Deccan and Khandesh, and while in this peripatetic office his knowledge of botany and agriculture allowed him, in

1838, to obtain the posts of superintendent and interim conservator of the botanical garden at Dapuri. There he paid special attention to the introduction and cultivation of exotic trees and plants, as well as food crops such as tapioca and potatoes; his successful efforts to procure several drugs for the use of the medical department received special commendation from the court of directors. In 1847 he was promoted to conservator of forests in the Bombay presidency. He held this position for fourteen years, showing considerable aptitude in the execution of his duties.

Gibson possessed a strong constitution, which enabled him to penetrate and to live in difficult jungle conditions. His reports were collected and published by the government, and on his retirement in 1860 he received from the governor in council a public acknowledgement of the beneficial results his work had secured for the state. He was elected a fellow of the Linnean Society on 19 April 1853. In addition to his reports, his works included a *Handbook to the Forests of the Bombay Presidency* (1863) and *Bombay Flora* (1861), which he produced and edited with Nicol Dalzell. Gibson died in Auchenreoch, Forfarshire, on 16 January 1867. B. D. JACKSON, *rev.* ALEXANDER GOLDBLOOM

Sources R. Desmond, *The European discovery of the Indian flora* (1992) · Desmond, *Botanists*, rev. edn, 276 · *Proceedings of the Linnean Society of London* (1866–7), 33 · d. cert. · H. J. Nottie, *The Dapuri drawings: Alexander Gibson and the Bombay Botanic Gardens* (2002)
Archives botanic gardens, Calcutta · RBG Kew

Gibson, Alexander Craig (1813–1874), folklorist, born at Harrington, Cumberland, on 17 March 1813, was the eldest son of Joseph Gibson, mariner, and his wife, Mary Stuart Craig, who was from Dumfriesshire, in which county Gibson spent part of his childhood. He trained in medicine in Whitehaven, and after studying at Edinburgh University began to practise in the villages of Branthwaite and Ullock in west Cumberland, where he remained about two years before moving to Coniston, Lancashire, in 1843. Here he married in May 1844 Sarah, daughter of John Bowman of Lamplugh, Cumberland. By 1849, when he moved to Hawkshead, he was serving as surgeon to the Coniston copper mines. In 1857, finding this work too heavy, he settled at Bebington, Cheshire, where he remained in practice until failing health forced him to retire in 1872.

From his youth Gibson had contributed to newspapers. His first separate book, *The Old Man, or, Ravings and Ramblings Round Coniston* (1849), was based on close observation of the local community and attempted to balance the romantic images of Lake District society promulgated by Wordsworth and others by providing a grass-roots portrait of folk life in the valley. His second volume, entitled *The Folk-Speech of Cumberland and some Districts Adjacent* (1869; 2nd edn, 1873), a collection of humorous stories and poems in the dialects of Cumberland, Furness, and Dumfriesshire, reflects his intimate knowledge of the dialect of those areas and the humour of their inhabitants. He also contributed widely to antiquarian and medical periodicals and wrote the geological outline for Harriet Martineau's *Guide to the Lake District*. He was FSA, MRCS (1846), licentiate of the Society of Apothecaries (1855), and licentiate in midwifery of the University of Edinburgh. He died at Bebington on 12 June 1874. His wife survived him.

ALBERT NICHOLSON, *rev.* ANGUS J. L. WINCHESTER

Sources *Whitehaven News* (18 June 1874), 4 · *Provincial Medical Directory* (1847) · *London and Provincial Medical Directory* (1849) · *London and Provincial Medical Directory* (1854) · *Medical Register* (1863) · parish register, Harrington, Cumbria AS, PR 77/4 · private information (1889) · *CGPLA Eng. & Wales* (1874) · *CGPLA Eng. & Wales* (1875)
Wealth at death under £3000: resworn probate, April 1875, *CGPLA Eng. & Wales* (1874)

Gibson, Sir Alexander Drummond (1926–1995), conductor, was born in Motherwell maternity home, Lanarkshire, on 11 February 1926, the son of James McClure Gibson, a butcher, and his wife, Williamina Williams. Educated at Dalziel High School, he was taken at the age of twelve to his first opera, *Madama Butterfly*, performed by the Carl Rosa company at the Theatre Royal, Glasgow. At fourteen he sang the Major-General in *The Pirates of Penzance*. He studied the piano at the Royal Scottish Academy of Music, where he was a prizewinner.

Gibson served in the Royal Corps of Signals (1944–8), and joined the Royal Signals band as solo pianist. Demobbed in 1948, he won a scholarship to the Royal College of Music in London. While there he conducted Mozart's *Così fan tutte* (1950) for the opera school, and won the Tagore gold medal. He also studied conducting at the Salzburg Mozarteum with Igor Markevich and in Siena at the Accademia Chirigiana with Paul van Kempen. In 1951 he entered an international conducting competition at Besançon, and won the Georges Enescu prize. He joined Sadler's Wells Opera as a répétiteur in that year, and conducted his first opera there, *The Bartered Bride*, in 1952. He then returned to Glasgow to become assistant conductor to Ian Whyte at the BBC Scottish Symphony Orchestra, and in 1954 conducted the Scottish National Orchestra in Gounod's *Faust* and Wolf-Ferrari's *The Jewels of the Madonna* for Glasgow Grand Opera Society. In the same year he returned to Sadler's Wells as a staff conductor, and during the next three seasons conducted *Tosca*, *Pagliacci*, *La traviata*, Menotti's *The Consul*, *La bohème*, *Die Fledermaus*, and other operas.

In 1957 Gibson became music director of Sadler's Wells, and conducted the world première of John Gardner's *The Moon and Sixpence*, based on the novel by Somerset Maugham. He also made his début at the Royal Opera House, Covent Garden, conducting *Tosca*. Other operas he conducted at Sadler's Wells included *Eugene Onegin*, *Gianni Schicchi*, *Falstaff*, *The Flying Dutchman*, and *Bluebeard's Castle*. He also conducted the Royal Philharmonic Orchestra, a connection that continued throughout his career, and recorded Sibelius's fifth symphony with the London Symphony Orchestra.

Leaving Sadler's Wells in 1959, Gibson became the first Scottish-born principal conductor of the Scottish National Orchestra (SNO), gaining particular praise for a cycle of Sibelius symphonies. In that year, on 21 February, he married (Ann) Veronica Waggett, a ballet dancer. There

Sir Alexander Drummond Gibson (1926–1995), by Sefton Samuels, 1970

were three sons and a daughter from the marriage. In 1961 he was one of a group of four—which also included Richard Telfer, an Edinburgh music teacher, Ainslie Millar, a chartered surveyor, and Ian Rodgers, a solicitor—who planned to give a week's season of opera at the King's Theatre, Glasgow, with the SNO in the pit and funded by Scottish Television and the Scottish Committee of the Arts Council of Great Britain. The first season had to be postponed, but on 5 June 1962 Scottish Opera (SO) was born. There were three performances of *Madama Butterfly* and three of *Pelléas et Mélisande* (it was the centenary of Debussy's birth). Gibson conducted all performances but one *Butterfly*. That autumn Peter Hemmings, then in charge of repertory and planning at Sadler's Wells, joined Scottish Opera as part-time administrator, later becoming full-time general manager. In 1963 there was a week in Edinburgh, at the King's Theatre, as well as the week in Glasgow. Gibson conducted a much admired production of Verdi's *Otello*, as well as the British première of Luigi Dallapiccola's *Night Flight*.

Over the next few years SO expanded its repertory as well as the length of the season and the number of places it visited: Aberdeen, Perth, Stirling, and later Newcastle upon Tyne were added to the tour. Mussorgsky's *Boris Godunov*, conducted by Gibson in 1965, was a major landmark, while *Die Walküre* in 1966 heralded the beginning of a cycle of Wagner's *Der Ring des Nibelungen*. In 1967, the year in which Gibson was appointed CBE, SO appeared for the first time at the Edinburgh Festival, with Stravinsky's *The Rake's Progress*. In October that year Gibson and the SNO played in Vienna. The soloists were the cellist Jacqueline du Pré and the mezzo-soprano Janet Baker. In 1969 Baker sang Dido in *The Trojans* by Berlioz, one of SO's greatest successes and also a personal triumph for Gibson.

The year 1970 brought a second appearance for SO at the Edinburgh Festival, with Hans Werner Henze's *Elegy for Young Lovers*. *Der Rosenkavalier* in 1971 scored another success, while a complete cycle of *Der Ring* was given in December, Gibson's finest achievement to date. Gibson continued to conduct at least two operas a year. In 1972 they were *Tristan und Isolde* and *The Merry Widow*; in 1974 the world première of Iain Hamilton's *Catiline Conspiracy* and Gluck's *Alceste*; in 1975 Verdi's *Un ballo in maschera* and Rimsky-Korsakov's *The Golden Cockerel*.

The Golden Cockerel was given not in the King's Theatre, Glasgow, but at the Theatre Royal, recently acquired and restored by SO, which finally achieved its own home. In 1976 Gibson conducted Verdi's *Macbeth* and Wagner's *Die Meistersinger von Nürnberg*. He was knighted in 1977 and a year later was awarded the Sibelius medal by the Finnish government. He demonstrated his versatility once again in 1980 with Berg's *Wozzeck* and *Tosca*. Gibson was principal guest conductor of the Houston Symphony Orchestra from 1981 to 1983, and retired from his position as chief conductor of the SNO, which no longer played in the pit for Scottish Opera, in 1984. He continued as music director of SO until 1987, then left to become a freelance.

Gibson's twenty-five years at SO had been very rewarding artistically, but he had not been able to take up many of the offers to conduct that flooded in from Europe and America. That now changed. He visited Los Angeles, where Peter Hemmings had become general manager of Music Center Opera. In 1988 he made the first of several guest appearances at Kentucky Opera in Louisville (where Thomson Smillie, once SO's press officer, was administrator), after which he returned annually until 1992. He visited the Bruckner Festival in Linz, where he conducted a concert performance of *Tristan und Isolde*. In 1993 he conducted Britten's *Peter Grimes* in Copenhagen.

Gibson was widely respected for his devotion to Scottish and English music, received six honorary doctorates, and was an honorary fellow of the major British musical institutions. He returned on several occasions to SO, and was president of the Royal Scottish Academy of Music and Drama in Glasgow from 1991 to 1995. In September 1994 he renewed his connection with English National Opera, as Sadler's Wells Opera had become known, conducting a new production of *Tosca* at the London Coliseum. Then on 14 January 1995 he died in St Mary's Hospital, Praed Street, London, following a heart attack. His funeral took place on 21 January in Glasgow. His wife, Veronica, survived him.

It is impossible to overstate the importance of Gibson's work in establishing in Scotland a home of international status for opera which at the same time encouraged local talent. He did not live to see the establishment of a new opera school at the Royal Scottish Academy of Music and Dance, which eventually opened in 1998; it was a fitting tribute that it should bear his name.

ELIZABETH FORBES

Sources C. Wilson, *Alex* (1993) · C. Wilson, *Scottish opera* (1972) · C. Oliver, *It is a curious story* (1987) · *The Times* (16 Jan 1995) · *The Independent* (16 Jan 1995) · *WW* (1993) · b. cert. · m. cert. · d. cert. · *Daily Telegraph* (16 Jan 1995) · *Glasgow Herald*

Archives NL Scot., corresp. and papers

Likenesses S. Samuels, photograph, 1970, NPG [*see illus.*] · C. Barda, photograph, 1982

Wealth at death £686,272 62*s*.: confirmation, 16 May 1995, *CCI*

Gibson [*née* Cullum], **(Susannah) Arethusa** (1814–1885), society hostess and political activist, was born on 11 January 1814 at Southgate Green, Bury St Edmunds, the only child of Revd Sir Thomas Gery Cullum, eighth baronet (1777–1855), and his first wife, Mary Anne, *née* Eggers (*d.* 1830). Much of her childhood was spent in Italy. On 23 February 1832 she married Thomas Milner *Gibson (1806–1884), whose radicalism she shared, even when their opinions on specific issues differed.

Witty and energetic, Gibson channelled her ability into conventional entertaining and charity work. She needed more stimulus, however, which she created in her eclectic salons, attended by diplomats, writers, politicians, and, after 1848, European exiles. Regular guests included Dickens, Thackeray, Hugo, Lady Morgan, the Disraelis, Cobden, and Louis Napoleon. Dickens in turn placed her, 'for Anti Corn Law Leaguality', among his own ideal guests (*Letters of Charles Dickens*, 4.106). Her hectic public life was for twenty-five years (1833–57) complicated by pregnancies, despite her husband's lengthy absences on his yacht, although characteristically she resumed her activities as quickly as possible. The early deaths of four of her eight children deeply depressed her. Allegedly in 1838–9 she had an affair with Sir George Wombwell, third baronet (1792–1855).

Gibson's rebelliousness and belief in individual freedom became focused after meeting Mazzini in 1844. Through her fund-raising skills, her many influential contacts, and her practical assistance with correspondence she helped for many years to promote Italian nationalism. She enlivened her frequent European travels with thrilling hints of conspiracies, and in 1857 dramatically appeared in a Genoa theatre wearing the Italian tricolour. In the 1850s she became an advocate of mesmerism and spiritualism, and in 1860 held an eventful séance for the spiritualist D. D. Home. Although she once described her latest child (1851) as 'This new enemy of the Pope' (Disraeli, *Letters*, 5.2084 n. 1), she later converted to Roman Catholicism. Her last years were spent mostly in Paris, which she found more stimulating than England. Her husband died (on board his yacht) in 1884. She outlived all but two of her children and died at her home, 11 avenue du Bois de Boulogne, Paris, on 23 February 1885; she was buried at Bury St Edmunds, Suffolk, on 3 March.

MARY S. MILLAR

Sources *Benjamin Disraeli letters*, ed. J. A. W. Gunn and others (1982–), vols. 3–5 • Bodl. Oxf., Dep. Hughenden D/III/C/830–906 • *The letters of Charles Dickens*, ed. M. House, G. Storey, and others, 4–6 (1977–88) • 'Gibson, Thomas Milner', *DNB* • *Mazzini's letters to an English family*, ed. E. F. Richards, 1 (1920) • *Mazzini's letters to an English family*, ed. E. F. Richards, 2 (1922) • Burke, *Gen. GB* (1875) • Burke, *Gen. GB* (1898) • *The Times* (25 Feb 1885) • *ILN* (7 March 1885) • A. C. Doyle, *The history of spiritualism* (1926) • C. Milbourne, *ESP, seers and psychics* (1970) • *DNB*

Archives Suffolk RO, Bury St Edmunds, travel journals

Likenesses photograph, repro. in Mazzini, *Mazzini's letters*, vol. 1, p. 292 • photograph, repro. in Mazzini, *Mazzini's letters*, vol. 2, p. 42 • photograph, Bodl. Oxf., Dep. Hughenden, D/III/C/889

Wealth at death £24,983 13*s*. 4*d*.: probate, 1 May 1885, *CGPLA Eng. & Wales*

Gibson, David Cooke (1827–1856), portrait painter, was born at Edinburgh on 4 March 1827, the son of David Gibson, miniaturist and engraver, and his wife, Ann. Gibson was first taught art by his father, who died early of consumption. After four years at the Edinburgh high school he was admitted to the Trustees' Academy. He passed through the ornamental class under Charles Heath Wilson, studied the collection of casts from the antique under Sir William Allan, and afterwards studied in the colour class and life class under Thomas Duncan. Before he was seventeen years old he was the chief support of his mother and sister, and he resigned all chance of a college career to devote himself to portrait painting as a means of providing their living. His mother, however, died soon after September 1844, and his sister on 2 December 1845 of consumption. Gibson had inherited the same disease and it was this that ultimately broke his own health, though there was an insinuation that this was due to a dissolute lifestyle, a claim supported by a perversion of his dying words. Of diminutive figure, he was a social favourite, fond of dancing, an excellent mimic, eminently handsome and graceful.

In January 1846 Gibson obtained three prizes at the Trustees' Academy. A month later, though, two of his small pictures were badly hung at the Royal Scottish Academy, and he asked to withdraw one of these. He later made a tour of London, Belgium, and Paris, studying in the great galleries. His copy of Van Dyck's *Charles I* was bought by Sir Edwin Landseer after Gibson's death. Returning to Edinburgh he worked hard at portraits and moved to London in April 1852, where he settled. At this time he wrote an immense quantity of easy and sometimes humorous verse, although he experienced disappointments and was discontented. He was interested in the views of socialists and sceptics, and was also attracted by the Pre-Raphaelites. His picture *The Little Stranger*, exhibited at the Royal Academy in 1855, was sold for £100. After revisiting Scotland he was advised to go abroad for his health, and passed the winter of 1855–6 at Malaga. Some of his Spanish pictures were exhibited in the Royal Academy in 1856, and a number were bought by John Phillips RA. After completing his painting Gibson visited the Alhambra in Granada in March 1856, and made many sketches. He returned to England in June, but unfortunately lingered there too long. He broke a blood vessel in September, and died in London on 5 October 1856, five months short of his thirtieth birthday. In the following May his *Gipsies of Seville* was exhibited at the Royal Academy. He bequeathed to Dr Tweedie his picture of the Alhambra towers with the Sierra Nevada in the distance, *A Pleasing Prospect*, and it was chromolithographed and published. His work was described as 'of much promise, careful in finish and strong in character' (Redgrave, *Artists*, 173).

J. W. EBSWORTH, *rev.* MARK POTTLE

Sources personal knowledge (1889) • *The exhibition of the Royal Academy* (1855–7) [exhibition catalogues] • W. Macduff, *Struggles of a young artist, being a memoir of David C. Gibson* (1858) • Redgrave, *Artists* • B. Stewart and M. Cutten, *The dictionary of portrait painters in Britain up to 1920* (1997) • Wood, *Vic. painters*, 2nd edn • P. J. M.

McEwan, *Dictionary of Scottish art and architecture* (1994) · Bryan, *Painters* (1903–5) · *Art Journal*, 17 (1855), 172 · *Art Journal*, 18 (1856), 68

Gibson, Sir Donald Edward Evelyn (1908–1991), architect, was born on 11 October 1908 at Northenden, Manchester, the second of three sons of Arnold Hartley Gibson (1878–1959), professor of engineering at the University of Manchester, and his wife, Amy, *née* Quarmby. His father was a pupil and biographer of Osborne Reynolds and a renowned authority on hydraulics. He was the author, among much else, of *Hydraulics and its Applications* (1908; 5th edn 1952) and *Internal-Combustion Engineering* (3rd edn 1938). Gibson inherited an ease with technology and an interest in scale-modelling, which his father used to study water-flow in projected dams, reservoirs, and barrages; he later listed his recreation in *Who's Who* as model railways. His education was at Manchester grammar school and the Manchester School of Architecture, where after a poor start he suddenly shone. He spent his fourth year at Harvard, gained American office experience, then returned to qualify professionally in 1932. On 19 October 1934 he married Winifred Mary (Winmary) McGowan (1911–1977), daughter of John Sinclair McGowan, physician and surgeon. They had three sons and a daughter.

Gibson soon gravitated to the public sector of architecture, just then opening up as a career path. His rise was rapid. He spent two spells at the government's Building Research Station, then still small and informal; as the sole architect there, he had to answer multifarious queries from correspondents about failures and puzzles in construction, which enriched his technical knowledge. In between he taught at Liverpool school of architecture, then full of excitement, and built a prefabricated nursery school at Chester. In 1936 he was appointed deputy county architect to the Isle of Ely, at March. There he gathered a handful of like-minded architects, committed to a socially directed modernism that could offer benefits to all. Among those he picked was a former Liverpool student, Stirrat Johnson-Marshall, who became Gibson's long-term friend and later ally. The team designed a few schools but was not stretched.

In 1938, still not yet thirty, Gibson was appointed by a fresh Labour council at Coventry to the new post of city architect. It was with Coventry that Gibson's name was memorably linked. His arrival was resented by the city engineer, Ernest Ford, and his infant department was confined to designing street furniture. Gibson hit on the ruse of inviting guest lecturers and instigating a wholly unofficial exhibition of how Coventry could be replanned, which drew notice. Six months later, in November 1940, came the Luftwaffe's destructive raid on Coventry. This was Gibson's chance; averring that 'like a forest fire the present evil might bright forth greater riches and beauty' (*Coventry Standard*, 7 Dec 1940), he with his depleted wartime staff now embarked on a more radical rebuilding plan for Coventry's centre. Approved over a rival submission by Ford in February 1941, it was endorsed by Lord Reith, and was soon drawn into the national propaganda for the post-war reconstruction of Britain. The key elements were a ring road (too close, it turned out, to the city's core) and a pedestrianized shopping centre—the first proposed in Europe, and audacious in a car-manufacturing city. To gain his ends, Gibson forged an alliance with the chairman of Coventry's planning committee, Alderman Hodgkinson.

In the post-war years Gibson's expanded department undertook an ambitious building programme for Coventry's suburbs, constructing a vast acreage of housing and schools, often with a tinge of technical experiment, and a modicum of public art where budgets allowed. The shopping centre at Tile Hill was to attract much notice. In the centre, things were harder. A revised plan for the centre was approved in 1946, but because of post-war economies took many years to implement, the first building completions being delayed until 1953. One consolation was the new Coventry Cathedral design, won in competition by Basil Spence in 1951 following the rejection of Sir Giles Scott's project; Gibson supported this and was involved in planning the cathedral's setting. But, increasingly frustrated by obstructions to Coventry's architectural progress, he resigned in 1955 and took up a post as Nottinghamshire's county architect. This unanticipated move convulsed the world of public-sector architecture.

Gibson was just three years at Nottinghamshire, but made his mark by turning a team that had fallen behind with its programme of schools into one of the leading public architects' departments. New staff were hired (with advice from Stirrat Johnson-Marshall, now chief architect to the Ministry of Education); and a special system of light-steel construction for schools was devised, to cope with Nottinghamshire's many sites affected by mining subsidence. The system soon spread to other counties with mining problems and, under the acronym CLASP (Consortium of Local Authorities' Special Programme), became the Ministry of Education's model for a national network of school-building 'consortia'—a term that came from the minister, Lord Hailsham. Though Gibson played a part in the technical development, his main contributions were the strategy and lateral thinking that were to win CLASP an international reputation.

Having consolidated his reputation as the leading local-authority architect, Gibson was appointed architect to the war department in 1958, with offices at Chessington, Surrey. There he eluded traditional hierarchies by twinning professionals with civil servants, and applied the then-fashionable methodology of 'light and dry' prefabricated construction to the army's estate of barracks at home and abroad. In 1962 he was knighted. In the same year Geoffrey Rippon persuaded him to become director-general of research and development in an enlarged Ministry of Public Building and Works, which now took over responsibility for military buildings. Gibson's major innovation in this post was the founding of the National Building Agency, which was intended to advise industry and local authorities on efficiency and productivity in building; this initiative soon ran into difficulties. Thereafter, the comradely methods of teamwork that Gibson relied on to get results were slowly stifled, and he was reduced to propagandizing for a livelier approach to the planning of British communities and cities. After 1967, when he became controller-general in the Ministry of Public Building and Works, he was distinctly unhappy. He received some cheer from his presidency of the Royal Institute of British Architects (1964–5) and from a spell as Hoffman Wood professor at the University of Leeds (1967–8). But, in a period of decreasing public building programmes, it was with visible relief that he retired in 1969, throwing his bowler hat into the Thames at his leaving party.

Gibson was among the best of the breed of chief architects who throve in public-sector Britain during the aftermath of the Second World War. A team man rather than a designer, he exuded a vision, a competence, and an integrity that inspired strong loyalties among his staff and persuaded those whom he dealt with face to face. He was without 'side', but could be guileful when he thought it necessary, and informal to the point of eccentricity. A good-looking man with prematurely silver hair and a Roman nose, he had a slight limp from a polio hip in childhood; he spoke quietly and succinctly, with much emphasis on practical sense. His first wife having died in 1977, he married second, on 16 August 1978, Grace Mary Haines (*b.* 1928), artist, and daughter of George William Royffe. With her he created a fine garden complete with model railway at his retirement house of Bryn Castell, Llanddona, Anglesey. He died there of cancer on 22 December 1991, and was survived by his second wife.

ANDREW SAINT

Sources P. Johnson-Marshall, *Rebuilding cities* (1966), 291–318 · A. Saint, *Towards a social architecture: the role of school-building in post-war England* (1987) · T. Mason and N. Tiratsoo, 'People, politics and planning: the rebuilding of Coventry's city centre, 1940–53', *Rebuilding Europe's bombed cities*, ed. J. M. Diefendorf (1990), 94–113 · *The Times* (26 Dec 1991) · *Daily Telegraph* (27 Dec 1991) · *The Independent* (3 Jan 1992) · *The Guardian* (7 Jan 1992) · personal knowledge (2004) · private information (2004) [Lady Gibson] · *Architects' Journal* (20 Jan 1953), 77 · *Architects' Journal* (26 June 1968), 1492–5 · *Architectural Design* (Dec 1958), 476–8 · tape from memorial meeting at *RIBA*, priv. coll. · D. Gibson, 'Buildings without foundations, a lecture on the problems of building on moving ground', *RIBA Journal*, 65 (1957–8), 47–59 · L. Campbell, *Coventry Cathedral: art and architecture in post-war Britain* (1996) · *WWW* · m. certs.

Archives Coventry Archives, reminiscences concerning architectural work in Coventry, ref 623 · priv. coll. | SOUND BL NSA, 'Interview/Gibson', 1984, C 447/11 01

Likenesses photographs, priv. coll. · portrait, RIBA

Wealth at death £208,225: probate, 13 Feb 1992, *CGPLA Eng. & Wales*

Gibson, Dwarf. *See* Gibson, Richard (1605/1615?–1690).

Gibson, Edmund (*bap.* **1669**, *d.* **1748**), bishop of London, was born at High Knipe, Bampton, Westmorland, and was baptized on 16 December 1669 at Bampton, the younger son of Edmund Gibson (*d.* 1703) of High Knipe and his first wife, Jane (*d.* 1689), daughter of John and Eleanor Langhorn of Hilton-end in the parish of Askham. He was educated at Bampton grammar school and then at Queen's College, Oxford, which he entered as batteler on 4 August 1686.

Edmund Gibson (*bap.* **1669**, *d.* **1748**), by Andrea Soldi, *c.*1740–45

Oxford and Lambeth On 17 July 1690 Gibson was elected BA on the foundation at Queen's, but he had scruples about the legality of the oaths to the revolutionary monarchy. Consequently, he did not take his degree until June of the following year, by which time 'he had satisfied himself, by comparing the Writings on both Sides, that *William* and *Mary* were King and Queen *de jure*, as well as *de facto*' (*Weekly Miscellany*, 70, 13 April 1734). By the time of his graduation he had produced his first publication, an edition of William Drummond's *Polemo-Middinia* and James V's *Cantilena rustica*, which revealed a knowledge of Old English, Gothic, and Norse as well as of classical authors. Gibson, indeed, was already emerging as a prominent member of the distinguished group of Oxford Anglo-Saxonists, centred on Queen's College, and including William Nicolson, White Kennett, and Edward Thwaites. Common interest in medieval studies transcended party allegiances, and all of this group were friendly with the nonjuror George Hickes. Gibson provided some assistance for Hickes in the revision of his Anglo-Saxon grammar, solicited subscriptions for the *Thesaurus* in 1698, and was entertaining him at Lambeth as late as 1706. Hickes also provided advice for Gibson in the preparation of his second work, the *Chronicum Saxonicum* (1692), in which he was encouraged by John Mill, principal of St Edmund Hall. By modern critical standards Gibson's edition was fundamentally flawed, conflating the various manuscripts and presenting the chronicle as a single continuous narrative. However, he utilized five manuscripts, three more than Abraham Wheloc for his edition of 1643, and Gibson's remained the standard edition until 1823.

Over the next few years a succession of scholarly works

flowed from Gibson's pen. Two, published in 1692 and 1698, were catalogues of manuscripts, the latter being an ambitious attempt by Gibson and Arthur Charlett to bring together the collections of the major public and private libraries in England and Ireland. He dabbled in classical studies with an edition of Quintilian's *De institutione oratoria* (1693), edited the posthumous works of Henry Spelman (1698), and produced two volumes about Roman antiquities in England, *Julii Caesaris Portus Iccius illustratus* (1694) and *A Treatise of the Roman Ports and Forts in Kent* (1694). His major work at this time, however, was a new English edition of Camden's *Britannia*, for which he had the assistance of numerous scholars, including Ralph Thoresby, Edward Lhuyd, and Samuel Pepys. It was finally published in 1695, with a second, expanded edition following in 1722. Gibson's *Camden* was superseded in 1789 by the edition of Richard Gough, but for a century it was held in high esteem:

> For tho' we here had liv'd some Ages past;
> We liv'd as Strangers on some Island cast,
> And scarce knew where we stood, till GIBSON drew
> *Britannia's Map*, and plac'd her all in View.
> (*A Congratulatory Poem*, 5)

In 1694, in order to pursue his researches on *Camden*, Gibson moved to London, where he lived with his uncle, Thomas Gibson, a nonconformist physician who had married a daughter of Richard Cromwell, the lord protector. He was tempted by a career in the law, which he briefly felt 'would be the much more eligible Profession to me' (Bodl. Oxf., MS Ballard 5, fol. 19), and was admitted to the Middle Temple on 4 May 1694. But by the end of the year he was writing to Thomas Tanner 'Divinity calls me, and that I resolve to follow' (Bodl. Oxf., MS Tanner 25, fol. 265). On 18 May 1695 he was ordained deacon by Bishop Hough, and significant preferment rapidly followed. Largely through the efforts of Charlett and William Wake, Archbishop Tenison offered Gibson the position of librarian at Lambeth Palace on 19 May 1696. He became a fellow of Queen's in August and was ordained priest on 30 May 1697. He declined the offer of a small living in the Isle of Thanet from Lord Somers, to whom he had dedicated *Camden*, but accepted the offer of the morning preachership at Lambeth from George Hooper. Then on 8 November 1698 the archbishop appointed him as one of his domestic chaplains.

Gibson now began to benefit from Tenison's patronage and influence. On 1 April 1700 he was instituted to the rectory of Sisted, Essex, a peculiar of the archbishop, where he was non-resident. In June 1703 he became precentor and canon of Chichester, where he resided every year from midsummer to Michaelmas. The wealthy rectory of Lambeth followed in October 1703. Here Gibson was an active parochial minister, establishing a religious society and producing two devotional tracts for his parishioners. These pamphlets, *Family Devotion* (1705) and *The Holy Sacrament Explain'd* (1705), became minor classics: both were later revised and expanded by Gibson, went through dozens of editions, and were still being reprinted well into the nineteenth century. They even circulated widely in the American colonies, and a service of prayer derived from *Family Devotion* was included in the 1789 American prayer book. Gibson was also acquiring a reputation as a preacher, which contributed to his appointment as lecturer at St Martin-in-the-Fields in March 1705. By this time he had married Margaret Jones (*d.* 1741), daughter of John Jones, rector of Selattyn, Shropshire, and the sister-in-law of John Bettesworth, dean of the arches. The marriage took place on 22 July 1704 and the Gibsons moved into a house in Lambeth. Their first child, a son, was born in 1705, but died two years later. Before her death in 1741 Margaret gave birth to ten more children, of whom one son, Thomas, became a clerk to the Treasury, and a daughter, Anne, married Christopher Wilson, bishop of Bristol.

Gibson's appointment as Tenison's domestic chaplain placed him at the heart of ecclesiastical affairs at a critical time. The publication of Francis Atterbury's *Letter to a Convocation Man* (1697) marked the beginning of the high-church campaign for a sitting convocation. The debates generated by the convocation controversy not only provoked bitter conflict between high- and low-churchmen, but also did much to widen the divisions between whigs and tories in the state. Gibson deprecated the tone of the controversy, wishing it 'had been manag'd in a more calm and Christian way' (Bodl. Oxf., MS Ballard 5, fol. 13). However, as a member of the archbishop's household he was inevitably drawn into the pamphlet war. As the debate shifted to high-church claims for the independence of the lower house of convocation, Gibson took over from Wake the main burden of developing the low-church response. Most notably, between 1701 and 1703 he produced three major pamphlets which provided detailed refutations of Atterbury's arguments: *The Right of the Archbishop to Continue or Prorogue the Whole Convocation, Asserted* (1701), *The Schedule Review'd* (1702), and *The Pretended Independence of the Lower-House upon the Upper, a Groundless Notion* (1703). These were all essentially controversial works, but Gibson's researches into the history of convocation also led to the publication of *Synodus Anglicana* (1702). This account of the body's constitution and proceedings came to be regarded as definitive, and was reprinted by Edward Cardwell shortly after its revival in 1852.

Gibson was widely perceived as a partisan low-churchman—Hearne claimed that 'he makes it his Business to cringe, flatter, write for the Whiggs' (*Remarks*, 2.46). Even so, as colleagues like Wake and Kennett were promoted, Gibson felt that he was being overlooked. Some reward came with his appointment on 6 June 1710, again by Tenison, to the archdeaconry of Surrey, 'a very good one, (tho' not soe good, as I believe it is generally thought)' (Bodl. Oxf., MS Ballard 6, fol. 109). He was a vigorous archdeacon, choosing to visit parochially, a practice which was far from universal. But, once more, much of his time was devoted to scholarly pursuits, in particular a collection of, and commentary on, the statutes, constitutions, canons, rubrics, and articles of the Church of England. This work, entitled *Codex juris ecclesiastici Anglicani*, was to be published by subscription. In the light of Gibson's reputation, it is hardly surprising that it was widely suspected to be 'a party-book', and the proposal was 'coldly received' (ibid., fol. 111). But gradually subscriptions came in, and the *Codex* finally appeared in two volumes in 1713. The importance of 'Gibson's *magnum opus*' (Sykes, 68) was immediately recognized, the lower house of convocation formally voting its thanks to the compiler. According to Stubbs it was 'still the standard work' in 1886 (Stubbs, 331), and even as late as 1947 the archbishops' commission described it as 'absolutely indispensable to any serious student of the law and constitution of the Church of England' (Baker, 106). It certainly entitles Gibson to an eminent place among English canonists.

Bishop of Lincoln The Hanoverian succession in August 1714 brought to an end four years of tory government, and, like many whig clergymen, Gibson greeted the new regime with a mixture of relief and expectation. In March he reinforced his whig credentials by preaching a strongly pro-Hanoverian and anti-tory sermon at the Surrey assizes, condemning that party 'who will not own the Church to be safe, till the State is well nigh undone, and *Popery* at our Doors' (Gibson, *Religion, the Best Security*, 22). He remained a close adviser of Tenison, sending regular bulletins about his health and opinions to friends. But the death of the archbishop in December 1715 dealt a blow to his hopes for rapid preferment, and the most he hoped for in the resulting promotions was a prebend of Westminster. In fact, Gibson had a strong advocate in Tenison's successor, William Wake, who, with the support of Lord Townshend, secured his nomination to the bishopric of Lincoln on 17 December 1715.

Like many post-revolutionary bishops, Gibson was acutely conscious of the pastoral 'crisis' facing the Church of England in the decades after the revolution of 1688. This sense of crisis was created partly by the effects of the Toleration Act in legalizing religious pluralism and partly by the perception that a tide of profaneness and immorality was sweeping the nation. One of the responses of reform-minded bishops, including Gibson, was to obtain far more detailed information about their dioceses, with the aim of improving pastoral oversight. The diocese of Lincoln was at the heart of this initiative. In 1706 Wake, Gibson's predecessor, had been the first bishop to issue a set of articles to his clergy, requesting information about the state of their parishes, in addition to the usual set of visitation articles sent to churchwardens. At his primary visitation in 1717–18 and at the triennial visitation of 1720–21 Gibson developed this practice, producing a more extensive set of articles and using the returns to compile a speculum, or diocese book, for his use and that of his successors, containing information about the size and population of each parish, the number of dissenters, the frequency of services, and so on.

With over 1300 parishes Lincoln was the largest diocese in the country, which created particular problems in the exercise of effective episcopal oversight. Gibson responded by splitting the work of visitation into two parts, visiting the southern archdeaconries in one year and the northern the next. Despite some criticism he also ended the practice of confirming during visitations, and instituted separate confirmation tours instead. Even so, he was overwhelmed by the demand, finding 700 candidates awaiting him at each centre on his 1718 tour. So he tried to limit the numbers to 400, requiring lists of candidates to be submitted in advance, and issuing a set of directions aimed at increasing the order and solemnity of the rite. Given the problems involved in administering such a large diocese, it is hardly surprising that Gibson became an advocate of the revival of suffragan bishops.

In January 1716 Gibson talked of his 'uncourtlike spirit' (Christ Church, Arch. W. Epist. 20, fol. 304). It is true that he was not a regular preacher at court, having been made a royal chaplain in only the previous September, nor was he a member of the princess of Wales's circle of clergymen. None the less, there was something disingenuous about this statement, since he was both politically acute and ambitious. Within weeks of his consecration as bishop of Lincoln, Gibson was already playing an important role in the episcopal opposition to the Select Vestries Bill of 1716, which was widely perceived as an anti-clerical attack on church power. It was Wake whose speech on the second reading was crucial in securing the bill's defeat, but he had been encouraged by Gibson's plea that he 'make a stand' (ibid., 15, fol. 405). On this occasion Gibson acted as his primate's lieutenant, but over the next two years he came to fear that Wake was abandoning 'a clear Whig bottom' (St Andrews University, Gibson MS 5219). Crucially, when George I quarrelled with his son at the end of 1717, Wake sided with the prince and princess of Wales. As a result, Gibson blamed Wake for leaving 'Church whigs' like him leaderless (Taylor, '"Dr Codex"', 22). He feared that the archbishop was allowing a vacuum to develop at court, into which radical whig churchmen like Benjamin Hoadly or Richard Willis would step. To Gibson, Wake's failings were never more apparent than during the Bangorian controversy. He believed that the latitudinarian doctrines advanced by Bishop Hoadly in his controversial sermon preached before the king in 1717 were pernicious. He fumed at the favour shown to Hoadly at court, and bombarded Wake with advice to attend more frequently in order to 'hinder mischief' (Christ Church, Arch. W. Epist. 20, fol. 437), but without effect.

Divisions among the whig bishops came to a head in the debates over the repeal of the Occasional Conformity Act in 1718. Although this measure had been passed by a tory parliament during the last years of Queen Anne's reign, Wake and some of his colleagues had come to see it, along with the Test Act, as one of the bulwarks of the church establishment. Gibson, however, believed that the maintenance of the protestant succession was the only way to 'preserve the Church', and that the 'Establishment in the State' was in far more danger from the tories than the 'Establishment in the Church' was from the dissenters (Bodl. Oxf., MS Add. A. 269, pp. 72–3). Repeal of the Occasional Conformity Act, therefore, by conciliating the dissenters, strengthened the parliamentary and electoral position of the whigs and so contributed to the security of both church and state. When the Bill for Strengthening the Protestant Interest had its second reading in the House of Lords on 18 December 1718, Gibson spoke strongly in its support. Rumours circulated that his vote had been bought by his uncle, who had threatened to cut him out of his will unless he voted in favour of relief for the dissenters. Wake felt deserted and betrayed, and the debate caused a breach between the two that was never healed. It also saw the alienation of Gibson from other old friends, such as William Nicolson, bishop of Derry, who had sided with Wake.

Despite his having joined Hoadly in supporting the religious policy of the Sunderland–Stanhope ministry, however, Gibson's own conscience was clear. He stressed that his support for the repeal of the Occasional Conformity Act was not based on Bangorian principles. Indeed, in his charge of 1720 he explicitly addressed the issues raised in the Bangorian and Trinitarian controversies, which were then agitating the clergy, in order to warn them against doctrines which 'Subvert the Christian Faith, and destroy the divine mission and authority of a Christian Church' (BL, Egerton MS 2073). None the less, his stand had marked him out as an important figure among the more junior whig bishops, and over the next few years he became ever more closely identified with first the Sunderland–Stanhope ministry and then its successor, led by Charles, Viscount Townshend, and Robert Walpole. Gibson's value to the whig ministry was recognized in 1721 by his appointment as dean of the chapels royal. In the same year he even became a ministerial pamphleteer, writing *The Causes of the Discontents* to justify the Quarantine Act passed in an attempt to prevent an outbreak of plague from reaching England. A tory critic dismissed it as 'a little scrub pamphlet … that he submits to for his hopes of London' (*Portland MSS*, 7.316). The prediction proved to be correct. On 11 April 1723, at the height of the investigation into Atterbury's Jacobite conspiracy by a secret committee of the House of Lords, of which Gibson was a member, Bishop Robinson died. The bishop of Lincoln was immediately nominated as his successor.

'Walpole's Pope' Robinson's death was followed, on 15 August 1723, by that of Charles Trimnell, bishop of Winchester. A close friend of Townshend and former tutor to the earl of Sunderland, Trimnell had retained the confidence of both whig factions even after the whig schism of 1717, and successive ministries had relied upon him for advice on ecclesiastical affairs. The leading ministers, however, had no doubt who his successor should be, and within days were writing to each other saying that 'Our Man must be the Bp of London' (BL, Add. MS 32686, fols. 316–19). Despite the fact that Townshend had been seeking advice from Gibson even before Trimnell's death, he appeared to be reluctant, proposing various alternatives, including that Trimnell's responsibilities should be shared by him, Lancelot Blackburne, and Richard Willis. However, as Walpole acutely observed, his protestations of '*nolo Episcopari*' were not to be taken seriously: he 'is a mortal man, wants to be ravish'd … He must be Pope, & would as willingly be *our* Pope as any Bodies' (ibid., fols. 326–7).

For the next thirteen years Gibson exercised considerable power and influence over church policy and patronage, probably as much as any bishop since William Sancroft in the latter years of Charles II's reign. The description of him as 'pope' quickly passed into common usage, but it is fundamentally misleading. He was given an office in the government buildings in the Cockpit; he was frequently referred to, and referred to himself, as 'Church minister'. But he held no official position, and, as he was well aware, his influence derived from the rather fragile basis of the confidence and trust of ministers. It was only enemies like John, Lord Hervey, who denounced Gibson's 'absolute power' (Hervey, 1.91). He himself far more realistically and accurately defined his role as 'the chief managing and conducting of Church-affairs *under the ministry*' (CUL, CH(H) P78/1c). And if Gibson was not 'pope', still less was he 'Walpole's Pope', a phrase popularized by Horace Walpole. In the 1720s it was Townshend, rather than Walpole, with whom he worked most closely, and it is unlikely that Gibson was ever comfortable with Walpole's reputation for religious indifference.

Part of Gibson's role as 'Church minister' was to organize the bishops in the House of Lords. He was seen by contemporaries as a ministerial whip for the bishops, his greatest triumph coming in the debates on the South Sea Company at the height of the excise crisis in 1733, when a solid block of twenty-four bishops voted for the court. The bishops' votes were crucial—on 1 June the ministerial majority was only five—and one pamphleteer depicted Gibson reminding Walpole that he owed the survival of his government to the support of the episcopate:

> Consider the Ch[u]rch is your *Rock of Defence*:
> Your *S[outh] Sea* Escape in your Memory cherish,
> When sinking you cry'd, help L[or]ds, or I perish.
> (Percival, 92)

Another part of his role was to act as a broker between the clergy and the ministry, passing on the 'Representations and Requests' of the former (CUL, CH(H) P78/1c) and returning the answers of the latter. But most importantly he exercised considerable influence over the formulation and implementation of the administration's religious policy.

In his own words Gibson's main objective was 'to bring the Body of the Clergy to a liking of a Whig-Administration, or at least to an acquiescence in it, and a disposition to be quiet and easy under it' (Hunt. L., Gibson MSS, bound vol., no. 13). One of the most important weapons in the pursuit of this policy was the church patronage in the hands of the crown. On the one hand Gibson tried to ensure that it was distributed only to whig clergymen, loyal to the Hanoverian monarchy and the revolution settlement in both church and state. He strongly disapproved of the favour shown by Queen Caroline to some tory clergy following her husband's succession to the crown in 1727, fearing in particular the consequences of the elevation to the episcopate of Thomas Sherlock. On the other hand Gibson recognized the importance of reassuring the clergy, especially perhaps the tory clergy, that the church was safe in whig hands. Thus, he insisted that preferments should be confined to men notable for their learning and morality, protesting to ministers against those whose only recommendation was their zealous whiggery. Another prerequisite which he demanded of candidates for crown patronage was religious orthodoxy. Indeed, after his resignation as 'Church minister' in 1736, he claimed that his first consideration was always 'the affection that the persons were known to bear to the Constitution of the Church' (St Andrews University, Gibson MSS 5312–5313). He reacted with horror to the proposal, again from the queen, that Samuel Clarke be made a bishop, warning Walpole that the promotion of a man whose views on the Trinity were widely regarded as Arian would be vigorously condemned by the whole body of the clergy.

In other ways, too, Gibson sought to demonstrate that the whig administration was concerned both to defend and to advance the interests of the church. He pressed for the prosecution of libertine authors, like Count Albert De Passaran, and in 1724 he secured a royal proclamation prohibiting public masquerades, which were widely seen as providing opportunities for people to engage in licentious and profane behaviour. More positively, the establishment of the regius professorships of modern history at Oxford and Cambridge was due largely to his initiative, as was the creation of the Whitehall preacherships. The latter offered minor, but prestigious, preferment for young fellows at the two universities, while simultaneously improving the quality of sermons in the Chapel Royal. In retrospect, these seem meagre achievements. Moreover, Gibson's schemes were often frustrated; an attempt to regulate the distribution of the crown's parochial patronage foundered on the opposition of Lord Chancellor King.

Gibson's lack of success, however, should not be allowed to obscure his ambition. He had been committed to the cause of church reform from early in his career. His *Codex*, published in 1713, was, in part, a manifesto for reform, highlighting issues worthy of consideration by convocation. During the last years of Queen Anne's reign he had supported many of the initiatives debated there, on which, contrary to the common impression, whig and tory clergymen often co-operated. In 1715, when he gave the address at the opening of convocation, he had urged that it pursue the reform of excommunication, a subject to which he returned in *Of Visitations Parochial and General*, published in 1717. It is clear that in the 1720s and 1730s Gibson hoped to use his relationship with the court and ministry to push through some long-cherished reforms. He produced a detailed set of proposals, many of which, like the reform of excommunication, the revival of rural deans, and the tightening up on the granting of marriage licences, had been discussed in convocation between 1702 and 1717. Others were far more radical, foreshadowing the work of the ecclesiastical commissioners in the nineteenth century by outlining a plan for the redrawing of diocesan boundaries. Nothing came of these proposals, but as late as 1740 Gibson was hoping for the revival of convocation to push through the programme of reform begun by its predecessors.

Gibson's 'resignation' Gibson was quite clear about the basis on which he had allied with Townshend and Walpole. He saw the government and himself as continuing the strategy developed by Archbishop Tenison. For Gibson this meant adhering to what he called 'the true Whig interest', which he defined as 'a Body made up of Lay-Whigs, Church-Whigs and Protestant Dissenters, united on the terms of maintaining the Protestant Succession, the Church Establishment, and the Toleration; as wisely fix'd and bounded at the Revolution' (Hunt. L., Gibson MSS, bound vol., no. 14). In the late 1720s and early 1730s, however, this alliance came under strain from two directions. First, the dissenters began to press for the repeal of the Test and Corporation Acts. In Gibson's view the character of the dissenting community had changed since the revolution of 1688—it was no longer interested in liberty of conscience, but wanted instead to pull down the church establishment. Second, there was a rising tide of anti-clericalism, an 'Antichurch Spirit' (ibid.), among whigs both inside and outside parliament. Through the early 1730s Gibson complained about the prevalence of anti-clericalism, and especially about the fact that the ministry seemed to be doing so little to combat it—it was well known that some of the most prominent pamphleteers against the church and clergy were in the pay of the court.

Gibson played a leading part in orchestrating the church's response. Once again he became a pamphleteer, writing an article in the *Whitehall Evening-Post* against the Tithe Bill of 1731, and then producing pamphlets against the ecclesiastical courts and church rates bills of 1733. He also made an influential contribution to the debate on the Test Act, arguing in *The Dispute Adjusted* (1732) that no time was proper for its repeal. Then, at the end of 1733, the news broke that Thomas Rundle, chaplain to Lord Chancellor Talbot, had been promised the bishopric of Gloucester. Rundle was suspected of Arianism and freethinking, and a major political crisis ensued. Gibson led a vigorous opposition to his promotion, making it clear that he would not participate in Rundle's consecration and threatening to resign as 'Church minister'. Talbot, however, refused to abandon Rundle, and the affair dragged on for a year while controversy raged in the press. Ultimately, Walpole sided with Gibson and Martin Benson became bishop of Gloucester. But Gibson had won only a pyrrhic victory. He could not prevent Rundle's being compensated with the bishopric of Derry, and the fact that he had found it so difficult to veto the promotion of a clergyman widely suspected of heterodoxy highlighted the extent to which his influence was declining.

During the controversy Gibson himself had been the focus of anti-clerical attacks. Increasingly pamphleteers focused on the bishop himself, attacking not only the power he exercised but also his churchmanship. The reputation he had acquired as a whig low-churchman during Anne's reign obscured the fact that he had many of the characteristics of a high-churchman. Most notably, in the

'Introductory discourse' to the *Codex* he had advanced a vigorous defence of the independence of church and state, claiming that the authority of the ecclesiastical courts, though it derived from the crown, was separate from, and equal to, that of the temporal courts. Gibson's vigorous assertion of the rights of the church was one reason why he made such a good 'Church minister' for a whig administration anxious to combat the cry of 'the church in danger'. But, in the eyes of anti-clerical whigs, such views were dangerous. Michael Foster produced a detailed rejoinder to the *Codex*, demonstrating that the ecclesiastical courts were 'an inferior jurisdiction' (Foster, 38). In the House of Lords, Lord Chief Justice Hardwicke claimed that it contained 'many things … contrary to law' (Hervey, 2.536). Gibson was frequently denounced as Dr Codex; he was even portrayed, as in the satirical print *The Parallel*, as a new Archbishop Laud.

Until 1736 Walpole adhered to his alliance with Gibson and refused to support any of the anti-clerical initiatives, and in that year he spoke against the repeal of the Test Act when it was debated in the Commons. But two further anti-clerical initiatives in that session, the Mortmain Bill and the Quaker Tithe Bill, did receive the backing of the ministry. The former was, in part, an attack on corporate Anglican philanthropy, but it did not threaten the rights and privileges of the church and clergy. The Quaker Tithe Bill, however, did. Gibson, increasingly sensitive to 'the charge of sacrificing the interests of Religion and the Established Church to my own private views' (St Andrews University, Gibson MS 5285A), mobilized the bishops and clergy against it. Petitions against the bill flooded into parliament and it was defeated on its second reading in the Lords, with fifteen bishops voting against it. Walpole believed that he had been betrayed by Gibson and denounced him as the '*Ringleader of Sedition*' (ibid., MS 5303). The bishop of London replied by informing the prime minister that henceforth he wanted 'no more share in the publick affairs of the Church, than the rest of my Brethren' (ibid., MS 5299). It had long been understood that Gibson would succeed Wake at Canterbury—though he had always insisted that his consent should not be taken for granted. In the event, it was no surprise that, when Wake died in January 1737, Gibson was passed over in favour of John Potter.

Bishop of London In spite of the demands of ecclesiastical politics, Gibson did not neglect his duties as a diocesan bishop. He conducted regular visitations, following the practice he had developed at Lincoln of sending questionnaires to the clergy. As at Lincoln, he undertook separate confirmation tours. He personally examined candidates for ordination, and was accessible to clergymen who wished to consult him. At his death he left his diocesan papers, containing 'a very clear & perfect detail of all particulars', to his successor (BL, Add. MS 35598, fol. 348). He also took a close interest in the pastoral problems of the capital and its surrounding area. He was a strong supporter of charity schools, the societies for the reformation of manners, and the Society for Promoting Christian Knowledge. He had joined the SPCK in 1700, two years after its foundation, and not only recommended its work to fellow clergy but also contributed works like *An Admonition Against Profane and Common Swearing* (3rd edn, 1723) and *The Sinfulness of Neglecting and Profaning the Lord's Day* (2nd edn, 1740) to its list of practical religious tracts.

In the late 1720s and early 1730s the problem which most engaged Gibson's attention was the growth of 'Profaneness and Impiety' in London (Gibson, *The Bishop of London's Pastoral Letter … Occasion'd by some Late Writings*, 2). The main cause of this, he believed, was the writings of 'Infidels', who were openly attacking Christianity with the aim of 'banishing' it from the nation (Gibson, *Charge*, 3). Gibson laid no claim to being a theologian, and he made no attempt to reply directly to deistical and freethinking books. Rather, he sought to deal with the pastoral problems created by these assaults on the Christian religion. In a charge delivered at his 1730 visitation he offered his clergy some hints about how best to respond to the claims of the 'Infidels'. Much more innovatory was his appeal direct to the inhabitants of the diocese in a series of three 'pastoral letters' published between 1728 and 1731. He sought to meet the criticism that most of the works published in defence of Christianity were 'too large and too learned' to be accessible to people 'of common Capacity'. His aim, therefore, was to draw up some simple 'Rules and Cautions' designed to strengthen the faith of 'sincere and unprejudic'd Christians' and to preserve them 'from these dangerous Infections' (Gibson, *The Bishop of London's Pastoral Letter … Occasion'd by some Late Writings*, 4). The first pastoral letter, 'occasion'd by some late writings in favour of infidelity', was followed by a second, published in 1730 and intended to counter the argument 'That reason is a sufficient guide in matters of religion, without the help of revelation'. The third, in 1731, was a defence of the divine inspiration of the New Testament. It is difficult to estimate the influence of these works, but they were undoubtedly a remarkable publishing success. Thirty thousand copies of the first were printed, 27,000 of the second, and 17,000 of the third. Such was the demand that 3000 copies were produced of a collected edition which appeared in 1732.

In the late 1730s Gibson's attention turned to a new threat to the church, the rise of Methodism and Moravianism. The opening of Methodist meeting-houses in London and Bristol in 1739 seems to have persuaded him that he needed to speak publicly about the movement. Three issues were prominent in Gibson's *Pastoral Letter* of 1739 and *Charge* of 1742. First, he highlighted Methodist theological errors in their doctrines of assurance, perfection, and imputed righteousness. Second, he was anxious to counter Methodist slanders against the clergy, though he also took the opportunity to encourage the clergy to disprove the allegations through their preaching and conduct. Third, he believed that the irregularities of the Methodists posed a threat to church discipline and order, which, he believed, were essential to the maintenance of religion. This last concern also explains much of his hostility to the Moravians. In his pastoral letter, however, Gibson balanced warnings against enthusiasm, the failure to distinguish 'aright between the *ordinary* and *extraordinary Operations of the Holy Spirit*' (Gibson, *The Bishop of London's Pastoral Letter … by Way of Caution*, 19), with a warning about the danger of lukewarmness, the belief that the duty of a Christian involved nothing more than going to church. True Christianity, he argued, lay in the middle way between these two extremes.

At this time Gibson's attitude to the Methodists was critical, yet moderate. He admitted that there was much that was good in their work, describing them as 'serious and well-meaning Christians' (Gibson, *The Bishop of London's Pastoral Letter … by Way of Caution*, 19). His early relations with John and Charles Wesley were friendly, though Charles's support for the practice of rebaptism did provoke a rebuke from the bishop. Indeed, judging by the quotations used in the 1739 *Pastoral Letter*, it was George Whitefield rather than the Wesleys who was Gibson's main target. However, while Gibson seems to have been prepared to turn a blind eye to the irregularities of the two brothers right up to his death, he gradually became more hostile to the Methodist movement. In 1744 he published anonymously *Observations upon the conduct and behaviour of a certain sect usually distinguished by the name of Methodists*, which was much more uncompromising in tone, and compared the Methodists with the sectaries of the seventeenth century who had brought confusion on the nation. This charge was repeated in Gibson's *Charge* of 1746–7, in which he confessed that his pastoral letter had been more gentle to the Methodists than they deserved.

As bishop of London Gibson also had responsibility for the Anglican church in the American colonies. Almost immediately after his translation he became aware of the problems of the colonial church—there was no provision for effective episcopal oversight, the laity were denied the rite of confirmation, and candidates for the ministry had to travel to England for ordination. Consequently, he began to advocate the creation of an American episcopate. About 1725 he laid before the privy council a detailed plan for the appointment of two suffragan bishops for the mainland colonies and two for the islands. However, nothing came of the initiative, and Gibson himself was forced to provide what supervision he could for the colonial church. He had discovered that the powers exercised by his predecessors had had no legal basis, and took out a commission from the crown to regularize his jurisdiction. There is no doubt that he took his responsibilities seriously, as the voluminous correspondence preserved among the Fulham papers at Lambeth Palace Library makes clear. But, despite appointing commissaries to exercise delegated jurisdiction in the colonies, he found it impossible to provide adequate supervision for the American church.

Last years After his resignation in 1736 Gibson withdrew from public affairs. He remained loyal to the administration, depositing his proxy with a reliable ministerial supporter in the House of Lords in every session from 1737 to 1748. During this period, however, he attended in person on only seven days. On three of these he was present to cast his vote against the ministry, opposing the Gin Bill in 1743 and the clause relating to episcopal orders in the Bill for Disarming the Highlands in 1748. To the end Gibson remained committed to his church-whig principles, a zealous supporter not only of whig government as the guarantor of the revolution settlement but also of the interests of the church and clergy.

After the resignation of Walpole in 1742, Gibson once more became involved in politics and policy. His relations with the Pelhams had always been good, and the duke of Newcastle turned to him at least occasionally for advice on preferments. His standing with the ministry was revealed clearly when he was offered the archbishopric of York in 1743 and then again in 1747, when, on the death of Potter, he was pressed to accept the primacy. On both occasions he declined, pleading his age and ill health. Certainly Gibson was coming to rely on younger colleagues for occasional assistance in discharging his episcopal duties. But he was well enough in 1745 to take the lead in mobilizing the church against the Jacobite rising. First he sent a circular letter to his clergy, exhorting them to raise in their congregations 'a just Abhorrence of *Popery*' (Hunt. L., Gibson MSS, bound vol., no. 27). Gibson's zealous missive was much approved by the ministry and compared favourably to Archbishop Potter's, 'the cold Phlegm of an Old man', as one commentator described it (BL, Add. MS 35598, fol. 51). Then he produced his fifth pastoral letter, reminding the people of his diocese—and many beyond it—of the 'mischiefs' of popery, warning them of the dangers posed by the rising and exciting them 'to a serious reformation of life and manners'. Gibson was, of course, returning to an old theme. The threat from popery had been the subject of one of his first published sermons in 1705, and, when fears about the spread of Catholicism had been raised again in the mid-1730s, he had edited a collection in three large folio volumes entitled *A Preservative Against Popery* (1738), which comprised the anti-popish tracts published in the reign of James II.

In other ways, too, Gibson returned to earlier interests during the last years of his life. In 1737 he had been infuriated by the judgment given by Lord Chief Justice Hardwicke in the case of *Middleton* v. *Crofts*, which ruled that post-Reformation canons were not binding on the laity. According to Richard Smalbroke, his first biographer, this prompted Gibson to return to the study of the law, examining the registers and records from the various cathedrals of England and Wales. The result of this labour, pursued over a number of years, was a treatise on the 'Ecclesiastical Common-Law' (Smalbroke, 13), reasserting the claims made in the *Codex* for the jurisdictional independence of the church. Fearing controversy, however, Gibson left it unpublished.

On 20 August 1748 Gibson went to Bath to seek 'relief under a weakness of the stomach' (Sykes, 387). He died there on 6 September and was buried, on 17 September, in a vault in Fulham churchyard, to which the remains of his wife were also removed in accordance with the wishes expressed in his will. At the height of his power in the

1720s and 1730s no one had any doubts about the importance of the man Walpole called his 'pope'. Gibson was also a major figure in the religious and intellectual life of the period—as an Anglo-Saxonist, as an antiquary, as a canonist, as a writer of books of popular piety, as an administrator. However, his historical reputation suffered from the deprecation of the Hanoverian church by Tractarians and evangelicals in the nineteenth century, while the fact that he was not a theologian ensured that he received little attention from writers like Mark Pattison and Leslie Stephen. Not until 1926 was Gibson accorded a full biography, by Norman Sykes, which helped to secure his reputation as 'the most influential of Georgian prelates' (Douglas, 85).

STEPHEN TAYLOR

Sources N. Sykes, *Edmund Gibson, bishop of London, 1669–1748: a study in politics & religion in the eighteenth century* (1926) • S. Taylor, '"Dr Codex" and the whig "pope": Edmund Gibson, bishop of Lincoln and London, 1716–1748', *Lords of parliament: studies, 1714–1914*, ed. R. W. Davis (1995), 9–28 • C. J. Abbey, *The English church and its bishops, 1700–1800*, 2 vols. (1887) • J. H. Baker, *Monuments of endlesse labours: English canonists and their work, 1300–1900* (1998) • W. Stubbs, *Seventeen lectures on the study of medieval and modern history* (1886) • Gibson–Nicolson correspondence, Bodl. Oxf., MS Add. A. 269 • R. E. G. Cole, ed., *Speculum dioeceseos Lincolniensis sub episcopis Gul: Wake et Edm: Gibson, AD 1705–1723*, Lincoln RS, 4 (1913) • Christ Church Oxf., Arch. W. Epist. 15, 20 • PRO, LC 3/63, 115 • CUL, Cholmondeley (Houghton) MSS, P78/1c • correspondence of the duke of Newcastle, BL, Add. MS 32686 • *The manuscripts of his grace the duke of Portland*, 10 vols., HMC, 29 (1891–1931), vol. 7 • John, Lord Hervey, *Some materials towards memoirs of the reign of King George II*, ed. R. Sedgwick, 3 vols. (1931) • [R. Smalbroke], *Some account of the Right Reverend Dr Edmund Gibson* (1749) • M. Percival, ed., *Political ballads illustrating the administration of Sir Robert Walpole* (1916) • M. Foster, *An examination of the scheme of church-power, laid down in the Codex juris ecclesiastici Anglicani, &c.* (1735) • LPL, Potter MSS, 1 • D. C. Douglas, *English scholars* (1939) • S. Taylor, 'Sir Robert Walpole, the Church of England, and the Quakers Tithe Bill of 1736', *HJ*, 28 (1985), 51–77 • S. Taylor, 'Bishop Edmund Gibson's proposals for church reform', *From Cranmer to Davidson: a Church of England miscellany*, ed. S. Taylor (1999), 169–202 • D. Fairer, 'Anglo-Saxon studies', *Hist. U. Oxf.* 5: *18th-cent. Oxf.*, 807–29 • C. J. Podmore, *The Moravian church in England, 1728–1760* (1998) • U. St Andr. L., Gibson MSS • *Weekly Miscellany*, 70 (13 April 1734) • E. Gibson and A. Charlett, correspondence, Bodl. Oxf., MSS Ballard 5, 6 • *A congratulatory poem on the translation of the right reverend father in God, Edmund, from the see of Lincoln, to the see of London* (1724) • Oxfordshire Archives, Oxf. Dioc. MSS d.106 • *IGI* • E. Gibson, *Religion, the best security to church and state: a sermon preach'd at the assizes held at Kingston in Surrey, March the 10th 1714/15* (1715) • Gibson's visitation charge, 1720–21, BL, Egerton MS 2073 • Hunt. L., Gibson papers • Bodl. Oxf., MSS Gibson • MSS, 1741–3, LPL, Gibson MSS, 2168 • LPL, Fulham MSS • BL, Herring–Hardwicke correspondence, Add. MS 35598 • E. Gibson, *The bishop of London's pastoral letter … occasion'd by some late writings in favour of infidelity* (1728) • E. Gibson, *The bishop of London's pastoral letter … by way of caution, against lukewarmness on one hand, and enthusiasm on the other*, 2nd edn (1739) • E. Gibson, *The charge of Edmund, lord bishop of London, to the clergy of his diocese … the 28th day of May, 1730* (1731) • M. E. Noble, ed., *Register of births, deaths, and marriages of the parish of Bampton* (1897) • M. E. Noble, *A history of the parish of Bampton* (1901) • PRO, PROB 11/765, fols. 141–4 • [T. Gordon], *A letter to Dr Codex* (1734) • Walpole, *Corr.*, vol. 17 • *A chorus of grammars: the correspondence of George Hickes and his collaborators on the 'Thesaurus linguarum septentrionalium'*, ed. R. L. Harris (1992) • *GM*, 1st ser., 18 (1748), 427 • W. Gibson, 'Bishop Gibson's *Codex* and the reform of the Oxford University Press', *N&Q*, 240 (1995), 47–52 • *Remarks and collections of Thomas Hearne*, ed. C. E. Doble and others, 11 vols., OHS, 2, 7, 13, 34, 42–3, 48, 50, 65, 67, 72 (1885–1921) • E. B. Fryde and others, eds., *Handbook of British chronology*, 3rd edn, Royal Historical Society Guides and Handbooks, 2 (1986)

Archives BL, notes for life of Henry Spelman, Add. MS 33751 • BL, visitation charge, Egerton MS 2073 • Bodl. Oxf., corresp. and MSS • GL, papers mainly relating to diocesan affairs • Hunt. L., corresp. and MSS • LPL, corresp. and papers relating to American colonies; also corresp. and papers relating to administration of the London diocese • LPL, corresp. and MSS • LPL, papers and collections • LPL, London, St Paul's Cathedral MSS • U. St Andr. L., corresp. and MSS | BL, corresp. with First Lord Hardwicke, Add. MSS 35585–35589, 35908, 36136, *passim* • BL, corresp. with White Kennett, Lansdowne MS 1017 • BL, corresp. with Philip Morant, Add. MS 37221 • BL, corresp. with duke of Newcastle and others, Add. MSS 32690–32715, *passim* • Bodl. Oxf., letters to Arthur Charlett; letters to William Nicolson • Bodl. Oxf., letters to Edward Lluyd, MSS Ashm 1829–1830 • Bodl. Oxf., corresp. with Thomas Tanner and others • CUL, Cholmondeley (Houghton) MSS, P78 • CUL, SPCK, Newman Society letters • CUL, letters to John Strype, Add. MSS 2–9 • CUL, letters to Sir Robert Walpole • GL, diocese book, MS 9550 • GL, visitation returns, MSS 25750–25755 • Lincs. Arch., Lincoln diocesan records, diocesan corresp.; speculum; visitation returns • LPL, American MSS and corresp., MS 1123 • LPL, Archbishops' papers, Potter 1 • LPL, Fulham MSS • LPL, Fulham MSS (colonial) • LPL, Secker MSS • NL Wales, letters to Humphrey Humphreys • PRO, State papers, domestic, corresp. and MSS, SP 35 and 36 • TCD, corresp. with William King • W. Yorks. AS, Leeds, letters to Ralph Thoresby, MSS 11–13 • Yale U., Lewis Walpole Library, Weston MSS, corresp. • Yale U., Osborn files, corresp. with Viscount Townshend

Likenesses J. Ellis, oils, *c.*1727 (probably a copy), Charterhouse, London • G. Vertue, engraving, 1728 (after J. Ellis), priv. coll. • oils, *c.*1731, Bodl. Oxf.; repro. in Sykes, *Edmund Gibson* • J. Vanderbank, oils, 1735, Queen's College, Oxford; version, Bodl. Oxf. • J. Vanderbank, oils, 1735, Sion College, London • caricature, engraving, 1735 (*The hierarchical skimington*), BM; repro. in P. Langford, *Walpole and the robinocracy* (1986) • caricature, engraving, 1736 (*The parallel*), BM; repro. in P. Langford, *Walpole and the robinocracy* (1986) • J. Faber, engraving, *c.*1737 (after J. Vanderbank) • A. Soldi, oils, *c.*1740–1745, subdeanery, Lincoln [*see illus.*]

Wealth at death approx. £15,000: Gibson, 'Bishop Gibson's Codex'

Gibson, Edward (1668/9–1701), portrait draughtsman, was perhaps the son of Richard *Gibson (1605/1615?–1690), miniature painter, and his wife, Anne, *née* Sheppard. According to Buckeridge and Vertue, he was the nephew of the miniature painter William *Gibson (1644–1703) [*see under* Gibson, Richard] from whom he received instruction in painting. He commenced painting portraits in oil, but subsequently found more employment in crayons. In this medium he showed some genius, and was making great progress when he died in January 1701 in his thirty-third year. He resided in Catherine Street, Strand, and was buried at Richmond, Surrey. He drew his own portrait in crayons twice, in one dressed as a Chinese, in the other as a Quaker. One self-portrait, dated 1690, was at Tart Hall near St James's Park, London, and was subsequently given to the National Portrait Gallery, London, in 1920. This was described by David Piper as 'evidence of a fresh and original talent' (Piper, 138). Another, dated 1696, was formerly in Sir Thomas Lawrence's collection, and was sold at Christies on 27 March 1866.

L. H. CUST, *rev.* ANNETTE PEACH

Sources M. Edmond, 'Limners and picturemakers', *Walpole Society*, 47 (1978–80), 60–242, esp. 109, 198 • D. Piper, *Catalogue of seventeenth-century portraits in the National Portrait Gallery, 1625–1714*

(1963), 137–8 • Vertue, *Note books*, 1.31; 5.3, 27 • [B. Buckeridge], 'An essay towards an English school of painters', in R. de Piles, *The art of painting, and the lives of the painters* (1706), 398–480 • D. Foskett, *Miniatures: dictionary and guide* (1987)

Likenesses E. Gibson, self-portrait, crayon drawing, 1690, NPG • E. Gibson, self-portrait, crayon drawing, 1696; Christies, 27 March 1866

Gibson, Edward, first Baron Ashbourne (1837–1913), lawyer and politician, was born in Dublin on 4 September 1837, the second son of William Gibson (*d.* 1872) of Rockforest, co. Tipperary, and his first wife, Louisa (*d.* 1853), daughter of Joseph Grant, barrister, of Dublin. Gibson, an ailing child, was educated privately and at Trinity College, Dublin, from which he graduated BA in 1858 with first-class honours in history and English literature. In 1860 he was called to the Irish bar; in 1872 he took silk, having developed a modest practice on the Leinster circuit over the previous years. He married on 4 April 1868 Frances Maria Adelaide (1849–1926), second daughter of Henry Cope Colles, a Dublin barrister, with whom he had four sons and two daughters.

Despite his intellectual promise, and his early commitment to the bar, Gibson emerged as an astute lawyer–politician rather than as a subtle legal commentator or scholar. Using the Conservative political resources of Trinity College, Gibson won national prominence in the 1870s as a political authority on Irish government. He responded to the home-rule movement by encouraging the development of Conservative associations in the small towns where he practised his advocacy; he assisted another prominent tory lawyer, David Plunket, in developing a network of Conservative graduate bodies. Gibson stood for Waterford city in 1874, but was defeated by two home-rulers; in 1875 he successfully contested Trinity College. As member for Trinity, Gibson occupied a position of some prominence in the House of Commons, and he quickly built upon this through his informed and mellifluous speeches on Irish matters. He accepted junior ministerial office, as attorney-general for Ireland, in 1877, and—against the context of developing agrarian poverty and violence—promoted a vision of firm Conservative government and a confident and controlled Dublin Castle administration. Unruffled by challenge, and persuasive in debate, Gibson won Disraeli's admiration and confidence; and in 1880–81 he was closely consulted and actively advanced by his leader.

The death of Disraeli in April 1881 and the eventual emergence of Lord Salisbury as Conservative leader were personal setbacks for Gibson. He was an intimate of Stafford Northcote, the defeated leadership contender, and was temperamentally and intellectually much closer to him than to Salisbury. As one of Northcote's closest lieutenants, and as a counter-weight to the maverick Lord Randolph Churchill, Gibson still merited a place in Salisbury's first cabinet, formed in June 1885. But, to the surprise of contemporaries, and against Salisbury's wishes, he insisted upon taking the relatively junior position of lord chancellor of Ireland. This was a deliberate retreat from the first rank of Conservative politics, and may be explained by Gibson's polite but cool relations with Salisbury, and by his desire to make financial provision for his large family (the chancellorship carried a salary of £8000 p.a., and a pension of £4000 p.a.).

Edward Gibson, first Baron Ashbourne (1837–1913), by Lafayette, 1906–7

Gibson took a peerage in 1885 and as Baron Ashbourne held the lord chancellorship of Ireland in every Conservative government until 1905. In July 1885 he drafted, virtually single-handedly, the Irish land act which bears his name, and which greatly extended the operation of land purchase in Ireland. However, this was his single legislative achievement. Increasingly he became entrapped in the minutiae of office: his name became a byword for genial jobbery, and he was renowned among senior ministers for the slippery defence of his own, often vulnerable, cabinet position. That he survived for so long within the Conservative leadership—he was a member of Bonar Law's shadow cabinet in 1912—reflected as much on his political dexterity as on his ministerial record.

Ashbourne died in St George's Hospital, London, on 22 May 1913. His ministerial career spanned almost thirty years, and he advised every Conservative leader from Disraeli to Bonar Law on Irish legal and political issues. He was at the first rank of Conservative politics in the early 1880s, and at the peak of his celebrity with the success of his land-purchase measure in 1885. But he lacked the ruthless political ambition of a Salisbury or a Randolph Churchill; and he lacked the remorseless physical and intellectual energy of a Gladstone or Lloyd George. The effort of climbing the greasy pole of Conservative politics between 1875 and 1885 appears to have exhausted his political energies. Or, perhaps, having made the ascent, he felt that the view was not worth the effort of sustaining.

ALVIN JACKSON

Sources A. B. Cooke and A. P. W. Malcomson, *The Ashbourne papers* (1974) • A. Gailey, *Ireland and the death of kindness* (1987) • A. Jackson, *The Ulster party* (1989) • *CGPLA Eng. & Wales* (1913)
Archives HLRO, corresp. and papers | BL, corresp. with Arthur James Balfour, Add. MS 49815, *passim* • CUL, letters to duke of Marlborough • Hatfield House, Hertfordshire, Salisbury MSS • HLRO, corresp. with fifth Earl Cadogan
Likenesses J. Russell & Sons, photograph, *c.*1892, NPG; repro. in *Our conservative and unionist statesmen*, 1 (1896–9) • Lafayette, photograph, 1906–7, V&A [*see illus.*] • J. Brown, stipple (after H. T. Wells; Grillion's Club series), BM, NPG • Spy [L. Ward], caricature, watercolour study, NPG; repro. in *VF* (4 July 1885)
Wealth at death £44,329 2*s.* 1*d.*: Irish probate sealed in London, 18 July 1913, *CGPLA Eng. & Wales* • £92,325 7*s.* 11*d.*: probate, 1 July 1913, *CGPLA Ire.*

Gibson, Francis (*bap.* **1752**, *d.* **1805**), mariner and collector of customs, was baptized at Whitby, Yorkshire, on 16 January 1752, the son of Joseph Gibson, commander of a merchant ship, and his wife, Mary, daughter of a customs controller at Whitby. He was sent to the day school run by Lionel Charlton, a man of considerable mathematical ability, as his father intended him for the merchant service. On his first voyage, under his cousin John Hudson, to Goldborough in New England, he drew the coast and harbour so competently that he received a generous reward from John Norman, whose goods they were carrying.

In 1775 Gibson married Alice, daughter of Thomas Fishburn, shipwright of Whitby, but she died in 1777, shortly after the birth of their daughter. Joseph Gibson had procured a ship for his son's command, but the latter, being newly married, did not wish to sail with troops to America; his refusal was fortunate as the ship was struck by lightning off the American coast and foundered. Another ship, the *Lord Howe*, was purchased, in which Gibson sailed to Russia in 1778 and again in 1779. That autumn he fell sick on the return voyage and was detained at a Russian port in the Gulf of Finland. When the American John Paul Jones attacked the Baltic fleet and volunteers were raised to defend the north-east coast, Gibson was commissioned as ensign in the Whitby force, and served until peace returned in 1783. He had by then acquired an interest in military science, read many books on the subject, and built a model fortress which was much admired.

Gibson married a second wife, Ann, daughter of Richard and Elizabeth Evans of Redhouse, Shropshire. Early in 1787 Lord Mulgrave recommended him to the collectorship of customs at Whitby, an office he held uneventfully through the years of slow physical and mental decline leading to his death. In 1790 he constructed a model of York Minster which was presented to the queen. He toured the seaboard of the Southern Netherlands, drew its harbours, and published descriptions of its ports in various provincial papers. He also contributed to the *Naval Chronicle*. His *Sailing Directions for the Baltic* (1791) were said to have served the Copenhagen expedition of 1801 under Sir Hyde Parker and Nelson. He also composed a play, translated Charpentier's collected papers from the Bastille, and wrote poetry.

Against her father's wishes his daughter married a Mr Ward who fell into debt, and Gibson offered himself as security. Ward sought to evade his creditors and their pressure on Gibson for payment worsened his illness. He died in Whitby on 24 July 1805. ANITA MCCONNELL

Sources W. Watkins, 'Essay on the life, writings, and genius of the late Francis Gibson', in *The poetical remains, with other detached pieces of the late F. Gibson* (1807), v–xiv

Gibson, George Stacey (**1818–1883**), botanist and philanthropist, was born on 20 July 1818 at Saffron Walden, Essex, the only child of Wyatt George Gibson (1790–1862) and Deborah, daughter of George Stacey of Alton, Hampshire. At the age of nine he was sent to Grove House School, Tottenham, Middlesex, where his mother's relatives lived. About 1836 he joined his father and uncles in the family firm, the Essex and Saffron Walden Bank, becoming a partner in 1840. In 1845 he married Elizabeth (1821–1890), daughter of Samuel Tuke of York; they had a daughter.

Gibson's family were members of the Society of Friends and, like so many in that sect, he was early encouraged in a taste for natural history and, through the influence of a much-loved aunt, developed a keenness for field botany in particular. In this he quickly won national prominence by finding five flowering plant species new to Britain in 1842–4, during which period he joined both national botanical societies, generously contributed specimens of newly discovered rarities to their annual exchanges, and began publishing notes and papers in the leading field botany periodical, *The Phytologist*. Blessed with ample means, he was able to travel widely and provided records from various counties for H. C. Watson's series of works on British plant distribution.

About 1843 Gibson conceived the idea of compiling a full-scale flora of Essex, but on hearing that the veteran Edward Forster already had one in hand felt obliged to desist. On the latter's death in 1849, however, no manuscript was found and Gibson accordingly revived his plan. The resulting book appeared in 1862 and in several respects was a notable advance on previous publications of its type, particularly in its impressively wide coverage of a large county with some areas of considerable remoteness and in its combing of the literature for earlier records stretching back three centuries.

At that point, however, the death of Gibson's father compelled much fuller attention to business and the assumption of a range of civic duties, including serving on the Saffron Walden council (he twice became mayor). He was left the bank's sole partner and brought in his brother-in-law and a cousin; the name thereupon changed to Gibson, Tuke, and Gibson, and the firm was ultimately one of the twenty which combined in 1896 to form Barclays Bank. Though he was still able to indulge his lifelong passion for book collecting and also continued to read extensively, Gibson's activities as a botanist were over, replaced by the time he gave unstintingly to numerous charitable commitments, especially those connected with the Society of Friends. To these he not only contributed munificently but brought to their affairs extreme conscientiousness and a scientist's (and banker's) stickling for precision: 'he grudged no amount of costly or toilsome research to verify a fact', his obituary in the *Journal of Botany* reported. Quiet and unobtrusive, ever considerate and ready to listen, he was predictably in very wide demand.

Gibson died at the Devonshire House Temperance Hotel, 12 Bishopsgate Street, City of London, from inflammation of the kidneys, on 5 April 1883. At the funeral in Saffron Walden 5000 people followed the coffin, testifying to the great respect in which he had been held. His herbarium passed to the Natural History Museum in London except for a small portion donated to the Essex Field Club. His wife survived him. D. E. ALLEN

Sources G. S. Boulger, *Journal of Botany, British and Foreign*, 21 (1883), 161–5 • G. S. Boulger, *Transactions of the Essex Field Club*, 4 (1885), 1–8 • *Annual Monitor* (1884), 34–43 • P. W. Matthews, *History of Barclays Bank Limited*, ed. A. W. Tuke (1926), 174ff. • S. T. Jermyn and J. K. Adams, *Flora of Essex* (1974), 17 • *CGPLA Eng. & Wales* (1883)
Archives Essex RO, Chelmsford, corresp. and MSS • NHM, herbarium • Passmore Edwards Museum, Newham, London, herbarium • RS Friends, Lond., corresp. • Saffron Walden Museum, corresp. and MSS
Likenesses photograph, repro. in *Journal of Botany, British and Foreign*, 21 (1883) • photograph, repro. in *Transactions of the Essex Field Club*
Wealth at death £342,456 18*s*. 0*d*.: probate, 5 Sept 1883, *CGPLA Eng. & Wales*

Gibson, Guy Penrose (1918–1944), air force officer, was born in Simla, India, on 12 August 1918, the second son and youngest of three children of Alexander James Gibson (1876–1968), of the Indian forest service, and his wife, Leonora (Nora) Mary Strike (1894–1939). The marriage was not happy, and in 1924 Nora Gibson returned to England with the children, who were placed in boarding-schools. In 1929 Alexander Gibson retired and likewise returned to England, but neither parent saw much of the children, who spent a good deal of their holidays with relatives.

Guy Gibson attended St George's preparatory school, Folkestone, Kent, from 1926 to 1932 and then St Edward's School, Oxford. Though not particularly gifted academically or physically he impressed as hard-working and determined, and this paid off when, after first being rejected as too short (at 5 feet 6 inches), he was in the summer of 1936 accepted for the RAF, and began pilot training at the Bristol Flying School, Yatesbury, on 16 November. Commissioned as acting pilot officer, after further flying training at 6 Flying Training School, Netheravon, from which he graduated on 31 August 1937 with a rating of 'average', Gibson was posted to 83 (bomber) squadron, at Turnhouse, near Edinburgh. In March 1938 the squadron, which was equipped with the attractive but entirely outdated Hawker Hind single-engined biplane bomber, moved to Scampton, near Lincoln, and in December was re-equipped with the Handley Page Hampden, a modern twin-engined monoplane.

Gibson remained with 83 squadron until September 1940, completing a tour of thirty-seven operations and (in July) being awarded the DFC, before being posted to instruct at 14 operational training unit, Cottesmore, Rutland. After two weeks, however, an acute shortage of night fighter pilots led to his posting to 29 squadron,

Guy Penrose Gibson (1918–1944), by Gordon Anthony, 1944

Digby, Lincolnshire, as a flight commander with flight lieutenant rank. 29 squadron was equipped with obsolescent Bristol Blenheims but was slowly re-equipping with the potent Bristol Beaufighter and getting to grips with airborne radar. Personally this was a time of happiness for Gibson, as on 23 November 1940, at Penarth, he married Evelyn Mary Moore (1911–1988), an actress, but it was a period of frustration for the squadron, which remained without success until 13 March 1941. The next night Gibson destroyed his first enemy bomber, adding three more after the squadron moved to West Malling, Kent, on 29 April. Promoted squadron leader in June 1941, he was awarded a bar to his DFC in September, but in December was posted 'tour expired' as chief flying instructor at 51 operational training unit, Cranfield.

Disliking instructing, and ill-suited to it, Gibson was again fortunate in being earmarked for promotion by Air Marshal Harris, commander-in-chief, Bomber Command, and at the beginning of April 1942 he assumed command of 106 squadron at Coningsby, Lincolnshire, with wing commander rank. It was a difficult time, since the squadron was equipped with the twin-engined Avro Manchester, an aircraft with an excellent airframe but handicapped by its unreliable and underperforming Rolls Royce Vulture engines, but Gibson's energy and, on occasion, ruthlessness quickly lifted the performance of the squadron. Conversion to the highly successful four-engined development of the Manchester—the Lancaster—followed, and within months 106 squadron was regarded as the top-performing 5 group squadron, on the evidence of target photographs. Gibson's achievement was acknowledged by a DSO in November 1942 and a bar in March 1943, on the completion of his tour, which brought his total bombing sorties to at least seventy-two.

After such prolonged operational service Gibson would normally have been rested but instead he was asked to form a new squadron to undertake a special project; the squadron was 617 and the special project was the 'Dambusters' raid of 16 May 1943. Of the raid itself, which was intended to disrupt industry in the Ruhr by destroying six key dams, much has been written, first by Gibson in his *Enemy Coast Ahead*; the raid, the squadron, and Gibson himself have become legendary. The propaganda success was huge. So too was the task facing Gibson when he arrived at Scampton on 21 March. The attempt to breach the Ruhr dams had to be made at the coincidence of a full moon and full dams—in mid May. In two months a squadron was formed and crews trained for an operation that required new and specialist skills. Only two of the dams (the Möhne and the Eder) were breached, insufficient seriously to disrupt production, and, since no other squadron had been trained, there was no possibility of a further raid. The fear that there might be another raid, however, led to the deployment of a large anti-aircraft defence force around German dams for the remainder of the war. For the attackers, too, the dams raid was costly: eight of the nineteen aircraft were lost, and of their fifty-six crew only three survived, to be taken prisoner.

Thirty-four aircrew were decorated for their part in the dams raid, Gibson himself, who, after dropping his mine, flew alongside other attacking aircraft to draw anti-aircraft fire, being awarded (28 May 1943) the Victoria Cross. A celebrity overnight, he was too valuable to be risked further on operations, and on 3 August he relinquished command of 617 squadron. Gibson travelled with Winston Churchill's party across the Atlantic, for talks with the Canadian prime minister, Mackenzie King, and President Roosevelt, but was released to carry out a continent-wide speaking tour, addressing air force and civic audiences in Canada and the United States. Now a protégé of Churchill as well as of Harris, he sought nomination as prospective Conservative parliamentary candidate for Macclesfield, in Cheshire. In March 1944 he won the nomination but within months came to the conclusion that he could not adequately fulfil his responsibilities, and on 14 August he resigned.

Having returned to Britain in December 1943 Gibson was posted to the directorate of accidents in the Air Ministry but spent most of his time working on a book, probably at the instigation of the Ministry of Information. The result was the best-selling *Enemy Coast Ahead*, published posthumously in 1946. There has been considerable debate over how much of it was actually written by Gibson but all the evidence, including that of the typescript, suggests that, though it was professionally edited, *Enemy Coast Ahead* is essentially as Gibson wrote (or probably dictated) it.

After a course at the RAF Staff College Gibson was posted in quick succession as a staff officer at two Lincolnshire bomber bases, no. 55 base, East Kirkby, and then, from 2 August 1944, no. 54 base, Coningsby. There he flew, semi-unofficially, three operations before wringing out of Air Marshal Harris permission to fly again, though only to a carefully selected soft target. That, on the night of 19/20 September, was the twin towns of Rheydt and Mönchengladbach, a few miles inside Germany's border with the Netherlands. Gibson appointed himself controller and directed the attack. He and his navigator, replacing one who reported sick at the last minute, had never flown together, and neither had flown a De Havilland Mosquito, a fast twin-engined type very unlike any that Gibson had previously flown operationally. The attack went well, with little opposition, and Gibson turned for home, flying at low level (against advice given at briefing) across the Netherlands. At 22.30 the Mosquito crashed on farmland near Steenbergen and exploded. The meagre remains of the two crew were buried the following day in the cemetery at Steenbergen.

Why Gibson's aircraft crashed cannot be ascertained. Morris concludes that 'five or six theories answer some of the facts' (Morris, 307) but inclines to the view that the Mosquito, perhaps damaged by enemy fire, suffered fuel starvation, which the crew, unused to the procedure for switching tanks, was unable to correct in time. This would account for eyewitness statements that the engines cut out. Whatever the explanation there can be no doubt that the inexperience of the crew and the fact that they had never flown together before contributed to their destruction. As Morris puts it: 'Nothing that happened … that evening could have been assisted by Gibson's overconfidence, inexperience, or neglect of the training that had been urged upon him' (ibid.).

The circumstances of Gibson's death in some respects typify the man. Scarred by his childhood, with a cold and remote father and a self-absorbed and alcoholic mother, he was emotionally insecure and seems to have felt a compulsion to assert or prove himself. When he had a role to play—as a commanding officer or, indeed, as a war hero on tour—he could be attractively modest but when he felt sidelined, as in desk jobs, he tended to act in ways that were ill judged and earned him a reputation as cocksure. Of aircrew he was warmly supportive, unless they failed his own high standards. With ground crew he never established as good a relationship, as the nickname Bumptious Bastard, which his 83 squadron ground crew gave him, indicates (Morris, 30). Gibson's attitude towards them was no doubt conditioned by his childhood in India, surrounded by servants, as were his political opinions, firmly rooted in ideas of class and empire.

Immediately following Neville Chamberlain's announcement that Britain was at war with Germany, Gibson's commanding officer remarked, 'Now's your chance to be a hero, Gibbo' (Morris, 37). This observation says much about how Gibson was then regarded. But it also proved accurate. The war did give Guy Gibson the chance to prove himself and to win fame. He did both, and though the dams raid seems, in retrospect, a greater success in propaganda terms than any other, through *Enemy Coast Ahead*—which, for all its inaccuracies, remains vivid and readable—and (in a memorable portrayal by Richard Todd that has largely replaced the actuality of Gibson himself) through the highly successful 1955 film *The Dam Busters*, he achieved near-legendary status.

DAVID GUNBY

Sources G. Gibson, *Enemy coast ahead* (1946) · R. Morris, *Guy Gibson* (1994) · S. Ottaway, *Dambuster: a life of Guy Gibson VC* (1994) · J. Sweetman, *Operation chastise: the dams raid* (1982); 2nd edn as *The dambusters raid* (1990) · *CGPLA Eng. & Wales* (1945)
Archives IWM, letters relating to his nomination as prospective conservative candidate for Macclesfield · Royal Air Force Museum, Hendon, papers, D 676/74/1324 | PRO, AIR 4/37 | FILM BFI NFTVA, 'US honours AVC', British News, 3 Jan 1944 [receiving the American Legion of Merit] · BFI NFTVA, documentary footage · BFI NFTVA, news footage · IWM FVA, 'Heroes all', British Movietone News, 28 June 1945, NMV 734-1 [decorated at Buckingham Palace] · IWM FVA, actuality footage · IWM FVA, documentary footage · IWM FVA, news footage | SOUND BBC WAC, *Desert island discs*, 19 Feb 1944 · BBC WAC, *The week's good cause*, 9 April 1944 · IWM SA, oral history interview
Likenesses photograph, 1943, Hult. Arch. · G. Anthony, photograph, 1944, IWM [*see illus.*] · C. Orde, oils, RAF Scampton, Lincolnshire, officers' mess · portrait, repro. in W. Rothenstein, *Men of the R.A.F.* (1942)
Wealth at death £2925 7*s.* 2*d.*: administration, 7 July 1945, *CGPLA Eng. & Wales*

Gibson, James (1799–1871), Free Church of Scotland minister and theologian, was born on 31 January 1799 at Crieff, Perthshire, the fourth son of Robert Gibson, public carrier, of Crieff, and Isabella Kemp. He was educated in Crieff, and entered the University of Glasgow aged twelve. He received his MA in 1817 and in 1820 was licensed to preach by the Church of Scotland's Hamilton presbytery. While at university he had worked as a private tutor in Lanarkshire, and after 1820 he tutored in Jedburgh, Roxburghshire, for over three years. In 1825 he became the travelling companion to a cousin of the earl of Minto, and they spent a considerable time living in Lisbon. On his return to Scotland, he was appointed assistant to the Revd Steel of the West Church, Greenock, but left two years later to resume his European travels, as a tutor to a young gentleman. His bitter opposition to Roman Catholicism was partly a result of these European journeys.

When Gibson returned from the continent, he was appointed assistant to Dr Lockhart in the College parish of Glasgow, being ordained in 1835. He was distinguished for accurate scholarship, a well-cultivated mind, and sincere piety, but by his own admission was not considered to be an attractive or effective preacher. He was, however, an effective controversialist and edited the *Church of Scotland Magazine* from 1834 to 1837. During the bitter disputes in the Church of Scotland over the principle of a national religious establishment, Gibson argued very effectively on behalf of the establishment position. As a result of this, some influential allies made it possible for him to receive a new church in Kingston, a destitute part of Glasgow, into which he was inducted in 1839. On 25 June that year he married Elizabeth Campbell, daughter of the Revd John Campbell of Edinburgh, and the couple had three children, John, Jane, and James.

Only four years later, however, came the Disruption of the Church of Scotland and Gibson, a staunch evangelical, was one of the hundreds of ministers who left the church. Within a week he was interdicted from entering his own church, but a new Free church was rapidly erected close by. He was the Free Church minister of Kingston from 1843 to 1856 and, having been elected unanimously to the position, he served as clerk to the Free Church Presbytery of Glasgow for several years. Following a long controversy over whether the Free Church should expand its number of theological colleges, in 1855 the Free Church general assembly agreed to proceed with the erection of a college in Glasgow. It was largely funded by a grant of £30,000 from William Clark of Wester Moffat, a friend of Gibson. In 1856 Gibson was elected professor of systematic theology and church history at the college.

Gibson was conspicuous as a debater in the courts of the Free Church, and strenuously opposed anything like innovation. He was a non-intrusionist, and an early opponent of union with the United Presbyterian church. But although a vigorous conservative he was a warm man, and it was said that he was 'the sturdy fighter, beneath whose somewhat rugged exterior there beat a generous heart' (Stewart and Cameron, 31). Besides contributing to volumes of lectures against infidelity, Roman Catholicism, and voluntaryism, he edited the *Scottish Protestant* (vols. 1 and 2, 1851–2), and wrote many treatises on various issues of ecclesiastical controversy. Gibson died, after three weeks' illness, of apoplexy, at 2 Greenvale Place, Cumberland Street West, Glasgow, on 2 November 1871.

JAMES LACHLAN MACLEOD

Sources *Fasti Scot.* · J. A. Wylie, *Disruption worthies: a memorial of 1843*, ed. J. B. Gillies, new edn (1881) · J. Forbes, *Free Church of Scotland Monthly Record* (Jan 1872) · A. Stewart and J. Cameron, *The Free Church of Scotland: a vindication* (1910) · A. L. Drummond and J. Bulloch, *The church in Victorian Scotland, 1843–1874* (1975) · W. Ewing, ed., *Annals of the Free Church of Scotland, 1843–1900*, 2 vols. (1914) · K. R. Ross, 'Gibson, James', *DSCHT* · *Free Church Monthly* (Jan 1872) · d. cert.
Likenesses etching, repro. in Gillies, ed., *Disruption worthies*, following p. 260
Wealth at death £951 16*s.* 0*d.*: inventory, 2 Feb 1872, NA Scot., SC 36/48/67/589

Gibson, Sir James Brown (1805–1868), military physician, studied medicine and graduated MD in 1826 at Edinburgh. He became MRCS, London, in the same year. He entered the military service in 1826 as a hospital assistant, and was promoted assistant surgeon in 1829 and surgeon in 1841. He served for nine years in the West Indies and three in Malta. He served in the Crimean War, where he was appointed body surgeon to the duke of Cambridge. He was present at the battles of Alma, Balaklava, and Inkerman, and was at the siege of Sevastopol. For his services he was awarded the campaign medal and the Turkish medal.

In 1860 Gibson was made director-general of the army medical department. His administration was generally considered to be disastrous. He was in office at a time of strong reaction against the privileges that had been granted to the medical service. He allowed many of these to be nullified and consequently 'had the pain of seeing his department fall into such disesteem in the profession that it was becoming necessary to resort to various shifts to recruit' staff (*BMJ*). Florence Nightingale summed up his effect on the service with the comment, 'Gibson was born to be our ruin' (Cantlie, 2.269). He was, even so, made KCB in 1865. Gibson retired in 1867, and died at Rome, where he had gone for his health, on 25 February 1868.

PATRICK WALLIS

Sources *Nomina eorum, qui gradum medicinae doctoris in academia Jacobi sexti Scotorum regis, quae Edinburgi est, adepti sunt, ab anno 1705 ad annum 1845*, University of Edinburgh (1846) • *BMJ* (7 March 1868), 331–2 • *The Lancet* (7 March 1868), 235 • N. Cantlie, *A history of the army medical department*, 2 vols. (1974) • *DNB* • *CGPLA Eng. & Wales* (1868)

Wealth at death under £16,000: probate, 16 May 1868, *CGPLA Eng. & Wales*

Gibson, James Young (1826–1886), translator, was born in Edinburgh on 19 February 1826, the fourth of the six sons of William Gibson (*d.* 1859?), a corn merchant, and his wife, Catherine Walker (*d.* 1836). He was educated at various schools in Edinburgh, Bathgate, and Chipping Ongar, and entered Edinburgh University in 1842 but did not take a degree. He was a student at the divinity hall of the United Presbyterian church, Edinburgh, between 1847 and 1852, and during one long recess in 1850–51 he attended the University of Halle in Germany, where he studied German and Hebrew. On 1 February 1853 the Edinburgh presbytery licensed Young as a preacher of the gospel. He was a private tutor for a year in the family of Henry Birkbeck at Keswick Hall, Norfolk, preached in a number of different places, and was ordained on 30 July 1856 after accepting a post as a Presbyterian minister in Melrose, Roxburghshire. After only three years, however, he resigned from the ministry, depressed and ill because of the strain of his duties, the dampness of the old church building, and the death of his father. From then on, in the words of his sister-in-law, 'he devoted himself to study, to foreign travel, and to the regaining of his lost health' (Smith, xxxiv). Gibson, who suffered nervous strain, was a tall, stalwart, broad-shouldered man with handsome features, keen blue eyes, and thick curly hair. Somewhat reserved in manner, he was nevertheless known for his gentleness and kindness.

Gibson spent the first half of 1863 in Italy, went with two friends on an adventurous journey in 1865 to the Middle East, and was present at the opening of the Suez Canal in 1870. Travelling through Spain in 1871 with his friend Alexander James Duffield, the translator and mining engineer, he was so smitten by its scenery, architecture, language, and literature that he stayed there for a time after Duffield returned to England, and made a first attempt to translate part of *Don Quixote*. One book that greatly influenced him was George Dennis's *The Cid* (1845, revised 1878). Illness, possibly rheumatic fever, accompanied by mental depression, struck him again at the end of 1878, when he was staying at the Westminster Palace Hotel in London. But he was encouraged three years later by the favourable reception of his translations of the poetical pieces in *Don Quixote* included in Duffield's translation (1881), which Gibson had proof-read. In 1883 he published a translation of Cervantes' *Journey to Parnassus*.

On 8 September 1883, after a three-year engagement, Gibson married Margaret Dunlop, *née* Smith [*see* Gibson, Margaret Dunlop], at a civil ceremony in the Hotel de Bellevue, Wildbad, Germany, followed by a religious ceremony in Stuttgart. In spring 1884 they settled near Surbiton, where Gibson completed his translation of Cervantes' tragedy *Numantia* (1885), 'a fascinating version which combines some of Cervantes' original simplicity with the more lurid expression of the penny dreadful' (Johnston, 417). Gibson died suddenly of pleurisy and possibly angina pectoris on 2 October 1886 at the Granville Hotel, Ramsgate, and was buried in the Dean cemetery, Edinburgh. An important posthumous publication was *The Cid Ballads and Other Poems and Translations from Spanish and German* (1887), which contains a memoir by his sister-in-law Agnes Smith.

DONALD HAWES

Sources A. Smith, 'Memoir', in J. Y. Gibson, *The Cid ballads and other poems and translations*, ed. M. D. Gibson, 2 vols. (1887), vol. 1, pp. xxiii–lv • *DNB* • *The Times* (15 Oct 1886) • *The Athenaeum* (16 Oct 1886) • Boase, *Mod. Eng. biog.* • H. A. Salmoné, 'In memoriam: James Y. Gibson', *Academy* (16 Oct 1886), 259 • D. Johnston, 'Spanish golden age drama', *Oxford companion to literature in translation*, ed. P. France (2000) • R. S. Rudder, *The literature of Spain in English translation: a bibliography* (1975) • R. U. Paine, *English translations from the Spanish* (New Brunswick, 1944) • d. cert.

Wealth at death £14,910 16*s.* 9*d.*: probate, 4 Jan 1887, *CGPLA Eng. & Wales*

Gibson, Sir John (1637–1717), army officer, was born in Alderston, Ratho, the son of Sir John Gibson of Pentland and Addisston, in Ratho parish, near Edinburgh, and younger brother of Sir Alexander *Gibson (*b.* before 1637, *d.* 1693), a principal clerk of session. A client of James Scott, duke of Monmouth, Gibson probably served in France between 1672 and 1674 with Monmouth's royal English regiment. From 1675 to 1687 he held a captaincy in the Anglo-Dutch brigade, despite attempts by James II in 1685 to have him dismissed on account of his whiggish politics (his father had been fined £50 Scots in 1676 for allowing field conventicles on his land). Promoted major, he accompanied the expedition of William of Orange to England in 1688 and was advanced to the lieutenant-colonelcy of Sir Robert Peyton's foot in 1689 and the colonelcy of a newly raised regiment of foot in 1694. From 1689 until his death he was also lieutenant-governor of Portsmouth. Gibson sailed, in April 1697, as commander of the land forces in John Norris's expedition to recapture Newfoundland which resecured St John's as a base for English fishermen. Gibson's regiment was disbanded in 1698 but re-formed in February 1702. Having retired from active service in 1704, he sold his regiment and settled in Portsmouth to administer his lieutenant-governorship, a duty dispatched with efficiency and effectiveness: he was knighted by Queen Anne on 6 September 1705. Heavy government patronage returned Gibson as MP for Portsmouth in 1696 and 1702. He left two sons at his death in

1717, Francis and James, and two daughters: Anne Mary, the eldest, married General Robert Dalzell (1662–1758). His brother, Thomas Gibson of Keirhill, was created baronet on 31 December 1702.

F. N. REID, *rev.* JOHN CHILDS

Sources C. Dalton, ed., *English army lists and commission registers, 1661–1714*, 6 vols. (1892–1904) • N. Luttrell, *A brief historical relation of state affairs from September 1678 to April 1714*, 6 vols. (1857) • J. Ferguson, ed., *Papers illustrating the history of the Scots brigade in the service of the United Netherlands, 1572–1782*, 1, Scottish History Society, 32 (1899), 157 • Journal of Captain Michael Richards, BL, Stowe MS 463 • *CSP col.*, 15, no. 1115 • J. C. R. Childs, *Nobles, gentlemen and the profession of arms in Restoration Britain, 1660–1688: a biographical dictionary of British army officers on foreign service* (1987), 36 • [J. Lauder of Fountainhall], *Historical notices of Scottish affairs* (1928), 124, 168 • GEC, *Baronetage*, 4.404–5
Archives Yale U., Beinecke L., letters to William Blathwayt

Gibson, John (*d.* 1787), historian, was a merchant in Glasgow. In 1777 he published *The history of Glasgow from the earliest accounts to the present time; with an account of the rise, progress, and present state of the different branches of commerce and manufactures now carried on in the city of Glasgow*. His was not the first history of Glasgow but it appeared at a time when Glasgow had evolved from a sleepy university city and was developing into the commercial and industrial heart of Scotland. While the city had been affected by the collapse of the tobacco trade, following the outbreak of the American war two years earlier, trade was recovering quickly. Thus while it is a creditable piece of historical scholarship much of its interest lies not in its description of the past but in its depiction of the contemporary scene—including such details as the cost of education and living—and in Gibson's passionate advocacy of herrings as a foodstuff. One third of the book was taken up by an appendix containing the text of charters and other documents, together with translations where necessary—for, as Gibson put it, 'I do not expect that this work will be read by the learned' (Gibson, *History of Glasgow*, vii). The volume was dedicated to Lord Frederick Campbell, member of parliament for the Glasgow burghs.

In 1778 Gibson started, apparently in addition to his other activities, to practise as an accountant, and established a partnership with Richard Smellie in 1784. On 10 March 1782 he married Janet Andrew, with whom he had a daughter, Jean (1785–1887), who was of note by virtue of her longevity. Gibson died in Glasgow on 17 August 1787 and was buried in the Ramshorn churchyard.

LIONEL ALEXANDER RITCHIE

Sources G. Macgregor, *The history of Glasgow* (1881), 360–63 • *A history of the chartered accountants of Scotland from earliest times to 1954* (1954), 11–13 • J. O. Mitchell, *Old Glasgow essays* (1905), 322–3 • *Scots Magazine*, 49 (1787), 415 • J. S. Fairie, *Transcriptions of monumental inscriptions in the Ramshorn burying grounds* (1983), 33

Gibson, John (1790–1866), sculptor, was born on 28 January 1790 at Gyffin, near Conwy, Caernarvonshire, and baptized in the same parish on 19 June, the eldest of the three sons of William Gibson (*d.* 1835), a gardener (himself the son of John Gibson, parish clerk of Llanidan in Anglesey), and his wife, Jane Roberts (*d.* 1835), of Fachleidiog. His brothers were Solomon *Gibson, sculptor and scholar,

John Gibson (1790–1866), by Sir Edwin Landseer, *c.*1850

and Benjamin Gibson (1811–1851), who became a sculptor and antiquary.

Early years in Liverpool When John Gibson was a child the family went to Liverpool; they had intended to emigrate to America, but, as Gibson recalled: 'When my mother saw the great ships in the docks, she formed the most determined resolution never to put her foot in any one of those', and they settled in Liverpool (Matthews, 5). As a schoolboy Gibson drew from memory the engravings displayed in shop windows, and later he was lent drawings and plaster casts to copy by John Turmeau (1777–1846), a miniature painter and printseller in Church Street. Although he had hoped to become apprenticed to a portrait painter, his father was unable to afford the premium required, and instead he was articled at the age of fourteen to the cabinet-makers Southwell and Wilson. After a year with the firm he was working as a woodcarver, ornamenting furniture.

When he was about sixteen Gibson visited the workshops of the marble masons Samuel and Thomas Franceys, at Brownlow Hill. The firm's principal carver at that time was the Prussian émigré sculptor F. A. Lege (1779–1837), who allowed Gibson to copy one of his works in clay. Afterwards he made his first piece in marble, a head of *Mercury*. The admiring comments that these works received from Samuel Franceys encouraged Gibson in his desire to be a marble carver, and he persuaded Franceys to buy him out of his apprenticeship. In the following years he worked for the firm as chief carver, designing ornamental objects such as vases, plaques, and chimney-pieces, as well as church monuments (drawings for some of which are in the V&A). One of his earliest monuments, which is signed with the name of Franceys, is the memorial to the art collector Henry Blundell (1813) in St Helen's Church, Sefton. In 1810, when the annual exhibitions of the Liverpool Academy were inaugurated, he began showing his drawings and terracotta models there.

At Franceys, Gibson met the man who was to be his Maecenas—the Liverpool banker, politician, historian, and art collector William Roscoe. Roscoe commissioned from the sculptor a bas-relief, *Alexander the Great Ordering the Works of Homer to be Placed in the Sarcophagus of Achilles* (terracotta, 1810; Hornby Library, Liverpool) for his library at Allerton Hall. Soon afterwards Gibson became a regular visitor to Allerton, where he copied old master drawings and engravings in the Roscoe collection. His most ambitious work of this period was a large pen-and-wash drawing, *The Fall of the Rebel Angels* (1808–11; Walker Art Gallery, Liverpool), inspired by Michelangelo's *Last Judgement*. However, Roscoe encouraged his protégé to turn his attention from high Renaissance models and to form his style 'upon the Greeks' simple actions and pure forms' (Matthews, 27), and Gibson began a study of casts, gems, and prints from the antique. On Roscoe's advice he also attended the lectures on anatomy given by Dr James Vose of the Liverpool Academy.

Roscoe introduced Gibson to friends of his in Liverpool, Solomon d'Aguilar and his son, General George d'Aguilar, and daughters, Rose Lawrence (*d.* 1857) and Emily Robinson (*d.* 1829). They became his patrons, cultivating his taste and inspiring him with the ambition to be a great sculptor. In 1814 they introduced him to the actor John Kemble, whose portrait bust (bronze, 1814; NPG) he made in Liverpool; two years later he sent his first contributions to the Royal Academy exhibition. Their primary aim, however, was to send their protégé to study in Rome—Gibson's own aspirations were prefigured in a dream in which he was carried there by an eagle—and, while it had been Roscoe's intention to fund this trip himself, the failure of his bank frustrated this plan. Instead a subscription was launched in Liverpool by Roscoe and Mrs Lawrence which eventually raised the £150 needed to maintain Gibson in Italy for two years.

In early 1817 Gibson travelled to London, taking with him introductions to the auctioneer James Christie the younger and the politician Henry Brougham (later first Baron Brougham and Vaux). Christie introduced him to the collector George Watson Taylor, of Erlestoke Park, who commissioned a portrait bust of William Roscoe (marble, 1819; Yale Center for British Art, Connecticut; copy, marble, *c.*1819; University of Liverpool Art Gallery) and busts of his family (including John Walter Watson Taylor, marble, 1816; V&A). Gibson also met the sculptor John Flaxman, who admired his drawings and encouraged him in his plans to go to Rome, the artists Henry Fuseli, Benjamin West, and William Blake, and the sculptor Joseph Nollekens. Though he received offers of further work to induce him to establish a career in London, Gibson was anxious to set off for Rome, even 'if I went there on foot', he remarked (Matthews, 41). In September 1817 he left England and, travelling via Paris, he reached Rome on 20 October.

A sculptor in Rome As one of the first of a new generation of British artists to arrive in Rome after the interruptions caused by the Napoleonic wars, Gibson was fortunate to begin his studies there when the celebrated neo-classical sculptor Antonio Canova (1757–1822) was still alive. Canova was known for his generosity to young artists, and Gibson lost no time in presenting to him his letters of introduction from his patrons in England. After examining Gibson's drawings Canova offered his support and gave him a place in his studio. Gibson also attended Canova's life academy before it was disbanded in 1820. His first work in Rome was a copy of a cast of Canova's *Creugas*, one of the Italian sculptor's two statues of Greek boxers in the Vatican Museum.

Early in 1818 Gibson took a studio of his own in via della Fontanella, near the piazza del Popolo. There, under Canova's supervision, he made his first original full-size work in Rome, *The Sleeping Shepherd Boy* (plaster model, 1818; RA). In the following year he began a large group, *Mars and Cupid* (marble, 1825; Chatsworth, Derbyshire) and, while modelling it, received a visit from William Spencer Cavendish, sixth duke of Devonshire. The duke, one of the leading collectors of modern sculpture in Rome, had been sent by Canova, and he ordered the work in marble. Though Gibson claimed to have undercharged for the work—'I did not make even a cup of coffee by it', he remarked (*Art Journal*, 28, 1866, 113)—nevertheless the commission effectively launched his reputation in Rome, and in the following years he enjoyed the patronage of some of the leading collectors of the day. These included Sir George Beaumont, for whom he carved the group *Psyche and the Zephyrs* (marble, 1822–7), and Lord George Cavendish, an uncle of the sixth duke of Devonshire, who commissioned a marble version of *The Sleeping Shepherd Boy* (1824). For Robert Vernon he made the group *Hylas and the Nymphs* (marble, 1826; Tate collection) and for Charles Anderson-Pelham, first earl of Yarborough, *A Nymph Preparing for the Bath* and *Venus and Cupid* (both marble, 1831; Usher Gallery, Lincoln). He also carved works in this period for, among others, John George Lambton, first earl of Durham, Sir John Johnstone, Sir Robert Peel, Count Schonbrun of Bavaria (*Female Dancer in Repose*, marble, *c.*1835), Prince Alessandro Torlonia (*Psyche and the Zephyrs*, marble, version, *c.*1839; Palazzo Corsini, Rome), and Grand Duke Alexander Nikolaevich of Russia, afterwards Tsar Alexander II (*Psyche and the Zephyrs*, marble, version, 1842–4; *Cupid Disguised as a Shepherd Boy*, marble, version, 1842–4; both Hermitage Museum, St Petersburg).

Gibson was deeply affected by the death in 1822 of his 'noble master' Canova, although he was fortunate afterwards to have 'recourse to Thorwaldsen for instruction', as he put it (Matthews, 111). The Danish sculptor Bertel Thorvaldsen (1770–1844), a generation younger than Canova and the other pre-eminent neo-classical sculptor, was to exert a strong influence on artists working in Rome in the early nineteenth century. Gibson's conception of his art followed closely that of his two masters: the representation of nature perfected according to the forms and recognized principles of antique sculpture (the notion of the 'ideal'). Although he never fully emerged from the shadow of his predecessors, his mature work is closer to the calmer, more austere classicism of Thorvaldsen than to Canova's more vigorous mode. Gibson's espousal of genre and of a low-key, sometimes sentimental, type of subject is also comparable to the work of Thorvaldsen and that of other neo-classical sculptors active in Rome in the mid-nineteenth century, such as Pietro Tenerani (1789–1869) and R. J. Wyatt.

In 1829 Gibson was elected an academician of merit of the Academy of St Luke, Rome, and in 1831 he became resident academician of merit. He was made an associate of the Royal Academy in 1833 and a Royal Academician in 1836. Professional recognition, gained within a relatively short time after his first arrival in Rome, was matched by a high demand for his work, and Gibson's studio account books (1822–65, RA archives) are a record of a prolific and wide-ranging practice. Throughout his career he received commissions not only for the marble 'ideal' statues on which his reputation was based, but also for bas-reliefs, 'fancy' busts derived from his own statues, portrait statues, and busts, as well as for numerous replicas of his most popular works. His designs were also reproduced in jewellery and cameos by Tommaso and Luigi Saulini and the Roman firm of Castellani, and his figure of *Narcissus* (marble, version, 1838; RA collection) was one of the earliest works of sculpture to be reproduced in the new ceramic medium of parian ware. With his increasing success, Gibson gradually enlarged his workshops, which by the mid-1840s occupied 4, 5, and 6 via della Fontanella. When the writer Anna Jameson visited Rome in the late 1840s, she found the sculptor in the same 'modest quiet little room' in which she had first seen him twenty-six years earlier, but 'around it extended lofty and ample ateliers crowded with models of works, already executed or in progress; and with workmen, assistants, students, visitors' (Jameson, 140). His studio assistants included Felice Baini, his chief carver, and many other named and unnamed workmen who appear in the account books in connection with a diversity of studio tasks, from pointing and carving to ornament cutting and marble polishing. In 1837 Benjamin Gibson joined his brother in Rome and worked in the studio, carving copies of John Gibson's works as well as some original designs; an authority on classical literature and antiquities, he also acted as his brother's 'classical dictionary' (Eastlake, 194). The Liverpool sculptor B. E. Spence was another who worked in Gibson's studio for a short time in the mid-1840s.

As the leading figure of the British art colony in Rome—he was described by a writer in the 1860s as the 'Nestor of British sculpture' (*Blackwood's Magazine*, 1861, 381)—Gibson was well known to a wide circle of artists, patrons, and visitors. In 1821–3 he had been a founder member, with the painters Charles Eastlake and Joseph Severn and the sculptors Richard Westmacott and Lawrence Macdonald, of the informal British Academy of Arts in Rome, and in 1829 he was one of the international group who set up the Società degli Amatori e Cultori delle Belle Arti, whose inaugural exhibition was held in 1830 on the Campidoglio. Among Gibson's expatriate contemporaries, his chief friendships were with the Welsh painter Penry Williams, who sometimes accompanied him on his travels, and the sculptors Macdonald, Spence, and Wyatt. Until his death in 1850, Wyatt was his friendly rival; the two would meet most mornings for breakfast at the Caffé Greco before taking a stroll on the Pincio. Like Canova, Gibson did not as a rule take on pupils, though he evidently gave help and advice to many of the young British sculptors who went to Rome to study. William Calder Marshall, for example, in Rome in the mid-1830s, referred to Gibson's kindness in helping him to measure and model his works (Marshall papers, RA archives). Gibson also assisted the studies of William Theed, the Irish sculptor John Hogan, George Gamon Adams, John Adams-Acton, Frederick Thrupp, Alfred Gatley, and others. The American sculptor Harriet Hosmer (1830–1908), who lived in Rome from 1852 and became a close friend, was, unusually, accorded the status of a 'pupil' (Matthews, 224). On several occasions Gibson helped to obtain commissions for British sculptors in Rome; for example, he recommended the work of Wyatt, Theed, Henry Timbrell, and Mary Thornycroft to the prince consort in the 1840s.

Though Gibson was often urged by his friends to return to London—where it was thought that he could succeed Sir Francis Chantrey as the leading national sculptor, and 'become a rich man' (Matthews, 65)—he steadfastly refused to do so. He considered Rome his 'battlefield' (ibid.) and once remarked, 'I thank God for every morning that opens my eyes in Rome' (Gunnis, 171). In England he thought his life 'would be spent in making busts and statues of great men in anti-sculptural dress' (Matthews, 65), whereas in Rome he had the opportunity to produce the more elevated ideal works for which commissions were readily given. Not least among Rome's attractions were the museums of antique sculpture, an international community of artists, skilled studio assistants, fine models, and a better climate. During the course of his career Gibson came to feel increasingly at odds with his artistic contemporaries in Britain, a disaffection frequently expressed in his memoirs and in his letters to friends. He deplored the widespread use of modern dress in public statuary—'the human figure concealed under a frock-coat and trousers is not a fit subject for sculpture', he remarked (ibid., 100)—and he disliked 'novelties' in sculpture, including the adoption of subjects 'drawn from modern poetry and novels' (ibid., 203). He speaks vehemently against the system of commissioning public sculpture in England, of the ignorance of those involved in judging competitions, and of the misleading opinions of the press, or 'scribblers on art' (ibid., 144). The absence of a national academy in Rome, funded by the British government, was one of his persistent complaints, and he corresponded on the subject in the 1840s and 1850s with the prime minister, Sir Robert Peel, and the politician Philip Henry, fifth earl of Stanhope. From the other point of view, Gibson's long-term residence abroad and his preoccupation with the classical world were sometimes regarded with bemusement. For example, Henry Weekes, professor of sculpture at the Royal Academy in the 1860s and 1870s, saw him inhabiting 'the centre of a system in that heaven of Art, far removed from, and having very little communication with ours' (Weekes, 315). To the sculptor Richard Westmacott, Gibson was an artist who 'confined himself to repeating the traditions of a bygone age ... rarely exercising his art upon subjects that could engage modern sympathies' (*The Builder*, 24 Feb 1866, 132).

In 1844 Gibson visited England for the first time after an absence of twenty-seven years. The purpose was to attend the placing of his second marble statue of the statesman William Huskisson (1836; Pimlico Gardens, London), which his widow, Emily Huskisson, had commissioned for the custom house in Liverpool; the first marble statue (1833) had been installed in the Huskisson mausoleum in St James's cemetery, Liverpool. However, Gibson disapproved of the location intended for the new statue, on account of its inadequate lighting and cramped situation, which led Mrs Huskisson to commission a third figure in bronze to be placed outside the custom house (now in the oratory, St James's Mount Gardens, Liverpool). Cast by the sculptor Ferdinand Muller at the royal foundry in Munich in 1846, it was unveiled on 15 October 1847, during Gibson's second visit to England, in the presence of Sir Robert Peel. During his visit in 1844 Gibson also received a royal commission to make a statue of Queen Victoria (1844–7; Royal Collection), an order that marked the beginning of a long friendship between the sculptor and the royal couple. The prince consort—who acquired several works by modern sculptors in Rome—communicated the queen's wish to have a portrait 'like a Greek statue' (Eastlake, 124). Gibson travelled to Windsor in November 1844 to model the bust, and he completed the statue in Rome. Exhibited at the Royal Academy in 1847, it was notable for being one of the sculptor's first essays in polychromy: he introduced red and blue colouring into the decorative border of the robe and tinted the diadem and sandals in yellow (see Darby, 38–9). The queen subsequently ordered a replica (unpainted; 1849) for Osborne House.

Gibson was in Rome in 1848 when the short-lived Roman republic was established. Though the habits of his daily life continued uninterrupted, he described vividly in his memoirs the events of that tumultuous period—the flight of Pope Pius IX, the entrance into the city of Garibaldi and his followers, the frequent political assassinations and stabbings in the streets. In April 1849, when the French army was preparing to bombard the city, Gibson and his brother Benjamin fled to Florence and remained for several months at Bagni di Lucca. It was there that Benjamin died, on a later visit, on 13 August 1851.

During the 1850s and 1860s Gibson resumed his visits abroad. Following a long-established custom he spent his summers in the Austrian Tyrol at Innsbruck, or in Switzerland, often travelling with his friends Penry Williams or Harriet Hosmer. He also returned to England on several occasions, for, having renewed links with friends in Liverpool, and encouraged by the support of certain loyal patrons—notably the royal family—he seems to have relished his new-found status as a visiting celebrity. In 1850 Prince Albert, as chairman of the commissioners on the fine arts, invited him to prepare a design for a new statue of Queen Victoria for the Palace of Westminster. Gibson worked on his sketch model during the summer and travelled to Osborne to take sittings for a new portrait bust. The statue, with the supporting figures symbolizing Justice and Clemency, was completed in Rome and installed in the prince's chamber in the House of Lords in 1856. In 1850 Gibson also received a government commission from the prime minister, Lord John Russell, to execute a statue of Sir Robert Peel (marble, 1852) for Westminster Abbey. In the following year he exhibited at the Royal Academy a statue of the engineer George Stephenson (marble, *c*.1851), prior to its installation in St George's Hall, Liverpool. However, Gibson was not always so successful in obtaining major public commissions in England, especially when he was required to compete with other sculptors. His austere neo-classical design for the monument to the duke of Wellington for St Paul's Cathedral, the model for which he submitted to the open competition held in 1857, failed to make the shortlist of prizewinning designs; the commission was eventually awarded to Alfred Stevens.

Throughout his life Gibson enjoyed great success with the neo-classical 'ideal' works on which his reputation was founded. However, the patrons of his early years, dominated by a group of leading English aristocratic collectors and connoisseurs, gave way in his later career to a broader base of collectors, many of them from the newly rich mercantile classes. The tendency for Victorian collectors to develop allegiances to artists with local connections was also reflected in Gibson's patronage, and many of his later commissions came from Liverpool buyers. The Liverpool West India merchant Henry Robertson Sandbach and his wife, Margaret (the granddaughter of William Roscoe and the sculptor's intimate friend and correspondent), purchased several of Gibson's marble and plaster works for their home at Hafodunnos Hall, north Wales (examples now in the Walker Art Gallery, Liverpool, and the NMG Wales). Other Liverpool buyers included the ironmaster and philanthropist Richard Vaughan Yates, the bankers Richard Naylor and John Naylor, and the manufacturers Richard Alison and Robert Preston. For Preston, Gibson executed the work for which he is best known, the coloured statue known as *The Tinted Venus* (1851–6; Walker Art Gallery, Liverpool). Preston visited the sculptor's studio in Rome around 1851 and commissioned a replica of a *Venus verticordia* (marble, 1833; FM Cam.) that Gibson had carved for the collector Joseph Neeld. He worked on the new statue for five years and then kept it in his studio for another four years, proudly showing it to the many visitors who came to see it. The statue finally left Rome and went on display at the London International Exhibition in 1862 in a polychrome temple designed by the architect Owen Jones, together with two other coloured statues by the sculptor, *Pandora* (marble, 1856–61; Lady Lever Art Gallery, Port Sunlight) and *Cupid Tormenting the Soul* (marble, *c*.1855–60; Cheltenham Art Gallery and Museum). The *Venus*, with its waxed and flesh-coloured body, blue eyes, gilt hair, coloured drapery borders, and real gilt-metal earrings, attracted huge publicity and mixed reactions from the English press and public. Some saw it as a striking departure for modern sculpture; others considered it unconvincing or vulgar. To Gibson, the statue represented a culmination of his researches into ancient Greek polychromy—a subject that had also occupied Canova—as well as an attempt to revitalize neo-classical sculpture, and, in particular, to draw attention to his own work at a time of waning interest. As Gibson is said to have remarked to the writer Charles Weld: 'Why do you find people looking more at pictures than at statues? Simply because the former are coloured and the latter are not' (Weld, 388). He made other coloured statues, including several replicas of the *Venus*, a *Hebe* (marble, 1862, for John Howard Galton of Hadzor, Worcestershire; marble repetition, tinted, *c*.1864, RA), and a *Nymph and Cupid* (marble, 1865) for Edward, prince of Wales.

Last years The prince of Wales's patronage marked the final chapter of Gibson's close association with the royal family, during the last few years of the sculptor's life. When the prince visited Rome in early 1859 Gibson took him to 'forty studios' (Matthews, 224). In November 1862 the royal party returned to Rome, and in the following summer Gibson travelled to England to model a bust of Alexandra, princess of Wales (two versions, marble, 1863; Royal Collection). He also journeyed to Osborne at the invitation of the queen, who consulted him over the design of the national memorial to her husband. However, Gibson declined to contribute to this project, as it would have meant remaining in England during the winter to undertake the work; his offer to make in Rome the model of *Europe*, one of the four allegorical corner groups, came too late.

This was Gibson's last visit to England. In the summer of 1864 he set out with Penry Williams for Switzerland, but the sculptor's fatigue caused their journey to be cut short at Leghorn. In the following winter he completed the bas-relief *Christ Blessing the Little Children* (marble, 1861–5; Walker Art Gallery, Liverpool), his only religious narrative subject. In spring 1865 Gibson fell ill but recovered sufficiently to work on a group of *Theseus and the Robber* in the autumn. On 9 January 1866 he was struck by paralysis which deprived him of speech, and he died, unmarried, in Rome, at via Babuino 144, nearly three weeks later, on 27 January 1866. He was buried on 29 January with French military honours in the protestant cemetery in Rome. In 1864 he had been made a chevalier of the French Légion d'honneur, and shortly before his death he was conferred with the Prussian order of Full Merit. He was elected a member of 'eleven Academies' (Matthews, 239)—St Luke in Rome, the Royal Academy, and those in Bologna, Urbino, Turin, Ravenna, Munich, Berlin, St Petersburg, Athens (the School of Art), and New York. In 1859 Ludwig I of Bavaria placed his portrait statue (designed by Brugger and executed by Lossow, the bust modelled by William Theed; destroyed) on the exterior of the Glyptothek in Munich, alongside figures of Canova, Thorvaldsen, and Tenerani and the German sculptors Rauch and Schwanthaler. Following the example of Canova and Thorvaldsen, who had left their studios to their own countries, Gibson bequeathed his remaining statues and models, as well as the bulk of his fortune, some £32,000, to the Royal Academy. The money was intended to be used for the 'reception and accommodation' of his works for the benefit of students and the public (*Art Journal*, 28, 1866, 115, citing Gibson's will, codicil dated 26 May 1865).

Gibson sat for many portraits, among the most notable being the paintings by Andrew Geddes (1830; Walker Art Gallery, Liverpool), Edwin Landseer (*c*.1850; RA), and Penry Williams (*c*.1844; Academy of St Luke, Rome), and the busts by William Theed (1852; Conwy parish church, Caernarvonshire; marble versions, *c*.1868, RA, NPG) and John Adams-Acton (1862; Walker Art Gallery, Liverpool). Gibson was of 'prepossessing appearance', with 'a peculiarly grave, immovable expression of countenance', according to a visitor who saw him in 1854 (Gunnis, 172). He features in the novel *The Marble Faun*, Nathaniel Hawthorne's celebrated tale of artistic life in nineteenth-century Rome, where he is described as 'a quiet, simple, elderly personage, with eyes brown and bright, under a slightly impending brow, and a Grecian profile, such as he might have cut with his own chisel.' Independent, unworldly, and famously absent-minded—as Harriet Hosmer once remarked: 'He is a god in his studio, but God help him when he is out of it!' (Eastlake, 231)—he nevertheless seems to have had a good business sense and made a great deal of money from his profession. While he was noted for his kindness, courtesy, and unassuming manner, he could be difficult in his professional dealings—'I am as obstinate as a Welshman, for I am one' (*Art Journal*, 28, 1866, 114), he himself once remarked—and he often put his own ideas before the wishes of his clients. Idealism, pride, and a certain naïvety combined to produce in him a defensive attitude on many subjects, particularly that of his own art, and, as his memoirs show, he could easily be upset by those whose opinions and practices differed from his own. A confirmed bachelor who had many friends, he was flattered by the attentions of people of rank, and seems to have reserved his strongest affections for a number of (usually married or widowed) women who played a central role in his life, and with whom he corresponded over the years. His work is carefully executed and technically refined, notable for its clarity of form and composition, subtle modelling, and delicate sentiment. In these qualities it stands out from that of most contemporary English sculptors, although his rigid views prevented him—his experiments in polychromy notwithstanding—from forwarding the cause of neo-classical sculpture in a way that Canova and Thorvaldsen had been able to do in their time. Gibson was nevertheless widely regarded as those sculptors' natural successor in Rome and enjoyed a formidable reputation in his lifetime. Substantial collections of his sculpture are on display at the Walker Art Gallery, Liverpool, the National Museum and Gallery of Wales, Cardiff, and Bodelwyddan Castle, north Wales (on loan from the National Portrait Gallery and the Royal Academy of Arts).

MARTIN GREENWOOD

Sources Lady Eastlake [E. Eastlake], ed., *Life of John Gibson, R.A., sculptor* (1870) [draws on the sculptor's MS autobiography (or 'memoirs') and on his correspondence with Margaret Sandbach in NL Wales; incl. personal recollection and work list] • T. Matthews, *The biography of John Gibson, R.A., sculptor, Rome* (1911) [draws on Eastlake's *Life*, using additional MS material; incl. work list] • A. Jameson, 'John Gibson', *Art Journal*, 11 (1849), 139–41 • *Art Journal*, 19 (1857), 273–5 • *Art Journal*, 28 (1866), 90–91, 113–15 • R. Gunnis, *Dictionary of British sculptors, 1660–1851* (1953); new edn (1968) • *DNB* • Graves, *RA exhibitors* • J. Turner, ed., *The dictionary of art*, 34 vols. (1996), vol. 12, pp. 597–9 • P. Curtis, ed., *Patronage and practice: sculpture on Merseyside* (1989), 32–59 • B. Read, *Victorian sculpture* (1982) • J. B. Hartmann, 'Canova, Thorvaldsen and Gibson', *English Miscellany*, 6 (1955), 205–35 • E. S. Darby, 'John Gibson, Queen Victoria, and the idea of sculptural polychromy', *Art History*, 4 (1981), 37–53 • H. Fletcher, 'John Gibson: an English pupil of Thorvaldsen', *Apollo*, 96/128 (Oct 1972), 336–40 • H. Le Grice, 'Gibson's studio', *Walks through the studii of the sculptors at Rome*, 2 vols. (1841), vol. 1, pp. 99–119 • *Imitations of drawings by John Gibson, R.A., sculptor, engraved by G. Wenzel and L. Proseda* (1851) • *Engravings from the original compositions of John Gibson, R.A., sculptor, drawn by P. Guglielmo* (1861) • E. Strutt, *The story of Psyche … with designs in outline by John Gibson Esq. R. A.* (1851) • C. R. Weld, *Last winter in Rome* (1865), 386–90 • H. Weekes, 'Chantrey, Behnes and Gibson', *Lectures on art* (1880), 294–317 • private information (2004) [Eric Forster] • *CGPLA Eng. & Wales* (1866)

Archives NL Wales, albums • RA, corresp. and papers | CUL, letters to Joseph Bonomi • Harris Museum and Art Gallery, Preston, J. B. Crouchley corresp. • Herts. ALS, letters to Lord Lyttelton • NL Wales, Mayer papers and corresp. • NL Wales, R. B. Preston papers and corresp. • NL Wales, letters to Henry Sandbach and his wife • V&A NAL, corresp. incl. letters to S. Horner • Walker Art Gallery, Liverpool, E. Lawrence corresp.

Likenesses J. Partridge, pencil drawing, 1825, NPG • A. Geddes, oils, 1830, Walker Art Gallery, Liverpool • C. Vogel, drawing, 1843, Staatliche Kunstsammlungen, Dresden, Küpferstichkabinett • W. Brockedom, chalk drawing, 1844, NPG • P. Williams, oils, *c.*1844, Academy of St Luke, Rome • J. G. Gilbert, oils, 1847, NG Scot. • E. Landseer, oils, *c.*1850, RA [*see illus.*] • W. Theed, marble bust, exh. RA 1852, Conwy parish church; versions, *c.*1868, NPG, RA • R. Lehmann, crayon drawing, 1853, BM • M. Carpenter, oils, 1857, NPG; repro. in R. Ormond, *National Portrait Gallery: early Victorian portraits* (1973), pl. 354 • F. Talfourd, drawing, 1859, BM • G. Scharf, pencil drawing, 1860, NPG • J. Adams-Acton, marble bust, 1862, Walker Art Gallery, Liverpool • Nadar [G. F. Tournachon], photograph, *c.*1862, NPG • W. Boxall, oils, 1864, RA • B. E. Spence, marble medallion, 1866, Gibson's tomb, protestant cemetery, Rome • J. Foubert, carte-de-visite, NPG • H. Hosmer, marble medallion, NPG • carte-de-visite, NPG • pencil drawing, NPG

Wealth at death under £40,000: probate, 3 May 1866, *CGPLA Eng. & Wales* • legacies incl. £32,000 to RA: *Art Journal* (1866), 115

Gibson, John (1793/4–1854), glass-stainer, was a native of Newcastle upon Tyne. He was probably the John Gibson who was baptized on 6 April 1794 at All Saints, Newcastle, the son of John Gibson and his wife, Elizabeth. He practised in Newcastle as an ornamental and house painter, and especially devoted himself to the art of enamelling in glass. Many of the churches at Newcastle and in the neighbourhood possess windows painted by him. Among them may be mentioned a figure *Jesus Christ with the Cup of the Last Supper* in the east window of St John's Church at Newcastle, and a figure *Jesus Christ Bearing the Cross* in the east window of St Nicholas's Church in the same city. Gibson dedicated himself ardently to the study and promotion of the fine arts, and formed an extensive and valuable gallery. His taste and judgement were appreciated in Newcastle. He was elected a town councillor for North St Andrews ward, and in 1854 served the office of sheriff of Newcastle. Shortly after vacating this office he died at his residence in Leazes Terrace, Newcastle upon Tyne, on 25 November 1854, aged sixty.

L. H. CUST, *rev.* HELEN CAROLINE JONES

Sources *GM*, 2nd ser., 43 (1855), 108 • *Newcastle Guardian* (2 Dec 1854) • *Newcastle Journal* (2 Dec 1854) • E. Mackenzie, *A descriptive and historical account of the town and county of Newcastle upon Tyne*, 1 (1827), 345; 2 (1827), 761

Gibson, John (1817–1892), architect, was born on 2 June 1817 at Castle Bromwich, Warwickshire, second son of Richard Gibson, a farmer and horse breeder, and his wife, Sarah Milward. He was educated at the King Edward VI Grammar School in Birmingham, and after a short training in joinery, under a Birmingham builder, entered the office of Joseph Aloysius Hansom, the architect of the Birmingham town hall. In 1835 he became an articled pupil of Sir Charles Barry and he remained with Barry until 1844. During this time he worked, first at Foley Place, London, and subsequently at Westminster, to which the staff were transferred during the designing of the Houses of Parliament, a project on which Gibson was employed. His move to independent practice coincided with the competition for the National Bank of Scotland in Glasgow (1844). Gibson won the competition with an Italianate design which was carried out in all its essential features. Other works rapidly followed, of which the earliest, and not the least important, was the Romanesque Bloomsbury Chapel (1847). Then in 1848 came the offices of the Imperial Insurance Company in Old Broad Street, and in 1849 the church in Charlecote Park, Warwickshire, which was built for Mary Elizabeth Lucy, whose family also entrusted Gibson with the restoration of Charlecote House, Warwickshire (1852–65), and secured for him, by introduction to Lady Willoughby de Broke, his most important ecclesiastical work, the designing of Bodelwyddan church, near St Asaph, Flintshire (1856–60). He also designed Shenstone church, near Lichfield, Hampshire (1862).

After designing the Brunswick Buildings, New Street, Birmingham (1852), Gibson built, in 1853, a house and studio for the painter Frederick Richard Pickersgill at Highgate, Combroke Schools, and in 1857 Myton Grange, the last two both in Warwickshire. The latter was an Elizabethan-style residence—a favourite class of work with Gibson, who specialized in country houses and banks. Alterations at Plas Power, near Wrexham, and Wroxton Abbey, near Banbury, were undertaken by him between 1858 and 1860, as was, later, the building of Woodcote, near Warwick, in 1861.

In 1864 Gibson began his long and successful connection with the National Provincial Bank of England, for which he immediately designed, in a dignified classic style, the head offices in Threadneedle Street (1864–5), described by Pevsner as 'one of the best banking buildings of the date in the City' (*London*, 1, rev. B. Cherry, 3rd edn, 1973, 220), and subsequently a national network of branch offices. The chief London branches designed by him were those in Baker Street and Piccadilly (1873).

Between 1865 and 1870 Gibson undertook various works in west Yorkshire for the Fielden family, or under their nomination, such as Dobroyd Castle (1866–8), and the Unitarian chapel (1865) and the town hall (1870) in Todmorden. In 1866 he designed the Molyneux mausoleum in Kensal Green cemetery; in 1868, the chancel of St Nicholas, Warwick; in 1871, Nutfield Priory, Redhill, and additions to Guy's Cliff, Warwick; in 1873, Bersham church and Imberhome, a house near East Grinstead, Sussex; in 1874, Bix church, near Henley-on-Thames, Oxfordshire; and in 1875 the City Bank, Exeter. In 1876 Gibson was engaged to build the offices of the Society for Promoting Christian Knowledge, in Northumberland Avenue (later Nigeria House), to which a top storey was subsequently added by Alfred Waterhouse. Among the last works he undertook were Child's Bank, Temple Bar (1879); the church and vicarage at Old Milverton, near Leamington Spa, Warwickshire (both 1878); and in 1883 the bank at Lincoln. After about 1883 Gibson appears to have retired from practice, but in 1890 he received, in recognition of his work as an architect, the gold medal of the Royal Institute of British Architects, a body to which he had been elected as an associate in 1849 and a fellow in 1853. He served at various periods on its council, and became a vice-president.

Gibson died, apparently unmarried, of pneumonia on 23 December 1892, at his home, 13 Great Queen Street, Westminster, and was buried in Kensal Green cemetery on 28 December.

PAUL WATERHOUSE, *rev.* JOHN ELLIOTT

Sources *The Builder*, 58 (1890), 448–9 • *The Builder*, 63 (1892), 524–5 • S. F. Clarkson, 'John Gibson, architect', *RIBA Journal*, 16 (1908–9), 13–32 • G. Worsley, 'One family, one architect: John Gibson and the Fieldens of Todmorden', *Country Life*, 179 (1986), 302–5 • *Dir. Brit. archs.* • *IGI* • *CGPLA Eng. & Wales* (1893)
Archives RIBA, biographical file • RIBA, nomination papers • RIBA, photographic collection • Warks. CRO, papers, plans, and elevations of proposed alterations to Woodcote House
Likenesses J. Underwood, bust (executed with H. Bursill), RIBA • photographs, RIBA • portrait, repro. in *Building News* (18 July 1890)
Wealth at death £52,429 9*s.* 2*d.*: resworn probate, Sept 1893, *CGPLA Eng. & Wales*

Gibson, John D. (*d.* **1852**), portrait painter, was born and worked in Glasgow. He exhibited eleven portraits at the Royal Scottish Academy between 1829 and 1842; all but one are unidentified. He also contributed to the exhibitions of the West of Scotland Academy. An oil portrait by him of the miniature painter Kenneth Macleay (1802–1878) is in the Scottish National Portrait Gallery, Edinburgh.

In October 1852 Gibson was actively engaged as a member of the hanging committee for the West of Scotland Academy, Glasgow. He was subsequently present at the private view on 7 October and attended the dinner afterwards. Later that evening he was found lying injured at the bottom of a flight of stairs. He died from his injuries the following night, at an advanced age.

L. H. CUST, *rev.* JILL SPRINGALL

Sources C. B. de Laperriere, ed., *The Royal Scottish Academy exhibitors, 1826–1990*, 4 vols. (1991), vol. 2 • *GM*, 2nd ser., 38 (1852), 551 • P. J. M. McEwan, *Dictionary of Scottish art and architecture* (1994) • B. Stewart and M. Cutten, *The dictionary of portrait painters in Britain up to 1920* (1997) • H. Smailes, *The concise catalogue of the Scottish National Portrait Gallery* (1990) • *Glasgow Chronicle* (13 Oct 1852)
Likenesses painted silhouette, Scot. NPG

Gibson, Sir John Watson (**1885–1947**), contracting engineer, was born on 9 August 1885 at 27 Pembroke Street, Middlesbrough, the second son of Robert Elwin Gibson, clerk and accountant, of Linthorpe, Middlesbrough, and his wife, Ruth Eleanor, *née* Hugill. Educated at Middlesbrough high school, he began his career in civil engineering as a pupil on contracts relating to the Middlesbrough Dock and one of the Huddersfield corporation reservoirs, working under John Scott from 1900 to 1908. Later, for another contractor, he was in charge of the construction of reinforced jetties at Southampton and near Tralee in Ireland.

On 11 November 1911 in the Primitive Methodist chapel, Gibson married Lillian (Lily) Gindle Armstrong (*b.* 1884), daughter of John Armstrong, a blacksmith in Linthorpe; they had two sons and three daughters. Gibson joined Lord Cowdray's organization (S. Pearson & Son Ltd), working on the construction of both the King George Dock, Hull, and the Metropolitan Water Board's Queen Mary Reservoir at Staines in Middlesex. He subsequently took charge of a huge project in the Sudan involving the construction of the Sennar Dam and some hundreds of miles of large irrigation canals from the Blue Nile.

During the First World War Gibson was loaned to the Ministry of Munitions. He worked on the production of small arms and went in 1916 to the United States with a small party of British officials dealing with munitions as director of shell and gun production. In March 1917 he accompanied Sir Frederick William Black, as his technical assistant, on a mission to India to advise the Indian government on its munitions service, following which, in June of that year, he became controller of aircraft requirements and review at the Air Ministry. He was appointed OBE for his wartime services in 1918.

After the war Gibson joined the firm of Lord Weir, under whom he had been working, but soon Lord Cowdray secured his services again, now as agent in charge of the completion of the Sennar Dam and irrigation works project. He was subsequently requested by the Sudanese government to carry out further schemes, this time on his own. Starting with a large excavation contract for the extension of the canalization, he was then joined by his brother Howard, and together, over the next few years, they constructed the Sennar Dam aprons, some considerable canalization extensions in the Gezira, and the salt works at Port Sudan. His next important contract, from 1933 to 1937, was for the construction of the Gebel Aulia Dam on the White Nile, over 3 miles in length, for the Egyptian government. To carry this out, the Gibsons linked up with the old-established firm of Pauling & Co. Ltd to form Gibson and Pauling (Foreign) Ltd, of which John Gibson was chairman. On completion of the project he joined the board of Pauling & Co. Ltd.

During the Second World War Gibson was controller of building construction at the Ministry of Supply from 1940 to 1941, in which capacity he was responsible for the construction of Royal Ordnance factories. He was a technical adviser to the president of the Board of Trade, and was subsequently engaged on the provision and layout of storage sites for colliery-produced coal and on initiating opencast coal workings. It was at this time that the Mulberry artificial harbours were being planned for the invasion of Normandy, and it was Gibson who advised the cabinet that the necessary work could be carried out chiefly in Britain. He undertook, as deputy director-general civil engineering (special) at the Ministry of Supply (1943–4), the direction at headquarters of much of the construction of the great artificial 'Phoenix' breakwater units for the Mulberry harbour used at Arromanches, Normandy. The work was carried out by many of the main British contracting firms, together with help from the United States. In recognition of his leadership and co-ordination in this enterprise Gibson was knighted in 1945.

After the war, in collaboration with the British Iron and Steel Federation, Gibson formed a group of contractors which, as British Steel Houses Ltd, erected over 30,000 houses. He was also chairman of Acton Bolt and Fine Thread Ltd. Away from business his interests included golf, cricket, and farming. His last work, with Pauling & Co., was undertaking the civil engineering works concerned with the ground nuts scheme in east Africa. Almost immediately, however, lung cancer developed and he died in St Mary's Hospital, London, on 19 March 1947. Twelve days earlier there had been a serious fire at his home, Stanwell Place, Stanwell, near Staines, which broke out in the room where he lay ill. He was survived by his wife.

HOWARD GIBSON and LEO D'ERLANGER, *rev.* ROBERT SHARP

Sources personal knowledge (1959) • private information (1959) • *WWW* • *The Engineer* (28 March 1947), 267 • *Engineering* (28 March 1947), 244 • *The Times* (21 March 1947), 7e • *CGPLA Eng. & Wales* (1947) • b. cert. • m. cert. • d. cert.

Likenesses photographs (at construction of Sennar Dam), Sci. Mus., S. Pearson & Son Ltd archive, PEA P12 and Q37

Wealth at death £61,136 13*s.* 6*d.*: probate, 23 Aug 1947, *CGPLA Eng. & Wales*

Gibson, Kennett (*bap.* **1729**, *d.* **1772**), antiquary, born at Paston, Northamptonshire, and baptized there on 30 October 1729, was the son of Thomas Gibson (1692–1758), rector of Paston, and his wife, Mary. His father was chaplain to Bishop White Kennett, after whom he may have been named. He was educated at Eton College (1743–8) and admitted a minor pensioner of Christ's College, Cambridge, on 7 May 1748. He graduated BA in 1752 as fourteenth junior optime, and was ordained deacon at Peterborough on 24 September 1752, and priest on 23 December 1753. In 1756 he became rector of Marholm in the soke of Peterborough, Northamptonshire, and also curate of nearby Castor in the same county.

For many years Gibson lived on the site of a Roman building at Castor and took a great interest in the Roman remains that were dug up in the area. His researches led him to identify Castor as Durobrivae (called Durocobrivae by Gibson), the seventh station recorded in iter v of the British section of the Antonine itinerary, which subsequent archaeological excavation in the nineteenth century by Edmund Tyrell Artis, agent to Lord Fitzwilliam at Milton, and more recent work by the Water Newton excavation committee have confirmed. Gibson intended to publish his findings, and on 3 July 1769 issued proposals to print, at a guinea subscription, a commentary on this part of the fifth route in the British section of the itinerary. However, his early death in 1772 at Paston, where he was also buried, prevented him from doing so. After his death his manuscript came into the possession of Daniel Bayley, fellow of St John's College, Cambridge, who in 1795 passed it to John Nichols. Nichols published it, with considerable additions, as the second volume of his *Miscellaneous Antiquities in Continuation of the 'Bibliotheca topographica Britannica'* under the title *A comment upon part of the fifth journey of Antoninus through Britain, in which the situation of Durocobrivæ, the seventh station there mentioned, is discussed; and Castor in Northamptonshire is shown, from the various remains of Roman antiquity, to have an undoubted claim to that situation*. Gibson's papers also included an account of the finding of a very interesting and rare 3 inch high Roman statuette of Jupiter, when extending his garden at Castor in 1765. Nichols published this in the same volume, but without an illustration. Unfortunately, the object has since been lost.

W. N. TERRY

Sources *DNB* • J. Nichols, 'Preface', *A comment upon part of the fifth journey of Antoninus through Britain*, 2nd edn (1819) • A. L. F. Rivet, 'The British section of the Antonine itinerary', *Britannia*, 1 (1970), 47–9 • E. T. Artis, *The Durobrivae of Antoninus* (1828) • H. I. Longden, *Northamptonshire and Rutland clergy from 1500*, ed. P. I. King and others, 16 vols. in 6, Northamptonshire RS (1938–52), vol. 5, pp. 219–20 • R. A. Austen-Leigh, ed., *The Eton College register, 1698–1752* (1927)

Gibson [*née* Smith], **Margaret Dunlop** (**1843–1920**), Arabic and Syriac scholar, was born on 16 April 1843 in Irvine, Ayrshire, the younger twin daughter of John Smith (*d.* 1866), writer to the signet, and his wife, Margaret, *née* Dunlop (*d.* 1843, three weeks after the twins' birth), both Scottish Presbyterians. Her father became wealthy on inheriting £200,000 from his distant cousin John Ferguson. Her life was inseparably linked with that of her identical twin sister, Agnes [*see* Lewis, Agnes Smith (1843–1926)]; almost indistinguishable, they were nicknamed 'the Giblews' (pronounced with a hard g), though her sister was the dominant twin. They were brought up by a nanny and governess and were taught Latin, French, and

German by their father, a keen linguist and traveller. They attended Irvine Academy and fashionable boarding-schools in Birkenhead, Cheshire, and Kensington, London (1858–63). Margaret later also received 'private tuition in classics and Oriental and modern languages by university men' (*WWW*, 403), but as a woman was then unable to attend a British university. Her inheritance from her father left her wealthy. The twins' fatherly mentor, the minister Dr William Robertson of Irvine, inspired their intellect and supported their desire to travel. After their father's death Margaret undertook, with Agnes and their friend and former teacher, Grace Blyth (*d.* 1917), several journeys to Greece, Turkey, Egypt, and Palestine. Margaret's personality was more romantic than her sister's. She was engaged for some time to James Young *Gibson (1826–1886), a minister of the United Presbyterian church, who was seventeen years her senior and a cousin of Grace Blyth. The engagement was broken off but she did eventually marry him on 8 September 1883 by which time he had left the ministry and had become a Spanish translator. They had no children, and lived at Swaynesthorpe, Ditton Hill, Long Ditton, near Surbiton, Surrey. He died suddenly on 2 October 1886. She edited his *The Cid Ballads and Other Poems and Translations from Spanish and German* (1887). After their husbands' deaths Margaret and Agnes lived and travelled together. Their home was Agnes's large Gothic revival house, built in 1890, Castle-brae, in Chesterton Lane, Cambridge. There they studied and entertained: at their garden parties a piper played on the lawn. Always loyal to Presbyterianism, they attended St Columba's Church and assisted in its Sunday school and other activities. Being rather forceful, they were considered eccentric. They dressed expensively if somewhat frumpishly, and wore white stockings. They owned one of the first cars in Cambridge.

Little is known about Margaret Gibson until her travels with her sister to Cairo, the monastery of St Catherine at Mount Sinai, the Coptic convent of St Mary Deipara at Deir al-Suriani in the Wadi al-Natrun in Egypt, and Palestine (1892, 1893, 1895, 1897, 1901, 1906), except that she learned Greek, Spanish, Hebrew, Syriac, Arabic, and Persian, and that she painted watercolours. To some extent, she was overshadowed by her sister. Margaret participated in many scholarly publications for which Agnes was acknowledged. She compiled the glossaries for several text editions of Christian Palestinian Aramaic (Palestinian Syriac). Probably due to her sister's lack of time she wrote *How the Codex was Found* (1893), based on Agnes's journals of 1892–3. Her task during the work on the manuscripts in the monastery of St Catherine was to study Arabic manuscripts and photograph them. The photographs and lantern slides were later left to Westminster College, Cambridge (many are now in the Bodleian Library, Oxford). She excelled in Arabic, whereas her sister was more proficient in Syriac and Christian Palestinian Aramaic.

Margaret's publications comprise text editions of Arabic. She began by describing the collection of Arabic manuscripts in the monastery of St Catherine with the help of J. Rendel Harris and published it as *Catalogue of the Arabic MSS. in the Convent of St Catharine on Mount Sinai* (1894). It was followed by a text edition of some New Testament epistles: *An Arabic version of the epistles of St. Paul to the Romans, Corinthians, Galatians with part of epistle to the Ephesians from a ninth century MS. in St Catharine's Convent on Mount Sinai* (1894), succeeded by another edition of similar contents: *An Arabic version of the Acts of the Apostles and the seven catholic epistles from an eighth or ninth century manuscript in the Convent of St Catharine on Mount Sinai: with a treatise on the triune nature of God* (1899). Noteworthy are also the editions of various Apocryphas and writings of the church fathers in Arabic, some of them in Syriac: *Apocrypha Sinaitica* (1896) and *Apocrypha Arabica* (1901). Her later works are text editions of Syriac manuscripts which were published as *The Didascalia apostolorum in Syriac* (1903) and the English translation, *The Didascalia apostolorum in English* (1903). Her final task was the reading and editing of a series of Bible commentaries written by the Syriac Bishop Ishodad of Merv: *The Commentaries of Ishodad of Merv, Bishop of Hadatha c. 850 AD* (1911), *Matthew and Mark in Syriac* (1911), *Luke and John in Syriac* (1911), *The Acts of the Apostles and the Catholic Fathers* (1913), and *The Epistles of St Paul* (1916).

She received for her scholarly achievements honorary degrees from St Andrews (DD, 1901), Heidelberg, (DD, 1904), and Dublin (LittD, 1911), and the triennial gold medal of the Royal Asiatic Society—the blue riband of oriental research—in 1915: it was presented by Austen Chamberlain, secretary of state for India. With her sister she was a benefactor of the Presbyterian theological college, Westminster College, Cambridge. They gave the money for its site and partly for its buildings, laid the foundation stone in May 1897, provided scholarships for Presbyterian students at Cambridge, and bequeathed their oriental manuscript and book collection to the college.

Margaret Gibson died suddenly of a cerebral thrombosis on 11 January 1920 at her home, Castle-brae, Chesterton Lane, Cambridge, survived by her sister. She was buried in Cambridge. She left the residue of her estate to the English Presbyterian church, mainly for Westminster College. Castle-brae became a hostel for Clare College students. CHRISTA MÜLLER-KESSLER

Sources A. W. Price, 'The ladies of Castlebrae', annual lecture to the Presbyterian Historical Society, Oct 1964, 1–23 · A. Whigham Price, *The ladies of Castlebrae* (1985) · M. D. Gibson, *How the codex was found* (1893) · M. D. Gibson, *Catalogue of the Arabic MSS. in the convent of St Catharine on Mount Sinai* (1894) · A. Smith Lewis, *In the shadow of Sinai: a story of travel and research from 1895 to 1897* (1898) · *DNB* · Boase, *Mod. Eng. biog.* · *WWW, 1916–28*

Archives Bodl. Oxf., photographs and lantern slides · Westminster College, Cambridge, Cheshunt Foundation, MSS and oriental books

Likenesses photograph, 1901?, repro. in Price, 'The Ladies of Castlebrae' · portrait, Westminster College, Cambridge

Wealth at death £48,290 6*s.* 5*d.*: confirmation, 2 Aug 1921, *CCI* · £908 16*s.*: additional estate, 4 Aug 1923, *CCI*

Gibson, Mathew (*d.* 1740/41), antiquary, was educated at Queen's College, Oxford, where he graduated BA on 9 December 1700 and proceeded MA on 26 June 1703. On 27

November 1722 he became rector of Abbey Dore, Herefordshire. He was both an acquaintance and a correspondent of Thomas Hearne, and reference to an amusing letter from him, dated 19 November 1709, is made in Hearne's *Letters from the Bodleian Library* (1813, 1.197). Hearne, however, was ambivalent about Gibson's character and noted in his diary in April 1734:

> Mr Mathew Gibson, rector of Abbey Dore, called on me. He said that he knew Mr Kyrle (the 'Man of Ross') well, and that he was his wife's near relation—I think her uncle. He said that Kyrle did a great deal of good but 'twas all out of vanity and ostentation. I know not what credit to give to Mr Gibson on this account, especially since he hath more than once spoken against that good worthy man, Dr Otley, late bishop of St David's. Besides this Gibson is a crazed man, and withal stingy, though he is rich and hath no child by his wife. (*Reliquiae*, 3.132)

In 1727 Gibson published a work on the churches of Abbey Dore, Holme Lacey, and Hempsted, which were all endowed by John, Viscount Scudamore. This also included memoirs of the Scudamore family together with an appendix of records and letters.

Gibson appears to have been married twice, secondly to Margaret, with whom he drew up a marriage settlement on 9 August 1739. He died at Abbey Dore in 1740 or 1741 and was buried in the churchyard there. He was succeeded as rector of Abbey Dore by the Revd Digby Coates, who was instituted on 21 July 1741, 'on vacancy caused by death of the last incumbent' (Hereford diocesan register). In his will, made on 31 January 1740 and proved on 1 April 1741, he left his property to his wife, and to his nieces and nephews. J. A. MARCHAND

Sources *Reliquiae Hearnianae: the remains of Thomas Hearne*, ed. P. Bliss, 2nd edn, 3 (1869), 132 • Nichols, *Lit. anecdotes* • Foster, *Alum. Oxon.* • *Remarks and collections of Thomas Hearne*, ed. C. E. Doble and others, 11 vols., OHS, 2, 7, 13, 34, 42–3, 48, 50, 65, 67, 72 (1885–1921), vol. 1, pp. 279; vol. 2, pp. 171, 311 • J. Duncumb and others, *Collections towards the history and antiquities of the county of Hereford*, 3 (1882), 112 • Hereford diocesan register, Hereford Cathedral • will, proved, 1 April 1741, PRO, PROB 11/708, sig. 90 • *DNB*

Wealth at death £300—in legacies: will, 31 Jan 1740; proved (with codicil amendment), 29 April 1741

Gibson, Matthew (1734–1790), vicar apostolic of the northern district, was born on 23 March 1734 probably at Stonecroft Farm, Warden, near Hexham, Northumberland, the fourth son of Jasper Gibson (*d.* 1752) of Stonecroft Farm and his wife, Margaret Leadbitter (*c.*1702–1777). He entered the English College at Douai on 29 September 1747, and was ordained priest about 1757 or 1758; he was appointed professor, first of philosophy, and afterwards of divinity.

In August 1768 Gibson returned to England for health reasons and was placed at Lartington Hall in the North Riding, as chaplain to the Maire family. In 1770 he was elected to the Old Chapter as archdeacon of Kent and Surrey. John Maire died in 1771 and two years later his widow, Mary, moved to Headlam Hall, co. Durham, taking Gibson with her. He was appointed vicar-general of the northern district by Bishop William Walton in 1776 and special vicar in 1777. At Walton's death in February 1780 Gibson was nominated to succeed him as vicar apostolic of the northern district, and on 3 September in London he was consecrated bishop of Comana *in partibus*. Mary Maire died in April 1784, bequeathing him £1000 and £40 p.a., but he was obliged to move, and he took up residence at Stella Hall, co. Durham, where his secretary Thomas Eyre was the tenant and missioner. A number of inaccurate catechisms were then current and Gibson, with the concurrence of his brother bishops, published an authoritative text: the *London* or *Little Catechism* (1784). It did not, however, supersede the *Douai Catechism* (1649 and innumerable subsequent editions) in popularity.

In May 1787 the Catholic Committee was reconstituted to draft a second Catholic relief bill, but the committee's aims differed from those of the vicars apostolic and relations between them became formal and cool. Gibson was particularly resistant to proposed infringements of episcopal prerogatives; he repudiated the committee's *Protestation* of 1789, and he led the opposition to the new oath and certain other terms embodied in the bill. In a joint pastoral letter the bishops unanimously rejected the draft bill and matters were unresolved at Gibson's death. Marmaduke Tunstall wrote that Gibson probably meant well but that he had 'extravagant notions of the power of the hierarchy, surely most strangely ill-timed and had he lived, might have embroiled his flock with many disagreeables' (Tunstall to W. Constable, 8 June 1790, English Letters C.29). But Gibson's successor, his younger brother William *Gibson (1738–1821), was equally intransigent and the bill enacted in 1791 was substantially that desired by the bishops. Gibson died at Stella Hall, co. Durham, on 17 May 1790 after a short illness lasting two weeks and was buried at Newbrough church, near Stonecroft, Northumberland. LEO GOOCH

Sources G. Anstruther, *The seminary priests*, 4 (1977), 111 • L. Gooch, *The revival of English Catholicism* (1995) • Gillow, *Lit. biog. hist.* • B. Ward, *The dawn of the Catholic revival in England, 1781–1803*, 1 (1909) • M. Tunstall, letter to W. Constable, 8 June 1790, Bodl. Oxf., MS Eng. lett. c.29

Archives Roman Catholic diocesan archives, Leeds, corresp. and papers • Ushaw College, Durham, corresp. and papers • Westminster Roman Catholic diocesan archives, London

Gibson, Patrick (1782?–1829), landscape painter and writer on art, was a native of Edinburgh. Although the parochial register of Dollar states that he died in 1829 'aged fifty-four years', the date of his birth is more probably that usually given, December 1782. Gibson attended the Trustees' Academy after John Graham had taken up his appointment there in 1798, and it would have been highly unusual to do so when older than twenty-three. Gibson was educated at the high school, Edinburgh, and in a private academy, and studied art under Alexander Nasmyth before attending the Trustees' Academy. From 1805 he lived in Lambeth, London, exhibiting at the Royal Academy between 1805 and 1807, and at the British Institution in 1811. In 1808 he was in Edinburgh, where he was a founding member of Scotland's first exhibiting society, the Associated Society of Artists, to whose exhibitions he contributed from then until 1814. He was represented in the exhibitions of the Institution for the Encouragement of the Fine Arts in Scotland in 1821 and 1822. In the earlier exhibition catalogues (for example at the Royal Academy) his name occasionally appears as Peter Gibson. In June 1818 he married Isabella, daughter of William Scott, a teacher of elocution. His wife is said to have been an accomplished musician and the composer of a tune, 'Comfort'.

In 1826 Gibson became a founder member of the Scottish Academy of Art, to whose exhibitions he contributed landscape and architectural subjects, both Scottish and foreign (1827–9). In 1824 he had been appointed professor of painting in Dollar Academy, Clackmannanshire, and he died in Dollar on 23 August 1829. His watercolours are delicate and careful, executed with washes of rather subdued and low-toned pigments. A volume of his drawings is in the National Gallery of Scotland, Edinburgh, and a self-portrait in watercolour is in the Scottish National Portrait Gallery, Edinburgh. He was a capable etcher, and published in 1818 a quarto series of etchings, *Select Views in Edinburgh, with Letterpress Descriptions*.

Gibson was a frequent and somewhat sharp critical essayist on contemporary art in Scotland. His articles appeared in a number of publications. He contributed a comprehensive article, 'Design' (this taken in its broadest sense to include painting and architecture) to the *Encyclopaedia Edinensis* (Edinburgh, 1827); and articles on drawing, engraving, and miniature painting to Dr Brewster's *Edinburgh Encyclopaedia*. His 'View of the progress and present state of the arts of design in Britain', in the *Edinburgh Annual Register* for 1816 (written in 1819 and published in 1820), is especially valuable for its perceptive notes on his Scottish contemporaries. He was the author of an anonymous essay on the Royal Institution's exhibition in Edinburgh in 1822; and, under the pseudonym Roger Roundrobin esq., of a 'Letter to the managers and directors' of the same institution, in 1826. A treatise entitled 'Perspective', written shortly before his death, was printed but not published. He also contributed to the daily press; the Edinburgh collector and antiquary David Laing (*Etchings by Sir David Wilkie and Andrew Geddes*, 1875) attributes to Gibson a review in the *Edinburgh Evening Courant* (15 December 1821), of Andrew Geddes's exhibition in Bruces' Great Room, Waterloo Place, Edinburgh.

J. M. Gray, *rev.* Mungo Campbell

Sources *Catalogue of paintings and sculpture*, National Gallery of Scotland, 51st edn (1957) • C. Thompson and H. Brigstocke, *Shorter catalogue: National Gallery of Scotland*, 2nd edn (1978) • H. Smailes, *The concise catalogue of the Scottish National Portrait Gallery* (1990) • Graves, *RA exhibitors* • Graves, *Brit. Inst.* • MS catalogues of the Associated Artists, Edinburgh, 1808–16, NG Scot. • W. D. McKay and F. Rinder, *The Royal Scottish Academy, 1826–1916* (1917); repr. (1975) • 'Gibson, Peter', Graves, *Artists* • file notes, NG Scot.

Likenesses P. Gibson, self-portrait, watercolour drawing, Scot. NPG

Gibson, Reginald Oswald (1902–1983), chemist, was born on 30 September 1902 in Dulwich, London, the only child of Samuel Gibson, civil servant, and his wife, Ethel Crowther. From Wilson's Grammar School in Camberwell he won a scholarship to St Dunstan's College, and from there in 1921 he entered the honours school of chemistry at University College, London. He obtained a first-class BSc degree and in 1925 took a junior research post at Leiden University. In the autumn of the following year he joined Brunner Mond & Co. as a research chemist at Winnington in Cheshire, and at about that time acquired his nickname, Hoot. (Hoot Gibson was a character in the Wild West films of the 1920s.)

In 1927 Gibson introduced his friend and research collaborator, Anton Michels of the University of Amsterdam, to his colleagues in what was by then ICI. This led to Gibson's being seconded in 1928 to work with Michels on the properties of gases at high pressures, and to ICI's becoming interested in the chemical effects of high pressures; this became the theme of Gibson's work on his return to Winnington in 1931.

Gibson was joined in this research by E. W. Fawcett. On Friday 24 March 1933 they set up an experiment in which ethylene and benzaldehyde were pressurized to 1900 atmospheres at 170 °C in the hope that they would combine together. They did not, but when the apparatus was dismantled on the Monday Fawcett noticed that the tip of a steel tube was coated with a waxy substance. This small deposit, less than half a gram, was the first solid polymer of ethylene ever made—polythene. However, Gibson and Fawcett's apparatus was primitive and the reaction could not be controlled. It was another two years before a different team took up the work again. Polythene finally went into production in 1939, and immediately played a crucial role, enabling radar equipment to be deployed effectively in the battle of Britain. In 1937 Gibson married Lesley Shena, daughter of William George Randles, barrister. They had a daughter and two sons.

During the Second World War, Gibson was in charge of process work at an ICI factory making anti-knock additives for aviation fuel. After the war this activity was transferred to the Associated Ethyl Company, and in 1948 Gibson left ICI to become that company's chief chemist. The post-war years saw an enormous expansion of the business, and Gibson became research and development manager with a team of some 150 staff. A long illness caused him to relinquish his management role, but he returned to work as scientific adviser until his retirement in 1963.

Gibson was a patient and thorough man. All his work was carefully thought out and executed with minute attention to detail. In addition to his research career he played a full part in local and professional affairs, holding office in the United Nations Association, the Chester Sailing Club, and the Royal Institute of Chemistry (RIC). His chairman's address to the institute's north-west section on the discovery of polythene became no. 1 in the RIC lecture series (1964). The highlight of Gibson's final year was the polyethylenes 1933–83 golden jubilee conference in London in June. He died the following month, at the Royal Naval Hospital, Plymouth, on 22 July 1983.

A. H. Willbourn, *rev.*

Sources *The Times* (28 July 1983) • ICI company records • private information (1993) • personal knowledge (1993)

Wealth at death £32,452: probate, 6 Sept 1983, *CGPLA Eng. & Wales*

Gibson, Richard [*called* Dwarf Gibson] (**1605/1615?–1690**), miniature painter, is generally said, but on unstated original authority, to have been born in Cumberland. More recently it has been proposed that he may have been the Richard, son of John Gibson, 'picturemaker', who was baptized in London at the church of St Dunstan-in-the-West on 7 July 1605 (Edmond, 107). Richard the miniaturist was a dwarf, 3 foot 10 inches in height, a fact of great significance for his whole career.

Gibson's first employment was as a page in the house of 'a Lady at Mortlack' (de Piles, 423). Noticing his talent for drawing she apprenticed him to Francis Cleyn (*c*.1582–1658), under whom he worked at the new Mortlake tapestry works (established 1619) until some time in the 1630s, when he entered the service of Philip Herbert, fourth earl of Pembroke, the lord chamberlain. The first reference to him in this capacity, and already painting miniatures, is in a memorandum by Abraham van der Doort, the keeper of the Royal Collection:

> the Picture of Adonis Venus Cupid and some doggs … done by Peter Oliver after Titian … tis pis auff ardonis was te noffember 1639 bij mi diliffert tu da kings hands inde Kabint and bij his Magen diliffert tu dick melort chamerlings dwarff vor tu kopit and den tu ristorit agn vorda kings us tu de Kabint. ('Abraham van der Doort's catalogue', 104)

Another member of Pembroke's household was Gibson's future wife, Anne Sheppard (*d*. 1707). Her birth date is unknown but she must have been considerably younger than her husband, since she seems to have been bearing children until 1662. She also was a dwarf; she appears in Van Dyck's portrait of Mary, duchess of Richmond, Pembroke's daughter-in-law, at her first marriage (Vertue, *Note Books*, 5.129; Davis, 1.44). According to Buckeridge both Richard Gibson and Anne Sheppard had by 1639 acquired appointments at court—Gibson as 'Page of the Back-Stairs'—and were so in favour with the king that he 'gave him his wife in marriage' (de Piles, 423–4). The marriage between Richard and Anne was one of the last great court festivities in London before the political situation of the monarchy deteriorated at the outset of the civil wars. It took place at the church of St Pancras, Soper Lane, on St Valentine's day, 14 February 1641.

Whatever his relationship with the king had been Gibson did not follow him to Oxford later in the year but remained firmly attached to Pembroke in London. He lived in Long Acre, on the north side, not far from Samuel Cooper and other miniaturists in this part of London. During the wars Gibson may also have been at Wilton House, Wiltshire, which notionally provides the Elysian setting for the famous double portrait of him and his wife by another member of the Pembroke circle, Sir Peter Lely (formerly in the Kimbell Art Museum, Fort Worth, Texas).

After Pembroke's death, in January 1650, Gibson became associated with Charles, second earl of Carnarvon, the grandson of Pembroke. It is from the extended Carnarvon family that many of the identifiable subjects of

Richard Gibson [Dwarf Gibson] (**1605/1615?–1690**), self-portrait, *c*.1658

Gibson's surviving miniatures were derived during the 1650s, such as the *Lady Katherine Dormer* of *c*.1658 (V&A). Some bear the monogram DG, for Dick or perhaps Dwarf Gibson; both had been familiar and affectionate names for him since his youth. The Carnarvon connection was maintained into the Restoration, but by that time the world, and evidently Gibson's estimation of himself, had changed.

As a man of means—for he had a reliable annuity from the Pembrokes—and of acknowledged talent—for Sanderson (p. 20) had called him one of the most eminent limners of the day—Gibson seems to have developed a much wider clientele. He was evidently busy:

> I cannot possibly prevail with Gibson the Painter to finish my Ladies picture by express from the King he is so take up in copying out 2 of the Countess of Castle Main that he will not intermeddle these 10 days with any other, and the great Picture must also waite his leisure without which he cannot worke. Mr ffranklin saith he will take care to send them as soon as the little one is finished. (John Booth, agent in London, to his principal, Henry Ingram, first Viscount Ingram, 7 Dec 1664, in Reynolds)

And, marking the enlarged circumstances of his life, in the late 1660s he changed the form of his signature, from DG to RG in monogram. The earliest known occurrence of the new form of the signature is on a chalk drawing of 1669 in the British Museum; it appears two years later on *Lady Elizabeth Dormer* (1671; V&A), and again on one of Gibson's last portraits of his long-standing patron Elizabeth, countess of Carnarvon (Yale U. CBA).

In May 1672 Gibson's even longer-standing relationship

with the crown was revived when he was appointed, two weeks after the death of Samuel Cooper, as 'picture-maker'—that is, king's limner (miniaturist), an appointment which he held, however, only until the next year, when he was succeeded by Nicholas Dixon (private information). Instead he was appointed drawing-master to the two young daughters of James, duke of York: Mary (*b.* 1662) and Anne (*b.* 1665). He remained close to Mary and accompanied her to The Hague on her marriage to Prince William of Orange in 1677. He took lodgings in Amsterdam, first at the house of Johan Nieulant, a silversmith in the Singel; then, in March 1679, he took a substantial house on the east side of the Boekhorststraat. He emerges from many references in the correspondence of Christiaan Huygens (1629–1695), the great mathematician and natural philosopher, as an active collector and dealer in the art market (*Œuvres complètes*).

Richard and Anne Gibson had five surviving children, of whom Susannah-Penelope *Rosse was a miniaturist of distinction in her own right, and Anne van Vrybergen (*b.* 1662) was the subject of a painful marital misunderstanding and breakdown, summarized in a detailed deposition by Richard Gibson to the Hof van Holland of 24 September 1681 (Bredius, 125). The sons, William, John, and Edward *Gibson, were evidently older and of substance, for when Gibson made his will in 1677, before departing for The Hague, he made provision for his daughters and their descendants or, failing them, for his brother Edward (buried apparently at St Martin-in-the-Fields on 25 August 1690), to the exclusion of his sons. In the absence of firm evidence to the contrary it seems sensible to suggest that William, the eldest son, was actually **William Gibson** (1644–1703), said by Buckeridge (de Piles, 425) to have been a miniaturist, connoisseur, and dealer in old-master drawings, to whom a portrait of Henry Cavendish, earl of Ogle, has been attributed (Goulding, 131). He was born in 1644, at about the time when Richard's eldest surviving son might have been born; he was the pupil of Richard Gibson and of Peter Lely, just as a son of Richard might have been; and he was a connoisseur-dealer, like Richard. He lived in the parish of St Giles-in-the-Fields, London, and was buried at Richmond in Surrey. John Gibson, perhaps named after his grandfather, is said to have been an army officer in the Netherlands. Edward, evidently named after his uncle, may be 'Mr. Edw. Gibson', said by Buckeridge (de Piles, 425) to be an oil painter and subsequently a pastellist, who died aged thirty-three and was buried at Richmond. It has been suggested in connection with a drawing, said to be a self-portrait, in the National Portrait Gallery, London, that he flourished from 1668 to 1701 and was resident in the Strand (Piper, 137–8). Dirck Gibson (*fl.* 1690–1712), who has even been suggested as the author of the 'DG' miniatures of the 1650s, and his possible brother Hendrick have also been suggested as sons (Foskett, 1.287) but they seem to be of a different family, and certainly are of a different generation from Richard's offspring.

Richard and Anne Gibson returned to London when Princess Mary and William of Orange acceded to the British throne in 1688. Gibson seems to have lived with his daughter Susannah-Penelope in the Henrietta Street house that had once been Samuel Cooper's. He died on 20 July 1690, as is attested by the signatures on his will (transcribed in Edmond, 109) of Susannah-Penelope, Anne, William, and Edward—John being presumably still in the Netherlands.

As a miniaturist Richard Gibson has only recently emerged from the confusion arising from his change of signature. The prime characteristic of his hand, clearly visible in the *Elizabeth Capell, Countess of Carnarvon* (V&A), in which the original bright-red cheeks of the sitter have survived unfaded, is the tendency of the hatching strokes in the flesh painting to move in diagonal parallel groups. This striation is combined with an impasto effect, visible under raking light, very different from the smooth transparency aimed at by the main seventeenth-century miniaturists. The impasto is not closely related to the basic pattern of hatching strokes, as it is in the blending process that Cooper and others adopted increasingly from *c.*1660, but it sweeps around the outlines of jaw, nose, and eyebrows, giving them a strong, painterly presence. These and other differences from the main technical tradition of miniature painting, such as the way in which the carnation ground is laid in and the way that white shirts or lace are painted, suggest that Gibson became a limner on the basis of the technical training that he had received as a designer and painter, reinforced by the encouragement of Lely, rather than in a miniaturist's studio in London. After about 1660, possibly under Cooper's influence, the composition and colouring of his miniatures change but the fundamental technique remains similar. None the less the sheer numbers of surviving later seventeenth-century miniatures that are in the Gibson manner suggest that more than one hand was responsible for them. The fact that at least three of Gibson's children seem to have been active in the art makes it likely that they were responsible for some of the work presently regarded as in Richard's general manner; perhaps new documents or improved connoisseurship will eventually make it possible to distinguish their hands. JOHN MURDOCH

Sources [B. Buckeridge], 'An essay towards an English school of painting', in R. de Piles, *The art of painting, with the lives and characters of above 300 of the most eminent painters*, 3rd edn (1754), 354–439 · G. Reynolds, *English portrait miniatures* (1952), 75; rev. edn (1988) · A. Bredius, 'Een en ander over Richard Gibson', *Oud Holland*, 28 (1910), 124–6 · *Œuvres complètes de Christiaan Huygens*, ed. Société Hollandaise des Sciences, 22 vols. (1888–1950) · R. W. Goulding, 'The Welbeck Abbey miniatures', *Walpole Society*, 4 (1914–15), esp. 131 [whole issue] · B. S. Long, *British miniaturists* (1929); repr. (1966), 171 · J. Murdoch and V. J. Murrell, 'The monogramist DG: Dwarf Gibson and his patrons', *Burlington Magazine*, 123 (May 1981), 282–9 · J. Murdoch, *Seventeenth-century English miniatures in the collection of the Victoria and Albert Museum* (1997) · private information (2004) [Katherine Gibson] · Lord Chamberlain's papers, LC3/27, fol. 72 · D. Foskett, *A dictionary of British miniature painters*, 2 vols. (1972) · A. Davies, *Dictionary of British portraiture*, 1 (1979), 44 · D. Piper, *Catalogue of seventeenth-century portraits in the National Portrait Gallery, 1625–1714* (1963) · *DNB* · M. Edmond, 'Limners and picturemakers', *Walpole Society*, 47 (1978–80), 60–242 · 'Abraham van der Doort's catalogue of the collections of Charles I', ed. O. Millar, *Walpole Society*, 37 (1958–60) • W. Sanderson, *Graphice: the use of the pen and pensil, or, The most excellent art of painting* (1658)

Likenesses P. Lely, double portrait, oils, *c*.1650–1660 (with his wife); formerly at Kimbell Art Museum, Fort Worth, Texas • R. Gibson, self-portrait, chalk drawing, *c*.1658, BM [*see illus.*] • oils (after P. Lely), NPG

Gibson, Richard (*b*. 1635, *d*. in or after 1712), naval official, was born in August 1635 in Great Yarmouth, the son of Robert Gibson, a shipmaster whose vessels traded with France, and his wife, Margaret. He entered the navy in April 1648, subsequently serving as purser on board *Assurance* in 1653–5 and *Sapphire* in 1655–65. By royal warrant dated 4 November 1665 he was appointed surveyor of the victualling at Great Yarmouth. From August 1667 until August 1670 he served the Navy Board as clerk to the clerk of the acts. The holder of this latter post was Samuel Pepys, with whom Gibson formed a close working relationship. Using his considerable knowledge of victualling and supply of the navy, Gibson framed a number of proposals that Pepys brought to the attention of his colleagues on the Navy Board. Pepys's *Diaries* note Gibson as having considerable enthusiasm for maritime history, and Pepys chose to employ his clerk to assemble notes for a planned history of the navy.

Proving himself one of the ablest and most industrious of Pepys's assistants, Gibson was recommended for further office in April 1668 and appointed to the post of purser general, Port Mahon, for the period of war against the Barbary corsairs (1670–72). After rejoining Pepys in 1672 Gibson continued to serve as chief clerk to two further clerks of the acts until March 1677 (Collinge, 22, 103). In addition he was appointed purser to the newly launched first-rate *Royal Charles* (1672–3) and entrusted with the supervision and control of all accounts relating to the quartering of sick and wounded seamen (1673–7). In 1677 he became a freeman of Great Yarmouth and began a brief period of service with Trinity House as chief clerk before recall to naval service and appointment to the post of clerk of the cheque at Deptford in 1679–80. In March 1680 he was once again appointed to the Navy Board serving as chief clerk to the comptroller (1680–86) until appointment to the office of clerk of the cheque to the victualling board. He subsequently moved to the Admiralty as chief clerk and remained there until 1693 when he appears to have gone out of office. During these later years he gave considerable thought to improving both naval victualling arrangements and the care of wounded seamen. Among papers presented to the Admiralty were recommendations for reduction of fraud (May 1693), opposition to victualling by contract (1694), and the establishment of a naval hospital at Greenwich (1691). This last project was adopted by Dr William Lower, who had been charged with bringing order to the medical affairs of the navy. Having originated the scheme for creating Greenwich Hospital, Gibson was unsuccessful in a bid to acquire stewardship of the hospital, a plan designed to secure him during his retirement. Instead he became a temporary auditor, inspecting the accounts previously kept by John Evelyn. Gibson was still living in 1712; the date and manner of his death and burial are unknown. PHILIP MACDOUGALL

Sources BL, Sloane MS 2572, fols. 79–87 • BL, Add. MS 11602 • Pepys, *Diary*, 10.155–6 • J. M. Collinge, *Navy Board officials, 1660–1832* (1978) • R. L. Ollard, *Pepys: a biography* (1974) • parish register (baptism), Great Yarmouth, 23 Aug 1635

Archives BL, Sloane MS 2572, fols. 79–87 • BL, Add. MS 11602

Gibson, Samuel (1793–1849), smith and naturalist, was born at Sowerby Bridge, Yorkshire. His father was a whitesmith and Methodist preacher at Butt Green chapel. Gibson attended Sunday school briefly before beginning to work as his father's apprentice. He soon became a skilled whitesmith and mechanic, and in 1814 was employed by a maker of spindles and flies in nearby Hebden Bridge. He set up his own whitesmith's shop in 1820 and was established as a 'tinman' in Hebden Bridge when Richard Spruce first consulted him about the botany of mosses in the late 1830s. Later, Gibson was more commonly described as a blacksmith. He married in 1812 and had a family of nine children.

Gibson became interested in botany in 1813 and pursued it his entire life, keeping, in later years, a much used and grimy copy of William Jackson Hooker's *British Flora* (1830) on his workbench. He soon established himself as an excellent discriminator of plants, particularly the difficult groups of sedges and mosses, as well as of insects and fossil shells. Gibson's skill was primarily manifested in his large collections. He was a lively and sometimes controversial contributor to the popular botanical magazine *The Phytologist* (1841–4). Most of his discoveries, however, were encompassed in the works of others, notably John Phillips's *Illustrations of the Geology of Yorkshire* (part 2, 1836); Henry Baines's *Flora of Yorkshire* (1840); Thomas Brown's 'Description of some new species of fossil shells', *Transactions of the Manchester Geological Society* (1, 1841, 212–35); Edward Newman's *History of British Ferns* (1844); and Richard Buxton's *Botanical Guide* (1849).

Gibson's local knowledge of botany and geology was sought by the surgeon and Methodist Robert Howard, and included in his publication *A history of the typhus of Heptonstall-Slack … together with a sketch of the physical condition of the hand-loom weavers* (1844), a pamphlet describing the harsh living conditions of working people of the area. By 1845 Gibson himself faced destitution when he had to abandon his craft following a fall from a building. His injuries were considered the cause of his subsequent poor health and cantankerous nature. Following his accident, he took over an inn in Mytholmroyd in which he established a museum.

Although living in an isolated area, Gibson associated with gentlemen and artisan naturalists from Manchester as well as from nearby Todmorden and Halifax. He also corresponded with several eminent botanists. The Manchester Geological Society elected him an honorary member in 1843. He had become more widely known to men of science in the previous year, when his fossil shells were exhibited at the Manchester meeting of the British Association for the Advancement of Science, which Gibson was allowed to attend, but in 1847 he was forced to sell this collection to the Manchester Natural History Society because his pub-museum failed to attract sufficient customers.

This sale allowed Gibson to leave the inn and move to a nearby cottage in early 1848. Probably suffering from heart disease, he soon became bedridden and during a long illness had to sell all his specimens of fossils, land and fresh-water shells, and birds. Edward William Binney, geologist and warm supporter of artisan naturalists, became aware of Gibson's plight in May 1849 and immediately made appeals for his support. By the end of the month Adam Sedgwick, William Buckland, and Lord Fitzwilliam had sent contributions and Binney was investigating ways of selling Gibson's remaining collections. In August 1849 Gibson's almost complete British herbarium was bought for £75 by Mark Philips, MP for Manchester from 1832 to 1847; his entomological collection, consisting of thirty-four boxes of insects, was retrieved by Binney (with Sedgwick's help) from a clergyman who had bought them from Gibson's wife for £2, and was resold for £45. These funds became Gibson's bequest to his family for he had died in Mytholmroyd on 21 May 1849; he was buried at Butt Green four days later. ANNE SECORD

Sources 'The late Mr Samuel Gibson, the naturalist', *Manchester Guardian* (7 July 1849) • J. Cash, *Where there's a will there's a way! or, Science in the cottage* (1873), 157–64 • R. Howard, *A history of the typhus of Heptonstall-Slack* [1844] • W. B. Crump and C. Crossland, *The flora of the parish of Halifax* (1904), lvi–lviii • 'The collections of the late Samuel Gibson, the naturalist', *Manchester Guardian* (11 Aug 1849) • 'Death of another of the old botanists', *Manchester Guardian* (30 May 1849) • R. Spruce, *Notes of a botanist on the Amazon and Andes*, ed. A. R. Wallace, 1 (1908), xxiii–xxiv • L. H. Grindon, *Country rambles, and Manchester walks and wild flowers* (1882), 166–7 • E. W. Binney, letter to W. J. Hooker, 23 May 1849, RBG Kew, directors' correspondence, vol. 27, letter 68 • Lord Fitzwilliam, letter to J. Phillips, 29 May 1849, Oxf. U. Mus. NH, J. Phillips MSS, 1849/10 • A. Sedgwick, letter to J. Phillips, 28 May 1849, Oxf. U. Mus. NH, J. Phillips MSS, Sedg./52

Archives Buile Hill Mining Museum, Salford, part of herbarium • Halifax Central Library, corresp. with R. Leyland • Manchester Museum, fossil collection • Warrington Library, corresp. with W. Wilson

Wealth at death £120—natural history specimens: Cash, *Where there's a will*, 162–3

Gibson, Solomon (1796/7–1866), sculptor, was born probably at Gyffin, near Conwy, north Wales, the younger son of William Gibson (*d.* after 1818), gardener and Baptist preacher, and his wife, Jane Roberts. About 1800 the Welsh-speaking family moved to Liverpool. It is possible that Solomon joined his elder brother, John *Gibson, in the firm of S. and F. Franceys, marble masons and sculptors.

In 1812, exhibiting for the first time at the Liverpool Academy, Gibson showed three works, including a freshly modelled terracotta *Venus Lamenting the Death of Adonis* (Walker Art Gallery, Liverpool). His seated *Mercury* was admired by the actor John Kemble, and by Thomas Lawrence who sent him a £10 note 'as an encouragement' (clay; exh. Liverpool Academy, 1813, price £1 5*s*., and Royal Academy, 1816; a version in biscuit earthenware cast, signed, and dated 1816 in Liverpool Museum). Listed for the first time as an artist in the Liverpool street directories of 1816, Gibson began to gain locally significant commissions, notably the marble monument to Dr Barrow (St Nicholas's, Liverpool; des.), who had died heroically during a typhoid outbreak; the commission was probably awarded in 1819. His exhibits at the Liverpool Academy show of 1824, which included a bust of Thomas Trail, a local celebrity, for the Liverpool Literary and Philosophical Society and a marble monument to Pudsey Dawson (Royal School for the Blind, Liverpool; des.), a philanthropist and former mayor, must have consolidated his reputation in that city. The latter, erected in 1817 at a cost of £126, showed 'Charity (*Pilgrim's Progress*) leading Blind Children to the Tomb of their Patron' (Royden, 104).

Never a regular exhibitor at the Liverpool Academy (1812–14, 1822, 1824, 1830), Gibson showed only once more at the Royal Academy (1822). Perhaps feeling overshadowed by his famous brother, he did not attempt to build on his early success as a figure modeller. He visited Rome, where John Gibson lived, probably only once (1826?–1830). Between 1834 and 1843 the Liverpool street directories list him as a marble mason and the design and production of monuments, usually in a neat, modest, neoclassical style, became his chief source of livelihood. These can be found in churches in Liverpool, north Wales, Shropshire, and Cheshire. Literary matters increasingly preoccupied him. He was an active member of the Liverpool Literary and Philosophical Society (1835–44), delivering papers on such diverse topics as the *Forum of Trajan at Rome* (1836), *The Symbolic Language used in Mathematics* (1837), and *The Improvements to the Mersey Channel* (none traced). He also belonged to the Liverpool Polytechnic Society (1843–9).

In 1848 Gibson designed for the Liverpool silversmith and antiquary Joseph Mayer a silver cradle presented to Mrs Horsfall, the mayor's wife, on the birth of her daughter (exh. Great Exhibition of 1851, London). He died in Paris on 24 January 1866 on his way to see his brother, John, under whose will he was to have received £100 a year, during the latter's final illness. Whether Mayer's assessment of him is fair—'There was an absence of purpose in the direction of his studies, and he passed through life a strange and useless though not commonplace man' (*DNB*)—is hard to judge until Mayer's manuscript biography reappears. TIMOTHY STEVENS

Sources E. Morris and E. Roberts, *The Liverpool Academy and other exhibitions of contemporary art in Liverpool, 1774–1867* (1998) • T. Matthews, *The biography of John Gibson, R.A., sculptor, Rome* (1911) • Lady Eastlake [E. Eastlake], ed., *Life of John Gibson, R.A., sculptor* (1870) • *Merseyside sculpture survey* (1976–7) [Walker Art Gallery, Liverpool, archive] • *DNB* • artist's file, archive material, Courtauld Inst., Witt Library • *ILN* (4 Nov 1848) • M. Royden, *Pioneers and perseverance: a history of the Royal School for the Blind, Liverpool (1791–1991)* (1991) • street directories, Liverpool • *Transactions of the Liverpool Literary and Philosophical Society* • *Transactions of the Liverpool Polytechnic Society* • letter from S. Gibson to H. Ellis, 6 July 1826, BL, Add. MS 41312, fol. 47 • standing committee minutes, 4 Jan 1826, BM • standing committee minutes, 11 Feb 1826, BM • letter from S. Gibson to G. Dunkerton, Feb 1819, Flintshire RO, Hawarden, Glynne-Gladstone MS 399 [copy] • *The exhibition of the Royal Academy* (1816); (1822) [exhibition catalogues] • *The Kaleidoscope* (5 Oct 1830), 111 [review] · two letters from S. Gibson to unknown correspondent and J. Foster, U. Lpool, Liverpool Royal Institution Archives, L.R.I. Arch 51.34–5 · *CGPLA Eng. & Wales* (1866)

Likenesses T. Griffiths, portrait

Wealth at death under £600: administration, 22 March 1866, *CGPLA Eng. & Wales*

Gibson, Thomas (*d.* 1562), printer and physician, was born at Morpeth, Northumberland. The Thomas Gibson who received an MB from the University of Cambridge in 1511 was probably the same man who was listed as a London barber-surgeon in March 1512; however, it is not clear whether this was the printer and publisher active in London between 1535 and 1539. Gibson's first publication was Coverdale's concordance of the New Testament which appeared in 1535; other publications included a plague tract, Lancelot Ridley's annotations on Jude, a corrected edition of the *Great Herbal*, an English primer, an English psalter, and an edition of the Tyndale Bible. On 21 July 1537 Bishop Latimer unsuccessfully recommended Gibson to Cromwell for the printing of *The Institution of a Christian Man*: 'He is an honest good man, and will set it forth in a good letter [typeface] and sell it good cheap, whereas others sell too dear, which lets many to buy' (*LP Henry VIII*, 12/2, no. 295, p. 122). The following year the city chamberlain paid Gibson 51*s.* 4*d.* for 'diverse papers and other bookes prynted by him concernynge the thamyse [Thames] and ward mote enquests', indicating that Gibson was the city printer at that time (Plomer, 17). Although the *Dictionary of National Biography* and other commentators have claimed that he wrote practically everything that he published *STC* credits him with only the authorship of *A Breve Cronycle of the Bysshope of Romes Blessynge*, published by John Day probably in 1548.

Gibson evidently fled England during Mary's reign as he, his wife, and daughter became members of the English protestant congregation at Geneva on 20 November 1557. He had returned by 1559, when he was granted a licence by the University of Cambridge to practise medicine. Bale claimed that Gibson's cures 'were almost incredible', and described him as a zealous defender of the Reformation (Hodgson, 438). John Hodgson, in his nineteenth-century history of Northumberland, remarked on the number of career parallels between Gibson and his much more famous contemporary and fellow native of Morpeth, William Turner. Gibson died in London in 1562.

I. GADD

Sources *STC, 1475–1640* · E. G. Duff, *A century of the English book trade* (1905) · H. R. Plomer, 'Notices of English stationers in the archives of the City of London', *Transactions of the Bibliographical Society*, 6 (1901), 13–27 · *LP Henry VIII*, 12/2.122 · *DNB* · Venn, *Alum. Cant.* · J. Hodgson, *A history of Northumberland*, 3 pts in 7 vols. (1820–58), vol. 2/2, p. 438

Gibson, Thomas (1648/9–1722), physician, the son of William Gibson, was born at High Knipe, in the parish of Bampton, Westmorland. After attending school at Bampton he was apparently created doctor of medicine by the archbishop of Canterbury on 16 May 1663; in 1671, aged twenty-two, he entered St John's College, Cambridge, where he incorporated his degree of MD in the same year. He later went to Leiden University, where he graduated MD on 20 August 1675.

Gibson was admitted a licentiate of the Royal College of Physicians on 26 June 1676, and became an honorary fellow on 30 September 1680. He was a presbyterian, and a visit which he and his second wife paid to his nephew John, provost of Queen's College, Oxford, is sourly described by Hearne. Gibson's religion and connections to the Cromwell family led to his being removed from the list of fellows of the College of Physicians when the college received a new charter under James II in 1687. After 1688 Gibson was reinstated and on 21 January 1719 he was appointed physician-general to the army. Gibson published *The Anatomy of Humane Bodies Epitomized* (1682; 6th edition, 1703), compiled for the most part from Alexander Read's work.

Gibson married first, Elizabeth (1646–1692), widow of Zephaniah Cresset of Stanstead St Margaret's, Hertfordshire, and third daughter of George Smith of that place; and second, on 16 June 1698, Anne (1659–1727), sixth daughter of Richard *Cromwell, the lord protector, who on meeting him thought Gibson 'modest to a beauty' (Butler, 172). There were no children of either marriage. Gibson died on 16 July 1722, and was buried in the ground adjoining the Foundling Hospital belonging to St George the Martyr, Queen Square, London. Edmund *Gibson (*bap.* 1669, *d.* 1748) was Gibson's nephew and heir.

GORDON GOODWIN, *rev.* PATRICK WALLIS

Sources Munk, *Roll* · Venn, *Alum. Cant.* · R. W. Innes Smith, *English-speaking students of medicine at the University of Leyden* (1932) · G. Clark and A. M. Cooke, *A history of the Royal College of Physicians of London*, 3 vols. (1964–72) · J. A. Butler, *A biography of Richard Cromwell, 1826–1712* (1994) · G. Atkinson, *The worthies of Westmorland*, 2 vols. (1849–50) · R. Clutterbuck, ed., *The history and antiquities of the county of Hertford*, 3 vols. (1815–27) · *Reliquiae Hearnianae: the remains of Thomas Hearne*, ed. P. Bliss, 2 (1857), 105

Gibson, Thomas (*c.*1680–1751), portrait painter, is of obscure origins. He was appointed a founder director of Godfrey Kneller's academy in London in 1711. According to the painter Thomas Highmore, Sir James Thornhill sometimes applied to Gibson to sketch for him in his large pictures figures in action. Vertue, who was on terms of great friendship with Gibson and who was one of his pupils at Godfrey Kneller's academy, recorded that other artists were offended with Gibson because he refused to raise his prices. He also stated that due to serious illness he was obliged to sell his pictures privately among his friends about 1729–30 and to retire from practice to Oxford. He subsequently returned to London about 1732 and is said to have resumed his practice. He died in London on 28 April 1751, aged about seventy-one. At the Society of Antiquaries there is a portrait of Vertue by Gibson, painted in 1723 (engraved by Vertue himself); at the Royal Society a portrait of John Flamsteed the astronomer. A number of his portraits are in Oxford, including portraits of Flamsteed and John Locke (Bodl. Oxf.) and a portrait of Archbishop Wake (Christ Church picture gallery). His last recorded works are a portrait of Augusta, princess of Wales, and a group portrait of her children, painted in 1742. Many of his portraits were engraved by J. Faber, J. Simon, G. White, G. Vertue, and others, including those of Sir Robert Walpole, Admiral Sir Charles Wager, Dr Henry Sacheverell (1710; Magdalen College, Oxford), Robert, Lord Molesworth, and the Revd Samuel Clarke. Further examples of Gibson's work are in the collections of the Society of Antiquaries, the National Maritime Museum, Lambeth Palace, the Royal Society, and Orleans House Gallery, London; and the Bodleian Library, Christ Church, and Magdalen College, Oxford. L. H. CUST, *rev.* SARAH HERRING

Sources R. Jeffree, 'Gibson, Thomas', *The dictionary of art*, ed. J. Turner (1996) · Vertue, *Note books*, vols. 1, 3–5; 6.32, 35, 37, 168 · Waterhouse, *18c painters*, 145 · B. Stewart and M. Cutten, *The dictionary of portrait painters in Britain up to 1920* (1997) · E. Einberg, *Manners and morals: Hogarth and British painting, 1700–1760* (1987), 57, 242 [exhibition catalogue, Tate Gallery, London, 15 Oct 1987 – 3 Jan 1988] · J. Kerslake, *National Portrait Gallery: early Georgian portraits*, 1 (1977), 9, 100, 203, 287, 342 · H. Walpole, *Anecdotes of painting in England: with some account of the principal artists*, ed. J. Dallaway, [rev. and enl. edn], 4 (1827), 45–6 · Mrs R. Lane Poole, ed., *Catalogue of portraits in the possession of the university, colleges, city and county of Oxford*, 3 vols. (1912–25), vol. 1, pp. 74, 85; vol. 2, pp. 177, 224, 252, 253; vol. 3, pp. 57, 60, 176, 261 · S. J. Hardman, *Lord Poulett's paintings in Georgia* (1978), 11

Likenesses attrib. G. Hamilton, group portrait (*An assembly of 'Virtuosi'*), AM Oxf.

Gibson, Thomas Hill [Tom] (**1893–1975**), Scottish nationalist, was born at 12 Whitevale Street, Glasgow, on 22 September 1893, the son of William Gibson, a mercantile clerk, and his wife, Mary, *née* Clement. He had a career in business, becoming secretary of the British Steel Federation and financial director of the British Iron and Steel Corporation.

Gibson became involved in politics before the First World War as a member of the Young Scots Society, a radical group associated with the Liberal Party. Home rule was a key part of the Young Scots programme, and after serving in the war Gibson returned to politics in the post-war era by joining the Scottish Home Rule Association (SHRA). The idea behind the SHRA was that it would act as a non-party umbrella organization to unite all those in favour of creating a Scottish parliament. As far as Gibson was concerned, the fact that most SHRA support came from the Labour Party and the Scottish Trade Union Congress meant that its political independence was compromised by virtue of the influence that these groups could bring to bear on association policy. Evidence of this was found in the way that home-rule Liberals were sidelined during by-elections in the early 1920s in favour of Labour candidates. After an official collection on association premises for the widow of the Clydeside revolutionary John Maclean in 1924, Gibson left in disgust and joined the hard-line Scots National League (SNL). This organization was modelled on Sinn Féin, and its uncompromising nationalism appealed to Gibson. Central to his political philosophy was the belief that Scottish interests could not be served by any British political organization because the numerical superiority of the English would always relegate Scottish interests to second place. It was this, he believed, which had caused the Liberals to fail in realizing Scottish home rule before the war and would subsequently lead the Labour Party to fail in the period afterwards.

A tireless and in many ways ruthless operator, Tom Gibson bent the SNL to his political will. As a minority organization on the fringes, the league was ideologically pure in that it had no contacts with any mainstream British political parties, and Gibson was determined to keep it that way. He pushed through a party constitution and set about instilling party discipline. Central to this objective was the belief that members of the league should not have anything to do with British political organizations or with groups dominated by them. He brought the league's president, Ruaraidh Erskine of Mar, to book for speaking at an SHRA rally. Gibson also worked hard to rid the league of its Celticist image. Writing in the *Scots Independent*, he focused on the economic policies that an independent Scotland could pursue. He also spent a great deal of time lambasting the SHRA for its misplaced trust in the Labour Party. Along with Iain Gillies, he propounded the belief that independence or home rule could be delivered only by an independent political party which secured an electoral mandate. This became the template for the National Party of Scotland (NPS) which was formed in April 1928.

Gibson was a central figure in the formation of the NPS and in its early development. His influence on the party began to waver after he moved to England in early 1932. This coincided with a period of traumatic upheaval in the NPS as the party split between hard-line separatists and the majority moderate devolutionists. Away from his power base and subject to conflicting appeals from both sides of the divide, Gibson was appalled both by the fundamentalists' lack of discipline and the leadership's wide-ranging expulsions. One reason for the expulsions was to pave the way for a merger between the National Party and the right-wing Scottish Party to form the Scottish National Party (SNP) in 1934. Gibson believed such a union to be a mistake as it would give the devolutionist wing too much power. His suspicions were confirmed when the SNP failed to maintain the ban on members joining other parties. This led to his disillusionment with the organization.

Gibson ceased to play an active part in nationalist politics until after the Second World War. The victory of the radical wing in the SNP over the moderate leadership in 1942 reaffirmed the main tenets of Gibson's policy, namely independence by contesting elections. During the war, his work as a civil servant prevented his active participation in party politics. In the late 1940s he re-entered nationalist politics, and with Robert McIntyre and Arthur Donaldson formed a leadership triumvirate which saw the SNP through to the mid-1960s. Appointed party chairman in 1955, with his tireless energy and passionate enthusiasm he set to work reactivating the movement and building up the organization. Latterly he lived at Auchencairn, near Rerrick, Kirkcudbrightshire. His wife,

Elma Campbell Gibson, and their son and daughter survived him following his death at the Royal Infirmary, Dumfries, on 23 April 1975. He was buried in Auchencairn cemetery. RICHARD J. FINLAY

Sources *Scotsman* (24 April 1975), 4 · *Glasgow Herald* (24 April 1975), 2 · b. cert. · d. cert. · R. J. Finlay, *Independent and free: Scottish politics and the origins of the Scottish national party, 1918–1945* (1994)

Gibson, Thomas Milner (1806–1884), politician, was born at Port of Spain, Trinidad, West Indies, on 3 September 1806, and baptized on 8 November, the only child of Thomas Milner Gibson and his wife, Isabella, daughter of Henry Glover of Chester. His father was the son of the Revd Thomas Gibson, of a family settled at Dovercourt-cum-Harwich and Ipswich, and was a major of the 37th foot. After serving in Trinidad he returned with his wife and son to England, where he died in May 1807. In July 1810 his widow married her second husband, Thomas Whiting Wootton, who died in 1844. Some time after the family's return to England in 1807 Gibson was sent to a Unitarian school at Higham Hill, Walthamstow, kept by Dr Eliezer Cogan, where he had Benjamin Disraeli for one of his schoolfellows. From this chance connection sprang many a later political combination. He was next at a school at Blackheath, then was entered at the Charterhouse in 1819, and five years afterwards was at a private tutor's in Nottinghamshire. At Trinity College, Cambridge, he was thirty-sixth wrangler in 1830, when he proceeded BA.

On 23 February 1832 Gibson married (Susannah) Arethusa (1814–1885) [*see* Gibson, (Susannah) Arethusa], only child of the Revd Sir Thomas Gery Cullum, eighth baronet, and his wife, Mary Anne, *née* Eggers. They had five sons and three daughters (only four of the children survived infancy). Gibson's illegitimate son, Thomas Gibson *Bowles, was also welcomed into their household. Arethusa Gibson was an important figure in literary and political society, making a greater splash than her husband.

Gibson was elected for Ipswich as a Conservative in July 1837, but in 1839, having become a convinced free-trader, he left the Conservative Party, resigned his seat, and, at the ensuing by-election, was defeated by seven votes. He was suspected of political opportunism. In the same year, on 7 February, he added by royal licence the name of Milner to his surname, in memory of Robert Milner of Ipswich. In September 1839 he unsuccessfully contested Cambridge City. He became active in the free trade movement and in the Anti-Corn Law League, though his presence was not always welcome. When he was selected as candidate for Manchester, Cobden wrote to Francis Place:

> As for the conduct of our men here in selecting Gibson, a young untried man and a Suffolk squire, to become member for Manchester, I am quite disgusted at it … We save our enemies the trouble of trampling on us, by very industriously kicking our own backsides. (McCord, 30)

Gibson won Manchester with Mark Philips at the general election in 1841. He continued to promote the league's cause, and gained some favour with Cobden, who had little option but to co-operate with him, the band of Anti-Corn Law League MPs being small.

Thomas Milner Gibson (1806–1884), by Charles Allen Du Val, 1843

When Russell formed his government in July 1846 following the Conservative split over free trade, Gibson became vice-president of the Board of Trade, the only leaguer to accept office. He was sworn of the privy council. He was unopposed in Manchester, and also at the general election in 1847, when John Bright became his co-MP. He chaired a select committee on the Navigation Acts in 1847, preparing the ground for their repeal. He ceased to be vice-president in April 1848, making notable speeches on the sugar duty question that year. In 1850 he became president of the Association for the Repeal of the Taxes on Knowledge, a cause he supported with success. In 1852 he held his seat in Manchester, but not comfortably. He was not included in the Aberdeen coalition in 1852, and on 15 April 1853, just before Gladstone's first budget, he defeated the government on the advertisement duties, with the support of radicals, Irish, and tories. In January 1854 he was a leading speaker for parliamentary reform at the reform banquet in Manchester. He opposed aspects of the Crimean War and criticized the navy's bombardment of undefended Baltic towns. In March 1857 he seconded Cobden's vote of censure on Palmerston's China policy and in the same month he and Bright, like many radicals elsewhere, were easily defeated at the general election, his opponent, Sir John Potter, being another member of the league. In December 1857, however, he was elected at a by-election for Ashton under Lyne, which he represented until 1868. It was Gibson's amendment to Palmerston's

Conspiracy to Murder Bill which brought down the latter's government in February 1858; once again, Gibson was supported by an odd coalition of radicals and tories.

It was at Gibson's house that were decided the tactics for the great meeting in Willis's Rooms on 6 June 1859, which brought together the elements of the Liberal Party. Palmerston, encouraged by Russell, invited Gibson and Cobden to join his government; Cobden declined, partly on the ground that Gibson 'represents entirely my views' (Steele, 119), and Gibson accepted, becoming president of the poor-law board, with a seat in the cabinet, and being almost at once transferred to his old department, the Board of Trade, as president. In cabinet he was one of three radicals, and more effective than the others, Villiers and Molesworth. Even so, Gibson's cabinet membership cramped his style, *The Times* remarking of one of his constituency speeches: 'There is not one syllable … that would lead an old lady to put down her tea cup and appeal to the higher powers' (Steele, 125). He formed his most effective combination not with his co-radicals, but with Gladstone. During Palmerston's government, Gladstone at the exchequer, rather than Gibson at the Board of Trade, was the driving force in the progress of free trade, and the establishment of a commercial department at the Foreign Office further reflected that department's partial decline, though Gibson and his department played some part in the commercial treaty with France of 1860 and the negotiation of reciprocity treaties with other continental countries. Gibson was a loyal ally of Gladstone over the question of retrenchment and military fortifications in the early 1860s. When the last of the 'taxes on knowledge' was repealed in October 1861, again more on the initiative of the exchequer than the Board of Trade, and after a battle with the Lords, Gibson was presented with gifts and a testimonial by his association; repeal of the taxes on knowledge was his chief political achievement.

Gibson retired with Russell's government in 1866. He had been unopposed in Ashton under Lyme since he was first elected in 1857, and in 1868, with a much extended franchise, he was easily defeated in what had become a marginal seat. He retired from politics, though remaining one of the most diligent of the public works loan commissioners, and devoted himself to his seat, Theberton House, Suffolk, and to yachting, being one of the leading amateurs of his day. He died on board his yacht, the *Resolute*, at Algiers on 25 February 1884 and was buried in Theberton churchyard on 13 March. Rich and landed as well as radical—he was a JP and deputy lieutenant for Suffolk—Gibson was a distinctive figure in the history of radicalism, his tradition maintained by persons such as Sir Wilfred Lawson.

H. C. G. MATTHEW

Sources *DNB* • *The Times* (26 Feb 1884) • *The Times* (13 March 1884) • J. Morley, *The life of Richard Cobden*, 2 vols. (1881) • M. Taylor, *The decline of British radicalism, 1847–1860* (1995) • E. D. Steele, *Palmerston and liberalism, 1855–1865* (1991) • J. B. Conacher, *The Aberdeen coalition, 1852–1855* (1968) • N. McCord, *The Anti-Corn Law League, 1838–1846* (1958) • Venn, *Alum. Cant.* • Burke, *Gen. GB* • A. Howe, *Free trade and liberal England, 1846–1946* (1997) • C. D. Collet, *History of the taxes on knowledge: their origin and repeal*, 2 vols. (1899) • Gladstone, *Diaries* • *CGPLA Eng. & Wales* (1884)

Archives Dorset RO, letter-book | BL, letters to John Bright, Add. MS 43388 • BL, corresp. with Richard Cobden, Add. MS 43662 • BL, corresp. with W. E. Gladstone, Add. MSS 44392–44783, *passim* • Bucks. RLSS, corresp. with first Baron Cottesloe • Bucks. RLSS, letters to duke of Somerset • PRO, corresp. with Lord John Russell, PRO 30/22 • U. Southampton L., letters to Lord Palmerston

Likenesses W. Holl, stipple, pubd 1842 (after J. Holmes), NPG • C. A. Du Val, watercolour drawing, 1843, NPG [*see illus.*] • S. Bellin, group portrait, mixed-method engraving, pubd 1850 (*The Anti Corn Law League*; after J. R. Herbert, 1847), BM, NPG • H. Daumier, lithograph cartoon, NPG; repro. in *Le Charivari* (25 Feb 1856) • Mayall, carte-de-visite, NPG • J. Phillip, group portrait, oils (*The House of Commons, 1860*), Palace of Westminster, London • S. W. Reynolds, mezzotint (after C. A. Duval), BM, NPG • W. Walker & Sons, photograph, NPG

Wealth at death £32,619 0s. 6d.: probate, 22 April 1884, *CGPLA Eng. & Wales*

Gibson, Walter (*b. c.***1645**, *d.* in or after **1717**), merchant and shipowner, was the eldest son of John Gibson (*d.* 1679), portioner of Newtoun (otherwise Overton or Overnewtoun), Lanarkshire. Walter Gibson's brothers John, Andrew, and Ninian were merchants, while another brother, James, was a ship's captain and agent in Amsterdam for the Company of Scotland Trading to Africa and the Indies during the first Darien expedition of 1698. He captained the *Rising Sun* on the second expedition of 1699 but after its failure in 1700 he perished with the ship during a hurricane off the coast of Charles Town. Walter Gibson became a merchant burgess and guild brother of Glasgow on 26 December 1670 as son-in-law of William Robertson (*d.* in or before 1670), merchant burgess, whose daughter Jonet (Janet) he had married. With the agreement of James VII and nomination of John Paterson, archbishop of Glasgow, he was 'elected' provost of Glasgow in January 1688, and in December that year was continued provost by royal instruction.

Gibson began as a malt maker but in the 1680s entered the more lucrative overseas trade. His interests were, at first, in herring, and he chartered Dutch ships to export fish to France, returning with wine, brandy, and salt. In addition, in April 1688, he acquired from the Royal Society of Fishing the valuable ten-year tack for duty charged on exported white fish and herring. He pioneered the smoking of red herrings in his smokeries at Gourock, his herrings being termed 'Glasgow magistrates'. By the late 1680s he had acquired three ships of his own and was also trading with Spain and Norway. He was also 'the first that brought [from Sweden] iron to Glasgow' (McUre, 207).

Gibson's involvement in Atlantic trade with Virginia and the West Indies was more dramatic and he joined other Glasgow merchants in evading the English navigation acts. In 1687 a cargo of sugar from the plantations was impounded for payment of customs as it appeared to be on a foreign ship. However, Gibson explained to the lords of exchequer that the false name *St Christopher* had been given to his own vessel, 'such a name being necessary, for other wayes all Scots shipps that trade to the plantations are confiscable' (NA Scot., warrants of exchequer, E 8.40).

He encouraged the Darien scheme but provided investment through his vessels and his brother, not as a subscriber to the Company of Scotland. In 1681 Gibson, having volunteered, was commissioned by the privy council to transport banished criminals and covenanters to America, and in 1684 transported at profit over thirty prisoners from the tolbooths of Edinburgh and Glasgow. He seems, however, to have been a religious pragmatist rather than an anti-covenanter, and counted presbyterians such as Henry Erskine, Lord Cardross, among his company and transported the emigrant Cardross to Carolina. None the less, Gibson's ambiguous religious position probably accounts for his removal as provost after the revolution of 1688.

Gibson and his wife had had several sons. He owned extensive property in and around Glasgow including the lands of Ballshagrie, Clayslopp, Whytinch, Hyndland, Partick, the fishings of Kelvin water, and the coalheughs of Camlauchie. Although apparently remaining wealthy, he was a prisoner in Glasgow tolbooth in 1708 after a dispute, dating back to 1695, over a debt of 5000 merks he owed to the burgh. Commercially combative, this has echoes of his bitter dispute with London merchants in 1690. Gibson's testament has not survived, and his date of death and place of burial are unknown, though he was alive in January 1717. A. J. MANN

Sources register of testaments, Glasgow, NA Scot., CC9.7/53–28/12/1728 • J. D. Marwick and R. Renwick, eds., *Extracts from the records of the burgh of Glasgow*, 6 vols., Scottish Burgh RS, 11–12, 16, 19, 23, 27 (1876–1909), vols. 3–4 • J. D. Marwick, ed., *Charters and other documents relating to the city of Glasgow*, 2 vols. in 3, Scottish Burgh RS, 14–15, 17 (1894–1906), 2.375, 402, 393, 396, 400, 634 • J. McUre, *A view of the city of Glasgow* (1736), 200–07 • J. R. Anderson, ed., *The burgesses and guild brethren of Glasgow, 1573–1750*, Scottish RS, 56 (1925), 189 • warrants of exchequer registers, NA Scot., E 8.38–41 • *Reg. PCS*, 3rd ser., vols. 7, 15 • *Journal of the Hon. John Erskine of Carnock*, ed. W. Macleod, Scottish History Society, 14 (1893), 69–72 • G. P. Insh, *The Company of Scotland trading to Africa and the Indies* (1932), 82–3 • G. P. Insh, *Scottish colonial schemes, 1620–1686* (1922), 278–9 • broadsides, tracts of Lord Fountainhall, NL Scot., Adv. Lib. AAA.77, fol. 54 • registers of deeds, NA Scot., RD 1675–1714

Gibson, Wilfrid Wilson (1878–1962), poet, was born on 2 October 1878 at Hexham, Northumberland, one of the younger children in the large family of John Pattison Gibson, chemist, of Hexham, an amateur archaeologist and photographer of note, and his wife, Elizabeth Judith Frances Walton. He was educated at private schools and by his half-sister, Elizabeth Cheyne Gibson, who wrote poetry and encouraged him in his wish to be a poet. He started writing in his early youth and, except for his war service, devoted his whole life to it. He never attended university. His early volumes of poetry were highly romantic. In *The Stonefolds* (1907) he first approached the central theme which characterizes his poetry: the lives of ordinary people. It was with *Daily Bread* (1910) that he achieved fame as the poet of the 'inarticulate poor'. After this, in some thirty books of verse-plays and long and short poems, he wrote of the poor of town and country in a plain idiom that reflected their plain speech; he spoke for and aroused sympathy for the northern people among whom he had grown up. He was admired by some of the best poets of his time—(Philip) Edward Thomas and Robert Frost, as well as Rupert Brooke.

In 1912 Gibson moved to London, which was crucial for his career, as he lived above Harold Monro's Poetry Bookshop and met John Middleton Murry and Katherine Mansfield, who introduced him to the patron Edward Marsh. Gibson became a contributor to Marsh's five volumes of *Georgian Poetry* (1912–22).

Through Marsh, Gibson met the young Rupert Brooke, and with him and others brought out the short-lived quarterly, *New Numbers*, which printed in December 1914 the 'War Sonnets' that made Brooke's reputation as a war poet. One result of this collaboration was that Brooke bequeathed to Gibson, Lascelles Abercrombie, and Walter de la Mare a third share each of his property, including the proceeds of his poems—which sold in unprecedented numbers in the decades following Brooke's death on the Greek island of Skyros in April 1915.

In 1915 Gibson married Geraldine Audrey Townshend (*d.* 1950), Monro's assistant in the Poetry Bookshop and daughter of Charles Uniacke Townshend, land agent, of Dublin. They moved to Gloucestershire soon after. Brooke's legacy enabled Gibson to live as a poet, never following another profession, although in later days his wife sometimes had to take in paying guests.

In the first years of the war Gibson made several attempts to enlist, but was turned down because of his poor eyesight. American enthusiasm for Brooke was partly reflected in an invitation to Gibson to lecture, and his US tour in 1917 was prolonged and successful. Macmillan, New York, published Gibson's *Collected Poems*. Also in 1917, he was accepted by the Army Service Corps, where he served until 1919. His writings of this time include the well-known war poem entitled 'Breakfast'. In this and 'The Return' he showed his compassion for the ordinary man and woman, and in 'The Lament' he wrote movingly of 'the heartbreak at the heart of things' (W. W. Gibson, *The Lament*).

Gibson's *Collected Poems* was published by Macmillan, London, in 1926, and this collection, based on twenty earlier books, is impressive for its variety, as well as for its length of nearly 800 pages. He published some fourteen more books—including four during the Second World War—with titles, like *The Alert* (1941), which showed his continued preoccupation with war.

After 1926 Gibson's literary standing fell: Robert Frost was concerned about it as early as 1928. He had built up his reputation as the spokesman for the inarticulate poor, and lived on into a time when a self-conscious working class preferred to speak for itself. He also tended to write too much and revise too little. Too many of his longer passages lack the liveliness of 'Hoops' (1914), or the sheer compulsion of 'Drove-road' (1917).

The Gibsons' marriage was a happy one, despite the tragic loss of their daughter Audrey in a landslide in Italy in 1939. They lived in Gloucestershire, in Pembrokeshire, and round about London, but never in Northumberland, the county that remained Gibson's inspiration. Geraldine

Gibson died in 1950, the year of Gibson's last book, *Within Four Walls*, and Gibson himself died at Holloway Sanatorium, Virginia Water, Surrey, on 26 May 1962. A second daughter, Jocelyn, survived him, as did a son, Michael, who published over thirty books, including some on his special subject, the history of roses.

R. N. CURREY, *rev.* SAYONI BASU

Sources *The Times* (28 May 1962) · M. Drabble, ed., *The Oxford companion to English literature*, 5th edn (1985)

Likenesses S. Schell, photograph, repro. in W. W. Gibson, *Collected poems* (1926), frontispiece

Wealth at death £10,401 6*s*. 0*d*.: probate, 4 Sept 1962, *CGPLA Eng. & Wales*

Gibson, William (*d.* 1542), judge and bishop, was the second son of Thomas Gibson of Durie in Fife. He was educated at the University of Glasgow, where he was incorporated in 1503 and graduated on 4 December 1507. He was elected bursar of the university in October 1507. Thereafter he evidently studied law at a university overseas.

By 1526, and probably in 1525, Gibson was appointed dean of Restalrig collegiate church near Leith. He did not always seem to have good relations with the prebendaries, for they later charged him with doctoring the text of a papal bull. He acted as a lord auditor of exchequer, certainly between 1527 and 1531, and as well as receiving a yearly fee of £10 for this work Gibson was granted an escheat worth £20 by the king in 1531. He seems to have maintained his links with the University of Glasgow. John Mair dedicated his *Octo libri physicorum* to Gibson and John Sproull, a colleague at Glasgow, and on 26 November 1529 Gibson was one of the subscribers of a testamentary donation to the university of the late Sir Archibald Calderwood, formerly its bursar. On 14 February 1531 Gibson was noted as being one of the fifteen spiritual lords of session, and his place on the bench was confirmed on 27 May 1532 at the foundation of the college of justice, when churchmen took up eight of the fifteen places on the session.

On 4 May 1540 James V petitioned the pope for Gibson's appointment as a suffragan to Cardinal David Beaton, with whom Gibson was closely associated. He was described by Beaton as being 'distinguished for knowledge of both laws and of theology as well as for his upright character' (Hay, 397). The pope was also asked to confirm Gibson in possession of the deanery of Restalrig, the rectory of Inverarity, and the vicarage of Gervock. On 16 July 1540 Gibson was accordingly provided to the titular see of Libaria and consecrated on 28 August 1541. He also became one of Beaton's vicars-general. Gibson does not appear on any surviving sederunt of the lords of session after May 1541, and he died on 7 July 1542. Details of his estate at death have not survived.

JOHN FINLAY

Sources manuscript register of testaments, NA Scot., commissary court of Edinburgh, C.C. 8 · manuscript books of sederunt, NA Scot., C.S. 1 · manuscript acts of the lords of council, NA Scot., C.S. 5 · manuscript acts of the lords of council and session, NA Scot., C.S. 6 · manuscript register of acts and decreets, NA Scot., C.S. 7 · register of deeds, NA Scot., RD1 · register house charters, NA Scot., RH6 · R. K. Hannay, ed., *Acts of the lords of council in public affairs, 1501–1554* (1932) · *APS, 1424–1567* · J. M. Thomson and others, eds., *Registrum magni sigilli regum Scotorum / The register of the great seal of Scotland*, 11 vols. (1882–1914), vol. 3 · M. Livingstone, D. Hay Fleming, and others, eds., *Registrum secreti sigilli regum Scotorum / The register of the privy seal of Scotland*, 1–2 (1908–21), vols. 1–2 · C. Innes, ed., *Munimenta alme Universitatis Glasguensis / Records of the University of Glasgow from its foundation till 1727*, 4 vols., Maitland Club, 72 (1854) · G. Brunton and D. Haig, *An historical account of the senators of the college of justice, from its institution in MDXXXII* (1832) · *LP Henry VIII*, vol. 15 · G. Donaldson, ed., *St Andrews formulare, 1514–1546*, Stair Society, 9 (1944) · D. E. R. Watt, ed., *Fasti ecclesiae Scoticanae medii aevi ad annum 1638*, [2nd edn], Scottish RS, new ser., 1 (1969) · M. H. B. Sanderson, *Cardinal of Scotland: David Beaton, c.1494–1546*, rev. edn (2000) · *The letters of James V*, ed. D. Hay (1954)

Gibson, William (1628/9–1684), Quaker leader, was born at Caton in Lancashire, but otherwise little is known of his background and parentage. During his early life he was a puritan and a soldier in the parliamentarian forces. While a member of the garrison at Carlisle he joined a party that went to abuse a Quaker meeting, but he was so attracted by the words of its preacher, Thomas Holme, that he attended other meetings and finally left the army.

In 1654 Gibson was committed to Lancaster gaol for the 'public testimony' he had proclaimed (Besse, 1.303). In 1655 and 1656 he was imprisoned for short periods on several occasions for the same offence, and is believed to have been recognized as a Quaker minister about this time. In 1660 he was again imprisoned at Lancaster for some months on account of his refusal to take the oaths of allegiance and supremacy, and in 1661 at Shrewsbury for some unknown cause. During the same year he was seized on the road near Stanton in Shropshire by a party of soldiers and sent to gaol with several other Quakers. They were all released at the assizes except for Gibson, who was kept in prison and cruelly treated by the gaolers; at one point he was thrown down a flight of stone steps, which caused him six months' illness. After being discharged he married Elizabeth Thompson (*d.* after 1683) of Crossmoor, Lancashire, in 1662, and they settled near Warrington, where he is believed to have engaged in trade. They appear to have had three children: John, William, and Patience.

Subsequently Gibson moved to London. In 1672 his name appears in a list of Quakers discharged from the king's bench prison under the general proclamation of Charles II. During 1676 and 1677, while living in Fenchurch Street, his goods were distrained several times for non-payment of tithes, and he was to suffer further losses of this kind in 1678, 1679, and 1682. In London Gibson played a prominent part in the centralized Quaker organization which began to develop in the 1670s. An important member of the meeting for sufferings, Gibson was a London correspondent for Lancashire, Cheshire, north Wales, and Ireland, and in May 1678 he and other leading Friends were appointed to speak to certain members of parliament on the issue of Quaker sufferings under the recusancy laws. He also played an important role in the second day morning meeting which was usually made up of London Quaker ministers. In 1675, for example, he was chosen to travel to the north with George Whitehead and other leading Friends in an attempt to sort out the Wilkinson–Story dispute. He also met frequently with William

Penn, Whitehead, and a few others to discuss the suitability of manuscripts for publication, and to edit and correct them.

Though not a prolific writer, Gibson nevertheless produced about nine tracts, a number of which were defences of Quakerism and of a theological nature, such as *A False Witness Examined and Rebuked* (1674) and *The Life of God* (1677), the latter an answer to the Anglican John Cheyney in which he outlines Quaker beliefs on the inner light, the church, ordinances, prayer, and scripture. His 1678 tract *Election and Reprobation* discusses the idea of universal salvation, and in this Gibson writes that Quakers 'deny that any man or woman is elect of God … without the sanctification of, or by the Spirit of Truth, and obedience unto it' (pp. 4–5).

In the early part of 1684 Gibson travelled to his native Lancashire, but on the return journey to London was taken ill at Coventry with an ague and fever. He managed to reach London, but died there some months later, aged fifty-five, on 23 November 1684. He was buried from a meeting in White Hart Court at the Quaker burial-ground, near Bunhill Fields, and his funeral was attended by over a thousand Quakers. His will, in which he described himself as a haberdasher, suggests that he was a man of some wealth for he bequeathed several hundred pounds to his wife and children as well as 500 acres of land in Pennsylvania.

A. C. Bickley, *rev.* Caroline L. Leachman

Sources J. Gough, *A history of the people called Quakers*, 4 vols. (1789–90), vol. 3 • D. Neal, *The history of the puritans or protestant nonconformists*, ed. J. Toulmin, new edn, 5 (1822) • J. Besse, *A collection of the sufferings of the people called Quakers*, 1 (1753) • C. L. Leachman, 'From an "unruly sect" to a society of "strict unity": the development of Quakerism in England, c.1650–1689', PhD diss., U. Lond., 1997 • J. Smith, ed., *A descriptive catalogue of Friends' books*, 1 (1867) • William Gibson's will, PRO, PROB 11/379, sig. 5, fols. 34*v*–35*v* • 'Dictionary of Quaker biography', RS Friends, Lond. [card index]
Archives RS Friends, Lond., portfolio MSS 16 and 17
Wealth at death £900; plus 500 acres of land in Pennsylvania: will, PRO, PROB 11/379, sig. 5

Gibson, William (1644–1703). *See under* Gibson, Richard (1605/1615?–1690).

Gibson, William (1719/20–1791), mathematician, was born at Bolton, near Appleby, Westmorland. He was orphaned early in life. Although his father was an agricultural labourer, the family was related to that of Edmund Gibson (1669–1748), bishop of London. After experience of farm work, Gibson rented a farm at Hollins, near Cartmel, Lancashire. Lacking all education, he taught himself to read an arithmetic book, and developed an extraordinary power of mental calculation, including computation of roots. He likewise taught himself to write, and studied all branches of mathematics, encompassing fluxions, spherical projection, astronomy, and navigation, becoming expert in all.

For many years Gibson sent in answers to all problems set in the *Gentleman's Diary*, the *Ladies' Diary*, and *The Palladium*; few were published, and then usually under other names. Even so, his fame spread, and he was consulted by mathematicians from various parts of the country and even from overseas. After living at a farm at Tarngreen for fifteen years Gibson finally settled at Blawith, east of Cartmel. He married probably some time in the early 1740s. In 1750 he opened a boarding-school for eight or ten pupils, also practising as a land surveyor and acting as inclosure commissioner. His many pupils studied accounting, surveying, and navigation, besides pure mathematics. John Barrow (1764–1848) was assisted by Gibson in his study of mathematics as a boy.

Gibson died as the result of a fall on 4 October 1791, aged seventy-one. His wife of nearly fifty years' standing and ten children survived him. A son of the same name, employed at the Bank of England, died at Pentonville on 13 February 1817.

[Anon.], *rev.* Ruth Wallis

Sources *GM*, 1st ser., 61 (1791), 1062–4 • F. W. Steer and others, *Dictionary of land surveyors and local map-makers of Great Britain and Ireland, 1530–1850*, ed. P. Eden, 2nd edn, ed. S. Bendall, 2 vols. (1997) • J. Barrow, *An auto-biographical memoir of Sir John Barrow* (1847) • A. Chalmers, ed., *The general biographical dictionary*, new edn, 15 (1814), 485–8

Gibson, William (1738–1821), vicar apostolic of the northern district, was born on 2 February 1738, the fifth son of Jasper Gibson (*d.* 1752) of Stonecroft Farm, Warden, Northumberland, and his wife, Margaret Leadbitter (*c.*1702–1777). Gibson entered the English College, Douai, in 1750. He taught three junior classes between 1757 and 1760 before beginning his own divinity course, financed by the Revell and Yates Fund. He was ordained priest in 1764, after only three of the usual four years' theology, so as to return home to assist his aged uncle, the Revd George Gibson, on the Tyneside mission. He went back to Douai at the end of the year, but a long illness following a skating accident prevented his completing the theology course, and he left in June 1765 to become chaplain to the Silvertop family at Minsteracres in Northumberland. He seems to have lived in London from 1775, though in what capacity is unknown.

Gibson's lack of academic distinction made him an unexpected choice to succeed Henry Tichborne Blount as sixteenth president of Douai College on 31 May 1781, but his exposure in the capital and the appointment of his elder brother Matthew *Gibson as vicar apostolic of the northern district in May 1780 may well have been advantageous. His administration was marked by a major refurbishment of the college fabric and a modernization of the syllabus, which drew high praise from the collegians, but many alumni in England deplored his extravagance, liberalizing tendencies, and snobbishness. Attempts to have him ousted failed and he held office until his election by *propaganda fide* on 19 July 1790 as vicar apostolic, in succession to his elder brother, despite opposition from the Catholic Committee and some priests who wished to establish their right to elect bishops.

Gibson was consecrated bishop of Acanthos *in partibus* at Lulworth Castle on 5 December 1790. He was immediately plunged into a fierce dispute between the bishops and the committee over the terms of the oath of allegiance to be embodied in the second Catholic Relief Bill, terms which would have taken the English Catholics into schism had the episcopal will not prevailed. He also had to deal with two consequences of the French Revolution in England: an influx of refugee French clergy and the repatriation of the exiled colleges and religious communities. The re-establishment of Douai College was the most problematic, and it revived the conflict between Gibson and the alumni. He procrastinated over its location and financing, and it was not until 2 October 1799 that an estate at Ushaw, co. Durham, was bought; however, the new college was still unfinished in July 1808 when the students moved in from their interim premises, Crook Hall, in north-west Durham. Gibson became autocratic and would accept no advice, but he presided over a substantial growth of the mission in his district, including the building of thirty new churches and numerous schools. He compiled a French grammar for use at Douai College, and published a translation, from the French of M. de Mahis, entitled *The Truth of the Catholic Religion Proved from the Holy Scriptures* (1799). *A Conversation between the Right Hon. Edmund Burke and the R R Dr Gibson*, in reference to the proposed government veto on the appointment of Catholic bishops, appeared at London in 1807. Gibson was also the author of a number of pastoral and other letters.

Gibson lived partly in York and partly in Durham and had a yearly salary of £200. He was continually gouty and suffered a stroke in 1798. When he hinted that he might ask for his younger brother Richard (1739–1801) to be his coadjutor, the Lancashire clergy told him that they would do all in their power to prevent it. Gibson desisted, but, though his health continued to deteriorate, he held out until 1807 before accepting the self-effacing and conciliatory missioner in Durham, Thomas Smith (1763–1831), his procurator at Douai and now his secretary, as coadjutor, but with no personal episcopal powers or freedom of action. The unrelenting opposition of many clerics and laymen after 1781 eradicated any progressive ideas from his mind, for, as Smith said, he became singularly averse to the introduction of novelties in religious matters and a strenuous advocate for ecclesiastical discipline. By 1819 Gibson had become so infirm and senile that his vicars-general petitioned for Smith to be given an independent mandate, but, before *propaganda fide* could accede, Gibson died at his residence, 33 Old Elvet, Durham, on 2 June 1821. He was buried at Ushaw College. LEO GOOCH

Sources Gillow, *Lit. biog. hist.* • B. Ward, *The dawn of the Catholic revival in England, 1781–1803*, 2 vols. (1909) • B. N. Ward, *The eve of Catholic emancipation*, 3 vols. (1911–12) • D. Milburn, *A history of Ushaw College* (1964), 1–121 • W. M. Brady, *The episcopal succession in England, Scotland, and Ireland, AD 1400 to 1875*, 3 (1877), 268–72 • L. Gooch, ed., *The revival of English Catholicism: the Banister–Rutter correspondence, 1777–1807* (1995) • G. Anstruther, *The seminary priests*, 4 (1977), 112 • P. R. Harris, ed., *Douai College documents, 1639–1794*, Catholic RS, 63 (1972) • J. Hodgson, *A history of Northumberland*, 3 pts in 7 vols. (1820–58)

Archives Leeds Roman Catholic diocesan archives, corresp. and papers • Northumbd RO, Hexham and Newcastle diocesan archives, corresp. and papers • Ushaw College, Durham, corresp. and papers • Westminster Roman Catholic diocesan archives, London

Likenesses W. M. Craig, portrait, repro. in *Catholic Miscellany* (Sept 1825) • J. Seal, oils, Ushaw College • Vowkes, lithograph (after W. M. Craig)

Wealth at death under £600; plus land in Hexham: Anstruther, *Seminary priests*

Gibson, William (1808–1867), minister of the Presbyterian Church in Ireland, was the only son of James Gibson, a merchant in Ballymena, co. Antrim, where he was born on 8 May 1808. He attended school in Ballymena and later at the Belfast Academical Institution, where he took the medal for classics in 1829. His collegiate training was obtained partly in Belfast and partly in Edinburgh. In 1833 he was licensed, and on 1 January 1834 was ordained minister of First Ballybay, co. Monaghan. In 1834 he married a daughter of Thomas Young of Ballymena and in 1842, presumably after the death of his first wife, he married a daughter of Joseph Cunningham of Crieve House, Monaghan. Further details of his wives and family are not known. On 2 November 1840 Gibson moved to Belfast to work with the Revd Samuel Hanna in Rosemary Street Church. In 1847 he was appointed professor of Christian ethics at the Presbyterian college, Belfast, a position which he retained until his sudden death in Dublin on 7 June 1867.

In 1835 Gibson contributed to the contemporary debate on the relations between the Presbyterian and established churches in Ireland with a widely circulated pamphlet entitled *The Position of the Church of Ireland and the Duty of Presbyterians in Reference to it*. Of more lasting significance, however, was his contribution to the establishment of the *Banner of Ulster*, a bi-weekly Presbyterian newspaper, which provided an important forum for the debate and dissemination of Presbyterian principles. In 1858 he visited the United States of America with a Presbyterian colleague, the Revd William McClure.

Gibson was moderator of the general assembly in 1859, the year of Ulster's great religious revival, and his major and best-remembered publication was his record of this event, *The Year of Grace: a History of the Ulster Revival of 1859*, which was written in response to a request from Boston for information on the revival and was published in Belfast in 1859. It immediately became an important source of reference, forming the basis of many subsequent histories of the revival. The book was heavily criticized by fellow Presbyterian Isaac Nelson in *The Year of Delusion* (1860), in which Nelson accused Gibson of exaggeration and inaccuracy. The second edition of *The Year of Grace* did indeed omit about 10 per cent of the original material, mostly that pertaining to the 'physical manifestations', which were the cause of much controversy and debate. Despite its faults, however, Gibson's work reflects the spirit of optimism and spiritual excitement which swept across most of Ulster in the summer of 1859, and as such is itself an important documentary source. The Gibson Chambers, a suite of dormitories in the Presbyterian college, was opened in his honour on 12 January 1869, two years after his death. MYRTLE HILL

Sources J. McConnell and others, eds., *Fasti of the Irish Presbyterian church, 1613–1840*, rev. S. G. McConnell, 2 vols. in 12 pts (1935–51) • *A*

history of congregations in the Presbyterian Church in Ireland, 1610–1982, Presbyterian Church in Ireland (1982) • A. R. Scott, 'The Ulster revival of 1859', PhD diss., TCD, 1962 • W. Gibson, *The year of grace: a history of the Ulster revival of 1859* (1859) • I. Nelson, *The year of delusion* (1860) • M. Hill, 'Assessing the awakening: the 1859 revival in Ulster', *Church and people in Britain and Scandinavia* [York 1995], ed. I. Brohed (1996)

Gibson, William Pettigrew (1902–1960), gallery curator, was born in Glasgow on 3 January 1902, the elder son of Edwin Arthur Gibson, a Scottish physician, and his wife, Ellen Shaw Pettigrew. He was educated at Westminster School and read natural sciences at Christ Church, Oxford, graduating in 1924 with a second in physiology. He was a contemporary and close friend of Humfry Payne, later director of the British School at Athens, and it was partly under his influence that Gibson abandoned plans for a medical career and turned to the study of the history of art. In 1927 he was appointed an assistant keeper of the Wallace Collection, London, and he remained there until 1936, when he became reader in the history of art in the University of London and deputy director of the Courtauld Institute of Art. In 1939 he was appointed keeper of the National Gallery under Sir Kenneth Clark, and he remained there for the rest of his life. In 1940 he married Christina Pamela, youngest daughter of Francis Ogilvy; they had no children. His wife's eldest sister had married Philip Hendy, Gibson's contemporary at Westminster and Christ Church, his predecessor at the Wallace Collection, and later his director at the National Gallery. The Gibsons settled soon after the war at Wyddiall Hall in north Hertfordshire, where Gibson took great delight in country pursuits, farming, and riding.

At the Wallace Collection Gibson was a good lecturer, and three of his lectures on French painting were published in 1930. He specialized in eighteenth-century French art, publishing occasional articles in art journals, including publications of the Vasari Society, and he prepared the catalogue *Miniatures and Illuminations* (1935) for the Wallace Collection. At the National Gallery during the Second World War he spent long periods on duty, and it was largely because of him that the buildings did not suffer more from incendiary bombs. In later years, under a new director, his experience was valuable; he was conscientious and exact in keeping before the board the rules of the National Gallery and the terms of the trusteeship, and his good manners, independence of judgement, and robust common sense lent weight to his advice. On what he considered a matter of principle he was determined, and could be obstinate.

Gibson was a tall, bulky man, of distinguished appearance, not athletic but physically very strong, having been an oarsman at Westminster and Christ Church. In personal relationships he was uncompromising, but most loyal to those who enjoyed his confidence and affection. A devout Catholic, Gibson died on 22 April 1960 in University College Hospital, London; his wife survived him.

James Byam Shaw, *rev.* Anne Pimlott Baker

Sources *The Times* (23 April 1960) • *WWW* • personal knowledge (1971) • private information (1971) • *CGPLA Eng. & Wales* (1960)

Wealth at death £26,366 12*s.* 2*d.*: probate, 30 June 1960, *CGPLA Eng. & Wales*

Gibson, William Sidney (1814–1871), writer, was born at Parson's Green, Fulham. He was for some years on the staff of a Carlisle newspaper. He entered Lincoln's Inn, and was called to the bar by that society in 1843. The previous year he had been appointed registrar of the Newcastle upon Tyne district court of bankruptcy. When the Bankruptcy Act of 1869 abolished this along with other similar courts, Gibson retired on a pension, and devoted himself to his literary pursuits.

By nature a recluse, Gibson's only local involvement seems to have been membership of the management committee of the homoeopathic dispensary at Newcastle. He spent his leisure writing articles on the ecclesiastical buildings of Northumberland and Cumberland, including an exhaustive monograph in two volumes on Tynemouth Priory (1846–7), still highly regarded. He also wrote for the *Quarterly Review*, *Colburn's New Monthly*, *Household Words*, *Notes and Queries*, the *Dublin Review*, *The Ecclesiologist*, *Chambers's Journal*, and *Bentley's Miscellany*; two collections of these articles were subsequently published in 1858 and 1863. In 1858 he was given an honorary MA by Durham University; he was also a fellow of the Society of Antiquaries of London, and many other learned societies.

Gibson died, unmarried, at the Grosvenor Hotel, London, on 3 January 1871. He was subsequently interred in the disused burial-ground of the Old Priory, Tynemouth, 'for which a special permission had been obtained from the Home Office during the lifetime of the deceased'.

Francis Watt, *rev.* C. M. Fraser

Sources R. Welford, *Men of mark 'twixt Tyne and Tweed*, 2 (1895), 286–92 • *New Monthly Magazine*, new ser., 148 (1871), 244 • *Solicitors' Journal*, 15 (1870–71), 200–01 • *N&Q*, 4th ser., 7 (1871), 48 • *N&Q*, 4th ser., 11 (1873), 28

Archives Oxf. U. Mus. NH, notes relating to Skipton Castle • U. Newcastle, Robinson L., letters to Sir Walter Trevelyan

Likenesses pen-and-ink sketch, repro. in Welford, *Men of mark*, 288

Wealth at death under £4000: administration, 30 Jan 1871, *CGPLA Eng. & Wales*

Giddy, Davies. *See* Gilbert, Davies (1767–1839).

Gideon, Samson (1699–1762), financier, was born in February 1699 at London Wall, in the City of London, the second son and one of five children of Rowland Gideon (or Abundiente) (*c.*1655–1722), a West India merchant of London Wall, and his second wife, Esther, the daughter of Domingo (Abraham) do Porto (*d.* 1690), a diamond buyer in Madras. He was circumcised on 5 March 1699. His grandparents were Jewish immigrants from Portugal and his father, who was born in Glückstadt, Denmark, lived first in Barbados, then in Boston, Massachusetts, Nevis in the West Indies, and finally London, where he was endenizened in 1679 and again in 1688. In 1697 he became a liveryman of the Painter–Stainers' Company and a freeman of the City of London.

Samson Gideon entered the Painter–Stainers' Company by patrimony and started in business on his own account as a general merchant in 1719, at the age of twenty, with a capital of £1500. In 1720 he contributed a commendatory English verse to Daniel Lopes Laguna's *Fiel espejo de la vida*; in that year he reckoned his fortune at £7900. He dealt in lottery tickets, but was not a significant holder of bank stock between 1719 and 1724. In September 1729 he bought one of the twelve broker's medals allowed to the Jewish community on the royal exchange and reckoned his fortune at that time to be £25,000. He underwrote insurance policies, made bottomry and respondentia loans (to be repaid on safe arrival of cargo) to the owners and officers of the East Indiamen, and occasionally imported rough diamonds from India. During the early eighteenth century many Portuguese Jews in the Netherlands became investors in the English funds, and Gideon formed investors' syndicates to subscribe for new issues of Treasury stock. In the early 1740s he married Jane (*d*. 1778), the daughter of Charles Ermell; they had two daughters and a son. Like their mother, their children were baptized and brought up as Anglicans. 'He breeds his children Christians', Horace Walpole wrote, correctly, in 1753 (Walpole, 35.178). Gideon never changed his own religion, but this marked the first step in his gradual alienation from the Jewish community.

In 1742 Gideon was consulted by Sir Robert Walpole and submitted a scheme, which was accepted, for raising £3 million at 3 per cent interest. He subscribed for £600,000 of the issue. In 1743 and 1744 his advice on the best method of floating an issue of Treasury stock was again sought, and followed, by Henry Pelham, the chancellor of the exchequer. In 1745 the East India Company voted him a fee of £200 for arranging the purchase of silver from Admiral George Anson. The initial successes of the Jacobite rising in that year so frightened the banker Thomas Snow that he wrote to ask for the immediate return of a £20,000 loan. Gideon sent him a bottle of smelling salts wrapped in twenty £1000 banknotes.

At this time the price of government stock collapsed, but Gideon underwrote new government loans and bought heavily while the stocks were still depressed. In consequence, with the defeat of the Jacobite rising and the recovery of the stock exchange, he doubled his fortune. In 1747 he received a grant of arms, and was also appointed bullion broker to the East India Company. By 1748 his fortune was worth about £156,000. In 1749 he got up a subscription in the City to give the aged and destitute Captain Coram of the Foundling Hospital a pension of 160 guineas a year. However, the most important service that he rendered to the government occurred in 1749–50, when he persuaded the South Sea Company, the East India Company, and the Bank of England to reduce the interest on their debt to 3 per cent in order to help Pelham to negotiate a reduction of the interest on government stock from 4 per cent to 3 per cent.

Gideon's ambition was to found a titled family. He bought estates at Spalding in Lincolnshire and at Erith in Kent, where his country home, Belvedere House, held his important collection of paintings, many from Sir Robert Walpole's collection at Houghton Hall. His own portrait was painted by Alan Ramsay. He was most annoyed when, in 1753, the agitation for the repeal of the Jews' Naturalization Act spoilt his plans. The act had been procured by Joseph Salvador, without consulting him, and led to his being pilloried in cartoons and in the press. He resigned his membership of the Bevis Marks Synagogue, but continued to subscribe to it anonymously. In 1754 he surrendered his Jews' broker's medal. In 1757 his daughter Elizabeth married the second Viscount Gage with a dowry of £40,000. His daughter Susannah (*d*. 1784) did not marry.

In 1758 Gideon wrote to the prime minister, the duke of Newcastle, listing his extensive services to the government and requesting a baronetcy. This was refused because of his religion. He modified the request the following year, and his son Sampson, then a schoolboy of fourteen at Tonbridge School, was made a baronet in May 1759, and then transferred to Eton College. In due course Sir Sampson Gideon, bt (1745–1821), inherited his father's estates, married Maria Marowe, the daughter of Sir John Eardley Wilmot, and was elected MP for Coventry. In 1789 he took the name and arms of Eardley and was granted an Irish peerage as Baron Eardley of Spalding. His coheirs were his three daughters, who married, respectively, the fourteenth Lord Saye and Sele, Sir Culling Smith, and J. W. Childers.

By the time of his death, from dropsy, on 17 October 1762 at Belvedere House, Samson Gideon's fortune was worth some £350,000, largely invested in land. Among other bequests, he left £1000 to the Spanish and Portuguese Jews' Congregation in London, on condition that they buried him with honour as a married man in their cemetery at Mile End; this was accordingly done. He left the residue of his estate to his descendants, and then, in default of heirs, to the duke of Devonshire, presumably because he was estranged from the families of his three sisters.

Gideon's command of the functioning of the financial market was unrivalled, but his rapid enrichment was resented. Horace Walpole complained that he was 'an engrosser' and unworthy of royal favour (Walpole, 16.42), but his reputation in the City for ability, integrity, and generosity was high. He was described as being 'of strong natural understanding, and of some fun and humour' (*DNB*). Gideon repeatedly gave the Treasury good service.

EDGAR SAMUEL

Sources L. S. Sutherland, 'Samson Gideon and the reduction of interest, 1749–70', *Economic History Review*, 16 (1946), 15–29 • L. S. Sutherland, 'Samson Gideon: eighteenth-century Jewish financier', *Transactions of the Jewish Historical Society of England*, 17 (1951–2), 79–90 • J. E. Wilmot, 'A memoir of the life of Samson Gideon', Nichols, *Illustrations*, vol. 6 • G. Yogev, *Diamonds and coral: Anglo-Dutch Jews and eighteenth-century trade* (1978) • R. D. Barnett and others, eds. and trans., *The circumcision register of Isaac and Abraham de Paiba, 1715–1775* (1991), suppl. no. 262 • *DNB* • J. Francis, *Chronicles and characters of the stock exchange* (1849) • J. A. Giuseppi, 'Early Jewish holders of Bank of England stock (1694–1725)', *Miscellanies of the Jewish Historical Society of England*, 6 (1962) • E. R. Samuel, 'The Jews in English foreign trade: a consideration of the *Philo Patriae* pamphlets of 1753', *Remember the days: essays on Anglo-Jewish history presented to Cecil Roth*, ed. J. M. Shaftesley (1966), 123–43 • W. S. Samuel, *A review of the Jewish colonists in Barbados in the year 1680* (1936) • Walpole, *Corr.*, 16.42; 35.178

Archives Beds. & Luton ARS • BL, corresp. with duke of Newcastle, etc., Add. MSS 32862–32938, 33055, *passim* • Lincs. Arch., papers regarding Bedford level estate
Likenesses cartoons, 1753 • A. Ramsay, portrait
Wealth at death approx. £350,000; largely invested in land; in 1759 he valued his estate after a fall in the stocks at £297,000: Wilmot, 'Memoir of the life of Sampson Gideon'

Gielgud, Sir (Arthur) John (1904–2000), actor and theatre director, was born on 14 April 1904 at 7 Gledhow Gardens, South Kensington, London, the third of the four children and youngest of three sons of Frank Henry Gielgud (1860–1949), stockbroker, and his second wife, Kate Terry Lewis (1868–1958), daughter of Arthur Lewis, director of the haberdashery firm Lewis and Allenby, and his wife, the actress Kate Terry. The actresses Dame Ellen Terry and Marion Terry were his great-aunts, and the actor Fred Terry was his great-uncle.

Family and education Also living at Gledhow Gardens when Gielgud was born were his two elder brothers, Lewis (1894–1953), later a senior official with the International League of Red Cross Societies and UNESCO, and Val Henry *Gielgud (1900–1981), later head of the BBC's radio drama department. At the time of Gielgud's birth his parents had been hoping for a daughter and, although on this occasion they were disappointed, three years later their last child, Eleanor (1907–1998), was born.

1904 also saw the birth of J. M. Barrie's *Peter Pan*, and it is tempting to see the real-life Gielguds as a counterpart to the Darling family—somewhat bohemian for the times, eccentric, often short of ready cash, but always extraordinarily theatrical and well connected. Although on his mother's side Gielgud came from what he called the 'Terry purple' of Victorian theatre, his father's family had been immigrants from Lithuania and Poland (the name Gielgud deriving from Gielgaudskis, a village in Lithuania), which is perhaps why Gielgud was in his early career among the first to introduce London audiences to such foreign playwrights as Chekhov, Maeterlinck, and Strindberg.

Gielgud's brother Val later wrote:

> The Terry family lay all about us in our infancy … [but] our parents looked distinctly sideways at the stage as a means of livelihood … What John possessed from the very beginning was singleness of heart and mind, together with a remarkable capacity for hard work. When he was not acting in the theatre, going to the theatre, or talking about the theatre, he was to all intents and purposes not living. (Morley, 9)

This obsessive love of the theatre showed itself early: a Christmas present of a toy theatre at the age of seven completely absorbed him, and with his brother Val he devised numerous plays. He later recalled vividly his first trip to the theatre—to see *Peter Pan*—and later visits with his great-aunt Ellen and others.

In 1912 Gielgud followed his elder brothers to Hillside preparatory school at Farncombe, near Godalming, Surrey. There he expanded his passion for the theatre, for both acting and scenic design. In his final year he, like his brothers, was head boy. He then went to Westminster School (1917–21), with opportunities to frequent Shaftesbury Avenue 'in time to touch the fringe of the great century of the theatre' (Gielgud, *Early Stages*, 46). Performing with the school's choir in Westminster Abbey also fed his sense of theatricality. Art and architecture were particular interests, and he developed a love for ballet, and for staging and scenery, possibly influenced by his second cousin Edward Gordon Craig, a notable designer and Ellen Terry's son by the architect Edward William Godwin.

Sir (Arthur) John Gielgud (1904–2000), by Howard Coster, 1935 [as Romeo, with Peggy Ashcroft as Juliet]

Early stages Forsaking possible careers as an architect or stage designer, Gielgud joined Lady Benson's private drama school on leaving Westminster in 1921. One of four boys in a class of thirty, he felt insecure about physical aspects of acting; Lady Benson said he walked 'like a cat with rickets' (Morley, 27). However, several amateur appearances were followed, in November 1921, by his professional, albeit inauspicious and unpaid, début as the Herald in Shakespeare's *Henry V* at the Old Vic, London, the theatre with which he was to have a lifelong association. More walk-on parts followed and a remarkable career was launched. His busy early years, influenced by numerous producers and actors, offered many and varied roles. Initially, 'the imaginative part of my playing came too easily, and the technical side was non-existent' (Gielgud, *Early Stages*, 63). His cousin Phyllis Neilson-Terry invited him to tour in J. B. Fagan's *The Wheel* (1922), as understudy and assistant stage manager and speaking a few lines. Then in 1923 he won a scholarship to the Royal Academy of Dramatic Art, London, where Claude Rains 'taught me a very great deal' (Morley, 32). Gielgud, the lead in its production of Barrie's *The Admirable Crichton*, impressed both the actor–manager Nigel Playfair, who cast him in two plays at the Regent Theatre, and Sybil Thorndike, an occasional teacher at the academy.

After a year at the Royal Academy of Dramatic Art Gielgud entered the real theatrical world in a Christmas season of Brandon Thomas's *Charley's Aunt* at the Comedy Theatre. He then joined J. B. Fagan's repertory company at the Oxford Playhouse; a tough apprenticeship of eighteen productions in twenty months, including works by European playwrights, boosted his confidence. His first successes included Valentine in Congreve's *Love for Love* (1924) and, especially, Trofimov in *The Cherry Orchard* (1925) by Chekhov, an author then little known in Britain but with whom Gielgud had a particular affinity. Between these two productions the manager Barry Jackson cast him as Romeo opposite Gwen Ffrangcon-Davies (a lifelong friend and frequent stage partner) at the Regent. Noël Coward chose him, partly because he could play the piano, as his understudy in his play *The Vortex*; Gielgud later played Nicky Lancaster, the drug-addicted son. His voice was becoming noticed, and success in Playfair's production of *The Cherry Orchard* at the Lyric Theatre, Hammersmith, in 1925 led to work for BBC radio, a medium he made his own for seventy years. He also made his film début, in *Who is the Man?* (1924), shortly before this.

'Intellectual theatre' was the poor relation of commercial theatre, but Gielgud sought opportunities in classical, foreign, even experimental roles, especially for numerous 'stage societies'. Performances in Chekhov's *The Seagull* (1925) and *Three Sisters* (1926) confirmed his reputation as an unequalled interpreter of Russian drama. The latter's renowned Russian director, Theodore (Komis) Komisarjevsky, taught him to study a part from the inside. Gielgud, now 'one of the most talked-about actors in town' (Morley, 43), again succeeded Coward, in Margaret Kennedy's *The Constant Nymph*, the hit of the 1926 season. With success he moved from home, leading a discreetly homosexual life; he found a partner, John Perry, an unsuccessful actor, later a playwright, who remained a lifelong friend and colleague. Although homosexuality conditioned Gielgud's life, his 'low-maintenance' partners did not interfere with his theatrical obsessions and ambitions.

Gielgud's New York début, in Alfred Neumann's *The Patriot* (1928), flopped, and back in London he was leading man in ten plays in eighteen months with scant success, despite acting with Mrs Patrick Campbell in Ibsen's *Ghosts*, and with Edith Evans and Ffrangcon-Davies in Reginald Berkeley's *The Lady with a Lamp* (1929). He also worked with the director Harley Granville-Barker, one of his 'greatest heroes', an important influence on his work and views. The elusive career-defining breakthrough eventually came when he was invited to the Old Vic by Harcourt Williams, recently appointed director of productions by Lilian Baylis. It was not the West End; it involved a cut in pay; but it was the place to learn Shakespearian technique and try new ideas. The fourth play, *Richard II*, was Gielgud's first undoubted triumph; 'many people felt that his interpretation of the role was the spearhead of a new kind of acting' (Brandreth, 32), taking Shakespeare out of the Victorian age with a style, less declamatory and frivolous than hitherto, which put up markers to the future. Singled out was his melodious verse speaking; Alec Guinness likened his voice to a 'silver trumpet muffled in silk' (Guinness, 66). His first Hamlet (1930), the youngest in memory, closed his first Old Vic season. Even the frequently acerbic critic James Agate expressed admiration.

Further success came at the Lyric, as John Worthing in Wilde's *The Importance of being Earnest* (1930) (a signature role, with *Richard II* and *Hamlet*), before Gielgud returned to the Old Vic as unchallenged, and influential, leading man—and matinée idol, despite a large nose and rapidly thinning hair. He played Hotspur to Ralph Richardson's Hal in *1 Henry IV* and Prospero to his Caliban in *The Tempest* (both 1930). Despite markedly different temperaments the two men complemented each other admirably, their friendship lasting fifty years. Gielgud had particular success as Benedick in *Much Ado about Nothing* (1931) but felt inadequate as Lear, his chosen farewell role. These seasons, characterized by teamwork, laid the foundations for his own companies.

Gielgud's first commercial success, in a long West End run, was as Inigo Jollifant in Priestley's *The Good Companions* (1931). He also played the role in a film version (1933), his third 'talkie'. Unlike Olivier, Richardson, and Redgrave, he felt he took years to learn the difference between stage and screen acting, and disliked the film-making process. Invited to direct *Romeo and Juliet* (1932) for the Oxford University Dramatic Society, Gielgud began another career. Peggy Ashcroft, another lifelong friend, played Juliet, and the Motley team of designers had a first opportunity; he subsequently worked with them on numerous productions, and was a crucial influence on their careers. A huge popular hit was *Richard of Bordeaux* by Gordon Daviot (Elizabeth Mackintosh) at the New Theatre (1932–4) and subsequently on tour (1934–5); his Richard II, a marvellous combination of vacillation, nobility, and embittered disillusion, took the town by storm.

The Hamlets … and Olivier Now a star with a large popular following, Gielgud played Hamlet at the New (1934) and directed; Agate felt it was 'Everest only half-scaled' (Morley, 113), but J. C. Trewin thought it 'the key Shakespearean revival of its period' (ibid.), and public acclaim was unanimous, the run of 155 performances bettered only by Henry Irving earlier and Richard Burton later. Seeking to direct as much as possible while preparing the next play could mean involvement in three plays simultaneously. At the New, Gielgud directed *Romeo and Juliet* (1935), alternating as Romeo and Mercutio with Laurence Olivier, whom he had given a classical chance in Daviot's *Queen of Scots* (1934). This was their sole stage appearance together. Gielgud's greater verse-speaking lyricism left Olivier feeling that victory was his rival's, perhaps causing perceived antagonism from Olivier throughout their careers, though Olivier's more masculine Romeo and his

Mercutio's greater dash and swagger drew excellent reviews. The play also made Ashcroft a major classical player and broke box-office records. During it Gielgud starred in Alfred Hitchcock's film *The Secret Agent* (1936), though he did not find this a particularly happy experience, self-consciously feeling that the camera identified his acting defects. Apart from *The Prime Minister* (1941), in which he played his only title role (as Disraeli), he made no more films until 1953. He did, though, readily embrace radio, performing new and classical work, encouraged by his brother Val; through the years he acted in over fifty plays and gave countless talks and poetry readings.

In 1936 Gielgud directed the Oxford University Dramatic Society in *Richard II*, and played Trigorin in Chekhov's *The Seagull*. The former began a deep lifelong friendship with Vivien Leigh; his acclaimed performance in the latter, the first Chekhov in the West End, was again directed by Komisarjevsky. Later that year his *Hamlet* opened in New York before Leslie Howard's version. Word of mouth overcame an initially cool reaction. Howard's reviews were poor and the 'battle of the Hamlets' was won. Gielgud was the toast of the town, and the production was moved from the Empire Theatre to the St James's Theatre to accommodate demand. The run took John Barrymore's record until broken by Richard Burton's in 1964.

Avoiding Hollywood, deciding against a film career at home, and during much debate about a national theatre, Gielgud formed a company to present a classical season (1937–8) at the Queen's Theatre: R. B. Sheridan's *The School for Scandal*, Chekhov's *Three Sisters*, and Shakespeare's *Richard II* and *The Merchant of Venice*. Happiest with Ashcroft as his leading lady, he gave chances to young talent while retaining veteran actors and notable directors. The season was mixed, although Michel Saint Denis's *Three Sisters* was memorable, and critics including Harold Hobson hailed the venture as a great achievement. Gielgud, as figurehead and driving force, was exhausted; but he was applauded for the courage of his conception, laying down the footprint for both the Royal Shakespeare Company and the National Theatre.

The war years Following the end of Gielgud's season at the Queen's, two commercial plays were put his way by Hugh (Binkie) Beaumont, who ran Tennents, the largest West End theatrical management. Beaumont promptly took over John Perry, although without acrimony, Perry becoming a partner at Tennents and remaining a close friend. In June 1939 Gielgud closed Henry Irving's Lyceum (due for demolition, but later reprieved) with a brief run of *Hamlet* before taking it, not without difficulty, to Elsinore itself. He then returned to *The Importance of being Earnest*, directing and playing John Worthing. With Edith Evans's definitive Lady Bracknell, it sold out through the summer of 1939. Interrupted by the outbreak of the Second World War, it returned, running into 1940.

After directing *The Beggar's Opera*, in which he briefly played (and sang) MacHeath during Michael Redgrave's loss of voice, Gielgud wanted something more serious for wartime London, and reopened the Old Vic with Shakespeare, with assistance from Harley Granville-Barker; critics were divided over his Lear, but his Prospero had greater maturity than in 1930. He then joined tours of military camps, using poems and extracts including lighter fare, for example from Coward's *Tonight at 8.30*, but usually ending with Henry V's Agincourt speech. These were very busy years for Gielgud, as actor and director, and included almost a year's touring with *Macbeth*, and entertaining troops in Gibraltar with ENSA. His revival of Congreve's *Love for Love* (1943) received rave reviews, but he turned down the film role of Shaw's Caesar opposite Vivien Leigh's Cleopatra, to his later regret. A Haymarket season for Beaumont included a Hamlet (1944) which many deemed his finest. John Webster's *The Duchess of Malfi* (1945) and the first major revival of *Lady Windermere's Fan* (1945) since Wilde's death were added to the season. But Olivier, with his film of *Henry V* (1944), and with Richardson at the Old Vic, was stealing much of Gielgud's thunder.

Uncertainty … and Stratford Through the autumn and winter of 1945–6 Gielgud toured the Middle and Far East with *Hamlet* and Coward's *Blithe Spirit*, again for ENSA, playing his last Hamlet in Cairo in February 1946. After the war he had doubts about the way forward, perhaps feeling that he had achieved the ambitions of youth; with the few new plays he was not good at sifting wheat from chaff. He revived old hits, albeit successfully, at home and in America. Although stimulated by New York's vibrant post-war theatrical scene, knighthoods for Richardson and Olivier dealt a blow to his pride. Success and mediocrity came equally. On Broadway he directed Judith Anderson to acclaim in Robinson Jeffers's adaptation of Euripides's *Medea* (1947), himself playing Jason. He declined a part in Terence Rattigan's *The Browning Version*, and there were directorial disappointments in London, but his reputation was re-established with his rescue of *The Heiress* (1949), Ruth and Augustus Goetz's adaptation of Henry James's novel *Washington Square*, and with *The Lady's not for Burning* (1949) by Christopher Fry. With Gielgud also playing Thomas Mendip, the latter made the London names of Richard Burton and Claire Bloom.

After directing a very successful *Much Ado about Nothing* at Stratford upon Avon, Gielgud was invited to the Shakespeare Memorial Theatre by Anthony Quayle, its resident director. The young director Peter Brook deconstructed certain of Gielgud's vocal and emotional effects, making him find a part's psychology and rely less on a magnificent voice, costumes, and sets. Breaking with his past, and reinventing Shakespeare for a public wanting more naturalism and fewer histrionics, Gielgud produced a stunning Angelo in *Measure for Measure* (1950), and developed confidence to proceed as the leading actor and director of Quayle's Stratford years. His Cassius in *Julius Caesar* (1950) was perhaps the performance of the season, his Lear deemed by both critics and audiences his best attempt at the role: the season broke all that theatre's records. Gielgud reunited with Brook to play Leontes in *The Winter's Tale* (1951) at the Phoenix Theatre, for the Festival of Britain.

He felt he was good in unsympathetic parts; here, his psychological approach produced the play's longest British run.

Hollywood success, London tragedy Gielgud did not make vast sums from his stage work, thanks to ties with Tennents. Offered the role of Cassius in Joseph L. Mankiewicz's *Julius Caesar* (1953) in Hollywood, he found a permanent agent, who relieved him from Beaumont's tight financial rein. The producer John Houseman wanted Gielgud, and also Marlon Brando after his triumph in *A Streetcar Named Desire*. Many studio technicians found their way to the supposedly closed set when Gielgud was working. Consensus was that Hollywood could do no better with Shakespeare. Gielgud enjoyed the California life (and its discreet homosexual community) for four months, though he was not tempted to stay. Back in London he took over management of the Lyric for a splendidly successful classical season (1952–3)—*Richard II*, Congreve's *The Way of the World*, and Otway's *Venice Preserv'd*—directing the first two and acting in the last two, as Mirabell and Jaffier, the last 'a dazzle of torment and nobility' (*The Guardian*). He was now what Kenneth Tynan called 'a theatrical possession, an inscription, a figurehead and a touchstone … the guarantee, rather than the product' (Morley, 231). The season was topped by a coronation knighthood (1953), which elicited a spontaneous declaration of affection from the audience at the theatre.

Then came the greatest tragedy. This was a time of official intolerance towards homosexuality, particularly suggestion of it on stage. Gielgud, usually most discreet regarding liaisons, was arrested about midnight on the evening of 20 October 1953 in Chelsea, and charged with soliciting. Fined in court the next day, he was told by the magistrate to 'see your doctor the moment you leave this court' (Morley, 246). A reporter recognized Gielgud's voice; it was soon front-page news. His company, especially Sybil Thorndike, proved solidly behind him, but felt as embarrassed as Gielgud himself. He bravely opened in Liverpool the following week, possibly owing to his brother Val's threat to Beaumont to 'out' those within his circle if Gielgud's position in the theatre were threatened. His first night entrance received a standing ovation. Fortunately his knighthood was safe, and a petition to eject him from Equity evaporated. It was, though, four years before he acted in America. With public opinion in his favour, newspapers soon left him alone. A few months later, however, he suffered a nervous breakdown, and he never thereafter spoke about the affair; nor did writers on Gielgud, such was their respect for him. He subsequently never gave public support to gay campaigns, but after his death it emerged that he had frequently given to gay charities.

Ups, downs … and heights Gielgud kept busy, directing revivals of *Charley's Aunt* (1953–4) and *The Cherry Orchard* (1954), and playing the disappointingly small role of Clarence in Olivier's film of *Richard III* (1954), before Quayle invited him back to Stratford to direct *Twelfth Night* (1955). This was a trying experience, not just because of an 'obstinate' Olivier's Malvolio, but also because Vivien Leigh was playing Viola, the Oliviers' marriage was crumbling, and Olivier resented Leigh's friendship with Gielgud. The latter, after playing *Much Ado about Nothing* and *King Lear* at the Palace Theatre, where *King Lear*'s Japanese sets and avant-garde music brought poor reviews, took both on a lengthy European tour. A big success directing Enid Bagnold's *The Chalk Garden* (1956) was balanced by disappointment as co-director and star of Coward's *Nude with Violin* (also 1956), but several modern plays enabled him to display new facets of his art. He had a cameo appearance in Mike Todd's film *Around the World in Eighty Days* (1956), was Mr Barrett in Sam Zimbalist's poor remake of *The Barretts of Wimpole Street* (1957), and directed an ambitious production of Berlioz's opera *The Trojans* (1957) at Covent Garden.

A great fillip came in 1957 at the Edinburgh Festival, with Gielgud's first presentation of George Rylands's Shakespeare anthology, *The Ages of Man*. For a decade this was the most successful solo Shakespeare show worldwide, and its Broadway triumph in 1958 won him a special Tony award. Attempts to find 'difficult' work still brought mixed results but Peter Shaffer's first play, *Five Finger Exercise* (1958), which Gielgud directed, received ecstatic reviews, winning him another Tony the following year. His American television début, in *The Browning Version* (1959), was deemed one of the performances of the year, even drawing praise from Olivier. His British television début, in N. C. Hunter's *A Day by the Sea* (also 1959), was less successful.

Although Gielgud's sister, Eleanor, had long been his secretary and gatekeeper, guarding his private life, he had by now met (Ferenc) Martin Hensler (1932–1999), a Hungarian exile and design manager. Hensler, a partner with expensive tastes, always encouraging Gielgud to work, could be extremely volatile and difficult, rarely fitting in with Gielgud's close friends. Yet their relationship lasted forty years, with Hensler looking after Gielgud and their home.

With his private life reorganized, Gielgud directed the first London performance of Britten's opera *A Midsummer Night's Dream* (1961) at Covent Garden, to considerable acclaim. Another Tony, for directing Hugh Wheeler's *Big Fish, Little Fish* (1961), was offset by Stratford failure in Franco Zeffirelli's *Othello* (also 1961). Gielgud found neither the jealousy nor the animal within the character; vocally and physically it was not his role. He bounced back with a memorable Gaev in *The Cherry Orchard* in Saint-Denis's Aldwych Theatre production (1961), and directed Richardson in *The School for Scandal* at the Haymarket Theatre (1962), himself playing Joseph Surface. On screen he won an Oscar nomination as Louis VII in *Becket* (1964), from Jean Anouilh's play. A minor but flashy role, this had considerable and long-lasting importance; his unrivalled theatrical dignity could greatly enhance a film. This was fortunate: with Olivier, at Chichester, soon to form the National Theatre, Shakespeare at Stratford moving towards realism and youth, and the West End shell-shocked by the revolution in theatrical tastes pioneered by the Royal Court Theatre, Gielgud was essentially now a jobbing actor. *Becket*'s star, Richard Burton, asked Gielgud to direct his modern-dress *Hamlet* on Broadway (1964). Burton had triumphed as Hamlet at the Old Vic (1953). He was a handful to direct, and had married Elizabeth Taylor during the pre-Broadway tour. But through the Burton–Taylor hysteria Gielgud kept *Hamlet* on the rails and it broke numerous records.

New directions Gielgud's subsequent work was mixed. Following the movie adventure of playing Henry IV in Orson Welles's Falstaff anthology, *Chimes at Midnight* (1966), his Mock Turtle in Jonathan Miller's *Alice in Wonderland* for television (1966) revealed a late-life talent for eccentric comedy. He began to establish himself in relatively minor but telling film roles. One of his best was his gently eccentric Lord Raglan in *The Charge of the Light Brigade* (1968). More frequently, film and television roles, sometimes not wisely chosen but often on foreign location, offered a mixture of companionship, egos, gossip, and loyalty, the things he missed from a theatre company.

At last came an invitation to the National, for a sequence of three productions in 1967–8. Nevertheless Olivier, who was unwell, could not co-star in Ibsen's *The Pretenders*, which was abandoned, and Molière's *Tartuffe* (1967), with Gielgud as Orgon, and Seneca's *Oedipus* (1968), directed by Peter Brook, were disappointing. Well-paid film cameos compensated, before his final opera, Mozart's *Don Giovanni* (1968), at the Coliseum, a 'terrible failure', despite set design by Derek Jarman. Then came a huge success as the headmaster in Alan Bennett's first play, *Forty Years On* (1968). In this work, based on an end-of-term play at a minor public school, Gielgud encountered a new world of satirical comedy. The lengthy run to capacity houses revitalized and redefined his late-life career. He and Hensler, wishing to leave London, moved to a country house, South Pavilion, at Wotton Underwood, near Aylesbury. His two worlds, of work and home, were kept separate, the latter virtually undisturbed. The need to finance the restoration of South Pavilion led to work on fifteen films in the 1970s including unwise remakes, telling co-starring roles, and Alain Resnais's 'muddled drama' *Providence* (1977); his roaring, randy, drunken, foul-mouthed, dying novelist Clive Langham in the latter won him the New York critics' award for best actor.

For some years Gielgud had been largely away from the London stage, aloof from the new movements, and to some now seeming overly traditional. But he reinvented himself, joining what he could not beat. The Royal Court was another world for him, but he bravely adapted to a new generation of writers and directors, and was inspired to a new style and by new challenges. David Storey's *Home* (1970), directed by Lindsay Anderson, reuniting Gielgud and Richardson as elderly inmates of a mental home, was a triumph for all, as it was when it moved to Broadway. He made his début at the Chichester Festival, as Caesar in Shaw's *Caesar and Cleopatra* (1971). The production was possibly too modern, and drew only average reviews, but he won the bulk of praise for Charles Wood's *Veterans* (1972) at the Royal Court. As a gossipy old actor–knight, getting his way with lethal charm, he gently parodied himself. He was fired (the only time in his career) from directing Debbie Reynolds's musical *Irene*, but had great success directing Coward's *Private Lives*, both in London (1972) and in America (1974). Pinero's *The Gay Lord Quex* (1975) was an ordinary end to his directorial career.

After Olivier left the National, Gielgud inaugurated Peter Hall's directorship, returning to a major Shakespeare role (Prospero) after sixteen years (1974). He played Shakespeare himself at the Royal Court in Edward Bond's *Bingo* (also 1974). He and Richardson again teamed up at the Old Vic for Harold Pinter's *No Man's Land* (1975), the last high-water mark of both their stage careers: Gielgud played Spooner, a seedy, garrulous, failed poet in what he later described as his happiest theatrical experience, effectively a year-long run before similar triumph in New York.

'Grand old man' Of Gielgud's three 'farewell' performances at the National, that as Sir Noël Cunliffe in Julian Mitchell's *Half-Life* (1977) drew the highest praise; he reprised the role at the Duke of York's Theatre in 1978 and on tour the following year, but no other stage role followed until 1988. Nevertheless film and television work flowed, including his most embarrassing professional appearance, in Playboy's film of Gore Vidal's *Caligula* (1979). Even then he was one of few involved who escaped relatively unmauled. He never left radio work for long, and a lengthy project covered every facet of his professional career. Among over twenty films in the 1980s, *The Elephant Man* (1980), *Chariots of Fire* and *Arthur* (both 1981), *Gandhi* (1983), *The Shooting Party* (1984), and *Plenty* (1985) were noteworthy. Gielgud could separate his reputation from the poorer films in which he appeared; he had little shame, believing, rightly, that poor reviews would not affect his stage career. For him, film was not a serious art form. With small roles, often shining in unpleasant ones, his presence frequently lent moments of charm and distinction to scripts little meriting them.

One film, *Arthur*, was an unexpected but total triumph, winning Gielgud an Oscar as supporting actor and other awards for his Hobson, the acid-tongued butler to the spoiled millionaire Arthur (played by Dudley Moore). Hollywood offered another lucrative butler role, in television commercials for Californian wines. Back in England, on a wave of success, he played Edward Ryder in John Mortimer's television adaptation of Evelyn Waugh's *Brideshead Revisited* (1982). His decision to take the role was a wise choice; Olivier had turned it down to play Lord Marchmain in the same series, but Gielgud won the plaudits. His choices were not always wise. Appearing with Olivier and Richardson in the mini-series *Wagner* (1983) was not a particularly happy experience, and he was incongruously dressed as a Hell's Angel in the film *Scandalous* (1983). Yet just after his eightieth birthday his recording of *The Ages of Man* won him a Grammy for the year's best spoken-word recording; he was the first non-American to receive this award. He remained a workaholic, for tax reasons and in order to vary the seclusion at home with Hensler. He ignored his age, thinking work might disappear should he stop. In 1985 he was awarded a special Olivier award for services to the theatre. As the 'grand old man', the living history of British theatre in his century, he was in demand for scholarly and archival projects, including obituaries as he began, through sheer longevity, to outlive many old friends.

Gielgud's final West End role, at the Apollo Theatre, was that of Sir Sydney Cockerell in Hugh Whitemore's *The Best of Friends* (1988). It was a gem, the production selling out as audiences anticipated his farewell stage performance. As Haverford Dawes in John Mortimer's television serial *Summer's Lease* (1989) he took the honours again, winning an Emmy. In 1991 came his last major film appearance. Having long wanted to film *The Tempest*, he now starred in *Prospero's Books* (1990), Peter Greenaway's daring adaptation of the play, speaking almost all the dialogue. Reviews were mixed but, as Greenaway said, 'whatever else is going on in the film, it is always Gielgud you watch' (Morley, 432). With roles finally dwindling he made guest appearances, of just a few days' shooting, in episodes of television series. His final films included Kenneth Branagh's *Hamlet*, *Dragonheart* (providing the voice of King Arthur), and *Shine* (as the doctrinaire piano teacher) (all 1996); and in *Elizabeth* (1999) there were still traces of the Gielgud magic. For Branagh he played his last Lear as BBC Radio 3 celebrated his ninetieth birthday, and he played St John Clarke in the television adaptation of Anthony Powell's *A Dance to the Music of Time* (1997) on television. He was also much in demand for the new medium of audio books.

Numerous honours came to Gielgud from the world of arts: the Theatre Museum, which he had long advocated, opened in Covent Garden, containing a Gielgud gallery; the Royal Academy of Dramatic Art, of which he was president from 1977 to 1989, made him its first honorary fellow; and in 1996 he was appointed to the Order of Merit (having already been made a Companion of Honour in 1977). When Shakespeare's Globe Theatre opened in 1995, the Globe in Shaftesbury Avenue was renamed the Gielgud—prompting him to remark that 'at last there is a name in lights on the Avenue which I actually recognise, even if it is my own' (personal knowledge). Occasionally he entertained Queen Elizabeth, the queen mother, and select guests with readings at Windsor; and notable actors used his *Ages of Man* recording as a masterclass.

Martin Hensler, Gielgud's companion of forty years, died of cancer in February 1999, and though theirs had been a volatile relationship Gielgud for a time seemed to lose his own will to live. But then, as so often, he rallied and decided to fire his agent in the hope of replacing him with one who could find him better employment. There was a role in a film of Beckett's short play *Catastrophe* (2000), and an interview for a BBC series on the theatre. He died peacefully at his home in Wotton Underwood, of cardiorespiratory failure, on 21 May 2000. Theatre lights were dimmed in the West End, and many leading players paid tributes in curtain speeches. He was cremated in Oxford; at his own request, there was no memorial service.

Assessment Gielgud was born into the most remarkable generation of classical actors in history. If Olivier was the soldier of that generation and Richardson its common man, Gielgud was its high priest. For him acting, guided by instincts and emotions, permitted a release which natural shyness did not allow. As both actor and director he displayed near-legendary inventiveness, seeking quality with intelligence and curiosity. He stressed the importance of a permanent ensemble, and became the age's greatest interpreter of Shakespeare with elegant style and inimitable clarity: Lee Strasberg said that 'when Gielgud speaks a line you can hear Shakespeare thinking' (Morley, 443). He also made a great mark in high comedy, having a sure feel for the Restoration period. Ever a keen pupil, he learned from success and failure alike and, reluctant to have a single off-stage hour, rushed on to new projects. Beneath the style and splendour was a radical vision. He was often at the centre of theatrical change. His enthusiasm for the theatre never diminished: it was 'more than an occupation or a profession; for me it has been a life' (Gielgud, *An Actor and his Time*, 220). Setting little store by his own reputation, he impressed all with his modesty and self-criticism. In his career as director of some ninety productions, what sometimes seemed to be indecision or constant change was more likely a quicksilver mind, brimming with ideas, reaching overload. He gave opportunities to many: the actors Michael Redgrave, Alec Guinness, and Paul Scofield, the designers the Motleys and Cecil Beaton, and the director Derek Jarman all owed a great deal to his early support. Passionate about design, ever striving for what worked best on stage, he always put the play before himself.

Gielgud lacked worldliness, but had a natural sense of humour, even mischievousness, loving to entertain verbally at parties. He was an incorrigible gossip (though never malicious) and famous for 'dropping bricks'; he once said to Elizabeth Taylor, about the Richard Burton he had discovered and she had married, 'I don't know what's happened to him—they say he has run off with some terrible movie star and lives in Hollywood' (private information). He 'strode, poker-backed, immaculately dressed, witty, generous and endearing, through thousands of private lives' (*The Guardian*). Respect and affection were his in equal proportion, as much for who he was as for what he achieved. His writings, on his life and on the theatre, including *Early Stages* (1939), *Distinguished Company* (1972), *An Actor and his Time* (1979), and *Backward Glances* (1989), added a wealth of information on the development of modern British theatre, to which his own magical presence had contributed so much.

Sheridan Morley and Robert Sharp

Sources S. Morley, *John G: the authorised biography of John Gielgud* (2001) • J. Croall, *Gielgud: a theatrical life* (2000) • R. Hayman, *John Gielgud* (1971) • G. Brandreth, *John Gielgud: a celebration* (1984) • J. Gielgud and others, *An actor and his time* (1979) • I. Herbert, ed., *Who's who in the theatre*, 1 (1981) • A. Guinness, *Blessings in disguise* (1985) • J. Gielgud, *Distinguished company* (1972) • R. Harwood, ed., *The ages of*

Gielgud: an actor at eighty (1984) • G. O'Connor, *Ralph Richardson* (1982) • www.uk.imdb.com, 28 Jan 2002 • J. Gielgud, *Early stages*, rev. edn (1953) • *The Times* (23 May 2000) • *The Guardian* (23 May 2000) • *The Independent* (23 May 2000) • *Daily Telegraph* (23 May 2000) • personal knowledge (2004) • private information (2004) • b. cert. • d. cert.

Archives BL, papers, Dep. 10007 • PRO, papers relating to his company's tour to Canada | Georgetown University, Washington, DC, letters to Elizabeth Jennings • King's AC Cam., corresp. with G. H. W. Rylands • NL Wales, corresp. with Emlyn Williams • Theatre Museum, London, corresp. with Christopher Fry • U. Reading L., corresp. with Edward Thompson of Heinemann | FILM BFI NFTVA, Omnibus, BBC 2, 12 April 1994 • BFI NFTVA, documentary footage • BFI NFTVA, performance recordings | SOUND BL NSA, documentary recordings • BL NSA, performance recordings

Likenesses L. Knight, charcoal sketch, 1924 (as Romeo), repro. in Croall, *Gielgud*, pl. 8 • caricature, 1927 (as Cassio), repro. in J. Gielgud and J. Miller, *Shakespeare: hit or miss?* (1991), following p. 52 • woodcut, 1929 (as Richard II), repro. in J. Gielgud and J. Miller, *Shakespeare: hit or miss?* (1991), following p. 52 • P. Lloyd, woodcut, 1930 (as Prospero), repro. in J. Gielgud and J. Miller, *Shakespeare: hit or miss?* (1991), following p. 52 • Y. Gregory, bromide print, 1930–39, NPG • Y. Gregory, bromide print, 1933, NPG • H. Coster, photograph, 1935, NPG [*see illus.*] • C. van Vechten, vintage print, 1936, NPG • A. McBean, photograph, 1959, NPG • A. Newman, bromide print, 1978, NPG • D. Remfry, oils, 1984, NPG • J. Swannell, Iris print, 1991, NPG • G. Adams, bromide print, NPG • C. Francis, caricature, repro. in Guinness, *Blessings in disguise*, following p. 130 • C. Francis, caricature (as John Worthing), repro. in J. Gielgud, *Stage directions*, new edn (1964), cover • R. Furse, caricature, repro. in J. Gielgud and J. Miller, *Shakespeare: hit or miss?* (1991), following p. 116 • D. Hockney, line drawing, repro. in Brandreth, *John Gielgud*, cover • photographs, repro. in Morley, *John G* • photographs, repro. in Croall, *Gielgud* • photographs, Hult. Arch.

Wealth at death £1,477,626—gross; £1,468,451—net: probate, 24 Oct 2000, *CGPLA Eng. & Wales*

Gielgud, Val Henry (1900–1981), radio executive and author, was born on 28 April 1900 at 36 Earls Court Square, South Kensington, London, the second of the four children and second of three sons of Frank Henry Gielgud (1860–1949), a stockbroker of Polish descent, and his wife, Kate Terry (1868–1958), daughter of Arthur Lewis. The family influences were strong. His Polish forebears, some of whom had been soldiers, had a romantic fascination for him and awakened his lasting passion for military history. From both his father and his mother, who was daughter of the actress Kate Terry and niece of Dame Ellen *Terry, he acquired a love of the theatre.

Though not such a scholar as his admired elder brother, Lewis (1894–1953), Val Gielgud was always a voracious reader and began early to write himself. In 1918 he went from Rugby School to the household brigade officers' cadet battalion. At the end of the war he took up a history scholarship at Trinity College, Oxford, where he 'read … talked and … began to learn how to think' (Gielgud, *Years of the Locust*, 26). He also directed some drama, but left after three years without taking his degree.

From 1921 to 1928 Gielgud worked briefly in various jobs before following his younger brother (Arthur) John *Gielgud (1904–2000) into acting. It amused him to say that while his brother had become arguably the best actor in Britain, he himself had undoubtedly been the worst. The claim reflected both his natural modesty and his excellent judgement. Throughout this period he continued to

Val Henry Gielgud (1900–1981), by Yvonne Gregory, 1930s

write, following a precept given to him by Michael Sadleir: that good fiction depended upon telling a good story. He wrote entertainingly for the rest of his life: over twenty novels, seven volumes of autobiography and essays, and eighteen plays and screenplays. Yet writing was never his primary occupation.

In May 1928 Gielgud's friend Eric Maschwitz, then editor of the *Radio Times*, invited him into the BBC as his assistant. The job was not arduous, and left time for such activities as an amateur production of a play by Ian Hay, *Tilly of Bloomsbury*, with Sir John Reith, the BBC's director-general, playing a drunken broker's man. Less than a year later, at the beginning of 1929, Gielgud was appointed director of productions, in succession to R. E. Jeffrey, with responsibility for all drama and variety.

It was a bold and unexpected appointment but it was inspired. Gielgud shared some of Reith's characteristics: vision, enthusiasm, and commitment to quality. He took over a small but diverse department with an annual output including only about twenty plays. Thirty-four years later, despite competition from television, he handed to his successor, Martin Esslin, the largest radio drama department in the world, with an output of over a thousand productions a year.

During those years Gielgud was widely involved in broadcasting and in the lively discussion that always surrounds it. His policy for drama was not only formative for radio but pioneered much that was later found on television. He fought, and won, the battle for drama of varying length, maintaining that plays should always be special events in the schedule. He made the serialization of classic novels one of the staple ingredients of broadcasting. He started series of popular plays, such as those heard on *Saturday Night Theatre* from 1943, which ran continuously to a cumulative audience of billions. In presenting the widest range of plays from all over the world, he could justly claim to have run a true national theatre long before there was one for the stage.

Like most pioneers Gielgud was often attacked for going too far or too fast, but he valiantly defended what he believed to be good. In 1941 his production of *The Man Born to be King*, by Dorothy L. Sayers, was almost prevented from reaching the air, but became one of radio's most triumphant and popular successes. Ten years later a parliamentary row over his own play *Party Manners* helped to reinforce the BBC's independence from direct political pressure.

Gielgud had taken part in early experiments with television yet, sadly, his period running television drama from 1949 to 1951 was not a success. He returned to radio, heading a lively department and producing many plays, until he retired in 1963. Like many shy people, Gielgud was sometimes mistaken for an autocrat. In fact, though firm in his beliefs, he often accepted the enthusiasm of others for work in which he saw little merit; honest to a fault, he would later take no credit for what he had allowed to happen. His achievements enriched the life of the country during a critical and formative period. He was appointed OBE in 1942 and CBE in 1958.

On 12 August 1921 Gielgud married Nathalie Mamontoff (*b.* 1902/3), daughter of Sergai Mamontoff, pianist; the marriage was dissolved in 1925. In 1928 he married the actress Barbara Dillon, daughter of Herbert Druce, actor. They had one son, Gielgud's only child. This marriage was dissolved and in 1946 he married Rita Vale, daughter of Samuel Weill, lawyer. After this marriage was dissolved, in 1955 he married Monica Joyce, daughter of Arthur Hammett Grey, company director of a Birmingham store. The marriage was dissolved in 1960 and in the same year he married (Vivienne) June (Judy), daughter of John Bailey, farmer.

Gielgud's retirement gave him more time to write and to travel, to watch polo, and to enjoy the company of his cats and many friends at the house near Lewes in Sussex to which he and his fifth wife moved from London in 1963. Gielgud died on 30 November 1981 at Springfield Nursing Home, 17 Prideaux Road, Eastbourne. His last wife survived him. RICHARD IMISON, *rev.*

Sources V. Gielgud, *Years of the locust* (1947) · V. Gielgud, *One year of grace* (1950) · personal knowledge (1990) · private information (1990) · *The Times* (1 Dec 1981) · *CGPLA Eng. & Wales* (1982) · A. Briggs, *The history of broadcasting in the United Kingdom*, 4 vols. (1961–79) · b. cert. · m. cert., 1921 · d. cert.

Archives FILM BFI NFTVA, documentary footage · BFI NFTVA, performance footage | SOUND BL NSA, documentary recordings · BL NSA, oral history interview · BL NSA, performance recordings · IWM SA, oral history interview

Likenesses Y. Gregory, photograph, 1930–39, NPG [*see illus.*]

Wealth at death £66,882: probate, 5 March 1982, *CGPLA Eng. & Wales*

Giesecke, Charles Lewis [*formerly* Johann Georg Metzler] (**1761–1833**), mineralogist and mineral dealer, was born on 6 April 1761 in Augsburg, Bavaria, the eldest surviving son of the six children of Georg Melchior Metzler (*d.* 1805), a protestant tailor, and his wife, Sibylla Magdalena Götz (1735–1794). Originally intended for the church, he studied at Göttingen from 1781 to 1783, but there his interests shifted to the law and to mineralogy, which science he pursued under Johann Friedrich Blumenbach (1752–1840). As a young man he had strong theatrical interests, writing plays and librettos, and himself performing. In 1781 he for some reason changed his name to Karl Ludwig Giesecke, and as such edited the *Regensburger Theater-Journal* between 1784 and 1786.

During the 1780s Giesecke resided in various south German towns and late in that decade he became established in Vienna, where he was associated with the theatre company of Emanuel Johann Schikaneder (1751–1812). For the company he prepared translations of foreign works, and he wrote the libretto for *Oberon der Elfenkönig*, staged in Vienna in 1790 with a musical score by Paul Wranitsky (1756–1808). In 1791 he took a minor role in *Die Zauberflöte* (*The Magic Flute*), and he evidently co-operated with Schikaneder and others in the writing of that opera's libretto. It has been reported that in 1817 he laid verbal claim to authorship of the entire libretto, but this was probably either braggadocio on Giesecke's part or else the false recollection of a conversation on the part of his auditor. In Vienna he, like Mozart, was an enthusiastic freemason.

The final decade of the eighteenth century saw Giesecke turn increasingly away from the stage and towards mineralogy. In 1801 he studied the science in Berlin and at Freiberg, he collected minerals widely in northern Europe, and he established a reputation as a mineral dealer and tutor in mineralogy. He collected in the Faeroes during August and September 1805, and in the following year the Danish government commissioned him to collect in Greenland. There he remained from May 1806 until the late summer of 1813. During his absence from Copenhagen his possessions there were destroyed in a fire following upon the British naval bombardment of September 1807.

Giesecke was a pioneer of the scientific study of Greenland, where he collected minerals, organic specimens, and ethnographical items. A Danish ship carrying some of the earliest of his Greenland materials became a British prize-of-war. She was taken into Leith, where his collection was sold in 1808, many of his specimens passing into the hands of the Scottish mineralogist Thomas Allan. In October 1813 Giesecke himself arrived in Leith. There he was befriended by Allan, and his portrait was painted by Henry Raeburn. He became a candidate for the vacant chair of mineralogy at the Dublin Society, and with Allan's help was elected, on 21 January 1814; he remained its occupant until the end of his life.

Giesecke's election is surprising. He confessed that, as yet, he lacked the ability to lecture in English, and in Robert Bakewell and Thomas Weaver the society would seem to have had two somewhat better qualified candidates.

The appointment smacks of partiality, and suggests the possibility that he may here have secured Irish benefit from his earlier association with Viennese freemasonry. Alternatively, it has been suggested that the society had purchased some of Giesecke's minerals at the Leith sale and was now anxious to offer him some redress for his lost collections.

Giesecke's relationship with the Dublin Society (it assumed the style Royal in June 1820) speedily became most cordial. In May 1817 the society presented him with a gold medal by William Stephen Mossop; that same year the society received the gift of his Raeburn portrait (a painting still in its possession); and Giesecke was allowed to spend the period from July 1817 until the autumn of 1819 travelling in Europe, among the fruits of which excursion was a mineral collection which he sent to Goethe in May 1819. His duties with the society were threefold. He delivered courses of lectures in mineralogy; he was responsible for its important mineral collection; and he conducted mineralogical surveys on its behalf. He investigated counties Galway and Mayo (1825), Donegal (1826), Antrim, Down, and Londonderry (1828), and Londonderry and Tyrone (1829). His projected book on Greenland was never completed. During 1816 he became a knight of the Danish order of Dannebrog, and henceforth he was always known as Sir Charles Giesecke. The mineral gieseckite was so named in his honour in 1817. He was elected a member of the Royal Irish Academy in 1816 and a fellow of the Geological Society of London in 1817, and was among the founders of the Zoological Society of Dublin in 1830 and of the Geological Society of Dublin in 1831. He died suddenly at Rutland Square West, Dublin, unmarried, on 5 March 1833, and was buried in St George's churchyard, Dublin. The Royal Dublin Society's museum was closed for two weeks in token of the esteem in which he was held.

MAURICE CRAIG, *rev.* GORDON L. HERRIES DAVIES

Sources G. Gugitz and M. Kirchmayer, 'Giesecke, Karl Ludwig', *Neue deutsche Biographie*, ed. Otto, Graf zu Stolberg-Wernigerode (Berlin, 1953–), 383–4 • H. F. Berry, *A history of the Royal Dublin Society* (1915) • T. de V. White, *The story of the Royal Dublin Society* (1955) • 'Biographical sketch of Sir Charles Lewis Metzler von Giesecke', *Dublin University Magazine*, 3 (1834), 161–75, 296–306 • R. L. Praeger, *Some Irish naturalists: a biographical note-book* (1949), 85–6 • W. V. Farrar, 'Thomas Allan, mineralogist: an autobiographical fragment', *Annals of Science*, 24 (1968), 115–20 • T. Ó Raifeartaigh, *The Royal Irish Academy: a bicentennial history, 1785–1985* (1985), 107 • J. Meenam and D. Clarke, *RDS: the Royal Dublin Society, 1731–1981* (1981) • J. Sweet, 'Robert Jameson and the explorers', *Annals of Science*, 31 (1974), 21–47, esp. 26–34 • A. Whittaker, 'Mineralogy and The magic flute', *Mitteilungen der Österreichischen Mineralogischen Gesellschaft*, 143 (1998), 107–34

Likenesses portrait, Royal Dublin Society; repro. in Meenam and Clarke, *RDS*, 158

Giffard. *See also* Gifford.

Giffard, Sir Ambrose Hardinge (1771–1827), judge in Ceylon, was born at Dublin, the eldest son of John *Giffard (1745–1819), high sheriff of Dublin in 1794, accountant-general of customs in Dublin, and a prominent loyalist, and Sarah (1750–1827), daughter of William Morton of Ballynaclash, co. Wexford. The Giffards were an ancient Devon family, but Ambrose Hardinge's grandfather John Giffard (*d.* November 1746), of Wotton and Great Torrington, who was the disinherited grandson of John Giffard (1639–1715) of Brightleigh, settled in Ireland. Giffard received his Christian names from his father's close friend Ambrose Hardinge. He was admitted at the Inner Temple and called to the bar. In 1808 he married Harriet, daughter of Lovell Pennell, of Lyme Regis, Dorset; they had five sons and five daughters.

Giffard was advocate-fiscal at Colombo, Ceylon, from 1811, puisne justice of the supreme court, Colombo, from September 1818, and chief justice from 1819, and he was knighted in 1819 (though this was not gazetted). In one of the court's clashes with the executive, the lieutenant-governor refused to produce a person in custody as the court ordered. As Giffard stated, its charters did not give it power to issue writs of habeas corpus. He criticized the lieutenant-governor's action, the issue was raised in the House of Commons, and in 1830 the court was given English powers of habeas corpus. Giffard also criticized the provincial court system and the high court of appeal. Sir Edward Cressy and others of the supreme court in 1866 agreed that 'for few judicial opinions did [the court] entertain so high a respect as for Sir Hardinge Giffard's' (Lewis, 350).

Giffard's leisure was devoted to literature, and one of his poems was published in Ceylon about 1822. An example, his translation of Catullus's 'Sirmio', is reproduced in the *Traditions and Recollections* of the Revd Richard Polwhele. Giffard's health failed and he was granted leave, but he died on 30 April 1827, on the homeward voyage, on the East Indiaman *Lady Kennaway*.

Giffard's third son was Admiral **Sir George Giffard** (1815–1895), naval officer, who was born at Colombo on 9 August 1815. He entered the navy as midshipman in June 1827 (lieutenant, October 1835), served in the 1840 Syrian coast operations (commander, November 1840), fought against pirates at Borneo in 1845, and was promoted captain (December 1845). In 1847 he married Magdalene Christian (*d.* 1888), daughter of Robert *Mushet, Royal Mint. He was a relief commissioner in Donegal in 1847, served in the Baltic and the Black Sea during the Crimean War (CB July 1855 and 4th class Mejidiye), and retired on half pay in December 1858 (retired vice-admiral, April 1870; admiral, January 1877). He was made KCB on 29 May 1875, and he was a Surrey JP. He died at his home, Brightleigh, Outwood, Redhill, Surrey, on 8 March 1895.

G. B. SMITH, *rev.* ROGER T. STEARN

Sources *GM*, 1st ser., 97/2 (1827), 367 • *GM*, 1st ser., 89/1 (1819), 481–5 • Burke, *Peerage* (1999) [Halsbury] • Boase, *Mod. Eng. biog.* • W. A. Shaw, *The knights of England*, 2 (1906) • O'Byrne, *Naval biog. dict.* • *Dod's Peerage* (1878) • W. L. Clowes, *The Royal Navy: a history from the earliest times to the present*, 7 vols. (1897–1903), vol. 7 • Kelly, *Handbk* (1894) • C. R. De Silva, *Ceylon under the British occupation, 1795–1833*, 1 (1941) • P. Lewis, 'Corrections of the *DNB*', *N&Q*, 12th ser., 12 (1923), 350 • L. A. Mills, *Ceylon under British rule, 1795–1932* (1933)

Archives BL, corresp. and papers

Giffard, Bonaventure (1642–1734), vicar apostolic of the London district, was born at Wolverhampton, the third son of Andrew Giffard (*b.* 1595), of a junior branch of the ancient recusant and royalist family seated at Chillington, Staffordshire, and Catherine, daughter of Sir Walter Leveson. He was educated at the English College, Douai (as Joseph Giffard), and at St Gregory's, Paris, whence he obtained a Sorbonne doctorate in June 1678. He had been ordained in 1667 as a secular priest for the English mission, to which he was assigned in July 1678. He appears to have ministered to the Arundells of Lanherne (Hemphill, 134) but the events surrounding the Popish Plot soon drove him overseas. Before returning to St Gregory's on 16 April 1679 he visited the English Poor Clare nuns of Rouen, their abbess being his cousin Winefride Giffard, whose successor was the subject of a manuscript memoir by him, drawn on in *A Short Account of the Life and Virtues of Mary of the Holy Cross, Abbess* (1767) by A. B. (Anne Bedingfield).

In June 1681, having taken the chapter oath, Giffard returned to England, where the secular clergy were governed by that body, which claimed jurisdiction while there was no Roman Catholic bishop in the country—a claim nullified by the appointment of one in 1685. In its last effective years, he acted as its secretary and served as capitular archdeacon of Essex and on a deputation to James II urging the chapter's view that the new prelate should be a bishop-in-ordinary, not a vicar apostolic. However, it was as the latter, a missionary bishop with a see *in partibus infidelium*, that John Leyburn took office, appointing Giffard his vicar-general in the large eastern district. The king, mindful of Giffard's talents and of his counsel to him when duke of York, chose him as one of two Romanist spokesmen opposing a pair of Anglican divines in a debate, the printed version of which was vetted by Giffard and reported in *A relation of a conference before his majesty and the earl of Rochester … concerning the real presence and transubstantiation, Nov 30, 1686* (1722).

Giffard, appointed a royal chaplain and court preacher, was concerned in July 1687 with a consignment of imported crucifixes, pictures, and altar requisites for the Chapel Royal, while sermons preached in that year, *On the Infallibility of the Church* and *On the Nativity of Our Lord*, were printed at the time. Chosen in the following January to govern the midland district, one of four vicariates into which England and Wales were then divided, he was consecrated bishop of Madaura *in partibus* on 22 April, the first and only half-yearly instalment of his £1000 *p.a.* stipend being entered in the secret service accounts. He and his confrères issued *A Pastoral Letter from the Four Catholic Bishops to the Lay-Catholics of England* (1688) and also formulated a ruling concerning usury. In the former, studiously non-triumphalist, they look forward to taking charge of 'our respective Provinces, where we are to devote ourselves to your spiritual improvement', and a newsletter of 31 July 1688 reported that Giffard had already set out for Oxford. He arrived there on 15 June as both vicar apostolic and president of Magdalen College, a royal appointment

Bonaventure Giffard (1642–1734), by Thomas Burford (after Hans Hysing)

affronting Anglican sensibilities and denounced by Bishop Leyburn. Giffard held a confirmation service in the romishly adapted college chapel on 10 July, while ventures further afield, supplementing many midland confirmations by Leyburn the year before, included the consecration of new popish chapels at Warwick and Birmingham.

However, such activities were terminated by the loss of Giffard's Oxford base in October and by his own flight and capture in Kent, where he was detained for much of December before being transferred (as Joseph Gifford) to Newgate, his downfall lampooned in *A dialogue between Father Gifford, the late popish president of Maudlin, and Obadiah Walker, master of university, upon their new college preferment in Newgate* (1689). Also in Newgate was the vicar apostolic of the western district, the Benedictine Bishop Ellis who subsequently fled the country, leaving Giffard to care for seven extra counties and the whole of Wales, a burden he shouldered for a quarter of a century rather than see another member of the regular clergy succeed to it.

Giffard was released in July 1690 and successive orders to quit the realm culminated in August 1691 in a warrant for his arrest and for the confiscation of his papers. Little record survives from the 1690s but when he was again able to supervise his vicariate, badly scarred by the no-popery vandalism of December 1688, he may have operated from a house in Cock Street, Wolverhampton, his birthplace. In the summer of 1699 he 'went confirming thro' Wales', according to *A letter to an honourable member of parliament concerning the great growth of popery and the treasonable practices of the Romish bishops and priests* (1700), whose author adds that, in the event of a Stuart and 'romanist' restoration, 'Bp. Gifford is ready to plant at Litchfield or Worcester'.

In 1702 Leyburn died and in the following year Giffard succeeded him in the metropolitan area, whence he relayed to Rome two decades of perils and privations. His translation to London followed close upon the passing of an act (11 and 12 Gul. III, c. 4) offering a reward of £100 for securing the conviction of a Roman Catholic cleric, and in September 1704, while living near Red Lion Square, he fell victim to an informer, was arrested, and was due to appear (as Joseph Giffard, or Fowler) at the Old Bailey, when, acceding to the pleas of spokesmen for his flock, he absconded, forfeiting his sureties' recognizances and becoming a fugitive for a year or more. By February 1706 he had found sanctuary with the Venetian ambassador but in October 1708 this ended and he resumed his precarious lifestyle. In 1711, however, he became temporarily responsible for the one area with which he had not already been associated, when the death of his northern colleague left him, as senior vicar apostolic, in charge of that district—a duty which fell to him again when a later vacancy embroiled him in 'a culinary schism in Lancashire' over Lenten observance (Bossy, 114). Also in 1711 he was in the western district where he visited Wardour, a major Roman Catholic centre in Wiltshire; travels further westwards, undetailed and undated, may, perhaps be inferred from mention of a 'Mr Giffard' confirming in Cornwall (Gilbert, 3.143).

To Giffard's anxieties over the Jacobite emergency of 1714–15, when, as Joseph Leveson, he was on the run from informers, including two ex-priests, were added unpleasantness of other kinds: charges that he was insufficiently anti-Jansenist; a campaign of denigration (rebutted by Giffard and his clergy) designed to gain John Talbot Stoner control over the London district, and some dissatisfaction with his attitude towards proposals involving an oath of fidelity to George I. This protracted project took a sinister turn in the summer of 1719 when its aggrieved advocate Thomas Strickland sought government collaboration in coercing his co-religionists through high-profile arrests, including that of Giffard, whose last minute escape spared him his fifth imprisonment.

At the end of that year Giffard nominated as his coadjutor Henry Howard, brother and heir to the duke of Norfolk, commending him as acceptable to both secular and regular clergy, an important consideration in view of the unresolved tensions between the vicars apostolic and the regulars over the latter's faculties to exercise their ministry in England. However, Howard died before he could take office and his diffident replacement, Benjamin Petre, disconcerted Giffard by repeatedly trying to resign; hence, perhaps, frequent praise of him for Roman consumption.

Giffard had long bewailed the poverty of the English mission and Rome's inadequate response to it, and in 1722 prophesied a dire outcome from Walpole's projected levy of £100,000 on Catholics and non-jurors. However, the high regard in which he was held never failed to attract benefactions, from the earl of Cardigan's gift and bequests while Giffard was midland vicar apostolic to support for later charities, including the Aged Poor Society founded shortly after his transfer to London. Even in the 1720s contributions were forthcoming not only for the benefit of needy priests and lay people but also towards two objectives very dear to him, the rebuilding of Douai College and the erection of a mass house at Wolverhampton. He himself had long given away most of his patrimony and his dedicated, discreet philanthropy was considered by Dodd to be his outstanding characteristic (Dodd, 3.469). Other facets of his long ministry were his concern to obey whenever possible the Tridentine command to preach, while his role as a spiritual counsellor is reflected in letters, dating back to his midland years, printed in *The Catholic Miscellany*, volumes 5–7 (1826–7).

Giffard's last active years, when his London residence was Stafford House, may have been characterized by that comparative freedom from molestation which Dodd unaccountably associates with his earlier career, remembered by the bishop himself, however, as having embraced 'much more difficult and dangerous times' (Hemphill, 76). Towards the end of his long life he moved to the chaplain's house attached to the semi-secret Hammersmith convent of the Institute of the Blessed Virgin Mary, with which he had long been associated and whose chaplain, William Crathorne, he had earlier commissioned to produce a collected edition of the works of John Gother.

Here on 12 March 1734 Giffard died after a long and painful illness; he was interred in St Pancras cemetery, having directed that his heart be preserved at his beloved Douai. His remains were later transferred to Old Hall, Ware, Hertfordshire. At his death some £3000 was available for religious purposes; he himself left provision for a second priest at Wolverhampton and for completing the house and chapel, and a short will dated 26 September 1733 and witnessed by Crathorne leaves bequests for poor Catholics in London and Wolverhampton and to his Stafford House manservant. At his death Giffard was in his ninety-second year and his forty-sixth as a bishop, having lived under eight rulers of England and twelve popes. His priests and people were for the most part devoted and supportive and his Anglican near-contemporary the Revd James Granger described him as much esteemed by persons of different religions, particularly those who knew him best (Granger, 459). A memorial tablet was erected to him in Magdalen College chapel in 1989. J. ANTHONY WILLIAMS

Sources B. Hemphill, *The early vicars apostolic of England, 1685–1750* (1954) • W. M. Brady, *Annals of the Catholic hierarchy in England and Scotland* (1877) • G. Anstruther, *The seminary priests*, 3 (1976) • J. A. Williams, 'Bishops Giffard and Ellis and the western vicariate, 1688–1715', *Journal of Ecclesiastical History*, 15 (1964), 218–28 • J. A. Williams, *Catholic recusancy in Wiltshire, 1660–1791* (1968) • J. A. Williams, 'Our patriarch: Bishop Bonaventure Giffard, 1642–1734: an introductory sketch', *Recusant History*, 26/3 (May 2003) • *Catholic Miscellany*, 5–7 (1826–7) • E. H. Burton, *The life and times of Bishop Challoner, 1691–1781*, 2 vols. (1909) • Birmingham Archdiocesan Archives, A9, A414, A475, A570, A1061 a and b • 'Bonaventure Giffard', B. C. Foley, *Some people of the penal times* (1991), chap. 8 • Gillow, *Lit. biog. hist.* • C. Dodd [H. Tootell], *The church history of England, from the year 1500, to the year 1688*, 3 (1742) • R. A. Beddard, 'James II and the Catholic challenge', *Hist. U. Oxf.* 4: *17th-cent. Oxf.*, 907–54 • R. Beddard, ed., *A kingdom without a king: the journal of the provisional government in the revolution of 1688* (1988) • L. Brockliss, G. Harriss, and A. Macintyre, *Magdalen College and the crown: essays for the tercentenary of the restoration of the college, 1688* (1988) • J. Sergeant, *An account of the chapter erected by William, titular bishop of Chalcedon*, ed. W. Turnbull (1853) • J. Bossy, *The English Catholic community, 1570–1850* (1975) • J. Granger, *A biographical history of England, from Egbert the Great to the revolution*, suppl. (1774)

Archives Birmingham archdiocesan archives, A9, A414, A475, A570, A1061 a and b • Westm. DA, *Epistolae variorum*; Kirk's transcripts (of 'Records of the vicars-apostolic under George I') and 'Paris seminary' archives, Series A and Series B

Likenesses R. van Bleeck, oils, archbishop's house, Westminster • T. Burford, mezzotint (after H. Hysing), BM, NPG [*see illus.*] • J. Russell, oils (after R. van Bleeck), Magd. Oxf.; repro. in Mrs. Reginald Lane Poole, *Catalogue of portraits in possession of the University, colleges, city, and county of Oxford*, Oxford Historical Society, 81 (1926), vol. 2, p. 221 • oils, Douai Abbey, Woolhampton

Wealth at death bequests: will, Hemphill, *Early vicars*, 182; Birmingham Archdiocesan Archives, A 570, A1061b, A1061a, A9, A475

Giffard, Diana Josceline Barbara. *See* Airey, Diana Josceline Barbara Neave, Baroness Airey of Abingdon (1919–1992), *under* Neave, Airey Middleton Sheffield (1916–1979).

Giffard, Sir George (1815–1895). *See under* Giffard, Sir Ambrose Hardinge (1771–1827).

Giffard, Sir George James (1886–1964), army officer, was born at Englefield Green, Surrey, on 27 September 1886, the eldest son of George Campbell Giffard, clerk of the journals, House of Commons, and his wife, Jane Mary Lawrence. Educated at Rugby School and at the Royal Military College, Sandhurst, he was commissioned into the Queen's Royal regiment in 1906.

Seconded to the King's African rifles in 1911, Giffard first saw active service in tribal warfare in east Africa during 1913–14; he remained with that regiment throughout the First World War and, from 1916 onwards, distinguished himself in the campaign against Colonel von Lettow Vorbeck in German East Africa. As temporary major in command of the 1st battalion 2nd King's African rifles he had to operate in very difficult country of bush, desert, and forest, with his men much exposed to malaria. In October 1917, when the Germans' offensive power broke and they set off in retreat, Giffard's battalion pursued them into Portuguese East Africa. Raised to the temporary rank of colonel while still only thirty-one, he was given command of a three-battalion column in February 1918 and again followed von Lettow Vorbeck through the bush, covering 435 miles in a month. With masterly skill the Germans avoided envelopment and maintained their guerrilla operations until the armistice. Giffard, who had been wounded in the campaign, was made a DSO. Besides four mentions in dispatches, he received the French Croix de Guerre and the Portuguese order of St Benedict of Aviz.

Giffard was selected for the first post-war course at the Staff College, Camberley, in 1919. In July 1920 he was appointed a staff officer to the inspector-general of the Royal West African frontier force, only returning to the Queen's Royal regiment in England in 1925. From 1928 to 1931 he was a GSO2 at the Staff College, Camberley, and after attending the Imperial Defence College in 1931–2 he took command of the 2nd battalion of his regiment at Aldershot as lieutenant-colonel. On promotion to full colonel in July 1933 he was posted to the 2nd division as GSO1 and played a prominent role in designing and carrying out the unconventional tactical exercises introduced by its commander, Archibald Wavell. In 1935–6 he was aide-de-camp to the king.

In 1936 Giffard, promoted major-general, became inspector-general of African colonial forces, which included, with other units, the Royal West African frontier force and the King's African rifles. He was appointed CB in 1938. Mid-1939 saw him in London as military secretary to the secretary of state for war, Leslie Hore-Belisha, but after seven months he was posted as general officer commanding under Wavell once more, in Palestine and Transjordan. In June 1940, after France had collapsed, he was appointed commander-in-chief west Africa, a new command set up because, with the closing of the Mediterranean, the area had become one of great strategic importance: a key staging-post for British convoys round the Cape and a link in the air route to Egypt, as well as a valuable source of raw materials.

In this post Giffard, who was promoted general and appointed KCB in 1941, successfully tackled a host of complex political and military problems with skill and zeal, carrying through a rapid expansion—indeed, transformation—of the army and organizing the training of some 200,000 Africans, many of them for service in fighting formations: two west African divisions and one from east Africa were later to serve under his command in Burma. When, in June 1942, Lord Swinton arrived as resident cabinet minister, he and Giffard worked in concord and mutual respect. 'No one but he could have accomplished what was done', Swinton wrote afterwards. 'With tireless energy and infinite patience he inspired his new officers with something of his own knowledge and genius for handling Africans' (P. Cunliffe-Lister, 199).

In the spring of 1943 the Mediterranean was reopened, west Africa's strategic importance declined, and it was possible to release Giffard to command Eastern Army, India, when Wavell asked for him in the post. Morale there was low, training inadequate, malaria rife. Setbacks since the loss of Burma had proved that British and Indian troops needed more self-confidence and new fighting methods before they could deal effectively with the triumphant Japanese. Throughout that summer Giffard supervised intensive training in jungle warfare and instituted strict anti-malaria precautions and other measures against tropical diseases.

When south-east Asia command was set up under Lord Louis Mountbatten, Giffard became commander-in-chief of the 11th army group, responsible to the supreme commander for all troops in Ceylon and the Indian Ocean bases and for the operations of the Fourteenth Army, which was formed in October 1943 under William Slim, later Viscount Slim. The 11th army group should have included the Chinese–American forces in northern Burma, but for largely personal reasons the American

General Stilwell (Vinegar Joe, as he was known) refused to place them under Giffard's command; however, he did consent to serve under Slim's individual control.

Since Giffard's prime task thus became to support the Fourteenth Army on the Arakan and central Burma fronts, it was fortunate that he and Slim worked so perfectly together. He reorganized the rear areas of an exceptionally wide and difficult front which was served by most inadequate roads and railways. With calm understanding and rock-like loyalty he backed Slim without interfering and shielded him at times of crisis. Slim paid many tributes to Giffard in *Defeat into Victory* (1956):

> he understood the fundamentals of war—that soldiers must be trained before they can fight, fed before they can march, and relieved before they are worn out. He understood that front-line commanders should be spared responsibilities in the rear, and that soundness of organization and administration is worth more than specious short-cuts to victory. (Slim, 164)

Unfortunately Giffard's relationship with Mountbatten was less satisfactory. Although the supreme commander liked him personally, and admired his professional ability and above all his integrity, and although he resisted strong American pressure to have Giffard removed, he came to criticize the general's caution, his slowness of reaction at certain crucial moments, and his failure to inform him in time of military developments and their implications. While the outcome of the desperate fighting at Imphal and Kohima was still uncertain, matters came to a head in May 1944 when Giffard told Mountbatten that he could not provide enough divisions for both monsoon and post-monsoon operations. Nor could he agree to Mountbatten's checking his programme to see if more troops could be extracted. Mountbatten thereupon told Giffard that he had lost confidence in him and must have a younger, more aggressive commander. In any case, he proposed to replace the 11th army group with a new command to be called allied land forces south-east Asia, for which Giffard would be acceptable neither to the Americans nor to Chiang Kai-shek.

Giffard took his dismissal without bitterness and with a clear conscience. Although in the difficult position of being 'under notice' for six months while negotiations for a successor dragged on, he behaved with exemplary courtesy, unselfishness, and loyalty. Once the Japanese invasion forces had been crushingly defeated at Kohima and Imphal, as Giffard had correctly forecast, it was possible, after June, to take greater risks in order to exploit success and, by fighting through the monsoon, to maintain unrelenting pressure on the Japanese retreating in disorder to the Chindwin River and beyond. Giffard, who was appointed GCB that year, eventually left for England in November 1944. Slim wrote: 'we saw him go with grief. I and others built on the foundations he laid' (Slim, 385).

Despite his great contribution to victory, Giffard remains probably the least known of all British generals who held high command in the Second World War. Genuinely disliking publicity, he was unspectacular in style, not at his best when making speeches or arguing a case at top-level allied conferences, but good at talking to individuals and small groups. He was a tall, erect, good-looking man with a firm but friendly look and a dignified presence.

In 1915 Giffard had married Evelyn Norah (*d.* 1964), second daughter of Richard Margerison FRCS, of Winchester; they had one daughter. He became aide-de-camp general to the king in 1945–6, and on his retirement in August 1946 he settled in Winchester. He served as president of the Army Benevolent Fund and from 1945 to 1954 as colonel of the Queen's Royal regiment, colonel commandant of the Royal West African frontier force, the King's African rifles, and the Northern Rhodesia regiment. With his usual enthusiasm and thoroughness he took up apple growing and turned a derelict orchard into a thriving, prize-winning concern. He also kept bees, watched birds, and fished on the Hampshire Avon. A man of high principles and deep religious faith, he spent his life trying to conform to what he saw as God's will; the letters he wrote to his wife, whose poor health prevented her from accompanying him on his many postings overseas, contain frequent heart-searchings over actions and decisions. In 1959 a coronary thrombosis obliged Giffard to curtail severely his physical activities, but with characteristic energy he took up tapestry and rug making. That someone with such large hands could produce such fine work was surprising. Giffard died at the Royal Hampshire County Hospital, Winchester, on 17 November 1964. His wife survived him by less than a fortnight.

ANTONY BRETT-JAMES, *rev.*

Sources *The Times* (19 Nov 1964) · G. J. Giffard, dispatches covering operations in Burma and north-east India and in Assam and Burma, *LondG* (13–30 March 1951) [suppl.] · [L. F. A. V. N. Mountbatten], *Report to the combined chiefs of staff by the supreme commander south-east Asia, 1943–1945* (1951) · S. W. Kirby and others, *The war against Japan*, 3–4 (1961–5) · W. Slim, *Defeat into victory*, new edn 1986 (1956), 164, 385 · P. Cunliffe-Lister, *I remember* (1949) · *Chief of staff: the diaries of Lt.-Gen. Sir Henry Parnall*, ed. B. Bond (1940–44), vol. 2 · P. J. Grigg, *Prejudice and judgement* (1948) · H. Moyse-Bartlett, *The king's African rifles* (1956) · private information (1981) · *CGPLA Eng. & Wales* (1965)

Archives NAM, corresp. with Alan Cunningham

Likenesses W. Stoneman, portrait, 1936, NPG · W. Stoneman, portrait, 1945, NPG · R. Guthrie, portrait, repro. in *Sunday Times* (18 Aug 1946)

Wealth at death £20,362: probate, 18 Jan 1965, *CGPLA Eng. & Wales*

Giffard, Sir George Markham (1813–1870), judge, was born at his father's official residence, Portsmouth Dockyard, on 4 November 1813, the fourth son of Admiral John Giffard, and his wife, Susannah, daughter of Sir John Carter. He was educated at Winchester College and at New College, Oxford, where he was made a fellow in 1832 and took the degree of BCL on 4 March 1841. He joined the Inner Temple and was called to the bar in November 1840. In 1853 he married Maria, the second daughter of Charles Pilgrim of Kingsfield, Southampton.

Giffard rose quickly in his practice, soon becoming a leading chancery junior counsel. In 1859 he became a queen's counsel, and attached himself to the court of Vice-Chancellor Sir William Page Wood, where, despite being ill for several months, he soon obtained a leading position. When Vice-Chancellor Wood became a lord justice of appeal in March 1868, Giffard succeeded him; and when Wood became lord chancellor in December, Giffard was promoted to the Court of Appeal and made a member of the privy council. Said to have been efficient, terse, and yet scholarly in his legal argumentation, he was well regarded by his colleagues. He was a Liberal in his politics, but never stood for parliament. He died after a lengthy illness on 13 July 1870 at his home, 4 Prince's Gardens, Hyde Park, London. J. A. HAMILTON, *rev.* HUGH MOONEY

Sources *Solicitors' Journal*, 14 (1869–70), 762–3 · E. Foss, *Biographia juridica: a biographical dictionary of the judges of England … 1066–1870* (1870) · *The Times* (16 July 1870) · *The Times* (20 July 1870)
Likenesses Disderi, carte-de-visite, NPG · wood-engraving (after photograph by J. Watkins), NPG; repro. in *ILN* (4 April 1868)
Wealth at death under £5150 effects in Ireland: probate, 11 Nov 1870, *CGPLA Ire.* · under £60,000: probate, 19 Aug 1870, *CGPLA Eng. & Wales*

Godfrey Giffard (1235?–1302), seal

Giffard, Godfrey (1235?–1302), administrator and bishop of Worcester, was the second son of Hugh Giffard of Boyton in Wiltshire, a royal justice, and Sybil, daughter and coheir of Walter de Cormeilles. His elder brother, Walter *Giffard (*d.* 1279), became archbishop of York, while his sisters Mabel and Juliana became abbesses of Shaftesbury and Wilton respectively. Hugh Giffard's position as constable of the Tower of London and guardian of the Lord Edward, and his wife's as nurse to the royal children and accoucheuse to Eleanor of Provence, ensured court connections for their children, and Godfrey was a member of the king's household from boyhood. Proceeding to university, he incepted at Oxford in 1251, but little is known of him before the 1260s, when he received both promotion at court and ecclesiastical preferment. Late in 1266, after a few months as chancellor of the exchequer, he followed Walter Giffard as chancellor of England, and remained so for two years. Meanwhile, preferments for Godfrey in the diocese of Bath and Wells, and subsequently at York, followed Walter's ecclesiastical promotion, first as bishop and then as archbishop, and complaints of favouritism ensued, together with allegations against Godfrey of pluralism and deficiency of learning and orders. Such circumstances presumably lay behind the archbishop of Canterbury's reported opposition to Godfrey's election to the see of Worcester in May 1268, but confirmation was granted. In June the king favoured him with a grant of the fruits of the vacancy. Consecrated at Canterbury on 23 September, he was enthroned at Worcester on Christmas day. There he remained bishop for over thirty-three years.

In common with many other bishops trained in royal service, Godfrey Giffard turned to diocesan work with zeal, and devoted himself largely to diocesan affairs throughout his long episcopate. Administrative ability was probably his greatest attribute (comment on academic or spiritual quality is rare), but contemporaries were undoubtedly impressed by his proud, forceful nature and quick temper, which was sorely aggravated by incapacitating attacks of gout in both feet. His massive bishop's register (nearly 500 folios) testifies to activity in pastoral, administrative, and judicial work, and is the first in the surviving series at Worcester. Other compilations relating to the possessions and privileges of the bishopric reveal his interest in the temporalities of the see. Detailed surveys of lands were carried out, as were building projects at Hartlebury, Withington, and Worcester.

During the 1270s Giffard was still involved in many matters unconnected with his diocese. In 1270 and 1271, for instance, he received several commissions relating to Welsh affairs. In 1272 he was among those appointed to settle disputes between the chancellor and scholars of Oxford, and the mayor and burgesses of the town. May 1273 saw him depart to France in company with the bishops of Winchester and Exeter to meet Edward I on his return from the Holy Land, and he was away from Worcester for six months. In 1278 his name headed the list of itinerant justices for Hertfordshire and Kent, though in the end he did not sit, and in 1279 he was one of those appointed to supply the king's place during Edward's absence on a journey to France. Health problems, however, were already evident—illness prevented Giffard from attending the Council of Lyons in 1275. At this time, too, he developed an interest in the mendicant orders: in 1279 he was conservator of the privileges of the Dominicans in England, and he was received into the Franciscan order in 1282, the result of an invitation extended in 1277. Giffard's family circumstances also changed, as he succeeded to extensive properties in 1279, on the death of Walter Giffard.

The 1280s were notable years of dispute. At the Benedictine priory of Great Malvern and at St Mary's collegiate church at Warwick exemption from diocesan jurisdiction was at issue. At Worcester a protracted quarrel arose between the bishop and chapter over plans to annex the most important churches in the bishop's patronage (and of the bishopric) to the collegiate church at Westbury-on-

Trym as new prebends there. The monks of the cathedral priory feared diminution of *sede vacante* rights and, perhaps, a rival capitular body, and steadfastly refused capitular assent to Giffard's plan; he attempted coercion, and relations deteriorated until concord was finally restored in 1291 through the mediation of Robert Burnell, the chancellor. The Westbury project was expressly omitted from the settlement, but effectively collapsed. On a wider horizon, Giffard was personally involved in bitter disputes between the Canterbury suffragans and Archbishop Pecham (*d.* 1292) about archiepiscopal encroachments upon diocesan jurisdiction. Giffard took a leading position in April 1282, considering himself heir to Thomas de Cantilupe (*d.* 1282) in this role, and claiming that there was no one else in the province who dared do anything about the archbishop's behaviour. Public enmity and personal bitterness ended in reconciliation in March 1284, but not without Giffard's comparing Pecham to the prodigal son.

Despite some continuing litigation, the final decade of Giffard's episcopate was comparatively peaceful, reflecting his declining health. From 1295 he increasingly delegated his episcopal work, and after 1297 committed to John of Monmouth (*d.* 1323), bishop of Llandaff, many duties that required episcopal orders. When Archbishop Winchelsey (*d.* 1313) conducted his metropolitical visitation at Worcester in 1301 Giffard was found to be ill, blind, and unable to look after his property. Characteristically, he did not submit to infirmity without a struggle: he arranged strenuous visitation itineraries, expressed opposition to the archbishop's visitation, and took measures to set the see to rights. He later attempted to reverse Winchelsey's deposition of certain officers of the cathedral priory, and refuted charges made against himself. By August 1301, however, further decline was marked by cessation of entries in his register. He made his will at Kempsey on 13 September, but lingered on until 26 January 1302, while the archbishop and the prior of Worcester exchanged letters about the ostentatious tomb which Giffard had prepared for himself, and controversy simmered over his property. He was buried in his cathedral on 4 February, by his friend the bishop of Llandaff, but his tomb, the subject of archiepiscopal disapproval, was subsequently moved, leaving decorative interlacing of pillars in the choir and lady chapel as his principal memorial at Worcester. SUSAN J. DAVIES

Sources Emden, *Oxf.*, 2.761–2 • J. W. W. Bund, ed., *Register of Bishop Godfrey Giffard, September 23rd, 1268, to August 15th, 1301*, 2 vols., Worcestershire Historical Society, 15 (1898–1902) [calendared edn, often inadequate in detail and fact] • S. J. Davies, 'Studies in the administration of the diocese of Worcester in the thirteenth century', PhD diss., U. Wales, 1971 • R. M. Haines, *The administration of the diocese of Worcester in the first half of the fourteenth century* (1965) • C. Dyer, *Lords and peasants in a changing society: the estates of the bishopric of Worcester, 680–1540* (1980) • R. Graham, 'Metropolitical visitation of the diocese of Worcester by Archbishop Winchelsey in 1301', *English Ecclesiastical Studies* (1929) • D. L. Douie, *Archbishop Pecham* (1952) • S. J. Davies, 'Giffard, Godfrey', *Dictionnaire d'histoire et de géographie ecclésiastiques*, ed. A. Baudrillart and others, 20 (Paris, 1983), 1275–9 • J. W. Willis Bund, ed., *Register of Bishop William Ginsborough, 1303 to 1307*, Worcestershire Historical Society (1907); rev. edn with introduction by R. A. Wilson, as *The register of William de Geynesburgh, Bishop of Worcester, 1302–1307* (1929) • C. Roberts, ed., *Calendarium genealogicum: Henry III and Edward I*, 1, PRO (1985), 281
Archives Worcs. RO
Likenesses seal, BL; Birch, *Seals*, 2279 [*see illus.*]
Wealth at death see will, Bund and Wilson, eds., *Register of Bishop William de Ginsborough*, 48–54; W. Thomas, *A survey of the cathedral church of Worcester with an account of the bishops thereof* (1736), appx, 77–81

Giffard, Hardinge Stanley, first earl of Halsbury (1823–1921), judge, was born at 12 Penton Street, Pentonville, London, on 3 September 1823. He was the third son of Stanley Lees *Giffard LLD (1788–1858) and his first wife, Susanna Meares, daughter of Francis Moran JP, of Downhill, Ballina, co. Mayo. His mother died when Hardinge was five years old and in 1830 his father married a second cousin, Mary Anne Giffard. Her stepchildren held her in deep affection. Educated by his father at home in the classics and in Hebrew, Hardinge entered Merton College, Oxford, in 1842. He rowed in the college eight, and spoke frequently at the Union, but he left university in 1845 with a disappointing fourth class in *literae humaniores*.

Journalism and early legal career Between 1845 and 1848 Giffard assisted his father as editor of *The Standard* newspaper, in which the tory cause was uncompromisingly advanced. He was admitted to the Inner Temple in 1848 and called in 1850, becoming a bencher in 1865. Initially joining the western circuit, he soon transferred to the south Wales circuit where his practice expanded. He also moved from the chambers of his brother John to those of Harry Bodkin Poland. Much of his early work was in chancery though he began to acquire an Old Bailey reputation. In 1859 he succeeded William Henry Bodkin as junior prosecuting counsel at the central criminal court, and he took silk in 1865. He featured in a number of celebrated cases during this period, including two separate proceedings as counsel for Governor Eyre (1867 and 1868), the Fenian conspiracy case (1869), and as second counsel for Arthur Orton, the Tichborne claimant, in one of the lengthy proceedings in the case (1871–2). His forte was his outstanding memory and his mastery of the facts of cases whose briefs he was quite likely not to have read.

MP and legal office Despite having failed to be elected as member of parliament for Cardiff in the general elections of 1868 and 1874, Giffard was appointed solicitor-general by Disraeli in November 1874 as replacement for Sir John Holker who had become attorney-general. A knighthood followed. Giffard became MP for Launceston in February 1877 and retained the seat at the general election of 1880. It was an unspectacular period of office, though he led for the crown in the important *Franconia* case (*R.* v. *Keyn*, 1876) which eventually resulted in the passage of the Territorial Waters Jurisdiction Act of 1878, and in *R.* v. *Staunton* (1877), the notorious Penge murder trial.

After the defeat of the Conservatives in 1880, Giffard became more prominent in parliament, while his practice at the bar also expanded. Perhaps his greatest forensic triumph was in the libel action of *Belt* v. *Lawes* (1882) in

Hardinge Stanley Giffard, first earl of Halsbury (1823–1921), by York & Son, 1890s

which, under difficult circumstances, he secured damages for the plaintiff, a sculptor whose creations had been dismissed as the work of others hired to execute his commissions.

Lord chancellor It is with his prolonged occupancy of the woolsack, however, that Giffard's reputation rests. He was first appointed as lord chancellor in 1885 in Lord Salisbury's first administration, taking the title Baron Halsbury, of Halsbury, in the parish of Parkham, Devon, which had been one of the former seats of the Giffard family. His first period on the woolsack lasted just eight months before the government went out of office in January 1886. He resumed the office in August 1886 for a six-year period and then held the post for a further ten years from June 1895 until December 1905, resigning shortly after his eighty-second birthday. He thus held the great seal for seventeen years, longer than anyone else except Hardwicke and Eldon. In 1898 he was created earl of Halsbury and Viscount Tiverton.

On his initial appointment in 1885 some observers had doubted whether Halsbury could occupy the post with distinction. There is no doubting that he possessed a strong and forceful personality, that he lacked any hint of self-doubt, that he would not be overawed on first acquiring the great seal by the reputations of his fellow House of Lords judges, and that he was a robust, indeed impatient, deliverer of rulings. But he was not a great lawyer. His judgments were not profound; they lacked substance, and the complexities and subtleties of legal principles played little part in the construction of his judicial opinions. They are rarely consulted for accurate and concise expositions of the law as he had a tendency to dispose of difficulties by taking a 'broad' view of the matter. Indeed, dogmatism characterized his later judgments. It is perhaps significant that Lord Lindley, a far more notable jurist who died two days before Halsbury, enjoyed a tribute in the *Law Quarterly Review*, whereas Halsbury's passing received no such acknowledgement.

Political patronage Halsbury's years as lord chancellor gave rise to two major controversies concerning his tenure of office. The first regarded his exercise of patronage and whether the trend of his appointments to the High Court, in particular, revealed that service to the Conservative Party rather than the possession of outstanding legal skills was for him the dominant criterion for preferment. The second was whether, in fulfilling his judicial functions (apart from appointments), he permitted political prejudices to interfere with the proper discharge of his duties.

Regarding the first issue, the facts are that Halsbury appointed thirty judges to the Supreme Court between 1885 and 1905. Of these thirty, eight had been members of parliament on their appointment, six as tories, one as a Liberal Unionist, and one as Liberal. Another appointee had been a Conservative member of parliament twenty years earlier. Three others had been unsuccessful tory candidates and two had been unsuccessful Liberal candidates at general elections during their previous careers. Thus fourteen out of thirty had been 'political lawyers', and of these ten had been tories, three Liberals, and one a Liberal Unionist. This in itself suggests political imbalance in appointments, though the numbers are extremely small from which to draw conclusive inferences. As regards the quality of Halsbury's appointments to the High Court, only about seven could be considered bad or unfortunate selections, and not in every case on the premiss that previous political service for the tory party was the motivating factor. Halsbury himself was prepared to deny preferment to tory lawyers whom he deemed unsuited for advancement or whom he considered were still required on the government benches. This was despite Lord Salisbury's writing to him in 1897 pointing out that 'there is no clearer statute in that unwritten law [of our party system] than the rule that party claims should always weigh very heavily in the disposal of the highest legal appointments' (Heuston, 52). Salisbury did, however, add two months later, apropos another proposed appointment, that, 'The judicial salad requires both legal oil and political vinegar; but disastrous effects will follow if due proportion is not observed' (Heuston, 57), prompting Halsbury to draw back from a potentially controversial appointment of another tory lawyer. Yet it was widely recognized that political experience could be of assistance to the judge faced with the task of assessing the character of litigants, witnesses, or prisoners in the dock. Overall, Halsbury made a small number of spectacular misjudgements in his appointments which tended to overshadow the solid, and on occasions, inspired promotions for which he was responsible. Whether his record compares particularly unfavourably with that of other lord chancellors in the last half of the nineteenth century and in the earlier part of the twentieth awaits systematic investigation.

Halsbury was also strongly criticized for the political partiality of his superintendence of the appointments of JPs; preventing a repetition of this was a special concern of Liberal governments after 1905. In evidence in 1910 to the royal commission on the selection of JPs he stated: 'There was some foundation for the complaint that the magistrates were more or less of one political complexion, which happened to be my own' ('Royal commission', 37.727).

Judicial decisions Regarding the second major allegation, that Halsbury's judicial duties were tainted with political bias, there are two strands to this claim. The first is that his own judgments, when closely scrutinized, did not consistently accord with the principle of *stare decisis* which he had notably and forcefully advanced in *London Street Tramways* v. *London county council* (1898). Instead, he ensured that there remained a large area for judicial discretion in decision making by invoking 'reason' and 'common sense' where he thought appropriate, and by retaining, in the words of one recent scholar, 'an armoury of devices for escaping the force of his own statements'. Thus legal formalism could be reduced to a mockery by stating, as Halsbury did in *Quinn* v. *Leathem* (1901), that 'a case is only an authority for what it actually decides. I entirely deny that it can be quoted for a proposition that may seem to follow logically from it'. The technique of narrowing the concept of a rule of law and of widening the concept of fact enabled Halsbury to shape the law as it suited him. The judicial function of the House of Lords under Halsbury could thereby be rendered legislative rather than expository or declaratory. Nowhere was this more clearly seen than in the trade union cases, especially the famous *Taff Vale case* (1901), but also in *Quinn* v. *Leathem* itself, an example of the ability of the Lords to 'distinguish the undistinguished', the latter referring to the previous ruling in *Allen* v. *Flood* (1898) in which Halsbury had dissented from the majority view that a threat to call out workers on strike without breaches of their contracts was not unlawful.

The trade union cases are also examples of the other strand of the accusation of Halsbury's political bias in respect to adjudication, the accusation of court-packing. In *Allen* v. *Flood*, he summoned the High Court judges to support his view of the law. On this occasion his efforts were in vain as the other House of Lords judges, including lords James and Davey, merely stiffened their resolve. In *Quinn* v. *Leathem*, however, his manipulation of the panel in order to exclude lords Davey and James from hearing the appeal produced the desired result. Similarly, in *Taff Vale* he arranged for a sympathetic panel of law lords, again omitting lords Davey and James, which overturned the Court of Appeal and restored the judgment of Mr Justice Farwell (a Halsbury appointee) that trade unions could be sued in tort for loss arising from a strike. This wholly unexpected interpretation of the law seriously undermined the reputations of the law lords hearing the appeal (lords Macnaghten, Shand, Brampton, and Lindley, as well as Halsbury) and hastened the transformation of British politics and the rise of the Labour Party.

Other, non-trade-union, cases which reinforced the criticism of Halsbury's judicial activities include *IRC* v. *Pemsel* (1891), in which he held up delivery of his decision for sixteen months in an effort to force the majority to shift towards his view. In the Free Church of Scotland case (1904), he omitted the most knowledgeable Scottish judge, Lord Kinnear, from the Lords' panel and secured the reversal of a unanimous Court of Session decision. Halsbury was not the only lord chancellor of his long generation to exploit his position in such fashion. Selborne before him and Loreburn after him were not unblemished in this regard. Halsbury's exploitation of his position was, however, more blatant and more frequent.

Halsbury was not a lord chancellor of the Eldon mould. He was sympathetic to ordinary working men seeking workmen's compensation. He was responsible for two important reforms, the Land Transfer Act of 1897 and the Criminal Evidence Act of 1898, by which persons accused of indictable offences and their spouses were made competent witnesses. He will also be forever associated with the monumental digest of *The Laws of England* (1905–16) which bears his name and reached its fourth edition in the late twentieth century under the editorship of a subsequent lord chancellor, Lord Hailsham of St Marylebone.

Final years Having vacated the woolsack in 1905, Halsbury continued to sit as a law lord, even delivering a judgment in his ninety-third year in *Continental Tyre and Rubber Co.* v. *Daimler Co.* (1916). Regarding the political work of the House of Lords, he deferred to the Conservative leader in the Lords, the marquess of Lansdowne, in the latter's reluctant acquiescence in the controversial legislative measures of the Liberal government such as the Trade Disputes Act of 1906 and the Finance Act of 1909. But during the constitutional crisis of 1910–11 he was the figurehead around whom the die-hard 'ditchers' organized their opposition to the Parliament Bill; he and Somerset sent a circular letter to the peers in March 1910 urging them to reject Lord Rosebery's proposals for reform of the Lords. Halsbury's simple faith led him to believe that it was constitutionally improper to interfere with the hereditary principle on which the House of Lords was hitherto based. As Lord Lindley, a fellow octogenarian, wrote to him in September 1911, one month after the momentous vote to approve the Lords' amendments had been lost by a small margin, the Liberals 'have the best cries to delude the masses who have votes and who do not care a straw for the constitution or for Home Rule or Welsh disestablishment or anything except more power, freedom to strike and higher wages' (BL, Add. MS 56375). Halsbury had no pretensions to being called a democrat and would heartily have concurred with such sentiments. Halsbury fulfilled a number of other duties over the next few years, occasionally sitting in court during the war years and presiding in 1913 over the House of Lords inquiry into the conduct of Arthur Murray, the master of Elibank, during the Marconi scandal.

Halsbury married, first, in 1852, Caroline Louisa, daughter of William Conn Humphreys of Wood Green, Middlesex, a partner in a solicitors' firm. The bride's half-brother was the father of the future Mr Justice Humphreys. Tragically, she died of shock in Switzerland in 1873 following a coach accident. There were no children of the marriage. He married, second, in 1874, Wilhelmina, daughter of Henry Woodfall of Stanmore, Middlesex. The latter was a fellow member of the bar and a relative of Henry Sampson Woodfall the publisher. There were three children of the marriage, Hardinge Goulburn (1880–1943), who became second earl of Halsbury; Lynie May Rohais, who died in childhood; and Constance Mary Evelyn, who married Edward Giffard, grandson of Halsbury's father's eldest brother who was chief justice of Ceylon.

In 1920, on the seventieth anniversary of his call to the bar, Halsbury received fulsome and warm congratulations from the bench and bar. However in his ninety-eighth year, his strength departed him. He died after three days' illness from influenza at his home, 4 Ennismore Gardens, London, on 11 December 1921 and was buried in Stanmore churchyard on 14 December. In physical appearance he was somewhat plain and unprepossessing. He had a broad body, and a large head without eyelashes and with an upraised nose. His short legs accentuated his dumpy and pugnacious appearance. But he exuded an expression of power and resolution. He was, therefore, a perfect model for the cartoonist's pen. G. R. Rubin

Sources R. F. V. Heuston, *Lives of the lord chancellors, 1885–1940* (1964) • R. Stevens, *Law and politics: the House of Lords as a judicial body, 1800–1976* (1979) • A. Wilson Fox, *The earl of Halsbury, lord high chancellor, 1823–1921* (1929) • Earl of Birkenhead [F. E. Smith], 'The earl of Halsbury', *Fourteen English judges* (1926) • A. A. Paterson, 'Judges: a political elite?', *British Journal of Law and Society*, 1 (1974), 118–35 • H. A. Clegg, A. Fox, and A. F. Thompson, *A history of British trade unions since 1889*, 1 (1964) • J. B. Atlay, 'Lord Halsbury and Lord Herschell', *The Victorian chancellors*, 2 (1908), 433–65 • *The Times* (12 Dec 1921) • *The Times* (15 Dec 1921) • G. D. Phillips, *The diehards: aristocratic society and politics in Edwardian England* (1979) • 'Royal commission on the selection of justices of the peace: minutes of evidence', *Parl. papers* (1910), 37.727, Cd 5358

Archives BL, corresp. and papers, Add. MSS 56367–56377 | Bodl. Oxf., corresp. with Lord Selborne • HLRO, letters to Lord Willoughby de Broke • PRO NIre., corresp. with Edward Carson • Suffolk RO, Ipswich, letters to Lord Cranbrook • U. Birm. L., corresp. with Joseph Chamberlain

Likenesses Spy [L. Ward], cartoon, 1874, repro. in Fox, *The earl of Halsbury* • photographs, 1874, repro. in Fox, *The earl of Halsbury* • York & Son, photograph, 1890–99, NPG [*see illus.*] • J. Collier, oils, 1897, Inner Temple, London; W. Menzies, copy, Merton Oxf. • A. Bryan, pen-and-ink drawing, NPG • O. Edis, photograph, NPG • Fry & Son, photograph, NPG; repro. in *Our conservative and unionist statesmen*, 3 (1896–9) • H. Furniss, two pen-and-ink sketches, NPG • S. P. Hall, pencil sketch, NPG • G. Reid, portrait, priv. coll. • J. Simpson, ink drawing, NPG • Spy [L. Ward], caricature, watercolour study, NPG; repro. in *VF* (22 June 1878) • photograph, repro. in Atlay, 'Lord Halsbury and Lord Herschell' • prints, NPG

Wealth at death £25,009 11*s*. 6*d*.: probate, 8 Feb 1922, *CGPLA Eng. & Wales*

Giffard, Henry (1694–1772), actor and theatre manager, the youngest of the eight sons of William Giffard (*d.* 1722) of Buckinghamshire, was born in London and educated at a private school. In 1716 he found employment as a clerk in the South Sea Company, but after three years he abandoned this position, moved to Bath, and joined an itinerant group of actors. About a year later he moved to the Smock Alley Theatre, Dublin, where he took a number of major roles, including Valentine in William Congreve's *Love for Love* and Sir Charles in Colley Cibber's *The Careless Husband*. Giffard's importance to the company at Smock Alley led to his being offered a part share in the management. While in Dublin he married Mary (Molly) Lyddal, an actress in the company. In either 1726 or 1727 she gave birth to a son, William, and a year later she died while giving birth to a daughter. In 1728 Giffard married Mary's sister, Anna Marcella (Nancy) Lyddal. The couple then moved to London, where they joined the company of Thomas Odell, who had recently opened a theatre at Goodman's Fields.

Giffard made his London début as Plume in George Farquhar's *The Recruiting Officer*, and he went on to play a number of leading roles in the 1729–30 season. His wife Nancy also made her London début around this time, and the two often appeared on stage together. Their roles as a dramatic couple included those of Bevil Junior and Indiana in Richard Steele's *The Conscious Lovers* and Altamont and Calista in Nicholas Rowe's *The Fair Penitent*. Following Odell's decision to relinquish control of Goodman's Fields in 1731, Giffard took over the management. He quickly drew up plans to erect a second, more spacious theatre near the site of the first, meeting the cost of over £2000 through a number of individual subscriptions. The new theatre, designed by Edward Shepherd, opened on 2 October 1732 with a performance of *1 Henry IV*. As well as managing the theatre, Giffard made regular appearances on stage until the end of the 1735–6 season, playing parts as diverse as Jaffeir in Thomas Otway's *Venice Preserv'd* and Loveless in John Vanbrugh's *The Relapse*. In September 1733, while still managing the theatre at Goodman's Fields, he purchased a share in the theatre at Drury Lane, and appeared on stage there several times at the beginning of the 1733–4 season before selling his share to Charles Fleetwood. In the summer of 1735 he toured Ireland with the company of the Aungier Street Theatre, Dublin.

In the autumn of 1736 Henry and Nancy Giffard moved to the vacant Theatre Royal at Lincoln's Inn Fields. In order to fill this older, larger house, Giffard offered subscribers the chance to purchase books of twenty tickets 'at half the expense' (*Daily Post*, 19 Nov 1736). He made only occasional appearances as an actor during the 1736–7 season, the majority of his time being taken up by the management of the theatre. In December 1736 he found himself in dispute with E. D. Cole, a dancer in the Drury Lane company. Cole accused him of causing a disturbance in the Drury Lane audience during a performance of *Tiddi-Doll*, a burlesque featuring Cole's daughter. Giffard rejected the charge. Gifford's counter-accusation, that Cole had employed a number of people to hiss performances at Lincoln's Inn Fields, was similarly denied.

In May 1737 Giffard attempted to sell his interest in

Goodman's Fields. However, the simultaneous introduction of Walpole's Licensing Act made the sale impossible. Walpole, who believed himself to have been unfairly lampooned by Fielding's players at the New Haymarket, found an ingenious way of persuading George II of the merits of the Licensing Act. He commissioned a two-act anti-government play, *The Vision of the Golden Rump*, and made sure that it found its way to Giffard at Lincoln's Inn. Giffard refused to stage the piece, but mistakenly attempted to earn Walpole's favour by surrendering the play to the government. Walpole was able to present the play to George II as the work of an anonymous player, and the king's fury was such that the Licensing Act was pressed through parliament with ease. The act prohibited the staging of theatrical performances in London beyond the confines of the city of Westminster, a measure that rendered Giffard's theatre at Goodman's Fields useless.

In June 1737 the Giffards left London to join the Smock Alley company in Dublin. The following summer Henry Giffard sold off the scenery, props, and costumes belonging to the theatre at Goodman's Fields. In autumn 1738 the Giffards accompanied the Smock Alley players on a tour of Carlow and Drogheda, and in the winter of the same year Henry Giffard led a company to Edinburgh. In March 1739, however, the Giffards returned to London, where they rejoined the company at Drury Lane. A year later Giffard successfully petitioned the lord chamberlain for permission to reopen the theatre at Goodman's Fields. He ran the theatre for two seasons, taking advantage of the summer break in 1741 to take his company to Ipswich.

Although by no means a great actor himself, Giffard was a keen student of the theatre and a diligent coach of his fellow players. His insistence upon the importance of thorough rehearsals brought the best out of the young actors in his company, chief among them David Garrick. In October 1741 Giffard gave Garrick his London début in the title role of Shakespeare's *Richard III*. For the 1742–3 season he returned to Lincoln's Inn Fields, but without the attraction of Garrick the theatre quickly began to lose money, and the company was soon disbanded. In the autumn of 1743 the Giffards joined the company at Drury Lane for a third time, where they remained until the summer of 1747. Henry Giffard's final performance, as Aimwell in Farquhar's *The Beaux' Stratagem*, was given at Covent Garden on 7 October 1748. Four days later Nancy Giffard made her final stage appearance, as Lady Fanciful in Vanbrugh's *The Provoked Wife*. Following their retirement from the stage the couple moved to New Brentford, Middlesex, where they lived for over twenty years. Henry Giffard died there on 20 October 1772, and was buried in the local cemetery five days later. He was survived by Nancy Giffard, who died on 21 January 1777.

William Giffard, Henry Giffard's son by his first wife, also made a career from the stage. He appeared as a child at Goodman's Fields in the early 1730s, and made his adult début at the same theatre in the 1740–41 season. He remained at Goodman's Fields for two years before moving with his father to the theatre at Lincoln's Inn. William Giffard's final London performance was on 5 May 1744, after which he appeared exclusively in the regional theatres. He finally retired from the stage towards the end of the 1760s, and died at Cockermouth, Cumberland, in 1807.

Charles Brayne

Sources W. R. Chetwood, *A general history of the stage, from its origin in Greece to the present time* (1749), 166–7 • *The thespian dictionary, or, Dramatic biography of the present age*, 2nd edn (1805) • D. Lysons, *The environs of London*, 2nd edn, 2/1 (1811), 35 • *London Daily Post and General Advertiser* (19 Nov 1736) • *GM*, 1st ser., 77 (1807), 382 • Highfill, Burnim & Langhans, *BDA* • A. H. Scouten, ed., *The London stage, 1660–1800*, pt 3: *1729–1747* (1961), lxxxi–lxxxii • W. S. Clark, *The Irish stage in the county towns, 1720–1800* (1965), 359

Likenesses satirical print, pubd 1743, repro. in *Catalogue of prints and drawings in the British Museum, division 1: political and personal satires*, vol. 3, pt 1 (1877), 475–9

Wealth at death owned freehold on twenty houses in Coventry Street, London, from which he received rent; also owned £750 of government stock: Highfill, Burnim & Langhans, *BDA*

Giffard, Henry Wells (1811–1854), naval officer, was born on 24 June 1811, in High Street, Portsmouth, the fourth of the eight children of John Giffard (1766–1855), admiral of the White, and his wife, Susanne, daughter of Sir John Carter of Portsmouth. The family had strong whig political connections. Giffard entered the Royal Naval College, Portsmouth, in April 1824 and passed out in March 1825 with the 'first medal', awarded to the volunteers who completed the course in the shortest possible time. He served as a midshipman in the *Asia*, flagship of Sir Edward Codrington, at the battle of Navarino (20 October 1827), and was made acting lieutenant in the *Shannon* in October 1830, being confirmed on 4 March 1831. After service in the *Volage* he was promoted to commander on 2 February 1838 and in 1839 travelled to Singapore to take command of the brig *Cruizer*, in which he took an active and distinguished part in the First Opium War of 1839–42. He was mentioned in dispatches three times and posted captain on 8 June 1841.

Too senior now to command a small brig, Giffard returned to Britain in 1842. On half pay for four and a half years, he gained his 'steam certificate' at Woolwich and from 1844 to 1846 studied steam at the Royal Naval College.

He married on 19 March 1846 Ella Emilia (1814–1906), daughter of Major-General Sir Benjamin Stephenson (1766–1839). They had two sons, George Augustus (1849–1924), who became an admiral, and Henry Rycroft (1850–1934).

On 13 October 1846 Giffard was appointed to command of the *Penelope*, often regarded as the first steam paddle frigate, on the west African station. He resigned this command, probably for health reasons, on 26 March 1848. On 3 August 1850 he was appointed to the steam paddle frigate *Dragon* and employed in the Mediterranean, before being transferred to the new steam frigate *Tiger* on 19 June 1852. The *Tiger* was involved in the naval operations in the eastern Mediterranean that preceded the outbreak of war with Russia in 1854. On 2 April she joined in the bombardment of Odessa. Sent to reconnoitre ten days later, she went aground in heavy fog a little to the south of Odessa and, unable to defend herself, was destroyed by Russian gunfire from the shore; her crew were taken prisoners. Giffard lost a leg in the action and died of gangrene in the quarantine centre at Odessa on 1 June. He was buried with military honours in a cemetery on Preobrazhenskaya in Odessa. An able officer, much liked by his contemporaries, Giffard's life was punctuated by ill health, probably benign tertian malaria, acquired early in his service.

J. K. LAUGHTON, *rev.* BASIL GREENHILL

Sources H. W. Giffard, personal notes, NMM, NMM JOD 30 • H. W. Giffard, midshipman's and lieutenant's logs, NMM • A. Royer, *The English prisoners in Russia* (1854) • B. Greenhill and A. Giffard, *Steam, politics and patronage* (1994) • log of surgeon of HMS *Tiger*, PRO, ADM 101/123/5 132735 • *United Service Magazine*, 3 (1854), 350–51 • Giffard family tree • F. C. A. Stephenson, *At home and on the battlefield: letters from the Crimea, China, and Egypt, 1854–1888 … together with a short memoir of himself*, ed. Mrs F. Pownall (1915)
Likenesses watercolour, 1846, priv. coll.

Giffard, John, first Lord Giffard (1232–1299), baron, was born on 19 January 1232, the son of Elias Giffard (*d.* 1248), holder of the castle and barony of Brimpsfield, Gloucestershire, and extensive lands in both Gloucestershire and Wiltshire. His mother was Alice, daughter of John Maltravers. His father formally betrothed him at Arrow in Warwickshire at the age of four years to Alberada (Aubrée) de Canville, daughter of Thomas de Canville of Arrow, who was his age. The arrangement did not proceed to marriage, and the girl later entered a nunnery. He was in the queen's wardship until 1253, and is found in 1256 having a respite of knighthood until his return from a journey to Ireland with John de Mucegros. He was active in the campaigns against Llywelyn ap Gruffudd in 1257–8 and 1260–61. In August 1262 he is found associated with the young aristocratic victims of the Savoyard purge of Edward's household, banned from tourneying or riding around in arms. Like them, he gravitated into the household of Simon de Montfort, earl of Leicester, leader of the opposition to 'alien' influences at court.

Giffard was active in Montfort's interest through most of the period of the baronial rebellion, being one of those who seized the alien bishop of Hereford, Peter d'Aigueblanche, in June 1263. In August he was given control of St Briavels and the Forest of Dean, and in December consolidated his power in the southern march with the keeping of the counties of Gloucester, Worcester, and Hereford. However, he had not forgotten his former attachment to Edward. In the same month, perhaps annoyed by Montfort's temporizing with Prince Llywelyn, he undertook to support Edward (saving his oath to support the provisions of Oxford). When his friends, the former associates of Edward, returned to the latter's household in October 1263, Giffard at first accepted a £50 money fee from Edward, but returned it after Christmas, and remained with Montfort. He was active in attacking Edward's supporters in the southern march in the winter of 1263, and, according to Robert of Gloucester, he assisted Montfort's capture of the town (but not castle) of Gloucester by secretly penetrating it dressed as a Welsh wool merchant. But when the time came to defend Gloucester against the Lord Edward in February 1264 he was unsuccessful. However, he captured Warwick and its earl for the Montfortians in April. He fought in Earl Simon's household at the battle of Lewes on 14 May 1264, when he was briefly taken prisoner, but himself took prisoner William de la Zouche.

It was immediately after the battle that Giffard left Earl Simon's retinue and entered that of Gilbert de Clare, earl of Gloucester and Hertford. The move made political sense for him, as Earl Gilbert was the dominant magnate in the southern march. But it led to ill feeling between Giffard and his former associates, as he took his prisoner, Zouche, with him, and also as he joined in the fighting between Earl Gilbert's brother, Thomas, and the sons of Earl Simon. The tournament at Dunstable arranged to settle the differences in February 1265 was prohibited, and Giffard and Earl Gilbert took this as their excuse to retreat to the southern march. Clare and Giffard concentrated their forces in the Dean area, uniting with the Lord Edward after his escape in late May, and assisting in his capture of the Severn valley. Giffard fought for the royalists at Evesham on 4 August 1265, taking a number of prisoners, and later accumulating great sums of money in ransoms and confiscated lands. He had pardon for his offences while with Montfort, and retained Dean until 1270.

In the aftermath of Evesham Giffard used his cash surplus to become a notable baronial player in the loan market. His adherence to Gilbert de Clare also brought him considerable gains, notably a grant in fee of a rent of £20 in the earl's borough of Burford, Oxfordshire, and manor of Badgeworth, Gloucestershire, and control of both places for life. His public career seems to have declined somewhat after Evesham, for reasons that are not immediately clear but which may have been perfectly innocent: a simple preference for rural pursuits, perhaps. The almost obsessional enthusiasm with which he devoted himself to the hunt, both in royal forests and his own parks, has been remarked upon. But he did not confine himself to hunting beasts of the chase. In October 1271 he caused a notorious scandal when he abducted from her house at Canford, Wiltshire, the (allegedly) unwilling Matilda Longespée, daughter and heir of Sir Walter de Clifford of Glasbury and widow of William (III) Longespée, sometime heir to the earldom of Salisbury. It seems that the two had already been negotiating a marriage contract, but Giffard became impatient and attempted a rough wooing. Giffard was heavily fined, but eventually managed to persuade the king to sanction the match. This marriage brought him the Clifford lordships and castles of Bronllys and Glasbury in Brecon, Llandovery in Deheubarth, and other manors in Shropshire for life, and brought him into the ranks of marcher lords.

Giffard's military skills and marcher connections remained much valued despite advancing years. He was still pursuing an enthusiasm for the tournament in 1274 (then aged forty-two), when he attended one at Newark with a large following. He played a full part in the campaigns of Edward I against Llywelyn ap Gruffudd, prince of Gwynedd, and was involved in the final campaign in which the prince was killed in December 1282. A year later he was rewarded with the lordship of Is-Cennen in west Wales, and in 1290 had the grant of the castle of Dynefwr (the royal seat of the dynasty of Deheubarth) for life, which greatly enhanced his position as a marcher baron. As such, he (with others) came into conflict with Humphrey (VI) de Bohun, earl of Hereford, in 1290–91. He was involved in dealing with the major Welsh uprising of 1294–5, commanding a force that relieved the castle of Builth in November 1294. King Edward showed his faith in Giffard by employing him as commander of the castle of Podensac, south of Bordeaux in Gascony, in the Anglo-French war of 1294–5. But the castle was surrendered by Giffard to Charles de Valois, which caused outrage among the Gascon nobility, and led to Giffard's trial and further trouble, when his troops mutinied.

John Giffard returned to England, and remained in favour, attending councils and parliaments up to the time of his death. He died at his house at Boyton, Wiltshire, on 29 May 1299, and was buried on 11 June at Malmesbury Abbey. His wife Matilda had died in or soon after 1281, and he had married in 1286 Margaret, widow of John de Neville (*d.* 1282). She died in 1338. Giffard left several children. He had three daughters with his first wife: Katherine, who married Nicholas Audley, Eleanor, and Matilda, still unmarried in 1299, who (with an elder half-sister) shared the Clifford inheritance from their mother. His only son, also John Giffard, was born to his second wife in or about 1287, and remained in wardship until 1308, when he inherited the lordship of Brimpsfield and the rest of his father's acquisitions.

The elder John Giffard's career is not without interest. His passionate involvement with the politics of the later Henrician monarchy, and his fitful relationship with the Lord Edward, dominated his young adulthood. His later years, following his final frenzied behaviour over Matilda Longespée, are a marked contrast. He settled into the mould of the Edwardian magnate, his career revolving around public service, the king's military ambitions, and his own financial and estate interests. His foundation of Gloucester Hall at Oxford (1283–4), as a Benedictine house within the university for students from the ancient abbey his family had long patronized, is an interesting manifestation of a new direction in aristocratic patronage, and is directly comparable with the patronage of Merton College by Sir Richard de Harcourt, another middle-ranking Edwardian aristocrat. DAVID CROUCH

Sources *Chancery records* • *CIPM*, vol. 3 • 'Hailes chronicle', BL, Cotton MS Cleopatra D.iii • W. H. Hart, ed., *Historia et cartularium monasterii Sancti Petri Gloucestriae*, 3 vols., Rolls Series, 33 (1863–7) • exchequer, forest proceedings, PRO, E32/188 • *Ann. mon.*, vol. 4 • [W. Rishanger], *The chronicle of William de Rishanger, of the barons' wars*, ed. J. O. Halliwell, CS, 15 (1840) • J. G. Edwards, ed., *Littere Wallie* (1940) • GEC, *Peerage* • J. N. Langston, 'The Giffards of Brimpsfield', *Transactions of the Bristol and Gloucestershire Archaeological Society*, 65 (1944), 105–28 • J. Birrel, 'A great thirteenth-century hunter: John Giffard of Brimpsfield', *Medieval Prosopography*, 15 (1994)

Giffard, John (1745–1819), politician and newspaper editor, was born on 14 February 1745 in Dublin, the son of John Giffard (*d.* 1746) of Wotton and Great Torrington, Devon, and his wife, Dorcas, *née* Murphy, of Oulart, co. Wexford, widow of Francis Robinson of Dublin. Though descended on his mother's side from the ancient Irish family the McMorroughs, and connected on his father's to the Giffards of Devon, Giffard's upbringing was decidedly modest. Educated, it was alleged, as a charity pupil at the famous Blue Coat Hospital in Dublin, he qualified as an apothecary in London, and he was made a freeman of the Apothecaries' Guild in Dublin in 1768. A year later, in June 1769, he married Sarah Morton (1750–1827), an heir of Ballynaclash, co. Wexford, and the first of their six children, Ambrose Hardinge *Giffard, was born in 1771.

Giffard was elected, as a representative of the Apothecaries' Guild, to the common council of Dublin corporation in 1774. His political orientation in the 1770s was towards opposition; in 1778 the first company of Dublin Volunteers was formed at his house, and in 1779 he joined with Napper Tandy and John Binns in advocating 'free trade'. However, political instinct and self-interest pulled him in the opposite direction, and the early 1780s were to witness his transformation into a conservative activist. His role in reporting the proceedings of the Irish parliament that resulted in the publication of the first volume of the *Parliamentary Register* (1782) attracted the notice of the Irish administration, and he was already a 'Castle scribbler' (Inglis, 58) when he publicly challenged the legality of an aggregate meeting convened in Dublin on 21 June 1784 to launch a campaign for parliamentary reform. His presence together with the attorney-general, John Fitzgibbon, when he embarked on a similar action three months later, emphasized his usefulness to the Dublin Castle authorities, and he confirmed his value during the mid-1780s by, among other services, reporting debates in the House of Commons in 1787. Already the beneficiary of a position in the customs service and a secret service pension of £300, Giffard's star rose further when Dublin Castle helped him secure the lease on the city's oldest newspaper, *Faulkner's Dublin Journal*, in 1788.

Dublin Castle's expectation was that Giffard would turn the *Dublin Journal* into a propaganda mouthpiece, and he did not disappoint. He used the paper and his membership of the growing 'castle party' on the common council to promote the administration's position during the late 1780s and early 1790s on such issues as the regency, the lord mayoralty dispute, the French Revolution, and Catholic relief. His egregious manner and assertive conservatism precipitated an unseemly altercation in 1790 with John Philpot Curran, but Giffard was unrepentant. Intolerant of those of opposite views and devoted to the maintenance of the political *status quo*, he was a member of the corporation committee that drafted the famous clarion call to protestants to rally to maintain 'protestant ascendancy' in January 1792. He further demonstrated his ardent conservatism by passing information from Thomas Collins, the United Irish spy, to Dublin Castle and by becoming a captain in the Dublin militia. As sheriff of Dublin in 1793–4 he zealously prosecuted radicals and, among other actions, conducted the raid upon Tailors'

Hall in May 1794 that brought the open phase of the United Irishmen to a close. His partiality and arrogant righteousness made him a hate figure in liberal circles and earned him the nickname the Dog in Office. Giffard resorted to the courts to protect his name, but despite his successful prosecution of the editor of the *Dublin Morning Post* in 1794 the sobriquet stuck. Indeed, its use by a rival newspaper in 1795 resulted in an assault by Giffard for which he was sentenced to six months' imprisonment, though high-level intervention secured his early release.

Just prior to this Giffard's career as a newspaper editor appeared finished when the lord lieutenant, Earl Fitzwilliam, 'dismissed' him and the *Dublin Journal* (Inglis, 61). The experience did nothing to temper his ultra-protestant activities, for following his restoration to favour on Fitzwilliam's recall he co-ordinated Dublin corporation's petition against Catholic emancipation and he was among the first members of the Orange order in the capital when a lodge was established there in 1797. Widely perceived in radical circles as a rabid bigot, he featured on several assassination lists in the run-up to the 1798 rising. He survived the rising unscathed but the death of his son William and his nephew Daniel Frederick Ryan left a deep mark. Convinced that protestant ascendancy and the British connection could be maintained only if Britain and Ireland were bound in a legislative union, he defied his colleagues in the Orange order and on Dublin corporation to support the measure. His political life thereafter was devoted to the twin causes of protestant ascendancy and the Union. To this end he sought at every opportunity to promote loyalty to the Hanoverian monarchy in Ireland, to popularize the Union, and, as befitted a deputy grand master of the Orange order, to oppose the enhancement of the position of Catholics. His procrustean commitment to the maintenance of protestant ascendancy meant relations with the Irish executive were often difficult. The earl of Hardwicke dismissed him from his place as accountant-general of the customs in 1805, but he was restored by the duke of Richmond, and successive tory administrations kept him on board until 1816 when he severed his connection with the *Dublin Journal*. Unable to accept that his brand of ultra-conservatism was no longer respectable, Giffard remained politically active in the cause he had done so much to promote until his death on 5 May 1819. JAMES KELLY

Sources A. H. Giffard, *Who was my grandfather? A biographical sketch* (privately published, London, 1865) • Burke, *Peerage* • B. Inglis, *The freedom of the press in Ireland, 1784–1841* (1954) • J. R. Hill, *From patriots to unionists: Dublin civic politics and Irish protestant patriotism, 1660–1840* (1997) • W. J. Fitzpatrick, *The Sham Squire and the informers of 1798* (1869) • W. J. Fitzpatrick, *Secret services under Pitt* (1892) • *GM*, 1st ser., 89/1 (1819), 481–4 • J. Kelly, *That damn'd thing called honour: duelling in Ireland, 1570–1860* (1995) • J. R. Hill, 'The politics of Dublin corporation', *The United Irishmen*, ed. D. Dickson and others (1993) • G. O'Brien, ed., 'Debate in the Irish parliament, 1787', *Analecta Hibernica*, 33 (1986) • J. T. Gilbert, R. M. Gilbert, and J. F. Weldrick, eds., *Calendar of the ancient records of Dublin*, 18 vols. (1889–1922), vols. 13–15 • *The life and surprising adventures of a dog, in which is given a true and faithful account of his birth and education, his various feats as a charity schooboy, a pilot to a blind man, an apothecary, a captain, an orator, an editor of a newspaper* (1803)

Archives BL, corresp. and MSS, Add. MS 56367 | NL Ire., Bolton MSS, MS 15883

Giffard, John Anthony Hardinge [Tony], **third earl of Halsbury (1908–2000)**, scientist and public servant, was born on 4 June 1908 at Ennismore Gardens, London. He was the only son and elder child of Hardinge Goulborn Giffard, second earl of Halsbury (1880–1943), barrister and recorder of Carmarthen, and his wife, Esme (1884–1973), daughter of James and Lucy Wallace. His father was English and his mother Scottish. Giffard was educated at Ludgrove School and Eton College. While Giffard was at Eton his grandfather Hardinge Stanley *Giffard, the first earl, who had been lord chancellor and editor-in-chief of Halsbury's *Laws of England*, died and Giffard became Viscount Tiverton. His intention was to read science at Oxford but his father, believing the financial reward of a scientific career insufficient to support an earldom, placed him in articles with the accountants Deloittes. Articles completed, Tiverton became a market clerk with a firm of chemical merchants. On 1 October 1930 he married Ismay Catherine Crichton-Stuart (*d.* 1989); their son, Adam Edward Giffard, was born in 1934; the couple divorced in 1936. Tiverton registered as an external student at London University in 1932 and, despite lack of money and spare-time private study, graduated with first-class honours in chemistry and mathematics in 1935.

In the same year Tiverton joined Lever Brothers as a chartered engineer, and quickly achieved substantial savings in the cost of producing margarine. He was transferred to a managerial post with Prices (Bromborough) Ltd, where he greatly improved profitability through the introduction of better chemical and manufacturing processes, including a new machine he designed and built from scrap, the output of which could meet the entire national demand for fatty alcohol. On 2 December 1936 he married Elizabeth Adeline Faith (Betty; *d.* 1983), daughter of Major Harry Crewe Godley. Their first daughter, Elizabeth Caroline Elinor Evelyn, was born in 1939, and their second, Clare Rohais Antonia Elizabeth, in 1944. Tiverton moved to the Brown–Firth Research Laboratories in Sheffield in 1942. In six weeks he turned himself into a metallurgist and was soon in charge of producing creep-resisting steels for jet engines. He also did much original work, including the development of high-temperature austenitic steels used in gas turbines and the first attempt to make ferritic creep-resisting steels.

Tiverton's father died in 1943 and he inherited the title. In 1947 Halsbury, as he now was, became director of research for the Decca Record Company and the family moved to 64 Barkston Gardens in London. The Decca works was plagued by strikes, and the records produced frequently deteriorated in storage. Halsbury soon added the duties of works manager to those of research director. Within six months the problems were solved, production more than doubled, and manufacturing costs had dropped dramatically. When he left in 1949 he had also

John Anthony Hardinge Giffard, third earl of Halsbury (1908–2000), by Lenare, 1955

produced full stereophonic sound on record and an almost indestructible vinyl long-playing disc.

In 1949 Halsbury was appointed the first managing director of the National Research Development Corporation established to protect and exploit inventions in the public sector. His approach was to seek and encourage invention with commercial potential and then to create public–private partnerships to enable exploitation. The impact on British universities in particular was considerable and led to today's network of university–industry collaboration. He enabled the development of the British computer industry, the hovercraft, the Bailey bridge, and a group of broad-spectrum antibiotics (cephalosporins). He left the corporation in 1959 and took several company directorships, including one with Joseph Lucas Industries. His championing of the development of laser technology by one of its subsidiaries, G. and E. Bradley Ltd, was important in establishing Britain's laser industry.

Halsbury was chairman of the Science Museum advisory council from 1951 to 1965, during which time the museum greatly extended its links with industry, reshaped its approach to education and training, and fostered the creation of the National Railway Museum in York, all projects close to his heart. He was chairman of the management committee of the Institute of Cancer Research from 1962 to 1977. Although convinced of the need to use animals in scientific experimentation, Halsbury was concerned that their conditions should be of a high standard. He introduced the Laboratory Animals Protection Bill in the House of Lords to regulate the conditions under which animals were kept.

In 1961 the government established a committee of inquiry into methods of decimalization of the currency, with Halsbury as its chairman. The committee was deeply divided over the 'core unit' of the new currency: should it be the equivalent of 10 shillings or the pound? The first was logical but Halsbury, concerned that abandonment of the pound might damage the international standing of sterling, argued tenaciously and successfully for its retention. He was interested in the design of the new coinage and proposed the seven-sided 50 pence piece, which was adopted. His experience as chairman of the government's review body on doctors' and dentists' pay (1971–4) was less happy. The government had instituted a 'social contract' to regulate all pay increases. Halsbury was reported as believing it foolish to recommend for doctors and dentists anything that required a government to violate its policy. He was accused of prejudging the issue and resigned.

Halsbury, a frequent contributor to debates in the House of Lords, introduced a number of bills, several of which related to the use of science for society's benefit. In 1986 he sought to prevent the teaching in schools of homosexuality as 'an acceptable family relationship'. The government incorporated the substance of his bill in the Local Government Act of 1988. Subsequently it became the subject of impassioned debate when the new Scottish parliament wished to repeal those provisions. With his appointment as its first chancellor in 1966, Brunel University acquired somebody who shared its aim of producing useful graduates and undertaking research that would have application in the 'real world'. Halsbury's questing mind, his willingness to debate with anybody who had something interesting to say, and his commitment to the university made him much respected and admired. He retired from office in 1997.

Tony Halsbury died on 14 January 2000 at Sherborne, aged ninety-one. He was an outstanding and innovative scientist and engineer, a capable manager, and a dedicated public servant. He was also a first-rate mathematician, poet, painter, and linguist. A modest man, proud of his noble Norman ancestry, he was reticent about his many distinctions, which included an FRS (1969), an FEng (1976), and honorary doctorates from Brunel and Essex universities. As a committed Christian, he was concerned that whatever he engaged in met high ethical standards. The qualities that most endeared him to those who knew him may also have denied him the wide public recognition his achievements merited. DAVID NEAVE

Sources O. Lindsay, 'The earl of Halsbury', *Biographical memoir for the Royal Society* [forthcoming] • *The Times* (11 Nov 1974) • *The Times* (13 Nov 1974) • *The Times* (18 Jan 2000), 2 • *Daily Telegraph* (18 Jan 2000) • *Chairman's Report, 1976–1977*, Institute of Cancer Research • *Hansard 5C*, 18 Dec 1986; 11 Feb 1987; 1 Feb 1988 • T. Dalyell, 'The earl of Halsbury', *The Independent* (18 Jan 2000), 6 • *WW* (2000) • Burke, *Peerage* (1999) • personal knowledge (2004)

Archives CAC Cam., corresp. with Francis Bacon • ICL, corresp. with Herbert Dingle; corresp. with Dennis Gabor

Likenesses Lenare, photograph, 1955, NPG [*see illus.*] • photograph, 1961, repro. in *Daily Telegraph* • photograph, 1967, repro. in Dalyell, 'The earl of Halsbury' • F. Skinner, bronze bust, 1981, Brunel University • D. Anderson, oils, 1997, Brunel University • photograph, repro. in *The Times*
Wealth at death £514,369—gross; £507,183—net: probate, 30 March 2000, *CGPLA Eng. & Wales*

Giffard [*née* Temple], **Martha, Lady Giffard** (**1639–1722**), letter writer, was the youngest child and only daughter of Sir John *Temple (1600–1677), master of the rolls in Ireland, and his wife, Mary Hammond (*d.* 1638). She was educated privately and shared her family's mistrust of religious extremism and 'the Great Rebellion' (Longe, xii). In February 1654 she visited her father in Dublin with her brother William. On 21 April 1662 she married Sir Thomas Giffard, bt, of Castlejordan, co. Meath, who came of a royalist family, related to Lord Halsbury. He died two weeks later (4 May) of natural causes; his funeral sermon at St Audoen's Church, Dublin, indicated his promise as soldier and statesman. Lady Giffard never remarried. In a letter of 22 May 1653 Dorothy Osborne, her future sister-in-law, noted that Martha was of her own brother Henry's 'humour' and shunned passion as a nuisance (*Letters of Dorothy Osborne*, 47).

Henceforth Lady Giffard lived much with her brother William and his wife, Dorothy, notably in Sheen and London during the plague year of 1665. At this time she began to correspond with Sir William Godolphin, a possible suitor (1665–8), Lady Sunderland ('Sacharissa', 1668–9), and a network of European acquaintances. Having acquired a useful knowledge of French and Spanish, she remained with her brother in Brussels in July 1667 when his wife and children fled the renewal of war, travelling with him, sometimes incognito, to Amsterdam and The Hague, where meetings with De Witt and the prince of Orange paved the way for the triple alliance and peace of Aix on 30 May 1668. In May 1674 she accompanied her brother, now ambassador, to The Hague, when the betrothal of the Princess Mary to William of Orange was suggested, although ladies were not usually received at The Hague on diplomatic occasions. By May 1675, during negotiations for the peace of Nimwegen, Colbert, respecting her influence, obtained permission from Louis XIV to offer her some advantage (D'Estrade, 165, 181).

Lady Giffard returned to England with her brother in 1679, and later resided with the Temples at Moor Park, Surrey, which Sir William purchased in 1685. It was there that she began writing her 'life' and 'character' of her brother and his only surviving son, Jack, after the latter's suicide in 1689—'All of us with our hearts broken' (Longe, 176). Parts of this manuscript were published in 1728. Jonathan Swift, Sir William Temple's secretary and literary executor, offended Lady Giffard by his manners, his demands for money (partly on behalf of Hester Johnson), and his selective and self-seeking use of her brother's correspondence and her own recollections in his edition of *Memoirs of Sir William Temple, Part 3* (1709) (Courtenay, 2.242). Swift, however, considered himself the injured party and justified his actions on the authority of his late patron (Swift, 1.154–7, 10 Nov 1709).

In later years Lady Giffard was 'always a doing' (*Correspondence of Edward Young*, 517). She regularly attended court and corresponded with family and friends. She died suddenly at her home in Dover Street, London, in mid-December 1722, aged eighty-three, possibly from pneumonia, leaving a London house and properties in England and Ireland. Although she had told Swift that she had no money, she made generous bequests to family, friends, and servants, including Mrs Hester Johnson (Swift's 'Stella'), and Swift's sister Mrs Fenton, her companion from 1711. Lady Giffard was buried in December 1722 in Westminster Abbey near Sir William Temple and his wife, having left money for a monument. Her correspondence sheds light on the changing society of her times and the role of women in diplomacy. V. E. CHANCELLOR

Sources J. G. Longe, *Martha, Lady Giffard, her life and correspondence, 1664–1722* (1911) • M. Giffard, *Life and character of Sir William Temple written by a particular friend* (1728) • J. Swift, *Journal to Stella*, ed. H. Williams, 2 vols. (1948) • T. P. Courtenay, *Memoirs of the life, works and correspondence of Sir William Temple*, 2 vols. (1836) • *The letters of Dorothy Osborne to William Temple*, ed. G. C. Moore Smith (1928) • *The works of Sir William Temple*, another edn, 2 vols. (1740) • G. D'Estrade, *Secret letters and negotiations* (1710) • *The correspondence of Jonathan Swift*, ed. H. Williams, 5 vols. (1963–5) • *The correspondence of Edward Young, 1683–1765*, ed. H. Pettit (1971) • T. Carte, *An history of the life of James, duke of Ormonde*, 3 vols. (1735–6) • J. Burke and J. B. Burke, *A genealogical and heraldic history of the extinct and dormant baronetcies of England, Ireland and Scotland*, 2nd edn (1841); repr. (1844) • 'Sir William Temple', T. B. Macaulay, *Essays* (1888), 415ff.
Archives BL, letters to Lady Berkeley, afterwards Lady Portland, 1705, fols. 9–36 • BL, Sir William Temple MSS • U. Southampton L., letter-books of Sir William Temple, etc.
Likenesses P. Lely, Broadlands, Hampshire; repro. in Longe, *Martha, Lady Giffard*, 8 • Netscher, double portrait (with Diana Temple), Broadlands, Hampshire; repro. in Longe, *Martha, Lady Giffard*, 148 • portrait, probably Broadlands, Hampshire; repro. in Longe, *Martha, Lady Giffard*, frontispiece
Wealth at death property valued at £2000 p.a.; also jewellery and furniture: Longe, *Martha Lady Giffard*, 345 ff.

Giffard, Roger. *See* Gifford, Roger (*d.* 1597).

Giffard, Stanley Lees (**1788–1858**), newspaper editor, was born on 4 August 1788 in Dublin, the youngest son of John *Giffard (1745–1819) of Dromartin, co. Dublin, and brother of Sir Ambrose Hardinge *Giffard. He was educated, initially, by Samuel Whyte, the schoolmaster of R. B. Sheridan and Thomas Moore, the poet. Giffard then studied at Trinity College, Dublin, where he obtained his BA in 1807, and took the degree of LLD in 1810. He entered the Middle Temple and was called to the bar in 1811, but made no progress as a barrister and became a political writer on the *St James's Chronicle*. After six years he was rewarded with the editorship by Charles Baldwin in 1819. As an editor, Giffard was in the true Baldwin tradition: violently anti-Catholic and bitterly opposed to emancipation. It was said that he regarded the Roman church as a political conspiracy carried on under the name of religion. He was also a leading supporter of the Irish church labouring under the distress of a tithe war. Coming from a protestant family—during the 1798 rising his father had been sheriff of Dublin and afterwards accountant-general of the Irish customs—he had never forgotten how his brother William, a serving officer, had been hacked to death while on leave in Dublin.

When, on 21 May 1827, Baldwin launched *The Standard*, Giffard was the obvious choice as editor. Within months of the launch, however, he was to be in trouble with the duke of Wellington over an article which caused the duke to exclaim: 'What can we do with these sort of fellows? We have no power over them, and for my part I will have no communication with any of them' (Griffiths, *Encyclopedia*, 263). And three months later, on 16 March 1829, the publication of a letter from Lord Winchilsea, criticizing the duke over King's College and Catholic emancipation, was to lead to Winchilsea and the duke fighting a duel in Battersea Fields. Fortunately, neither party was injured and two days afterwards Giffard published an apology in *The Standard*, plus the full correspondence—some eighteen letters.

The continuing outspokenness of Giffard meant that he was now a person to be reckoned with, but he was not without his critics, as John Gibson Lockhart wrote in 1835: 'But McGinnis's [Maginn's] superior in *The Standard* is a man of a different cast and calibre and *he* really is worth thinking of. He, too, is poor—often embarrassed, and thence, irritable, sulky and dangerous' (Griffiths, *Encyclopedia*, 263). Despite this criticism, Giffard was a proud man, and in 1828 had even refused a gift of £1200 from the duke of Newcastle, who had been impressed by one of the editor's leaders. As the father of ten children, who in the autumn of 1840, as a result of vast debts, was forced to send his family to France to live on £3 a week, this was self-sacrifice of the highest order. His first wife was Susannah Meares Moran, daughter of Francis Moran JP, of Downhill, co. Mayo. His third son by this marriage, Hardinge Stanley *Giffard, was raised to the peerage as earl of Halsbury in 1885 on first becoming lord chancellor, and was promoted to an earldom during his third tenure of the chancellorship, which he retained until 1905. His second wife was Mary Anne, daughter of Henry Giffard RN.

Giffard's life was almost entirely bound up with *The Standard*, although he had contributed articles to *Blackwood's Magazine* and written a *Life of the Great Duke of Ormonde*; and in 1846 he had even stood as a tory parliamentary candidate for Trinity College, Dublin, but withdrew before the poll. Throughout this period Giffard had been heavily involved in opposing the repeal of the corn laws, and was attacked by name in John Bright's speech at the famous meeting in Covent Garden Theatre in 1845. With Charles Baldwin having been succeeded by his son Edward Baldwin as proprietor, Giffard was now also engaged in editing the *Morning Herald*, which had recently been purchased.

Giffard was fortunate during this period to have his son Hardinge as assistant editor. However, for more than a decade Giffard had suffered bouts of ill health—at one time his close friend Alaric Watts had stood in for him as editor—and in the spring of 1855 he was bedridden for three months. After more than forty years' service to the Baldwin family, Giffard realized that his heart was not with the new owner, James Johnstone, and he retired and moved to Folkestone, where he died of cancer on 6 November 1858.

In Giffard's obituary notice in *The Standard* on 9 November 1858, it was noted:

> In the obduracy of his sympathies and anticipation in politics he was a man after Dr Johnson's own heart; and with him departed perhaps the last of the school of Georgian political writers, who brought so great a fund of learning to the pursuit of the press.

D. M. Griffiths

Sources priv. coll., Halsbury archives · D. Griffiths, *Plant here The Standard* (1996) · D. Griffiths, ed., *The encyclopedia of the British press, 1422–1992* (1992) · A. Aspinall, *Politics and the press, c.1780–1850* (1949) · British Newspaper Library, *The Standard* files · GL, manuscripts section, *St James's Chronicle* files · British Newspaper Library, *Morning Herald* files · private information (2004) · *The Standard* (9 Nov 1858)

Archives BL, corresp. and papers, Add. MSS 56368–56369 | BL, letters to P. Bliss, Add. MSS 34570–34572 · BL, corresp. with Sir Robert Peel, Add. MSS 40377–40577, *passim* · priv. coll., Halsbury archives · U. Southampton L., corresp. with Wellington

Likenesses line drawing, priv. coll.

Giffard, Walter (*c*.1225–1279), archbishop of York, was the son of a royal justice, Hugh Giffard of Boyton in Wiltshire, and his wife, Sybil, daughter and coheir of Walter de Cormeilles. Probably their eldest son, he was the older brother of Godfrey *Giffard, a member of Henry III's household and later royal chancellor (1266–8) and bishop of Worcester (1268–1301). Although Walter was a member of one of the most influential clerical dynasties in mid-thirteenth-century England, and a relative of Archbishop Walter Gray of York, little is known of his early life. At some stage a student at Cambridge University, for which he long retained affection, it was at Oxford that he eventually (in 1251) became a master of arts in the company of his brother Godfrey. Henry III himself helped to subsidize Walter's inception feast on that occasion; and five years later Oxford Castle was assigned to Walter Giffard and his mother as their (no doubt temporary) residence. It was in the early 1250s, and presumably while still at Oxford, that Giffard attracted the favourable attention of Friar Adam Marsh who commended his academic talents to another university luminary, Robert of St Agatha.

Walter Giffard was already a papal chaplain as well as a favourite royal clerk by August 1250, and as early as June 1245 he had already been dispensed to hold an additional incompatible benefice. In 1247 he was presented to the rectory of Newland in Gloucestershire and was later canon and prebendary of Wells Cathedral. However, it was only after his election to the bishopric of Bath and Wells on 22 May 1264, an election approved by Henry III six days later, followed by restitution of temporalities on 1 September, that Giffard at last became a prominent figure in national political and ecclesiastical affairs. A committed supporter of the king's cause in his struggle against Simon de Montfort and his baronial allies, Giffard took an oath to support Henry III on the occasion of a visit to Paris, where he received consecration as bishop at Notre Dame on 4 January 1265. During the bishop's absence abroad, many of his manors were allegedly wasted by the king's enemies; and when he returned to England, Giffard was instructed by the archbishop of Canterbury, Boniface of Savoy, to excommunicate Montfort and his supporters. Immediately after the king's victory at the battle of Evesham on 4 August 1265, Giffard received the highest possible rewards for his loyalty to his king. Within six days (on 10 August 1265) he was appointed royal chancellor, an office he held until he became archbishop of York in October of the following year. Throughout the closing years of the reign of Henry III, while Archbishop Boniface was usually abroad, Giffard became the effective leader of the English church as well as one of the king's most influential clerical counsellors. In August 1266 he became one of the commissioners appointed under the dictum of Kenilworth; and on 13 October 1269 he officiated at the second translation of St Edward the Confessor in Westminster Abbey. As the senior ecclesiastic in the kingdom when the Lord Edward left Dover for the Holy Land in August 1270, Giffard was not only the first English prelate to swear allegiance to the new king over Henry III's dead body in 1272, but during the following two years probably did more than anyone, including his two fellow regents, to ensure an untroubled accession for Edward I.

By 1274, however, Walter Giffard had long been strenuously committed to his responsibilities as archbishop of York. Provided to the metropolitan see of St Peter by Pope Clement IV on 15 October 1266, Giffard was enthroned in York Minster—with remarkable speed—only two weeks later. There can be no doubt that the new archbishop owed his elevation to strong pressure from Henry III himself, who succeeded in quashing the formidable rival claims of both Dean William Rotherfield, the York chapter's own favourite candidate, and the celebrated Bonaventure (later St Bonaventure; *d.* 1274). The temporalities were restored on 26 December. Though by no means a continuous or comprehensive record of his pontificate, Giffard's surviving episcopal register not only marks the decisive transition from roll to book form in the York registry, perhaps in emulation of the current practice within the archbishop's previous see of Bath and Wells, but also gives a vivid impression of the immense complexities of diocesan organization in one of the largest sees in medieval England. Perhaps the most serious of Walter Giffard's many problems were financial ones. To judge from the archbishop's frequent letters on the subject, the expenses of his translation to York and of ceaseless litigation, particularly at the Roman curia (that 'whirlpool of usury'), forced him into the voracious clutches of Italian usurers. In 1270 he argued that he was too deeply in debt to visit the apostolic see; and as late as 1275 he still owed £648 to merchants from Lucca. Admittedly Giffard's register also confirms the Lanercost chronicle's comment that the archbishop was exceptionally liberal as well as 'elegant, chaste and sociable' (Maxwell, 19). His role as a generous paterfamilias to his most favoured clerks and especially to the members of his family is extremely well documented. In 1267, for example, he collated the archdeaconry of York to his brother Godfrey in the face of considerable opposition. More happily, it was Giffard's financial support which aided the university studies of two of his successors as archbishop, John le Romeyn and his own young relative, William Greenfield.

In many ways Walter Giffard's success in creating a large network of talented Yorkshire and north Lincolnshire clerks, many of whom progressed from his own administrative service at York to the chancery and privy seal office of the royal government, proved to be his most enduring achievement. Less fortunate were his attempts to preserve the jurisdictional liberties of his archbishopric. By insisting on having his primatial cross carried before him outside as well as within his own province, he not only revived a tediously long-standing dispute between the churches of York and Canterbury but also prejudiced his own attendance at Edward I's coronation in Westminster Abbey on 19 August 1274. More seriously, he took the opportunity of a vacancy in the see of Durham created by the death of Bishop Robert Stichill to conduct (on 30 October 1274) a visitation of the Benedictine monks who formed the cathedral chapter there. Although the archbishop, who no doubt saw such a visitation *sede vacante* as his canonical duty, seems to have behaved with considerable tact when at Durham, in practice his visit inaugurated the most tempestuous period in the long turbulent history of the relationship between the church of York and its powerful suffragan. However, Giffard himself, whether or not now 'fretful and feeble because of his corpulence' (*Chronicle of Lanercost*, 19), remained active in national and diocesan affairs until his death at York on 24 or 25 April 1279. He was buried in York Minster, probably in the choir, although Archbishop John Thoresby (*d.* 1373) later moved his remains to a long-vanished tomb in the retrochoir. None of his books seems to survive; and there is no evidence that he wrote anything except—highly eloquent—letters. R. B. DOBSON

Sources register of Walter Giffard, Reg. 2, Borth. Inst. • *The register of William Giffard, lord archbishop of York, 1266–1279*, ed. W. Brown, SurtS, 109 (1904) • T. S. Holmes, ed., *The registers of Walter Giffard, bishop of Bath and Wells, 1265–1266, and of Henry Bowett, bishop of Bath and Wells, 1401–1407*, Somerset RS, 13 (1899) • W. H. Dixon, *Fasti Eboracenses: lives of the archbishops of York*, ed. J. Raine (1863), 302–17 • R. Brentano, *York metropolitan jurisdiction and papal judges delegate, 1279–1296* (1959) • R. B. Dobson, 'The political role of the archbishops of York during the reign of Edward I', *Thirteenth century England: proceedings of the Newcastle upon Tyne conference* [Newcastle upon Tyne 1989], ed. P. R. Coss and S. D. Lloyd, 3 (1991), 47–64 • H. Maxwell, ed. and trans., *The chronicle of Lanercost, 1272–1346* (1913), 19–20 • *CEPR letters*, vol. 1 • F. M. Powicke, *King Henry III and the Lord Edward: the community of the realm in the thirteenth century*, 2 (1947) • G. E. Aylmer and R. Cant, eds., *A history of York Minster* (1977), 47, 75, 77–81 • Emden, *Oxf.*
Archives Borth. Inst., register, Reg. 2

Giffard, William (*d.* **1129**), bishop of Winchester, was the elder brother of Walter Giffard, earl of Buckingham (*d.* 1164). He had begun his ecclesiastical career first as canon, and later as subdean, of the cathedral at Rouen, remaining in only deacon's orders throughout. However, the real basis of his rise to prominence was his position as king's clerk under the Conqueror, and as chancellor under

Rufus. His reward for supporting Henry I in 1100 was immediate elevation to the wealthy see of Winchester, which had been vacant since 1098. He is first recorded attesting as bishop-elect in charters issued on 5 August 1100, only three days after Rufus's death. It was his curial connection, not his family background, which was really the explanation for this. William of Malmesbury paints a traditional picture of a pious Giffard reluctantly receiving high office: nevertheless there is a late tradition, reported by Matthew Paris, of simony being involved. Giffard probably secured access to the temporalities of his see in that year, though there are no surviving documents issued in his name which date from this period, when he would have been styled *electus*, bishop-elect. Inevitably his consecration became one of the bones of contention between Anselm and Henry I in their struggle over investitures. Bishop William took part in the Council of Westminster in September 1102. In February 1103, however, for reasons unclear, he caused a sensation by refusing consecration at the hands of Archbishop Gerard of York at a public ceremony in St Paul's. Giffard was apparently banished by the king for his pains, though this may not have taken place immediately. John of Worcester implies that Bishop William accompanied Anselm into exile: if this was so he would have arrived at Wissant on 27 April 1103, and in Rome by 10 November of that year. There are a number of letters in Anselm's correspondence which imply close relations between the saint and the bishop, but Giffard's zeal for Rome must have been qualified, to say the least. One letter shows the saint exhorting Giffard not to abandon this good resolution. The precise cause and occasion of his reconciliation with Henry I is uncertain, but Giffard was certainly back in England by February 1105, when he was one of those who wrote to Anselm urging him to make peace with the king. Once this had been achieved, Giffard's long-delayed consecration, and advancement to the priesthood, could take place. This occurred at Canterbury on 11 August 1107, when he, along with Roger of Salisbury, Reinhelm of Hereford, William de Warelwast of Exeter, and Urban of Llandaff, was consecrated by Anselm, assisted by Gerard of York and six other bishops. He made his profession like any other bishop.

Giffard had a reputation as a reformer and a supporter of the new monasticism, based primarily on his series of foundations and refoundations. Right at the end of his life he gave crucial support to the fledgeling Cistercian house of Waverley in Surrey, the first house of that order in England. According to the Waverley annals, the abbey was founded on the episcopal manor of Farnham on 24 November 1128: in fact this probably did not occur until 28 October 1129, that is, after Giffard's death, but some preliminary steps were clearly taken before then. Giffard's main interest seems to have been the Augustinians. About 1120 he obtained five canons from the new Augustinian abbey of Merton in Surrey, where he had consecrated a wooden chapel for the founder, Gilbert Norman, the local sheriff, some three years earlier, for the decaying secular minster at Taunton in Somerset. He transformed that, too, into an Augustinian abbey, and he also made a substantial donation, which caused him to be styled 'founder'. The canons of St Mary Overie, Southwark, also later called him 'founder', but the bishop's surviving *acta* in favour of Southwark, which in any case grant nothing of any obvious significance, may well be spurious, since they both survive only in royal charters of *inspeximus*, issued in the fourteenth century or later. His designation as founder was more probably a consequence of his generosity towards the building of the nave of the priory church in 1107. He was also involved with reformed monasticism originating in Normandy—apparently he founded the priory of Hamble in Hampshire, of the order of Tiron, about 1109. Charters recording his generosity to Hamble once existed, being referred to in confirmations issued by his episcopal successors, Henry de Blois (1129–1171) and Richard of Ilchester (1174–1188), but they were not among the muniments which made their way to Winchester College on Hamble's demise in 1392. Giffard had some uncertain involvement with the Augustinian priory of Southwick, in Hampshire, in its first incarnation at Porchester, and also, possibly, with the tiny Benedictine nunnery of St Mary at Ivinghoe in Buckinghamshire.

It would appear that Giffard had a high conception of the importance of episcopal authority, as, indeed, is implied by his stand on the issue of investitures in 1103. His destruction of the Saxon New Minster, and the removal of its community from a position next to his cathedral to a new home at Hyde, for which he allegedly paid 800 marks to Henry I, can be interpreted as a move intended to enhance the status of the cathedral, and with it that of the bishop, in the city and diocese. His famous (though not certainly authentic) grant to the cathedral priory of the oblations of Pentecost from all priests and parishioners in Hampshire, Surrey, and the Isle of Wight, can be seen in a similar light. The extensive building programme in the nave of Winchester Cathedral, begun under his predecessor Walkelin, seems to have been concluded about 1121, and was the occasion for the renewal of the quarrel between the bishop and the monks of his cathedral priory concerning the patronage of the priory's churches, originally set aside for the building fund, but which William had been using to fund his *familia*. Twentieth-century historians have described him as an assiduous diocesan, with a high reputation for piety among his monks, but in fact so little is known of his activities that this cannot be certain. He was with the king in Normandy in 1119 and was one of those chosen to attend the council of Rheims in that year. In January 1121 he conducted the marriage of Henry I to Adela at Winchester. William Giffard died, clothed as was common at the time, in the monastic habit, on 23 January 1129, and he was buried in his cathedral church two days later.

M. J. FRANKLIN

Sources M. J. Franklin, ed., *Winchester, 1070–1204*, English Episcopal Acta, 8 (1993) • M. J. Franklin, 'The bishops of Winchester and the monastic revolution', *Anglo-Norman Studies*, 12 (1989), 47–66 • *Willelmi Malmesbiriensis monachi de gestis pontificum Anglorum libri quinque*, ed. N. E. S. A. Hamilton, Rolls Series, 52 (1870) • *Eadmeri*

Historia novorum in Anglia, ed. M. Rule, Rolls Series, 81 (1884) • Dugdale, *Monasticon*, new edn • *The letters of Saint Anselm of Canterbury*, ed. and trans. W. Fröhlich, 3 vols. (1990–94), vol. 1, p. 333; vol. 2, pp. 86–9, 93–4, 114–21, 146–8, 154–8, 162–3, 166–9; vol. 3, pp. 251, 362 • C. W. Hollister, 'The strange death of William Rufus', *Speculum*, 48 (1973), 637–53 • J. H. Round, *Feudal England: historical studies on the eleventh and twelfth centuries* (1895); repr. with foreword by F. M. Stenton (1964) • D. Whitelock, M. Brett, and C. N. L. Brooke, eds., *Councils and synods with other documents relating to the English church, 871–1204*, 1 (1981) • *Florentii Wigorniensis monachi chronicon ex chronicis*, ed. B. Thorpe, 2 vols., EHS, 10 (1848–9) • *Fasti Angl., 1066–1300*, [Monastic cathedrals] • *Matthaei Parisiensis, monachi Sancti Albani, Historia Anglorum, sive … Historia minor*, ed. F. Madden, 3 vols., Rolls Series, 44 (1886–9)

Giffard, William (*d.* 1731), man-midwife, about whose early life nothing is known, practised in Brentwood, Essex, before moving to Westminster, London, in 1724. From 1725 he began recording some of his midwifery cases, with a view to publication. Giffard recorded the use of the forceps from 8 April 1726. He called them his 'extractor'. The blades were straight, not conforming to the pelvis though curved to fit the foetal head, whereas those depicted by Edmund Chapman in 1735 in the second edition of his book, *A Treatise on the Improvement of Midwifery*, also showed a curve to match that of the pelvis.

Giffard wrote his only work, *Cases in Midwifry*, at Brentwood, to where he had retired. The place is significant because it is near to Woodham Mortimer, where Peter Chamberlen, a member of the family of refugee Huguenots, who had invented the obstetric forceps, had prudently retired during the civil war. Chamberlen took his then secret instrument—the obstetric forceps—with him but about the beginning of the eighteenth century they became known to a few practitioners living nearby, Giffard included. Giffard's book was published posthumously in 1734 by Edward Hody, who wrote that it was 'an account of 225 mostly difficult cases and to which he had been summoned by midwives'. Giffard believed that 'midwives should summon a male practitioner as soon as they encountered any difficulty in the birth; failure to do so he criticized as "self-sufficiency"' (Wilson, 98). The book has a frontispiece engraving of Giffard's forceps and of the forceps as 'improved' by John Freke, surgeon at St Bartholomew's Hospital.

Giffard once used the forceps on a face presentation. He removed the placenta (afterbirth) manually after the birth of the baby. He recorded a case of the uterus turning inside out (inversion) when he had pulled on the cord attached to the placenta when it was still inside the womb. In breech deliveries he brought down the arms. For the after-coming head in breech presentations he used a finger in the mouth, and fingers over the shoulders to pull the head out of the pelvis. The manoeuvre was later attributed to William Smellie, though Giffard predated him by several years. He also supported the perineum at birth with his hand. This became known much later as von Ritgen's manoeuvre after he described it in 1828.

Giffard also recorded a case which was probably a tumour of the placenta (choriocarcinoma), and he early described the manner of stopping the ante-partum haemorrhage of placenta praevia (placenta in front of the presenting part of the foetus) by turning the presentation to that of the breech using a hand inside the uterus (internal version), then drawing down a leg so that the bleeding site could be compressed.

In his numerous cases Giffard described many obstetric complications dealt with in competent and practical fashion. He was among the first to write about them. Following the diffused knowledge of the forceps, many obstetricians in London evolved newer methods of coping with obstetric difficulties and taught their methods to students and medical practitioners. Giffard was in the forefront of these movements in ideas and practice. Hody described him as 'a plain man, remarkable for an honest, frank behaviour, of strong judgment, skilful and experienced in his profession and very charitable to the poor, averse to all kinds of flattery, and a generous and judicious practitioner' (Spencer, 18). Giffard died at Brentwood towards the end of 1731. PHILIP RHODES

Sources H. R. Spencer, *The history of British midwifery from 1650 to 1800* (1927) • H. Graham, *Eternal Eve* (1950) • H. Speert, *Obstetric and gynecologic milestones* (1958) • W. Smellie, *A treatise on the theory and practice of midwifery* (1752) • E. Chapman, *A treatise on the improvement of midwifery*, 2nd edn (1735) • W. Giffard, *Cases in midwifry* (1734) • W. Radcliffe, *The secret instrument* (1947) • A. Wilson, *The making of man-midwifery: childbirth in England, 1660–1770* (1995)

Giffen, Sir Robert (1837–1910), economist and statistician, born on 22 July 1837 at Strathaven, Lanarkshire, was the younger son of Robert Giffen, a village grocer and an elder of the Presbyterian church, and his wife, Janet Wiseman. Giffen was educated at the village school. He read all the books he could find and, with his elder brother, John, wrote short articles and poems anonymously for a Hamilton newspaper. In 1850 he was apprenticed to a lawyer in Strathaven. Three years later he moved to a lawyer's office in Glasgow, and remained in that city seven years, attending lectures occasionally at the university. William Black, the novelist, was one of his closest Glasgow friends. After two years in a commercial house, in 1860 Giffen turned to journalism as a career by becoming a reporter and sub-editor of the *Stirling Journal*. In 1862 he moved to London, where he became a reporter and sub-editor for *The Globe*, a Palmerstonian paper owned by the economist Robert Torrens. He appears to have moved to the *Daily News* in 1866, but also acted as assistant editor for John Morley's *Fortnightly Review* before joining *The Economist* in 1868; there he became City editor (1870–76) and was a leading contributor under Walter Bagehot, by whom he was much influenced. He was also City editor for the *Daily News* (1870–73), as well as occasional contributor to *The Times* and *The Spectator*. In 1877 he was offered the succession to Bagehot at *The Economist*, but, having failed to agree terms with its proprietors, he went on instead to found in 1878 *The Statist*, the leading rival to *The Economist* in this period and a venture which throve thanks to Giffen's intimate practical knowledge of the workings of the City of London.

Giffen's economic journalism was accompanied by a growing mastery of statistics. In 1868 he valuably assisted

Sir Robert Giffen (1837–1910), by Sydney Prior Hall, pubd 1897

Goschen in compiling the historical and statistical materials for his classic *Report on Local Taxation* (1871), and in 1872 he wrote a pioneering study of the costs of the Franco-Prussian War. His statistical interests now determined a further change of career, and in 1876 he was appointed chief of the statistical department and controller of corn returns at the Board of Trade, although he secured permission to continue to publish his economic views. In 1881 his injudicious journalism led to his temporary suspension but, as he later wrote to his head at the board, 'a good deal of the literature I have done was really conducive to the objects of my department which would not have been so successful if I had not done the literature' (R. Giffen to Sir Thomas Farrer, 15 May 1886, Surrey RO). In 1882, despite his indiscretions, Giffen was appointed an assistant secretary at the board when the statistical department was merged with the reformed commercial department on the latter's returning to the board from the Foreign Office. In 1886 he took over supervision of the work of the new labour statistics bureau but he later resisted the creation of a Ministry of Labour (whose potentially interventionist role he deprecated). Instead, in 1893 a new labour department was set up, with Giffen now appointed controller-general of the commercial, labour, and statistical departments. In 1896 his first wife, Isabella, daughter of D. McEwen of Stirling whom he had married in 1864, died. On 25 November 1896 he married Margaret Anne, daughter of George Wood of Aberdeen, who survived him. There were no children from either marriage. He retired from the board in 1897, and moved to Chanctonbury, Haywards Heath.

At the board, building on the work of G. R. Porter and Richard Valpy, Giffen's main professional ambition was to create an efficient central statistical office, 'a department which publishes statistics for statistical purposes alone, the statistics not being required for daily administration' (Memorandum, 18 July 1889, PRO, BT12/27). His influence is also to be seen in a wide variety of legislative proposals (for example, the Bankruptcy Bill of 1882), in numerous cabinet memoranda, and in parliamentary debate, with Giffen remembered for remarking on one occasion, 'The debate was very interesting and *all* the arguments were my own' (F. S. Hopwood to G. W. Balfour, 26 June 1903, Balfour of Whittingehame MSS, NA Scot., M118/4). He also served on various departmental committees, was a member of the royal commissions on the depression of agriculture in Great Britain (1893–7), and on the port of London (1900–02), and gave important statistical and economic evidence before numerous royal commissions, notably on the depreciation of silver (1876), the London stock exchange (1878), the depression in trade and industry (1886), gold and silver (1886–8), and local taxation (1898–9).

Outside the board, Giffen acquired an unrivalled reputation for practical statistical work. He served on the council of the Royal Statistical Society, edited its journal (1876–91), and acted as its president (1882–4). He was twice president of the economic and statistical section of the British Association (1887 and 1901) and helped set up the International Statistical Institute in 1885. From 1877 he was a pillar of the Political Economy Club and in 1890 a founder member of the Royal Economic Society, to whose *Economic Journal* he frequently contributed, including for many years its 'City notes'. He was also an important contributor to the study of index numbers and to monetary debate (especially through his *Stock Exchange Securities*), while *The Growth of Capital* (1889) pioneered the use of income tax returns to estimate the national capital stock. He proved one of the most forthright and influential critics of the proposed bimetallic standard, and *The Case Against Bimetallism* (1892) was held by the *cognoscenti* to have 'practically snuffed out bi-metallism as a practical project for this country' (*The Economist*, 16 April 1910, 835). Giffen, while still a civil servant, also proved a stern critic of financial aspects of Gladstone's home-rule proposals for Ireland, and his indictment of them in 1893 contributed to the appointment of the royal commission on the financial relations between Great Britain and Ireland (1895–6), before which he was a witness. Regarding Ireland as overtaxed, he also urged the reduction of its representation in the House of Commons and promoted the visionary idea of a tunnel under the Irish Sea.

However, Giffen's greatest political influence came through the dissemination of his statistical defence of free trade through newspapers, tracts (including his own *The New Protection Cry*, 1879), and the popular economic literature of the Cobden Club. More than any other economist, Giffen firmly linked free trade with the prosperity of the nation and above all of the working classes, especially in his paper 'The progress of the working classes' (1883), itself the foundation for many subsequent optimistic interpretations of the impact of industrialization in Britain. Through these writings—many of which were collected in his *Essays in Finance* (1880, 1886) and *Economic Enquiries and Studies* (1904)—Giffen became the most persuasive and influential opponent of the fair-trade movement in the late 1870s and early 1880s. In similar vein, in 1903 he publicly exposed the statistical fallacies of Chamberlain's case for tariff reform. By then, however, he was ready to admit that imperial preference and a colonial *Zollverein* might be supported on political, if not economic, grounds. For, despite their early radical and democratic flavour, Giffen's political views now separated him from his Liberal friends as he proposed increased armaments expenditure (as a deterrent to the even greater costs of warfare), supported compulsory military service, and ultimately was ready to broaden the basis of taxation by import duties rather than through direct taxation. He was a strident critic of Lloyd George's 1909 budget and in January 1910 was to support the Unionist Party, for now protection was preferable to 'socialism', that is, Liberal collectivist legislation. Such collectivism, he believed, undermined the ethic of individual self-help which his own career had exemplified.

Giffen was made an honorary LLD of Glasgow University in 1884 and was created CB in 1891 and KCB in 1895. He died of heart failure at the Lovat Arms Hotel, Fort Augustus, Inverness-shire, on 12 April 1910, while on a visit to Scotland, and was buried at Strathaven.

A prolific writer on economic, financial, and statistical subjects, Giffen

> possessed a luminous and penetrating mind, great stores of information, an intimate acquaintance with business matters, and shrewd judgment. His instructive handling of statistics and his keen eye for pitfalls contributed greatly to raise the reputation and encourage the study of statistics in this country, though he did not develop its technique by the higher mathematical treatment. (*DNB*)

His *Handbook of Statistics* (edited by H. Higgs and G. Yule) was published in 1913 but stands more as a testimony to his own past achievements than a pointer to future methods. Nevertheless, Giffen, acknowledged by Alfred Marshall as the 'Prince of Statisticans' (Marshall to Giffen, 2 July 1895, Giffen MSS), has acquired a considerable posthumous reputation for the 'Giffen paradox' or 'Giffen goods'. This holds that, especially among the poor, a rise in the price of certain goods will produce an increase in demand, the only widely acknowledged exception to the law of demand. This paradox, although its exposition owed more to Marshall than Giffen himself, has ensured the survival of Giffen's name among modern economists.

A. C. Howe

Sources BLPES, Giffen MSS • *DNB* • R. S. Mason, *Robert Giffen and the Giffen paradox* (1989) • R. S. Mason, 'Robert Giffen and the tariff reform campaign, 1865–1910', *Journal of European Economic History* (1996), 171–88 • A. E. Bateman, 'Sir Robert Giffen', *Journal of the Royal Statistical Society*, 73 (1910) • F. Y. Edgeworth, 'Sir Robert Giffen', *Economic Journal*, 20 (1910) • *The Times* (13 April 1910) • *Glasgow Herald* (13 April 1910) • *The Statist* (16 April 1910) • *The Economist* (16 April 1910) • *Economic Bulletin* (June 1910) • Board of trade and cabinet memoranda, PRO • Glos. RO, Hicks Beach MSS • J. C. Wood, *British economists and the empire* (1983) • R. Davidson, *Whitehall and the labour problem in late Victorian and Edwardian England* (1985) • R. D. Edwards, *The pursuit of reason: The Economist, 1843–1993* (1993) • J. K. Whitaker, 'The economics of defense in British political economy, 1848–1914', *Economics and national security*, ed. C. D. Goodwin (1991), 37–59

Archives BLPES, corresp., papers, press cuttings | Glos. RO, earl of St Aldwyn MSS • Glos. RO, corresp. with Sir Michael Hicks Beach • U. Birm. L., corresp. with Joseph Chamberlain

Likenesses S. P. Hall, drawing, repro. in *The Graphic* (16 Oct 1897) [*see illus.*] • double portrait (with Lady Giffen), repro. in *The Graphic* (16 Oct 1897) • portrait, repro. in Bateman, 'Sir Robert Giffen', 528

Wealth at death £9645 7*s.* 11*d.*: probate, 18 May 1910, *CGPLA Eng. & Wales*

Gifford. *See also* Giffard.

Gifford. For this title name *see* individual entries under Gifford; *see also* Hay, Helen Selina, countess of Gifford (1807–1867).

Gifford, Adam, Lord Gifford (1820–1887), judge and benefactor, eldest son of James Gifford, administrator, and his wife, Catherine Ann, *née* West, teacher, was born at Edinburgh on 29 February 1820. His sister Mary married the Congregationalist minister Alexander Raleigh, and was the mother of Sir Walter Alexander Raleigh, first professor of English literature at Oxford. His father, who had risen from a comparatively humble position, became treasurer and master of the Merchant Company, an elder in the Secession church, and a zealous Sunday school teacher. His mother was vigorous in body and mind, and a very independent thinker. She was the only teacher of her sons Adam and John until Adam was eight years old, when the boys were sent to learn Latin and Greek at a small school kept by John Lawrie in West Nicolson Street. Adam Gifford was afterwards a pupil at the Edinburgh Institution, founded in 1832. In early life he became a Sunday school teacher in the Cowgate, besides sometimes taking a service on a Sunday forenoon with the poor children of Dr Guthrie's ragged school.

In 1835 Gifford was apprenticed to his uncle, a solicitor in Edinburgh; at the same time he attended classes in the university, and became a member of the Scots Law Debating Society. He soon became managing clerk in the office, but decided to become an advocate, and in 1849 was called to the bar. He was clear-headed, persevering, and had good connections but, from unwillingness to push himself, advanced slowly. He acquired by degrees an extensive practice. As a radical politician he expected nothing from the government, but in 1861 he was appointed an advocate-depute. In that capacity he conducted on behalf of the crown, in 1863, the prosecution against Jessie McLauchlan in the Sandyford murder case. On 7 April 1863 he married Maggie, daughter of James Pott, writer to the signet. She died on 7 February 1868. In 1865 he was appointed to succeed W. E. Aytoun as sheriff of Orkney and Shetland; but he continued his practice as an advocate, having appointed a resident sheriff-substitute.

On 28 January 1870 Gifford was nominated a judge, and

on 1 February he took his seat in the Court of Session as Lord Gifford. From 1872 he suffered from progressive paralysis, but he worked on until 25 January 1881, when he retired with a pension. He died at his home, Granton House, near Edinburgh, on 20 January 1887. On the 27th he was buried in the old Calton cemetery, Edinburgh. He was survived by one son, Herbert James Gifford.

Gifford was an able judge, with great common sense and little respect for technicalities. He often lectured to literary and philosophical societies. By his will, recorded on 3 March 1887, a sum estimated at £80,000 was bequeathed to found lectureships on natural theology, £25,000 being assigned to Edinburgh, where Gifford was curator, £20,000 to Glasgow and Aberdeen, and £15,000 to St Andrews. The object was to found 'a lectureship or popular chair for promoting, advancing, teaching, and diffusing the study of natural theology, in the widest sense of that term, in other words, the knowledge of God', and 'of the foundation of ethics' (will, 1887, proved at Edinburgh). All details and arrangements were left to be settled by the accepting trustees in each town, subject only to certain leading principles and directions stated in the will. The first appointments were made and lectures delivered in 1888. JAMES TAIT, *rev.* ERIC METCALFE

Sources private information (1889) · *The Scotsman* (1870) · *The Scotsman* (21 Jan 1887) · will, General Register Office for Scotland, Edinburgh [proved 1887] · Irving, *Scots.*
Archives NL Scot., notes on books read
Likenesses J. Moffat of Edinburgh, carte-de-visite, NPG
Wealth at death £189,338 7*s.* 3*d.*: confirmation, 10 March 1887, *CCI*

Gifford, Andrew (1700–1784), Baptist minister and numismatist, was born on 17 August 1700 in Bristol, the son of Emmanuel Gifford (1673–1723), a Baptist minister, and his wife, Eleanor Lancaster (1662–1738), and grandson of Andrew Gifford, also a Bristol Baptist minister. Educated first at Samuel Jones's academy, Tewkesbury, he left in 1719 to study with Dr John Ward at Gresham College from 1720. He then served as a Baptist minister in Nottingham (1725–6). He assisted Bernard Foskett at Broadmead, Bristol, from February 1727. In 1729 he married Martha Ware of Chesham; their two sons died in infancy, and Martha died in December 1732 and was buried at Chesham. His second wife, Grace Paynter, whom he married in 1737, died on 28 November 1762. She brought him a fortune of £6000, and their one child died in infancy.

In January 1730 Gifford became Baptist minister at Little Wild Street, London. In 1735 a member of the congregation accused Gifford of sodomy in his youth; the charge was never proved, but it led to his ostracism by other London Baptists. On 17 February 1736 Gifford, with many former Little Wild Street members, formed a new congregation in Eagle Street. Unusually for a Baptist minister he was also a chaplain, to Sir Richard Ellys, and after Sir Richard's death to Lady Ellys from 1731 to 1745. In 1754 he received the degree of DD from Marischal College, Aberdeen.

Gifford had a great knowledge of coins and his own collection was purchased by George II for his private cabinet. He was a fellow of the Society of Antiquaries and his handwritten notes are entered in the British Museum's copy of Martin Folkes's *A Table of English Silver Coins from the Norman Conquest to the Present Time* (1745), together with details of his own coin collection. He edited Folkes's *Tables of English Silver and Gold Coins*, which was published in two volumes in 1763. The influence of friends during his chaplaincy to Ellys and the fact that his former tutor, John Ward, was one of the trustees, led to his appointment as assistant librarian in the British Museum in 1757, where he frequently gave lectures on numismatics. In 1780 Gifford gave £100 to the Bristol Education Society to erect over their former library a new room for a museum to house his valuable collection of bibles, books, manuscripts, pictures, and curiosities, given to the Bristol Baptist College in his will of 13 July 1782. Among the bibles was a complete first edition (1526) of William Tyndale's New Testament, which in 1995 was purchased from Bristol Baptist College by the British Library. As pastor of Eagle Street congregation until his death, Gifford bequeathed £400 to it, making the six deacons his executors. Of his printed sermons, that on 'the Great Storm in 1703' (1734) went through several editions. He edited *Eighteen Sermons* (1771), by George Whitfield, which sold widely in England and America.

Gifford died on 19 June 1784 at his home in Brunswick Row, Queen Square, Ormond Street, London, and was buried in Bunhill Fields on 2 July 1784. The Revd John Ryland spoke at the interment, and a funeral sermon was given in Eagle Street by the Revd John Rippon; both addresses were published together in 1784. Gifford's biographer, L. G. Champion, states that his significance was in his determination to provide an educated Baptist ministry through Bristol Baptist College, and his unusual combination of a Calvinist theology with evangelical passion, by no means a universal Baptist conviction in his early years, but increasingly so after his death.

EDWIN CANNAN, *rev.* ROGER HAYDEN

Sources Bristol Baptist College, Terrill collection, Gifford MSS · minute book, Broadmead Baptist Church, Bristol · L. G. Champion, *Farthing rushlight: the story of Andrew Gifford, 1700–1784* (1961) · *GM*, 1st ser., 7 (1737), 637 · *GM*, 1st ser., 32 (1762), 600 · *GM*, 1st ser., 54 (1784), 478, 485, 595 · J. Rippon, *A sermon occasioned by the death of … A. Gifford, D.D. with an address delivered at his interment by J. Ryland, etc.* (1784) · Nichols, *Lit. anecdotes*, 5.461; 6.367 · A. W. Light, *Bunhill Fields: written in honour and to the memory of the many saints of God whose bodies rest in this old London cemetery*, 2nd edn, 2 vols. (1915–33) · J. Gill, *Sermons and tracts*, 2 (1815), 372ff. · minute book, Eagle Street Baptist Church, London, Regent's Park College, Oxford, Angus Library
Archives Bristol Baptist College, MSS | Regent's Park College, Oxford, Angus Library, church minute books for Little Wild Street, London, and Eagle Street, London
Likenesses J. Russell, oils, 1755, BM · R. Houston, mezzotint, pubd 1774 (after J. Russell), BM, NPG · mezzotint, pubd 1774 (after J. Russell), BM, NPG · engraving, repro. in *Gospel Magazine* (May 1774)
Wealth at death left £400 to Eagle Street deacons: *DNB* · £100 to Bristol Academy, and 'museum' of bibles, books, paintings, curios etc.: will, extract in Bristol Baptist College, Terrill collection, Gifford MSS

Gifford, (Thomas Johnstone) Carlyle (1881–1975), lawyer and investment trust manager, was born at Ingleston,

Twynholm, Kirkcudbrightshire, on 14 January 1881, the son of Patrick Gifford, a farmer, and his wife, Barbara Sloan Grierson. He was educated at George Watson's College, Edinburgh, and Edinburgh University. On 11 June 1907 he married Maud Oriel Riata, the daughter of the Hon. Charles Henry Pearson, fellow of Oriel College, Oxford; they had one son.

Gifford undertook his legal apprenticeship with W. J. Cook, writer to the signet, and spent a period as private clerk to Sir Henry Cook. He himself became a writer to the signet on 29 March 1905. He then accepted an offer from Augustus Baillie to go into partnership, and the firm of Baillie and Gifford, writers to the signet, was formed in 1906. Its legal practice was quite small, but the partners had some contacts in the rubber plantation business, from where their future growth was to come. In 1909 the Straits Mortgage and Trust Company was set up to lend money to planters, with Baillie and Gifford as managers and secretaries. Four years later its name was changed to the Scottish Mortgage and Trust Company. Baillie's role was to bring in new business, while Gifford ensured that it was conducted properly.

Gifford specialized in two areas of law: land law, and the rules and regulations of the stock exchange. His talents in these areas led him to be invited to serve on the boards of several investment trusts, and by 1925 he was present on the boards of companies run by all of the Edinburgh fund management groups. On the outbreak of the Second World War he served on the boards of twenty-two companies. As well as investment companies and trusts, these included the Scottish Widows Fund and Life Assurance Society. By 1957 Baillie, Gifford & Co. had become the largest of the Scottish investment trust managers—a position they retained at the time of Gifford's death in 1975. By then he had been semi-retired for several years.

In building up the investment side of the business Gifford was aware of the need to employ non-lawyers. His solution was to split the business between investment and law. Two firms were created, one consisting of lawyers, the other of fund managers, and by 1970 there were no common partners. Gifford's business interests were not confined to Edinburgh, and he set up two investment trusts in London in 1929. His great involvement in the trust business led him to become closely involved in the setting up of the Association of Investment Trust Companies in 1929. Elected the first deputy chairman of this organization, he also served as chairman between 1934 and 1936.

During the Second World War Gifford was called into government service. He served on the committee which advised on the requisition and disposal of overseas investments, and by 1940 he was described in *The Times* as 'special British Treasury Agent in charge of the sale of British holdings of American securities' (*DSBB*). He spent almost two years in the USA, and was involved in the disposal of other British assets. The only controversy was over the sale of American Viscose, which was owned by Courtaulds: Winston Churchill later claimed that it had been sold at too low a price (ibid.).

Gifford's sojourn in the USA reinforced an already strong belief in the free enterprise system, and in the immediate post-war years he remained opposed to nationalization and state regulation. It also reaffirmed his view that the USA was likely to be at the forefront of world economic growth. In the post-war years, despite the expense of acquiring overseas investment funds, he invested heavily in the USA, and was rewarded with the growing pre-eminence of his firm among British investment managers.

Beyond the investment world Carlyle Gifford, as he was popularly known, had many other interests. As a lawyer he had a reputation for pleading successfully in tax cases. He also served on the court of Edinburgh University. The owner of a small farm at Humbie in East Lothian, he was a not very successful breeder of Hereford cattle. On 4 May 1960 he married Sophia Mary Wharton Millar; they had one son. Gifford loved sport and played tennis, including real tennis, and golf. He was a member of the Honourable Company of Edinburgh Golfers and an enthusiastic bridge player. He was an atheist, and was given to occasional acts of charity.

Gifford died on 24 January 1975 from heart failure at his home, 24 Rothesay Terrace, Edinburgh, survived by his second wife. CHARLES W. MUNN

Sources *DSBB* · *The Times* (27 Feb 1975) · *The Society of Writers to His Majesty's Signet with a list of the members* (1936) · d. cert.
Likenesses photograph, repro. in A. Muir, *The Fife Coal Company* (1953?), 87
Wealth at death £317,190.42: confirmation, 13 March 1975, *CCI*

Gifford, Denis (**1927–2000**), cartoonist and film historian, was born on 26 December 1927 at 1 Bampton Road, Forest Hill, London, the son of William Thomas Benjamin Gifford, a lithographic printer, and his wife, Amelia Emma Rachel, *née* Hutchings. From his early pre-school years he showed his talent for drawing, and he claimed that from the age of three he had begun to collect and cherish comics. He was educated in south-east London, first at St Bartholomew's Church of England primary school and then at Dulwich College, where he formed a long-standing friendship with a fellow student, Bob Monkhouse (the future professional comedian), who shared Gifford's passion for comics, animation and vintage cinema, and radio programmes.

While still a pupil at Dulwich, in co-operation with Monkhouse, Gifford produced and circulated to his schoolmates at a penny a time a magazine printed by the primitive and laborious heated gelatine-and-hectograph ink process. By the time he was fourteen Denis was contributing sketches to professional publications such as D. C. Thomson's comic *Dandy*, for which he was paid a half-crown each time. By the time he left Dulwich College he had decided on a career as a writer and cartoonist. His first job was as a junior cartoonist on a national Sunday newspaper, *Reynolds News*. Just after the ending of the Second World War he was called up and joined the Royal Air Force.

After demobilization Gifford set up a small studio with Monkhouse, producing comics for minor publishers towards the end of the 1940s. He was then commissioned to take over the drawing of already established strips, for example 'Our Ernie' and 'Stonehenge Kit the ancient Brit' for the Amalgamated Press's *Knockout Comic*, and began to create characters of his own such as 'Steadfast McStaunch' for the Amalgamated Press and a variety of publishers. Gifford continued to produce comic strips throughout his life, contributing to well over 100 different comics, boys' weeklies, and newspapers.

By the 1950s Gifford was well known not only as an illustrator but as a 'nostalgist', keenly concerned with preserving the particularly British type of comic, which was becoming swamped by the distribution of imported slicker (but arguably cruder) American cartoon publications. His profound interest in popular culture, particularly of the 1930s and 1940s, influenced many publishers, who consequently brought out reprints and reappraisals of different aspects of the subject. Gifford began to establish a reputation as a lecturer and broadcaster, and in the 1950s he wrote comedy scripts for BBC radio shows and comedians, including Derek Roy and Morecambe and Wise. He was probably best known in the 1960s for devising the long-running nostalgic celebrity radio quiz show *Sounds Familiar*, which began in 1966. This was followed by *Looks Familiar* from 1972, a television programme of a similar nature which he also devised.

Gifford's research into films, both British and American, was prodigious, and it was while working for Pathé Films that he met and married on 3 August 1963 Angela (Angeliki) Kalagias (*b.* 1944/5), who was then employed in the Pathé offices. They had one child, Pandora Jane, but the marriage had ended in divorce by the 1970s. From then until his death Gifford lived alone, surrounded by what was almost certainly the largest ever collection of British comics, in his small south-east London home: he was estimated to possess over a quarter of a million comics, his collection weighing some 12 tons when it was put up for auction after his death.

Gifford continued to broadcast regularly about films, comics, and vintage radio programmes and in the 1970s founded the Association of Comics Enthusiasts and established the Ally Sloper award for British comics, as well as becoming a founder member of the Society of Strip Illustrators and organizing the first British Comics Convention in London. He was invited to lecture widely in Britain and abroad and from the 1960s produced a series of meticulously researched books about his favourite aspects of popular culture, which reached a wide and varied audience. He published more than thirty-five books, of which perhaps the most valuable are *The British Comic Catalogue, 1874–1974* (1975); *The Great Cartoon Stars; a Who's Who* (1979); *The Golden Age of Radio* (1985); *The International Book of Comics* (1984); *The Encyclopaedia of Comic Characters* (1987); and, surely his greatest publishing achievement, *The British Film Catalogue, 1895–1970* (1973), which listed and described every British entertainment film of that period. This took him some fifteen years to compile: it was reprinted and updated in 1986, and he prepared a further reprint and update in the year before he died (this final edition of the book appeared in 2001).

Denis Gifford continued his campaign for recognition of the strength and skill of British cartoonists until his death in 2000. He remained, despite severe illness, active to the end of his life, and well deserved the title bestowed upon him by other writers and enthusiasts: 'guardian of the nation's nostalgia'. He died, alone in his home, 80 Silverdale, Sydenham, London, on 20 May 2000 from a pulmonary embolism, deep vein thrombosis, and the cancer from which he had been suffering for some time.

MARY CADOGAN

Sources personal knowledge (2004) · B. Doyle, *Story Paper Collectors' Digest*, 642 (June 2000) · T. Vallance, *The Independent* (24 May 2000) · Programme notes, 'A tribute evening to Denis Gifford, 2000', National Film Theatre, London (2000) · S. Holland, *The Guardian* (26 May 2000) · b. cert. · m. cert. · d. cert. · *The Times* (30 May 2000) · *Daily Telegraph* (25 May 2000) · R. Stummer, 'Art of Dennis the Menace and Billy Bunter expected to raise £250,000 at auction', *The Independent* (4 Feb 2001)

Likenesses photograph, before 2000, repro. in Holland, *The Guardian* · photograph, repro. in *Daily Telegraph* · photograph, repro. in *The Times* · photograph, repro. in Vallance, *The Independent*

Gifford, Edwin Hamilton (1820–1905), biblical scholar, was the sixth son of Richard Ireland Gifford (*d.* in or before 1873) and his wife, Helen, daughter of William Davie of Stonehouse, Devon. He was born at Bristol on 18 December 1820. He was educated at Queen Elizabeth's Grammar School, Plymouth, and from 1837 at Shrewsbury School. In 1839 he went on to university at Cambridge, where he won a scholarship at St John's College; in 1842 he also won the Pitt university scholarship. In 1843 he graduated with a BA as senior classic and fifteenth wrangler in the mathematical tripos, and won the chancellor's medal. Gifford was elected a fellow of St John's College on 4 April 1843 but resigned his fellowship on 20 March 1844 upon marrying Ann, the daughter of John Yolland of Plymouth. He was ordained in the same year. He proceeded to an MA in 1846, and a DD in 1861. In 1843 he returned to Shrewsbury as second master. In 1848 he was appointed Headmaster of King Edward's School, Birmingham. He proved to be a worthy successor to the famous headmaster James Prince Lee, and remained in the post for fourteen years until ill health made him resign in 1862.

Gifford had held the position of honorary canon of Worcester from 1853 and became in 1865 chaplain to Francis *Jeune, bishop of Peterborough, who presented him to the rectory of Walgrave, Northamptonshire. His first wife having died, in 1873 he married Jeune's daughter Margaret Symons, sister of Francis Henry Jeune. They had one daughter. He subsequently held the post of examining chaplain to two successive bishops of London, Jackson and Temple. In 1875 he accepted the benefice of Much Hadham, Hertfordshire, and in 1877 ceased to be honorary canon of Worcester to become honorary canon of St Albans. In 1883 he was nominated to the prebend of Islington in St Paul's Cathedral, and the following year he succeeded Piers Calverley Claughton as archdeacon of London and canon of St Paul's.

Gifford was chosen as select preacher at the University of Cambridge in 1864 and 1869 and at the University of Oxford in 1879 and 1890–99, but he was not an effective preacher and had a better reputation as a scholar than as an ecclesiastic. His contributions to biblical and patristic scholarship, which were marked by insight and accuracy, included: *Voices of the Past* (1874), the Warburtonian lectures delivered at Lincoln's Inn 1870–74; *The Epistle to the Romans* (1881) in the Speaker's Commentary; *Baruch and the Epistle of Jeremy* (1888) in the same series; *Authorship of Psalm CX* (1892); *The Catechetical Lectures of St Cyril of Jerusalem* (1894), a revised translation in volume 7 of the Nicene and Post-Nicene Library; and Eusebius's *Præparatio evangelica* (1903, 5 vols., text, and translation).

On 24 April 1889 Gifford resigned as archdeacon and retired to Arlington House, Oxford, where he continued his academic pursuits. In 1903 he was elected an honorary fellow of St John's College, Cambridge. He died at 14a Upper Wimpole Street, London, on 4 May 1905.

G. S. Woods, *rev.* Joanna Hawke

Sources *The Times* (6 May 1905) • *Guardian* (10 May 1905) • *Church Times* (12 May 1905) • J. E. B. Mayor, *The Eagle*, 26 (1905), 372–4 • E. W. Bowling, *The Eagle*, 26 (1905), 374–7 • W. A. C. [W. A. Cox], *The Eagle*, 26 (1905), 377–87 • W. A. C. [W. A. Cox], *The Eagle*, 26 (1905), 387–8 [unsigned extract from Dr Sanday's sermon at Christ Church, Oxford, Sunday 7 May] • E. Schürer, 'Eusebii Pamphili evangelicae praeparationis libri XV ed. Gifford, IV tomi', *Theologische Literaturzeitung* (24 Oct 1903), 28–2, cols. 595–600 • Allibone, *Dict.*, suppl. • J. Davson, 'Critical and conservative treatments of prophecy in nineteenth-century Britain', DPhil diss., U. Oxf., 1991 • m. certs. [Ann Yolland, Margaret Jeune]

Archives LPL, corresp. with Frederick Temple

Wealth at death £686 17*s.* 10*d.*: probate, 2 June 1905, *CGPLA Eng. & Wales*

Gifford, George (1547/8–1600), Church of England clergyman and author, was the son of Boniface Gifford of Dry Drayton, Cambridgeshire, perhaps servant to John Hutton, MP for Cambridgeshire in 1563. Dedicating his first published sermon to Hutton, Gifford observed: 'I was brought up under you, my parents receiving benefits daily from you' (*A Sermon on the Parable of the Sower*, 1582, sig. A2*v*).

Gifford is unlikely to have been the man of these names who studied at Hart Hall, Oxford, in the early 1560s but the possibility cannot be conclusively refuted. He graduated BA, however, from Christ's College, Cambridge, in 1570, proceeding MA in 1573.

On 21 April 1572 Gifford married Agnes, or Anne, Lennard of Taunton, Somerset, at St Mary Woolnoth, London. His appointment as an under-master at Brentwood School, Essex, he probably owed to William Fulke, rector of neighbouring Great Warley, since in 1573 he published an English translation of Fulke's *Praelectiones*. In November 1575 he and Agnes were summoned before the official of John Walker, archdeacon of Essex, for not receiving communion in their parish church of Mountnessing. Gifford admitted that for a full year they had done so instead 'at my Lord Rich's'—presumably the chapel at Leighs Priory, Rich's principal seat. Further accused of telling his auditory during 'a prophesy in the pulpit' to do 'as some ministers teach and not as they do' he claimed that he 'spake it not to the slander of any ministers' (Essex RO, D/AEA 9, fol. 13*v*). When in July 1576 Elizabeth demanded the suppression of such clerical exercises, expressing her dislike of lay participation in them, Walker nevertheless defended Gifford: allowed to speak only when an appointed clergyman failed to attend, he was a learned graduate 'and therefore doth well teach' (LPL, MS 2003, fol. 12*r*).

On 15 December 1578, now aged thirty, Gifford was ordained deacon and priest by John Aylmer, bishop of London, thereafter serving as curate of All Saints-with-St Peter, Maldon, a centre of advanced protestantism. Aylmer's investigations into the borough's affairs in 1581 led to the resignation of the vicar, Fabian Withers. Despite his association with Withers, Gifford was on 30 August 1582 instituted by Aylmer as his successor, on the presentation of Richard Francke.

Gifford was probably chief organizer at about this time of the clandestine conference of ministers that met 'about Brayntree side' (Bancroft, 84). On 7 October 1583, following Aylmer's episcopal visitation, he was called into consistory for nonconformist practices and then interviewed by Aylmer personally. The case dragged on until Easter 1584, by when it had been overtaken by events. John Whitgift, archbishop of Canterbury, was now demanding subscription to three articles which enshrined the proposition that the prayer book contained nothing contrary to the word of God. One of several leading Essex clergy interviewed by Aylmer on 5 March 1584 and confronted with these, Gifford was given until 20 March to subscribe and was then suspended. A petition against the articles, probably organized by the Braintree conference, was signed by Gifford and twenty-six other Essex ministers. Lord Burghley intervened on Gifford's behalf, but after consulting Aylmer, Whitgift informed him on 29 May that as 'a ringleader of the rest' Gifford's 'deserts may be such as will deserve deprivation' (BL, Lansdowne MS 42, fol. 105*r*). Gifford duly became the sacrificial victim of the subscription crisis in Essex: he was deprived by the high commission in June or July.

It was probably Burghley's well-advertised dislike of Whitgift's proceedings that led to Gifford's swift rehabilitation. Although the exact circumstances remain obscure, compromise was effected and he remained in Maldon as town preacher until his death. He also continued to lead the Braintree conference: in February 1585 he and Robert Wright were seconded to the 'national synod' which gathered in London to lobby MPs on behalf of ecclesiastical reform.

In an attempt to have Gifford fully reinstated in Maldon, Mark Wiersdale, his successor as vicar (possibly chosen by Richard Francke solely for the purpose), offered to resign in Gifford's favour. But Aylmer refused to institute him and in the episcopal visitation of July 1586 Gifford was amongst those who were suspended for refusing the surplice.

It was perhaps this discouraging train of events that prompted Gifford to join the earl of Leicester in the Low Countries as a chaplain to the English troops. Possibly present at the battle of Zutphen on 22 September 1586, when Sir Philip Sidney was fatally wounded, Gifford was summoned to Sidney's deathbed on 30 September and remained with him until the end. As Sidney was evidently troubled about his former relationship with Penelope, Lady Rich, the 'Stella' of his sonnets, it was presumably Gifford's connection with the Riches which determined his selection. Left £20 in his will, Gifford thereafter wrote *The Manner of Sir Philip Sidney's Death*. Despite some striking personal details this was designed primarily to edify the reader and, unpublished at the time, was perhaps commissioned by Lady Rich herself as a private *memento mori*.

In March 1587, with five other members of the Braintree conference, Gifford petitioned parliament for restoration to his public ministry. The chief result of this initiative seems to have been the deprivation in May of two of the three beneficed petitioners, William Tunstall of Great Totham and Giles Whiting of Panfield. Gifford himself was restored by early 1589 and that year attended the last provincial synod to be held, at St John's College, Cambridge.

Aylmer and Whitgift made no further serious attempt to pursue Gifford. Although Aylmer's 1589 visitation administered the *coup de grâce* to the conference movement in Essex, Gifford was not summoned for nonconformist practices. Whilst his name was frequently mentioned during the Star Chamber trials of 1590–91 which followed the exposure of the conference movement and the pursuit of both Martin Marprelate and the separatist leaders, Gifford was not himself examined.

The main reason, no doubt, was that despite his troubles Gifford had emerged during the 1580s as one of the most prolific and influential of godly writers. His works blended practical piety with common sense and the level-headed defence of a moderate, evangelizing protestant tradition. In 1581 he dedicated to Ambrose Dudley, earl of Warwick, *A briefe discourse of certaine points of the religion, which is among the common sort of Christians, which may be termed the countrie divinitie*. Presented as a dialogue, this influential exposition of popular protestant belief inspired Arthur Dent to write *The Plaine Mans Path-Way to Heaven* (1601).

A stream of works followed: until the year of Gifford's death in 1600, those of 1585, 1588, and 1592 were the only ones in which a new volume or a new edition is not known to have left the London presses. In *A Dialogue betweene a Papist and a Protestant* (1582), dedicated to Thomas Radcliffe, earl of Sussex, Gifford coined the phrase 'church papist'. *A Catechisme Conteininge the Summe of Christian Religion* (1583) was an informed discussion between 'Q' and 'A' rather than a catechism in the true sense. *A Discourse of the Subtill Practices of Devilles by Witches and Sorcerers* (1587), dedicated to the master of the mint, Sir Richard Martin, and *A Dialogue Concerning Witches and Witchcraftes* (1593) have appealed both to social historians for their wise moderation and to literary critics for their possible influence upon Shakespeare. The *Dialogue* was reprinted as the first of the Shakespeare Association Facsimiles in 1931. *A Treatise of True Fortitude* (1594), dedicated to Robert, earl of Essex, high recorder of Maldon from 1584, discussed current notions of manliness and revenge.

What above all carried Gifford through the crisis years of 1589–91 was his uncompromising denunciation of separatism. From 1588 he conducted a personal campaign against John Greenwood and Henry Barrow, in 1590 publishing *A Short Treatise Against the Donatists of England, whome we Call Brownists* and *A Plaine Declaration that our Brownists be Full Donatists*, both dedicated to Burghley. *A Short Reply unto the Last Printed Books of Henry Barrow and John Greenwood* appeared in December 1591. Meanwhile, on 30 May, Gifford had preached at Paul's Cross, sounding a call for Christian unity and pointedly emphasizing obedience to the godly magistrate.

Gifford's numerous treatises were complemented by a succession of more than forty sermons, published singly or in bulk. *Sermons upon the Whole Booke of the Revelation* (1596) and *Fifteene Sermons upon the Song of Salomon* (1598) were both dedicated to Essex.

Although the 1590s saw a running battle in Maldon between Gifford's supporters and those of Robert Palmer, whom in May 1587 Aylmer had imposed as vicar in succession to Wiersdale, Gifford and Palmer did not become personal enemies. Palmer died within days of Gifford and his successor was Ralph Hawden, a friend whom Gifford remembered in his will. He made it on 8 May 1600, appointing Agnes sole executrix and remembering his sons John, Daniel, Samuel, Jeremy, George, and William; his daughters Mary and Martha; and 'the child whereof my wife now goeth' (LMA, DL/C/359, fol. 210r). Probate was granted on 31 May 1600.

John Gifford (*d.* 1650), George Gifford's eldest son, graduated BA from Emmanuel College, Cambridge, in 1601, proceeding MA in 1604 and DD in 1616. He was rector of St Michael Bassishaw, London, from 1607 until ejected by parliament in 1642. He married Eliza, daughter of Thomas Skellthorne of Derbyshire, and they had three sons and three daughters. The son of George Gifford the younger, another George (*d.* 1686), was Gresham professor of divinity in 1661 and president of Sion College in 1677.

BRETT USHER

Sources *The visitation of London, anno Domini 1633, 1634, and 1635, made by Sir Henry St George*, 1, ed. J. J. Howard and J. L. Chester, Harleian Society, 15 (1880), 314 • Foster, *Alum. Oxon.*, 1500–1714, 2.563 • Venn, *Alum. Cant.*, 1/2.213 • J. M. S. Brooke and A. W. C. Hallen, eds., *The transcript of the registers of … St Mary Woolnoth and St Mary Woolnoth Haw … 1538 to 1760* (1886) • *Miscellaneous prose of Sir Philip Sidney*, ed. K. Duncan-Jones and J. van Dorsten (1973) • A. Peel, ed., *The seconde parte of a register*, 2 vols. (1915) • R. G. Usher, ed., *The presbyterian movement in the reign of Queen Elizabeth, as illustrated by the minute book of the Dedham classis, 1582–1589*, CS, 3rd ser., 8 (1905) • D. D. Wallace Jr, 'George Gifford, puritan propaganda, and popular religion in Elizabethan England', *Sixteenth Century Journal*, 9 (1978), 27–49 • P. Collinson, *The Elizabethan puritan movement* (1967) • W. J. Petchey, *A prospect of Maldon 1500–1689* (1991) • act book of archdeacon of Essex, Essex RO, D/AEA 9 • GL, MS 9535/2, fol. 4r–v, ordination; MSS 9537/5–7, call books of visitation • vicar-general's books, LMA, DL/C/333 and 334 • S. Adams, ed., *Household accounts and disbursement books of Robert Dudley, earl of Leicester, 1558–1561, 1584–1586*, CS, 6 (1995) • *The writings of John Greenwood, 1587–1590*, ed. L. H. Carlson (1962) • *The writings of John Greenwood and Henry Barrow, 1591–1593*, ed. L. H. Carlson (1970) • registered will, LMA, DL/C/359, fol. 210r •

[R. Bancroft], *Daungerous positions and proceedings* (1593) • A. Macfarlane, *Witchcraft in Tudor and Stuart England* (1570) • S. Anglo, ed., *The damned art: essays in the literature of witchcraft* (1977)

Wealth at death unquantifiable; modest bequests to children: will, LMA, DL/C/359, fol. 210r

Gifford, George (*fl.* 1632–1635), engraver, is principally known from an interesting portrait of Bishop Hugh Latimer, engraved as frontispiece to the edition of Latimer's sermons published in 1635. Gifford also engraved a portrait of John Bate as frontispiece to the second edition of his *Mysteries of Art and Nature*, published in the same year, and a title-page for the 1632 edition of Matthew Mainwaring's *Vienna*. Of what was evidently a set of the four apostles, only St Peter survives: it is known in two states, the second being a restrike by Peter Stent.

L. H. CUST, *rev.* ANTONY GRIFFITHS

Sources A. M. Hind, *Engraving in England in the sixteenth and seventeenth centuries*, 3, ed. M. Corbett and M. Norton (1964), 261–2 • A. Globe, *Peter Stent, London printseller circa 1642–1665: being a catalogue raisonné of his engraved prints and books* (1985), cat. 397

Gifford, Gilbert (1560–1590), spy, was the son of a recusant, John Gifford (*d.* 1613), of Chillington in Staffordshire. He went abroad while still in his teens and on 31 January 1577 entered William Allen's college for the training of missionary priests at Douai. He seems to have been a difficult, truculent young man and is said to have challenged a fellow student to a duel. In April 1579 he transferred to the English College at Rome, where he first became involved in the feuding between the secular priests and the Jesuits. He was expelled at some time prior to September 1580 and after leaving Rome spent several months wandering between England and the continent. On 3 March 1582 Allen wrote offering to give him another chance, and on 23 June he returned to the Douai College, now at Rheims; but he did not settle, and Allen began to give up all hope of him.

In September 1582 Gifford left again for England, but a month later he was back in France and on his way to Rome. Finally, in October 1583, he turned up at Rheims penniless and penitent and, in spite of his misgivings, the charitable Allen took him in once more. This time he stayed for two years, an apparently reformed character, and on 5 April 1585 was admitted to the diaconate. Nevertheless, it was during this period that he became friendly with another student, John Savage, and discussed with him a plan to assassinate Queen Elizabeth. In October 1585 Gifford left Rheims for the last time and made for Paris, where he got in touch with Thomas Morgan, an agent of Mary, queen of Scots, and Charles Paget, both leading members of the secular party. In December he crossed over to England, landing at the port of Rye. He was immediately detained and escorted to London for a private conference with Sir Francis Walsingham.

Gifford may or may not have already been employed by Walsingham's secret service, but from this point there can be no doubt about his double dealing. According to his own account, his intention had been merely to pursue the secular priests' campaign against the Jesuits; but he also carried instructions from Thomas Morgan to try to find a way of reopening communications with the queen of Scots, now confined at Chartley in Gifford's own county of Staffordshire and, under the guardianship of Sir Amias Paulet, effectively cut off from the outside world. It appeared that Walsingham also wanted to re-establish Mary's private post office, but under his supervision, and Gifford was to play a vital part in its operation. Beer for the household at Chartley was delivered once a week by a local brewer and, with his connivance, letters could be smuggled in and out concealed in the bung-hole of the beer barrels. Gifford would collect Mary's mail from the French embassy, where it had been accumulating for the past two years, and pass it on to Walsingham. While it was being deciphered and translated, he would travel up to Chartley and wait for the originals to be returned to him by Paulet. He would then take them to the brewer who, unknown to him, took them back to Paulet who checked that nothing had been added to the package, which was then sent in as arranged. The outgoing post would work in reverse order, and in due course Gifford would hand Mary's replies to the French ambassador.

The first delivery was made in January 1586 and Gifford, who had come warmly recommended by Morgan, was quickly trusted by the queen of Scots. Once the system was in place a substitute could sometimes be used as letter carrier and in June Gifford paid a visit to France, where he helped Edward Grateley, an old associate from college days, to put the finishing touches to a book of anti-Jesuit propaganda—chiefly, it seems, to keep up his reputation among the seculars. He returned to England in July, just as the details of the Babington plot began to emerge from the beer barrels, but did not wait to see the outcome. He left the country again, hurriedly and in secret, before the end of the month, fearing possibly damaging revelations when the arrests and trials began. He did not inform Walsingham, who wrote on 2 August 1586: 'Sorry I am that G. G. is absent. I marvel greatly how this humor of estranging himself cometh upon him' (Read, 3.45 n. 6).

Gifford has been accused by some Catholic writers of having acted throughout as Walsingham's *agent provocateur* and of manufacturing the evidence which brought the queen of Scots to the scaffold; but although he was undoubtedly acquainted with several of the Babington conspirators and may well have been more deeply involved with them than he cared to admit, these charges have never been satisfactorily proved. The only certain thing about him is that he was thoroughly untrustworthy and ready, without hesitation, to betray any person or cause in order to survive in the murky world he inhabited. Arrived at Paris in August 1586 he told Mendoza, the Spanish ambassador recently expelled from London, all about Babington's plans to release the queen of Scots and asked his approval for the intended murder of Elizabeth. Gifford had been granted a pension of £100 a year by Walsingham and he continued to keep in touch with Walsingham's assistant, Thomas Phelippes. On 14 March 1587 he was ordained priest and talked of returning to Rome. Instead, he stayed on in Paris and in October made some serious allegations against the English ambassador, Sir Edward

Stafford, who retaliated by describing Gifford as 'the most notable double treble villain that ever lived, for he hath played upon all the hands in the world' (Pollen, 126).

In December 1587 Gifford was arrested in a brothel and, as a priest, consigned to the archbishop's prison. His papers were seized and a copy of the controversial book he had written with Grateley fell into the hands of the authorities. He was brought before the papal nuncio's tribunal in February 1588, but Walsingham had been careful to keep Gifford's name out of the published proceedings against Babington, and no conclusive evidence of his treachery came to light, despite the strong suspicions of the other Catholic exiles. No verdict against Gifford is recorded, but his enemies ensured that he stayed in prison in Paris, and he died there in November 1590.

ALISON PLOWDEN

Sources J. H. Pollen, *Mary queen of Scots and the Babington plot*, Scottish History Society, 3rd ser., 3 (1922) • C. Read, *Mr Secretary Walsingham and the policy of Queen Elizabeth*, 2 (1925) [337]; 3 (1925), chap. 12 • G. Anstruther, *The seminary priests*, 1 (1969), 132 • *The letter-books of Sir Amias Poulet*, ed. J. Morris (1874) • H. Foley, ed., *Records of the English province of the Society of Jesus*, 6 (1880), 15–16 • J. Morris, ed., *The troubles of our Catholic forefathers related by themselves*, 2 (1875) • *The letters and memorials of William, Cardinal Allen (1532–1594)*, ed. T. F. Knox (1882), vol. 2 of *Records of the English Catholics under the penal laws* (1878–82) • T. F. Knox and others, eds., *The first and second diaries of the English College, Douay* (1878)

Gifford [*née* Galpin], **Hannah** (*fl.* **1629–1668**), schoolmistress, was one of at least five children of Bernard Galpin (*b.* *c.*1565) of Dorchester, Dorset, shoemaker. In 1629 she married Robert Gifford, also of Dorchester and, like her family, a member of the town's self-consciously 'godly' community. When her father, several siblings, and numerous kin sailed on the *Mary and John* to New England in 1630, Hannah and her husband remained behind. They brought up several children in some degree of poverty: in the 1640s Robert Gifford was a recipient of Richard Bushrod's bequest, distributed annually to the godly poor.

As part of its drive for spiritual and moral reformation in the town, in October 1651 the corporation of Dorchester decided to establish a school for the education of poor children. Hannah was selected as teacher, and allocated a salary of £10 a year if there were fewer than thirty children attending and £12 if there were more. In the event, the school was instantly popular, and numbers had to be restricted to sixty, although a few dropped out once they had received free new clothing. Hannah proved a conscientious schoolmistress: 'she taught reading and later the catechism, being commended by the Corporation for her "extraordinary pains" in this' (Underdown, 225). The school, supplied by local booksellers John Long and William Churchill with books and bibles paid for by the corporation from donations given at gunpowder treason anniversary services, 'was one of the most striking achievements of puritan Dorchester' (ibid., 226). It was still functioning with Hannah as teacher in 1668, but by 1676 it seems to have discontinued. It is not known when Hannah died.

VIVIENNE LARMINIE

Sources D. Underdown, *Fire from heaven: life in an English town in the seventeenth century* (1992)

Gifford, Humphrey (*fl.* **1580**), poet, was probably the second son of Anthony Gifford of Halsbury, Devon. He may also have been the Humfrey Jeffert who was headmaster of Barnstaple grammar school and who died in 1589 (Darton, xix–xxi). In 1580 Gifford published *A Posie of Gilloflowers, Eche Differing from other in Colour and Odour, yet All Sweete*. One section of the work is in prose, the other in verse. The prose is prefaced by a dedicatory epistle 'To the worshipfull his very good maister, Edward Cope of Edon, esquier', whom Gifford describes as 'the onely maister that ever I served' and whose daughter Dorothy is thought to have been Gifford's wife (Darton, xi). The poems are dedicated 'To the Worshipfull John Stafford of Bletherwicke, Esquier'. The prose chiefly consists of translations from the Italian and French, while the verse is Gifford's own.

Gifford's work was reprinted twice in the nineteenth century by Alexander B. Grosart, first in 1870 in his *Miscellanies of the Fuller Worthies' Library* and again in 1875 in his Occasional Issues of Unique or Very Rare Books. F. J. Harvey Darton produced a new edition in 1933, following the discovery in 1930 of a second copy of the *Posie of Gilloflowers*. That copy, unlike the one from which Grosart worked, contained a second title-page, reading: 'A Comfortable Recreation: Containing in it matter both of Pleasure and Profit'.

A. H. BULLEN, *rev.* ELIZABETH GOLDRING

Sources A. B. Grosart, introduction, in [H. Gifford], *Posie of gilloflowers*, Occasional Issues of Unique or Very Rare Books, 1 (1875) • A. B. Grosart, 'Memorial-introduction', *Miscellanies of the Fuller Worthies' library*, 1 (1870), 3–24 • F. J. H. Darton, 'Introduction', in H. Gifford, *A posie of gilloflowers, eche differing from other in colour and odour, yet all sweete*, ed. F. J. H. Darton (1933), v–xxii

Gifford, James, the elder (*bap.* **1739**, *d.* **1813**), religious writer, eldest son of James Gifford, mayor of Cambridge in 1757, and his wife, Martha Hylen, was born at Cambridge and christened there at All Saints' Church on 19 December 1739. Educated at Rugby School, he entered the army at the age of eighteen, and as captain of the 14th foot served in Canada during the Seven Years' War. In 1766 or 1767 he married in Boston, Massachusetts, Elizabeth Cremer (*c.*1746–1840), a native of Nova Scotia. They had seven sons and one daughter. All the sons served as officers in either the army or the navy; the eldest, James *Gifford the younger (1768–1853), became a rear-admiral, and William (*b.* 1770), a major-general. Gifford meticulously supervised the religious and moral training of each of his children, issuing written instructions for this purpose and composing special prayers for family events. It is not clear when he resigned his commission but by 1788 he was residing at Girton, near Cambridge, where he continued to live until his death.

Gifford became an influential figure in the Unitarian movement, having been converted to Unitarian beliefs after reading the works of John Jebb. He was a friend of some of the leading Unitarians of his time, including Theophilus Lindsey, George Dyer, William Frend, and T. Fyshe Palmer; Mrs Elizabeth Rayner, a munificent patroness of the Unitarians, left him a considerable legacy on her death in 1800. It was Gifford's written works which brought him to the attention of the Unitarian movement at large. His first publication in 1781 was *A Short Essay on the Belief of an Universal Providence*, but by far his most important work was *An Elucidation of the Unity of God, Deduced from Scripture and Reason* (1783). An enlarged fifth edition (1813), edited and annotated by his son William, and containing as an appendix an earlier work entitled 'A letter to the archbishop of Canterbury', was heralded as a work of 'incalculable importance' and an admirable justification of Unitarian beliefs (*Monthly Repository*, 144).

Gifford died at Girton on 21 January 1813 and was buried in All Saints' Church, Cambridge, where a monument was erected to his memory and that of his parents. His widow moved to St Helier, Jersey, where she died on 16 April 1840. ALEXANDER GORDON, *rev.* M. J. MERCER

Sources *Christian Reformer, or, Unitarian Magazine and Review*, new ser., 1 (1845), 821 • *Christian Reformer, or, Unitarian Magazine and Review*, new ser., 10 (1854), 21–2 • E. Kell, 'Memoir of Miss Gifford', *Christian Reformer, or, Unitarian Magazine and Review*, new ser., 14 (1858), 729–36 • *Monthly Repository*, 11 (1816), 143–5 • Allibone, *Dict.* • *IGI*

Gifford, James, the younger (1768–1853), naval officer, was born at Halifax, Nova Scotia, on 20 November 1768. He was the son of James *Gifford the elder (*bap.* 1739, *d.* 1813) and his wife, Elizabeth, *née* Cremer (*c.*1746–1840). Having entered the navy in October 1783, Gifford served under the broad pennant of Sir Charles Douglas on the Halifax station. He was afterwards in the West Indies, the channel, and the Mediterranean; during the occupation of Toulon he served in the *St George*, flagship of Rear-Admiral John Gell. In October 1793 he was promoted lieutenant, and shortly afterwards was appointed to the frigate *Lutine* (32 guns, Captain James Macnamara), in which he narrowly escaped capture by the French squadron under Richery off Cadiz, on 7 October 1795. After serving in the *Pompée* with Captain Vashon, and in the *Prince* and the *Prince George*, flagships of Sir Charles Cotton, he was promoted commander on 7 May 1802.

For a short time in 1803 Gifford was acting captain of the frigate *Braave*; then in 1804 he was appointed to command the brig *Speedy*, part of the squadron off Boulogne and Calais during that and the succeeding year. In 1808 he was appointed to the sloop *Sarpen*, for service in the Baltic and North Sea, and in February 1812 to the sloop *Sheldrake*, from which, on 12 August, he was promoted captain. He had no further service afloat, and, following his father's example, devoted himself from this time to religious studies and labours in the cause of Unitarianism.

After his father's death (21 January 1813), Gifford seems to have lived for some time at Swansea, where he wrote his *Remonstrance of a Unitarian, Addressed to [Burgess] the Bishop of David's* (1818; 2nd edn, 1820), which was highly regarded by Unitarians, and which earned two replies, *Unitarianism Indefensible: a Letter … to … James Gifford* (1818, by J. Garbett) and *An examination of the remonstrance addressed to the bishop of St David's, with answers to the questions addressed to Trinitarians generally* (1822).

Gifford afterwards moved with his sister and mother to Jersey, where he lived very modestly, devoting most of his small income to benevolent works and to the cause of Unitarianism. In 1845 he published a pamphlet, *Letter of a Unitarian to the Rev. S. Langston, Minister of St James's Church, Jersey*; but his principal work was in his silent, unpretending but effective devotion to Unitarianism. In October 1846 he became rear-admiral on the retired list, but the promotion made no change in his life, beyond increasing his income and ability to give. He never married, and died at Mont Orgueil Cottage, near St Helier, Jersey, on 20 August 1853. His mother had died, at the age of ninety-four, on 16 April 1840; his sister, Juliana Elizabeth, who had lived with him, survived him a few years, and died on 19 April 1858 aged eighty-four.

J. K. LAUGHTON, *rev.* ROGER MORRISS

Sources O'Byrne, *Naval biog. dict.* • J. Marshall, *Royal naval biography*, suppl. 3 (1829), 97–8 • J. Gifford, 'A prayer by Captain Gifford', *Christian Reformer, or, Unitarian Magazine and Review*, new ser., 1 (1845), 821 • E. Kell, 'Memoir of Rear Admiral James Gifford', *Christian Reformer, or, Unitarian Magazine and Review*, new ser., 10 (1854), 21–31 • E. Kell, 'Additions to the memoir of Rear Admiral Jas. Gifford', *Christian Reformer, or, Unitarian Magazine and Review*, new ser., 10 (1854), 98–101 • E. Kell, 'Memoir of Miss Gifford', *Christian Reformer, or, Unitarian Magazine and Review*, new ser., 14 (1858), 729–36 • *Monthly Repository*, 20 (1825), 499 [obit. of Major-General W. Gifford] • A. B. Rodger, *The war of the second coalition: 1798–1801, a strategic commentary* (1964) • R. Muir, *Britain and the defeat of Napoleon, 1807–1815* (1996) • O. Chadwick, *The Victorian church*, 1 (1966) • *GM*, 2nd ser., 41 (1854), 648

Gifford, John (*d.* 1650). *See under* Gifford, George (1547/8–1600).

Gifford, John (*d.* 1655), Independent minister, was best known as the minister who inspired John Bunyan, author of *The Pilgrim's Progress*. Nothing is known about Gifford's birthplace or parentage, but his arrival in Bedford, conversion, and ministry are described in 'A brief account of the 1st gathering of the Church of Christ at Bedford' included in the modern edition of the minutes of the church.

Gifford, the account records, was a Kentish man who served as a major in the king's army during the civil war and was taken prisoner by Fairfax's forces after fighting at Rochester in 1648. He was condemned to die but escaped, with the help of his sister and divine intervention, first to London then to Bedford, only to embark on a life of debauchery while he practised as a physician. He would later recall his murderous fantasies against 'brother Harrington, meerly from that great antipathy that was in his heart against the people of God and the holyness of the Gospell' (Tibbutt, 16). His conversion is recorded as following a conventional pattern. After losing heavily at gambling and having 'desperate thoughtes against God', Gifford was convinced of his sinfulness by reading a holy book by a Mr Bolton (ibid.). He subsequently sought the acquaintance of a group of puritan believers in Bedford who shared a dislike for 'the bishops and their superstitions' (ibid., 15) but had not yet separated from the open communion of the parish. These included John Grew, John Eston, and Anthony Harrington. Initial scepticism among the godly about Gifford's conversion from sinner to believer was overcome by his skill as a preacher. It is recorded that he made a convert, Sister Cooper, during his first public sermon.

Gifford was a prime mover in organizing the Bedford puritans into a gathered church and was chosen as its first pastor in 1650 by his eleven fellow 'foundation stones', three men and eight women. The unprecedented religious freedoms of the 1650s, under the Commonwealth and protectorate, allowed this collective or congregational church to enjoy a brief period of toleration. In 1653 Gifford, who had never been ordained, was admitted to the mastership of the hospital and rectory of the church of St John the Baptist in Bedford.

The only extant writing by Gifford is a letter sent to his congregation from his deathbed in 1655. The letter exhorts the faithful to avoid divisive arguments and disputes about matters like baptism, psalm singing, or 'any externalls', to follow the scriptures, and to 'submit to one another in love' (Tibbutt, 19). It also rejects discrimination on the basis of wealth or social status, advocates that leading members of the church act as examples in their 'faith, love and zeale', and reminds the congregation of the need for orderly behaviour (ibid., 20). Gifford's letter was traditionally read aloud to the congregation on new year's day until the twentieth century, including the more turbulent times of persecution under the Restoration regime.

Gifford's ecumenism and insistence on equality and order may have influenced the thinking of his most famous successor as minister of the Bedford church, John Bunyan, who had been baptized and made a full member of the church just before Gifford's death. After Gifford's death the congregation nominated John Burton as minister, and after pressure was put on the mayor and corporation by Oliver Cromwell he was granted the living of St John the Baptist. Burton was in turn succeeded by Bunyan in 1672.

There is little evidence of Gifford's life or family. He died on 21 September 1655 and was buried in St John the Baptist Church, having made a will on 2 August. His will designated his 'loving wife' Margaret as his sole executrix and established bequests to each of three children: to his eldest daughter, Mary, £55 on the day of her marriage or at the age of twenty-one, to his daughter Elizabeth £50 on the same conditions, and £50 to a child as yet unborn. This child was born the following year and named Martha. Gifford also seems to have had a son who died before him: a register in St Paul's Church in Bedford records the burial of John, son of John Gifford, on 30 June 1651.

TAMSIN SPARGO

Sources H. G. Tibbutt, ed., *The minutes of the first Independent church (now Bunyan meeting) at Bedford, 1656–1766*, Bedfordshire Historical RS, 55 (1976) • J. Brown, *John Bunyan (1628–1688): his life, times, and work*, rev. F. M. Harrison, rev. edn (1928) • C. Hill, *A turbulent, seditious, and factious people: John Bunyan and his church* (1988) • PRO, PROB 11/257, fol. 186*v*

Wealth at death small bequests, but no overall value of estate: will, PRO, PROB 11/257

Gifford, John [*formerly* John Richards Green] (**1758–1818**), tory political writer, was the only son of John Green, a lawyer in Worfield, Shropshire. His mother and father died shortly after his birth, whereupon he lived with his grandparents, from whom he inherited a large property in 1772. Green was educated at Repton School and entered St John's College, Oxford, on 28 April 1775, becoming a student of Lincoln's Inn at the same time. By the age of twenty-three, with his fortune spent, he found it expedient to retire to France in 1781 or 1782, and to change his name to Gifford. According to one account he became the delight of the British embassy at Paris; an apparently more authentic narrative, in the *Gentleman's Magazine*, states that he never went to Paris at all, but lived at Lille and Rouen.

About 1788 Gifford returned to England and soon established himself as a historian, publishing a two-volume *History of England* (1790), a four-volume *History of France* (1791–3), and in 1794 *The Reign of Louis XVI: a Complete History of the French Revolution*. In addition he wrote a number of works on contemporary British politics and was a vigorous supporter of Pitt's government. He published *A Plain Address to the Common Sense of the People of England*, to which was annexed 'An abstract of Thomas Paine's life and writings' (1792), and his *Short Address to Members of Loyal Associations* (1798) is said to have sold 100,000 copies. In the 1790s he translated several anti-French-revolutionary pamphlets written by émigré noblemen.

Gifford reputedly became the editor of a morning and an evening paper in 1796. Following the decline, in 1798, of *The Anti-Jacobin, or, Weekly Examiner*, edited by his namesake William Gifford, John Gifford started *The Anti-Jacobin Review and Magazine, or, Monthly Political and Literary Censor*, which ran from 1798 to 1821. Gifford and Andrew Bisset were its chief writers, and the political philosopher James Mill was employed as a reviewer. On Pitt's death, Gifford wrote a laudatory *Political Life*, published in six volumes in 1809. He was rewarded for this by an appointment as a police magistrate, first in Worship Street, Shoreditch, and afterwards in Great Marlborough Street.

On his return from France, Gifford lived much in Bromley in Kent, to be near a trusted physician. He was twice married: after the death of his first wife in 1805 he married a Miss Galleper and, according to his obituary, left several children at his own death in Bromley, Kent, on 6 March 1818.

LESLIE STEPHEN, *rev.* ADAM I. P. SMITH

Sources *GM*, 1st ser., 88/1 (1818), 279, 403 • *Annual Biography and Obituary*, 3 (1819), 311–37 • W. Jerdan, *The autobiography of William Jerdan: with his literary, political, and social reminiscences and correspondence during the last fifty years*, 4 vols. (1852–3)

Gifford, Richard (**1724/5–1807**), Church of England clergyman and writer, was baptized on 27 December 1725 at Bishop's Castle, Shropshire, the second son of the Revd John Gifford of Bishop's Castle and his wife, Elizabeth. He entered Balliol College, Oxford, in 1744 as a batteler, and graduated BA in 1748. He was described as 'in principle a sound Whig of the Old School, a zealous friend of the House of Hanover' (*GM*) in a college full of tories, which was accounted the reason why he did not continue in his college. Soon after his graduation, in 1748, he published a pamphlet, *Remarks on Mr Kennicott's Dissertation on the Tree of Paradise*, on an early work by the distinguished Hebraist and Old Testament scholar Benjamin Kennicott, who was also one of the university's principal supporters of the Pelham ministry. In 1753 Gifford published a poem, *Contemplation*, which Samuel Johnson subsequently quoted in his dictionary under the definition of wheel.

After ordination Gifford served as curate of Richard's Castle in Herefordshire and then as morning preacher at St Anne's, Soho, in London, and in 1758 he became chaplain to John, marquess of Tweeddale. In 1759 Bishop Cornwallis of Lichfield presented him to the vicarage of Duffield, near Derby, where his eloquence 'edified and delighted crowded audiences' (*GM*). Derby was then a major centre of cultural, intellectual, and industrial activity, with such residents as Jedidiah Strutt, Richard Arkwright, the painter Joseph Wright, and Erasmus Darwin, who founded Derby Philosophical Society in 1782. Gifford appears to have been in touch with the intellectual life of Derby. In 1782 he published *Outline of an Answer to Dr Priestly's Disquisition* in response to Joseph Priestley, the distinguished Birmingham dissenting minister, polymath, and scientist. Gifford also translated the Leicestershire section of *Domesday Book* for Nichols's *History and Antiquities of the County of Leicester*, published in 1775, and was an occasional contributor to 'Mr Urban's Miscellany' in the *Gentleman's Magazine*, under the name R. Duff.

In 1772, on the recommendation of Hugo Meynell, whose tutor he had been, Thomas Browne presented Gifford to the rectory of North Ockenden in Essex. He subsequently spent the summer months there and the rest of the year in Duffield until the climate of the Essex marshes so adversely affected his health that he ceased to visit North Ockenden during the last five or six years of his life. To compensate for his modest pluralism he was said to have gratuitously officiated in poorly endowed parishes in the neighbourhood of Duffield for extended periods. On 26 February 1763 he married Elizabeth Woodhouse, cousin and heir of Thomas Alleyne of Loughborough; she died on 15 January 1793. Gifford died, aged eighty-two, at Duffield on 1 March 1807. He was survived by an only daughter. W. M. JACOB

Sources *DNB* • Foster, *Alum. Oxon.* • *GM*, 1st ser., 77 (1807), 477 • E. G. Rupp, *Religion in England, 1688–1791* (1986) • *Hist. U. Oxf.* 5: *18th-cent. Oxf.*

Archives Derbys. RO, corresp. and papers

Gifford, Robert, first Baron Gifford (1779–1826), judge, was born in Exeter on 24 February 1779, the youngest son of Robert Gifford of Exeter, a prosperous general dealer, and his second wife. He was educated first at a school kept by a dissenting minister in Exeter, and then at the grammar school of the neighbouring village of Alphington. He showed an early interest in the law, regularly attending assizes, and was articled to a solicitor by the name of Jones in Exeter. Disappointed at not being taken into partnership after articles, he entered Middle Temple in 1800, where he was able to read with two eminent special pleaders, Robert Bayley and Godfrey Sykes. In 1803 he took chambers in Essex Court, where he practised as a special pleader for several years. He was called to the bar on 12 February 1808, and joined the western circuit, where his Exeter connections helped him to find work quickly.

Gifford's knowledge of property law was matched by few on the western circuit, and his rise was exceptionally rapid. In 1812 he was elected to the recordership of Bristol, made vacant by the resignation of Sir Vicary Gibbs, and his portrait was commissioned by the corporation; the full-length portrait, painted by Sir Thomas Lawrence, was placed in the town hall. In 1816 he married Harriet Maria, daughter of the Revd Edward Drewe, rector of Broadhembury, Devon. They had seven children, including a son, Robert Francis, who succeeded his father.

On 9 May 1817 Gifford was appointed solicitor-general and duly knighted. On 16 May he was elected MP for Eye in Suffolk, and the same day was chosen a bencher of the Middle Temple. In June he made the reply for the crown in the case of James Watson, on trial for the offence of imagining the king's death, but the jury acquitted the prisoner. Gifford also appeared for the crown at Derby on 16 October prosecuting rioters, who were convicted of treason and executed.

At the general election of 1818 Gifford retained his seat and on 24 July 1819 was appointed attorney-general. As such he conducted the prosecution of the Cato Street conspirators in April 1820, and in the following August addressed the House of Lords in support of the bill of pains and penalties against Queen Caroline. As government prosecutor in various cases of seditious libel he was thought at the time to have showed moderation. His private practice was confined to the court of chancery and the House of Lords, where he had almost the monopoly of Scottish appeals. On 6 January 1824 he became serjeant-at-law and on 9 January he was appointed lord chief justice of the common pleas and sworn in as a member of the privy council. On 31 January 1824 he was raised to the peerage as Baron Gifford of St Leonards, Devon. On 19 February he was commissioned to stand in for the lord chancellor in the House of Lords during his absence, while Lord Eldon was presiding in the court of chancery. This office of deputy speaker of the House of Lords Gifford continued to hold even after he was created master of the rolls on 5 April 1824, discharging its duties without fee.

It was generally believed that Gifford would succeed Eldon as lord chancellor, but death supervened. He had gone to his house on the Marine Parade, Dover, for the summer of 1826 when a liver disorder followed by cholera caused his death on 4 September 1826. He was buried in the Rolls Chapel on 10 September.

As a lawyer, Gifford's abilities were high rather than brilliant. As a political speaker, he had no conspicuous success. In private life, he was courteous and amiable.

J. M. RIGG, *rev.* HUGH MOONEY

Sources E. Foss, *Biographia juridica: a biographical dictionary of the judges of England … 1066–1870* (1870) • *GM*, 1st ser., 87/1 (1817), 358 • *GM*, 1st ser., 89/2 (1819), 85 • *GM*, 1st ser., 94/1 (1824), 79, 175 • *GM*, 1st ser., 96/2 (1826), 367–9 • *Bracton Law Journal*, 26 (1994), 43–4

Archives BL, corresp. with Sir Robert Peel, Add. MSS 40299–40370, *passim*

Likenesses T. Lawrence, portrait, after 1812; commissioned by the Recordership of Bristol • T. Wright, stipple, pubd 1821 (after

A. Wivell), BM, NPG · H. Meyer, stipple, pubd 1829 (after C. Penny), BM, NPG · G. Hayter, drawing (study for *The trial of Queen Caroline, 1820*), NPG · G. Hayter, group portrait, oils (*The trial of Queen Caroline, 1820*), NPG · C. Hullmandel, lithograph (after M. Gauci), NPG

Gifford [Giffard]**, Roger** (*d.* **1597**), physician, was the son of Ralph Gifford of Steeple Claydon, Buckinghamshire, and his wife, Mary, daughter of Sir Edward Chamberlain, of Woodstock, Oxfordshire. His sister, Fredesmund, married Richard Barnes (1532–1587), bishop of Durham. Gifford was educated at Christ Church, Oxford (BA 1556), and became a fellow of Merton College in 1557. He proceeded MA in 1560. Gifford was Linacre lecturer at Oxford between 1561 and 1563. On 8 April 1562 he was elected junior university proctor, and was re-elected on 21 April 1563. He received the degree of bachelor of medicine in 1563, and became a fellow of All Souls in that year. In 1566 he was created MD by Walter Bayley and Henry Bayley, by virtue of a commission directed to them by the convocation, which had selected him to dispute before Queen Elizabeth on her intended visit to the university in the following September. Gifford was afterwards appointed physician to the queen.

Gifford was censor of the College of Physicians from 1570 to 1572, consiliarius from 1585 to 1587, and again in 1591, and president from 1581 to 1584. He was MP for Old Sarum in 1584 and 1589. He was precentor of St David's with the prebend of Llanbedr Pont Steffan (Lampeter) in 1592. Judging by his library, Gifford was a cultured man, well read in French, Italian, and Flemish literature. He was married, and with his wife, Frances, had at least three children: a son, Thomas, a daughter, Mary, mother of the royalist Sir Francis Ottley, and another daughter who married Thomas Harries. He owned land in Durham and the lease of a farm in Essex.

Gifford died of haematemesis on 27 January 1597, and was buried in St Bride's Church, Fleet Street, London; he was survived by his wife. His will, made on the day of his death, was not proved until 1 August 1597. He left to lord keeper Sir Thomas Egerton 'the Jewell wherein the Quenes picture is which he vsed to weare aboutes his necke … in remembrance of my duty and unfeigned affection towards his lordship'. To Merton College he bequeathed 'suche of his bookes as Mr. Henry Savill should choose to be placed in the Librarye of the same Colledge for the use of the Fellowes and Schollers of the same howse'. An anonymous report dated 30 January 1576 claimed that Gifford was among the Roman Catholic members of the College of Physicians.

GORDON GOODWIN, *rev.* SARAH BAKEWELL

Sources Munk, *Roll* · Foster, *Alum. Oxon.* · B. V. Henderson, *Merton College* (1899), 89–90 · G. Lewis, 'The faculty of medicine', *Hist. U. Oxf.* 3: *Colleg. univ.*, 213–56 · HoP, *Commons, 1558–1603*, vol. 2 · will, 1 Aug 1597, PRO, PROB 11/90, sig. 77

Wealth at death owned land in Durham: will, 1 Aug 1597, PRO, PROB 11/90, sig. 77

Gifford, William [*name in religion* Gabriel of St Mary] (**1557/8–1629**), archbishop of Rheims, was described as being twenty-one years of age and belonging to the diocese of Winchester when he was received as a student at the English College at Rome in 1579. His exact place in the ancient and distinguished Gifford family is not clear but he is usually considered the second son of John Gifford who owned property in Gloucestershire but who died on 1 May 1563 and was buried at Crondall, Hampshire. His mother was Elizabeth, the daughter of Sir George Throckmorton of Coughton, Warwickshire. She married a second time in 1569, and placed her son under the care of John Bridgewater at Lincoln College, Oxford, for his early education. When Bridgewater's religious opinions led to his dismissal, Gifford was transferred to the school of another Catholic sympathizer, George *Etheridge.

About 1573 Gifford left Oxford for Louvain where he gained the degree of MA and came into contact with Robert Bellarmine who was lecturing in divinity. After four years the troubled state of the Low Countries led him to depart to Paris whence he was invited by William Allen to become a member of the college founded at Douai but now transferred to Rheims. On 20 July 1579 Allen sent him to Rome and on September 5 he was received as an alumnus of the recently opened English College. He continued his theological studies and was ordained priest in the college chapel on 13 December 1581. Although 'little more than 22 years of age' (Dodd, 2.359), he showed much promise and at Allen's request in March 1582 he was summoned to Rheims to teach theology. It was during his period in Rome that he made the acquaintance of Charles Borromeo. Probably, like others completing their studies in Rome, he visited him at Milan on his way north.

Gifford arrived in Rheims on 23 June 1582, and on 11 July began to lecture on the first part of the *Summa theologica* of Thomas Aquinas. Under Allen's moderation he prepared himself for the doctorate in divinity and in the presence of Cardinal Guise, archbishop of Rheims, and four other bishops and many of the nobility he took his degree at Pont-à-Mousson in Lorraine some time in the second half of 1584. His brilliance led many to think he was a mature man of forty whereas 'he was not much above 26' (Dodd, 2.359). His talent was recognized but doubts were raised as to the firmness of his character and loyalty to the Catholic cause. A kinsman, Gilbert *Gifford, had been expelled from the college in Rome and was working as a spy in the service of the English government. Allen was anxious to protect his disciple from harmful influences. When he was created cardinal in 1587, Gifford spent time with him in Rome and was later referred to in a list of members of Allen's household as 'doctor in theology, very noble and very learned, theologian to the Lord Cardinal' (Knox, *Letters and Memorials*, 377). However, he did not give up lecturing at Rheims and he sometimes acted for the college on official business with Innocent Malvasia, the nuncio in Brussels.

After the death of Allen, Gifford in May 1595 was nominated dean of the collegial church of St Peter in Lille by Pope Clement VIII. His view for the future of Catholicism in England differed from that of Robert Persons, especially in regard to the succession to the English throne. He was one of those English Catholics in Flanders who in 1596 refused to endorse the work of the Jesuits, and this alarmed Barret, the new rector at Rheims, who wrote to Persons:

> It seems that this seminary will be nothing else than a house for those Englishmen who are inimical to the Spaniards and to the fathers of the Society and that it will obtain support from Charles Paget, Dr Gifford and all that faction. (Renold, *Letters*, 273)

At Lille, Gifford was able to complete the controversial treatise begun by William Reynolds, *Calvino-Turcismus*, which drew parallels between Calvin and Muhammad. As dean it fell to him on 5 February 1600 to make the official address of welcome to the archdukes Albert and Isabel when they made their entrance into Lille.

Through the nunciature at Brussels, Gifford sought to influence the Holy See's attitude towards the claims of James VI to the English throne. When the Scottish king succeeded Elizabeth in 1603 Gifford was sent on a special mission to him pleading the cause of the English Catholics. The new oath of allegiance destroyed these hopes. In 1606 the archduke banished Gifford from the Low Countries. Some say that the Jesuits brought about his departure because he supported the Benedictines in their proposal to set up a house at Douai. It would seem more likely that his friendship with Sir Thomas Edmondes, the English ambassador in Brussels, heightened a suspicion that he was acting as an informer for the English government. However, due to the delicacy of the relationships between England, Spain, and the Holy See, the reasons for his expulsion were never disclosed either to Gifford or to Frangipani the nuncio. At Rheims he was offered a chair in theology and was elected rector of the university in 1608.

Gifford's decision to become a Benedictine monk was no sudden flight from the world. Several students had left the English seminaries in Spain and Rome to take the habit, and the order was engaged in missionary activity in England. In 1606 Gifford had used his influence with the cardinal of Lorraine to grant the English Benedictines the collegiate church of St Laurence at Dieulouard, and in 1607 a Benedictine, Augustine Bradshaw, proposed Gifford for a bishopric in England should the Holy See decide to restore the hierarchy. He became a Benedictine on 11 July 1608 at St Remigius's Church in Rheims. He went to Dieulouard and twelve months later he was professed and took the name Gabriel of St Mary; he was often referred to thenceforth as Father Gabriel. He became prior and regent of studies. In 1611 a new convent of the English Benedictines was opened at St Malo and Gifford was appointed its first prior. He remained in this post until 1618 although for the last eighteen months of office he resided in Paris and was instrumental in founding a house there. In 1617 he was elected one of the nine definitors whose task it was to draw up terms of union between the old English and Spanish congregations. In June 1617 he was elected first president of the united congregation.

For many years Gifford had been close to the Guise family; they had supported him with an annual pension when he was teaching at the English College in Rheims. In 1618 the cardinal-archbishop of Rheims, Louis of Lorraine, petitioned the Holy See for a coadjutor and nominated Gifford. He was ordained bishop on 17 September 1618 with the title bishop of Archidalia. When the archbishop died Gifford, who gave the funeral oration, succeeded him. The second son of the duke of Guise was destined for this honour but, as he was yet an infant, and in order to safeguard family interests, Gifford was promoted and the Guises provided him with the necessary pension. Thus an Englishman became bishop of the most distinguished see in France and thereby the country's first peer and duke of Rheims. He took possession of his see in February 1623 and received the pallium on 6 March 1623. Few details are known about his life as a bishop. Shortly after taking office he suffered a stroke. The records use glowing terms to describe his works of charity and pastoral zeal. There is a tradition that when commended for his personal austerities he replied ''Tis nothing to what I have seen in my great master St Charles, Archbishop of Milan' (Allanson, 16). Chaussy has modified his reputation as a preacher not by denying his Latin eloquence but by questioning his fluency in the French language. He died at Rheims on 11 April 1629 and was buried behind the high altar in the cathedral at Rheims without any epitaph or inscription. Following his own request his heart was interred before the lady altar in the convent of St Peter of the Benedictine nuns, Rheims. He was succeeded by the son of the duke of Guise, now aged fifteen, who never took orders, amassed several benefices, and after twelve years resigned and married.

Gifford remains a controversial figure. He was attached to the French rather than the Spanish faction and on the death of Cardinal Allen this led to conflict with Robert Persons and later to his dismissal from Lille. His attitude to the Society of Jesus is not easy to determine. He studied under the Jesuits but his real mentor was Allen and it was due to his favour that he was able to advance his academic career. Other superiors—Alfonso Agazzari in Rome and Richard Barret at Rheims—were not so favourable towards him. MICHAEL E. WILLIAMS

Sources A. Fane, 'The family of Gifford of Boyton', *Wiltshire Archaeological and Natural History Magazine*, 2 (1855), 100–08 • 'Church notes', *Collectanea Topographica et Genealogica*, 7 (1841), 223–4 • J. H. Smith, 'The Giffards of Chillington', *Herald and Genealogist*, 7 (1873), 68–9 • *The letters and memorials of William, Cardinal Allen (1532–1594)*, ed. T. F. Knox (1882), vol. 2 of *Records of the English Catholics under the penal laws* (1878–82) • T. F. Knox and others, eds., *The first and second diaries of the English College, Douay* (1878) • C. Dodd [H. Tootell], *The church history of England, from the year 1500, to the year 1688*, 3 vols. (1737–42) • *Dodd's Church history of England*, ed. M. A. Tierney, 5 vols. (1839–43), vol. 4, appx 5, pp. lx–lxi; vol. 5, appx 6, pp. xx–xxvii • Gillow, *Lit. biog. hist.*, 2.457–61 • G. Anstruther, *The seminary priests*, 1 (1969), 132–3 • P. Guilday, *The English Catholic refugees on the continent, 1558–1795* (1914), 230–34 • E. Hautcoeur, *Histoire de S. Pierre de Lille*, 3 vols. (1899) • *Gallia Christiana in provincias ecclesiasticas distributa*, 9, ed. F. Hodin, E. Brice, and Father Duplessis (1751), c 159 [Maurists] • W. Kelly, ed., *Liber ruber venerabilis collegii Anglorum de urbe*, 1, Catholic RS, 37 (1940) • L. Hicks, *An Elizabethan problem: some aspects of the careers of two exile-adventurers* (1964) • L. Hicks, 'The exile of Dr William Gifford from Lille in 1606', *Recusant History*, 7 (1963–4), 214–38 • P. Renold, ed., *The Wisbech stirs, 1595–1598*, Catholic RS, 51 (1958), 226 • *Letters of William Allen and Richard Barret, 1572–1598*, ed. P. Renold, Catholic RS, 58 (1967), 41, 244–5 • Y. Chaussy, 'Gifford', *Dictionnaire de spiritualité ascétique et mystique: doctrine et histoire*, ed.

M. Viller and others (1937–95) · Y. Chaussy, *Les bénédictins anglais réfugiés en France au XVII*[e] *siècle (1611–1669)* (Paris, 1967) · Y. Chaussy, 'New evidence on the English Benedictines', *Downside Review*, 88 (1970), 49–56 · J. McCann, *Ampleforth & its origins* (1952), 137–60 · D. Lunn, *The English Benedictines, 1540–1688* (1980) · W. B. Patterson, *King James VI and I and the reunion of Christendom* (1997) · A. Allanson, *Biography of the English Benedictines* (1999) · A. F. Allison and D. M. Rogers, eds., *The contemporary printed literature of the English Counter-Reformation between 1558 and 1640*, 1 (1989), 595–604 · J. Pits, *Relationum historicarum de rebus Anglicis*, ed. [W. Bishop] (Paris, 1619), 809 · *DNB*

Gifford, William (1756–1826), satirist and editor, was born in April 1756 in Ashburton, Devon, the first of the two sons of Edward Gifford (*d.* 1767), glazier and house painter, and his wife, Elizabeth, formerly Cain (*d.* 1768), the daughter of a local carpenter. Gifford's early life and his rise from highly unpromising beginnings to an Oxford education and aristocratic patronage are set out in the autobiographical sketch prefaced to his translation of Juvenal (1802). This is a moving document of hardship and self-improvement (admired even by Gifford's bitter enemies Leigh Hunt and William Hazlitt), which is written in a sparse and understated prose style and lacks the splenetic and acerbic tone evident in much of his later writing. Though Gifford's great-grandfather, in the writer's own words, had 'possessed considerable property', his 'extravagant and dissipated' grandfather had managed to render himself indigent. Gifford's father, who as a schoolboy had distinguished himself by running away to sea and later absconding to travel with Bamfylde Moor Carew, the 'King of the Gypsies', was similarly given to drunkenness and riotous behaviour. After his marriage he set up in business at South Molton. However, such stability was short-lived, as in the mid-1750s Edward Gifford fled Devon to avoid a charge of attempting to incite a riot in a Methodist church, and returned to sea. The pregnant Elizabeth returned to Ashburton and was there delivered of William, her first child. The boy was a physically unprepossessing youth, weak and so small that some contemporary antipathetic descriptions of the adult Gifford label him, inaccurately, a dwarf.

Apprenticeship and education In 1764 Gifford's father returned and set up as a glazier and house painter in Ashburton. William was enrolled in Hugh Smerdon's free school at Ashburton. In 1767, however, his father, who was not yet forty, 'fell a martyr' to drink. Gifford's widowed mother, soon embezzled by journeymen employees of the little money left to her, died in the following year and the penniless William and his infant brother were left to the scant protection of his godfather Carlile. Gifford's brother was placed in a workhouse and later sent to sea, where he died while still a boy. William initially remained at school, but, 'sickened of the expense', Carlile set him to work as a ploughboy. This was an occupation to which Gifford's diminutive stature and physical infirmities little suited him, and he was consequently sent to be a ship boy. Gifford's depredations at sea raised grumbling among the people of Ashburton and Carlile was eventually persuaded to put the boy back to school. He made good progress, qualifying as an assistant to the master. However,

William Gifford (1756–1826), by John Hoppner, *c.*1800 [replica]

Gifford's hopes of becoming a schoolmaster were shattered at the age of fifteen, when Carlile apprenticed him as a shoemaker. Gifford 'hated [his] new profession with a perfect hatred'. The young cobbler obtained a few ill-assorted books which he hid from his master, a small-minded and eccentric Presbyterian 'whose reading was entirely confined to the small tracts published on the Exeter controversy'. He also began to write satirical verse, 'lamentable doggerel' on local and quotidian circumstances. When he discovered his treasures, Gifford's master confiscated them and forbade him further composition. The boy's lowest point came soon afterwards when he heard of the election of another to the post left by the death of Smerdon.

Gifford's fortunes changed when his poetical efforts came to the attention of an Ashburton surgeon, William Cookesley. Cookesley raised a subscription to have the boy's apprenticeship bought out and he returned to school. By 1779 he had made progress enough to enter Exeter College, Oxford, as a Bible clerk; he matriculated on 16 February 1779 and graduated BA on 10 October 1782. He worked on his translation of Juvenal while still at Exeter and sent out proposals for publishing the whole by subscription in January 1781. Cookesley died in December 1781 and Gifford, much depressed, felt himself unable to make much progress on his translation, returning what subscriptions he could. However, another piece of good fortune restored his spirits. A letter of his to the Revd William Peters, sent under cover to Lord Grosvenor, came into the hands of the nobleman himself. Grosvenor took up Gifford (who had truthfully told him that he had 'no prospects'), letting the young man live in his house and engaging him as a tutor for his son. Most of the 1780s saw

Gifford in Grosvenor's employ, working once again on his Juvenal and engaged in grand tours on the continent with his pupil which 'occupied many years'. It was not until the next decade that he finally established a more independent career.

The Baviad and Antijacobin During the 1790s Gifford established a name as a verse satirist in *The Baviad* (1791) and *The Maeviad* (1795), 'the first satires of the day' to Lord Byron's mind, neo-classical imitations of Persius and Horace in the manner of Alexander Pope which savagely attacked (both on poetic and political grounds) the then voguish Della Cruscan school of Robert Merry, Hannah Cowley, Edward Jerningham, Mary Robinson, Thomas Vaughan, John Williams, and others. The members of this grouping have tended to live in literary history more as a result of their representation in satire rather than as a consequence of the particular merits of their work. This is mainly attributable to the *Baviad's* merciless onslaught on their mannered sentimentality and proclivity for mutual praise. Much of the *Baviad* relies on acerbic defamatory tirades against the likes of 'snivelling Jerningham', although there are moments, such as the splendid Popean set piece of Merry's visit to Mrs Piozzi's tea party and the footnotes' highly effective use of verbatim parody in a manner derived from the *Dunciad*, where the comic range widens. Late in 1797 one of Gifford's victims, the satirist Williams ('Anthony Pasquin'), unsuccessfully sued him for a supposed libel contained in a note to the *Baviad* (a trial gleefully recorded in succeeding editions of Gifford's satires). Throughout the *Baviad* Gifford's heart, in the true Juvenalian manner, 'burns dry with rage'. Paradoxically, the very success of the *Baviad* has hindered appreciation of the work. The eclipse of the Della Cruscans, for which Gifford was primarily responsible, has left a sense that he was breaking butterflies on the wheel. The likes of Robinson and, in particular, Merry were enthusiasts for the French Revolution, an event hymned in the latter's 1790 *The Laurel of Liberty* (which the *Baviad* describes as a 'philosophical rhapsody on the French Revolution'), and Gifford's attack has highly ideological motivations.

The *Baviad* was seen in its day as the greatest contemporary exercise in classical satire. However, it has been less admired in more recent times. Gifford's intemperate tone (exemplified in the poem's description of Joseph Weston as a 'filthy toad'), misogyny, rancorous toryism, and personal spite which seems to go beyond formal Juvenalianism, have won him few admirers. However, these issues should not blind readers to the effectiveness of his performance. The *Maeviad*, which is ultimately an inferior production, saw Gifford returning to the fruitful subject of the Della Cruscans, in further baiting of Merry, Cowley, and, most memorably, Vaughan. However, the poem also attacks the corruption of the contemporary English stage in its brackish handling of the likes of Thomas Holcroft and John O'Keefe.

Gifford's high reputation as a tory satirist made him a logical choice for the editorship of the *Antijacobin, or, Weekly Examiner*, a journal which brilliantly combines partisan polemic with satire. Sponsored by the tory government of Pitt the younger, and published between 20 November 1797 and 9 July 1798, the *Antijacobin* campaigned vigorously against whiggism and Jacobinism. Gifford's main contribution took the form of a weekly section uncompromisingly entitled 'MISTAKES, MISREPRESENTATIONS AND LIES' in which he offered intemperate repudiations of the liberal press and of anti-governmental writing in general. The principal contributors to the paper, Gifford apart, were three tory MPs who were all gifted comic writers: George Canning, George Ellis, and John Hookham Frere. The weekly 'Poetry of the Antijacobin' section, which uses satire and parody to lambaste liberal and radical politicians (the likes of Fox, Grey, and Thelwall) and writers (Samuel Taylor Coleridge, Payne Knight, William Godwin, Robert Southey, and others), was immediately recognized, with its verve and panache, as the most innovative part of the magazine and was collected and edited by Gifford in 1799 as the *Poetry of the Anti-Jacobin*, a volume which remains a hugely important document in the development of English parody. The *Antijacobin* is also significant in that it is one of the earliest critical documents to be sensitive to the emergence of a nascent English Romanticism. In the very first issue Canning writes of a 'NEW SCHOOL' of poetry and the early numbers parody the new poetical spirit of the age, attacking Southey's millenarianism, metrical experiments, and philanthropic animadversions on the injustices of the poor. Literary significance apart, editing the *Antijacobin* also had more utilitarian consequences for Gifford, allowing him to cultivate notable tory grandees, and he was rewarded by governmental patronage, receiving the sinecures of appointments as paymaster of the gentleman-pensioners and a commissioner of the state lottery, with stipends of £1000 and £100 per year respectively.

The *Antijacobin* was succeeded by the often scurrilous, equally ultra-tory *Anti-Jacobin Review* edited by John Gifford (who was no relation to William), though none of the contributors to the original journal was actively involved in this periodical. However, the oppositionalist satirist John Wolcot ('Peter Pindar'), believing that William Gifford was responsible for an attack on him in the *Review* which was actually published by John Gifford, physically assaulted William at Wright's bookshop in Piccadilly. Gifford retaliated in *An Epistle to Peter Pindar* (1800), a denunciatory biography of Wolcot from 'noxious childhood to pernicious age', which assaults both his work (described as 'vomit') and morals (Wolcot is a 'prodigy of drunkenness and lust'). The decline in Gifford's powers evident in a comparison between the *Baviad* and the *Maeviad* is even more apparent here. Wolcot is a 'bloated mass', a 'slimy toad' who spews out the 'crude abortions of his loathsome muse'. Wolcot replied, in similarly acidulous manner, in *Out at Last* (1801), which describes Gifford as being 'sprung from a dunghill' (as the later attacks by William Hazlitt and Leigh Hunt also demonstrate, liberal satirists were never slow to jeer at Gifford's humble antecedents) and argues that his main service to Grosvenor was the procurement of an endless stream of harlots.

Editor of the *Quarterly Review* The *Epistle* was Gifford's last significant satirical poem, and it was as an editor and translator that he spent his remaining years. In 1802 *The Satires of Juvenal Translated* was finally published. The work was successful, though it received adverse notice in the *Critical Review*, to which Gifford, never one to give up the opportunity for literary bloodsports, stingingly replied in *An Examination of the Strictures of the Critical Reviewers on the Translation of Juvenal* (1803; supplemented 1804). Late in his life Gifford published another significant translation, returning to the figure whom he had imitated so effectively in the *Baviad*'s 'paraphrastic imitation of the first satire of Persius', in *The Satires of Persius Translated* (1821).

Gifford's editorial work involved him both as a literary journalist and as a textual scholar. From 1809 to 1824 he was editor of the *Quarterly Review*, a magazine founded in large part as a tory rival to the highly successful, but whiggish, *Edinburgh Review*. Periodical journalism of this period was almost invariably partisan, and Gifford of the *Quarterly* and Francis Jeffrey of the *Edinburgh* came to be seen as figureheads of the rival literary tribes of tories and whigs. Gifford had an impressive roster of contributors which included J. W. Croker, a reviewer of real, if intemperate, critical flair, Walter Scott, and the quondam *Antijacobin* whipping boy Robert Southey. After an uncertain start the *Quarterly* built up a circulation of about 14,000 by 1818, by which time Gifford was being paid £900 a year for his services as editor. He did not write extensively for the *Quarterly*, but was a highly interventionist editor, as both Lamb's and Southey's complaints about the mutilation of their copy demonstrate. Southey had been a principal contributor from 1809 and was perhaps minded to let Gifford's mangling pass for financial reasons, given that he was paid at the rate of £100 per article.

When Gifford did contribute, his prose criticism was often as ferocious as his poetical satire, as the politically motivated attack on Hazlitt's *Political Essays* in the July 1819 number demonstrates. Hazlitt is described as a 'death's head hawk-moth' whose 'favourite object is, always, the plunder of a hive, and its sole safeguards in accomplishing its purpose are its startling appearance and disagreeable noise'. The essayist replied in kind in 'A letter to William Gifford, Esq' (1819), which sourly characterizes Gifford's relationship with his patrons: 'To crawl and lick the dust is all they expect of you, and all you can do' (*Complete Works*, 9.15) and returned to the subject in *The Spirit of the Age* (1825): 'The low-bred, self-taught man, the pedant, and the dependent on the great contribute to form the Editor of the *Quarterly Review*' (ibid., 11.114). Leigh Hunt, who had also suffered under the lash of the *Quarterly*'s most acerbic contributors, attacked Gifford in *Ultra-Crepidarius: a Satire on William Gifford* (1823) which portrays him as a shoe personified, 'A thing made for dirty ways, hollow at heart' (p. 15). Often the anonymous attacks which provoked such radical anathemas were not by Gifford himself; the 'Editor of the Quarterly Review' had come to be seen as a symbol of reaction and of the worst kind of toryism.

Gifford's editorial work as a textual scholar is accomplished. He produced various editions of English dramatists—Philip Massinger's *Plays* (4 vols., 1805; revised 1813), Ben Jonson's *Works* (9 vols., 1816), John Ford's *Dramatic Works* (2 vols., 1827)—and his notes were used in the edition of William Shirley's *Dramatic Works and Poems* published after Gifford's death by Alexander Dyce (6 vols., 1833). The editorial apparatus of these collections often manifests that peculiarly Giffordian mixture of scholarship leavened with personal vitriol. Gifford's most notable textual work was on Jonson, of whom he was a fierce partisan. His edition contains forthright attacks on bardolators who had dared to speak evil of Jonson as well as the customary splenetic condemnations of the flaws of rival scholars. Such a manner led *Blackwood's Edinburgh Magazine* to comment that:

> Mr Gifford is the most acute, learned, and judicious, of all the Commentators or Editors of our dramatic literature. But the temper of his mind is scornful and intolerant. He often treats the most venial errors—the slightest mistakes—the very semblance of ignorance in his predecessors, with unmitigatable ferocity.

A Menippean satire, *The Illiberal! Verse and Prose from the North* (1822), has sometimes been attributed to Gifford. Gifford certainly shared the political views which led the author of this work to heap maledictions on Byron, Percy Bysshe Shelley, and the 'cockney school', but it is improbable that the by then ailing Gifford, who never deviated from heroic couplets in his extended satires and whose powers were waning as early as the turn of the century, should have returned to the fray with such acerbic vigour, and in a radically different satirical genre from that which he had hitherto employed.

Gifford never married, reserving what affection his heart could muster for his long-term servant Anne Davies who died aged forty-two on 6 February 1815 and whom he elegized in 'I wish I was where Anna lies'. Gifford relinquished the editorship of the *Quarterly* in September 1824 and was succeeded by John Gibson Lockhart in 1825. He died at his house at 6 St James's Street on 31 December 1826 and was buried in Westminster Abbey on 18 January 1827.

Throughout his career Gifford was concerned to uphold traditional poetical proprieties and to anathematize political subversion. A man more famed than admired, Gifford was a 'good hater', and his enemies were not slow to return the compliment. His achievement as a journalist was considerable; editing two of the most important journals to be founded in the Romantic period is no small accomplishment. Despite his often acrimonious tone, Gifford was also a textual editor of real distinction, and as an advocate of Jonson did great service to the restoration of the dramatist's reputation. Of his output as a classical satirist, the role in which he was most celebrated for much of his life, his *Baviad* alone deserves to be remembered. After that work, his poetry's venomous wit is too often displaced by venom pure and simple. Perhaps Gifford knew after the *Epistle to Peter Pindar* that his satirical vein was mined to exhaustion, and, despite Byron's imploring in

English Bards and Scotch Reviewers, he was wise to concentrate on the *Quarterly* in the latter part of his career, where he became, for better or worse, the iconic figure of Romantic period literary toryism. JOHN STRACHAN

Sources W. Gifford, 'introduction', in *The satires of Decimus Junius Juvenalis*, trans. W. Gifford (1802) • *GM*, 1st ser., 97/1 (1827), 105–12 • *Annual Biography and Obituary* (1828), 159–200 • 'A letter to William Gifford, Esq.' and 'Mr Gifford', *The complete works of William Hazlitt*, ed. P. P. Howe, 21 vols. (1932), vols. 9, 11 • J. Leigh Hunt, *Ultra-crepidarius: a satire on William Gifford* (1823) • *Blackwood*, 2 (1817–18), 497–501 • J. Wolcot, *The works of Peter Pindar*, 4 vols. (1816), 3.386 • *The satires of Decimus Junius Juvenalis*, trans. W. Gifford (1802)
Archives NL Scot., letters | BL, letters to G. Ellis, Add. MS 28099 • Bodl. Oxf., letters to Isaac Disraeli • Devon RO, letters to E. Copleston • NL Scot., letters to Sir Walter Scott
Likenesses J. Hoppner, oils, *c.*1800 (replica), NPG [*see illus.*] • line engraving, BM, NPG; repro. in *GM* (1827)

Gift, Theo. *See* Boulger, Dorothy Henrietta (1847–1923).

Gigli, Giovanni (1434–1498), papal official, diplomat, and bishop of Worcester, was born at Bruges, the son of Carlo Gigli, a member of the Lucchese merchant community there, and his wife, Camilla Cagnoli. His father had had links with England since 1451, and was resident in London during 1461–4, so that Giovanni may have passed some of his early life there. Pietro Griffo, his near successor as collector, credits him with fluent English and an Oxford education and, writing to Oxford on 27 April 1490, Gigli called himself a member of that university. In papal documents from 1476 onwards he is doctor of canon and civil law.

By February 1476 Gigli was prior of Sant' Alessandro in Lucca; on 1 April Sixtus IV appointed him papal collector to the realm of England; he was already papal subdeacon. He was in London in April 1477, when he wrote to William Sellyng, prior of Canterbury; he was granted letters of denization on 12 December.

Gigli was admitted rector of St George's, Southwark, on 24 October 1477; later he was archdeacon of London and Gloucester, and canon and prebendary of Wells, St Paul's, London, Lichfield, Lincoln, Chichester, York, Salisbury, and St Mary's, Warwick, besides holding several livings. On 25 January 1485 he was reappointed papal collector by Innocent VIII; by 1488 he was protonotary apostolic. His eloquence on 21 March 1480 failed to secure from convocation financial aid to defend Rhodes, and in 1481 he employed William Caxton to print indulgences for contributors to this. As one of the commissaries for the crusade that Henry VII ordered to be proclaimed in England in 1488–9, he again employed Caxton.

Gigli's diplomatic and rhetorical skills made him useful to the English crown. On 17 April 1479 Edward IV appointed him one of a mission to Sixtus IV to discuss a peace treaty with France; he attended a meeting of the king's council in August 1482. In December 1485 he wrote to Innocent VIII in approval of Henry VII's proposed marriage with Elizabeth of York, and in January 1486 was made one of Henry's proctors for the legatine hearing on the dispensation required for the wedding. Henry commended Gigli to the pope in July 1488, and appointed him to assist in negotiating peace between France and Brittany in March 1489. In October he was one of the English delegates to meet Charles VIII's ambassadors at Calais, and a few months later in London retorted tauntingly to the French humanist Robert Gaguin in Henry's presence.

Perhaps in response to Henry's wish to be well represented with the papacy, Gigli asked to be relieved of his collectorship; his successor was nominated in 14 October 1489. On 1 July 1490 Henry made him the first of a series of Italians to be royal ambassadors resident in Rome; the hope he expressed of Gigli's return to England may have been more than conventional.

His journey slowed by an attack of gout in Lyons, Gigli had reached Milan in October 1490. In Rome on 14 June 1492, he greeted John Shirwood, the English ambassador, and accompanied him in September to convey Henry's obedience to the new pope, Alexander VI. Towards the end of the same year he gave Alexander information on the English peace with France.

A member of the confraternity of the English hospice of St Thomas the Martyr in Rome from 3 May 1491, Gigli was its chamberlain in 1494 and 1496. He was appointed bishop of Worcester by Alexander VI on 30 August 1497, being consecrated at Rome on 10 September. He never resided, employing Thomas Wodyngton as his vicar-general and his nephew Gian Paolo Gigli, merchant of Lucca, as his agent. His temporalities were restored on 5 December 1497 and he was installed *in absentia* at Worcester on 12 April 1498. On 11 May 1498 Lodovico il Moro in Milan instructed Agostino Spinola, his agent in London, to assure Henry VII that he would further the king's wish to obtain a cardinalate for Gigli. At Lodovico's prompting Cardinal Ascanio Sforza, his brother, promised support.

The attempt was frustrated by Gigli's death at Rome, hastened by his gout, on 25 August 1498. A carpet and pair of red bishop's gloves, lent him by the hospice, were not returned, the gloves having been interred with him. His monument in the hospice chapel, where he was buried, was erected by his nephew Silvestro Gigli, his assistant and successor as English ambassador in Rome, who also succeeded him as bishop of Worcester. No longer extant, its inscription gave his age at death as sixty-four. A sixteenth-century portrait in oils of Gigli hangs in the deanery of San Michele in Foro, Lucca.

Gigli's few extant writings, all in polished Latin and mostly composed in England, were undertaken with an eye to advancement rather than recreation. They survive almost exclusively in manuscript. Besides his *dispacci*, they comprise the letter to Sellyng; dedicatory letters; brief poems on flyleaves, inscribing to Cambridge a copy of Cicero's *Tusculan Disputations* (Venice, 1472) and to Lady Margaret Beaufort a pretty Italian lectionary (BL, Add. MS 33772); an epithalamium for Henry VII and Elizabeth; epigrams on the birth, nativity, and name of Prince Arthur; and further epigrams to his book, and to Richard Fox, then royal secretary (1486; BL, Harley MS 336). Bernard André wrote verses on Gigli and reports his wit at Gaguin's expense. Two ecclesiological tractates are extant. *Quaestiones de observantia quadragesimali* ('Matters concerning Lenten observance') was originally dedicated to John

Russell, bishop of Lincoln, about 1480–83, though compiled earlier; an illuminated copy was made for Fox (Yale University, Beinecke MS 25; BL, Harley MS 336). About 1485–6 Gigli dedicated to John Morton, as bishop of Ely, *Libellus de canonizatione sanctorum* ('A little book on canonization of the saints'), composed about 1480–83 (BL, Arundel MS 366). A treatise addressed to Maximilian, against the marriage of Charles VIII and Anne of Brittany, also survives (Rome, Biblioteca Casanatense, MS 4377).

J. B. Trapp

Sources Emden, *Oxf.* • R. Weiss, 'Lineamenti di una biografia di Giovanni Gigli, collettore papale in Inghilterra e vescovo di Worcester (1434–1498)', *Rivista di Storia della Chiesa in Italia*, 1 (1947), 379–91 • *Il 'De officio collectoris in regno Angliae' de Pietro Griffi da Pisa, 1469–1516*, ed. M. Monaco (1973) • *CPR, 1476–85*, 74 • *CEPR letters*, 10.553; 13.197–201, 208, 262–3, 281–2, 705, 859; 14.3, 14–17, 34, 54, 56; 17.59, 1335–7 • *CSP Milan*, 48, 62, 56, 113, 237n., 261–2, 264, 266, 323, 343, 345, 348 • *CSP Venice, 1202–1509*, nos. 506, 520, 531, 535, 550–51, 553, 573, 576–8, 582–3, 620, 626, 751, 771 • P. O. Kristeller, *Iter Italicum*, 7 vols. (1963–97), vol. 2, no. 104; vol. 4, nos.131a, 154b–155a; vol. 5, no. 275b; vol. 6, no. 229a • *Letters of Richard Fox, 1486–1527*, ed. P. S. Allen and H. M. Allen (1929) • A. Kenny, 'From hospice to college', *The Venerabile*, 21 (1962), 218–73, 269–70 [sexcentenary issue: *The English hospice in Rome*] • D. R. Carlson, *English humanist books: writers and patrons, manuscript and print, 1475–1525* (1993) • Archivio Vaticano, Vatican City, Div. Cam. 50, fol. 70 • English College Archivio, Rome, Lib. 17, fols. 21–26v • G. Tournoy and G. Tournoy-Thoen, 'Giovanni Gigli and the renaissance of the classical epithalamium in England', *Myricae: essays on neo-Latin literature in memory of Jozef IJsewijn*, ed. D. Sacré and G. Tournoy (Leuven, 2000), 133–93 • D. R. Carlson, 'Three Tudor epigrams. 2. Giovanni Gigli on the *Tusculanae quaestiones …*', *Humanistica Lovaniensia*, 45 (1996), 192–6

Archives Biblioteca Casanatense, Rome, MS 4377 • BL, Add. MS 33772 • BL, Arundel MS 366 • BL, Harley MS 336 • Yale U., Beinecke L., MS 25

Likenesses portrait, exh. 1945, San Michele, Lucca, Deanery

Wealth at death see Archivio Vaticano, Vatican City, Div. Cam. 50, fol. 70; English College at Rome, Lib. 17, fols. 21–26v

Gigli, Silvestro (1463–1521), diplomat and bishop of Worcester, was born in Lucca in 1463, perhaps on 1 January, to Ser Nicolao Gigli (*c.*1410–1489) and his wife, Francesca (*b.* *c.*1433, *d.* after 1489), daughter of Giusfredo Rapondi. His patrician family exerted significant political power in Lucca, with wealth accumulated from trading interests that extended to Bruges, Paris, and London, and from the church through presentation rights and landholdings. On 2 February 1472 Silvestro was tonsured and ordained acolyte, thereby enabled to make presentations to ecclesiastical offices, to hold church lands and benefices, and, if so desired, become a priest. Such a ceremony was unexceptional for a patrician boy on the Italian peninsula; however that the ceremony was in Rome, rather than Lucca, probably testifies to the influence of his cousin, Giovanni Gigli, then at the Roman curia: Giovanni proved a determining factor in Silvestro's career. A law graduate, probably of Bologna University, by mid-June 1483 Silvestro was living in London as Giovanni's 'servant', probably his secretary; Giovanni had been papal nuncio and collector of Peter's Pence in the kingdom since 1476, a denizen since 1477. From 1490 Giovanni was Henry VII's resident orator at the court of Rome, and Silvestro probably was in his entourage, for certainly by 1494 he was one of Giovanni's *familia*; from 1496, if not earlier, he was a chamber clerk, assisting his cousin with English crown business.

In 1494 Giovanni Gigli resigned to Silvestro the revenue of the abbey of Cantignano. The next year, following a contested election to a canonry of the cathedral of San Martino, Lucca, it passed to Silvestro's elder brother, Marcantonio, who on 7 September resigned it expressly to Silvestro, with the approval of Bishop Sandonnino of Lucca, a relative of the Gigli and Giovanni's personal friend. That same year Cardinal Borgia resigned to Silvestro a significant portion of the revenues of the priory of San Michele in Foro, Lucca, and those of the associated rectory of San Giorgio. Backed by his cousin and by Sandonnino, thereafter Silvestro rapidly accumulated further prestigious ecclesiastical benefices and offices. When Giovanni died in Rome on 25 August 1498 Silvestro arranged his funeral and burial in the English Hospice's church of St Thomas. In 1492 Giovanni had been instrumental in the appointment as cardinal protector of England of Sandonnino's friend, Francesco Todeschini Piccolomini. Following Giovanni's death and the cardinal's commendation to Henry VII, Silvestro became orator in his cousin's stead. On 1 December he was admitted *in absentia* to his uncle's see of Worcester, nomination being accepted by the pope on 24 December at Piccolomini's presentation (Giovanni's death at the papal court enabled the pope to nominate the successor); enthronement by proxy came the following 16 April. Gigli administered his diocese through officials like his chancellor Thomas Bagard, and through a series of vicars-general, among whom John Bell, who held the office from 1518, was particularly active. He also enjoyed the co-operation of successive heads of Worcester Cathedral priory, notably John Wednesbury from his election in 1507. Wednesbury died on 23 August 1518 on a pilgrimage to Rome, and was buried in the church of the English Hospice, with a tombstone and epitaph provided by Gigli. In the autumn of 1505 Gigli appeared before the court of Star Chamber at Westminster regarding a contested election and riot in Stratford upon Avon within his diocese, a rare instance of his involvement in diocesan affairs.

After Sandonnino's death in 1499 Gigli, while still royal orator, represented Lucca's interests to the pope, particularly in August–September 1504 during his native city's dispute with Florence. Circumstances at the curia continued to favour Gigli, with the election in November 1503 of Julius II, generally hostile to former associates of Alexander VI. Among the latter was Gigli's professional rival Adriano Castellesi, briefly cardinal protector of England in 1503, whose influence was diminished. About 17 March 1505 Gigli was appointed legate to take to England the papal dispensation permitting Prince Henry's marriage to Katherine of Aragon, with personal honours for Henry VII: the papal sword and cap, awarded to a sovereign annually. Andrea Ammonio of Lucca, later Henry VIII's Latin secretary, probably accompanied Gigli to England, though Baldassare Castiglione's hopes of doing so were dashed. In England Gigli, created a royal chaplain, on occasion acted as a royal functionary over the next seven years.

In February 1512 Gigli was commissioned, perhaps at Wolsey's suggestion, as the king's special representative at the Fifth Lateran Council; he reached Rome only in late October during its second session, thereafter attending sporadically. A guardian of the conclave that elected Leo X in March 1513, as he had been in 1503 at the elections of Pius III and Julius II, by September 1513 he was once more a royal English orator at the curia, serving under Christopher Bainbridge, who was effectively cardinal protector of England. By then the latter's diplomatic endeavours were self-evident failures, and quarrels with Gigli over policy ensued. On 31 December Gigli wrote to Wolsey taking credit for the award to Henry VIII of the papal sword and cap. Apparently by then Gigli was Wolsey's client, employed deliberately to undermine Bainbridge; it was Gigli who in February 1514 obtained the services of Giulio de' Medici as cardinal protector of England. On 20 May Bainbridge retaliated by writing to the king detailing Gigli's intrigues with the French.

On 14 July 1514 Bainbridge died of poison, which one of the cardinal's household confessed under torture to having administered at Gigli's behest. Claiming diplomatic immunity, and supported by Wolsey, Gigli escaped arrest; probably this episode occasioned the oration delivered in Gigli's defence by the Lucchese humanist Niccolò Tegrimi. Testifying to his rehabilitation on 3 September Gigli sang mass in the church of Santa Maria del Popolo to celebrate the peace between England and France sealed by the marriage of Mary Tudor to Louis XII. In December the pope formally absolved Gigli of Bainbridge's murder, but the affair effectively doomed his ambition to become a cardinal.

As Wolsey's agent in Rome, Gigli successfully promoted Wolsey for the cardinalate in 1515 and the English legation in 1518, while simultaneously working with Wolsey to effect Castellesi's final disgrace. In spring 1516 he obtained initial papal approval for conferment on Henry VIII of the title agreed in 1521 as 'Christianae Fidei Defensor', but the pope shelved the award in the face of opposition from François I, who was on the peninsula with an army. Gigli's reward in late August 1517 from Wolsey was the English collectorship of Peter's pence, once his cousin's; Castellesi's sub-collector, was the already displaced Polydore Vergil, who chose not to mention Gigli in his *Anglica historia*. Between 1516 and 1520 Gigli assisted Erasmus with several papal dispensations, and in January 1521 Erasmus dedicated to him his paraphrase of the epistle of Paul to the Hebrews. Shortly before Giovanni Gigli's death Henry VII had brought the English Hospice in Rome under royal authority; responsibility for it partially passed to Silvestro. He was admitted one of its *confratres* on 16 July 1499, and played a part in its subsequent administration, being one of its two *camerarii* from 1500 to 1504, as again in 1518. On 29 March 1521, fearing dismissal as orator at Cardinal Giulio de' Medici's prompting, in a bid for royal favour Gigli sent the king his anti-Lutheran pamphlet when Henry was himself engaged in writing an attack on Luther, published as the *Assertio septem sacramentorum* in July. On receiving his congé, before his replacement reached Rome, Gigli was taken ill (probably a stroke). He died in Rome on 18 April and was buried the next day in the church of St Thomas at the English Hospice. On 11 May 1521 the pope authorized Gigli's heirs to transfer his remains to the church of San Michele, Lucca, where he had founded a side chapel dedicated to San Silvestro for that purpose, where an impressive tomb was erected, sculpted by Baccio di Montelupo and his son Raffaello; all that remains is its relief of the Madonna and child.

CECIL H. CLOUGH

Sources S. Tabacchi, 'Gigli, Silvestro', *Dizionario biografico degli italiani*, 54 (2000), 690–93 · T. B. Deutscher, 'Silvestro Gigli', *Contemporaries of Erasmus*, ed. P. G. Bientenholz and T. B. Deutscher, 2 (1986), 97–8 · M. Creighton, 'The Italian bishops of Worcester', *Historical essays and reviews*, ed. L. Creighton (1902), 211–20 · W. E. Wilkie, *The cardinal protectors of England* (1974) · D. S. Chambers, *Cardinal Bainbridge in the court of Rome, 1509 to 1514* (1965) · U. Bittins, *Das Domkapital von Lucca im 15. und 16. Jahrhundert* (1992), 236, 243–8 · M. Underwood, 'The pope, the queen and the king's mother', *The reign of Henry VII* [Harlaxton 1993], ed. B. Thompson (1995), 65–81 · A. Adorni-Braccesi, *'Una città infetta': la repubblica di Lucca nella crisi religiosa del cinquecento* (1994), 14–18, 35, 53, 56 · A. Giustinian, *Dispacci*, ed. P. Villari, 3 (1876), 218–19, 530–33 · N. H. Minnich, *The Fifth Lateran Council (1512–1517)* (1993), item 1, 187 no. 173 · *The English Hospice in Rome*, 21 (1962) [sexcentenary issue] · M. Gigli, 'Descrizione della famiglia dei Gigli … copiata 1618', Biblioteca Statale, Lucca, MS 1008, fols. 23–25v · J. L. Bolton, ed., *The alien communities of London in the fifteenth century: the subsidy rolls of 1440 and 1483–4* (1998), 85–6 · I. S. Leadam, ed., *Select cases before the king's council in the star chamber, commonly called the court of star chamber*, SeldS, 16 (1903), 230–34, · C. Dyer, *Lands and peasants in a changing society: the estates of the bishopric of Worcester, 680–1540* (1980), 154, 202 · C. Eubel, *Hierarchia catholica medii aeri, sive, summorum pontificum, S.R.E. cardinalium ecclesiorum antistitum*, ser. 2–3, 2nd edn, ed. L. Schmitz-Kallenberg (1914–23) · *LP Henry VIII*, vols. 1–3 · P. Paschini, *Tre illustri prelati* (1957)

Archives BL, Cotton MSS, letters to T. Wolsey and Henry VIII · diocesan RO, Worcester, episcopal register compiled by his vicars-general · PRO, official MSS rel. to diplomatic mission

Gil [Gill], **Alexander, the elder** (**1565–1635**), headmaster, was born in Lincolnshire on 27 February 1565. He was admitted scholar of Corpus Christi College, Oxford, in September 1583, graduated BA in 1586, and proceeded MA in 1589. Anthony Wood believed that he was then a schoolmaster at Norwich, where he was living in 1597 when he wrote his *Treatise Concerning the Trinity*, an attack on the Anabaptist Thomas Mannering, which was published in 1601.

On 10 March 1608 he was appointed high master of St Paul's School, London, in succession to Richard Mulcaster. Milton was among his pupils from 1620 or earlier to 1625. 'He had', says Wood:

> such an excellent way of training up youth that none in his time went beyond him; whence 'twas that many noted persons in church and state did esteem it the greatest of their happiness that they had been educated under him. (Wood, *Ath. Oxon.*, 2.597–600)

Less deferential recollections were long enshrined in irreverent songs (quoted by Aubrey) about his enthusiasm for flogging boys, though it is possible that the actions of Alexander *Gil the younger (1596/7–1642?) were, with the passage of time, wrongly attributed to the father who shared his name.

Gil and his wife, Elizabeth, had three sons and two

daughters. His sons all attended Trinity College, Oxford, though Alexander migrated to Wadham. George matriculated at Trinity on 13 December 1616, aged fourteen, graduated BA in 1620, and proceeded MA in 1624; he was under-usher at St Paul's School from 1628 to 1637 and surmaster from 1637 until his death in 1640. Nathaniel matriculated on 17 January 1623, aged seventeen, graduated BA in 1625, and proceeded MA in 1629; he subsequently became rector of Burgh St Mary and Burgh-next-Aylsham in Norfolk. Gil's two daughters were Anna Banister, who was still alive (as a widow) in 1673, and Elizabeth, who married a pewterer, Gabriel Bouchier. The escapade of his son Alexander in 1628 distressed Gil greatly, and he successfully exerted himself—supplicating 'on his knees' (*Brief Lives*, 1.263)—to obtain at the hands of Laud, with whom he was on friendly terms, a remission of the punishment inflicted by the Star Chamber.

Gil was not only famous as a schoolmaster, but was, as Wood attests, 'esteemed by most persons to be a noted Latinist, critic and divine'. His *Sacred Philosophie of the Holy Scripture* (1635) attempted to defend the truth of the apostles' creed against the rival creeds of Muslims, Jews, atheists, and heretics. He also wrote a dedicatory poem for John Speed's *Theatre of the Empire of Great Britaine* (1611) and a preface (in Latin) to Francis Anthony's *Apologia veritatis illucescentis, pro auro potabile* (1616) thanking him for curing his infant daughter and one of his sons by the administration of potable gold. His most important book was *Logonomia Anglica* (1619; rev. 1621), which champions a phonetic system of English spelling which may have influenced Milton's individualistic spelling: Gil's 'sutl' (instead of subtle or subtil), for instance, may account for Milton's 'suttle'. In his section on grammatical and rhetorical figures Gil quotes freely from English authors such as Daniel ('our Lucan'), Dyer, Harington ('our Martial'), Jonson, Sidney ('our Anacreon'), Wither ('our Juvenal'), and especially Spenser ('our Homer'). Gil died at his house in St Paul's Churchyard, London, on 17 November 1635, and was buried on 20 November in Mercers' Chapel. A transcript of his will, dated 30 July 1634, is among Wood's papers at the Bodleian Library (D. 11). Gil's widow, Elizabeth, received a pension from the Mercers' Company until 1648. GORDON CAMPBELL

Sources Wood, *Ath. Oxon.*, new edn, 2.597–600 • *Brief lives, chiefly of contemporaries, set down by John Aubrey, between the years 1669 and 1696*, ed. A. Clark, 1 (1898), 263 • R. B. Gardiner, ed., *The admission registers of St Paul's School, from 1748 to 1876* (1884), 32 • *Alexander Gill's Logonomia Anglica*, ed. O. Jiriczek (Strassburg, 1903) • D. L. Clark, 'Milton's schoolmasters: Alexander Gil and his son Alexander', *Huntington Library Quarterly*, 9 (1945–6), 121–47 • D. L. Clark, *John Milton at St Paul's School* (1948), 65–83 • W. R. Parker, *Milton: a biography*, ed. G. Campbell, 2nd edn, 2 vols. (1996), vol. 2, p. 711 • A. Barker, 'Milton's schoolmasters', *Modern Language Review*, 32 (1937), 517–36 • E. J. Dobson, *English pronunciation, 1500–1700*, 2nd edn (1968), 131–55 • H. F. Fletcher, *The intellectual development of John Milton*, 1 (1956), 169–81 • R. Baldwin, 'Alexander Gill, the elder, high master of St Paul's School: an approach to Milton's intellectual development', PhD diss., University of Illinois, 1955 • D. Dixon, 'Alexander Gil's *Logonomia Anglica*, edition of 1621, translated with an introduction and critical and explanatory notes', PhD diss., University of Southern California, 1951 • will, 30 July 1634, Bodl. Oxf., MS Wood D. 11

Gil, Alexander, the younger (1596/7–1642?), headmaster and poet, eldest son of Alexander *Gil the elder (1565–1635), schoolmaster, and his wife, Elizabeth (*d.* 1648?), was born either in London, as recorded in Oxford sources, or in Norwich, where his parents were living in 1597. At St Paul's School he was taught by the under-usher William Sound and, in the upper school, by his father. He was admitted to Trinity College, Oxford, as an exhibitioner on 26 June 1612 at the age of fifteen, but on 20 April 1613 migrated to Wadham, where he was admitted as an *aedituus*, or Bible clerk (a status which obliged him to read lessons in chapel and say grace in hall); on 24 February 1615 he was granted a scholarship by the co-founder, Dorothy Wadham. He graduated BA from Wadham on 26 February 1616 and proceeded MA from Trinity on 9 November 1619 (incorporated at Cambridge in 1623), BD on 27 June 1627, and DD on 9 March 1637; he was licensed to preach on 15 July 1637.

Gil's teaching career began in Thomas Farnaby's school, London. On 26 January 1622 he succeeded Oliver Smythe as under-usher of St Paul's but retained his links with Farnaby, to whom he sent at new year 1624 a poem and canary wine. Some of Gil's other early poetry had a less friendly purpose. The death of some ninety Catholic worshippers when a secret chapel close to St Paul's collapsed on 15 November 1623, for example, drew a compassionate response from some protestants, but Gil celebrated by composing an exultantly vindictive poem, *In ruinam camerae papisticae*, in which he depicts the accident as God's revenge for the Gunpowder Plot (15 November in the protestant Julian calendar was 5 November in the Catholic Gregorian calendar). Similarly, Gil took revenge on Ben Jonson's slighting of his father in *Time Vindicated* (1623) by mocking Jonson's 'bed-ridden wit' (Jonson had been paralysed by a stroke), abusing him for the failure of *The Magnetic Lady*, and suggesting that he go back to bricklaying (Bodl. Oxf., MS Ashmole 38). Jonson retaliated with another abusive poem, and Zouch Townley weighed in with a defence of Jonson against Gil's attack.

In September 1628, in a tavern in Oxford with friends, Gil drank the health of John Felton, who had assassinated the duke of Buckingham a week earlier. Two days later, while drinking in the cellar of Trinity College, Oxford, he imprudently disparaged King Charles and his late father. William Chillingworth, who was present, reported Gil's actions to his godfather William Laud, then bishop of London. On 4 November Gil was arrested at St Paul's School on Laud's orders, and imprisoned in the Gatehouse at Westminster. The rooms of Gil's friend William Pickering in Trinity College were searched, and incriminating 'libels and letters' by Gil were found (PRO, SP 16/117). On 6 September Gil was examined by Laud, who reported his findings to the king, and on 6 November the court of Star Chamber sentenced him to be degraded from the ministry, dismissed from his ushership at St Paul's, deprived of his university degrees, fined £2000, to lose one ear in the pillory at Westminster and the other in Oxford, and to be imprisoned in the Fleet prison at the king's pleasure. Gil's father successfully petitioned for a mitigation of the fine and a remission of the corporal punishment, but Gil seems to have been imprisoned for about two years. He was given notice of a royal pardon on 18 October 1630 and received the pardon on 30 November 1630. He had lost his official teaching post at St Paul's, but for the next few years the school employed him unofficially.

In 1632 Gil collected his Latin verse (and a few Greek poems) in a small volume entitled *Parerga* ('Incidental Poems'). The volume seeks to make amends and to reaffirm his loyalty to king and church with a fulsome dedication to the king, a profoundly respectful poem addressed to Laud, and congratulatory verses on the birth of Princess Mary; it also contains poems to potential patrons such as the diplomat Sir Paul Pindar and the earl of Denbigh.

Gil was, in Anthony Wood's words, 'accounted one of the best Latin poets in the nation' (Wood, *Ath. Oxon.*, 3.42–3), a judgement in which Gil's friend Milton concurred in praising one of Gil's poems for its poetic majesty and Virgilian genius. In 1634 Gil and Milton exchanged poems. Gil had written a bawdy 75-line hendecasyllabic epithalamium for the wedding of Elizabeth Noel, daughter of the second Viscount Campden, on 20 November 1634, and sent a copy to Milton, who replied on 4 December with a Latin letter and a copy of his recently composed translation of Psalm 114 into Greek verse. After the publication of *Parerga* Gil never again collected his poems, though a manuscript of poems and letters now in the East Sussex Record Office (FRE 690) may have been intended for the press. His later poems, both English and Latin, are all occasional pieces, such as an English poem on the victories of Gustavus Adolphus (1632) and congratulatory Latin verses on the return of Charles from Scotland (1641).

Gil succeeded his father as high master of St Paul's ten days after the latter's death on 17 November 1635. The acts of the court of assistants of the Mercers' Company, which was the governing body of St Paul's, show that Gil had a difficult relationship with the governors. These problems culminated on 5 February 1639, when a petition was lodged on behalf of a boy named John Bennett alleging that Gil had lifted him up by the jaws, beaten him, and kicked him up and down the school. After months of argument arising out of this incident and subsequent allegations of drunkenness and unauthorized absence, Gil was finally dismissed from the high mastership.

On 28 January 1640 Gil lodged an appeal to the king against dismissal (PRO, SP 16/443). The king referred Gil's petition to Archbishop Laud and 'some other lords'. The court of assistants argued that it enjoyed the prerogative to deal with Gil as it judged appropriate. Laud, in defending Gil, appealed to canon law in formulating his view that Gil's bishop would have to be party to any decision to dismiss him. Laud's appeal to canon law not only failed to save Gil from dismissal but also contributed to his own fate, in that it formed the last of the ten supplementary charges brought against Laud at his trial in 1644.

Gil shared with his father a reputation for what Aubrey described as 'whipping fits'. His savage temper and fondness for corporal punishment became the stuff of legend, and in the process these same characteristics were also attributed to his father (who shared his name).

After his dismissal Gil managed to secure the post of headmaster of Oakham School, in Rutland; an entry dated 30 April 1644 in the decrees of Oakham School records that Richard Swann had been appointed master 'in the place of Dr Gil, deceased'. Gil had probably secured this post through the patronage of the Noel family, as Gil was a friend of Baptist Noel, third Viscount Campden. He did not stay in Rutland for long: tax records for St Botolph, Aldersgate, for 1641 and 1642 show that Gil had returned to London, where he became a neighbour of Milton. Wood says that he died in this parish in 1642, but this cannot be verified because the burial entries between 13 February 1642 and 18 June 1643 are missing from the surviving registers. GORDON CAMPBELL

Sources M. McDonnell, *The annals of St Paul's School* (privately printed, Cambridge, 1959), 202–20 • M. McDonnell, ed., *The registers of St Paul's School, 1509–1748* (privately printed, London, 1977), 117–22 • Wood, *Ath. Oxon.*, new edn, 3.42–3 • acts of the court of assistants, 1634–49, Mercers' Hall, London • acts of the court of assistants, 1637–41, Mercers' Hall, London • GL, MSS 1503 and 3854/1 • R. B. Gardiner, ed., *The registers of Wadham College, Oxford*, 1 (1889), 18, 480 • D. L. Clark, *John Milton at St Paul's School* (1948), 65–9, 83–99 • W. R. Parker, *Milton: a biography*, 2nd edn (1996), 2.711–12, 754, 807, 884, 1216, 1223 • L. Miller, 'On some of the verses by Alexander Gil which John Milton read', *Milton Quarterly*, 24 (1990), 22–5 • L. Miller, ed. and trans., unpublished edition of the poems of Alexander Gil, University of Colorado at Boulder, Leo Miller Collection • PRO, SP 16 • Bodl. Oxf., MS Ashmole 38

Archives E. Sussex RO, FRE 690 • Harvard U., Houghton L., MS Latin 114 | BL, Burney MS 368 • Bodl. Oxf., MS Ashmole 36.37 • Bodl. Oxf., MS Rawl. Poetical 84 • Bodl. Oxf., MS Tanner 306 • Bodl. Oxf., MS Wood F34

Gilbart, James William (1794–1863), banker and author, was born in London on 21 March 1794, descended from a Cornish family. In 1813 he began work as a junior clerk with a London bank, which stopped payment on account of the panic of December 1825. He was for some time after this engaged as cashier in the employment of a Birmingham firm, but soon returned to London, where, early in 1827, he published *A Practical Treatise on Banking*. This contained an account of the London and country banks, and also discussed the joint stock banks of Scotland and Ireland. The work went through a number of editions, and was highly esteemed as a standard treatise. Gilbart wrote a number of articles for popular periodicals, and was also connected with the Union Club, a debating society founded by J. S. Mill, of which T. B. Macaulay was a member.

In 1827 Gilbart went to Ireland, and gained six and a half years' experience of joint-stock banking. During that time he managed, in succession, the branches of the Provincial Bank of Ireland at Kilkenny and Waterford. He nevertheless continued his literary activity, and became so well known that when joint-stock banks were established in London he received offers of employment from two of them. In the event he became manager of the London and Westminster Bank on 10 October 1833. The bank opened its doors on 10 March 1834 and, both before and after, Gilbart had hard and delicate work to pilot the new institution through the real early difficulties faced by joint-stock banks in England.

The Bank of England was determined to hamper the London and Westminster's operations, however, and resisted its request to open a drawing account. The bank was also in 1836 prohibited from accepting any bills drawn at less than six months after date. This seemed likely to kill the bank's country connection, but Gilbart skilfully evaded the danger by getting the country banks to draw upon his bank bills 'without acceptance' (Michie, xiii). He took this plan from the method adopted by the Bank of Ireland in drawing bills upon the Bank of England. He was also faced with the refusal of the private banks to let the London and Westminster use the facilities of the London Clearing House. Gilbart wrote on the subject, gave evidence before various parliamentary committees, and played a key role in the Association of Joint-Stock Banks, which was formed in 1838. He saw the complete success of his labours when, in 1844, Sir Robert Peel's Bank Charter Act enacted, *inter alia*, that joint-stock banks could sue and be sued by their public officers, and could accept bills at six months after date. In 1854 the joint-stock banks were also finally admitted to the London Clearing House.

An austere and frugal bachelor, Gilbart keenly felt the disadvantages of his position at the London and Westminster Bank. He complained incessantly to his directors that he was underpaid, and that his social position was inferior to that of a private banker. In public estimation, Gilbart argued, he was 'considered as holding an office analogous to that of chief clerk in a private bank' (Kynaston, 1.120).

Elected a fellow of the Royal Society in 1846, Gilbart was a member of a number of other learned societies, including the Statistical Society, to whose *Transactions* he contributed various papers. In addition, he took part in the International Statistical Congress held in July 1860. Gilbart's writings on banking continued to be highly regarded throughout his lifetime, and a sixth edition of his *Practical Treatise* was published in 1859. His writings were collected and republished in six volumes in 1865.

Gilbart's interest in his profession was shown in 1851 by his giving a prize of £100 for the best essay on the subject 'The adaptation of recent inventions, collected at the Great Exhibition of 1851, to the purposes of practical banking' (Michie, xiv). In 1859 he retired on a pension of £1600 per annum from the bank. Gilbart died at his home, 56 Brompton Crescent, London, on 8 August 1863.

ROBERT BROWN

Sources A. S. Michie, 'Biographical notice of the author', in J. W. Gilbart, *The history, principles, and practice of banking*, rev. A. S. Michie, rev. edn, 1 (1882), i–xv · D. Kynaston, *The City of London*, 1 (1994) · *GM*, 3rd ser., 15 (1863), 385 · *CGPLA Eng. & Wales* (1863)

Likenesses W. J. Taylor, bronze medal, 1853, NPG · H. Adlard, stipple (after G. B. Black), NPG · S. Hollyer, engraving (after photograph by T. R. Williams), repro. in J. W. Gilbart, *Works*, 6 vols. (1865) · D. J. Pound, stipple (after photograph by Mayall), NPG · G. Zobel, mezzotint (after photograph by T. R. Williams), NPG · lithograph, BM · portrait, repro. in *A record of the proceedings of the London and Westminster Bank during the first thirteen years of its existence*) (1847) · portrait, repro. in 'The laws of the currency as employed in the circulation of country bank notes in England since the passing of the act of 1844', *Statistical Society Journal* (1855) [reprinted] · portrait, repro. in J. W. Gilbert, *Moral and religious duties of public companies* (1856)

Wealth at death under £35,000: probate, 17 Oct 1863, *CGPLA Eng. & Wales*

Gilbert [Gilbertus; *called* Gilbert the Universal] (*d.* **1134**), bishop of London, was a Breton by birth, and kinsman of Hervey, first bishop of Ely. In early life his closest links seem to have been with Auxerre, where he was a canon of the cathedral. Here he witnessed charters of 1100, 1120, and probably also 1126—in 1120 with his nickname as 'Magister Gillebertus Universalis'. His title 'magister', as well as his known writings and his fame as a scholar, suggest that he was in charge of the cathedral school. Gilbert was elected bishop of London, as successor to Richard de Belmeis, late in 1127 and was consecrated on 22 January 1128. Henry of Huntingdon claims that at the time of his election he was master of the schools of Nevers, and other sources confirm some connection with Nevers. But a short account of his career by one of his nephews makes no mention of the place. Furthermore, a charter of the bishop of Nevers of 1130 (by which time Gilbert was bishop of London) was witnessed by 'Gillebertus doctor', canon and probably master of the schools of Nevers, and there may have been confusion between the two. According to John of Worcester, Gilbert was also a canon of Lyons, but there is no supporting evidence for this. Invectives by Peter Abelard against the teaching of a Burgundian theologian and incidental allusions to a Master Gilbert cannot safely be taken to refer to Gilbert the Universal.

It seems clear that Gilbert enjoyed a considerable reputation as a canon lawyer, and it may well have been his involvement in a legal battle, rather than his distinction as a theologian, that gained him the see of London. Hugh the Chanter, in his *History of the Church of York* complains bitterly that Gilbert, 'a wise clerk and famous advocate', changed sides, even though he had promised to support the archbishop of York at the papal curia against the claim of Canterbury to primacy over York (*History*, ed. and trans. Johnson, 214–5). Hugh accused him of betraying justice for the prospect of better pay from the wealthier archbishop of Canterbury. Whenever York suffered a check in this protracted struggle Hugh becomes an untrustworthy witness, but it is credible that Gilbert was giving legal support to Canterbury and it is known that Henry I, who certainly had a hand in the appointment of Gilbert, favoured Canterbury. Little is known about Gilbert's six years as bishop. The affairs of the diocese and cathedral probably remained firmly in the hands of the men of his predecessor, among them at least two sons and four nephews of Bishop Richard serving as dean, archdeacons, and canons of St Paul's. But there were limits to what Gilbert would accept. Against the claims of Richard de Belmeis (*d.* 1162), who had been given the archdeaconry of Middlesex by his uncle when still a minor, Gilbert upheld Richard's vicar in this office. He himself established two nephews as canons of St Paul's, and one of them so fully identified himself with his church that he wrote an ardent account of the miracles of Earconwald, the saintly seventh-century bishop of London, to propagate his cult. At Westminster Abbey Gilbert tried to assert what he believed to be his right as diocesan, by celebrating a mass on the feast of St Peter and Paul and taking the oblations. But he supported the abbey in the foundation of a nunnery at Kilburn (Middlesex), and the backing of his authority, as that of an eminent theologian, was sought by Osbert de Clare, prior of Westminster, for the contested Anglo-Saxon tradition of celebrating the feast of the Immaculate Conception of the Virgin Mary. According to Henry of Huntingdon, Gilbert knew how to exploit the resources of his office but lacked the munificence becoming to a bishop and devoted himself to avarice. On the other hand St Bernard of Clairvaux, a friend of Gilbert, praised the bishop for his life of voluntary poverty and for his charity. He died early in August 1134.

Contemporaries praised Gilbert for his immense learning in the liberal arts and theology, and for his work on glossing the Bible. His fame had almost completely faded when Beryl Smalley rediscovered him in the 1930s, and showed him to have been one of the leading scholars behind the *Glossa ordinaria* of the Bible. In its developed form in the late twelfth century this became the standard gloss for the complete Vulgate. In essence a compilation of earlier authorities, with a sprinkling of new explanations, the *Glossa* grew out of a collaborative effort which is generally believed to have been initiated by Master Anselm at Laon (*d.* 1117). In a work like this it is difficult to assess individual contributions, but there are portions which are consistently ascribed to Gilbert in the manuscripts. At the end of the gloss on Lamentations, Gilbert, 'deacon of the church of Auxerre', names himself as the author. A copy of the book of Lamentations with Gilbert's gloss, written in the priory of Augustinian canons at Riechenberg near Goslar in 1131, is the earliest datable manuscript of any part of the *Glossa* known today. Other parts of the *Glossa* attributed to Gilbert are the gloss on the Pentateuch and the prophets, and, more tentatively, the gloss on the seven historical books from Joshua to the second book of Kings. There is also a commentary on the Psalms attributed to him. It is in the nature of Gilbert's known writings that they give little direct insight to his thinking, but they show him to have been a dedicated teacher in full command of the vast tradition of earlier biblical scholarship. John of Salisbury tells us that in a controversy in 1148 Gilbert was still cited as a leading authority, for his opinion on a fundamental point of theology.

FALKO NEININGER

Sources B. Smalley, 'Gilbertus Universalis, bishop of London, 1128–1134, and the problem of the *Glossa ordinaria*', *Recherches de Théologie Ancienne et Médiévale*, 7 (1935), 235–62; 8 (1936), 24–64 • B. Smalley, 'Glossa ordinaria', *Theologische Realenzyklopädie*, ed. G. Krause, G. Müller, and S. Schwertner, 13 (Berlin, 1984), 452–7 • F. Neininger, ed., *London, 1076–1187*, English Episcopal Acta, 15 (1999) • E. G. Whatley, *The saint of London: the life and miracles of St Erkenwald. Text and translation* (1989) • C. N. L. Brooke, 'The earliest times to 1485', *A history of St Paul's Cathedral and the men associated with it*, ed. W. R. Matthews and W. M. Atkins (1957), 1–99, 361–5, esp. 24–6 • W. Petke, 'Eine frühe Handschrift der Glossa ordinaria und das Skriptorium des Augustiner-Chorherrenstifts Riechenberg bei Goslar', *Papstgeschichte und Landesgeschichte: Festschrift für Hermann Jakobs zum 65. Geburtstag*, ed. J. Dahlhaus and A. Kohnle (Cologne, 1995), 255–96 • *Hugh the Chanter: the history of the church of York, 1066–1127*, ed. and trans. C. Johnson (1961) • Henry, archdeacon of Huntingdon, *Historia Anglorum*, ed. D. E. Greenway, OMT (1996) • *The Historia pontificalis of John of Salisbury*, ed. and trans. M. Chibnall, rev. edn, OMT (1986), 19 • *Sancti Bernardi opera*, ed. J. Leclercq and others, 7 (Rome, 1974), 24, 76–7 • *Biblia latina cum glossa ordinaria: facsimile reprint of the Editio princeps, Adolph Rusch of Strassburg, 1480/81*, 4 vols. (1992) [introduction by Karlfried Froehlich and Margaret T. Gibson] • *Fasti Angl., 1066–1300*, [St Paul's, London], 1, 15, 27, 57 • F. Barlow, *The English church, 1066–1154: a history of the Anglo-Norman church* (1979) • J. Laurent, ed., *Cartulaires de l'abbaye de Molesme, ancien diocèse de Langres, 916–1250*, 2 (Paris, 1911), p. 482, no. 642 [charter of 1126, not cited by Smalley] • *Florentii Wigorniensis monachi chronicon ex chronicis*, ed. B. Thorpe, 2, EHS, 10 (1849), 89 • *Gallia Christiana in provincias ecclesiasticas distributa*, 12, ed. P. Henri and J. Taschereau (1770), instrumenta 339–40, no. 48 [charter of 1130, Nevers, not cited by Smalley] • P. Labbe, ed., 'Gesta abbatum S. Germani Autissiodorensis', *Nova bibliothecæ manuscriptorum: librorum tomus primus*, 1 (Paris, 1657), 570–93, esp. 577 • M. T. Gibson, 'The twelfth century glossed Bible', *Studia patristica 23: papers presented to the Tenth International Conference on Patristic Studies held in Oxford 1987*, ed. E. A. Livingstone (1989), 232–44 • M. T. Gibson, 'The place of the *Glossa ordinaria* in medieval exegesis', *Ad litteram: authoritative texts and their medieval readers*, ed. K. Emery jun. and M. D. Jordan (1992), 5–27 • *The chronicle of John of Worcester, 1118–1140*, ed. J. R. H. Weaver (1908), 26 • J. Lebeuf, *Memoires concernant l'histoire ecclésistique et civile d'Auxerre*, 2 vols. (1743) [2nd edn in 4 vols., 1848] • E. O. Blake, ed., *Liber Eliensis*, CS, 3rd ser., 92 (1962), 279 • A. Vidier and L Mirot, eds., *Obituaires de la Province de Sens*, 3 (1909), 239, 261 • Ordericus Vitalis, *Eccl. hist.*, 6.478 • *The letters of Osbert of Clare, prior of Westminster*, ed. E. W. Williamson (1929), 11–13, 65–8 • W. Holtzmann, ed., *Papsturkunden in England*, 1/2 (Berlin), Abhandlung der Gesellschaft der Wissenschaften zu Göttingen, new ser., 25/2 (1931), no. 17 • *Petri Abaelardi opera theologica*, ed. E. M. Buytaert, 3, ed. C. J. Mews (Turnhout, 1987), 218–19, 439–40 • *Radulfi de Diceto … opera historica*, ed. W. Stubbs, 1: *1148–79*, Rolls Series, 68 (1876), 245 • M. Prou and A. Vidier, eds., *Recueil des chartes de l'abbaye de Saint-Benoît-sur-Loire*, 1 (1900–07), 267–9 no. 107 [charter of 1110, cited by Smalley from Lebeuf] • L. A. Muratori, ed., *Antiquitates Italiae medii aevi*, 4 (Milan, 1741), 1097 [Richard of Cluny] • E. Martène and U. Durand, eds., *Veterum scriptorum et monumentorum historicorum, dogmaticorum, moralium, amplissima collectio*, 5 (1729), 1172 • B. Smalley, 'La *Glossa ordinaria*: quelques prédécesseurs d'Anselm de Laon', *Recherches de Théologie Ancienne et Médiévale*, 9 (1937), 365–400 • B. Smalley, 'A collection of Paris lectures of the later twelfth century in the MS. Pembroke College, Cambridge 7', *Cambridge Historical Journal*, 6 (1938–40), 103–13, esp. 112 • F. Stegmüller, ed., *Repertorium biblicum medii aevi*, 2 (Madrid, 1950), 351–5, nos. 2536–78 • F. Stegmüller, ed., *Repertorium biblicum medii aevi*, 9 (Madrid, 1977), 29–33, nos. 2541–73 • E. Mason, J. Bray, and D. J. Murphy, eds., *Westminster Abbey charters, 1066–c.1214*, London RS, 25 (1988), nos. 155, 249 • M. A. Zier, 'The medieval Latin interpretation of Daniel: antecedents to Andrew of St Victor', *Recherches de Théologie Ancienne et Médiévale*, 58 (1991), 43–78

Wealth at death immense wealth: Henry of Huntingdon, *Historia Anglorum*

Gilbert [Gille, Gilli, Gillebertus; *called* Gilla Espaic] (*d.* **1145**), bishop of Limerick, was called Gilla Espaic ('Bishop's Servant', or 'Bishop's Devotee') on the authority of the seventeenth-century Gaelic scholar Geoffrey Keating, but is referred to as Gille and Gillebertus both by himself and by the seventeenth-century antiquarian Sir James Ware, and is named as Gilli in his annalistic obit recorded in the *Chronicum Scotorum*. He was papal legate to Ireland for almost all his episcopate, the first person, according to Bernard of Clairvaux, to have held the position 'per universam Hiberniam', contradicting a late Irish source assigning the role of first legate to Máel Muire Ua Dúnáin (unless the latter's jurisdiction did not extend to the entire country).

Nothing is known of Gilbert's early life, including whether he was of Irish or Norse extraction, and, unlike other bishops of Hiberno-Norse towns, there is no evidence that he studied in England. His first appearance is his brief letter, styling himself Gillebertus, 'Lumnicensis episcopus', to Anselm of Canterbury (*c.*1107), congratulating the latter on the outcome of his quarrel with Henry I and enclosing a gift of twenty-five pearls. Anselm replied, thanking him, and recalling their earlier acquaintance at Rouen. No clue is provided regarding the circumstances of their meeting, but the fact that Anselm says that 'I now learn' of Gilbert's consecration indicates that the latter had been at Rouen in some other capacity, perhaps as a student, and, unlike his contemporary Hiberno-Norse bishops, had apparently not been consecrated at Canterbury. The archbishop, however, expresses no dissatisfaction at this, and no doubt that the election was canonical; neither does he claim to be Gilbert's metropolitan, and merely encourages him to attend to 'the correction of abuses among that people', and to work 'with your king and the other bishops' in doing so (Ussher, 4.513).

The king in question was Muirchertach Ó Briain, whose capital was Limerick, and who had earlier promoted Canterbury's involvement with the Hiberno-Norse sees. While Gilbert's apparent consecration elsewhere may indicate moves to exclude Canterbury, Gilbert's successor was consecrated there, and one of Gilbert's few later appearances is in the *Historia novorum* of Eadmer, the Canterbury monk, whose list of the suffragans present at Westminster on 19 September 1115, assisting Archbishop Ralph in the consecration of a new bishop of St David's, ends with 'Gislebertus Lumniensis de Hibernia'.

Gilbert is best known as author, while legate 'apud Hibernos', of the treatise *De statu ecclesiae*, which survives in at least two manuscripts, preceded by a prologue, *De uso ecclesiastico*, which also occurs alone in another manuscript. Both tracts were published by Archbishop James Ussher in 1632, in an edition reissued among Ussher's complete works in 1847. The prologue is essentially a letter to the bishops and priests of all Ireland. Gilbert, styling himself 'Gille Lumnicensis', states that many of them have asked him to write a guide to the proper canonical recitation of the hours and 'the fulfilment of the duties of the whole ecclesiastical order', so that 'those diverse and schismatic orders with which nearly all Ireland has been deluded may give place to one Catholic and Roman office' (Ussher, 4.500). It is a plea for liturgical uniformity, whereas the accompanying treatise is concerned with ecclesiastical organization, suggesting perhaps that Gilbert wrote elsewhere on liturgical use. *De statu ecclesiae* is a commentary on a diagram contained in the manuscripts, in the form of an elaborate pyramid, intended to illustrate the hierarchical structure of the church, and the interrelations between its members, with Christ at the apex, the pope below him, then the prelates, and so forth (and their lay equivalents, the emperor, kings, and so on), the homiletic text instructing each grade as to its duty. Little is known of the sources upon which Gilbert relied and it may be unfair to assume his tract's out-datedness on the basis of his (somewhat critical) reference to Amalarius of Metz (*d. c.*850).

The diocesan structure which Gilbert outlines was introduced at (and may, in his capacity as legate, have been especially prepared for) the Synod of Ráith Bressail in 1111, over which, according to Keating, he presided. Although the surviving annals fail to mention his role, the synodal enactments, which usually define the newly established dioceses by four boundary points, give thirteen in the case of Limerick, also note that its cathedral church is St Mary's, and then pronounce a curse on those who question Limerick's boundaries, suggesting its bishop's personal involvement in their drafting.

Gilbert does not appear to have been an active legate thereafter, his only contribution being his conjunction with Máel Ísu of Lismore in persuading Máel Máedóc Ó Morgair (St Malachy) to accept the vacant see of Armagh in 1129. St Bernard of Clairvaux is the source for this and for the fact that Ó Morgair was appointed legate to Ireland in 1140, Bishop Gilbert having just then relinquished the office 'by reason of age and infirmity of body' (*Life of St Malachy*, 73), at which point, too, his successor to Limerick was elected. Gilbert's death is noted in *Chronicum Scotorum* for 1145 (the sole reference to him in the Irish annals), where he is called simply 'Gilli, bishop of Limerick'.

SEÁN DUFFY

Sources J. Ussher, 'Veterum epistolarum Hibernicarum sylloge', in *The whole works of … James Ussher*, ed. C. R. Elrington and J. H. Todd, 17 vols. (1847–64), vol. 4, pp. 383–572 • G. Keating, *Foras feasa ar Éirinn / The history of Ireland*, ed. D. Comyn and P. S. Dinneen, 3, ITS, 9 (1908), 298–307 • 'De praesulibus Hiberniae', *The whole works of Sir James Ware concerning Ireland*, ed. and trans. W. Harris, 1 (1739) • Bernardus Claraevallensis, 'Vita S. Malachiae', *Patrologia Latina*, 182 (1854), 1073–118 • *Eadmeri Historia novorum in Anglia*, ed. M. Rule, Rolls Series, 81 (1884), 236 • W. M. Hennessy, ed. and trans., *Chronicum Scotorum: a chronicle of Irish affairs*, Rolls Series, 46 (1866), s. a. 1145 • J. F. Kenney, *The sources for the early history of Ireland* (1929), 763–4, no. 651 • A. Gwynn, *The Irish church in the eleventh and twelfth centuries*, ed. G. O'Brien (1992) • A. Gwynn, 'The diocese of Limerick in the twelfth century', *North Munster Antiquarian Journal*, 5 (1946–7), 35–48 • *St Bernard of Clairvaux's Life of St Malachy of Armagh*, ed. and trans. H. J. Lawlor (1920)

Archives CCC Cam., MS 66, 98–9 • CUL, MS Ff.1.27, pp. 239–42 • Durham Cath. CL, MS B.II.35

Gilbert [*called* Gilbert the Great] (*d.* **1167**), abbot of Cîteaux and theologian, is said to have been English by origin. He went to France and became a Cistercian there. In 1143 he was made abbot of Ourscamp, while in 1163 he succeeded the eighth abbot, Fastradus, as abbot of Cîteaux. As abbot he was responsible in 1164 for composing the statutes for the knights of Calatrava. In 1165 Pope Alexander III gave the Cistercian order exemption from all episcopal jurisdiction, probably at Gilbert's instigation. In 1166, in the course of his quarrel with Thomas Becket, and resenting the support the Cistercians had given to the exiled primate, Henry II brought pressure to bear on the general council of the order, with the result that Gilbert had the task of conveying to the archbishop, who was then at Pontigny, the suggestion that he should go elsewhere.

Gilbert's career seems to show him to have been an able administrator. His claims to scholarly eminence rest on shakier foundations. He is credited with works of scriptural commentary (Bodl. Oxf., MS Auct. D.4.6), and with a collection of *distinctiones theologicae* (Bodl. Oxf., MSS Bodley 29 and 45), but these cannot be attributed to him with any certainty. Bale says that he wrote a commentary on the Song of Songs, beginning 'varii sunt affectus amantium quia'. There also survive three short letters from him to Louis VII of France. Although his sobriquet, 'the Great', is contemporary, no reason for his being so designated is provided by twelfth-century sources, and the title remains puzzling. Gilbert died on 17 October 1167.

G. R. EVANS

Sources Bale, *Index* • F. Barlow, *Thomas Becket* (1986)
Archives Bodl. Oxf., MS Auct. D.4.6 • Bodl. Oxf., MSS Bodley 29, 45

Gilbert of Hoyland. *See* Holland, Gilbert of (*d.* 1172).

Gilbert of Moray (*d.* **1243/1245**), bishop of Caithness, is of uncertain parentage. In the sixteenth century he was thought to have been of the noble house of Moray (de Moravia), which acquired the earldom of Sutherland during his episcopate, but no family relationship is ever stated in charters in which he is named along with members of that family.

Gilbert is styled master from between 1207 and 1211, and the later Aberdeen breviary states that he was educated and given up to studies, although it is not known where. Although Walter Bower identifies him as the young Scottish clerk, Gilbert, who made an eloquent speech at the Council of Northampton in 1176 in defence of the independence of the Scottish church, the identification has been firmly repudiated. Similarly there is no evidence to support Bower's statement that Gilbert was made chamberlain by Alexander II, although he does appear to have been relied on as an administrator in the north by both Alexander's father, William, and by Alexander himself. Before about 1206 Gilbert became archdeacon of Moray, and while he held that office reproved Bishop Brice for extortions and other scandalous acts, complaining by letter to the pope. But he was also later remembered as being concerned with the building of castles, and it must have been his position as a royal officer which explains the substantial grant of land, to be held in full hereditary right, which Hugh Freskin, who probably held all of Sutherland at this date, made to Gilbert while the latter was still archdeacon (*c.*1211).

The original grant survives, with a confirmation by King William the Lion (*c.*1212), a new charter confirming the original grant by Hugh Freskin's son William, lord of Sutherland (*c.*1214), and a confirmation by Alexander II of a gift of the same lands made by Gilbert, now bishop, to his brother Richard (1235). The importance of the lands seems to lie in their frontier location, extending westwards from Skelbo on the east coast to Invershin and the borders of Ross. The purpose of such a grant must have been strategic, and points to Gilbert's skills as an administrator on behalf of the crown, which at this time was making determined efforts to extend its authority north of the River Oykell and detach Sutherland from Caithness. It does give some support to Bower's statement that Gilbert was King William's 'closest confidant in his more secret business' (Bower, 4.331).

It was not until 1222 or 1223 that Gilbert was made bishop of Caithness, however, after the disastrous episcopates of John and Adam. According to Bower he was elected 'in the presence of the lord king and the chief men of his army' (Bower, 5.115), during Alexander's expedition north to Caithness when retribution for the murder of Bishop Adam in 1222 was meted out. It had finally been realized that a tough cleric was needed for the difficult situation existing in this most northerly diocese. The new bishop moved his episcopal seat away from the previous bishop's church at Halkirk, the scene of the slaughter of his predecessor, to Dornoch, in the south of the diocese, close to his own land and castle of Skelbo. There Gilbert built a new cathedral, at his own expense. He was also responsible for devising a constitution for the cathedral chapter, an adaptation of the Lincoln model, but one which diverted revenues from every parish in the diocese for the support of the bishop and canons.

Bishop Gilbert was active outside his diocese on ecclesiastical matters; he attended at least two church councils, was appointed a papal mandatory on a number of occasions, and possibly visited Rome. He made his will (which has not survived) in 1242, and died on 1 April in either 1243 or 1245, perhaps at Scrabster. A powerful and effective prelate, he brought the church in the province of Caithness firmly into the sphere of Scottish influence, finally breaking the links with the northern, Scandinavian, world which had been the underlying cause of the violence suffered by his two episcopal predecessors. His relics at Dornoch came to be venerated, but he was never formally canonized a saint.

BARBARA E. CRAWFORD

Sources D. E. R. Watt, *A biographical dictionary of Scottish graduates to AD 1410* (1977), 414–17 • W. Blew, ed., *Breviarium Aberdonense*, 2 vols., Bannatyne Club, 96 (1854) • W. Bower, *Scotichronicon*, ed. D. E. R. Watt and others, new edn, 9 vols. (1987–98), vols. 4–5

Gilbert of Rothbury. *See* Rothbury, Gilbert (*b.* in or before 1260, *d.* 1321).

Gilbert of St Lifard. *See* St Leofard, Gilbert de (*c.*1230–1305).

Gilbert of Sempringham [St Gilbert of Sempringham] (**1083–1189**), monastic reformer, was the son, probably the eldest, of Jocelin, a Norman knightly tenant of Alfred of Lincoln, and an unnamed Anglo-Saxon mother, through whom his father presumably came into his estates, most of which were concentrated in Lindsey. He had at least one brother, Roger, and a sister, Agnes, both of whom supported their brother's monastic foundations.

Early life and foundations Because of an unspecified deformity Gilbert was unable to follow a knightly profession, and it was probably for this reason that he was sent to school, first locally, perhaps at Lincoln, and then to France, probably Paris, though he may have gone to Laon to study with Master Anselm. On his return his father gave him two churches, Sempringham and West Torrington, both in Lincolnshire, though he was not yet a priest and still wore costly secular dress, and he established a small school for boys and girls of the neighbourhood, perhaps run on quasi-monastic lines. Gilbert, who had the aid of a chaplain, originally lodged with a family in Sempringham, but they later built themselves a house in the churchyard. His attempts to reform the parish, insisting on the payment of tithes and curbing drinking feasts, though resented, were, according to his biographer, largely successful.

Some time before 1123 Gilbert entered the household of Robert Bloet, bishop of Lincoln. Following Robert's death in that year he remained in the service of his successor, Alexander (*d.* 1148). Alexander persuaded Gilbert to be made priest, and while serving as an episcopal chaplain his reputation for ascetic piety led Alexander to make him a diocesan penitentiary and later to offer him an archdeaconry, which Gilbert refused. Shortly afterwards he decided to return to Sempringham: he sold his goods and distributed them to the poor, like many contemporary reformers looking to follow the path of poverty. About 1131 he became spiritual director to a small community of anchoresses living in cells around a cloister attached to the parish church of Sempringham. Here they were enclosed by Bishop Alexander. Initially their temporal care was undertaken by female servants. These, however, were soon replaced—perhaps on the advice of Abbot William of Rievaulx (*d.* 1145)—by lay sisters. These were followed by the introduction of lay brothers, another development which may have been inspired by the Cistercians. The first recruits included escaped serfs and beggars. During this early period the community attracted and encouraged few endowments and was probably supported from Gilbert's own resources, including his two churches, while one of their first patrons was his brother, Roger. In 1139, however, Bishop Alexander established another community of women a few miles north of Sempringham at Haverholme (where he had originally intended to establish a Cistercian monastery), which he placed under Gilbert's supervision. This may have followed a version of the Cistercian rule: however, neither Sempringham nor Haverholme at this point had any formal structure, and though they may have been influenced by Cistercian customs they had as yet no written institutions, nor is there any indication that Gilbert wished to found a religious order: indeed, the saint's life suggests a marked reluctance to undertake leadership.

This reluctance may have led Gilbert in 1147 to journey to Cîteaux, and there attempt to persuade the Cistercian general chapter to assume control of his communities. In this he was unsuccessful. The chapter of 1147 oversaw the takeover by the white monks of two other orders, those of Savigny and Obazine; Gilbert's small communities, lacking as they did a secure organizational structure and directed primarily at the care of women, had little appeal for the Cistercians whose attitude to the role of women in the religious life was at best ambivalent, at worst hostile. However, there is some evidence that he was encouraged and advised by Bernard of Clairvaux, although the latter's influence may have been exaggerated by Gilbertine writers keen to deflect criticism of their order at the end of the twelfth century when double communities came under attack. Certainly, Gilbert was already familiar with Cistercian practice through his friendship with Abbot William of Rievaulx, and his presence at Cîteaux gave him the opportunity to observe Cistercian organization at first hand. On his return to England in 1148 the first codification of the Gilbertine order was made: the nuns' institutions followed the Benedictine model; those of the lay brothers were heavily dependent on the Cistercian rule; a new rule was devised for the lay sisters, while in the early 1150s Gilbert introduced canons, who followed a version of the Augustinian rule, for the spiritual care and temporal management of his communities. This period also saw the foundation of virtually all of the Gilbertine double houses, for nuns and canons, and also two (Malton in Yorkshire and St Katherine's, Lincoln) for canons only.

Growing pains But at the same time the emergent order was faced with a sequence of crises. A notorious sexual scandal at the east Yorkshire priory of Watton demonstrated the fragility of the Gilbertine structure, and was only resolved through the intervention of Ailred, abbot of Rievaulx (*d.* 1167), who, towards the end of his life some ten years later, recorded the episode of the nun of Watton in his *De sanctimoniali de Wattun*. At about the same time Gilbert aided Archbishop Thomas Becket in his escape to France. Two Gilbertine brothers accompanied Becket in his flight from the Council of Northampton (1164), and the archbishop stayed at two Gilbertine houses on his way to the channel. As a consequence of his support for Becket, Gilbert was cited to appear before royal justices to account for his actions, and he was additionally accused of providing the exile with funds. However, after Henry II had personally intervened and Gilbert had declared his innocence, the case was dropped.

This matter had not been finally resolved when Gilbert was faced with a serious revolt among the lay brethren, who seemingly resented the shift of control away from them to the canons, a cause of complaint that is also found at about the same time at Grandmont. The rebellion was led by two *conversi*—lay brothers—to whom Gilbert had entrusted the oversight of all the communities. In 1165 they appealed to Pope Alexander III claiming mistreatment and scandalous behaviour in the order. Alexander ordered Becket to undertake an inquiry, and the archbishop wrote to Gilbert advising him to reform his communities and requiring his presence to answer the charges on 2 February 1166. On his failure to comply Becket wrote to Gilbert in stronger terms, urging him to moderate the rigour of his rule. At the same time Gilbert was mobilizing support, and the king, as well as a number of leading prelates including Henry de Blois, bishop of Winchester, wrote on his behalf to the pope in praise of the order. Henry II himself threatened that unless the pope supported Gilbert and confirmed the authority of the Gilbertine canons he and his magnates would take back all properties granted to the order. Alexander responded by setting up two inquiries, in the provinces of Canterbury and York, to settle the issues. These centred on the nature of the lay brothers' profession and status, and charges of sexual misconduct they had brought against the canons. Both inquiries reported in Gilbert's favour, and he was finally cleared in the Roman curia of all charges against him. In 1169 papal privileges were issued reinforcing the authority of Gilbert and the canons, and though some *conversi*, notably one of their leaders, Ogger, continued their struggle for many more years, the revolt was to all intents and purposes over. While towards the end of his life Gilbert did make a few concessions regarding the brothers' food and clothing, the balance of power within the order had shifted irrevocably in favour of the *magister* and his canons.

Later years and death The rebellion had demonstrated the degree to which Gilbert was a revered establishment figure. He enjoyed the patronage of Henry II, who founded the Gilbertine priory of Newstead, Lincolnshire, and of Queen Eleanor, and the royal court is reported to have visited him in his lodgings, perhaps in London. He was also a friend of Archbishop Hubert Walter (*d.* 1205), to whom his life—contained in the *Liber sancti Gilberti*—was later dedicated. He continued to attend the episcopal court of Lincoln, although, interestingly, there is little evidence of any close friendship with his saintly contemporary Hugh, bishop of Lincoln (*d.* 1200).

Gilbert was by now a very old man, although he continued to travel around his communities and also acted as spiritual adviser to other groups of nuns. In the late 1170s he handed over control of the order to his successor, Roger, prior of Malton, although even after this he retained ultimate authority within it. At about the same time he reluctantly assumed the monastic habit and formally joined the order, probably at the urging of his communities, who feared that on his death the order might fall into the hands of an outsider. Gilbert's last years were marked by increasing weakness and blindness. Nevertheless he both maintained the asceticism which he had practised throughout his life, and continued to work for the unity and discipline of his order. He received the last sacraments at Newstead at Christmas 1188, and was then moved back to Sempringham by his household, who feared that if he died away from the community his body would be seized as a relic by others. After being visited by all the Gilbertine priors, and having commended the order to Roger, he died early on the morning of Saturday 4 February 1189.

Canonization Gilbert was buried shortly afterwards in Sempringham Priory, in the wall dividing the nuns' part of the church from the canons', so that both women and men might approach the tomb. Miracles had been reported even before his death, and they increased markedly afterwards. Yet there was no formal attempt to canonize Gilbert until 1200. The canonization process, the first to be carried through according to the new centralized rules established by Pope Innocent III (*r.* 1198–1216), is fully recorded in the *Liber sancti Gilberti* (*The Book of St Gilbert*). It was carefully orchestrated by Archbishop Hubert Walter and King John—the latter was present when the first inquiry into miracles was held on 9 January 1201. Its report, together with supporting letters from many English prelates and a short life, was forwarded to the Roman curia which ordered a further inquiry, held on 26 September. Its evidence was transmitted to Innocent, who issued the bull of canonization on 30 January 1202, and the body of Gilbert was finally translated to its new shrine on 13 October 1202. Shortly afterwards a new life was produced, dedicated to Hubert Walter and corrected by William de Montibus (*d.* 1213), chancellor of Lincoln and a supporter of the Gilbertines. This was probably written by Ralph de Lisle, sacrist of Sempringham, and included the corpus of miracles presented at the canonization inquiries. Many miracles were associated with members of the Gilbertine communities, several of them seemingly recorded with a didactic purpose to reinforce good discipline. Most of the other cures were visited on members of the local laity. After the canonization no further miracles are recorded, and although the shrine survived until the dissolution, the cult was never more than a minor one. The fate of Gilbert's relics is unknown: Waltham Priory possessed a bone of the saint given in the thirteenth century, while the relics currently exhibited at St Sernin, Toulouse, seem to be misidentified.

Of Gilbert's character little can be recovered other than what is recorded in the hagiographic tradition and which was intended to construct an image of sanctity. Such evidence is liable to distortion. On the one hand it stresses Gilbert's affable temper and playfulness, his eloquence and generosity, and his readiness to help his communities in menial tasks, but it also presents an autocratic disciplinarian who was at once both reluctant to take and to relinquish authority. Virtually nothing is left of his own writings. His autobiographical account, written after 1167, known either as the *De constructione monasteriorum* or the *De fundatatione monasteriorum* is almost wholly lost, though fragments are embedded in the life and in the opening, autobiographical section of the rule. Of the letters he wrote to his communities shortly before his death urging unity and condemning dissension, only that to the canons of Malton survives.

Sources Knowledge of Gilbert's life and the early history of the order is therefore largely confined to the so-called *Liber sancti Gilberti*, an English translation of the life completed in 1451 by John Capgrave, the autobiographical fragments, and the Gilbertine rule. The *Liber*, which survives in three manuscripts (BL, Cotton MS Cleopatra B.i and Harley MS 468, and Bodl. Oxf., MS Digby 36), is a compilation seemingly assembled as the canonization dossier and containing the life, material relating to the lay brothers' revolt, and canonization process, together with the miracle collections. Capgrave's translation of the life was requested by the order's master for those Gilbertine nuns who did not understand Latin. It is based upon the life and *lectiones*, as well as incorporating oral testimony from within the order.

The rule survives in a single manuscript (Bodl. Oxf., MS Douce 136) and dates from between 1220 and 1223. It incorporates revisions made after Gilbert's death, but the manuscript also includes the decisions of Gilbertine general chapters held in the later middle ages. Like all monastic rules it was constantly being revised and it is difficult to reconstruct arrangements as they stood during Gilbert's lifetime. Control of the communities was personal rather than institutional. Gilbert was responsible for the disciplinary visitations of his communities and for the pastoral supervision of the nuns, and provided the only link between Sempringham and its daughter houses, while the incident of the nun of Watton suggests that the structure of the order was then far more fluid and informal, and also less segregated, than it was to be in the last years of Gilbert's life and following his death: indeed, the crises of the 1160s may well have been the catalyst towards the emergence of a more rigid rule.

The saint and his order By the time of Gilbert's death there were said to be 700 men and 1500 women in the order—almost certainly an exaggeration, though some of the communities were substantial. The priories of Sempringham, Watton, and Bullington, Lincolnshire, are all reported to have contained 200 nuns in the late 1240s. Nine double houses and four houses for canons only had been founded. Most of these were in Gilbert's native Lincolnshire, or in Yorkshire. Thereafter the pace of foundation slowed and there was only one more double house (Shouldham, Norfolk), which reflected growing suspicion of double religious communities for women and men. At the dissolution there was a total of twenty-three Gilbertine communities: an additional six (including one each in Normandy, Scotland, and Rome) had failed. None of the Gilbertine priories was very wealthy. Only three double houses (Watton, Sempringham, and Chicksands, Bedfordshire) had a net income over £200 in 1535. Yet these were prosperous, by comparison with other nunneries. The Gilbertines undoubtedly appealed to local benefactors, notably to members of the lesser aristocracy, such as the Kyme family (who founded Bullington) and Eustace fitz John (*d.* 1157), who founded Watton and Malton. In Lincolnshire the order also attracted support from the free peasantry, whose small grants contributed to the gradual expansion and consolidation of Gilbertine estates. The priories received sons and daughters of their patrons as recruits and provided a burial for benefactors and their families. Some communities, such as Clattercote, Oxfordshire, and St Katherine's, Lincoln, also functioned as hospitals, and the Lincoln house continued to receive bequests for its eleemosynary work until the dissolution.

According to the late twelfth-century Augustinian chronicler, William of Newburgh, Gilbert was 'of singular grace in the care of women' (William of Newburgh, *Historia rerum Anglicarum*, ed. R. Howlett, Rolls Series, 1884, 55). But he was not alone. The mid-twelfth century witnessed the emergence of a number of small communities of religious women, grouped around a *magister*, and often associated with a few clerics and lay brothers. Perhaps the majority were found in Lincolnshire and Yorkshire, the region where Gilbert was most active, and several claimed to be Cistercian and followed Cistercian customs, just as Gilbert's early foundation at Haverholme had done. Only Gilbert's communities, however, developed into a new order. Indeed, patriotic nineteenth-century hagiographers emphasized Gilbert as the founder of the only English order. This is misleading. The Gilbertines, concentrated as they were in the eastern half of England, represent the sole example in England of a phenomenon common in twelfth-century western Europe, the regional order. Like many other contemporary monastic reformers, such as Étienne d'Obazine in the Massif Central or Robert d'Abrissel, the founder of Fontevrault, Gilbert owed much to the eremitical tradition. Though not himself a hermit, he acted as spiritual director or *magister* to the first anchoretic community of women at Sempringham. Gilbert, like his eremitic contemporaries, was noted for his personal asceticism and the rigour of his rule, a rigour clearly indicated in the complaints of his *conversi* in the 1160s. It is in this context of eremitic experimentation which typifies twelfth-century monasticism and spirituality that Gilbert should be placed. BRIAN GOLDING

Sources R. Foreville, ed., *The book of St Gilbert*, ed. and trans. G. Keir, OMT (1987) • B. Golding, *Gilbert of Sempringham and the Gilbertine order, c.1130–c.1300* (1995) • R. Graham, *St. Gilbert of Sempringham and the Gilbertines* (1901) • Dugdale, *Monasticon*, new edn, vol. 6 • R. Howlett, ed., *Chronicles of the reigns of Stephen, Henry II, and Richard I*, 1, Rolls Series, 82 (1884), 55 • *John Capgrave's Lives of St Augustine and St Gilbert of Sempringham*, ed. J. J. Munro, EETS, 140 (1910)
Archives BL, Cotton MS Cleopatra B.i • BL, Harley MS 468 • Bodl. Oxf., MS Douce 136 • Bodl. Oxf., MS Digby 36

Gilbert the Englishman [Gilbertus Anglicus, Gilbertus de Aquila, Gilbert de l'Egle] (*d. c.***1250**), priest and medical writer, was the author of the most important medical and surgical work of the English middle ages, the *Compendium medicinae*. Originally written in Latin, the *Compendium* survives in a number of manuscripts and at least one printed edition. Translated excerpts were made into New High German, Hebrew, Catalan, and Middle English. Its English translation was one of the most popular, if not the most popular, of all vernacular medical texts circulating in medieval England.

Little is known for certain about Gilbert's life, and he has been confused with several other contemporaries of the same name, both in England and on the continent. A manuscript of the *Compendium* dated 1271 (Bruges, Bibliothèque Publique, MS 469) refers to him as Gilbertus de Aquila, Anglicus, which may link him with the family of Aquila or L'Aigle, which held the honour of Pevensey, Sussex, in the twelfth and early thirteenth centuries. He is probably the Gilbert del Egle, physician, who, along with masters Henry Lafaitie and Jordan, also physicians, witnessed a charter of Hubert Walter, archbishop of Canterbury, just before the latter's death in 1205. Similarly, he is likely to have been the Magister Gillbertus del Egle who, according to the chronicler Ralph of Coggeshall, attended the archbishop on his deathbed, along with Henricus le Afaitie, doubtless the same physician who had witnessed the archbishop's charter. Coggeshall described Hubert Walter's last illness as a severe fever accompanied by carbuncle (in Latin, *anthrax*). Master Gilbert feared bloodletting, lest the poisonous matter be drawn from the carbuncle into the blood vessels, and instead admonished the archbishop to confess. He also recommended—unnecessarily—that Walter should make a will. Gilbert seems to have heard the archbishop's confession himself, implying that like his near-contemporary Nicholas of Farnham (*d.* 1257), he acted simultaneously as physician and confessor. Upon the administration of the eucharist, the fervour of the sick man's passion caused the moistness of his brain to dissolve in a flood of tears. Much relieved, the archbishop finished sundry items of worldly business and died at last, beyond the help of friends or medicines.

Other documents suggest that Gilbert was at about that time in the service of Robert de Breteuil, earl of Leicester (*d.* 1204). In 1207 he received an ecclesiastical income from Stithed, Kent, which had passed from the archbishop to King John at Hubert Walter's death, and he may be the E. Aquila who witnessed a charter as the king's physician at about the same time. He remained faithful to his royal patron during John's troubles with Innocent III (1198–1216): one Gilbertus de Aquila appears among clerics called to Rome in 1214 to answer for having officiated during the interdict. Gilbert may have remained on the continent after that time, perhaps wisely, in light of the difficult conditions in England. The composition of the *Compendium*, which his use of Arabic sources indicates cannot have been completed before about 1230–40, suggests Gilbert's attendance at a more sophisticated centre of medical and philosophical learning than could be found in England at that time. The place and year of his death are unknown, but cannot have been much after 1250.

Gilbert's medical and philosophical erudition were unequalled by any English scholar of his time, yet his university associations, if any, are unknown. Oxford and Cambridge had yet to develop medical faculties of any note, but Paris, Montpellier, and Salerno were all centres of medical learning, as was the papal court. Gilbert is probably the author of a commentary on the uroscopy of Montpellier writer Gilles de Corbeil (*d.* 1224) and in his *Compendium medicinae* he mentions a certain Master Richardus, probably his near-contemporary Richard of Wendover (*d.* 1252), as 'of all the doctors the most learned and experienced' (*Compendium*, 1510, fol. 47). Richard himself had associations with Montpellier, Bologna, Spoleto, and possibly with the papal court. Gilbert's very early use of Averroes, as well as his associations with Gilles and Richard, point to his own presence at Montpellier, but the question remains open.

Gilbert's *Compendium* covers all of learned medicine and surgery, as well as many aspects of religious healing and the use of prayers and charms. It is divided into seven books, beginning with fevers, which affected the entire body. Other books concern the head, sense organs, organs of respiration (including the heart), organs of digestion, the humours, and, in the last book, diseases of women, advice for travellers, how to light fires, and antidotes to poisons. His sources range from Latin translations of Hippocrates, Aristotle, and Galen, through their Arabic commentators, up to the best authorities of his own time. The clerical surgeon Teodorico da Lucca cited Gilbert in his work (*c.*1267), but the Montpellier surgeon Gui de Chauliac derided him for his use of charms and folk cures (1363). In the general prologue to the *Canterbury Tales* (line 434), Geoffrey Chaucer names Gilbert among the three leading authorities of the poet's time (the others are John Gaddesden and the French physician Bernard de Gordon). By the early modern period Gilbert had become something of a hero to medical practitioners desiring English remedies. John Partridge cited a recipe from him in 1573, while Henry Stubbs (*d.* 1676) in 1671 praised his bloodletting technique as the equal of Avicenna's.

FAYE GETZ

Sources Gilbertus Anglicus, *Compendium medicinae* (1510) • *Healing and society in medieval England: a middle English translation of the pharmaceutical writings of Gilbertus Anglicus*, ed. F. M. Getz (1991) • C. H. Talbot and E. A. Hammond, *The medical practitioners in medieval England: a biographical register* (1965) • H. E. Handerson, *Gilbertus Anglicus: medicine of the thirteenth century* (1918) • C. H. Talbot, *Medicine in medieval England* (1967) • F. M. Getz, 'Charity, translation, and the language of medical learning in medieval England', *Bulletin of the History of Medicine*, 64 (1990), 1–17 • L. Thorndike and P. Kibre, *A catalogue of incipits of mediaeval scientific writings in Latin*, rev. edn (1963) • M. Kurdzialek, 'Gilbertus Anglicus und die psychologischen Erörterungen in seinem Compendium Medicinae', *Sudhoffs Archiv*, 47 (1963), 106–26 • *Radulphi de Coggeshall chronicon Anglicanum*, ed. J. Stevenson, Rolls Series, 66 (1875) • F. Getz, 'Medical practitioners in medieval England', *Social History of Medicine*, 3 (1990), 245–83 • *Ann. mon.*, vol. 3 • E. Wickersheimer, *Dictionnaire biographique des médecins en France au moyen âge*, 2 vols. (Paris, 1936)
Archives Public Library, Bruges, MS 469

Gilbert, Sir Alfred (1854–1934), sculptor and goldsmith, was born on 12 August 1854 at 13 Berners Street, off Oxford Street in London, the eldest of the four children of Alfred Gilbert (1828–1902), an organist and editor of eighteenth-century musical texts, and his wife, Charlotte (1824–1909), a singing teacher and performer, daughter of James Cole, organist of Tarrington church, Hereford.

Education Although Gilbert was later to describe his childhood as tense and unhappy, both his stern father and his ambitious mother found it natural to encourage their children's musical and artistic abilities. After two miserable years at the Mercers' School in London (1863–5) the pugnacious and unruly boy was sent to Aldenham, a minor public school in Hertfordshire where their father taught music and which was unusual for its time in offering its boys scope to develop their creative talents.

Although not academic by nature, when he was eighteen Gilbert applied, at his father's suggestion, for an open scholarship to Middlesex Hospital, intending to become a surgeon. After failing to win his scholarship he was allowed to pursue his real interest, sculpture. He attended the Thomas J. Heatherley School of Art in London (1872–3)

Sir Alfred Gilbert (1854–1934), by Ralph W. Robinson, 1889

and then entered the Royal Academy Schools (1873–5). At Burlington House he quickly discovered that the Royal Academy trained painters, not sculptors. Many years later he told his first biographer, Joseph Hatton, that 'the Academy school of modelling was only … make-believe' (Hatton, 20).

Dissatisfied with his formal training at the Royal Academy, Gilbert worked part-time in the studios of the sculptors Matthew Noble and William Gibbs Rogers. In 1872 he became an assistant to the Hungarian-born sculptor Edgar Boehm, in whose studio he gained experience in pointing, carving, casting, and chasing, and was allowed to work on full-length statues, equestrian monuments, and portrait busts. The highly realistic way in which Boehm manipulated marble and bronze, his emphasis on delineating the intricate folds and swirls of a dress or robe, and his ability to suggest in stone the textures of flesh, fur, fabric, and metal represented the antithesis of the neo-classical taste prevailing in England at that time. In this early exposure to the idea of sculpture as a sensuous, tactile medium lay the origins of Gilbert's mature style. He was to call Boehm and another assistant in the studio, the French sculptor Édouard Lantéri, his real teachers.

By 1875 Gilbert had no more to learn from the older men. Boehm encouraged him to go to Paris, to study at the École des Beaux-Arts under the sculptor Pierre-Jules Cavelier. He thus became the first British sculptor to benefit from the rigorous training which was then available in Paris but not in London. The decision to leave England was forced on Gilbert: he was in love with his first cousin Alice Jane Gilbert (1847–1916) and when he learned that they were expecting a child, the couple eloped on 3 January 1876, marrying the same day. In Paris they lived in the rue Humboldt, where their first son, George, was born on 9 May 1876. The rest of their children were all born during the nine years the family lived on the continent at this time: Mary (*b.* 1877), Francis (*b.* 1879), Alfredo (*b.* 1880), and Charlotte Emily (Caprina; *b.* 1881).

Early works At the École des Beaux-Arts, Gilbert continued to draw and to model in clay, but gained no more experience in carving and casting. In his first major sculpture, *The Kiss of Victory* (1878–81, Minneapolis Institute of Arts), a young Roman soldier, dying, sinks back into the arms of the Genius of Victory. At just under 5 feet high, it was meant to be seen close-up, in the setting of a drawing-room. Although its vocabulary of heroic gesture is found in similar works in the Beaux-Arts style of Gustave Doré and Antonin-Jean Mercié, its sensuality and refinement owe more to the example of Antonio Canova's *Cupid and Psyche* (1783–93, Musée du Louvre, Paris) than to the work of any contemporary French artist.

To carve *The Kiss of Victory* in marble, Gilbert moved in October 1878 with his young family to Rome. For him the lure of Italy was not that of the antique, as it had been for English artists of the eighteenth century and early nineteenth, nor even the medieval painting and architecture which had attracted John Ruskin in the mid-nineteenth century, but the opportunity to see works in bronze by Renaissance sculptors, particularly Donatello, Verrocchio, Cellini, and Giambologna. His first visit to Florence in 1880 inspired his first statue in bronze, *Perseus Arming* (1882; a cast in the Fitzwilliam Museum, Cambridge), a male nude created in emulation of Donatello's *David* in the Museo del Bargello and, by Gilbert's own account, Cellini's *Perseus with the Head of Medusa* in the Loggia dei Lanzi.

In 1903 Gilbert explained to Joseph Hatton that three of his large bronze statues, *Perseus Arming*, *Icarus* (1884, National Museum and Gallery of Wales, Cardiff), and *Comedy and Tragedy: 'sic vita'* (1891–2; a cast in the National Gallery of Scotland, Edinburgh), formed a trilogy symbolizing aspects of his own life. In *Perseus Arming*, the first of the series, the untried adolescent who gracefully turns to check his winged sandals symbolizes the artist as a fledgeling hero, testing his equipment for the battle of life. For his English début in 1882 Gilbert sent *Perseus Arming* to the Grosvenor Gallery and *The Kiss of Victory* to the Royal Academy. Critics praised both, but *Perseus Arming* was to have particular importance to the generation of artists who would learn from it in the coming decades, and whose work would be called the New Sculpture. Not only was its casting method of *cire perdue* (or lost wax) novel in England, but so was its scale. At 29 inches high, it was too big for the category of bibelot, yet neither was it the usual life-sized plaster or marble monument.

For the next statue—and the next instalment in the symbolic autobiography he was writing through his art—Gilbert chose another male nude. Exhibited in 1884, *Icarus* shows the son of Daedalus about to take flight and so to compete with nature itself—just as Gilbert saw himself poised to soar over all earthly obstacles at the beginning of his career as an artist. The statue created a sensation at the Royal Academy in 1884.

Major commissions On Gilbert's return to England later in 1884, he did not at once try to repeat its success. His first important public commission in England was the Fawcett memorial (1885–7, Westminster Abbey), in which seven symbolic Virtues line up for the viewer's inspection beneath the portrait head of Fawcett. These disarming miniature figures, all intricately detailed, highly coloured, and (at one time) inset with semiprecious stones, represented something new in Gilbert's art, his adaptation of the slightly old-fashioned Gothic revival to the refined sensibility of the 1880s. The scale, too, was new. At about 15 inches high, the allegorical figures on the Fawcett memorial are comparable to those on Peter Vischer the elder's tomb of St Sebald (1508–19) in Nuremberg.

Gilbert's next commission, the Winchester jubilee memorial to Queen Victoria (1887, Great Hall of Winchester Castle, Winchester), had the sweep and grandeur of Bernini's tomb of Urban VIII (1628–47) in St Peter's, Rome. He clothed the queen in rivers of cascading bronze drapery, quite unheard of in English sculpture where drapery more usually hung limp over the shoulder or fell in syrupy folds around the sitter's feet. Not content to give the queen a 'real' crown on her head, he added a second crown, this one a symbolic confection of tendrils and lilies suspended over her throne. At the age of thirty-three he had made one of the most impressive of all portraits of the queen.

During this period of astonishing creativity Gilbert was teaching himself the arts of the goldsmith as well as those of the sculptor. The Winchester memorial was followed by commissions for a mayoral chain for the city of Preston (1888–92, town hall, Preston, Lancashire) and a magnificent epergne presented to Queen Victoria as a jubilee gift by the officers of the army (1887–90, Royal Collection; on loan to the Victoria and Albert Museum, London). By the early 1890s he was at work on spoons, keys, seals, and sword hilts; his materials now included ivory, sea shells and crystal, and he learned to use enamel and ormolu as well as the technique of damascening.

In his work both as a goldsmith and as a sculptor Gilbert became fascinated by new materials and techniques. Working with the metallurgist Sir William Chandler Roberts-Austen, he experimented with Japanese casting techniques in an attempt to achieve effects of polychromy in bronze hitherto unknown in England. When in the later 1880s it became possible to cast aluminium cheaply, he was the first artist to employ this new alloy to create the soaring figure of Eros—the light, silvery, buoyant nude symbolic of selfless love which crowns his next important sculptural commission, the Shaftesbury memorial in Piccadilly Circus, London, unveiled in 1893.

Although Gilbert fully expected that the successful execution of an important public monument in the very heart of London would make his career, in fact the Shaftesbury memorial marks the beginning of the decline in his fortunes. At the time of the initial commission in 1886 he had contracted to create the memorial for a certain sum, on the promise that he would be given used gunmetal to cast. When the government reneged on its promise, he was compelled to procure copper at an inflated price because a lengthy delay in casting would destroy the moulds. Instead of costing £3000, therefore, the fountain ended up costing £7000 and Gilbert was held personally responsible for the difference. He was plunged into debt at the outset of his career.

The use of copper, however, enabled Gilbert to create spectacular effects with the patination. When the memorial was unveiled the *Daily Telegraph* spoke of 'the green and golden bronze, the one contrasting and relieving the other, while the winged genius shooting an arrow, which is the crown and apex of the work, is of aluminium' (30 June 1893). Nevertheless, it was heavily criticized on the grounds that it was ugly and pretentious, while the nude figure of Eros was mistaken for Cupid (a highly dubious god to preside over an area of London notorious for prostitution). More legitimately, Gilbert was accused of not providing an adequate basin to catch the water, which drenched passers-by and, in the words of one critic, left Piccadilly a 'dripping, sickening mess' (H. Hubbard, *The Times*, 17 July 1893). It was not until the First World War that the fountain—comprising sea shells, flying fish, and rollicking babies grasping slippery fishtails, all of which are topped by Eros who wears his fluttering loincloth and eccentric helmet—became dear to flower girls, music-hall singers, and tommies as the symbol of London itself.

The most productive part of Gilbert's life was crammed between the years 1885 and 1898. The amount and the quality of what he did in that time surpass that of the life's work of most artists and includes such masterpieces of imaginary portraiture as the bronze bust of the eighteenth-century physician John Hunter (1893–1900, St George's Hospital medical school, Tooting, Surrey) and the full-length bronze monument to the prison reformer John Howard (1890–94, Market Square, Bedford). Among his many enchanting portraits of children is the little boy in his night-shirt as part of the memorial to Randolph Caldecott in bronze and aluminium (1887–95, St Paul's Cathedral, London) and the bronze bust of Thoby Prinsep (1898, priv. coll.).

Of the many honours bestowed upon Gilbert, the most important were that of Royal Academician in 1892; an honorary degree from the University of Durham in 1893; election to the consulting committees of the New Gallery, London, in 1890, and to the International Society of Sculptors, Painters and Gravers in 1898; and the gift of the Royal Victorian Order of the fourth class in 1897 as a reward for personal services to the sovereign. He was elected professor of sculpture at the Royal Academy Schools in 1901.

While all this was happening, however, Gilbert's private life fell into disarray. After the relative happiness of his penurious years in Italy, he felt overwhelmed and seduced by commissions with which English patrons inundated him. 'In rashly making the exchange [of England for

Italy]', he wrote, 'I had fatally closed for ever, the gate to Idealism, and peaceful contentment, to enter the ever open portal to materialism and feverish unrest. I was not long in discovering my error, and bitterly regretting it' (A. Gilbert, 'Answers to questions', 10 Dec 1924, Windsor Castle, Royal Archives, Add./x/215).

Unable to refuse any commission, Gilbert became the darling of aristocratic society. His friendship with Princess Louise, one of the daughters of Queen Victoria, would make him the favourite sculptor of the royal family during the final years of the queen's reign. After Boehm's death in 1890, Gilbert emerged as the most famous sculptor in England. A man about town, first-nighter, member of the Athenaeum and Garrick clubs and close friend of Henry Irving, Frederic Leighton, G. F. Watts, and Edward Burne-Jones, he was a picturesque character of the 1890s in his flamboyant black cape, felt sombrero, and walking-stick.

As the foremost sculptor of his age Gilbert could reasonably expect to earn huge sums from his art. He therefore built a large house and studio at 16 Maida Vale, north London. But he was a perfectionist. The simplest portrait bust would take him four or five years to execute, whereas for anything really ambitious the client could expect to wait eight or ten years. He was extravagant and generous, both with his money and with the bronze casts he gave to friends. Gradually worries over money came to dominate his life. In addition, Alice Gilbert, the young cousin with whom he had eloped to Paris in 1876 found it difficult to cope with his London social life. She remained as much as possible in the house the family rented in Gomshall, Surrey, soon after their return to England, and as a consequence began to feel lonely and neglected. A few days after the disastrous unveiling of the Shaftesbury memorial, she had a mental breakdown and was sent to a private nursing home. The title of one of Gilbert's earlier works, a bronze roundel showing a knight in armour pursuing the siren figure of fame and fortune, at whose back rides the shrouded figure of Anxiety, proved all too prophetic: *Behind the Rider Sits Dark Care* (c.1883–7; a cast of 1899 in the Victoria and Albert Museum, London).

The third statue of the autobiographical bronzes, *Comedy and Tragedy*, was exhibited at the Royal Academy in 1892 when Gilbert was at the height of his fame but otherwise unhappy. It represents a young actor or prop-boy carrying a comic mask. Seen from one side, the boy appears to be laughing, but the reality, visible only as the viewer moves around to the other side, is a face contorted by the pain of a bee sting.

The world knew nothing of Gilbert's dual life. In January 1892 the prince and princess of Wales asked him to make the tomb for their eldest son, Prince Edward, duke of Clarence, the recently deceased heir to the throne of England (1892–1901, with additions of 1926–8; St George's Chapel, Albert memorial chapel, Windsor Castle). Gilbert created a recumbent effigy of the prince wearing the uniform of the 10th hussars, carried out in marble, bronze, brass, and aluminium. He erected a bronze grille surrounding the tomb and punctuated by eighteen uprights, twelve of which held ivory and bronze figures of saints. Dominating all, a great aluminium angel, bowed down in sorrow, held an overscaled crown above the prince's head.

Later years In 1898, overwhelmed with debts and burdened by clamorous patrons desperate for memorials and portraits they had paid for but never received, Gilbert allowed himself to be side-tracked by another royal commission, the mortuary chapel of Prince Henry of Battenberg, husband of Queen Victoria's youngest daughter, Princess Beatrice (1898; St Mildred's, Whippingham, Isle of Wight). This added to delays. Gradually clients began to feel cheated. Later he wrote of the enormous house and studio in Maida Vale, 'the very walls and beams, at times, seemed to be closing in, and ready to crush me' (A. Gilbert, 'Answers to questions', 10 Dec 1924, Windsor Castle, Royal Archives, Add./X/215). In August 1901 he declared himself bankrupt. He sent his family to Bruges while he saw to the selling of the contents of his house and studio. On the night before leaving his studio for ever, in order to prevent the wholesale exploitation of his work, he destroyed many of his plaster casts.

At this time, the tomb of the duke of Clarence still lacked five of the twelve saints. Not wishing to add to Gilbert's misfortunes, the prince of Wales lent the sculptor a studio at Windsor Castle. But the tomb remained unfinished and his royal patron's patience had worn thin. In 1903 Gilbert asked Edward VII for permission to publish photographs of the statues from the Clarence tomb in a monograph Joseph Hatton was writing on Gilbert for the Easter number of the *Art Journal* that year (the *Easter Art Annual*). The king replied unequivocally on 3 February 1903 through his equerry Sir Deighton Probyn that he would not sanction any photographs to be taken of the tomb: 'why publish a "discredit" which the unfinished condition of the memorial certainly is?' (Windsor Castle, Royal Archives, Z 475/261).

As though to destroy any hope of reconciliation with the royal family, Gilbert went ahead and published photographs of statues for the tomb which he labelled 'working models'. In fact, the photographs clearly showed the original ivory and bronze statues of Saint Elizabeth of Hungary and the Virgin which he had taken off the tomb and sold to an art dealer in 1899 and had then replaced with the all-bronze casts which are still on the tomb. Since the king had paid for statues in ivory and bronze, and since the article also noted the private collection of which these chryselephantine figures were now a part, their publication put an end to any further dealings between the artist and the king. At court, Gilbert was accused of dishonesty.

Resident in Bruges, Gilbert returned frequently to London where he lectured as the Royal Academy's professor of sculpture during the winters of 1901–3 and in 1905. In 1904 he separated from Alice Gilbert. She returned to England and died there on 2 December 1916. Gilbert's decline accelerated after an affair with a client, Eliza Macloghlin, the beautiful but deranged widow of a Blackpool doctor, Percy Plantagenet Macloghlin. When Gilbert refused to surrender *Mors janua vitae* (1905–9, London, Royal College of Surgeons), the bronze and marble cinerarium she had commissioned from him (and in which she intended to deposit her own ashes along with those of her husband and Gilbert), she threw stones at the glass windows of his studio in Bruges until he complied. In 1908 she wrote a mad and insulting letter to Edward VII, begging him to have compassion for Gilbert. Because their handwriting was remarkably similar, at court this letter was misattributed to Gilbert and his chances of reinstatement grew ever more remote.

Another client, Mrs Julia Frankau, further damaged Gilbert's reputation when the monument she had commissioned to her husband's memory failed to materialize. On 15 and 22 March 1906 the gossip magazine *Truth* ran two articles outlining not only her allegations against him but also those of other disappointed clients. Gilbert was called a 'liar' and a 'rogue', 'his actions indistinguishable from theft', and, worse, the story was picked up by the national newspapers.

Two years later the duke of Rutland complained to Edward Poynter, the president of the Royal Academy, about a similar case in which Gilbert took money for a memorial which he failed to produce. For conduct which the president characterized as 'dishonourable and unworthy of a member of the Royal Academy', Gilbert was asked to resign or else face expulsion (Royal Academy minutes of council, cxxi, 1901–6 fol. 471). On 24 November 1908 he resigned. At the same time, he also resigned from the Victorian order. The art school he had started in 1901 in Bruges was a failure, and he seems not to have been capable of finishing or casting any large-scale new work. When his son Francis visited him in November 1908 he found him starving and without warm clothes. Although few more commissions came to him at his studio at Bruges, an exception is the bizarre chimney-piece *A Dream of Joy during a Sleep of Sorrow* (1909–11, Leeds City Art Gallery), commissioned by the industrialist Sam Wilson, which like many of his later works is filled with obscure and highly personal symbolism. It is also executed in a much freer and more expressionistic style than works from this English period.

Gilbert stayed in Bruges throughout the First World War and married his Flemish housekeeper Stéphanie Quaghebeur, a lace maker, on 1 March 1918. For two years they lived in Rome (1924–5) and returned to England in July 1926. Largely through the efforts of a stubborn Scottish journalist, Isabel McAllister, Gilbert was forgiven by George V, the second son of Edward VII and brother of the duke of Clarence. The 72-year-old artist was summoned home and allowed to work in a studio, first at St James's Palace and then at Kensington Palace. While McAllister wrote Gilbert's biography, he finished the five missing figures for the tomb of the duke of Clarence and was given the prestigious commission for the memorial to his old friend Queen Alexandra. The finished monument, unveiled at Marlborough Gate in London on 8 June 1932, shows three crowned female figures, personifying Faith, Hope, and Charity, guiding a nearly nude adolescent girl across a low fountain of falling water, symbolic of the stream of life. The elegiac shrine is the quintessence of the symbolist movement which had bloomed and died thirty years before the monument's completion. Just before it was unveiled Gilbert was reinstated as a member of the Royal Academy, and on 9 June 1932 he was knighted. For the next two years he lived in his studio at Kensington Palace. He died on 4 November 1934 in Cromwell Nursing Home, 198 Cromwell Road, London, and was cremated. Although an atheist who disliked all organized religion, his memorial service was held on 13 November in St Paul's Cathedral, where a memorial tablet to him was erected in the crypt. At the time of his death he was one of the best-known figures in England and plans to make a film based on his colourful life had been under discussion. The last statue on which he worked, which was uncompleted, was *Atalanta*. Continuing to record his life in his art, Gilbert saw an appropriateness in giving form to the story of the maiden who lost the race because she allowed herself to be distracted by glittering gold apples strewn in her path.

In 1935 the Fine Art Society in London held an exhibition of Gilbert's bronzes, followed by a commemorative retrospective at the Victoria and Albert Museum in 1936 with an accompanying catalogue by E. Machell Cox. Then for three decades his name was almost forgotten. Lavinia Handley-Read, in her catalogue for an exhibition of Victorian sculpture at the Fine Art Society and in three seminal articles in *Connoisseur*, all published in 1968, may be said to have written him back into the history of British art. Richard Dorment published the first modern biography of Gilbert in 1985, and a full-scale exhibition at the Royal Academy of Arts in 1986 confirmed his position as the most original sculptor of the late Victorian era.

RICHARD DORMENT

Sources R. Dorment, *Alfred Gilbert* (1985) [incl. extensive bibliography] · R. Dorment and others, *Alfred Gilbert: sculptor and goldsmith* (1986) [exhibition catalogue, RA, 21 March – 29 June 1986] · I. McAllister, *Alfred Gilbert* (1929) · A. Bury, *Shadow of Eros: a bibliographical and critical study of the life and works of Sir Alfred Gilbert, RA, MVO, DCL* (1954) · J. Hatton, 'The life and work of Alfred Gilbert', *Easter Art Annual* (1903) [whole issue]

Archives Henry Moore Institute, Leeds, corresp. · Royal Arch., corresp. and papers | Bodl. Oxf., letters to Elizabeth, Lady Lewis · NL Ire., letters to Alice Stepford Green · RA, letters to Sir Frederick Fry · RA, letters to the Royal Academy · RA, corresp. with Marion H. Spielmann · RIBA BAL, letters to E. P. Dawbarn

Likenesses J. E. Boehm, plaster, *c.*1885, repro. in Dorment, *Alfred Gilbert* (1986), fig. 37; priv. coll. · J. McClure Hamilton, chalk drawing, 1887, NPG · photograph, *c.*1887–1890, NPG · photographs, *c.*1887–1939, repro. in Dorment, *Alfred Gilbert* (1985), frontispiece, fig. 175, fig. 193 · R. W. Robinson, photograph, 1889, NPG [*see illus.*] · M. Beerbohm, pencil and chalk cartoon, *c.*1896, NPG, V&A · photograph, *c.*1906, Grundy Art Gallery, Blackpool · W. H. Bartlett, group portrait, oils (*Saturday night at the Savage Club*), Savage Club, London · B. Partridge, pencil and chalk caricature, NPG; repro. in *Punch* (8 May 1929) · A. Toft, life mask, priv. coll. · photograph, NPG

Wealth at death £920 9*s.* 10*d.*: probate, 16 March 1935, *CGPLA Eng. & Wales*

Gilbert, Ann (1782–1866). *See under* Taylor, Jane (1783–1824).

Gilbert, Ashurst Turner (1786–1870), bishop of Chichester, was born on 14 May 1786 near Burnham Beeches, Buckinghamshire, the son of Thomas Gilbert (*d.* 1844), a captain in the Royal Marines, and his wife, Elizabeth, daughter of William Long Nathaniel Hutton, rector of Maids Moreton, Buckinghamshire. He was educated at the Manchester grammar school from 1800 until 1805, when he matriculated at Brasenose College, Oxford. He took a first class in *literae humaniores* in 1808, graduating BA in 1809 and MA in 1811. He was awarded a BD in 1819 and a DD in 1822. Gilbert was elected a Hulme exhibitioner of Brasenose in 1809 and Frankland fellow in the same year. He served as a college tutor, and as public examiner for the university during 1816–18; in 1818 he was a select preacher. On 2 February 1822 Gilbert was elected principal of Brasenose, after the premature death of Frodsham Hodson. On 31 December 1822 he married Mary Anne, only child of the Revd Robert Wintle, vicar of Culham, Oxfordshire. They had eleven children, of whom the second daughter, Elizabeth Margaretta Maria *Gilbert, was blind.

As principal of Brasenose, Gilbert was regarded as a man of charm and culture, and gained the reputation of being a protestant high-churchman of the old school, hostile to both evangelicalism and religious liberalism. In the first years of the Tractarian movement he supported the authors of the Tracts for the Times as learned defenders of church and university against whig latitudinarianism. Newman, who regularly dined with him, reciprocated the compliment, describing Gilbert early in 1836 as 'a very right minded man' (Newman to H. J. Rose, 19 Feb 1836; *Newman*, 4.138). In the same year Gilbert was an active opponent of the appointment of R. D. Hampden to the regius chair of divinity at Oxford, being one of the four heads of houses in favour of bringing Hampden's works before the convocation of the university for censure. As principal of Brasenose, he discouraged, if not prevented, members of his college from attending Hampden's divinity lectures. Gilbert was vice-chancellor of the university from 1836 to 1840. In the last year of his vice-chancellorship he turned against the Tractarians, when he took offence at a sermon which appeared to advocate the doctrine of the mass preached by the Tractarian J. B. Morris of Exeter College in October 1839. Gilbert now confided to the duke of Wellington that he considered the Tractarians to be pioneers of a reintroduction of popery. The Tractarians responded to Gilbert's opposition by challenging his renomination as vice-chancellor in 1839 (normally a formality), though in the resulting scrutiny only two votes were cast against him.

Gilbert resigned the principalship of Brasenose, after being nominated by Peel, on the recommendation of the university chancellor, the duke of Wellington, to the vacant bishopric of Chichester on 24 January 1842. He was consecrated at Lambeth Palace on 27 February 1842. His elevation by the Conservative ministry of Sir Robert Peel was viewed rightly as a reward for his services to the University of Oxford. Gilbert's Tractarian critics, however, mistakenly assumed that he had been selected merely 'as a man who has distinguished himself by opposing the Tracts' (Churton to Copeland, 1 Feb 1842; Churton Papers). They overlooked Gilbert's high-church credentials and his known antipathy to low-churchmen; he had considered depriving Thomas Townson Churton of his college tutorship at Brasenose because of dislike of Churton's evangelicalism.

As bishop, Gilbert was zealous in his performance of diocesan duties, taking a close interest in the foundation of Lancing College and other educational institutions in the diocese. He was bountiful in his personal contributions to church and school building. At Oxford he had gained the reputation of being a modest Old Testament scholar; in the early part of his episcopate Gilbert hoped to renew and extend his study of Hebrew, but was prevented from engaging deeply in such scholarly pursuits. As his examining chaplain, H. B. W. Churton, lamented, the bishop's time 'was fully occupied in endeavouring to lessen party feeling and in appeasing often perhaps needless strife and suspicion, which might otherwise more happily and peacefully, and perhaps more profitably, have been spent upon yet deeper study of the Word of God'.

Gilbert's authoritarian inclinations, combative character, and legalistic cast of mind were not designed to defuse controversy or allay opposition. His personal relations with his first two archdeacons, the liberal Julius Hare (Lewes) and high-church Henry Manning (Chichester)—both of whom idolized his predecessor but one, Bishop Otter—appear to have been strained. In 1844 Manning felt unable to request the publication of his diocesan's charge, and at the visitation in 1847 Hare's toast to the bishop turned into a panegyric on Otter, with Gilbert's response being no less pointed and robust.

Gilbert's difficulties stemmed from his attempts to contain theological polarization in his diocese. As a moderate high-churchman he was suspect in the eyes of a vociferous protestant lobby in Brighton, which subjected him to relentless pressure to intervene against suspected 'Puseyites'. On the other hand, his own suspicions of high-church extremism led him to exert his full episcopal authority against recalcitrant Tractarian clergy. These included A. D. Wagner, William Gresley, John Mason Neale (whom he took to the court of arches for 'debasing the minds of these poor people with his spiritual haberdashery'), and R. W. Randall. The proceedings which he instituted in 1868 against the ritualist clergyman John Purchas of Brighton led to the famous Purchas judgment (1871).

Gilbert was not without some sympathy for aspects of the Catholic revival in the Church of England. He was often irritated by the misleading and mischievous nature of accusations brought by protestant extremists in the diocese against Tractarians and ritualists. He raised no objection to the formation of the Sisterhood of St Margaret at East Grinstead, approved the rule, and acted as visitor to the sisterhood for a number of years. He had a good working relationship with the superior of the community, Mother Ann. By 1864 Gilbert had rescinded his inhibition against Neale. His strictness and severity in episcopal dealings were tempered by personal kindness, courtesy, and charm of manner, though the latter traits may have been more apparent in his private, as opposed to public, persona. He could be an entertaining and witty public speaker. During the grand agricultural meeting held in Oxford in July 1839, as vice-chancellor he delighted his audience by an exuberant and amusing speech.

Gilbert died at the Episcopal Palace, Chichester, on 21 February 1870, and was buried at Westhampnett church, Sussex, on 25 February 1870. His wife had predeceased him on 10 December 1863. PETER B. NOCKLES

Sources H. B. W. Churton, *Our rulers in the Lord of loving remembrance: a sermon preached in the Cathedral Church of Chichester, on Sunday February 27, 1870* (1870) · Brasenose College register · Foster, *Alum. Oxon.* · *ILN* (5 March 1870), 259 · *ILN* (28 May 1870), 563 · *Guardian* (23 Feb 1870), 215 · A. Burns, *The diocesan revival in the Church of England, c.1800–1870* (1999) · M. Chandler, *The life and work of John Mason Neale* (1995) · BL, Peel MSS · LPL, Neale & Golightly MSS · U. Southampton L., Wellington MSS · priv. coll., Churton MSS · W. R. Ward, *Victorian Oxford* (1965), 114–15, 118 · *The letters and diaries of John Henry Newman*, ed. C. S. Dessain and others, [31 vols.] (1961–), vol. 4, p. 310; vol. 5, pp. 237–8; vol. 6, pp. 331, 335, 339; vol. 7, pp. 171–3, 176–7, 417 · G. V. Cox, *Recollections of Oxford*, 2nd edn (1870), 308–9

Archives BL, letters to Philip Bliss, Add. MSS 34568–34581, *passim* · BL, Peel MSS · Bodl. Oxf., corresp. with H. E. Manning · Lancing College, corresp. with Nathaniel Woodard · LPL, Golightly MSS, Neale MSS · LPL, corresp. with A. C. Tait and related papers · U. Southampton L., letters to first duke of Wellington · W. Sussex RO, letters to J. C. Hare; letters to Duke of Richmond

Likenesses A. Edouart, silhouette, 1827, NPG · T. Phillips, oils, exh. RA 1835, Brasenose College, Oxford · caricature, woodcut, NPG; repro. in *Punch* (1868)

Wealth at death under £12,000: will, 31 March 1870, *CGPLA Eng. & Wales*

Gilbert, Sir Bernard William (1891–1957), civil servant, was born at 58 Bunbury Street, Nottingham, on 28 September 1891, the son of Harry Gilbert, a hosiery warehouseman, and his wife, Mary Ellen Atkin. He was educated at Nottingham high school and at St John's College, Cambridge, where he graduated first class in part two of the mathematical tripos in 1913.

Gilbert entered the Treasury in 1914, but his career was interrupted by the war, during the last two years of which he served with the Royal Horse Artillery and Royal Garrison Artillery. He then returned to the Treasury for the remainder of his career, save during 1920–21 when he was seconded to Dublin during the final attempt to prevent the seceding of southern Ireland from the union, and where he worked under the direction of Sir John Anderson. On 12 December 1925 he married Janet Maud Fison (*b.* 1895/6), daughter of Alfred Henry Fison DSc, a lecturer on physics, of Cricklewood. They had one son and three daughters.

Making steady progress through the ranks of the Treasury between the wars, Gilbert became principal assistant secretary in 1934, under-secretary in 1939, joint second secretary in 1944 with responsibility for supply services (to which was added responsibility for home finance during 1952–3), and finally from 1953 until retirement in 1956, deputy to the permanent secretary, by which time he had become the most senior official co-ordinating economic advice to the chancellor. His retirement had in fact been delayed for five years beyond the normal age upon the insistence of Sir Edward Ettingdene Bridges, Treasury permanent secretary. Bridges rated Gilbert's ability so highly that he insisted he would not continue at the Treasury himself unless his most senior secondary secretary did so also. Consequently Gilbert retired when Bridges did. He was made CB in 1937; KBE, 1943; KCB, 1946; and GCB, 1950.

Of the supply services Gilbert acquired particular expertise in the social services, but his experience extended across the full range of spending activities; during the late 1930s he was much involved in the financing and management of the rearmament effort. Here he was a stalwart defender of the Treasury view that finance was the fourth arm of defence. He was known to have joked that 'I have always found that with the female members of my own family, the only way to stop spending money is to see that they don't have it' (Jay, 172). Peden, in his history of the Treasury, places him firmly in the tradition of officials who sought to maintain Gladstonian attitudes in public finance in face of the *Realpolitik* of post-war big government and Keynesian demand management (Peden, 38, 531). There was, however, much more to him than mere candle-ends and conservatism. For Hugh Dalton, when chancellor (1945–7), he was 'the wisest of my advisers' (Pimlott, 426), while even Douglas Jay, one of the first Keynesian professional economists to sit on the Treasury bench in the Commons, mused: 'Occasionally, the unworthy thought crept into my mind that there might be as much truth in his outmoded wisdom as in the advanced thought of the Keynesian economists surrounding me' (Jay, 172). On the other hand, the government's principal economic adviser, Sir Robert Hall, had no such reservations—to him Gilbert represented all that was wrong with the Treasury of the early 1950s (Hall, 2.71, 80). Among later historians there is the view that the hangover of Gilbert and his cohort delayed the modernization of the Treasury, with disastrous results for economic policy and thus, ultimately, the British economy. But this was not the predominant view within the Treasury at the time, far from it. Perhaps Edwin Plowden comes closest to a balanced assessment with his verdict that Gilbert was 'a pessimist in the finest Treasury tradition' (Plowden, 137), especially when it is remembered that only in this most peculiar of British institutions could pessimism be a much-prized attribute. Gilbert died from lung cancer at his home, Cherry Tree Corner, North Road, Chesham Bois, Buckinghamshire, on 7 November 1957. He was survived by his wife. ROGER MIDDLETON

Sources G. C. Peden, *The treasury and British public policy, 1906–1959* (2000) · D. Jay, *Change and fortune: a political record* (1980) · *The Robert Hall diaries*, ed. A. Cairncross, 2 vols. (1989–91) · E. Plowden, *An industrialist in the treasury* (1989) · *The Times* (9 Nov 1957), 8f · *The Times* (13 Nov 1957), 13d · B. Pimlott, *Hugh Dalton* (1985) · b. cert. · m. cert. · d. cert. · *WWW*

Archives PRO, Treasury MSS

Wealth at death £6003 4*s.* 3*d.*: probate, 3 Jan 1958, *CGPLA Eng. & Wales*

Gilbert, Charles Sandoe (1760–1831), druggist and topographer, the son of Thomas Gilbert, was born in Kenwyn, near Truro, Cornwall. With a Mr Powell he earned considerable sums travelling throughout Devon and Cornwall selling medicines. Calling himself Dr Gilbert he continued the business alone after Powell retired. He had premises at 29 Market Street, Plymouth, and at Fore Street, Devonport, and also sold his drugs through eight or nine travellers. A Mr Parrot afterwards became his partner and later entirely took over the running of the business. In the belief that he was descended from the Gilberts of Compton Castle, Devon, about 1810 Gilbert began to study history, genealogy, and heraldry and ultimately undertook a general history of Cornwall. He and his travellers and, after 1812, the artist Henry Perlee Parker took notes about and made drawings of local scenes and events. Gilbert's *Historical Survey of the County of Cornwall* (2 vols., 1817–20) proved useful and popular, not least for its heraldic engravings. Gilbert's neglect of his business and the fact that the *Survey* cost almost double the estimate led him into financial troubles and, although he was patronized by successive dukes of Northumberland and obtained a number of subscribers, he was declared bankrupt on 29 October 1825 and his effects were auctioned. In 1826 he moved to London where he opened a chemist's shop at 27 Newcastle Street, Strand. He died in his bed on 30 May 1831, according to contemporary accounts, from apoplexy. He was unmarried and childless. At his request he was buried in the churchyard of the Savoy. While not in actual want, he none the less died poor and it was his friend Parker, who had illustrated his book, who erected a headstone to his memory. Parker described him as warm-hearted and the friend and patron of many young men who were later prominent figures in science and the arts. The Cornish gentry, who at first looked askance at him because of his broad Cornish dialect, later came to admire his knowledge of the county. ELIZABETH BAIGENT

Sources J. Maclean, 'Notes on C. S. Gilbert', *Journal of the Royal Institution of Cornwall*, 6 (1878–81), 343–9 • *N&Q*, 4th ser., 9 (1872), 141 • D. Giddy, *The parochial history of Cornwall*, 1 (1838), xiii–xiv • *DNB*

Wealth at death died poor but not in material distress: McLean, 'Notes'

Gilbert, Claudius, the elder (*d.* 1696?), Church of Ireland clergyman, is of unknown parents and background. He entered St Catharine's College, Cambridge, as a pensioner in 1642, and graduated BA in 1648. He appears next in Ireland, as a preacher paid by the state in the important garrison of Limerick in 1652. He had probably been lured there by his uncle, Colonel Henry Markham, important alike in the military establishment and civilian administration of the reconquered island. Sir Hardress Waller, major-general in the army in Ireland and a prominent landowner in the environs of Limerick, had also influenced his decision. Gilbert's salary, raised from £150 to £200, suggested the high repute in which he was held. It put him among the best remunerated preachers in interregnum Ireland. This reputation was also shown by his inclusion in the panel which adjudicated on aspirant preachers in co. Cork. Often he was required to perform a similar function outside Cork. He was also one of three ministers entrusted in 1655 with finding more acceptable fellows of Trinity College, Dublin, where he was incorporated BA in that year.

Gilbert's role as a champion of orthodoxy was demonstrated in four sermons which he published in London between 1657 and 1658. In *The Libertine School'd* (1657) he upheld the rights of civil magistrates to intervene in religious matters. Those who opposed such intervention were likened to the Anabaptists in sixteenth-century Münster and accused of 'levelling, ranting and quaking principles' (sig. B1*v*). He invoked the examples of Arnhem and Amsterdam after 1535 to argue the necessity of strict magisterial oversight. Gilbert was particularly exercised by the threat from the Quakers, recently arrived in Limerick (as in other Irish towns), whom he saw as agents of popery and atheism. He urged nominal compliance with the worship prescribed by the state as a first and essential step to salvation. He returned to similar themes in *A Sovereign Antidote Against Sinful Errors*, *The Blessed Peace-Maker and Christian Reconciler*, and *A Pleasant Walk to Heaven*, all published in 1658. He decried the tendency of the various protestant sects in Ireland to quarrel rather than co-operate. To correct this habit, he supported schemes to unite ministers in associations and have them subscribe to a confession of faith. This outlook inclined him to the more conservative approach of Henry Cromwell, nominal ruler of Ireland between 1655 and 1659, to whom *The Libertine School'd* was dedicated. Gilbert's value as a fluent exponent of these socially and theologically conservative opinions may have led to his transfer to the church of St Michael in Dublin in 1658. But the restoration of Charles II in 1660 soon ended the appointment.

Whatever initial misgivings Gilbert may have felt towards the restoration of episcopacy after 1660, he conformed to the re-established Church of Ireland, and in 1666 was presented to the prebend of Ballymore in the diocese of Armagh. More substantial preferment, as vicar of Belfast, came from Arthur Chichester, first earl of Donegal, owner of much of the town. Donegal showed sympathy towards protestant dissent which, as a result, flourished in Belfast. Gilbert, as minister in the town from about 1671 until his death, did little to check the local presbyterians. He retained strong links with colleagues from the 1650s who had not subsequently conformed to the Church of Ireland. Thomas Emlyn, a chaplain of the Donegals, sometimes deputized for Gilbert in the parish church. In 1683 he published a translation of Pierre Jurieu's riposte to Jacques-Benigne Bossuet, *A Preservative Against the Change of Religion*, intended to counter an increasingly fashionable Catholicism. He may have been responsible for a sermon preached in Dublin on 5 November 1686 which displeased the government with its uncompromising hostility towards Catholicism. Gilbert probably died in 1696; he had married, but nothing is known of his wife. His son, Claudius *Gilbert the younger (1670–1742), was a noted collector of books and medals;

some volumes in his library of over 13,000 titles, bequeathed to Trinity College, may have belonged to his father. TOBY BARNARD

Sources St J. D. Seymour, *The puritans in Ireland, 1647–1661* (1921); repr. (1969) • T. C. Barnard, *Cromwellian Ireland* (1975) • Longford to Clarendon, 14 March 1686–14 March 1687, Bodl. Oxf., MS Clarendon 89, fols. 50v, 52v • J. Agnew, *Belfast merchant families in the seventeenth century* (1996), 64 • P. Kilroy, *Protestant dissent and controversy in Ireland, 1660–1714* (1994) • J. B. Leslie, *Clergy of Dublin and Glendalough*, ed. W. J. R. Wallace (2001), 661–2 • Venn, *Alum. Cant.*

Gilbert, Claudius, the younger (1670–1742), benefactor, was born in Belfast, the only son and heir of Claudius *Gilbert the elder, minister at Limerick and Belfast. He received his early education in Belfast and entered Trinity College, Dublin, on 23 March 1686. He became a fellow of the college in 1693, and received the degrees of doctor of laws and doctor of divinity in 1706. Gilbert was for some time professor of divinity at Trinity and was appointed vice-provost in 1717. He is mentioned favourably in a satirical pamphlet, *The Conclave Dissected* (c.1726), which attacked the provost and other fellows of the college for their arrogance and frivolity. He obtained the rectorship of Ardstraw in co. Tyrone in 1735, and died in October 1742. He bequeathed considerable sums to various charities, and gave about 13,000 volumes of printed books to Trinity College along with a catalogue compiled by himself. Gilbert's donation is commemorated by an inscription over his collection in the library of the college.

J. T. GILBERT, *rev.* PHILIP CARTER

Sources J. W. Stubbs, *The history of the University of Dublin, from its foundation to the end of the eighteenth century* (1889) • R. B. McDowell and D. A. Webb, *Trinity College, Dublin, 1592–1952: an academic history* (1982) • Burtchaell & Sadleir, *Alum. Dubl.*

Likenesses S. Vierpyl, white marble bust, 1758, TCD

Gilbert [*formerly* Giddy], **Davies** (1767–1839), scientific administrator and applied mathematician, was born on 6 March 1767 at St Erth, Cornwall, as Davies Giddy, the son of Edward Giddy (1734–1814), curate, and Catherine (1728–1803), daughter and heir of John Davies of Tredrea, St Erth. He was educated at Penzance grammar school, from about 1775 to 1779, at home by his father, and at Benjamin Donne's mathematical academy in Bristol before matriculating at Pembroke College, Oxford, as a gentleman commoner on 12 April 1785, whence he proceeded MA in 1789. At Oxford, Giddy assiduously studied mathematics, astronomy, and other sciences, forming a close friendship with Thomas Beddoes, reader in chemistry. Giddy advised Beddoes on the latter's Pneumatic Medical Institution in Bristol in which a young Cornish chemist whom Giddy had encouraged, Humphry Davy, was employed for a time. Beddoes and Giddy shared sympathy with the first blush of revolution in France but their political paths subsequently diverged.

After Oxford, Giddy began a decade of county service in maintenance of public order, preparations to repel invasion, and control of food supplies. He served as high sheriff of Cornwall in 1792–3 and was appointed deputy lieutenant in 1795. At this time, as president of the Penzance Agricultural Society, he contributed a paper on the use of

Davies Gilbert [Giddy] (**1767–1839**), by Thomas Phillips, 1833

sea salt as manure to Arthur Young's *Annals of Agriculture*. His agricultural interests were sustained through his election to the board of agriculture in 1809 and in the extensive improvements which he later made on his Sussex estates. His mathematical skills were deployed in calculating the efficiency of Jonathan Hornblower's compound steam engine, in advising on the design of his rotary engine, and subsequently on that of Richard Trevithick's high-pressure steam engine. In this he was allied with those Cornish interests, including those of his parliamentary patron, Sir Francis Basset, who sought to break the stranglehold of James Watt and Matthew Boulton on the Cornish steam engine business. However, Giddy acknowledged the great debt owed to Watt's innovations.

Serving as member of parliament first for Helston (1804–6) and then for Bodmin (1806–32) Giddy refused office under successive ministries but chaired numerous parliamentary committees, drafting and shepherding many items of legislation. Finance, commodity prices, public works, weights and measures, the *Nautical Almanac*, the board of longitude, and the establishment of an astronomical observatory at the Cape of Good Hope were among the issues with which he dealt. While Cornish concerns and scientific matters were paramount, he also entered debate on major political questions, including agricultural protection and currency reform, publishing *A Plain Statement of the Bullion Question* in 1811. During the Corn Bill riots of March 1815 his London house at 6 Holles Street was attacked by the mob. Giddy had become a firm opponent of measures to extend the franchise, voting against them consistently. However, in the debates on the

1832 Reform Bill, which ended his own parliamentary career, he conceded the need for, and advocated, its passage while still voting against the bill as a final gesture of support for a long held political credo. Gilbert collaborated with William Sandys on a collection of Cornish ballad carols, part of the oral tradition which he saw in danger of disappearing. Their *Christmas Carols Ancient and Modern* (1822) set the agenda for the rediscovery of this ancient form.

Gilbert married, on 18 April 1808 at Northiam, Sussex, Mary Ann (1776–1845), daughter of Thomas Gilbert of Eastbourne and heir to substantial estates in Sussex. These estates passed to Giddy on the death of his wife's uncle in 1814 with a condition that the name of Gilbert be perpetuated. By royal sign manual Davies Giddy became Davies Gilbert on 10 December 1817 and the family names of his children were changed on 7 January 1818. Gilbert also inherited property in Cornwall on the death of his father. The marriage was Gilbert's resolution of intolerable problems created by the infatuation with him of Anna Beddoes, the wife of his best friend. She had declared her love for Gilbert some years earlier but he loved her as a sister. The fact that Gilbert became guardian to the Beddoes's children on her husband's death further complicated matters. But he willingly executed that trust, especially in the case of Thomas Lovell *Beddoes, whom he regarded as a son. Of the eight children from Gilbert's marriage, four predeceased him. The first child, Mary, was born on 14 February 1809 without a dura mater and lived a vegetative existence until her death on her seventeenth birthday. Their first son, Charles Davies, died in 1813 aged three, and their fifth child, a boy, died hours after birth the following year. Another daughter, Mary Susanna (*b.* 1816), died in 1834.

Gilbert was a significant figure in the scientific community of his day, though he published little of major importance. In the *Quarterly Journal of Science* (1821) and the *Philosophical Transactions* (1826, 1831) he published his mathematical investigations into the catenarian curve and suspension bridge design. Thomas Telford's plans for the Menai suspension bridge, and the strength of the bridge itself, were improved thanks to Gilbert's theoretical calculations of the relationship between the maximum tension in the main chains and the depth of curvature of the suspension. His methods remained in use for a century. Gilbert also published on other mathematical topics and on the efficiency of steam engines, producing some thirteen scientific papers in all.

Elected a fellow of the Royal Society in 1791, Gilbert became a member of the Linnean Society in the following year. He was also a supporter of the Royal Institution, recommending Humphry Davy to its employ and maintaining close contact with Davy's work there. In 1814 he was a founder and first president of the Geological Society of Cornwall. His tireless parliamentary efforts on behalf of science and his service to the Royal Society persuaded its long serving president, Sir Joseph Banks, to appoint Gilbert as one of the vice-presidents of the society in 1819 and to nominate him as his successor in 1820. Forces of reform rumbled in the Royal Society too, and in Banks's view Gilbert seemed the man to resist them. But Gilbert's diffidence and the greater scientific claims of his protégé, Sir Humphry Davy, saw Davy elected president in 1820 with Gilbert serving as treasurer. Not until 1827, after Davy's resignation because of illness and after an unsuccessful attempt to interest Robert Peel in the presidency, did Gilbert take the chair. His presidency was dogged by infighting over reform and attacks upon the administration of the society, not least by Charles Babbage in his *Reflections on the Decline of Science in England* (1830). Finally the duke of Sussex (a son of George III) was elected president in 1830, an election which Gilbert had engineered amid cries of 'borough-mongering' from the reformers. As president, Gilbert had also been charged in the will of Francis Henry Egerton, eighth earl of Bridgewater, with the nomination of the authors of the Bridgewater treatises and his choices became another source of controversy.

In his declining years Gilbert was involved in the affairs of the newly founded British Association for the Advancement of Science. Just before the 1833 meeting at Cambridge the university gave him an honorary doctorate of laws. He was considered as a possible president for the Bristol meeting in 1836; the leaders of the association thought him still potentially useful in lobbying government. He had received an honorary DCL from Oxford in 1832.

Gilbert's importance to the development of science in the early nineteenth century lay in his faith that science provided the best means to tackle practical problems and in his facility as a parliamentary promoter of scientific ventures. Elected a fellow of the Society of Antiquaries in 1820, he also pursued antiquarian, literary, and historical research. He edited and published a number of works in the Cornish language. His four-volume *The Parochial History of Cornwall* (1838) was not well received.

By temperament Gilbert pursued the dutiful and usually the middle course. In political maturity he positioned himself between the forces of radicalism and reaction and he bore personal tragedies with stoicism. Gilbert states in a letter in 1830 to Charles Babbage that 'My most earnest endeavour through the whole of my life has been to please and gratify everyone—a fruitless endeavour as I have found in numerous circumstances' (Gilbert to Babbage, 8 July 1830, BL, Add. MS 37185, fol. 254). This echoes the judgements of his contemporaries who found him indecisive and irresolute as president of the Royal Society. Gilbert's repeated refusal of political office and his predilection for behind-the-scenes administrative work were much in character. A portrait by John Opie depicts Gilbert, who was tall, fair, and blue eyed, as a strikingly handsome young man. He died at Eastbourne on 24 December 1839 and was buried on 29 December in Eastbourne church. He was survived by his wife, three daughters, Catherine (*b.* 1813), Anne (*b.* 1817), and Hester Elizabeth (*b.* 1818), and a son, John Davies Gilbert FRS (1811–1854).

David Philip Miller

Sources A. C. Todd, *Beyond the blaze: a biography of Davies Gilbert* (1967) • M. B. Hall, *All scientists now: the Royal Society in the nineteenth* *century* (1984) • D. P. Miller, 'The cultural politics of scientific organization: the Royal Society, 1800–35', PhD diss., University of Pennsylvania, 1981 • *DNB* • A. C. Todd, 'Davies Gilbert—patron of engineers (1767–1839) and Jonathan Hornblower (1753–1815)', *Transactions* [Newcomen Society], 32 (1959–60), 1–13 • T. W. Horsfield, *The history, antiquities, and topography of the county of Sussex*, 2 vols. (1835) • *Catalogue of scientific papers*, Royal Society, 1–6 (1867–72) • *GM*, 2nd ser., 13 (1840), 208–11 • pedigree, Cornwall RO, Gilbert papers, CRO/DG/116 • W. H. Brock, 'The selection of the authors of the Bridgewater treatises', *Notes and Records of the Royal Society*, 21 (1966), 162–79 • R. McGrady, *Traces of ancient mystery: the ballad carols of Davies Gilbert and William Sandys* (1993)

Archives Cornwall RO, corresp. and papers • Royal Institution of Cornwall, Truro, corresp. | BL, letters to Charles Babbage, Add. MSS 37182–37185, 37205 • BL, letters to H. Boase, Add. MS 29281 • BL, corresp. with Sir Robert Peel, Add. MSS 40347, 40394, 40397, 40411 • Cornwall RO, letters to John Hawkins • NL NZ, letters to Gideon Algernon Mantell • Royal Cornwall Museum, Truro, corresp. with Richard Trevithick • RS, letters to Sir John Herschel; letters to Sir John Lubbock • W. Sussex RO, Hawkins MSS • Yale U., Beinecke L., letters to Sir Samuel Egerton Brydges

Likenesses S. Cousins, mezzotint, 1828 (after H. Howard), BM, NPG; repro. in Horsfield, *History, antiquities* • T. Phillips, oils, 1833, RS [*see illus.*] • R. Westmacott jun., marble bust, exh. RA 1833, Pembroke College, Oxford • W. Brockedon, pencil drawing, 1838, NPG • Graf, lithograph (after E. F. H.), NPG • J. Opie, portrait, repro. in Todd, *Beyond the blaze* • J. F. Skill, J. Gilbert,and E. Walker, group portrait, pencil and wash (*Men of science living in 1807–08*), NPG • R. Westmacott, marble bust, RS

Gilbert, Edmund William (1900–1973), geographer, was born on 16 October 1900 in Hemsworth, Yorkshire, the only child of the Revd Robert Henry Gilbert (1868–1922), rector of Hemsworth, and his wife, Mabel Billinton. After attending St Peter's School, York, he matriculated from Hertford College, Oxford, as an exhibitioner in 1919, graduating BA in modern history in 1922 with second-class honours.

Gilbert's interest in geography was aroused when he attended the summer school held at the University of Oxford's school of geography, in 1922. He subsequently followed the diploma course, gaining the Oxford diploma in geography with distinction in 1924. His study of the Pontefract and Doncaster area of Yorkshire was judged to be of exceptional merit. His first geographical paper, on Pontefract, was published in 1925. He proceeded BLitt in 1928, having undertaken further work in historical geography. As a diploma student he was the instigator and a founder member in 1924 of the Herbertson Society, the Oxford undergraduate geographical society, named after Andrew Herbertson, professor of geography at Oxford.

Between 1923 and 1926 Gilbert was junior lecturer in geography at Bedford College for Women in London, during which time he toyed with the idea of becoming a barrister. As a member of the Middle Temple he was placed in the first class in criminal law and procedure in the bar examination. But his interest in geography was restored after hearing an inspirational lecture on geography and world peace by Professor Percy Roxby of the University of Liverpool. In 1926 he moved to the University of Reading as lecturer in historical geography and was much happier there, remaining ten years and playing the leading part in setting up an honours school of geography. In 1927 he married a fellow Oxford diploma student, Barbara Maud

Edmund William Gilbert (1900–1973), by unknown photographer [left, with James Alfred Steers]

Flux Dundas (*b.* 1902), who gave him support over the next forty-six years, caring for him with understanding during his occasional bouts of depression. There were no children of the marriage.

Gilbert returned to Oxford in 1936 as research lecturer in human geography, to work on a survey of social services in the Oxford district financed by the Rockefeller Foundation. In the war years he worked for the naval intelligence division of the Admiralty on the production of the Geographical Handbook series, writing most of the volumes on Spain and Portugal. He was appointed reader in human geography in 1943 and subsequently professor of geography in 1953, a position he held until 1967. The chair carried with it a fellowship at his old college, Hertford, for which he had considerable affection and of which he was emeritus fellow from 1967. Throughout his career Gilbert maintained close links with the Royal Geographical Society, serving three times on its council. He also served on the council of the Hakluyt Society and on committees of the British Association, section E (geography) and the Geographical Association.

Publication of *The Exploration of Western America, 1800–1850* (1933) while he was at Reading reflected Gilbert's early interest in historical geography. His social conscience later found expression in his work on Oxford where, influenced by the writing of Vaughan Cornish, he also became involved in the activities of the Oxford Preservation Trust, serving as a trustee. His publications in the 1940s on English regions as a basis for administrative reform were pioneering and attracted attention beyond the geographical profession. In all his writing he stressed the importance of the past as a clue to understanding the present, a philosophy that found particular expression in his publications on university towns and seaside resorts. *Brighton: Old Ocean's Bauble* (1954) illustrates well his ability to blend geography and social history. His last book, *British Pioneers in Geography* (1972), paid tribute to, among others, his predecessor, Sir Halford Mackinder, with whom he shared a belief in geography as 'an humane study'.

All Gilbert's writing, like his lectures, was elegant and carefully crafted, and he drew on novelists and painters to assist in the description and interpretation of regions that he regarded as central to geography. He was a skilled photographer, preferring black and white to colour. He was especially fond of visiting the capital cities and university towns of western Europe, and took many pictures of these places.

Billy Gilbert, as he was called by his friends, was a shy but kindly man, more at home at the school of geography in Oxford or the Royal Geographical Society than at geographical conferences and, for that reason, not as widely known as he deserved to be. He raised the status of geography within Oxford, securing fellowships in the colleges for his younger colleagues, and planning a major extension to the school of geography. He also recognized the need to encourage graduate studies, and a growing number of graduate students benefited from his encouragement and the ready hospitality which he and Barbara accorded them at their cottage in Appleton, near Oxford. He retired there in 1967 and in the same year was awarded the Murchison grant by the Royal Geographical Society in recognition of his contribution to urban studies and the history of geography. In 1968 he was presented with *Urbanization and its Problems*, a collection of essays by colleagues and former pupils. He died at his home, Old Cottage, Appleton, on 2 October 1973, having suffered a stroke in the previous year. He was buried at Appleton on 5 October 1973. The geography society at Hertford College is named after him. IAN SCARGILL

Sources T. W. Freeman, 'Edmund William Gilbert 1900–1973', *Geographers' Bibliographical Studies*, 3 (1979), 63–8 • *WWW*, *1971–80* • *The Times* (5 Oct 1973) • T. W. Freeman, *Geography*, 59 (1974), 68 • I. Scargill, 'The Oxford School of Geography, 1899–1999', *School of Geography Research Papers*, 55 (1999) • *GJ*, 140 (1974), 176–7 • *Geographical Magazine*, 46 (1973–4), 151 • *Oxford Mail* (4 Oct 1973) • *Oxford Times* (5 Oct 1973) • R. P. Beckinsale and J. M. Houston, eds., *Urbanization and its problems: essays in honour of E. W. Gilbert* (1968)

Archives Bodl. Oxf., corresp., lecture notes, and papers • Hertford College, Oxford • U. Oxf., school of geography and the environment, papers and photographs

Likenesses J. Pannett, pencil drawing, 1962, Hertford College, Oxford; photographic copy, school of geography and the environment, U. Oxf. • photograph, U. Oxf., school of geography and the environment [*see illus.*]

Wealth at death £13,179: probate, 2 Jan 1974, *CGPLA Eng. & Wales*

Gilbert, Elizabeth Margaretta Maria (1826–1885), campaigner for blind people, born at Oxford on 7 August 1826, was the second of eight daughters and third of the eleven children of Ashurst Turner *Gilbert (1786–1870), principal of Brasenose College, Oxford, and afterwards bishop of Chichester, and his wife, Mary Anne (*d.* 1863), only surviving child of Robert Wintle, vicar of Culham, Oxfordshire. She was at an early age a fine child, with flashing black eyes, but when only three years old she was blinded by a bad attack of scarlet fever. Her parents decided that she should be brought up with her sisters, though she was vulnerable to the hazards of everyday life—she once fell and badly burnt her hands on the firegrate. When young she romped and played happily, and she grew to be intelligent and capable, with a strong interest in poetry, music, birds, and nature generally. At the age of twenty she could understand French, German, and Italian, and had been thoroughly educated.

At twenty-one Gilbert inherited half her godmother's estate, and, prompted by her sister Mary and a friend, she became keenly interested in the state of poor blind people. In 1851 she acquired a Foucault frame, a newly invented device which, inserted under a sheet of paper, guided handwriting, and she began to correspond with William Hanks Levy, a young blind teacher employed by the London Society for Teaching the Blind to Read at its school in St John's Wood. In May 1854 she hired a cellar in Holborn, London, at the cost of 1*s.* 6*d.* a week, for the sale of the work of seven blind men who worked at their own homes, and were paid the full selling price, less the cost of material. Levy was engaged as manager. The institution developed into the Association for Promoting the General Welfare of the Blind, and attracted the support of Queen Victoria, Gladstone, and Dickens. In accordance with Levy's wish, none but blind persons were employed, although Gilbert disapproved of their isolation. As the work developed there were many moves, especially in the early years. At the end of the twentieth century, the association had a head office and two factories in London and another factory in Luton, with residential accommodation for some employees in both places.

Gilbert proposed in a thoughtful paper the establishment of a school for training teachers for blind pupils and later took much interest in the founding and work of the Royal Normal (now the Royal National) College for the Blind. Finding that much time might be saved by the use of blocks upon which baskets could be modelled, she sent Levy to France to obtain the necessary tools. She took a leading part in compiling a memorandum to government in connection with the 1870 Education Act, which helped pave the way for the admission of blind children to mainstream schools in the 1890s.

Gilbert materially assisted Levy in writing a book on *Blindness and the Blind* (1872), a remarkably detailed work of over 500 pages, which Levy dedicated to her. In November 1874 she sent a paper to a special committee appointed by the Charity Organization Society to consider means of helping blind people, but was too ill to attend the meeting. Her work for the association diminished, although her interest remained until the end. After very great suffering from a number of serious ailments, but without complaint, and with constant concern for those nursing her, she died very peacefully on 7 February 1885, at 5 Stanhope Place, Hyde Park, London.

GORDON GOODWIN, *rev.* KENNETH R. WHITTON

Sources F. Martin, *Elizabeth Gilbert and her work for the blind* (1891) • F. Martin, 'Elizabeth Gilbert and her work for the blind', *The Athenaeum* (17 Dec 1887), 818–19

Likenesses W. Boxall, oils, *c.*1850; copy, formerly at General Welfare for the Blind, Tottenham Court Road, London, *c.*1977

Wealth at death £14,894 5*s.* 8*d.*: probate, 23 March 1885, *CGPLA Eng. & Wales*

Gilbert, George (*d.* 1583), Roman Catholic layman, was born in Suffolk, the son of Ambrose Gilbert (*d.* 1554) and Grace Townsend. His grandfather was William Gilbert of

Clare, Suffolk. He was educated in London and Cambridge. At an early age he succeeded, on his father's death, to extensive landed estates. While under royal licence on the continent he met Thomas Darbyshire in Paris, and was converted to the Roman Catholic church by Robert Persons at Rome in 1579.

On Gilbert's return to London he and Thomas Pound of Belmont formed a group of twenty-six Catholic young men of birth and property without wives or offices. They promised 'to content themselves with food and clothing and the bare necessities of their state, and to bestow all the rest for the good of the Catholic cause'. The members of the association lodged together in the house of Norris, the chief pursuivant, in Fetter or Chancery Lane. Norris had great credit with John Aylmer, bishop of London, and was liberally paid by Gilbert. At Fulham the bishop's son-in-law, Adam Squire, was in Gilbert's pay. Through the connivance of these men the members of the association were able to receive priests and to have masses celebrated daily in their house until, after the arrival of the Jesuits Persons and Campion in England, the persecution grew more severe.

In 1581 Gilbert deemed it prudent to withdraw to the English College at Rheims, where he was cordially welcomed by William Allen, who described him as 'summus patrum presbyterorum patronus' ('the greatest patron of the Catholic clergy'). Proceeding afterwards to Rome, Gilbert entered the English College as a pensioner and devoted himself to promoting the Catholic cause in England. This included writing an essay in Latin, *A way to deal with persons of all sorts so as to convert them and bring them back to a better way of life*. Pope Gregory XIII ordered Gilbert to France on diplomatic business. However, he died of a fever at Sant Andrea, Rome, on 6 October 1583. While on his deathbed he was admitted into the Society of Jesus. The pope declared his death a serious blow to Catholicism in England.

Gilbert incurred great expense by covering the walls of the English College at Rome with frescoes of the English martyrs. He left the superintendence of this work to William Good, who had the pictures engraved and published in Rome in 1584 under the title of *Ecclesiae Anglicanae trophaea*. Gilbert's portrait was engraved by W. P. Kiliam from a drawing by J. G. Hemsch.

THOMPSON COOPER, *rev.* THOMAS H. CLANCY

Sources H. More, *Historia missionis Anglicanae Societatis Iesu* (St Omer, 1660) • *The Elizabethan Jesuits: Historia missionis Anglicanae Societatis Jesu (1660) of Henry More*, ed. and trans. F. Edwards (1981) • H. Foley, ed., *Records of the English province of the Society of Jesus*, 3 (1878), 658–704 • T. M. McCoog, ed., *Monumenta Angliae*, 2: *English and Welsh Jesuits, catalogues, 1630–1640* (1992), 330 • L. Hicks, ed., *Letters and memorials of Father Robert Persons*, Catholic RS, 39 (1942), 331–40 • M. Questier, 'Like locusts all over the world', *The reckoned expense: Edmund Campion and the early English Jesuits*, ed. T. M. McCoog (1996), 265–84, esp. 272, 280–81 • J. H. Pollen, *The English Catholics in the reign of Queen Elizabeth* (1920), 342

Likenesses W. P. Kiliam, engraving (after drawing by J. G. Hemsch) • engraving, repro. in Foley, ed., *Records*

Wealth at death left 800 scudi to sustain the novitiate of Sant Andrea in Rome; evidently had very little when he died: Foley, ed., *Records*, 3.683 ff.

Gilbert, Sir Humphrey (1537–1583), explorer and soldier, was born in Greenway, near Dartmouth, Devon between January and May 1537, the second son of Otho Gilbert of Compton, Devon (*d.* 1547), landowner, and Katherine, daughter of Sir Philip Champernoun of Modbury, Devon. Following Otho Gilbert's death Katherine married Walter Ralegh (1496?–1581), a gentleman from Hayes Barton in the same county. Sir Walter *Ralegh (1554–1618) was a child of this second marriage and was therefore Humphrey Gilbert's half-brother.

Education and early career According to John Hooker of Exeter, the main source of information on Gilbert's early life, Gilbert was educated at Eton College and Oxford and then entered the service of Princess Elizabeth about 1554–5 through the good offices of his aunt Katherine Ashley, the future monarch's governess. In 1558 he attended New Inn, an inn of chancery. His military career began with a commission held during the Newhaven expedition of 1562–3. The earl of Warwick, his superior officer in this exploit, warmly praised Gilbert for the quality of his service. On his return to England Gilbert turned his attention to the possible discovery of a direct route by sea to the Far East, and in late 1565 he petitioned Queen Elizabeth for a commission to achieve this end. About this time, in the presence of the queen and some of the privy council, Gilbert advocated the case for a north-west passage over America to the Pacific in contradiction of Andrew Jenkinson, a supporter of the idea of a north-east passage. Accordingly he wrote the first version of his *Discourse of a Discoverie for a New Passage to Cataia* in 1566, a work that was published ten years later with a commentary by George Gascoigne and which subsequently featured in the first edition of Hakluyt's *Principall Navigations*. This treatise, as well as pointing out the damage that might be inflicted on Spanish and Portuguese interests if the English discovered such a route, also advocated the colonization of the New World by the English in order to alleviate vagrancy and poverty in the mother country. Gilbert's attempts to undertake this project were frustrated by the breakdown of negotiations with the Muscovy Company concerning the terms under which such an expedition would be undertaken.

Ireland, Westminster, and the Netherlands In 1566 Gilbert began his notorious association with Ireland when he went to Ulster as a military captain to assist Henry Sidney, the lord deputy of Ireland, in the campaign to defeat Shane O'Neill. In the aftermath of O'Neill's assassination in 1567 Gilbert, as well as travelling between Ireland and England, became involved in the planning of plantation schemes in Ireland, one in Ulster and one with Sir Warham St Leger in Munster. Even later, in 1572, Gilbert and his uncle Sir Arthur Champernoun were petitioning Sir John Perrot, president of Munster, with plans for a plantation. However, the turmoil caused in 1569 by the uprisings of James fitz Maurice Fitzgerald and Edmund Butler ensured Gilbert's return to military action. In September 1569 he was made colonel of the army in Munster and became military governor of the province with a commission of martial law. With only 500 troops in the field Gilbert subdued a force perhaps eight times larger in six weeks. He forced the earl of Clancar, MacDonagh, and the white knight into submission in early December and James fitz Maurice Fitzgerald only narrowly eluded his grasp.

The ruthlessness of Gilbert's campaign, largely remembered for Thomas Churchyard's gory account of 1579 as well as Gilbert's frank and brutal letters from the field, has often tended to conceal the calculated political motivation of his intention to terrorize the Irish. The colonel on principle refused to recognize the rebels through direct or indirect contact. Neither would he give anyone protection unless they first submitted to him, swore an oath to the queen, and entered into pledges of good behaviour. According to Churchyard, those who submitted to Gilbert had to approach him through a lane marked by decapitated heads. He boasted of his disregard for the liberties of the chartered towns of Munster, stating 'that the Prince had a regular and absolute power, and that which might not be done by the one, I wolde do it by the other in Casez of necessitie' (Churchyard, sigs. Qi–Ri; PRO, SP 63/29, 82–3). Even as late as 1581 Sir Walter Ralegh, his half-brother, could assert that he 'never heard nor read of any man more feared than [Gilbert] is amonge the Irish nation' (Edwards, 2.12). In recognition of his service Gilbert was knighted by Lord Deputy Sidney in Drogheda in January 1570 and returned to England, citing pressing business as the cause of his absence. In the same year he married Anne Aucher, an heiress from Kent who bestowed considerable landed wealth upon him, wealth that Gilbert almost entirely consumed through supporting various maritime projects. The union produced six sons and a daughter.

Gilbert was returned to the parliament of 1571 as member for Plymouth. His most notable contribution to the Commons was an extremely unpopular speech defending the queen's prerogative against an attack on royal licences of purveyance previously made by Robert Bell. Having branded Bell 'an open enemy' Gilbert urged caution, stating that the queen might look to her own power and therefore find cause to suppress parliament for good. He cited continental European precedents to support this assertion. Gilbert was subsequently subjected to personal attack by Peter Wentworth and was denied right of reply by the house three times. Gilbert was later returned for Queenborough to the parliament of 1572–81, although it seems that he only attended the session of 1581. In 1571 he also became receiver-general of fines resulting from the enforcement of statutes prohibiting unlawful games and guaranteeing maintenance of armaments and horses for defence of the realm. His considerable favour in high places at this time is indicated by his co-operation with Sir William Cecil, the earl of Leicester, and Sir Thomas Smith in sponsoring William Medley's ill-fated alchemical project to change iron into copper.

In the early 1570s Gilbert wrote a tract entitled *The erection of an achademy in London for educacion of her maiestes wardes, and others the youth of nobility and gentlemen*. This aimed to secure the education of wards and the younger sons of gentlemen in 'matters of accion meet for present practize, both of peace and warre'. Gilbert asserted that 'suche as governe Common weales ought rather to bend themselves to the practizes thereof, then to the bookish Circumstances of the same' (Gilbert, 1–12). For that reason the cursus envisaged by Gilbert not only contained the usual rhetorical and physical exercises advocated by sixteenth-century pedagogues, but also advocated the study of natural philosophy in an empirical manner, the teaching of surgery, and the application of mathematics to the study of warfare by land and sea. Gilbert's views on the teaching of humanities and letters aimed at the immersion of the student in what he termed 'Chivallric pollicy'. He envisaged that the academy would produce a host of capable and vigorous crown servants. Other innovations recommended by Gilbert included the provision of a copyright library and the publication of findings, in the vernacular, stemming from the institution's studies and research.

From July to November 1572 Gilbert led a force of 1100 supposed volunteers to Flushing in an expedition, with clandestine royal approval, to support the Dutch states against the Spaniards. After a period spent skirmishing with the Spanish garrison and unsuccessfully besieging Goes, Gilbert returned to England in pretended disgrace. During the next five years he predominantly attended to his personal concerns in Devon, Kent, and London. But in 1577 he seized the opportunity afforded by increasing hostility at court towards the Spanish empire to put proposals before Elizabeth for a scheme to 'annoy the King of Spayne' by destroying the Spanish and Portuguese fishing fleets of Newfoundland and establishing an English colony in the West Indies in order to plunder Spanish shipping.

Gilbert receives letters patent On 11 June 1578 Gilbert became the recipient of letters patent that entitled him for six years to search out 'remote heathen and barbarous landes' not already in the possession of a Christian prince, which, when found, he and his heirs could have, hold, occupy, and enjoy forever. Gilbert was to wield legislative and jurisdictional power in these lands as well as the right to grant tenures to colonists licensed to leave England. His continued and various attempted applications of this royal grant constitute the dominant motif of the remainder of his life. However, his plans to capitalize upon the letters patent by immediately embarking upon an expedition were successively stalled until November 1578. Disagreements between Gilbert and Henry Knollys, a participant in the proposed voyage, led to a split within the fleet from the start. As a result Knollys left with three ships the day before Gilbert set sail with the remaining seven. The motive and course of this venture is unknown. D. B. Quinn suggests that Gilbert aimed to fulfil his aforementioned ambitions in the West Indies. Although little is known of the details of Gilbert's voyage, it is certain that he was back in England by the end of April 1579.

In the summer of that year Gilbert, under commission,

patrolled the southern coast of Munster with three ships to ward off James fitz Maurice Fitzgerald's anticipated return to Ireland with continental allies. This service proved particularly costly as his sailors, once their pay had ceased, absconded with two ships causing him losses of £2000. Gilbert subsequently attempted to generate revenue by farming out privileges under his patent to others: for example he handed over all rights to discoveries above the fiftieth line of latitude to John Dee. However he ran into trouble with the privy council for using his patent to issue licences to transport victuals out of England; in truth, he only had the right to issue licences to transport victuals to lands he had himself discovered.

Gilbert next used his letters patent in November 1582 to gather a joint-stock mercantile company around him in Southampton in order to support his planned maritime venture. The members of this corporation were to have exclusive rights to freedom of trade with whatever lands might be gained under his patent, and landowning privileges in those newly discovered areas. At the same time Gilbert entered into agreements with a group of Catholics led by Sir George Peckham and Sir Thomas Gerrard to enable them to set up a colony in the New World, thus evading England's increasingly severe recusancy laws. Originally intending to accompany them on their voyage Gilbert assigned them at least 8,500,000 acres in the Americas for their proposed settlement in 1582–3. This scheme foundered largely because of the privy council's requirement that the departing Catholics should pay their recusancy fines before leaving the realm.

Gilbert's final voyage With the support of the Southampton company Gilbert finally left Plymouth with a fleet of five ships—the *Delight*, the *Bark Ralegh*, the *Golden Hind*, the *Swallow*, and the *Squirrel*—on 11 June 1583. An eyewitness account of this, Gilbert's final voyage, was written by Edward Hayes, captain and owner of the *Golden Hind*. According to Hayes, the intention of the voyage was to make for Newfoundland and then move southwards along the coast. The *Bark Ralegh*, however, lacking sufficient victuals, returned to port within two days. By the end of July Newfoundland had been sighted. On 3 August Gilbert entered the harbour of St John's, facing down opposition from the Newfoundland fishing fleet by showing his letters patent. He landed two days later and claimed the harbour and all land within 200 leagues' radius of it in Queen Elizabeth's name, in accordance with his commission of 1578, thus establishing the first English possession in the New World since John Cabot's expedition in 1497. Soon afterwards the arms of England engraved in lead were hoisted nearby on a wooden pillar. Gilbert imposed his authority on the local fishing fleet by leasing out drying grounds to them in fee farm, securing promises that they would pay him a rent.

Gilbert then set out on 20 August with the *Squirrel*, the *Delight*, and the *Golden Hind* on a reconnaissance trip southwards along the coast to reach Sable Island where, it was thought, livestock might be found. The *Swallow* remained in the hands of sailors who refused to follow Gilbert any further, preferring to return to England as soon as possible. On 29 August the *Delight* struck aground and sank, taking mineral specimens from Newfoundland and some newly charted maps with it. The crews of the remaining ships then insisted on returning home. According to Hayes, Gilbert was, by contrast, optimistic, anticipating generous royal support for a broader-based voyage to the Americas in the future. However, about midnight on 9 September 1583, and having encountered a fierce storm around the Azores, the *Squirrel*, with Gilbert on board, was engulfed by the sea. According to Hayes, Gilbert was last seen standing on deck with a book in his hand. His final words, shouted over to the *Golden Hind*, were 'We are as near to heaven, by sea as by land' (Hakluyt, 3.679–97).

Reputation and posterity Gilbert's posthumous fame as a pioneer and mariner owes much to the innovative nature of his patent of 1578 and Hakluyt's inclusion of both Hayes's eyewitness account and Gilbert's work on the north-west passage in his 1589 edition of *Principall Navigations*. Ironically, even Elizabeth remarked that Gilbert was 'of not good happ by sea' (Quinn, 1.82). Certainly his picturesque death prevented his return to England as a disgraced and demoralized debtor and gave him something of the allure of a tragic hero, an image enhanced by the fact that the personal mottoes he assumed were *Quid non?* ('Why not?') and *Mutare vel timere sperno* ('I scorn to change or to fear'). Late nineteenth- and early twentieth-century treatments of Gilbert's life, notably those by J. A. Froude and William Gosling, stressed this adventurous aspect of his personality, casting him as the 'father of English colonization' (Gosling, 9). D. B. Quinn's thorough work on Gilbert, although stressing his status as pioneer of English transatlantic projects, places more weight on Gilbert's being symptomatic of the social context and economic pressures of his time.

This understandable maritime emphasis has, however, meant that contemporary assertions that he was a man of considerable intellectual sophistication have often been neglected. Thomas Churchyard, George Gascoigne, and William Camden all paid tribute to his intellectual capabilities. Hooker, in particular, highlighted Gilbert's interest in 'studies pertaining to the state of government' (Hooker, 133). Certainly the tenor of his views about the nature of his authority in Munster in 1569, coupled with his daring interventions in the parliament of 1571, indicate that Gilbert was a 'prerogative man', one who had a fundamental belief that all authority within the realm ultimately belonged to the monarch. Moreover, marginalia to Gabriel Harvey's copy of Livy's *Discourses* refer to Gilbert's reading Livy in the company of Sir Thomas Smith, whose pursuits included the examination of forms of government. The resulting debate compared the forward strategy of Marcellus to the cunning delaying tactics of Quintus Fabius Maximus. Gilbert, recently returned from suppressing rebellion in Ireland, argued for Marcellus. However, he eventually yielded to Sir Thomas Smith's advocacy of Fabius. Significantly, the somewhat Machiavellian conclusion Harvey reached, having heard them debating, was that 'each [is] as indispensible as the other in his place. There are times when I would rather be Marcellus, times when Fabius' (Grafton and Jardine, 40–42). Gilbert also had a lively interest in the occult which is best shown by an account, in the first person, of 'straung visions' he witnessed between 24 February and 6 April 1567. These tumultuous and violent visions, laden with dragons, angels, and books of archaic lore, reflect intriguingly on his psyche. Perhaps the most telling detail of these hallucinations is that of Gilbert, splendidly dressed and fully armed, receiving the homage of both Solomon and Job who promise him access to secret mystical information.

Gilbert's sexuality was a matter of contemporary speculation; both Sir Thomas Smith and Medley indicate that he may have been a pederast. In physical appearance he was, according to John Hooker, 'of higher stature than of the common sort, and of complexion cholerike' (Hooker, 132). His difficulties, though inspiring the loyalty of those who served with him, as attested by both Sir Roger Williams and Edward Hayes, proved to be a grave impediment to his success in both maritime and military exploits. Although many contemporaries pointed to his courage, intelligence, and enthusiasm, they also indicated that he was indiscreet, abrasive, and financially imprudent.

RORY RAPPLE

Sources D. B. Quinn, ed., *The voyages and colonising enterprises of Sir Humphrey Gilbert*, 2 vols., Hakluyt Society, 2nd ser., 83–4 (1940) • R. Hakluyt, *The principall navigations, voiages and discoveries of the English nation* (1589) • J. Hooker, 'Chronicles of Ireland', *The chronicles of England, Scotland and Ireland*, ed. R. Holinshed and others, 2nd edn, ed. J. Hooker, 2 (1586) • H. Gilbert, *Queene Elizabethes Achademy*, ed. F. J. Furnivall, EETS, extra ser., 8 (1869), 1–12 • T. Churchyard, *A generall rehearsall of warres* (1579) • 'Anonymous journal, 2–21 April, 1571', *Proceedings of the parliaments of Elizabeth I*, ed. T. E. Hartley, 1 (1981) • R. Rapple, 'The political thought of Sir Humphrey Gilbert', MPhil diss., U. Cam., 1998 • A. Grafton and L. Jardine, '"Studied for action": how Gabriel Harvey read his Livy', *Past and Present*, 129 (1990), 30–78 • W. G. Gosling, *The life of Sir Humphrey Gilbert* (1911) • J. A. Froude, 'England's forgotten worthies', *Short studies on great subjects*, 2 (1867), 136–45 • E. Edwards, *The life of Ralegh*, 2 vols. (1868) • PRO, SP 63/29/82–3 • HoP, *Commons, 1558–1603* • BL, Add. MS 36674 [account of Gilbert's visions] • *The works of Sir Roger Williams*, ed. J. X. Evans (1972)

Likenesses W. and M. van de Passe, line engraving, BM, NPG; repro. in H. H. [H. Holland], *Herωologia Anglica*, 2 vols. (Arnhem, 1620) • portrait (posthumous), repro. in Quinn, *Voyages*, frontispiece; priv. coll.

Wealth at death Estate of Minster with Ridge marsh, worth approx. £3000: will, Quinn, *Voyages and colonising enterprises*, 2.335–9

Gilbert, Sir Jeffray (1674–1726), judge and legal writer, was born at Burs, near Lamberhurst, Kent, and baptized at Goudhurst on 10 October 1674, the son of William Gilbert (*d.* 1674) and Elizabeth, his wife. Nothing is known about his parents, except that his father was buried on 1 November 1674. Gilbert was closely connected to the Gybbon or Gibbon family of Hole Park, Rolvenden, a Kentish Cromwellian and later whig family. He shared with Phillips Gybbon (MP for Rye 1707–62), who was his first-named executor, an aunt, a Mistress Gibbon who was housekeeper of Whitehall under Cromwell. Phillips Gybbon's

Sir Jeffray Gilbert (1674–1726), by Michael Dahl, 1723

father, Robert, was steward and executor to Sir Matthew Hale. The connection thus located Gilbert in both whig politics and Hale's approach to the common law; he certainly had access to Hale's manuscript writings.

Gilbert's early life is obscure. His works make clear that he must at some point have acquired the elements of a classical education, and he shows some familiarity with the civil law, but he did not matriculate at either of the English universities, or at Leiden. He was admitted to the Inner Temple in 1692, and called to the bar in 1698. He seems to have practised on the home circuit, in king's bench, and in equity, but he was not among the leaders of the bar, and his family and political connections were not strong enough to mark him for English preferment. He seems not to have married, and left no children.

On 4 February 1715 Gilbert was appointed a puisne judge of the Irish king's bench, and on 5 July of that year he was promoted to chief baron of the Irish exchequer, on the recommendation of Lord Cowper. Like the English exchequer, the Irish had an equity as well as a common law jurisdiction, and Gilbert seems also to have been commissioned to hear chancery causes *vice* Alan Brodrick, Viscount Midleton, the chancellor, during his absences. Gilbert was said to have been offered and refused the Irish chancellorship, presumably in the early 1720s, when the administration was seeking a replacement for Midleton.

Gilbert's most notable judicial act in Ireland, and the turning point of his career, was in the case of *Annesley* v. *Sherlock* in 1716–20. The case turned on the issue of whether appeals from equity jurisdictions in Ireland lay to the Irish, or the British, House of Lords, a matter of some sensitivity. Gilbert led the Irish exchequer in following the orders of the British Lords in preference to those of the Irish, at one point arranging a special session of the court at his house to reverse a conciliatory decision of the other two barons. The Irish Lords in 1719 ordered the arrest of Gilbert and other barons. The British Lords retaliated in 1720 with a resolution supporting the barons' action, an address to the crown recommending that they should receive 'some Mark of his Royal Favour' (*JHL*, 21.214), and an act declaring that the British parliament had full legislative power over Ireland, and that the Irish House of Lords had no appellate jurisdiction.

Gilbert had thus made his name as a politically reliable whig judge deserving preferment in England. In 1722 he was rewarded with the post of puisne baron of the English exchequer (appointed 7 June). On the fall of the chancellor, Macclesfield, Gilbert was appointed to the commission for the English Great Seal, and at the same time he was knighted (7 January 1725). The appointment of Sir Peter King as chancellor led to a general reshuffle of judges, and Gilbert was promoted on 3 June 1725 to be chief baron. On 7 May 1726 he was elected a fellow of the Royal Society, an honour at this period sometimes conferred on senior judges. By this time, however, he was probably terminally ill; he does not seem to have sat in court in Trinity term 1726, and he died after a long illness at Bath on 14 October. He was buried in the abbey church, Bath, on 17 October, but a more elaborate monument was erected by his executors in the Temple Church.

Both a contemporary obituarist and the monument in the Temple identify Gilbert as having a high reputation both as a lawyer and as a judge, and for interests in mathematics and the arts. The evidence for these wider interests is limited. As a judge he displayed the whig biases of most members of the bench at this period; but his judgments were neither widely reported nor frequently cited later, and those that survive say more about legal history than about current applicable law. Gilbert's later reputation came from his posthumously published legal treatises, and these provide the reason to see him as more than a political placeman.

Gilbert seems to have been engaged around 1700 and shortly thereafter in the production of a general treatise on English law on the 'Institutional' model, divided into *Persons*, *Things* (*Personal Property* and *Real Property*), and *Actions*; the text was probably intended for publication. A complete, though imperfect, manuscript draft of *Personal Property* survives in Columbia University Library, as do the plan and a large number of fragments of *Actions*, which included a general section on the jurisdiction of courts and common law and equity procedure, as well as treatments of the particular forms of action. The work was a collective one involving at least three hands, though Gilbert shaped the overall structure, wrote the majority of the text, and edited other contributions. The remains of the other sections, *Persons* and *Real Property*, are more fragmentary.

If the work had been completed and published in this form it would have been of high importance. It anticipated the method of Sir William Blackstone's *Commentaries* (1765–9) by fifty years, and presented English law from a rigorously whig standpoint strongly influenced by John Locke; both history and the civil law were used for explanatory purposes. Gilbert's analytical and historical method was derived from Hale, but he innovated both in the politics of his account of the common law, and in his use of civil law materials. However, Gilbert abandoned work on the project some time before 1710. Shortly after 1720 he rewrote and updated the material on equity procedure and added new material on substantive equity doctrine, and in 1724–5 he produced an expanded and updated version of the text on the exchequer; these are probably preparations for his judicial responsibilities in England. During his life Gilbert published only *Abstract of Locke's 'Essay Concerning Human Understanding'* (1709), and that anonymously. By his will he left 'all my law manuscripts to Charles Clarke Esq. under special Trust that none should be printed' (Lofft, xliv), either following Hale's example, or thinking that his reputation would not be well served by their publication.

Significant parts of the draft treatise, however, were already in manuscript circulation. The section entitled *Evidence* was already in circulation in 1710, and some of Gilbert's own manuscripts seem to have been left in Ireland. Between 1730 and 1763 twelve separate fragments or groups of fragments were published as free-standing treatises: *A Treatise of Tenures* (1730); *The Law and Practice of Ejectments* (1734); *The Law of Uses and Trusts* (with *A Treatise of Dower*) (1734); *The History and Practice of Civil Actions in the Court of Common Pleas* (including an introduction, 'The constitution of England'; 1737); *A Historical View of the Practice of the Exchequer* (1738); *An Historical Account of … Devises, and Revocations* (1739); *The Law of Evidence* (1754); *The Law and Practice of Distresses and Replevins* (1755); *Two Treatises on the Proceedings in Equity and the Jurisdiction of that Court* (1756); *A Treatise on Rents* (1758); *A Treatise on the Action of Debt* (1760); and *The Law of Executions* (including *The History and Practice of the Court of King's Bench*; 1763). In addition, substantial parts of the *New Abridgment* (5 vols., 1736–66) usually attributed to Mathew Bacon were certainly drawn from Gilbert's manuscripts, though it is clear that Bacon did not have a complete set, that he did not follow Gilbert's general organization, and that he adapted and updated Gilbert with a free hand.

The circumstances of the publication of Gilbert's works mean that a number of works have been more dubiously attributed to him. *Reports of Cases in Equity … by a Late Learned Judge* (1734) include some of Gilbert's draft judgments, but also some reports which cannot be by him. *Cases in law and equity … from the original manuscript of the late lord chief baron Gilbert* (1760) could be by Gilbert, but the case is not compelling. Later attributions to Gilbert of *The Law of Evidence* (1717), *General Abridgment of Cases in Equity* (1732), and *A Treatise of Equity* (1737) are clearly wrong.

By comparison with contemporary practitioners' books Gilbert's writings are relatively lucid and well organized (though these features are purchased at the expense of accuracy and complete coverage of the law). Their clarity gave them a considerable reputation. Blackstone described *Evidence* as 'a work which it is impossible to abstract or abridge without losing some beauty and destroying the chain of the whole' (*Commentaries*, 3.367) and this book not only continued to be edited down to 1801, but also shaped the form of other treatments of the law of evidence down to the mid-nineteenth century. *Uses* continued to be edited down to 1811, *Distresses* to 1823, and *Tenures* to 1824.

As a judge Gilbert was a fairly minor figure. His writings, however, cast light both on early eighteenth-century whig views of the law, and on the process of transition from the 'abridgement style' of much seventeenth-century legal writing to the modern legal treatise. M. MACNAIR

Sources M. Macnair, 'Sir Jeffrey Gilbert and his treatises', *Journal of Legal History*, 15 (1994), 252–68 • C. Lofft, 'Preface and account of the author', in Gilbert, *The law of evidence*, 5th edn, 1 (1792), 1–45 • *JHL*, 20–21 (1714–26) • F. G. James, *Ireland in the empire, 1688–1770* (1973), 99–107 • W. Blackstone, *Commentaries on the laws of England*, 16th edn, 3 (1825), 367 • J. N. Adams, G. Averley, and F. J. G. Robinson, eds., *A bibliography of eighteenth century legal literature* (1982) • Col. U., Diamond Law Library, Singleton MSS, 21, 26, 28, 33–4, 54–5, 57, 61–3, 66 • Harvard U., law school, MSS 1002, 1064, 1163, 2107, 5141 • Sainty, *Judges*, 97, 128

Archives Col. U., law school, Singleton MSS • Herts. ALS, corresp. with first Earl Cowper

Likenesses M. Dahl, oils, 1723, Lincoln's Inn, London [*see illus.*] • J. Faber jun., mezzotint, 1725 (after M. Dahl), BM, NPG

Wealth at death total legacies at least £3000; Burs estate approx. 110/120 acres, passed as part of a one third share: Lofft, 'Preface and account', xlii–xlv

Gilbert, John (*b.* 1658/9), Church of England clergyman, was the son of John Gilbert of Salisbury. He matriculated aged fifteen from Hart Hall, Oxford, on 9 April 1674, graduating BA in 1677 and proceeding MA in 1680. He was incorporated at Cambridge in 1687, following the publication the year before of his critique of Jean Bénigne Bossuet, *An answer to the bishop of Condom (now of Meaux), his exposition of the Catholic faith … wherein the doctrine of the Church of Rome is detected, and that of the Church of England expressed* (1686), with which was published 'Reflections on his pastoral letter'. In 1688 Gilbert became vicar of St John the Baptist, Peterborough. Two other works have been ascribed to him: *A Sermon on the Sin of Stealing Custom, and the Duty of Paying Tribute* (1699), which is almost certainly by a namesake with whom he has sometimes been confused, a prebendary of Exeter Cathedral (*d.* 1722), and, on no very clear grounds, *Reflections on Dr Fleetwood's essay upon miracles: shewing the absurdity, falshood and danger of his notions* (1706). Gilbert's date of death is as yet unknown.

J. M. RIGG, *rev.* CAROLINE L. LEACHMAN

Sources Wood, *Ath. Oxon.*, new edn, 4.794 • Wood, *Ath. Oxon.: Fasti* (1820), 360, 372 • Foster, *Alum. Oxon.*

Gilbert, John (1693–1761), archbishop of York, was born on 18 October 1693, and baptized on 24 October at Christ Church Greyfriars, London. He was the son of John Gilbert of London, a warehouse keeper for the East India Company, and his wife, Martha, and grandson of John Gilbert, fellow of Wadham College, Oxford, and prebend of Exeter. He was educated at Merchant Taylors' School, London, until 1712, then Magdalen Hall, Oxford, before migrating to Trinity College, where he graduated BA on 5 May 1715. He proceeded MA from Merton College on 1 February 1718 and was granted the degree of LLD at Lambeth on 8 January 1725. Gilbert married Margaret Sherard, daughter of Bennet Sherard of Whissendine, Rutland, and Dorothy, daughter of Henry, Lord Fairfax, and sister of Philip, second earl of Harborough, on 2 May 1726 at St James's, Westminster. They had one daughter, Emma.

He began his ecclesiastical career in the diocese of Exeter, being appointed to the chapter living of Ashburton in 1721. He became chaplain-in-ordinary to George I in the same year, probably through the influence of his bishop, Lancelot Blackburne, a favourite of the king. He then became rector of St Peter Tavy, and canon of Exeter in 1723 on the death of his grandfather, and subdean of Exeter on 24 June 1724, a post he vacated on being elected dean on 27 December 1726. In January 1726 he received a canonry of Christ Church from the crown, having narrowly failed to be selected as bishop of Chester despite the efforts of his patron, Blackburne, then archbishop of York. While visiting Christ Church in 1728 Gilbert drew attention to himself by riding 'with pistols, with holsters that would become a major-general' preceded by a black servant carrying a long gun (Portland MSS, 7.461).

Gilbert's promotion to the episcopal bench had been expected for some years: he had preached a very moving sermon for the king on Christmas day, 1737, following the death of Queen Caroline, and he was mentioned as a possible candidate for the bishoprics of Exeter and St Asaph before he became bishop of Llandaff on 28 December 1740. Viscount Percival had been convinced that Gilbert would be rewarded with a bishopric as he had behaved particularly graciously towards Mrs Skillet, Sir Robert Walpole's 'whore', and later wife, although earlier his 'obsequious behaviour' towards her had apparently given offence, as had his 'familiarity and jocular discourses with the nobility' (*Diary*, 2.250, 476). Gilbert retained the canonry of Christ Church *in commendam*. He was translated to Salisbury in October 1748, expressing delight at leaving his 'most disagreeable situation' at Llandaff (BL, Add. MS 32717, fol. 210). Apparently he had been made many promises of preferment, and had received many disappointments. Gilbert became the chancellor of the Order of the Garter in 1750, clerk of the closet in October 1752, and archbishop of York in 1757, the last on the express wishes of George II. He was also appointed lord high almoner at this time. According to Horace Walpole, Gilbert's promotion to York was so unpopular in the diocese that 'the bells were rung backwards in detestation of him' when they heard the news. However he 'opened a great table there, and within six months they thought him one of the most Christian prelates that had ever sat in that see' (Walpole, 2.245).

While at Salisbury, Gilbert was involved in a dispute with the mayor over the separate jurisdictions of city and cathedral. He refused to allow the mace to be carried before the mayor in the church precincts and was apparently involved in a scuffle with the mace-bearer on one occasion. Gilbert was also noted for introducing a new practice in confirmations, first recorded by Dr Thomas Newton at St Mary's, Nottingham. Instead of laying hands on two or four people and repeating the prayer over them,

> he went round the whole rail at once, laid hands upon the head of every person severally … then drew back to the Communion table, and in as audible and solemn manner as he could pronounced the prayer over them all.

This method 'commanded attention', 'raised devotion', and the ceremony was performed with more order and regularity (Newton, 2.105). This was an important consideration at this time as bishops frequently confirmed several thousands within a few weeks; in the first two weeks of August 1758 the bishop of St Asaph, Drummond, confirmed 15,000 people in the West Riding on Gilbert's behalf, as the latter was suffering from extremely painful feet and ankles.

As archbishop of York, Gilbert seems to have been concerned not to promote those with Methodist tendencies. He was also known not to favour those who were too forward in their applications to him. The Revd George Woodward of East Hendred, Wiltshire, wrote that 'he is a man not to be solicited too much, and I have heard him say, that he would never do anything sooner for being asked' (*Parson in the Vale*, 39). However, several of his relatives benefited from his patronage. Although Gilbert's contributions to the debates of the House of Lords are unknown, he was generally considered a government supporter. He did vote against the government, however, on the clause relating to episcopal orders in the bill for disarming the Scottish highlands in 1748, and he absented himself the day the vote on the Spirituous Liquors Act took place in February 1743, when all the bishops present voted against the government.

Views of Gilbert's character differ widely. Lord Egmont described him as having 'little learning, but great merit' (*Diary*, 2.476). Thomas Newton found him 'a kind friend and a generous patron' but with 'some appearance of haughtiness to others' (Newton, 2.105). Horace Walpole, noted for his acerbity, claimed Gilbert was 'composed of that common mixture of ignorance, meanness, and arrogance' (Walpole, 2.245). Another commentator decried Alexander Pope's description of Gilbert as 'leaden', 'since the unanimous opinion of all those, who recollect this Prelate, fully contradicts the splenetic poet's intimation' (Rastall, 328).

Gilbert's health was already failing by the time he was appointed to the archbishopric, and he 'rather languished than lived, through a pontificate of four years, when he sunk under a complication of infirmities' (Rastall, 328). He died at his house in Twickenham on 9 August 1761, attended by Thomas Newton, three days after his daughter was married there to George, third Baron Mount-Edgcumbe. He was probably buried at Grosvenor Chapel, South Audley Street, London. His wife had died many years earlier.

M. E. CLAYTON

Sources *IGI* • H. Walpole, *Memoirs of King George II*, ed. J. Brooke, 2 (1985), 245 • *Manuscripts of the earl of Egmont: diary of Viscount Percival, afterwards first earl of Egmont*, 3 vols., HMC, 63 (1920–23), vols. 1–2 • *Parson in the Vale of the White Horse: George Woodward's letters from East Hendred, 1753–61*, ed. D. Gibson (1982), 39, 97 • W. D. Rastall, *History of … Southwell in … Nottingham* (1787) • *The manuscripts of his grace the duke of Portland*, 10 vols., HMC, 29 (1891–1931), vol. 7 • N. Sykes, *Church and state in England in the XVIIIth century* (1935) • S. L. Ollard, 'Confirmation in the Anglican communion', *Confirmation, or, The laying on of hands*, 1 (1926), 60–245, esp. 226 • S. H. Cassan, *Lives and memoirs of the bishops of Sherborne and Salisbury, from the year 705 to 1824*, 3 (1824), 273–4 • C. J. Robinson, ed., *A register of the scholars admitted into Merchant Taylors' School, from AD 1562 to 1874*, 2 (1883), 6, appx 668 • Cobbett, *Parl. hist.*, 12.1426; 14.272 • Foster, *Alum. Oxon.* • BL, Add. MS 32717, fol. 210 • BL, Add. MS 32716, fols. 379–80 • BL, Add. MS 32721, fol. 109 • Herts. ALS, D/EP.F 259 • T. Newton, 'The life of Dr Thomas Newton', in L. Twells and S. Burdy, *The lives of Dr Edward Pocock … Dr Zachary Pearce … Dr Thomas Newton … and of the Rev. Philip Skelton*, 2 (1816), vol. 2 • *DNB* • *GM*, 1st ser., 31 (1761), 382

Archives Borth. Inst., corresp. and papers | BL, corresp. with duke of Newcastle, Add. MSS 32713–32872

Likenesses J. Wills, oils, *c*.1740–1749, Christ Church Oxf.; version, Bishopthorpe, York • portrait (in robes of chancellor of the order of the Garter), palace of Salisbury • portrait, Mount Edgcumbe House, Cornwall

Wealth at death £1000 in trust to faithful nurse; £100 to brother and sister: will, proved 18 Aug 1761; Cassan, *Lives and memoirs*

Gilbert, John (1812–1845), zoological collector and explorer in Australia, was born on 14 March 1812 in Newington Butts, London, the son of William Gilbert (*b*. *c*.1793), a carpenter, and his wife, Ann (*b*. *c*.1792); they were from villages in Kent just 3 miles apart. As a teenager Gilbert was apprenticed to John Gould (1804–1881), who was then employed as taxidermist to the Zoological Society of London but later became an illustrious publisher and bird artist. Gould taught him the principles of the art of taxidermy, a specialist skill of which he became a master. Very little is known about his private life; he seems to have married twice, to a widow, Catherine Alice Crump, on 6 September 1829, and to Esther Sadler on 29 November 1836. He may have had a daughter, though clear evidence of any offspring is lacking. He apparently had two younger brothers (William (*b*. 1813), and Thomas (*b*. 1818)) and a sister, possibly called Rachel.

Gilbert became the first curator of the Shrewsbury Museum in 1836, but was dismissed after only a few months for trying to install his wife in his rooms at the museum. After applying to his former employer for help he was hired as field assistant on Gould's much-heralded 1838 expedition to Australia. He soon proved his worth as a collector and naturalist. At first Gould and he worked together in Tasmania, but soon Gould became so sure of his capabilities that, in early 1839, Gilbert was sent on his own to Western Australia. He also collected on the Cobourg peninsula of Northern Territory, at that time a totally unexplored area, between 1840 and 1841.

In 1841 Gilbert returned to Britain, but such had been his success in Australia that Gould almost immediately sent him back. Gilbert worked his old patches in Western Australia for a time, having many adventures, such as nearly being shipwrecked on the notorious Houtman Abrolhos islands. He eventually moved on to New South

Wales, working his way overland to the lush Darling Downs of southern Queensland. Here he had a fateful encounter with the German explorer Ludwig Leichhardt. In October 1844 he joined Leichhardt's overland expedition from Brisbane to Port Essington (north of Darwin); after many trials and tribulations the party was ambushed by Aborigines at Dunbar Creek near Mitchell River, Cape York peninsula, on 28 June 1845, and Gilbert died almost instantly when a spear pierced an artery in his neck. He was buried at the scene of the attack the next day.

Gilbert collected more new species of Australian birds and mammals than any other collector, past or present. Of the 785 or so species of Australian birds or mammals that are known to exist, Gilbert was the first collector of fifty-nine (7.5 per cent). There are Gilbert specimens in museums all over the world, but the most important are in Liverpool, London, and Philadelphia. Among the many bird species he discovered were the paradise parrot, *Psephotus pulcherrimus*, which is now probably extinct; the Gouldian finch *Chloebia gouldiae*, possibly the most colourful bird in the world; and Gilbert's whistler (otherwise known as Gilbert's thickhead) *Pachycephala inornata gilbertii*, first collected by Gilbert in Western Australia. Of a long list of mammals which he discovered, perhaps the most appropriate to mention is Gilbert's rat-kangaroo *Potorous tridactylus gilbertii*, which was rediscovered at Two Peoples Bay in Western Australia in November 1994, after having been thought to be extinct since the 1870s. No photographs or pictures of Gilbert have been located, but he is said to have been short, dark, and spare; he was a good bushman, a crack shot, an excellent zoologist and taxidermist, and could turn a neat phrase with his pen. He seems to have been an industrious and efficient soul who did not suffer fools at all. CLEMENCY THORNE FISHER

Sources A. H. Chisholm, *Strange journey: the adventures of Ludwig Leichhardt and John Gilbert*, rev. edn (1973) • C. T. Fisher, 'The importance of early Victorian natural historians in the discovery and interpretation of the Australian fauna, with special reference to John Gilbert', PhD diss., CNAA/Liverpool Polytechnic, 1992 • A. H. Chisholm, 'The story of John Gilbert', *Emu*, 40 (1940), 156–76 • A. H. Chisholm, 'Birds of the Gilbert diary', *Emu*, 44 (1944), 131–50 • A. H. Chisholm, 'Birds of the Gilbert diary', *Emu*, 45 (1945), 183–200 • H. M. Whittell, 'The visit of John Gilbert to the Swan river colony', *Western Australia Historical Society*, 4/1 (1949), 23–53 • H. M. Whittell, *The literature of Australian birds: a history and a bibliography of Australian ornithology* (1954) • H. S. Torrens, 'John Gilbert (1812–1845) … New light on his work in England', *Archives of Natural History*, 14 (1987), 211–9 • G. C. Sauer, *John Gould the bird man: a chronology and bibliography* (1982) • H. J. Frith and J. H. Calaby, eds., *Fauna survey of the Port Essington district* (1974), 28.1–19 • parish register (baptism), 25 Oct 1812, Clerkenwell, Lady Huntingdon's Chapel, PRO, RG4/4171 • parish register, London, St Leonards, 6 Sept 1829, GL [marriage] • parish register (marriage), 29 Nov 1836, London, St Dunstan and All Saints, Stepney • journal of Ludwig Leichhardt, Mitchell L., NSW

Archives Mitchell L., NSW • Queensland Museum Library, Brisbane | CUL, Gould MSS • Liverpool Central Library, thirteenth earl of Derby MSS • Mitchell L., NSW, Gould and Leichhardt MSS • National Museum and Galleries of Merseyside, thirteenth earl of Derby • NHM, Gould MSS

Wealth at death £100: administration, PRO, PROB 6/223, fols. 1–99

Gilbert, Sir John (1817–1897), illustrator and painter, was born on 21 July 1817 at Blackheath, London, one of six children of George Felix Gilbert, a retired militiaman and a land and estate agent, and his wife, Elizabeth. Upon leaving school in 1833 Gilbert took a position in the firm of Dickson and Bell, estate agents in Charlotte Row. He had little interest in being a clerk and spent much of his time sketching the colourful spectacle of city life continuously unfolding outside his office window. Military displays, fashionable coaches, and the showy costumes of the populace captured his fancy and provided him with a wealth of motifs that served him throughout his artistic career. After two undistinguished years as a clerk Gilbert's parents allowed him to pursue a career as an artist. Failing to enter the classes of the Royal Academy, he was largely self-taught, taking only a few lessons from the still-life painter George Lance. He became skilled in a variety of techniques, but was most proficient in drawing on paper and wood, watercolours, and oil painting, earning considerable recognition in these fields during his long career.

Gilbert first exhibited his work in 1836, sending a watercolour, *The Arrest of Lord Hastings*, to the Society of British Artists. This was followed in 1837 by two oil paintings at the British Institution. In all he exhibited sixty oils at these venues, most of them depicting historical and literary subjects. Gilbert also exhibited at the Royal Academy from 1838 to 1851, when he stopped because his pictures were badly hung. The organization with which he became most closely associated was the Old Watercolour Society. On 9 February 1852 Gilbert was elected an associate and on 12 June 1854 he became a full member. He remained connected to that institution until his death, exhibiting approximately 270 works in the society's gallery, including numerous themes from *Don Quixote* and the works of Shakespeare. He was instrumental in the inauguration of regular winter exhibitions there in 1862, and in June 1871 was elected its president. Soon thereafter, on 14 March 1872, Gilbert was given a knighthood, which both honoured his own achievements and indicated royal recognition of watercolour's importance as a branch of art.

Gilbert's professional advancement continued in the ensuing years. On 29 January 1872 he was elected an associate of the Royal Academy, having begun sending his paintings there again in 1867 after a sixteen-year break. On 29 June 1876 he was made a full academician; his diploma picture was *Richard II Resigning the Crown to Bolingbroke* (Walker Art Gallery, Liverpool). He contributed more than fifty works to Royal Academy exhibitions throughout his career, including *Fair St. George* (exh. RA, 1881; Guildhall Art Gallery, London) and *Ego et rex meus* (exh. RA, 1889; Guildhall Art Gallery, London). In 1878 he sent *Doge and Senators of Venice* to the Universal Exhibition in Paris, where it was highly regarded and secured for Gilbert the Légion d'honneur.

Gilbert worked assiduously at history painting, longing to earn acclaim in this most prestigious art, but his primary occupation during these years was in the more remunerative fields of book illustration and pictorial journalism. Encouraged by William Mulready, who had

Sir John Gilbert (1817–1897), self-portrait, 1892

seen great promise in the twenty-year-old's pen-and-ink drawings, Gilbert worked steadily as an illustrator, beginning in 1838 with a book of nursery rhymes. In addition to illustrating many editions of English poets, including Longfellow (1858), Scott (1857), Wordsworth (1859), and Milton (1864), he illustrated religious and literary works such as *The Pilgrim's Progress* (1860), and *Don Quixote* (1872).

It was Gilbert's association with Shakespeare that earned him his greatest fame as an illustrator. Howard Staunton's impressive edition of Shakespeare, issued in three volumes in 1860, contains 829 designs by Gilbert, many depicting scenes never before illustrated. His original blocks for this work, now in the print room of the British Museum, were engraved by the Dalziel brothers. Gilbert also expressed his passion for Shakespeare in a large, multi-figured oil on canvas called *The Plays of William Shakespeare* (exh. British Institution, 1850; Dahesh Museum of Art, New York).

Gilbert supplied numerous wood-engraved illustrations to periodicals such as the *London Journal*, *Punch*, and the *Leisure Hour*, but it was his vast contribution to the *Illustrated London News*—approximately 30,000 drawings over a period of thirty years—that ensured his place among the originators of pictorial journalism. His association with the *Illustrated London News* began with the first issue in May 1842, which contained eight engravings of guests at a Buckingham Palace ball. Gilbert's love of pageantry, pomp, and picturesque costumes came to the fore in such designs, and the quickness and ease with which he executed them became legendary. It is an oft-repeated anecdote that Gilbert was able to compose and draw directly on the woodblock—with no preliminary sketches—any subject his editor requested in about an hour while a messenger waited.

In 1885, perhaps to avoid the embarrassment of his decreasing popularity and prices, Gilbert resolved no longer to sell his work. He announced in April 1893 that he was presenting a collection of his pictures to the nation. This major gift was divided between the municipal galleries of London, Birmingham, Liverpool, and Manchester. In recognition, Gilbert was given the freedom of the City of London, the first artist to be so honoured. He also gave a collection of his sketchbooks to the Royal Academy.

Gilbert died, an avowed bachelor, at his home, Ivy House, Vanbrugh Park in Blackheath, London, where he lived his entire life, on 5 October 1897 and was buried in Lewisham cemetery. Although his oil paintings and watercolours are characterized by lively colour and well-handled groups of figures, he did not explore the artistic possibilities of this medium or make bold compositional choices. His main interest was narrative, which certainly explains his great success as an illustrator. Indeed, Gilbert is remembered primarily as an incredibly fertile illustrator, whose naturalistic, sketchy, and spirited designs captured both the elevated realm of poetry and the everyday world of the popular press. LISA SMALL

Sources M. H. Spielmann, 'Sir John Gilbert: a memorial sketch', *Magazine of Art*, 22 (1897–8), 53–64 · R. Davies, 'Sir John Gilbert', *Old Water-Colour Society's Club*, 10 (1932–3), 20–43 · 'Sir John Gilbert's gift to the City of London', *Art Journal*, new ser., 13 (1893), 199–200 · R. Ormond, 'Victorian story-teller in paint: Sir John Gilbert', *Country Life*, 140 (1966), 400–03 · R. Ormond, 'Private life of a Victorian painter', *Country Life*, 140 (1966), 462–5 · *DNB* · *CGPLA Eng. & Wales* (1897)

Archives Greenwich Local History Library, London, corresp. and receipts · Lewisham Library, London, Lewisham Local Studies Centre, corresp., family papers, etc. · priv. coll., diaries | BL, corresp. with A. D. Fripp, Add. MS 46445

Likenesses H. Nelson O'Neil, group portrait, oils, 1869 (*The billiard room of the Garrick Club*), Garr. Club · J. Gilbert, self-portrait, oils, 1892, Guildhall Art Gallery, London [*see illus.*] · Cundall, Downes & Co., photograph, carte-de-visite, NPG · H. Furniss, caricature, pen-and-ink sketch, NPG · Lock & Whitfield, photograph, woodburytype, NPG; repro. in T. Cooper and others, *Men of mark: a gallery of contemporary portraits*, 2 (1877) · Smeeton and Tilly, woodcut (after A. Gilbert), BM, NPG; repro. in *L'Art* (1875) · W. Walker & Sons, carte-de-visite, NPG · J. & C. Watkins, photograph, carte-de-visite, NPG · wood-engraving (after photograph by J. Watkins), NPG; repro. in *ILN* (16 March 1872) · woodcuts, BM, NPG

Wealth at death £231,928 6*s.* 9*d.*: probate, 30 Dec 1897, *CGPLA Eng. & Wales*

Gilbert, John Graham (1794–1866), painter and art collector, was born John Graham in Glasgow on 26 March 1794, the son of David Graham (1761/2–1827), a West India merchant, and Agnes McAslan (*b.* 1767). He attended the grammar school in Glasgow and worked with his father for a short period before moving to London in 1818 to train as an artist at the Royal Academy Schools. In 1819 he was awarded the first silver medal for the best drawing from the antique, and he received the gold medal for historical painting two years later. In London he established himself as a portrait painter, and sent 'fancy' subjects and portraits to the Royal Academy's exhibitions from 1820 to

1823, and exhibited at the Glasgow Institution for Promoting and Encouraging the Fine Arts in 1821 and 1822. He spent two years in Italy where he studied and copied old masters and was particularly influenced by the Venetian school. In 1827 he returned to Scotland and lived in Edinburgh, contributing works to the Institution for the Encouragement of the Fine Arts, and the Scottish Academy, with which he was involved, and where he was elected academician in 1829. He also exhibited at the Glasgow Dilettanti Society's exhibitions from its foundation in 1828 and became an extraordinary member of the society in 1829. A major exhibition of 103 of his pictures was held at the society's rooms in 1833 and consisted of portraits, 'fancy subjects', history paintings, and a landscape painted in 1816.

On 9 September 1834 Graham married Jane Gilbert (*d.* 1877), a wealthy Glasgow heiress, and they moved to Glasgow. She inherited her uncle's Yorkhill estate, to the west of the city, in 1838 and the terms of the settlement required him to assume the surname of Graham Gilbert.

Graham Gilbert's most notable work was done in portraiture although he was known to prefer subject and 'fancy' pictures, in particular those of beautiful young women portrayed as peasants or Gypsies in Scottish, Italian, and Greek country dress. He made a number of copies after the old masters including Correggio's *Madonna della Scodella* (Glasgow Art Gallery and Museum). His sitters encompassed a cross-section of predominantly Scottish society from scientists and professors, writers and artists, to the aristocracy, businessmen, industrialists, and politicians. The Royal Society of Edinburgh commissioned him to paint *Sir Walter Scott* (1829; Royal Society of Edinburgh) and he retained a replica which his widow presented to the National Portrait Gallery in London in 1867. Other sitters included the chemist Thomas Graham (1837; University of Strathclyde), Archibald McLellan the coach builder and founder of Glasgow's civic art collection (1839; Trades' Hall, Glasgow) and fellow artists John Gibson (1847; National Gallery of Scotland, Edinburgh), described as 'intimately conceived and subtly characterised' (Caw, 87), and Sir John Watson Gordon (1854; Scottish National Portrait Gallery, Edinburgh). His reputation as a portrait painter is considered to rest on his portrayal of women such as Anne Scott (1828; Abbotsford, Roxburghshire), Sir Walter's daughter, and Mrs James Scott of Kelly (1850; Glasgow Art Gallery and Museum). His handling of rich fabrics and textures is sensual but, as in many of his male portraits, the underlying structure can appear weak.

Graham Gilbert formed a particularly fine collection of Dutch, Flemish, and Italian old masters including Rembrandt's *A Man in Armour*, *Nature Adorned by the Graces*, by Rubens and Jan Brueghel the elder, and Giovanni Bellini's *Madonna with the Child Blessing*. They were bequeathed to the city of Glasgow in 1877 by his widow and are now in Glasgow Art Gallery and Museum, Kelvingrove, along with some of his copies of the old masters, 'fancy' and biblical subjects, and the life-size statue of him by William Brodie which Jane Graham Gilbert presented in 1870.

John Graham Gilbert was closely involved with Glasgow's art life and co-founded the West of Scotland Academy of the Fine Arts, which mounted its first annual exhibition in 1841; he was its president and a regular exhibitor. He was a trustee of the Glasgow Government School of Design when it opened in 1845, and on the general council of the Glasgow Institute of the Fine Arts at its creation in 1861. In 1857 he was appointed an extraordinary director of the Union Bank of Scotland and the following year a trustee of the Andersonian University, the precursor of Strathclyde University in Glasgow. He narrowly lost the election to the presidency of the Royal Scottish Academy in 1864. He died of heart disease at Yorkhill on 4 June 1866 and was buried at the Glasgow necropolis on 8 June. One biographer commented that many who met him saw:

> the modest diffidence that characterized him in public, give way to the brightened eye and the earnest voice with which he would discourse of his art, point out the beauties of his gallery, or tell of some acquisition at Christie's, or urge some plan, as he was ever doing, for the happiness of those he loved. (Mitchell and others, 148)

Examples of his work are in Glasgow Art Gallery and Museum, the Hunterian Art Gallery, University of Glasgow, the Royal Scottish Academy, the National Galleries of Scotland, Edinburgh City Art Centre, and the National Trust for Scotland.

R. E. Graves, *rev.* George Fairfull Smith

Sources *Glasgow Herald* (5 June 1866) • *Art Journal*, 28 (1866), 217 • [J. O. Mitchell, J. Guthrie Smith, and others], 'John Graham Gilbert, RSA', *Memoirs and portraits of one hundred Glasgow men who have died during the last thirty years*, ed. J. MacLehose, 1 (1886), 145–8 • *Catalogue of Mr Graham's pictures, Glasgow 1833* (1833) [exhibition catalogue, Dilettanti Society, Glasgow, March 1833] • *Catalogue of oil paintings forming the Graham-Gilbert bequest to the corporation of Glasgow*, Glasgow Corporation Galleries of Art (1877) • W. Roberts, *Six pictures by John Graham-Gilbert, RSA* (c.1921) • W. D. McKay, *The Scottish school of painting* (1906) • J. L. Caw, *Scottish painting past and present, 1620–1908* (1908) • Graves, *RA exhibitors* • W. D. McKay and F. Rinder, *The Royal Scottish Academy, 1826–1916* (1917) • C. B. de Laperriere, ed., *The Royal Scottish Academy exhibitors, 1826–1990*, 4 vols. (1991), vol. 2 • R. Billcliffe, ed., *The Royal Glasgow Institute of the Fine Arts, 1861–1989: a dictionary of exhibitors at the annual exhibitions*, 4 vols. (1990–92), vol. 2 • C. Waterson, *The Royal Society of Edinburgh portrait prowl* (1997) • private information (2004) [family] • D. Irwin and F. Irwin, *Scottish painters at home and abroad, 1700–1900* (1975) • Glasgow town council minutes, 1867, Mitchell L., Glas. • Glasgow town council minutes, 1870, Mitchell L., Glas. • E. Gordon, *The Royal Scottish Academy of painting, sculpture and architecture, 1826–1976* (1976) • *IGI* • *CGPLA Eng. & Wales* (1866)

Archives Royal Scot. Acad., corresp. | University of Strathclyde, Glasgow, Dilettanti Society corresp.

Likenesses Tonney?, photograph, c.1854, Royal Scot. Acad. • W. Brodie, marble relief on monument, c.1867, Glasgow necropolis • W. Brodie, marble statue, 1870?, Glasgow Art Gallery and Museum • A. Edouart, silhouette, Scot. NPG • J. Graham Gilbert, self-portrait, oils, Royal Scot. Acad. • Maclure & Macdonald, engraving (after photograph), repro. in MacLehose, ed., *Memoirs and portraits*, vol. 1 • photograph, Royal Scot. Acad.

Wealth at death £83,090 17*s.* 1*d.*: confirmation, 2 July 1866, NA Scot., SC 36/48/55/710–716

Gilbert, Sir John Thomas (1829–1898), historian and antiquary, was born at 23 Jervis Street, Dublin, on 23 January

Sir John Thomas Gilbert (1829–1898), by unknown photographer

1829, the son of John Gilbert (*d.* 1833), an English protestant of Devon origin, who had established himself in Dublin in the Spanish wine trade, and who for many years held the post of consul at Dublin for Portugal and Algarve. Gilbert's mother Eleanor, daughter of Henry Costello of Dublin, was an Irish Roman Catholic, who brought up her son in her own communion. His childhood was spent for the most part at Branackstown, co. Meath, where he acquired a deep love of nature. He was educated at St Vincent's Seminary, Usher's Quay, Dublin, Bective College, Dublin, and Prior Park College, near Bath.

Gilbert showed an early interest in antiquarianism. In 1851 he contributed to the *Irish Quarterly Review* an essay entitled 'Historical literature of Ireland', which was followed in 1852, by 'The streets of Dublin'. The latter work, which was expanded into his well-known *History of the City of Dublin*, published in 1861, became the main printed source of information on the topography of the city, and won for him the Cunningham gold medal of the Royal Irish Academy in 1862.

In 1855 Gilbert became, in conjunction with James Henthorn Todd, honorary secretary to the Irish Celtic and Archaeological Society. In the work of this society he associated with an eminent group of students of Irish antiquities, which included such men as Sir William Wilde, Eugene O'Curry, John O'Donovan George Petrie, Charles Graves (afterwards bishop of Limerick), and Sir Thomas Larcom. According to Graves (as quoted in an obituary of Gilbert in the *Proceedings of the Royal Irish Academy*) it was mainly owing 'to the exertions of the two secretaries … that that society was for many years able to continue its publication of various works of the utmost importance in the history of Ireland'.

In 1863 Gilbert published a series of papers under the *nom de plume*, 'an Irish archivist', in which he called attention to the defects in the treatment of Irish historical documents in the *Calendars of Patent and Close Rolls of Chancery in Ireland*, published under the authority of the Treasury. His campaign for archival professionalism led to the setting up of a small but high-powered committee of inquiry by the Treasury. The legitimacy of Gilbert's criticisms was indirectly acknowledged by his association shortly afterwards with Sir Thomas Duffus Hardy in organizing the new Public Record Office at Dublin. On the constitution of this office in 1867 Gilbert was, with the general approval of the public, appointed secretary, and he retained this post until 1875, when it was abolished.

Gilbert's works as a historian, *History of Dublin* (3 vols., 1854–9) and *History of the Viceroys of Ireland* (1865), have retained only limited value, but his achievements as archivist and editor have endured. From the mid-1860s he committed himself to editing a large number of manuscript sources for Irish history, producing works including *Facsimiles of the National Manuscripts of Ireland* (5 vols., 1874–84), *Documents Relating to Ireland, 1795–1804* (1893), and the seven-volume *History of the Irish Confederation* (1882–91), used by W. E. Gladstone. Although his work was not free from error, its value has been acknowledged by succeeding generations of historians of Ireland.

A considerable part of Gilbert's time was given to the affairs of the Royal Irish Academy, of which he became a member in 1855, and was for more than thirty-four years librarian. At his suggestion the council of the academy began the publication, under his editorship, of their collection of ancient Irish manuscripts. He also acted for many years as an inspector under the Historical Manuscripts Commission, reporting on many public and private collections, and editing for that commission some of the papers of the marquess of Ormond. He also edited for the corporation of Dublin the valuable *Calendar of Ancient Records of Dublin* (7 vols., 1889–98), which had reached the year 1730 at the time of his death.

Gilbert held many honorary offices of public trust, such as the vice-presidency of the Royal Irish Academy. In 1880 he became a trustee of the National Library of Ireland. The Royal University conferred on him the honorary degree of LLD in 1892. In 1897 he was knighted. Gilbert's life for nearly fifty years was passed at his house, Villa Nova, Blackrock, near Dublin, where he formed a unique collection of Irish historical and archaeological works; after his death this was acquired by the corporation of Dublin.

Gilbert married, in 1891, Rosa, second daughter of Joseph Stevenson Mulholland MD, of Belfast, who survived him; they had no children. He died on 23 May 1898 in Dublin, of heart failure.

C. L. Falkiner, *rev.* Colm Lennon

Sources *Proceedings of the Royal Irish Academy*, 3rd ser., 5 (1898–1900), 309–12 [minutes] · D. Hyde and D. J. O'Donoghue, *Catalogue of the books and manuscripts comprising the library of the late Sir John*

T. Gilbert (1918) • G. Ó Dúill, 'Sir John Gilbert and archival reform', *Dublin Historical Record*, 30/4 (1976–7), 136–42 • R. M. Gilbert, *Life of Sir John T. Gilbert* (1905)

Archives Gilbert Library, Dublin • NL Ire., corresp., papers, and transcripts • PRO, corresp. as an HMC inspector, HMC 1 | University College, Dublin, letters to D. J. O'Donoghue

Likenesses J. Lavery, portrait, 1910, NG Ire. • photograph, NPG [*see illus.*]

Wealth at death £2046 3s.: probate, 7 July 1898, *CGPLA Eng. & Wales*

Gilbert, Joseph (1732?–1820/21), seaman and hydrographer, was baptized on 1 June 1732 in Kirton in Holland, near Boston, Lincolnshire, the eighth and youngest child of John Gilbert (*bap.* 1697, *d.* 1782), farmer, and his wife, Elizabeth (*bap.* 1695, *d.* 1759), daughter of Thomas and Elizabeth Armstrong of Bicker. Nothing is known of Gilbert's early life, except that soon after he was born his father moved from Kirton to Freiston, about 6 miles to the north-east. On 16 November 1758 at Freiston he married Frances Plant (*d.* 1784).

It is not known at what age Gilbert went to sea, but from 1764 to 1769 he was master of HMS *Guernsey* (32 guns), one of the ships engaged under Hugh Palliser in the hydrographical survey of the coasts of Newfoundland and Labrador which consolidated the reputation of James Cook and which for over a century served as a model of hydrographical accuracy under the most adverse conditions. Gilbert River and Gilbert Lake in Labrador (lat. 52°41′N, long. 56°10′W) still bear witness to Gilbert's part in this great work; some of his charts, together with those of Cook, Michael Lane, and others, were engraved and published by Thomas Jefferys, later reappearing in *The North American Pilot* (1775).

Gilbert subsequently became master of HMS *Pearl* (32 guns), in which he surveyed Plymouth Sound in 1769 (BL, Maps M.T.11.h.1(8)), and of HMS *Asia* (64 guns), until at the unusually advanced age of forty he was selected by Cook to serve as master of the *Resolution* on his second great Pacific voyage (1772–5). Cook thought highly of Gilbert both as a seaman and as a surveyor and draughtsman, paying tribute particularly to his judgement ('whose judgement and assiduity in this [surveying] as well as every other branch of his profession is exceeded by none'; letter to Philip Stephens, secretary to the Admiralty, 22 March 1775; PRO, ADM 1/1610) and named after him Gilbert Isle (lat. 55°20′S, long. 71°15′W), a small island off Tierra del Fuego, 'the most desolate coast I ever saw' (*Journals*, 2.589–90), although a compliment was presumably intended. During the voyage, Gilbert produced not only a terse log (PRO, ADM 55/107), but many finely executed charts, as well as a number of charming watercolour drawings and perspective views. Perhaps the most vivid is on the largest scale, a chart of the Pacific and Southern oceans showing the track of the *Resolution* (NMM, G201, 3/4 (HO A859)), but Gilbert's charts of Table Bay and Dusky Sound (PRO, ADM 55/107) are better evidence of his skill as a hydrographer.

On his return to England, Gilbert was rewarded with the gift of Cook's watch and, on the recommendation of Palliser, with the position of master attendant at Sheerness Dockyard, whence he soon moved, briefly to Woolwich, and then to the more prestigious equivalent position at Portsmouth, where he served from 1776 to 1791. This was a period of great change and modernization in the dockyards and Gilbert earned praise from the controller of the navy, Sir Henry Martin, for his 'diligence and activity' (NMM, Portsmouth Dockyard records F/18, 1783). His last post, a promotion, was as master attendant at Deptford from 1791 until 1803. He then retired, with his unmarried daughter Frances (*b.* 1764), to Fareham, Hampshire. Surviving letters of this period show him as a touchingly humble man in affectionate awe of his learned nephew, the Congregational minister Revd Joseph Gilbert.

Joseph and Frances Gilbert had at least four children, all born in Freiston. Two further children, Matthew and Barzena, born to Frances in 1774 and 1775 while her husband was in the south seas were illegitimate. Gilbert's eldest child, George (1759–1786), sailed with Cook on his third voyage and produced a journal (now in BL, Add. MS 38530) which supplements that of Cook himself; having served as a lieutenant in the West Indies, he died of smallpox on the threshold of a promising naval career. Joseph Gilbert's second son, Richard (1767–1845), also entered the navy, apparently retiring as a post captain; Richard Gilbert's daughter Emma married the writer John Doran. Joseph Gilbert died, a man of modest affluence, probably at Fareham, aged eighty-eight or eighty-nine, and was buried at Fareham on 20 January 1821. ROBIN TAYLOR GILBERT

Sources A. David, R. Joppien, and B. Smith, eds., *The charts and coastal views of Captain Cook's voyages*, 2: *The voyage of the Resolution and Adventure, 1772–1775* (1992) • T. Jefferys, *A collection of charts of the coasts of Newfoundland and Labradore drawn from the original surveys taken by James Cook and Michael Lane, surveyors, Joseph Gilbert, and other officers in the king's service* (1770) • T. Jefferys, *The North American pilot for Newfoundland, Labradore, the Gulf and River St Lawrence drawn from original surveys taken by James Cook and Michael Lane, surveyors, and Joseph Gilbert* (1775) • R. J. B. Knight, *Portsmouth dockyard papers, 1774–1783: the American war* (1987) • *The journals of Captain James Cook*, ed. J. C. Beaglehole, 4 vols. in 5, Hakluyt Society, extra ser., 34a, 35, 36a–b, 37 (1955–74), vols. 2–3 • J. A. Rupert-Jones, 'Five fellow workers of Captain Cook', *N&Q*, 152 (1927), 111–15 • parish registers of Aswarby, Bicker, Kirton in Holland, and Freiston, Lincolnshire, and of Fareham, Hampshire • *GM*, 1st ser., 56 (1786), 352 [George Gilbert] • unpublished correspondence, priv. coll. • private information (2004) • J. C. Beaglehole, *The life of Captain James Cook* (1974) • 'Doran, John', *DNB* • will, PRO, PROB 11/1639

Archives BL, Add. MSS 15500, 38530, Maps M.T.11.h.1 • PRO, MSS, ADM 55/107, 1/1610 | NMM, Portsmouth dockyard records, F/18; G201, 3/4 (H.O. A859)

Wealth at death see will, PRO, PROB. 11/1639

Gilbert, Joseph (1779–1852), Congregational minister, born in the parish of Wrangle, Lincolnshire, on 20 March 1779, was son of John Gilbert, a farmer who had come under the influence of John Wesley, and his wife, Sarah. After receiving some education at a free school on the boundaries of the parishes of Wrangle and Leake, he was apprenticed to a general shopkeeper at Burgh. On the expiration of his term he became assistant in a shop at East Retford, Nottinghamshire, of which he eventually became proprietor. Here he began to associate with a small body of Congregationalists, for whom he sometimes preached.

On 7 May 1800 he married Sarah Chapman, daughter of a surgeon from Burgh. Following her death he married, on 24 December 1813, Ann (1782–1866), daughter of Isaac Taylor of Ongar, with whom he had several children including the agricultural chemist Sir Joseph Henry *Gilbert. Ann *Gilbert [*see under* Taylor, Jane] was well known as the author of poetry for children.

In 1806 Gilbert gave up business and entered Rotherham Independent college. In 1808, at the request of Dr Edward Williams, its principal, he published his first book, a reply to a work by William Bennet, entitled *Remarks on a recent hypothesis respecting the origin of moral evil, in a series of letters to the Rev. Dr Williams, the author of that hypothesis*. His college course finished, he became minister at Southend, Essex. After a residence of eighteen months there he was appointed classical tutor in Rotherham College. On 8 December 1818 he was ordained pastor of the Nether Chapel, Sheffield, still retaining his tutorship, spending Sundays and Mondays in Sheffield and the rest of the week at Rotherham. In July 1817 he became minister of Fish Street Chapel, Hull, and in November 1825 moved to James Street Chapel, Nottingham. A new meeting-house was built for him in April 1828 in Friar Lane, Nottingham. In London in 1835 he delivered the course of Congregational lectures by which he became best-known, entitled *The Christian atonement, its basis, nature, and bearings, or, The principle of substitution illustrated as applied in the redemption of man* (1836). He continued his work until November 1851, when he resigned his charge owing to poor health, and he died at St James's Street, Nottingham, on Sunday 12 December 1852. He was buried in Nottingham. The following year his widow published a biographical sketch of Gilbert, to which one of his sons contributed recollections of Gilbert's later sermons.

THOMAS HAMILTON, *rev.* J. M. V. QUINN

Sources A. Gilbert, *A biographical sketch of the Rev. Joseph Gilbert* (1853) • d. cert. • *IGI*

Likenesses M. Gauci, lithograph, pubd 1833 (after T. Barber), BM • J. Cochran, stipple (after J. Gilbert), NPG • I. Taylor, miniature, priv. coll.

Gilbert, Joseph Francis (1792–1855), landscape painter, was the second son of Edward Gilbert, 'an inventor of several ingenious plans for firing bombs' (*Art Journal*, 305). Gilbert pursued his interest in art amid family difficulties and by 1813 he lived at 137 High Street, Portsmouth, from where he exhibited *Landscape and Figures* at the Royal Academy, and in the following year, *The Rustic Traveller Crossing the Style*. Subsequently he moved to Sussex, and resided for many years at Chichester. He continued to exhibit at the British Institution, the Society of British Artists in Suffolk Street, and at the Royal Manchester Institution. He primarily painted the scenery of Sussex, although occasionally he worked in other areas such as Wales and the Lake District. Some of his works were up to 6 feet long, and many were engraved, including two views reproduced in the *Art Union* in its prize annual, and *A View of the Ruins of Cowdray* by T. Clark. The fifth duke of Richmond was a patron, for whom work included scenes from his racecourse such as *Priam Winning the Gold Cup* and *The Goodwood Race-Course*. In 1847 he was a competitor at the Westminster Hall exhibition with an oil painting, *Edwin and Emma*, from a poem by Mallet. He died on 25 September 1855, at 17 Hoptons almshouses, Green Walk, Southwark, London.

L. H. CUST, *rev.* L. R. HOULISTON

Sources M. H. Grant, *A dictionary of British landscape painters, from the 16th century to the early 20th century* (1952) • *Art Journal*, 17 (1855), 305 • Redgrave, *Artists* • T. Smith, *Recollections of the British Institution for Promoting the Fine Arts in the United Kingdom* (1860) • Bryan, *Painters* • Thieme & Becker, *Allgemeines Lexikon* • Bénézit, *Dict.* • Wood, *Vic. painters*, 3rd edn • J. Johnson, ed., *Works exhibited at the Royal Society of British Artists, 1824–1893, and the New English Art Club, 1888–1917*, 2 vols. (1975) • Graves, *Brit. Inst.* • Graves, *RA exhibitors* • Graves, *Artists* • *Checklist of British artists in the Witt Library*, Courtauld Institute, Witt Library (1991) • D. T. Mallett, *Mallett's index of artists* (1935) • d. cert. • *The Post Office London directory* (1842)

Gilbert, Sir Joseph Henry (1817–1901), agricultural chemist, was born on 1 August 1817, in Hull, Yorkshire, one of the seven children of Joseph *Gilbert, Congregationalist minister, and his wife, Ann *Gilbert, known as Ann Taylor (1782–1866) [*see under* Taylor, Jane], a successful children's writer. In 1825 the family moved to Nottingham where Gilbert spent his childhood. In 1832 he suffered a gunshot accident which caused the loss of one eye and severely impaired vision in the other. He was educated privately and at Mr Long's school in Mansfield.

In 1838 Gilbert entered the University of Glasgow, specializing in analytic chemistry under Professor Thomas Thomson. This was followed by a period (1839–40) at University College, London, where he probably met his later associate John Bennet Lawes (1814–1900), heir to the manor of Rothamsted (near Harpenden, Hertfordshire). In the summer of 1840 he worked in the laboratory of Justus Liebig in Giessen, where he was awarded a PhD. Among his fellow students at Giessen were Lyon Playfair and Augustus Voelcker. Returning to London, Gilbert became an assistant to Anthony Todd Thomson at University College (1840–41) before moving to the Manchester area to work on the chemistry of calico printing and dyeing.

On 1 June 1843 Gilbert took up an appointment at Lawes's agricultural estate at Rothamsted, where he was to help set up and supervise an experimental programme on crop and animal nutrition. He and Lawes used the results of their experiments to show that plants, other than legumes, required a supply of nitrate and ammonium ions in the soil. This position was diametrically opposed to Liebig's view that plants acquired their nitrogen directly from the atmosphere. Liebig kept up a long (twenty years) and frequently acrimonious debate with Gilbert and Lawes on this issue in published papers and pamphlets. Later however, Liebig conceded that Gilbert and Lawes's well-marshalled case for nitrogenous fertilizers was correct. The Rothamsted programme of research was also used to make the case for applying generous amounts of readily available phosphorus and potassium to the frequently impoverished soils of nineteenth-century England. This led to another controversy with Liebig, who had declared that it was only necessary to replace the amounts removed in the harvested crops. The vigour with which these disputes were pursued was partly due to their immediately practical economic consequences for farmers, who needed to decide on the type of fertilizers to use; both Liebig and Lawes held patents on fertilizing products.

In August 1850 Gilbert married Eliza Forbes Laurie, daughter of George Laurie. She died on 15 February 1853. On 2 October 1855 he married Maria Smith of Heyford, daughter of Benjamin Smith. There were no children from either marriage.

Gilbert's association with Lawes, which lasted for fifty-seven years, was one of the longest and most productive scientific partnerships on record. Their experiments demonstrated that crop productivity could be maintained by either organic manures or chemical fertilizers but that the latter would be needed to maintain a food supply for the increasing population of the late 1800s. Equally important was their finding that the source of fat in animals was carbohydrate in the diet. In agricultural circles their names are for ever linked. Though Lawes was the more practical agriculturalist, the quality of the experimental results owed much to Gilbert. Everything he undertook was performed with scrupulous accuracy and attention to detail. He kept up his interest in the experiments even in old age; he and Lawes were still publishing papers on their results in the late 1890s.

Gilbert was a member of many learned societies both at home and overseas. He joined the Chemical Society in 1841 and was its president in 1882–3. He was elected a fellow of the Royal Society in 1860, was awarded its royal medal in 1867, and served on its council in 1886–8. In 1883 he was elected an honorary member of the Royal Agricultural Society, in whose journal many of the results of the Rothamsted experiments were published. From 1884 to 1890 he was Sibthorpian professor of rural economy at the University of Oxford. In 1893, the fiftieth year of the Rothamsted experiments, he was knighted, and in the same year he lectured on them at the Chicago Exhibition. In the following year he (together with Lawes) received the Albert gold medal of the Royal Society of Arts. He was awarded honorary degrees by the universities of Glasgow (1883), Oxford (1884), Edinburgh (1890), and Cambridge (1894).

Eight of the experiments that the two men started between 1843 and 1856 were still running 150 years later. With many of the original treatments unaltered, they were then the oldest continuous agricultural experiments in the world, and were still providing unrivalled practical and scientific information for both agriculture and ecology. Most probably on Gilbert's insistence, samples of crops and soils from these experiments were collected and stored; these form the basis for a unique scientific archive of samples which stretches back over 150 years, and is of great value for agricultural and ecological research. Gilbert died at West Common, Harpenden, on 23 December 1901 and was buried in the churchyard there. His second wife, who survived him, was granted a civil-list pension of £100 in 1904.

ERNEST CLARKE, *rev.* A. E. JOHNSTON

Sources *Journal of the Royal Agricultural Society of England*, 62 (1901), 347–55 • *PRS*, 85, 236–42 • J. A. V., *JCS*, 81 (1902), 625–8 • *Nature*, 65 (1901–2), 205–6 • A. E. Johnston, 'The Rothamsted chemical experiments', *Long-term experiments in agricultural and ecological sciences*, ed. R. A. Leigh and A. E. Johnston (1994), 9–38 • personal knowledge (1912) • private information (2004) • d. cert. • m. certs. • d. cert. [Eliza Forbes Gilbert]

Archives Rothamsted Experimental Station Library, Harpenden, corresp. and papers | CUL, letters to Sir George Stokes

Likenesses J. Gilbert, oils, *c.*1840, NPG • F. O. Salisbury, oils, 1900, Rothamsted Experimental Station, Harpenden, Hertfordshire • J. E. Clutterbuck, mezzotint (after oil painting by F. O. Salisbury), NPG • Maull & Co., sepia photograph, RS • photograph, NPG

Wealth at death £4781 19*s*.: probate, 13 Feb 1902, *CGPLA Eng. & Wales*

Gilbert, Nicolas Alain (1762–1821), Roman Catholic priest, born at St Malo in Brittany, was ordained for the diocese of Rennes in 1785 and subsequently became parish priest of Saint-Pern. During the French Revolution he was several times imprisoned, having refused the oath of allegiance in 1791. After escaping to England he was stationed from 1796 to 1802 at Wooler, Northumberland, and from 1803 to 1815 at Whitby, Yorkshire, where he built a church and presbytery and published several works of controversy against Presbyterianism and Methodism. Following the restoration of Louis XVIII in 1815 he returned to France, and became noted for his zeal in preaching missions in Brittany and Touraine, during which he vigorously attacked the doctrines of the revolution. He died at St Laurent-sur-Sèvre on 25 September 1821.

THOMPSON COOPER, *rev.* G. MARTIN MURPHY

Sources T. de Morembert, 'Gilbert, Nicolas Alain', *Dictionnaire de biographie française*, ed. J. Balteau and others, 16 (Paris, 1985), 9 • Gillow, *Lit. biog. hist.* • D. A. Bellenger, *The French exiled clergy* (1986) • J. Gillow, *The Haydock papers* (1888), 223–8 • W. J. Nicholson, 'Nicholas Alain Gilbert, French émigré priest', *Northern Catholic History*, 12 (1980), 19–22 • D. A. Bellenger, 'Nicholas Alain Gilbert', *Northern Catholic History*, 15 (1982), 13–14

Gilbert, Richard (*c.*1794–1852), printer and editor of reference works, was born in St John's Square, Clerkenwell, London, the second son of Robert Gilbert, printer. His mother's name is not known. He had at least one sister, whose name is unknown. He began his working life as an accountant for the Society for Promoting Christian Knowledge (SPCK), a position he continued to hold until at least 1820. On the death of his father (buried 17 January 1815) he joined his brother Robert as a printer at St John's Square. The firm was then known as R. and R. Gilbert. On the death of his brother in 1818 he took over the business.

Gilbert was a laborious compiler of information for the clergy, notably the *Clerical Guide* (1817, 1822, 1829, 1836) and the pocket-sized *Clergyman's Almanack* (first edition, 1819).

On 11 September 1823 he married Anne, only daughter of the Revd George Whittaker, curate of Northfleet in Kent, and sister of George Byrom *Whittaker (1793–1847), bookseller and publisher. Gilbert devised and edited the *Liber scholasticus* (1829), an account of the fellowships, scholarships, and exhibitions at universities and other corporate educational bodies (a second edition entitled *The Parents' School & College Guide* appeared in 1843).

Active in the religious life of Clerkenwell, he was a vestryman of St John's and contributed to the building of the new churches of St Mark's and St Philip's. He was a governor of Christ's and St Bartholomew's hospitals, a liveryman of the Stationers' Company, and an auditor of the Royal Literary Fund for the Relief of Authors.

In 1830 William Rivington became a partner in Gilbert's business and thereafter the firm was known as Gilbert and Rivington. Richard Gilbert died, probably from a liver disorder, at his home, 70 Euston Square, London, on 26 February 1852, and was buried in the vaults of St John's Church on 4 March. He was survived by his widow, who received his share of the English stock of the Stationers' Company. His son Robert was left his property in St John's Square, having already inherited the business of his uncle, George Byrom Whittaker. His nephew, Edward Bracebridge, son of a fellow vestryman, was made executor and was left £200.

Gilbert's long connections with the SPCK and Rivington suggest that he was a devout high-churchman. Although little is now known about his personal life, he was a greatly respected inhabitant of Clerkenwell, who used his business skills in the service of the established church and of philanthropy. ANNE STOTT

Sources *DNB* • *GM*, 2nd ser., 37 (1852), 525–6 • W. J. Pinks, *The history of Clerkenwell*, ed. E. J. Wood, 2nd edn (1881) • J. Storer and H. S. Storer, *History and description of the parish of Clerkenwell* [n.d.] • W. B. Todd, *A directory of printers and others in allied trades, London and vicinity, 1800–1840* (1972) • S. Rivington, *The publishing family of Rivington* (1919) • parish register, Clerkenwell, St John [birth] • parish register, Northfleet, Kent, 11 Sept 1823 [marriage] • parish register, Clerkenwell, St John, 4 March 1852 [burial] • will, PRO, PROB 11/2149, fols. 87*v*–92*v*

Wealth at death see will, PRO, PROB 11/2149, fols. 87*v*–92*v*

Gilbert, Samuel (*d.* 1692?), writer on horticulture, was chaplain to Jane, wife of Charles, fourth baron Gerard of Gerard's Bromley, and rector of Quatt, Shropshire. In 1676 he published a pamphlet entitled *Fons sanitatis, or, The healing spring at Willowbridge in Staffordshire, found out by … Lady Jane Gerard*. He himself vouched for some of the cures recorded in this work, and it may be that he also practised as a doctor. He married Minerva, daughter of John Rea, gardener, of Kinlet, near Bewdley, Worcestershire. As his own writings contained many verses, it is likely that Gilbert also wrote those in Rea's *Flora, Ceres, and Pomona* (1676). Gilbert seems to have lived with his father-in-law and he inherited Rea's collection of flowering plants after his death in 1681.

In 1682 Gilbert published the *Florist's vademecum*, calling himself 'Philerimus' on the title page. The work is a month-by-month guide to what to do in the flower garden, and it includes a plan for a tulip garden. When the second edition appeared in 1683 it was bound together with the *Gardener's Almanack*, a monthly calendar for 1683–7 with the signs of the zodiac and phases of the moon. Gilbert believed in the importance of astrology to gardeners, and the *Almanack* contained advice such as not to graft trees when the moon is waning or prune vines when the moon is full.

Gilbert had one son, Arden, and four or five daughters. The exact date of his death is unknown, but he probably died between 1692 and 1694. ANNE PIMLOTT BAKER

Sources J. Jacob, 'Two early English flower books', *The Garden*, 77 (4 Jan 1913), 5–6 • 'Early writers on English gardening, no. 10: Rev. Samuel Gilbert', *Journal of Horticulture, Cottage Gardener and Country Gentleman*, 30 (1876), 172–3 • 'Florist's vade mecum', *Cottage Gardener*, 2 (1851), 107, 6/138

Likenesses R. White, line engraving, pubd 1683, repro. in R. White, *Journal of Horticulture and Cottage Gardener*, 55 (1876), 172–3

Gilbert, Thomas (1609/10–1673), clergyman and ejected minister, whose parentage and origins are unknown, may have been the Thomas Gilbert who graduated MA at Edinburgh on 25 July 1629, becoming a minister of the word. The university register marked him as 'Anglus': Englishman. However, Edmund Calamy called Gilbert a Scottish divine, and he may have spent the next years in that country, while in his later years Gilbert himself certainly identified himself as Scottish.

Gilbert's first certain appearance is in Cheshire when 'an ordinance of the Parliament of the 26th March 1644, sequestered the rectory of Cheadle … from Dr Nicholls, for his delinquency, to the use of Thomas Gilbert, a godly and orthodox divine'; recalling this in September 1646 the committee for plundered ministers ordered that, 'Mr Gilbert do officiate the said cure of the said church as Rector and preach diligently to the parishioners there, and that he shall have for his pains therin, the parsonage house, glebelands and profits of the said rectorie' (Earwaker, 1.221). This proved easier said than done. Earlier Nicholls seems to have fought and won a protracted lawsuit concerning a neighbouring estate against one Captain Humphrey Buckley, who at or before the rector's sequestration seized all his property and refused to hand it over to his successor. Efforts to enforce Gilbert's possession seem to have had little practical effect, and the struggle was still continuing on 6 October 1647, when the committee once again ordered that Gilbert, as 'minister of the church of Cheadle' be granted quiet possession of the rectory.

It seems that Gilbert eventually prevailed. It was as minister of Cheadle that he preached in October 1650 that 'the Scots do well to stand to their covenant' and opposed Cromwell's invasion of their country. He is also reported to have said that 'if Cromwell loose the day all that have taken the Engagement will be proceeded against as traitors and rebels', yet the local magistrates were relaxed enough to release him—on condition that he took the Engagement (Morrill, 255–6). Gilbert was succeeded at Cheadle by Peter Harrison DD, whose name appears in the parish register in 1653. Gilbert had already been presented in 1651 to the rectory of Ealing, Middlesex, and he wrote from there on 23 April 1653 to Lord Wharton to recommend a young man to his service who 'is admitted by our Societie to the Sacrament' (*Calamy rev.*, 221). Gilbert was appointed an assistant to the Middlesex commission of ejectors under the ordinance of 28 August 1654. In October 1660 he was convicted at the Middlesex sessions of refusing to read from the Book of Common Prayer and was ordered to find pledges for his appearance at the next sessions to hear judgment. He was ejected from his living before 4 January 1661, when his successor was instituted.

Gilbert emigrated to Massachusetts, arriving in Boston on the *Prudent Mary* in July 1661. He initially settled at Charlestown, from where he was called to become the first pastor of the church at Topsfield, on 4 November 1663. His ministry was not a happy one, beset by the hostility of a faction gathered around William Perkins, who had been responsible for the original organization of the church and building its meeting-house but who had been passed over in favour of Gilbert when the congregation was formally gathered, and undermined by his own words and actions. In March 1666 Perkins appeared before the Essex county quarterly court to charge that Gilbert had 'in public prayers and sermons at several times … uttered speeches of a high nature, reproachful and scandalous to the King's Majesty and his government' (Dow, 3.310). He provided twenty-seven instances of such speeches. Gilbert had lamented how the divisions between presbyterians and Independents had undermined the godly cause: 'What a brave day had wee in Ingland … but wee fell a quarrelling each wth other, & have lost all' (ibid.). Praying for the people of God in old England who had lost their godly ministers he called on God to avenge the elect. Above all he condemned the king as a covenant breaker and an idolater. 'Tis better to bee heere poore, & to live in the wildernesse being Covenant keepers, then to sit on the Throne & bee Covenant breakers' (ibid., 3.311). His sympathy for the Scots in 1650 who had stood by the covenant was now echoed in his fierce attacks on the king, who had at that time signed the covenant but long ago reneged on it. Edmund Bridges reported that Gilbert had declared that:

> God was avenging the breach of that blessed covenant by visiting the land with sword and pestilence, speaking of Charles I, and also used this expression 'Good lord be intreted for the son thoue thow [though thou] wouldst not for the father'. Also that there was a blessed covenant made between the King and Scotland, which the King had broken and which God would never let go unpunished.
> (ibid., 3.312–13)

The quarterly court, 'apprehending the case to be extraordinary, both in its nature and tendency' (Dow, 3.310) referred the matter upwards to the next general court of election, binding Gilbert over in £1000. Gilbert survived these charges but remained at odds with leading members of his congregation gathered around Perkins and his family, and was frequently before the quarterly court. In 1667 Perkins sued him for defamation, and Gilbert admitted in court that he had indeed said the preceding Sunday, 'that men must repent of what they had done or else go to hell and he prayed that the necks of all who opposed the ministers of the Gospel should be broken' (ibid., 3.445). In May 1670 a series of witnesses lined up to accuse him in graphic detail of drunkenness both in and out of the pulpit, his defenders claiming that these were symptoms of sickness rather than intoxication; he received a warning from the court. The following April he was accused of using his sermons and prayers to revile members of his congregation and to scorn the authority of the quarterly court itself. He had said in a sermon that, 'thay that sat to Judge would say et was the scotties blod and the scoties fumes that fumeed up into his head', yet if ever the court came to Heaven, 'thay shall bles god that ever thay did see the Scot man' (ibid., 4.370). The court delivered a second stern reprimand: if he could not behave in a more sober and Christian-like manner, they 'do thinke it more convenient for him to surcease from the exercise of any publick imployment' (ibid., 4.366).

In September 1671 Gilbert made his last appearance before the quarterly court, for defamation and threatening assault. Shortly afterwards he ceased to be pastor of Topsfield: his successor was ordained pastor the following year. He died in Charlestown at the house of its minister, Zechariah Symmes, on 26 October 1673, aged sixty-three, and was buried in the church there two days later. By his will, dated 2 June 1673, he left everything to his wife, Elizabeth, including £30 due to him for his pains in the ministry at Topsfield. Nothing more is known of his wife, and there is even a little uncertainty about her name: the records which report her admission to the Charlestown church name her Sarah. Cotton Mather chose to remember Gilbert not for his last turbulent years but, drawing on the words of his epitaph, as 'that Reverend, Sincere, Zealous, Devout and Faithful Minister of Jesus Christ, Mr Thomas Gilbert … the Proto-Martyr, the first of the Ministers that suffered Deprivation in the Cause of Non-Conformity in England' (Mather, 3.221).

STEPHEN WRIGHT

Sources *Calamy rev.* • J. P. Earwaker, *East Cheshire: past and present, or, A history of the hundred of Macclesfield*, 2 vols. (1877–80) • C. Mather, *Magnalia Christi Americana*, 7 bks in 1 vol. (1702), bk 3, p. 221 • *Walker rev.* • J. Morrill, *Cheshire 1630–1660: county government and society during the English revolution* (1974) • D. Laing, ed., *A catalogue of the graduates … of the University of Edinburgh*, Bannatyne Club, 106 (1858) • BL, Add. MS 15671 • G. F. Dow, ed., *Records and files of the quarterly courts of Essex county, Massachusetts*, 8 vols. (1911–21), vol. 3, pp. 3, 151, 310–13, 394, 445; vol. 4, pp. 244–50, 367–70, 419–21 • J. Savage, *A genealogical dictionary of the first settlers of New England*, 4 vols. (1860–62), vol. 2, p. 252 • C. Porter, 'The pastors of the congregational church of Topsfield', www.members.mva.net/cct/pastors.html

Gilbert, Thomas (*bap.* **1613**, *d.* **1694**), clergyman and ejected minister, was baptized on 17 January 1613 at Prees, Shropshire, the parish in which his father, William Gilbert, lived; his mother's name is unknown. On 13 November 1629 he matriculated at St Edmund Hall, Oxford, aged sixteen; he graduated BA on 28 June 1633 and proceeded MA on 7 November 1638. Philip, Lord Wharton, presented Gilbert to the vicarage of Nash, Monmouthshire, in 1635, and it can be presumed that it was at about this time that he was also appointed through Wharton's influence to the vicarage of Upper Winchendon, Buckinghamshire. Gilbert then appears to have served in Ireland, perhaps as a minister in Connaught, during the later 1630s and early 1640s. On 27 June 1643 a minister of his name was referred by the House of Commons to the committee for plundered ministers for appointment to a vacant parish.

In 1646 Gilbert became vicar of St Laurence, Reading. During the parliamentary visitation of Oxford University he was created BD on 19 May 1648. The tale of Gilbert's presentation to the rectory of Edgmond, Shropshire, in 1649 is tangled, but he was in possession of the living by May 1650 and rapidly became one of the most active government supporters in the region. He became assistant to the commission for ejecting insufficient ministers in Shropshire in 1654; he corresponded with Secretary Thurloe about the county's JPs in 1655, and with Henry Scobell about organizing the county's representatives to the Savoy conference in 1658. Although he was resident in Shropshire, several authorities state that Gilbert was a chaplain to Magdalen College, Oxford, between 1656 and 1660. In a letter to Thurloe of 11 April 1660, addressed from Shropshire, Gilbert explained that although he had never behaved 'incivilly in the least toward the cavalier party, my best and surest friends tell me, I am so much threatened by them, that I cannot (as they apprehend) be long safe among them' (Thurloe, 7.895). In June 1660 John Hall successfully petitioned the House of Lords for the living of Edgmond, although it appears that Gilbert had already withdrawn. He retired to the vicarage of Upper Winchendon, but he knew that his nonconformity would cost him this living. In a letter to Wharton of 4 August 1662 Gilbert remarked that patrons with 'any thing of Religion' in them would have to find the best conformist they could to serve their livings (Cliffe, 43). On his ejection from Winchendon, Gilbert moved to Oxford.

Gilbert married at least once (his widow was named Anna), and he had several children: one, Thomas, became a bookseller in Oxford; one of his daughters married John Sproston, his successor as vicar of Upper Winchendon; another daughter, Elizabeth, married a Church of England minister called Benyon. Once settled in St Ebbe's parish, Oxford, Gilbert and his wife apparently took in the sons of nonconformists as boarders and sent them to Magdalen School. Gilbert also undertook tasks for Lord Wharton. In April 1663 he reported on the suitability of Hungerford Dunch as a possible match for one of Wharton's daughters, and in 1670 he advised Wharton about the best tutor at St Edmund Hall for his nephew. He apparently continued to preach in Oxford. In 1663 the earl of Clarendon, as chancellor of the university, instructed Gilbert, Henry Cornish, John Conant, and Christopher Rogers to quit Oxford because 'he had heard very foule things of them in keping conventicles and meetings in their houses' (*Calamy rev.*, 221). But none of them seem to have heeded the order. In 1664 John Owen and others may have proposed Gilbert for the presidency of Harvard, but on his own evidence Gilbert believed 'were I worthy that dignity I think I ought rather at present to frame myselfe to suffer in Old, than to reign in New England' (ibid.). Gilbert maintained his connections in Shropshire and visited occasionally; he preached at Whitchurch in 1669. Under the 1672 declaration of indulgence he took out a preaching licence as a congregationalist, yet his closest associates seem to have been three presbyterians, Dr Henry Langley, Henry Cornish, and John Troughton, with whom he established a congregation.

After the withdrawal of the indulgence Gilbert served no congregation and suffered financial hardship. He turned down Lord Wharton's offer of the curacy of Ravenstonedale, Westmorland, because his conscience would only allow him to administer the sacraments to a gathered congregation. In 1678 he explored the possibility of becoming a minister at Great Yarmouth. Gilbert seems to have suffered little harassment for his nonconformity until the 'tory reaction' of Charles II's last years, when he was bound over at the 1684 Oxford assizes. However in August 1687, thanks to the more tolerant atmosphere of James II's reign, he was retained, despite his congregationalist principles, by the presbyterian Sir John Thompson to preach to a presbyterian conventicle in his house in St Peters in the East. In the early 1690s, after the establishment of toleration, Gilbert, like other Oxford nonconformists, attended two Sunday services, one conducted by John Hall, bishop of Bristol and master of Pembroke College, and the other by the presbyterian minister Joshua Oldfield. In 1692 Bishop Hall allowed Gilbert to read to eight scholars of Pembroke College who scrupled to wear gowns. It seems clear that Gilbert, like a considerable number of other ejected ministers, found it difficult initially to resist the call to exercise his ministry, and that he was prepared to co-operate with godly ministers whether Independent or presbyterian. Towards the end of his life he appears to have become comfortable, especially as a worshipper, with a loosely defined partial or semi-conformity.

Gilbert wrote on a wide variety of topics. He published in Latin and English on soteriology, particularly the nature of satisfaction for sin, and on the numerology of 666; he also wrote Latin and English poetry, some of it an excruciating attempt to awaken the English to their sins and the need for amendment. Anthony Wood called him 'the common epitaph-maker for dissenters' (Wood, *Ath. Oxon.*: *Fasti*, 2.180). Edmund Calamy, who knew Gilbert in 1691–2, described him as 'very purblind', and as 'the completest schoolman' he ever knew, but also remarked that Gilbert was sometimes 'very facetious and pleasant in conversation' (*DNB*). The aged Gilbert seems to have depended upon the munificence of patrons like Wharton and the earl of Anglesey, and on the support of various Oxford dons. At various times, he was familiar with several fellows and heads of houses, including Hall, Bathurst, Aldrich, Wallis, Jane, Barlow, and Fell, and according to White Kennett 'did partake of their Civility and Bounty to him, for his many old Stories, and some rare Books and Papers that he pick'd up for them' (Kennett, 919). Gilbert died at Oxford on 15 July 1694 and was buried in the chancel of St Aldates Church. JOHN SPURR

Sources *Calamy rev.*, 221–2 • *Walker rev.*, 305 • Wood, *Ath. Oxon.*, new edn • Wood, *Ath. Oxon.*: *Fasti*, new edn • Foster, *Alum. Oxon.* • W. Kennett, *A register and chronicle ecclesiastical and civil* (1728) • Thurloe, *State papers* • *Calendar of the correspondence of Richard Baxter*, ed. N. H. Keeble and G. F. Nuttall, 2 vols. (1991) • J. T. Cliffe, *The puritan gentry besieged, 1650–1700* (1993) • PRO, PROB 6/71, fol. 50v • PRO, PROB 6/85, fol. 144v • *DNB* • *IGI*

Gilbert, Thomas (*bap.* **1713**, *d.* **1766**), satirist and rake, was baptized on 18 December 1713, at St Mary's, Whitechapel, the son of Thomas Gilbert, gentleman, and his wife, Susanna, of Stepney in London. He was educated at Eton College from 1725 to 1728, and at Trinity College, Oxford (where he matriculated on 29 October 1729, aged sixteen). He took his Oxford BA in 1733, but a quarrel with George Huddesford, president of Trinity (obscurely alluded to in Gilbert's satires) resulted in his migration to Cambridge. He was admitted to Peterhouse on 12 April 1735, took his Cambridge MA in 1737, and was fellow of Peterhouse from 1736 to 1744.

Gilbert's first verse satire, *A View of the Town* (1735), attacks such targets as epicurean clergy, fops, and sodomites. *The World Unmasked* (1738) and *A Panegyric on a Court* (1739) are more political and specific, and *The First Satire of Juvenal Imitated* (1740) is a powerful attack on Walpole. Several of Gilbert's poems were printed in Benjamin Loveling's *Latin and English Poems* (1738).

Gilbert possessed an estate at Skinningrove, near Whitby, Yorkshire, where he periodically enjoyed the company of Laurence Sterne and John Hall-Stevenson in a friendship probably dating from their Cambridge days. He was a prominent member of Hall-Stevenson's club of Demoniacks at Skelton Castle. The obscene fabliau, *A Poet's Tale, or, The Cautious Bride*, in Hall-Stevenson's *Works* (1795, 3.154–6), seems intended for him.

Though in 1746 Gilbert congratulated himself on

> an independent life,
> Where *Delia* serves instead of wife
> (Gilbert, 257)

he was married to a woman named Ann at the time of his death. She died on 15 June 1801, aged seventy-five. Gilbert's last publication was *A Satire on All Parties* (1749; 3rd edition revised with additions, 1750), but he may be the Thomas Gilbert whose unpublished and unacted tragedy *Jugurtha* was shown between 1759 and 1763 to the earl of Bute, George III, and David Garrick. Gilbert died on 23 November 1766; he was buried at Petersham, Surrey.

James Sambrook

Sources T. Gilbert, *Poems on several occasions* (1747), preface, dedications, and notes • Venn, *Alum. Cant.* • Foster, *Alum. Oxon.* • *N&Q*, 3rd ser., 5 (1864), 263–4, 349 • R. A. Austen-Leigh, ed., *The Eton College register, 1698–1752* (1927) • *Letters of Laurence Sterne*, ed. L. P. Curtis (1935), 226n. • L. Hartley, 'Sterne's Eugenius as indiscreet author: the literary career of John Hall-Stevenson', *P.M.L.A.*, 86 (1971), 428–45 • *The letters of David Garrick*, ed. D. M. Little and G. M. Kahrl, 1 (1963), 375n. • L. C. Jones, *The clubs of the Georgian rakes* (1942), 155–63 • two letters (signatures missing) to the earl of Bute, 1759 and 1762, said to be from Thomas Gilbert, BL, Add. MS 5726D, fols. 222–3 • *IGI* • will, PRO, PROB 11/924, sig. 453

Wealth at death over £10,000; £1900 in various bequests; annuity of £200 p.a. to widow; plus jewels, household furniture, plate, chinaware, horses, books, manuscripts; also an unspecified residue in trust for family of sister: will, PRO, PROB 11/924, sig. 453

Gilbert, Thomas (*bap.* **1720**, *d.* **1798**), land agent and poor law reformer, was baptized on 26 January 1720 in Cotton, Staffordshire, the eldest son of Thomas Gilbert, a small landowner engaged in farming and mining, and his wife, Elizabeth. He was admitted to the Inner Temple in 1740 and was called to the bar in 1744.

The Gilbert family had some ties to the family of Lord Gower through the elder Thomas Gilbert's estate. The earliest record of a connection with young Thomas is his acceptance of a commission in Lord Gower's regiment, formed at the time of the Jacobite rising in 1745. Soon afterwards he undertook legal work connected with Gower properties, and by 1754 he was reviewing the Gower electoral expenses. In 1758 he became Lord Gower's chief land agent. In 1763 he was elected to parliament for the family seat of Newcastle under Lyme, and in 1768 he was returned for the Gower-controlled seat at Lichfield. Gilbert held this seat until his retirement in 1794, when he vacated it to make room for Lord Granville Leveson-Gower.

Thomas Gilbert (*bap.* **1720**, *d.* **1798**), by unknown artist, *c.*1790

Gilbert was a valuable agent, less for his knowledge of farming than for his skills in the legal, commercial, industrial, and political aspects of management. The Gower estate was on its way to becoming one of England's wealthiest, and the work of Gilbert in the later eighteenth century was no small part of that process. He was well rewarded for his efforts: as well as a stipend of £300 as agent he was made paymaster for the charity for relief of widows of naval officers, a post he held for the rest of his life. This was a fund established in the Admiralty in 1732, disbursing moneys withheld from officer's wages, plus other funds provided by parliamentary grants. His patron Lord Gower may have promoted him for this, and he definitely placed him in the more prestigious post of comptroller of the great wardrobe when, in 1763, Gower was made keeper; he kept this position until it was abolished in 1782. Holding this lucrative sinecure, Gilbert in parliament, apart from the period July 1765 to December 1767, when the duke of Bedford's party was in opposition, was a supporter of government until the end of North's ministry in 1782. He later supported the ministries of Shelburne and William Pitt, who made him chairman of the committee of ways and means in 1784, which carried a salary of £500, perhaps even £800, per annum.

Gilbert began his campaign as a poor law reformer with a bill for the 'better relief and employment of the poor' in 1765. The bill promised to assist the poor, reduce the cost of poor relief, and improve society. This measure was a generalized version of the numerous local acts over the previous seventy years. Gilbert's plan was to choose commissioners in every county who would draw up combined parish districts for poor relief and select guardians, or local administrators, who in turn would choose directors for each area, and they would purchase land and build workhouses where needed. The bill passed the Commons but was rejected (66 to 59) in the Lords. Gilbert's next effort was an omnibus bill in 1768, aimed at consolidating all poor law legislation and adding the right of all parishes to combine, but omitting the elaborate procedures of the previous bill. This proposed overhaul was more ambitious and comprehensive than the first effort but it never reached the committee stage in the Commons.

The next attempt to advance the cause of poor law reform was a survey of parochial information. Instead of the packaged solutions already attempted, Sir Walden Hanmer initiated an act to require overseers to submit data on the operation of the laws (16 Geo. III c. 40). Gilbert had sat on the Commons committee (1775–6) that reviewed, abstracted, and reported on the data, and he presented its second report. This immersion in evidence may have prompted his bill in 1777 to elicit information regarding charitable donations for the poor. During this phase of his work Gilbert published pamphlets on the subject, beginning with his *Observations upon the Orders and Resolutions of the House of Commons with Respect to the Poor* (1775), followed by *A bill intended to be offered to parliament for the better relief and employment of the poor in England* (1775). In May 1781 he introduced another bill for 'the better relief and employment of the poor', and in June he presented a bill for amending the laws relating to houses of correction. These bills made little progress, in spite of an assiduous pamphlet campaign, which included three pamphlets written by Gilbert himself.

Gilbert's next proposal became his signal effort, that which became known as Gilbert's Act of 1782. By this point he had divided his subject into three areas: relief and employment of the poor; houses of correction; and rogues and vagabonds. He introduced three bills; the first (relief and employment, 22 Geo. III c. 83) and second (houses of correction, 22 Geo. III c. 64) became law, the third (on rogues and vagabonds) did not. The two acts provided for the creation of parish unions, and for workhouses to shelter the aged, sick, and orphans only. Guardians were to find work for the able-bodied and otherwise to 'cause such person or persons to be properly maintained, lodged and provided for, until such employment shall be procured'. Sidney and Beatrice Webb called his relief act 'the most carefully devised, the most elaborate and perhaps the most influential, for both good and evil, of all the scores of Poor Law statutes between 1601 and 1834' (Webb, 171, n. 1). While they observed that 'for years it scarcely worked at all' (ibid., 275) and that the sixty-seven unions formed under it were a 'relatively trifling' outcome, the act endorsed the controversial practice of outdoor relief, which would overtax the system in the next generation.

Evidently Gilbert had not finished his campaign in 1782, for he continued to produce pamphlets and he made one more legislative foray. In 1786 he published a second edition of his *A Plan of Police; with Objections Stated and Answered*, first published in 1781. In 1787 he produced *A Collection of Pamphlets Concerning the Poor*, which included one by Thomas Firmin from 1678 and other older works. In the same year he also published *Heads of a bill for the better relief and employment of the poor and for the improvement of police*. Gilbert's final effort for poor law reform came with a bill in 1788 that only had a first reading, though it prompted considerable comment. This measure combined the matter that had been separated in 1782, and it would have made parish unions mandatory, requiring quarter sessions to appoint commissioners to unite parishes, but evidently it never reached the committee stage.

The poor law was only one dimension, albeit the main one, in Gilbert's work as a reforming and improving land agent. He authored legislation in many other areas, the most important of which was work related to highways. He sponsored many local acts and also a general act for the improvement of highways, the last in 1773 (13 Geo. III c. 78). He was also involved with canal building and was acquainted with the engineer James Brindley; he was said to have advised the duke of Bridgewater to hire him. Gilbert and Brindley together purchased an estate in Staffordshire. Gilbert himself was a supporter of canal projects, including the grand trunk scheme. He sponsored legislation in a wide range of areas that affected his employer and were meant to improve the moral economy of landed society: punishing deer stealing (1775); supporting resident clergy (1776 and 1777); protecting child apprentices (1780); he was also interested in restricting country alehouses, abolishing imprisonment for small debts, and supporting friendly societies.

Gilbert presents a contradictory picture as an economical reformer. While he held sinecures, in 1778 he proposed a 25 per cent tax on government places and pensions as a measure to support war expenditure with the resources of the crown. It was carried in committee, against the wishes of Lord North, but on report it was rejected by six votes. When the debates on economical reform occurred a year later Gilbert defended his own sinecure in the wardrobe, claiming that he and Lord Gower had introduced savings of £900 per annum; he thought the king should be allowed to make needed reforms without the interference of parliament. In 1782 Lord Shelburne asked Gilbert to make an inquiry into places and pensions, and Gilbert claimed that this led to the abolition of many sinecures and the reduction of many salaries. It also led to a payment of £700 to Gilbert for his efforts.

Gilbert had not made a career at the bar but in his later years he was active in the affairs of the Inner Temple: he was made a bencher in 1782, a reader in 1788, and he was treasurer of the inn in 1789. He had two sons by his first marriage, in 1761 or 1762, to a Miss Philips, who died on 22 April 1770. He later married Mary, daughter of Lieutenant-Colonel George Crauford; he retired to Cotton with her in 1795 and devoted himself to improving his estate. He died there on 18 December 1798. RICHARD S. TOMPSON

Sources J. Brooke, 'Gilbert, Thomas', HoP, *Commons, 1754–90* • S. Lambert, *Sessional papers of the eighteenth century* (1975) • J. R. Wordie, *Estate management in 18th century England* (1982) • S. Webb and B. Webb, *English local government*, 7/1: *English poor law history* (1927) • F. M. Eden, *The state of the poor*, 3 vols. (1797), 1.362–6, 389–95 • *GM*, 1st ser., 54 (1784), 460 • *GM*, 1st ser., 68 (1798), 1090, 1146 • P. D. G. Thomas, *The House of Commons in the eighteenth century*, rev. edn (1992) • S. Smiles, *Lives of the engineers*, 3 vols. (1861–2), 1.347–51, 432–9 • *DNB* • *IGI*

Archives Birm. CA, letters to Matthew Boulton • BL, corresp. with Charles Jenkinson, Add. MSS 38201–38220, 38307–38308, *passim* • PRO, letters and accounts to Earl Gower, PRO 30/29

Likenesses miniature, *c*.1790, NPG [*see illus.*]

Gilbert, Sir Walter Raleigh, first baronet (1785–1853), army officer in the East India Company, was born on 18 March 1785 at Bodmin, Cornwall, third son of the Revd Edmund Gilbert (*d*. 1816), vicar of Constantine and rector of Helland, Cornwall, and his wife, the daughter of Henry Garnett of Bristol. He belonged to the Devon family of Gilbert of Compton to which Sir Humphrey *Gilbert also belonged. Sir Humphrey's mother was by a second marriage mother of Sir Walter Raleigh. In 1800 Gilbert obtained a Bengal infantry cadetship. In September 1801 he was posted as ensign to the 15th Bengal native infantry, and arrived in India in October, where he became lieutenant, on 12 September 1803, and captain on 16 April 1810. In that regiment, under Colonel John Macdonald, he was present at the defeat of Perron's brigades at Koil, Aligarh, the battle of Delhi, the storming of Agra, the battle of Laswari, and the four desperate but unsuccessful attacks on Bharatpur, where he attracted the favourable notice of Lord Lake. Afterwards he was in succession barrack-master and cantonment magistrate at Cawnpore, commandant of the Calcutta native militia, and commandant of the Ramgarh local battalion. He was promoted major on 12 November 1820, lieutenant-colonel of the 39th Bengal native infantry, then just formed, in 1824, and colonel of the 35th native infantry in 1832. He became major-general in June 1838, and lieutenant-general in November 1851. He commanded a division of the army under Sir Hugh Gough in the First Anglo-Sikh War, at the battles of Mudki and Ferozeshahr (December 1845), and at Sobraon (10 February 1846). Gough in his dispatch spoke highly of Gilbert's services. Gilbert commanded a division of Gough's army in the Second Anglo-Sikh War, at the battles of Chilianwala (13 January 1849), and Gujrat (21 February 1849). After Gujrat, Gilbert with his division crossed the Jhelum in pursuit of the remains of the Sikh army, part of which surrendered to him on 3 March, while the rest, 16,000 fine troops with forty-one guns, surrendered to him at Rawalpindi three days later. He pursued their Afghan allies to the entrance of the Khyber Pass. Gilbert, who had been made KCB in April 1846, was appointed GCB in June 1849. He was military member of the supreme council from December 1852 to February 1853. He was made a baronet in December 1850. In 1832 he was appointed colonel of the 1st Bengal European fusiliers.

Gilbert was well known as a sportsman in India, and a supporter of the turf. He married at Calcutta, on 1 June 1814, Isabella Rose, daughter of Major Thomas Ross, Royal Artillery; they had at least one child. Gilbert died at Stevens' Hotel, Bond Street, London, on 12 May 1853. A memorial obelisk was erected on the Beacon at Bodmin. The baronetcy became extinct on the death at Cheltenham, on 17 November 1863, of his son Sir Francis Hastings Gilbert, second baronet (*b*. 1816), British consul at Scutari, Albania. H. M. CHICHESTER, *rev.* ROGER T. STEARN

Sources J. Maclean, *The parochial and family history of the deanery of Trigg Minor in the county of Cornwall*, 1 (1873) • *East-India Register and Army List* • P. R. Innes, *History of the Bengal European regiment* (1885) • L. Shadwell, *The life of Colin Campbell*, 2 vols. (1881) • E. J. Thackwell, *Narrative of the Second Seikh War, in 1848–49* (1851) • V. C. P. Hodson, *List of officers of the Bengal army, 1758–1834*, 2 (1928) • *GM*, 2nd ser., 39 (1853) • B. Bond, ed., *Victorian military campaigns* (1967) • H. C. B. Cook, *The Sikh wars: the British army in the Punjab, 1845–1849* (1975) • T. A. Heathcote, *The military in British India: the development of British land forces in south Asia, 1600–1947* (1995) • P. Lawson, *The East India Company* (1993) • Boase, *Mod. Eng. biog.*

Archives BL, corresp. with Lord Camelford and Lady Camelford, Add. MSS 69298–69300, 69341 • Duke U., Perkins L., corresp. with Lord Dalhousie

Likenesses T. Lupton, mezzotint, pubd 1852 (after G. F. Atkinson), NPG • wood-engraving, NPG; repro. in *ILN* (1846)

Gilbert, William (1544?–1603), natural philosopher, was almost certainly born in Colchester, Essex, the first of four children of Jerome Gilbert (*d*. 1583), lawyer and recorder of Colchester, and his first wife, Elizabeth Coggeshall. Jerome's father William was a weaver, appointed sewer (server) to the chamber to Henry VIII, who lived in Clare, Suffolk. Jerome moved to Colchester by the 1520s, and by 1558 he had married as his second wife Jane Wingfield, with whom he had nine more children. Excepting official records of Gilbert's university and medical career, biographical information about him is sparse. No record survives of Gilbert's baptism, but evidence converges strongly upon the year 1544. A later nativity relied upon the time and date of 2.20 p.m., 24 May 1544. The inscription on a monument erected in Holy Trinity Church, Colchester, by his stepbrothers Ambrose and William states that he 'was born in the town of Colchester', but unreliably gives his age at death as sixty-three (Munk, *Roll*; Gilbert, *De magnete*, xxiii).

Education and medical career Nothing is known of Gilbert before he matriculated from St John's College, Cambridge, in May 1558. He might have attended the Royal Grammar School, Colchester, although his family was wealthy enough to employ a private tutor. His university career was unexceptional for an aspiring scholar and

William Gilbert (1544?–1603), by R. Clamp (after Harding, after unknown artist, 1591)

physician. He graduated BA and was admitted to the fellowship of the college in March 1561, proceeded MA in 1564, and served in the junior position of mathematical examiner in 1565 and 1566, before graduating MD in 1569. He was senior bursar in January 1570, but he subsequently left Cambridge to pursue a medical career in London. There is no evidence for Wood's oft-repeated claim that he first travelled or studied medicine abroad (Wood, *Ath. Oxon.*, 1.737). There are likewise few clues as to why he came to reject much of the orthodox science (more properly, natural philosophy) of his day in his great work *De magnete* ('On the lodestone', 1600).

Gilbert must have built up a successful clientele among London's gentry and aristocracy during the 1570s. The inscription on his monument states that he practised 'for more than thirty years at London' (Munk, *Roll*; Gilbert, *De mundo*, xxiii). His place of residence in these early years is not known. Gilbert obtained a grant of arms in 1577, and was moving in court circles by January 1580 when, as was common for physicians in noble households, he acted as a trusted emissary from the earl of Leicester to the earl of Shrewsbury. About 1580 he was elected to one of the thirty odd fellowships of the College of Physicians in London, for he held the post of censor, regulating standards of practice, for eight years between 1581 and 1590.

By 1595 Gilbert had acquired and moved into Wingfield House in St Peter's Hill, a substantial property near St Paul's Cathedral possibly inherited from his stepmother. He moved from there to the court in February 1601, when he was selected to become one of the royal physicians. They were generally highly esteemed fellows of the College of Physicians, although court patronage and acceptance were also important. Gilbert had risen to become treasurer of the college (1587–94, 1597–9), elect (1596–7), consiliarius (1597–9), and finally president in 1600. He had also added to his patrons the powerful Cecil family. He attended at the deaths of William Cecil, Lord Burghley, Elizabeth I's chief counsellor, and his wife. A medical report to Robert Cecil, William's son and political successor, may be in Gilbert's hand (Roller, 81). The connections surely facilitated his formal appointment for life in April 1601 as a physician to Elizabeth I, with the usual stipend of £100 per year. She did not favour him especially, and there is no evidence for the scene painted by A. A. Hunt of Gilbert demonstrating experiments before her. He was re-appointed royal physician to James I, but died a few months afterwards.

Personal life Very little is known of Gilbert's personal life. He did not marry. Judging from his will (printed by Houston) he was close to his family, especially to his half-sisters and half-brothers, one of whom edited his manuscript remains. His will mentions one godson, and two 'good ffrends', a Mr Harwood and, more significantly, John Chamberlain. Chamberlain, the famous gossipy correspondent, lodged with Gilbert in Wingfield House between *c.*1595 and 1601, and mentioned him respectfully. Gilbert, Chamberlain, and other *habitués* of Wingfield House made up a sociable circle or informal 'college' of uncertain composition. One candidate is Gilbert's fellow physician and defender of his magnetic philosophy, Mark Ridley. Ridley, to whose home Chamberlain moved, claimed that he was Gilbert's friend and had experimented with his apparatus (Ridley, preface; *Letters of John Chamberlain*, 1.5). Thomas Blundeville the mathematician was another 'good friend' and popularizer of Gilbert's discoveries. Lancelot Browne, the father-in-law of William Harvey, was a close acquaintance of both Gilbert and Blundeville. Browne's medical career paralleled Gilbert's, and he possessed an autographed copy of *De magnete*. Finally, Gilbert worked very closely with the mathematician Edward Wright (*bap.* 1561, *d.* 1615). The Wingfield 'society' must have discussed Gilbert's research, and probably also discussed religion. Giving the only available insight into Gilbert's private opinions, Chamberlain wrote, concerning outspoken preachers, that 'yt is not good *irritare crabrones*, or to meddle with these pulpit-hornets, as our Doctor was wont to call them' (*Letters of John Chamberlain*, 1.396). Gilbert's firm belief that theologians of all confessions had obstructed the development of true science and Copernican astronomy meant that his books did not follow this Erasmian counsel.

In his texts and in conversation Gilbert exhibited biting wit. This moderates the judgement of Thomas Fuller, who, relying on a relative and other sources some forty years after Gilbert's death, recounted that '[o]ne saith of him, "that he was stoical but not cynical", which I understand reserved but not morose'. Fuller added (presumably of Gilbert's intellect) that he had 'the clearness of Venice glass, without the brittleness thereof; soon ripe, and long lasting, in his perfections'. 'His stature was tall, complexion cheerful; an happiness not ordinary in so hard a student and retired a person' (Fuller, *Worthies*, 1.515). Wood responded identically to a portrait he saw in Oxford. Although it was destroyed, an engraving was made, from which derive modern reproductions of Gilbert in formal dress.

Maritime interests Apart from his professional success, Gilbert's medical career seems unusual—though significantly so for a philosopher of magnetism—only in his connections with London's maritime community and naval explorers. In 1588 he and Browne were approached by the privy council to administer drugs to sailors struck down by an epidemic, being two of four 'very fytt persons to be employed in the said Navye to have care of the helthe of the noblemen, gentlemen and others in that service' (Roller, 79). If he was not one of the two selected, Gilbert nevertheless became acquainted with nautical practitioners, and wrote proudly of conversations with England's heroic circumnavigators Francis Drake and Thomas Cavendish. To Richard Hakluyt, the chronicler of Elizabethan voyages, he offered to compile a book on tropical medicine. He also advised Sir Francis Walsingham, Elizabeth's security chief during the hostilities with Spain, that a sick petitioner should be allowed to leave for a hot, dry country. His experience, unusual for an élite Galenic physician, of drug-based mass medicine might explain Gilbert's involvement between 1589 and 1594 in the college's first, controversial, and aborted attempts to produce a pharmacopoeia, which finally appeared in 1618.

Gilbert's acquaintance with English mariners and navigation experts was surely facilitated by his medical duties and interests, but it was also a crucial source of his burgeoning knowledge of terrestrial magnetism for which, far more than his medical career, he is remembered. A major achievement of Gilbert's magnetic philosophy was that it provided the first comprehensive and satisfactory explanation of the behaviour of the nautical magnetic compass. The correct recording and use of compass bearings made possible the 'age of exploration', and its concomitants of trade, naval capability, colonial imperialism, and missionary work. Recent naval successes had shaped the identity of Gilbert's England. Francis Bacon, Gilbert's contemporary both as courtier and as reformer of natural philosophy, made the compass, with printing and gunpowder, one of the three technologies that defined a modern age of progress beyond classical achievements. The new importance of the compass, the new availability of magnetic data, the new status of navigation experts in Elizabethan England, and a growing belief among the London scientific community that university learning was outdated, help to explain why Gilbert was the founder of a new science of magnetism.

The most important collaborator upon whose technical expertise Gilbert relied was Edward Wright, a mathematician who, under the patronage of the earl of Cumberland, had left Cambridge and theory for London and practical mathematics. He was an expert lecturer on navigation, and the author of the classic *Certaine Errors in Navigation* (1599), and of *The Havenfinding Art* (1599), a translation of a work by his Dutch counterpart Simon Stevin. Gilbert also exchanged knowledge of magnetism with William Barlow, a court chaplain and compass expert, who deferred to Gilbert's advanced research in his book *The Navigators Supply* (1597). In controversial terms that Bacon echoed, Gilbert asserted that navigational practitioners, metalworkers, and even farmers had a better knowledge of the nature of the earth than did professors of natural philosophy.

De magnete Gilbert's enduring significance is secured by the one work published in his lifetime, *De magnete, magneticisque corporibus, et de magno magnete tellure; physiologia nova, plurimis & argumentis, & experimentis demonstrata* ('A new natural philosophy of the lodestone, magnetic bodies, and the great lodestone the earth, proved by many reasonings and experiments'). It was printed by Peter Short of Bread Street, London, in 1600. The full title, announcing a new science of the earth, corrects the impression given by its universally used incipit *De magnete* that it was a treatise 'on the magnet'. Unusually for a work of its period and genre, *De magnete* has no dedicatory epistle, suggesting that Gilbert did not seek, or failed to gain, patronage for his natural philosophical researches.

Evidence of Gilbert's long-standing and broad interests in natural philosophy comes from his other work. His half-brother William edited two more or less finished manuscripts into a handsome manuscript book entitled *De mundo nostro sublunari, nova philosophia contra Aristotelem* ('A new philosophy of our sublunary world in opposition to Aristotle'), which he presented to Prince Henry, a patron of Barlow, Wright, and navigation in general. Previously placed in the Royal Library, it (or possibly a copy) is now in the British Library. A version found with some of Francis Bacon's manuscripts was published in Amsterdam in 1651. By then some of Gilbert's philosophical principles and style, though not his magnetic experiments and discoveries, were outmoded, and *De mundo* received limited attention. Nevertheless, the lack of evidence about how Gilbert came to produce *De magnete*, coupled with *De mundo*'s very different style, makes the latter an invaluable source.

Despite the conventional success of his medical career, Gilbert's natural philosophy was at odds with conservative institutions such as Cambridge University and the College of Physicians that defended orthodox Aristotelian natural philosophy and Galenic medicine. He deplored the excessive authority accorded to Galen's texts, and emphasized the importance of experience. He rejected the traditional physician's habitual diagnosis of disease as a humoral imbalance of the qualities of heat, cold, wetness, and dryness, although he was also critical of the emerging alternative of Paracelsian or chemical medicine. He was especially hostile to the Galenic theory of attraction in which, significantly, Galen had explained the body's faculties by analogy with the magnet; both were apparently able to attract similar substances and to repel or expel harmful ones.

There is insufficient evidence to trace or explain the sources of Gilbert's profound hostility to Aristotelian and Galenic theory of matter. The Italian nature philosophers Bernardino Telesio and Francesco Patrizi both published self-consciously new and anti-scholastic natural philosophies during his formative period. They were influences, despite Gilbert's characteristic dismissals. He was more impressed by Giordano Bruno, whose advocacy of a vitalist, infinite universe contributed to his execution in Rome in 1600. But Gilbert certainly did not share Bruno's 'Hermetic' position that true philosophy was revealed in very ancient, pre-Hellenic texts. Indeed, Gilbert (and Bacon) pioneered the iconoclastic modern positions that knowledge progressed, and that science needed to begin anew on empirical and experimental foundations.

The philosophical core of Gilbert's hostility was, as for Patrizi and Bruno, his rejection of the traditional division by Christian Aristotelians of the cosmos into a superior celestial world and an inferior terrestrial one alone composed of the four elements. Gilbert particularly objected to the low status accorded to the terrestrial sphere of earth. Unlike the heavens, earthy matter was supposedly corrupt, and informed by the inactive qualities of coldness and dryness. Together with Aristotelian theories of gravity these properties explained why the earth had to be gathered as a motionless ball at the centre of the universe, maximally separated from the perfect heavens in which, according to a dominant theory, the planets were moved in endless circular orbits by indwelling motor souls. Gilbert was one of the very few sixteenth-century thinkers to promote a Copernican philosophy of the earth as a planet that was an integral part of a harmonious solar system. Proving this was the aim and climax of *De magnete*. Having rejected the authority of almost all previous natural philosophers, Gilbert set out to prove it with a brilliant series of magnetic experiments and inferences from them.

First, Gilbert established the modern science of magnetism by showing that magnetic attraction was a pervasive property of matter, specifically of all 'true' terrestrial and lunar matter. This challenged the dominant Aristotelian theory that elemental earth was cold, dry, and inert. To do so Gilbert distinguished magnetism from a plethora of highly specific occult sympathies, such as the electrostatic attraction of amber for chaff, or drugs for poisons, within which Renaissance philosophers had classified the pairing of lodestone and iron. Second, he discovered the foundations of geomagnetism, according to which the earth behaves like a giant dipole magnet. Third, he developed his geomagnetic theory into the first satisfactory explanation of the nautical compass. Since England and other European countries were fighting for military and commercial dominance on the seas, *De magnete*'s applications to the problems of finding latitude and especially longitude were very attractive. Fourth, Gilbert provided controversial, if subsequently vindicated, arguments that magnetism was an immaterial force. Within their 'sphere of activity', magnets were capable of attracting and repelling ferrous bodies across empty spaces and through solid matter according to fixed laws.

Despite his claim to have broken with Renaissance philosophical traditions, Gilbert concluded from the lawlike and immaterial nature of terrestrial magnetism that it emanated from something akin to a magnetic soul in the earth. This fifth claim provoked the most criticism. To progressive seventeenth-century followers of Descartes, animate explanations were outdated. Galileo criticized Gilbert's 'reasons' for lacking mathematical rigour (*Dialogue Concerning the Two Chief World Systems*, trans. S. Drake, 1962, 406). Conservative opponents on the other hand did not object to planetary souls—they had been a standard explanation of the regular orbits of heavenly bodies. They opposed the principal thesis of Gilbert's magnetic philosophy, that the earth was not a passive, motionless body inferior to the planets, but a noble, self-moving equal.

Sixth, and in the controversial final book of *De magnete*, Gilbert argued that magnetism was the cosmic force that moved the earth. In doing so he was the first to offer a physical, dynamical rather than mathematical, astronomical proof of Copernicanism. This aspect of it was rendered unnecessary by seventeenth-century theories of inertia. As an adherent of disproofs of solid celestial spheres by the Danish astronomer Tycho Brahe, Gilbert was one of the first to assert that the earth moved effectively in a vacuum. He therefore argued that the fixed orientation of the earth's axis of daily rotation was also caused magnetically. He was almost certainly a thoroughgoing Copernican, but all his writings concerning the earth's annual rotation were skilfully evasive. He may have decided that there was no magnetic proof of it, or may have been restrained by theological concerns. English Copernicans like Gilbert and Thomas Harriot had reason to fear public ridicule and suspicion, if not religious persecution. In 1612 John Owen published two hostile epigrams about Gilbert. One read:

> Stare negas terram; nobis miracula narras;
> Haec cum scribebas, in rate forsan eras.
> (You deny that the earth stands still; you tell us a miracle;
> Perhaps you were in a boat when you wrote this. Roller, 89)

Although a magnetic dynamics of celestial motion was rejected by post-Newtonian physicists, it was the most discussed aspect of magnetic philosophy in the first half of the seventeenth century.

The enthusiasm of scientists like Kepler and Galileo shows that Gilbert's Copernicanism, if not his animism, was treated as a reasonable inference from his magnetic experiments. Modern commentators have tended to agree more with Francis Bacon. While Bacon shared Gilbert's impatience with traditional natural philosophers, his admiration for the knowledge of low-status practitioners such as metalworkers and navigators, and his interest in applied science, Bacon repeatedly reproved Gilbert for an approach that generalized and speculated too readily upon too narrow an observational base. The force must be conceded of Bacon's judgement that Gilbert 'made a philosophy out of a few experiments of a lodestone' (Bacon, *Works*, 1857, 1.169).

Although Gilbert did not articulate a formal scientific method of the kind explicit in Bacon's writings or implicit in Galileo's work, *De magnete*'s experimentalism has impressed most readers from its publication to the present day. Gilbert's use of experiments was unprecedentedly thorough and innovative. As Gilbert himself noted, he surpassed the Italian natural magician Giambattista della Porta, whose unsystematic, over-spectacular, and sometimes unreliable collection was the previous fullest source for magnetic phenomena. He generally followed his rule to include nothing 'that has not been investigated and again and again done and repeated under our eyes' (Gilbert, *De magnete*, xlix), and he intended readers to replicate the experiments that he had performed or commissioned.

Gilbert's work on electricity, in book 2, chapter 2 of *De magnete*, is a typical example of his approach. He began, in Aristotelian fashion, with a review of past opinions, but with the post-Renaissance aim of ruthlessly exposing their inadequacy and ignorance of experimental facts. He then described apparatus and procedures for generating and detecting what is called electrostatic attraction. He indicated in the margin his many new discoveries. Key among these was identification of the numerous substances besides the traditional occult pair of amber and jet that would attract; the inability of electrostatic attraction to act through solid media; and its vulnerability to variables such as heat and humidity. Equally typically, Gilbert confidently and misguidedly explained that the cause of electrostatic effects was a ubiquitous aqueous humour or vapour. For coining the word *electricitas* (derived from the Greek word for amber) and for expanding the range of electrics and electrostatic experiments, Gilbert has been called the father of electricity. The designation misses the point that Gilbert's purpose was to distinguish succinctly magnetic attraction from its traditional occult partner by showing that electricity was a material property of many substances, whereas magnetism was immaterial and unique.

De magnete provided a huge repertory of experiments investigating the composition, shape, and strength of different magnets, but Gilbert's most important series used apparatus that he called *terrellae* and *versoria*. A *terrella* was a naturally occurring lodestone turned into a sphere. The name, meaning 'little earth', encapsulates his conclusion that a laboratory magnet reproduced terrestrial phenomena. The lack of experimental science before Gilbert is partially explained by the Aristotelian principle that a man-made object could not substitute for a natural one. Gilbert's success significantly weakened that objection. His concept of the *terrella* was almost certainly inspired by a few extraordinary experiments with a spherical magnet described in a letter of 1269 by a French engineer, Pierre de Maricourt, and in print in 1562. For Maricourt, however, the sphere imitated the heavens not the earth.

Gilbert modelled his innovative *versorium*, or 'turn detector', on the nautical compass. The miniature needle was mounted so that it could rotate freely in three dimensions. In modern terms it indicated the magnetic field vector. Gilbert moved *versoria* over the surface of his *terrellae*, in explicit imitation of ships' compasses travelling over the earth. His unprecedented strategy was to replicate and synthesize in the laboratory all the magnetic phenomena recorded by navigators, and hence to prove by analogy that the earth was a giant lodestone. Gilbert's intimate acquaintance with and respect for navigators and their skills were crucial.

A good example was Gilbert's use of the discovery of geomagnetic 'dip', or inclination, announced by the London compass maker Robert Norman in 1581. Unlike flat-mounted compasses, Gilbert's *versorium* indicated this vertical component of the earth's field. His method for identifying a magnet's poles was to find the places where the *versorium*'s needle stood vertically. He discovered that dip increased steadily from 0° at a *terrella*'s equator to 90° at its poles. Applied to the earth, this dip-latitude relation offered an alternative to astronomical methods for determining latitude, and *De magnete* included the description and instructions for use of such a dip instrument. Although the method was rarely tested or used at sea, its basic validity established the theoretical and practical credentials of magnetic philosophy.

Gilbert conducted similarly impressive investigations of magnetic variation. That compass needles rarely pointed true north was known to Europeans from the fourteenth century. Data gathered by 1600 had made the cause and geographical distribution of this bane of navigators into a major problem. Gilbert presented persuasive, though not reliably replicable, experiments using *terrellae* with prominences and depressions that modelled continents and oceans. These also generated variation, the needle seemingly attracted slightly away from the poles towards the 'continents'. Gilbert concluded that variation was an artefact of geology, of the earth's slight departures from a perfect, homogeneous magnetic sphere. While only partially correct, it was the first convincing explanation, and it accorded with the empirical survey of variation published by Stevin in 1599. Gilbert's magnetic philosophy gave new and scientifically rigorous direction to Stevin's and other late sixteenth-century proposals for a solution to the longitude problem using compass observations. This, together with magnetic latitude finding, was a compelling practical reason for interest in Gilbert's work. Research into magnetic position finding continued for over a century, even after 1635 when a follower of Gilbert's, the Gresham professor Henry Gellibrand, presented evidence that variation changed over time. The inference was soon drawn that the earth's magnetic poles were separate from the geographical poles, and rotating around them.

Gilbert had rejected the theory of separate poles, because his magnetic astronomy required the earth's axis of rotation to be magnetically stabilized. Consequently, he interpreted variation as a circular motion away from true north. It was one of five magnetic motions. Dip was another, as was the basic rotation of any small magnet into alignment with the field of a larger one. The primary motion was the attraction of one magnet for another, although Gilbert coined the term 'coition' as a better description of the mutual interaction by which two magnets come into contact. He observed 'attraction' (he claimed never to see repulsion) using two magnets in water on floats, when they do appear to circle each other as if in a mating ritual.

These four 'circular' motions made more credible Gilbert's claim to a fifth magnetic rotation—that of the whole earth. Unlike Maricourt, Gilbert explicitly denied that he had seen carefully suspended *terrellae* imitate the earth's diurnal motion. Nevertheless, from the other four observable circular motions, he inferred that the earth's substance was capable of natural rotation, a possibility denied by Aristotelians and other geostatic astronomers. For Gilbert, the immateriality of the earth's magnetic virtue further confirmed that it did actually perform planet-like rotations.

De mundo The posthumous compilation of the five books of *De mundo* means that it cannot be established when Gilbert wrote or revised their elements, or if he intended to publish them. Notwithstanding, the first two books comprise a 'Physiologia nova contra Aristotelem' ('A new natural philosophy in opposition to Aristotle') that is for the most part organized, polished, and built upon *De magnete*. Arranged according to scholastic natural philosophical topics (the four elements, qualities, place, light, the earth, moon, other heavenly bodies and their motions, etc.), it forms a complete natural philosophy in the same genre as Patrizi's. Gilbert developed his explanations of magnetism and electricity into a theory of sublunary matter that replaced the four elements with true magnetic earth and compounds of aqueous and oily humours. In his cosmology the magnetic virtues of the earth and moon, together with other specific planetary virtues, were excited by the sun's luminous virtue into harmonious Copernican orbits. A diagram, as deliberately ambiguous as his writings, strongly suggested that the earth moved in an empty, infinite universe. Because Gilbert concluded that the moon, as the earth's satellite, was also magnetic, he was especially interested in it: *De mundo* included the first map of the moon. Gilbert also proposed that the earth's tides were caused by the moon's magnetic attraction of water. In this, and in his general theory that the attractive power of the earth's and other virtues decreased with distance, his dynamic theory of cosmic attractions anticipated Newton's gravitational solution. Kepler freely acknowledged that it underpinned his magnetic explanation of the elliptical planetary orbits he discovered. But Gilbert believed that the complex interactions of the solar and planetary virtues would defeat mathematicians. This helps to explain why Gilbert maintained the conservative view that astronomers, even Copernicus, did not plot real orbits.

The most puzzling aspect of *De mundo* is its almost total lack of new experiments, experimental reasoning, instruments, and practical knowledge, especially practical mathematics—features that made *De magnete* impressively novel. One hypothesis is that Edward Wright ensured their prominence in *De magnete*. Mark Ridley wrote that Wright had admitted an editorial role, and authorship of parts of *De magnete* dealing with the mathematics and use of the dip instrument. Ridley also confided that Gilbert needed help with astronomy from a Joseph Jessop. It might be that the philosophical *De mundo* was the book that Gilbert wanted to write, while the influential combination in *De magnete* of theory and practice, natural philosophy and mathematics, was the synthesis of two men, sympathetic to each other's interests, but working in different disciplines.

De mundo's last three books make up a 'Nova meteorologia contra Aristotelem' ('A new meteorology in opposition to Aristotle'). This too is organized around scholastic topics derived from Aristotle's own *Meteorology*. Gilbert discusses winds, rivers, and seas (the phenomena of elemental air and water that control the weather) as well as conventionally 'aerial' phenomena such as rainbows, shooting stars, and comets, in comparatively conventional ways. It declines into fragments. The 'New meteorology' does, however, afford some clues to the development of Gilbert's ideas. Dated weather observations suggest that in the late 1560s Gilbert had begun to seek new, anti-Aristotelian causes of the weather and its astrological correlation with planetary positions. The 'New meteorology' was most likely composed in the early 1580s and, while there are no references to magnetic experiments or compass observations, Gilbert did mention his big idea of the earth as a magnetic sphere. It may have originally occurred to him as a substitution for Maricourt's heavenly magnetic sphere. Wright claimed in his 'laudatory address' at the beginning of *De magnete* that Gilbert had held back his magnetic philosophy for eighteen years. This may refer to a prolonged period of experimental research and proofs, and collation of navigational data. Barlow wrote in 1597 that Gilbert 'many years hath laboured in the consideration of the properties of that [lode] Stone' (Barlow, *The Navigators Supply*, sig. C3r).

Last years Between 1600 and his death Gilbert collaborated with grateful practical mathematicians to ensure that navigation was enhanced by his magnetic science. In 1602 Blundeville published a tract introducing English seamen to latitude-finding using a dipmeter sent to him by Gilbert. Tables calculated by Henry Briggs, the first professor of geometry at Gresham College, were appended by Wright, purportedly at Gilbert's suggestion. Gilbert also corresponded with Barlow, who, in order to establish his own credentials as a magnetic philosopher, published Gilbert's only surviving letter, which contained some praise of him. Gilbert told Barlow of his continuing magnetic research, a proposed addition to *De magnete*, and his receipt of a letter from Giovanni Sagredo, the Venetian friend of Galileo, who 'reporteth wonderfull liking of my booke' (Barlow, *Magneticall Advertisements*, appx).

This is the only evidence that Gilbert was aware before his death of the excitement *De magnete* was stimulating among continental philosophers. The English exile Nicholas Hill was the first to publish support for Gilbert's magnetic Copernicanism in 1601. In January 1603 Kepler wished he 'had wings with which to travel to England to confer with him. I certainly think I can demonstrate all the motions of the planets with these same principles' (J. Kepler, *Gesammelte Werke*, 1938, 14.352). The last generation of occult philosophers like Robert Fludd and Athanasius Kircher also used *De magnete* in doomed defences of a rational and experimental basis to magic.

Kepler's and Galileo's use of Gilbert's principles in their promotion of Copernicanism ensured that the cosmological aspects of *De magnete* were seriously discussed in the seventeenth century. Magnetic Copernicanism was controversial, and divided Gilbert's erstwhile colleagues Barlow and Ridley, who vied to communicate Gilbert's ideas in English. While Ridley was even more radical than his mentor, the clergyman Barlow admitted that only his respect for Gilbert's work had restrained him from theological criticism of the cosmology. After 1628, when pirate editions of *De magnete* first appeared, the most prolific magnetic philosophers were Catholic philosophers in the Society of Jesus, who were determined to harness magnetic science to their defence of the earth's immobility. Some surviving copies of *De magnete* have the Copernican book 6 mutilated or missing, according to the Roman inquisition's censorship practices, and Gilbert was cited as a perverse heretic in its prosecution of Galileo. The charge was not based on any particular knowledge. However, *De mundo* expanded upon Gilbert's hints in *De magnete* that theologians held primary responsibility for the erroneous state of contemporary natural philosophy. This was particularly true of the doctrine of solid celestial spheres which, in Gilbert's opinion, had begun as astronomers' calculating devices, had been given a spurious solidity by Aristotle, and was turned into virtual articles of faith by theologians. He wrote that 'the theologians will cry out that I am impious and irreligious, but I show them to be insane and foolish, who defend this opinion borrowed from the Peripatetics' (Gilbert, *De mundo*, 239).

According to his stepbrothers' inscription, Gilbert died on 30 November 1603: his will was proved on 3 December. He probably died in the severe plague epidemic in London that year. Sir Michael Hicks, the Cecils' secretary, recorded how, on 6 December 1603:

> I heard as I was writing hereof that Doctor Gilbert, the physician, is dead, who was my neighbor at St. Peter's Hill. He was a learned physician, and an honest. The sickness is greatly decreased in London, and the citizens do return daily in great numbers. (Roller, 90)

He died a wealthy man. He bequeathed, mainly to Ambrose and William, his stepbrothers, nine houses with lands attached, five lots of real estate, and other tenements and leases. William junior also inherited his 'heade house' in Colchester, almost certainly the Tudor mansion called 'Tymperley's' that is now a Colchester museum. He passed Wingfield House to his sister Agnes, wife of William Smith (PRO, PROB 11/102, fol. 408*r–v*). In 1646 it was purchased for £500 as a hall for the Worshipful Company of Upholders, and was destroyed in the fire of 1666. Fittingly, Crane Court, the future home of the Royal Society, was erected on the site. More seriously for Gilbert scholars, the fire also claimed the College of Physicians, to which Gilbert had bequeathed 'all my bookes in my Librarye, my Globes, and Instrumentes, and my cabinet of myneralles'. The collection must have been substantial, because Gilbert willed £6 to cover their relocation to the college, almost as much as his bequest for a dinner for its fellows.

Reputation Gilbert has remained a heroic figure through many changes of fashion in the history and philosophy of science. To an early fellow of the Royal Society like Sir Christopher Wren he was, with Galileo, the liberator of natural philosophy from Aristotelianism. With the rise of positivism in the early nineteenth century William Whewell and others read him as the pioneer of an inductive experimental method who thereby founded the modern sciences of magnetism and electricity. This interpretation, which persists, struggles to explain his broader concern with natural philosophy and cosmology. Some analysts have attempted unsuccessfully to separate his 'modern' experimentalism from his 'medieval' speculation, although the Marxist historian Edgar Zilsel argued well that he was indebted to progressive craftsmen for his experimental method. By the 1960s the popularity of the 'hypothetico-deductive' school of scientific method saw Gilbert and his cosmological theories claimed as exemplary by this philosophical school too. In the early twenty-first century, historians are less confident of finding the origins of modern science in Gilbert's era, and have begun to locate him as a man of his time and place in the Elizabethan metropolis, and to explore his relationship with Renaissance magic. Our concern with context, however, should not obscure the revolutionary impact of Gilbert's magnetic experiments, hypotheses, and navigational applications. John Dryden, praising 'th' asserters of free reason', was half right when he versified in 1663 that

> Gilbert shall live till loadstones cease to draw,
> Or British fleets the boundless ocean awe.
> (Gilbert, *De magnete*, xxvii)

STEPHEN PUMFREY

Sources D. H. D. Roller, *The 'De magnete' of William Gilbert* (1959) • S. Pumfrey, 'William Gilbert's magnetic philosophy, 1580–1684: the creation and dissolution of a discipline', PhD diss., U. Lond., 1983 • S. Pumfrey, *Latitude & the magnetic earth* (2002) • S. Kelly, *The 'De mundo' of William Gilbert* (1965) • W. Gilbert, *De magnete*, trans. P. F. Mottelay (New York, 1958) • W. Gilbert, *De mundo nostro sublunari philosophia nova* (1651) • S. P. Thompson, 'The family and arms of Gilbert of Colchester', *Transactions of the Essex Archaeological Society*, new ser., 9 (1903–6), 197–211 • Munk, *Roll* • *The letters of John Chamberlain*, ed. N. E. McClure, 2 vols. (1939) • M. Ridley, *Magneticall animadversions made by Mark Ridley, doctor in physicke, upon certain magneticall advertisements, lately published, from Maister William Barlow* (1617) • W. Barlow, *The navigators supply: conteining many things of principall importance belonging to navigation* (1597) • W. Barlow, *Magneticall advertisements* (1616) • W. Barlow, *A breife discovery of the idle animadversions of Marke Ridley doctor in phisicke, upon a treatise* *entituled, 'Magneticall advertisements'* (1618) • *CSP dom.*, 1595–1601; 1603–10 • Fuller, *Worthies* (1662) • Venn, *Alum. Cant.* • Wood, *Ath. Oxon.*, new edn, vol. 1 • J. F. Houston, *Featherbedds and flock bedds: notes on the history of the Worshipful Company of Upholders of the City of London* (1993), pt 2

Archives BL, Royal MS 12 F XI

Likenesses A. A. Hunt, oils, *c.*1900, Colchester town hall, Essex • F. Daniell, oils, *c.*1902, Colchester town hall, Essex • L. J. Watts & Co.?, marble statue, *c.*1902, Colchester town hall, Essex • R. Clamp, stipple (after Harding, after unknown artist, 1591), NPG [*see illus.*] • Clamp?, engraving (after seventeenth-century portrait, now lost), repro. in Gilbert, *De magnete*, frontispiece • statue, St John Cam.

Wealth at death substantial: will, Houston, *Featherbedds and flock bedds*

Gilbert, William (*b.* in or after **1760**, *d. c.***1825**), poet, was born in Antigua, the son of Nathaniel Gilbert, speaker of the house of assembly there, and initiator of the first Methodist society formed in the West Indies. He was educated for the bar, and came to England about 1784 as counsel for the defence in a court martial. Gilbert was placed in a Bristol asylum in 1787, after a mental collapse, but was released after a year's confinement, and disappeared until 1796, when he reappeared in Bristol. He then published 'The Hurricane: a Theosophical and Western Eclogue', a poem which illustrates both his poetic abilities and his madness. He became acquainted with Coleridge and Southey, both of whom he deeply respected and in whose company he tried to control his excesses. Even so, Southey described him in an unpublished letter to William Sidney Walker as 'the most insane person I have ever known at large, and his insanity smothered his genius'. However, Southey continued, 'that genius, when it appeared, was of a high order, and he was not more an object of pity than of respect to all who knew him'.

In 1798 Gilbert mysteriously disappeared. He had often talked of the 'Gilberti', an African people mentioned in James Bruce's *Travels* (1790), whom he believed to exist, and to be closely related to his own family. Southey, conjecturing that he had gone in search of this nation, caused enquiries to be made of captains in the African trade but no trace was found of him. Writing to Sidney Walker in 1824, Southey therefore spoke of Gilbert as long dead. In fact he had made his way to Charleston in America, where he survived until about 1825, restored to reason and in good circumstances having recovered some litigated property.

Southey thought so highly of Gilbert's poetical power that he assured Cottle, on the first publication of Landor's 'Gebir', that 'the poem is such as Gilbert, if he were only half as mad as he is, could have written' (Cottle, 219). In fact, in 'The Hurricane', Gilbert gives little evidence of insanity where he keeps to descriptive writing. The notes to his poems are far more bewildering than the texts themselves although Wordsworth in his notes to *The Excursion*, quotes one of them as 'one of the finest passages of modern English prose' (Wordsworth, 428). Read in this context it may have inspired Keats with the Darien simile in 'On First Looking into Chapman's Homer'. Montgomery also appears to be indebted to Gilbert for the idea of his 'Pelican Island'. Gilbert also wrote two works entitled 'The Law of Fire' and 'The Standard of God Displayed', as well as a poem in praise of Garrick.

RICHARD GARNETT, *rev.* S. C. BUSHELL

Sources J. Cottle, *Reminiscences of Samuel Taylor Coleridge and Robert Southey* (1847), 42–6 • R. Southey, *The life of Wesley and the rise and progress of Methodism*, 2nd edn, 2 vols. (1820), 466–7 • R. Southey, manuscript letter to W. Sidney Walker • J. Gorton, *A general biographical dictionary*, 3 vols. (1841) • W. Beckett, *A universal biography*, 3 vols. (1835–6) • W. Wordsworth, *The excursion* (1814); facs. edn (1991), 428 • T. Southey, *Chronological history of the West Indies*, 2 (1827); facs. edn (1968), 340, 429 • P. Kaufman, '"The hurricane" and the Romantic poets', *English Miscellany*, 21 (1970), 99–115 • Allibone, *Dict.* • Watt, *Bibl. Brit.* • private information (2004) [Paul Cheshire]

Gilbert, William (**1804–1890**), writer, was born on 24 May 1804 in London, the eldest son of William Gilbert (*d.* 1812), a prosperous grocer (or perhaps cotton broker), and his wife, Catherine Mathers (*d. c.*1810). Early orphaned, William, his brother, and sister were affectionately brought up by their mother's married sister Mary Mathers Schwenck. She was also godmother to their sons, William's being the well-known dramatist William Schwenck *Gilbert (1836–1911).

In early life Gilbert evidently spent three years in the East India Company's 'brutal' service, from which he drew materials for his fiction, especially *Sir Thomas Branston* (1869), *Memoirs of a Cynic* (serialized 1873), and *King George's Middy* (1869). He then travelled in Italy, which also provided incidents for his novels, and on 3 December 1830 became a member of the Royal College of Surgeons. He seems not to have practised, except perhaps briefly as an assistant naval surgeon. On 5 September 1832 Gilbert married Mary Ann Skelton, a minor, who died very young without children, and on 12 February 1836 he married Anne Mary Bye Morris (1812/13–1888). Their first child, William Schwenck, was born the following November, followed by three daughters: Jane Morris, Mary Florence, and Anne Maude. The Gilbert family travelled in Europe before finally returning to London. Gilbert and his wife led an increasingly quarrelsome life there and separated informally in 1876. After a serious illness, Gilbert went to Salisbury to live with his married daughter Jane.

Between 1857 when his first pamphlet was published (*On the Present System of Rating for the Poor in the Metropolis*) to 1882 when his last book (*Legion, or, The Modern Demoniac*) appeared, Gilbert published a number of novels and works of non-fiction as well as writing stories and articles for many journals, including the *Cornhill Magazine*, *Temple Bar*, *The Fortnightly*, and *Good Words*. In a number of instances he borrowed heavily from himself as in 'The English demoniac' (*Good Words*, February 1867), which used material from his *Cornhill* article 'A visit to a convict lunatic asylum' (October 1864) and lent material to the book *Legion, or, The Modern Demoniac*. All of these dealt with the danger of alcohol, especially adulterated alcohol, for Gilbert constantly attacked gin (sin) and gin palaces owned by the Church of England. In 1869 one of Gilbert's works, *Margaret Meadows: a Tale for the Pharisees* (1859), was plagiarized by Tom Taylor, who adapted it as a successful drama, *Mary Warner*. On arbitration, Taylor was ordered to pay Gilbert £200 and add his name to the playbill. Gilbert accepted the money but refused the attribution.

The publisher William Tinsley remarked that Gilbert always had 'a craze of some kind, or something or some-one to dispute about or with' (Tinsley, 2.314). Foremost among his 'crazes' were a dedication to exploring the lives of the 'social deposits', that is, the poorest of the poor, and an interest in abnormal psychology as studied by French psychologists. These 'crazes' overlapped in the relationships observed between alcoholism and the mental afflictions of the impoverished, sometimes manifesting themselves in 'hauntings' and 'phantoms'. These hallucinations of dead loved ones are sometimes represented as tender and comforting as in *Shirley Hall Asylum, or, The Memoirs of a Monomaniac* (1863) and *Martha* (1871). A recurrent alcoholic phantom is even used to produce a comic effect in 'How Brother Jonas, the Sub-cellerer, was Haunted by an Evil Spirit' (*Britannia*, April 1869); but this use is the exception to a more sinister envisioning, as when the perpetual image of a shepherd in a red cap drives Jones, a murderer, to suicide in *Nothing but the Truth* (1877). Gilbert collected statistics showing that strong drink was not a help in typhus, could not prevent cholera, was not necessary for manual labourers, and could cause sudden impulsive murder for no motive. Irrational urges to kill might, however, overtake non-drunkards, and against them, prayer was the only safeguard. Fantastic, but on the whole harmless, monomanias appear in *Shirley Hall Asylum* and its sequel, *Dr Austin's Guests* (1866).

Gilbert never wearied, nevertheless, of inveighing against the establishment and firmly believed that environment, not heredity, caused children to become thieves and prostitutes. He disliked capitalists who profited from the poor. He called for housing and sanitary reform of the poorest areas of London, insisting that the poor should have fresher or 'atmospheric' air. He also believed that, unlike parish officers, the 'social deposits' were truly good to their fellows: crones such as he described in 'Poor old women' (*Good Words*, April 1867) could be beautiful in self-sacrifice. He was anti-Catholic in his dislike of Roman 'millinery', anti-vivisectionist, and pro-Semitic, repeatedly pointing out the well-ordered, extraordinary charity of Jews even to gentiles. As an honorary secretary for the Society for Relief of Distress, Gilbert did not take his duties lightly. He investigated cases, visited prisons, wrote about what he had observed, and adjured the government to pay attention as in, for instance, 'Our discharged convicts' (*Good Words*, September 1867). Having an entrée to hospitals he described the proximity of refuse bins and dead-houses to sick wards (*Contrasts: Dedicated to the Rate Payers of London*, 1873).

The second large group of Gilbert's works, fantastic tales, included children's stories, such as 'The Seven-Leagued Boots' (December 1869) and 'Mrs Blunderbore's Trials' (January 1870), both in *Good Words for the Young*, and interlocking tales in *The Magic Mirror* (1866 [1865]) and *The Wizard of the Mountain* (1867). William Schwenck Gilbert illustrated the first and third as he did *King George's Middy*. In these narratives magic or the supernatural is explicit, even overlapping Gilbert's 'realistic' fiction. For example, *'Them Boots'* (1877) is organized around a pair of magic boots, which carry each woman who wears them willy-nilly into a real public house. In *The Magic Mirror* a Venetian looking-glass grants wishes which lead only to trouble, as when one person wants a glass brain, which enables him to make money, but renders him completely detached from humanity.

Gilbert also wrote an anti-defamatory life of Lucrezia Borgia (1869), which reviewers praised chiefly for its rendering of setting and descriptive details. Detail was indeed the author's great advantage in whatever work he produced, and critics frequently compared him to Defoe for his plain but very specific style. The reformed hero of *The Landlord of the Sun* (1871) suggests Hugo's Jean Valjean, and there are Dickensian touches as well as anticipations of Zola, the former particularly in *Dives and Lazarus, or, The Adventures of an Obscure Medical Man in a Low Neighbourbood* (1858), the latter in *The Weaver's Family* (1860), and both in the rendering of the filthy streets and overcrowded habitations in which Gilbert's characters perforce move, live, and frequently die.

William Gilbert himself died of paralysis in Salisbury on 3 January 1890, and was buried three days later in the cloister. His will insisted on a plain, inexpensive funeral.

JANE W. STEDMAN

Sources J. W. Stedman, '"A peculiar sharp flavour": the contributions of Dr. William Gilbert', *Victorian Periodicals Review*, 19 (1986), 43–50 • H. A. Page [A. H. Japp], 'Psychology in art: William Gilbert', *Contemporary Review*, 12 (1869), 437–44 • 'Review of *Lucrezia Borgia, duchess of Ferrara: a biography*', *The Athenaeum* (20 Feb 1869), 267–8 • W. Tinsley, *Random recollections of an old publisher*, 2 vols. (1900) • J. M. Bulloch, 'W. S. Gilbert's father', *N&Q*, 171 (1936), 435–8 [an incomplete, annotated bibliography] • [S. Edwards], *Daily News* (4 Jan 1890), 3 • H. Frye, ed., *The royal guide to the London charities for 1866–7* (1866) • *DNB* • Royal College of Surgeons, list of fellows and members • *IGI* • d. cert. • private information [F. Pascoe]

Likenesses oils, repro. in C. Hibbert, *Gilbert and Sullivan and their Victorian World* (New York, 1976), 28 • oils, repro. in L. Baily, *The Gilbert and Sullivan book*, 4th edn (1956), 38

Wealth at death £2632 9s. 6d.: resworn probate, Sept 1890, *CGPLA Eng. & Wales*

Gilbert, Sir William Schwenck (1836–1911), playwright, the eldest child and only son of William *Gilbert (1804–1890), author and surgeon, and his second wife, Anne Mary Bye Morris (1812/13–1888), was born on 18 November 1836 at 17 Southampton Street, London, the home of his maternal grandfather, Dr Thomas Morris.

Early years, education, and legal career At first Gilbert was nicknamed Bab for 'Baby', a name he later used as a signature for his verses and drawings. Within the family he was called Schwenck, the surname of his great-aunt who had acted as mother to William Gilbert when he was early orphaned. Bab/Schwenck had three younger sisters: Jane Morris, who married Alfred Weigall, a miniature painter; and Mary Florence and Anne Maude, neither of whom married.

Dr William Gilbert, though he qualified as a surgeon, soon ceased practice and travelled *en famille* in France, Germany, and Italy. Bab learned French well and at the age of seven went to school in Boulogne. Afterwards he attended Western Grammar School, Brompton, London, and the prestigious Great Ealing School where, although by his own admission lazy and unpopular, he rose to be head boy and to write plays for performance by his schoolfellows and himself. He also painted scenery.

In March 1853 Gilbert enrolled as an 'occasional student' at King's College, London, and after six months entered the department of general literature and science as a regular student. He was instrumental in temporarily changing the college Engineering Society into a Shakespearean Reading and Dramatic Society, of which he became secretary. Having completed work for his BA in 1856, he read for a competitive examination to become an officer in the Royal Artillery. The Crimean War was being waged, but fortunately for Victorian drama it ended abruptly and the examination was indefinitely postponed. Three years later he compensated for his disappointment by joining the volunteers—first the Civil Service Rifles, then the West Yorkshire militia, and finally the Royal Aberdeenshire Highlanders as a lieutenant, and later captain, from which he retired in 1878 with the honorary rank of major.

After taking his BA in 1857, Gilbert became an assistant clerk in the education department of the Privy Council Office. Upon inheriting £300, he left to become a barrister, having already entered the Inner Temple as a student. He was called to the bar on 17 November 1863 and wrote a short story about his first brief for the *Cornhill Magazine* in December. After practising in London, he joined the northern circuit in March 1866, but without much success. In 1861, however, he had become a contributor to a new comic weekly, *Fun*, edited by H. J. Byron, which at its height would rival *Punch's* circulation.

Fun and works of the 1860s Gilbert had already appeared in print, having in 1858 translated the laughing song from Scribe's and Auber's *Manon Lescaut*. His childhood friend Euphrosyne Parepa (later Madame Parepa-Rosa) was singing it in French at Promenade Concerts and had asked him to render it in English for the playbill.

For some dozen years of *Fun* Gilbert turned out fillers, squibs, puns, biting social criticism, grotesque drawings, verses including the 'Bab Ballads', illustrated burlesque playlets (which were really shrewd reviews of current plays), and two long series of character sketches by the Comic Physiognomist, also illustrated. Under Tom Hood the younger, editor from 1865 to 1874, Gilbert's work became a leading feature of *Fun*. He occasionally contributed drawings and verse to *Punch* until its editor, Mark Lemon, rejected 'The yarn of the *Nancy Bell*' (*Fun*, 3 March 1866) as 'too cannibalistic' and insisted that Gilbert sever all connections with *Fun* without the promise of a permanent position on *Punch*. Gilbert refused. In the 1860s, however, he continued to publish stories, articles, and reviews in the *Cornhill Magazine*, *London Society*, *Tinsley's Magazine*, and *Temple Bar*; to be London correspondent for *L'Invalide Russe*; and to be drama critic for the *Illustrated London Times* and briefly for the *Daily News*, *Sunday Times*, and *The Observer*, which in 1870 was to send him temporarily to France as a war correspondent reporting on the Franco-Prussian War. In the 1860s he also contributed to Tom Hood's Christmas annuals, to *Saturday Night*, the *Comic News*, and the *Savage Club Papers*. In 1869 his first collection of *The*

Sir William Schwenck Gilbert (1836–1911), by Frank Holl, 1886

'Bab' Ballads was published by John Camden Hotten, who proved to be much less than forthright; so Gilbert turned to George Routledge & Sons, who published successive collections of the ballads until the end of the century, after which Macmillan took them over. During this decade Gilbert also illustrated works written by his father, who had commenced publishing in 1857. These included 'The Seven-Leagued Boots' in *Good Words for the Young* (1869), *The Magic Mirror* (1866), and *King George's Middy* (1869).

Meanwhile, Gilbert had been writing plays, which first found a stage when *Uncle Baby* (1863), a comedietta, was produced at the Lyceum Theatre in London on 31 October. It was neither a failure nor a noticeable success, but at Christmas 1866 his first acknowledged burlesque proved decidedly popular. This was *Dulcamara! or, The Little Duck and the Great Quack*, performed at the St James's Theatre (29 December 1866) under the lesseeship of Miss Herbert to whom the dramatist Tom Robertson had recommended Gilbert. The plot was a travesty of Donizetti's opera *L'elisir d'amore*, while many lines satirized Dr Robert Hunter, who had very recently brought a well-publicized libel suit against the *Pall Mall Gazette* and had been awarded a contemptuous farthing. Gilbert charged 30 guineas, which W. S. Emden, the acting manager, reduced to pounds with the advice never again to sell so good a piece for so little. Gilbert never did. He continued to write burlesques: *La vivandière* (Liverpool, 15 June 1867; Queen's Theatre, London, 22 January 1868), a travesty of Donizetti's *La figlia del reggimento*, was followed by *The Merry Zingara, or, The Tipsy Gypsy and the Pipsy Wipsy* (Royalty Theatre, London, 21 March 1868), a play drawn from Bunn and Balfe's *The Bohemian Girl*. *Robert the Devil, or, The Nun, the Dun, and the Son of a Gun*, a parody of Weber's opera, was first performed at the opening of the Gaiety Theatre on 21 December 1868, with Nellie Farren as Mercury. A Gilbertian version of Bellini's *Norma*, entitled *The Pretty Druidess, or, The Mother, the Maid, and the Mistletoe Bough*, was produced for the opening of the Charing Cross Theatre on 19 June 1869. These met with varying degrees of approval, being well received by most reviewers, who praised their use of operatic airs rather than the more customary popular songs such as 'Skidamalink'. Like the Bab ballads, the burlesques provided suggestions for the librettos Gilbert would write. He also experimented with an innovative 'respectful perversion' of Tennyson's long poem *The Princess* (Olympic Theatre, 8 January 1870), highly regarded by critics and forming the basis for the later libretto of *Princess Ida*.

Having already written anonymously some portion of Charles Millward's Astley pantomime *Hush-a-bye, baby, on the tree top, or, Harlequin fortunia, King Frog of Frog Island, and the magic toys of Lowther Arcade* (Christmas 1866), Gilbert essayed a pantomime of his own. Hastily flung together, half-rehearsed on the stage of the Lyceum Theatre by E. T. Smith on 26 December 1867, *Harlequin Cock Robin and Jenny Wren, or, Fortunatus and the water of life, the three bears, the three gifts, the three wishes, and the little man who woo'd the little maid* introduced the cancan to England. The press praised Gilbert but was outraged by the dance. The playwright, however, derived some articles from the experience, including 'My pantomime' (*Era Almanack*, 1884), but he resolved from then on to control any stage on which his works might be performed. He also wrote farces: *A Colossal Idea* (unperformed); a translation of a French comedy entitled *Allow me to Explain* (Prince of Wales's Theatre, 4 November 1867); and *Highly Improbable* (Royalty Theatre, 5 December 1867). The first two are conventional, but the third anticipates a more individual style.

On 6 August 1867 Gilbert married Lucy Agnes Blois Turner (1847–1936), the posthumous daughter of Captain Thomas Metcalfe Blois Turner. Her mother was Herbertina Compton, whose father, Sir Herbert Compton, was lord chief justice of Bombay. Lucy was not Gilbert's first love, however; in 1866 he had proposed marriage to Annie Thomas, a prolific 'advanced' novelist with a keen sense of humour. She rejected him, presumably at her mother's behest, and instead married a curate. Gilbert and his wife had no children, but he was much loved by the offspring of his friends.

Plays from 1869 to 1884 Two years later Gilbert began a satisfying association with Thomas German Reed and his wife, Priscilla Horton Reed, at their Gallery of Illustration. This tiny theatre in Regent Street carefully avoided all theatrical terminology; for instance, roles were termed 'assumptions'. Limiting itself to very small casts, it attracted both sophisticated playgoers and those who would not visit theatres. Gilbert wrote six entertainments for the Reeds: *No Cards* (29 March 1869); *Ages Ago* (22 November 1869), the most popular piece in the gallery's repertory, and revived many times; *Our Island Home* (20 June 1870); *A Sensation Novel* (30 January 1871); *Happy Arcadia* (28 October 1872); and *Eyes and No Eyes* (St George's Hall, 5 July 1875). The casts included the Reeds, Fanny Holland, Arthur Cecil, and Corney Grain. In most cases German Reed himself provided original music, but Frederic Clay set *Ages Ago* and *Happy Arcadia*. These works, too, prefigured elements of Gilbert's more famous librettos. Clay also collaborated with Gilbert on two longer works: *The Gentleman in Black* (Charing Cross Theatre, 26 May 1870), the plot of which ended with one of Gilbert's favourite time juggles; and *Princess Toto* (Nottingham, 1 July 1876; Liverpool, 24 July 1876; London, Strand Theatre, 2 October 1876), which was not a great success in London because of miscasting.

The decade of the 1870s was Gilbert's most prolific one. He went briefly to Paris as *The Observer*'s correspondent for the Franco-Prussian War and had the farce 'A Medical Man' published in a collection called *Drawing-Room Plays and Parlour Pantomimes* (1870). He began collaborating with Arthur Seymour *Sullivan (1842–1900), whom he had met at the Gallery of Illustration in 1869, when *Cox and Box* by Sullivan and Francis Burnand was the Reeds' second most popular entertainment. (Although both remembered being introduced by Clay, it is likely that they met earlier, albeit briefly.) Together they wrote *Thespis, or, The Gods Grown Old* for John Hollingshead, performed at his Gaiety Theatre (26 December 1871) with Nellie Farren and J. L. Toole. Typical of Gilbert's 'invasion plots', in which characters 'invade' another society and alter it, usually for the worse, *Thespis* features a troupe of actors taking over from the Olympian gods. It was a successful enough play after it had shaken down, but musician and author did not come together again until *Trial by Jury* four years later.

Instead, Gilbert's most imposing work in the early 1870s lay in his fairy comedies, blank verse plays in which magic is an essential ingredient. The enchantment of *The Palace of Truth* (19 November 1870), for instance, was followed by the vivification of a marble statue in the enormously popular *Pygmalion and Galatea* (9 December 1871). Fairies themselves were featured in *The Wicked World* (4 January 1873), a bitter sexual comedy in which love invades and nearly destroys fairyland, and a magic veil provides an important plot element in *Broken Hearts* (Court Theatre, 9 December 1875). Except for the last, these were staged at the Haymarket Theatre, managed by John Baldwin Buckstone, who played the comic lead in each, with Madge Robertson (Mrs Kendal) and W. H. Kendal as romantic leads. A charge that *The Wicked World* was indecent led to Gilbert's libel suit against the *Pall Mall Gazette* in which the jury declared both parties innocent. It also led to a burlesque, *The Happy Land*, under the *nom de plume* F. Tomline (later F. Latour Tomline), with assistance from Gilbert À Beckett. Originally intended for merely private performance, it was, instead, performed at the Court Theatre (3 March 1873). Gilbert had substituted politics for love, and the male characters were made up to resemble the prime minister, William Gladstone, and two cabinet members. The lord chamberlain ordered *The Happy Land* closed, but after the make-up was changed, and some lines altered, it was reopened to the great delight of audiences who flocked to the theatre. Gilbert then adapted Meilhac's and Halévy's *Le roi Candaule* as *The Realm of Joy* (Royalty Theatre, 18 October 1873), in which he satirized the lord chamberlain as 'The Lord High Disinfectant'.

Concurrently, Gilbert worked for the Court Theatre, newly opened by the actress Marie Litton, for whom he wrote *Randall's Thumb* (25 January 1871), *Creatures of Impulse* (15 April 1871), *Great Expectations*, an adaptation of Dickens's novel (29 May 1871), *On Guard* (28 October 1871), *The Wedding March* (15 November 1873), and *The Blue-Legged Lady* (4 March 1874). The first two were dramatizations of two of his short stories, and *Creatures of Impulse* was considered innovative because it did not end with a romantic pairing off. The last two were adapted from the French of Labiche and Marc-Michel, *The Wedding March* proving one of Gilbert's often revived pieces; *The Blue-Legged Lady* was a failure and Gilbert forgot all about it.

The Haymarket next staged a Gilbert problem play, which antedated those by Arthur Wing Pinero but was not a success in spite of a good cast. *Charity* (3 January 1874) attacked the sexual double standard and included a thief/prostitute whom Gilbert depicts as a victim of environment, a favourite theme of his. Another, *Ought we to visit her?* (Royalty Theatre, 17 January 1874), adapted from a novel by Mrs Edwardes, emphasized the good-heartedness of an actress and the bad-heartedness of the self-righteous community which rejects her. It too was unsuccessful. Gilbert also twice adapted Meilhac's and Halévy's *Le réveillon*, first as *Committed for Trial* (Globe Theatre, 24 January 1874) and then as *On Bail* (Criterion Theatre, 3 February 1877). Later in 1874 he made a great hit with a little sentimental play, *Sweethearts* (Prince of Wales's Theatre, 7 November 1874), in which the accomplished actress Mrs Bancroft surpassed herself. Gilbert returned to farce with the three-act *Tom Cobb* (St James's Theatre, 24 April 1875) and with *Engaged* (Haymarket Theatre, 3 October 1877), his most cynical comedy, in which characters profess high-flown motives but are really actuated by money. Some reviewers were shocked; some compared him to Jonathan Swift.

Gilbert continued to experiment with serious drama. *Dan'l Druce* (Haymarket Theatre, 11 September 1876), its initiating incident drawn from George Eliot's *Silas Marner*, was applauded; *The Ne'er-do-Weel* (Olympic Theatre, 25 February 1878), even when revised as *The Vagabond*, did not hold the stage; and *Gretchen* (Olympic Theatre, 24 March 1879) was a failure. 'I called it *Gretchen*, the public called it rot', Gilbert supposedly said (Dark and Grey, 56). In 1877 Gilbert also found himself in a pamphlet war with Henrietta Hodson, an actress, who accused him of persecuting her by interrupting rehearsals, and talking loudly to friends while she was on stage. She also maintained that he was fond of humiliating actresses, vain, and, in an earlier letter, capable of forgery. This has often been taken as evidence of Gilbert's intolerable temper, but many of Hodson's so-called 'facts' prove false when examined dispassionately, especially since Gilbert had kept pressed copies of his letters. All of the written evidence favours him.

More pleasantly, Gilbert wrote one of the acts for a charity pantomime, *The Forty Thieves*, given in February, March, and April of 1878. He loved to act and played Harlequin in it, learning to do 'trips' and 'window-leaps' and to dance a hornpipe for his role. After the 1870s he wrote fewer plays, though his short *Comedy and Tragedy* (Lyceum Theatre, 26 January 1884) was an admirable vehicle for the beautiful American actress Mary Anderson. His 1881 comedy, *Foggerty's Fairy* (Criterion Theatre, 15 December 1881), was judged too complicated for its audience.

Collaboration with Sullivan and others During the late 1870s and until 1889, Gilbert concentrated on librettos for the Savoy operas, as they were called, after the theatre which Richard D'Oyly Carte built for them in 1881. Carte brought 'Gilbert and Sullivan' together to furnish a short piece for the Royalty Theatre, where he was business manager for Selina Dolaro. Gilbert had already expanded his 'Trial by Jury' in *Fun* (11 April 1868) to be set by Carl Rosa, but the premature death of his wife, Euphrosyne Parepa-Rosa, caused him to disband his company for some time. Arthur Sullivan now wrote a score rapidly, and the piece was first performed on 25 March 1875 before an enthusiastic audience. Fred Sullivan, Arthur's brother, played the comic lead, and *Trial by Jury* proved far more popular than Offenbach's *La périchole*, the full-length piece it accompanied.

Gilbert and Sullivan then collaborated on a longer opera, *The Sorcerer* (Opera Comique, 17 November 1877), in which a love potion added to the communal teapot scrambles the relationships of the characters. Fred Sullivan had died and was replaced by George Grossmith, making his professional début. When Mrs Howard Paul was engaged for Lady Sangazure, she brought with her a young member of her touring company, Rutland Barrington, whose stolidity proved an amusing contrast to the mercurial Grossmith. Together they and Richard Temple, a bass, appeared in most of Gilbert and Sullivan's operas as continuing favourites. On 11 October 1884 a somewhat revised *Sorcerer* was revived and greeted happily.

For the original *Sorcerer* a Comedy Opera Company (Limited) had been formed with Carte as manager, which also produced *HMS 'Pinafore', or, The Lass that Loved a Sailor* (25 May 1878). After a slow start the opera became immensely popular, running for over 500 performances and pirated widely by amateur and professional companies in the United States, which underwent a *'Pinafore'* mania. Carte sent out three touring companies and began a kind of Carte 'empire' in the provinces.

Since American productions brought no profit to Carte, Sullivan, or Gilbert, they determined to go to New York, arriving in November 1879 to mount their own 'legitimate' *'Pinafore'* and to première their new opera, *The Pirates of Penzance, or, The Slave of Duty*. Blanche Roosevelt, an American soprano, Jessie Bond (who had entered the company for *'Pinafore'*), Alfred Cellier, the musical director, and other English singers went too. After a disagreement with the New York orchestra over payment, *'Pinafore'* opened on 1 December and *Pirates* on new year's eve 1879 at the Fifth Avenue Theatre, to a fashionable and appreciative audience. In England one of Carte's touring companies mounted an almost impromptu performance of *Pirates* in Paignton, Devon, for copyright purposes. In the United States the works of Gilbert and Sullivan recurrently suffered from copyright disputes and unauthorized productions, especially of *The Mikado*, in which American judges found there was no infringement.

In London, Carte was now free of the Comedy Opera Company; *Pirates* opened at the Opera Comique on 3 April 1880 with Grossmith, Barrington, Temple, and Marion Hood. This was followed by *Patience, or, Bunthorne's Bride* (23 April 1881), a comic treatment of both the much satirized Aesthetes and their supposed opposites, a chorus of military men. Gilbert's even-handed satire was unique among that of *Punch* and others who attacked the Aesthetes alone. Six months later, on 10 October, *Patience* transferred to Carte's new Savoy Theatre, the first in the world to be lit entirely by electricity. After more than 500 performances of *Patience* came *Iolanthe, or, The Peer and the Peri* (25 November 1882), political satire mixed with a band of fairies, and *Princess Ida, or, Castle Adamant* (5 January 1884), a more muted work, dealing with women's education as had Tennyson's *The Princess*. In it, Rosina Brandram took over the contralto roles permanently from Alice Barnett.

For the next opera Gilbert constructed a 'lozenge plot', as Sullivan called it, in which by taking a lozenge or using some such magic device, people either became what they pretended to be or revealed their hidden selves. Although Gilbert had been successful with 'lozenge plots' earlier, Sullivan considered them lacking in human interest and consistently rejected them, which led to quarrels. Fortunately Gilbert found another subject, and the opera which now burst upon a delighted public was *The Mikado* (14 March 1885), which ran for two years in London and was frequently revived, reaching more than 1000 performances before Sullivan's death in 1900. It is the happiest of the Savoy operas, even though it deals with the threat of execution, and proved inexhaustible throughout the twentieth century. When *The Mikado* finally ended its run, *Ruddygore* replaced it (22 January 1887). This was much less popular, being a satire on melodrama with the noble sentiments of the genre turned to the cash nexus and self-interest. The title was respelt *Ruddigore* and changes made in text and music, but it was not revived in London until 1921, a year after the first revival of *Princess Ida*. Nevertheless, Gilbert said that he made £7000 from this 'failure'. It was followed by a splendid revival of *HMS 'Pinafore'* and after that by first revivals of *The Pirates of Penzance* and *The Mikado*.

After another proffered and rejected 'lozenge plot', Gilbert and Sullivan produced a more serious opera in *The Yeomen of the Guard* (3 October 1888), which they considered their best work. The public preferred more fun, but it ran for 423 performances, and its bitter jester, Jack Point, is one of Gilbert's best creations. 'There is a Shakesperian halo about the whole', was the comment of the *Morning Post*. During 1888 Gilbert was also building a new theatre, the Garrick, on Charing Cross Road and preparing a serious drama, *Brantinghame Hall* (29 November) for the St James's Theatre, now managed by Barrington. This may have been an old unacted play, revised for Gilbert's dark, Amazonian protégée, Julia Neilson. It was the worst failure of his career; Clement Scott, the leading reactionary critic, attacked both author and actress. Although Scott had often been the object of libel suits, the press took his part, and only one reviewer praised *Brantinghame Hall*. Gilbert resolved to write no more serious plays, though in 1897 he did *The Fortune Hunter* for Miss Fortescue, who played it in Edinburgh and the provinces without great success.

In Edinburgh, Gilbert gave an interview which led to a contemptuous *Era* editorial; he sued the proprietor for libel, but the jury failed to agree. On 16 September 1889 *The Brigands*, which Gilbert had adapted from Offenbach's opera in 1871 but which had not been performed, was now played in Plymouth and in London (Avenue Theatre) in a debased version. This elicited an unsuccessful legal appeal from Gilbert. A more ebullient opera, *The Gondoliers* (7 December 1889), followed, Sullivan having once more rejected the 'lozenge plot'. Sparkling and happy, it ran for well over a year at the Savoy Theatre but was a virtual failure in the United States.

Gilbert and his wife now went to India for a long visit, he leaving behind a volume of short stories, *Foggerty's Fairy and other Tales*, to be published for the Christmas trade.

When they returned in April 1890 he discovered that preliminary expenses for *The Gondoliers* had reached an astonishingly high figure, which included a new carpet for the front of the house. This precipitated the so-called 'carpet quarrel', which drew Sullivan in on Carte's side. Far more than the carpet was involved, and Gilbert eventually took legal action. An erroneous affidavit from Sullivan to which the composer stubbornly clung lost the case for Gilbert and maintained the breach between them, even after Carte and Gilbert had become reconciled. Nevertheless, Gilbert dedicated his *Songs of a Savoyard* to Sullivan.

During this time Gilbert bought a country estate, Grim's Dyke in Harrow Weald, Middlesex; he became a justice of the peace for Middlesex, unusual in refusing to assume that a policeman's evidence was invariably accurate. In 1902 he became a deputy lieutenant of Middlesex. He did not collaborate with Sullivan again until *Utopia (Limited)* (7 October 1893), but in 1891 he and Alfred Cellier worked together on *The Mountebanks* (Lyric Theatre, 4 January 1892). It had a moderate success in England and abroad in spite of Gilbert's having to make hasty revisions because of Cellier's dilatoriness and death in late December 1891. Later in 1892 Gilbert's travesty of *Hamlet*, *Rosencrantz and Guildenstern*, formed part of a triple bill at the Court Theatre, and he turned *The Wedding March* into *Haste to the Wedding*, with a simple score by George Grossmith (Criterion Theatre, 27 July 1892). It did not succeed. By early 1893 Gilbert was reconciled with Sullivan and had begun to consider a new libretto for the Savoy: *Utopia (Limited)*, his most elaborate political satire produced at great expense and with great éclat. The leading soprano, Nancy McIntosh, an American, was a Gilbert discovery; Sullivan, however, was of two minds about her voice and eventually refused to have her in another opera. In spite of initial enthusiasm, *Utopia (Limited)* ran for only 245 performances. Gilbert turned next to Osmond Carr as collaborator and staged *His Excellency* (Lyric Theatre, 27 October 1894), originally intended for Sullivan and the Savoy. Barrington, Grossmith, Bond, and McIntosh were in the cast, but despite a hilarious chorus of dancing hussars, it ran only until April 1895. Gilbert himself, who at times suffered from migraine and gout, now became very ill and could not work on a new opera (*The Grand Duke*) until August 1895. It began a run of 123 performances on 7 March 1896, a failure by Savoy standards. Neither *Utopia (Limited)* nor *The Grand Duke* has, at the time of writing, been revived professionally except for one fully staged version of the first and one concert version of the second during the D'Oyly Carte centenary celebration in 1975. Amateurs in the twentieth century, however, staged both.

Final years, personality, and significance Sullivan died in 1900; after that Gilbert continued to write, but less frequently and never again for a long run. *The Fairy's Dilemma* (Garrick Theatre, 3 May 1904), however, has been called the best satire on pantomime ever written (M. Booth, ed., *English Plays of the Nineteenth Century*, 1976, 5.52). Other works by Gilbert during this time include *The 'Pinafore' Picture Book* (1908); *The Story of 'The Mikado'* (1921); and a pamphlet, *My Case Against the Rev. J. Pullein Thompson*, protesting a clergyman's mismanagement of a charity in which Gilbert had interested himself. His last libretto, *Fallen Fairies* (Savoy Theatre, 15 December 1909), based on *The Wicked World*, with music by Edward German, failed utterly but not altogether deservedly. His last play was a short, grim prison drama for the Coliseum (27 February 1911) in which James Welch played a weak-minded coster boy convicted of murder. Another example of his views on the importance of environment, it out-Galsworthyed Galsworthy as critics exclaimed with surprised approbation.

In 1907 Gilbert was knighted, the first dramatist ever to receive that accolade, and in 1908–9 he took part in the unsuccessful attempt by dramatists to modify or abolish theatrical censorship. He was elected to the Garrick Club in 1906, having long been a member of the Beefsteak and Junior Carlton clubs.

Like many other Victorians, Gilbert's nature was litigious; he was quick-tempered, but not so irascible as legend has made him. He objected to blood sports and was a generous though often anonymous contributor to charity. He continued to direct revivals of the Savoy operas for Helen D'Oyly Carte, an astute businesswoman long associated with her husband in theatre management, and he continued to coach actresses and to examine for the Academy of Dramatic Arts. Nancy McIntosh lived with the Gilberts at Grim's Dyke, fulfilling the duties of a daughter of the house and acting as companion to Lady Gilbert until the latter's death in 1936. Gilbert died of heart failure at Grim's Dyke on 29 May 1911, having swum too rapidly to save a girl who mistakenly supposed she was drowning in his artificial lake. After being cremated, his ashes were buried on 2 June in the churchyard of St John the Evangelist in Great Stanmore, Middlesex.

During his fifty years of dramatic life Gilbert had helped to raise the income, the status, and the literary standards of playwrights. He had taken a leading part in turning an actor's theatre into a director's theatre and in establishing the respectability of the stage. He was scrupulous in acknowledging the indebtedness, if any, of his own pieces. His use of the comic was so individual as to create the adjective 'Gilbertian', and he has never been successfully imitated. He believed that 'all humour, properly so called, is based upon a grave and quasi-respectful treatment of the ridiculous and absurd' (P. H. Fitzgerald, *The Savoy Opera and the Savoyards*, 1899, 14n.). His political wit has seldom or never been equalled by librettists:

> I always voted at my party's call,
> And I never thought of thinking for myself at all.
> (*HMS 'Pinafore'*, 1878, act I)

> I often think it's comical
> How Nature always does contrive
> That every boy and every gal,
> That's born into this world alive,
> Is either a little Liberal,
> Or else a little Conservative.
> (*Iolanthe*, 1882, act II)

> Government by Party! Introduce that great and glorious element ... and all will be well! No political measures will

endure, because one Party will assuredly undo all that the other Party has done; and while grouse is to be shot, and foxes worried to death, the legislative action of the country will be at a standstill. Then there will be sickness in plenty, endless lawsuits, crowded jails, interminable confusion in the Army and Navy, and, in short, general and unexampled prosperity! (*Utopia (Limited)*, 1893, act II)

Although he was not a revolutionary satirist, he satirized both Conservatives and Liberals, and indeed all political principles, from the middle ground of common sense.

Gilbert's mordant sense of irony and his lively sense of the absurd therefore mingle with and balance each other. In his comic works three elements constantly meet: the invasion theme, the 'lozenge plot', and topsyturvydom, the principles of which he enunciated in a Bab ballad, 'My Dream' (*Fun*, 19 March 1870), and in an extravaganza, *Topsy-Turvydom* (Criterion Theatre, 21 March 1874). This is essentially an inversion in which physical laws are subservient to logic and moral opposites change places. Gilbert hated hypocrisy, and his operatic characters freely and innocently admit their own deficiencies, which non-Gilbertian persons would try to hide.

In creating librettos Gilbert's approach was akin to writing a brief, always with the intention of ultimately expressing his meaning in as few words as possible. He began by writing out the plot as a narrative, which he laid aside and wrote out again, comparing the two versions. He might continue to do so. Next he wrote individual scenes with what he called 'epitomes' (rough outlines) of dialogue; and after this, lyrics as the mood took him. The final text was discussed with Sullivan for appropriate musical situations, and even after the first night they might together make changes. Gilbert constantly reused and reworked elements of his earlier prose and verse until they reached a state of perfection, usually in the final form of the Savoy operas. His early work as a drama critic emphasized clear enunciation and accuracy in costumes, sets, and other elements of staging, and his own plays and librettos were as precise as he could make them. From Tom Robertson, whose stagecraft he admired, he learned to use small, illuminating bits of stage 'business' and insisted on sufficient rehearsal time, preferably four or five weeks. He worked out positions on a miniature stage with wooden markers for characters. Perhaps his most significant innovations were his dictate that comic characters should take themselves seriously on stage, and his transformation of the chorus into a corporate character who participated in the action rather than being a mere musical echo. At times he designed costumes for his works, and thus was the most complete *homme du théâtre* that the English stage had ever known.

JANE W. STEDMAN

Sources J. W. Stedman, *W. S. Gilbert: a classic Victorian and his theatre* (1996) • R. Allen, *W. S. Gilbert: an anniversary survey and exhibition checklist* (1963) • W. S. Gilbert, 'An autobiography', *The Theatre*, 4th ser., 1 (1883), 217–24 • J. W. Stedman, 'Gilbert's stagecraft: little blocks of wood', *International conference on Gilbert and Sullivan* [Lawrence, Kansas May 1970], ed. J. Helyar (1971), 195–211 • R. Allen, ed., *The first night Gilbert and Sullivan* (1958) • J. W. Stedman, 'From dame to woman: W. S. Gilbert and theatrical transvestism', *Suffer and be still: women in the Victorian age*, ed. M. Vicinus (1972), 20–37 • C. Rollins and J. Witts, *The D'Oyly Carte Company in Gilbert and Sullivan operas: a record of productions, 1875–1961* (1962) • S. Dark and R. Grey, *W. S. Gilbert: his life and letters* (1923) • W. O. Skeat, *King's College London, Engineering Society, 1847–1957* [1957] • J. W. Stedman, 'Introduction', *Gilbert before Sullivan: six comic plays*, ed. J. W. Stedman (1967) • J. Ellis, ed., introduction, in W. S. Gilbert, *The Bab ballads*, ed. J. Ellis (1970) • J. R. Stephens, *The censorship of English drama, 1824–1901* (1980) • A. Jacobs, *Arthur Sullivan: a Victorian musician* (1984) • W. Archer, *Real conversations* (1904) • H. How, *Illustrated interviews* (1893) • P. Fitzgerald, *The Savoy opera and the savoyards* (1899) • T. Rees, 'introduction', in W. S. Gilbert, *'Uncle Baby': a comedietta*, ed. T. Rees (1968) • H. Pearson, *Gilbert: his life and strife* (1957) • BL, W. S. Gilbert MSS, Add. MSS 49289–49353, 54315, 54999 • Morgan L., Gilbert and Sullivan collection • J. W. Stedman, *W. S. Gilbert's theatrical criticism* (2000) • d. cert. [William Gilbert] • d. cert. [Anne Mary Bye Gilbert] • b. cert. [Lucy Agnes Blois Turner] • d. cert. [Lucy Agnes Blois Gilbert]

Archives BL, corresp. and papers, incl. literary MSS, Add. MSS 49289–49353, 54315 • Hunt. L., letters; marked copies of *Fun* • Morgan L., collection • NRA, corresp. and literary papers | BL, corresp. with Macmillans, Add. MS 54999 • NYPL, Berg Collection, Isaac Goldberg MSS • Theatre Museum, London, D'Oyly Carte MSS, letters to Lord Chamberlain's licensee • U. Reading L., letters to George Bell

Likenesses Window & Grove, photograph, *c.*1871 • Elliott & Fry, photograph, *c.*1883 • F. Holl, oils, 1886, NPG [*see illus.*] • Barraud, photograph, 1890, NPG • R. Lehmann, drawing, 1893, BM • Langfier, photograph, *c.*1899 • H. G. Herkomer, oils, 1908, Garr. Club • G. Frampton, bas-relief head on bronze tablet, 1913, Victoria Embankment, London • H. Furniss, three pen-and-ink sketches, NPG • A. Lucchesi, bronze statuette, probably Bushey Heath Cottage Hospital • Spy [L. Ward], chromolithograph, caricature, NPG; repro. in *VF* (21 May 1881) • Walery, photograph, NPG; repro. in *Men and Women of the Day*, 3 (1890) • T. W. Wilson and F. Walton, oils, W. Sussex RO, Goodwood collections • chalk drawing (in middle age), Theatre Museum, London • oils (as young man), repro. in L. Baily, *The Gilbert and Sullivan book*, new edn (1966)

Wealth at death £118,028 2*s.*: resworn probate, 9 Aug 1911, *CGPLA Eng. & Wales*

Gilbertson [*née* Brown], **Jenny Isabel** (**1902–1990**), film-maker, was born on 28 October 1902 at 29 Falkland Mansions, Kelvinside, Glasgow, the second of three children of William Brown (1865–1952), an iron and steel merchant, and his wife, Mary Dunn Wright (1872–1957). She attended Laurel Bank School, where she became head girl. After Glasgow University she trained as a teacher at Jordanhill Training College, Glasgow, but decided that the regular hours of the profession were not for her. Uncertain about what to do with her life, she spent a year in the USA as au-pair to the family of Professor Merriman, head of the history department at Harvard University. After a year back in Glasgow, in 1929 she ventured south to do a secretarial course, with journalism, in London. While trying to be a freelance journalist she saw an amateur film of friends on holiday by Loch Lomond and immediately decided that film-making was the career for her. She wanted to make educational films and lecture with them in schools: at this time the educational value of film was starting to be recognized.

Jenny Brown bought a 16 mm camera, and after practising by filming in a park with two 50 foot rolls of film she went to Shetland to film life through the seasons. She arrived in January 1931 and by the autumn had made *A*

Crofter's Life in Shetland. After cutting the film together she was advised to invite John Grierson, the pioneering documentary film-maker, to view her film, and was amazed at his enthusiasm. He advised her on techniques to improve her documentary making and recommended that she buy a professional camera. Though reluctant at first, she bought a 35 mm Eyemo camera and, back in the Shetland Islands, made five films. Grierson bought them all for the General Post Office film library; he then advised her to make a documentary with a story in it. This resulted in *The Rugged Island*, a story of the harsh life of crofting families in the 1930s. She married blacksmith-farrier Johnny Gilbertson, who had played the 'romantic hero' in *The Rugged Island*, on 30 June 1934 at the City of Westminster register office.

During a lecture tour of Canada in 1934–5 with *Rugged Island*, Jenny Gilbertson made *Prairie Winter* with Evelyn Spice; she subsequently used this in a lecture tour of Britain. Between 1936 and 1939 she made three Shetland films. By now she had two daughters, Helen and Ann, Johnny was in the Royal Army Service Corps, and the Second World War had started. She sold her camera and from 1940 ran a small Shetland hosiery business. Realizing in 1947 that she had no head for business she reluctantly accepted an offer of teaching in the local school for one year, and stayed for twenty. During this time she broadcast several fifteen-minute radio talks and wrote scripts for schools radio and two one-hour radio plays.

While Jenny Gilbertson was still teaching, her friend Elizabeth Balneaves, artist and film-maker, suggested that they make a film together for BBC Northern Service, Aberdeen. Jenny bought a camera, and *People of many Lands: Shetland* was broadcast on BBC television in October 1967. She had retired from teaching when her husband died in March 1967, and with both daughters married she was able to devote more time to film-making. She had started in 1965 to collect material of the cyclical life of the ponies on Shetland, and after several attempts to film the mares foaling—'I was always in the wrong place at the wrong time', she remarked—*Shetland Pony* was finished in 1969.

This was an extraordinary 'retirement'. Jenny Gilbertson left Shetland for long periods to film in Canada. In 1970, at the suggestion of a Shetlander teaching in the Arctic, she and Elizabeth Balneaves prepared to film there, but Elizabeth became ill, and so Jenny went alone. Over the next seven years she made many films of Arctic life: *People of many Lands: the Eskimo* was commissioned by the BBC and bought by the National Film Board of Canada, and *The Museum of Man* was made for the Canadian National Museum; *Jenny's Arctic: Part 1* was made for the Canadian Broadcasting Company (CBC) in 1972. To film *Jenny's Dog Team Journey* in 1975 four adults and a three-month-old baby travelled 300 miles in two weeks over inhospitable terrain from Igloolik to Repulse Bay, sleeping in an igloo every night. It was broadcast by CBC in 1976 and by the BBC in 1978; the other major Canadian broadcasting companies also bought the film. In 1977–8, now aged seventy-six, she spent thirteen months in Grisefiord, Ellesmere Island, 900 miles north of the Arctic circle, to make *Jenny's Arctic Diary*, recording a cyclical year in the life of the Inuit community.

Jenny Gilbertson was remarkable in that all her films were what she described as a 'one-woman job'; she did all the script-writing, filming, sound, lighting, and direction herself. They were so successful because they had a very special quality derived from the intimacy with the subject; in these works she identifies with and is clearly accepted by the people being filmed. She has not received the acclaim that she deserves for her achievement as a pioneering solo woman film-maker; her work bears comparison with more famous documentarists such as Robert Flaherty in its simple style of showing the truth of her subjects in their daily life.

Jenny Gilbertson died at Iglooga, Exnaboe, Virkie, her home in Shetland, on 8 January 1990; she was cremated in Aberdeen and her ashes were buried in Shetland, with her husband in Esha Ness churchyard. ANNE R. WADE

Sources R. Crichton, *Jenny Gilbertson: documentary film-maker* (1999) • J. McBain, draft obituary of Jenny Gilbertson, Scottish Screen Archive, Glasgow • private information (2004) [J. Gilbertson, J. McBain] • J. Gilbertson, autobiographical notes, Scottish Screen Archive, Glasgow

Archives Scottish Screen Archive, Glasgow, Gilbertson collection, diary, diaries of Arctic travels, press cuttings, photographs, unpublished autobiographical notes | FILM Scottish Screen Archive, Glasgow

Likenesses photograph, 1930–33, repro. in Crichton, *Jenny Gilbertson*, front cover

Wealth at death £28,590.73: confirmation, 1991, *CCI*

Gilbey, Alfred Newman (1901–1998), Roman Catholic priest, was born at Mark Hall, Latton, Harlow, Essex, on 13 July 1901, the fifth son and youngest among the seven children of Newman Gilbey and his Spanish wife, Maria Victorina de Ysasi. His paternal grandfather had founded a wine business and it is from the family associated with the Gilbeys in that enterprise that Alfred derived his second name. He was educated at the Jesuit Beaumont College, near Windsor (1914–20), and Trinity College, Cambridge (1920–24), where he read history. Having decided to become a priest, he was sent to the Beda College in Rome (1925–9) and was ordained on 15 August 1929 at Mark Hall 'on his own patrimony', an arrangement then possible in the Roman Catholic church, whereby a priest could look for pastoral work in what diocese he chose, but no diocese had responsibility for his upkeep. In fact he was personal secretary to Bishop Arthur Doubleday of Brentwood from 1929 to 1932, before being appointed as chaplain to Catholic undergraduates at the University of Cambridge. This post, which has no official standing so far as the university is concerned, had been created by the Catholic bishops of England and Wales in 1895, the arrangement being special to Oxford and Cambridge. However the lack of endowment or any adequate funding for the chaplaincy meant that only a priest with a private income could be appointed. During all his years at Cambridge, Gilbey received no salary and paid most of the chaplaincy's running costs out of his own pocket.

In 1932 Gilbey thus began a period of pastoral work for which his gifts were particularly well suited. The warmth and vitality of his personality, inherited from his Spanish mother, gave a unique character to his hospitality. Lightly carried erudition marked his devotion to the history of Cambridge, its university and colleges. His sense of humour, wit, and elegance completed a personality which made its mark in Cambridge during the thirty-three academic years and one term when he was in residence. The sight of Gilbey in the streets of Cambridge, attired in frock coat and broad-brimmed ecclesiastical hat, remains a memory of that period. All this served the ministry of the priesthood, to which he gave his wholehearted service. He was remarkably successful in extending the chaplaincy's influence beyond the small group of Catholic students; although he never proselytized, he received as chaplain 170 members of the university into full communion with the Catholic church.

When students returned to Cambridge in large numbers after the Second World War, Gilbey resumed the tradition of an open house at the chaplaincy, and integrated into his flock students from state schools funded by grants from local authorities. However the material existence of Fisher House, the chaplaincy's buildings in Guildhall Street (formerly the Black Swan), was threatened from 1948 onwards by successive plans to develop the city centre. Gilbey led a long-drawn-out campaign to highlight the importance of Fisher House for the Catholic body in England; it was not until 1964 that the house and its curtilage were definitely left out of the Lion Yard scheme, which destroyed Petty Cury, the oldest street in Cambridge. Without Gilbey's persistence and influence Fisher House would probably also have vanished, to the great detriment of the chaplaincy's work.

Women students were not technically full members of the University of Cambridge until 1948; a separate chaplaincy for Catholic women students had been created which from 1937 operated at Lady Margaret House, whereas at Oxford the two chaplaincies had merged in 1941. Gilbey was no misogynist and had many women friends but, although he had the gifts to make an excellent chaplain to a mixed body of students, he preferred to maintain unchanged the arrangements that he had found when he became chaplain. Already in 1949 there had been requests among students for a mixed chaplaincy at Fisher House. By the 1960s opposition to the Cambridge situation was becoming more vocal and the board which represented the Catholic hierarchy in its relation to the Oxford and Cambridge chaplaincies received objections to the continuing segregation at Cambridge, both from Catholic senior members of the university and from students, the latter led to a considerable extent by young priests and graduate students from St Edmund's House. As a result Gilbey, who had announced his intention of retiring in the summer of 1966, brought the date forward to December 1965. It was seen as regrettable by many that someone who had done so much for the chaplaincy was not allowed to complete his term of office. The manner of his departure from Cambridge left a legacy of division to the small Catholic community. This was exacerbated by the way Fisher House was stripped of the furniture and memorabilia, which Gilbey had collected. It exemplified the damage done to many Catholic churches at the time through ill-considered attempts to implement the Second Vatican Council's decisions. Gilbey suffered keenly from what had happened, but he was exemplary in charity, treating those who opposed his policy with unfailing courtesy and consideration.

Gilbey went to live in London at the Travellers' Club, where he began a second apostolate as long and, in its own way, as effective as his first. He became the unofficial chaplain to former members of his Cambridge flock, their wives, children, and grandchildren. Cardinal Heenan had obtained permission from Rome for him to continue saying the Tridentine mass and, at a time of liturgical upheaval, he helped many to remain within the Catholic church. He also continued to instruct numerous would-be converts. His instructions were recorded by a friend and published as *We Believe, by a Priest* (1983), a book which enjoyed unexpectedly wide success. At a time when there was considerable confusion in catechetical programmes, Gilbey reaffirmed that to be a Catholic implies acceptance of the teaching authority of the church and illustrated that teaching with clarity and the resources of a well-stocked mind, including extensive quotations from the documents of the Second Vatican Council. He also distinguished between essential teaching and the vagaries of ecclesiastical policy in the application of the council, thus enabling many traditionally minded Catholics to remain within the church and to avoid the schism of Archbishop Lefebvre.

As the years passed, Gilbey became more and more of a cult figure for those who were fascinated by the manners and diction of a bygone age, and by his critique of contemporary society. The centre of his life continued to be the exercise of his priesthood. He celebrated mass daily at the Brompton Oratory, twice a month for his wider flock. At the Travellers' Club he had obtained the use of a small room at the top of the building for his private oratory, where he was able to reserve the blessed sacrament. There he would spend much time in prayer and sometimes say mass. There were many telephone calls for Mgr Gilbey, and the club porter, tired of walking from his lodge to the oratory, asked that there should be a telephone extension. The telephone was concealed under the altar, so that those who were invited to share Gilbey's orisons were sometimes surprised to see him dive behind the altar frontal in response to the telephone bell.

'There is always time for the sacraments' was a favourite phrase of Gilbey's (Watkins, 76, 82), and he continued this ministry almost to the end of his life, grateful for having exercised for so long 'the sublime and aweful gift of the priesthood' (*Fisher House Newsletter*, 1979, 15). Because of failing health, he moved from the club to the Poor Sisters of Nazareth, Hammersmith Road, Brook Green, a few days before his death, which occurred on 26 March 1998 at Charing Cross Hospital, Fulham. He was buried on 6 April in the courtyard of Fisher House at Cambridge.

In 1950 Gilbey was made a prelate of honour, in 1964 a protonotary apostolic, and in 1981 an honorary canon of

Brentwood Cathedral. He had been a chaplain of the order of Malta since 1947, and in 1982 was promoted to grand cross conventual chaplain *ad honorem*.

M. N. L. Couve de Murville

Sources P. Gregory-Jones, *A history of Cambridge Catholic chaplaincy, 1895–1965* (Cagliari, 1986) · D. Watkins, ed., *Alfred Gilbey: a memoir by some friends* (2001) · *Fisher House Newsletter* (1979) · *Fisher House Newsletter* (2000) · *The Tablet* (4 April 1998) · *The Tablet* (11 April 1998) · *The Tablet* (18 April 1998) · *The Times* (27 March 1998) · *Daily Telegraph* (27 March 1998) · *The Independent* (28 March 1998) · *The Guardian* (31 March 1998) · b. cert. · d. cert.
Archives priv. coll.
Likenesses G. Maxwell, oils, 1949, Fisher House, Cambridge · A. Festing, oils, 1981–2, priv. coll. · S. Aarons, photograph, 1990, Hult. Arch. · photograph, repro. in *The Times* · photograph, repro. in *The Independent* · photograph, repro. in *The Guardian* · photograph, repro. in *Daily Telegraph*
Wealth at death £1,288,637: probate, 8 June 1998, *CGPLA Eng. & Wales*

Gilbey, Sir Walter, first baronet (1831–1914), wine merchant and horse breeder, was born on 2 May 1831 at Bishop's Stortford, Hertfordshire, the sixth son of Henry Gilbey, coach proprietor, and his wife, Elizabeth, daughter of William Bailey of Stansted, Essex. Educated at Bishop's Stortford grammar school, Gilbey was briefly apprenticed to an estate agent cousin before taking employment with a parliamentary agent in London. At the outbreak of the Crimean War he joined his brother Alfred in applying for a civilian post in the War Office, and the two men travelled to the front, where they were engaged in administrative duties throughout the hostilities. In 1857, several years after their return to England, the brothers established themselves in the wine trade.

On the advice of their elder brother, Henry, himself a prosperous wine merchant, the junior Gilbeys acquired premises on the corner of Berwick Street and Oxford Street in London and, with the assistance of a generous injection of capital from their brother, embarked on a course which, by 1860, was to make them the third largest importers of wine in Britain. Despite Gladstone's equalization of duties on colonial and foreign wines (to the disadvantage of the Gilbeys, who dealt solely in colonial products), the business flourished by means of direct sales to retail grocers via a country-wide system of local agencies. By 1869 the Gilbey holdings included a warehouse complex and gin distillery in Camden Town, London, while the 1880s witnessed the purchase of whisky distilleries in Scotland and a vineyard complex in the Médoc.

The operation of this highly lucrative business was due in no small measure to Walter Gilbey's organizational skills. Intelligent delegation, allied to great care in staff selection and attention to market research, ensured a smoothly efficient business, whose financial returns afforded Gilbey the leisure to concentrate on cultivating his own interests. Indeed, by the late 1860s it was no longer necessary for him to be involved in day-to-day company affairs and, although he retained an active financial and management interest until his retirement in 1905, he became increasingly a country gentleman, and less of a wine merchant, as the years went by.

Six years after his marriage in 1858 to Ellen (*d.* 1896), daughter of John Parish of Bishop's Stortford, Gilbey purchased Hargrave Park, not far from his native town, and he lived there for the next ten years. By 1874 an increasing family and a growing interest in land management prompted the sale of Hargrave Park and the purchase of the 8000 acre Essex estate of Elsenham Hall, where Gilbey was to remain for the rest of his life. Here his restless, and apparently boundless, energies were expended in the development of the estate, establishing the celebrated Elsenham jams and promoting fruit and lavender growing on the home farm. He proved a characteristically generous landlord and a pillar of strength to many charities; at the same time, he was widely celebrated as a host, both at Elsenham and at his London residence, Cambridge House in Regent's Park. A staunchly anti-tory supporter of home rule, Gilbey resisted the blandishments of W. E. Gladstone and refused to stand for parliament, being content to restrict his public life to the magistracy and deputy lieutenancy of Middlesex. For all his professions of socialism in his later years (which were probably little more than contrived eccentricities), he appears to have had little genuine political interest.

Gilbey's tastes were essentially those of a country gentleman. He assembled one of the richest libraries of sporting and agricultural works in Britain, and was an avid collector of paintings and engravings reflecting his love of country life and, more especially, of the horse. His lengthy biographies of Moreland and Stubbs both attracted critical acclaim; he also wrote a variety of books, pamphlets, and articles, dealing primarily with equine matters, though not without the occasional foray into the worlds of cockfighting and poultry keeping. His general interest in rural affairs led to the endowment, in 1896, of the Gilbey lectureship in the history and economics of agriculture at the University of Cambridge.

Respected throughout the agricultural world for his enormous practical knowledge of animal husbandry, Gilbey had been one of the first to recognize the essential importance of breeding superior livestock to meet the needs of an agricultural economy which was assuming an increasingly pastoral character by the 1870s. Moreover, his speeches and writings on the dangers of over-reliance upon overseas supplies of cavalry-type horses did much to resuscitate British horse breeding from the doldrums into which it had recently descended. He was closely instrumental in the foundation of the Shire Horse Society and the Hackney Horse Society, respectively in 1878 and 1883, and of the Hunters Improvement Society in 1885, and in the establishment of the royal commission on horse breeding in 1888.

A practical man first and foremost, Gilbey built up his own stud of shire horses, and also set about assembling quality horses of the hackney breed. An exacting critic of horseflesh, his almost encyclopaedic knowledge of breeding and stud management and his unerring judgement brought him into personal contact with several members of the royal family. He regularly advised the prince of Wales on equine matters, and it was due largely to the intercession of the prince that he was created baronet in 1893. To his various honours, including the presidency of the Shire and Hackney Horse societies, was added the presidency of the Royal Agricultural Society of England in 1896.

Selfless service to the cause of agricultural and equine improvement over a period of some forty years was the hallmark of this tall, slim man, of genial and unaffected manner and fastidious tastes. His ample generosity, natural courtesy, and hatred of injustice endeared him to all with whom he came into contact. Although deeply distressed by the death of his wife in 1896, he continued to pursue his many interests and did not finally retire from the wine business until 1905. Walter Gilbey had never enjoyed the soundest of health, and a lower than normal body temperature meant that he was regularly the victim of colds, bronchitis, and kindred maladies. Laid low with bronchitis once again in late October 1914, he died on 12 November 1914 at his home, Elsenham Hall, Essex. He was buried in St Michael's Church, Bishop's Stortford, on 19 November, mourned by his four sons and four daughters. The baronetcy, and the bulk of his property passed to his eldest son, Walter. R. J. MOORE-COLYER

Sources *Journal of the Royal Agricultural Society of England*, 75 (1914), 136–46 · *Livestock Journal*, 13 (1914), 492 · K. Chivers, *The shire horse* (1976) · H. Maxwell, *Half-a-century of successful trade: being a sketch of the rise and development of the business of W. A. Gilbey, 1857–1907* (1907), 74–5 · J. Unwin, *Wine and the vine: an historical geography of wine and the wine trade* (1991), 333 · *Essex Review*, 24 (1915), 30–33 · *The Times* (13 Nov 1914) · *The Times* (23 Feb 1915) · E. P. Loder, *Bibliography of the history and organisation of horse racing and thoroughbred breeding in Great Britain and Ireland: books published … 1565–1973* (1978)

Likenesses N. Q. Orchardson, oils, 1891, priv. coll.

Wealth at death £425,156 2*s*. 7*d*.: probate, 18 Feb 1915, *CGPLA Eng. & Wales*

Gilburne, Samuel (*fl.* 1605), actor, is listed as one of the 'Principall Actors' in the preliminaries of the first folio of William Shakespeare's work (1623). In the will of Augustine Phillips, another member of Shakespeare's company, which is dated 4 May 1605, Phillips names Gilburne as his one-time apprentice. '[To] Samuell Gilborne my Late Aprentice the some of Fortye shillinges and Taffety dublet A blacke Taffety sute my purple Cloke sword and dagger And my base viall' (Honigmann and Brock, 73). Nothing is known of Gilburne's origins; there is no further evidence of a stage career and it has therefore been suggested that he may not have been apprenticed to Phillips as an actor but as a musician. A copy of the first folio, held at the Folger Shakespeare Library, carries what is thought to be Gilburne's signature. EVA GRIFFITH

Sources E. A. J. Honigmann and S. Brock, eds., *Playhouse wills, 1558–1642: an edition of wills by Shakespeare and his contemporaries in the London theatre* (1993), 73 · E. K. Chambers, *William Shakespeare: a study of facts and problems*, 2 (1930), 85–6 · G. E. Bentley, *The Jacobean and Caroline stage*, 7 vols. (1941–68), vol. 2, p. 443

Gilby, Anthony (*c*.1510–1585), religious writer and Church of England clergyman, a native of Lincolnshire, graduated BA from Christ's College, Cambridge, in 1531–2, before proceeding MA in 1535. Converted to protestantism while still a young man, at the university he was noted for his skill in the biblical languages of Latin, Greek, and Hebrew, which he employed to good effect in his refutation of the bishop of Winchester's defence of the mass, *An Answer to the Devillish Detection of Stephane Gardiner* (1548). He seems to have begun his ecclesiastical career as a preacher in Leicestershire in the reign of Edward VI. Closely associated with such evangelicals as Latimer, Lever, Hooper, Becon, and Horne, he joined with them in denouncing the corruptions of the age, writing at this time *A Commentarye upon the Prophet Mycha* (1551) and *A Commentarye upon the Prophet Malaky* (1553?), 'the which Treatise by the rage of persecution, partly perished' (Gilby, *A Briefe Treatice of Election, and Reprobation*, [1556], introduction).

On the accession of Mary, Gilby fled with his wife, Elizabeth, and son, Goddred [*see below*], to Frankfurt, where in the early months of 1555, with Knox, Whittingham, Foxe, and Thomas Cole, he helped devise a reformed liturgy for the English church. On the arrival of Richard Cox, who insisted on reimposing the Book of Common Prayer, in October 1555 he moved with his family to Geneva where in 1556 and 1558 two daughters were born, though only the second, Ruth, survived. At Geneva the English church chose Knox and Christopher Goodman as its pastors, Gilby deputizing for Knox during the latter's absence in France. During the subsequent three years Gilby took a major part in the translation of the Geneva Bible, which appeared in 1560. He also wrote *A Briefe Treatice of Election, and Reprobation* (n.d. [1556]) and *An Admonition to England and Scotland to Call them to Repentance* (1558). When news of Mary Tudor's death reached the continent Gilby was one of the signatories of the letter from the Geneva church to the English congregations in Aarau and Frankfurt exhorting them to make common cause for the restoration of protestantism in England.

On his return Gilby and his family re-established themselves in Leicestershire, though they may have lived for a time in London, where his schoolboy son, **Goddred Gilby** (*fl.* 1561), in July 1561 published a translation of *An Epistle … by Marcus Tullius Cicero, to his Brother Quintus*, and some months later a translation of a work by Calvin, *An Admonicion Against Astrology*. However, nothing further is known of Goddred, and it seems likely that he died young. In Leicestershire, Anthony Gilby found a patron in Henry Hastings, a one-time companion of Edward VI, who had succeeded to the earldom of Huntingdon on the death of his father in June 1560, and spent the last twenty-five years of his life as a lecturer at Ashby-de-la-Zouch. In gratitude for his protection Gilby produced in 1570 the *Commentaries of that divine John Calvine, upon the prophet Daniell, translated into Englishe, especially for the use of the family of the ryght honorable earle of Huntingdon*, following this in 1580 by a dedication to the countess of Huntingdon, the earl of Leicester's sister, 'mine especial good Lady', of a translation of Beza entitled *The Psalmes of David, Truely Opened*.

Huntingdon seems from the beginning to have intended that Gilby should evangelize not only his household but the entire county, where for the first years of the reign his Geneva colleague William Whittingham was acting as a roving preacher. By 1570 Gilby had set up exercises at Ashby to improve the learning of the local clergy, while his appointment by Huntingdon as a feoffee of the Ashby grammar school in 1567 gave him the opportunity of ensuring the education in godliness of the next generation.

From Leicestershire, Gilby kept in close touch with his friends from the exile, rebuking Thomas Bentham, the new bishop of Coventry and Lichfield, for not dealing severely enough with backsliding ministers in his diocese, and admonishing Robert Beaumont, when vice-chancellor of Cambridge, for enforcing the wearing of the surplice. On the side of the radicals during the vestiarian controversy, he published in 1566, probably at Emden, an epistle *To my Lovynge Brethren that is Troublyd abowt the Popishe Aparrell*, which ended with a prayer that 'we may serve the Lord of hostes in synglenes of hart, and laboure to rote out all stomblinge blockes in religion that Christes glorie maye nakydly shyne of yt sealve, without all tradicions or invencions of men'.

On the emergence of the presbyterian movement in 1570, Thomas Wood, Gilby's fellow elder in Geneva, who had subsequently settled at Groby, in Leicestershire, provided a link between Gilby at Ashby and Field and Wilcox in London. Having encouraged Thomas Cartwright in his campaign to extirpate the dregs of popery still remaining in the church, even if it resulted in his imprisonment or banishment, Gilby felt impelled at this juncture to publish *A Pleasaunt Dialogue betweene a Souldior of Barwicke and an English Chaplaine*, which he had written at the time of the vestiarian crisis, but held back for seven years in the hope that parliament might have implemented further reform. This seminal tract, which contained a table of '120 particuler corruptions yet remaining in our saide Church', anticipated the appeal to the populace made in both *The Admonition to the Parliament* of 1572 and the Marprelate tracts of the next decade.

In 1576 John Aylmer, then archdeacon of Lincoln, complained that Gilby, labouring unceasingly in the interests of reform, had come to wield the influence of a bishop in Leicestershire. When the bishop of Lincoln threatened to suppress the exercises Gilby and the other ministers at Ashby protested vociferously. Although they failed to prevent the ban, they contrived to substitute fasts for the exercises, at which Gilby was frequently invited to preach. He almost certainly inspired the stand made in 1584 against Whitgift's three articles by no fewer than 300 Leicestershire ministers, who consented only to a conditional subscription.

Despite Field's eagerness to publish anything he might write, in his last decade Gilby confined himself to translations, bringing out in 1574 *The Testaments of the Twelve Patriarches*, originally translated from Greek into Latin by Robert Grosseteste, and in 1581 *A Paraphrastical Explanation or Opening of Fourteene Holie Psalmes*, from Beza's original. In his old age he was assisted at Ashby by the preacher Thomas Wydows, who had married his daughter Esther in 1570. Gilby's wife was buried at Ashby-de-la-Zouch on 6 November 1584, and little more than a month later, on 28 December, Gilby made his will, in which he expressed at length his thankfulness that 'in all alterations and persecutions God hath geven me grace to professe Jesus Christe our onely sufficient savior, and both publickly and privately to detest all the inventions and traditions of the Romishe Antichriste'. He then went on to commend his surviving sons, Richard and Nathaniel, his three daughters, 'and all that I have' to the earl of Huntingdon, 'my very good Lord and master' (Leicester County RO, wills series IV, 1584, 99). He died in January 1585 and was buried at Ashby-de-la-Zouch.

Huntingdon more than fulfilled the obligations placed upon him. Nathaniel, Gilby's younger son, while still at the university in 1592, presented his translation of a work by Sohn, *A Brief and Learned Treatise … of the Antichrist*, to the countess of Huntingdon, whose favour, together with that of her husband, had been 'comfortable to many of God's children, and especially vouchsafed to my father, my selfe and other friendes'. In the autumn of 1595 the earl performed a final kindness by summoning Nathaniel Gilby to serve as his chaplain at York, so making possible the election of Joseph Hall, another scholar of the Ashby school, to Nathaniel's fellowship at Emmanuel College, Cambridge. Gilby ministered to Huntingdon in his last illness in December 1595 and soon after wrote a moving account of the earl's death. In 1600 he acquired the rectory of St John's, in Bedford, dying in London in July 1606.

CLAIRE CROSS

Sources Leics. RO, wills series IV, 1584, 99 • A. G., *Commentaries of that divine John Calvine, upon the prophet Daniell, translated into Englishe, especially for the use of the family of the ryght honorable earle of Huntingdon, to set forth as in a glasse, how one may profitably read the Scriptures, by consideryng the text, meditatyng the sense therof, and by prayer* (1570) • A. Gilby, *The Psalmes of David, truely opened, set foorth in Latine by that excellent learned man Theodore Beza, and faithfully translated into English by Anthonie Gilbie* (1580) • [A. Gilby], *A pleasaunt dialogue betweene a souldior of Barwicke, and an English chaplaine, wherein are largely handled & laide open, such reasons as are brought in for maintenaunce of popishe traditionss in our Eng. church* (1581) • [W. Whittingham?], *A brief discourse of the troubles at Frankfort*, ed. E. Arber (1908) • *An epistle or letter of exhortation written in Latyne by Marcus Tullius Cicero, to his brother Quintus the proconsull or deputy of Asia, wherin the office of a magistrate is connyngly and wisely described, translated into englyshe by G[oddred] G[ylby]* (1561) • *An admonicion against astrology judiciall … by John Calvine and translated into Englishe by G[oddred] G[ylby]* (*c.*1561–*c.*1562) • G. Sohn, *A briefe and learned treatise, contening a true description of the Antichrist … translated into English*, trans. N. Gilby (1592) • C. Cross, 'The third earl of Huntingdon's death-bed: a Calvinist example of the *ars moriendi*', *Northern History*, 21 (1985), 80–107 [incl. transcript of MS by N. Gilby] • A. Peel, ed., *The seconde parte of a register*, 1 (1915) • Venn, *Alum. Cant.* • C. H. Garrett, *The Marian exiles: a study in the origins of Elizabethan puritanism* (1938) • L. Lupton, *A history of the Geneva Bible*, 5 (1973) • T. Fuller, *The worthies of England*, ed. J. Freeman, abridged edn (1952) • P. Collinson, *The Elizabethan puritan movement* (1967) • P. Collinson, *Godly people: essays on English protestantism and puritanism* (1983) • P. Collinson, *Archbishop Grindal, 1519–1583: the struggle for a reformed church* (1979) • P. Collinson, *The religion of protestants* (1982) • P. Collinson, *The birthpangs of protestant England: religious and cultural change in the sixteenth and seventeenth centuries* (1988) • M. M. Knappen, *Tudor puritanism: a chapter in the history of idealism* (1939) • C. Cross, *The puritan earl: the life of Henry Hastings, third earl of Huntingdon* (1966)

Wealth at death £87 0s. 10d.: inventory, 4 Feb 1585, Leics. RO, wills series IV, 1584, 99 (Gilby)

Gilby, Goddred (*fl.* 1561). *See under* Gilby, Anthony (*c.*1510–1585).

Gilby, William Hall (1793–1835), geologist and physician, was born on 19 July 1793, the son of William Gilby, surgeon, of Yardley, Birmingham, and Clifton, Bristol, and his wife Eliza Gilby. He studied under Professor Robert Jameson at Edinburgh, where he graduated MD in 1815. His thesis, *Disceptatio … de mutationibus quas ea, quae e terra gignuntur, aëri inferent*, was published in 1815, at which time he was annual president of the Royal Society of Medicine in Edinburgh.

Gilby's interest in geology began while he was living at Clifton, from where he was able to examine the sequence of rocks exposed in the Severn Gorge and encountered elsewhere on his travels in Gloucestershire and mid-Wales. He was a member of the Geological Society before its formal incorporation. From 1814 he published a number of articles describing the limestones which rested unconformably on inclined coal measures. He also examined the fossils and performed chemical analyses on the limestones. His last paper, in 1821, reported his experiments on the respiration of plants, performed during his student years.

Latterly Gilby moved to Wakefield, and was among the first subscribers to the British Association for the Advancement of Science, established in 1832. He subsequently moved back to Clifton, and was resident at Hotwells when he died on 18 June 1835. He was unmarried, and administration of his estate was granted to his father. B. D. Jackson, *rev.* Michael Bevan

Sources W. H. Gilby, *Disceptatio …* (1815) • *GM*, 2nd ser., 4 (1835), 220 • PRO, PROB 6/211, fol. 148r

Wealth at death under £3000: PRO, PROB 6/211, fol. 148r

Gilchrist, Alexander (1828–1861), biographer, was born on 25 April 1828 at Newington Green, Middlesex, the son of James Gilchrist, author of *The Intellectual Patrimony* (1817), and his wife, Deborah Champion. In 1829 his father resigned as a General Baptist minister and moved to an old watermill on the Thames at Mapledurham, near Reading. James Gilchrist died in 1835 and his widow moved with her children to London. At the age of twelve Alexander was sent to University College School, leaving it at sixteen to study law. He entered the Middle Temple in 1846, and was called to the bar in 1849, but never practised as a barrister. Instead, he tried to make a living as an art critic. His talents were eventually recognized by Dr Price, editor of the *Eclectic Review*. All his writings for three or four years appeared in the *Eclectic*, and an article about William Etty, published in 1849 and reissued separately, brought him a commission from David Bogue to write Etty's life. On 4 February 1851, after a difficult courtship and long engagement, Gilchrist married Anne Burrows (1828–1885) [*see* Gilchrist, Anne], also a biographer and essayist, at Earl's Colne, Essex. The first of their four children was born later that year. Their eldest son became the metallurgist Percy Carlyle *Gilchrist. Gilchrist then collected materials for the *Life of Etty*, which appeared in 1855. Carlyle read it in January and, in a letter to Gilchrist, called it 'a book done in a vigorous sympathetic vivacious spirit'. William Rossetti reviewed the book in *The Spectator*. Gilchrist afterwards wrote lives of artists for an edition of *Men of the time*.

In 1853 the family settled near Guildford. In a visit to London, Gilchrist saw some of Blake's illustrations to the book of Job. He had previously only known the illustrations to Blair's *Grave* and Allan Cunningham's life of the artist, but now resolved to write a full life of Blake. In 1856 he settled in Chelsea, having the previous year met Carlyle and provided materials to help with *Frederick the Great*. Gilchrist's account of this visit has been often quoted and called the best thing he ever wrote (Wilson, 227). The two now became next door neighbours. Gilchrist was for two years afterwards chiefly occupied in winding up the business affairs of a brother who had died suddenly, but after this he devoted himself to Blake, contributing also to the *Literary Gazette* and *The Critic*. In the spring of 1861 he made the acquaintance of D. G. Rossetti, whose brother William later wrote of Gilchrist in the preface to *Anne Gilchrist: her Life and Writings*: 'He was then regarded, in my own circle, as the best equipped and ablest of the various art-critics on the periodical press'. Gilchrist had not finished *Blake* but was establishing a growing reputation and circle of friends, including Walter White, when he died of scarlet fever on 30 November 1861 at Cheyne Row in London. He was buried at Kensal Green cemetery. His loss called forth strong expressions of sympathy from Ford Madox Brown and D. G. Rossetti—the latter calling him 'a far-sighted and nobly honest writer'. The *Life of Blake* was completed by his widow, with the assistance of the Rossettis, and published in 1863. Anne Gilchrist also edited a second edition in 1880, and prefixed to it a *Memoir of Alexander Gilchrist*. H. H. Gilchrist, *rev.* Michael Thorn

Sources M. W. Alcaro, *Walt Whitman's Mrs G.: a biography of Anne Gilchrist* (1991) • H. H. Gilchrist, ed., *Anne Gilchrist: her life and writings* (1887) • W. M. Rossetti, *Some reminiscences*, 2 vols. (1906) • D. A. Wilson, *Carlyle to threescore-and-ten (1853–1865)* (1929), vol. 5 of *Life of Carlyle* (1923–34)

Archives priv. coll., family MSS

Gilchrist [*née* Burrows], **Anne** (1828–1885), writer, was born at 7 Gower Street, London, on 25 February 1828, the daughter of Henrietta Carwardine (1786–1875) and John Burrows (in or before 1788–1839), a solicitor. Her grandfather the Revd Thomas Carwardine had been a friend of Romney and Hayley. One of three children, Anne lost a sister in infancy in 1831. She developed a close bond with her younger brother, John, who saved her from falling into an uncovered well when she was ten years old.

Anne's father died in 1839, after a fall from a horse. Mrs Burrows and the two children moved to Highgate, Middlesex, where Anne was already being educated by the Cahusac sisters. She completed her education in 1844, at the age of sixteen. Two years later the family moved from Highgate, and rented a house in Heathcote Street, London. The owner of the property was Mrs James Gilchrist, very probably her future mother-in-law. Anne was naturally inclined to think deeply about spiritual matters, a characteristic reinforced by the death of her brother from a malignant fever in 1847. As a teenager she was already reading the transcendentalists, and in 1848 said of Emerson, '[His] writings are treated with a good deal of contempt and ridicule now, but I think the next generation will call him a great man' (Gilchrist, 29).

On 4 February 1851 Anne married Alexander *Gilchrist (1828–1861), biographer and art critic. Their first child, Percy Carlyle *Gilchrist, was born on 27 December, at Lyme Regis, and by 1853 they were settled near Guildford, where a second child, Beatrice, was born. In 1856 they moved to Chelsea, living next door to the Carlyles, having made their acquaintance through Alexander's *Life of Etty*. During the next five years Alexander prepared his *Life of William Blake* and Anne gave birth to two more children—Herbert in 1857, and Grace in 1859. She also began to write essays. 'A glance at the vegetable kingdom' was published in *Chambers* in 1857, and 'Whales and whalemen' in the same publication in 1860. The following year a more autobiographical piece, 'Lost in the Wood', appeared in *Magnet Stories*.

Alexander was consolidating his reputation as an art critic, assisted by his association with the Rossettis. Anne was managing to combine some degree of intellectual independence with maternal and domestic demands. Her home-made bread was the envy of Jane Carlyle. The family appeared to be poised to take up a prominent position in the intellectual and social life of Victorian London. However, towards the end of 1861, Beatrice and Percy caught scarlet fever. In due course, all the children became infected. They survived, but Alexander succumbed and died at the end of November. His funeral took place on 4 December. He was buried at Kensal Green cemetery. Anne immediately took her children away from London and in April 1862 settled at Brookbank, a small cottage at Shottermill, near Haslemere, Surrey. A scientific essay, 'The indestructibility of force', was accepted by *Macmillan's Magazine*, but Anne announced 'That will be the last thing I shall attempt for many a long day, as I have fully made up my mind to give myself up wholly to educating the children' (Gilchrist, 153).

None the less, Anne did complete her husband's *Life of William Blake* in 1863. While doing so she was given valuable support by her husband's associates. This collaboration required frequent visits by the Rossetti brothers to the isolated Shottermill. Christina Rossetti was also a visitor, and 'Maidensong' was composed at Anne's cottage. She also received visits from the Tennysons, who were looking for land on which to build. Anne gave a good deal of assistance in this enterprise, through to attending the foundation stone ceremony at Aldworth, on land previously known as Green Hill. Anne's comments about Emily Tennyson, in conversation with William Rossetti in the spring of 1871, were perceptive and critical, concerning Emily's tendency to attach a great importance to position and appearance. Anne was at this time recovering from several months of prostration. Was her state of physical and nervous exhaustion brought on by her efforts on behalf of the Tennysons? Her biographer, Marion Walker Alcaro, thinks it just as possible that it was attributable to disappointment at a lack of reaction from Walt Whitman to her effusive defence of his poetry. The review—valuable for its feminine acceptance of sexuality—had appeared in the May 1870 edition of *The Radical* (a Boston monthly), entitled 'An Englishwoman's estimate of Walt Whitman (from late letters by an English lady to W. M. Rossetti'.

On 3 September 1871 Anne composed a long, intensely personal, and confessional letter to Whitman, telling him that she had never truly loved her husband, that her own sexuality had been 'slumbering—undeveloped', and openly declaring her love for the strong divine soul of the man who had at last embraced hers with passionate love, through his poems. Whitman eventually replied in November, after two further letters from Anne. His response was courteous, brief, and cautious. Anne was undeterred, and a mutual correspondence was begun. The two met face to face in September 1876, Anne having set sail for Philadelphia on 30 August from Liverpool. She rented a house at 1929 North 22nd Street and Whitman, who had suffered a stroke three years earlier, immediately began visiting. 'She must have known within a very few minutes that the man who stood before her was not the great Adamic lover she had dreamed of' (Alcaro, 162). Whitman would not have been so comfortable enjoying the comforts of what he called 'the best room in the house, breezy and cool' if Anne had continued to press her romantic designs. Anne's own creativity, for so long stifled by her long-distance infatuation with the poet, became active again. While in Philadelphia she worked on a translation of Hugo's *La légende des siècles* and while travelling in Massachusetts wrote 'Three glimpses of a New England village', later published in *Blackwood's Magazine*.

Anne returned to England in 1879, bought a house in Hampstead, prepared a memoir of her husband to be prefixed to the second edition of the *Life of William Blake* (1880), and wrote a *Life of Mary Lamb*. She suffered increasingly from emphysema, and her daughter Beatrice committed suicide in August 1881, while undergoing medical training in Edinburgh. Anne had planned a life of Dorothy Wordsworth, but died from breast cancer at her home, 12 Well Road, Hampstead, London, on 29 November 1885 and was buried at Kensal Green cemetery, beside her husband. Her son Percy developed a career as a metallurgist, and Herbert, who drew together the materials for *Anne Gilchrist: her Life and Writings* (1887), was a painter.

MICHAEL THORN

Sources M. W. Alcaro, *Walt Whitman's Mrs G.: a biography of Anne Gilchrist* (1991) • H. H. Gilchrist, ed., *Anne Gilchrist: her life and writings* (1887) • W. M. Rossetti, *Some reminiscences*, 2 vols. (1906) • T. B. Harned, ed., *The letters of Anne Gilchrist and Walt Whitman* (1918) • E. P. Gould, *Anne Gilchrist and Walt Whitman* (1900) • K. Jones, *Learning not to be first: the life of Christina Rossetti* (1991) • J. Kaplan, *Walt Whitman: a life* (1980) • P. J. Ferlazzo, 'Anne Gilchrist, critic of Walt Whitman', *South Dakota Review*, 10/4 (1972–3), 63–79 • *CGPLA Eng. & Wales* (1885)

Archives priv. coll., collection | BL, letters to Macmillan & Co., Add. MSS 55253–55257, *passim*

Likenesses photograph, 1874, repro. in Alcaro, *Walt Whitman's Mrs G*, 152; priv. coll. • H. Gilchrist, portrait, 1882–4, University of Pennsylvania, Department of Special Collections, Van Pelt Library • H. Gilchrist, group portrait, 1884 (*The Tea Party*), University of

Pennsylvania, Department of Special Collections, Van Pelt Library · H. Gilchrist, portrait, 1885, University of Pennsylvania, Department of Special Collections, Van Pelt Library

Wealth at death £3333 8*s*. 3*d*.: resworn administration, April 1886, *CGPLA Eng. & Wales* (1885)

Gilchrist, Ebenezer (*bap.* **1708**, *d.* **1774**), physician, baptized at Dumfries on 30 September 1708, was possibly the son of John Gilchrist (*d.* 1733), merchant, and his wife, Lilias Maxwell. He studied medicine at Edinburgh, London, and Paris, and graduated at Rheims. In 1732 he returned to practise in Dumfries. On 17 September 1744 he married Grizzel Corrie, daughter of James Corrie, provost of Dumfries; they had daughters and a son, John Gilchrist (*d.* 1830), also a physician in Dumfries.

Gilchrist was widely known and often consulted by letter; he corresponded with Edinburgh physicians. He followed conventional treatments, but with some scepticism, doubting if bloodletting 'did much good' in fevers, or that blistering was useful (Gilchrist, 1752, 291). He advocated exercise, and considered that overcrowding and poor nutrition could lead to disease, especially consumption. His major work, *The Use of Sea Voyages in Medicine* (three editions, each longer than its predecessor, 1756, 1757, 1771; French translation 1770), considers asthma and scrofula (tuberculosis of the neck glands), as well as consumption. It is clearly written, with detailed case notes. Although he advocated sea voyages and a good diet with more confidence than anything else, by the third edition he envisaged sanatoria of small detached villas for the treatment of consumption. He was mistakenly credited with suggesting, but not attempting, treating consumption by artificial pneumothorax (collapsing a lung). Gilchrist's publications, mainly on infectious diseases, show a keen interest in treatment. He deplored the absence of a rule by which the effect of a treatment could be judged. When assessing results, he insisted that all cases, whatever the outcome, should be considered: 'The first step, in order to be right, is to know that we are wrong' (Gilchrist, 1757, 166).

Gilchrist died in Dumfries on 3 June 1774, and was buried in St Michael's, the old parish churchyard of Dumfries. JEAN LOUDON

Sources *Medical and Philosophical Commentaries*, 2 (1774), 327, 433–7 · W. McDowall, *Memorials of St Michael's, the old parish churchyard of Dumfries* (1876), 15–16 · *GM*, 1st ser., 68 (1798), 175 · E. Gilchrist, *The use of sea voyages in medicine* (1756) · E. Gilchrist, *The use of sea voyages in medicine*, 2nd edn (1757) · E. Gilchrist, *The use of sea voyages in medicine*, new edn (1771) · E. Gilchrist, 'An essay on nervous fevers', *Medical Essays and Observations*, 4 (1752), 280–326 · J. Avalon, 'Un médecin du XVIIIe siècle: Gilchrist précurseur de Forlanini', *Bulletin de la Société Française d'Histoire de la Médecine*, 16 (1922), 409–12 · D. A. Wittopkoning, 'A letter from Boerhaave to Ebenezer Gilchrist', *Janus*, 48 (1959), 258–63 · parish register (baptism), 30 Sept 1708 · parish register (marriage), 17 Sept 1744 · T. Dormandy, *The white death: a history of tuberculosis* (1999), 252

Gilchrist, James (*d.* **1777**), naval officer, went to sea in 1728, was promoted lieutenant on 28 August 1741, and in 1749 was serving with the *Namur* when, on 12 April, she was lost with all hands. Gilchrist escaped as he was on shore, possibly with his admiral, Boscawen, to whom he was probably flag-lieutenant. With confirmation of the peace Gilchrist returned home in command of the *Basilisk* (a bomb-vessel), bringing the *Namur*'s few survivors, and arrived at Plymouth on 17 April 1750.

On 18 July 1755 Gilchrist was advanced to post-rank and appointed to the *Experiment* frigate, in which in September he was sent first to the coast of France and then, early in 1756, into the Mediterranean, where he joined Admiral Byng. He was present at the action off Minorca on 20 May, and subsequently gave evidence, unfavourable to the admiral, at Byng's court martial, for which he was described by Augustus Hervey as 'the most fawning sycophant that ever cringed to power' (*Hervey's Journal*, 234). In the Mediterranean he was appointed by Sir Edward Hawke, in rapid succession to the *Chesterfield*, the *Deptford*, and the *Trident*. After returning home in April 1757 he was appointed to the *Southampton*, a 32-gun frigate, in which, off Portland, on 25 July, he fought off two French frigates of superior force and, on 12 September, captured the French frigate *Émeraude*. In 1758 he captured two large privateers in the channel; and on 28 March 1759 in the North Sea, in company with Captain Hotham in the *Melampe*, he took the 40-gun French frigate *Danae*. In this hard-fought action Gilchrist was shot through the shoulder by a 1 lb ball, a wound that rendered his arm permanently useless; he never served again, and from this time lived in retirement at his family seat of Hunsfield in Lanarkshire. He died at Hunsfield in 1777.

Gilchrist had married Ann Robertson, and they had two daughters, Grizel and Anne (1755–1784); Anne married Archibald Cochrane, ninth earl of Dundonald, on 17 October 1774, and was the mother of Thomas Cochrane, the tenth earl. J. K. LAUGHTON, *rev.* ROGER MORRISS

Sources J. Charnock, ed., *Biographia navalis*, 6 vols. (1794–8) · PRO, ADM 107/3 · PRO, PROB 11/1037 · *Augustus Hervey's journal*, ed. D. Erskine, 2nd edn (1954) · GEC, *Peerage*

Gilchrist, John Borthwick (**1759–1841**), philologist, was born in Edinburgh on 19 June 1759. His parentage is unknown, but as he was educated at the charitable institution of George Heriot's Hospital in Edinburgh, it is likely that he was the son of a deceased freeman of the city. It is likely too that Heriot's Hospital paid for his education at Edinburgh University, where he graduated in medicine in 1774, at the age of fifteen, with a thesis entitled *De febre anomala inter Dumfrisienses epidemica anno 1767*.

After several years in the West Indies, where he mastered the principles of indigo manufacture, Gilchrist arrived in Bombay early in 1782 as an assistant surgeon with the Royal Navy. In February 1782 he was appointed an assistant surgeon with the East India Company's Bengal army and shortly afterwards marched with a detachment of the army from Surat, north of Bombay, to Fatehgarh in upper India. The journey revealed to him the extent to which the language of Hindustani could be understood in different regions of India, and it surprised him to discover that his employers neither required nor encouraged him to learn it. Subsequent experience in combat confirmed his belief that officers should be able to converse in Hindustani with their soldiers, and in April 1785 he obtained leave to further his understanding of the language, which he defined as the 'grand living popular speech of all Hindoostan' (*A Dictionary, English and Hindoostanee*, pt 1, 1787, preface, p. iv).

Hindustani had grown out of the Indo-Aryan language of Hindi–Hindavi and existed in its purest form in upper India, north-west of Calcutta. For months Gilchrist traversed this region, settling for a time at Fyzabad, near Lucknow, in search of the best poets and scribes. By 1787 he was ready to call for subscriptions for a proposed dictionary and grammar of Hindustani, but the work of printing it proved tedious and expensive and the project was not to be completed for eleven years. Midway, in an effort to raise funds, he embarked on indigo, sugar, and opium production in Ghazipur, a business that boomed for a while and then slumped, further depleting his finances and energies. *A Grammar of the Hindoostanee Language* finally appeared in 1796, while *A Dictionary, English and Hindoostanee*, which had been issued in parts, was not ready for binding (in two volumes, dated 1787 and 1790) until 1798. It had been a massive labour, the difficulties of which Gilchrist enumerated in his 1798 preface to the dictionary. It is a kind critic, however, who does not think that Gilchrist must have brought some of these difficulties on himself. Alternately rambling and forthright, self-pitying and aggressive—indeed, at times downright abusive—the preface set the tone of scholarly martyrdom that was to pervade many of his later publications.

Gilchrist could not complain of lack of government patronage. He had been promoted to surgeon in October 1794 and his leave from medical duties had been extended virtually indefinitely. In 1798 the government agreed to purchase 300 copies of his *Oriental Linguist*, a primer for learners of Hindustani. It also accepted his offer of cheap daily tuition in Hindustani and Persian for the company's junior servants, and in 1800 the governor-general, Lord Wellesley, appointed him the first professor of Hindustani at Fort William College. The college was Wellesley's personal scheme for improving the intellect of the company's servants and he lavished money on its appointees; Gilchrist's salary was a healthy Rs 1500 per month—about £1800 per year.

At the college Gilchrist gathered together Hindustani scribes from around Lucknow and Delhi and set them to translating stories into Hindustani from Persian. Modern Urdu scholars consider the best of these translations to be Mir Amman's *Bagh o bahar* ('Garden and Spring', 1801), a collection of five romantic stories similar in structure to the *Arabian Nights*. As Gilchrist was intent on teaching Hindustani for administrative purposes, the style of prose he encouraged was direct and smooth-flowing, shorn of the floral ornamentation favoured in the northern court cities whence his writers had come. It was a long time, therefore, before the prose works he had fostered were taken up by non-European readers; no one of taste, asserted critics from Lucknow, would ever write so baldly. With another band of hand-picked assistants, Gilchrist turned to producing ideal specimens of Hindi prose, which were printed in the Devanagari character. His *Hindee Story Teller* (1802) was the first example of Khari Bholi Hindi ever to be printed, while Lalluji Lal's *Prem sagar* ('Ocean of love', 1803) was perhaps the college's most famous Hindi production; it remained a standard in civil service language tests for decades to come.

Philologists dispute the significance of Gilchrist's work at Fort William College, in particular his role in the distillation of the two modern languages of Urdu and Hindi from the Hindustani–Hindavi cauldron. Some Hindi specialists have accused him of practising a linguistic version of divide and rule. They argue that, by standardizing typefaces, vocabulary, and rules of grammar, he pigeonholed Hindi as the language of the Hindus and Hindustani (or Urdu) as the language of the Muslims. In contrast, modern Urdu scholars have tended to play down his contribution to their language. At their most dismissive, they argue that his work 'stands outside the main current of Urdu prose and … has no place in its evolution' (Sadiq, 290). Neither judgement seems fair. From Gilchrist's writings it is apparent that he was struggling to clarify a linguistic difference that was already in existence when he began his work. In the milder assessment of the Hindi scholar Amrit Rai (Rai, 8–17) Gilchrist may have hastened the division between Hindi and Urdu, but he did not create it, nor was he sufficiently master of the culture around him so to dictate its future. Likewise, a less extreme position on the Urdu side of the debate would allow that Gilchrist and his scholar-assistants played an initiatory, if artificially motivated, role in the development of Urdu prose literature. Gilchrist may also be given credit for acknowledging the labours of the *munshis* and pandits who worked with him; this was not the case in many of the literary ventures undertaken by colonial officials.

Gilchrist's fiery temperament involved him in numerous scrapes at the college, and eventually led to his premature resignation. Early in 1804, when planning the college's annual public disputation, he unwittingly kicked up a storm by directing his students to debate the proposition that Indians would embrace Christianity as soon as they were enabled to compare Christian precepts with those of their own religions. The Muslim scholars employed at the college were outraged by the theme and rumours of forced conversion, which were of a perennial nature in Calcutta, were soon doing the rounds again. In response to the public alarm, Wellesley directed that the disputation topic be changed, a decision that so offended Gilchrist that he resigned his post on 23 February 1804 and sailed almost immediately for Britain.

On arrival home Gilchrist settled in Edinburgh. He married Mary Ann, daughter of John Coventry of Douglas, on 11 May 1808 and took a house on the north side of Nicholson Square, where, to the delight of locals, he established a large aviary, whose colourful and exotic inhabitants were visible to passers-by. He resigned the company's service in 1809, but failed to get more than an ordinary surgeon's pension from the directors, a source of lasting grievance to him. In partnership with James Inglis, he set up a bank in Edinburgh under the title of Inglis, Borthwick Gilchrist & Co., but the enterprise crumbled, apparently because investors doubted the soundness of its management. Eventually this and some of his other investments did prove to be profitable, but Gilchrist prefaced his books, advertisements, and appeals to the company with tales of such financial woe that it is easy to miss the fact that he died a wealthy man and for many years lived comfortably in the fashionable locality of Clarges Street, London.

While still in Edinburgh, Gilchrist achieved notoriety as an outspoken political radical, a reputation that was boosted by his publication in 1815 of *Parliamentary reform on constitutional principles, or, British loyalty against continental royalty*. The tenor of his political views and also the impetuosity of his nature are compactly displayed in the opening lines of an introductory letter he wrote to Jeremy Bentham, a private hero who subsequently became a friend:

> I have hitherto refrained from paying my personal respects to an individual whom I would much rather see, than all the potentates who have ever been, now are, or ever will be, strutting on the face of the earth, with weak heads and hollow hearts, glaring enough to sicken everything except the reptiles which bask in the sunshine of royalty and fatten on the degrading offals from a throne. (Falconer, 7)

With the loud and repeated expression of such views it is not surprising that Gilchrist made enemies. In 1816 he and his wife left Edinburgh for ever, accusing Scottish tories of political persecution.

Back in London, Gilchrist began offering private language tuition for young men destined for India. He had never slackened in his publication of textbooks and constantly revised his earlier works for the consumption of new generations of civil servants. His *British Indian Monitor* (2 vols., 1806–8), for example, was a compression of earlier publications, including the *Antijargonist* (1800), *Strangers East Indian Guide* (1802), and *Oriental Linguist* (1798). In 1816 he published *The Orienti-Occidental Tuitionary Pioneer to Literary Pursuits*, a curious compilation of old reports on oriental education and the numerous memorials of complaint that he had presented to his former employers. It also included a 'Panglossal diorama for a universal language and character', which a modern editor has called 'a contribution to phonetics of unacknowledged importance' (Note to the Scolar Press facsimile of Gilchrist's *Grammar of the Hindoostanee Language*, 1970). Remarkably, the unfriendly tone of the *Tuitionary Pioneer* did not prevent the company from rehiring Gilchrist to teach Hindustani and Persian to its newly recruited medical officers. From 1818 the company paid him £200 a year, plus £150 for providing a lecture room in his Oriental Institution in Leicester Square, on the understanding that he would take no more than 3 guineas from each student. Gilchrist got round this by requiring the students to purchase textbooks from his publishers totalling £10 to £15, a profitable but unpopular scam. The textbooks themselves raised hackles because, perhaps as a result of his republicanism, he had conceived a dislike of capital letters and refused to admit them to his publications. Matters eventually came to a head when Gilchrist tried to manoeuvre the company into sending all its new appointees to him, not just the assistant surgeons. In 1825 the company withdrew its support for his classes and in the following year he handed over the Oriental Institution to Duncan Forbes and Sandford Arnot. He subsequently quarrelled with them as well; the first annual report of the London Oriental Institution (1828) revealed that he had tried to set up rival classes nearby.

Beyond the field of oriental languages Gilchrist was committed to increasing popular education. He counted Joseph Hume and George Birkbeck among his friends, and in 1823 he helped Birkbeck found the London Mechanics' Institution. He was also involved in the foundation of the University of London. No likenesses of him survive from this period, but something of the vividness of his personality is preserved in a description of him in Chambers's *Biographical Dictionary*:

> his bushy head and whiskers were as white as the Himalayan snow, and in such contrast to the active expressive face which beamed from the centre of the mass, that he was likened to a royal Bengal tiger—a resemblance of which he was even proud. (Chambers, 2.107)

Gilchrist's final years were spent in Paris, where he died, on 8 January 1841, and was buried. There had been no children from his marriage and in 1850 his widow married General Guglielmo Pépé of Naples. In his will Gilchrist had left her a comfortable allowance, but he directed that the bulk of his capital be placed in an educational trust 'for the Benefit, Advancement, and Propagation of Education and Learning in every part of the World as far as circumstances will permit'. Joseph Hume was among the trustees he nominated. For twenty-five years the trust was tied up in litigation as the result of a suit brought by a nephew of Gilchrist's, but the House of Lords eventually found in favour of the trustees. The delay was unexpectedly beneficial, for during the case a tract of land in Australia called Balmain, adjoining Sydney town, which Gilchrist had bought in 1801 for £17 10*s*., had rocketed in value to over £70,000. Once operational, the trust was faithful to Gilchrist's aims and for many years it sponsored scholarships to Britain for students from India, Canada, and Australia; scholarships and fellowships for women at Oxford and Cambridge; travelling studentships for secondary school teachers; an annual series of public lectures in British industrial centres; and grants to the Workers' Educational Association and for university extension courses. With hindsight, the innovatory work of the trust can be seen as a more faithful memorial to Gilchrist's political and educational ideals than anything he—hampered by a notoriously impetuous and mercurial temperament—was able to effect himself.

KATHERINE PRIOR

Sources U. J. Kaye-Shuttleworth, Baron Shuttleworth of Gawthorpe, *Gilchrist Educational Trust: pioneering work in education* (1930) • R. Falconer, 'The Gilchrist scholarships: an episode in the higher education of Canada', *Proceedings and Transactions of the Royal Society of Canada*, 3rd ser., 27 (1933), section 2, pp. 5–13 • Chambers, *Scots.* (1855) • S. Kidwai, *Gilchrist and the 'language of Hindoostan'* (1972) •

D. G. Crawford, ed., *Roll of the Indian Medical Service, 1615–1930* (1930) • personal records, BL OIOC, O/6/1, 401–2; o/6/6, 459–65 • *List of the graduates in medicine in the University of Edinburgh from MDCCV to MDCCCLXVI* (1867) • *GM*, 2nd ser., 34 (1850), 650 [for widow's remarriage] • A. Rai, *A house divided: the origin and development of Hindi/Hindavi* (1984) • M. Sadiq, *A history of Urdu literature*, 2nd edn (1984) • *IGI* • m. reg. Scot.

Archives BL, letters

Likenesses C. F. Voight, bronze medal, 1841, NPG • medallion-style sketch (after medal by C. F. Voight, 1841), repro. in Shuttleworth, *Gilchrist Educational Trust*

Wealth at death over £100,000: Kaye-Shuttleworth, *Gilchrist Educational Trust*; Falconer, 'Gilchrist scholarships'

Gilchrist, Marion (1864–1952), physician, was born on 5 February 1864 at Bothwell Park, Lanarkshire, the daughter of William Gilchrist (*d.* 1903), a well-to-do tenant farmer, and his wife, Margaret Williamson. Marion was a pupil at the nearby Hamilton Academy, but left school at the age of fourteen to work on the farm. Not content with supervising milking and butter and cheese making, she secretly enrolled in a correspondence course in English and attended evening classes at her old school. In 1887 she matriculated as an arts student from Queen Margaret College for the Higher Education of Women, Glasgow, probably aiming to become a teacher. At the end of her first year she began to take the exams leading to a LLA (lady literate in arts) awarded by the University of St Andrews, which she sat first at Paisley and then at Queen Margaret College itself. This qualification allowed many women throughout the United Kingdom to embark on professional careers. In 1888 Marion Gilchrist passed in physiology, French, and botany, in 1889 in logic and metaphysics and with honours in English and in education, and in 1890 in natural philosophy. She gained her LLA in that year and immediately enrolled along with thirteen other women in the newly opened medical school at Queen Margaret College.

By this time Marion Gilchrist was taking an active part in student politics as a member of the Liberal Club. Since the college was not allowed to present candidates for professional exams, in 1891 she applied on behalf of herself and her fellow students for entry to the University of Glasgow under the terms of the 1889 Universities (Scotland) Act which sanctioned the admission of women. In the following year the first women students matriculated and Marion Gilchrist, with fifty-five other women, entered the medical faculty. So as to be able to graduate as quickly as possible, she took classes in the summer of 1893 at the Royal Hospital, the military hospital in Dublin. She graduated in July 1894 along with her fellow student Alice Lilian Louisa Cumming. Because Marion Gilchrist gained a high commendation she was technically the first woman graduate of the university. In the same year (Elizabeth) Dorothea Lyness (later Dr Chalmers Smith) also graduated. Along with her fellow women students, Marion Gilchrist had to overcome considerable hostility from some quarters of the male medical establishment and from male students. Despite her remarkable achievement in completing the course in four and a half years, she found time to be vice-president of the Queen Margaret College Student Union, vice-president of the Literary and Debating Society, and convener of the Queen Margaret College committee of the Glasgow University Liberal Club.

After qualifying, Marion Gilchrist assisted in a general practice in the west end of Glasgow, developing an interest in diseases of the eye. The death of her father in 1903 gave her the means to set up in practice at 5 Buckingham Terrace, where she remained for the rest of her life. She never married, but shared her home and consulting rooms until 1928 with **Katherine Mary Chapman** (1883–1948), who had first matriculated from Glasgow University in 1894. The daughter of John Henry Chapman, a barrister in Cheltenham, Katherine Chapman did not graduate until 1903 when she gained the triple qualification from the Faculty of Physicians and Surgeons in Glasgow. Later she worked in the electrical department at Glasgow Royal Infirmary, the first radiography department in the world. She became head of department—the first woman to achieve such a position in a major Scottish teaching hospital—and university lecturer in radiology, electrotherapy, and diagnosis. She retired from these positions in 1928 and set up practice in the West End of London. She died unmarried at Cardross in Dunbartonshire in May 1948. Marion Gilchrist wrote a touching notice in the *Glasgow Herald* in which she praised her friend's pastoral care as much as her clinical skills. Their relationship had remained formal to a fault. To the end they never addressed each other than as Dr Gilchrist or Dr Chapman.

Financial and professional independence allowed Marion Gilchrist to become politically active more openly. During 1903—encouraged by her friends Janie Allan, the daughter of the owner of the Allan Line, and Margaret Irwin—she joined the Glasgow and West of Scotland Association for Women's Suffrage, formed the previous year. Frustrated by the association's lack of progress, in 1907 all three supported a call for more militant action from Grace Paterson, who had been actively involved in establishing Queen Margaret College and was one of the first two women elected to the Glasgow school board. She had also been involved in setting up Redlands Hospital for Women in Glasgow in 1903. Dissatisfied with the committee's response, the four women resigned and joined the Glasgow branch of the Women's Social and Political Union. Unlike Janie Allan and her fellow student Dorothea Chalmers Smith, Marion Gilchrist did not take part directly in militant protest, although she became a member of the Glasgow branch of the Women's Freedom League. She preferred instead to devote her voluntary energies to the Invalid Children's School of the Queen Margaret College Settlement for which she acted as physician from 1903 to 1911. In 1914 she was appointed assistant surgeon for diseases of the eye at the Victoria Infirmary on the south side of the city. From 1916 until 1918, while Hugh Walker, the surgeon for diseases of the eye, was away on war work, Marion Gilchrist took over his duties. She resigned from the infirmary in 1930 as she found it difficult to share the position with that of ophthalmic surgeon at Redlands Hospital for Women to which she had been appointed three years before. She continued to serve Redlands Hospital until the end of her life, not just as a clinician but also assisting with fundraising events.

As Marion Gilchrist became less engaged with the suffrage movement, she became more involved in medical politics. She was among the first members of the Medical Women's Federation, which she supported actively throughout her life. She was a prominent member of the British Medical Association and the first woman chairman of the Glasgow division. She was a trustee of the Muirhead Trust, which had been established in 1889 with the initial purpose of establishing a medical school in the west of Scotland for women. She used these positions to advance the careers of medical women within the male-dominated medical institutions in the west of Scotland. She was an enthusiastic early motorist and traveller. Above all she was a medical practitioner with a fierce sense of duty—a quality which she expected others to share. When a newly qualified woman doctor was visiting her for tea during the war and the air-raid warning sounded, she told her young colleague that she must return at once to her hospital on the other side of Glasgow even though bombs were falling outside. Marion Gilchrist died at her home in Buckingham Terrace, Glasgow, on 7 September 1952.

MICHAEL S. MOSS

Sources b. cert. • d. cert. • U. Glas. • *Medical Directory* • *The Post Office directory of Glasgow* • L. Leneman, *A guid cause: the women's suffrage movement in Scotland* (1991) • private information (2004)
Wealth at death £112,735 3*s*. 11*d*.: confirmation, 6 Nov 1952, *CCI*

Gilchrist, Octavius Graham (1779–1823), literary scholar, was born at Twickenham, one of sixteen children of Stirling Gilchrist, lieutenant and surgeon in the 3rd dragoon guards, who left the service when his regiment returned to England, and retired to Twickenham. A brother, R. A. Gilchrist, later made his name as an artist. Octavius was educated at Magdalen College, Oxford, but left early without a degree, in order to assist a relative (Alderman Joseph Robinson, grocer) in business at Stamford. In 1803 he was elected FSA, and in 1804 he married Elizabeth, daughter of James Nowlan, merchant, of the Hermitage, Wapping.

In 1805 Gilchrist printed, privately, a little volume *Rhymes*, and in 1807 published a full and valuable edition of the poems of Richard Corbet (1582–1635), bishop of Oxford and of Norwich. To his friend William Gifford he addressed in 1808 *An examination of the charges maintained by Messrs. Malone, Chalmers, and others of Ben Jonson's enmity towards Shakespeare*, and in 1811 *A Letter … on the Late Edition [by H. Weber] of Ford's Plays*. Gifford, in his editions of Jonson and Ford, acknowledged the help received from Gilchrist's investigations. In the *Quarterly Review* for June 1812 Gilchrist severely criticized Stephen Jones's edition of Baker's *Biographia dramatica*. Jones replied in *Hypercriticism Exposed* (1812). Early in 1814 Gilchrist considered publishing *A select collection of old English plays in 15 vols. 8vo, with biographical notices and notes critical and explanatory*, but abandoned this owing to the appearance of Dilke's *Old English Plays*. Notes of Gilchrist are included in the third edition (by J. P. Collier) of Dodsley's *Old Plays* (1825–7). The *Quarterly Review* for October 1820 had some uncomplimentary remarks on William Lisle Bowles, in a review of *Spence's Anecdotes*. Bowles replied in *The Pamphleteer* (vol. 17), attributing the *Quarterly* article to Gilchrist, who (while disclaiming the authorship) published a vigorous *Letter to the Rev. William Lisle Bowles* (1820). An acrimonious controversy followed. Gifford (in his introduction to Ford's *Works*) declared that 'in the extent and accuracy of his critical knowledge' Gilchrist was 'as much superior to the Rev. Mr. Bowles as in good manners'. In 1819 Gilchrist befriended the poet John Clare, and hosted a meeting with Clare's publisher, John Taylor. He presented Clare to the public in the *London Magazine* (January 1820), and accompanied him on his first visit to London.

On 30 June 1823 Gilchrist died at his house in the High Street, Stamford, after long suffering from consumption. His will stated his desire to be buried in his father's grave at Twickenham. His library, which contained some choice Elizabethan and early printed books, was sold by auction on 5–11 January 1824. Gilchrist probably supplied much of the material for Drakard's *History of Stamford* (1822).

A. H. BULLEN, *rev.* JOHN D. HAIGH

Sources *GM*, 1st ser., 79 (1809), 53 • *GM*, 1st ser., 91/1 (1821), 291–4, 533–4 • *GM*, 1st ser., 93/2 (1823), 278 • private information (1889) • J. Gorton, *A general biographical dictionary*, 3 vols. (1841) • J. Clare, *John Clare's autobiographical writings*, ed. E. Robinson (1983), *passim* • *The letters of John Clare*, ed. J. W. Tibble and A. Tibble (1951) • will, PRO, PROB 11/1685, sig. 293
Archives Stamford Public Library, Stamford, letters and MSS | BL, letters to John Clare, Egerton MSS 2245–2246, 2250 • BL, letters to Philip Bliss, Add. MSS 34567–34568, *passim*
Likenesses Freeman, stipple, pubd 1810 (after J. Lonsdale), NPG; repro. in *Monthly Mirror* (Aug 1810)
Wealth at death see will, PRO, PROB 11/1685, sig. 293

Gilchrist, Percy Carlyle (1851–1935), metallurgist, was born in Lyme Regis on 27 December 1851, the elder son (there were also two daughters) of Alexander *Gilchrist (1828–1861), barrister and writer, and his wife, Anne *Gilchrist, *née* Burrows (1828–1885), biographer and essayist, daughter of John Parker Burrows, solicitor. His boyhood was first spent in Guildford and then, from 1856 to 1862, in Chelsea, in the house next door to Thomas and Jane Carlyle, who became close friends. Despite his literary and artistic upbringing Percy Gilchrist embarked upon a scientific career. Unlike his cousin, Alexander's nephew Sidney Gilchrist *Thomas (1850–1885), with whom he was to collaborate, Gilchrist received a complete education, first at Felsted School, and then at the Royal School of Mines (1868–71), where he trained as a metallurgist and analytical chemist and was Murchison medallist in July 1870. He subsequently gained membership of the institutes of civil and mechanical engineers. His first post was that of analytical chemist at an ironworks at Cwmafon in Glamorgan. In 1876 he took a similar position at the Blaenafon ironworks in Monmouthshire under the management of Edward Martin.

In 1875 Thomas hit upon a way of removing phosphorus from iron ores in the process developed by Henry Bessemer for the manufacture of steel. To test his idea, Thomas persuaded Gilchrist to carry out experiments during his leisure hours at the Blaenafon works. On learning their secret, Martin agreed to pay for further development and the cost of the patents taken out on the dephosphorization process in 1877 and 1878. On publication of the process in 1879 Gilchrist moved to Middlesbrough to help perfect the dolomite (magnesium limestone) liner for the converter in the works of Bolckow, Vaughan & Co. In 1881 Gilchrist and Thomas developed their own steelworks, North Eastern Steel Company, at Middlesbrough. When this was sold to Dorman, Long & Co. in 1903 Gilchrist retired from active work in metallurgy. Between 1882 and 1894 he was also chairman of the Basic and Dephosphorizing Patents Company, which was set up to safeguard the many patentees with interests in the dephosphorization process and the agricultural disposal of the phosphorus-rich basic slag.

Gilchrist was elected FRS in 1891. He was a vice-president of the Iron and Steel Institute (1891), a member of the Society of Chemical Industry, a fellow of the Royal Society of Arts, and a chevalier of the Légion d'honneur. In 1887 he married Norah Augusta Mara, the second daughter of Captain Lewis Roper Fitzmaurice RN. They had a son and daughter. Although when awarded the Bessemer medal in 1883 Thomas acknowledged Gilchrist's 'unwearied exertions, conspicuous energy and ability', Gilchrist was always overshadowed by his romantic, inventive cousin, his vivacious mother, and his talented brother, the painter Herbert Harlakenden Gilchrist. In later life he was an invalid.

Gilchrist died at his home, The Grove, Pinner, Middlesex, on 15 December 1935, having survived his cousin by fifty years. His wife outlived him. W. H. BROCK, *rev.*

Sources H. C. H. Carpenter, *Obits. FRS*, 2 (1936–8), 19–24 • *DBB* • *The Times* (18 Dec 1935), 14c • *CGPLA Eng. & Wales* (1936)
Likenesses photograph, repro. in Carpenter, *Obits. FRS*
Wealth at death £1468 6*s*. 3*d*.: administration, 20 April 1936, *CGPLA Eng. & Wales*

Gilchrist, (Andrew) Rae (1899–1995), physician and cardiologist, was born on 7 July 1899 at the manse, Holywood, co. Down, Northern Ireland, the only son of Andrew Gilchrist (1871–1954), Presbyterian minister, and his wife, Catherine Hill, *née* Witherow (1879–1955). His parents were Scottish. He was educated at George Watson's Boys' College in Edinburgh, Campbell College in Belfast (1913–16), and the University of Edinburgh (1917–21), where he qualified in medicine. He became a fellow of the Royal College of Physicians of Edinburgh when only thirty, and received a gold medal for his MD thesis in 1933.

After junior appointments at Addenbrooke's Hospital, Cambridge, the Princess Elizabeth Hospital for Children, London, and a year at the Rockefeller Hospital in New York, Gilchrist was appointed to the consultant staff of the Royal Infirmary of Edinburgh in 1930 at the early age of thirty-one. In those days this was the ultimate aim for an ambitious young clinician. Gilchrist always said that he was lucky because three more senior physicians had died before the age of fifty. This early security permitted him to develop his lifelong interest in heart disease, leading to the establishment of a dedicated department of cardiology in the Royal Infirmary of Edinburgh in 1953. His particular interest was in cardiac arrhythmias, heart block, paediatric cardiology, and cardiac problems associated with pregnancy. He published many papers on these subjects.

In 1930 Gilchrist reported in the *Edinburgh Medical Journal* the first seven cases of coronary thrombosis recorded in Europe. As an alert young physician, working in acute medical wards of the Royal Infirmary, this was his total experience of the previous four years. It was a seminal report, ignored by almost all his seniors—most of whom had not heard of the condition or did not believe that it was compatible with survival. Recognizing that his contemporaries were excellent physicians and that it was unlikely that they would fail to make the correct diagnosis, Gilchrist was firmly of the view years later that coronary heart attacks (first described in 1911) were a new disease.

Gilchrist was the founder of cardiology in Scotland. During and after the Second World War, the Edinburgh clinical school of medicine was particularly strong, and possibly the leading teaching centre in Britain. Together with Sir Stanley Davidson, professor of medicine, and Sir Derrick Dunlop, professor of therapeutics, Gilchrist influenced the learning and clinical judgement of medical students and young graduates for more than thirty years. As a teacher he would brook no equivocation. An ambiguous answer, even if it concealed real doubt, to one of his commanding bedside questions would be met by scorn. This bred a discipline and orderliness of mind in his students, undergraduate or postgraduate, that few other teachers achieved. It also bred an extraordinary loyalty and respect from all who worked closely with him. He was a large and formidable figure, but magnanimity and humour were never far away.

Gilchrist was a founder member in 1959 of the British Heart Foundation. He recognized that the amount of money available for research into heart and circulatory diseases from official sources was very limited—the Medical Research Council budget totalled about two-thirds of one per cent of the whole cost of the National Health Service, and the amount spent on heart and vascular disease did not exceed about £50,000 a year. For these reasons the British Heart Foundation made an appeal directly to the public, and in the 1990s the sums accumulated allowed the expenditure of up to £50 million per year on support for research into heart disease, with most directed towards coronary disease. One outcome of this was the establishment in 1986, with the University of Edinburgh, of the Duke of Edinburgh chair of cardiology.

Gilchrist welcomed new advances, though always with appropriate critical appraisal, and always with the question, 'Will this help my patients?' He encouraged his young staff to develop new ideas, while strict in his assessments of their contributions: to be prolix was fatal, to vacillate was nearly as bad, and to dissemble in any way was unacceptable. However, when new ideas were being developed he was excited and gave all his considerable influence to their study. Although clinically oriented, Gilchrist recognized the need to encourage studies of clinical physiology and biochemistry, particularly into the pathogenesis of atherosclerosis and coronary heart disease.

Gilchrist was president of the Royal College of Physicians of Edinburgh from 1957 to 1960 and was made an honorary fellow in 1990. He was also a fellow of the Royal College of Physicians, London, from 1944. He was appointed CBE in 1961 and received many other honours worldwide. He retired in 1964, ironically after a major coronary thrombosis, but survived another thirty years—an unusually long survival, which Gilchrist himself had thought impossible when he was in active consultant service. He was married twice: first, on 16 September 1931, to Emily Faulds Slater (1906–1967), younger daughter of W. Work Slater, of Edinburgh and Innerleithen, Peeblesshire, with whom he had one son and one daughter; and secondly, on 27 September 1975, to Elspeth Martin Wightman, *née* Scott (1904–1995), widow of his colleague Arthur Wightman. He died at his home, 16 Winton Terrace, Fairmilehead, Edinburgh, on 1 March 1995, and was cremated at Mortonhall crematorium, Edinburgh, on 4 March. He was survived by his son and daughter, and by his second wife, who died on 27 June 1995. M. F. Oliver

Sources personal knowledge (2004) · private information (2004) [family] · *WWW* · *The Times* (19 April 1995)
Likenesses photograph, repro. in *The Times*
Wealth at death £937,910.31: confirmation, 5 June 1995, NA Scot., SC/CO 840/35

Gildas [St Gildas] (*fl.* **5th–6th cent.**), writer, is remembered for his principal extant work, known as *De excidio et conquestu Britanniae* ('On the ruin and conquest of Britain'). His name is of obscure derivation. It is difficult to see to which sub-group of the Celtic languages it belongs: linguistically it is not close to that of the Breton saint Gweltas. It may derive from Ireland. The notion that Gildas is a pseudonym has also been advanced. There is no contemporary evidence for his family. The name of his father appears in later Welsh genealogies: Caw of Britain, or Caunus in the eleventh-century life of Gildas, written by a monk of the Breton abbey of St Gildas-de-Rhuis (Morbihan). The latter source also names four brothers and a sister, and the genealogies credit Gildas with two sons. These late testimonies are beyond proof. In the eighteenth century, scholars posited the existence of two Gildases: Gildas Albanicus, whose death was dated to the beginning of the sixth century, and Gildas Badonicus, supposedly born at about that time.

The life of Gildas is deeply obscure. He himself says that he was born in the year of the siege of 'Mons Badonicus', forty-three years and one month before the time at which he wrote *De excidio*. Both the date and the location of this siege have been hotly contested. An entry in the *Annales Cambriae*, probably dating from the late eighth century, ascribes it to 516. But Bede gives 493; and modern scholars have offered a range of dates. The composition of *De excidio* has been variously dated, most recently to between 479 and 484 (N. Higham) and to between 515 and 530 (T. D. O'Sullivan), giving Gildas a birth date at some time in the middle of the fifth century, though others have placed it rather later, *c.*500 (D. Dumville). The date of 570 given by the *Annales Cambriae* for his death must be regarded as, at best, traditional. While the eleventh-century life gives his place of birth as Arecluta (Dumbarton), most modern scholars locate his origins further south. The place of his death is given by his earlier life as the island of Houat, off Morbihan, and as Llanilltud Fawr (Llantwit Major, Glamorgan) by the later life, a twelfth-century Welsh production of the school of hagiography associated with Caradog of Llancarfan. It may be less important to modern eyes, however, than where he was educated and lived. This is no more certain than any other fact of his life. The earlier life, written in Brittany, puts him at the monastery of St Illtud at Llanilltud Fawr, then in Ireland with a certain king, Ainmericus, then at Rome and Ravenna, and finally in Brittany. Some modern scholars have defended the notion that St Gildas-de-Rhuis existed at that time and that Gildas ended his life in Brittany (L. Fleuriot). But, as the product of the monastery dedicated to him, the Breton life had good reason to place him there. Others have located Gildas in northern Britain (E. A. Thompson, M. Miller), in Wales (J. Morris), and in the south-west, in Dorset or Wiltshire (N. Higham).

It may be that Gildas spent part of his life in a monastic environment. He had already become a deacon when he wrote *De excidio*, a work which demonstrates its author's monastic sympathies. In a letter to Pope Gregory the Great written *c.*600, Columbanus refers to correspondence on points of monastic discipline between Gildas and Uennianus, the saintly Finnian, who may be identified with Finnian of Clonard, or with Findbarr of Movilla, or with the single figure who may lie behind both cults. Gildas was an orthodox Christian who severely criticized the moral laxity of his fellow countrymen. The British milieu in which he lived was still heavily romanized. Following a familiar medieval hagiographical scheme, the earliest life says that his parents entrusted him to the monk Illtud to learn the scriptures and the liberal arts, in a school in south Wales where his fellow pupils included the future saints Samson and Paul Aurelian. This is almost certainly a fiction. The high standard of Gildas's Latin suggests that he was educated in a secular Romano-British school, of a kind which could still have existed in southern Britain, rather than in a purely monastic establishment.

A late ninth-century manuscript contains fragments from Gildas's letters, most of which were included in the Irish canon collection *Collectio canonum Hibernensis*, compiled *c.*700. Fragments 4 and 5 are parts of the letter to Finnian to which Columbanus refers. A short penitential of twenty-seven canons, surviving in two ninth- or tenth-century continental manuscripts, is also attributed to him. By far Gildas's most famous work, however, is that of which the original title is unknown, but which has traditionally been called *De excidio et conquestu Britanniae*. This survives in full in four manuscripts, the earliest dating from the eleventh century (BL, Cotton MS Vitellius A.vi). The work falls into two parts, which may be called *Historia* (chaps. 2–26) and *Epistola* (chaps. 27–110). The *Historia*, a review of British history beginning before the Roman conquest, takes the form not of ordered chronology, but of providential history of a kind which had a number of precedents in late antique Christian literature. Gildas saw a causal relationship between the Britons' morality and God's response to it. God visited upon them 'damages and afflictions' because of their sinfulness, but would bring them success if they were obedient to him.

For the modern historian, Gildas's account of British history is frustratingly oblique. There are few proper nouns from Britain in the work: for the sub-Roman period before his own lifetime, only two people and one place. Yet scholars have picked over every word, since *De excidio* remains by far the longest remotely contemporary source for the Britain of the late fifth and early sixth century which witnessed the momentous *adventus Saxonum*—the coming of the Saxons. That Gildas's sequence of events is defective is clear from, for instance, his ascription of the building of Hadrian's Wall to the era after the formal withdrawal of the Romans when, he says, they returned at the request of the British to help them against marauding Picts and Scots. His narrative continues with a further appeal, to the Roman commander Agitius, who, largely because Gildas says he was addressed as 'thrice-consul', has been identified with the emperor Valentinian III's general Aëtius, who was killed in 454. This appeal was rejected, but the Britons attained some success on their own, which won them a period of peace and, according to Gildas, luxury. There then followed a plague, and the rumour of renewed attack from the Picts, which the British countered with an invitation to the Saxons to come to their aid. After 'a long time' the Saxons, settled in the east of Britain, complained that the supplies they had been granted were insufficient and plundered the whole island. The British recovered and, under the leadership of Ambrosius Aurelianus, defeated the Saxons in battle. From then on, victory went now to the British, now to their enemies, until the British won nearly 'the last defeat of the villains, and certainly not the least' (*Ruin of Britain*, trans. Winterbottom, 26), at Mons Badonicus in the year of Gildas's birth.

The *Historia* serves as an introduction to the *Epistola*, a long admonition to the kings and clerics of his time, supported by biblical citations, especially from the Old Testament prophets. Gildas names five kings, whose identity has been much discussed. Three are associated with identifiable areas: Constantine with 'Damnonia' (probably Dumnonia, roughly modern Devon and Cornwall); Vortipor, 'tyrant of the Demetae', a British tribe which had inhabited south-west Wales since before the Roman era; and Cuneglasus, linked with 'Din Eirth' (the Dinarth Rhos peninsula). The other two are Aurelius Caninus and Maglocunus, whose prestige, if not his sins, is accorded a higher status than that of the others. Echoing his attack on these kings, Gildas's complaint against contemporary churchmen also concerns their moral and spiritual laxity. He summons up broad biblical knowledge to offer a lengthy criticism of 'imperfect shepherds' (*Ruin of Britain*, trans. Winterbottom, 60), urging them to penitence.

Gildas's Latin is unique, but most closely resembles that of Latin writers of late fifth-century Gaul like Ennodius of Pavia and Avitus of Vienne, while his most prominent sources, apart from the Bible, are earlier Christian writers, especially Orosius, Jerome, and John Cassian. He employs few syntactical innovations, but introduces into his prose certain forms derived from poetry. His language might be called 'colonial Latin'. His style is pompous, but not without a certain splendour. Modern studies have revealed that the structure of *De excidio* is 'on the grand scale, conscious and calculated' (*Ruin of Britain*, trans. Winterbottom, 6), and clearly the work of a single author, confounding the notion that only the *Epistola* dates to the beginning of the sixth century, while the *Historia* is a later forgery composed by an Anglo-Saxon. The hymn *Lorica*, traditionally attributed to Gildas, is probably the work of the seventh-century Irish writer Laidcenn.

In the time between Patrick and Columbanus, Gildas is the only witness of any stature to give information about the still little-known world of sub-Roman Britain. Bede calls him 'their [the Britons] own historian' (Bede, *Hist. eccl.*, 1.22), and drew on him extensively for his own, influential, account of the period. In an important sense, the history of the English language begins with Gildas, for he says that the Saxons' word for the ships in which they arrived in Britain is *cyule*: almost certainly the earliest extant example of Old English. More substantially, Gildas's work provides evidence for the high standard of Latin culture and education still surviving in Britain *c.*500. He also enjoyed a high reputation in the middle ages. As well as being described by Columbanus as *auctor elegans*, by the ninth century he was accorded, like other insular writers versed in the scriptures and Latin letters, the epithet Sapiens ('Wise'). In addition to Bede, his work was used by Alcuin at the end of the eighth century and by the late ninth-century Breton monks of Landevennec, Uurdisten, and Uurmonoc.

Included among the list of saints commemorated in the Stowe missal, written in Ireland in 792, Gildas was never widely venerated in the British Isles, though he appears also in Irish martyrologies of *c.*800 and in Anglo-Saxon calendars from the ninth century to the eleventh, in all of which his feast day is given as 29 January. His cult spread chiefly in Brittany, where it may have replaced that of Gweltas. The monastery dedicated to him at Rhuis was probably not founded until the early eleventh century. Gildas reappeared in British literature early in the twelfth century, in the work of William of Malmesbury and in Geoffrey of Monmouth's influential, if legendary, elaboration of the Arthurian story. Roughly contemporaneously with the latter, and probably in the same context, a second, entirely fictional, life was written by Caradog of Llancarfan or one of his school, designed solely to associate Gildas with Glastonbury Abbey.

FRANÇOIS KERLOUÉGAN

Sources *Gildas: 'The ruin of Britain', and other works*, ed. and trans. M. Winterbottom (1978) · 'Gildae sapientis De excidio et conquestu Britanniae', *Chronica minora saec. IV. V. VI. VII.*, ed. T. Mommsen, 3, MGH Auctores Antiquissimi, 13 (Berlin, 1898), 1–

85 · 'Vita Gildae in Monasterio regionis Aremoricae Ruyensi', *Gildae de excidio Britanniae*, ed. H. Williams, Honourable Society of Cymmrodorion, Cymmrodorion Record Series, 3 (1899–1901), 322–88 · Vita sancti Gildae, *Gildae de excidio Britanniae*, ed. H. Williams, Honourable Society of Cymmrodorion, Cymmrodorion Record Series, 3 (1899–1901), 390–413 · M. Lapidge and D. N. Dumville, eds., *Gildas: new approaches* (1984) · L. Fleuriot, *Les origines de la Bretagne* (1980) · N. J. Higham, *The English conquest: Gildas and Britain in the fifth century* (1994) · F. Kerlouégan, *Le De excidio Britanniae de Gildas: les destinées de la culture latine dans l'Île de Bretagne au VIe siècle* (Paris, 1987) · T. D. O'Sullivan, *The De excidio of Gildas: its authenticity and date* (1978) · A. de la Borderie, 'La date de la naissance de Gildas', *Revue Celtique*, 6 (1883–5), 1–13 · J. Loth, 'Le nom de Gildas dans l'île de Bretagne en Irelande, et en Armorique', *Revue Celtique*, 46 (1929), 1–15 · Bede, *Hist. eccl.*, 1.22 · M. Lapidge and R. Sharpe, *A bibliography of Celtic-Latin literature, 400–1200* (1985) · P. Sims-Williams, 'Gildas and the Anglo-Saxons', *Cambridge Medieval Celtic Studies*, 6 (1983), 1–30 · E. A. Thompson, 'Gildas and the history of Britain', *Britannia*, 10 (1979), 203–26 · E. A. Thompson, 'Gildas and the history of Britain', *Britannia*, 11 (1980), 344 · M. Miller, 'Bede's use of Gildas', *EngHR*, 90 (1975), 241–61 · J. Morris, *The age of Arthur* (1973) · F. W. H. Wasserschleben, ed., *Die irische Kanonensammlung*, 2nd edn (1885)
Archives BL, Cotton MS Vitellius A.vi

Gilderdale, John (1802–1864), Church of England clergyman and religious writer, was educated at Howden grammar school in Yorkshire. As a youth, he hoped to follow a seafaring life, but he eventually adopted a literary and scholastic profession. On the completion of his school career he matriculated from St Catharine's College, Cambridge, where he graduated BA in 1826, proceeded to his degree of MA in 1830, and to that of BD in 1853. He proceeded 'ad eundem' in the University of Oxford on 25 June 1847. After leaving Cambridge he was (1842–7) lecturer of the parish church of Halifax, Yorkshire. In 1848 he became curate of Upper Clapton, London, and from 1849 to 1863 he was principal of Forest School, Walthamstow. He and his wife, Rebecca, had at least one child (their son John Smith Gilderdale was also a teacher at the school).

Gilderdale published *An essay on natural religion and revelation, considered with regard to the legitimate use and proper limitation of reason* (1837), a book of family prayers (1838) and a pamphlet on education (1838). He was made incumbent of Staunton Caundle, Dorset, in 1863 and died there on 25 September 1864.

W. F. Wentworth-Shields, *rev.* H. C. G. Matthew

Sources *GM*, 3rd ser., 17 (1864), 661 · Venn, *Alum. Cant.* · Foster, *Alum. Oxon.* · Boase, *Mod. Eng. biog.* · Crockford (1864)
Wealth at death under £2000: probate, 14 Oct 1864, *CGPLA Eng. & Wales*

Gildon, Charles (*c.*1665–1724), writer, was born at Gillingham, Dorset, the son of Richard Gildon (*d. c.*1674), gentleman; his mother's name is unknown. The family was Roman Catholic and royalist. Gildon's grandfather Richard Gildon (*d.* 1679) lost three-quarters of an estate, worth £140 p.a., by sequestration in 1645; Gildon's cousin Joseph Gildon (*d.* 1736) was a Roman priest.

After an early education in Gillingham, under a Mr Young, Gildon spent five years at the English College in Douai, but did not enter the Roman priesthood as his family had intended. He returned to England, aged nineteen, and two years later went to London, where he spent or was tricked by lawyers out of the greatest part of his paternal estate, and, aged about twenty-three, he imprudently married a woman of no fortune. Her name is unknown and no reference to her after 1703 has been found.

Financial need forced Gildon to become a versatile professional writer, producing translations, biographies, essays, plays, verse, fictional letters, tales, and criticism as required. His earliest identifiable work was a flattering *History of the Athenian Society* (1692), commissioned by John Dunton. (The Athenian Society was a 'notes and queries' periodical founded by Dunton.) Dunton continued to employ Gildon, and in 1705 wrote that he:

> is well acquainted with the Languages, and writes with a peculiar Briskness, which the common *Hacks* can't boast of, in Regard, they want the Life and Spirit, and the same *Liberty*, and Extent of *Genius*. He was always very just in the Engagements where I had any Concern and his Performances were done, as well as the *Designs* wou'd admit. (Dunton, 241)

Gildon maintained a standard well above the common hacks for some thirty years of copious and varied output. He was received into the company of John Dryden, William Wycherley, and Aphra Behn; John Dennis became his mentor in literary criticism.

After discarding Roman Catholicism, Gildon adopted deism for a while. He twice edited the works of the notorious deist Charles Blount (*d.* 1693), adding writings of his own in *Oracles of Reason* (1693), and, in 1695, published an account of Blount which justified his suicide. Daniel Defoe fulminated that Gildon 'Lampoons the Deity' and is 'a First Rate *Rake*', who 'keeps six whores and starves his modest wife' (Defoe, 10), but, whether or not Gildon changed his behaviour, he soon reformed his religion to Anglicanism, converted by the *Method with Deists* (1698) of Charles Leslie (1650–1722). Gildon's vindication of orthodoxy, *The Deist's Manual* (1705), dedicated to the archbishop of Canterbury, was prefaced by Leslie's congratulations on his conversion.

Four heroic blank-verse tragedies by Gildon, influenced by Nathaniel Lee, Thomas Otway, and Dryden, and Gildon's adaptation of Shakespeare's *Measure for Measure* were performed with little success between late 1696 and December 1702. His dramatic criticism extended over most of his writing life, from a relatively modernist defence of Dryden against Rymer in *Miscellaneous Letters and Essays* (1694) to a rehash of old neo-classical writings in his *Complete Art of Poetry* (1718). Of more interest today perhaps are Gildon's collections of short tales, *The Post-Boy Robb'd of his Mail* (1692–3), *The Golden Spy* (1709), and *All for the Better* (1720), each series arranged ingeniously on a different thread.

In so far as he was involved in politics Gildon was a whig, but in 1706 he was used as a cat's-paw by tories to publish and review controversial letters recommending that Queen Anne's successor, the electress Sophia, should visit England (implying that she wished to be on hand in case of Anne's sudden death). The government prosecuted him for publishing a seditious libel, tending to create misunderstanding between queen and electress; he was tried on 12 February 1707 and on 17 May was fined £100, being lucky to escape pillory or prison. Influential whigs helped him: Sir Richard Steele drafted his petition before sentence and Arthur Mainwaring paid his fine.

Gildon dedicated his *Life* of the actor Thomas Betterton (1710) to Steele and Steele wrote a preface to Gildon's *Grammar of the English Tongue* (1711), published by John Brightland (*d.* 1717), a manager of the Sun Fire Office, who also enrolled Gildon as company clerk and editor of the company's journal, the *British Mercury*, at a salary of £80 p.a. Gildon edited the *Mercury* for seven months from December 1711 until, his salary having been reduced to £52, then £40 p.a., he resigned, but not before pursuing a feud with Jonathan Swift and Alexander Pope in the pages of that journal. Gildon disliked Pope probably because they were rivals for Wycherley's favour; Swift was detested by Gildon's patron Mainwaring and in addition Gildon believed that Swift had plagiarized his own scheme for an English academy. Gildon renewed his attacks on Pope in *A New Rehearsal* (1714) and *Memoirs of the Life of William Wycherley* (1718). Pope responded immediately in several short poems and, after Gildon's death, annihilated his reputation in *The Dunciad* and the *Epistle to Arbuthnot*.

By the beginning of 1719 Gildon was poverty-stricken, living in a garret in Chichester Rents, Chancery Lane; he was blind (owing to syphilis according to Pope, *Correspondence*, 2.3), and dependent for reading and writing upon an amanuensis named Lloyd. Gildon's abject condition was partly relieved in February 1721 by gratuities from the duchess of Buckingham, dedicatee of his *The Laws of Poetry* (1721), and from Lord and Lady Harley, forwarded by their intermediary Mathew Prior. Gildon was now living slightly more salubriously in Bull Head Court, Jewen Street, Aldersgate, but lameness and ill health had added to his miseries. He so resented his dependence that when he received no answer to an appeal for help in July 1721 he accused Prior of ungentlemanly conduct towards 'a gentleman, as I may say I am both by birth and education' and a scholar (*Bath MSS*, 3.507). However, he was awarded £100 'as of Royal Bounty' (PRO, T.38/225) on 24 November 1721, apparently thanks to his appeal to Harley through Prior. He was also probably the intended beneficiary of a performance of Thomas Southerne's *Oroonoko* at Lincoln's Inn Fields on 12 December 1723 for the 'Benefit of a Gentleman under Misfortune' (Avery, 1.469). If so, his respite from misfortune was brief: Gildon died in London on 12 January 1724. JAMES SAMBROOK

Sources [C. Gildon], *The lives and characters of the English dramatick poets … first begun by Mr Langbain* [1699], 174–6 • R. Shiels, *The lives of the poets of Great Britain and Ireland*, ed. T. Cibber, 3 (1753), 326–30 • *The manuscripts of his grace the duke of Portland*, 10 vols., HMC, 29 (1891–1931), vol. 8, pp. 232, 349, 353 • *Calendar of the manuscripts of the marquis of Bath preserved at Longleat, Wiltshire*, 5 vols., HMC, 58 (1904–80), vol. 3, pp. 496–7, 506–7 • C. Gildon, *Robinson Crusoe examin'd and criticis'd*, ed. P. Dottin (1923), 5–53 • H. B. Wright, 'Prior and Gildon', *N&Q*, 201 (1956), 18–20 • *The correspondence of Richard Steele*, ed. R. Blanchard (1941), 523–4 • A. Boyer, *The political state of Great Britain*, 27 (1724), 102–3 • *The critical works of John Dennis*, ed. E. N. Hooker, 2 (1943), 374 • J. Honoré, 'Charles Gildon, rédacteur du *British Mercury*, 1711–1712: les attaques contre Pope, Swift, et les wits', *Études Anglaises*, 15 (1962), 347–64 • E. L. Avery, ed., *The London stage, 1660–1800*, pt 2: *1700–1729* (1960), vol. 1, p. 469 • BL, Add. MS 32686, fol. 352 • R. H. Griffith, 'Isaac Bickerstaff's "Grammar"', *N&Q*, 194 (1949), 362–5 • P. Rogers, *Grub Street: studies in a subculture* (1972), 35–6, 300–01 • J. Spence, *Observations, anecdotes, and characters, of books and men*, ed. J. M. Osborn, new edn, 1 (1966), 71–2 • J. Hutchins, *History of Dorset*, 3rd edn (1868), 3.637 • J. Dunton, *The life and errors of John Dunton … written by himself* (1705), 241 • D. Defoe, *More reformation* (1703) • *The correspondence of Alexander Pope*, ed. G. Sherburn, 1 (1956), 73; 2 (1956), 3, 334 • N. Ault, *New light on Pope, with some additions to his poetry hitherto unknown* (1949), 101–19 • A. Pope, *The Dunciad*, ed. J. Sutherland (1943), vol. 5 of *The Twickenham edition of the poems of Alexander Pope*, ed. J. Butt (1939–69); 3rd edn [in 1 vol.] (1963); repr. (1965) • J. Foster, *The register of admissions to Gray's Inn, 1521–1889, together with the register of marriages in Gray's Inn chapel, 1695–1754* (privately printed, London, 1889) • Gillow, *Lit. biog. hist.*, 2.466 • will, 2 June 1679, Dorset RO [Richard Gildon, grandfather] • *The works of Aphra Behn*, ed. J. Todd, 7 vols. (1992–6), vol. 1, pp. ix–x • L. Welsted, *One epistle to Mr. A. Pope* (1730), 22n.

Archives BL, letters to Harley and letter to his brother Edward, Add. MS 4163, fols. 255–7 • BL, assignment of *Measure for measure*, Add. MS 38730, fol. 1046

Giles, Francis John William Thomas (1787–1847), civil engineer, was born on 10 October 1787 and baptized at Walton-on-Thames parish church on 21 October, the son of Samuel and Mary Giles. He came from a large family, and was trained as a surveyor by his elder brother Netlam (1775–1816) from about 1803, and after six years' pupillage became his partner. By that time they employed a small staff including Alexander Comrie and James Brazier as assistant surveyors. In the late eighteenth century Netlam was working as a land surveyor, and he bought a half-share in the publication of a map of Surrey of 1799 by Joseph Lindley and William Crossley. Although such work continued, with the two brothers publishing a map of Leeds in 1815, and issuing a prospectus for a map of Lancashire in 1816, from the time Francis joined his brother they were largely involved in civil engineering surveys on behalf of John Rennie (1761–1821).

Francis Giles's first job was to assist in the survey of the London and Portsmouth Canal in 1803; this was followed by other surveys, notably for the Weald of Kent Canal in 1803, Dymchurch wall in 1804, Shorncliffe Canal in 1804, the Royal Military Canal in 1804–5, Dover harbour in 1805, the Loch Erne and Perth Canal in 1806, and for improvements of the Birmingham Canal in 1807. These early surveys were generally conducted in conjunction with his brother, and from about 1810 printed plans were published bearing both their names. Surviving examples include plans of Seaton and Beer Bay in 1810, Boston harbour in 1811, the Weald of Kent Canal in 1811, and the Arundel and Portsmouth Canal in 1817. Although precise responsibility for the various surveys undertaken by the brothers is now difficult to determine, there can be no doubt that before his brother's death, Francis Giles had established a formidable reputation as a civil engineering surveyor. This was reflected in John Rennie's decision about 1813 to entrust to him the training of his son John in surveying.

The young Rennie assisted Giles in surveys of harbours in both south-west Scotland and Ulster, in addition to surveys of the Tyne, of a proposal for a Stockton and Darlington canal and railway, of an eastern extension of the

Kennet and Avon Canal, and of the Thames near Woolwich Dockyard. These works formed only a small part of the surveys undertaken by Giles generally involving John Rennie senior. In addition Giles was involved in surveys of most of the main rivers and estuaries of the United Kingdom, as well as of John Rennie's major bridge schemes over the Thames at Southwark, London Bridge, and Waterloo, where he was responsible for setting out the foundations.

By the time of John Rennie's death in 1821 Giles had a well-established reputation and maintained a London office. He had a young family of his own to support, in addition to having responsibility for his brother Netlam's family. His wife, Mary Ann Wyer (*b.* *c.*1790), whom he married at St Martin's, Birmingham, on 14 April 1814, gave birth to their first child, Francis George, in 1815, and their family grew to include four sons and four daughters. From 1821 Giles was a notable civil engineer on his own account, working from his offices in Salisbury Street, Adelphi, rather than as a surveyor working with the Rennies. In addition to his consultancy work he acted as county surveyor in Bedfordshire from 1825, a position he retained until his death.

Giles's first independent work was to survey the extension of the Ivel navigation to Shefford in 1821. His early works almost exclusively concerned canal proposals, including the Hertford (Lea) Union Canal in 1823–4, the Basingstoke Canal extension to Newbury in 1825, the extending of the Sankey navigation in 1830, and the St Helens Canal to Widnes in 1833. Inevitably there were also surveys for schemes which were never built, including his work for the Rennies on the London and Portsmouth Ship Canal in 1825. Giles continued to work on inland navigation schemes until his death; among his last reports was one on improvements to the Lea navigation in 1844, which were carried out after an act of parliament in 1850.

By this time Giles had become heavily involved in railways. He is perhaps best-known for his criticisms of George Stephenson's route for the Liverpool and Manchester Railway, particularly across Chat Moss. 'No engineer in his senses', he maintained, 'would go through Chat Moss if he wanted to make a railway from Liverpool to Manchester' (*DNB*). Despite his parliamentary opposition to this scheme he was soon employed by railway companies in search of an experienced engineer. He was asked by the proprietors to carry out an independent survey of the Newcastle–Carlisle railway following the passage of its parliamentary act in 1828, and in 1829 he was appointed engineer. In many ways this can be regarded as the triumph of his civil engineering career—involving the Cowran cutting, 102 ft deep, and impressive bridges across the Eden, the Gelt, and Corby Beck. It is possible that Giles's printed specifications of work on this line were the first to be issued for railway contracts. In 1833 Giles became consultant to the company building that line, though there were concerns about the amount of time he was able to devote to the work. His assistant John Blackmore became engineer in charge of the scheme.

Giles was heavily involved with plans for the London–Southampton railway, for which he had been engineer since 1831 and which obtained its act of parliament in 1834. Giles was increasingly criticized for his management of the project, particularly by a group of shareholders from Lancashire, who brought in the civil engineer Joseph Locke to report on progress; in the face of Locke's findings, in January 1837 Giles resigned on six months' notice. Giles was to some extent a victim of circumstance, as some delays arose from problems in acquiring land, and rising costs owing to the railway boom of the time. However, Giles had preferred to deal with small contractors, dividing the line into small lots, which added to the difficulties.

This set-back had little effect in the demand for Giles's services. In the 1830s he was involved in surveys for other lines associated with the Southampton scheme, such as the Portsmouth Junction Railway, the Basing–Bath railway, and later the Reading–Reigate railway (in 1846). Elsewhere he surveyed the London–Greenwich project, the South Midland Railway, and a route for a London–Holyhead railway, and he reported on the Great North of England Railway. Overseas he reported on the Altona, Hamburg, and Lübeck railways.

Execution of the Hamburg railway was supervised by two of Giles's former assistants, William Lindley, son of Netlam's former partner, and his brother George's son, George Giles (1810–1877), both of whom had been trained by Francis Giles in the 1820s, as was his nephew Francis (1806–1884). Two of his own sons—the eldest, Francis George, and Alfred (1816–1895)—joined their father. In Alfred's case this was because of the pressure of his father's railway work in the early 1830s rather than his own wishes. Alfred was largely responsible for the supervision of one of his father's most important works, Southampton docks.

Giles's initial involvement with Southampton docks coincided with his work for the London–Southampton railway. Work began in 1838, but financial problems dogged progress and construction did not really proceed until the 1840s. It was the chief achievement of the last decade of Giles's life. Earlier, Giles had been responsible for harbour works at Bridport and Courtown, completed to the plans of Alexander Nimmo after his death, in addition to many harbour surveys. Throughout the 1820s he was involved with work in the Mersey area for Liverpool corporation, and he designed the embankment at Leasowe in the Wirral. He was also responsible as engineer for many important road bridges including Hayward Bridge, Dorset, and Warwick Bridge, Cumberland. One of his last proposals concerned a cable-stayed crossing of the Bristol Channel at Aust passage; it comprised four main spans of 1100 feet and two side spans of 550 feet, a design he developed in connection with his South Wales Railway proposal of 1845.

Giles died at his home, 9 Adelphi Terrace, London, on 4 March 1847, and was survived by his wife. He is best remembered for his skill as a surveyor. Despite being involved in many railway schemes he did not seem to meet successfully the new challenge of railway civil engineering, and his reputation was consequently overshadowed by the standing of the canal engineers who preceded him and the railway engineers who followed. His name was associated with many subsequently forgotten projects. However, he left an important legacy of Giles-trained engineers—Sir John Rennie, William Lindley, and his own son Alfred, who was to become president of the Institution of Civil Engineers, an institution which Giles himself did not join until 1842. MIKE CHRIMES

Sources *PICE*, 7 (1848), 8–9 · *DNB* · *GM*, 2nd ser., 27 (1847), 449 · Walton-on-Thames parish records, Surrey CRO · *IGI* · parish register (birth), Walton-on-Thames, Surrey, 10 Oct 1787 · parish register (baptism), Walton-on-Thames, 21 Oct 1787
Archives Inst. CE, Telford MSS · NL Scot., Rennie MSS · W. Yorks. AS, Leeds, Yorkshire Archaeological Society, Lindley MSS

Giles, Herbert Allen (1845–1935), Sinologist, was born at Oxford on 8 December 1845, the fourth son of the editor and translator John Allen *Giles (1808–1884), and his wife, Anna Sarah Dickinson (*d.* 1896). He was educated at Charterhouse, and in 1867 joined the China consular service as a student interpreter. He made steady progress through the service, reaching the level of vice-consul at Pagoda island in 1880 and at Shanghai in 1883. He was appointed consul at Tamsui (Danshui) in 1886 and at Ningpo (Ningbo) in 1891. He left China late in 1892, formally resigning from the consular service in October 1893.

Giles was twice married: first, in 1870, to Catherine Maria (*d.* 1882), daughter of Thomas Harold Fenn, of Nayland, Suffolk; second, in 1883, to Elise Williamina (*d.* 1921), daughter of the biblical scholar Alfred *Edersheim. With his first wife he had six sons and three daughters, and with his second wife one daughter. One son, Lionel, also became a distinguished Sinologist and was keeper of the department of oriental printed books and manuscripts at the British Museum.

Giles began to write on Chinese history, language, and literature in the early 1870s, and within a few years had completed a Mandarin phrase book, a language guide in the Swatow dialect, further guides to Mandarin, and a large number of translations and historical and descriptive works on China. By the end of the 1870s he had published more than a dozen works on Chinese subjects. In 1874 he began work on a Chinese–English dictionary, which was finally published in 1892, and on which rested most of his subsequent reputation. Building on the work of Sir Thomas Wade, the transliteration system Giles set out in his dictionary became accepted as standard. The 'Wade–Giles' system was abolished for external use by China only in 1979 and until the early 1990s was still used by many Western institutions.

Following his return from China, Giles lived in Aberdeen until 1897 when he replaced Wade as professor of Chinese at Cambridge. Contemporaries differed in their views of Giles's success as a professor. There was little student interest in Chinese studies at Cambridge, and it has been suggested that Giles's personality—'naturally combative'—alienated many, and limited the support he received from colleagues or the university (Marshall, 524–5).

Giles's clearest contribution to Chinese studies was his ability through his writings to 'humanize' China for a Western audience. His clear and flowing style and his understanding of China meant, said one contemporary, that he was 'able to breathe life' into his subjects (Shang-Ling Fu, 85), and his translations were praised for capturing the spirit of the original works. Yet he was also criticized for what even his supporters admitted was his lack of attention to small details. This remained a major criticism of Giles, perhaps put most harshly by E. G. Pulleybank, who said that Giles's work 'suffers very much from the disease of amateurism, a fundamental lack of serious scholarly discipline' (Pulleybank, 3). Despite this, Giles was a highly significant Sinologist, both for the long-lasting impact of his transliteration work and for the fundamental part he played in kindling interest in Chinese studies in the West. In an eightieth birthday tribute, a colleague said that Giles's 'most notable work has been that of making the study of Chinese language and literature easier for students … We are all his debtors' (Ferguson, 2).

Giles was punctual and methodical, and regarded as an excellent conversationalist, yet his most remembered characteristic was always his readiness to enter into an argument, leading one writer to call him a 'fanatical type … always furiously taking sides no matter right or wrong' (Moule, 577). Between the 1870s and the 1920s Giles published nearly sixty works on China. He received honorary degrees from the universities of Aberdeen (1897) and Oxford (1924), was awarded the order of Jiahe by the Chinese government and the gold medal of the Royal Asiatic Society, and twice awarded the prix St Julien by the French Academy. He resigned from his professorship in 1932 and died at his home, 10 Selwyn Gardens, Cambridge, on 13 February 1935. JANETTE RYAN

Sources A. C. Moule, 'Herbert Allen Giles', *Journal of the Royal Asiatic Society of Great Britain and Ireland* (1935), 577–9 · *The Times* (14 Feb 1935), 7 · *WWW* · Shang-Ling Fu, 'One generation of Chinese studies at Cambridge', *The Chinese Social and Political Science Review*, 15 (1931–2), 78–91 · P. R. Marshall, 'H. A. Giles and E. H. Parker: Clio's English servants in late nineteenth-century China', *The Historian*, 46 (1983–4), 520–38 · E. G. Pulleybank, *Chinese history and world history* (1955) · D. E. Pollard, 'H. A. Giles and his translations', *Renditions: a Chinese-English Translation Magazine*, 40 (autumn 1993) · *Cambridge Review* (22 Feb 1935) · J. C. Ferguson, 'Dr Giles at 80', *China Journal of Science and Arts*, 4/1 (1926) · *FO List* (1903), 123 · A. J. Arberry, *British orientalists* (1943), 46 · B. Hook, ed., *The Cambridge encyclopedia of China*, 2nd edn (1991), 337 · I. L. Legeza, *Guide to transliterated Chinese in the modern Peking dialect*, 1, 2 (1968), 17
Archives CUL, unpublished typescript and MSS
Likenesses photograph, repro. in Ferguson, 'Dr Giles at 80'
Wealth at death £23,614 12*s.* 8*d.*: probate, 1 April 1935, *CGPLA Eng. & Wales*

Giles, James (1801–1870), landscape painter, was born at Glasgow on 4 January 1801, the son of Peter Giles, a calico designer, artist, art teacher, and native of Aberdeenshire, and his wife, Jean Hector. At thirteen Giles was painting the lids of snuff-boxes, by fifteen he had begun to take pupils, and at nineteen he was teaching public drawing classes in Aberdeen. His summers were spent on sketching tours of the highlands. In 1824–5 he made a tour through Europe. In Italy he made drawings from the old masters. He painted and drew buildings and ruins and developed his interest in watercolour. His continental watercolours are distinguished by a breadth and freedom and an interest in the effects of light and weather conditions. On his return home Giles was introduced to George Hamilton-Gordon, fourth earl of Aberdeen, who became a significant patron and commissioned a series of paintings of eighty-five Aberdeenshire castles from 1835 to 1855. It was at the suggestion of Lord Aberdeen that Giles painted a number of watercolours of Balmoral Castle which were Queen Victoria's first views of Balmoral; the royal couple subsequently took over the lease of Balmoral Castle. Queen Victoria became a patron of Giles and commissioned a number of works including eight interiors of Balmoral. Giles also assisted the prince consort in laying out and planting the grounds of the new Balmoral in 1855. He was employed in a similar capacity by William Gordon at Fyvie Castle and for Lord Aberdeen at Haddo House. He also enjoyed a local reputation as a portraitist.

Giles was twice married: first to Clementina Farquharson, who died at the age of twenty-one and with whom he had a son, and secondly to Margaret Walker, who survived him and with whom he also had a son. He first exhibited at the Royal Institution for the Encouragement of the Fine Arts in Scotland, but in 1829 he became an academician of the Royal Scottish Academy, and exhibited there every year from 1830 until 1870 (except 1834). He also exhibited at the Royal Glasgow Institute of the Fine Arts and the Royal Hibernian Academy of Arts. In London he exhibited at the British Institution, the Royal Academy, and the Society of British Artists. His picture *The Weird Wife* is in the National Gallery of Scotland, Edinburgh. His last work was a painting of himself, his wife, Margaret, and his younger son, which he left unfinished. He died at his home, 62 Bon Accord Street, Aberdeen, after a lingering illness, on 6 October 1870.

R. E. Graves, *rev.* Jocelyn Hackforth-Jones

Sources D. Irwin and F. Irwin, *Scottish painters at home and abroad, 1700–1900* (1975) • P. J. M. McEwan, *Dictionary of Scottish art and architecture* (1994) • W. D. Simpson, ed., *James Giles: drawings of Aberdeenshire castles* (1936) • *The Scotsman* (8 Oct 1870) • Graves, *RA exhibitors* • Graves, *Brit. Inst.* • C. B. de Laperriere, ed., *The Royal Scottish Academy exhibitors, 1826–1990*, 4 vols. (1991) • J. Johnson, ed., *Works exhibited at the Royal Society of British Artists, 1824–1893, and the New English Art Club, 1888–1917*, 2 vols. (1975); repr. (1993) • R. Billcliffe, ed., *The Royal Glasgow Institute of the Fine Arts, 1861–1989: a dictionary of exhibitors at the annual exhibitions*, 4 vols. (1990–92) • A. M. Stewart and C. de Courcy, *Royal Hibernian Academy of Arts: index of exhibitors and their works, 1826–1979*, 3 vols. (1985–7) • J. Halsby and P. Harris, *The dictionary of Scottish painters, 1600–1960* (1990) • Redgrave, *Artists*, 2nd edn

Wealth at death £9892 8*s.* 9*d.*: confirmation, 1871, Scotland

Giles, John Allen (1808–1884), translator and literary editor, son of William Giles and his wife, Sophia, *née* Allen, was born on 26 October 1808 at Southwick House, in the parish of Mark, Somerset, the home of his father and grandfather. Aged sixteen he entered Charterhouse as a Somerset scholar. From Charterhouse he was elected to a Bath and Wells scholarship at Corpus Christi College, Oxford, in November 1824. In the Easter term of 1828 he obtained a double first class, and shortly afterwards graduated BA. In a pamphlet of 1829 he opposed Catholic emancipation, but argued that Irish absentee landlords should be compelled to return to their estates and improve the lot of the peasantry. He was awarded a Vinerian scholarship in 1830, and took his MA in 1831 and DCL in 1838. His election to a fellowship at Corpus on 15 November 1832 followed his college scholarship as a matter of course.

Giles wished to become a barrister, but his parents persuaded him (to his regret then and later) to take orders. He was ordained deacon in 1832 and priest in 1835, and held the curacy of Cossington, Somerset, jointly with the headship of Bridgwater School. On 17 December 1833 he married Anna Sarah Dickinson (*d.* 1896), and vacated his fellowship. His *Scriptores Græci minores* had been published in 1831, and his *Latin Grammar* in 1833. In 1834 he was appointed to the headmastership of Camberwell College School, and on 24 November 1836 was elected headmaster of the City of London School. He had imaginative and sometimes advanced ideas for the school's development, but lacked the personality to gain the confidence of staff and pupils, and failed to keep discipline; on 8 January 1840 the school committee asked him to resign. He retired to Windlesham Hall, Surrey, which he had built, and there took pupils, and engaged in literary work.

In 1846 Giles became curate of Bampton, Oxfordshire, where he continued taking pupils, and edited and wrote many works. By 1848 he was printing several of these on his own press at his house at Bampton; he trained local girls in typography, and by the early 1850s the press was expanding to take on more ambitious work. In 1847 he applied unsuccessfully for the chair of modern languages and literature at Oxford, stating that since 1828 he had spent 'a very large portion' of his time in the Netherlands, Belgium, France, Switzerland, and so on (BL, Add. MS 34576, fol. 507).

In 1854 Samuel Wilberforce, bishop of Oxford, required Giles, on pain of losing his curacy, to suppress his *Christian Records*, which argues that the gospels were put together around AD 150. Giles complied under protest, but printed the correspondence in a pamphlet, *The Bishop of Oxford's Letters*, in which he observes that he has 'no wish to become a martyr, even though my becoming so would probably do me more worldly good than ever the church has done me', and complains 'that the bishop denies to me that liberty of thought which he claims for himself'. Disaffection with the church helps to explain his disastrous act of good nature on 5 October 1854, when he performed the marriage of one of his printing girls (who had requested secrecy to avoid 'rough music') outside the legal hours, falsified its date in the parish register, falsely entered that it was performed by licence, and forged the mark of a witness who was not present. Local reactions show an irritation with his conduct as curate—one of the vicars wrote to Wilberforce rejoicing 'that we are freed for ever from the ministrations of one who for many reasons was quite unfitted for his office' (Oxon. RO, CPZ 1/22)—and Giles's wild attempts to influence witnesses and obscure the facts made matters worse. On 6 March 1855 he was tried at Oxford assizes. He spoke on his own behalf; Wilberforce also spoke for him, though for the rest of his life Giles was to blame him as a malicious instigator of the prosecution. Giles was found guilty, but strongly recommended to mercy; Lord Campbell sentenced him to a year's imprisonment in Oxford Castle. There was much sympathy for him in the university and county, and after three months' imprisonment he was released by royal warrant on 3 June.

Giles moved to Notting Hill, and in 1857 took the curacy, with sole charge, of Perivale in Middlesex. In 1861 he became curate of Harmondsworth, but resigned after a year and went to live at Cranford, where he took pupils, subsequently moving to Ealing. In 1867 he bought the living of Sutton in Surrey, which he held for seventeen years. He died at the rectory there on 24 September 1884 and was buried at Churchill, Somerset. His wife survived him, and he left two sons, one in the Bengal police, the other, Herbert Allen *Giles, professor of Chinese at the University of Cambridge. He also left two daughters: Anna Isabella, married to Dundas W. Cloeté of Churchill Court, Somerset, and Ellen Harriet, unmarried.

Giles is described as 'a very short, wiry little man, with iron-grey hair' (Magdalen College, Oxford, MS 800 (i)). Estimates of his personality are very consistent: warm-hearted, considerate, convivial, but lacking practical sense and dignity of manner. His memoirs convey an omnivorous curiosity and a strong sense of humour. Both he and others thought that he was unsuited to be a clergyman, and certainly his advanced and frankly expressed views on the gospels harmed his career. He produced about 180 published works, including several books on the New Testament and on early British history, such as *History of the Ancient Britons* (1847), *The Life and Times of Alfred the Great* (1848), and *The Story-Book of British History* (1851); he also wrote long series of school books called Dr Giles's Juvenile Library and Dr Giles's Keys to the Classics. He had a remarkable memory, especially for poetry, and his enthusiasm for medieval texts is obvious from his memoirs and letters, but his prodigious output of editions has not lasted well. He lacked critical rigour and much of his writing was done as task work for booksellers, so that his texts are careless, badly organized, and lack proper apparatus. They include editions of most of the major English medieval chroniclers, including *The British History of Geoffrey of Monmouth* (1842), *Bede's Ecclesiastical History* (1847), and *The Whole Works of King Alfred the Great* (1858), many of them in the publications of the Caxton Society and in his own series Patres Ecclesiæ Anglicanæ. After the scandal which drove him from Bampton, he largely abandoned editing and original writing, but kept up a steady stream of translations from Greek, Latin, and medieval authors. His *History of Bampton* (1847) and *History of Witney* (1852) show his usual faults, but have their own interest as early single-parish local histories containing well-observed details of topography and popular culture.

John Blair

Sources *DNB* • *The diary and memoirs of John Allen Giles*, ed. D. Bromwich, Somerset RS (2000) • *Proceedings of the Somersetshire Archaeological and Natural History Society*, 30/2 (1884), 166–8 • J. A. Giles, *The Bishop of Oxford's letters to the Rev. Dr. Giles for suspending the publication of Christian records, with Dr Giles's letters in reply*, 2nd edn (1854) • *The Times* (7 March 1855), 11–12 • *The Times* (7 June 1855), 10 • T. Hinde, *Carpenter's children: the story of the City of London School* (1995), 25–32 • H. R. Plomer, 'Some private presses of the nineteenth century', *The Library*, new ser., 1 (1900), 407–28, esp. 421–2 • *CGPLA Eng. & Wales* (1884)

Archives BL, letters to Philip Bliss, Add. MSS 34572–34580, *passim* • Bodl. Oxf., MSS Eng. b. 2097–2102 • Bodl. Oxf., corresp. with Sir Thomas Phillipps • Magd. Oxf., MS 800 (i) • Oxon. RO, CPZ 1 • U. Newcastle, Robinson L., letters to Sir Walter Trevelyan

Likenesses portrait, 1837–1840?, City of London School • J. D. Miller, mezzotint (after G. Richmond), BM • photograph (later in life), repro. in Bromwich, ed., *Diary and memoirs*, frontispiece • portrait (in later life), repro. in Hinde, *Carpenter's children*, 26

Wealth at death £217 11*s*. 8*d*.: probate, 22 Oct 1884, *CGPLA Eng. & Wales*

Giles, Nathaniel (*c*.1558–1634), choirmaster and composer, was born in or near Worcester, the son of William Giles, of a well-known local family—that he was the son of Thomas Giles has been disproved. Giles became a clerk of Magdalen College, Oxford, for the year 1577—the claim that he was a chorister of Magdalen from 1567 to 1571 has also been refuted. He may have been a pupil of John Colden, master of the choristers at Worcester Cathedral, whom he succeeded in 1581. Giles proceeded to the degree of bachelor of music at Oxford on 26 June 1585. On 14 June 1587 he married Anne (*d*. 1635), eldest daughter of John Stayner of Worcester, with whom he had four sons and five daughters. He is said to have been noted for his religious life and conversation.

On 8 June 1585 Giles was appointed organist and master of the choristers at St George's Chapel, Windsor, at the 'request and desire' of the dean and canons as it is put in the indenture (St George's Chapel archives, XI.B.30). The position was to be for life and, apart from duties as organist, included complete responsibility for the finding, welfare, and training of the chorister-boys of the chapel. Giles must have acquired a considerable reputation as a choir trainer for on 9 June 1597, while still retaining his place at Windsor, he was sworn in as master of the children at the Chapel Royal, in succession to William Hunnis. His predecessor at Windsor, Richard Farrant, had been closely associated with the Elizabethan 'choirboy-plays'. Giles carried on production of these plays involving choristers and, with a partner, continued to use the theatre at Blackfriars established by Farrant.

Nathaniel Giles supplicated for the degree of DMus in

1607 but the doctorate was not conferred on him until 5 July 1622 owing to his failure to submit a required exercise. Giles was a highly competent composer of liturgical and devotional works. In spite of his involvement with the theatre, he seems not to have composed any secular music but its influence may be seen in his compositions, especially in the twenty 'verse' anthems that constitute the major part of his output. Further works include two services, three motets, and three full anthems. Although well constructed and eminently functional, his compositions are unexceptional. Giles did not exhibit the same originality and melodic inspiration as some of his contemporaries, several of whom were his associates at the Chapel Royal including Byrd, Morley, and Orlando Gibbons.

Nathaniel Giles died at Windsor on 24 January 1634 and was buried on 29 January having held his position at Windsor for forty-nine years, thirty-seven of those years jointly with his mastership at the Chapel Royal. In St George's Chapel a memorial tablet to him, which may be found in the floor of the Rutland Chapel, was placed there by his son Nathaniel who had been elected a canon of St George's on 2 March 1624. NEVILLE WRIDGWAY

Sources E. H. Fellowes, *Organists and masters of the choristers of St George's Chapel in Windsor Castle* (1939) • A. Ashbee, ed., *Records of English court music*, 9 (1996) • P. Le Huray, *Music and the Reformation in England, 1549–1660* (1967) • E. F. Rimbault, ed., *The old cheque-book, or book of remembrance, of the Chapel Royal, from 1561 to 1744*, CS, new ser., 3 (1872) • S. Bond, ed., *The chapter acts of the dean and canons of Windsor: 1430, 1523–1672* (1966) • *New Grove*

Peter Giles (1860–1935), by Lafayette, 1933

Giles, Peter (1860–1935), philologist and college head, was born at Strichen in the district of Buchan, Aberdeenshire, on 20 October 1860, the eldest son of Peter Giles (*d.* *c.*1865), a factor, and his wife, Margaret Eddie Brown (*d.* 1905), who on her mother's side was of highland descent from Inverness-shire. He was educated first at the parish school of Strichen. In 1878 he proceeded with a Middleton bursary to King's College in the University of Aberdeen, graduating with first-class honours in 1882. He went directly with a classical scholarship to Gonville and Caius College, Cambridge, where he obtained first classes in both parts of the classical tripos (1884, 1887) with distinction in comparative philology and history in part two; in the historical tripos he was awarded a second class (1885) after only a year of study; he was Browne medallist (1884), and Whewell scholar for international law and Lightfoot scholar for ecclesiastical history (1885). In 1887 he was elected a fellow of his college, but in 1890 he migrated to Emmanuel College as fellow and classical tutor. In July 1893 he married Elizabeth Mary Dunn (1872–1965), eldest daughter of Thomas William Dunn, headmaster of Bath College, and they had one son and four daughters, one of whom predeceased her parents.

Giles possessed wide learning, but his chief interest was in comparative philology, a field at Cambridge in which he followed John Peile, master of Christ's College. In 1886 at Freiburg, and again in 1887 at Leipzig, he attended the lectures of Karl Brugmann, who was then expounding the doctrines of the *Neo-Grammatiker*. This led Giles to produce his only book, the *Short Manual of Comparative Philology for the Use of Classical Students* (1895), which brought the new ideas to England in a wide survey. It was translated into German and a second edition appeared in 1901, but a projected third edition and other translations were not completed. From 1891 until his death Giles held the readership in comparative philology vacated by Peile.

Giles also wrote many papers on linguistic, classical, and miscellaneous subjects, especially in large collaborative surveys; these are fully enumerated in the British Academy memoir (Dawkins, 406–32). His views on linguistics appear most clearly in an essay which he contributed to the commemorative volume *Darwin and Modern Science* (ed. A. C. Seward, 1909). Much time was devoted to an edition of Theocritus in collaboration with Arthur Bernard Cook, but it was finally abandoned. Indeed, after his election as master of Emmanuel in 1911, his energies were increasingly diverted from scholarship to administration, in both college and university. In addition to many lesser tasks, he had to deal with the effects of the First World War, an arduous term as vice-chancellor in 1919–21, and membership of the statutory university commission of 1923–7. In later years physical weakness hampered him.

Giles took the degree of LittD at Cambridge in 1910 and received honorary degrees from the universities of Aberdeen (1903) and Harvard (1927); he was elected an honorary fellow of Caius (1913), and a fellow of the British Academy (1927). He died at Emmanuel College on 17 September

1935 after a long illness, and was cremated on 20 September. His ashes were interred in the Emmanuel College chapel. R. M. DAWKINS, *rev.* JOHN D. PICKLES

Sources R. M. Dawkins, 'Peter Giles, 1860–1935', *PBA*, 21 (1935), 406–32 • 'Peter Giles', *Emmanuel College Magazine*, 29 (1934–5), 150–73 [suppl.] • [L. H. G. Greenwood], *Cambridge Review* (11 Oct 1935), 5 • Venn, *Alum. Cant.*

Archives CUL, papers relating to academic concerns • CUL, papers relating to Theocritus | Emmanuel College, Cambridge, MSS incl. letters to R. M. Dawkins

Likenesses photograph, 1910, repro. in *Emmanuel College Magazine* • Lafayette, photograph, 1933, NPG [*see illus.*] • A. Hayward, oils, 1934, Emmanuel College, Cambridge; repro. in *Emmanuel College Magazine*, 29/1 (1933–4) • G. Owst, cartoon, repro. in *Granta* (April 1920)

Wealth at death £6383 0s. 8*d*.: resworn probate, July 1938, *CGPLA Eng. & Wales* (1935)

Giles, Ronald [Carl] (**1916–1995**), cartoonist, was born on 29 September 1916, at 413 City Road, near the Angel, Islington, London, the youngest son (there was a younger daughter) of Albert Edward Giles (*b*. 1881/2), tobacconist, 'a conscientious, decent and much-liked man' (Tory, *A Life*, 28), and his wife, Emma Edith, *née* Clarke (*b*. 1886/7), dressmaker. His paternal grandfather was Alfred Edmund 'Farmer' Giles of Newmarket, Suffolk, a jockey who had ridden for Edward VII. His mother came from a Norfolk farming family. Giles's birth certificate registered him as Ronald. Known as Carl—because his childhood haircut echoed that of the actor Boris Karloff—the extrovert, already bespectacled Giles was educated at Barnsbury Park School, where his mischief was restrained by the sarcastic, skeletal Mr Chalk, a teacher who, as Chalky, later became one of his most enduring cartoon creations. On leaving school, aged about fourteen, Giles began work first as an office boy for 10s. a week and then as an animator at Superads in Charing Cross Road, London. Between 1930 and 1935 at Alexander Korda's studios in Elstree he was a principal animator, under the artist Anthony Gross, on *The Fox Hunt*, the first British animated colour cartoon with sound. He also helped to animate versions of Roland Davies's *Sunday Express* strip 'Come on Steve' (Steve was an amiable carthorse). Later, during the Second World War he helped to animate cartoons for the Ministry of Information.

In 1937, following the death of his brother Bert, Giles returned to London. There, at twenty-one, he joined the left-wing *Reynolds News*, for which, without any specific art training, he drew cartoons, illustrations and 'Young Ernie', a strip. The *Sunday Express* editor John Gordon attempted to entice the reluctant artist—'I would be very unhappy if I changed' (Gordon)—to his richer, then hugely successful, right-wing paper whose owner, Lord Beaverbrook, had recognized Giles's burgeoning genius. Eventually hooked, Giles was indeed briefly miserable, but when readers began expressing their enthusiasm for his work his confidence and enthusiasm returned.

On 14 March 1942, at St John's Church, East Finchley, Giles married (Sylvia) Joan Agnes Clarke (1918–1994), his first cousin and childhood sweetheart. They had no children. She was a charming, practical woman of long but not unlimited patience. The couple moved from Islington to Edgware to Ipswich. Just after the war Giles bought Hillbrow Farm, a gloomy seventeenth-century farmhouse, soon to be brightly transformed, in the village of Witnesham, Suffolk. This was to be their permanent home.

Giles's first drawing for the *Sunday Express* was published on 3 October 1943. Later that month he became not only deputy cartoonist to Sidney Strube on the *Daily Express* but also, perhaps surprisingly, the paper's war correspondent. Captain Giles, as he temporarily became, was an unmilitary figure, classified unfit for military service because of partial deafness caused some years before when, in a near fatal accident, his Panther 600 motorcycle had collided with an oncoming truck. Giles admired the First World War cartoons of Captain Bruce Bairnsfather, the creator of popular cartoons based on firsthand frontline experiences. With perky optimism Giles also drew on firsthand experience, a distillation which 'epitomised the

Ronald [Carl] **Giles** (**1916–1995**), by Jane Bown, 1986

spirit of the hour' (Tory, *The Ultimate Giles*, 64). In the aftermath of war Giles drew the grim interior of Fort Breendouk punishment camp, near Antwerp. The dark, uncharacteristic sketches are examples of unvarnished, visual reporting which at the artist's request were not published until 1994. In spite of editorial requests Giles could not bring himself to record the horrors of Belsen. He witnessed scenes which affected him profoundly for the rest of his life, and was brought to a deeper maturity. Although less meaningful to later generations, Giles's wartime cartoons were among his funniest, particularly his 'GI Joes', for whom in real life he had a strong (and reciprocated) affection.

Strube left the *Daily Express* in 1948. Thereafter Giles, dealing with social subjects, alternated with the young right-wing political cartoonist Michael Cummings. During the fifties Giles's work grew in strength. Here was artist, architect, and jokester who drew, among many excellent things, landscapes—particularly snow scenes—of a high and, for his fellow cartoonists, enviable order. Panoramic settings filled with accurate detail of place, people, and atmosphere brought new qualities and a wider vision to British cartooning, influencing his contemporaries including Jak (Raymond Jackson; 1927–1997) and Mac (Stanley McMurtry; *b*. 1936). Giles fits comfortably into a tradition stretching from Rowlandson to Dicky Doyle. He was also influenced by Pont (Graham Laidler; 1908–1940), whose famous series in *Punch*, 'The British character', was based on upper middle-class types, benignly but unerringly observed. In his short life Pont was always the amused spectator rather than angry satirist, an attitude Giles took to heart. The artist's most-loved creation, the Giles family, made its first appearance in the *Sunday Express* on 5 August 1945. The family's common humanity—children's mischief, for example, is not limited by class—had a wide social appeal. For four decades Mother, Father, young Ernie, daughter Ann and her terrible twins, bookworm George (Sartre and Orwell) and his sniffling, aspirin-riddled wife Vera and their son, George junior, Ann's younger sisters Bridget and Susan, their Airedale Butch (and a permanent visitor, young Stinker with his ever present camera and wet-mop haircut) were dominated by their granite-tough, invincible Grandma, who invariably wore ankle-length black bombazine and an alarming frown. She clutched a parrot-knobbed brolly and a padlocked handbag, both of which could be used as weapons if needed. Grandma, among other things, was irascible, pugnacious, fearless, bloody-minded, a 'small c' conservative socialist, outrageous yet patriotic, anarchic and somehow endearing. Friends noted Giles's spiritual resemblance to his creation, a likeness later compounded in photographs taken in his later years revealing a facial resemblance both touching and quietly comic. The family remained unaltered for forty years: the kids did not grow up and Grandma and the others did not grow older. Instead, the world changed around them while they observed and reacted to it.

The making of three large cartoons a week, taking from eight to ten hours each, required a self-discipline not always manifest in Giles's life. They were drawn in a large studio suite in Ipswich and when finished were forwarded, often late, by train to London or by taxi if the trains were not running or by helicopter if the weather put both beyond reach. Deadlines were held in contempt, an attitude which did not endear Giles to the frantic newspaper staff trying to put the paper to bed.

Joan Giles once admitted that marriage to this complex, contradictory man was like having 'at least five husbands': the cartoonist, the engineer, the designer and builder, the pig-breeder, and the car enthusiast. She added, 'All my husbands have one thing in common—fairly regular lapses into vagrancy' (J. Giles, 1955). With fame and a much-increased income he was able to indulge himself. For a time he motored, mostly around the UK, in a huge mobile studio-cum-caravan which he designed and built himself. He bought and raced a Jaguar XK120 at Silverstone in 1952; he owned a Bentley Mulsanne, a Range Rover, a Land Rover, and a much-loved Nicholson 38 yacht. Although shamelessly hedonistic—a man's man, and apparently irresistible to women—his warmth and humour were often overwhelmed by an abrasive grumpiness. 'A sometimes dark and snarling beast' (Tory, *A Life*, 36) seemed to lurk behind these sudden, surprising, often unwarranted outbursts of irascibility. He was severely critical of authority and authoritarian figures—of anything or anyone who hampered him in his pursuits. Generous by nature, Giles nevertheless had difficulty in expressing the compassion which formed the bedrock of his nature and which came across so clearly in his cartoons. A genuinely modest man, Giles avoided talking about himself or his work, which he believed spoke for itself. He was a left-winger who bought expensive grown-up toys, smoked huge cigars, yet never abandoned his roots—to which he returned often and noisily, travelling from pub to pub to do so. His friendships ranged from the many eccentrics, acquaintances, and drinking companions near home to Prince Philip, Prince Charles—the royal family owns a large collection of Giles originals—and Max Aitken (Lord Beaverbrook's son) away from it. He enjoyed the company of the famous and successful if they were honestly forthright in their views and could share his love of horses, cars, and sailing.

Giles drew more than 7000 cartoons for the *Daily Express* and *Sunday Express* and a Giles annual appeared every year from 1946. It was on the covers of his annuals, and in the ornate, coloured Christmas cards he drew for his favourite charity, the Royal National Lifeboat Institution (RNLI)—of which he was made president for life—and for the Royal National Institute for the Blind that he was able to produce comic masterpieces in which he returned to the pleasures of drawing at a more leisurely pace than newspaper deadlines allowed him, with accurate detail and superbly composed crowd scenes. Of Giles's entire output it has been said: 'For the historian of the second half of the 20th century his work will be indispensable' (L. Lambourne, *Giles: Mirror of an Age*, 1993, exhibition catalogue).

During his last decade Giles suffered seriously from

encroaching physical disabilities. Weakening eyesight, increasing deafness, and worsening blood circulation, the latter brought on by heavy smoking, inevitably affected his work, although Giles at his weakest was better than many cartoonists at their best. He was treated to typical Fleet Street insensitivity in his final months with the *Express*, and in 1989, after forty-seven years, he quit with a succinct: 'I just thought, sod this.' In the following year further problems with his circulation resulted in both legs being amputated just below the knee.

Giles was appointed OBE in 1959. He was a founder member in 1966, and later president, of the British Cartoonists' Association (BCA); in 1990 he was awarded a senior fellowship of the Royal College of Art, and in 1993 a large retrospective exhibition was organized by the Cartoon Art Trust (CAT): collections of his work are held by the trust, and at the Cartoon Study Centre at the University of Kent. When guest of honour at a luncheon at London's Garrick Club on 24 March 1993, given by the BCA to honour his fifty years in the business, Giles, in his wheelchair—attended always by his 'minder' Big Louis—chatted amiably throughout the meal. His afflictions were never mentioned, except once, when he gazed at his then less than flexible fingers and said, 'I hope I can begin to draw again'. His words were spoken wistfully and without self-pity and were painful to hear. At the end of the meal the chairman rose to speak but Giles interrupted. 'Forget the speeches', he said. 'Let's go to the pub'.

At seventy-eight Carl Giles—who had given (and taken) so much pleasure in his lifetime, an active man living a physically diminished life—was grief-stricken when his wife Joan died on Christmas day 1994. In spite of the consolation offered by his many friends Giles died eight months later at Ipswich Hospital on 27 August 1995. His funeral was held at Tuddenham church, Suffolk, and there was a memorial service in London at St Bride's, Fleet Street. A statue of Grandma, Vera, and Butch the dog was unveiled in Ipswich in 1993, while at Felixstowe the support and rescue boat *Grandma* was launched in May 1999.

JOHN JENSEN

Sources M. Bryant, *Dictionary of twentieth-century British cartoonists and caricaturists* (2000) • P. Tory, *Giles: a life in cartoons* (1992) • J. Giles, introduction, *Giles Annual*, 8th ser. (1955) • J. Gordon, introduction, *Giles Daily Express and Sunday Express Cartoons* [annual], 1st ser. (1946) • P. Tory, *The Giles family* (1993) • P. Tory, *The ultimate Giles* (1995) • W. Feaver, *Giles: fifty years at work* (1994) • A. Doran and L. Lambourne, eds., *Giles: a celebration: 50 years of work for Express Newspapers* [1993] • J. B. F. Allison, bibliography (privately printed, Nottinghamshire, [n.d.]) • A. Christiansen, 'A Babel of people', *Headlines all my life* (1961), 247–9 • R. Beaumont, *Grandma: the biography of Giles's infamous cartoon character* (1999) • A. Lunn, 'British humour', *Graphis* (March–April 1946), 145–59 • M. Horn, ed., *The world encyclopedia of cartoons* (1980), 257–8 • B. Hillier, *Cartoons and caricatures* (1970) • J. Geipel, *The cartoon: a short history of graphic comedy and satire* (1972), 257–8 • *The Guardian* (29 Aug 1995) • *The Independent* (30 Aug 1995) • personal knowledge (2004) • private information (2004) • b. cert. • m. cert. • d. cert. • b. cert. [Joan Giles]
Archives priv. coll., corresp., photographs, and MSS | FILM BFI, 'Portrait of Giles', ITV (17 Sept 1995), documentary • IWM, 'Work and war front', short animated film by Giles
Likenesses R. Giles, self-portraits, cartoons, 1948–9, repro. in Doran and Lambourne, eds., *Giles: a celebration*, endpapers • J. Bown, photograph, 1986, NPG [*see illus.*] • M. Cummings, caricature, repro. in order of service for memorial service, 5 Dec 1995 • R. Giles, self-portrait, caricature, repro. in Tory, *Ultimate Giles*, 143 • photographs, repro. in Tory, *Giles: a life in cartoons*, 55, 94, 160

Giles, William (1872–1939), colour printmaker, was probably born on 19 November 1872 in Reading, Berkshire, the second son of William John Giles (*c*.1835–1924), carver and gilder; his mother is unknown.

Giles received art tuition from the age of eleven through the Government School of Art, Reading, where he later gained a free place (1891–2) before winning a royal exhibition to the National Art Training School, South Kensington (1892–5). He spent time in Paris before returning to Reading to complete his art master's certificate (*c*.1897–1900) and to study the art of creating woodblock colour prints in the Japanese manner under Frank Morley Fletcher. His first colour woodcut, *September Moon* (1901), was innovative in omitting the key block and in treating the composition as an arrangement of colours. Time spent during the next few years cycling and camping in Sweden, Denmark, and Germany established his habit of being in direct contact with nature when travelling in search of new landscape subjects. On 7 September 1907 at the British consulate in Venice, Giles married Ada Matilda Shrimpton (1856–1925), a talented watercolour painter many years his senior. They lived in London and by 1911 had settled at 183 Kings Road, Chelsea. They enjoyed a close, mutually supportive, professional as well as personal relationship, and Ada Shrimpton, who continued to exhibit under her maiden name, devoted her energy and personal wealth to helping him achieve his artistic aims. There were no children.

Giles exhibited sporadically at the Royal Academy and with several art societies, but his principal association was with the Society of Graver-Printers in Colour (SGPC), of which he was an early member and president from 1925 until his death; he participated in every exhibition from 1910 to 1938. In 1911 he exhibited one of his finest woodcuts, *Swan and Cygnets*, for which he and his wife had spent six weeks in a punt observing and befriending a swan family while making preparatory sketches. He was particularly drawn to the coastal landscape of the Vejle Fjord in Denmark, and returned frequently for lengthy summer visits. It inspired his most important subject, *Midsummer Night* (1912), his first work in the Giles method, which was subsequently reworked and published in 1919. Giles donated a signed proof to the Victoria and Albert Museum, London, together with the plates, a set of progressive proofs, and an explanation of his technique. He employed the Giles method almost exclusively from 1912 until 1926; *October Mist* (exh. Liverpool autumn exhibition, Walker Art Gallery 1919), *A Break in the Storm—Jura* (exh. SGPC 1922), and two peacock subjects, *When Winter Wanes* (exh. SGPC 1924) and *Sic transit gloria mundi* (exh. SGPC 1925), are also among the finest metal prints.

In 1924 with his wife's help Giles produced and edited

the *Original Colour Print Magazine* to encourage the collection of original colour prints but found it difficult to continue after her death; there were only two further editions, in which he paid tribute both to her work and to her generous gift, the A. M. Shrimpton and William Giles bequest, left jointly to the Victoria and Albert Museum and the British Museum specifically to encourage the development of printing in colours by relief processes. Giles subsequently set up the Colour Print Club (*c.*1927) and edited its shortlived journal (1931–3). He returned to the medium of wood with *The Bathing Pool* (exh. SGPC 1926) and after 1927 abandoned the Giles method altogether. He remained active until shortly before his death, and good examples from the second woodblock phase are *Spring* (exh. SGPC 1928) and *The Haunt of the Jay* (exh. SGPC 1932). By 1929 he had left Chelsea and moved to Essex and from 1932 lived at The Studio, Newport, Essex. He took an active interest in village affairs and was a well-liked local figure, with silver hair and a moustache. He died at home on 24 February 1939 and was buried at Hemsdean Road cemetery, Caversham, next to his wife.

Giles was a leading exponent of the original colour print, known principally for landscapes and bird subjects, and much admired for the sensitivity of his colouring. His development of the Giles method, by etching zinc plates and printing from their cameo relief surfaces, transferred the basic principles of the woodcut to metal. Giles was a popular president of the Society of Graver-Printers in Colour and tirelessly dedicated to promoting the original colour print, an art which demanded the artist's personal execution of every part of the creative process: composing the design, cutting the woodblock or etching/engraving the metal plate, and printing each impression by hand. His prints were usually signed with a monogram WG in the block or plate and below, in pencil, 'W. Giles', often followed by 'In. Sc. et Imp.', and sold for approximately 5 guineas if unframed. In addition to a few early paintings he created approximately forty original colour prints from wood, thirty-four from metal, and some bookplates. Although his own work is little known today, his importance lies in the terms and conditions he laid down for the bequest, which prompted both young and established artists to experiment with techniques of relief printing in colours and which stimulated the acquisition by both museums of contemporary colour relief prints directly from the artists themselves. The largest collection of his works is held at the Victoria and Albert Museum; others are at the British Museum, the Gallery of Modern Art, Edinburgh, the Manchester City Galleries, the Walker Art Gallery, Liverpool, and the Hunterian Art Gallery, Glasgow. His papers contain the unfinished manuscript for a book, 'The epic of art and folklore'.

RUTH WALTON

Sources M. C. Salaman, *Masters of the colour print*, 4 (1928) · W. Giles, ed., *Original Colour Print Magazine*, 2 (1925) · W. Giles, ed., *Original Colour Print Magazine*, 3 (1926) · M. C. Salaman, 'Great Britain', *The Studio* [special issue, *Modern etchings, mezzotints and drypoints*, ed. C. Holme] (1912–13), 4–12, 39 · M. C. Salaman, *The modern colour-print of original design* (1920) · exhibition catalogues (1910–39) [Society of Graver–Printers in Colour] · private information (2004) [P. Hviid, S. Gold, H. Chapman] · registered papers, V&A, VA 110/3 · Giles bequest competition, 1909–54, V&A · Giles bequest competition, 1955–8, V&A, pt 1 · Giles bequest competition, 1959–71, V&A, pt 2 · autumn exhibition catalogues (1897–1930) [Walker Art Gallery, Liverpool] · b. cert. [Ada Shrimpton] · d. cert. [Ada Shrimpton] · census returns, 1891 · register of deaths, Saffron Walden, Essex, General Register Office for England, 27 Feb 1939, no. 17 · *Government School of Science and Art, 30th Annual Report* (1890–91) · *Department of Science and Art Calendar*, 1893–5 (1899–1900) · *Reading Standard* (7 Nov 1898) · *Who's who in art* (1929)

Archives NL Wales, corresp. and MSS | V&A, Giles bequest competition, part 1; part 2, VA 110/3

Likenesses photograph, V&A, Department of Drawings and Paintings, photograph no. 2–1950

Wealth at death £7196: V&A, VA 110/3; Giles bequest competition, 1909–54

Gilfillan, George (1813–1878), minister of the United Presbyterian church and author, was born on 30 January 1813 in Comrie, Perthshire, the eleventh of twelve children of Revd Samuel *Gilfillan (1762–1826) and his wife, Rachel Barlas (*b.* 1770/71). His mother was a minister's daughter, and his father was minister of the Comrie Secession congregation. Father and son were very close, and it was assumed from an early age that he would enter the ministry. Samuel Gilfillan died suddenly in 1826, just as George was entering his second year at Glasgow University (after attending Mr Drummond's school in Comrie). At Glasgow he was strongly influenced by the arrival (in the same year) of the poet Thomas Campbell as rector, and he read widely and enthusiastically in English and Scottish poetry while continuing his theological studies. Reading the works of Shelley and William Godwin led him into a period of religious doubt which he ultimately dispelled by renewed study of the Bible in Hebrew and Greek, but the experience left its mark on him: while deeply attracted to literature, he came in later life to suspect that it was irrelevant and perhaps even inimical to one's spiritual life. For much of his life he strove to unite the two. His last university year (1832–3) was spent in Edinburgh, where he studied moral philosophy under John Wilson (1785–1854), who wrote under the pen-name of Christopher North. Wilson's loose, unstructured 'Noctes Ambrosianae' columns from *Blackwood's Magazine* had a major impact on Gilfillan's own literary style.

In 1835 Gilfillan was granted his minister's licence from the Edinburgh presbytery, and in 1836 he was ordained and installed in the School Wynd congregation in Dundee, a position he held for the rest of his life. On 9 November of that year he married Margaret, daughter of Robert Vallantine, the factor of the nearby Burn estate; they took up residence in a house in Paradise Road, Dundee, where they lived until their deaths (they had no children). Gilfillan became a popular preacher due to his impassioned and imaginative sermons, and he was sought after as a speaker by many civic groups in the area. His first book, *Five Discourses* (1840), was a set of his sermons, polished and expanded; although quite orthodox in content, the book was remarkable for its sophisticated style and tone. In that same year the poet Thomas Aird invited him to contribute literary essays to the *Dumfriesshire and Galloway Herald*—analyses of contemporaries such as Wordsworth, Francis

Jeffrey, and Thomas De Quincey; these essays, appealingly idiosyncratic and highly rhetorical, were well received, and in 1845 he published them in book form as *A Gallery of Literary Portraits*, a work which created for him a reputation as notable critic. There were two sequel volumes in 1849 and 1854.

While his literary reputation was on the rise, Gilfillan also wrote on theological topics. His 1842 *Hades, or, The Unseen* caused some controversy by its statement that not everything accepted as truth by the church need be believed. He was called before the presbytery to explain himself, and though he acquitted himself well the experience strengthened his evolving theological liberalism, and he continued to maintain that church doctrine was not infallible. Toward the end of his life, in 1870, he was once again called before the presbytery for having publicly questioned several doctrines (such as predestined damnation), and again he avoided censure.

In 1843 Gilfillan read Thomas Carlyle's *Sartor Resartus* and met the author, whom he at first saw as a modern prophet; but the two men fell out after Gilfillan criticized Carlyle in his 1850 work *The Bards of the Bible*, and he later came to see the sage as a pernicious influence; Carlyle, in turn, saw Gilfillan as too fixed in his orthodoxy. *The Bards of the Bible* is one of Gilfillan's most striking performances: he treated the prophets in much the same way that he had treated poets in his *Gallery* series, creating intense, impressionistic portraits of them in an attempt to convey their essential spirit and message. The book's opening sentence—'The language of the imagination is the native language of man'—declared his intent to read the prophets as poets, another example of the liberalism that sometimes alarmed the presbytery. Gilfillan's fame and influence were at their height from 1845 to 1855, and he was visited in Dundee by the poet Ralph Waldo Emerson, the American slave-born journalist and diplomat Frederick Douglass (Gilfillan was passionately anti-slavery), and numerous young writers and poets.

Gilfillan enjoyed a wide circle of admirers, although it would be exaggeration to say he was at the head of a 'school' of literature. Nevertheless he was portrayed thus in a devastating satire, *Firmilian* (1854), by the poet William Edmondstoune Aytoun. Aytoun deftly depicted Gilfillan as Apollodorus, the charlatan leader of the Spasmodic school. *Firmilian* was a success, and Gilfillan became the subject of lampoons and attacks in *Blackwood's* and elsewhere, which severely damaged his reputation. Aytoun had been motivated by Gilfillan's attack on him in the 1852 *Martyrs, Heroes and Bards of the Scottish Covenant*, but Aytoun's satire was close enough to the mark to obscure his motivation: Gilfillan's too-warm, undisciplined prose invited a term like 'spasmodic'.

Though personally hurt by Aytoun's satire, Gilfillan continued to produce literary work, editing some forty-eight volumes of the Library Edition of British Poets (1853–60), with prefaces and biographical sketches of British poets from Chaucer to Scott. And in 1856 he published his *History of a Man*, a thinly disguised autobiography which was meant as a companion and corrective to *Sartor Resartus*. At this period, both his Christian commitment and his distrust of the ultimate value of imaginative literature were growing. Acutely aware of the deepening rift between Christianity and the *Zeitgeist*, visible in both science and literature, he produced in 1857 *Christianity and our Era*: he argued that Christianity is not static but evolving, and that it would soon reach its ultimate manifestation, in which all the conflicts between faith and modernity would be resolved. This reconciliation was the theme also of the single book-length poem he wrote, *Night* (1867). The rambling, discursive blank verse of *Night* prophesied the redemption of this corrupted world through the imminent return of Christ. An unfinished novel, *Reconciliation*, worked with similar ideas.

Gilfillan was prolific in his last years, giving public lectures, delivering two or three sermons a week, and writing biographies of Scott (1870), the journalist and poet William Anderson (1873), and Burns (1878). His last Sunday sermon, occasioned by the drowning of a local man, was on the topic of sudden death. Ironically, on Tuesday 13 August 1878, Gilfillan suffered a heart attack and died within hours at 3 Clerk Street, Brechin. Although by then his larger fame had long passed, dissolving in the laughter aroused by the satires of the 1850s, he was revered locally: over 1000 people attended his burial service on 17 August at Balgay cemetery, Dundee. His florid prose has kept him out of fashion, perhaps unfairly, but he deserves to be remembered as a liberalizing churchman torn between Athens and Jerusalem, earnestly struggling to reconcile the two. RAYMOND N. MACKENZIE

Sources R. A. Watson and E. S. Watson, *George Gilfillan: letters and journals, with a memoir* (1892) • D. Macrae, *George Gilfillan: anecdotes and reminiscences* (1891) • W. Walsh, *George Gilfillan* (1898) • G. Gilfillan, *The history of a man* (1856) • b. cert. • m. cert. • d. cert. • J. Gross, *The rise and fall of the man of letters: aspects of English literary life since 1800* (1969), 190–93 • G. Pursglove, 'George Gilfillan', *Nineteenth-century British literary biographers*, ed. S. Serafin, DLitB, 144 (1994), 117–26

Archives BL, letters, as sponsor, to Royal Literary Fund, loan 96 • NL Scot. • U. Edin. L.

Likenesses D. O. Hill and R. Adamson, photograph, 1844 (with Dr Samuel Brown), U. Texas, Gernsheim Coll. • W. B. Lamond, oils, Dundee City Art Gallery • W. B. Lamond, print, Dundee City Art Gallery • J. Valentine, carte-de-visite, NPG • photograph, repro. in Watson and Watson, *George Gilfillan* • photograph, repro. in Macrae, *George Gilfillan*, frontispiece • two prints, NPG

Wealth at death £5174 14*s*. 2*d*.: confirmation, 7 Dec 1878, *CCI*

Gilfillan, James (1797–1874), minister of the United Presbyterian church, was born at Comrie, Perthshire, on 11 May 1797, eldest son of the Revd Samuel *Gilfillan (1762–1826), a leading United Secession minister, and his wife, Rachel Barlas (*b.* 1770/71). He was the brother of George *Gilfillan (1813–1878). James Gilfillan received his early education at a school in his native village, and entered Glasgow College in 1808, when only eleven and a half years old. After spending six sessions there he entered the Divinity Hall of the Anti-Burgher synod in Edinburgh, and in 1821 was licensed by the Edinburgh presbytery of the United Secession church. He was ordained on 24 December 1822 as minister of the Stirling United Secession Church.

Gilfillan was a good preacher, but was better known as the author of *The Sabbath, Viewed in the Light of Reason, Revelation, and History* (1861), on which he had been working for twenty laborious years. This contribution to the nineteenth-century sabbatarian debate in Scotland (then about to reach a climax in the 1865–6 controversy over the running of Sunday trains) was a restatement of the conservative position also held by the Free Church and the Church of Scotland: recent commentators have opined that 'little attention was paid to [the] book except among those who agreed with it already' (Drummond and Bulloch, 308). In 1866 the University of Glasgow conferred on him the degree of DD. Resigning his duties in 1869, he moved to Portobello, near Edinburgh, where he died on 28 January 1874.

THOMAS HAMILTON, *rev.* ROSEMARY MITCHELL

Sources Boase, *Mod. Eng. biog.* • W. Blair, 'Memoir of the late Rev. James Gilfillan, DD, Stirling', *United Presbyterian Magazine*, new ser., 18 (1874), 401–6 • A. L. Drummond and J. Bulloch, *The church in Victorian Scotland, 1843–1874* (1975), 308

Wealth at death £1072 10s. 7d.: confirmation, 1874, Scotland

Gilfillan, Robert (1798–1850), poet and songwriter, was born on 7 July 1798 in Dunfermline, Fife, the son of Robert Gilfillan (*d.* 1834), a master weaver, and Marion Law (1770–1844), daughter of a small manufacturer in Dunfermline. They had three sons, James, Robert, and Henry, and one daughter, Margaret. Robert's great-grandfather had been a farmer in Stirlingshire and his grandfather, also Robert, captain of a merchant ship. His childhood could not have been easy if, according to one account, his father was unable to provide for the family through ill health (*Whistle-Binkie*, 38). His early education was rudimentary but it was at this time he discovered in himself a juvenile talent for songwriting: on a guising (mummering) expedition one Christmas he performed some verses on the death of General Ralph Abercromby.

In 1811 Gilfillan's family moved to Leith, where he was apprenticed to the firm of Thomson and Muir, coopers. During his seven-year apprenticeship, by the chance find of some money, he bought a one-keyed flute which he taught himself to play and in 1816 began to write poetry, with the stanzas beginning 'Again let's hail the cheering spring' (based on the air 'For a' that'). He returned to Dunfermline in 1818 and worked for three years as an assistant in Provost Wilson's grocery shop. He read avidly in his spare time and attended meetings of like-minded young men for mutual improvement in literature, science, and art, where he would read his early attempts at verse. He moved back to Leith in 1821 where he remained for the rest of his life. He was employed as a clerk in the warehouse of Smith and Muir, oil and colour merchants, and then as a confidential clerk to Thomas McRitchie, wine merchant. For two winters he attended evening classes in mechanics, chemistry, and the physical sciences at Edinburgh School of Arts.

Gilfillan began contributing poems and songs (always first heard by his mother and sister) to the press and attracted favourable notice, even being quoted by James Hogg in *Blackwood's Magazine* as the '"fine chiel" down at Leith'. Encouraged, in 1831 he brought out a small volume, *Original Songs*, with a typically modest preface: 'Had my education been better than it is, this little Work would probably have presented fewer inelegancies of language, and fewer violations of grammar'. Whatever inelegancies it possessed did not stop it enjoying a wide circulation and a second edition, enlarged by fifty pieces, was published in 1835, simply titled *Songs*. This included what is probably Gilfillan's best poem, 'The Tax-Gatherer' (written in 1828), an amiable satire on tax collecting based on Peter McCraw, the Leith poor rate collector:

> O do ye ken Peter, the taxman an' vriter?
> Ye're weel aff wha ken naething 'bout him ava.

Gilfillan was consequently given a public dinner in his honour in Edinburgh at which a large silver cup was presented to him by his admirers. In reply he said he had made poetry a pastime, not a profession and he would rather forgo the fame of the poet than do anything to lower the character of the man. He was also honoured to be made grand bard to the grand lodge of freemasons of Scotland at the centenary meeting of the grand lodge on 30 November 1836. In 1837 Gilfillan became a tax gatherer himself when he was appointed collector of police rates for Leith, an office he discharged faithfully until his death. A third edition of his work appeared in 1839, with an additional sixty songs. A fourth edition, *Poems and Songs*, with a memoir by William Anderson, was published posthumously in 1851. He contributed to the *Dublin University Magazine* and the anthology *Whistle-Binkie*; he was theatre critic for the *Edinburgh Chronicle* and for twenty years was Leith correspondent for *The Scotsman*.

Amid all this busy life Gilfillan never married. His brother James's daughter Marion kept house for him. He ventured abroad a few times but was restless and unhappy until he was home again. He seems to have been universally liked, a kind, simple, affable, unobtrusive soul who shone in convivial company.

In his time Gilfillan was talked of in the same breath as Ramsay, Fergusson, and Burns, but his range was much narrower, concentrating on Scottish domestic sentiments and manners—indeed, he himself claimed no higher ambition. With one or two exceptions, which have crept into the twentieth century in Scottish song albums, his songs have not stood the test of time. Perhaps if he had given more rein to the satiric than the sentimental he would be included in more Scottish anthologies. Certainly 'The Tax-Gatherer' ('Peter McCraw') is worth reviving, as are the humorous poems 'There cam' to our village a stranger' and 'Write, Write, Tourist and Traveller'.

In April 1850 Gilfillan organized a successful subscription to repair the monument to Robert Fergusson which Burns had erected in Canongate churchyard. On the morning of 4 December 1850 Gilfillan was struck with a fit of apoplexy. He rallied for a while but suffered a second attack and died that evening at his home in Hermitage Place, Leith Links. He was buried in South Leith cemetery.

HAMISH WHYTE

Sources W. Anderson, 'Memoir', in R. Gilfillan, *Poems and songs* (1851) • *Whistle-binkie, or, The piper of the party: being a collection of songs* *for the social circle*, new edn, 1 (1878), 38–43 • Chambers, *Scots.* (1835) • J. G. Wilson, ed., *The poets and poetry of Scotland*, 2 (1877), 177–8 • C. Rogers, *The modern Scottish minstrel, or, The songs of Scotland of the past half-century*, 3 (1856), 261 • J. Ross, ed., *The book of Scottish poems: ancient and modern* (1878)

Archives NL Scot., letters and poems

Likenesses Wallace, engraving, repro. in Gilfillan, *Poems and songs*, frontispiece • silhouette, Scot. NPG

Gilfillan, Samuel (1762–1826), United Secession minister, son of a small shopkeeper in the village of Buchlyvie, Stirlingshire, was born there on 24 November 1762. He was the youngest of a family of fifteen children. As a child he displayed an enthusiasm for reading, and the habit was encouraged by his mother, who wanted him to enter the ministry. After receiving a rudimentary education in a country school, in November 1782 he went to the University of Glasgow, attended the arts course, and afterwards studied theology under William Moncrieff of Alloa and Archibald Bruce of Whitburn. During his studies Gilfillan supported himself mainly by teaching.

Gilfillan was licensed to preach by the Associate Presbytery of Perth in June 1789, and shortly afterwards received calls from the congregations at Barry in Forfarshire, and Auchtergaven and Comrie in Perthshire. The synod sent him to Comrie, a small village in the upper part of Strathearn, where he was ordained on 12 April 1791. In July 1793 Gilfillan married Rachel (*b.* 1770/71), eldest daughter of the Revd James Barlas of the adjacent parish of Crieff. A highly attractive woman, she was known locally as 'the star of the north'. Gilfillan himself was a handsome man: his son George described his 'manly figure, tall and erect, [with] long dark hair … a lofty forehead, a quick and restless eye' (G. Gilfillan, 32). The couple had twelve children, of whom eight survived to adulthood; they included James *Gilfillan (1797–1874) and George *Gilfillan (1813–1878).

Despite his happy family life, Gilfillan faced considerable difficulties at Comrie. His initial stipend was a mere £50 a year, and his congregation numbered only sixty-five members. Moreover, Gilfillan did not understand Gaelic, while two-thirds of his parishioners did not speak English. However, he later preached in both Gaelic and English to great effect, holding to strict Calvinist doctrine. His congregation increased, and his stipend eventually rose to £100. With other ministers of his church, Gilfillan in 1819 planned and put into action a scheme for building lending libraries in the highlands, with a stock largely of religious works; fourteen were eventually established.

Gilfillan's published writings included many articles for the *Christian Magazine*, which were signed Leumas (Samuel reversed). A number of these were also included in 1822 in a volume of *Short Discourses on Various Important Subjects for the Use of Families*. His *Essay on the Sanctification of the Lord's Day* (1804) passed through ten English editions, and was translated into several foreign languages. Another small treatise, *Domestic Piety*, was published in 1819, and an enlarged edition in 1825. In 1826 he published his most significant work, *Discourses on the Dignity, Grace, and Operations of the Holy Spirit*. Gilfillan also contributed some articles to the columns of *The Student*, a Glasgow University periodical, in 1817. A posthumous work giving a collection of his letters, to which a memoir was added, was published in 1828 by his eldest son, James. According to John M'Kerrow, Gilfillan's published works—like his sermons, from which they were often derived—were 'plain and simple, without any pretensions to ornament', nevertheless exhibiting 'an intimate acquaintance with the human heart' (M'Kerrow, 912); his son George confirms that he was a widely read and imaginative writer, but no great scholar.

Samuel Gilfillan died at Comrie on 15 October 1826, reputedly from a bowel inflammation caused by eating sloes. He was buried in the parish churchyard, close beside the River Earn, four days later. He was survived by his wife. HENRY PATON, *rev.* ROSEMARY MITCHELL

Sources J. Gilfillan, 'Memoir', in S. Gilfillan, *Letters chiefly to afflicted friends* (1828) • G. Gilfillan, *Remoter stars in the church sky* (1867), 26–38 • J. M'Kerrow, *History of the Secession church*, rev. edn (1841), 910–13 • R. Cochrane, *The treasury of modern biography* (1879) • R. Small, *History of the congregations of the United Presbyterian church from 1733 to 1900*, 2 (1904), 612, 624

Wealth at death £255 10*s.* 11*d.*: inventory, 1833, Scotland

Gilkes, Arthur Herman (1849–1922), headmaster, was born on 2 November 1849 at Leominster, Herefordshire, the fourth child of William Gilkes (1813–1866), chemist and ink maker, and his wife, Mary (*née* Heming). He had six brothers and four sisters. The family was Anglican with a Quaker ethos. Gilkes was educated at Shrewsbury School, for which he always felt a deep affection. Elected to a junior studentship at Christ Church, Oxford, in 1868, he gained first classes in classical moderations and *literae humaniores*. He was one of the founders of the Oxford University association football club and a member of the Christ Church cricket eleven. He returned to Shrewsbury as an assistant master in 1873 and remained there until 1885, when he was appointed master of Dulwich College in succession to J. E. C. Welldon.

During the twenty-nine years of his mastership, Gilkes secured Dulwich's position as one of the leading public schools of the period, particularly by its scholarship successes at Oxford and Cambridge. He had unshakeable convictions about education: he thought little of success in examinations or games, and attached prime importance to the moral training of the boys under his care, striving to instil into them a reverence for what is good, an instinct for doing right rather than wrong, and an appreciation of beauty. At first his hesitant manner, apparent mildness, and slight stammer led staff and boys to underrate his moral strength, but they soon learned that behind the diffidence was an iron determination. He was involved in every aspect of the school, knew every boy by name, and had a workload which would have broken a lesser man. Himself a noted classical scholar, he taught classics and divinity to the sixth forms. Plato was one of his favourite authors, and he adopted a Socratic method of moral instruction. He also introduced many of the ideals that he

Arthur Herman Gilkes (1849–1922), by Samuel Melton Fisher

had admired at Shrewsbury: thriving science and engineering sides were established; he founded a school mission on Walworth Road; a rifle corps came into being; and the prefect system was reformed. Sport of all kinds was encouraged, but participation was voluntary. He punished little—a Board of Education inspector's report in 1909 spoke of 'his kindly severity'—and he had a natural simplicity which gave him a strong insight into the minds of his charges. Gentle as his manner was, however, his sarcasm could be withering. He once said, defending his habitual attitude of reserve, 'You know, I have to be very careful: I was meant by nature for a buffoon.' Many of his ideas were embodied in a series of semi-fictional books, which are virtually unreadable because the message, the paramount importance of goodness, takes precedence over everything else.

As Gilkes grew older his immense stature (he was 6 feet 5 inches tall and weighed 18 stone), habitual air of gravity, and long beard ('Did he sleep with it inside or outside the bedclothes?', his younger pupils sometimes wondered) made him a formidable figure. In 1892 he married Millicent Mary (*d.* in or after 1922), daughter of B. M. Clarke of Sydenham; they had four sons. In his latter years at Dulwich, Gilkes increasingly suffered from poor health and resigned in the summer of 1914. He incurred temporary unpopularity at the start of the war by a letter to the *Daily Mail* criticizing the recourse to arms as 'miserable nonsense'. In 1915 he was ordained, serving as curate at St James's, Bermondsey. Christ Church, Oxford, appointed him in 1919 vicar of St Mary Magdalene, Oxford, where he remained until his death of a heart attack at his house, 53 Broad Street, Oxford, on 13 September 1922.

Gilkes's third son, **Christopher Herman Gilkes** (1898–1953), followed his father as master of Dulwich College from 1941 to 1953. He had himself been educated there before going on to Trinity College, Oxford. His first wife, Eleanor Benson, whom he married in 1921, died in 1938, and in the following year he married Kathleen Josephine Gaston Murray (1906–1960). Dulwich was one of the few schools which continued to function in London during the Second World War, and when Christopher Gilkes took over as master it was in a desperate state: no part of the buildings had escaped bombing; the numbers of pupils and the academic level had plummeted; and it was on the verge of bankruptcy. Gilkes restored it to its former eminence with vision and single-minded purpose, though not without raising some hackles. His greatest achievement was the expansion, after the 1944 Education Act, of a scheme begun early in the century, under which the fees of particularly clever boys were paid for by their local authority. By 1961 just over 86 per cent came into this category—more than in any comparable school. As a result, not only did the academic level become very high, but the college acquired a rare classlessness, enabling many children from deprived backgrounds to receive a first-class education which would otherwise have been denied them. Christopher Gilkes died of a heart attack at Nolton Haven, Pembrokeshire, on 2 September 1953.

SHEILA HODGES

Sources S. Hodges, *God's gift: a living history of Dulwich College* (1981) • W. R. M. Leake, ed., *Gilkes and Dulwich, 1885–1914* (1938) • private information (2004) • *The Times* (14 Sept 1922) • *WWW* • *The Times* (4 Sept 1953)

Archives Dulwich College, London • priv. coll.

Likenesses S. M. Fisher, portrait, Dulwich College [*see illus.*] • bust, Dulwich College • portrait (Gilkes, Christopher Herman), Dulwich College

Wealth at death £2469 15*s.* 10*d.*: administration with will, 17 Nov 1922, *CGPLA Eng. & Wales* • £21,351 4*s.* 11*d.*—Christopher Herman Gilkes: probate, 4 Nov 1953, *CGPLA Eng. & Wales*

Gilkes, Christopher Herman (1898–1953). *See under* Gilkes, Arthur Herman (1849–1922).

Gill, Alexander, the elder. *See* Gil, Alexander, the elder (1565–1635).

Gill, Alexander, the younger. *See* Gil, Alexander, the younger (1596/7–1642?).

Gill, Alfred Henry (1856–1914), trade union leader and politician, was born on 3 December 1856 at 36 Oldham Road, Rochdale, the son of John Gill, a cotton spinner, and his wife, Mary Stott. He received an elementary education, curtailed from the age of ten when he was employed as a half-timer in a local cotton mill; full-time work began at thirteen. On 4 January 1876 he married Sarah Ellen (*b.* 1855/6), daughter of John Greenwood of Rochdale, painter. In 1879 he moved to Oldham, still as a cotton operative, and in 1887 to Pendlebury to take up a better position.

Gill's upbringing imbued him with a desire for self-improvement. He was raised as, and remained a Wesleyan Methodist. He joined the Band of Hope at the age of twelve, and stayed true to its temperance principles; he took part in the co-operative movement, becoming chairman of his local society; and in 1896, after attending evening classes in scientific and technical subjects, he was appointed assistant secretary of the Bolton and District Operative Spinners' Association. Eight months later he progressed to the post of secretary, which he held for the remainder of his life. As a full-time trade union official, Gill was known for his mastery of the complicated system of wage rates then operating in cotton mills, and for a conciliatory approach to industrial relations. His moderation made him acceptable as a member of the Bolton magistrates' bench, to which he was appointed in 1899, and as a representative on a number of other local bodies.

The Amalgamated Association of Operative Cotton Spinners, in which the Bolton district was prominent, sent Gill as one of its two delegates to the founding conference of the Labour Representation Committee in 1900. The long-established unions in the cotton industry occupied an influential, somewhat cautious, position within the labour movement, but the election of David Shackleton as a member of parliament in 1902 gave the impetus to independent political activity among the leaders of Lancashire's textile workers. Gill was already a member of the committee of the United Textile Factory Workers' Association (UTFWA), one purpose of which was to lobby on political issues of concern to the various trade unions in the textile industry. When in 1903 the UTFWA affiliated to the Labour Representation Committee it became the largest body in that organization. Gill was adopted in 1903 as a parliamentary candidate, sponsored by the textile workers, for the Bolton constituency, which returned two MPs and came within the pact made by Herbert Gladstone and Ramsay MacDonald to ensure electoral co-operation. At the general election of 1906 Gill and the Liberal George Harwood were returned. A similar arrangement ensured his success in the general elections of 1910.

In parliament, like other Labour MPs from the trade union wing of the party, he maintained a role in the affairs of his union. In 1903 he had been elected as one of the thirteen members of the parliamentary committee of the Trades Union Congress, a term of office that continued until 1907 when he presided over the congress of the TUC held that year in Bath. He again sat on the TUC's parliamentary committee in 1913–14. In the House of Commons he called for better ventilation of factories, a more efficient system of inspection, and measures to reduce accidents. He made the practice of 'time-cribbing', by which employers added on a few minutes to the working day, the subject of regular questions. He was especially concerned to improve workmen's compensation, and it was on this issue that he spoke for the last time in the House of Commons, on 20 May 1914.

Gill suffered a heart attack in June 1913, and although he recovered sufficiently to resume his parliamentary duties, he never regained full health. He died on 27 August 1914 at his home, 61 Hampden Street, Bolton. After a funeral service at Halliwell Road Wesleyan Church, Bolton, on 31 August, he was buried in the nonconformist section of Heaton cemetery. He was survived by his wife and by a son and four daughters. D. E. MARTIN

Sources *DLB* · *WWBMP* · *WWW* · D. E. Martin, '"The instruments of the people"? the parliamentary Labour party in 1906', *Ideology and the Labour movement*, ed. D. E. Martin and D. Rubinstein (1979), 125–46 · K. D. Brown, ed., *The first labour party, 1906–1914* (1985) · A. Fowler and T. Wyke, eds., *The barefoot aristocrats: a history of the Amalgamated Association of Operative Cotton Spinners* (1987) · P. F. Clarke, *Lancashire and the new liberalism* (1971) · B. C. Roberts, *The Trades Union Congress, 1868–1921* (1958) · E. Hopwood, *A history of the Lancashire cotton industry and the Amalgamated Weavers' Association* (1969) · m. cert. · census returns, 1881

Wealth at death £3693 7*s*. 3*d*.: probate, 6 Oct 1914, *CGPLA Eng. & Wales*

Gill, Sir David (1843–1914), astronomer, was born at 48 Skene Terrace, Aberdeen, on 12 June 1843, the eldest son of David Gill (1789–1878), a watchmaker with a well-established business in Aberdeen, and his wife, Margaret Mitchell (1809–1870). He was educated at Dollar Academy and at Marischal College, Aberdeen, where he was inspired by the lectures of James Clerk Maxwell. In response to his stern father's wishes he entered the watchmaking business at the age of seventeen without taking a university degree. What at the time seemed to the young Gill a disappointing end to his studies turned out to be providential. After two years' apprenticeship in Switzerland and England he became not only an outstanding watchmaker but a first-class engineer who loved to create and use instruments of the highest possible precision. He became his father's partner and eventually head of the firm, devoting his spare time to physics and chemistry in a small laboratory which he had kept at home since his schooldays.

Interest in astronomy Gill's active interest in astronomy began in 1863. It occurred to him that a time service similar to that established by Charles Piazzi Smyth in Edinburgh might usefully be installed in Aberdeen. An introduction to Smyth by David Thomson, professor of natural philosophy at Aberdeen, followed, when Gill was shown the time ball and time gun as well as the instruments at the observatory in Edinburgh. With Thomson's help, a small transit circle was unearthed and mounted, and a solar clock added, to establish a time service for Aberdeen on the Edinburgh pattern. Gill also acquired a 12 inch reflector, on an equatorial mounting of his own design, with a driving clock made by his own hands, and accurate enough for long-exposure astronomical photography. Assisted by the Aberdeen photographer George Washington Wilson, he obtained some excellent photographs of the moon which brought him to the attention of professional astronomers.

On 7 July 1870 Gill married Isobel Sara (1849–1919), the daughter of John Black, a farmer of Linhead, Aberdeenshire. Two years later the opportunity came to devote his time exclusively to scientific pursuits. This arose out of

Sir David Gill (1843–1914), by unknown photographer

the friendship he had formed with Lord Lindsay (afterwards twenty-sixth earl of Crawford), an amateur astronomer who was attracted by Gill's enthusiasm and skill. Gill was offered the charge of a private observatory which Lord Lindsay was setting up on the family's country estate at Dun Echt, 12 miles west of Aberdeen. He accepted eagerly, though the move involved a considerable sacrifice of income. The years 1872–4 were busily occupied in equipping this observatory with a range of first-class astronomical instruments, modelled on those of Pulkovo observatory near St Petersburg, then considered the best-appointed observatory in the world. In this connection Gill paid a visit to Pulkovo in 1873, and afterwards to Germany, where he met many of the leading astronomers of the day. The level of Gill's activity at this period was phenomenal, as he was at the same time in charge of the building operations at Dun Echt, assisted only by the local estate workers.

Expeditions Preparations were next made for an expedition to the island of Mauritius to observe the transit of Venus of December 1874. The rare occurrences of transits, when the planet passes directly in front of the sun, were events of major astronomical importance since they were the means of determining the sun's distance, a fundamental unit in astronomy. The practical task required observations to be made from widely separated points on the surface of the earth. The Dun Echt team of Lindsay, Gill, and Ralph Copeland took part in this great international effort. They observed the transit with a formidable array of instruments, including a 4 inch heliometer, an instrument little used in Britain, which Lord Lindsay had acquired from the firm of Repsold of Hamburg specially for the purpose. The heliometer, a double-image instrument originally designed to measure the angular diameter of the sun's disc, could also be used to determine separations between objects in the sky as far apart as 2 degrees. The outcome of these and of all other observations of the transit of Venus, carefully planned and executed at great expense of time and money by expeditions all over the world, did not live up to expectations. However, the Dun Echt efforts in Mauritius were far from wasted, as they included Gill's inauguration of an alternative independent method of determining the sun's distance. This, the so-called diurnal parallax method, consisted of observing a planet when close to opposition in the evening and in the morning. Gill, who had noticed that the minor planet Juno would be in opposition around the time of the transit of Venus, employed the heliometer to track its position over a period of fifteen nights. The result gave the value of the distance of the sun correct to 1 part in 200, and convinced Gill of the superiority both of the method and of the heliometer as a high-precision instrument.

Gill left Dun Echt in 1876. He borrowed the heliometer from Lord Lindsay and, with funds obtained from the Royal Society and the Royal Astronomical Society, made an expedition to the island of Ascension in order to measure the distance of Mars when it came exceptionally close to the earth in 1877, using the same technique by which he had observed Juno on Mauritius. On this difficult and adventurous expedition he was accompanied by his wife, who published an interesting account of their experience, *Six Months on Ascension* (1878). The expedition was crowned with success, the sun's distance being determined with much greater accuracy than had previously been attained. The work earned for Gill the gold medal of the Royal Astronomical Society in 1882.

Astronomer at the Cape Gill now looked around for a professional appointment. He applied for the post of Radcliffe observer at Oxford—where the observatory possessed a magnificent but little-used heliometer—but was unsuccessful. Shortly afterwards, in 1879, with the support of a number of leading scientists and particularly of Lord Lindsay, he was elected to fill the post vacated by the new Oxford appointee, Edward J. Stone, that of her majesty's astronomer at the Cape of Good Hope. The choice of Gill, a man without formal academic qualifications, in preference to a rival candidate, William M. Christie, chief assistant at the Royal Greenwich Observatory, caused some surprise and, on Christie's part, a certain amount of resentment. As a result, Gill's later relations with Christie, who became astronomer royal in 1881, were less than cordial. Time showed, however, that Gill was undoubtedly the ideal person for the post.

The Cape observatory had been founded and equipped in 1820 by the Admiralty to provide for the southern hemisphere, for the benefit of navigators, similar observations to those made at Greenwich of the northern skies. This 'fundamental astronomy' was the main work at the Cape, but by the time of Gill's appointment the observatory had fallen into a sad state of neglect. His first task, attacked with characteristic vigour, was to restore the instruments and to reduce and publish observations of thousands of stars left unreduced by his predecessors.

Gill's own special instrument was, once again, the heliometer. He used, first, the Dun Echt one, which he purchased from Lord Lindsay, and later a 7 inch one, also made by the firm of Repsold, installed in 1887—the most productive heliometer ever constructed. By means of these instruments, the distances of several bright southern stars were measured with an accuracy that marked an era in the determination of stellar distances. Gill's most outstanding achievement with the large heliometer was the redetermination of the solar distance, based on observations of the minor planets Iris, Victoria, and Sappho when they approached near the earth in 1888–9. The result was a value of the solar distance, determined to 1 part in 1000, which was adopted as definitive for half a century. This high precision was due as much to Gill's great personal skill as to the admirable design of his heliometer.

Photographic astronomy The application of photography to astronomy made great strides at the close of the nineteenth century, and Gill was one of the pioneers in this field. Long-exposure photographs on dry plates which he obtained of the Great Comet of 1882, using an improvised camera attached to an equatorial telescope, revealed a striking number of faint stars, a fact that impressed on him the power of photography for mapping the stars and its superiority over visual observations. In 1885 he installed a 6 inch lens for the purpose of making a photographic survey of the southern heavens, the Cape Photographic Durchmusterung (CPD). In the same year Jacobus Kapteyn, who had no observational facilities of his own in the Netherlands, offered to measure all the photographic plates taken with this instrument. The happy collaboration between Gill and Kapteyn resulted in the publication between 1896 and 1900 of the positions and magnitudes of 455,000 stars, used by Kapteyn himself in his researches in stellar statistics, and by many later workers.

In 1887 an international conference on astronomical photography was convened in Paris under the presidency of the director of the Paris observatory, Admiral Ernest Mouchez. Driven largely by Gill's enthusiasm, an ambitious plan was launched to produce photographic charts of the entire sky, the *Carte du ciel*, recording stars to magnitude 15, and an astrographic catalogue of positions of stars to magnitude 12. The task was to be shared between eighteen observatories throughout the world, using identical astrographs of 13 inches aperture. The Cape observatory's allotted portion of the sky was photographed under Gill's supervision between 1892 and 1906.

In the international *Carte du ciel* project, Gill was over-optimistic. The effort continued well beyond his lifetime, interrupted by two world wars. It was not until 1964 that the last volumes of the catalogue were published under the auspices of the International Astronomical Union, by which time the work was largely redundant. Nevertheless, the exercise stands out as an important early example of large-scale international collaboration in science.

Gill's flair for planning comprehensive schemes is well illustrated in the geodetic survey of South Africa. His first experience of geodetic work had been in Mauritius in 1874, when he established the geographic co-ordinates of his own and other observing stations. As the telegraph did not reach these distant places it was necessary to transport chronometers, of which no fewer than fifty were assembled by Gill and maintained for the duration of the expedition. When sailing homewards through the Indian Ocean, Gill determined the longitudes of a number of other locations, including Aden, where he set up a telegraph link with Berlin, thus connecting the longitudes of the various stations with Europe. In Egypt also, at the request of the khedive, he measured a base-line for the projected survey of that country. Soon after arriving in South Africa he outlined a system of principal triangulation for the Cape Colony, Natal, the Orange Free State, and the Transvaal, which was carried through for the Cape and Natal between 1883 and 1896, and for the Transvaal and the Free State after the close of the Second South African War. He further saw that these operations might be made the starting point of a chain of triangulation stretching the whole length of Africa, approximately on the 30th meridian. In 1897 he organized this scheme and saw the chain eventually carried to within 70 miles of Lake Tanganyika.

Retirement Gill, who was elected a fellow of the Royal Society in 1883 and created KCB in 1900, left the Cape in 1907 after twenty-eight years of service. When he went there the observatory was comparatively small and possessed but one instrument of value. He left it well equipped with modern instruments, including a new transit circle installed in 1897 and the Victoria 24 inch photographic refractor, the gift of Frank McClean FRS, an amateur astronomer and patron of astronomy. During his career he had received numerous civil and academic honours, among them the German order of merit and the French Légion d'honneur.

After his retirement Gill settled in London and took an active share in its scientific life. The Royal Astronomical Society awarded him his second gold medal in 1908 and chose him as president for the period 1910–12. He was president of the British Association at the Leicester meeting in 1907. He continued to carry out his duties on the committee of the *Carte du ciel* in Paris and was the British representative on the international bureau of weights and measures.

At home, nothing gave him greater pleasure than to invite his astronomical friends to his house, especially if an occasion was provided by the visit of a distinguished foreign astronomer to 'have a talk with astronomers about astronomy'. Much of his time was given to completing his *History and Description of the Cape Observatory* (1913), which also recorded his own early life and experiences. In that history Gill mentions the delight with which he read

Struve's history of the Pulkovo observatory: 'the author had the true genius and spirit of the practical astronomer, a love of refined and precise methods of observation, and the inventive and engineering capacity' (Gill). These words were as true of Gill as of Struve. His profound understanding of the theory and practice of scientific instruments is strikingly revealed in his beautiful articles on the telescope and the heliometer in the eleventh edition of the *Encyclopaedia Britannica* (1911). His enthusiasm communicated itself to his colleagues and assistants, and his kindness of heart made them devoted to him. His force of character enabled him to triumph over difficulties and carry out great projects, even if it meant, as happened more than once, financing his researches with his own money. He had a happy married life, tempered only by anxieties about his wife's health. The Gills had no children, but brought up from 1893 three orphan sons of Gill's only sister. In South Africa, Gill was at the centre of intellectual and social life. His home was always hospitably open to visiting colleagues. He took a lively interest in political matters and was well acquainted with many of the men who helped shape that country's history.

In December 1913 Gill contracted pneumonia, and he died at his London home, 34 De Vere Gardens, Kensington, on 24 January 1914. He was buried on 28 January in the ancient graveyard of St Machar's Cathedral in Aberdeen.

F. W. DYSON, *rev.* HERMANN A. BRÜCK

Sources D. Gill, *A history and description of the Royal Observatory, Cape of Good Hope* (1913) • G. Forbes, *David Gill, man and astronomer* (1916) • B. Warner, *Astronomers at the Royal Observatory, Cape of Good Hope* (1979), chap. 5 • H. A. Brück, 'Lord Crawford's observatory at Dun Echt, 1872–1892', *Vistas in Astronomy*, 35 (1992), 81–138 • A. S. E. [A. S. Eddington], *Monthly Notices of the Royal Astronomical Society*, 75 (1914–15), 236–47 • J. C. Kapteyn, *Astrophysical Journal*, 60 (1914), 161–72 • F. W. D. [F. W. Dyson], *PRS*, 91A (1915), xxvi–xlii • R. H. Stoy, 'Gill, Sir David', *DSB* • C. A. Murray, 'David Gill and celestial photography', *Mapping the sky*, ed. S. Débarbat, J. A. Eddy, H. K. Eichhorn, and others (1988), 143–8 • I. Gill, *Six months in Ascension* (1878) • F. Becker, *Geschichte der Astronomie* (1968), 181–2 • *CCI* (1914)

Archives CUL, corresp. and papers • RAS, corresp. and papers • RGS, corresp. and papers • Royal Observatory, Edinburgh, corresp. and papers | BLPES, letters to Violet Markham • CUL, corresp. with Lord Kelvin • CUL, letters to George Stokes

Likenesses G. Reid, oils, *c.*1833, RAS • photograph, *c.*1865, repro. in Forbes, *David Gill* • photograph, *c.*1900–1907, South African Astronomical Observatory • G. Henry, oils, exh. RA 1912, RS • Elliott & Fry, photograph, repro. in Forbes, *David Gill* • Elliott & Fry, photograph, repro. in H. Macpherson, *Astronomers of today* (1905) • photograph, RAS, Add. MS 91, 3 [*see illus.*]

Wealth at death £6022 4*s.* 7*d.*: confirmation, 18 June 1914, *CCI*

Gill, (Arthur) Eric Rowton (1882–1940), artist, craftsman, and social critic, was born at 32 Hamilton Road, Brighton, Sussex, on 22 February 1882, the eldest son and second of the thirteen children of the Revd Arthur Tidman Gill (1848–1933), minister of the Countess of Huntingdon's Connexion, a Calvinist Methodist church, and his wife, (Cicely) Rose King (*d.* 1929), formerly a professional singer of light opera under the name Rose le Roi. Arthur Tidman Gill, who came from a long line of Congregational missionaries and had been born in the South Seas, had himself been a Congregational minister, but had recently

(Arthur) Eric Rowton Gill (1882–1940), self-portrait, 1927

left the church of his forebears, after doctrinal disagreements, to join the connexion. Eric Gill was brought up in an atmosphere of religious controversy and holy poverty that helped shape his own valiant, if not totally successful, ambition 'to make a cell of good living in the chaos of our world' (Gill, *Autobiography*, 282).

Gill became the greatest artist–craftsman of the twentieth century: a letter-cutter and type designer of genius, whose Gill Sans and Perpetua typefaces have continued in world-wide use for many decades; a sculptor whose powerful work initiated a return to the directness of hand carving; a draughtsman and wood-engraver of consummate subtlety and skill. In any one of these crafts Gill would be considered a prime practitioner. He was also a copious essayist and a vociferous polemicist. The energy and spread of his activity, underpinned by a fervent belief in the values of making by hand as a bastion against the dehumanizing forces of industrialization, make his achievement comparable with that of William Morris in the century before.

Brighton and Chichester, 1882–1899 Eric, named after the hero of Dean Farrar's moralistic school story *Eric, or, Little by Little*, later wrote affectionately of his early childhood, spent in a succession of small, tightly packed houses near the railway line in Brighton where Eric—always to be an admirer of functional engineering design—watched and drew the trains. He went intermittently to a local kindergarten kept by the Misses Browne, sisters of the Dickens illustrator Hablot K. Browne (Phiz). He then spent seven years at Arnold House, a traditional boys' preparatory school in Hove where he was 'fairly happy', although poor to mediocre in all academic subjects except arithmetic. In retrospect the uninspired regime at Arnold House quite suited his developing iconoclasm: 'I was taught nothing in such a way as to make it difficult to discard' (Gill, *Autobiography*, 24).

Gill's unashamed fascination with the bodily functions, especially the sexual, surfaced early. Towards the end of his schooldays, he discovered the splendours of the male erection: 'how shall I ever forget the strange, inexplicable rapture of my first experience? What marvellous thing was this that suddenly transformed a mere water tap into a pillar of fire—and water into an elixir of life?' (Gill, *Autobiography*, 53). His struggles to reconcile the flesh and spirit determined his later life, his writings, and his art.

In 1897 the Gill family moved to 2 North Walls, Chichester. Arthur Tidman Gill had now joined the Church of England. Eric enrolled at the Chichester Technical and Art School, where he was befriended and encouraged by the art master George Herbert Catt, winning a queen's prize for perspective drawing. But the examination-dominated art school training, designed to produce more art teachers, was irksome to a student of Gill's wide-ranging curiosity. He learned more from his explorations of Chichester itself, the serene historic city, 'clear and clean and rational', contained within its Roman walls (Gill, *Autobiography*, 81). Chichester became Gill's model of the ideal city. The architecture of Chichester Cathedral entranced him. The two famous early Norman relief panels set into the interior have an obvious influence on the linearity of Gill's own later sculpture. At the age of seventeen he fell precociously in love with the cathedral sacristan's daughter Ethel Hester Moore (1878–1961), a fellow student at the Art School, and they embarked on a long engagement, which was not without its tensions.

London, 1900–1907 Gill described the next few years, in which he moved to London to train as an architect in the office of W. D. Caroë, architect to the ecclesiastical commissioners, as 'a period of all-round iconoclasm' (Gill, *Autobiography*, 94). His discontent was exacerbated by his lingering grief over the death in 1897 of his favourite sister, Cicely. His disillusionment with architecture as experienced in Caroë's prosperous complacent Anglican church practice in Whitehall Place, Westminster, was profound. The lack of contact between gentlemen architects and artisan builders offended his ideas of human dignity and contravened the theories of creative integration he was already formulating at this time.

Gill found relief in agnosticism, socialism, and the crafts, escaping from the recommended evening lectures in architecture to take classes in masonry at the Westminster Technical Institute and calligraphy at the Central School of Arts and Crafts, a school founded in 1896 on revolutionary principles of practical training in technical skills. The co-principal was W. R. Lethaby, whom Gill was to acknowledge as one of the great men of the nineteenth century, one of the few whose minds were enlightened directly by the Holy Spirit.

Gill's enthusiasm for lettering dated back to his childhood: early drawings of trains (in West Sussex Record Office) show how meticulously he drew out the engine names. These skills had been developed in Caroë's office, where he provided lettering for architectural drawings. But Gill's sense of the real possibilities of letters was awakened only when he joined Edward Johnston's classes at the Central School. His first sight of the skilful, dedicated Johnston writing in script, using a quill pen, came as a revelation: 'I was struck by lightning, as by a sort of enlightenment. It was no mere dexterity that transported me; it was as though a secret of heaven was being revealed' (Gill, *Autobiography*, 119).

In 1902 Gill moved out of his lodgings in Clapham to join Edward Johnston in his bachelor rooms at 16 Old Buildings, Lincoln's Inn. By 1903 a number of commissions for inscriptional carvings on tombstones and memorial tablets convinced him that he could make a living from letter-cutting and monumental masonry: 'I managed to hit on something which no one else was doing and which quite a lot of people wanted' (Gill, *Autobiography*, 117). He gave up his pupillage with Caroë and confidently married Ethel, known lovingly as Ettie, in the sub-deanery church of St Peter in Chichester on 6 August 1904. His father officiated at the ceremony.

'Eric Gill, Calligrapher', as he was entered in the register, started married life in a small tenement flat in Battersea Bridge Buildings, moving in 1905 to 20 Black Lion Lane in Hammersmith, close to Kelmscott House, once the home of William Morris, and to Morris's Kelmscott Press. Hammersmith was still an enclave of the arts and crafts, and especially the printing crafts. The Gills' move had been precipitated by the birth of their first child, Elizabeth (Betty), on 1 June 1905; a second daughter, Petra, followed on 18 August 1906.

Gill had acquired an important German client, Count Harry Kessler, a connoisseur of printing, who commissioned him to design the title-pages for a special edition of Goethe's *Schiller*, to be published by Insel Verlag, Leipzig. This and subsequent commissions from Kessler brought Gill a new involvement with fine print. In 1906 he started wood-engraving. He returned to the Central School, this time as a teacher, and was also giving classes in masonry and lettering to stonemasons at the Paddington Institute.

In this hopeful period of relative prosperity, Gill took on his first apprentice, Joseph Cribb, and he and Ethel felt able to afford a maid-of-all-work, Lizzie, whose duties soon included sleeping with her master. 'First time of fornication since marriage', runs a characteristically accurate and candid entry in his diary for 14 June 1906 (diary, University of California, Los Angeles). He also acquired the first of many mistresses, Lillian Meacham, with whom in 1907, in spite of Ethel's disapproval, he set off on an ecstatic architectural visit to the cathedral in Chartres.

Though by now well known in London art and socialist circles, a member of the Fabian Society, the Arts and Crafts Exhibition Society, the Art Workers' Guild, Gill's iconoclasm and uncouthness set him apart from the cliquish craftsman followers of Morris. He remained to a great extent an outsider, an extremist—in his own later words, the stranger in a strange land. In the summer of 1907 he struck out on his own again, resettling his workshop, wife, and children in the countryside, acting out his conviction that 'life and work and love and the bringing up of a family and clothes and social virtues and food and houses and games and songs and books should all be in the soup together' (Gill, introduction to *Engravings*, 1929). Gill's move to Sussex was the first of several attempts to create the idyllically integrated life.

Ditchling village, 1907–1913 Gill's first six years in Ditchling were spent at Sopers, a small brick house in the main street of the village. He set up his workshop alongside the house. At this period Gill branched out from letter-cutting to sculpture. His first carving in stone, *Estin Thalassa*, of the maiden of the eternal seas, was made in late 1909, a time of 'comparative continence' while Ethel was pregnant with their third daughter, Joanna, born on 1 February 1910. Gill regarded the creation of his substitute woman of stone as a natural development from inscriptional carving: this new job was the same job, only the letters were different ones. 'A new alphabet—the word was made flesh' (Gill, *Autobiography*, 159).

Gill's approach to sculpture was essentially a craftsman's in its directness and its feeling for materials. He rejected the usual 'modelling-and-pointing machine' techniques, whereby the sculptor's clay model was enlarged by mechanical means by an artisan assistant, disliking the division of labour this entailed. The primitive power of Gill's early carvings drew admiration not only from Count Kessler but also from Roger Fry and William Rothenstein. Through Rothenstein, Gill met the philosopher and critic Ananda Coomaraswamy, expert in the arts and crafts of India, and eagerly absorbed Coomaraswamy's theories of the essential sacredness of sensual art. Coomaraswamy's aphorism 'An artist is not a special kind of man, but every man is a special kind of artist' (*The Transformation of Nature in Art*, 1934, 64) was quoted by Gill so often most people have imagined Gill originated it.

Count Kessler had arranged for Gill to become an apprentice–assistant to the famous French sculptor Aristide Maillol. Gill went to visit Maillol in Marly-le-Roi but realized quickly that their methods were incompatible. His allegiances were now with Jacob Epstein, Augustus John, and a small group of radical young London artists anxious to form a community based on the 'new religion', with quasi-primitive emphasis on sun worship and worship of the fecund female body. Until it exploded into the acrimony that ended many of Eric Gill's male relationships, his friendship with Epstein was particularly close, and together they planned a sequence of immense carved human figures looming over the Sussex landscape like a twentieth-century Stonehenge. This grandiose configuration did not materialize.

Gill himself, with his peculiar combination of the mischievous and solemn, was pushing out the boundaries between the acceptable and unacceptable, in personal behaviour as in art. His sister Gladys and her husband, Ernest Laughton, were the models for the realistic carving which Gill entitled *Fucking* (1911). (This work, retitled *Ecstasy*, is now in the Tate collection.) While the sculpture was in progress, Gill was embarking on the incestuous relationship with Gladys that continued for most of his adult life. It is almost certain he had sexual relations with his sister Angela, and possibly with other sisters too. Another carving of this period, *Votes for Women* (1910), shows the act of intercourse with woman ascendant, man kneeling to receive her. It was bought for £5 by Maynard Keynes. When his brother asked him how his staff reacted, Keynes replied, 'My staff are trained not to believe their eyes' (MacCarthy, 104).

In January 1911 Eric Gill's first one-man exhibition of stone carvings was held at the Chenil Gallery in Chelsea. It was well reviewed. Gill's small mother-and-child figures made an especially strong impression on the critic Arthur Clutton-Brock, who praised the 'simplicity and force' with which Gill expressed the instinct of maternity (*The Times*, 17 Jan 1911). Two relief carvings—*Crucifixion* and *A Roland for an Oliver*—were purchased by the Contemporary Art Society. The following year Gill received a commission from Madame Strindberg for designs for her soon notorious new night-club, the Cave of the Golden Calf, off Regent Street. His spectacularly phallic calf was the motif recurring on the membership card and the bas-relief hung at the entrance of the club, finally appearing in three-dimensional form, gilded and mounted on a pedestal. Gill's resplendent Golden Calf was among seven of his sculptures shown in Roger Fry's 'Second Post-Impressionist Exhibition'.

Gill had growing misgivings about his success in the London 'high art' world, which he came to regard as a corrupt and, to a serious artist, a demeaning system dependent 'upon the ability of art dealers, assisted by art-critics, to preserve a hot-house culture in the midst of an inhuman and anti-human industrialism' (Gill, *Autobiography*, 177). It offended his religious sensitivities. Gill was now emerging from his period of strident agnosticism followed by Nietzscheism, and gradually moving towards Roman Catholicism. In 1911 he visited the abbey of Mont César in Louvain, where his first experience of hearing monastic plainchant brought him to an overwhelming moment of religious certitude: 'I knew, infallibly, that God existed and was a living God—just as I knew him in the answering smile of a child or in the living words of Christ' (ibid., 187). On 22 February 1913 he and his wife—who now took the name of Mary—went to Brighton to be received into the Roman Catholic church.

Ditchling Common, 1913–1924 In the year of his conversion Gill and his family moved out to Ditchling Common, 2 miles north of the village. Here their house, Hopkins Crank, had outbuildings and farming land. Gill was intent on a life of medieval self-sufficiency in which the family produced its own food, baked its bread, made its own clothes, and educated its daughters at home. Gill's apprentice Joseph Cribb also became a Roman Catholic. As other Catholic craft workers were attracted to the common, it became an enclave of determinedly unworldly attitudes to life, combining fervent work and worship. As described by one resident, Gill at Ditchling had reverted to 'a fascinating sort of communal early Christianity' (P. Anson, *Aylesford Review*, spring 1965).

Gill's new Catholic credentials qualified him for the substantial commission, in 1913, for the fourteen carved stone stations of the cross for Westminster Cathedral. These occupied him for the next five years, exempting him from service in the First World War. The Westminster stations, controversial in their day on account of their painful rawness, now appear among the most impressive of Gill's large-scale sculptural works. He was his own model for Christ in the tenth station, having drawn his portrait in the mirror. Gill was to carve further sequences of stations for St Cuthbert's Church in Bradford, commissioned by his friend Father John O'Connor in 1921, and for St Alban's, Oxford, in 1938.

The early years on Ditchling Common saw a surge of activity in the graphic arts. Gill was stimulated, first, by the arrival in Ditchling of Edward Johnston, with whom he co-operated in the development of sans serif lettering for London Underground, precursor of Gill's own famous sans serif type design. In 1915 they were joined by Douglas (later Hilary) Pepler, whom both had known in Hammersmith. Pepler brought with him a Stanhope hand press, which had once belonged to William Morris, and in 1916 founded St Dominic's Press, the most ebullient if not the most technically sophisticated of the private presses of the period. It drew much of its character from Gill's engravings and his marvellous dexterity in combining the type and the image on the page. Together he and Pepler printed books and pro-Catholic, anti-capitalist pamphlets, which they distributed by hand, and combined in producing the idiosyncratic magazine *The Game*. It was, for a time, an all-involving friendship. 'Those are pleasant days', wrote Gill, 'when young men and men in the prime of their life argue and debate about the divine mysteries and concoct great schemes for the building of new societies, and they were pleasant days for us' (Gill, *Autobiography*, 206).

Eric Gill, with his intense respect for the male hierarchies, was anxious for a son. After a history of miscarriages, Mary was now unlikely to conceive, and in the autumn of 1917 the Gills took in an eight-month-old boy, an illegitimate child from an infants' home in Haywards Heath. He was not legally adopted, but was known as Gordian Gill and brought up as the Gills' son.

The following summer Gill was finally called up and spent the last few months of the war as a driver in the RAF mechanical transport camp at Blandford, Dorset, enduring military service with a tolerance curiously at odds with his later pacifist stance. From the end of the First World War, war memorials formed the staple of Gill's major sculptural commissions, the most impressive being those at Bryantspuddle (1918), Chirk and South Harting (1919), Trumpington, near Cambridge, and the huge lettered wall panel recording 228 names of the fallen in the ante-chapel at New College, Oxford (both 1921).

Over the war years Gill had become closely involved with the Dominican order, and in particular with Father Vincent McNabb, a forceful Dominican priest whom he first met at a luncheon party in Edinburgh in 1914. Influenced by Father Vincent, Eric Gill, his wife, Mary, Hilary Pepler, and Gill's new protégé-apprentice Desmond Chute, became members of the third order of St Dominic, the lay order of the Dominicans. In January 1919 at Hawkesyard Priory, Gill 'put on the habit' for the first time. He took to wearing the girdle of chastity with his monastic dress. 'Much good it did him', said a cynical friend (MacCarthy, 143).

The Catholic craft community at Ditchling now developed energetically, in accordance with Father Vincent's dictum that there can be no mysticism without asceticism. Ditchling Common was marked out as a place of austere holiness by the Spoil Bank Cross, a large wooden calvary erected on a hillock beside the London to Brighton railway line. At the centre of the complex of workshops was the chapel, designed by Gill, now prior of the order, where the office was said at regular intervals through the working day.

Philosophically, Ditchling was underpinned by the theories of the French Roman Catholic intellectual Jacques Maritain, great twentieth-century interpreter of St Thomas Aquinas, whose *Art et scolastique* was published in its new English translation as *Art and Scholasticism* at the St Dominic's Press. The craft Guild of Sts Joseph and Dominic was founded on the premise that all work is ordained by God and is therefore divine worship. The members, obeying distributist tenets of individual responsibility, owned their own tools, workshops, and the products of their work. By 1922 forty-one Catholics were living and working on the common. Some were professional craftspeople. Some were lost young men of the post-war generation, in search of a vocation. Among these was the artist David Jones.

Ditchling became a place of pilgrimage, an inspiring demonstration of Catholic family values. One visitor was convinced he saw a nimbus around Gill's head and shoulders as he sat at table. The realities of Ditchling life were not so reassuring. Entries in Gill's private diaries, made public in 1989, show repeated incidents of incest with his elder daughters Betty and Petra, a pattern of behaviour also said to have been present in his father, Arthur Tidman Gill. At this same period Gill was making a series of nude drawings of his teenage daughter Petra which were the basis of the most exquisite of his wood-engravings. One of Gill's favourite sayings was 'It all goes together' (E. Gill, *Last Essays*, 1942, 176). But there was an increasingly obvious dichotomy between his public persona and private morality.

Gill's justification for sexual latitude was that sexual pleasure was an aspect of worship. 'Man is matter and spirit—both real and both good' (E. Gill, *In a Strange Land*, 1944, 152). He developed an elaborate theory of human love as the participation in and glorification of divine love. The erect phallus had a powerful symbolism as the image of God's potency. Gill's own holy pictures acquired a new sexual candour alarming to many of his previous admirers: especially scandalous was his wood-engraving

The Nuptials of God (1922), depicting Christ on the cross in the voluptuous embrace of his bride, the Roman Catholic church. Gill courted further controversy with his Leeds University war memorial *Christ Driving the Moneychangers from the Temple* (1923), a blatantly tactless attack on capitalist commercialism.

In 1924 Gill resigned from the Guild of Sts Joseph and Dominic and the family left Ditchling, peremptorily and finally. The ostensible reason was that Gill had found so many visitors intrusive. Stronger motivations were a bitter quarrel with Pepler over guild finances, and Gill's resentment of the love affair between his daughter Betty and Pepler's son David, to whose marriage he finally, reluctantly assented in 1927.

Capel-y-ffin, 1924–1928 In August 1924 the Gills and a small entourage of followers and animals arrived at the former Benedictine monastery at Capel-y-ffin in the Black Mountains of Wales. The place had been chosen by Gill for its beauty and remoteness, 14 miles from Abergavenny and 10 from the nearest railway station. The rural isolation gave scope to Eric Gill's contemplative and analytic urges: he began to articulate the views on art and society, religion and sex, that poured out into his writings over the next decade. If Ditchling had been the period of his 'spiritual schooldays', then Capel represented 'spiritual puberty' (Gill, *Autobiography*, 223).

Gill, in his early forties, had lost the youthful scrubbiness that alienated some of his contemporaries and was already taking on the appearance of the patriarch, customarily dressed in a belted knee-length rough tweed tunic, which many mistook for a monk's habit, and often to be seen in the stonemason's traditional square folded paper hat. Count Harry Kessler, resuming the collaboration with Gill that had been severed by the First World War, now found him 'a Tolstoy-like figure in smock and cloak, half monk, half peasant' (H. Kessler, *Diary of a Cosmopolitan*, 1971, entry for 20 Jan 1925). Gill's special form of rational dress, the charm and persuasiveness of his personality, and his extraordinary quality of concentration come over in a series of portrait photographs taken at Capel-y-ffin by Howard Coster and now in the National Portrait Gallery.

Artistically, the four years at Capel were productive. Although facilities for carving large works were non-existent, and the monolithic female figure named *Mankind* (1928) was made in a borrowed studio in Chelsea, some of Gill's most beautiful and engaging smaller carvings emanate from Capel. They include the lovely sequence of naiads with frondy hair; the vulnerable image of *The Sleeping Christ* (1925); the black marble torso entitled *Deposition* (1925), now at King's School, Canterbury, described by Gill as 'about the only carving of mine I'm not sorry about' (Gill, *Autobiography*, 219). In Wales he also completed his only substantial carving in wood, the war memorial altarpiece in oak relief for Rossall School (1927).

Gill's wood-engraving burgeoned in the mid-1920s. At Capel he began printing his own engravings, experimenting with a copperplate press, and he started an enormously successful and enjoyable collaboration with Robert Gibbings, proprietor of the Golden Cockerel Press, and his wife, Moira. With Gill's insistence on the merging of work with leisure, this became a tripartite amatory collaboration too. The most important Golden Cockerel editions for which Eric Gill provided the engravings were *The Song of Songs* (1925), *Troilus and Criseyde* (1927), *The Canterbury Tales* (1928), and *The Four Gospels* of 1931—Gill's and Gibbings's *tour de force*. No other wood-engraver of the period comes near to Gill's originality and verve. But, once again, the explicit eroticism of *The Song of Songs* and of Gill's later illustrations for E. Powys Mather's *Procreant Hymn* of 1926 shocked many of his former supporters and drew puzzled reproaches from the Dominicans.

The most influential of Gill's commissions at Capel-y-ffin came from his fellow Catholic Stanley Morison, typographic adviser to the Monotype Corporation. The typefaces designed by Gill for Monotype—Perpetua (1925), Gill Sans-serif (1927 onwards), Solus (1929)—remain his greatest achievement: ironically so, since they were designed for the machine production Gill so despised. Gill Sans can be considered the first truly modern typeface, and it had a lasting impact on twentieth-century European type design.

Gill, devotee of the excursion, made long-ranging expeditions out from the Black Mountains: to Rome in 1925, to Paris in 1926. He made several visits to Salies-de-Béarn, a spa town in the Pyrenees. The family spent winter 1926–7 there, staying in the house belonging to Gill's current secretary–mistress–model, Elizabeth Bill. Miss Bill and her elderly fiancé were also of the household. Salies-de-Béarn became established in Gill's pantheon as an ideal little city, active, religious, decorous, of a kind that, in Britain, was ceasing to exist.

Pigotts, 1928–1940 In October 1928 Gill made his final move: to Pigotts, near Speen, 5 miles from High Wycombe. The quadrangular assembly of local redbrick farm buildings, with an ancient pigsty in the centre, made a more practical environment than Capel-y-ffin for work that now derived increasingly from London. Gill's 1928 solo exhibition at the Goupil Gallery was critically and financially successful, and he had recently been commissioned by the architect Charles Holden to lead the team of sculptors working on the London Underground headquarters at St James's Park. The regime at Pigotts was less that of the formalized religious community, more that of the devout extended family, with its chapel and resident chaplain. The Gills' second daughter, Petra, lived at Pigotts after her marriage, in 1930, to Denis Tegetmeier, the engraver and cartoonist, as did their youngest daughter, Joanna, and her husband, René Hague. Gill set up the Hague and Gill press with his son-in-law in 1931.

The Pigotts years were dominated by a number of large-scale commissions for sculpture which brought Gill increasingly into the public eye. The popular press identified his ambiguity, referring to him as 'the Married Monk'. In 1931 he began his famous series of carvings for the new

BBC building in London, culminating in the giant figures of Shakespeare's Prospero and Ariel above the portals, transformed by Gill into God the Father and Son. After public complaints to the BBC governors about the size of Ariel's genitals, the headmaster of a well-known public school was brought in to adjudicate, and Gill was instructed to reduce them in scale. In 1933 he provided decorations for Oliver Hill's modernist Midland Hotel at Morecambe: the big stone relief for the dining room, *Odysseus Welcomed from the Sea by Nausicaa*, shows Gill in his most supple and inventive mid-1930s mode.

In 1934 Gill travelled to Jerusalem, to carve reliefs on the new archaeological museum; his first visit to the Holy Land impressed him deeply. In 1935 the British government commissioned him to carve a large relief for the assembly hall of the new League of Nations building in Geneva. His original proposal, for an international version of his controversial Leeds *Moneychangers* carving, did not find favour, and Gill substituted a grandiose but no less politically charged design influenced by Michelangelo, depicting the 're-creation of man by God' (Collins, 211). He finished the 9 metre three-panel relief *in situ* and attended the unveiling in August 1938.

The nature of Gill's workshop had altered fundamentally. Laurie Cribb, brother of Joseph, a supremely skilled letter-cutter who had come with Gill from Capel, remained his much-valued personal assistant. But there was now a changing population of pupil–assistants, not necessarily Catholic. The structure was more formal. Gill called them by their forenames; they called him Sir. Visitors compared the atmosphere to that of a Renaissance atelier. Many of Gill's apprentices—notably Donald Potter, Walter Ritchie, David Kindersley, and Ralph Beyer—became well-known sculptors and letter-cutters in their own right. Gill's nephew, the sculptor John Skelton, joined the workshop as a trainee in the final months before Gill's death.

In the 1930s Gill designed five more typefaces: Golden Cockerel Roman (1930) for Robert Gibbings; Joanna (1930), designed originally for Hague and Gill, later adapted for machine production by Monotype; Aries (1932) for Fairfax Hall's private Stourton Press; Jubilee (1934) for Stephenson Blake; and Bunyan (1934) for Hague and Gill, a version of which was issued under the name Pilgrim by Linotype in 1953. Joanna, named in honour of his youngest daughter, is considered by many specialists to be the finest of all Gill's type designs. He also designed Hebrew and Arabic typefaces. His informative and sprightly *Introduction to Typography* was published in 1931. The Post Office commissioned Gill to provide lettering for stamps of the values ½d. to 6d. issued for George VI's coronation in 1937. He continued wood-engraving, Gill's bookplates for his friends being among the most delightful of his works.

Eric Gill had an unusual ability for working in both two and three dimensions, and on variable scales. At this same period he returned to architecture, replanning and rebuilding with the boys of Blundell's School at Tiverton a chapel with a central altar (1938), designed with the aim of democratizing churchgoers' participation in the mass—a radical and influential innovation. The same plan was adopted for St Peter's, Gorleston-on-Sea, in Norfolk, the only complete building designed by Eric Gill. This austere and quasi-primitive Roman Catholic church was built in brick by local craftsmen, with curved arches forming an octagonal centre space.

Gill's published essays and lectures, spasmodic in his early days, became a steady stream, beginning with *Art-Nonsense* in 1929. The frontispiece of this book is designed around a version of Gill's *Belle sauvage* wood-engraving, showing a nude woman emerging from a thicket, for which the model was Mrs Beatrice Warde, American-born publicity manager to Monotype. Warde, for years Gill's intellectual sparring partner and his lover, was the most sophisticated of the women in his life.

Gill's next books *Art and a Changing Civilisation* and *Money and Morals* followed in 1934; *Work and Leisure* in 1935; *The Necessity of Belief*, Gill's most considered and convincing argument of faith, in 1936; *Work and Property* in 1937. Eric Gill's *Last Essays* was published posthumously in 1942, and a further collection, *In a Strange Land*, in 1944.

In a sense, these books were all the same book, imbued with Gill's peculiar blend of Ruskinian morality, William Morris utopianism, Thomist philosophy, and bumptious common sense, whether arguing pro-nudity and sunbathing or anti-contraception ('masturbation *à deux*') and the wearing of trousers on the grounds that these constricted and dishonoured 'man's most precious ornament' (E. Gill, *Trousers*, 1937). Though Gill's private conversation could be gentle and delicious, his forceful repetitiousness in public was compared by D. H. Lawrence to that of a workman 'argefying' in a pub (*Book Collector's Quarterly*, October 1933).

In the mid-1930s Gill's views moved further leftward, driven by his sense that the logical conclusion of Catholicism could only be a form of communism. He joined the Artists' International Association, the Christian Arts International, PAX, the Peace Pledge Union, becoming a familiar figure on the anti-fascist protest platforms of the period, 'speaking in a light voice, with a dry wit, above his Biblical beard' (*News Chronicle*, 8 Jan 1938). Gill's support for workers' control of the means of production and, as the Second World War drew nearer, his high profile support for pacifism brought him into direct confrontation with the Roman Catholic church.

Gradually, Gill's health was breaking down. In 1930 he spent several weeks in hospital following a mysterious nervous collapse. A succession of illnesses and accidents assailed him after his return from Jerusalem, exacerbated by his arduous workload and growing financial worries in supporting his multitude of dependants: the Gills had eleven grandchildren by the end of the decade. His son Gordian had disappointed Gill's expectations, and a permanent rift arose between them after Gordian discovered by accident that he had been adopted. Domestic dramas were intense as Gill fell in love again—with Daisy Hawkins, teenage daughter of the Gills' housekeeper, an affair he pursued in tandem with a longer-standing sexual relationship with May Reeves, the schoolmistress at Pigotts.

Gill's passionate and yearning love for Daisy, who was eventually banished by Mary to Capel-y-ffin, is captured in the many drawings he made of her, published in *Twenty-Five Nudes* (1938) and *Drawings from Life* (1940).

Gill became an honorary associate of the Royal Institute of British Architects in 1935, a royal designer for industry in 1936, an associate of the Royal Academy in 1937. His acceptance of honours from just the establishment art institutions he had formerly despised can be read as symptomatic of his increasing exhaustion. He drove himself in his work on the sculptures for his friend Sir Edward Maufe's new cathedral at Guildford, carving the figure of St John the Baptist *in situ* on the scaffold from October to December 1939.

Through summer 1940 Gill was seriously ill, first with German measles, then with congestion of the lung. He had been (and remained) an inveterate smoker, demonstrating working-class solidarity by rolling his own cigarettes. The onset of the Second World War depressed him beyond measure. In bed or in a deckchair in the garden, wrapped in a rug, he wrote his *Autobiography* (1940), an endearing, nostalgic ramble through his life that only hinted at facts he had earlier seemed on the brink of disclosing: 'I do not see how my kind of life, which is not that of a big game hunter, could be written without intimate details', he had told his publisher in 1933 (MS, Cape archive, University of Reading).

Lung cancer was diagnosed in October 1940. He refused the proposal of a pneumectomy and died in Harefield Hospital, Uxbridge, in the middle of a heavy air raid in the early morning of 17 November 1940. The funeral was held four days later at Pigotts, in the Gills' family chapel. Requiem mass was said according to the Roman rites. Gill's body was then transported in a farm cart for burial in the churchyard of the Baptist church at Speen, a curious reconnection with his dissenting ancestors. He had left characteristically exact instructions for his gravestone, allowing space for Mary. The inscription was cut by Laurie Cribb.

Gill's last major work of sculpture, the stone altarpiece for the English martyrs in St George's Chapel, Westminster Cathedral, was incomplete at his death, remaining at Pigotts through the war. In 1947, when it was eventually set in place, the small carved monkey, mischievously placed by Gill clinging to the bottom edge of the robes of Sir Thomas More, had been removed, presumably on the instructions of Westminster Cathedral authorities.

Reputation Gill's declared intention was to 'have done something towards reintegrating bed and board, the small farm and the workshop, the home and school, earth and heaven' (Gill, *Autobiography*, 282). The energy and solemnity with which he pursued his ideals of integration were not negated by Gill's fallibilities and contradictions.

After the initial shock, especially within the Roman Catholic community, as Gill's history of adulteries, incest, and experimental connection with his dog became public knowledge in the late 1980s, the consequent reassessment of his life and art left his artistic reputation strengthened. Gill emerged as one of the twentieth century's strangest and most original controversialists, a sometimes infuriating, always arresting spokesman for man's continuing need of God in an increasingly materialistic civilization, and for intellectual vigour in an age of encroaching triviality.

Gill's reinvention of a 'holy tradition of workmanship', in the sense of a return to ideals of hand making and personal responsibility, helped to shape the individual workshop movement as it developed in Britain from the early 1970s, Gill's influence being particularly obvious on the flourishing craft of letter-cutting. His reputation as a sculptor was much strengthened by a series of exhibitions in the 1990s, in particular by his first large-scale retrospective, held at the Barbican Art Gallery in 1992. This finally defined Gill not simply as the twentieth century's leading British Roman Catholic artist, but as a key figure in early modernism, a superb advocate for the techniques of 'direct carving' later taken up by such sculptors as Frank Dobson, Barbara Hepworth, and Henry Moore.

FIONA MACCARTHY

Sources E. Gill, *Autobiography* (1940) · F. MacCarthy, *Eric Gill* (1989) · R. Speaight, *The life of Eric Gill* (1966) · D. Attwater, *A cell of good living: the life, work and opinions of Eric Gill* (1969) · M. Yorke, *Eric Gill: man of flesh and spirit* (1981) · E. Gill, *Bibliography of Eric Gill* (1953) · J. Collins, *Eric Gill, the sculpture: a catalogue raisonné* (1998) · C. Skelton, *The engravings of Eric Gill* (1983) · E. Gill, *The inscriptional work of Eric Gill: an inventory* (1964) · R. Harling, *The letter forms and type designs of Eric Gill* (1976) · D. Peace, *Eric Gill, the inscriptions: a descriptive catalogue* (1994) · *Pax* (spring 1941) · *Blackfriars* (Feb 1941) [Eric Gill memorial number] · *The Tablet* (30 Nov 1940) · R. Heppenstall, *Four absentees* (1960) · D. Kindersley, *Eric Gill: further thoughts by an apprentice* (1982) · D. Potter, *My time with Eric Gill* (1980) · W. Shewring, 'Considerations on Eric Gill', *Making and thinking* (1957) · J. K. M. R. [J. K. M. Rothenstein], *Eric Gill* (1927) · J. Thorp, *Eric Gill* (1929) · R. Brewer, *Eric Gill: the man who loved letters* (1973) · S. Carter, 'Eric Gill', *Twentieth century type designers* (1987) · b. cert. [Ethel Moore, wife] · m. cert. · d. cert. [Mary Ethel Gill, wife]

Archives Blackfriars, George Square, Edinburgh, Dominican archives · Boston PL, corresp. and papers · St Bride Institute, London, St Bride Printing Library · U. Cal., Los Angeles, William Andrew Clark Memorial Library, corresp., diaries, and papers · U. Cal., San Francisco, corresp. and papers · U. Texas, collection, incl. important notes of work · W. Sussex RO, collection | BL, corresp. with G. K. Chesterton, F. A. Chesterton, and others, Add. MS 73195, fols. 86–115 · BL, corresp. with Sir Sydney Cockerell, Add. MS 52716 · Centre for the Study of Sculpture, Leeds, Henry Moore Institute, letters to Joseph Cribb · Harvard U., Houghton L., letters to Sir William Rothenstein · NL Scot., letters to André Raffalovich · Tate collection, list of books printed by him and René Hague, and papers · V&A NAL, questionnaire completed for Kineton Parks | FILM BFI NFTVA, 'Eric Gill, 1882–1940', J. Muir, LWT (1983) | SOUND BBC, Eric Gill sound archives

Likenesses E. Gill, self-portrait, pen and ink, 1908, U. Cal., Los Angeles, Clark Library · photograph, *c.*1908–1909, Ransom HRC · E. Gill, two self-portraits, wood-engraving, 1908–27, V&A · W. Rothenstein, oils, *c.*1913, NPG · W. Rothenstein, chalk drawing, 1921, NPG · H. Coster, photographs, 1927, NPG · E. Gill, self-portrait, engraving, 1927, Ransom HRC [*see illus.*] · E. Gill, self-portrait, pencil, 1927, NPG · E. Gill, self-portrait, wood-engraving, 1927, NPG · D. Jones, watercolour and pencil drawing, 1930, NMG Wales · H. Coster, photographs, 1935, NPG · D. Chute, pencil drawing, *c.*1938, NPG · photographs, repro. in *The Bystander* (30 Oct 1940) · steel medal, NPG

Gill, John (1697–1771), Particular Baptist minister and theologian, was born of poor parents, Edward Gill, a woollen merchant, and Elizabeth Walker, at Kettering, Northamptonshire, on 23 November 1697. He spent a very short time at Kettering grammar school, and his formal education ended at the age of eleven. Soon after his baptism on 1 November 1716, Gill began preaching. He spent a few months in 1718 helping the Baptist congregation at Higham Ferrers, Northamptonshire, where he met and married that year Elizabeth Negus (*d.* 1764). In 1719 he moved to the Baptist congregation at Horselydown, Southwark, where he was ordained on 22 March 1720.

By 1740 Gill was fast becoming the leading theological spokesman for the Particular Baptists in both Great Britain and America. Critical in establishing his reputation were his *Exposition of the Book of Solomon's Song* (1728); *A Treatise on the Doctrine of the Trinity* (1731), that was designed to check the spread of Sabellianism, a heresy among the Baptists that asserted that the Trinity was one person, not three; and *The Cause of God and Truth* (4 vols., 1735–8), which was a major defence of the five points of Calvinism. Cementing that reputation was his *magnum opus*, the *Exposition of the Old and New Testaments*, which employed his extensive rabbinical learning. The New Testament portion appeared in three volumes in 1746–8; the Old Testament, in 6 folio volumes, was completed in 1766. This work and his *Body of Doctrinal and Practical Divinity* (1769–70) became a standard part of the library of most Baptist ministers of the day. In 1748 he received a DD from Marischal College, Aberdeen. Gill died at Gracechurch Street, Camberwell, where he lived, on 14 October 1771, and was buried in Bunhill Fields. His successor as minister to his congregation was John Rippon, whose *Memoir* of Gill was published in 1838. MICHAEL A. G. HAYKIN

Sources J. Rippon, *A brief memoir of the life and writings of the late Rev. John Gill, D.D.* (1838) • M. A. G. Haykin, ed., *The life and thought of John Gill (1697–1771): a tercentennial appreciation* (1997) • T. George, 'John Gill', *Baptist theologians*, ed. T. George and D. S. Dockery (1990)

Archives Metropolitan Tabernacle, London, church minute books, Horselydown Baptist Church

Likenesses G. Vertue, engraving, 1748 (after J. Highmore junior), BM, NPG • J. Wright, mezzotint, pubd 1770 (after M. Chamberlain), BM • portrait, Metropolitan Tabernacle, London

Gill, Joseph (1675–1742), builder and Quaker minister, was born on 10 March 1675 at Skelton, in Cumberland, to Quaker parents, William Gill, who may have been a builder, and Margaret, daughter of Robert Warton of Cumberland. From an early age he found himself torn between the desire to play with other children and the 'connections of the spirit or Grace of God in my own heart' (Gill), which he considered incompatible with the playing of ball games or of cards. At the age of sixteen he implored his father to remove him from the temptations of the town, and the family settled on an estate at How, near Castlesowby, in Cumberland.

Aged twenty Gill began his travels and was encouraged by George Bewley, a Quaker living in Ireland, to go to that country to establish himself in business. He found employment with a leading Dublin builder, Benjamin Crawley, where he was able to use the building skills acquired from his father's employees. He supervised workmen in Wexford and subsequently worked on the construction of Burton Hall, in co. Carlow. During this time he was concerned that his spiritual well-being was under threat. While supervising the construction of barracks at Carlow, Tullow, and Athy he felt tempted by the behaviour of the soldiers and, as a result, quit his position as building supervisor and was put in charge of his employer's timber yard in Dublin.

On 24 June 1702 Gill married Isabel Robinson (*d.* 1714), of Cumberland, in the new Quaker meeting-house at Carlisle, following which they set up a grocer's shop in Dublin's Meath Street. Finding this too great a tie Gill established a timber yard nearby, in Cole Alley, and organized it in such a way that he could leave it and travel without the business suffering. He often accompanied English Quakers on their travels in Ireland, at one time being confined to gaol in Dublin for three days because one of his companions had been preaching in the street.

About 1706 Gill became concerned that his business was hindering his spiritual development and his potential to be of service to Quaker preachers. He also began to develop a calling to travel in the ministry but was consumed with doubts as to his abilities, though he was encouraged by a number of older Quakers, including William Edmondson. In the meantime he continued to visit Friends' meetings throughout Ireland and in England, often as a representative of Irish Quakers.

In 1711, when Gill was thirty-six, he had a profound spiritual experience, after which he overcame his reticence and began to preach. His travels in Ireland and England continued, usually in the company of other Quakers, and with every tour he undertook he noted the mileage that he travelled and the number of Friends' meetings that he visited. Early in 1714 he was called back from a tour of Ulster, as his wife was ill; she died soon afterwards, on 8 February, leaving five children. Gill married again on 24 July 1716, his second wife being Anna Durrance (*d.* 1736), of Cumberland; over the next twelve years they had six children, three of whom died young.

Up to the year 1724 Gill wrote an account of his travels, itemizing the places visited but not setting down his beliefs in any detail. In 1723, however, he published a response to an Anabaptist minister who had written a pamphlet condemning Quaker beliefs in relation to baptism by water. Gill's publication demonstrates his breadth of knowledge of the scriptures and of the writings of many key religious commentators.

In the 1730s Gill visited the eastern colonies of North America, and reported back to Friends in Ireland in May 1736. During this tour he had travelled more than 5500 miles and visited almost 400 meetings. He died in Dublin on 28 January 1742, at the age of sixty-six, and was buried there on 30 January. In his will he left property to the value of £817, which included six houses in Cole Alley and two at Frenchay, as well as the house and timber yard in Earl Street, Dublin. ROB GOODBODY

Sources J. Gill, 'Journal, 1697–1724', *c.*1724, Friends Historical Library, Dublin, SR 31D P1 • birth, marriage, and death records of Religious Society of Friends in Ireland, Friends' Historical Library, Dublin • will, NA Ire., T. 6224 • J. Rutty, *A history of the rise and progress of the people called Quakers in Ireland* (1751) • G. J. Willauer, 'Irish Friends report on their missions to America', *Quaker History*, 59 (1970), 15–23 • O. C. Goodbody, 'Irish Quaker diaries', *Journal of the Friends' Historical Society*, 50 (1962–4), 51–64 • P. B. Eustace and O. C. Goodbody, eds., *Quaker records, Dublin: abstracts of wills* (1957)
Archives Religious Society of Friends, Dublin, journal
Wealth at death house and timber yard in Earl Street; two houses at Frenchay; six houses at Cole Alley (Gill Square); a quantity of furniture and other contents; approximately £200 cash; value of property disposed of £817: will, 1742, NA Ire., T. 6224; Eustace and Goodbody, eds., *Quaker records*

Gill, Thomas Patrick (1858–1931), journalist and politician, was born at Ballygraigue, Nenagh, co. Tipperary, on 25 October 1858, the son of Robert Gill, a civil engineer. He was educated by the Christian Brothers in Nenagh and entered Trinity College, Dublin, in January 1876, but he appears not to have graduated. In early life he was greatly influenced by his uncle Peter E. Gill, the founder and proprietor of a Nenagh paper, the *Tipperary Advocate*, and a member of the National Brotherhood of St Patrick, a Fenian organization. Through his uncle's influence, Gill became secretary of the North Tipperary Farmers' Association, a forerunner of the Land League. While still at college, he was sent by E. Dwyer Gray, the owner of the *Freeman's Journal*, to visit the west of Ireland, and he wrote a series of articles, 'The famine fever in the west'. He subsequently worked as associate editor with William O'Brien of *United Ireland*, and in 1881 founded *Tipperary*, a nationalist paper in Thurles, co. Tipperary. After the suppression of the Land League in 1881, Gill went to America and worked in New York as editor of the *Catholic World*, and was hired by the *North American Review* to study land tenure in the United States. He subsequently wrote a series of articles for the *Review* called 'Landlordism in America'.

Gill returned to Ireland in 1885 when, under the patronage of Charles Stewart Parnell, he became home-rule MP for Louth South. In November 1889 Gill went to America with John Dillon, William O'Brien, and Timothy Harrington to raise funds, and at this moment Parnell published his *Manifesto to the Irish People*, which precipitated the split in the Irish party. On his return, Gill took part in negotiations held in Boulogne in an attempt to repair the rift. However, these failed and he decided not to seek re-election in 1892. During this period, he met Horace Plunkett, and became a key figure in Plunkett's work to establish agricultural co-operatives and assistance for industry. In 1895 Gill worked with Plunkett on the recess committee (so-called because it met during parliamentary recess), whose task was to study the Irish economy. Gill reported on developments in state assistance in continental Europe, and as its secretary he wrote the committee's report recommending a system of financial and administrative backing for Irish agriculture. His skilful drafting ensured that the report was adopted unanimously.

In 1898 Plunkett bought the Dublin *Daily Express* and appointed Gill as editor. Here he provided a platform for the Irish literary revival, publishing articles by W. B. Yeats, John Eglinton (W. K. Magee), Lady Gregory, and 'AE' (George Russell); James Joyce reviewed regularly for the paper. In May 1899 Gill was the host of a Dublin banquet for the Irish Literary Theatre, which was satirized by George Moore in *Hail and Farewell*, likening Plunkett and Gill to Flaubert's clerks, Bouvard and Pecuchet. The experiment with the *Daily Express* lasted just over a year, for, in 1900, Gill was appointed secretary to the newly formed department of agriculture and technical instruction, again headed by Plunkett, where he remained until 1923. During the last ten years of his life, he was a member of committees that considered various aspects of Irish agriculture and forestry. He negotiated the removal of the American government's embargo on the import of Irish potatoes, and during the First World War was a member of war committees for the supply and distribution of food and materials for agricultural and industrial production. He ended public life as president of the Irish Free State central savings committee.

Gill's background and his linguistic ability (he spoke French and Italian fluently) led to his appointment as one of the original members of the general assembly of the International Institute of Agriculture in Rome. He was a member of the council of the Ligue Internationale pour l'Éducation Familiale in Brussels, and a corresponding member of the French Academy of Agriculture. He wrote a pamphlet on the constitutions of the British empire, and his translation of a book by L. Paul-Dubois on the Irish question was published in 1934. Plunkett described Gill as 'a practical Thomas Davis' (quoted in West, 42); Gill's political connections provided Plunkett with an essential link with the nationalists. He was called 'neutral Gill' because of his tendency to go with the majority, and although his politics were on the moderate wing of nationalism he was frequently attacked by Unionists, who prevented his appointment to the constitutional convention of 1917 chaired by Plunkett.

In 1882 Gill married Annie, daughter of John Fennell; they lived in Dún Laoghaire, co. Dublin. He died on 19 January 1931 in the Whitworth Hospital, Dublin.

MARIE-LOUISE LEGG

Sources *WW* • T. West, *Horace Plunkett: co-operation and politics* (1986) • *The Times* (20 Jan 1931) • *Irish Independent* (20 Jan 1931) • G. Moore, *Hail and farewell! A trilogy: ave, salve, vale*, 3 vols. (1911–14) • R. B. O'Brien, *The life of Charles Stewart Parnell*, 2 vols. (1898)
Archives NL Ire., corresp. and papers • TCD, corresp. and papers | NL Ire., letters to John Redmond • Plunkett Foundation, Long Hanborough, Oxfordshire, Plunkett MSS • TCD, corresp. with John Dillon
Likenesses S. Purser, oils, 1898, NG Ire. • S. P. Hall, pencil sketch, NG Ire.
Wealth at death £82 14*s*. 7*d*.: administration, 17 Aug 1931, *CGPLA Éire*

Gill, William John (1843–1882), explorer and army officer, son of Major Robert Gill, Madras army, was born at Bangalore. He is known to have had one brother and one sister. He was educated at Brighton College, where one of his contemporaries was Augustus Margary, later his precursor in travel from China to the Irawadi. From Brighton he went to the Royal Military Academy at Woolwich, and obtained a commission in the Royal Engineers in 1864. Between September 1869 and March 1871 he served in India, and was then stationed until 1876 at Aldershot, Chatham, and Woolwich; but just before his return to England in 1871 a relative left him a considerable fortune, which enabled him to become an explorer.

Gill first became known as a traveller when he joined Colonel Valentine Baker's journey to Persia, described by Baker in 1876 in *Clouds in the East*. Between April and December 1873 the party travelled to Tiflis and Baku, and thence across the Caspian to Asterabad, intending to explore the Atrak valley. Disappointed in this, they went to Tehran and explored the Alborz Mountains north of that city, crossing the range by a pass at 12,000 feet; then skirting Mount Damavand they descended into the dense forests of Mazandaran, and, recrossing the mountains to Damghan, followed the northern border of the desert of Khorasan, and after visiting Mashhad struck north to Kalat. From here they passed on to the Dar-e-gaz district and, recrossing the great frontier range, explored the upper course of the Atrak, and thence went south-west to Emamrud, and rejoined the high road from Mashhad to Tehran. The survey made by Gill under great difficulties in this expedition considerably added to the geographical knowledge of the area, and was described by him at the Belfast meeting of the British Association in 1874, and published in the *Geographical Magazine* (1874).

In 1874 Gill stood unsuccessfully for Hackney as a Conservative. Six years later he stood for Nottingham, but was again unsuccessful. In 1876 he was ordered to Hong Kong, and while there obtained leave to travel in China. He reached Peking (Beijing) in September. After a trip in the north of Pecheli to the borders of Liaotung (Liaodong) and the sea terminus of the Great Wall, he ascended the Yangtse as far as Chungking (Chongqing) in Szechwan (Sichuan), with Evelyn Colborne Baber. From Chungking he travelled to Chengtu (Chengdu), the capital of Szechwan, from where he visited the mountains to the north of Szechwan. No European traveller had preceded Gill in that part of China. The journey of some 400 miles brought him into contact with the Mantzu and Xifan people. On his return to Chengtu, Gill started with a Mr Mesny for eastern Tibet and the Irawadi. From Tachienlu (Dajianlu) (8340 feet) he ascended to the summit level of the great Tibetan plateau continuing his journey by Litang (18,280 feet) to Batang (8546 feet) in a tributary valley of the Kinsha; and then, crossing that river, he turned south, travelling parallel to the river to Talifu (Dalifu), the western capital of Yunnan. The route thence to the Irawadi had been already surveyed by Valentine Baker. Having descended the Irawadi, Gill went to Calcutta and back to England, after twenty months of travel. The story of this journey was published in *The River of Golden Sand* (2 vols., 1880), but the scientific results were published in the *Journal of the Royal Geographical Society* (1878), and in a map of forty-two sheets on a scale of half an inch to one mile. In recognition of these he was awarded the gold medal of the Royal Geographical Society in 1879, and that of the Paris Geographical Society in 1880.

On his return to England, Gill was appointed to the intelligence branch of the War Office. In 1879 he was sent to Constantinople as assistant boundary commissioner for the new boundary between Turkey and Russia, consequent on the Berlin treaty. He obtained leave to go to India to join Sir Charles Macgregor, as a survey officer, in his expedition against the Maris, and was mentioned in dispatches. At the end of the expedition Gill embarked at Karachi for Bandar-e-ʿAbbas, and travelled by Sirjan, Kerman, Yazd, and Tehran, to Mashhad. He hoped to get to Merv, but complaints from M. de Giers of English officers haunting the frontier brought about a recall, and he returned to England by Russia, reaching London on 1 April 1881.

In October 1881 Gill was granted leave of absence to explore the provinces between Tunis and Egypt. After waiting in vain in Tripoli for some months for a travel permit he set off without it. He made several interesting journeys from his base in Tripoli, but his plans to travel through the Cyrenaica to Egypt were stopped by the Turkish authorities, and he returned to England via Constantinople, arriving in London on 16 June 1882.

On 21 July 1882 Gill started for Egypt on special service as deputy assistant adjutant-general. While in England he had been employed collecting information for the Admiralty on the Bedouin in the Suez Canal zone, the occupation of which was to be the primary objective of any military intervention in Egypt—a mission not to be prejudiced by Bedouin in the area. After the British bombardment of Alexandria in July 1882, Gill was sent to join Admiral Hoskins at Port Said as an officer in the intelligence department. He was ordered to cut the telegraph wire from Cairo which crossed the desert to al-Arish and Syria and thence to Constantinople, and which was being used by Arabi Pasha, the nationalist leader, to galvanize opposition to British intervention in Egypt, and to the khedive and his supporters. On 6 August, Gill went to Suez, by then under British control, where he met Professor Palmer and Lieutenant Charrington (the flag-lieutenant of the admiral commanding), and they went together into the desert, Palmer and Charrington to go to Nakhl to meet a sheikh from whom they were to purchase camels, and Gill to cut the telegraph. Palmer, who had with him £3000 in English sovereigns, had engaged Meter Abu Sofieh (who falsely claimed to be a head sheikh) to conduct them. Meter planned to rob, if not to murder, them. On their arrival in Wadi Sudr they were attacked by Bedouin, made prisoners, and murdered the next day, 11 August. The knowledge of what took place, the punishment of the murderers, and the recovery of the fragmentary remains of the murdered men were due to Colonel Sir Charles Warren. The remains were sent to England and buried in the crypt of St Paul's Cathedral on 6 April 1883. A stained-glass window was placed in Rochester Cathedral in Gill's memory and his sister founded the Gill Memorial at the Royal Geographical Society for the encouragement of exploration.

R. H. VETCH, *rev.* ELIZABETH BAIGENT

Sources *Parliamentary blue book*, C 3494 (1883) · records of the royal engineers · *CGPLA Eng. & Wales* (1882) · H. R. Mill, *The record of* *the Royal Geographical Society, 1830–1930* (1930) • A. Schölch, *Egypt for the Egyptians: the socio-political crisis in Egypt, 1878–1882* (1981); trans. of *Ägypten den Ägyptern! Die politische und gesellschaftliche Krise der Jahre 1878–1882 in Ägypten* (1972)

Archives RGS, journals in Africa and the East

Likenesses T. B. Wirgman, etching, NPG

Wealth at death £160,563 15*s*. 0*d*.: probate, 6 Dec 1882, *CGPLA Eng. & Wales*

Gilla Cóemáin (*fl.* **1072**), Gaelic poet, was one of the most important medieval Irish learned poets; his floruit derives from a reference within one of his poems, but otherwise practically nothing is known about him apart from his verse. In the last stanza of his longest poem he is called son (or grandson) of Gilla Samthainne ('servant of Samthann'). St Samthann was the saint of Clúain Brónaig (modern Clonbroney, in co. Longford). His own name, which translates as 'servant of Cóemán', probably refers, therefore, to St Cóemán Brecc, of Russagh, Westmeath, which is some 27 miles to the east of Clonbroney. He may thus have belonged to one or other of the midland kingdoms of Mide and Tethbae. Neither his name nor that of his father is attested in the genealogies.

Five poems have been attributed to Gilla Cóemáin with high probability. *Hériu ard inis na rríg* ('Lofty Ireland, island of the kings') catalogues the names of the legendary pre-Christian kings of Ireland, giving the duration of their reigns and the manner of their deaths. The matter of the poem lies close to the eleventh-century stage in the development of the Irish origin-legend, *Lebor Gabála Érenn* ('The book of the taking of Ireland'). Although this legend had been in existence since the late seventh century, the first full version comes from the century before the Norman settlement of Ireland. *At-tá sund forba fessa* ('Herein is the Apex of Knowledge') is effectively a continuation of *Hériu ard*: it catalogues the names of the Christian kings of Ireland from the time of Lóegaire (*fl.* 5th cent.) until that of Brían Bóruma (*d.* 1014), together with the duration of their reigns and the dynasties to which they belonged.

Both these poems perceived the history of Ireland as a sequence of overkings. They thus endorsed the claims of the kings of Tara to be rulers of Ireland. The next poem, *Annálad anall uile* ('All the computation heretofore'), has a wider scope, relating the regnal chronology of pre-Christian Ireland to that of the Near East. The kings of Ireland were thus aligned with the chronological works of Eusebius and Bede. The poem then goes on to set out Irish regnal chronology, together with famous battles, up to 1072, the date of its composition. It is a striking feature of these poems on the kings of Ireland that they do not continue beyond the reign of Máel Sechnaill mac Domnaill (*d.* 1022). After his death the principal kingdom of the southern Uí Néill, Mide, declined in power permitting other provincial kings to assert claims to the high-kingship. Gilla Cóemáin's omission of any names after Máel Sechnaill mac Domnaill allowed him to avoid passing any judgement on such contemporary issues, but it also meant that he did not have to reveal the calamitous decline of Cland Cholmáin, the ruling kindred of Mide, which may have been his own kingdom.

The other two poems securely attributed to Gilla Cóemáin are both concerned with the legendary pre-history of the Irish. *Góedel Glas ó tát Goídil* ('Góedel Glas from whom are descended the Goídil') sets out the movements of the descendants of Goídel son of Scota (a name artificially composed from two names for the Irish, Goídil and Scotti) from north Africa to Asia Minor, and thence to Spain and Ireland. *Tigernmas mac Follaig aird* ('Tigernmas son of noble Follach') celebrated the reign of one particular legendary king, Tigernmas, and his victories in battle. Both of these poems formed part of the Irish origin-legend, *Lebor Gabála Érenn*, and demonstrate the importance of Gilla Cóemáin in the final stages of the evolution of that text before the earliest surviving manuscript version (the mid twelfth century).

Two important prose texts have been associated with Gilla Cóemáin. *Lebor Bretnach* is a translation of the *Historia Brittonum*, a text which, in its original early ninth-century form, is one of the first witnesses to the Irish origin-legend. The other is in both prose and verse and presents an account of the Six Ages of the World. Neither attribution is secure; Gilla Cóemáin's range of interests makes them at least plausible, while the attribution to him of *Lebor Bretnach* has more support in the tradition of the text.

The importance of Gilla Cóemáin, therefore, is as one of the main figures in the history of the Irish origin-legend, working at a period when one of the traditional supports of that legend, the Uí Néill kingship of Tara, was slipping into the hands of rival dynasties. PETER J. SMITH

Sources R. I. Best and others, eds., *The Book of Leinster, formerly Lebar na Núachongbála*, 6 vols. (1954–83), vols. 1, 3 [incl. edns of the five securely attributed poems] • D. Dumville, 'Nennius and the *Historia Brittonum*', *Studia Celtica*, 10–11 (1975–6), 78–95 • D. Dumville, 'The textual history of Lebor Bretnach: a preliminary study', *Éigse*, 16 (1975–6), 255–73, esp. 270, 272 • M. Herbert, 'The Irish *Sex aetates mundi*: first editions', *Cambridge Medieval Celtic Studies*, 11 (1986), 97–112 • G. Lehmacher, 'Goedel Glass', *Zeitschrift für Celtische Philologie*, 13 (1919–21), 151–63 • B. Mac Carthy, *The Codex Palatino-Vaticanus, No. 830* (1892) • R. A. S. Macalister, ed. and trans., *Lebor gabála Érenn: the book of the taking of Ireland*, 2, ITS, 35 (1939); 5, ITS, 44 (1956) • C. O'Conor, 'Chronologia metrica regum Hiberniae', *Rerum Hibernicarum Scriptores Veteres*, 1 (1814), xxxi–xlii, proleg., pt 2 • D. Ó Cróinín, ed., *The Irish 'Sex Aetates Mundi'* (1983) • H. P. A. Oskamp, 'On the author of *Sex aetates mundi*', *Studia Celtica*, 3 (1968), 127–40 • R. M. Scowcroft, '*Leabhar Gabhála*: part 2: the growth of the tradition', *Ériu*, 39 (1988), 1–66 • P. J. Smith, 'Three poems ascribed to Gilla Cóemáin: a critical edition', DPhil diss., U. Oxf., 1996 • W. Stokes, 'Gilla Cóemáin's chronological poem', *The tripartite life of Patrick, with other documents relating to that saint*, ed. and trans. W. Stokes, 2; Rolls Series, 89 (1887), 530–41 • R. Thurneysen, 'Zu *Nemnius (Nennius)*', *Zeitschrift für Celtische Philologie*, 20 (1933–6), 97–132 • H. L. C. Tristram, *Sex Aetates Mundi* (1985) • *Lebor Bretnach: the Irish version of the Historia Britonum ascribed to Nennius*, ed. A. G. van Hamel (1932) • P. J. Smith, 'Early Irish historical verse: the evolution of a genre', *Irland und Europa im früheren Mittelalter / Ireland and Europe in the early Middle Ages: texts and transmission* [Konstanz 1998], ed. P. Ní Chathaín and M. Richter (Dublin, 2002), 326–41 • J. Carey, *A new introduction to Lebor gabála Érenn* (1993)

Gilla meic Liac [Gelasius] (**1087–1174**), archbishop of Armagh, was an important exponent of ecclesiastical reform in twelfth-century Ireland. He was a member of the Cenél nEógain of the northern Uí Néill, but his precise genealogical affiliation has been a matter of some ambiguity. He is called Gilla meic Liac mac Ruaidrí or mac meic Ruaidrí ('son or grandson of Ruaidrí') in some chronicles, though it has been suggested that this was Gilla meic Liac mac Annaid meic Flaithbertaig meic Ruaidrí of the Síl nÁeda Ollain. However, another source calls him mac Diarmata meic Ruaidrí, while notes to the list of successors of Patrick call him *mac ind fhir dana* ('son of the poet') of Uí Birn (possibly Clann Birn of Cenél nEógain). He became abbot or *erenagh* of Derry in 1121, probably on the resignation of Finn Ua Conaingen, and held the post for sixteen years.

In 1137 Gilla meic Liac was chosen by Máel Máedoc Ó Morgair (St Malachy) to follow him as archbishop, or *coarb* ('successor of Patrick'), of Armagh against the traditional hereditary line of Clann Sínaig, possibly indicating that he had been an advocate of reform during his tenure at Derry. Hints in one chronicle suggest that his succession was not as smooth as traditional accounts imply and that the Clann Sínaig claimant Niall mac Áeda meic Máel Ísu had briefly succeeded in 1136. Whatever the exact turn of events, the succession of Gilla meic Liac in 1137 marked a victory for the reformers; and in the 1150s and 1160s he presided over a series of clerical assemblies and synods which sought to implement ecclesiastical reform and bring the Irish church into closer association with developments in the rest of Europe. For example, in 1152 he convened, with Cardinal Giovanni Paparo, a synod attended by 300 ecclesiastics which laid down new rules for clerical behaviour including the putting away of concubines, prohibition of demands for payment for anointing and baptizing, and legislation against simony. In 1158 Gilla meic Liac convened the Synod of Breemount, Meath, attended by twenty-five bishops and the papal legate Gilla Críst Ua Connairche, which passed further reform legislation as well as confirming Flaithbertach Ua Brolcháin as head of all Columban churches in Ireland. This last provision was an attempt to bring the traditional system of monastic federations in line with standard diocesan structures. A further synod was held in 1162 at Clane, Kildare, which, in addition to 'enjoining rule and morality upon the Irish', reaffirmed the primacy of Armagh.

Gilla meic Liac was indeed active in maintaining the jurisdiction of Armagh. In 1140 he made his first circuit (*cuairt*) of Connacht, obtaining jurisdiction over the churches in that province from the king Toirdelbach Ua Conchobair. He made further circuits of Connacht in 1151 and 1172, and of Cenél nEógain in 1150 and 1162. In 1162 he consecrated Lorcán Ua Tuathail, *coarb* of St Caemgen, as archbishop of Dublin. Gilla meic Liac also had close relations with secular rulers, particularly Muirchertach Mac Lochlainn, king of Cenél nEógain and later high-king of Ireland. In 1157 he presided over the consecration of Mellifont, Louth, on which occasion generous donations were made by Mac Lochlainn as well as by Donnchad Ua Cerbaill, king of Airgialla, and Derbforgaill, wife of Tigernán Ua Ruairc. The same event also witnessed the excommunication (presumably at the instigation of Gilla meic Liac) of Donnchad Ua Maíli Shechlainn, king of Meath, who had earlier slain Cú Ulad Ua Coindelbáin, king of Loegaire, while under the protection (*comairge*) of the archbishop and others. It also seems likely that he presided over a number of peace negotiations between Irish kings. Gilla meic Liac was among the Irish bishops addressed in a letter of 20 September 1172 by Pope Alexander III, urging them to support Henry II in governing Ireland and to excommunicate those who would violate the oath they had sworn. He died two years later, on 27 March 1174 (the Wednesday after Easter), and was succeeded by Conchobar Ua Conchaille (*d.* 1175), and, in the following year, by Gilla in Coimded Ua Caráin (*d.* 1180).

DAVID E. THORNTON

Sources W. M. Hennessy and B. MacCarthy, eds., *Annals of Ulster, otherwise, annals of Senat*, 4 vols. (1887–1901), vol. 2 • *AFM*, 2nd edn • H. J. Lawlor and R. I. Best, 'The ancient list of the coarbs of Patrick', *Proceedings of the Royal Irish Academy*, 35C (1918–20), 316–62 • *Sancti Bernardi opera*, ed. J. Leclercq and others, 8 vols. (Rome, 1957–77) • M. Herbert, *Iona, Kells, and Derry: the history and hagiography of the monastic familia of Columba* (1988) • A. Gwynn, *The Irish church in the eleventh and twelfth centuries*, ed. G. O'Brien (1992) • T. W. Moody and others, eds., *A new history of Ireland*, 9: *Maps, genealogies, lists* (1984)

Gillan, Robert (1799–1879), Church of Scotland minister, was born at Hawick, Roxburghshire, on 1 October 1799. His father, the Revd Robert Gillan (*d.* 1824), formerly minister of Ettrick, was minister there. His mother was Marion, daughter of the Revd William Campbell. Gillan studied at Edinburgh High School and University, where he was noted for his scholarship and oratory.

On 7 July 1829 Gillan was licensed to preach by the presbytery of Selkirk, and ordained minister to the congregation at Stamfordham, Northumberland, in October 1830. From 1833 he was minister of South Shields. In the month that he arrived there, on 7 October, he married Anne, daughter of George Green, the minister of Carmunnock. They had two daughters and three sons. In 1837 he transferred to Holytown in Lanarkshire, where he remained until 1842. He served at Wishaw in the same county for six months, then accepted the parish of Abbotshall, Fife, after the Disruption in 1843, before being transferred on 25 February 1847 to St John's, Glasgow. On 23 January, a month before his arrival in Glasgow, his wife died. He was married a second time, on 13 June 1848, to Laura, daughter of John Buttery of Woodville; there were no children of this marriage. Gillan remained at St John's for fourteen years, building up a good following in the congregation. He took an active interest in all religious and social movements, and was an early opponent of the law of patronage. The University of Glasgow conferred on him the degree of DD in 1853.

The incessant activity of Gillan's Glasgow charge finally told on his health, and on 10 January 1861 he accepted charge of the small church of Inchinnan, Renfrewshire. He was, however, still able to work and, being appointed one of Glasgow University's first two lecturers on pastoral theology, he prepared a course of lectures, which were on two separate occasions delivered at the four Scottish universities. On 11 October 1870 he was publicly entertained in Glasgow, and presented with his portrait. He adhered firmly to the established church of Scotland, and as moderator presided over the general assembly of 1873. Gillan was the author of several works, including *A General Fast Sermon* (1832) and *The Decalogue* (1856). He died at the manse, Inchinnan, on 1 November 1879. His second wife survived him, dying in November 1885.

G. C. BOASE, *rev.* ROSEMARY MITCHELL

Sources *Fasti Scot.* · Irving, *Scots.* · J. Smith, *Our Scottish clergy*, 1st ser. (1848) · *Church of Scotland Home and Foreign Missionary Record*, 1 Dec 1879

Wealth at death £10,751 16*s*. 1*d*.: probate, 19 March 1880, *CCI*

Gillard, Francis George [Frank] (**1908–1998**), broadcaster and war correspondent, was born on 1 December 1908 at 20 Silver Street, Tiverton, Devon, the elder child and only son of Francis Henry Gillard (*c*.1880–1953), master butcher, and his wife, Emily Jane, *née* Burridge (1882–1958). A west countryman by birth, upbringing, and conviction, he contrived to pursue a career which took him to the summit of his profession while never having to uproot himself. For all but a dozen of his ninety years his home was in Devon, Somerset, or Bristol. He was educated at Wellington School, Somerset, and St Luke's College, Exeter, whose students took London University external degrees, in his case a BSc. He became a schoolmaster, but from 1936 began to contribute items to the BBC's west region, and in 1941 was taken on to the staff. From its headquarters in Bristol, west region then covered an area stretching along the channel coast as far as Brighton. One of its responsibilities was to assign a war correspondent to the army's southern command. Gillard was nominated, and thereby became the only radio reporter to accompany the Dieppe raid, launched from southern command. In later years he regretted that he had not been franker, and more critical of what was generally regarded as a disaster, though survivors of the raid who subsequently took part in the Normandy landings were certain that the lessons so painfully learned in 1942 paid off in 1944.

Meanwhile, Gillard's instinctive grasp of the nature of battle had been noted and in December 1942 he was sent to north Africa to join Godfrey Talbot on the final stages of the Eighth Army's epic advance from El Alamein to Tripoli. He struck up a friendly relationship with General Montgomery and went on to cover the landings in Sicily and Italy. But after Montgomery had departed to prepare for the invasion of northern Europe, he fell foul of General Alexander, the allied supreme commander, who accused him of slipping uncleared information past the censors. The BBC sent its newly appointed editor-in-chief, William Haley, out to Italy to investigate. Gillard was exonerated. Alexander apologized and suggested Gillard might like to show Haley around the battlefront while the latter awaited a flight home. This he did, and it can hardly have been unhelpful to Gillard's subsequent BBC career to have spent ten days in the company of someone soon to become its director-general. Gillard himself returned to London in time to join the war report team which would cover the D-day landings and subsequent campaign. His friendship with Montgomery thrived again, and one of his most celebrated broadcasts came from an open-air church service in Normandy at which the general read the lesson, pausing when fighters roared overhead. At the end the bells of the church rang out to celebrate the village's liberation.

The war over, Gillard went back to west region as head of programmes and into battle again, now as a combatant. Within the BBC the whole future of regional broadcasting was being questioned. Until 1939 there had been only regional services plus the National Programme. During the war the regions retained their identity but put out a shared programme called the Home Service, while the National Programme became the Forces Programme. This arrangement still held, except for the designation 'Light' instead of 'Forces'. Regional items were broadcast on the local Home Service wavelength as variants on, or 'opt-outs' from, the central dispensation. Now there was a proposal to add a third, highbrow, national programme. Would there still be a need for regional broadcasting? Gillard argued forcefully and successfully so, not only because it served particular communities but also because it favoured the kind of radio he liked, and which war reporting had fostered. 'Our policy in Bristol,' he declared, 'will be to get away from the artificial atmosphere of the studio … and take the microphone among the people' (Briggs, 97). In the first full year of peace he increased locally originated programming from twelve hours a week to nineteen.

Already, though, a fresh threat had arisen. Because the low-frequency emissions then in use interfered with each other unless they were carefully spaced apart, European countries were restricted to a few wavelengths each. If the BBC was to launch its promised Third Programme, it had to find a wavelength from its existing allotment. The proposal was to do this by merging west region with the midland region. It was fought at political level as well as professional, and in the end was resolved by filching a British forces' frequency from occupied Germany instead. Gillard continued to strengthen west region's identity by getting its programmes on to the national services, most enduringly in the case of *Any Questions*. He also kept himself in the public ear by acting as a radio commentator on state occasions or royal tours abroad. He even suggested that he might stand in for the BBC's wayward American correspondent Alistair Cooke when Cooke was due three months' home leave. Cooke smartly quashed such a threat, as he saw it.

In 1955 Gillard was transferred briefly (as it turned out) to London, as chief assistant to the director of sound broadcasting, with the rank of controller. Next year the controllership of west region fell vacant, and Gillard was recalled to Bristol to fill the post. Unlike some old radio hands, he took a keen interest in the fast-growing medium of television, and was soon promoting the region's contribution to the television service as assiduously as he had steered *Any Questions* on to the Light Programme. He held a competition for new television plays, won by Peter Nichols, gave the future film director John Boorman his first chance to strike out, and encouraged the specialist departments which were to endow Bristol with a virtual monopoly in BBC wildlife and antiques programmes. He was made a CBE in 1961.

Gillard was by now a confirmed bachelor whose name, as far as his relations knew, had been linked with a woman's only once, and that when he went off to war. His sister, Doreen, had married an Exford farmer, William Bawden. In 1956 they acquired Poole Farm in Taunton Vale, near Wellington, where Gillard helped with the purchase, was a partner in the farm, and regularly stayed. Their daughter Gillian and son Peter became, in a sense, his family too. 'He was like a third parent', Gillian later said (private information). Seven years passed happily until in 1963 he was appointed to the top job of director of sound broadcasting—or managing director, radio, as it became.

This was another spell of seven years, and Gillard's longest exile from his beloved west country. On routine visits to London he had always stayed at the Farmers' Club; required now to be in his office in Broadcasting House most days, he took a flat in Langham Place, close by. His major task as director was in a way a sequel to the reorganization campaigns he had fought on behalf of Bristol, except that he had now to be the instigator. The advent of frequency modulation (FM) broadcasting had largely removed the old wavelength shortage. The BBC was free to add a fourth nationwide service. Meanwhile the post-war trio of Home, Light, and Third seemed hopelessly unfocused in name, if not in fact. The Reithian ideal that every programme should be addressed to every listener was crumbling, and the title of a popular programme surviving from wartime, *Music while you Work*, was a tacit admission that not everyone listened in reverent silence; for many, radio was an adjunct to other activities. It was necessary to cater for audiences of different brow heights and varying levels of attention, but without condescension. Gillard's prescription was brilliantly simple—radios 1, 2, 3, and 4. Listeners might privately think of them as radios Pop, Cosy, Highbrow, and Everything Else, but they didn't have to feel inferior if they chose a low number.

Also made possible by FM were local radio stations serving individual towns and counties. It had been assumed that these would be commercial stations drawing their revenue from local advertisers. Gillard made the bold decision to set up BBC local stations as well. Though they nibbled into his already precarious budget—radio reception no longer required a licence and BBC radio was dependent on a grace-and-favour share of the television licence revenue—he believed it was important to keep a BBC presence in all strata of broadcasting. His two most unpopular deeds were to axe *Children's Hour* and wind up the talks and features department, which had gained much lustre over the years. The first of these was in fact sensible. Children had switched to teatime television; the old radio equivalent mourned by elderly critics was now attracting a mere 25,000 listeners. The other was so resented within Broadcasting House that when, under BBC age rules, Gillard retired in 1970 his leave-taking was not entirely cordial. In the opinion, however, of Gerard Mansell, first controller of Radio 4 and later deputy director-general, Gillard was the most creative and positive radio chieftain with whom he worked.

Gillard settled in his last and best-loved home, Trevor House, only a short walk from Poole Farm. He had his main meals with the family, looked after himself otherwise, was house-proud, and loved tending his garden. But he had not quite finished with broadcasting. Almost immediately he was lured to the United States to act as a 'distinguished fellow' (that is, consultant) to the nascent public broadcast system. It was Gillard who suggested, after they had successfully shown the BBC's version of *The Forsyte Saga*, that they might now raid the backlog of British classic serials. Under the title of *Masterpiece Theatre*, and introduced by Alistair Cooke, this became an institution.

In Britain, Gillard picked up a new career as the unseen narrator of a number of outstanding television documentaries. Some of these, such as two series of *The Commanders* devoted to the likes of Rommel, MacArthur, and Yamamoto, arose naturally from his own Second World War experiences, but his warm and trusty voice also enhanced *Hospital 1922*, the near perfect account of everyday routine in the old Charing Cross Hospital as reconstructed (by Peter Goodchild and Brian Gibson) fifty years later. His last, self-ordained project was to record, either on audio tape or film, the memoirs of his fellow grandees of the BBC. These, he made clear, were for use only when all were dead, or otherwise on the BBC's centenary in 2022.

Back on the farm Peter Bawden was now sharing the management with his father, and Gillian helped. After their mother died in 1983, and then their father in 1994, the farm was divided. Peter moved with his wife and children to another house. Gillian and her husband, Ian Cubitt, and their children, born in the 1980s, took over as Gillard's surrogate family. As before, he took his lunch and tea with them every day when at home. In London he stayed again at the Farmers' Club in Whitehall Court, amused to learn that during the war it had been part-requisitioned as accommodation for senior officers. Room 23 had been reserved for his friend Montgomery and Room 24 for the commander who trusted him less, Alexander. Gillard often entertained distinguished latter-day guests in the club, always immaculate in evening dress. At other times he held court in the bar. He was respected, popular, and loved good company. It was at the club that he died of a heart attack, in his sleep, on 21 October 1998. He was cremated at Taunton crematorium eight days later and his ashes were scattered over Poole Farm.

PHILIP PURSER

Sources L. Miall, *Inside the BBC* (1994) · A. Briggs, *The history of broadcasting in the United Kingdom*, 4 (1979) · N. Clarke, *Alistair Cooke: the biography* (1999) · D. Hawkins and D. Boyd, eds., *War report* (1946) · *Sunday Telegraph* (7 Oct 1973) · *Daily Telegraph* (23 Oct 1998) · *The Times* (23 Oct 1998) · *The Guardian* (23 Oct 1998) · *The Independent* (23 Oct 1998) · *WWW* · private information (2004) · personal knowledge (2004) · b. cert. · d. cert.

Archives FILM BBC Television Archive | SOUND BBC Sound Archive

Likenesses photograph, 1944, repro. in *The Independent* • photograph, 1945, repro. in *Daily Telegraph* • photograph, repro. in *The Guardian*

Wealth at death £602,424—gross; £598,103—net: probate, 7 May 1999, *CGPLA Eng. & Wales*

Gille. *See* Gilbert (*d.* 1145).

Gillespie, George (1613–1648), Church of Scotland minister and theologian, was born at Kirkcaldy, Fife, on 21 January 1613, the second son of John Gillespie (*b. c.*1579, *d.* in or before 1627), minister of Kirkcaldy, and Lilias (1590/91–1627), daughter of Patrick *Simson (1556–1618), minister of Stirling. Raised in a staunch presbyterian family, as a child George was 'somewhat dull and soft-like', neglected by his mother in favour of his younger and more spirited brother Patrick *Gillespie (1617–1675). His father, however, recognized the boy's latent abilities and is reported to have prophesied that he would become a 'great man' in the Church of Scotland (Wodrow, 3.110). He was educated at the University of St Andrews and, according to his cousin Patrick Simson, he graduated MA in 1629, when only sixteen; however, this may have been the year he entered the university (*Fasti Scot.*, 1.58). The minutes of the presbytery of Kirkcaldy record that from 1629 to 1631 he was maintained at St Andrews by the presbytery as a 'bursar of Theology', though it is unclear whether this was in the capacity of an undergraduate or a continuing student of theology (W. Stevenson, 8).

After leaving the university, unwilling to receive ordination from a bishop, Gillespie was appointed domestic chaplain to John Gordon, Viscount Kenmure, probably through the influence of Samuel Rutherford, Kenmure's parish minister. This appointment marked the beginning of Gillespie's lifelong friendship with Rutherford and his association with what has been termed the kirk's radical party—a group of militant ministers who were implacably opposed to episcopacy, championed divine right presbyterianism, defended the practice of godly conventicling, and deprecated all set forms and liturgies (D. Stevenson, 24). Upon Kenmure's death in September 1634 Gillespie became chaplain to the great presbyterian nobleman, John Kennedy, sixth earl of Cassillis, and tutor to his eldest son, Lord Kennedy. During this period he wrote his first work, a scathing polemic against the episcopalian 'innovations' being imposed on the kirk by Charles I, entitled *A Dispute Against English Popish Ceremonies*. It was published anonymously in the Netherlands and appeared in Scotland in the summer of 1637, just as the entire kingdom was in uproar over the introduction of the new Scottish Book of Common Prayer. The *Dispute* created such a sensation that in October of the same year the Scottish privy council ordered all copies of his book to be collected and burnt by the common hangman.

Through the influence of his friends, on 5 January 1638 Gillespie was presented to the parish of Wemyss in Fife by the town council of Edinburgh and, despite opposition from Archbishop Spottiswoode, the preliminaries to his ordination were undertaken by the presbytery of Kirkcaldy. In March all but three members of the presbytery subscribed the national covenant and, on 26 April, in a calculated act of defiance to episcopacy, the presbytery ordained Gillespie to Wemyss, this being only the second instance of non-episcopal ordination since the 1610 general assembly. In the summer Gillespie published his second anonymous contribution to the struggle against episcopacy, a brief vitriolic tract entitled *Reasons for which the Service Book, Urged upon Scotland Ought to be Refused* (Edinburgh, 1638). Soon after, his authorship of this tract and the *Dispute* became generally known, causing his colleagues to marvel that works of such exceptional ability had been penned by a mere 'youth'. 'I think', Robert Baillie observed in a letter to William Spang, 'he may prove amongst the best wits of this isle' (*Letters and Journals of Robert Baillie*, 1.90). In November 1638 he was invited to preach at the famous Glasgow general assembly that abjured episcopacy—a singular honour for one so young and a measure of the high esteem in which he was held. In his sermon, however, based on the text 'the king's heart is in the hand of the Lord', he was deemed by the moderate covenanters to encroach too far on the king's prerogatives, prompting the earl of Argyll to admonish the assembly's more radical members 'to let authority alone' (*Letters and Journals of Robert Baillie*, 1.146).

During the second bishops' war Gillespie served as a chaplain in the covenanting army, and following the treaty of Ripon in October 1640 he was chosen as one of the ecclesiastical commissioners to the treaty of London. While there he and his fellow ministers acted the part of presbyterian propagandists, making contacts with influential English puritans, preaching to large, enthusiastic congregations, and advocating religious unity and uniformity in church government between England and Scotland. Upon his return to Scotland he took the opportunity to publish an exposition and defence of presbyterian government, *An Assertion of the Government of the Church of Scotland* (Edinburgh, 1641). Soon thereafter, he was called by the town council of Aberdeen to be one of the city's ministers, but the 1641 general assembly, at his request, refused to translate him. Overtures were also made for his settlement at St Andrews, but they too were declined, and he was eventually translated to Greyfriars Kirk, Edinburgh, on 23 September 1642.

Following the approval of the solemn league and covenant by the general assembly and the convention of estates on 17 August 1643 Gillespie was named, along with Rutherford, Baillie, and Alexander Henderson, as one of the kirk's commissioners to the assembly of divines at Westminster. He took his seat at the assembly on 16 September 1643. During the course of the next four years he returned to Scotland only once, when, in January 1645, he and Robert Baillie presented the directory for public worship to the general assembly. Although, at the age of thirty-one, he was the assembly's youngest member, he quickly distinguished himself in its deliberations by his zeal, learning, and debating acumen. He gained particular distinction in the 'Grand Debate' between presbyterians and Independents on church government, engaging in detailed battles of scriptural exegesis with eminent Independent divines such as Thomas Goodwin, Philip Nye, and William Bridge. After witnessing Gillespie's performance on the assembly floor Robert Baillie was so impressed that he declared, 'there is no man whose parts in publick dispute I doe so admire' (*Letters and Journals of Robert Baillie*, 2.160). Gillespie also played a leading role in the assembly's Erastian controversy, at one point giving a speech on excommunication that so confounded the learned lawyer John Selden that he is reported to have exclaimed, 'That young man, by this single speech, has swept away the learning and labour of ten years of my life!' (Hetherington, xxiii).

While in London, Gillespie also acted the part of the Scots' pamphleteer, publishing, as part of a controversial exchange with Thomas Coleman, three tracts against Erastianism—*A Brotherly Examination* (1645), *Nihil respondes* (1645), and *Male audis* (1646). He also published anonymously a discussion of current affairs, *A late dialogue betwixt a civilian and divine concerning the present condition of the Church of England* (1644), and two tracts against Independency and religious toleration—*A Recrimination in Defence of Presbyterianism* (1644), and *Wholesome Severity Reconciled with Christian Liberty* (1645). In what little spare time he had he produced what many scholars consider to be his *magnum opus*, an elaborate examination of the entire Erastian controversy entitled *Aaron's Rod Blossoming, or, The Divine Ordinance of Church Government Vindicated* (1646).

After helping to frame the Westminster confession of faith, Gillespie took his final leave of the assembly on 16 July 1647. In August he presented the confession to the Scottish general assembly, together with his report, a piece that has been described as 'the best succinct account of the work at Westminster given by a contemporary divine' (Campbell, 67). Under his watchful eye the general assembly speedily approved the confession of faith. It also ordered the printing of his *One Hundred and Eleven Propositions Concerning the Ministry and Government of the Church* (Edinburgh, 1647), termed by Baillie, his 'Theses against Erastianism' (*Letters and Journals of Robert Baillie*, 3.20), and directed that copies be sent down to the presbyteries.

With his reputation greatly enhanced, Gillespie now assumed the role of Scotland's leading divine. Consequently, on 22 September 1647 he was chosen to replace the recently deceased Alexander Henderson as minister of the prestigious first charge of St Giles, Edinburgh. Despite a rapidly worsening tubercular condition circumstances allowed him but brief respite from his labours. From January to August 1648 he was called upon to exert all his energies in opposing the state backed alliance of moderate covenanters and 'malignant' royalists known as the engagement. On 12 July he was elected moderator of the 1648 general assembly, taking an active part in all its deliberations, including its official condemnation of the engagement and its approval of the shorter and larger catechisms. On 12 August he was given the further honour of being elected moderator of assembly's commission but, within a matter of days, was forced by ill health to retire to his native Kirkcaldy.

From his deathbed Gillespie issued two 'dying testimonies', which were published posthumously by his brother Patrick in early 1649 (reprinted in *The Works of Mr George Gillespie*, 1–3). In them he warned against confederacies with 'malignants' and urged the kirk to 'purge' itself of all 'enemies to God and his cause'. In the years that followed, these testimonies were to have a profound influence on the course of the covenanting movement, paving the way for the political and military 'excommunication' enjoined by the 1649 Act of Classes and, ultimately, the division of the kirk between radicals and moderates during the protester–resolutioner controversy. Gillespie died at Kirkcaldy on 17 December 1648, aged thirty-five, and was buried there. He was survived by his wife, Margaret Murray, of whom no other details are known.

K. D. Holfelder

Sources W. M. Hetherington, 'Memoir', *The works of Mr. George Gillespie*, 2 vols. (1846), 1.ix–xxxvi • W. M. Campbell, *The triumph of presbyterianism* (1958), 51–72 • R. Wodrow, *Analecta, or, Materials for a history of remarkable providences, mostly relating to Scotch ministers and Christians*, ed. [M. Leishman], 4 vols., Maitland Club, 60 (1842–3), vol. 1, pp. 154–60; vol. 3, pp. 109–12 • *Fasti Scot.*, new edn, 1.38, 58–9; 5.120 • *The letters and journals of Robert Baillie*, ed. D. Laing, 3 vols. (1841–2) • W. D. J. McKay, *An ecclesiastical republic: Church government in the writings of George Gillespie* (1997) • R. S. Paul, *The assembly of the Lord: politics and religion in the Westminster assembly and the 'Grand debate'* (1985) • D. Stevenson, *The Scottish revolution, 1637–44: the triumph of the covenanters* (1973) • W. Stevenson, ed., *The presbyterie booke of Kirkcaldie* (1900), 8

Archives NL Scot., letters and papers

Likenesses oils, Kirkcaldy old parish church, Fife

Gillespie, James, of Spylaw (1726–1797), tobacconist and benefactor, was born in 1726, probably at Roslin, near Edinburgh. He had one sister and a younger brother. His family were members of the Cameronians, or reformed Presbyterians, a strict nonconformist sect. Gillespie began his career as a tobacconist and, in partnership with his brother, John, he opened the Gillespie Tobacco Shop at 231 High Street, Edinburgh. The brothers prospered, and in 1759 built a snuff mill at the nearby village of Colinton. By 1768 they had acquired the Spylaw estate and in 1773 added the adjoining Bonaly and Fernielaw estates. John continued to manage the Edinburgh business while James moved to Spylaw, where he supervised the snuff mill.

As laird of Spylaw, Gillespie was remembered for his kindness towards his small tenants, with whom he enjoyed a close, patriarchal relationship. An unassuming man, he lived frugally with few comforts. Neither he nor his brother married. Gillespie survived his brother by five years and continued to run the business until his death at Spylaw on 8 April 1797. He was buried with his brother in Colinton churchyard.

Shortly before his death, Gillespie was offended by the young relative who had been his prospective heir. The youth was disinherited and, besides small annuities to servants, Gillespie made two major charitable bequests. He set aside £2700 to found a school in Edinburgh for the education of 100 poor boys. The remainder of his estate, some £12,000, plus land valued at over £30,000, was left to build and endow a hospital for the elderly. The governors, including members of the Merchant Company of Edinburgh, town council, and city ministers, were incorporated by royal charter in 1801 and James Gillespie's Hospital completed four years later. The building was sold in 1870 and a trust established to provide annual pensions for the elderly. JAMES TAIT, *rev.* CHRISTINE CLARK

Sources A. Heron, *The rise and progress of the Company of Merchants of the city of Edinburgh, 1681–1902* (1903) • J. Paterson, *Kay's Edinburgh portraits: a series of anecdotal biographies chiefly of Scotchmen*, ed. J. Maidment, 2 vols. (1885) • *Memorials of his time, by Henry Cockburn*, 2 vols. (1872) • T. Somerville, *My own life and times, 1741–1814*, ed. W. Lee (1861)

Likenesses J. Kay, double portrait, caricature, etching, 1797 (with John Gillespie), NPG • J. Foulis, portrait; formerly in possession of Edinburgh Merchant Company, 1889 • bust; formerly in possession of Edinburgh Merchant Company, 1889

Gillespie, Lilias. *See* Skene, Lilias (1626/7–1697).

Gillespie, Patrick (1617–1675), Church of Scotland minister, was born in 1617 and baptized on 2 March, the third son of John Gillespie (*b. c.*1579, *d.* in or before 1627), minister of Kirkcaldy, Fife, and his wife, Lilias Simson (1590/91–1627), and younger brother of George *Gillespie (1613–1648). He was educated at the University of St Andrews, where he graduated MA in 1635. Between this date and September 1641 he married Sara, widow of James Stewart of Nether Horsburgh, and daughter of Sir John Cockburn of Ormiston (*d.* 1626) and his second wife, Elizabeth Bellenden. Gillespie was presented to St Mungo's, Glasgow, on 15 November 1641, but declined, owing to opposition from the town council. On 14 April 1642 he was ordained to the second charge of Kirkcaldy. Soon afterwards he was appointed a member of the general assembly's powerful standing committee, the commission for the public affairs of the kirk, on which he served without interruption until 1650. In early 1648 he was translated to the newly established Outer High Kirk, Glasgow.

In March of the same year Gillespie joined with the assembly's commission in condemning the royalist engagement led by the duke of Hamilton. Following the defeat of Hamilton's forces at Preston in August 1648 he supported the overthrow of the government which had sanctioned the engagement, and joined with the kirk's radical party in advocating that all royalist 'malignants' be barred from public office and military service. Soon after the premature death of his brother George in December 1648 he was appointed by the commission to publish some of his papers in which he denounced confederacies with malignants. These were printed at Edinburgh in 1649 under the titles *An Usefull Case of Conscience*, and *A Treatise of Miscellany Questions*. In February 1650 he joined with like-minded radicals in kirk and state in opposing the treaty of Breda, maintaining that no commission should be sent to the exiled future Charles II until he had first exhibited some evidence of a genuine repentance. Following the Cromwellian invasion of Scotland in late June 1650 Gillespie became an outspoken critic of the government, denouncing the king for his manifest insincerity, and calling upon the committee of estates to purge the covenanting army of all known malignants and former engagers.

In the ensuing division between moderate and radical covenanters Gillespie emerged as a leading radical. He was instrumental in reviving the army known as the western association and in October 1650 he joined with the association's officers and other prominent radicals in drafting the infamous western remonstrance. In this document Gillespie and his associates announced their intention to withhold support from Charles until he evinced clear and unmistakable signs of repentance. When the moderate controlled commission condemned the remonstrance on 28 November 1650 Gillespie joined the radical ministers in a complete boycott of its meetings. From December 1650 to June 1651 he denounced the public resolutions in which the commission conceded to parliament that acts barring malignants and former engagers from military service and public office might legally be lifted. During the July 1651 general assembly, which saw the national kirk irreparably divided between resolutioners and protesters, he joined with the latter party in protesting against the assembly's proceedings and declining its authority. Subsequently Gillespie and two other leading protesters were deposed from the ministry. Ignoring the assembly's sentence he returned to his ministerial charge and in early October induced the synod of Glasgow–Ayr to issue a 'Testimony' which approved the protestation, condemned the public resolutions, and declared the 1651 general assembly to be null.

During the Cromwellian occupation of Scotland, Gillespie continued as one of the leading protesters, although, unlike his more conservative colleagues, he favoured closer civil and ecclesiastical relations with the English. In appreciation for his willingness to treat with the government he was appointed principal of Glasgow University by the English in February 1653, and in March 1654 was invited by Cromwell to London in order to develop a new ecclesiastical settlement for Scotland. The result of his consultations with the English was a council ordinance dated 8 August 1654, popularly known as Gillespie's charter, which circumvented the authority of the kirk's presbyterian courts in favour of a system of provincial certifiers, or triers, who were to oversee the admittance of ministers to particular parishes. Although never fully implemented the charter gave Gillespie the leverage he needed to carry out his agenda of purging unfit resolutioner ministers from their parishes, and planting their vacant charges with 'godly' protesters. The power that this afforded him, particularly within the environs of the synod of Glasgow–Ayr, prompted his fellow protester, Sir Archibald Johnston, Lord Wariston, to refer to him as 'not only Archbishop of Glascow but Metropolitan and Patriarch of Scotland' (*Diary of Sir Archibald Johnston*, ed. Ogilvie, 44).

Throughout the remainder of the 1650s Gillespie continued to work closely with the English. He actively courted the favour of Lord Broghill and the new Scottish council in the autumn of 1655, and on 14 October became the first Scottish minister to pray publicly for the lord protector. In January 1657, soon after the English council's decision to abandon his charter, he travelled to London, along with Wariston and James Guthrie, in order to petition Cromwell for a new ecclesiastical settlement. During their time in London, in putting their case against that of the resolutioners' agent, James Sharp, Gillespie and his colleagues were backed by leading army officers around Cromwell, including major-generals Lambert and Fleetwood, and by leading Independent ministers, John Owen, Philip Nye, and Joseph Caryl. Although Gillespie and Wariston's designs for a new ecclesiastical settlement ultimately failed, they did succeed in having an amendment, or proviso, added to 'The humble petition and advice' which prohibited all former engagers and their malignant supporters from voting or holding public office in Scotland. Soon after his return to Scotland, Gillespie attempted to use the proviso to influence the Glasgow burgh elections, but was opposed by General Monck, who convinced the English council to drop the proviso's enforcement. With the recall of the Rump on 7 May 1659 Gillespie again proceeded to London, and joined with Wariston and the marquess of Argyll in another abortive attempt to secure an ecclesiastical settlement favourable to the protesters.

Soon after the Restoration, Gillespie was arrested on the charge of treason and imprisoned in Stirling Castle. When he was brought to trial in May 1661 he threw himself on the mercy of the court, renounced the western remonstrance, his protestation against the general assembly, and his compliance with the Cromwellians. On 5 July 1661 he was pardoned and set at liberty, but was confined to within 6 miles of Ormiston, in Haddingtonshire.

The same year Gillespie published at London the first instalment of what was intended to be a five-volume work on federal theology, *The Ark of the Testament Opened, or, A Treatise of the Covenant of Grace*. In preparing this work he used his brother George's unpublished manuscripts, casting 'his matter in another mold' (Wodrow, *Analecta*, 1.169). The second volume, *The Ark of the Covenant Opened, or, A Treatise of the Covenant of Redemption*, was published posthumously at London in 1677 with a preface by his old friend John Owen. The remaining three volumes, 'finished by himself, and made just ready for the press' (ibid.), were all subsequently lost.

Little is known of Gillespie's activities after 1661, and nothing of his wife. He preached occasionally, but never again obtained full-time employment in the ministry. His friend Lord Sinclair wished to have him appointed to Dysart, but his old adversary, James Sharp, now archbishop of St Andrews, maintained that one metropolitan was enough for Scotland, and two for the kingdom of Fife would be too many. He is mentioned in the will of one Alexander Carmichael as having been 'sometime minister' of Yester, but this can relate only to a temporary appointment during the absence of the parish's full-time minister, Laurence Charteris (*Fasti Scot.*, 1.399). Gillespie died in relative obscurity at Leith in February 1675.

K. D. Holfelder

Sources *The letters and journals of Robert Baillie*, ed. D. Laing, 3 (1842) • *Fasti Scot.*, new edn, 3.162; 1.399 • R. Wodrow, *Analecta, or, Materials for a history of remarkable providences, mostly relating to Scotch ministers and Christians*, ed. [M. Leishman], 1, Maitland Club, 60 (1842), 168–9 • *Diary of Sir Archibald Johnston of Wariston*, 2, ed. D. H. Fleming, Scottish History Society, 2nd ser., 18 (1919) • *Diary of Sir Archibald Johnston of Wariston*, 3, ed. J. D. Ogilvie, Scottish History Society, 3rd ser., 34 (1940) • W. Stephen, ed., *Register of the consultations of the ministers of Edinburgh*, 2 vols., Scottish History Society, 3rd ser., 1, 16 (1921–30) • A. F. Mitchell and J. Christie, eds., *The records of the commissions of the general assemblies of the Church of Scotland*, 3 vols., Scottish History Society, 11, 25, 58 (1892–1909) • A. Peterkin, ed., *Records of the Kirk of Scotland* (1838) • R. Wodrow, *The history of the sufferings of the Church of Scotland from the Restoration to the revolution*, ed. R. Burns, 1 (1828), 204–5 • D. Stevenson, *Revolution and counter-revolution in Scotland, 1644–1651*, Royal Historical Society Studies in History, 4 (1977) • F. D. Dow, *Cromwellian Scotland, 1651–1660* (1979) • general register of sasines, NA Scot., 43/185, 43/211, 44/83

Archives NL Scot., letters and papers • U. Glas., papers

Gillespie, Sir Robert Rollo (1766–1814), army officer, descended from an old Scottish family which acquired property in co. Down, Ireland, early in the eighteenth century, was born in Comber, co. Down, on 21 January 1766, the only child of Robert Gillespie (*d.* 1791) of Comber. His father was married three times, twice without issue, and Robert was the child of the third marriage with a sister (*d.* in or after 1796) of James Bailie of Innisharrie, co. Down, member for Hillsborough in the Irish House of Commons.

Robert went to Norland House, a private school in Kensington, London, and afterwards to the Revd Tookey of Exning, near Newmarket, Suffolk, to prepare for entry into Cambridge. He chose instead a military career, and on 28 April 1783 was appointed to a cornetcy in the 3rd Irish horse (later the 6th dragoon guards, Carabiniers). Three years afterwards, on 24 November 1786, he contracted a clandestine marriage in Dublin with Annabell, fourth daughter of Thomas Taylor of Taylors Grange, co. Dublin, whom he had met at the deanery at Clogher a few weeks previously.

Soon after his marriage, Gillespie was second to an officer named Mackenzie in a duel with a brother of the lawyer Sir Jonah Barrington. It was proposed that the matter should end after the opponents had fired twice fruitlessly, but a quarrel then arose between Barrington and Gillespie. Gillespie drew a handkerchief from his pocket and challenged Barrington to fight across it. Shots were fired, and Barrington fell dead. Gillespie fled, and took refuge with some of his wife's relatives. Afterwards he and his wife escaped to Scotland, but he later returned and surrendered to be put on trial. He was tried on a charge of wilful murder at Maryborough, Queen's county, at the summer assize of 1788. Despite the adverse summing-up of Judge Bradstreet, the jury, which included several half-pay officers, brought in a verdict of justifiable homicide, and Gillespie was discharged upon his own recognizance to plead the king's pardon in the court of king's bench at Dublin during the ensuing term.

Gillespie refused to settle down on his estate, having

inherited it on his father's death in 1791. Instead, he resolved to see active service, and thus accepted promotion in 1792 to a lieutenancy in the newly raised 20th (Jamaica) light dragoons. At Madeira, on the voyage out to the West Indies, the ship in which Gillespie was travelling was driven out of its anchorage by a violent storm, and Gillespie and some others escaped to shore in an open boat across a tumultuous sea. After arriving in Jamaica he contracted yellow fever, from which he recovered, and when the French planters in San Domingo applied to Jamaica for aid, he offered his services as a volunteer, his regiment (in which he got his troop in January 1794) remaining in the colony. He was present at the capture of Tiburón in February 1794, and afterwards at Port-au-Prince, where he was fired at while swimming ashore with a flag of truce to demand the surrender of the town. He displayed much gallantry at the capture of Fort Bizotten and received several wounds in the attack on Fort de l'Hôpital. After the fall of Port-au-Prince he took advantage of a temporary cessation of hostilities to return home.

Gillespie rejoined his wife in Ireland and travelled about at home for a time. Appointed major of brigade to General Wilford, he re-embarked for the West Indies in 1796 and became regimental major that year. He accompanied Wilford to San Domingo, where he was appointed adjutant-general and was much feared by the republicans. At San Domingo a gang of eight desperadoes broke into Gillespie's quarters, murdered his slave-boy, and attacked him. However, he defended himself with his sword, killing six of his assailants; the two others, after firing at him and wounding him, fled. The patrol heard the sound of the shots and came to the scene of the incident, the news of which reached Europe and appears to have hastened his mother's death. When he attended a levee years later, George III at first expressed surprise at Gillespie's boyish appearance. 'Eh, eh, what, what', said the king, looking at his diminutive stature, 'is this the little man that killed the brigands?'

Gillespie returned to Jamaica and assumed command of his regiment, and in 1799 was recommended by the lieutenant-general and house of assembly for the rank of lieutenant-colonel. At the peace of Amiens in 1802 the 20th light dragoons were transferred from Jamaica to the English establishment. Gillespie returned home in command, having been awarded by the house of assembly 100 guineas to purchase a sword 'as testimony of the high esteem in which he is held by this house' (*Journals of the House of Assembly, Jamaica*, 9 Dec 1801). Soon after his arrival in England allegations that he signed false returns were made against him by Major Allen Cameron of the 20th light dragoons, who had been tried in Jamaica for mutiny and sedition. Gillespie applied for inquiry by a court martial. After two years' delay he was tried at Colchester on 29 June 1804, by a general court martial, of which the Hon. John Hope was president and Lord Henry William Paget, Hussey Vivian, and others were members. He was fully acquitted, and Cameron, his accuser, was removed from the service.

Gillespie's financial position became sorely embarrassed by his open-handedness and misplaced trust, and he was compelled to exchange to India. He joined the 19th light dragoons, of which Sir Robert Wilson had just become lieutenant-colonel. Gillespie, intending to travel to India overland, went via Hamburg, where, as a fellow countryman, he was warned by Napper Tandy that he was in danger from French spies. He escaped in disguise to nearby Altona, and afterwards travelled via Vienna and the Danube to Greece, from where he made his way via Aleppo and Baghdad to India.

Once in India, he was appointed commandant of Arcot, where the 19th light dragoons were stationed, and he had not been there many days when, riding before breakfast on 10 July 1806, he was met by an officer who reported an uprising at Vellore. Vellore was a place 14 miles distant where the family of the late Tipu Sultan and their retainers were confined. Gillespie immediately hurried there with a squadron of the 19th and some Indian cavalry, and directed the rest of the dragoons with their 'galloper' guns to follow. Upon arriving, he found that the Sepoy troops had massacred the Europeans and that the survivors of the 69th foot had spent their ammunition and were making their last stand. With the aid of a rope he had himself hoisted into the fort, where he rallied and encouraged the 69th until the arrival of the guns from Arcot, which blew open the gates and allowed the dragoons to enter and cut down more than 800 of the mutineers. His gallant conduct at Vellore proved of immense importance to British prestige in India. After removing the captive princes to Madras, he was employed at Wallajabad and other stations where symptoms of disaffection appeared.

When the 19th dragoons were ordered home, in April 1807, Gillespie exchanged to the King's Royal Irish light dragoons (later the 8th hussars). Early in 1809 he commanded the cavalry and horse artillery against the Sikhs under Ranjit Singh, until Sir Charles Metcalfe ended the dispute in April. In January 1809 Gillespie transferred to the 25th light dragoons, at which time the non-commissioned officers and men of the 8th presented him with a costly sword, 'the gift of the Royal Irish', and the officers solicited his restoration to the regiment. He was subsequently commandant of Bangalore, and afterwards commanded the Mysore division of the Madras army.

In 1811 an expedition against Java was mounted in India, commanded by Sir Samuel Auchmuty, who was accompanied for part of the time by the governor-general, Lord Minto; Gillespie, as a brigadier-general, commanded the advance guard. After Batavia surrendered Gillespie led the way south, but shortly before setting out he and his staff were poisoned by some drugged coffee; luckily, however, they were not disabled. He led the assault on the strongly fortified Dutch lines at Cornelis on 26 August. Although suffering from fever, he led the storming column, was wounded, and at one stage fainted from exhaustion. Nevertheless, he cut a horse out of an enemy limber, mounted, and led his dragoons in a charge against the retreating enemy, totally routing them. Six thousand prisoners, including two generals, were taken. After the subsequent capture of Java, Auchmuty left Stamford Raffles as civil governor and gave Gillespie command of the troops.

In March 1812 Gillespie was dispatched from Batavia to the island of Sumatra (which had been tributary to the Dutch in Java), as the sultan of Palembang had murdered Europeans there. He quickly deposed the sultan, placed his brother on the throne, secured the cession of the island of Banca (Bangka) to the British, and returned to Java. When he found out that a confederacy of Javanese chiefs had taken up a position at Jogjakarta, a powerful stockaded fort defended by 100 guns and 30,000 men, he promptly attacked and carried it with 1500 troops, thereby, in all probability, saving the lives of all the Europeans in the island. Gillespie had disputes with Raffles respecting the military establishment requisite for the safety of the European population, and a massacre of Europeans soon proved the soundness of his judgement. He also preferred charges against Raffles in regard to the sale of lands. To these charges the court of directors of the East India Company devoted a prolonged inquiry and finally, after Gillespie's death in 1814, decided the main issue against Raffles.

Gillespie became major-general on 1 April 1812, and in October of that year gave up his Java command, in which he was succeeded by Sir Miles Nightingale. He returned to India, where he was appointed to a command at Meerut. In 1814 he commanded the Meerut division of the Bengal troops in the war against Nepal. Among the frontier defences was the fort of Kalunga (Kalanga), near Dehra Dun, perched in an almost inaccessible position in the Siwalik foothills of the Himalayas, and having stockaded approaches. An attack on Kalunga was fixed for 31 October 1814, the troops being told off in four small columns to attack the four faces of the fort. Three of the columns had to make long detours over difficult ground, and a preconcerted signal was agreed upon. Meanwhile the Gurkha garrison made a sortie, and Gillespie, who thought to follow them in after their repulse, made a failed attempt to rush the fort with a dismounted party of the 8th dragoons. Without waiting for the other columns, he renewed the attack with some companies of the 53rd foot, which also failed, in the course of which Gillespie, who was in front encouraging the men, was shot through the heart. The disasters at Kalunga are said to have been caused by a panic in an unidentified British regiment, and Gillespie's death was the result of his desperate endeavours to restore confidence. His body was taken back to Meerut for burial, and an obelisk was erected to his memory in the cemetery there.

The news of Gillespie's death not yet having reached England, he was included in the KCB list on new year's day 1815. A public monument (1820) by the sculptor Francis Chantrey was erected in St Paul's Cathedral, London, and a cenotaph was placed in Calcutta Cathedral. A commemorative column was also set up at Comber, his birthplace in Ireland. As a commanding officer, Gillespie inspired his men with confidence. He was a keen sportsman, and once killed a tiger on the racecourse at Bangalore. Sir John Fortescue describes him as 'the bravest man that ever wore a red coat but also extremely capable and resourceful' (Fortescue, *Brit. army*, 11.129).

H. M. CHICHESTER, *rev.* JAMES LUNT

Sources W. Thorn, *A memoir of Major-General Sir Robert Rollo Gillespie* (1816) • W. Thorn, *Memoir of the conquest of Java* (1815) • H. H. Wilson, *The history of British India*, 4th edn, 7 (1845–6) • R. Cannon, ed., *Historical record of the eighth, or the king's royal Irish regiment of hussars* (1844) • [S. Raffles], *Memoir of the life and public services of Sir Thomas Stamford Raffles* (1830) • *Colburn's United Service Magazine*, 3 (1873) [19th and 20th light dragoons] • *Colburn's United Service Magazine*, 3 (1876) [19th and 20th light dragoons] • Fortescue, *Brit. army*, vols. 7, 11 • E. G. Phythian-Adams, *The Madras regiment, 1758–1958* (1958) • D. C. Boulger, *The life of Sir Stamford Raffles* (1897) • 'Papers relating to the origin and termination of war in Nepal', *Parl. papers* (1817), 11.389, no. 2 • R. Cannon, ed., *Historical record of the fifty-third, or the Shropshire regiment of foot* (1849) • M. C. Hill, *A guide to the Shropshire records* (1952)

Archives NL Scot., corresp. with Lord Minto

Likenesses F. Chantrey, monument, 1820, St Paul's Cathedral, London • H. R. Cook, stipple (after W. Haines), BM, NPG; repro. in *Military Panorama*, 4 (1814), facing p. 395 • cenotaph, Calcutta Cathedral, India • commemorative column, Comber, co. Down • commemorative obelisk, Meerut cemetery, India • engraving, repro. in Thorn, *Memoir of Major-General Sir Robert Rollo Gillespie*

Gillespie, Thomas (1708–1774), Church of Scotland minister and a founder of the Relief church, was born at Clearburn, Duddingston, Edinburgh. Gillespie was the only son of a second marriage, his father, details of whom are unknown, having at least two previous children, a son Robert, and a daughter. The family owned a farm and a brewing business which his mother kept on after his father's death during Gillespie's childhood. His mother encouraged him to attend a communion season in the Scottish borders to hear the preaching of Thomas Boston the elder. It was in this company that, aged about nineteen or twenty, Gillespie passed through a conversion experience which radically altered his outlook on life. Involvement in the family business meant that Gillespie did not enter Edinburgh University until 1732. He appears to have completed the three year course in philosophy, and to have been nearing the end of a further three years of tuition in divinity when, in 1738, he left to study under William Wilson at the newly formed Secession Church Divinity Hall in Perth. However, the theological atmosphere there did not prove conducive to scholarship and he departed after only ten days. In 1740 Gillespie entered Philip Doddridge's academy at Northampton where he completed his theological education.

Gillespie was licensed at Northampton as a preacher of the gospel on 30 October 1740, and was ordained on 22 January 1741. After a short ministry in an independent congregation at Hartbarrow, Lancashire, he returned to Scotland and became the Church of Scotland minister of Carnock, Fife, on 4 September 1741. In the following year he became involved in the revival movement, 'one of the most remarkable effusions of the Spirit … since the Reformation', in the neighbouring parishes of Cambuslang and Kilsyth (*Dunfermline Sermons for 1746*). James Robe, minister of Kilsyth, who held him in high regard, asserted that 'of all others, the Rev Thomas Gillespie, Minister of the Gospel at Carnock, was most remarkably God's send to me' (Robe, 96). Gillespie was one of four leading evangelical ministers in Scotland who edited the testimonies of converts at Cambuslang, compiled by William McCulloch, which provide a wealth of material about the religious experiences of those who came under the influence of the revival. At about this time Gillespie also wrote his *Essay on the continuance of immediate revelations of facts and future events in the Christian church* which was not published until 1771. In this work he was concerned that an acceptance of immediate revelations and other strange phenomena should lessen the authority of scripture. Gillespie was convinced that all extraordinary gifts of the Holy Spirit had ceased to exist following the days of the apostles and the completion of the canon of scripture. On 19 November 1744 he married Margaret Riddell (*d.* 1787); the couple had no children.

From 1749 until 1752 Gillespie, along with other members of the evangelical party within the presbytery of Dunfermline, supported the rights of the Inverkeithing congregation in opposing the settlement of Andrew Richardson as their minister. They consistently refused to obey the general assembly of the Church of Scotland to perform an induction service. Several members of the emerging moderate party within the Church of Scotland were determined to use the Inverkeithing case to uphold ecclesiastical law and order by disciplining those who refused to obey the orders of the assembly. By a vote of ninety-three to sixty-five, the general assembly of 1752 determined on the deposition of one of the six ministers of the Dunfermline presbytery who refused to induct Richardson to Inverkeithing. When the assembly met on the following day Gillespie made a further statement in which he amplified his objection to the law of patronage. This action may have led some people to feel aggrieved because, when it came to a vote, the majority called for Gillespie to be deposed. When the sentence was read out, Gillespie accepted it in a spirit of meekness and returned to Carnock, never again to preach within the parish church where he had worked so faithfully. The decision of the general assembly to discipline Thomas Gillespie confirmed the power of the moderates within the Church of Scotland.

In the winter of 1752–3 Gillespie's congregation moved to Dunfermline. Despite the efforts of many within the Church of Scotland, the general assembly of 1753 refused to rescind the sentence of deposition. Following further disputed settlements, Thomas Boston the younger, minister of Jedburgh, joined Gillespie at the induction of Thomas Colier to the newly formed congregation at Colinsburgh in Fife, on 22 October 1761. After the induction services the three ministers and an elder from each of the three congregations met to form the presbytery of Relief to fulfil the same purpose as that of 'members of the Established Church' and to act 'for the relief of oppressed Christian congregations' (Struthers, 160). They believed that each individual, regardless of social status or educational attainment, was of equal value in the eyes of God and should have a voice in the affairs, including the selection of ministers, of a church not controlled by the crown or by aristocratic patrons. Gillespie believed that, although the Relief church should embrace a defined set of doctrinal standards grounded in scripture, it should not allow its own specific beliefs to result in a narrow sectarianism or a withdrawal from communion with other Christian denominations. On the contrary, Gillespie's insistence upon open communion with all who hold the headship of Christ represents the beginnings of ecumenical outreach in the Scottish reformed tradition.

The final years of Gillespie's life witnessed the growth and consolidation of the presbytery of Relief. From the three congregations which existed in 1761 the presbytery grew to nineteen congregations by the time of his death. However, he also witnessed divisions within the Relief church. He discovered that some of his ministerial colleagues did not share his vision of open communion and he came to see many of his ideals undermined by dispute. Perhaps not surprisingly, in latter years he became quick tempered and inflexible in his call for a reunion of the Relief church and the Church of Scotland. Gillespie died, aged sixty-five, on 19 January 1774 'with undiminished serenity of mind, and … enjoyed a good hope through grace of a blessed and glorious immortality' (Lindsay, 299). He was buried in Dunfermline Abbey. Following his death, a group within the Dunfermline congregation led by his brother Robert requested that the general assembly recognize them as a chapel of ease, free to issue a call to a minister of their own choice and retain some measure of independence in doctrine and discipline. The Relief church subsequently continued to expand until 1847 when, with 136 congregations, it joined with the United Secession church to form the United Presbyterian church in Scotland, and became the largest single denomination in Glasgow and accounted for slightly under one-fifth of churchgoers in Scotland. KENNETH B. E. ROXBURGH

Sources *Fasti Scot.*, new edn, 5.11 • *A speech concerning the reponing of the Reverend Mr. Gillespie* (1753) • *Case of the donors for purchasing and building the meeting-house occupied by the late Reverend Mr Thomas Gillespie* (1774) • J. Baine, *Memoirs of modern church reformation* (1766) • J. Baine, *The case of the Rev. Mr. Thomas Gillespie reviewed in a letter to The Rev. Dr. Webster* (1770) • I. D. L. Clark, 'From protest to reaction: the moderate regime in the Church of Scotland, 1752–1805', *Scotland in the age of improvement*, ed. N. T. Phillipson and R. Mitchison (1970), 200–24 • W. Lindsay, *Life and time of the Rev. Thomas Gillespie* (1849) • W. Mackelvie, *Annals and statistics of the United Presbyterian church*, ed. W. Blair and D. Young (1873) • K. B. E. Roxburgh, *Thomas Gillespie and the origins of the Relief church in eighteenth-century Scotland* (1999) • R. B. Sher, *Church and university in the Scottish Enlightenment: the moderate literati of Edinburgh* (1985) • L. Schmidt, *Holy fairs: Scottish communions and American revivals in the early modern period* (1989) • R. Small, *History of the congregations of the United Presbyterian church from 1733 to 1900*, 2 vols. (1904) • G. Struthers, *The history of the rise, progress, and principles of the Relief church* (1843) • J. Robe, *A short and true account of the wonderful conversion at Kilsyth* (1742) • U. Edin., New Coll. L., McCulloch MSS, MCC 6.1–2 • T. Gillespie, 'Sermons for 1746', Dunfermline Public Library, Dunfermline

Archives Dunfermline Public Library, sermons • New College, Edinburgh, sermons • U. Aberdeen, sermons

Gillespie, Thomas (1778–1844), Church of Scotland minister and writer, was born at Dunn's Yett, Gilchristland, Closeburn, Dumfriesshire, on 21 February 1778 and educated at Wallace Hall Academy, Dumfries Academy, and Edinburgh University. At the university he distinguished himself as a classical scholar and as a debater; at the conclusion of his college course he was licensed as a preacher on 4 January 1810. He had married in 1809 Elizabeth, daughter of John *Hunter (1745–1837), professor of humanity at St Andrews; they had four daughters and two sons. On leaving college he acted as tutor in the family of Sir James Hay of Dunragit. In 1813 he was presented by the United College, St Andrews, to the living of Cults, Fife, where he devoted his leisure to literature. Following the death in 1821 of his first wife, he married in 1823 Janet, elder daughter of George Campbell, parish minister of Cupar, and sister of John Campbell, the lord chancellor.

In 1824 Gillespie received the degree of LLD from Glasgow. In 1828 he was appointed assistant and successor to his father-in-law as the professor of humanity at St Andrews, and in 1836 he was elected to the professorship. He died at Dunino, near St Andrews, East Fife, on 11 September 1844. He contributed numerous articles in both prose and verse to leading periodicals, including essays in *Blackwood's Magazine*, the *Scots Magazine*, and *Constable's Miscellany*, and sketches in John Mackay Wilson's *Tales of the Borders*. In 1822 he published a volume of sermons, entitled *The Seasons Contemplated in the Spirit of the Gospel*. An *Analecta* for the use of his class appeared in 1839.

WILLIAM BAYNE, *rev.* M. C. CURTHOYS

Sources Chambers, *Scots.* (1835) • M. F. Conolly, *Biographical dictionary of eminent men of Fife* (1866) • *Fasti Scot.* • *Wellesley index*
Archives NL Scot., letters to Blackwoods • NL Scot., corresp. with John Lee • U. Edin., New Coll. L., letters to Thomas Chalmers

Gillespie, William (1776–1825), Church of Scotland minister and poet, was the eldest son of the Revd John Gillespie (1730–1806), minister of Kells in Galloway, and his wife, Dorothea, daughter of Robert M'Kean, shoemaker and bailie of Kirkcudbright. He was born in Kells manse on 18 February 1776. He attended the parish school, and also received private instruction from the schoolmaster, who lived in the manse. In 1792 he entered Edinburgh University, where he studied theology and also, as a secondary subject, medicine. He was a member of the Academy of Physics, a club whose members included Henry Brougham and Francis Jeffrey. From early years he was interested in painting, poetry, and music. A popular print of a view of Kenmure Castle was executed from a drawing made by him when about fourteen years of age. While at Edinburgh he wrote a poem entitled 'The Progress of Refinements' (1805) which was published in a collection some years later; he found subjects for some of the poems that were published with it in a tour through the western highlands, which he took with Alexander, son of Sir Alexander Don of Newton Don, to whom he was tutor.

At the end of his university course Gillespie was licensed as preacher by the presbytery of Kirkcudbright (1 August 1798), and on 7 August 1800 he was ordained assistant and successor to his father. In April 1806 his father died, having served as minister of Kells for forty-two years, and he became sole minister. During this period he engaged in little literary activity, except occasional contributions to periodicals such as the *Scots Magazine* and the communication of information to the Highland Society, of which he was a member. In 1815, however, he published a second volume of poetry entitled *Consolation*, with other poems.

Gillespie's sole involvement in public life took place in 1820, when he was chaplain to the stewartry of Kirdcudbright yeomanry cavalry. The commandant wrote to him, asking whether in his service before the force he would pray for the queen. He replied evasively, but in the prayer for the royal family he inserted the words, 'Bless also the queen.' On this the commandant ordered him to consider himself under arrest and not at liberty to go out of the county (30 July). Gillespie then published the sermon 'The rebellion of Absalom' which he had preached before the yeomanry, with appendices explaining the circumstances, and proving the illegality, of his arrest. He was released and received an apology from the commandant.

On 26 July 1825 Gillespie married Charlotte Hoggan, third daughter of Major George Hoggan of Waterside, Kells. While on his wedding tour he was attacked by erysipelas, and he died on 15 October 1825. He was said to have been of a pleasing appearance, with a musical voice and winning manners, and he was remembered in his parish for his refined taste and his hospitality. But as a poet he lacked any distinction and his publications enjoyed a very limited success.

EDWIN CANNAN, *rev.* ROSEMARY MITCHELL

Sources *Fasti Scot.* • Anderson, *Scot. nat.* • Chambers, *Scots.* (1835) • private information (1888)

Gillett, Joseph Ashby (1795–1853). *See under* Gibbins family (*per. c.*1770–1919).

Gillett, Martha (1798–1882). *See under* Gibbins family (*per. c.*1770–1919).

Gilliam, Laurence Duval (1907–1964), radio producer, was born on 4 March 1907 in Fulham, London, the younger son of Ernest William Gilliam (*d.* 1943), a businessman, and his wife, Beatrice Bishop (*d.* 1946). Educated at the City of London School (1918–25) and Peterhouse, Cambridge (1925–8), Laurence Gilliam worked first with the Gramophone Company in various capacities, and later as a freelance journalist, actor, and producer before joining the editorial staff of the *Radio Times* in 1932. He transferred to the BBC drama department a year later, where he worked on the development of special feature programmes which wove sound, words, and music together to create an aural picture. From 1933 until the end of his life he was responsible for the world-wide Christmas day programmes which preceded the monarch's address. These programmes were the BBC's technically most complicated assignment, linking the Commonwealth outposts with Broadcasting House in London via elaborate world-wide link-ups. Another notable example of Gilliam's early technical ambition was *'Opping 'Oliday*—a 'sound picture' of hop picking in Kent—which he produced in 1934 using the newly established mobile recording van.

Val Gielgud, head of drama, transferred responsibility for features to Gilliam in May 1936, though features really came into their own during the Second World War. While much of the BBC saw broadcasting as a means of escaping from the blitz, Gilliam saw the possibilities for the medium to reflect the reality of war. In his major topical series *The Shadow of the Swastika*, which documented the rise of Nazism, Gilliam demonstrated the power of the factual documentary for propaganda purposes and offered the first challenging piece of work from the BBC since the outbreak of war. Gilliam had a natural sympathy for the journalistic approach to broadcasting, and his war work reflected these instincts. As one of the two editors (with Donald Boyd) of *War Report*, he helped to create a revolutionary technique on which all news reporting has since been based, taking the microphone to the fighting line to report back to the people at home nightly, in record time. In recognition of this outstanding war record, features became a separate department at the end of the war, with Laurence Gilliam as its head, and Gilliam himself was appointed OBE.

Throughout the post-war period—the 'golden age of radio'—Gilliam did more than anyone in the BBC to recruit and encourage poets and writers to contribute work for the BBC features department. He maintained proudly that the feature was the one unique form that radio had achieved in its short history; and it was largely due to him that features came to stand for so much that was vital, contemporary, experimental, and above all 'pure radio'. He showed a gift for leadership which inspired devoted loyalty in a group of the most talented writers and producers in radio history, including Louis MacNeice, Douglas Cleverdon, Leonard Cottrell, Jennifer Wayne, Christopher Sykes, W. R. Rodgers, Francis Dillon, Nesta Pain, Wynford Vaughan Thomas, Alan Burgess, and D. G. Bridson. As Douglas Cleverdon discovered, Gilliam would always rather back a project that had a chance of success than reject one that might fail: 'He was also a *bon viveur*, unpunctual, extremely good company, and a tower of strength to his subordinates' (Cleverdon, 'The art of radio').

Large, ebullient, and generous-minded, with his wiry grey hair Gilliam was broad in every sense of the word, a man of inspiring integrity whose approach to programme making, as to all things, was larger than life. There was a flamboyance about Gilliam which impressed everyone who came into contact with him and quickly earned him the nickname Lorenzo the Magnificent. He combined a lack of respect for authority with a supreme confidence in the value of the work for which he was responsible. While his tastes were catholic and he enjoyed the good things of life, he was always more interested in people than in things.

In 1940 Gilliam married Marianne Helweg (1914–1976), a Dane whose father, Jacob Helweg, had immigrated to Britain in the 1920s to take up a lecturing position at the University of London. The couple met at the BBC, where Marianne had been a plays reader. She and Laurence had three sons and one daughter; the eldest was found at the age of four to have a mental handicap and was committed to a mental home soon after the war. They lived in Highgate, Middlesex, until the marriage was dissolved in 1952, when Marianne moved in with Bertie (W. R.) Rodgers, who worked for Gilliam. Rodgers, the engaging poet-minister from Armagh who had become a features producer in 1946, resigned from the features department in 1952 as a result of the relationship.

By the early 1960s the features department was under threat from the BBC managers as television began to encroach upon radio and Gilliam was offered early retirement. For twenty years he had acted as the buffer between his team of idiosyncratic producers and the administrators, keeping his team on a very loose rein. Gilliam still maintained his faith in radio, but as the end of features department was being discussed, his health was deteriorating. Laurence Gilliam died of cancer of the kidneys on 15 November 1964 in St Andrew's Hospital, Dollis Hill, Middlesex, where he was convalescing after an operation.

The development of features by the BBC, if not actually the creation of Laurence Gilliam, owed more to him than to any other single individual. In the early days of broadcasting he was among those who championed the possibilities of the medium as new, exciting, almost limitless in its possibilities. And throughout his life he maintained his belief in radio and its importance in linking world-wide communities. The establishment and direction of BBC features were Gilliam's life's work—and became very largely his life. Unfortunately, early in 1965, a few months after his death, the BBC's features department was disbanded. JEANETTE THOMAS

Sources L. Gilliam, ed., *BBC features* (1950) • D. Hawkins, ed., *BBC war report* (1946) • P. Scannell and D. Cardiff, *A social history of British broadcasting*, [1] (1991) • D. G. Bridson, *Prospero and Ariel: the rise and fall of radio* (1971) • B. Coulton, *Louis MacNeice in the BBC* (1980) • J. Stallworthy, *Louis MacNeice* (1995) • A. Briggs, *The history of broadcasting in the United Kingdom*, 4 vols. (1961–79), vols. 1–3 • P. H. Newby, *Feelings have changed* (1981) • T. D. Cleverdon, 'Radio features and drama at the BBC', *TLS* (26 Feb 1970), 229 • T. D. Cleverdon, 'The art of radio in Britain, 1922–1966', BBC WAC • staff files, programme files, press cuttings, BBC WAC • J. Gilliam, address for the funeral of Nina Gilliam, BBC WAC • E. L. E. Pawley, *BBC engineering, 1922–1972* (1972) • *CGPLA Eng. & Wales* (1965)

Archives BBC WAC | SOUND BBC WAC • BL NSA, documentary recordings • BL NSA, performance recordings

Likenesses F. Man, group photograph, 1943, Hult. Arch. • photograph, repro. in Gilliam, ed., *BBC features*

Wealth at death £23,577: probate, 11 May 1965, *CGPLA Eng. & Wales*

Gilliat, Sir Martin John (1913–1993), army officer and courtier, was born on 8 February 1913, the younger son and second of the three children of Lieutenant-Colonel John Babington Gilliat (1868–1949), army officer and landowner, of Hertfordshire, and his wife, Muriel Helen

Sir Martin John Gilliat (1913–1993), by Walter Bird, 1962

Lycette, *née* Grinnell-Milne. Both parents came from banking families and Gilliat's paternal grandfather, John Saunders Gilliat (1829–1912), was governor of the Bank of England. Gilliat was educated at Eton College and the Royal Military College, Sandhurst, before joining the King's Royal Rifle Corps in 1933. He became his father's heir when a tiger killed his brother in India in 1935.

During the Second World War, Gilliat served in the British expeditionary force and was mentioned in dispatches, before being captured at Calais in 1940. Until 1945 he was a prisoner of war, escaping four times. His first two escapes were from the marching column, heading to Germany. On his third attempt he remained free for a fortnight, almost reaching Hamburg. In 1943 he tunnelled his way out of Eichstadt, to be recaptured near the River Danube. He was then imprisoned in Colditz Castle, serving as adjutant to the senior British officer. A fellow prisoner, David Walker, noted his qualities of wit and unflappability. Though he remained in touch with his old comrades Gilliat avoided Colditz reunions in later life and was haunted by his memories and the experiences of his fellow prisoners. He suffered recurring nightmares for the rest of his life. He was appointed MBE in 1946.

Gilliat served in 1947 as deputy military secretary to Lord Mountbatten when he was viceroy and subsequently governor-general of India. He witnessed scenes of inhuman cruelty during the Delhi riots that preceded independence. In September 1947 he was wounded in the ear-pate and back when shots hit his car at point-blank range, during a night-time visit to a trouble spot in the Pahargunj area after dining with Mountbatten. He was invalided back to Britain. In due course he was delighted to be appointed comptroller to Malcolm Macdonald, high commissioner for the United Kingdom in south-east Asia, serving from 1948 to 1951, enjoying Macdonald's relaxed intelligence in contrast to Mountbatten's fussing about protocol and his 'ferocious flapping' (Gilliat to D. Walker, 16 Dec 1949, Walker papers). He then served as military secretary to Field Marshal Sir William Slim, governor-general of Australia from 1953 to 1955. As such he was to the fore during the visit of the queen and the duke of Edinburgh in February 1954, and was appointed CVO.

On the advice of his friend and contemporary Martin Charteris, a fellow green jacket, Gilliat was appointed private secretary and equerry to Queen Elizabeth the queen mother in 1956, slipping into the job, as Charteris described it, 'like a prawn into aspic' (Charteris, memorial address). For nearly forty years he was responsible for all the queen mother's official duties, and he was one of the mainstays of her hospitable and almost Edwardian court. Relish for life permeated every quarter of the building, emanating from Queen Elizabeth, whom he invariably called 'my employer'. All invited visitors were made to feel special, and if the hour of the day was appropriate their nerves were relaxed by what Charteris described as 'a fortifying drink pressed into their hands', poured out by Gilliat (Charteris). He was responsible for many aspects of the queen mother's horse-racing career, and was himself an owner, training with Ryan Price. He was also the animateur of many private parties at Royal Lodge. He was particularly energetic at ensuring that Queen Elizabeth met and entertained leading figures from the worlds of the arts, business, the services, and racing, while Ruth, Lady Fermoy, one of her ladies-in-waiting, brought in musicians. He and Lady Fermoy were the leading lights of the queen mother's August house parties at the castle of Mey.

Gilliat was promoted KCVO in 1962, and GCVO in 1981. He was deputy lieutenant of Hertfordshire from 1963 (vice-lieutenant from 1971 to 1986), and a JP for that county, living for many years at Appletrees, near Welwyn. He was made an honorary bencher of the Middle Temple, and an honorary doctor of laws of the University of London, both in 1977. He held his alma mater, Eton, in high esteem, visiting the college regularly and paying for the painting of three leaving portraits, two by Derek Hill and one by Andrew Festing. He was a steward at Windsor racecourse, and at Kempton Park (later patron). He sat as a magistrate on the bench at St Albans crown court. He was also an 'angel', backing at least thirty plays on the London stage, and to him fell the sometimes complicated task of finding a suitable play for his employer to attend on her birthday.

By 1979 the possibility of Gilliat retiring was mooted by his friends, but he felt that since he was working for someone thirteen years his senior, he could not do so unless she wanted him to. She did not, and he was soon joking that she looked at him with amazement when at times his energy flagged. When the queen mother celebrated her ninetieth birthday in 1990 he predicted on television that she would reach her century, but wondered how many of the household would still be with her. He continued to serve even after his health collapsed, and he died, in office, of liver cancer, in London on 27 May 1993. He was unmarried. HUGO VICKERS

Sources *The Times* (29 May 1993) • *Daily Telegraph* (29 May 1993) • *The Independent* (1 June 1993), 20 • Lord Charteris of Amisfield, memorial service address, St Martin-in-the-Fields, London, 8 July 1993 • letters from Martin Gilliat to David H. Walker, University of New Brunswick, David H. Walker papers • D. Walker, *Lean, wind, lean* (1984) • *WWW, 1991–5* • Burke, *Gen. GB* (1965) • personal knowledge (2004) • private information (2004) [A. Windham; N. Jaques, Eton College; L. Murphy, Clarence House] • private diaries of Sir Charles Johnston, priv. coll.

Archives University of New Brunswick, letters to David H. Walker

Likenesses W. Bird, photograph, 1962, NPG [*see illus.*] • photograph, repro. in *The Times* • photograph, repro. in *Daily Telegraph* • photograph, repro. in *The Independent*

Wealth at death £1,379,768: probate, 19 July 1993, *CGPLA Eng. & Wales*

Gilliat, Sidney (1908–1994), film director and screenwriter, was born on 15 February 1908 at 12 Torkington Street, Stockport, Cheshire, the first of the four children of George Gilliat (1882–1980), journalist and newspaper editor, and his wife, Annie Mary, *née* Stone (1883–1966), daughter of a Northampton lace manufacturer. His brother Leslie (*b.* 1917) followed him into the film industry, ultimately serving as a producer. The family moved south to New Malden, Surrey, in 1915. Following education in local schools, Gilliat studied English and history at London University. A career in journalism was expected, but in 1928 Gilliat—a quiet, diffident youth with a taste for continental films—found employment instead at British International Pictures, Elstree, Hertfordshire, as assistant to the studio's new scenario chief, Walter Mycroft, formerly film critic of the London *Evening Standard* (a newspaper edited by Gilliat's father from 1928 to 1933). Motley, unrewarding work was followed by a useful period assisting the director Walter Forde, learning about comic timing and the new problems of talking pictures. Gilliat's breakthrough to prominence came in 1932 with his script for Forde's thriller *Rome Express*, widely admired at the time for its bright dialogue and technical expertise. On 21 December 1933 he married Beryl Maud (1909–1981), daughter of Stanley Percival Brewer, furniture dealer; they had two children, Joanna in 1935 and Caroline in 1938.

In 1935 Gilliat collaborated with Frank *Launder on another thriller script, *Seven Sinners*. Gilliat and Launder became lifelong professional partners, working together as writers, producers, and directors, and somehow staying firm friends in the process. In temperament each balanced the other: Gilliat, shy beneath his bluff exterior, was the gloomy hypochondriac and pessimist; Launder was the carefree, outgoing optimist. Their interests outside films also varied: where Launder might have been found at the racetrack, Gilliat preferred the opera house at Glyndebourne. In the 1930s the pair made a speciality of sprightly thrillers, influenced by the flippant, fast style of Hollywood, but with a characteristic English regard for eccentricity and the ability to endow even minor characters with individuality. *The Lady Vanishes* (1938), directed by Alfred Hitchcock, was a particular success, and the characters of Charters and Caldicott—fond caricatures of the imperturbable Englishman abroad—found a place in further scripts by the team, including *Night Train to Munich* (1940).

The coming of war, and the resulting shake-up of film personnel, provided a first opportunity for Launder and Gilliat to direct. *Millions Like Us* (1943), based on their own original script, painted a vivid portrait of the home front in England. This was the only time the team directed a film side-by-side on the studio floor; subsequently, each directed their separate projects. Gilliat's speciality was dry social comedy, best typified by *The Rake's Progress* (1945), an excellent satire about a profligate charmer who finds his feet in the Second World War. This was Gilliat's favourite among his films. *The Rake's Progress* was the first product of Launder and Gilliat's own company, Individual Pictures, one of several independent outfits grouped under the Rank Organisation's umbrella during the late 1940s. Gilliat found further success with *Green for Danger* (1946), an agreeably sardonic adaptation of Christianna Brand's thriller, and *State Secret* (1950), his own story about a surgeon's enforced involvement in central European intrigue, and the first of several productions for Alexander Korda following the disbandment of the Rank group.

By the 1950s Launder and Gilliat were firmly established as reliable and versatile makers of intelligent, middlebrow cinema. Launder concentrated successfully on farce with *The Happiest Days of your Life* (1950), and *The Belles of St Trinian's* (1954) and its sequels. Gilliat found it harder to find satisfactory outlets for his more literate, cynical wit; while *The Constant Husband* (1955) and *Left, Right and Centre* (1959) had many charms, both just failed to come to the boil. Creative life became circumscribed by increasing managerial responsibilities once he and Launder joined the board of the British Lion Film Corporation in 1958. Unpretentious and unlikely film moguls, the pair managed to stay well-respected in the industry. Gilliat's fortunes rose again with *Only Two Can Play* (1962), a vigorous and popular adaptation of Kingsley Amis's novel *That Uncertain Feeling*, which displayed his old flair for mordant detail. His passion for opera found an outlet when he wrote the libretto for Malcolm Williamson's *Our Man in Havana* (1963), based on the novel by Graham Greene. But as the 1960s advanced administrative burdens at British Lion and Shepperton Studios, where he served as chairman, again weighed heavily. *Endless Night* (1971), based on an Agatha Christie whodunnit, was his last film.

In contented retirement from the industry, Gilliat worked on a novel about nineteenth-century railway fraud, *Catch me Who Can*, an ebullient stylistic exercise, exhaustively researched, and left incomplete at his death. In addition, his sharp recall of British film history was plundered gratefully by numerous film researchers and historians. He died on 31 May 1994, at Embrook, Hilcott, Wiltshire, his home since 1936. He was survived by his two daughters, his wife having predeceased him in 1981. A memorial service was held at St James's Church, North Newnton, near Pewsey, Wiltshire, on 10 July 1994.

GEOFF BROWN

Sources G. Brown, *Launder and Gilliat* (1977) · *The Times* (1 June 1994) · *The Times* (11 July 1994) · *The Independent* (2 June 1994) · *The Independent* (11 June 1994) · personal knowledge (2004) · private information (2004) · b. cert. · m. cert.
Archives FILM BFI NFTVA, documentary footage | SOUND BL NSA, documentary recording · BL NSA, performance recording
Likenesses photograph, repro. in *The Times* (1 June 1994)
Wealth at death £510,475: probate, 5 Oct 1994, *CGPLA Eng. & Wales*

Gilliatt [*née* Conner], **Penelope Ann Douglass** (1932–1993), journalist and novelist, was born at 16 Eldon Road, Kensington, London, on 25 March 1932, the elder daughter of Cyril Conner, barrister, and his wife, Mary Stephanie, *née* Douglass. Both parents came from Newcastle and were connected with shipping, her mother's family as owners and her father's on the artisan side; as a boy her father begged in the street for the money to take a train to Haileybury, where he was given a scholarship. After practising as a barrister he joined the BBC, and eventually became head of radio in Belfast. Later he was appointed a quarter sessions judge. He and his wife, Mary, divorced when Penelope was eleven and a half, abandoning the house in Studland, Dorset, which had been a haven for all the family. Penelope and her younger sister, Angela, moving from one place to another round the country, were at one point taught by their mother under the Parents National Educational Union system. Penelope then spent brief periods in various schools before going to Queen's College, Harley Street, London, where she finished her secondary education. From there she went to New York to train at the Juilliard School of Music, but became anorexic; it was soon realized that the emotional strains of a concert pianist's life would be too much for her, and she went instead to Bennington College, Vermont. She returned to London as a winner of the *Vogue* talent contest, which carried an automatic appointment to a job with Condé Nast (dogsbody to the needlework section, in her case). She quickly moved on to writing features for *Vogue* itself. On 18 December 1954 she married Roger William Gilliatt (1922–1991), a distinguished neurosurgeon, and son of Sir William *Gilliatt, obstetrician. They set up house in a chic flat in Knightsbridge.

From the late 1950s Penelope Gilliatt wrote for the *New Statesman*, *The Guardian*, *The Spectator*, *Queen*, *Encounter*, the *London Review of Books*, and many other newspapers, magazines, and journals. Chic, petite, almost pixie-like, with a wicked smile, vivid wit, and 'outstanding red-headedness' (*The Independent*, 14 May 1993), she became a star of the media scene that was just emerging as 'swinging London'. She was a member of the Labour Party, and walked with her husband, Roger, for at least a short part of anti-nuclear marches. Nevertheless, by the early 1960s the marriage had cooled; she became involved with the playwright John *Osborne (1929–1994), son of Thomas Godfrey

Penelope Ann Douglass Gilliatt (1932–1993), by unknown photographer

Osborne, advertising copy writer; she moved with him into an old mill house in Hellingly, Sussex, and married him on 25 May 1963. This move came in for a good deal of public disapproval, apparently not so much because Osborne had abandoned his previous wife, the actress Mary Ure, without seeing their three-week-old son, as because Penelope had walked out on someone who had been best man at a royal wedding: that of Princess Margaret to Lord Snowdon in 1960. The gossip columnists made a meal of this, delighted to get back at her for a searing article entitled 'The friendless ones' she had written for *Queen* in which she attacked them for the inaccuracy and scurrilous nature of their columns. The article had prompted Lord Rothermere, owner of the *Daily Mail*, to discontinue the Paul Tanfield column.

The Osbornes did not stay in the country long, but moved into an impressive Georgian house in Chester Square, Belgravia, which Penelope's sister Angela, by then a celebrated sculptor, gutted and dramatized in true 1960s style: an immense refectory table dominated the ground floor, walls were removed, and shapes were changed. Meanwhile Penelope (as Penelope Gilliatt) continued her career in journalism, becoming features editor of *Vogue* and alternating as film critic with Kenneth Tynan in *The Observer* (1961–5 and 1966–7). She began to write novels and short stories: *One by One* in 1965, and *A State of Change* in 1967, getting up at five each morning to write. She was devoted to Osborne—with whom she had a daughter,

Nolan—but marriages to him seldom lasted, and in 1968 he left her for the actress Jill Bennett.

Gilliatt felt she could no longer continue in London and moved with Nolan to New York, where she wrote film reviews for the *New Yorker*, contributed to the magazine *Grand Street* and other publications, and wrote a highly successful film script, *Sunday Bloody Sunday* (1971, starring Peter Finch and Glenda Jackson). This was nominated for an Oscar for best original screenplay, and won awards for best original screenplay from the New York Film Critics' Circle and both British and American film critics. She made a glittering place for herself on the New York scene, as she had in London, occupying a large flat overlooking Central Park, cooking excellently for her friends, and writing prolifically: profiles, reviews, novels, a libretto, a play, short stories, and several further film scripts, though no more films were actually made. But increasingly she kept up the level of her vivacity with drink. After an occasion when, writing a profile of Graham Greene, she muddled his words with her own to a lamentable extent, the job with the *New Yorker* came to an end—though the editor, still a great friend, continued to print her writing under a different name. Increasingly, she relied on drink, denied that it was a problem, and failed at various attempts to give it up. She returned to Britain, where she died on 10 May 1993 at her home, 29 Burnham Court, Moscow Road, Westminster, of postural asphyxia and cirrhosis of the liver. She was survived by her daughter, Nolan. As a critic and journalist she was one of the most sparkling personalities of her time. KATHARINE WHITEHORN

Sources *The Independent* (14 May 1993) · *The Times* (12 May 1993) · *The Times* (20 May 1993) · *WWW, 1991–5* · personal knowledge (2004) · private information (2004) [Angela Conner, sister] · b. cert. · m. certs. · d. cert.

Archives Bodl. Oxf., notebooks and scripts | SOUND BL NSA, performance recording

Likenesses photograph, News International Syndication, London [*see illus.*] · photograph, repro. in *The Independent*

Wealth at death £197,534: probate, 5 Aug 1994, *CGPLA Eng. & Wales*

Gilliatt, Sir William (1884–1956), obstetrician, was born on 7 June 1884 at Boston, Lincolnshire, son of William Gilliatt, farmer, and Alice Rose. The father later abandoned farming to run his own chemist shop in Boston. William, fourth in a family of five, was educated at Kirton village school and Wellingborough College. His headmaster, impressed by his ability, persuaded him to give up the idea of farming in favour of medicine. In 1902 he entered University College Hospital, but after a year transferred to the Middlesex, where he won several scholarships. After qualifying in the London MB, BS, in 1908, he was awarded the Lyell gold medal in 1909 and went on to hold various resident house appointments, taking the London MD in 1910 and winning the gold medal in obstetrics and gynaecology. Two years later he was made FRCS and graduated MS (London) while holding the post of registrar and tutor in obstetrics and gynaecology at the Middlesex Hospital.

In 1914 Gilliatt married Anne Louise Jane, daughter of John Kann, stockbroker of Lyne, Surrey. She was a doctor and practised for several years as an anaesthetist. They had one daughter, and a son, Roger William (1922–1991), who became professor of neurology at the National Hospital for Nervous Diseases.

In 1912 Gilliatt was appointed first assistant resident medical officer at Queen Charlotte's Maternity Hospital, and later pathologist and registrar. In 1916 he was appointed assistant obstetric and gynaecological surgeon and lecturer in the medical school of King's College Hospital and physician to outpatients at Queen Charlotte's Hospital, and in 1919 obstetric surgeon to in-patients. But in 1920, unable properly to discharge his obligations in two large departments, he resigned from Queen Charlotte's to give more time to King's College Hospital, where he had much teaching and was senior obstetric and gynaecological surgeon from 1925 to 1946. He also worked as an honorary member of the staff of the Bromley, the Maudsley, and St Saviour's hospitals and the Samaritan Hospital for Women.

Gilliatt was a notable teacher with a clear and concise method. He was a skilful and dexterous obstetrician, a painstaking but not spectacular surgeon. Above all, he was an astute diagnostician with remarkably good judgement and common sense. He wrote little, but made valuable contributions on the subject of maternal mortality and morbidity. He contributed to the *Historical Review of British Obstetrics and Gynaecology* (1954) and contributed to successive editions of the *Ten Teachers* series in obstetrics and gynaecology.

Gilliatt was a foundation fellow of the British (later Royal) College of Obstetricians and Gynaecologists in 1929. He was elected to the council in 1932, served as president (1946–9), and remained active in college affairs until the day of his death. His clear and logical thought and argument made him an ideal committee member, and he effectively chaired many committees in the college and at King's College Hospital.

Gilliatt developed a considerable private practice especially in obstetrics within the constraints passed by his other professional responsibilities and this allowed him to maintain homes at 2 Hyde Park Crescent and 100 Harley Street. He delivered Princess Marina, duchess of Kent, of all her children and Princess Elizabeth of Prince Charles and Princess Anne. After Princess Elizabeth became queen, Gilliatt was appointed her surgeon-gynaecologist. He was appointed CVO in 1936, knighted in 1948, and promoted KCVO in 1949. In 1947 he was elected FRCP and in 1953 was made an honorary master of midwifery of the Society of Apothecaries. In 1954–6 he was president of the Royal Society of Medicine.

When young Gilliatt played football for the Corinthian Casuals, and later became a keen and very good golfer. In later life he was a regular visitor to and member of many racing clubs including Ascot and Kempton Park. He was a keen freemason. Although shy, Gilliatt had a strong character and sense of duty, a stern self-discipline, and a single-minded determination, which at times gave the impression of ruthlessness. He did not waste words, but was always willing to advise. His quiet dignity, courtesy, and sincerity made him a successful elder statesman of many professional institutions. Gilliatt died in a motor accident at Langcross Road, Chertsey, on 27 September 1956. JOHN PEEL, *rev.* ELIZABETH BAIGENT

Sources W. R. Brain, *Annual address delivered to the Royal College of Physicians, 1957* (1957) · *WWW* · *The Times* (28 Sept 1956) · *CGPLA Eng. & Wales* (1956) · G. Gordon-Taylor, 'In memoriam Sir William Gilliatt', *Annals of the Royal College of Surgeons of England*, 19 (1956), 394–6 · J. Peel, *The lives of the fellows of the Royal College of Obstetricians and Gynaecologists, 1929–1969* (1976)
Archives Royal College of Obstetricians and Gynaecologists, London, corresp. and papers
Likenesses D. Alison, oils, *c.*1950, Royal College of Obstetricians and Gynaecologists, London · E. I. Halliday, oils, after 1956 (posthumous; after photograph), Royal Society of Medicine · portrait, repro. in Gordon-Taylor, 'In memoriam Sir William Gilliatt'
Wealth at death £50,712 7*s.* 2*d.*: probate, 24 Dec 1956, *CGPLA Eng. & Wales*

Gillie [*married name* Smith], **Dame Annis Calder** (**1900–1985**), general practitioner and medical politician, was born in London on 3 August 1900, the eldest daughter and first of the four children of Dr Robert Calder Gillie, a minister in the Presbyterian church, and his wife, Emily Japp. She was proud to be a daughter of the manse and equally proud of her family, which included a number of distinguished journalists. She was educated at Wycombe Abbey School, University College, London, and University College Hospital, graduating MB BS in 1925 and taking the membership of the Royal College of Physicians two years later. The attitude of the staff and students at University College Hospital did not make things easy for her. With a fellow student she

> was for ever trying to avoid the constant jibes and criticism. They would sit at the very back of the out-patients clinics and feel safer there; on ward rounds, to avoid being questioned and inevitably taunted, they would 'hide behind the rest of the students and quietly slip away un-noticed at the first opportunity'. (Merrington, 239)

Gillie entered general practice in London as assistant to a partnership of three women, one of whom, Christine Murrell, was a well-known figure in medical politics. When one senior partner died and the others retired Gillie worked single-handed from her London home in Connaught Square. During the Second World War she moved out of London to her country cottage at Pangbourne whence she drove in and out of London and over a wide area of countryside visiting patients. She resumed in partnership in 1954 until her retirement in 1963.

Annis Gillie played a predominant part in the renaissance of general practice that began after the Second World War. She was a member of the General Medical Council in 1946–8 and was president of the Medical Women's Federation in 1954–5. She became a member of several statutory bodies concerned with general practice including the medical practices committee, the executive council of London, the standing medical advisory committee, and the Central Health Services Council. She was a member (and for some years vice-chairman) of the British Medical Association's central ethical committee and a member of its council in 1950–64.

Gillie was a founder member of the Royal College of General Practitioners, an early member of its council, and its chairman in 1959–62. This was a period of intense depression within general practice. Recruitment was falling, general practitioners were leaving the country in large numbers, more and more areas lacked a general practitioner, and all the advantages, particularly financial, lay with medical careers other than general practice. It was also a time of difficult relationships between the new college and the British Medical Association. In 1961 the standing medical advisory committee set up a subcommittee, chaired by Gillie, to predict the course along which general practice should develop over and beyond the next decade. Its report, 'The field of work of the family doctor', was published in 1963. It was unusual in that the chapters were written by members of the committee rather than departmental officials but it provided a statement of confidence in the future drawn from a strong factual base. It made its mark on practice throughout the English-speaking world and profoundly influenced the 'charter' agreed between the British Medical Association and minister of health in 1964 which restored the fortunes of general practice. It had also a major effect upon the report of the royal commission on medical education which, appearing in 1968, recognized general practice as a separate speciality and gave pride of place to its separate postgraduate training.

During the time that Gillie held office in the College of General Practitioners, first as chairman of council and then president in 1964–7, many important decisions were taken, such as the institution of an examination for membership and the purchase of 14 Princes Gate, London, the college's subsequent home. This period was crowned with the award to the college of the royal charter. Gillie had a strong personality and a very tough centre. She dealt with patients in a gentle, firm, authoritarian manner. In meetings she was able when necessary to silence unconstructive contributions but always did this with courtesy. On public occasions she never failed to find the right words. She was not an original thinker nor an innovator. Her skills were those of facilitating, encouraging, and promoting others, and persuading committees to produce sensible and balanced conclusions. She was a medical politician and as one of her contemporaries said, was an 'Attlee' rather than a 'Bevan' and was always nearer to the political than the academic side of her discipline.

Gillie was appointed OBE in 1961 and DBE in 1968. In 1964 she was elected FRCP and was awarded an honorary MD by Edinburgh University (1968). She was elected a fellow of the British Medical Association in 1960 and in 1968 was elected a vice-president of the association in recognition of her valuable service, the first woman to be so honoured.

In 1930 she married Peter Chandler Smith (*d.* 1983), an architect. His practice was destroyed by the war and he was rejected for military service, and she was for many years the breadwinner. They had a daughter, who died in 1974, and a son. Her husband became incapacitated with a chronic illness that made him very dependent upon her for the last fifteen years of their life together. Annis Gillie died on 10 April 1985 at her home in Bledington, Oxfordshire. V. W. M. DRURY

Sources personal knowledge (2004) · *WWW* · W. R. Merrington, *University College Hospital and its medical school: a history* (1976)

Gillie [*née* Reeves], **Cecilia Grace Hunt** (**1907–1996**), radio executive, was born on 18 August 1907, at 16 Alma Road, Sheerness, on the Isle of Sheppey, Kent, the second of two daughters of Albert Robert Reeves, a naval engineer, and his wife, Ella, *née* Hunt. She was brought up in Birmingham and educated at King Edward VI High School for Girls, and later at Newnham College, Cambridge, where she graduated in modern languages. She joined the BBC's foreign department in 1933, working in the foreign liaison office, a small offshoot of the BBC that enabled foreign broadcasters to transmit material to their home countries. In 1937 she was particularly concerned with arrangements for the new European director of the Columbia Broadcasting System in New York, Edward R. Murrow. In March 1938 he had been sent to Vienna to cover Hitler's *Anschluss*. On Murrow's return Cecilia Reeves immediately arranged for his report to be transmitted, uncensored, to the United States. Afterwards she listened to Murrow's own personal account of the horrors he had witnessed. That experience, and her contact with the less formal American broadcasting practices, were to be crucial to her later role.

In 1939 Reeves helped Richard Marriott, the foreign liaison officer, to set up the BBC's Paris office, but events forced them to return to London after only a brief period in France. She was responsible for French talks during summer 1940 when, after a speech on 17 June by Marshal Pétain suing for peace, and another the next day by General de Gaulle urging resistance, it became urgent to set up a formal framework for broadcasting by the BBC to occupied France. This was the start of a most effective propaganda operation which lasted for the rest of the war.

Cecilia Reeves was asked to form a team of French broadcasters and journalists to handle the necessary expansion of the service. She enlisted the services of Michel Saint-Denis, a French stage director, whom she persuaded not to accept a commission in the British army, but to serve his country through broadcasting. He agreed, and this led to the creation of a nightly broadcast entitled *Les Français parlent aux Français*, using a flexible multi-voiced formula which owed something to the American informal style introduced to Cecilia Reeves through her contact with Ed Murrow.

Reeves was conscious of the French passion for discussion and so, in addition to *Les Français parlent aux Français*, she encouraged Michel Saint-Denis, broadcasting as Jacques Duchesne, to become the first member of a group known as *les trois amis*. He was joined by, among others, Pierre Maillaud and Jean Oberle, who broadcast regularly for the rest of the war. Raymond Mortimer, head of French broadcasting at the Ministry of Information, wrote subsequently: 'Their work, which sprang from a happy collaboration between Frenchmen of very various professions and opinion, is likely to rank as a classic of propaganda in the best sense of the word' (*The Independent*, 24 April 1996). Using Gallic wit, sarcasm, and derision, determined to broadcast the truth, however grim, but always pleading convincingly the case for hope and patience, they succeeded in gaining the confidence of the sceptical French public, so that when hope of eventual victory first dawned, the BBC was implicitly believed. As one French resistance leader put it: '*Les Français parlent aux Français* were the words which, in the silence of occupation, when every mouth was gagged, helped the French to surmount the lies of the enemy and saved them from despair' (*The Times*, 6 May 1996).

By the end of the war Cecilia Reeves had become head of the unit in the European liaison office in London, and in 1947 she was appointed the BBC's representative in Paris. She held this post until 1958, when with the increasing interest in television Robin Scott was appointed representative. Cecilia Reeves remained in charge of radio talks until 1967. The post-war years saw a much increased interest in French cultural life on the part of BBC radio, with the newly created Third Programme providing an outlet for many distinguished French voices. This owed much to Cecilia Reeves's unparalleled network of contacts among French intellectuals, journalists, and politicians, who came to the studios on avenue Hoche to make their contribution to Anglo-French understanding. Through her auspices Jean Cocteau painted a mural on the wall of the BBC office on avenue Hoche.

During the war Reeves had worked closely with Darsie Rutherford Gillie (1903–1972), who was the BBC's French news editor, and who after the war returned to the *Manchester Guardian* as the paper's French correspondent. He and Cecilia Reeves were married in 1955, and entertained a vast circle of French and English intellectuals at their apartment on the rue Casimir Perrier in Paris. They retired to Provence in 1967 because of Darsie's ill health, and welcomed an ever-increasing circle to their house in Mirabeau. Darsie died in 1972 after a long illness, and Cecilia stayed on in Mirabeau teaching English to scientists and writing a cookery book. She suffered a severe and disabling stroke in 1987, and died nine years later on 20 April 1996 in Warsaw, where she had been cared for by an old Polish friend. She was cremated, and her ashes were scattered over the English Channel. SUSAN PHELPS

Sources C. Gillie, history of the BBC's wartime French service, BBC WAC, ref. 550 · *The Guardian* (24 April 1996) · private information [Mme Maud Vidal] · *The Times* (6 May 1996) · *Daily Telegraph* (27 April 1996) · *The Independent* (24 April 1996) · b. cert.

Gillies, Adam, **Lord Gillies** (**1760–1842**), judge, was born in Brechin, the youngest son of Robert Gillies of Little Keithock, Forfarshire, and his wife, Margaret, *née* Smith, daughter of a merchant. He was brother to John *Gillies, the historian. Adam Gillies was educated for the law and was admitted an advocate on 14 July 1787. On 20 March 1806 he became sheriff-depute of Kincardineshire. On 30

November 1811 he succeeded Lord Newton as an ordinary judge of the college of justice, and in March 1812 he succeeded Lord Craig as a lord of justiciary. Following Lord Meadowbank's death he was appointed, on 10 July 1816, a lord commissioner of the jury court. In 1837 he resigned his seat as a lord of justiciary, and was appointed a judge of the court of exchequer in Scotland. He took little part in politics; in early life his views were whig, but subsequently they became tory. He died at Leamington Spa, Warwickshire, on 24 December 1842.

J. A. HAMILTON, *rev.* ERIC METCALFE

Sources Irving, *Scots.* • G. Brunton and D. Haig, *An historical account of the senators of the college of justice, from its institution in MDXXXII* (1832) • Anderson, *Scot. nat.*
Archives NRA Scotland, priv. coll., letters to William Adam, etc.
Likenesses J. Kay, two etchings, NPG; repro. in H. Paton, ed., *A series of original portraits and caricature etchings by the late John Kay*, 2 (1842) • T. Lupton, mezzotint (after C. Smith), NPG
Wealth at death £7469 10s. 6d.: inventory, 16 March 1843, NA Scot., SC 70/1/63, p. 601

Gillies, Duncan (1834–1903), politician in Australia, was born in January 1834 at Overnewton, a suburb of Glasgow, the second son of Duncan Gillies, a market gardener, and his wife, Margaret. He left Glasgow high school around the age of fourteen and worked as a clerk in the Post Office until 1852, when he emigrated to Australia under the sponsorship of James Russell Thompson, a colonial official whom he had met while both were working at the Post Office in Glasgow. Both men soon after joined the gold diggings at Ballarat, Victoria, and later worked together at the Great Republic Mine, of which Gillies became a working partner. Thompson was said to have trained Gillies in the art of public speaking after seeing the 'ambitious' young man's potential (*Ballarat Courier*, 14 Sept 1903, 4). Short, sturdy, and dapper, Gillies first became publicly known as an advocate of miners' rights, and was elected by his fellow miners to the local mining court in 1854. He was, however, absent from the events surrounding the Eureka stockade rebellion by miners that December.

Gillies first stood for parliament in 1859, but was not elected until the February 1861 poll, in the Ballarat West constituency. He was re-elected to this seat in the following three elections, but in this time was steadily moving towards a more conservative political stance, while also gathering a reputation as a master debater in the house. He accepted a ministerial post in the Sladen government after the 1868 election, but was defeated in the resulting by-election.

Gillies re-entered parliament at the election of March 1870 for the seat of Maryborough, and from 1872 to 1877, under the Francis, Kerferd, and McCulloch administrations, held portfolios in the areas of railways and roads, lands, and agriculture. He was elected for the seat of Rodney in May 1877, but a new election was called after a court found that officials of the lands department, for which Gillies was the responsible minister, had influenced the result through the issue of leases to electors during the contest. Gillies was cleared of personal blame, and won the new election in November.

In parliament, Gillies had by then become a leading member of the 'conservative' grouping and a supporter of James Service in his opposition to the liberal and protectionist Berry government. When Service took office in February 1880, Gillies became minister for railways for six months, and returned to this position when Service and Berry formed a coalition government in March 1883. When they stepped down in February 1886, the conservative–liberal coalition was continued, with Gillies and Alfred Deakin taking the respective party leadership positions; Gillies became premier and treasurer.

Geoffrey Serle has described Gillies as 'perhaps the most crucial premier in Victorian history, for he was to preside over Victoria's self-destruction' (Serle, 40)—that is, the unsustainable economic expansion of the late 1880s, which culminated in severe depression in the 1890s, and the end of the state's long period of prosperity.

Despite his parliamentary abilities and considerable self-confidence, Gillies was a poor administrator. His government over-extended the finances of the state through large borrowings and public works, particularly railway construction and irrigation, and this intensified the existing boom conditions. Though he was apparently not involved himself, Gillies's government did little to curb the financially precarious and often fraudulent activities of the land syndicates, building societies, and banks fuelling the boom. *The Economist* asserted that the government acted 'incompetently and indolently' in this period (Serle, 259), and Gillies himself, a persistent sabre-rattler in the dispute with France over the New Hebrides, showed little understanding of Anglo-French relations.

The government was returned in March 1889, when Gillies transferred to the seat of Eastern Suburbs in Melbourne. But growing unemployment, increasingly obvious difficulties in funding the state's committed works, and resentment over the government's handling of industrial disputes intensified discontent with his government. In mid-1890 his effigy was being beheaded at demonstrations of the unemployed. By the end of October the opposition was able to pass a no-confidence motion. Gillies resigned on 5 November 1890, and led the opposition until 1894. During this time he maintained the strong support for the federation of the Australian colonies that he had shown in government, and he represented Victoria at a number of intercolonial conferences promoting this issue. In January 1894 he reluctantly became Victoria's agent-general in London, and remained there until early 1897. Just before leaving London, on 15 January 1897 he entered into a short-lived marriage with a 37-year-old widow, Harriett Turquand Fillan, *née* Theobald, who stayed with Gillies only briefly on his return to Australia before leaving for, and remaining permanently in, Johannesburg.

In October 1897 Gillies was again elected to the Victorian parliament, this time as the member for Toorak. He was voted speaker of the house of assembly in 1902, and remained in that position until his death.

Gillies has been described as a 'ladies' man' (Serle, 40), on the basis of a perhaps ironic portrayal of him in *The Bulletin* as a 'Lothario' of whom the future premier Tommy Bent had said that he shouldn't let 'a daughter of his be seen on the same side of the street with him' (23 Jan 1886, 6). But Gillies's public manner was universally noted as exceedingly cold and formal. A brilliant debater, however, he ultimately owed his rise to prominence to the respect he had gained in parliament rather than among the populace.

Gillies died of heart failure in his apartments at Parliament House, Melbourne, on 12 September 1903, following a stroke the previous December, and was buried at Melbourne general cemetery on 14 September.

MARC BRODIE

Sources *Ballarat Courier* (14 Sept 1903) · *Ballarat Courier* (15 Sept 1903) · *The Age* [Melbourne] (14 Sept 1903) · *The Argus* [Melbourne] (14 Sept 1903) · G. Serle, *The rush to be rich: a history of the colony of Victoria, 1883–1889* (1971) · K. Thompson and G. Serle, *A biographical register of the Victorian parliament, 1859–1900* (1972) · *AusDB*, 4.250–52 · H. J. Gibbney and A. G. Smith, eds., *A biographical register, 1788–1939: notes from the name index of the 'Australian dictionary of biography'*, 2 (1987) · *The Bulletin* (23 Jan 1886), 6 · *The Age* [Melbourne] (17 Dec 1887), 13 · B. Scates, 'A struggle for survival: unemployment and the unemployed agitation in late nineteenth-century Melbourne', *Australian Historical Studies*, 24 (1990–91), 41–63 · W. Bate, *Lucky city: the first generation at Ballarat, 1851–1901* (1978)

Likenesses photograph, *c*.1885, repro. in Serle, *The rush to be rich*, facing p. 37 · J. M. Maut, portrait, Parliament House, Melbourne, Australia · P. Tennyson Cole, oils, National Gallery, Melbourne, Australia

Gillies, Sir Harold Delf (1882–1960), plastic surgeon, was born in Dunedin, New Zealand, on 17 June 1882, the youngest of the six sons of Robert Gillies, a contractor and noted amateur astronomer, and his wife, Emily Street. His great-uncle was Edward Lear, author of the *Book of Nonsense*. He was educated at Wanganui College, where he was captain of the cricket team, and at Gonville and Caius College, Cambridge, where he played golf (1903–5) and also rowed (1904) for the university; he obtained a second class in part one of the natural sciences tripos in 1904. From Cambridge he moved for his clinical studies to St Bartholomew's Hospital, London, where he qualified in 1908 and became FRCS in 1910. After a brief period in general surgery he became interested in otorhinolaryngology and worked with Milsom Rees.

Gillies's great opportunity came with the war of 1914–18. He joined the Royal Army Medical Corps in 1915, went to France, and was enormously impressed by the work of French and German surgeons in the field of reconstructive surgery for patients with facial injuries. Such was his enthusiasm that a centre for the treatment of these patients was started at Aldershot later in the same year, and Gillies was placed in charge of it under Sir Arbuthnot Lane. In 1918 the centre moved to Queen Mary's Hospital, Sidcup, and was eventually administered by the Ministry of Pensions, to which Gillies became honorary consultant. The collective experience the unit had in the reconstruction of facial wounds was rapidly expanded, and soon it covered the whole field of reconstructive surgery to include such afflictions as burns, limb injuries, and congenital malformations.

After the war many of the surgeons trained by Gillies returned to their native lands. William Kelsey Fry remained at Guy's Hospital to continue as the great dental collaborator and Ivan Magill stayed at the Westminster Hospital as the pioneer of intra-tracheal anaesthesia. Gillies and T. P. Kilner, who had joined him in 1918 as his assistant, now took up private practice as specialists in plastic surgery. After a difficult start conditions improved, and Gillies became plastic surgeon to St Bartholomew's and other hospitals, to the London county council, and to the Royal Air Force. In 1924 he treated a number of Danish casualties in Copenhagen following the premature explosion of a phosphorous bomb, and he was subsequently made a commander of the order of Dannebrog. He had been appointed CBE in 1920 and was knighted in 1930.

When war broke out in 1939 most of Gillies's trainees were in other countries. There were in the United Kingdom only four plastic surgeons of experience: Gillies, his cousin Archibald *McIndoe, and another New Zealander, Rainsford Mowlem, who were already in partnership; and Kilner, who was now working independently. It fell to these four men rapidly to train a number of other surgeons in the field of plastic surgery at the same time as dealing with the many thousands of patients pouring into their units. Gillies's team worked in Rooksdown House, near Basingstoke, and, while the centre did not receive all the publicity which perhaps it deserved, it nevertheless became famous for plastic surgery.

In 1946 Gillies became the first president of the newly formed British Association of Plastic Surgeons. In 1948 he was awarded an honorary fellowship of the American College of Surgeons and made a commander of the order of St Olaf for training Norwegian surgeons during the war. In 1955 he was elected the first president of the International Plastic Surgery Society at Stockholm. He received honorary degrees from Ljubljana (1957) and Colombia (1959), and in 1960 he was given the special honorary citation of the American Society of Plastic and Reconstructive Surgery. In their journal of January 1961 Dr Jerome P. Webster wrote:

> He was a giant pre-eminent in his chosen field of endeavor. The ideas engendered by his fertile brain have spread and are being spread afar, and generations of plastic surgeons will be affected by what he gave forth to the world. His memory may perish but his influence is immortal.

An indefatigable worker, Gillies wrote many papers and was in great demand as a lecturer. He published two notable books: *Plastic Surgery of the Face* (1920), which recorded his experiences in the war, and *The Principles and Art of Plastic Surgery* (with D. Ralph Millard, 2 vols., 1957) which remained a classic.

In versatility Gillies was a Renaissance figure. He was a noted athlete in his younger days, an excellent artist, and one of the best dry-fly fishermen in England. He played golf for England against Scotland in 1908, 1925, and 1926, and won the St George's Grand Challenge Cup in 1913. He thoroughly and unashamedly enjoyed being in the limelight and his famous high golf tee, which he was finally requested not to use by the St Andrews golf club, afforded him enormous pleasure and not a little publicity as an eccentric. Until the end of his days he retained a Peter Pan streak and enjoyed practical jokes; on occasions such as formal dinners he could behave in such a way as to upset the more dignified and often much younger members of his profession. His zest for painting and his proficiency in oils were exemplified in 1959 by a second one-man show at Foyles of 132 paintings, of which at least a third were sold. His first exhibition was in 1947 and a posthumous one was held at Walker's Galleries in 1961.

In 1911 Gillies had married Kathleen Margaret (*d.* 1957), daughter of Josiah Jackson, a brick manufacturer; they had two sons and two daughters. In 1957 he married Marjorie, daughter of John T. Clayton, a jeweller; she had worked with him in the operating theatre for many years. Gillies died at the London Clinic, 20 Devonshire Place, Marylebone, London, on 10 September 1960.

RICHARD BATTLE, *rev.*

Sources R. Pound, *Gillies, surgeon extraordinary* (1964) • personal knowledge (1971) • private information (1971) • *CGPLA Eng. & Wales* (1960) • *The Times* (12 Sept 1960), 14a • *The Times* (15 Sept 1960), 14b, 18c • *BMJ* (17 Sept 1960), 866–7; (24 Sept 1960), 948–50 • *The Lancet* (19 March 1960), 655–6
Archives RCS Eng., lecture notes
Likenesses B. Adams, oils, 1939?, Queen Mary's Hospital, Roehampton, London • W. Stoneman, photograph, 1940, NPG • H. Barron, oils, 1963?, RCS Eng. • B. Adams, oils, priv. coll. • H. Furniss, pen-and-ink drawing, NPG • H. Tonks, group portrait, pen-and-ink drawing, RCS Eng. • photograph, repro. in *The Times* (12 Sept 1960)
Wealth at death £21,161 13*s.* 3*d.*: probate, 11 Nov 1960, *CGPLA Eng. & Wales*

Gillies, Iain (1903–1989), Scottish nationalist, was born at 48 Dartmouth Park Hill, Islington, London, on 28 August 1903, his name at birth being registered as Ian Yothre Gillies, the son of William *Gillies (1865–1932), export merchant and Scottish nationalist, and his wife, Mary Dott (*née* Black). His foremost political influence was his father, whose Celticist and nationalist principles he took up at an early age. He worked with his father in promoting the Scots National League (SNL), which was founded in 1920 as a political organization dedicated to securing Scottish independence. Like his father, he was heavily influenced by the activities of Sinn Féin in Ireland, and his early propaganda work targeted the British army during the Anglo-Irish War. Although imbued with Celtic romanticism, he was more pragmatic than most of the early members of the SNL, and his objective was to tie nineteenth-century nationalist idealism with more modern political ideologies in order, as he believed, to give it mass appeal.

Gillies was a radical, in favour of land reform and an open proponent of socialism, which made him somewhat removed from both his father and his Irish nationalist allies. He believed that an independent Scotland was the best way to achieve socialism and social justice in Scotland, and was influenced by the popular Edwardian Scottish Liberal dictum that Conservative England held back radical Scotland. Gillies believed that socio-economic policies had to be brought on board if Scottish nationalism was to have mass appeal and win support among the working class, which he believed was an essential prerequisite for Scottish independence. Together with framing a socio-economic case for Scottish independence, he worked with Tom Gibson to ensure that the Scots National League made itself independent of other political parties and laid down a blueprint to contest elections to secure a mandate for independence through the ballot box. In short, he was the co-author of Scottish nationalist political strategy.

Although a seminal idea, this strategy never got off the ground because the SNL was prone to fissures and personality clashes. All this helped to affirm Gillies's conviction that the nationalist movement ought to be a broad church. In 1927 he wrote what would become the blueprint for the modern Scottish National Party, 'Scotland's need: a national party' (published in the *Scots Independent*, September 1927), in which he urged members of the Scottish Home Rule Association, the Scottish National Movement, the Glasgow University Scottish Nationalist Association, and any other like-minded people to pool their resources into one party. He backed up this call for nationalist unity with a pragmatic programme designed to enhance the electoral credibility of the nationalist cause by promoting distinctive social and economic policies. It was a key element of his philosophy that independence had to make sense to the man in the street and that its advantages had to be spelled out in bread-and-butter terms. This represented a waning of the predominantly romantic vision of Scottish nationalism. The result was the formation of the National Party of Scotland (NPS) in April 1928.

Due more to his pedigree than to the reality of his philosophy, Gillies was located on the party's fundamentalist wing, which believed in complete independence and would have no truck with devolution. Although the NPS contained a broad range of opinions on the preferred constitutional settlement, Gillies believed that they would be won over by argument to the case of complete independence. To this end the party journal, the *Scots Independent*, of which he was editor, printed many articles to back up his position. The failure of the NPS to mobilize much electoral support, however, brought the latent divisions within the National Party increasingly out in the open. For Gillies and fellow fundamentalists, the party's timidity was the reason why electoral success was elusive. The solution, he argued, was to be more forceful about independence and to adopt more radical policies; he was a proponent of Douglas social credit as a means of achieving greater economic redistribution. Perhaps most controversial of all was his use of the argument that Scotland was held under English colonial domination. The increasingly republican, radical, and separatist tendencies of the fundamentalists were believed by moderates to be the cause of the party's poor electoral showing as they were frightening away potential support.

Gillies was ousted as editor of the *Scots Independent*, and the moderates pushed through a programme of reform which toned down the National Party's separatism and paved the way for a merger with the right-wing Scottish Party in April 1934 to form the Scottish National Party (SNP). He fought tooth-and-nail against this development and was expelled from the party for his pains in 1933. Although marginalized, he continued to work for the nationalist cause from the sidelines. He was vindicated by the fact that the SNP eventually returned in 1942 to the strategy he first proposed in 1927. Gillies was married to Mary Kyle Cathie. He died on 16 July 1989 at his home, 327 Albert Drive, Glasgow, survived by his wife. His death certificate described him as a retired hospital administration officer.

RICHARD J. FINLAY

Sources R. J. Finlay, *Independent and free: Scottish politics and the origins of the Scottish national party, 1918–1945* (1994) • b. cert. • d. cert.
Wealth at death £65,214.87: confirmation, 5 Oct 1989, *CCI*

Gillies, John (1712–1796), Church of Scotland minister, was born at the manse of Careston, near Brechin in Forfarshire, the son of John Gillies (1681–1753), minister at Careston, and Mary Watson (*d.* 1779), who was descended from a respectable family in Galloway. After finishing his literary and divinity studies at Glasgow University and serving as a tutor in the families of Brisbane of Brisbane, Macdowell of Castle-Semple, and John, earl of Glasgow, he was ordained minister of Blackfriars Church in Glasgow on 29 July 1742, where he remained until his death. His first wife, Elizabeth, who died on 6 August 1754 as a result of complications connected with the birth of their seventh child, was the eldest daughter of John Maclaurin, celebrated minister of St David's, Glasgow, whose biography Gillies wrote for Maclaurin's *Sermons and Essays* (1755). Gillies's second wife, Joanna Stewart (*d.* 1792), whom he married on 19 January 1756, was the twin sister of Sir Michael Stewart of Blackhall and youngest daughter of John Stewart of the Blackhall family. Their only child, Rebecca, married the Hon. David Leslie, second son of the earl of Leven.

Gillies is best-known for his lengthy and influential pastoral ministry and his religious works. He preached three times each Sunday and for a time delivered midweek lectures from which he published a weekly abstract called *An Exhortation to the Inhabitants of the South Parish of Glasgow*, which was also issued as a two-volume book in 1750–51. In 1754 he published, also in two volumes, his groundbreaking history of revival, *Historical Collections Relating to Remarkable Periods of the Success of the Gospel*, which was augmented by an appendix in 1761 and a supplement in 1796, and proved a catalyst for the Scottish revivals of the late eighteenth and early nineteenth centuries. As a means of encouraging his parishioners in the exercise of true religion, he published in London in 1769 two volumes of *Devotional Exercises on the New Testament*. Of an open temperament (although he opposed the repeal of legal restrictions on Roman Catholics in 1778), he was free from the prejudice of party spirit and opened his pulpit to the Methodists George Whitefield and John Wesley. Commenting on Gillies's invitation, Wesley exclaimed, 'Who would have believed, five and twenty years ago, either that the minister would have desired it or that I should have consented to preach in a Scotch kirk' (*Journal*, 4.63). Gillies also enjoyed Whitefield's friendship and wrote the first account of his life, *Memoirs of the Life of the Reverend George Whitefield* (1772). He was a leading member of the popular party in the general assembly, and joined the unsuccessful attempt to urge the assembly to encourage a conciliatory government policy towards the American colonists in 1776–8. Edinburgh University awarded him the LLD in 1778. He died on 29 March 1796 at his home in Dunlop Street, Glasgow.

W. G. BLAIKIE, *rev.* C. W. MITCHELL

Sources *Fasti Scot.*, new edn, 3.399 • J. Erskine, 'Account of the Revd Dr Gillies', in J. Gillies and J. Erskine, *A supplement to two volumes … of historical collections* (1796) • W. Nicol, 'Memoir', in J. Gillies, *The New Testament … with devotional reflections* (1810) • A. Fawcett, *The Cambuslang revival: the Scottish evangelical revival of the eighteenth century* (1971) • *The journal of the Rev. John Wesley*, ed. N. Curnock and others, 8 vols. (1909–16)

Gillies, John (1747–1836), ancient historian and classical scholar, was born in Brechin, Forfarshire, on 18 January 1747, the eldest son in the large family of Robert Gillies, a merchant in Brechin and proprietor of Little Keithock, and his wife, Margaret Smith, the daughter of a Brechin merchant. His paternal grandfather was John Gillies (1681–1753), minister of Careston; John *Gillies (1712–1796), minister of the South Parish, Glasgow, was his uncle; and the Scottish judge Adam *Gillies (1760–1842) was his youngest brother. He was educated at Brechin and at Glasgow University, where he matriculated in 1760 and graduated MA in 1764. Among the distinguished staff at Glasgow his principal teacher was the professor of Greek, James Moor. During term Gillies lived with his uncle; when at home he passed the day (according to a local source) 'studying in his father's garret' (Jervise and Gammack, 275). Before he was twenty he was selected to teach the Greek class in the university during a period of Moor's ill health. At this period Gillies published anonymously *An inquiry, whether the study of the ancient languages be a necessary branch of modern education* (1769). Soon afterwards he went to London to follow literature, but gave up his engagements on going abroad to Germany and other parts of Europe as tutor to the Hon. Henry Hope, fifth son of John Hope, second earl of Hopetoun. Hope died in 1776, and the following year the earl settled an annuity on Gillies.

In 1778 Gillies published his first work under his own name, a translation of some of the orations of Lysias and Isocrates with a historical introduction, the whole designed as a commentary on the history of the first half of the fourth century BC. In that year he was awarded the degree of LLD by the University of Edinburgh. He was a fellow of the Royal Society, the Society of Antiquaries, and the Royal Society of Edinburgh, and a corresponding member of the Institut de France and of the Königliche Gesellschaft der Wissenschaften, Göttingen. In 1784 he made a further visit to Germany as tutor to two of the earl of Hopetoun's younger sons, John, later general and fourth earl, and Alexander, later Sir Alexander, general and MP; this occasioned his *A view of the reign of Frederick II of Prussia: with a parallel between that prince and Philip II of Macedon* (1789). This work was later criticized by William Smyth, in his *Lectures on Modern History* (1840), for being more a panegyric than a history. Otherwise Gillies lived in London, carrying on his scholarly work.

Gillies's principal work was a history of ancient Greece published in two parts, each of two stout quarto volumes, in 1786 and 1807, respectively titled *The history of ancient Greece, its colonies, and conquests; from the earliest accounts till the division of the Macedonian empire in the east* and *The history of the world, from the reign of Alexander to that of Augustus, comprehending the latter ages of European Greece, and the history of the Greek kingdoms in Asia and Africa from their foundation to their destruction*. The first part was immediately translated into French and German, and both were reprinted until the 1820s. Gillies was thoroughly acquainted with modern works in several languages and with the ancient literary sources, both histories and other genres, and he constructed from them (with rather arbitrary choice or amalgamation where they differed) a continuous narrative of events, including sections on cultural matters. His style was readable but somewhat pompous and was described by the *Edinburgh Review* as 'diffuse and overcharged' (pp. 55–6). However their usefulness and popularity—highly praised in *Public Characters of 1800–1801*—did not outlive their author. The revolution in ancient history brought about by source analysis, epigraphy, and archaeology, together with changes in literary taste, brought total oblivion to both books and their author.

In 1793 Gillies was appointed historiographer royal for Scotland on the death of William Robertson. In the same year he published a translation of two of Aristotle's works, *Nicomachean Ethics* and *Politics*; the second edition of 1804 added a reply to criticism by the Platonist Thomas Taylor. On 25 September 1794 Gillies married, at Ealing, Catharine Beaver, 'an amiable and accomplished woman' (*Public Characters*, 233), the daughter of the Revd James Beaver, curate of Lewknor, Oxfordshire; they settled in a pleasant house in the vicinity of Portman Square, London. In 1807 he lived in Upper Seymour Street. His last publication was a translation of Aristotle's *Rhetoric* in 1823. From 1830 he lived in retirement at Clapham, Surrey, where he died on 15 February 1836 in his ninetieth year. 'He had no disease of any kind, and departed without a pang … or the change of a single muscle' (*GM*, 437). Mathias says that Gillies was 'a man of good intentions, a passable scholar, an indefatigable reader, and of most respectable character', but there was no touch of genius in his writings (Mathias, *Second Dialogue*, 118, 120). Fanny Burney found him in conversation 'very communicative and informing' (*Diary and Letters of Mme. D'Arblay*, 1842–6, 5.225). He is described as a man of about middle height, with a handsome figure, and a countenance 'open, ingenuous and expressive—rather of sagacity and cheerfulness than of any keen activity of passion' (*Public Characters*, 235). W. W. WROTH, *rev.* I. C. CUNNINGHAM

Sources *GM*, 2nd ser., 5 (1836), 436–7 • A. Jervise and J. Gammack, *The history and tradition of the land of the Lindsays* (1882), 224, 275–6 • *Public characters of 1800–1801* (1801), 250–62 • T. J. Mathias, *The pursuits of literature, second dialogue* (1796), 118, 120 • T. J. Mathias, *The pursuits of literature, third dialogue* (1796), 143 • Allibone, *Dict.* • W. I. Addison, ed., *The matriculation albums of the University of Glasgow from 1728 to 1858* (1913) • W. I. Addison, *A roll of graduates of the University of Glasgow from 31st December 1727 to 31st December 1897* (1898) • D. Laing, ed., *A catalogue of the graduates … of the University of Edinburgh*, Bannatyne Club, 106 (1858) • *Scots peerage*, vol. 4 • Chambers, *Scots.*, rev. T. Thomson (1875) • *EdinR*, 11 (1807–8), 40–61

Archives NL Scot., letters to R. P. Gillies

Likenesses J. Caldwell, line engraving, 1788 (after J. Boyle), BM, NPG; repro. in J. Gillies, *History of Greece* (1788) • J. Opie, oils, Scot. NPG • engravings (after J. Opie), Scot. NPG • engravings (after J. Boyle), Scot. NPG

Wealth at death fortune sufficiently equal to moderate plan of expense; annuity from earl of Hopetoun; profits from books; £200 p.a. as historiographer royal: *Public characters of 1800–1801*

Gillies, John MacDougall (1855–1925), player and teacher of the highland bagpipe, was born on 20 May 1855 at 126 Gallowgate, Aberdeen, eldest of the three sons of John MacDougall Gillies (*b.* 1825), marble polisher from Glendaruel, Argyll, and his wife, Isabella Smith (*b.* 1825), from Glasgow. On 30 December 1881 he married Margaret Grieve Low (1859–1890), a dressmaker. Following her early death, he moved from Aberdeen to Glasgow, where on 11 September 1891 he married Margaret McCulloch. They had two sons, Alastair and Ian. His first job was as a house painter, and he played with the Aberdeen Volunteers under Pipe-Major Alex Fettes (later to be six times mayor of Port Elizabeth in South Africa), who composed the classic 6/8 march 'The Glendaruel Highlanders' in the family's honour. He received his higher instruction in piping from Alexander Cameron the younger (1848–1923), then piper to the marquess of Huntly at Aboyne Castle, and they remained close until Cameron's death in 1923. Gillies went on to win all the top piobaireachd awards, including the Braemar gold medal in 1875, the Inverness prize pipe in 1882, the Oban gold medal in 1884, and the gold medal for previous winners at Inverness in 1885. He was the first winner of the clasp for former gold medallists at Inverness in 1896. Contemporaries attested to his outstanding refinement and subtlety as an interpreter of *ceòl mór*.

In 1886 Gillies became first piper to the marquess of Breadalbane at Taymouth Castle in Perthshire. It was probably the biggest private piping establishment in Scotland. His distinguished predecessors John Bàn MacKenzie (1796–1864) and Duncan MacDougall of Aberfeldy (*c.*1837–1898) had been able to turn out more than twenty pipers for lavish 'highland' entertainments where guests had included Queen Victoria, Prince Albert, and Prince Leopold of the Belgians. It was related how

> he and … Sandy Cameron used to adjourn to the Tower and there play to their hearts' content. Mr. Gillies used to say he never heard anything finer than Sandy's playing of 'The Ribean Gorm' on a fine summer evening with a gentle breeze carrying it far up the glen. Variation after variation of this most symmetrical and beautiful tune, rolled around singlings, doublings, and treblings, embedding the urlar in the crunluath-a-mach as even as a wheel on a mill-lade. (*Oban Times*, 26 Dec 1925)

But conditions of employment for pipers in the landed sector were becoming less attractive as the expectation grew that they should perform a range of menial functions in addition to their musical duties. A defining moment came when Lady Breadalbane arrived at Taymouth from her Park Lane residence in 1888:

> Her Ladyship, not in the best of moods, had heavy gambling losses. … On her last night in London she had lost £72,000 on the turn of a card.
>
> She sent for the factor and ordered all those pipers doing nothing but playing pipes to sweep the drive. MacDougall Gillies … fetched his pipes and belongings and left. (MacAulay, 4.10)

In Glasgow, Gillies continued to work as a painter, sharing lodgings with Sandy Cameron (then piper to the lord provost) at 61 Grove Street, Cowcaddens. From about 1905 until a week before his death, he was manager for Peter Henderson's, the bagpipe makers. In Glasgow he became an outstanding teacher, a focus for the city's development as 'the centre of the piping world' (Donaldson, 195). Many gifted young players studied with him, including William Gray, George Yardley, and Robert Reid. He served from 1891 as honorary pipe-major of the 1st (later 5th) volunteer battalion Highland light infantry, pioneering competitive ensemble play and winning the first Cowal open pipe band championship in 1906, with a further four wins up to 1912. He was pipe-major of the Glasgow Highland Club and president of the Scottish Pipers' Association, formed in 1920.

Gillies had acted as professional adviser and instructor to the Piobaireachd Society (formed in 1903 by a group of gentlemen enthusiasts), whose early competition scores (1905–12) were mostly published by his firm. The society's socially exclusive and authoritarian approach created much disquiet, however, and led to the formation in November 1910 of the Scottish Pipers' and Dancers' Union, with Gillies on the committee. The union aimed to regain control of the way the music was played by providing knowledgeable judges and ending the requirement to play the Piobaireachd Society's 'official' scores in competition. The First World War intervened, and the problems which the union sought to address went unresolved. The Piobaireachd Society's powerful music editor, Archibald Campbell (1877–1963), had lessons from Gillies and later invoked his name to justify the arrangements in the society's second series of publications (from 1925). But these differed greatly from the elegant stylings in Gillies's manuscript collection (begun in 1879, and containing some seventy tunes), which remained unpublished and little known at the end of the twentieth century.

John MacDougall Gillies died at his home at 409 Great Western Road, Glasgow, on 17 December 1925 and was buried with full military honours. The *Oban Times* obituary described him as 'one of the finest and most cultured of players … Even to the initiated he could express piobaireachd in a manner which created astonishment and admiration'.

William Donaldson

Sources W. Donaldson, *The highland pipe and Scottish society, 1750–1950* (2000) • J. Campbell, *Highland bagpipe makers* (2001) • U. Glas., J. MacDougall Gillies MS, Gen. 1457 • 'The late Mr J. MacDougall Gillies: a famous piper', *Oban Times* (26 Dec 1925) • A. Fairrie, *The Northern Meeting, 1788–1988* (1988) • A. MacAulay, 'The art and history of the MacDougalls of Aberfeldy', *Piping Times*, 16/4 (1963–4), 7–10; 16/5 (1963–4), 9–14 • J. Campbell, 'Patrons of piping', *Piping Times*, 51/6 (1998–9), 16–22 • D. Ross, 'Some of the old pipers I have met', *Piping Times*, 26/4 (1973–4), 9–17 • D. Sinclair, *The history of the Aberdeen volunteers* (1907) • A. Chatto, 'The Cowal highland games: part 1', *The Voice*, 27/3 (1998), 34–5 • A. Campbell, 'Togail nam bo, or, The MacFarlanes gathering', *Piping Times*, 7/12 (1954–5), 6–7 • A. Campbell and others, eds., *Piobaireachd Society Collection*, 1–8 (1925–39) • b. cert. • d. cert.

Archives U. Glas., MS Gen. 1457

Likenesses photograph, repro. in Fairrie, *Northern Meeting*

Gillies, Margaret (1803–1887), painter, was born on 7 August 1803 in Throgmorton Street in the City of London and baptized on 6 February 1804 at St Benet Fink, Threadneedle Street, the fourth of the five children of William Gillies (1761–1845), corn merchant, and his wife, Charlotte Hester Bonnor (*d.* 1811), daughter of the Gloucestershire engraver and topographical artist Thomas *Bonnor. After the death of their mother in 1811 and as a result of their father's precarious position as a corn merchant in London, the Gillies children were brought up by relatives in Scotland: at first in Brechin, Forfarshire—where they associated with their cousin, the portrait painter Colvin *Smith—and subsequently in Edinburgh, when they were under the guardianship of their uncle, Adam *Gillies, Lord Gillies. Judge at the court of session, lord of the justiciary, and lord commissioner of the jury, Lord Gillies occupied a prominent position in Edinburgh society and his nephews and nieces were introduced to the literary and legal circles frequented by Sir Walter Scott, Lord Jeffrey, Lord Erskine, Lord Eldon, and Lord Skene. Margaret Gillies displayed an early interest in art. About 1819, having refused an offer of marriage, she and her elder sister Mary Gillies returned to their father's house in London, both determined to earn a living as painter and writer respectively. In the 1820s Margaret became a pupil of Frederick Cruikshank, a Scottish miniature painter who worked in the style of Andrew Robertson.

In London, Margaret Gillies either renewed or began an acquaintance with Thomas Southwood *Smith (1788–1861), a physician, pioneer of health reform, and formerly a Unitarian minister. Through him, in the 1830s, she became associated with the set which formed around William Johnson Fox, editor of the Unitarian periodical the *Monthly Repository*, and whose members included Richard Henry Horne, Sarah and Eliza Flower, Robert Browning, Leigh Hunt, John Stuart Mill, Harriet Taylor, and William Macready. The Gillies sisters attended the new Finsbury Unitarian Chapel in South Place where Fox, also a Unitarian minister, preached. By the late 1830s relationships had developed between Margaret Gillies and Southwood Smith (who had separated from his second wife) and between Mary Gillies and Richard Henry Horne; about 1838 or 1839 all four were sharing the same accommodation at 31 Upper Montague Street. Southwood Smith lived with Margaret Gillies until the end of his life.

During the first two decades of her career Margaret Gillies exhibited large miniature portraits (and some subject compositions), chiefly in watercolour and gum on ivory, at the Royal Academy (1832–61), the Society of British Artists (1834–42), the Royal Scottish Academy (1834–52), and the Liverpool Academy (1839–49). Her ideal of portraiture was highly motivated and corresponded with the educative artistic credo of writers on art in the *Monthly Repository*. She wrote:

> Artists in general seize every opportunity of painting the nobility of wealth and rank. It would be far more grateful to me to be able to paint what I conceive to be true nobility, that of genius, long, faithfully, earnestly and not without suffering labouring to call out what is most beautiful and refined in our nature and to establish this as the guide and standard of human action. (Brewer, 232)

Her sitters—many of whom were writers, intellectuals, and social reformers—included William Johnson Fox, Harriet Martineau, Southwood Smith (priv. coll.), Horne (National Portrait Gallery, London), Rammohun Roy, Jeremy Bentham, Mary Leman Grimstone, Leigh Hunt (National Portrait Gallery, London), Charles Dickens, and William Wordsworth (versions Wordsworth Trust, Dove Cottage, Grasmere, and priv. coll., Cumberland), at whose house, Rydal Mount in the Lake District, she spent about two months in 1839, painting several portraits of the poet and others of his family and friends.

By February 1841 the Gillies sisters and Southwood Smith had moved to 5 Fortess Terrace, Kentish Town, London. Southwood Smith's granddaughter Gertrude Hill, whose mother was Caroline Hill (a writer on education), came to live with them at this time for financial reasons. In 1840, Southwood Smith had become one of four commissioners on the children's employment commission, whose first task was to examine the employment of children in mines and collieries. The first report, published in May 1842 (the first illustrated government report), included twenty-six wood-engravings, many of which were based on drawings (some drawn 'on the spot') by Margaret Gillies. From 1844 to 1854 the Gillies/Southwood Smith household lived at Hillside, Millfield Lane, Highgate. Portraits of William and Mary Howitt (Castle Museum, Nottingham), Anna Mary Howitt, Ebenezer Elliott, Edwin Chadwick, Matilda Hays, and Anne Marsh date from these years. In 1844 *A New Spirit of the Age*, edited by Richard Henry Horne, included engravings from four portraits by Margaret Gillies—of Charles Dickens, Southwood Smith, William Wordsworth, and Harriet Martineau. Two years later the *People's Journal of Popular Progress* published 'A People's Portrait Gallery', with engravings after Gillies's portraits of the same individuals and in addition Leigh Hunt, among others. Engraving was an important factor in the realization of Margaret Gillies's ideal of educating the public through the example of men and women of 'genius'.

From the 1840s Margaret Gillies specialized increasingly in larger subject pictures—mainly in watercolour, to a lesser extent in oil. These she exhibited not only at the above-mentioned institutions but also at the British Institution (1846–53), the National Institution (1851–4), the Royal Manchester Institution (1852–69), the Old Watercolour Society (1852–87), and the Society of Female Artists (1858–65), as well as at national and international exhibitions (Paris Universal Exhibition, 1855; Paris Universal Exhibition, 1878; Manchester Art Treasures Exhibition, 1857; International Exhibition, London, 1862 and 1871; Royal Jubilee Exhibition, Manchester, 1887). In 1852 she was elected a member of the Old Watercolour Society. Women were her principal subjects and edification remained a primary aim. A series of paintings which she exhibited in the 1830s on the theme of The Captive Daughter of Zion, which suggested the importance of suffering for spiritual benefit (a Unitarian concept), was thematically typical. In the 1840s she portrayed suffering heroines from the Bible, literature, and history. After 1851, the year in which she studied in Paris under Henri and Ary Scheffer, her major works became increasingly religious in tone and allegorical in subject. Her most successful and lucrative period was from 1855 to 1861, when she showed such works as *The Past and the Future* (exh. Royal Manchester Institution and Old Watercolour Society, 1855), *Vivia Perpetua* (exh. Society of Female Artists, 1859), *Trust* (exh. RA, 1860; Victoria and Albert Museum, London), and *Beyond* (exh. Old Watercolour Society, 1861). She had always received praise for her rendering of intellectual and emotional expression. In 1861 a reviewer referred to 'that quasi-classic kind of art in which she seems to stand without a competitor' (*Art Journal*, 23, 1861, 173). In 1862 a street in St Pancras, London, was named after her on the basis of the location of her studio.

Southwood Smith died in 1861 while on a visit to his daughter in Italy. Since 1854 he, the Gillies sisters, and Gertrude had lived at The Pines in Weybridge, Surrey, the departure from Hillside resulting from a need to economize. After his death the sisters moved for the last time, to 25 Church Row in Hampstead where they attended the Rosslyn Hill Unitarian Chapel. Gertrude remained with the Gillieses (and with Margaret after the death of Mary Gillies in 1870) even after her marriage in 1865 to Charles Lee Lewes (the son of the writer George Henry Lewes), until 1878; it was through her that the sisters became acquainted with George Eliot. Gertrude modelled for many of Margaret Gillies's paintings.

Gillies travelled widely during this last period, not only all over the British Isles (Scotland in particular) but also in France and Italy; numerous rural genre scenes were the result, the majority of which were exhibited at the Old Watercolour Society. She was also represented at the Glasgow Institute (1867–77), the Liverpool autumn exhibitions (1875–80), and the Grosvenor Gallery, London (1877–81). Her larger paintings remained allegorical in nature, though many—such as *Desolation* (exh. Society of Female Artists, 1864) and *The End of the Pilgrimage* (exh. Old Watercolour Society, 1873; Cheltenham Art Gallery and Museum)—alluded simultaneously to her personal experience, specifically the death of Southwood Smith. In a major group of pictures on medieval themes she combined the two main tenets of her essentially Unitarian faith. In works such as *Sorrow and Consolation* (exh. Old Watercolour Society, 1866; priv. coll.), *Doubt not; Go Forward!* (exh. Old Watercolour Society, 1870; ex Christies,

London, 18 October 1977), and *Christiana by the River of Life* (exh. Royal Society of Painters in Water Colours, 1887; priv. coll.), the knight came to represent the intellectual and reforming heroes she had portrayed in the 1830s and 1840s among whom Southwood Smith was her paradigm. The knights' ladies, mothers, and nurses, usually sorrowful or grieving, symbolized the suffering necessarily undergone by the modern hero, and by everyone, in the cause of human advancement and spiritual fulfilment.

Margaret Gillies exhibited at least 461 works during her lifetime. In the year of her death she contributed *A Mother and Child* (Royal Collection) to the jubilee album presented to Queen Victoria. She died of pleurisy at The Warren, Crockham Hill, near Edenbridge, Kent, on 20 July 1887 and was buried on 23 July in the churchyard at Crockham Hill. She is also commemorated on the tomb of her sister Mary in Highgate cemetery, London. An obituarist, who met her two weeks before her death, wrote of 'the venerable Miss Gillies, a pleasant-looking lady in gray satin' (*The World*).

Charlotte Yeldham

Sources C. Yeldham, *Margaret Gillies RWS: Unitarian painter of mind and emotion, 1803–1887* (1997) • A. Ainger, 'Margaret Gillies', *Hampstead Annual* (1899), 59–69 • Lady Lindsay, 'Some recollections of Miss Margaret Gillies', *Temple Bar*, 81 (1887), 265–73 • Mrs C. L. Lewes, *Dr. Southwood Smith: a retrospect* (1898) • F. N. L. Poynter, 'Thomas Southwood Smith—the man (1788–1861)', *Proceedings of the Royal Society of Medicine*, 55 (1962), 381–92 • *Men of the time* (1856) • E. C. Clayton, *English female artists*, 2 vols. (1876) • J. L. Roget, *A history of the 'Old Water-Colour' Society*, 2 vols. (1891) • A. Blainey, *The Farthing Poet: a biography of Richard Hengist Horne, 1802–1884* (1968) • L. A. Brewer, ed., *My Leigh Hunt library: the holograph letters* (1938) • *The George Eliot letters*, ed. G. S. Haight, 9 vols. (1954–78) • R. H. Horne, ed., *A new spirit of the age*, 2 vols. (1844) • *Mary Howitt: an autobiography*, ed. M. Howitt, 2 vols. (1889) • *The letters of William and Dorothy Wordsworth: the later years*, ed. E. De Selincourt, 3 vols. (1939) • *CGPLA Eng. & Wales* (1887) • *The World* (27 July 1887), 18 • *The Times* (26 July 1887) • *IGI* • records of Rosslyn Hill Unitarian Chapel, DWL, MS 38, fols. 152–4

Archives BM, department of prints and drawings • Mitchell L., NSW, R. H. Horne MSS • Rydal Mount, Rydal, Cumbria • Wordsworth Trust, Grasmere, Cumbria, Wordsworth Library and Dove Cottage

Likenesses M. F. Field, portrait, repro. in *Hampstead Annual*, frontispiece • photograph, Wordsworth Trust, Dove Cottage, Grasmere

Wealth at death £1659 15*s*. 2*d*.: probate, 12 Nov 1887, *CGPLA Eng. & Wales*

Gillies [*née* Rede; *other married name* Grimstone], **Mary Leman** (*b*. *c*.**1800**, *d*. in or after **1851**), writer and social reformer, was one of the five children of Leman Thomas Rede (*d*. 1810), writer. She was probably born in Hamburg about 1800. She had two sisters, about whom little is known, and two brothers, Leman Thomas *Rede and William Leman *Rede, both of whom enjoyed some fame as playwrights. The family returned to England (from which they appear to have fled to escape Leman Rede's debts) following the death of her father.

Mary Leman Rede began writing for publication in 1815, and had many of her pieces accepted by *La Belle Assemblée*. During the 1820s she published poems under the pseudonym Oscar. About 1824 or 1825 she married, becoming Mary Leman Grimstone, the name by which she is best known. Nothing is known about her husband, and it is possible that she was soon widowed, for she left England for Hobart, Van Diemen's Land, at the end of 1825 with her sister and brother-in-law, Lucy and Stephen Adey. She remained in Hobart until 1829; while she was there she wrote most of a novel, *Women's Love* (1832), which, despite its English setting, was probably the first novel written in Australia. Her residence in Hobart provided her with material for a number of her future novels and short stories.

Grimstone's first novel had been published in 1825, and four more were to follow, including *Character, or, Jew and Gentile* (1833) and *Cleone, a Tale of Married Life* (1834). *Woman's Love*, however, with its lengthy polemical postscript on women's rights, was her most important novel, and gave notice of a theme that was to dominate her life and work. As she explained to Charles Cowden Clarke, the 'master-motive of my mind [is] the elevation of my own sex in the social scale' (Gleadle, 143). In the early 1830s she was given the opportunity to develop her feminist ideas when she came into contact with the radical Unitarian circle which revolved around William Johnson Fox at South Place Chapel in London. Fox's periodical, the *Monthly Repository*, was one of several journals which published a great many of her articles, often over the initials M. L. G. (Others included *Tait's Edinburgh Magazine* and the *Tatler*.) The predominant theme of these essays was that of women's rights. Grimstone argued passionately for the improvement of women's education and for the extension of women's employment opportunities. She called both for the recognition of women's political rights and for a revolution in marriage. Her reforming fervour also led her to champion religious toleration, political radicalism, and improvements in the condition of the working classes. She canvassed for the People's International League, and became involved in Samuel Wilderspin's campaign for infant education, which had been inspired in part by her friend Mary Gaskell.

It was probably during 1835 that Mary Grimstone became the third wife of a Scottish businessman, William Gillies (1761–1845). Gillies, a 'perennial bankrupt' (Blainey, 96), was the father of Margaret *Gillies, artist, and Mary Gillies, author, both important figures in the South Place circle. During the next ten years Mary Leman Gillies seems to have temporarily retired from her active career, possibly because she gave birth to a son. When she resumed writing in 1846 her feminism had a more conciliatory tone. In her work for Mary and William Howitt's *People's Journal* she sometimes now extolled women's moral qualities and their unique contribution as mothers.

Despite her close professional associations with progressive circles, Mary Leman Gillies seems to have held herself somewhat aloof from her peers: personal references to her are extremely rare, and there are hints that people found her exasperating. Yet her work was of considerable importance to contemporary radicals. Her stories, articles, and poems were reprinted and quoted in a whole range of publications, from the *Leeds Times* to the secularist *Reasoner*; her novels were favourably reviewed.

Her writing was particularly popular in the Owenite press, and her own political philosophy was revealed in her vigorous championing of the co-operative cause.

Claims that Gillies remained active in the 1850s and 1860s probably stem from confusion with her stepdaughter, Mary Gillies. Scholars have been unable to trace a record of her death, and reliable references to her cease with the closure of the *People's Journal* in 1851.

KATHRYN GLEADLE

Sources M. Roe, 'Mary Leman Grimstone (1800–1850?): for women's rights and Tasmanian patriotism', *Tasmanian Historical Research Association, Papers and Proceedings*, 36 (1989), 8–32 • K. Gleadle, *The early feminists: radical Unitarians and the emergence of the women's rights movement, 1831–51* (1995) • E. M. Miller, *Pressmen and governors: Australian editors and writers in early Tasmania* (1952) • *New Monthly Magazine*, new ser., 80 (1847), 102–9 [obit. of William Leman Rede] • A. Blainey, *The Farthing Poet: a biography of Richard Hengist Horne, 1802–1884* (1968)
Archives Fondazione Giangiacomo Feltrinelli, Milan, Archivio Linton | U. Leeds, Brotherton L., Novello-Cowden Clarke collection
Likenesses M. Gillies, self-portrait, repro. in M. L. Grimstone, *Louisa Egerton, or, Castle Herbert: a tale from real life* (1830)

Gillies, Robert Pearse (**1789–1858**), poet and writer, was born on 9 November 1789 at or near Arbroath, a member of the Forfarshire family of Gillies, and the son of Dr Thomas Gillies (*d.* 1808), wealthy landowner, and Jean Cruikshank. On his father's death in 1808 Gillies inherited the family property, which allowed him to indulge in literary interests, including writing poetry, amassing a substantial book collection, and studying law under Dugald Stewart and Playfair at the University of Edinburgh. He was admitted advocate in 1813, but, after losing most of his fortune in consequence of a rash speculation, settled in Edinburgh in 1815, where he devoted himself to writing. Another factor in his settling in Edinburgh was his subsequent marriage to Amelia Mary McDonald on 1 February 1815, at St Cuthbert's Church in Edinburgh.

Gillies was one of the early contributors to *Blackwood's Magazine*, and figures as Kemperhausen in Christopher North's *Noctes Ambrosianae*. He was a well known figure among the literary men who frequented the Ballantynes, and was a special friend of Scott. Reminiscences of his intercourse with Scott were published by Gillies in 1837. Like Scott, Gillies was drawn to German and Danish literature, many examples of which he translated and published in *Blackwood's Magazine* between 1820 and 1826 under the pseudonyms Horae Germanica and Horae Danica. He resided in Germany for a year, and met Goethe and Tieck. Gillies also corresponded with Wordsworth, who encouraged him in his early pecuniary difficulties in a sonnet commencing:

> From the dark chambers of dejection freed,
> Spurning the unprofitable yoke of care,
> Rise, Gillies, rise: the gates of youth shall bear
> Thy genius forward like a wingèd steed.
> (W. Wordsworth, *Miscellaneous Sonnets*, pt 2, no. 4)

Gillies likewise attracted the attention of Byron, who in his diary (23 November 1813) remarks on his work:

> The young man can know nothing of life; and if he cherishes the disposition which runs through his papers will become useless and perhaps not even a poet, which he seems determined to be. God help him! No one should be a rhymer who could be anything else.

Most of Gillies's remaining means disappeared in the commercial panic of 1825, and he became involved in a series of lawsuits. Scott assisted him in various ways, and finally suggested to him the idea of a journal of foreign literature. Gillies succeeded in inducing the London firm of Treuttel and Würtz, Treuttel junior, and Richter to take up the project, and the result was the foundation of the *Foreign Quarterly Review* in July 1827. Gillies as editor was to receive £600 per annum, but he was to pay the contributors out of this. Contributors to the first number included Scott (who declined to receive remuneration for his work), Robert Southey, G. R. Gleig, W. Maginn, and others.

Gillies now moved to London, where he led a somewhat chequered life. His affairs remained hopelessly involved, and consequent difficulties forced him to evade his mounting debts by moving overseas in 1840 to Boulogne, where he remained for seven years. On his return to London in 1847 he was at once thrown into prison, and not released until 1849.

On his release Gillies turned to account his acquaintance with famous men in his *Memoirs of a Literary Veteran* (3 vols., 1851), where he gives personal reminiscences of many. Among the most notable besides Scott were James Hogg, Lord Jeffrey, Thomas De Quincey, John Kemble, Mrs Siddons, and John Galt. Selections from this work with a biography were subsequently edited by Richard Henry Stoddard, as the tenth volume of the Bric à Brac series (1876). Other works of Gillies included a range of poetry collections, novels, and German and Danish translations. He died at his home, 4 Upper Holland Street, Kensington, London, on 28 November 1858; his wife predeceased him and he was survived by at least one daughter.

FRANCIS WATT, *rev.* DAVID FINKELSTEIN

Sources *DNB* • R. Inglis, *The dramatic writers of Scotland* (1868) • *IGI* • *CGPLA Eng. & Wales* (1859) • bap. reg. Scot.
Archives NL Scot., corresp., letter-books | NL Scot., letters to Robert Anderson; letters to Blackwoods; letters to Sir Walter Scott • U. Newcastle, letters to Sir Walter Trevelyan
Wealth at death under £100: administration, 21 Oct 1859, *CGPLA Eng. & Wales*

Gillies, William [Liam MacGille Iosa] (**1865–1932**), Scottish nationalist and Gaelic cultural activist, was born at 16 Upper Berkeley Street West, Paddington, London, on 23 December 1865, the son of Robert Gillies (1836–1909), a draper in the City of London, and his wife, Agnes, *née* Clark (1836–1922), a sea captain's daughter. Gillies spent most of his life in London, working at one time as an export merchant, but made many trips to Maxwelltown in Dumfries, the family's ancestral home. He was drawn to radical Liberal politics and at seventeen befriended John Murdoch, the leader of the Highland Land League. He worked as a propagandist for Murdoch's newspaper, *The Highlander*, which drew him into the world of highland politics, Gaelic culture, and contacts with Irish nationalism. Impressed by the efforts of Irish nationalists to revitalize Gaelic culture, Gillies believed similar efforts would pay dividends in Scotland. He was secretary of the Gaelic Society in 1904–5 and argued strenuously that the language had to be treated as a living one and not as the overly scholastic one then in vogue with many members. To this end he wrote five plays in his adopted language which were staged in London between 1904 and 1908, and argued that similar modern media should be used to give the language contemporary meaning. An indication of Gillies's politics can be gauged from the title of one of his plays: *The Four Scourges of Gaeldom: Feudalism, Militarism, the Church and Whisky*. He was a founder of the London Gaelic Choir and gave sermons in the London Gaelic church. He was married to Mary Dott (*née* Black), and had at least two sons and a daughter.

The Easter rising of 1916 in Dublin confirmed many of Gillies's assumptions regarding the relationship between the Anglo-Saxon and the Celt. He denounced the government's handling of the rising and booed (James) Ian MacPherson, the chief secretary of Ireland (1919–20), at a public meeting of the London Gaelic Society. Although little documentary evidence survives and sources are ambivalent, Gillies was important in helping Irish nationalists in London during the Anglo-Irish War. He prayed with Irish nationalists outside the walls of Wormwood Scrubs for Terence MacSwiney, the lord mayor of Cork, who died on hunger strike. His service to Irish nationalism was rewarded with an honorary membership of the Irish Self Determination League (a legal offshoot of Sinn Féin). In 1920 Gillies worked with his son Iain *Gillies and John MacArthur to produce a broadsheet, *Liberty*, which as well as promoting Scottish nationalism acted as a vehicle for Irish propaganda during the Anglo-Irish War.

Gillies's politics were greatly influenced by the Irish example, and he gave primacy to culture and language as weapons for political change. He was inclined to believe that a political strategy which engaged with politics from a narrow social and economic perspective would fail, and that Scottish cultural independence was a necessary prerequisite for political independence. With this aim in mind he joined with Ruaraidh Erskine of Mar, John MacArthur, and, for a short time, the Clydeside revolutionary John Maclean to found the Scots National League (SNL) in 1920. The SNL was a hard-line nationalist organization, modelled on Sinn Féin, which eschewed all contact with British parties. It refused to recognize the legitimacy of the Westminster parliament and advocated complete independence from England. The league made little impact on Scottish politics during the early 1920s, largely because the bulk of the membership and leadership lived in London. Furthermore, the baseline of SNL politics, a belief in the 'Celtic bedrock' of Scottish nationality, together with the constant pursuit of readings of history and culture which were ethnically determined, failed to cut much ice with the Scottish public. Although Gillies was not the most ardent proponent of a Celtic vision of Scottish nationalism, his association with this school of thought led pragmatists within the SNL to marginalize his influence. He was made honorary president of the league, along with Erskine of Mar, in June 1926, which had the effect of removing him from policy decisions. The league began to devise a strategy of contesting elections for a mandate for independence under the direction of Tom Gibson.

In spite of his promotion upstairs, Gillies remained an important figure in nationalist circles. He had always been more of a cultural activist than a politician, and through the nationalist journals the *Monthly Intelligencer* (1922–6) and the *Scots Independent* (1926–) he constantly broadcast his views on Scottish culture. As the forces of nationalism coalesced into the National Party of Scotland in April 1928, Gillies's message of cultural independence and his ideals of Celticism became increasingly marginalized as the National Party sought to project itself as a more up-to-date political organization by focusing on socio-economic policy. Latterly he lived in Kent, and his occupation was described as house furnisher at the time of his death at Beckenham Hospital on 23 July 1932.

Richard J. Finlay

Sources *Scots Independent* (Sept 1932), 166–7 • R. J. Finlay, *Independent and free: Scottish politics and the origins of the Scottish national party, 1918–1945* (1994) • b. cert. • d. cert.

Wealth at death £1110 2s. 10d.: probate, 24 Sept 1932, *CGPLA Eng. & Wales*

Gillies, William (1884–1958), political organizer, was born on 5 December 1884 at 79 Grove Street, Glasgow, the fourth of six children of James Gillies (*b.* 1839), journeyman marble cutter, and his wife, Agnes Wilson (1852–1943). He received elementary education and started his political career with the Glasgow Fabians. He was briefly secretary to this group in 1910, organizing a meeting at which one of the speakers was the leading Fabian Sidney Webb.

Gillies joined the Labour Party research staff in 1912. His position gave him exemption from service in the First World War, and he rose to the secretaryship of the information bureau. On the creation of an international department in January 1922, he was appointed its head, at a salary of £525 p.a., to serve both the Labour Party and, until 1925, the Trades Union Congress. He was also a member of the Labour Party international and imperial advisory committees, both of which reported to the international department. Collating information from these sources, and from the Labour and Socialist International, he reported directly to the national executive committee of the Labour Party. His expertise was reflected in his membership of the committee of the Royal Institute of International Affairs, Chatham House.

The successful re-formation of the Second International was the basis for Gillies's powerful position in the Labour Party. When in the research department, he helped with arrangements for convening the rump of the International, which had collapsed during the First World War. He was present with Arthur Henderson at the conference in Hamburg in May 1923, which was the occasion for the International's re-formation and its acquisition of the title Labour and Socialist International. The British Labour Party provided its secretariat and formed its administrative committee, to which Gillies was co-opted. When the Labour and Socialist International moved to Switzerland in 1925, he became the most regular British delegate, and was often the only one. He was appointed in 1929 to the International's executive committee and in 1930 to its bureau, the major decision-making forum. He consolidated his position at the International through alliance with its 'Scandinavian', anti-communist wing and became a leading opponent of collaboration with the Third, Communist, International, which was the policy of the 'Latin' wing. Gillies was strongly in favour of armed resistance to fascism, while central European affiliates preferred neutrality. A member of the International Socialist Committee for Labour Palestine, he propounded the British Labour Party's pro-Zionist position in opposition to the secretary of the International, Friedrich Adler. Gillies's championship of these various causes meant that he was viewed as obstructive, but he never departed from British Labour Party policy.

Gillies had been a founder member of the 1917 Club formed to 'Hail the Russian Revolution', but his experience of Third International activities in Europe fostered a virulent anti-communism. He blamed German communists for weakening German social democracy and coined the term 'communazis' to express their culpability. Communist international ancillary, or 'front', organizations, purporting to have political neutrality, were his especial *bêtes noires*, and he built a huge collection of information on such bodies. This collection resulted in the publication in 1933 of *The Communist Solar System*; its authorship is open to doubt, but it may be judged a team effort to which Gillies substantially contributed. His work here led him to identify the organizations which he suggested, often successfully, for proscription by the Labour Party at its annual conference.

In the 1930s Gillies's work with refugees increased. He was helpful in making cases for immigration and in arranging payment for articles in labour movement periodicals. His single most dramatic act was to help with the evacuation of refugees from Prague in March 1939, when the German invasion was under way. As a member of the Workers' Travel Association, whose activities included running cruise ships, plus excursion trains in Czechoslovakia, he was in a position to make an ambitious programme of refugee evacuation.

As well as to *The Communist Solar System*, Gillies contributed to Labour Party publications on international affairs and produced *International Service*, a brief account of Labour and Socialist International activities, and Aids for Study in International Relations, a series of annotated bibliographies for local Labour parties.

The final stages of Gillies's career were unhappy. His memoranda about the future of Germany, expressing scepticism about the possibility of rebuilding social democracy there, offended German Social Democrats in exile and, with his judgement rendered suspect, he took early retirement in 1944. His ill temper was as legendary as his expertise. Denis Healey, who succeeded him as international secretary, remembered him as 'a cantankerous Scot who distrusted foreigners and hated all Germans' (D. Healey, *The Time of my Life*, 1990, 57). However, Gillies's assistant, Christine Howie, worked for him from 1922 until her retirement. Gillies joined the Transport House (Labour Party and Trades Union Congress headquarters) social club and was admired by the leader of the Transport and General Workers' Union (and later Foreign Secretary) Ernest Bevin.

Gillies remained unmarried; he was close to his younger sister Agnes, and lived with his mother. He enjoyed walking tours and claimed to drink the juice of three oranges daily. Photographs show him as a short man; in 1918 Beatrice Webb referred to him as 'that little dwarf Gillies' and summarized his character as 'an honest, oversensitive and obstinate minded but well informed little Glaswegian Fabian' (N. Mackenzie and J. Mackenzie, eds., *The Diary of Beatrice Webb*, 1983, 326). Gillies died on 26 January 1958, from pneumonia, influenza, and generalized atheroma, at his home, 113 Bourne Way, Beckenham, Kent.

CHRISTINE COLLETTE

Sources William Gillies correspondence, JRL, labour party archives • International sub-committee minutes, JRL, labour party archives • Labour and Socialist International papers, JRL, labour party archives • Sozialistische Arbeiter-Internationale papers, Internationaal Instituut voor Sociale Geschiedenis, Amsterdam • C. Collette, *The international faith: labour's attitudes to European socialism, 1918–1939* (1998) • C. Collette and S. Bird, eds., *Jews, labour and the left* (2000) • D. Warriner, 'Winter in Prague', *Slavonic and East European Review*, 62 (1984), 209–40 • *The Labour who's who* (1924) • b. cert. • d. cert.

Archives JRL • Labour History Archive and Study Centre, Manchester, papers relating to Germany, India, Italy, Japan, Malta, and Palestine | Bodl. Oxf., corresp. with Attlee • Internationaal Instituut voor Sociale Geschiedenis, Amsterdam, Sozialistische Arbeiter-Internationale papers • Labour party archives, international subcommittee MSS, Labour and Socialist International MSS

Likenesses photographs, People's History Museum, Manchester

Gillies, Sir William George (1898–1973), painter and art teacher, was born on 21 September 1898 in Haddington, East Lothian, the second of the three children of John Gillies (1857–1921), tobacconist, and his wife, Emma (1864–1963), fourth daughter of William Smith of Kirriemuir, Forfarshire. His early childhood was spent in a flat above his father's shop in Haddington's High Street. Later the family moved to Westlea, a newly built house in Meadow Park on the outskirts of the town. Together with his two sisters, Janet (1895–1960) and Emma (1900–1936), Gillies was educated at Haddington's local preparatory school and then at the Knox Institute, where he was awarded the Dux medal in 1916. His youthful enthusiasm for art was encouraged by his uncle, William Ryle Smith, art teacher at the Grove Academy, Broughty Ferry, and by Robert Alexander Dakers, editor of the *Haddington Courier*, collector of Scottish art, and an amateur painter. As a boy Gillies accompanied both on painting expeditions into the picturesque closes of Haddington and the neighbouring countryside, beginning a lifelong habit of working out of doors. He enrolled at Edinburgh College of Art in the autumn of 1916 and in April 1917 was called up, serving with the Scottish Rifles in France. Wounded and gassed on the western front in 1918, he was sent back to Scotland to recuperate. Recalling these times more than half a century later he described his war experience as 'Two wasted years … when I'm asked my age I always subtract these two' (Richardson, 21). Gillies returned to Edinburgh College of Art in the autumn of 1919, graduating in 1922. On completion of a postgraduate year at the college he was awarded a travelling scholarship, enabling him to go to Paris in 1923 where he studied at the Académie Montparnasse under the cubist painter André Lhôte.

From Paris, Gillies travelled to Italy, visiting Florence, Padua, Ravenna, and Venice. On his return to Scotland in 1924 he was appointed to a teaching post at Inverness Royal Academy, but returned to Edinburgh in 1925 to begin his long teaching career at his former college. Gillies quickly became a central figure in the artistic community of Edinburgh, moving there in 1929 with his mother and sisters to a house at 162 Willowbrae Road. In 1931 he took a studio in Edinburgh at 45 Frederick Street, which he shared with the painter William MacTaggart. Gillies's paintings dating from the mid- to late 1920s are indebted to Lhôte's form of cubism (for example, *Florence*, 1924; Royal Scottish Academy, Edinburgh) but he later criticized the instruction he had received in Paris, which he considered programmatic and stifling. He recalled:

> What started off as appearing to be a new and exciting way of producing pictures in the end turned out to be a dismal cul-de-sac. I did not long employ Lhôte's principles in my painting … The hours were long and constant, so that we came into contact with no other French painters … We went to exhibitions or out sketching at the weekends … that was all. (Dickson, 20)

In 1931 an exhibition was held in Edinburgh of late paintings by the Norwegian artist Edvard Munch: these expressionist works greatly impressed Gillies, whose subsequent landscape paintings were executed with an emotional response not evident in his previous work (for example, *Near Durisdeer*, *c*.1932; Scottish National Gallery of Modern Art, Edinburgh). About 1930 Gillies began to make regular painting trips around Scotland, frequently in the company of John Maxwell, a fellow lecturer at Edinburgh College of Art. Gillies found the Scottish landscape an ideal subject for the loose, fluid, expressive style he was then developing. His output on these expeditions was prodigious. The painter David McClure recounted how 'Gillies would complete half-a-dozen watercolours before lunch, while Maxwell would still be contemplating some suitable aspect of his subject' (McClure, 17). In the mid-1930s Gillies experimented briefly with abstraction, but rejected this in favour of observed subject matter, and this remained the basis of his art. He painted mainly landscapes and still lifes, although he also executed several fine portraits and large-scale figure compositions, showing his immediate family and friends in domestic surroundings, such as *Family Group, Willowbrae* (1937; Royal Scottish Academy, Edinburgh). In his more formal oils his style was eclectic, particularly in his still-life painting, which was influenced by Bonnard, Vuillard, Matisse, and, latterly, Braque. In his landscapes in watercolour, painted directly from nature, he responded freely and intuitively to his subject matter, producing works of great insight and originality, such as *In Ardnamurchan* (*c*.1936; Scottish National Gallery of Modern Art, Edinburgh). Together with his Scottish contemporaries Maxwell, MacTaggart, and Anne Redpath, Gillies's work exemplifies the painterly approach and use of bold colour strongly associated with the so-called Edinburgh school painters, who flourished from the 1930s. In 1939 Gillies, his mother, and sister moved to the village of Temple in Midlothian, 10 miles from Edinburgh. This was to remain Gillies's home and the village and borders countryside to the south became a favourite subject for his art. In contrast to the mountainous Scottish highlands, which featured predominantly in his landscapes of the 1930s, the gentler character of the borders landscape contributed to a stylistic shift from the painterly expressionism of his earlier work to an approach based on careful use of line and refined colour, as in *Landscape with Houses* (mid-1940s; Scottish National Gallery of Modern Art, Edinburgh). This would remain a defining characteristic of his subsequent landscape painting.

In 1946 Gillies was made head of the school of drawing and painting at Edinburgh College of Art (succeeding his former teacher David Alison) and in 1959 was appointed principal, retiring in 1967. As such he influenced several generations of students. While his teaching responsibilities meant he was able to give less time to his own work, he always enjoyed college life, commenting:

> Far from being a burden … my teaching career has been a real delight to me … I feel that my contact with the attitudes of so many young and enthusiastic and idealistic students has prevented me from becoming the old fossil you might have expected me to grow into. (Scott-Moncrieff, 25)

One student remembered him thus:

> He was of small wiry build. His hair—so strong, upgrowing and crisp, full of vitality and energy—always seemed to me to epitomise the character of the man. It was nearly white but with that yellowed bloom from the nicotine of the cigarettes he smoked almost constantly. His voice was fairly high pitched, his speech slightly clipped and rapid with a narrow-vowelled 'educated' Scots accent. Sometimes he seemed to ham his own personality and accentuate his idiosyncrasies of speech and phrase. He scampered around the room uttering words that got right to the point of any obvious, unresolved—or unnoticed flaw—'the feet are too big' or, as he moved to the next student, 'the head's too wee'. (Gordon Smith, 90)

A self-portrait dating from 1940 is in the collection of the Scottish National Portrait Gallery, Edinburgh. In spite of his teaching commitments Gillies was an immensely prolific painter and exhibited regularly throughout his career. As a student at Edinburgh College of Art he had been a founding member of the exhibiting society the 1922 Group and his work was included in their annual exhibitions held in Edinburgh from 1923 to 1929. In 1931 he was invited to join the Society of Eight, a prestigious exhibiting group whose membership included the painters Sir John Lavery and the Scottish colourists S. J. Peploe and F. C. B. Cadell. He showed regularly with the Society of Scottish Artists, the Royal Scottish Academy (of which he was made a member in 1947), and the Royal Scottish Society of Painters in Watercolour (of which he was president from 1963 to 1969). He also held numerous solo exhibitions at the Scottish Gallery, Edinburgh. Gillies's most important patron was Dr Robert Lillie, who on his death in 1977 owned 372 works by Gillies: many of these were bequeathed to the Scottish National Gallery of Modern Art. Gillies was appointed CBE in 1957, received an honorary doctorate of letters from the University of Edinburgh in 1966, and in the same year was elected a fellow of the Educational Institute of Scotland. In 1970 he was knighted in recognition of his services to art in Scotland and in 1971 was elected a Royal Academician. A large retrospective exhibition of his work was held at the Royal Scottish Academy and Scottish Arts Council Galleries in Edinburgh in 1970. He died at his home in Temple on 15 April 1973, and was cremated at Mortonhall crematorium on 19 April. He never married. He bequeathed his estate, including many pictures, to the Royal Scottish Academy.

PHILIP LONG

Sources J. Soden and V. Keller, *William Gillies* (1998) · T. E. Dickson, *W. G. Gillies* (1974) · W. Gordon Smith, *W. G. Gillies* (1991) · P. Long, *William Gillies* (1994) [exhibition catalogue, NG Scot.] · Royal Scot. Acad., William Gillies papers · S. Richardson, 'W. G. Gillies: the artist reminisces', *Christian Science Monitor* (12 March 1970) · D. McClure, *John Maxwell* (1976), 17 · G. Scott-Moncrieff, 'Fresh aspects of beauty', *Times Educational Supplement* (6 Feb 1970) · *DNB*
Archives Royal Scot. Acad., drawings, papers, photographs, etc.
Likenesses W. G. Gillies, self-portrait, oils, 1940, Scot. NPG · E. Schilsky, bronze bust, Scot. NPG · group portrait (*Gathering at 7 London Street*), Scot. NPG

Gilligan, Arthur Edward Robert (1894–1976), cricketer, was born at Witherhurst, Grove Park, Camberwell, London, on 23 December 1894, the second of three sons (there was also a daughter) of Willie Austin Gilligan (*b*. 1864), a manager for Liebig's Extract of Meat Co., and his wife, Alice Eliza Kimpton. He attended Fairfield School before entering Dulwich College (1906–14), where he excelled in cricket and athletics. In 1913 all three of the Gilligan brothers played for the Dulwich College cricket eleven; in their subsequent contribution to first-class cricket they were a public-school sporting phenomenon to rival the Lytteltons of Eton, the Fosters of Malvern, and the Ashtons of Winchester. Their father was a member of the committee of the Surrey county club, for whose second eleven Arthur played during his school holidays in 1913 and 1914.

Gilligan's undergraduate career at Pembroke College, Cambridge (1914, 1919–20), was interrupted by war service in France as a captain with the 11th battalion of the Lancashire Fusiliers. In 1919 he won his cricket blue for Cambridge, ensuring a Cambridge victory by taking six for 52 in Oxford's second innings. It was an outstanding display of fast bowling. A few days earlier, representing Cambridge against Sussex, he had put on 177 in 65 minutes with J. N. Naumann for the last wicket, scoring 101 batting at number eleven. In 1920 he went down from Cambridge to join the firm in which his father had become a senior partner, Gilbert Kimpton & Co., general produce merchants, of Monument Street in the City of London. On 6 April 1921 he married Cecilia Mary, only daughter of Henry Noble Mathews.

Gilligan played three games for Surrey in 1920, but in the following year was registered for Sussex, and represented the county as an amateur for the next ten years. He captained Sussex from 1922 to 1929, producing a strong all-round side known for their attractive play and fine fielding, inspired by his own acrobatic ability in the field at mid-off. Although not noted as a tactician, he was an inspiring captain, who laid emphasis on blooding young talent. During his first year as captain he made great strides as a bowler and took 135 wickets (at 18.75). He was picked for the Gentlemen and toured South Africa with MCC in the winter of 1922–3. In 1923 he performed the 'double' (1000 runs and 100 wickets). He was chosen to captain England in 1924 in the first test at Edgbaston, where he and M. W. Tate combined to bowl out South Africa for 30, with Gilligan taking six for 7. When South Africa followed on he took a further five for 83 to secure an England victory by an innings. Tate and Gilligan became the most feared opening attack of the time, bowling out many of the best sides in the county championship cheaply. At Lord's, Sussex dismissed Middlesex for 41, with Gilligan taking eight for 25.

In Gilligan's period of greatest success disaster struck. When batting for the Gentlemen against the Players at the Oval in July 1924, he was struck by a ball over the heart. Shrugging off his injury, he went on to make 112, but he was seriously hurt and had done himself irreparable damage. He was never able to bowl fast again and became almost a passenger in the MCC team he captained in the following winter in Australia, though his captaincy and fielding remained an inspiration. Although the series was lost, he led England to victory at Melbourne in February 1925, their first victory against Australia since 1912. That effectively was the end of his career as a test cricketer, though he became a selector in 1926 and captained MCC in India the following winter. He retired from the first-class game in 1932 with career figures of 9140 runs (at 20.08) and 868 wickets (at 23.20).

Gilligan became popular as one of the earlier radio commentators on test matches and was a stickler for sporting behaviour. He wrote on cricket regularly for the *News Chronicle* and was the author of several books on cricket, including an account of the 1954–5 MCC tour of Australia, *The Urn Returns*. He was president of MCC in 1967–8 and was much sought after as a lecturer and after-dinner speaker. An outstanding golfer, he became president of the English golf union in 1959. He was also a talented skier and met his second wife, Katharine Margaret Fox (1902–1998), whom he married in 1934, in Wengen, his first marriage having ended in divorce. A new stand opened at the Sussex county cricket ground at Hove in 1971 was named in his honour. Gilligan died at his home, Cherry Trees, Tudor Close, Mare Hill, Pulborough, Sussex, on 5 September 1976 and was buried at Stopham, Sussex.

The youngest of the Gilligan brothers, **(Alfred Herbert)**

Harold Gilligan (1896–1978), cricketer, was born at Denmark Hill, London, on 29 June 1896, and educated at Fairfield School and Dulwich College. He was in the Dulwich eleven for three years and captain in 1915. During the First World War, as a pilot in the Royal Naval Air Service, he was the first person to fly over the German fleet at Kiel. After joining his father's firm he went on to have a highly successful career in business as co-director of Carltona. He played cricket for Sussex from 1919 to 1931 and often captained the county in Arthur's absence. He toured South Africa with S. B. Joel's unofficial side in 1924–5 under Lord Tennyson, and replaced his brother, who had to withdraw on health grounds, as captain of MCC in New Zealand (1929–30). An impetuous batsman, who loved to play his strokes, he never quite fulfilled his early promise; he averaged just 17 for Sussex and scored only one century (143 against Derbyshire). His record, however, of playing 70 first-class innings in a season (1923) has never been challenged. In later years he served on the Surrey County Cricket Club committee. On 1 June 1933 he married Marjorie Winifred White; their daughter Virginia married Peter May, captain of Surrey and England. He died at Stroud Common, Shamley Green, Surrey, on 5 May 1978.

The eldest of the Gilligan brothers, **Frank William Gilligan** (1893–1960), cricketer, was born on 20 September 1893, and was at Fairfield School (1900–1906) and Dulwich College (1906–13) before going on to Worcester College, Oxford (1913–14; 1919–20). He was a captain in the 12th battalion, Essex regiment, during the First World War. After the war he won two cricket blues at Oxford, one as captain, and graduated with honours in English. On 6 August 1921 he married Clara Elizabeth, second daughter of James Brindle of Craven Park, Preston, Lancashire. Between 1919 and 1929 he played seventy-nine matches for Essex, keeping wicket with considerable success and averaging 23.62 with the bat. He was a career schoolmaster and became a housemaster at Uppingham School, where he taught from 1920 to 1935, before taking on the headmastership of Wanganui Collegiate School in New Zealand (1936–54). For his services to education he was appointed OBE in 1955. He died in Wanganui, Wellington, New Zealand, on 4 May 1960. D. R. W. Silk

Sources B. Green, ed., *The Wisden book of obituaries* (1986) • *Wisden* (1924) • private information (2004) [Katharine Margaret Gilligan] • personal knowledge (2004) • *WWW* • T. L. Ormiston, *Dulwich College register, 1619 to 1926* (1926) • C. Lee, *From the sea end: the official history of Sussex county cricket club* (1989) • b. cert. • *CGPLA Eng. & Wales* (1960) • *CGPLA Eng. & Wales* (1976) • *CGPLA Eng. & Wales* (1978)
Archives FILM BFI NFTVA, news footage
Likenesses photograph, repro. in *Wisden* (1924) • photograph, repro. in *Wisden* (1939) • photograph, repro. in *Wisden* (1977)
Wealth at death £29,555 6*s*. 6*d*. in England; Frank William Gilligan: New Zealand probate sealed in England, 15 Sept 1960, *CGPLA Eng. & Wales* • £36,645: probate, 18 Nov 1976, *CGPLA Eng. & Wales* • £53,223—Alfred Herbert Harold Gilligan: probate, 26 Sept 1978, *CGPLA Eng. & Wales*

Gilligan, Frank William (1893–1960). *See under* Gilligan, Arthur Edward Robert (1894–1976).

Gilligan, (Alfred Herbert) Harold (1896–1978). *See under* Gilligan, Arthur Edward Robert (1894–1976).

Gilliland, Thomas (*fl.* 1804–1816), writer on the theatre, was of obscure origin; the surname is associated with Ulster. In 1804 he produced *A Dramatic Synopsis*, an essay with remarks on contemporary playwrights and 'strictures' on the actors of the London theatres. The *Monthly Mirror's* reviewer thought it the work of 'a man of sense and liberality, judgment and taste'. Two pamphlets published by Gilliland in 1804 criticized John Philip Kemble and the management of the Covent Garden Theatre.

In 1806 Gilliland contributed two pamphlets, under the pseudonym Philo-Veritas, to a controversy over the relations between Nathaniel Jefferys and the prince of Wales. In the first of these, *Diamond Cut Diamond*, he wrote that he 'could not fight in a better cause, than that of an injured and libelled Prince'. *The Diamond New Pointed* was a 'supplement' to the earlier pamphlet, and printed three letters from Jefferys to the earl of Moira.

Gilliland clearly made himself enemies. His next work, *The Dramatic Mirror*, is dated on the title-page 1808, but may have appeared in 1807. An expansion of *A Dramatic Synopsis*, it contained a history of the stage, with accounts of actors from the time of Shakespeare onwards, and of playwrights from 1660. It was dedicated to the prince of Wales, and was venomously reviewed in *The Satirist* of January 1808. The reviewer's charges included plagiarism ('The original matter … would lay in as small a space as its author's brains') and inconsistency, since Gilliland now praised Kemble. The review claimed that Gilliland, 'during a recent season … was wont to intrude himself into the greenroom of Drury-lane theatre', until he desisted in the face of a petition to the managers calling for his exclusion, 'signed by the most spirited of the performers' headed by Charles Mathews. Gilliland's alleged purpose was to spy 'upon the private conduct of public men' and to use their talk in his journalism, 'as he at that time had not been dismissed from the newspapers for want of talent'. The review called him the 'cast-off fag' and 'ci-devant scout' of Anthony Pasquin (pseudonym of John Williams).

1808 also saw the publication of Gilliland's *The Trap: a Moral, Philosophical, and Satirical Work* on the subject of love. Gilliland there referred to himself as a single man. The book was attacked in *The Satirist* of December that year, the reviewer expressing astonishment that Gilliland could write for a living. A jibe that his 'trash' might be countenanced by 'his Grace the Duke of Piccadilly' (William Douglas, duke of Queensberry), Matthew Gregory Lewis, and Thomas Moore, all at that time associated with Charles James Fox or the prince of Wales, suggests that *The Satirist*'s animosity arose from political as well as literary principles.

Little is known of Gilliland's subsequent career. He appears to have been living in the Tottenham Court Road in 1808. His name and the bibliographical details of three of his works are included in *A Biographical Dictionary of the Living Authors of Great Britain and Ireland* (1816), but without comment. John Wells

Sources 'The dramatic mirror: by Thomas Gilliland, author of dramatic synopsis etc.', *The Satirist, or, Monthly Meteor*, 1 (1 Jan 1808),

Thomas Gilliland (*fl.* **1804–1816**), by Thomas Cheesman, pubd 1807 (after Samuel De Wilde)

418–24 • 'Review of Gilliland's "The Trap"', *The Satirist, or, Monthly Meteor*, 3 (1 Dec 1808), 532–40 • Philo-Veritas [T. Gilliland], *Diamond cut diamond…* (1806) • [J. Watkins and F. Shoberl], *A biographical dictionary of the living authors of Great Britain and Ireland* (1816) • *The Monthly Mirror*, 17 (June 1804), 405 [review of subject's 'A dramatic synopsis' 1804] • Adams, *Drama*

Likenesses T. Cheesman, stipple, pubd 1807 (after S. De Wilde), BM, NPG [*see illus.*] • print, Harvard TC

Gilling, Isaac (*bap.* **1663**, *d.* **1725**), Presbyterian minister, was born at Stogumber, Somerset, and baptized on 22 August 1663 at Bicknoller, near Stogumber, the elder son of Richard Gilling, baker, and his wife, Elizabeth Sully. His father had been reported as holding conventicles in his house in 1669, and in 1672 took out a licence under Charles II's indulgence for a Presbyterian minister to preach there. After attending grammar school, perhaps at the boarding-school conducted by George Hammond, minister of Pauls Meeting, Taunton, Isaac Gilling was probably educated for the ministry at the nonconformist academy in Taunton conducted by Hammond's colleague Matthew Warren. He was among the young ministers pressed into early service during the first years of toleration. He subsequently claimed 'Some of us entred young, and raw upon our Work' (Gilling, 10). He was ordained with seven others at Lyme Regis, Dorset, by four Presbyterian ministers on 25 August 1687. At the time he was described as curate of Barrington and of Seavington St Mary's, Somerset. His relative and biographer, John Fox (1693–1763), wrote that Gilling first 'preached often in churches, though he was never a regular conformist' ('Memoirs', 327). According to the Common Fund survey, by the early 1690s he was one of a number of itinerant preachers who supplied places in Somerset. After working as an usher at a Latin school in Axminster, Devon, where he also preached to a nonconformist congregation, he became minister of the Presbyterian congregation at Silverton, Devon, and on 27 August 1691 married Mrs Sarah Baker of Bramford Speke, described by Fox as 'somewhat deformed' and by whom he acquired an estate (ibid., 327). They had a son, Isaac, and a daughter, Elizabeth.

Some time before September 1697 the Presbyterian congregation at Newton Abbot called Gilling as William Yeo's successor. His wife died shortly afterwards. He then married Mrs Jane Atkins, the widow of the Revd Samuel Atkins of Exeter. 'He was passionately fond of her, and afraid of her; for she governed absolutely' ('Memoirs', 328). Gilling's earliest published works were his funeral sermons for her husband and her son. At Newton Abbot he kept a successful Latin school in his house, with at one time nineteen boarders from Exeter and other places, besides scholars from Newton Abbot and the surrounding parishes. Among his pupils was Dr John Huxham (1692–1768), the physician. During Anne's reign Gilling met with considerable trouble from the incumbent of the parish, Walter Elford, who prosecuted him for keeping a school without a bishop's licence. He was forced more than once to abscond to avoid arrest; the last occasion was in 1712, when he went to Plymouth in disguise 'in a long wig' to stay with Fox's family because a process was out against him for illegally keeping a Latin school (ibid., 327). Gilling retired to London, taking Fox with him, having promised to do all in his power to remove Fox's aversion to the ministry. At the end of a fortnight Gilling returned to Newton Abbot with Fox, who remained with him as his pupil for three-quarters of a year (1712–13). Fox fell in love with Gilling's daughter, whom he later married. He was greatly pleased with the situation of Gilling's house and gardens, and his great collection of books. Gilling 'had a polite taste both in Greek and Latin, especially in the classics', and 'was a great lover of critical learning'. He also had considerable ability as an editor, and prepared the works of Walter Moyle for the press, though they were 'unhandsomely taken from him' and published by another (ibid., 329). He did publish an abridgement and continuation of George Trosse's autobiography, first published by Joseph Hallett (1656–1722). Gilling's copy of Hallett's edition, with his annotations, formed part of the New College collection now at Dr Williams's Library, London.

Gilling was a strong supporter of the Exeter assembly of ministers in Devon, and frequently acted as its scribe. His own manuscript notebook, preserved in Dr Williams's Library, provides a detailed record of the business of the assembly up to 1718, when the Exeter controversy broke out over orthodox fears concerning the spread of Arian opinions. The sermon Gilling preached at the young men's lecture in Exeter in September 1718 for the right of Christians 'to stick to the Bible as the rule of Faith', rather than to any Trinitarian subscription, provoked 'a most fearful Outcry … as if we went about to sap the very Foundations of Christianity' (I. Gilling, *The Mischief of Rash and Uncharitable Judging*, 1719, Preface). As a result of joining with the minority who refused to subscribe, he was excluded from the assembly, and more than half his congregation left to form a new meeting in 1719, leaving him with 'little more or better than the walls to talk to' ('Memoirs', 328), whereas previously, according to the Evans List, he had a meeting of 380 hearers in 1715. Other disappointments followed. In spite of having had a handsome income from his school, property, and meeting, he lived too well after his second marriage and ran into debt. He had educated his son as a physician at Paris and Leiden (entered 4 October 1723) at some cost, but he did not turn out well. The loss of his congregation struck him particularly hard; 'he thought it a terrible disgrace to be deserted' (ibid.). Gilling died at Newton Abbot on 21 August 1725. He had asked to be buried in the church at Newton Abbot, but the parish being a peculiar, the ordinary, Sir William Courtenay, refused, saying 'they might bury him in one of the marshes' (ibid.). He was therefore buried in his meeting-house at Newton Abbot.

ALEXANDER GORDON, *rev.* DAVID L. WYKES

Sources 'Memoirs of himself, by Mr John Fox … with biographical sketches of some of his contemporaries; and some unpublished letters [pts 1, 5]', *Monthly Repository*, 16 (1821), 126–35, esp. 132–5; 325–31, esp. 327–9 • 'The Fox memoirs: worthies of Devon', *Report and Transactions of the Devonshire Association*, 28 (1896), 129, 157 • A. Brockett, ed., *The Exeter assembly: the minutes of the assemblies of the United Brethren of Devon and Cornwall, 1691–1717*, Devon and Cornwall RS, new ser., 6 (1963) • 'Gilling's transactions', DWL, MS 38.24; published as *The Exeter Assembly … as transcribed by the Reverend Isaac Gilling*, ed. A. Brockett (1963) • E. Calamy, *A continuation of the account of the ministers … who were ejected and silenced after the Restoration in 1660*, 2 (1727), 419 • M. Smith, 'A presbyterian survivor: Richard Bryan, rector of Silverton, Devon, 1657–1688', *Devon and Cornwall Notes and Queries*, 37 (1992–6), 121–8 • I. Gilling, *The qualifications and duties of ministers. A sermon preach'd at Taunton, May the 27th 1708. Before an assembly of the united ministers of Somerset and Devon. Publish'd at the request of the assembly* (1708) • G. L. Turner, ed., *Original records of early nonconformity under persecution and indulgence*, 1 (1911), 8, 312 • A. Gordon, ed., *Freedom after ejection: a review (1690–1692) of presbyterian and congregational nonconformity in England and Wales* (1917), 94, 270 • J. Evans, 'List of dissenting congregations and ministers in England and Wales, 1715–1729', DWL, MS 38.4, 27 • 'The diary (1705–1726) of Rev. Samuel Short, dissenting minister at Uffclume, Devon', *Devon and Cornwall Notes and Queries*, 23 (1947–9), 221–40, 251–3 • J. Huxtable and A. Snow, *Our fathers that begat us: the story of the protestant dissenters of Newton Abbot, 1662–1984* (1985) • parish register, Upton Helions, Devon, 27 Aug 1691 [marriage, Sarah Baker] • parish register, Bicknoller, Somerset, 22 Aug 1663 [baptism] • parish register, Bicknoller, Somerset, 8 May 1649 [marriage, R. Gilling and E. Sully]

Archives DWL, notebook

Gillingwater, Edmund (*bap.* **1736**, *d.* **1813**), topographer, the fourth son of Edmund Gillingwater (*c.*1693–1772) and Alice Frary (*c.*1706–1784), was baptized on 29 December 1736 at St Margaret's, Lowestoft, where his father had been churchwarden in 1734. He was a pupil of the Revd John Bellward (1726–1792) before being apprenticed to a barber, but after working as a hairdresser, first in Lowestoft and then for two years in Norwich, he moved permanently to Harleston in Norfolk in December 1761 to set up as a stationer and bookseller in the old market place. He was overseer for the poor of Harleston when he published *An Essay on Parish Work-Houses* in 1786, written as a well-

Edmund Gillingwater (*bap.* **1736**, *d.* **1813**), by H. S. Turner (after Henry Walton)

informed and conscientious guardian. He kept in touch with kindred spirits in Norwich by becoming an active member of the United Society of Friars, founded in 1785, where he read papers on saving the lives of shipwrecked sailors and on the causes of idiocy. Other members included William Wilkins, John Sell Cotman, Humphry Repton, and the Norfolk topographer Mostyn Armstrong. At about this time he met and married Mary Bond (*d.* 1802), a widow of his own age with sufficient means to enable him to retire from business and to write; they had no children.

Gillingwater's elder brother Isaac (1732–1813), who lived and worked as a barber opposite the old chapel in Lowestoft High Street, made extensive collections for a history of that town. He sent Richard Gough a printed prospectus which named himself as author and promised publication in one volume, priced half a guinea, in August or September 1789. But a second copy of the sheet has 'Isaac' at 'Lowestoft', changed to 'Edmund' at 'Harleston'. This seems to confirm contemporary allegations that Edmund published his brother's work over his own name as *An historical account of the ancient town of Lowestoft, … the adjoining parishes … and the island of Lothingland*, undated. George Ashby had lent him his own copy of John Ives's fragment of a printed history and was irritated to find it reproduced without permission. Perhaps it is not surprising that Gillingwater's dedicatory preface, dated 15 November 1790, is ambiguous about the authorship. The substantial volume contains much factual and statistical information, but the many maps and illustrations which Isaac Gillingwater had collected for it, the finest by Richard Powles of Lowestoft, were not included. Instead, Isaac Johnson of Woodbridge extra-illustrated a small number of copies with watercolours and wash drawings for such wealthy collectors as John Gage Rokewood. Gillingwater's next work was his *Historical and Descriptive Account of St Edmunds Bury … and the Abbey*, which went through two editions (1804 and 1811); it breaks little new ground.

The Gillingwaters were as good at gathering and arranging material as many of their contemporaries, but Edmund, who aspired to be a historian of the whole county, was insufficiently widely travelled or knowledgeable. His collections for a county topography in thirteen folio volumes consist largely of handwritten excerpts from works in print on slips of paper. The calligraphic title-page, with a quotation dated 1796, indicates that the work was to have had a Norwich printer, but the project came to nothing. Occasional original observations are to be found only under those north-east Suffolk parishes which he knew at first hand; the first drafts of most of these are in the Suffolk Record Office. These volumes were bought after Gillingwater's death by Henry Jermyn of Sibton, who died later the same year; whereas Jermyn's Suffolk collections are in the British Library, Gillingwater's papers, after passing through many hands, are still in private possession.

From 1806 to 1810 Gillingwater served as churchwarden of Redenhall with Harleston. A staunch and devout Anglican, he worked hard to develop Sunday schools, and was a regular visitor to the one in his own parish. An amateur student of theology, the ideas he sent Samuel Burder over several years earned that writer's gratitude. After losing his wife on 18 May 1802, his health declined, steeply during his last years. He died on 13 March 1813 in Harleston and was buried six days later next to Mary on the path leading to the west entrance to Redenhall church. The headstone for his father, Edmund, mother, Alice, and brother Isaac, who died on 14 May 1813, in Lowestoft churchyard mistakenly proclaims the father 'The historian of Lowestoft', whereas Isaac deserved the title. Isaac continued recording local history at least until 1807 as if for a second edition of *Lowestoft*. Towards the end of his life he became very poor, and to raise money sold some of his antiquarian papers, despite their poor condition, to Robert Reeve of Lowestoft; they are now in the British Library.

J. M. Blatchly

Sources Nichols, *Illustrations*, 3.200; 6.545 • S. Tymms, ed., *The East Anglian, or, Notes and Queries on Subjects Connected with the Counties of Suffolk, Cambridge, Essex and Norfolk*, 4 (1869–70), 253–5, 276 • Bodl. Oxf., MS Bodley Gough Gen. Top., vol. 3, fols. 363–6 [materials for third edn of *Anecdotes of British topography*] • Suffolk RO, Lowestoft, Gillingwater MSS, 193/2/1; 193/1/1–3 • parish register (baptism), Lowestoft, St Margaret's, 1736 • *DNB* • memorial inscriptions, Redenhall churchyard, Lowestoft

Archives Suffolk RO, Lowestoft, papers, incl. collections relating to Bungay and plans

Likenesses H. S. Turner, lithograph (after H. Walton), BM, NPG; Suffolk RO [*see illus.*] • H. Walton, oils

Gillis, James (1802–1864), vicar apostolic of the eastern district, was born in the parish of Notre Dame, Montreal, Canada, on 7 April 1802. He was the only son of a prosperous Banffshire Scottish Catholic migrant, Alexander Gillis, *maître de pension*, and his Episcopalian wife, Elizabeth Langley. She became a Catholic shortly before her death in 1850. Educated at the French Sulpician college in Montreal before the family returned to Scotland in 1816, he acquired a considerable command of the French language which served him throughout his life. The family settled permanently at Fochabers and Gillis went to study at Aquhorties seminary in Aberdeenshire in October 1817. In December 1818 he entered St Nicholas's seminary, Paris, where he was a fellow student with the future bishop of Orléans, Dupanloup. In October 1823 he transferred to the Sulpician seminary of Issy-les-Moulineaux. Three years later in February 1826 ill health forced him to return to Scotland. Here he continued his studies in Glasgow under Revd Andrew Scott, later vicar apostolic of the western district, and was ordained at Aquhorties on 9 June 1827.

Gillis had a zest for grandees and grand gestures. While spending the summer and autumn of 1827 at Blairs seminary he became a close friend of the wealthy Catholic patron John Menzies of Pitfodels. On the death of Bishop Alexander Cameron (1747–1828) of the lowland district his successor, Bishop Alexander Paterson (1766–1831), took Gillis to Edinburgh, where he was largely responsible for the highly visible, lavish funeral of Cameron. He went on a fund-raising mission to France from 1828 and witnessed the 1830 revolution. Early in 1831 he became secretary to Bishop Paterson, whose funeral shortly after was graced by the presence of the exiled Charles X. Gillis subsequently spent much time with the exiled Bourbons in Holyrood Palace: he had a royal pew fitted out on the right of the sanctuary at St Mary's, Broughton Street, Edinburgh, and took letters of recommendation from the royal family on his next fund-raising tour of France, Spain, and Italy in 1831–2.

Gillis was a rising star. Menzies of Pitfodels and many eastern district clergy wanted Gillis to succeed Paterson, but the vicars apostolic felt his youth and inexperience were too great. He brought a more exuberant European expression of Catholicism to Scotland: he bought a site for the first convent in Scotland since the Reformation in February 1834 and recruited Ursuline nuns from France, including the recent Scottish convert Agnes Xavier Traill (1798–1872). St Margaret's Convent opened on 16 June 1835. Gillis wished to provide education for Catholics of all social conditions, as well as medical assistance and an orphanage. Like several other of his enterprises these enthusiastic ambitions exceeded his resources and proved short-lived in their original form. In 1858 he recruited Sisters of Charity from Limerick and, after introducing the Oblates of Mary Immaculate in 1852, he encouraged Jesuit establishments in Edinburgh and the borders (1859). Bishop James Kyle, vicar apostolic northern district, invariably urged calmness and caution upon him in the face of possible popular bigotry.

In 1837 Gillis became coadjutor in the eastern district as

bishop of Limyra *in partibus*: here considerable Irish immigration put pressure on his slender financial resources. An approach to the association for the Propagation of the Faith in Lyons proved unsuccessful, so Gillis and influential friends organized L'oeuvre du Catholicisme en Europe. Rome soon ordered the two bodies to merge and Gillis won his financial support. He also secured the return to Blairs of the remnants of the library of the Scots College, Paris. When Carruthers, vicar apostolic of the eastern district, retired to Blairs in Easter 1840 Gillis was left in effective control. He immediately made considerable alterations to the cathedral of St Mary's: new pews, ornate pulpit, organ, and an extravagant oak rood screen. But his new responsibilities did not curtail his peripatetic energies. In 1843 he went to investigate the Bavarian government threat to the Scottish seminary at Regensburg; four years later he was again in Europe, and another visit followed in 1848.

At his death in 1845 Menzies left his considerable fortune to the church in Scotland to pay off church debts, build a new church in Aberdeen, and provide spare cash for the bishops. Once again Gillis's zeal outran resources: he bought an old Episcopal college at Crieff to use as a seminary but the plan soon withered. The same fate befell the infant academy at Wellburn. Other schemes proved more successful. In 1840 to assist the poor he founded the Holy Gild of St Joseph, a Catholic mutual benefit organization to provide relief in sickness and old age, encourage hygiene, award prizes for the cleanest homes, and lay on a huge annual Christmas gathering. Within five years Gillis could claim 350 members, and it soon spread to other parts of Britain and to Australia. In 1845 he introduced the lay St Vincent de Paul Society to assist poorer Catholics, and five years later he began the St Andrews Society to aid less fortunate parishes in the vicariate. In 1853 he introduced the Sodality of the Sacred Heart into all parishes and began the first retreats for his clergy. He also acquired a Catholic cemetery and began episcopal visitations in 1861.

But Gillis's active restless imagination produced still more projects. In 1850 he got his friend A. W. Pugin to design a gigantic cathedral for his Greenhill site in Edinburgh: revived Catholicism was to be made a permanent feature of Scotland. Once more his zeal exceeded his resources and the scheme collapsed, but Gillis's architectural interests did not die. He was closely associated with the architect Gillespie Graham, partly responsible for Edinburgh's New Town, and with J. A. Hanson in an abortive effort to found an art institute in Leith.

Gillis preached at many significant Roman Catholic occasions, including the opening of Cheadle church in 1846 and at the opening of St George's, Southwark, in 1848. A year before his death he preached his last sermon at the opening of the Italian church, Moorfields (1863). Although a very popular preacher he was not outstanding. John Henry Newman was scathing in his description of his performance at the opening of Pugin's Cheadle church in 1846: 'Dr Gillis is an able man—at the opening of Cheadle Church he preached a sermon half screaming and bellowing and half whining—and Lady Dormer and the ladies of quality were in raptures with it' (J. H. Newman to H. Wilberforce, 28 Dec 1850, *Letters and Diaries*, 14.183). A prolific pamphleteer, he rarely let protestant criticism go unanswered.

Gillis succeeded as vicar apostolic of the eastern district on the death of Bishop Carruthers in 1852. His episcopate saw the conversion of several major landowners and substantial families who were able to provide money, land, churches, and schools. A further windfall helped in 1858: it came from Miss Maxwell, the daughter of Dr William Maxwell, Burns's revolutionary medical friend. Gillis was himself responsible for the conversion of Lord and Lady Fielding. Intending to establish a Scottish intellectual presence and a major college, Gillis brought Henry Caswall and others to Edinburgh, although J. B. Dalgairns refused the invitation. Despite his lack of success in founding a college, Gillis left his vicariate in a healthy condition, with 54 priests, 67 churches and stations, and 36 schools.

Gillis's constant activities, travels, and worries took their toll on his health, and in June 1852 he was injured in a train crash *en route* from London. The following year, on a fund-raising visit, he spent six weeks at the Ax hot springs. But illness did not limit his activities. Five years later, after visiting Vichy, he preached impressively on Jeanne d'Arc in Orléans to raise funds. He returned with the heart of Henry II from Chinon (1857), and from the queen of Spain he brought relics of St Margaret (1862). Even when seriously ill in 1862 he travelled to Rome for the canonization of the Japanese martyrs. Gillis died in Edinburgh on 24 February 1864. His funeral appropriately had a Jesuit preacher and a Mozart requiem mass and was held at St Mary's, Edinburgh, a church greatly extended and improved by him. He was buried at St Margaret's Convent on 1 March 1864.

Gillis's sense of occasion, history, and drama, and his inexhaustible energy, made him a powerful purveyor of ultramontane zeal in the Scottish Catholic church: there can be no doubt that he was a major figure in the Scottish Catholic revival. However his enthusiasm and his position as an outsider did lead to misjudgements: his close associations to wealth and power, Scottish and continental, encouraged him to attempt visionary schemes on all too slender resources.

BERNARD ASPINWALL

Sources Scottish Catholic archives, Edinburgh · Scots College archives, Rome · Archivio Vaticano, Vatican City · *The letters and diaries of John Henry Newman*, ed. C. S. Dessain and others, [31 vols.] (1961–) · J. Darragh, *The Catholic hierarchy of Scotland: a biographical list, 1653–1985* (1986) · W. M. Brady, *Annals of the Catholic hierarchy in England and Scotland* (1877) · J. F. S. Gordon, *Ecclesiastical chronicle for Scotland*, 4 vols. (1867), vol. 3, pp. 480–91 · C. Johnson, 'Scottish secular clergy: the northern and eastern districts', *Innes Review*, 40 (1989), 24–68 · d. cert.

Archives Archivio Vaticano, Vatican City, archives of Propaganda Fide · Blairs College, Aberdeen, collections · Scots College, Rome · Scottish Catholic Archives, Edinburgh, notes, sermons, and papers | Birmingham Oratory, Newman MSS

Likenesses J. le Conte, stipple (after J. Archer), BM · portrait, Archbishops House, 42 Greenhill Gardens, Edinburgh · portrait, Gillis Centre, Whitehouse Loan, Edinburgh

Gillmore, David Howe, Baron Gillmore of Thamesfield (1934–1999), diplomatist, was born on 16 August 1934 at 70 Bath Road, Swindon, Wiltshire, the eldest of the three sons of Air Vice-Marshal Alan David (Peter) Gillmore (1905–1996), an RAF officer, and his wife, Kathleen Victoria (Kate), *née* Morris. He was educated at St Dunstan's preparatory school in Burnham-on-Sea and then Trent College in Long Eaton, Nottingham. He was head boy at both schools, a successful scholar, and an above average athlete, playing both cricket and rugby for Trent College first teams. At King's College, Cambridge (1953–6), he read Russian and French, both of which languages were to mark his later life.

On leaving university Gillmore took some time to decide what to do. He worked briefly for Reuters and then in a plastics factory outside Paris before taking a year off to live in the seaside village of Nerja in Andalusia, where he wrote a novel, *A Way from Exile* (1967), about the Cathars in medieval France. He returned to London having in 1964 married Lucile Sophie Morin, a Frenchwoman then working for UNESCO. Their sons, Julian and Paul, were born in 1967 and 1970. Gillmore's marriage was at the centre of his life, and he remained devoted to Lucile; she was an anchor of stability and later the source of much quiet but shrewd and practical advice on a whole range of questions, including the problems of spouses in an increasingly pressurized foreign service. In London, Gillmore spent four years teaching in the East End, which was both a challenging experience for him and a revealing one for his pupils.

Gillmore entered the Foreign and Commonwealth Office (FCO) by a special late entrants' examination in 1970. He was considered old for a new entrant, and at his first interview the head of the personnel department informed him that his career expectation would be to reach the rank of counsellor in a medium-sized consulate somewhere in western Europe. Notwithstanding this slightly unencouraging appraisal, and having served a brief apprenticeship in London, Gillmore and his family left in 1972 for Moscow, where he spent the next two years as first secretary in the economic section. This grounding in the way the country worked, and the Soviet obsession with secrecy and security, stood him in good stead for the next stage of his career as an arms control expert. In Vienna from 1975 to 1978 the Francophone Gillmore family became acquainted with the German language and Austrian culture, while Gillmore himself joined (as a counsellor) the negotiations on mutual and balanced force reductions, a complex attempt to scale back the vast quantity of conventional forces facing each other across the line separating the Warsaw pact and NATO.

In 1979 Gillmore was appointed head of the defence department at the FCO. He was then forty-five and had in nine years made up for the 'lost' fifteen years prior to his joining the office. He was promoted in 1981 to assistant under-secretary of state in charge of defence. The subject remained at the top of the list of priorities with which the

David Howe Gillmore, Baron Gillmore of Thamesfield (1934–1999), by unknown photographer

FCO had to deal and brought Gillmore into close contact with the prime minister, Margaret Thatcher, who typically wished to know the detail of the complex and highly sensitive negotiations between the Americans and Russians over strategic nuclear arms limitations in which the UK, as a nuclear power, had a vital national interest. There were only a few people in the FCO, Ministry of Defence, and intelligence communities who were privy to the information on which decisions were made, and it was critical that they should win the trust of an equally small circle of advisers in Washington. The fact that Gillmore was known to have the confidence of, and access to, Mrs Thatcher was a great help in his dealings with his American counterparts. He was also a key figure in helping to allay European concerns about American policies and maintaining support for them in NATO in the face of determined efforts at wedge driving by the Soviet Union.

In 1983 Gillmore was posted to Kuala Lumpur for his only spell as an ambassador or high commissioner. The Malaysian prime minister, Dr Mohatir Mohammed, had devised the policy of 'buy British last' as a way of expressing post-colonial resentment at the power and influence of Britain in Malaysia. It was a sensitive situation, and Gillmore played a leading role in keeping things under control. He returned to London in 1986 as a deputy under-secretary of state to join the inner group of six or so senior officials whose task it was to supervise and co-ordinate policy and advice to ministers. His area of responsibility was wide and included the Far East. He was in charge of developing closer contacts and a better understanding with Japan and for shaping policy towards China while bearing in mind British interests in Hong Kong.

Appointed CMG in 1982 and KCMG in 1990, Gillmore was informally notified that his final job would be as the British permanent representative to the United Nations. But a last-minute change of plan occurred, and in 1991, after spells as a visiting fellow at Harvard and the Western European Union (WEU) Institute of Strategic Studies in Paris, he became permanent under-secretary of state and head of the diplomatic service. He was fortunate in that the foreign secretary was Douglas Hurd, whom he knew well. He brought to his new post a thoroughly modern approach. Before business management jargon had become fashionable in Whitehall, he put in place systems which accurately informed senior decision makers in the FCO about the cost of the policies they were discussing. He also brought to the task of running the service a warmth and a genuine concern for the welfare and careers of those who were not destined to fill the top positions in Washington or Paris. Douglas Hurd, writing after Gillmore's death, commented, 'I have never known a public servant who was more completely liked and trusted by those with whom he dealt' (*The Independent*). He was promoted GCMG in 1994, his last year as permanent secretary.

On retirement Gillmore followed a wide range of interests, becoming chairman of the Ditchley Foundation, a governor of Birkbeck College and of the English-Speaking Union, and a non-executive director of Vickers plc and of the Prudential Corporation. He was also involved in many charities. In 1996 he was created Baron Gillmore of Thamesfield and took his place on the cross-benches of the House of Lords, where he was a member of the select committee on public service. He died of cancer on 20 March 1999 at his home, 19 Ashlone Road, Putney, London, and was buried following a funeral service at All Saints' Church, Fulham, London, on 29 March. He was survived by his wife and their two sons.

Gillmore was highly gifted—an intellectual excited by ideas, music, and art. He was a Francophone who knew and loved France, but also a loyal Englishman who served his country in an exemplary manner. He was never pompous, never over-impressed by his own achievements and position. His honesty, kindness, and humour were unfailing, and his courage in the last few months of his illness, which he knew to be incurable, was a testament to a remarkable man. NIGEL BROOMFIELD

Sources *The Times* (22 March 1999) · *Daily Telegraph* (23 March 1999) · *The Independent* (26 March 1999) · *The Guardian* (30 March 1999) · *WWW* · *Diplomatic Service List* (–1995) · private information (2004) [Squadron Leader James Gillmore] · personal knowledge (2004) · b. cert. · d. cert.

Likenesses photograph, 1984, repro. in *Daily Telegraph* · photograph, c.1996, repro. in *The Guardian* · photograph, repro. in *The Times* · photograph, repro. in *The Independent* · photograph, Foreign and Commonwealth Office, London [*see illus.*]

Gillott, Joseph (1799–1872), steel pen maker and art patron, the son of a workman in the cutlery trade, was born at Sheffield on 11 October 1799. He became a working cutler, acquiring a reputation as a 'noted hand' at forging and grinding knife blades. About 1821, in need of work, he moved to Birmingham, taking up employment in the 'light steel toy trade', the technical name for the manufacture of steel buckles, chains, and other works and ornaments of that kind.

Gillott married Maria Mitchell, a sister of John and William Mitchell, the steel pen makers; and he himself about 1830 began the manufacture of such pens. These were then laboriously cut with shears out of the steel, and trimmed and fashioned with a file. Gillott was determined to speed up the process, and adapted a hand-press for the making of pens. With much ingenuity, unflagging perseverance, and his wife's help, he experimented in his attic with different qualities of steel, and the various ways of preparing it for use. In 1831 Gillott registered his first patent for the manufacture of pens.

One of Gillott's chief problems was the extreme hardness of the pens. This he obviated by cutting side slits in addition to the centre slit, which had been solely in use up to that period. To this was afterwards added the cross grinding of the points; and these two processes imparted an elasticity to the pen, making it in this respect nearly equal to a quill. His pens achieved world fame, and it was said to be doubtful if any article of such wide and universal use was ever so identified with the name of one man.

For some years Gillott kept his method of working secret, fashioning his pens with his own hand, assisted by a woman, his first pens being 'blued' in a frying pan over a garret fire. At first he worked for others, selling his pens for a shilling each to a firm of stationers called Beilby and Knott. Along with other Birmingham pen makers like Josiah Mason, his business rapidly increased. This was because of the quality of his goods, their increasing cheapness, and the demand for them from a growing population, which was becoming more literate. He moved his manufactory first to Bread Street, Birmingham, then to Church Street, then to 59 Newhall Street, and finally, in 1859, to his great factory in Graham Street, the Victoria works. His operations were distinguished by the subdivision of labour and the mechanization of production. A workforce of 450 produced upwards of 5 tons per week, and the price of pens was reduced from 5*s* per gross (144) in the late 1830s to as low as 1½*d.* per gross in the mid-1860s. An enlightened and paternalistic employer, Gillott ensured that the works afforded much convenience and comfort to his employees, most of whom were women. He established a benevolent society among the workpeople, to which he subscribed liberally. He seldom changed his managers, and apparently never had a dispute with his workforce.

Gillott began to buy paintings from an early age, and his collection, housed in his homes in Westbourne Road, Edgbaston, and at Great Stanmore, near London, contained many gems of English art. Its great strength lay in paintings by J. M. W. Turner and William Etty, the latter being a special friend of the collector. Gillott appreciated Turner's talents before they had been generally recognized, and purchased his paintings when others doubted their worth. The collection was also very rich in the work of John Linnell, David Roberts, and others. After the owner's death the paintings were sold for £170,000. His collection of violins, on which he much prided himself, was also sold, fetching £4000.

For many years Gillott was a familiar figure at the Birmingham Theatre Royal, after which he would adjourn to the Hen and Chickens Hotel to smoke a 'churchwarden' and converse with friends. Until about ten days before his death failing eyesight was the only sign he gave of old age. On Boxing day 1871 he entertained as usual some of his children and their friends; the next morning he was attacked by a complication of pleurisy and bronchitis, and he died at home at Westbourne Road, Edgbaston, Birmingham, on 5 January 1872. G. C. BOASE, *rev.* CARL CHINN

Sources S. Timmins and J. T. Bunce, 'Joseph Gillott, 1799–1872: sketch of his life', *Birmingham Daily Post* (6 Jan 1872) • P. M. F., 'Joseph Gillott, 1799–1872: recollections of his pictures', *Birmingham Daily Post* (15 Jan 1872) • E. Edwards, *Personal recollections of Birmingham and Birmingham men* (1877) • E. Burritt, *Walks in the Black Country and its green border-land* (1868) • R. B. Prosser, *Birmingham inventors and inventions* (1881) • S. Timmins, 'The Birmingham steel pen trade', *The resources, products and industrial history of Birmingham and the midland hardware district*, ed. S. Timmins (1866) • *Birmingham Faces and Places*, 4 (1892), 30–32 • G. H. Wright, 'A general survey of the trades', *A handbook for Birmingham and the neighbourhood*, ed. G. A. Auden (1913) • D. Cannadine, 'Joseph Gillott and his family firm: the many faces of entrepreneurship', *From family firms to corporate capitalism: essays in business and industrial history in honour of Peter Mathias*, ed. K. Brulard and P. O'Brien (1998), 247–68 • C. Chinn, *Birmingham: the great working city* (1994)

Archives Getty Center for the History of Art and the Humanities, California

Wealth at death under £250,000: *DNB* • £350,000: Cannadine, 'Joseph Gillott and his family firm', 260

Gillow family (*per. c.*1730–*c.*1830), cabinet-makers and upholsterers, came to prominence with Richard [ii] Gillow (1733–1811), the son of Robert [i] Gillow (1702/3–1772) [*see below*], the founder of the firm. Gillows's reputation as one of the leading British cabinet-making firms of the eighteenth and nineteenth centuries was established by contributions from some ten members of the family over three generations. The business was established about 1728; in 1813 probably for both economic and social reasons, the Gillow family sold the firm to three partners, Redmayne, Whiteside, and Ferguson, who retained the name Gillow & Co. Succeeding partnerships such as Waring and Gillows Ltd (founded 1897), Waring and Gillow (1932) Ltd, and other concerns also incorporated the name until the end of the twentieth century. During the eighteenth century the Gillow firm established a reputation for producing quality furniture at moderate prices, made from the best woods, by competent workmen, in elegant but practical styles, which sometimes incorporated ingenious devices. Some of Gillows's designs were based on plates from eighteenth- and nineteenth-century pattern books, while others were provided by Wyatt. However, in some instances Gillows were using designs several years before they appeared in pattern books, for example, shield, on escutcheon back chairs. Gillows produced good, solid, well-made furniture, and were the only eighteenth-century cabinet-makers to establish and maintain a branch in both London (opened 1770) and the provinces. The Gillow Archives (now in the City of Westminster Archives Centre) comprise mainly the Lancaster branch's business records from about 1728 to 1932, and include estimate sketch and memorandum books from 1759 to 1905. Although incomplete, they are the longest and largest cabinet-makers' records to have survived in the world. The Lancaster branch also stamped their name on some of their furniture from about 1789, thereby enabling some of their output to be identified and dated via the firm's estimate sketch books.

Members of each generation became involved in the day-to-day running of the family business and from an early age represented the firm; waited on customers to take their orders; gained experience in the Oxford Street, London, shop; and became equal partners in the firm. The social status of members of the Gillow family changed with their wealth and influence, from that of successful artisan craftsman in the 1740s to established members of the squirearchy by the early nineteenth century. No clearer illustration of the Gillows' rise in status can be cited than that, whereas Robert [i] Gillow provided furniture for Lord and Lady Gerard from the 1740s, in 1801, his grandson Richard [iii] Gillow married an heiress, Elizabeth Stapleton, the cousin of another Lady Gerard.

Robert [i] **Gillow** (1702/3–1772), the founder of the firm, was the son of Richard [i] Gillow (*d.* 22 Dec 1717), a yeoman of Great Singleton, Lancashire, and his wife, Alice Swarbrick (*d.* 1721). His father was, like former and subsequent generations of the family, a devout Roman Catholic, and he suffered imprisonment for his faith. Robert was apprenticed in March 1721 to John Robinson, a Lancaster joiner, and after completing his apprenticeship in 1727 or 1728 he became a freeman of Lancaster and set up a cabinet-making business. From about 1731 to 1735 he was in partnership with another Roman Catholic joiner, George Haresnape. He entered the West Indies trade as a merchant in 1741 and the Baltic trade in 1742. Robert [i] Gillow married Agnes Fell (1709–1757), daughter of James Fell of Swarthmore, Ulverston, in 1731. Robert and Agnes Gillow had nine children, of whom only one daughter and three sons survived infancy. Alice, their first child, born in 1731, married Thomas Worswick (*c.*1730–1804), a watchmaker, on 26 April 1756, at the priory church of St Mary, Lancaster. Worswick, who founded one of the first banks in Lancaster, supplied some clocks to fit Gillows cases, and Gillows supplied cases for his clocks. The Worswick family were also devout Roman Catholics from Singleton, and like the Gillows became merchants. Of Robert and Agnes Gillow's three sons two, Richard [ii] Gillow and Robert [ii] Gillow [*see below*], became cabinet-makers. John [i] Gillow [*see* Gillow, John (1753–1828)], their youngest son, was sent to Douai in 1766 and became president of Ushaw College. In the 1740s Robert [i] Gillow began to make some furniture for the gentry, probably through the patronage of another Lancastrian, William Bradshaw (1700–1775), an eminent London tapestry weaver and upholsterer. In January 1757, Robert [i] Gillow took his eldest son, Richard [ii]

Gillow, into equal partnership; and in 1769 he retired leaving his share of the partnership to his second son, Robert [ii] Gillow. Robert [i] Gillow died at Church Street, Lancaster, and was buried at St Mary's Church, Lancaster, on 3 December 1772. He left property in the town to his sons, but his main legacy was a firm foundation for the business on which his sons, nephews, and grandsons subsequently built.

Robert [i] Gillow's son **Richard** [ii] **Gillow** (1733–1811) was born in Lancaster on 29 December 1733. He was apprenticed in London to a Mr Jones, an architect, during the 1750s, and in 1753 was sent by his father on a voyage to Barbados in the West Indies. In 1754 he subscribed to Thomas Chippendale's *Gentleman and Cabinet-Maker's Director*. In 1754–5 he became a freeman of Lancaster, and on 1 January 1757 he joined his father as an equal partner in Robert Gillow & Son. From September 1758 all the firm's apprentices were bound in his name, and from the late 1750s he also prepared new furniture designs based on sketches supplied from London by his cousin James Gillow (*b. c.*1732) [*see below*]. He married Sarah Haresnape (1734/5–1783), said to be the daughter of Robert Haresnape of Thurnham, on 11 February 1761 at the priory church of St Mary, Lancaster. Richard and Sarah had eight children, five daughters and three sons; Robert [iii] Gillow; George [ii] Gillow; and Richard [iii] Gillow [*see below*], all joined the family firm. When Richard [ii]'s father retired from business in 1769 and his brother Robert [ii] joined him as a partner, the brothers declared their intention: 'to equal (if not to surpass) the port of London, or any other in the export of furniture' (GA, 344/161, 26 Feb 1769). During Richard [ii] Gillow's long period with the firm, Gillows developed from thriving provincial cabinet-makers to one of the best London upholsterers. His main role was to run the Lancaster business, but he encouraged and advised his cousin Thomas Gillow [*see below*] when in 1769 he declared his intention to start a London cabinet-making business. Richard [ii] also informed customers of the latest London fashions, and counselled them wisely and tactfully on matters of taste and practicality in furniture and interior design. In 1807 Clarke recommended 'Mr Gillow's extensive ware-rooms' in Lancaster 'stored with every article of useful and ornamental mahogany furniture', as 'well worth the attention of the stranger; as they are said to be the best stocked of any in this line, out of the metropolis' (Clarke, 64). Richard [ii] Gillow acquired a house in Margate and established the first Roman Catholic mission in the town, and a small chapel was erected by his generosity in 1801. He retired from the firm in 1800, and died at his Lancaster house in Thurnham Street 'of dropsy' on 14 August 1811, aged seventy-seven. In his obituary he was described as 'formerly a cabinet-maker and upholsterer; a man who spent a long life of business with honour and integrity, and as a son, husband, and member of society, in the performance of every Christian duty' (*Lancaster Gazette*, 17 Aug 1811). He was buried in St Mary's churchyard near the tomb of his brother Robert [ii] Gillow.

Richard [ii] Gillow's brother **Robert** [ii] **Gillow** (1746/7–1795) was born in Lancaster. He appears to have attended school in the Fylde area of Lancashire, like his younger brother John Gillow. In May 1762 his father paid a small sum to John Calvert for 'Bob's learning' (GA, 344/31, p. 197, 26-5-1762). He probably learned the cabinet-maker's trade from his father and brother. In 1766–7 he became a freeman of Lancaster, and in January 1769 his father left him his equal share in the firm, which became known as Messrs Richard and Robert Gillow. He took equal responsibility for the Lancaster firm's apprentices from March 1770. Robert [ii] Gillow married Jane Shaw (*d.* 1783) by licence on 24 June 1771 at St Mary's Church, Lancaster, and they had a son, Robert [iv] Gillow [*see below*] and a daughter, Jane, in 1775. One of the partners in the London firm, Gillows and Taylor, William Taylor, died in 1775, and in January 1776 Robert [ii] Gillow left Lancaster to take charge of the business in London, assisted by his cousin Thomas Gillow, who had been Taylor's partner. Thomas Gillow also became ill in 1778, and died the following summer. Thus ten years after the London branch was established it was in the hands of the Lancaster brothers. Robert's wife, Jane, also died in London in June 1783. Two years later on 12 September 1785 Robert Gillow, widower, of Oxford Street, married again at Holy Trinity Church, Keswick. His second wife was Mary, widow of William Newby late of Horncop Hall, Kendal. In July 1791 Robert [ii] Gillow made a will in which he mentioned a son, Robert [iv] Gillow, then a minor. His daughter Jane had decided to become a nun in 1791, much to her father's dismay, as he considered she should enjoy the pleasures of life which, as a result of his successful industry, he could give her. Although Robert [ii] Gillow took charge of the London business, he returned to Lancaster regularly, calling on customers on his journey north. He sent orders from London customers to his brother Richard [ii] in Lancaster and obtained services and material unavailable in Lancaster, in addition to advising him about the latest fashions. Robert [ii] Gillow died in Lancaster on 22 September 1795 aged forty-eight. He was buried appropriately by his own firm in a grave in the churchyard of St Mary's, Lancaster, on 26 September. His sister, Sarah, was buried in the same grave in 1801. Their epitaph reads: 'they lived respected and beloved, may our end be like unto them' (Tombstone, St Mary's churchyard).

James Gillow (*b. c.*1732) was the second of six sons and one daughter of George [i] Gillow (*d. c.*1759), a yeoman farmer of Great Singleton, near Kirkham, Lancashire, and his wife, Alice. He was apprenticed on 8 September 1746 to his uncle, Robert [i] Gillow, and after completing his apprenticeship he continued to work for Gillows as a journeyman in Lancaster; however, by January 1759 he was working in London. He lodged in St Martin's Lane, in the same area as eminent cabinet-makers such as Thomas Chippendale, William Vile & Co., and John Cobb. James Gillow's employer is unknown, but letters from his cousin Richard [ii] Gillow show that he was used as an errand-boy for the Lancaster firm and procured materials unobtainable in Lancaster. He suffered from ill health and returned to Lancashire, where he had been offered 'light work' by his cousins during the summer of 1759. On his return to

London, Richard [ii] requested that James send him furniture designs and published design books such as 'Chippendale's additional number' (GA, 344/164, 5-7-1760). He was last mentioned in Gillow correspondence in November 1765, when he was newly married. He was almost certainly the Roman Catholic cabinet-maker of that name who was living in Marlborough, Wiltshire, with his wife, Hannah, in August 1767. After the death of his brother Thomas, he may have returned to London to help his cousin Robert [ii] Gillow run the Oxford Street shop, since between 1781 and 1785 the firm was listed in some directories as Robert, Richard, and James Gillow (Beard and Gilbert, 341).

Thomas Gillow (*c*.1736–1779) was the third of the seven children of George [i] Gillow and his wife, Alice. By 1748 he was, like his brother James, also living with his uncle Robert [i] Gillow to whom he was apprenticed in November 1750. He worked as a journeyman for Robert [i] Gillow but by July 1760 he had moved to Liverpool. It may be no coincidence that by January 1766, shortly after his brother James moved from London to Marlborough, Thomas was working in the capital, and living in Marshall Street, Carnaby Market. Thomas played a similar role to his brother in supplying his cousins in Lancaster with materials. His neighbours were the celebrated cabinet-makers William Ince and John Mayhew, whose book *The Universal System of Household Furniture* was published in parts from 1759 to 1761. In April 1769 Richard Gillow wrote to Thomas that he 'was glad to find by what you hinted that you intend beginning for yourself in London' (GA, 344/166, 16-4-1769). He went into partnership with William Taylor (*d.* 1775), another Lancaster cabinet-maker, and they became the first London partners of the firm in Oxford Street known as Gillows and Taylor, and Richard and Robert Gillow entered into an agreement to supply them with cabinet wares, including billiard tables. In January 1771 Thomas married Ann Cannon, at St James, Westminster. Taylor died in the autumn of 1775, and Thomas's cousin Robert [ii] Gillow joined him to run the London shop in January 1776. Thomas Gillow, like his brother James, suffered from ill health; he made his will in April 1778, and it was proved in July 1779. He had no children and left his estate to his 'beloved wife Ann' (will).

John [ii] **Gillow** (*b.* 1756/7) was the son of Edward Gillow (*b. c.*1702), a yeoman of Westby in the parish of Slaidburn, Yorkshire, and his wife, Ann (*b.* 1715). Edward Gillow was the brother of Robert [i] Gillow. John [ii] Gillow was apprenticed to his cousins Richard [ii] and Robert [ii] Gillow in Lancaster from 19 March 1770 for seven years, and worked as a journeyman for the firm before becoming a cabinet-maker in Liverpool from about 1784 to 1794.

Robert [iii] **Gillow** (1764–1838) was born on 9 October 1764, the eldest son of Richard [ii] Gillow (1733–1811), and the brother of George [ii] and Richard [iii] Gillow who also became cabinet-makers. During the 1770s Robert [iii] Gillow and George [ii] were educated at Roman Catholic boarding-schools, by Mr Pennington of Robert Hall, near Hornby, then by Mr Peter Newby of Eccleston, who was probably a kinsman. In 1781 his father paid the expenses of sending Robert [iii] to London; by December 1786 Robert was acting as a commercial traveller for the firm, and the following year he became a freeman of Lancaster when he was described as an 'upholsterer' (Freemen rolls, 130). He married Anne Parker (1764–1841), daughter and heir of Edward Parker, esquire, at Preston in 1797. Robert [iii] and Anne Gillow had four daughters, all coheirs who married into the gentry, his two eldest daughters in the private chapel at Clifton Hill, Forton, Lancashire. Robert [iii] Gillow and his family moved to the Clifton Hill estate after December 1817 and before October 1822, and he died there on 11 July 1838, aged seventy-five. He was a generous patron of the Roman Catholic church. He also amassed a library of about 700 volumes and was in possession of the residue of his late brother George's collection of paintings and drawings which had remained unsold after Christies auction of April 1824. In his will he mentioned his furniture, plate, linen, pictures, and books, which—apart from specific items bequeathed to his wife and daughters—were all to be auctioned on his wife's death.

George [ii] **Gillow** (1765/6–1822) was the second son of Richard [ii] Gillow. He was born in Lancaster and educated in Lancashire during the 1770s with his elder brother Robert [iii] Gillow, first by William Pennington of Robert Hall, a Roman Catholic institution near Hornby, then by Peter Newby of Eccleston, near Kirkham. Their education included social graces such as learning to dance. George [ii] Gillow became a freeman of Lancaster in 1782–3, and joined his uncle Robert [ii] Gillow as a partner in the London shop restyled Robert and George Gillow & Co. from March 1791. At about this date he married Judith Gildon (*d.* 1843), member of an ancient Dorset and Wiltshire Roman Catholic family. George and Judith had eight daughters. By January 1796 George [ii] Gillow had been joined in London by his younger brother, Richard [iii] Gillow, and their cousin, Robert [iv] Gillow. In 1813 the Gillow family retired from active participation in the cabinet-making business and sold the firm to Redmayne, Whiteside, and Ferguson. The agreement was that the new partners should purchase the firm in instalments, the final instalment being due in 1821, and that the proceeds were to be divided equally between the three remaining partners (the sons of Richard [ii] Gillow). George [ii] Gillow amused himself by forming a large collection of European paintings and drawings, 'at great expense', which included a 'grand gallery picture by P. Veronese' and other works by Masaccio, Bellini, Caravaggio, and Leonardo da Vinci, described in Christies sale catalogue of April 1824. George [ii] Gillow would not have had long to enjoy his share, since he died at Hammersmith on 1 December 1822, aged fifty-six, leaving his eight daughters as his coheirs. Judith, his wife, died on 2 March 1843.

Richard [iii] **Gillow** (1772–1849) was born on 8 March 1772, the third and youngest son of Richard [ii] Gillow. He married Elizabeth Stapleton (1780–1848) on 31 May 1801 at St Mary's Church, Marylebone, Middlesex. Elizabeth was the daughter and eventual heir of a Preston doctor, Charles Stapleton, younger son of Nicholas Stapleton of Carlton Hall, Yorkshire, heir to the barony of Beaumont, subsequently restored. Richard and Elizabeth had thirteen children, one of whose baptismal sponsors was Elizabeth's cousin Lady Gerard, whose forebears had patronized Richard [iii] Gillow's grandfather, Robert [i] Gillow, the founder of the firm during the 1740s. In three generations, therefore, the Gillow family had risen in status from serving the gentry as tradesmen to claiming kinship with them by marriage. Richard [iii] Gillow was described as a 'cabinetmaker and upholsterer' in 1796–7 when he became a Lancaster freeman (Freemen rolls, 132). He was an active partner in the Oxford Street shop. In May 1800 Richard [iii] Gillow of London patented an expanding dining table which was a great success and large numbers were manufactured by the firm. He lived in London for many years at Little Holland House, Campden Hill, Kensington, where many of his children were born, while others were born at Ellel Grange, near Lancaster, a property owned by one of his Worswick cousins. In February 1822 Worswick's Bank was declared insolvent; and in December 1823 both Leighton Hall and Ellel Grange were offered for sale by order of the high court of chancery. Leighton Hall was purchased by Richard [iii] Gillow, and after some renovations in April 1824, the family moved their furniture from Ellel Grange to Leighton. From 1825 'Richard Gillow Esq.' purchased more furniture from the new partners in their old family firm (GA 344/102, p. 3457, 25-11-1825). Elizabeth Stapleton died on 18 November 1848, and Richard [iii] Gillow died at Leighton on 16 December 1849; they were both interred in the family mausoleum at Leighton Hall. Richard Thomas Gillow (1806–1905), eldest son of Richard and Elizabeth, is said to have been the last family member to be associated with the firm, but he, and his father, retired from trade in 1830.

Robert [iv] **Gillow** (1771x4–1798) was the son of Robert [ii] Gillow and his first wife, Jane Shaw. His date of birth is unknown but it must have been between 1771 and before 1775 when his sister Jane was born. By January 1796 (a few months after his father's death) he had joined his cousins George [ii] Gillow and Richard [iii] Gillow as a London partner. However, Robert [iv] Gillow died unexpectedly at the English College, Lisbon, Portugal, on 10 March 1798, having outlived his father by less than three years.

Gillow furniture originally graced a vast number of town and country houses owned by the artistocracy and gentry; some collections still remain in private ownership today, although most commissions have inevitably been dispersed over the centuries. The number of provenanced or marked Gillow examples to be seen in country houses open to the public today vary considerably from one or two, to over 150 pieces at Tatton Park, near Knutsford, Cheshire. Broughton Hall, near Skipton, Yorkshire, has probably the largest private collection, and Leighton Hall, near Carnforth, home of Richard [iii] Gillow, naturally has a good collection of furniture by the family firm. Many other houses and institutions in north-west England have mainly smaller but notable collections, or a few pieces by the firm including: Sizergh Castle, Cumbria; Abbot Hall Art Gallery, Kendal; Levens Hall, near Kendal; Dalemain, near Penrith; Mirehouse, near Kendal; the Judge's Lodgings Museum; Lancaster Castle; Lancaster City Museums; Lancaster Town Hall, Lancaster; Browesholme, Lancashire; and Tabley House, Cheshire. Houses outside the north-west region with some Gillow furniture in their collections include: Ardgowan, Renfrewshire, Scotland (open to special interest groups by arrangement); Berrington Hall, Hertfordshire; Dyrham Park, Gloucestershire; Raby Castle, near Darlington; Normanby Hall, near Scunthorpe; Belvoir Castle, Leicestershire; Stonor Park, near High Wycombe; Belton House, Lincolnshire; and Erddig Park, near Wrexham, north Wales. Over the three generations that Gillows were involved in the cabinet-making trade, they changed from artisan craftsmen to entrepreneurial manufacturing upholsterers and cabinet-makers employing a large workforce with prestigious showrooms in London and Lancaster. The firm were enabled to develop, expand, and probably to help finance their furniture making ventures, by becoming, from the 1740s, West Indies and European import and export merchants. Indeed their furniture rarely accounted for more than a small proportion of their exports, because it took up too much space on board ship in proportion to the profits to be made out of it. Therefore their furniture was also used as storage space for more profitable small British manufactured goods such as jewellery, brass and iron wares, textiles, shoes, and felt hats; and other perishable provisions for the colonies were also exported by the firm. Imports varied according to the state of the British markets but sugar, cotton, rum, and fine wines as well as mahogany and other timber were often included. Gillows promoted their furniture at every opportunity, and constantly sought new markets both at home and abroad. The Gillow family's contribution to furniture history remains to be fully evaluated. However, Gillows's designs were aimed at the gentry and growing upper middle classes; they occupied the middle ground between fashionable whimsy and boring conservatism. The firm adapted the latest London designs to suit their customers' taste, as well as creating some ingenious designs of their own, which they were anxious not to let other cabinet-makers copy. Research has also indicated that Gillows were making some furniture styles years before similar designs were published in design books by, for example, A. Hepplewhite & Co. and Thomas Sheraton. In 1817 Gillows work was described as 'all the fashion in the houses of the first Nobility and Gentry in England' and 'Mr. Gillow at Lancaster' as 'the first Upholsterer in the Kingdom' (D. McInnis and R. A. Leath, pp. 137–74, ref. p. 142). The success of the Gillow family firm was mainly due to sound business management and the manufacture of good quality practical furniture made from the best wood, by competent workmen, at the cheapest prices. It was, in essence, as the firm wrote to a customer in 1797, made to stand 'the test' of time (GA, 344/173, 20-9-1797). SUSAN E. STUART

Sources 26 Jan 1766, City Westm. AC, Gillow Archives, GA 344/165, p. 70 • 26 Feb 1769, City Westm. AC, Gillow Archives, GA 344/161 • 26 May 1762, City Westm. AC, Gillow Archives, GA 344/31, p. 197 • 5 July 1760, City Westm. AC, Gillow Archives, GA 344/164 •

16 April 1769, City Westm. AC, Gillow Archives, GA 344/166 • E. S. Worrall, ed., *Returns of papists, 1767*, 2 vols., Catholic RS, occasional publications, vols. 1–2 (1980–89), vol. 1, p. 126 • J. P. Smith, ed., *The Lancashire registers*, 3, Catholic RS, 20 (1916), 34, 64 • *Lancaster Gazette* (17 Aug 1811) • Lancaster apprentice register (1735–54) • Lancaster apprentice register (1752–83) • K. Docton, *Directory of Lancaster* (1766) • extracted from window tax, Lancaster, 1766, Lancs. RO, DDca 15/3 • G. Beard and C. Gilbert, eds., *Dictionary of English furniture makers* (1986) • J. Brownbill and others, eds., *Marriage bonds for … part of the archdeaconry of Richmond now preserved at Lancaster*, 4: 1729–34, Lancashire and Cheshire RS, 81 (1932), 80 • C. Clarke, *An historical and descriptive account of the town of Lancaster* (1807), 64 • W. B. Kendall and T. C. Hughes, eds., *The rolls of the freemen of the borough of Lancaster, 1688 to 1840*, Lancashire and Cheshire RS, 87 (1935) • L. Boynton, *Gillow furniture designs, 1760–1800* (1995) • Christies auction catalogue, 9 April 1824 • D. McInnis and R. A. Leath, 'Beautiful specimens, elegant patterns: New York furniture for the Charleston market, 1810–1840', *American furniture*, ed. L. Beckerdite (Hanover, NH, 1996), 142 • S. Stuart, 'Was Squire Bradshaw of Halton Hall Robert Gillow's first London connection?', *Quarto* [Abbot Hall, Kendal, journal], 32/2 (1994), 8–11 • parish register, Kendal, Cumbria AS, Kendal, WPR 38

Archives City Westm. AC, business records, incl. estimate sketch and memorandum books, mainly for Lancaster shop, accessions no. 344, 735 • Lancaster City Museums, MS plans for collection of room settings • V&A, MS plans for collection of room settings | Lancs. RO, Preston, records relating to Waring & Gillow and associated firms

Likenesses W. Hudson?, portrait (Richard [ii] Gillow), priv. coll. • A. Ramsay?, portrait (Robert [i] Gillow), priv. coll. • portrait (Richard [iii] Gillow), priv. coll.

Gillow, George (1765/6–1822). *See under* Gillow family (*per. c.*1730–*c.*1830).

Gillow, James (*b. c.*1732). *See under* Gillow family (*per. c.*1730–*c.*1830).

Gillow, John (1753–1828), Roman Catholic priest and college head, was born on 25 March 1753, son of Robert *Gillow (1702/3–1772) [*see under* Gillow family], a furniture manufacturer, of Westby, Lancashire, and his wife, Agnes Fell. His parents were both from Lancaster, and they had four other sons and one daughter. After early education at the dame-school at Fernyhalgh, Preston (Anstruther, 4.113), Gillow was sent in 1766 to the English College at Douai, where he was ordained priest on 18 December 1779, and taught in succession rhetoric, philosophy, and theology. Each year the college lecturers printed theses summarizing their courses: Gillow's courses in philosophy for 1784–6 survive in this form at Ushaw.

In 1791 Gillow returned to England to take charge of the mission at York, where Roman Catholics had worshipped for five decades in a house in Little Blake Street. In 1793, after the Douai college had been forced to close in the aftermath of the French Revolution, Gillow briefly looked after a small group of students until more lasting arrangements could be made for a continuation of the college's work in England. In 1802 he was able to replace the chapel with one built in the same street by public subscription, with Gillow himself as a principal contributor (Minskip, 10). Some of the incidents that occurred in the course of this missionary work were related in *Footsteps of Spirits* (1859), published anonymously by the Revd James Augustine Stothert.

John Gillow (1753–1828), by Charles Turner, pubd 1814 (after James Ramsay)

On 11 June 1811 Gillow was installed president of Ushaw College, near Durham, in succession to Thomas Eyre (1748–1810). After fourteen years in temporary accommodation, Ushaw had opened in 1808 as the northern continuation of the Douai college. Following Douai tradition, Ushaw printed annual theses: Gillow's courses in theology for 1813–20 are preserved in this form at Ushaw. Although he was sometimes styled 'doctor', he was never granted a papal doctorate: what he took to be the grant of a doctorate was notice of his election as an associate of the Catholic Academy in Rome (Ushaw Archives, Lingard Letters 633). During his presidency the original quadrangle was completed by the addition of a west wing to accommodate an increase in the number of students, but the burden of unpaid debt on the original building meant that 'the 1820s were years of poverty and retrenchment' (Milburn, 120). He was considered by his students and contemporaries to be a model priest of the old school and looked to his own training at Douai as a pattern for Ushaw. He was tall, stout, and dignified in appearance. A student remembered his white hair 'rendered whiter still by the use of hair powder' and the edifying impression made by his refraining altogether from taking snuff until after he had celebrated mass and commenced his thanksgiving (*Records and Recollections*, 157).

Gillow was highly esteemed not only by Roman Catholics but by members of all denominations, and his opinion was often solicited by the vicars apostolic during the agitation which preceded the passing of the Catholic Emancipation Act of 1829. He died at Ushaw College on 6 February 1828, and was buried in the college's cemetery, 'of all Ushaw presidents the most mourned' (Milburn, 126). His memorial tablet at Ushaw was composed by John Lingard.

THOMPSON COOPER, *rev.* MICHAEL SHARRATT

Sources J. Gillow, 'Theses philosophicae', Ushaw College, Durham · J. Gillow, 'Theses theologicae', Ushaw College, Durham · D. Milburn, *A history of Ushaw College* (1964) · D. Minskip, *A history of St Wilfred's mission, York* (1989) · Gillow, *Lit. biog. hist.* · P. R. Harris, ed., *Douai College documents, 1639–1794*, Catholic RS, 63 (1972) · A. H., *Orthodox Journal* (19 Oct 1833), 49–50 · *Records and recollections of St Cuthbert's College, Ushaw … by an old alumnus* (1889) · letters of J. Lingard, Ushaw College, Durham · G. Anstruther, *The seminary priests*, 4 (1977) · P. Morgan, 'The Gillows and the growth of Catholicism in the north of England in the nineteenth century', MA diss., U. Lpool, 1996 · *Miscellanea, V*, Catholic RS, 6 (1909) · gravestone, Ushaw College cemetery, Ushaw, co. Durham · [J. A. Stothert], *Footsteps of spirits* (1859)

Archives Ushaw College, Durham, corresp. and papers

Likenesses C. Turner, mezzotint, pubd 1814 (after J. Ramsay), BM, NPG [*see illus.*] · J. Ramsay, oils, Ushaw College, Durham · C. Turner, engraving (after J. Ramsay), repro. in *Orthodox Journal* · stained glass, St Wilfred's Roman Catholic Church, York

Wealth at death under £100: Anstruther, *The seminary priests*

Gillow, John (*b.* 1756/7). *See under* Gillow family (*per.* c.1730–c.1830).

Gillow, Joseph (1850–1921), biographical lexicographer and genealogist, was born on 5 October 1850 at Frenchwood House, Preston, Lancashire, the son of Joseph Gillow (1801–1872), a magistrate, and his wife, Jane Haydock, *née* Smith (1805–1872), of Lea. The Gillows were a long-established Roman Catholic yeoman family who could trace an unbroken pedigree back to Conishead Priory in 1325. Gillow's father was a benefactor to the Catholic cause, and his mother was descended, by her mother, from the Haydocks of Cottam, another recusant family.

Joseph Gillow was educated at Sedgley Park, near Wolverhampton (1862–3), and St Cuthbert's College, Ushaw (1864–6), where his uncles and brothers had studied for the priesthood, and discovered there an abiding interest in Lancashire and family genealogy, resulting in his publication of *The Tyldesley Diary* in 1873, edited from a Lancashire diary kept during the years 1712–14, and in 1888 of *The Haydock Papers*, a survey of Catholic life in Lancashire as seen through generations of a local family, compiled from family papers and other records.

On 11 September 1878 Gillow married Ella (1850–1945), daughter of John McKenna, a brewer, of Dunham Massey, and secured a private income for the rest of his life. This left him free to pursue his literary studies unimpeded, and he conceived the idea of producing a continuation of Dodd's *Church History*, covering the period from 1688 onwards and making use of later material collected by the Revd John Kirk and George Oliver, the Catholic directories, and various manuscript sources from Catholic archives. This was followed by a formal commission from the Catholic publishers Burns and Oates to produce the *Biographical and Bibliographical Dictionary of the English Catholics* in five volumes—volume one appearing in 1885.

As work progressed on the new dictionary, however, it became evident that seven volumes were required, but the publishers were inflexible, insisting that it be completed in five as agreed. To this Gillow reluctantly complied, giving them, in 1902, the last volume, heavily excised and abbreviated. In spite of this the dictionary is still one of the landmarks of Catholic history, particularly useful for the bibliographies of eighteenth- and nineteenth-century Catholics, for which Gillow drew extensively from his own library of 4000 volumes. Cardinal Gasquet described the dictionary as a 'veritable storehouse of information' (Gasquet, vii), but as no index was available until 1986, much of the anonymous and pseudonymous literature that Gillow had identified remained locked within its pages.

Gillow's sadness at the inglorious end of his great undertaking was somewhat alleviated by the foundation of the Catholic Record Society in 1904, when he was appointed honorary recorder. He contributed much material to the first twenty volumes of the society's published transactions, especially transcriptions of Lancashire's Catholic registers, and was an energetic and valued member.

After his marriage Gillow lived at his wife's home in Dunham Massey, until he moved to Alderley Edge in 1913 and then to Westholme, Hale, where he died on 17 March 1921. He was interred in the family vault at The Willows, Kirkham. He left six sons and a daughter. The family were cousins of Richard Gillow of Leighton Hall, who was the grandson of Robert Gillow of Lancashire, the founder of the firm of furniture makers that became Waring and Gillow. Joseph Gillow's large collection of books was presented to the Catholic Record Society and set up as a reference library in Duke's Lane, Kensington, during the 1930s. After many moves and depletions the remainder was housed at Downside Abbey.

Joseph Gillow was essentially a compiler and editor rather than a historian in the modern sense, and his interpretation of history was always coloured by his own proud Catholicism. He was inclined on occasion to make assumptions where the facts were wanting and to repeat information from other sources without verification; nevertheless, the dictionary can still be regarded as a cornerstone of any Catholic library and is the first and easiest work of reference. His friend Father Thomas Bridgett rightly called him 'the Plutarch of the English Catholics' (Burnand, 1908).

J. F. X. BEVAN

Sources J. F. X. Bevan, *Index and finding list to the bibliographical dictionary* (1986) · F. C. Burnand, ed., *The Catholic who's who and yearbook* (1907–21) · F. A. Gasquet, *Catholic Record Society Transactions*, 1 (1905) [introduction] · M. Whitehead, 'The Gillows and their work in Georgian Lancaster', *Catholic Englishmen*, ed. J. A. Hilton (1984), 21–7 · J. F. X. Bevan, 'Joseph Gillow and his dictionary', *North West Catholic History*, 13 (1986), 14–17 · *The Tablet* (2 April 1921) · *Ushaw Magazine* (July 1921) · *Laity's Directory* (1758–1839) · *Catholic Directory* (1838) · private information (2004) · parish register, Preston, St Augustine, 7 Oct 1850, Lancs. RO [baptism]

Likenesses A. M. Rossi, oils, 1910, priv. coll.

Wealth at death £11,538 9s. od.: probate, 20 June 1921, *CGPLA Eng. & Wales*

Gillow, Richard (1733/4–1811). *See under* Gillow family (*per.* c.1730–c.1830).

Gillow, Richard (1772–1849). *See under* Gillow family (*per. c.*1730–*c.*1830).

Gillow, Robert (1702/3–1772). *See under* Gillow family (*per. c.*1730–*c.*1830).

Gillow, Robert (1746/7–1795). *See under* Gillow family (*per. c.*1730–*c.*1830).

Gillow, Robert (1764–1838). *See under* Gillow family (*per. c.*1730–*c.*1830).

Gillow, Robert (1771x4–1798). *See under* Gillow family (*per. c.*1730–*c.*1830).

Gillow, Thomas (*c.*1736–1779). *See under* Gillow family (*per. c.*1730–*c.*1830).

Gillow, Thomas (1769–1857), Roman Catholic priest, was born on 23 November 1769 at Singleton, Lancashire, the fourth son of Richard Gillow, of Singleton, and Isabel, the sister and heir of Henry Brewer of Moor House, Newton-cum-Scales. He was admitted to the English College at Douai on 22 May 1784. When the professors and students of the college were imprisoned during the French Revolution he succeeded in escaping to England with Thomas Penswick in October 1793. After spending a brief period at home and at St Edmund's College, Old Hall Green, Gillow arrived at Crook Hall, co. Durham, on 6 December 1794, where he continued his studies and was ordained priest on 1 April 1797. While at Crook Hall, on 15 July 1795, he was obliged to subscribe to the Act of Toleration in Durham. He remained at Crook Hall as a professor until 21 August 1797, when he was appointed to the chaplaincy of Callaly Castle, home of the Catholic family of Clavering. Here his duties were light; he founded a school in the adjacent village of Whittingham. In 1817 he was selected as bishop over the vicariate of the West Indies, with the title of bishop of Hysopoli in Asia *in partibus*, but he declined for reasons of health.

On 11 June 1821, Gillow left Callaly to take charge of a new mission at North Shields. The church, erected by his cousin, Revd James Worswick, had only a small congregation, which Gillow increased substantially. He is said to have received nearly a thousand converts to Catholicism during his ministry. He had a reputation as an eloquent preacher, whose oratory was of 'a pleasing and persuasive character', even though his appearance was 'rather deficient in graceful and easy bearing, and his voice [had] little music in it' (*Catholic Miscellany*, 199). He erected a presbytery and several schools and founded a new chapel and mission at South Shields, despite losing much of his private fortune through the failure of the Union Bank in Newcastle. With John Lingard and Thomas Penswick, he was proposed as candidate for coadjutor for the northern district in 1823, but Penswick was appointed. In 1842, Gillow's nephew, Richard Gillow, was appointed to assist him. He became blind in his later years, and died at the church of St Cuthbert, North Shields, on 19 March 1857.

Rosemary Mitchell

Sources Gillow, *Lit. biog. hist.* • J. Kirk, *Biographies of English Catholics in the eighteenth century*, ed. J. H. Pollen and E. Burton (1909), 103 • P. R. Harris, ed., *Douai College documents, 1639–1794*, Catholic RS, 63 (1972), 403 • W. M. Brady, *The episcopal succession in England, Scotland, and Ireland, AD 1400 to 1875*, 3 (1877), 273–6 • 'Pulpit sketches III: the Rev. Thomas Gillow', *Catholic Miscellany*, new ser., 3 (1830), 193–200 • *DNB*

Gillray, James (1756–1815), caricaturist, was born in Robinson's Lane, Chelsea, Middlesex, near London, on 13 August 1756, the third of the five children of James Gillray (1720–1799) of Culter, Lanarkshire, Scotland, and his wife, Jane Coleman (1716–1797), of Long Hope, Gloucestershire. The elder Gillray, after some experience as a blacksmith, enlisted in the cavalry and, as a trooper in the Queen's dragoons, lost an arm at the battle of Fontenoy (1745). He became in 1748 a pensioner at the Royal Hospital, Chelsea. In the following year he joined the Moravian Brethren, an extreme protestant sect which, persecuted in Bohemia and then Germany, had fled to England in the 1730s and 1740s, setting up communities at Fetter Lane in the City of London and at Chelsea. As a strict Calvinist James Gillray senior had much in common with the Moravians; his wife was admitted to the brethren in 1751, and for over forty years he acted as sexton of their burial-ground at Chelsea.

Education, training, and early work The Moravians believed in the fundamental depravity of man, the worthlessness of life, and death as a welcome release from life's afflictions. Such a dark theology did not prevent the brethren from providing for their children an excellent and wide-ranging education, although it involved separating the children from their parents at five and subjecting them to stern discipline and hard conditions. James Gillray followed his elder brother Johnny to the Moravian school at Bedford in 1762, aged five and a half. Johnny died some months later (none of Gillray's siblings survived beyond the age of ten) and James was returned to his parents at Chelsea after the Bedford school was disbanded in December 1764 for financial reasons.

It is not known what further education Gillray received, but the evidence of his work and the opinion of a German reporter who described him as 'an extremely well-informed and widely read man' (*London und Paris*, 1, 1798, 196) argue its merits. Yet it is doubtful whether life in a Moravian household, enforcing a code of behaviour which forbade games and insisted upon introspection, could have offered much joy. To sad soul-searching must be added the grief Gillray would have experienced from the death of his brother and sisters.

Gillray's lively and well-observed sketch in pen and ink and watercolour of a goldfinch, made when he was twelve or thirteen and now in the British Library, is the earliest surviving demonstration of his skill in art. Although his talent was obvious, his background and family situation prevented his entering the artistic profession by way of an expensive apprenticeship to one of the better-known artists. Instead he was apprenticed to Harry Ashby (1744–1818), a lettering engraver whose shop in Holborn, London, produced trade cards, banknotes, certificates, scripts, stationery, and maps. The penmanship and

James Gillray (1756–1815), self-portrait, *c.*1800

engraving techniques he learned from Ashby greatly benefited Gillray in later life.

It is not surprising to learn from the same German reporter quoted above that such an individualist as Gillray 'did not really enjoy this work' but more surprising, in view of his upbringing, to hear that he left it 'to join a company of strolling players' (*London und Paris*, 1, 1798, 196). However, his vagabond acting career was apparently short-lived, for on 25 October 1775 William Humphrey, a printseller of Soho, London, published *Six-Pence a Day*, one of twenty-five plates ascribed to Gillray before 1780 (Hill, *Mr Gillray*, 19). These satires, which Draper Hill describes as 'primarily political; a distinct flavour of pornography tinges the remainder' (ibid., 13), are all attributed to Gillray on stylistic grounds since his early work, strongly influenced by the grotesque imagination and spindly figures of John Hamilton Mortimer (1741–1779), was either anonymous or signed with a pseudonym.

In 1778 Gillray was admitted into the Royal Academy Schools, London, to study engraving under Francesco Bartolozzi (1728–1815), the master of the stipple or 'dot' method. The president of the Royal Academy, Sir Joshua Reynolds (who had painted caricature portraits in his youth but long since abjured them), advocated history painting in the 'grand manner', a branch of art which Gillray in later years parodied with superb effect in such caricatures as *Shakespeare Sacrificed* (1789), *Titianus Redivivus* (1797), and *The Apotheosis of Hoche* (1798). From the date of his entry into the Royal Academy Schools his draughtsmanship showed a marked improvement. Among his contemporaries there was William Blake.

Over the next few years Gillray alternated between satires, illustrations—two stipple engravings for Fielding's *Tom Jones* in Bartolozzi's style (1780) and a further pair for Goldsmith's *The Deserted Village* (1784)—reproductive engravings, including two shipwreck scenes after James Northcote RA, and portraits in miniature. On a trade card probably dating from this time he described himself as 'Gillray Portrait Painter' (Hill, *Mr Gillray*, 28). For two and a half years, from 1783, he issued very few satires in a concentrated effort to establish himself as a reproductive engraver. Failing, because his style was too idiosyncratic, too inclined to distortion, he returned in 1786 to caricature, producing between 1786 and 1789 some of his finest work. One of his last attempts at 'straight' engraving was a portrait of William Pitt for the Piccadilly-based publisher Fores (1789) which, being too uncomplimentary, was speedily withdrawn by the publisher and replaced by another version only slightly less offensive.

Caricature By the time of Gillray's emergence as a caricaturist in the 1780s the word 'caricature' had come to mean pictorial comedy of every description—jokes, distorted portraits, political and social satires. Caricature existed in Europe, but to no significant extent; the main conditions which favoured the growth of political caricature—freedom of expression, party faction, and a sizeable market—were to be found only in England. Caricaturists had taken advantage of their liberties to savage Sir Robert Walpole but Hogarth, although immensely advancing the range and status of comic art in general, had been little concerned with politics, his cautionary tales being designed for moral purposes. Marquess Townshend and the anonymous artists working for such periodicals as the *Oxford Magazine* revived political satire, but its appeal was limited to the initiated, relying as it did on the extensive use of hieroglyphs and symbols. The way forward at the start of the 1780s—politicians transformed into instantly recognized 'characters'—was indicated by James Sayers, whose approach, while lacking nothing in bite, was handicapped by feeble drawing. However, the appetite for political caricature, as witness the Westminster election of 1784, was growing all the time.

Social satires had dispensed with moralizing. In the years leading up to Gillray they consisted of Henry Bunbury's mild depiction of modes and manners, John Collet's genre scenes, sometimes with erotic implications, and Matthew Darly's portraits, often suggested or sketched by amateurs—altogether an innocuous collection. There was little in the way of scandal; the spicy 'Têtes à têtes' published in the *Town and Country Magazine* from 1769 were accompanied by uncaricatured portraits. The royal family was not yet caricatured in a personal capacity. Gillray was to change all that.

Yet Gillray, with all these opportunities at his disposal and with an unequalled aptitude to exploit them, was slow to commit himself exclusively to caricature. As a profession it paid poorly by comparison with what he could have earned as a successful reproductive engraver. It entailed some danger of prosecution, as he would himself later discover, and there was also the question of status. Caricature was regarded by the art establishment as a low form of artistic life. Francis Grose, the antiquary, wrote in

1788: 'the art of drawing Caricatures is generally considered as a dangerous acquisition, tending rather to make the possessor feared than esteemed' (*Rules for Drawing Caricatures*, 1788, 2). Gillray was not the man to covet social position but like most people he was sensitive to disapproval of his métier.

Having decided to devote himself to caricature, Gillray revealed powers that no other artist except Thomas Rowlandson approached remotely. Abandoning the spidery line of Mortimer, he launched in his finest work into a bounding baroque style which had echoes of his hero, Rubens. To draughtsmanship of a high order (as revealed also in sketches and preparatory drawings) he added compositional skills and a mastery of engraving techniques—etching, engraving, stippling, and aquatinting—used in combinations that were innovatory and spectacular. Most remarkable of all were his powers of invention: caricature presented in scenes of fantasy, parody, and burlesque.

Gillray was the artist who introduced wit (as opposed to humour) into English caricature. His wit, sometimes playful, more often dark, is observable in the captions and speech 'bubbles', over which he took great care, as well as in the image. But the wit is frequently impregnated with cruelty and bawdy to an extent that some of his contemporaries, let alone the Victorians, found repellent. Gillray's critics were equally worried by the irony and consequent ambivalence of much of his work. They concluded that his genius was nourished by a scorn for the human race.

Party political satires From 1780 until 1789 Gillray was occupied mainly by English party politics. It was a highly exciting and volatile time, encompassing the Gordon riots, the loss of the American colonies, the start of Pitt's premiership, the opening of Warren Hastings's trial, the king's madness, and the outbreak of the French Revolution. Among the leaders of the parties were men of outstanding gifts, memorable presence, and caricaturable habits: Fox, Burke, and Sheridan on the whig side, Pitt on the tory. In Gillray's hands Fox became 'Black Charlie', a devious demagogue, Burke a bespectacled Jesuit, and Sheridan a red-nosed sot, while Pitt became 'Bottomless'—or in one celebrated print of 1791, 'An excrescence—a fungus—alias a toadstool upon a dunghill'.

Gillray's cynicism about politics and politicians, together with a keen appreciation of his commercial interest, ruled out a party allegiance until 1797, when Pitt secured his temporary loyalty with a pension. Even thereafter he was a loose cannon. The only consistent attitude discernible in his work was a detestation of 'French principles' once the extremists had taken control of the revolution. Ridiculing and reviling the French meant for Gillray administering the same treatment to their traitorous sympathizers in Britain, most notably Charles James Fox.

Gillray etched for a considerable number of printseller–publishers. In 1786 much of his best work went to William Holland, whose radical sympathies were well known; a year or two later he transferred to Fores, who inclined more towards the government and in 1788 advertised 'all the works of Bunbury and Gillray to be had of W. Fores No. 3 Piccadilly'. But in September 1791 he ceased to be a freelance and started to work exclusively for Hannah Humphrey (*d.* 1818), sister of his first publisher, who had sold his plates intermittently since 1779. She was a maiden lady of no known political affiliation, some fifteen to twenty years his senior. He went to lodge over her shop at 18 Old Bond Street in 1793, and in 1798 followed her to 27 St James's Street, the famous shop he depicted in *Very Slippy Weather* (1808), to stay there for the rest of his life. She appears (with her maid Betty) in his caricature *Two-Penny Whist* (1796).

Settling in with Mrs Humphrey was one turning point in Gillray's life: another was the friendship, starting in the early 1790s, with the Revd John Sneyd, an amateur caricaturist who often supplied him with ideas and sketches and, more importantly, was a close friend of George Canning, a future prime minister, but in 1795 a rising tory MP who had attracted the favourable attention of Pitt. Intensely ambitious, Canning thought that his inclusion in a caricature by Gillray would give a fillip to his career and, through Sneyd, a meeting was arranged which bore fruit in *Promised Horrors of the French Invasion* in 1796, followed by *The Giant-Factotum Amusing Himself* (1797). During the latter year Canning with some friends launched *The Anti-Jacobin*, a weekly magazine aimed at discrediting the opposition and boosting the war effort. Although it was unillustrated, the magazine's editors obtained Gillray's support in producing sympathetic prints, for which he was awarded a pension of £200 per annum. *The Anti-Jacobin* lasted only eight months but its renown, especially the verse contributions of Canning, encouraged a publisher in 1800 to issue a prospectus for *Poetry of the Anti-Jacobin*, for which Gillray was contracted to provide a series of engravings. Canning, a subscriber, wanted moral satires, not personal caricatures; personal caricatures were Gillray's forte, and he would not be dictated to, so they quarrelled. Eventually Gillray agreed to destroy his plates—'6 months labour'—and Canning compensated him handsomely with a cash payment of £150. The quarrel was over.

The two men needed each other. From Gillray, Canning got propaganda to unsettle his political opponents; from Canning, Gillray, directly or more often through an intermediary like Sneyd, got valuable information and ideas. It was essential for the relationship to be kept clandestine. In 1804 Canning gave Gillray £50 and may have helped him on other occasions; according to Cobbett (*Political Register*, 30 May 1818) Gillray's pension was renewed in 1807 when Canning regained cabinet office.

When Pitt resigned in 1801, mainly over the king's refusal to grant emancipation to Irish Catholics, Canning followed suit and Gillray, his pension terminated, joined him in assailing the comparatively feeble administration of Addington, the shortcomings of whom were summed up in the jingle 'Pitt is to Addington as London is to Paddington'. Addington, 'the Doctor', and his colleagues became the target of memorable caricatures like *Lilliputian Substitutes* (1801). Pitt (and Canning) returned to office in 1804, but when Pitt died, early in 1806, Canning disdained an invitation to join the 'ministry of all the talents' under Lord Grenville, dubbed by Gillray the 'Broad Bottoms' partly in grateful acknowledgement of the target offered by the Grenville posteriors. He laid into it with relish, his caricature *More Pigs than Teats* (1806), with its depiction of a 'new litter of hungry grunters'—politicians fighting for office and perquisites—affording much amusement to the king.

It was Gillray's last great flourish. When in 1807 the 'Talents' were replaced by the Portland ministry with Canning as foreign secretary, Gillray's powers were waning and perhaps his enthusiasm too. Fox and Pitt, the stars of his show, had both died in 1806. Much of the high drama of English politics departed with them.

The French Revolution and Napoleon As the son of a soldier who lost an arm in the course of a war against France, Gillray could have been expected to nurse more than the normal level of prejudice against the national enemy. In common with many of his fellow countrymen he hailed the downfall of the *ancien régime* in 1789, responding with the print *France Freedom, Britain Slavery* (July 1789). His engraving of the capture of the Bastille after Northcote (1790) was dedicated 'à la Nation Françoise—par leurs respectueux admirateurs James Gillray & Robert Wilkinson' (a reference to the publisher).

Gillray also reflected public opinion in changing his mind as events took a more bloodthirsty turn. *The Hopes of the Party* (July 1791) showed Fox, assisted by others, decapitating George III, a gross libel somewhat softened by the king saying, characteristically, 'What! What! What! What's the matter now?'. In the following year, after the September massacres, Gillray published *Un petit souper à la Parisienne* which depicted a cannibal feast and was perhaps the most bestial and horrifying caricature he ever etched. On 18 January 1793 Louis XVI was guillotined, evoking from Gillray on 12 February *The Zenith of French Glory—the Pinnacle of French Liberty*, a brilliant fantasy dominated by the unforgettable image of a sans-culotte, balanced on a lantern and playing a violin. More terrifying but also more obvious was the blood-bespattered close-up of the execution in *The Blood of the Murdered Crying for Vengeance* (1793).

Gillray's assaults on the sans-culottes, which have scarcely ever been paralleled in their ferocity, were matched in venom by his onslaught on Fox, the chief supporter of France in parliament. Once the French had declared war in February 1793, Fox was seen as a traitor. Out of his plump figure and swarthy visage, Gillray conjured a villain, constantly inciting or practising sedition: see *A Democrat* (1793), *The Republican Rattle-Snake* (1795), and *Daily Advertiser* (1797). In 1797, when Ireland and England were threatened with invasion, the villain turned into a hairy monster, as in *Republican Hercules* and *Le coup de maître*. It was too extreme an image of evil to carry conviction with those who knew Fox to be a libertarian statesman with many attractive qualities, a true if perhaps misguided friend of the people. There was always a suspicion of ironic intent in Gillray's work.

After Fox had gone into self-imposed exile from the House of Commons (see *Stealing Off, or, Prudent Secession*, 1798), he was replaced as the arch-enemy personified by Napoleon Bonaparte. *Little Boney* was Gillray's greatest creation. Gaunt, diminutive, and manic, he bore scant relation to the original except in the constant menace he represented. In *Fighting for the Dunghill* (1798), *The First Kiss this Ten Years* (1801), *Maniac Ravings, or, Little Boney in a Strong Fit* (1803), *The Hand-Writing upon the Wall* (1803), *The Plumb-Pudding in Danger* (1805), and *Tiddy-Doll the Great French Ginger-Bread Baker Drawing out a New Batch of Kings* (1806), he mocked Napoleon in a series of classic caricatures that reverberated around Europe. It is by this display of reduction, defiance, and patriotism that Gillray is best remembered; by this and by his denigration of the royal family.

Royalty and John Bull The habit of traducing members of the royal family in caricature was not invented by Gillray, but he brought to it a wit that had not been seen before, and a coarseness and viciousness that no rivals attempted and which amazed observers from abroad. George III, who according to the clerihew 'ought never to have occurred', invited retribution by his entry into the party political arena, the crucial role he played in the loss of the American colonies, and his continuing attempts to use the vast powers of the crown against the whig interest in parliament. In 1787 appeared *Monstrous Craws at a New Coalition Feast*, a colossally rude print showing the queen as a hideosity, the prince of Wales as a dunce, and the king as an old peasant woman, filling the goitres that dangled from their necks with golden guineas from a bowl labelled 'John Bull's Blood'. This accusation of royal greed was also an accusation of miserliness, a charge renewed in 1792 in *Anti-Saccharrites* and *Temperance Enjoying a Frugal Meal*. In 1792 too appeared *Taking Physic*, in which the king and queen are shown seated on their privies, terrified by the news that the king of Sweden has been assassinated. Echoing the satires of John Wolcot (Peter Pindar), the king says: 'What? Shot? What? What? What? Shot! Shot! Shot!'

But in 1793, under the stimulus of war with France, Gillray's attitude to his sovereign began to change. In *The French Invasion* the body of George III as a map of England is shown bombarding French 'bumboats' with a massive expulsion of wind and turds. Gradually he was transformed into the father of his people. In 1795 he appears as Farmer George in *Affability*. The transformation was confirmed as a condition of Gillray's pension in 1797, and was revived in *The King of Brobdingnag and Gulliver* (1804). It reached a triumphant conclusion in *St George and the Dragon* (1805), in which George III as St George rescues Britannia from the coils of Napoleon as a winged python. Why Queen Charlotte, apart from the fact that she was German, should have so aroused Gillray's spite is somewhat mysterious. By general consent she was no beauty, but that seems an inadequate reason for his representation of her in print after print as a hag with libidinous tendencies. *Sin, Death and the Devil* (1792) in which the queen appears as Sin is a demonstration of Gillray at his nastiest.

There was no mystery about the cause of his assaults on the prince of Wales and his *louche* companions. The prince was adulterous, spendthrift, indolent, fickle, and a friend of Fox. *Wife and No Wife, or, A Trip to the Continent* (1786) revealed, inaccurately, the prince's illicit marriage to Mrs Fitzherbert; *The Morning after Marriage* (1786) suggested, salaciously, the consequences. In *Bandelures* (1792) the prince of Wales, now corpulent and evidently debauched, idles away his time with a yo-yo while Sheridan fondles Mrs Fitzherbert. *Fashionable Jockeyship* (1796) alludes to his affair with Lady Jersey with her husband's compliance. The results of the prince's debauchery are shown in one of the most graphic and potent of Gillray's caricatures, *A Voluptuary under the Horrors of Digestion* (1792) There were other caricatures of the prince but none of the same hostility: *The Lover's Dream* (1795) shows him—ironically—anticipating a future with his debts paid and happily married to a beautiful woman.

There was a limit to royal or perhaps political tolerance; on 23 January 1796 Gillray was arrested, along with several printsellers—all being charged with selling Gillray's *The Presentation, or, The Wise Men's Offering*, published by Mrs Humphrey two days after the birth of Princess Charlotte to the princess of Wales. This relatively innocuous print showed Fox and Sheridan fawning as the infant was displayed to her tipsy father. It was, however, a storm in a teacup; Gillray and the printsellers were all released on bail, and the matter never proceeded. Curiously perhaps, both George III and the prince of Wales were collectors of caricatures, including Gillray's. The king sent caricatures of himself to the University of Göttingen Library in Hanover; his son had an account with Mrs Humphrey and bought the prints partly for gratification and partly in order to suppress those which he found most objectionable. Most of the royal collection of caricatures, including many rare examples, was sold in 1920 to the Library of Congress in Washington, DC.

Whereas the prince of Wales's debauchery provoked Gillray's puritan disgust, he was more indulgent to the prince's brothers, the dukes of York and Clarence, no paragons of virtue themselves. *Fashionable contrasts, or, The duchess's little shoe yielding to the magnitude of the duke's foot* (1792), referring to the duke of York's recent marriage, is a marvellously economical expression of wit. More brutal and explicit in its sexuality is *Lubber's Hole—alias—the Crack'd Jordan* (1791), exposing Clarence's affair with the actress Dorothy Jordan, who is depicted as a chamber-pot, for which her name was a popular synonym. Altogether kinder to Mrs Jordan was *La promenade en famille* (1797), in which the duke takes his illegitimate family for a stroll in the park.

The duke of York, however, was a soldier, and Gillray seldom missed an opportunity to mock Britain's military might (see *March to the Bank*, 1787; *Supplementary Militia*, 1796; *St George's Volunteers*, 1797; and *Hero's Recruiting at Kelsey's*, 1797), even when it was most needed for the defence of the realm—another puzzle for foreign observers. In 1793 an army commanded by the duke of York was sent to Flanders to assist the Dutch in their struggle against the French. Gillray, true to form, found the expedition risible. *Fatigues of the Campaign in Flanders* (1793) shows soldiers and camp followers carousing, the duke amiably supporting a Flemish woman on his knee. As part of the campaign, the British laid siege to the fortress of Valenciennes, which capitulated after six weeks. Philip de Loutherbourg RA (an occasional caricaturist himself) was commissioned to celebrate this success in a large painting, and in August 1793 he took Gillray to France with him to make sketches. They spent about a month touring the battle area in what was probably Gillray's only trip abroad. On their return they showed their work to the king who, according to Henry Angelo, complained that he did not understand Gillray's sketches (*Reminiscences*, 1.297). It is noteworthy that he was prepared to receive Gillray at all.

However deplorable Gillray found the English, foreigners were as bad. It was not only the French that he pilloried; *Germans Eating Sour-Krout* (1803) portrayed a deeply unattractive spectacle. Foreign royalty, like the prince of Orange in *The orangerie, or, The Dutch Cupid Reposing* (1796) and the prince of Württemberg in that magnificent print *The Bridal Night* (1797), looked no more edifying than British royalty. The English nation was represented by John Bull, for whom George III occasionally stood proxy. Very far from heroic—almost the only heroic figure in Gillray's *œuvre* was Nelson—John Bull was usually shown as an obese, shambling, simple-minded yokel in a parlous state of bewilderment. But he has a countryman's cunning. Fox and his gang try to convert him in *Alecto and his Train at the Gate of Pandaemonium* (1791), and a Frenchman does the same in *French-Taylor fitting John Bull with a Jean de Bry* (1797); he resists both their blandishments. *Begging No Robbery* (1796) shows how put-upon he is by the government in the matter of taxation, but in *Opening the Budget* (1796) he declares that if necessary he will give it his last penny, even his breeches. Uncouth he may be, but he is obstinate and stalwart, although Pitt frightens him horribly with invasion scares in *John Bull Bother'd* (1797). All in all, Gillray is telling his compatriots (and anyone on the continent who may be listening) not to be misled by Tom Paine, Joseph Priestley, or malcontents in parliament, nor dismayed by rebellion in Ireland, mutinies in the navy, or shortages of bread. John Bull grumbles—his right as a free Englishman—and is easily alarmed, but threaten his liberties and he will fight like a lion. It was a message that would have been more convincing in the mouth of a more impressive spokesman and unaccompanied by sallies at the expense of British troops. When John Leech and John Tenniel re-created John Bull for a later generation, they portrayed a figure who commanded respect.

Social and personal satires Although it is for his political prints that Gillray is most renowned, about a third of his lifetime's output of approximately 1000 caricatures consists of social and personal satires, a proportion that rose sharply in his last years.

In this work, as with all contemporary caricaturists, his concern was not social justice. Private customers for his prints wanted something to amuse them, preferably something which, when coloured by hand, looked attractive and could be kept in portfolios, hung in the less grand rooms of houses, or cut up and used to decorate screens.

Trade customers pasted them on the walls of taverns, coffee houses, and barber-shops. In neither case did the customers want subjects that stirred the conscience. They wanted jokes.

Gillray's own jokes covered a wide range of subjects from scenes of domesticity to extremes of fashion and often included word play and literary allusions in the captions. The humour, as in *Harmony before Matrimony* and *Matrimonial Harmonics* (1805), was often tinged with cynicism. However, many jokes were based on ideas or sketches supplied to Gillray by amateurs like Sneyd, Brownlow North, or Charles Lorraine-Smith. What George Cruikshank was to call 'washing of other peoples' dirty linen' (W. Bates, *George Cruikshank: the Artist, the Humourist and the Man*, 1878, 3) provided a useful addition to his income. These social satires, although seldom among his finest artistic creations, showed a more gentle side of Gillray's nature.

Very different were some of the personal caricatures. Gillray, whether of his own volition or responsive to a paymaster, had a striking capacity for vendetta. Among those who became objects of his merciless ridicule were Alderman John Boydell (against whom Gillray bore a grudge for being invited to engrave prints after the pictures in his *Shakspeare Gallery*) in *Shakespeare Sacrificed* (1789), Philip Thicknesse (a quarrelsome and unpopular writer) in *Lieutenant Governor Gall-Stone* (1790), the earl of Derby and Miss Farren in *A Peep at Christies* (1796), General Davies (an amateur caricaturist who was believed to have spoken slightingly of Gillray) in *The Military Caricaturist*, Emma Hamilton in *Dido in Despair* (1801), and Sir William Hamilton in *A cognoscenti Contemplating ye Beauties of ye Antique* (1801). He seemed to hate the 'Ton', especially female leaders of fashion pictured in *La belle assemblée* (1787) and *Dilettanti Theatricals* (1803).

Life and character Considering that Gillray was the son of a trooper turned sexton and nothing other than a professional caricaturist, occupying a place in society on a par with Grub Street journalists and pamphleteers, it is to be expected that information about his life should be sparse. Apart from the few letters from and to him that have been preserved, and the brief journal he kept during his trip to Valenciennes (in which he showed marked sensitivity to the quality of the wine and food), most of what is known about him derives from the German magazine *London und Paris* between 1798 and 1806 (see Banerji and Donald) and *The Reminiscences of Henry Angelo*, first published in 1830 and reprinted in two volumes with copious illustrations in 1904.

Frederick A. Wendeborn, a German pastor working in London, wrote of the great quantity of prints exported to Germany and beyond, adding that 'very few of those who pay dearly for them know any thing of the characters and transactions which occasioned such caricatures' (*A View of England towards the Close of the Eighteenth Century*, 1791, 2. 213–14). This appetite had been stimulated by the popularity of Hogarth's engravings, and made for the deficiency that *London und Paris*, based in the cultured dukedom of Weimar, addressed from 1798. Every issue contained reproductions of prints accompanied by lengthy explanations, and among English caricatures Gillray's predominated by far. Johann Christian Huttner (1766–1847), the journal's sensible and well-informed correspondent in London, who knew Gillray over a long period, wrote:

> His extensive knowledge of every kind; his extremely accurate drawing; his ability to capture the features of any man, even if he has only seen him once; his profound study of allegory; the novelty of his ideas and his unswerving, constant regard for the true essence of caricature; these things make him the foremost living artist in his genre, not only amongst Englishmen, but amongst all European nations. (*London und Paris*, 18 July 1806)

It is not known when Gillray left the family home in Millman's Row, Chelsea, nor where he lived before moving in with Mrs Humphrey in 1793. Apart from his trip to Valenciennes, a visit to the Revd John Sneyd's house at Elford, Staffordshire, in 1795, and a visit to that of Viscount Bateman (a former courtier, MP, patron of the arts, and strong supporter of Pitt) in 1798, he does not seem to have strayed far from home. He went to the gallery of the House of Commons to obtain likenesses of politicians, and he visited taverns; otherwise he led an uneventful, hard-working life. As a general rule, to which Sneyd, Lord Bateman, and the associates of Canning on *The Anti-Jacobin* were exceptions, his friends were drawn from his own class—shopkeepers, master craftsmen, and fellow caricaturists, most notably Rowlandson and Isaac Cruikshank. But even George Cruikshank, his devoted disciple, who called him 'the prince of caricaturists', said he was 'never admitted to personal familiarity with him' (Grego, *Rowlandson*, 1.16).

Gillray's relations with Mrs Humphrey, which started as a working arrangement, developed into a fondness which in 1793 caused him to inscribe a firescreen he gave her decorated with his caricatures, 'For his old friend and Publisher H. Humphrey, as a mark of respect and esteem'. Over the subsequent years their friendship, which is assumed to have been chaste, became deep enough for them to agree upon marriage, but Gillray took fright at the door of St James's Church and they returned home (as recounted in *The Caricatures of Gillray*, 1824). Certainly Mrs Humphrey's livelihood depended on Gillray, yet her letters reveal a motherly affection for him that far transcended commercial advantage. She looked after all his needs and took unremitting care of him in his later madness.

As to Gillray's character, opinions differed. *London und Paris* described him as 'pleasant in company with an effervescent wit … a simple, fundamentally honest man and a wonderful son who supports his aged father in every way he can' (*London und Paris*, 1, 1798, 196). On the other hand the memoirist Henry Angelo (1756–1835), though an admirer of Gillray's work, wrote that:

> many stories related of him, too well authenticated to leave a doubt of the facts, declare him to have been a stranger to the feelings of friendship, and sometimes meanly mischievous in his contracted circle … he was a careless sort of cynic, one who neither loved nor hated society. (*Reminiscences*, 1.301)

Most accounts agree that Gillray was shy, reserved, enigmatic, melancholic, hyper-sensitive, and excitable, causing Draper Hill to suggest that in temperament he was a manic-depressive (Hill, *Mr Gillray*, 142). 'This gaunt, bespectacled figure' was how Huttner described him (*London und Paris*, 18 July 1806). Angelo referred to Gillray's 'slouching gait and careless habits' (*Reminiscences*, 1.299). The self-portrait he painted in miniature (*c.*1795–1800; NPG), the engraving from which by Charles Turner was published in 1819, shows a spare, grey man with thin hair combed forward to disguise baldness. He has a chilling expression.

Gillray's health, apart from an attack of rheumatism in 1795, appears for most of his life to have been unremarkable. In all probability he drank excessively although not enough to justify a later charge that he was a habitual drunkard. By 1807 his eyesight was starting to deteriorate, and in that year he experienced a mental and physical breakdown which obliged him to convalesce in Margate. In 1808 his touch as well as his imagination was failing and in 1809 he signed the last plate as one of his own invention. He lapsed into insanity in the following year, and in 1811 attempted to commit suicide by throwing himself out of the window. On 1 June 1815 'he was seen for the last time, naked and unshaven at mid-day, standing in the shop where his caricatures were sold' (*The Athenaeum*, 1 Oct 1831). He was led upstairs to his room in 72 St James's Street and died there the same day. He was buried in St James's churchyard, Piccadilly, Westminster, on 7 June. Mrs Humphrey followed his coffin to the grave accompanied by George Cruikshank, his heir apparent, who had great pride in completing his unfinished plates. Gillray had produced nothing for five years; only the *Gentleman's Magazine* recorded his death and there were no full obituaries. In his will, composed eight years before his death, Gillray left everything he had to Mrs Humphrey—'at her disposal' (PRO, PROB 11/1569, fol. 313). His estate was valued at under £2000 including £1285 in 5 per cent navy bonds.

Reputation During his lifetime Gillray was, although inconspicuous, a celebrity. A Frenchman, visiting London in 1802 during the peace of Amiens, described the posting of a fresh batch of his caricatures in the shop window: 'the enthusiasm is indescribable when the next drawing appears; it is a veritable madness. You have to make your way in through the crowd with your fists' (C. R. Ashbee, *Caricature*, 1928, 47). His fame was international: Jacques-Louis David, the great French painter, knew his work and tried to rival it; so did Hieronymus Hess in Switzerland, calling himself Gilray junior; and Johann Gottfried Schadow in Germany, who used the pseudonyms Gillray, Gilrai-Paris, and Gilray-London (Broadley, 2.107, 113, 114). Gillray's own caricatures had enough staying power for collections to be issued by Miller and others in 1824, and in 1830 by Thomas McLean from the original plates. McLean, the leading caricature publisher of the day, knew that he was taking a risk, for the public mood had reacted against the scurrility of Georgian satire; McLean himself advertised in 1828 the work of the political caricaturist John Royle (HB) as 'entirely free from whatever would offend the most scrupulous or wound the most susceptible'. The reaction gathered momentum in the 1830s when the sale of the old prints dwindled to extinction.

In October 1831 an anonymous writer in *The Athenaeum* described Gillray as 'a caterpillar on the green leaf of reputation … a sort of public and private spy … who insults inferiority of mind and exposes defects of body'. It was not the cruelty of Gillray to which the Victorians objected so much as the coarseness. A generation inclined to cover up the legs of pianos in the interests of modesty was hardly likely to welcome pictures of nude ladies dancing behind a gauze screen in *Ci Devant Occupations* (1805), still less French fishwives thrashing the bare bottoms of nuns in *A Representation of the Horrid Barbarities Practised upon the Nuns* (1792). When Joseph Grego came to making a selection for *The Works of James Gillray, the Caricaturist* (1873), he made a virtue of 'suppressing these subjects which, from their vulgarity, have injuriously reflected their coarseness upon the choice examples of graphic humour by which they are accompanied' (p. 7).

Yet Gillray was not forgotten. The publisher Henry Bohn issued his works in 1851 in two atlas folios, the slimmer one containing the less respectable prints. Reference books increasingly stressed his wit and powers of delineation, applauded his patriotism, and excused the bawdy element in the context of his age. The gradual process of establishing Gillray as perhaps the greatest of all political cartoonists, if compassion is ruled out of the reckoning, was advanced by Low in his book *British Cartoonists, Caricaturists and Comic Artists* (1942). It was substantiated by Draper Hill in his biography *Mr Gillray, the Caricaturist* (1965) and endorsed by the exhibition at Tate Britain in 2001, 'James Gillray: The Art of Caricature' (large permanent collections of his original work are at present held at the British Museum, the House of Lords Library, the Library of Congress in Washington, DC, and the New York Public Library). The Tate exhibition in 2001, curated by Richard Godfrey, was designed to 'bring a wider appreciation of his achievements as satirist, technician and draughtsman, and to re-affirm his importance, and that of caricature, in the history of British art' (Godfrey, *Gillray*, 7). It also demonstrated the influence of Gillray on living British cartoonists and caricaturists such as Steve Bell, Peter Brookes, Martin Rowson, and Gerald Scarfe. Reviewing the exhibition, the historian Andrew Roberts drew attention to Gillray's 'disturbing sexual and scatological imagery … scenes of buggery, groping, excretion and flagellation recur far more frequently in Gillray's work than in the work of his contemporaries, raising questions it is difficult to ignore'. But he concluded that Mrs Humphrey 'always believed he was a genius—at last we have the chance to see why she was right' (*Sunday Telegraph*, 3 June 2001). ANITA MCCONNELL and SIMON HENEAGE

Sources D. Hill, *Mr Gillray, the caricaturist: a biography* (1965) • M. D. George, *British Museum catalogue of political and personal satires*, 5–8 (1935–47) • R. Godfrey, *James Gillray: the art of caricature* (2001) [exhibition catalogue, Tate Britain, London] • C. Banerji and

D. Donald, *Gillray observed: the earliest account of his caricatures in 'London und Paris'* (1999) · *The reminiscences of Henry Angelo*, 2 vols. (1904) · J. Grego, *The works of James Gillray, the caricaturist*, ed. T. Wright (1873) · D. Donald, *The age of caricature: satirical prints in the reign of George III* (1996) · M. D. George, *English political caricature: a study of opinion and propaganda*, 2 vols. (1959) · D. Hill, *The satirical etchings of James Gillray* (1976) · D. Bindman, *The shadow of the guillotine: Britain and the French Revolution* (1989) · D. Low, *British cartoonists, caricaturists and comic artists* (1942) · A. M. Broadley, *Napoleon in caricature, 1795–1821*, 2 vols. (1911) · R. Godfrey, *English caricature, 1620 to the present* (1984) [exhibition catalogue, V&A] · J. Grego, *Rowlandson the caricaturist*, 2 vols. (1880) · R. L. Patten, *George Cruikshank's life, times, and art*, 1 (1992)

Archives BL, corresp. and papers, Add. MS 27337

Likenesses J. Gillray, self-portrait, watercolour on ivory, *c.*1800, NPG [*see illus.*] · watercolour, *c.*1810, NPG · C. Turner, mezzotint, pubd 1819 (after J. Gillray), BM, NPG; repro. in Banerji and Donald, *Gillray observed* · J. Gillray, self-portrait, pencil drawing, BM · coloured etching, BM, NPG

Wealth at death under £2000: will

Gilly, William Stephen (1789–1855), Church of England clergyman, born on 28 January 1789 at Hawkedon, Suffolk, was the son of William Gilly (1761/2–1837), rector of Hawkedon and of Wanstead, Essex, and his wife, Anne, daughter of Stephen Oliver of Long Melford. In November 1797 he was admitted at Christ's Hospital, London, from where he proceeded in 1808 to Caius College, Cambridge; he migrated in the same year to St Catharine's College, where he graduated BA in 1812. He graduated MA in 1817 and DD in 1833. Ordained as deacon in 1812 and priest in 1814, he was presented by Lord Chancellor Eldon to the rectory of North Fambridge in Essex in 1817. In December 1825 he married Jane Charlotte Mary, only daughter of Major Colberg. They had at least two sons.

In 1823 Gilly paid the first of many visits to the Vaudois, a persecuted Christian community in north Italy, which had long attracted the support of continental protestant churches. During the following year Gilly published a *Narrative of an excursion to the mountains of Piedmont, and researches among the Vaudois, or Waldenses* (1824), which awoke much sympathy for the Vaudois in England. The *Narrative* reached a third edition in 1826, and a subscription, headed by the king and Shute Barrington, bishop of Durham, was started for the relief of the Vaudois; it was devoted in part to the endowment of a theological college and library at Torre Pellice in Piedmont. The book also influenced the decision of J. C. Beckwit (1789–1862), a former army officer, to settle among the Vaudois as an evangelical missionary.

On 13 May 1826 Gilly was collated to a prebendal stall in Durham Cathedral. In the following year he became perpetual curate of St Margaret, Durham, and in 1831 vicar of Norham, near Berwick upon Tweed. In 1853 he was appointed canon residentiary of Durham. With a view to improving the condition of the agricultural labourers in north Northumberland, he wrote *The Peasantry of the Border: an Appeal in their Behalf* (1841), in which he called the attention of landowners to the miserable state of the labourers' accommodation. Gilly also published a further work on the Vaudois, *Waldensian Researches* (1831); a memoir of the French protestant clergyman Felix Neff (1832); *Our Protestant Forefathers* (1835); and several works on the gospels. He contributed a preface to *Narratives of Shipwrecks of the Royal Navy, between 1793 and 1849*, by his son William O. S. Gilly, and to J. L. Williams's *Short History of the Waldensian Church* (1855). His three letters on the *Noble Lesson* and Waldensian manuscripts, which appeared in the *British Magazine* in 1841, were reprinted in the appendix to J. H. Todd's *Books of the Vaudois* (1865). Gilly died at Norham on 10 September 1855.

Gordon Goodwin, *rev.* Mari G. Ellis

Sources Venn, *Alum. Cant.* · *GM*, 2nd ser., 44 (1855), 437–9 · *Clergy List* (1847) · F. L. Cross, ed., *The Oxford dictionary of the Christian church*, 2nd edn, ed. E. A. Livingstone (1974), 1454–5

Archives Suffolk RO, Bury St Edmunds, papers relating to his life [copies]

Likenesses J. Jackson, oils, 1833, University College, Durham · J. G. Lough, statue, 1858, Durham

Gilman, Harold John Wilde (1876–1919), painter, was born on 11 February 1876 in Rode, Somerset, the second son of the seven children of John Gilman (1840–1917), curate of Rode, and his wife, Emily Purcell Gulliver (1850–1940). In 1890 the Revd John Gilman secured the livings of Snargate with Snave in Romney Marsh, Kent, and his son was enrolled as a boarder at Tonbridge School, where a year later he injured his hip in a heavy fall. Confined to bed for nearly two years and on crutches for a third, Gilman was educated privately, read a great deal, and began to sketch. In October 1894 he matriculated as a non-collegiate student at the University of Oxford but after one term left to take up a post as tutor to the children of an English family in Odessa. He enrolled in 1896 at the Hastings School of Art in Sussex, moving on to the Slade School of Fine Art in London in 1897, where he studied until 1901. His long training as an artist culminated in a visit to Spain from 1901 until 1903, where he copied paintings by Velázquez and Goya in Madrid's Museo del Prado. In the Prado in 1901 he met Grace Cornelia Canedy (*c.*1864–*c.*1957), daughter of a wealthy Chicago industrialist and some twelve years his senior, who was also on a pilgrimage to copy Velázquez. They married on 2 February 1902 in the garden of the United States consulate in Toledo, Spain. Grace was about forty when their first child, Elizabeth, was born (19 January 1904) in England. The couple had three more children over the next five years.

The murals painted by Gilman in a Canadian government building in Ottawa in 1904 before he joined his wife in Chicago, where their daughter Hannah was born (4 February 1905), are lost, and few paintings of this early period have been traced. However, the influence of Velázquez is apparent in the cool silvery harmonies, fluent liquid brushwork, and sensitive grasp of tonal values of his earliest extant paintings (*c.*1905–1908). His subjects—at this period repeated studies of his wife and their young family in domestic settings—were found closer to hand. From the outset he revealed an impressive mastery of formal compositional structure.

In February 1907 Gilman met Walter Sickert. Together with his Slade contemporary Spencer Gore, he became a founder member of the group which, under the formula

'Mr Sickert at home', rented premises at 19 Fitzroy Street in London to discuss, exhibit, and sell their work to discriminating patrons. In 1908, 1909, 1910, and 1912 he exhibited at the non-jury Salon des Indépendants in Paris, and from 1908 at its newly formed London counterpart, the Allied Artists Association. Meanwhile, the Fitzroy Street group expanded to incorporate Lucien Pissarro, Robert Bevan, and Charles Ginner. For Gilman, who in 1908 had moved from his parents' home in Romney Marsh to the new garden city of Letchworth, Hertfordshire, the opportunity Fitzroy Street afforded to develop his art and his ideas in collaboration with like-minded metropolitan colleagues was crucial. After 1909, when Grace Gilman, debilitated by childbirth and anaemia, took their three surviving children to Chicago and was subsequently unable to return, Gilman spent more time in London.

Between 1910 and 1914 Gilman transformed his execution. Within Fitzroy Street, the example of Gore and Pissarro had first persuaded him to adopt a crusty, broken touch and fuller, richer colour. Then, prompted by the overwhelming selection of key works by Gauguin, Cézanne, and Van Gogh included in the exhibition 'Manet and the post-impressionists' masterminded by Roger Fry at the end of 1910, Gilman undertook a more radical overhaul of his style and technique. His passion for French post-impressionism, and above all for Van Gogh, was consolidated on a visit to Paris in the company of Ginner in 1911. On summer visits to Sweden (1912) and Norway (1913) he experimented with vivid colour, forcefully applied, sometimes in striated slashed strokes, sometimes in thickly encrusted broken touches, and sometimes in a patchwork of flat, simplified areas of paint. However daring his execution, he never lost control of the compositional structure of the land and townscape. A prime example is *The Canal Bridge, Flekkefjord* (1913, Tate collection), the first of his paintings to enter a British public collection (in 1922).

Throughout this period Gilman pursued the politics of the art world with single-minded passion. While Sickert was the actor–manager and Gore the mediator, Gilman, with his more truculent personality, was the driving force behind the creation in 1911 of the *Camden Town Group and in 1913 of the London Group (of which he was first president). Sickert's portrait of about 1912 (Tate collection) captures his fiercely uncompromising character. His didactic temperament also found expression in his teaching, from 1912 to 1915 at the Westminster Technical Institute (where he took over Sickert's evening classes until the latter abruptly reclaimed his post) and in 1916–17, with Ginner, at a private school they established in Soho.

While Gilman had appropriated the vocabulary of subjects developed in Fitzroy Street under Sickert's leadership—dingy bed-sitters, shabby London streets, and nudes on metal bedsteads—he rejected the dinginess of Sickert's palette. Instead he preached the gospel of pure, clean colour applied with no dilutant. He also brought a warmer humanity to his treatment of Sickertian themes. This is well seen in the series of interiors painted from 1914 to 1917 at 47 Maple Street, his first permanent London address, where from 1916 he found the ideal sitter in his landlady, Mrs Mounter (versions include those in the Ashmolean Museum, Oxford, Tate collection and Leeds City Art Gallery). Because he painted from drawn studies rather than directly from nature, Mrs Mounter is also the subject of many intricately worked reed-pen-and-ink drawings (a technique he brilliantly adapted from Van Gogh's example). Gilman's paintings of women, whether nude or clothed and of whatever age and class, reveal a rare tenderness. In portraits of his first wife, their nursemaid, his mother in Snargate rectory, his friends such as Mrs Bevan, and his second wife nursing their child, he achieved a perfect harmony between subject and treatment. The respect and affection with which Gilman portrays Mrs Mounter is sustained by the loving laboriousness of his handling, whether in paintings constructed from infinite touches of undiluted paint or drawings defined in myriad dots and dashes of ink.

In 1915 Gilman asked Grace for a divorce. He wished to marry his pupil at Westminster, (Dorothy) Sylvia Hardy, formerly Meyer (1892–1971), daughter of Arthur Reginald Hardy, company director. Their son was born in December 1917. On 20 April 1918, on learning that the interlocutory phase of the divorce had been accomplished in California, they married. Later that year Gilman visited Halifax, Nova Scotia, where he worked with unrelenting dedication, in all weathers, to fulfil a commission from the Canadian war records. His large painting, *Halifax Harbour at Sunset* (1918), is now in the National Gallery of Canada, Ottawa.

On 12 February 1919, a day after his forty-third birthday, Harold Gilman died in the French Hospital, Shaftesbury Avenue, London, a victim of the virulent post-war influenza epidemic. A memorial exhibition held that year at the Leicester Galleries was the first devoted to his work. Two earlier substantial shows at the Carfax Gallery in London had been shared, first with Gore (1913) and then with Ginner (1914). Ginner's catalogue introduction in 1914 had announced their credo as 'neo-realists', a term that encompassed the dedicated range of their art but not the resonant brilliance of Gilman's means of expression.

In 1921 Sylvia married Leofric Gilman, Harold's brother. She lived to witness growing appreciation of her first husband's achievement. An Arts Council retrospective exhibition was held in 1954–5 and over the following years Gilman's work was acquired by major public galleries throughout the United Kingdom and the Commonwealth. WENDY BARON

Sources *DNB* • A. Causey and R. Thomson, eds., *Harold Gilman, 1876–1919* (1981) [exhibition catalogue, Arts Council of Great Britain] • B. Fairfax Hall, *Paintings and drawings by Harold Gilman and Charles Ginner in the collection of Edward le Bas* (1965) • W. Lewis and L. F. Fergusson, *Harold Gilman: an appreciation* (1919) • private information (1993) • J. Rothenstein, 'Harold Gilman', *Modern English painters*, 1: *Sickert to Smith* (1952), 146–59 • W. Baron, *The Camden Town Group* (1979) • b. cert. • m. cert. [Harold Gilman and Sylvia Hardy] • d. cert.

Likenesses W. Sickert, oils, *c.*1912, Tate collection • W. Sickert, pen-and-ink, 1912, V&A • Beresford?, photograph, repro. in Lewis and Fergusson, *Harold Gilman*, frontispiece

Wealth at death £857 11*s.* 1*d.*: administration with will, 17 July 1919, *CGPLA Eng. & Wales*

Gilmore [*née* Morris], **Isabella** (1842–1923), philanthropist and Church of England deaconess, was born on 17 July 1842 at Woodford Hall, Essex, the eighth of the ten children of William Morris (1797–1847), City billbroker with Messrs Sanderson & Co., and his wife, Emma (1805–1894), daughter of Joseph Shelton. Her siblings included, most famously, William *Morris (1834–1896), artist, poet, and designer, but also Emma (1829–1895), who in 1850 married Joseph Oldham, a former curate of Walthamstow, and Henrietta (1833–1902), who was converted to Catholicism about 1870.

After the death of William Morris senior in 1847, the family moved to Water House, Walthamstow, in 1848, then to Leyton House, Leyton, Essex, in 1856. The Morris children were described as being 'most simply brought up' regarding food and clothes but as having a 'happy healthy childhood', ideal 'for children with healthy outdoor tastes' (*Deaconess Gilmore*, 1–2). 'Issy's' brother Edgar (1844–1924) recalled her as 'a bit of a tomboy' (Edgar Morris to Ada Morris, 1923, Morris family letters, Church of England Record Centre, CWMC/IG/2). By contrast with William Morris's later disparaging remarks about his 'bourgeois' home and family religion, Archbishop Randall Davidson claimed in Isabella's memorial sermon that her love for the poor could be traced to 'that constant personal communion with our Lord from her early life outward to its close' and to 'the unconscious influence of her early days, among what were then regarded as socialistic surroundings' (*Deaconess Gilmore*, 54).

Isabella was educated at home by a governess, went to a private school in Brighton, and then a finishing school in Clifton until the age of seventeen. She 'came out' in 1860, and reputedly met her future husband, Lieutenant Arthur Hamilton (Archy) Gilmore RN (1832–1882), at the Beacontree Assembly Rooms, Wanstead. They were married at St Mary's Church, Leyton, on 18 September 1860. On 1 November 1882 Commander Archy Gilmore died of tubercular meningitis at Lyme Regis. They had no children.

In spite of the opposition of her family (except for William and Emma), Isabella trained as a nurse from 1882 to 1886 at Guy's Hospital, where she worked as a ward sister and recalled being 'extremely happy' ('Reminiscences', 1). After the death of her brother Thomas Rendall (1839–1884) she took on financial and other responsibility for his eight children, aged two upwards, who called her mother, and spent holidays with them where possible.

Victoria Jones, matron of Guy's, who in 1923 described Gilmore as 'a very capable nurse and a first-rate sister' (*Deaconess Gilmore*, 6), recommended her in 1886 to Bishop Thorold of Rochester as a suitable person to found a deaconess order in his diocese. Initially reluctant, Gilmore 'received the call' on holiday that year. She subsequently worked closely with Thorold to revive the ancient order of deaconesses which existed in the early church, and which had its parallel in the male order of deacons. By contrast to the practice in Anglican sisterhoods and existing deaconess houses, Gilmore believed that the deaconess, once trained, should 'owe obedience' only to the bishop and the priest of the parish in which she worked, but could regard the head deaconess as an adviser or friend. Randall Davidson, bishop of Rochester from 1890 to 1896, later recalled that she had been 'a trusted counsellor and attached friend' to three successive bishops (*Deaconess Gilmore*, 53): Thorold, himself, and Edward Stuart Talbot.

To oversee the affairs of the institution, Bishop Thorold formed a council, of which he was head, with a warden, secretary, and treasurer. The first deaconess house, where Gilmore was ordained by Bishop Thorold on 16 April 1887, was at 11 Park Hill, Clapham; the second, The Sisters, 83 North Side, Clapham Common, taken in 1891, was extended and altered in 1896 to include a new chapel designed by Philip Webb. The trouble Gilmore expended on the decoration of this and the other two chapels illustrates her love of 'gorgeous colour' and fine craftsmanship (Stirling, 139).

Gilmore was described as 'handsome', when young; when older as having the same pronounced features as her brother William, and an expression both 'stern and benevolent' (Stirling, 139). Although she later recalled how happy she was in her work, she encountered initial opposition, from some clergy, and also from her mother. She considered she was only 'lent to the work' until her mother's death in 1894 ('Reminiscences', 9).

Gilmore wished her deaconesses to be 'well-educated gentlewomen', 'widows or virgins', preferably the former, but not married (Gilmore, 'Deaconesses', 2). Deaconesses and probationers wore a special (blue) dress, so they could be instantly recognizable, and as a sign of dedication. Trainees had to live in the deaconess institution for three months as visitors, then for one year (later two) as probationers. Finding suitable women was difficult initially, but by the autumn of 1889 there were three, and by 1890, seven. Five were ordained in Southwark Cathedral in 1892, and by 1906 forty-five had been ordained. Although unused to public speaking, Gilmore addressed numerous meetings throughout the diocese explaining the aims of the institution, and recruiting associates, Anglican communicants who were pledged to support the institution through prayer and financially.

Gilmore obtained a reputation for 'standing no nonsense' ('Reminiscences', 50), which she believed was necessary to deter the wrong kind of applicant. In her view, the essential quality was 'absolute devotion to Christ' (Deaconess Institution, *11th Annual Report, 1897*, LPL, 3). Worship, with chapel services, usually taken by Gilmore, held five times daily, was central to the life of the institution. Theological training initially consisted of Bible study, prayer book, and church history, including written papers, then 'Elementary Dogmatics', added in 1893. From 1898 instruction was given by specialist lectures, with classes in Greek for those who wished.

Gilmore emphasized the importance of visiting the poor in a spirit of friendship, and of offering immediate practical help. Probationers therefore had to become proficient in housework, cooking, and plain sewing, and attend a course of nursing, some of them at Guy's for six months. Parochial visiting with a trained deaconess took place most days in the poorest districts of the Battersea parishes of St Mary's and St John's with St Paul's, then St Peter's. Besides visiting homes and nursing the sick, the deaconesses established a Sunday ragged school, taught in Sunday (and later, day) schools, and took mothers' meetings. Gilmore's practice was to talk about religion where opportunity presented itself, not to try to force the poor to go to church. She arranged baptism services on weekday evenings (the first was attended by ninety-four children) and cottage meetings in poor districts, which deaconesses had to learn to address. Deaconesses also had to liaise with different agencies: the relieving officer, the school attendance officer, the local doctor, local hospitals, and charities.

William Morris reputedly said to Gilmore 'I preach socialism—you practise it' (*Deaconess Gilmore*, 37), and other contemporaries were impressed by Gilmore's skill and sympathy in visiting. She recalled that 'the people soon became very dear to me and it was agony to find how terrible their condition was' ('Reminiscences', 27). She was a member of the first executive of the National Union of Women Workers, established in 1895. However, her concern was with the spiritual as much as the material needs of the poor. While recording that the question of relief was extremely difficult, she established many heavily subsidized forms of philanthropic organization, such as the provision of clothing for small loans, provident clubs, an industrial society, and girls' preventive home (founded in 1893). Deaconesses had to learn simple bookkeeping, and she regarded club-collecting as a useful means of entry into poor homes. She hated alcohol and deaconesses were expected to break up fights.

From 1901 deaconesses had to be over thirty but a system of licensed lay workers, who had the same training, was established. By Gilmore's retirement in 1906 there were many Rochester-trained deaconesses working both overseas and in Britain, such as Helen Barnes, working with the navy, who was based on HMS *Pembroke* at Chatham from 1895 to 1916. Katherine Beynon did a year's training (1895–6) and then founded St Hilda's Deaconess House, Lahore.

After retiring Gilmore lived with her nieces Ada and (from 1920) Effie at Reigate (until 1914), Kew (until 1921), then Parkstone, Dorset. At the archbishop's request, she wrote a pamphlet called 'The deaconess', which she revised in 1908. She kept in close contact with deaconesses she had trained, addressed numerous conferences, including the women's committee of the Pan-Anglican Congress in 1908, and was consulted by the Association of Head Deaconesses, founded that year. The status of the deaconess order was enshrined in the statutes of the Lambeth conferences of 1920 and 1930.

Isabella Gilmore made a valuable contribution to the work of the Church of England by establishing, in principle and practice, that trained deaconesses and lay workers could work with a parish priest, licensed by the bishop, but independent of any religious community. The Sisters, known as Gilmore House after 1934, remained a training institution until 1970. Arguably, the acceptance of the ordained ministry of deaconesses was an important step towards the eventual admission of women to the Anglican priesthood in November 1992. Gilmore's insistence on rigorous standards in training, and on the independent status of ordained deaconesses, who were paid (her own services were given free), had important implications for the professionalization of women's work from *c.*1890.

Gilmore died at her home, Kingston, Sandecotes Road, Parkstone, Dorset, on 15 March 1923, of myocardial degeneration and heart failure. Her memorial service, addressed by Randall Davidson, archbishop of Canterbury, was held on 20 March 1923 at Lambeth parish church, and she was buried at St Michael's Church, Lyme Regis, beside her husband, on 21 March. A memorial fund paid for a bas-relief portrait of her in white marble in Southwark Cathedral in 1924; the remainder went towards bursaries for deaconesses.

MARY CLARE MARTIN

Sources 'Reminiscences of Isabella Gilmore from 1886', Church of England Record Centre, CWMC/19/4 • *Deaconess Institution for the Diocese of Rochester, Annual Reports of the Head Deaconess*, 1888–1902, LPL, G4423.R6 • *Deaconess Gilmore: some memories collected by Deaconess Elizabeth Robinson* (1924) • I. Gilmore, 'Deaconesses: their qualifications and status', in *Pan-Anglican papers*, Pan-Anglican Congress (1908) • J. Grierson, *Isabella Gilmore: sister to William Morris* (1962) • *Deaconess Institution for the Diocese of Rochester, Annual Reports* (1888–1906, 1908–9, 1911–12, 1914–15, 1917–22), LPL, G 4423.R6 [esp. *11th Annual Report, 1897*; *19th Annual Report, 1905*, 25–35] • b. cert. • m. cert. • d. cert. • A. M. W. Stirling, *The merry wives of Battersea, and gossip of three centuries* (1956) • Morris family tree, William Morris Gallery, Walthamstow, general Morris file 5A • Church of England Record Centre, Rochester and Southwark Diocesan Deaconess Institution MSS, CWMC/IG/7 [including *Constitution and rules* (1884)] • *The Rochester and Southwark Diocesan Deaconess House, 1887–1937*, Church of England Record Centre • *The Gilmore Memorial Committee, 1923–5*, Church of England Record Centre, CWMC/IG/8 [loose sheet] • Edgar Morris to Ada Morris, 1923, Church of England Record Centre, Morris family letters, CWMC/IG/2 • Isabella Gilmore to Effie Morris, 27 April 1891, Church of England Record Centre, Morris family letters • some notes on the work of deaconesses, partly in the hand of Gilmore, LPL, Gilmore House MSS, MS 3464 • G. Lister and E. Lister, 'Old Leytonstone: some memories', pamphlet, 1934, Waltham Forest Archive and Local History Library, L96 [typescript], 4 • H. P. Adam, *Women in council* (1945)

Archives Church of England Record Centre, London, corresp. and MSS | LPL, Gilmore House MSS • William Morris Gallery, Walthamstow, London, letters and photographs, general Morris file 5A

Likenesses photograph, *c.*1860, William Morris Gallery, Walthamstow • photograph, after 1865, William Morris Gallery, Walthamstow • photograph, *c.*1887, William Morris Gallery, Walthamstow • A. G. Walker and Mr Comper, marble bas-relief, 1924, Southwark Cathedral • C. B. Leighton, pastel drawing; formerly at Gilmore House • photograph (of Leighton drawing), Church of England Record Centre • photographs (in retirement), William Morris Gallery, Walthamstow

Wealth at death £6066 1*s.* 4*d.*: probate, 10 May 1923, *CGPLA Eng. & Wales*

Gilmour, Douglas Graham (1885–1912), engineer and aviator, was born at Dartford, Kent, on 7 March 1885, the elder son of the large family of East India merchant David Gilmour (*d.* 1907), formerly of Shanghai, and his wife, Margaret Jane Muirhead (*d.* 1910). His paternal grandfather, J. B. Gilmour, was a Glasgow merchant and the family were proud to trace their ancestry back to Grahame Claverhouse, Viscount Dundee. Gilmour was sent, with his younger brother Stanley Graham Gilmour (*b.* 1888), to Clifton College, entering the school in January 1899. He was already interested in engineering and spent much of his spare time in the school workshop, his other enthusiasm being the volunteer cadet force. He shot at Bisley in 1901 as one of two cadets representing the school in the cadets challenge trophy. In July 1902 he was in the school squad of eight, competing for the Ashburton challenge shield. Before leaving the college Gilmour had begun to acquire and work on a collection of motorbicycles, at one time owning nineteen, which he tested on the Surrey slopes above the family home at Mickleham downs. He became an engineering student at the Central Technical College, later Imperial College, London, and had considerable success in motorcycle hill-climbing competitions.

By the time Blériot had flown the channel in July 1909 Gilmour was already fascinated by the possibility of using his motor engineering skills to seek a career in powered flight. He made immediate application to the Aero Club, and was elected a full member in September 1909. In Paris he joined a group of pioneer aviators, including Claude Grahame-White, and followed the aviators and engineers of the Blériot school south to Pau, in search of good flying weather. He had acquired a Blériot machine, which was damaged in transit to Pau. After restoration it was ready to fly, but was then seriously damaged by the collapse of a hangar, so Gilmour was occupied for much of the winter in repair work. He took the flight tests for his French Aero Club pilot's licence no. 75 at Pau on 29 March 1910.

Gilmour had invented an aircraft anchor slip device to enable pilots to run an engine up and take off without assistance, and this was already being produced by a Bedford manufacturer. He returned to England with his machine and took over the tenancy of hangar no. 7 at Brooklands. Early in May he crash-landed close to the paddock end of the motor track, and was lucky to avoid serious injury. However he was soon flying again and experimenting with a more powerful engine. For the next twenty-one months, until his untimely death in a flying accident, Gilmour's flying activities and occasional 'escapades' were frequently recorded in the national press, and he drew large crowds of admirers. He took part in the first all-British aviation meeting at Dunstall Park racecourse, Wolverhampton, and in early August went up to Lanark for the international meeting. A new railway station had to be specially constructed alongside the racecourse to cope with the arrival of an estimated 30,000 visitors a day.

By September, Gilmour had joined forces with L. D. Gibbs & Co. and was flying their two-seater Blériot—the Big Bat—but contravened royal parks regulations by descending without permission among a herd of deer near Hampton Court. At Brooklands on 5 October, Gilmour and the same aircraft won the duration prize of £60 and a cup for remaining aloft for a flight of almost three hours. He was now continuously under pressure to take passengers for short pleasure flights in this two-seater machine. One of his passengers was General Cummings, the first British general to evaluate the military possibilities of a powered aircraft at first hand, and Gilmour hoped he would make his opinion known to the War Office.

The War Office had just leased flying rights to the British and Colonial Aeroplane Company of Bristol and a site for hangars at Lark Hill, Salisbury Plain. Serving military officers were already seeking instruction in flying training and two Bristol aircraft had taken part in the army's autumn manoeuvres on the plain. Gilmour commenced flying the new Bristol Boxkite biplanes at Lark Hill, and the company lent him an aircraft to compete for the 1910 British Michelin cup. He fitted his own ENV engine and made several attempts but had to concede victory to Cody at the end of the year. The company appointed him their demonstration pilot as the most daring and skilful British pilot, attributes which he exhibited throughout 1911.

Like many other enthusiastic motorists of the time Gilmour had already collected a batch of police court summonses for speeding and driving a motor car to the danger of the public. On his first appearance at Woking the chairman of the magistrates imposed a nominal fine, but was so impressed with the charm of the young aviator that he

Douglas Graham Gilmour (1885–1912), by unknown photographer

invited him home for tea. He had amassed ten convictions, including three for dangerous driving, by March 1911, was fined again, and had his licence suspended for three months. On this occasion he had been driving rather fast from Brooklands to Brighton, keeping up with his fellow aviator Oscar Morison who was making the first ever cross-country flight to Brighton.

Gilmour and five aviators from Hendon attracted the attention of the crowds which had assembled to watch the university boat race on 1 April 1911 by flying over the river. Gilmour was especially prominent by his weaving and gliding over the course while the race was in progress, and at the finish ran out of petrol and had to land in a nearby field. Newspaper coverage of the aviation far exceeded that of the boat race. A week later he and E. Gordon England inaugurated a new way of travelling—an aerial tour of Wiltshire and Dorset, making numerous landings to call on friends and putting up at a hotel overnight. Local press reports of their aerial progress stated that it was the first aircraft that had ever been seen in the area.

Gilmour competed in the first Brooklands to Brighton air race in early May, but Gustav Hamel beat him into second place. He was the first aviator to fly to Portsmouth, over-fly Royal Navy warships, and demonstrate their vulnerability to air attack. He 'bombed' Fort Blockhouse, the submarine depot's headquarters, with oranges, before landing in the grounds of the Haslar Royal Naval Hospital.

Accused of manslaughter in one traffic accident, Gilmour was summoned to Wiltshire assizes at the end of May 1911. News spread of his intention to fly to court and thousands of Salisburians were on the look-out for his aircraft. He flew from Shoreham to Salisbury, circling the cathedral spire several times *en route* for the assizes. Although exonerated at the inquest he was later sent for trial following disclosure of driving while disqualified; he was acquitted.

At Henley regatta, while racing was in progress, Gilmour flew with his wheels almost touching the water. On 7 July he followed the Thames, flying past the houses of parliament and round St Paul's Cathedral. These 'stunts' brought him into conflict with the Royal Aero Club, which had already cautioned him over the Salisbury Cathedral flight. The club suspended his pilot's licence, but since it was a French one a Court of Appeal judgment ruled against them. Gilmour was excluded from the Circuit of Britain, the forerunner of the king's cup air race, in which he had been entered as pilot for the British and Colonial Aeroplane Company.

Gilmour's publicity made him even more popular with the public. In August he gave exhibition flights at Sherborne Castle and attended local charity fêtes and flower shows in the west country as the special attraction. In the autumn he was flying and testing aircraft on Salisbury Plain in preparation for an attempt on the Michelin no. 1 trophy for 1911. In December at Brooklands he was frequently seen flying a Martin-Handasyde monoplane purchased from T. O. M. Sopwith, and demonstrated his flying skills to weekend crowds. He also flew it at Hendon in January and early February 1912. On 17 February 1912, in perfect flying weather, after taking off from Brooklands for a cross-country flight in the Martin-Handasyde, Gilmour's plane crashed in the Old Deer Park, Richmond, and he died of a fractured skull, aged only twenty-seven.

Gilmour anticipated the possibility of dying in an air accident and in April 1911 had lodged a letter with a friend setting out his wishes, especially requesting no bell be tolled. He was buried on the 21st at Mickleham church beside his parents. He donated his Blériot to Clifton College and it was fixed to rafters in the gym. Although so well known for his enthusiasm and feats of daring flying, he was a most careful pilot, always using a safety belt. His obituary in *Flight* recorded 'he was one of those pilots whom the science and practice of heavier-than-air locomotion could little afford to lose'. SYLVIA ADAMS

Sources *The Aero* [London] · *Flight* · C. G. Grey, *The Aeroplane* (22 Feb 1912), 183 · *The Times* · *Surrey Herald* · *Portsmouth Times* · *Western Gazette* (23 Feb 1912) · *Sussex Daily News* · *Brighton and Hove Herald* · *Evening Argus* · *The Sketch* (9 April 1913), 27 · d. cert.

Likenesses photograph, repro. in Grey, *The Aeroplane* · photograph, priv. coll. [*see illus.*]

Wealth at death £22 10s.: administration with will, 21 May 1912, *CGPLA Eng. & Wales*

Gilmour, Sir John, of Craigmillar (*bap.* **1605**, *d.* **1671**), judge, was the son of John Gilmour of Craigmillar, Edinburghshire, writer to the signet. Having been educated at Edinburgh University, he graduated MA on 26 July 1625. He was admitted a member of the Faculty of Advocates on 12 December 1628. As an advocate he acquitted himself so much to the satisfaction of those who supported royal policies in Scotland that in 1641 he was appointed by the committees of estates counsel for the earl of Montrose. He subsequently gained a very extensive practice. As a reward for his constant allegiance to the crown, he was knighted about 1650 or 1651. In 1659 he made the second of four marriages, this time to Margaret, daughter of Sir William Cockburn of Langton; the name of his first wife is unknown.

Following the re-establishment of the court of session after the restoration, Gilmour was appointed lord president on 13 February 1661; his appointment, for which he received a pension of £500 a year, was approved by parliament on 5 April, and the sittings of the court were resumed on 1 June. In the parliament of that year he was elected a commissioner for the shire of Edinburgh, which he continued to represent until his death, and at the same time was appointed a lord of the articles. He obtained the clause in the Militia Act that the kingdom should not be obliged to maintain any force levied by the king otherwise than as it should be agreed by parliament or a convention of estates. During the trial of the marquess of Argyll, Gilmour made a noble but ineffectual attempt to save the accused by rising in his place in parliament and declaring that, having studied the case against him, 'the greater part of the house were as guilty as he' (Wodrow, *Analecta*, vol. 3, January 1712). As a supporter of the earl of Lauderdale's party, Gilmour was called to London for a personal audience with the king. The concerns he expressed regarding the misgovernment of Scotland were instrumental in the fall in 1663 of Lauderdale's rival John Middleton, earl of Middleton.

In 1664 Gilmour became a member of the court of high commission, and exerted his influence without success to mitigate the severity of the bishops who were also members. In the privy council he refused to vote for the execution of the insurgents taken at Pentland in 1666, to whom quarter had been promised. On 22 December 1670 he resigned his judgeship in consequence of ill health, and died the next year. He had had twenty children, but only his third marriage, to Margaret, daughter of Sir Alexander Murray of Blackbarony, produced a surviving son—Sir Alexander Gilmour of Craigmillar, who was commissioner to parliament for Edinburghshire between 1690 and 1701. Sir John's reports for 1661 to 1666 were published with those of Sir David Falconer for 1681 to 1686 as *A Collection of Decisions of the Lords of Council and Session* (1701). Sir George Mackenzie, who had served alongside Gilmour at the bar, described him in his *Idea eloquentiae forensis* as a man of rough eloquence and powerful common sense, but little learning.

J. A. Hamilton, *rev.* Gillian H. MacIntosh

Sources Burke, *Gen. GB* (1871), vol. 1 • G. Brunton and D. Haig, *An historical account of the senators of the college of justice, from its institution in MDXXXII* (1832) • *APS*, 1661–9 • D. Laing, ed., *A catalogue of the graduates … of the University of Edinburgh*, Bannatyne Club, 106 (1858) • J. Nicoll, *A diary of public transactions and other occurrences, chiefly in Scotland, from January 1650 to June 1667*, ed. D. Laing, Bannatyne Club, 52 (1836) • R. Wodrow, *Analecta, or, Materials for a history of remarkable providences, mostly relating to Scotch ministers and Christians*, ed. [M. Leishman], 2, Maitland Club, 60 (1842), Jan 1713
Archives BL, letters to duke of Lauderdale and Charles II, Add. MSS 23116–23131 • Buckminster Park, Grantham, corresp. with duke of Lauderdale • U. Edin., letters to duke of Lauderdale
Likenesses attrib. L. Schuneman, oils, Parliament Hall, Edinburgh • Scougal, portrait; known to be at Inch, near Edinburgh, in 1889

Gilmour, Sir John, of Lundin and Montrave, second baronet (1876–1940), politician, was born at Montrave in Fife, on 27 May 1876, the second but eldest surviving son of Sir John Gilmour (1845–1920), who was created baronet in 1897 when he was president of the Scottish Union of Conservative Associations, and his wife, Henrietta (*d.* 1926), daughter of David Gilmour of Quebec. He was educated at Trinity College, Glenalmond, Edinburgh University, and Trinity Hall, Cambridge. Soon after leaving college Gilmour served with distinction in the Second South African War; he was twice mentioned in dispatches and reached the rank of major in the imperial yeomanry, and he actively continued thereafter in the Fife and Forfar yeomanry, of which he became lieutenant-colonel. He married, on 9 April 1902, Mary Louise (*d.* 1919), eldest daughter of Edward Tiley Lambert, of Telham Court, Battle, Sussex. They had one daughter and one son.

Gilmour had determined from the start on a political career on the Conservative side: he joined the Fife county council, stood unsuccessfully in 1906 against Asquith in his native East Fife, where his father had three times been the Conservative candidate, and then gained the Liberal seat of East Renfrewshire in January 1910. He remained MP for East Renfrewshire until migrating to Glasgow, Pollok, in 1918, a seat he held until his death. Jack Gilmour was soon popular in the parliamentary ranks, and when he was made a whip in January 1913 the chief whip noted that he had chosen 'a ginger-headed soldier who will be useful and whose appointment will be popular', while fellow whip Robert Sanders delighted at the promotion of 'a very good fellow' (*Crawford Papers*, 304; *Real Old Tory Politics*, 59). At the start of the First World War he interrupted his political career by becoming one of the first to re-enlist. He was present at the Gallipoli landings, served later in Egypt and Palestine, until wounded, and won the DSO and bar. His first wife died in January 1919 and on 17 April 1920 he married her younger sister Violet Agnes Lambert, with whom he had a daughter. He succeeded to his father's baronetcy in July 1920.

Gilmour returned to the whips' room in 1919, formally joined the government in April 1921 as a junior lord of the Treasury, and was sworn of the privy council in 1922. He had, though, a real conflict of loyalty in the party crisis of 1922. He threatened to resign in May because the whips' advice was so consistently ignored, took part in the 'under-secretaries' revolt' of July–August (but then voted with Austen Chamberlain at the Carlton Club meeting in October), and from loyalty to Chamberlain twice refused Bonar Law's invitation to accept the Scottish Office in his new government.

It was not until the Conservative rift was healed in 1924 and the ex-coalitionists rejoined the front bench that Gilmour's career could resume its upward course, but in November he joined Baldwin's cabinet as secretary for Scotland (he resumed in 1926 the ancient title of secretary of state for Scotland, the first to hold it since 1746). On the latter occasion his popularity across the political divide was marked by a ceremony in which members of both houses presented his portrait to the Scottish Office. During the later 1920s he also received the freedoms of Edinburgh (1928), Dundee (1928), and Glasgow (1929), was lord rector of Edinburgh University (1926–9), brigadier of the Royal Company of Archers (the king's Scottish bodyguard), and captain of the Royal and Ancient Golf Club of St Andrews (1927).

Gilmour was a well-informed and well-prepared Scottish secretary, in

> a most arduous post, for the work involves a great number of departments, such as health, education and agriculture … Sir John Gilmour was thoroughly familiar with Scottish problems, particularly those concerned with agriculture, for he had long been a practical and experienced farmer and taken a leading part in agricultural societies. (*The Times*, 1 April 1940)

Gilmour sought to transfer staff, authority, and practical decision-making from London to Edinburgh, a reform that promoted both greater rapidity in executing policies and more responsiveness to Scottish opinion. This approach was further pursued in the reorganization of Scottish departments in 1939, on the recommendation of a committee that he had chaired in 1937. Within cabinet he was generally a calming influence, for example by seeking to mediate between Churchill and Neville Chamberlain in their epic battle over de-rating in 1928–9. William Bridgeman assessed him in November 1929 as having been

> a very industrious and successful Secretary for Scotland, [who] won respect from all sides by straightforwardness in speech and conduct. He never shirked a difficult job and always spoke plainly and expressed his opposition to any proposal in direct and unmistakeable language without giving offence. He has a quick temper, but controls it well, and was always loyal to those he was working with and ready to take his share of any unpopular course of policy. (*Modernisation*, 229)

On the formation of the National Government in 1931 Gilmour went to the Ministry of Agriculture, another post for which he had specialist qualifications (he was a noted stock breeder), and in that capacity took part in the British delegation to the Ottawa conference of 1932. He did not carry out the policy consequences of Ottawa, however, for in September 1932 he was moved to the Home Office, specifically to tackle corruption and low morale in the Metropolitan Police, but once again with relevant experience from his days at the Scottish Office. He therefore found himself taking charge of the forces of law and order during a difficult time, when unemployment marches and other such protests were producing the threat of civil disorder. The rise of Oswald Mosley's British Union of Fascists presented the home secretary with more political difficulties, for example after the excessive violence displayed by stewards at the 1934 Olympia rally. Gilmour did well under these trying circumstances, and his reputation for fairness did not suffer, but he also found time for more traditional Home Office business, as with a reform of the gambling laws.

When Baldwin returned to the premiership in June 1935 Gilmour willingly retired from the cabinet, and by vacating the Home Office for Sir John Simon enabled Baldwin also to get a new foreign secretary. He was happy to devote himself more directly to Scottish affairs, by becoming high commissioner in 1938 and 1939 of the general assembly of the Church of Scotland, but when war broke out in September 1939 he was again recalled to the colours, this time politically. Neville Chamberlain made Gilmour minister of shipping, an appointment of which there was much criticism since it seemed to symbolize the government's turning only to old and unthreatening faces. This time Gilmour had no special skills in a key wartime post, but threw himself into the office unstintingly, and overwork may indeed have contributed to his sudden death, in London, on 30 March 1940, aged only sixty-three. *The Times*, offering a leader as well as an obituary, concluded that Gilmour was 'the first casualty of the war in the ranks of the Government' (1 April 1940).

Gilmour was clearly a capable man with most of the political and administrative gifts required for a solid ministerial career, and he was devoted in particular to his native Scotland, its countryside, its traditional sports (he was keen on both golf and curling), and its national church. He was always loyal to his party and its leader, but at the same time mainly devoid of the partisanship which alienates opponents. He was not perhaps the most dynamic British politician of the age—Leo Amery thought his speeches of 1930 'feeble', and Lord Crawford, having dined in 1925 with Willie Bridgeman, Gilmour, and Lord Peel, concluded that 'if politics are indeed as dull as these three cabinet ministers, the peaceful outlook of these realms is indeed assured' (*Amery Diaries*, 60; *Crawford Papers*, 501)—but *The Times* felt able to conclude in 1940, as could be said of very few politicians of cabinet rank, that 'it is difficult to suppose that he had an enemy in the world' (1 April 1940).

JOHN RAMSDEN

Sources *The Times* (1 April 1940) • *The Scotsman* (1 April 1940) • *DNB* • *WWW*, 1929–40 • *Real old tory politics: the political diaries of Robert Sanders, Lord Bayford, 1910–35*, ed. J. Ramsden (1984) • *The modernisation of conservative politics: the diaries and letters of William Bridgeman, 1904–1935*, ed. P. Williamson (1988) • *The Crawford papers: the journals of David Lindsay, twenty-seventh earl of Crawford … 1892–1940*, ed. J. Vincent (1984) • *The empire at bay: the Leo Amery diaries, 1929–1945*, ed. J. Barnes and D. Nicholson (1988) • M. Cowling, *The impact of labour, 1920–24* (1971) • A. T. C. Pratt, ed., *People of the period: being a collection of the biographies of upwards of six thousand living celebrities*, 2 vols. (1897) [on Sir John Gilmour, first baronet] • *CCI* (1940)

Archives NA Scot., personal and political corresp., GD 383 | FILM BFI NFTVA, news footage

Likenesses W. Stoneman, photograph, 1922, NPG • portrait, 1926, Gov. Art Coll. • J. Guthrie, oils, 1934, Gov. Art Coll.

Wealth at death £116,736 16*s*. 11*d*.: confirmation, 27 June 1940, *CCI*

Gilmour, John Scott Lennox (1906–1986), botanist and horticulturist, was born on 28 September 1906 at 1 St John's Wood Road, London, the youngest in the family of one daughter and three sons of Thomas Lennox Gilmour, Edinburgh lawyer, and his wife, Elizabeth, daughter of Sir John Scott *Keltie (1840–1927), geographer. He was educated at Uppingham School, where he showed an early interest in botany, and then went to Clare College, Cambridge, to read natural sciences, in which he obtained a second class in both parts of the tripos (1928 and 1929). His first appointment (1930) was as curator of the university herbarium and botanical museum in the botany school, where he and other colleagues, notably Thomas Tutin and William Stearn, were enthusiastic students of that remarkable teacher Humphrey Gilbert-Carter, the first scientific director of the university botanic garden. These lifelong friendships were largely responsible for a considerable rebirth of interest in taxonomic botany in Britain during the expansion of universities after the Second World War.

Gilmour displayed early qualities of ability, tact, and charm, which undoubtedly helped his rapid promotion, in 1931, to the post of assistant director of the Royal Botanic Gardens at Kew. His career, interrupted by wartime service in the Ministry of Fuel and Power (1940–45), took him to the directorship of the Royal Horticultural Society's garden at Wisley (1946–51) and then, on the retirement of Gilbert-Carter in 1951, back to Cambridge as director of the botanic garden and a fellow of Clare College. He held the directorship until his retirement in 1973.

The post-war years in Cambridge saw the expansion of the botanic garden: a golden age made possible by a very generous private bequest and by the talents of the young director, whose sympathetic and humane administration educated many young people, some of whom became leading horticulturists. In this happy academic environment Gilmour made his mark on national and international botanical and horticultural science, in two particular directions. One of these concerned the philosophy of classification and its relevance to biology, a subject in which he had shown a surprisingly early interest, as evinced by his presentation in 1936 to the annual meeting of the British Association in Blackpool of a paper entitled 'Whither taxonomy?'

An early friendship with Julian Huxley bore fruit, not least in the publication of Gilmour's most important paper in this field in Huxley's *The New Systematics* (1940), a book that stimulated much-needed discussion involving botanists and zoologists in the newly formed Systematics Association. Radical ideas on the desirability of making a logical distinction between so-called 'natural classifications' and evolutionary (phylogenetic) ones underlay Gilmour's whole approach and, although most biologists remain unconverted, the impact of his ideas is still evident in modern academic controversies. His 1940 paper is suitable for modern students interested in this area of scientific activity. Among his other publications were *British Botanists* (1944), *Wild Flowers of the Chalk* (1947), *Wild Flowers* (jointly with S. M. Walters, 1954), and *Some Verses* (1977).

Unusually for philosophers of science, Gilmour remained throughout a pragmatist with an abiding interest in encouraging people to work out by rational argument how they should collectively proceed. These talents were much exercised in the field of horticultural nomenclature and taxonomy, where his second great contribution was made. In 1950 he and William Stearn represented the Royal Horticultural Society in the nomenclature sessions of the seventh International Botanical Congress held in Stockholm; from these meetings arose his book *International Code for the Nomenclature of Cultivated Plants* (1953). His skill as a chairman was widely appreciated. A Dutch colleague, Frans Stafleu, who ran the International Association of Plant Taxonomy during those years, wrote in 1986 that 'for many of his contemporaries and colleagues Gilmour was the world's most charming botanist'.

Music and books were Gilmour's main hobbies, both enjoyed best in the company of family and friends. He was a founder editor of the New Naturalist series of books published by Collins from 1945, and put his considerable knowledge of the second-hand book market to use in building the rich horticultural library in the Cambridge Botanic Garden. He became a fellow of the Linnean Society in 1932 and was awarded the Royal Horticultural Society's Victoria medal of honour in 1957.

Gilmour fervently believed that formal religion was on balance 'a bad thing', though characteristically his criticisms of religious colleagues and friends were full of charity. He was a founder member of the Cambridge Humanists in 1955, and enjoyed nothing so much as a tolerant, rational discussion of religion. He was dark haired and exceptionally handsome. Athletic in his youth, he became stocky later. In 1935 he married Molly, daughter of the Revd Maurice Berkley, an Anglican vicar. It was a singularly happy marriage and they had three daughters. Gilmour was troubled by incapacity and illness in his later years and died on 3 June 1986 at his home, 25 Fitzwilliam Road, Cambridge. S. MAX WALTERS, *rev.*

Sources *Plant Systematics and Evolution* [memorial volume], 167 (1989) · W. T. Stearn, *The Garden*, 112 (1987) · M. P. Winsor, 'Species, demes, and the Omega taxonomy: Gilmour and the new systematics', *Biology and Philosophy*, 15 (2000), 349–88 · P. Marren, *The new naturalists* (1995) · private information (1996) · personal knowledge (1996)

Archives Botanic Garden, Cambridge, notes · CUL, corresp. and papers · NHM, corresp. and papers | NHM, corresp. with Norman Douglas Simpson, letters · Rice University, Texas, Woodson Research Center, corresp. with Sir Julian Huxley

Likenesses photographs, repro. in Marren, *The new naturalists*

Gilpin, Bernard (1516–1584), Church of England clergyman and preacher, was a younger son of Edwin Gilpin, who came from a family of well-established Westmorland gentry settled at Kentmere, and his wife, Margaret, daughter of William Layton of Delamain, Cumberland, and niece of Cuthbert Tunstall, bishop of Durham; George *Gilpin (*d.* 1602) was one of his elder brothers. These family connections were to stand him in good stead throughout his career. In 1533, aged seventeen, Gilpin entered Queen's College, Oxford, where he later became a fellow, graduating BA on 24 February 1540 and proceeding MA on 21 March 1542. In 1547 he migrated to Christ Church and made supplication for the degree of BTh in 1549.

According to his first and principal biographer, George Carleton, bishop of Chichester, who had been a pupil at his school, at this time Gilpin 'seemed a great upholder of the Popish religion', though he was an adherent of the 'liberal' interpretation of the faith favoured by Tunstall and Pole. Consequently, when in 1549 he became involved in a series of debates with John Hooper, at that time leader of advanced protestants in London, and Pietro Martire Vermigli (known as Peter Martyr) he began to have doubts and 'the zeal which I had for the Popish religion began to cool in me every day more and more' (Marcombe, 22). This cooling did not arise from reading the writings of Martin Luther but from a study of the Bible and the ancient fathers of the church. Gilpin concluded not only that the Catholic church was outwardly corrupt, but also that it had usurped the authority of God by creating false doctrine in matters such as transubstantiation and salvation by good works. The process of alienation, culminating with the notion that the pope was Antichrist, was completed by pronouncements from the Council of Trent, which did no more than reinforce the traditional doctrinal pattern. With opinions such as this Gilpin emerged as a prominent preacher under Edward VI. He preached before the court at Greenwich in 1552 and obtained a general preaching licence in 1553. His court sermon illustrates not only his powerful rhetoric but also the fact that, like Hugh Latimer, he was a man who saw an intimate connection between Christianity and the everyday world. As well as attacking clerical abuses, rack renting, engrossing, and enclosure came in for criticism, avarice being seen as the root cause of most of the ills that beset the state.

Shortly before the death of Edward VI Gilpin was sent overseas by his patron, Bishop Tunstall, to arrange for the publication of Tunstall's book on the eucharist. During this time he visited his brother George at Malines; worked in the library of the Franciscans at Louvain; spent some time at Antwerp; and lodged with the printer Vascosanus in Paris. It was an experience that not only broadened his horizons but also enabled him to avoid the traumas of Tunstall's imprisonment, the succession plot, and the Catholic restoration under Mary. His studies were funded by his presentation to the rectory of Thornton in the Moors, Cheshire, in 1553 and to the vicarage of Norton, Durham, in 1554, though his non-residence caused him pangs of conscience. On his return to England in 1556 he resigned Norton, and Tunstall made him archdeacon of Durham, an appointment that carried with it the rich rectory of Easington. Although by this time Gilpin was clearly reconciled to Catholicism, enough of his earlier reputation survived to make his tenure of the archdeaconry a testing and uncomfortable experience. He continued to preach against clerical corruption and some suspect doctrinal pronouncements, over the sensitive issues of salvation and clerical marriage, suggested to some that he remained a closet protestant. John Tunstall, rector of Haughton-le-Skerne and another relative of the bishop, was 'very hot' against the archdeacon and complaints were presented to Bishop Tunstall on two occasions (Marcombe, 24–5). The bishop did his best to protect his protégé but in 1558 the allegations reached the ears of Edmund Bonner, bishop of London, and Gilpin anticipated his trial and martyrdom, instructing his servant, William Airey, to procure a long and comely garment for the stake. Happily for Gilpin, Queen Mary's death and the accession of Elizabeth in 1558 ushered in a regime much more in line with his moderate doctrinal views. Nevertheless, he had some doubts about specific aspects of the church settlement and when his kinsman Edwin Sandys, bishop-elect of Worcester, invited him to preach at the royal visitation at Durham in 1559 Gilpin had a sleepless night and confessed 'I did never feel such a want of utterance' (Carleton, 131–2). Having unsuccessfully attempted to avoid subscription, he was co-opted onto the visitorial commission and travelled with it to Cumberland, Westmorland, and Lancashire. Despite his reluctance, he was an important convert and, more than most, represented the continuity of the protestant tradition in the north.

In 1560 Gilpin resigned the archdeaconry and the rectory of Easington in order to concentrate on his rectory of Houghton-le-Spring, co. Durham, to which he had been presented by Tunstall in 1557. Houghton was the wealthiest living in the diocese, with 286 households in 1563. It was worth about £400 per annum and his splendid rectory 'seemed like a bishop's palace' (Carleton, 107). It was this, coupled with his unhappy experiences as archdeacon, that caused him to turn down the bishopric of Carlisle when it was offered to him through the earl of Bedford's influence in 1560 and the provostship of Queen's College, Oxford, in 1561. Sandys made an unsuccessful effort to persuade him to accept Carlisle (which he himself had also declined and there were those who thought that his preference for 'the peaceful tranquillity of private life' was 'blameworthy'. But others were more sanguine. On his return from Scotland at about this time the secretary of state William Cecil paused at Houghton, where he was impressed by Gilpin's hospitality and courteous welcome. Climbing to the top of Rainton Hill he surveyed the huge parish and commented 'What doth he want that a bishopric could more enrich him withall? Besides that he is free from the greater weight of cares' (ibid., 111–15).

As a former archdeacon with powerful friends at court Gilpin was indeed in a unique position. Moreover, after the death of his patron, Bishop Tunstall, he established a close friendship with the new bishop, James Pilkington, enthroned on 10 April 1561, and gradually any doubts that may have lingered about the settlement of 1559 were resolved. Certainly he owned books by Calvin, though he escaped the vestiarian charges that involved some of the Durham clergy in the 1560s and he appears to have had little sympathy with advanced nonconformity. At Houghton he set the example of a model incumbent in caring for his benefice and parishioners. He spent about £300 on the repair of the parsonage, kept open table for all his parishioners on a Sunday, and provided a pot of boiled meat for the poor on Thursdays. Stories of individual acts of charity abound, such as Gilpin's spontaneous gift of a horse to a poor husbandman when he saw the man's plough horse drop dead in its traces. His main concern was with Catholics and the likelihood that recusants, especially those sent to him for conversion, might undermine the beliefs of his parishioners. 'A mischief doth increase easily and spread and creep further in one day than good lessons in a whole month' (Carleton, 73).

Gilpin's influence spread far beyond his parish in all sorts of ways. The most celebrated example of this is the preaching tours that he carried out during the winter months in Tynedale and Redesdale, the most desolate and godless parts of the diocese. During these expeditions, made necessary by the shortage of adequate clergy in Northumberland, he showed great personal courage and fortitude. At Rothbury when two armed factions arrived at church during his sermon he pacified them and went on to preach against the deadly feud 'that barbarous and bloody custom of theirs' (Carleton, 117). At another Northumberland church a glove hung as a silent challenge to anyone who dared remove it. Not only did Gilpin take it down, he went on to preach against 'these inhuman challenges … and so laboured to persuade them to a reconciliation and to the practice of mutual love and charity amongst themselves' (ibid., 118). A more permanent solution to the lack of clergy lay in education. Probably from

1560, at least, Gilpin educated deserving pupils on a private basis at Houghton and in 1570 there was an abortive attempt to found a school there. Eventually on 2 April 1574 Kepier School was established by letters patent, the project being a partnership between Gilpin and John Heath, a London merchant who had purchased the estates of the dissolved hospital of Kepier. Heath was persuaded to transfer part of his property to the school and more was purchased by Gilpin and added to the endowment. Despite some difficulties over the title to the tithes and pensions with which the school was endowed, it appears to have flourished, and it produced some notable scholars, among them Henry Airey, later provost of Queen's College, Oxford, and George Carleton. The fact that the school received no statutes underlines Gilpin's intention to maintain a personal, active involvement and it is clear that he had a close interest in his scholars, who were often supported in their university studies or when difficulties beset them in later years. For example, in the mid-1570s he persuaded a former pupil, John Robson, to return to Durham to take on the poorly endowed curacy of St Andrew's, Auckland. When in 1581 Robson began to encounter opposition from the impropriator, Christopher Pickering, Gilpin wrote on his behalf to the chancellor of the exchequer, Sir Walter Mildmay, and was instrumental in obtaining the crown vicarage of Hart for Robson in 1584. He regarded himself primarily as an educationist and once stated that if he lost his living a teaching post would be more congenial to him in any case.

Gilpin's last years were blighted by a well-publicized quarrel with Bishop Pilkington's successor, Richard Barnes, consecrated in 1577. Barnes was broadly unsympathetic to anyone who had been close to Pilkington but the immediate cause of the dispute was visitation fees levied by the bishop's brother and commissary, John Barnes, rector of Haughton-le-Skerne, who had been significantly involved in episcopal business. Another dimension was provided by Hugh Broughton, a former pupil of Gilpin, who had returned to the diocese from Cambridge and was enjoying the patronage of Barnes. Broughton and Gilpin had never seen eye to eye and the fact that both he and John Barnes had interests in the next advowson of Houghton gave them a prime motive for wanting to see Gilpin removed so that their own financial ambitions might be achieved.

Gilpin's troubles began when he was suspended for failing to appear at a visitation that coincided with one of his preaching tours in Northumberland. Despite his suspension he was required to appear at the next visitation at Chester-le-Street and, at the last moment, to preach. Gilpin, who had not prepared a sermon, returned to a familiar theme and roundly condemned the corruption of the bishop's administration, adding that it was no good Barnes feigning ignorance, as he usually did, because now all of the issues had been brought before him in as direct a manner as possible. Gilpin's friends were dismayed and believed 'you have … put a sword into his hand to slay you', but the tough talking apparently had the opposite effect (Carleton, 154). Travelling home with him to Houghton, Barnes accompanied Gilpin into his parlour and famously declared:

> Father Gilpin, I acknowledge you are fitter to be Bishop of Durham than myself to be parson of this church of yours: I ask forgiveness for errors past … so long as I shall live Bishop of Durham, be secure, no man shall injure you. (ibid., 155)

Barnes's unexpected reaction was probably not wholly altruistic. There were those who wrote down all that was said during the sermon and Gilpin still had powerful friends at court who might have made Barnes's position uncomfortable.

After 1580 Gilpin's health was failing and following a collision with an ox in Durham market place he was left weakened and lame. He died, probably at Houghton-le-Spring, on 4 March 1584, when he was described as aged sixty-six, and was buried beneath a simple altar tomb at Houghton on the following day. Though he was a supporter of clerical marriage he had remained celibate and apparently lived simply. Carleton says 'He was tall of stature and slender, being hawk-nosed. His clothes were ever such as cost not very dear … In all things belonging to his own body he was very frugal and retained the austerity of the ancient'. He wrote his will on 17 October 1582 during a visitation of the plague at Houghton, most of the bequests going to the benefit of Kepier School and its scholars, his parishioners, family, and friends. The parish gained a fund of £60 thanks to Gilpin, the interest on which was distributed annually to the poor by the churchwardens. In 1626 his pupil George Carleton published his *Vita Bernardi Gilpin*, which contains much firsthand material written by Gilpin himself. Further studies have followed. The result of these was to create a legend of Gilpin as the Apostle of the North and 'an Elizabethan saint'. Although Carleton was both a relative and a pupil of Gilpin, writing more than forty years after his death, his thoughts on his mentor are broadly confirmed by what little documentary evidence has survived and by Carleton's own reputation as a meticulous scholar. Certainly Gilpin was highly regarded in his own time and has continued to be so ever since. His reputation superseded mere hagiography. The fact that he sometimes fell short of his own self-imposed standard was a matter of concern to him, just as it was to others, who, with little justification, sometimes called him a hypocrite. DAVID MARCOMBE

Sources G. Carleton, *Vita Bernardi Gilpin* (1628); C. Wordsworth, *Ecclesiastical biography*, 4 (1818) [repr. (in translation)] • D. Marcombe, 'Bernard Gilpin: anatomy of an Elizabethan legend', *Northern History*, 16 (1980) • C. S. Collingwood, *Memoirs of Bernard Gilpin* (1884) • W. Gilpin, *Life of Bernard Gilpin* (1753) • G. Battiscombe, *Bernard Gilpin* (1947) • Foster, *Alum. Oxon.* • *The registers of Cuthbert Tunstall … and James Pilkington*, ed. G. Hinde, SurtS, 161 (1952) • [W. Greenwell], ed., *Wills and inventories from the registry at Durham*, 2, SurtS, 38 (1860) • C. Sturge, *Cuthbert Tunstall* (1938) • M. Lewins, *Life of Bernard Gilpin, Apostle of the North* (1850) • G. H. Ross-Lewin, *Father Gilpin* (1901) • G. Every, 'Letters of an Elizabethan saint', *Church Quarterly Review*, 127 (1937), 82–99

Archives Bodl. Oxf., letters and papers • LPL, family papers

Likenesses portrait, repro. in Collingwood, *Memoirs of Bernard Gilpin*, frontispiece

Gilpin [*married name* Sadler], **Eva Margaret** (1868–1940), headmistress and educationist, was born on 25 March 1868, at Nottingham, the second daughter of Edmund Octavius Gilpin, a stockbroker, and his wife, Margaret, *née* Binns. Her parents, who were Quakers, could claim some distinguished forebears: three clergy, two artists, an MP, a diplomat, and a headmaster of Cheam School. Eva's younger brother, Edmund Henry (Harry) Gilpin (1876–1950), became director of a large engineering firm, was active in the Liberal Party, and was knighted. She was educated at Ackworth School, a Quaker boarding-school near Pontefract, Yorkshire; its curriculum concentrated on Bible study and the learning of texts, together with penmanship, plainness, clarity of speech and, above all, reverence for the truth. History was particularly well taught, while art consisted of mechanical or representational drawing, and craftsmanship. She left school about 1883, and became a pupil-teacher at a private school in Holland Park, London, run by the Misses Lecky, sisters of the historian William E. H. Lecky.

In 1892 Gilpin went as governess to her Quaker cousins, William and Anna Harvey of Ilkley, Yorkshire, to take charge of the education of five of their seven children. Among the many guests were two cousins, Mary Harvey and her husband, the educationist Michael Ernest *Sadler (1861–1943), who brought their son Michael Thomas Harvey Sadler (later Sadleir) to live with the Harvey family and be placed under the care of Eva Gilpin during term time. The imaginative and articulate children in the Harvey nursery-cum-schoolroom were captivated by Gilpin's enthusiasm and inventiveness.

In 1895 Gilpin moved with the Sadler family to Weybridge. She had for some time been 'cherishing a vague aspiration to start a children's school'. Having passed her London matriculation in mathematics and Latin in August 1897, she opened and began to run a small school, later to be known as the Hall School, initially in a single room in Weybridge village hall in 1898. Sadler expressed admiration of her work, encouraged his acquaintances to send their children to her school, made reference to it in public lectures, and quite possibly co-financed it with the Harvey family. Two successful years later Gilpin was able to move into her own home, Chesterton, in Prince's Road, Weybridge.

Slowly the school expanded to encompass the entire building and the curriculum developed, with Latin and French added in the early 1900s. In 1906 Gilpin travelled to Rome with the Sadler family and in subsequent years she visited the Loire valley, Paris, and Germany. While on a trip to an educational conference in Leipzig she and a Slade-trained colleague saw examples of the use of linocuts in schools. On their return tools were made out of umbrella spokes, and thereafter books—which were to become such a feature of life at the school—contained linocuts, woodcuts, and later lithographic illustrations. By 1912 Gilpin had visited the experimental institute of Jacques Dalcroze in Hellerau, Germany, after receiving ecstatic accounts from M. T. H. Sadleir and her cousin John Wilfred Harvey (1889–1967), who had coined the word 'eurhythmics' to translate the German 'rhythmische Gymnastik', which was Dalcroze's own name for his teaching. At the Hall School, Dalcroze's teachings, which were promoted by Michael Sadler, informed not only music but also drama by giving pupils a new medium of expression.

In 1915 Gilpin produced 'The Village Hall, Weybridge', the first book made and bound by pupils with woodcut, stencil, etching, and hecto-ink copy illustrations. A school parliament, called the 'Court', was introduced, where children could raise issues of the day and debate topics of import relating to the running and future planning of the school. A student from later years, Primrose Boyd (Hubbard), described Gilpin as looking like Mrs Noah:

> The hair was brown, parted in the middle and drawn back into a small bun placed high at the back of her head. Her cheekbones were high, and she had a patch of red on each cheek. Her mouth was tight and small, her chin abrupt and firm, but her nose was not a Noah nose, it was long and enquiring. Her eyes were small and grey with hooded lids. Her figure was like Mrs Noah's, robust, buxom and well-corseted. As she walked she held herself very upright and her head was held high up from her neck. (Sharwood-Smith, 49)

Gilpin's teaching methods were ahead of their time. Children were taught in mixed ability classes and parts of the curriculum were aimed 'at a living synthesis'. This form of 'integration' was partially achieved through subject specialists teaching unfamiliar subjects. Another novel form of learning was the expeditions—visits to places around London or Oxford, that informed the facts and figures learned in school. Skills were also taught, foremost the skills of communication. The co-operative rather than the competitive approach of the school facilitated communication, with groups working together on projects such as enacting scenes from history or collating cuttings about current affairs. Younger pupils attracted bonus points for their group if they became first-time speakers.

Subjects such as French, Latin, and maths were taught in classrooms in a more formal manner. French language and culture, with history, were the intellectual passions of Gilpin's life. In addition to eurhythmic dancing, there were also art, nature study, and games. Visiting teachers included the artist John Nash, probably through the good offices of Michael Sadler, who collected pictures by both John and his brother Paul; some of Sadler's collection of paintings, by artists such as Paul Gauguin, adorned the walls of the Hall School. Gilpin's feelings about games can be summed up by a pupil's recalling her attempt to persuade the games mistress 'that cricket would be a much better and faster game if bowling took place indiscriminately from both ends' (Sharwood-Smith, 23). E. M. Forster, who lived in Weybridge, often attended the Hall School plays, which in the case of 'The Ballad of Sir Patrick Spens' (1920) he favourably reviewed for the *Times Educational Supplement*. In 1920 the school also took part in a rally of local schools celebrating the foundation of the League of Nations, with children dressed in the national costumes and holding flags of the various countries. The school was also, atypically for the period, open to children with physical or mental disabilities.

After attending a youth conference, in 1926, at the Château de Bierville in France, which had been turned into a peace centre by its owner Marc Sangnier, Eva Gilpin formed an idea for bringing English, French, and German children together to improve their love and respect of one another's language and as a means to foster understanding between the three most powerful nations of Europe. In her pioneering and typically meticulous manner she set about creating what became known as 'international gatherings'; the first was held in Bierville in 1927. There 150 children from the three nations met for seventeen days preparing in the mornings various entertainments to be performed in each other's mother tongue in the evenings, while the afternoons were devoted to sport or excursions. The helpers included John Harvey, who had by then become a professor of philosophy. Thereafter, 'gatherings' took place in locations in each country in turn, until 1937 when the aggressive militarism and anti-Jewish climate of Germany brought them to a close.

In 1931 Mary Harvey, Michael Ernest Sadler's wife, died. In autumn 1934 Sadler proposed marriage to Eva Gilpin, and was accepted. They were married on 18 December 1934, the year she handed over the running of the Hall School to her niece, Monica Brooks. For five years Sadler and Gilpin entertained, sketched, and toured. After suffering peritonitis of the abdomen, followed by an operation, she died of heart failure at their home, The Rookery, Headington, Oxford, on 23 September 1940. She was buried at Rose Hill cemetery, Oxford.

Although many of Eva Gilpin's former pupils have kept her name alive through reunions, continuing friendships, and publications, she remains a relatively unknown figure in the world of education. Her innovations at the Hall School, and her life and pioneering teaching methods, deserve to be re-assessed and celebrated by a wider audience. Child-centred teaching never goes out of fashion. As she recalled in her farewell speech at Weybridge in December 1934, 'education … is an art as well as a science and the supreme thing in it is, I feel, what I may call the kindling of the spark—the quickening touch which makes things live and glow' (Henderson, 27).

ADRIAN GLEW

Sources J. Henderson and others, eds., *A lasting spring: Miss Gilpin and the Hall School, Weybridge, 1898–1934* (1988) • J. Sharwood-Smith, 'Miss Gilpin and the village hall', 1991, Tate collection • J. MacGibbon, *I meant to marry him* (1984) • *The Friend* (11 Oct 1940) • M. Sadleir, *Michael Ernest Sadler … 1861–1943: a memoir by his son* (1949)
Archives Bodl. Oxf., Sadler papers • priv. coll. • Tate collection, TGA 2000/1. 33; TGA 2001/1. 17 • Tate collection, Sadler papers, TGA 8221 | U. Leeds, Brotherton L., Sadler papers | SOUND priv. coll.
Likenesses M. Sadler?, photograph, 1938, repro. in Henderson and others, eds., *Lasting spring*, frontispiece
Wealth at death £9613 18*s*. 6*d*.: probate, 1941, *CGPLA Eng. & Wales*

Gilpin, George (*d.* 1602), diplomat and translator, was the second son of Edwin Gilpin of Kentmere, Westmorland, and Margaret Layton of Dalemain, Cumberland, and the elder brother of Bernard *Gilpin (1516–1584). He apparently studied civil law at Malines in the early 1550s, and converted to protestantism not long thereafter. He is noted as a merchant in the Low Countries in the 1550s, and became more involved in the political scene once Queen Elizabeth acceded. Speaking Dutch as few other Elizabethans did, he first appears officially as Sir Thomas Gresham's secretary during the latter's activities, diplomatic and financial, in the Low Countries in 1560. Gilpin provided continuity in the post as Gresham perambulated between London and Antwerp between 1560 and 1563. He subsequently performed the same duties for John Shers, Gresham's replacement, in the first half of 1564. Gresham and the earl of Bedford were Gilpin's earliest patrons. In 1561 the queen in a letter to Sir Thomas Gresham promised to be a friend to his secretary Gilpin in any reasonable suit, and he seems to have become a formal servant of the English government shortly afterwards.

Financial dealings were a fitting internship for Gilpin, since he frequently served as the agent for procuring and repaying Elizabeth's loans in both Germany and the Low Countries during the rest of the reign, as well as being something of a paymaster for various diplomatic agents. Besides having substantial financial responsibilities, it is also clear that he was a primary source of intelligence. He was highly conversant with Dutch affairs, reporting judiciously and comprehensively in his frequent dispatches. This was certainly the report of Valentine Dale in 1564, and others later in the reign, although it was also alleged that Gilpin was too venal to do the queen's business properly. In 1564 he played a leading role in the short-lived effort to remove the English cloth mart from Antwerp to Emden. Gilpin remained until his death one of the queen's principal sources of information and advice on the Low Countries, and was an increasingly visible intermediary in Anglo-Dutch relations.

By 1564 Gilpin had become the secretary for the Merchant Adventurers in Antwerp, from where he continued news-gathering and periodic diplomatic employment. In essence he was the English chargé d'affaires (at a time before this term was widely used), for his diplomatic responsibilities were continuous, serving as a backdrop to the steady stream of English special ambassadors to the area. This matched the queen's clear predilection for using Englishmen abroad at someone else's expense for diplomatic objectives. One of Gilpin's more specific duties was an association with William Davison in his mission from 1577 until 25 May 1579. In June 1582 the queen dispatched Gilpin to the imperial diet and emperor at Augsburg to protect the interests of the Merchant Adventurers in the Hanse towns. While the diet voted to ban the English merchants from the empire, the emperor Rudolph apparently refused to publish the decree—thus neutralizing it. Gilpin's energetic remonstrations are given credit for the successful dénouement. He also apparently undertook to secure the release of Daniel Rogers, his own predecessor as secretary to the Merchant Adventurers. Rogers had been imprisoned by mistake while undertaking royal service and then languished in captivity for four long years while awaiting a ransom. Gilpin was less successful in this endeavour, though he intermittently pursued a resolution over the next several years. He returned from the emperor to Antwerp in October 1582.

Gilpin's more formal diplomatic employment began in March 1586, when he became the English secretary on the Dutch council of state. He also served as a secretary to its required English councillor, in a role comparable to being the secretary of a diplomatic legation. About 30 June 1593 he replaced Sir Thomas Bodley as the accredited English councillor, at 20*s*. a day, and served in that role for the rest of his life. In this post he acted as an intelligence agent for both Lord Burghley and Robert, earl of Essex.

Gilpin spent little time in England during Elizabeth's reign. Besides his official remuneration, he benefited from the small perquisites that accrued to a lower-level official: a monopoly for making an oven 'more economical of using wood', and possibly, in 1577, a patent for arrearages on certain concealed lands. In 1585 and then again in 1587 he may be the George Gilpin noted as a JP for Westmorland. He had, by the late 1580s, apparently moved into the earl of Essex's orbit, since much of his correspondence from the Low Countries, which had previously gone to Sir Francis Walsingham, now went to the earl.

Gilpin was also an accomplished translator. He published a (now rare) translation from the Dutch of the *Apiarium Romanum* (1571) by Philip von Marnix, seigneur de St Aldegonde. The first edition of 1579 was entitled *The bee-hive of the Romishe churche, wherein the author, a zealous protestant, under the person of a superstitious papist, doth so driely refell the grose opinions of popery, and so divinely defend the articles of Christianitie, that (the sacred scriptures excepted) there is not a booke to be founde either more necessarie for they profite, or sweeter for they comforte*. It was dedicated to Philip Sidney. The second edition followed in 1580. These translations, plus a lively interest in the religious and literary controversies of the day, brought him into the circle of poets and patrons in the Low Countries that at times included Sidney, Daniel Rogers, the earl of Leicester, Hotman, Dousas, and others. Gilpin died in service, probably in the Netherlands, in late September 1602, a fact announced in a letter to Dudley Carleton, a relative, and was presumably buried there. A will has not been discovered. GARY M. BELL

Sources J. Buxton, *Sir Philip Sidney and the English Renaissance*, 2nd edn (1966) • J. van Dorsten, *Poets, patrons and professors* (1962) • Baron Kervyn de Lettenhove [J. M. B. C. Kervyn de Lettenhove] and L. Gilliodts-van Severen, eds., *Relations politiques des Pays-Bas et de l'Angleterre sous le règne de Philippe II*, 11 vols. (Brussels, 1882–1900) • T. Lloyd, *England and the German Hanse, 1157–1611* (1991) • C. Wilson, *Queen Elizabeth and the revolt of the Netherlands* (1970) • R. B. Wernham, *After the Armada: Elizabethan England and the struggle for western Europe, 1588–1595* (1984) • R. B. Wernham, *The return of the armadas: the last years of the Elizabethan war against Spain, 1595–1603* (1994) • *CSP for.*, 1559–89 • *CSP dom.*, 1547–80, i–vi • PRO, E403/2560, 2597, 2655–2658, 2674, 2721 • BL, Cotton MSS, Galba c.vii, c.ix • BL, Harley MS 285 • PRO, SP 80/1, SP 83, and 84 • G. D. Ramsay, *The City of London in international politics at the accession of Elizabeth Tudor* (1975) • P. E. J. Hammer, *The polarisation of Elizabethan politics: the political career of Robert Devereux, 2nd earl of Essex, 1585–1597* (1999) • *DNB*

Archives PRO, corresp., SP 83–84 | CKS, letters to earl of Leicester • Lincs. Arch., corresp. with Lord Willoughby

Gilpin, Randolph [Randall] (**1593/4–1661/2**), Church of England clergyman, may have been born into the Gilpin family living at Bungay, Suffolk, or at Aldingham, Lancashire. He was educated at Eton before matriculating aged seventeen on 4 July 1611 at King's College, Cambridge. He was awarded a fellowship from 1614, graduated BA the following year, and proceeded MA in 1618. He served as minister of St Benet's, Cambridge, in 1625–6 and held university office in 1627.

When the fleet sailed to the relief of the protestants of La Rochelle in 1628 Gilpin acted as their chaplain. Either that year or in 1629, when he relinquished his fellowship, Francis Gilpin, probably a kinsman, presented him to the rectory of Barningham, Suffolk. Gilpin lived unharmoniously with his parishioners. Disputes about alleged tithing customs led to multiple suits in 'Chancery, in the Court of Arches, in the Court of Requests, and two suits at law' (*CSP dom., 1637*, 478–9). On 17 October 1637 Gilpin petitioned the king, requesting that the whole matter might be referred to the archbishop of Canterbury and the bishop of Norwich. When the case was heard in Star Chamber on 24 January 1636 an order was made adjusting the tithes, but Gilpin and his parishioners received a lecture from Archbishop William Laud on their duty to 'frame themselves to live in a more quiet and peaceable manner' (*CSP dom., 1637*, 478–9).

Gilpin claimed, when petitioning in 1660, that he had been ejected from his living fourteen or fifteen years earlier. During the Commonwealth he composed a work dedicated to Eton School entitled *Liturgica sacra; Curru Thesbitico, i.e. Zeli inculpabilis vehiculo deportata, & via devotionis regia deducta a Rand. Gilpin, sacred, vel, Opsonia spiritualia omnibus vere Christianis, etiam pueris degustanda* (1657). At the Restoration he was created DD by royal mandate. He also obtained from the king the rectory of Worlingham, Suffolk, on 10 May 1661. His will, dated 9 November that year, requested that he be buried in St Mary's Church, Bungay, Suffolk, and named his brother Richard as the chief beneficiary. He died within the next two months, the will being proved on 11 January 1662.

GORDON GOODWIN, *rev.* S. L. SADLER

Sources *CSP dom., 1637–8*, 183 • will, PRO, PROB 11/307, fol. 44 • *Seventh report*, HMC, 6 (1879), 106a • W. Kennet, *A register and chronicle* (1728) • Venn, *Alum. Cant.*, 1/2.218 • *Walker rev.*, 335 • Wing, *STC* • T. Harwood, *Alumni Etonenses, or, A catalogue of the provosts and fellows of Eton College and King's College, Cambridge, from the foundation in 1443 to the year 1797* (1797), 213

Wealth at death left numerous cash bequests to friends and family: will, PRO, PROB 11/307, fol. 44

Gilpin, Richard (**1625–1700**), nonconformist minister and physician, was born in October 1625 in Strickland Ketel township, Westmorland, and baptized on 23 October in the parish church at Kendal, the second son of Isaac Gilpin (*d*. in or after 1649) of Strickland and his wife, Ann (*d*. in or after 1664), daughter of Ralph Tunstall of Coatham Mundeville, Durham. Bernard *Gilpin (1516–1584) was his great-uncle. He may have been a chorister at Durham Cathedral before studying medicine and then divinity at Edinburgh University, from where he graduated MA on 30 July 1646.

By this time Gilpin's family had been scattered as a result of the civil war. His father and a brother (probably Henry (*bap.* 1623)) took up arms for parliament, although Isaac was active for only six months. Following the seizure of his house and destruction of some of his goods, for which he blamed orders from the royalist commander, the earl of Newcastle, Isaac was by 1645 resident in Durham and an elder in the local classis. Briefly keeper of the Bear Park outside the city, he had lost this post by July 1646, when he petitioned the committee for compounding for its return. He was subsequently assistant master at Durham Cathedral grammar school, for which he received a £10 salary in 1649. At least one source suggests that Richard Gilpin also taught at the school, but like much of the evidence for his early career, this cannot be substantiated. At some point he was ordained, but it is not clear by whom or with what rite. Edmund Calamy claimed that he began his ministry at Lambeth and continued it at the Savoy under John Wilkins, afterwards bishop of Chester. By 1 May 1649 he was administering the sacrament in Durham Cathedral and by 2 October 1650, when he was described as a minister of Durham, he was receiving arrears on £150 owed him from former dean and chapter lands.

In late 1652 or early 1653 Gilpin became rector of Greystoke, Cumberland. The living, from which William Morland had been sequestered in 1650, was one of the richest in the county and worth £300 a year. Gilpin supplied its four chapels with preachers and organized the parish on the congregational model with an inner circle of communicants and a staff of deacons. He would probably have preferred a presbyterian system, but this was not adopted in Cumberland. Like Westmorland, the county was perceived by Gilpin and others as particularly notable for its religious ignorance and its profanity. In 1653 he was instrumental in organizing local clergy and their congregations into an association similar to that contemporaneously promoted by Richard Baxter in Worcestershire; its terms, published as *The agreement of the associated ministers & churches of the counties of Cumberland and Westmorland* (1656), gave the clergy somewhat larger powers than Baxter approved. In 1654 Gilpin was assistant to the commission for the four northern counties, and his name appears on many ministerial licences throughout the 1650s.

Gilpin's *The Temple Rebuilt* (1658), a sermon preached at Keswick on 19 May 1658 in celebration of the association, hints at the fissiparous pressures it struggled to contain, Gilpin stating that it was not the intention 'to cut off the liberty of particular Congregations' (Nightingale, 1.106). From the beginning the local implementation of Gilpin's conception of parish reformation was threatened by missionary effort by Quakers. In the 'Explication' of *The Agreement of the Associated Ministers* they are highlighted as the 'supremum malum' (greatest evil), and Gilpin was sorely troubled with 'this impetuous wild spirit' (ibid., 1.101–2, 2.1266). They disturbed him in the pulpit during worship and subjected him to aggressive cross-questioning, drawing away some of his parishioners. One of the earliest reconversion narratives is that of his kinsman, John Gilpin of Kendal, dated 4 July 1653 and published as *The Quakers Shaken, or, A Firebrand Snach'd out of the Fire*, while the defection of one Henry Winder caused him and his friends particular distress. In 1658 the Cumberland Quaker Joseph Helling singled out Gilpin from among the 'parish masters' who filled 'up the measures of both Scribes and Pharisees and the papists, persecuting and fighting themselves', as one who 'pushed me with his hand, calling me a simple foole and threatening me with prison and clapping by the heeles' (ibid., 1.321). The friction was to last several decades.

On 16 September 1656 at Thursby Gilpin married Susanna Brisco (1625–1715) of Crofton; they had thirteen children between 1657 and 1677. At some point in the 1650s he bought Scaleby Castle, north of Carlisle, formerly the property of the royalist Musgrave family. Under patent dated 15 May 1657 he was appointed visitor to the college at Durham, newly established by Oliver Cromwell.

The Restoration at first made little difference to Gilpin's career. He preached an assize sermon at Carlisle on 10 September 1660, and was subsequently offered the see of Carlisle. He declined, motivated according to Calamy by modesty, reinforced by the recollection that Bernard Gilpin had refused a bishopric under Elizabeth I. However, on 2 February 1661 he resigned his living in favour of the sequestered Morland; Thomas Gibbon of Greystoke suggested in 1707 that Gilpin would have stayed in the rectory and conformed to the 1662 settlement had he managed to persuade Morland to 'quit his claim' (Nightingale, 1.369–70). He does not seem to have been rigid on issues of church government, and continued to frequent prayer-book services and to speak favourably of the Church of England. A Baxterian, his concern was always for a pastoral ministry, and his 'close adherence to Scripture-revelation made him disrelish those wanton and idle speculations, which bold witts he saw venturing on more and more' (*Ambrose Barnes*, 147). Retiring to Scaleby Castle, he ministered to the medical and spiritual needs of his poor neighbours, whom he called 'on Sundays into a great arched hall in his castle, which he had fitted up as a chapel' (Gilpin, *Memoirs*, 6). He also preached at Penruddock, where John Noble gathered a congregation in his own house.

By 1663 the persecution of nonconformists in Cumberland had escalated under the administration of Sir Philip Musgrave and Gilpin seems to have spent more time in Newcastle. On 1 November he led a 'congregation of saints' in worship at the Barber Surgeons' hall in the town. That year the bishop of Durham, John Cosin, complained about him. Gilpin apparently disregarded the conventicle acts, but although he was presented, he escaped with fines. Following the Five Mile Act, Gilpin lodged in Newcastle with Ambrose Barnes, who persuaded the magistrates to let him stay in the town because of his usefulness as a doctor. Despite a prohibition from the mayor, Gilpin continued to hold meetings at the Barber Surgeons' hall, where he attracted 500 people on All Saints' day 1668, as well as in private houses. As Bishop Cosin noted, on 25 November that year the dissenters held a fast 'from eight a clock in the morning till four in the evening, the work being held forth by their four chief leaders and abettors, Mr Gilpine, Mr Durant, Mr Leaver and Mr Pringle' (*Ambrose Barnes*, 405). Cosin upbraided the corporation for its reticence in prosecuting such offenders, and it is clear that several members were sympathetic to the meetings. The bishop was told on 7 April 1669 that Gilpin also held 'frequent assemblies', avoiding both civil and ecclesiastical jurisdiction, by 'flitting between Newcastle and Carlisle, situate in 2 dioceses' (*CSP dom., 1668–9*, 268–9). Informed on for holding a meeting in his house at White Friars, Newcastle, that summer, Gilpin's last arraignment for holding a conventicle was on 4 August; after that he seems to have been left alone.

In Newcastle, Gilpin became prosperous as a result of appreciative congregations and patients. Having possibly arrived in the town with relatively little medical experience, he apparently acquired knowledge from one Dr Tonstall, probably one of his mother's kin. To regularize his medical practice he went to the University of Leiden in the Netherlands. He was awarded the MD on 6 July 1676, following a disputation before Professor Spinaeus (with whom he lodged), published as *Disputatio medica inauguralis de hysterica passione* (1676). His research was focused on the medical understanding of enthusiasm and melancholy; some of his letters on the subject appear in Timothy Rogers, *A Discourse Concerning Trouble of the Mind, and the Disease of Melancholy* (1691).

The year after gaining his doctorate, Gilpin published *Daemonologia sacra, or, A Treatise of Satan's Temptations* (1677), composed six years earlier in Newcastle. The title is somewhat misleading. Its literary topos is not that of continental demonology, with its emphasis on *malleus*, a rebellion against God and an all-pervasive witchcraft which had to be extirpated. Nor, unlike works by Joseph Glanville, Richard Baxter, and Increase Mather, is it concerned with that other literary form, the collection of wonders and illustrious providences. On the other hand, it shares the aims of Glanville and Henry More to combat atheism by proving the existence of witchcraft and the devil. It perhaps most resembles the work of William Perkins, being above all a manual of puritan self-examination, although it also echoes the *Religio medici* of his fellow physician Sir Thomas Browne. While paying the attention to phenomenological evidence appropriate to a man charged with curing bodies, Gilpin constructs a providential model in which God permits a strong Satan to chastise weak and sinful mankind; external human agency in the form of *maleficium* is conspicuous by its absence. The battleground is the human soul. Satan exploits not only spiritual and moral failings but also psychological and medical weaknesses: he works on passions, humours, and obsessions; corrupts reason and promotes enthusiasm; utilizes spiritual fascinations, spiritual sadness, melancholy, and the peculiar puritan anxiety, fears about non-election.

Meanwhile Gilpin retained his residence at Scaleby and was still influential in Cumberland. In 1669 he survived an attempt by the Musgrave family to regain part of their former property, including Scaleby, possibly through the legal acumen of his father-in-law; he rebuilt the castle about 1680. It is clear that the Musgraves loathed Gilpin. Sir Christopher Musgrave described him on 19 February 1672 as 'a great phanatique & ye most dangerous person in ye ffoure northern Countys' (Nightingale, 1.469). Both Scaleby and Gilpin's house in Newcastle were licensed on 5 September that year as presbyterian meeting-places, and he also preached in the dissenting congregations of Cumberland, for instance on 1 October 1676 at Cockermouth, Cumberland. A case was brought against him in the court of corrections, Carlisle, on 5 December 1684.

On the other hand, Gilpin himself continued to combat Quakerism. In 1674 he defended the reconverted Henry Winder against accusations lodged by some Quakers at Carlisle assizes, supplying the court from documents he had to hand with 'a full account of … all their Revelations, Accusations and miserable Events' (Winder, 12). The Quaker evangelist Thomas Story, who had had youthful links with the Gilpin family, was invited to Scaleby Castle in 1691, having been asked by Gilpin to send him Quaker books. Story's fears that his host sought his reconversion were confirmed when Gilpin animadverted on the Quakers' denial of the Lord's supper, baptism, and the role of prayer. Yet, according to Story, they 'parted in Friendship' and Gilpin was afterwards 'much more free and familiar with me than before, or than I expected' (*Journal*, 41–5). However, Gilpin could also be irascible and combative. At a subsequent meeting on 15 October 1696, they had 'some discourse about matters of religion; in which [Gilpin] discovered more passion and prejudice than became his high profession or years, and could not bear any contradiction' (*Ambrose Barnes*, 447).

Following the death of William Durant in 1681, Gilpin received his Newcastle congregation into communion with his own. Integrating these Independents proved a challenge and Calamy noted Gilpin's skill 'in managing a numerous congregation of very different opinions and tempers' (*Ambrose Barnes*, 444). In 1687 Gilpin accepted James II's declaration of indulgence and addressed the king. He supported the Happy Union of congregationalists and presbyterians begun in London in the early 1690s. A survey of 1690–92 describes Gilpin and Mr Gill as having a substantial meeting-house which was both well-attended and well-endowed. John Pringle, the last of Gilpin's colleagues from the 1650s, died in 1692. Two years later William Pell, formerly ejected from the rectory of Great Stainton, Durham, joined Gilpin as his assistant. After the final breakdown of the Happy Union in London in 1695, Gilpin's congregation experienced tension.

According to Gilpin, in 1698 'a small party' who were the 'few remainders of Mr Durant's congregation' were persuaded by Ambrose Barnes to choose his youngest son Thomas, recently returned from London, as their minister. Gilpin allowed him to preach in the meeting-house, but the group then seceded and used the Baptist premises instead. Concluding that the group wanted to get legal title to the meeting-house and that Barnes contradicted his teaching about preparation to conversion and preached the antinomian tenets of Tobias Crispe, Gilpin publicly rebuked him. Gilpin wrote gloomily to Richard Stretton on 13 December 1698 that the dissenting interest in the north depended greatly on the state of his own congregation and that episcopalians hoped that his death would mark its demise in Newcastle. It was not that he wanted to protect his own corner to the exclusion of others, but rather that division was detrimental to all: as he observed elsewhere, differences among and between conformists and nonconformists 'daily produce effects as must needs be very pleasing to the devil' (Gilpin, *Daemonologia sacra*, 133).

Gilpin's last years were dogged by his failure to unite the various protestant dissenting factions in Newcastle and to ensure ministerial continuity for his congregation. Following the death of Pell on 2 December 1698, Timothy Manlove of Leeds was called to succeed him as Gilpin's assistant, but he too died on 3 August 1699. In his two funeral sermons for Manlove, published as *The Comforts of Divine Love* (1700), Gilpin again voiced his concerns for the future. In the next few months he wrote a preface to and published a treatise by Manlove on the immortality of the soul, and issued an updated version of an assize sermon he himself had first preached on 10 September 1660, reminding civil magistrates of their duties and commending the work of the Societies for the Reformation of Manners. By February 1700 he was seized with a feverish cold. He died of pneumonia on 13 February and was buried on 16 February in All Saints' Church, Newcastle, having asked for the funeral rites of the established church. His wife retired to Scaleby and continued to pay off the mortgage on the property. She died on 18 January 1715 on a visit to her married daughter Anne Sawrey (1660–1745) at Broughton Tower, Lancashire, and was buried at Broughton three days later. Among the Gilpins' other surviving children were: William (1657–1724), a barrister and JP, who became recorder of Carlisle in 1718 and was noted for his artistic and antiquarian tastes; Isaac (1658–1719); Dorothy (1668–1708), who married first Jabez Cay, a Newcastle physician, and secondly Eli Fenton; and John (1670–1732), a merchant at Whitehaven who made a fortune in the Virginia trade.

On his contemporaries' assessment, Gilpin was the most significant protestant dissenting minister in the four northern counties in the period 1660–1700, and a living link between the association movements of the 1650s and the 1690s. Ambrose Barnes, by no means an impartial observer, attributed to this to his longevity: he 'outlived all the ministers of his own age and time, many his superiors and most of them his equals' (*Ambrose Barnes*, 147). He depicted an old style puritan, Calvinist and evangelical, a frequent and attentive listener to sermons. Calamy noted that Gilpin himself 'preached wholly extempore, with graceful and expressive gestures … [and] from his very heart he would with pathos plead with sinners', while 'in prayer he was solemn and fervent, using scripture language extensively and with a flood of affection which often forced him to silence until he had vented it in tears' (*Ambrose Barnes*, 443–4). He 'kept, and he left [his congregation] in Peace' (Calamy, 415), but within three years, Thomas Bradbury, the assistant who arrived just before his death, had precipitated the split in his church that he had so much feared. JONATHAN H. WESTAWAY

Sources B. Nightingale, *The ejected of 1662 in Cumberland and Westmorland: their predecessors and successors* (1911), 2 vols. • R. Gilpin, *Daemonologia sacra, or, A treatise of Satan's temptations in three parts*, ed. A. B. Grosart (1867) • *Memoirs of the life of Mr Ambrose Barnes*, ed. [W. H. D. Longstaffe], SurtS, 50 (1867) • *A journal of the life of Thomas Story: containing an account of his remarkable convincement of, and embracing the principles of truth, as held by the people called Quakers*, ed. J. Wilson and J. Wilson (1747), 41–5 • *DNB* • *Calamy rev.*, 223–4 • H. Winder, *The spirit of Quakerism, and the danger of their divine revelation laid open* (1696), 12 • E. Calamy, ed., *An abridgement of Mr. Baxter's history of his life and times, with an account of the ministers, &c., who were ejected after the Restauration of King Charles II*, 2nd edn, 2 vols. (1713), 415 • E. Calamy, ed., *An abridgement of Mr. Baxter's history of his life and times, with an account of the ministers, &c., who were ejected after the Restauration of King Charles II*, 2nd edn, 2 vols. (1713), vol. 2, pp. 154 ff • E. Calamy, *A continuation of the account of the ministers … who were ejected and silenced after the Restoration in 1660*, 2 vols. (1727), 1. 226 • W. Gilpin, *Memoirs of Dr. Richard Gilpin, of Scaleby Castle in Cumberland*, ed. W. Jackson, Cumberland and Westmorland Antiquarian and Archaeological Society, extra ser., 2 (1879) • H. Winder, *A critical and chronological history of the rise, progress, declension, and revival of knowledge, chiefly religious*, ed. G. Benson, 2 vols. (1756) • J. Westaway, 'Scottish influences upon the reformed churches in north-west England, *c.* 1689–1829: a study of the ministry within the congregational and presbyterian churches in Lancashire, Cumberland and Westmorland', PhD diss., University of Lancaster, 1997, 150–205 • R. W. Innes Smith, *English-speaking students of medicine at the University of Leyden* (1932) • E. Peacock, *Index to English speaking students who have graduated at Leyden University*, Index Society (1883), 40 • *CSP dom.*, 1668–9, 73, 268–9, 342 • J. H. Colligan, 'Penruddock presbyterian meeting-house', *Transactions of the Cumberland and Westmorland Antiquarian and Archaeological Society*, new ser., 4 (1905), 150–71 • G. Whitehead, 'Brampton XVIIth century presbyterians', *Transactions of the Cumberland and Westmorland Antiquarian and Archaeological Society*, 8 (1886), 348–72 • R. Welford, *Men of mark 'twixt Tyne and Tweed*, 3 (1895), 302–9 • G. F. Nuttall and R. S. Paul, 'Editorial', *Congregational Historical Society Transactions*, 16/4 (July 1951), 163 • *The correspondence of John Cosin D.D., lord bishop of Durham*, ed. [G. Ornsby], 2, SurtS, 55 (1872), 121 • R. L. Greaves, *Enemies under his feet: radicals and nonconformists in Britain, 1664–1677* (1990), 149 • *Calendar of the correspondence of Richard Baxter*, ed. N. H. Keeble and G. F. Nuttall, 2 vols. (1991), 131, 658, 674 • J. Sharpe, *Instruments of darkness: witchcraft in England, 1550–1750* (1996), 235–51 • F. Nicholson and E. Axon, *The older nonconformity in Kendal* (1915), 250 • J. F. Curwen, *The castles and fortified towers of Cumberland, Westmorland, and Lancashire North-of-the-Sands, together with a brief historic account of Border warfare*, Cumberland and Westmorland Antiquarian and Archaeological Society, extra ser., 13 (1913), 236 • J. Hunter, *Familiae minorum gentium*, ed. J. W. Clay, 1, Harleian Society, 37 (1894), 1100 • *The journal of George Fox*, ed. N. Penney, 1 (1911), 141, 418, 422 • Bishop of Barrow in Furness, 'Bishop Nicolson's diaries', *Cumberland and Westmorland Antiquarian and Archaeological Society Transactions*, 1

(1901), 1–51 • J. Wilson, 'The earliest registers of the parish of Thursby', *Cumberland and Westmorland Antiquarian and Archaeological Society Transactions*, 14 (1897), 121–33

Archives BL, portions of deeds, incl. a deed relating to Hanslope, Add. MS 37070, A. 21, fol. 75 • BL, invitation to T. Manlove, Add. MS 38856, lot 456, fol. 114 • BL, Thoresby MSS

Likenesses engraving, BL, Hodgkin MSS • portrait, repro. in A. Chalmers, ed., *The general biographical dictionary*, vol. 15 (1814), 521 • portrait, repro. in Gilpin, *Daemonologia sacra*; priv. coll.

Gilpin, Sawrey (1733–1807), animal painter, was born at Scaleby, near Carlisle, Cumberland, on 30 October 1733, the seventh child of Captain John Bernard Gilpin (1701–1776), landscape painter, and his wife, Matilda, *née* Langstaffe (1703–1773), and younger brother of the writer on art William *Gilpin. He was a promising pupil of his father, who in 1749 sent him to London to study with the marine painter Samuel Scott. Although apprenticed for seven years and an assistant for two, the young artist was more interested in the market carts, horses, and other animals in the streets. This enthusiasm was supported by William Augustus, duke of Cumberland, ranger of Windsor Great Park in 1758, when he employed Gilpin to draw at his stud at Newmarket and at Windsor. About 1759 he made a set of expressive etchings of horses' heads to illustrate a manuscript by his brother William entitled 'On the characters of horses'; some of them were eventually published in the latter's *Remarks on Forest Scenery, and other Woodland Views* (1791). A recent historian noted that 'this work indicates that Gilpin's grasp of the problems of visual representation of the emotions of animals was as sophisticated as Stubbs's, but he never exploited it fully' (Deuchar, 'Gilpin', 646). From 1786 the artist lived in Knightsbridge, London, with his wife, Elizabeth, *née* Broom, whom he married on 6 June 1759, and with whom he had six children, including William Sawrey *Gilpin (1761/2–1843), watercolourist and landscape gardener. Gilpin exhibited with the Incorporated Society of Artists from 1762 to 1783, becoming a director in 1773 and its president in 1774. Only one excursion breaks this pattern, a tour about 1768 of the Scottish highlands, with Colonel Thornton of York and Gilpin's son-in-law George Garrard, the sculptor and painter. In 1786 Gilpin began to exhibit at the Royal Academy and this continued until his death. While the horse was his principal subject, he painted a variety of other animals; his *Death of the Fox* (engraved by John Scott) was acquired by Colonel Thornton in 1788. In 1795 he was elected ARA, and RA in 1797.

Gilpin was overshadowed by George Stubbs, ten years his senior, throughout his career. The first Earl Grosvenor, for instance, commissioned five paintings from Gilpin but eleven from his rival. Both artists, however, suffered from the low status of animal painting compared to other genres. To raise this status Stubbs explored the range of passions which the horse was capable of expressing, while Gilpin went further by means of analogy in suggesting that, like man, the horse had a personality. His source was Jonathan Swift's *Gulliver's Travels* (1726). He chose three episodes, not four (as Deuchar says), from 'A Voyage to the Houyhnhnms': (1) *Gulliver Addressing the Houyhnhnms Believing them to be Conjurors* (1768, Yale U. CBA; variant version, Government Art Collection; variant version, ex Sothebys 9 April 1997); (2) *Gulliver reprimanded … when Describing the Horrors of War* (1772, York Art Gallery; variant version, ex Sothebys 3–4 April 1978); (3) *Gulliver Taking his Final Leave of his Master, the Sorrel Nag* (1771, Yale U. CBA; variant version, ex Lenygon *c.*1919). Two of these paintings were engraved. Since each work was exhibited in a separate year, it is possible that they were not conceived originally as a series. Apart from *The Election of Darius* (1770, York Art Gallery), the subject from *The Histories* by Herodotus, Gilpin never followed up the successful Gulliver set. The demands of his large family required a steady income and thus a return to 'the meaner employment of horse-portrait painting' (Cunningham, 242). His election to the Royal Academy in 1798 gave him the opportunity, more than twenty years later, to revive his interest in anthropomorphism in his diploma work *Horses Frightened in a Thunderstorm* (1798, Royal Academy of Art, London). Unlike Stubbs, Gilpin was less interested in the anatomy of the horse than in portraying the horse in motion, as exemplified in his diploma work. In his lifetime and later Gilpin was criticized, as was Stubbs, as being incapable of adding landscape or figures to his compositions. This is transparently not the case in any of his figure paintings.

When Gilpin's wife died, probably in 1802, he was invited by his friend and patron the philanthropist Samuel Whitbread the younger to stay at Southill, Bedfordshire, where he was effectively in retirement. In 1805 he returned to London to live with his daughters at 16 Brompton Crescent until his death there on 8 March 1807.

L. H. Cust, *rev.* Peter Tomory

Sources S. Mitchell, *The dictionary of British equestrian artists* (1985) • J. Burke, *English art, 1714–1800* (1976) • E. Waterhouse, *Painting in Britain, 1530–1790*, 5th edn (1994) • artist's file, archive material, Courtauld Inst., Witt Library • O. Millar, *Southill: a regency house* (1951) • S. Deuchar, *Sporting art in eighteenth century England* (1988) • M. Pilkington, *A general dictionary of painters: containing memoirs of the lives and works*, ed. A. Cunningham, new edn (1840) • P. A. Tomory, *Sir George Beaumont and his circle* (1953) [exhibition catalogue, Leicester Museums and Art Gallery, June–July 1953] • S. Deuchar, 'Gilpin, Sawrey', *The dictionary of art*, ed. J. Turner (1996)

Archives Bodl. Oxf., corresp. and papers

Likenesses W. Sherlock, watercolour drawing, *c.*1780–1789, NPG • G. Dance, pencil drawing, 1798, RA • G. Garrard, plaster bust, 1803, Burghley, Northamptonshire • G. Dance, pencil drawing, BM • G. Garrard, marble bust, Southill, Bedfordshire

Gilpin, William (1724–1804), writer on art and headmaster, was born on 4 June 1724 at Scaleby Castle, near Carlisle, Cumberland, and baptized on 7 June, the son of Captain John Bernard Gilpin (1701–1776) and Matilda Langstaffe (1703–1773). His father was considered one of the best amateur painters of the time and included among his pupils John 'Warwick' Smith and the painter Robert Smirke. His younger brother was the animal painter Sawrey *Gilpin. He attended school at Carlisle and subsequently at St Bees School, near Whitehaven, Cumberland. In 1740 he entered Queen's College, Oxford, where he regarded the system of teaching as 'no better than solemn trifling' (Gilpin, 110). He graduated BA in 1744 and was

William Gilpin (1724–1804), by Henry Walton, 1781

ordained deacon in 1746 by George Fleming, bishop of Carlisle, and appointed to the curacy of Irthington in Cumberland. He shortly afterwards returned to Oxford to take his MA in May 1748, and in June of that year received full orders. In 1747 he preached a sermon at Buckingham, and it was probably during that period that he visited the famous gardens at Stowe, which became the subject of his anonymous *A Dialogue upon the Gardens of the Right Honourable the Lord Viscount Cobham at Stowe* (1748). In the *Dialogue* he broached, for the first time in his writings, distinctions between moral and aesthetic beauty in natural scenery and ruined buildings, and thereby laid the foundations for his later writings on the picturesque. There followed a brief period in London during which he prepared a biography of his Elizabethan ancestor Bernard Gilpin, the liberal 'Apostle of the North': this was published as *The Life of Bernard Gilpin* (1752). Gilpin was a prolific biographer and an engaging autobiographer, publishing lives of (among others) Bishop Hugh Latimer (1755), John Wycliffe (1765), and Thomas Cranmer (1784). He composed *Memoirs of Dr. Richard Gilpin … and of his posterity … together with an account of the author, by himself: and a pedigree of the Gilpin family* (ed. W. Jackson, 1879).

In 1751 or 1752 Gilpin married his first cousin, Margaret Gilpin (1725–1807), and by 1753 he had taken over the management of Cheam School for Boys, in Surrey, where he had been an occasional assistant teacher for two or three years. He was a very able teacher and an enlightened disciplinarian. Corporal punishment was largely replaced under his regime by detention and fines: the proceeds from these went to the maintenance and improvement of the school's resources as well as to charity. Vegetable and ornamental gardening was encouraged as part of a recreational programme, and from time to time the boys kept little shops at the school. The broad aim was to promote 'uprightness and utility' and 'to give them a miniature of the world they were afterwards to enter' (Gilpin, 127–8). In matters of religious instruction he concentrated on a variety of ways of making the New Testament more accessible to and valued by his pupils. This enterprise issued many years later in his publication *An Exposition of the New Testament* (1790). His addresses to the boys on church catechism were collected and abridged by him and published as *Lectures on the Catechism of the Church of England* (1779): five editions appeared over the following twenty years.

In 1777 Gilpin left Cheam to become vicar of Boldre in the New Forest, Hampshire, a living presented to him by William Mitford, which gave him an income of £600 a year. In his *Memoirs* he claimed that there were 'only two transactions of his life' which could fairly claim the attention of posterity: 'his mode of managing his school at Cheam, which was uncommon—& his mode of endowing his parish-school at Boldre, from the *profits of his amusements*, wh. was also, as far as he knows, intirely new' (Gilpin, 147–8). It is for these '*amusements*' that Gilpin is now best-known, for he is referring, somewhat slightingly, to his picturesque writings.

In 1768 Gilpin's *Essay on Prints* was published (anonymously) and received excellent reviews. His aim, as the title-page indicates, was to outline 'the Principles of picturesque Beauty, the Different Kinds of Prints, and the Characters of the most noted Masters'. The third edition in 1781 revealed the name of the author. The *Essay* defines 'picturesque' as 'a term expressive of that peculiar kind of beauty, which is agreeable in a picture' (*Essay on Prints*, 2), but does not develop the definition. That challenge was met in the series of books published between 1782 and 1809, all of which bore the same title format: *Observations on* [various regions of Britain] *relative chiefly to picturesque beauty*. He travelled widely in Britain, with his notebook and sketching materials, in order to identify locations which offered that particular kind of beauty in landscape 'which is agreeable in a picture'. Picturesque tourism constituted 'a new object of pursuit', as he wrote in the first of these books, *Observations on the River Wye* (1782): the practice recommended was 'that of not merely describing; but of adapting the description of natural scenery to the principles of artificial landscape' (*Wye*, 2). Further picturesque books, with aquatint reproductions of Gilpin's pen-and-wash drawings, included *Observations* on Cumberland and Westmorland (2 vols., 1786), the Scottish highlands (2 vols., 1789), south-west England and the Isle of Wight (1798), and the eastern counties of England and north Wales (1809). *Remarks on Forest Scenery* (1791), illustrated with etchings by his brother, Sawrey, concentrated on the New Forest, where he lived. *Three Essays* of a more analytical kind, on the nature of picturesque beauty, picturesque travel, and on the sketching of landscape, together with a poem on landscape painting, appeared in 1792. In 1804 *Two Essays* described his methods and principles in making his sketches.

In 1791, with the proceeds from his first three picturesque books (amounting to about £400), Gilpin built and endowed two little schools at Boldre. He established a fund for the maintenance and operating expenses of the schools, and in 1802 a sale of his drawings, which realized about £1500, handsomely supplemented the fund and enabled him to extend financial help to the neighbouring school at Brockenhurst. The popularity of his picturesque writings and drawings—though it enabled him to be a greater benefactor to his parish than he might ever have imagined—did not sit comfortably with him. In 1802 he asked his publishers to promote his religious writings more strongly: 'I have figured so much lately as a picturesque man, that I should be glad to redeem my character as a clergyman' (Andrews, 56).

William Gilpin died at Boldre on 5 April 1804 and was buried on 13 April in the churchyard there. He was survived by his wife. His two daughters had died in infancy; his eldest son, John Bernard, came to be appointed British consul for Rhode Island; and his younger son, William, succeeded his father at Cheam School.

MALCOLM ANDREWS

Sources W. Gilpin, *Memoirs of Dr. Richard Gilpin … and of his posterity … together with an account of the author, by himself: and a pedigree of the Gilpin family*, ed. W. Jackson (1879) • W. Templeman, *The life and work of William Gilpin (1724–1804), master of the picturesque and vicar of Boldre* (1939), vol. 24, nos. 3–4 of Illinois Studies in Language and Literature • C. P. Barbier, *William Gilpin: his drawings, teachings, and theory of the picturesque* (1963) • R. Warner, *Literary recollections*, 2 vols. (1830) • M. Andrews, *The search for the picturesque: landscape aesthetics and tourism in Britain, 1760–1800* (1989) • *GM*, 1st ser., 74 (1804), 388 • parish register, 1724, Cumbria AS [baptism] • Foster, *Alum. Oxon.* • monumental tablet, Boldre church, Hampshire

Archives Bodl. Oxf., notebook containing draft remarks on forest scenery • Bodl. Oxf., corresp. and papers • Bodl. Oxf., 'Hints for sermons' • Bodl. Oxf., notebooks and volume 1 of 'Observations on natural history' • Hants. RO, family archives • Surrey HC, notebook containing sketches and notes on gardens, architectural features • V&A NAL, journal of imaginary tour | Bodl. Oxf., letters to Mrs Delaney; letters, mostly to Sir Harry Bernard Neale and Lady Neale • East Riding of Yorkshire Archives Service, Beverley, corresp. relating to education of John Grimston's sons at Cheam • FM Cam., MS of 'Instructions for examining landscape' • Magd. Oxf., watercolours and text, 'On sunsets' • V&A NAL, fragment of 'Description of the Thames from London to Windsor' with drawings by Sawrey Gilpin

Likenesses H. Walton, oils, 1781, NPG [*see illus.*] • G. Clint, engraving, 1805 (after H. Walton), repro. in Templeman, *Life and work of William Gilpin*

Wealth at death approx. £1000—1804 sale: H. Walpole, *Anecdotes of painting*, ed. R. N. Wornum (1849), 3.829n.

Gilpin, William Sawrey (1761/2–1843), landscape painter and landscape gardener, was the second of six children of Sawrey *Gilpin (1733–1807), animal painter, and Elizabeth Broom. Gilpin's uncle, his father's older brother, was the author and schoolmaster the Revd William *Gilpin (1724–1804). Both Gilpin's great-grandfather William Gilpin (1657–1724) and his grandfather Captain John Bernard Gilpin (1701–1776) were eminent amateur artists. Details about Gilpin's life, and about his earlier years in particular, are sparse. His youth was probably spent in Windsor and London where his father, at that time working under the patronage of Henry Frederick, fourth duke of Cumberland, was based. Gilpin is also believed to have attended his uncle's school in Cheam, Surrey.

Following in his father's footsteps Gilpin took up a career as a painter and established himself as a drawing master at Paddington Green near London. In his early twenties he provided the illustrations for some of the Revd William Gilpin's popular writings on the picturesque, including *Observations on the River Wye* (1782). Many years later, in 1818, Gilpin was to produce his own lavishly illustrated (though unpublished) 'Tour through part of north Wales', an account of a journey undertaken a year or two earlier, from Cheltenham through Wales to north Yorkshire (priv. coll.). Although Gilpin did paint in oil the majority of his works were executed in watercolours. His landscapes depicted scenes in and around Hampshire, Surrey, Killarney, and Glamorgan. Mallalieu describes Gilpin as 'an eclectic painter who worked in a number of styles at different periods of his career. At times he is close to Nicholas Pocock, at others to Humphry Repton and later to Girton' (Mallalieu, *Watercolour artists*, 2.387). Gilpin first exhibited at the Royal Academy in 1797, a watercolour painting of the village of Rydal in Westmorland. Westmorland was also the address given for him at three subsequent exhibitions (1799, 1800, and 1801), indicating that Gilpin spent some years away from London. At the exhibition of 1799 Gilpin's work caught the attention of the art patron Sir George Beaumont, who, upon visiting him shortly afterwards, introduced Gilpin to his close friend Sir Uvedale Price, author of *Essays on the Picturesque* (1794). This introduction was to prove crucial to Gilpin's later career as a landscape gardener.

It is not known when Gilpin married, but in 1785 a son was born to him and his wife, Elizabeth Paddock (1766/7–1841). More than fifteen years later they had a second son, and possibly a third (sources differ on this matter). One of their sons, probably because of some disability, was dependent on his father possibly for all his life and certainly as late as 1835. This might account for the 'difficulties of longstanding' with which Gilpin was said to be struggling by his wife, Elizabeth, in a letter dated 1822 (Piebenga, 9).

By 30 November 1804 Gilpin was back in London, where he was elected the first president of the Society of Painters in Water Colours, a position from which he resigned in March 1806. Richard and Samuel Redgrave suggest that the reason for this resignation was the inferiority of Gilpin's work, apparent at the society's first exhibition in the spring of 1805 (*A Century of Painters of the English School*, 1, 1866, 470). This seems unlikely as Gilpin continued to exhibit at the society until 1815. Another, more plausible, explanation for Gilpin's resignation may be his commencement, on 8 March 1806, of a teaching post as third drawing master at the Royal Military College in Marlow, Buckinghamshire (which moved in 1812 to Sandhurst, Surrey).

A series of letters held at the Royal Military College at

Sandhurst reveal Gilpin to be a difficult character. However, later letters describe him as 'an amiable gentleman-like man' (Ralph Sneyd of Keele, Piebenga, 8); 'a more excellent, conscientious and religious man exists not' (ibid., Elizabeth Gilpin); while Sir Uvedale Price referred to Gilpin's 'many good & amiable qualities' (ibid.).

At the end of the Napoleonic wars, numbers of staff at the college were reduced, and in May 1820 Gilpin received notice of his discharge, regarded by him as 'unprecedented and therefore unanticipated' (Piebenga, 8). In a letter addressed presumably to one of the lieutenant-governors of the college, Gilpin complains of the 'cruelty of suddenly tearing me from my means of livelyhood, which I had every reason to rest upon as secure … abandoned at that age [nearing sixty] to begin the world again in search of a precarious support' (ibid.). It was at this point that Gilpin turned to landscape gardening.

After his discharge from the Royal Military College, Gilpin moved to Painesfield in East Sheen, Surrey, where two of his numerous Gilpin cousins lived and owned property. Gilpin also had a London address at 50 Upper Berkeley Street, Portman Square, Paddington Green, the house of the artist George Barret junior, a close friend of Gilpin. From these bases (and later, also Sedbury Hall in the North Riding of Yorkshire) Gilpin travelled all over the country, advising landowners on the improvement of their properties. During the 1820s and 1830s he managed to establish himself as a respected landscape gardener. By 1837 he had been involved, in his own words, with 'some hundreds' of properties ('House of Commons: committee on the Edinburgh & Glasgow Railway Bill: promoters' evidence', 1838, NA Scot., BR/PYB(S)1/7, 59). Most of his landscape works, of which only seventy have been identified so far, are in England and the southern half of Scotland, with a small number in Ireland and one in Wales. The vast majority of Gilpin's employers were members of the aristocracy and of the landed gentry. It would appear that on a number of occasions Gilpin acted as a kind of gentleman adviser to the owner of a property, steering the ideas of his employer and assisting with staking out plantations and drives—hence Ralph Sneyd at Keele referring to Gilpin as 'my man of taste' (Piebenga, 23).

Just as in Gilpin's earlier occupation as drawing master, where he had taught his pupils the art of (landscape) drawing, so now in his later profession, he would instruct his employers in the art of landscape gardening and assist them in their endeavours. This pupil–master relationship and this method of operating explains, in part, the fact that documentation by Gilpin detailing his work is sparse and that the little documentation that does exist is of a poor quality, often unsigned and undated.

In his work as a landscape gardener Gilpin professed to be a follower of Sir Uvedale Price. Price advocated the application of the principles of painting to the improvement of landscapes, and had long called for a painter to take up landscape gardening. Gilpin had not taken up this suggestion when the two men had met some years earlier but in 1820, upon renewing their acquaintance, Price wholeheartedly endorsed Gilpin's new undertaking as landscape gardener and strongly recommended his services to his friends.

Gilpin set out and illustrated his theories on landscape gardening in a book entitled *Practical hints upon landscape gardening: with some remarks on domestic architecture, as connected with scenery* (1832; 2nd edn 1835). Improving scenery with a painter's eye and referring constantly to the art of painting Gilpin considered connection, variety, and intricacy as the leading principles of landscape gardening. This style of improvement could very well be described as 'picturesque improvement', a term coined by the horticultural author John Claudius Loudon in 1806 (*A Treatise on Forming, Improving and Managing Country Residences*, 355). In Gilpin's proposals, variety and intricacy are reflected especially in highly irregularly shaped plantations with bold projections and recesses. The element of intricacy is also to be found in the architectural details of Gilpin's terrace walls with overhanging copings, vases, and protruding buttresses. Following the principle of connection, in order to unite an artificial building with its natural surroundings, Gilpin called for 'the principle of an architectural foreground to be established' (Gilpin, 35), typified in his proposals by terrace walks, parterre gardens, and balustrades. Working in the 1820s and 1830s Gilpin was at the forefront of this reintroduction of formality into the garden. Good examples of his work can be seen at Gorhambury, Hertfordshire, Wolterton Hall, Norfolk, and Sudbury Hall, Derbyshire.

The prolific and influential horticultural author J. C. Loudon recommended Gilpin's services to his readers (*The Suburban Gardener, and Villa Companion*, 1838, 673), while other fellow professionals referred to Gilpin, posthumously, as 'a man of … great taste and practical experience' (J. Major, *The Theory and Practice of Landscape Gardening*, 1852, 22); 'one of our best landscape-gardeners' (C. MacIntosh, *The Book of the Garden*, 1, 1853, 605). Gilpin's particular role in the history of landscape design lies in the fact that, at a time when gardening was dominated by horticultural innovations and exotic plant introductions, he almost singly adhered to the picturesque principles advocated by Sir Uvedale Price.

In 1825 a cousin of Gilpin, the Revd John Gilpin (*d.* 1844), bought Sedbury Hall, near Gilling West in the North Riding of Yorkshire. From that date onwards Gilpin divided his time between Sedbury and Painesfield. It was at Sedbury that William Sawrey Gilpin died on 4 April 1843, aged eighty-one, barely one and a half years after his 'beloved' wife Elizabeth (inscription on tombstone). Although Gilpin died intestate it would appear that his second career had procured him a comfortable income, judging by the not inconsiderable amount of money he left on his death (£1500). Gilpin was buried on 8 April 1843 at the churchyard of St Agatha's Church in Gilling West.

Sophieke Piebenga

Sources S. Piebenga, 'William Sawrey Gilpin (1762–1843): a review of his work as a landscape gardener', DPhil diss., University of York, 1995 [incl. extensive bibliography] • I. A. Williams, 'The artists of the Gilpin family with special reference to William Sawrey Gilpin', *Old Water-Colour Society's Club*, 29 (1951), 16–24 •

W. Jackson, ed., *Memoirs of Dr Richard Gilpin of Scaleby Castle in Cumberland, and of his posterity in the succeeding generations* (1879) • Mallalieu, *Watercolour artists*, 2nd edn, vol. 1 • W. S. Gilpin, *Practical hints upon landscape gardening*, 2nd edn (1835) • d. cert.
Archives Bowhill, Borders, sketches, memorandum, plans • Gorhambury House, Hertfordshire, sketches, memorandum, plans • PRO, letter, memorandum, plan • Royal Military Academy, Sandhurst, material relating to his employment as drawing master • Wembury, Devon, family papers, illustrated travelogue, 'Tour through part of North Wales' • Wolterton Hall, Norfolk, Wolterton papers, sketches, letters, memoranda
Wealth at death £1500: administration, 10 June 1845, PRO, PROB 12/252

Gilson, Julius Parnell (1868–1929), librarian and palaeographer, was born at Worksop, Nottinghamshire, on 23 June 1868, the younger son of Henry Robert Gilson, of Worksop, and his wife, Mary Anne, daughter of George Quilter, vicar of Canwick, near Lincoln. He was educated at Haileybury College (1881–6), and at Trinity College, Cambridge (BA, 1889; MA, 1893), where he was a scholar. He was placed in the first class of both parts of the classical tripos. After a period of study at Cambridge, Bonn, Hanover, and elsewhere, and briefly teaching at Sherborne School under F. B. Westcott, Gilson in 1894 was appointed assistant in the department of manuscripts at the British Museum. He was promoted assistant keeper (a title afterwards changed to deputy keeper) in 1909, and keeper of the department and Egerton librarian on the retirement of Sir George Frederic Warner in 1911. In 1899 Gilson married Helen Georgina, fourth daughter of Frank Joseph Pearce, of Ledwell House, Oxfordshire. They had no children.

As well as his administrative tasks, Gilson made a substantial scholarly contribution to the museum through the production with Warner of *A Catalogue of Western Manuscripts in the Old Royal and King's Collections* (1921). Gilson provided many of the descriptions and also the wide-ranging and important introduction to the work.

Gilson wrote widely in a number of other fields of scholarship. He was a classical, and particularly Greek, scholar, and also had a wide knowledge of the medieval world and thought. Additionally he was an accomplished palaeographer. From 1903 he edited the *Facsimiles of Ancient Manuscripts*, published by the New Paleographical Society; he became one of the joint editors of the society's publications in 1910. In 1905 he edited the *Mozarabic Psalter* for the Henry Bradshaw Society; in 1906 *Gulliver's Travels and other Works* of Swift; in 1910, for the Roxburghe Club, *The Correspondence of Edmund Burke and William Windham*; and in 1916, for the same club, *Lives of Lady Anne Clifford and of her Parents*. He contributed to the transactions of the Bibliographical Society an account of the library of Sir Henry Savile of Banke (vol. 9, 1908). In 1925 he wrote *A Description of the Saxon Manuscript of the Four Gospels in the Library of York Minster* (privately printed). He also began to edit, with W. W. Greg, the series English Literary Autographs, and before his death he had just produced for the museum trustees, in honour of the Monte Cassino celebrations, a reproduction of *An Exultet Roll* (1929). For several years before his death Gilson had been preparing for a work on manorial history: and in 1933 there was published, in memory of him, an edition of the thirteenth-century legal and manorial formularies in the British Museum's Additional Manuscript 41201.

In 1920 Gilson wrote the small *Guide to the Manuscripts of the British Museum* in the Help for Students of History series, and it was recognized by contemporaries that one of his greatest contributions to the museum and the public was the help and benefit of his broad knowledge, which he was always willing to offer to all students and others who visited the museum in his time. 'Only the writer of footnotes acknowledging his help, and there are many of those', wrote one contemporary, could know how great that help was across many areas of scholarship (*The Times*, 17 June 1929, 19).

A quiet man devoted to scholarly study, Gilson also found enjoyment as a skilled alpine climber. He died at the Cottage Hospital, Weybridge, Surrey, on 16 June 1929, and was buried at Weybridge, where he had been living, on 19 June, survived by his wife.

A. J. K. ESDAILE, *rev.* MARC BRODIE

Sources *The Times* (17 June 1929) • *The Times* (20 June 1929) • Venn, *Alum. Cant.* • *WWW* • L. A. Speakman, *Haileybury register, 1862–1922*, 5th edn (1922) • private information (1937) • *CGPLA Eng. & Wales* (1929)
Archives BL, letters to Idris Bell, Add. MS 59511
Wealth at death £10,695 17*s*. 4*d*.: probate, 31 July 1929, *CGPLA Eng. & Wales*

Gilstrap, Sir William, baronet (1816–1896), maltster, was born on 20 December 1816 at The Hotel, Kirkgate, Newark-on-Trent, Nottinghamshire, the eldest surviving son of the eight children of Joseph Gilstrap (1785–1869), wine merchant and maltster, and his first wife, Elizabeth, second daughter of William Welsh, of Leake, Lancashire. William and his brother George (1822–1864) were educated locally before joining the family business. William worked initially in the wine trade, but was soon attracted to his father's newest venture, malting.

Situated on the River Trent, and at the heart of prime barley land, Newark had for long been an important malting centre, but the coming of the railways and the parallel expansion of the brewing industry in Burton upon Trent underpinned a rapid rise in the demand for malt. Few exploited the new opportunities better than Gilstrap. The first malting was purchased in 1834. Eight years later, Gilstrap & Sons acquired the substantial business of William Brodhurst, with maltings at Newark and Mansfield. Large modern maltings were built at Newark, and others leased at Lincoln, Retford, Wakefield, and Grimsby. Then in 1880, after the death of its senior partner, George Harvey, Gilstrap acquired the Newark business of Harvey and Earp. The new partnership of Gilstrap, Earp & Co. (of which Thomas Earp became managing partner), producing around 100,000 quarters of malt a year, was the largest in Britain. In the jubilee honours of 1887, Gilstrap was created a baronet for his services to the malting industry.

Gilstrap was enterprising and ambitious. He remained as senior partner in Gilstrap, Earp & Co. until his death in

1896 but, from the 1860s, adopted the lifestyle of a landowning gentleman. In 1847 he married Elizabeth (1822–1891), fourth daughter of Thomas Haigh of Colnebridge House, Huddersfield, and lived in some style in South Parade, Newark. Eight years later he purchased a country house and 20 acres at nearby Winthorpe; in 1862 he bought from Lord John Manners for £85,000 the 1600 acre Fornham Park estate near Bury St Edmunds, Suffolk. The following year he added the nearby Herringswell estate—2400 acres of light land, which he developed as a fine shoot—and in 1868 acquired a further 600 acres at Fornham All Saints. Gilstrap threw himself wholeheartedly into Suffolk life; he was appointed a JP, deputy lieutenant, and, in 1867, high sheriff of the county. That same year, Fornham was the venue for the Royal Agricultural Society's annual show. He was a genial host, and his wife, Elizabeth, was renowned for her charm and wit. The estate became famous for its shooting parties, and a favourite with the prince of Wales and his brothers, who for many years were regular visitors.

Although never deeply involved in politics, Gilstrap broke with family tradition and became a lifelong supporter of the Liberal cause. He was a generous benefactor, supporting many charities and institutions, including the Newark and Bury hospitals, the National Society for the Prevention of Cruelty to Children (NSPCC), the Imperial Institute, and Bury Athenaeum Council. On its formation in 1882 he gave £3500 to the Royal School of Music to found the Suffolk scholarship, and in same year donated £16,000 to build and endow the Newark Free Library and create the Castle Gardens.

William and Elizabeth Gilstrap were childless. When in 1889 his niece Isabella (1861–1949), second daughter of his deceased brother George, married John, second son of Duncan MacRae of Karnes Castle, Bute, MacRae became a partner in Gilstrap, Earp & Co. Under the terms of Gilstrap's will, MacRae assumed the additional name of Gilstrap and inherited his business interests. The Fornham estate eventually passed to Isabella's sister, Anna, and her husband, George Espee Manners, nephew of the duke of Rutland. Gilstrap died at his home, Fornham Park, on 15 February 1896, and was buried at Fornham St Martin church on 20 February. CHRISTINE CLARK

Sources *Newark Advertiser* (19 Feb 1896) • *Bury Free Press* (22 Feb 1896) • G. Hemmingway, 'The Gilstraps of Newark', 1982 • J. Bateman, *The great landowners of Great Britain and Ireland* (1878) • *WWW* • P. Stephens, *Newark, the magic of malt* (1993) • W. White, *History, gazetteer, and directory of Suffolk*, 3rd edn (1874) • W. White, *History, gazetteer, and directory of Suffolk*, 5th edn (1891) • W. White, *History, gazetteer, and directory of Suffolk* (1900)

Likenesses W. H. Cubley, oils, Gilstrap Heritage Centre, Newark-on-Trent • J. McLeod, photograph, repro. in Stephens, *Newark*

Wealth at death £194,466 18s. 1d.: probate, 1 May 1896, *CGPLA Eng. & Wales*

Gim. *See* Gimson, Alfred Charles (1917–1985).

Gimpel, Jean Victor (1918–1996), cultural historian and historian of medieval technology, was born in Paris on 10 October 1918. Of Jewish descent, he was the third son of René Gimpel (*d.* 1944), a leading art dealer and friend of Renoir and Proust, and his English wife, Florence (*d.* 1978), sister of Joseph Duveen, an even more famous art dealer. Gimpel was educated in England and Switzerland, then at the Lycée Louis Le Grand in Paris. He failed his *baccalauréat*, so never went to university—but he was always proud of being an autodidact. In 1939–40 he was in the French army, then joined the resistance where he became a saboteur, blowing up factories. For this he was awarded the Croix de Guerre, médaille de la Résistance and the Légion d'honneur. He met another resistance worker, Paul-Denise (Cathérine) Corre (*b.* 1921), from Brittany, whom he married in 1946.

In Paris after the war he at first shared the family's passion for art, and founded a laboratory for the study of Old Masters. Then for a while he was a diamond broker, combining this with writing. His gradual revulsion against art—a key episode in his life—came when he was researching for his first book, *Les bâtisseurs des cathédrales* (1958), which made him realize that the great architects, engineers, and craftsmen who designed and built the medieval cathedrals were undervalued and 'treated as mere workmen', as compared with the vain artists of the Renaissance who basked in glory. Published in English as *The Cathedral Builders*, the book became an international best-seller.

Gimpel pursued its theme in two further influential books. In his diatribe *Contre l'art et les artistes* (*The Cult of Art*) (1968) Gimpel argued that art had been allowed to usurp the place of religion, and he attacked the concept of the artist as a special individual deserving privileges. The 'deification' of Picasso was 'a disgrace to our civilisation'. The book aroused acute anger in some quarters: the *Times Literary Supplement* devoted a two-column editorial to denouncing its author. Then in *The Mediaeval Machine* (1976), translated into twelve languages, Gimpel sought to demonstrate that the technological revolution of the middle ages, based on mills, watermills, and so on, was as remarkable as that of the industrial revolution.

In 1963 Gimpel moved with his wife and three small children to London, where his two elder brothers had an art gallery. From London he developed what became the major work of his later life—the practical application of medieval technology to the needs of the 'third world'. Visiting countries such as Nepal, Kenya, and Senegal, he saw how modern machinery was often woefully unsuited to their rural life. So in 1977 he set up a charity, Models for Rural Development, funded entirely by himself. This enabled him to take scale-models of early inventions around many third world villages, so that local craftsmen could copy them for use. The models were, for example, of pumps, sawmills, and water-wheels, or the Archimedean screw used for raising water from one level to another. Gimpel sometimes received United Nations grants for his work.

A lifelong socialist, and ever mistrustful of modern capitalism, Gimpel published in 1995 *The End of the Future*, a Cassandra-like prediction of the decline of America, with a Wall Street crash that would bring down western civilisation. The French press dubbed him 'the Nostradamus of the twentieth century'. The book was less scientifically researched and argued than his earlier works, and, though serious at heart, its provocative tone left some critics feeling that prejudice had got the better of cool judgement.

Gimpel was a man of great physical energy and zest for life. He had a fast-talking wit and a restless manner that could disconcert: at a dinner party he would not stay still but keep getting up from table. At their London home in Chelsea he and his wife for many years ran a 'salon' on certain Sunday afternoons. Writers, academics, scientists, and others would eagerly attend and for some it provided a focus for their social lives. With typical cheekiness Jean would say, 'I hate nature as I hate art, so the salon's aim is to deter Londoners from going into the country'. He would go round the room, busily shuffling his guests, talking volubly in his French accent. 'I am for women and technology, in that order', he would often say; 'women are superior to men'—and his delight in their company was palpable. 'Give me once more your lovely smile', he said to one woman friend on his deathbed in 1996.

Gimpel was in the true French line of the intellectual who became also a man of action. He easily bestrode the 'two cultures' of arts and science, and was once praised by C. P. Snow for this. Generous and warm hearted, with a real feeling for the world's poor, he owed much to the patient and loving support of his wife, Cathérine. Despite his own dislike of art she worked for many years in the family's Mayfair art gallery, Gimpel Fils, while he spent the mornings writing in bed. Gimpel died from cancer at his home, Flat 5, 11 Chelsea Embankment, London, on 15 June 1996, and was buried the same month in Treflez, Finistère, Brittany. JOHN ARDAGH

Sources personal knowledge (2004) • private information (2004) [C. Gimpel] • *The Times* (1 July 1996) • *The Guardian* (18 June 1996) • *The Independent* (26 June 1996) • *Daily Telegraph* (17 June 1996) • d. cert.

Gimson, Alfred Charles [Gim] (**1917–1985**), phonetician, was born on 7 June 1917 at 587 Garratt Lane, Wandsworth, London, the son of Charles Edmund Gimson, munition factory fireman, and his wife, Kate Louise Derbyshire. He was educated at Earlsfield primary school in Wandsworth, London, and, from 1928 to 1936, at Emanuel School, Wandsworth, where he was school captain, editor of the school magazine, and captain of tennis. He entered University College, London (UCL), in October 1936 to study for a BA degree in French; he graduated with first-class honours in 1939. As part of his course he took classes in French and English phonetics under the tutelage of Hélène Coustenoble (1894–1963) and Daniel Jones—events that were to shape his future career. Gimson spent the Second World War in the army intelligence corps, mainly as a liaison officer with the French and Polish allied forces, and rose to the rank of major. He was known familiarly as Gim.

In 1945 Gimson was appointed to a temporary lectureship in phonetics at UCL, the post being made permanent the following year. In 1961 he was appointed reader, and in 1966 professor. Between 1971 and 1983 (the year of his retirement) he was head of department. In 1973 he was made a fellow of UCL. His published work focused mainly on the pronunciation of modern English, though his range of expertise included French, Serbo-Croat, Norwegian, and the history of English. His most significant publication, the *Introduction to the Pronunciation of English*, first published in 1962 and revised on several occasions since, remains the standard authoritative work on the pronunciation of British English, written, as the title indicates, ostensibly for the beginner, but including a good deal of more advanced material as well. His *Practical Course of English Pronunciation* (1975) is a well-respected course, especially among teachers of English as a foreign language.

The International Phonetic Association benefited greatly from Gimson's administrative and managerial support from 1949 onwards, when he took on the post of secretary and, later, treasurer. He was made a life president of the association in 1984. His involvement with the profession of speech and language therapy was marked by his appointment to the examinations board of the Royal College of Speech and Language Therapists in 1949, and by the award of an honorary fellowship of the college in 1958. He acted as chairman of the college from 1965 to 1972.

Gimson was a founding member in 1967 of the academic advisory committee of Linguaphone, and his name is associated with many self-study language courses produced by the company. His skills as a phonetician came to the attention of a wider public with his short talks on BBC radio on aspects of current English pronunciation ('Changing English'), and his role as the pronunciation adviser to the *Longman Dictionary of Contemporary English* (Proctor and others, 1978) and to the *Oxford Advanced Learner's Dictionary of Current English* (Hornby and others, 1974). In 1967 Gimson took over the editorship of the *English Pronouncing Dictionary*, begun by Daniel Jones in 1917, and made various necessary changes to its content and style of presentation. It is still one of the standard academic reference works on British pronunciation.

Gimson was regarded by students and colleagues worldwide as not only a talented lecturer and tutor, but also a humane, kind-hearted, and supportive person. He and his wife, Margaret Dilys Muir, had a daughter. Gimson died suddenly of a heart attack in his sleep at his home, 50 Princes Avenue, Petts Wood, Orpington, Kent, on 22 April 1985; his wife survived him. M. K. C. MACMAHON

Sources S. Ramsaran, ed., *Studies in the pronunciation of English: a commemorative volume in honour of A. C. Gimson* (1990) • B. Collins and I. M. Mees, *The real Professor Higgins: the life and career of Daniel Jones* (Berlin and New York, 1999) • 'Professor A. C. Gimson: authority on pronunciation of English', *The Times* (27 April 1985) • J. C. Wells, 'Professor A. C. Gimson', *British Journal of Disorders of Communication*, 20 (1985), 117–18 • J. C. Wells, 'Professor A. C. Gimson, 1917–1985', *Journal of the International Phonetic Association*, 15 (1985), 2–4 • b. cert. • d. cert. • private information (2004) [G. M. Furlong, library, UCL; T. Jones, Emanuel School; W. Kirkby, UCL; E. Smith, Linguaphone Company; J. C. Wells, UCL]

Gimson, Ernest William (**1864–1919**), craftsman and architect, was born in Leicester on 21 December 1864, the fourth child and second son in the family of three sons and four daughters of Josiah Gimson (1818–1883), iron-

Ernest William Gimson (1864–1919), by unknown photographer, *c.*1900–10

founder, engineer, and industrial entrepreneur, who established the Vulcan works in Leicester, and his second wife, Sarah Ansell (1828–1899). Josiah Gimson's father was a carpenter. From an early age Gimson's interest in buildings was obsessive; as a young man he was quoted as saying 'I am thinking of architecture all the time I am awake' (Lethaby, Powell, and Griggs, 2).

After leaving Franklin's School, Stoneygate, Leicester, in 1881 Gimson was articled to a local architect, Isaac Barradale, and also attended Leicester School of Art, where he won national medals for suburban housing and for furniture design. His father was a leading freethinker, founder member and president of the Leicester Secular Society, and a Liberal member of the city council. Gimson's view of life—which was always to be that of the 'idealist individualist' (Lethaby, Powell, and Griggs, 1)—was formed more by the mood and the standards of that crowded, argumentative, intellectually zealous, middle-class, provincial household than by his formal education.

In 1884 Gimson went to listen to William Morris lecturing to the Leicester Secular Society on 'Art and socialism'. Afterwards he met Morris, who suggested the way that he should go in combining his radical conscience with his practical abilities in making and designing. It was Morris who encouraged him to move to London, recommending him to J. D. Sedding, a 'freestyle' church architect himself involved in the practice of the crafts.

Gimson was a deeply solitary man with a contradictory need for close male friendships. In the mid-1880s in Sedding's office, he joined the small convivial group of young Arts and Crafts architects, satellites around Morris and Philip Webb, becoming a member of such early architectural action groups as the Art Workers' Guild and the Society for the Protection of Ancient Buildings.

In 1890 Ernest Gimson was prime mover in establishing an individualistic London decorating firm, a brotherhood of architects designing and supervising the making of their furniture by cabinet-makers. The other members were W. R. Lethaby, Sidney Barnsley, Mervyn Macartney, Reginald Blomfield, and a less active partner, Colonel Mallet, each contributing £100 of capital. This short-lived but enthusiastic enterprise was called Kenton & Co., after a neighbouring street in Bloomsbury, and was obviously modelled on Morris's own firm.

Gimson subscribed to the arts and crafts principle that '*doing* is Designing' (Lethaby, Powell, and Griggs, 4). He was fascinated by the practicalities of a new approach to traditional crafts. Before Kenton & Co. opened he had travelled to Bosbury in Herefordshire to learn the craft of turned rush-seated chair making from an old man, Philip Clissett, who had been bodging chairs since 1838. His own versions of these, soon given their own generic title 'Gimson chairs', were still being made at the end of the twentieth century.

Gimson also learned the techniques of moulded and modelled plasterwork from the London trade firm of Whitcombe and Priestley, having admired the plaster ceilings at such historic houses as Speke Hall, Lancashire, Haddon Hall, Derbyshire, and Chastleton, Oxfordshire. In the William Morris manner of reviving ancient crafts in a new creative spirit, Gimson's plasterwork drew on natural motifs—pinks, roses, trailing strawberry plants. These images recur in his designs for embroidery made at the same time. As his furniture workshops expanded Gimson was less able to take part in actual processes of making: his chief role became that of director and designer. But plasterwork was the one craft he continued all his life.

Ernest Gimson was a ruminative character, 'a thinker, an explorer, a teacher', as described by his colleague W. R. Lethaby (Lethaby, Powell, and Griggs, 9). Having private means as a young man he travelled widely in England and Italy, making closely observed Ruskinian architectural drawings, watching with dismay the despoliation of the countryside, and gradually evolving his singular philosophy of craftsmanship and the environment.

In 1893 Gimson left London with Sidney Barnsley and went to live at Ewen in Gloucestershire. It was a move rich in symbolic overtones, true to Gimson's conviction that to do good work one must live near to nature in uncorrupted, incorruptible surroundings. Sidney's brother, the architect Ernest Barnsley, joined them with his family. In 1894 they all moved to Pinbury, a hamlet in a then remote and heavily wooded area five miles west of Cirencester. Here Gimson converted a stone farm building to make a cottage.

> The room was large, and the floor flagged with white stone … A large black dresser, hung with gay and well-used crockery, a large settle at the fireside, and oak armchair and

other rush-bottom chairs made by himself on his pole lathe, were its furniture. (Lethaby, Powell, and Griggs, 18)

Gimson used one of the outbuildings of Pinbury Park as a workshop for plaster and ladder-back chair making. He and Ernest Barnsley entered into a partnership as furniture makers, starting to employ cabinet-makers of their own.

In 1900 Gimson married Emily Ann Thompson (*d.* 1940), an enthusiastic amateur sketcher, daughter of the vicar of Skipsea in the East Riding of Yorkshire. Two years later the Gimsons and the Barnsleys moved to Sapperton, barely a mile away from Pinbury, where Gimson built himself a large new cottage, high-roofed with straw thatch. They established workshops and a showroom at Daneway House, a rare example of a medieval Cotswold house, leased from Earl Bathurst. (In the mid-twentieth century Daneway was occupied by the modernist architect Oliver Hill.) Tensions arose between the three families. By 1905 the partnership between Gimson and Ernest Barnsley broke up in bitterness. Sidney Barnsley and Gimson were only able to continue their friendship outside their homes. But their work retained recognizable stylistic affinities: a clear respect for techniques and materials, a strong love of tradition, and a belief in the vernacular which had a considerable impact on both theory and practice of British twentieth-century industrial design.

Gimson's furniture has long been regarded as his supreme achievement, the only relatively modern work to bear comparison with that of the great English cabinet-makers of the eighteenth century. It was highly perfectionist furniture, made by skilled craftsmen under Gimson's expert Dutch foreman, Peter van der Waals, using the minimum of machinery. Though Gimson so solemnly espoused the simple life much of his furniture was elaborate in concept and rich in its materials, using such timbers as ebony, rosewood, and English walnut with carved and inlaid detailing.

Gimson's furniture was made to commission for wealthy and discriminating clients, notably Sir Ernest Debenham and C. H. St John Hornby, owner of W. H. Smith & Sons. Gimson's woodwork and metalwork—the wrought-iron architectural fixtures, fire-irons, candlesticks and sconces made by his craftsmen in the blacksmiths' shop at Sapperton—were commissioned for their buildings by other arts and crafts architects true to the ideal of the union of crafts. Prime examples are Gimson's ebony choir stalls in J. F. Bentley's Roman Catholic cathedral in Westminster and his massive timberwork at St Andrew's Church, Roker, designed by Edward Prior.

Within and beyond his own lifetime Ernest Gimson was regarded primarily as a furniture designer. In 1936 Nikolaus Pevsner described him as 'The greatest of the English artist-craftsmen' (*Pioneers of the Modern Movement*, 1936, 146). The originality and integrity of his few completed buildings had long been recognized, particularly his craggy stone-built cottages at Markfield near Leicester, buildings that themselves seem rooted in their landscape, and the magnificent timbered library at Bedales School, built posthumously. But for many decades Gimson's architecture was considered as an interesting sideline. Only in the 1990s did more concentrated study of the drawings for Gimson's architectural projects, less than half of which were realized, reveal the continuing centrality of his architecture in Gimson's creative life. His designs for the Port of London Authority headquarters and his masterplan for the new city of Canberra show great reserves of visionary energy. He was the most faithful of William Morris's followers and, besides two pairs of stone cottages at Kelmscott, was commissioned by May Morris to design her father's Memorial Hall, opened by Ramsay MacDonald in 1934.

With his tall well-built frame, his broad and rather florid features, his heavy hobnail boots and country yeoman's tweeds, Gimson seemed the rural Englishman personified. Beneath his bluff exterior was an immense austerity and the will-power to demonstrate what he believed in. When he led the country dances in the village hall at Sapperton it was reported 'there were no idle feet' (Lethaby, Powell, and Griggs, 32). Gimson's verbal uncommunicativeness and his wife's *de haut en bas* approach to village life worked against the achievement of his ambitions for a national resurgence of the crafts. He had bought land at Sapperton to set up a craft village, model for other villages to come. Plans had not developed far when Ernest Gimson died at his home of cancer on 12 August 1919. He was buried in Sapperton churchyard, under the yews. Peter van der Waals took over Gimson's workshop, continuing to make fine furniture which lacked the inspiration of his master's. Gimson's philosophical and practical influence on the twentieth-century craft workshop movement has been considerable particularly in the small furniture workshops which burgeoned from the 1970s. Collections of Gimson's furniture are in Cheltenham Art Gallery and Museum, Gloucestershire, Leicester City Museums, Belgrave Hall, and the Arts and Crafts Collection, Owlpen Manor, Uley, Gloucestershire. FIONA MACCARTHY

Sources W. R. Lethaby, A. H. Powell, and F. L. Griggs, *Ernest Gimson: his life and work* (1924) • M. Comino, *Gimson and the Barnsleys* (1980) • N. Jewson, *By chance I did rove*, privately published (1973) • M. Greensted, ed., *The arts and crafts movement in the Cotswolds* (1993) • private information (2004) [Edward Barnsley] • D. J. Pendery, 'The architectural works of Ernest Gimson, 1864–1919', PhD diss., University of Sheffield, 1998 • A. Carruthers, *Ernest Gimson and the Cotswold group of craftsmen*, Leicestershire Museums Publication, no. 14 (1978) [catalogue of works in the collections of Leicestershire Museums]

Archives Cheltenham Art Gallery and Museum, collection • Leicester City Museums, Belgrave Hall, collection • Owlpen Manor, Uley, Art and Crafts collection, papers

Likenesses photograph, *c.*1900–1910, Cheltenham Art Gallery and Museum [*see illus.*] • group portrait, photograph, Edward Barnsley Educational Trust, Petersfield, Hampshire

Wealth at death £8936 6*s.* 3*d.*: probate, 26 Feb 1920, *CGPLA Eng. & Wales*

Ginckel, Frederik Christiaan van Reede-, second earl of Athlone (1668–1719). *See under* Ginckel, Godard van Reede-, first earl of Athlone (1644–1703).

Ginckel, Godard van Reede-, first earl of Athlone (1644–1703), army officer, was born on 4 June 1644 at Amerongen Castle, Utrecht, the Netherlands, the only son of Godard Adriaan, first Baron van Reede (1621–1691), head of an old feudal family and a leading Dutch diplomat, and his wife, Margaretha, or Brilliana (*d.* 1700), daughter of Captain George Turnor, an English gentleman serving in the Netherlands during the Thirty Years' War, and his wife, Salomé van Meetkerchen. Having embarked on a military career in the cavalry, he was appointed captain in 1658, promoted major in 1663, and became colonel of a regiment in 1665. In 1666 he married Ursula Philippota van Raesfelt (*d.* 1721), daughter and heir of Reinier van Raesfelt (*d.* 1650), lord of Middachten, and his wife, Margaretha van Leefdael. Six sons and eight daughters were born of the marriage. Serving under William of Orange in the war against the French, he was wounded at the battle of Senef in 1674, but recovered. In 1675 he was appointed commissary-general of cavalry and in 1683 promoted to lieutenant-general.

Ginckel accompanied William to England in 1688. In March 1689, at Swaton Common in Lincolnshire, he suppressed a mutiny of the Royal Scots regiment with a force of Dutch horse and dragoons. He subsequently commanded the armed forces in the north of England at Berwick. He served in Ireland during William's 1690 campaign, fighting by the king's side at the battle of the Boyne and playing an active role during the siege of Limerick. As senior lieutenant-general, he became commander of the army in Ireland in September 1690. He was regarded as a stopgap, and it was expected he would be replaced by a soldier of more authority and reputation. William, however, preferred his Dutch compatriot to any of the alternative candidates, and Ginckel retained his command. His headquarters were at Kilkenny. He proved a cautious soldier, but painstaking and competent in his conduct of operations, and possessed of considerable diplomatic skill. He overcame initial difficulties in controlling unco-operative British subordinates, and thereafter preserved unity in his army of many nationalities by listening to all points of view. He also opened communications with the Jacobites in pursuit of William's overriding objective of ending the war as quickly as possible so that military resources could be redeployed to Flanders. His initial peace overtures were unsuccessful, but the process helped lay the foundation for the final surrender, which came, however, only after military victory.

During the winter of 1690–91 the Williamite army's quarters were much troubled by the depredations of Irish rapparees, or guerrilla bands, which the revival of a protestant militia helped to contain. Every effort was made to ensure the army was well equipped for the 1691 campaign. The arrival of an artillery train, consisting of thirty-two heavy guns and six mortars, enabled him to open his offensive in early June. The immediate objective was to capture Athlone, the fortified town on the mid-Shannon which was the key to Connaught, the remaining territory under Jacobite control. The Jacobite outpost at Ballymore fell on 8 June. Ginckel was joined there by his forces from

Godard van Reede-Ginckel, first earl of Athlone (1644–1703), by Sir Godfrey Kneller, 1692

the south of Ireland, which brought his field army to a strength of approximately 20,000. On 19 June he advanced to Athlone. The part of the town located east of the river was only lightly defended and fell to an assault the next day. However, the Jacobite field army, equal in size to Ginckel's force and commanded by the French general the marquis de St Ruth, advanced to support the defence of west Athlone. Over the next week the Williamite artillery reduced the west town to rubble, firing off more than 12,000 cannon balls. The spirit of the defenders remained unbroken, and they thwarted efforts by the Williamites to cross the river via the old stone bridge and a pontoon bridge. On 30 June west Athlone finally fell to a well-managed Williamite assault across the old ford in the centre of the town, which routed the defending Jacobites, who were caught by surprise. On 9 July Ginckel took advantage of the victory to publish a proclamation of the Irish lords justices offering a pardon to Jacobite officers on certain conditions. Although of little immediate effect, this eventually provided the basis for the discussions that led to the treaty of Limerick.

St Ruth rallied the Jacobite army to make a stand against Ginckel at Aughrim in co. Galway, where a major pitched battle was fought on 12 July. A marsh protected the Jacobite centre, and his continental troops were at first unable to overcome the determined resistance of the Jacobite right wing. Attempts by his infantry to cross the marsh were also repulsed. However, the death of St Ruth by a chance cannon shot coincided with an opportune advance by Williamite cavalry along a narrow causeway into the heart of the Jacobite left wing, which the Irish cavalry failed to check. The new pressure on their flank forced the infantry of the Jacobite centre to give ground. Ginckel renewed his attack on all fronts, and the Jacobite infantry was overborne and then massacred as its resistance crumbled. More than a fifth of the 40,000 troops engaged at Aughrim were casualties, three-quarters of them on the Jacobite side. His complete victory, achieved by characteristic perseverance, broke the will of the Jacobite army to resist and heralded the end of the war. On 21 July Galway surrendered to him on generous terms. Recrossing the Shannon with his army, in August he invested Limerick, the last Jacobite stronghold. He bombarded the city with artillery, including guns brought ashore from a naval squadron in the Shannon estuary, but avoided a formal siege, rightly judging that the mood of the Jacobites was defeatist. They offered little resistance to the erection of a pontoon bridge upstream of Limerick. On 22 September he personally led a strong force across it into co. Clare, which cut the garrison's communications with the Irish cavalry. A detachment of Jacobite infantry posted outside the fortifications suffered heavy casualties at Thomond Bridge.

Ginckel had previously issued a declaration giving a final extension to the July offer of terms, and on 23 September the Jacobites asked for a capitulation and a ceasefire. He treated the Jacobite negotiators with great courtesy. The military articles, which he regarded as entirely within his own responsibility, were quickly settled with Sarsfield, the senior Irish general. Limerick was to be surrendered, but those of the Irish army who wished to accompany Sarsfield to France were to be permitted to do so in shipping provided by the Williamites. The civil articles, which provided for the fate of the Jacobites who remained in Ireland, involved hard bargaining. Again Ginckel took a leading role in the negotiations, but the lords justices had an input into the final settlement, which was signed on 3 October. It was agreed that Jacobites who still held out, together with those under their protection, were to be pardoned if they swore allegiance to William, and there were assurances of religious freedom to Catholics. Ginckel's son was given the honour of bringing the signed treaty to England. He was criticized for the generosity of the terms granted at Galway and Limerick, but a settlement best served William's wider strategic needs. It was to his credit that in 1692 he intervened with William to give the benefit of the Limerick articles to the Irish who had been under the Jacobite army's protection, an important clause in the terms of surrender omitted, perhaps inadvertently, from the signed version. In 1697 he intervened again to support an interpretation of the Galway articles which was favourable to the Catholics.

With hostilities over, Ginckel, who succeeded his father as second Baron van Reede in October 1691, travelled to Dublin, where he was received by the corporation and lords justices, before sailing for Chester on 6 December. He travelled in triumph to London, where on 4 January 1692 he was formally thanked by the speaker of the House of Commons for his good service, naturalized by act of parliament on 24 February, and on 4 March raised by William to the Irish peerage as baron of Aughrim and earl of Athlone. He was also rewarded with 40,000 acres of Irish land, forfeited from William Dongan, earl of Limerick, and Christopher Fleming, Lord Slane. In 1695 this grant was confirmed by the Irish parliament. His Irish property was managed by Bartholomew van Homrigh, the former commissary-general of the army who was a prominent figure in the commercial and civic life of Dublin and father of Swift's Vanessa. All William's grants of Irish land were reversed in 1700 by the English parliament, but before this Ginckel sold his Irish property at a knockdown price. In March 1692 he accompanied William to Flanders for the campaign against the French, throughout which he commanded the Dutch cavalry. In July 1692 King Christian V of Denmark made him a member of the order of the elephant. In August he presided over the court martial which tried and condemned the sieur de Grandval for his plot to assassinate William. He participated in the unsuccessful operations to relieve Namur that summer, but in 1695 had the satisfaction of taking part in its recapture by the elector of Bavaria. He was present in the battles of Steenkerke (1692) and Landen (1693), in which he narrowly escaped drowning. In 1696 he supported Coehoorn in the successful destruction of the extensive French magazines at Givet.

When not on campaign Ginckel lived mainly at Utrecht or The Hague. He held the office of *ridderschap* of Utrecht in succession to his father from 1693 to 1701. In the 1690s, with his wife, he rebuilt her castle at Middachten, which had been destroyed by the French. His own castle at Amerongen, also rebuilt after destruction by the French, was decorated with frescoes of his victories in Ireland. In 1702, on the outbreak of the War of the Spanish Succession, he again took the field with the Dutch army, but was obliged to yield overall command of the allied forces in Flanders to the earl of Marlborough, which he did with good grace. In June, at Nijmegen, he thwarted the duc de Bourgogne's offensive against the republic. He succeeded the count of Nassau-Ussingen as field marshal of the Dutch army on 19 October, but died, after a brief illness, of apoplexy at Utrecht on 11 February 1703. He was buried at Amerongen, as was his wife, who died in 1721.

Frederik Christiaan van Reede-Ginckel, second earl of Athlone (1668–1719), his eldest son, succeeded him. He served in the Dutch cavalry, rising in 1709 to the rank of lieutenant-general. In 1710, while guarding a convoy on the River Lys, he was defeated and taken prisoner by the French. In 1713 he was made governor-commandant of Mons, and in 1718 governor of Sluys. On 2 March 1715 he married Henrietta, youngest daughter of William Henry de Nassau-Zulyestein, a Dutch diplomat and soldier, created earl of Rochford by William in 1695. He died at Sluys on 15 August 1719 and was buried at Amerongen. His two sons were successively third and fourth earls of Athlone. His grandson, Frederik-Christiaan Reinhart, fifth earl of Athlone (1743–1819), fled from the Netherlands during the French occupation in 1795. He took his seat in the Irish

House of Lords, which in 1800 granted him an annuity as a poor peer. The line became extinct with the death without issue of the ninth earl at The Hague in 1844.

HARMAN MURTAGH

Sources P. C. Molhuysen and P. J. Blok, eds., *Nieuw Nederlandsch biografisch woordenboek*, 3 (Leiden, 1914), 1007–9, 1017–21 • GEC, *Peerage*, new edn, vol. 1 • J. Lodge, *The peerage of Ireland*, rev. M. Archdall, rev. edn, 2 (1789), 153–7 • *Fourth report*, HMC, 3 (1874), 317–25 [de Ros MSS] • G. Story, *An impartial history of the wars of Ireland* (1693) • J. G. Simms, *Jacobite Ireland, 1685–91* (1969) • J. G. Simms, *The Williamite confiscation in Ireland, 1690–1703* (1956), 26–9, 56–9, 66–71, 76–8, 85, 88–9, 101–2, 125, 139–41 • K. Danaher and J. G. Simms, eds., *The Danish force in Ireland, 1690–1691*, IMC (1962) • W. Troost, 'William III and the treaty of Limerick, 1691–1697', Doctor in de Lettern diss., University of Leiden, 1983 • K. P. Ferguson, 'The army in Ireland from the Restoration to the Act of Union', PhD thesis, University of Dublin, 1980, 22–49 • W. Troost, ed., 'Letters from Bartholomew van Homrigh to General Ginkel, earl of Athlone, 1692 to 1700: from the Huisarchief Amerongen, Amerongen Castle, near Utrecht', *Analecta Hibernica*, 33 (1986), 59–128 • J. C. R. Childs, *The British army of William III, 1689–1702* (1987), 22–3, 28 • J. C. R. Childs, *The Nine Years' War and the British army, 1688–1697: the operations in the Low Countries* (1991), 222, 224, 269, 271, 275, 281–2, 289, 310–11, 348 • J. A. Gravin Ortenburg-Bentinck and N. W. Conijn, *Kasteel Middachten* (1986)

Archives Huisarchief Amerongen, Amerongen Castle, Utrecht | Boston PL, letters to William Blathwayt • Leics. RO, corresp. with earl of Nottingham and related material • PRO NIre., letters to Lord Coningsby and some to the lords justices • TCD, corresp. with George Clarke and other material

Likenesses J. Ovens, oils, *c.*1665, Amerongen Castle, Utrecht, Netherlands • R. White, line engraving, 1691, BM, NPG • G. Kneller, oils, 1692, NG Ire. [*see illus.*] • P. Schenk, mezzotint, 1703, BM, NPG • J. de Baen?, oils, Amerongen Castle, Utrecht, Netherlands • J. Houbraken, line engraving (after countess of Athlone), BM, NPG • F. Van der Leyden, portrait, Amerongen Castle, Utrecht, Netherlands • portrait, Middachten Castle, Geldereland, Netherlands • two portraits, Amerongen Castle, Utrecht, Netherlands

Wealth at death Amerongen Castle and estate; also Middachten Castle and estate, which he owned with wife

Gingold, Hermione Ferdinanda (1897–1987), actress, was born in London on 9 December 1897, the elder daughter (there were no sons) of James Gingold, stockbroker, who had emigrated from Austria, and his wife, Kate Walter. She claimed Viennese, Turkish, and Romanian blood on her father's side. Her mother was Jewish.

La Gingold, or Herman or Toni, as she was often called in the theatre, first appeared on stage at the age of ten as the herald in *Pinkie and the Fairies*, produced by Herbert Beerbohm Tree. She later played the title role on tour and was cast by Tree as Falstaff's page in *The Merry Wives of Windsor*. In 1912, aged fifteen, she played Cassandra at Stratford upon Avon in *Troilus and Cressida*, adventurously produced by William Poel. Edith Evans was Cressida. For an actress who was subsequently to achieve fame for her flamboyant personality, her wit, her sophisticated but often grotesque comedy, and her basso profundo voice, described by J. C. Trewin as 'powdered glass in deep syrup', her surprising billing in the actors' directory *Spotlight* in the 1920s and early 1930s read 'Shakespearean and soprano'. She lost her high notes after suffering nodules on her vocal chords: 'One morning it was Mozart and the next "Old Man River".'

Gingold played many parts in the theatre and on radio

Hermione Ferdinanda Gingold (1897–1987), by Francis Goodman, 1945

in the 1930s; but she found her true métier in revue. She was in *Spread it Abroad* at the Saville in 1936, *The Gate Revue* in 1939 which transferred to the Ambassador's Theatre, and its sequel *Swinging the Gate* (1940). Her legendary partnership with Hermione Baddeley [*see* Baddeley, Hermione Youlanda Ruby Clinton (1906–1986)] ('the two Hermiones'), which was shorter lived than memory usually allows, began at the Comedy Theatre in 1941 with *Rise above it* (two editions), and continued in *Sky High* at the Phoenix Theatre. It was during this show that their rivalry escalated in the press into a famous feud. She moved back to the Ambassador for *Sweet and Low* (1943), *Sweeter and Lower* (1944), and *Sweetest and Lowest* (1946). Gingold became a special attraction for American soldiers and 'Thanks, Yanks' was one of her most appropriate numbers. During the astringent, name-dropping 'Sweet' series she played 1676 performances, before 800,000 people, negotiating 17,010 costume changes.

Gingold followed with *Slings and Arrows* at the Comedy in 1948 and appeared in cameo roles in English films, notably in *The Pickwick Papers* (1952), capturing a wider radio following with her weekly show *Home at Eight*, which featured Sid Colin's Addams-like family, the Dooms. However, in spite of success with Baddeley in 1949 in *Fallen Angels*, by Noël Coward, achieved despite the author's disapproval of their overdoing the comic effects, she was determined to renew her American friendships. Her first significant appearance in New York was in John Murray Anderson's *Almanac* (Imperial, 1953). For the rest of her career she was based in America and became particularly well known on talk shows. She made other appearances in revue, and toured in a number of plays and musicals—taking over from Jo Van Fleet the role of Madame Rose Pettle in Arthur Kopit's *Oh Dad, poor Dad, Mama's hung you in the closet and I'm feelin' so sad*. She made many cameo appearances on television and in films, notably *Around the World in Eighty Days* (1956), *Bell, Book and Candle* (1958), and *The Music Man* (1962). She joined the San Francisco Opera to play the Duchess of Crackenthorp in Donizetti's *La fille du régiment* in 1975 and attacked the concert platform as a narrator.

There were two milestones in this period. Gingold appeared with Maurice Chevalier in the film *Gigi* (1958), in which they sang Alan Jay Lerner and Frederick Loewe's song 'I remember it well' with exquisite wit and pathos. In 1973 she played Madame Armfeldt in Stephen Sondheim's *A Little Night Music*, triumphing with 'Liaisons', the memoirs of a grande horizontale. Once again she reminded audiences of her gift for pathos and the power of her acting.

In 1977 Gingold took over the narrator's role in *Side by Side by Sondheim* on Broadway. Over eighty, she stayed with it gallantly on the gruelling 'bus and truck' tour of one-night stands, travelling over 30,000 miles and visiting sixty cities until she tripped over an iron pole on Kansas City railway station in the small hours. A shattered knee and a dislocated arm effectively ended her performing career.

Hermione Gingold was an artist whose style and wit were unmistakable and who always held the promise of laughter and outrage. Adored as an icon and often underestimated as an actress, she is secure in her reputation as a queen of revue and one of the essential sights of London during the Second World War. She was a statuesque woman who exaggerated her gargoyle features for comic effect on the stage; but she could achieve a handsome aspect in repose.

In 1918 Gingold married Michael *Joseph (1897–1958), publisher, the son of Moss Joseph, diamond merchant. They had two sons, the younger of whom, Stephen Joseph, pioneer of theatre in the round in Scarborough, later Alan Ayckbourn's base, died in 1967. They were brought up by her husband. The marriage was dissolved in 1926, and in the same year she married (Albert) Eric *Maschwitz (1901–1969), playwright, lyricist, and television executive, son of Albert Arthur Maschwitz, of Edgbaston. The marriage was dissolved in 1940. Hermione Gingold died of pneumonia and heart disease in the Lennox Hill Hospital, New York, on 24 May 1987.

NED SHERRIN, *rev.*

Sources H. Gingold, *How to grow old disgracefully* (1989) · *The Noël Coward diaries*, ed. G. Payn and S. Morley (1982) · G. Bordman, *American musical theatre* (1978) · personal knowledge (1996)

Likenesses photographs, 1943–87, Hult. Arch. · F. Goodman, photograph, 1945, NPG [*see illus.*]

Ginkel, Godert de. *See* Ginckel, Godard van Reede-, first earl of Athlone (1644–1703).

Ginner, (Isaac) Charles (**1878–1952**), painter, was born in Cannes, France, on 4 March 1878, the third of the four children of Isaac Benjamin Ginner (*d.* 1895), who had moved to Cannes from Hastings, Sussex, and established a pharmacy there, and his Scottish wife, Lydia Adeline Wightman. The first Ginner son died in infancy; the second, Ernest Wightman Ginner, became a doctor who established a successful practice on the Riviera; and the youngest child, Ruby Mary Adeline Ginner (later Dyer), became an honoured exponent of the revival of Greek dancing.

Ginner attended the Collège Stanislas in Cannes but left at sixteen, after a serious illness, to sail the Mediterranean and the south Atlantic in a tramp-steamer belonging to his uncle, Charles Harrison. Because of family opposition and shortage of money after his father's death in 1895, he came late to the study of painting. He worked in an architect's office in Paris from 1899 until 1904, when financial support from his uncle and occasional commissions for magazine illustrations enabled him to enrol at the Académie Vitti and, for a time (*c.*1905), at the École des Beaux-Arts.

From about 1911 until 1947 Ginner kept manuscript notebooks in which he recorded his pictures, their dates and measurements, where and when they were exhibited, and to whom they were sold and for how much. Several works are retrospectively recorded for 1908, when he left the Académie Vitti to launch his career by sending work to London for exhibition at the first show of the non-jury exhibiting society, the Allied Artists' Association. In 1909 he visited Argentina, where in September he and Dora Erichsen held a joint exhibition at the Salón Costa in Buenos Aires. Towards the end of that year he moved to London (where his sister and his mother, following her remarriage, lived) and took a studio in Chelsea. In 1910 he again exhibited with the Allied Artists' Association, where, because of his surname, he was brought together with Harold Gilman and Spencer Gore to serve on the alphabetically selected hanging committee. The three formed an immediate kinship. Ginner, with his French looks and manners and firsthand knowledge of French post-impressionism, was an exciting addition to the Saturday 'at homes' at 19 Fitzroy Street, cradle of the *Camden Town Group. About 1911 he moved to 3 Chesterfield Street, near King's Cross on the fringes of Camden Town.

Ginner's earliest works of 1908–11, brilliantly coloured and vehemently executed in thick worms of oily paint, betray an exuberant admiration for Van Gogh. However, by 1912 he had established the basis of his mature, lifelong, and unmistakable style: the application of loaded paint in small, tightly juxtaposed touches of rich, deep-toned colour to build up a crustily woven surface comparable in texture to silk embroidery. Urban subjects represent his especial contribution to the vocabulary of Camden Town painting, influencing in particular the work of Malcolm Drummond (*Portrait of Ginner*, 1911, City Art Gallery, Southampton). His innate feeling for pattern brought coherence and strength to his views of city roofs and bustling city centres (*Piccadilly Circus*, 1912, Tate collection). He used a hand-held viewfinder to select the precise boundaries of his motif, transcribed in meticulous, annotated drawings from nature on which he based the intricate paintings created in the studio.

Although a key participant in the creation of the

Camden Town group in 1911, of the London group in 1913, and of the Cumberland Market group formed by Robert Bevan in 1915, Ginner was not a political activist like his friend Gilman. His only foray into polemics was 'Neo-realism', a cogent essay first published in the *New Age* on 1 January 1914 and in April as a manifesto prefacing the catalogue of his joint exhibition with Gilman at the Goupil Galleries. The basis of his creed was that only art based on the objective study of nature had value; formulaic art was without worth. This declaration suggests that he did not esteem the three stylized murals (*Tiger Hunting*, *Birds and Indians*, and *Chasing Monkeys*; all now lost) which he painted on commission in 1912 to decorate the 'Cave of the Golden Calf' at the avant-garde Cabaret Theatre Club in London.

Ginner was profoundly affected by the death of his two closest colleagues, Gore in 1914 and Gilman (who caught his influenza when tending Ginner) in 1919. He moved to Hampstead and became increasingly reclusive. Having seen the woman he loved marry another, he remained a bachelor. Despite his adventurous youth he seldom went abroad, apart from an official war artist posting to Marseilles in 1917–18. Instead he went on painting trips around Britain—to Chester, Leeds, Belfast, Cornwall, and the Isle of Wight.

Ginner took every opportunity to exhibit his work in London and elsewhere in England, and in later life was especially successful in the north. He was appointed an official war artist during the Second World War, became an associate of the Royal Academy in 1942, and was appointed CBE in 1950. Untouched by fashion, he never wavered from the unique style and vision he established at the beginning of his career. Opulent in texture, meticulously crafted, bold in pattern, and rich in colour, his paintings were less literal and more adventurous than realized at the time. However, his art was self-contained and had little influence on other artists after 1914. He died at the Belgravia Chelsea Nursing Home, Chelsea, London, from pneumonia on 6 January 1952. His work is represented in nearly every public art gallery in the United Kingdom. WENDY BARON

Sources B. F. Hall, *Paintings and drawings by Harold Gilman and Charles Ginner in the collection of Edward le Bas* (1965) • J. Rothenstein, 'Charles Ginner', *Modern English painters*, 1: *Sickert to Smith* (1952), 188–93 • M. Easton, 'Charles Ginner: viewing and finding', *Apollo*, 91 (1970), 204–9 • *CGPLA Eng. & Wales* (1952)

Archives Tate collection, notebooks detailing his paintings and drawings | Tate collection, letters to Stanislawa de Karlowska • Tate collection, letters to Basil Geighton and Frances Creighton

Likenesses M. Drummond, oils, 1911, Southampton Art Gallery • C. Ginner, self-portrait, pen, ink, and watercolour drawing, 1940–49, NPG • C. Ginner, self-portrait, oils, 1942; formerly in possession of Edward le Bas

Wealth at death £7485 18*s*. 2*d*.: probate, 10 March 1952, *CGPLA Eng. & Wales*

Ginnett, (John) Frederick (1825–1892), equestrian performer and circus proprietor, was born in Lambeth, the eldest son of Jean Pierre Ginnett (*d*. 1861), the founder of Ginnett's circus, and his wife, Anne, *née* Partridge (*d*. 1877). (A John Frederick Jannett was baptized in Lambeth on 2 October 1825.) He made his first recorded public appearance at Astley's Amphitheatre, London, in December 1830, described as 'an entirely new prodigy … the infant non pareil'. In 1832 he appeared in a command performance before the king and queen at Brighton with Andrew Ducrow's equestrian company. By 1851 he had become director of Franconi's Cirque National from Paris, and in 1861, following the death of his father, he took over control of the family circus, and was responsible for its enormous success. He built a number of permanent circus buildings, including those at Portsmouth, Plymouth, Dublin, and Cork (the Portsmouth building was used only as a music-hall).

With his first wife, Sarah (*d*. 1866), the daughter of William Savage, a Warwick corn dealer, whom he married on 20 February 1855, Ginnett had three sons, Frederick, Claude, and Bertie, all of whom went into the profession, Frederick with considerable success. On 17 September 1874 Ginnett married Anne Maria (1853–1915), the daughter of John Snape, a Leamington Spa decorator; they had four daughters (including the equestrian performer Ida Iona) and two sons. Ginnett died from bronchitis and asthma on 12 January 1892 at his residence, 27 Wellington Road, Brighton, and was buried in the Brighton parochial cemetery three days later.

At the time of his death, Ginnett owned three circus buildings, the Eden Theatre (later the Grand) in North Road, Brighton, the Hippodrome, Belfast, and the Hippodrome, Torquay. His estate, valued in March 1892 at some £36,000, included 274 horses and a large tenting circus with associated paraphernalia. JOHN M. TURNER

Sources A. H. Saxon, *The life and art of Andrew Ducrow* (1978) • R. M. Sanders, *The English circus* (1932) • H. A. A. Whiteley, *Memories of circus, variety, etc.* (1981) • *Brighton Examiner* (15 Jan 1892) • parish register (baptisms), St John the Evangelist, Lambeth, Surrey, 2 Oct 1825 • m. cert. • d. cert. • F. Foster, *Pink coat, spangles and sawdust* (1948) • C. B. Cochran, *Showman looks on* (1945) • C. W. Montague, *Recollections of an equestrian manager* (1881) • G. Ginnett, *The sawdust ring* (1936) • R. Croft-Cooke and W. S. Meadmore, *The sawdust ring* (1951) • J. Lloyd, *My circus life* (1925)

Likenesses photographs, priv. coll.

Wealth at death £36,334 15*s*. 0*d*.: probate, 17 March 1892, *CGPLA Eng. & Wales*

Ginsberg, Morris (1889–1970), sociologist and philosopher, was born in Lithuania on 14 May 1889, the son of Meyer Ginsberg, tobacco manufacturer. He migrated to Britain, where he attracted attention as a talented undergraduate while reading philosophy at University College, London (UCL), which he entered in 1910. Such a migration was common enough at that time but, as Maurice Freedman (his junior colleague, friend, and admirer as joint editor of the *Jewish Journal of Sociology*) remarked, 'there can have been few Talmudic scholars, entirely Yiddish-speaking until their adolescence, who transformed themselves into members of the austere English middle class' (Fletcher, 269). Part of the interest of Ginsberg's life and an essential key to his character lies in the long bridge he successfully crossed from an obscure Lithuanian Jewish community and a childhood education in classical Hebrew to a prominent position in British social studies at the

Morris Ginsberg (1889–1970), by Claude Rogers, 1960

London School of Economics (LSE). Much of his early life will probably remain obscure: for he was determinedly reticent about his youth, refused to record his personal memories, and clearly wished to be remembered mainly, even exclusively, through his writing and teaching.

Ginsberg's unusual quickness of mind and lucidity of expression earned him recognition at UCL before the First World War, when he was a Martin White and John Stuart Mill scholar. He obtained his BA in philosophy with first-class honours in 1913, and his MA in 1915. His philosophical career began there as assistant to Professor G. Dawes Hicks. While the connection with UCL and the grounding of his life's work in philosophy was maintained, it is with sociology and the LSE that Ginsberg is mainly associated from 1914, when he was first invited to be a part-time assistant to L. T. Hobhouse. Permanent tenure did not come to him until 1922, but his service to the school continued thereafter for more than forty further years as reader (1924), successor to Hobhouse in the Martin White chair of sociology (1929), and as an emeritus professor (1954) who undertook part-time teaching well into the 1960s. He was prevented from active service by poor eyesight in the First World War, but the legend and indeed truth is that he stood in for four of the regular teaching staff, including Major Clement R. Attlee and Sergeant R. H. Tawney.

Ginsberg's association with and devotion to Hobhouse began while he was at UCL, where he collaborated in a comparative anthropological study which became a classic—L. T. Hobhouse, G. C. Wheeler, and M. Ginsberg, *The Material Culture and Social Institutions of the Simpler Peoples* (1915). Subsequently and throughout his working life Hobhouse was the dominant influence and Ginsberg devoted himself to the same essential problems of the liberal tradition, the understanding of the evolution of mankind, materially, socially, culturally, and morally. At the centre of this tradition was a preoccupation with the idea of moral progress and its economic and social correlates: and around that central problem he undertook wide exploration of how variations in social structure were related to moral belief and behaviour, steadily searching on the one hand for the basis of a rational ethic and, on the other, for a definition of the prospects for social institutions expressing reason and justice.

The pursuit of these intellectual concerns required both philosophical sophistication and an immense knowledge of social history. Ginsberg acquired both and demonstrated them in a long series of books, essays, and lectures. His prose style was economical and unpretentious, carrying lightly a vast erudition. The titles convey the theme of these sustained interests—*Moral Progress* (1944), *The Idea of Progress: a Revaluation* (1953), *On the Diversity of Morals* (1953), and *Reason and Unreason in Society* (1947). His last published work, *On Justice in Society*, which appeared in 1965, is a characteristic essay in analysis of the concepts of justice, equality, rights, and duties and their application in criminal law, contract, and international relations.

Ginsberg's contribution to these difficult and enduring problems of ethics in society gives him a permanent place in twentieth-century scholarship. Dahrendorf appraised him as 'the wise social philosopher' (Dahrendorf, 204). His reputation as a sociologist is, however, less secure. After Hobhouse he was the major British sociologist between the wars. But the rapid development of the subject after the Second World War passed him by and he was absent from the reading lists of the LSE *Calendar* in 1996–7. Attention shifted mainly to American work, towards which he was gently but firmly dismissive, regarding most of its leading exponents as verbose and pretentious. It was not that his own erudition was in any way limited. On the contrary, he was familiar with the major and minor European authors, appreciated the importance of Max Weber in Germany and Emile Durkheim in France, and was quick to provide a critical introduction of Vilfredo Pareto to the English-speaking world. He was aware of and lectured on German phenomenology a generation before it became fashionable in America and Britain.

Yet the weight of Ginsberg's teaching continued to rest on the interests he inherited from Hobhouse and conceded little or nothing to the eagerness of his post-war students to come to grips with the growing volume of American empirical sociology, the development of quantitative methods, and, later, of Marxist and phenomenological approaches to sociological theory. A rapidly expanding profession of sociology with diverse methods and theories replaced the coherent blend of moral philosophy and social inquiry of which Ginsberg had succeeded Hobhouse as the leading scholar. The question of the relation between moral and social evolution, which they both addressed with painstaking scholarship, remained important but no longer occupied the centre of the subject.

As an academic notable, Ginsberg was widely recognized and admitted to fellowship of the British Academy in 1953. He also held honorary degrees from London, Glasgow, and Nottingham universities, and was an honorary fellow of LSE.

On a personal level, Ginsberg won and kept strong affection from colleagues and students. He was respected for his integrity, loved for his gentleness, and admired for his informed intellectual power. But he also had enemies, notably Karl Mannheim. Fletcher affects to know nothing of this animosity, which the director of the LSE described as the Mannheim–Ginsberg problem (Fletcher, 6; Dahrendorf, 295), but both Dahrendorf and Shils (pp. 215–16) offer objective accounts of it. Ginsberg's humility and academic assurance were often remarked. Both were real in him and appeared to others as a paradoxical character—a kind of self-effacing arrogance. Although he held a chair in a subject held suspect by many scholars, his own standards were of the highest demanded by academic tradition. He was remembered by his contemporaries professionally through his writing, personally as 'a small, quiet, serious yet friendly man, curled up in an old armchair, surrounded by walls of books, looking as if he had grown out of them' (Fletcher, 265).

A private and rather lonely man, Ginsberg was seldom exuberant, often sad, and sometimes despairing. He remained something of an outsider, having travelled far from his East European origins without alienating himself from the religion of his forebears. In 1931 he married Ethel, daughter of Arthur William Street, fellmonger. They had no children. They lived in Highgate, where she died in 1962. He also died there, at his home at 5 Millfield Lane, on 31 August 1970. A. H. Halsey

Sources R. Fletcher, ed., *The science of society and the unity of mankind: a memorial volume for Morris Ginsberg* (1974) • *The Times* (1 Sept 1970) • *The Times* (14 Sept 1970) • R. Dahrendorf, *LSE: a history of the London School of Economics and Political Science, 1895–1995* (1995) • E. Shils, *Portraits: a gallery of intellectuals* (1997) • personal knowledge (2004)

Archives BLPES, corresp. and papers; further papers | Bodl. Oxf., corresp. relating to Society for Protection of Science and Learning • Keele University Library, LePlay Collection, corresp. and minute books

Likenesses W. Stoneman, photograph, 1957, NPG • C. Rogers, pencil, 1960, NPG [*see illus.*] • C. Rogers, oils, London School of Economics • photograph, repro. in Fletcher, ed., *Science of society and the unity of mankind*

Wealth at death £140,951: probate, 8 Dec 1970, *CGPLA Eng. & Wales*

Ginsburg, Christian David (1821–1914), Bible scholar and missionary, was born on 25 December 1821 in Warsaw, Poland, to Baruch Ginsburgh (or Güntzberg). Little is known about his Jewish family of birth. Family tradition maintains that his parents lived in Spain before migrating to Warsaw before Ginsburg's birth; that an ancestor was in the court of the Spanish monarchs Ferdinand and Isabella; and that his mother was English. One older brother is mentioned in an account of his conversion to Christianity.

In Poland, Ginsburg pursued Bible studies and was a cotton spinner, working at Ozorkow for some years. On 7 October 1845 he married Teiszer Mala Berkewicz according to Jewish rites; they had one child. After several years of contact with the Warsaw mission of the London Society for Promoting Christianity Amongst the Jews, Ginsburg was baptized by the Revd F. W. Becker on 3 October 1846 and took the name 'Christian'. Leaving his wife and child behind, he travelled to England under the auspices of the London Society and moved into the London Society's Operative Jewish Converts' Institution. He applied, unsuccessfully, in 1849 to its Hebrew College (opened in 1840), but enrolled instead in July 1850 (on probation) in the Jews' College in London, the British Society missionary school (founded in 1847). There he studied a curriculum based on Bible Hebrew and Greek that was designed to prepare students to become missionaries. He studied with Benjamin Davidson, the first principal of the college and the first missionary employed by the British Society, and he established what became a lifelong friendship with Isaac Salkinson, later a missionary in Vienna and a translator into Hebrew of the New Testament and of the works of Shakespeare and Milton.

After completing his course Ginsburg was in 1853 appointed a missionary for the British Society in London, and in 1857 he was transferred to Liverpool. In the same year he also published his first book, a translation and commentary on the Song of Solomon. In 1858 he became a naturalized British subject. It is not clear what happened to his first wife, but on 19 October he married Margaret Ryley, *née* Crosfield, the daughter of William Crosfield, a Liverpool sugar refiner. His wife's family, who were Quakers, actively supported the work of the British Society and promoted his own scholarship. There were two children: Benedict William Ginsburg, born in October 1859, and Ethel Margaret. In 1867 Margaret died, and in the following year Ginsburg married Emilie, *née* Hausburg, daughter of F. Leopold Hausburg of Woolton. They had three daughters: Emilie Catherine, Hildegarde Beatrice, and Sybil Gwendolyn.

Ginsburg's scholarly interests grew and deepened. In 1861 he published his translation and commentary on Ecclesiastes. He became an active member of the Literary and Philosophical Society of Liverpool, giving papers and publishing articles in their *Proceedings*, including histories of the Karaites in 1862 and of the Kabballah in 1865. In February 1863 he was awarded an honorary LLD degree from the University of Glasgow.

In 1863 Ginsburg retired from missionary work because of his health and in order to devote his full energy to his scholarship. In 1864 he published a history of the Essenes, a Jewish ascetic sect in the 'Second Temple' period, and joined the committee of the British Society. In 1867 he published an annotated translation of Jacob ben Chayim's *Introduction to the Rabbinic Bible* and of Elias Levita's *Masoret Ha-Masoret*. In 1870 he was invited to be one of the original members of the Old Testament Revision Company, and he subsequently moved to a new home at Binfield, Berkshire, to be closer to his work in London.

In 1870 Ginsburg published a book on the Moabite

stone, including a transcription, a translation, and a commentary. The Moabite (or Mesha) stone was a monument of the mid-ninth century BC, containing an inscription by King Mesha of Moab which was written in ancient Canaanite letters. In 1872 Ginsburg participated in an expedition to Moab. His most important scholarship, however, focused on his work on the text of the Hebrew Bible and the Masorah. Working with sixty manuscripts he collected and collated textual variants and notes to prepare his Masoretico-critical edition of the Hebrew Bible, which was published in 1894 by the Trinitarian Bible Society. In his 'Introduction' he described the Masoretic enterprise of counting letters, words, and verses and developing an extensive apparatus of notes to preserve the text. He also collected and collated these Masoretic notes, publishing them in his magnum opus *The Massorah* (4 vols., 1880–86), a work of great importance for subsequent Masoretic and biblical scholars. In 1904 Ginsburg was elected editor of the British and Foreign Bible Society's *New Critical Hebrew Bible*, eventually published in 1926. Before his death in 1914 he completed the Pentateuch, the Prophets, and part of the Writings.

Ginsburg was recognized as an authority on biblical and Hebrew matters. In 1883, when the British Museum was offered a manuscript of Deuteronomy written in the same ancient Canaanite script as the Moabite stone, officials asked him to evaluate the fragments. He published the text and translation and then declared the fragments forgeries. In this celebrated incident of the Shapira manuscript, Ginsburg was portrayed as saving the British from financial and scholarly humiliation. Among the first modern Bible critics to recognize and use textual variants and notes, he set the stage for subsequent scholars who have built upon his foundations. Although his work would have benefited more from a critical appreciation of stemmatic types—probing the reliability of independent evidence that one manuscript can bring to another—his careful collation of variants, and his determination to bring these notes, variants, and manuscripts to light, changed the course of biblical scholarship.

Ginsburg also was active in scholarly and political circles. He delighted in social situations and was a member of the Liberal Club, which appointed him to its library committee and which continued to display his portrait. He collected Bibles and engravings, sat as a justice of the peace for Surrey and Middlesex, was a close associate of William Aldis Wright and A. E. Cowley, and was a friend of William E. Gladstone. Ginsburg died at Oakthorpe, Palmers Green, Middlesex, on 7 March 1914, and was buried, after a service in Southgate parish church, at Southgate cemetery, Middlesex, on 10 March; he was survived by his wife, Emilie.

FRED N. REINER

Sources J. Dunlop, *Memories of gospel triumphs among the Jews during the Victorian era* (1894) • F. J. Exley, *Our hearts' desire: the story of the British Society for Propagation of the Gospel among the Jews* (1942) • J. F. A. de le Roi, *Die evangelische Christenheit und die Juden* (1892), vol. 3 • I. Singer and others, eds., *The Jewish encyclopedia*, 12 vols. (1901–6) • J. Klatzkin, ed., *Encyclopaedia Judaica: das Judentum in Geschichte und Gegenwart*, 10 vols. (Berlin, 1928–34) • C. Roth, ed., *Encyclopaedia Judaica*, 16 vols. (Jerusalem, 1971–2) • *Jewish Intelligence* (Dec 1846), 440–41 • *Jewish Intelligence* [other issues] • *Jewish Herald* • *Proceedings of the Literary and Philosophical Society of Liverpool* (1862) • *Proceedings of the Literary and Philosophical Society of Liverpool* [other issues] • H. M. Orlinsky, 'The Masoretic Text: a critical evaluation', in C. D. Ginsburg, *Introduction to the Massoretico-critical edition of the Hebrew Bible* (1966) [Prolegomenon] • birth, marriage and death records, Warsaw, 38 (1845) • *The Times* (11 March 1914)

Archives BL, journal of expedition to Moab, Add. MSS 41291–41292, 41294 • BL, corresp. relating to M. W. Shapira's forged MS of Deuteronomy, Add. MS 41294 | BL, memorandum and letters to W. E. Gladstone, Add. MSS 44482–44789, *passim* • British and Foreign Bible Society, Swindon, archives

Likenesses A. C. Gould, oils, 1914, National Liberal Club, London • Elliott & Fry, photograph, repro. in Dunlop, *Memories of gospel triumphs among the Jews*, 369

Wealth at death £8993 17*s*. 5*d*.: probate, 30 June 1914, *CGPLA Eng. & Wales*

Giolo, Prince (*fl.* **1690**). *See under* Exotic visitors (*act. c.*1500–*c.*1855).

Giordani, Giuseppe (*fl.* **1745–1767**). *See under* Giordani, Tommaso (*c.*1733–1806).

Giordani, Nicolina (*fl.* **1753–1774**). *See under* Giordani, Tommaso (*c.*1733–1806).

Giordani, Tommaso (*c.***1733–1806**), composer, was born probably in or near Naples, Italy, the son of **Giuseppe Giordani** (*fl.* 1745–1767), librettist, and his wife, Antonia (*d.* 1764), a singer, who formed a travelling opera company in Naples in the 1740s. The company included Tommaso, his brother Francesco, a dancer, and his sisters Nicolina and Marina, both singers. The company played in Ancona and Pesaro in 1745 before moving north to Graz in 1747, Frankfurt and Salzburg in 1750, Amsterdam in 1752, and Paris in 1753, and reached London by the end of 1753. There they performed the comic opera *Gli amanti gelosi*, with Giuseppe's libretto, on 17 December 1753 at Covent Garden Theatre. A great success, it was followed by three other comic operas during the winter season. The company performed at the Little Theatre in the Haymarket in 1755 in Giuseppe's new comic opera *L'albergatrice*, for which Francesco created the dances, and on 12 January 1754 put on *La comediante fatta cantatrice*, with music by Tommaso, at Covent Garden. Nothing more is heard of the family until 1764, when they were invited to Dublin to perform at the Smock Alley theatre. Despite the death of Antonia in Capel Street, Dublin, in October, they opened the season on 24 November 1764 with a new version of *Gli amanti gelosi*, with new dances created by Francesco and an overture and three airs composed by Tommaso (the rest of the music was by Galuppi). The cast included Nicolina and Marina. Francesco also contributed the dances for Thomas Arne's *Artaxerxes*, first performed in Dublin at Smock Alley in February 1765. The family remained in Dublin, performing at the Crow Street theatre until 1767.

Tommaso composed the music for several comic operas at the Smock Alley theatre between 1765 and 1767, including *Don Fulminone* (1765), *The Maid of the Mill* to Isaac Bickerstaff's libretto (1765), and *Love in Disguise* (1766). *Phyllis at Court*, his first *opera seria*, had its first performance on 25 February 1767 at the Crow Street theatre. Giordani remained in Dublin until 1768, when he moved to London following charges of plagiarism, although he returned to Dublin to conduct the 1769 season at the Rotunda.

Giordani settled in London and became closely involved with the King's Theatre, Haymarket, where he directed operas and musical entertainments and composed three new operas: the comic operas *Il padre e il figlio rivali* (1770) and *Il bacio* (1782), and *Il re pastore* (1778), an *opera seria*. He also composed songs for Richard Brinsley Sheridan's *The Critic*, first performed at Drury Lane on 29 October 1779, and wrote popular songs for the concerts at the Vauxhall Pleasure Gardens, many of which he published. He was also a prolific composer of instrumental music, especially for the keyboard; his works included a set of quintets for harpsichord and string quartet (1771), six keyboard concertos, op. 14 (1776), and his very popular overture to *The Elopement*, a pantomime performed at Drury Lane in 1767, which was published in parts about 1770.

Tommaso Giordani returned to Dublin in the summer of 1783 for the season at the Rotunda. With the countertenor Michael Leoni he then created the English Opera House at the Little Theatre in Capel Street in December 1783, opening on 18 December with *Gibraltar* and *The Haunted Castle*. They intended to put on operas with librettos by Irish writers and music by Giordani, but although the season included seven new works, including his burlesque opera *Orfeo et Euridice* and the musical entertainments *The Enchantress* and *The Dying Indian*, the venture was a financial disaster, and they were declared bankrupt in July 1784.

In 1784 Giordani married one of the daughters of Tate *Wilkinson (1739–1803), the actor and theatre manager, and he remained in Dublin as composer at Smock Alley for the 1784–5 season and as music director at the Crow Street theatre in 1788. He continued to write for the stage, his compositions including music for the pantomime *The Island of Saints*, put on at Smock Alley in 1785. His last opera, *The Cottage Festival*, was performed at Crow Street in 1796. Giordani was also a teacher, and his pupils included John Field (1782–1837) and Thomas Cooke (1782–1848). Field's début as a pianist was in one of the 'spiritual concerts' organized by Giordani at the Rotunda in March 1792. Giordani was president of the Irish Music Fund from 1794.

Tommaso Giordani died in February 1806 at his home, 201 Great Britain Street, Dublin. The exact date of his death is unknown, but it is recorded that on 24 February the Irish Music Fund made a payment of 5 guineas for his funeral.

Giordani's sister **Nicolina Giordani** (*fl.* 1753–1774) won fame in her role as La Spiletta in *Gli amanti gelosi*, first performed at Covent Garden on 17 December 1753, and from then on she took the name Signora Spiletta. In 1764 she accompanied her family to Dublin, where she was very popular, repeating her success in *Gli amanti gelosi* at the Smock Alley theatre. She was in London in the 1770s, singing at the King's Theatre, Haymarket, in 1774, and had a reputation as an excellent comic actress. Horace Walpole wrote that 'besides being pretty' she 'has more vivacity and variety of humour than ever existed in any creature' (Walpole, *Corr.*, 35.160).

ANNE PIMLOTT BAKER

Sources *New Grove*, 2nd edn · T. J. Walsh, *Opera in Dublin, 1705–1797: the social scene* (1973) · Highfill, Burnim & Langhans, *BDA* · R. Fiske, *English theatre music in the eighteenth century* (1973) · B. Boydell, *Rotunda music in eighteenth-century Dublin* (Dublin, 1992) · C. Price, J. Milhous, and R. D. Hume, *Italian opera in late eighteenth-century London, 1: The King's Theatre, Haymarket, 1778–1791* (1995) · S. McVeigh, *Concert life in London from Mozart to Haydn* (1993) · Walpole, *Corr.*

Likenesses portrait (Nicolina Giordani as Spiletta in *Gli amanti gelosi*), repro. in Walsh, *Opera in Dublin*

Gipps, Sir George (1791–1847), colonial governor, born in Ringwould in Kent, was the son of George Gipps, rector of the parish. He was educated at the King's School, Canterbury, and at the Royal Military Academy, Woolwich, then joined the Royal Engineers and saw duty in Portugal, Spain, and Flanders (1809–17). After travelling in Europe and being employed at Chatham, he was in the West Indies (1824–9), where by his reports on slavery and possible emancipation he displayed considerable administrative ability. In 1830 he married Elizabeth, the daughter of Major-General George Ramsay. The couple had one child, later General Sir Reginald Gipps GCB.

In the early 1830s Gipps was a member of two commissions inquiring into English electoral boundaries. He was appointed private secretary to Lord Auckland in 1834. Then, in 1835, he went to Canada as a member of the Gosford commission, which inquired into administration and land tenure. In the same year he was made KCB. On his return to England in 1837, Gipps was offered the governorship of New South Wales; he arrived at Sydney in February 1838.

Gipps found a colony experiencing rapid change, and therefore full of tensions. The position of Aborigines in law remained undefined. Pastoralism was expanding rapidly, particularly in the Port Phillip district (Victoria). Free immigration had grown speedily through the 1830s. Following the report of the Molesworth committee (1838), the imperial government discontinued convict transportation to eastern mainland Australia in 1840. In 1842, responding to local pressure, it instituted a legislative council, one-third nominated, two-thirds elected on a property franchise. A heterogeneous population demanded religious toleration, and education for its children.

Quiet dignity and steady application of principle marked Gipps's approach to these and other issues. He recognized the inevitability of pastoral expansion:

> as well might it be attempted to confine the Arabs of the Desert within a circle, traced upon the sands, as to confine the Graziers or Woolgrowers of New South Wales within any bounds that can possibly be assigned to them. (*Historical Records of Australia*, 1st ser., 21, 1924, 127)

However, by licence fees and a levy on stock to pay for a border police, he tried to bring some order to it. Following Colonial Office instructions, he sought to extend the law's protection to Aborigines; and, in the face of considerable public opposition, he saw that some of the white stockmen responsible for the Myall Creek massacre of June

1838 were punished. In conjunction with Charles Joseph La Trobe, with whom he enjoyed a remarkable rapport, he oversaw the administration of the Port Phillip district, including a protectorate system. He vigorously supported immigration. While not really in sympathy with the project, he sanctioned Alexander Maconochie's penal experiments at Norfolk Island. Always concerned to be financially prudent—'my whole official experience teaches me, that in Downing Street at least the governor who keeps his government out of debt is the best' (quoted in *AusDB*)—he kept a tight rein on colonial expenditure.

Opposition to Gipps's policies increased steadily in the 1840s. When he attempted to augment the money available for immigration, by altering land-granting and -selling policies and insisting on the payment of quit-rents, he united the pastoralists against him; they first voiced their opposition in the new legislative council, and then appealed (ultimately successfully) to London. Because it involved forced relocation and regimentation according to the dictates of an alien culture, and because the protectors lacked effective powers, the protectorate system failed the Aborigines of Victoria miserably. There was otherwise little improvement in the lot of Aborigines, with the border police essentially acting as a military force protecting Europeans and their property rather than as one keeping peace between the races. Gipps found it impossible to reconcile the competing educational requirements of Anglicans, Catholics, and nonconformists; and he failed to persuade the legislative council that it should support his proposal for a comprehensive, non-denominational system, paid for by the government. Newspaper editors demanded that the legislative council, rather than an austere official whose loyalty was to a distant authority, control the colony's finances. On Gipps's quitting office, the *Sydney Morning Herald* (4 July 1846) stated that 'from the matured observation of eight years … Sir George Gipps *has been the worst Governor New South Wales ever had*'. History shows this assessment to be false.

The portrait of Gipps in the state library of New South Wales presents a handsome man, reserved but intense. Contemporary accounts indicate that, while he answered questions frankly, he asked few himself; and he withheld from the public the warmth and humour he showed his family and in his letters to Governor La Trobe. He worked very hard, and was able to command both general issues and myriad details. He argued his views logically and honestly; what he lacked was political cunning. Given his character and outlook, it was inevitable that he should meet opposition in the colony he came to govern. Between 1838 and 1846, by birth and migration, the European population of New South Wales almost doubled, to reach *c.*190,000. From 1840 the proportion of convicts in it shrank rapidly. Together with judicial and administrative reforms, these developments meant that the society was rapidly transformed into a free one, whose citizens were eager to exercise full political rights. Even so, Gipps brought much order to the governance of New South Wales, and the colony benefited from his firm control even as the people deprecated it.

Gipps left Sydney and returned to England in July 1846, with advanced heart disease. He died on 28 February 1847, at St Martin's Hill House, Canterbury, Kent; there is a monument to him in the cathedral. ALAN FROST

Sources S. C. McCulloch, 'Gipps, Sir George', *AusDB*, vol. 1 • S. C. McCulloch, 'Sir George Gipps and Captain Alexander Maconochie', *Historical Studies*, 27 (1955–7), 387–405 • *Gipps–La Trobe correspondence, 1839–1846*, ed. A. G. L. Shaw (1989) • d. cert.
Archives Mitchell L., NSW, speeches | Auckland Public Library, Melbourne, letters to Sir George Grey • Lpool RO, letters to Lord Stanley • RBG Kew, letters to Sir William Jackson Hooper • State Library of Victoria, Melbourne, corresp. with C. J. La Trobe
Likenesses attrib. H. W. Pickersgill, portrait, *c.*1840, State Library of New South Wales, Australia • H. Weekes, marble bust, *c.*1849, Canterbury Cathedral • oils, Mitchell L., NSW

Gipps, Sir Richard (*bap.* **1659**, *d.* **1708**), topographer, second son of John Gipps (*c.*1620–1707) of Great Whelnetham, near Bury St Edmunds, Suffolk, and his second wife, Mary (*d.* 1665), daughter of David Davidson, alderman of London, was baptized at Great Whelnetham on 15 September 1659. After seven years under Edward Leeds at Bury grammar school he matriculated at Gonville and Caius College, Cambridge, in September 1675. The following February he was admitted to Gray's Inn where, despite one lapse of discipline, he was made master of the revels on 3 November 1682. The revels enjoyed the patronage of royalty, and on 27 November the new master was knighted by Charles II at Whitehall. Two months later Gipps invited the king, queen, and court to a masque to be performed next Candlemas (2 February) at the inn.

After this early climax to his career in high society, Gipps retained chambers at the inn, but spent most of his time on his Suffolk estate. He is notable as an early field archaeologist, drawing and using considerable insight to describe coin and pottery finds near his home. His widely dispersed manuscripts include 'Antiquitates Suffolcienses' (BL, Add. MS 20695), valuable accounts of the origins of over three hundred Suffolk families, edited for publication in 1894. Some of his most interesting papers survive from the library of the Suffolk antiquary Cox Macro (1683–1767).

About 1690 Gipps married Mary, daughter and heir of Edward Giles of Bowden, near Totnes, Devon; she brought him a large estate and they had three sons and a daughter between 1692 and 1700; she died in 1703. Exercising his rights over fishing at Ashprington there in 1695, it was alleged that Gipps and two servants broke into a poacher's house doing damage and taking goods worth £100. In June 1702 his Ickworth whig neighbour John Hervey came to complain that Gipps had cut down trees of his for the Whelnetham maypole, but the moment was ill-judged, for that morning Gipps had heard that he and other tories were put out of the commission for the peace of the county. A court case between the two men ensued.

Gipps died on 21 December 1708 and was buried on 24 December in his wife's grave in Great Whelnetham church. His son Richard succeeded to the estate, but his fine library was disposed of in 1729 when it was one of the first to be sold by means of a priced catalogue rather than at auction. J. M. BLATCHLY

Sir Richard Gipps (*bap.* 1659, *d.* 1708), by John Smith, 1687 (after John Closterman)

Sources S. H. A. Hervey, ed., *Great and Little Whelnetham parish registers*, Suffolk Green Books, 15 (1910) · *Letter books of John Hervey, first earl of Bristol*, ed. S. H. A. H. [S. H. A. Hervey], 1 (1894) · F. Haslewood, 'Ancient families of Suffolk', *Proceedings of the Suffolk Institute of Archaeology and Natural History*, 8 (1892–4), 121–214 · Suffolk RO, Ipswich, Gipps MS collections, HD 695 · *DNB* · will, 1709, PRO, PROB 11/506, sig. 34

Archives BL, commonplace book, Egerton MS 3880 · BL, Suffolk collections, Add. MS 20695 · BL, Suffolk collections, Harley MS 4626 · Bodl. Oxf., Tanner MSS · Suffolk RO, Ipswich, notes relating to the history of Suffolk probably by him

Likenesses J. Smith, mezzotint, 1687 (after an oil painting by J. Closterman), BM, NPG [*see illus.*] · J. Closterman, oils

Gipps, Ruth Dorothy Louisa (1921–1999), conductor and composer, was born on 20 February 1921 at 14 Parkhurst Road, Bexhill, Sussex, one of three children of Gerard Cardew Bryan Gipps, examiner at the Board of Trade, and his wife, Hélène Bettina Johner, piano teacher. Known from childhood as Wid, Gipps was educated at Brickwall School, The Gables, and, finally, Bexhill county school, which she left at the age of twelve. Her precocious musical talent was cultivated by her mother, and she appeared as a pianist in public from an early age: in 1925 she played Grieg's waltz in A minor at a student concert at the Grotrian Hall, London; in 1929 she performed her first published composition, *The Fairy Shoemaker*, at the Brighton Festival; in 1931 she was the soloist in Haydn's keyboard concerto in D major at the Colonnade, Bexhill; and in 1936 she performed Beethoven's piano concerto no. 5 ('Emperor') at the Hastings Festival. Though gifted, Gipps had difficulty in gaining early formal recognition for her talents: she failed the performer's licentiate of the Royal Academy of Music on three occasions, finally obtaining the diploma of associate of the Royal College of Music at Christmas 1936. In the following year she entered the college as a full-time student and studied composition (with R. O. Morris, Gordon Jacob, and Ralph Vaughan Williams), the piano (with Herbert Fryer, Arthur Alexander, and Kendall Taylor), and the oboe (with Leon Goossens and Harold Shepley). But the college failed to satisfy fully her passion for knowledge, so she undertook an external BMus degree at the University of Durham, which she completed successfully in 1941.

In 1942 Gipps left the Royal College of Music; attended the Matthay Piano School; married (on 19 March) Robert George Hugh Baker (*b.* 1920/21), the principal clarinettist of the City of Birmingham Symphony Orchestra (CBSO); and heard her tone poem *Knight in Armour* performed at the last night of the Promenade Concerts under Sir Henry Wood. Although she was a talented composer, Gipps's skills did not provide a living wage, so she worked as a freelance oboist and pianist, playing with, among others, the BBC Symphony Orchestra and the Carl Rosa Opera. Like many other artists she juxtaposed her activities as a musician with her duties as a citizen: she served as an air-raid warden and gave recitals at the National Gallery. In November 1943 George Weldon conducted the first performance of her tone poem *Death on a Pale Horse* with the CBSO, and in the following year she became a full-time member of the orchestra, playing the oboe and cor anglais. Attracted to Gipps both personally and professionally, Weldon, the orchestra's permanent conductor, was keen to draw fully upon her diverse talents: he agreed to her deputizing for indisposed concert pianists, and at a remarkable concert in March 1945 she played the solo part in Glazounov's piano concerto no. 1 in the first half and rejoined the orchestra to play the cor anglais for the première of her symphony no. 1 in the second.

Encouraged by Weldon, Gipps became increasingly interested in conducting: in 1948 she was appointed chorus director of the City of Birmingham Choir and in 1949 she was engaged as conductor of the Co-op Orchestra and the CBSO Listeners' Club ladies' choir. But when Weldon was dismissed in 1951 she could no longer draw upon his support, so she decided to seek work elsewhere. Having completed an external DMus at the University of Durham in 1948, she hoped to secure an academic post locally. This was not forthcoming, so she applied for a post at BBC Midland. Her application failed, but she secured part-time work with the Oxford extra-mural delegacy. Though passionate about education, she remained a committed performer, and in September 1954 she conducted a fully professional orchestra for the first time: the Boyd Neel Orchestra at the Birmingham Town Hall.

When she moved to London in 1954, Gipps was keen to build on her experiences in Birmingham. Drawing upon her abilities as both executant and educator, she founded the London Repertoire Orchestra in 1955. The orchestra's aims were to establish a venue at which unemployed musicians could practise their skills and provide an environment where young and inexperienced performers could get to know the standard orchestral repertory. Known increasingly as a composer–conductor, she directed her cantata *The Cat* and Beethoven's symphony no. 9 ('Choral') with the Pro Arte Orchestra at the Royal Festival Hall in 1957. She was the first woman to conduct at the hall, and though the reviews of the concert were ambivalent, she returned there later that year to direct a performance with the then all-male London Symphony Orchestra. In 1959 she travelled to the USA on a Ford Foundation travel award from the English-Speaking Union and conducted a broadcast performance of her *Coronation Procession* op. 41 with the New York Orchestral Association.

After her return from North America, Gipps's career flourished: in 1959 she was appointed professor at the Trinity College of Music, London; in 1961 she founded the Chanticleer Orchestra; in 1967 she became chair of the Composers' Guild and a professor at the Royal College of Music; and in 1969 she was the first woman to conduct a symphony of her own creation—the symphony no. 3, composed in 1965—in a BBC broadcast. But her career suffered through her antagonism towards modern compositional trends: refusing to modify her views, she left the Royal College of Music in 1977. Her career now went into sharp decline. Her appointment as senior lecturer at Kingston Polytechnic between 1977 and 1979, along with the BBC's ambivalence towards her symphony no. 5 in 1982, did little to improve her flagging fortunes. But the corporation did not abandon her totally, and in 1983 a performance of her symphony no. 4 by Sir John Pritchard and the BBC Symphony Orchestra was broadcast. In 1986 she resigned from the London Repertoire Orchestra and was appointed musical director of the Heathfield Choral Society. Two years later she conducted a concert at St John's, Smith Square, London, that traced the development of music written by women composers during the previous 300 years; this was her last significant engagement as a conductor.

Gipps composed more than seventy works, including five symphonies, six concertos, and one ballet. Her music is not iconoclastic but it is appealing and often colourful. Some have suggested that her career suffered from gender discrimination. But with the subsequent interest in women composers her works were reassessed and a recording of her symphony no. 2 was released. She was made an honorary member of the Royal Academy of Music in 1966 and a fellow of the Royal College of Music in 1972, and was invested as an MBE in 1981. Ruth Gipps died, survived by her husband, at the Eastbourne District General Hospital, Eastbourne, Sussex, on 23 February 1999.

RAYMOND HOLDEN

Sources M. Campbell, 'Ruth Gipps: a woman of substance', *Signature*, 1/3 (1996), 15–20, 32–4 • A. I. Cohen, *International encyclopedia of women composers*, 2nd edn, 1 (1987) • *The Composer*, 4 (March 1960), 40 • *Daily Telegraph* (30 March 1999) • N. Kenyon, *The BBC Symphony Orchestra: the first fifty years, 1930–1980* (1981) • Grove, *Dict. mus.* (1954) • *The Guardian* (30 March 1999) • J. Halstead, 'A study of Dr. Ruth Gipps illustrating her musical development through detailed reference to symphonies two to five', MPhil diss., University of Sheffield, 1991 • b. cert. • m. cert. • d. cert. • *The Independent* (3 March 1999) • *The Macmillan dictionary of women's biography* (1999) • *New Grove* • *New Grove*, 2nd edn • *Who's who in music*, 3rd edn (1950) • *The Penguin biographical dictionary of women* (1998) • C. Pluygers, 'Discrimination: the career of Ruth Gipps', *Winds*, 7/1 (spring 1992), 14–15 • *Baker's biographical dictionary of musicians*, rev. N. Slonimsky, 8th edn (1992) • *The Times* (9 April 1999) • D. C. F. Wright, 'Ruth Gipps', *British Music*, 13 (1991), 3–13

Likenesses D. Miller, photographs, 1957, Hult. Arch.

Gipps, Thomas (*d.* 1709), Church of England clergyman, was apparently born in Leicestershire, to parents whose names are as yet unknown. He was educated at St Paul's School, London. On 23 February 1655 he was admitted a sizar at Trinity College, Cambridge, where he matriculated in 1656, graduated BA in 1659, was made a fellow in 1661, and proceeded MA in 1662. On 22 September 1667 he was ordained deacon and priest at Peterborough, and in 1668 became curate of Bottisham, Cambridgeshire. He subsequently became chaplain to the earl of Derby, who, as patron of Bury rectory, presented Gipps with the living in 1674.

Gipps was hostile to all dissent. In July 1696 he preached in Manchester *A Sermon Against Corrupting the Word of God*. He accused Presbyterians of corrupting biblical text by altering Acts 6: 3 from 'whom we might appoint' to 'whom ye might appoint' to endorse their doctrine of the right of the congregation to appoint ministers, tracing this alteration to a bible printed in 1638. To Gipps, who associated religious dissent with political disloyalty, this was a highly significant date, linking this textual change to a Cambridge puritan plot in the prelude to civil war. Publication of the sermon brought a caustic response from James Owen, the Presbyterian minister at Oswestry. An ill-tempered exchange of pamphlets followed of which *Testamentum novum* (1696), which defiantly reasserted the apostolic origins of bishops, and *Remarks on Remarks* (1698), which more emphatically stated his arguments about Cambridge subversion and the textual distortion of 1638, were Gipps's contributions.

Gipps was apparently an acerbic character. A small notebook containing his description of the glebe and the parish of Bury survives in the archives at Manchester central reference library; his comments on the character of his curate and some of the parishioners were not flattering. He also published *Three Sermons Preached in Lent and Summer* in 1683. There is no evidence to suggest that he ever married. He died at Bury on 11 March 1709 and was buried there on 13 March. His will was proved at Chester in May 1710. After the payment of bequests to friends, servants, and the poor, the residue of his estate was bequeathed to his brother, nephew, and two great-nieces, one of whom, Ann Dan, was appointed executor.

CATHERINE NUNN

Sources T. Gipps, *A sermon against corrupting the word of God* (1697) • Venn, *Alum. Cant.* • F. Howarth, *I remember: some notes on old Bury* (1917) [incl. complete transcript of Gipps's MS notebook] • E. Baines and W. R. Whatton, *The history of the county palatine and duchy of Lancaster*, new edn, ed. J. Croston and others, 2 (1889) • F. R. Raines, *The vicars of Rochdale*, ed. H. H. Howorth, 2 vols., Chetham Society, new ser., 1–2 (1883), vol. 1 • *The Rev. Oliver Heywood … his* *autobiography, diaries, anecdote and event books*, ed. J. H. Turner, 2 (1883) · will, Lancs. RO, WCW 1710 · notebook of Thomas Gipps, Man. CL, LI/34/2 · parish register, Bury, Lancashire, 13 March 1707, Lancs. RO [burial]

Wealth at death £192 1*s*. 4*d*.: will, Lancs. RO, WCW 1710

Giraldus Cambrensis. *See* Gerald of Wales (*c*.1146–1220x23).

Girardus Cornubiensis. *See* Gerard of Cornwall (*supp. fl. c*.1350).

Giraud, Herbert John (1817–1888), surgeon and botanist, was born at Faversham, Kent, on 14 April 1817, the second son and youngest child of John Thomas Giraud (1764–1836), surgeon, and his wife, Mary Chapman, daughter of William Chapman of Badlesmere Court, Kent. His grandfather, Francis Frederick Giraud (1726–1811), was born of Waldensian protestant refugee parents at Pinache, Württemberg, and was brought to England by his uncle, the Revd William Henry Giraud, vicar of Graveney, Kent, in 1736.

Herbert John Giraud was educated at the University of Edinburgh, where he graduated MD in 1840. In 1842 he married Christina Shaw, daughter of Dr David Shaw of the Bombay medical service. They had two daughters. Entering the medical service of the East India Company in 1842, he became professor of chemistry and botany in 1845 and then principal of the Grant Medical College, Bombay; at this time he was also chief medical officer of Sir Jamsetjee Jeejeebhoy's Hospital, chemical analyst to the Bombay government, surgeon-major and deputy inspector-general of the Bombay army medical service, and, in 1863, dean of the faculty of medicine in Bombay University. As a prominent physician in Bombay, Giraud was often consulted as an expert in medico-legal cases in the Bombay presidency.

Giraud wrote on a variety of botanical and chemical subjects, publishing ten papers before his retirement in 1867. The most valuable and interesting of these are on the embryo of Tropaeolum, and his work with Robert Haines, *Analysis of the Mineral Springs and Various Well and River Waters in the Bombay Presidency* (1860). Giraud died on 12 January 1888 at Shanklin, Isle of Wight, where he had lived since his retirement in 1867.

G. T. Bettany, *rev.* Jeffrey S. Reznick

Sources *Men of the time* (1875) · *Men of the time* (1884) · *The Times* (13 Jan 1888) · private information (1889)

Likenesses wood-engraving, NPG; repro. in *ILN*, 92/142 (1888)

Wealth at death £6483 2*s*. 5*d*.: probate, 20 Feb 1888, *CGPLA Eng. & Wales*

Girdlestone, Charles (1797–1881), biblical scholar, the second son of Samuel Rainbow Girdlestone (1766–1836), a chancery barrister, and his wife, Caroline Roberts Powell, was born in London in March 1797. His younger brother was Edward *Girdlestone, canon of Bristol. He was educated at Tonbridge School, under Vicesimus Knox, and in 1815 he was entered as a commoner at Wadham College, Oxford, where he held two exhibitions, one for Hebrew, the other for botany. In 1818 he graduated BA, with a first class in classics and a second in mathematics. His contemporaries at Wadham included Richard Bethell (afterwards Lord Westbury). In the same year he was elected to an open fellowship at Balliol, which had then begun (under Dr John Parsons, afterwards bishop of Peterborough) its era of reform and prominence. He was appointed catechetical, logical, and mathematical lecturer in the college. He was ordained deacon in 1820 and priest in 1821, when he also became MA. About this time he became tutor to the twin sons of Sir John Stanley of Alderley Park; it was this connection which led to his being appointed rector of Alderley some years later. In 1822 he was curate at Hastings, and in 1824 at Ferry Hinksey, near Oxford. He was classical examiner for degrees at Oxford in 1825–6, and select preacher to the university in 1825 and 1830. In 1826 he married Anne Elizabeth, only daughter of Baker Morrell, solicitor to the University of Oxford; she survived him by about a year. They had one daughter, who died in infancy, and eight sons, of whom seven survived him.

Charles Girdlestone (1797–1881), by George Richmond, 1830s

Shortly after his marriage Girdlestone was presented by Lord Dudley and Ward, on the recommendation of Edward Copleston (then provost of Oriel), to the vicarage of Sedgley, a district of about 20,500 inhabitants, forming one parish, in the mining district of south Staffordshire. Here, with the assistance of his patron, he built several district churches, schools, and parsonages. The place suffered severely from its first cholera epidemic, in 1832.

Immediately after the epidemic was over, Girdlestone published *Seven Sermons Preached during the Prevalence of Cholera*, with a map of the district, and a preface giving an account of the epidemic and of the religious impressions produced by it at the time upon the people. Girdlestone henceforth took a keen interest in sanitary reform. In 1843–4 he was one of the earliest supporters of the Metropolitan Association for Improving the Dwellings of the Industrial Classes, and in 1845 he published twelve *Letters on the Unhealthy Condition of the Lower Class of Dwellings*, founded on the official reports recently issued by the poor-law commissioners, and by the commission on the health of towns. Girdlestone combined effectively with nonconformists on non-establishment questions.

In 1837, when Edward Stanley was appointed bishop of Norwich, Girdlestone accepted the living of Alderley, Cheshire, which the bishop had vacated. The offer was made to him through the influence of his former pupil, Edward John Stanley, then under-secretary for foreign affairs. But the advantages of comparative rest at Alderley after his severe work at Sedgley were marred by protracted litigation with the first Lord Stanley (patron of the living) and other landowners of the parish, caused by the Tithes Commutation Act of 1836. Girdlestone largely won his point, but the result was the complete alienation of the Stanley family.

Girdlestone passed part of 1845 and 1846 in Italy and elsewhere on the continent in the hope of improving his delicate health. On his return to England he accepted the important rectory of Kingswinford in the Staffordshire mining district, offered him by Lord Ward, afterwards earl of Dudley, cousin of his former patron. Here Girdlestone had to face the second great cholera epidemic of 1849, when Kingswinford suffered severely. He resigned in 1877; at the time one of his sons was his *locum tenens*. He had himself for many years resided at Holywell House, Weston-super-Mare, on account of his health, where he died on 28 April 1881. His son, Robert Baker Girdlestone, was principal of Wycliffe Hall, Oxford, from 1877 to 1889; Gathorne Robert *Girdlestone was his grandson.

Girdlestone was a man of sincere piety, and an energetic and enlivening preacher. Both as a politician and as a churchman he chose in early life the *via media*—reflected in his sermon, *Affection between Churchmen and Dissenters* (1833). But after middle age he sided with the evangelicals and conservatives, though always an advocate of church reform and reform of convocation, of revision of the prayer book and also of the Authorized Version of the Bible. In later life he spoke of 'those noxious errors, Tractarian and Neological'. His principal work was his commentary on the Bible, which occupied him for several years. The New Testament was first published in two volumes between 1832 and 1835, and the Old Testament in four volumes, in 1842. It was intended for family reading and is an excellent specimen of an explanatory and practical commentary written in the early period of modern biblical criticism and addressed especially to the moderate evangelical school. In later life Girdlestone employed himself in thoroughly revising it on more distinctly protestant principles, and a new edition, in six volumes, was published in 1873. He published also eleven small volumes of sermons and several single ones; these were once very popular. On one occasion he heard one of them read from the pulpit by a preacher who was quite unconscious of the author's presence. Girdlestone also published numerous other works, including two on family devotions (2 vols., 1835) and hymns (2 vols., 1835), twenty-eight *Sedgley Church Tracts* (1831–6), several other works on the Bible, a concordance to the Psalms (1834), and *Thoughts on Dying Daily* (1878). W. A. Greenhill, *rev.* H. C. G. Matthew

Sources Boase, *Mod. Eng. biog.* • Foster, *Alum. Oxon.* • Crockford (1876) • *CGPLA Eng. & Wales* (1881) • R. H. Trainor, *Black Country élites: the exercise of authority in an industrialised area, 1830–1900* (1993)
Likenesses G. Richmond, drawing, 1830–39, priv. coll. [*see illus.*]
Wealth at death £1692 9*s.* 4*d.*: probate, 1 July 1881, *CGPLA Eng. & Wales*

Girdlestone, Edward (1805–1884), Church of England clergyman, was born in St Pancras, London, on 6 September 1805, the third and youngest son of the four children of Samuel Rainbow Girdlestone (1766–1836), a chancery barrister, and his first wife, Caroline Roberts, daughter of James Powell. Charles *Girdlestone was his elder brother. His father was financially ruined and spent time in the Fleet prison in 1814 after standing security for a failed venture, but he was able to return to legal practice. Edward matriculated from Balliol College, Oxford, in 1822, was elected to a scholarship in 1823, and graduated BA, having taken second-class honours in classics in 1826, proceeding MA in 1829. He was ordained to the curacy of Deane, Lancashire, in 1828, and was presented to the vicarage of Deane in 1830 by the lord chancellor. He married in 1832 Mary (*d.* 1891), eldest daughter of Thomas Ridgway of Wallsuches, Lancashire, with whom he had four daughters and seven sons between 1833 and 1850.

Girdlestone was an effective minister to his Lancashire parish, near Bolton, which had a large population of miners and hand-loom weavers. His success in levying a church rate was evidence of his popularity, while he trained graduate ordinands in the duties of the clergy towards industrial parishes. In 1833 he restored Deane church, installing stained glass in 1845, and he built church schools. He foresaw that finding the money to run elementary schools was in the long run more of a problem than raising funds to build them, and recognized the need for assistance from the state, even where this involved an element of lay control. He argued this point in *The Committee of Council on Education: an Imaginary Enemy, a Real Friend* (1850), which attacked the position of G. A. Denison and other high-churchmen within the Anglican National Society who sought to defend clerical control at all costs. His *Sermons on Romanism and Tractarianism* (1851) further marked him out as an opponent of Puseyites within the Anglican church.

In 1854 Lord Cranworth, the lord chancellor, appointed Girdlestone canon residentiary of Bristol Cathedral, where he became a prominent evangelical preacher. Though he took a literal view of the Bible and preached the universality of sin, his theology differed from many of his low-church contemporaries in drawing also upon the works of the early fathers and orthodox Anglicans such as Richard Hooker. He published *Apostolical succession neither proved matter of fact nor revealed in the Bible nor the doctrine of the Church of England* (1857) and *Reflected Truth, or, The Image of God Lost in Adam Restored in Jesus Christ* (1858). In 1861 he was a critic of *Essays and Reviews*. He meanwhile held a succession of livings in the gift of the dean and chapter of Bristol. At St Leonard, Bristol, which he held from 1855 to 1858, he was an active founder of schools, and he more controversially reformed the parish charities. He then moved to the prosperous rural parish of Wapley-with-Codrington, Gloucestershire (1858–62), before becoming vicar of Halberton, Devon (1862–72).

At Halberton, where the landowners were absentees, Girdlestone encountered extreme rural poverty. His exposure, both in sermons and letters to the press (notably *The Times*), of the miserable wages paid by the farmers, the appalling housing of the labourers and their families, and the poor sanitation of the villages made a considerable impression on contemporaries (see F. G. Heath, *The English Peasantry*, 1874) and continue to be of interest to historians of the English countryside. He was particularly associated with schemes to enable labourers to migrate to regions where wages were higher, especially the north of England, and was reckoned to have helped over 400 families to move out of Devon. His desire to place the labourers in a more independent position led him to suggest, at the British Association meeting in 1868, the establishment of agricultural trade unions. At the church congress in 1873 he urged the clergy to take a sympathetic view of the movement to organize the labourers and to take up social questions, arguing that the breakdown of the old paternal relations in the countryside was a critical moment for the established church. His article on agricultural trade unions in *Macmillan's Magazine* (28, 1873) was, however, critical of strikes. He distanced himself from the agricultural labourers' union as it increasingly assumed an anti-clerical tone, though he was still known by, and proud of, his contemporary sobriquet, the Agricultural Labourers' Friend.

Girdlestone's outspoken campaigning on behalf of the labourers made him unpopular among some of his Halberton parishioners, the farmers especially, who pointed to his own position as a tithe receiver and his reliance on underpaid curates to undertake much of his parochial work. He and his family were boycotted, and his attempt to introduce drainage in the village led to opposition in the vestry and a law suit. In March 1872 he became vicar of Olveston, near Almondsbury, enabling him to resume an active role at Bristol Cathedral, where he resided on his canonry for three months each year. He was chairman of the Bristol Athenaeum and was on the committee of the Bristol General Hospital. Theologically he increasingly took a liberal position, having declined to join the opposition within the Exeter diocese to the installation of Frederick Temple as bishop in 1869. He gave evidence in August 1884 to the royal commission on the housing of the working classes, stressing that poor housing undermined the beneficial moral and social effects of elementary education, which it had been his lifelong aim to extend. Girdlestone caught a cold while on his way to visit the prince of Wales at Sandringham, and died of pneumonia at the Canon's House, Deanery Road, Bristol, on 4 December 1884. He was buried in the graveyard of Bristol Cathedral.

M. C. Curthoys

Sources P. J. Perry, 'Edward Girdlestone, 1805–84: a forgotten evangelical', *Journal of Religious History*, 9 (1976–7), 292–301 · R. B. Girdlestone, *Genealogical notes on the Girdlestone family* (1904) · *Men of the time* (1875) · Boase, *Mod. Eng. biog.* · Foster, *Alum. Oxon.* · G. Kitson Clark, *Churchmen and the condition of England, 1832–1885* (1973) · G. E. Mingay, ed., *The Victorian countryside*, 2 vols. (1981) · B. Heeney, *A different kind of gentleman: parish clergy as professional men in early and mid-Victorian England* (1976)

Likenesses portrait, repro. in *Church of England photographic portrait gallery* (1859) · portrait, repro. in *Church Portrait Journal* (Aug 1884)

Wealth at death £2271 9*s.* 4*d.*: probate, 10 Jan 1885, *CGPLA Eng. & Wales*

Girdlestone, Gathorne Robert (1881–1950), orthopaedic surgeon, was born on 8 October 1881 at Wycliffe Hall, Oxford, the only son of the principal, the Revd Robert Baker Girdlestone, later an honorary canon of Christ Church, and his second wife, Mary Matilda, daughter of John Wood, of Thedden Grange. He was the grandson of Charles *Girdlestone. He was educated at Charterhouse School and at New College, Oxford, where he obtained a second class in natural science (physiology) in 1904. He entered St Thomas's Hospital as a university scholar and qualified in 1908. After holding resident appointments at St Thomas's he settled in 1911 at Oswestry in Shropshire as a general practitioner and surgeon. He became attracted to the work of Robert Jones (whose notice he wrote for the *Dictionary of National Biography*) at the orthopaedic hospital at Baschurch which had been founded by Dame Agnes Hunt. From being a spectator Girdlestone became an assistant and quickly grasped the significance of the endeavours to make the hospital the centre of a group of orthopaedic aftercare clinics in the surrounding counties.

Between 1915 and 1919 Girdlestone served in the Royal Army Medical Corps and was placed in charge of a military orthopaedic centre established at the Wingfield Convalescent Home in Headington, Oxford. When in 1919 the hospital came under the supervision of the Ministry of Pensions, Girdlestone remained in charge of it. Later, beds were reserved for crippled children, and as the work for pensioners diminished so, in 1922, the Wingfield Orthopaedic Hospital emerged. After the war Jones and Girdlestone embarked on their national campaign for the relief of 'cripples' and in 1920 the Central Council for the Care of Cripples was formed. Together they worked out a plan on the Oswestry model to serve as a guide for developments elsewhere. Girdlestone's own scheme was based at the Wingfield and served Oxfordshire, Buckinghamshire, and Berkshire.

During the following decade Sir William Morris (later Viscount Nuffield) became aware of Girdlestone's pioneer work and his ambition to rebuild the Wingfield. He provided the money and in 1933 the new Wingfield–Morris Orthopaedic Hospital was opened (it was later renamed the Nuffield Orthopaedic Centre). Girdlestone, now a close friend of Lord Nuffield, was also concerned in the negotiations which led up to Nuffield's gift of £2 million to the University of Oxford for the establishment of professorial clinical departments. Again with Lord Nuffield's generous aid Girdlestone established orthopaedic schemes for Northern Ireland and for South Africa, which he visited in 1937. From 1937 to 1939 Girdlestone was professor of orthopaedic surgery in Oxford, the first to hold such a chair in this country; he was not, however, a scientist, and was disturbed by the growth in medicine of experimental investigation.

The war called for an extension of the Wingfield, but as regional orthopaedic consultant in the Emergency Medical Service, Girdlestone wisely persuaded the Ministry of Health to erect a separate hospital; its design, far better than that of the standard emergency hospital, was largely his own work. It was named the Churchill Hospital and, at Girdlestone's suggestion, was first occupied by an orthopaedic unit from the United States called the American Hospital in Britain. The hospital, despite its 'temporary' buildings, became a valuable part of the United Oxford Hospitals. Thus Girdlestone helped to give Oxford two of its premier hospitals. In 1940 he became consulting orthopaedic surgeon to the Ministry of Pensions, honorary consultant to the army, and in 1942–3 he was president of the British Orthopaedic Association.

Girdlestone wrote with clarity and elegance and a number of his papers have an abiding value; so also has his book, *Tuberculosis of Bone and Joint* (1940). He was a handsome man, whose portrait by Sir William Rothenstein did not do him full justice. He also gave and inspired great affection and his life was governed by deeply religious feelings. It was his passionate belief in the importance of his mission rather than cool statesmanship which accounted for the success of his enterprises and for his great influence. Essentially an autocrat, he was uncompromising and, in consequence, sometimes came into conflict with those whose ideas differed from his own. In 1909 Girdlestone married Ina Mabel (*d.* 1956), daughter of George Chatterton, JP and civil engineer, of Wimbledon; there were no children. They lived latterly at Fir Corner, Frilford Heath, Berkshire. Girdlestone died at St Bartholomew's Hospital, London, on 30 December 1950.

H. J. SEDDON, *rev.*

Sources *BMJ* (13 Jan 1951), 93–5 • *The Lancet* (13 Jan 1951) • personal knowledge (1959) • private information (1959) • *CGPLA Eng. & Wales* (1951)

Likenesses F. Eastman, print, Nuffield Orthopaedic Centre, Headington, Oxford • W. Rothenstein, chalk drawing, NPG

Wealth at death £57,633 2*s.* 9*d.*: probate, 15 March 1951, *CGPLA Eng. & Wales*

Girdlestone, John Lang (1756–1825), translator and schoolmaster, was the fourth child and second son of the seven children of Zurishaddai Girdlestone (*bap.* 1719, *d.* 1767), rector of Baconsthorpe, Norfolk, and Sarah (1725/6–1795), daughter of John and Elizabeth Hewitt. He attended schools in Baconsthorpe and Scarning near East Dereham, entered Gonville and Caius College, Cambridge, of which his father and brothers were members, in 1779, and proceeded BA in 1785, and MA in 1789. He was junior fellow of the college from 1786 to 1789, and was ordained priest at Norwich in June 1787. He became rector of Swainsthorpe, Norfolk, in 1788, and in 1813 vicar of Sheringham, Norfolk, and held both livings until his death. On 30 September 1791 he married at Holt, Norfolk, his first cousin Maria Hewitt, who survived him with their three daughters, Maria, Ann, and Rebecca, all of whom were to die unmarried.

Girdlestone was appointed master of the endowed Beccles School at Beccles, Suffolk, in 1794 and remained until December 1813, being noted as a sound scholar but severe disciplinarian, although he could sometimes be diverted from lessons in winter, for he was a passionate ice-skater. He gained a reputation for eccentricity and 'rarely was he seen except clad in a short blue spencer, worn through all kinds of weather' (Rix, 40) and carrying a cane that never touched the ground. Among his pupils was Joseph Arnold. He published *All the Odes of Pindar*, the first complete English translation, in 1810, an ambitious rendering of a difficult original; a *Sketch of the Foundation of the Christian Church* (1817); and an anonymous poetical miscellany, *The Amusement of a Recluse*, published posthumously (1825). A work on the authorship of Junius by Thomas Girdlestone was misattributed to him during his lifetime. He died on 22 January 1825 at Sheringham and was buried in the churchyard there on 26 January.

JOHN D. PICKLES

Sources R. B. Girdlestone, *Genealogical notes on the Girdlestone family* (1904) • J. Venn and others, eds., *Biographical history of Gonville and Caius College*, 2: 1713–1897 (1898), 103 • S. W. Rix, *The Fauconberge memorial: an account of Henry Fauconberge* (1849) • [J. Watkins and F. Shoberl], *A biographical dictionary of the living authors of Great Britain and Ireland* (1816) • review of Pindar, *Monthly Review*, new ser., 63 (1810), 34–47

Girdlestone, Thomas (1758–1822), physician and writer, was born at Holt, Norfolk, probably the son of Henry Girdlestone and his wife, Margaret Cooper. He entered the army as a surgeon's mate, and served for some time under the command of Colonel Sir Charles Stuart, governor of Minorca, to whose friendship he attributed his success in life. After passing some years with the army in India he returned home with his regiment in 1785 when it was disbanded, and he was placed on half-pay. In 1787 he was entered at Leiden to study medicine. He then settled in Great Yarmouth, Norfolk, where he succeeded John Aikin MD, and practised with great success for the rest of his life. He married the widow of the Revd John Close, and daughter of Robert Lawton of Ipswich, Suffolk, and they had one son.

Girdlestone's main medical works were his *Essays on the Hepatitis and Spasmodic Affections in India* (1787) and *A Case of Diabetes, with an Historical Sketch of that Disease* (1799). His other writings included a translation of *The Odes of Anacreon* (1803) and an essay maintaining that Arthur Lee was the author of *Junius*, entitled *Facts tending to prove that General Lee was never absent from this country for any length of time …* (1813). In person, Girdlestone was tall, slender, and upright. Scrupulously dressed in black, and with silk stockings and half-gaiters, a white cravat, an ample shirt-frill, and a powdered head and pigtail, he could be seen daily, strolling in town with his gold-headed cane. In 1803 Girdlestone was one of the promoters of the public library at Great Yarmouth. He died suddenly at Great Yarmouth, Norfolk, on 25 June 1822.

GORDON GOODWIN, *rev.* CLAIRE L. NUTT

Sources E. Peacock, *Index to English speaking students who have graduated at Leyden University* (1883) • *GM*, 1st ser., 92/1 (1822), 643 • C. J. Palmer, *The perlustration of Great Yarmouth*, 3 vols. (1872–5) • *DNB*

Giric mac Dúngal [Gregory] (*d. c.*890), king in Scotland, called Grim in Fordun's chronicle, is credited in later medieval sources as liberator of the Scottish church from Pictish exactions, and as conqueror of Ireland and 'almost all England'. Although the military successes attributed to him are patently imaginary, some truth has been claimed for his freeing of the church. It cannot be assumed with certainty, however, that it is any more factual than his conquests. Both originate as a note in king-lists whose archetype is no earlier than 1214.

Giric, who may not have been of royal lineage, appears to have competed for dominance over the shattered remains of the Pictish kingdom after the viking occupation of 875–6 and death in battle of Constantine I. A rival was Constantine's brother Aed, in whose death in 878 at the battle of Strathallan Giric may have played a part. Another rival was Eochaid, son of Rhun, king of Dumbarton, and grandson of Kenneth mac Alpin. It is probably indicative of the political turmoil in the region following the disasters of 875–6 that there is no certainty about whether Giric ruled with Eochaid or whether one followed the other. The earliest source, the old Scottish chronicle (as it stands no earlier than the late tenth century), gives two options: either Eochaid reigned for eleven (or perhaps nine) years or Giric reigned as Eochaid's 'foster-father and guardian'. It also states that both Giric and Eochaid were expelled following an eclipse (which, if true, would be the eclipse on 16 June 885). However, Giric is mentioned alone in later Scottish king-lists, whose archetype can be dated to at least as early as 1093–4. Invoked as a protector against heathens in the Dunkeld litany, a text whose original core was probably composed during his reign, Giric is said to have died at Dundurn in Strathearn, where he had probably been living, in a year which may have been 889; according to a late and doubtful source he was buried on Iona. It has been argued that Giric had a brother, Constantine, who succeeded him, but this is based principally on a king-list miscopied (probably in England) in the thirteenth century.

DAUVIT BROUN

Sources A. O. Anderson, ed. and trans., *Early sources of Scottish history, AD 500 to 1286*, 1 (1922), 363–8 • M. O. Anderson, *Kings and kingship in early Scotland*, rev. edn (1980), 249–53, 265–89 • A. Macquarrie, 'The kings of Strathclyde, *c.* 400–1018', *Medieval Scotland: crown, lordship and community: essays presented to G. W. S. Barrow*, ed. A. Grant and K. J. Stringer (1993), 1–19 • M. Miller, 'The last century of Pictish succession', *Scottish Studies*, 23 (1979), 39–67 • M. O. Anderson, 'Dalriada and the creation of the kingdom of the Scots', *Ireland in early mediaeval Europe*, ed. D. Whitelock, R. McKitterick, and D. Dumville (1982), 106–32 • *John of Fordun's Chronicle of the Scottish nation*, ed. W. F. Skene, trans. F. J. H. Skene (1872)

Girling [*née* Clouting], **Mary Ann** (1827–1886), founder of the Children of God, was born on 27 April 1827 at Little Glemham, Suffolk, the daughter of William Clouting, a small farmer. The details of her formal education, if any, are not known. On 2 May 1843 she married George Stanton Girling, a mariner who later worked as a fitter in an iron foundry and as a general dealer in Ipswich. They had at least two children, including a son named William, who was born about 1856, and one daughter. The couple, who were married in an Anglican church, were also members of the Methodist Connexion until Mrs Girling was expelled for disturbing the rest of the congregation. It is not clear whether or not she left the Methodist community alone: an article in the *Secular Review* (11 April 1885) claimed that she ran away from her lawful husband about 1860, and various reports confirm that he afterwards lived apart from her in Ipswich.

In late December 1864, as she afterwards explained to a number of journalists, Mary Ann Girling developed the stigmata, or the signs of Christ's wounds, on her hands, feet, and side. This development, along with other purportedly visionary and mystical experiences, convinced her that she was a new incarnation of the deity. She gathered around her a band of mainly working-class men and women who met for worship in at least two places in London: 107 Bridge Road, Battersea (where they attracted press attention in 1870), and under a railway bridge at Queen's Road, Chelsea. They were generally described as Shakers by outsiders, but styled themselves the Children of God, and called Mrs Girling 'Mother'. Among their tenets was the belief that they would never die, that the divinity of Mrs Girling would eventually be acknowledged, and that she would rule over a peaceful world. In her only known publication, a four-page tract of 1883 entitled *The Close of the Dispensation: the Last Message to the Church and the World*, Girling claimed that she was 'the second appearing of Jesus, the Christ of God, the Bride, the Lamb's Wife, the God-mother and Saviour, life from heaven', and that as soon as she was accepted 'the full power of God w[ould] come, and be revealed among men' (*Secular Review*, 11 April 1885). The tract was signed 'Jesus First and Last (Mary Ann Girling), Tiptoe, Hordle, nr. Lymington, Hants, 1883'.

On 2 January 1872 the Children of God moved from Chelsea to a residence and farm called New Forest Lodge, near Lymington in Hampshire. The lodge had been bought for them by an admirer, Miss Julia Wood, who gave £2250 for the property, on which there remained a mortgage of £1000. The community, which then consisted of about 20–30 men and 111 women and children, failed to pay the interest due on the mortgage. The property was repossessed on 15 December 1874 and Girling was arrested, although soon released on a certificate of insanity. The evicted Children of God camped on the roadside with their belongings, singing and praying in snow and heavy rain. Their plight was reported sympathetically in the *Pall Mall Gazette* and the story was taken up by *The Times* (17 December 1874; 28 December 1874) and other newspapers. Public indignation was particularly aroused by an inquest concerning a baby reported to have died from exposure.

A local dignitary, the Hon. Auberon W. E. M. Herbert (youngest son of the third earl of Carnarven), wrote to *The Times* on 27 December 1874 to protest at what he considered to have been the unduly harsh treatment of a deluded, but harmless, sect and to solicit money to help them. The sheriff's officer at Andover, who described his enforcement of the repossession as 'one of the most disagreeable' tasks of his career, responded that the eviction had been fully justified and that some members of the community had been violent (*The Times*, 28 Dec 1874). Herbert then invited the community to stay in a barn on his own property at Ashley Arnewood Farm, Lymington, insisting, however, that Girling sign a statement, which she did on 2 January 1875, to promise to 'prevent any dances without clothes taking place among any of the brothers, sisters or children' under her care. On 11 February 1875 the clerk of Lymington Union Rural Sanitary Authority informed Herbert that the overcrowding of his barn was in contravention to the provisions of the Nuisances Removal Act and the Children moved to a nearby field. When this lease expired the community again turned to the road for about five weeks before finding land to rent at Tiptoe Farm, near Hordle, Lymington.

In what was to become their permanent settlement at Tiptoe Farm, the Children of God soon became a tourist attraction. In 1876 Lady Florence Herbert measured their popularity by the number of charabancs which came to Hordle and by the 'huge waggon of beer every Saturday night and Monday morning' which was sold to the public house nearest to the settlement (Harris, 178). A correspondent for the *Irish Monthly* reported in 1878 that advertised attractions in Hampshire included, amid day trips to see Corfe Castle and the Rufus Stone, excursions every Friday by a special charabanc to see the 'Shakers' at Hordle.

The settlement at Tiptoe consisted of six wooden shacks which served as dormitories (with separate quarters for men, women, and children), a school, and a communal building. Services took place in the grandest of these buildings, which boasted a wooden gallery and a harmonium and could seat about 150. The form of worship was said to be similar to that of other 'conventicles', except that Girling, apparently in a 'mesmerised state', spoke in 'doggerel rhymes'. The climax of the service came when worshippers broke into 'a simple hob-nail dance, consisting of one figure only, a bang of the left foot followed by a double-stroke with the right-heel and flat-foot' (*Secular Review*, 25 April 1885).

Girling, at about the age of fifty, was described as tall and thin 'but by no means feeble', with 'plenty of black hair' which she wore back, but uncovered, making her look 'much younger at a distance' (*Secular Review*, 25 April 1885). She was generally considered to be shrewdly intelligent and her own letters, although full of spelling and grammatical errors, reveal some theological subtlety. She died at Tiptoe of cancer on the morning of 18 September 1886 and was buried in Hordle churchyard on 22 September. She left behind her a small and disillusioned community of about twenty members. MARY HEIMANN

Sources *DNB* • J. O'R, 'A visit to the Shakers in Hampshire', *Irish Monthly*, 6 (1878), 555–64 • *The Times* (17 Dec 1874) • *The Times* (26 Dec 1874) • *The Times* (28 Dec 1874) • *The Times* (20 Sept 1886) • *Secular Review* (11 April 1885) • *Secular Review* (18 April 1885) • *Secular Review* (25 April 1885) • *Secular Review* (9 Jan 1886) • *Secular Review* (2 Oct 1886) • *Pall Mall Gazette* (18 Sept 1886) • *Pall Mall Gazette* (27 Sept 1886) • S. H. Harris, *Auberon Herbert: crusader for liberty* (1943) • I. Wilson, *The bleeding mind* (1988) • E. D. Andrews, *The people called Shakers* (1953) • m. cert. • d. cert.

Girodias, Maurice (1919–1990), publisher, was born in Paris in 1919, the first of four children. His father was Jonas (Jack) *Kahane (1887–1939), an Englishman who founded and ran the Obelisk Press in Paris in the 1930s, and his mother was Marcelle Eugénie Girodias, of Spanish origin. Girodias used his family name, Kahane, until the German occupation of Paris, when he adopted his mother's maiden name to disguise his Jewish origins. After the Second World War he retained the name Girodias although the rest of his family, including his own daughters, used Kahane.

The death of his father in 1939 left the youthful Girodias the sole breadwinner for his family. He managed to raise money and established a publishing firm called Éditions du Chêne which specialized in illustrated books. In 1945 Girodias married Laure (Laurette) Buzon (1917–1994) and the couple had two children, Valerie and Juliette. But neither the marriage nor Girodias's business affairs prospered and he fell into debt and lost Éditions du Chêne to Hachette. However, by 1953 he had restored his fortunes sufficiently to launch the Olympia Press that was to give birth to some of the most celebrated novels of the twentieth century and to be the first publisher of many subsequently standard works which British and American publishers were unwilling or unable for legal reasons to publish. Girodias's first books were drawn from his father's Obelisk list, notably works by Henry Miller, and new commissions which included a number of erotic novels, translated from the French.

Olympia attracted the attention of the editors and writers of *Merlin*, a small avant-garde literary magazine, who persuaded him to co-publish Samuel Beckett's novel *Watt*, which had been rejected by other publishers. Girodias later published three more of Beckett's novels—*Molloy*, *Malone Dies*, and *The Unnamable*—thus playing a major role in bringing the Irish writer's work to the English-speaking world.

Following his father's publishing strategy, Girodias signed up some of the *Merlin* group to write 'dirty books'—he called them 'DBs'—to help finance Olympia's literary list. Other impoverished expatriate writers living in Paris joined the team of pornographers. Salacious titles—*White*

Thighs, *Helen and Desire*, *The Sexual Life of Robinson Crusoe*, *Lust*, and *The Loins of Amon*—were accompanied by colourful pseudonyms such as Count Palmiro Vicarion (the English poet Christopher Logue), Carmencita de las Lunas (the Scottish writer Alexander Trocchi), and Akbar del Piombo (the American painter Norman Rubington). Girodias published the 'DBs' in distinctive green covers in a special Traveller's Companion series, and sold them with great commercial flair and success.

In 1954 Girodias received two unsolicited manuscripts from authors who had been repeatedly rebuffed in Britain and the USA. One was *The Ginger Man* by J. P. Donleavy, an expatriate American living in Ireland, and the other *Lolita* by Vladimir Nabokov, then teaching at Cornell University in the United States. Girodias's decision to publish both novels played an important part in breaking down the walls of censorship in the countries which had rejected them, as well as bringing their authors notoriety and fame, mental anguish and artistic salvation, and great wealth. The books lifted Girodias to the zenith of his publishing career, and *Lolita* produced his largest financial bonanza.

The Ginger Man was published in Paris in June 1955 in the pornographic Traveller's Companion series. This upset Donleavy so much that he decided to find his own British and American publishers and thus began a legal struggle with Girodias that was to last more than two decades. The novel itself became a best-seller and was published worldwide. *Lolita*, appearing three months later, was not an immediate success but sprang into the limelight when it was praised by Graham Greene in Britain and banned in France. Girodias, who loved to tilt his lance at the establishment, fought valiantly for the novel and had the verdict reversed. He sold the American rights of *Lolita* handsomely to Putnams and the novel was published in the USA in 1958, where it immediately became a best-seller.

At the Frankfurt book fair in 1959 Girodias found himself a celebrity as the most renowned avant-garde publisher of the day. He added to his kudos and to his coffers by publishing *Candy*, a sexual satire by Terry Southern and Mason Hoffenberg; *The Naked Lunch*, William Burroughs's seminal novel on drug addiction; and the first English version of *The Story of O* by the mysterious author Pauline Réage, who is now known to have been the French *dame de lettres* Dominique Aury. Simultaneously, Girodias kept up a steady production of 'DBs'. But instead of ploughing his profits into his firm, he invested in an ambitious nightclub, bar, restaurant, and theatre complex called the Grande Séverine. For a brief time, this elegant establishment became the toast of Paris before going bankrupt and pulling down the Olympia Press with it.

Behind the scenes the legal feud with Donleavy continued and culminated with the purchase of the Olympia Press at a Paris auction in 1970 by Donleavy's wife, whom the author had sent across to Paris to act incognito on his behalf. Girodias pursued the matter in the courts but a final decision in 1978 went against him and Donleavy became the owner of the press that had published his first and greatest novel.

Girodias moved to New York and launched a new Olympia Press. But the climate had changed; pornography was widespread and persecuted talented novelists in short supply. Girodias, whose first marriage had ended in divorce, married Lilla Cabot Lyon, an American physician, in 1974 and published a number of books before going under once again. He returned to Paris and wrote his memoirs which were published in France just before he died of a heart attack during a radio interview on 3 July 1990. He was buried in Père Lachaise cemetery, Paris. His second wife, from whom he had separated, survived him.

JOHN DE ST JORRE

Sources M. Girodias, *The frog prince: an autobiography* (1980) · M. Girodias, *L'arrivée* (1990), vol. 1 of *Une journée sur la terre* · M. Girodias, *Les jardins d'Éros* (1990), vol. 2 of *Une journée sur la terre* · M. Girodias, ed., *The Olympia reader* (1965) · P. Kearney, *The Paris Olympia Press* (1987) · J. de St Jorre, *Venus bound: the erotic voyage of the Olympia Press and its writers* (New York, 1996) · E. De Grazia, *Girls lean back everywhere: the law of obscenity and the assault on genius* (1992) · J. P. Donleavy, *The history of the 'Ginger man'* (1994) · V. Nabokov, *On a book entitled Lolita: the annotated Lolita*, ed. A. Appel jnr (1991) · B. Boyd, *Vladimir Nabokov: the American years, 1940–1977* (1991) · T. Morgan, *Literary outlaw: the life and times of William Burroughs* (1991) · private information (2004) [L. L. Girodias, J. Kahane, E. Kahane]

Likenesses photographs, repro. in de St Jorre, *Venus bound*

Girouard, Désiré (1836–1911), jurist and politician in Canada, born at St Timothy, co. Beauharnois, Lower Canada, on 7 July 1836, was the son of Jérémie Girouard and his wife, Hippolite Piccard. He was descended on his father's side from Antoine Girouard, private secretary to De Ramezay, governor of Montreal in 1720. After attending Montreal College he studied law at McGill University, Montreal, obtaining the first prize three years consecutively, and graduating BCL in 1860 and DCL in 1874; he was also LLD of Ottawa University. He was called to the bar of Lower Canada in October 1860, and was appointed QC in October 1880. He attained great distinction at the bar, especially in commercial cases, and was a well-known writer on legal and international questions. In 1860 he published a useful treatise on bills of exchange. He also wrote on the civil laws of marriage (1868) and on the Insolvent Act (1865). He was one of the chief collaborators in *La Revue Critique*, which in 1873–4 voiced the dissatisfaction of the Montreal bar with the then Quebec court of appeals and led to the reconstitution of that court in 1874.

Girouard first stood for the Canadian parliament in 1872, but was not successful until 1878, when he became Conservative member for the constituency of Jacques Cartier. He held the seat for seventeen years, until the close of his political career. In parliament, where he proved a good debater, he carried in 1882 a bill legalizing marriage with a deceased wife's sister and with the widow of a brother. Later, in 1885, along with several French-Canadian Conservatives, he opposed the government's decision to proceed with the execution of Louis Riel, but he did not abandon the Conservative Party. He was chairman of the standing committee on privileges and elections, presiding in the famous *Langevin–McGreevy* case. He was offered a seat in the dominion cabinet, but preferred a judgeship, and was appointed in September 1895 to the bench of the supreme court of Canada, where he rose to be senior puisne judge.

Girouard was an authority on the early settlement of Montreal, and in recognition of this was presented by the governor-general with the confederation medal in 1895. In 1893 his historical papers, translated by his son D. H. Girouard, were collected at Montreal under the title *Lake St Louis, Old and New, and Cavalier de la Salle*. He also published his own family history (1902).

Girouard was married three times: first, in 1862, to Marie Mathilde, the daughter of Jean-Baptiste Prat (John Pratt) of Montreal; she died in 1863; second, in 1865, to Essie, the daughter of Dr Joseph Cranwill of Ballynamona, Ireland; she died in 1879; and third, on 6 October 1881, to Edith Bertha, the youngest daughter of Dr John Beatty of Cobourg, Ontario. He left four daughters and six sons. One of his sons from his second marriage was Sir (Édouard) Percy Cranwill *Girouard. He died at Ottawa as the result of a carriage accident on 22 March 1911.

C. P. Lucas, *rev.* Elizabeth Baigent

Sources *The Times* (23 March 1911) • *Montreal Daily Star* (22 March 1911) • *Canadian who's who* (1910) • J. Tassé, *Le 38me fauteuil ou souvenirs parlementaires* (1891) • H. J. Morgan, ed., *The Canadian men and women of the time* (1898) • *The Canadian parliamentary guide* (1901) • *DNB*

Girouard, Sir (Édouard) Percy Cranwill (1867–1932), railway engineer and colonial governor, was born on 26 January 1867 in Montreal, the son of Désiré *Girouard (1836–1911) and his second wife, Essie (*d.* 1879), daughter of Dr Joseph Cranwill of Ballynamona, Ireland. The Girouard family had been prominent in Quebec administration and politics from the early 1700s, and his father was a Conservative member of the Canadian parliament from 1878 to 1895, and thereafter judge of the supreme court of Canada until his death in 1911. Girouard grew up fluent in both French and English. He was educated at the seminary at Trois-Rivières, and at Montreal College before entering, aged fifteen, the Royal Military College at Kingston, Ontario, from which he graduated in 1886 with a diploma in engineering. He then worked for two years on the engineering staff of the Canadian Pacific Railway. This proved to be important training for his future. In a sense Girouard's career can be seen as a conduit whereby Canadian railway technology and experience was transferred to British Africa, where low costs and speed of construction were equally important to imperial expansion. In 1888 Girouard accepted, much against his father's wishes, a commission in the British Royal Engineers, and from 1890 to 1895 served as railway traffic manager at the Royal Arsenal in Woolwich.

Girouard's African career began with his secondment to the Egyptian army in 1896, as part of the preparations for Kitchener's invasion of the Sudan to forestall the French expedition to Fashoda. As director of the Sudan railways from 1896 to 1898, his construction of the railway bypassing the Nile cataracts made possible Kitchener's victory over the Mahdists at Omdurman. Girouard's reward was appointment as president of the Egyptian railway and telegraph board in 1898. His railway skills were so highly regarded that with the outbreak of the Second South African War in 1899 he became director of South African Railways, charged with making maximum use of the railways in waging war against the Boers. He wrote an account of this in his *History of the Railways during the War in South Africa, 1899–1902*, published in 1903. He was appointed KCMG in 1900, and at the end of the war took charge of reconstructing the railways of Transvaal and Orange River Colony, a position he resigned in 1904 after prompting from Lord Milner, who was responding to Afrikaner hostility against Girouard.

In 1903 Girouard married Mary Gwendolen, only daughter of Sir Richard Solomon, agent-general in London for the Transvaal Colony. They had one son. The marriage was dissolved in 1915. Returning to England to serve in regular army posts, first as a staff officer at Chatham, and then in 1906 as assistant quartermaster-general, western command, in Chester, Girouard soon found his railway skills again placed him in demand in Africa. In 1907 he accepted an offer from the Colonial Office to become the high commissioner (governor from 1908) of Northern Nigeria, succeeding Sir Frederick Lugard. His task was to carry construction of the railway, already built from Lagos to the Niger, into the north and up to Kano. This he planned and began, though the line reached Kano only in 1911 under his successor.

A successful colonial governorship entailed more than railway expertise, however, and later critics have suggested that Girouard lacked political skills. He was from the first a devoted disciple of Lugard's ideology of 'indirect rule', but without Lugard's vision that British overrule could gradually lead to social change, including educational expansion, in the feudal regimes of the Fulani emirs. Girouard left the development of the indirect rule system almost entirely in the hands of the British resident agents in the capitals of each emirate, accepting their wish to allow each to establish 'native treasuries', with the result that the system tended to become one of ossified local conservatism, with emirs and residents often allied together to resist change. Girouard was also much interested in land reform designed to protect Africans against a possible influx of Europeans demanding land for plantations. He seems to have been influenced by the radical ideas of Henry George concerning the nationalization of land. Girouard saw this as a means to prevent the development of freehold property and the alienation of African communal land. It was Girouard's initiative which set up a committee in London on Northern Nigerian land questions. Following its report the governor issued the land and native rights proclamation of 1908, in which the entire land of Northern Nigeria, occupied or not, was declared to be 'Native Land' under the control of the governor, who alone could grant rights of occupancy, but not freehold. The decree was much criticized by educated African lawyers, who pictured this as an attempt to seize the land. Girouard had plans to tax the land on Henry George principles but the Colonial Office was dubious and never permitted these ideas to be implemented.

In 1909 Girouard accepted the governorship of the British East Africa Protectorate. The Colonial Office was much concerned at the military costs and violence of 'pacification', an inevitable consequence of policies favouring white settlers in the protectorate. Girouard's Nigerian experience was thought to be a reassuring check on such activities. But even more it was his reputation as a railway administrator that once again won him the job, for east Africa was burdened by the large capital costs of the railway from the coast at Mombasa, completed in 1901. This was constructed largely for military motives to bind landlocked Uganda to the British empire. The railway's costs far exceeded receipts, however, and the search to solve this problem had already led to the somewhat desperate remedy of settling white men with capital in the Kenya highlands in the hope that they would develop agricultural crops for export and import goods from Europe, which might make the railway solvent. Girouard, whatever his ideas in Nigeria, became convinced that in east Africa increased white settlement was the only solution to make the railway pay, and the protectorate's finances viable. At the same time he wanted to develop African traditional institutions towards some kind of 'indirect rule', and to prune those officials whom he regarded as dead wood. He thus won considerable settler support, unlike most of his predecessors. When Girouard initiated a mass removal of Maasai herdsmen there was missionary opposition, and opposition in Britain from humanitarian lobbies fed with information by disgruntled local officials. Girouard proved stubborn when the Colonial Office attempted to rein in his pro-settler actions. Finally, in 1912, the Colonial Office, convinced that Girouard had misled them about promises of Maasai land to white settlers, forced his resignation.

This was the end of Girouard's career as an imperial proconsul. He joined the board of directors of the armaments firm Armstrong-Vickers. In 1915 he took a government post as director-general of munitions supply, with a brief period in Belgium on munitions procurement and railway organization, but he resigned in 1917 to return to Armstrong-Vickers, resigning from that, too, into retirement from public life in 1919. Girouard died at 2 Beaumont Street, Marylebone, London, on 26 September 1932.

JOHN FLINT

Sources A. H. M. Kirk-Greene, 'Canada in Africa: Sir Percy Girouard, neglected colonial governor', *African Affairs*, 83 (1984), 207–39 • G. H. Mungeam, *British rule in Kenya, 1895–1912: the establishment of administration in the East Africa Protectorate* (1966) • M. Bull, 'Indirect rule in Northern Nigeria, 1906–1911', in K. Robinson and F. Madden, *Essays in imperial government, presented to Margery Perham* (1963) • I. F. Nicholson, *The administration of Nigeria, 1900–1960: men, methods and myths* (1969) • R. Heussler, *The British in Northern Nigeria* (1968) • A. Clayton and D. C. Savage, *Government and labour in Kenya, 1895–1963* (1974, [1975]) • *CGPLA Eng. & Wales* (1933) • d. cert. • K. J. King, 'The Kenya Masai and the protest phenomenon, 1900–1960', *Journal of African History*, 12 (1971), 117–37 • *DCB* • *DNB*

Archives Bodl. RH, corresp. with F. D. Lugard • Tyne and Wear Archives Service, Newcastle upon Tyne, letters to Lord Rendel

Wealth at death £1648 8s. 1d.: administration, 29 March 1933, *CGPLA Eng. & Wales*

Girtin, Thomas (1775–1802), watercolour painter, was born at Great Bandy Leg Walk, Southwark, on 18 February 1775, the son of a brushmaker of Huguenot descent, John Girtin (1738–1778), and his wife, Rosehanna (*née* Lawley). He was baptized at St Saviour's, Southwark, on 17 March. In 1778 Girtin's father died and Mrs Girtin moved the business to 2 St Martin's-le-Grand in the City of London; she later married the pattern draughtsman Thomas Vaughan.

Early years Girtin is said to have been taught drawing by a Mr Fisher of Aldersgate Street before being apprenticed to the topographical watercolourist Edward Dayes on 15 May 1789. He learned Dayes's technique of undershadowing in grey-blue wash, then adding accents of local pastel colours to views of Gothic cathedrals and castle ruins. Although Girtin seems to have worked out his seven-year apprenticeship, there are (unconfirmed) legends that master and pupil quarrelled, and that Dayes had Girtin put in prison as a refractory apprentice. Dayes wrote slightingly of Girtin in 'Professional sketches of modern artists' in *Works of the Late Edward Dayes* (1805): 'Had he not trifled away a vigorous constitution he might have arrived at a very high degree of excellence as a landscape painter' (*Works*, 329). Dayes undoubtedly started the rumours of Girtin's rakish life: 'Intemperance and irregularity have no claim to longevity', thundered Edward Edwards (Edwards, 280).

From about 1792 Girtin produced finished watercolours from the antiquarian sketches of James Moore FSA, a wealthy Cheapside linen draper who was also a patron of Dayes. In 1794 he undertook a tour of the midlands with Moore, concentrating on the great Gothic cathedrals. Girtin's first watercolour exhibit at the Royal Academy, in 1794, *Ely Cathedral* (Ashmolean Museum, Oxford), was based on a drawing by Moore. Slightly later drawings, such as *Peterborough Cathedral*, 1794 (exh. RA, 1795; Ashmolean Museum, Oxford), reveal Girtin's sense of drama and a masterly play of light on the complex façade.

From mid-1794 to 1797 Girtin and J. M. W. Turner were employed in the evenings to copy drawings by John Robert Cozens in the possession of Dr Thomas Monro, the well-known specialist in mental illness, at Adelphi Terrace. According to the artist and diarist Joseph Farington, 'Girtin drew in outlines and Turner washed in the effects' (Farington, *Diary*, 11 Nov 1798). A large number of these drawings survive in the Turner bequest (Tate collection). Girtin also copied drawings by Monro's Adelphi Terrace neighbour John Henderson, who bought many of his mature drawings (later bequeathed to the British Museum). He honed his architectural drawing skills by copying works by Canaletto, Marco Ricci, and Thomas Malton.

Tours, 1795–1799 In 1795 Girtin probably made a tour of the Cinque Ports with James Moore. The next year, free of his apprenticeship, he made his first independent tour, to the north of England, visiting York, Ripon, Durham, and Newcastle, and crossing into the borders, where he made a pencil sketch, *Jedburgh* on 11 (or 2) October (BM).

Thomas Girtin (1775–1802), by John Opie, *c*.1800

Girtin responded to the sublime scenery of the north by creating his sonorous and influential watercolour palette of warm browns, slate greys, indigo, purple, and through panoramic, dramatic compositions. *Durham Cathedral and Bridge from the River Wear*, of 1799 (Whitworth Art Gallery, Manchester), derived from a sketch of 1796, emphasizes the massiveness of the medieval architecture with a pared-down, vertiginous composition which vigorously rejects the pastel picturesqueness of Dayes.

Girtin showed nine northern views at the Royal Academy exhibition of 1797; by that date he had left his mother's house and was living at 35 Drury Lane. That summer he toured the west country, visiting Somerset, Dorset, and Devon, journeying along the coast from Weymouth to Devonport, and gaining patrons such as the Bluetts of Holcombe Rogus. Girtin responded to the sunny climate of the west with a brighter palette, experimenting with glittering highlights of Chinese white (gouache). Watercolours like *A Devonshire Farm* (Yale U. CBA) respond to the fecundity of nature by catching up buildings, figures, and trees in exuberant broken brushwork.

In 1798 a tour to north Wales, partly funded by a young man from Norwich called Moss (probably an amateur artist), introduced Girtin to mountain landscape and resulted in two monumental watercolours, *Beddgelert* (exh. RA, 1799, nos. 347 and 381). Girtin also went to Yorkshire again and stayed with his most important patron, Edward Lascelles (son of the first earl of Harewood) at Harewood House near Leeds. Lascelles paid Girtin for tuition on 21 November (Lascelles, Personal Account Books). Tradition has it that Girtin and Turner sketched together at Harewood. In the watercolour *Warkworth Castle, Northumberland* (*c*.1798; Yale U. CBA), Girtin's palette of russet browns, dramatic lighting, and complex brushwork show him at his closest to Turner.

By 1799, when Girtin moved lodgings again to 6 Long Acre, the boldness and attack of his watercolours had attracted sophisticated champions such as his pupils Amelia Long (later Lady Farnborough) and Lady Sutherland, as well as the art collector Sir George Beaumont. Farington recorded: 'Mr Lascelles as well as Lady Sutherland are disposed to set up Girtin against Turner,—who they say effects his purpose by industry—the former more genius—Turner finishes too much' (Farington, *Diary*, 9 Feb 1799). On 29 April the *True Briton* reported that Girtin's large watercolour *Beddgelert* at the Royal Academy had all the 'bold features of genius'.

Girtin broadened his artistic horizons by joining the Brothers, a sketching society of professional artists (Robert Ker Porter, Louis Francia, George Samuel) and well-heeled amateurs (Thomas Worthington, John Charles Denham, Thomas Richard Underwood). They first met on 20 May 1799 'for the purpose of establishing by practice a school of Historic landscape, the subjects being designs from poetick passages' (inscription on the back of Francia's *Landscape Composition—Moonlight*; V&A). The drawings were made in a couple of hours before supper, using monochrome wash; the host for the evening was president and kept the results. Girtin attended until 1801 and his style dominated the group.

Girtin's (justifiable) view of his rising status as an artist is evident in his refusal of an offer in 1799 from Lord Elgin to accompany him as draughtsman on his mission to Constantinople. Girtin was offered only £30 a year, less than half the salary of Elgin's valet.

Late tours, 1800–1801 In 1800 Girtin again went to Wales—probably visiting Sir George Beaumont at Benarth—as well as Devon, Harewood, and the border country round Dryburgh, where he stayed with that champion of Romantic art, the eleventh earl of Buchan, David Steuart Erskine, in late summer. From 1800 Girtin produced his finest mature watercolours, stripping down landscape to essentials in compositions of austere power such as *The Ouse Bridge, York* (1800; Yale U. CBA). Works like *Lydford, Devon* (1800; priv. coll.) show acute naturalistic observation allied to sweeping panoramic composition, and use a pure watercolour palette (strong greens, indigo, purple, warm brown, ochre), which lifts the medium far beyond the topographical tradition in which Girtin had been trained.

Girtin exhibited three views at the Royal Academy in 1800 from 11 Scott's Place, Islington, the address of a wealthy Aldersgate Street goldsmith, Phineas Borrett. Girtin married Borrett's sixteen-year-old daughter, Mary Ann (*b*. 1783/4) at St George's, Hanover Square, on 16 October 1800. Presumably bankrolled by Borrett, the young couple set up home at fashionable St George's Row, Hyde Park, next to the painter Paul Sandby. From that address Girtin sent to the Royal Academy in 1801 his first oil painting, a now-lost view, *Bolton Bridge*, which *The Porcupine* praised for its 'impressive grandeur, very much in the manner of [Richard] Wilson' (28 April) and the *Monthly Mirror* for its 'solemn twilight' (June). *The Sun* noted: 'There seems to be some sort of competition between this artist [Girtin] and Mr. Turner' (Girtin and Loshak, 29 n. 1).

Girtin made summer tours to Yorkshire and Northumberland, possibly also to the west country: the dashing panoramic *plein-air* sketch *Estuary of the River Taw, Devon* (Yale U. CBA), with its naturalism and directness, was probably made that year. He stayed at Harewood, later completing four large (24¾ x 38½ in.) watercolours of Harewood and its environs: *Harewood House from the South-East* (priv. coll.); *Harewood House from the South-West* (priv. coll.); *A Distant View of Knaresborough* (1801; Whitworth Art Gallery, Manchester); and *Plompton Rocks* (V&A).

With professional success increasing, Girtin's health was deteriorating. In a letter of 27 June Edward Lascelles mentions the price for the watercolours painted in and around Harewood—20 guineas, Girtin's top price—and adds that he is sorry that Girtin may be obliged to go to 'another climate' for his health (Roget, 1.110). That summer Girtin also stayed with another important patron, Lord Mulgrave, at Mulgrave Castle near Whitby, North Riding of Yorkshire. The charm which had made Girtin a popular teacher of aristocratic pupils like Lady Sutherland was also in evidence in Girtin the country-house guest. Mulgrave thought him 'a good-natured, open-dispositioned man', but added 'he laboured under the Symptoms of an Asthma which not long afterwards killed him' (Farington, *Diary*, 24 March 1807).

Paris On 17 October 1801 Girtin wrote to Mr Harrison at Alderman Boydell's 'I am so very ill that I am advised to go into the country for a little while' (Roget, 1.110–11). Instead, just after being an unsuccessful candidate for associate of the Royal Academy on 2 November (surprisingly, not garnering a single vote), Girtin went to Paris, which was suddenly accessible to English visitors after the signing of the preliminaries of the peace of Amiens.

Girtin left his wife, who was eight months pregnant (their son Thomas Calvert Girtin was born on 10 December), and journeyed to Paris, which, in November, seems an odd place for an asthmatic to visit. It was business—and perhaps a tangled emotional life—that sent Girtin abroad. Two days after he was supposed to have departed for the Dover packet, he was met by Mr Jackson, father-in-law of John, Girtin's engraver brother, in London. Girtin sheepishly explained that he had 'only returned to take a farewell of a Lady who he had forgotten to take leave of at the time of his departure' (Jackson quoted by the Girtin collector Chambers Hall whom J. J. Jenkins interviewed on 12 July 1852, Royal Watercolour Society, MS RWS J 39/14).

Girtin probably went to Paris to explore the feasibility of exhibiting his panorama of London there, and perhaps of making sketches for a panorama of Paris. He had begun preparatory pen-and-ink and watercolour sketches for the panorama of London, taken from the British Plate Glass Manufactory at the south end of Blackfriars Bridge, in 1800–01. The scheme for exhibiting the London panorama in Paris proved unrealistic: 'I think the panorama here does not answer', Girtin wrote to his brother John on 9 April 1802, about a fortnight before he left the city (T. Girtin to J. Girtin, Whitworth Art Gallery, Manchester).

Girtin filled his five and a half months in Paris making highly sophisticated watercolours such as *La rue St Denis* (1802; priv. coll.), an atmospheric evocation of urban architecture. It was used as the design for a backdrop for a Thomas Dibdin pantomime back in London. Girtin 'coloured on the spot' (T. Girtin to J. Girtin, Whitworth Art Gallery, Manchester) from hackney coaches; despite the huge number of English visitors who flocked to Paris during the peace, artists could still be regarded as spies.

The main fruits of Girtin's Paris tour were the pencil sketches (BM) for *Twenty Views in Paris and its Environs*, panoramic views of sombre power etched in softground by Girtin on his return to London (June–October), aquatinted by specialists, and published as a set after Girtin's death by his brother in 1803. The playwright and former treason trial radical Thomas Holcroft accompanied Girtin on a three-day excursion in the countryside around Paris, visiting Marly, Charenton, and Versailles. Holcroft gives a unique glimpse of Girtin's artistic philosophy and practice: he recorded that the artist drew with immense sureness and speed, looking for a panoramic prospect, objects which formed masses, and water to light up a composition (Holcroft, 488–98).

The London panorama Back in England in late April or early May 1802, Girtin worked hard to paint the *Eidometropolis*, a circular panorama of London, 18 ft high and 108 ft in circumference, which was to open at Wigley's Great Room, Spring Gardens, on 2 August, 'If Mr. Girtin's health permits' (*The Times*). Panoramas were a lucrative public spectacle patented by Thomas Barker in 1787. Girtin's was ground-breaking in its naturalistic treatment of urban light and atmosphere, from the sunlit Temple Gardens to the smoky forges and factories of Southwark. It was appreciatively reviewed and well attended.

However, Girtin's professional success was undermined by his declining health. On 25 October Sir George Beaumont approved a plan for Girtin to recuperate in Madeira, but it was too late. Girtin died on 9 November 1802 at his painting room at Mr Norman's, a framemaker in the Strand, with his wife at his side. The cause of death was either asthma or, according to Mary Ann's best friend Miss Hog, 'ossification of the heart' (notes made by J. J. Jenkins of an interview with Miss Hog in 1852, Royal Watercolour Society, MS RWS J 39/10). He was buried on 17 November at St Paul's, Covent Garden. J. M. W. Turner, Sir William Beechey, and Sir George Beaumont were among the mourners.

Reputation Girtin, with Turner, initiated the Romantic watercolour in the 1790s. He abandoned the topographical practice of undershadowing in grey wash before adding pastel tints of local colour, instead using broad washes of strong colour such as browns, slate blue, mossy green, sometimes adding accents with pen and brown ink or brush tip, and varnish to achieve deeper shadows. Sublime mountainous landscapes, open-ended, panoramic compositions, and the glorification of humble vernacular buildings—an austere Yorkshire stone mill on a wind-swept moor, for example—brought a new sensibility to the practice of watercolour.

Large (24¼ x 37½ in.) watercolours like the brooding sunset *Bridgnorth* of 1802 (BM), aspire to the emotive power and status of oil painting, paving the way for the ambitious 'exhibition' watercolours of the nineteenth century.

Girtin's austere, highly controlled, but seemingly casual compositions influenced the work of John Sell Cotman, John Varley, Peter DeWint, and Richard Parkes Bonington. John Linnell wrote in 1811 that Girtin 'was reckoned the greatest genius in Water-Colour painting' and Turner was 'the inheritor of all that Girtin had discovered' (Crouan, vii). Certainly Turner, who survived Girtin by forty-nine years, achieved much more—but Turner still had lessons to learn from him as late as 1840, when he scribbled 'Girtin White House' on an alpine drawing (CCCLII-66*v*, Turner bequest, Tate collection) to remind himself of a brilliant compositional device in Girtin's drawing *The White House at Chelsea* (1800; Tate collection).

SUSAN MORRIS

Sources T. Girtin and D. Loshak, *The art of Thomas Girtin* (1954) [catalogue raisonné] · J. L. Roget, *A history of the 'Old Water-Colour' Society*, 2 vols. (1891) · Farington, *Diary* · T. Holcroft, *Travels from Hamburg, through Westphalia, Holland and the Netherlands to Paris*, 2 vols. (1804) · *The works of the late Edward Dayes*, ed. E. W. Brayley (privately printed, London, 1805) · E. Edwards, *Anecdotes of painters* (1808); facs. edn (1970) · personal account books of Edward Lascelles jun., 1798–1801, W. Yorks. AS, Leeds · J. J. Jenkins, 'MSS notes for a history of the Old Water-Colour Society: file on Girtin', 1852–8, Royal Watercolour Society, Bankside Gallery, London SE1, RWS J 39, 1–22 · T. Girtin, letter to John Girtin, 9 April 1802, Whitworth Art Gallery, Manchester · 'Recollections of the late Thomas Girtin', *Library of the Fine Arts*, 3 (1832), 307–19 · 'Anecdotes of artists of the last fifty years', *Library of the Fine Arts*, 4 (1832), 27–8 · F. Hawcroft, *Thomas Girtin* (1975) [exhibition catalogue, Whitworth Art Gallery, Manchester and V&A] · S. Morris, 'Thomas Girtin', PhD diss., Courtauld Inst., 1990 · S. Morris, *Thomas Girtin, 1775–1802* (1986) [exhibition catalogue, Yale U. CBA] · D. Hill and S. Morris, *Genius in the north* (1999) [exhibition catalogue, Harewood House, Yorkshire] · K. Crouan, *John Linnell: truth to nature* (1982) [exhibition catalogue, Martyn Gregory Gallery, London, 8–20 Nov 1982, and Davis and Langdale and Co., New York, Feb, 1983] · L. Binyon, *Thomas Girtin: his life and works* (1900) · R. Davies, *Thomas Girtin's watercolours* (1924) · M. Hardie, 'A sketchbook of Thomas Girtin', *Walpole Society*, 27 (1938–9), 89–95 · H. J. Pragnell, *The London panoramas of Robert Barker and Thomas Girtin* (1968) · apprenticeship duty records indentures, PRO · parish register, London, Hanover Square, St George's, 16 Oct 1800 [marriage]

Archives BM, department of prints and drawings, family archive

Likenesses G. Dance, pencil drawing, 1798, BM · T. Girtin, pencil drawing, *c*.1800, BM · J. Opie, oils, *c*.1800, Whitworth Art Gallery, Manchester · J. Opie, oils, *c*.1800, NPG [*see illus.*] · S. W. Reynolds, mezzotint, 1817 (after J. Opie) · W. Daniell, soft-ground etching (after pencil drawing by G. Dance, 1798) · H. Edridge, pencil drawing, BM

Wealth at death £600: administration, 12 May 1804, PRO, PROB 6/179, fol. 616

Gisa. *See* Giso (*d.* 1088).

Gisborne, John (1770–1851), poet, was born at St Helens, Derby, on 26 August 1770, the youngest son of John Gisborne (*d.* 1779) and his wife, Anne Bateman (*d.* 1800), both of St Helens and of Yoxall Lodge, Staffordshire. He was the younger brother of Thomas *Gisborne (1758–1846). John Gisborne was educated at Harrow School and at St John's College, Cambridge, where he graduated BA in 1792. In the same year, on 13 October, he married Millicent Pole, daughter of Colonel Edward Sacheverell Chandos Pole of Radbourne, Derbyshire, and they went to live at Wootton Hall, Derbyshire. In 1815 they moved to Blackpool on account of Millicent's health. Afterwards Gisborne shifted the family residence constantly, partly on account of pecuniary losses, and they lived at Darley Dale, Shirland, Wyaston Grove, and Willington, all in Derbyshire.

Gisborne had a keen eye for nature and he was complimented by Wordsworth upon his descriptions of scenery, but his modesty induced him to destroy this and all other letters of congratulation on the publication of his works. His piety caused him to be called the Man of Prayer. At Blackpool and elsewhere he worked for the welfare of the inhabitants and he also did much for the prosperity of Blackpool. His geniality, humility, and sympathy made him universally popular as a country gentleman. Gisborne's principal works are *The Vales of Wever*, written during his residence at Wootton Hall and published in London in 1797, and *Reflections*, a poem written and published during his residence at Darley Dale between 1818 and 1835. He also kept a diary showing strong religious sentiments, from which extracts have been published with a memoir by his daughter Emma Nixon. He died at Pentrich in Derbyshire on 17 June 1851, leaving his wife and several grown-up sons and daughters. He was buried on 23 June 1851 in Breadsall, near Derby.

R. M. BRADLEY, *rev.* REBECCA MILLS

Sources E. Nixon, ed., *A brief memoir of the life of John Gisborne, esq., to which are added, extracts from his diary* (1852) · *IGI* · Venn, *Alum. Cant.*, 2/3.60 · *GM*, 1st ser., 62 (1792), 960 · Watt, *Bibl. Brit.*, vol. 1

Archives Bodl. Oxf., notebooks · Derby Local Studies Library, extracts from diary · Duke U., Perkins L., diary [portion] | Bodl. Oxf., journals and notebooks · Bodl. Oxf., letters to Robert Finch · UCL, letters to Joseph Parkes [copies]

Gisborne [*née* James; *other married name* Reveley], **Maria** (1770–1836), friend of William Godwin and Mary and Percy Shelley, was probably born in England, the daughter of an English merchant whose surname was James and who abandoned his wife and infant daughter to a penurious existence in England and went to Constantinople. When Maria was eight her mother took her to Constantinople in order to remind Mr James of his paterfamilial duties—only to find him in concubinage with the wife of one of his skippers. Mr James managed to kidnap Maria, with whom he was delighted, and to hoodwink his wife, with whom he was less than delighted, into returning to England *sans* daughter and *sans* the annuity he had promised her. To his credit, however, James saw carefully to his daughter's education, and she quickly matured into a young woman with social graces beyond her years who entered into the society of European merchants and diplomats. Mary Shelley's account of Maria's early years is intriguing and suggestive in its ambiguity: 'Having no proper chaperone, she was left to run wild as she might, and at a very early age had gone through the romance of life' (Paul, 1.82). Given this testimony, it is possible that the free-thinking Maria had an affair before reaching her majority.

When she was fifteen Maria and her father moved to Rome. Maria had demonstrated a talent for painting and engaged to study under the tutelage of Angelica Kauffman. Her studies were cut short, however, by her marriage about 1788 to William Reveley (*d.* 1799), a young English architect. Reveley, a political liberal and friend of William Godwin and Thomas Holcroft, had been travelling in Greece and Italy, and it was in Rome that he and Maria met. Maria's father was against the marriage and refused to help the young couple financially, and Reveley's allowance from his father was only £140 p.a. The income from Reveley's business was at first modest and uncertain; he received his first professional commission (£10) about 1791 from Jeremy Bentham (whom Maria had met in 1785) for his assistance with Bentham's Panopticon scheme. By this time, however, Maria had given birth to two children, and their income was inadequate to maintain the desired appearance of gentility. These factors, as well as the proverbial 'temperamental differences' between William and Maria, put a strain on the Reveleys' marriage, in which Maria was decidedly unhappy. The sudden death of William Reveley on 6 July 1799, therefore, though at first a terrible shock, must have in retrospect occasioned in Maria mixed feelings. Of the two offspring of their marriage, there is record only of Henry Willey Reveley, who was educated in Italy, became a marine engineer, proposed marriage to Claire Clairmont in 1820 and was refused, married a sister of Copley Fielding in 1824, and settled ultimately in western Australia.

Maria and William Reveley had moved in the 1790s in liberal political circles and were friends with William Godwin and, briefly, with Godwin's wife at the time, Mary Wollstonecraft, with whom Maria exchanged a few letters concerning their children. Holcroft had introduced Godwin to Maria on 21 September 1793, and the two—as Mary Shelley later observed—took to one another: 'There was a gentleness, and yet a fervour in the minds of both Mrs. Reveley and Godwin that led to sympathy. He was ready to gratify her desire for knowledge, and she drank eagerly of the philosophy which he offered' (Paul, 1.82–3). Godwin continued to pay social visits to Maria over the next six years despite the growing disapproval of her husband (especially after the death of Wollstonecraft in 1797), and it has been suggested that the two might have had an affair. Whatever the truth of the matter, Godwin remained fascinated by Maria throughout his life, and she confessed later that she had loved him for years.

It is hardly surprising, therefore, that within less than a month after her husband's death in 1799, Mrs Reveley had a new proposal of marriage from William Godwin, then a widower with two children in his keeping. Godwin's earlier philosophical stand against the institution of marriage had apparently by this time completely faded from his memory—obscured, no doubt, by Maria's great attractiveness and his need for a mother for the two children in his charge, whom Maria had temporarily taken into her care after the death of Wollstonecraft. Perhaps not wanting to violate the decorum of a period of mourning (as Godwin's near-hysterical letters appealing to her to see reason and marry him suggest); perhaps not wanting to add Godwin's two children, Fanny Imlay and Mary Wollstonecraft Godwin, permanently to her charge; or perhaps simply because as a suitor, Godwin did not take her fancy—Maria refused his repeated epistolary proposals over the summer and early autumn of 1799. In May 1800, however, and much to the surprise of Godwin, she married John Gisborne (*d.* 1835/6). Maria and Godwin severed ties for the time being, but after a hiatus of some two decades they did manage to re-establish their friendship, which lasted until their deaths within about two weeks of each other. The Gisbornes moved to Rome in 1801 and nothing is known of their activities until they moved to Livorno (Leghorn) in 1815, where John Gisborne attempted an abortive business enterprise.

On 9 May 1818 Mary and Percy Shelley arrived at the Gisbornes' home at Livorno, the Casa Ricci in the via Genesi, and thus began the friendship for which Maria Gisborne is primarily remembered. The Shelleys were no doubt predisposed to like the woman who had been a friend of Mary's mother, admired by her father, and nurse to Mary herself in her infancy. The first month of their adult acquaintance was spent in visiting and taking walks, after which the Shelleys left Livorno, a town which Percy felt was redeemed only by the presence of Maria Gisborne. Mary and Maria began a correspondence that was interrupted only by a brief period of estrangement from the Shelleys and the years they both lived in London. Mary's letters to Maria were at first abundant, somewhat chatty, and exhibited an affection which Mary desperately needed reciprocated from Maria, whom Mary cast as her surrogate mother in a strange land. For her part, Maria's letters—though familiar and even at times showing a protective solicitude—tended to be a bit more restrained. Nor did Maria write as often, a fact for which she expressed some contrition and tried to remedy by writing a few longer letters to bring her friends up to date. As their friendship matured, and the Gisbornes began helping the Shelleys with their business matters (and vice versa), the earlier chattiness of Mary's letters gradually gave way to hurriedly written letters about urgent business that needed doing and some that aired the worries and concerns that began to weigh down the Shelleys.

The Shelleys returned to Livorno on 17 June 1819, where, grieving for the death of their son William, they were comforted by the Gisbornes. Maria, widely read in Spanish and Italian literature, took this opportunity to share her knowledge with the Shelleys. It was she who alerted the Shelleys to the story of the Cenci by showing them a manuscript of the narrative, which Mary copied and Percy used for his famous play. Maria also began teaching Percy Spanish and helped him read the plays of Calderón. On their side, the Shelleys helped finance Henry Reveley's project to build a steamboat. Unbeknownst to Mary, Percy also asked for and received aid from the Gisbornes in the delicate matter of his illegitimate child, Elena Adelaide Shelley.

The Gisbornes left Livorno for a visit to England in May 1820. Probably at Mary's suggestion, Maria kept during this period a journal which reads as though meant to be read by the Shelleys. In London they visited Godwin (to whom they presented the manuscript of Mary's short novel *Mathilda*, per Mary's request), the Hunts, Keats (whom Maria described in the 12 July 1820 entry of her diary as 'under sentence of death from Dr. Lamb[e]' and 'emaciated'), Hogg, and others in the Shelley circle. The Shelleys, meanwhile, took up residence in Casa Ricci, where Percy wrote 'To a Skylark' and 'Letter to Maria Gisborne'. The Gisbornes returned to Livorno in October 1820 with an altered attitude towards the Shelleys, particularly Percy, owing to the unflattering descriptions of him received from Godwin. They announced to the Shelleys their intention of moving back to England and abandoning the steamboat project. The Gisbornes' proposed terms of repayment to the Shelleys after liquidating the saleable remains of the project, however, angered Percy and he resolved to have nothing more to do with them. The terms of the actual repayment must have been better than Percy expected, however, and that, along with the Gisbornes' appreciation of his newly printed *Adonais*, facilitated a reconciliation between the Shelleys and Gisbornes, whom, by 19 July 1821, Percy was again addressing as 'My Dearest Friends'.

The Gisbornes set out once again for England on 29 July 1821 and, after reaching London, continued to correspond regularly with the Shelleys; John Gisborne even acted as a quondam literary agent for Percy. After Percy was drowned in July 1822, it was to Maria Gisborne that Mary wrote on 15 August a long account of their last days together and the aftermath of her husband's death. Maria again comforted the young widow, and their friendship and correspondence continued to the end of Maria's life.

The Gisbornes made one last trip to Italy in 1827, but lived out their last years in England, retiring to Plymouth some time before 1832. John Gisborne was buried at Plymouth on 16 January 1836; Maria herself was buried there on 23 April of the same year. DAVID KALOUSTIAN

Sources *Maria Gisborne and Edward E. Williams, Shelley's friends: their journals and letters*, ed. F. L. Jones (1951) • C. Kegan Paul, *William Godwin: his friends and contemporaries*, 2 vols. (1876); repr. (New York, 1970) • *The letters of Mary Wollstonecraft Shelley*, ed. B. T. Bennett, 3 vols. (1980–88) • *The journals of Mary Shelley, 1814–1844*, ed. P. R. Feldman and D. Scott-Kilvert, 2 vols. (1987) • R. Holmes, *Shelley: the pursuit* (1975) • D. Locke, *A fantasy of reason: the life and thought of William Godwin* (1980) • *Collected letters of Mary Wollstonecraft*, ed. R. M. Wardle (1979) • *The letters of Mary W. Shelley*, ed. F. L. Jones, 2 vols. (1944) • *Mary Shelley's journal*, ed. F. L. Jones (1947) • *The letters of Percy Bysshe Shelley*, ed. F. L. Jones, 2 vols. (1964) • E. Dowden, *The life of Percy Bysshe Shelley* (1966) • *DNB* • P. H. Marshall, *William Godwin* (1984)

Archives BM, journal, Ashley MS 3262 | Bodl. Oxf., MSS Abinger, notebooks of John Gisborne

Gisborne, Thomas (*bap.* 1725, *d.* 1806), physician, was baptized at Staveley, Derbyshire, on 18 October 1725, the second of the four sons of James Gisborne (*d.* 1759), rector of Staveley and prebendary of Durham, and Anne, his wife. After attending Staveley School, Gisborne was admitted at St John's College, Cambridge, aged eighteen, on 28 June 1744. He proceeded BA in 1747, MA in 1751, and MD in 1758. On 24 January 1757 he was elected physician to St George's Hospital, London, an office which he resigned in 1781. He was admitted a candidate of the College of Physicians on 30 September 1758, and a fellow on 1 October 1759. He delivered the Goulstonian lectures in 1760, was censor in 1760, 1768, 1771, 1775, 1780, and 1783, elect on 28 June 1781, and president in 1791, 1794, and from 1796 to 1803. Gisborne was also physician-in-ordinary to George III. He was elected FRS on 16 November 1758. Gisborne died at Romiley in Stockport, Cheshire, on 24 February 1806. He was at the time the senior fellow of St John's College.

GORDON GOODWIN, *rev.* MICHAEL BEVAN

Sources Venn, *Alum. Cant.* • Munk, *Roll* • S. C. Lawrence, *Charitable knowledge: hospital pupils and practitioners in eighteenth-century London* (1996) • *GM*, 1st ser., 76 (1806), 287 • will of Revd J. Gisborne, PRO, PROB 11/849, sig. 326 • *IGI*

Gisborne, Thomas (1758–1846), Church of England clergyman and religious writer, was born on 31 October 1758 at Derby, the eldest son of John Gisborne (*d.* 1779), landowner, and Anne Bateman, daughter of William Bateman of Derby. He was educated privately for six years by the Revd John Pickering, vicar of Mackworth, near Derby, before going to Harrow School at the age of fourteen. Three years later, in 1776, he was admitted to St John's College, Cambridge. He graduated BA as sixth wrangler and senior chancellor's medallist in 1780 and MA in 1783; he was made a deacon in 1781 and ordained priest in 1782. In the autumn of 1783 he was presented by the dean of Lichfield to the perpetual curacy of Barton under Needwood, Staffordshire, and in the same year he moved into Yoxall Lodge, Staffordshire, inherited from his father, which was 3 miles from his church, where he lived until his death sixty-three years later. On 1 March 1784 he married at Ampthill, Bedfordshire, Mary Babington (*b.* 1760), daughter of Thomas Babington, of Rothley Temple in Leicestershire, and his wife, Lydia Cardale. In 1786 Joseph Wright of Derby painted a fine double portrait of the young husband and wife. Together they had six sons and two daughters; the eldest son, Thomas *Gisborne (1794–1852), became a member of parliament and the fourth son, James, a clergyman who succeeded his father as perpetual curate of Barton in 1820.

Gisborne had the intellect and connections to secure himself an eminent and distinguished public career in parliament or on the episcopal bench, but he chose the quiet life of a country parson and writer. He was a central figure in the influential group of evangelical Anglicans known as the Clapham Sect, and Yoxall 'became almost a second Clapham' (Howse, 18). His closest friends were

Thomas Babington, his brother-in-law, and William Wilberforce. His friendship with Wilberforce, begun when they were fellow students at Cambridge, was renewed when both became involved in the campaign to abolish the slave trade. Wilberforce was a frequent visitor to Yoxall Lodge and it was there that much of the work on the anti-slavery campaign was done. In 1792 Gisborne published his *Remarks on the late decision of the House of Commons respecting the abolition of the slave trade*, but generally he acted behind the scenes, doing the research and sitting in the Commons gallery with Babington when Wilberforce introduced the 1792 abolition bill.

As a writer, Gisborne was an astute critic of William Paley. His *Principles of Moral Philosophy* (1789) was the most direct and forcefully argued of evangelical assaults on Paley's utilitarianism. Paley's *Principles of Moral and Political Philosophy* (1785) had been adopted as a student text at Cambridge and was soon widely read at Oxford. This immensely influential work viewed moral philosophy from a latitudinarian and utilitarian standpoint and was criticized from both the Catholic and the evangelical wings of the Church of England. Gisborne regarded Paley's book as an Erastian work with a calculating, rationalist spirit. Gisborne saw morality as a categorical imperative imposed by God and revealed by him to man in the Bible, not as a human perception of what was expedient. Both Paley and Gisborne were criticized by George Croft, the Bampton lecturer and friend of Lord Eldon in 1797; Paley remained in the Cambridge syllabus for over sixty years, but the evangelical case had been made. As late as the 1830s, Paley's defenders, like Latham Wainewright, still felt the need to address Gisborne's argument.

Gisborne was no mere controversialist. He was a poet, a preacher, and a naturalist. In 1794 he published *Walks in a Forest*, a volume of poems describing the scenery of Needwood Forest, which bordered his estate at Yoxall. To him, his most important works were those written as a Christian pastor. His *Enquiry into the Duties of Men* (1795) and *Enquiry into the Duties of the Female Sex* (1797) were written for the educated classes and focused on the Christian subject's duties rather than his or her rights. They not only stressed subordination and acceptance of the divinely imposed social hierarchy at a time of potential unrest, but also recognized that most people did not believe wholeheartedly the Christian revelation and so were not bound by its strictures.

Gisborne was appointed prebendary of Durham Cathedral in 1823 and moved from the fifth to the first stall in 1826. He died at Yoxall Lodge on 24 March 1846 at the age of eighty-seven and left a clear £1000 for charities in the Durham diocese, as well as small sums for worthy causes in and around Staffordshire. ROBERT HOLE

Sources E. M. Howse, *Saints in politics: the 'Clapham sect' and the growth of freedom* (1952) · *GM*, 1st ser., 54 (1784), 234 · *GM*, 2nd ser., 25 (1846), 643–5 · Venn, *Alum. Cant.* · R. Hole, *Pulpits, politics and public order in England, 1760–1832* (1989) · T. P. Schofield, 'English conservative thought and opinion in response to the French Revolution, 1789–1796', PhD diss., U. Lond., 1984, 73–7 · G. Croft, *A short commentary, with strictures, on certain parts of the moral writings of Dr. Paley and Mr. Gisborne* (1797) · L. Wainewright, *A vindication of Dr Paley's theory of morals from the principal objections of Mr. Dugald Stewart; Mr. Gisborne; Dr. Pearson; and Dr. Thomas Brown* (1830) · *DNB* · *IGI*

Archives Sandon Hall, Staffordshire, Harrowby Manuscript Trust, corresp. · U. Durham L., letters to his publisher · William Salt Library, Stafford, account books and papers relating to the administration of his estate | Bodl. Oxf., corresp. with William Wilberforce · NL Scot., letters to Lord Muncaster · Trinity Cam., letters to Thomas Babington

Likenesses J. Wright, double portrait, oils, 1786 (with Mary Gisborne), Yale U. CBA · C. R. Smith, bust, 1814, U. Durham · J. Hoppner, oils, exh. Ehrich Gallery, New York 1933 · H. Meyer, stipple (after an oil painting by J. Hoppner), BM, NPG; repro. in *The British gallery of contemporary portraits* (1814) · J. Wright, oils; Sothebys, 1956 · engraving, BM, NPG · engraving, BM · oils, University College, Durham

Wealth at death over £1000; incl. charitable bequests: *GM* (1846), 25.643–5

Gisborne, Thomas, the younger (1794–1852), politician, was the eldest son of Thomas *Gisborne (1758–1846), prebendary of Durham, and his wife, Mary, daughter of Thomas Babington, of Rothley Temple, Leicestershire. The younger Gisborne's first wife was Elizabeth (*d.* 20 June 1823), daughter of John Fyshe Palmer of Ickwill, with whom he had four children, and his second, whom he married in 1826, was Susan, widow of Francis Dukinfield Astley of Dukinfield, Cheshire. Gisborne was a person of some substance in Derbyshire, with a seat at Howick House, and was deputy lieutenant of the county. He also had business interests in Manchester.

Gisborne's political career was so unsettled that it was hard for him to make any real mark. He was elected unopposed for Stafford in 1830, and again in 1831, as a supporter of the Reform Bill. From 1832 until 1837 he represented North Derbyshire. In 1839 he stood for Carlow, and, though beaten at the poll, was seated on petition. In 1841 he stood unsuccessfully for both Newport (Isle of Wight) and South Leicestershire. In 1842 he unsuccessfully contested Ipswich. At last, in 1843, he was elected for Nottingham, but was defeated in 1847. In 1849 he was unsuccessful at Kidderminster. He was 'a whig, and a good deal more' (cited in Ward, *Men of the reign*), and supported the ballot, the abolition of church rates, and the extension of the suffrage; he was also a strong supporter of the Anti-Corn Law League. He was a vigorous speaker, with much humour, and spoke frequently at the free-trade gatherings in Drury Lane, London. He published some speeches and pamphlets; and in 1854 he published *Essays on Agriculture*, three of the four of which had already appeared in the *Quarterly Review* (nos. 168, 171, 173). He died at his family's home, Yoxhall Lodge, Staffordshire, on 20 July 1852. H. C. G. MATTHEW

Sources *Dod's Parliamentary Companion* · *GM*, 2nd ser., 38 (1852), 315 · Ward, *Men of the reign* · *DNB*

Gisleham, Sir William of (*c.*1230–1293), justice, was probably born *c.*1230 in the village of Gisleham in north-east Suffolk. He was the son of a minor landowner, Richard son of Moses of Gisleham, and his first known appearance in surviving records is an appointment in 1259 to act as his father's attorney. The pattern of his appointments to act as an attorney for other litigants suggests that he may have become a professional lawyer by 1260. He had almost certainly entered the small élite of professional serjeants by 1271. During the 1270s he may have been a serjeant in the common bench and may also have regularly appeared for litigants at local assize sessions.

There was a major reorganization of the general eyre in the summer of 1278. This established what were intended to be two permanent eyre circuits, and added to their jurisdiction the receipt of claims to franchises in each of the counties they visited, and the determination of royal challenges to such claims. There is no evidence that Gisleham attended the first eyre on the 'southern' eyre circuit held in Hertfordshire in the autumn of 1278, but he did act as the king's serjeant on the circuit's second eyre, which opened in Kent in January 1279. Thereafter he acted either on his own or sometimes with a junior colleague in each eyre of the 'southern' circuit before the Wiltshire eyre of 1289, aggressively challenging claims to franchises on behalf of the king, and also making property claims on the king's behalf. During the same decade he seems also to have regularly acted for private clients on the same eyres, and to have managed to fit in a number of appearances in the common bench, on behalf both of private clients and of the crown. He was appointed one of the justices of the common bench in mid-January 1290, as one of the replacements for the justices who had been disgraced during the 'state trials' which began in 1289. From the summer of 1290 he also served as a regular assize justice in East Anglia. A number of surviving law reports of the period show him at work in the common bench, most often by himself but sometimes with his senior colleague, John of Mettingham (*d.* 1301), and less commonly with his fellow justice, Robert of Hartforth. Knighted by January 1292, Gisleham served as a royal justice for just three years before dying suddenly in a boat, perhaps one carrying him from Westminster to his home in London, in mid-February 1293.

Gisleham's first wife, Agnes, was the daughter and one of the heirs of the London merchant and alderman, Walter of Winchester, and the widow of Adrian Eswy, who had also belonged to London's mercantile élite. They were married by 1260, and she brought him property in London and a claim to dower lands in Surrey and Middlesex. By 1285 he was married to a second wife, Alice, who may have brought him property at Barking and Dagenham in Essex. Gisleham left no sons and the manor he had reassembled in Kessingland, the next village to Gisleham, and a second major holding at Ilketshall and three other Suffolk villages, passed to his heirs. They were his daughter Clemencia and another Clemencia, the daughter of Agnes, probably his granddaughter, who later married William Tivetshall. PAUL BRAND

Sources P. A. Brand, ed., *The earliest English law reports*, 2, SeldS, 112 (1996), xli–xlvi • D. W. Sutherland, *Quo warranto proceedings in the reign of Edward I, 1278–1294* (1963) • PRO SCI/27 no. 191

Giso (*d.* **1088**), bishop of Wells, was a Lotharingian by birth. In the short history of Wells Cathedral previously attributed to him (the *Historiola de primordiis episcopatus Somersetensis*) he is described as being from the village of St Truiden or St Trond in the region of Hesbaye, in modern Belgium. It is not known where he went to school, but he was described by the author of the life of Edward the Confessor as well educated. Before 1061 he became chaplain to Edward the Confessor; he therefore belongs to the sizeable group of Lotharingian clerics invited to England by Edward to serve at his court. On the death of Duduc, bishop of Wells, on 18 January, probably (according to Dorothy Whitelock) in 1061, Giso was appointed to succeed him, and, since he wished to avoid consecration at the hands of Stigand, then archbishop of Canterbury, he travelled to Rome with another new episcopal appointee, Walter of Hereford, to be consecrated by Nicholas II at his Easter synod. The ceremony took place on 15 April 1061 'in the basilica of the patriarch' (*English Historical Documents*, 2.601). A few days later, on 25 April, Giso requested a bull from Nicholas to confirm the properties of the see of Wells. He and Walter then left Rome in a large company of English pilgrims, headed by Earl Tostig; but almost immediately after its departure the party was ambushed and had to return to Rome.

Giso eventually reached England between 17 and 24 June. His first preoccupation was to enlarge the cathedral community at Wells, which numbered about four or five clerks, and to construct the buildings necessary for a communal existence. To provide the financial basis for expansion, he persuaded Edward the Confessor to grant property at Wedmore; Queen Edith added to the grant members of the manor at Mark and Mudgley and also granted land at Milverton. Giso tried to recover land at Winsham which had been leased by one of his predecessors, by anathematizing the current holder, but to no avail. He even considered anathematizing Earl Harold for depriving Wells of various lands, though he decided against this when the latter became king in 1066. He also bought land at Litton.

After the Norman conquest Giso quickly established friendly relations with William I, from whom he hoped for support in his drive to increase the lands of the see. He occurs as witness or addressee in several undisputedly genuine charters and writs of William. He assisted at Lanfranc's consecration on 29 August 1070 and attended the Council of Windsor at Whitsun 1072 and the Council of London in 1075. At yet another church council, between 1077 and 1088, Giso brought complaints against the abbots of Muchelney and Athelney that they were disregarding his episcopal authority, but Abbot Thurstan of Glastonbury successfully counterclaimed that such cases ought to be heard in his chapter. Glastonbury Abbey was considerably richer than the see of Wells and made it difficult for Giso to maintain strong control over his diocese. Meanwhile, however, Giso was making steady progress in his fight to build up the estates of the church of Wells. William I granted Winsham to the canons of Wells and approved Giso's purchase of Combe from Azor, son of Thored. The latter transaction was conducted in the gallery of Wilton church, at a gathering presided over by Queen Edith on 28 February 1072, recorded in one of the last extant Old English landbooks.

Giso began the process of separating the lands of the bishop from those of the chapter. The *Historiola*, which was probably written by the clergy at Wells after Giso's death, shows which properties belonged to the cathedral clergy and which to the bishop, though the section describing the episcopal acquisitions is missing. With the money thus raised, Giso built a cloister, refectory, and dormitory for his canons and commanded them to live under a canonical rule (perhaps the rule of Aachen, though this is not specified). The cathedral church seems to have been left untouched under Giso, though the chapel of St Mary lying to the east was enlarged. The canons chose one of their number, Isaac, to administer their revenues. With the cathedral chapter now brought up to strength, Giso was able to introduce liturgical ideas from the continent, notably numerous saints' cults popular in Germany, Flanders, and Burgundy, all recorded in his calendar (Aldegund, Bavo, Hubert, Remaclus, Servatius, Gertrude, Gereon, Ursula and the eleven thousand virgins, Pantaleon, Florian, Maiolus, Mary Magdalen, Faith, and Giles). He also appointed the first archdeacon of the see, Benselin, before 1086, granting him the church of Yatton with some land. This suggests that Benselin lived apart from the cathedral chapter and it is likely that he formed part of Giso's household, another prominent member of which would have been the bishop's nephew, Osmund, the tenant of the episcopal estate of Winsham. Giso died in 1088 and was buried at Wells Cathedral. His remains were exhumed in 1979, revealing him to have been a tall, deep-chested man.

JULIA BARROW

Sources J. Hunter, ed., *Ecclesiastical documents*, CS, 8 (1840) • A. Farley, ed., *Domesday Book*, 2 vols. (1783), 1.89b–d • D. Whitelock, M. Brett, and C. N. L. Brooke, eds., *Councils and synods with other documents relating to the English church, 871–1204*, 2 vols. (1981), pt 1, 545–50, 552–4; pt 2, 585n, 588, 604, 612, 615, 630–31 • F. M. R. Ramsey, ed., *Bath and Wells, 1061–1205*, English Episcopal Acta, 10 (1995), xxi–xxiii, xxxix • F. E. Harmer, ed., *Anglo-Saxon writs* (1952), 35, 39n., 55, 57, 59, 61, 229, 270–86, 288–9, 561 • John of Worcester, *Chron.*, 2.586–9 • *Willelmi Malmesbiriensis monachi de gestis pontificum Anglorum libri quinque*, ed. N. E. S. A. Hamilton, Rolls Series, 52 (1870), 39, 194, 251 • *The early history of Glastonbury: an edition, translation, and study of William of Malmesbury's De antiquitate Glastonie ecclesie*, ed. J. Scott (1981), 155 • F. H. Dickinson, 'The sale of Combe', *Proceedings of the Somersetshire Archaeological and Natural History Society*, 22/2 (1876), 106–13 • F. Wormald, ed., *English kalendars before AD 1100*, 1, HBS, 72 (1934) • *English historical documents*, 2, ed. D. C. Douglas and G. W. Greenaway (1953), 600–01 • W. Rodwell, 'The Anglo-Saxon and Norman churches at Wells', *Wells Cathedral: a history*, ed. L. S. Colchester (1982), 1–23 (at 10–12, 14, 18, 20–21) • V. Ortenberg, *The English church and the continent in the tenth and eleventh centuries* (1992), 5, 8n, 18, 19, 37, 58, 63–4, 72, 74–6, 117, 120–22, 153, 162, 169, 171, 174, 211, 226, 246, 247, 250, 253, 255, 256 • W. Holtzmann, ed., *Papsturkunden in England*, 2 (Berlin), Abhandlung der Gesellschaft der Wissenschaften zu Göttingen, 3rd ser., 14–15 (1935–6), 131–2 • *Reg. RAN*, 1.7, 26, 28, 64, 125, 160, 187, 194 • *ASC*, s.a. 1060; s.a. 1061 [text D; text E] • F. Barlow, ed. and trans., *The life of King Edward who rests at Westminster* (1962), 52–6 • S. Keynes, 'Giso, bishop of Wells (1061–88)', *Anglo-Norman Studies*, 19 (1996), 203–71

Likenesses tomb effigy, 13th cent., Wells Cathedral; repro. in Rodwell, 'Anglo-Saxon and Norman churches at Wells', pl. 8

Gisors, John (I) de (*d.* 1282), merchant and mayor of London, laid the foundations for the success of a family, probably of Norman origin, who can be traced in London for nearly three hundred years. The son of Peter de Gisors, John married a sister of Arnold Fitzthedmar, alderman and chronicler. He was sheriff in 1240–41 and 1245, and alderman of the ward of Vintry from 1243 to *c.*1263. He lived on the riverside in the parish of St Martin Vintry, and acquired extensive property elsewhere in the city and nearby counties.

Gisors traded chiefly in wines, often transported in his own ships. His sales, and his purchases of wines as butler for the royal household, as well as other services, led to a profitable association with Henry III. The king entrusted the shrievalty of London to him in December 1245, and the custody of the city in 1254. The royalist group among the aldermen was strong enough to elect Gisors as mayor from January to October 1246 and again for the year from 28 October 1258, and 'that, too, even in his absence' wrote the chronicler (Riley, 42). But by that time the king's position had deteriorated, and the city's approval of the provisions issued by the Oxford parliament was required by the baronial reformers. Although the king was again in control by 1261—he appointed Gisors master of the exchange in 1262—rioting in London and a populist mayor in office allowed Simon de Montfort to establish himself at the Tower of London in 1263, despite an attempt by Gisors and his friends to trap him. Gisors headed a list of men the rebels planned to kill, but he was saved by the news of the royalist victory at Evesham in August 1265. In poor health in 1263, he died in 1282. A will, enrolled before the court of husting on 27 April 1282, conveys little impression of his wealth.

Gisors's eldest son, John (II) de Gisors (*d.* 1296), alderman of the ward of Vintry in 1282–96, was in turn the father of **John (III) Gisors** (*d.* 1351), mayor of London. Of this John's four brothers and four sisters, Anketin, alderman (1312–36) and six times MP, was the most prominent. John (III) married twice, first Isabella, who was dead by 1350, and second Alice. Possibly knighted, he inherited valuable properties in and near London; part of Gisors Hall, built by his father in the parish of St Mildred, Bread Street, was to survive until the mid-nineteenth century. A vintner and rentier, not a pepperer, he probably lived in the parish of St Martin Vintry.

Gisors was alderman from 1306, from 1310 for the ward of Vintry, when conflicting personalities and shifting interests both in London and the kingdom seriously threatened Edward II's control of his turbulent capital. He held the mayoralty from 28 October 1311, soon after the king had been forced to accept reforms proposed by the lords ordainer, until October 1313, and again from 1314 to 1315. He maintained the traditional protection of London's liberties, defending the franchise, and resisting both levies of tallage and investigation by royal justices of misdeeds of officials.

Gisors's family interests in the wine trade, harmed by royal favour to Gascon importers, drew him at first into opposition to the king. But while all citizens were agreed on protection of their monopoly of retail trade, not all supported Gisors's vigorous anti-alien policy, which in the spring of 1312 he pressed through in assemblies to which representatives of wards had been added. Conflicting objectives divided both leading merchants and retailers within trades. A year later an assembly, which included representatives from each trade, decreed that craft regulations, then implicitly recognized, should be publicized and enforced. All became alarmed by the city's growing lawlessness, of which Gisors had personal knowledge when in September 1312 unruly crowds surrounded the Guildhall and insisted on seeing for themselves that he was not under arrest. By the summer of 1313 Gisors and his friends were ready to co-operate with more conservative aldermen whose leader, William Leyre, was, with Gisors, elected on 10 August 1314 to represent the city at the York parliament. Attempts were made to check the uproar that had accompanied civic elections by a decree of 1313, repeated in 1315, that only 'the more discreet and powerful citizens' should take part (Sharpe, *Calendar of Letter Book D*, 25).

By 1320, when Edward and Hugh Despenser the younger moved to tighten control of London, Gisors was coming under attack. When royal justices sat at the Tower of London from 13 January to 20 May 1321 to challenge privileges and investigate grievances, Gisors was found guilty of having in 1312 predated the grant of the freedom to a committed felon so that he could release him on bail, a privilege restricted to freemen. Such use of his powers as an elected mayor, and other complaints against him, provided the king with the pretext he needed to suspend the mayoralty and appoint a royal warden. Gisors was arrested, fined, and removed from his aldermanry.

By 1323 Gisors was supporting Roger Mortimer, whose escape from the Tower he assisted, and in November 1326, when Queen Isabella with her son and Mortimer were welcomed in London after violent scenes, the Tower was surrendered to him. He led the city's delegation to see the king at Kenilworth in January 1327. But by March 1327 Gisors was no longer constable of the Tower, and he played no part in public life in later years. He died in 1351, leaving three sons and one daughter and his widow, Alice; his will, dated 5 January 1351, was enrolled before the court of husting on 19 January 1351. He left bequests for a chantry to be set up in the church of St Martin Vintry, where he and other members of the family were buried.

ELSPETH VEALE

Sources R. R. Sharpe, ed., *Calendar of letter-books preserved in the archives of the corporation of the City of London*, [12 vols.] (1899–1912), vols. A, E • 'The French chronicle of London, 1259–1343', *Chronicles of the mayors and sheriffs of London, AD 1188 to AD 1274*, ed. and trans. H. T. Riley (1863), 229–95 • A. Fitz-Thedmar, 'Liber de antiquis legibus', *Chronicles of the mayors and sheriffs of London, AD 1188 to AD 1274*, ed. and trans. H. T. Riley (1863) • W. Stubbs, ed., 'Annales Londonienses', *Chronicles of the reigns of Edward I and Edward II*, 1, Rolls Series, 76 (1882), 1–251 • W. Stubbs, ed., 'Annales Paulini', *Chronicles of the reigns of Edward I and Edward II*, 1, Rolls Series, 76 (1882), 253–370 • *Chancery records* • H. M. Cam, ed., *The eyre of London, 14 Edward II, AD 1321*, 1, SeldS, 85 (1968) • A. H. Thomas and P. E. Jones, eds., *Calendar of plea and memoranda rolls preserved among the archives of the corporation of the City of London at the Guildhall*, 1 (1926) • R. R. Sharpe, ed., *Calendar of wills proved and enrolled in the court of husting, London, AD 1258 – AD 1688*, 1 (1889), 57, 643–5 • A. B. Beaven, ed., *The aldermen of the City of London, temp. Henry III–[1912]*, 2 vols. (1908–13) • G. A. Williams, *Medieval London: from commune to capital* (1963) • P. Nightingale, *A medieval mercantile community: the Grocers' Company and the politics and trade of London, 1000–1485* (1995) • S. L. Thrupp, *The merchant class of medieval London, 1300–1500* (1948), appx • J. Stow, *A survay of London*, rev. edn (1603); repr. with introduction by C. L. Kingsford as *A survey of London*, 2 vols. (1908); repr. with addns (1971)

Wealth at death will, Sharpe, ed., *Calendar*, vol. 1, p. 57 • John Gisors III; £100 to wife; property in thirteen London parishes: will, Sharpe, ed. *Calendar*, vol. 1, pp. 643–5

Gisors, John (**III**) (*d.* **1351**). *See under* Gisors, John (I) de (*d.* 1282).

Gissing, Algernon Fred (**1860–1937**), novelist, was born on 25 November 1860 at 55 Westgate, Wakefield, Yorkshire, the third son of Thomas Waller Gissing (1829–1870), a pharmaceutical chemist, and Margaret (1832–1913), the daughter of William Bedford, a solicitor's managing clerk. There Gissing attended Back Lane School; then, following his father's death in 1870, he became a boarder at Lindow Grove School, Alderley Edge, Cheshire, together with his brothers William Gissing and George Robert *Gissing (1857–1903). After receiving his LLB from London University in 1882 Algernon Gissing set up as a solicitor in his native town, playing a modest part in local cultural affairs. Clients failing to present themselves, he boldly opted for literature a few years later, living on a small legacy from a paternal great-aunt. On 8 September 1887 he married Catherine (1859–1937), daughter of James Bennett Baseley, an outfitter with Wakefield connections, and they settled in Broadway, Worcestershire. For fifty years they lived in rural areas of the midlands and the north, invariably used as settings in his fiction. Although he published thirty books, none brought him in more than a mere pittance; nor did his half-hearted attempts at securing some other remunerative employment ever succeed. To the end of his life he eked out his meagre earnings by borrowing from his relatives and friends money which he rarely repaid. The birth of five children increased his difficulties, and his son Alwin in old age equated his father's clinging to unsuccessful novel-writing with a curse on the family. Five times between 1904 and 1918 he received grants from the Royal Literary Fund. Penury and seclusion were unpropitious to a badly needed renewal of inspiration.

Besides Gissing's booklets on Broadway (1904) and Ludlow (1905), and *The Footpath Way in Gloucestershire* (1924), his published work consists of twenty-five novels, ten of them in multi-volume form, and two collections of short stories. Very few went into a second edition. He ceased writing fiction just before the First World War, but his undying interest in country life led him to contribute a series of 'New rural rides' to the *Cornhill Magazine* in the 1920s. While no book of his roused critical enthusiasm, his artistic conscientiousness was acknowledged, and his true feeling for nature, as reflected in his descriptions of north-country scenery, duly praised. So were his rustics, occasionally likened to Thomas Hardy's. His experimentation with Meredithian complexity, notably in *A Masquerader* (1892), met with little favour, however, and his style was criticized for its affectation and grammatical oddities. The weaknesses of his plots and sometimes unconvincing characterization were found trying by many reviewers as well as by his brother George, with whose superior novelistic achievements his stories constantly invited comparison. By common consent his better work is to be found in *A Moorland Idyl* (1891), *The Scholar of Bygate* (1897), and *A Secret of the North Sea* (1900). After a pathetic twenty-five-year struggle he acknowledged himself beaten as a novelist, as repeated assurance that one was above the average was no passport to posterity. Algernon Gissing died of heart disease at Bloxham, near Banbury, Oxfordshire, on 5 February 1937, his invalid wife surviving him by barely three months. He was buried in the Bloxham cemetery on 9 February.

PIERRE COUSTILLAS

Sources *The collected letters of George Gissing*, ed. P. F. Mattheisen, A. C. Young, and P. Coustillas, 9 vols. (1990–97) · 'Mr A. Gissing: Johnsonian and novelist', *The Times* (9 Feb 1937), 16 · *Evesham Journal* (13 Feb 1937), 9 · priv. coll. · P. Coustillas, 'An uphill, unrewarding struggle: the letters of Algernon Gissing to James B. Pinker', *Gissing Journal*, 31/2 (1995), 15–34 · D. Shrubsall, 'Don't let poor Alg starve', *Gissing Newsletter*, 23/3 (1987), 30–35 · D. Shrubsall and P. Coustillas, eds., *Landscapes and literati: unpublished letters of W. H. Hudson and George Gissing* (1985) · b. cert. · General Register Office for England · Clifford Brook, 'The baptism records of George Gissing and his brothers and sisters', *Gissing Newsletter*, 13/1 (Jan 1977), 17–19

Archives NRA, priv. coll., corresp. | NYPL, Berg collection · U. Leeds, Brotherton L., letters to Clement Shorter · Yale U., Beinecke L., letters to James B. Pinker and others

Likenesses photograph, *c*.1863 (group portrait), repro. in Mattheisen, Young, and Coustillas, eds., *Collected letters of George Gissing*, 1 · photograph, June 1884, repro. in Mattheisen, Young, and Coustillas, eds., *Collected letters of George Gissing*, 2 · photograph, 1905, repro. in Mattheisen, Young, and Coustillas, eds., *Collected letters of George Gissing*, 9 · photograph, 1929, repro. in J. Korg and C. Korg, *George Gissing on fiction* (1978)

Gissing, George Robert (1857–1903), novelist, was born on 22 November 1857 at 55 (now 60) Westgate, Wakefield, Yorkshire, the eldest of the five children of Thomas Waller Gissing (1829–1870), a pharmaceutical chemist, and Margaret Bedford (1832–1913), the daughter of William Bedford, who at the time of his early death in 1832 had risen to be managing clerk in the office of Thomas Gale Curtler, a solicitor in Droitwich, Worcestershire. On the paternal side Gissing was the great-grandson and grandson of humble Suffolk shoemakers, while his Worcestershire ancestors on the maternal side had for generations had some land or other solid property to hand down to their offspring. Of the four other children, William, a music teacher, died of consumption at the age of twenty; Algernon *Gissing (1860–1937) earned for himself a very modest reputation as a regional novelist; and Margaret and Ellen grew into genteel old maids with conservative views.

Education and juvenilia Deeply influenced by his father, who watched with admiring attention his promising intellectual development, George Gissing showed a remarkable appetite for literary, historical, and artistic knowledge, reading the carefully chosen volumes in the family's library, and opting at an early age for his father's agnosticism against the traditional faith of his mother.

George Robert Gissing (1857–1903), by Sir William Rothenstein, 1897

Until his father's death he attended Back Lane School, Wakefield, where he was a pupil of Mary Susan Milner and then of the Revd Joseph Harrison, winning prizes in his stride, happier at work than at play. The juvenilia that have been preserved, now largely collected in *The Poetry of George Gissing* (1995), offer varied specimens of his precocious literary talent. His capacity and enthusiasm for work, coupled with an unflagging mental curiosity, impressed all about him, parents, teachers, and schoolfellows alike. However, with the death of his father, the sole controlling agent and truly enlightened guide in his early life, Gissing lost his best chance of smooth progress towards adulthood. Friends of the family, who had associated with Thomas Gissing as a Liberal town councillor and in the many cultural societies then flourishing in Wakefield, helped his impoverished widow to find a boarding-school where her three sons could be placed until their personal emancipation through employment. George Gissing stayed for two years (1871–2) at Lindow Grove School, a Quaker establishment at Alderley Edge, Cheshire, where he was the pride of the principal, James Wood, with whom he kept casually in touch throughout his life. His brilliant results in the 1872 Oxford local examinations—he passed first in the Manchester district and twelfth in the kingdom—to which were attached three years' free tuition and scholarships offered by Owens College (now the University of Manchester), enabled him to pursue studies under such teachers, subsequently of national reputation, as A. W. Ward and A. S. Wilkins. At Owens College, as its calendars testify, Gissing distinguished himself, winning a great many prizes in the humanities, in particular the English poem prize with 'Ravenna' (1873), and the Shakspere scholarship (1875), scoring another great success in 1874, when he came out first in England in both English and Latin at the intermediate BA examination of the University of London.

Early career An academic career seemed to be in store for Gissing, but such a prospect was ruined in the winter of 1875–6. He had until then been entirely absorbed in the acquisition of learning, but at this time became acquainted with a parentless girl of the streets only a few months his junior, Marianne Helen Harrison (1858–1888), known as Nell. Having fallen in love with her and convinced himself that she was a social victim, he gave her whatever money he could spare; and, in his desperate efforts to save her, began to rifle the pockets of the students' coats in the locker rooms. On 31 May 1876 a detective hired by the college authorities caught him red-handed; he was expelled from the establishment and sentenced on 6 June to one month's imprisonment with hard labour, which he served in Bellevue Prison, Manchester. He never recovered from this disgrace, although he lived it down as an adult of pathetic honesty. Supported by a few Wakefield friends and the college staff, who, seriously embarrassed by the whole affair, collected some money to help him materially, his mother sent him off to start a new life in the United States. He sailed to New York in September; but neither in Boston, where he arrived with a few letters of recommendation to local personalities, nor in the mixed school in nearby Waltham, in which he taught for two months, did he succeed in taking root. On 1 March 1877 he abruptly left for Chicago, where until the summer he supported himself by writing short tales, most of which he sold to local papers, notably the *Chicago Tribune*, then edited by Samuel Medill. His American experiences, echoed in chapter 28 of *New Grub Street* (1891), included assisting an itinerant photographer for a time.

Defeated by circumstances, Gissing sailed back to England in September 1877, and promptly settled in shabby London lodgings, where Nell soon joined him. Until the mid-1880s he lived mainly on the meagre income he drew from private tuition, at first also supplemented by occasional odd jobs for S. Vincent Mercier, secretary of St John's Hospital. Simultaneously Gissing turned to fiction writing, his first completed long narrative (title unknown and manuscript lost) being ready as early as July 1878. His first published novel, *Workers in the Dawn* (1880), was practically finished, when, with typical masochism, he married Nell on 27 October 1879, although he had by then lost all hope of redeeming her. Despite some obvious flaws *Workers* offers a notable picture of lower-class London life as seen by a young *déclassé* idealist divided between social and artistic commitments. Because publishers spurned his manuscript, he had to bring it out at his own expense, a bold venture made possible by a small legacy from a great-aunt, Emily Waller Williams. The history of Gissing's next novel, 'Mrs Grundy's Enemies', accepted and paid for by Bentley & Son in late 1882, was to become a *cause célèbre* in English publishing. Frightened by its naturalistic strains, George Bentley cravenly eschewed publication, though after reading over two-thirds of the proofs Gissing obligingly revised the whole book.

By the time *The Unclassed*, which was admired by both George Meredith and Thomas Hardy, appeared in 1884, Gissing had separated from his wife, whose inveterate drinking and disorderly habits caused her death in a Lambeth slum about four years later. Partly thanks to Frederic Harrison, the positivist leader and writer to whom he had sent a copy of *Workers in the Dawn*, Gissing was able to find more pupils, including Harrison's own sons, Bernard and Austin, and to keep his head above water. His quarterly contributions to *Vestnik Evropy* (*Le Messager de l'Europe*, 1881–2), arranged through E. S. Beesly and Turgenev, also resulted from Harrison's unobtrusive determination to assist him.

Although *The Unclassed* achieved a *succès d'estime* with the intelligentsia, Gissing's stark realism and pessimistic view of human affairs, which put off publishers until the mid-1880s, prevented him from becoming popular. Yet the power and originality of his work did not go unnoticed, and his poverty was somewhat relieved when Smith, Elder & Co. became his main publishers from 1886, with the anonymously published *Demos*, to 1891, which saw the publication of *New Grub Street*. It was with *Demos*, subtitled 'A Story of English Socialism', that Gissing unquestionably made his mark. *Isabel Clarendon* (1886) and *A Life's Morning* (1888), both written before *Demos*, depicted middle-class life, and were indebted to the artistically invigorating influence of the wealthy Gaussens of Broughton Hall, Lechlade.

Gissing returned, however, to the mores of the proletariat in *Thyrza* (1887) and *The Nether World* (1889), respectively the gentlest and the darkest of his pictures of poverty in London. In *The Nether World* his personal and philosophical despair, intensified by Nell's death, reached a peak, resulting in a work of particular power. The sale of the book's copyright to Smith, Elder for £150 enabled him to indulge his long-thwarted desire to visit Italy in the winter of 1888–9—a desire fostered by his passionate interest in the classics. His life was intense and lonely in those years; his only two soulmates were Morley Roberts (1857–1942), a former college friend, who became a prolific writer and Gissing's first biographer in a slapdash *roman-à-clef* entitled *The Private Life of Henry Maitland* (1912), and Eduard Bertz, a German socialist exile, later a man of letters. Gissing met him in 1879 and they remained permanently in touch after Bertz's return to his native country in 1884.

The middle years The late 1880s and early 1890s were for Gissing times of instability; although culturally enriching, they were marked by emotional frustrations. After his prolonged stay in France and Italy in the autumn and winter of 1888–9 he went south again, visiting Greece and once more Naples. His quest for an educated wife having failed, he perversely convinced himself that only a lower-class girl would accept him; so on 25 February 1891 he married another uneducated young woman, Edith Alice

Underwood (1867–1917), a stonemason's daughter, who proved to be as unsuitable a partner as Nell had been. Two children, Walter (1891–1916) and Alfred (1896–1975), were born of this union, which turned into a domestic inferno once the apparently meek and docile Edith revealed all her shrewish potentialities. By the time they separated, in the autumn of 1897, she had evinced undoubted symptoms of insanity, which made it necessary to confine her to an asylum some four years later.

Domestic circumstances notwithstanding, this second spell of married life was, artistically, Gissing's most productive. With *The Emancipated* (1890), a satirical study in moral and spiritual emancipation set in Naples and Yorkshire, he launched into a wide-ranging discussion of the main political and societal problems with which England was confronted in the last years of Victoria's reign. He also first exposed the commercialization of literature resulting from the spread of education in *New Grub Street*, his strongest book, an acknowledged classic. Its main characters have become recognized symbols of the many shades of professional integrity and adaptability in the literary world, shades not substantially affected by the passing of the years. Discussing the story in later life, Gissing admitted personal affinities with the two defeated younger writers Edwin Reardon and Harold Biffen, proudly adding, however, that unlike them he had not failed. Equally characteristic was his next novel, *Born in Exile* (1892), in which he pitted scientific rationalism against superannuated religious dogma. Its memorable central figure, Godwin Peak, bears comparison with such protagonists of European fiction as Robert Greslou, Bazarov, Raskolnikov, and Niels Lyhne. *The Odd Women* (1893) dealt with the impact of turn-of-the-century demographics on the larger debate then raging concerning women's rights and social status, a subject Gissing had broached in *Denzil Quarrier* the year before.

Gissing's concern for wider cultural problems was further illustrated, and more stridently so, in *In the Year of Jubilee* (1894), a quasi-Hogarthian picture of new mental and commercial developments in suburban life, which he chose to view more humorously, yet just as devastatingly, in *The Paying Guest* (1895). *The Whirlpool* (1897) concluded this series. Alongside the baneful attraction of urban effervescence, he dealt in it with such of his favourite themes as the corruption of art by the lust for fame and money, women's emancipation, and, with Kipling's influence in mind, the danger of the more blustering forms of imperialism. By this time Gissing was commonly regarded, together with Meredith and Hardy (whom he knew personally), as one of the three leading English novelists. He had achieved this enviable position not only by the intellectual distinction of his work, but by stringent artistic integrity.

After two and a half years of provincial seclusion in Exeter, from January 1891 to June 1893, Gissing moved closer to the centre of the literary arena, settling with his family in Brixton, where he was attracted by the recently founded Henry Tate Library. In this new home, which he transferred to Epsom in the autumn of 1894, he was within easy reach of publishers and editors, and his work, as witnessed by the increasing amount of international comment, was considered with greater attention than in the previous decade. This evolution in public opinion was facilitated in 1893 by Gissing's embarking on a second career as a short-story writer. His work in that field was collected in *Human Odds and Ends* (1898) and several posthumous volumes, and he was assisted in publishing it by his successive literary agents, William Morris Colles and James B. Pinker. In a less measurable manner, his rising fame benefited from his association with a number of well-known figures in the journalistic and literary worlds, notably C. K. Shorter, Henry Norman, John Davidson, J. M. Barrie, Edmund Gosse, and Edward Clodd.

But Gissing's health began to fail and simultaneously his domestic life went from bad to worse. In April 1896, in order to protect his elder son from Edith's violent conduct, he had to entrust him to his two sisters, who had just opened a preparatory school in Wakefield. Barely a year later, his doctor having diagnosed a moist spot in his right lung, he 'fled' from Edith and went to recuperate for a few months at Budleigh Salterton. During an abortive attempt at reconciliation with his wife in the summer of 1897 he succeeded in writing the most Dickensian of his novels, *The Town Traveller* (1898), a social farce he soon repudiated as unworthy. His more solid fictional work had now been done; but following the collapse in 1894 of the established system, previously supported by the circulating libraries, of publishing fiction in three volumes, he showed a remarkable capacity for tailoring his work to the demands of publishers and editors alike. *Eve's Ransom*, a tongue-in-cheek satire of a self-seeking young woman, and *Sleeping Fires*, a novella, partly set in Greece, about the renewal of love in middle age, were commissioned stories which testify to this.

The work Gissing went on to produce showed further diversification of his achievements, somehow foreshadowed by his decision to leave for Italy in September 1897. Relieved by his final separation from Edith, who kept Alfred with her, and was, when need arose, pacified by his two staunch, forward-looking friends Eliza Orme and Clara Collet, Gissing wrote at Siena his *Charles Dickens: a Critical Study*, which stands as a landmark in the movement towards a rational appreciation of his great predecessor. Then in November he journeyed to the extreme south, recording impressions that gracefully found their way into his much admired travel book *By the Ionian Sea* (1901). After a short halt at Monte Cassino he settled in Rome for some months, collecting material for his long-planned sixth-century romance of Roman and Goth, *Veranilda* (1904). There he lived in a cosmopolitan atmosphere, on which he passed humorous judgements, and was joined by H. G. Wells and his wife, prior to returning to England via Potsdam, the home of his old friend Bertz. The visit was cut short by Gissing's horror of the rampant militarism prevailing in Germany.

Life in France The course of Gissing's life was entirely reshaped in July 1898, when, having rented a house at

Dorking, he was visited by a cultured middle-class Frenchwoman of twenty-nine, Gabrielle Marie Edith Fleury (1868–1954), who sought his permission to translate *New Grub Street*. Their subsequent love affair developed into a common-law marriage from May 1899 onwards. Gissing lived from that time in France: first in Paris, with intervals at St Honoré-les-Bains and Couhard in central France; then from late 1901, on account of his impaired health, at Arcachon; and finally in the Basque villages of Ciboure and Ispoure, respectively near St Jean-de-Luz and St Jean-Pied-de-Port. Early on, the presence of Gabrielle's mother in their home was, mainly for dietary reasons, a source of temporary difficulties between the couple, which came to a head in the summer of 1901, when, on the advice of English doctors, Gissing had to stay for some six weeks in the newly opened East Anglian Sanatorium at Nayland, Suffolk. After that his life ran more smoothly; he had no opportunity to visit England again, but nostalgia for his native country cropped up increasingly in his correspondence, notably with Edward Clodd and Dr Henry Hick, a childhood friend.

Despite temptations to turn to other genres, fiction remained Gissing's principal literary medium, essentially because it was the most remunerative. *The Crown of Life* (1899), which he wrote while waiting to join Gabrielle Fleury across the channel, was partly inspired by his love for her, but the story, with its strong anti-imperialist plea for pacifism, also links up thematically with *The Whirlpool*. 'Among the Prophets', a novel satirizing the spiritual crazes fashionable at the turn of the century, is supposed to have been destroyed at his request by his agent James B. Pinker. With *Our Friend the Charlatan* (1901) Gissing turned again to political mores, with a Meredithian outlook on the comedy he briskly staged. His last full-length story of modern life, *Will Warburton*, published posthumously in 1905, is imbued with the resignation which came through in his later letters to his friends and occasional correspondents. Interspersed with these works were further writings on Dickens, resulting from the success of Gissing's critical study in the Victorian Era series. These writings included articles for newspapers and journals, but were composed mainly of an abridged and revised version of John Forster's biography of Dickens and of introductions to the ill-fated Rochester and Autograph editions. However, to a larger audience than he had hitherto commanded, Gissing's most striking book published before his death was the unclassifiable *Private Papers of Henry Ryecroft* (1903), first serialized in the *Fortnightly Review* as 'An author at grass'. Half-reminiscential, half-speculative, these idiosyncratic essays, lovingly composed in 1900 and 1901, for half a century put all Gissing's non-belletristic titles in the shade. They are obviously the work of an ageing man whose physical strength was ebbing away, and their valetudinarian tone and refreshing candour on controversial matters of life and death enchanted the Edwardians.

Gissing was not given time to complete his historical novel *Veranilda*, five chapters of which remained unwritten. During a walk in early December 1903 he caught a cold which quickly developed into broncho-pneumonia; his condition at Christmas was so serious that Gabrielle Fleury telegraphed for H. G. Wells and Morley Roberts. Wells rushed to Ispoure and found Gissing still alive; however, remembering that his friend had been underfed in his Paris days, he made him consume so much that—according to Gabrielle—he precipitated his death at Maison Elguë, Ispoure, on 28 December. Medical opinion, however, attributed it to myocarditis. There was a dispute about a conversion supposed to have taken place while the patient was delirious, but the weak-minded Anglican clergyman Theodore Cooper, who had set the false news afloat, was indignantly contradicted in print by Morley Roberts. Although Roberts reached Ispoure only after Gissing's death, his enquiry enabled him to restore the truth that Gissing had been a consistent agnostic to the end. Having escorted the coffin to St Jean-de-Luz, he attended, together with the English colony there, the Anglican funeral service arranged out of regard for Gissing's relatives, and saw his friend laid to rest on 30 December in his grave at the top of the local cemetery.

Gissing's was a genial personality, shy and altruistic, deeply marked by the traumatic experience of his youth. Convinced that all avenues to happiness were closed to him after the Manchester scandal, he contracted two mortifying unions, taking it for granted that no educated girl in sympathy with his artistic aims would ever agree to marry him. Material cares, even in the last decade of his career, when his annual income fluctuated between £180 and £720, never ceased to weigh on his mind. The contrast between his critical reputation and his income drew from him many sarcastic remarks. Yet he was not naturally a gloomy man, and he impressed his friends and acquaintances as a brilliant conversationalist when in congenial company. A demanding artist, he was rarely satisfied with public assessments of his works—works which were none the less held in high esteem by the more enlightened critics. Equipped with a formidable knowledge of literature, ancient and modern, English and foreign, he was fundamentally a humanist at odds with the modern way of life, as well as a pacifist opposed to all forms of violence. He was a writer who placed his artistic principles above financial reward, hence the number of his completed manuscripts that he destroyed.

The continued relevance of Gissing's work (which the Japanese intelligentsia of the inter-war and post-war years, responding to the humane qualities apparent in his volumes of short stories and *belles-lettres*, was first to recognize) is undoubted, and his finest interpreters now tend to view him as an intellectual who rose to be the conscience of his time. An apt analyst of the female mind, Gissing was perhaps at his strongest, as he himself declared in 1895, when he described 'a class of young men distinctive of our time—well educated, fairly bred, but *without money*' (letter to Morley Roberts, 10 Feb 1895, *Collected Letters*, 5.294–7). His unremitting cultural commitment has endeared him to successive generations of discerning readers. However unpalatable a particular truth was, he courageously voiced it, and his lucid, if pessimistic, judgements on human affairs, as well as the sterling originality of his art, have secured his place in the history of the English novel.

PIERRE COUSTILLAS

Sources *The collected letters of George Gissing*, ed. P. F. Mattheisen, A. C. Young, and P. Coustillas, 9 vols. (1990–97) • P. Coustillas, ed., *London and the life of literature in late Victorian England: the diary of George Gissing, novelist* (1978) • P. C., 'George Gissing', *The Cambridge bibliography of English literature*, ed. J. Shattock, 3rd edn, 4 (1999), cols. 1535–52 • P. Coustillas, 'Gissing's reminiscences of his father: an unpublished manuscript', *English Literature in Transition, 1880–1920*, 32 (1989), 419–39 • B. Postmus, ed., *George Gissing's American notebook: notes—G. R. G.—1877* (1993) • P. Coustillas, *George Gissing at Alderley Edge* (1969) • P. Coustillas, 'Gissing's academic feat reconsidered', *Gissing Newsletter*, 15/4 (1979), 12–15 • Owens College calendars, 1872–6 • unpublished letters concerning Gissing's exclusion from Owens College, University of Manchester • R. L. Selig, ed., *George Gissing: lost stories from America* (1992) • P. Coustillas and C. Partridge, *Gissing: the critical heritage* (1972) • *Church Times* (8 Jan 1904), 33 • M. Roberts, 'The late George Gissing', *Church Times* (15 Jan 1904), 61 • G. M. Adams, 'How and why I collect George Gissing', *The Colophon*, 5/18 (1934) [incl. facs. of Gissing's account books, 1880–98] • b. cert. • parish register, All Saints' Church, Wakefield, Yorkshire [baptism] • m. certs. • d. cert.

Archives BL, letters to his son Walter, Add. MS 59790 • Boston PL, letters • Col. U., letters and literary papers • Colgate University, Hamilton, New York, letters and literary MSS • Dartmouth College, Hanover, New Hampshire, letters and literary papers, incl. one notebook • Hunt. L., letters and literary MSS, memorandum book • Indiana University, Bloomington, Lilly Library, letters, papers, and literary MSS • Morgan L., letters and literary MSS • NL Scot., MS essay on Robert Burns • NYPL, Carl H. Pforzheimer Collection of Shelley and His Circle, letters and papers, incl. literary MSS • Ransom HRC, letters and literary MSS • U. Leeds, Brotherton L., letters • University of Illinois, letters and literary papers • University of Pennsylvania, Philadelphia, letters and literary papers • Yale U., Beinecke L., letters, notebooks, and literary MSS | BL, letters to Henry Hick, Add. MS 49993 [typescript] • Royal Society for the Protection of Birds, Sandy, letters to William Henry Hudson; fragment of 'A Life's Morning' • U. Warwick Mod. RC, letters to Clara Collet [photocopies]

Likenesses photograph, *c*.1862, Wakefield Public Library, West Yorkshire • print, 1884, Yale U. • W. Rothenstein, engraving, 1897, BM, NPG [*see illus.*] • W. Rothenstein, sketch, 1897, NPG • C. Rook, portrait, 1901, Berg Coll., NPG • photographs, repro. in Mattheisen, Young, and Coustillas, eds., *Collected letters*

Wealth at death £1052 2*s*. 6*d*.: probate, 15 Nov 1904, *CGPLA Eng. & Wales*

Gittings, Robert William Victor (1911–1992), poet and writer, was born on 1 February 1911 at Southsea, the son of Surgeon-Captain Fred Claude Bromley Gittings and Dora Mary, *née* Brayshaw. He attended St Edward's School, Oxford, where he was influenced by an outstanding teacher, George Mallaby. While at school he had poems published, bringing him into contact with Christopher Fry, who became a lifelong friend. In 1930 he went to Jesus College, Cambridge, as a history scholar, and gained a first in 1933. During his undergraduate years his literary interests developed and he received encouragement from Sir Arthur Quiller-Couch, whose college rooms were adjacent to his. In 1931 he was awarded the chancellor's gold medal for English verse. In 1933 he was made a research fellow of the college and in 1934 he married Katherine (Kay) Edith Cambell, a former student at Girton College. They had two sons. Gittings was history supervisor from 1938 until 1940, when he moved to the BBC as writer and producer. During his twenty-three years with the BBC his output was prolific and of consistently high quality. His schools broadcasts—dramatized history and literary programmes—are classics of their kind. He was a regular contributor to long-running and highly regarded programmes including *Poets and Poetry*, *World History Series*, *Poetry Now*, and *The World of Books*. His marriage ended in divorce and in 1949 he married again; his second wife was Joan (Jo) Greville Manton, a colleague at the BBC, and herself a distinguished biographer and later collaborator with Gittings. They had one daughter.

Gittings would probably wish to be remembered as a poet. His first major book of verse, *Wentworth Place* (1950), was well received and held to be rich in promise and achievement with 'lines that hold fast in the memory' (*TLS*, 31 March 1950). Here and in *Famous Meeting* (1953) he showed a rare ability to bring alive the past. He published twelve volumes of poetry, disciplined and graceful in the Georgian tradition, but later volumes did not develop the earlier promise. Gittings was a good, minor poet of real talent and sound craftsmanship, a keen observer of the natural scene and the human condition capable of finely tuned and evocative verse, but not rising to the highest levels of perception and imagination.

In 1954, Gittings's *John Keats: the Living Year* was published and received with acclaim. In this book of freshness, originality, and excitement Gittings displayed the skills he was to refine in his later biographies—meticulous scholarship combined with a keen literary sensitivity, an appreciation of social and historical context, and an infectious sense of the joys of detection. *The Mask of Keats* followed in 1956, and an excursion into Shakespeare studies in 1960 (*Shakespeare's Rival*).

Gittings left the BBC in 1964 and in the years that followed he established his reputation as a major authority on both Keats and Hardy. *John Keats* (awarded the W. H. Smith literary award) was published in 1969. Gittings's studies of Hardy, though conscientious, scholarly, and eminently readable, are perhaps marred by a certain lack of respect for Hardy the man. In this Gittings did not wholeheartedly apply his own dictum that 'biography begins, in one sense or another, with praise' (*The Nature of Biography*, 1978, 19). But as a literary biographer Gittings is masterly and he well illustrates his own definition of biography as 'poetry with a conscience' (ibid., 10), in his combination of clear observation, enthusiasm, search for truth, and felicity with words. *The Young Thomas Hardy* appeared in 1975, followed by *The Older Hardy* in 1978 and *The Second Mrs Hardy* (with Jo Manton) in 1979.

As playwright, Gittings was a master of radio drama. Less well known were the plays he wrote over several years for women's institutes. *Son et lumière* (*This Tower my Prison*, 1961, and *Conflict at Canterbury* for the 1970 Canterbury Festival) were much acclaimed while *Introducing Thomas Hardy*, his brilliant double act with Frances Horowitz, first performed in 1971, was in demand throughout the country until Horowitz's death in 1978.

In 1985 Gittings turned to the Wordsworths and with Jo

Manton wrote *Dorothy Wordsworth*, an engaging and revealing study. He also published his last collection of poems, *People, Places, Personal*, a title which fairly describes the wide range of his poetry. In the short poems 'The Bell Tolls' and 'In the Car Park', he digs below the surface of the mundane to expose human fragility and insecurity.

Gittings was always an enthusiast for games—squash, golf, and real tennis—and was a dependable middle-order batsman until well into his seventies. He regularly recruited actors from the Chichester Theatre to play in cricket matches. Tall and trim, he had the high, bald dome of an intellectual, with a warm, friendly, and expressive face, always enquiring and slightly quizzical. He had an attractive personality. A man of strong principles, he was, nevertheless, unfailingly considerate and generous, with a gift for friendship and a warm sense of humour.

Appointed CBE in 1970, Gittings was awarded the honorary LittD by Cambridge in 1970 and by Leeds in 1981. His election as honorary fellow of Jesus College in 1979 gave him particular pleasure.

Robert Gittings died at Chichester on 18 February 1992. On the morning before he died, he read the first copy of his last book, *Claire Clairmont and the Shelleys*, fresh from the publishers. He commented: 'It's all right. It'll do, I think' (*Jesus College (Cambridge) Report*, 47). The cremation took place on 24 February at Chichester crematorium.

G. Tolley

Sources *TLS* · BBC WAC · *Jesus College (Cambridge) Report* (1992) · *The Times* (21 Feb 1992)

Archives W. Sussex RO, verse, corresp., diaries, and working papers · Wordsworth Trust, Dove Cottage, Grasmere, library | SOUND BBC Archives

Gittins, Charles Edward (1908–1970), educational administrator, was born on 24 January 1908 at Rhostyllen, Esclusham, Wrexham, Denbighshire, the son of Charles Thomas Gittins, a colliery engine fitter, and his wife, Susannah Frances Rabbitt. He was educated initially at Bersham boys' council school and Grove Park county school, Wrexham. His undergraduate years (1925–8) were spent at the University College of Wales, Aberystwyth, where he graduated in 1928 with a first-class honours degree in history. The following year he obtained his teaching diploma and took up a postgraduate research studentship from 1929 to 1931 in the same college. He was awarded his MA degree in 1934, his subject being education in the early years of the French Revolution. Proud of his debating prowess, he became president of debates as well as treasurer and president of the students' union. His future wife, Margaret Anne Davies, also born in 1908, was a fellow student who became a teacher. They married on 28 December 1934 and had two children, John (*b.* 1938) and Margaret (*b.* 1942).

From 1931 to 1938 Gittins was senior history master at St James Grammar School, Bishop Auckland, co. Durham, where his headmaster regarded him as an outstanding teacher. He was also deputy headmaster from 1937 to 1938. He combined his teaching career with lecturing for the Workers' Educational Association (1932–5) and the extramural department of Durham University (1935–8).

In 1938 Gittins was appointed assistant education officer in the Durham county education authority, where he headed an investigation particularly pertinent to the period—the relationship between intelligence and undernourishment. In 1942 he was appointed administrative assistant to the county education committee of the West Riding of Yorkshire, where he was responsible for school meals, emergency feeding centres, nursery education, and post-war development schemes. A. L. Binns, the education officer, whose word mattered, counted him among the best ever administrative assistants in his department.

In 1944 Gittins was appointed to the post of director of education in Monmouthshire, where he was responsible for primary and secondary education as it evolved after the major education legislation of that year. Following R. A. Butler's Education Act each county was required to submit a development plan for the reorganization of school education from a parallel system of elementary and secondary schools to a sequential system of primary, secondary, and further education. The system which emerged under Gittins's direction followed the standard bipartite pattern of grammar and secondary modern schools. He served on the usual variety of outside committees, including the Burnham Technical Committee (1946–53), the Schools' Broadcasting Council (Wales) from 1947, the Welsh committee of the Arts Council (1947–55), and, most important, the Central Advisory Council for Education (Wales) from 1956. He supported the founding of the National Youth Orchestra of Wales and a village college movement in Monmouthshire.

In 1956 Gittins was appointed professor, head of the department, and dean of the faculty of education at the University College of Swansea. As head of department he presided over the expansion of both postgraduate teacher training and in-service courses. He inaugurated diploma courses in educational psychology, special needs, and counselling, areas in which the Swansea department acquired a national reputation. Though he published little himself, he fostered research, and from the early 1960s his department's work on compensatory education acquired international significance. The department's work in identifying the effect on pupils' educational progress of material, social, and emotional disadvantage gained an international reputation. In the same period faculties of education—university departments, training colleges, and local schools—were developing an important role under the aegis of the four Welsh university colleges. Gittins stimulated a comprehensive programme of courses for teachers, including the new master of education degree, and secured the use of a dedicated college building for faculty use. He was a highly effective head of department. His spare, grey-haired, medium-height figure exuded charm and dignity of manner, and inspired respect among colleagues and students. His conduct of committees was crisp and efficient. His colleagues remembered his integrity and courtesy, administrative abilities, and loyalty to them. He was also active in the local community and in the city of Swansea. Brought up a Methodist, he later attended Anglican worship and served as churchwarden in Bishopston, Swansea. In 1964 he was chairman of the arts and crafts committee of the national eisteddfod in Swansea.

Although Gittins had been a member of the Local Government Boundary Commission for Wales in 1958, his most notable committee work was as chairman of the Central Advisory Council for Education (Wales) from 1964 to 1967. In one of the more significant post-war acknowledgements of a distinctive Welsh education, the Welsh committee was required by Sir Edward Boyle to produce a general report on primary education and the transition to secondary schooling which exactly paralleled that of Lady Plowden's Central Advisory Council for Education (England). Gittins served as the crucial link, as a member of the English committee and chairman of the Welsh. Just as the 'Plowden report' is one of the landmarks in primary education in England in the post-war period, so is the 'Gittins report', published in 1967, of central importance in the history of Welsh education, as much for what it symbolized as for what it advocated. *Primary Education in Wales* ran to 646 pages and echoed the progressive, child-centred approach of the English committee. Gittins recommended the reorganization of primary education in Wales, with part-time nursery provision from age three, infant schools from five to eight (to be renamed first schools), middle schools from eight to twelve plus, then transfer to the secondary school. There were enlightened recommendations to ease the transition from primary to secondary schools, and a firm recommendation that the class should not form the essential teaching group but be broken down into flexible groupings to meet differing needs, with no streaming. The fixed timetable in junior schools was to be replaced by programmes of work which broke down traditional subject barriers. There was considerable controversy within the committee and in Wales over recommendations to make religious education and corporate worship non-statutory. The report was prescient in recommending ubiquitous teaching of Welsh with the aim of making pupils bilingual by the end of the primary stage. In 1968 Gittins was made CBE for his services to education.

The final phase in Gittins's career came with his appointment as vice-principal of University College, Swansea, in 1967, in which his abilities as an administrator were particularly evident. From 1967 to 1968 he combined this work with the headship of the department of education. Then the mounting problems of universities, both financially after the dramatic expansion of the previous decade, and in relations with students, decreed that he devote himself full-time, deanship of the faculty of education apart, to his duties as vice-principal. In years of unprecedented campus militancy, he was left to take the main responsibility at Swansea for fraught negotiations with students.

Gittins was anxious to become permanent vice-principal, though this involved a break with tradition. Despite prevarication by the principal, the appointment was agreed in the summer of 1970. Shortly afterwards one of his university colleagues suggested a boating trip. It turned to tragedy. In Oxwich Bay, off the Gower peninsula, the boat capsized. Gittins died of heart failure, due to the shock of immersion in the sea, on 6 August 1970 at Singleton Hospital, Swansea. He was cremated and his ashes scattered in the grounds of Bishopston parish church, Swansea. A memorial volume of essays was published in 1972, and a regular lecture in his memory was instituted at the University of Wales, Swansea.

GARETH ELWYN JONES

Sources M. Chazan, ed., *Aspects of primary education* (1972) [incl. tribute by F. L. Jones, 1–6] · F. Ll. J. [F. Ll. Jones], *Annual Report* [University College of Swansea], 50 (1969–70), 133–5 · R. Aldrich and P. Gordon, *Dictionary of British educationists* (1989), 95 · Schools Council Committee for Wales, *Aspects of primary education: the challenge of Gittins* (1970) · G. E. Jones, *Which nation's schools* (1990) · D. G. Lewis, *The university and the colleges of education in Wales, 1925–1978* (1980) · curriculum vitae of C. E. Gittins, 1956, University College, Swansea · newspaper cuttings, Swansea Central Library · *Annual Report* [University College of Swansea] (1956–70) · b. cert. · d. cert. · m. cert.

Archives priv. coll.

Wealth at death £19,946: administration, 29 Dec 1970, *CGPLA Eng. & Wales*

Gittins, John Stanley (1910–1996), educationist, was born on 1 March 1910 in Hinckley, Leicestershire, the son of Albert Harold Gittins (1886–1943), a manager of the Co-operative Society, and his wife, Lily, *née* King (1883–1917). He was educated at Hinckley grammar school (1920–27); University College, Leicester (1927–31), where he graduated BSc in chemistry; Cambridge University (1931–2), where he was awarded a diploma in education; and the University of London Institute of Education (1932–3), where he graduated MA. He married Elizabeth Lewis (*b.* 1909), schoolteacher and approved school matron, on 2 August 1934. They had two children, Ann (*b.* 1939) and Christopher (*b.* 1946).

Gittins served as a science master at Whitgift Middle School, Croydon, between 1932 and 1936, and was then appointed lecturer in education and psychology at the University College of the South West, Exeter, between 1937 and 1938. From 1938 to 1942 he worked as an inspector in the children's department of the Home Office. His duties during the Second World War entailed the inspection of possible sites for new approved schools in rural areas away from cities under threat of bombing and intended for the increasing number of young people identified as delinquent or at risk because of the social and geographical dislocations wrought by the war. One such site, formerly a hostel owned by the Ministry of Works, was at Aycliffe, near Darlington. When Gittins declared it suitable in 1942, he was invited by the Home Office to establish and administer the new school, and he remained its principal until his retirement.

Gittins brought an evolving amalgam of themes to his new post: a natural scientific bent acquired as an undergraduate chemist; an admiration for psychology acquired as a graduate student in education; a stress on the superiority of experience and 'common sense' over academic theory; and a personal commitment to teaching. Professing—as in the *Northern Echo* of 1 June 1954—that very little was known about the causes or cures of delinquency, he nevertheless maintained a cautious optimism about the possibility of changing the young by exposing them to improving influences, including community service, hiking, art, drama, 'good films', and classical music. He once told Ron Clarke, sometime head of the Home Office research unit, that he was wasting his time on 'all that "kiddlepumph"' about absconding from approved schools, the subject of Clarke's PhD dissertation, and that he would do better to examine the successful methods employed at Aycliffe (private information). Delinquency, Gittins said, is 'a malaise of society', a form of social incompetence compounded by unsatisfactory, unstimulating, and unstable homes (*Evening Dispatch*, 31 Jan 1947). Aycliffe itself combined practical activity with therapy and education broadly conceived in 'a kind of crucible in which one is carrying out an experiment using ingredients in a concentrated form'.

In common with many other post-war penologists, Gittins became persuaded that successful rehabilitation rested on early intervention and a proper classification of the young into categories for allocation to different regimes. Aycliffe was the first classifying school approved by the Home Office, the biggest and the best in the country according to the *Evening Standard*, designed to observe, assess, and place children in local training schools in the north-east. Gittins was perhaps most celebrated for the classifying methods he devised at Aycliffe and subsequently publicized in a Home Office report of 1952. Those methods were represented as pragmatic and simple, intended for purposes of action, and based on the limited knowledge of the time, rather than as scientific or precise measures of complex phenomena. Boys were transferred to a training school after a comprehensive report had been compiled on tests for educational attainment and intelligence, observations of health, and descriptions of family background and present conduct.

As Aycliffe's founder, long-standing principal, and trainer of new staff, Gittins, who was described by Professor Roger Hood as a 'tall and imposing man' and by others as 'charismatic' (private information), came to exert a considerable authority over thinking about penal policy. He was appointed OBE in 1962 and retired from Aycliffe in 1970. He died of heart failure at the Freeman Hospital, Newcastle upon Tyne, on 27 October 1996, and was cremated in Newcastle the following month. He was survived by his wife, daughter, and son. PAUL ROCK

Sources V. Bailey, *Delinquency and citizenship* (1987) · priv. coll., Gittins MSS · *The Independent* (7 Nov 1996) · private information (2004) [family]

Archives priv. coll., MSS

Likenesses photograph, repro. in *The Independent*

Giudice, Filippo del (1892–1962), film producer, was born in Trani, Italy. He studied at Rome University and established a successful law practice. By 1932 his anti-Fascist views made his position untenable and he fled to England (ironically his one film appearance was as a boastful Fascist air marshal in Leslie Howard's *The First of the Few*, 1942). Living in a basement flat in South Kensington, London, del Giudice made a living giving Italian lessons and established contact with the large community of European exiles working within the British film industry. In 1937 he set up Two Cities Films with fellow Italian Mario Zampi. The company's first film, *French without Tears* (1939), typified del Giudice's approach, bringing together a promising young playwright, Terence Rattigan, with a promising young director, Anthony Asquith, and allowing them untrammelled creative freedom to make a film they were enthusiastically committed to.

Two Cities' progress was halted by the outbreak of the Second World War. Early in 1940 del Giudice and Zampi were interned on the Isle of Man as enemy aliens. Zampi was shipped out to Canada but del Giudice was released in September. He brought in Anthony Havelock-Alan, a successful producer of 'quota quickies', to help him revive the fortunes of Two Cities and approached Noël Coward with the idea of making a film about the Royal Navy. Coward's experience with screen adaptations of his plays had been less than happy but del Giudice's willingness to allow him complete creative control tempted him to write a screenplay based on the naval experiences of his friend Lord Louis Mountbatten. Despite the opposition of the Ministry of Information to a film centring on a lost battle and a sunk ship, it was turned into a highly successful film—*In Which We Serve* (1942)—directed by Coward in collaboration with David Lean.

In Which We Serve was the top British box-office film of 1942 and was more successful in America than any other British film during the war. Del Giudice had had to struggle hard to raise the budget—a much bigger one than that of any previous Two Cities film—but he and his company were now firmly established. Critically and commercially successful films such as Leslie Howard's *The Gentle Sex* (1943), Carol Reed's *The Way Ahead* (1944), and David Lean's *This Happy Breed* (1944), triumphantly vindicated del Giudice's policy of choosing talented film-makers and allowing them the freedom to make the best films they were capable of with as little interference as possible. In this he was fortunate in receiving the financial support of J. Arthur Rank who was pursuing a similar policy with his Independent Producers' company. Rank initially offered a distribution guarantee for Two Cities' films, but as del Giudice became more ambitious, he came to rely increasingly on Rank's financial support, and when the budget for Olivier's *Henry V* (1944) soared towards £500,000 he was forced to cede control of Two Cities to Rank.

Del Giudice remained at the helm of his company but the lavishness of his film budgets made him highly vulnerable to the criticisms of Rank's right-hand man, the accountant John Davis. In 1947, after protracted disputes over Olivier's second Shakespeare adaptation, *Hamlet* (1948), del Giudice resigned to set up his own independent company, Pilgrim Pictures. Two Cities continued as a Rank subsidiary but produced very little of interest before being merged into the Rank Organization at the end of 1949. Pilgrim also fared badly. After two interesting and modestly successful films—the Boulting brothers' *The Guinea Pig* (1948) and Peter Ustinov's *Private Angelo* (1949)—

Pilgrim produced a film written and co-directed by Bernard Miles, *A Chance of a Lifetime* (1950). Its story, about a workers' co-operative, was hardly more radical than an Ealing comedy, but it fell foul of the cinema circuit bookers who decided it was too political and it was given a lukewarm and poorly publicized release. Pilgrim tilted into bankruptcy and del Giudice, disgusted with the way in which the British film industry operated, returned to Italy in 1950.

Though in the early 1950s del Giudice was full of plans to make films with his friends Roberto Rossellini, Ingrid Bergman, and Errol Flynn, he was never able to re-establish himself and he died in poverty in Fiesole, near Florence, on 31 December 1962. Del Giudice's generosity and flamboyance had their counterparts in indulgence and extravagance. Rank's biographer, Alan Wood, presents an unforgettable image of del Giudice boating down the river to his luxury mansion in Buckinghamshire, imperiously ordering other craft out of his way. But an extraordinary number of British wartime classics were Two Cities films. Del Giudice's arguments for quality cinema, and his rage against the rigid exhibition system which allowed films only three days or a week in a cinema, before being moved on, fundamentally challenged the idea of film as ephemeral entertainment. The increasing erosion of cinema's mass audience as television continued to take hold lent weight to del Giudice's case for films which would attract discerning audiences to art house cinemas, and the approach he advocated can be seen as a viable and attractive option which might well have proved more fruitful than the inflexible course that the production, distribution, and exhibition of film in Britain actually pursued. ROBERT MURPHY

Sources A. Wood, *Mr Rank: a study of J. Arthur Rank and British films* (1952) • G. Macnab, *J. Arthur Rank and the British film industry* (1993) • S. Street and M. Dickinson, *Cinema and state* (1985) • BFI, Filippo Del Giudice special collection
Archives BFI

Giustinian, Sebastian (1460–1543), diplomat, was born in Venice, the son of Marino Giustinian of a patrician family associated with Istria, and his wife, the daughter of Piero Gradenigo. Sebastian married first a daughter of Doge Francesco Foscari, and second a relative of Agostino Agostini, Thomas Wolsey's physician. The Christian names of his wives are unrecorded. He had three sons. As Venetian ambassador to Hungary (1500–03) he delivered a Latin oration, later published, urging King Ladislaus to attack Sultan Bajazet. He was briefly ambassador to Poland in 1505, was governor of Brescia when it fell to the French in 1509, and in July 1511 became governor of Illyria, where he successfully subdued factional violence and rebellions.

In December 1514, by now holding the rank of *eques*, Giustinian was appointed ambassador to England, a crucial post with twin tasks of developing commercial links and, more urgently, discouraging the forthcoming Anglo-Habsburg alliance against France and Venice, and promoting Anglo-Venetian-French relations. His diplomatic style was highly personal, involving frequent meetings with the king, Wolsey, and influential people, and being generously hospitable. He cultivated Richard Fox, who opposed the imperial alliance, and used the papal nuncio Francesco Chieregati as his principal source of confidential information. Giustinian's dispatches of June 1515 praise Henry VIII, but later and more secret letters to the council of ten express wariness. His dispatches document the increasing tension between François I and the emperor Maximilian and England's fluctuating position. After 1516, when the League of Cambrai weakened, the dispatches concentrate on his efforts towards peacemaking between France, England, and Venice.

Giustinian's elegant prose style contains abundant social observation. He describes the nobility's genealogies and conspicuous displays of tapestries and gold plate, especially noting Wolsey's theatrical show of power and wealth. He skilfully wove diplomatic news into social contexts: a single dispatch of February 1516 reports the death of Ferdinand of Aragon, and tells how the news was kept from Queen Katherine, then in labour, and how Giustinian delayed formal congratulations by a few hours because her child was a daughter. A letter to Erasmus in March 1517 distinguishes between the 'elegant foolery' of humanist literary style and the serious business which it serves.

Giustinian's 226 consecutive letters from England reflect a complex and manipulative world of diplomacy. A connoisseur of paradox, he assesses Wolsey with mixed antagonism and admiration, describing him in January 1516 as 'rex et autor omnium', accurately indicating his importance but misjudging other political forces. Giustinian also describes Wolsey's efforts to intimidate and upset him, Henry's cynical opinion of Franco-Venetian relations, and his own suspicions of other ambassadors.

Giustinian returned from 'exile' to Venice in October 1519, after receiving from Henry and Wolsey the customary gold chain amid congratulatory speeches on his efforts towards the Anglo-French treaty of London (1518). He became councillor superior in 1519, and ambassador to France in 1526, a post later filled by his son Marino. The signory made him procurator of St Mark in 1540. He died at Venice on 13 March 1543, aged eighty-three, and was buried there. BARRY COLLETT

Sources S. Giustinian, letter books, 12 Jan 1515–26 July 1519, Biblioteca Marciana, Venice, MS It. VII 1119 (7449) • *CSP Venice, 1509–19*, 219–563 • *Four years at the court of Henry VIII: selection of despatches written by the Venetian ambassador Sebastian Giustinian, and addressed to the signory of Venice, January 12th 1515, to July 26th 1519*, ed. and trans. R. Brown, 2 vols. (1854) • Biblioteca Marciana, Venice, MS It. VII, 228–286 [diaries of Marin Sanuto] • *I diarii di Marino Sanuto*, ed. F. Stefani and others, 19–28: *1514–1519* (Venice, 1887–90) • Biblioteca Marciana, Venice, MS It. VII 1233, fols. 114–21 [Giustinian's report to the senate, 1519] • *The correspondence of Erasmus*, ed. and trans. R. A. B. Mynors and others, 22 vols. (1974–94), vol. 4, no. 559, pp. 294–8 • *La oration del Magnifico … Misier S. Justiniano orator Veneto: facta Al Serenissimo Signor Verladislao Re di Ongaria … Adi cinque de Aprile. M.CCCCC*, 1 (Venice, 1500) [repr. in F. Sansovino, *Delle orationi volgarmente scritte* (Venice, 1562), a 44–9] • E. Gurney Salter, *Tudor England through Venetian eyes* (1930) • 'Venetian dispatches', *QR*, 96 (1854–5), 354–93
Archives Biblioteca Marciana, Venice, MS It. VII 1119 (7449)

Gizycka, Countess Krystyna [*née* Countess Krystyna Skarbeka; *alias* Christine Granville] (**1915–1952**), secret operations officer, was born on 1 May 1915, probably at Mlodziesyn, some 30 miles from Warsaw, Poland. Her father, Count Jerzy Skarbek, had married in 1899 Stephanie Goldfeder, daughter of a Jewish banker, and they already had a son. The estate was soon overrun by the German army, and her infancy was spent under German occupation. In 1920 the family moved to another estate, at Trzebnica, near Piotrków, where she learned to ride; she later learned to ski. 'She was recalcitrant to any form of discipline' (Masson, 9). In 1930 her father died of tuberculosis; her mother moved to Warsaw and let Krystyna leave her convent school to work as a clerk for a motor dealer. She had dark hair, small bones, and graceful movement. She was a boisterous teenager, who hated office work and was strongly attractive to young men. She liked to spend holidays round Zakopane, on the Czechoslovak border, skiing, and smuggling tobacco for fun. In 1933 she was briefly and unsuccessfully married to Karol Getlich, a wealthy Polish businessman of German origin; they divorced promptly by mutual consent.

By accident, Krystyna met on a skiing slope near Zakopane a Polish diplomat, Jerzy Gizycki, who was captivated by her, and married her in Warsaw on 2 November 1938. He took up a post as consul in Addis Ababa, and introduced Krystyna to Africa; but that marriage too soon became one of incompatibles. On hearing of the German invasion of Poland in 1939 they at once moved to London, and Krystyna was engaged that autumn by George Taylor as an agent for the British secret service. From that time onwards she was known as Christine Granville. She travelled to Budapest, whence she set out to cross Slovakia into Poland, intending to deliver leaflets to sustain the morale of the Poles. She made three journeys into Poland that winter, and once got as far as Warsaw; she returned with several Polish officers who wanted to continue fighting, and with valuable information. Her friendships with the locals made these crossings feasible; but they seemed suspicious both to the Polish and to the British secret authorities. The Polish government in exile asked the British not to employ her again. She failed to persuade her mother to leave Poland, and never saw her again; Countess Skarbeka was later murdered by the Nazis.

While in Budapest, Christine renewed friendship with an acquaintance of her gentry childhood, Andrzeij Kowerski (called Andrew Kennedy later, in the Special Operations Executive, or SOE). They became strongly attached to each other, and travelled together to Constantinople, later to Cairo. Though devoted to him, she detested housework and preferred living in single rooms in hotels, and eating in cafés, to keeping house. Eventually (1 August 1946) she divorced Gizycki, who had settled in Canada.

SOE found both her and Kennedy office jobs, successively in Constantinople and in Cairo. Entirely fluent in French from childhood, she was accepted as an agent by AMF section of SOE, which worked from Algiers, and parachuted into France on 6–7 July 1944 to act as courier to Francis Cammaerts ('Roger'), who was in charge of all subversive activities east of the Rhône. She arrived just in time to be at Cammaerts's elbow during the fighting in the Vercors in mid-July, and evaded capture with him—by marching 70 miles in twenty-four hours—when the Germans reconquered the plateau. She next crossed into Italy, beyond Briançon, and made contact with a band of Italian partisans in the Alps; then, at the Col de Larche farther south, she talked a unit of Polish conscripts in the Wehrmacht into changing sides.

On 13 August, at a chance road control, Cammaerts, his other courier, Xan Fielding, and a Gaullist officer called Sorensen were arrested and imprisoned in Digne. Christine, bold as brass, called on Max Waem, a Belgian, the local Gestapo interpreter, indicated what would happen to him if he did not release the prisoners promptly, secured (by parachute from Algiers) a bribe of 2 million francs and on 17 August drove Waem and all three prisoners away into the country. Waem was saved from any prosecution. For this feat she was awarded a George Medal by the British and a Croix de Guerre by the French. She was also commissioned into the Women's Auxiliary Air Force; but plans to parachute her back to Poland were cancelled. She was appointed OBE instead.

At the end of the war Christine quarrelled with Kennedy and drifted from job to job, mainly in London, sometimes in Kenya; always short of money. She was granted British citizenship on 23 November 1946. She settled in May 1951 to be a stewardess on Shaw Savill liners plying to Australia. On her first liner she met a sailor, Dennis George Muldowney, whose advances she resisted. He pursued her closely, even when she switched to the Union Castle Line, and in a frenzy knifed her to death in the hall of a small hotel in South Kensington on 15 June 1952. He was hanged ten weeks later. She was buried in Kensal Green cemetery. M. R. D. Foot

Sources M. Masson, *Christine, a search for Christine Granville, GM, OBE, croix de guerre* (1975) • X. Fielding, *Hide and seek: the story of a wartime agent* (1954) • private information (2004)
Archives PRO, SOE papers
Likenesses photographs, repro. in Masson, *Christine*

Gladman, John (*fl.* **1644–1685**), parliamentarian army officer and conspirator, is of unknown parents and background, though he claimed in 1683 to be related to the former parliamentarian soldier and plotter Richard Rumbold. He succeeded James Berry as captain-lieutenant in Oliver Cromwell's Ironsides regiment in 1644, and was promoted captain when his troop was incorporated into Sir Thomas Fairfax's horse regiment the following year. Gladman, who commanded Fairfax's own troop, was active in the New Model Army's defiance of parliament over the planned military expedition to Ireland in spring 1647. By 1648, however, he had apparently concluded that radical activity had gone as far as was practicable or perhaps desirable, for on 24 April he and his fellow Baptist captain William Packer took the initiative in breaking up an attempt to revive Leveller agitation in the ranks at St Albans. One of the 'moderate or conservative officers close to Fairfax', he attended a number of meetings of the army council and its committees between late 1648 and early 1649 (Gentles, 269). The following April he was sent to investigate the Digger colony at St George's Hill, Surrey, but found that 'the business is not … worth the taking nottis of'. According to Gladman, 'I cannot heare that there hath beene above twentie of them together' and William Everard, one of the Digger leaders, was 'no other than a madd man' (*Clarke Papers*, 2.212).

Gladman was wounded at Musselburgh during the New Model's Scottish campaign in 1650, and continued in service until he was cashiered by Cromwell in 1658 for opposing the protector's increased authority under 'The humble petition and advice', and still more the establishment of the 'other house'. In May 1659 the restored Rump Parliament reinstated him with his old regiment and promoted him to the rank of major. With William Packer, now his colonel, Gladman joined the army coup led by John Lambert in October, and supported Lambert in his eleventh-hour attempt to maintain the republic in April 1660. Like many other former Cromwellian officers he was a constant subject of surveillance, and often of detention, in the immediate Restoration period. He was arrested, along with Packer, in the dragnet that followed the failure of Venner's Fifth Monarchist rising in January 1661. On 10 April he and Packer were among fifteen former officers and soldiers whose detention was ordered as a precautionary measure for Charles II's coronation, even though he appears to have still been in gaol. He was released eight days later after posting a bond of £500 for good behaviour, at which time he was described as of Cripplegate parish, London. Alongside the other discharged officers he was ordered to quit the City within twenty-four hours and to remain at a distance of at least 20 miles until 20 May.

With the government preparing for the mass ejection of nonconformist ministers in 1662, Gladman was confined in the Fleet prison, then on 18 May transferred with Packer to the Gatehouse, and later to king's bench. In September he was ordered to be transported from London on the *Colchester*, and by October he and Packer were being held in Dublin Castle. However, by the following year he was free and described as the commander of projected rebel forces in Nottinghamshire and Staffordshire in the abortive northern rising of October. In September 1664 he was arrested for his alleged part in the rising.

Gladman is next known to have been associated with Thomas Blood, whose various projects culminated in an attempt to kidnap and hang the duke of Ormond, and, in May 1671, to steal the royal crown and sceptre from the Tower of London. When Blood shortly afterwards sued for pardon and turned agent and informer, Gladman sought private audiences with Charles II and the government's spymaster, Joseph Williamson, but there is no record of whether he was similarly employed.

Gladman was reported to be a member of a political club with ties to the duke of Buckingham that met at the Salutation Tavern during the exclusion crisis, and whose fifty-odd members also included the veteran plotter Colonel Henry Danvers, Lieutenant-Colonel Ralph Alexander, and the radical printer Francis Smith. He was again placed under surveillance, and was reported in April 1683 to be making armour, presumably his trade, with Alexander. Meanwhile he was instrumental in gathering a group of dissidents which met at his home in St Botolph without Bishopsgate and included old Cromwellian officers such as his kinsman Rumbold and Rumbold's brother William; Lieutenant-Colonel Abraham Holmes, like Gladman a Baptist; Captain Anthony Spinage, a former associate of Lambert's; and the Baptist minister Daniel Dyke.

Gladman was implicated in the Rye House Plot to assassinate Charles and the duke of York that was disclosed to the government in June 1683, and one of whose principals was Rumbold. Arrested on 23 August, Gladman denied any connection to the plot: 'I cannot help being related to Rumbold', he was reported to have said; 'I am not related to his wicked designs and, I hope, never shall be' (Zaller, 11). Apparently he was believed, for he was released on the same day, though on £1000 bail and with two sureties for £500 apiece. In 1685 he was again arrested in a round-up of Cromwellian officers after the failed rebellions of the duke of Monmouth and the earl of Argyll. Rumbold was executed in July for his part in Argyll's rising; Gladman was released on bail in November. It is the last that is heard of him.

ROBERT ZALLER

Sources R. Zaller, 'Gladman, John', *Biographical dictionary of British radicals in the seventeenth century*, 2 (1983), 11 · C. H. Firth and G. Davies, *The regimental history of Cromwell's army*, 1 (1940) · *CSP dom.*, *1660–61*, 569; *1661–2*, 376, 476; *1664–5*, 663–4; *Jan–Sept 1683*, 320, 322, 325, 333, 336–7, 355 · R. L. Greaves, *Deliver us from evil: the radical underground in Britain, 1660–1663* (1986) · R. L. Greaves, *Enemies under his feet: radicals and nonconformists in Britain, 1664–1677* (1990) · R. L. Greaves, *Secrets of the kingdom: British radicals from the Popish Plot to the revolution of 1688–89* (1992) · I. Gentles, *The New Model Army in England, Ireland, and Scotland, 1645–1653* (1992) · *The Clarke papers*, ed. C. H. Firth, [new edn], 2 vols. in 1 (1992) · R. Morrice, 'Ent'ring book', DWL, Morrice MS P, 492

Gladney, John (1839–1911), conductor and brass-band trainer, was born in Belfast on 12 August 1839. His father, also John Gladney, was the bandmaster of the 30th regiment, and in consequence he had an itinerant childhood, moving with his father's postings. He was, however, exposed to a range of musical experiences, and had lessons from a number of eminent teachers. His father taught him the piccolo when he was four. By 1850 he was living in Manchester, where he appeared as a child soloist with Louis Jullien's orchestra. A year later his father's regiment was moved to Cephalonia, where Gladney received piano lessons from Zanin, a pupil of Czerny. At about this time he also started learning the clarinet, the instrument with which he was to be professionally associated. Other military postings took the Gladneys to Turkey and Gibraltar, where they remained until 1854; then, at the start of the Crimean hostilities, they returned home to attachments in Lincoln, Portsmouth, Fermoy, and London.

At an early age Gladney decided that he had no inclination for a musical career in the army, declined a personal invitation from the bandmaster Charles Godfrey to join the Coldstream Guards band, and also refused a place at the newly established Military School of Music at Kneller

Hall. Instead, he toured with a number of opera companies and became leader of the Harrogate Spa Band. In 1861 he joined the Hallé Orchestra, where he remained as a clarinettist for most of his playing career. However, his most important achievements were as a conductor and trainer of brass bands.

Gladney had been introduced to brass instruments in his father's bands, but his first post as a conductor of a brass band appears to have been in the late 1850s, with the Tower Hamlets Band. His major successes, however, were with the great bands of the north of England, which he began conducting in the 1860s. He was said to have conducted and trained 105 bands in all. His most influential collaboration was with the Meltham Mills Band, with which he won the British Open Contest in three consecutive years (1876–8), an achievement he repeated with the Kingston Mills Band between 1885 and 1887. These and other successes made him the most sought-after brass-band conductor of his time. He always maintained that the Meltham Mills Band was 'unequalled in perfection', and it was the instrumentation he devised for this band that became the basis for the standard instrumentation of all brass bands.

With two of his contemporaries, Edwin Swift and Alexander Owen, Gladney was the most important influence on the brass-band movement in the nineteenth century. It was their vision and intelligence that nudged this amateur, working-class pastime into a coherent musical movement with playing styles, standards, and a repertory that made it a uniquely British phenomenon. Gladney was the most urbane and gifted of the three, and was genuinely ambitious to raise the standards and tastes of his amateur musicians. In later life he said that his highest achievement was to have provided a means of self-improvement for the working classes and to have created a desire for classical music 'in places that would [otherwise] have remained in ignorance of it'.

Gladney died of heart failure at his home, 36 Camp Street, Broughton, Manchester, on 12 December 1911 and was buried in Ardwick cemetery three days later, leaving a widow and an adult family. He had lived in Broughton for the previous fifty years, and was a regular worshipper at Bury Road Congregational Church. According to his obituary, he was 'in politics, an ardent conservative'.

Gladney's was a sophisticated musical talent, and he arranged many pieces for his bands; most were not printed and several have been lost. During his lifetime he was often described as 'the father of the brass band movement'. Though he modestly disclaimed this title, he has been recognized as the most articulate and influential force on brass bands in the nineteenth century.

TREVOR HERBERT

Sources *British Bandsman* (23 Dec 1911), 622–33 · *Salford Chronicle* (16 Dec 1911), 5 · *British Bandsman* (1 May 1899), 133–4 · d. cert.

Likenesses photograph, repro. in *British Bandsman* (1 May 1899), facing p. 133

Wealth at death £3098 3*s*. 1*d*.: resworn probate, 25 Jan 1912, *CGPLA Eng. & Wales*

Gladstanes, George. *See* Gledstanes, George (*c*.1562–1615).

Gladstanes, John (*d*. 1574), judge, possibly belonged to the family of Gladstanes of Cocklaw in Roxburghshire, though little is known of his immediate family origins. He may have been related to John Gladstane of that ilk and his wife, Margaret Jardine, but positive evidence is lacking. He certainly had a brother, William ('of Arthursheill'), who had two children, Elizabeth and William, but no other siblings are known. In 1506 a Johannes Gledstains was incorporated as a student at the University of St Andrews and was listed as a licentiate in 1509. If this was Gladstanes the advocate then it is likely that he subsequently spent some time studying abroad, where he gained a licentiate in civil and canon law.

Early in his career Gladstanes worked as a chancery scribe, receiving £3 from the fees of the privy seal in December 1532. He moved from this to acting as an advocate in the years following the foundation of the college of justice in 1532. In February 1533 he and his cousin Robert Fraser petitioned the king and the lords of council for licence to travel abroad, to France and elsewhere, for purposes of study. They sought, and received, a formal declaration that they were of noble status. It is not clear, however, whether they did go abroad, and in any case they are unlikely to have done so immediately, since Gladstanes appeared before the lords as a procurator in June 1533. In March 1535 he was appointed with Thomas Marjoribankis as one of the advocates for the poor. It seems likely that he was junior to Marjoribankis, the latter agreeing that it was Gladstanes who should receive the £10 annual fee.

In 1539 Gladstanes was appointed by Archbishop James Beaton as civilist at the new St Mary's College in the University of St Andrews. He was later appointed a lord of session, being first recorded on the bench on 30 January 1542. On 3 September 1546 his colleagues on the bench appointed him their factor to ensure execution of the papal bulls which had ratified the foundation of the college of justice against those churchmen who owed an annual contribution towards judicial salaries. He was specifically granted power to receive these contributions and to grant receipts. On 1 and 4 February 1549 the accounts were audited; a sum of £40 was available for each of the judges, and a surplus of £17 7*s*. 10*d*. was divided equally between the king's advocate and Gladstanes. As a gift from the court the latter likewise obtained certain arrears of the contribution. Gladstanes attended as a member of the privy council on only two recorded occasions, in 1550 and 1561. He ceased attending the court in 1570 and died in April 1574, leaving as executors of his small estate of only £368 his brother William and one George Gladstone.

JOHN FINLAY

Sources R. K. Hannay, ed., *Acts of the lords of council in public affairs, 1501–1554* (1932), 558–9 · Acts of the lords of council and session, NRA Scotland, CS6/1 fol. 89, 17 fol. 127*v* · register of testaments, NRA Scotland, CC8/8/13 · M. H. B. Sanderson, *Cardinal of Scotland: David Beaton, c.1494–1546* (1986) · P. G. B. McNeill, 'Senators of the college of justice, 1569–1578', *Juridical Review*, new ser., 5 (1960), 120–24 · M. Livingstone, D. Hay Fleming, and others, eds., *Registrum secreti sigilli regum Scotorum / The register of the privy seal of Scotland*, 2 (1921) · register of deeds, NRA Scotland, RD1/7 · *Reg. PCS*, 1st ser. · J. M. Thomson and others, eds., *Registrum magni sigilli regum*

Scotorum / The register of the great seal of Scotland, 11 vols. (1882–1914), vols. 3–4

Wealth at death £368: NA Scot., commissary court of Edinburgh, manuscript register of testaments CC8/8/13

Gladstone [*née* Glynne], **Catherine** (**1812–1900**), philanthropist and wife of William Ewart *Gladstone, was born on 6 January 1812 at Hawarden Castle, Flintshire. She was the third child and elder daughter of the four children of Sir Stephen Glynne, eighth baronet (1780–1815), and his wife Mary, *née* Neville (*d.* 1854), daughter of the second Baron Braybrooke and his wife, Catherine. Sir Stephen Richard *Glynne, ninth baronet (1807–1874), was her brother. Catherine Glynne's father died when she was three and she was reared by her mother, who schooled her well in literature and foreign languages. She was taught the piano by Franz Liszt during her visit to Paris in 1829. From the age of three she was known in the family as Pussy (in later life Aunt Pussy) and had a reputation for flirtatiousness. She had blue eyes and, in her youth, brown hair. Well connected to the Pittite aristocracy (she was related by birth to four prime ministers—William Pitt the Elder, Pitt the Younger, Sir Richard Grenville, and Lord Grenville), she travelled and made the usual social round. She had many serious suitors (her husband made a list of nine such after their marriage), and was jilted by Colonel Francis Harcourt about 1835. In 1834 Lady Glynne had a stroke and for the rest of her life she suffered bouts of depression, during which she was nursed by Catherine and her younger sister, Mary.

In 1838 Catherine, Stephen, and Mary Glynne travelled to Rome, where they met W. E. Gladstone, who had been at Christ Church, Oxford, with Stephen. Catherine was courted in the moonlight in the Colosseum, at Naples, and by letter; after considerable initial misgivings, she became engaged to Gladstone, then a young tory MP of slightly eccentric reputation, on 8 June 1839. She quickly was married in a double wedding on 25 July 1839, her sister Mary marrying George Lyttelton at the same ceremony. Catherine was quite well prepared by her background for political life, but little prepared for domestic life with Gladstone, whose tempestuous nature and severe sexual temptations in the first thirty years of their marriage required a spouse of unusual character, determination, and forbearance.

Between 1840 and 1854 Catherine Gladstone bore eight children and suffered at least one miscarriage. All her confinements were difficult. One daughter, Jessy, died in 1850, aged five, and her first son, William Henry, died from a brain tumour in 1891. Among her surviving children were Mary *Drew, Helen *Gladstone, Henry Neville *Gladstone, and Herbert John *Gladstone. She ran a political household in London, helped to cover for her incompetent brother Stephen's mismanagements at Hawarden, looked after her mother, and was the mainstay of her sister, Mary, who bore fourteen children in sixteen years before dying after childbirth in 1857. Catherine Gladstone played a large part in the Lyttelton household, before and after Mary's death, acting as mother to the younger children, especially to Lucy *Cavendish [*see under* Cavendish, Lord Frederick Charles (1836–1882)]. In these years she rarely flagged, although she sometimes became ill from overwork, and was seriously thrown off balance by her sister's death.

Catherine Gladstone (**1812–1900**), by Cyril Flower, Baron Battersea, 1890s

Between 1852 and 1894 Catherine Gladstone's husband was four times chancellor of the exchequer and four times prime minister. She entertained idiosyncratically, sometimes disconcerting guests at 10 Downing Street with oblique comments and odd costumes. Her reputation for dottiness was probably in part self-encouraged. She was a consistent defender of her husband but made no attempt to assist by acting as a political hostess. She believed her husband and her family were happiest when he was in office and she strongly resisted his various suggestions of retirement. She sometimes acted as his amanuensis and on occasion as political go-between; in the 1890s she had a little success in diminishing the acrimony Queen Victoria felt towards Gladstone. He respected his wife's judgement and confidentiality and always kept her in touch with the details of political developments (when apart, he wrote to her daily, she replying rather less frequently). He relied on her heavily in moments of stress and her quite frequent absences tending sick relatives often coincided with his sexual, and sometimes with his political, crises. She was, on the whole, 'skilful in the management of her husband' (Lee, 213), seeing to his dietary needs and curbing his propensity to overwork. She provided the little bottles of egg-and-sherry drink that he consumed when giving a long speech in the Commons or on the platform, and her estimate of the length of the speech—shown by the number of bottles—became a famous guide to reporters and political opponents.

In public Catherine Gladstone presented herself as the devoted wife: W. L. Watson, for example, observed 'the soft face, high-coloured as a girl's, and tremulous mouth; intent on one thing only in this life—her husband' (Pratt, 41). But in fact she had a good eye for the details of political presentation, waving from windows and from trains when her husband was too tired to do so, and checking that reporters were ready when he was about to speak. She was one of the first political wives regularly to sit by her husband on political platforms and on occasion she spoke at public meetings. The Gladstones presented themselves at extra-parliamentary political occasions as a pair and Catherine Gladstone became something of a political icon, featuring on political plates and memorabilia. In 1887 (aged seventy-five) she became first president of the Women's Liberal Federation, her aim being to 'guide, purify, and stimulate great political movements' (Pratt, 226). Her presidency was regal rather than executive in tone, and she found the details of political business difficult. She was unable to prevent the secession of a group within the federation, led by Rosalind, Lady Carlisle, which found her modest acceptance of women's suffrage excessively timid, and, after the federation split on the question, she resigned from it in October 1892.

As her family commitments eased in the 1860s, Catherine Gladstone involved herself in philanthropy, initially with the House of Charity in Greek Street, Soho, London, then in 1864 founding the Newport Market refuge for vagrants, in Seven Dials, London, to which she later added an industrial school. During the cholera epidemic of 1866 and its aftermath she set up an orphanage and a series of convalescent homes at Snaresbrook and Woodford. For these institutions she was an unembarrassable fund-raiser. Like her husband, she was also much involved in 'rescuing' prostitutes; she sometimes sought to restore their sense of self-respect by entertaining them to tea at 10 Downing Street.

This active life took its toll. She, even more than her husband, suffered from insomnia from about 1880 and her memory, always somewhat selective, deteriorated in the 1890s. On her husband's advice she declined the offer of a peerage when he retired as prime minister in 1894. She was the chief mourner at his state funeral in 1898. Catherine Gladstone died from pneumonia at Hawarden Castle on 14 June 1900. She was buried on 17 June next to her husband in their double grave in Westminster Abbey: his will had made this provision a condition of his being buried there. H. C. G. MATTHEW

Sources E. A. Pratt, *Catherine Gladstone* (1898) · G. Battiscombe, *Mrs Gladstone* (1956) · M. Drew, *Catherine Gladstone* (1919) · A. T. Bassett, *Gladstone to his wife* (1936) · Gladstone, *Diaries* · H. C. G. Matthew, *Gladstone*, 2 vols. (1986–95); repr. in 1 vol. as *Gladstone, 1809–1898* (1997) · J. Marlow, *Mr and Mrs Gladstone* (1977) · P. Gladstone, *Portrait of a family: the Gladstones, 1839–1889* (1989) · E. Lee, *Wives of the prime ministers, 1844–1906* (1918)

Archives BL, corresp. and papers, Add. MSS 44247–44752, 46222–46229, *passim* · Flintshire RO, Hawarden | BL, letters to John Bright, Add. MS 43385 · BL, H. J. Gladstone MSS · BL, Mary Gladstone MSS · BL, W. E. Gladstone MSS · BL, letters to Sir Edward Walter Hamilton, Add. MS 48611 · BL, corresp. with Lord Ripon, Add. MS 43515 · BL, letters to Earl Spencer · Bodl. Oxf., letters to H. W. Acland · CUL, letters to Lord Acton · LPL, letters to Laura Thistlethwayte · NL Scot., corresp. with Lord Rosebery · Royal Arch. | FILM National Film Archive, film of W. E. Gladstone's funeral, 1898

Likenesses L. Macdonald, bust, 1839, Hawarden Castle · W. Bradley, oils, 1842, Hawarden Castle · G. Richmond, watercolour, 1843, Hawarden Castle · J. Adams-Acton, bust, 1884?, Hawarden Castle · H. von Herkomer, portrait, 1888, probably Hawarden Castle · C. Flower, Baron Battersea, photograph, 1890–99, NPG [*see illus.*]

Wealth at death £10,834 12*s*. 1*d*.: probate, 14 Dec 1900, *CGPLA Eng. & Wales*

Gladstone, Helen (1849–1925), educationist, was born in London on 28 August 1849, the sixth of the eight children of William Ewart *Gladstone (1809–1898), who was four times British prime minister, and his wife, Catherine (1812–1900), daughter of Sir Stephen Glynne, bt, of Hawarden, Flintshire, and his wife, Mary. An elder sister having died in childhood, Helen was the youngest of three girls in the lively crowd of seven children growing up at Hawarden Castle—their number often doubled and more by an influx of their favourite cousins, the Lytteltons of Hagley in Worcestershire. On a generally crowded canvas Helen's childhood is all but invisible, and it is not until 1873, when her eldest sister left home on marriage, that she seems to emerge as an individual. As one of the cousins then noted, there was now scope for 'the two unmarried'. Mary effectively freed her mother for charitable work by running the household; Helen was involved with the village schools and no doubt would have gone on like that had not her more dynamic sister faced her, after a visit to Cambridge, with the surprising proposition that she should study at Newnham Hall (soon to become a women's college). Fired by those pioneers of women's education Henry Sidgwick and his wife Nora, Mary was eager to persuade her father that Helen should try it for a year. Helen was compliant but apprehensive. She had a keen desire to study but her schoolroom days were remote and had been governess-led, at home. She doubted if she could master political economy, felt ashamed that her memory was bad, and worried lest Newnhamites should be given to over-free discussion of the Christian faith. Still, in 1877 she went to Newnham: the oldest (at twenty-eight) of its twenty-five students, and probably the most diffident.

Being in this 'pie of girls', as she wrote, seemed queer at first but Helen came to enjoy it. She did not wish to go in for the tripos but passed the higher local examination with distinction in political economy. In 1880 she became secretary to Nora Sidgwick (then vice-principal) and succeeded her two years later, proud of having this part to play in moulding the life of the new community. No one cherished the highlights of the college's early years more: whether the day that Philippa Fawcett was placed above the senior wrangler, the visit of Mr and Mrs Gladstone to Newnham to plant a tree there in 1887, or the university's solemn tribute on the death of Miss Clough, its first principal. It seemed a hopeful time for women. When Helen asked her father in 1892 to add his signature to a memorial that women should be allowed to take degrees, she could not have guessed it would be fifty years before the university made this concession.

In July 1886 Helen was invited to become first principal of the new Royal Holloway College. This immediately exposed a question of the relative claims of work and home which had been implicit since she went to Newnham but gained new immediacy from the fact that her sister Mary had recently married and could not be assumed to stay at Hawarden for ever; also that it would have been out of the question to combine Royal Holloway with 'home duties'. Though she canvassed opinions widely Helen seems to have been clear from the start that to take the post would be morally wrong. The moment of truth came ten years later, in 1896, when she resigned from Newnham to look after her parents (by then well in their eighties). It was a wrench to leave the work she loved for duties which she had never performed as well as Mary, or in a way that pleased her mother. Her father died in 1898 and Mrs Gladstone in 1900. For several years afterwards Helen was warden of the Women's University Settlement in Southwark. In 1910 she left London for Hawarden, where she lived at Sundial until her death there on 19 August 1925, happily near to her extended family but still in touch with Newnham, whose students recalled her open-hearted interest as well as her habit of overdoing the anecdotes of Mr Gladstone. She was buried in Hawarden church. SHEILA FLETCHER

Sources corresp. between Helen Gladstone and her sister Mary, BL, Add. MS 46231 • obituary of Helen Gladstone by her sister Mary, BL, Add. MS 46270, pt 2 • 'Newnham Letter', Newnham College, Cambridge, archive [reminiscences] [dates *passim*] • A. Phillips, ed., *A Newnham anthology* (1979) • P. Jalland, *Women, marriage and politics, 1860–1914* (1986) • R. McWilliams-Tullberg, *Women at Cambridge* (1975)

Archives Newnham College, Cambridge, MSS • St Deiniol's Library, Hawarden, family corresp. and MSS | BL, corresp. with her brother, Lord Gladstone, Add. MS 46046 • BL, corresp. with her sister Mary, Add. MS 46231 • CUL, letters to Lord Acton

Likenesses photograph, repro. in Phillips, ed., *Newnham anthology* • photograph, Newnham College, Cambridge; repro. in 'Newnham Letter'

Wealth at death £28,256 6*s*. 3*d*.: probate, 29 Sept 1925, *CGPLA Eng. & Wales*

Gladstone, Helen Jane (1814–1880), Roman Catholic convert, was born on 28 June 1814 at 62 Rodney Street, Liverpool. She was the second daughter, and youngest of the six children, of Sir John *Gladstone, first baronet (1764–1851), and his second wife, Anne, *née* Robertson (1771/2–1835). William *Gladstone, the future prime minister, was the next youngest child. Much of her unhappy life was to be spent attempting to break away from the powerful personalities of her brother and her father. Her mother's illnesses meant that she was reared mainly by her elder sister, Anne, an intense evangelical. From an early stage she was regarded by members of her family as self-indulgent and perverse, possibly with an element of freethinking. Even so, she formed a close and confidential bond with her brother William; they often corresponded at length on religion, even when living in the same house. At the

Helen Jane Gladstone (1814–1880), by unknown sculptor

age of fourteen she began to show signs of compulsive eating (a disorder later defined as *bulimia nervosa*) and was given a course of galvanism by Dr Lebeaume. Like her mother and sister, though not suffering from consumption as they did, she became an invalid. Following a decade of suffering she was sent, in 1838, to Ems, initially accompanied by her brother William. Once on her own Helen became engaged to Count Leon Sollohub of a Polish-Russian family; she prepared to be received into the Greek Orthodox church, but his family prevented the marriage. She emerged from a period as a recluse to attend Roman Catholic church services and in June 1842 she was received into the Roman Catholic church in a well-advertised conversion—one of the first of the 'wave' of the 1840s—to the fury of her brother William. Sent to Baden-Baden, she became an opium addict, and after a traumatic visit in 1845 from William was brought back to Britain. Her family prevented attempts by her Roman Catholic friends to have her declared a lunatic and thus removed from her family's restraint. With £10,000 settled on her by her father, she subsequently moved between Britain and the continent, became a tertiary of the order of St Dominic, and eventually settled in Cologne. She died there, in the Hotel Disch, Brückenstrasse, on 16 January 1880, her brother William, at least, convinced that she rejected the pope's infallibility and died an Old Catholic. She was buried in the Gladstone family vault in St Andrew's Chapel, Fasque, Scotland, but without the commendatory prayer. H. C. G. MATTHEW

Sources S. G. Checkland, *The Gladstones: a family biography, 1764–1851* (1971) • Gladstone, *Diaries* • H. C. G. Matthew, *Gladstone, 1809–1874* (1986) • H. C. G. Matthew, *Gladstone, 1875–1898* (1995)

Archives Flintshire RO, Hawarden

Likenesses bust, repro. in Checkland, *Gladstones*, 240 • bust, priv. coll. [*see illus.*]

Wealth at death under £8000: administration with will, 29 April 1881, *CGPLA Eng. & Wales*

Gladstone, Henry Neville, Baron Gladstone of Hawarden (1852–1935), businessman and financier, was born on

2 April 1852 at 6 Carlton Gardens, London, the third son and seventh child of William Ewart *Gladstone (1809–1898), the prime minister, and his wife, Catherine *Gladstone, *née* Glynne (1812–1900). He was educated at the Revd William Montagu Higginson's church preparatory school in Hunstanton, Norfolk, and then at Eton College, Windsor. In 1870 he attended lectures at King's College, London, at the same time acting (as on later occasions) as private secretary to his father. In the following year he entered the London office of Gladstone, Wylie & Co., the firm founded by his paternal grandfather, Sir John *Gladstone.

In 1874 Gladstone was sent by the family firm to Calcutta as an assistant to work in its piece-goods department on a salary of £360 p.a. Although impressed by the company's 'palatial office' on Clive Street and the 'hot meals with champagne' provided daily, he found his first year in India frustrating as he was given little responsibility. Gladstone, Wylie & Co. had, by this time, passed its peak and its major interests—indigo, piece-goods, and shipping—were not prospering. He was dismissed within the year and sent back to England.

This inauspicious beginning did not diminish Gladstone's determination to pursue a commercial career in India. In 1876 he took a position with another Indian firm, Gillanders, Arbuthnot & Co., which having been founded in 1833 by business partners of his grandfather John Gladstone, was the oldest British merchant house in Calcutta. Here he was soon put in charge of the firm's shipping business and, in 1881, he was made a junior partner in the firm. In 1883 his father gave him £4000 with which to buy a senior partnership.

Gladstone's connections through his father proved useful to the firm from the very beginning. In 1876 he was sent to Rangoon to improve the company's poor relations with the colonial authorities of Lower Burma, which believed, correctly, that Gillanders had been abusing their teak concessions. He was able to soothe official ire and the firm was allowed to maintain this lucrative trade. His father's friendship with Sir Donald Currie, the Scottish business magnate, helped to revive the firm's flagging shipping business.

As well as making use of his father's influence and connections, Gladstone also possessed some entrepreneurial flair. Realizing that the nature of economic opportunity in India was changing, he abandoned the company's traditional fields of piece-goods, indigo, and the consignment trade, and embraced manufacturing. Under his auspices the firm successfully floated two very profitable jute mills, managed the Darjeeling-Himalayan Railway Company, and provided lucrative loans to the Indian aristocracy. His financial acumen was recognized by his appointment as director of the Bank of Bengal in 1886.

Gladstone was unusual among British businessmen in India for his political liberalism. While not opposed to imperialism as such and a strong advocate of the annexation of Upper Burma (which he regarded as 'a splendid thing for trade'), he was liberal in his attitude to racial issues, and his name made him suspect in Indian circles. In 1884 he was one of the few British businessmen to offer public support to Lord Ripon during the notorious 'Ilbert controversy', when Ripon proposed to bring British expatriates under the jurisdiction of Indian judges. Throughout, his father used material from his son's letters on the Ilbert issue for parliamentary debates in London.

In 1889 Gladstone returned permanently to Britain, although he continued to be involved with the firm and acted as senior partner from 1900 to 1931, becoming increasingly conservative in his attitudes. On 30 January 1890 he married Maud Ernestine (1865–1941), second daughter of Stuart *Rendel, afterwards Baron Rendel (1834–1913), Liberal MP for Montgomeryshire and one of his father's closest friends. They had no children. He managed the Hawarden estate for his eldest brother, William Henry Gladstone, and after his death in 1891 was a trustee. Following his father's death in 1898 he looked for a residence of his own, and in 1902 purchased the Burton Manor estate in Cheshire. He practically rebuilt the house, and made many improvements to the estate.

After the owner of Hawarden, his nephew, William Glynne Charles Gladstone, was killed in action in April 1915, Gladstone purchased the succession to the estate. He paid off the outstanding mortgage and improved the house, which from 1921 was his home for the rest of his life. The Burton Manor estate was sold in 1924.

Gladstone succeeded his nephew as lord lieutenant of Flintshire, and was an alderman on Flintshire county council and a magistrate for both Flintshire and Cheshire. He chaired the appeal committee of the disestablished church in Wales, to which he personally contributed £20,000. He was treasurer of the National Library of Wales and president of the University College of North Wales, Bangor. In 1932 he was created Baron Gladstone of Hawarden.

Gladstone inherited from his father, whom he closely resembled, financial acumen and a deep religious faith. He did not have his father's literary interests, but shared with his wife a deep love of music. Although a lifelong Gladstonian Liberal, he never stood for parliament. He, like his brother Herbert *Gladstone, first Viscount Gladstone, was devoted to the memory of his father. The brothers gave their father's diaries to the archbishop of Canterbury (*ex officio*) and his political papers to the British Museum. In 1927 Henry encouraged his brother in his successful legal action against a journalist named Peter Wright who in his book, *Portraits and Criticisms*, had claimed that it had been their father's custom 'to pursue and possess every sort of woman'.

Gladstone died of a heart attack at Hawarden Castle on 28 April 1935, and was buried on 1 May at Hawarden parish church. His title died with him, his widow surviving him until 1941. C. J. WILLIAMS and A.-M. MISRA

Sources I. Thomas, *Gladstone of Hawarden*, 1st edn (1936) · A.-M. Misra, *Enterprise and empire* (1997) · J. S. Gladstone, *A history of Gillanders, Arbuthnot & Co.*, 1st edn (1910) · *The Times* (29 April 1935) · A. Maybrey, 'The Gladstone era', *Burton in Wirral: a history*, ed. P. H. W. Booth (1984), 191–205

Archives BL, corresp., Add. MSS 46045–46046 · St Deiniol's Library, Hawarden, corresp. and papers | BL, letters to Sir Edward Walter Hamilton, Add. MS 48611 · BL, corresp. with Macmillans, Add. MS 55243 · Bodl. Oxf., letters to Sir Matthew Nathan · LPL, corresp. and papers relating to W. E. Gladstone
Likenesses A. van Anzooy, oils, Hawarden Castle, Flintshire · C. H. Thompson, oils, Hawarden Castle, Flintshire · photograph, repro. in Thomas, *Gladstone of Hawarden*, frontispiece
Wealth at death £473,274 3*s*. 7*d*.: probate, 4 July 1935, *CGPLA Eng. & Wales*

Gladstone, Herbert John, **Viscount Gladstone** (**1854–1930**), politician and governor-general of the Union of South Africa, was born on 7 January 1854 at 12 Downing Street (now known as no. 11), then occupied by his father as chancellor of the exchequer. Named after Sidney Herbert, his parents' friend, and his grandfather, Sir John *Gladstone, he was the youngest child of the four sons and four daughters of William Ewart *Gladstone (1809–1898) and his wife, Catherine *Gladstone (*née* Glynne). Henry Neville *Gladstone and Mary *Drew (*née* Gladstone) were among his siblings.

Herbert John Gladstone, Viscount Gladstone (**1854–1930**), by George Charles Beresford, *c*.1902

Education and early political career In 1866 Gladstone went to Miss Evans's house at Eton College, along with his brothers and his cousins, the sons of George Lyttelton. At Eton he was popular, high-spirited, and a fair football player, but did not greatly distinguish himself. In 1872 he went to University College, Oxford, obtaining a third class in classical moderations in 1874 and a first class in modern history in 1876. From 1877 to 1880 he was history lecturer at the newly founded Keble College, where his relative Edward Talbot was the first warden. Gladstone lectured, among other things, on medieval economic history.

W. E. Gladstone was keen for his children to follow him into politics. All his sons were apprenticed by acting as his political secretary, both in Downing Street and at the family home, Hawarden Castle. Herbert showed particular interest, and more ability than the eldest son, William, already an MP. At the 1880 general election Herbert Gladstone unsuccessfully contested Middlesex, but was returned unopposed at a by-election for Leeds in May 1880 (the seat becoming vacant because his father chose Midlothian rather than Leeds, having been elected for both). He sat for Leeds (after 1885 West Leeds) until 1910, always winning it comfortably except in 1892, 1895, and 1900, when his majority fell markedly. In 1881 he was appointed a Liberal whip and made the first of several visits to Ireland, subsequently in April 1882 negotiating with Frank Hugh O'Donnell, a home rule MP, about the 'new departure' in Irish politics (a series of talks parallel to the notorious negotiations between Joseph Chamberlain and W. H. O'Shea).

The 'Hawarden kite' Gladstone became an important conduit between his father and Irish politicians. He was decidedly sympathetic to home rule and in the autumn of 1885 knew of his father's view that home rule coupled with a land purchase scheme offered the best settlement for Ireland. On 12 December 1885 Herbert Gladstone's letter supporting home rule was published in *The Times* and, with 'the whole position … on the boil' (Gladstone, *Diaries*, 11.662) he went to London and told Henry Labouchere, Thomas Wemyss Reid, and others of his father's support for the policy. These conversations were immediately and sensationally reported in the press. Whether this flying of the 'Hawarden kite'—as the episode became known—was a deliberate (but ham-handed) attempt to force his father's hand or a naïve action by an inexperienced politician is unclear from Herbert Gladstone's own accounts (Gladstone, *Diaries*, 11. appx I, D).

Politics, 1886–1905 In his father's third government (February–July 1886) Gladstone was financial secretary to the War Office and thus distanced from the making of the Irish settlement. In the opposition years, 1886–92, he came more to the fore and in his father's last government, 1892–4, was under-secretary at the Home Office to H. H. Asquith. He was thus well positioned to play a central role in the Liberal Party after his father finally retired. Made a privy councillor in 1894, he was Lord Rosebery's first commissioner of works in 1894–5, and as such was responsible for controversial negotiations which eventually placed the statue of Oliver Cromwell outside the House of Commons.

Herbert Gladstone with his brother Henry was a chief organizer of his father's state funeral in 1898, and in 1899 was appointed chief Liberal whip by Sir Henry Campbell-Bannerman: his first real chance for independent political initiative. Gladstone was an outstanding whip, the first in the Liberal Party to attempt a strategy which looked beyond day-to-day business. He played an important part in preventing a split in the party over the Second South African War; he attempted to introduce a more modern constituency structure; he urged local Liberal associations to adopt working-class candidates; and by a series of secret meetings in 1903 he made what became the famous Gladstone–MacDonald pact by which, especially in two-member constituencies, local agreements would be engineered so that Liberal and Labour candidates did not split the anti-Unionist vote. His reward was the Liberal triumph in 1906, the party's best result since 1832, with 400

MPs and a majority over the Unionists of 243. The pact bound the nascent Labour Party to the Liberals, though by the election of 1906 it had ceased, at least in the short term, to be necessary in order for the latter to hold power.

Character, recreations, and marriage Gladstone appeared a placid, straightforward fellow, amiable and sensible. In the family, however, he was known also for irritability. As a young man, and perhaps later, he suffered from asthma. Even so, he was a keen fly-fisher and a very keen golfer. Of medium height and sporting a moustache, he was also a gymnast, cyclist, and mountaineer, and was for many years president of the Physical Recreation Society. He was a keen supporter of Leeds United Football Club. A competent musician and glee singer, he was on the council of the Royal College of Music. Gladstone was comfortably off, having had a higher allowance from his father than his brothers, and a settlement in 1896 of £27,000; but, except when in office, he had no income of his own. He and his brother Henry acted in close co-operation in managing the Hawarden estate and guarding their father's reputation. In 1901, aged forty-seven, Gladstone married Dorothy Mary (*d.* 20 June 1953), youngest daughter of Sir Richard Horner Paget (1832–1908) and his wife, Caroline Isabel (*d.* 1946), daughter of Henry Edward Surtees. The marriage was childless but brought Gladstone balance and contentment.

Home secretary, 1905–1910 When the Liberals returned to office in December 1905 Campbell-Bannerman made Gladstone home secretary, though he had asked to return to the commission of works. The Gladstones lived in his birthplace, 11 Downing Street, as Asquith, though chancellor, did not wish to reside there. Gladstone was neither a 'new Liberal' nor an old *laissez-faire* Liberal in his father's mould. His co-operation with Ramsay MacDonald seemed to point the way to radical legislation, but Gladstone was cautious and, as home secretary, often had to be encouraged by his cabinet colleagues. Even so, he carried through twenty-two bills, many of them controversial and important. The Workmen's Compensation Act (1906) and the Eight Hours Act (1908) dealt with matters long outstanding in the party. The Trade Boards Act (1909) was passed with Winston Churchill, president of the Board of Trade, the dominant partner in the making of the legislation. Gladstone interested himself especially in the introduction of the borstal system for young offenders and of children's courts (brought in by the Probation of Offenders Act (1907) and the Children Act (1908)). When Churchill succeeded him as home secretary he complained to him that Churchill had not fairly acknowledged the important legislation he had drafted but not had time to introduce (Churchill, 2.387). Gladstone also wrote the daily report on the Commons for the king, a duty his father had punctiliously discharged as prime minister.

As home secretary Gladstone was responsible for public order and the prison service. He dealt well with various minor episodes, such as the case of the Revd Shapurji Edalji, Anglican clergyman and mutilator of horses, but he was slow to control the controversy in 1908 which blew up over a procession through London by the papal legate accompanied by the host. Asquith, badgered by the king, had to step in to persuade the Roman Catholics not to process the host in the face of a potentially violent protestant opposition, and the matter led to Lord Ripon's resignation from the cabinet. His colleagues generally blamed Gladstone for the episode and the king wanted him replaced. Gladstone half offered resignation, turned down the sinecure of the lord presidency, and stayed another year at the Home Office, during which time the question of women's suffrage starkly faced him. That movement placed Gladstone in a very difficult position. He had become a supporter of women's suffrage and advocated the change publicly and in cabinet. But he was responsible for the security of ministers, including Asquith, the prime minister, who opposed women's suffrage, and for women imprisoned as a result of the acts of violence encouraged by the Women's Social and Political Union (WSPU). Gladstone tried to act moderately, for example reducing the sentence on Teresa Billington in 1906. In October 1906 he announced that suffragists would no longer be imprisoned in the first division (the more stringent prisons) and he ordered the police not to arrest for mere technical obstruction. In 1908 he was subpoenaed by Mrs Pankhurst and was described by her daughter Christabel, who conducted the WSPU's defence, as 'rather a timid person' (Rosen, 112). In 1909 women suffragists began hunger strikes on a significant scale and Gladstone ordered them to be force-fed. He wrote to Emily Hobhouse on 9 November 1909:

> My duty is unpleasant & distasteful enough, but that is no reason why I shd. shirk it … forcible feeding is not punishment. To let women starve wd not only be inhuman but in the event of death wd expose all concerned to a charge of manslaughter. (Rosen, 128)

Gladstone's approach of avoiding confrontation when possible had short-term success, for when he left the Home Office no suffragettes were in prison. He believed, rightly, that the extension of the suffrage to women would only be settled by a coalition government.

Governor-general of South Africa, 1910–1914 In September 1909 Asquith, against the strongly expressed opposition of Edward VII, offered Gladstone the governor-generalship of the new Union of South Africa; he ceased to be home secretary on 19 February 1910, becoming Viscount Gladstone of the county of Lanark. Gladstone had visited South Africa in 1877 (and India in 1886). Through acting as his father's secretary he had intimate knowledge of its complex political and social history. In the Second South African War of 1899–1902 he had, like Campbell-Bannerman, moderately opposed the British government's policies. Soon after his arrival, the Union of South Africa was formally constituted on 31 May 1910 and he chose Louis Botha, one of the erstwhile Boer generals, to be first prime minister. Gladstone found Botha 'one of the most attractive men I have ever known' (Mallet, 232). The South Africa Act represented the successful withdrawal of direct imperial rule, leaving the country with a unitary constitution, the two white cultures more reconciled than theretofore, and the future of 'native', racial policy undetermined. The role of the governor-general was thus chiefly ceremonial, but with an implied obligation to safeguard the imperial interest and to see that the new political system was stabilized. Gladstone consistently supported Botha through a series of political crises, including the dismissal of General J. B. M. Hertzog when the government was reconstituted in December 1912. His support for Botha was unpopular among sections of the English-speaking community and with the separatists among the Afrikaners, but the successful integration of the majority of the Afrikaners into the union was a clear imperial interest.

Gladstone toured the country, made speeches, and superintended the visit of the duke of Connaught (*vice* George V) in October 1910 to open the new parliament. Lord and Lady Gladstone proved adept at establishing a liberal etiquette in the new country. In the matter of labour and race relations Gladstone had an awkward responsibility. He encouraged legislation on Indian immigration, which was eventually passed in 1913, but it failed to satisfy Indian opinion, M. K. Gandhi leading major demonstrations in Transvaal and the viceroy of India complaining of the Botha government's recalcitrance. General Jan Smuts's negotiations with Gandhi reached a compromise conclusion in 1914. In the major strike in the summer of 1913 Gladstone strongly supported his ministers and called out imperial troops. He worked daily in the government building in Pretoria even when the strikers pulled down its union jack and substituted the red flag, and his personal courage played some part in ending the strike. He was also high commissioner of Northern and Southern Rhodesia and commissioner for Swaziland, Bechuanaland, and Basutoland. In Northern Rhodesia he had direct responsibilities, but in Southern Rhodesia his authority was uncertain and ineffectual, as he found when he exhorted the white community there to fairer treatment of Africans.

Lady Gladstone's health was poor, requiring the Gladstones to return to Britain in 1912 for a while, and by 1914 Gladstone was determined to retire, with the possibility of becoming viceroy of Ireland, the first under the home rule legislation about to be passed. The Gladstones sailed from Cape Town on 11 July 1914, arriving in Britain just before war was declared. Gladstone was made GCB in recognition of his work (he might have expected to be promoted to earl).

Later years and death During the First World War Gladstone was treasurer of the war refugees committee, and with Lady Gladstone devoted himself to assisting Belgian refugees in Britain, being made GBE, a grand officer of the crown of Belgium, and a knight of grace of the order of St John of Jerusalem (and Lady Gladstone correspondingly a dame of that order). The post of importance which a person of his name and experience might have expected in a war conducted by a predominantly Liberal government did not come his way. Gladstone none the less selflessly returned to work for the Liberal Party in what had been his most effective role, for he set its organization on as sound a footing as was possible in the circumstances of the Asquith–Lloyd George split after 1917, especially working at Liberal headquarters in 1922–3. He supported Lord Grey of Fallodon on the Liberal Council formed in December 1926. He was active also on foreign policy, attacking the government's wartime policies in the Near East, visiting Bulgaria in 1924 (where the name of Gladstone ensured a tumultuous reception), and working for the League of Nations Union.

The Gladstones lived from 1915 at Dane End, a property of Lady Gladstone's family, near Ware in Hertfordshire; they also had a London house, 4 Cleveland Square, left to Gladstone by his father's crony, Lord Armitstead. Gladstone pursued his pastimes of fishing and golf (at which in the 1890s he had been almost obsessive). He became increasingly interested in his family's past. In 1918 he wrote a memoir of his nephew, W. G. C. Gladstone (1885–1915), the heir to Hawarden Castle, killed in action. After his father's death he, his brother Henry, and their sister Mary had taken the decision to invite John Morley to write their father's biography, published in 1903. Morley used W. E. Gladstone's diaries selectively, with no reference to the many passages of sexual guilt which they contained. In 1925, Captain Peter E. Wright claimed in *Portraits and Criticisms* that W. E. Gladstone's custom was to 'pursue and possess every sort of woman'. Herbert Gladstone cleverly provoked Wright to sue him for libel, his defence being that the charges he publicly made against Wright's character were justified because Wright's comments on his father were a calumny. Gladstone intended to submit his father's diaries as evidence, but was wisely dissuaded from this by Charles Russell, the family's solicitor. Gladstone was successfully defended by Norman Birkett. In 1928 Gladstone and his brother Henry gave the diaries to the archbishop of Canterbury to own *ex officio*. The same year Gladstone published *After Thirty Years*, with much detail on his father and a strong attack on what he saw as G. E. Buckle's unscrupulous editing of the second series of *The Letters of Queen Victoria*; this led to a violent exchange in the correspondence columns of *The Times*.

Gladstone made notes for an autobiography in his declining years, but, like his father, did not publish them. Having suffered from heart trouble, he died of pneumonia at Dane End on 6 March 1930 and was buried on 10 March in the churchyard of Little Munden, near Dane End. A large memorial service was held in Westminster Abbey on 11 March.

Herbert Gladstone was a sturdy and convinced Liberal, whose life almost exactly spanned the effective years of his party. To follow his father's profession had hardly been an easy choice, for comparison dogged him at almost every point. He was a more determined character than his mild manner suggested and was only the second prime minister's son to reach the cabinet since William Pitt the younger.

H. C. G. MATTHEW

Sources C. Mallet, *Herbert Gladstone: a memoir* (1932) • Gladstone, *Diaries* • H. C. G. Matthew, *Gladstone, 1875–1898* (1995) • T. O. Lloyd, 'The whip as paymaster: Herbert Gladstone and party organization', *EngHR*, 89 (1974), 785–813 • D. Marquand, *Ramsay MacDonald* (1977) • R. Jenkins, *Asquith* (1964) • P. Rowlands, *The last liberal governments: the promised land, 1905–1910* (1968) • R. S. Churchill, *Winston S. Churchill*, 2: *Young statesman, 1901–1914* (1967) • A. Rosen, *Rise up, women! The militant campaign of the Women's Social and Political Union, 1903–1914* (1974) • L. M. Thompson, *The unification of South Africa, 1902–1910* (1960)

Archives BL, corresp., diaries, and papers, Add. MSS 45985–46118, 46474–46486 • NL Scot., corresp. • St Deiniol's Library, Hawarden, family corresp., diaries, and papers • University of Bristol, corresp. | BL, corresp. with Sir Herbert Campbell-Bannerman, Add. MSS 41215–41217 • BL, Drew MSS • BL, W. E. Gladstone MSS • BL, letters to Sir Edward Walter Hamilton, Add. MS 48611 • BL, corresp. with Macmillans, Add. MS 55244 • BL, corresp. with Lord Ripon, Add. MS 43543 • BLPES, letters to A. G. Gardiner • Bodl. Oxf., corresp. with Herbert Asquith • Bodl. Oxf., letters to Margot Asquith • Bodl. Oxf., corresp. with Sir William Harcourt and Lewis Harcourt • Bodl. Oxf., corresp. with Sir Donald Maclean • Bodl. Oxf., corresp. with Lord Ponsonby • Bodl. Oxf., corresp. with Lord Selborne • CUL, corresp. with Lord Hardinge • Devon RO, letters to Sir Thomas Dyke Acland, etc. • HLRO, corresp. with Herbert Samuel • JRL, letters to C. P. Scott • LPL, corresp. and papers relating to W. E. Gladstone • Lpool RO, letters to Sir Edward Evans • NL Ire., letter to John Redmond • U. Newcastle, corresp. with Walter Runciman

Likenesses M. Beerbohm, caricature drawing, 1900, U. Cal., Los Angeles, William Andrews Clark Memorial Library • G. C. Beresford, photograph, *c*.1902, NPG [*see illus.*] • W. Stoneman, photograph, 1918, NPG • P. Tennyson Cole, oils, 1930, Government House, South Africa; watercolour replica, Keble College, Oxford • H. Adlard, stipple, BM • Barraud, photograph, NPG • A. Garratt, watercolour, repro. in Mallet, *Herbert Gladstone* • J. R. Herbert, oils, Hawarden Castle, Flintshire • A. M. Severn, watercolour, Hawarden Castle, Flintshire • Spy [L. Ward], watercolour study, NPG; repro. in *VF* (6 May 1882) • B. Stone, two photographs, NPG • lithograph, NPG; repro. in *West London Advertiser* (9 Dec 1882) • two photographs, NPG

Wealth at death £64,138 18*s*. 6*d*.: probate, 6 June 1930, *CGPLA Eng. & Wales*

Gladstone [Gladstones], **Sir John, first baronet** (**1764–1851**), merchant and politician, was born John Gladstones on 11 December 1764 in Leith, the eldest son of the sixteen children (four dying in infancy) of Thomas Gladstones (1732–1809), a merchant in Leith, and his wife, Nelly (1739–1806), daughter of Walter Neilson, a merchant in Springfield, near Edinburgh. Jack (as he was known in the family in his early years) Gladstones left school aged thirteen and served an apprenticeship to Alexander Ogilvy, manager of the Edinburgh Roperie and Sailcloth Company, from which he was discharged on 18 May 1781. He was very tall, big-boned, and gangly, with big feet and hands. With some familiarity with the Baltic trade from his apprenticeship, he entered his father's already burgeoning corn-chandling business. Trading in grain and vitriol in the Baltic, he impressed Edgar Corrie of Liverpool with his acumen and in 1786 moved to Liverpool to work with Corrie, entering into a fourteen-year partnership of £4000 with him and Jackson Bradshaw on 1 May 1787, Gladstones providing £1500. That year, on Corrie's advice, he became John Gladstone, though his legal name remained Gladstones until 10 February 1835. Gladstones sent the first

Sir John Gladstone, first baronet (1764–1851), by David Octavius Hill and Robert Adamson, 1844

ship to Calcutta when trade resumed. The successful partnership quickly diversified into Virginian tobacco and it was on a combination of American grain and tobacco that Gladstone's fortune was based (though his initial foray, in 1789–91, was ruined by flying weevil in the grain). By June 1799 Gladstone was worth £40,000; by 1812, £145,600; by 1820, £333,600; by 1828, £502,550. He ended his partnership with Corrie in 1801, on bad terms, and started another with his brother Robert, gradually involving his other five brothers. He entered shipping insurance, shipowning, and Liverpool real estate, owning warehouses and suburbs. In 1811 he built Seaforth House on the Litherland estate outside Liverpool. His success was based on ready money, excellent market intelligence, and the natural advantage of the Liverpool market in the period of the American and French wars. In 1813 he published two letters to Lord Clancarty, president of the Board of Trade, attacking importation of American cotton during the war with America.

Gladstone began sugar and cotton trading in the West Indies in 1803, that year also purchasing the Belmont estate in Demerara, the first of several, the largest being Vreedenhoop in Demerara, with 430 slaves, acquired in 1826 for £80,000. In the 1820s Gladstone increased his sugar estate holdings, adding estates in Jamaica and disregarding the growth of the anti-slavery movement. Unwilling to invest significantly in British manufacturing, he saw West Indian estates as the best outlet for his substantial surplus capital. He never visited the West Indies, though from 1809 he was chairman of the Liverpool West Indian Association. As such he energetically defended the interests of the planters, markedly in a controversy with

James Cropper, the abolitionist, in the *Liverpool Courier* in October 1823, Gladstone writing as 'Mercator' (republished as *The Correspondence between John Gladstone … and James Cropper*, 1824). In 1830 he published *Statement on the Present State of Slavery*, which opposed total abolition while acknowledging the slave owners' responsibilities. His son W. E. *Gladstone's maiden speech in the Commons defended the management of the Vreedenhoop estate against the charges of Lord Howick, the colonial under-secretary. Gladstone remains a common name in the West Indies.

Gladstone was reared in the strict Scottish religious tradition and he took it with him to Liverpool, where initially he attended the Renshaw Street Unitarian Chapel, where he met William Roscoe and William Ewart. With Ewart and others he built a Scottish church and school in Oldham Street. But Gladstone's first wife, married in 1792, was Jane Hall (*b.* 1765?), daughter of Joseph Hall of Liverpool, an Anglican merchant; they built 1 (later 62) Rodney Street as their home in 1792. Jane Gladstone died childless on 16 April 1798. On 29 April 1800 in Liverpool, Gladstone married Anne Mackenzie Robertson (1771/2–1835), daughter of the Episcopalian Andrew Robertson (1720–1796), sheriff of Dingwall, and his wife, Annie. Anne Gladstone was sickly and a strict evangelical, a friend of Thomas Chalmers, who several times visited the family and praised Gladstone's Christian initiative in *The Christian and Civic Economy of Large Towns*, 3 vols. (1821–6). John and Anne Gladstone had six children, of whom W. E. Gladstone was the fourth son and fifth child.

Broadening his religious base and using his substantial funds, John Gladstone made his way in Liverpool politics, initially in whig radicalism as a supporter of William Roscoe and a founder of the *Liverpool Courier*, increasingly in Canningite toryism and Anglican religion. He managed George Canning's election campaigns for the Liverpool seat in 1812, 1816, 1818, and 1820. In 1815 he built St Andrew's Episcopal Church in Renshaw Street, Liverpool, and St Thomas's at Seaforth; he was also a founder of Liverpool Collegiate Institution. (His last charitable undertaking in Liverpool was the building of St Thomas's Church, Toxteth, in 1840.) In 1818 he was returned for Lancaster, spending £12,000. In 1820, with Lancaster too costly, he bought one of the Woodstock seats from the duke of Marlborough for £877. The duke wanted more in 1826 and Gladstone transferred to Berwick upon Tweed, winning the seat but being unseated on petition in 1827. He did not stand again, and had not been an active MP, but he pursued a political career vicariously through the three of his sons—Thomas, John Neilson, and William Ewart—who became MPs after 1830. His son Robertson carried forward the family business. John Gladstone hoped to found a political rather than a business dynasty, and had a partial, but comparatively a considerable, success. Thomas and John Neilson Gladstone found the pressure of their father's expectations almost impossible to withstand; neither made any significant political impact. But he successfully dissuaded his son William from taking holy orders and arranged with the duke of Newcastle for his first constituency. John Gladstone was the first of four generations of Gladstones in the Commons.

Gladstone lived nomadically among the English spas as his wife and elder daughter took the waters; this partially impeded supervision of his scattered business interests. His daughter Anne Mackenzie Gladstone, a strict evangelical and an important influence on the household, died in 1829; his other daughter, Helen *Gladstone, found the prevailing protestant piety unsustainable and began to turn to Roman Catholicism. In 1833 he returned to Scotland, buying the estate of Fasque and Balfour for almost £80,000, becoming a director of the Royal Bank of Scotland, and investing in canals and railways. Encouraged by his son William, he put up much of the money to found Trinity College, Glenalmond, an Anglican boarding-school in Perthshire. He enlarged the house at Fasque and laid down a fine wine cellar. His second wife died there on 23 September 1835 after many years of illness. His children took turns to attend the ageing widower.

With slavery ended in the West Indies, Gladstone sold most of his property there and invested in Bengal sugar; he developed his interest and put money into Gillanders, Ogilvy, which became one of the chief agency firms in Calcutta, the family retaining an interest in the firm well into the twentieth century, H. N. *Gladstone, John Gladstone's grandson, being a partner.

Gladstone strongly opposed corn-law repeal, though supporting a sliding scale, and in 1843 attacked Richard Cobden in *A Review of Mr. Cobden's Corn Politics*; in 1846 he strongly criticized Peel's government in *Plain Facts*, and in 1849 in letters to the *Montrose Standard* denounced his son William's support for repeal of the Navigation Acts. Despite this, Peel made him a baronet on 18 July 1846.

Sir John Gladstone was a classic entrepreneur, but he left his interests diverse and unconsolidated; he founded many businesses, but only a small proportion of these survived him as family concerns. After bearing many losses in the 1840s as his energy and control diminished, after bailing out the Glynne family into which his son William had married, and after distributing £324,000 to his children, he was worth £745,679 in 1848 (Checkland, 415). A demanding and bitter old man, he died at Fasque on 5 December 1851 and was buried in the vault of St Andrew's Chapel, Fasque, the Episcopalian chapel he had founded in 1846. H. C. G. Matthew

Sources S. G. Checkland, *The Gladstones: a family biography, 1764–1851* (1971) • Gladstone, *Diaries* • H. C. G. Matthew, *Gladstone, 1809–1874* (1986) • D. B. Davis, 'James Cropper and the British anti-slavery movement', *Journal of Negro History*, 45 (1960), 241–58; 46 (1961), 154–73 • J. S. Gladstone, *History of Gillanders, Arbuthnot and Co., and Ogilvy Gillanders and Co.* (1910) • wine catalogue (1972) [Christies, 15 June 1972] • will, PRO, PROB 11/2151, sig. 307

Archives BL, corresp. and papers, Add. MSS 44357–44739, *passim* • Flintshire RO, Hawarden • Lpool RO, letters to Lord Stanley; South American trade bills and receipts • NRA Scotland, priv. coll., business accounts and corresp. with Fraser family • NRA Scotland, priv. coll., business, Fasque estate, and personal corresp. • St Deiniol's Library, Hawarden, business, family, social corresp.; estate and financial papers • U. Glas., Archives and Business Records Centre, letter-books relating to West Indian estates and trade with India | BL, corresp. with William Huskisson, Add. MSS 38739–38758 · Derbys. RO, Matlock, letters to Sir R. J. Wilmot-Horton · NRA Scotland, priv. coll., letters to Sir John Sinclair · U. Edin., New Coll. L., letters to Thomas Chalmers · corresp. with Sir Robert Peel, Add. MSS 40401–40594, *passim*

Likenesses D. O. Hill and R. Adamson, calotype, 1844, U. Glas. L. [*see illus.*] · S. W. Reynolds, mezzotint, pubd 1844 (after W. Bradley), BM, NPG · T. Gladstone, oils, NPG

Wealth at death approx. £746,000: Checkland, *The Gladstones*, 416

Gladstone, John Hall (1827–1902), physical chemist, was born on 7 March 1827 at 7 Chatham Place West, Hackney, Middlesex, the eldest son of John Gladstone and his wife, Alison Hall. His younger brother, George (1828–1909), was a prominent educationist and for many years chairman of the school board of Hove, Sussex. His father came from Kelso, where the family had been established since 1645, and after a successful career as a wholesale draper and warehouseman retired from business in 1842. After being privately educated, in 1844 Gladstone entered University College, London, where he attended the chemistry lectures of Professor Thomas Graham, gaining a gold medal for original research. In 1847 he went to Giessen University, where he was a pupil of Liebig, and after graduating PhD he returned to London in 1848.

From 1850 to 1852 Gladstone was lecturer on chemistry at St Thomas's Hospital. He sat on the royal commission which inquired into lighthouses, buoys, and beacons from 1859 to 1862, and on the committee which the War Office appointed in 1864 to investigate questions regarding gun cotton. He succeeded Michael Faraday as Fullerian professor of chemistry at the Royal Institution in 1874, but resigned in 1877. His *Michael Faraday* (1872), a biography inspired by close personal friendship, was frequently reprinted. Gladstone was elected a fellow of the Royal Society in 1853 and was awarded its Davy medal in 1879. He was a founder member of the Physical Society and served as its president (1874) and as president of the Chemical Society (1877–9). In 1892 he was made an honorary DSc at Trinity College, Dublin.

Gladstone was twice married: in 1852, to Jane May (*d.* 1864), only child of Charles *Tilt, the publisher, with whom he had one son and six daughters; in 1869, to Margaret, daughter of David *King, and niece of William Thomson, Baron Kelvin. She died in 1870, leaving a daughter, Margaret Ethel *MacDonald (1870–1911), a socialist and suffragist who married (James) Ramsay MacDonald in 1896.

The death of his father-in-law Charles Tilt in 1861 left Gladstone independently wealthy, enabling him to devote himself to science and philanthropy. He contributed extensively to learned journals; his papers (one hundred and forty as sole author and seventy-eight with collaborators), established his position as one of the founders of physical chemistry. He was particularly interested in relationships between the chemical composition of substances and their optical properties. A pioneer in spectroscopy, he was among the first to recognize its potential in chemical analysis. He also published several articles,

John Hall Gladstone (1827–1902), by Spy (Sir Leslie Ward), pubd 1891

including one with Sir David Brewster, on the absorption lines of the solar spectrum. With the Revd Thomas Pelham Dale (1821–1892), he measured the relationship between temperature and refractive index for numerous liquids. They also correlated the refractive and dispersive powers of various substances with their chemical compositions, showing that the molecular refractivity of a compound was an additive property, reducible to the individual atomic refractivities of its component elements. Gladstone published valuable work on fluorescence, phosphorescence, the polarization of light, and on chromatic phenomena. Using various solution reactions whose end product (ferric thiocyanate) has a strong red colour, he attempted to quantify the dynamics of chemical change (1855–62), partly anticipating the more successful researches of the Norwegian chemists C. M. Guldberg and P. Waage.

Besides his contribution to physical chemistry, Gladstone did significant work in other branches of the subject. His paper 'On the relationship between the atomic weights of analogous elements' (*Philosophical Magazine*, 5, 1853, 313–20) extended suggestions made by J. B. Dumas, partly anticipating the periodic law subsequently proposed by J. A. R. Newlands and fully developed by D. I. Mendeleyev. In 1872, with his assistant Alfred Tribe, he discovered that zinc covered with spongy copper would decompose water. Further experiments indicated the value of the copper–zinc union as a reducing agent for both organic and inorganic compounds. The results were published in the *Journal of the Chemical Society* between 1872 and 1875. Papers on a similar subject, 'The chemistry of the secondary batteries of Planté and Faure', which were communicated to *Nature* (1882–3), appeared in 1883 in volume form.

An ardent Liberal in politics, Gladstone was frequently invited to stand for parliament, and did so once, unsuccessfully, at York in 1868. He intended, if elected, to contribute to the national debate over state education (which eventually culminated in the passage of the Forster Act in 1870). However, membership of the London school board was his only public office. He sat on the board from 1873 to 1894, serving as vice-chairman from 1888 to 1891, and giving his time and thought liberally. As chairman of the school management and the books and apparatus committees, he was responsible for many of the changes in the curriculum and improvements in the methods of education, described in the memorandum he contributed to Leonard Huxley's *Life and Letters of Thomas Henry Huxley* (1.350). Gladstone was a pioneer of technical education and manual instruction, and one of the earliest advocates of the introduction of science into elementary schools. He was an ardent supporter of the Spelling Reform Association, which was founded in 1879 after a meeting in his house, and he published several works on this and other educational topics.

Gladstone was active in philanthropic and charitable work, and keenly interested in Christian endeavour, organizing devotional meetings and bible classes among educated men and women. He was a vice-president of the Christian Evidence Society, and wrote and lectured frequently for it on Christian apologetics. He also published several books and articles on religious topics and a few hymns. He was one of the earliest collaborators with Sir George Williams in the work of the Young Men's Christian Association, with which he was connected from 1850; he was especially active in its international relationships.

Gladstone died at 17 Pembridge Square, Notting Hill, London, on 6 October 1902, and was buried in Kensal Green cemetery on 10 October. MICHAEL A. SUTTON

Sources W. A. T. [W. A. Tilden], *JCS*, 87 (1905), 591–7 · T. E. T., *PRS*, 75 (1905), 188–92 · *DSB* · *Nature*, 66 (1902), 609–10 · J. P. Partington, *A history of chemistry*, 4 (1964) · A. Morgan, *J. Ramsay Macdonald* (1987) · Lord Elton [G. Elton], *The life of James Ramsay MacDonald* (1939) · L. Huxley, *Life and letters of Thomas Henry Huxley*, 1 (1900)

Archives RS, corresp. and papers | CUL, letters to Sir George Stokes · Som. ARS, corresp. with Arthur Bulleid

Likenesses Lock & Whitfield, woodburytype photograph, NPG; repro. in T. Cooper, *Men of mark: a gallery of contemporary portraits* (1880) · A. Lucas, sepia photograph, RS · Maull & Co., sepia photograph, RS · Maull & Polyblank, sepia photograph, RS · Spy [L. Ward], cartoon, chromolithograph, NPG; repro. in *VF* (14 Nov 1891) [*see illus.*] · H. J. Whitlock, carte-de-visite, NPG

Wealth at death £73,383 2*s*. 8*d*.: probate, 5 Nov 1902, *CGPLA Eng. & Wales*

Gladstone, Mary. *See* Drew, Mary (1847–1927).

Gladstone, William Ewart (1809–1898), prime minister and author, was the fifth child and fourth and youngest son of Sir John *Gladstone, first baronet (1764–1851), and his second wife, Anne, *née* Robertson (1771/2–1835). His parents named him William Ewart after their radical friend of that name, who, like them, was part of the Scottish commercial community in Liverpool. John Gladstones (he dropped the 's' informally in 1787 and by letters patent in 1835) had established himself as a leading member of that community and it was at the fashionable address of 62 (formerly 1) Rodney Street, Liverpool, that his fourth son was born on 29 December 1809.

Family, early religion, and Eton Gladstone was born into an evangelical family, his mother and his sister Anne (who was his godmother) both combining prolonged illnesses with intense evangelical pietism. His mother was of Scottish Episcopal origins, and his father joined the Church of England, having been a Presbyterian when he first settled in Liverpool. William was thus baptized into the Church of England, in St Peter's Church, Liverpool. But the Scottish ties of the family remained strong: William probably first visited that country in 1814, aged four, recalling in old age having heard the guns of Edinburgh Castle fired, probably to celebrate the abdication of Napoleon that spring. Gladstone's upbringing in the Liverpool area rooted him in northern England, midway between the metropolitan south, which was to be the centre of his political and intellectual life, Scotland, whither his father retired in 1830, Ireland just across the sea, and Wales, where his family home was to be from 1839. Gladstone recalled, 'I was not a devotional child' (Morley, 1.13), but this may have been a self-deprecation arising from the reverence in which he held the religiosity of his mother and sister Anne. From an early age he read copiously—he later recalled the 'great and fascinating hold' (ibid.) that Bunyan's *Pilgrim's Progress* took upon him and remembered weeping profusely at the description of the life and death of William Wallace in Jane Porter's *Scottish Chiefs*.

By the 1810s the Gladstones were a rich family, their fortune based on transatlantic corn and tobacco trade and on the slave-labour sugar plantations they owned in the West Indies. William attended the small school at Bootle near Liverpool kept by William Rawson, a moderate evangelical, previously private tutor in the Gladstone household. He thought he learned little from Rawson. In 1821 John Gladstone sent his son to Eton College, where the eldest son, Thomas, was already a pupil. John Gladstone was determined that at least one of his children should succeed in the political world, and he saw an education at Eton and Christ Church, Oxford, as the best preparation for that success. William, who was an Oppidan, roomed with Thomas, their 'dame' being Mrs Shurley. Already well exposed to tory politics, for his father was George Canning's chief supporter and political organizer in Liverpool, Gladstone at Eton also met whigs, notably Arthur

William Ewart Gladstone (1809–1898), by Sir John Everett Millais, 1879

Henry *Hallam [*see under* Hallam, Henry], for whom in 1824 he formed a close affection. For Gladstone, Hallam, and others such as Francis Doyle and James Milnes-Gaskell, the chief focus of their Eton life was the Eton Society (later 'Pop') which they ran as an intellectual and debating club, and from whose coterie was published the *Eton Miscellany* (1827), edited by Gladstone (writing as Bartholomew Bouverie) and George Selwyn (later the noted bishop). In the Eton Society, Gladstone learned that readiness of public speaking which never left him. Gladstone's tutor at Eton was the whiggish H. H. Knapp, but E. C. Hawtrey was the master whose intellectual encouragement Gladstone especially valued. He was flogged at least once by John Keate; he occasionally played cricket and was a competent sculler. Gladstone left Eton at Christmas 1827, proficient in Greek and Latin, competent in French, barely adequate in mathematics, and largely ignorant of the sciences. Yet his self-education in English literature, history, and theology was already considerable, and the school had achieved his father's objective of grafting him onto the metropolitan political élite. However, Gladstone had privately maintained his evangelical religion; this was a subject he rarely discussed with his friends. He found Eton's religion arid, though he was confirmed there by Bishop Pelham on 1 February 1827. He quickly became a regular communicant, a practice he maintained for the rest of his life, and he also broadened his evangelicalism by an unusual interest in Roman Catholicism.

While a boy at Eton, Gladstone became a diarist. The first entry, dated 16 July 1825 and written during a heat-wave while on holiday at Gloucester, begins: 'Read Ovid …'. He maintained his diary daily and almost unbroken until 1894, then spasmodically until 29 December 1896 (about 25,200 entries). Its terse first entry established its usual format: lists of reading, correspondence, and activities both religious and secular, only exceptionally fleshed out with reflections or comments, and these usually telegraphic in form. It was, Gladstone told his son Herbert in 1872, 'an account-book of the all-precious gift of Time' (Morley, 1.205). We are, therefore, exceptionally well informed about Gladstone's day-to-day activities.

Christ Church, Oxford Gladstone matriculated from Christ Church, Oxford, on 28 January 1828: his father's plan (from 1824) was that he should take a degree at Oxford's chief political college, then read for the bar, and subsequently enter politics.

By the end of his Eton days Gladstone was clearly promising; by the end of his time at Christ Church he was a rising star of British public life. He prepared for Oxford by being crammed in mathematics at Wilmslow by J. M. Turner (another moderate evangelical), for he hoped to take a double first. At Christ Church he helped to found an Essay Club—intended to match the Cambridge Apostles of which Arthur Hallam was a member—which became known as the WEG, meeting in his rooms in Canterbury quadrangle. His ability was recognized by Dean Smith, who got him elected a 'student' of Christ Church in 1829. In the university he was active in the newly formed Oxford Union Society, of which he was president in 1830.

As well as enlarging his contacts and standing with the future political class which was being educated with him, Gladstone tried to maintain his evangelical religion. He dabbled in the extreme Calvinism of H. B. Bulteel and the St Edmund Hall set and reacted strongly against it. He never experienced an identifiable moment of religious conversion, and at Oxford, like many of his generation, began to feel that evangelicalism offered an inadequate ecclesiology. However, he found Christ Church Cathedral almost as arid in its religion as Eton chapel. After he became its 'prickbill' (recorder of compulsory attendance) he was beaten up in his rooms on 23 March 1830, probably for excessive and officious zeal in his duties: some contemporaries found Gladstone something of a prig. In August that year, while attending a reading party at Cuddesdon, near Oxford, Gladstone decided to tell his father that he felt a duty to ask his permission to offer himself for ordination. He wrote knowing his father would attempt to dissuade him. The strength of his determination is hard to assess. Certainly, he relied considerably on John Gladstone's judgement, which was decisively hostile to the idea. Gladstone lacked a clear call and may have been relieved to be persuaded into politics. He told his father: 'I do not now see my own view can or ought to stand for a moment in the way of your desires' (Matthew, *Gladstone, 1809–1874*, 28). No lingering regret attended this decisive moment, and Gladstone did not subsequently refer much to it.

Gladstone also followed his father politically. On 29 December 1831 he noted in his diary: 'This has been my debating society year, now, I fancy, done with. Politics are fascinating to me; perhaps too fascinating.' He was a Canningite in supporting Catholic emancipation and opposing parliamentary reform, though on the latter question his position during the crisis of 1830–32 had some ambivalence. On 11 November 1830 he dramatically carried in the Oxford Union a motion of no confidence in Wellington's government. His speech was partly opposed to aspects of reform, but it was also opposed to Wellington's total rejection of it. Gladstone wanted modest change co-ordinated by tories. Lord John Russell's sweeping bill frustrated that objective, Gladstone recalling: 'the Reform bill frightened me in 1831, and drove me off my natural and previous bias. Burke and Canning misled many on that subject, and they misled me' (Morley, 1.70). Gladstone's speech caught the attention of Lord Lincoln, son of the fourth duke of Newcastle, and many others: it was the first of thousands of his speeches to achieve national comment and it set him aside in his generation.

There remained the matter of examinations. After coaching from Charles Wordsworth, which failed to gain him the Dean Ireland scholarship (Gladstone failed to win any of the university prizes for which he entered), his finals results in 1831 became famous. Like Peel twenty-three years earlier, he obtained first classes in *literae humaniores* (in November) and in mathematics and physics (in December). Gladstone characteristically complained that the examination had been insufficiently wide-ranging. When during the *viva voce* part the examiner attempted to change the subject, Gladstone declared, 'No, sir; if you please, we will not leave it yet' and declaimed further upon it (Morley, 1.79).

Early political career and marriage Gladstone left Oxford on 15 December 1831, and stayed at Trinity College, Cambridge (Christ Church's sister college), meeting its master, William Whewell, through Christopher Wordsworth, father of his coach, and visiting Arthur Hallam, by then closer to Alfred Tennyson than to Gladstone and soon to be the subject of the latter's *In Memoriam*. John Gladstone's plans had been realized as much as he could have wished and perhaps more than he expected.

On 1 February 1832 Gladstone and his brother John left for a continental tour, visiting Belgium, France, Savoy, Italy, and Austria. He was struck by the stamina and stoicism rather than by the distinction of the protestant Waldensians, but the chief import of the tour was his first extended experience of Roman Catholicism, which both attracted and repelled him. He as yet knew no Roman Catholics in Britain, and he elaborately examined and annotated the habits of continental Catholics. He at once distinguished between the illegitimacy of the pope's temporal power and the mystique of Catholicism. Entering St Peter's, he noted: 'most deeply does one feel the pain and schism which separates us from Rome—whose guilt … rests … upon Rome itself' (Gladstone, *Diaries*, 31 March 1832).

While abroad (in Milan), Gladstone received an invitation from the duke of Newcastle (prompted by his son, Lord Lincoln) to stand as member of parliament for Newark, which the duke, a strong tory and protectionist, largely controlled. Despite his father's plans for him to read for the bar, Gladstone quickly accepted, and was elected after a smart contest at the head of the poll with 887 votes at the general election following the Reform Act in December 1832. He took his seat on 29 January 1833 (as an insurance he ate the required dinners at Lincoln's Inn, but was never called to the bar). In March he moved into L2, Albany, Piccadilly—his home until his marriage.

Although he had made an earlier intervention in the Commons, Gladstone's maiden speech was given on 3 June 1833 on the terms of the emancipation of slaves in the West Indies, where his father was a substantial slave owner. He became a prominent spokesman for the West Indian interest, which was trying to extract better terms of reparation for emancipation, though he did not defend the principle of slavery. He also became known as a defender of the Anglican establishment in Ireland and a pronounced opponent of the whigs' plan for concurrent endowment (indiscriminate state financial support for religious denominations). Opposition to concurrent endowment was his most consistently held political position. In Peel's short minority government in 1834–5 he was briefly a commissioner of the Treasury—that is, a whip—(December 1834 – January 1835) and then under-secretary for war and the colonies (January 1835 – April 1835). Lord Aberdeen being his chief, he handled colonial business in the Commons. He was returned unopposed for Newark at the general election in January 1835.

This apparently easy political start was not mirrored in Gladstone's personal or intellectual life, though when Benjamin Disraeli met him at dinner at the lord chancellor's on 17 January 1835, he (Disraeli) reported: 'we had a swan very white and tender, and stuffed with truffles, the best company there' (*Lord Beaconsfield's Correspondence with his Sister*, 1886, 30). Even so, for Gladstone London political society was a series of awkward religious hurdles. The young bachelor with strong religious principles found himself ill at ease in London society. Moreover, like many Oxonians in his generation, he found that the Canningite Conservatism learned in his youth only partially equipped him to answer the vital questions of the organization of civil and religious society which the march of events and the reforms of the whig governments of the 1830s posed. In opposition from 1835 to 1841, Gladstone had time to try to work out his own response, which was published in two books, *The State in its Relations with the Church* (1838) and *Church Principles Considered in their Results* (1841). The first sought to define the role of the state as the agent of religious principle: the state necessarily had a moral role as the agent in secular affairs of the established church. Influenced especially by Plato, Coleridge, and the idealist school, it attempted an awkward combination of thoroughgoing theocratic argument leavened with English practicality. The second was a more comfortable statement of how Gladstone saw the role of the church. Taken together, the books offered an interesting reassertion of theocratic Anglicanism in a period when religious pluralism was fast gaining ground.

Gladstone prepared for writing *The State* while at Fasque, the Scottish house in the Mearns, in Kincardineshire, bought by his father, where he spent many parliamentary recesses until his father's death in 1851. He discussed the contents and proofs of the book with his two closest friends at that time, Henry Edward *Manning and James Hope (later Hope-*Scott), both of them, like Gladstone, broadening an evangelical youth into a high-church early manhood. Gladstone knew many of those involved in the Tractarian movement, and was strongly influenced by it. He attended church daily when possible and communicated frequently. He drew up plans in 1838 for a Third Order (a lay brotherhood of persons in public life). He was closely involved in Bishop C. J. Blomfield's Metropolitan Churches Fund from 1836, and in 1838, on Blomfield's suggestion, joined the National Society for the Education of the Poor. He was active in the founding of the Additional Curates Society in 1837. As an MP in the 1830s, Gladstone was principally interested, and involved, in a variety of aspects of Anglicanism. Stays in Scotland increased his interest, shared by many involved in the Tractarian movement, in the non-established Episcopal Church in Scotland. Gladstone's interest had a practical outcome, for his contacts with Scottish gentry convinced him of the need for provision for Anglican education in Scotland; from this sprang Trinity College, Glenalmond, planned in detail with Hope from 1840, and in part financed by Gladstone's father.

In 1838 Gladstone again made a continental tour, spending much time in Italy, especially Rome, Naples, and Sicily, visiting the latter with Arthur Kinnaird (Gladstone's diary account was later incorporated in Murray's *Handbook to Sicily*). In Milan, Gladstone met Alessandro Manzoni, author of *I promessi sposi*. In Rome he met Manning, who with Hope helped him with the proofs of *The State*, which was published in December 1838 while he was abroad.

Equally importantly, Gladstone fell in love in Rome with Catherine Glynne (1812–1900) [*see* Gladstone, Catherine]. His awkwardness with respect to women had shown itself earlier in two inept attempts at marriage. In 1835–6 he courted—mainly by letter—Caroline Farquhar, a well-known society beauty, the sister of Walter Farquhar, one of his political friends at Christ Church. His epistolary barrage met with no success. He then rather suddenly, and with an even more rapid rejection (in January 1838), courted Lady Frances Douglas, daughter of the earl of Morton. Catherine Glynne responded more favourably, but with caution, to meetings in the moonlight in the Colosseum. Once back in England, she agreed to an engagement on 8 June 1839 and they were married on 25 July 1839 in Hawarden parish church, with Francis Doyle as best man; it was a double wedding, Catherine's sister Mary being married at the same ceremony to George *Lyttelton. The marriage linked Gladstone to the Hawarden estate in north Wales and to a minor aristocratic family, well established in that area and embodying Pittite political values, represented by Sir Stephen *Glynne, Gladstone's brother-in-law.

The end of the period of Conservative opposition in 1841 thus found Gladstone apparently more settled. But the publication of *The State* had led to puzzlement among Peelite Conservatives (it was said that Sir Robert crossed the street so as to avoid having to speak to Gladstone about the book), enthusiasm among high-churchmen and Tractarians (who looked to Gladstone as the political leader of intransigent Anglicanism), and fury among the whigs. Macaulay memorably denounced the book in the *Edinburgh Review* (April 1839), famously dubbing its author 'the rising hope of those stern and unbending Tories'. J. S. Mill, with some alarm, thought Gladstone 'the man who will probably succeed Peel as the Tory leader, unless [Gladstone's connection with the Oxford Movement] prevents him' (Matthew, *Gladstone, 1809–1874*, 45). But the toryism of which Gladstone was seen as the rising hope was a creed of whose absolute character Gladstone himself was becoming increasingly uncertain. Moreover, his marriage unleashed Gladstone's sexuality rather than containing the difficulties he already felt about it.

The Peel government, 1841–1846: Conservatism in crisis When Peel formed his government in September 1841, Gladstone hoped to be Irish secretary, so as to buttress the position of Anglicanism in Ireland. This was by no means Peel's view of how to improve the political situation in Ireland, and he made Gladstone vice-president of the Board of Trade. In June 1843 Peel appointed him to succeed Lord Ripon as the board's president, with a seat in the cabinet; as president he was also master of the Royal Mint. Gladstone was thus the central figure in the department vitally involved in fiscal policy, the most controversial subject in a controversial government. He had not previously been associated with the free-trade question, despite his family's business background. In the 1830s he was, following his father, a moderate tariff reformer, and he was not sympathetic to the Anti-Corn Law League, for the tory party in the 1841 election did not support repeal of the corn laws (in that election, Gladstone declined a public debate at Walsall with Richard Cobden). John Gladstone increasingly defended protection, but his son, once at the Board of Trade, moved rapidly in the other direction as he assisted Peel, who acted almost as his own chancellor of the exchequer, in the preparation of budgets.

Gladstone quickly showed that command of fiscal detail which was to be an anchor and a hallmark of his political character for the rest of his career. He provided the figures and the detailed arguments for the tariff-reform budgets of 1842 and 1845. Increasingly persuaded of the case for free trade, Gladstone favoured a step-by-step approach, gradually reducing tariffs across the board (he explained his view in his anonymous article 'The course of commercial policy at home and abroad', *Foreign and Quarterly Review*, January 1843). His gradualist approach was thus the opposite of that of the Anti-Corn Law League, which attacked the corn laws as a chief bastion of protectionism whose fall would mean a general surrender to free trade. The railway boom of the late 1830s and early 1840s produced unmanageable quantities of private bill legislation. Gladstone's Railway Act of 1844 tidied up the process and, though the railway network remained largely unplanned, introduced the social safeguard of the 'parliamentary train' (one train to run daily on each route at 1*d*. per mile) and provided, under certain stated terms of compensation, for the ultimate acquisition of the railways by the state should the national interest be felt to require it—a remarkably far-seeing and unprecedented provision.

Experience at the Board of Trade persuaded Gladstone that the future of Conservatism lay in an increased acceptance of commercial and industrial progress in a free market. His religious writings of the 1830s had implied a civil society organized according to very different criteria. The conflict between the two began to close like a pincer movement on the tory party, with Gladstone caught between the groups. Peel's Irish policy implied an integration of the Roman Catholic propertied class as a means towards political stability in Ireland. Gladstone's writings had defended Anglican exclusivity in Ireland. When Peel proposed an extended grant and a sum to endow the Roman Catholic seminary at Maynooth, Gladstone felt he must resign from the government. He did so, after about a year of attempting to have the proposal reconsidered, on 3 February 1845, but voted for Peel's policy soon after, thus further puzzling those of his colleagues without theological interests. He had, he told J. H. Newman, 'clung to the notion of a conscience, in the state, until that idea has become in the general mind so feeble as to be absolutely inappreciable in the movement of public affairs' (Matthew, *Gladstone, 1809–1874*, 69). Slow to take up the question of free trade, Gladstone found himself during the 1841–6 government emerging as one of its chief exponents; quick to spot a deviation from right church and state relations and initially eager to instruct the party leadership in correct ecclesiastical arrangements, he found himself during that government following rather than leading the prime minister.

1845 was a very unsettling year for Gladstone. Soon after his resignation, he became involved in the Engagement, a secret lay religious group—mostly composed of Tractarian Oxonians living in London—which was the context of the start of his lifetime's 'rescue' work with prostitutes. He underwent severe sexual temptation, which was compounded by a visit to Germany in October 1845 to his sister Helen [*see* Gladstone, Helen Jane], who, having been exiled by her family (and especially by her brother William) following her conversion to Roman Catholicism, was suffering a nervous illness and opium addiction. The visit prompted her brother to further nervous difficulties of his own. Gladstone steadied himself by publishing *Remarks upon Recent Commercial Legislation* (1845) and *A Manual of Prayers from the Liturgy, Arranged for Family Use* (1845).

Even so, when Peel reconstructed his government in December 1845 on the understanding that the corn laws would be repealed, Gladstone became secretary of state for war and the colonies. As such, he had to stand for re-election, but the strong protectionism of the duke of Newcastle, his patron in Newark, meant that he could not stand there and no other seat was available. Throughout the corn law crisis of 1846, therefore, Gladstone was in the highly anomalous and possibly unique position of being a secretary of state without a seat in either house and thus unanswerable to parliament. As colonial secretary, succeeding Lord Stanley, Gladstone encouraged—as he had done in earlier speeches in the 1830s on the Canada question—the development and where possible exercise of local colonial opinion as the best base for the settled empire, particularly in Canada and New Zealand. He controversially recalled J. Eardley Wilmot, governor of Van Diemen's Land, and suspended convict transportation thither, but he encouraged the employment of convicts for public and private service in New South Wales, Canada, Gibraltar, and elsewhere. He developed an abiding interest in the colonial church, planned new bishoprics for Australia and the Cape, and was later treasurer of the Colonial Bishoprics Fund. He opposed the occupation of Labuan. Gladstone left office in June 1846 when Peel's government resigned, the Conservative Party split on the corn laws and the ministry defeated on Ireland.

In opposition, 1846–1852 Opposition in the 1830s had produced books and an emerging if somewhat puzzling reputation. Opposition in the 1840s encouraged a further search for political identity, but in a context which was intellectually clearer if politically more complex. Most of Gladstone's policy positions and most of his votes pointed away from traditional Conservatism. He himself saw the experience of governing in 1841–6 as decisive, and the identification of experience rather than theory as the basis for action—a major change of view from the 1830s—led to his abiding interest in the theology of Joseph Butler, the eighteenth-century theologian and bishop of Durham, on whom he began serious study in 1845. At the general election of December 1847 Gladstone was elected one of the two burgesses (MPs) for Oxford University, supported especially by the Anglo-Catholics and by the Liberals of the university (the electorate comprised all Oxford MAs who turned up to vote). In certain respects the university seat seemed natural for Gladstone, but it was a fairly constant source of difficulty to him, for a burgess from Christ Church could not neglect tory opinion in the university, and the crisis of Conservatism affected Anglican Oxford as much as it did Gladstone. From December 1847 Gladstone supported the removal of Jewish civil disabilities (which he had previously opposed); when given an honorary degree at Oxford on 5 July 1848, he was greeted in the Sheldonian Theatre by shouts of 'Gladstone & the Jew Bill' (Gladstone, *Diaries*, 5 July 1848).

The period was personally unsettling in several respects. In 1847 a company partly owned by the Glynne family—the Oak Farm brick and iron works near Stourbridge—went bankrupt in the crash of that year. The Glynnes nearly went under also, and were forced for a time to leave Hawarden Castle. John Gladstone provided enough capital to avoid complete catastrophe, though William Gladstone was examined in the Birmingham court of bankruptcy in 1848. For thirty years after, Gladstone spent considerable time—in and out of office—on the mortgaged Hawarden estates, many of which were held in his name.

Gladstone's sexual difficulties increased. Catherine Gladstone had nine pregnancies between 1839 and 1854 (including one miscarriage). Their children were: William Henry (1840–1891); Agnes (1842–1932), who married Edward Charles *Wickham (1834–1910) in 1873; Stephen Edward (1844–1920), rector of Hawarden from 1872; Catherine Jessy (1845–1850); Mary (1847–1927), who married the Revd Harry Drew in 1885 [*see* Drew, Mary]; Helen *Gladstone (1849–1925), educationist; Henry Neville *Gladstone (1852–1935), businessman; and Herbert John *Gladstone (1854–1930), Liberal politician. Happy though Gladstone was with his family, his wife's pregnancies and her frequent absences to help her sister Mary through her own fourteen childbirths led to severe sexual frustration for her husband, who was also greatly affected by the death of their daughter Jessy, aged five, in April 1850. Tempted by pornography and the prostitutes whom he began attempting to redeem under the terms of the Engagement, he began to flagellate himself as a spiritual and physical punishment. He recorded many instances of flagellation in his diary between October 1845 and May 1859, almost all inflicted after an encounter with a prostitute. As he noted, he 'courted evil' (Gladstone, *Diaries*, 19 July 1848).

The frustrations of the public and private crises of the 1840s were sharply elided on the occasion of the Gorham case, which racked the Church of England from 1847 to 1850. Gladstone published *Remarks on the Royal Supremacy* (1850; reissued 1865, and 1877 with new preface) on the case, opposing the view that the judicial committee could adjudicate on an ecclesiastical case which seemed to turn on theology (the validity of infant baptism). Several members of the Oxford Movement, including his friends Manning and Hope, joined the Roman Catholic church following the judgment. Gladstone, though not tempted to do likewise, was 'unmanned' by this episode—he briefly lost his moral sense—for, ever since his sister Helen's conversion, Roman Catholicism had repelled him emotionally despite his high-Anglican and strong apostolic theological position. He removed Hope from the list of executors of his will.

This crisis coincided with Gladstone's return from a visit to Naples, made between October 1850 and February 1851 for the health of his daughter Mary. While there he met Italian liberals and made a brief visit to the notorious prison, the Vicaria. On his return to London he published two letters to Lord Aberdeen (April and July 1851) on the conditions in Naples, the first describing the kingdom of the Two Sicilies as 'the negation of God erected into a system of government'. He answered his critics in *An Examination of the Official Reply of the Neapolitan Government* (1852). Gladstone also translated (as *The Roman State*, 4 vols., 1851) L. C. Farini's *Lo stato Romano*, a liberal Catholic work critical of the pope's temporal authority. He was helped in the translating by his cousin Anne Ramsden, who later converted to Catholicism. Gladstone's writing on Neapolitan politics gained him a European reputation and associated him, more than was then really the case, with European liberalism.

In September 1851 Gladstone returned to Scotland for his autumnal attendance on his father—his last visit, as it turned out, to Fasque as a home, for his father died that December with William at his bedside ('I thrice kissed my Father's cheek & forehead before & after his death: the only kisses that I can remember'; Gladstone, *Diaries*, 13 Dec 1851). While awaiting that event he wrote *A Letter to … William Skinner … on Functions of Laymen in the Church* (published in 1852), an interesting advocacy of the importance of the laity in an episcopal church. Fasque became the property of William's eldest brother, Sir Thomas Gladstone, a staunch tory, and visits there were subsequently infrequent.

The years 1850–51 were thus a time of adjustment, unease, sometimes even of despondency for Gladstone. He mourned 'The rending & sapping of the Church, the loss of its gems, the darkening of its prospects; as well as the ill fruit this has meant for me individually' (Gladstone, *Diaries*, 31 Dec 1851). The uncertainty of his political position was further emphasized by the formation of Derby's government in February 1852, which, with the other Peelites, he declined to join. In the general election of that year he was re-elected at Oxford after a sharp campaign by his followers, in which by convention he did not himself participate. When parliament reassembled in November 1852, Disraeli, Derby's chancellor of the exchequer, presented an innovative budget which included a controversial proposal to differentiate income tax. At the end of the debate on 16 December, when Disraeli had, as he thought, rounded off the discussion, Gladstone leapt to his feet and, in a brilliant speech while a thunderstorm shook the windows of the new House of Commons, denounced Disraeli's budget, and especially income tax differentiation, as irresponsible and socially divisive. His speech was followed by the defeat of the tory government and the formation of Aberdeen's Peelite–whig–Liberal coalition. Gladstone had thus prominently participated in the moment that united the various progressive forces in British politics and consequently left the tories isolated. His reputation as the man who slew the tories exaggerated his association with progressive politics, but it pointed to what was to be a vital aspect of his popular appeal: an ability at certain critical political moments to promote himself—only partly self-consciously—as the champion of liberal causes.

Chancellor of the exchequer, 1852–1855 When Lord Aberdeen discussed his possible cabinet with the queen, he mentioned Gladstone for the exchequer or the Colonial Office; crown influence, according to Prince Albert, tipped the balance towards the exchequer. Gladstone began the first of his four chancellorships on 28 December 1852. Both his predecessors, the whig Wood and the tory Disraeli, were held to have failed in that office: politically they left a major opportunity to whomsoever could grasp it. Gladstone appreciated this and set out to use the exchequer (as Disraeli had tried to do) as the co-ordinating domestic office of the ministry.

Politically, the presentation and passing of a budget were vital to the coalition as well as to Gladstone. His first budget was presented on 18 April 1853, in a speech of four and three-quarter hours. It was ambitious and successful. Gladstone made the reduction of tariffs, and hence the furtherance of the free-trade cause, the central feature, abolishing 123 tariffs and reducing 133. The future of the income tax—introduced as a peacetime tax for the first time by Peel for three years in 1842 and subsequently periodically renewed, but never for more than three years—was a nettle the chancellor had to grasp. Gladstone did so with apparent boldness: he continued income tax, which he characterized as 'an engine of gigantic power for great national purposes', for seven years to finance the tariff abolitions and reductions (and, following Disraeli's proposal, extended it to Ireland). But he accompanied this with a plan for step-by-step reduction and then abolition on 5 April 1860. He reduced the starting level of its payment from £150 to £100, thus increasing its yield, broadening its base, and making its value to any government greater. Planned abolition of income tax made its differentiation, which was an important issue for the professional class, unnecessary. Gladstone thus created a fiscal and administrative context in which the deviation from Peelite orthodoxy of which he had accused Disraeli in 1852 became subsidiary. He further softened the blow by extending succession duty, another cause favoured by J. S. Mill and the differentiationists. His speech 'not only obtained universal applause from his audience at the time, but changed the convictions of a large part of the nation' (Northcote, 185). Gladstone's budget speech of 1853 set the tone for many of his subsequent performances: the presentation of the annual account of the nation's financial health was like one of Charles Dickens's readings of his novels, a dramatic rendering of an intriguing plot. Gladstone made the annual financial budget report and reckoning a central occasion of the British parliamentary year: his battered dispatch box was symbolically used by the chancellor of the exchequer on budget day for most of the twentieth century.

A quite different question also preoccupied Gladstone in 1852–4—the reform of Oxford and Cambridge universities, in which his constituents expected him to take a close interest; he was himself fascinated by the task, not least as a way of keeping the legislation out of the hands of whigs and secularist Liberals. The Oxford and Cambridge bills of 1854 secured moderate reform; Liberal plans for professorially directed universities were set aside; the collegiate structure was retained but reformed by provision for adequate statutes, with the colleges represented through elected university boards. Gladstone worked closely on the legislation with Benjamin *Jowett, then a tutor at Balliol College. Allied to these reforms and prompted by Jowett and Frederick Temple, Gladstone asked Stafford *Northcote (formerly his secretary) and C. P. *Trevelyan to report on recruitment to the civil service, thus eliciting the Northcote–Trevelyan report, which gradually led to a university-dominated civil service with an administrative grade largely composed of classically educated Oxford and Cambridge men. Gladstone, who described the seventeenth century as an age of rule by prerogative and the eighteenth century as one of rule by patronage, believed the nineteenth century to be one of rule by virtue. His fiscal and institutional reforms were intended to provide the context in which such virtue could flourish.

The Crimean War was an important set-back to Gladstonian finance, though a fillip to administrative reform. Gladstone did not play a prominent role in the process by which diplomacy slipped into combat in 1854 but he responded to it boldly. His intention was to pay for the war out of current taxation. His second budget on 6 March 1854 anticipated war and raised income tax to a new height of *1s. 2d.*; on 8 May a further budget increased indirect taxes. The attempt to finance a European war without increasing the national debt was unprecedented and unsuccessful, but it showed both the confidence of the Treasury in Britain's dominance in the world economy and Gladstone's determination that voters should know through the weight of taxes the consequences of war; if war taxation was deflationary to the economy, the citizens should be aware of the results of their government's actions. Gladstone's mentor, Aberdeen, and his closest political friend, the fifth duke of Newcastle (as Lord Lincoln had become), were the cabinet members especially blamed for the mishandling of the war. Condemned by a vote in the Commons on J. A. Roebuck's hostile motion—Gladstone being the chief defender of the government—Aberdeen and his ministers resigned on 30 January 1855. Gladstone, the Peelites, and Palmerston (acting in concert) declined to join a government led by Lord Derby; Gladstone also declined to serve in the whiggish Lord Lansdowne's proposed government, which refusal he later considered 'a serious and even gross error of judgment' (Morley, 1.529). On 6 February, encouraged by Aberdeen, Gladstone joined Palmerston's government as chancellor of the exchequer but soon—on 21 February 1855—resigned from it with most of the Peelites (some, such as Gladstone's friend Argyll, remaining in office). It was an inconclusive end to a period of ministerial office which began so brightly with the budget of April 1853.

In opposition, 1855–1859 Unexpected opposition led to a return to the unease of the 1846–52 years, although the Peelites without Peel lacked the cohesion of that period. Gladstone disliked Palmerston's tone but was uneasy with the whigs: he had quite often differed with them during the Aberdeen coalition, and these differences were exacerbated by a personal row involving T. F. *Kennedy (1788–1879) and Lord John Russell. He sympathized with aspects of some of the radicals' case against the war, but did not forswear his support for its chief objective, the maintenance of Turkish integrity against Russia (though Turkey he already felt 'full of anomaly, full of misery and full of difficulty … a political solecism of the Mahomedan faith' (speech made in Manchester, 11 Oct 1853; Hirst,

156)). He criticized Palmerstonian finance (though Lewis's budget of 1855 was largely prepared by Gladstone before leaving office) and, in 'The declining efficiency of Parliament', an unfinished article for the *Quarterly Review* (BL, Add. MS 44745), he deplored the condition of parliament and of the party system. To contemporaries he seemed tetchy and unpredictable. His filibustering opposition to the Divorce Bill in 1857 was a contrast to the accommodating adaptability to religious questions which he had come to show since the early 1840s and provided a cheerful point of reference for tories and Irish home-rulers when they filibustered Gladstonian bills in the 1880s.

Classicism, *Studies on Homer*, and the Ionian Islands Unsettled in his role in British politics, Gladstone turned to classical studies. He felt that the moral role of the classics in a Christian education had been poorly developed both at Eton and Oxford, as he showed in 'On the place of Homer in classical education and in historical inquiry' (*Oxford Essays for 1857*, 1857). He had studied Homer at Oxford, but not compulsively. He read the *Iliad* and the *Odyssey* occasionally in the 1830s and 1840s, but regularly from August 1855 onwards; in November 1886 he was reading the *Iliad* for, he thought, the thirty-fifth time (his diary records him reading it once more after that). His first instalment of Homeric publication in 1857 culminated in *Studies on Homer and the Homeric Age*, published by Macmillan for the Clarendon Press, Oxford, in three volumes in 1858 (its total royalties were £58). The proofs were checked by Connop Thirlwall, the broad-church bishop of St David's, and the book was translated into German by Dr A. Schuster in 1863. These volumes diverged sharply from contemporary scholarship. They asserted the Homeric poems to be a single body of work (probably by a single author) which offered a glimpse of human society at the unspoilt dawn of its existence. Subsequent Greek experience had, in Gladstone's view, been a gradual corruption rather than—as his contemporaries mostly thought—an evolution towards the higher civilization of Aristotelian Athens. Gladstone saw 'a relative parallel between the oldest Holy Scripture and the works of Homer', the latter constituting and offering 'an original similitude' with 'the best ideas of our European and our British ancestry'—an interpretation that many mid-Victorians, who looked to Anglo-Saxon origins, would hardly have shared.

This interest in Homer was followed up in two ways. Gladstone for the rest of his life regularly contributed articles on Homeric subjects to the serious popular journals, such as the *Fortnightly* and *Contemporary* reviews. He did not publish in scholarly journals—though many of his articles on Homeric grammar and epithet might appropriately have been placed in them—because he believed his articles, however technical, maintained public interest in an essential text of European citizenship and public life. He published several books popularizing and developing the arguments of *Studies on Homer*—*Juventus mundi: the Gods and Men of the Heroic Age* (1869), *Homeric Synchronism: an Enquiry into the Time and Place of Homer* (1876), *Homer* (1878) for J. R. Green's Literature Primers (a series published by Macmillan), and *Landmarks of Homeric study, together with an essay on the Assyrian tablets and the Homeric text* (1890). From 1861 he worked at a trochaic translation of the *Iliad*, sufficiently full to be shown to Alfred Tennyson in July 1862, but never published; and from 1867 he compiled a Homeric thesaurus (never sufficiently completed for publication in full, though sections were published as articles). A good translator, he published, with his brother-in-law, Lord Lyttelton, *Translations* (1861), from Homer, Dante, Horace, and other authors; he became preoccupied with Horace in later life, publishing various translations including *The Odes of Horace* (1894). Classical scholarship in its various forms became for Gladstone almost as ingrained into his routines as churchgoing. He recognized its value as a balance to restlessness (Gladstone, *Diaries*, 31 Dec 1861) and, in the great struggle for self-control in which the Manichaean forces in Gladstone's personality were countered by hard work and the deliberate assertion of virtue, Homer and allied intellectual activities were important. But Gladstone took more from Homeric work than the acquisition of self-control: 'along with an outline of sovereignty and public institutions highly patriarchal, we find the full, constant and effective use, of two great instruments of government, since and still so extensively in abeyance among mankind; namely, publicity and persuasion' (*Studies on Homer*, 3.7). Gladstone was not to leave them much in abeyance after 1859.

Soon after the publication of *Studies on Homer*, Lord Derby, briefly prime minister of a minority tory government, invited Gladstone to go to the Ionian Islands (a British protectorate since 1815) as commissioner-extraordinary. To the surprise of the political world and the alarm of his friends, Gladstone accepted, and arrived in November 1858 with his family, via Dresden, Prague, Vienna, and HMS *Terrible*. He toured the islands and visited Albania and Greece (attracting approbation for kissing the ring of the Orthodox bishop of Athens—his piety was unintentionally balanced by his catching the prelate's chin with his head as he stood up). Gladstone ran a semi-Ruritanian court on Corfu and addressed the Ionian assembly in classical Greek, perfectly orated but incomprehensible to his Italian-speaking audience. But he learned valuable lessons in dealing with the Enosis (freedom) movement, for his elaborate attempt to counter the movement for union with Greece was unsuccessful.

At the beginning of 1859, on Gladstone's recommendation, Sir John Young, lord high commissioner of the Ionian Islands, was recalled to Britain, Gladstone temporarily taking his place. By holding the lord high commissionership Gladstone vacated his Commons seat. Most Peelites saw the whole Ionian episode as a Disraelian plot to draw Gladstone into a by-election in Oxford which he might lose, and consequently they expedited the arrival of Sir Henry Storks, Gladstone's successor as lord high commissioner. By the time the writ for the by-election was moved, Storks was in post, and Gladstone was no longer lord high commissioner. He was unopposed when re-elected for the university seat in February 1859.

Return to the exchequer, 1859 The Gladstones returned to Britain on 8 March 1859, visiting Venetia and Piedmont *en* *route*, William Gladstone twice meeting Cavour and other Risorgimentist leaders for discussions of the rapidly shifting situation in northern Italy. Immediately on his return he met with Antonio Panizzi to assist the recently liberated Neapolitan liberals. His immediate action, however, removed him from this liberal context, for, speaking from the government's side of the house, he opposed Lord John Russell's resolution on reform on 29 March, and on 31 March voted with the tory government when its Reform Bill was defeated. Unopposed at Oxford in the ensuing general election—though his induction with Acton as the first honorary fellows of All Souls on 11 May reminded his constituents of his tory credentials—Gladstone republished his Neapolitan letters of 1852 and wrote 'Foreign affairs: war in Italy' for the *Quarterly Review* (April 1859), which drew on his Italian meetings; it showed a moderate sympathy for an enlarged Piedmont in northern Italy and his abiding dislike of the pope's temporal power.

Unlike his close political friend and fellow Peelite Sidney Herbert, Gladstone did not attend the famous meeting of progressive forces in Willis's Rooms on 6 June and on 10 June he voted with the tories in the confidence debate. But three days later and with apparent paradox he wrote: 'Went to Ld P[almerston] by his desire at night: I accepted my old office' (Gladstone, *Diaries*, 13 June 1859). Palmerston would have preferred to continue with Lewis, his previous chancellor, and make Gladstone colonial or Indian secretary. Gladstone saw Palmerston, knowing that Lewis would cede the exchequer, and insisted on it. He told Herbert that he would have accepted nothing but the exchequer. It was Gladstone's lingering and over-punctilious support for the tories which was out of place. Unless he anticipated a career spent permanently on the back benches—and few people in public life were more naturally executive politicians—membership of Palmerston's government, whose chances looked fair with or without Gladstone, was at the least the natural consequence of the elimination of alternatives and, better, an opportunity to put through the extensive and remarkable programme of exchequer-led financial and administrative reform which he had drawn up in 1856 in the post-Crimean doldrums.

John Morley's classic analysis of Gladstone's behaviour at this time still has merit:

> It seems a mistake to treat the acceptance of office under Lord Palmerston as a chief landmark of Mr. Gladstone's protracted journey from tory to liberal … I am far from denying the enormous significance of the party wrench, but it was not a conversion. Mr. Gladstone was at this time in his politics a liberal reformer of Turgot's type, a born lover of government. (Morley, 1.631)

As Gladstone told Samuel Wilberforce in 1857, 'I greatly felt being turned out of office, I saw great things to do. I am losing the best years of my life out of my natural service' (Matthew, *Gladstone, 1809–1874*, 106). As in 1853, his acceptance of the chancellorship ended years of political and personal uncertainty.

The high noon of Gladstonian finance, 1859–1866 Army and navy expenditure had spoiled the plan of 1853 for step-by-step abolition of income tax. Gladstone was determined that foreign and military affairs should not again disrupt the establishment of a fiscal order whose well-being he thought central to the health of the body politic: 'Finance is, as it were, the stomach of the country, from which all the other organs take their tone', he wrote in 1858 (Matthew, *Gladstone, 1809–1874*, 113).

In February 1856 Gladstone had set out in a memorandum of twenty-one points the reforms which the chancellor might introduce (Gladstone, *Diaries*, 16 and 20 Feb 1856). Such programmatic initiative was very rare in Victorian politics, and provided Gladstone with a plan of action for his chancellorship. Central to it was 'to complete the construction of a real department of Finance'. This he did through encouraging the energetic scrutiny by the Treasury of all aspects of domestic and defence expenditure through Treasury control of the civil service; the better co-ordination, presentation, and audit of estimates of finance; and, at the constitutional level, through the committee of public accounts which he established in 1864, and the Exchequer and Audit Act of 1866, which had been the first point on his memorandum of 1856. 'To bring all really public accounts under the control of the Treasury' was an objective remarkably achieved, and one which placed free-trade probity, balanced budgets, and retrenchment at the heart of British public finance. Dramatically presented to parliament, the ethos and principles of Gladstonian finance were to endure despite the changing needs of a very different economy. The application of this ethos of finance was contested as to some of its details, but it built upon, received, and developed a wide inter-party agreement in the mid-Victorian years. Strict retrenchment and the absence of governmentally provided welfare would be balanced by welfare provision through voluntary associations of a variety of sorts, whose financial probity would be safeguarded by a system of state registration and public checking of their accounts.

The Gladstonian system of finance and welfare presupposed the existence of the active citizen and a strong general sense of public duty. Gladstone practised what he preached about charitable financial transfers: he normally gave 12–14 per cent of his income in charitable bequests. He maintained a priority for retrenchment with what Morley called 'a boldness sometimes bordering on improvidence' (Morley, 2.54). The chancellor should, he remarked in 1879,

> boldly uphold economy in detail; and it is the mark of … a chicken-hearted Chancellor of the Exchequer, when he shrinks from upholding economy in detail … He is ridiculed, no doubt, for what is called saving candle-ends and cheese-parings. No Chancellor of the Exchequer is worth his salt who is not ready to save what are meant by candle-ends and cheese-parings in the cause of the country. (W. E. Gladstone, *Political Speeches in Scotland*, 1879, 148)

These cheese-parings took the form of reused envelopes and labels and suchlike, the detailed probing of the need for every appointment and post, and the nurturing of a 'Treasury mind', focused on the details of expenditure rather than on its overall pattern and with no interest whatsoever in investment, whose habits of thought continued throughout much of the subsequent century. On the other hand, when there was a large and exceptional undertaking to be faced—such as the votes of credit in the 1880s and the land-purchase scheme of 1886—Gladstone was bold in the scale of his proposals.

Gladstone succeeded in his financial measures in embodying the aspirations of both the income-tax paying propertied classes of his time, and the non-voters whose contribution through indirect taxation was proportionately markedly lower than any of their European contemporaries. He articulated in an attractive, even beguiling way, the details of taxation and associated them with a general, thoroughgoing conception of good government and social as well as economic progress, claiming for them a world as well as a national significance. Joseph Schumpeter, the great Austrian economist, identified the British public finance of this period as the epitome of a particular form of state organization: 'Gladstonian finance … translated a social, political, and economic vision which was comprehensive as well as historically correct, into clauses of a set of co-ordinated fiscal measures' (J. A. Schumpeter, *History of Economic Analysis*, 1954, 403).

When Gladstone took up his chancellorship in 1859, he was opposed at the consequent by-election by Lord Chandos, who was beaten on 1 July by 1050 votes to 859. Gladstone quickly prepared a holding budget, presented on 18 July, which raised income tax from 5*d.* to 9*d.* to meet the deficit of £5 million left by Disraeli and the Third Anglo-Chinese War. He then began to plan the financial settlement of 1860. It had two parts: the budget, and a treaty with France. On 12–13 September 1859 Richard Cobden visited Hawarden to discuss the idea of a tariff treaty with France. Gladstone noted that they discussed 'Tariffs and relations with France. We are closely & warmly agreed' (Gladstone, *Diaries*, 13 Sept 1859). Gladstone thus formed a notable public partnership with a leading radical. Cobden negotiated the treaty in Paris; Gladstone handled its cabinet and parliamentary presentation. The purpose of the treaty—criticized by some free-traders because it was a treaty of reciprocity—was not primarily a trading gain, but the 'desired fruit in binding the two countries together by interest and affection' (Matthew, *Gladstone, 1809–1874*, 113): military and naval rivalry and the need for defence against France were to be diminished by commercial harmony.

The treaty was signed on 23 January 1860 and presented to parliament together with Gladstone's budget (delayed by several days because of his cold) on 10 February. He spoke from 5.00 until 9.00 p.m. 'without great exhaustion: aided by a great stock of egg & wine' (Gladstone, *Diaries*, 10 Feb 1860). 'He came forth', Charles Greville recorded, 'and *consensu omnium* achieved one of the greatest triumphs that the House of Commons ever witnessed' (Hirst, 182). Abolishing all protective tariffs except the shilling duty on corn, Gladstone removed duties from 371 articles, substantially reduced indirect taxation, and left only fifteen indirect taxes of importance, almost all on food. This simplification, a central objective of Peel–Gladstone finance, created an intentional political difficulty to those wishing to increase central government expenditure, because any increase of indirect taxation would be almost as obvious as an increase of direct. Income tax was raised in the 1860 budget to 10*d.* to balance the books. Gladstone had proposed the paper duty for abolition—the remaining 'tax on knowledge': the tories in the Lords, surreptitiously encouraged by Palmerston, threw out the proposal. This advantaged Gladstone in the party in the country, but it drew him into a series of cabinet rows with Palmerston and various of the whigs. He was also in dispute with the prime minister, the army, and the navy on military fortifications against France, which he believed had been made less urgent by the 1860 treaty. The abolition of the paper duty was got through the Lords by reviving it in the 1861 budget (presented on 15 April) and by making it part of a consolidated Finance Bill (the first such). But many of Palmerston's forts were built and naval expenditure increased. Gladstone several times threatened resignation, and his day-to-day opponent was his close friend Sidney Herbert, who died under the strain. In 1863–4 increased yield and a reduction in expenditure growth enabled income tax to be reduced, reaching 4*d.* in the budget just before the 1865 general election.

Liberal politics in the 1860s Gladstone's relations with the gradually consolidating Liberal Party were straightforward on the principle of free trade, less easy on a wide range of other issues. Even his proposals as chancellor were quite often challenged and defeated, and he felt his campaign for the reduction of central government spending had been frustrated (though in fact central government expenditure declined from £70 million (10 per cent of gross national product) in 1860 to £67.1 million (7.9 per cent) in 1865). His Savings Bank Monies Bill was defeated in 1860 and in 1863 his budgetary proposal to make charities subject to income tax had to be dropped (Gladstone regarded charitable exemption as a gift from the taxpayer to bodies which were mostly poorly run and often corrupt). In 1864 his bill establishing Post Office Savings Banks was much opposed by trustee savings banks and friendly societies, which feared state invasion of their territory; however, the bill passed and the idea of using post offices for services other than postal was one of Gladstone's enduring legacies. Although his initiatives as chancellor did not all come to fruition, the tour of Tyneside by William and Catherine Gladstone in October 1862 was a great success, exemplifying the alliance of free trade, industrialism, and popular Liberalism. In Newcastle, Gladstone made a famous speech, in which he said:

> We may have our own opinions about slavery; we may be for or against the South; but there is no doubt that Jefferson Davis and other leaders of the South have made an army; they are making, it appears, a navy; and they have made what is more than either, they have made a nation.
> (Morley, 2.79)

Gladstone's remarks were less out of line with British opinion than was subsequently claimed, but they caused a furore. In 1896 he noted that he had made a mistake 'of incredible grossness' (ibid., 2.82); his public comments probably made British mediation for an agreed partition between the North and the South—already under cabinet consideration—more rather than less difficult, and they certainly encouraged the Americaphilia which was a pronounced feature of the later Gladstone, though, despite various invitations from Harvard University and elsewhere, he never crossed the Atlantic.

Religion remained politically problematic for Gladstone; he differed from many Liberals in supporting church rates and his high-Anglicanism sharply distinguished him from the nonconformists. From 1864 he developed links with London nonconformists through meetings organized by C. Newman Hall and he began to modify his opposition to the abolition of church rates. He was also prominent in the celebrations attending Garibaldi's visit to England in April 1864 (though behind the scenes he worked to limit it). Gladstone's gathering association with political Liberalism and radicalism was exemplified by his reply for the government on 11 May 1864 on Baines's private member's Reform Bill, which electrified the political world and infuriated Palmerston:

> I venture to say that every man who is not presently incapacitated by some consideration of personal unfitness or of political danger, is morally entitled to come within the pale of the constitution. Of course, in giving utterance to such a proposition, I do not recede from the protest I have made against sudden, or violent, or excessive, or intoxicating change. (Morley, 2.126)

Gladstone hoped that such persons, many of them nonconformists, would elect parliaments serious about retrenchment—so strong was his belief in the anti-state views of the 'labour aristocracy' whose enfranchisement he was coming to support and whom he courted (though he denied that he so did) in a tour of Lancashire in October 1864.

At the general election of 1865 Gladstone was defeated at Oxford University, coming a poor third in the poll to his friend Sir William Heathcote and G. Gathorne-Hardy. Gladstone was the last Liberal—and in 1865 he was not fully that—to hold one of the Oxbridge seats and his defeat was no surprise; he had been quite strongly opposed at the by-election following his appointment to office in 1859 and new legislation had allowed the non-resident MAs a postal vote. Charles Dodgson's anagrams of Gladstone's names caught the tone of rejection: 'A wild man will go at trees; Wild agitator! Means well; Wilt tear down all images?' (M. Cohen, *Lewis Carroll*, 1995, 251). However, Gladstone was returned instead for South Lancashire, where he launched his candidacy on 18 July in Manchester's Free Trade Hall, famously announcing: 'At last, my friends, I am come among you "unmuzzled"' (Morley, 2.146). In the three-member, notoriously protestant constituency he scraped in, third in the poll behind two tories. When John Russell succeeded Palmerston on the latter's death in October 1865, just after a great general election victory, Gladstone worked with the new prime minister on a Reform Bill intended to produce a modest extension of the urban electorate by enfranchising, Gladstone intended, artisans of probity who would further the cause of retrenchment and broaden the base of anti-militarism in the Commons. The bill failed in 1866 amid extensive division and recrimination in the Liberal Party, part of which wanted more than Gladstone and Russell offered, and a larger part less; redistribution of seats was, controversially, to be separately dealt with. Gladstone was leader of the house as well as chancellor of the exchequer and bore the brunt of the unpopularity caused by the bill's failure. The government resigned following its defeat on 18 June 1866 and his long chancellorship thus ended almost as bathetically as that of 1852–5.

Steps to the premiership, 1866–1868 Gladstone's unpopularity among Westminster Liberals was probably not reflected in the country, where, strongly supported by the *Daily Telegraph*, which he sedulously briefed, he was becoming known as 'The People's William' (the phrase was its editor's, Levy Lawson). This was despite the fact that until 1870 he described himself in *Dod's Parliamentary Companion* as a 'liberal conservative'. The Gladstones wintered in Rome in 1866–7, where he had an important audience with Pope Pius IX on 22 October 1866.

On his return, Gladstone was the Liberal Party's opposition leader in the Commons (the only other time he was in this position was in 1886–92) against the Reform Bill proposed by the minority tory government in 1867. The Derby–Disraeli Reform Bill initially trapped Gladstone, as Disraeli had intended. Accustomed to instigating rather than opposing legislation, and with the Liberals still divided on franchise reform, Gladstone failed to carry his party with him when he moved an amendment on rating, the government surviving by 310 votes to 289. He thought it 'A smash perhaps without example' (Gladstone, *Diaries*, 12 April 1867) and considered resigning the party leadership in the Commons. He did not resign, though further defeats followed and he felt unable to speak on the third reading of the bill for fear of provoking a reaction from his own side. The 1867 Reform Act in fact liberated Gladstone in the longer term: it created the extended but still limited electorate within which his later career flourished.

Gladstone quickly escaped from the imbroglio of 1867. While the minority government was entangled in the complexities of redistribution and Irish and Scottish reform, Gladstone opened an attack from a different angle, encouraged by Lord Russell's statement at Christmas 1867 that he would not again take office, and thus, despite the difficulties, leaving the way clear for Gladstone if he could show a capacity to lead the party. In February 1868, just as Disraeli succeeded Derby as prime minister, Gladstone moved and carried a bill to abolish compulsory church rates, an issue which consolidated radicals, libertarians, nonconformists, and those quite numerous Anglicans keen to abandon undefendable outposts of what had come to be seen as privilege. He followed this by carrying with a majority of sixty-five votes the first of three resolutions to abolish the Anglican establishment in Ireland, and then by passing a suspensory bill through the Commons (in 1866 he had favoured action over Irish land rather than the church). The Liberal Party, so fractured over parliamentary reform, reunited over changes in church–state relations as the majority party and, with Gladstone in the Commons often seeming more the prime minister than the leader of the opposition, the party under his leadership faced the general election on the new franchise with confidence and enthusiasm.

Gladstone defended what seemed to some a *bouleversement* on Irish establishment in *A Chapter of Autobiography*, published just after the 1868 election. He claimed in that pamphlet a long-term, private, and principled hostility to Irish disestablishment dating from his political self-reorientation in the mid- and late 1840s. He came to see his decision publicly to advocate Irish disestablishment as an example of 'a striking gift' endowed on him by Providence, which enabled him to identify a question whose moment for public discussion and action had come. This quality occasioned Henry Labouchere's famous *mot*: he 'did not object to the old man always having a card up his sleeve, but he did object to his insinuating that the Almighty had placed it there' (Lord Curzon, *Parliamentary Eloquence*, 1913, 25).

The Liberals won the general election in November–December 1868 with a majority of 112. Gladstone was, as anticipated, defeated in South-West Lancashire, largely by a powerful anti-popery reaction to the proposal for Irish disestablishment, but he had already been returned for Greenwich. On 1 December, while tree-felling with Evelyn Ashley in Hawarden Park, he was brought a telegram from the queen announcing the impending arrival of her secretary with her commission to form a government. Gladstone read the telegram and continued tree-felling. A few minutes later, he stopped, 'looked up, and with deep earnestness in his voice, and great intensity in his face, exclaimed: "My mission is to pacify Ireland." He then resumed his task, and never said another word till the tree was down' (Ashley's obituary of Gladstone, quoted in Matthew, *Gladstone, 1809–1874*, 147). His means of pacification was to be primarily legislative: he intended to show that there was no reasonable Irish demand which the Westminster parliament could not fulfil.

On 3 December 1868 Gladstone kissed hands as first lord of the Treasury and prime minister for the first (and he expected the last) time. He was also by convention leader of the House of Commons. A distinctive characteristic of all his premierships was quickly apparent: Gladstone led his government from the front by taking personal responsibility for bills which would usually be seen as departmental. He believed that 'big bills', as he called them, kept the party together and, more generally, legitimized parliament and its procedures to the nation.

In 1869 he played the chief part in drawing up the Irish Church Bill, a measure bristling with technical complexities which could easily go wrong, for the bill disendowed as well as disestablished the Anglican church in Ireland. He declined to use the Church of Ireland's property to fund the concurrent endowment of all churches in Ireland, the proceeds (after various existing interests had been provided for) instead going to a poor relief fund. He got the bill through the cabinet early in February 1869 and through the Commons in the spring with majorities of over 100. The tories in the Lords resisted the bill, forcing a compromise on the financial terms but without rejecting it in principle. Exhausted by his efforts, Gladstone left the final negotiations to Lord Granville, who from the 1860s to the 1880s eased Gladstone's way in many a difficulty with the Lords and the court. Just as Disraeli's 1867 Reform Bill aided Gladstone long term, so Irish establishment was, ironically, a convenience to English tory establishmentarians. Disestablishment in Ireland removed a major religious and civil grievance of Irish Roman Catholics and Presbyterians.

Disestablishment was followed by an Irish Land Bill in 1870 prepared from August 1869, in which Gladstone took an equally prominent role. His hope was to use the Ulster tradition of tenant right as a way of recognizing customary rather than contractual land relationships in Ireland generally, and thus establishing a more settled set of rural relationships. In approaching the land question in this way he acknowledged the importance of a sense of custom and history in social relationships, something of a shift from the a-temporal approach of free-market contract. Opposed by the whigs in the cabinet Gladstone backtracked, and the bill as published offered tenant right for Ulster, compensation for disturbance for the rest of Ireland. The fact of the passing of the bill was important, but its complexity bewildered as much as appealed; it alarmed the propertied classes but did not gain the sort of enthusiastic Irish response of the church bill a year earlier.

1870 also saw Gladstone in dispute with sections of his party on the religious provisions of the Elementary Education Bill, whose drafting by Earl de Grey and W. E. Forster he commissioned in October 1869. From the start Gladstone favoured the maintenance of the existing church schools, with the state providing ancillary board schools; though a fateful decision for English education, the retention of church schools was necessary if a bill was to pass the Lords. But, as with concurrent endowment, he bitterly opposed a state-funded compromise on the teaching of religious truth in the classroom. He preferred state provision of secular teaching, and the funding of religious teaching by the various churches. The Cowper-Temple amendment, with its ill-defined compromise providing for latitudinarian religious instruction in all schools, was thus a major disappointment for Gladstone, though its implications were not immediately publicly apparent. Even so, the passing of the act was notable; no government since the 1832 Reform Bill had succeeded in carrying a thoroughgoing reform of English education. The bill was matched with a statute passed for Scotland in 1872.

Foreign policy of the first government Gladstone believed in a system of states relating to each other through diplomacy and in the context of congresses: he did not, as did some free-traders such as Richard Cobden, see such arrangements as unnatural, second-best, or corrupt. In

1869 he began to encourage the idea of international arbitration as a means of settling the claim of the United States for damages caused during the civil war to Northern shipping by the Southern gunboat the *Alabama*, built on the Mersey and permitted by the British government to be sold to the Confederacy. That Hamilton Fish, the American secretary of state, proposed as recompense the annexation of Canada to the USA, showed the degree of American injury. Gladstone encouraged his foreign secretaries Lord Clarendon and Lord Granville (who succeeded Clarendon on the latter's death in June 1870) towards arbitration, the preliminary treaty of Washington being signed in 1871. Gladstone cut through delays caused by the extent of new American claims, by directly and personally negotiating with Robert Schenck, the American minister in London from 1872, and the case went forward to successful arbitration at Geneva, Britain paying out after various modifications £3,200,000 in 1873. Gladstone's huge exculpatory letter to Schenck—for the whole episode was to an extent an atonement for his speech of 1862—was published in *Harper's New Monthly Magazine* in 1876.

Strong political will and money enabled Gladstone to make a fresh start to Anglo-American relations. Continental Europe was less straightforward. Gladstone did not oppose German unification, indeed he saw the naturalness of the union of 'our Teutonic cousins'. He recognized the role of military and naval force in right circumstances. In 1869–70 the 'rightness' of both French and German action was, as Bismarck intended, peculiarly difficult to gauge. Gladstone and his cabinet initiated various moves to maintain European peace in June–July 1870 but, beyond Gladstone's preparation of an expeditionary force of 30,000 men to defend Belgian neutrality, made no attempt to go beyond diplomatic means of influence. He arranged a treaty, finally signed on 9 August 1870, with France and Prussia by which Britain would co-operate with either if the other invaded Belgium. His statement on it to the Commons on 8 August 1870 was the basis for Britain's declaration of war in August 1914. He took the extraordinary step of writing an anonymous article 'Germany, France, and England', in the *Edinburgh Review* (October 1870), asserting the primacy of international law and right; his authorship was quickly revealed. He strongly opposed Germany's annexation of Alsace-Lorraine, but was prevented by his cabinet on 30 September from organizing a campaign by neutral European states against annexation by mere military force and without a plebiscite. Almost as great a blow against 'civic individuality', Gladstone thought, was the declaration of papal infallibility made at the Vatican Council of 1870, whose proceedings were brought to a rapid conclusion as French troops maintaining the integrity of the Vatican state were withdrawn to fight at home and the Italian army occupied the city. Gladstone energetically encouraged European action to prevent the declaration, but without success, the leader of 'the madmen of the Council', as he dubbed the ultramontanists, being his former close friend H. E. Manning. Gladstone's dismay at the declaration was suppressed but not forgotten, as we shall see. However, he provided a warship to rescue the pope should he have to flee Rome.

Domestic affairs: the army and the court Gladstone and his cabinet pressed forward, though not perhaps as energetically as they might, on the question of meritocratic and egalitarian reform. In 1870 open competition by examination for entrance to the civil service, begun in 1854, was achieved for all departments except the Foreign Office; university religious tests were largely abolished in 1871; and in 1872 (after earlier rejections by the Lords) voting by ballot throughout the United Kingdom was established, though Gladstone was personally cautious about both the abolition of tests and the introduction of the ballot. Following the Franco-Prussian War, he advocated 'complete and definite' reform of the British, Indian, and colonial army and militia, but Cardwell's Army Regulation Bill of 1871, abolishing promotion by purchase, was as far as Gladstone could get the court and the War Office to go. The bill was bitterly opposed, and wrecked the government's programme in the Commons. Gladstone cut the knot by a royal warrant which withdrew the exceptions to an act of 1809 by which almost all commissions were purchased; officers thus risked losing the compensation which the 1871 bill offered and it was then quickly passed. Gladstone's action seemed high-handed, even bullying, and, though the abolition of purchase was quickly recognized as desirable, he confirmed the enmity towards Liberalism of the majority of the officer class.

The episode reflected a growing distrust between Gladstone and the court. Quite a close friend of Victoria and Albert (especially the latter) in the 1850s, in his first government Gladstone found himself in frequent dispute with the queen. His plan, persistently proposed, to employ the prince of Wales in Ireland was rejected by Victoria, who also objected to some of the choices for membership of his cabinet. Gladstone was determined to counter incipient republicanism within the Liberal Party (and not least in his own constituency of Greenwich) by getting the near-reclusive Victoria to resume official duties. He had little success, except in persuading her to attend the service of thanksgiving at St Paul's in 1871 for the recovery of the prince of Wales from typhoid. The queen resented Gladstone's tone, which she found hectoring but which he intended as persuasion by exhaustive argument. 'He speaks to me as if I was a public meeting' was the queen's famous comment, probably enunciated at this time (reported in G. W. E. Russell, *Collections and Recollections*, 1898, chap. 14), Russell noting that Gladstone paid 'to everyone, and not least to ladies, the compliment of assuming they are on his own intellectual level'.

Governmental disarray and defeat, 1872–1874 By the end of 1872 the government was faltering. Bruce's bold Licensing Bill of 1871—the government's response to considerable pressure for temperance reform within the Liberal Party and to a longer-term bipartisan requirement—had to be dropped, for the Liberals were split between reformers and abolitionists. Bruce's more modest proposal of 1872 was enacted, infuriating the drink trade without satisfying the reformers. From 1871 the drink trade, hitherto by no means anti-Liberal, saw a Liberal victory as dangerous. Even topics that seemed disposed of, such as the trade union legislation of 1871, reappeared, the latter in the gas stokers' judgment of December 1872 and the failure quickly to counter it, which earned the Liberals extensive trade union hostility. A series of small episodes gave the opposition opportunity to exploit the prime minister's reputation for sharp practice in the use of detail ('Jesuitical' was a frequent tory epithet). Gladstone in December 1871 appointed William Wigan *Harvey (1810–1883), an Eton contemporary who had gone to King's College, Cambridge, to the crown living of Ewelme, whose incumbent had to be an Oxford MA (Harvey became one by incorporation before being appointed); Gladstone was accused of evading the spirit of the act and the Commons debated the affair on 14 March 1872. Gladstone was also accused of evasion when he appointed his attorney-general, Robert Porrett *Collier (1817–1886), to a vacancy on the judicial committee of the privy council which had to be held by a former judge. Collier was made a judge and became an ex-judge in only three days, a manoeuvre which only just escaped condemnation in debates in both houses in February 1872. Disraeli's speech in Manchester on 3 April 1872 contained one of the great similes of political invective, as prophetic of his own fate as it was devastating about the Liberal front bench:

> Ministers reminded me of one of those marine landscapes not very unusual on the coasts of South America. You behold a range of exhausted volcanoes. Not a flame flickers on a single pallid crest. But the situation is still dangerous. There are occasional earthquakes, and ever and anon the dark rumbling of the sea. (W. F. Monypenny and G. E. Buckle, *The Life of Benjamin Disraeli*, 1910–20, 5.191)

In 1873 the third of Gladstone's Irish bills, a bill to reform Irish universities by broadening the basis of Roman Catholic attendance, was opposed both by Liberal secularists such as Henry Fawcett and by many of the Irish MPs, encouraged by the Roman Catholic bishops. Like many of the Liberal government's proposals, it did too much for some and too little for others. On 11 March 1873 the bill, which Gladstone had made a point of asserting as a measure of government confidence, was defeated by three votes. An Irish demand had not been adequately met by the Westminster parliament. He offered his resignation to the queen on 13 March, who accepted it and summoned Disraeli. The latter's policy was to let the Liberals swing in the wind; he coolly declined to form yet another tory minority government (this was the last occasion in British politics on which the opposition has declined office when it was offered). Gladstone carried on, resuming office on 16 March (as seals were not returned, his period of office is treated as uninterrupted). The government was further weakened by a variety of sleazy scandals in the summer of 1873.

Even Liberal finance came adrift and on 9 August 1873 Gladstone replaced Robert Lowe and became his own chancellor of the exchequer. This provoked a further embarrassing episode—a prolonged and unresolved dispute as to whether he had vacated his seat by taking office, in which case he would have to be re-elected at a by-election. Gladstone sought to regain the political initiative by a daring and dramatic financial plan: 'abolition of Income Tax and Sugar Duties with partial compensation from Spirits and Death Duties. This *only* might give a chance' (Matthew, *Gladstone, 1809–1874*, 220). The exchequer's surpluses resulting from the inflationary boom of the early 1870s opened a unique window, to be propped open by some new property tax. Gladstone intended income tax abolition to consolidate retrenchment, which he thought the income tax endangered by its quick and certain revenues. To balance the books for income tax abolition, he needed some defence savings, which the army and navy cabinet ministers would not yield. He therefore, on 21 January 1874, wrote to the queen requesting a dissolution, informing his cabinet of this two days later. The row with the defence departments being secret, many assumed Gladstone was escaping from the prospect of having to fight a by-election in Greenwich. It was the first dissolution in the recess without prior announcement since 1780. His manifesto published on 24 January revealed his financial plan, Disraeli immediately responding by supporting income tax abolition.

The Liberals lost the general election after a short campaign in which Gladstone made only three speeches. Gladstone held his Greenwich seat but came second in the poll behind a tory, a brewer, the other Liberal candidate being defeated. 'We have been borne down in a torrent of gin and beer', Gladstone wrote to his brother Robertson on 6 February, in a phrase that later became famous; 'Next to this', he added, 'has been the action of the Education Act of 1870, and the subsequent controversies' (Morley, 2.495). On 17 February 1874 he resigned without meeting parliament, the first leader of the party of progress to lose a general election since 1841, and the first since that year to cede office to a majority tory government. Like 1855 and 1866 the early months of 1874 were a curious conclusion to a notable start.

Gladstone in 1874–1875 Whatever the causes of Liberal defeat in 1874—and they ranged from Gladstone's impetuous dissolution and personal unpopularity through immediate issues such as drink and education to much wider, long-term shifts in British voting patterns—he himself felt liberated, but estranged from his party and politically drained. He had been in high office almost continually since 1859 and he had led his government in as physically demanding a way as could be imagined, for as well as being prime minister and chancellor of the exchequer he was leader of the Commons and thus responsible for the details and day-to-day business of the welter of Liberal legislation which his approach to party management encouraged.

Gladstone was sixty-four when he startled the ex-cabinet by telling it on 16 February 1874 that he would 'no longer retain the leadership of the liberal party, nor resume it, unless the party had settled its difficulties', a resignation publicly confirmed in December 1874 (Gladstone, *Diaries*, 16 Feb 1874). It would be wrong to suggest, however, that Gladstone was in any sense played out. He was fit, spare, and sprightly. He stood 5 feet 10½ inches and had an abnormally large head, with eagle-like eyes. He had accidentally shot off his left forefinger while shooting in September 1842 and always wore a fingerstall. A trim 11 stone 11 pounds, he ate and drank moderately, and did not smoke. Remarkable physical resilience made him, despite his occasional illnesses (some of them diplomatic), one of the fittest of prime ministers. Tree-felling, begun in 1852 and maintained until 1891, was a demanding and invigorating activity; it kept him fit and spry. In September 1873 he walked 33 miles in the rain through the Cairngorm mountains from Balmoral to Kingussie (a dramatic escape from the *longeurs* of court attendance!).

His relentless energy meant that the life of 'mental repose' which Gladstone planned for himself was never likely to be sufficient, sincerely though the retirement of 1874 was intended. Restlessness, interest, and perhaps something more, had led Gladstone into an *amitié curieuse* with an ex-courtesan, Laura *Thistlethwayte, whom he had met, probably through the duke of Newcastle, in 1865. Unlike the prostitutes whom Gladstone energetically continued throughout his premiership to attempt to redeem, Laura Thistlethwayte was already saved from sin and was converted. Gladstone was at first intrigued and soon obsessed with her tale. In 1869 and 1870, especially, he was constantly in touch, by letter and visits, even visiting her at her home near Boveridge in December 1869. His intense letters to her are printed as appendices to volumes 7 and 13 of *The Gladstone Diaries*. This was in effect a platonic extra-marital affair, Catherine Gladstone knowing of Mrs Thistlethwayte but not meeting her until 1887. By 1874 the most intense phase of their relationship had passed, and the repose Gladstone sought was perhaps personal as well as political. On the third finger of his right hand he often wore a ring given him by Laura Thistlethwayte (shown in many of his later portraits).

Repose was not to last long. The Gladstones prepared to sell their London house, 11 Carlton House Terrace, and moved wholly to Hawarden, where William had built a study–library known as the Temple of Peace; it had two desks, one for Homeric and one for other work. Retirement did not prevent him during 1874 from intervening by speech and pen on the Scottish Church Patronage Bill and from vigorously opposing Archbishop Tait's anti-ritualist Public Worship Regulation Bill.

In September 1874 Gladstone visited in Bavaria his old friend J. J. I. von Döllinger, excommunicated for opposition to papal infallibility. Papal infallibility had encouraged Gladstone, like many high Anglicans at that time, to closer association with other apostolical churches such as the Old Catholics (with which Döllinger was associated) and the various Orthodox churches: Gladstone had contacts in both the Greek and the Russian varieties. Incensed by Rome's handling of Döllinger, Gladstone added to the proof of his article 'Ritualism and ritual' in the *Contemporary Review* (October 1874), a stinging attack on British Roman Catholics for their supine reaction to the Vatican decrees, and followed it up by a pamphlet, *The Vatican Decrees in their Bearing on Civil Allegiance: a Political Expostulation*, published in November 1874. The pamphlet, which sold over 100,000 copies, attacked the implications of the infallible rulings of a universalist pope for the civil allegiance of British citizens. It elicited replies from H. E. Manning, J. H. Newman, and many others, to which Gladstone replied in *Vaticanism: an Answer to 'Reproofs and Replies'* (1875).

Return to political action, 1876–1880 In February 1876, at the same time as attacking Disraeli's purchase of the Suez Canal shares and the Royal Titles Bill which made the queen empress of India, Gladstone bought 73 Harley Street, London, a harbinger of political return. Deep in Homeric and ecumenical theological studies and publications at Hawarden in the summer of 1876, he was a little slow to see the full implications of the rising protest against Turkish massacres of Orthodox Christians in the Balkans, but on 6 September 1876 he published the most famous of his pamphlets, *The Bulgarian Horrors and the Question of the East*, whose call for Turkish withdrawal 'bag and baggage' quickly entered the language (the pamphlet was translated into Russian by K. P. Pobedonostsev, later the fervent apologist for tsarist rule). As Lord Derby, the foreign secretary, immediately noticed, Gladstone's vehement invective in fact had a tame conclusion, a 'simple recommendation of autonomy for the disturbed provinces' (*A Selection from the Diaries of Edward Henry Stanley … between September 1869 and March 1878*, ed. J. R. Vincent, CS, 5th ser., 4, 1994, 324). A speech at Blackheath on 9 September, a tour of the north-east, and further meetings and publications made Gladstone the leader of a popular front of moral outrage. The man who had been a special constable during the Chartist meeting in 1848 was now the chief speaker at huge gatherings attempting to change government policy. Granville and Hartington, leaders of the party in the Lords and Commons respectively, tried to carry on the normal business of opposition while Gladstone developed a new form of evangelical mass politics. Co-operation with the party in the Commons was difficult, for moderate Liberals disapproved of Gladstone's policy on the Eastern question and disliked his extra-parliamentary activities. When on 7 May 1877 he gave notice to the house of five resolutions on the Eastern question, moderate Liberal MPs rebelled, and only the first resolution was moved.

Gladstone addressed the inaugural meeting of the National Liberal Federation (NLF) in Birmingham in May 1877 but the politics he was developing was based much more on a relationship between a charismatic oratorical leader and the extended electorate than on the caucus organization which Joseph Chamberlain's NLF represented. The tory response to the Gladstonian campaign on the Eastern question was bitter, especially in London, where the Gladstones' windows in Harley Street were broken by a Jingo mob on a Sunday evening; 'This is not very sabbatical' was Gladstone's comment (Gladstone, *Diaries*, 24 Feb 1878). The hostility earlier evident towards Gladstone in military circles became explicit, the duke of Cambridge (the commander-in-chief) now refusing to shake his hand on meeting. What began as a campaign on a particular question of Eastern policy broadened into a personalized and general indictment of 'Beaconsfieldism', carried out in a remarkable series of journal articles (especially 'Aggression on Egypt and freedom in the East', 'The peace to come', 'The paths of honour and of shame', and 'England's mission', published in the *Nineteenth Century* in 1877 and 1878). These attacked imperialism and warned of the dangers of a bloated empire with worldwide responsibilities which in the long run would become unsustainable.

From 17 October to 12 November 1877 Gladstone made his only substantial visit to Ireland (he had planned one in 1845, and made a very brief stop, during a sea voyage, on 29 August 1880). Staying with wealthy Anglo-Irish families in co. Wicklow, he was prevented from visiting the west—'But not enough of *Ireland*', he noted (Gladstone, *Diaries*, 20 Oct 1877); but he visited Maynooth and received the freedom of Dublin on 7 November.

A growing anti-metropolitanism was reflected in Gladstone's announcement in March 1878 that he would not again stand for Greenwich—a decision long contemplated. Negotiations with the Liberals of Midlothian, eased by Lord Rosebery and by Gladstone's comfortable victory in an election for the lord rectorship of Glasgow University in November 1877, led to a decision in January 1879 to contest the tory seat of Midlothian (whose incumbent, Lord Dalkeith, was son of Gladstone's colleague in 1841–5, the duke of Buccleuch). He had been much in the city as first lord rector of Edinburgh University in 1859–65.

In 1879 and 1880 Gladstone's Midlothian campaigns captured the seat and astonished the political world. (It was from them that Max Weber derived his analysis of the charismatic in popular politics: Weber saw 'Ein cäsaristisch-plebiszitäres Element' in Gladstone's behaviour (Matthew, *Gladstone, 1875–1898*, 50)). In the 1879 campaign he noted giving thirty substantial speeches, heard, he estimated, by 86,930 persons, and in the 1880 campaign, eighteen speeches. The verbatim reporting of Gladstone's speeches ensured that they were available to every newspaper-reading household the next morning. The Midlothian campaigns were thus campaigns both for and from the constituency. The constituency itself was a rather corrupt country seat with proportionately far fewer electors than the new borough seats: Buccleuch made generous creations of faggot votes, which the Liberals matched. Gladstone defeated Dalkeith on 5 April 1880 by 1579 votes to 1368 (just the margin his advisers had forecast eighteen months earlier). He was also elected for Leeds, topping the poll with 24,622 votes (his son Herbert was unopposed at its subsequent by-election).

Gladstone's Midlothian speeches attempted to articulate principles of foreign policy as well as a critique of Beaconsfieldism. They engaged popular political opinion in a wide range of complex questions and thus, in Gladstone's view, restored a harmony between popular opinion and the Commons which Disraeli had endangered. But much propertied opinion took alarm: 'In a word, everything is overdone' remarked *The Times* (29 Nov 1879), a view shared not only by the tories but also by a proportion of the Liberal intelligentsia.

The queen unsuccessfully sought to avoid the obvious consequence of the election: another Gladstonian premiership. He responded by requiring the two party leaders whom she had consulted—Granville and Hartington—to agree that they had 'unitedly advised the Sovereign that it was most for the public advantage to send for me' (Matthew, *Gladstone, 1875–1898*, 101). This they did. Gladstone thus kissed hands on 23 April 1880 with the whigs acknowledging his supremacy and the public good of his premiership. Gladstone had become something of a loose cannon in the Liberal Party. In some respects he was an essential link between factions within it which were otherwise irreconcilable. But he had also begun the process by which Liberalism and Gladstonianism became fused into a political movement, which could be seen both as awkwardly over-personalized and as a unique and beneficent political crusade whose character derived from one person's remarkable capacity to absorb and resolve within himself the self-contradictions of the Liberal movement.

The second government, 1880–1885 The Midlothian campaigns gave Gladstone a strong start to his second government. Yet from the beginning he stressed the short-term character of his leadership of it. He had protested since 1876 that his return to politics was temporary: once the detritus of Beaconsfieldism—the problems of the Near East, Afghanistan, South Africa, the national finances—had been swept up, he would retire from the premiership and from the chancellorship of the exchequer (which office he took up in 1880). Gladstone seriously considered so acting in the autumn of 1881, in the summer of 1882, in 1883, and in the spring of 1885; but on each occasion outstanding problems, and the protests of his colleagues, obliged him, he felt, to remain in office. His personal position was thus the opposite of a normal politician's: he stayed in office as the servant of events and of his colleagues. The latter had little option but to want him to soldier on, for he had made the party unleadable during his active lifetime save by himself, and the whigs, despite their complaints at aspects of his politics and policies, looked to him for protection against the radicals. The result was a rather unsettled cabinet. But the achievements of the 1880 government, though falling short of the sweeping expectations of some radicals, were more substantial than is often allowed. In foreign and colonial matters, however, the 1880–85 cabinet required Gladstone with striking frequency to agree to policies which he had initially opposed. He had a non-expansionist view of empire, approving of the empire of settlement, but very cautious about any further expansion of it, and opposing quite consistently the view that Britain needed to occupy non-settlement territories to keep other European powers out. On the other hand, his long experience of cabinet government accustomed him to accept cabinet responsibility for frequent wars, interventions, and occupations, and to defend them vigorously in the Commons. Unlike

John Bright, the policy changes imposed upon him never, in his first and second governments, made him think of resignation. Moreover, unlike Bright, Gladstone was by no means opposed to using foreign policy for interventionist purposes, and he attempted to articulate principles on which such intervention might be undertaken.

Foreign and colonial policy, 1880–1885 Gladstone's six principles of correct international behaviour, based on nations reconciling differences through the Concert system, avoiding secret alliances ('needless and entangling alliances'), and acknowledging the 'equal rights of all nations', were stated in Midlothian on 27 November 1879. They seemed of general application, but were directed 'especially to the Christian nations of the world'. But it was in the Islamic area of the Near and Middle East that Gladstone's chief difficulties lay. The removal of Beaconsfield's government by no means meant the end of foreign and imperial problems. The government had considerable success in establishing sufficient stability in Afghanistan. Negotiations to partition it were ended and internal order secured. 'Mervousness' (the duke of Argyll's word for anti-Russianists' anxieties) was discounted and Russia was allowed to advance through Merv up to the Afghan border but no further: stopping her there led to the Panjdeh incident of 1885 and the threat of war.

Much less straightforward was the crisis in the Near East. Gladstone in opposition had criticized Turkish brutality, but he had always stopped short of demanding a dissolution of the Ottoman empire. He resolutely used the threat of force to end disputes over the Montenegrin frontier in the autumn of 1880. In Egypt the nationalist movement led by Arabi Pasha initially appealed to him. Encouraged by Wilfrid Scawen Blunt he wrote: '"Egypt for the Egyptians" is the sentiment to which I should wish to give scope: and could it prevail it would I think be the best, the only good solution of the "Egyptian question"' (letter to Granville, 4 Jan 1882, Ramm, *Political Correspondence … 1876–1886*, 1.326). But in 1882 Gladstone abandoned this view and came to see Egyptian nationalization as a dangerous rather than a stabilizing force in Egyptian affairs. Riots in Alexandria on 11 June 1882 led to the city's bombardment by the British fleet. Gladstone and Granville tried to earn French support for a dual intervention on behalf of the Concert of Europe. When this failed, Gladstone reluctantly agreed with the rest of his cabinet, of whom all—save John Bright, who resigned—were more eager than Gladstone for action to invade Egypt. By September 1882 the country was in British hands, and Gladstone was making the first of the many British attempts between 1882 and 1918 to disengage. Gladstone turned harshly against Arabi, on whom he now heaped blame, and had him imprisoned in Ceylon. From late in 1882 until the spring of 1885, the settlement of Egypt, both politically and financially, was a central preoccupation: 'the Egyptian flood comes on us again and again, like the sea on the host of Pharaoh', Gladstone wrote in January 1885 (Matthew, *Gladstone, 1875–1898*, 141). Regularization was achieved in March 1885, just before the government fell. Egyptians found it hard to see how Gladstone's fifth principle—that the 'foreign policy of England should always be inspired by the love of freedom'—had been applied to them.

An unanticipated consequence of the invasion of Egypt was responsibility for the Sudan, where a rising against the khedive, the nominal authority, was being led by *Muhammad Ahmad, the Mahdi. The sending of Charles George *Gordon to evacuate the Sudan was unwisely left by Gladstone to his colleagues departmentally responsible—Hartington, Northbrook, and Granville—and indeed Gladstone warned that Gordon would be difficult to handle. But it was Gladstone who bore the public obloquy of the Gordon débâcle. He delayed agreeing to a relief expedition, and especially one mounted by means of a railway constructed from Suakin on the Red sea, because he feared a strong British military presence would lead, as in 1885 it very nearly did, to permanent occupation rather than withdrawal. Moreover, it was of the Mahdists that Gladstone enunciated one of his most famous sayings: 'Yes; these people are struggling to be free; and they are struggling rightly to be free' (*Hansard* 3, 288, 12 May 1884, col. 55).

Gladstone did not handle the dénouement of the fall of Khartoum and Gordon's probable death in 1885 sensitively, and he survived a censure motion on 27 February 1885 by only fourteen votes. Gladstone's failure to rescue the maverick and flagrantly disobedient Gordon entered British folk memory and M. O. G. (Murderer of Gordon) became the tory response to the Liberals' G. O. M. (Grand Old Man), the acronym coined by Henry Labouchere in April 1881.

In the rest of Africa, likewise, Gladstone's objective was to avoid imperial expansion. He was successful in this in east Africa, but elsewhere found himself superintending significant British expansion. In southern Africa (and in the Pacific) he favoured a German presence, partly as he had no objection to other nations' colonial enterprises, partly because he saw a German presence as a useful way of keeping increasingly truculent white colonists in order. British–Boer relations were at a critical stage when he took office. Gladstone initially hoped to maintain the confederate objective of the outgoing tory government; this plan collapsed in June 1880 and Bartle Frere, the governor, with whom Gladstone was already publicly at odds, was recalled. The Transvaal declared its secession and began an armed rebellion. On 27 February 1881 news reached London of the death of Sir George Colley and ninety-two British troops at Majuba Hill ('Sad Sad news from South Africa: is it the Hand of Judgment?', Gladstone noted; Gladstone, *Diaries*, 28 Feb 1881); this was a public relations disaster, though the military consequences were quickly quashed, and an accommodation reached by the convention of Pretoria in August 1881 (later renegotiated by the convention of London in 1884). Gladstone was unable to prevent his cabinet dispatching Sir Charles Warren's expedition to declare a protectorate over Bechuanaland in 1884.

In foreign and imperial policy for 1880 to 1885, Gladstone confirmed the forecast that he had made in opposition before 1880, that Britain was being drawn into ever wider imperial responsibilities with long-term strategic and economic consequences whose future form and cost could only be guessed at. These obligations, in his view, were a deflection from Britain's true mission and interest, which was the nurturing of the domestic economic base and of a self-sufficient, settled empire. He deplored all these further responsibilities, but, even as prime minister, he found he could do no more than occasionally slow their growth.

Aspects of domestic policy: the exchequer and the Bradlaugh affair Unlike 1868, Gladstone became prime minister in 1880 with no great programme of legislative reform, though various Liberal groups had different ideas about how the large parliamentary majority should be used, and there was a general assumption, shared by Gladstone, that local government legislation was necessary and that the county franchise would need reform towards the end of the parliament. His fury against 'Beaconsfieldism' produced no general constitutional reform proposals to prevent its repetition. As his own chancellor of the exchequer, Gladstone had immediate departmental obligations: these he discharged effectively if fairly conservatively. In 1880 he successfully abolished the malt tax, a long-standing farming grievance, the removal of which was a technically complicated operation. In 1881 he increased spirits duties, reformed the probate and legacy duties, and lowered income tax. In 1882, in his final budget, he ironically had to increase income tax; on 12 December 1882, under severe strain and suffering from insomnia, he ceded the chancellorship to H. C. E. Childers.

The parliament opened with an unusual controversy, in May 1880, as the secularist Charles Bradlaugh claimed the right to make an affirmation rather than to swear the oath of allegiance, and when the former was not permitted, to take the oath itself. Gladstone, as leader of the house, was at once involved in what became a prolonged dispute of the sort of theological church–state wrangling which Victorians of all forms of belief especially valued. Gladstone's own position was simple and consistent: he intensely deplored Bradlaugh's atheism and its public consequences, but parliament was no longer legally an exclusively Christian assembly; it was not for the Commons to judge whether those swearing the oath were sincere or not; it was not possible to draw distinctions between pantheists and atheists; if Bradlaugh had broken the law, that was a matter for the law courts. This position was not popular with the opposition and despite the introduction of several Affirmation bills and Bradlaugh's victory in several by-elections, the matter was resolved only in January 1886, when the new speaker (A. W. Peel), proposed by Gladstone after winning the general election, took Gladstone's position, ignored the previous debates and resolutions, and allowed Bradlaugh to take the oath. Gladstone was active in 1891 in getting the original resolution of June 1880 repealed as Bradlaugh lay dying. Gladstone's Liberalism sometimes seems ambivalent; on no question was his position more classically Liberal than on the Bradlaugh affair.

Ireland, 1880–1882 Gladstone in 1880 was surprised to find himself dealing with a major crisis of public and social order in Ireland as the Land League's campaign spread rapidly. Here, as in 1868–74, he intervened firmly, although his Irish secretary, W. E. *Forster, was a stronger character than Chichester Fortescue had been in the earlier government. Gladstone at once set up, in June 1880, the Bessborough royal commission to inquire into the working of the 1870 Land Act. The tories in the House of Lords threw out the government's Compensation for Disturbance Bill in August 1880. On 30 September 1880 Parnell and the other home-rule MPs were imprisoned, their prosecutions failing in January 1881. As the home-rule and Land League movement burgeoned, Gladstone's initial reaction was to meet it by some form of local government devolution, for he always believed that self-responsibility was the key to social and political order. However, the exigencies of the land crisis in Ireland persuaded him to agree with Forster that another Land Act was needed to achieve social order more quickly than self-government could do. The league's objective of tenant right and the three Fs (fair rent, fixity of tenure, and free sale) was profoundly conservative, however revolutionary its methods.

The Irish Land Bill of 1881, hammered out in cabinet over the winter of 1880–81, readjusted social and financial relationships by court arbitrations. But it left the landowner still technically owning the land: Gladstone disliked government-financed programmes of land purchase. The duke of Argyll resigned from the government on 31 March 1881, but the bill passed with less whiggish outrage than might have been expected, though its passage in the Commons was a major battle, with Gladstone handling most of the prolonged committee stage. The bill successfully undercut the league and Gladstone drove home his advantage by goading Parnell, telling him in a great speech in Leeds on 7 October 1881 that 'the resources of civilization are not yet exhausted' (Matthew, *Gladstone, 1875–1898*, 197). Parnell was incarcerated in Kilmainham gaol on 12 October and the Land League proscribed on 20 October. Thus far Gladstone had balanced various forms of conciliation with a determined use of state force. With the league broken, he was intent on a longer-term political reconciliation. Parnell was to be the focus of constitutionalism in Irish politics, and was released on 6 May 1882 after what became called the Kilmainham treaty (though Gladstone's cabinet minute of 1 May read: 'There has been *no* negotiation. But we have obtained information. The moment is golden' (Gladstone, *Diaries*, 1 May 1882)). Gladstone refused to be deflected by the Phoenix Park murders on 6 May, and an Arrears Bill was passed as planned. Later in May, Katharine O'Shea [*see* Parnell, Katharine] began to act as go-between for Gladstone and her lover, Parnell.

Gladstone continued to favour a devolution and democratization of government in the United Kingdom generally, through the introduction of elected local government. The lack of success of the many plans and bills which his cabinet considered was the chief failure of his second government. Even the plan for administrative devolution to Scotland through the re-creation of the Scottish secretaryship of state was left to the tories to introduce in 1885. In 1871 in a speech at Aberdeen Gladstone had declared: 'There is nothing that Ireland has asked and which this country and this Parliament have refused' (Matthew, *Gladstone, 1809–1874*, 201); the course of the second government, during which home rule became more and more a clear, though as yet (as Gladstone pointed out) still rather unspecific Irish demand, showed that that claim was increasingly hard to sustain. Not long before making his new assumptions about Parnell, Gladstone noted: 'Conversation with H.J.G[ladstone] on "Home Rule" & my speech: for the subject has probably a future' (Gladstone, *Diaries*, 10 Feb 1882).

Parliamentary reform, 1883–1884 In the autumn of 1883 Gladstone changed the cabinet's tack, as he began planning a package of political reform, though one which would have vital consequences for Ireland. As in 1866, redistribution of seats was to follow rather than accompany franchise reform, and as in 1866 this was a chief focus of hostility to the proposals, though in 1884 the bill passed in the Commons without a Liberal split.

Gladstone focused rigorously on a Franchise Extension Bill. The bill's chief change was to extend the 1867 household suffrage to the counties, thus considerably increasing the electorate (though still leaving over 40 per cent of adult males unfranchised). Gladstone refused to accept a female suffrage amendment. For the first time England, Wales, Scotland, and Ireland were all included in a single franchise bill, with the large franchise increase for Ireland's largely rural population consequently tacked onto the proportionately less dramatic increase for the mainland. Gladstone moved the bill's introduction on 28 February 1884 and saw it through the Commons. On 8 July the Lords summarily rejected it. In September Gladstone made a spectacular tour of Scotland, which proved to be both the apogee and the last hurrah of nineteenth-century constitutional Liberalism. Back in London, a compromise between the two houses was arranged in a series of meetings in November 1884, Gladstone and Sir Charles Dilke representing the Liberals, and Lord Salisbury and Stafford Northcote the tories; the Liberals agreed to many of the tories' demands on redistribution, the tories agreed to the franchise changes. Gladstone and Dilke both seem to have underestimated the advantage to the tories of the ending of most of the two-member constituencies.

The fall of the government, the events of 1885, and the move towards home rule The spring of 1885 was taken up with the legislative enactment of the reform compromise. It was punctuated by the public disaster of the death of Gordon, the Panjdeh incident in Afghanistan, the vote of credit on 21 April of £11 million to deal with the Sudan and with Russia, and the disintegration of the cabinet over proposals for local government legislation for Ireland.

Gladstone's second government is usually seen as a disappointment after the legislative achievements of the first; even so, the Liberal Party held together better in the second than in the first. By 1885 the cabinet was riven by threats of resignation, but apart from Argyll in 1881, and Forster and Bright in 1882, none occurred. The extended crisis over reform kept the party together in 1884 and in the first four months of 1885, and the home-rulers in tow. With the passing of the Redistribution Bill on 11 May the need for unity ceased, and on 8 June the home-rulers voted with the tories to defeat the government on Hicks Beach's amendment to the budget on indirect taxation, seventy Liberals abstaining or absent. As in 1873 Gladstone resigned but, unlike Disraeli in 1873, Lord Salisbury accepted office and formed a minority tory government (dependent on home-rule votes). Gladstone left office on 24 June 1885, but continued as leader of the Liberal Party, a general election on the new franchise and distribution being imminent, though control of the exact timetable was now in Salisbury's hands.

The wide spectrum which the Gladstonian Liberal Party covered was becoming wider still, as the 'radical programme' of 1885 broadened its objectives. Gladstone, aged seventy-five, retained a remarkable capacity for innovation and surprise, but he was unlikely to move in the direction of the radical programme, for he saw it as representing in the Liberal Party that 'leaning of both parties to Socialism which I radically disapprove' (letter to Argyll, Gladstone, *Diaries*, 30 Sept 1885). He now saw the Irish problem as his reason for staying in active political life, but leading a united party into the election was his immediate duty. He took action on several different fronts, studying colonial legislative precedents for devolved authority and asking Parnell to define what he wanted in an Irish constitutional settlement. Suffering from a serious throat condition which prevented him from making speeches, Gladstone took a cruise to Norway on Thomas Brassey's yacht, the *Sunbeam*; while on board he drafted a lengthy party election manifesto which tried to unify the party on parliamentary procedure, land reform, electoral registration reform, and local government reform. In September 1885 he noted: 'I have long suspected the [Irish] Union of 1800 … this was like Pitt's Revolutionary war, a gigantic though excusable mistake' (ibid., 19 Sept 1885). On 1 November Gladstone received from Parnell the latter's 'Proposed Constitution for Ireland' which linked the home-rulers to a stated objective. On 14 November, staying at Dalmeny House for the Midlothian election campaign, Gladstone drafted the structure of an Irish Home Rule Bill which closely followed the paper Parnell had sent a fortnight earlier (itself based on colonial, chiefly Canadian, precedents).

Gladstone and the Liberals won the general election of November 1885, their second in a row, with a majority of seventy-two over the tories, unless the eighty-six home-rulers voted with the latter. Gladstone comfortably beat C. Dalrymple for the Midlothian seat.

Gladstone believed a home-rule solution would best come through a bipartisan measure promoted from the right (thus solving the difficulty of a rejection by the Lords of a bill approved by the Commons). On 15 December he met Arthur Balfour and floated this idea, confirming it in a letter of 20 December. On 17 December Herbert Gladstone's announcement of his father's home-rule views was published in the press (the 'Hawarden kite', as it became known); the initiative of a bipartisan solution came to nothing and the political world was ablaze with excitement.

The third government and the proposed pacification of Ireland, 1886 In the early morning of 27 January 1886 the Liberals and the home-rulers voted together to defeat the government and on 30 January 1886 Gladstone received the queen's commission to form his third government (Victoria having first tried G. J. Goschen). He was unopposed for Midlothian at the ensuing by-election. He formed his government with no formal commitment to home rule, and he formed his cabinet on the understanding that it would inquire into a home-rule solution. He had prepared neither the party nor the country for the dramatic legislation which he introduced in the spring of 1886, and he paid a high price for that. On the other hand the character of the party and the nature of the political timetable of 1885–6 would have made it impossible for him to lead a united party into the election on a home-rule programme. Gladstone's technique of using 'big bills' to unite the Liberal Party through legislative action offered a chance of retaining the whiggish wing of his party, though when Lord Hartington declined to join the new cabinet that chance was already slim.

Gladstone's plan was bold and broad. He drafted, with the help of Treasury officials and Sir Robert Hamilton, the home-rule permanent under-secretary in Dublin, a third Land Bill; unlike the first two, it was based on a transfer of land enabled by state funds, initially costed at £120 million (that is, more than the annual budget) but reduced to £50 million in the published bill. By this measure the landlord class could leave Ireland and social order in the countryside could be established as the preliminary to a stable political settlement. He next planned a Government of Ireland Bill establishing a legislative body of two houses in Dublin; the bill was to include a financial settlement (which was negotiated with Parnell). Irish MPs were no longer to sit at Westminster. Gladstone saw this proposed settlement as the best way to conserve a degree of union; he wished to impose responsibility on the Irish, who since 1800 had had representation with no prospect of power.

On 13 March 1886 the Land Bill was explained to the cabinet; on 26 March Joseph Chamberlain and G. O. Trevelyan walked out of the cabinet room, resigning. On 8 April Gladstone introduced the Government of Ireland Bill to the Commons. It was soon in difficulties and the accompanying Land Bill was introduced by Gladstone on 16 April but taken no further. Gladstone offered to withdraw, reconstruct, and reintroduce in the autumn the Government of Ireland Bill if it passed its second reading. He concluded his speech early on the morning of 8 June with a prophetic commendation:

> This, if I understand it, is one of those golden moments of our history; one of those opportunities which may come and may go, but which rarely return, or, if they return, return at long intervals, and under circumstances which no man can forecast. (W. E. Gladstone, *Speeches on the Irish Question in 1886*, ed. P. W. Clayden, 1886, 165)

The bill was beaten by 341 votes to 311, and that afternoon Gladstone drove through an uncertain cabinet a decision to dissolve parliament rather than resign. In a confused general election, he tried to lead a disorganized party by an outpouring of public letters and telegrams in addition to his usual speeches. So dedicated was Gladstone to the campaign that he agreed to break the habit of the previous forty years and cease his attempts to convert prostitutes, for fear, for the first time, of causing a scandal (Liberal agents had heard that the Unionists were monitoring Gladstone's nocturnal movements in London with a view to a press exposé). In the election the number of Liberal MPs fell from 333 in 1885 to 196, though no party gained an overall majority. The Liberal Party was divided, with the whiggish section seriously and probably permanently disrupted. Gladstone was unopposed in Midlothian and was also returned unopposed for Leith burghs (for which he stood at the last minute on the request of local Liberals; the position on home rule of the former Liberal MP, William Jacks, was uncertain and he withdrew when Gladstone stood). Gladstone chose Midlothian. On 20 July the cabinet decided to resign without meeting parliament to be voted out, Gladstone formally ceasing to be prime minister on 30 July. The queen thought him 'pale and nervous' at his final audience (*Letters of Queen Victoria*, ed. A. C. Benson and Lord Esher, and G. E. Buckle, 3rd ser., 1930–32, 1.168).

Gladstone had pursued his plan for an Irish settlement with exceptional energy (even for him) and with what seemed to many of his largely unprepared colleagues mulish obstinacy. Gladstone's third government hardly lasted long enough for any substantial legislative achievements, though the Crofters' Act was a notable and long-lasting innovation in Scottish land tenure. 'An old man in a hurry' was Lord Randolph Churchill's jibe as he 'played the Orange card' in Ulster (it was soon seen that it was Lord Randolph who was really hurried). Incomprehension at Westminster did not necessarily mean rejection in the country. For every tory who thought Gladstone mad there was a Liberal who thought him great. Certainly Gladstone felt that part of his mission was to represent the 'masses against the classes' on the Irish question as on others, and the extent of support for home rule was probably much more extensive than the organs of Unionism and a disaffected Liberal intelligentsia made out. In the United States and the empire (and especially in Australia and India) home rule was a popular and populist movement (Swaraj—the name of Gandhi's movement—being a direct translation of 'home rule').

The later Gladstone's intellectual and cultural context Gladstone retained many of the intellectual characteristics of his earlier life, but he applied them in striking new ways. His study of Bishop Butler, which he renewed in opposition, was intended to give those in public life a philosophy based on probability and experience; that is, to permit adaptation and to allow change, though change in politics as a second order activity which could only dimly reflect the certainties of theology. His intellectual friends were persons such as Lord Acton, whom he had boldly ennobled in 1869 and who especially prized liberal individualism in public life. Gladstone moved also among political economists, as a member of the Political Economy Club, at which he gave the address at the celebrations marking the centenary of Smith's *The Wealth of Nations* on 31 May 1876, and he had many contacts in the Victorian coterie of the Metaphysical Society. Like a number of his scholarly contemporaries, he dabbled in spiritualism, in his case in the mid-1880s; in 1885 he agreed to become an honorary member of the Society for Psychical Research. He engaged in intellectual disputes (mostly good-humoured) with a wide range of Victorian opinion through his many articles in the *Nineteenth Century*, and the *Contemporary*, *Fortnightly*, and other reviews, most of which were written for his friend the journal editor and owner J. T. Knowles. Some of these, such as 'The evangelical movement, its parentage, progress, and issues' (*British Quarterly Review*, July 1879) and '"Locksley Hall" and the jubilee' (*Nineteenth Century*, January 1887), a powerful attack on Tennysonian pessimism, were important contributions to the historiography of the century. He was a strong defender of moderate Christian Darwinism, publishing his views in articles, including a dispute with T. H. Huxley in 1890, and in *The Impregnable Rock of Holy Scripture* (1890; 2nd edn, 1892). He was always willing to help a new journal get started (for example, the *English Historical Review* in 1886) with an article or a book review. He wrote the substance (though he did not take the credit) for the articles on his father, E. C. Hawtrey, and Sir Stephen Glynne in the *Dictionary of National Biography*. His long book reviews, notably those of Tennyson's *Maud* and *Idylls of the King*, J. R. Seeley's *Ecce homo*, G. Cornewall Lewis's *Influence of Authority on Matters of Opinion*, G. O. Trevelyan's *Macaulay*, Lecky's *History of England*, and Mary Ward's *Robert Elsmere*, are important texts of Victorian cultural history.

Tennyson stayed several times at Hawarden, Gladstone and the family politely listening to the poet reading his unactable plays. Gladstone got Tennyson the first poetic peerage, in 1883, and was rewarded by a sonnet published in *The Times* calling on the Lords to reject the Franchise Bill. Ruskin also visited Hawarden, in 1878, Gladstone's daughter Mary noting that 'the experienced Ch. of Ex. and [the] visionary idealist came in to conflict' (L. Masterman, *Mary Gladstone*, 1930, 142). Ruskin, in his campaign to succeed Gladstone as lord rector of Glasgow University, remarked that he cared for Disraeli and Gladstone no more than he did for two old bagpipes. Gladstone's artistic tastes were pronouncedly pre-Raphaelite; he was a modest but significant patron of their works, and supported the Grosvenor Gallery from 1879. Burne-Jones's memorial window to Gladstone in Hawarden church was based on personal knowledge, and G. F. Watts and J. E. Millais both painted more than one portrait of him (see below). Gladstone was professor of ancient history at the Royal Academy in the 1880s, but never seems to have lectured (a rare abstinence); he always attended the opening day of the academy summer show.

Gladstone was always an energetic theatregoer, at home and on the continent. He enjoyed the company of actors and actresses and invited them to 10 Downing Street. He invited Henry Irving to Hawarden, and tried but failed to get him a knighthood in 1883 (it was through Irving that Gladstone met Lillie Langtry, who made a great deal of their brief friendship in 1882–5). He publicly supported a plan for a national theatre (*The Theatre*, 13 March 1878, 103). He also enjoyed opera, including Wagner. In old age, as his sight and hearing failed, he usually sat on the stage.

Gladstone read widely in European literature. Next to Shakespeare, Molière was his most frequently read dramatist. He worked energetically, if idiosyncratically, on Dante, whom he had first read in the mid-1830s but to whom he specially turned from 1874 onwards. He engaged in extensive correspondence with European scholars on classical, literary, theological, and economic topics, and he read and spoke fluently in Latin, Greek, Italian, French, and German, got by in Spanish, and learned enough Norwegian to say a few words during a visit. His cultural range in the European context was exceptional, exemplified by an honorary degree from Bologna during its eighth centenary celebrations and membership of the Académie des Sciences Morales et Politiques in Paris. He was elected fellow of the Royal Society in 1881 (though election during his first premiership would have been more usual).

Few people in British public life, and certainly no prime minister, succeeded in publicly articulating his opinions or in determining the agenda of public life over such a range of subjects or so long a time. In 1879 Gladstone collected a selection of his articles and addresses in *Gleanings of Past Years* (7 vols.), which he supplemented by *Later Gleanings* (1897). His gallimaufrous abilities and his voluminous capacity for general intellectual discussion of all sorts (except on science), were ideally matched by the high journalistic culture of his later life.

To an extent Gladstone wrote for money, for from the 1870s, with many of his adult children still financially dependent on him, he believed himself strapped for cash. In 1896 he calculated his literary earnings at £18,826 (see Matthew, *Gladstone, 1875–1898*, 374). But he declined an offer of £100,000 in 1887 for his autobiography, which he wrote privately and episodically between 1886 and the end of his life. This remarkable offer was probably engineered by his friend Andrew Carnegie, the Scottish-American steel magnate, who had a penchant for helping British Liberals financially. Carnegie also, using Gladstone as intermediary, saved Acton from bankruptcy by buying his library, and in 1887 offered Gladstone an interest-free loan of any sum, cancellable on death if there were insufficient funds to pay it back (Gladstone politely declined, asking Carnegie to finance home rule instead).

Much of Gladstone's private spending was on books. Up

to the 1870s he also collected pictures and china; his collection was partly dispersed by sale in 1875, the remaining china being given to the South Kensington and Liverpool museums. In the course of a lifetime of haunting bookshops, Gladstone built up a large library, cataloguing it in 1845 and on subsequent occasions. In his diaries more than 21,000 works by over 4500 authors are noted as read. Sir Walter Scott was his favourite novelist, Émile Zola the most deplored (though not the least read). From 1886 Gladstone planned to make his books publicly available, especially but not exclusively for the benefit of the clergy. He built an iron hut at Hawarden for this purpose, which in 1889 he decided to name St Deiniol's Library, and endowed it with a trust deed signed on 1 January 1896. He invented a system of rolling-stack bookcases, advising the Bodleian Library in Oxford in 1888 to adopt it; it can be seen as the origin of much modern library design (see his *On Books and the Housing of them*, 1898, and E. W. Nicholson, *Mr. Gladstone and the Bodleian*, 1898).

Much though Gladstone enjoyed books and intellectual conversation, he was equally happy with his businessman cronies Stuart *Rendel and George Armitstead, who provided the châteaux in France and much of the physical support that the Gladstones enjoyed in their old age, and whose regular duty was to play backgammon with Gladstone each evening. As he aged, tree-felling became too demanding a form of exercise, and regular walks predominated. Gladstone was not interested in sport, and did not attend cricket or football matches, unlike many other political leaders of the 1880s and 1890s. (Under pressure from Granville he once attended the Derby, in 1870.)

In opposition, 1886–1892 The six years after 1886 were Gladstone's only period of what might be called normal opposition leadership. He used them chiefly to assert the primacy of home rule, putting this above the reunification of the party which some expected after the 1886 election defeat. A few whigs and several radicals returned severally, encouraged by Gladstone, but he did not play a leading part in the abortive 'round table' talks of 1886–7. Gladstone published widely and combatively on Ireland in these years, gathering some of his articles in *The Irish Question* (1886) and *Special Aspects of the Irish Question* (1892); the latter included his article on Daniel O'Connell—an interesting reappraisal of his own as well as O'Connell's views, first published in the *Nineteenth Century* (January 1889). He spoke at the annual meetings of the National Liberal Federation (NLF) (except in 1890), with the aim of making home rule seem a natural solution, presenting the home-rulers as thoroughgoing constitutionalists. In this he had considerable success, especially as the unionist alternative led to scandals such as the Michelstown shootings in September 1887 and the extraordinary duplicities exposed by the special commission of 1888–9 on the Pigott forgeries. Two meetings with Parnell in March 1888 and December 1889 suggested that the Liberal–home-rule alliance was harmonious, and all seemed set fair for a Liberal majority after the next election.

The divorce of Katharine O'Shea, with Parnell as co-respondent, in November 1890 dramatically altered this expectation. Gladstone, under strong pressure from religious opinion, decided that the cause of home rule must take precedence over Parnell's leadership of the Home Rule Party, but the muddled process by which this information failed to be privately conveyed to the Home Rule Party meeting on 25 November 1890 led to a public demand by Gladstone for Parnell's resignation; the Home Rule Party then split, the majority following Gladstone's lead, the minority Parnell. At the 1891 NLF meeting in Newcastle, Gladstone continued to assert that home rule came first, but added to it a list of reforming measures for the mainland, quickly known as the 'Newcastle programme'.

As party leader Gladstone paid little attention to the details of organization, relying as always on great speeches to link the electorate directly to good argument and a charismatic leader. He recognized, however, the importance of greater labour representation, met such Labour MPs as there were, and devised a scheme of payment for MPs to promote their increase. His agenda of constitutional reform, home rule, and free trade, was one on which the nascent labour organizations could enthusiastically co-operate with the Liberal Party, and proved the basis for a 'Lib–Lab' partnership which subsisted for much of the next century, as Gladstone anticipated in a remarkable article, 'The rights and responsibilities of labour' (*Lloyd's Weekly Newspaper*, 4 May 1890).

Although his physical and mental powers were waning, Gladstone remained a powerful force in politics and intellectual life. When he stayed at All Souls College, Oxford, early in 1890, one of the young tory fellows, Charles Oman, noted: 'I was far from suspecting, till I had seen him close, what vigour there still was in the old man' (C. Oman, *Things I have Seen*, 1937, 77). He attended the centenary celebrations of the French Revolution, making several speeches in French, including one at the top of the Eiffel Tower.

Gladstone traded somewhat on his age, and easily beguiled a new generation of politicians with tales of pre-1832 politics. To have met George Canning and to be still seeking office in 1892 was phenomenal by any standard, though privately he recognized just before his last general election: 'Frankly: for the condition (*now*) of my senses, I am no longer fit for public life: yet bidden to walk in it. "Lead thou me on"' (Gladstone, *Diaries*, 15 July 1892).

The fourth government, 1892–1894 The Liberals won the general election of July 1892, being the largest party with 272 MPs and 49 per cent of the English votes. Gladstone's own vote in Midlothian, where he was opposed by A. G. Wauchope, fell sharply; his majority was only 690 (but he was unopposed at the by-election consequent on his taking office). He was hit on the left eye (his good one) while campaigning in Chester, his sight being affected for several months and his campaigning capacity considerably diminished. Aged eighty-two, he received on 15 August the queen's commission to form a government, a process not aided by a quite severe injury when he was knocked down by a mad cow in Hawarden Park on 29 August. He is the only person in British history to begin a premiership over the age of eighty. Disappointed by the election result, which gave a majority for home rule insufficient to force acceptance on the Lords, Gladstone considered dealing with Ireland by resolution rather than a bill, so as to have more time for British bills. He was dissuaded from this course by Lord Spencer and John Morley. He was initially preoccupied by the inaugural Romanes lecture, which he gave at Oxford on 24 October 1892 on medieval universities, and by a cabinet crisis over Buganda, Gladstone's support for British withdrawal being eventually frustrated by adroit manoeuvring by Lord Rosebery, the foreign secretary, and the appointment of Gerald Porter to write a report.

Gladstone prepared his second Government of Ireland Bill (this time there was no accompanying land bill) and brought it in on 17 February 1893. The financial clauses of the bill were bungled by the Treasury and had to be restructured, but the bill passed the Commons on 1 September 1893 after eighty-two sittings and an extended session. Gladstone personally took the bill through the committee stage in a remarkable feat of physical and mental endurance. In some respects this was a futile gesture—the bill was, as expected, summarily rejected by the Lords—but the passing of the bill, like the existence of the Liberal government itself, was an important reminder that imperial Britain was not inevitably unionist. Gladstone was keenly aware of this contribution, and used his last cabinet to give experience more rapidly than previously to men such as H. H. Asquith and James Bryce. To Gladstone's surprise Salisbury used the tory majority in the Lords not merely against home rule but significantly to alter or reject almost every major Liberal bill in the 1893 session. Gladstone initially hoped to dissolve on the question of the Lords' rejection of the Irish bill, but there was no support in cabinet for this course of action. He fussed more than in previous governments about small matters—the poet laureateship (for which John Ruskin was his somewhat bizarre preferred candidate), a dukedom for Lord Lansdowne—and his relations with the queen were worse than ever, despite his help to her over the royal grants question in 1889. Concern at what he saw as her maltreatment of him became a major Gladstonian preoccupation.

In December 1893 Gladstone was appalled by the draft defence estimates for 1894, which provided for a large expansion of the navy. Very close to resigning because of his inability to persuade the cabinet to reduce the navy estimates, he agreed to withdraw to Biarritz in January 1894, his colleagues hoping that he would there decide to retire. He returned in February without retiring and with no success on the estimates. His eyesight poor, his political position isolated, and the queen refusing to ease his way, Gladstone chaired the last of his 556 cabinets on 1 March 1894. It became known as the 'blubbering cabinet' from the tears of his colleagues, but Gladstone, John Morley noted, 'sat quite composed and still. The emotion of the Cabinet did not gain him for an instant' (Morley's diary, 1 March 1894; Matthew, *Gladstone, 1875–1898*, 354). He spoke for the last time in the Commons that afternoon—attacking the Lords—and resigned office on 3 March 1894. The queen did not ask his advice as to his successor. Gladstone declined a peerage, as he had also done in 1874 and 1885, and advised his wife to decline one also, as she did.

Final years and death Retired at last, Gladstone completed his edition of *The Works of Joseph Butler D.C.L.* in two volumes, published by the Clarendon Press in 1896 together with his *Studies Subsidiary to the Works of Bishop Butler*. An unsuccessful operation for cataract in his right eye in May 1894 prevented him having to decide whether to attend Laura Thistlethwayte's funeral. Gladstone's final crusade was on behalf of the Armenians, with a speech in Liverpool on 24 September 1896, which drove Lord Rosebery to resign the leadership of the Liberal Party. At the end of that year Gladstone divided much of his capital between his children, as he had done at several earlier points in his life, for he agreed with Andrew Carnegie that property should be divested not inherited (though he clashed with Carnegie in excepting landed property from this maxim). Having done this, he made a new will and also a written declaration for his children's benefit recording his marital fidelity. He did this so as to deny rumours past and future about himself, Laura Thistlethwayte, and the rescue cases. On his birthday, 29 December 1896, he wrote the final entry of his diary. Suffering from as yet undiagnosed cancer of the palate, he wintered with Catherine Gladstone in Cannes in 1897–8, returning to Britain in March 1898. The cancer being diagnosed and publicly announced, Gladstone began a rather public death at Hawarden. He died there on Ascension day, 19 May 1898. The family accepted the offer of a state funeral and, after Gladstone's body had lain in state for three days in Westminster Hall, he was buried in the statesman's corner of Westminster Abbey on 28 May (Catherine Gladstone was buried in the double grave in 1900), simultaneous services being held in many British and overseas villages, towns, and cities. The ceremonies at Westminster were resolutely religious and civilian, with no imperial echoes. This last great set piece of Victorian Liberalism sent its own echo through the waning Liberal world.

Gladstone and Victorian public life Gladstone had touched Victorian public life at many points. Most important, from his own point of view, was his ownership and stewardship of the advowsons of St Thomas's, Toxteth, and St Thomas's, Seaforth; in 1890 he bought the advowson of Liverpool. He was a trustee of the British Museum from 1853, resigning as a personal trustee in 1881; a trustee of the Colonial Bishoprics Fund, and at times its treasurer, from 1841; a trustee of the Radcliffe Trust from 1855 to 1888, and its chairman from 1861 to 1888 (during which time the trust gave the Radcliffe Camera to the University of Oxford to be part of the Bodleian Library); a trustee of the Dee Embankment Trust from 1857, and of the River Dee Trust from 1856; and one of the two trustees appointed to handle the chaotic affairs of his friend the fifth duke of Newcastle. Gladstone was lord rector (an elected position) of the universities of Edinburgh (1859–65) and Glasgow (1877–80); he was on the council of King's College,

London, from 1838, and of Trinity College, Glenalmond, from its foundation in 1845; and he was a governor of the Charterhouse and of Guy's Hospital, London. He was a freeman of Aberdeen (1871), Cardiff (1889), Dingwall (1853), Dublin (1877), Edinburgh (1853), Glasgow (1865), Hamilton (1879), Inverness (1853), Kirkwall (1883), Liverpool (1892), Newcastle (1891), and Perth (1879); as a freeman of the City of London (1876) through membership of the Turners' Company, he could not be an honorary freeman. He wrote the inscription for the Eros statue in Piccadilly and for various other public monuments and he restored the Mercat Cross in Edinburgh in 1885.

Gladstone in perspective Gladstone's chief legacy was threefold. First, his financial priorities in the areas of free trade, retrenchment, and the tax structure, shaped the relationship of the Treasury to the rest of British government and the economy long after the type of economy they were designed to serve had passed away.

Secondly, Gladstone's attempt through home rule to modify Britain's unitary constitution was, apart from county and borough local government, the approach for Ireland, Scotland, and Wales preferred by Liberal and Labour governments throughout the twentieth century. The bill of 1886 set the terms of discourse for major constitutional change in the United Kingdom for more than a century and was the basis of the Government of Ireland Act of 1920 (ironically enacted only with respect to Northern Ireland), and the Government of Scotland Acts of 1978 and 1998, the latter finally achieving Gladstonian home rule for a significant part of the United Kingdom.

Thirdly, the idea of a party of progress broadly based, willing to accommodate and conciliate varying interests, committed to causes and campaigns as well as programmes of reform, was of world-wide importance, as was the idea of executive politicians justifying their policies through public as well as parliamentary speeches. The Gladstonian Liberal Party was fractious, argumentative, and sometimes self-destructive, but it had a comprehensive role unique among its European contemporaries; even when, late in Gladstone's career, labourist groups began to appear, they did so as developments from the Liberal Party, not as enemies of it. When Gladstone died, the TUC central committee adjourned its meeting. His earnestness infuriated opponents and, largely unintentionally, he raised the temperature as well as the tone of politics by the nature of his personality. He tantalized and mesmerized his opponents and many of his supporters, for he had the rare quality of investing the most anodyne of topics with controversy; the public attention which most politicians strive to create came to Gladstone like a bee to honey. With this capacity to act as a political lightning rod went a high level of political tolerance; Gladstone's thick skin, especially at the end of his active political years, enabled him to absorb with a good deal of equanimity the bolts of lightning which he attracted so easily. The ill temper, sometimes evident in the Commons in his middle years, was much less seen in 'The old Parliamentary hand', as he was wont in his later years to describe himself. Gladstone's angry eye was politically famous, and feared by those, even quite senior politicians, against whom it was turned; but it was the eye of political rebuke, not of loss of temper.

Less clear than his public achievements were the answers to the personal questions Gladstone had posed himself. He had maintained sufficient self-control in a personality that quite often, both to contemporaries and to Gladstone himself, seemed in danger of losing its balance. But the notion that sustained the last twenty years of his political life—that his reappearance was merely temporary, the result of immediate 'special causes'—wore thin and took a heavy toll on his colleagues, his wife, and his family, though it gave Gladstone himself a free-ranging and exhilarating political role. He himself felt that he had failed to sustain an adequate level of retrenchment in public finance, to prevent undesirable imperial expansion, and to find a satisfactory solution to the question of the relationship of national religion and Anglican truth to an increasingly secularizing society. When in 1886 he listed 'the actual misdeeds of the legislature during the last half-century' they were all religious: the Ecclesiastical Titles Act 1851, the Divorce Act of 1857, the Public Worship Regulation Act 1874. He violently deplored birth control and contemplated a public crusade against it. At the end of his long political career, Gladstone found much of civic, political, and economic progress to praise, but the Christian state which as a young MP he had set out to sustain and develop was even less of a reality in the 1890s than it had been in the 1830s.

Remnants for the future Gladstone left many artefacts for posterity. His vast collection of papers, carefully assembled from Eton onwards, is the central archive for nineteenth-century British public life (it is now divided between the British Library, Lambeth Palace Library, and St Deiniol's Library). His voice was recorded several times, one probably authentic recording of 1888 being held by the National Sound Archive at the British Library, the earliest cogent recording of any public figure. His funeral procession was filmed. He was often painted, drawn, and photographed. J. E. Millais painted four portraits of Gladstone (1879, 1884, 1885, 1889), of which that in Christ Church, Oxford, is the most characteristic. George Richmond's drawing (1843) for Grillion's Club catches the high-minded religiosity of the young MP. F. von Lenbach's unfinished joint portrait of Gladstone and Döllinger, begun in September 1886, is an excellent likeness, more attractive than any of those by Millais. G. F. Watts painted three portraits of Gladstone (1859, 1861, 1874), destroying the face in the third in frustration. Gladstone offered baronetcies to Millais and Watts, the latter declining. Gladstone cartoons in *Punch*, including many by Tenniel, for whom he was a favourite as well as a required subject, are collected in *The political life of … W. E. Gladstone, illustrated from 'Punch'* (3 vols., 1897). His was not an easy face for cartoonists, who usually got round this difficulty by an emphasis on the context of the cartoon (Homeric volumes, axes, and so on). Gladstone's old age and flashing eye was brilliantly caught in Phil May's cartoon of 1893. Gladstone photographed stiffly when taken by men, though the series by F. von Lenbach (taken in Munich in 1879 in preparation for a not very good portrait) is striking; but photographs by Eveleen Myers (1890) and Sarah Acland (1892) show the relaxed charm for which he was known in private company. Thomas Woolner's larger-than-life-sized bust with Homeric plinth (1863–7) is the best contemporary statue, given to the University of Oxford by his constituents and now in the Ashmolean Museum, Oxford. Representations of Gladstone on plates and cups (and the bottom of chamber pots for tory households) were common; he personally took an interest in seeing that the many cartes-de-visite sold to Liberal supporters were cheaply priced. After his death many towns erected statues of him. The Gladstone National Memorial Fund, set up in June 1898, erected three statues: at Aldwych, London (by Hamo Thornycroft, 1905), in St Andrew's Square, Edinburgh (by James Pittendrigh Macgillivray, 1917, moved in 1955–6 to Coates Crescent, Edinburgh), and at Hawarden (by John Hughes, planned for Dublin but declined by its corporation until an adequate memorial to Parnell had been erected). The fund also extended and rebuilt the unique residential St Deiniol's Library, Hawarden, and established a Gladstone Memorial Trust to award prizes and bursaries at Oxford University and other educational establishments. Cities and towns are named for him in several states in the USA and in many Commonwealth countries, and few British cities are without a Gladstone Street.

Historical representation Gladstone suffered little of the eclipse which almost all Victorians underwent in the first part of the twentieth century. Popularly, 'Mr Gladstone' (as he continued to be called) remained a substantial figure, generations of schoolchildren in Britain and the empire being told to chew their food thirty-two times to the mouthful, as he was alleged to have done. 'Gladstone claret', introduced by his wine-duty reductions in 1860, did not retain its name for long, but the 'Gladstone bag' (a portmanteau bag midway between a doctor's bag and a cricket bag), was quite common in the twentieth century. Politically, his free-trade and constitutional legacy remained an important, even foremost, part of the Liberal creed, and the Liberal Party, at least until the 1940s, nurtured his memory. It was also maintained by the presence in politics of two further generations of Gladstones: Herbert Gladstone, the cabinet minister, and William Glynne Charles Gladstone (son of the prime minister's eldest son, Willy), a whip in Asquith's government and killed in action in 1915. Herbert Gladstone and his brother Henry carefully nurtured their father's memory through their own and commissioned publications, and Herbert gained the jury's exoneration for his father at the end of the Wright case in January 1927, when Herbert provoked Captain Peter Wright into suing him for libel. Herbert's defence was that Wright was shown to be no gentleman through his comment that the prime minister's custom was 'to pursue and possess every sort of woman'; Charles Russell, the family's solicitor, had prudently dissuaded the brothers from submitting their father's diaries as evidence.

At his death, Gladstone was already well treated in G. Barnett Smith's two-volume life (1879) and A. F. Robbins, *The Early Public Life of William Ewart Gladstone* (1894), as well as being the subject of many brief lives. R. Masheder's hostile religious biography (1865) was a sharp attack and Walter Bagehot's essay (1860) a perceptive analysis. Gladstone published several volumes of his speeches, but an attempt at a complete edition by A. W. Hutton and H. J. Cohen produced only two volumes. However, the scrapbook of newspaper reports of speeches, systematically maintained at Hawarden by Gladstone and his family, is part of *The Papers of William Ewart Gladstone* in the Prime Ministers' Papers on Microfilm series (edited by H. C. G. Matthew, 1994–). The diaries or memoirs of four of Gladstone's secretaries—Edward *Hamilton, George Leveson-Gower, Arthur *Godley (Lord Kilbracken), and Algernon *West—have been published, and Hamilton also published *Mr. Gladstone: a Monograph* (1898). The diaries of Hamilton and West are important sources, as are those of Stuart Rendle and the reminiscences of Lionel Tollemache.

Many contemporaries published studies of Gladstone just before or after his death, T. Wemyss Reid editing a still useful compilation in 1899; several others also remain of importance, including those by G. W. E. Russell (1891), James Bryce (1898), Sydney Buxton (1901), and Goldwin Smith (1904). Herbert Paul's biography (n.d.) was the original, longer version of his memoir in the *Dictionary of National Biography*. John Morley was appointed biographer by the Gladstone family shortly after Gladstone's death. Assisted by F. W. Hirst—whose *In the Golden Days* (1947) describes the making of the biography—Morley published his three-volume life in 1903; an acute and still relevant study for the years up to c.1880, it was, not surprisingly, discreet about later Liberal politics and, following the conventions of its time, silent on the sexual aspects of Gladstone's private life. Morley's own diary shows him to have been much more critical of the later Gladstone than his biography suggests.

Morley's biography included many original documents, sometimes defectively edited, but D. C. Lathbury's *Correspondence on Church and Religion* (2 vols., 1910) was excellently done. It set the standard for the various editions of Gladstone's papers which have punctuated the twentieth century, culminating in Agatha Ramm's four volumes of the Gladstone–Granville correspondence (1952–62) and the publication of *The Gladstone Diaries*, authorized by Archbishop Fisher and edited by M. R. D. Foot and H. C. G. Matthew (14 vols., 1968–94), the later volumes including the minutes of his cabinets and a generous selection of his prime-ministerial correspondence.

F. W. Hirst, Francis Birrell, Paul Knaplund, F. E. Hyde, Erich Eyck, J. L. Hammond, and others wrote studies between the wars of various aspects of Gladstone's career; Hammond's *Gladstone and the Irish Nation* (1938) remains a central text, identifying Gladstone with the European mind and the League of Nations tradition. Gladstone's religion was brilliantly analysed in Alex Vidler, *The Orb and the Cross* (1945). Philip Magnus used the family papers to good advantage (but without the diaries) for his popular biography (1954), as did S. G. Checkland in his detailed account, *The Gladstones: a Family Biography, 1764–1851* (1971).

The publication of the diaries led to a revival of interest in Gladstonian religion, finance, and politics, exemplified in H. C. G. Matthew's two-volume reprint and amplification of his introductions to volumes of the diaries (1986–95; reprinted as a single volume with additions, 1997). Among other recent studies and biographies of scholarly and interpretative importance are those by Derek Beales (1961), John Vincent (1966), David Hamer (1972), Peter Stansky (1979), R. T. Shannon (1963, 1982–99), Deryck Schreuder (1969), R. Kelley (1969), Michael Barker (1975), Owen Chadwick (1976), Perry Butler (1982), T. A. Jenkins (1988), Agatha Ramm (1989), Peter Jagger (1991), David Bebbington (1993), and Travis Crosby (1997). Roy Jenkins (1995) made aspects of recent research popularly accessible. Peter Gay's *The Bourgeois Experience* (1984) placed Gladstone's private life in a general context. There is a very large number of scholarly articles about Gladstone. Biographers usually treat Gladstone with a mixture of sympathy, awe, and irritation. The multiplicity of books and articles on Gladstone reflects his omnipresence in nineteenth-century historiography; he was both a chief protagonist and a chief observer of his age.

H. C. G. MATTHEW

Sources EDITIONS OF MANUSCRIPTS Gladstone, *Diaries* • *Correspondence on church and religion of William Ewart Gladstone*, ed. D. C. Lathbury, 2 vols. (1910) • *Gladstone and Palmerston: being the correspondence of Lord Palmerston with Mr Gladstone, 1851–1865*, ed. P. Guedalla (1928) • P. Guedalla, ed., *The queen and Mr Gladstone*, 2 vols. (1933) • *The Gladstone papers* (1930) • *Gladstone to his wife*, ed. A. T. Bassett (1936) • *The political correspondence of Mr Gladstone and Lord Granville, 1868–1876*, ed. A. Ramm, 2 vols., CS, 3rd ser., 81–2 (1952) • *The political correspondence of Mr Gladstone and Lord Granville, 1876–1886*, ed. A. Ramm, 2 vols. (1962) • *Gladstone–Gordon correspondence, 1851–1896*, ed. P. Knaplund (1961) • *W. E. Gladstone*, ed. J. Brooke and M. Sorensen, 4 vols. (1971–81) • *The papers of William Ewart Gladstone*, ed. H. C. G. Matthew (1993–8) [microfilm]
BIBLIOGRAPHIES L. March-Phillips and B. Christian, eds., *Some Hawarden letters* (1917) • P. M. Long, ed., *A bibliography of Gladstone publications at Saint Deiniol's Library* (1978) • C. J. Dobson, ed., *Gladstoniana: a bibliography of material relating to W. E. Gladstone at St Deiniol's Library* (1981) • A. T. Bassett, ed., *Gladstone's speeches: a descriptive index and bibliography* (1916) • Gladstone, *Diaries*, vol. 14 [incl. bibliography of Gladstone's reading]
BIOGRAPHIES AND STUDIES J. Morley, *The life of William Ewart Gladstone*, 3 vols. (1903) • T. W. Reid, ed., *The life of William Ewart Gladstone* (1899) • H. C. G. Matthew, *Gladstone, 1809–1874* (1988) • H. C. G. Matthew, *Gladstone, 1875–1898* (1995) • P. M. Magnus, *Gladstone: a biography* (1954) • S. H. Northcote, *Twenty years of financial policy: a summary of the chief financial measures passed between 1842 and 1861, with a table of budgets* (1862) • S. C. Buxton, *Finance and politics, an historical study, 1783–1885*, 2 vols. (1888) • F. W. Hirst, *Gladstone as financier and economist* (1931) • D. H. Macgregor, *Public aspects of finance* (1939) • M. Drew, *Acton, Gladstone and others* (1924) • *William Ewart Gladstone in Glasgow* (1902) • H. Friedrichs, *In the evening of his days: a study of Mr. Gladstone in retirement, with some account of St Deiniol's Library and Hostel* (1896) • *The passing of Gladstone: his life, death and burial* (1898) • D. M. Schreuder, *Gladstone and Kruger: Liberal government and colonial 'home rule', 1880–85* (1969) • J. Vincent, *The formation of the liberal party, 1857–1868* (1966) • T. A. Jenkins, *Gladstone, whiggery and the liberal party, 1874–1886* (1988) • J. P. Parry, *Democracy and religion: Gladstone and the liberal party, 1867–1875* (1986) • R. T. Shannon, *Gladstone and the Bulgarian agitation, 1876* (1963) • A. P. Saab, *Reluctant icon: Gladstone, Bulgaria, and the working classes, 1856–1878* (1991) • J. Loughlin, *Gladstone, home rule and the Ulster question, 1882–93* (1986) • A. B. Cooke and J. Vincent, *The governing passion: cabinet government and party politics in Britain, 1885–86* (1974) • O. Chadwick, *Acton and Gladstone* (1976) • P. Butler, *Gladstone, church, state, and Tractarianism: a study of his religious ideas and attitudes, 1809–1859* (1982) • M. J. Lynch, 'Was Gladstone a Tractarian? W. E. Gladstone and the Oxford Movement, 1833–45', *Journal of Religious History*, 8 (1974–5), 364–89 • J. Vincent, *Gladstone and Ireland* (1978) • D. Nicholls, 'Gladstone and the Anglican critics of Newman', *Newman and Gladstone: centennial essays*, ed. J. Bastable (1978) • C. Matthew, 'Gladstone, evangelicalism and "the Engagement"', *Revival and religion since 1700: essays for John Walsh*, ed. J. Garnett and C. Matthew (1993), 111–26 • G. M. Young, 'The schoolman in Downing Street', *Victorian essays* (1962) • R. Deacon, *The private life of Mr. Gladstone* (1965) • J. L. Hammond, *Gladstone and the Irish nation* (1938) • S. C. Buxton, *Mr. Gladstone as chancellor of the exchequer* (1901) • F. E. Hyde, *Mr. Gladstone at the board of trade* (1934) • G. J. Shaw-Lefevre, *Gladstone and Ireland: the Irish policy of parliament from 1850–1894* (1912) • A. F. Robbins, *The early public life of William Ewart Gladstone* (1894) • A. Shaw, *Gladstone at the colonial office, 1846* (1986) • R. E. Robinson and J. Gallagher, *Africa and the Victorians* (1961) • R. W. Seton-Watson, *Disraeli, Gladstone, and the Eastern question* (1935) • A. Schölch, *Egypt for the Egyptians: the socio-political crisis in Egypt, 1878–1882* (1981); trans. of *Ägypten den Ägyptern! Die politische und gesellschaftliche Krise der Jahre 1878–1882 in Ägypten* (1972) • A. Warren, 'Gladstone, land and social reconstruction in Ireland, 1881–87', *Parliamentary History*, 2 (1983), 153–73 • A. F. Thompson, 'Gladstone's whips and the general election of 1868', *EngHR*, 63 (1948), 189–200 • M. Pointon, 'W. E. Gladstone as an art patron and collector', *Victorian Studies*, 19 (1975–6), 73–98 • M. R. D. Foot, 'Morley's Gladstone: a reappraisal', *Bulletin of the John Ryland's Library, Manchester*, 51 (1968–9), 368–80 • G. Veysey, *Mr. Gladstone and Hawarden* (1982) • H. Lloyd-Jones, *Blood for the ghosts* (1982) • I. Guest, *Dr. John Radcliffe and his trust* (1991)
Archives BL, Add. MSS 44086–44835 • BL, Add. MSS 44900–44901 • BL, Add. MS 46221 • BL, Add. MSS 56444–56453 • BL, loan 73 • LPL • St Deiniol's Library, Hawarden | Balliol Oxf., Morier MSS • BL, Aberdeen MSS, Add. MSS 43070–43071 • BL, Bright MSS, Add. MS 43385 • BL, Campbell-Bannerman MSS, Add. MS 41215 • BL, Dilke MSS, Add. MSS 43875–43885 • BL, Gladstone MSS, Add. MS 46044 [H. J. Gladstone] • BL, Hamilton MSS, Add. MS 48607A, B • BL, Panizzi MSS, Add. MSS 36715–36726 • BL, Peel MSS, Add. MSS 40469–40470 • BL, Ponsonby MSS, Add. MS 45724 • BL, Ripon MSS, Add. MSS 43513–43515 • BL, Stanmore MSS, Add. MS 49209 • Bodl. Oxf., Acland MSS • Bodl. Oxf., Bryce MSS • Bodl. Oxf., Clarendon MSS • Bodl. Oxf., Disraeli MSS • Bodl. Oxf., Harcourt MSS • Bodl. Oxf., Kimberley MSS • Bodl. Oxf., Thorold Rogers MSS • Bodl. Oxf., Taylor MSS • Bodl. Oxf., Tupper MSS • Bodl. Oxf., Wilberforce MSS • Chatsworth House, Derbyshire, Devonshire MSS • Co-operative Union, Holyoake House, Manchester, Holyoake MSS • CUL, Acton MSS • CUL, Childers MSS • Cumbria AS, Carlisle, Graham MSS • Duke U., Primrose MSS • HLRO, Brand MSS • Keble College, Oxford, Keble MSS • London School of Economics, Broadhurst MSS • LPL, Selborne MSS • LPL, Tait MSS • Lpool RO, Derby MSS • NL Scot., Blackie MSS • NL Scot., Hope-Scott MSS • NL Scot., Rosebery MSS • NL Wales, Lewis MSS • NL Wales, Rendel MSS • NPG, Watts MSS • Oriel College, Oxford, Hawkins MSS • PRO, Cardwell MSS, 30/48 • PRO, Granville MSS, 30/29 • PRO, Russell MSS, 30/22 • PRO, Russell MSS, FO 918 [Odo Russell] • PRO NIre., Ingram MSS • Pusey Oxf., Pusey MSS • Som. ARS, Carlingford MSS • Suffolk RO, Ipswich, Gurdon MSS • U. Birm., Chamberlain MSS • U. Edin., Chalmers MSS • U. Southampton, Palmerston MSS • University of Sheffield, Mundella MSS • University of York, Halifax MSS • W. Sussex RO, Cobden MSS • West Glamorgan Archive Service, Swansea, Aberdare MSS | FILM BFI, film of funeral, 1898 | SOUND BL NSA, speech, 1888

Likenesses G. Hayter, oil sketch, 1833, Hawarden Castle, Flintshire • W. Bradley, oils, 1838, Hawarden Castle, Flintshire • J. Lucas, oils, 1843, Hawarden Castle, Flintshire • G. Richmond, chalk drawing, 1843, Gov. Art Coll. • Maull & Polyblank, photograph, 1857, NPG • G. F. Watts, oils, 1859, NPG • J. Adams-Acton, marble bust, 1864?, National Liberal Club, London • T. Woolner, marble bust, 1866, AM Oxf. • G. L. Dickinson, oils, 1871, Liverpool College, Liverpool • F. von Lenbach, oils, 1874, Lenbachhaus, Munich • F. von Lenbach, oils, 1879, Scot. NPG • J. Millais, oils, 1879, NPG [*see illus.*] • photographs, 1879, Lenbachhaus, Munich • T. Woolner, bronze bust, 1882, NPG • Bassano, photograph, 1883, NPG • J. Millais, oils, 1884, Eton • R. Potter, photograph, 1884, NPG • J. Millais, oils, 1885, Christ Church Oxf. • F. von Lenbach, double portrait, oils, 1886 (with J. J. I. von Döllinger), Lenbachhaus, Munich • J. Millais, oils, 1889, Hawarden Castle, Flintshire • J. M. Hamilton, oils, 1890, Louvre, Paris • E. Myers, photograph, 1890, NPG • S. Acland, photograph, 1892, Bodl. Oxf. • S. P. Hall, drawings, *c.*1893, NPG • P. May, pen-and-ink caricature, 1893, NPG • M. Beerbohm, eleven caricature drawings, 1898, Carlton Club, London • W. Richmond, pencil drawing, 1898 (posthumous), NPG • W. Nicholson, coloured woodcut, 1899, NPG • H. Thornycroft, statue, 1905, Aldwych, London • W. B. Richmond, memorial tomb, 1906, Hawarden parish church, Flintshire • J. P. Macgillivray, statue, 1917, Edinburgh • H. Furniss, cartoons, NPG • M. Grant, marble bust, All Souls Oxf. • J. Hughes, statue, Hawarden • P. Troubetzkoi, oils, Scot. NPG

Wealth at death £59,506 17*s.* 8*d.*: probate, 1898

Gladwin, Francis (1744/5–1812), Persian scholar, was born the elder of two known sons of an otherwise unidentified F. Gladwin. He went to a school in Islington kept by John Shield. The whole of his adult life was spent in India. In 1765 he was reported to have been working for 'some time' in the office of the secretary to the East India Company's council in Bengal, although he is also described as having 'come out a cadet' in the company's army (*Fort William–India House Correspondence*, 4.321, 452). Gladwin made a good impression on Robert Clive, who pressed the directors of the company at home to give him the valuable appointment of writer in the company's Bengal civil service. He was to hold a variety of employment in that service. During the 1770s he was concerned with revenue administration in rural Bengal. In the 1780s and 1790s he was posted to Calcutta with responsibility for the city's revenue. He took over the management of the company's printing press, paying a considerable sum for it to his predecessor, and launched from it the weekly *Calcutta Gazette, or, Oriental Advertiser* in 1784. In 1801 he was appointed first professor of Persian at the new college for the company's junior servants at Fort William. Although he presented the college with 'valuable Fonts of Types in the Oriental Characters' (Roebuck, 27), he appears to have spent little time there, being transferred in 1802 to Patna, in Bihar, where he was managing the company's commercial concerns at the time of his death ten years later. Gladwin was twice married: on 3 December 1769 to Ann Proctor, who, permitted to leave India in a vain attempt to restore her health, died at sea on 5 February 1773. A report circulated in the *Annual Register* for that year, that she and her two children had been poisoned by their Indian servants, appears to be unfounded. Gladwin married Sarah Alexander on 3 July 1782. With her he had a son, Francis William Ulrick. A natural daughter by an unknown mother was christened Isabella in 1776.

Gladwin was clearly a man of wide intellectual interests—he accumulated a remarkable library—and with a passion for learning languages and for making translations, above all from Persian. He published a large number of his translations. In 1775 he produced a specimen of a 'vocabulary' of words in various Asian languages, a project that he was later to realize in several different formats. Two years later he published proposals in London for his most ambitious undertaking, *Ayeen Akbery*, a translation of the *A'in-i-Akbari* of Abu'l-Fazl, minister of the Mughal emperor Akbar. This work was widely esteemed by contemporaries as embodying, in the words of Gladwin's generous patron Warren Hastings, 'the original constitution of the Mogul Empire', knowledge of which would enable British administration to return to 'first principles' (*Ayeen Akbery, or, The Institutes of the Emperor Akbar*, 3 vols., Calcutta, 1783–6, 1.ix). Gladwin's translation was not to be superseded for another hundred years, one of the new editors then expressing surprise that 'he has on the whole succeeded so well' (Blochman and Jarrett, ix). A stream of other publications followed, making Gladwin the most frequently published author in late eighteenth-century Calcutta. Gladwin was responsible for dictionaries and vocabularies, translations of Persian histories, collections of stories and revenue accounts, treatises on medicine and rhetoric, and a Persian version of an abridgement of the biblical history. He also edited a series of miscellanies, chiefly consisting of translations.

None of this activity is likely to have been lucrative. Gladwin confessed to spending heavily in acquiring manuscripts. Publication costs in India were notoriously high and the market was very restricted. Success depended largely on the willingness of the East India Company to purchase multiple copies. The company was generous in this respect, while Hastings was not only assiduous in canvassing support for Gladwin, but he personally paid for a dozen sets of the *Ayeen Akbery*. The extent of Gladwin's patronage and 'the tender regard … payed to his circumstances' (Shaw, 26) aroused the envy of rivals, but it could not save him from bankruptcy. By 1787 his property had been assigned to his creditors and in his later years he wrote that his financial circumstances did not permit him to leave India. Gladwin died at Patna and was buried in the military cemetery at nearby Dinapore on 19 September 1812, which was probably also the day of his death. P. J. Marshall

Sources G. Shaw, *Printing in Calcutta to 1800: a description and checklist of printing in late eighteenth-century Calcutta* (1981) • Gladwin to Warren Hastings, BL, Add. MSS 29168–29170, 29172, 29179 • K. K. Datta and others, eds., *Fort William–India House correspondence*, 21 vols. (1949–85) • inventory of Gladwin's estate, BL OIOC, L/AG/27/48 • Bengal burials, BL OIOC, N/1/9 • Bengal marriages and baptisms, BL OIOC, N/1/2, N/1/4 • Gladwin's father to the directors of the East India Company, 4 June 1784, BL OIOC, E/1/74 • T. Roebuck, *Annals of the college of Fort William* (1879) • *Bengal Past and Present*, 28 (1924), 206–7 • *The Ain i Akbari by Abul Fazl 'Allami*, trans. H. Blochmann and H. S. Jarrett, 3 vols. (1873–94) • Nichols, *Lit. anecdotes*, 6.637–8 • R. C. Sterndale, *An historical account of the Calcutta collectorate*, 2nd edn (1958) • J. S. Grewal, *Muslim rule in India: the assessments of British historians* (1970) • *Annual Register* (1773), 110–11 • East India Company record of service, BL OIOC, L/F/10

Archives BL OIOC, 'Account of the rise of Mahratta states, translated from original papers', MS Eur. B 92 | BL, corresp. with Warren Hastings, Add. MSS 29168–29170, 29172, 29179
Wealth at death library: inventory, BL OIOC, L/AG/27/48 • bankrupt in 1787: Sterndale, *Calcutta collectorate*, 23–4 • in 1790, creditors remitted two thirds of claims: BL, Add. MS 29172, fol. 46

Gladwyn. For this title name *see* Jebb, Cynthia, Lady Gladwyn (1898–1990); Jebb, (Hubert Miles) Gladwyn, first Baron Gladwyn (1900–1996).

Glaisher, James (1809–1903), astronomer and meteorologist, was born on 7 April 1809 in Rotherhithe, London, the son of James Glaisher, watchmaker, and his wife, Mary. The family moved to Greenwich shortly afterwards. Glaisher visited the Royal Observatory in 1829, where he expressed interest in the scientific instruments, and his brother John (*d.* 1846) became a computer there. His own first employment was in Ireland in 1829 on the principal triangulation of the Ordnance Survey in co. Galway and the Keeper Mountains, near Limerick, but, made ill by exposure, he returned to England at the end of 1830. He later traced his meteorological interests to this period, when he reportedly spent much time surrounded by clouds.

In 1833 Glaisher joined the Cambridge University observatory, then under Professor George Airy, and as assistant made a series of observations of the position of Halley's comet at its return in 1835. This was the beginning of forty years' association between the two men. When Airy became astronomer royal at Greenwich, in June 1835, he appointed Glaisher as his assistant in the astronomical department, and in December Glaisher moved to Greenwich. He was succeeded at Cambridge by his brother John, who later was astronomical assistant to John Lee at Hartwell House, Aylesbury.

In 1838 Airy put Glaisher in charge of the new magnetical and meteorological department which he superintended until his resignation in 1874. Glaisher's account of the new department was published in the *Illustrated London News* on 16 March 1844. The observations, made every two hours, day and night, provided the basis for his published tables of *Corrections to Meteorological Observations for Diurnal Range*. Scientific meteorology was in its infancy, and his first task had been to standardize the instruments and to systematize the collection of observations. Charles Dickens launched the *Daily News* in 1846, and from 1848 Glaisher sent him daily weather reports, the first telegraphic reports and weather maps of their kind. In 1847 he communicated to the Royal Society the result of three years' experiments on the nocturnal radiation of heat. His *Hygrometrical Tables Adapted to the Use of the Dry and Wet Bulb Thermometer* (1847 and later editions), remained the accepted authority by British meteorologists for many years, and possibly led to his investigations in the late 1840s with Dr William Farr into the theory that the evaporation of miasmatic substances from the Thames caused cholera.

On 31 December 1843 Glaisher married Cecilia Louisa (1829–1892), the youngest daughter from the first marriage of John Henry Belville, a well-respected assistant at

James Glaisher (1809–1903), by Negretti & Zambra, 1862 [left, with Henry Tracey Coxwell]

Greenwich observatory, who was of French descent. At the time of her marriage in All Souls' Church in the parish of St Marylebone, Cecilia's age was given as sixteen years, although she was in fact only fourteen. A talented amateur artist with an interest in nature, she drew the illustrations for her husband's published studies of snow crystals. They had three children: James Whitbread Lee *Glaisher (1848–1928), fellow and lecturer at Trinity College, Cambridge, and the author of many important contributions to mathematical literature; Cecilia Appelina, who migrated with her husband, Dr F. E. Hunt, to New Zealand in 1880; and Ernest (*d.* 1887), a naturalist who travelled in South America, wrote books on butterflies, and was the curator of the Georgetown Museum in British Guiana.

About 1846 Glaisher began collecting meteorological observations from approximately forty centres in various parts of the country for inclusion in the registrar-general's *Quarterly Returns of Births, Marriages, and Deaths*. He established meteorological stations, inspected them regularly, tested the instruments, and trained sixty volunteers (mostly medical men and clergy) to take daily weather notes. His meteorological contributions to the *Quarterly Returns* continued until his death. He received no payment for these services until 1853 when the Treasury sanctioned a small annual allowance, but this was discontinued in 1875. Thereafter he continued unpaid, but with the help of an assistant paid by the council of the Meteorological Society.

Glaisher joined the Royal Astronomical Society in 1841, and was elected a fellow of the Royal Society in 1849. By 1850 he was the recognized authority in Britain for the verification of meteorological instruments, and he served as a juror for the class of philosophical instruments at the International Exhibition in 1851. In 1850 he joined ten fellows of the Royal Society and the Royal Astronomical Society at Hartwell House to found the British Meteorological Society. Elected the society's first secretary, Glaisher held that office until 1873, except for 1867–8 when he was president. He edited the society's publications for many years. From 1848 to 1876 he regularly contributed papers to the Royal Society, the Meteorological Society, and the British Association for the Advancement of Science (BAAS). In a meteorological report for the General Board of Health in 1854 he sought to define the relations between the weather and the cholera epidemics in London in 1832, 1849, and 1853–4. A member of the board of directors of several gas and water companies, Glaisher often gave evidence before parliamentary committees on bills dealing with the water supply, and in 1863 he prepared an official report on the meteorology of India. He was a member of the royal commission on the warming and ventilation of dwellings, appointed in 1857, and he wrote its report. Glaisher regularly attended BAAS annual meetings and he served on several committees, including the committee on observations of luminous meteors, to which he was appointed in 1860, and which he chaired for more than twenty years.

In 1861 the British Association appointed a balloon committee to oversee the collection of meteorological observations at high altitudes. A large balloon was constructed by Henry Coxwell, a popular aeronaut. Glaisher and Coxwell made eight ascents in 1862, including some for public exhibition at Crystal Palace. Glaisher employed volunteers to record the balloon's path and its height, and himself made observations every 20 seconds on his instruments, which were tied to a board attached to the basket. On 5 September 1862 Glaisher became unconscious at a height he later determined as 29,000 feet. Coxwell temporarily lost the use of his limbs, but with his teeth seized the cord which opened the valve, and this allowed the balloon to descend from an altitude of 37,000 feet. Neither Glaisher nor Coxwell suffered permanent injury. Their misadventure in the service of meteorological science became a major news topic in its day, a subject of widespread praise and satire, and occasioned a poem in *Punch*. Glaisher made many later ascents with Coxwell and other aeronauts under the auspices of the British Association between 1863 and 1866, publishing his balloon observations in the BAAS *Reports* (1862–6). After his relationship with Coxwell deteriorated following a riot that resulted in the destruction of Coxwell's balloon, Glaisher ascended in a captive balloon at Chelsea, and made low altitude observations. He edited an account of his own ascents, with essays by French astronomers who had promoted balloon meteorology, as *Travels in the Air* (1871). In 1866 he helped to found the Aeronautical Society and served as its treasurer. He frequently lectured and wrote articles to promote the balloon as a 'philosophical instrument' instead of in its traditional form, as a vehicle of entertainment.

Glaisher played a leading role in several British scientific societies. In 1856 he was elected fellow of the Microscopical Society of London, and was its president from 1865 to 1868, the period in which the society received the royal charter. An avid photographer with an interest in the scientific applications of the camera, he served as president of the Photographic Society from 1869 to 1892, with the exception of one year. Glaisher maintained his interest in astronomy and mathematical science in the 1870s. In 1875 he joined the BAAS committee on mathematical tables of which his son, Dr J. W. L. Glaisher, was reporter. Supported by a grant from the association he completed for this committee, and published in three volumes, the *Factor Tables* (1879–83) begun by J. C. Burckhardt in 1814 and continued by J. N. Z. Dase in 1862–5.

Following a disagreement with Airy, Glaisher, who had a reputation for being autocratic and intolerant of criticism, retired from the Royal Observatory in 1874. He continued to supply his quarterly report to the registrar-general until the last year of his life. For many years he was a member of the Palestine Exploration Fund, serving as chairman in 1880, and contributing fifteen papers on meteorological observations made in Palestine. Glaisher's relationship with his wife deteriorated about 1866, the time of their daughter's marriage, which he strenuously opposed. Glaisher broke off communication with his daughter and the two were never totally reconciled, although she attempted a reconciliation in 1900 when he was living in Trinity College, Cambridge, with his eldest son.

His wife having died in 1892, in 1893 Glaisher moved from Dartmouth Terrace, Blackheath, to Shola, 2 Heathfield Road, Croydon, where he had his own meteorological station. Apart from periods of time spent with his son at Trinity College, Cambridge, he lived there until his death from a cerebral haemorrhage on 7 February 1903.

H. P. Hollis, *rev.* J. Tucker

Sources W. Marriott, 'James Glaisher', *Quarterly Journal of the Royal Meteorological Society*, 29 (1903), 115–21 • 'James Glaisher', *Quarterly Journal of the Royal Meteorological Society*, 30 (1904) • *Daily Telegraph* (Feb 1903) • W. Marriott, 'The earliest telegraphic daily meteorological reports and weather maps', *Quarterly Journal of the Royal Meteorological Society*, 29 (1903) • J. Glaisher and others, *Travels in the air*, ed. J. Glaisher (1871) • H. T. Coxwell, *My life and balloon experiences*, [vol. 1] (1887) • *Monthly Notices of the Royal Astronomical Society*, 64 (1903–4), 280–87 • W. C. N., *The Observatory*, 26 (1903), 129–32 • J. Glaisher, 'An account of meteorological and physical observations in eight balloon ascents', *Report of the thirty-second meeting of the British Association for the Advancement of Science, held at Cambridge in October 1862* (1863), *Reports*, 376–503 • J. Glaisher, 'An account of meteorological and physical observations in five balloon ascents', *Report of the thirty-third meeting of the British Association for the Advancement of Science, held at Newcastle-upon-Tyne in August and September 1863* (1864), *Reports*, 426–516 • J. Glaisher, 'An account of meteorological and physical observations in nine balloon ascents', *Report of the thirty-fourth meeting of the British Association for the Advancement of*

Science, held at Bath in September 1864 (1865), *Reports*, 193–326 • J. Glaisher, 'An account of meteorological and physical observations in three balloon ascents', *Report of the thirty-fifth meeting of the British Association for the Advancement of Science, held at Birmingham in September 1865* (1866), *Reports*, 145–92 • m. cert. • d. cert. • private information (2004) • *CGPLA Eng. & Wales* (1903)

Archives Meteorological Office, Bracknell, Berkshire • National Museum of Photography, Film and Television, Bradford, Royal Photographic Society collection, photographs • RAS, corresp. and papers • RAS, letters to Royal Astronomical Society | Inst. EE, corresp. with Sir Francis Ronalds [archives] • RAS, letters to John Lee • Wellcome L., letters to Henry Lee

Likenesses Negretti & Zambra, carte-de-visite, 1862 (with Henry Coxwell), NPG [*see illus.*] • bust, *c.*1887, Royal Meteorological Society • T. R. Annan, photogravure (after J. E. Mayall), NPG • S. A. Walker, carte-de-visite, NPG • H. J. Whitlock, carte-de-visite, NPG • photograph, Royal Aeronautical Society • photographs, RAS • woodcut, repro. in Glaisher, Flammarion, de Fonvielle, and Tissandier, *Travels in the air*

Wealth at death £36,037 11*s.* 9*d.*: probate, 9 March 1903, *CGPLA Eng. & Wales*

Glaisher, James Whitbread Lee (1848–1928), mathematician, was born at Dartmouth Terrace, Lewisham, Kent, on 5 November 1848, the elder son of James *Glaisher (1809–1903), astronomer and meteorologist, and his wife, Cecilia Louisa Belville (1829–1892). He was sent to St Paul's School, London, in 1858. In 1867 he went to Trinity College, Cambridge, where he was elected a scholar the following year, and in 1871 he graduated second wrangler. He was elected a fellow of Trinity in October 1871 and was at once appointed a lecturer and assistant tutor. He remained in residence at Trinity for the rest of his life.

Glaisher's lectureship continued for thirty years until 1901, a special extension having been made by the college council; he was a tutor of the college from 1883 to 1893, then the customary period of tenure. He proceeded to the newly established Cambridge degree of ScD in 1887. He never held any permanent appointment outside Cambridge and he refused the official invitation to become astronomer royal in 1881 on the retirement of Sir George Airy.

Glaisher was much involved in the scientific organizations of his time. He was elected a fellow of the Royal Society at the early age of twenty-seven in 1875, served on its council for three periods (1883–4, 1890–92, 1917–19), and was awarded the Sylvester medal in 1913. His earliest original paper (dealing with numerical tables of some non-evaluable integrals), written while he was still an undergraduate, was communicated to the society in 1870 by Arthur Cayley. Glaisher joined the London Mathematical Society in 1872, was a member of its council continuously until his retirement in 1906, served as president in 1884–6, and was awarded the De Morgan medal in 1908. His presidential address of 1886 gave an interesting history of the Cambridge mathematical tripos and anticipated some of the changes made in 1909, when the Order of Merit and the title of wrangler were abolished. He joined the Royal Astronomical Society in 1871, was on its council from 1874 until 1928, served twice as president (1886–8 and 1901–3), and for thirty-three years presided over the Royal Astronomical Society club. Like his father, he was active in the British Association for the Advancement of Science, as secretary of Section A for a number of years, as president of the section at the Leeds meeting of 1890, and as a member of many of the committees dealing with numerical tables, and of those reporting on the contemporary state of mathematical science. He used his address to the Leeds meeting of 1890 to call for greater recognition of pure mathematics as a subject in its own right. Among other societies to which he belonged were the Royal Society of Edinburgh and the Manchester Literary and Philosophical Society, and he was also a foreign member of the National Academy of Sciences in Washington.

The main part of Glaisher's published work consists of his papers on mathematics and astronomy. In later life he wrote papers on ceramics and he also contributed an appendix on Wrotham ware to *English Pottery* (1924), by B. Rackham and H. Read. The number of his mathematical papers amounts to nearly four hundred, few of which are of lasting interest. Mention should, however, be made of his contributions to definite integrals, differential equations, elliptic functions and their developments, and, significantly for Cambridge, to the theory of numbers particularly in connection with elliptic functions. He devoted much attention to the calculation of mathematical tables such as those of the Theta-functions; and from the beginning to the end of all his work he maintained a productive interest in the history of mathematics. His historical writings ranged from the origins of the plus and minus signs to the work of Napier and Briggs on logarithms in the seventeenth century and H. J. S. Smith's work on numbers and elliptic functions in the nineteenth century. For many of the later years of his life he provided finance for the *Messenger of Mathematics* and the *Quarterly Journal of Pure and Applied Mathematics*, both of which ceased to exist at Cambridge after his death.

In middle life Glaisher began his study of ceramics which developed into the dominant pursuit of his remaining years and resulted in his becoming one of the leading collectors of his day. The elaborate catalogue of his collection, in forty manuscript volumes, is a valuable addition to the literature of the subject. He bequeathed his collection and a substantial cash legacy to the Fitzwilliam Museum, Cambridge.

Very tall, and spare in frame, Glaisher was fond of walking and cycling. Even in his early seventies he maintained the vitality and the geniality of youth, and it was only in the last years of his life that his health gave way. He died in his college rooms in New Court on 7 December 1928 and was buried at Cambridge. He never married.

A. R. Forsyth, *rev.* J. J. Gray

Sources J. J. Thomson, *Cambridge Review* (25 Jan 1929), 212–13 • G. H. Hardy, 'Dr Glaisher and the Messenger of Mathematics', *Messenger of Mathematics*, 58 (1929), 159–60 • H. H. T. [H. H. Turner], *Monthly Notices of the Royal Astronomical Society*, 89 (1928–9), 300–08 • A. R. Forsyth, *Journal of the London Mathematical Society*, 4 (1929), 101–12 • B. Rackham, *The Glaisher bequest* (1931) [Fitzwilliam Museum pamphlet] • personal knowledge (1929) • b. cert. • d. cert.

Archives Brown University, Providence, Rhode Island, John Hay Library, corresp., letters and papers • RGS | Air Force Research Laboratories, Cambridge, Massachusetts, letters to Sir George Strutt • CUL, Stokes MSS

Likenesses Maull & Fox, photograph, 1891–2, RS · F. Dodd, pencil drawing, Trinity Cam. · Maull & Fox, two photographs, RS
Wealth at death £43,223 18s. 8d.: probate, 15 April 1929, *CGPLA Eng. & Wales*

Glaister, John (1856–1932), expert in medical jurisprudence and public health, was born on 9 March 1856 in the county town of Lanark, the eldest of four children born to Joseph Glaister (1830–1871) and Marion Hamilton Weir (1832–1871), small property owners, grocers, and spirit merchants. Glaister was educated at Hugh Brown's School, Westport, and Lanark grammar school before entering into a legal apprenticeship at the age of fifteen. After the death of his parents the family business was bought by an uncle, who became his guardian. Glaister then turned his back on the law and entered Glasgow University, in 1873, to study medicine. He proved a gifted student, gaining many prizes, and completed his studies in less than four years, though he was refused permission to sit the final MB examinations immediately because he was still some months under the age of twenty-one.

Undeterred, in 1877 Glaister obtained licences from both the Royal College of Physicians and the Royal College of Surgeons of Edinburgh, and after a brief period as assistant to a practitioner in Carluke he set up practice in the then affluent Townhead district of Glasgow. An archetypal young man in hurry, he married in 1878 Mary Scott Clarke, daughter of Robert Clarke, of Wishaw. The first of their six children was born in 1879. In the same year Glaister graduated MD at Glasgow. With a young family to support and no medical connections or continental study to further his career, he augmented his income by obtaining the post of police surgeon for the St Rollox division, an industrial district on the banks of the Forth and Clyde Canal. The foundations of Glaister's ensuing medico-legal career were laid in this period. He rapidly became acquainted with a wide range of wounds caused by crimes and industrial accidents. The canal provided him with material to differentiate between injuries caused to bodies by the screws of passing steamers before and after death. By 1893 he had seen 300 dead bodies as part of his duties.

Glaister's wide circle of medical friends included the rising surgeon William Macewen, then a part-time extramural lecturer on medical jurisprudence at Glasgow Royal Infirmary medical school. In 1881 Glaister succeeded Macewen in this post, the latter having obtained the infirmary lectureship in surgery, and he also became a fellow of the Faculty of Physicians and Surgeons of Glasgow. In the mid-1880s he added lectures in public health to his course, responding to the demand for suitably qualified medical officers of health. He was appointed, in 1887, as special lecturer in public health at the Royal Infirmary, with a laboratory which he equipped at his own expense. Glaister took the Cambridge diploma in public health in 1889. His was the sole laboratory in Glasgow and the west of Scotland to offer sufficient tuition for the Cambridge diploma.

Glaister was appointed professor of forensic medicine and public health in 1889 when the Glasgow Royal Infirmary school merged with St Mungo's medical school. At this point public health appeared the more important field to Glaister. He published a book and several articles on the subject but it is doubtful whether he shared James Burn Russell's ideology: Glaister's writings on sanitary failings are tinged more with nature than with nurture. During the 1890s he campaigned for improved standards in death certification. With Russell he toured public health laboratories throughout the United Kingdom for Glasgow University. In 1899 he was elevated to the university's regius chair of forensic medicine and public health; he taught female students separately at the nearby Queen Margaret College. In 1903 Glaister introduced postgraduate degrees for BSc and DSc in public health. By 1907 Glaister had successfully acquired custom-built and specially equipped laboratory facilities for both forensic medicine and public health within the university's latest extension.

John Glaister (1856–1932), by William Somerville Shanks, 1917

When the sheriff of Lanarkshire appointed him a crown medical witness in 1899, Glaister resigned his police position and sold his private practice. From that time onwards he derived his income mainly from his professorial salary and his medico-legal fees, and he styled himself 'medico-legal examiner in crown cases'. He lived in some comfort, with a small country estate in Dumfriesshire, where he indulged his leisure pursuits of golf, fishing, and motoring.

Glaister became a household name as his appearances increased in the busy Glasgow high courts. Like his Edinburgh counterpart, Henry Littlejohn, Glaister considered himself the complete medical detective: a forensic pathologist, toxicologist, serologist, psychiatrist, and ballistics and fingerprint expert, who dealt with all theatres of death. Notorious trials such that of Oscar Slater in 1909 for the murder of Marion Gilchrist by assault with a hammer, and of Donald Merrett in 1926 for the murder by shooting of his mother, secured Glaister's position in a forensic firmament later inhabited by Bernard Spilsbury and Sydney Smith, with whom he did battle, or so it seemed to his medical students and the average Glaswegian.

Unlike Littlejohn, however, Glaister was a full-time academic who also wrote valuable textbooks. His first, published in 1902, conjoined the two subjects professed from his chair: *A Textbook of Medical Jurisprudence, Toxicology and Public Health*. Thereafter, subsequent editions were restricted to medical jurisprudence and toxicology, with one edition of *A Textbook of Public Health* in 1910. He dedicated each edition to his wife under the acronym MSG. Glaister's was the first British textbook to use photographic evidence to illustrate violent death and other aspects of forensic medicine, each further edition amplified by his latest cases. In court his textbook was often quoted back at him by defence counsels, notably the eminent Craigie Aitchison. It pleased Glaister enormously to gain student recognition through the affectionately scurrilous 'Ballad of John Glaister', which encapsulated many of his lecture and textbook themes. The ballad's fame crossed the Atlantic to Harvard medical school, whose students thought Glaister to be a fictional character similar to Sherlock Holmes. In his lifetime Glaister published five editions of his textbook. John Glaister the younger, his son and successor in the chair, continued with further editions.

Glaister carried his forensic skills beyond the criminal courts and into the arena of industrial disease and death. He was the specialist medical referee in industrial diseases for the counties of Lanark, Ayr, Renfrew, Bute, Stirling, and Dumbarton. He made a unique study of accidental arsine poisoning through the triggering of the Marsh test effect, which produces arseniuretted hydrogen.

During the First World War Glaister carried the bulk of teaching and examination in public health and forensic medicine at Glasgow. The post-war growth of the subjects' specialisms forced him to recognize what had been accepted in Edinburgh in 1897—that the traditional Scottish teaching of both subjects in tandem was no longer viable. In 1923 one of Glaister's friends, the industrialist Sir Henry Mechan, endowed a separate chair of public health. Glaister continued as professor of forensic medicine until 1931. When he retired the university conferred upon him the honorary degree of LLD. Until the end of his career Glaister's idiosyncratic court attire consisted of the silk top hat, long frock-coat, and Gladstone high collar of his younger days.

Between 1907 and 1909, when Glaister was president of the Faculty of Physicians and Surgeons of Glasgow, the faculty applied for and was granted the title 'Royal'. In his time Glaister was also elected president of the Royal Glasgow Philosophical Society, vice-president of the Medico-legal Society of Great Britain, the Medico-legal Institute of New York, and academician and gold medallist of the Royal Chemico-Physico Academy of Palermo. He was a member and fellow of many societies including the Edinburgh Royal Society, the Chemical Society, and the Royal Sanitary Institute. Closer to home Glaister was a member of the management board of the Royal Infirmary and a long-time member of the Southern Medical Club. He also worked enthusiastically for the British Medical Association: he was joint secretary at the 1888 annual general meeting in Glasgow, president of the section of industrial diseases and forensic medicine at the 1922 meeting, and, shortly before his death, vice-president of the section on forensic medicine at the centenary meeting in 1932. He was a staunch member of the St Rollox Conservative Association, and for fifty-six years he was a member and senior deacon at the Elgin Place Congregational Church. Glaister was a moving force in the foundation of the Scottish Burial Reform and Cremation Society, of which he was a medical referee, director for thirty years, and chairman from 1922 to 1932.

In December 1932 Glaister and his wife succumbed to an influenza epidemic sweeping Glasgow. On 18 December they died within four hours of each other at their home in Newton Place. Their joint funeral service was held on 23 December in the university chapel, Glaister's coffin distinguished by his scarlet robe. They were cremated at the Maryhill crematorium, Glasgow, and their ashes interred in the family grave in Lanark. BRENDA M. WHITE

Sources *BMJ* (31 Dec 1932), 1215–16 • *The Lancet* (31 Dec 1932) • *Glasgow Medical Journal*, 119 (1933) • *Scots Law Times: News* (7 Jan 1933) • *The Times* (19 Dec 1932) • *The Times* (23 Dec 1932) • *Glasgow Herald* (19 Dec 1932) • *Glasgow Herald* (23 Dec 1932) • 'University memory XX: John Glaister, senior … professor of forensic medicine, 1898–1931', *College Courant: Journal of the Glasgow University Graduates Association*, 10/20 (1958), 85–92 • J. Glaister, 'History of the Glaister family of Lanark', U. Glas., Glaister papers • J. Glaister, *Final diagnosis* (1964) • M. A. Crowther and B. White, *On soul and conscience: the medical expert and crime* (1988) • *Glasgow Herald* (13 March 1964) • *Glasgow Herald* (18 March 1964) • 'Ballad of John Glaister', U. Glas., Glaister MSS • *The Bailie* (16 March 1898)
Archives U. Glas.
Likenesses W. S. Shanks, oils, 1917, Hunterian Museum and Art Gallery, Glasgow [*see illus.*] • T. R. Annan and Sons, photograph, Wellcome L.
Wealth at death £7212 11s.: confirmation, 21 Feb 1933, *CCI*

Glamis. For this title name *see* Lyon, Sir John, lord of Glamis (*d.* 1382); Lyon, Patrick, first Lord Glamis (*c*.1400–1460); Lyon, Alexander, second Lord Glamis (*c*.1430–1486?) [*see under* Lyon, Patrick, first Lord Glamis (*c*.1400–1460)]; Lyon, John, third Lord Glamis (*c*.1432–1497) [*see under* Lyon, Patrick, first Lord Glamis (*c*.1400–1460)]; Douglas, Janet, Lady Glamis (*c*.1504–1537); Lyon, John, seventh Lord Glamis (*b.* *c*.1521, *d.* in or before 1559); Lyon, John, eighth Lord Glamis (*c*.1544–1578); Lyon, Sir Thomas, of Auldbar, master of Glamis (*c*.1546–1608).

Glancy, Sir Bertrand James (1882–1953), administrator in India, was born in Ireland on 31 December 1882. His father, Lieutenant-Colonel Thomas Glancy, was an officer in the Royal Engineers who spent most of his life working abroad, and his mother, Helen, moved from hotel to hotel on the French riviera, with the result that Bertrand was brought up by a maiden aunt in Roscommon. He met his sister, Ethel, only at a tennis party when he was seventeen. His education began at a school for the sons of army officers at Westward Ho!. He soon moved on to Clifton College as a day boy, where he experienced the trauma of the death of one of his elder brothers. This may have contributed to a further removal to Monmouth, another minor public school more renowned for its rugby than classics, where Bertrand completed his studies before going up to Exeter College, Oxford, as a commoner at the age of nineteen.

Bertrand followed in the footsteps of his elder brother, Sir Reginald Isidore Robert Glancy (1874–1939), when he entered the Indian Civil Service in 1905. Like Reginald, he was to spend many years in the political department working in the princely states of India, although he received his initial training in the prestigious Punjab cadre of the Indian Civil Service. This latter experience reinforced his natural disposition towards unending work, born of social unease and a desperate need to please the ambitions of his 'martinet of a mother'. In later years Glancy overcame his shyness by developing a reputation as a brilliant wit and raconteur. He remained anxious to please his mother, however, keeping up a regular weekly correspondence until her death at the age of ninety-one.

In the year before his posting as first assistant to the agent to the governor-general in Rajputana in 1915 he married Grace Steele in Mount Abu, a hill station in Bombay presidency. Only one of their four children, Terence, was to survive; all the others died in infancy. From 1918 to 1921 Glancy was posted to the residency in Kashmir. After a brief spell at the political department in Delhi in 1921 his services were 'lent' to the state of Jammu and Kashmir for five years.

On his return from home leave in 1926 Glancy returned to the political department in Delhi. In 1929 however he re-entered the world of the princely states. From then until 1932 he was president of the Jaipur council of state, before beginning his third and final spell of duty in Kashmir. After a home leave Glancy became resident and agent to the governor-general in the princely states of central India in 1933, and was stationed at Indore.

Glancy's dealings with Tukoji Rao Puar III (1888–1937), the ruler of the tiny Maratha princely state of Dewas Senior, some 350 miles north-west of Bombay, were years later held up by the novelist E. M. Forster in his memoir, *The Hill of Devi* (1953), as symptomatic of British insensitivity in relationships with Indians. Tukoji's dispute with the political department, which culminated in his flight to French Pondicherry, was occasioned by gross financial mismanagement. The workaholic Glancy certainly had little personal sympathy with the effete ruler and his court, but Tukoji's claim that he acted vindictively in revenge for an earlier humiliation of his brother Reginald is untenable. Forster's account is also tendentious: it was largely prompted by romantic memories of the Christmas house parties at Dewas between 1909 and 1914, which Tukoji put on for his former guardian, Sir Malcolm Darling (1880–1969), and his set of highbrow British friends.

Glancy's pre-eminence as an administrator in princely India was recognized by his appointment in 1934 as political secretary and, from 1938, political adviser to the crown representative. This period was marked by the ultimately futile attempts to secure the princes' accession to a future all-India federation as envisaged by the 1935 Government of India Act. Many of the princes were unaware of the wider issues at stake; they were also disquieted by the increasing agitation for reform within their domains supported by the Indian National Congress, although it did not formally operate within the princely states. The failure of the federation scheme led ultimately to the collapse of the princely order on the British departure in 1947, and the transfer of power to the two democratic governments of India and Pakistan. Glancy, along with colleagues in the political department, greatly regretted this outcome and regarded it as a desertion of allies and dereliction of Britain's treaty obligations to the states, as the paramount power on the continent.

Glancy was equally disillusioned by the British treatment of the ruling Unionist Party in the Punjab. It had traditionally adopted a loyalist stance and had actively encouraged recruitment to the Indian army. By the time that he became governor of the province in 1941 the first cracks were appearing in the cross-communal Unionist Party as a result of the dislocations brought by the war and the Muslim League's growing campaign for Pakistan in the province, which raised tension among the non-Muslim population. Glancy shared the Unionist leaders' opposition to the Pakistan demand because of its impact on the unity of the Punjab. He encouraged the Muslim Unionist leaders, Sikandar Hayat (premier in 1937–42) and Khizr Tiwana (premier in 1942–6), in their stand against Jinnah, the Muslim League leader who was demanding Pakistan. Indeed, he stretched his constitutional powers to the limit to secure the dismissal of the minister for public works, the pro-Muslim League Shaukat Hayat, on 26 April 1944 to prevent him embarrassing the Unionist government by resigning.

Glancy's relations with Khizr were especially cordial and reproduced those he had earlier established with the princes. When Glancy left India in April 1946 Khizr declared: 'I can never adequately thank you for all your many kindnesses … I never deserved all I got.' Given this relationship, it is unsurprising that Khizr discounted the possibility that the British would desert their Unionist allies. The Muslim League triumph in the rural Punjab constituencies in the 1946 provincial elections surprised both Glancy and his prime minister. The outgoing governor became embroiled in controversy amid claims by the Punjab Muslim League president, the Nawab Iftikhar Husain Khan of Mamdot (1906–1969), that Glancy had denied his party the fruits of its victory by encouraging the formation of a Unionist–Akali–Congress coalition government. There is no evidence however that he paved the way for Khizr to resume office on 7 March 1946.

Glancy retired to Kenya, which held far more appeal

than attempting to live off an 'inflation-ravaged pension' in austerity Britain. He was kept informed by Khizr of developments within the Punjab. He was greatly saddened by the growing communal violence which culminated in the holocaust which accompanied the partition. He had warned his superiors of such an eventuality, but his voice had gone unheeded. He saw the rapid decision to divide and quit in 1947 as a 'betrayal of friends' in which 'all values were twisted out of shape'. He was appointed CSI in 1933, KCIE in 1935, and GCIE in 1946.

Time hung heavily on Glancy's hands during retirement: he had been so immersed in his work that he had never taken up any hobbies. He took pride in his collection of Indian coins, which were placed on display in London and New Delhi. He also began writing his memoirs. Unfortunately these remained unpublished at the time of his sudden death in Nairobi on 17 March 1953. He was survived by his wife.

Sir Bertrand Glancy was the ablest administrator of his generation in the political department of the government of India. His hallmarks were industry, wisdom, charm, and a 'wonderful way with words' which hid his lingering insecurity. Glancy retained, until the end of the raj, the paternalistic ethos of the Punjab school of administration, preferring rural allies to Indian politicians under the dominance of the Indian National Congress.

IAN TALBOT

Sources I. Talbot, *Khizr Tiwana, the Punjab unionist party and the partition of India* (1996) • I. Talbot, *Punjab and the raj, 1849–1947* (1988) • E. M. Forster, *The hill of Devi* (1983) • N. Mansergh and others, eds., *The transfer of power, 1942–7*, 12 vols. (1970–83) • A. Jalal, *The sole spokesman: Jinnah, the Muslim League and the demand for Pakistan* (1985) • *Wavell: the viceroy's journal*, ed. P. Moon (1973) • C. Dewey, *Anglo-Indian attitudes: the mind of the Indian civil service* (1993) • E. P. Moon, *Divide and quit: on the partition of India and Pakistan in 1947* (1961) • I. Copland, *The British raj and the Indian princes* (1982) • P. N. Furbank, *E. M. Forster: a life* (1979) • D. Gilmartin, *Empire and Islam: Punjab and the making of Pakistan* (1988) • private information (2004) • *CGPLA Eng. & Wales* (1953)

Archives BL OIOC • priv. coll. | BL OIOC, Linlithgow MSS • BL OIOC, Moon MSS • U. Cam., Centre of South Asian Studies, Darling MSS • U. Southampton L., corresp. with Sir Malik Tiwana

Likenesses photographs, priv. coll.

Wealth at death £2151 12s. 3d.: probate, 16 Dec 1953, *CGPLA Eng. & Wales*

Glanvill, John (1663/4–1735), poet and translator, was born at Broad Hinton, Wiltshire, the third of five children of Julius Glanvill (1631/2–1710) of Lincoln's Inn, and Anne Bagnall (*c*.1637–1702). His exact date of birth is not known, but the birth records of his siblings reveal that it would have been in 1663 or 1664. His grandfather and namesake was Sir John *Glanville (1585/6–1661). After attending Marlborough College, he became a commoner of Trinity College, Oxford, in 1678, was elected scholar in 1680, and proceeded BA in 1682 and MA in 1685. In 1683 he competed for a fellowship at All Souls, but the fellowship was awarded to the translator Thomas Creech, and in a fit of pique Glanvill declaimed in the schools 'Contra translatores' (*Life and Times of Anthony Wood*, 3.88). Allegedly expelled from Trinity (*Remarks*, 1.265), Glanvill entered Lincoln's Inn, and was in due course called to the bar.

In spite of his proclaimed dislike of translations, much of Glanvill's work took such a form. He translated parts of Seneca's *Agamemnon* for *Miscellany Poems and Translations by Oxford Hands* (1685). He also translated, from the French of Fontenelle, *A Plurality of Worlds* (1688), an influential popularization of current scientific thinking. His œuvre also includes numerous pieces of panegyric, such as *Some Odes of Horace Imitated with Relation to his Majesty and the Times* (1690), and a *Poem … Lamenting the Death of her Late Sacred Majesty from the Small-Pox* (1695). Other panegyric verse to members of the royal family followed. It is also possible, but not certain, that Glanvill was the 'J. G.' who wrote *Damon* (1696), a pastoral lamenting the death of Henry Purcell. His *Poems, Consisting of Originals and Translations* (1725) includes most of his surviving work. Francis Gregor's edition of Sir John Fortescue's *De laudibus legum Angliae* (1737) includes two letters written to Gregor by Glanville in 1730. Because of the early deaths of his two elder brothers Glanvill had inherited the family estates at Kingston, Surrey, and about 1728 he acquired a large estate at Catchfrench, near St Germans, in Cornwall. He died there a wealthy bachelor on 12 June 1735, and his will was proved by his nephew and heir, John Glanvill, citizen and apothecary of London, on 16 June 1735.

MATTHEW STEGGLE

Sources W. U. S. Glanville-Richards, *Records of the Anglo-Norman house of Glanville* (1882) • *Remarks and collections of Thomas Hearne*, ed. C. E. Doble and others, 11 vols., OHS, 2, 7, 13, 34, 42–3, 48, 50, 65, 67, 72 (1885–1921) • *The life and times of Anthony Wood*, ed. A. Clark, 5 vols., OHS, 19, 21, 26, 30, 40 (1891–1900) • *DNB* • will, PRO, PROB 11/671/122 • will, PRO, PROB 11/513/33 [Julius Glanvill, father]

Wealth at death large Cornish estate: will, PRO, PROB 11/671/122; will of Julius Glanvill, proved Feb 1710, PROB 11/513/33

Glanvill [Glanville], **Joseph** (1636–1680), Church of England clergyman, was born in Plymouth, the third of three sons of the puritan merchant Nicholas Glanville (*b.* 1597) of Halwell, Whitchurch, Devon, and his wife, Joan. The only member of his family to drop the terminal 'e', Glanvill matriculated at Exeter College, Oxford, on 2 April 1652 and graduated BA on 1 October 1655, migrating to Lincoln College, Oxford, in 1656, and proceeding MA from Lincoln in 1658. He found the puritanism of his family, along with Oxford's scholastic Aristotelianism, increasingly uncongenial. Although there is no evidence that Glanvill attended the meetings of the experimentally minded natural philosophers at Oxford led by John Wilkins and Robert Boyle, he was aware of their work. After graduating MA Glanvill became chaplain to Francis Rous, the Cromwellian provost of Eton College. Following Rous's death in 1659, Glanvill returned to Oxford where he remained until the Restoration.

Scepticism The ambitious Glanvill adapted easily to the Restoration and was ordained in the Church of England in the winter of 1660 by Bishop Robert Sanderson. Glanvill's brother Benjamin, a London tin merchant, purchased the advowson of Wimbish, Essex, for him, and presented him to the rectory. There Glanvill published his first book, *The*

Joseph Glanvill (1636–1680), by William Faithorne the elder, pubd 1681

Vanity of Dogmatizing (1661). Influenced by Henry More, *The Vanity of Dogmatizing* attacked Aristotle and praised 'that wonder of men, the Great Des-Cartes' (p. 28) as an opponent of outmoded dogma, while criticizing Cartesian physics and psychology. It also included the story of the scholar Gypsy, who learned from the Gypsies how to employ the power of his imagination to perform wonderful feats, including controlling the wills of others without their being aware of it, a tale later to inspire a poem by Matthew Arnold.

Glanvill asserted the unknowability of the inner workings of the universe, arguing that certain knowledge of nature was possible only in Eden. The fall, by limiting human sensory awareness, made it impossible for humans truly to understand the cosmos. Glanvill was neither a system builder nor a profound student of philosophical texts, understanding Greek thought mainly through translations. He saw scepticism as a solvent of dogmatism rather than as an adequate philosophy in itself. A passage in *The Vanity of Dogmatizing* attacking the idea of a necessary connection between a cause and an effect prefigures David Hume's argument about the nonintrinsic nature of the causal relationship, although there is no discernible direct influence from Glanvill to Hume. The connection between Glanvill and Hume on causality was first made in the late eighteenth century, and led to revival of interest in Glanvill as a philosopher.

Glanvill's second book, *Lux orientalis* (1662), drew on Plato, Origen, and Henry More to demonstrate the pre-existence of the human soul before conception. The same year Glanvill left Wimbish, having been presented by Sir James Thynne in November to the vicarage of Frome Selwood, Somerset, in place of John Humphrey, who had been ejected for nonconformity. About this time Glanvill married Mary Stocker (*d.* 1679), with whom he had five children, Joseph who died in infancy, Maurice who followed Glanvill into the church, becoming rector of Wimbish in 1681, Sophia, Henry, and Mary. To each of the last three he left in his will an annuity of £40. Glanvill had another son, Charles, with his second wife, Margaret Selwyn, to whom he was married briefly between his first wife's burial on 30 April 1679 and his own death in 1680, and who survived him.

The Vanity of Dogmatizing led to a controversy, the first of many for Glanvill. The *Sciri, sive, Sceptices et scepticorum a jure disputationis exclusio* (1663) by the Catholic priest and Aristotelian philosopher Thomas White, published in English as *An Exclusion of Sceptics from All Title to Dispute* (1665), asserted that many positions denied by sceptics could be logically demonstrated. Glanvill's rebuttal was *Scepsis scientifica* (1664), a reworking of *The Vanity of Dogmatizing* with two appended sections, one addressing White's criticisms and entitled 'Scire\i tuum nihil est, or, The author's defense of *The Vanity of Dogmatizing*', the other 'A letter to a friend concerning Aristotle'. Reissuing his books under a variety of titles and formats was Glanvill's habit throughout his career. Generally speaking, his prose evolved to a less ornamented and baroque style, and he was a leader in the development of plain prose.

Scepsis scientifica was shorn of much of the praise of Descartes, as, probably under More's influence, Glanvill had become disenchanted with Cartesian mechanical reductionism as materialistic. It included a new dedication to the Royal Society. The book was presented to the society by Lord Brereton on 7 December 1664. Brereton proposed Glanvill for membership, and he was elected to the society the following week. Glanvill was also secretary to a short-lived Somerset natural philosophical society that corresponded with the Royal Society. He made some contributions on local mines and baths to the society's journal, *Philosophical Transactions*, in the late 1660s and traced the missing manuscripts of Samuel Foster, the deceased astronomy professor at Gresham College, for the society. Glanvill's major writings related to the society were *Plus ultra, or, The Progress and Advancement of Knowledge since the Days of Aristotle* (1668) and *Philosophia pia, or, A discourse of the religious temper and tendencies of the experimental philosophy which is profest by the Royal Society* (1671). *Plus ultra* began in a conflict with a local puritan minister and Aristotelian, Robert Crosse. This conflict was much less civil than that with White. Crosse even composed anti-Glanvill ballads to be sung in alehouses. Conceived as a supplement to Thomas Sprat's *History of the Royal Society* (1667), *Plus ultra*, an early attempt at a history of science, praised the new philosophy of the Royal Society as the most productive yet found. Conceived in one conflict, it led to another, an elaborate pamphlet war with Glanvill and Thomas Sprat defending the society against the attacks of Crosse's associate, the Aristotelian physician Henry Stubbe, author of *Legends no histories, or, A specimen of some animadversions upon the history of the Royal Society ... together with the 'Plus ultra' reduced to a 'non plus'* (1670), which accused the society of being intellectually elitist and crypto-Catholic. Glanvill responded in *A Prefatory Answer to Mr. Henry Stubbe, the Doctor of Warwick* (1671) and *Philosophia pia*, defending the religious functions of the new natural philosophy. Glanvill argued that science glorified God in his works and confuted atheism, materialism, and superstition. Glanvill, whose public life was one of untiring controversy, also recommended natural philosophy as an aid against 'the Humour of Disputing' (p. 28).

The writings on witchcraft There was no incompatibility between Glanvill's beliefs in the progress of science and in witchcraft. Glanvill was less concerned with witchcraft *per se* than with the reality of spirits and their interaction with matter. Like other Restoration natural philosophers, Glanvill believed that devils were real and could intervene in the natural world, and he corresponded about supernatural matters with such major figures as Robert Boyle, Henry More, and Richard Baxter. Opponents of witchcraft belief who denied the reality of demons and their effects on the world, he held, were contributing to the menace of atheistic materialism. Glanvill attempted to refute atheism and materialism through the collection and compilation of stories of witches and other supernatural phenomena. Since the stories had to be believable, Glanvill was careful to credit witnesses, and recount his own investigations, as in the famous case of the phantom drummer at the house of Mr Mompesson in Tedworth, Wiltshire, which Glanvill visited in 1663. After Mompesson had a wandering drummer arrested and his instrument confiscated, his house was regularly shaken by the beating of a phantom drum and he, his family, and visitors were subjected to poltergeist-type phenomena such as the throwing of furniture. Glanvill's recounting of this story became celebrated, inspiring Joseph Addison's play *The Drummer*.

An avid user of dedications, gift copies, and flattery to gain patronage and notoriety, Glanvill sent a copy of his first witchcraft book, *A Philosophical Endeavour towards the Defense of the being of Witches and Apparitions* (1666), with a flattering letter to the aristocratic natural philosopher Margaret Cavendish, duchess of Newcastle. They entered into a correspondence, and several of Glanvill's letters on philosophical subjects were printed in *Letters and Poems in Honour of the Incomparable Princess, Margaret, Dutchess of Newcastle* (1676). The first edition of *A Philosophical Endeavour* was mostly destroyed in the fire of London in 1666, but two subsequent editions appeared in 1667, the second as *Some Philosophical Considerations Touching the being of Witches* and the third, including the Mompesson story, as *A Blow at Modern Sadducism*.

The physician John Webster published *The Displaying of Supposed Witchcraft* in 1677, asserting that God prevented evil spirits from making compacts with witches. Webster made Glanvill the main target of his attacks. Glanvill responded in the final version of his witchcraft book, posthumously published with material added by Henry More as *Saducismus triumphatus* (1681). Glanvill asserted that Webster, despite his proclaimed piety, was aiding materialists who denied a spiritual world. Glanvill was widely considered to have vanquished his opponent. After his death he continued to be seen in England, New England, and Europe as one of the greatest champions of the belief in witches. *Saducismus triumphatus* went through several editions through the first quarter of the eighteenth century, and was published in German in 1701.

The Anglican controversialist On 23 June 1666 Glanvill became rector of the abbey church in Bath. He lived in Bath and retained the living for the rest of his life, although he continued to accumulate other desirable church posts, exchanging Frome Selwood for the rectory of Streat and Walton in Somerset on 26 July 1672, becoming a chaplain in ordinary to Charles II the same year, and receiving a prebend at Worcester Cathedral on 22 June 1678 through the influence of the marquess of Worcester. Though a pluralist, Glanvill was a conscientious if not always popular or happy parish clergyman in an area where protestant dissent was very strong. His manual for communicants, *An Earnest Invitation to the Sacrament of the Lord's Supper* (1673), went through several editions in the seventeenth and early eighteenth centuries. Glanvill's religious position, as stated in *Logou threskeia, or, A Seasonable Recommendation and Defence of Reason in Affairs of Religion against Infidelity* (1670) and other writings, was one of support for a comprehensive Church of England emphasizing basic Christian doctrines, and allowing a wide range of opinions and practices. He opposed toleration of dissent, although he had friendly relations for several years with the presbyterian Richard Baxter, to whom he sent manuscripts of his books for comment before publication.

As an Anglican controversialist Glanvill published an anonymous attack on Andrew Marvell's *The Rehearsal Transprosed* titled *An apology and advice for some of the clergy, who suffer under false, and scandalous reports written on the occasion of the second part of 'The rehearsal transprosed'* (1674). Defending the Anglican clergy from Marvell's scurrilous assaults, Glanvill found himself on the same side as his old enemy Stubbe, and preached Stubbe's funeral sermon in Bath in 1676, albeit without much commendation of the deceased. Glanvill's attacks on dissenters as enemies of reason drew a response from Robert Ferguson. Ferguson's *The Interest of Reason in Religion* (1675) argued that dissenters accepted reason in its proper place in religious affairs. Glanvill and William Sherlock, also attacked by Ferguson, replied in *An Account of Mr. Ferguson his Common-Place-Book* (1675), ignoring Ferguson's arguments but charging him with extensive plagiarism of Glanvill and other authors. Glanvill also published several sermons.

Glanvill's most significant work was collected in *Essays upon Several Important Subjects in Philosophy and Religion* (1676), dedicated to his wife's relative and his own patron, the marquess of Worcester. Only the last of the seven essays included was entirely original. The others were reworkings of *Scepsis scientifica*, 'Scire\i tuum', *Plus ultra*, *Philosophia pia*, *A Seasonable Recommendation*, and *Some Philosophical Considerations*. The seventh essay, 'Anti-fanatical religion and free philosophy', was an intellectual history and encomium of the Cambridge Platonists and latitudinarians, in the form of a continuation of Francis Bacon's *The New Atlantis*.

During the Popish Plot crisis beginning in 1678 Glanvill wrote his most partisan Anglican book, published posthumously as *The Zealous, and Impartial Protestant* (1681). He attacked toleration of dissenting religious practices, while asserting that mere beliefs should not be persecuted. A Church of England more flexible on liturgical and ceremonial practices could bring moderate dissenters into the church, uniting protestants to more effectively combat Catholicism. Glanvill's calls for more rigorous enforcement of the anti-dissenter laws pained his old friend Baxter, who reprinted a flattering letter introducing himself which Glanvill had written to him in 1661 in *A Second True Defense of the Meer Nonconformist* (1681). Glanvill died at Bath of a fever on 4 November 1680 and was buried in the abbey church there five days later. A funeral sermon preached by the Reverend Joseph Pleydell was included in *Some Discourses, Sermons, and Remains of the Reverend Mr. Jos. Glanvil* (1681).

Glanvill was a prominent and untiring advocate of the new philosophy in science and of an Anglican church tolerant of a broad range of opinion within itself but intolerant of dissenting churches. He was an equally zealous opponent of Aristotelianism and materialism. Glanvill embodied many of the features of the eighteenth-century latitudinarian compromise in the Church of England, but his defence of witch belief and an intolerant state church mark him as a man of the Restoration.

WILLIAM E. BURNS

Sources F. Greenslet, *Joseph Glanvill: a study in English thought and letters in the seventeenth century* (1900) • J. I. Cope, *Joseph Glanvill: Anglican apologist* (1956) • *DNB* • A. J. Jewers, ed., *The registers of the abbey church of SS Peter and Paul, Bath*, 2 vols., Harleian Society, Register Section, 27–8 (1900–01) • Wood, *Ath. Oxon.*, new edn • R. H. Popkin, 'The development of the philosophical reputation of Joseph Glanvill', *Journal of the History of Ideas*, 15 (1954), 305–11 • S. Talmor, *Glanvill: the uses and abuses of scepticism* (1981) • W. E. S. Glanville-Richards, *Records of the Anglo-Norman house of Glanville* (1882) • S. Clark, *Thinking with demons: the idea of witchcraft in early modern Europe* (1997) • PRO, PROB 11/364, fols. 312r–313r [quire 164]

Archives RS, corresp. | DWL, corresp. with Richard Baxter • University of Chicago

Likenesses W. Faithorne the elder, line engraving, BM, NPG; repro. in J. Glanvill, *Some discourses, sermons and remains* (1681) [*see illus.*]

Glanville, Bartholomew de. *See* Bartholomaeus Anglicus (*b.* before 1203, *d.* 1272).

Glanville [*née* Goodricke; *other married name* Ashfield], **Eleanor (1654–1709)**, entomologist, was the elder of the two daughters of Major William Goodricke (*d.* 1666) and his wife, the widow Eleanor Poyntz, *née* Davis (1617–1664). Her father left £1000 to Mary, his younger daughter, and to Eleanor the estates which her mother had brought to the marriage in 1652. Thus, Eleanor found herself a very rich woman in her own right having inherited several properties, including Tickenham Court in Somerset where she established her home. On 14 April 1676 she married Edmund Ashfield (*d.* 1679), an artist from Lincolnshire, with whom she had three children, Forest Edmund (*b.* 1677) and in 1678 twins, Mary, and Katherine, who died at birth. Following the death of her first husband, she married Richard Glanville (*b.* *c.*1644) in November 1685. Four more children were born; two died in infancy but were survived by Richard (*b.* 1687) and Eleanor (*b.* 1688). Glanville proved to be a violent husband and by 1698 the marriage had failed. He began desperately trying to lay hands on Eleanor's fortune, circulating stories of her madness and forcing her children to sign affidavits against their mother, but his bid was unsuccessful; Eleanor had shrewdly turned over her properties to trustees while retaining the right to direct her own affairs. Problems with her husband and children seem to have encouraged stories in the local neighbourhood of her insanity, or at least eccentricity, not helped by her interest in collecting butterflies—a practice thought to be odd.

Eleanor had begun her interest in butterfly collecting at an early age, but started to make a serious collection soon after separation from her husband. Collecting insects became an obsession and she paid her servants to collect for her. She taught them how to pack specimens in folded papers and to preserve and transport them safely back to her. Eleanor's payments were generous, as long as the specimens were handed over in perfect condition—6*d.* per specimen in most cases, but for a special butterfly and caterpillar even 1*s.*

Eleanor became a correspondent of James Petiver (1660–1718), a London apothecary, naturalist, and insect collector, Joseph Dandridge (*c.*1664–1718), silk-screen printer and owner of one of the finest butterfly collections of the time, and the botanist Adam Buddle (*bap.* 1662, *d.* 1715), whom she described as a cousin. They introduced her to other naturalists with whom she exchanged information. Petiver used many of her specimens and information received from her in his great work *Gazophylacium naturae artis* (1703). He described *Callophrys rubi* (hairstreak butterfly) from her specimens and gives her credit in his text. Many of her butterflies and moths provided new records for Britain, including the now famous Glanville fritillary (*Melitaea cinxia*). The common name was first given to the species by James Dutfield in *A New and Complete Natural History of English Moths and Butterflies* (1748–9). Eleanor Glanville published nothing, but the earliest record of a local list of insects, made by E. Glanville on the insects of the Bristol area, may be from her hand. When she went to London in 1703 taking with her a large collection of butterflies her visit caused some excitement among naturalists in the capital. A few of her specimens exist in the Natural History Museum, as part of the Petiver collection.

No doubt her husband's behaviour and that of her children drove Eleanor to distraction. She bequeathed her estate to her second cousin Sir Henry Goodricke, except for some small legacies to her children. Her estates were left in the hands of her trustees, and there were legacies for her trustees and her executor. Her son Forest contested the will, mainly on the grounds of his mother's lunacy; in 1712 he won his case and the will was set aside. Eleanor Glanville died in the early part of 1709 at Tickenham Court; the exact date of death is not known.

PAMELA GILBERT

Sources W. S. Bristowe, 'The life of a distinguished woman naturalist, Eleanor Glanville, *c*.1654–1708', *Entomologist's Gazette*, 18 (1967), 202–11 • R. S. Wilkinson, 'Elizabeth Glanville, an early English entomologist', *Entomologist's Gazette*, 17 (1966), 149–60 • W. S. Bristowe, 'More about Eleanor Glanville, 1654–1708', *Entomologist's Gazette*, 26 (1975), 107–17 • BL, Sloane MSS, 4063, fol. 188; 4066, fol. 349; 3324, fol. 90, 17–20 • PRO, will, PROB 11/506 sig. 3 • C. A. Goodricke, ed., *History of the Goodricke family* (1885)

Archives NHM, Petiver collections, Glanville specimens | BL, Sloane MS, letters to Petiver

Wealth at death £6000–£7000—estates, manors, and lordships in Tickenham, Rodneystoke, Cheddar, and Backwell: will, PRO, PROB 11/506, sig. 3; Bristowe, 'The life'; Bristowe, 'More about Eleanor Glanville'

Glanville, Gilbert de (*d.* **1214**), bishop of Rochester, may have been a kinsman of the justiciar Ranulf de Glanville (*d.* 1190), though this has not been established with certainty. The Rochester chronicler, Edmund Hadenham, claims that Glanville came from Northumbria, but there seems to be no other evidence to support this. His education is equally obscure, though since Herbert of Bosham later described him as a master of both canon and civil law, it may be conjectured that he studied in Paris or Bologna. Herbert states that Glanville was the last to join the group of *eruditi* surrounding Becket, but also one of the most faithful. He is glimpsed undertaking a mission for the archbishop to the curia in 1164, and interceding for Jocelin de Bohun and Reginald of Salisbury in 1167. On the eve of the archbishop's martyrdom, Becket dispatched Glanville on a mission to the pope. He then entered the service of Bishop Arnulf of Lisieux (*d.* 1184), becoming archdeacon of Lisieux some time before 1179. But at the time of his appointment to the see of Rochester, he is referred to as clerk to the recently enthroned Archbishop Baldwin, who engineered his election on 16 July 1185. He was ordained priest on 21 September and consecrated at Canterbury on 29 September.

Bishop Glanville was zealous in defence of his episcopal rights. His unhappy relations with his monastic chapter were long remembered. Like archbishops Baldwin and Hubert Walter, and Bishop Hugh of Coventry (*d.* 1198), he sought unsuccessfully to substitute for monks a college of secular canons. It was under his auspices, moreover, that in 1197 the monks of Rochester Cathedral priory agreed to exchange with the archbishop of Canterbury their church and manor of Lambeth for those of Darenth, thus contributing to the possibility of Hubert Walter's cherished but ultimately frustrated plan of establishing a college of secular canons there. The bishop was further accused by the Rochester monks of appropriating to himself the rights of presentation to vacant benefices which belonged to them, and of usurping the right of appointing monastic lay officials and servants. In particular he was charged with encroaching on monastic property for the endowment of his foundation in 1192–3 of the hospital of St Mary at Strood, intended for the reception of the poor, the infirm, and travellers, and to pray for the restoration of Christianity in the kingdom of Jerusalem and for King Richard's release from captivity.

A protracted lawsuit between bishop and convent followed, and it was finally settled only in 1205–6, largely to the bishop's advantage. Glanville also built a stone quay, a chapel, and houses at the Strood end of the bridge over the Medway; the rents were to go to the hospital to pay for its share in the upkeep of the bridge. The rebuilding of the eastern side of the cathedral cloister has been attributed to him, together with the rebuilding or repair of various episcopal dwellings, and he also made generous gifts of vestments, ornaments, and books to the convent. Within the wider life of the church, Glanville served as papal judge-delegate on a number of occasions between 1192 and 1210, notably in the dispute between the archbishop of York and the bishop of Durham in 1192, and in 1206 to investigate the dispute between the abbey of Evesham and the bishop of Worcester. In 1188, as vicar of Archbishop Baldwin, he assisted in preaching the crusade at Geddington in Northamptonshire and in the same capacity he was charged with the administration of spiritualities and temporalities of the diocese of Canterbury when the archbishop departed on crusade in 1190. He himself evidently made a pilgrimage to Santiago de Compostela at some time before 1205.

Glanville was also intermittently engaged in secular affairs. He was employed by Henry II on a mission to Philip Augustus of France at Noyon in 1186, he served as a justice in England in 1187 and 1188, and he was present at the conference of La Ferté-Bernard in May 1189. He returned to England in August 1189 and attended Richard I's coronation and the Council of Pipewell in September of that year. He was frequently in attendance on the king in England and France, and between 1194 and 1197 he acted as a justice both on eyre and at Westminster.

During Richard's absence on crusade, Glanville attempted to mediate in the dispute between Count John and William de Longchamp, the chancellor. He was present at Longchamp's trial and escorted him to Dover when he fled the country in October 1191. He was involved in the election of Archbishop Hubert Walter in 1193, and was one of the bishops who excommunicated John on 10 February 1194. His request to Pope Innocent III in 1206 for permission to relinquish his bishopric on account of his advanced age was kindly but firmly refused. He remained loyal to John despite the interdict, and the king seems to have respected his claim to act as deputy of the absent Archbishop Stephen Langton. He was one of the last bishops to leave the country when John was excommunicated in 1209. He took refuge in Scotland (at Roxburgh according to the Melrose chronicler) with the goodwill of the Scottish king, and appears to have returned to England in 1213. He died on 24 June 1214, eight days before the lifting of the interdict, and the Rochester chronicler records, with undisguised satisfaction, that he was therefore denied Christian burial. Nevertheless he was buried in Rochester Cathedral; his tomb survives on the north side of the high altar in the presbytery.

M. N. BLOUNT

Sources J. Moule, 'Gilbert Glanvill, bishop of Rochester, 1185–1214', MA diss., University of Manchester, 1954 • H. R. Luard, ed., *Flores historiarum*, 3 vols., Rolls Series, 95 (1890) • *The historical works of Gervase of Canterbury*, ed. W. Stubbs, 2 vols., Rolls Series, 73 (1879–80) • J. Thorpe, ed., *Registrum Roffense, or, A collection of antient records, charters and instruments … illustrating the ecclesiastical history and antiquities of the diocese and cathedral church of Rochester* (1769) • R. Mortimer, 'The family of Rannulf de Glanville', *BIHR*, 54 (1981), 1–16 • *The letters of Arnulf of Lisieux*, ed. F. Barlow, CS, 3rd ser., 61 (1939) • J. C. Robertson and J. B. Sheppard, eds., *Materials for the history of Thomas Becket, archbishop of Canterbury*, 7 vols., Rolls Series, 67 (1875–85) • A. O. Anderson and M. O. Anderson, eds., *The chronicle of Melrose* (1936) • *The letters of John of Salisbury*, ed. and trans. H. E. Butler and W. J. Millor, rev. C. N. L. Brooke, OMT, 2: *The later letters, 1163–1180* (1979) [Lat. orig. with parallel Eng. text] • *The letters of Pope Innocent III (1198–1216) concerning England and Wales*, ed. C. R. Cheney and M. G. Cheney (1967) • D. M. Stenton, ed., *Pleas before the king or his justices, 1198–1212*, 3, SeldS, 83 (1967) • M. N. Blount and M. Brett, eds., *Rochester*, English Episcopal Acta [forthcoming] • R. V. Turner, *The English judiciary in the age of Glanvill and Bracton, c.1176–1239* (1985)

Archives BL, Rochester monastic registers • Canterbury Cathedral, archives, cartae antiquae, R 70 A • CKS, Rochester episcopal and other registers • Medway Archives and Local Studies Centre, Rochester, Kent, Rochester dean and chapter MSS

Likenesses seal, 1193, Medway Archives and Local Studies Centre, Rochester, Kent, Rochester dean and chapter MSS, MS DRc/T 572/11

Glanville, John (1542–1600), judge, second or third son of John Glanville (*d.* 1580), a Tavistock merchant, and Thomasine Browne, is said to have been bred an attorney; if so, he was the first attorney who is recorded to have reached the bench. He entered at Lincoln's Inn on 11 May 1567, was called to the bar on 24 June 1574, and was made bencher on 29 June 1587. He was reader there in Lent 1589, and again in the autumn, having been called serjeant in the meantime. He was member of parliament for Launceston in 1584, for Tavistock in 1586, and for St Germans in 1593. He was a justice of the stannaries in 1592, and was in 1594 interested in St Margaret's tin works in Cornwall. He owned substantial estates in Devon and Cornwall. On 30 June 1598 he was made a judge of the common pleas, where he gained a reputation for even-handedness. A corpulent man, he died on 27 July 1600 after a fall from his horse. He was buried in Tavistock church, where there is an elaborate tomb with a recumbent statue of him in his robes (engraved in Polwhele's *History of Devonshire*). His wife, Alice, daughter of John Skerret of Tavistock, survived him; she later married Sir Francis Godolphin. The Glanvilles had seven children, of whom the second son was John *Glanville, speaker of the House of Commons in 1640. Glanville, who had built the mansion of Kilworthy, near Tavistock, died a rich man.

J. A. HAMILTON, *rev.* DAVID IBBETSON

Sources W. U. S. Glanville-Richards, *Records of the Anglo-Norman house of Glanvill* (1882) • HoP, *Commons, 1558–1603*, 2.193 • W. P. Baildon, ed., *The records of the Honorable Society of Lincoln's Inn: the black books*, 1 (1897) • R. Polwhele, *The history of Devonshire*, 3 vols. (1793–

John Glanville (1542–1600), by unknown artist

1806), vol. 3, pp. 440, 442 • R. Polwhele, *The history of Cornwall*, 7 vols. (1803–8), vol. 5, pp. 137, 138 • J. Prince, *Danmonii orientales illustres, or, The worthies of Devon* (1701), 326–8 • Baker, *Serjeants*, 514 • Sainty, *Judges*, 1598 • Wood, *Ath. Oxon.* • *Report and Transactions of the Devonshire Association*, 8 (1876), 381 • *CSP dom.*, *1591–4*, 441 • PRO, C142/271/158 [inquisition post mortem] • PRO, PROB 11/62, m. 54 [father's will]

Archives Lincoln's Inn, London, legal notebook

Likenesses effigy, Tavistock church; repro. in Polwhele, *History of Devonshire*, 3 (1806), facing p. 441 • oils, Lincoln's Inn, London [*see illus.*] • portrait, repro. in Glanville-Richards, *Records*, facing p. 94

Wealth at death value of lands p.a. £115: PRO, C 142/271/158

Glanville, Sir John, the younger (1585/6–1661), lawyer and politician, was born in Kilworthy, Devon, the second son of John *Glanville (1542–1600), judge of common pleas, and his wife, Alice (*d.* 1632), daughter of John Skerret of Tavistock, Devon, who later married Sir Francis Godolphin (*d.* 1608). Glanville, who was said to be aged thirty-four in 1620, was reputed to have turned to study the law by utilizing his father's notes, but he was admitted to Lincoln's Inn on 7 February 1603, and called to the bar on 6 February 1610. By 1615 he had married Winifred (*d.* 1676), daughter of William Bourchier of Barnsley, Gloucestershire. They had four sons, one of whom predeceased him, and three daughters.

Glanville was elected to parliament in 1614 for the borough of Liskeard, where he was fee'd counsel of the borough. He made an impact as a speaker almost immediately. By 1617 he was standing counsel for Plymouth, and he was recorder by 11 December 1620, when he was elected to parliament for that borough. When the parliament met in 1621, Glanville was a keen supporter of the bill for a free fishery which was an attack on Sir Ferdinando Gorges's patent for a plantation in New England, which adversely affected west country fishing interests. His most notable contribution was to the debate on 6 February 1621 on the decrease of money in the kingdom. Glanville was re-elected on 28 January 1624, when his address was given as Tavistock. During this parliament he was a very active contributor to debates and he was elected to the chair of the committee of privileges. Thus, he oversaw the widening of the franchise in a number of parliamentary boroughs, which provided the material for the collection of election cases known as *Glanville's Reports*, which were subsequently published in 1775 by John Topham. Glanville was also a prominent supporter of war with Spain during the debates in March 1624.

Following the death of James I, Glanville was re-elected to the parliament on 23 April 1625. Although not now chairman of the committee of privileges, he was again concerned in election disputes, most notably that of Sir Thomas Wentworth for Yorkshire, which was declared void by the house on 5 July 1625. He also steered the Bill for Free Fishing through the Commons. Glanville attended the parliament following its adjournment to Oxford, contributing to the debate on supply on 10 August and drafting the Commons' declaration on the 12th protesting against a dissolution, which was adopted with black rod at the door of the chamber. By way of punishment, when Glanville visited Plymouth in September 1625 in his capacity as recorder to attend the city's reception of Charles I, he was pressed into service as secretary to the military expedition to Cadiz under Edward Cecil, Viscount Wimbledon. As he rather plaintively wrote in protest, his wife and six children were currently dispersed over six counties, and following illness he had had no time to put his affairs in order. As 'a mere lawyer' he was unfitted for the task, and he faced the loss of his livelihood if separated from his practice for a long period. The fleet sailed from Plymouth in early October and put back into Kinsale on 11 December. Glanville left for a visit to the earl of Cork at Lismore on 24 December, where he fell ill with a 'long and dangerous sickness' (Glanville, 121–2). He returned to England in March 1626.

Despite Glanville's absence from England when new parliamentary writs were issued in December 1625, he was re-elected for Plymouth on 29 January 1626. In April 1626 Glanville was named to the select committee reviewing the proceedings against Buckingham, and he reported on it on occasion, particularly on procedural points. On 8 May 1626 Glanville presented to the Lords at a conference the charges relating to the delivery of English ships to the French and their subsequent use against the Huguenots of La Rochelle, and the extortion of money from the East India Company.

The next parliament was elected in February and March 1628, and Glanville was a leading proponent of the petition of right, making a set-piece speech at a conference with the Lords on 23 May in which he located the supreme authority in the state in the law, not the king:

> there is no trust reposed in the King's sovereign power, or prerogative royal, to enable him to dispense with them, or take from his subjects that birthright and inheritance which they have in their liberties, by virtue of the common law and these statutes. (Russell, 363)

In the second session of the parliament, which took place in 1629, Glanville was concerned to find a way to avoid confrontation with Charles I over his collection of tonnage and poundage without parliamentary sanction, while gaining redress for those merchants that had refused to pay it.

Glanville's growing eminence in the legal profession was noted by Star Chamber in 1635, when he was deputed along with Henry Rolle to end the dispute between Lord Poulett and the Revd Richard Gore. In 1635 or 1636 Charles I vetoed the recommendation of Lord Chief Justice Finch that he be made a serjeant-at-law, but through the mediation of the queen and the earl of Holland he was made a serjeant in June 1637, his patrons being the queen, the archbishop of Canterbury, William Laud, and the earl of Coventry. By this time he was the leader of the chancery bar.

Glanville had become recorder of Bristol in 1630, and he was elected to parliament in 1640 for the city. According to Whitelock, Glanville 'had engaged to be a better servant to the King' (Whitelock, 1.97), and on 13 April 1640 he was elected speaker of the Commons, and escorted to the chair by the treasurer, Henry Vane, and the secretary, John Windebank. During a committee of the whole house on 4 May 1640 Glanville spoke of his opinion that ship money was not legal and that parliament should declare it so. On the following morning Glanville did not appear to chair the session, and when the Commons was summoned to the Lords they found Glanville already there, and the king ready to dissolve parliament.

On 6 July 1640 Glanville was appointed king's serjeant, with a special dispensation that he could retain the recordership of Bristol. Glanville was not elected to the Long Parliament, but on 3 December 1640 he was named to assist the Lords with the examinations against Lord Strafford. He was knighted on 7 August 1641. In 1642 Glanville and John Tailer replaced the MPs for Bristol, who were expelled as monopolists. Glanville followed the king to Oxford, and in December 1643 he presided over the trial at Salisbury of the earls of Pembroke, Northumberland, and Salisbury, but the jury did not find a true bill. He also sat in judgment at Exeter Castle on Captain Turpen, who was executed. On 31 January 1644 he was created a DCL at Oxford. On 14 June 1644 he surrendered to parliament, and on the 20th he was imprisoned in the Tower.

Glanville was impeached by the Commons on 22 July 1644, but on the 27th he petitioned the Lords as their assistant, 'having already sustained as much damage in his possession and estate as any man of his degree' (*House of Lords MSS*), and praying that his estate not be sequestrated until after his trial. In May 1644 he had been required to pay an assessment of £3000, which he complained of in August because he lived in Wiltshire not London. In December 1644 he was allowed by the Commons to compound for his delinquency, arguing in January 1645 that he had not joined the king in Oxford voluntarily, but following capture. On 25 September 1645 he was disabled from sitting in the Commons for delinquency.

On 17 August 1646 Glanville petitioned from the Tower asking to attend the committee for sequestrations in order to protect his property, and again on 1 September for bail. In March 1647 the committee of safety of the Tower reported Glanville fit to be bailed, and in April he was allowed to go to Bath for his health. In August 1648 Glanville finally paid off all his composition money for his delinquency and was released from his bail.

In March 1654 the council of state discussed admitting Glanville to his legal practice. In July 1654 he was at Broad Hinton, but residing in the gatehouse, as his house had been destroyed by royalist forces on 14 May 1645 to prevent it being garrisoned by parliamentarian forces. On 14 January 1659 Glanville was elected to parliament for St Germans, but a new election was ordered on 12 February as he was deemed not qualified to sit in the house.

At the Restoration, Glanville was reappointed a king's serjeant on 6 June 1660, and was designated prime serjeant. He died at Broad Hinton, Wiltshire, on 2 October 1661, and was buried there the following day.

STUART HANDLEY

Sources J. P. Ferris, HoP, *Commons, 1604–29* [draft] • J. L. Vivian, ed., *The visitations of the county of Devon, comprising the herald's visitations of 1531, 1564, and 1620* (privately printed, Exeter, [1895]), 411–13 • Baker, *Serjeants* • Sainty, *King's counsel* • W. U. S. Glanville-Richards, *Records of the Anglo-Norman house of Glanville from A.D. 1050 to 1880* (1882), 95–168 • C. Russell, *Parliaments and English politics, 1621–1629* (1979) • J. Glanville, *The voyage to Cadiz in 1625*, ed. A. B. Grosart, CS, new ser., 32 (1883) • M. A. E. Green, ed., *Calendar of the proceedings of the committee for compounding … 1643–1660*, 2, PRO (1890), 408–11 • *CSP dom., 1631–40* • *Sixth report*, HMC, 5 (1877–8), 230, 284–5, 517; vol. 2, pp. 121, 366 [House of Lords (1643–7)] • B. Whitelocke, *Memorials of English affairs*, new edn, 4 vols. (1853), vol. 1, pp. 97–8 • will, PRO, PROB 11/306, fol. 145r–v • *JHL*, 10 (1647–8), 422 [7 Aug 1648] • W. R. Prest, *The rise of the barristers: a social history of the English bar, 1590–1640*, 2nd edn (1991) • *DNB*

Archives Lincoln's Inn, London, reports of cases in King's Bench • Northants. RO, speech in parliament relating to petition of right

Likenesses portrait, Lincoln's Inn, London; repro. in Baker, *Serjeants*, pl. ix

Glanville [Glanvill], **Ranulf de** (1120s?–1190), justiciar, was born in Suffolk. His foundation at Butley Priory preserved the tradition that his birthplace was Stratford, probably Stratford St Andrew near Saxmundham. The family name comes from a Norman village in Calvados, near Pont-l'Évêque, north-west of Lisieux, and Ranulf's ancestors arrived in Suffolk in or shortly after 1066. Although his father, Hervey, was not from the family's eldest line, he was prominent in the shire court of Norfolk and Suffolk, and a man of that name was also one of the four leaders of Anglo-Norman forces who in 1147 attacked Lisbon, then under Muslim control. Several of Ranulf's brothers and sisters appear in the sources. His only known wife was Bertha, daughter of Theobald de Valognes, whom he married before 1170. Theobald held lands in Suffolk, including the neighbouring lordship of Parham, and also in Yorkshire. By the marriage Glanville acquired various lands including the site of Butley, the earliest of his religious foundations. Bertha's sister Matilda married Hervey Walter, father of the future justiciar and archbishop, Hubert *Walter (*d.* 1205), who was, therefore, Glanville's nephew by marriage. If he had any sons, certainly any legitimate sons, they did not survive him, but he was survived by three daughters, Matilda, Amabilla, and Helewise, between whom his estates were divided after his death.

Glanville first appears about 1144, in a writ addressed by Nigel, bishop of Ely, to Hervey de Glanville and Ranulf his son, ordering them to give up to the monks the land of Bawdsey in Suffolk, and promising to do them justice if they claimed anything in the land. About 1150 with several of his relatives he witnessed various gifts by his uncle Bartholomew to Broomholme Priory, and in the late 1150s he witnessed two Suffolk charters of King Stephen's son William. A Ranulf de Glanville is mentioned in the 1161/2 pipe roll, while in his famous account of his lawsuit of the early 1160s, Richard of Anstey mentions an approach to Glanville, perhaps indicating that he already had some influence in legal matters.

Sheriff and justice Between 1163 and 1170 Glanville was sheriff of Yorkshire. His sole connection with the area seems to have been through his wife's family, but he took with him in his household various men to whom he was connected by kinship and locality. In the meantime he was at least sometimes involved in central administration, as when he witnessed a charter sealed before Richard de Lucy and the other barons of the exchequer in 1168. In 1170, however, he was replaced as sheriff of Yorkshire by Robert (III) de Stuteville, being thus one of the many sheriffs who fell in connection with the inquest of that year, but in Glanville's case, as in several others, the fall from grace was limited. Charters show him to have been with the king on the continent in June or July 1171 and in Ireland in October of that year. In 1171 he became keeper of the honour of Richmond in Yorkshire, following the death of Earl Conan. In 1173–4 he was sheriff of Lancashire, a position he may have been given for military reasons as the likelihood of rebellion increased. The civil war of 1173–4 certainly brought Glanville to greater prominence. First he succeeded in capturing an English ally of the Scottish king, Hamo de Massy, and then he enjoyed still more spectacular success against the invasion of William the Lion, king of Scots, in July 1174. According to the metrical chronicle of Jordan Fantosme, it was Glanville who took the vital decision to send a scouting expedition in front of the main English force as it advanced towards Alnwick. Aided by mist, they surprised the enemy on 13 July, winning a decisive victory and capturing the king; indeed Jordan Fantosme attributes the capture of William to Glanville personally, making it the happiest day of his life. On Henry II's orders Glanville took William to Southampton, and was then commanded to take him to Normandy.

Such military activities must have helped Glanville's rise in royal favour. For example, from June to July 1175 a final concord records him sitting as a royal justice at Woodstock, and charters show him to have been frequently with the king and other leading men, particularly in the north of the realm. In 1175–6 he was restored to the shrievalty of Yorkshire, a position which he held until the end of the reign. In 1177 he rendered account as sheriff of Westmorland, a position which he had held for three years, discharging his duties partly through his steward, Reiner, and the 1179/80 pipe roll stated that the account of Westmorland was not to be demanded from Glanville as Henry II had granted it to him at the royal pleasure to maintain himself in the king's service. The revenues of Westmorland were largely devoted to the restoration of the king's castles in the north of England, but considerable profit could also be reaped from such shrieval duties. The 1176–7 pipe roll records him as accounting for a debt from Westmorland of over £1570, in addition to various jewels, horses, and other possessions, and goods taken by his servants. As well as indicating the scale of what many must have regarded as administrative oppression, and the sources of administrators' wealth, the case also reveals the benefits of royal favour, for Glanville and his men were pardoned their debts in return for two gerfalcons.

At Michaelmas 1175 account was rendered for pleas held by Glanville, together with Hugh de Cressy, in Bedfordshire, Buckinghamshire, Cambridgeshire, Derbyshire, Essex, Hertfordshire, Huntingdonshire, Lincolnshire, Norfolk, Northamptonshire, Nottinghamshire, Oxfordshire, Suffolk, Yorkshire, and Northumberland. Following the assize of Northampton in January 1176 he was one of three justices appointed to hear pleas in Yorkshire, Lancashire, and counties further north, and the pipe rolls account for their having done so in Northumberland and Yorkshire. He was probably one of the five justices appointed by Henry in 1178, and in 1179, at the Council of Windsor, Henry placed him in charge of the eyre to the north of the Trent, during which, according to Howden, the justices were to listen to the claims or complaints (*clamores*) of the people. This initial plan was modified in practice, and Glanville heard pleas in Derbyshire, Herefordshire, Nottinghamshire, Oxfordshire, Shropshire, Staffordshire, Worcestershire, and Yorkshire. His importance in royal administration at this time is confirmed by Gerald of Wales's story of Roger of Asterby, a Lincolnshire knight, whom mysterious voices urged to bring complaints against the regime of Henry II; the voices mentioned Glanville as one of those to whom the complaints should be addressed.

Justiciar of England Glanville's duties were not restricted to the judicial or shrieval. He may have travelled to Flanders in 1176, and certainly in 1177 he acted as an ambassador there, hearing the count swear that he would not marry his nieces to anyone without Henry's consent. In February 1180 he was present at the Council of Oxford, where the king devised new plans for the currency. In the same year Henry addressed two letters to him concerning peace with Philip Augustus, king of France, and with the count of Flanders. It was also in 1180 that Glanville became chief justiciar, in succession to Richard de Lucy who had retired in 1178. Immediately, as the pipe roll of the twenty-sixth year of Henry's reign (1179/80) shows, a mass of acts and payments were undertaken by writ of Ranulf de Glanville, acting with his vice-regal powers. As when he became sheriff of Yorkshire, Ranulf's entourage as justiciar displays East Anglian and family connections. Most notable among these was his nephew Hubert Walter.

In 1182 Glanville appeared as an executor in the king's will. He was present, and claimed no right for the king, when the archbishop of Canterbury invested the new bishop of Rochester with the *regalia* of the see. He also led an army against the Welsh, which marks the beginning of a period when he was highly involved in Anglo-Welsh affairs. In 1183, after making peace with his son Geoffrey, the king sent to England for his youngest son, John, and for John's master, Glanville, and they duly joined the king in Normandy. In 1184 Glanville was again involved in Welsh business, he and the archbishop of Canterbury acting as royal envoys when Rhys ap Gruffudd came to a conference at Hereford. In the same year he held a council at London, which refused to permit the papal envoys to raise aid in England, and which promised to recompense the king for any aid which he gave to the pope. In 1185 he accounted for the farm of Northumberland for half a year. Then in 1186 he negotiated a peace in the Welsh marches, between on the one side Rhys ap Gruffudd and certain Welsh knights and on the other the men of Hereford and Chester. In the same year he went on a mission to France, and with some difficulty negotiated a truce with Philip Augustus.

Glanville's success was closely associated with that of his royal master, and in the last year of Henry's reign the justiciar crossed several times between England and Normandy, striving to secure the old king's power. After Henry's death he was present at Richard I's coronation, and was sent by the king to repress the attacks on the Jews that followed it, but with little success. Then in 1190 Glanville ceased to be justiciar. According to Richard of Devizes he was deposed for having taken advantage of his closeness to Henry II, and was fined £15,000, a payment for which there is no evidence on the pipe rolls (*Chronicon*, ed. Appleby, 5). William of Newburgh tells a different story, stating that Glanville resigned because he was old, because Richard consulted him less than had Henry, and because he wished to go on crusade (Newburgh, 1.302; see also Howlett, *Chronicles*, 1.302; see also *Gesta regis Henrici secundi*, 2.87, 90, 2.87, 90). Certainly other members of his family seem to have shared his fall in 1190, though Hubert Walter continued to prosper. Together with Walter and others with whom he had a close connection, Glanville duly set out on crusade. He accompanied the king as far as Marseilles, and eventually reached the Holy Land. He died on 21 October 1190 at the siege of Acre, his death caused by the climate, not by battle.

Contemporary reputation Glanville is an outstanding example of a royal servant of Henry II, to whom his personal tie is made very clear by his fate under Richard. He combined service in a wide variety of fields. Benefits of office followed his successes. In 1175/6 the king gave him land at Leiston in Suffolk, where Glanville soon founded a Premonstratensian abbey. He also received the manor and church of Upton in Norfolk. His relatives too benefited by his prominence, with, for example, five kinsmen becoming sheriffs while he was justiciar. There is occasional evidence that he abused his power. In addition to his dismissal as sheriff of Yorkshire in 1170 there is the case of Gilbert of Plumpton. According to Roger of Howden, Glanville hated Plumpton, and 'attempted to hand him over to death' by accusing him of abducting an heiress who was in the king's gift and of related offences of theft and robbery. Glanville had wanted to give the heiress as wife to his man Reiner. He succeeded in getting Plumpton condemned to death, but on the intervention of the bishop of Worcester and with divine aid, the sentence was postponed. The episode ended with Glanville's keeping Plumpton imprisoned for the rest of his life.

In general, however, contemporaries viewed Glanville favourably, even once death had made criticism less unwise. According to Richard of Devizes he was the 'eye of the kingdom and the king'. When he was in power, no one was more eloquent, although after his fall in 1189–90 'he became so stupid through grief that his son-in-law Ralph of Arden lost through Ranulf's pleading what he had been awarded in judgment through his own pleading' (*Chronicon*, ed. Appleby, 5–7). Gerald of Wales places in his mouth pointed criticisms of Cluniacs and Cistercians when considering his foundation of houses of canons at Butley and Leiston. Gerald also records his own discussion with Glanville late in Henry II's reign concerning recent failings in the defence of Normandy against France compared with earlier successes. Glanville, 'wise and eloquent', maintained that France's earlier weakness stemmed from the loss of the flower of French youth in two great battles, one between Charlemagne's son Louis and Gurmund, the other involving Raoul de Cambrai. His view of the past, it would seem, was based on the *chansons de geste*. Walter Map also noted his forthright views on why clerical officials were usually more oppressive than laymen, and on the speediness of royal, compared with ecclesiastical, justice.

Glanville and 'Glanvill': the law book and its authorship Later tradition ascribed to Glanville the invention of the assize of novel disseisin and the action of replevin. This association must be connected with the attribution to him of the *Tractatus de legibus et consuetudinibus regni Anglie* (commonly called *Glanvill*), a manual concerning royal judicial procedures, composed, or at least completed, between 1187 and 1189. Roger of Howden, under the year 1180, mentions the appointment as justiciar of Glanville, 'by whose wisdom the laws written below were established [*conditae*]'. There follow the so-called *Ten Articles of William I*, the *Leges Edwardi Confessoris*, the *Tractatus de legibus*, and certain decrees of Henry II. Since Glanville had no connection with the composition of the ten articles or the *Leges Edwardi*, Howden's statement is no proof that he was the author of the *Tractatus*. Likewise, the work's incipit, which may belong to the original text, and is certainly present in manuscripts within a decade, states only that the treatise was 'composed in the time of King Henry the Second when justice was under the direction of the illustrious Ranulf Glanvill, the most learned of that time in the law and ancient customs of the realm'. Again the connection stated is not one amounting to authorship, although it does suffice to explain the later attribution to Glanville.

Other prominent candidates for authorship have been suggested, most notably two men who later became justiciars, Hubert Walter and Geoffrey fitz Peter. Yet objections are open to these names too, not least the unlikelihood of their authorship's having been so quickly forgotten as to have left no trace and to have permitted the rapid emergence of a false attribution. The most likely type of candidate is a royal clerk, quite possibly with some academic training in law, but of such a status, at least at the time of writing, that his identity is now unlikely to be certain. What is wellnigh certain, however, is that the author came from the following of Glanville and of his nephew Hubert Walter; and the originality of the *Tractatus*'s exposition, its clarity, and its praise for the laws and justice of the royal court remain as a monument to that circle.

JOHN HUDSON

Sources *Tractatus de legibus et consuetudinibus regi Anglie qui Glanvilla vocatur*, ed. G. D. G. Hall, rev. edn (1993) • R. Mortimer, 'The family of Rannulf de Glanville', *BIHR*, 54 (1981), 1–16 • J. S. Falls, 'Ranulf de Glanville's formative years', *Mediaeval Studies*, 40 (1978), 312–27 • *Pipe rolls* • R. C. van Caenegem, ed., *English lawsuits from William I to Richard I*, 2 vols., SeldS, 106–7 (1990–91) • J. Fantosme, *Chronicle*, ed. R. C. Johnston (1981) • W. Stubbs, ed., *Gesta regis Henrici secundi Benedicti abbatis: the chronicle of the reigns of Henry II and Richard I, AD 1169–1192*, 2 vols., Rolls Series, 49 (1867) • *Chronica magistri Rogeri de Hovedene*, ed. W. Stubbs, 4 vols., Rolls Series, 51 (1868–71) • *Gir. Camb. opera* • R. Howlett, ed., *Chronicles of the reigns of Stephen, Henry II, and Richard I*, 4 vols., Rolls Series, 82 (1884–9), vols. 1–2 • *Radulfi de Diceto … opera historica*, ed. W. Stubbs, 2 vols., Rolls Series, 68 (1876) • *Chronicon Richardi Divisensis / The Chronicle of Richard of Devizes*, ed. J. T. Appleby (1963) • *DNB* • W. Stubbs, ed., *Chronicles and memorials of the reign of Richard I*, 2: *Epistolae Cantuarienses*, Rolls Series, 38 (1865) • *Radulphi de Coggeshall chronicon Anglicanum*, ed. J. Stevenson, Rolls Series, 66 (1875), 29

Glanville, Stephen Ranulph Kingdon (1900–1956), Egyptologist, was born on 26 April 1900 in Westminster, London, the elder son of Stephen James Glanville, deputy editor of the *Daily Telegraph*, and his wife, (Nannie) Elizabeth, daughter of Francis Kingdon; she was a hospital matron and became first president of the Catholic Nurses' Guild.

Glanville was educated at Marlborough College (1914–19), and from 1919 at Lincoln College, Oxford, winning a scholarship to read modern history; later he changed to *literae humaniores*, graduating with a fourth in 1922. He then went to Egypt to teach English at Mansura government school, devoting his spare time to learning the principles of archaeology and visiting the ancient sites, including the newly discovered tomb of Tutankhamun. In 1923 he joined the Egypt Exploration Society's archaeological expedition to Tell al-Amarna and began to study hieroglyphs under F. Ll. Griffith. He returned to London in 1924 and continued his studies under A. H. Gardiner. He was appointed assistant (later assistant keeper, 1930–33) in the department of Egyptian and Assyrian antiquities at the British Museum, where he became the pupil and friend of Sir Herbert Thompson, under whom he specialized in the late cursive script called demotic, and began the catalogue of the museum's demotic papyri.

In 1925 Glanville married Ethel Mary, eldest daughter of J. B. Chubb, of Froyle, Hampshire; they had two daughters. He returned to Egypt to excavate at Tell al-Amarna (1925) and Armant (1928). From 1929 to 1935 he was Laycock student of Egyptology at Worcester College, Oxford. He used part of the money attached to the studentship on an extensive tour of North American museums from September to December 1932. In 1933 he was appointed reader in Egyptology at University College, London, and from 1935 he was Edwards professor of Egyptology there. One of his main tasks was to arrange and catalogue the important Petrie collection. This was interrupted by the outbreak of war in 1939; Glanville served on the air staff, reaching the rank of wing commander. His brief return to University College ended in 1946, when he was elected to the new chair of Egyptology at Cambridge, endowed by Thompson with the aim of furthering demotic and Coptic studies.

Glanville was equally at home with archaeological and philological aspects of Egyptology, as shown by the bibliography of his publications in the *Journal of Egyptian Archaeology* (57, 1971, 181–4). His experience with excavations and museum collections was apparent in his 1929–30 Royal Institution Christmas lectures for children, subsequently published as *Daily Life in Ancient Egypt* (1930), and in his editing of *The Legacy of Egypt* (1942), which he managed to complete despite his war duties. He was honorary keeper of the Fitzwilliam Museum, Cambridge, from 1950. After Thompson's death in 1944, Glanville was the foremost demotic scholar in Britain; his most important work in this field was on the first two volumes of the *Catalogue of Demotic Papyri in the British Museum* (1939–55). In 1946 he was elected FBA, and the following year he gave the Schweich lectures for the British Academy, 'The contribution of demotic to the study of Egyptology'.

In addition to his academic talents, Glanville was a gifted administrator, widely admired for his ability to grasp the essentials of a problem and its solution; this was supplemented by his fair-mindedness and his warmly generous and gregarious nature. These qualities were fully exercised during the war, when he was entrusted with the delicate task of liaison between the Air Ministry and the allied air forces based in Britain; his success was rewarded by an MBE (1946), as well as by Dutch, Czechoslovak, and Yugoslav decorations. In later years these qualities resulted in his election not only as provost of his Cambridge college, King's (1954), but also as master of the Worshipful Company of Grocers (1952), to which he had belonged since 1922. He died suddenly of a heart attack at King's on 26 April 1956; his wife survived him.

R. S. Simpson

Sources I. E. S. Edwards, 'Stephen Randulph Kingdon Glanville, 1900–1956', *PBA*, 44 (1958), 231–40 · R. M. Janssen, *The first hundred years: Egyptology at University College London, 1892–1992* (1992), 27–53 · *Journal of Egyptian Archaeology*, 42 (1956), 99–101 · *Annual Report of the Council* [King's College, Cambridge] (1956), 1–5 · *Annales du Service des Antiquités de l'Égypte*, 54 (1957), 289–94 · *Nature*, 177 (1956), 1013–14 · *The Times* (28 April 1956), 10 · *The Times* (3 May 1956), 14 · *The Times* (5 May 1956), 10 · *The Times* (7 May 1956), 12, 16 · *The Times* (12 May 1956), 10 · *The Times* (16 May 1956), 15 · W. R. Dawson and E. P. Uphill, *Who was who in Egyptology*, 3rd edn, rev. M. L. Bierbrier (1995), 168–9 · *WWW*, *1951–60* · E. P. Uphill, *Journal of Egyptian Archaeology*, 57 (1971), 181–4 [bibliography] · *CGPLA Eng. & Wales* (1956)

Archives Egypt Exploration Society, London, corresp. with the Egypt Exploration Society · U. Oxf., Griffith Institute, corresp. with Jaroslav Corny

Likenesses photograph, *c*.1930, repro. in Janssen, *First hundred years*, 29 · A. C. Barrington Brown, photograph, 1954, repro. in *Journal of Egyptian Archaeology*, pl. 7 · Lafayette Ltd, photograph, U. Oxf., Griffith Institute; repro. in Janssen, *First hundred years*

Wealth at death £11,545 19*s*. 11*d*.: probate, 2 July 1956, *CGPLA Eng. & Wales*

Glanville, Sir William Henry (1900–1976), civil engineer, was born on 1 February 1900 at 75 Kempe Road, Willesden, Middlesex, the only son and second of three children of William Glanville, a London builder of Cornish origins, and his wife, Amelia, *née* Venning. He was educated at Kilburn grammar school and, after a brief period of service at the end of the First World War, studied civil engineering at East London College, University of London. He graduated with first-class honours in 1922, later gaining the degrees of PhD (1925) and DSc (1930). Rather than gaining practical experience on site or in the office of an engineer, he took the unusual step of directly entering a research establishment.

All Glanville's working life was spent in the scientific civil service, the greater part in the Department of Scientific and Industrial Research (DSIR). In November 1922 he entered the Building Research Station (BRS) as an engineering assistant. This laboratory had been established in East Acton in April 1921 for the building materials research committee to provide research regarding new materials and construction methods connected with the government's planned large housing schemes. R. E. Stradling was appointed director of building research in 1924. Glanville first investigated the permeability of concrete and established the importance of controlling water content. He then assisted Professor A. J. S. Pippard on a paper regarding primary stresses in timber roofs. In 1925 the BRS moved to new premises at Garston, near Watford, where he supervised a series of classic studies in reinforced concrete such as the causes of the adhesion of concrete to steel, and the causes and effects of shrinkage of concrete. Such investigations were written up usually as Building Research Technical Papers.

On 20 June 1930 Glanville married Millicent Patience Carr, daughter of Eli John Carr, a railway official; they had a son, who also became a civil engineer, and a daughter.

In 1931 London county council sought recommendations towards establishing a code of practice for the use of reinforced concrete in building. The Building Research Board set up a committee whose report, drawing heavily on the researches of Glanville and his team, was published in 1933, and became incorporated in the British standards code 114. At this time Glanville was also carrying out tests on continuous beams and small portal frames as well as on the driving of concrete piles.

In 1936 Glanville left the BRS to become deputy director of the DSIR Road Research Laboratory (RRL) at Harmondsworth. He now became increasingly involved in administration and the directing of research, but an early task was a detailed study of factors relating to the performance and life of concrete roads. This complemented work he had done at the BRS on the behaviour of concrete road slabs. He soon also appreciated the need for a separate section devoted to the emerging discipline of soil mechanics. This was set up under A. H. D. Marwick in 1938. In 1939 Glanville succeeded Stradling as director of the RRL but, at the outbreak of war, was attached to the research and experiments department of the Ministry of Home Security at Princes Risborough; he was put in charge as chief scientific adviser. When enemy air attacks did not materialize he returned to the RRL, where staff were furnishing technical advice to the Air Ministry and the Ministry of Aircraft Production on the construction of concrete runways and, particularly, less orthodox airfields. For example, where soil was soft, a special bitumen-impregnated hessian, known as prefabricated bituminized surfacing, was developed, as were special laying machines. The soil mechanics section came into its own, analysing soils so that they could be treated, thereby enabling both aircraft and armed forces to move on difficult terrain. This affected tank design, leading to the reduction in failure owing to traction loss. Glanville also worked on the effects of explosives, an area about which little was known; he co-operated with Barnes Wallis in preparing for the attack on the Möhne and Eder dams in May 1943. Glanville oversaw the development of plastic protective plating, a stone-filled bituminous material in a thin steel casing which not only gave increased protection against bomb and shell fragments, but also reduced the demand on steel supplies. This plating was eventually used to protect bridges and gun positions on most allied merchant ships.

After the war Glanville's work concentrated on the problems of the roads. In examining tar and bitumen compounds the RRL adopted a radical new approach to the problem of the specification of bituminous mixtures: the road itself was to be the laboratory, with experiments carried out on a uniform length of road. Such experimentation had been begun in 1939 on the Colnbrook bypass where 800 different compositions were studied. Close co-operation was maintained with industry and with practising highway engineers. New research was in areas as diverse as substituting tar for imported bitumen, devising an alternative traffic-line paint, and developing safer, non-skid road surfacings. By late 1947 these interests and topics were represented on an elaborate but effective system of fourteen committees. That experimental results could thereby be applied quickly and confidently was a tribute to Glanville's scientific method and his grasp of diverse issues in practical engineering.

With the soils section after the war, Glanville emphasized research based on soil types rather than detailed study of individual soils. A wide range of British soils was studied, and this led to classic textbooks, *Soil Mechanics for Engineers* (1952) and *Concrete Roads, Design and Construction* (1955). Classification of road aggregates according to strength, abrasion, and skidding resistance led to *Sources of Road Aggregates in Great Britain* (1948).

In 1946 the laboratory was enlarged to take a wider role in aspects of road safety and traffic flow. Glanville took the opportunity to apply scientific method to such problems, and sought to evaluate the influence of particular road features on accident rates. Skidding was specifically investigated, leading to the use of high hysteresis rubber in tyre treads. Research into the nature of injuries provided much information which led eventually to legislation on the wearing of helmets and seat belts. Other areas studied included headlight dazzle, braking performance, pedestrian crossings, which led to the introduction of the zebra marking in 1951, and traffic speed, which led to specific speed limits. The behaviour of road users was not forgotten, and studies were jointly undertaken by the RRL and the Medical Research Council.

Glanville appreciated that much of his work had direct applications abroad, especially in developing countries. Initially he appointed a colonial liaison officer at the laboratory. He then realized that a simple transfer of technology was not sufficient, and persuaded the Colonial Office to support the colonial section, later the tropical section, which researched problems related specifically to developing countries. Glanville always sought to spread the results of the laboratory's work. He chaired a committee of the Institution of Civil Engineers (ICE) which organized a biennial conference on civil engineering problems overseas. He responded to numerous overseas invitations, and had close ties with many other foreign road research bodies. He was on the organizing committee of a number of international road-related conferences over many years, as well as that of the International Society for Soil Mechanics (1957) and those of the ICE conference on civil engineering problems overseas from 1952 to 1970. He served on the British standards codes of practice committee from 1940 to 1965, on the Royal Engineers' advisory board from 1950 to 1965, and on the board of the British Nuclear Energy Conference from 1953 to 1958. For many years he was a member of the Civil Engineering Research Council and its later incarnations, and served on its council. He was latterly chairman of its information committee. In

1969 he was president of the Smeatonian Society of Civil Engineers.

Glanville remained just as active after his retirement from the directorship in 1965. He set up a consulting practice, and acted as arbitrator in technical legal cases and as an expert witness for the Ministry of Transport and the Department of the Environment. He was also asked by the president of the International Road Federation to serve as a consultant, which he did for ten years.

Many honours came to Glanville. He was knighted in 1960, having been made a CBE in 1944 and a CB in 1953. He was president of the ICE in 1950–51, the youngest ever elected, was its James Forrest lecturer in 1959, and received its Ewing gold medal in 1962. He also received the gold medal of the Institution of Structural Engineers, of which he was a fellow, in 1961. He received the Viva shield and gold medal of the Worshipful Company of Carmen in 1965. He was an honorary member of the institutions of Municipal Engineers, Highway Engineers, and Royal Engineers, and of the Concrete Society. He was a fellow and a governor of Queen Mary College, London, and almoner and governor of Christ's Hospital. He was elected a fellow of the Royal Society in 1958. The day after participating in a meeting on the future of concrete technology, Glanville died suddenly of a stroke, on 30 June 1976, at his home, Langthwaite, 13 Kewferry Drive, Northwood, Middlesex. ROBERT SHARP

Sources *DNB* · Lord Baker, *Memoirs FRS*, 23 (1977), 91–113 · *WWW* · *The Times* (1 July 1976), 18f · *The Times* (6 July 1976), 16g · b. cert. · m. cert. · d. cert.

Likenesses G. Argent, photograph, repro. in *Memoirs FRS*, facing p. 91

Wealth at death £64,751: probate, 16 Feb 1977, *CGPLA Eng. & Wales*

Glanystwyth. *See* Hughes, John (1842–1902).

Glapthorne, Henry (*bap.* **1610**), playwright and poet, was baptized on 28 July 1610 at Whittlesey, Cambridgeshire, the son of Thomas Glapthorne and his third wife (*d.* 1625), a daughter of Thomas Hatcliffe; his father was bailiff to Lady Hatton, the redoubtable wife of Sir Edward Coke. Glapthorne matriculated at Corpus Christi College, Cambridge, in 1624 and seems to have moved to London when he left the university. In 1642 Lovelis, daughter of Henry Glapthorne and his wife, Susan, was baptized at St Bride's, Fleet Street; Susan died the following year, on 22 March 1643, in Fetter Lane.

Glapthorne became a minor figure on the literary scene, enjoying a modest success as a playwright and poet. Six of his plays are extant and three others are known by title; he published two collections of his own poetry and edited the poems of Thomas Beedome. His surviving works were collected and edited in 1874.

From the dedications and allusions of Glapthorne's poems the reader can form some sense of his social milieu. He was a good friend of Charles Cotton sen. and of Aston Cockayne; Richard Lovelace was his 'noble friend and gossip' (H. Glapthorne, *Whitehall*, 1643) and he was an acquaintance and admirer of Ben Jonson. It has been suggested that he authored entertainments for Lady Hatton in the 1630s (Butler). He dedicated work to Thomas Wentworth, earl of Strafford, in hope of patronage, but he also wrote elegies on the fourth earl of Bedford and on the earl of Manchester, both of whom were opposed to court policies. The Latin verses prefixed to the 1640 edition of his tragedy *Wallenstein* are by Alexander Gill jun. (the son of Milton's headmaster at St Paul's School), who was something of a protestant radical. Glapthorne's poem *Whitehall*, dated 4 March 1642 and published in 1643, takes an elegiac view of the deserted palace and reflects on the vanished literary glories of the place, including appreciative recollections of the masques. Glapthorne was probably the 'Glapthorne who lived in Fetter Lane' who wrote the tract 'His majesties gracious answer to the message sent from the honourable citie of London, concerning peace', for which the printer Richard Herne was summoned to the House of Lords on 12 January 1643 and committed to the Fleet prison; it is not known whether Glapthorne joined him there. After 1643 he disappears from the record.

Glapthorne's plays belong to the 1630s and form a varied and not easily classifiable group. He did not settle to any one company but wrote for the King's Men, the Queen's Men, the King's Revels, and Beeston's Boys. *Argalus and Parthenia* (published in 1639), a Neoplatonic romantic pastoral derived from an episode in Sidney's *Arcadia*, is characteristic of the refined courtly taste associated with the queen in the 1630s. It enjoyed several revivals in the early Restoration years, although when Pepys saw it in October 1661 he remembered it not for the Neoplatonic sentiments but for the actress playing Parthenia, who 'had the best legs that I ever saw' (Pepys, 27 Oct 1661). *Wit in a Constable*, a city comedy about the intrusion of local by-laws into citizens' lives—played in 1639, published in 1640, and dedicated to Strafford—was also revived at the Restoration, when Pepys declared that 'so silly a play I never saw I think in my life' (ibid., 23 May 1663).

The Tragedy of Albertus Wallenstein (written after 1634, published in 1639) was perhaps Glapthorne's most popular play. It was acted at the Globe and appealed to the protestant sympathies of the audience for it depicted, in tragicomic mode, the violent downfall of the Catholic general Wallenstein, who was one of the leaders of the imperial armies in the Thirty Years' War. Wallenstein is represented both as a domestic tyrant and as a political monster, and his murder is gruesomely enacted, to the evident satisfaction of London audiences. Glapthorne's other published plays are *The Ladies Priviledge* (written *c.*1637, published in 1640), a work set in Italy and containing debates about women and performance that were topical in the period of Henrietta Maria's sponsorship of court theatricals, and *The Hollander* (written in 1635–6, published in 1640), another London city comedy. The text of another play, 'The Lady Mother', was found in the manuscript collection BL, Egerton MS 1994. Unattributed, it was ascribed to Glapthorne on account of verbal similarities to other of his extant plays, and this attribution has never seriously been challenged (Bullen). It was licensed on 15 October

1635 and topical references within the play place it after 1632. Its sub-plot, involving a drunken steward who fantasizes about a social and sexual liaison with his mistress, is indebted to *Twelfth Night*. Three other plays by Glapthorne were entered in the Stationers' register but were never published; these were the tragedies 'The Dutchess of Fernandina' and 'The Vestal' (both entered on 9 September 1653) and 'The Parricide, or, Revenge for Honor' (entered on 29 November 1653). This last play may be identical with the play published as George Chapman's in 1654, *Revenge for Honor*, which turns on the story of a parricide. Glapthorne's plays have slipped from notice but they remain strong examples of Caroline drama and of the age's sensibility and taste. JULIE SANDERS

Sources A. Harbage, *Cavalier drama: an historical and critical supplement to the study of the Elizabethan and Restoration stage* (1936) • A. H. Bullen, *Old English plays*, 4 vols. (1883) • H. Glapthorne, *The plays and poems*, ed. R. H. Shepherd, 2 vols. (1874) • H. Glapthorne, *The lady mother*, ed. A. Brown (1958) • M. Butler, *Theatre and crisis, 1632–1642* (1984) • M. T. Burnett, *Masters and servants in English Renaissance drama and culture* (1997) • G. Langbaine, *An account of the English dramatick poets* (1691) • J. O. Halliwell, *A dictionary of old English plays* (1860) • Pepys, *Diary* • *DNB* • M. Heinemann, *Puritanism and theatre* (1980) • J. H. Walter, 'Henry Glapthorne', *TLS* (19 Sept 1936), 748 • M. Butler, 'Entertaining the palatine prince: plays on foreign affairs, 1635–1637', *Renaissance Historicism*, ed. A. F. Kinney and D. S. Collins (1987)

Glas, George (1725–1765), mariner, was born probably at Dundee, one of fifteen children of John *Glas (1695–1773), founder of the Glasite or Sandemanian church, and his wife, Katharine Black (*d.* 1749). One account suggests that he was trained as a surgeon and in that capacity made several voyages to the West Indies, where he made a fortune and lost the best part of it and was captured and imprisoned nine times. Another report suggests that he served as a midshipman in the Royal Navy. He was put in command of a ship which traded to Brazil and in it made several voyages to the west coast of Africa and the Canary Islands. On one such trip he discovered a river which, according to his own account, lay between Cape Verde and Senegal, though this does not accord with the probable location of the settlement he later established. The river was navigable some way inland and he concluded that it would be a good site for a trading settlement.

Glas returned home and proposed to the Board of Trade and Plantations that he be given an exclusive grant of the country for all trading purposes for thirty years. This was refused as it conflicted with the act to abolish the African company which stipulated that trade on that coast was to be left free. Glas finally agreed with the board that he would have £15,000 if he obtained a free cession of the country by its rulers to the British crown. He therefore fitted out a ship with trading goods, and with his wife, Isabel Miller (1723–1765) of Perth, whom he had married in 1753, and their daughter Catherine (1754–1765) sailed from Gravesend in August 1764. He arrived at his destination, which he named Port Hillsborough after Wills Hill, first earl of Hillsborough, president of the Board of Trade and Plantations. Its location has been impossible to establish unequivocally, but it was probably at Santa Cruz de Mar Pequeña (Puerto Causado) (Monod, figure 11). It must have been on the west coast of Africa opposite the Canary Islands, that is far north of Cape Verde and Senegal. According to his own report, if not those of others, he easily persuaded the local headmen to sign a treaty giving up their lands.

Glas then sailed in a long boat for Tenerife to obtain supplies, leaving his ship anchored off the mainland. He arrived at Lanzarote and finding there an English ship, by it sent his treaty to the British authorities. However, his activities in a part of Africa subject to competing political claims had aroused the suspicions of the Spanish authorities and shortly after his arrival he was arrested and imprisoned in Tenerife under severe conditions. Attempts made by the British authorities to secure his release were unsuccessful, and meanwhile, in March 1765, the local people attacked the settlers at Port Hillsborough, killing some and forcing others to flee. Among the latter were Glas's wife and child, who arrived by boat in Tenerife to learn of Glas's imprisonment. In October 1765 Glas was finally released and the following month the family embarked for home on the English brig *The Earl of Sandwich*.

Some of the crew of the ship became aware that there was treasure on board and on the night of 30 November 1765, when the vessel was off the south coast of Ireland, they murdered the captain and loyal crew members. They then killed Glas with his own sword as he came on board on hearing the noise and flung his body overboard before sending his wife and daughter after him. The murderers then scuttled the ship and escaped with their booty to the shore; but the ship, instead of sinking, drifted on shore and was discovered still laden with rich cargo but with no living person on board. A link was made to the murderers, who had been spending their gains over-freely, and they were arrested in Dublin, tried, and executed after having confessed their guilt.

Glas was a cultivated man. His translation from a manuscript of J. Abreu de Galinda, a Franciscan of Andalusia, then recently found at Palma, *An Account of the Discovery and History of the Canary Islands*, was published in 1764. Later editions carry a biographical sketch of Glas. He left a manuscript on the Arabs living between the Atlas and Senegal (Bibliothèque Ste Geneviève, Paris, under the name of John Glas). ELIZABETH BAIGENT

Sources T. Monod, 'Notes sur George Glas (1725–1765), fondateur de Port Hillsborough (Sahara Marocain)', *Annario de Estudios Atlanticos*, 22 (1976), 409–517 • *GM*, 1st ser., 35 (1765), 545–7 • 'A short account of the life of Capt. Glas', J. A. de Galinda, *The discovery and history of the Canary Islands*, trans. G. Glas, 2nd edn, 2 vols. (1767), i–viii • *DNB*

Glas, John (1695–1773), founder of the Glasite or Sandemanian church, was born on 21 September 1695, at Auchtermuchty, Fife, and baptized there on 3 October the only son of Alexander Glas (*c.*1653–1725), minister of Auchtermuchty and later of Kinclaven, Perthshire, and Christian, daughter of John Duncan, minister of Rerrick, Kirkcudbrightshire. He was educated at the village school

John Glas (1695–1773), by James Macardell (after William Millar)

in Kinclaven, Perth grammar school (to 1709), and St Leonard's College, St Andrews, where he graduated MA on 6 May 1713. He proceeded to prepare for the ministry at the University of Edinburgh. Despite a feeling of inadequacy he began his trials for licence in October 1717, finally achieving his aim in May 1718. He was ordained on 6 May 1719 to the parish of Tealing, a community of about 800 people near Dundee. There were no indications of any anxiety about his attitude to church government or doctrine at this stage, and his preaching became very popular.

Glas soon began to be concerned for what he regarded as the spiritually impoverished state of his parishioners. He was opposed by those who sought to maintain the covenants, and who allied themselves with the Cameronians, and also by those who were made uncomfortable by his insistence on rigid Presbyterian discipline. Desiring to build a community of saints, he gathered about seventy parishioners into an ecclesiola, with its own rules and monthly celebrations of the Lord's supper, and thus began a journey towards independency. This was noticed unfavourably by local ministers, especially the evangelical John Willison. In correspondence with Francis Archibald of Guthrie, Glas was drawn into controversy over the place of covenants and covenanting in Scotland, and forced further into adopting an independent stance. By 1725 he had developed a spiritualized concept of the church, distinct from the state, and composed of true believers. In 1729 when presbytery and synod were taking proceedings against him, Glas published *The Testimony of the King of Martyrs Concerning His Kingdom* (1729), which attempts to define the nature, extent, and purpose of Christ's kingdom, based on his exposition of the gospel of John 18: 36–7. As a source, Bishop Hoadly's 1717 sermon, *The Nature of the Kingdom or Church of Christ*, seems to be the most likely predecessor, although John Owen's writings may have been influential. After long debates in the general assembly and its commission, and despite defence by Duncan Forbes, the lord advocate, and several of the more moderate ministers who did not want to lose a promising young man from the church, Glas was deposed from the ministry of the Church of Scotland on 12 March 1730. He was charged with having departed from the doctrines and principles of the national church in several particulars, especially concerning subscribing to the formula, and those passages of the confession of faith relating to the magistrates' power circa sacra (that is, when exercised in spiritual or church matters), and that he had continued to exercise his ministry, and followed divisive and schismatical courses in setting up meeting-houses in Tealing and Dundee. In 1739 the assembly revoked the sentence of deposition, but by that time Glas was no longer interested in reconciliation.

Glas moved to Dundee, where he had many supporters, and with them and a number from Tealing he formed the Glasite church, 'subject to no jurisdiction under heaven', the title of a work published in 1728. Francis Archibald joined him for a few years, and George Byres, minister of St Boswell's, became a Glasite elder in Galashiels. Later two Fife clergymen, Robert Ferrier of Largo and James Smith of Newburn, were influenced by him, and Ferrier associated himself with the Glasites in the later 1760s. Otherwise, Glas had little clerical support. He did however find a small but devoted following in Dundee, where the Baxter family, who moved from Tealing to establish themselves as mill owners, were church members for several generations. A list of members from 1746 records forty-eight men, including John Baxter and John Glas, as the teaching elder, and sixty-two women. In later lists it is evident that most of the members were involved in the weaving industry, and it is in towns where that trade flourished, such as Perth (1733), Galashiels (1738), Arbroath (1742), and Paisley (1767), that Glasite societies were founded, as well as in the bigger cities of Edinburgh (1734), Aberdeen (1750), Glasgow (1762), and London (1762). Adherents were also found in the Lake District, where some of the followers of Benjamin Ingham became Glasites. It is there that the most famous of all Glasites, Michael Faraday, had his origins. Glas spent most of his ministry in Dundee, conducting a large correspondence with his churches. He had two spells as elder in Perth, between 1736 and 1737, and 1764 and 1769.

In comparative isolation from other Scottish churches the Glasites developed a distinctive theology and liturgy. Glas was a very competent biblical and patristic scholar, and wrote extensively on controversial issues of the day, as well as on the text of scripture. His churches became increasingly exclusive, partly through the contentious writings of his son-in-law, Robert *Sandeman, who had married Glas's daughter Katharine in 1737. By the time of Glas's death the church had withdrawn from contact on spiritual matters with all other Christians. Glas remained a Calvinist, and opposed to overt evangelism. He held that the apostolic office had ceased with the first apostles, and new adherents were recruited through reading Glasite literature. An intellectual view of faith evolved, so that the contemporary appeal to feelings and emotions was excluded. A bare belief in the fact of the resurrection became the basis of church membership, and later Glasites debated the nature of Christian assurance. With the developing study of scripture came new ideas of church order and worship, central to which was the separation of church and state. Glasite thinking also questioned the necessity of trained ministers, and soon 'unlearned' elders were ordained whose duties included preaching. Deacons were appointed to care for the poor, and deaconesses to look after women in the congregation. After long discussion it was decided to celebrate the Lord's supper every Lord's day afternoon, a notable deviation from Presbyterian practice. Close attention to the New Testament, especially the Acts of the Apostles, led to the church's adopting a love feast between Sunday services, at which hymns were sung, and for which the earliest Scottish hymnbook, *Christian Songs*, was produced in 1749. The kiss of peace and the washing of feet were ordained at suitable occasions; the eating of blood was forbidden; strict unanimity was required for every decision. Each church, to be properly set in order, required at least two elders. Infant baptism was performed in households. In the Sunday liturgy, the whole Bible was read in order; chapters from each section of the scriptures were interspersed with prayers, and psalms were read at each service. Sermons were exhortations in biblical language. Underpinning all this was the sense that Christendom had gone astray from the New Testament church order, and that Glas had been raised up to restore the church. Exclusiveness arose from the rejection of false charity, and Glasites were attacked by Andrew Fuller in his *Strictures on Sandemanianism* as much for their exclusiveness as for their doctrine of faith. To their critics it was a matter of concern that Glasites, following their founder, had a relaxed attitude to public entertainments such as the theatre, although they were fanatically opposed to anything that appeared to be governed by chance. Members were expected to care for their own poor, and to hold their material possessions at the disposal of the church, to create a potential community of goods.

In 1721 Glas married Katharine (*d.* 1749), daughter of Thomas Black, minister of Perth. They had fifteen children, all of whom Glas outlived. Glas's wife died of consumption in December 1749. Their son Alexander produced several sacred poems before his death aged twenty-two. Another son, George *Glas, achieved fame as an explorer and author and was brutally murdered off the coast of Ireland in 1765. Glas was above ordinary height, strong and robust, very healthy, fond of children, and with an informal manner, quite unlike the clergymen of his day: 'there was nothing of the fanatic, far less the priest, about him' (Ferrier, 16–17). He was well educated and a talented and prolific writer: the *Works of Mr John Glas* was first published in four volumes in Edinburgh in 1761 and appeared at Perth in five volumes in 1782. He was a strong influence in the churches of the Glasite order, which, although nominally independent, were dominated by him as long as he lived. Glas's influence extended beyond the small churches that bore his name, and which still, very tenuously, exist. In the 1760s both the Old Scots Independents and the Scotch Baptists had many of the characteristics of the Glasite theology and liturgy. Glas died at Dundee on 2 November 1773 and was buried there in the Old Howff cemetery. His writings later influenced James Haldane, and Thomas Campbell and the Churches of Christ. His ideas on independency, and on the spiritual nature of the church, along with his intellectual Calvinism, keep recurring on the fringes of evangelicalism, and the desire to reconstruct a church after the New Testament pattern continues to haunt Independent churches.

DEREK B. MURRAY

Sources *DNB* • J. Glas, *A continuation of Mr Glas's narrative* (1729) • J. T. Hornsby, 'The case of Mr John Glas', *Records of the Scottish Church History Society*, 6 (1936–8), 115–37 • J. T. Hornsby, 'John Glas: his later life and work', *Records of the Scottish Church History Society*, 7 (1939–41), 94–113 • G. N. Cantor, *Michael Faraday: Sandemanian and scientist* (1991) • D. B. Murray, 'The influence of John Glas', *Records of the Scottish Church History Society*, 22 (1984–6), 45–56 • *Fasti Scot.*, new edn • D. B. Murray, 'Glas, John', *DSCHT* • R. Ferrier, 'Preface', in J. Glas, *The testimony of the king of martyrs*, ed. R. Ferrier, new edn (1777)

Archives St Andrews Church, Dundee, Glasite MSS • University of Dundee, papers | University of Dundee, Baxter MSS

Likenesses J. Macardell, mezzotint (after W. Millar), NPG [*see illus.*] • portrait, priv. coll.

Glascock, William Nugent (1787?–1847), naval officer, entered the navy in January 1800 on the frigate *Glenmore* with Captain George Duff. He followed Duff in 1801 to the *Vengeance*, in which he served in the Baltic, on the coast of Ireland, and in the West Indies. In 1803 he was appointed to the *Colossus* and afterwards to the *Barfleur*, in which he was present in the action off Cape Finisterre on 22 July 1805, and later at the blockade of Brest under Admiral Cornwallis. In November 1808 he was promoted lieutenant of the *Dannemark*, and served in her at the capture of Flushing in August 1809; in 1812 he was a lieutenant of the *Clarence* in the Bay of Biscay. He afterwards served in the frigates *Tiber*, *Madagascar*, and *Meander* on the home station, and in the *Sir Francis Drake*, flagship of Sir Charles Hamilton, on the Newfoundland station; he was promoted from her to the command of the sloop *Carnation* (18 guns) in November 1818. In 1819 he commanded the brig *Drake* (10 guns), from which he had to be invalided out.

In 1830 Glascock was appointed to the sloop *Orestes*, which he commanded on the home station during 1831. In 1832 he was sent out to the coast of Portugal, and during the latter months of the year was stationed in the Douro, for the protection of British interests in the then disturbed state of the country [*see* Sartorius, Sir George Rose]. He continued in the Douro as senior officer for nearly a year, during which time his conduct under troublesome and often difficult circumstances won him Admiralty approval and promotion to post rank, on 3 June 1833, accompanied by a special complimentary letter from Sir James Graham, the first lord. He did not, however, leave the Douro until the following September, and on 1 October he paid off the *Orestes*. From April 1843 to January 1847 he commanded the frigate *Tyne* on the Mediterranean station, and during the following months was employed in Ireland as an inspector under the Poor Relief Act. He was married and had at least one child.

Glascock devoted long intervals on half pay, as both commander and captain, to literary labours, and produced between 1826 and 1838 several volumes of naval novels, anecdotes, reminiscences, and reflections, which are weak enough as novels, and of little historical value, but are occasionally interesting as social sketches of naval life in the early part of the century. His *Naval Service, or, Officers' Manual* (2 vols., 1836), on the other hand, was a useful manual for young officers; it was reprinted several times, and also translated, and was used in foreign navies. While working in Ireland, Glascock died suddenly at Baltinglass on 8 October 1847.

J. K. LAUGHTON, *rev.* ROGER MORRISS

Sources O'Byrne, *Naval biog. dict.* • J. Marshall, *Royal naval biography*, 4/2 (1835), 490–525 • *Colburn's United Service Magazine*, 3 (1847), 465–6 • R. Muir, *Britain and the defeat of Napoleon, 1807–1815* (1996) • H. V. Livermore, *A new history of Portugal* (1976)

Glasgow. For this title name *see* Boyle, George Frederick, sixth earl of Glasgow (1825–1890).

Glasgow Boys (*act.* **1875–1895**) was the name adopted by a group of twenty or so young artists associated with new developments in painting in Glasgow who were more formally known as the Glasgow school of painters. The majority of these painters came from Glasgow and the west of Scotland, but some were from Edinburgh and the east coast, and one, Joseph Crawhall [*see below*], was English. What drew them together was a shared admiration for James McNeill Whistler, the naturalist paintings of Jules Bastien-Lepage, a shared objection to the tired genre and history painting of many Glasgow-based painters (whom the Boys dubbed 'The Gluepots'), a strong sense of ambition, and a shared aim of dismantling the stranglehold of Edinburgh and its Royal Scottish Academy over artistic life in Scotland.

The Boys first appeared as a coherent force in Scottish painting at the annual exhibition of the Glasgow Institute of the Fine Arts in 1885. They never spoke with one voice and they drew upon three distinct branches of adherents. The first group comprised **William York MacGregor** (1855–1923) and his friend James Paterson [*see below*], who painted together from the mid-1870s. Macgregor was born in Finnart, Dunbartonshire, in September 1855, the son of John MacGregor, a shipbuilder, and his wife, Margaret, *née* York. He studied painting as a pupil of James Docharty in Glasgow and then at the Slade School of Fine Art, London, under Alphonse Legros. This more formal training, combined with his private means and a certain *gravitas* in his manner, gave him the sobriquet 'Father of the School', but in artistic terms he was eclipsed by the events of 1885 and took only a minor role in later years. He was crippled by asthma, and left Glasgow for the cleaner air of Bridge of Allan in 1886 as well as visiting South Africa in 1888 in the hope of a cure. On 30 April 1918 he married Jessie Watson, a nurse, and they lived at Albyn Lodge, Bridge of Allan, Stirlingshire. He died on 28 September 1923 at the Great Western Hotel, Oban, and was buried at Logie, near Bridge of Allan. His friend Paterson wrote that 'he relished a good sermon, loved savoury food, drank little or nothing, smoked fine cigars … [was] an omnivorous reader, keenly interested in classical music … always shy with women, [with] a cordial contempt for "Swells"' (Paterson).

James Paterson (1854–1932) was born on 21 August 1854 in Hillhead, Glasgow, the son of Andrew Paterson, a cotton and muslin manufacturer, and Margaret Hunter. He studied at Glasgow School of Art from 1871 to 1874 and then with various masters in Paris, including Jacquesson de la Chevreuse (1877–9) and Jean Paul Laurens (1879–83). On 24 April 1884 he married Eliza Grier Ferguson (*b.* 1856/7) and settled in Moniaive, Dumfriesshire, thus removing himself from the centre of the artistic developments in Glasgow post-1885, although he was deeply involved in the launch and production of the *Scottish Art Review* from 1888 to 1890. He became a member of most of the artistic bodies in Scotland (Royal Scottish Society of Painters in Watercolour, 1885; associate member of the Royal Scottish Academy, 1896; full member of the Royal Scottish Academy, 1910; president of the Royal Scottish Society of Painters in Watercolour, 1922–32). He died on 25 January 1932 at 12 Randolph Crescent, Edinburgh, and was buried there in Dean cemetery.

Paterson and MacGregor met at school and from 1877 to 1883 they painted together, mainly on the east coast of Scotland. MacGregor's pursuit of the tonal values found in the more consistent light of the east of Scotland, his honesty of technique, and Paterson's French training all combined to lead them towards the naturalism of Bastien-Lepage. Landscape watercolours became Paterson's forte, painted *en plein air*, for example *Moniaive* (1885; Hunterian Art Gallery, University of Glasgow), while MacGregor concentrated on both landscape and pictures of contemporary life, such as *Crail* (1883; Smith Art Gallery, Stirling) and his masterpiece *The Vegetable Stall* (1883–4; National Galleries of Scotland, Edinburgh), a painting which he substantially altered after seeing the works of James Guthrie and John Lavery in 1885 and which he never exhibited publicly. MacGregor's private income enabled him to run a large studio in Glasgow, where he entertained many of his colleagues in the early 1880s and where many of the group's ideas and beliefs were honed, but any artistic leadership MacGregor offered waned after 1885.

The second group consisted of painters who made more sustained visits to France, particularly to Grez-sur-Loing, an artists' colony where many followers of naturalism congregated. John *Lavery (1856–1941) was the most important of these, but others such as Thomas Millie Dow (1848–1919) and **William Kennedy** (1859–1918) joined him. Kennedy was born on 17 July 1859 at 89 Hospital Street, Glasgow, the son of John Kennedy, master baker, and his wife, Lillian, *née* Shedden. He studied at Paisley

School of Art and possibly also at Glasgow School of Art, probably at the evening classes. From 1880 to 1885 he spent much of his time in France, studying in Paris under William-Adolphe Bouguereau and A. F. Fleury and later working with Bastien-Lepage, L. J. R. Collin, and Gustave Courtois. By 1884 he was painting in a proficient naturalist manner, as in, for example, *Spring* (1884; Paisley Museum and Art Gallery), and making drawings and taking photographs of French peasants at work in the fields, which were later translated into paintings. On his return to Scotland he settled near Stirling, where he was attracted by the army camps in Queen's Park. For the rest of his life the daily routine of the military, not its grand set-piece pageants, became his principal subject matter, painted in a much more immediate and colourful manner than his earlier naturalist paintings. Examples include *In the Cooking Trenches*, *Waiting to Mount Guard*, *The Canteen—Mid-Day*, all exhibited at the Glasgow Institute of the Fine Arts in the 1890s. Although never so united in drawing up a constitution as the contemporary New English Art Club in London, the Glasgow Boys, when they did toy with a formal association around 1887, proposed Kennedy as president. The venture was short-lived, however, and never had any real meaning in the development of the school. On 21 September 1898 Kennedy married Helena Fife Scott (Lena) (*b.* 1867/8), also a painter, and soon they began to pay extensive visits to Berkshire, where Kennedy underwent a change of style and subject matter, much influenced by the rural charm of its gentle villages. Kennedy's health caused him to settle in 1912 in Tangier, where Lavery had a house and where he died on 11 December 1918. He was buried in the British section of Tangier cemetery.

Many of the key naturalist works of the school were painted by the three members of the third group, James *Guthrie (1859–1930), Edward Arthur *Walton (1860–1922), and **Joseph Crawhall** [*known as* Joseph Crawhall the third] (1861–1913). Guthrie and Walton painted together from the late 1870s, developing a strong interest in Bastien-Lepage's work, which they encountered not just at the Glasgow Institute but also in a series of exhibitions in London in 1882 and 1883. Bastien-Lepage strongly recommended that a painter become part of a local community, as he had at Damvillers, painting its daily life without resorting to the great set pieces which formed so many of the exhibits at the Paris Salon and its British equivalents. Peasants in the fields and tradesmen in the street seen going about their daily tasks became Bastien-Lepage's standard subject matter, which he painted without the symbolism with which Jean-François Millet had imbued his similar paintings a generation before. The Scots took to spending summers in single locations in emulation of Bastien-Lepage, such as Crowland, Lincolnshire, and Cockburnspath, Berwickshire (where Guthrie lived and worked for almost three years, 1883–5). Their paintings of these rural locations were seen to best advantage in 1885 at the Glasgow Institute and they were recognized as the virtual leaders of an identifiable new school. Crawhall was related to Walton through marriage and began to paint alongside him and Guthrie from about 1879. He was born on 20 August 1861 at Wansbeck House, Newgate Street, Morpeth, Northumberland, the son of Joseph *Crawhall (1821–1896), a wood-engraver and arts promoter, and his wife, Margaret, formerly Boyd (*c.*1833–1928). The young Crawhall attended King's College School in London from 1877 to 1879 but he had no formal art training other than two months in the studio of Aimée Morot in Paris in 1882. He developed his own natural and considerable talents through the example of both Guthrie and Walton, who had each received a varied formal training. He became one of the most accomplished watercolourists of his generation, specializing in horses, birds, and other animals, in preference to purely figurative subjects. A close friend of Lavery, he spent much of his time from 1884 to 1893 in Morocco, where many of his best watercolours were produced. The Glasgow shipowner and collector William Burrell became his chief patron, acquiring over 140 of his pictures, including masterpieces such as *The Aviary, Clifton* (1888) and *The Flower Shop*. From 1907 he lived in Yorkshire and died at 92 Redcliffe Gardens, South Kensington, London, on 24 May 1913, following an operation for emphysema. He was buried at St Mary's, Morpeth.

Arthur *Melville (1855–1904) was another outsider, born and brought up in the east of Scotland, but at an early stage in his career he left Edinburgh to study in the ateliers of Paris, where he adopted the pursuit of tonal values which became an integral part of the style of the Glasgow Boys. He also visited Grez-sur-Loing but then travelled on through Spain and Morocco to the Middle East. His earlier, more naturalist works had a considerable influence on Guthrie, Walton, Lavery, and Crawhall but his watercolours of Spain and of Arab life (for example, *A Mediterranean Port*, 1892; Glasgow Museums and Art Galleries), with their strong colours and bold technique, had a greater appeal to a younger generation of painters associated with the Boys, particularly George Henry and Edward Atkinson Hornel [*see below*].

George Henry (1858–1943) was born on 14 March 1858 at Irvine, Ayrshire, the son of William Hendry, brewer, and his wife, Ann, *née* Fisher. Though his name was recorded at his birth as Hendry, he used the name Henry. Hardly anything is known of his early life. By the early 1880s he was employed as a clerk in Glasgow but he also enrolled for classes at Glasgow School of Art in 1882 and 1883. He was working at Brig o'Turk in 1882, probably alongside Guthrie and Walton, and his early works show a clear interest in tonal values and are much influenced by the work of the older men. When Guthrie settled in Cockburnspath in 1883 Henry joined him and rapidly adopted a naturalist manner. It was probably in Cockburnspath that he met Arthur Melville, whose use of strong, clear colour was to divert Henry away from naturalism. He showed a fascination with the symbolic use of colour and with his friend Hornel began to experiment with looser and more emotional compositions. This culminated in *The Galloway Landscape* (1889; Glasgow Museums and Art Galleries), a painting which seems to owe much to the Pont-Aven painters centred on Paul Gauguin. Henry was certainly in France in the late 1880s and Scottish painters such as Charles Mackie were in touch with Gauguin. An interest in Japan and *japonaiserie* took over, however, encouraged by Hornel, and in 1893 Henry travelled with Hornel to Japan, where he stayed for eighteen months. By the time he returned to Glasgow many of the Boys had left the city and Henry followed several of them to London, where he established himself as a successful portrait and landscape painter. He died on 23 December 1943 at 132 Fulham Road, London, and was buried in Cathcart cemetery, Glasgow.

Edward Atkinson Hornel (1864–1933) was born on 17 July 1864 at Bacchus Marsh, Australia, the son of William Lidderdale Hornel (*b.* 1822), a bootmaker, and Ann Elizabeth Habbishaw (*b. c.*1832), who had recently emigrated there from Kirkcudbright. The family returned to Kirkcudbright in 1866 and Hornel made the town his home for the rest of his life. He studied at the Trustees' Academy, Edinburgh (1880–83), and then at the Académie Royale des Beaux Arts in Antwerp under Charles Verlat (1883–5). He appears to have met Guthrie, who was visiting Kirkcudbright, in 1885 and almost immediately adopted a naturalist manner in his painting. Guthrie may have introduced him to Henry but however they met, the two became close friends, sharing ideas and even canvases for the next decade. Hornel was keenly interested in folklore and local history, which began to appear in his paintings in a change of subject matter, rural peasantry giving way to druids, as in *The Druids: Bringing Home the Mistletoe* (1890, with George Henry; Glasgow Museums and Art Galleries), and goblins. Melville's intense colours were a profound influence but the heavily worked impastoed surface of his paintings was a unique aspect of Glasgow school painting. His fascination with Japan, inspired by J. A. M. Whistler, was reflected in the changing subject matter of his paintings. The Galloway milkmaids were now dressed in kimonos and chased butterflies with silk bandannas (for example *Midsummer*, 1892; Walker Art Gallery, Liverpool). Eventually, aided by funds from William Burrell and Alexander Reid, Hornel set out with Henry to visit Japan. His Japanese paintings are more a record of life in Japan than an assimilation of Japanese art; their bright colours and sometimes crude impasto seem the antithesis of Japanese art. Hornel remained in Kirkcudbright, refusing to move to London, and certainly not to Edinburgh (he refused membership of the Royal Scottish Academy in 1901). His later paintings concentrate on a repetitive formula (sustained by the use of photographs) of groups of young girls playing in bluebell woods or on the shores of the Solway Firth. They were extremely successful and he was able to afford the life of a country gentleman, indulging his interests in foreign travel and rare books. He died, unmarried, on 30 June 1933 at his home, Broughton House, 12 High Street, Kirkcudbright.

The exhibition at the Glasgow Institute in 1885 brought together all of the different aspects of the Glasgow school, and the painters were recognized as having common aims (the sobriquet Glasgow Boys was preferred by the artists themselves as they found the use of the term Glasgow school pretentious and stuffy). Just as soon as they came together, however, they began to drift apart. By the time their work was shown at the Grosvenor Gallery, London, in 1890 several of the artists had left Glasgow or were busy developing new styles. Their exhibition was the final show at the Grosvenor Gallery and so attracted much press attention. This in turn caught the eyes of several of the new exhibiting bodies in Europe, principally secessionist, where naturalism was becoming accepted as a logical compromise between academic painting and the avant-garde work of the Impressionists. The Grosvenor Gallery exhibition was taken to Munich and from there the Boys began to exhibit throughout Europe and beyond—Berlin, Vienna, Venice, Rome, Barcelona, Budapest, Turin, Moscow, St Petersburg—and then in America—in Pittsburgh, St Louis, Chicago, Cincinnati, and New York. The Boys also began individually to send their work to the Paris Salon and similar institutions in Europe. Gradually they were assimilated into the establishment which they had railed against in 1880.

There were other naturalist movements in Britain, principally in Newlyn, Cornwall, but most of these painters were simply dressing up high Victorian sentimentality in modernistic clothes (as, of course, was John Lavery). Guthrie, Henry, Walton, Paterson, and Kennedy (and several other artists associated with the Boys) more fully understood the motives and aspirations of Bastien-Lepage. Their paintings were by no means social realism on the scale of Courbet, but they painted everyday life in its uneventfulness, without social or political comment and without trivializing the sometimes mean existences of their subjects. In this they echoed the work of Sir George Clausen and his circle in London and East Anglia, but their achievement was more than just pictorial or artistic. In 1875 the visual arts in Scotland were dominated by the Royal Scottish Academy and social institutions such as Glasgow Art Club. The Boys were ambitious enough to want to join these bodies, but not on the terms laid down to them: 'paint as we do, don't rock the boat'. The academy even went so far as to exclude from membership any artist who did not take up residence in Edinburgh. By 1890 the Boys had broken all of these barriers and had shown that Glasgow was a major artistic centre, which had been concealed by the status quo of the academy for fifty years. Glasgow could not, however, sustain the Boys, or at least not satisfy their growing success, and gradually they left, usually retaining some formal link with the city such as teaching at the Glasgow School of Art or retaining a portrait practice there. They brought Glasgow to national and international attention, extended the boundaries of contemporary British painting, and gave an encouraging example to the coming generations of young Scottish painters such as the Scottish colourists. More immediately, their fame within the European Secessionist movement eased the path of Charles Rennie Mackintosh and his contemporaries, who began to exhibit in Europe in the late 1890s. Their star waned after 1918 and by the 1950s their paintings had been consigned to the basements of museums before being reappraised by a new generation of art historians and curators who recognized the power of the contribution they had made.

ROGER BILLCLIFFE

Sources R. Billcliffe, *The Glasgow Boys: the Glasgow school of painting, 1875–1895* (1985) · *The Glasgow Boys*, Scottish Arts Council, 2 vols. (1968–71) · D. Martin, *The Glasgow school of painting* (1897) · V. Hamilton, *Joseph Crawhall, 1861–1913* (1990) · W. Smith, *Edward Atkinson Hornel* (1998) · b. certs. [Crawhall, Kennedy, Henry, Hornel] · m. certs. [MacGregor, Paterson, Kennedy] · d. certs. [MacGregor, Paterson, Crawhall, Henry, Hornel] · *CGPLA Eng. & Wales* (1913) [Joseph Crawhall] · *CGPLA Eng. & Wales* (1943) [George Henry] · J. Paterson, 'William York Macgregor and the Glasgow school, a manuscript history of Macgregor's involvement with the Boys including transcripts of several letters from Macgregor to Paterson', priv. coll.

Archives NL Scot., corresp. and papers [E. A. Walton] · Tate collection, corresp., papers, and picture registers [John Lavery] | NL Scot., letters to J. P. McGillivray [James Guthrie] · NL Scot., letters to J. P. McGillivray [George Henry] · NL Scot., letters to R. B. Cunninghame Graham [John Lavery]

Wealth at death £6188 17*s.* 2*d.*—Joseph Crawhall: probate, 8 July 1913, *CGPLA Eng. & Wales*

Glasgow Girls (*act.* **1880–1920**), were a group of women artists in Glasgow. The name, conferred on the group by twentieth-century scholars, deliberately alludes to the contemporary group of Scottish male artists known as the *Glasgow Boys. The impetus to identify, record, and exhibit the work of women artists in Glasgow at the end of the nineteenth century came from the exhibition 'Scottish Painting' held at the Glasgow Art Gallery in 1961: this featured the work of 'the Boys' in abundance but did not include a single work by a woman. The earliest recorded reference to the Glasgow Girls appears to be that in William Buchanan's essay in the catalogue to the Scottish Arts Council exhibition 'The Glasgow Boys' in 1968, the year in which the exhibition 'Founder Members and Exhibitors' was held at the Lady Artists' Club. The founding of the Glasgow Society of Lady Artists in 1882, the first residential club of its kind in Scotland, provided a meeting place for women artists and opportunities and a space to exhibit their work. It was, however, the encouragement and enlightened approach to teaching that Francis (Fra) *Newbery, the exceptional headmaster of the Glasgow School of Art from 1885 to 1917, showed to his women students during that period that provided the foundation of their success. All of the Glasgow Girls studied at the school and several went on to become members of staff.

At the school students came into contact with, and became practitioners within, the contemporary art movement known as the Glasgow style, an avant-garde design development that was influenced by the arts and crafts movement and an understanding of art nouveau. The revival of Celtic designs also contributed to this innovative style. Alongside these developments in design the Glasgow Girls worked within the context of the movement in painting known initially as the Glasgow school and later by the name given to the group of painters involved, the Glasgow Boys. The burgeoning prosperity of Glasgow ensured not only that there were local patrons willing to buy art, but that funding was available to support the education of women as well as men at the Glasgow School of Art. In 1897 the school moved from the top floor of the Corporation Buildings to a new building designed by the architect and designer Charles Rennie *Mackintosh, whose work was in that year the subject of an important article in *The Studio*. The enlarged school provided better facilities for artisans attending early morning and evening classes in manufacturing design. Day classes were also held for middle-class women and paid for initially by their families.

Four years after his appointment as headmaster, on 28 September 1889 Fra Newbery married Jessie Wylie Rowat, an embroiderer. **Jessie Wylie Newbery** (1864–1948) was born in Paisley, near Glasgow, on 28 May 1864, one of the four children of William Rowat and his wife, Margaret Downie Hill. William Rowat was a shawl manufacturer and later tea importer who had strong views on the education of women. Like her father, Jessie had an independent nature. At the age of eighteen she visited Italy, where she became interested in mosaics, textiles, pottery, and 'peasant crafts'. Throughout her life she collected textiles from Italy, Russia, and the Balkans. In 1884 she enrolled as a student at the Glasgow School of Art, and ten years later she became head of the school's department of embroidery, which she had established earlier. Her work raised the status of embroidery to that of a creative art form. She evolved

> a characteristic linen appliqué … worked on linen ground, with applied simple stylized flowers and leaves, cut out of coloured linens and held down by satin stitch in silk … the stems coiled into strong lines, outlining the shape of the article. (Swain, 'Mrs J. R. Newbery', 105)

She 'liked the opposition of straight lines to curved; of horizontal to vertical … I specially aim at beautifully shaped spaces and try to make them as important as the patterns' (ibid.). The Glasgow rose, emblem of the Glasgow style, 'is believed to have evolved from her circles of pink linen, cut out freehand and applied with lines of satin stitch to indicate folded petals' (ibid.). She introduced lettering, mottoes, and verses as part of her designs, and also taught needleweaving and dress design. In an interview with Gleeson White she commented, 'I believe in education consisting of seeing the best that has been done. Then, having this high standard thus set before us, in doing what we like to do: that for our fathers, this for us' (G. White, 48). She was a fine teacher and inspired many of her students.

At the same time Mrs Newbery managed her mercurial husband and brought up two daughters, Elsie and Mary, for whom she designed artistic yet practical dresses, as she designed and made her own attractive clothes. Her original and individual designs for dresses incorporating embroidery set a style for her students which was emulated by many of the Glasgow Girls, including the Macdonald sisters, Margaret and Frances. Like women in other artistic circles, for example, Jane and May Morris, Jessie Newbery wore dresses of an Italian Renaissance appearance, though she also believed that dress should be practical as well as beautiful. At a school at-home in November 1900

> her black merve [*sic*] gown was slightly trained and had the long sleeves puffed at intervals to correspond with the simply fashioned bodice which was finished with a narrow collar of old lace, and on the shoulders bows of reddish gold velvet. (Burkhauser, 148)

It was later noted that 'she never wore a corset in her life ... she deplored the tight lacing imposed by the current fashion' (ibid., 50), a comment that reveals her interest in rational dress (she possessed a 'rational' skating costume with red flannel bloomers). In 1918 she retired with her husband to Eastgate, Corfe Castle, Dorset, where she died on 27 April 1948.

Jessie Newbery's most talented student, **Ann Macbeth** (1875–1948), was born at 41 Chorley Old Road, Little Bolton, Lancashire, on 25 September 1875, the eldest of the nine children of Norman Macbeth, a mechanical engineer, and his wife, Annie MacNicol. Her grandfather was the portrait painter Norman *Macbeth RA. She attended a dame-school in St Anne's, whither her family had moved, and was influenced by her parents' active support of the local church. (Though Scottish Presbyterians, they attended a Congregational church, there being no Presbyterian church nearby.) Owing to a childhood attack of scarlet fever, Ann had the use of only one eye. In 1902, while still a student, Ann Macbeth joined Jessie Newbery as a teacher in the embroidery department of Glasgow School of Art. That year she won a silver medal at the Turin Esposizione Internazionale d'Arte Decorativa, and a silk cushion she had worked with the floral attributes of the four countries of Britain was presented to Queen Alexandra in commemoration of the coronation. She taught needlework, embroidery, and appliqué, and from 1909 to 1912 also taught metalwork and bookbinding. About 1911 she succeeded Jessie Newbery as head of the embroidery department at Glasgow School of Art, where she had become a member of the school council in 1908. Like her teacher, she made and embroidered her own dresses and also executed fine works of embroidery such as *The Sleeping Beauty* (1902; Glasgow Museums and Art Galleries) and a pictorial work, *Elspeth* (1904; priv. coll.). Her works often incorporate panels of figures worked on satin. Their 'billowing elongated skirts with ... decorated borders are romantic but still functional' (Swain, 'Ann Macbeth', 8). She was a fine draughtswoman and an influential teacher at her Saturday classes for teachers run by the school. Macbeth reached a wider public with a series of lectures across Scotland, England, and Wales. Her books included *Educational Needlework* (1911, with Margaret Swanson), *Embroidered Lace and Leatherwork* (1924), and *Countrywoman's Rug Book* (1926; repr. California, *c.*1990). Over a long period examples of her work were on exhibition at Miss Cranston's tea-rooms in Glasgow. She designed for Liberty's and Knox's Linen Thread Company, and embroidered a frontal for the communion table of Glasgow Cathedral. Fra Newbery praised 'her very practical outlook' and noted of her work 'how stuffs, plain, yet of sound quality and good colour could be beautified by the addition of embroidery and other decoration' (ibid.). She was awarded diplomas in art from institutions in Paris, Tunis, Ghent, Budapest, and Chicago. In 1928 she retired to Patterdale, Westmorland, where she 'was quickly recognized by her long flowing cape, her skirt possibly vivid scarlet and emerald green, wearing long necklaces' (Ives, 6). Ann Macbeth died, unmarried, at 8 Eden Mount, Carlisle, on 23 March 1948. As a foreword to Anne Knox Arthur's *Embroidery Book* (1920) she wrote: 'One may embroider poems, another may embroider prayer and praises for her church, another may beautify a woman's garments or sing a little song in stitches for a baby's robe' (ibid.). Her embroidery of *The Nativity* is in Glasgow Museum and Art Gallery; that of *The Good Shepherd* remains in Patterdale church.

Following their move to Glasgow in 1890, Margaret Macdonald [*see* Mackintosh, Margaret Macdonald] and her sister Frances Eliza *Macdonald [*see under* Mackintosh, Margaret Macdonald] attended Glasgow School of Art. Noticing a similarity in style between their work and that of two evening students, Charles Rennie Mackintosh and Herbert McNair, Fra Newbery introduced them, a meeting that led to the development of the Glasgow style and then to the marriages of Frances to McNair and Margaret to Mackintosh in 1899 and 1900 respectively. While they were still students, some of their work appeared in 'The Magazine', a manuscript periodical edited by a fellow student, Lucy Raeburn (1869–1952), which appeared from 1893 to 1894. The work of the Glasgow Four as they came to be known is seen to represent the core of the Glasgow style. Both sisters were members of a group at the school known as the Immortals.

The bookbinder and illustrator Jessie Marion *King also studied at the Glasgow School of Art, where her vivid imagination and fine linear style were encouraged by Fra Newbery. From 1900 to 1908 she taught in the school's department of book decoration, which became the department of bookbinding and design. In 1902 she was awarded a gold medal at the Scottish section of the international decorative arts exhibition at Turin for her binding of *L'enfance de l'évangile*. She illustrated many books, including *The High History of the Holy Grail* and *The Defence of Guinevere*, two of her finest works.

Annie [Anne] **French** (1872–1965) was another illustrator who used a fine linear technique. Born at 5 Calder Street, Govan, Glasgow, on 6 February 1872, she was the daughter of Andrew French, a colliery clerk and later metallurgist, and his wife, Margaret Weir. Unlike Jessie King, her interest in art was encouraged by her family, and she was a student at the Glasgow School of Art from 1886 to 1889. She taught at the school's department of ceramic decoration from 1908 to 1912. Her black and white illustrative work, for example *The Picture Book* (reproduced in *The Studio*, 14 July 1906) and *The Plumed Hat* (*c.*1900; reproduced in Burkhauser, 142), shows some similarity in style to that of Aubrey Beardsley: it was imaginative and full of fantasy, but was little published although well reviewed in the prestigious art journal *The Studio*. In 1914 she married the ceramic artist George Wooliscroft Rhead (1867–1920) and settled in London. She died at The Limes, a nursing home in St Helier, Jersey, on 27 January 1965. Examples of her work are held in private collections and a few are in the collection of Glasgow Museums and Art Galleries.

Though Katharine *Cameron illustrated many books, she was better known as a watercolour painter of flowers (especially roses) and landscapes. As a student at the Glasgow School of Art from 1888 to 1895 she was friendly with C. R. Mackintosh and the Macdonald sisters, and a member of the Immortals group. She contributed to 'The Magazine' and in 1949 presented its four issues to the Glasgow School of Art.

Among Fra Newbery's many innovative ideas was the establishment of craft studios and the appointment of many women teachers of design on his staff. **De Courcy Lewthwaite Dewar** (1878–1959), metalwork designer, was born on 12 February 1878 in Kandy, Ceylon, the daughter of a tea planter, John Lewthwaite Dewar, and his wife, Amelia Cochran. Her unusual first name had been passed down through several generations in her family, by whom she was known as Kooroovi, the Tamil word for a small bird. She was one of three surviving daughters of the family. From 1891 until 1908 or 1909 she studied part-time at the Glasgow School of Art. Her enamel and metalwork, which included jewellery, clock surrounds, mirror surrounds, plaques, caskets, buttons, and sconces, was frequently illustrated in *The Studio*. She also painted, engraved, and produced designs for bookplates, calendars, tea-room menus, and cards, as well as costumes for masques. For thirty-eight years Dewar taught design in the metalwork department of the school, during some of that period with Peter Wylie Davidson, in whose *Applied Design in the Precious Metals* (1929) her *Presentation Casket* (*c.*1910; Glasgow Society of Women Artists, on loan to Glasgow Museums and Art Galleries) is illustrated. 'Dewar's enamel and graphic work is characterized by strong colour and vigorous outline and the Glasgow Style designs from her student and tutorial phase gradually evolved to a more geometric and boldly coloured Czechoslovakian folk-art influenced style' (Burkhauser, 163). She was president of the Society of Lady Artists' Club, whose history she wrote (privately printed, 1950). Her sketchbooks of *c.*1895–1910 (priv. coll.), letters, and journals provide 'a rare account of a woman designer of the Glasgow Style era' (ibid.). Dewar was involved with the women's suffrage movement, for whom she designed bookplates, programmes, and calendars. She compiled files on women artists for the National Council of Women in London providing biographical information and reproductions of works. She did not marry and lived with her sister, Katharine, at 15 Woodside Terrace, Glasgow, until her death there on 24 November 1959.

Of a talented family, Helen Walton (1850–1921) joined the staff of the Glasgow School of Art in 1894 to teach ceramic design and decoration. The designer and architect George Henry *Walton was her brother. Helen's sister Hannah (1863–1940) decorated china and glass, and another sister, Constance, like their brother Edward Arthur *Walton, was a painter. Later, in 1902, Dorothy Carleton Smyth (1880–1933) and her sister Olive (1882–1949) were both on the school's staff and taught in a variety of applied art media and techniques such as sgraffito, gesso panels, illumination on vellum, and woodblock printing on textiles. Dorothy is now chiefly remembered for her costume illustrations and Olive for her stylized scenes in watercolour on vellum of subjects from legends.

Four of the Glasgow Girls were painters in oils and worked more independently than the designers and decorative artists. **(Richmond Leslie) Stansmore Dean** (1866–1944), painter, was born at 105 Breadalbane Terrace, Hill Street, Glasgow, on 3 June 1866, the youngest of the six children of Alexander Davidson Dean, an engraver and a co-founder of the printing firm of Gilmour and Dean, and his wife, Jean Leslie. From 1883 Stansmore Dean studied at the Glasgow School of Art, where she became friends with Margaret Rowat, the sister of Jessie Newbery, and was a fellow student of C. R. Mackintosh and Bessie MacNicol. She was the first woman student to win the school's Haldane travelling bursary in 1890, and went to the Académie Colarossi in Paris to study under August Courtois. At the beginning of the twentieth century she established her own studio in Glasgow and exhibited at the Glasgow Institute, in Paisley, and in Liverpool. She showed twice with the International Society in London; her work, for example *Meditation* (*c.*1899; Glasgow Museums and Art Galleries) and *Girl in a Straw Hat* (*c.*1910; priv. coll.), shows the influence of J. A. M. Whistler, president of that society. When exhibiting work her masculine-sounding name, which was a family one, may have been an advantage. An active member of the Lady Artists' Club and a forceful personality, she put forward Mackintosh as the man to carry out alterations and redecoration of the club's premises in Blythswood Square. His distinctive black entrance porch was erected before the club's council overrode her recommendations as convenor of the decorating committee. On 30 April 1902 she married the artist Robert Macaulay Stevenson (1854–1952). He was a widower, and she helped to bring up his young daughter, Jean. This left her with fewer opportunities to develop her own career, and financial worries obliged them to let Robinsfield, their large house by Bardowie Loch to the north of Glasgow, where each had their own studio. They went to live at Montreuil-sur-Mer in northern France, where they both worked throughout the First World War with the Church of Scotland huts helping the soldiers. They returned to Robinsfield in 1926 but left again in 1932 to live in Kirkcudbright, then home to several Scottish painters, and Borgue. Stansmore Dean died at Castle Douglas, Kirkcudbrightshire, on 15 December 1944. Her portrait of the writer Neil Munro (*c.*1905) is in the Scottish National Portrait Gallery, Edinburgh.

Bessie MacNicol [*see* MacNicol, Elizabeth] studied at the Glasgow School of Art from 1887 to 1892. In 1896 she painted a portrait of Edward Atkinson Hornel, one of the Glasgow Boys, in his studio in Kirkcudbright and was subsequently much influenced by his use of colour and interest in paint textures. So much did she share stylistically with 'the Boys' that many members of the Glasgow Art

Club (which did not then admit women painters) attended her funeral and left a wreath mourning 'the loss of a true artist' (Burkhauser, 197).

Eleanor Allen Moore (1885–1955), painter, was born on 26 July 1885 at Glenfield, Glenwherry, co. Antrim, Northern Ireland, the daughter of Hamilton Moore (1856–1927), an Irish Presbyterian minister, and his wife, Annie Kinnear Stephen (1860–1940) of St Cyrus, Kincardineshire. Her childhood was spent at Newmilns in Ayrshire, where her father was minister of Loudoun parish. She studied at the Glasgow School of Art from 1902 to 1907. As a daughter of the manse she was dependent on bursary assistance, and was encouraged by Fra Newbery, who was still teaching painting classes himself until 1906, when Maurice Grieffenhagen joined the staff. Since she was unable to afford models, her earlier work consisted of large richly painted self-portraits in various guises, for example, *Marmalade* (*c*.1913; priv. coll.) and *The Silk Dress* (*c*.1919; priv. coll.). On 29 June 1922 she married Robert Cecil Robertson (1889–1942), a doctor of medicine, and their daughter was born in 1923. In 1925 the family sailed for Shanghai, where her husband took up an appointment in public health. Eleanor Moore continued to paint portraits of British army and naval officers, but with the help of the Shanghai Art Club was also able to paint Chinese men, women, and children of all ages. As anti-foreigner riots began to die down she was able to explore the Yangtse delta by houseboat and visited the walled cities of Soochow and Wusih. She painted landscapes and townscapes, but her preference was to paint portraits of Chinese people. A good example is *The Letter Writer* (*c*.1936; priv. coll.). Though she loved Chinese art, her own remained uninfluenced by it. With other British women and children she was evacuated from Shanghai in 1937 and went to live in Hong Kong. Following her husband's death there on 4 August 1942 she returned to Scotland and died at the Western General Hospital, Edinburgh, on 17 September 1955. Her ashes were interred in Loudoun cemetery, Ayrshire.

Norah Neilson Gray (1882–1931), painter, was born on 16 June 1882 at Carisbrooke, 108 West King Street, Helensburgh, Dunbartonshire, the second youngest daughter among the seven children of George William Gray, a Glasgow shipowner, and his wife, Norah Neilson. She first studied locally at The Studio with Miss Park and Miss Ross, but the family moved to Glasgow, where she was a student at the Glasgow School of Art from 1901 to 1906. She taught fashion-plate design at the school and also taught art to the girls of St Columba's School, Kilmalcolm, before establishing her position as a portrait painter with her first solo exhibition in 1910 at Warneuke's Gallery, Glasgow. During the First World War she painted several important pictures, including *The Belgian Refugee* (1916; Glasgow Museums and Art Galleries) and *The Country's Charge*, bought by the manufacturer Joseph Bibby and presented to the Royal Free Hospital, London. In 1918 she went as a voluntary aid detachment nurse to the Abbaye de Royaumont, near Paris, which was staffed by women of the Scottish Women's Hospitals, and in her free time painted the arrival of the wounded in the old vaulted hall of the abbey. She was later commissioned to paint the surgeon Frances Ivens, with hospital staff and patients in the abbey cloisters. *The Scottish Women's Hospital* (1920) is now in the Imperial War Museum, London. After the war Gray resumed portrait painting and excelled particularly with young children. *Little Brother* (1920–22, exh. RA, 1922; Glasgow Museums and Art Galleries) was bought by Glasgow corporation at the memorial exhibition of her work in Glasgow in 1932. Gray exhibited annually at the Paris Salon des Artistes Français and was awarded their silver medal in 1923; she was better known abroad than in her own country. Her watercolours, for example, *July Night, Loch Lomond* (*c*.1922; priv. coll.), were notable for their modernist approach and pointilliste technique. Gray died of cancer at the height of her career at 1 St James Terrace, Glasgow, on 27 May 1931.

In 1988 the Glasgow School of Art mounted the exhibition '"Glasgow Girls": Women in the Art School, 1880–1920'. This was well received, and the work of this talented group of designers and painters was recognized, in some cases for the first time. The exhibition led to the publication of *'Glasgow Girls': Women in art and design, 1880–1920* (1990; rev. edn, 1993), edited by Jude Burkhauser.

AILSA TANNER

Sources J. Burkhauser, ed., *'Glasgow girls': women in art and design, 1880–1920* (1990); rev. edn (1993) • D. L. Dewar, *A history of the Glasgow Society of Lady Artists' Club* (1950) • A. Tanner, *The centenary exhibition of the founding of the Glasgow Society of Lady Artists in 1882* (1982) [exhibition catalogue, Glasgow Society of Women Artists, Glasgow, 1982] • H. Ferguson, *Glasgow School of Art: the history* (1995) • G. White, 'Some Glasgow designers and their work, III', *The Studio*, 12 (1898), 47–51 • G. Rawson, *Fra H. Newbery: artist and art educationalist, 1855–1946* (1996) [exhibition catalogue, Glasgow School of Art, 1996] • M. Swain, 'Mrs J. R. Newbery, 1864–1948', *Embroidery*, 24 (1973), 104–7 • M. Swain, 'Ann Macbeth', *Embroidery*, 25 (1974), 8–11 • M. Ives, *The life of Ann Macbeth of Patterdale* [n.d., *c*.1981] • J. Helland, *The studios of Frances and Margaret Macdonald* (1996) • R. Billcliffe, *Charles Rennie Mackintosh: the complete furniture, furniture drawings and interior design* (1979); 3rd edn (1986) • G. White, 'Some Glasgow designers and their work, I', *The Studio*, 11 (1897), 86–9, 222–35 • C. White, *The enchanted world of Jessie M. King* (1989) • B. Smith, *D. Y. Cameron: the visions of the hills* (1992) • *Margaret Macdonald Mackintosh, 1864–1933* (1983), 6 [exhibition catalogue, Hunterian Art Gallery, 1983] • A. Tanner, *Stansmore Dean Stevenson, 1866–1944* (1984) [exhibition catalogue, Lillie Art Gallery, Milngavie, 1984] • A. Tanner, *Bessie MacNicol: new woman* (privately printed, 1998) • A. Tanner, *My parents* (1997) • typescript autobiography of Tina Gray, sister of Norah Neilson Gray, priv. coll. • K. Moon, *George Walton: designer and architect* (1993)

Likenesses photograph (Stansmore Dean), repro. in Tanner, *Stansmore Dean* • photograph (Eleanor Allen Moore), repro. in Tanner, *My parents* • photographs (nine of the Glasgow Girls), repro. in Burkhauser, ed., *Glasgow girls*, 18

Wealth at death De Courcy Lewthwaite Dewar: Scottish confirmation sealed in London, 11 March 1960, *CGPLA Eng. & Wales* • £28,948 14*s*. 10*d*.—Jessie Wylie Newbery: probate, 3 Aug 1948, *CGPLA Eng. & Wales* • £2066 13*s*. 7*d*.—Annie Macbeth: probate, 29 July 1948, *CGPLA Eng. & Wales*

Glasgow, Raymond Charles Robertson- (1901–1965), cricketer and journalist, was born on 15 July 1901 at Murrayfield, Edinburgh, the younger son of Colonel Robert Purdon Robertson-Glasgow (1868–1937), and his wife, Muriel Barbara Holt-Wilson (*d*. 1946). The family owned an estate at Craigmyle, Aberdeenshire, which his father could no longer afford to keep (it was sold to Thomas Shaw, Baron Craigmyle), and they moved south during Raymond's childhood. He was educated first at Hindhead preparatory school in Surrey, then won a scholarship to Charterhouse, where he showed an early aptitude for ball games, especially cricket. Excellent classics teaching, an impressive headmaster in Frank Fletcher, and all-round success on the cricket field made Charterhouse increasingly congenial to him, and he flourished in the sixth form; he became head of his house and won an open classical scholarship to Corpus Christi College, Oxford, where he went into residence in October 1919. He took a second in classical moderations (1921) and only a fourth in *literae humaniores* (1923), but won blues at cricket, representing Oxford for four years (1920–23).

Robertson-Glasgow's good performances against the counties as a university player attracted the attention of the Somerset captain, John Daniell, and on the tenuous qualification of having cousins who lived at Hinton Charterhouse, one of whom was MP for Bath, he began the long and happy association with Somerset that lasted all his life. He played seventy-seven matches for the county between 1920 and 1935. In all first-class matches he took 464 wickets at 25.77 each, bowling fast medium away-swingers, and scored 2102 runs (average 13.22). He appeared five times for the Gentlemen against the Players between 1924 and 1935. His nickname, Crusoe, came out of a match between Essex and Somerset. C. P. McGahey, out first ball, complained that he had succumbed to 'a chap named Robinson Crusoe' (*Wisden*, 971).

After Oxford Robertson-Glasgow went back to teach at Hindhead, and played for Somerset in the holidays. His health deteriorated, and he gave up teaching in 1933 to concentrate on cricket writing. He became cricket correspondent of the *Morning Post* in that year and later wrote for the *Daily Telegraph*, *The Observer*, and the *Sunday Times*, and he contributed also to *Wisden*, *The Cricketer*, and *Punch*. He read more widely than ever and developed a style which brought a new distinction to the literature of cricket. His work combined a degree of scholarship with a lightness of touch and sense of humour that transformed the old cliché-ridden prose of the Edwardian period. Like Neville Cardus, he used imagery—in his case from the classics, especially Virgil—but unlike Cardus he had played a great deal of first-class cricket, which gave him an advantage when he wrote of the lesser professionals, the foot soldiers of first-class cricket whom he understood and with whom he had served. 'I knew nearly all the cricketers about whom I was to write, many of them intimately,' he later recalled, 'and in writing, I fancied myself to be among them on the field, listening to the comments and quips and complaints which are the unreported life of cricket' (Robertson-Glasgow, 169). He wrote admirable pen portraits of many of the great players of his day. His cricket books included *Cricket Prints* (1943), *More Cricket Prints* (1948), *46 Not Out* (1948), *Rain Stopped Play* (1948), *The Brighter Side of Cricket* (1933), *All in the Game* (1952), and *How to Become a Test Cricketer* (1962).

On 7 August 1943 he married Elizabeth Edward Hutton (*b.* 1898/9), medical nursing sister, who had nursed him during a period of illness; she was a widow, daughter of Alexander Powrie, businessman. Through Robertson-Glasgow's life bleak moods of depression lay behind the 'reverberating laugh' and 'infectious conviviality' which were his outward characteristics (Ross, 14). In the last phase of his life these fits of depression and claustrophobia deepened and became more frequent. He felt himself fortunate to find a home at the preparatory school St Andrew's, Pangbourne, run by his brother. He died by his own hand, of barbiturate poisoning, at Prospect Park Hospital, Reading, Berkshire, on 4 March 1965, a much loved figure in the cricket world. His wife survived him.

D. R. W. SILK

Sources R. C. Robertson-Glasgow, *46 not out* (1948) · *Wisden* (1966) · A. Ross, 'Introduction', *Crusoe on cricket: the cricket writings of R. C. Robertson-Glasgow* (1966) · P. Roebuck, *From Sammy to Jimmy: the official history of Somerset county cricket club* (1991) · Burke, *Gen. GB* (1937) · *WWW* · m. cert. · d. cert.

Likenesses photograph, repro. in Robertson-Glasgow, *46 not out*, frontispiece

Wealth at death £33,948: probate, 25 June 1965, *CGPLA Eng. & Wales*

Glasier, John Bruce (1859–1920), politician, was born (according to his accounts) on 25 March 1859 in Glasgow. He was the second of eight children of John Bruce of Irvine, a farmer and cattle dealer, and Isabella McNicoll of Shiskine, Arran, daughter of Alexander McNicoll, fisherman, crofter, and Gaelic poet. Bruce had left his wife and family to live with the much younger Isabella, so John Bruce Glasier, his brother, and six sisters were all born out of wedlock.

John Bruce Glasier grew up in the Ayrshire countryside, herding sheep and reading Burns's poetry, when not attending the parish school of Newton Ayr. After his father's death in December 1870, his mother adopted the surname Glasier (for reasons unknown). When Glasier was thirteen, she moved the family to Glasgow (where some of her relatives lived). This could have been to improve the employment prospects of her children. Glasier was soon apprenticed as an architectural draughtsman and his sisters entered office work. The family lived for several years at 250 Crown Street, near the Gorbals.

In Glasgow, Glasier initially came under the influence of his mother's uncle Neil Robertson. Robertson, a cabinet-maker, a strict Calvinist, and owner of a good collection of books, imbued his great-nephew with religious zeal: so much so, that Glasier at fourteen pledged himself to become a minister. However, Glasier's avid reading of Huxley and Darwin, as well as Burns, Byron, and Shelley, led him first to a crisis of faith and then to radical ideas.

Glasier was artistic by temperament. Like so many of his generation of socialist pioneers, he aspired to be a poet and long wrote verse. His architectural work gave way to work as a designer in ornamental ironwork. Like William Morris, he often spoke of the rights of men and women under socialism to enjoy and express themselves through art.

John Bruce Glasier (1859–1920), by unknown photographer

By the early 1880s Glasier was a notable advocate in Glasgow of land nationalization and socialism. He spoke at numerous radical and literary meetings as well as on soapboxes on Glasgow Green. His early socialism was fiery, even revolutionary. It drew on his experiences of being unemployed and on his reading. He and his friend Shaw Maxwell joined the Land League after hearing Michael Davitt speak in Glasgow in December 1879. Maxwell edited, and Glasier wrote for, a Glasgow Land League newspaper. Later, they both joined the Scottish Land Restoration League, and attended the inaugural meeting held by Henry George in Glasgow in February 1884. In the summer of 1884 Glasier was a founder member of the Social Democratic Federation (SDF).

Throughout his life Glasier was influenced by hero-figures. After Davitt came William Morris, and then Keir Hardie. Glasier was entranced when he heard Morris speak in Edinburgh and Glasgow in November 1884. When Morris and his associates left the SDF and founded the Socialist League, Glasier became secretary of its Glasgow branch, a post he held until 1889, when he moved to Alloa to work in a foundry. Glasier preached an ethical and Utopian socialism, and about this time, like Morris, was influenced by the anarchist ideas of Prince Kropotkin. He wrote much for Morris's newspaper *Commonweal*. In these years and later Glasier looked the part of the romantic politician, the vagabond poet, or the Pre-Raphaelite aesthete. After the disintegration of the Socialist League, Glasier remained a nominal member of Morris's Hammersmith Socialist Society, but otherwise resumed his role of lone socialist propagandist until he joined the Independent Labour Party in late 1893. On 21 June 1893 he married Katharine St John Conway [*see* Glasier, Katharine St John Bruce (1867–1950)]. The Glasiers were to be an effective socialist partnership. Unlike the Webbs, the Glasiers had children: Jeannie, Malcolm, and John Glendower.

For much of the Independent Labour Party's first twenty-five years Glasier was one of its 'Big Four' leaders, along with Keir Hardie, James Ramsay MacDonald, and Philip Snowden. He served on the party's national administrative council from 1897 to 1909, when the Big Four resigned over the annual conference's failure to back them fully in a dispute concerning Victor Grayson, and again from 1910 to 1919. Glasier succeeded Hardie as party chairman (1900–03). After editing *ILP News* for several years, he took on editing the *Labour Leader* (January 1905 – April 1909) after Hardie sold the paper to the Independent Labour Party. Although sales rose from 13,000 to a peak of 43,000 in 1908, Glasier's editorship came under growing criticism, particularly for his proneness to defend the increasing pragmatism of the party's leadership. Stanley Pierson has commented that after 1900 Glasier's socialism 'lost much of its inspirational quality and became apologetic' (Pierson, *British Socialists*, 197).

Glasier was at his best as the socialist evangelist. He and his wife, Katharine, made very great financial and physical sacrifices for the socialist cause. The Glasiers' finances were rescued in 1909 by a trust fund of $15,000 set up for them by a wealthy Boston widow, Elizabeth Glendower Evans. Glasier rarely put himself forward for public office. He served as a Chapel-en-le-Frith parish councillor for a period from 1903, having, to his surprise, topped the poll. He stood unsuccessfully for Birmingham, Bordesley Green, in the 1906 general election. Otherwise, he stood aside and supported Hardie and, for a period, MacDonald. He attended the Second International's congresses from 1896 and delighted in opposing Marxists, both British and continental European. Like Hardie, Glasier condemned both the Second South African War and the First World War.

John Bruce Glasier suffered cancer of the bowel from 1915. After brave attempts to contain the disease by diet and by Christian Science, he became housebound in 1919. In his last months he wrote *The Meaning of Socialism* (1919) and *William Morris and the Early Days of the Socialist Movement* (1921) and compiled a collection of his verse, *On the Road to Liberty*. He died at 37 Windsor Road, Levenshulme, Lancashire, on 4 June 1920.

CHRIS WRIGLEY

Sources W. Whitely, ed., *Memorial to Bruce Glasier* (1920) · L. Thompson, *The enthusiasts: a biography of John and Katharine Bruce Glasier* (1971) · J. B. Huffman, 'Glasier, John Bruce', *BDMBR*, vol. 3, pt 1 · E. P. Thompson, *William Morris: romantic to revolutionary* (1955) · H. Pelling, *The origins of the labour party, 1880–1900* (1954) · S. Pierson, *Marxism and the origins of British socialism* (1973) · S. Pierson, *British socialists: the journey from fantasy to politics* (1979) · S. Yeo, 'A new life: the religion of socialism in Britain, 1883–1896', *History Workshop Journal*, 4 (1977), 5–56 · R. Kenney, *Westering: an autobiography* (1939) · U. Lpool L., special collections and archives, Bruce Glasier MSS · d. cert.

Archives BLPES, corresp. and papers • Labour History Archive and Study Centre, Manchester, letters • U. Lpool L., special collections and archives, corresp., diaries, and MSS | BLPES, corresp. with William John • JRL, letters to James Ramsay MacDonald • People's History Museum, Manchester, Labour party MSS • University of Toronto, Thomas Fisher Rare Book Library, letters to James Mavor

Likenesses photograph, NPG [*see illus.*]

Glasier, Katharine St John Bruce [*née* Katharine St John Conway] (**1867–1950**), socialist and politician, was born on 25 September 1867 in Stoke Newington, London. She was the second of seven children of Samuel Conway, a Congregationalist minister based at Ongar, Essex, and his wife, Amy (*née* Curling), of a well-to-do Stoke Newington family. The classical scholar Robert Seymour *Conway was her elder brother. She was christened Katharine St John (pronounced 'Saint John') Conway.

The family moved to the Congregationalist manse in Walthamstow when Katharine was young. Although by middle-class standards her father's income was low, she and her brother and sisters were brought up with the assistance of servants. She was taught by her mother until ten, when she went to Hackney High School for Girls. In 1886 she went to Newnham College, Cambridge, with a clothworkers' scholarship in classics. There she was influenced by Helen Gladstone, who held strong high-church and feminist views. In 1889 she was placed in the second class of the classical tripos. Although Cambridge University refused to award degrees to women, Conway thereafter usually listed BA after her name in defiance of this sexual discrimination.

Conway went to Bristol to teach at Redland high school. While senior classics mistress there, she became a socialist after witnessing striking female cottonworkers demonstrating during a service in All Saints, Clifton, in November 1890. She was briefly a member of the Bristol Socialist Society, an offshoot of the Marxist Social Democratic Federation (SDF). After leaving Redland high school, having either resigned or been sacked for attending a socialist meeting, she taught briefly, from autumn 1891, at a board school in the working-class St Phillips area of Bristol. That autumn she went to live with Dan Irving, a leading Bristol socialist, his invalid wife, and their children.

Conway joined the Clifton and Bristol branch of the Fabian Society, a branch which before 1891 had been a Christian socialist society. As a daughter of Congregationalist manses, she found the views of this group more congenial than the class-war beliefs of the SDF. Edward Pease, the secretary of the Fabian Society, later commented of such early branches that they were 'from the first "ILP" in personnel and policy and were Fabian only in name' (*The History of the Fabian Society*, 1916, 102).

Conway was soon put on the national panel of Fabian lecturers by W. S. De Mattos, the society's lecture secretary. She lectured for the Fabians from the autumn of 1891, and did so on a regular basis from April 1892; she received 5*s.* a lecture plus travel and other expenses. She was a Bristol delegate at the Fabian Society's first annual conference in February 1892. Afterwards she became a member of a group of provincial Fabians, who were

Katharine St John Bruce Glasier (1867–1950), by unknown photographer

among the founders of the Independent Labour Party, a group started by S. G. Hobson, a fellow member of the Bristol Socialist Society. Conway's speaking engagements in 1892 included general election meetings in support of Ben Tillett in Bradford, the Manchester Labour church, and fringe meetings at the Trades Union Congress (TUC) held in September in Glasgow (where she first met John Bruce Glasier).

At a separate meeting held during the TUC, she was one of six appointed to an arrangements committee to organize a conference to found a national Independent Labour Party (ILP). At the resulting conference held in Bradford in January 1893 she was one of fifteen elected to the ILP's first national administrative council. Although she did not stand for re-election, she remained a leading figure. Of the ILP's early days, Henry Pelling has observed that 'the "new woman" was almost as important an element in the leadership as the new unionist' (Pelling, 164). Katharine Conway, like Caroline Martyn, Enid Stacy, Isabella Ford, and Emmeline Pankhurst, was an able middle-class propagandist for the party. Her speeches were highly emotional, preaching an ethical 'Come-unto-Jesus' style of socialism. She was much influenced by Edward Carpenter and William Morris. Of the former she wrote that 'he gave me Jesus Christ's teaching in its wholeness and truth for the first time'.

She continued making lengthy speaking tours after her marriage on 21 June 1893 to John Bruce *Glasier. Both she and her husband were great favourites of socialists in west

Yorkshire, Nottinghamshire, and elsewhere. She also campaigned for nursery schools, pithead baths, poor-law reform, and, later, the Save the Children Fund.

Katharine Glasier edited the *Labour Leader* from mid-1916, after Fenner Brockway left to oppose conscription, until April 1921. She took over when its anti-war stance had reduced its circulation. Under her editorship it reached a new peak of 51,000 in 1917 and by early 1918 its circulation was over 62,000, but from 1920 it fell steeply. Her editorship was notable for a clash with Philip Snowden, with Glasier dissociating herself from his anti-Bolshevik writings. The strains of the editorship plus the delayed stress of nursing her terminally ill husband led to a nervous breakdown in April 1921. After her recovery she was appointed national ILP propagandist. When the ILP disaffiliated from the Labour Party in 1932, she left it and continued her propaganda work for the Labour Party.

Katharine Glasier combined her activities as socialist propagandist with family life. She had three children: Jeannie, Malcolm, and John Glendower (Glen). She was much hurt by the deaths of her mother (1881), her husband (1920), and her younger son, Glen (1928). Like her husband, she aspired to be a poet. As well as socialist pamphlets she published three novels (*Husband and Brother*, 1894; *Aimee Furniss, Scholar*, 1896; and *Marget*, 1902–3) and a collection of short stories (*Tales from the Derbyshire Hills*, 1907). In later life she found support not only in her socialist faith but in her memberships of the Society of Friends and the Theosophical Society. Her home, Glen Cottage, Earby by Colne, Lancashire, where she lived from 1922 until her death on 14 June 1950, was preserved in her memory by the labour movement. CHRIS WRIGLEY

Sources L. Thompson, *The enthusiasts: a biography of John and Katharine Bruce Glasier* (1971) • J. B. Huffman, 'Glasier, Katharine St John Conway', *BDMBR*, vol. 3, pt 1 • *The Labour who's who* (1927) • S. Pierson, *Marxism and the origins of British socialism* (1973) • S. Pierson, *British socialists: the journey from fantasy to politics* (1979) • H. Pelling, *The origins of the labour party, 1880–1900* (1954) • D. Howell, *British workers and the independent labour party, 1888–1906* (1983) • S. Yeo, 'A new life: the religion of socialism in Britain, 1883–1896', *History Workshop Journal*, 4 (1977), 5–56 • S. G. Hobson, *Pilgrim to the left: memoirs of a modern revolutionist* (1938)

Archives BLPES, corresp. and papers • U. Lpool L., Sydney Jones Library, corresp. and papers | BL, George Bernard Shaw MSS

Likenesses photograph, NPG [*see illus.*] • photographs, repro. in Thompson, *Enthusiasts*

Wealth at death £1271 13*s*. 6*d*.: probate, 26 Oct 1950, *CGPLA Eng. & Wales*

Glass, Ann Catherine. *See* Elwell, Ann Catherine (1922–1996).

Glass, David Victor (1911–1978), sociologist and demographer, was born in the East End of London on 2 January 1911, the elder child of Philip Glass, a journeyman tailor who was the son of immigrants from eastern Europe, and his wife, Dinah Rosenberg. He was educated at a public elementary school and Raine's Grammar School. In 1928 he entered the London School of Economics (LSE) as an undergraduate, specializing in economic and social geography.

On graduating in 1931, Glass was appointed research assistant to Sir William Beveridge, the then director of LSE. The development of his thinking was greatly influenced by his association with Lancelot Hogben, who was professor of social biology at LSE, and his collaborators. From them he acquired an interest in the relationship between social and biological problems and a conviction, which was to last throughout his life, of the importance of quantitative research in the social sciences. Hogben encouraged him to work on population problems and his work turned increasingly in that direction. When in 1936 the population investigation committee was founded under the chairmanship of A. M. Carr-Saunders, Glass was appointed its first research secretary. For the next five years of his life he was engaged in full-time demographic research and rapidly established a reputation as one of the most promising young scholars in that field. His work was concerned with demographic trends and policies in European countries and culminated in the publication, early in 1940, of his doctoral thesis, *Population Policies and Movements in Europe*, which has remained the standard work on this subject.

During the war Glass entered government service and worked as deputy director of the British petroleum mission in Washington and for the Ministry of Supply in London. In 1942 he married Ruth Durant [*see* Glass, Ruth Adele (1912–1990)], previously married to Henry Durant, and daughter of Eli and Lilly Lazarus, and herself a sociologist of repute. They had a son and a daughter. Glass returned to academic life in 1945, when he became reader in demography at LSE. He was promoted to a chair of sociology in 1948 and became Martin White professor in 1961.

Between 1944 and 1949 Glass's work was actively associated with that of the royal commission on population. Though not himself a member of the commission, he served on its statistics committee and its biological and medical committee and directed the family census of 1946 on its behalf. He could thus exercise considerable influence on the commission's thinking and conclusions. In the family census he pioneered the use of the method, which has been widely adopted since, of cohort analysis for the study of fertility. But his interests extended beyond demography. As research secretary of the population investigation committee, he stimulated and encouraged a number of social research projects, the most important of which were: the first nationwide inquiry in Britain, carried out by Dr Lewis Faning, into the prevalence of contraceptive practice; the repeat survey on the intelligence of Scottish schoolchildren conducted by Dr J. Maxwell, which established that apprehensions of a decline in national intelligence which had been voiced by a number of scholars were unfounded; and the national survey of health and development of children, directed by Dr J. W. B. Douglas, in which extensive information was collected on environmental and other factors related to the development of a group of children born in March 1946, who were interviewed at different periods of their lives. Although the actual direction of this work was left to others, Glass took a close interest in it and served on steering committees; many of his ideas were incorporated in the surveys. He also became the UK delegate to the newly founded Population Commission of the United Nations and helped shape the policies and work of that body. In 1947 he founded the journal *Population Studies*; he subsequently served as its editor or joint editor until his death.

Another of Glass's major interests was in the study of social mobility. Very little factual information about the extent of social mobility in Britain was available at the time of Glass's appointment to his chair and he set about to remedy this. He organized a number of inquiries, and his study *Social Mobility in Britain*, published in 1954, not only provided new facts and insights into the subject, but also pioneered methods which have become standard. During the last twenty years of his life he continued working on these topics, but he also became increasingly interested in historical demography, a subject to which he made important contributions.

Glass's scientific work brought him many academic honours. He was elected FBA in 1964 and in 1971 achieved the rare distinction for a social scientist of election to the Royal Society. He was a foreign associate of the United States National Academy of Sciences and received honorary degrees from a number of universities. His demographic colleagues honoured him by electing him to the presidency of the International Union for the Scientific Study of Population.

Glass's work was within the tradition of British empirical social research. His early association with workers in the biological sciences resulted in an approach to social problems which had more in common with that of the experimental scientist than of the social philosopher. His emphasis on the need for quantitative information in the discussion of social problems and his suspicion of generalization were not universally shared by his fellow sociologists at the time and led him to stand somewhat apart from the profession. None the less, his influence was considerable, not only in Britain but also in the less economically developed countries, and particularly in India, a country to which he became greatly attached and which he visited regularly during the later years of his life.

Glass was a keen bibliophile and amassed an outstanding collection of books and pamphlets on the subject of population. He was no mere collector, however, but was familiar with the contents of all items of his library. As one of his colleagues remarked of him: 'He seemed incapable of forgetting anything that he had ever read'. Glass died in London on 23 September 1978.

E. Grebenik, *rev.*

Sources W. D. Borrie, 'David Victor Glass, 1911–1978', *PBA*, 68 (1982), 537–60 • E. Grebenik, *Population Studies*, 33/1 (1979), 5–17 • *The Times* (27 Sept 1978) • *CGPLA Eng. & Wales* (1979)
Archives BLPES, population MSS
Likenesses photograph, repro. in Borrie, 'David Victor Glass', facing p. 537 • photograph, repro. in *Population Studies*, facing p. 5
Wealth at death £35,276: probate, 9 Jan 1979, *CGPLA Eng. & Wales*

Glass, Joseph (1791/2–1867), philanthropist and inventor of machinery for sweeping chimneys, was born at Colchester and spent his early years in Manningtree, where he became a convinced teetotaller. He moved to London and worked as a bricklayer. He married Margaret, who was a year younger than Glass and from Gloucestershire. By the 1820s he was established at 2 Moor Lane in the City of London, running a chimney-sweeping business. He was the inventor of a mechanical chimney-sweeping device; a less successful machine, the scandiscope, had been invented in 1805 by George Smart but until Glass's invention those campaigning for the abolition of chimney sweeping by 'climbing boys' made little headway. Glass's machine had an efficient means of connecting the flexible rods needed to navigate the bends in the chimneys and was operated from below (previous machines having been operated from the top of the chimney). It was adopted in 1828 by the Society for Superseding the Necessity of Climbing Boys in Cleaning Chimneys, of which Glass then became agent. Sir Robert Peel, as home secretary, ordered Glass's machine to be used in government offices from 1829 and by the end of that year it was being quite widely used. Glass received a medal and a prize of £200 but he never patented his machine. In 1834 he gave evidence to the select committee on the bill of that year. Legislation in 1834, 1840, and 1864 diminished but did not wholly abolish the use of climbing boys. Glass remained active in the campaign and prosecuted those who tried to evade the provisions of the legislation. In 1861 he was living in Brixton, but with his business still in Moor Lane, employing four men. He died at his home in Barrington Crescent, Brixton, London, on 29 December 1867, in his seventy-sixth year, his invention having significantly improved the human lot. His wife probably survived him; they had at least two sons, Henry, a newspaper editor, and Joseph, a Congregational minister. His death was noticed in the *Court Circular*, Queen Victoria being interested in the fate of the climbing boys.

H. C. G. Matthew

Sources G. L. Phillips, *England's climbing-boys: a history of the long struggle to abolish child labor in chimney-sweeping* (1949) • *GM*, 4th ser., 5 (1868), 259 • *The Times* (1 Jan 1868) • *The Athenaeum* (11 Jan 1868), 160 • *CGPLA Eng. & Wales* (1868) • *Mechanic's Magazine*, 9 (1828), 181–5 • J. Glass, *Reminiscences of Manningtree* (1855) • *Report of the Society for Superseding the Necessity of Climbing Boys* (1826); (1829) • *DNB* • d. cert.
Wealth at death under £1500: probate, 23 March 1868, *CGPLA Eng. & Wales*

Glass, Sir Richard Atwood (1820–1873), telegraph cable manufacturer, was born at Bradford-on-Avon, Wiltshire, the son of Francis Glass and his wife Mary, *née* Canning, of Marlborough, Wiltshire. He had a brother, Francis. He attended King's College School, 1833–5, before entering an accountant's office in London, where in the course of his duties he met George Elliott, who was associated with the wire-rope manufactory of Kuper & Co., and whose partner he became. For some years the partners traded as Glass, Elliott, and in 1852 Glass, who had a mechanical as well as a financial turn of mind, saw the advantage of adapting the wire rope as a protection for gutta-percha insulated submarine cables. This armouring was first applied to the partially completed Dover–Calais cable. On

9 November 1854 Glass married Anne, daughter of Thomas Tanner of Tidcombe, Wiltshire.

After their experience with other cables, Glass, Elliott received an order for 1250 miles of armoured cable for the first transatlantic submarine telegraph, which was made at their works at Morden Wharf, Greenwich. The completion of this task was celebrated in July 1857 with a festivity at Belvidere House, near Erith, Kent. Speaking about the problems of manufacturing the cable, the other half of which had been manufactured by R. S. Newall of Gateshead, Glass delighted in pointing out that the two firms had laid the twist of their cable in opposite directions; but as he had already manufactured 100 miles before Newall started, the latter was clearly at fault.

The early failure of the 1857 cable served to encourage projects for its replacement and for other long-distance cables. Glass, Elliott, by this time amalgamated with John Pender's Telegraph Construction and Maintenance Company (Telcon), manufactured the Atlantic cables of 1865 and 1866. Glass was on board ship to supervise their laying, and, 'after ten years of unremitting labour' (according to *The Times*, 28 Nov 1866) he was knighted. In 1867 he retired from Telcon, retaining an interest in submarine telegraphy through his chairmanship of the Anglo-American Telegraph Co., and in 1868 stood as Conservative parliamentary candidate for Bewdley, Worcestershire. He was returned, and sat from December until the following March, when he was unseated on petition. In later years he bred and showed cattle, winning various awards.

Glass succumbed to chronic Bright's disease, and died at his home, Moorlands, Bitterne, South Stoneham, Hampshire, on 22 December 1873. ANITA MCCONNELL

Sources *ILN* (3 Jan 1874), 22 • *The Engineer*, 37 (1874), 4 • *The Times* (28 Nov 1866), 4a • *The Times* (25 Dec 1873), 8c • *The Times* (24 July 1887), 5e • K. R. Haigh, *Cableships and submarine cables* (1968), 28, 41, 348 • E. B. Bright and C. Bright, *The life story of the late Sir Charles Tilston Bright*, 2 vols. (1899?) • m. cert. • d. cert.

Likenesses wood-engraving (after photograph by Mayall), NPG; repro. in *ILN* (8 Dec 1866)

Wealth at death under £120,000 (in England): probate, 24 Jan 1874, *CGPLA Eng. & Wales*

Glass [*née* Lazarus; *other married name* Durant], **Ruth Adele** (**1912–1990**), sociologist, was born on 30 June 1912 in Berlin, Germany, the second of three daughters (there were no sons) of Eli Lazarus, described on her marriage certificate as a factory burner, a member of a distinguished Jewish family with a long rabbinical tradition, and his wife, Lilly Leszczynska. She embarked on a degree in social studies at the University of Berlin, and published a study of youth unemployment in Berlin in 1932 (reprinted in *Clichés of Urban Doom*, 1989), but following the rise of the Nazis she left Germany in 1932 before completing her degree. She studied at the University of Geneva and in Prague before arriving in London in the mid-1930s, where she resumed her sociological studies, at the London School of Economics. *Watling*, a study of a new London county council cottage estate in Hendon, on the outskirts of London, published in 1939, established her reputation as a social scientist. Meanwhile, in 1935 she had married Henry William Durant, statistician and pioneer of public opinion surveys, and son of Henry William Durant, foreman in a grain mill. They were divorced in 1941, and in 1942 she married David Victor *Glass (1911–1978), demographer, the son of Philip Glass, journeyman tailor. There were one son and one daughter of this second marriage, which was a very close one.

From 1940 until 1942 Ruth Glass was senior research officer at the Bureau of Applied Social Research, Columbia University, New York, and was awarded an MA degree, but she returned to Britain in 1943 and became involved in town planning, as lecturer and research officer at the Association for Planning and Regional Reconstruction. From 1947 to 1948 she was a research officer for PEP (Political and Economic Planning), and she then spent two years (1948–50) at the Ministry of Town and Country Planning, in charge of the new towns research section. She returned to academic life in 1950, to University College, London, which remained her academic base for the rest of her life. Her husband had become professor of sociology at the London School of Economics in 1948, and together they became known at the University of London as the Heloïse and Abelard of sociological research. For many years they edited jointly a series entitled Studies in Society.

In 1951 Ruth Glass became director of the social research unit at University College, working under William Holford, professor of town planning, and she founded the Centre for Urban Studies in 1951, becoming director of research in 1958, a post she retained until her death. In addition, she was visiting professor at University College (1972–85), and at the University of Essex (1980–86). She was chairman of the urban sociology research committee of the International Sociological Association (1958–75). She was also on the editorial board of several journals, including *Sage Urban Studies Abstracts* and the *International Journal of Urban and Regional Research*.

During the earlier part of Ruth Glass's career her interests centred on town planning, and *The Social Background of a Plan: a Study of Middlesbrough*, based on a survey done in 1944, appeared in 1948. She was always concerned with the social aspects of town planning, constantly anxious that planners should not forget human needs, especially those of people being rehoused because their homes had been destroyed during the Second World War. She studied housing problems in London, editing *London, Aspects of Change* in 1964, and publishing *London's Housing Needs* (1965) and *Housing in Camden* (1969). She gave evidence to several government committees and inquiries, most notably the royal commission on local government in Greater London (1957–60). She invented the term 'gentrification' in 1962, giving warnings about the squeezing of the poor out of London and the creation of upper-class ghettos.

Ruth Glass became interested in the consequences of immigration and the position of minorities in British society. In *Newcomers: the West Indians in London* (1960) she started from the premiss that racial discrimination is an intolerable insult both to the human dignity of an individual, and to the dignity of the society in which it is practised. She did a study of the Notting Hill riots of 1958, and in the 1960s she campaigned against the new immigration laws. She was also concerned with social change in the 'third world'. In 1968 she set up a one-year postgraduate course on urbanization in developing countries. She was particularly drawn by India, which she visited for two months every year from 1958 onwards.

Although she was a key figure in establishing urban sociology as an academic discipline, publishing *Urban Sociology in Great Britain* in 1955, Ruth Glass opposed the idea of research for its own sake, believing that the purpose of sociological research was to influence government policy and bring about social change, and to this end she involved herself in political debate. A Marxist all her life, she was never a member of the Communist Party, and after the compromises made by the Labour Party over immigration in the 1960s she felt that radicals had no place in any political party in Britain.

Abrasive and confident, with a powerful intellect, Ruth Glass could be devastating in argument, especially where she detected sloppy thinking. She had no time for jargon and clichés. She had a passion for justice and fought hard for those she believed to be oppressed. She was a distinctive figure, very short, always dressed in blue, with a strong German accent. She was made an honorary fellow of the Royal Institute of British Architects in 1972 and was awarded an honorary LittD by Sheffield in 1982. She never recovered from her husband's death in 1978, and in the last ten years of her life, although she continued to lecture and to work, she became increasingly lonely. Her final few years were marred by illness. She died on 7 March 1990 in Willow Lodge Nursing Home, Sutton, Surrey.

Anne Pimlott Baker, *rev.*

Sources *The Independent* (13 March 1990) • R. Glass, *Clichés of urban doom and other essays* (1988) • K. Leech, *The birth of a monster*, 2nd edn (1990) • *The Times* (9 March 1990) • *CGPLA Eng. & Wales* (1990)
Likenesses photograph, repro. in *The Times*
Wealth at death £609,907: administration, 20 Dec 1990, *CGPLA Eng. & Wales*

Glass, Thomas (1709–1786), physician and medical writer, was born on 14 May 1709 in Tiverton, second of the nine children of Michael Glass, dyer, of Tiverton, Devon, and Elizabeth, daughter of John Handford. He was educated first at Tiverton by Revd John Moore, and secondly at Exeter by André de Majendie, an emigré Huguenot pastor. He became a medical student at Leiden on 29 October 1728, and graduated MD in July 1731. On 10 February 1737 he married Mary (1715–1783), daughter of Sir Nathaniel Hodges. They had four daughters. Born a Baptist, about 1742 he joined the Anglican church. He and his wife resided first at Tiverton Castle, then moved in 1740 to Exeter, leasing part of Bedford House; in 1773 they moved to Bartholomew Yard, Exeter.

Glass first practised at Tiverton; then, after moving to Exeter, he became a physician of the Devon and Exeter Hospital on its foundation. He also imparted a process of

Thomas Glass (1709–1786), by John Opie, *c.*1780–83

preparing magnesia alba to his brother Samuel, a surgeon at Oxford. Magnesia alba, an absorbent antacid and mild purgative, was particularly recommended for infants, and Samuel Glass perfected the preparation to his great benefit, and published in 1764 an essay on its use. He ultimately sold the secret of its formula to Peter Delamotte. However, in the summer of 1771 Thomas Henry, a Manchester apothecary, communicated to the College of Physicians an 'improved' method of preparing magnesia alba, and his paper was printed in the college *Transactions*. After Samuel Glass's death on 25 February 1773, Henry published in the following May *Strictures* on the magnesia sold 'under the name of the late Mr. Glass', alleging that it was inferior and advertising his own preparation as 'genuine'. Thomas Glass replied in *An Examination of Mr. Henry's 'Strictures' on Glass's Magnesia* (1774), and was petulantly answered by Henry the same year.

Glass's principal work was *Commentarii duodecim de febribus ad Hippocratis disciplinam accommodati* (1742), published as *Twelve Commentaries on Fevers* in 1752. He also published works on smallpox and was considered the greatest English authority after Sir William Watson on inoculation for smallpox. A German translation of their papers was published at Halle in 1769. Among his other writings were *Meditations upon the Attributes of God and the Nature of Man* (1770) and *An Essay on Revealed Religion* (1772).

In 1776 Glass was elected a foreign associate of the Royal Medical Society of Paris. He left unpublished a 'new edition' of the *De Medicina* of Celsus, based on the Rotterdam edition (1750) and including a comprehensive commentary. Four large volumes of manuscript notes were subsequently kept in the Bodleian Library. Glass died at Exeter on 5 February 1786 and was buried on 12 February in St David's churchyard. In his will, dated 8 November 1783, he bequeathed to the dean and chapter of Exeter all his 'medical printed books', to be placed in their library for the use of any physician of the city. He also made provision for the education of poor children in Exeter.

Glass was regarded very highly by his peers. In 1783 he received a laudatory address from eleven members of the Exeter Medical Society, who presented the hospital with his portrait, painted by John Opie. He was further honoured by election, uniquely for a physician, as president of the hospital in 1785. A less generous note was struck by Bartholomew Parr, who succeeded him at the hospital, when he addressed a 'society of gentlemen' in Exeter in 1795, scarcely losing any opportunity to damage his reputation. This may have been because he disapproved of Glass's admiration for Boerhaave and the 'Ancients', or because Glass failed to pass on any of his wealthier patients when Parr succeeded him.

GORDON GOODWIN, *rev.* ALICK CAMERON

Sources B. Parr, 'Biographical anecdotes of the late Dr Glass of Exeter', 1795, RCP Lond. • A. Cameron, *Thomas Glass, MD: physician of Georgian Exeter* (1996) • University of Leiden, ASF 14, 41 • University of Leiden, ASF 415, 300 • J. D. Harris, *The Royal Devon and Exeter Hospital* (1922), 48–51, 61 • Minutes of General Court of Governors of Devon and Exeter Hospital, 24 Sept 1741, Devon RO, 1260 F HM1 • Minutes of General Court of Governors of Devon and Exeter Hospital, 18 March 1785, Devon RO, 1260 F HM3 • T. Henry and R. Warren, 'An account of an improved method of preparing magnesia alba', *Medical Transactions of the Royal College of Physicians* (1771), 226–34 • *Medical and Philosophical Commentaries*, 4/3 (1776), 348 [list of lately named foreign members of the Royal Society of medicine (Paris)] • *GM*, 1st ser., 43 (1773), 155 • Devon RO, 49/9/6/210 [marriage settlement] • parish records, Exeter, St David, Devon and Cornwall Record Society

Archives Bodl. Oxf.

Likenesses T. Hudson, oils, *c.*1750, priv. coll. • J. Opie, oils, *c.*1780–1783, Royal Devon and Exeter Hospital [*see illus.*] • E. A. Ezekiel, engraving (after J. Opie, *c.*1780–1783), Royal Albert Museum, Exeter

Wealth at death £13,744 9*s*. 7*d*.: will, Devon RO, 2309B/W111 (b); PRO, PROB 11/1138, sig. 90

Glasse, George Henry (1761–1809), classical scholar and Church of England clergyman, the son of Dr Samuel *Glasse (1734–1812), was born at Harrow, Middlesex. He was sent to Christ Church, Oxford, in 1775, and graduated BA on 28 April 1779 and MA on 14 January 1782. He took holy orders, and in 1785 his father resigned to him his living of Hanwell, Middlesex. He was also domestic chaplain to the earl of Radnor, the duke of Cambridge, and the earl of Sefton successively. In 1783 he married Anne Fletcher of Ealing.

Glasse's intellectual attainments were impressive. In 1781 he published a Greek and Latin translation of William Mason's *Caractacus*, which was very favourably reviewed. In 1788 appeared Glasse's rendering in Greek verse of Milton's *Samson Agonistes*. The ease with which Glasse handled the classical languages is illustrated by his Latin version of George Colman's *Miss Bayley's Ghost*, which was sung by Tom Moore at a masquerade given by Lady Manvers, and afterwards published in the *Gentleman's Magazine* (1st ser., 75, 1805, 750). He also published a large number of sermons.

The most popular of Glasse's works was *Louisa: a narrative of fact supposed to throw light on the mysterious history of the Lady of the Haystack* (1801), translated from *L'inconnue, histoire véritable*. This work, which quickly reached a third edition, was an attempt to prove that a mysterious refugee at Bristol was identical with Félix-Julienne de Schonau, otherwise Freulen, who declared herself to be the natural daughter of the emperor Francis I, and who was the unnamed heroine of the anonymous French work *L'inconnue*. Glasse frequently contributed to the *Gentleman's Magazine*, and wrote a paper in *Archaeologia* in 1787.

After his first wife's death in June 1802, which took place within a few days of the death of their eldest daughter, Glasse married in May 1805 Harriet, daughter of Thomas Wheeler. He soon found himself in considerable financial difficulty, having run through a large fortune in sixteen years. Glasse, who was described as 'short and fat, his face full and rather handsome, with an expression of benevolence and intelligence', hanged himself on 30 October 1809 in the Bull and Mouth inn, St Martin's-le-Grand, London. At the inquest his solicitor testified that his financial embarrassments were so great as to fully account for mental derangement.

ALSAGER VIAN, *rev.* MARI G. ELLIS

Sources Nichols, *Lit. anecdotes*, 9.131–3 • Foster, *Alum. Oxon.* • *GM*, 1st ser., 79 (1809), 1082–3 • *St James's Chronicle* (31 Oct 1809)

Archives BL, letters to Lord Spencer and to Charles Poyntz

Glasse [*née* Allgood], **Hannah** (*bap.* **1708**, *d.* **1770**), writer on cookery and costumier, born at Greville Street, Hatton Garden, London, was baptized at St Andrew's Church, Holborn, on 24 March 1708, the daughter of Isaac Allgood (1683–1725) and Hannah Reynolds. The Allgoods were a Northumberland family of good standing, and Isaac Allgood was married at the time to Hannah Clarke (*d.* 1724), daughter of a London vintner. Hannah Reynolds was Isaac Allgood's mistress, with whom he lived in London, and whom he subsequently took back to Hexham; their other two children died in adolescence. Isaac's only legitimate child was Lancelot Allgood (1711–1782), born on 11 February 1711, later high sheriff and member of parliament for Northumberland, and knighted in 1760.

Mrs Reynolds was banished from Hexham but she and Isaac Allgood were living together again in London in 1713 and 1714; when he was 'in liquor' on 10 February 1714 he signed a deed transferring most of his London property to Mrs Reynolds. When he realized what he had done he turned her out, but it was too late, and his foolish act was to trouble Hannah Glasse for many years to come. Allgood's family tried to sort out the affair but it was not until 1740 that it was finally settled by his son and Hannah was provided with annuities as well as some capital.

When Allgood's wife died in 1724 Hannah, then sixteen, went to live in London with her grandmother; the latter was very strict and would not allow her to attend social events. It is not clear how or when she met John Glasse, but they were married by special licence on 4 August 1724. This was not discovered until the following month when she left her grandmother and went to live with Glasse in lodgings in Piccadilly. The Allgood family, furious, had enquiries made; it appeared that John Glasse was Irish and had been on the staff of Lord Polwarth, lord chancellor of Scotland. His letters were well written, rather smug and sanctimonious, and full of evasions.

Hannah wrote to her aunt apologizing for the secrecy but not for the marriage. Friendly exchange of letters recommenced between Hannah and the Allgoods in 1728, when Hannah was living at New Hall, Broomfield, Essex, residence of the earl and countess of Donegal, where John Glasse was probably estate steward. In November 1734 Lord Donegal went to his mother in Surrey and the Glasses returned to London, taking lodgings until 1738 when Hannah returned to Greville Street. Ten children were born to the Glasses, of whom five died in infancy. Hannah was anxious that they should have a good education; her daughters, Hannah (*b.* 1728), Margaret (*b.* 1729), and Catherine (*b.* 1734), attended excellent schools in the vicinity and her sons went to Eton College and Westminster School. However, money was her constant worry; her annuities were often late in arriving, so she began to devise schemes for making money in other ways.

Hannah Glasse's first project was to sell Daffy's elixir, believing she had the secret prescription, but nothing came of this. In October 1745 she mentioned that her husband had set up two looms for cloth making, and in November she had begun writing the *Art of Cookery* and was collecting subscriptions. By January 1746 the book was in press, and it was published on 16 August. There were 202 subscribers for the first edition, somewhat more for the second and third editions. In the preface Hannah expressed the hope that ladies would read the book in its entirety, but her declared aim was to assist the middle and lower classes to cook in a simple manner. The book was issued anonymously, an action which led, after Hannah's death, to the suggestion that a pharmacist, Dr John Hill, was the author, writing under the *nom de plume* of Hannah Glasse. The true identity of the author was re-established by M. H. Dodds in 1938.

The Art of Cookery, Made Plain and Easy … by a Lady was certainly a success, but before the second edition appeared in 1747 John Glasse died, and was buried on 21 June 1747 at St Mary's Church, Broomfield. Earlier in the year Hannah and her daughter Margaret had opened a costumier's shop in Tavistock Street, a smart shopping area, where she attracted custom from the princess of Wales. Bubb Dodington's *Journal* recorded a visit in December 1749 with the prince and princess of Wales and their retinue to view a display of Hannah's costumes interspersed by conjurors and other entertainments, while the coaches of the aristocracy at her door suggested that business was flourishing. Behind this expensive façade, however, Hannah was borrowing money in quantities far in excess of her ability to repay.

On 27 May 1754 a docquet of bankruptcy was granted against Hannah for debts of over £10,000. The commissioners of bankruptcy did not auction her stock as it was held in Margaret Glasse's name, but on 29 October 1754 the copyright of *The Art of Cookery* and the printed sheets of the fifth edition were sold to Andrew Miller and his conger (a partnership of booksellers), who were to be responsible for the *Art* for the next fifty years. The *London Gazette* of 17 December 1754 stated that Mrs Glasse would be issued with a certificate of conformity on 11 January 1755; that is, she was discharged from bankruptcy.

The Glasses were at this time still living at Tavistock Street but in 1757 Margaret Glasse paid the rates and the next year the house was empty, for on 22 June Hannah was consigned as a debtor to Marshalsea prison and transferred to the Fleet prison on 7 July. No record survives of her release, but on 12 December 1757 she registered three shares in *The Servants' Directory*. This venture was not a success, although pirated editions were popular in America. She also wrote *The Compleat Confectioner*, which was undated, but probably appeared about 1760. It was reprinted on several occasions; a Maria Wilson produced a new edition in 1800.

Of Hannah's five surviving children, Isaac (1735–1773) went out to Bombay in 1754, where he died, and George (1740–1761) entered the navy, and was drowned in the shipwreck of HMS *Sunderland* off Pondicherry in January 1761. Her daughters had all assisted with the costumier's business; Margaret died unmarried in Jamaica in the late 1760s, Catherine married a Mr Hart, had a son, and was widowed, and Hannah vanished from sight. Nothing is known of the last ten years of their mother's life. There was only a brief announcement in the *London Magazine* and the *Newcastle Courant* that Mrs Hannah Glasse, sister to Sir Lancelot Allgood, had died in London on 1 September 1770. No will has been found. A. H. T. Robb-Smith

Sources *A history of Northumberland*, Northumberland County History Committee, 15 vols. (1893–1940), vol. 15 • *The political journal of George Bubb Dodington*, ed. J. Carswell and L. A. Dralle (1965), 33 • M. H. Dodds, 'The rival cooks: Hannah Glasse and Ann Cook', *Archaeologia Aeliana*, 4th ser., 15 (1938), 43–68 • A. Cook and R. Burnet, *Ann Cook and friend* (1936) • J. Boswell, *The life of Samuel Johnson*, 2 vols. (1791) • CLRO, Estates of insolvent debtors' MSS, Glasse 1757 • M. J. P. Weedon, 'Richard Johnson and the successors to John Newbery', *The Library*, 5th ser., 5 (1950–51), 25–63 • Northumbd RO, Allgood MSS

Archives Northumbd RO, Allgood MSS

Glasse, Samuel (1734–1812), Church of England clergyman, was born and baptized on 18 June 1734 at Purton rectory, Purton, Wiltshire, the son of the Revd Richard Glasse (1700–1748), rector of Purton, and his wife, Elizabeth (*d.* 1747). Glasse was a scholar of Westminster School from 1749 to 1752, when he was elected a junior student of Christ Church, Oxford, on 4 June. He took the degrees of BA in 1756 and MA in 1759, and he accumulated the degrees of BD and DD on 7 December 1769. In 1764 Glasse became a fellow of the Royal Society and he became chaplain-in-ordinary to George III in 1772.

Though academically able Glasse's first priority was always his parochial work. In 1769 he was appointed by

Bishop Terrick of London to the rectory of St Mary's, Hanwell, Middlesex (resigned 1785). The parish church was rebuilt while he was incumbent and he contributed generously towards the costs. Glasse there began the practice of taking private pupils from fashionable families. Between 1782 and 1785 he was also vicar of Epsom, Surrey; he resigned the post in favour of his friend and fellow high-churchman Jonathan Boucher, an American loyalist. Glasse moved in 1786 to Wanstead, Essex, on the nomination of Sir James Tylney Long, bt, and he remained there until death. His arrival coincided with a decision to build a new parish church to accommodate increasing numbers. Glasse was again one of the main instruments behind the plan; he also started a church school in 1786 and rebuilt the rectory in 1794.

Glasse had a long wait for preferment outside the parish, despite his support of William Pitt and his connection with the first Lord and Lady Camelford, who were related to the premier. Hopes of a stall at Worcester or Gloucester came to nothing and it was not until 15 April 1791 that he was collated to the prebend of Shalford in Wells Cathedral; to that he added the prebend of Oxgate in St Paul's Cathedral, collated 29 November 1797. He died in Sackville Street, Piccadilly, London, on 27 April 1812, and was buried at Wanstead. He was survived by his son, George Henry *Glasse, though Samuel's marital details are unknown.

Glasse was a strong churchman, at home in the circle of George Horne and William Jones of Nayland; he shared their monarchism and was a fervent loyalist during the 1790s. With Jones, Glasse had a keen appreciation of music. As a popular and eloquent preacher—especially on behalf of special charities including the Sons of the Clergy, the Marine Society, and Brethren of Trinity House—many of Glasse's sermons were printed between 1773 and 1803. In 1801 his *Six Lectures on the Church Catechism* appeared to much acclaim. He also took part in many of the public debates of the late eighteenth century on moral issues; his *The Piety, Wisdom, and Policy of Promoting Sunday Schools* (1786) reflected his keen sympathy with Robert Raikes in that work (see also *GM*, 1st ser., 58, 1788) and his own ambition for serious observance of the sabbath. At Wanstead he took particular pleasure in encouraging the observance of neglected festivals in the Church of England with 250 people attending his Ascension day service in 1788. He published in 1787 *A narrative of proceedings tending towards a national reforming previous to, and consequent upon, his majesty's royal proclamation for the suppression of vice and immorality: in a letter to a friend, &c. by a country magistrate* (1787). An active magistrate, Glasse produced *The magistrate's assistant, or, A summary of those laws which immediately respect the conduct of a justice of the peace* (1784).

NIGEL ASTON

Sources J. Welch, *The list of the queen's scholars of St Peter's College, Westminster*, ed. [C. B. Phillimore], new edn (1852), 349, 358, 359, 534 • *GM*, 1st ser., 56 (1786), 719 • *GM*, 1st ser., 61 (1791), 686 • Venn, *Alum. Cant.*, 1/2.222 • Foster, *Alum. Oxon.* • Nichols, *Illustrations*, 9.131 • E. M. Richardson, *The story of Purton* (1919) • *Fasti Angl., 1541–1857*, [Salisbury], 81 • *Fasti Angl., 1541–1857*, [Bath and Wells], 79 • *Fasti Angl., 1541–1857*, [St Paul's, London], 49 • O. Manning and W. Bray, *The history and antiquities of the county of Surrey*, 2 (1809), 623 • W. Eastment, *Wanstead through the ages*, 3rd edn (1969) • J. E. Tuffs, *The story of Wanstead and Woodford from Roman times to the present* (1962), 62, 65 • D. Lysons, *The environs of London*, 2 (1795), 553 • J. P. Malcolm, *Londinium redivivum, or, An antient history and modern description of London*, 4 vols. (1802–7), vol. 3, p. 20 • parish register, Purton, Wilts. & Swindon RO • *VCH Middlesex*, vol. 3 • *VCH Essex*, vol. 6 • F. C. Mather, *High church prophet: Bishop Samuel Horsley (1733–1806) and the Caroline tradition in the later Georgian church* (1992)

Archives BL, Add. MS 39311, fols. 76, 133, 136, 139, 153, 219, 240 | BL, corresp. with Lady Camelford, Add. MS 69306 • BL, Dropmore MSS, 39312, fols. 271–8; 69306 • BL, letters to Lady Spencer and Charles Poyntz

Likenesses W. Bond, stipple, pubd 1803 (after G. F. Joseph), NPG • M. N. Bate, stipple (after D. B. Murphy), BM, NPG • D. B. Murphy, portrait

Glassford, James (1771–1845), advocate and legal writer, was born on 12 February 1771, the son of John *Glassford (1715–1783) of Dougalston, and his third wife, Lady Margaret Mackenzie (*d.* 1773), sixth daughter of George *Mackenzie, third earl of Cromarty. He was admitted as a member of the faculty of advocates on 3 December 1793, and was sheriff-depute of Dunbartonshire from 1805 to 1815. On 28 September 1808 he married Isabel (*d.* 4 July 1809), daughter of Sir William Murray of Ochtertyre. His second wife was Jane (*d.* 13 Oct 1840), daughter of Colin Mackay.

Glassford succeeded to the family estate at Dougalston on the death of his elder brother, Henry, in 1819. In 1824 he was appointed one of the commissioners for the state of education in Ireland, and in that capacity visited Ulster, Leinster, Munster, and Connaught. He published a letter to the earl of Roden on the state of popular education in Ireland in 1829, and an account of his travels in Ireland in 1838. He also acted as one of the commissioners for inquiring into the duties and emoluments of the clerks and other officers of the courts of justice in Scotland, having published in 1812 some remarks on the constitution and procedure of the Scottish courts. In his *Essay on the Principles of Evidence* (1820), Glassford was one of the first legal writers to treat evidence as a distinct subject, advancing a holistic, as opposed to atomistic, approach to the evaluation of testimony and evidence. As well as writing about the law, Glassford also translated into English the Latin writings of Francis Bacon (1823) and the Italian poems of Ariosto, Sannazaro, and others (1834). Glassford died at Edinburgh on 28 July 1845.

W. F. WENTWORTH-SHIELDS, *rev.* JONATHAN HARRIS

Sources F. J. Grant, ed., *The Faculty of Advocates in Scotland, 1532–1943*, Scottish RS, 145 (1944), 82 • *Scots peerage*, 3.81 • D. M. Walker, *The Scottish jurists* (1985), 400 • W. L. Twining, *Theories of evidence: Bentham and Wigmore* (1985), 3–4, 26 • G. Moir, review of Glassford's *Lyrical compositions selected from the Italian poets* (1834), *EdinR*, 60 (1834–5), 353–63 • D. H. Akenson, *The Irish education experiment: the national system of education in the nineteenth century* (1970), 94–8 • S. Waddington, ed., *The sonnets of Europe* (1886), 257–8 • Allibone, *Dict.*

Archives NL Scot., commonplace book

Glassford, John (1715–1783), tobacco merchant, was the third son of James Glassford, a merchant and burgess in Paisley, Renfrewshire, and Euphan Smyllie. He is said to have begun in business as a textile manufacturer, and became a burgess of Edinburgh by right of his father in 1733, and four years later a burgess and guild brother of the burgh of Glasgow. It was probably during the late 1730s that he first became involved in the tobacco trade.

Trade with Britain's American colonies opened up to Scottish merchants after the Act of Union of 1707. From 1750 to 1775 Glasgow merchants dominated the United Kingdom's trade in tobacco with Virginia and Maryland, having developed the sophisticated 'store system' in the colonies whereby the merchant's factor established a store in a tobacco-growing area, offering linen, clothing, and other manufactured goods for sale on credit against the security of the grower's crop. Like his fellow merchants, Glassford spread his interests in the trade through a number of business partnerships, most importantly John Glassford & Co. and Glassford, Gordon & Co., but also Glassford, Ingram & Co., Archibald Henderson & Co., James Gordon & Co., Henderson, McCall & Co., and George Kippen & Co.

With William Cunningham and Archibald Speirs, Glassford was one of the city's foremost 'tobacco lords', and the companies in their groups controlled over half of the Clyde's tobacco trade by 1775. In *The Expedition of Humphry Clinker* (1771), Tobias Smollett's character Matthew Bramble wrote from Glasgow that:

> I conversed with Mr G——ssf——d, who I take to be one of the greatest merchants in Europe. In the last war [1756–63?], he is said to have had at one time five and twenty ships, with their cargoes, his own property, and to have traded for above half a million sterling a year. (1990 edn, 239)

In 1772 alone, when 49,000 hogsheads (nearly 44 million lb) of tobacco were imported to Scotland by forty-six Glasgow firms, John Glassford & Co. alone imported 4506 hogsheads.

Like the other great tobacco lords, Glassford established a wide range of business interests in Scotland. During the 1760s he became a director of the Prestonpans Vitriol Company, and he had interests in the Glasgow Tanwork Company, the Dyeing and Calico Printing Company, the Cudbear Works, and the Anderston Brewery in Glasgow. He was one of the founders of the Glasgow Arms Bank in 1750 and the Thistle Bank in 1761, a founder subscriber of the Tontine Coffee Hall in 1782, and a founder member of the Glasgow chamber of commerce in 1783.

In 1745 Glassford purchased a mansion house on the outskirts of Glasgow, at Whitehill, in Dennistoun. He sold the house in 1759, and the following year purchased the old Shawfield Mansion, off Glasgow's Argyle Street, where he lived until his death in 1783; a new thoroughfare, Glassford Street, was subsequently laid out on the site of the house and garden. In keeping with the spirit of the times, Glassford and other Scottish merchants and industrialists acquired country estates, and introduced the fashionable ideas of the agricultural improvers. In 1767 he purchased the estate of Dougalston in Dunbartonshire, and commenced an extensive programme of planting, building, and other improvements there. He purchased nearby estates, liming the soil, laying out fields, and making a cut from the Forth and Clyde Canal (he was one of the original subscribers in the canal company) to bring up dung. The improvement work was left largely in the hands of others—Glassford confessed, 'I know very little myself of the proper management of a farm'.

On 24 April 1743 Glassford married Anna Coats (*d.* 1751), the daughter of a Glasgow merchant, with whom he had five children. After her death he married, on 12 November 1752, Anne (*d.* 1766), the daughter of Sir John Nisbet of Dean; they had two sons and four daughters. After Anne's death he married, on 24 November 1768, his third wife, Lady Margaret Mackenzie (*d.* 1773), the daughter of George *Mackenzie, earl of Cromarty, a union which produced a further three children, including the advocate and legal writer James *Glassford. He was survived by two sons and six daughters.

The American War of Independence (1775–83) ruined Glasgow's trade in American tobacco. The city's was predominantly an entrepôt trade, importing and then re-exporting tobacco to Europe, and especially to France. With independence the Americans became free to trade directly with countries outside the British empire. During and after the war the Glasgow merchants encountered great difficulty in recovering debts and forfeited lands and property. One of Glassford's companies, John Glassford & Co., was said to have been left with £20,000 owing from the colonists, although an agent was able to recover and realize some of the firm's property by the time the company's claims for compensation were presented to the British government in 1790. According to James Gourlay, in *A Glasgow Miscellany*, Glassford had opposed the war with the colonists and refused to put his ships at the disposal of the British government; he may have suffered less through confiscations and repudiated debts in Virginia and Maryland than through imprudent investment in the funds and a cavalier attitude towards the financial management of his businesses. Whatever the reason, when Glassford died, at his home, Shawfield Mansion, on 27 August 1783, he had debts, according to Gourlay, of over £93,000 (including provisions made in his will for members of his family) and assets of just £40,000. He was buried in Ramshorn kirk, Glasgow.

Little is known of Glassford's private life and interests. Some historians have suggested that he matriculated at the University of Glasgow in 1728, though the evidence is inconclusive. In 1737 he and his future brother-in-law Archibald Ingram published *The Doctrine of Regeneration*, a theological work which appears to have been his first and last venture into print. He did retain some interest in the world of books and publishing, however, and in 1754 helped, with John Coats Campbell and Ingram, to provide financial support for the Foulis brothers' Academy of Fine Arts in Glasgow. Another enthusiasm is suggested by the popular name for the large building he erected near his mansion at Dougalston, which he called the Banqueting House and others referred to as the Gaming House.

Glassford is commemorated by little more than the name of Glassford Street, but his contributions to the mercantile history of Glasgow, to agricultural improvement schemes, and to the financing of fledgeling industries in the central belt of Scotland deserve wider recognition. IAIN F. RUSSELL

Sources [J. Gourlay], *A Glasgow miscellany* [n.d.] • T. M. Devine, *The tobacco lords: a study of the tobacco merchants of Glasgow and their trading activities, c.1740–1790* (1975) • W. R. Brock, *Scotus Americanus: a survey of the sources for links between Scotland and America in the eighteenth century* (1982) • G. Stewart, *Curiosities of Glasgow citizenship* (1881) • A. Henderson, letterbook, 1760–64, Mitchell L., Glas., Strathclyde regional archives, TD 168 [xerox copy] • Claims of American loyalists, PRO, evidence in the case of John Glassford & Co., 1790, AO 12/9 • J. M. Price, 'The rise of Glasgow in the Chesapeake tobacco trade', *William and Mary Quarterly*, 11 (1954), 179–99

Archives L. Cong., Neil Jamieson MSS

Likenesses A. McLauchlan, group portrait, oils, *c.*1770, Art Gallery and Museum, Glasgow; repro. in Devine, *Tobacco lords* • group portrait (with his third wife and family), probably priv. coll. • group portrait (with family and servant), repro. in J. Fisher, *The Glasgow encyclopaedia* (1994), 123

Wealth at death much property and debts in USA, delaying settlement of affairs; British unentailed assets over £40,000, but debts and provisions for family by will £93,130: [Gourlay], *Glasgow miscellany*, 48

Glasspool, Richard Louveteau (1884–1949), businessman and philanthropist, was born on 8 June 1884 at the Junction Hotel, Eastleigh, Hampshire, the third of four children of Richard Glasspool (*d.* 1904), hotelier and later nurseryman, and his wife, Elizabeth Deborah Wells (*d.* 1937). At the age of nineteen, following the early death of his father, he took over the failing family business, and on his own death he was the owner of nurseries at Flamstead End and Russell's Ride, Cheshunt, Goff's Oak, and Hillingdon. He was a pioneer of the steam-heating apparatus for cultivating mushrooms. He owned and part-owned racehorses, one of which, White Cockade, won the Wokingham Stakes at Ascot in 1948. He kept detailed ledgers on his bets on horses which earned him up to £13,000 per annum.

On 23 January 1939 Glasspool's agents placed an advertisement in the *Daily Telegraph* inviting charities to apply for free housing or housing at nominal rents for needy pensioners or others. A Sunday newspaper then reported that he wanted to give away all his money and he was inundated with letters. Initially he, his sister (Mrs Victoria Culff), and niece (Miss Peggy Culff) sorted through 800 letters in office space provided by Edward Culff, estate agent. Miss Audrey Greenstock was then seconded from Edward Culff & Co. and became the trust's first secretary and a trustee, and she was later chair of the trust until shortly before her death in 1987.

Glasspool had already come to the conclusion that 'indiscriminate donations to multitudinous Charitable Organisations' (Greenstock) were unsatisfactory and decided to set up his own charity to save on income tax and on the proportion of donations spent on fund-raising by recipients. He endowed the R. L. Glasspool Charity Trust with six freehold properties and two mortgage debts and stocks and shares with a face value of £10,000 (actual value at time of gift not known), yielding an initial income of £2000 p.a. by a deed of trust dated 22 July 1939:

> for the relief of such poor sick or necessitous persons without regard to any question of nationality or religion as they [the trustees] shall consider at their absolute discretion to be in need and deserving of help having special regard in granting such help to the purpose of overcoming their temporary misfortunes. (ibid.)

Under the terms of the trust deed, the trust could make grants only to individuals. All Glasspool's gifts to organizations had to be done privately and little is now known, but, for example, he presented the gates to the Hoddesdon football club and supported local hospitals.

Grants were soon restricted to the immediate area of the office (Walthamstow) so that personal contact could be made. Several of the first grants were to enable people to purchase goods to carry on small businesses, including £3 3*s.* 0*d.* to a gentlewoman who was selling needlework pictures. The aim was always to help people to become independent where possible, which Glasspool described as 'helping a lame dog over a stile' (private information). Total expenditure from 1939 to 1947 was £20,396 3*s.* 0*d.*

In 1944 Glasspool sought advice on his wish that the trust build housing for rental to needy people at reasonable rents. To his abiding disappointment, both the Charity Commission and queen's counsel advised that the terms of the deed precluded letting properties at 'uneconomic' rents. In a private capacity, he bought properties for housing the elderly poor which were managed by the Fellowship Homes Scheme—Dartnell Park House in West Byfleet, Surrey, a house in Surbiton, Lamellan in Plymouth—and rented Fleethurst in West Byfleet for temporary use during the blitz years.

By 1946 the trust was regularly overspending its annual income. By a supplemental deed of trust on 29 July 1948 Glasspool made over a further £25,400 in stocks and shares, increasing the trust's income to £8000 per annum. On his death the following year he left £60,144, with the residue to the trust after various personal bequests.

Glasspool was an unassuming man with considerable business acumen and he actively avoided publicity for his charitable giving. He could be very mean with his personal expenditure, to the point where his housekeeper, Franceska Leeb, felt impelled to replace his underwear from her income from selling eggs. The trust remains national in scope, in the top 2 per cent of registered charities, and continues to abide by the spirit of its founder's intentions. In his own words:

> There is the necessity of collaboration with all other sorts of Organisations but I hope the collaboration will not result in our slavishly following the recognised system of social work, and that we shall always be just that little bit different in our approach. (Greenstock)

He did not marry, had no children, and lived at Howfield, Ware Road, Hoddesdon, in Hertfordshire. Glasspool died of heart failure, aged sixty-five, on 8 April 1949 at the Bull Hotel, Barton Mills, Mildenhall, Suffolk, after playing golf during a week's holiday attending Newmarket races. He was buried on 13 April in the family grave at Great Amwell churchyard, Hoddesdon. FRANCES MOORE

Sources A. Greenstock, 'History of the R. L. Glasspool Trust, 1939–1947', R. L. Glasspool Trust, Walthamstow, London • *Cheshunt*

Telegraph (15 April 1949) • *Evening Standard* (23 Sept 1949) • b. cert. • d. cert. • gravestone, Great Amwell parish churchyard, Hertfordshire • private information (2004)

Wealth at death £60,144 0s. 2d.: probate, 20 Sept 1949, *CGPLA Eng. & Wales*

Glastonbury, John of (*fl. c.*1400), Benedictine monk and chronicler, is known for certain only as the author of the *Cronica sive antiquitates Glastoniensis ecclesie*, a history of his abbey, Glastonbury, from the legendary foundation of the first church by St Joseph of Arimathea until the succession of Abbot Walter Monington in 1342. At the end of the fifteenth century a brief continuation to 1497 was composed or commissioned by another Glastonbury monk, William Wyche. The *Cronica* and Wyche's continuation were first edited by Thomas Hearne in 1726 from the late fifteenth-century manuscript, now Princeton University, MS Robert Garrett 153. In 1978 James P. Carley edited the *Cronica*, basing his text on the only known early copy, now Cambridge, Trinity College, MS R.5.16. (He did not include Wyche's continuation, which is found only in later copies of the *Cronica*.) Carley issued a revised and enlarged edition, with an English translation, in 1985.

John specifies some of his sources, and describes how he has treated them, in the prologue to the *Cronica*. He based his narrative, successively, on the *De antiquitate Glastonie ecclesie* by William of Malmesbury, revising and expanding it, and from 1126 to 1290 (actually 1291) on the chronicle of Adam of Damerham, which he abbreviated. Then, he claims, he continued to *c.*1400. The view has been advanced that because John ends in 1342 he wrote in the mid-fourteenth century, and that the chronicler should be identified with John Seen, a monk of Glastonbury who probably died before 1377. It seems more probable, however, that either the prologue was composed before the completion of the *Cronica*, which was subsequently left unfinished, or that the surviving text is a truncated version of the original. In either case, Trinity College, MS R.5.16, would have to be dated *c.*1400, a not improbable date. Furthermore, if the date of *c.*1400 in the prologue is authentic, then John Seen lived too early to be the *Cronica*'s author. A large number of Glastonbury monks were called John. On the present evidence, a firm judgement on both the date and the authorship of the *Cronica* must be reserved.

John's continuation of Adam of Damerham is a factual record of each abbacy, evidently compiled from the abbey's archives, with scarcely any references to general history, and, therefore, mainly of value for local history. More remarkable is the legendary content of the *Cronica*'s early chapters. For this John drew material (as he states in the prologue) 'from various books, saints' lives and other ancient writings' (*Chronicle of Glastonbury Abbey*, 7). Carley lists a number of those that have been identified, and John himself names Gerald of Wales and Ranulf Higden as among his authorities. He immediately takes issue with Higden, who stated in the *Polychronicon* that the St Patrick (allegedly) buried at Glastonbury was not the apostle of Ireland, but another, lesser Patrick. John retaliated by 'proving' that the apostle of Ireland was indeed buried at Glastonbury and was the first abbot.

John's principal objective was to demonstrate the great antiquity and holy associations of the church at Glastonbury. He synthesized and wonderfully embellished the legends concerning its origins and early history. He linked the legend of St Joseph of Arimathea with the Arthurian legend, by a genealogy tracing Arthur's descent from Joseph, and began his narrative with the statement that Joseph was the founder of Glastonbury's first church, in AD 63. This was of inestimable value to Glastonbury's prestige: it gave its church priority of foundation over all other monasteries in England, and, therefore, enabled the abbot to claim precedence over all other heads of religious houses at national assemblies. Moreover, it had wider implications. By establishing England's apostolic conversion, the legend improved the standing of Henry IV and Henry V at general councils of the church, starting with the Council of Pisa in 1409, because the precedence of the 'nations' at the councils was determined by the date of a country's conversion. ANTONIA GRANSDEN

Sources *The Chronicle of Glastonbury Abbey: an edition, translation and study of John of Glastonbury's Cronica sive antiquitates Glastoniensis ecclesie*, ed. J. P. Carley, trans. D. Townsend, rev. edn (1985) • *Johannis … Glastoniensis Chronica, sive, Historia de rebus Glastoniensibus*, ed. T. Hearne, 2 vols. (1726) • A. Gransden, 'The date and authorship of John of Glastonbury's *Cronica sive antiquitates Glastoniensis ecclesie*', *Legends, traditions, and history in medieval England* (1992), 289–98 • J. A. Robinson, *Two Glastonbury legends: King Arthur and St Joseph of Arimathea* (1926) • *The early history of Glastonbury: an edition, translation, and study of William of Malmesbury's De antiquitate Glastonie ecclesie*, ed. J. Scott (1981) • J. Taylor, *English historical literature in the fourteenth century* (1987), 45 • A. Gransden, 'The growth of the Glastonbury traditions and legends in the twelfth century', *Journal of Ecclesiastical History*, 27 (1976), 337–58; repr. in A. Gransden, *Legends, traditions and history in medieval England* (1992) • F. Riddy, 'Glastonbury, Joseph of Arimathea and the grail in John Hardyng's Chronicle', *The archaeology and history of Glastonbury Abbey: essays in honour of … C. A. Ralegh Radford*, ed. L. Abrams and J. P. Carley (1991), 317–31 • John of Glastonbury, *Cronica, sive, Antiquitates Glastoniensis ecclesie*, ed. J. P. Carley (1978)

Archives Princeton University, New Jersey, MS Robert Garrett 153 • Trinity Cam., MS R.5.16

Glazebrook, James (1744–1803), Church of England clergyman, was born on 11 October 1744 at Madeley, Shropshire, the son of William Glazebrook and his wife, Elizabeth. His parents were known only as respectable, but not affluent. A witty and robust young man, Glazebrook laboured as a collier. Having experienced a religious conversion as a youth of sixteen, he was later drawn toward the ministry under the influence of the Revd John Fletcher of Madeley. In 1768 he entered the newly opened Trevecca College (the countess of Huntingdon's college) in south Wales. While a student, his studies were frequently interrupted by itinerant preaching. Despite his affiliation with well-known revivalists Glazebrook maintained his loyalty to the established church. He was ordained deacon in 1771 by Dr Brownlow North, bishop of Lichfield and Coventry, and priest in 1777 by Dr Richard Hurd, bishop of Worcester. After serving in numerous curacies he moved in 1779 to Warrington, where he became incumbent of a new church, St James's, Latchford. That same year he married Dorothy Kirkland, daughter of the medical writer Dr Thomas *Kirkland. Their son, Thomas *Glazebrook, was born in 1780.

Glazebrook was not a man to shy away from controversy. While a travelling preacher for Selina, countess of Huntingdon, he encountered considerable opposition from settled clergymen who lacked appreciation for young, uninvited revivalists who presumed to preach in their parishes. In the same period Glazebrook was involved in theological disputes between evangelicals who divided into Calvinist and Arminian camps. A committed Calvinist, Glazebrook maintained a tense, but civil, relationship with Wesleyan preachers; but in time the genuine differences led him into an open quarrel. With characteristic humility, gusto, and self-revelation, Glazebrook described his meeting with John Wesley in 1772: 'He and those with him were very civil, but I confess my wicked heart would scarcely admit of my being so to them' (Cheshunt archives, F1/176).

As a settled minister in Warrington, Glazebrook joined in a sharp controversy on infant baptism with the nonconformist scholar Gilbert Wakefield. Wakefield afterwards acknowledged that his opponent was 'a man of talents, very superior in his education and advantages, and deserves the warmest commendations for the pains which he must have taken with the cultivation of his understanding in very untoward circumstances' (*DNB*). Inspired by this disputation, he published *A Defence of Infant Baptism, &c.* (1781). In 1796 Glazebrook was appointed vicar of Belton, Leicestershire, though he retained his incumbency at St James's. He was in bad health, however, and died at Belton on 1 July 1803.

In 1794 Glazebrook published *The Practice of what is Called Extempore Preaching Recommended*, arising out of his solid roots in the eighteenth-century evangelical revival. His other publications were sermons or collections of sermons and included *The Minister's Enquiry into the State of his People: a Sermon* (1798).

C. W. SUTTON, *rev.*
DOROTHY EUGENIA SHERMAN BROWN

Sources Westminster College, Cambridge, Cheshunt archives • 'Biographical sketches: Rev. James Glazebrook', *Evangelical Register* (March 1836), 73–8, 113–118 • 'Biographical sketches: Rev. James Glazebrook', *Evangelical Register* (1837), 302–6 • J. P. Rylands, *Genealogies of Bate and Kirkland* (1877) • D. E. S. Brown, 'Evangelicals and education in eighteenth-century Britain', PhD diss., University of Wisconsin-Madison, 1992 • G. Ormerod, *The history of the county palatine and city of Chester*, 3 vols. (1819) • J. Glazebrook, *Sermons on various important subjects*, ed. T. W. Whitaker (1805) • A. H. New, *The coronet and the cross, or, Memorials of the right hon. Selina, countess of Huntingdon* (1858) • *IGI*
Archives Westminster College, Cambridge, Cheshunt archives, corresp. with Lady Huntingdon

Glazebrook, Michael George (1853–1926), headmaster and Church of England clergyman, the eldest of the five children of Michael George Glazebrook, merchant, and his wife, Margaret Elizabeth, daughter of Alfred Tapson, was born in London on 4 August 1853. He was educated at Brentford grammar school, Blackheath proprietary school, and Dulwich College, where he became head of the school, and in 1872 entered Balliol College, Oxford, as a mathematical scholar. He obtained first classes in mathematical and classical moderations in 1873 and 1874 respectively, a second class in the final mathematical school (1876), and a first class in *literae humaniores* (1877). He represented Oxford against Cambridge in the hundred yards and high jump: at the latter in 1875 he was amateur champion. At Balliol he was a close friend of Arnold Toynbee, of whose social work he was afterwards a strong supporter.

After a year of adventurous travel in Mexico and elsewhere Glazebrook in 1878 accepted an invitation from H. M. Butler to go to Harrow as an assistant master. There he produced school editions of Aeschylus and Euripides. He married in 1880 Ethel, fourth daughter of the chemist Sir B. C. *Brodie, and elder sister of the wife of his Balliol contemporary Sir T. H. Warren. She shared his life and work, serving on diocesan committees and as a poor-law guardian. She published verse, an edition of Dante, and a school edition of Robert Browning's poetry.

In 1888 Glazebrook was appointed high master of Manchester grammar school, where he set himself the task of planting the corporate activities of public boarding-schools in soil which was hardly ready for them. Perhaps Glazebrook was rather too conscious of being a disciple of Jowett and Butler, but the later development of this great school owed much to his energy and organizing ability. In 1891 he was appointed headmaster of Clifton College. Under John Percival and J. M. Wilson, Clifton had gone from strength to strength, but the original impetus was beginning to die. The masters of the heroic age of Percival were leaving or else passing their prime. Without waiting to get public opinion on his side, Glazebrook began his work of reorganization and development. His stern manner and almost brutal candour prevented his ever being popular with the masters, the boys, or the old boys, and he was not an inspiring preacher. But although there was a considerable decline in numbers, which caused him to offer his resignation in 1897 and 1898, there was none in efficiency. He strengthened the staff where it had before been weak, especially in modern languages and music. In music he made Clifton a pioneer school by appointing A. H. Peppin director of music and giving him a free hand. The encouragement which he gave to music was perhaps Glazebrook's most important contribution to English education. He resigned in 1905.

In the same year Glazebrook, who had been ordained deacon and priest at Manchester in 1890, was appointed canon of Ely Cathedral, where he became a leader of the Modern Churchmen movement. His passion for sincerity and truth found a congenial task in the interpretation of the Bible and the Christian religion to a scientific age. Already he had written a school edition of the Old Testament—*Lessons from the Old Testament* (1890; rev. edn, 1922)—which was widely used. It enabled many schoolmasters to teach the Old Testament with a new sincerity. He himself regarded his Warburton lectures at Lincoln's Inn (1907–11) as most fully representing his mature views. They were collected under the title *The End of the Law* (1911). His *Faith of a Modern Churchman* (1918; rev. edn, 1925), although it brought him into conflict with his diocesan bishop, Frederic Henry Chase, made clear to the ordinary layman the results of other men's researches in biblical scholarship. In 1914 Glazebrook became chairman of the Modern Churchmen's Union. He took an active part in the annual conferences of Modern Churchmen, where his firmness and moderation made him an admirable chairman. He was elected chairman of the council of Ripon Hall when it opened at Oxford in 1919. In his later days Glazebrook found it much easier to show the humanity and sympathy which some had always discerned behind his rather frigid public manner. He was especially loved by and devoted to children, though he had none himself. His wife's fatal illness occasioned his own death, which took place at The College, Ely, on 1 May 1926, fifteen days before hers. He was buried at Ely. N. WHATLEY, *rev.* M. C. CURTHOYS

Sources *The Times* (3 May 1926) · *The Times* (21 May 1926) · *The Cliftonian* (June–July 1926) · D. Winterbottom, *Clifton after Percival* (1990) · private information (1937) · *The Modern Churchman*, 16 (1926), 57 · A. M. G. Stephenson, *The rise and decline of English modernism* (1984) · *WWW* · *CGPLA Eng. & Wales* (1926)
Likenesses H. de T. Glazebrook, oils, Dulwich College, London · W. Strang, oils (after Richmond), Clifton College, Bristol
Wealth at death £1878 5*s*. 6*d*.: probate, 20 Aug 1926, *CGPLA Eng. & Wales*

Glazebrook, Sir Richard Tetley (1854–1935), physicist, was born on 18 September 1854 at West Derby, Liverpool, the eldest son of Nicholas Smith Glazebrook, surgeon, and his wife, Sarah Anne, daughter of Richard Tetley, also of Liverpool. He was educated at Dulwich College, Liverpool College, 1870–72, and Trinity College, Cambridge, from 1872, where he was elected a major scholar in 1875 and a fellow in 1877. He was fifth wrangler in the mathematical tripos of 1876 and after graduation he studied physics under James Clerk Maxwell in the newly opened Cavendish Laboratory. When Lord Rayleigh succeeded Clerk Maxwell as director in 1880 Glazebrook was appointed as a demonstrator at the Cavendish, a post he held alongside a college lectureship in mathematics and physics and a university lectureship in mathematics. His research became increasingly concerned with electrical standards and in recognition of this work he was elected a fellow of the Royal Society in 1882 at the age of twenty-eight. He married Frances Gertrude Atkinson of Leeds in 1883; they had three daughters and a son.

When Rayleigh retired from the Cavendish professorship in 1884 Glazebrook hoped to be appointed as his successor but he was passed over in favour of Sir J. J. Thomson. This was a serious disappointment to Glazebrook, who had been Rayleigh's choice as his successor, but he remained at Cambridge, becoming assistant director of the Cavendish in 1891 and, four years later, bursar of Trinity College. In 1898 he was offered the post of principal of University College, Liverpool, which he accepted on the understanding that he would resign should the current campaign for a National Physical Laboratory be successful

Sir Richard Tetley Glazebrook (1854–1935), by Olive Edis, 1915

and he was to be offered the position of director. The following year the National Physical Laboratory was created under the control of the Royal Society, supported financially by a Treasury grant in aid, and Glazebrook accepted the post of its director in June 1899.

The National Physical Laboratory was to be based at Kew observatory but public opposition to an extension of that site meant that much of Glazebrook's time was spent at first in finding alternative accommodation. Eventually the offer of Bushy House, Teddington, was accepted and the ground floor and cellars were converted into laboratories while the upper parts became the Glazebrooks' private residence. In the early years of the laboratory's existence Glazebrook's efforts were frequently directed towards persuading a reluctant Treasury that a higher level of funding was required if all the demands placed on the new institution were to be met. The Treasury view was that the laboratory should become financially self-supporting and this inevitably meant that large volumes of routine, commercial testing were undertaken in order to generate income. Glazebrook fought hard to ensure that such work did not displace more fundamental, industrially oriented research but the tension between short- and long-term research lasted throughout his directorship. None the less, progress was made, often thanks to substantial gifts from individuals which a reluctant Treasury was persuaded to match. New buildings were provided for electrical work, metrology, and engineering and in 1908 Alfred Yarrow funded a tank for pioneering experimental work on models of ships which provided important data for the shipbuilding industry. The embryonic aeronautics industry also benefited from work at the laboratory which began in 1909, at the request of R. B. Haldane, then secretary of state for war.

By the outbreak of the First World War Glazebrook's leadership had established the National Physical Laboratory as a permanent feature of the scientific landscape. New buildings to accommodate work in optics and metallurgy meant that the range and scale of the laboratory's activities were now considerable. In the face of Treasury indifference and, on occasion, outright opposition to certain aspects of the work of the laboratory this was a significant achievement. The war brought fresh challenges. In the first months Glazebrook lost one-quarter of his staff and the work of the laboratory became increasingly dominated by the demands of the war: gauges for munitions production had to be tested in growing numbers (over one million by the end of the war) while fundamental research had to be undertaken on the production of optical glass and other products formerly obtained from Germany, on aeronautical problems arising from the introduction of new types of aircraft, and on radio communications. The laboratory grew rapidly as a result of these activities. Glazebrook realized that the scale of its work was such that the Royal Society could no longer be financially responsible for it and towards the end of the war discussions were held with the newly created Department of Scientific and Industrial Research (DSIR) with a view to the laboratory being funded in future through the department while the Royal Society continued to advise on its scientific programme. Glazebrook was particularly closely involved in what were often difficult negotiations with the DSIR as he attempted to ensure that financial control by the new department did not lead to control of the laboratory's scientific programme. Although he achieved some success relations between Glazebrook and officials of the DSIR were frequently strained. On reaching retirement age in 1919 he decided to stand down from the directorship of the laboratory although he let it be known that in other circumstances he would have been prepared to remain in post and guide the laboratory into the post-war era.

At the age of sixty-five Glazebrook's energies were undiminished. From Bushy House he moved to Cambridge, where he edited the *Dictionary of Applied Physics*, and then to London where from 1920 to 1923 he was Zarahoff professor of aviation at Imperial College. In 1924 he settled at Limpsfield in Surrey. His involvement with the National Physical Laboratory was maintained through his membership of its general board and, from 1925 to 1932, the chairmanship of its executive committee. His work for the Royal Society included two periods as vice-president (1919–20 and 1924–8) as well as serving as its foreign secretary between 1926 and 1929; the society awarded him the Hughes medal in 1909 and a royal medal in 1931. He was appointed CB in 1910 and after being knighted in 1917, KCB in 1920, and KCVO in 1934. He was awarded honorary degrees by the universities of Manchester, Oxford, Edinburgh, and Heidelberg.

Glazebrook was one of the foremost scientific figures of his day. He was, at various times, president of the Physical Society, the Optical Society, the Faraday Society, the Institution of Electrical Engineers and the Institute of Physics. Although he continued to publish throughout his life—two papers on electrical standards were received by the *Proceedings of the Physical Society* only nine days before his death—his place in late nineteenth- and early twentieth-century physics owes more to his vision of the role and application of science in a modern industrial society and his ability to put that vision into practice. His contemporaries recalled Glazebrook as a tall, spare figure: 'the precise and curiously clipped diction … the steel spectacles removed with a sudden, almost nervous, jerk and used to emphasise a point in the argument' (*Proceedings of the Physical Society*, 933). His commitment to his work left little time for recreation although he enjoyed an annual mountaineering holiday in Switzerland and he played golf until the end of his life. He died at Limpsfield on 15 December 1935. RUSSELL MOSELEY

Sources Lord Rayleigh [R. J. Strutt] and F. J. Selby, *Obits. FRS*, 2 (1936–8), 29–56 · *Proceedings of the Physical Society*, 48 (1936), 929–33 · R. Moseley, 'Science, government and industrial research: the origins and development of the National Physical Laboratory, 1900–1975', DPhil diss., U. Sussex, 1976 · *DNB* · *The Times* (17 Dec 1935) · *CGPLA Eng. & Wales* (1936)

Archives ICL, corresp. and papers relating to Imperial College · PRO, corresp. and papers, DSIR10/20 · RS · U. Lpool, corresp. and papers relating to University of Liverpool | BL, corresp. with Macmillans, Add. MSS 55215–55217 · Bodl. Oxf., notes relating to supply of munitions and corresp. with Viscount Addison · CUL, corresp. with Lord Kelvin · CUL, corresp. with Lord Rutherford · CUL, letters to Sir George Stokes · U. Cam., Trinity College, corresp. with Joseph John Thomson · UCL, corresp. with Sir Oliver Lodge

Likenesses O. Edis, photograph, 1915, NPG [*see illus.*] · H. de T. Glazebrook, oils, 1919, National Physical Laboratory, Teddington, Middlesex · W. Stoneman, two photographs, 1919–31, NPG · J. E. Cluysenaar, bas-relief, National Physical Laboratory, Teddington, Middlesex · O. Edis, prints, NPG · photograph, repro. in *Obits. FRS*, 28 · photograph, National Physical Laboratory, Teddington, Middlesex · photograph, RS

Wealth at death £30,835 12s. 10d.: probate, 2 March 1936, *CGPLA Eng. & Wales*

Glazebrook, Thomas Kirkland (1780–1855), glass manufacturer and writer, was born on 4 June 1780 at Ashby-de-la-Zouch, Leicestershire, the son of the Revd James *Glazebrook (1744–1803) and his wife, Dorothy, *née* Kirkland (*d.* 1834). Glazebrook lived for many years at Warrington, where he supervised his glass manufacturing business. He married Elizabeth Twanbrook (*d.* 1844) in 1801, and they had a large family. He was the captain of a local volunteer corps in 1803, and was always an ardent supporter of the tory party.

Glazebrook was a man of wide-ranging interests. He was a keen composer, particularly fond of Handel and organ music, and published a translation of Virgil's first eclogue in English verse in 1807. In 1809 he wrote the first local history of Southport: *A Guide to Southport, North Meoles, in the County of Lancaster*. He also published an *Alphabetical and Chronological List of Companies, Trades &c* in 1831. During the cholera epidemic of 1833 he served as secretary to the local board of health. Glazebrook settled in Southport in 1835 and lived there until his death, from influenza, on 18 January 1855 in Manchester Road, Southport. He was buried in Wallasey parish church, Cheshire, on 23 January. MEGAN A. STEPHAN

Sources J. Kendrick, ed., *Profiles of Warrington worthies*, 2nd edn (1854), 6 · E. Glasgow, *Thomas Kirkland Glazebrook: Southport's first local historian* (1955) [1973] · J. P. Rylands, *Genealogies of the families of*

Bate and Kirkland of Ashby-de-la-Zouch, Leics. (1877), 6 • d. cert. • H. Fishwick, *The Lancashire library* (1875), 176 • *DNB*
Likenesses silhouette, repro. in Kendrick, *Profiles*

Glazier [Oxford], **Thomas** (*d.* in or before **1427**), glass painter, is first recorded in 1386 in Oxford, where his workshop was located. It was the usual small-scale enterprise, numbering at least one assistant in addition to Glazier himself. He enjoyed the patronage of William Wykeham, bishop of Winchester, on whose foundations of New College, Oxford, and Winchester College he was employed. Substantial quantities of his chapel windows survive in both establishments. The New College chapel glazing seems to have been executed in two phases. The Old Testament figures and saints in the antechapel are closely comparable with English manuscripts of the 1380s and were evidently inserted during the main construction period of the college (1380–86). The Jesse tree formerly in the west window (since the eighteenth century in York Minster) is much closer in style to the Winchester College glass, upon which Glazier was engaged in 1393.

These two works signal a new phase in Thomas Glazier's *œuvre*. Every aspect of design, from treatment of figures to canopies, from borders to backgrounds, is transformed. Together with one of the hands in the Carmelite missal (BL, Add. MSS 29704, 29705, 44892) and the Wilton diptych (London, National Gallery), the Winchester College chapel windows and the New College Jesse mark the emergence of indigenous variants of the so-called international Gothic style. In a craft where the initial designs were often carried out by painters rather than glaziers, it is conceivable that Glazier was following the innovations of others. In view of the affinities between Winchester and slightly later north-German panel painting, the presence of a painter named Herebright of Cologne in Wykeham's service may be significant. None the less, Glazier was one of the leading English exponents of this style working in this medium.

Thomas Glazier, who is known to have been married, remained active into the 1420s but had died by 1427. Although none of his other documented commissions has survived, there are several extant works which can be linked with him on stylistic grounds. These include some figures in the east window of Merton College chapel, Oxford, and some displaced glass from the nave clerestory of Winchester Cathedral; and the St Christopher and St Anne teaching the Virgin to read panels in the parish church of Thenford, Northamptonshire, are exquisite essays in line and shading, executed almost exclusively in white glass. RICHARD MARKS

Sources C. Woodforde, *The stained glass of New College, Oxford* (1951) • J. H. Harvey and D. G. King, 'Winchester College stained glass', *Archaeologia*, 103 (1971), 149–77 • J. D. Le Couteur, *Ancient glass in Winchester* (1920) • R. Marks, *Stained glass in England during the middle ages* (1993), 171–8
Archives New College, Oxford, glazing • Winchester College, glazing • York Minster, glazing
Likenesses image (after lost original by Thomas), Winchester College Chapel

Gledstanes [Gladstanes], **George** (*c.*1562–1615), archbishop of St Andrews, was a son of Herbert Gladstanes (*d.* 1569?), town clerk and bailie of Dundee. He was educated at Dundee grammar school and at the University of St Andrews, where he graduated MA in 1580, probably aged about eighteen. He may subsequently have studied theology under Andrew Melville at St Mary's College, St Andrews. He then taught languages in the grammar school at Montrose and was appointed reader in the parish kirk there in 1585. He was ordained to his first charge at Ecclesgreig, or St Cyrus, in the presbytery of Fordoun before 23 July 1587. In the following year, the kirk still being short of recruits, he briefly also held the charge of Aberlethnot, or Marykirk. At about this time he was the object of a number of violent attacks by armed followers of William Douglas, son of the laird of Glenbervie. The general assembly of February 1588 stated that Douglas had 'onbesett, at syndrie tymes … Mr George Gladstaines … with armed men' (Thomson, *Acts and Proceedings*, 2.718). On one occasion Gledstanes is said to have escaped death only narrowly. He moved to the parish of Arbirlot in the presbytery of Arbroath in 1592, where he remained for five years. He married Christian Durie (*d.* 1617); the date of the marriage is unknown.

Between king and kirk Gledstanes is first recorded as attending the general assembly at Edinburgh in August 1590. In 1595 he was named in a commission to advise James VI in his choice of a new minister for the royal household. In the autumn of the following year he became involved in a major confrontation between the kirk and the king over the return from exile of the Catholic earls of Huntly and Erroll and the inflammatory preaching of David Black, minister of St Andrews. The kirk appointed a standing commission to sit in Edinburgh to lobby the crown and Gledstanes was one of the four commissioners for the north of Scotland. As with so many others who had been similarly appointed, his allegiance appears to have been transferred to the crown following a riot in Edinburgh on 12 December 1596 which led to James VI resolving to take firm control of the kirk. At a general assembly at Perth in March, Gledstanes was appointed to confer with Huntly regarding his religion; at another, held at Dundee in May, he was appointed to the king's commission of the general assembly. This body, ostensibly designed to improve communication between king and kirk, increasingly became a means for royal control. Gledstanes remained a member of that commission right through to its final reappointment in 1608. He attended every general assembly after 1596 and was named on a number of specific commissions relating to such issues as ecclesiastical finance and Catholicism.

In July 1597 the new commission of the general assembly appointed Gledstanes as minister of St Andrews to replace David Black, who was transferred to Gledstanes's former charge at Arbirlot. On 15 July the presbytery was commanded to accept him, and James Melville, another member of the commission of the assembly, admitted Gledstanes who was soon accepted by the rest of the presbytery. As 'the maist gracious of their number in court' he and Melville were appointed to travel to Edinburgh on 4 August to ask the king that theology students be allowed to participate in the presbytery's exercise of doctrine, the commission of the general assembly having excluded them in July (Register of St Andrews presbytery, fol. 81*v*). On 8 September his ministry in St Andrews was formally approved by the whole presbytery; he and Melville were again appointed to discuss the matter of the theology students with James VI, and in December he and four others were elected commissioners to go to Edinburgh at the time of parliament in case a general assembly was called.

In January 1598 Gledstanes was involved in planting new ministers in Edinburgh, replacing incumbents who had been deposed for their alleged part in the riot of December 1596. In the general assembly at Dundee in the following March he argued in favour of ecclesiastical representation in parliament, on the grounds that the kirk was one of the estates of the realm. Perhaps as a result he was one of three commissioners chosen by the synod of Fife in June, allegedly under pressure from royal commissioners, to discuss parliamentary representation with the delegates of other synods. In July 1599 he was made vice-chancellor of the University of St Andrews during a visitation by the king and commissioners of the general assembly, and he became chancellor, replacing the late earl of Montrose, in 1608.

Bishop of Caithness Meetings to discuss ecclesiastical representation in parliament between the king and delegates from the kirk continued into 1600, and at one such gathering in October Gledstanes was one of the first bishops to be appointed to a vacant see since 1585. He was given that of Caithness while David Lindsay received Ross and Peter Blackburn Aberdeen. In spite of this Gledstanes retained his parochial charge at St Andrews and continued to live there. A few weeks later he attended parliament at Edinburgh for the first time. He regularly attended parliaments and conventions of estates thereafter, being appointed to the committee of the articles on five occasions and serving on a number of parliamentary commissions, including the commission to negotiate closer union with England in 1604. At the next meeting of the synod of Fife in February 1605, he was challenged over his attendance at the previous parliament and he admitted that he had sat as a bishop 'but against his will … becaus they would not name him otherwise' (Calderwood, 6.101). The kirk had favoured some form of parliamentary representation for years, but there were fears that the use of the word 'bishop' might be turned to the crown's advantage as a means towards the restoration of a full-blown episcopal system. In spite of such fears the general assembly of 1601 had granted Gledstanes powers of visitation over his diocese of Caithness, while that of July 1602 had renewed the commission following his report of his first year's performance, including a written record of his visitation. On 24 November 1602 he was admitted to the privy council, and he was a regular member until four months before his death.

In 1604 growing resentment of their minister-bishop came to the surface within the presbytery of St Andrews. Some of the ministers protested in writing against the fact that Gledstanes had been 'advancit to honour to sit in counsaill, parliament and [ex]checker' (Register of St Andrews presbytery, fol. 123*v*). The matter was referred up to the synod and nothing more is recorded. Three weeks later, in what appears to have been a thinly veiled attack on their only member who was regularly absent on crown business, a system of fines for absence from presbytery meetings was instituted: double penalties were to be applied to those living in St Andrews. In the following August the presbytery resolved to have all of its members subscribe the confession of faith and acts of parliament of 1592 securing the presbyterian system. The signature of Gledstanes, either keen to placate their fears or under pressure to prove his support for presbyterianism, is the first on the list after the moderator's.

Archbishop of St Andrews In his *Autobiography and Diary* James Melville claims that Gledstanes had sworn that he had no desire to become archbishop of St Andrews 'becaus his predicessouris thairin had so evill succes and wer so evill haitit' (p. 644). It must then have been with considerable trepidation that Gledstanes returned to St Andrews in January 1605, having been appointed to the archiepiscopal see on 12 October 1604. In an attempt to pre-empt any outcry, he 'declarit in presens of the haill brethrene that as he departit a brother sa he returnis usurping na superioritie over them' (Register of St Andrews presbytery, fol. 131*v*). It is noteworthy that he would not use the title 'archbishop', always referring to himself as merely 'bishop of St Andrews'.

Gledstanes attended the meetings between the king and eight leading Scottish dissident divines at Hampton Court in the autumn of 1606, and on his return from England he was appointed constant moderator of the presbytery of St Andrews at the general assembly at Linlithgow in December. He was not well received by his brethren, who resisted the imposition of an unelected moderator, as did numerous other presbyteries. Although the assembly at Linlithgow had not introduced constant moderation for synods, the government claimed that it had and made strenuous efforts to impose the same. In June 1607 three royal commissioners came to the synod of Fife along with Gledstanes in an attempt to ensure his acceptance as constant moderator. They faced stout resistance and ordered the synod to adjourn on pain of horning. It refused to adjourn and threatened excommunication of Gledstanes if it was horned. In August Gledstanes turned up with four royal commissioners, but the synod found fault with him for his ministry at St Andrews. According to James Melville, he was 'scharplie censurit for absenting himselff from the doctrine [presbytery meetings] … At the quhilk wordis the great Bischope kendelit sua in a raige of foull flyting [abuse], that … he was unworthie to be in the number of ministeres', let alone constant moderator of the synod (*Autobiography and Diary*, 718). As a result of its resistance, four ministers of the synod of Fife were put to the horn by the privy council: these included Gledstanes's own brother-in-law, John Dykes, who had written to James Melville in June that Gledstanes was 'foolishlie fordward' in pressing for the acceptance of constant moderators (Calderwood, 6.664).

In 1609 Gledstanes participated in the conference between bishops and ministers at Falkland which vainly tried to resolve the increasing problems in the kirk. That autumn, along with other Scottish bishops, he travelled to England where he is said to have discussed fundamental alterations to the constitution of the general assembly, and also to have planned the establishment of two courts of high commission to supersede the general assembly as the highest court of ecclesiastical appeal under the king. The latter duly proceeded, and on 15 February 1610 Gledstanes was named as the head of the new court of high commission for the province of St Andrews. He was also appointed to a number of commissions for the peace in November. In the following December he was consecrated at St Andrews by John Spottiswoode, archbishop of Glasgow, Andrew Lamb, bishop of Brechin, and Gavin Hamilton, bishop of Galloway, who had been consecrated by English bishops earlier in the year so that the apostolic succession could be restored to the Scottish episcopate.

Last years Gledstanes does not seem to have courted controversy in the last years of his life, but remained dedicated to his see, regularly holding synods and visitations. In 1613 he moved into the bishop's castle in St Andrews, having had it repaired. In 1614 he arrested the Jesuit James Moffat at the same time as his counterpart in Glasgow, John Spottiswoode, arrested John Ogilvie. Both were tried, but unlike Ogilvie, Moffat saved his skin by acknowledging James VI's supremacy in ecclesiastical affairs within his own realm. On 2 May 1615 George Gledstanes died in his castle at St Andrews. He was buried soon after his death in the south-east corner of Holy Trinity parish kirk in St Andrews. His 'funeral', paid for to the tune of 10,000 merks (£6666 13*s.* 4*d.* Scots) by James VI, was not held until 7 June, when an empty coffin was carried under a black canopy. Gledstanes was survived by his wife and probably two children, one of whom, Alexander, was archdean of St Andrews.

A number of administrative letters survive in printed sources, none of which sheds much light on Gledstanes's life or character. Calderwood describes the archbishop as 'both ambitious and covetous', saying that 'Papists and haynous offenders were winked at for bribes' (Calderwood, 7.197). But to his archiepiscopal colleague and successor John Spottiswoode, he was 'a man of good learning, ready utterance and great invention'. Perhaps finding the finances of the archbishopric in some disarray in 1615, Spottiswoode also describes his predecessor as 'of an easy nature, and induced by those he trusted to do many things hurtful to the see' (*History of the Church*, 3.227).

Alan R. MacDonald

Sources *Fasti Scot.*, new edn, vol. 5 • D. Calderwood, *The history of the Kirk of Scotland*, ed. T. Thomson and D. Laing, 8 vols., Wodrow Society, 7 (1842–9) • T. Thomson, ed., *Acts and proceedings of the general assemblies of the Kirk of Scotland*, 3 pts, Bannatyne Club, 81 (1839–45) • *APS*, *1567–1625* • *The autobiography and diary of Mr James Melvill*, ed. R. Pitcairn, Wodrow Society (1842) • presbytery book of St Andrews, 1585–1605, U. St Andr., MS 23 • J. Spottiswood, *The history of the Church of Scotland*, ed. M. Napier and M. Russell, 3 vols., Bannatyne Club, 93 (1850) • *Reg. PCS*, 1st ser. • Edinburgh commissary court register of testaments, NA Scot., CC8/8/2 • St Andrews commissary court register of testaments, NA Scot., CC20/4/6 • diocesan synod of St Andrews beneath Forth, 1610–36, NA Scot., CH2/154/1 • J. Kirk, *Patterns of reform: continuity and change in the Reformation kirk* (1989) • J. Wormald, 'No bishop, no king: the Scottish Jacobean episcopate, 1600–1625', *Miscellanea historia ecclesiasticae VIII* [Strasbourg 1983], ed. B. Vogler (Brussels, 1987), 259–67 • D. G. Mullan, *Episcopacy in Scotland: the history of an idea, 1560–1608* (1986) • A. R. Macdonald, *The Jacobean kirk, 1567–1625: sovereignty, polity and liturgy* (1998)

Archives NA Scot., records of the diocesan synod of St Andrews beneath Forth, CH2/154/1 • U. St Andr., St Andrews presbytery book, MS 23

Wealth at death £15,104 4*s.* 0*d.* Scots: St Andrews commissary court register of testaments, NA Scot., CC20/4/6

Glees, (Franz) Paul (**1909–1999**), anatomist, was born on 23 February 1909, at Cologne, Germany, the son of Joseph Glees, a silk merchant. His family were Roman Catholics but he 'fell out with his Catholic inheritance at an early age, considering it unscientific' (*The Times*, 23). From a school in Bad Godesberg he won a place to study mathematics and then medicine at the University of Bonn, and while still a student was appointed assistant to one of the professors (Stoehr), a noted anatomist; he graduated MD in 1935. His future wife, Eva Antonia Maria Löb (*b.* 1909), was a dental student at Bonn, and graduated in 1936. Paul had for long been dismayed by the seemingly unstoppable rise of Nazism, and Eva was Jewish; so in 1936 he left Germany for Amsterdam, then moved to London, where he and Eva married in St Agnes's Catholic Church, Cricklewood, on 3 July 1936. They had two daughters and two sons.

Glees worked for a time at the Strangeways Laboratory in Cambridge. In 1940 he moved to Oxford, at first in the department of anatomy under Wilfred Le Gros Clark and then in physiology under E. G. T. Liddell. In the war years, despite being an 'Aryan' German, he was not interned. He 'gave whatever help he could to Britain's war effort … and was proud to be included on the Gestapo's list of important refugees to arrest after the hoped-for invasion of England' (*The Times*, 23). He taught histology in Oxford for some twenty years. His pupils from those days report that he was a good teacher, stimulating, and broader in outlook than most of the dons. He also spent six months as visiting scientist at the National Institutes of Health, Bethesda.

There were some forays into neuropathology, but for the most part Glees's researches were into the anatomy of the normal nervous system. In broad terms his career spanned the last third of the era of classical micro-anatomy that was made possible by the development of the compound light-microscope and by the multitude of new dyestuffs and other substances produced by the rise of chemistry and the chemical industry. Much had already been discovered about the grosser connections of nerve fibres ('wiring diagrams'), especially of those fibres which, having fatty (myelin) sheaths, were relatively easy to stain, whether in health or when degenerating.

Finer details remained elusive because the terminal branches, even of myelinated fibres, are unmyelinated and were therefore undetectable by the older staining methods. Glees's great achievement was to devise a technique that made it possible to trace the terminal branches. His method, with modifications, proved of great value in others' hands, but it is hard to escape the judgement that, by temperament, Glees himself was not patient enough to make best use of the technique. The Glees method was of great importance until the next phase in studying the nervous system: the era of multidisciplinary neuroscience.

Glees wrote two books, *Neuroglia, Morphology and Function* (1955) and *Morphologie und Physiologie des Nervensystems* (Stuttgart, 1957); the latter was too difficult for students and too wide-ranging and superficial to help specialists but, being written with exceptional clarity, was helpful to English-speaking experts in neural science who wished to improve their knowledge of technical German. In 1961 the Oxford University Press published Glees's own English translation.

While Glees's students at Oxford found him friendly and stimulating, most of his colleagues did not. Many thought him over-sure of himself, prickly, even pig-headed. His feeling that he was undervalued was an important factor in his move, in 1961, to a chair in a specially built institute at Göttingen. There

> he was appalled to discover that, before drawing his salary, he was required to certify that he was not a Jew. He made a huge fuss about this Third Reich law (which was quickly rescinded) but was horrified that it had been accepted without question by all the existing professors. He took time in his medical lectures to expose Nazi thinking, and did not shy from naming colleagues who had used their scientific skills to underpin racist ideas. His students regarded him as very unGerman, but he insisted he was merely a good German. (*The Times*, 23)

His first marriage ended in divorce in 1970, and in the same year he married Frauke Schulmeyer (*b.* 1940), with whom he had one daughter.

After his retirement Glees returned to Cambridge in 1978, where, to the surprise of Hans Kuypers, who arrived in the mid-1980s as head of the department of anatomy, he had a toehold in the department and also did some college teaching. After about nine years he went back to Göttingen to live near a married daughter, a doctor. Retaining a clear mind to the last, he died on 18 July 1999, aged ninety, survived by his second wife, Frauke, his first wife, Eva, with whom he kept in close touch, and by three daughters and two sons. GORDON WRIGHT

Sources *The Times* (4 Aug 1999) • private information (2004) • m. cert. [Eva Löb] • A. A. Straus and W. Röder, eds., *International biographical dictionary of central European émigrés, 1933–45*, 2/1 (1983), 381–2

Likenesses photograph, repro. in *The Times*

Gleichen. For this title name *see* Victor, prince of Hohenlohe-Langenburg [*known as* Count Gleichen] (1833–1891).

Gleichen, Lady Feodora Georgina Maud (1861–1922), sculptor, was born in London on 20 December 1861, the eldest daughter of Admiral Prince *Victor Ferdinand Franz Eugen Adolf Constantin Friedrich of Hohenlohe-Langenburg (1833–1891), a naval officer and, from 1866, a sculptor, the son of Prince Ernest of Hohenlohe-Langenburg and Queen Victoria's half-sister Feodora. Her mother was Laura Williamina, youngest daughter of Sir George Francis *Seymour, admiral of the fleet. Feodora's father assumed the family title Gleichen following his morganatic marriage in 1861 and used it until 1885. In 1917, when George V decided to relinquish the royal family's German titles, Countess Feodora and her siblings abandoned theirs and assumed the courtesy titles of the children of a marquess; she then became known as Lady Feodora Gleichen.

Feodora studied art in her father's studio and then for four years under Alphonse Legros at the Slade School of Fine Art, University College, London; she completed her studies in Rome, from 1891 taking a studio there for several winters. Neither particularly innovative nor merely amateurish, Lady Feodora exhibited regularly at the Royal Academy from 1892 and worked seriously at her art, right up to the year of her death, with no diminution in quality or quantity of exhibitions and commissions. Her obituary in *The Times* (23 February 1922) accorded her an 'unassuming' character, yet she was represented worldwide with works which ranged from monumental public ones to more intimately scaled pieces. An important early commission, for the children's hospital in Montreal, Quebec, was the life-size group of Queen Victoria surrounded by children (1895).

Lady Feodora was successful in open competitions: for example, her decorative relief (signed and dated 'Countess Feodora Gleichen sc. 1906'), which won first prize, was selected for the exterior of the National Art Gallery of New South Wales in Sydney, Australia; and she won the anonymous competition for the Edward VII memorial at Windsor (1912, outside the King Edward VII Hospital) entirely on her merit, not, as might be inferred, through family connections—a fact stressed by her younger sister, the painter Helena Emily Gleichen (1873–1947), in her book *Contacts and Contrasts: Reminiscences* (1940). Her statue of Florence Nightingale (1914) is outside the Royal Infirmary at Derby; and her memorial to the fallen of the 37th (British) division (which had been commanded by her brother, Lord Albert Edward Wilfred Gleichen), at Monchy-le-Preux in France, was unveiled in October 1921. The First World War memorial at the Royal Military College, Sandhurst, Berkshire, is a reproduction of the one in France.

Lady Feodora's only public work in London is the Diana fountain in Rotten Row, Hyde Park, a bronze figure of the nude goddess shooting an arrow; it was originally made

Lady Feodora Georgina Maud Gleichen (1861–1922), by unknown photographer

for Sir Walter Palmer's garden at Frognal, Ascot, Berkshire, in 1899 and was presented to Hyde Park by Lady Palmer in 1906. Lady Feodora also produced medals, and a number of portrait busts, including two of Queen Victoria, and among her last works was a head of the king of Iraq, Feisal I (1921; location in 1940 Museum of Baghdad, Iraq). Besides modelling for bronzes and carving in stone and marble, she experimented with combinations of materials, as in a bronze, enamel, and ivory looking-glass (exh. RA, 1897; illustrated in *The Studio*, May 1898, 264) and bas-reliefs (some of children), for example *Musica celesta* (date unknown, Much Marcle church, Herefordshire), a slate panel incorporating ivory. Her sculpture, including another hand-mirror in jade and bronze, won a bronze medal at the Paris Universal Exhibition of 1900. Shortly before her death the French government made her a member of the Légion d'honneur for her work at Monchy-le-Preux. She died, unmarried, on 22 February 1922 in her grace-and-favour apartment in Engine Court, St James's Palace, London, put at the disposal of her parents by Queen Victoria. Posthumously, she was made the first woman member of the Royal Society of British Sculptors.

ANDREA GARRIHY

Sources Lady H. Gleichen, *Contacts and contrasts: reminiscences* (1940) • *Life and work of Feodora Gleichen* (privately printed, 1934) • *The Times* (23 Feb 1922) • M. H. Spielmann, *British sculpture and sculptors of to-day* (1901), 161 • Graves, *RA exhibitors* • 'Studio-talk', *The Studio*, 13 (1898), 262–77, esp. 262, 264, 266 • P. Dunford, *A biographical dictionary of women artists in Europe and America since 1850* (1990), 110–11 • *CGPLA Eng. & Wales* (1922) • *DNB*

Archives Courtauld Inst., photographs • Royal Society of British Sculptors, London, file relating to award | Royal Collection, London, index

Likenesses K. Thomson, oils, 1882, Osborne House, Isle of Wight • photograph, NPG; repro. in *Life and work of Feodora Gleichen* [*see illus.*] • photograph, repro. in Gleichen, *Contacts and contrasts* • photograph

Wealth at death £18,302 2*s*. 5*d*.: probate, 12 May 1922, *CGPLA Eng. & Wales*

Gleig, George (1753–1840), Scottish Episcopal bishop of Brechin, was born on his father's farm at Boghall, in the parish of Arbuthnott, Kincardineshire, on 12 May 1753. His family, about which no further details are known, was Scottish episcopalian, and had suffered for its attachment to the Stuart cause. After some instruction at the school in Arbuthnott he entered King's College, Aberdeen, aged about thirteen. He there won first prizes in mathematics and the moral and physical sciences, and graduated MA on 29 March 1773. In the same year he took orders in the Scottish Episcopal church and was appointed to the charge of Crail and Pittenweem, Fife. With light parochial duties Gleig had time to write contributions to the *Scots Magazine* and other periodicals from 1776.

Gleig was foremost among those working for relaxation of the penal laws operating against the Episcopal church, and he also sought much closer ties with the Church of England. His friend and ally in that campaign was George Berkeley, vice-dean of Canterbury, whom Gleig had first met in 1781 when Berkeley brought his son to study at St Andrews University, and who preached in 1784 in Pittenweem, where the upper floor of a dwelling house was used for worship. Gleig found the Stuart claims to the throne (which he accepted intellectually) an embarrassing obstacle to achieving reconciliation with the Church of England. In 1786 he went to London, chiefly to negotiate for the speedy repeal of the penal laws, and appears to have obtained from Archbishop Moore a draft of a bill to which the government might assent. However, it involved having to pray for George III by name which the Scottish bishops were unwilling to do while Charles Edward Stuart, the Young Pretender, was still alive. The Stuart claimant's death in January 1788 reduced the tension and ended Gleig's plan to organize a petition of Scottish nobles and gentry to lobby parliament for his scheme. Gleig later described his effort as a 'foolish attempt'. It brought upon him the distrust of Bishop John Skinner, already resentful of Gleig's criticism of his consecration sermon in the *Gentleman's Magazine* for 1785 (p. 438) and fearful that Gleig would jettison the Scottish communion office. Though Gleig was elected by the clergy as bishop of Dunkeld in 1786 and 1808, Skinner's hostility voided the result.

In 1787 Gleig moved from Pittenweem to Stirling. Two years later he married Janet (*d*. 1824), widow of a Dr Fulton, and youngest daughter of Robert Hamilton of Kilbrackmont. The couple had one daughter and three sons, all but one of whom predeceased their father. Gleig took part in the campaign of 1790–92 leading to the abolition of the penal laws, and became a frequent contributor to the

Monthly Review, the *Gentleman's Magazine*, the *British Critic*, and the *Anti-Jacobin Review*. He also penned several articles for the third edition of the *Encyclopaedia Britannica*, and was engaged to edit the six remaining volumes on the death of the editor, Colin Macfarquhar, in 1793. He wrote the substantial articles 'Instinct', 'Metaphysics', and 'Theology' himself. The two supplementary volumes, which appeared in 1801, he wrote almost unaided. King's College, Aberdeen, awarded him the degree of LLD in January 1796. He was elected a fellow of the Royal Society of Edinburgh, contributed to their *Transactions*, and also became a fellow of the Society of Antiquaries of Scotland. In addition to various sermons and charges Gleig was the author of *Some account of the life and writings of William Robertson … late principal of the college of Edinburgh* (1812), prefixed to an 1819 edition of Robertson's works, and *Directions for the study of theology in a series of letters from a bishop to his son on his admission into holy orders* (1827). He edited Jerome Lobo's *Voyage to Abyssinia* (1789) and Thomas Stackhouse's *History of the Holy Bible* (1817). Gleig was attacked for lax views upon original sin as expressed in his edition of Stackhouse. His uncompromising anti-Calvinism was well known in his church and had led to charges of Pelagianism, originally levelled after he had published some controversial articles in the *British Critic* (vol. 31, January 1808). The issue resurfaced in the early 1820s and drew him into an acrimonious exchange with the Revd Edward Craig, of the Edinburgh diocese. English high-church sympathizers also felt Gleig had erred too far towards Pelagianism, but they esteemed the regard for the primitive church which was always his ideal.

At Stirling in 1795 Gleig led his congregants to occupy their first regular church building, and his pastoral success assisted his prospects of finally becoming a bishop. On 28 September 1808 Gleig was unanimously chosen coadjutor to John Strachan in the Brechin diocese and, having bound himself to maintain the Scottish office as primus, as Bishop Skinner required, he was consecrated in St Andrew's Church, Aberdeen, on 30 October. He at once drew up a long circular letter addressed to the clergy (18 November) stressing the importance of strictly conforming to the English liturgy in every office except holy communion; Gleig referred to the 1662 prayer book as a 'collection of the most perfect liturgical offices that ever was used in the Christian world' (Lochhead, 56). In 1810 he suggested a scheme to improve the clergy's education, and helped prepare the code of canons of 1811 promulgated in synod at Aberdeen. Gleig had connections with H. H. Norris, the Watsons, and other members of the high-church Hackney Phalanx. In recognition of his services to Anglican unity Gleig was proposed for an Oxford LLD degree in 1810, but he declined the honour.

Having succeeded Strachan as bishop of Brechin in 1810 Gleig was elected primus of the Scottish Episcopal church on 20 August 1816, following Bishop Skinner. During the next twenty-one years the church grew considerably. Gleig's principal achievement came in 1828 when the general synod of the Episcopal church finally ordered the adoption of the English liturgy for morning and evening prayer and gave bishops the right to insist on their clergy using the 1662 communion service. In 1825 he agreed to consecrate Matthew Luscome as bishop with responsibility for Anglicans living in France and Belgium. Otherwise, Gleig largely failed to fulfil the promise of his appointment; his persistent and abortive interference in diocesan elections was much resented. In his own diocese, he made a triennial visitation. In June 1823 he went to London to try to pursue a measure to secure the *regium donum* grant for the Episcopal church. From 1830 age and infirmity greatly hindered Gleig from taking an active part in running the diocese; the visitation of 1831 was his last. By then he was deaf, and had become increasingly obstinate and autocratic. He finally resigned the primacy on 15 February 1837 and received a coadjutor bishop at Brechin a few months later. Gleig died on 9 March 1840 and was buried in a chapel attached to the Greyfriars Church, Stirling. His wife had predeceased him on 15 June 1824. Gleig was survived by his youngest son, George Robert *Gleig, who wrote of his father:

> I know that his brethren feared more than they loved him; but he was a true man, and if hasty at times and somewhat impatient of mediocrities, he was generous and even tender in his feelings. (Lochhead, 60)

NIGEL ASTON

Sources W. Walker, *Life of the Right Reverend George Gleig, bishop of Brechin and primus of the Scottish Episcopal church* (1878) · *GM*, 1st ser., 55 (1785), 437–40, 776–9 · J. P. Lawson, *History of the Scottish Episcopal church* (1843) · G. Grub, *An ecclesiastical history of Scotland*, 4 vols. (1861), vol. 4, pp. 99, 124–35, 174–89 · F. Goldie, *A short history of the Episcopal church in Scotland: from the Restoration to the present time*, 2nd edn (1976), 106–8 · F. C. Mather, 'Church, parliament and penal laws: some Anglo-Scottish interactions in the eighteenth century', *EngHR*, 92 (1977), 540–72 · E. L. de Montluzin, *The anti-Jacobins, 1798–1800: the early contributors to the 'Anti-Jacobin Review'* (1988), 97–9 · G. T. S. Farquhar, *Three bishops of Dunkeld: Alexander, Rose and Watson, 1743–1808* (1915) · M. Lochhead, *Episcopal Scotland in the nineteenth century* (1966), 52–60 · *Correspondence between the Right Rev. Bishop Gleig, &c. and the Rev. Edward Craig, respecting an accusation lately published* (1820) · G. Gleig, *The constitution of the Scottish Episcopal church, concisely stated* (1829) · P. J. Anderson, ed., *Officers and graduates of University and King's College, Aberdeen, MVD–MDCCCLX*, New Spalding Club, 11 (1893), 250, 253

Archives NL Scot., corresp. and family papers | BL, letters to George Berkeley, vice-dean of Canterbury, Add. MS 39312 · BL, letter to John Douglas, bishop of Salisbury, Egerton MS 2186 · BL, letters to Alexander Henderson of Edinburgh, Add. MS 28960 · LPL, Moore MSS

Likenesses H. Adlard, stipple, NPG, Scot. NPG · W. Walker jun., mezzotint (after S. B. Cadlip), BM, Scot. NPG

Gleig, George Robert (1796–1888), chaplain to the armed forces and author, was born on 20 April 1796 at Stirling, the son of George *Gleig, bishop of Brechin, and his wife, Janet Hamilton of Kilbrackmont, Fife. He had two brothers and one sister who survived childhood. He was first taught by his father before going to the local grammar school in Stirling. He entered Glasgow University in 1809. Two years later he was awarded a Snell exhibition to Balliol College, where he remained until 1812. He then secured an ensigncy in the 85th regiment, much against his father's wishes. He readily took to military life, and

George Robert Gleig (1796–1888), by Daniel Maclise, pubd 1875

after a short tour of duty in Ireland, during which time he was promoted to lieutenant, his regiment was ordered in 1813 to join Wellington's army in Spain, which was in pursuit of Marshal Soult's forces. Gleig saw action at the crossing of the Bidassoa, at the siege of Bayonne, at Orthez, and at Toulouse. The 85th was then dispatched to North America where Gleig was present at the attacks on Washington, Baltimore, and New Orleans. He was wounded on several occasions, though accounts differ as to the number of times.

At the end of the Napoleonic wars, Gleig was pressured by his father to resign on half pay and return to Magdalen Hall, Oxford, to continue his studies with the intention of entering the church. Gleig later referred to this decision as a sacrifice of his hopes of an army career, made to satisfy his father. He graduated BA in 1818 and MA in 1821. In 1819 he married the daughter of Captain Cameron of Kinlochleven, with whom he had eight children. He spent most of 1819 in Cumberland preparing for ordination. He was appointed curate of Westwell in Kent, which was worth only £70 per year, and in 1821 the archbishop of Canterbury, who had ordained him in 1820, preferred him to the perpetual curacy of Ash, worth £130 per year. To these the archbishop added in 1822 the rectory of Ivychurch in Romney Marsh, Kent, valued at £250 per year. His initial attempts to supplement his income by taking on students failed and he soon turned to writing to support his growing family. A pamphlet in 1823 attacking the evangelical leanings of the Church Missionary Society was shortly followed by a novel, *The Stranger's Grave*. The novel was a commercial failure, though the pamphlet did mark him out as a staunch conservative in ecclesiastical matters. William Blackwood published three articles by Gleig on church affairs in 1824 and 1825 and these were followed by the serialized account of Gleig's service in the Peninsular campaigns, *The Subaltern*. It was a great success and well written, though some critics thought that it was too preoccupied with the comforts and conditions of a junior officer. Blackwood rushed a book version into press in 1825, and a revised edition was offered in London by John Murray in 1826. While Gleig later complained that he did not gain much financially from *The Subaltern*—he sold the copyright to Blackwood for £150—it did provide the foundation for a long and prolific literary career. By the time he died in 1888, Gleig had written fifty-eight books, including edited collections and revised editions, and he has been identified as the author of 138 articles in contemporary literary journals. Few of his later works achieved the literary acclaim of *The Subaltern*. Instead, Gleig came to be viewed as a sturdy workhorse, a writer of the cut-and-paste school who, by identifying and ordering scraps of information, could dash off articles and books at short notice, especially on military, church, and imperial affairs. Gleig sought to inculcate in his readers a conservative, loyalist, and patriotic appreciation of Britain's character and destiny. An acquaintanceship with James Cumming of the Board of Control resulted in several articles on India under the pseudonym 'An Old Indian'. Cumming also introduced Gleig to the widow and literary executor of Major-General Thomas Munro, who commissioned Gleig to write a three-volume life of Thomas Munro, published in 1830.

The success of *The Subaltern* also provided Gleig with an introduction to the duke of Wellington who was subsequently the recipient of Gleig's numerous political recommendations and pleas for patronage. Wellington was at best a half-hearted patron, though he was godfather to at least two of Gleig's children. Gleig firmly identified with Wellington over questions of church and state, though the two would later differ over military affairs. Gleig unsuccessfully pressed upon Wellington in 1831 that opponents of parliamentary reform should purchase rural newspapers to combat the whigs and their supporters. Gleig himself was briefly editor and part proprietor of the *Kentish Gazette*, through which he countered calls for political reform. He was also active as a justice of the peace in Kent during the agrarian protests of 1830–31. Lord John Russell appointed Gleig chaplain of Chelsea Hospital in 1834 with an annual salary of £300, though Gleig's public opposition to the whigs made this a controversial appointment.

Gleig's writing output continued with the publication of a four-volume *History of India* (1830–35), the *Chronicles of Waltham* (1834), *The Hussar* (1837), *Chelsea Hospital, and its*

Traditions (1838), the *Sketch of the Military History of Great Britain* (1845), *Sale's Brigade in Afghanistan* (1847), the *Story of the Battle of Waterloo* (1847), and biographies of Clive and Hastings. He also produced for soldiers' use several catechisms and collections of his sermons. T. B. Macaulay described his *Memoirs of the Life of the Right Honourable Warren Hastings* (1841) as the 'worst book ever written' (Wilson, 156), alleging that it was the product of an alliance of Hastings's supporters who 'bound themselves to furnish papers' and Gleig who 'bound himself to furnish praise' (Macaulay, *Warren Hastings*, 1843, 1). There is evidence in his lives of Munro and Hastings that Gleig deliberately altered or fabricated original correspondence in his pursuit of an instructional story, offering some support to Macaulay's complaint that Gleig suffered from 'Furor Biographicus', a condition that transformed the biographer into the hagiographer.

Gleig was appointed chaplain-general of the forces in 1844, upon the recommendation of Henry Hardinge, the secretary for war, and two years later he added the office of inspector-general of military schools. Meanwhile he retained the office and salary of chaplain of Chelsea Hospital. However, Gleig had eyes on the see of Calcutta; when he was not made bishop he blamed Hardinge, and in retaliation penned an article (1846) on the conduct of the Anglo-Sikh War that praised General Hugh Gough's handling of the campaign and held Hardinge responsible for the initial setbacks. Gleig also complained to Peel, protesting that the office of chaplain-general was 'of small repute or influence, and remunerated at a rate not quite equal to the pay of a double-entry clerk'. Known for his tactlessness and ambition, Gleig was described by Hardinge at this time as 'a disappointed man and not at all times a very discreet man' (*Letters of … Hardinge*, 186). Differences of opinion over army education with the secretary of war, Lord Panmure, led to Gleig resigning the office of inspector-general in 1857, though he continued as chaplain-general until 1875. From 1848 until his death he was prebendary of Willesden in St Paul's Cathedral. As chaplain-general and especially as inspector-general of military education, Gleig argued that reforming the religious and educational life of regiments would make for a better disciplined and more popular army. He instituted regulations to govern military schoolmasters and barrack libraries and introduced a normal school to train regimental teachers, where a combination of spiritual and useful knowledge was emphasized. Yet Gleig's commitment to reform had its limits, and he spoke out in 1848, 1857, and 1867 against those who favoured raising soldiers' pay and improving their diet.

Old age and several bouts of bronchitis led to Gleig's death on 9 July 1888 at Bylands, a cottage in the grounds of Stratfield Saye that had been set aside for his use by the second duke of Wellington. He was buried in the churchyard of Stratfield Saye. DOUGLAS M. PEERS

Sources G. R. Gleig, *Personal reminiscences of the first duke of Wellington*, ed. M. Gleig (1904) • D. R. Jones, 'The Reverend G. R. Gleig and early Victorian army education', MA diss., Queen's University, Belfast, 1983 • A. C. E. Jarvis, 'My predecessors in office, the Rev. G. R. Gleig', *Quarterly Journal of the Royal Army Chaplains' Department*, 4 (1931), 14–77, 320–58; 5 (1935), 9–29 • E. B. Hamley, 'The death of Mr Gleig', *Blackwood*, 144 (1888), 311–14 • W. Bates, *The Maclise portrait gallery of illustrious literary characters*, new edn (1898) • Boase, *Mod. Eng. biog.* • *The Greville diary*, ed. P. W. Wilson, 2 vols. (1927) • *The letters of the first Viscount Hardinge of Lahore … 1844–1847*, ed. B. S. Singh, CS, 4th ser., 32 (1986) • G. R. Gleig, 'Memoirs of a long life of four score years', NL Scot., MS 3872 • D. M. Peers, '"Those noble exemplars of the true military tradition": constructions of the Indian army in the mid-Victorian press', *Modern Asian Studies*, 31 (1997), 109–42

Archives BL, corresp., etc., Add. MSS 28510, 29233, 29240 • Bodl. Oxf., corresp. • NL Scot., corresp. and reminiscences, MS 3869–3872 • S. Antiquaries, Lond., notes and sketches relating to Richborough | BL, corresp. with Sir Robert Peel, Add. MSS 40396, 40398, 40422, 40559 • BL IOIC, letters to Lady Munro, MSS Eur F 151/197 • BL OIOC, Thomas Munro MSS • Bodl. Oxf., letters to Joseph Murray • Lpool RO, letters to fourteenth earl of Derby • NL Scot., corresp. with Blackwoods; corresp. with Sir George Brown; corresp. with Archibald Constable; letters to J. G. Lockhart; corresp. with second Lord Panmure • PRO, Russell MSS • U. Southampton L., letters to first duke of Wellington

Likenesses D. Maclise, lithograph, pubd 1875, NPG [*see illus.*] • W. Drummond, lithograph (after E. U. Eddis), BM; repro. in *Athenaeum portraits*, 31 (1836) • D. Maclise, drawing (after lithograph, pubd 1875), V&A • drawing, Royal Army Chaplain's Department • pen-and-ink sketch, repro. in Bates, *Maclise portrait gallery*

Wealth at death £1629 5*s*.: resworn administration, April 1889, *CGPLA Eng. & Wales* (1888)

Gleitze, Mercedes (1900–1981), swimmer, was born at 124 Freshfield Road, Brighton, on 18 November 1900, the youngest of three daughters (there were no sons) of Heinrich Gleitze, journeyman baker, and his wife, Anna Kurr, a language teacher. She spent her childhood partly in Brighton and partly with her grandparents in Herzogenaurach, Bavaria, and was educated in both countries, including two years at the Maria Stern Convent School, Nördlingen. In the early 1920s, while working as a bilingual secretary in Westminster, she spent her spare time training in the Thames to become a long-distance swimmer. In 1923 she set a British ladies' record for Thames swimming (10 hr 45 min.). In 1927 she swam the 120 miles from London to Folkestone in stages; and on 7 October 1927, at her eighth attempt, she became the first Englishwoman to swim the channel (from France to England in 15 hr 15 min.). In 1928 she became the first person ever to swim the Straits of Gibraltar (in 12 hr 50 min.). Between 1927 and 1932 she also swam the Wash, Lough Neagh, from Portstewart in Ulster to Moville in the Irish Free State, Loch Ryan, the Firth of Forth, around the Isle of Man (100 miles) in stages, the Hellespont (from Europe to Asia Minor), the Sea of Marmora, Wellington harbour, Galway Bay, and from Cape Town to Robben Island, both ways (the first person to complete the double), as well as many more swims in South Africa, New Zealand, and Australia. During these years she also held the British record for endurance swimming, extending it from 26 hr in January 1930 to 44 hr 30 min. by the end of the year, then to 45 hr in 1931, and finally to 46 hr in 1932. These swims were mainly in municipal baths, and she was supported by the community singing of the thousands of people who filed in to see her perform. She retired in 1932.

Mercedes Gleitze (1900–1981), by J. P. Bamber

Driven by an urge to alleviate poverty during the depression, Gleitze worked hard to secure sponsorship for her swims and in 1928 set up a trust fund to finance the Mercedes Gleitze homes for destitute men and women. She purchased a large eight-bedroomed house in Leicester, and had it converted into flats, which were then made available to homeless families. These homes were run under the caretakership of the Leicester Rotary club, which was involved in a scheme to move families from distressed areas in the north of England to Leicester; the Mercedes Gleitze homes provided temporary accommodation until employment and permanent lodgings could be found. The homes were used for this purpose from 1933 until the outbreak of war in 1939, when they were used by the Leicester Committee for Refugees from Czechoslovakia. Although her homes were destroyed by enemy action in November 1940, her charity is still active under the trusteeship of the Family Welfare Association. In keeping with the spirit of the founder's intention, its funds are targeted towards grants to alleviate need arising from homelessness—the demand for such support being as great at the start of the twenty-first century as when she first set up the trust.

On 9 August 1930, at St Paul's Roman Catholic Church, Dover, Mercedes Gleitze, whose occupation was recorded as professional swimmer, married Patrick Joseph Carey (1904–1983), originally of Dublin, a sheet metal engineer and later a technical representative, the son of Patrick Carey, also a sheet metal engineer. They had two daughters and a son. Gleitze died at Colindale Hospital, London, on 9 February 1981, and was cremated three days later at Hendon crematorium.

Doloranda Hannah Pember

Sources swimming logs and maritime charts certified by pilots and other witnesses, priv. coll. [in the possession of Gleitze's daughter] • documents relating to the establishment of a trust fund for the purpose of maintaining the Mercedes Gleitze homes for destitute men and women, charity commission no. 252248 (A107738) • b. cert. • m. cert. • d. cert. • personal knowledge (2004)
Archives priv. coll., MSS | FILM BFI NFTVA, documentary footage
Likenesses photograph, 1928, Hult. Arch. • J. P. Bamber, photograph, NPG [*see illus.*] • photographs, priv. coll.

Glemham, Edward (*d.* in or after **1594**), privateer, was from Benhall in Suffolk. Although he was described as 'esquire', nothing is known of his parents or his early life, but in the summer of 1590 he was of sufficient means to fit out the 240 ton ship *Edward Constance* at his own expense. As recounted in an anonymous pamphlet of 1591, he left his wife and the 'pitteous mone of his sweet children' (*The Honourable Actions*, sig. A2v) and sailed from Gravesend that August for the Canaries. After two months of fruitless cruising he ran short of victuals and so resolved to head for the Azores where, with eighty-six men, he effected a landing on the island of St George. However, after surprising the Spanish there he was unable to hold the island and so concluded a truce with the governor; in exchange for 1000 crowns and supplies for his ship, he agreed to depart.

After leaving the island Glemham met with six Spanish galleons which pursued him. Becalmed, he was forced to do battle before escaping to Algiers for repairs. There he agreed to escort a French vessel home but the small convoy was assailed by four Spanish ships off Gibraltar. Although the French ship managed to avoid serious damage Glemham was forced to retire again to Algiers for more repairs. After refitting, he decided to sail the Mediterranean where, on 4 December 1591, he seized a Venetian ship, the *Manicella*, laden with 200 chests of sugar and other valuable commodities, in flagrant breach of Queen Elizabeth's decree that Venetian shipping ought not to be molested. When Glemham reached England some months later he discovered that the Venetian agent in London had lodged a complaint against him in the admiralty. Although Glemham claimed that the goods he had taken belonged to a Portuguese merchant on the ship, and he had forced the latter to subscribe a statement to this effect, his goods and ship were sequestered. The judgment of the admiralty court was against Glemham and in September 1592 he tried unsuccessfully to sell the *Edward Constance*.

Glemham embarked on a second voyage in February 1594, described in *Newes from the Levane Seas* (1594), as general of a fleet of three ships. But after searching for the pope's treasure ship and harassing shipping in the western Mediterranean for several months, to little avail, he sailed to Algiers to resupply. Short of money, he sent eight mariners ashore as pledges for future payment; when he returned several months later for more supplies he sent another eight men ashore, departing without them under cover of a storm. Shortly after returning to England in late 1594, Glemham died in poverty; what few assets remained were promptly sold to repay his creditors. In March 1598 his son, Thomas, became an apprentice to Francis Cockaine of the Skinners' Company.

From 1595 to 1600 the privy council made efforts to raise money to ransom the men Glemham had pawned in Algiers, although half of them had, by 1596, converted to Islam and been released. Though a national appeal by the bishops of the country failed to raise the necessary sum, the master and wardens of Trinity House in London eventually provided the difference and the men were freed in 1600. RICHARD RAISWELL

Sources H. R., *Newes from the Levane Seas* (1594) [repr. in *Illustrations of Old English literature*, vol. 1, ed. J. P. Collier (1866)] • *The honourable actions of that most famous and valiant Englishman, Edward Glemham* (1591) • *Miscellanea genealogica et heraldica*, ed. J. J. Howard, vol. 1, ser. 3 (1896), 150 • N. A. M. Rodger, *The safeguard of the sea: a naval history of Britain*, 1: *660–1649* (1997), 345 • *VCH Suffolk*, 2.215 • *APC*, *1591–2, 1595–1600* • *List and analysis of state papers: foreign, Elizabeth*, vol. 3 (June 1591–April 1592), no. 816; vol. 6 (Jan 1595–Dec 1595), no. 458 • *CSP Venice*, *1592–1603*, 20 • *CSP dom.*, *1591–4*, 221, 264–5

Glemham, Sir Thomas (1595–1649), royalist army officer, was the son and heir of Sir Henry Glemham (*d.* 1632), deputy lieutenant and MP, of Glemham Hall, Suffolk, and his wife, Anne Sackville, eldest daughter of Thomas *Sackville, Lord Buckhurst and later first earl of Dorset, and his wife, Cicely. Sir Henry Glemham inherited extensive lands in Suffolk, Norfolk, Lincolnshire, Nottinghamshire, and Kent, and Clarendon reflected that 'Sir Thomas Glemham was a gentleman of noble extraction and a fair fortune' (Clarendon, *Hist. rebellion*, 1888, 2.286). After matriculating at Trinity College, Oxford, in 1610, he left the university to pursue a military career and was knighted by James I on 10 September 1617. About 1620 he married Katherine Vanlore, daughter of Sir Peter *Vanlore of Fenchurch Street, London, a wealthy Dutch merchant; in or close to 1630 he married Mary Soame.

Glemham, who spent much time with his cousin, the third earl of Dorset, was MP for Reigate (1621–2) and Aldeburgh (1625–6). He was taken prisoner during the disastrous Isle de Ré expedition, and was later present at the siege of 's-Hertogenbosch in 1629. On returning to England he served as a JP and deputy lieutenant for Suffolk. He was implicated in the soap monopoly, and was 'a fierce presser of the recusancy laws from which he hoped to profit' (Newman, 158), yet he was also noted as a supporter of common rights against enclosure in Suffolk. During the second bishops' war he commanded a west country regiment of 1200 foot, three quarters of whose officers joined Glemham in his subsequent royalist allegiance in the civil war.

On his way to York on 17 March 1642 the king discussed with Glemham a strategy to cut off the water supply of the rebellious town of Hull, and in August Glemham was appointed to command the Yorkshire gentry's cavalry resisting incursions from parliamentarian Hull. Although a commissioner of array for Suffolk, he was appointed governor of York and second-in-command to the earl of Cumberland. He was unable to dislodge the parliamentarian blockade of the city until the arrival in York of the earl of Newcastle's royalist army in December 1642. He remained as colonel of foot and governor until November 1643, when Newcastle appointed him colonel-general of Northumberland to prepare defences against the Scots. In April 1644 he was recalled to govern York during the ensuing siege. After the battle of Marston Moor he held the city for two weeks before negotiating generous terms for surrender on 16 July.

As colonel-general of the royalist northern army's remnants, Glemham reassembled 3000 men in Cumberland in August 1644, but he was forced into another siege, defending Carlisle from the Scots, where 'he was the first man that taught soldiers to eat cats and dogs' (D. Lloyd, ed., *Memoires of … Excellent Personages*, 1668, 552). After enduring much extremity he surrendered the town on honourable terms on 25 June 1645, and was escorted by the Scots to Hereford. With his 200 survivors he joined the king at Cardiff in August, but he went unrewarded while Charles Gerard was given 'unseasonable preferment' (Clarendon, *Hist. rebellion*, 1888, 4.76–7) and created Baron Gerard of Brandon in Suffolk, despite Glemham's being an heir of the Brandons and already holding claim to the land. Glemham's regiment briefly formed the king's life guard before he was appointed governor of Oxford on 2 October 1645. He was created DCL by Oxford University and he greatly improved the fortifications and defences. He was personally opposed to surrender when the king ordered him to do so on 19 May 1646, but he finally surrendered the city on terms on 24 June 1646.

Imprisoned in the Fleet for about a month, Glemham petitioned the speaker on 16 August that this was in breach of Oxford's terms of surrender. The House of Commons ordered his release on 21 August, but as he was not merely a prisoner of state, being also confined for debt, parliament had to indemnify the sheriffs to release him. Clarendon implied that Glemham's fortune had diminished owing to his lengthy military service overseas (Clarendon, *Hist. rebellion*, 1888, 2.286). His son, Sackville, compounded for his estates on his behalf for the sum of £951 15*s*, and his estate was noted as discharged from sequestration only in March 1648. Nevertheless Glemham was active during the second civil war, and English parliamentary commissioners failed in their demand for his surrender from the parliament of Scotland on 31 March 1648. Having been reported on the streets of Edinburgh on 5 April, he assisted Sir Philip Musgrave's capture of Carlisle on 29 April. Early in May royalist sympathizers in York mistook parliamentarian cavalry for royalist insurgents, shouting 'Glenham was come, Glenham was come' (Ashton, 367), but he seems to have taken no further part in the war.

One historian has assessed him as a commander of 'remarkable competence and resilience' (Newman, 158), and he was certainly adept at defending towns beyond hope of relief against high odds. Having made his will on 22 January 1648 he went into exile in France, where he died in 1649. Although his exact date of death is uncertain, his brother Dr Henry Glemham proved his will on 13 March 1650 and arranged for his body to be buried at Little Glemham, Suffolk. ANDREW J. HOPPER

Sources P. R. Newman, *Royalist officers in England and Wales, 1642–1660: a biographical dictionary* (1981) • Foster, *Alum. Oxon.* • A. Fletcher, *The outbreak of the English civil war* (1981) • M. C. Fissel, *The bishops' wars: Charles I's campaigns against Scotland, 1638–1640* (1994) • J. E. Mousley, 'Glemham, Sir Henry', HoP, *Commons, 1558–1603*, 2.196–7 • W. C. Metcalfe, ed., *The visitations of Suffolk* (1882) • C. V. Wedgwood, *The king's war, 1641–1647* (1958) • I. Tullie, *A narrative of the siege of Carlisle, in 1644 and 1645*, ed. S. Jefferson (1840) • Wood, *Ath. Oxon.* • H. Cary, ed., *Memorials of the great civil war in England from 1646 to 1652*, 2 (1842) • R. Ashton, *Counter-revolution: the second civil war and its origins, 1646–8* (1994) • M. A. E. Green, ed., *Calendar of the proceedings of the committee for compounding … 1643–1660*, 2, PRO (1890) • private information (2004) [G. Blackwood] • *The diaries of Lady Anne Clifford*, ed. D. J. H. Clifford (1990) • *CSP dom., addenda, 1625–49* • GEC, *Peerage*, new edn • GEC, *Baronetage* • G. R. Smith and M. Toynbee, *Leaders of the civil wars, 1642–1648* (1977) • W. Emberton, *The English civil war day by day* (1995) • will, PRO, PROB 11/2211, sig. 39

Archives BL, Add. MSS 5497, fol. 133; 18982, fol. 75; 39245, fols. 160–61

Glen, Andrew (1665/6–1732), botanist, was born at Hathern, Leicestershire. He graduated BA from Jesus College, Cambridge, in 1683, and MA in 1687. According to Pulteney he was a fellow of St John's College, but Baker does not give his name in his list of fellows; according to the *Graduati Cantabr.* he was fellow of Jesus College. Glen was a friend of John Ray and it was probably through him that he became interested in botany. In 1685 he formed a herbarium of 700 native and 200 foreign plants, some of which were collected on a tour of the continent. He afterwards travelled in Sweden and spent some time in Turin, where in 1692 he collected a further 200 specimens. In 1694 he returned to Hathern as rector, after which time he seems to have paid little attention to botany. His wife, Elizabeth, whom he married before 1699, died in 1705, leaving three daughters, Elizabeth, Mary, and Margaret. Glen himself died at Hathern, where he was buried, on 1 September 1732. His only published work was an assize sermon, dated 1707. G. S. Boulger, *rev.* P. E. Kell

Sources R. Pulteney, *Historical and biographical sketches of the progress of botany in England*, 2 (1790), 63–4 • J. Nichols, *The history and antiquities of the county of Leicester*, 3/2 (1804), 846 • A. R. Horwood and C. W. F. Noel, *The flora of Leicestershire and Rutland … with biographies of former botanists (1620–1933)* (1933), clxxxvii–clxxxviii • Nichols, *Lit. anecdotes*, 8.196

Glen, David (1853–1916), bagpipe maker and publisher of highland bagpipe music, was born on 3 April 1853 at 30 St Andrew Square, Edinburgh, one of the nine children of Alexander Glen (1801–1873), bagpipe maker, and his second wife, Ann Marshall (*b. c.*1816). He married Catherine Stewart in 1876, and they had five children, including sons, Alexander (1877–1951) and David (1883–1958). David Glen was born into a prominent musical dynasty founded by his father and his uncle Thomas Glen (1804–1873), whose sons John (1833–1904) and Robert (1835–1911), of the firm J. and R. Glen, were also important instrument makers and early music scholars. David Glen was taught piping by Gilbert Gordon, piper to Lord Panmure, and was apparently an excellent player. His firm David Glen & Sons was an important pipe-making company and the leading publisher of bagpipe music in Scotland during the later nineteenth and early twentieth centuries.

Glen came at a critical point in the transition of pipe music from an oral to a predominantly written form. Written canntaireachd, the traditional syllabic notation system, had long been in use, but to record piobaireachd—the classical music of the pipe—using the staff notation conventions pioneered by Donald MacDonald (1767–1840) and his successors made for bulky and expensive volumes and the music continued to be transmitted mainly by oral–aural processes well into the nineteenth century. But piping flourished in the new urban environment and Glen responded to the demand for affordable scores by being the first to publish in a variety of formats. His titles included *David Glen's Collection of Highland Bagpipe Music* (1876–1900), the definitive collection of light music for the pipe of its period, and one of the musical treasures of Victorian Scotland. The seventeen parts eventually contained more than 1000 tunes. Some 80,000 copies were sold and it remained in print for nearly a century.

Glen's *Collection of Ancient Piobaireachd or Highland Bagpipe Music* (1880–1907) was issued in seven parts and contained 100 tunes, covering the classic heart of the repertory. The collection could be bought as a bound volume with historical notes by 'Fionn' (the journalist and Celtic scholar Henry Whyte (1852–1913)), in separate parts, or as single tunes. In 1900 Glen issued *Music of the Clan MacLean*, which included a number of little-known piobaireachds which he transcribed from the playing of John Johnston of Coll, a musical heir of the Rankins of Mull. Glen's final large work was *The Edinburgh Collection of Highland Bagpipe Music: Pibrochs, Marches, Quicksteps, Strathspeys, Reels & Jigs*, which contained more than 500 tunes and was issued in eleven parts (1903–8).

Glen was a tireless collector of piobaireachd, and his manuscript collection (NL Scot. 22120) was one of the largest ever assembled. He was at the centre of a group of like-minded people, friends and fellow pipe-music editors Charles Bannatyne (1867–1924), John McLennan (1843–1923), and Charles Simeon Thomason (1833–1911), who gave him access to the historically important unpublished collections, and leading players such as Colin Cameron (1843–1916) and John MacDougall Gillies (1855–1925), who also supplied him with material. By the early years of the twentieth century they had published among them virtually the whole piobaireachd repertory in a variety of formats, faithfully edited to reflect its traditional idiom and stylistic variety. But in 1903 the Piobaireachd Society was founded by a group of influential gentlemen amateurs possessed by fears about the well-being of tradition, who felt called upon to rescue piobaireachd from the pipers. Although few of them could actually play the pipes, they quickly took control of judging at the major competitions and issued prescribed scores for these events, edited by themselves. Glen offered to supply the music at reduced price but the society decreed that only its own settings would be acceptable, advertising, 'To pipers. Caution … This is the only Edition authorised … and from which the competitors will be judged' (*Oban Times*, 1 April 1905). The society continued to publish its own scores, ignoring protests from players about their inaccuracy and departure from traditional idiom. By 1956 the society's editor, Archibald Campbell of Kilberry (1877–1963), could declare that 'we are absolutely the only suppliers of such music today' (Piobaireachd Society papers, NL Scot., Acc. 9103/11, correspondence, 1955–7, 5 Jan 1956). Although they were musically the poorest of all the published sources, the institutional power of the Piobaireachd Society ensured that their settings became the standard twentieth-century text.

Glen's piobaireachd scores remained in esteem among expert performers—John MacDonald of Inverness (1865–1953) described them in 1940 as 'the most reliable we have today' (Donaldson, 444)—but they became increasingly difficult to obtain. By the end of the twentieth century few of even the greatest libraries had copies of all Glen's publications and his major contribution to Scottish traditional music had still to receive appropriate recognition. Glen died of a stroke at 5 Brunton Place, Edinburgh, on 25 June 1916. WILLIAM DONALDSON

Sources W. Donaldson, *The highland pipe and Scottish society, 1750–1950* (2000) • D. Glen, ed., *David Glen's collection of highland bagpipe music*, 17 vols. (1876–1900) • D. Glen, ed., *Collection of ancient piobaireachd or highland bagpipe music*, 7 vols. (1880–1907) • D. Glen, ed., *Music of the clan MacLean* (1900) • D. Glen, ed., *The Edinburgh collection of highland bagpipe music: pibrochs, marches, quicksteps, strathspeys, reels & jigs*, 11 vols. (1903–8) • D. Glen, 'The Piobaireachd Society of Scotland', *Oban Times* (26 Sept 1903) • D. Glen, 'Piobaireachd movements', *Oban Times* (16 April 1910) • D. Glen, 'Piobaireachd Society's music', *Oban Times* (28 May 1910) • R. D. Cannon, *A bibliography of bagpipe music* (1980) • J. Campbell, *Highland bagpipe makers* (2001) • correspondence, 1955–7, NL Scot., Piobaireachd Society MS Acc. 9103/11 • R. D. Cannon, 'The Glen family', *Piping Times*, 21/11 (1968–9), 7–9 • D. Johnson and A. Myers, 'Glen', *New Grove*, 2nd edn • J. Campbell, 'Notices of bagpipe makers, part 5', *Piping Times*, 50/10 (1997–8), 17–22 • 'To pipers. Caution', *Oban Times* (1 April 1905) • 'The late Mr David Glen, bagpipe maker', *Oban Times* (8 July 1916) • b. cert. • d. cert.

Archives NL Scot., MS 22120

Wealth at death £4191 13s. 4d.

Glen, James (1701–1777), colonial governor, was born in Linlithgow, the first of the eight children of Alexander Glen (*d.* 1722?), provost of Linlithgow, and Marion, the daughter of James Graham of Edinburgh. Alexander Glen owned Longcroft, a 114 acre estate in Linlithgow, and a liferent from the Bonnytoun estate, all of which he bequeathed to James. Like numerous other Scots, James Glen studied law at the University of Leiden, where he became more interested in Roman law than the common law. Although he was a member of St Michael's Presbyterian Church in Linlithgow, Glen did not show interest in predestination or theology in general. He made a valiant effort later as royal governor of South Carolina to administer the Anglican church there.

In Scotland, Glen like his father served as provost of his native Linlithgow, a burgh between Edinburgh and Stirling, from 1724 to 1726 and from 1730 to 1736. As provost, or chief magistrate, he exercised complete control over the burgh; it was a lucrative post that required very little responsibility. He did not favour Scottish independence, participated in the selection of members of parliament, and made official trips to London. In London, he mixed with the British aristocracy. He became friends with Spencer Compton, earl of Wilmington, and later married his illegitimate daughter, Elizabeth Wilson, who was also the granddaughter of Sir William Wilson. He served as keeper of the royal palace of the Stuarts in Linlithgow and keeper of Blackness Castle on the Scottish coast. In 1738 he became both watchman of the salt duty at the port of Bo'ness and Scotland's inspector of state-seized prohibited and untaxed goods. These appointments brought him prestige and an annual salary of £30 sterling.

Although the crown appointed Glen governor of South Carolina, a post secured by Wilmington in 1738, he delayed going there until 1743, after he had resolved a dispute over his salary. He argued that his inherited income would not be enough for him to maintain the life of a planter and that the provincial assembly could not be trusted to pay him. The crown finally agreed to an annual salary of £800 and permission for the assembly to provide him a house or house rent. Glen's sixteen-page commission gave him a royal council of twelve members and the right to call and dismiss general assemblies, make and veto laws, supervise public money, issue land grants, appoint judges, and raise and command military forces.

Glen enjoyed a long and successful tenure in South Carolina from 1743 to 1756. The elaborate ceremony, which included two fifteen-gun salutes, that greeted his arrival in Charles Town on 17 December 1743 disguised the tension that existed between royal officials and the colonists. Although the governor and council thought they should rule with the assistance of the Commons house of assembly, the Commons acted otherwise. It welcomed harmony with the royal officials as they attempted to govern the 25,000 white citizens and 40,000 slaves who lived in South Carolina. Yet, it encroached upon royal prerogatives by selecting the public treasurer, printing paper money, denying the governor the right to make Anglican religious appointments, and setting times for elections. Glen had to make concessions to the Commons in order to raise money.

Despite his weakened position, Glen had some notable accomplishments. He fortified the city of Charles Town and the ports of Beaufort and George Town. He excelled at diplomacy with American Indians, particularly with the neighbouring Cherokee nation, by travelling into dangerous territory for face-to-face negotiations and sometimes entertaining their leaders at his home in Charles Town. Under his leadership the province enjoyed good relations with the Cherokees, Creeks, and Chickasaws, though he could not persuade them to undertake major campaigns against the French. He also controlled licences for Indian traders, sometimes profiting personally from that trade.

Glen struggled to maintain the royal prerogative against the increasing power of the common house of assembly, but he wisely compromised and attempted to persuade the Board of Trade in London to make concessions. He aligned himself with the planters and sometimes showed great compassion for the province. Finding him too sympathetic to South Carolina, the Board of Trade decided to replace him in 1755. His most valuable historical legacy as governor was his account of life and government of the colony, *Descriptions of South Carolina* (1761). His other legacy, good American Indian relations, was quickly demolished by his successor, William Henry Lyttelton.

Glen remained in the province until 1761. He negotiated with Indians who were friendly to the British and participated in the early military campaigns of the Seven Years' War in America (the French and Indian War), including the 1758 campaign led by his cousin, John Forbes, against Fort Duquesne. He made money from the American Indian trade and purchased a small rice plantation and nineteen African slaves. He formed a partnership with John Drayton of Drayton Hall, and later supervised the education of Drayton's four sons in England.

Glen returned to Britain in 1761. He maintained and improved the estates he had inherited from his father in Scotland, but he passed much of his time in London, living at Golden Square. An extrovert, he gave elaborate dinner parties, enjoyed an active social life, and gambled with cards. A widower by the mid-1770s, the surviving portrait of him suggests a man of medium stature with delicate hands and facial features. Although he had no children of his own, he cared for his younger siblings, his nieces, and his nephews. He avoided jeopardizing his comfortable place in royal society, but he appeared to understand and sympathize with American patriots on the eve of their independence.

James Glen died on 18 July 1777. He left an estate worth £1939 sterling to his oldest niece. He was buried at St Michael's Presbyterian Church, adjacent to Linlithgow Palace; his grave is no longer identifiable. A copper replica of his grave marker hangs in the South Carolina state capitol in Columbia. E. STANLY GODBOLD JR.

Sources W. S. Robinson, *James Glen: from Scottish provost to royal governor of South Carolina* (Westport, Connecticut, 1996) · M. E. Sirmans, *Colonial South Carolina: a political history, 1663–1763* (Chapel Hill, NC, 1966) · J. P. Greene, *The quest for power: the lower houses of assembly in the southern royal colonies, 1689–1776* (1963) · R. M. Wier, *Colonial South Carolina: a history* (Millwood, New York, 1983) · D. D. Wallace, *The history of South Carolina*, 4 vols. (1934) · E. McCrady, *The history of South Carolina under the royal government, 1719–1776* (1899) · W. S. Robinson, *The South Carolina colonial frontier, 1607–1763* (Albuquerque, New Mexico, 1979) · C. Hudson, *The southeastern Indians* (Knoxville, Tennessee, 1976)

Archives LUL, answers to the trade commissioners · NA Scot., corresp. and papers · NRA Scotland, priv. coll., papers · University of South Carolina, Columbia, corresp. and papers | PRO, Colonial Office papers, 5 · University of South Carolina, Columbia, South Caroliniana Library, Lady Elizabeth Glen Ramsay collection

Likenesses P. Syners, oils, 1743, priv. coll.

Wealth at death £1939: Robinson, *James Glen*, 131

Glen, William (1778–1849), missionary and biblical translator, was born in Lochwinnoch, Renfrewshire, on 30 January 1778, the son of William Glen, tailor. He matriculated at Glasgow University in 1797 but left without a degree and studied at the theological college of the Associate Synod in Selkirk, under George Lawson. He was ordained minister of a newly formed congregation of Burgher seceders in Annan, Dumfriesshire, on 15 April 1807.

On 28 September 1810 Glen married Margaret Scott of Annan; they had five sons, the eldest two being twins. Glen and his wife provided lodgings in their house for Thomas Carlyle, then mathematics master at his old school, Annan Academy. Carlyle praised Glen in his *Reminiscences* (1881) as 'a most pure and excellent man, of correct superior intellect, and of much modest piety and amiability', and described his wife as 'a handsome, brave, and cheery-hearted woman'.

Glen resigned from Annan in November 1816; his discouragement was partly caused by the friction created in trying to raise sufficient funds to carry on the work of the congregation. He offered his services to the Edinburgh Missionary Society as an overseas candidate, thus fulfilling a youthful ambition. After training, Glen, accompanied by his wife, went as a missionary to Astrakhan in southern Russia, where he remained for five years. He achieved little in the way of conversion but was more successful in his efforts to master the Persian, Arabic, and Turkish languages. About 1823 he began what was to be his principal life's work, the translation of the Old Testament from Hebrew into Persian. He began with Psalms and Proverbs, his translations being published separately by the British and Foreign Bible Society. By the time he returned to Scotland in 1834 his reputation as a Persian scholar was already established.

Glen continued working on his translation in Scotland until 1837, when he was sent to Persia, by the synod of the United Secession church, to complete his labours. He lived in Tabriz and Tehran; in 1843 he returned to Scotland, taking his completed manuscript with him. It was printed by Thomas Constable of Edinburgh and published in 1845, the cost met by the mission board of the United Secession church, aided by a grant of £500 from the British and Foreign Bible Society. In 1845 he was awarded the degree of DD by the University of St Andrews.

Glen volunteered to supervise the distribution of his work in Persia and to circulate with it a new edition of the Persian translation of the New Testament by Henry Martyn. Glen and his son Andrew sailed for Persia by way of Constantinople in 1847. In January 1848 they were received by the shah, who was presented with copies of the Old and New testaments and a translation of *Sketch of the Evidence from Prophecy* (1823) by Alexander Keith. After a short illness Glen died of dysentery in Tehran on 12 January 1849 and was buried there in the Armenian cemetery.

GRAYSON CARTER, *rev.*

Sources *Missionary Record of the United Presbyterian Church* (May 1849), 73–7 · F. Miller, 'Carlyle's missionary friend', *Record*, new ser., 23 (1923), 97–8 [home and foreign mission work of the United Free church of Scotland] · W. Glen, *Journal of a tour from Astrachan to Karass* (1823)

Glen, William (1789–1826), poet, was born in Queen Street, Glasgow, on 14 November 1789, the son of Alexander Glen, a Russia merchant from an old Renfrewshire family, and his wife, Jean Burns. After leaving school Glen, at about the age of seventeen, entered a firm trading with the West Indies. When he had become familiar with the business he went for some years to one of the islands as representative of the firm. On his return to Glasgow he started business for himself, but retired, after going bankrupt, in 1814. An uncle in Russia now supported him, and his mode of life became rather unsettled. For some time he would appear to have lived entirely on his poetic gifts and his social instincts. As a boy Glen eagerly learned of the fallen house of Stuart, and his pathetic song 'Wae's me for Prince Charlie', which is charged with the true Jacobite spirit, constitutes the recognized dirge of the lost cause. Several other songs of Glen's are on occasional themes—such as 'The Battle of Vittoria', 'The Battle Song', and three on Napoleon—and there are love songs and narrative pieces, all more or less meritorious. The Jacobite lament, however, which has made the tune of 'Johnnie Faa' its own, stands out so clearly above all the others that Glen is generally known only as the writer of this one song. He published in 1815 a volume of *Poems, Chiefly Lyrical*.

In 1818 Glen married Catherine Macfarlane, daughter of a Glasgow merchant, and joint tenant with her brother of a farm at Port Monteith, Perthshire. During most of his remaining years Glen lived here, dependent on his wife's resources and his uncle's generosity, and a general favourite in the district. His old weakness for social amusement and late hours still haunted him, and it may have hastened the disease that ultimately proved fatal. Feeling his end approaching, Glen induced his wife to accompany him to Glasgow, on the conclusive plea that it was 'easier to take a living man there than a dead one' (*Political Remains*), and they were not long settled when he died there, in December 1826. His wife and only daughter afterwards managed an orphanage at Aberfoyle. In 1874 Charles Rogers edited his *Poetical Remains*, with a memoir.

T. W. BAYNE, *rev.* S. R. J. BAUDRY

Sources *Poetical remains of William Glen*, ed. C. Rogers (1874) • A. Whitelaw, ed., *The book of Scottish song*, another edn (1867) • J. G. Wilson, ed., *The poets and poetry of Scotland*, 2 vols. (1876–7) • *IGI* • bap. reg. Scot.

Glenalmond. For this title name *see* Patton, George, Lord Glenalmond (1803–1869).

Glenavy. For this title name *see* Campbell, James Henry Mussen, first Baron Glenavy (1851–1931); Campbell, Beatrice Moss, Lady Glenavy (1883–1970); Campbell, Patrick Gordon, third Baron Glenavy (1913–1980).

Glenavy, Beatrice. *See* Campbell, Beatrice Moss, Lady Glenavy (1883–1970).

Glenbervie. For this title name *see* Douglas, Sylvester, Baron Glenbervie (1743–1823).

Glencairn. For this title name *see under* Cunningham family (*per. c.*1340–1631) [Cunningham, Alexander, first earl of Glencairn (1426?–1488); Cunningham, Cuthbert, second earl of Glencairn (*c.*1470–1540/41); Cunningham, William, fifth earl of Glencairn (*b. c.*1526, *d.* in or before 1580); Cunningham, James, sixth earl of Glencairn (*c.*1552–1630); Cunningham, William, seventh earl of Glencairn (*b.* in or after 1575, *d.* 1631)]. *See also* Cunningham, William, third earl of Glencairn (*d.* 1548); Cunningham, Alexander, fourth earl of Glencairn (*d.* 1574/5); Cunningham, William, eighth earl of Glencairn (1610/11–1664); Cunningham, James, thirteenth earl of Glencairn (1749–1791).

Glencorse. For this title name *see* Inglis, John, Lord Glencorse (1810–1891).

Glendenning, Raymond Carl (1907–1974), sports broadcaster, was born on 25 September 1907 at 13 Rugby Road, Newport, Monmouthshire, the son of Robert James Samuel Glendenning, a commercial clerk and later a company director, and his wife, Mathilde Anna Elise, *née* Deveridge. He was educated at Newport high school and the University of London, where he took a BCom. In 1931 he qualified as a chartered accountant and he practised for a short time before joining, in 1932, the BBC as the Cardiff organizer of the radio programme *Children's Hour*. He moved to Belfast in 1935 as outside broadcasts assistant and in 1939 transferred to London; there in 1942 he became assistant director of outside broadcasts.

Glendenning later remembered the special difficulties of broadcasting under wartime censorship restrictions. A ban on any live description of the weather, which might be picked up by the enemy and used to direct bombing raids, called for particularly inventive commentary. His vivid narrative of one particular football match, which went ahead despite thick fog, startled those living close to the ground. His varied tasks as a broadcaster during the war included providing commentary on the enthronement of the bishop of Coventry in the ruined shell of his own cathedral. It was, by Glendenning's own estimation, 'the most impressive and moving' scene that he was ever called upon to describe (Glendenning, 66).

Glendenning married on 11 September 1945 Sheilagh Dundee Millar (*b.* 1913/14), daughter of Thomas Millar, a company director. That year he left the permanent staff of the BBC to work as a freelance sports commentator and reporter, but he remained until 1963 the corporation's principal commentator on football, boxing, racing, and tennis. He possessed a voice that was 'both powerful and mellow' and which was well suited to his 'effervescent style' of commentary. Never at a loss for words, he could work himself into a high pitch of excitement: 'But his enthusiasm was authentic, as was his love of sport, and he could set with great skill the scene of a great sporting occasion' (*The Times*, 25 Feb 1974). He gave a memorable commentary on the FA cup final of 1953, in which Blackpool defeated Bolton 4–3 after two decisive interventions from Stanley Matthews, who made the winning goal in the last minute of normal time: 'Taylor to Matthews on the right … Matthews beats one man, beats two … moves in … he centres … it's Perry … Perry has scored, Perry has scored!' (Keating).

As a pioneer in the art of live commentary Glendenning had his share of mishaps. His 'hoodoo' event was the Cambridgeshire race. In 1951 he managed to describe this from start to finish without once mentioning the winner, the aptly named Fleeting Moment. He had, though, a less than ideal vantage point in the stands and struggled to distinguish between forty-five riders, three of whom, including the winner, wore different combinations of the same colours, orange and purple. More serious was the criticism surrounding his commentary of the world middleweight title fight between Britain's Randolph Turpin and the great American champion Sugar Ray Robinson at Earls Court in July 1951. Few in Britain expected Turpin to win, and Glendenning's commentary inevitably reflected this. But the British boxer grew in strength with every round and won the title to achieve one of the great upsets in boxing history. Glendenning was afterwards privately satisfied with his blow-by-blow account, but the BBC was flooded with complaints accusing him of bias in favour of Robinson. Glendenning found himself vilified in the press and the uproar grew until the BBC took the unprecedented step of rebroadcasting the commentary, to give listeners a second opportunity to judge for themselves. Callers afterwards were equally divided between praise and blame. It was a sobering experience for Glendenning, who detected more than a trace of hypocrisy in some of his critics. He at least could point to an article in the *Sunday Graphic* in which he had given Turpin 'a great chance' in the fight, which was more than some in Fleet Street had done.

In appearance Glendenning was as gloriously individual as his commentary. Large horn-rimmed glasses, which did not altogether hide 'a twinkling pair of eyes', were offset by a luxuriant handlebar moustache (*The Times*). He was a sociable man and in April 1947 was one of the ten founder members of the Handlebar Club, a convivial gathering that included the entertainers Jimmy Edwards and Frank Muir, and which raised money for charitable causes. Glendenning published a characteristically amusing memoir of his career in broadcasting, *Just a Word in your Ear* (1953), and he later produced *A Sportsman's Who's Who* (1957) with Robert Bateman. As his broadcasting career came to an end he became a director of Reading Standard Group Ltd (1961–7) and an editorial director of *Golf News* (1963–7). He died on 23 February 1974 at Wycombe General Hospital, High Wycombe, of cardiac failure. MARK POTTLE

Sources *WWW* • R. Glendenning, *Just a word in your ear* (1953) • *The Times* (25 Feb 1974) • R. Glendenning and R. Bateman, *A sportsman's who's who* (1957), 384 e. 101 • F. Keating, 'Death of a legend', *The Guardian* (24 Feb 2000) • b. cert. • m. cert. • d. cert.
Archives FILM BFI NFTVA, advertising film footage • BFI NFTVA, documentary footage • BFI NFTVA, performance footage • BFI NFTVA, sports footage | SOUND BL NSA, documentary recordings • BL NSA, performance recordings
Likenesses H. Magee, photograph, 1949, Hult. Arch. [*see illus.*]
Wealth at death £5940: probate, 30 April 1974, *CGPLA Eng. & Wales*

Raymond Carl Glendenning (1907–1974), by Haywood Magee, 1949

Glendoick. For this title name *see* Murray, Sir Thomas, of Glendoick, baronet, Lord Glendoick (*c*.1633–1684/5).

Glendyne. For this title name *see* Nivison, Robert, first Baron Glendyne (1849–1930).

Glenelg. For this title name *see* Grant, Charles, Baron Glenelg (1778–1866).

Glenesk. For this title name *see* Borthwick, Algernon, Baron Glenesk (1830–1908).

Glenie, James (*bap.* **1750**, *d.* **1817**), soldier and mathematician, baptized on 7 October 1750 at Leslie, Fife, was the son of John Glenie, army officer, and his wife, Margaret Smith. He went from a parochial school to the University of St Andrews where he made good progress in classics and divinity, being intended for the church, but soon showed a talent for science and mathematics. He joined the army, and on the outbreak of the American War of Independence in 1775 he embarked with his regiment for North America, becoming second lieutenant in the artillery in November 1776. He was transferred to become practitioner engineer and was commissioned second lieutenant in the engineers in February 1779.

In 1774, while in the army, it seems that Glenie discovered the 'antecedental calculus', and wrote 'a small performance' of it in Latin which was printed in July 1776. He sent a paper on this to the Royal Society, which was read in 1777 and published the following year. At much the same time Glenie wrote papers entitled 'The division of right lines, surfaces and solids' and 'The general mathematical laws which regulate and extend proportion universally', printed in the society's *Philosophical Transactions* in 1776 and 1777. These publications, with his book, *The History of Gunnery with a New Method of Deriving the Theory of Projectiles* (1776), secured Glenie's election to the Royal Society on 18 March 1779, while he was still in Quebec. He returned to England in 1780 and married Mary Anne Locke, daughter of the military storekeeper at Plymouth, with whom he had three children.

When in 1783 Sir Joseph Banks, newly installed president of the Royal Society, sought to oust the mathematician–engineer Charles Hutton from his post as foreign secretary to the society, Glenie was one of those fellows who opposed the move; his vigorous speech, made at a meeting in February 1784 in defence of the mathematical fellows, was published in the account of this confrontation.

The duke of Richmond, appointed master-general of the ordnance in 1783, consulted Glenie about his plans to fortify all naval arsenals and to create lines of defence along the British coast. Glenie's somewhat tactless declaration that these plans were absurd and impracticable was ill received and led to a flurry of pamphleteering on both sides. (Even though the duke's proposals were rejected by parliament in 1786 Glenie later published *Observations on the Duke of Richmond's Plans*, 1805, which was followed by his own ideas, as *Observations on the Defence of Great Britain*, 1807.) Glenie had been promoted first lieutenant in 1787 but, having incurred the duke's displeasure, resigned his commission and emigrated with his family to New Brunswick, Canada, where he purchased a tract of land and was elected a representative of the house of assembly. He set up as a contractor for ships' timber and masts, but his speculation failed and Glenie and his partner were financially ruined. He was eventually also a political failure and he returned to England in 1805 (see F. G. Stanley in *Collections*, 42, 1942, 145–73).

In 1794 Glenie published a new booklet on the antecedental calculus. Newton's approach to the calculus had used the notion of limit unclearly, and also drew upon velocity; Glenie wished to avoid all this, so as an alternative he defined the derivative of a function algebraically by using the binomial theorem in order to express the ratio of the increments of two functions as a power series in the incremental variable h, and then blithely deleting terms containing powers of h above the first. A related work was a letter from Glenie to Francis Maseres, containing 'A demonstration of Sir Isaac Newton's binomial theorem'. This, and other papers by Glenie, were published by Maseres in his *Scriptores logarithmici* (6 vols., 1791–1807).

Glenie was elected fellow of the Royal Society of Edinburgh on 27 January 1794, and several of his papers were published in Edinburgh. Glenie now had no employment but the earl of Chatham paid him a retainer as 'engineer-extraordinary', and later found him an appointment as instructor in artillery to the East India Company, with a reasonable income of £400 per annum. The earl also secured his appointment in 1797 as inspecting engineer to some of the West Indian islands. This good fortune was, however, of short duration. He was summoned to testify for the crown at the prosecution of G. L. *Wardle MP, but his evidence provoked severe censure from chief justice Lord Ellenborough, and led to his dismissal from his existing posts.

In 1812 Glenie went to Copenhagen to negotiate the purchase of a large plantation in Denmark for a member of parliament, but no agreement had been made before hand and on return his claim for compensation was disputed. It was referred to arbitration, but the arbitrators themselves could not agree and so Glenie was once more left destitute. His attempts to recruit some mathematical pupils failed. He died of apoplexy in Chelsea on 23 November 1817; he was buried at St Martin-in-the-Fields, Westminster, and later reburied in an unknown place.

W. Johnson

Sources Chambers, *Scots.* (1856) • *GM*, 1st ser., 87/2 (1817), 571–2 • *Army List* (1770–87) • D. R. Fisher, 'Wardle, Gwyllym Lloyd', HoP, *Commons* • J. M. Anderson, ed., *The matriculation roll of the University of St Andrews, 1747–1897* (1905), 17 • N. Guicciardini, *The development of Newtonian calculus in Britain, 1700–1800* (1989) • W. Johnson, 'An introduction to the works of James Glenie', *International Journal of Impact Engineering*, 19 (1997), 515–29 • W. Johnson, 'James Glenie in Canada and "America" and new aspects of his life and work', *International Journal of Impact Engineering*, 21 (1998), 203–24 • bap. reg. Scot.

Glenkinglas. For this title name *see* Noble, Michael Antony Cristobal, Baron Glenkinglas (1913–1984).

Glenlee. For this title name *see* Miller, Sir Thomas, first baronet, Lord Glenlee (1717–1789); Miller, Sir William, second baronet, Lord Glenlee (1755–1846).

Glenny, Alexander Thomas (1882–1965), immunologist, was born in Camberwell, London, on 18 September 1882, the third son among the five children of Thomas Armstrong Glenny, a stockbroker's clerk and Plymouth Brethren minister, and his wife, Elizabeth Foreman. He was educated at Alleyn's School, in Dulwich, and at Chelsea Polytechnic, where he attended evening classes and later graduated BSc (Lond.). On leaving Alleyn's School in 1899, he joined the Wellcome Physiological Research Laboratories, then at Herne Hill, to work as a technician. There he became closely involved in work associated with the immunization of horses for the production of antitoxins, and his meticulous care and efficiency led to his appointment in 1906 as head of the immunology department. In this capacity he was responsible for the production, control testing, and potency assays of all the antitoxins produced by the Wellcome laboratories—a heavy responsibility, particularly during the First World War when the demand for antitoxins became immense. When war broke out again in 1939, Glenny was responsible for meeting even greater demands, particularly for tetanus and gas-gangrene antitoxins. To these were added vast requirements for diphtheria toxoid, for the diphtheria immunization campaign launched throughout Britain in 1941, as well as for tetanus toxoid, for the active immunization of all members of the British armed forces.

In addition to his routine commercial work in supplying

therapeutic and prophylactic immunological products, Glenny was engaged in fundamental research, particularly in relation to the mechanisms of antibody production. His work on the primary and secondary responses in immunized animals was one of his most outstanding contributions. Through experiments on guinea-pigs, rabbits, goats, sheep, horses, and humans, using diphtheria toxin/antitoxin mixtures as antigens, Glenny and his colleague H. J. Südmersen worked out the pattern of the primary and secondary antibody responses, which were shown to be slow and small for the primary while rapid and large for the secondary, and demonstrated how, by altering the time interval between the primary and secondary antigenic stimuli, the secondary response could be considerably modified. These findings formed the basis for schedules of immunization both of people and of animals and applied to virtually all responses to antigenic stimuli. Another outstanding contribution was the discovery that diphtheria toxin which had lost its toxicity by formalin treatment, and was referred to as toxoid, still retained its ability to induce the formation of antitoxin when injected into animals. There was some controversy at the time as to whether Glenny or Gaston Ramon, working in France, could claim priority for this discovery; nevertheless Glenny was the first to demonstrate the efficacy of toxoid in humans, a finding which formed the basis for the highly effective products used in the active immunization of people against both diphtheria and tetanus. A third outstanding contribution was his discovery that alum-precipitated toxoids were considerably more powerful in their antigenic activity than toxoids alone. As a result, aluminium salts were employed as adjuvants in many of the prophylactic antigens used for the protection of humans and animals against infectious diseases. All three of these discoveries laid the foundations for new immunization procedures, particularly for those in which toxoids were used.

Other researches undertaken by Glenny included the development of the concept of avidity, by demonstrating that the firmness of binding of antitoxin to toxin depended on the particular antitoxin used and on the discrimination of toxins produced by bacteria (particularly the gas-gangrene organisms), on the basis of the different antibodies they induced in animals.

Glenny had an exceptional intellect and was full of new ideas, and he had an original approach to experimentation. His passion for organization enabled him to carry out fundamental research in addition to the routine duties demanded by his employer. He was a great stimulus to the young people who worked under him and who respected him highly, though he was by no means easy to get on with. He was not a very happy man and was somewhat disappointed that his work did not receive the attention he felt it deserved, but this was probably due to his lack of interest in publishing his results. When he did publish, his papers were somewhat complicated and difficult to follow. Nevertheless, recognition came, though rather late in life, when Glenny was elected to the Royal Society in 1944; he was also awarded the Addingham gold medal and the Jenner medal, both in 1953.

Glenny was married in 1910, to Emma Blanche Lilian Gibbs; they had two sons and one daughter. After his retirement from the Wellcome laboratories in 1947, Glenny spent much of his time writing up his unpublished work. However, in 1960 his memory began to fail and he died at 21 South Park Hill Road, Croydon, on 5 October 1965.

David Evans, *rev.*

Sources C. L. Oakley, *Memoirs FRS*, 12 (1966), 163–80 · personal knowledge (1981) · probate

Likenesses W. Stoneman, photograph, 1944, NPG · W. Stoneman, photograph, 1946, RS archives · two photographs, Wellcome L.

Wealth at death £6224: probate, 19 Jan 1966, *CGPLA Eng. & Wales*

Glenny, George (1793–1874), landscape gardener and writer on horticulture, was born on 1 November 1793 one of at least two sons of a watch-case maker in Clerkenwell, London. Apprenticed in the same trade as his father, in 1815 Glenny married the daughter of a watch-case maker. He worked at this craft at home in Clerkenwell from 1815 to 1820, when he became secretary of a new insurance company in the City which provided benefits for workers. His wife died in 1823, leaving him with two children. In 1825 he founded the Royal Union Association, a friendly society and charity, which survived until 1839. He also became a wine merchant in 1826, but subsequently went bankrupt. Following his second marriage in 1828 to Louisa Whiting, Glenny moved to Twickenham. There were seven children from this second marriage.

Glenny became interested in gardening at an early age, after seeing a bed of tulips in Walworth, and helped by his father he started a garden in Spitalfields and began to grow tulips, hyacinths, and auriculas. In 1832 he helped to found the Metropolitan Society of Florists and Amateurs, and in 1833 he became a fellow of the Horticultural Society. He began to exhibit flowers at the Chiswick shows, with great success. The story was told that he once entertained fifty-seven guests at his table, and was able to set before each individual a silver cup won as a prize for showing auriculas, dahlias, tulips, and roses as an amateur.

However, because Glenny criticized the judging at the Chiswick show in 1838 he was censured by the council of the Horticultural Society in 1839. He also organized shows himself for the Metropolitan Society and in his own garden at Worton Lodge, Isleworth, where he had moved in 1835. Glenny was bankrupt again in 1839, after three shows in his newly built floricultural hall at Stafford House, Chiswick, failed to attract many people. Glenny spent many years trying to improve the English tulip, publishing details of the ideal tulip towards which growers should aspire; during his lifetime, probably as a result of his efforts, the appearance of the English tulip changed dramatically.

Glenny's first writings appeared in the *Antigallican Monitor*, and he subsequently edited a number of other journals. With the consent of Queen Adelaide he started the *Royal Ladies' Magazine* in 1830. He began to write seriously on horticultural subjects in 1832, when he started the

Horticultural Journal, which was published until 1839. He also began the papers entitled 'Properties of flowers', originally published in the *Horticultural Journal* between 1832 and 1835. These were reprinted in 1864, and were his most important works. Glenny started the *Gardener's Gazette*, the first weekly gardening newspaper, in 1837, and edited various other periodicals, including the *Garden Journal*, the *Practical Florist*, and *Glenny's Journal*.

After his bankruptcy in 1839 Glenny was forced to sell the *Gardener's Gazette*; but he remained as editor for a time. From 1841 he earned his living by writing on horticulture and did much to popularize gardening among the working population. He was the first garden journalist to have a column in a popular newspaper, *Lloyd's Weekly London Newspaper*, for which he wrote from 1852 until his death in 1874. In addition to journalism, Glenny was engaged in publishing many books, including *Gardening for the Million* (1838), which went into its seventeenth edition in 1849, *Cottage Gardening* (1847), *Glenny's Handbook to the Flower Garden and Greenhouse* (1851), and *The Gardener's Every-Day Book* (1863). Glenny was one of the founders of the Royal Gardeners' Benevolent Institution in 1839, and he subscribed the first 20 guineas.

Glenny died at his home, Paxton Villa, Colby Road, Gipsy Hill, Norwood, Surrey, on 17 May 1874. His son, George Glenny, a gardener at Paxton House nurseries, Fulham, continued to publish *Glenny's Almanac*, which his father had started in 1837. ANNE PIMLOTT BAKER

Sources W. Tjaden, 'George Glenny: horticultural hornet', *The Garden: Journal of the Royal Horticultural Society*, 3 (1986), 318–23 • *Gardeners' Chronicle*, new ser., 1 (1874), 676 • *Gardener's Magazine* (23 May 1874) • *Journal of Horticulture, Cottage Gardener and Country Gentleman*, 26 (1874), 429 • A. Amherst, *A history of gardening in England*, 2nd edn (1896), 252–4 • J. Wright, 'Champions of the English tulip', *Country Life*, 149 (1971), 1148–9 • Desmond, *Botanists* • A. Simmonds, 'Glenny's "golden rules"', *Journal of the Royal Horticultural Society*, 69 (1944), 307–8 • W. Roberts, 'Garden annals', *Gardeners' Chronicle*, 3rd ser., 30 (1901), 425 • *CGPLA Eng. & Wales* (1874) • Boase, *Mod. Eng. biog.*

Likenesses Maull and Co., photograph, repro. in *Gardener's Magazine*, 269 • oils, Royal Horticultural Society, London • portrait, repro. in *Journal of the Royal Horticultural Society*, 7 (1986), 321

Wealth at death under £100: probate, 2 June 1874, *CGPLA Eng. & Wales*

Glenny, Michael Valentine Guybon (1927–1990), Russian scholar and translator, was born at 45 Devonshire Street, London, on 26 September 1927, the only child of Arthur Willoughby Falls Glenny (*d.* 1947) and his wife, Avice Noel Boyes. His father was an RAF officer, rising to the rank of air commodore, and his mother, a South African, drove ambulances in the Second World War. After preparatory school in Suffolk, he was educated at Radley College and then at Christ Church, Oxford, where he gained a second in Russian and French in 1951. Called up for national service, he was commissioned into the Royal Horse Guards, holding the rank of captain, and found himself in Berlin at the height of the cold war. On 20 December 1952 he married Juliet Mary Crum (*b.* 1934), the daughter of John Alexander Stewart Crum, an army officer; they had a daughter and three sons (one being the broadcaster Misha Glenny). He contemplated a professional career in the army, and also seems to have considered a move into intelligence, but this came to nothing. He left the army in 1954 and returned to London, where he worked first in insurance and subsequently as an export manager for Wedgwood in Europe. It was as a representative of Wedgwood that he made his first trip to the USSR in the early 1960s to advise on the restoration of the Wedgwood Room in the Russian royal palace at Tsarskoye Selo (in the Soviet years known as Pushkin). By this time, through friendship with the publisher George Weidenfeld, he had already begun a part-time career as a translator, though his first published translations were from German.

Glenny's career as a translator from Russian took off during the second half of the 1960s. The post-Stalin thaw had already begun to cool, but there was still a major body of work discovered or written during that period, but as yet inaccessible to the English-speaking world. For such a reading public the two great revelations of the 1960s were Solzhenitsyn and Bulgakov and it is with these two writers that Glenny's name will always be associated. The first ever publication in Russia in 1966–7 of *The Master and Margarita*, the work of an author who had died quarter of a century previously, was a major literary event. Glenny's translation appeared within the year and has remained in print, ensuring that Bulgakov's novel remains part of the literary canon of the twentieth century. But Glenny had a broader interest in Bulgakov, producing in quick succession English-language versions of three of his earlier works: *Black Snow (a Theatrical Novel)* (1967), *The Heart of a Dog* (1968), and *The White Guard* (1971). Glenny's other major contribution of this period was his 1972 translation of Solzhenitsyn's *August 1914*. Less well known is his involvement in one of the two 1968 translations of *First Circle* where the name 'Michael Guybon' represents the joint work of Glenny, Max Hayward, and Ronald Hingley.

As he began to make his name as a translator, Glenny left Wedgwood and joined the staff of *The Observer* newspaper as advertising and special projects manager, organizing a landmark exhibition on the Masada. In 1972 he made a somewhat belated entry into academic life as a lecturer in Russian at Birmingham University. But academia was not his main focus of interest and indeed his work as popularizer and proselytizer of Russian literature remains far more significant than anything he might have achieved as a formal teacher of Russian. He left Birmingham in the mid-1970s to spend two years as visiting professor at the University of Southern Illinois, working with the film historian Herbert Marshall translating and editing Eisenstein's theoretical writings. Thereafter, for the rest of his life he earned his living entirely from freelance translating and reviewing, and though some of the works he translated have worn better than others, he always sought to tackle only works of genuine literary quality or proven topical interest. In this respect he is perhaps unique in his field, since his career was based entirely on his ability to convey the substance and significance of contemporary (or, as in the case of *The Master and Margarita*, for instance, recently discovered) Russian writing. He never seems to have sought the comfort zone of a new translation of Dostoyevsky, Tolstoy or Chekhov, which would have brought in a guaranteed income.

Glenny's constant search for new and interesting works of literature resulted in a number of trips to the Soviet Union, during which he built up many contacts among the Russian intelligentsia. Like most of his fellow Russianists in the West, he was no fan of the Soviet regime, but recognized that good work could often result from the very constraints under which Soviet artists worked. However, he was also well aware of the contribution made by writers forced into exile and emigration, and was equally at home, for instance, translating the émigrés Georgii Vladimov (*Faithful Ruslan*, 1979) and Zinovii Zinik (*The Mushroom-Picker*, 1987—later to be dramatized for television), the exiled Vasilii Aksionov (*The Burn*, 1984) or the Moscow-based Yurii Trifonov (*Another Life* and *The House on the Embankment*, 1983). It was no doubt his unwillingness to confine himself to what the Soviet authorities regarded as 'acceptable' writers that led to his being banned from the Soviet Union at about the time of the Moscow Olympics. But once perestroika got under way, he was back again, despite worsening health, seeking fresh sources with the renewed enthusiasm of someone who saw the dream of a free Russia coming true. Indeed, he and his partner were warmly received as the first foreigners to visit the formerly closed city of Tambov when they arrived for a performance of *Sarcophagus*, a play which Glenny was to translate. His lifelong interest in the theatre bore fruit during this period with the publication in 1989 of his *Five Plays from the Soviet Union*. He took an active interest in the staging of plays which he had worked on and notably in the second half of the 1980s he was often called upon on radio or television to comment on the Russian cultural scene. In collaboration with Norman Stone he also put together a collection of reminiscences of emigration (*The other Russia*, 1990). Ironically, perhaps, his final contribution was, in terms of its sheer volume and public importance, his mightiest effort: the 100,000 words of Boris Yeltsin's memoirs, which he completed in two months in 1990. Back in Moscow on yet another search for material, on 1 August 1990 he suffered a fatal heart attack. He was buried at Paston church, near his home town of North Walsham, Norfolk.

Michael Glenny was an outstanding practitioner of the difficult art of translation. He had a natural feel for language. He could make the occasional mistake—one might argue that, of necessity, he at times took on too much too quickly—but he was always readable and convincing in the English version. But he was not just a skilled technician. He was also a great Russophile, generally a fine judge of literary merit, and someone who by example contributed much to the growing interest in Russian culture in the second half of the twentieth century. A gregarious, sociable personality, he enjoyed music and the theatre by way of relaxation. His first marriage was dissolved in 1972 and he married on 23 August 1975 Valerie Forbes Hartley-Brewer, a medical student, whose previous marriage had also been dissolved; she was the daughter of Robert Moon, a shopkeeper. The last five years of his life were spent in Norfolk with his partner, Elizabeth Purdy.

MICHAEL FALCHIKOV

Sources private information (2004) [Juliet Sydenham; Elizabeth Purdy; Misha Glenny] · *The Times* (3 Aug 1990) · R. Crane, *The Guardian* (3 Aug 1990) · F. Williams, *The Guardian* (3 Aug 1990) · b. cert. · m. cert. [Juliet Mary Crum] · m. cert. [Valery Forbes Hartley-Brewer]

Archives priv. coll., MSS · U. Leeds, Leeds Russian Archive · UCL, school of Slavonic and east European studies, corresp. and papers | SOUND BL NSA, current affairs recording · BL NSA, performance recording

Wealth at death under £115,000: probate, 12 Nov 1990, *CGPLA Eng. & Wales*

Glenorchy. For this title name *see* Campbell, Willielma, Viscountess Glenorchy (1741–1786).

Glisson, Francis (1599?–1677), physician and philosopher, was most probably born in 1599 in Bristol, the third of at least thirteen children of William Glisson, tailor, and his wife, Mary, daughter of John Hancock of Kingsweston, Somerset, and South Perrott, Dorset. He attended the school at Rampisham in Dorset for seven years, where his family had moved at the beginning of 1600. Glisson entered Gonville and Caius College, Cambridge, in 1617, graduated BA in 1621 and proceeded MA in 1624. He was a fellow from 1624 to 1634. He was incorporated MA at Oxford on 25 October 1627. In 1626 he was nominated lecturer in Greek, and dean of Caius College in 1629. In 1634 he obtained his degree of MD at Cambridge, where in 1636 he was appointed regius professor of physic. He held this post until his death, although in 1675, owing to the pressure of old age, he appointed his pupil Robert Brady, master of Caius, as his deputy as physic professor. Upon Glisson's death Brady went on to become regius professor.

From the time of his appointment in Cambridge and during the civil war Glisson frequently spent time in London, living in Fleet Street. From a comment in a letter we know that Glisson was married to Maria Morgan. He took an active role in the scientific life of London in three different ways: he was a prominent member of a group of friends, all physicians, who would gather to discuss the results of their research; he set up a connection with the College of Physicians of which he became a fellow; he took part in the meetings of the so-called '1645 group' which can be considered as one of the original nuclei of the Royal Society.

The result of Glisson's work in the informal group of physicians was his first treatise *De rachitide sive morbo puerili* (1650), translated into English by Philip Armin in 1651. As stated in the preface, these medical meetings were attended by George Bate, Nathan Paget, Assuerus Regimorter, Thomas Sheaf, Edmund Trench, and Robert

Francis Glisson (1599?–1677), by unknown artist, *c.*1670

Wright. During the meetings they exchanged results in the form of papers and then discussed the content. Originally, the treatise on rickets was to be written by Glisson, Bate, and Regimorter, but since Glisson had already completed the part concerning the essence of the disease along with a wealth of original observations, it was agreed that the treatise should be published under his name. Further Latin editions appeared in 1660 and 1671 (London), in 1671 (Leiden), and in 1682 (The Hague). Unlike Daniel Whistler's *Disputatio medica inauguralis de morbo puerili Anglorum* (1645), which is based on information already available at the time, Glisson's important treatise on rickets stands out for its careful description of the symptoms, its clinical observations, and the originality of its explicative framework. The aetiological hypothesis already alludes to Glisson's typical notion of life, with the emphasis placed on spirits and tissue irritability in the determination of the disease.

Glisson became a fellow of the College of Physicians on 30 September 1635. In 1639 he was elected reader in anatomy and Goulstonian lecturer the following year. In 1655 he was appointed elect, then censor in 1656 and president in 1667 (a post to which he was re-elected in both 1668 and 1669). From 1666 until the time of his death he held the position of consiliarius. Under his presidency Glisson had the difficult task of raising funds for the reconstruction of the College of Physicians building after its destruction by fire in 1666. As a result of the anatomical lectures given at the College of Physicians beginning in 1641, he published *Anatomia hepatis* in 1654, which contains an excellent description of the anatomy, normal and morbid, of the liver and a section on the lymphatic vessels (the aqueous ducts, as Glisson named them). The work, which is notable for the dissection techniques employed, was immediately recognized as a major achievement in the field of anatomical investigation. It also stands out for the clear identification of the fibrous sheath of the portal tracts which still today bears the name Glisson's capsule. Further editions of *Anatomia hepatis* came out in 1659 (Amsterdam), 1665 (Amsterdam), and 1681 (The Hague). From the large amount of anatomical and physiological notes scattered throughout Glisson's manuscript archive in the British Library it is apparent that, above all during the course of the 1650s, Glisson was working on a project of anatomizing the organs of nutrition and digestion. What remains of his Goulstonian lectures at the College of Physicians and of the numerous disputations at the University of Cambridge conducted under his guidance emphasizes the relevant place given to such organs as the stomach, gut, liver, spleen, and gall bladder.

From 1645 Glisson started having meetings with George Ent, Jonathan Goddard, Christopher Merrett, Charles Scarborough, John Wallis, a former pupil of Glisson's at Cambridge, and John Wilkins, in order to discuss natural philosophy. They usually gathered at Jonathan Goddard's rooms at the Mitre in Wood Street or at his rooms in Gresham College. In the turmoil of the civil war the group split up. Wallis, Wilkins, and Goddard moved to Oxford and they joined with other people who were likewise interested in natural philosophy including Robert Boyle and Christopher Wren. All these scientific groups ultimately led to the foundation of the Royal Society. Glisson was not present at the meeting at Gresham College (28 November 1660) at which the Royal Society was officially proclaimed, but he was one of its original fellows.

From the 1660s Glisson devoted himself to an in-depth philosophical investigation on the notions of being, life, and matter. The outcome of this investigation were the unfinished manuscript treatises 'De inadaequatis rerum conceptibus' and 'Disquisitiones metaphysicae' and, above all, the published treatise *De natura substantiae energetica, seu, De vita naturae* (1672). All the published and manuscript evidence points to the fact that Glisson's original theoretical plan was to write a real metaphysics, of which the main parts were to be gnoseology and logic (BL, Sloane MS 3314), ontology (BL, Sloane MSS 3313/3308) and metaphysical physics (the published treatise on the energetic nature of substance). In Glisson's philosophy, substance (which he calls *biousia*) is an undifferentiated entity that can appear to our intellect as either being or energy. In its ultimate essence it is a living and perceptive principle of movement (natural perception). Matter too, being substance, is inherently endowed with life and perception. This philosophical view raised the anxieties of some Cambridge Platonists. It was criticized as hylozoistic atheism by Ralph Cudworth, master of Clare College and regius professor of Hebrew, while Henry More, fellow of Christ's College, in his refutation of Spinozism, associated Glisson's philosophy to that of Spinoza. Glisson's philosophy, however, was highly esteemed by Richard Baxter. In the absence of a direct profession of faith,

Glisson's tolerant and conciliatory outlook in matters of thought and his scarce interest in the theological questions (rational soul, nature of angels, and divine providence) pertinent to his medical concerns raise the suspicion of an agnostic attitude and of no identification with particular religious sects.

Little is known about Glisson's professional activity as a physician. He was probably practising in London in 1631, since a condition of admission to the College of Physicians was a four-year period of practice. He enjoyed some renown as an orthopaedic surgeon thanks to his invention of a sling to reduce the deformity of the spine caused by rickets. We know that among his patients were Matthew Hale and Anthony Ashley Cooper, first Baron Ashley and first earl of Shaftesbury, to whom the treatise on the energetic nature of substance is dedicated. Locke, who was under the patronage of Shaftesbury in the same period, consulted Glisson before carrying out the famous operation on the suppurating hydatid abscess of Shaftesbury's liver (1668). Prior to this Glisson had suggested a purge, which proved to be ineffective.

According to the short autobiographical sketch contained in the preface to his fourth published work, *De ventriculo et intestinis*, an earlier version of a planned treatise on the abdominal organs had been written around the years 1661–2, but it had been neglected because of growing philosophical interest in the need to clarify the speculative notions underlying the theory of reactive tissue. Glisson resumed and finished his treatise on the intestines during the last years of his life. It was published in 1677, the year of his death. *De ventriculo* is divided into two treatises, the first regarding the structure of the various abdominal organs, and the second more specifically devoted to the stomach and intestine, and especially to the physiology of their fibres. An appendix on fermentation concludes the whole work. The philosophical investigation on the life of nature led Glisson to rethink his own conception of anatomy. In fact, while the first part of the *De ventriculo* follows the usual paths of the anatomy of the macrostructures of the body, in the second part Glisson tried to work out an anatomy of the irritable fibres, that is, a kind of anatomy which moves from the organic patterns to the primitive structures of matter with its innumerable motions and forms. Glisson's philosophical and physiological notion of the irritability of tissues was taken up in the following century by Albrecht Haller and enjoyed great success throughout the eighteenth century, up to the German *Natürphilosophie*.

Glisson died on 14 October 1677 at his house in Fleet Street, near Shoe Lane, and was buried in St Bride's Church on 22 October. In his will, dated 14 December 1674 and proved by his executor, Paul Glisson, on 27 November 1677, he had provided for the division of his properties among his brothers, sisters, nephews, and nieces.

GUIDO GIGLIONI

Sources R. M. Walker, 'Francis Glisson and his capsule', *Annals of the Royal College of Surgeons of England*, 38 (1966), 71–91 • R. M. Walker, 'Francis Glisson', *Cambridge and its contribution to medicine* [Cambridge 1969], ed. A. Rook (1971), 35–47 • W. Pagel, 'Harvey and Glisson on irritability, with a note on Van Helmont', *Bulletin of the History of Medicine*, 41 (1967), 497–514 • J. Henry, 'Medicine and pneumatology: Henry More, Richard Baxter, and Francis Glisson's *Treatise on the energetic nature of substance*', *Medical History*, 31 (1987), 15–40 • O. Temkin, 'The classical roots of Glisson's doctrine of irritation', *Bulletin of the History of Medicine*, 38 (1964), 297–328 • G. Giglioni, 'Anatomist atheist? the "hylozoistic" foundations of Francis Glisson's anatomical research', *Religio medici: medicine and religion in seventeenth-century England*, ed. O. P. Grell and A. Cunningham (1996), 115–35 • H. Marion, 'Francis Glisson', *Revue Philosophique de la France et de l'Étranger*, 14 (1882), 121–55 • C. de Rémusat, *Histoire de la philosophie en Angleterre depuis Bacon jusqu'à Locke* (1875), 2.163–8 • F. Glisson, *Philosophical papers 1672*, ed. G. Giglioni (1996) • F. Glisson, *From Anatomia hepatis*, ed. A. Cunningham (1993) • J. Venn and others, eds., *Biographical history of Gonville and Caius College*, 1: *1349–1713* (1897) • parish register (burial), 22 Oct 1677, London, Fleet Street, St Bride

Archives BL, corresp. and papers, Sloane MSS • RCP Lond., letters and papers

Likenesses oils, *c*.1670, RCP Lond. [*see illus.*] • W. Faithorne, portrait, before 1672, RCP Lond. • W. Dolle, engraving (after W. Faithorne, before 1672), Wellcome L.; repro. in F. Glisson, *De natura substantiae energetica* (1672), title page • W. Faithorne, engraving (after his portrait, before 1672), Wellcome L.; repro. in F. Glisson, *Tractatus de ventriculo et intestinis* (1677) • W. Faithorne, line engraving (after an oil painting, *c*.1670), BM, NPG; repro. in F. Glisson, *De natura substantiae energetica* (1672)

Gloag, James (*bap.* **1795**, *d.* **1870**), teacher of mathematics and educationist, was baptized on 5 October 1795 at Gretna, Dumfriesshire, the second of six children of Andrew Gloag (*b.* 1761), a cotton hand-loom weaver at Rigg in that parish, and his wife, Agnes Gordon. Though details of Gloag's early schooling are unknown it was adequate to prepare him for the arts and philosophy course at United College, St Andrews, which he studied in 1814–18. His attendance at the first session of the divinity course at St Mary's College, St Andrews (1818–19), together with the tutoring he undertook to finance his studies, reveals Gloag's original intention to become a Church of Scotland minister. After an unsuccessful attempt in 1820 to become rector of Dundee Academy he became mathematics master at George Heriot's Hospital in Edinburgh, and taught there from 1820 to 1824.

With the creation of the new and progressive Edinburgh Academy in 1824 Gloag submitted his printed *Testimonials in Favour of James Gloag*, which contained references from no fewer than five professors and from the ministers of eight of the most important Edinburgh churches. Henry (later Lord) Cockburn, in an annotation to his own copy, wrote of Gloag that he was 'A sensible looking man with a pale face and hoarse voice. Gentle and amiable'; the latter point was debatable as Gloag was repeatedly censured for his use of excessive corporal punishment. He was nevertheless appointed as the academy's first master of the mathematical and geometrical school, a post which he held with distinction for exactly forty years until his retirement in July 1864, when his former pupils established the Gloag medal for mathematics in his honour. A born, though irascible, teacher—the rector's annual report for 1833 described him as 'most honest, zealous and energetic'—the quantifiable successes of his mathematical pupils at Cambridge University alone included ten wranglers, most importantly James Clerk Maxwell (second wrangler, 1854) and Peter Guthrie Tait (senior wrangler, 1852), both of whom were also first Smith's prizeman. At a dinner celebrating Tait's success Gloag 'could hardly divest himself of the idea that *he* was the hero of the occasion, such credit did he take to himself' (Fergusson, 85). While most writers on Maxwell and Tait have noted Gloag's early influence, George Davie cites Gloag directly (though he misnames him John) as one of the last of a type of Scottish schoolmaster, himself taught at a Scottish university, who brought a distinctively Scottish, metaphysical approach to the teaching of mathematics and science (Davie, 197). Indeed it has been suggested that 'The Directors dreamed of a great classical school and accidentally [in Gloag] founded a great mathematical one' (Harris).

Gloag was a founder member, in 1847, of the Educational Institute of Scotland, of which he was also a fellow. He was secretary to its board of examiners for many years, and its president in 1855–6, having already received an honorary degree of LLD in 1848 for his legendary educational prowess. In an uncharacteristically apologetic presidential address, on 20 September 1856, Gloag bewailed the failure of the institute to make a sufficient impact on the Scottish teaching profession while at the same time applauding the efforts of the lord advocate, James Moncrieff, in acknowledging, for the first time, the institute's essential and professional role.

In appearance Gloag was:

> a heavy, broad, square-shaped man of average height; with a long oval face; keen, deep-set, black eyes under bushy black eye-brows, and … at first, short, black hair and close-cut whiskers—not an ill-looking man. His voice had a peculiarly deep sound, very impressive. (Fergusson, 36–7)

With an impenetrable Dumfriesshire accent, which he never lost, Gloag was an iron disciplinarian and a legendary flogger, presenting his tawse to one of the school clubs after his retirement. In the many anecdotal recollections of him by his eminent pupils he comes across as fair, though strict—'outwardly playful, but fraught with concealed severity'—but well respected by his pupils (Fergusson, 46).

On 28 September 1832, at St Cuthbert's Church, Edinburgh, James Gloag married Elizabeth (1793–1869), daughter of James Muir, a burgess of the Merchant Company of Edinburgh, and his wife, Janet Black. They had one daughter, Janet (Jessie) Black Gloag, later Shepherd (1835–1873), whose two daughters both died in infancy. Gloag himself died, of influenza and bronchitis, at 32 Tower Street, Portobello, Edinburgh, on 21 January 1870. He was buried two days later in Warriston cemetery, Edinburgh, where his headstone survives.

PETER BELL

Sources J. Gloag, ed., *Testimonials in favour of James Gloag* (1824) • A. Fergusson, *Chronicles of the Cumming Club* (1887) • M. Magnusson, *The clacken and the slate: the story of the Edinburgh Academy, 1824–1974* (1974) • *Prize list of the Edinburgh Academy* (1833) • report of 10th general meeting, Educational Institute of Scotland, 1856 • G. E. Davie, *The democratic intellect: Scotland and her universities in the nineteenth century* (1961), 197 • parish register, Gretna, 5 Oct 1795 [baptism] • parish register, Edinburgh, St Cuthbert, 28 Sept 1832 [marriage] • d. cert. [Elizabeth Muir] • d. cert. • NA Scot., SC 70/1/147/692–699 • matriculation roll, U. St Andr. • Warriston cemetery, Edinburgh, records • G. Harris, 'Enlightenment and empire? The foundation of the Edinburgh Academy', lecture, 29 Oct 1999

Likenesses photograph, *c*.1864, Edinburgh Academy

Wealth at death £7012 4*s*. 10*d*.: confirmation, 29 March 1870, NA Scot., SC 70/1/147/692–699

Gloag, Paton James (1823–1906), Church of Scotland minister and theologian, was born in Perth on 17 May 1823, the eldest son of William Gloag (1778/9–1856), a banker in Perth, and Janet (Jessie) Burn (1785/6–1864). William Ellis *Gloag, Lord Kincairney, was a younger brother. Gloag was educated at Perth Academy up to 1839, and from 1840 at the University of Edinburgh, where he distinguished himself, especially in mathematics. His intention, however, was to become a minister in the Church of Scotland and his studies were therefore inevitably and profoundly affected by the Disruption of 1843. Many of his fellow divinity students left the established church to join the Free Church, and as a result Gloag transferred to St Andrews University. There he became part of a small but distinguished theology class, with four out of the eight students subsequently going on to become moderators of the Church of Scotland. He successfully completed his studies, and was licensed by the presbytery of Perth on 10 June 1846.

From 1846 Gloag served the congregation of Dunning, Perthshire, first as assistant to the Revd James Russell and then from 1848 until 1860 as the minister. During his time there he introduced hymns into the Sunday school and a system of 'district visitation' by the women of the congregation, of which his biographer commented that he was 'probably the first minister in the Church of Scotland to adopt either of these methods now so general' (Gloag, 38). From 1860 to 1871 he served as minister to the congregation of Blantyre, Lanarkshire, where his parishioners included the family of Dr David Livingstone: Gloag met the famous explorer and missionary, and visited Livingstone's mother during her final illness. While minister at Blantyre Gloag's energy and originality were again in evidence as he helped to provide a new parish church, established a savings bank, and attempted to preach to the unchurched mining community through open-air and cottage meetings. At the same time he continued to produce a steady stream of theological works, and St Andrews University made him an honorary DD in 1867. He moved again in 1871, to the parish of Galashiels, where he served until his resignation in 1892. During that time he was a Baird lecturer (1879) and moderator of the general assembly of the Church of Scotland (1889).

In 1896, following a rebellion by Aberdeen University students against what they saw as the incompetence of Professor Johnson, Gloag was appointed as the interim professor of biblical criticism. He filled that role with some distinction until 1899, when he retired and received the honorary degree of LLD from a grateful university. As well as being, in the words of the general assembly tribute, 'a faithful and energetic parish minister, wherever he was placed' (*Church of Scotland General Assembly Records*, 157), Gloag was a theologian of international reputation who wrote prodigiously. He was deeply influenced by F. D. Maurice, but although liberal on some issues, he was popular with many figures more conservative than himself. He did, for example, carry on a long and friendly correspondence with B. B. Warfield, and Warfield used Gloag's *Introduction to the Pauline Epistles* as a textbook for his classes at Princeton. His position on the fundamentals of Christianity he once summarized as follows:

> To me the reality of Christianity is founded on the truth of Christ's resurrection, and hence objections to Christianity do not much perplex me. As to the mysterious doctrines contained in it these I accept as forming part of a divine revelation. I do not profess to explain them. (Gloag, 106–7)

Gloag's ministry took place during a time when confessional subscription was an extremely contentious issue both in Scotland and around the world, and his position on this was unambiguous. As someone who objected deeply to what he saw as the harshness of the Calvinism of the Westminster confession of faith, Gloag was firmly opposed to the mandatory subscription to the confession that the Church of Scotland demanded. Accordingly he was in 1887–8 at the forefront of the efforts to change the rules on subscription, and although dissatisfied with the results, he did succeed in making subscription easier for those who shared his objections.

On 23 January 1867 Gloag married Elizabeth Stobie Lang (1840–1914), third daughter of the Revd Gavin Lang of Glasford; the couple had no children. After suffering a stroke in late 1898 Gloag never walked or held a pen again, although he did continue to write, using dictation and a typewriter. His health continued to fail and he died at his home, 28 Regent Terrace, Edinburgh, on 9 January 1906. He was buried at St Serf's Church, Dunning, and a memorial window to him was placed in St Paul's Church, Galashiels. The general assembly paid their old moderator the warmest of tributes, concluding that 'best of all Dr Gloag was a humble Christian, a good and deeply religious man, loving and beloved … [whose] steadfast aim was to glorify God' (*Church of Scotland General Assembly Records*, 158).

JAMES LACHLAN MACLEOD

Sources E. S. Gloag, *Paton J. Gloag DD. LLD.: a memoir* (1908) • tribute to Gloag, *Church of Scotland general assembly records* (1906) • *Fasti Scot.*, new edn, vols. 2, 4 • *Life and Work* (Feb 1906) • A. L. Drummond and J. Bulloch, *The church in late Victorian Scotland* (1978) • S. J. Brown, *Thomas Chalmers and the godly commonwealth in Scotland* (1982) • *DNB* • 'Dunning St Serf's Church graveyard survey', www.dunning.uk.net/gstart.html

Likenesses two photographs, repro. in Gloag, *Paton J. Gloag*

Wealth at death £23,050 11*s.* 1*d.*: confirmation, 7 March 1906, *CCI*

Gloag, William Ellis, Lord Kincairney (1828–1909), judge, was born at Perth on 7 February 1828, the son of William Gloag, a banker in Perth, and his wife, Jessie, the daughter of John Burn, writer to the signet in Edinburgh. His eldest brother was Paton James *Gloag, a theological writer, and his eldest sister, Jessie Burn Gloag, established in Perth one of the first ragged schools in Scotland. Educated at Perth grammar school and Edinburgh University, William Gloag was called on 25 December 1853 to the Scottish bar, where he enjoyed a fair practice. In 1864 he married Helen Stark, daughter of James Burn, writer to the signet in Edinburgh; they had one son, William Murray *Gloag, professor of law at Glasgow University, and three daughters.

A Conservative in politics, Gloag was not offered promotion until 1874, when he was appointed advocate-depute on the formation of Disraeli's second ministry. He became sheriff of Stirling and Dumbarton in 1877, and of Perthshire in 1885. He was raised to the bench in 1889, when he took the title of Lord Kincairney, and his career as a judge was successful. Gloag died at Kincairney, Murthly, Perthshire, on 8 October 1909, and was buried at Caputh. His wife survived him.

G. W. T. OMOND, *rev.* ERIC METCALFE

Sources *The Scotsman* (9 Oct 1909) • Roll of the Faculty of Advocates, Edinburgh • D. Laing, ed., *A catalogue of the graduates … of the University of Edinburgh*, Bannatyne Club, 106 (1858) • The Juridical Society, records • [W. M. Watson], ed., *The history of the Speculative Society, 1764–1904* (1905), 32, 145, 201

Likenesses G. Reid, portrait, Kincairney, Murthly, Perthshire

Wealth at death £17,639 0*s.* 7*d.*: confirmation, 16 Dec 1909, *CCI*

Gloag, William Murray (1865–1934), jurist, was born at 27 India Street, Edinburgh, on 15 March 1865, the eldest in the family of one son and three daughters of William Ellis *Gloag, Lord Kincairney (1828–1909), judge, and his wife, Helen Stark, daughter of James Burn, writer to the signet, Edinburgh. He was educated at Edinburgh Academy and Balliol College, Oxford, where he obtained a first class in modern history in 1887. He attended law classes at Edinburgh University and became an advocate in 1889. Success as a pleader eluded him and, like many counsel in that position, Gloag became a law reporter. With J. M. Irvine he published *Law of Rights in Security Heritable and Moveable Including Cautionary Obligations* (1897) and the future direction of his career was set. Two years later Gloag became assistant in Scots law at Edinburgh University and in February 1905 he was appointed regius professor of law at Glasgow University. Gloag moved to Glasgow, where, with an unmarried sister, he set up home in the university. In 1909 he was made a KC.

A dedicated scholar, Gloag was an inspired teacher, even for students attending lectures at 8 a.m. He spoke without notes and sprinkled his trenchant remarks with a dry wit which some claim to glimpse in *Carmina legis, or, Verses Illustrative of the Law of Scotland* (1920). Though reserved, he was popular with his students. To the best among them he offered opulent breakfasts that ended with stronger drink than coffee. He was a founder of the student law society. During term Gloag's life centred on the university. He acted as dean of the law faculty and served on the court. Outside the university, in July 1915 he became a chairman of the Glasgow munitions tribunal, but he proved ill suited to handling its rowdy proceedings and was dismissed the following year. Spells as a subcommissioner under the national service scheme and as assessor to the

Glasgow dean of guild court (from 1926) were successful. His leisure was spent at the Western Club and, on Saturday afternoons, at Prestwick Golf Club. Vacations found him at his estate at Murthly, Perthshire, or, after its sale in 1921, on Speyside and in St Andrews. Gloag was an assiduous golfer and bridge player. He achieved a hole in one at Troon in 1907.

In 1914 Gloag published *The Law of Contract* (2nd edn, 1929), the principal Scottish monograph on the subject and his lasting memorial. He assembled, organized, and analysed a mass of authorities, both Scottish and English. The resulting exposition is so authoritative that practitioners and the courts departed from it only rarely unless subsequent developments made this necessary. In 1917 he received the LLD degree from Edinburgh University. Ten years later, with Professor R. Candlish Henderson, he produced an *Introduction to the Law of Scotland* (10th edn, 1995), a succinct and accurate statement of the law.

Gloag had a deformity of the right arm and a somewhat high-pitched voice, but overall made a forceful impression. He was unmarried. Having become ill in Prestwick, he was admitted to Park Nursing Home, Glasgow, where he died two days later, on 5 February 1934.

A. F. RODGER, *rev.*

Sources D. M. Walker, *The Scottish jurists* (1985) • G. R. Rubin, *War, law and labour* (1987) • *CGPLA Eng. & Wales* (1934)

Glock, Sir William Frederick (1908–2000), music administrator, was born on 3 May 1908 at 21 Woolstone Road, Catford, London. His father, William George Glock, the headmaster of a school in south London, was a musical enthusiast, who inspired his son with the love of music from his earliest years. Of his mother, Gertrude Annie, *née* Maltby, Glock later wrote that she 'perhaps bequeathed an element of persistence and determination'. In 1920 (aged eleven) he won a scholarship to Christ's Hospital School. He had been learning the piano since the age of five, and at nine he had played in concerts before his father's pupils. Now he was able to continue under an enterprising teacher who introduced him to a wider repertory, including some Debussy, Rachmaninoff, and even Busoni. At fifteen he took up the viola, and thus was able to enjoy the experience of orchestral playing. He had started to study the organ at thirteen, and he won an organ scholarship to Gonville and Caius College, Cambridge, in 1926. He took a degree in history in 1929. At Cambridge he encountered for the first time some of the masterpieces of twentieth-century music, partly through Boris Ord (with whom he took part in a two-piano arrangement of Stravinsky's new piano concerto) and especially with Edward Dent, who remained a counsellor and mentor in the years ahead.

Early career In February 1930 Glock heard the pianist Artur Schnabel play Schubert and Beethoven in Oxford, and decided he wanted to study with him. Despite some hostility from the insular English musical establishment, he spent nearly three years between 1930 and 1933 in Berlin studying with Schnabel. It was a formative experience, of which he left an eloquent account in his autobiography. These Berlin years also gave Glock the chance to hear Fürtwangler, Kleiber, and Klemperer conduct, as well as to attend performances by the Busch and the Rosé quartets.

While in Berlin, Glock had written articles for the *Monthly Musical Record*. Its editor Richard Capell was now chief music critic of the *Daily Telegraph* and asked him to write concert notices for that paper. In the spring of 1934 a meeting with A. H. Fox Strangways led to an invitation to write for *The Observer*, which he did for the next eleven years, taking over as chief music critic on Fox Strangways's retirement in 1939. Both his reservations about the then-deified Toscanini and his enthusiasm for Bruckner (in England virtually unknown) aroused hostility among the senior critical fraternity.

Meanwhile, Glock was increasingly drawn to the music of the twentieth-century masters—in the first instance Bartók and Hindemith. He had got to know Vaughan Williams's fourth symphony, Walton's viola concerto, and the earliest works of Britten. Visits to Morley College fostered a lively friendship with Michael Tippett; Britten's return from the USA with *Hymn to St Cecilia* and the *Serenade for Tenor, Horn and Strings* initiated a not uncritical admiration for his music. Glock had also got to know a number of Stravinsky's neo-classical scores during the 1930s: but Stravinsky did not really overtake Bartók in his critical esteem until he heard *Symphony in Three Movements* (1945). An isolated chance meeting in the dining car of a train with Stravinsky and his son Soulima in 1935 anticipated their much closer acquaintance twenty years later.

In 1941 Glock joined the RAF; he somehow managed to combine service on various Bomber Command airfields in Lincolnshire and Leicestershire with continuing to write a fortnightly column for *The Observer*, often at the cost of his sleep. But his confidently expressed espousal of the modern caused difficulties after the theatre critic Ivor Brown became general editor. A flamboyant sentence from his obituary notice of Bartók ('no great composer had ever cared how "pleasant" his music sounded') was too much for Brown: Glock left *The Observer* in October 1945, but he continued to write for *Time and Tide* and for the *New Statesman*.

On 16 May 1944 Glock married Clemency (Clement) Davenport, *née* Hale (*b*. 1913/14), a set designer and scenery painter at Covent Garden. They had one daughter, who died in 1980 at the age of thirty-four. The marriage ended in divorce, and on 21 November 1952 Glock married Anne Genevieve Balfour (*née* Geoffroy-Dechaume; 1910/11–1995). He had a close relationship with his four stepchildren.

New opportunities soon came up: in 1946 the BBC Third Programme was inaugurated, and Glock was soon on its list of preferred speakers for broadcast talks on music. More immediately, he was in 1947 sent on a prolonged European tour to gather information for the BBC about how continental musical life was reviving after the Second World War. The tour took in Munich, Vienna, Prague,

Berlin, Hamburg, and Copenhagen (where the International Society for Contemporary Music festival was taking place). Glock met the conductors Hans Rosbaud and Georg Solti; the composers Karl Amadeus Hartmann, Shostakovich (briefly in Prague); and, in Berlin, Boris Blacher. In Berlin, too, he heard Fürtwangler conduct once again.

Dartington summer school A summer school of music, to focus upon the classical piano repertory, was to be held at Bryanston in Dorset in 1948. The sponsor, Gwynn Jones, approached his friend Artur Schnabel, who put forward Glock's name as director. The opportunity was seized. The first year was an exciting artistic success, a financial failure: Gwynn Jones, who had undertaken to be financially responsible, now withdrew his support. Other financial backers were found, and the summer school became an annual event. Schnabel's original conception had been to provide first-rate professional performances, alongside classes and lectures for the public. Glock defined this further when he later wrote that it should 'appeal equally to students and young professionals, to teachers, and to ordinary concert-goers'. From the beginning twentieth-century music played a leading part in the summer school programmes. In 1948 the four weeks featured works by Stravinsky; a lecture by Erwin Stein on Schoenberg, Berg, and Webern, not accompanied by performances; Hindemith (who himself came to give composition classes); and works by Bartók. The lecturers in this first year included Nadia Boulanger and Imogen Holst. Nor were other arts neglected: literature, theatre, painting, philosophy. There were lectures from Wyndham Lewis, Canetti, V. S. Pritchett, and E. M. Forster. Glock worked himself to the limit: he gave lectures and he performed, on top of all the planning and administration. The programmes devised in these early years were extraordinary for their time. That their range and their taste now seem agreeable but nothing extraordinary is the most telling tribute to the way in which Glock managed almost single-handedly to transform British musical life and culture.

In 1953 the summer school moved to Dartington Hall, where it continued to develop, increasingly enriched by cross-fertilization from the growing number of Glock's other activities. In 1949 he had founded *The Score*, a serious music magazine whose range of interest was wide but which prominently featured twentieth-century music. Many memorable controversies were aired in its pages: it ran to twenty-eight issues and survived for twelve years. Between 1954 and 1958 Glock was chairman of the music section of the Institute of Contemporary Arts, which was itself linked to the International Society for Contemporary Music. Both these activities brought Glock into even closer contact with the European and American world of new music. The Dartington programmes were thus enriched by music by Elliott Carter, Boulez, Nono, and many younger composers.

Musicians from around the world gathered at Dartington. The Amadeus Quartet, newly formed, were there from the beginning; later came the Juilliard and Hollywood quartets, the Kolisch Quartet, and the Lindsay Quartet. Pianists in early days included Noel Mewton-Wood and Monique Haas; Vlado Perlemuter was a regular. Later came Barenboim, Ashkenazy, Brendel, and the young Postnikova. Composition teaching was done by Alan Bush, Blacher, Elliott Carter, Roberto Gerhard, Nono, and Lutoslawski. Two visits stood out for all who were there: that in 1953 of the virtuoso and visionary *extraordinaire* Georges Enesco; and the residence in 1957 of Igor Stravinsky. For generations of young musicians growing up in the second half of the twentieth century, this mixture of high art and summer holiday, of professional endeavour and private enjoyment that William Glock had created and sustained, played a decisive part in their musical education.

Controller of music at the BBC For some time Glock had been on friendly terms with the controller of music at the BBC, Richard Howgill, who now suggested that Glock might like to become his successor in the post. The decision was publicly announced on 13 February 1959, drawing from the impresario Walter Legge the comment: 'I feel rather as though I were a citizen of Wittenberg in 1536 and Luther had just been elected Pope'. The enterprising days of the early 1930s when Adrian Boult and Edward Clark had variously led the BBC towards an adventurous music policy were long gone, and the corporation had settled into one of its recurring periods of intellectual stagnation and mediocrity. Glock was considered by many as 'a quixotic outsider', and a few probably were already aware of two things: that he knew far more about all kinds of music than any of them did, and that he was prepared temperamentally to upset any number of apple-carts in order to forward the process of renewal and reform. What they did not realize was that his appointment was in one sense a return to austere and uncompromising Reithian values. When Glock was later called before the Pilkington committee, its chairman asked him what he wished to offer listeners. 'What they will like tomorrow' has all his great predecessor's Caledonian intransigence and assurance about it.

The first battle was over the promenade concerts—in the BBC's gift since 1927 but since Sir Henry Wood's death increasingly occasions of inordinate length and unimaginative dullness; their camel-like physiognomy predictable since they had been designed by a committee. Glock insisted, against much opposition, on personal direction; the results were immediate and (despite a temporary dip in audiences) permanent. Innovations flowed from his imagination: there were evenings of complete operas; more young composers were commissioned; foreign orchestras were invited to take part. The proms became a great international music festival.

The BBC Symphony Orchestra itself needed immediate attention. Brought in a few years after its foundation in 1930 to a high pitch of perfection by Adrian Boult, it was highly esteemed among world orchestras by Toscanini. After Boult's absurdly enforced retirement in 1950 it had fallen on hard times. It was depleted in membership and depressed in spirit by low salary scales and inferior working conditions. The appointment in 1963 of Antal Dorati as chief conductor saw a resumption of first-rate orchestral training, and the orchestra's raised morale was confirmed by the success of two foreign tours, to the east coast of the USA in 1965 and to the USSR in 1967. Dorati was followed by two very different personalities: Colin Davis in 1967 and Pierre Boulez (already much involved with the BBC) in 1971.

Glock's talent for programme-making was at full strength during these years. Another innovation was that of the Tuesday invitation concerts. The originality of their format—much derided on first appearance—left a permanent mark on the building of good programmes in general. Basically, it consisted of the juxtaposition of old and new: the first concert sandwiched Boulez's *Le marteau sans maître* between two Mozart string quintets. But the 'old' element often went much further back in time—Machaut's *Messe de nostre Dame*, for instance, or a Byrd motet. The 'new' could be Stockhausen or Elliott Carter.

From the beginning Glock had found allies inside the corporation, notably Eric Warr and Peter Gould. But it was also necessary to recruit like-minded new blood. David Drew and Alexander Goehr worked part-time; Leo Black and Stephen Plaistow became full-time BBC employees. But the chief acquisition was that of Hans Keller, with whom Glock enjoyed a predictably stormy relationship, cemented only by their shared passion for the Viennese classics. Glock was the very reverse of the faceless public servant, and it is not surprising that day-to-day administration was not his forte. His artistic policy he splendidly described as one of 'creative imbalance', and this phrase was thrown in his face by opponents and by all who felt that they had been unfairly passed over, especially British composers born in the 1920s and 1930s. In the reaction against his policies which followed his retirement in 1972, the *salon des refusés* had something of a field day: drabness once again overcast British musical life, and some very dull pieces of music were pulled belatedly into the light of day.

Retirement On his retirement there was much to occupy Glock's abundant energies and imagination. For nine years (1975–84) he was, at Michael Tippett's invitation, director of the Bath Festival, which emphasized seventeenth- and eighteenth-century music. Nor indeed had this music ever been neglected at Dartington. So there continued at Bath to be much Monteverdi, Purcell, Handel, and J. S. Bach—as well as Haydn string quartets and Mozart wind music. But Kurtág, Elliott Carter, Maxwell Davies, Tippett, and Birtwistle also appeared, and many younger composers were encouraged by performances.

Glock's talents as a music administrator continued to be sought. He was a member of the board of the Royal Opera House, Covent Garden (1968–73), and chairman of the London Orchestral Concerts Board (1975–86). The passion for programme planning continued into his eighties. He organized the Music of Eight Decades Festival of contemporary music, and in 1989–90 he was responsible for a celebration of the music of Haydn, a composer he had always admired. He took up teaching again. Having been deeply involved in the late 1960s with the Leeds Piano Competition, he now went up to Manchester to coach piano pupils in masterclasses at the Royal Northern College of Music. In 1972 he ventured into book publishing, as general editor of a new series called Eulenburg Books which produced both valuable reprints such as Edward Dent's classic biography of Busoni and newly commissioned books—studies of Debussy, Boulez, Tippett, and Elliott Carter. He published in 1991 his autobiography, *Notes in Advance*, which, although it offers a somewhat muted self-portrait, contains fascinating pages about his tuition by Schnabel, his understanding and love of Mozart, and an account of his friendship with Pierre Boulez. Honours had come his way: he was appointed CBE in 1964 and knighted in 1970. In 1971 he became an honorary member of the Royal Philharmonic Society and also received the Albert medal of the Royal Society of Arts. He received honorary degrees from the University of Nottingham in 1968, from York in 1972, from Bath in 1984, and from Plymouth in 1993. Sir William Glock died in Oxford on 28 June 2000.

HUGH WOOD

Sources W. Glock, *Notes in advance* (1991) [autobiography] · *The Times* (29 June 2000) · *Daily Telegraph* (30 June 2002) · *The Guardian* (29 June 2000) · *The Independent* (1 July 2000) · *The Scotsman* (7 July 2000) · N. Kenyon, *BBC Symphony Orchestra* (1981) [history] · D. Cox, *The Henry Wood proms* (1980) · H. Carpenter, *The envy of the world: fifty years of the BBC Third Programme and Radio 3, 1946–1996* (1996) · b. cert. · m. certs.

Archives BL, music collections, corresp. and papers, 2000/23 | FILM BFI NFTVA, documentary footage

Likenesses N. Libbert, photograph, repro. in *The Guardian* · photograph, repro. in *The Times* · photograph, repro. in *Daily Telegraph* · photograph, repro. in *The Scotsman*

Wealth at death £822,854—gross; £752,160—net: probate, 17 Nov 2000, *CGPLA Eng. & Wales*

Gloucester. For this title name *see* Robert, first earl of Gloucester (*b.* before 1100, *d.* 1147); William, second earl of Gloucester (*d.* 1183); Isabella, *suo jure* countess of Gloucester (*c.*1160–1217); Clare, Gilbert de, fifth earl of Gloucester and fourth earl of Hertford (*c.*1180–1230); Clare, Richard de, sixth earl of Gloucester and fifth earl of Hertford (1222–1262); Clare, Gilbert de, seventh earl of Gloucester and sixth earl of Hertford (1243–1295); Joan, countess of Hertford and Gloucester (1272–1307); Audley, Hugh, earl of Gloucester (*c.*1291–1347); Clare, Gilbert de, eighth earl of Gloucester and seventh earl of Hertford (1291–1314); Clare, Margaret de, countess of Gloucester (1291/2?–1342); Thomas, duke of Gloucester (1355–1397); Humphrey, duke of Gloucester (1390–1447); Eleanor, duchess of Gloucester (*c.*1400–1452); Henry, Prince, duke of Gloucester (1640–1660); William, Prince, duke of Gloucester (1689–1700); Mary, Princess, duchess of Gloucester (1776–1857) [*see under* George III, daughters of (*act.* 1766–1857)]; Henry, Prince, first duke of Gloucester (1900–1974).

Gloucester, Benedict of (*fl. c.*1150), Benedictine monk and hagiographer, was a member of his order's house of St Peter's Abbey, Gloucester. He records this of himself in the prologue to his only known work, a life of St Dyfrig (Dubricius), which survives as folios 71–77 in BL, Cotton

MS Vespasian A.xiv, part of a collection of lives of Welsh saints assembled about the end of the twelfth century, perhaps at Monmouth. The same collection (fols. 58*v*–61) contains another, shorter, life of Dyfrig, identical with that contained in the Book of Llandaff, an early twelfth-century compilation made to document the rights and properties claimed by the diocese of Llandaff. Benedict uses this as the basis for his own work, but extends it with borrowings from the *Historia regum Britanniae* of Geoffrey of Monmouth, which was probably in circulation by 1138. He declares his motive for writing as essentially indignation that so little should be known of Dyfrig's life and holiness. But although Benedict illustrates the latter with miracle stories taken from the earlier life, these are overshadowed by his borrowings from Geoffrey, chosen to show Dyfrig as associated with the great deeds of Ambrosius Aurelianus, Uther Pendragon, and Arthur, from the time he was consecrated archbishop of Caerleon to the day he resigned his primacy to become a hermit. In Geoffrey's pages Dyfrig is the outstanding prelate of his time; Benedict takes glorification a stage further, by claiming that Arthur's affairs and wars had prospered only for as long as the king had the support of the archbishop's prayers, and that when that support ceased, misfortune followed.

Although Gloucester Abbey had an obvious motive for wanting to know about the lives of Welsh saints, arising from the substantial grants of lands and churches which the monastery received as a result of Anglo-Norman inroads into central and southern Wales after 1066, Benedict's main purpose in thus lauding St Dyfrig was probably to promote the latter's cult at Llandaff, initiated by the translation of his relics thither in 1120. Links between Llandaff and Gloucester were close. In 1148 Nicholas ap Gwrgan, a Gloucester monk, became bishop of Llandaff, and occupied the see for thirty-five years. Not only did he maintain a connection with his former monastery, but some time between 1150 and 1166 he issued a charter for Margam Abbey which was witnessed by three Gloucester monks, one of them named Benedict—without much doubt the hagiographer. The praise of the holy Dyfrig, represented (in a passage not matched in the earlier life) as adding substantially to the endowment of his see, was far from irrelevant to the concerns of Bishop Nicholas, engaged in consolidating the achievement of his predecessor, Bishop Urban, who had done much to recover Llandaff's lost possessions.

How far Benedict's life of Dyfrig circulated in the middle ages is unknown. However, Vespasian A.xiv was known to the mid-fourteenth-century hagiographer John Tynemouth, who uses Benedict, albeit in heavily abbreviated form, as the basis for the account of Dyfrig in his own *Sanctilogium*. After the Reformation the manuscript passed via Sir John Price of Brecon (a strong believer in the historicity of Geoffrey of Monmouth) and Sir Henry Sidney to Archbishop Matthew Parker, whose secretary noted Benedict's life of Dyfrig as being among its contents. Early in the seventeenth century it came into Sir Robert Cotton's collection. Most of the life of Dyfrig by Benedict was printed in 1691 by Henry Wharton, in the second volume of his *Anglia sacra*, though he omitted a few miracle stories.

HENRY SUMMERSON

Sources BL, Cotton MS Vespasian A.xiv, fols. 58*v*–61, 71–77 · [H. Wharton], ed., *Anglia sacra*, 2 (1691), 654–61 · N. K. Chadwick and others, *Studies in the early British church* (1958) · D. Crouch, ed., *Llandaff episcopal acta, 1140–1287*, South Wales and Monmouth RS, 5 (1988), no. 25 · A. W. Wade-Evans, ed. and trans., *Vitae sanctorum Britanniae et genealogiae* (1944), viii–ix · J. S. P. Tatlock, *The legendary history of Britain: Geoffrey of Monmouth's Historia regum Britanniae and its early vernacular versions* (1950) · 'De sancto Dubricio episcopo et confessore', *Nova legenda Anglie, as collected by John of Tynemouth, J. Capgrave, and others*, ed. C. Horstman, 1 (1901), 267–72
Archives BL, Cotton MS Vespasian A.xiv, fols. 58*v*–61, 71–77

Gloucester, Miles of, earl of Hereford (*d.* **1143**), magnate, was the third generation of a family which had grown powerful in royal administration. His grandfather, Roger de Pîtres, a protégé of William fitz Osbern, was sheriff of Gloucestershire and castellan of Gloucester Castle. His estates in Gloucestershire and Herefordshire, with smaller tenures elsewhere, formed the honour of Caldicot. Roger died before Domesday Book was compiled, and in 1086 his brother, Durand, was sheriff of Gloucestershire. That office, with the office of castellan of Gloucester Castle, passed to Roger's son, Walter of Gloucester, perhaps *c.*1097; like his father he held the castle directly from the king. He was given a wide range of duties, including responsibilities in south Wales, and he acquired the office of royal constable, probably in 1114. He died at Llanthony Priory *c.*1126. Miles succeeded to his father's offices; in Gloucestershire he served as sheriff and, almost certainly, as local justiciar. Father and son left their mark on Gloucester. Walter was responsible for building the tower keep of Gloucester Castle; in 1129–30 Miles accounted for work on the keep, and in Stephen's reign he continued to build the outer defences of the castle and strengthened the defences of the borough. William of Malmesbury claimed in a confused sentence that Miles held Gloucester from Robert, earl of Gloucester, but there is no other evidence for such a change of tenure.

In 1121 Henry I gave Miles as his wife Sybil, the daughter of Bernard of Neufmarché, lord of Brecon. She brought to the Gloucester family her father's lands. Marriage in 1121 and the assumption of his hereditary offices by 1127 suggest that Miles must have been born in the last years of the eleventh century. By 1130 he was also sheriff of Staffordshire. He was closely associated with another *curialis*, Pain fitz John, sheriff of Herefordshire and Shropshire. Between them they dominated local administration in the west midlands and south Wales 'from the Severn to the sea'. The extent and harshness of their 'rule' may be gauged from the pipe roll for 1129–30.

In the first days of 1136, like other magnates and royal officials, Miles had to come to terms with the *fait accompli* of Stephen's coronation. He joined Stephen at Reading, where the king and his barons had gathered for Henry I's funeral on 4 January. There he did homage and received confirmation of his lands and hereditary offices. His prompt adhesion was important for the king; it ensured that Stephen would enjoy the normal income from Gloucestershire, and in an area dominated by one of the potential rivals for the succession, Robert, earl of Gloucester, he would have the support of an experienced and influential administrator. For the next three years Miles was actively engaged as sheriff, as a royal justice, and as a curial figure, responding to royal writs, attesting the king's charters, and receiving tangible rewards for his services. The clearest indication of the close links between king and constable is to be found in the marriage, approved by the king, between Miles's son, *Roger, earl of Hereford, and Cecily, the daughter of Pain fitz John. She brought to the Gloucester family her father's inheritance and his claims to estates belonging to the Lacy family, an endowment which extended their estates and interests in Herefordshire. Some incidents in Miles's career in the marches in these years stand out sharply. In 1136 Richard de Clare, travelling through south-east Wales, was ambushed and killed near Crickhowell; in west Wales his widow was besieged in Cardigan Castle. Stephen sent Miles to rescue her, and in a brief but dangerous foray he brought her and her companions to safety. He received Stephen at Gloucester in May 1138, and in August he joined the king at the siege of Shrewsbury. In February 1139 Stephen appointed as abbot of St Peter's, Gloucester, Gilbert Foliot, who was a kinsman of Miles and owed his appointment to Miles's influence. During these years there is no hint that Miles was an unwilling adherent, or that his loyalty was suspect. When, in 1138, Robert, earl of Gloucester, rebelled, Miles remained loyal.

But behind Stephen's apparent security there remained the uncomfortable fact that Matilda's claim to the English throne was technically the stronger. In the late summer of 1139 she landed in England under Earl Robert's direction. Her arrival meant that problems of loyalty which had been forced into the shadows by Stephen's *coup d'état* in 1135, and which had begun to surface in 1138, now re-emerged as major political factors. Earl Robert left Matilda at Arundel and travelled to Gloucestershire where he persuaded Miles to declare for the empress. For the rest of his life he was unswerving in his devotion to her cause. In the months of sieges and strikes against enemy strongholds which followed, Miles played a full part. Stephen laid siege to Wallingford and then moved westward to capture Miles's castle at South Cerney. To relieve pressure on Gloucestershire, Humphrey (II) de Bohun (at Miles's instigation) garrisoned Trowbridge, and Stephen was drawn to Wiltshire to counter that threat. This enabled Miles to relieve Wallingford, to attack the king's supporters at Worcester, and to regain South Cerney. He forced the royalists out of Winchcombe, although the town suffered heavily. He failed to take Sudeley Castle, where he suffered a number of casualties. During this phase of the conflict he secured Hereford. In February 1141 he was involved in the battle of Lincoln, where Stephen was taken prisoner, to be held first at Gloucester and later at Bristol. This victory gave Matilda the opportunity to enter London. Her domineering manner alienated the citizens and she abandoned the city and fled to Gloucester. Miles restored her confidence and persuaded her to use Oxford as an advance base. There, on 25 July 1141, she conferred on him an earldom, and since Gloucester was already the earldom of her half-brother, Robert, he took the title of Hereford. With his own interests in Herefordshire and in the neighbouring lordship of Brecon, and his son's possessions in Herefordshire, it was an appropriate choice. At the end of July Matilda moved in what proved to be a critical attack against Winchester. There she met with a prompt and vigorous response by Stephen's queen, Matilda, and his mercenary captain, William of Ypres. The empress's forces were caught between the garrison of Wolvesey Castle, the citizens of Winchester, and the troops commanded by William of Ypres; she was outmanoeuvred and forced to retreat. As she withdrew under the protection of Reginald, earl of Cornwall, Earl Robert and Earl Miles had the difficult task of covering the retreat, harassed by William's mercenaries. Robert was captured, while Miles escaped, discarding arms and armour in the process.

Miles saw himself as the most loyal of Matilda's supporters, declaring that she had been dependent on his generosity throughout her stay in England. There was much truth in that, certainly until she was settled at Devizes in 1142, although it does not do justice to Earl Robert's support for her cause. Miles's loyalty was acknowledged by those most opposed to her claims; even the writer of the *Gesta Stephani* saw him as a father figure on whom she could depend. In 1142 and 1143 he was actively involved in local affairs in Gloucestershire and in attendance on Matilda at Bristol, Oxford, and Devizes. One extension of her patronage was permission to hold Brian fitz Count's lordship of Abergavenny. There were signs that these were difficult years. In June 1142, in preparation for a journey to Normandy, Earl Robert, apparently concerned for the loyalty of his associates in his absence, demanded that they should each hand over a son as a hostage. The resulting treaty of friendship scarcely disguised Robert's open assertion of authority. Robert provided a group of knightly tenants as guarantors of his good faith, but Miles had to give his son, Mahel, as hostage.

In 1143 Miles found the task of providing fighting men for the empress beyond his resources, and he made heavy demands on local churches and on the bishop of Hereford who, supported by the bishop of Worcester, imposed censure on him. Miles had never been a generous patron of the church. The monks of Gloucester and Brecon owed little to him; his benefactions were reserved primarily for the canons of Llanthony. When they left Wales to seek refuge in England, he gave them land outside Gloucester (May 1136) to build a new monastery and church (consecrated on 10 September 1137). On Christmas eve 1143 Miles was hunting in the Forest of Dean; a companion loosed an arrow at a deer, but it hit and killed the earl. The canons of Llanthony Priory near Gloucester made ready to bury him, but the right was claimed by the monks of St Peter's, Gloucester. The immediate dispute was settled in favour of Llanthony. Miles was succeeded by his eldest son, Roger, who later founded an abbey for the Cistercians at Flaxley, allegedly at the place where his father died.

DAVID WALKER

Sources *Reg. RAN*, vols. 2–3 • K. R. Potter and R. H. C. Davis, eds., *Gesta Stephani*, OMT (1976) • D. Walker, ed., 'Charters of the earldom of Hereford, 1095–1201', *Camden miscellany, XXII*, CS, 4th ser., 1 (1964), 1–75 • D. Walker, ed., 'A register of the churches of the monastery of St Peter's, Gloucester', *An ecclesiastical miscellany*, Bristol and Gloucestershire Archaeological Society Records Section, 11 (1976), 1–58 • D. G. Walker, 'Miles of Gloucester, earl of Hereford', *Transactions of the Bristol and Gloucestershire Archaeological Society*, 77 (1958), 66–84 • M. Chibnall, *The Empress Matilda* (1991) • E. King, ed., *The anarchy of King Stephen's reign* (1994)

Gloucester, Robert of (*fl. c.*1260–*c.*1300), chronicler, was author of part of an English metrical chronicle that survives in two versions and is the work of at least two authors. Both versions begin with the legendary founding of Britain by Brutus, with the longer (*c.*12,000 lines) ending in 1270, and the shorter (*c.*10,000 lines) ending in 1272 with the accession of Edward I. The two are similar from their beginnings until the death of Henry I (1135). The continuation covering events after 1135 consists in the longer version of *c.*3000 lines, in the shorter of *c.*600 lines. Robert refers to himself near the end of the continuation in two manuscripts of the longer version: in telling of the darkness that fell on the area around Evesham at the time of the battle, on 4 August 1265, he adds that 'Robert who first made this book' was frightened by it (*The metrical chronicle*, 2.765–6). Although this could refer to a scribe, it is usually interpreted as a reference to the author. Robert could have written the part to 1135 and had copies sent to libraries before writing the continuation in which his name appears; but an anonymous chronicler could have written the early part and Robert only the continuation. Another author must have revised the original chronicle that ended in 1135, adding to the early part about 800 lines derived from Geoffrey of Monmouth and Layamon, and also its continuation to 1272. Since the two continuations have accounts of the reign of King Stephen that are different but of approximately the same length, they were presumably written by different authors.

Wright believed that the early part of the chronicle was written after 1294, during the reign of Edward I, since in its account of Edward the Confessor the author remarks that the later Edward treated the clergy with less generosity; after that date Edward I began exacting half the clergy's revenues. The continuation in which Robert's name appears was at least revised *c.*1300, since it includes a reference to the canonization of St Louis, which occurred in 1297.

Most of what has been presented as biographical information about Robert is speculative. John Stow (*d.* 1605) first referred to him as Robert of Gloster in a list of authors in the third edition of his *Summarie of English Chronicles* (1570). A doctor of canon law named Robert of Gloucester, who lived between *c.*1252 and about January 1322, was associated with Oxford, but there is no evidence that he wrote a chronicle. Although the dialect of the work has been described as that of Gloucestershire, or of the south-west, or of the south-west midlands, studies of the manuscripts indicate that the author's dialect would in fact be difficult to determine. Robert was, however, familiar with Oxford and Gloucester: the author's knowledge of some details, in, for example, his accounts of the town and gown riots of Oxford in 1263, of the royalist sheriff of Gloucester's seizing his baronial rival by the hair and dragging him through the streets of Gloucester in 1261, or of Sir John Giffard's breaking into the city through the abbot's unguarded orchard in 1263, indicate that he may have witnessed some of the events described.

John Weever, in his *Ancient Funerall Monuments* (1631), first described Robert as 'Monke of Gloucester', and Thomas Hearne assumed that he was a monk of St Peter's Abbey, Gloucester, who studied at Oxford. He may have been a monk: the chronicle shows interest in both Gloucester and St Peter's; its support of the barons against Henry III in the conflicts of the thirteenth century is typical of monastic chronicles; and its author's use of several chronicles and saints' lives as sources suggests access to a monastic library. No evidence, however, associates him with the Gloucester monks who studied at Oxford. The only interest that the chronicle shows in a religious order at Oxford is with the Augustinian priory of St Frideswide, which Henry III visited in 1263. Robert could possibly have been a secular clerk associated with both Oxford and Gloucester rather than a monk: none of the twelve manuscripts known to Aldis Wright, whose edition of the chronicle for the Rolls Series appeared in 1887, originated in monastic libraries; the chronicle, which was influenced by French Arthurian romance, is concerned primarily with lay, rather than ecclesiastical, matters and, written in English, would have been intended for the unlearned. It has been plausibly argued that it may have been written for a powerful layman, Sir Warin of Bassingbourn, whose exploits are several times presented in a flattering light. Robert may have become a monk of St Peter's late in life, having earlier been a layman at Oxford, where he could have met Sir Warin.

The chronicle was well known in the middle ages and later. Fourteen medieval manuscripts of the two versions survive, as well as two different fifteenth-century prose adaptations. Three transcripts were copied in the seventeenth and eighteenth centuries, and it was a source for sixteenth- and seventeenth-century antiquarians like Stow, Camden, Selden, Weever, Dugdale, Fuller, and Wood. Hearne's edition (1724) made it available to many more readers. No one has admired the chronicle as poetry, but it has been valued for linguistic evidence, and for the historical information it provides concerning the barons' war. It was the first chronicle written in English after Layamon's *Brut*, and the first English vernacular chronicle to add the legendary history of Britain to an account that told of Anglo-Saxon and post-conquest England. By incorporating this legendary material into the whole history of England, it legitimized it as history for many in the middle ages.

EDWARD DONALD KENNEDY

Sources E. D. Kennedy, *A manual of the writings in Middle English, 1050–1500*, 8: *Chronicles and other historical writings*, ed. A. E. Hartung

(1967), 2617–22, 2798–807 [incl. list of MSS and transcripts] • A. Gransden, *Historical writing in England*, 1 (1974), 432–8 • *The metrical chronicle of Robert of Gloucester*, ed. W. A. Wright, 2 vols., Rolls Series, 86 (1887) • A. Hudson, 'Robert of Gloucester and the antiquaries, 1550–1800', *N&Q*, 214 (1969), 322–33 • A. Hudson, 'Tradition and innovation in some Middle English manuscripts', *Review of English Studies*, new ser., 17 (1966), 359–72 • Emden, *Oxf.*, 2.273–4 • *DNB* • D. D. Brown, 'Robert of Gloucester's chronicle and the life of St Kenelm', *Modern Language Notes*, 41 (1926), 13–23

Gloucester, William of (*d.* 1269). *See under* Moneyers (*act.* *c.*1180–*c.*1500).

Gloucester and Edinburgh. For this title name *see* Maria, duchess of Gloucester and Edinburgh (*bap.* 1736, *d.* 1807) [*see under* William Henry, Prince, first duke of Gloucester and Edinburgh (1743–1805)]; William Henry, Prince, first duke of Gloucester and Edinburgh (1743–1805); William Frederick, Prince, second duke of Gloucester and Edinburgh (1776–1834).

Glover, Boyer (*fl.* 1758–1771), member of the Muggletonians, may have been the son of Richard and Elizabeth Glover who was baptized Bowyer Glover on 10 January 1713 at St Andrew's, Holborn. He was a watch- and clockmaker in Leadenhall Street, London. With one exception he made his mark on the sect's life by his music rather than by his politics. Seven of his songs are in a collection, *Songs of Gratefull Praise*, of 1794; to them are added another forty-two in *Divine Songs of the Muggletonians* of 1829, which included one song contributed by his wife, Elizabeth, also known as Daisy Glover. The exception was important, however. In 1656 the founder prophets, Lodowicke Muggleton and John Reeve, had published *A Divine Looking Glass*; after Reeve's death in 1658 Muggleton steered the small sect on a different, more quietist, course. Integral to this was his revision of that pamphlet in 1661. Both in 1719 and 1760 the 1656 edition was republished; in the latter case against Glover's wishes. Glover's championship of the 1661 edition was taken up in the nineteenth century by Joseph Frost. When Frost gifted the prophets' works to the British Museum, a letter to the trustees in 1853 justified his reinstatement of Muggleton's revised work in the 1846 edition. The recent recovery of the Muggleton Archive shows that as late as 1933 the debate over the editions continued.

Alexander Gordon, *rev.* William Lamont

Sources BL, Add. MSS 60168–60256 • priv. coll., Noakes MSS • BL, Add. MS 61950 • C. Hill, B. Reay, and W. Lamont, *The world of the Muggletonians* (1983) • W. Lamont, 'The Muggletonians, 1652–1979: a "vertical" approach', *Past and Present*, 99 (1983), 22–40 • W. Lamont, 'A new Jerusalem: the elusive dream', *Living and learning*, ed. M. Chase and I. Dyck (1996), 10–24 • *IGI*
Archives BL, Add. MSS 60168–60256

Glover, Brian (1934–1997), actor, was born on 2 April 1934 at the Women's Hospital, Sheffield, the son of Charles Glover, grocer and all-in wrestler (under the name of the Red Devil), and Ida Fell, formerly Drake, a domestic housekeeper, of 70 The Dale, Sheffield. His parents, who did not marry until Glover was twenty, moved to Lundwood, outside Barnsley, in 1937; there his mother ran a beauty salon-cum-lending library. Glover won a scholarship to Barnsley grammar school and he was a member of the Barnsley Boys soccer team that won the English schools trophy in 1949. He went on to Sheffield University, but as a Yorkshireman with a keen, and even comic, sense of the value of money, he succumbed to wrestling when he realized that a £200 a year grant could be superseded by fees of £100 a night. In his first bout he took the place of Leon Arras, a Frenchman who had failed to turn up, and the name stuck. On 10 July 1954 he married Elaine Foster (*b.* 1934/5), a General Post Office telephonist and daughter of Willie Foster, colliery deputy, of Barnsley. The birth of their daughter Maxine persuaded him to attend teacher training college and for a decade Mr Glover taught French and English at Barnsley grammar school, while Leon Arras flew to wrestle in Paris, Milan, Zürich, and Barcelona.

In 1969 a novel written by Glover's teaching colleague Barry Hines was filmed by Ken Loach as *Kes*, and Hines suggested Glover for the part of Mr Sugden, the games master overtaken by a Bobby Charlton fantasy. A huge acting personality was instantly apparent: the stocky, bald, battered appearance, the bluster that was not afraid to be pathetic, the ripe Yorkshire tones, the comic bluntness that masked kindness and a well-read, well-travelled mind. In 1970 he gave up teaching to play Captain Hardy in Terence Rattigan's *A Bequest to the Nation*, and he found his significant home when the director Bill Bryden took him to the Royal Court Theatre for Keith Dewhurst's plays *Pirates* and *Corunna!* In 1971 he worked for Lindsay Anderson for the first time in David Storey's *The Changing Room* and in 1972 he made his first television appearance in Peter Terson's *The Fishing Party* for David Rose's regime at BBC Birmingham, where Glover's own later television plays were produced. Glover had a shrewd sense of how to accommodate himself to different directors and managements, and in 1973 he joined the Royal Shakespeare Company, playing Falstaff and the Wrestler in *As You Like It*. On television he was in the popular prison sitcom *Porridge* and in the cinema he was in Anderson's *O Lucky Man!* (1973) and *Brannigan* (1975), in which he took a punch from John Wayne. In the theatre he worked for Richard Eyre at Birmingham and for Anderson in David Storey's *Life Class* and Joe Orton's *What the Butler Saw*. In 1977 he became a founder member of Bill Bryden's Cottesloe Company, in which his gift for epic popular theatre saw its fullest expression as God in *The Mysteries* (1977 and *passim*), in Keith Dewhurst's *Lark Rise* (1978) and *The World Turned Upside Down* (1978), and in several plays by Eugene O'Neill.

Glover's generation had profited from government encouragement of the arts during the Second World War and from the spread of secondary education thereafter. It was natural for him to believe that artistic work could be both popular and profound, and his acting embodied that notion. Wrestling taught him to perform clear and simple actions that would be intelligible to the entire audience, while his own taste and knowledge of life told him that these actions need not be vulgar. Thus it was that his great performance as God in *The Mysteries* led to his immense popularity in the 1980s when he appeared in commercial theatre hits such as *La cage aux folles* and *The Canterbury*

Tales, highbrow pieces such as Tony Harrison's *Trackers of Oxyrinthus*, films such as *An American Werewolf in London*, *Britannia Hospital*, and *Aliens 3*, and as the voice of many television commercials.

In his private life Glover had a vast acquaintance, most of whom relished his comic sexual escapades and his particular wit. In his teaching days a teacher of some airs and graces complained to the common room that she did not know how to spend her summer holiday. 'Go to Blackpool,' advised Glover, 'get drunk and get tattooed!' (private information)—a pungent remark, yet kind in its way, and typical of his sallies at the Chelsea Arts Club or in his favourite Greek restaurant on Fulham Road in London. When he knew that his brain tumour was mortal he married, on 2 October 1996, his companion Tara Angleen Kamla Prem (*b*. 1945/6), film producer, and daughter of Bakhshi Prem, actor. (His first marriage had ended in divorce.) He died at the Trinity Hospice, Clapham, London, on 24 July 1997. He was survived by his second wife, Tara Prem; their son, Gus; and Maxine, the daughter of his first marriage. At his funeral in Brompton cemetery on 30 July, attended by hundreds of people, he was played to his rest by the folk musicians with whom he had worked at the Cottesloe Theatre. As he once said to me about a play that I had written there: 'Don't worry. T'band'll carry it.'

KEITH DEWHURST

Sources *Daily Telegraph* (25 July 1997) • *The Times* (25 July 1997) • *The Guardian* (25 July 1997) • *The Independent* (25 July 1997) • *The Independent* (28 July 1997) • personal knowledge (2004) • private information (2004) [Richard Hines] • b. cert. • m. cert. • d. cert.
Archives priv. coll., television scripts, personal memorabilia
Likenesses photograph, repro. in *The Times* • photograph, repro. in *The Independent* (25 July 1997) • photograph, repro. in *Daily Telegraph* • photograph, repro. in *The Guardian*
Wealth at death £650,816: probate, 22 Dec 1997, *CGPLA Eng. & Wales*

Glover, Charles William (1806–1863), composer, was born in February 1806 in London. After studying with T. Cooke he went on to play the violin in the orchestras of Drury Lane and Covent Garden theatres, and in 1832 was appointed musical director at the Queen's Theatre, Tottenham Street, a post which he retained for some years. He composed numerous songs, duets, and piano pieces, and made several arrangements. Some of the vocal pieces, which range from the comic to the sentimental, were very popular, notably 'Jeannette and Jeannot', 'Sing not that song to me, sweet bird', and 'Of love, pretty maidens, beware'. Glover died on 23 March 1863. His younger brother, Stephen Ralph *Glover, was also a composer.

L. M. MIDDLETON, *rev.* DAVID J. GOLBY

Sources J. D. Brown, *Biographical dictionary of musicians: with a bibliography of English writings on music* (1886), 273–4 • Grove, *Dict. mus.*

Glover, Edmund (1813–1860), actor and theatre manager, was the eldest son of Samuel Glover and the actress Julia *Glover, *née* Betterton (1779/1781–1850). His brother was the composer and writer William Howard *Glover. He occupied for a time a leading position in London at the Haymarket Theatre, and then went to Edinburgh, where, under W. H. Murray, he played leading business. He appears to have joined the company about 1841 and remained until 1848. He was a man of diverse talents, a sound though not a brilliant actor, a good dancer, fencer, and pantomimist, and a fairly skilled painter. He was well regarded in Scotland, and his salary in 1842 was 3 guineas a week. The parts he played included Richelieu, Rob Roy, Creon in *Antigone*, Jonas Chuzzlewit, Othello, Macbeth, Richard III, Iago, Shylock, and Cardinal Wolsey. On 16 January 1848 he played Falkland in *The Rivals*—his first appearance after a severe accident.

In 1847 Glover engaged Jenny Lind to sing in Edinburgh, Glasgow, and Perth, and cleared £3000 by the transaction. Emboldened by this success he took a large hall in West Nile Street, Glasgow, which he opened as the Prince's Theatre in January 1849. In 1852 he undertook the management of the Theatre Royal, Glasgow. He became lessee also of the Theatres Royal at Paisley and Dunfermline, and in 1859 opened a new theatre at Greenock. Glover maintained his connection with Edinburgh during this successful period as a theatre manager. In March 1850 he was Othello to W. C. Macready's Iago, and he played Falkland at Murray's farewell benefit in October 1851. In March 1856 he began to alternate with Thomas Powrie, the Scottish tragedian, in the parts of Macbeth and Macduff. In February 1857 he played alongside Henry Irving. His last appearance at the Edinburgh Theatre Royal was in May 1859. He had been ill for some time, and died on 24 October 1860 of dropsy, at 3 Gayfield Place, Edinburgh, in the house of Robert Wyndham, later manager of the city's Theatre Royal.

Glover's wife, Elizabeth Peperall (1809–1895), was also on the stage and was seen in Glasgow as Lady Teazle (1852), Katherine in *The Taming of the Shrew* (1853), Helen in Sheridan Knowles's *The Hunchback*, and Mrs Simpson in John Poole's *Simpson and Co.* (1858). Of their children, William was said to have inherited his father's talents as a painter, Samuel became a well-known Scottish comic actor and died abroad, and Phyllis married Thomas Powrie.

JOSEPH KNIGHT, *rev.* NILANJANA BANERJI

Sources P. Hartnoll, ed., *The Oxford companion to the theatre* (1951); 2nd edn (1957); 3rd edn (1967) • J. C. Dibdin, *The annals of the Edinburgh stage* (1888) • Adams, *Drama* • J. Parker, ed., *Who's who in the theatre*, 6th edn (1930) • NA Scot., SC 36/48/46, 833–7
Wealth at death £3640 19*s*. 10*d*.: confirmation, 9 Jan 1861, NA Scot., SC 36/48/46, 833–7

Glover, Edward George (1888–1972), psychoanalyst, was born on 13 January 1888 at Lesmahagow, Lanarkshire, the third son of Matthew Glover, a country schoolmaster, and Elizabeth Smith Shanks, who was of a farming family. His eldest brother, James, who died early, in 1927, was regarded as the genius of the family, taking after his father, whereas Edward was regarded as being more pedestrian. The middle brother died when Edward was four. Edward's intellectual capacities only appeared at fourteen when his father became his teacher. Before that he was 'a reluctant, rebellious, contumacious and obstinate schoolboy' (Kubie, 86). He followed James into medicine and qualified MB ChB Glasgow, aged twenty-one. Four years of good academic medicine (under a cardiologist, Professor

John Cowan) honed his scientific bent, though his awareness of psychological forces when treating children brought to his attention the clash between the strictly organic approach to medicine and the scope of actual clinical experience.

Glover spent some years in tuberculosis medicine, publishing some papers, until his elder brother James introduced him to psychoanalysis. Glover recognized both his identification with James and also the need of the young brother to copy and surpass his older sibling rival. Later, when they were both psychoanalysts they worked together without incapacitating rivalry, each acting as foil for the mind of the other. The brothers both went to Germany at the end of the First World War to study with Karl Abraham, the outstanding figure of the new Berlin Psychoanalytic Institute. Edward, then thirty-two, was honorary medical officer to an English Quaker relief commission. Both James and Edward were luminaries in early British psychoanalysis but James's life came to a sudden end from diabetes.

Glover spent many years as the collaborator of Ernest Jones, the dominating life president of the British Psycho-Analytical Society, which he had formed in 1919. Successively he was director of research, later director, and chairman of the training committee of the Institute of Psychoanalysis. Glover was regarded as Jones's crown prince and successor but finally broke with him over his political manipulations within the Psycho-Analytical Society.

Between 1926 and 1929 Jones and Glover represented the Psycho-Analytical Society on the British Medical Association's committee investigating the status of psychoanalysis, which was formed following public disquiet at its possible harmful effects. Together, against strong opposition, they received the association's recognition of psychoanalysis as a technique requiring professional training. During these years Glover took over Jones's functions in the society as Jones was grief stricken following the death of his daughter Gwenith.

Glover described himself in adolescence as 'a little prig and have remained so' (Kubie, 86). He was very critical of his own writings and those of others as he had learned from his father how to aim for high academic standards and insisted on the importance of distinguishing metapsychology from metaphysics. His writing style was clear and fluent and he held no respect for persons in authority. He insisted that basic Freudian principles should be respected and tested before developing new ideas. Thus, though he had been a supporter of Melanie Klein's speculations on the early development of mind, he later launched trenchant criticisms on her work. In this he was joined by Melanie Klein's daughter, Melita Schmideberg, who had entered analysis with him; their alliance raised considerable hostility. He considered that Klein's speculations about the infant's early mental development were unscientific and incompatible with Freud's theories and that, therefore, the society, which he alleged was being taken over by Mrs Klein's followers, was no longer a Freudian society. His many contributions to the controversial discussions of the British Psycho-Analytical Society show his considerable polemical skills which he did not hesitate to use when challenged. Schmideberg was so exaggerated and hostile in her attacks that it was not possible to differentiate real causes for concern from mischief making. Glover himself, according to the psychoanalytic historian R. Steiner, became out of touch with historical reality, his forecasts being apocalyptic and ferociously one-sided.

Glover resigned from the British Psycho-Analytic Society in 1944, no longer able to accept what he considered major deviations of Freudian psychoanalysis, particularly from the Klein school. Playing second-in-command to Jones for decades, his ambition to succeed Jones as president of the society was doomed by his polemics against those who did not agree with his views on what constituted Freudian psychoanalysis. He became a member of the Swiss Psychoanalytic Society and an honorary member of the American Psychoanalytic Association.

Glover's achievements lay in four areas. First he pioneered psychoanalytic research on delinquency and criminology and was a founder of the Institute for Scientific Treatment of Delinquency, later the Portman Clinic. His *Diagnosis of Delinquency* appeared in 1944. He was also the founder and editor of the *British Journal of Criminology*. Second, he insisted on psychoanalysis taking a serious attitude to research, both theoretical and technical. His 1932 enquiry into the practice of the British Psycho-Analytical Society, not published until 1940, revealed a great variability of theory and technique within the society. His important text, *The Technique of Psycho-Analysis*, was published in 1928. Third, he argued for high standards in psychoanalytic training and was active nationally and internationally, being vice-president and honorary secretary of the International Psycho-Analytical Association. He was chairman of the training committee of the British Psycho-Analytical Society and acting chairman during the Second World War. Fourth, he attempted prematurely to develop a psychoanalytic diagnostic schema for mental disorders. His most original contribution was his theory of the early development of mind in which he postulated ego nuclei of experience gradually coalescing and integrating into a unitary ego. This work predated many later ideas in this area. His writings also included *War, Sadism and Pacifism* (1933), *Psychoanalysis: a Handbook for Medical Practitioners and Students of Comparative Psychology* (1939), and *Exceptional Children* (1960).

Glover's first marriage was in 1918 to Christine Margaret Speir, who died in childbirth the same year with a still-born son; his second marriage, on 15 July 1924, was to Gladys (1887/8–1966), daughter of Robert Blair; their one daughter was born mentally handicapped. Her parents gave her great devotion, which, however, led them into a considerable degree of social isolation. Gladys Glover died in 1966 after three years of painful illness from a brain tumour.

Glover and Ernest Jones fought for the acceptance of psychoanalysis within the scientific community of Great Britain; the British Medical Association report of 1929 achieved partial recognition. Glover's most permanent achievement, outlasting his polemics against Jung and Klein, was the establishment of psychoanalytic investigation and treatment of delinquency which was the origin of forensic psychotherapy. A formidable figure to those who knew him only in public, in private Glover was known for his kindness, cordiality, and Scottish humour. He died in London on 16 August 1972.

MALCOLM PINES

Sources L. S. Kubie, 'Edward Glover: a biographical sketch', *International Journal of Psycho-Analysis*, 54 (1973), 85–93 · M. N. Walsh, 'The scientific works of Edward Glover', *International Journal of Psycho-Analysis*, 54 (1973), 95–102 · E. Glover, 'The position of psychoanalysis in Great Britain', *British Medical Bulletin*, 6 (1949), 27–31 · E. Glover, 'Psychoanalysis in England', *Psychoanalytic pioneers*, ed. F. Alexander, S. Eisenstein, and M. Grotjahn (1966) · C. W. Wahl, 'Edward Glover: theory and technique', *Psychoanalytic pioneers*, ed. F. Alexander, S. Eisenstein, and M. Grotjahn (1966) · V. Brome, *Ernest Jones: Freud's alter ego* (1982) · P. King and R. Steiner, eds., *The Freud–Klein controversies, 1941–1945* (1991) · m. cert. · *CGPLA Eng. & Wales* (1972)

Wealth at death £23,217: probate, 26 Sept 1972, *CGPLA Eng. & Wales*

Glover, George (*fl.* **1634–1652**), engraver, was, after John Payne, the best of the native English engravers working in London in the reign of Charles I. Nothing is known of his life except what can be deduced from his engravings, and it is these that determine the span of his career. The catalogue of his output compiled by Margery Corbett and Michael Norton on the basis of the notes of A. M. Hind shows that most of his work consisted of title-pages or portraits, and that most of the latter served as the frontispieces to books.

Glover's main patrons, therefore, were London publishers. Other plates were made for specialist print publishers, among them Robert Peake, Thomas Banks, John Hinde, and Peter Stent. The most interesting are perhaps the five series Glover made for William Peake and William Webb. They show half-length women dressed in highly fashionable costumes, representing by the attributes they hold the four complexions (that is, temperaments), the five senses, the seven liberal arts, the seven deadly sins, and the nine women worthies. These are among the best of a genre that was extremely popular during the Caroline period, but of which very few impressions survive at the end of the twentieth century. Whether Glover designed them himself, or whether he copied them from some unidentified French original, is still unclear.

During these years the immigrant Dutchman Robert van Voerst dominated print-making commissioned by members of the court. Glover's only attempt to raise his art to this level was in a portrait of Queen Henrietta Maria after a painting by Van Dyck, engraved in 1640, and dedicated to her by Glover himself. How he obtained permission to do this is unclear, and mysterious. It is the only plate that Glover published himself, and is now rare.

ANTONY GRIFFITHS

Sources A. M. Hind, *Engraving in England in the sixteenth and seventeenth centuries*, 3, ed. M. Corbett and M. Norton (1964), 225–50 · A. Griffiths and R. A. Gerard, *The print in Stuart Britain, 1603–1689* (1998), 103–4, 108–9 [exhibition catalogue, BM, 8 May – 20 Sept 1998]

Glover, Sir James Malcolm (**1929–2000**), army officer, was born on 25 March 1929 at 7 St Andrews Road, Portsmouth, son of Major-General Malcolm Glover (1897–1970) of the South Lancashire regiment and of the 14th Punjab regiment, Indian army, and his wife, Jean Catharine Ogilvie, daughter of Colonel J. Will of the Royal Army Medical Corps. He therefore had the army in his blood on both sides of the family. Jimmy, as he was known, had a brother and sister. Educated at Wellington College and the Royal Military Academy, Sandhurst, he was commissioned in 1949 into the Royal Artillery with whom he served until transferring to the rifle brigade in January 1957.

At that time the battalion was in Malaya fighting communist terrorists. Operating against small numbers of very experienced Chinese guerrillas hiding in thick jungle was an exacting and physically demanding business which gave Glover his first experience of combating insurgents. On 11 September 1958 he married Janet Diones De Pree (*b.* 1937/8)—from another army family—who was his unfailing support thereafter: they had a son and a daughter. He spent 1959 at the Staff College, and then became brigade major of 48 Gurkha infantry brigade in Hong Kong.

In 1963 Glover returned to 1st rifle brigade as a company commander in Cyprus. When Greek Cypriots attacked Turkish Cypriots there was a danger that war might break out between Greece and Turkey. British battalions were therefore interposed between the combatants and Glover found himself running a sector of Nicosia. In the coming weeks he discovered how to use bluff in the absence of a clear mandate. He also discovered the meaning of civil control of the military when the minister of defence personally told him to move six men from one place to another.

After attendance at the joint services Staff College, Glover returned to the army Staff College as an instructor. In 1970 he was given command of the 3rd battalion Royal Green Jackets, a mechanized battalion in West Germany. In the course of the next two years it moved into the strategic reserve from where it was sent at short notice to Northern Ireland for eighteen crucial days at the height of the protestant marching season. Soon afterwards it joined the United Nations peacekeeping force in Cyprus for six months. Maintaining efficiency and morale in the face of these rapid changes proved no problem for Glover, though disbanding the battalion at the end of his period of command as part of government cutbacks must have appalled him. A highly intelligent man above medium height and with an athletic figure, Glover achieved success as a commander because his men respected his professionalism and judgement; he had no need for play-acting.

For the next two years Glover was a colonel in the Ministry of Defence, responsible for the operational deployment of all army units. He was then promoted brigadier commanding 19 airportable brigade in England, the main role of which was to reinforce 1st British corps in Germany in war. In the event it went to Cyprus to reinforce the British bases there when the Turks invaded in July 1974. The bases were being swamped by Greek and Turkish refugees.

Glover's next appointment was as a brigadier in the defence intelligence staff, a job which involved putting together intelligence concerning Northern Ireland gathered from a variety of sources. While there he wrote a paper on future terrorist trends, which was leaked to the republican press. In it he pointed out that the IRA, having changed their organization to make it more difficult to penetrate and having assembled a large quantity of weapons, men, and money, was preparing for a lengthy war. The current British view was too optimistic.

In February 1979 Glover became commander land forces, Northern Ireland. He arrived at a time when government policy required raising the profile of the Royal Ulster Constabulary and lowering that of the army. This was complicated by differences of opinion between the general officer commanding and the chief constable, as a result of which Glover had a difficult task. The disaster at Warrenpoint when eighteen soldiers were killed by IRA bombs also occurred at this time. He left the province in October 1980 just before the IRA 'dirty protest' turned into a hunger strike.

Glover's next appointment, in the rank of lieutenant-general, was deputy chief of the defence staff (intelligence) with a seat on the joint intelligence committee. He was now the senior service officer dealing with intelligence, a particularly exacting task during the Falklands War. In May 1993 he became vice chief of the general staff and a member of the army board. He was also colonel commandant Royal Green Jackets (1984–8).

In 1985 Glover was promoted full general and appointed commander-in-chief United Kingdom land forces. With two lieutenant-generals under him, one commanding the field army and one the individual training organization, he was able to concentrate on the tri-service aspects of planning overseas operations and securing the home base from interference during the opening stages of war when, it was assumed, vast numbers of British and American troops would be passing to the continent. In maintaining good relations with the civilian population, he took a particular interest in forging links with the business community.

Soon after retiring, Glover in an interview with the BBC said that the provisional IRA could never be defeated militarily. This is an indisputable fact, as insurgency which consists of a mixture of violence with other measures can be beaten only by the government using a similar mixture of military force with other forms of coercion and persuasion. The implication of his statement was that he did not expect an adequate mixture to be forthcoming. Instead he recommended negotiation. Although subsequently proved right, his statement was not universally welcomed.

On retirement he joined the board of BP and became chairman of the royal armouries and of Merlin Communications International. Glover was awarded the MBE in 1964 and the KCB in 1981. In 1997 he was appointed deputy lieutenant for Hampshire. He died of a heart attack at his home, West End Farm House, near Medstead, Hampshire, on 4 June 2000. FRANK KITSON

Sources *WWW, 1961–70*, 432 • *WW* (2000), 775 • *The Times* (6 June 2000) • *Daily Telegraph* (8 June 2000) • *The Guardian* (16 June 2000) • *Army List* (1984), pt 3, biographical • D. Hamill, *Pig in the middle, the army in Northern Ireland* (1985), 238–41 • P. Taylor, *Brits, the war against the IRA* (2001), 218–20 • personal knowledge (2004) • b. cert. • m. cert. • d. cert.

Likenesses photograph, 1979, repro. in *Daily Telegraph* • photograph, 1985, repro. in *The Times*

Wealth at death £353,292—gross • £350,060—net: probate, 2000, *CGPLA Eng. & Wales*

Glover, Jean (1758–1801), actress, was born in Kilmarnock, Ayrshire, on 31 October 1758, the third child of James Glover, a weaver, and his wife, Jean, *née* Thomson. At an early age she joined a band of strolling players, and reputedly married their leader, a man named Richard, described by the poet Robert Burns as 'a sleight-of-hand blackguard' (Stenhouse). Glover was reputedly the best singer and actress in the company, and was used to attract customers by dressing in gaudy costume and playing the tambourine in the street. One observer described her in her player's finery as 'the brawest woman that had ever been seen to step in leather shoon' (*DNB*). She is recorded as having performed in a public house in Muirkirk and at Irvine in 1795. Her sole claim to fame is that Burns recorded a song she composed, 'O'er the muir among the Heather', transcribing it directly from her own performance. He published it in the *Scots Musical Museum* (4, 1792; song no. 328), to an earlier tune, and it was featured widely in nineteenth-century collections. Burns observed that Glover was 'not only a whore but also a thief; and in one or other character has visited most of the correction houses in the west' (Lindsay). If she composed other songs, they have not been preserved. Glover died at Letterkenny, co. Donegal, Ireland. T. W. BAYNE, *rev.* K. D. REYNOLDS

Sources W. Stenhouse, *Illustrations of the lyric poetry and music of Scotland* (1853) • D. Baptie, ed., *Musical Scotland, past and present: being a dictionary of Scottish musicians from about 1400 till the present time* (1894) • R. Burns and others, *The Scots musical museum*, ed. J. Johnson and W. Stenhouse, new edn, 4 vols. (1853); repr. (1991) • *The life and works of Robert Burns*, ed. R. Chambers, 4 vols. (1851–4) • S. Tytler and J. L. Watson, *The songstresses of Scotland*, 2 vols. (1871) • b. cert. • M. Lindsay, *The Burns encyclopedia*, 2nd edn (1970) • *The poems and songs of Robert Burns*, ed. J. Kinsley, 3 (1968)

Glover, John (1713/14–1774), preacher and writer, was born in Norwich, and under his mother's influence showed religious concerns from an early age. Apprenticed to an unspecified trade in 1728, he lost almost all his religious impressions and indulged in reading plays and novels. About 1736 strict religious people influenced him to attend church regularly, receive the sacrament, and practise private devotions, though he continued to delight in plays and novels. He was married about 1741. Some four years later his uncle died, leaving him a legacy which later often supplied his sole income.

Though devoted to the Church of England, Glover felt that contemporary Anglican preaching on moral obedience as sufficient for salvation contradicted the liturgy. About 1751–2 he heard 'Methodists' in Norwich (probably followers of James Wheatley, a preacher recently dismissed for immorality by John Wesley) speak of saving faith, and felt he needed this. Driven by ill health and distaste for worldly concerns, from 1756 Glover concentrated on his spiritual life. He was led to evangelical Calvinism by reading puritan and Calvinist writers including John Owen and James Hervey. Walter Marshall's *Gospel Mystery of Sanctification* (1692) convinced him that salvation is 'a free gift … without any regard to our works as the procuring cause' (*Memoirs*, 37). Though comforted by the doctrine of final perseverance (that those saved by grace cannot fall away), he warned against the risk of antinomianism (disregard of moral law). He emphasized Christian experience for confirming biblical teaching, though remained wary of feelings as proof of salvation.

From 1764 Glover kept a diary of his religious experiences, gave up his business, corresponded with religious friends, notably the Calvinist writer Anne Dutton, and wrote devotional works. He founded a religious society in Mattishall, Norfolk, on the pattern publicized by Josiah Woodward and built a chapel for his followers there. They formed a congregational church and ordained Glover's convert John Carter as minister in 1772. Carter published Glover's autobiography (1774) and extracts from his diary (1779).

Carter's own memoir makes clear Glover's lifelong Anglicanism. John Glover's career illustrates how evangelistic zeal could provoke a faithful Anglican into irregular activity—even to the unintended foundation of a dissenting congregation. Glover's wife lost her reason in 1770 and died in 1771. Glover himself died, aged sixty, on 5 May 1774, and was buried in Norwich Cathedral graveyard on 9 May. His tombstone was later removed, as its outspoken statement of salvation by Christ's merits alone was deemed 'scandalous', 'nonsensical', and to reflect on the clergy (*Memoirs*, 105). HENRY D. RACK

Sources *Some memoirs of the life of John Glover … written by himself* (1774) [with sermon on him by John Carter] · *The hidden and happy life of a Christian … exemplified in extracts from the diary of Mr J[ohn] G[lover]* (1779) · J. Browne, *A history of Congregationalism and memorials of the churches in Norfolk and Suffolk* (1877), 351–3 · 'Memoir of the late Rev. John Carter', *London Christian Instructor, or, Congregational Magazine*, 1 (1818), 617–28 · E. J. Bellamy, *James Wheatley and Norwich Methodism in the late 1750s* (1994), 27–32

Glover, John (1767–1849), landscape painter, was born at Houghton on the Hill near Leicester on 18 February 1767, and baptized there on 22 February, the youngest of three children of William Glover, a small farmer, and his wife, Ann, *née* Cole. Little is known of his early years or education, but in 1786 he was appointed writing-master at the free school, Appleby. There he began to paint professionally and to pay visits to London, where he viewed exhibitions and received lessons from William Payne (*c.*1760–1830) and possibly from John 'Warwick' Smith (1749–1831). On 25 July 1790 at Houghton on the Hill he married Sarah Young (1758–1853) and their first child was John Richardson Glover (1790–1868), who himself later became a landscape artist.

In 1794 Glover moved to Lichfield, where he set up as a teacher of painting and drawing; Henry Curzon Allport (1789–1854) was among his pupils. Glover joined the circle of Anna Seward, for the second edition of whose *Odes Paraphrased from Horace* (1799) he designed a title-page vignette. Although at this time he experimented with etching and portraiture, his growing reputation was founded almost exclusively on landscape watercolours. He first exhibited at the Royal Academy in 1795, but the next four years were largely taken up with a series of sketching tours through Britain and it was only in 1799 that he began to exhibit regularly (five pictures in 1801; six in 1803; two in 1804). Encouraged by success, he moved to London in 1805 and took a house at 3 Montagu Square. The market for watercolours was buoyant at this period and Glover's numerous contributions (seldom fewer than twenty pictures) fetched high prices at the annual exhibitions of the Society of Painters in Water Colours, of which he was an early member and of which he served as president in 1807–8. By 1812, however, Glover was becoming ambitious to excel in oil painting (he had begun to exhibit large canvases at the British Institution in 1810) and he was probably among the instigators of the divisive reconstruction of the Old Watercolour Society as the Society of Painters in Oil and Water Colours. He remained a productive member of the society until 1817 when he resigned, perhaps in the vain hope of election to the Royal Academy. Shortly after his resignation he moved to Blowick Farm, his property near Ullswater, but in 1818 he set out on a tour of Switzerland and Italy (he had previously travelled to Paris in 1814, where his large oil *The Bay of Naples* was exhibited at the salon and awarded a gold medal by Louis XVIII). In 1820 he held at 16 Old Bond Street, London, the first of a series of successful exhibitions devoted to his own work, though in 1823 and 1824 he included a few landscapes by his son William (*fl.* 1813–1833) and his former pupil Edward Price (1801–1899). In 1823 he became a founder member of the Society of British Artists, with whom he was also a prolific exhibitor. Advancing years, however, saw decreasing sales and Glover began to talk of permanent retirement to Ullswater. Instead, in 1830 he decided to emigrate to Van Diemen's Land, whither he had been preceded in the previous year by his three younger sons, James, Henry, and William. He auctioned most of his paintings, sold the house at 61 Montagu Square which he had occupied since 1812, and, accompanied by his wife and eldest son (two married daughters, Mary Bowles and Emma Lord, remained in England), embarked on the *Thomas Lawrie* in September 1830.

The Glovers arrived in Hobart on 1 April 1831 and took a house in New Town. Later in the same year Glover acquired a free grant of 2560 acres on the Nile River to which he moved in March 1832 and which he reminiscently named Patterdale. Here he began once again to paint regularly and in 1835 his son-in-law John Lord exhibited sixty-eight of Glover's pictures at 106 New Bond

Street, London, including thirty-eight views of Van Diemen's Land. A number of these Australian scenes included groups of Aborigines, for whom Glover expressed a marked sympathy ('one seldom sees such gaiety in a Ball Room, as amongst these untaught Savages'; McPhee, *The Art of John Glover*, 38) and in 1840 he presented two such paintings, *A Corroboree of Natives in Van Diemen's Land* and *Ben Lomond, Sunset*, to Louis Philippe of France (Louvre, Paris). By this time, however, his sight was failing and in his last years he painted little and spent much time in devotional reading. He died at Patterdale on 9 December 1849 and was buried in the grounds of the protestant chapel at Deddington.

In his watercolours (of which the Victoria and Albert Museum holds a comprehensive selection) Glover sought to convey light and atmosphere rather than precise topographical detail. His technique was developed (under Payne's influence) to suggest spontaneous facility (foliage, for example, was executed with a split brush to give 'a clever lightness'; Redgrave and Redgrave, 210), but it frequently produces an effect only of blandly monotonous charm. Hostile contemporaries referred sneeringly to his 'annual manufactory' (Long, 19). The large oils with which he hoped to establish himself as the 'English Claude'—a title which Constable, for one, bestowed ironically (Beckett, 6.133)—follow their model sedulously. *Landscape with Ruins and a Distant View of the Sea* (exh. Society of British Artists, 1829?; Art Gallery of New South Wales, Sydney) is a characteristic example, with its receding plains and diffused golden light. They are too often indifferently executed, however, and texturally thin. By contrast, Glover's late Australian landscapes, of which the largest concentrations are held by the Tasmanian Museum and Art Gallery, Hobart, and the Queen Victoria Museum and Art Gallery, Launceston, although romanticized, are also genuinely responsive to his new environment and register with sharp observation the particularity of its contours, its trees, and its people. ROBERT DINGLEY

Sources *DNB* • J. McPhee, *The art of John Glover* (1980) • B. S. Long, 'John Glover', *Walker's Quarterly* [whole issue], 15 (1924) • J. McPhee, *John Glover* (1977) [exhibition catalogue, Queen Victoria Museum and Art Gallery, Launceston, Tasmania] • *John Glover, 1767–1849* (1986) [sale catalogue; exhibition catalogue, Rex Irwin Art Dealer, London, Oct 1986] • T. Bonyhady, *Images in opposition: Australian landscape painting, 1801–1890* (1985) • R. Redgrave and S. Redgrave, *A century of British painters*, new edn, ed. R. Todd (1947) • *John Constable's correspondence*, ed. R. B. Beckett, 6, Suffolk RS, 12 (1968) • B. Smith, 'Glover, John', *AusDB*, vol. 1 • *IGI* • survey office records, Hobart, Tasmania • supreme court records, Hobart, Tasmania

Archives Mitchell L., NSW | Bodl. Oxf., corresp. with Sir Thomas Phillipps

Likenesses M. M. Allport, watercolour on ivory, *c.*1840, Allport Library and Museum of Fine Arts, Hobart, Tasmania • J. S. Prout, drawing, 1845, Mitchell L., NSW • J. Glover, self-portrait, oils, Queen Victoria Museum and Art Gallery, Launceston, Tasmania • woodcut, BM, NPG; repro. in *Art Journal* (1850)

Wealth at death £10,000: Long, 'John Glover', 15.23

Glover, John (1817–1902), chemical manufacturer, was born in Newcastle upon Tyne on 2 February 1817, the son of Robert Glover, a cooper, and was brought up in humble circumstances. He was apprenticed to a plumber at thirteen and followed that trade for fourteen years, during which he acquired a taste for study and an interest in science. He studied chemistry at Newcastle Mechanics' Institute in the 1830s.

On 19 September 1837 Glover married Elizabeth, daughter of William Kelly, a gardener. They had three sons and one daughter. Two of the sons, William and Henry, assisted their father at the Carville works, designing towers for acid plants. In 1841 Glover went to work at the Felling chemical works, where he maintained the lead chambers of the sulphuric acid plant. Here he conceived the idea for his invention of a tower in which the oxides of nitrogen, the catalyst in the lead-chamber process, would be retained and returned to the process for reuse. In 1852 he was employed by H. L. Pattinson at the Washington chemical works, where large-scale trials of his tower were made about 1859. It was found to improve the efficiency of the process by extracting the oxides of nitrogen and facilitating the reaction before the hot gases reached the lead chambers. After eighteen months' successful operation at the Washington works, Glover set up his own chemical works at Carville, Wallsend, in 1861, with W. F. Clark and J. W. Mawson as partners. In 1868 the works became the Carville Chemical Company. He continued to develop his invention but took out no patent and freely explained its operation to visitors. Other chemical manufacturers were thus able to install the tower. Glover and his partners manufactured sulphuric acid, alkali by the Leblanc process, and bleaching powder, but competition from the Solvay process, introduced by Brunner, Mond & Co. at Gateshead in 1873, led to the decline of the Leblanc process on Tyneside and the Carville works closed in 1882.

Glover was genial, modest, and always eager to improve himself. He read extensively in science, social economy, and religion, became involved in local charitable activities, and was especially interested in the *Wellesley* training ship for boys on the Tyne. He was a member of many local societies, including the Newcastle Literary and Philosophical Society and the Newcastle Historical Society. He was president of the Newcastle Chemical Society (1871–2) and a vice-president until 1882, when it became the Newcastle section of the Society of Chemical Industry, in which he continued to take an active interest. He received the first gold medal awarded by the Society of Chemical Industry for 'conspicuous service to applied science' at its fifteenth annual meeting in 1896. He died at his home, 20 Holly Avenue, Jesmond, Newcastle upon Tyne, on 30 April 1902. N. G. COLEY, *rev.*

Sources D. W. F. Hardie, 'Chemical pioneers 13: John Glover', *Chemical Age*, 78 (1957), 816 • 'John Glover', *Journal of the Society of Chemical Industry*, 21 (1902), 595–6 • F. Hurter, 'Presidential address', *Journal of the Society of Chemical Industry*, 15 (1896), 510–11 • 'John Glover', *Journal of the Society of Chemical Industry*, 50 (1931), 95 • *Newcastle Weekly Chronicle* (3 May 1902) • m. cert. • d. cert.

Wealth at death £482 5*s.* 1*d.*: probate, 24 May 1902, *CGPLA Eng. & Wales*

Glover, Sir John Hawley (1829–1885), naval officer and colonial administrator, was born at Yately, near Farnborough, Hampshire, on 24 February 1829, the son of the Revd Frederick Robert Augustus Glover (*d.* 1881) and his first wife, Mary Broughton (*d.* 1841), second daughter of Admiral Broughton. His father's family claimed descent from Ecgberht, king of the West Saxons, and through the Plantagenets from Charlemagne and Hildegarde of Swabia; and his mother's family claimed descent from Katherine Parr, sixth wife of Henry VIII. F. A. Glover was an infantry officer who served in the First Anglo-Asante War (1826), took holy orders, and after English livings was Anglican chaplain at Cologne until 1861. He believed the English were 'the remnant of Judah', wrote books on the great pyramid, invented an ambulance, and died in August 1881 in his eighty-second year.

When he was three years old, John Hawley Glover was kidnapped at Bath by Gypsies but rescued. He entered the navy in 1841 on the *Queen*, flagship of Sir Edward Owen in the Mediterranean. On 24 October 1851, while serving on the *Penelope* off the west coast of Africa, he was promoted lieutenant, and in May 1852 was appointed to the *Royalist* in the East Indies. Moved to the *Sphinx*, he took part in the disastrous action near Donabew in Burma on 4 February 1853 [*see* Loch, Granville Gower], where he was severely wounded, a ball entering under his right eye and passing out at his ear. In the summer he returned to England and in October was appointed to the *Royal George*; then in February 1854 first lieutenant of the paddle-sloop *Rosamond*, in which he served in the Baltic in the Crimean War. From 1855 to 1857 he commanded the *Otter*, a small steamer. Religiously motivated and enthusiastic for the evangelization of Africa, he volunteered for Dr William Balfour Baikie's second ascent of the River Niger in 1857. The expedition vessel, the *Dayspring*, was wrecked upriver near Jebba in October 1857 and Glover had to travel overland three times to Lagos. His unfortunate experiences with the Egba turned him against them and apparently caused his rejection of the British pro-Egba policy. In 1861 he returned to England and was appointed to the *Arrogant*, going out as flagship off the west coast of Africa, where for the next year he commanded her tender *Handy*, a small wooden *Clown*-class screw gunboat, largely in the vicinity of Lagos. On 24 November 1862 he was promoted commander, and his sea service ended.

In 1861 Palmerston had annexed Lagos. It depended on trade to and from its hinterland, where the Yoruba successor states after the old Oyo empire fought wars which disrupted trade. Glover joined the new colonial administration under the first governor (Henry Stanhope Freeman), initially as harbour master, though administering the government when the governor was on leave. From 1864 he was secretary, and from 1866 to 1872 administrator. A domineering, dynamic 'man on the spot', Glover (known as 'Golobar' by Africans) was the dominant influence in the new colony and its relations with African states. Disregarding, as far as possible, the intentions of successive colonial secretaries of both parties, and of the 1865 select

Sir John Hawley Glover (1829–1885), by Maull & Co.

committee on the west African settlements—which criticized his interference in Yoruba affairs and recommended withdrawal from Lagos—Glover followed his own policy. According to Pope-Hennessy, he asked, 'What does the Government mean by interfering with my policy?' (Newbury, 453).

Glover's aims were to maximize trade with the hinterland, keeping routes open and establishing new routes, and ending the Yoruba wars; to expand the Lagos protectorate, establish British supremacy over Yoruba through a series of client states, and to prevent French expansion from Porto Novo, a French protectorate in 1863–4; and to suppress the slave trade. Reversing the former British policy of favouring the Egba of Abeokuta—his *bêtes noires* whom he saw as monopolizing and blocking trade to the interior—his policy was anti-Egba and pro-Ibadan. He formed an effective Hausa armed police force and also used British naval and military (West India regiment) units, diplomacy, and blockade. Expansionist, he intervened in Yoruba and extended the Lagos protectorate, and by his 1863 agreement with them blocked the expansion of the French from Porto Novo. Following the French withdrawal he attempted to gain control of Porto Novo, and in 1872 he blockaded it and proposed annexation; Lord Kimberley, the colonial secretary, refused. Glover attempted mediation in the Yoruba wars and posted police beyond the Lagos boundaries. In March 1865, when the Egba threatened Ikorodu, Lagos's British-protected port on the lagoon for the Ibadan trade, Glover took unauthorized military action. With a force of British sailors, soldiers from the West India regiment, Hausa police, and Ikorodu Yoruba, he defeated and drove away the Egba. He attempted to open and maintain an eastern trade route through Ondo and, after this failed, in 1872 tried to subdue the Egba by blockade. His forward, interventionist policies—and also the refuge given to escaped slaves in Lagos—provoked mistrust among the Yoruba and increased Egba hostility. Glover favoured missionaries, especially those of the Church Missionary Society, but his policies antagonized missionaries trying to work in the interior and they protested to, and apparently influenced, the Colonial Office.

Since colonial secretaries largely refused to back his initiatives, Glover had only limited success. Colonial secretaries repeatedly criticized him. In 1863 the duke of Newcastle considered that Glover was 'too ready to enlarge his territory and draw the sword' (McIntyre, 'Commander Glover', 65), and in 1867 the duke of Buckingham stated his disapproval of Glover's attempt to enlarge Lagos territory, 'entirely on his own motion, without leave, and contrary to what he must well know to be the policy of H. M. G.' (Newbury, 366). In 1872 Kimberley decided to restrain Glover but was against recalling him. He instructed the new governor-in-chief of the west African settlements, the impetuous, quarrelsome, and controversial John Pope-Hennessy, an arrogant little man, to caution him. Pope-Hennessy, who favoured the 1865 committee's withdrawal policy, went to Lagos in April 1872. He quickly formed an antipathy to Glover and told him, 'You know nothing of the country, the place or the people' (Pope-Hennessy, 135). While criticizing Glover for disobeying government instructions, Pope-Hennessy himself exceeded Kimberley's instructions by sending Glover home in June and, in haste and with evident animus, reversing anti-Egba policy. Kimberley disapproved but decided Glover should not return; effectively he was dismissed, though the Colonial Office denied it. Glover had envisaged Lagos as the great port not only for Yoruba but also for western Sudan, and under him it had grown and changed; according to H. M. Stanley, he 'enriched the country beyond belief' (Glover, xxvii).

In 1873, following the Asante invasion of the Gold Coast protectorate, the imperial government decided to send a military expedition to invade the Asante kingdom. Glover offered his services to the Colonial Office, proposing to raise an African force in the Accra and Volta region to attack Asante in the flank and rear. The government, however, decided that Glover's flank attack, by the Volta route to the east, should be subsidiary to Wolseley's offensive against Kumasi. In August 1873 Glover was appointed special commissioner to the eastern district of the Gold Coast. Relations between Glover and Wolseley were formally correct, but privately they were rivals and, according to Winwood Reade, then a war correspondent, 'they both wished each other at the devil' (Lloyd, 144). Glover took a few British officers and a force of Hausa police, and raised an army of tribesmen. In January 1874 he crossed the Pra and threatened the Asante left flank, so facilitating Wolseley's advance. Glover's force was not severely engaged, though there was some skirmishing; and the main fighting was by Wolseley's force, which captured Kumasi on 4 February. Glover's force reached its smouldering ruins on 12 February, then followed Wolseley's force to the coast. The Second Anglo-Asante War was much publicized in the British press—graphically portrayed in the *Illustrated London News* [*see* Prior, Melton]—perceived as a brilliant success, and popular. Although war correspondents thought his Volta expedition a mistake, Glover himself had favourable press coverage, including from G. A. Henty and from H. M. Stanley, who described him as 'really a great man' (ibid., 146). He gained some celebrity, the thanks of parliament, and a GCMG (8 May 1874).

From 1876 to 1881 Glover was governor of Newfoundland. On 7 November 1876 he married Elizabeth Rosetta, the eldest daughter of William James Butler Scott of Anne's Grove Abbey, Mountrath, Queen's county, Ireland. In November 1877 he was put on the naval retired list with the rank of captain, and from 1881 to 1883 he was governor of the Leeward Islands. From 1883 until his death in 1885 he was again governor of Newfoundland where, according to Judge D. W. Prowse, 'No more honourable, generous, kind-hearted, or active ruler ever presided over our Government' (Prowse, 501).

Harmed by his African service, Glover's health deteriorated and, diagnosed as 'suffering from an over-strained heart' (Glover, 311), in 1885 he went on sick leave to England. He stayed in London in Harley Street for medical treatment, and died at 35 Harley Street, Cavendish Square, on 30 September 1885; his wife survived him. He was buried at Kensal Green cemetery, London, and commemorated by memorials in the crypt of St Paul's Cathedral, London, and in the Anglican cathedral, St John's, Newfoundland, and at Lagos by a bronze statue by Boehm and by the Glover Hall. Sir William Butler described him as 'one of the most remarkable' of the British in Africa and 'before his time' (*Butler: an autobiography*, 155). Many years later, from the 1960s, revived study of west African history led to new research into and reappraisals of his career.

ROGER T. STEARN

Sources E. R. Glover, *Life of Sir John Hawley Glover*, ed. R. Temple (1897) • *The Times* (2 Oct 1885) • H. Brackenbury, *The Ashanti war*, 2 vols. (1874) • W. D. McIntyre, 'Commander Glover and the colony of Lagos, 1861–73', *Journal of African History*, 4 (1963), 57–79 • W. D. McIntyre, *The imperial frontier in the tropics, 1865–75* (1967) • C. W. Newbury, ed., *British policy towards west Africa: select documents*, 2 vols. (1965–71); repr. (1992) • J. D. Hargreaves, *Prelude to the partition of west Africa* (1963) • E. A. Ayandele, *The missionary impact on modern Nigeria, 1842–1914* (1966) • B. Bond, ed., *Victorian military campaigns* (1967) • A. Lloyd, *The drums of Kumasi: the story of the Ashanti wars* (1964) • *Dod's Peerage* (1878) • D. W. Prowse, *A history of Newfoundland from the English, colonial, and foreign records* (1895) • J. Pope-Hennessy, *Verandah: some episodes in the crown colonies, 1867–1889* (1964) • *Sir William Butler: an autobiography*, ed. E. Butler (1911) • Burke, *Peerage* (1879) • Boase, *Mod. Eng. biog.* • *CGPLA Eng. & Wales* (1885) • *DNB*

Archives CUL, Royal Commonwealth Society Library, corresp. and papers | Bodl. Oxf., corresp. with Lord Kimberley
Likenesses Bosch, photograph, repro. in Prowse, *History of Newfoundland*, frontispiece • Maull & Co., photograph, NPG [*see illus.*] • engraving, repro. in *ILN*, 64 (1874), 384–6 • photograph, repro. in Glover, *Life of Sir John Hawley Glover*, frontispiece
Wealth at death £5950 6*s*. 0*d*.: probate, 27 Oct 1885, *CGPLA Eng. & Wales*

Glover [*née* Betterton or Butterton], **Julia** (**1779/1781–1850**), actress, was born in Newry, co. Down; her birth date is given variously as 8 January 1779 and 8 February 1781. Her father, Thomas William Betterton or Butterton (*d*. 1834), an actor, claimed descent from the seventeenth-century actor Thomas Betterton. Her mother was the widow of Wingfield Palmer, also an actor; she had married Betterton on 21 December 1778, and died in 1793. Julia's father put her on the stage at an early age—it was said that she had made more histrionic attempts by the age of six than many had done by sixty—and exploited her financially until his death at an age of more than eighty. After touring throughout Ireland, about 1789 she and her father joined Tate Wilkinson's York circuit, and she appeared as Page in Otway's *The Orphan*. She also played the duke of York to George Frederick Cooke's Richard III and Tom Thumb to his Glumdalca. She toured the provinces with her father, and in 1794 appeared with Watson's company in Hereford. In 1795 'Miss Betterton from Liverpool' was at Bath, playing Marianne in Frederick Reynolds's *The Dramatist*. Between 1795 and 1797 she took many important roles in both tragedy and comedy at the Bath theatre, including Desdemona to Henry Siddons's Othello, Lady Macbeth, and Lady Amaranth in John O'Keeffe's *Wild Oats*.

In 1797 Julia Betterton was engaged by Thomas Harris for Covent Garden for five years, on the substantial rising salary of £15 to £20 a week. Her father was also taken on. She made her London début on 12 October 1797 as Elwina in Hannah More's *Percy*. Her performance as Charlotte Rusport in *The West Indian* so pleased its author, Richard Cumberland, that he gave her the part of the heroine, Emily Fitzallan, in his new play, *False Impressions*, in November 1797. On 3 November that year she had performed before the king, choosing to play Portia in *The Merchant of Venice*. In March 1799 she was the original Maria in Thomas Dibdin's *Five Thousand a Year*, and took many other comic parts, including Lydia Languish and Lady Amaranth. Under pressure from the management, who preferred another actress in these roles, she undertook serious characters, such as Queen Elizabeth in *Richard III*, in which she was less successful.

Julia Betterton had fallen in love with a Drury Lane actor, James Biggs, whom she had met at Bath, but he died in December 1798. Her father, who continued to take her salary and to treat her with great brutality, then sold her into marriage with one Samuel Glover, the supposed heir to a large fortune. Glover was in fact cut off by his father, and Betterton never received the £1000 he had been offered for his daughter. The marriage, which took place on 20 March 1800, merely added to the burdens on the young actress: to her rapacious father's demands were added the extravagance of and persecution by a neglectful husband and the need to maintain a family of eight children, four of whom survived to adulthood. She at once returned to the stage as Mrs Glover, appearing on 27 March 1800 as Letitia Hardy in Hannah Cowley's *The Belle's Stratagem*.

In October 1802 Julia Glover made her début at Drury Lane, as Mrs Oakley in George Colman's *The Jealous Wife*. The following season she was back at Covent Garden, where she remained for four years. In 1810 she returned to the Drury Lane company, then playing at the Lyceum as their own theatre had been destroyed by fire, and returned with them to their home in 1812–13. In January 1813 she was the original Alhadra in Coleridge's *Remorse*; it appears that later this year her son Edmund *Glover was born. In 1814 she played Queen Elizabeth to Edmund Kean's Richard III and Emilia to his Othello. On 16 September 1816, on the first appearance of W. C. Macready at Covent Garden, she played Andromache to his Orestes, after an absence of ten years from that theatre.

In 1817 Samuel Glover, from whom Mrs Glover was by now estranged, attempted to use the law to claim custody of their children, and to have her salary paid directly to himself so that he could use it to maintain another (illegitimate) family and his French mistress. In both these attempts he was unsuccessful, and apparently he eventually died in the Marshalsea prison for debtors. In 1818 Julia Glover was at Drury Lane again, and the following year a son, William Howard *Glover, was born. In 1822 she played with Thomas Dibdin at the Surrey Theatre, before returning once more to Drury Lane. She seems not to have performed there between 1824 and 1829—her appearance as Mrs Subtle in John Poole's *Paul Pry* in the latter year was announced as her first appearance there for five years. At the Haymarket in 1830 she was the original Ariette Delorme in *Ambition, or, Marie Mignot*. In 1833 she played Falstaff at that theatre, her figure having 'expanded into rotundity'. In 1849 she joined William Farren at the Strand, where she played a series of her best characters, including Widow Green in Sheridan Knowles's *The Love Chase*, which part she had created at the Haymarket in 1837. A 'professional farewell' took place at her benefit at Drury Lane on 12 July 1850, where she took the stage for the last time as Mrs Malaprop. She had been ill for some weeks and was so unwell that she could not take her curtain calls; she died before the receipts of the house could be given to her, on 16 July 1850 at 21A Soho Square. She was buried near her father in the churchyard of St George the Martyr, Queen Square, Bloomsbury.

Julia Glover was an actress of considerable talents, fair, blue-eyed, and of medium height; in later life she was described as 'monstrously fat'. In middle age she was probably the first comic actress of the period, and was renowned for her great memory. Her Mrs Simpson in John Poole's *Simpson & Co.* was one of the most successful of her original parts; Estifania, Mrs Malaprop, and Mrs Subtle were also characters in which her admirable vein of comedy and her joyous laugh won high recognition.

Joseph Knight, *rev.* J. Gilliland

Sources Highfill, Burnim & Langhans, *BDA* • J. W. Cole, *Life and times of Charles Kean* (1859) • Mrs C. Baron-Wilson, *Our actresses*, 2 vols. (1844) • *Oxberry's Dramatic Biography*, 4/50 (1826), 19–35 • *The biography of the British stage, being correct narratives of the lives of all the principal actors and actresses* (1824) • Adams, *Drama* • R. Pogson, *Enciclopedia della spettacolo*, ed. G. C. Sansoni, 5 (Rome, 1958), col. 1380 • T. Gilliland, *The dramatic mirror, containing the history of the stage from the earliest period, to the present time*, 2 vols. (1808) • Genest, *Eng. stage*, vol. 2 • *Era* (21 July 1850) • Hall, *Dramatic ports.*
Likenesses W. Ridley, engraving, 1802 (after watercolour, 1802), repro. in Highfill, Burnim & Langhans, *BDA*, 236 • watercolour drawing, 1802, Harvard TC • Clint, portrait, exh. RA 1831, V&A • S. De Wilde, watercolour, BM • S. Drummond, pastel drawing, Garr. Club • W. S. Lethbridge, watercolour drawing (as Lady Allworth), Garr. Club • Rogers, engraving (as Mrs Candour in *The school for scandal*; after T. Wugeman), repro. in *Oxberry's Dramatic Biography* • O. Smith, engraving (in *Temperance*; after drawing by P. Egan, junior, 1837), repro. in B. Webster, ed., *The acting national drama*, 1 (1837), frontispiece • prints, BM, NPG • sketch (as Roxalana), repro. in *Biography of the British stage*, 83
Wealth at death £450: Genest, *Eng. stage*

Glover, Mary (*b.* 1587/8), demoniac, was the daughter of Timothy Glover, a shopkeeper in the parish of All Hallows-the-Less, Thames Street, London. She was fourteen when, according to the account of her affliction by Stephen Bradwell, she was sent on an errand to the house of an old charwoman, Elizabeth Jackson. The latter disliked Mary, says Bradwell, 'for discovering to one of her Mistresses a certain fashion of her subtle and importunat begging'. Elizabeth locked the door and railed at Mary, saying, 'it had byn better that you had never medled with my daughters apparrell', an accusation that Bradwell does not explain (Bradwell, 3). An hour later she released Mary, who went home feeling ill. The next Monday Elizabeth went into Mary's father's shop and glared at her while she was drinking a posset. When Elizabeth left Mary felt unable to eat, her throat and neck swelled, she could not speak, and the affliction continued in 'fittes' for eighteen days. In this time she ate almost nothing; her parents believed that she would die.

Dr Robert Shereman, of the College of Physicians, was asked to treat Mary Glover, and believed that she had tonsillitis. But new symptoms appeared: her belly swelled, there was something moving inside her breast, and on occasion she became blind and dumb. Shereman began to suspect supernatural causes. He eliminated, to his own satisfaction, the possibility of hysteria, but Mary's parents wanted a second opinion and Dr Thomas Moundeford, an authority on melancholy, treated her for a further three months. He concluded that the disease was natural, but not hysterical. Thus medical opinion remained divided. Mary remained sick.

Meanwhile Elizabeth Jackson had been heard saying, 'I thanck my God he hath heard my prayer, and stopped the mouth and tyed the tongue of one of myne enemies', a statement she repeated in the house of Mary Glover's kinsman Alderman William Glover (Bradwell, 4). Indeed, Mary's illness worsened: whenever she saw Jackson or tried to eat or rest, she would convulse, her body stiff and bending backwards hoop-like, a classic symptom of demonic possession. She fell into trances in which she would move as if automatically, for example playing invisible musical instruments. Mary screamed and wrestled with those who tried to hold her, convulsions from which she would recover to offer fervent prayers.

Mary Glover also convulsed at the words 'deliver us from evil', a significant phrase held to be one which witches were often unable to utter. At last Mary confidently stated that 'Goodwife Jackson had hurt her, and they should see som token of it' (Bradwell, 20). Mary and Elizabeth were brought before Alderman Glover in his capacity as a magistrate. Insensible, she stiffened and tumbled towards the 'witch': a voice emerged from her closed mouth saying 'hange her'. This was one of four staged confrontations between the girl and the old woman in the presence of divines and physicians. In another the recorder of London, Sir John Croke, carried out tests, disguising Elizabeth to see whether Mary still reacted to her, burning Mary to test whether she was indeed insensible during her trances, and making Elizabeth recite the Lord's prayer. She missed out the words 'deliver us from evil'. Elizabeth Jackson was indicted at the Old Bailey on 1 December 1602 for bewitching Mary.

During the trial familiar patterns were repeated. When Mary Glover was brought into court, not seeing Elizabeth Jackson in the dock, she 'felt a commanding power seaze upon her, and therefore, as interrupted in her purposed speech cryed, "Where is shee? where is she?"' (Bradwell, 22). Sceptics on the bench accused her of counterfeiting and ordered her to carry on with her evidence, but before she had got forty words out she had fainted, with her body grotesquely contorted; 'Now also was the accustomed voice, hang her, hang her, audible in her nostrils' (ibid.). Mary was taken to a chamber, where the judges and court officers tested her by trying to terrify her out of her trance, loudly threatening to burn her on the cheek with hot irons as a counterfeit; the recorder burnt her on the hand with a burning paper until she blistered. When Elizabeth Jackson was brought into the room the words 'Hang her' spoken through Mary's nostrils rose so loud as to be audible in the next chamber, and when Jackson touched Mary the latter writhed violently. Again Elizabeth was unable to get through the Lord's prayer and the creed, and when she spoke certain words from them Mary's convulsions grew worse.

In court there were witnesses to testify to Elizabeth Jackson's witchcraft. Elizabeth Burges, who had once spoken on Mary Glover's behalf, had been threatened by Elizabeth; she spoke of the vomitings and visions which had followed, and while giving her testimony was struck dumb. A preacher who had visited Elizabeth to admonish her for her lewd tongue had been struck dumb and fallen to his knees under her gaze. 'Witch's marks' were found on her body.

The case of Mary Glover had become part of the ecclesiastical battle over the reality of demonic possession fought between 1599 and 1603 in a pamphlet war between the supporters of the sceptical bishop of London, Richard Bancroft, and the supporters of the puritan exorcist John Darrell. The testimony of physicians on both sides as to whether Mary's disease was supernatural formed an important part of the trial. Edward Jorden, a sceptic, conceded that he did not believe that Mary's disease was counterfeit but could provide no medical explanation for it. 'Then in my conscience', the judge, Sir Edmund Anderson, concluded, 'it is not naturall: for if you tell me neither a Naturall cause of it, nor a naturall remedy, I will tell you, that it's not naturall' (Bradwell, 28). Elizabeth Jackson was convicted and sentenced to a year's imprisonment and to be pilloried, the maximum penalty that could be inflicted upon her at that point because her supposed victim had not died, although she was soon released because of the intense controversy. Mary's supporters continued to believe her possessed, and dispossessed by the 'puritan' method of prayer and fasting on 14 December 1602. She used the same words at her deliverance that her grandfather, the protestant martyr Robert *Glover, had used at his execution in 1555. She had not only beaten her enemy Elizabeth Jackson and been cured of her affliction (and perhaps dramatized in her possession elements of sexual, generational, and religious conflict), but had clearly established her godliness and presumably returned to the normal life of a fourteen-year-old girl in Elizabethan London.

Mary Glover's case prompted Jorden to write *A Briefe Discourse of a Disease called the Suffocation of the Mother* (1603), in which he argued that apparent victims of demonic possession were likely to be suffering from hysteria. He referred only obliquely and in passing to the case, but in response his fellow physician Stephen Bradwell produced his partisan but very full manuscript narrative of Mary's possession. Nothing more is known of Mary Glover's life.

MARION GIBSON

Sources M. MacDonald, ed., introduction, *Witchcraft and hysteria in Elizabethan London: Edward Jorden and the Mary Glover case* (1991) • S. Bradwell, 'Mary Glovers late woeful case, together with her joyfull deliverance', 1603 [transcribed in M. MacDonald, ed., *Witchcraft and hysteria*, 1991, with separate pagination, from BL, Sloane MS 831] • J. Swan, *A true and breife report of Mary Glovers vexation, and of her deliverance by fastings and prayer* (1603) [repr. in M. MacDonald, ed., *Witchcraft and hysteria*, 1991] • E. Jorden, *A briefe discourse of a disease called the suffocation of the mother* (1603) [repr. in M. MacDonald, ed., *Witchcraft and hysteria*, 1991] • D. P. Walker, *Unclean spirits* (1981) • J. Sharpe, *Instruments of darkness: witchcraft in England, 1550–1750* (1996) • S. Connor, *Dumbstruck: a cultural history of ventriloquism* (2000)

Glover, Moses (*fl.* 1622–1635), map maker, was described in 1622 as a painter–stainer living in Isleworth, Middlesex, when the bishop of London issued a licence for him to marry Juliana Gulliver, the widow of Richard Gulliver, a painter, at St Botolph's, Aldersgate. At least two of their children were buried at All Saints', Isleworth, between 1625 and 1628.

In 1635 Glover was employed by Algernon Percy, tenth earl of Northumberland, to map the hundred of Isleworth and manor of Sion. The map, now at Syon House, is notable for its wealth of topographical detail, drawn at a scale of one inch to one mile. Fields, buildings, and roads are named, notable landowners are given, and acreages are stated, together with the depth of the River Thames. Buildings are shown in perspective, and the map is decorated with scenes of everyday life. The many additional notes describing features and owners and giving their histories form a distinctive feature of the map. It is decorated with coats of arms, including those showing the descent of the Percy family. Glover describes himself on his map as 'paynter and architectur', and the earl of Northumberland as 'my noble lord and master'. His later career is not known.

SARAH BENDALL

Sources J. L. Chester and G. J. Armytage, eds., *Allegations for marriage licences issued by the bishop of London*, 2, Harleian Society, 26 (1887) • *Syon House: a seat of the duke of Northumberland* (1987) • E. Startin, 'The evolution of Isleworth: mapping of the area, 1607–1746', *c.*1988, GL • F. W. Steer and others, *Dictionary of land surveyors and local map-makers of Great Britain and Ireland, 1530–1850*, ed. P. Eden, 2nd edn, ed. S. Bendall, 2 vols. (1997) • [W. Papworth], ed., *The dictionary of architecture*, 11 vols. (1853–92)
Archives Syon House, Isleworth, Syon MSS

Glover, Richard (1712–1785), writer and politician, was born in St Martin's Lane, Cannon Street, London, the son of Richard Glover, a Hamburg merchant, and his wife, Mary. He was educated under Mr Sanxay at Cheam School, where he was 'permanently imbued with a taste for the learning of antiquity' (Aikin), then joined his father's business. In 1728 his 'Poem on Sir Isaac Newton' was prefixed to Henry Pemberton's *View of Sir Isaac Newton's Philosophy*. As a prominent City merchant opposing Walpole's pacific foreign policy, Glover allied himself with the group of 'patriot' whigs led by George Lyttleton, with Frederick, prince of Wales, as figurehead. In the 1730s Glover worked on *Leonidas*, a high-minded epic on the virtuous resistance by the Spartan king (perhaps an optimistic portrait of Frederick) to the effeminate and treacherous Persian army. It was published in nine books early in 1737, with a dedication to Lord Cobham, already eulogized by Alexander Pope for his opposition to Sir Robert Walpole. The poem was praised for its devotion to freedom and public spirit by Lyttleton in *Common Sense* (no. 10, 9 April 1737), as well as in a poem, 'To Mr. Glover, on his Poem of Leonidas'. Jonathan Swift wrote to Pope on 31 May 1737, 'Pray who is that Mr. Glover, who writ the Epic Poem called Leonidas, which is re-printing here, and hath great vogue' (*Correspondence*, 5.42). Henry Pemberton puffed it in *Observations on Poetry* (1738), and Glover was ever after known by the sobriquet Leonidas. The poem engendered an envious satirical extravaganza on Glover's wedding night from Richard Savage; ministerial response came in John Henley's *Hyp doctor* of 12 April 1737.

On 21 May 1737 Glover married Hannah Nunn, a wealthy heiress, in a ceremony performed by Thomas Rundle in St Martin's Lane. In 1739 Glover published *London, or, The Progress of Commerce*, a whig panegyric identifying England's destiny as commercial capital of the world. In 1740 'Admiral Hosier's Ghost' appeared anonymously as a broadside ballad, but in engraved form and with a highly polished illustration. It recalled a disastrous failure of naval activity in 1726, in the context of renewed calls for war. Francis Conway told Walpole, 'The Patriots cry it up and the Courtiers cry it down and the hawkers cry it up and down 'till they make one deaf … I like it extremely and think it mighty solemn and mighty poetical'. Walpole was disposed to be slighting and satirical about Glover, calling him in 1742 'the greatest oaf' and casting aspersions about the prince of Wales's patronage (Walpole, *Corr.*, 37.64–9, 13.249, and 17.353–4). In that year Glover made a long, much reprinted speech summing up the complaints of the merchant community concerning the lack of military protection against Spain. After Walpole's fall Glover continued to involve himself in political affairs as a spokesman for the merchants. Frederick is alleged to have sent Glover an expensively bound set of the classics, and to have provided him with money. He corresponded with Sarah, duchess of Marlborough, who in her will commissioned Glover and David Mallet to write a biography of her husband, at a premium of £500, on condition that none of it was in verse; the 'capricious restrictions' (Glover, 55) led Glover to turn the offer down, and Mallet hardly began the task. In 1751 Glover was asked to stand against Thomas Harrison for the office of chamberlain of the City of London, but lost, making a respectable speech on the occasion.

Glover had known David Garrick since 1741, and his tragedy *Boadicia* was accepted for Drury Lane in 1753. Davies tells how Glover insisted on reading the play to the cast himself, despite his harsh and disagreeable voice and Garrick's polite attempts to take over. The play was premièred on 1 December 1753 with Garrick as Dumnorix, the Trinobantian chief, and Hannah Pritchard in the title role, which she evidently performed with much passion. The music was by Boyce. It was performed ten times that month. Arthur Murphy declared, 'I cannot but remark that the applause it met with, was scarcely warm enough for such fine writing … I am convinced that this Tragedy will prove an elegant Closet-companion to every reader of taste' (*Gray's Inn-Journal*, 8 December, quoted in Stone, 1.397). Walpole found it ranting and absurd, but 'the parts are so well acted, the dresses so fine, and two or three scenes pleasing enough, that it is worth seeing' (Walpole, *Corr.*, 9.157–8). Paul Hiffernan denounced the title character as a 'monster well deserving what she suffers' and claimed that even Garrick's 'continued and vigorous exertion' sometimes failed to make the piece intelligible (Stone, 1.401). Despite praise from Pemberton in *Some Few Reflections on the Tragedy of Boadicia* (1753), it was never revived.

Glover was still active in politics. In October 1755 he was being used by the opposition to foment the City against Hanoverian subsidies; he was called 'Dodington's trumpeter' (HoP, *Commons, 1754–90*). In 1756 he provided William Pitt with a statement of the conditions upon which he should consent to form a cabinet. In the same year Glover began writing his political memoirs, expressly in a mood of depression about the fate of the nation. He regarded this secret history as an alternative to the national history he might have written in the biography of Marlborough. Glover was returned for Weymouth and Melcombe Regis on Dodington's interest in 1761 and sat until the dissolution of parliament in 1768. He spoke at great length and in great detail on 10 December 1761 to oppose the German war. On 13 May 1762 he spoke to oppose a subsidy to Portugal and was answered by Pitt. Glover apparently made a great deal of money out of the subscription to the government loan of 1763. In March 1763, however, he opposed the cider tax, making a bizarre speech against excises and incurring the suspicions of the king. Thereafter he seems to have acted independently, being counted as a friend of the administration but often voting against it.

Glover had read his tragedy *Medea*, loosely based on Seneca's version of the story and retaining a classical chorus at the end of each act, at a dinner at Dodington's house in February 1753. It was published in 1761, and was chosen by Mary Yates for benefit performances at Covent Garden on eight occasions between 24 March 1767 and 25 March 1779 (and once more by Elizabeth Pope on 26 March 1792). She was 'inimitably great' and 'fine in her Character; but the Play is too heavy and will not do' (Stone, 3.1393; Hogan, 1.30). Mrs Siddons is said to have regarded the part as unfeminine, but a cut of her in the character was affixed to Bell's edition of the play (1792). Glover's two plays exalt resistance to political tyranny; but both also focus on passionate women and demonstrate a concern with the preservation of a pair of sons, casting some light on Glover's troubled marriage, which ended in divorce by act of parliament in 1756. There were two sons, the younger of whom eloped in 1777 with a daughter of Solomon Dayrolles (Walpole, *Corr.*, 28.288). In 1770 Glover republished *Leonidas* in twelve books; lacking political momentum, it passed without great notice. Glover remained in contact with politicians such as Lord Temple, and in 1774 he again appeared on behalf of the merchant community, summing up grievances in relation to the linen trade to Germany and the Netherlands. In the following year he performed the same service for the plantation owners in the West Indies, receiving plate worth £300 as a sign of their appreciation.

In June 1785 Glover sang 'Hosier's Ghost' to a company including Hannah More, who found it 'very affecting', and Horace Walpole, who listened 'with complacency' (Walpole, *Corr.*, 31.229). Glover died at his home in Albemarle Street, Piccadilly, on 25 November 1785. In an obituary Richard Brocklesby commended his 'exemplary simplicity of manners' and claimed that 'he lived as if he had been bred a disciple of Socrates' (Chalmers). Glover made his will (PRO, PROB 11/23/599) on 28 February 1785. He left over £11,000 to his son Richard, together with the family pictures and all his books. His second wife, Eleanor, received an income of £150, with the use of the household goods and plate; she was residuary legatee and sole executor. Glover left his 'natural daughter' Mary Glover over £8000, together with all his papers. A complicated codicil assigning several manors in the home counties from the marriage settlement of his deceased son Bonouvrier (*b.* 1739) was added. Among his papers were a sequel to *Medea* called *Jason*, too elaborate to stage, but published in 1797, and *The Athenaid*, a thirty-book epic about the wars between Athens and Persia. This was published by his daughter, by then Mrs Halsey, in 1787. Glover's *Memoirs* was published in 1813 by Richard Duppa as part of an unconvincing attempt to prove that Glover wrote *The Letters of Junius*.

PAUL BAINES

Sources J. G. Schaaf, *Richard Glover: Leben und Werke* (Leipzig, 1900) · G. E. Kelley, 'Richard Glover', *Eighteenth-century British poets: first series*, ed. J. Sitter, DLitB, 95 (1990), 101–6 · M. M. Drummond, 'Glover, Richard', HoP, *Commons, 1754–90* · [R. Glover], *Memoirs of a celebrated literary and political character*, ed. R. Duppa (1813) · A. Chalmers, *The works of the English poets*, 17 (1810), 3–12 · N. Rogers, *Whigs and cities: popular politics in the age of Walpole and Pitt* (1989) · C. Gerrard, *The political opposition to Walpole: politics, poetry, and national myth, 1725–1742* (1994) · Walpole, *Corr.* · G. W. Stone, ed., *The London stage, 1660–1800*, pt 4: *1747–1776* (1962) · C. B. Hogan, ed., *The London stage, 1660–1800*, pt 5: *1776–1800* (1968) · Allibone, *Dict.* · *The letters of David Garrick*, ed. D. M. Little and G. M. Kahrl, 3 vols. (1963) · *The political journal of George Bubb Dodington*, ed. J. Carswell and L. A. Dralle (1965) · *The correspondence of Jonathan Swift*, ed. H. Williams, 5 vols. (1963–5) · J. Aikin and others, *General biography, or, Lives, critical and historical of the most eminent persons*, 10 vols. (1799–1815)

Archives BL, letters and poems

Likenesses B. Granger, stipple engraving, BM, NPG; repro. in Cooke, *Poems*, ed. R. Glover (*c.*1800) · T. Holloway, line engraving (after N. Hone), BM, NPG; repro. in *European Magazine* (1786) · bust, repro. in R. A. Davenport, *A dictionary of biography* (1831)

Wealth at death £20,000; plus land and household goods: will, 28 Feb 1785, PRO, PROB 11/23/599

Glover, Richard (1837–1919), Baptist minister, was born on 6 January 1837 in South Shields, one of ten children (and the youngest of eight sons) of Terrot Glover (1802–1885), a prosperous Scottish businessman, active Liberal, and respected civic leader, and his wife, Anne, *née* Reaveley (1798–1858). The family had links with the sea: Terrot Glover had money in ships and two of his sons were shipowners (one son, John, becoming chairman of Lloyds), and in his youth Richard voyaged widely. They were also Presbyterian, Terrot Glover serving for nearly sixty years as elder of the English Presbyterian church.

In 1846 Richard Glover became one of the first pupils at a sessional day school linked to St John's Presbyterian Church, South Shields. From 1853 to 1855 he studied arts at Edinburgh University, without taking a degree. From 1855 to 1856 he took evening classes at King's College, London, in the Old and New testaments, English language and composition, history, and geography. In 1856 he began training for the ministry at the Presbyterian college, London, completing his course in 1860. While training, however, Glover became convinced of the case for believer's baptism and self-governing local churches. Encouraged by a friend, and with a letter of introduction from his tutor, he visited William Landels, minister of the Regent's Park Baptist Chapel. Soon after, Landels baptized him, recommending him to the small Blackfriars Street Church in Glasgow's east end. On preaching there, Glover was at once invited to the pastorate, starting in January 1861. During eight years' ministry he became known as a thought-provoking preacher, at ease with all kinds of people, notable especially for his Sunday evening lectures for young men on subjects such as science and religion. He spoke often at meetings of the Baptist Association of Scotland and helped initiate a new Baptist Union in Scotland. He also began a lifelong campaign to promote worldwide evangelism, making his mark with an inspirational sermon, preached at Landels's suggestion at the May meetings of the Baptist Missionary Society (BMS) in 1867. He married Anne Finlay (1838–1924) of Glasgow on 26 March 1866. Of their three children, Dorothy was the first woman to chair the BMS, while Terrot Reaveley *Glover became a distinguished Cambridge classicist and leading Baptist layman, perhaps best known for his influential *The Jesus of History* (1917).

Glover's main ministry was at Bristol, however, where in April 1869 he became the first minister of Tyndale Baptist Church, newly formed to serve the fast-growing and wealthy suburbs of Clifton and Redland. Glover remained at Tyndale until his retirement in 1911, assisted from 1908 by Herbert Burdett. The first twenty years saw Tyndale's membership multiply tenfold, a lecture hall and classrooms added, and a mission church founded. As secretary to the Bristol Baptist college from 1873 to 1919, Glover befriended and influenced generations of ministerial students. Patriarchal in appearance, with a mane of white hair and well-trimmed beard, he became well known in the city. He was a governor of the city's infirmary and an honorary secretary of the convalescent home, founded at his suggestion to mark Queen Victoria's diamond jubilee. In this last, as in other projects, he could count on the backing of wealthy and influential church members: in its first twenty-five years the church was said to have raised some £40,000 for good causes, excluding buildings.

Within the wider Baptist denomination Glover was active, influential, well liked and respected, and known for his geniality, deep personal faith, wide interests, and freshness of approach. He championed the closer integration of home and overseas mission work, and as Baptist Union president in 1884 urged the need for evangelism. When the down-grade controversy shook the union, Glover managed to stay on good terms with all the protagonists. He himself was progressive in theology. Repelled by Calvinism's judgemental aspects, he was open to modern scientific teaching and Biblical criticism, confident that they could not threaten Christianity.

Glover took part in the ecumenical discussions at Grindelwald in 1891 and spoke at the second Free Church congress in 1894. His great passion, however, was overseas mission. In 1879, to much relief at Tyndale, he declined to become the BMS Indian secretary, but from 1873 until his death he was an influential member (and from 1907 an honorary member) of the society's committee, chairing the China subcommittee from 1884 to 1912. Resisting firmly any suggestion that finance should dictate missionary work, Glover raised funds effectively for the BMS and sister societies. His own church gave significantly, both in money and workers. Glover stressed the need for missionaries to understand the culture and respect the beliefs of the people among whom they worked. He travelled widely for the BMS, most notably to China with Thomas Morris of Ipswich in 1890. This visit, the first ever 'home deputation' to the China mission field, was described by Morris in *A Winter in North China* (1892), for which Glover wrote the introduction. Shortly after his return from

China, in 1891, Glover received an honorary DD from Edinburgh University. This was followed, in 1912, by an LLD from Bristol University.

Glover's published works included teacher's commentaries on the gospel of St Mark (1884) and the gospel of St Matthew (1889); lectures on the Lord's prayer (1881), the Beatitudes (1888), and the fourteenth chapter of the gospel of St John (1908); a biography, *Herbert Stanley Jenkins, Medical Missionary, Shensi, China* (1914); and—reflecting his love of children—several sets of 'Notes for teachers' in the *Sunday School Chronicle*. Glover died on 26 March 1919 at 15 Westfield Park, Clifton, Bristol, after some years of failing health. He was buried in Bristol's Canford cemetery.

ROSEMARY CHADWICK

Sources J. S., 'The Rev. Richard Glover', *Baptist Magazine*, 79 (1887), 433–8 • H. G. Wood, *Terrot Reaveley Glover: a biography* (1953) • *Shields Daily Gazette* (27 March 1919) • *Baptist Times and Freeman* (4 April 1919) • *Western Daily Press* (27 March 1919) • *Western Daily Press* (31 March 1919) • *Missionary Herald* (May 1919) [memorial supplement] • T. D. Landels, *William Landels, a memoir* (1900) • D. T. Roberts, 'Mission, home and overseas: Richard Glover of Bristol', *Baptist Quarterly*, 35 (1993), 108–120 • *Shields Daily Gazette* (24 Feb 1885) • *Shields Daily News* (24 Feb 1885) • B. Stanley, *The history of the Baptist Missionary Society, 1792–1992* (1992) • L. G. Champion, ed., *Tyndale Baptist Church, Bristol, 1868–1968* (1968) • T. H. Robinson, *Terrot Reaveley Glover, MA, DD, LLD, of Cambridge* (1943) • G. B. Hodgson, *The borough of South Shields* (1903) • *Ward's north of England directory* (1859–60) • d. cert.

Archives Bristol Baptist College • St John Cam. • Tyndale Baptist Church, Bristol

Likenesses London Stereoscopic Photographic Co. Ltd, photograph, Regent's Park College, Angus Library • bust, Baptist House, Didcot • cartoon, repro. in *Clifton Society* (April 1903), supp.

Glover, Robert (*d.* 1555), protestant martyr, came of gentry stock in Warwickshire. He was one of three brothers, each of whom was attracted to protestant views under Henry VIII. The youngest brother, William, was probably the author of an adulatory letter to Anne Boleyn. John (the eldest) was the most remarkable, according to John Foxe, with whom he was acquainted in the 1540s. Having been 'called by the light of the Holy Spirit to the knowledge of the gospel', John became haunted by the fear that he had sinned against the Holy Ghost, and despaired of his salvation. Denying himself all manner of bodily comforts 'by the space of five years', John's mortification gave him a celestial mien, as if he were 'like one placed in heaven already, and dead in this world' (*Acts and Monuments*, 7.384–6, 390–93).

Robert Glover, meanwhile, was educated first at Eton College, and was then elected to King's College, Cambridge, in 1533. He proceeded BA in 1538, and MA in 1541, and he held a fellowship until 1543. His Cambridge connections and interest in reform may have brought him to Latimer's attention, and thus led to his marriage (by 1545) to Mary (*d. c.*1568), whose surname is unknown, but whose mother was one of Latimer's six sisters. Orphaned young, Mary was fostered by her uncle, whose household she ran. Robert and Mary settled at Baxterley in Warwickshire (near John and his wife, Agnes, at Mancetter). Latimer stayed with the Glovers so frequently that it was said that he formed the greater part of her dowry. Of their four children, the eldest son was named Hugh.

Marriage to Latimer's favourite niece was not without its dangers. Latimer was in eclipse, having been levered out of the bishopric of Worcester in 1539 following the passage of the Act of Six Articles. When he ran the danger of being burnt during the sacramentarian crisis of 1546, the Glovers' residence was searched. But Edward VI's accession the following year brought greater security. Latimer was among the leading preachers at the young king's court in 1549 and 1550. Robert's position at the heart of a network of reformers in the west country was enhanced, and his circle included John Careless, a Coventry weaver. A constellation of prominent preachers who enjoyed the Glovers' support orbited between London and Coventry and elsewhere, including Augustine Bernher, John Bradford, Laurence Nowell, John Olde, and Laurence Saunders. A Christmas sermon delivered by Latimer at Baxterley survives.

The ferocity with which the Marian regime moved to suppress the Glovers is a testament to their prominence in the protestant movement. Latimer was arrested at Baxterley in September 1553. In 1555 the Glovers became targets in their turn. Bishop Ralph Baynes sent a commission to the mayor and officers of Coventry to arrest John and his brothers. Warned, John and William fled, but according to Foxe, Robert was lying ill in bed 'sick of a long disease' (*Acts and Monuments*, 7.386) when the searchers rushed in. Examined by Baynes, Robert denied that the mass was a sacrament. In an interrupted letter to Mary, Robert wrote that he refused 'to pull my own neck out of the collar' (ibid., 7.390), and he shared Latimer's conviction that to surrender one's life was an honour not accorded to even the highest angels.

Robert Glover was burnt in the same fire with Cornelius Bungey, a capper, at Coventry on 19 September 1555. Latimer went to the flames in the next month. They were comforted at the stake by Bernher. John's sorrow that Robert was arrested in his stead was intense, and when renewed searches were initiated for him late in Mary's reign, he took refuge in the woods, caught an ague, and died. His wife, Agnes, was arrested and forced to abjure. When William Glover died at Wem in Shropshire, Baynes refused to permit his body to be buried in consecrated ground, and according to Foxe, he was interred in a 'broom-field'. Likewise, Mary informed Foxe of plans to disinter John's body and cast it 'into the highway' (*Acts and Monuments*, 7.400–01).

Letters survive from Robert Glover to his wife, to the mayor and brethren of Coventry, and to Bernher. In addition to Foxe's account of the Glovers, ballads written by Mary's second husband, Richard Bott, are also important sources for Robert Glover's martyrdom.

SUSAN WABUDA

Sources *The acts and monuments of John Foxe*, ed. S. R. Cattley, 8 vols. (1837–41), vol. 7, pp. 384–402 • two ballads by R. Bott, BL, Stowe MS 958, fols. 2v–3r, 8r–17r • S. Wabuda, 'Shunamites and nurses of the English Reformation: the activities of Mary Glover, niece of Hugh Latimer', *Women in the church on the eve of the dissolution*, ed. W. J. Sheil and D. Wood, SCH, 27 (1990), 335–44 • John Careless to Mary Glover, BL, Add. MS 19400, fols. 69*r*–70*r* • Robert Glover to Augustine Bernher, BL, Add. MS 19400, fols. 80*r*–81*r* • *Sermons and remains of Hugh Latimer*, ed. G. E. Corrie, Parker Society, 20 (1845), 84–96 • *DNB*

Glover, Robert (1543/4–1588), herald, was the elder son of Thomas Glover (*d.* 1556), of Ashford, Kent, and his wife, Mildred Bate. He was still only a child when his father died; he was bequeathed £20. With his mother he then lodged in Canterbury, where he went to school, presumably at King's (or Cathedral) School. After this he was 'much beyond the seas' (Ramsay, xi); it may be inferred that his formal education had now stopped and that he went to the continent in some mercantile capacity. Later he certainly proved fluent in French besides being an accomplished Latinist.

Glover's career had begun by March 1568, when he was appointed Portcullis pursuivant of arms. This was a junior position in the College of Arms, but it assured him of reasonable prospects in the long term, since promotion within the heraldic hierarchy was usually by seniority. Within a few years, if not already, he was married to Elizabeth Flower, daughter of William Flower, Norroy herald (Norroy being one of the three kings of arms or principal heralds). As Norroy, Flower had particular responsibility for the northern counties of England, and in 1570 he deputed Glover to visit throughout the northern province. Over the next fifteen years Glover held visitations in co. Durham, Cheshire, Yorkshire, and other counties, alone or with his father-in-law. Glover's visitation books increasingly set a standard for his heraldic colleagues to emulate; quite apart from drawing on the evidence of charters and seals, he was the first to represent pedigrees in these books by the rectilinear form (as still universally used today) in place of the medieval form of circles and radiating lines.

In December 1570 Glover was promoted to the office of full herald, Somerset, and in 1580 Flower obtained for himself a new patent as Norroy whereby that office would automatically pass on his death to Glover. During these years Glover was also attached to two missions of Garter king of arms: to Denmark in 1582 and France in 1584. He enjoyed the patronage of both William Cecil, Lord Burghley, and Queen Elizabeth's principal secretary, Sir Francis Walsingham.

Glover was the heralds' heraldist. He had a vision of what needed to be done for heraldic and genealogical studies, and he rapidly set about fulfilling it. In the ten years to 1588 he succeeded in locating and copying most of the medieval English rolls of arms; he also made innumerable drawings of medieval armorial seal impressions and other medieval coats of arms, and he then arranged these in the heraldists' order, as an ordinary of arms. Glover's ordinary was assembled in its first form in 1584; with its 15,000 coats it was soon recognized as being of unprecedented accuracy and fullness. It came to form the basis of all subsequent ordinaries, and only in 1992 did it start to be superseded, with the publication of a new medieval ordinary that returns to the original sources.

Glover was evidently a perfectionist, and none of his historical works was printed in his own lifetime. His 'Defence of the title of Queen Elizabeth to the English crown', against the book by John Lesley, bishop of Ross, in favour of Mary, queen of Scots (1569, etc.), was never published. His very substantial collection of biographies and genealogies of the English kings and nobility was printed only in 1608 by his nephew Thomas Milles, as *Nobilitas politica et civilis*, and then in English translation, and enlarged, as *The catalogue of honor, or, Treasury of true nobility, peculiar and proper to the isle of Great Britaine* (London, 1610). Nearly a century after its compilation, it was justly praised by Sir William Dugdale:

> I have a great reverence for the memory of Glover, Somerset; and though what he hath done in his Booke of Nobility may in some things deserve correction; yet I think I may say he did it *with great exactnesse*, I mean as great as such a worke may probably be done by one man, from such light as he could have. (Ramsay, x)

Glover's work was valued in his own lifetime and subsequently because he was dependable: he made his notes from the original sources, and he had a very fair grasp of how to sift and weigh conflicting historical evidence. He gathered together a substantial collection of medieval charters, cartularies, and chronicles, as well as many transcripts; and since he realized that many of the English noble families had French origins or connections that had been investigated and published by French scholars, he also acquired French books of local history.

Glover's hopes and expectations were cut short when he was only forty-four, by his falling mortally ill. 'Sicke of bodie but of good memorie, the Lorde be praysed', he made his will on 4 April 1588; he asked Thomas Randolph, master of the queen's posts, and Robert Beale, clerk of the council, to be overseers.

> And for that it maye be that my bookes and other thinges which I have painefully and derely gotten may be sowghte by others to the great prejudice of my saide wife and children, beinge the principall part of my substance that I shall leave unto them,

he asked Sir Francis Walsingham to act as protector and friend in all just causes (PRO, PROB 11/23, fol. 53*r*). He died six days later, on 10 April 1588. His collections were divided up, some passing first to Thomas Milles and others, then later to another nephew, John Philipot, while most were sold, to Lord Burghley and others; they are now scattered throughout Britain and North America. Glover was buried, without any ceremonies (by direction in his will), in the church of St Giles without Cripplegate, London. He was survived by his widow, Elizabeth, and two sons and three daughters. NIGEL RAMSAY

Sources N. L. Ramsay, introduction, *The kings of England ever since it was so called, by Robert Glover and Thomas Milles*, ed. D. Parker (1995), ix–xviii • BL, Add. MS 74253, fols. 57*v*–58*r* • W. H. Godfrey, A. Wagner, and H. Stanford London, *The College of Arms, Queen Victoria Street* (1963), 156 [biographical notice by H. S. London] • N. J. Philipson, ed., *The heraldic visitatione of the countye palatyne of Durham in 1575* (1820) • *The visitation of Cheshire in the year 1580, made by Robert Glover, Somerset herald*, ed. J. P. Rylands, Harleian Society, 18 (1882) • J. Foster, ed., *The visitation of Yorkshire made in the years 1584/5 … to which is* *added the subsequent visitation made in 1612* (privately printed, London, 1875) • P. M. Selywn, '"Such speciall bookes of Mr Somersettes as were sould to Mr Secretary": the fate of Robert Glover's collections', *Books and collectors, 1200–1700: essays presented to Andrew Watson* (1997), 389–401 • prerogative court of Canterbury, wills, PRO, PROB 11/23, fol. 53 • J. Weever, *Funerall monuments* (1767)

Archives BL, heraldic visitations and papers, Harley MSS • Bodl. Oxf., extracts from his collections and visitations • Bodl. Oxf., heraldic papers • Bodl. Oxf., historical and genealogical collections • Bodl. Oxf., notes • Coll. Arms, pedigrees and evidences, his baronage, etc. • Devon RO, copy by Glover of 1564 visitation of Devon • JRL, armorial • NL Wales, transcript by Glover of *Libellus de officio militari* (1458) • Norfolk RO, book of pedigrees and arms of knights of the Garter • Norfolk RO, heraldic papers • S. Antiquaries, Lond., visitation of Staffordshire [contemporary copy] • W. Yorks. AS, Leeds, Yorkshire Archaeological Society, pedigree of Lacy of Folkston • Yale U., Beinecke L., heraldic miscellany

Glover, Sarah Anna (1786–1867), music teacher, was born on 13 November 1786 at Norwich, the eldest daughter of the Revd Edward Glover, incumbent of St Lawrence's Church, Norwich. At the age of six she began receiving music lessons from Dr John Beckwith, the organist of Norwich Cathedral, eventually becoming 'an accomplished pianist'. Studious, resolute, and devout, she never married. In her early twenties she ran a local Sunday school with her younger sister Christiana, and there she began making tentative efforts to produce a simplified system of musical notation.

Glover's first experiment involved pasting guide-letters on the piano keys to help unmusical teachers pick out unknown tunes. She later used both alphabetical and sol-fa names for the purpose, and from that point can be traced the evolution of her novel notation using the initials of the sol-fa syllables—D, R, M, F, S, L, T—to represent the rising major scale. She had Anglicized *do*, *re*, *mi*, *fa*, *sol*, *la*, *si* as Doh, Ra, Me, Fah, Sole, Lah, and Te, renaming the seventh degree to avoid confusion between the identical initials of *sol* and *si*. All these ideas sprang jointly from careful study of Burney's *General History of Music* and her experiences while teaching young children in local charity schools.

By 1827 Glover had drawn up a complete method in manuscript form and was using it as part of her daily teaching in a girls' school of her own founding in Black Boy Yard, Colegate Street, Norwich. Instead of following tradition by first memorizing orthodox musical symbols, her pupils sang from the outset, learning by means of sol-fa notes pointed out on a chart, her 'Norwich sol-fa ladder'. Soon they were singing short phrases in canon and hymn tunes harmonized in two parts. All these were sung from a sol-fa tune book printed in Glover's 'Norwich sol-fa' notation, comprising sol-fa initials and a few additional symbols to represent accent and duration.

A choir enrolled from Glover's pupils now sang each Sunday at the services in St Lawrence's Church, and there were many enquiries as to how such young children had learned to sing so skilfully. She was repeatedly pressed by visitors to publish an account of her training methods. But it was not until 1835, when her pupils' singing had made St Lawrence's Church widely celebrated, that she found a publisher in Jarrold & Sons of Norwich and was able to produce a detailed summary of her method in print, under the allusive title *Scheme for rendering psalmody congregational, comprising a key to the sol-fa notation of music, and directions for instructing a school*.

In 1841 a copy of Glover's *Scheme* was lent to John Curwen, a young Congregationalist minister deeply interested in educational practice who was then examining various systems of teaching singing with a view to synthesizing a method suitable for general use. Excited by Glover's account, Curwen impulsively adopted, even modified, several of her devices as the basis of what became known as tonic sol-fa, but without seeking her permission. Despite Curwen's hastily expressed apologies and his repeated public acknowledgement of indebtedness to her, the strained relationship that understandably arose between them was resolved only during Glover's last years. She died of a stroke at Malvern on 20 October 1867 and was buried at Hereford, where she had retired only a few years earlier to live with her sister Christiana.

BERNARR RAINBOW

Sources S. A. Glover, *A manual of the Norwich sol-fa system for teaching singing in schools and classes, etc.*, 3rd edn [1845] • B. Rainbow, 'Introduction', in S. Glover, *Scheme for rendering psalmody congregational* (1982) • J. Curwen, 'History and statistics', *The art of teaching, and the teaching of music: being the teacher's manual of the tonic sol-fa method* (1875), 377–86 • J. S. Curwen, *Memorials of John Curwen* (1882) • L. Brown, 'Reminiscences of Miss Glover', in J. S. Curwen and J. Graham, *Tonic sol-fa jubilee: a popular record and hand book* [1891], 1–10 • d. cert.

Archives Royal College of Music, London, Curwen archive

Likenesses photograph, *c.*1856 (at Reading); copy, glass lantern slide (for John Curwen's lectures) • oils, *c.*1879 (after photograph, *c.*1856), Royal College of Music • engraving (after photograph, *c.*1856), repro. in Curwen, 'History and statistics' • print (after lantern slide), repro. in B. Rainbow, *The land without music* (1967), facing p. 48

Wealth at death under £800: probate, 6 Dec 1867, *CGPLA Eng. & Wales*

Glover, Stephen (*bap.* 1794, *d.* 1869), publisher and topographer, was baptized on 20 February 1794 at Long Clawson, Leicestershire, the son of William and Jane Glover. He moved to Derby as a young man and was apprenticed for five years to an iron-founder, Thomas Wheeldon. After a period studying navigation with a view to a naval career, Glover was employed by a bookseller, Marriott of Derby, before setting up as a printer in Full Street, Derby. He published directories and guidebooks, such as the *Peak Guide* (1830), and collected materials for a county history. To this end, Glover transcribed a version of a then unpublished early eighteenth-century 'History of Derbyshire' by William Woolley, which, with additions, formed the basis of the second and last published volume of Glover's *History of the County of Derby Drawn up from Actual Observation and from the Best Authorities* (2 vols., 1829–31).

Glover's more ambitious publishing ventures were unsuccessful and his doubtful financial dealings earned him the distrust of antiquarian colleagues and collaborators such as Thomas Bateman (1821–1861). He died in poverty at Leasowe, near Birkenhead, on 26 December 1869 and was buried at Moreton, Cheshire. Many of his Derbyshire historical notes and transcripts, including his version of Woolley's 'History of Derbyshire', were sold and some now form part of the Bemrose collection in Derby Public Library. Glover's reputation is that of 'a compiler of directories and guidebooks and in no sense an antiquary of any standing' (*William Woolley's History*, xlix), but the topographical information he accumulated remains of local interest. MARGARET O'SULLIVAN

Sources 'The history and gazeteer of the county of Derby', *Derbyshire Miscellany*, 1 (1956), i–ii · *William Woolley's history of Derbyshire*, ed. C. Glover and P. Rideu (1981) · *DNB* · parish register (baptism), Long Clawson, Leicestershire, 20 Feb 1794

Archives CUL, copy of William Woolley's *History of Derbyshire* with MS notes and additions by Glover · Derby Central Library, papers relating to Derbyshire · Derbys. RO, corresp. with J. J. Briggs · Derbys. RO, genealogical notes; pedigree of the Tempest and Radford families

Glover, Stephen Ralph (1813?–1870), composer, was born in London, probably on 7 December 1813, the brother of Charles William *Glover (1806–1863). He was a popular and prolific composer, and many of his nearly 1500 works were published. His most important pieces include twelve *Songs from the Holy Scriptures* (1848), a setting of Longfellow's 'Excelsior' (1855), and *Beauty and the Beast* (1863), a chamber opera, though he also produced songs, ballads, duets, piano pieces, and transcriptions. He died in London on 7 December 1870. DAVID J. GOLBY

Sources L. Middleton, 'Glover, Stephen', Grove, *Dict. mus.* (1954)

Glover, Terrot Reaveley (1869–1943), classical scholar and historian, was born at 10 Belgrave Road, Cotham, Bristol, on 23 July 1869, the eldest child and only son of the Revd Richard *Glover (1837–1919), Baptist minister, and his wife, Anna Finlay (1838–1924). Educated at Bristol grammar school, he was admitted to St John's College, Cambridge, as a £50 minor scholar in 1888. In *Cambridge Retrospect* (1943), published just before his death, Glover recalled some characteristics of the teaching and the teachers, Leonard Whibley, J. E. Sandys, William Emerton Heitland, and others, of his undergraduate years. After gaining the Browne medal twice, the chancellor's medal, and the Porson prize as well as first classes in both parts of the classical tripos (1891, 1892), Glover was elected into a fellowship of his college in 1892. Four years later he left to become professor of Latin at Queen's University, Kingston, Ontario, at a stipend of C$2000. He married on 11 May 1897 Alice Emily Cornelia, second daughter of Harry Gleaves Few, corn merchant, of Cambridge, with whom he had two sons and four daughters. In 1901 he returned to his own college as a teaching fellow; in 1911 he was appointed university lecturer in ancient history, and Cambridge was his home for the rest of his life.

Thus, on the face of it, Glover's life might seem to have been just that of a college don and in many of his writings he displayed much of the humour and whimsicality which have been commonly associated with donnishness. His genius for composing light verse in English and Latin was manifestly encouraged by H. R. Tottenham (1856–1937), fellow and lecturer at St John's, who in a parody of Juvenal, i.79 thought out 'facit indigestio versum'. When he became orator of the university in 1920 he was able to display his epigrammatic ingenuity to full advantage: 'Dat vitam vitaminando' was one of his phrases in presenting Sir Frederick Gowland Hopkins, the biochemist, for an honorary degree. But, in fact, Glover was much more than an academic figure. 'I modestly claimed', he once wrote, 'to understand irrelevance', and in his university lectures, as elsewhere, he covered a wide range of digression. 'It's a poor subject', he said, 'that cannot be brought into an ancient history lecture.' Meanwhile a restless mind and a fluent pen quickly led him to authorship. His first substantial work was *Life and Letters in the Fourth Century* (1901); this was followed by *Studies in Virgil* (1904) and *The Conflict of Religions in the Early Roman Empire* (1909); and to the end of his life Glover was a prolific author of books and essays on classical themes. Among them were *Herodotus* (1924), *Democracy in the Ancient World* (1927), and *Greek Byways* (1932), and in all of them he showed first, an abiding faith in the value of a classical education; second, an intense delight in the byways as well as in the highways of literature; and third, a rebellious protest against philology, textual criticism, and the stricter canons of classical scholarship. Indeed, he combined with his deep love of Cambridge a scornfully sceptical attitude towards the Cambridge tradition of accurate learning. His own books, he said, were too readable to win the approval of the purists. In dedicating *Greek Byways* to F. J. Foakes Jackson he wrote:

> I send you my *Byways*, to be sure of one reader who is not a candidate for a Tripos and who will realize that they were written for people bred like you and me on the Classics, and fond of them, and in no great hurry to do something else. What a world the others miss!

But Glover could not rest content with purely classical subjects. Puritan as he was by training and conviction, his literary taste was truly catholic. The romantics, the adventurers, the buccaneers made an immediate appeal to him; he loved Don Quixote as well as Bunyan, Erasmus as well as Luther; in his *Poets and Puritans* (1915) there is an essay on James Boswell.

Glover was a deeply religious man, inheriting from his father a loyalty to the Baptish church which never faltered. He became president of the Baptist Union in 1924. Furthermore, his influence as a preacher extended beyond his own denomination. He preached in the chapel of his own college from time to time and also in the church of St Edward, King and Martyr, Cambridge. For him, the central point in the history of the ancient world was the life of Jesus Christ, and his aim both as historian and as Christian was 'to see the Founder of the Christian movement and some of his followers as they appeared among their contemporaries'. In 1915 college and university authorities granted Glover permission to spend a year in India, working for the YMCA. Before going he was to spend a month in Le Havre in a camp for soldiers with venereal disease. His proctorial experiences had given him sympathetic insight into the temptations faced by undergraduates. *The Jesus of History* (published in 1917 with a foreword by the archbishop of Canterbury, Randall Davidson), which grew out of lectures delivered in Indian cities in 1915–16, was the most popular exposition of this theme, making Glover's name known to thousands of non-classicists.

Glover's five years in Ontario imbued him with a deep love of Canada: his Cambridge lectures were conspicuous for digressions on the prairies, the mountains, the Great Lakes, and forest fires. This affection for the dominion sprang in part, perhaps, from his highland descent of which he was inordinately proud and Heitland once told him that he had taken to Canada 'as a duck to green peas'. Canada was for Glover a land of high romance and in *A Corner of Empire: the Old Ontario Strand* (1937), written in collaboration with his friend Dilbert Calvin, he demonstrated his vital interest in Canadian history. He made twenty return trips across the Atlantic, fifteen between the two world wars; he preached and lectured in many American as well as Canadian universities, was Lowell lecturer at Boston in 1922 and Sather professor in classics in the University of California in 1923. Both at home and abroad other universities honoured him with degrees: he was LLD of Queen's (1910), McMaster (1917), and Glasgow (1930); DD of St Andrews (1921); and LittD of Trinity College, Dublin (1936). He was also president of the Classical Association in 1938. In Cambridge he twice (1914–15, 1919–20) held the office of proctor, and recalled that he had once fined Prince Albert (afterwards George VI) for smoking in academical dress; similarly, he was proud, as orator, to have presented for degrees six prime ministers, two kings, and one god (the crown prince of Japan). He was described accurately by his pupil Professor Emeritus S. E. Smethurst as 'a burly man whose square jaw and piercing eye gave him a formidable appearance' (private information). He retired in 1939, becoming orator emeritus, and died at his home, 67 Glisson Road, Cambridge, on 26 May 1943. He was survived by his wife.

SYDNEY C. ROBERTS, *rev.* HERBERT H. HUXLEY

Sources T. R. Glover, *Cambridge retrospect* (1943) · *TLS* (13 Oct 1945) · H. G. Wood, *Terrot Reaveley Glover* (1953) · R. Kilpatrick, *T. R. Glover at Queen's (1896–1901)* (1997) · E. Miller, *Portrait of a college: a history of the College of Saint John the Evangelist, Cambridge* (1961) · private information (2004) · personal knowledge (1959, 2004) · *CGPLA Eng. & Wales* (1943)

Archives CUL, corresp. and papers · CUL, lecture notes on ancient history · CUL, transcript of John Johnson's record of William Cowper's dreams · St John Cam., papers | FILM BFI NFTVA, news footage

Likenesses G. Owst, pen caricature, 1920, St John Cam.; repro. in *Old Cambridge Magazine* · W. Fisk-Moore, charcoal drawing, *c.*1940–1943, St John Cam. · Mrs Lipscomb, portrait, Christ's College, Cambridge; repro. in *Old Cambridge Magazine* · H. Wilkinson, portrait, priv. coll. · photograph, repro. in Wood, *Terrot Reaveley Glover* · photographs, St John Cam.

Wealth at death £35,447 7*s.* 2*d.*: probate, 4 Oct 1943, *CGPLA Eng. & Wales*

Glover, Thomas Blake (1838–1911), merchant, was born on 6 June 1838 at 15 Commerce Street, Fraserburgh, in Aberdeenshire, the fifth of the eight children of Thomas Berry Glover (1805–1878), a civilian chief officer of the coastguard at Fraserburgh, and his wife, Mary, *née* Findley (1807–1887), of Fordyce, Banffshire. He probably attended the parish school at Fraserburgh, and his name appears on the register of Channonry House School (The Gymnasium), Old Aberdeen, for the year 1854.

Glover arrived in Nagasaki via Shanghai on 19 September 1859, soon after the opening of Japan to foreign trade. In May 1861 he became established as a general commission agent, representing among others Jardine, Matheson & Co., and in February 1862 he formed Glover & Co. At first he mainly exported refined Japanese tea, but this was not profitable.

Glover's fortunes began to change in late 1863, when he started to take advantage of the business opportunities offered by the domestic political rivalries of late Tokugawa Japan. With funds loaned from Jardine, Matheson & Co., he switched his major interests to more speculative activities, such as the sale of ships, and arms and ammunition. Glover & Co. became the biggest Western firm in Nagasaki, opening branches in Shanghai and Yokohama in 1864. In 1865 Glover ordered munitions from Armstrong & Co. on behalf of the shogunate; he sold ships and even arranged for some domains to have ships built in Britain. Such orders were generally made through Glover Brothers, the Aberdeen firm of his brother Charles (1830–1877).

Glover later claimed that he had been the most rebellious of all the rebels against the Tokugawa shogunate. Although he had dealings with the shogunate, and there is no contemporary evidence as to his political convictions, his links with the Satsuma domain did grow closer as it developed an increasingly pro-trade and pro-British stance. He arranged for young samurai from Satsuma, some of whom played prominent roles in the early Meiji government, to study in England in 1865, and persuaded Sir Harry Parkes to visit the capital of Satsuma in July 1866.

Ironically, Glover & Co. found it difficult to adjust to the changes in trade which occurred with the Meiji restoration of 1868, including the economic decline of Nagasaki. Glover attempted to shift to entrepreneurial activities, constructing a patent slip dock and developing the Takashima coalmine. He also started branches in the newly opened Hyogo and Osaka, anticipating good trading prospects. However, he was seriously undercapitalized and his new ventures did not produce results quickly enough. The firm was declared bankrupt in August 1870 and the Netherland Trading Society acted as trustees. This failure is attributable to a lack of managerial ability, probably linked to his optimistic outlook on life, as well as to the disappearance of the circumstances which had earlier brought him prosperity. After the bankruptcy he continued to work at the Takashima coalmine, which was eventually bought by Mitsubishi. Mitsubishi was founded by Yataro Iwasaki, a former Tosa samurai, who had had business dealings with Glover before the restoration. Glover acted as a consultant for Mitsubishi in various ways, playing a crucial role in the founding of what became the Kirin Brewery Company.

Glover was married, probably in 1867, to Tsuru Awajiya (1848–1899), who is said to have been one of the models for Arthur de Long's "Madam Butterfly". Although this story was the inspiration behind Puccini's opera, Tsuru was never a geisha and it is unlikely that the character of Lieutenant Pinkerton was based on Glover. They had two children, Hana (1868–1938) and Tomisaburo (1870–1945). In 1908 he was awarded the order of the Rising Sun (second class) by the Japanese emperor for his contribution to the establishment of the Meiji government.

Glover's residence in Nagasaki became a famous tourist spot and he remains a well-known historical figure in Japan, although his role in the Meiji restoration has been exaggerated. He is criticized for his arms-dealing activities and praised for his attempts to introduce Western technology. In Britain his behind-the-scenes role in liaising with anti-shogunate domains before the restoration was valued by Lord Redesdale, a diplomatic contemporary (Redesdale, 377), but he was largely forgotten. In the late 1980s, however, local historians in the Aberdeen area, aware of his fame in Japan, began to revive his memory. Glover died of Bright's disease on 16 December 1911 at his home, 8 Fujimi-cho, Azabu, Tokyo. He was buried at Sakamoto international cemetery in Nagasaki beside his wife, Tsuru.

S. SUGIYAMA

Sources S. Sugiyama, *Meiji ishin to Igirisu shonin: Thomas Glover no shogai* (1993) [British merchants and the Meiji restoration of 1868: the life of Thomas B. Glover] • S. Sugiyama, 'Thomas B. Glover: a British merchant in Japan, 1861–70', *Business History*, 26 (1984), 115–38 • T. B. Glover, 'Cho-satsu-ei no kankei' [Relations between Choshu, Satsuma, and Great Britain], *Bocho Shidankai Zasshi*, 27 (1912) • Lord Redesdale [A. B. Freeman-Mitford], *Memories*, 2 vols. (1915) • NA Scot., Old parochial register 196/2 • A. S. Maxwell, ed., *The registers of the Episcopal congregation, Fraserburgh, 1766–1884* (privately printed, Aberdeen, 1985) • *Japan Times* (19 Dec 1911) • A. Shewan, *Spirat adhuc amor* (1923) • H. Noda, *Glover fujin*, revised edn (1991) [[Mrs Glover]] • *Japan directory* (1863–1911)

Archives CUL, Jardine Matheson MSS • Nationaal Archief, The Hague, Nederlandsche Handel–Maatschappij 5935

Likenesses group portraits, photographs, Nagasaki Prefectural Library, Japan

Glover, William Howard (1819–1875), conductor and music critic, was born in Kilburn, Middlesex, on 6 June 1819, the second son of the actress Julia *Glover. At the age of fifteen he joined the Lyceum Opera orchestra as a violinist and also took lessons from the conductor, William Wagstaff. He continued his studies on the continent, and was soon afterwards employed as an accompanist and solo violinist in London and the provinces. With his mother, he founded the Musical and Dramatic Academy in Soho Square, and was encouraged by its success to open a season of opera at Manchester and Liverpool, his pupils forming the nucleus of the company. He conducted and occasionally sang in the company, and was joined in the enterprise by his elder brother Edmund *Glover and Emma Romer. After returning to London he gave annual 'monster' concerts at St James's Hall and Drury Lane Theatre. Many first-rate artists appeared, and the length of the entertainments inspired more than one foreign critic with philosophical reflections upon the English amateur's capacity for endurance. Glover performed Beethoven's 'Pastoral' symphony with pictorial and choreographic illustrations in 1863 and Mendelssohn's *Israel in Egypt* with scenery, dresses, and poses in 1865.

Glover was music critic of the *Morning Post* from about 1850 to 1865, and wrote appreciative reviews of Berlioz's 1852 concerts. Berlioz conducted Glover's cantata *Tam o' Shanter* on 4 July 1855, later describing it as 'très piquante de style, mais difficile, qui m'a fait suer jusqu'à grossir le ruisseau du Strand' ('very piquant in style, but difficult, which made me sweat enough to overflow the gutters in the Strand'). His opera *Ruy Blas* was successfully produced on 24 October 1861 at Covent Garden; however, after a week the management announced that it was so exhausting for the singers that they could only give it three times a week. It was revived in 1863. Glover also wrote several operettas—*Once Too Often* (Drury Lane, 20 January 1862), *The Coquette*, *Aminta*, and, in New York, *Palomita*—as well as songs and piano music. He went to the USA in 1868 and became conductor of the orchestra at Niblo's Garden. He died in New York on 18 October 1875.

L. M. MIDDLETON, *rev.* JOHN WARRACK

Sources *New Grove* • Grove, *Dict. mus.* • Brown & Stratton, *Brit. mus.* • A. W. Ganz, *Berlioz in London* (1950) • *Correspondence générale: Hector Berlioz*, ed. P. Citron, 5 (Paris, 1989) • H. Rosenthal, *Two centuries of opera at Covent Garden* (1958) • *Musical World* (1855–75), passim

Glubb, Sir John Bagot [*known as* Abu Hunaik; *called* Glubb Pasha] (**1897–1986**), army officer and Arabist, was born on 16 April 1897 in Preston, Lancashire, the only son and younger child of Sir Frederic Manley Glubb, a major in the Royal Engineers, and his wife, Frances Letitia Bagot. Jack Glubb was educated at Cheltenham College and passed second into the Royal Military Academy, Woolwich, in 1914. He was commissioned in the Royal Engineers on 20 April 1915 and joined a field company of the Royal Engineers in France in November. He served there throughout the First World War, being three times wounded, once nearly fatally in the jaw, and was awarded the MC (1917).

In 1920 Glubb was posted to Mesopotamia, where he later became a ground intelligence officer with the Royal Air Force. This was the beginning of his connection with the Arabs, for whom he formed an instant sympathy, so much so that in 1926 he left the army to join the British administration in Iraq. At that time the Iraqi Bedouin and shepherd tribes in the southern desert were being terrorized by raids by Ibn Saʿud's Wahabis (al-ikhwan). Glubb was posted there in 1928 as administrative inspector.

Partly by persuading the Bedouin to join his armed police, and partly with RAF support, Glubb had ended the raiding by 1930, when he was invited to join the Arab Legion in Transjordan, with a similar mission. This he accomplished within three years, raising a force of Bedouin camel police, which became famous as the desert patrol. In 1939 Amir Abdullah appointed him to command the Arab Legion as *feriq* (lieutenant-general), although he was better known perhaps as Abu Hunaik (Father of the little jaw), a reference to his 1917 war wound.

Glubb was probably the first man to succeed in turning

Sir John Bagot Glubb [Glubb Pasha] (**1897–1986**), by Howard Coster, 1954

the Bedouin into disciplined soldiers. Previously they had been considered untameable. Glubb was, however, careful to train his Bedouin in accordance with their age-old customs. In 1941 he led them alongside the British army in Syria and Iraq, and was appointed to the DSO. His contribution to the capture of Baghdad in 1941 and the subsequent capture of the desert fortress of Palmyra in Syria was decisive, for it denied the eastern flank of the Middle East to Hitler. Later he formed a complete mechanized brigade, almost entirely Bedouin. He was now known as Glubb Pasha, 'pasha' being an Ottoman honorific title.

On 15 May 1948 Glubb led the Arab Legion across the Jordan to occupy the West Bank, as laid down by the United Nations partition resolution of November 1947. He did not expect to have to fight for it, which is what actually happened. When the fighting ended with an armistice in March 1949, Glubb had the responsibility for defending the West Bank, but with far too few troops with which to do it. The Arab Legion had to be expanded with British financial support, but with the proviso that the British officers serving in the Arab Legion should be increased in number. They occupied all the important posts, which gave rise to resentment among many Jordanian officers. Glubb shared their disquiet, but the subsidy was vital. He was greatly reliant on King Abdullah's support, which vanished when the king was assassinated on 20 July 1951. His son Talal reigned only a few months before abdicating, and was succeeded by his son, Hussein, still only sixteen and a schoolboy at Harrow. Although Hussein respected Glubb, the gap between their ages proved impossible to bridge and they soon fell out. Military and political developments were rapidly outgrowing Glubb, and the influential foreign adviser to an oriental monarch was becoming an anachronism.

Hussein, who came of age in 1953, particularly disagreed with Glubb's plan for the defence of the West Bank. Glubb sought to gain time by a planned withdrawal until Britain intervened in accordance with her treaty with Jordan. Hussein refused to countenance any withdrawal. The two views were irreconcilable and resulted in Hussein's dismissal of Glubb Pasha on 1 March 1956. The order giving him twenty-four hours to leave the country was intended to forestall any attempt to reinstate him. Glubb had in fact forbidden any bloodshed and had told his British officers to calm the situation. Soon they too were on their way. Glubb's abrupt dismissal caused a furore in Britain, and shocked many in Jordan.

Although Glubb was deeply hurt by the manner of his dismissal he behaved with exemplary dignity. Neither then nor later did he blame the king. He arrived in Britain with only £5, and was not awarded a general's pension by either Britain or Jordan. He was appointed KCB (1956) on his arrival and thereafter the British government washed its hands of him. He had been appointed OBE in 1925 and CMG in 1946. Glubb turned to his pen, and to lecturing, to provide for himself and his family of two sons and two daughters. He had married in 1938 Muriel Rosemary, daughter of James Graham Forbes, physician. They had a son in Jerusalem in 1939, whom they named Godfrey, after the Crusader king. In 1944 they adopted a baby Bedouin girl, and, after the death of another son who was born prematurely in 1947, adopted another daughter and son, both Palestinian refugees. Glubb was not impressive in appearance and was almost diffident in manner, speaking in rather a high-pitched voice. Yet there was about him an unmistakable air of authority, and when in uniform he wore no fewer than five rows of medal ribbons.

Glubb wrote twenty-two books, mostly on the Arabs, and lectured in Britain and the USA. His best book is perhaps *War in the Desert* (1960), which tells of his Iraq service. He had a soldier's aversion to politics—and to politicians. He had tried hard not to become involved, but as commander of Jordan's security forces some involvement was unavoidable. His dismissal was a political act, supported by Hussein's prime minister, Samir Rifai. Glubb remained nevertheless throughout his life a staunch supporter of Jordan and King Hussein. He was a devout Christian, an Edwardian in both manner and values. A servant of both Britain and Jordan, he was the last in the long line of powerful British proconsuls. He died from aplastic anaemia on 17 March 1986 in Mayfield, Sussex.

JAMES LUNT, *rev.*

Sources J. Glubb, *The changing scenes of life* (1983) • J. D. Lunt, *Glubb Pasha: Lieutenant-General Sir John Bagot Glubb, commander of the Arab legion, 1939–1956* (1984) • T. Royle, *Glubb Pasha* (1992) • personal knowledge (1996) • *CGPLA Eng. & Wales* (1986)

Archives Royal Engineers, Brompton barracks, Chatham, Kent, diaries • St Ant. Oxf., Middle East Centre, papers relating to Iraq and Jordan | King's Lond., Liddell Hart C., corresp. with Sir B. H.

Liddell Hart • St Ant. Oxf., Middle East Centre, corresp. with Cecil Edmonds

Likenesses photographs, 1951–70, Hult. Arch. • H. Coster, photograph, 1954, NPG [*see illus.*] • A. G. Davidson-Houston, portrait, headquarters, Royal Engineers

Wealth at death £205,843: probate, 25 June 1986, *CGPLA Eng. & Wales*

Gluck, Hannah [*real name* Hannah Gluckstein; *known as* Gluck] (**1895–1978**), portrait painter, was born on 13 August 1895 in Canfield Gardens, West Hampstead, London, the elder child of Joseph Gluckstein (1854–1930) and his American wife, Francesca Hallé (1875–1958). She pronounced her chosen name with a short vowel sound (to rhyme with 'duck'). On the backs of photographic prints of her paintings, sent out for publicity, she always wrote 'please return in good condition to Gluck, no prefix, suffix, or quotes'. The Glucksteins were a patriarchal, dynastic Jewish family. Joseph's father, Samuel, an immigrant in 1880 from Rheinberg, Prussia, built up a tobacco business in the East End of London with his cousins and brother, calling the partnership Salmon and Gluckstein. His sons then created J. Lyons & Co.—the catering empire of tea-shops, Corner House restaurants, and the Trocadero, Strand, Regent Palace, and Cumberland hotels. The Glucksteins married their cousins and second cousins, the Salmons, Josephs, and Abrahams, out of trust and business acumen. From the 1880s they all pooled their capital in the family fund. They moved from the East End first to West Hampstead and then to St John's Wood. The fund paid for everything: houses, health care, education, carriages, servants. When any of the family died their capital and assets reverted to the fund. Socially they dined together, worshipped at the same synagogue, and lived in the same neighbourhood.

Expectations for Hannah Gluckstein were that she should marry and define her life through the family's values. She was taught at home by a governess, and at a dame-school in Swiss Cottage. Then in 1910, aged fifteen, she went to St Paul's Girls' School in Hammersmith, where she excelled at art and music. She then went to St John's Wood Art School near the family home. Regarding her time there, she said: 'As far as I was concerned there was nothing taught that could be considered training' (autobiographical notes, n.d., priv. coll.). She paired up with another art student, E. M. Craig, and went to Lamorna in Cornwall with her. Encouraged by Alfred Munnings and Laura Knight, she lived and painted there. In 1924 she held her first exhibition at the Dorien Leigh Gallery, South Kensington, and her second, in 1926, was at the Fine Art Gallery in Bond Street, the venue of all her subsequent exhibitions. Gluck painted aspects of her life: Cornish landscapes, self-portraits, her mother, the women who were her lovers, stage scenes from C. B. Cochran's revues of the twenties. Her father was mortified by her lesbianism and rebelliousness but did not penalize her financially. She received Gluckstein money in trust, and in 1926 she bought Bolton House, a Georgian house in Windmill Hill, Hampstead. The architect Edward Maufe converted an outbuilding into a model studio in 1931.

Gluck disliked abstract painting, showed her work only in solo exhibitions, and shunned comparisons with other artists. Lovers influenced her work more than art theories. From 1932 to 1936 she had a relationship with Constance *Spry, florist to royalty and the aristocracy, and she painted white flowers arranged in the Constance Spry manner. Spry's clients, including Syrie Maugham and Molly Mount Temple, commissioned work from Gluck. In the thirties Gluck was at the height of her success. Her androgynous clothes were designed by Elsa Schiaparelli and Victor Steibel. She herself designed and patented the Gluck frame consisting of three symmetrically stepped panels. The arrangement was such that 'Instead of the outer edge of the frame dominating it was made to die away into the wall' (autobiographical notes, n.d., priv. coll.). She first used her frame in her 1932 exhibition at the Fine Art Society.

In 1936 Gluck fell in love with Nesta Obermeyer, *née* Ella Ernestine Sawyer (*b.* 1894), an elegant socialite married to a wealthy American. She painted *Medallion* (priv. coll.), a portrait of their merged profiles, and called it the YouWe picture. Intending to start life afresh, she destroyed diaries, letters, and portraits of past lovers. 'Anything even vaguely smelling of the past stinks in my nostrils', she wrote to Nesta (Gluck to Obermeyer, 1936, priv. coll.). Embittered when this love failed, she did very little work in the forties and fifties. She had a breakdown and feuded with her brother and the Gluckstein trustees over the management of her affairs.

In 1944 Gluck moved to the Chantry House, Steyning, Sussex, the home of the sisters Nora Heald and Edith Heald (1885–1976). Nora was editor of *The Lady* from 1930 to 1953, and Edith wrote the *Evening Standard*'s 'Londoner's diary' in the 1920s and opinion pieces for the *Express* newspapers. Tension and scenes followed Gluck's arrival and after two years Nora, then sixty-three, moved out. Gluck and Edith Heald lived together at the Chantry House until Edith died in 1976. Gluck did not recapture her pre-war success and became embittered and litigious. Furthermore, she did not get on with Edith, she fell out with her brother, and her mother developed Alzheimer's disease. Her sense of injustice found expression in a series of formal portraits of judges, including Wilfrid Arthur, Lord Greene, and Sir Raymond Evershed, both masters of the rolls. From 1953 on she fought with the Board of Trade and the manufacturers of artists' materials for better quality paints and canvases and for an agreed standard for defining pigments in oils. For a decade she spent one-third of her annual income on this campaign. Her efforts were successful but at great cost to her career.

In 1972 Gluck went again to the Fine Art Society. 'As my last show was here in 1937 I think it is time we considered another', she told the gallery directors Andrew McIntosh Patrick and Tony Carroll (Gluck to A. McIntosh Patrick, 4 May 1972, The Fine Art Society). They looked at photographic records of her exhibitions, went to the Chantry House, saw that she had reacquired many of her best paintings, and offered her another exhibition. Reviewers praised her sense of harmony and form and perfectionist use of colour and brushwork. Her exhibition included exquisite flower paintings, landscapes of Cornwall, and the best of her portraits, and showed how she linked objective observation to inner feeling. It also included her latest painting premonitory of death, *Rage, Rage Against the Dying of the Light*, an image of a fish's head with hollowed eyes washed up by the tide. She worked on it for three years with special oils handmade for her by Rowney & Son. Gluck died of a stroke at the Chantry House, Steyning, on 10 January 1978 at the age of eighty-two. Following her cremation, her ashes were scattered in the garden of her studio there. DIANA SOUHAMI

Sources D. Souhami, *Gluck, 1895–1978: her biography* (1988) • archive of family MSS, priv. coll. • Gluck MSS, The Fine Art Society, London [including photographs of her paintings]
Archives Fine Art Society, London, MSS • priv. coll., family MSS | Tate collection, corresp. with Lord Clark
Likenesses H. Gluck, self-portrait, oils, 1925; stolen • R. Brooks, oils, 1926, Smithsonian Institution, Washington, DC, National Collection of Fine Arts • E. A. Hoppé, photograph, 1926, Fine Art Society, London • H. Gluck, double portrait, self-portrait, medallion, oils, 1936 (with Nesta Obermeyer), priv. coll.; reproduction, The Fine Art Society, London • H. Gluck, self-portrait, oils, 1942, NPG
Wealth at death £91,322: probate, 19 April 1978, *CGPLA Eng. & Wales*

Glück, Louis [*pseud.* Louis Glück Rosenthal] (**1804–1874**), artist and Hebrew scholar, was born in Posen in Prussia. His father, Pielte Elimelech Glück (*d. c.*1840), a furrier, was a prominent (*hakham*) member of the Jewish community. Nothing is known of Louis's mother, and little of his early life in Prussia, except that he married about 1830 a woman by the name of Malé (1810–1844). They had two children.

In 1836 Glück emigrated to Great Britain, leaving Malé and the children behind until he was settled. After landing originally at Leith, from Stettin, he soon took lodgings in the East End of London, and started to make a name for himself as an artist, working in oils, watercolours, and—his speciality—micrography. These are engravings in which the subject is delineated by a minutely inscribed text amounting to a biography of the subject. Not surprisingly this work brought on considerable eyestrain, for which he was admitted to the London Hospital in 1840. He has since fallen into obscurity as an artist as has the medium that he favoured. His only works that are known to survive are micrographic portraits of Queen Victoria (in the Royal Collection, Windsor, in the Victoria and Albert Museum, and in private hands) and the duke of Sussex (in the British Museum).

Glück composed the texts of his micrographic portraits after a succession of interviews with the prince consort and the duke. He also published them in book form: *Biographical Memoir of Her Most Gracious Majesty Queen Victoria* (1844) and *A Biographical Memoir of his Late Royal Highness, the Duke of Sussex* (1846). The latter, for which he used the pen-name 'L. Glück Rosenthal', served as source material for the *Dictionary of National Biography* entry on the duke, and is quite widely quoted in works on that subject.

Glück was also a Hebraist and 'professor of languages', and in the early 1840s was engaged by the duke as his Hebrew tutor. Shortly after the duke's death, Glück was invited to let his name go forward for appointment as the first rabbi in St Thomas, Virgin Islands, who would use the new liturgy developed by the reform movement in England. Perhaps because of complications in his private life, however, the appointment did not materialize.

In 1843 his wife Malé arrived from Prussia with the children, and Glück deserted a gentile girl in Bethnal Green, Sarah Gregory (*b.* 1818), who had by then borne him three children. Malé, however, died of consumption on 28 December 1844. Glück was negotiating for the hand of Rebecca Levy (1818–1898) in 1846 (they married on 5 August) when he had another child with another gentile girl, Sarah Brown. Rebecca was the daughter of Nathan Levy, a wealthy jeweller and man of property in Woolwich whose family had settled in England a century before. The marriage, which produced five children, gave Glück new respectability and domesticity. The family lived at 3 Prospect Place, Woolwich, for the next ten years; then at 1 King's Place, St George-in-the-East, until the early 1860s, when they moved to 100 (and later 112) Devonshire Street, Sheffield.

In his later life Glück won respect as a learned community leader who worked for closer understanding between Jews and Christians. In this he was perhaps taking a leaf out of the book of his earlier patron, the duke of Sussex, who had been an eminent advocate of inter-communal understanding. Contemporary newspapers refer to Glück's maintaining through his lifetime an energetic correspondence with distinguished Jews and Christians alike (which he carefully preserved, but which is now sadly lost); and to the bridge-building spirit in which he led the community at the opening of Sheffield's new synagogue at North Church Street in 1872. Glück died, after long years in pain, from gout syncope at 112 Devonshire Street, Sheffield, on 27 April 1874, and was buried on 28 April at the Jewish burial-ground in Ecclesfield, near Sheffield. PETRA LAIDLAW

Sources *Jewish World* (8 May 1874) • *Voice of Jacob* (26 Nov 1841) • *Sheffield Daily Telegraph* (5 Jan 1872) • *Jewish Chronicle* (10 Oct 1873) • L. Glück Rosenthal, *A biographical memoir of his late royal highness, the duke of Sussex* (1846) • L. Glück Rosenthal, *Biographical memoir of her most gracious majesty, Queen Victoria* (1844) • ships' records, census data, PRO • m. cert. • d. cert.
Likenesses oils, 1840–60, priv. coll.
Wealth at death under £300: will, proved, 1874

Gluckman, (Herman) Max (**1911–1975**), social anthropologist, was born in Johannesburg, South Africa, on 26 January 1911, the second child in the family of three sons and one daughter of Emmanuel Gluckmann, a lawyer of strong liberal views, and his wife, Kate Cohen, who was a leading personality in the Zionist movement. Proud of their Russian-Jewish background, the family, except for Max, emigrated to Israel after the establishment of the state. From King Edward VII School, Johannesburg, Gluckman (who dropped the final *n* from the family name) went to the University of the Witwatersrand in 1928. He intended specializing in law, but attendance at Winifred Hoernlé's lectures diverted him to social anthropology. A first-class honours degree, combined with an excellent athletic and sporting record and prominence in extra-curricular student activities—he was a powerfully built six-footer gifted with boundless energy and holding strong principles all his life—gained him the Transvaal Rhodes scholarship for 1934, which took him to Exeter College, Oxford.

Gluckman was drawn in Oxford into the new 'functionalist' movement in British social anthropology. Most importantly for his career he also developed a friendship with E. E. Evans-Pritchard. Awarded his DPhil in 1936 Gluckman returned to South Africa for two years of field research in Zululand (three significant papers published in 1940 and 1942 presented the germs of later key ideas). Thus enriched by his first field study of a changing African society, he returned to Oxford in 1938. Influenced by A. R. Radcliffe-Brown, newly appointed to the Oxford chair, Evans-Pritchard, Meyer Fortes, and B. Malinowski, he established the framework of theory that guided all his research thereafter. In 1939 Gluckman married Mary (*d.* 1973), the only child of Giuseppe Brignoli, an attorney. A gifted linguist, she worked regularly with Gluckman both in the field and in his later researches, and helped to make their home a centre of genial hospitality. They were to have three sons.

In September 1939 Gluckman was appointed to the staff of the Rhodes-Livingstone Institute in Northern Rhodesia at the insistence of the director, Godfrey Wilson, in the teeth of some settler and official antisemitic and anti-liberal opposition. Prevented from enlisting in the armed forces and after daunting initial obstructions Gluckman began in Barotseland the fieldwork that became the ethnographic foundation of all his later researches. When Wilson resigned in 1941, Gluckman became temporary director of the institute, and then director in 1942. At once he began to implement single-handedly the research, advisory, and educational programmes that later made the institute famous. He expanded, himself largely producing, the institute's publications, developed collaboration with government departments, drew officials and other residents into its activities, and, above all, ensured the goodwill and support of government and industry. In 1945, with the war over and with funds from the Colonial Development and Welfare Fund, he recruited and trained a group of research officers, most of whom subsequently attained professorial rank in Britain or abroad. A series of outstanding monographs on both tribal and industrialized communities resulted from this programme.

In 1947, concluding that he had demonstrated the importance of locally based social research for both practical and academic purposes, Gluckman accepted a lectureship at Oxford. Two years later he moved to Manchester to the chair established specially for him, and he remained there (after 1971 as Nuffield research professor) until his death. Gluckman continued for fifteen years to work with the Rhodes-Livingstone Institute, notably by providing facilities for the staff to write up their field research in his department. He assumed British nationality in 1950.

Indefatigable, outspoken, and passionately committed to the advancement of sociological science, Gluckman created a centre of vigorous and innovative research and teaching which quickly gained international recognition. Defining social anthropology as a comparative science of social systems and institutions, he promoted research in contexts ranging from factory floor and rural village organization in Britain to both tribal and modern urban communities abroad, notably in Israel. His celebrated research seminar was frequented not only by his students and staff but by other eminent professors of philosophy, politics, and economics (such as his friend and collaborator Ely Devons) and by the distinguished visiting scholars, mostly from abroad, whom he brought to Manchester with the help of the Simon Trust. Many later publications bear the stamp of this seminar's influence. Throughout Gluckman also served on various university and national bodies concerned with the social sciences, and he participated in non-academic activities that brought him into contact with the Manchester public. In 1960, while on a visit to the Australian National University, ignorant political intervention barred him from New Guinea, much to the later embarrassment of the responsible ministry. In 1965 the newly independent Zambian government invited him to visit, and it was partly dismay over changes in tribal life he then observed that led him to concentrate on Israel thereafter.

Gluckman's impressive scholarly output ranges over all aspects of social anthropology. Often frankly personal in developing an argument, he sought always to elicit general principles from a close examination of empirical data. His semi-popular books—*Custom and Conflict in Africa* (1955) and *Politics, Law and Ritual in Tribal Society* (1965)—indicate well where his chief interests lay. Maintaining that tribal society is invariably built up on a balance of criss-crossing ties (for example, of kinship) and cleavages (such as those of political allegiance) between individuals and groups, he argued that conflict, inducing either social change or redressive response, is intrinsic to it, and this became the cornerstone of the research theory of the Manchester school. However, Gluckman's main claim to fame rests on his masterly researches in legal anthropology and comparative jurisprudence, which revitalized these studies. In *The Judicial Process among the Barotse* (1955, 1967) Gluckman demonstrated his method of analysing directly observed court cases and showed that tribal judges followed procedures and applied standards (for example, of 'the reasonable man') wholly comparable to those of western judges. *The Ideas in Barotse Jurisprudence* (1965, 1972) reconsiders these findings with impressive and felicitous learning in the widest context of historical and theoretical jurisprudence, shows how tribal law is dominated by the law of persons and status, and emphasizes the idea of debt as against right, in conformity with theories of power and responsibility in social organization. Other jurisprudential issues were dealt with in publications elsewhere.

A meticulous scholar, Gluckman gave careful editorial

attention to his own and his students' publications. Spontaneous, sociable, and self-assured, he attracted a following wherever he went. An unswervingly loyal friend, colleague, and teacher, he gave generously of his time and support. Ever ready to answer—or advance—criticism without acrimony, he was punctilious in his tributes to his predecessors and his acknowledgements of his contemporaries. Strenuous country walks, golf, and cricket, and attending Manchester United football games with his sons, gave outlet to his abundant physical vitality.

Gluckman was elected FBA in 1968 and foreign honorary member of the American Academy of Arts and Sciences in 1970. An honorary DSocSci of the Free University of Brussels (1965), he held visiting lectureships at some dozen universities abroad and was Lady Davis visiting scholar at the Hebrew University, Jerusalem, at the time of his death. Among many other awards and honours he particularly prized his appointment to give the Storrs lectures in jurisprudence at Yale in 1963 and the Radcliffe-Brown lecture at the British Academy in 1974. He contributed notably to the work of the International African Institute as a member of council (1956–65), consultative director (1966–74), and vice-chairman (1974), and likewise to the development of the Association of Social Anthropologists of the British Commonwealth as honorary secretary (1951–7) and chairman (1962–6). Among a number of academic and non-academic public positions held by him were his membership of the social studies subcommittee of the University Grants Committee (1966–70) and of the advisory committee to the Sports Council (1974) which gave him special pleasure. Gluckman died in Jerusalem on 13 April 1975. M. FORTES, *rev.*

Sources *The Times* (21 April 1975) · R. Firth, 'Max Gluckman, 1911–1975', *PBA*, 61 (1975), 479–96 · M. J. Aronoff, *Freedom and constraint* (1976) · private information (1986) · personal knowledge (1986)
Archives CUL, corresp. with Meyer Fortes · JRL, letters to A. P. Wadsworth
Wealth at death £1979: probate, 9 July 1975, *CGPLA Eng. & Wales*

Glyde [*formerly* Glide], **John** (1823–1905), social commentator and antiquary, was born at 9 Eagle Street, Ipswich, in December 1823, the second son of John Glide (1800/01–1880), a hairdresser, and his wife, Mary (1793/4–1844). Glide first worked in his father's shop, and entertained the customers by retailing the contents of the newspapers, of which he was an avid reader. At fifteen he joined the Ipswich Mechanics' Institute, and at eighteen won a prize for an essay on social conditions in Ipswich. In 1843 he spent a year in London, and on his return opened a hairdresser's shop at 35 St Matthew's Street, Ipswich, changing the spelling of his name to Glyde. He was still described as a hairdresser in White's *Directory of Suffolk* in 1855, though by that time he had largely abandoned the trade in favour of a bookshop, a circulating library, and a domestic agency. He was also a busy author.

In the intervening years Glyde had been active in radical politics. He was the secretary and a pamphleteer of an Owenite group in 1841, and corresponded with John Goodwyn Barmby, the Christian socialist. He was then close to the Ipswich Chartists, and joined their Utilitarian Society when he returned from London in 1844, but he was a Unitarian, and had attended William Johnson Fox's chapel in Finsbury. By the end of the decade he had become a moderate Liberal, critical of Chartist beliefs and concerning himself increasingly with practical social reform. At the same time he was expanding his prize-winning essay into an enterprising study, which he published in 1850 as *The Moral, Social, and Religious Condition of Ipswich in the Middle of the Nineteenth Century*.

The work opens conventionally with a historical sketch, but then turns to discuss the contemporary town. An account of trade is followed by chapters on sanitary conditions, poverty, education, intellectual life, and religious observance. As far as he could Glyde illuminated local and national statistics with his own careful observation. His object was to record, but with a didactic purpose. He hoped for social and economic amelioration through education, but also through improvements in the physical environment. He reprobated drunkenness and the ill effects of sensational literature, but he saw crime as a product of social dislocation, and the spread of literacy as a desirable end in itself. At large he combined precept with practical action, campaigning for improvements in the water supply, for the closure of the town's churchyards for further burials and the establishment of a cemetery, and for the effective direction of philanthropic work. In 1866 he promoted a district nursing association, which foundered on sectarianism, and in 1868 worked for Foster Barham Zincke's National Educational League.

In examining the churches and their congregations Glyde anticipated the inquiries into religious observance in the census of 1851. In the following years he expanded his book into a general survey of the county, published in 1856 as *Suffolk in the Nineteenth Century: Physical, Social, Moral, Religious, and Industrial*. That work was said to have prompted the registrar-general to appoint him registrar of marriages in Ipswich, a post which he held until his death. His local standing was also enhanced by a series of studies of the clergy, entitled 'The Ipswich pulpit', which appeared in the *Suffolk Chronicle* in 1857, and were followed by a larger biographical collection published as *Suffolk Worthies* in 1858. Glyde's later works included *The Autobiography of a Suffolk Labourer* (1894), a sympathetic composite portrait compiled from a wide range of material, and antiquarian and literary studies. In 1897 he argued that the best memorial to Queen Victoria's jubilee would be a free public library, and subsequently left a bequest of £500 to buy books for the reference collection.

Glyde was twice married; first, on 4 March 1849, to Eliza Taylor (*b. c.*1829), daughter of Robert Taylor, a builder, and the second time, in or about 1860, to Mary (*b. c.*1840), a stationer's assistant (her surname is unknown), who outlived him. Both marriages seem to have been childless. He died on 14 June 1905 at his home, 22 St Nicholas Street, Ipswich, and was buried in Ipswich cemetery on 17 June.

Glyde invites comparison with the Colchester radical William Wire (*d.* 1857). Both had little schooling, but both developed distinctive intellectual tastes. Wire made an important contribution to archaeological studies in

Essex, but laboured under a heavier burden of social disapproval than Glyde. Glyde, longer-lived, equally pertinacious but more adroit, gained social esteem in a no less conservative town, and promoted some useful changes. The originality of his interests may have helped him; they still stand to his credit. G. H. MARTIN

Sources *East Anglian Daily Times* (15 June 1905) • J. Glyde, *The moral, social, and religious condition of Ipswich*, ed. A. F. J. Brown (1971) • *Suffolk county handbook* (1906) • census returns, 1851, 1891 • d. cert. [Mary Glide] • m. cert. • d. cert. [John Glide, father] • Ipswich cemetery records

Archives Suffolk RO, Ipswich, historical notes, papers, and collections relating to Suffolk • Suffolk RO, Ipswich, biographical notes relating to J. S. Henslow

Wealth at death £3426 2*s*. 7*d*.: probate, 11 Aug 1905, *CGPLA Eng. & Wales*

Glyn [*née* Sutherland], **Elinor** (**1864–1943**), novelist and screenwriter, was born in Jersey on 17 October 1864, the younger daughter of Douglas Sutherland (1838–1865), civil engineer, and his wife, Elinor, *née* Saunders (1840/41–1937). Douglas Sutherland died three months after Elinor was born. The family soon returned to Guelph, Ontario, in Canada, where her mother had been born; she remarried in 1871. With her second husband, David Kennedy, the family settled again in Jersey, a few years later. Elinor's childhood was relatively lonely. Her strong will and the incompetence of the governesses hired by her parsimonious stepfather meant that she was mostly self-taught. As a young girl she immersed herself in mythology and the history of France, exhibited some skill in drawing, wrote stories, and kept a diary. Although the family had little money, they socialized with the 'Government House' set on the island. Elinor feared her strikingly red hair made her ugly, but in her teens and twenties she attracted a number of admirers, especially during a series of visits to relatives and friends in France and England. By the mid-1880s she was spending most of her time away from Jersey.

Elinor's background had not prepared her for any life beyond marriage, and she was determined to find a place in upper-class society, but with no dowry and few connections her opportunities were limited. Moreover, she rejected several suitors who did not fulfil her romantic ideals. Finally, on 27 April 1892, she married (Henry) Clayton Glyn (1857–1915). Although Elinor entered this marriage with high hopes of achieving the romance and status she craved, it soon began to disappoint. Clayton Glyn was more interested in food, drink, and gambling than in his wife's romantic effusions over scenic views and ruins. He did not share her nascent leanings towards belief in reincarnation and mysticism, nor her delight in high fashion. Neither, however, did he attempt to curb her spending on clothes and home decoration. Elinor's first daughter, Margot, was born in 1893; her second child, Juliet [*see* Williams, Juliet Evangeline Rhys], was born in 1898. During her second pregnancy, Elinor wrote a series of fashion and beauty articles for *Scottish Life*. After the birth of Juliet, Elinor developed post-partum depression compounded by a series of physical illnesses including rheumatic fever. But, she wrote, 'one day I had a fit of rebellion against the idea of dying young', and began putting her pre-marriage diaries and letters to her mother into 'a readable form' (*Romantic Adventure*, 92–3). The resulting book, *The Visits of Elizabeth* (1900), was serialized in *The World* and published by Gerald Duckworth. It was an immediate success, and Elinor enjoyed her royalties and the attention she received as the author of a best-selling *roman à clef*. Four more novels followed quickly; all of them expressed her beliefs in romantic love and the natural superiority of the aristocracy.

Elinor's marriage to Clayton Glyn, however, continued to deteriorate. Although they remained married until his death in 1915, Elinor soon began to seek romance in a series of friendships with other men. A particularly intense relationship with Lord Alistair Innes Ker provided the impetus for her most famous book, *Three Weeks* (1907). *Three Weeks* is centred on the Lady, an exotic Balkan queen who seduces Paul, a younger British aristocrat, to ensure that she bears Paul's child, not her degenerate husband's, as next ruler of her country. The Lady also teaches Paul about love and his duty as an aristocrat. Glyn always argued for the novel's purity of purpose and defended it against charges of immorality, but readers focused on the detailed descriptions of the Lady's romantic techniques—such as her sensual writhing on tiger skins and her numerous creative caresses—rather than on the development of Paul's sense of *noblesse oblige*. Despite uniformly negative reviews, millions of copies were sold. Later editions of *Three Weeks* include the photoplay edition (1924) with pictures from the 1923 Metro-Goldwyn-Mayer film version and a 1974 edition with an introduction by Cecil Beaton. *Three Weeks* has remained a piece of cultural shorthand parodied and alluded to in high and popular culture. It also influenced the subsequent development of the woman's romance. Glyn's example led to a modification of traditional plots, encouraging the emphasis on women's sexuality and a point of view tightly centred on the female protagonist.

Despite the financial success of *Three Weeks*, and a new but very discreet relationship with George, Lord Curzon, Glyn found it necessary to continue to write at least a novel a year to cover her husband's debts and her own spending. She was invited to the Russian imperial court to write a novel; the result, *His Hour* (1910), was one of her most successful. She also visited and wrote about Spain and Hungary, and her lifelong affection for France led her to work there during the First World War as a newspaper correspondent. Her relationship with Curzon and a friendship with Alfred, Lord Milner, provided her with access that enabled her to write detailed reports of military and political events.

Glyn visited the United States several times, and worked for several years in the Hollywood film industry. In 1927 she developed *It*, a film for Clara Bow. She had first described 'it' in *The Man and the Moment* (1923); but it was the film that made the term famous as a synonym for sex appeal. Despite many successes, Glyn's extravagances and financial ineptitude made her economic situation constantly difficult, and she was compelled to continue writing to support herself for the rest of her life. At least thirty-eight different volumes appeared, including a book on how to avoid wrinkles, and with her last novel, *The Third Eye* (1940), she attempted to write a thriller. She never remarried; Curzon ended their relationship in 1916, and her long friendship with Lord Milner never became more than that.

Early in her life Glyn had rejected conventional religious beliefs. Later, she was at various times involved in 'new thought' and spiritualism, but turned against all those ideas, retaining only her long-standing belief in reincarnation. Elinor Glyn died in London at 39 Royal Avenue, Chelsea, on 23 September 1943 after a short illness. JoAnn E. Castagna

Sources J. Hardwick, *Addicted to romance: the life and adventures of Elinor Glyn* (1994) • M. Etherington-Smith and J. Pilcher, *The IT girls: Lucy, Lady Duff Gordon, the couturière 'Lucile', and Elinor Glyn, romantic novelist* (1986) • *Romantic adventure: the autobiography of Elinor Glyn* (1937) • A. Glyn, *Elinor Glyn* (1955) • M. Fowler, 'High priestess of "It"', *The Beaver*, 74/5 (1994), 18–25 • J. Tully, 'My interview with Elinor Glyn', *Vanity Fair* [New York], 25/6 (1926), 80 • *The Times* (24 Sept 1943) • *New York Times* (24 Sept 1943) • M. R. Rinehart, '"Three weeks" by Elinor Glyn', *Georgia Review*, 7/4 (1953), 370–72 • J. Bettinotti and M.-F. Truel, 'Lust and dust: desert fabula in romances and the media', *Para Doxa*, 3/1–2 (1997), 184–94 • N. Brooks, 'Fitzgerald's "*The great Gatsby*" and Glyn's "*Three weeks*"', *The Explicator*, 54/4 (1996), 233–6 • J. Sexton, 'Brave new world, the feelies, and Elinor Glyn', *English Language Notes*, 35/1 (1997), 35–8 • *CGPLA Eng. & Wales* (1944)

Archives U. Reading, corresp., papers, literary MSS | BL, corresp. with Society of Authors, Add. MS 56710 • Theatre Museum, London, letters to Lord Chamberlain's licensee

Likenesses P. Tanqueray, photograph, *c*.1932, NPG • A. Mason, oils, 1942, NPG • Szekely, photograph, NPG

Wealth at death £6588 11*s*. 1*d*.: probate, 17 Feb 1944, *CGPLA Eng. & Wales*

Glyn, George Carr, first Baron Wolverton (1797–1873), banker, was born on 27 March 1797, the fifth but fourth surviving son of Sir Richard Carr *Glyn, first baronet (1755–1838), and his wife, Mary (1760/61–1832), daughter of John Plumptre of Fredville, Kent. Glyn was educated at Westminster School, and entered his father's bank, Glyn, Mills, Hallifax, Glyn, Mills & Co., straight from school. He became a partner in 1819 but did not become senior partner until after the death of his elder brother Sir Richard Plumptre Glyn in 1863. On 17 March 1823 Glyn married Marianne, third daughter of Pascoe *Grenfell [*see under* Grenfell family] of Taplow, Buckinghamshire. His wife's sister Frances married Charles Kingsley, and another sister, Charlotte, married J. A. Froude. The Glyns had nine sons and two daughters; the eldest son, George Grenfell *Glyn, succeeded to the title. Two sons entered the army, a third the navy, one was called to the bar, and another, Edward, became bishop of Peterborough in 1897.

Personally, and through the medium of his family bank, Glyn made a significant contribution to the development of railway transport, not only in Great Britain but in many other parts of the world. By the 1850s his bank was known as the railway bank and probably had the largest business of any of the London banks. In all, some one hundred and thirty British railway companies and eighty foreign ones banked with it, and at the time of his death railway company credit balances with his bank exceeded a quarter of its total deposits. His bank also acted as London agent for about sixty country banks and played an important part in the development of investment trusts. One of the earliest, the Foreign and Colonial Government Trust, was formed in 1868, with Glyn, Mills, Currie & Co. (as his bank had become in 1864) as its bankers.

Glyn was treasurer of the company formed by act of parliament in 1824 for the construction of St Katherine's Dock in London, his father-in-law, then MP for Penryn, acting as one of the promoters. In 1833 he became a member of the London board for the London and Birmingham Railway Company, becoming chairman in 1837. The company amalgamated with the Grand Junction Railway Company and the Manchester and Birmingham Railway Company in 1846 to form the London and North Western Railway Company, of which he remained chairman until his resignation in 1852 on grounds of ill health. He took much interest in the details of the construction of the railway and in the running of the company, and it was at his suggestion that it built a school at the new town of Wolverton, in north Buckinghamshire, which was its creation and where Glyn Square was named after him. According to his obituary in *The Economist*, 'his speeches at the half-yearly meetings of the company became epochs in the railway history of the time. There was no affectation of oratory, but in simple dignity and force and in luminous arrangement they have never been excelled.' He was chairman of the Bankers' Clearing House and, inspired by this example, he founded the Railway Clearing House in January 1842, remaining chairman until his death.

Glyn became Liberal member of parliament for Kendal in 1847, retiring at the 1868 election. He rarely spoke in the House of Commons, but he was an early supporter of free trade and served on numerous committees and commissions. He gave evidence before a parliamentary committee in 1832, strongly opposing joint-stock banks. Private banks, he thought, could deal with individual clients with a speed and secrecy beyond that of a public establishment. He always remained strongly opposed to the Bank Charter Act of 1844. He succeeded his father as treasurer of the Globe Insurance Company. He became a governor of Harrow School, a commissioner of lieutenancy for London, a governor of the Hudson Bay Company, and a joint high commissioner for Canada.

In 1837 Glyn's bank, together with Baring & Co., became the London agents for the provincial government of Canada, and together with Barings it advanced considerable sums, eventually arranging for Canadian government securities to be quoted on the London stock exchange. In 1852 he joined with Thomas Baring as promoter of the Grand Trunk Railway of Canada. This project ran into serious financial difficulties and it was twelve years before it became financially sound. Throughout this period Glyn acted with exemplary rectitude, meeting many claims from his own pocket. He was created Baron Wolverton on

14 December 1869, taking his title from the town which was the creation of the London to Birmingham Railway. He died on 24 July 1873 at his house, 1 Upper Eccleston Street, London. His widow died in 1892.

Glyn's obituary in *The Times* records that 'throughout his life the quick vigour of his character was remarkable', and his obituarist in *The Economist* wrote that he was 'energetic, sagacious, affable, intelligent, [and] an almost unerring judge of character'. MICHAEL REED

Sources *The Times* (25 July 1873) • *The Economist* (26 July 1873) • GEC, *Peerage* • R. Fulford, *Glyn's, 1753–1953: six generations in Lombard Street* (1953) • R. A. Ashbee, 'George Carr Glyn and St Katherine dock', *Three Banks Review*, 129 (1981), 49–54 • 'George Carr Glyn and the railways', *Three Banks Review*, 46 (1960), 34–47 • *CGPLA Eng. & Wales* (1873)
Archives Royal Bank of Scotland, London, business records | BL, corresp. with W. E. Gladstone, Add. MSS 44368–44527, *passim* • BL, corresp. with Sir Robert Peel, Add. MS 40591 • U. Durham L., corresp. with Lord Grey
Likenesses F. Grant, portrait; formerly in Euston, 1953 • portrait (after pastel), repro. in Fulford, *Glyn's*, facing p. 145
Wealth at death under £1,000,000: probate, 14 Aug 1873, *CGPLA Eng. & Wales*

Glyn, George Grenfell, second Baron Wolverton (1824–1887), politician and banker, was born in London on 10 February 1824, the eldest son of George Carr *Glyn. He was educated at Rugby and University College, Oxford, where he matriculated on 26 May 1842. On coming of age he became a partner in the metropolitan banking firm of Glyn, Hallifax, Mills, & Co., and continued in the business until his death. On 22 June 1848, he married Georgiana Maria, daughter of the Revd George Frederick Tuffnell of Uffington, Berkshire (she died, aged sixty-eight, on 10 January 1894).

Glyn was chairman of the Railway Clearing House from 1876 until his death, and was a lieutenant of the City of London. He sat as Liberal MP for Shaftesbury from 1857 to 1873, when he succeeded his father in the peerage. He nominally succeeded Henry Brand as Liberal chief whip in December 1866 but the two men worked together until Gladstone took office in November 1868, when Brand finally stood down. Glyn fused the whips' office and the Liberal Registration Association into a single party headquarters, linking the Liberal leaders in parliament with local party associations. Through his control of the party's funds during the general election of 1868, he brokered the secret deal with the radicals George Howell and W. R. Cremer by which Liberal candidates received Reform League support in marginal borough constituencies. He was joint secretary to the Treasury from 1868 to 1873, during which period he was an energetic whip, though unable to prevent the party's disintegration over the Irish University Bill. He was then sworn of the privy council. In the Liberal ministry of 1880 to 1885 he was paymaster-general, and his zealous adherence to Gladstone's home-rule proposals was rewarded by the appointment of postmaster-general (February to July 1886). Wolverton during the remainder of his life gave valuable support, both oratorical and pecuniary, to the home-rule cause,

George Grenfell Glyn, second Baron Wolverton (1824–1887), by London Stereoscopic Co.

remaining a Liberal when much of the city went Unionist. On 2 October 1887 he presided at a great 'anti-coercion' demonstration at Templecombe, Dorset, when he was presented with an address from eight parliamentary districts. Both while chief whip and after, Glyn was one of Gladstone's closest political confidants. In any crisis he was at hand with advice, and he always discouraged Gladstone's attempts to retire from politics.

Wolverton was a model landlord and a staunch supporter of fox-hunting in Dorset. At Iwerne Minster in that county, one of his country seats, he and his wife supported two orphanages in connection with the Home Boy Brigade originated by her. He gave his salary as postmaster-general to secure beds in a convalescent home for sick London postmen. Wolverton died suddenly and childless in the Bedford Hotel, Brighton, on 6 November 1887. Gladstone noted in his diary: 'A great grief came to us today in the death of our warm and generous friend Lord Wolverton.' L. C. SANDERS, *rev.* H. C. G. MATTHEW

Sources GEC, *Peerage* • Gladstone, *Diaries* • *The Times* (7 Nov 1887) • *Daily News* (7 Nov 1887) • A. F. Thompson, 'Gladstone's whips and the general election of 1868', *EngHR*, 63 (1948), 189–200 • F. M. Leventhal, *Respectable radical: George Howell and Victorian working class politics* (1971) • R. Harrison, *Before the socialists: studies in labour and politics, 1861–1881* (1965)
Archives BL, corresp. with W. E. Gladstone, Add. MSS 44347–44349 • BL, corresp. with Lord Ripon, Add. MSS 43621–43630, *passim* • NRA, priv. coll., letters to Joseph Levy • PRO, corresp. with Lord Cardwell, PRO30/48

Likenesses J. Brown, stipple (after photograph by Mayall), BM; repro. in *Baily's Magazine* (1875) • London Stereoscopic Co., photograph, NPG [*see illus.*] • chromolithograph caricature, NPG; repro. in *VF* (24 Feb 1872)
Wealth at death £1,817,725 11*s*. 11*d*.: resworn probate, Aug 1889, *CGPLA Eng. & Wales* (1887)

Glyn, Isabella [*real name* Isabella Gearns] (**1823–1889**), actress, was born in Edinburgh on 22 May 1823, the daughter of an architect named Gearns, of strong Presbyterian views and a turn for preaching, and his wife, whose maiden name was Glyn. Her parents opposed her theatrical ambitions, but, having taken part in amateur theatricals in London, she went to Paris with her first husband, Edward Wills, to study acting under Michelet. After being widowed she returned to England in 1846, and, on the advice of a friend, had an audition with Charles Kemble, who gave her lessons.

Isabella Wills made her professional début under the name of Glyn at the Theatre Royal, Manchester, on 8 November 1847, as Constance in *King John*, a role she followed with Lady Macbeth and Hermione. Her first London appearance took place at the Olympic under Spicer in *Lady Macbeth* on 26 January 1848. After some months on Pritchard's York circuit, she appeared at Sadler's Wells as Volumnia in *Coriolanus* opposite Samuel Phelps (27 September 1848); she remained there until 1851, winning recognition in characters such as Cleopatra, the Duchess of Malfi, and the new role of Garcia in F. G. Tomlins's *The Noble Error*. She toured the provinces in 1851, and that September gave the first of a series of Shakespearian readings. She then moved to Drury Lane, under Bunn's management, where she made her first appearance as Bianca in Dean Milman's *Fazio* on 26 December. In October 1854 she was the original Miss Stewart in *The King's Rival* by Tom Taylor and Charles Reade. After performing at the Standard, she reappeared at Sadler's Wells in 1859, and in May 1867 played Cleopatra at the Princess's. It was said of her in this latter role that 'Antony might well lose the world for such a woman'.

From this period Isabella Glyn's appearances on the stage were infrequent, and her time was occupied principally with theatrical tuition, mainly at the School of Dramatic Art, and with Shakespearian readings (Blanchard considered her *Othello* 'clever but dreary'). She had much success with a series of such readings in Boston in 1870, and again in 1878 and 1879 in London, at the Steinway and St James's halls.

In December 1853 Glyn had married the journalist Eneas Sweetland *Dallas (1828–1879) in Edinburgh, and the marriage was resolemnized at St George's, Hanover Square, London, on 12 July 1855; the couple separated shortly afterwards and in 1874 she petitioned for divorce. She was sent to Holloway Prison for contempt of court for refusing to produce documents relevant to the case, but her petition was granted on 10 May 1874. Her later years were beset by financial misfortunes: in 1862 her house in Hanover Square burnt down, and she lost all her property. She was awarded a pension of £200 a year by the Salisbury government, and a subscription for her benefit was raised

Isabella Glyn (1823–1889), by Henry Wyndham Phillips [as Constance in *King John* by William Shakespeare]

by her friends shortly before her death, from the cancer from which she had been suffering for some years, on 18 May 1889, at her London home, 13 Mount Street, Grosvenor Square. She was buried on 22 May 1889 at Kensal Green cemetery.

Isabella Glyn had a voluptuous figure, latterly inclined to stoutness, a melodious voice, dark complexion and eyes, and strong and expressive features. She was short of inspiration, however, and her success was most pronounced in characters in which her commanding figure was of advantage. JOSEPH KNIGHT, *rev.* J. GILLILAND

Sources F. Hays, *Women of the day: a biographical dictionary of notable contemporaries* (1885) • *The life and reminiscences of E. L. Blanchard, with notes from the diary of Wm. Blanchard*, ed. C. W. Scott and C. Howard, 2 vols. (1891) • *St James's Gazette* (20 May 1889) • W. M. Phelps and J. F. Robertson, *Life of Samuel Phelps* (1886) • S. D'Amico, ed., *Enciclopedia dello spettacolo*, 11 vols. (Rome, 1954–68) • E. Stirling, *Old Drury Lane*, 2 vols. (1881) • H. G. Adams, ed., *A cyclopaedia of female biography* (1857) • J. A. H., 'Portrait Gallery (no II) Miss Glyn', *Tallis's Dramatic Magazine* (1850), 37–40 • C. E. Pascoe, ed., *The dramatic list*, 2nd edn (1880) • Adams, *Drama* • Boase, *Mod. Eng. biog.* • Hall, *Dramatic ports.* • *The Athenaeum* (29 Jan 1848) • *Manchester Courier* (23 May 1889)

Archives Theatre Museum, Covent Garden, London, letters
Likenesses Paine of Islington, seven engravings, repro. in J. A. H., 'Portrait Gallery (no II) Miss Glyn' • H. W. Phillips, portrait, Garr. Club [*see illus.*] • eight prints, Harvard TC • portrait (as Duchess of Malfi), repro. in Boase, *Mod. Eng. biog.* • portrait, repro. in *Tallis's drawing-room table book of theatrical portraits, memoirs and anecdotes*, John Tallis & Co. (1851) • portrait, repro. in *The players*, 3 (1861), 291, 408 • portrait, repro. in *Theatre*, 4th ser., 14 (1889), 215
Wealth at death £250: probate, 12 Dec 1891, *CGPLA Eng. & Wales*

Glyn, Sir Richard, first baronet (*bap.* **1711**, *d.* **1773**), drysalter and banker, was baptized on 13 June 1711 at the

Sir Richard Glyn, first baronet (*bap.* 1711, *d.* 1773), by Johan Zoffany, 1769

church of St Andrew, Holborn, London, the second son of Robert Glyn (1673–1746), an oilman and drysalter of Hatton Garden, London, and his wife, Ann, *née* Maynard. He was educated at Westminster School before joining his father in his business as a wholesaler of the salt and chemicals used as preservatives and dyestuffs. He took his freedom by patrimony in the Salters' Company on 31 May 1733, and assumed control of the business in the following month, continuing after his father's death with Thomas Baskerfield as his partner.

Glyn married on 8 June 1736 Susannah (*d.* 1751), the only child and heir of George Lewen of Ewell, Surrey, former MP for Wallingford, Berkshire, to whom he was distantly related. They had three sons, Robert (1737–1743), George (1739–1814), and Richard (*d.* 1741). Susannah died on 5 February 1751, and he married secondly, on 23 March 1754, Elizabeth, the daughter of Robert Carr of Hampton, Middlesex, a silk mercer of Ludgate in the City, and an important connection for Glyn's trade in dyestuffs. Their two sons, Richard Carr *Glyn (*b.* 1755) and Thomas Glyn (*b.* 1757), both followed him as bankers. By the time of his second marriage Glyn was rising to modest prominence in the City; he later bought a country seat at Gaunts House, near Wimborne, Dorset. He was master of the Salters' Company in 1751, alderman for Dowgate ward from 1750 to 1772, and sheriff jointly with Charles Asgill in 1752–3. After delivering a loyal address to George II on his return from Hanover, he and Asgill were knighted in 1752. He was lord mayor in 1758.

This relationship with Asgill probably introduced Glyn to Joseph Vere, Asgill's banking partner. In December 1753 Vere and Glyn formed a partnership with Thomas *Hallifax, chief clerk at Martin's Bank, and in January 1754 opened in Lombard Street, as Vere, Glyn, and Hallifax, bankers. Glyn provided £10,000 of the total capital of £24,000, and remained a partner, in what was to become one of London's most successful private banks, until his death in 1773. He had no previous banking experience, but was able to introduce custom from the many rich silk merchants trading nearby. By 1757 the bank had prospered sufficiently to move into larger premises in Birchin Lane. During its early years the bank was hardly troubled by bad debt. It was the extension of trading on borrowed capital, linked to the geographical expansion of business into the provincial silk districts of Coventry and Derby, and particularly its involvement with the Scottish iron-foundry of Carron, that brought Glyn and Hallifax (Vere having died in 1766) to the brink of disaster.

In 1754 Glyn unsuccessfully contested parliamentary elections for one of the four City of London seats, but in 1758 was elected as MP for the City of London, which he represented for ten years. A moderate tory, opposed to John Wilkes during the 1760s, in 1768 he was defeated in London and, after a controversial campaign, elected as MP for Coventry. He was created baronet on 25 September 1759. In addition he served as president of Bethlem and Bridewell hospitals (1755–73); vice-president (1762–4) and president (1764–8) of the Equitable Life Assurance Society; colonel of the Orange regiment of the city militia (1762–73); and treasurer (1763–70) and vice-president (1770–73) of the Honourable Artillery Company. He was fervently anti-French, being a prominent member of an Anti-Gallican Society, and was awarded an honorary degree by Oxford University in July 1759.

Glyn died on 1 January 1773 of a slow fever. However, since his death followed so quickly after a disastrous few weeks in the summer of 1772 when Glyn and Hallifax's bank stopped payment, his doctor was obliged to issue a public statement to scotch rumours of suicide. Sir Richard's second son by his first marriage, George Glyn, succeeded as second baronet. ALISON TURTON

Sources A. B. Beaven, ed., *The aldermen of the City of London, temp. Henry III–[1912]*, 2 vols. (1908–13) · HoP, *Commons* · parish register, St Andrew's, Holborn, London · R. Fulford, *Glyn's, 1753–1953: six generations in Lombard Street* (1953) · notes compiled for publication of Fulford history, Royal Bank of Scotland archives, London · L. S. Pressnell, *Country banking in the industrial revolution* (1956)

Likenesses J. Zoffany, portrait, 1769, King Edward's School, Whitley, Surrey [*see illus.*]

Glyn, Sir Richard Carr, first baronet (1755–1838), banker, was born in London on 2 February 1755; he was the eldest son of Sir Richard *Glyn, first baronet (*bap.* 1711, *d.* 1773), banker, and his second wife, Elizabeth, daughter and coheir of Robert Carr, a silk mercer of Ludgate in the City

Sir Richard Carr Glyn, first baronet (1755–1838), by John Hoppner

of London. He was educated at Westminster School. Glyn's father, a prosperous dry-salter, was the second partner in the bank of Vere, Glyn, and Hallifax, which opened for business on 5 January 1754. Richard Glyn's first wife was Susannah, only child and heir of George Lewen of Ewell, in Surrey, who died in 1751. They had three sons, only one of whom survived into manhood, and who succeeded to the baronetcy and to the Ewell estate. Richard Glyn married again in 1754, and was made a baronet in 1759.

During the financial crisis of 1772 the bank stopped payment between 22 June and 6 August. All creditors were eventually paid in full and no financial assistance was offered by the Bank of England. Following his father's death on 1 January 1773, Richard Carr Glyn entered the bank. He became a partner at the age of eighteen, and the bank changed its name to Hallifax, Mills, Glyn, and Mitton. In 1788 the bank moved into new premises at 12 Birchin Lane, London, and the death of Sir Thomas Hallifax early in 1789 meant that Richard Carr Glyn became the senior partner; the bank's name now changed to Glyn, Mills, and Mitton. The steady expansion in the bank's business in the following decades led to its acquisition of adjacent properties. This was matched by an increase in the number of clerks which it employed, nine in 1793, thirty-six by 1815. This growth was due first of all to an increasing involvement in government finance. A consequence of the wars with France was a rising demand on the part of government for loans, a number of which were placed by the bank. At the same time government had to raise money by taxation. Several receivers-general of taxes kept their accounts with Glyns, and some of the first receipts of the new income tax were paid into the bank in July 1799.

The second cause of the growth of the bank was the rapid rise in the numbers of country, or provincial, banks. In 1797 there were 230, by 1808/9 there were 800. Glyns bank acted as London agent for at least forty of these. The growth of this network of agencies was based at first upon personal ties in Northumberland, Cornwall, Dorset, and Kent, but it eventually came to embrace most parts of the kingdom. Richard Carr Glyn gave evidence before a parliamentary committee in 1797 in which he explained the nature of the relationship between a country bank and its London agent. He said that country bank bills were drawn on Glyns and that country banknotes were payable there. He either charged a commission based upon the turnover of business or else he insisted that the bank keep a minimum balance with his bank. In December 1825 a crisis suddenly broke in the financial markets. Six London banks and over sixty country banks failed. Glyns came through this crisis comparatively unaffected, since only two of the failed banks had accounts with it, and it took over the business of several country banks which had had accounts with those London banks that had failed.

Richard Carr Glyn held a number of senior positions in the City of London. He was chosen alderman for Bishopsgate ward in September 1790 and became sheriff in the following year, when he was also knighted. Glyn was elected to parliament in the tory interest for St Ives, in Cornwall, in 1796, but did not stand again in 1802. During that time he spoke in support of the Seditious Meetings Bill and of the Act of Union with Ireland of 1800. He served as lord mayor of London in 1798, and was made a baronet on 22 November 1800. He was president of Bridewell and Bethlem hospitals, like his father before him, and was elected a fellow of the Society of Antiquaries of London on 26 November 1795. Glyn was also a member of the Committee of Six set up in 1805 to recommend improvements in the Bankers' Clearing House (which had existed since 1770).

On 2 July 1785 Glyn married Mary (1760/61–1832), the only daughter of John Plumptre of Fredville in Kent. They had six sons, one of whom died in infancy and two others during Glyn's lifetime, and two daughters, of whom one also died in infancy. In 1809 Glyn began to rebuild Gaunts, a mansion house on the Dorset estate of Hinton Martell, acquired by his father in 1770. William Evans of Wimborne was employed to transform this country retreat by building a villa of five by five bays, and laying out a park of some 200 acres. Glyn hoped that the estate would form the basis for a landed family and he left it in his will to his eldest son, Richard Plumptre Glyn. These hopes were not to be realized, however, since this son died a bachelor. His fourth surviving son, George Carr *Glyn, became a partner in the bank in 1819, and later became Baron Wolverton. Sir Richard Carr Glyn died at his house in Arlington Street, London, on 27 April 1838. The motto to his coat of arms was 'Firm to my trust'. MICHAEL REED

Sources *GM*, 2nd ser., 10 (1838), 211–12 • R. Fulford, *Glyn's, 1753–1953: six generations in Lombard Street* (1953) • J. Hutchins, *The history and antiquities of the county of Dorset*, 3rd edn, ed. W. Shipp and J. W. Hodson, 3 (1868), 246 [family pedigree] • 'Committee of secrecy appointed to examine … outstanding demands on the Bank of England', *British Sessional Papers: Reports*, 19 (1796–7), 66, no. 134c • *An inventory of historical monuments in the county of Dorset*, Royal Commission on Historical Monuments (England), 5 (1975), 30 • HoP, *Commons*

Archives Royal Bank of Scotland, London, business MSS | CUL, letters to R. J. Buxton

Likenesses W. Say, mezzotint, pubd 1804 (after J. Hoppner), AM Oxf., BM, NPG • H. Cook, line engraving, pubd 1830 (after bust by Baily), NPG • T. L. Busby, line engraving, pubd 1835, AM Oxf., BM, NPG • J. Hoppner, oils, unknown collection; copyprint, Thomas Agnew's & Sons, London [*see illus.*]

Glyn, William (1504x10–1558), bishop of Bangor, was born in Heneglwys parish in Anglesey, probably in 1504; Foxe, however, says that he was forty-one years old in 1551. The most reliable pedigree shows that he was the son of John Glyn, rector of Heneglwys, and his second wife, Annes, daughter of Meredydd ap Gwilim of Ceinmeirch, Denbighshire. (The church's rule of celibacy was but little regarded among the Welsh parochial clergy.) He had one brother, Jeffrey Glyn, who was a distinguished advocate in the court of arches and founder of the Friars' School, Bangor. He also had two half-sisters and four half-brothers, one of whom, John Glyn, was dean of Bangor between 1508 and 1534, and on his death in the latter year made William his executor and heir.

Glyn was educated at Queens' College, Cambridge. He graduated BA in 1527, MA in 1530, BD in 1538, and DD in 1544. He became a fellow of his college in 1530, junior bursar in 1533, senior bursar in 1534, and dean in 1540. In 1544 he vacated his fellowship and became Lady Margaret's professor of theology, 'being', as Sir John Wynn says, 'a great scholar and a great hebrician', though Hebrew was 'rare at that time'. He was one of the original sixty fellows of Trinity College, named in the charter of foundation (19 December 1546), and he became the first vice-master of the new college, an office he held from 1546 to 1551. He was opposed to the protestant innovations of Edward VI's reign, and being inhibited from lecturing, resigned his professorship in June 1549. He was one of the disputants who maintained the doctrines of transubstantiation and the eucharistic sacrifice before the royal commissioners for the visitation of Cambridge, also in June 1549: 'The sacrifice and offering of Christ's body in the sacrament of the altar … I will defend even to the effusion of blood' (*Acts and Monuments*, 6.320), he declared. The voluminous arguments at the three disputations are all given by Foxe (ibid., 6.306–7, 319–20, 332–3).

Glyn's institution on 7 March 1550 to the rectory of St Martin Ludgate, on the presentation of Bishop Thirlby (whose chaplain he became in 1551), and his appointment to his father's living of Heneglwys on 13 February 1552, show that he must have conformed to the new services. He was also instituted rector of Rhoscolyn, in Anglesey. After Mary's accession, however, in December 1553 he was instituted to the livings of Cilrhedyn and Llanbedr Felffre in Pembrokeshire; and he was made president of Queens', his old college, where the spirit of Erasmus was more powerful than anywhere at Cambridge, except St John's. At Queens' he gathered a group of promising young clerics, including two future bishops, about him. In April 1554 he was one of the six delegates sent to Oxford to dispute with Cranmer, Latimer, and Ridley. He arrived at Oxford on 13 April and lodged at The Cross inn. He was now incorporated DD of Oxford. In 1554 Glyn became vice-chancellor of Cambridge, but before the end of the year he was called away by state business and was succeeded by Cuthbert Scott, the master of Christ's College.

In 1555 Glyn was sent with Thirlby and others on a mission to Rome, to obtain a confirmation of Pole's acts as legate. He arrived there on 24 May, and returned to London on 24 August. He was already destined for the bishopric of Bangor, the *congé d'élire* for his election being issued as early as 4 March 1555. His election duly followed, but his final appointment was due to papal provision. According to Stubbs, he was consecrated on 8 September 1555 at London House by Bonner, although Machyn says this happened at St Paul's. Glyn assisted at the consecration of Pole, and was enthusiastically greeted by the Welsh poet, Siôn Brwynog. He held several diocesan synods, which he compelled his clergy to attend, as a means of enforcing his doctrines upon them. However, Glyn may have been sympathetic towards married clergy, since his father and grandfather were priests. He resigned his headship of Queens' College, Cambridge, only in the latter part of 1557.

Glyn died at Bangor on 21 May 1558, as his register notes, and was buried in his cathedral on the north side of the choir, where a brass plate existed in Browne Willis's day, but has since disappeared. It described him as a distinguished preacher in his native tongue and very learned. His will, with its Catholic-style preface, survives and has been published. Sir John Wynn describes him as 'a good and religious man after the manner of that time' (Wynn, 62). He was, says Fuller, 'an excellent scholar, and none of the papists pressed their arguments with more strength and less passion. Though constant to his own he was not cruel to opposite judgments, as appeareth by there being no persecution in his diocese' (Fuller, *Worthies*, 2.571). It is said that the house of Trefeilyr, which belonged to his ancestors, remained in his family until 1775. Glyn must be distinguished from his senior contemporary, Dr William Glyn, archdeacon of Anglesey, who belonged to a different family. T. F. TOUT, *rev.* F. G. COWLEY

Sources *The acts and monuments of John Foxe*, ed. S. R. Cattley, 8 vols. (1837–41), vol. 6, pp. 242, 306–7, 319–20, 332–3, 439 • J. E. Griffith, *Pedigrees of Anglesey and Carnarvonshire families* (privately printed, Horncastle, 1914), 239 • J. Wynn, *The history of the Gwydir family and memoirs*, ed. J. G. Jones (1990), 62 • J. B. Mullinger, *The University of Cambridge*, 2 (1884), 45, 84, 114 • *The diary of Henry Machyn, citizen and merchant-taylor of London, from AD 1550 to AD 1563*, ed. J. G. Nichols, CS,

42 (1848), 93–4 · Rymer, *Foedera*, 2nd edn, 15.415 · W. M. Brady, *The episcopal succession in England, Scotland, and Ireland, AD 1400 to 1875*, 1 (1876), 83 · W. Stubbs, *Registrum sacrum Anglicanum*, 2nd edn (1897), 81 · Fuller, *Worthies* (1811), 2.571 · W. G. Searle, *The history of the Queens' College of St Margaret and St Bernard in the University of Cambridge*, 2 vols., Cambridge Antiquarian RS, 9, 13 (1867–71), vol. 1, pp. 245–63 · B. Willis, *A survey of the cathedral church of Bangor* (1721), 30, 47, 104–5 · A. I. Pryce, *The diocese of Bangor in the sixteenth century, being a digest of the registers of the bishops' registers, AD 1512–1646* (1923), 14–16, 50–51 · D. Wilson-Reid, 'William Glyn, bishop of Bangor, 1555–58', *Transactions of the Anglesey Antiquarian Society and Field Club* (1950), 87–90 · W. Hughes, *Recollections of Bangor Cathedral* (1904), 33–4 · 'Extracts from old wills', *Archaeologia Cambrensis*, 4th ser., 14 (1883), 237–9 [gives Noodes, fol. 32, pob. 3.7.1558] · *DWB*

Archives NL Wales, register for Bangor diocese

Wealth at death see will, *Archaeologia Cambrensis*, 237–9

Glyn Dŵr [Glyndŵr]**, Owain** [Owain ap Gruffudd Fychan, Owen Glendower] (*c*.**1359**–*c*.**1416**), rebel leader in Wales, declared prince of Wales on 16 September 1400, was the acknowledged leader of the most serious and widespread rebellion against English authority in Wales since the conquest of 1282–3.

Lineage and estates Born possibly in 1359, or earlier (an event later invested by Shakespeare with supernatural significance), Owain Glyn Dŵr's upbringing and early career reflect many of the conflicting forces at work in fourteenth-century Welsh society. Through his father, Gruffudd Fychan, lord of Glyndyfrdwy and Cynllaith, and his mother, Elen, daughter of Owain ap Thomas ap Llywelyn, coheir with Margaret, her sister, of the half-commotes of Iscoed Uwch Hirwen and Gwynionydd Is Cerdyn, Cardiganshire, he was descended of impeccable Welsh princely stock. The poet Iolo Goch (*fl.* 1345–1397), in a celebrated *cywydd* composed almost certainly before the rebellion, traces his pedigree in the paternal line to *Bleddyn ap Cynfyn, prince of Powys (*d.* 1075), and in the maternal line to *Rhys ap Tewdwr, prince of Deheubarth (*d.* 1093), refers to the descent of his great-grandmother Gwenllian from the house of Gwynedd, and recites the common ancestry of these lineages in the legendary kings of early British tradition. Despite the family's native Welsh origins, however, marriage connections were also established with English or Anglo-Welsh families of the border. Glyn Dŵr's paternal grandmother was Elizabeth, daughter of John (V) Lestrange of Knockin; his sister Lowri married Robert Puleston, while Glyn Dŵr himself married Margaret Hanmer, daughter of Sir David Hanmer (*d.* 1387), king's serjeant and judge in king's bench, whose family, of English origin, had settled in Maelor Saesneg, the detached portion of Flintshire, and had long intermarried with Welsh families. His father's estates, to which Glyn Dŵr succeeded some time before 1370–71, when his mother is described as 'lately (*jadis*) the wife of Gruffudd of Glyndyfrdwy' (Shrewsbury Public Library, MS 5923), consisted of the lordship of Glyndyfrdwy, a relatively inhospitable terrain situated in the Dee valley between Corwen and Llangollen, and a moiety of the commote of Cynllaith, a fertile lordship to the south of the Berwyn range and bordering the Tanat valley. He inherited also his mother's estates in the county of Cardigan, for following his rebellion his lands in both north and south Wales were declared forfeit and he may have claimed part of the estate of his maternal grandmother at Trefgarn in the hundred of Pebidiog. His great-great-grandfather *Gruffudd Fychan (Gruffudd ap Gruffudd ap Madog) [*see under* Madog ap Gruffudd Maelor], coheir of the principality of Powys Fadog, was one of the few princely survivors of the conquest of 1282–3, and by the early fourteenth century Gruffudd's son, Madog, was holding the lordships of Glyndyfrdwy and Cynllaith of the king in chief by Welsh barony, a landed estate that provided an income of some 300 marks. There is a contemporary note of Owain's 'fine dwelling and park' (Nicolas, ed., *Proceedings … of the Privy Council*, 2.61) in Glyndyfrdwy (or Glyn Dŵr: the lordship by whose name he was known), which may refer to a domestic establishment at Carrog, but his residence at Sycharth in Cynllaith, a modern, half-timbered, tiled, and chimneyed house, set on a motte, with chapel, bakehouse, and mill adjacent, is described in admiring if extravagant detail by Iolo Goch.

Owain Glyn Dŵr [Owen Glendower] (*c*.**1359**–*c*.**1416**), seal [as prince of Wales]

Career to 1400 Although early connections between Owain Glyn Dŵr and both Henry Bolingbroke and Richard II have been suggested, documentary evidence points clearly to the family's close associations with the Fitzalans, earls of Arundel, and lords of Bromfield and Yale (from 1347) and Oswestry and Chirk, the latter including the other half of the commote of Cynllaith. Glyn Dŵr's grandfather, described as Gruffudd, lord of Glyndyfrdwy, witnessed the charter granted by Edmund Fitzalan, earl of Arundel, to the lordship of Chirk, on 1 October 1324 (L. B. Smith, 162). His father, Gruffudd Fychan, was the earl of Arundel's steward of the lordships of Chirk and Oswestry and is described as such in deeds and account rolls, while the Arundel connection may have been strengthened by Glyn Dŵr's marriage to Margaret Hanmer, whose father served on the earl's marcher council in 1386–7. Owain and his brother Tudur are named among the esquires of the retinue of Richard (III) Fitzalan, earl of Arundel, mustered on 13 March 1387, and Owain's name headed the list of Arundel's esquires mustered for overseas service in May 1388, although he may not have served on the expedition. No evidence of a direct connection with Richard II has yet been produced. Glyn Dŵr's 'Tudor' cousins, however, Rhys ap Tudur and Gwilym ap Tudur, sons of Margaret, his mother's sister, from her second marriage, to Tudur ap Goronwy of Penmynydd in Anglesey, had close links of service with the king [*see* Ednyfed Fychan].

Owain Glyn Dŵr's upbringing and career were, in so far as they may now be reconstructed, typical of a young man of gentle birth. English chroniclers noted his training as apprentice-at-law and record sources reveal his military service. As Howeyn Glyndourde and Tedyr Glynderde he and his brother served under Sir Gregory Sais at Berwick in 1384 (Glyn Dŵr's exploits there were commemorated in verse by Iolo Goch), in Scotland, and under Richard (III) Fitzalan at the blockade of Sluys in 1387. He had some knowledge of heraldry and, described as aged 'twenty-seven years and more' (Nicolas, ed., *Scrope and Grosvenor*, 1.254–5), gave evidence, along with Tudur, his brother, and John Hanmer and Robert Puleston, his brothers-in-law, to a court of chivalry held at Chester on 3 September 1386, when the rival claims of Richard, Lord Scrope, and Robert Grosvenor were ventilated. His legal training and his Hanmer connections are shown by his appointment in 1387 as joint feoffee of the Hanmer lands for the term of life of Sir David's widow, Angharad.

Outbreak of the revolt Contemporary evidence for the causes of Glyn Dŵr's uprising is exiguous, but there is little doubt that for Glyn Dŵr himself, and for many of his adherents from among the Welsh *uchelwyr*, or squirearchy, the rebellion represented a significant breach with family traditions of loyalty and service to the crown and to marcher dynasties. The *Annales Henrici quarti*, of St Albans provenance, claimed that the rebellion was instigated by a territorial dispute, which parliament failed to redress, between the lord of Dyffryn Clwyd who succeeded in 1388, Reynold *Grey (*d.* 1440), and Glyn Dŵr, a conflict subjected to much later embellishment when the land in question is identified as common land called Croesau in the parish of Bryneglwys. The *Vita Ricardi secundi*, a work connected with Evesham, and a brief fifteenth-century Welsh tract recount the withholding by Grey of a summmons to a general muster addressed by the king to Glyn Dŵr. The harsh fiscal policies pursued by the crown and by marcher regimes, which caused tenant recalcitrance and opposition among local officials, the few opportunities for professional advancement available to ambitious laymen and churchmen, and resentment of privileged English settlers, especially those in the towns of the crown lands and the marcher lordships of north-east Wales, helped to fuel a broader support for armed insurrection. Less convincing is the alleged tide of support for Richard II, although his deposition in 1399 may have been instrumental in fomenting rebellion among the Tudurs in Anglesey.

A Shropshire jury, sworn on 25 October 1400, recited that an assembly of men, including Glyn Dŵr's brother, his son Gruffudd, his Hanmer and Puleston brothers-in-law, Hywel Cyffin, dean of St Asaph, and Crach Ffinant, described as 'their prophet' (*eorum propheta*), and many other Welshmen, had gathered at Glyndyfrdwy on 16 September, intending the death and disherison of Henry, king of England, and the prince of Wales, and the obliteration of the English language. They had 'elevated … Owain as their prince' and had proceeded 'in warlike fashion like enemies' to the town of Ruthin which they had plundered and burned, thence turning to attack the 'English towns' of Denbigh, Rhuddlan, Flint, Hawarden, Holt, Oswestry, and Welshpool which were likewise plundered and despoiled (Sayles, 114–15). Corroborative evidence of the gravity of the assault on Ruthin is provided by the lordship's court records which testify that the attack was launched on 18 September, the Saturday preceding the town's St Matthew fair, and that some 270 men were involved of whom, on the evidence of locational names, the largest number were drawn from surrounding Welsh lordships, notably the lordship of Denbigh. Although a brief but valuable near contemporary Welsh chronicle suggests that Grey was himself in the neighbourhood, it is unlikely that he took the field against Glyn Dŵr until the launch of a second attack upon Ruthin in the early months of 1402. Henry IV, hearing at Leicester of the Welsh rising, and making his way towards Shrewsbury, summoned on 19 September 1400 the levies of the midland and border counties of England, while on 24 September the rebels received a summary check, near the town of Welshpool 'on the river Severn', by Hugh Burnell, commanding the troops of the counties of Shropshire, Staffordshire, and Warwickshire. According to the Welsh chronicler Glyn Dŵr himself 'escaped into the woods' (Lloyd, 150) and little is known of his whereabouts over the winter. Early in October the king made a circuit of the whole of north Wales, arriving at Bangor on 7 October and at Caernarfon two days later. On 15 October an order was given that, although various men in north Wales had lately risen in insurrection, the king's lieges in south Wales should be allowed none the less to come and go into England provided they were of good behaviour. Offers of pardon were made to rebels over a wide area of north Wales including the lordship of Ellesmere (where Glyn Dŵr's father had once acted as keeper) and the lordship of Whittington, but excepting Glyn Dŵr himself and Rhys and Gwilym ap Tudur. Glyn Dŵr's lands in north and south Wales were declared forfeit in November 1400, together with those of his kinsmen. By May 1401 it was said that 'the country of North Wales' (*le paiis de Northgalez*; *Proceedings … of the Privy Council*, 1.150–51) was well intendant and obedient in all points to the law, except for rebels in the castle of Conwy, and that the people of the counties of Caernarfon and Merioneth were prepared to submit and to pay substantial payments for pardon.

Progress of the revolt, 1401–1404 Despite the illusion of containment there were, however, several portents of continued resistance. Although the military activity focused on Glyn Dŵr himself had all but abated by the autumn of 1400, the island of Anglesey had witnessed resistance by Rhys and Gwilym ap Tudur, cousins of Glyn Dŵr. Early in 1401 parliament heard that Welsh scholars at Oxford and Cambridge were leaving their studies to join Glyn Dŵr, and Welsh labourers in England were likewise returning to Wales and preparing for war. Several petitions emphasized the gravity of the situation in Wales and six punitive statutes were enacted, followed on 18 and 22 March by further supplementary measures taken on account of 'the late insurrection in north Wales' (*CPR*, *1399–1401*, 469). The Tudur brothers, in a bold and unexpected stroke, were able to attack and to take the castle of Conwy on Good Friday (1 April) 1401 and hold it for some eight weeks, although it is not certain that this initiative or their earlier defiance was waged in association with Glyn Dŵr. Despite suffering a heavy defeat at the hands of John Charlton, who, it was said in a letter of 4 June 1401, had 'discomfited Glyn dŵr' (*Proceedings … of the Privy Council*, 1.153) and had killed many rebels, Glyn Dŵr won a signal victory 'in the uplands of Ceredigion' (Lloyd, 150) at Hyddgen Mountain, according to the Welsh chronicler, possibly at a spot marked to this day by two stones of quartz known to local tradition as the 'covenant stones of Owain Glyn Dŵr'. It was a success that, so the same chronicler maintained, transformed Glyn Dŵr's fortunes such that 'a great number of youths and fighting men [*direidwyr*] from every part of Wales rose and joined him, until he had a great host behind him' (ibid., 150). A letter, known only from a late manuscript sent by Glyn Dŵr styling himself Owain ap Gruffudd, lord of Glyndyfrdwy, to Henry Dwn, a leading landowner, soldier, and administrator of the Lancaster lordship of Kidwelly, exhorting him to join in the movement to liberate the Welsh from their bondage, may belong to this period, although it may pertain to the events of 1403. Glyn Dŵr's appearance in 'the marches of Carmarthen' (*Proceedings … of the Privy Council*, 2.55) before the end of May signalled the opening up of a new sphere of hostilities and an escalation of the rebellion into a movement led by himself and which, it was now emphasized, posed a serious danger to the realm of England, its people, and its language.

By the anniversary of the first act of defiance the rebel cause, despite the initial setbacks, had taken firm root. A summons, dated 18 September 1401, to a general muster at Worcester stressed that Owain Glyn Dŵr and other rebels had risen in no small number, a view given substance by the alleged adherence of many landowners of the crown lands of the south-west to the rebellion. A royal expedition in the following month wrought considerable damage to the abbey of Strata Florida while a renewed attack on Welshpool, *caput* of the Charlton lordship of Powys, by Glyn Dŵr, signalled the return of the rebel leader to the northern parts. There was talk at this juncture, possibly encouraged by the Percys, that Glyn Dŵr was prepared to enter into a treaty, but no peace was concluded. The chronicler Adam Usk describes the siege of Caernarfon Castle and the town in November 1401 by the rebel army with Glyn Dŵr at its head, where his standard, a golden dragon on a white field, was unfurled. Although unable to take the castle, the administrative and military headquarters of English rule in the crown lands of north Wales, Glyn Dŵr began to seek external alliances, addressing letters in French to the king of Scotland and in Latin to the Gaelic lords of Ireland. Early in 1402, according to Adam Usk, a second attack was launched on the town of Ruthin and Reynold Grey, who had been appointed one of Prince Henry's five lieutenants in north Wales on 15 January, and who was almost certainly in the lordship on 21 February, was himself captured some time before 18 April and a ransom of 10,000 marks was demanded for his release. A foray into Maelienydd in the middle march of Wales in June resulted in a bloody slaughter of English troops led by Sir Edmund (IV) Mortimer, uncle of the young earl of March, Edmund (V) Mortimer, at Bryn Glas near the village of Pilleth, and the capture of Mortimer. A letter written at the end of 1402 by Mortimer to Sir John Greyndor, guardian of the Mortimer lordship of Radnor, and others, expressed the former's adherence to the cause of Glyn Dŵr (an alliance cemented by his marriage to Catherine, Glyn Dŵr's daughter), the intention of placing the earl of March on the throne if Richard II were not alive, and of restoring to Glyn Dŵr his right in Wales. Meanwhile a tripartite attack, directed from Shrewsbury, Chester, and Hereford and set in motion on 31 July, achieved little military success. However, parliament, when it assembled on 30 September 1402, enacted a series of statutes prohibiting public assemblies, the bearing of arms by the Welsh, the importation of victuals or armour, and the keeping of castles or the holding of office by Welshmen. Especial mention was made of those of the amity or alliance of 'Owen ap Glendourdy, traitor to our sovereign lord and king' (Luders and others, eds., 2.140–41), who, together with Englishmen married to Welshwomen, were likewise denied office in Wales. The appointment of Prince Henry as royal lieutenant in Wales on 8 March 1403, with the promise of financial support from the exchequer, although it presaged an increasing emphasis on paid military service, did little to assuage the grave military position. Glyn Dŵr had been seen in the region of Hopedale, but did not engage in hostilities. In early May, however, an expedition by Prince Henry destroyed and burned Glyn Dŵr's house at Sycharth, proceeded to Glyndyfrdwy, where the lodge and park were also razed, and advanced to 'the fine and well-inhabited land of Edeirnion' (*Proceedings … of the Privy Council*, 2.62) which met a similar fate before the army returned to headquarters at Shrewsbury.

By the summer of 1403 the activities of Glyn Dŵr himself, hitherto largely hidden from view, are revealed in a number of mainly undated letters which may reliably be ascribed to the month of July. The abortive siege of the castle of Brecon by the Welsh forces was followed by Glyn Dŵr's arrival in person in the Tywi valley, where he had been expected as early as 16 June, on account, it was said, of 'want of victuals' (*CPR*, *1401–5*, 280). A number of responsible and prominent men of the region were named as his supporters. A letter written by John Fairford, receiver of the lordship of Brecon, referring to news sent to him by Jenkyn Havard, constable of the castle of Dinefwr, relates that Glyn Dŵr with a following of 300 men laid siege to the castle of Llandovery on Tuesday 3 July, was assured of the men of the district, except for those in the castle, and had spent the night at Llandeilo where the people of the county of Carmarthen and the lordships adjacent were 'assured and sworn' (*assurez et jurrez*; Hingeston, 139) to him. Although a march towards the town of Brecon was feared, his presence at the castle of Dryslwyn is attested on 4 July when John Scudamore, constable of Carreg Cennen Castle, who according to later report married Glyn Dŵr's daughter Alice, had spoken with the rebel leader under truce, and, in vain, had sought his safe conduct to remove members of his family from the castle. The castle of Carmarthen with its town (where about fifty inhabitants had died) and the castle of Newcastle Emlyn were ceded to him between 4 and 7 July, whence Glyn Dŵr proceeded to St Clears and to Laugharne, avoiding a pitched battle with forces led by Thomas, Lord Carew, who nevertheless inflicted heavy losses on the rebels. While he was still at Carmarthen it was said that Glyn Dŵr, true to his devotion to prophecy, had consulted a 'maister of Brut', named as Hopcyn ap Thomas ab Einion of Ynysdawe in Gower (*fl.* 1337–1408), a noted literary patron and connoisseur of manuscripts, who had forewarned him of his imminent capture between Carmarthen and Gower. The rebellion of Henry Percy (Hotspur), with whom it is possible that Glyn Dŵr had established an understanding as early as April 1403, was declared at Chester on 10 July. Percy, joined by a number of Welshmen, including men from the lordships of Denbigh and Dyffryn Clwyd and the county of Flint, and marching south to Shrewsbury, engaged and was defeated by royal forces on 21 July. Although there is no evidence that Glyn Dŵr was himself in the region when the battle was fought, the encounter may have served to divert his forces eastwards. There were fears of a Welsh attack on Shrewsbury and an invasion of Shropshire (a danger realized by the destruction of several manors in 1403) and the southern march was, likewise, under threat. A royal expedition was planned, to set out from Worcester on 3 September. The brief campaign that ensued passed through the valleys of the Usk and the Tywi, reaching Carmarthen by the end of September, while commissioners were appointed to receive the submitting Welshmen of Brecon, Cantref Selyf, and neighbouring lordships. The appearance of French and Breton ships off Kidwelly on 3 October and off Caernarfon in the following month, and the assaults made on both castles and towns, not only signalled the intervention of hostile foreign powers in the Welsh rebellion but also augured the conclusion of a formal treaty of alliance between Glyn Dŵr and Charles VI of France.

The apogee of revolt, 1404–1406 The years between 1404 and 1406 are generally regarded as the high-water mark of the Glyn Dŵr rebellion, but the movements and personal influence of the rebel leader himself on the formulation of policy remain as elusive as ever. The fall of Aberystwyth and Harlech castles, long under threat, into Welsh hands during 1404 (the castle of Aberystwyth was garrisoned by the English from March to November 1404) confirmed Glyn Dŵr's influence over a large swathe of western Wales, and endowed him with two key coastal fortresses and a refuge for family members after the destruction of Sycharth and Carrog. Glyn Dŵr's request for armed aid was conveyed to the French court in May 1404 by two proctors, John Hanmer, his brother-in-law, and the cleric Gruffudd Young, described as his chancellor, in a document sealed with Glyn Dŵr's privy seal and dated in the fourth year of his principate. The ensuing treaty, dated 14 July 1404, ratified on 12 January 1405, 'in the sixth year of our principate' (Matthews, 39) at the castle of Aberystwyth, and sealed with his great seal, bound king and prince in a bond of true covenant and friendship against Henry of Lancaster, both parties promising that neither would enter into a separate peace with Henry and that disputes arising between their subjects on land or sea should be amicably settled. No formal promise of military assistance was given or received although a French chronicler recorded that a list of ports and seaways had been provided by Glyn Dŵr. In 1404, according to Adam Usk's derisory comment, Glyn Dŵr assembled the first of his known parliaments at Machynlleth, while to the second, held at Harlech in Ardudwy in August 1405, according to contemporary report, he had summoned four good men from each commote of Wales that acknowledged his rule. The so-called tripartite indenture, a document of uncertain authenticity, concluded between emissaries of Glyn Dŵr, Edmund Mortimer, and Henry Percy, earl of Northumberland (*d.* 1408), agreed the division of England and Wales, with Glyn Dŵr taking as his share a greatly extended Wales which stretched to the source of the Trent and to the Mersey. A document dated at Pennal on 31 March, 'in the sixth year of our rule' (1406) and reciting the deliberations of an assembly that included the 'proctors of the nobles and prelates of our principality and others', committed the Welsh, a nation 'oppressed by the fury of the barbarous Saxons' (Matthews, 53), to the obedience of the Avignon pope, Benedict XIII (*r.* 1394–1417), and pressed for the advancement of a number of specific proposals concerned with the status of the church of Wales. They included the restoration of the church of St David's to its original dignity as metropolitan church, and the institution not only of the Welsh dioceses but also those of Exeter, Bath, Hereford, Worcester, and Lichfield as its suffragans, the provision of clergy who knew the Welsh language to ecclesiastical office in Wales, and the establishment of two universities, one in north Wales and the other in south Wales in places to be determined by Glyn Dŵr's ambassadors. References to letters patent and close, to a council, chancellor, secretary, notaries, and proctors, to the prince's privy seal (a quartered shield charged with the four lions rampant of the princes of Gwynedd), to his great seal (with, on its obverse, a ruler enthroned and sceptred and, on its reverse, a warrior on horseback, in armour and surcoat), suggest a prince of an emerging state who could call on the services of a trained and experienced bureaucracy. A like impression is conveyed by the formal and elegant diplomatic language of the documents issued in his name, his intitulation as 'prince of Wales by the grace of God' (Matthews, 42), and by the formal holding of parliaments. The advent of increasing numbers of churchmen from 1404 onwards to the rebel cause may have influenced the formulation of policy and strengthened the administration of the nascent Welsh state.

Creative and imaginative endeavours in state-building did not, however, eliminate the need for opportunistic assault and prudent defensive measures. In the south-east, raids on the town of Newport in 1403, the fall of the town and castle of Cardiff (one of whose residents, John Sperhauke, had earlier been executed for his support for Glyn Dŵr) to Welsh troops in 1404, and the attack on Coety Castle where its lord, Sir Lawrence Berkerolles (*d.* 1411) was besieged for some weeks, betokened the serious threat to English power and to the revenues of baronial holders of marcher lordships in the region. In June 1404 the Welsh rebels in great number attacked Archenfield in the county of Hereford. The Welsh defeat on Campstone Hill in the parish of Grosmont, an event assigned by the Welsh chronicler to this year, was answered by a Welsh victory at Craig-y-dorth near Monmouth, where the English were chased to the town gate. In the northern march punitive raiding expeditions were launched into Shropshire, whose inhabitants complained of the destruction wrought by the rebels and concluded a truce with 'the land of Wales' (*Proceedings … of the Privy Council*, 1.236). The French dispatched troops, which landed at Milford Haven early in August 1405, and the south-western regions came under assault with the attack on the castle of Haverfordwest and the capture of the town by the Welsh, followed by assaults on Carmarthen and Cardigan which, according to French sources, also fell into Welsh hands. Combined Welsh and French forces were at Woodbury Hill outside Worcester by the end of the month, at a place which according to Camden was known in the seventeenth century as 'Owen Glyndŵr's camp', but, although strong English forces were mustered under the king's command, no battle was fought and the Welsh troops withdrew into Wales. The seizure of the king's baggage train, loaded with provisions and jewels, by the rebels as a royal expedition advanced to attempt the relief of Coety Castle, and the conclusion of a truce with the men of the county (*comitatus*) of Pembroke, who yielded up £200 of silver, brought welcome financial windfalls to the rebel cause. Despite the apparent success of the rebels, however, there were also Welsh losses. In a battle fought at Pwll Melyn near Usk against Richard, Lord Grey of Codnor (*d.* 1419), Welsh troops were heavily defeated, Glyn Dŵr's son Gruffudd was taken prisoner, and, according to legend, Glyn Dŵr's brother Tudur was killed. The turning tide of rebellion in 1405 was graphically portrayed by the Welsh chronicler who noted that at this time 'Glamorgan made its submission to the English, except a few who went to Gwynedd to their lord' (Lloyd, 152).

The final years, 1406–1415 To characterize the course of the rebellion from 1406 onwards as one of inexorable decline obscures not only the serious structural weaknesses exposed even in the years of apparent triumph but also the capacity for resistance that Glyn Dŵr continued to command. At no point during the rebellion could he claim the entire support of his people. Although his movement had attracted adherents from prominent, respectable, and interrelated families, the successes enjoyed in the summer of 1403 coupled with the Percy rebellion, which also commanded support in north Wales, confirmed the movement's appeal to influential members of the class of *uchelwyr*. But committed adherents were balanced by intransigent foes drawn not only from townsmen and English families settled in Wales but from native Welsh lineages. In geographical terms, the area under his direct command was a limited one while his power outside a western zone stretching roughly from Ceredigion to Anglesey, despite the fact that his supporters were widely disseminated, was confined to brief shows of strength as he and the crown competed for the allegiance and loyalties of communities. His financial base was at all times uncertain, given the demands on his income, although it is likely that ransoms, such as those demanded and paid for the release of Reynold Grey and Dafydd Gam of Brecon (*d.* 1415), payments for negotiated truces, and the profits of pillage and plunder may have helped fill his coffers. Lines of communication, running mainly from east to west, tended to favour the English invader more than a Welsh ruler hoping to impart a measure of geographical unity. Sea power, in which the Welsh (apart from sporadic French aid and the efforts of individual rebels) were deficient, had long been identified as the key to the conquest and retention of Wales by the English and was instrumental once more in combating the Glyn Dŵr rebellion. With the exception of Aberystwyth and Harlech the English-built castles stood firm or were lost only briefly, and those of south Wales and the march were deployed as headquarters of mounted troops capable of offensive sallies on the Welsh rebels. On the other hand, the rebels' reluctance to commit their troops to pitched battle, preferring instead the lightning strikes and the raids of a guerrilla campaign, enhanced their capacity to resist final defeat and frustrated English attempts to contain the rebellion. Moreover, despite the formal submission in 1406 of the communities of Gower, Ystrad Tywi, Ceredigion, and Anglesey, followed in the ensuing years by those of several north-eastern lordships, pacification was by no means complete. In 1409 Glyn Dŵr with a large following of rebels was said to be devastating far and wide. A great raid was launched on the Shropshire borders about the same time, while in 1412 Welsh rebels in the lordship of Brecon were able to take captive and ransom no less a person than the redoubtable warrior Dafydd Gam. As late as 1415 Welsh rebels were present in the county of Merioneth, an area long identified as a source of disturbance. The imprisonment of two Scottish merchants at Caernarfon in 1410, and the evidence contained in an undated letter referring to assemblies in desolate places and expected landings of men from the outer isles of Scotland at Barmouth and Dyfi, suggest persistent Welsh hopes of rekindling external alliances.

A number of forces combined to effect the rebels' ultimate defeat. The castle of Aberystwyth, besieged by troops led by Prince Henry, fell to the English by the end of 1408. By February 1409 not only had Harlech fallen to troops led by Gilbert Talbot and his brother, John, but Glyn Dŵr's own family, including his wife, two of his daughters, and his granddaughters lodged in the castle had been taken prisoner and dispatched to London. The loss of several of his loyal adjutants, including a Tudur kinsman, in the ill-fated Shropshire raid, coupled with the loss of one of his sons who, according to the *Annales Henrici quarti*, met his death in an earlier encounter on St George's day, depleted his inner core of support. Meanwhile a determined and dogged English campaign was achieving its aims. A regular money supply from a healthier exchequer, the creation of a defensive bulwark in the march, the safeguarding of supply routes to the English while, at the same time, those of the Welsh were severed, ensured, at length, the success of the military response. On the wider political front the beginnings of negotiations for truce between England and France, from which Glyn Dŵr was specifically excluded, stilled any hopes that might have remained of a positive French intervention. In the north of England the defeat of the earl of Northumberland who, it was said, had been in collusion with the Welsh rebels early in 1406, removed from the scene a potential source of support, while the heir to the Scottish throne was held captive in England. The exceptionally hard winter of 1407–8 may also have helped to reduce to still further misery a countryside already depleted and ravaged by war.

Glyn Dŵr's own influence on the turn of events in these final years of rebellion is a matter of uncertain conjecture. The Welsh chronicler, on doubtful authority, records that he went into hiding on 'St Matthew's day in harvest' (Lloyd, 152)—21 September—1415 and a brief fifteenth-century memorandum associated with the lordships of Oswestry and Chirk and which relates material of local interest gives the 'day of St Matthew, apostle, 1415' (ibid.) as the day of Glyn Dŵr's death. An agreement concluded between the men of Powys, Gwynedd, and Deheubarth which is dated in 'the sixth year after the revolt of Owain ap Gruffudd, the year of Christ, 1421' (NL Wales, Peniarth MS 86, fol. 186) suggests that the year 1415 was later regarded as the end of the rebellion if not the year of Glyn Dŵr's death. On 5 July 1415 Gilbert Talbot was appointed to receive Owain Glyn Dŵr and other rebels into the king's obedience and it is possible that Glyn Dŵr was believed to be alive at that date. On 24 February 1416 a second commission was given to Talbot to negotiate with Glyn Dŵr's son Maredudd, and to receive Glyn Dŵr and any other rebel who sought pardon, but there is no mention of the father in the pardon offered to Maredudd on 30 April 1417 and it may be presumed that, by then, Glyn Dŵr was dead. His refuge in his final days and the place of his burial were matters of great speculation. Two, possibly three, daughters survived him, of whom the marriages of two, namely Alice, who married John Scudamore of western Herefordshire, and Gwenllian, said to be an illegitimate daughter who married Philip ap Rhys of Cenarth in Gwrtheyrnion, are known from contemporary evidence. Several local traditions connect his last days with Herefordshire locations. It is possible that his surviving son, Maredudd, had already assumed the leadership of the faltering rebellion before his father's death. An undated letter, almost certainly of 1411, written by the outlaw Gruffudd ap Dafydd ap Gruddudd to Reynold Grey, refers to the fact that he was under the protection of Maredudd ab Owain and suggests that, when it was written, Glyn Dŵr, if indeed he was still alive, had retired from active leadership of the movement. Maredudd himself may have served with the king in Normandy and in April 1421 received letters patent granting him pardon for all offences, 'as on the testimony of the Holy Writ, the son shall not bear the iniquity of the father' (*CPR*, 1416–22, 335).

Posthumous reputation Although much of the credit for Owain Glyn Dŵr's rehabilitation as a national hero has been accorded to Thomas Pennant, who in his *Tours in Wales* (1778) searched out the legends and topographical detail associated with his name, the centuries since his death had not been without sympathetic portrayals of his endeavours. If the nineteenth-century writer William Owen of Caernarfon is to be believed, an Anglesey physician, David Bulkeley, had, as early as 1520, written an account of Glyn Dŵr, although no trace of the manuscript survives. Shakespeare's portrayal, perhaps the most influential in shaping Glyn Dŵr's image among an English public, presented him not only as a fierce warrior endowed with supernatural powers, but also as a cultured and dignified figure 'not in the roll of common men' (*1 Henry IV*, III.i). George Owen (1552–1613), the Elizabethan antiquary of Henllys in Pembrokeshire, while he regretted the rebellion's stultifying consequences for the well-being of pre-union Wales, nevertheless emphasized that Glyn Dŵr had opposed a usurper whose actions had generated the dynastic conflicts of fifteenth-century England. While the comments of seventeenth- and eighteenth-century writers (with some significant exceptions) are largely censorious, the renascent patriotism of the last decades of the nineteenth century encouraged a more positive and approving assessment. For the exponents of Welsh liberal ideals Glyn Dŵr was identified as the prime inspiration of their own cherished aims—a Welsh parliament, a reformed and liberated church, and a national university—while a number of studies aimed at a popular audience depicted him as a leader of a peasant movement and as the hero of the common man. The publication in 1931 of the biography by Sir John Edward Lloyd (1861–1947), with its avowed intention of removing the 'undergrowth of legend and error' that had gathered around the name of Glyn Dŵr, not only signalled the advent of an authoritative, scholarly study but also established the rebel's credentials as a national hero and as a Welsh statesman of vision and imagination. LLINOS SMITH

Sources PRO · NL Wales, Peniarth MSS 26, 86, 135 · *Chancery records* · *RotP* · I. Bowen, ed., *Statutes of Wales* (1908) · H. Ellis, ed., *Original letters illustrative of English history*, 2nd ser., 4 vols. (1827) · N. H. Nicolas, ed., *Proceedings and ordinances of the privy council of England*, 7 vols., RC, 26 (1834–7) · F. C. Hingeston, ed., *Royal and historical* *letters during the reign of Henry the Fourth*, 1, Rolls Series, 18; repr. (1965) • 'Annales Ricardi secundi et Henrici quarti, regum Angliae', *Johannis de Trokelowe et Henrici de Blaneforde … chronica et annales*, ed. H. T. Riley, pt 3 of *Chronica monasterii S. Albani*, Rolls Series, 28 (1866), 155–420 • G. B. Stow, ed., *Historia vitae et regni Ricardi Secundi* (1977) • *The chronicle of Adam Usk, 1377–1421*, ed. and trans. C. Given-Wilson, OMT (1997) • T. Matthews, ed., *Welsh records in Paris* (1910) • J. E. Lloyd, *Owen Glendower* (1931) • G. Williams, *Owain Glyndŵr* (1993) • R. R. Davies, *Conquest, coexistence, and change: Wales, 1063–1415*, History of Wales, 2 (1987) • R. R. Davies, *The revolt of Owain Glyndŵr* (1995) • A. E. Goodman, 'Owain Glyndŵr before 1400', *Welsh History Review / Cylchgrawn Hanes Cymru*, 5 (1970–71), 67–70 • R. I. Jack, 'New light on the early days of Owain Glyndŵr', *BBCS*, 21 (1964–6), 163–6 • R. I. Jack, 'Owain Glyn Dŵr and the lordship of Ruthin', *Welsh History Review / Cylchgrawn Hanes Cymru*, 2 (1964–5), 303–22 • R. A. Griffiths, 'Some partisans of Owain Glyn Dŵr at Oxford', *BBCS*, 20 (1962–4), 282–92 • R. A. Griffiths, 'Some secret supporters of Owain Glyn Dŵr', *BIHR*, 37 (1964), 77–100 • R. A. Griffiths, 'The Glyn Dŵr rebellion in north Wales through the eyes of an Englishman', *BBCS*, 22 (1966–8), 151–68 • R. R. Davies, 'Owain Glyn Dŵr and the Welsh squirearchy', *Transactions of the Honourable Society of Cymmrodorion* (1968), 150–69 • R. Griffiths, 'Prince Henry's war: armies, garrisons and supply during the Glyndŵr rebellion', *BBCS*, 34 (1987), 165–74 • J. B. Smith, 'The last phase of the Glyndŵr rebellion', *BBCS*, 22 (1966–8), 250–60 • J. R. S. Phillips, 'When did Owain Glyndŵr die?', *BBCS*, 24 (1970–72), 59–77 • K. Williams-Jones, 'The taking of Conwy Castle, 1401', *Transactions of the Caernarvonshire Historical Society*, 39 (1978), 7–43 • *Iolo Goch: poems*, ed. and trans. D. Johnston (1993) • Shrewsbury Public Library, Shrewsbury, Shropshire, MS 5923 • L. B. Smith, 'The Arundel charters to the lordship of Chirk in the fourteenth century', *BBCS*, 23 (1968–70), 153–66 • N. H. Nicolas, ed., *The Scrope and Grosvenor controversy*, 1 (privately printed, London, 1832) • G. O. Sayles, ed., *Select cases in the court of king's bench*, 7, SeldS, 88 (1971) • A. Luders and others, eds., *Statutes of the realm*, 11 vols. in 12, RC (1810–28), vol. 2

Likenesses A. Turner, portrait, 1916, City Hall, Cardiff • seal, NMG Wales [*see illus.*]

John Glynn (*bap.* 1722, *d.* 1779), by unknown engraver, *c.*1769

Glynn, John (*bap.* **1722**, *d.* **1779**), lawyer and politician, the second son of William Glynn (*b. c.*1692) of Cardinham, and his wife, Rose, the daughter of John Prideaux of Padstow, both in Cornwall, was baptized at Cardinham on 3 August 1722. He entered Exeter College, Oxford, in 1738, but failed to graduate; he was called to the bar at the Middle Temple in 1748. By the time he inherited the family estate on the death of his lunatic nephew in December 1762 he had established himself as a foremost London barrister. In January 1763 he was created a serjeant-at-law, and was rated the first man in Westminster Hall for legal knowledge. But his legal career took second place to, and suffered from, his involvement in radical politics after he undertook the role of counsel to John Wilkes, and he never received any official appointments in the patronage of government. He came to political prominence in the first Wilkes case of 1763, when he pleaded successfully against the validity of general warrants, and thereafter he often acted on behalf of Wilkes, the radical publisher John Almon, and other critics of government. In 1763 Glynn found time to marry, on 21 July, Susanna Margaret (1744–1816), the daughter of Sir John Oglander, fourth baronet, of Nunwell in the Isle of Wight; they had three sons and a daughter. That Glynn cherished his own political ambition was signified by his unsuccessful candidature, on his father-in-law's interest, for the Isle of Wight borough of Newtown at the general election of 1768. He was the immediate Wilkite choice for a Middlesex by-election that followed soon after the controversial return of Wilkes for that county in 1768, and won the seat in December by 1542 votes to 1278 after supporters of the ministerial candidate had violently interrupted the poll. This victory, achieved at a cost of £12,000, demonstrated the Wilkite hold on the county better than the success of the popular hero, for Glynn was merely his lawyer.

In the House of Commons, Glynn naturally challenged the ministry's decision to deprive Wilkes of his Middlesex seat. In the debate of 3 February 1769 on the expulsion, so Horace Walpole recorded, 'Serjeant Glynn gained great fame by the candour of his conduct on the whole proceeding; owning that, as counsel for Wilkes, he had maintained points which he would not assert in the House' (Walpole, 3.219). Outside parliament Glynn presided over the public meeting that decided on 20 February 1769 to establish the Society of Supporters of the Bill of Rights in support of Wilkes; he later chaired that society's fund-raising committee. In the City of London the Wilkite-dominated common council transferred the City's legal business from the official recorder to Glynn in 1770, and on 17 November 1772 he was himself narrowly elected recorder by the court of aldermen, when the salary was raised from £600 to £1000.

Glynn seems to have been a man who created a good

impression on all who knew him. Even the sharp-penned Horace Walpole could find no fault in 'a man of unexceptionable character' (Walpole, 3.190). When during the Falkland Islands crisis of 1770 the obstruction of naval press warrants by London radicals was criticized by Lord Chatham, Glynn went to see the great man and devised a compromise solution of offering bounties for volunteers. 'I find him a most ingenious, solid, pleasing man, and the spirit of the constitution itself', Chatham wrote. 'I never was more taken by a first conversation in my life' (*Correspondence of William Pitt*, 3.483). But Glynn's impact on the House of Commons was limited. Although he spoke about fifty times in the six-year parliament elected in 1768, he rarely did so other than on legal matters and the Middlesex election. His hobby horse was the rights of juries, especially in libel cases, and his most notable parliamentary performance was a long speech on 6 December 1770 in which he moved unsuccessfully for an inquiry into the administration of justice, with particular reference to the liberty of the press and the role of juries. Matters close to radical hearts would bring him to his feet, as when in 1771 he spoke in favour of press freedom to report parliament. Rarely did he venture outside his self-imposed brief to matters of national policy. He spoke only once on America in 1774, but he voiced all the prejudices of London radicals against the Quebec Bill. Three times he rose on the second reading on 26 May 1774, attacking the measure for putting English subjects under French law, for not giving the colony a representative assembly, and for not safeguarding the protestant religion. He spoke twice more at the report stage on 10 June, to urge the merits of jury trials.

At the general election of 1774 Wilkes and Glynn were elected without opposition for Middlesex, and, from 1775 until he was too ill to do so in 1779, Glynn seconded Wilkes's annual motion to reverse the 1769 resolution declaring him ineligible to sit in the previous parliament. He had been troubled by gout for at least a decade, and faded from the political scene long before he died, on 16 September 1779. He was buried at Cardinham on 23 September. His widow survived him by many years, and died at Catharine Place, Bath, on 20 May 1816. A man of moral and political rectitude, Glynn had never found Wilkes a kindred spirit. The two men were merely associates, as Wilkes explained to George III after the king had enquired about his friend. 'Sir, rejoined Wilkes, he was my counsel—one must have a counsel; but he was no *friend*; he loves sedition and licentiousness, which I never delighted in. In fact, Sir, he was a Wilkite, *which I never was*' (Twiss, 2.356).

PETER D. G. THOMAS

Sources P. D. G. Thomas, *John Wilkes: a friend to liberty* (1996) • HoP, *Commons* • parliamentary diary of Henry Cavendish, 1768–74, BL, Egerton MSS 215–263, 3711 • H. Walpole, *Memoirs of the reign of King George the Third*, ed. G. F. R. Barker, 4 vols. (1894) • *Correspondence of William Pitt, earl of Chatham*, ed. W. S. Taylor and J. H. Pringle, 4 vols. (1838–40) • *The public and private life of Lord Chancellor Eldon, with selections from his correspondence*, ed. H. Twiss, 3 vols. (1844) • H. W. Woolrych, *Lives of eminent serjeants-at-law of the English bar*, 2 vols. (1869) • *IGI*

Archives Cornwall RO, corresp.

Likenesses R. Houston, group portrait, oils, *c*.1768, NPG • engraving, *c*.1769, NPG [*see illus.*] • double portrait (with John Wilkes), repro. in H. Bleachly, *Life of John Wilkes* (1917); priv. coll. • line engravings, BM, NPG

Glynn, Joseph (1799–1863), mechanical and civil engineer, was born on 6 February 1799, in Hanover Square, Newcastle upon Tyne, one of at least two sons of James Glynn. He was taught by John Brace, a noted mathematician, at the Percy Street Academy; he was then his father's assistant at the Ouseburn iron foundry, until 1820. After erecting a steam engine for the earl of Carlisle to drain the Talkin colliery at Brampton, Cumberland, he designed and erected a gasworks at Berwick upon Tweed in 1821. This was so successful that he was asked to erect another at Aberdeen; he drew up the plans and reports but turned down the actual execution, because he had accepted the offer of a position as engineer to the Butterley Company, Ripley, Derbyshire.

The official history of the Butterley Company by R. H. Mottram and C. Coote concentrates on the lives of its financiers, the Wright family, and never mentions Glynn, even though he succeeded William Brunton as chief engineer in 1821 and held that post for at least twenty-five years. Today Glynn is remembered for his land drainage work, while his other contributions to the development of the steam engine, particularly in shipping, and of bridges and other civil engineering structures, have been forgotten.

The commissioners for Deeping Fen near Spalding invited tenders in 1823 for two engines to drive scoopwheels at Pode Hole. The Butterley Company won the order for the larger 80 hp one. Following this introduction to fen drainage, Glynn developed a standard design with a low boilerhouse on one side of a tall building for the single-cylinder beam engine, with the scoopwheel on the further side. Glynn erected one engine at Misterton Soss, on the Trent, and then about a dozen more, before 1847, in the fens. Of these the most important was the 'Hundred Foot' engine for Littleport and Downham district. The Stretham engine was subsequently preserved. Although Glynn did not pioneer this application of steam engines, on 8 February 1836 he was awarded the Gold Isis medal of the Society of Arts for his communication on draining land by steam power. The following November he was elected to this society, and he subsequently served as a member of council and as vice-president.

While Glynn was building the engine for Pode Hole, the Butterley Company supplied the winding engines which hauled the wagons up the inclines of the Cromford and High Peak Railway. One of these was subsequently preserved at Middleton Top. Powerful engines for both winding and pumping were supplied to collieries around Ripley as well as in co. Durham. Familiarity with steam power helped the Butterley Company to build engines for steam boats such as the *Royal Sovereign*, for the Royal Navy, and for export.

Glynn's connection with land drainage covered other schemes beyond the fens, both in Britain and overseas in the Netherlands, Hamburg, and British Guiana. This interest in raising water extended to the reverse, its fall, in generating power. Glynn executed some large water-wheels and wrote the *Rudimentary Treatise on the Power of Water* (1853). He also published his *Rudimentary Treatise on the Construction of Cranes and Machinery* (1849), for among its other products the Butterley Company supplied cranes and dredgers. The introduction of this second book shows his concern to improve the welfare of the working man.

The Butterley Company undertook the ironwork for a variety of civil engineering structures, but in how much of this it acted as a contractor and in how much it used designs by Glynn remains unknown. He supplied much of the ironwork for the Royal Naval establishment at Sheerness as well as for many bridges, such as Vauxhall Bridge, the road bridge over the Ouse at Ely, and later railway bridges. Glynn was also involved with constructing the Midland Counties Railway and others. He became chairman of the Eastern Counties Railway for a couple of years and gave evidence before committees of both houses of parliament on such railway matters as the use of iron in structures.

Glynn became a member of the Institution of Civil Engineers in 1828 and was elected a fellow of the Royal Society on 8 February 1838. He contributed papers to both—one in 1847 to the 'Civils' on a canal to join the Atlantic and the Pacific, for which he was awarded the Telford medal, and another in 1851 concerning the future Suez Canal. Glynn died at his home, 28 Westbourne Park Villas, London, on 6 February 1863, well respected in his profession. RICHARD L. HILLS

Sources *Journal of the Society of Arts*, 11 (1862–3), 230–32 • J. Glynn, 'Draining land by steam power', *Transactions of the Society of Arts*, 51 (1838), 3–24 • R. L. Hills, *Machines, mills and uncountable costly necessities, a short history of the drainage of the fens* (1967) • J. Glynn, *Rudimentary treatise on the construction of cranes and machinery for raising heavy bodies* (1849) • P. Riden, *The Butterley Company, 1790–1830*, 2nd edn, Derbyshire RS (1990) • R. H. Mottram and C. Coote, *Through five generations: the history of the Butterley Company* (1950) • C. Hadfield and A. W. Skempton, *William Jessop, engineer* (1979) • *PICE*, 23 (1863–4), 492–8 • J. Glynn, *Rudimentary treatise on the power of water, as applied to drive flour mills and to give motion to turbines* (1853) • *CGPLA Eng. & Wales* (1863) • d. cert.
Archives Derbys. RO, Butterley Company records
Wealth at death under £40,000: resworn probate, Oct 1863, *CGPLA Eng. & Wales*

Glynn, Prudence Loveday [*married name* Prudence Loveday Hennessy, Lady Windlesham] (**1935–1986**), fashion writer, was born on 22 January 1935 at 34 Evelyn Gardens, Kensington, London, the youngest child in the family of two sons and two daughters of Lieutenant-Colonel Rupert Trevor Wallace Glynn, a retired Royal Artillery officer, of Poplar Farm House, Cold Ash, Newbury, Berkshire, and his wife, Evelyn Margaret Vernet. She grew up in Tetsworth, and was educated at Downe House, Berkshire, leaving school for a job in advertising. After working for Frank Usher, the dress company, she turned to writing for women's magazines, and became fashion editor of *Women's Mirror*. On 22 May 1965 she married David James George Hennessy, third Baron Windlesham (*b.* 1932), Conservative politician and later managing director of the ATV television network: they had one son and one daughter.

In 1966 Prudence Glynn was appointed the first fashion editor of *The Times*, a post she held until 1980. The editor, Sir William Haley, wanted to change the image of the paper, and appointed a women's editor, Susanne Puddefoot, to introduce a daily women's page. She recruited Prudence Glynn, whose first article launched the new women's page on 3 May 1966, the first time in the history of *The Times* that news appeared on the front page. After the new editor William Rees-Mogg introduced personal bylines in 1967, she became very well known. Her articles were stylish and witty, though some felt they were too witty, and made fun of the serious world of fashion. She championed British designers, including Jean Muir, and after attending his first fashion show in 1966 was instrumental in the rise to fame of the pop designer Ossie Clark (1942–1996), whom she regarded as one of the most talented fashion designers ever produced in Britain: she chose his chiffon and satin trouser suit as the 1968 dress of the year for the Museum of Costume in Bath. Glynn was passionate about British fashion, and she crusaded through her articles to raise it to the level of French fashion; this led to government initiatives to promote the manufacture and export of British designs. She enjoyed the glamour of the fashion scene, and the power that she wielded at the height of her influence as a *grande dame* of fashion. Highly respected as a fashion journalist, she was regarded as authoritative because she wrote for *The Times*, and to be mentioned by her was of enormous importance to designers. She was an excellent journalist, writing beautifully and at length, and it was a standing joke that her sentences were even longer than those of her fellow journalist Bernard Levin. Many people read her articles not because they were interested in fashion, but because they were fun to read. But she found it hard to get on with her female colleagues at *The Times*, and after several difficult years from the mid-1970s onwards she was removed from the post of fashion editor, and given a weekly column. Her first piece, on 16 October 1980, was 'Fourteen years and positively no regrets'.

Glynn published two books, both lavishly illustrated. *In Fashion: Dress in the Twentieth Century* (1978), a social history of fashion, puts the work of designers into the context of their times, and traces the ways in which fashion reflects society. It is full of witty observations, such as her comment on the contradiction involved in buying a pair of blue jeans by Yves St Laurent: 'that is one problem of wearing pioneer dress in the richest country in the world' (p. 59). The book covers sporting fashion, royal fashion, theatrical fashion, and utility clothes, as well as *haute couture*. *Skin to Skin: Eroticism in Dress* (1982) begins by asking why people wear clothes at all, and agrees with Robert Burton that 'The greatest provocations of our lust are from our apparel'. Recalling that Hardy Amies once told her that the most erotic sight he ever saw was nuns playing tennis, making the point that sexual excitement can be caused as much by concealment as by revelation, she concludes that 'Eros, god of love, depends from every coathanger' (p. 16).

During the 1970s Prudence Glynn was very influential in the design world as a member of the council of the Royal College of Art from 1969 to 1977, and the Design Council from 1973 to 1979. She was also on the Council for National Academic Awards committee for art and design from 1972, and a member of the Crafts Council from 1977 to 1980. She was elected a fellow of the Royal Society of Arts in 1974.

Glynn was very tall, slim, and elegant, and described herself as having a face like a currant bun. In her later years she began to suffer psychiatric problems; she separated from her husband, and the quality of her journalism became uneven. She died on 24 September 1986 in the St Charles Hospital, Kensington, London.

ANNE PIMLOTT BAKER

Sources J. Grigg, *The history of The Times*, another edn, 6: *The Thomson years 1966–1981* (1995) • *The Ossie Clark diaries*, ed. H. Rous (1998) • *The Times* (26 Sept 1986) • Burke, *Peerage* (2000) • *WW* • private information (2004) [Lord Windlesham and others] • b. cert. • m. cert. • d. cert.

Likenesses D. Daines, portrait, exh. Grafton Gallery, London 1976 • K. Green, portrait, exh. Grafton Gallery, London 1976 • D. Remfry, portrait, exh. Grafton Gallery, London 1976 • photograph, repro. in *The Times*

Glynn [*later* Clobery], **Robert** (1719–1800), physician, was born at Brodes, near Bodwin, Cornwall, on 5 August 1719, and baptized at Helland church on 16 September 1719. He was the eldest and only surviving son of Robert Glynn and his wife, Lucy, daughter of John Clobery of Bradstone, Devon. After some teaching from a local curate, he was placed on the foundation at Eton College. In 1737 he was elected a scholar of King's College, Cambridge, where he took the degrees of BA in 1741, MA in 1745, and MD in 1752, and became a fellow. His medical tutor at Cambridge was the elder William Heberden of St John's College. Glynn himself announced in March 1751 a course of lectures at King's College on the medical institutes, and the following year gave a second course on anatomy. For a short time he practised at Richmond, Surrey, but soon returned to Cambridge, never to leave the university. In 1757 Glynn competed successfully for the Seatonian prize, to prevent a man called Bally from gaining it a third time. It was unfairly insinuated that Glynn was not the author of his own poem, but 'The Day of Judgement' was printed in several editions and included in anthologies.

On 5 April 1762 Glynn was admitted a candidate, and on 28 March 1763 became a fellow, of the Royal College of Physicians. He accepted no further distinctions, though William Pitt the younger offered him the chair of medicine at Cambridge in 1793. Glynn had attended Pitt in the autumn of 1773, when Lord Chatham wrote a letter of congratulation on his son's recovery from sickness, with the hope that he was 'enjoying the happy advantage of Dr Glynn's acquaintance, as one of the cheerful and witty sons of Apollo, in his poetic not his medical attributes'.

Glynn was eccentric in manner and dress. Professor Pryme describes him as usually wearing 'a scarlet cloak and three-cornered hat; he carried a gold-headed cane. He also used pattens in rainy weather' (Pryme, 46). Another contemporary, Sir Egerton Brydges, records the doctor's pride 'on saying whatever came uppermost into his mind'. To William Cole he was a 'solitary savage' (Venn, *Alum. Cant.*). Glynn's tea-parties were famous, and frequented by many undergraduates. As a physician he showed judgement and attention, but with characteristic eccentricity he resolutely refrained from prescribing opium, cathartics, or bleeding. He recommended and practised an open-air life. He attended Thomas Gray in his last illness. Richard Watson (1737–1816), bishop of Llandaff, was one of his patients in 1781, when Glynn gave his opinion that recovery was hopeless.

Glynn gave free advice to patients from the fens, who constantly battled with malaria, and would take no fee from a Cornishman or an Etonian. His kindness to one of his poor patients was celebrated by a younger son of Robert Plumptre, president of Queens' College, in verses called 'Benevolus and the Magpie'. Glynn had treated a little boy, who was too ill to travel, at his own expense and much trouble. When the child recovered, he sent his favourite magpie to Glynn as a present. Glynn diplomatically sent his thanks, and asked the boy to take care of the bird for him, which he then paid him to do.

In 1778 Glynn became involved in the controversy over the authorship of the poems said to be by Thomas Rowley, a fifteenth-century monk. The poems were 'discovered' by Thomas Chatterton, and before long it was believed by most that Chatterton had forged the poems. Chatterton committed suicide in 1770, but the controversy was still current when Glynn became convinced of the poems' authenticity. William Barrett relied credulously on material supplied by Chatterton for his *History and Antiquities of the City of Bristol* (1789), and in the preface to the work includes a Latin letter, said to have been written by Glynn, encouraging him to complete the work. On Barrett's death in 1789 the original forgeries by Chatterton were presented to Glynn, who bequeathed them to the British Museum (Add. MSS 5766, A, B, and C). At the close of his life Glynn was the acknowledged head of the medical profession in Cambridge and his medical services were highly respected at Ely, where he regularly attended every week. Late in life Glynn inherited a considerable property from a maternal uncle, and adopted the name of Clobery because of it. He died at his rooms in King's College, Cambridge, on 8 February 1800, and, according to his wishes, was buried in the vault of the college chapel by torchlight, between the hours of ten and eleven at night on 13 February, in the presence of members of the college only. A tablet to his memory was placed in the chapel, in a little oratory on the right hand after entering its south door. Though Glynn had had a large practice and lived economically, he was too generous to be rich. He left his lands in Helland to the Revd John Henry Jacob, whom he knew at King's College, and who was the son of John Jacob of Salisbury, a particular friend. The college received a legacy of £5883 6*s*. 8*d*. in stock. It was chiefly spent on some improvements, carried out between 1825 and 1830; but a prize of £20 a year, annually divided between two scholars 'for learning and regularity of conduct', was also provided. To the Revd Thomas Kerrich of Magdalene College, Cambridge, his friend and executor, he bequeathed the sum of £5000. His library was sold in 1800, and many of the books were said to abound 'with MS notes by the late learned possessor'.

W. P. Courtney, *rev.* Claire L. Nutt

Sources Munk, *Roll* • B. Hill, 'A Cambridge eccentric', *The Practitioner*, 206 (1971), 149–53 • A. Rook, 'Robert Glynn (1719–1800), physician at Cambridge', *Medical History*, 13 (1969), 251–9 • H. Rolleston, 'Some worthies of the Cambridge medical school', *Annals of Medical History*, 8 (1926), 335–6 • Nichols, *Lit. anecdotes*, 7.211–15, 520, 632; 9.687–8 • *GM*, 1st ser., 70 (1800), 276–8 • E. Brydges, *The autobiography, times, opinions, and contemporaries of Sir Egerton Brydges*, 1 (1834), 64 • G. Pryme, *Autobiographic recollections of George Pryme*, ed. A. Bayne (1870), 46 • Venn, *Alum. Cant.* • J. H. Jesse, *Memoirs of celebrated Etonians*, 2 vols. (1875) • L. Kelly, *The marvellous boy* (1971), 48–9, 55, 92

Likenesses J. Facius and G. Facius, stipple (after T. Kerrick), Wellcome L. • J. Page, line engraving (after his portrait), NPG, Wellcome L.

Wealth at death over £10,000: *DNB*

Glynne, Sir John (1603–1666), judge and politician, was born at Glynllifon, Caernarvonshire, the third son of Sir William Glynne (*b.* 1578) of Glynllifon and his wife, Jane, daughter of John Griffith of Caernarfon. The Glynnes were a long-established and prominent Caernarvonshire family yet John's elder brother Thomas Glynne was, in 1624, the first family member to sit in the House of Commons, even though his mother's antecedents had often been returned local MPs. John Glynne entered Westminster School in 1615 and subsequently matriculated at Hart Hall, Oxford, on 9 November 1621. However, as a younger son a career in the law had been designed for him and on 27 January 1621 Glynne was admitted a member of Lincoln's Inn; he was called to the bar in 1628 and was to rise to seniority as a bencher in 1641. Glynne married on 2 May 1633 at St Margaret's, Westminster, Frances (*d.* 1646), daughter of Arthur Squibb, later Clarenceux king of arms, of Henley Park, Surrey; the marriage produced two sons and five daughters, two of whom died in infancy. His second marriage, about 1647, was to Anne Lawley (*d.* 1668), widow of Sir Thomas Lawley (*d.* 1646), baronet, of Spoonhill, Shropshire, and daughter of John Manning of London, with whom he had another son and a daughter. Anne was coheir of her late brother, John Manning (*d.* 1633), of Cralle Place in Warbleton, Sussex.

Public office Glynne's first recorded experience of public office was as a commissioner of sewers for Middlesex in 1632, and in Hilary term the following year he argued his first reported case. Appointment as a Westminster JP, and as deputy steward and recorder of Westminster, followed in 1636. In 1638 he also obtained the reversion of the office of keeper of the records in common pleas. But it was the summoning of the Short Parliament of 1640 that finally brought Glynne national recognition as a lawyer and politician. Glynne was returned to this parliament both for Westminster, his settled residence, and Caernarfon Boroughs and apparently opted for the former constituency.

Sir John Glynne (1603–1666), by unknown artist, *c.*1655–60

Despite being a total newcomer to parliament his growing reputation as a lawyer, and presumably his political association with fellow MPs who led criticism of Charles's government, equipped him for a prominent role. He was appointed chairman of the committee of the whole house for the courts of justice on 16 April and the next day was added to the committee of privileges. Nomination to three other committees (for the Apparel Bill, the Ecclesiastical Courts Bill, and the general committee of grievances) came shortly afterwards. Glynne was also appointed on 24 April one of the managers of a conference with the Lords about safeguarding parliamentary privilege. His opinions and priorities were soon made plain. In the committee of privileges debate about a disputed election in Great Bedwin, Glynne supported a popular franchise, a view he was to maintain in the Long Parliament when there was a similar dispute in Tewkesbury. In the latter case he was to conclude 'that the more general the election was the freer' (D'Ewes, 138n.). He seconded the proposal to investigate the stormy end of the 1628–9 parliament, which ushered in the eleven years of Charles's personal rule, and strongly supported Pym's insistence that grievances must be redressed before the house would grant the king his urgently needed subsidies. In the 2 May debate Glynne identified these grievances as concerning religion and the property of the subject, citing ship money and coat and conduct money in the latter instance. By the end of the parliament he had identified himself as both a leading contributor to parliamentary debate and a prominent critic of the court.

Glynne was again returned MP for Westminster in elections to the Long Parliament and soon became one of its most active members sitting on, and reporting from, numerous committees concerned with a wide variety of matters, helping to draft crucial measures and actively contributing to debate. By the time of his suspension from the house in June 1647 he had been appointed to more than 800 committees, with a particularly heavy commitment in the pre-civil war period, and regularly made reports to the house. He was frequently chosen to manage conferences with the Lords, and to report on them to the Commons, and to serve on joint committees of both houses. His committee and other commitments included enquiring into the activities of papists in the capital and the operation of the laws against them; debating and helping to prepare the Subsidy Bill; denouncing the new Laudian canons for church discipline as illegal; beginning work on the indictment of Archbishop Laud for treason; and reporting on the London wine monopolists.

However, it was Glynne's role in the treason trial of the earl of Strafford in spring 1641 which brought him the most immediate recognition as a member of an inner circle of MPs who were heading the offensive against the accumulated grievances of the personal rule. He was involved at an early stage with a fellow lawyer MP, John Maynard, in the management of Strafford's impeachment, helping to prepare many of the articles against him and later assisting Pym in managing a conference with the Lords about the trial. On 13 April Glynne gave a lengthy reply at the bar of the House of Lords to the earl's closing speech in his defence, arguing that, when viewed in their entirety, Strafford's actions constituted treasonable intent. An abbreviated version of Glynne's speech was subsequently published under the title *The replication of Master Glynne … to the general answer of Thomas, earl of Strafford … to the several charges exhibited against him* (Thomason tracts, E 207/10). Working again alongside Maynard he helped secure the reading of Strafford's bill of attainder on 15 April.

On 23 April Glynne assisted in drafting the protestation oath to defend the protestant religion, parliament, and the rights and liberties of the subject. During the following summer Glynne helped investigate the second army plot against parliament, urging that the plotters be charged with treason. He was appointed to the house's committee for the recess with its extensive executive powers on 9 September. Towards the end of the year the debate on the grand remonstrance, Irish affairs (in the aftermath of the 1641 rising), the impeachment of the bishops who had protested that parliament was not free, and the campaign against the earl of Bristol and his son, Lord Digby, were some of the more important matters commanding Glynne's active attention.

During the first half of 1642 Glynne distinguished himself as one of the most active and energetic MPs and over the year as a whole he accumulated a formidable committee membership. After the king's attempted coup against the five members on 4 January, Glynne was appointed to the committee to vindicate the privileges of parliament and was subsequently named to the Commons committee which sat in the City during parliament's adjournment. The eight breaches of privilege identified by the committee in their declaration against the attempted coup were published as a speech purportedly made by Glynne (*A speech made in parliament by Mr. Glynne on Wednesday, the 5 January 1642, concerning the breaches of the privileges thereof*, Thomason tracts, E 200/3). As political tensions mounted Glynne keenly backed the Militia Bill and was added to the deputy lieutenancy for Middlesex. His support for parliament's war effort in the following June was demonstrated by a £100 subscription and the maintenance of a horse in its cavalry.

Civil war After the outbreak of war Glynne moved into a close association with those leading politicians who occupied the broad middle ground between the peace and war parties, working for a negotiated settlement with the king but maintaining military preparedness should negotiations fail. He was also a firm supporter of the earl of Essex as commander-in-chief of parliament's forces, and opposed attempts by City militants to give Sir William Waller a more independent military authority. Glynne's religious views were similarly measured and moderate: he saw little problem with a reformed episcopacy in a national church and he acted as a majority teller in July 1643 against the sequestration of St Mary-at-Lambeth from its moderate rector, Daniel Featley. Yet, nominated to the assembly of divines, by 1644 Glynne was prepared to accept a presbyterian settlement provided that any clericalist pretensions were reined in. His main practical contribution to the parliamentarian cause in the early part of the conflict was to act as the draftsman of parliamentary orders, declarations, and letters, to give legal advice, and to conduct investigations. For example, he was responsible for drawing up the April 1643 ordinance for the City's weekly assessment towards the war effort and the next month was one of those named to examine suspects implicated in Waller's plot for an alleged royalist rising in London.

After being elected recorder of London on 30 May 1643 Glynne became a familiar conveyor of messages between parliament and the City. He took the covenant on 3 October 1643. Appointed to the committee of both kingdoms in February 1644 he was named in May as one of the committeemen to treat with the Scots and subsequently became a frequent reporter of war news from the committee to the Commons. Although shortly to be identified as a political presbyterian, he incurred the wrath of the high presbyterians by helping to defeat an attempt to secure a Commons vote on 1 November 1644 recognizing presbyterian church government as being *jure divino* (divinely ordained and hence deriving its legitimacy from God). In August 1645 he also invited enmity from the future Leveller leader, John Lilburne, when he informed the house of the latter's controversial publication, *A Letter to a Friend*, and was put in charge of arrangements for Lilburne's trial.

Fall and recovery With the civil war entering its final phase, on 30 January 1646 Glynne was named to the committee given the task of drafting peace proposals to be sent to the king. The latter having surrendered to the Scots in May, in the following September Glynne was one of the joint committee charged with reaching agreement with Scots commissioners about the disposal of the king's person. He was again to become involved in negotiations with the Scots commissioners in December–January 1646–7. However, by summer 1647 he had become involved with Sir Philip Stapilton, Denzil Holles, and other leading political presbyterians at Westminster in the counter-revolutionary attempt to disband the army. As a result he was one of the eleven members impeached by the army in June 1647; in the following September he was unseated from the Commons and committed to the Tower. The charges raised against him focused in particular on his role in London helping to foment a new war, encouraging the riotous invasion of the houses on 26 July and scheming with the committee of safety and the new presbyterian-dominated city militia committee. He was released from custody by the Commons on 23 May 1648. Having been discharged from any proceedings on the vote for his impeachment he was restored to his Commons seat on 7 June in response to a petition from his Westminster constituents and once again immersed himself in committee work. Back in favour he was trusted enough to be appointed on 1 September a commissioner to negotiate terms with the king at Newport, in the Isle of Wight, and on 12 October he was made a serjeant-at-law.

Pride's Purge and the trial and execution of the king brought a renewed eclipse on Glynne's elevated career. He wisely kept away from Westminster on 6 December, thus avoiding arrest, and did not return to the house subsequently. He was replaced in July 1649 as recorder of London by the radical lawyer William Steele yet not without £300 in compensation from the City for his agreeing to relinquish the office. There was also a rare whiff of possible corruption: Glynne was accused of having concealed in 1643 jewels, plate, and furniture belonging to the Catholic royalist marquess of Worcester but investigations by the committee for advance of money cleared him of the charge. Glynne spent the next few years in relative obscurity in Lincoln's Inn, where he rented chambers, and in Caernarvonshire. In 1653 he purchased properties in Flintshire, including the castle and manor of Hawarden, which had formerly belonged to the earl of Derby, an executed royalist.

Glynne's return to favour began in May 1654 when he became the lord protector's serjeant and shortly afterwards prosecuted three men who had been conspiring to kill Cromwell. Returned for Caernarvonshire in 1654 to the first protectorate parliament he soon resumed his energetic committee work dealing with a variety of matters including the regulation of chancery and other legal reforms. After Penruddock's rising in the west Glynne conducted the trial of the rebels at Exeter in April 1655 and in the following June his valuable service was recognized with promotion to chief justice of the upper bench. In November he was added to the committee considering proposals for the readmission of the Jews, giving his judgment that there was no legal objection to their return. In the elections of 1656 to Cromwell's second parliament he was returned for both Caernarvonshire and Flintshire, eventually deciding to sit for the latter. During the life of this parliament he was nominated to fifty-two committees with a wide variety of concerns. Although no friend to the Quakers, and strongly in favour of their legal suppression, in December 1656 Glynne opposed the imposition of the death sentence for blasphemy on James Nayler and voiced concern over the legal and constitutional implications of parliament assuming a judicial role. In the following February he was responsible for the trial and conviction for treason of Miles Sindercombe, another plotter against Cromwell's life.

Glynne was one of the leading supporters of the 1657 humble petition and advice and in April was named to the committee given the task of justifying the assumption of kingship by Cromwell. At a conference with Cromwell at Whitehall, Glynne advanced seven major reasons for his acceptance of the crown beginning with the fact that kingship was known to the law, and emphasizing that it had parliamentary sanction and ancient custom on its side, while a protectorship was a new office not known to the law and would create uncertainty. Glynne's pro-monarchical views, and those of his fellow commissioners, were to be conveniently published at the Restoration in *Monarchy asserted to be the best, most ancient, and legal form of government* (*Scarce and Valuable Tracts … Lord Somers*, 6.346–71). On 10 December 1657 Glynne was called to the new second chamber, characteristically becoming a regular attender, and he sat in Richard Cromwell's upper chamber after Oliver's death. The restored Rump purged him from office but in December 1659 he resumed his seat in parliament with other secluded MPs and recommenced his committee work.

Final years At the Restoration, Glynne was returned to the Convention Parliament for Caernarvonshire but neither that county nor Flintshire would return him to the Cavalier Parliament in 1661. Nevertheless he was again made serjeant-at-law in June 1660 and in November became king's serjeant and was knighted as Sir John Glynne of Henley Park, Surrey. Higher judicial office, however, eluded him as he paid the price for his previous political record. At the king's coronation in 1661 Glynne suffered a near fatal fall from his horse and onlookers were reported to have jeered at him. As king's serjeant in June 1662 he helped prosecute his former political ally Sir Henry Vane for regicide.

Glynne died on 15 November 1666 at his house in Portugal Row in Lincoln's Inn Fields and was buried in the chancel of St Margaret's, Westminster, after an impressive funeral, the cost of which he had previously stipulated should not exceed £400. This great political survivor was believed to have made £100,000 in the last nineteen years of his life. Under his will, made on 15 August 1664 and proved on 12 January 1667, his eldest son and heir, Sir William Glynne, bt (*c*.1638–1690), was left the castle and manor of Hawarden and property at Bicester and elsewhere in Oxfordshire. The house and estate at Henley Park and property in Lincoln's Inn Fields was to come to his son John after his wife's death. Other properties in north Wales were bequeathed to his son Thomas. Clearly this was the will of a man who had prospered greatly in the world as is confirmed by the references to jewels and silver plate, expensive items of furniture and wall hangings, studies of books and a best coach and horses in addition to his landed estates and other properties. His enemies might have been ready to dismiss him as an unprincipled time-server, and he was no doubt a man of ambition ready to seize opportunities to further his career and accumulate wealth. Yet he was also a firm believer in strong and stable government, and a consistent champion of legality, during a period of exceptional political turmoil, and successive regimes were able to rely upon his skills as a lawyer and judge, a phenomenal committeeman and skilled negotiator. KEITH LINDLEY

Sources HoP, *Commons, 1640–60* [draft] • will, PRO, PROB 11/323/5 • *DNB* • *Old Westminsters*, 1.377 • *The diary of Bulstrode Whitelocke, 1605–1675*, ed. R. Spalding, British Academy, Records of Social and Economic History, new ser., 13 (1990), 124–6, 132, 155, 171, 193–4, 198–9, 205, 222, 464 • Foss, *Judges*, 6.434–40 • 'Boyd's Inhabitants of London', Society of Genealogists, London, 58778 • J. Rushworth, *Historical collections*, new edn, 8 vols. (1721–2), vol. 7, pp. 803–5, vol. 8, pp.706–7 • *The Short Parliament (1640) diary of Sir Thomas Aston*, ed. J. D. Maltby, CS, 4th ser., 35 (1988), 5, 14, 60, 126, 147, 149 • V. A. Rowe, *Sir Henry Vane the younger: a study in political and administrative history* (1970), 19, 27, 32, 73, 263, 266 • W. Scott, ed., *A collection of scarce and valuable tracts … Lord Somers*, 2nd edn, 13 vols. (1809–15), vol. 6, pp. 346–71 • *A speech made in Parliament by Mr. Glynne on Wednesday, the 5 January 1642* [Thomason tract] • *The replication of Master Glynne … to the general answer of Thomas, earl of Strafford* [Thomason tract] • *The journal of Sir Simonds D'Ewes from the beginning of the Long Parliament to the opening of the trial of the earl of Strafford*, ed. W. Notestein (1923), 138n. • GEC, *Baronetage*, 3.199 • Foster, *Alum. Oxon.*, *1500–1714*, 1.573 • *IGI* • *CSP dom.*, 1666–7, 263 • D. Underdown, *Pride's Purge: politics in the puritan revolution* (1971), 64, 69, 147 • *VCH Oxfordshire*, 6.17, 23 • *VCH Surrey*, 3.342

Likenesses portrait, *c.*1655–1660, Hawarden Castle, Flintshire [*see illus.*] • P. Caldwell, line engraving, NPG • group portrait, oils (with his family), Lincoln's Inn, London • print, NPG

Wealth at death believed to have made £100,000 in last nineteen years; estates in Surrey, Oxfordshire, Middlesex, north Wales; houses in Lincoln's Inn Fields; jewels, silver plate, library: will, 15 Aug 1664, PRO, PROB 11/323/5; HoP, *Commons*

Glynne, Sir Stephen Richard, ninth baronet (**1807–1874**), antiquary, was the eldest son of Sir Stephen Richard Glynne, eighth baronet, of Hawarden Castle, Flintshire, and Mary, daughter of Richard *Griffin, second Lord Braybrooke, of Audley End, Essex. The Glynnes were a junior branch of the Glynne family of Glynllifon, Caernarvonshire, descended from Sir John Glynne, who had purchased the sequestered Hawarden Castle and estate in 1653 from the trustees of the executed James, seventh earl of Derby. Sir John's son William (*d.* 1690) was created a baronet on 20 May 1661. Stephen Glynne was born on 22 September 1807 and succeeded as ninth baronet in 1815. He was educated at Eton College and at Christ Church, Oxford (BA 1828, MA 1831). From 1832 to 1837 he sat as a Liberal in the House of Commons as MP for Flint Boroughs, and from 1837 to 1847 as MP for Flintshire in the Conservative interest. He later stood unsuccessfully as an

Sir Stephen Richard Glynne, ninth baronet (1807–1874), by unknown photographer

independent in the 1857 election with the support of his brother-in-law W. E. Gladstone, who had married his elder sister, Catherine [*see* Gladstone, Catherine], in July 1839. He was for many years lord lieutenant of the same county, where the family estates lay.

W. E. Gladstone described Glynne as 'a man of singular refinement and of remarkable modesty' and his powers of memory as 'on the whole decidedly the most remarkable known to me of the generation and country' (*DNB*). Quiet and reserved, as a child Glynne was precocious, 'as good as a pocket peerage' in knowing the names and family details of all the members of the House of Lords; he could also list 500 Eton schoolboys in order. His maternal uncle, Thomas Grenville, encouraged a love of books. From an early age he indulged a passion for music and church architecture which continued all his life. At thirteen he was riding 20 miles or more in search of churches, and four years later on a south Wales excursion he covered 930 miles in forty-eight days during which time he inspected eighty-four churches, forty-three castles, and five cathedrals and ruined abbeys. He was considered to be 'one of the most accurate of observers' and Gladstone thought his knowledge of church architectural history was 'such as to be probably without example for extent and accuracy' (*DNB*). His manuscript notes on the architectural details and fittings of more than 5500 churches, which he inspected from 1824 until a few days before his death, are written in 106 volumes, now kept in St Deiniol's Library, Hawarden. They cover England and Wales, the Channel Islands, and a small number in Scotland and Ireland, and are particularly valuable as many of the buildings were seen and described before their Victorian restorations. Sir Stephen approved of the Gothic style and disliked the introduction of pews, galleries, and monuments. None of his notes were published during his lifetime, but an increasing number have since appeared, beginning with those on Kent churches (now missing), edited by his nephew, W. H. Gladstone, in 1877.

Glynne was a committee member, and later one of the honorary secretaries, of the Ecclesiological Society, and helped to edit the *Hand-Book of English Ecclesiology* published in 1847. He was also the first president of the Cambrian Archaeological Association founded in that year. He did not support many of his brother-in-law's Liberal policies, and was not really interested in politics. He was not an energetic or an effectual landowner, and Gladstone acquired much financial and business expertise in sorting out his estate affairs resulting from the disastrous attempt to develop the Oak Farm estate near Stourbridge, Staffordshire, in the late 1840s. Parts of the Hawarden estate had to be sold, and Glynne lived on a reduced income for many years. Hawarden Castle was closed in 1848 and only reopened four years later when Glynne, as a bachelor, made financial arrangements to share the family home with his sister and brother-in-law, whom he called 'the Great People'. Gladstone often asked his advice and opinion, especially on church appointments and particularly on the important vacancy for the bishopric of St Asaph in 1870.

Glynne collapsed and died suddenly in Shoreditch, London, on 17 June 1874, and was buried at Hawarden, where there is a memorial to him by Matthew Noble in the church. He was unmarried and the baronetcy became extinct. His will (27 September 1855) and later settlement deed (16 December 1867) left the Hawarden estate and castle to his sister's eldest son, William Henry Gladstone (1840–91). It later passed to the descendants of the Revd Stephen Gladstone (1844–1920), the second son of W. E. Gladstone. A. GEOFFREY VEYSEY

Sources A. G. Veysey, 'Sir Stephen Glynne, 1807–74', *Flintshire Historical Society Journal*, 30 (1981–2), 151–70 • *Notes on the churches of Kent*, ed. W. H. Gladstone (1877) • J. Morley, *The life of William Ewart Gladstone*, 3 vols. (1903) • Gladstone, *Diaries* • *DNB* • St Deiniol's Library, Hawarden, Glynne–Gladstone MSS

Archives Flintshire RO, Hawarden, business, family, and personal papers • Hagley Hall, letters and Worcestershire antiquarian papers • NL Wales, corresp. and papers; letters to Cambrian Archaeological Association • St Deiniol's Library, Hawarden, corresp. and papers

Likenesses G. Hayter, portrait, *c.*1832, Hawarden Castle, Flintshire • W. T. Roden, portrait, 1874, Hawarden Castle, Flintshire • G. Hayter, group portrait, oils (*The House of Commons, 1833*), NPG • M. Noble, marble effigy, Hawarden church, Flintshire • S. C. Smith, chalk drawing, V&A • photograph, Hawarden Castle, Flintshire [*see illus.*] • portrait, repro. in *Outlook*, 55 (1978)

Wealth at death under £25,000: resworn administration, Aug 1876, *CGPLA Eng. & Wales*

Goad, Charles Edward (1848–1910), cartographer and civil engineer, was born on 15 March 1848 at High Street, Camberwell, Surrey, the second son of Charles Goad, plumber, of London, and his wife, Caroline Ann (*née* Nagel). He was educated locally and became an associate of arts of the newly created University of Oxford local examinations board. He moved to Canada in 1869 and was employed until 1873 as an engineer in the construction of the Toronto, Grey, and Bruce Railway. Without formal qualifications, his 'on-the-job' training in engineering and surveying stood him in good stead. He worked for the Montreal Northern Colonial Railway in building a line from Montreal to Ottawa, and in 1876 was appointed chief engineer of the Halifax and Cape Breton Railway.

Goad's most significant work was his series of insurance surveys of cities in Canada, Great Britain, and elsewhere. In 1875 he realized that fires, which were destroying many buildings and even entire city districts, created a demand for street maps and detailed plans showing the width of streets and delimiting every building. Fire insurance companies needed to know details of construction, building materials (and hence flammability), and the exact size of buildings; the nature of the water-works system and the location of fire appliances; and the spatial concentration of policy holders so as to limit a company's losses in the event of a conflagration.

The Charles E. Goad Company was established in Montreal in 1875. With teams of surveyors he mapped streets and measured each building in detail, noting its use and room arrangement, the thickness of the walls, construction material, type of roof, and location of doors and windows. The first city to be mapped was Levis, Quebec, but insurance companies were slow to buy Goad's plans and he continued to work for the Halifax Railway. In 1881 he started a magazine, *The Insurance Society*, in which he quoted statistics to prove the high profits earned by companies which used his plans. His impressive advertising had its effect, and in 1885 he moved to Toronto. An advertisement of 1884 indicated his diversity: 'Railway Surveys, Estimates and Construction, Corporation, and Water Works, Real Estate Plans and Street Profiles, Insurance Surveys, Diagrams and Views'. Over the next decade he extended his series of large-scale insurance plans to more than 1300 places in Canada.

In 1885, with the company firmly established in Canada, Goad returned to Britain and in London opened what was to become, after his death, the company's head office. The Goad fire insurance plans were first produced for towns and cities within the British Isles in 1886, and within ten years the central parts of all the major towns and industrial districts were covered. The large-scale plans (1:3600) depict, by means of colour and symbol, impressive information on land use and building construction. London became the hub of Goad's extending international involvement with plans produced for France and Denmark, Egypt and Turkey, the West Indies, Venezuela, Chile, and South Africa. The plans contributed significantly to the development of fire insurance procedures and London's primacy in that business, and Goad's London office was strategically located at 56 Crouch Hill, near the head offices of the major London insurers, in the City.

Insights into Goad's fine organizational skills, his achievements in developing and standardizing survey, cartographic, and reprographic techniques, and his methods of gaining access to various buildings, are afforded by the company's correspondence books, in the British Library. Letters between Goad and Bram Stoker, author of *Dracula*, are revealing. In 1886 Stoker, then manager of the Lyceum Theatre in London, refused access to a Goad surveyor intent upon undertaking internal surveys and drawings of the Lyceum. Goad wrote immediately threatening the possibility of 'exorbitant insurance premiums'. Stoker quickly acquiesced and allowed the detailed internal inspection to proceed.

In 1877 Goad married Caroline Madeleine (*d.* 1941), a Montreal woman of French-Canadian extraction; they had three sons and one daughter. A man of wide interests and considerable vitality, Goad was a member of the American Society of Civil Engineers, the Canadian Society of Civil Engineers, the London chamber of commerce, the Engineers' Club of New York, a fellow of the Statistical Society of London, and a life fellow of the Imperial Institute. He used his engineering skills to drain the swamps that then characterized Toronto Island and the present park on the island owes much to his ingenuity and vision. During his later years, accompanied by his family, he would spend winters on his plan business in London and summers in Toronto.

Goad was well-built and bearded, and of above average height. He was a respected family man in Toronto and London society, an active freemason, an Anglican, and a longtime member of St Thomas's Church, Toronto. He died following a paralytic seizure at his home, 80 George Street, Toronto, on 10 June 1910 and was buried in the family vault at Mount Pleasant cemetery, Toronto. His three sons continued the London-based business that survived as an independent operation until 1974. GWYN ROWLEY

Sources R. J. Hayward, *Fire insurance plans in the national map collection / Plans d'assurance-incendie de la collection nationale de cartes et plans* (Ottawa, 1977) • G. Rowley, *British fire insurance plans* (1984) • H. J. Morgan, ed., *The Canadian men and women of the time* (1898) • 'Charles E. Goad dead', *The Globe* [Toronto] (11 June 1910), 8 • private information (2004) • b. cert.

Archives BL

Likenesses photograph, repro. in Rowley, *British fire insurance plans* (1984), vi

Wealth at death £1717 10s.: confirmation, 21 Jan 1911, *CCI*

Goad, George (*bap.* **1603**, *d.* **1671**), headmaster, was baptized on 6 November 1603 at Windsor; his father's name is unknown, but his mother was Jane (*d.* 1627x32), and he was the younger brother of Thomas *Goad (*d.* 1666). Educated at Eton College as a king's scholar from 1616 to 1620, Goad entered King's College, Cambridge, in 1620 as a scholar, graduated BA in 1624, and proceeded MA in 1627. He was a fellow of King's from 1623 to 1647, and senior proctor in the year 1637–8. He wrote Latin verses for *Ducis Eboracensis fasciae* (1633) and William Hawkins's *Varia corolla* (1634), and is described as 'a good Limner, and an excellent Scholar and Preacher' (Cole). He was chaplain to the chief justice of common pleas, Sir John Bankes, and subsequently, from 1646 to 1649, rector of Horstead and Coltishall, Norfolk. Goad returned to Eton, and was headmaster from 1647 to 1649 and also bursar. On 19 November 1648 he was elected fellow in place of the ejected John Cleaver. From 1655 he was rector of Southmere, Norfolk. At an unknown date he had married Jane Woodhall, sister of his brother Thomas's wife, Mary. She died aged thirty-four in 1657, leaving four children.

After the Restoration, Goad retained the Southmere rectory and his fellowship's legality was confirmed, despite the objection of a rival claimant, Nicholas Cordell, that Goad was 'a rich man, and a complier with the late times' (*CSP dom.*, *1660–61*, 175). Goad continued, for the years 1621–46, Thomas Hatcher's manuscript catalogue of scholars elected to King's. He died in 1671 and was buried at Eton College on 10 October. He bequeathed to his three sons, George, Christopher, and Thomas, land in Berkshire and other valuable items, and to his daughter, Jane, a £1000 portion. HUGH DE QUEHEN

Sources W. Sterry, ed., *The Eton College register, 1441–1698* (1943) • Venn, *Alum. Cant.* • W. Cole, 'George Goad', BL, Add. MS 5816, fol. 86 • parish register, Windsor (Berkshire), Society of Genealogists, London [transcript] • BL, Add. MS 33577 [will of J. Goad], fol. 39 • burials register, Eton College, Society of Genealogists, London [transcript] • *CSP dom.*, *1653–4*

Archives BL, biographical notices of members of King's College, Add. MSS 5814–5817, 5955 • Bodl. Oxf., biographical notices of members of King's College, MSS Rawl. B. 274, 276 • Bodl. Oxf., catalogue of scholars going from Eton College to King's College, Wood MS E.3

Wealth at death estate was valuable, with property at Bray, Buckinghamshire, and Eton; also valuable silver

Goad, John (**1616–1689**), headmaster and meteorologist, was born in Bishopsgate Street, London, on 15 February 1616, the son of John Goad. Educated at Merchant Taylors' School, he was then admitted to St John's College, Oxford, in 1632, graduating BA in 1636 and proceeding MA in 1640. In 1643 Goad became the vicar of St Giles', Oxford, where he performed services under cannon-fire during the parliamentary siege. On 23 June 1646 he was presented by the university to the vicarage of Yarnton, Oxfordshire, which he retained throughout the interregnum and where he tutored Anthony Wood and his brother Christopher. He proceeded BD in 1647. On 12 July 1661 he was appointed headmaster of Merchant Taylors' School, where he remained for the next twenty years.

The breadth of Goad's interests is represented in his varied writings. In addition to several printed sermons, some preached at St Paul's between 1662 and 1664, and 'A treatise concerning plagues, their natures, numbers, kinds' (destroyed in press during the great fire of London in 1666), he published *Genealogicum Latinum: a Previous Method of Dictionary of All Latin Words* (2nd edn, 1676), *Comment on the Church of England Catechism* (n.d.), 'Declamation, on whether monarchy be the best form of government' (in William Richards's *The English Orator*, 1680), and *Autodidactica, or, A Practical Vocabulary … to Attain to the Knowledge of the Latin Tongue* (1690). However, the principal interest of his life, in addition to his vocation and religion, was reflected in his *magnum opus*, *Astro-meteorologica, or, Aphorisms and discourses of the bodies coelestial, their natures and influences, discovered from the variety of the alterations of the air … collected from the observation … of thirty years* (1686). A shorter version in Latin, entitled *Astro-meteorologia sana* and anonymously edited by Edward Waple, a former pupil of Goad's, appeared posthumously in 1690.

As the last title reflects, Goad's efforts comprised a consciously Baconian programme to reform astrology by using experimental natural philosophy to save its rational and useful core, and discard its superstitious accretions. He foresaw great potential gains, not only in terms of weather prediction but indirectly for agriculture, medicine, and so on. In line with earlier as well as contemporary astrological reformers—including Goad's close friend (and fellow crypto-Catholic) John Gadbury—the most promising testing-ground, given its empirically accessible nature, seemed to be the weather. Goad's working assumption was that the planets (each with a specific and unique nature) influenced the earth's atmosphere, particularly through certain of their angular separations along the ecliptic (which again were held to be qualitatively distinct). These relationships, called 'aspects', also had the advantage of being precisely and mathematically specifiable.

Accordingly Goad began keeping a weather diary in 1652, and continued until 1685. In it he recorded observations (the majority non-quantitative, like most of those at the time) of the temperature, precipitation, and wind; he then compared these to the planetary aspects at the time, and attempted to analyse the results. In addition, between 1677 and 1689 he sent monthly weather predictions, using the same methodology, to his friend Elias Ashmole. Goad was a true Baconian, refusing to cede the weather to chance, since 'Casualty is inconsistent with Science, so inconsistent that it is not to be pleaded by any lovers of Learning' (Goad, *Astro-meteorologica*, 15). However, his attempt to arrive at decisive conclusions was defeated by the sheer complexity of weather, together with his unavoidably primitive methodological and statistical tools. As he complained to Ashmole about an unexpectedly wet day, 'Upon a quadrate of the Sun to Jupiter sometimes we hear [of] it in July, but sometimes will not make an Aphorisme' (MS Ashmole 368, fol. 303b).

The response to Goad's work was mixed. Among members of the Royal Society, who were its chief audience, Robert Hooke was unimpressed, and the approbation of Thomas Henshaw and Robert Plot was countered by Jonas Moore's citation of John Flamsteed's supposedly negative opinion, although a letter by the latter (dated 4 July 1678) states that Goad's 'conjectures I find come much nearer the truth than any I have hitherto met with' (RS, MS 243, no. 35). A review of *Astro-meteorologica* in *Acta Eruditorum* (January 1688) accused Goad of excessive ambition. In the end, notwithstanding his long labours, his uncertain results combined with the unsavoury reputation of astrology in post-Restoration England to consign them to near-oblivion.

In the furore surrounding the Popish Plot, Goad had been charged by the grand jury of London in March 1681 with writing and teaching 'certain passages savouring of popery' (Wood, *Ath. Oxon.*, 4.268) and on 13 April the Merchant Taylors' Company found him guilty. He was dismissed from his post as headmaster but awarded £70 as a recognition of past services. Goad then opened a private school in Piccadilly, which continued until shortly before his death. In 1686, taking advantage of James II's religious sympathies, he openly declared himself Catholic. He died, unmarried, in London on 28 October 1689, and was buried in the church of St Helen, Bishopsgate.

PATRICK CURRY

Sources Wood, *Ath. Oxon.*, new edn, 4.267–9, 711 • J. Goad, *Astro-meteorologica* (1686) • J. Goad, 'Diary of the weather', Bodl. Oxf., MS Ashmole 367 • J. Goad, letters, Bodl. Oxf., MS Ashmole 368 • 'Dr Goad's diary', BL, MS Sloane 1731 • P. Curry, *Prophecy and power: astrology in early modern England* (1989), 67–74 • John Flamsteed to John Goad, 4 July 1678, RS, MS 243, no. 35 • *Acta eruditorum* (Jan 1688) • *DNB*

Archives BL, weather diary, Sloane MS 1731 • Bodl. Oxf., weather diary, MS Ashmole 367 | Bodl. Oxf., letters to E. Ashmole, MS Ashmole 368

Likenesses R. White, line engraving, 1686 (aged sixty-two), BM, NPG; repro. in Goad, *Astro-meteorologica*

Goad, Roger (1538–1610), college head, was born at Horton, Buckinghamshire. He attended Eton College and took up a scholarship at King's College, Cambridge, matriculating at Michaelmas 1555. He was admitted a fellow of King's in 1558, and graduated BA in 1559/60 and MA in 1563. Ordained priest in the diocese of Ely on 29 July 1565, he took his BTh in 1568/9, and was awarded his doctorate of theology in 1576. He is reported to have been at Guildford School in 1569, perhaps as usher. Goad's wife, Katherine (*bap.* 1554), survived him, having borne at least six sons (all Cambridge alumni, including Thomas *Goade), and two daughters.

In December 1565 Goad and other fellows of King's College wrote to William Cecil to complain of the neglect of religion in their college. On 9 September 1569 Bishop Grindal wrote to Cecil, drawing attention to the continuing 'miserable state of that house, through the misgovernment of an evil provost', Philip Baker (Nicholson, 308). Baker, a Catholic sympathizer who had enriched himself at the college's expense, was deprived and fled to Louvain. The fellows' choice of successor was Roger Goad, and they wrote on 28 February 1570 commending 'his piety, prudence and equity' (Strype, *Whitgift*, 1.36). On 19 March Goad was admitted to the provostship of King's, a position he held for more than forty years.

Despite his support among the fellows Goad encountered his full share of the troubles which beset religion at Cambridge. He was one of the nine college heads who in December 1570 deprived the puritan Thomas Cartwright of his Lady Margaret professorship. The advanced protestant party were probably not impressed by Goad's own appointment to that post on 3 November 1572. By 1576 the visitor of King's, Bishop Cooper, was reporting 'many evils broken in by intestine jars' and 'sundry great and enormous disorders' at the college (Strype, *Annals*, 2/2.36–7).

Goad was accused of continuing his predecessor's religious and administrative policies, to the detriment of the college. He retorted (correctly) that he had provided for the erection of a new library and founded a Hebrew lecture, to be given by 'one Baro a Frenchman', which cost the college nothing. (The employment of this Frenchman undoubtedly became for Goad a matter of regret.)

In 1580 Goad was on the panel charged to examine members of the Family of Love imprisoned in Wisbech Castle. He may also have been the editor of a version of their *Supplication*, issued in 1606, with acidic editorial 'examinations' inserted in the text. College heads, including Goad, were expected to defend the Church of England, to which they were bound by their convictions—and by material interests. On 6 March 1577 Goad was instituted as chancellor of the diocese of Wells. On 7 March 1587 he was collated to the second prebend of Wedmore. He resigned both these positions before 23 December 1589, in favour of the prebend of St Decuman in the diocese of Bath and Wells. But Goad, and other moderate puritans in high office, though unimpeachably loyal to the established church, were anxious not to press too far the case against the advanced party within it. He was aware of dangers both from the gathering forces of counter-reformation abroad, and from conservative Anglicans. Goad was one of those appointed in 1581 to confer with the captured Jesuit Edward Campion, debating alongside William Fulke on 18 and 23 September. *A True Report of the Disputation* was published in 1583. It was also in that year that Goad, a party in Cartwright's earlier deprivation, now combined with other moderate masters to encourage their critic to undertake his *Confutation* of the Catholic New Testament, recently published in Rheims. From 1589 the drive against more radical spirits increasingly threatened the moderates' natural allies. On 27 February 1592 Goad complained to Cecil that while papists had 'grown bold and dangerous to the state, divers of the true friends and lovers of the gospel' had been treated with 'hard severity' (Strype, *Whitgift*, 3.265–6). In later controversies over doctrine a recurrent theme of Goad and his allies was the popish views and sympathies which their opponents were said to hold.

Goad was becoming increasingly involved in defending not only the established practices of the church, but also the Calvinist theology which was coming to predominate at its highest levels, and in the universities. He played a central role in the famous cases of those two Arminans *avant la lettre*, Peter Baro and William Barrett. On 29 April 1595, in a sermon at Great St Mary's, Barrett attacked Calvin openly, asserting that it was possible for the elect to fall away, and made other pronouncements alarming to orthodox predestinarians. Goad was one of those who presided in May 1595 at three long meetings with Barrett, who was eventually persuaded to sign a harshly worded retraction. But on 9 October Barrett gave a sermon which repeated some of his earlier assertions, and he probably never signed a second recantation presented by Goad.

Baro owed to Goad his first position at Cambridge, although as early as 1583 his teaching was condemned by a clandestine synod held at Goad's house in London. When the Lambeth articles arrived in Cambridge in November 1595 Goad, now vice-chancellor of the university, urged college heads to 'take knowledge and warning' of them; to 'some particular persons, of whom I doubted, as namely Dr Baro the Frenchman, I gave knowledge and caveat … that nothing should be publicly taught to the contrary' (Porter, 378–9). On 12 January 1596 at St Mary's, before several college heads and Vice-Chancellor Goad himself, Baro preached a sermon which blatantly ignored this advice. But in the absence of active support from Whitgift and Burghley, Goad could take no action against him.

The argument resurfaced in 1599, when it was the turn of John Overall, elected regius professor of divinity in 1595, to threaten the citadel of orthodoxy. Goad was again prominent in the case, heading the committee to which Vice-Chancellor Jegon referred it. It was at the provost's lodge at King's College that the first examination of Overall was conducted in early September 1599. It is clear that the argument ranged more freely than hitherto over a range of issues connected with the eternal decrees, and that Overall, a subtle disputant, sensibly prevaricated when asked to commit his views to paper. In December, Goad and Laurence Chaderton produced an extended confutation of Overall's positions, but for a time the heads shrank from further action against him. Overall's remarks early next year on the real presence of Christ in the eucharist opened a new front, and seem to have provoked Goad to a virulent assault. In a sermon in March 1600 he attacked as 'a popish opinion, that justifying grace might be lost by mortal sins', affirming that 'perpetuity of justifying grace once given, and certainty of salvation, was our freehold, and therefore in no case to be let go' (Porter, 402). In reply Overall stressed that repentance was a necessary condition of salvation: it was 'a vain fancy and dangerous presumption' for a man to think himself exempt from this. Bad-tempered exchanges during the commencement disputations on 30 June and 1 July marked the end of the affair.

In his own college, Goad's enforcement in the early years of his provostship of certain neglected college statutes had the effect of increasing the number of clerical and preaching fellows. His new library was financed partly by sale of vestments and ornaments of the old religion in the possession of King's. The regularity of lectures in philosophy and Greek was much improved, and Goad himself gave a lecture in divinity three times a week. In 1595, as vice-chancellor, he laid down a strict dress code, issuing prohibitions against the 'hurtful and unscholarly exercise' of football, fishing, and bull and bear baiting, and the practice of bathing in public. In 1594, however, the visitor Bishop Wickham reported 'most strange insolencies and immodesties' perpetrated by fellows and scholars against college officials, and other notable breaches of discipline. In spring 1602 many fellows expressed dissatisfaction with the management of college property, partly because of the meagre subsistence they received. Their petition was rejected by Goad.

In May 1603, Goad invited Bishop Chaderton to make a

new visitation. It revealed that the authorities were held in such widespread contempt that breaches of discipline had become rife: fellows were found to have taken up gambling, lent money at interest, continued in their fellowships when disentitled, and spoken publicly against the college management; the bachelors complained of over-strict imposition of petty rules and of favouritism in allocating chambers. Angry fellows and juniors decided to appeal to the king; the provost and seniors chose to inform Robert Cecil of this drastic move before it happened. Goad readied himself to ride to London, but on arrival at the college stables he discovered that two of the juniors' spokesmen had risen from their beds at 4 a.m., stolen the horses, and were well on the way to Westminster. A brief lull in hostilities then followed, but when plague appeared in Cambridge in August 1604 the authorities at King's decided to close the college: despite some provision for the fellows' loss of commons, this raised resentment to a yet higher level, and many refused for some weeks to leave. Eventually King James intervened, furious at the example that such rowdy scenes might have in Cambridge and elsewhere, and admonished the luckless Chaderton for his leniency and negligence.

Not all the charges levelled against Goad were without foundation. It had been alleged that he had improperly profited from property held in trust for the college. At about the time of his election, King's College had acquired a large new property at Sampford Courtenay in Devon where, it was said, Goad 'had the commodities for fines of copyholders for himself' (Leigh, 80). It is clear that during these years of inflation Goad rented for a fixed amount the college's farm at Grantchester and kept the profits, despite being warned against this by the visitor. One Henry Howgrave, hearing a report that Goad was soon to be made dean of Windsor, commented that the provost 'had been a thief all his life, and would now be a Dean of thieves' (Leigh, 84). For this sally he found himself discommuned, which may indicate Goad's extreme sensitivity in the matter.

Goad contributed much to King's College, especially in the early part of his provostship. In later years, however, his efforts to impose strict discipline aroused growing resentment, and he seems to have become a remote figure, lacking in sympathy for the young men of the college. Among his bequests to King's was the rectory of Milton, Cambridgeshire, to which he had been instituted in 1597. He died on 25 April 1610 and was buried in the chapel of King's College. STEPHEN WRIGHT

Sources H. C. Porter, *Reformation and reaction in Tudor Cambridge* (1958) • A. A. Leigh, *King's*, University of Cambridge College Histories (1899) • J. Strype, *Annals of the Reformation and establishment of religion … during Queen Elizabeth's happy reign*, new edn, 4 vols. (1824) • J. Strype, *The life and acts of John Whitgift*, new edn, 3 vols. (1822) • *Fasti Angl.*, 1541–1857, [Bath and Wells] • C. R. Fay, *King's College Cambridge* (1907) • P. Lake, *Moderate puritans and the English church* (1983) • P. Collinson, *The Elizabethan puritan movement* (1967) • W. Nicholson, ed., *The remains of Edmund Grindal*, Parker Society, 9 (1843) • *VCH Surrey*, 2.169 • C. W. Marsh, *The Family of Love in English society, 1550–1630*, another edn (1994) • Venn, *Alum. Cant.*

Goad, Thomas. *See* Goade, Thomas (1576–1638).

Goad, Thomas (*c.*1595–1666), jurist, was probably born at Windsor, Berkshire, and was baptized at New Windsor on 18 May 1595. His father's first name is not known; his mother was Jane Collins (*d.* 1627x32), sister of Samuel Collins, provost of King's College, Cambridge, and regius professor of divinity at Cambridge. Educated at Eton College, as were his brothers George *Goad and Christopher and several of his cousins, sons of Roger Goad, provost of King's College, Goad was admitted a scholar at King's College on 24 August 1611 and matriculated on 17 December 1611. He took the BA degree in 1613 and was admitted to Gray's Inn the same year. In 1614 he was elected to a fellowship at King's, and incorporated as MA at Oxford in 1617. He was appointed university reader in logic in 1620, proproctor in 1621, and 'poser' (an examiner) in 1623. He was senior proctor in 1629–30. He took the LLD degree in 1630 and on 7 May 1631 was admitted to full membership of Doctors' Commons and as an advocate of the court of arches. He was first bursar of King's College 1629–30, and vice-provost 1633–4. He married Mary, daughter of Edmund Woodhall of Saffron Walden, Essex, fellow of King's College 1600–03, and subsequently registrar of the prerogative court of Canterbury; she survived him. They had two daughters, Grace and Mary, who married respectively John Byng, fellow of King's College, and John Clenche.

In 1635 Goad was commissioned to hear a case in the high court of delegates, and in the same year became regius professor of civil law at Cambridge in succession to George Porter. With other leading members of the university he contributed verse to a number of collections published to mark royal occasions in the 1630s and early 1640s. He was archidiaconal official for Cambridgeshire, and is said to have been a friend of Archbishop Laud and a great sufferer at parliamentary hands during the civil war and Commonwealth, though he avoided expulsion, and died in office between 16 April and 11 June 1666, leaving his wife as executor of his will and the recipient of a life interest in his lands in New and Old Windsor. He was buried on 11 June 1666 at Grantchester, Cambridgeshire, where he also owned land. N. G. JONES

Sources B. P. Levack, *The civil lawyers in England, 1603–1641* (1973) • W. Sterry, ed., *The Eton College register, 1441–1698* (1943) • D. N. Griffiths, transcript of the register of the parish of New Windsor, 1976, Society of Genealogists • Venn, *Alum. Cant.* • protocollum books 1577–1627 and 1627–78; list of bursars; catalogue of provosts, fellows, and scholars, King's Cam. • G. D. Squibb, *Doctors' Commons: a history of the College of Advocates and Doctors of Law* (1977) • matriculations, 1544–1613; subscriptions, 1613–38; grace book E, CUL, department of manuscripts and university archives • R. Bowes, *A catalogue of books printed at or relating to the university, town and county of Cambridge from 1521 to 1893* (1894) • H. Pigot, *Hadleigh* (1860) • probate register of the Eton peculiar court, 1600–43, Eton, archives • T. Harwood, *Alumni Etonenses, or, A catalogue of the provosts and fellows of Eton College and King's College, Cambridge, from the foundation in 1443 to the year 1797* (1797) • Wood, *Ath. Oxon.: Fasti* (1815) • W. C. Metcalfe, ed., *The visitations of Essex*, 2, Harleian Society, 14 (1879) • D. Lloyd, *Memoires of the lives … of those … personages that suffered … for the protestant religion* (1668) • parish register, Grantchester, Cambs. AS, P79/1/41, 11 June1666 [burial]

Goadby, Robert (1720/21–1778), printer and bookseller, was the son of Samuel Goadby, a member of the Founders' Company in London. He had a brother, Samuel, who was probably the London stationer Samuel Goadby (1719–1808), and he had possibly two sisters, one of whom, Joanna, married William Lee on 6 January 1749. He may have been educated at Repton School: in 1740 he established a bookselling business in Wade's Passage, Bath, from where he published two translations of humorous novels by Cervantes, dedicated to his masters at Repton. By 1744 he had moved to Yeovil, where he published on 30 July 1744 the first issue of a provincial newspaper known as the *Western Flying Post, or, Yeovil Mercury*. In January 1749 Goadby and Hannah Bettison, the printer of the *Sherborne Mercury, or, Weekly Advertiser*, agreed to unite their two newspapers under a new title; the result was called the *Western Flying Post, or, Sherborne and Yeovil Mercury*, but was widely known as the *Sherborne Mercury*. In the same year, on 22 May, Goadby was freed by patrimony into the Founders' Company. Eight years later, on 4 October 1757, he transferred into the Stationers' Company and was received into the company's livery on the same day. Over the next twelve years he bound five apprentices with the company.

Goadby continued as sole printer of the new paper, on a weekly basis, until his death in 1778, by which time the distribution had extended westwards from Sherborne through the counties of Dorset, Somerset, Devon, and Cornwall with further agencies in Bristol and London. Two of the London agencies were headed by Samuel Newbery (who held shares in the *Sherborne Mercury*) and William Owen, both well-known London printers and booksellers: the acquittal of the latter in July 1752 over the publication of *The Case of Hon. Alex Murray, Esq.*, a pamphlet describing the events concerning the arrest of the Jacobite Alexander Murray in 1751, was greeted in Sherborne with general joy. A third London agency belonged to the stationer Samuel Goadby.

Goadby's house and printing office both lay in Long Street, Sherborne, and the value of the business at his death was £1000. His social standing in the town was sufficient for him to be elected in 1760 to the governing body of the town's grammar school, in which capacity he served for the statutory period of ten years. He survived the founding in 1764 of a rival paper, the *Sherborne Journal*, by William Cruttwell, and in 1765 he added to his business by opening a lending library in Cheap Street, Sherborne, with 1900 volumes. Goadby was also involved in provincial book printing, including numerous sermons and a popular work, *An Apology for the Life of Mr Bampfylde Moore Carew* (Carew was commonly called the King of the Beggars). Together with William Owen, Goadby published a list of all English and Welsh fairs as well as a book of roads. Perhaps his most notable works were his religious volumes, principally *The Illustration of the Holy Bible* (1769).

A key figure in the book trade of the west of England, Goadby was known as a man of modesty and integrity and a strong whig:

> Few men have been more generally known in the West than he was, and few had more friends or more enemies. To the freedom of his sentiments on religious and political subjects, and to the openness with which he declared them, he was indebted for both. (Nichols, *Lit. anecdotes*, 3.723)

He died at Long Street, Sherborne, on 12 August 1778 aged fifty-seven 'a victim to an atrophy' (*GM*), and was buried in the churchyard at Oborne, a village just outside Sherborne. It is not clear when and where he married his wife, Rachel, but they left no children. In his will he left the printing house, with its equipment and stock of books, to his nephew and his brother; the will also included 5 guineas for 'my old Friend Mr Owen'. As testament to his enduring interest in botany and natural history, in a codicil he left an endowment of £2 per annum for the vicar of Sherborne to preach an annual sermon on the first Sunday in May 'on the Wisdom and Goodness of God in the Works of Creation' (fol. 212*v*). His wife continued the business.

GEORGE TATHAM

Sources Nichols, *Lit. anecdotes*, 3.431–5, 723–6 • C. H. Mayo, *Bibliotheca Dorsetiensis* (1885), 74–8 • will, PRO, PROB 11/1045, sig. 357 • J. Feather, *The provincial book trade in eighteenth-century England* (1985) • *DNB* • R. Wells, *Newsplan: report of the pilot project in the south-west*, Library and Information Research Report, 38 (1986), 164–6 • J. Beard, *Unitarian Herald* (11 July 1873) • G. Tatham, 'The *Sherborne Mercury* in the eighteenth century: a regional newspaper', priv. coll. • Sun Fire Insurance policy no. 402594, GL • *GM*, 1st ser., 54 (1784), 93–5 • C. H. Timperley, *A dictionary of printers and printing* (1839), 743–4 • C. H. Timperley, *Encyclopaedia of literary and typographical anecdote*, 2nd edn (1842), 833 • GL, MS 6336/2, fol. 24*r* • H. R. Plomer and others, *A dictionary of the printers and booksellers who were at work in England, Scotland, and Ireland from 1726 to 1775* (1932), 104 • D. F. McKenzie, ed., *Stationers' Company apprentices*, [3]: 1701–1800 (1978) • *IGI*

Wealth at death £2800 in legacies; plus £25 p.a. and half clear profits of the *Sherborne Mercury* in year after death; also share in hotel, Weymouth and value of the *Sherborne Mercury* books and print materials: will, PRO, PROB 11/1045, sig. 357

Goade [Goad], **Thomas** (1576–1638), theologian, was the second son of Roger *Goad (1538–1610), provost of King's College, Cambridge, and Katherine or Katharine (*bap.* 1554), daughter of Richard Hill of London, merchant, and his wife, Elizabeth; he had at least five brothers and six sisters. Like his brothers, Goade was sent to King's sister foundation, Eton College. Between 1588 and 1592 he was first a commensal and then a king's scholar there, and continued to King's College first as a scholar, and then from 1595 as a fellow. He graduated BA in 1596, proceeded MA in 1600, was ordained priest in 1606, and proceeded BD in 1607. He served as bursar of his college from 1609 and dean of divinity in 1611. He gained a reputation as a scholar with a great breadth of learning, a historian and theologian, and a precise critic, who all his life delighted in writing poetry. According to Thomas Fuller, 'he had a *commanding* presence, an uncontrolable spirit, impatient to be opposed, and loving to steere the discourse … of all the Company he came in' (Fuller, *Worthies*, 1.159).

Goade was influenced by the strong Calvinism of his father, who in his will left him the rectory of Milton, Cambridge, with instructions that his brother Matthew should present him. In 1611 he resigned his fellowship. That year

George Abbot, who had been Roger Goad's pupil at Guildford Free School, became archbishop of Canterbury, and soon afterwards appointed Thomas as one of his chaplains. Having proceeded DD in 1615 and been admitted to Gray's Inn in 1616, Goade accumulated preferments, becoming in 1617 rector of Merstham, Surrey, and in 1618 precentor of St Paul's Cathedral, London, and rector of the archiepiscopal living of Hadleigh, Suffolk; he held both the latter appointments until his death.

In 1619, because illness prevented Bishop Joseph Hall from participating in the Synod of Dort, on Abbot's initiative Goade replaced him in the English delegation. The original records of the debates, over Calvinist and Arminian theologies of salvation, show that Goade shared Abbot's Calvinist view that Christ died only for the elect. During the 1620s he was deeply involved in anti-Arminian moves. Bishop Richard Mountague thought that Goade, with Daniel Featley, assisted by Joseph Hall and John Prideaux, had drawn up the articles against him which were presented to the 1624 parliament, and had evidently accused him of Arminianism and popery. When in 1626 Samuel Ward preached in the university church at Cambridge an extended attack on Mountague's views, Goade licensed its publication, as that of other anti-Arminian literature. These activities were accompanied by further preferment. He became prebendary of Wolverhampton in 1620, perhaps through the influence of the evangelical Bishop Thomas Morton of Coventry and Lichfield, and prebendary of Winchester in 1621 through that of Bishop Lancelot Andrewes, who regarded ability more than theology.

Goade's position in Abbot's household, which was deeply hostile to any rapprochement with Spain and especially to a royal marriage alliance, probably led him to publish anti-recusant literature. He translated works of the former Roman Catholic, Archbishop Antonio de Dominis, altering some of his inconveniently ecumenical views in the process. Goade wrote *The Dolefull Even-Song* (1623), derived from eyewitness accounts of the collapse of rooms in the French embassy where recusants were worshipping. He uses the sermon given to stress man's hardness of heart and need for forgiveness, and the preservation of many from death as a divine sign that they should turn from error to the Church of England. He contrasts the frailty of buildings with the enduring nature of human temples of the Holy Spirit, and urges readers to sorrow with rather than to judge the victims. He also appears to have edited *The Friers Chronicle* (1623), dedicated to the countess of Devonshire. This is a compendium of widely scattered and vile incidents, largely drawn from Huguenot sources, designed to blacken the Roman church. It ends with an appeal to those sheltering priests to return to the true church. He chose the theme and some of the contents of John Gee's *The Foot out of the Snare* when the latter returned to the Anglican church from Roman Catholicism. He also participated in debates with Jesuits, like that with John Fisher in 1623. He continued to add to his preferments, acquiring in 1623 Black Notley, Essex, through the patronage of Sir John Leveson, with licence to hold it in plurality for life. He was twice proctor for Cambridge in the Canterbury provincial convocation, and in 1625 was prolocutor of the lower house.

About 1627 Goade took up residence at Hadleigh, and perhaps wrote there *Stimulus orthodoxus: a disputation concerning necessity and contingency in the world, in respect of God's eternal decree*, not published until 1661. In it he argues that to believe God predestinates everything is fatalistic, and makes God the author of sin. He has ordered the world so that all animate creatures have freedom of action, and eternally foreknows the consequences. Thus nothing happens accidentally. God ensures, by influencing people's hearts, only that important events happen by necessity, so that the overall effect reflects His mercy and justice. Nevertheless, Goade does not hold 'the proud Error concerning *Free-will*' (p. 19), because he sees some events as both contingent upon and the result of God's special decision. Free will and grace are both essential to moral good.

Though such views are compatible with those expressed at Dort, they can be interpreted as closer to Arminianism than to Calvinism, as Bishop Laurence Womack appears to have thought in publishing them after the Restoration. Perhaps they explain why in October 1633 Archbishop William Laud made Goade, jointly with John Barkham, rural dean of Bocking. Probably Goade's decoration of Hadleigh church and rectory with wall-paintings and mottoes was a concession to Laud's beauty of holiness policy, and helps explain why he became an ecclesiastical commissioner in December 1633, and a prebendary of Canterbury in 1636. In this year he was a commissioner for Bishop Matthew Wren's visitation of Norwich diocese. He referred distastefully to the puritan tribe, and at Bury St Edmunds enforced the use of the prayer book by hitherto notable nonconformists, removed a huge reading-desk obscuring the chancel, and recommended the railing of what he called the altar. Thus he was going beyond an insistence on the legal liturgical position, and tending to ceremonial Arminianism. He established a library in the former south chapel of Hadleigh church, and the name, though not the books, survived ninety years later. It is uncertain if Goade married, but neither wife nor child survived him. He died at Hadleigh on 8 August 1638 and was buried next day in the chancel. He left an endowment for library books for King's College, and legacies to many relatives, but chiefly to his beloved brother Matthew. ELIZABETH ALLEN

Sources W. Sterry, ed., *The Eton College register, 1441–1698* (1943), 140–1 • N. Tyacke, *Anti-Calvinists: the rise of English Arminianism, c.1590–1640* (1987), 47, 92, 96–9, 148–9 • *DNB* • will, BL, Add. MS 19088, fols. 75r–75v, 167 • M. C. Questier, 'John Gee, Archbishop Abbot, and the use of converts from Rome in Jacobean anti-Catholicism', *Recusant History*, 21 (1992–3), 347–60, esp. 350–51 • Fuller, *Worthies* (1662), 1.159 • Bodl. Oxf., MS Tanner 68, fols. 45–45v • PRO, PROB 11/116, fols. 134B, 135A • K. Fincham, *Prelate as pastor: the episcopate of James I* (1990), 198, 253–63 • PRO, SP 105/95, fol. 48v • H. Pigot, *Hadleigh* (1860), 166–76 • Venn, *Alum. Cant.* • D. MacCulloch, *Thomas Cranmer: a life* (1996), 109–10 • R. Newcourt, *Repertorium ecclesiasticum parochiale Londinense*, 2 (1710), 443

Wealth at death landowner: will, BL, Add. MS 19088, fols. 75r–75v; PRO, PROB 11/116, fols. 134B, 135A

Gobat, Samuel (1799–1879), bishop in Jerusalem, was born on 26 January 1799 in Crémine, near Moutier, in the canton of Bern, Switzerland (at that time under French rule; today known as Canton Jura), the son of David Gobat, farmer, and his wife, Susanne. Gobat himself acknowledged that in his early years his 'heart was full of the love of the vanities of the world' and that he spent his time in 'frivolities, especially in card-playing' (Thiersch and Gobat, 9–10). Not until he was nineteen did he decide to change direction, and in 1821 he entered the renowned missionary seminary in Basle, the Basler-Mission. He remained there for two years, and in 1824 was sent to Paris for oriental studies, particularly Arabic. In 1825 he went to England, entered into the service of the Church Missionary Society (CMS), and spent nine months in the society's missionary college at Islington (at this time many emissaries of the German and Swiss missionary societies joined the more wealthy British mission societies).

In the following year Gobat embarked on an evangelical mission among the people of Ethiopia but on arrival in Egypt he found that no foreigners were permitted to enter Ethiopia. He remained in Egypt for three years, acquiring a mastery of spoken Arabic and Amharic. Only in October 1829 did he finally arrive in Ethiopia, where he worked until January 1833, and then returned to England. On 23 May 1834, he married Maria Christine Régine (1813–1879), daughter of the renowned German missionary Christian Heinrich Zeller (1779–1860), of Beuggen, in Baden. Maria gave birth to five sons and five daughters.

On his second visit to Ethiopia, which began in June 1834, Gobat contracted a form of chronic dysentery and was confined to his bed for two years. At length he was forced to return home, and left Ethiopia in September 1836. His recovery was effected in Switzerland, Germany, and England from the beginning of 1837 until 1839. He was then posted under the CMS in Malta. He remained on the island, engaged in revising the Arabic Bible until 1842 and from then to 1845 lived in Switzerland and Germany, working for the society. In summer 1845 he spent three months in London, and in August was ordained deacon by Bishop Blomfield, of London. This allowed him to accept nomination as vice-principal of the new protestant college in Malta established by the CMS for the benefit of youth in the Levant.

In the meantime (1841) Britain and Prussia had established the joint protestant bishopric in Jerusalem to improve the condition of protestants in the Holy Land. The first bishop, nominated by Queen Victoria, was the converted rabbi Michael Solomon Alexander, who died in December 1845. Friedrich Wilhelm IV, king of Prussia, called on Gobat (according to the guiding principles of the bishopric) to fill the vacant see, thanks to the reputation that Gobat had already achieved as an outstanding missionary to the East. At the beginning of July 1846 he was ordained priest at Fulham, and on 5 July, at Lambeth, he was consecrated bishop of the Church of England and Ireland in Jerusalem by the archbishop of Canterbury. The new bishop arrived in Jaffa on Christmas eve 1846, on board the steamer *Hecla*, and entered Jerusalem on 30 December.

In his new position Gobat gradually changed the mandate given to the bishop, which was 'directed to the conversion of the Jews, to their protection, and to their useful employment' (*Statement of Proceedings Relating to the Establishment of a Bishopric … in Jerusalem*, 1841, 7). As an emissary of the CMS, which did not operate among the Jews, he shifted his efforts mainly to the 'wise and to the ignorant, Greeks [Orthodox], Romanists [Catholics], Armenians, Turks [Muslims], &c' (Thiersch and Gobat, 216). Thus, in the words of his numerous opponents, practising 'unheard Christian mission among Christians'. He concentrated his efforts on setting up a network of educational institutions throughout Palestine that were intended for the Christian Arab population, especially that of the dominating Greek Orthodox community. Thousands of Christian Arab members of the eastern churches, as well as a few Muslims and Jews, were educated in these fine institutions. This fact forced Gobat's opponents, especially the heads of the orthodox church in Palestine, to establish schools of their own alongside his institutions.

Besides his own efforts among the local Christian Arab population Gobat encouraged and even initiated the work of other protestant institutions in Palestine. The first institution that hastened to take advantage of his appointment to Jerusalem, as early as September 1846, was the Basle Pilgrim Mission of St Chrischona. In April 1851 the Deaconess Sisterhood of Kaiserswerth (near Düsseldorf) followed suit and began its activities in Palestine, on Gobat's initiative. But above all else Gobat did much to help the Church Missionary Society in the Holy Land. He proposed that the society make Palestine the springboard for its activities in the East, and during the 1870s, towards the end of his term of office, he gradually began to transfer his educational institutions around the country into CMS hands. During his thirty-three years in office, thanks to his strong character and outstanding talent, he deeply influenced the development of nineteenth-century Palestine.

In his eightieth year Gobat visited his family and friends in Europe for the last time. In September 1878, during his stay in Switzerland, he suffered a slight attack of apoplexy and returned in December to Jerusalem, where he wanted to die. On Easter day 1879 his illness entered a new phase, and on 11 May he died. He was buried under an olive tree in the protestant cemetery (which he had helped to acquire in 1848) on Mount Zion. His wife, Maria, died three months later and was buried alongside him. His daughters Dora (and her husband, Heinrich Rappard), Maria (and her husband, Paul Kober), and Hanna (and her husband, Johannes Zeller) later themselves became prominent for their missionary work in Palestine as well as in Basle.

YARON PERRY

Sources H. W. J. Thiersch and S. Gobat, *Samuel Gobat, bishop of Jerusalem: his life and work* (1884) • A. Carmel, *Christen als Pioniere im Heiligen Land: ein Beitrag zur Geschichte der Pilgermission und des Wiederaufbaus Palästinas im 19. Jahrhundert* (Basel, 1981) • Y. Perry,

British mission to the Jews in nineteenth-century Palestine (2002) • State Archive of the Canton of Basle (Staatsarchiv des Kantons Basel-Stadt), Gobat MSS, private archive 653 [C. F. Spittler archive] • U. Birm. L., special collections department, Church Missionary Society archive, Gobat MSS, Africa (Group 3) Mission, Mediterranean and Palestine, C M/O 28/1-115 • A. Kober, *Samuel Gobat: vom Juradorf nach Jerusalem* (Basel, 1968) • E. Veiel-Rappard, *Mutter: Bilder aus dem Leben von Dora Rappard-Gobat* (Giessen und Basel, 1925) • M. Kober-Gobat, *Skizzen aus meiner Jugendzeit* (Basel, 1917) • E. Stock, *The history of the Church Missionary Society: its environment, its men and its work*, 3 vols. (1899) • [H. Abeken], *The protestant bishopric in Jerusalem: its origin and progress. From the official documents published by command of His Majesty the King of Prussia and from other authentic sources* (1847)

Archives Bodl. Oxf., corresp. and papers • LPL, corresp. and papers • State Archive of the Canton of Basle, Spittler archive, papers, private archive 653 • U. Birm. L., corresp. and papers | BL, letters to Lord Strathnairn, Add. MS 42798 • LPL, corresp. with A. C. Tait

Likenesses drawing, repro. in Thiersch and Gobat, *Samuel Gobat*

Wealth at death under £8000 in England: probate, 18 Feb 1880, *CGPLA Eng. & Wales*

Gobbán Sáer (*supp. fl.* **7th cent.**). *See under* Mo Ling (*d.* 697).

Gobnait (*fl.* **6th cent.**?). *See under* Munster, saints of (*act. c.*450–*c.*700).

Godber, Frederick, Baron Godber (**1888–1976**), petroleum executive, was born in London on 6 November 1888, the third son and youngest of the five children of Edward Godber, carpenter, of Camberwell, and his wife, Marion Louise Peach. He attended the local school and left at the age of fifteen, when he joined the Asiatic (later Shell) Petroleum Company in March 1904 as a clerk.

In 1906–7 Godber was fortunate to be a member of the small secretarial group under G. S. Engle while the long and complex negotiations were under way for the merger in 1907 of Shell Transport and Trading Company and Royal Dutch Petroleum. From 1912 to 1919 he was head of the newly formed American department, looking after the rapidly growing involvement in the western hemisphere. He spent the years 1919 to 1929 in the USA, and in 1922 was appointed president of Roxana Petroleum, a Royal Dutch–Shell subsidiary company, in St Louis. In this position he was intimately involved in the detailed negotiations which resulted in the acquisition of the Union Oil Corporation of Delaware and the creation of Shell Union Corporation, the predecessor of Shell Oil and the foundation of Shell's fortunes in the USA.

Godber was recalled to London in 1929 to become a managing director of the Royal Dutch–Shell Group in one of its principal operating companies. From then until the outbreak of war he travelled widely to visit all parts of Shell's steadily expanding empire throughout the world. During the Second World War he was chairman of the overseas supply committee of the Petroleum Board. This committee, composed of senior executives of international oil companies, co-ordinated supplies of petroleum from all sources to all war fronts and also dealt with home-country needs. Godber's wide contacts in both Britain and the USA, together with his capacity for getting on

Frederick Godber, Baron Godber (1888–1976), by Walter Bird

with people, enabled him to weld it into a very effective instrument. For this and other war work he was knighted in 1942.

After the war Godber succeeded, in 1946, to the chairmanship of the Shell Transport and Trading Company, following the retirement of the second Viscount Bearsted. While this relieved him of detailed day-to-day involvement in company activities, he turned himself wholeheartedly to raising money for relief work in the Netherlands, as chairman of the Help Holland Fund. For this and other services to Anglo-Dutch relations he was created in 1947 a grand officer of the Order of Orange Nassau. In 1946 he also became chairman of Shell Petroleum Company Ltd.

Godber's career spanned the period in which two small, relatively unknown, companies, mainly engaged in producing and selling oil in the Far East, merged and developed into a worldwide corporation. In the post-war years he played an important part in reconstructing the group's affairs, expanding its activities, and modifying them to cope with the new nationalism in large producing countries. Unlike Sir William Fraser, his opposite number at British Petroleum, Godber maintained excellent relationships with Whitehall. Shell's efficiency and success under his chairmanship was symbolized not only by its well-known petrol station logo, but also by Shell Centre, a corporate headquarters building constructed on London's South Bank. He retired in 1961 from both the chairmanships he held at Shell, having served the group for fifty-seven years, but he continued until 1968 as chairman of the Commonwealth Development Finance Corporation, which he had served since 1953.

To all the tasks he faced Godber brought to bear a formidable battery of intelligence, appetite for work, prodigious memory, and a talent for dealing with people. He had a tall, erect figure, a kindly smile, and an invariably courteous manner. In his private life at Cranesden in Mayfield, Sussex, he farmed and was a keen gardener. Godber was raised to the peerage as Baron Godber in 1956. He was also an honorary bencher of the Middle Temple (1954), Cadman medallist (1957), a trustee of Churchill College, Cambridge (1958), an honorary liveryman of the Leathersellers' Company (1962), and an honorary fellow of the Institute of Petroleum (1965). He married in 1914 Violet Ethel Beatrice, daughter of George Lovesy, chartered accountant, of Cheltenham. They had two daughters. Godber died at his home in Mayfield on 10 April 1976 and the barony became extinct. DAVID BARRAN, *rev.*

Sources V. Rady, 'Godber, Frederick', *DBB* • private information (1986) • J. H. Bamberg, *The history of the British Petroleum Company*, 2: *The Anglo-Iranian years, 1928–1954* (1994), 327 • *The Times* (12 April 1976), 16g • *Shell Magazine*, 34 (1954), 92 • *Shell World*, 4 (1976), 27
Archives Shell Archives, London
Likenesses W. Bird, photograph, NPG [*see illus.*] • J. Gunn, portrait, Shell Centre, London
Wealth at death £982,437: probate, 7 June 1976, *CGPLA Eng. & Wales*

Godber, Joseph Bradshaw, Baron Godber of Willington (1914–1980), politician, was born at Willington Manor, Bedfordshire, on 17 March 1914, the son of Isaac Godber (*d.* 1957), a farmer, and his wife, Bessie Maud, *née* Chapman. He had two distinguished brothers: Sir George Edward Godber (*b.* 1908), a physician, who became chief medical officer to three government departments, and Geoffrey Chapman Godber (*b.* 1912), a solicitor, who became chief executive of West Sussex county council. His family ran a thriving horticultural business and, after attending Bedford School, Godber joined the firm in 1932. But the energetic young man needed more to occupy him; he was active in the National Farmers' Union, and in 1946 was elected to Bedfordshire county council. He had married on 17 April 1936 Miriam (*b.* 1910/11), the daughter of Haydn Arnold Sanders, captain in the Royal Navy, also of Willington; they had two sons.

With a practical background in small business and obvious negotiating skills, Godber was an ideal recruit for the post-war Conservative Party. At his first attempt, in 1951, he was elected for parliament. The only surprise was that he strayed outside his home county, winning Grantham in Lincolnshire for the Conservatives. He held the seat until 1979. He kept up his work for the family firm until he became joint parliamentary secretary to the ministry of agriculture in 1957. For the two previous years he had been an assistant government whip.

Godber remained at agriculture until October 1960, when he became an under-secretary at the Foreign Office. The foreign secretary, Lord Home, had noted his qualities, and in June 1961 Godber was promoted to minister of state. In this capacity he played a prominent role in the negotiations at Geneva which led to the 1963 nuclear test ban treaty. Although Godber received little public credit, he was active in seeking a compromise with the Russian delegation. His achievements were recognized by a further promotion in June 1963, when he became secretary of state for war (outside the cabinet).

In October 1963, when Home became prime minister, Godber was well placed for further preferment, his unblemished reputation being an additional recommendation in the aftermath of the Profumo affair. Having proved both able and adaptable, he was moved to the Ministry of Labour to tackle the increasingly restive trade unions. Since this was becoming a key post it was surprising that Godber was not given a place in the cabinet, unlike his successor John Hare. If this reduced status were not a sufficient handicap, Godber was denied the time to make a mark; the government fell only a year after his appointment. In that time he had tried to conciliate the unions, without noticeable success, though the government refused union demands to reverse the *Rookes* v. *Barnard* judgment which undermined their legal immunities. Industrial unrest in 1964 was persistent rather than seriously disruptive; yet this was a poor return for recent government attempts to foster a constructive relationship with the unions. Sensing that the government was weak on industrial relations, Harold Wilson tried to make political capital out of Godber's discomfort. Before the general election of 1964 he was forced to deny Wilson's claim that Conservative businessmen were deliberately provoking strikes in the hope of discrediting the opposition.

When Edward Heath succeeded Home as leader in 1965, Godber remained on the front bench, but he was moved back to agriculture. He maintained his interest in union policy, but the initiative passed to more vigorous spokesmen. While Godber worked on the premise that reasonable people could always reach a compromise, it was now felt that union power would have to be restrained under a new legal framework. When the Conservatives returned to office in 1970, Godber was asked to undertake a second stint as minister of state at the Foreign Office, an appointment which reunited him with Alec Home. Only in 1972 did he finally reach the cabinet as secretary of state for agriculture, just before Britain joined the European Economic Community. He could not cajole his colleagues into reforming the common agricultural policy, but the bulk of the negotiations had already been completed by Geoffrey Rippon. Godber did set out British proposals for change, but he was unfairly criticized through his association with an unpopular policy.

This was an unfortunate end to a notable political career. Godber had never been a candidate for the highest offices; indeed, he had climbed far higher than he had expected. He was a quiet, unobtrusive, self-effacing man; his single quirk—a refusal to wear socks for many years—attracted some notice only because in other respects he was so conventional. As a speaker he was regarded as rather dull and matter-of-fact. After the general election of February 1974 Godber resumed his business career, taking several directorships. He was made a life peer in July 1979 after the general election of that year, but he was given little chance to give the Lords the benefit of his long and varied experience because he died of a heart attack at his home, Willington Manor, on 25 August 1980.

MARK GARNETT

Sources *The Times* (30 Aug 1980) • *WWW* • b. cert. • m. cert. • d. cert. • J. Ramsden, *The winds of change: Macmillan to Heath, 1957–1975* (1996) • J. Campbell, *Edward Heath: a biography* (1993) • W. D. Rubinstein, *The biographical dictionary of life peers* (1991)
Likenesses M. Lawn, photograph, 1972, NPG
Wealth at death £195,126: probate, 19 Feb 1981, *CGPLA Eng. & Wales*

Godbolt, John (*bap.* **1583?**, *d.* **1648**), judge and law reporter, was probably baptized at Tannington, Suffolk, on 21 July 1583, the son of Thomas Godbold (*d.* 1622) and his wife, Agnes. After a brief period at Barnard's Inn he was admitted to Gray's Inn in November 1605. He was called to the bar in 1611, elected a member of the Grand Company in 1622, and was appointed reader in 1627. By 1632 he was recorder of Bury St Edmunds. In 1635 he was executor to the deceased Gray's Inn preacher Richard Sibbes. Godbolt was a capable lawyer and he was created serjeant-at-law in 1637 and the following year he became chief justice of the Isle of Ely. He represented Bury St Edmunds in the Short Parliament of 1640. In 1647 he rode the western circuit with Henry Rolle and the same year he was made a judge of common pleas, but he held office for only one year. He died at his house in St Andrew's, Holborn, London, on 3 August 1648, and was survived by his wife, Dorothy.

Like many contemporary lawyers he had reported cases, and his notes were used by fellow lawyers. The *Reports of certain cases, arising in the severall courts of record at Westminster, in the raignes of Q. Elizabeth, K. James, and the late K. Charles, collected by very good hands, and lately reviewed by Justice Godbolt*, published in his name in 1652, were not of his making, although he may have been responsible for collecting and editing them.

DAVID IBBETSON

Sources J. Foster, *The register of admissions to Gray's Inn, 1521–1889, together with the register of marriages in Gray's Inn chapel, 1695–1754* (privately printed, London, 1889) • R. J. Fletcher, ed., *The pension book of Gray's Inn*, 1 (1901) • *N&Q*, 7th ser., 2 (1886), 182 • Baker, *Serjeants* • Sainty, *Judges* • *The obituary of Richard Smyth … being a catalogue of all such persons as he knew in their life*, ed. H. Ellis, CS, 44 (1849) • F. Crisp, *Registers of Tannington, Suffolk* (1884) • *Members of parliament: return to two orders of the honorable the House of Commons*, House of Commons, 2 vols. (1878) • M. E. Allen, ed., *Wills of the archdeaconry of Suffolk, 1625–1626* (1995) • PRO, PROB 6/24, fol. 95*v* • J. S. Cockburn, *A history of English assizes, 1558–1714* (1972) • W. R. Prest, *The rise of the barristers: a social history of the English bar, 1590–1640* (1986) • ER

Godby, James (*fl.* **1790–1815**), printmaker, worked in London in the early part of the nineteenth century. In 1800 his address was 25 Norfolk Street, London. Apart from his work little is known of his life. Simply signed 'Godby Sculp', his first engraving is a portrait of Edward Snape (1791) after William Whitby. Between 1799 and 1800, this was followed by two atlas-sized biblical subjects after Henry Singleton's *Adam Bearing the Wounded Body of Abel* and the *Departure of Cain*. Godby specialized in stipple engraving and favoured the subjects of mythology, sentimental literary genre, and female portraiture that were invariably associated with this medium. He engraved after old masters and work by his contemporaries. He was also competent in the crayon manner and aquatint and frequently worked in conjunction with the publisher Edward Orme. Along with Swaine and Vivares, Godby was one of the team of engravers to work on Orme's eye-catching and novel *Essay on Transparent Prints and on Transparencies in General* (1807), a gimmicky volume of designs for stained-glass window cut-outs. Godby also provided stipple engravings for Orme's commercially led *Graphic History of the Life, Exploits and Death of Horatio Nelson* (1806); notably, he engraved a coloured aquatint view of Nelson's funeral procession after the design of W. M. Craig. Godby's ambitious and confident nature can be judged from his engraving in 1812 of a version of Raphael's *Miraculous Draft of Fishes*. But at the same time he also worked on a modest scale for publications such as the *Literary Magazine* and *The Fine Arts of the English School*.

L. H. CUST, *rev.* LUCY PELTZ

Sources A. W. Tuer, *Bartolozzi and his works*, 2nd edn (1885) • Redgrave, *Artists* • T. Dodd, 'Memoirs of English engravers, 1550–1800', BL, Add. MS 33/401

Goddard, Arabella (**1836–1922**). *See under* Davison, James William (1813–1885).

Goddard, Charles (**1769/70–1848**), Church of England clergyman, was born in Westminster, the son of Charles Goddard, though rumour attributed his paternity to Charles Lloyd, secretary to Lord Grenville. He was educated at Christ Church, Oxford, where he matriculated in November 1787 aged seventeen. He left Oxford in the summer of 1789 without taking a degree. In August 1789 he was appointed to a clerkship in the Home Office, which he held until October 1794, and he became personal secretary and précis writer to Grenville, the home secretary. When Grenville was foreign secretary, Goddard, as the minister's protégé, was made collector and transmitter of state papers in that department, with a salary of £500, and subsequently received a pension of £850 a year when he relinquished the office. He served as a midshipman at the battle of Trafalgar, was later a prisoner in France, and was freed through the influence of Charles James Fox.

About 1813 Goddard was ordained and served for seven years as curate of Hitcham, Buckinghamshire, where Joseph Goodall, the headmaster of Eton College, was rector. As a curate he established district committees at High Wycombe and Aylesbury of the Society for Promoting Christian Knowledge (SPCK), and supported the National Society for Promoting the Education of the Poor in the Principles of the Established Church, the Society for the Propagation of the Gospel, and the Incorporated Church Building Society. In 1814 Sir George Pretyman-Tomline, the bishop of Lincoln, made him prebendary of Louth in Lincoln Cathedral, and further promoted him to the archdeaconry of Lincoln (1817). He was additionally presented by Bishop Howley of London to the rectory of St James Garlickhythe, London, in 1821. In that year he received an

Oxford MA by decree and proceeded BD and DD. He delivered the Bampton lectures at Oxford in 1823, later published as *The Mental Condition Necessary to a due Inquiry into Religious Evidence* (1824). Although a pluralist (see J. Wade, *The Extraordinary Black Book*, 1832, 107) who owed his advancement to the notorious nepotist Pretyman-Tomline, he was a conscientious clergyman associated with the Hackney Phalanx, the reformist circle of traditional high-churchmen.

Goddard was an energetic archdeacon. Between 1817 and 1822 he visited about 400 of the 516 parishes in his archdeaconry. His visitations were rigorous. At Leake in 1820 he ordered all the bells to be rung to test their soundness, causing the parish clerk to comment, 'Archdeacon you call him. I think he is the Archdevil' (letter from Dr Parkinson of Ravendale; Binnall, 158–9). Where he found a dilapidated church he required the churchwardens to summon a vestry to levy a rate to pay for repairs. If they refused he threatened legal action. He encouraged the establishment of clerical lending libraries at each visitation centre in his archdeaconry, conducted on the basis of the rules for such libraries drawn up by Thomas Bray, one of the founders of the SPCK. On financial grounds he ceased to undertake further routine visitations in 1827; his archdeaconry was worth only £30 a year and his prebend £14.

Goddard worked closely with John Kaye, bishop of Lincoln from 1827. He urged Kaye to reintroduce rural deans into the diocese and recommended as candidates competent, locally respected, resident incumbents whose ecclesiastical opinions conformed to his own. He saw non-residence as the great evil in the church, although he recognized pluralism as an economic necessity for many clergy. In his 1833 charge to the clergy in his archdeaconry he admitted the need to augment benefice incomes, and in his 1836 charge supported the ecclesiastical commissioners' policy, which he had previously opposed, of diverting cathedral endowments to this purpose, acknowledging parliament's moral right to redistribute endowments intended for public objects. But he criticized the Church Discipline Bill of 1839 for interfering with bishops' spiritual jurisdiction, and opposed proposals for government inspection of church schools.

In 1844 Goddard resigned the archdeaconry and accepted the subdeanery of Lincoln Cathedral in order to allow the establishment of a new canonry under the Dean and Chapter Act (1840) linked to the archdeaconry and thus provide an adequate income for future archdeacons. In 1836 he had exchanged his London rectory for that of Ibstock, Leicestershire. He died at Ibstock on 21 January 1848 aged seventy-eight and was buried there. He had intended that his charges, beginning with the second (published in 1819), should provide his clergy with a manual of ecclesiastical discipline and clerical duty, but he did not complete the task. W. M. Jacob

Sources P. B. G. Binnall, 'A formidable archdeacon', *Lincoln Diocesan Magazine*, 79 (1963), 158–9 • *GM*, 2nd ser., 29 (1848), 555 • Foster, *Alum. Oxon.* • F. Knight, *The nineteenth-century church and English society* (1995) • D. M. Thompson, 'Historical survey, 1750–1949', *A history of Lincoln Minster*, ed. D. Owen (1994), 210–318 • *Letters and correspondence of John Henry Newman during his life in the English church*, ed. A. Mozley, 2 vols. (1891) • BL, Peel MSS, Add. MS 40417, fols. 235–7 • P. Jupp, *Lord Grenville, 1759–1834* (1985) • J. C. Sainty, ed., *Home office officials, 1782–1870* (1975) • J. M. Collinge, ed., *Office-holders in modern Britain*, 8: *Foreign office officials, 1782–1870* (1979)

Archives BL, corresp. with Lord Grenville, Add. MSS 58981–58982, 69045

Goddard, George Bouverie (1832–1886), sporting and animal painter, was born at Salisbury on 25 December 1832. When he was only ten his drawings were in demand as the products of youthful genius, yet he received no artistic training, and it was in the face of much opposition that he adopted art as a profession. He moved to London in 1849 and settled near the zoological gardens, where he spent upwards of two years making studies of animal life. During this time he supported himself mainly by drawing on wood sporting subjects for *Punch* and other illustrated periodicals. He returned to Salisbury in 1851, where his work was warmly supported by the county gentry, who gave him many valuable commissions. He nevertheless found this sphere of work too limiting and he returned to London in 1857. Goddard began to exhibit at the Royal Academy in 1856, sending a painting of hunters, but his first work of note was *The Tournament* in 1870. This was followed in 1872 by *Sale of New Forest Ponies at Lyndhurst*, and in 1875 he exhibited the picture by which he was best known, a 14 foot long canvas representing Lord Wolverton's bloodhounds. This was praised in the hunting enthusiast Whyte-Melville's *Riding Recollections* as a 'spirited and truly artistic' painting. It depicted the hounds 'in chase, sweeping like a whirlwind over the downs … One could almost fancy, standing opposite this masterpiece, that one heard the cry' (Whyte-Melville, 205). It was followed in 1876 by *Colt-Hunting in the New Forest*, in 1877 by *The Fall of Man*, from Milton's *Paradise Lost*, and in 1879 by *The Struggle for Existence*, now in the Walker Fine Art Gallery in Liverpool. In 1881 he sent to the Royal Academy *Rescued*; in 1883 *Love and War: in the Abbotsbury Swannery*; and in 1885 *Cowed!*

Goddard was a lover of all field sports, and equally at home in the covert and the hunting field. He died at the early age of fifty-three at his residence at 37 Brook Green, Hammersmith, London, on 6 March 1886, after a very short illness, from a chill caught during a visit to his dying father, whom he survived only by a few hours. His son James Arthur Goddard, a banker's clerk, also of 37 Brook Green, was his executor; nothing is known of James's mother. R. E. Graves, *rev.* Mark Pottle

Sources *Art Journal*, new ser., 6 (1886), 158 • *The Times* (18 March 1886) • *The Times* (29 March 1886) • J. Johnson and A. Greutzner, *The dictionary of British artists, 1880–1940* (1976), vol. 5 of *Dictionary of British art* • Mallalieu, *Watercolour artists*, vol. 1 • S. H. Pavière, *A dictionary of British sporting painters* (1965) • G. J. Whyte-Melville, *Riding recollections* (1985) • *The exhibition of the Royal Academy* (1856–86) [exhibition catalogues] • *CGPLA Eng. & Wales* (1886)

Wealth at death £939 13*s*. 1*d*.: administration, 2 April 1886, *CGPLA Eng. & Wales*

Goddard, Guybon (1612–1671), lawyer and parliamentary diarist, was the only son of Thomas Goddard of Stanhoe and his wife, Mary, daughter of William Guybon of Watlington; both families were of long standing in Norfolk. He matriculated at Peterhouse, Cambridge, in 1629, entered Lincoln's Inn on 5 February 1631 (by which time his father had died), and was called to the bar in 1639. In 1642 Goddard married Mary, daughter of John Greene, serjeant-at-law, a match that brought him useful connections, notably with Edward Bysshe, who was appointed Garter king of arms by parliament in 1646.

In pursuit of a professional legal career Goddard was prominent in the affairs of King's Lynn over three decades—freeman in 1645, deputy recorder from 1645 to 1651, and then recorder (succeeding Miles Corbet) until the Restoration. In 1656 he secured from the protector a new charter for the borough. During the 1650s he sat on various commissions, including the commission for the assessment in Norfolk and the commission for oyer and terminer in London. A bencher of Lincoln's Inn in 1657, he became a judge in the sheriff's court of London in 1659. Ten years later he was appointed a serjeant-at-law.

Something of an antiquary, Goddard collected a great deal of (chiefly) Norfolk documents upon which later historians were to draw, notably Francis Blomefield (1705–1752) for his classic *History* (1739) of the county. In common with many contemporary lawyers he also combined this taste with a concern for current politics. He was elected to the first protectorate parliament in 1654 for King's Lynn, and again to the second in 1656, this time on a double return which was rejected. Returned for Castle Rising 'without any seeking or soliciting' on his part to Richard Cromwell's parliament in 1659, again on a double return, he was allowed to sit but was inactive until the election was overturned a few days before the dissolution in April. He did not sit in any subsequent parliament. For both the 1654 and the 1659 Commons he kept a sort of diary. That for 1654 was printed in 1828 by J. T. Rutt as an introduction to his edition of the diary of Thomas Burton MP. Rutt also drew upon the 1659 record to annotate, supplement, and modify Burton's. Into his transcript of the 1654 diary he slipped brief extracts from the Commons journals while silently omitting—largely on grounds of illegibility—'a great variety of phrases, borrowed from the ancients' (p. cxcii), interspersed in the speeches.

For 1654 Goddard produced not a plain 'on-the-spot' piece of reporting, but rather more of a compilation, in which he summarized proceedings and debates, naming very few participants, but indicating the general drift of attitudes and conclusions, occasionally at length but often very briefly. Compared with the diaries of Burton or of Sir John Gell for 1659, his diary is somewhat slight, but as the only internal account and commentary on the debates it has unique value. Goddard gives the impression of a house working seriously and in accordance with traditional procedures towards the performance of its roles, especially the legislative one. Though in the event this was an addled parliament, it was by no means fainéant: a good many bills, public and private—quite apart from the major one intended to revise in a parliamentary way the 'Instrument of government'—were introduced and pursued, as Goddard, who was a conscientious attender, suggests, mostly without acrimony, though references to 'the court party' and 'the soldiery and courtiers' indicate underlying partisanships. Unfortunately and inexplicably, he breaks off in mid-sentence (about finance) on 18 December, leaving the reader uninformed on the major discussions leading to the abrupt dissolution on 22 January 1655.

The diary is rather colourless, no doubt like its author, but there are some shrewd comments and occasional lively touches. On the first day some members cry 'sit still' when summoned to the painted chamber to hear the protector. In November they are making 'themselves a little merry with puns'. Tearing into the instrument, some behave 'as if they had been in the schools, where each man had liberty to propose his own *Utopia*, and to frame commonwealths according to his own fancy'. Goddard himself seems to have leaned towards 'the more moderate sort' in these matters, as is shown by his reaction to the protector's requirement of a written recognition by MPs on 12 September that government by a single person and a parliament was an unalterable fundamental. He and fellow Norfolk members dined together and decided (most of them) to comply with 'the breach of privilege' rather than to risk putting 'the nation into another combustion and confusion'. Guybon Goddard, oddly for a scribacious lawyer, died intestate in 1671. IVAN ROOTS, *rev.*

Sources congregation books, King's Lynn archives • BL, Add. MS 5138 • W. Rye, ed., *The visitacion of Norffolk … 1563 … 1613*, Harleian Society, 32 (1891) • H. J. Hillen, *History of King's Lynn* (1907) • *Diary of Thomas Burton*, ed. J. T. Rutt, 4 vols. (1828); repr. (1974) • Wilts. & Swindon RO, Savernake papers
Archives Wilts. & Swindon RO, parliamentary diaries

Goddard, John (*fl.* 1631–1663), engraver, the son of Robert Goddard, citizen of London and member of the Cordwainers' Company, was apprenticed to the prolific early engraver Robert Vaughan for a term of nine years on 17 January 1631 and became a freeman of the Merchant Taylors' Company on 4 September 1639. His modest output consisted mainly of engraved title-pages, portraits, book illustrations, and similar works, of which representative examples are his portrait of the writing master Martin Billingsley (1651), the title-page to Sylvanus Morgan's *Horologiographica Optica* (1652), and an undated set of plates of *The Seaven Deadly Sins*. Goddard also undertook calligraphic engraving for Richard Gething's *Chirographia, or, A Booke of Copies* (1645) and Thomas Shelton's *Zeiglographia, or, A New Art of Short Writing* (1650). He engraved John Farrer's map of Virginia (1651), as well as further maps for Thomas Fuller's *A Pisgah-Sight of Palestine* (1650) and Peter Heylyn's *Cosmographie in Foure Bookes* (1652). His most impressive piece was perhaps the undated broadside allegory *The Tree of Mans Life*. A John Goddard junior recorded as an engraver in the 1660s can be presumed to be Goddard's son; he can probably be identified with the John Goddard made free of the Merchant Taylors' Company by patrimony on 31 August 1664, and one or other of these men was recorded by the company as working as an engraver in Fetter Lane in 1663. Examples of Goddard's works may be found in the British Museum.

LAURENCE WORMS

Sources A. M. Hind, *Engraving in England in the sixteenth and seventeenth centuries*, 3, ed. M. Corbett and M. Norton (1964) · GL, Merchant Taylors' Company MSS · A. Griffiths and R. A. Gerard, *The print in Stuart Britain, 1603–1689* (1998), 110; 148–51 [exhibition catalogue, BM, 8 May – 20 Sept 1998]

Goddard, Jonathan (*bap.* 1617, *d.* 1675), physician, chemist, and anatomist, was baptized at St Mary, Chatham, Kent, on 2 February 1617, the son of Henry Goddard, a wealthy Deptford shipbuilder. Goddard entered Magdalen Hall, Oxford, as a commoner in 1632 and for four years 'he applied himself to physic', though left without a degree in 1637. As a consequence he took the bachelor's degree in physic at Cambridge as a pensioner of Christ's College on 26 June 1637. In the following year he became MB and in 1643 he took his doctorate in medicine, both of which brought him into contact with Francis Glisson, the regius professor of medicine and disciple of William Harvey. In November 1640 Goddard qualified for the licence of the College of Physicians and eventually proceeded to election as a fellow on 4 November 1646. This led to an association with the college that would include delivering the anatomy lectures the following March, being named as reader in anatomy in the Barber–Surgeons' Hall, appointed Goulstonian lecturer, made censor on eight occasions after 1660, and finally chosen as one of the eight elects in 1672. In this regard one striking dimension of his career was to defend, in a work composed in 1665, *Discourse on the Unhappy Condition of the Practice of Physic in London* (1670), the college, and the medical establishment more generally, against the increasing advances of the apothecaries. This very public role was combined with a successful general practice, a fact borne out in the autobiographies and diaries of eminent contemporaries.

The mathematician and divine John Wallis mentions Goddard as among those 'worthy persons, inquisitive into natural philosophy' who met together in London in 1645 'sometimes at Dr Goddard's lodgings in Woodstreet (or some convenient place near) on occasion of his keeping an Operator in his house for grinding Glasses for Telescopes and Microscopes' (Wallis, 7–9). Goddard was a very active and ambitious physician at the time, wanting no doubt to confirm his credentials as a leading advocate of the new philosophy and able as a bachelor to offer his lodgings as a location for the 1645 Group. The group has generally been regarded as something of a precursor to both the Oxford Experimental Philosophy Club of the 1650s and the later Royal Society. As Wallis suggested, the group showed the desire of experimental physicians to broaden their scientific remit and this is expressed in the group's convergence of physical sciences, such as astronomy, geometry, navigation, statics, magnetism, and mechanics, with medicine, anatomy, and chemistry.

The London group was to remain relatively cohesive until the parliamentary commission began to inaugurate the first wave of ejections from Oxford, the former centre of royalist operations in the civil war. Not surprisingly, as this substantially reduced the academic ranks, prominent members of the London group who had parliamentary sympathies were selected for preferment. The virtuoso and divine John Wilkins, for example, was appointed warden of Wadham College from where he would oversee Oxford science in the early 1650s, while John Wallis became Savilian professor of geometry. Goddard himself was invited by Cromwell in 1648 to accompany him to Ireland as physician-in-chief to the army and, in the following year, went with Cromwell to Scotland where he helped him get through a serious illness. When they returned to London in 1651 after the victory of Worcester, Goddard was rewarded with appointment in Oxford on 9 December as warden of Merton College, where he was incorporated DM the following January. Goddard's continuing favour with Cromwell can be seen after the dissolution of the Long Parliament in April 1653 when the subsequent Barebone's Parliament in November confirmed Goddard as the sole representative of his university. Similarly, in 1655 Goddard's association with Cromwell helped him to succeed Thomas Winston as professor of physic at Gresham College, London, where he enjoyed in common with the other professors free accommodation and a salary of £50 per annum. It was a position complementing Goddard's continuing association with the Oxford club, which remained until Goddard's move to London in 1658, despite his continuing as warden of Merton until July 1660. Indeed, it is a testament to Goddard's political adroitness that when Gresham College was taken over as a barracks in 1659 no suspicion was cast on Goddard while all the other professors were ejected. Similarly, Charles II at the Restoration did not eject Goddard from Merton despite his nine years' tenure during the Commonwealth.

Goddard's notable sympathies for those who wished to see more radical medical improvement for the population during the Commonwealth are demonstrated by his involvement with the two state hospitals, Ely House and the Savoy. Established initially for limited military purposes they became venues for the appointment of practitioners who took an active interest in iatrochemistry and experimental science. The American iatrochemist and associate of the Hartlib circle George Starkey mentions in his *Natures Explication and Helmonts Vindication* (1657) 'Dr Goddard of Oxford' as one of those 'chymically given' and averse to Galenic medical practices (fols. 4*v*–5*r*). In fact Goddard had been added to the hospital management committee as early as 1653 and had considered leaving Oxford to become master of the Savoy in 1658, in the event the year he took up his position at Gresham College. During the optimistic period of the Saints' Parliament, Goddard was also to sit on a substantial committee for lunatics which had been established.

Goddard is usually recognized as one of the group that founded the Royal Society in 1660 and frequently provided his own quarters for the meetings at Gresham. Goddard and other Gresham professors informally underpinned what would rapidly transform itself into a more formal organization and, ultimately, a national institution by dint of royal charter in 1662 and 1663. It would be characterized by its enthusiasts as the legitimate heir of Bacon's *Instauratio magna*. Goddard was appointed a member of council in both charters, and the later historian of the Royal Society, Thomas Birch, recounted that there were few meetings where Goddard failed to replicate experiments and convey observations. An entry dated 20 December 1672 in the diary of Robert Hooke, the society's curator of experiments, notes that 'At Dr Godderds tryd spectacles, found them help sight' (R. Hooke, *The Diary of Robert Hooke*, ed. H. W. Robinson and W. Adams, 1935, 17).

Though there is only intermittent documentation of Goddard's collaborative scientific work in the early years of the Royal Society, evidence suggests that Goddard assumed an active role in this period. For example, he was involved in research into the nature and function of respiration initiated by the eminent Anglo-Irish chemist, Robert Boyle. An extensive series of respiration trials involving a duplicate of Boyle's air pump began in August 1662 and lasted for almost a year. Perhaps the most significant line of research explored the possible relationship between respiration and combustion. In October 1662 John Wilkins proposed the experiment 'of sinking a lamp in a glass-vessel under water, to see how long it would burn there' (Frank, 151). Goddard, who a few weeks earlier had designed an experiment to measure the maximum volume of human lungs, was now requested to aid Wilkins with his enquiry. On 29 October they reported that a lamp burning under water in a vessel containing 4 gallons would last eleven minutes and that they hoped to replicate the experiment several times and to use it on living creatures. However, the trials did not resume until the following January when Boyle returned to Gresham. Unfortunately Boyle's speculative hopes that the air pump would show clear similarities between combustion and respiration failed, although Hooke's experiments between February and June on the respiration of fish which involved Goddard's observations were more fruitful. Goddard was again a key observer, along with the society's secretary, Henry Oldenburg, on 7 November 1664 when Hooke, on Boyle's suggestion, used Nathaniel Highmore's open thorax experiment to see whether air travelled to the heart and to test further the mechanical theory of respiration. Goddard also sat on a Gresham committee appointed to replicate transfusion trials set up by the Oxford physiologist Richard Lower in the autumn of 1666. In the event this was aborted until November of that year. Goddard's catholic interests are also expressed in a short paper put before the Royal Society in 1667 and contained in Sprat's *History of the Royal Society* (1667). Goddard's 'A proposal for making wine from sugar' considered 'whether good Wine may not be made out of the Juyce of sugar-canes' (p. 193) with the wider aim of using sugar from the plantations in Barbados to help compensate for its falling market price.

In the postscript to the *Discourse* of 1670 Goddard informed his readers that it was composed five years before with 'at first little thought or inclination to publish' (p. 57). The reason for its publication five years later was at bottom the continuing warfare between physicians and the ever increasing numbers of apothecaries in London, a warfare that had temporarily abated only because of the plague and fire. The struggle can be dated back to 1664 when a fellow, Timothy Clarke, managed to get a resolution passed by the college that physicians should make their own medicines. This is indeed the starting point for Goddard's work, which concedes that over time 'that part of the Art of Physick, which concerns the Preparation and Composition of Medicaments' was increasingly left to apothecaries while physicians 'became strangers to the Materials and Preparations of Medicines' (J. Goddard, *Discourse*, 1670, 8). Though Goddard stresses that this division of labour had much to commend it significant numbers of apothecaries were now taking advantage of the untutored public and making 'ostentation of being Masters of, or knowing all the Secrets and Practice of all the Physicians in London' (ibid., 12). Goddard's line of defence is staunchly orthodox on this issue. He insists that 'a manifold greater proportion of Judgement and Skill is requisite to discover the Disease, than to apply the Remedy' (ibid., 14–15). While Goddard is perfectly prepared to argue for prescriptions that 'avoid complicated compounds' in favour of 'a judicious choice of a few Ingredients' (ibid., 27) there is little direct suggestion that the medical establishment itself was frequently guilty in prescribing such compounds for apothecaries to make up. This was something which Robert Boyle, for example, pointed to in some of his medical writings. The similarly optimistic suggestion from Goddard that physicians were less likely to charge unreasonable rates for their prescriptions was also rejected by Boyle, as well as by Paracelsian empirics, and not without good reason. However, Goddard's points in defence of the medical establishment are generally well made and lacking in the polemics of many comparable works dealing with the controversy. The work throws into sharp relief the well-known fact that he used his own laboratory for compounding his own 'arcana' or secret remedies, most famously the *Guttae Anglicanae*, Goddard's drops, the secret of which may have been sold to Charles II for as much as £6000 if Martin Lister is to be believed in his *Journey to Paris in 1698*. Lister thought the drops were nothing more than volatile spirit of raw silk rectified with oil of cinnamon but it is highly likely that they were more potent. The drops only underline the reality for many in the college that compounding their own medicines at least had the virtue of aborting attempts by apothecaries to copy and sell them. It should be noted that there was speculation that Goddard had written an earlier book in 1668 with the same theme as the *Discourse*, titled *Discourse Concerning Physick and the many Abuses Thereof by Apothecaries*. It would seem, however, that this was due to a confusion with a similar work published in 1669 by Christopher Merrett titled *A Short View of the Frauds Committed by Apothecaries*.

Goddard died from apoplexy at the corner of Wood Street, Cheapside, London, on the evening of 24 March

1675, on his way home from a meeting of virtuosi which had been held at The Crown in Bloomsbury. Three days later he was buried without inscription in the chancel of St Helen's Church in Bishopsgate, near his colleague and friend Robert Hooke. He died unmarried, leaving no will. His library and a substantial sum of money went to his sister's son, a scholar at Gonville and Caius College, Cambridge. Two posthumous accounts of his medicines were published: *Medicamenta Goddardiana* (1688) and *Arcana Goddardiana* (1691). MALCOLM OSTER

Sources R. G. Frank, *Harvey and the Oxford physiologists* (1980) • W. S. C. Copeman, 'Dr Jonathan Goddard', *Notes and Records of the Royal Society*, 15 (1960), 69–77 • C. Webster, *The great instauration: science, medicine and reform, 1626–1660* (1975) • R. S. Roberts, 'Jonathan Goddard. *Discourse concerning physick and the many abuses thereof by apothecaries*, 1668: a lost work or a ghost?', *Medical History*, 8 (1964), 190–91 • J. Wallis, *A defence of the Royal Society* (1678) • T. Birch, *The history of the Royal Society of London*, 4 vols. (1756–7), vol. 1 • *DNB* • private information (2004) [C. Richards]
Archives BL, papers, Sloane MSS 1139, 1159 • RS, papers
Wealth at death library; 1000 guineas; 300 broad pieces: Copeman, 'Dr Jonathan Goddard', p. 76

Goddard, Joseph (1840–1900), architect, was born on 11 April 1840 in Leicester, the younger of the two children of Henry Goddard (1792–1868) and his wife, Ann, *née* Gardiner (1806–1885). He is the best-known figure in a dynasty of local architects spanning six generations, still in practice at the end of the twentieth century, and the longest-surviving in Britain in a father-to-son line. His grandfather Joseph (1751–1839) had migrated, as a young man, some 5 miles from Kirby Muxloe to Leicester, where he prospered as a carpenter, builder, and property speculator. By 1827 he and his son Henry were styling themselves 'architects' as well as 'surveyors' and 'appraisers'. The architectural side of the practice increased and, by the time the younger Joseph was established, the family's professionalization was complete.

Goddard was educated at Mr Packer's school in Nottingham, which specialized in technical training, before being articled to his father in 1856. He became a partner in 1862. He greatly increased the output of the practice and capitalized on the boom in church building and restoration. His most notable achievement in the 1860s was Tur Langton church, Leicestershire (1865–6), which shows the strong influence of G. E. Street's important St James-the-Less, Pimlico (1859–61). Much of this church work was in the prime hunting country of south Leicestershire, where he also developed a thriving practice for houses and stables.

On 6 October 1864 Goddard married Annie Wright (1839–1933) from Pontefract, Yorkshire, whose connections provided a commission for the church and parsonage at nearby Skelbrooke (1871–2). This was one of the few jobs outside Leicestershire where the volume of work available meant that, like many other provincial architects, he had little need to seek commissions elsewhere. An active social life brought him into contact with potential clients in town and country, and success in the Leicester clock tower competition (1868), followed by the impressive Gothic premises of the Leicestershire Banking Company (1872–4) in Granby Street, sealed his reputation.

In 1871 Goddard became a fellow of the Royal Institute of British Architects, and in 1874 he took on a partner, A. H. Paget (1848–1909). The practice prospered and in 1886 Goddard moved from Beausite, a spacious house he built in 1875–6, to an even larger residence, Knighton Spinneys in the leafy suburb of Stoneygate, where he built numerous houses for Leicester's successful middle classes. The 1880s produced two of the practice's most striking Leicester buildings, Melbourne Hall (1880–81), a large octagon based on the Union Chapel in London, and St John the Baptist (1884–5), probably Goddard's best work, an ingenious reinterpretation of J. L. Pearson's great church of St Augustine, Kilburn, London.

In 1888 Henry Langton Goddard (1866–1944), the second of Joseph's six children, became a partner and, like his father a quarter of a century before, brought new dynamism to the practice. The firm followed the trend of the time by providing well-designed buildings in a great variety of styles. Joseph's success was epitomized by his move about 1898 to the Manor House at Newton Harcourt, south of Leicester. Here he died of apoplexy on 10 October 1900, aged sixty. GEOFFREY K. BRANDWOOD

Sources G. Brandwood and M. Cherry, *Men of property: the Goddards and six generations of architecture* (1990) • Newton Harcourt Manor House, Leicestershire, Goddard family MSS • *CGPLA Eng. & Wales* (1901) • d. cert.
Archives Newton Harcourt Manor House, Leicestershire, family MSS
Likenesses photograph, Newton Harcourt Manor House, Leicestershire, Goddard family MSS; repro. in Brandwood and Cherry, *Men of property*, p. 27
Wealth at death £62,659 17*s*. 8*d*.: probate, 1 Jan 1901, *CGPLA Eng. & Wales*

Goddard, Julia Bachope (1825/6–1896), children's writer and animal welfare campaigner, was the eldest daughter of Samuel Aspinwall Goddard, an American merchant and United States consul in Birmingham. Her early life is obscure. In 1863 she published her first children's book, *Karl and the Six Little Dwarfs*; more than twenty-five others were to follow. Clearly written and well presented, they earned Goddard considerable popularity among contemporaries. Since her death, however, her writing has rarely even merited a mention in bibliographical reference works. She also wrote a number of pieces for contemporary journals and magazines and was a frequent contributor to the *Birmingham Daily Post*.

Many of Goddard's children's books, such as *The Four Cats of the Tippertons and other Stories about Animals* (1881), focused upon the treatment of animals, reflecting her lifelong endeavour to improve their condition. She was, according to one contemporary animal welfare publication, 'one of the hardest and yet most unpretentious workers the movement has yet possessed' (*Animals' Friend*). Goddard does not appear to have been associated with the more radical elements in the animal rights' movements or anti-vivisection campaigns: she was not herself a vegetarian, arguing instead for more humane methods of animal slaughter. Indeed, she personified a particular brand of moderate humanitarianism, advocated by publications such as the *Animals' Friend*, which applauded her work, and to which she contributed.

Goddard's abiding aim was to ensure that all children were instructed in the correct and humane treatment of animals, arguing that 'The subject must be taught as much as any other subject of education' (Goddard, 87–8). She believed that such a move would not only contribute greatly to an improvement in animal welfare but also have a dramatic effect in uplifting the morality of the young. She persistently urged the Department of Education to make the proper treatment of animals a compulsory element in the school curriculum; while she did not achieve this goal, the department did recommend teachers to include such lessons in their pupils' reading courses. Goddard encouraged and publicized the works of writers such as the Revd J. G. Wood and F. H. Harkwell, who wrote books designed for teachers' use on natural history and kindness to animals.

Goddard was best remembered for her establishment of an annual prize to school pupils in her home town, Birmingham, from 1876 onwards. This was in keeping with her philosophy that positive inducements and not merely punitive measures were required if a sea change was to be effected in the country's treatment of animals. The scheme, which she devised with the assistance of J. A. Langford, a former secretary of the Birmingham Co-operative League, was awarded on the basis of essays on the subject of animal welfare and *viva voce* examinations. It involved Goddard in the judging of up to two thousand essays each year and the organization of large public meetings to award the prizes. Such local dignitaries as John Bright and George Dawson publicly endorsed the scheme. Goddard was also known locally for her establishment of a competition to improve the treatment and conditions of horses and donkeys for hire in Sutton Park.

From 1894 Goddard suffered from extremely poor health following a severe attack of influenza. This, combined with her failing eyesight, forced her to give up her work. She died unmarried of a cerebral haemorrhage on 30 September 1896 at her cottage in Little Aston, near Sutton Coldfield, which she shared with her sister, Fanny Goddard. Her funeral took place on 5 October at Edgbaston church. KATHRYN GLEADLE

Sources *Birmingham Daily Post* (2 Oct 1896) • *Animals' Friend* (Nov 1896) • *The Times* (3 Oct 1896) • J. Goddard, 'Teach the children', *Animals' Friend* (Dec 1897), 87–8 • letters to J. A. Langford, Birm. CL, MS 135 • d. cert. • *CGPLA Eng. & Wales* (1897)
Archives Birm. CL, letters to J. A. Langford
Likenesses photograph, repro. in *Animals' Friend*, 28–9
Wealth at death £3259 7s. 9d.: resworn probate, Dec 1897, *CGPLA Eng. & Wales*

Goddard [*née* Egan], **Mary** (*bap.* **1717**, *d.* **1752**), poet and milliner, was baptized on 12 July 1717 at St Nicholas Within, Dublin, the daughter of Mary, whose maiden name was probably Colwell, and Terence Egan, variously styled 'Mr.' or 'Gent.' in the parish registers. Egan seems to have been a Catholic who conformed under the act of 1709 to safeguard a place in the legal profession, in this case as a clerk or low-level functionary in the nearby court offices of king's bench, School House Lane, or exchequer, Kennedy's Lane, adjacent to the parish church. The entry 'Terence Egan, gent., 24 Dec. 1709' appears in a list of oath-takers appended to the calendar of convert rolls (O'Byrne, 304), and in 1748 the subscribers' list to his daughter's *Poems on Several Occasions* (advertised as available from 'Mr. Egan at the King's Bench Office' is flush with the names of minor court officials and attorneys, including his 25-year-old son 'Mr. John Egan, Attorney'. A few foreign-language translations in the *Poems* suggest that Mary's education included some French and Latin. At the age of seventeen, on 29 September 1734, she married the assistant curate of her parish, the Revd Valentine Goddard (*d.* 1745), then a widower of seven years' standing. To judge by her later poems in praise of him as Fidelio or Valentine, the match proved unusually happy. Between 1735 and 1741 she bore five children, all but one of whom survived infancy.

After Valentine Goddard died on 28 November 1745—still curate at St Nicholas Within—Mary Goddard supported their family as a milliner in Hoey's Court adjoining the parish, moving a few streets south-eastwards to Digges Street in 1747. By that time, to judge by his surviving letters, she was presiding over a small literary circle including Edmund Burke, then in his final year at Trinity College, and his friends Richard Shackleton, the future author Beaumont Brenan, and William Dennis. All contributed verse to her *Poems* volume along with 'W. K.', who was probably the elderly miscellaneous writer Walter Kennedy, a Catholic military man turned attorney who was memorialized a few months later at his death, in the *Dublin Courant* for 23–27 February 1748. As she frankly admitted in her preface, publishing her *Poems* was meant to supplement her millinery income, to 'ease the Wants' of 'the Infant Objects of my Care'. Boasting a large, middle-class subscription list, the book finally appeared in July 1748, without her name on the title-page but clearly advertised as hers in the press: 'Poems on several Occasions by Mrs. Goddard', announced as published 'This Day' in the *Dublin Journal* for 19–23 July. Mainly lyrics and short topical pieces about her friends—assured if conventional in their prosody—her contributions demonstrate a forthright poetic voice, direct in its expressions of emotion, modest about herself, occasionally witty, and sometimes feminist in tone. The dates of composition go back as far as 1737, well before her husband's death, but apparently only one poem had been printed before, an anonymous epigram in praise of the former viceroy Lord Chesterfield, which appeared in the *Dublin Journal* for 19–22 April 1746. Her subsequent work, if any, has not been traced. Mary Goddard died in Dublin and was buried on 16 February 1752 at her home church, St Nicholas Within.

A. C. ELIAS JR.

Sources parish registers, 1671–1788, St Nicholas Within, Dublin, Representative Church Body Library, Dublin, MS P.154.1.1 • [M. Goddard], *Poems on several occasions* (1748), preface • *The correspondence of Edmund Burke*, 1, ed. T. W. Copeland (1958) • A. C. Elias Jr, 'Male hormones and female wit: the sex appeal of Mary Goddard and Laetitia Pilkington', *Swift Studies*, 4 (1994), 5–16 • *Dublin Journal*

(1746–8) • *Dublin Courant* (1746–8) • A. P. I. Samuels, *The early life, correspondence and writings of the Rt. Hon. Edmund Burke, LL. D.* (1923) • E. O'Byrne, ed., *The convert rolls*, IMC (1981)
Likenesses P. Hussey, drawing
Wealth at death poor

Goddard, Mary Katherine (1738–1816), printer and postmaster, was born on 16 June 1738 in either Groton or New London, Connecticut, the eldest surviving child of Giles Goddard (*c.*1703–1757), a physician, and **Sarah Goddard** [*née* Updike] (*c.*1700–1770), printer and newspaper publisher.

As one of five daughters of an affluent Rhode Island landowner, Lodowick Updike (1646–1737), and his wife, Abigail Newton (1654–1745), Sarah Updike was of higher social standing than Giles Goddard, whom she married on 11 December 1735. While her daughter Mary Katherine grew up in comfortable circumstances in New London, Connecticut, on reaching adulthood she found her economic situation bound up with the fortunes of her younger brother William Goddard (1740–1817). After he had completed an apprenticeship in New Haven, Connecticut, the by then widowed Sarah Goddard in 1762 helped to finance his establishment of a printing press in Providence, Rhode Island. Both Sarah and Mary Katherine moved to Providence in order to assist William with the printing in 1762 of its first newspaper, the *Providence Gazette*; this began Mary Katherine's long career in printing and newspaper publishing. In May 1765, at the time of the Stamp Act crisis, William Goddard sought to secure a more advantageous business partnership, first in New York city and then in Philadelphia, Pennsylvania, leaving Sarah and Mary Katherine to supervise the Providence press and, in August 1766, to resume publication of the *Providence Gazette*.

At William's request in November 1768, Sarah Goddard sold the Providence printing press to her assistant, John Carter, and she and Mary Katherine joined William at his new printing press, in Philadelphia. There Sarah Goddard died, on 5 January 1770, and was buried in Christ Church. Following her mother's death Mary Katherine supervised the printing press during her brother's frequent and prolonged absences. In February 1774 she moved to Baltimore to oversee yet another new printing press, while William set off on a quest to supplant the imperial postal system with one to be controlled by newly emerging revolutionary organizations. In August 1775 Mary Katherine Goddard was appointed postmaster of a new, 'constitutional' postal office in Baltimore. William continued to travel extensively to establish the independent new postal system throughout the northern and southern colonies, while Mary Katherine helped to develop new post offices in other towns within the state of Maryland.

In January 1777 Mary Katherine Goddard was chosen by the continental congress to print the first broadside copy of the Declaration of Independence that listed the names of the signers. Meanwhile she continued to publish the *Maryland Journal*, in one case appealing to the Baltimore committee of safety after being threatened by a local tory, and in two cases sidestepping political controversies instigated by her fractious brother William. William having wrested control of the *Maryland Journal* from his sister in January 1784, their sibling rivalry became a public scandal in November 1784, when they published competing almanacs in the same month. The editorial preface to William's almanac referred to Mary Katherine as a 'hypocritical character', an insult that effectively ended any amicable relations between sister and brother. In May 1786 Mary Katherine did not attend her brother's marriage, to Abigail Angell of Providence, and in August 1792 she stayed behind in Baltimore when William moved permanently to Rhode Island. In 1785 she published an almanac for the last time, and withdrew from the printing business to concentrate on bookselling.

Mary Katherine Goddard's public service ended on her dismissal as postmaster of Baltimore in November 1789. Her abrupt removal by the new federal government prompted more than 200 prominent men of Baltimore to petition the postmaster-general for her reinstatement. No response was made until she herself petitioned President George Washington on 23 December 1789. With Washington's noncommittal intercession the postmaster-general responded not to Goddard but to the male petitioners from Baltimore, and defended his decision to replace her with an inexperienced outsider to Baltimore (John White, who had been based in Annapolis as a commissioner of army accounts during and after the American War of Independence). On 29 January 1790 Goddard sought redress from the United States senate, but it took no action beyond reading her petition on 18 February, which effectively closed the door to her reinstatement and ended her public career.

Ousted from printing in 1785 and removed from the post office in 1789, Mary Katherine Goddard continued to operate a bookstore in Baltimore but gradually turned to the sale of other dry goods. The 1796 Baltimore city directory listed her as a bookseller, but from 1802 to 1807 she was listed as a 'store-keeper' or 'shop-keeper'. She finally retired at some point about her seventieth year, since the next published city directory, for 1810, listed her as a 'gentlewoman'. On 12 August 1816 Mary Katherine Goddard died, never having married. Her will provided for the manumission of her slave, Belinda Starling, to whom she left all her property. KONSTANTIN DIERKS

Sources W. L. Miner, *William Goddard: newspaperman* (Durham, NC, 1962) • L. C. Wroth, *A history of printing in colonial Maryland, 1686–1776* (Baltimore, 1922) • J. T. Wheeler, *The Maryland press, 1777–1790* (Baltimore, 1938) • S. Henry, 'Sarah Goddard: gentlewoman printer', *Journalism Quarterly*, 57 (1980), 23–30 • N. F. Chudacoff, 'Woman in the news, 1762–1770: Sarah Updike Goddard', *Rhode Island History*, 32 (1973), 99–105 • L. C. Wroth, 'The first press in Providence: a study in social development', *Proceedings of the American Antiquarian Society*, 51 (1941), 351–83 • C. S. Humphrey, 'Goddard, Mary Katherine', *ANB* • W. Goddard, *The partnership, or, The history of the rise and progress of the Pennsylvania Chronicle, &c.* (Philadelphia, 1770) • *William Goddard's Pennsylvania, Delaware, Maryland, and Virginia almanack and ephemeris, for the year of our Lord, 1785* (Baltimore) [1784] • P. Force, *American Archives*, 4th ser., 6

(1846), 1460–61 [Washington] · 'Journal of the committee of observation of the middle district of Frederick Co., MD', *Maryland Historical Magazine*, 11 (1916), 237–60, esp. 239 · W. W. Abbott and others, ed., *The papers of George Washington: presidential series*, 4, ed. D. Twohig (1993), 426–8 · L. G. De Pauw and others, ed., *Documentary history of the first federal congress of the United States of America, March 4, 1789–March 3, 1791*, 14 vols. (Baltimore, 1972–97), 1.243; 3.415; 8.231–9 · [W. Thompson] and Walker, *The Baltimore town and Fell's Point directory* (Baltimore) [1796] · C. W. Stafford, *The Baltimore directory* (1802) · C. W. Stafford, *The Baltimore directory* (1803) · J. Robinson, *The Baltimore directory* (1804) · J. McHenry, *Baltimore directory, and citizens' register* (1807) · W. Fry, *The Baltimore directory* (1810)

Archives Maryland Historical Society, Baltimore, papers
Wealth at death all property left to slave, Belinda Starling

Goddard, Rayner, Baron Goddard (1877–1971), judge, was born on 10 April 1877 at Bassett Road, Notting Hill, London, the second of three sons and third of the five children of Charles Goddard (1842–1922), solicitor, and his wife, Janet Gertrude (1853–1934), daughter of John Jobson, an ironmaster of Derby. Named after his paternal grandmother, whose maiden name was Rayner, he was educated at Marlborough College and at Trinity College, Oxford, graduating in 1898 with a second-class degree in jurisprudence and gaining a full blue in athletics. As a member of the Inner Temple he was called to the bar in 1899. In 1906 he married Marie Linda (1884–1928), daughter of the banker Sir Felix Otto *Schuster. They had three daughters, Pamela (*b.* 1908), Janet (*b.* 1909), and Ruth (*b.* 1912).

Rayner Goddard, Baron Goddard (1877–1971), by Sir James Gunn, 1949

Early professional life Immediately after call, Goddard joined the western circuit chambers of Sir A. Clavell Salter at 1 Mitre Court Buildings, Temple. Through consistent application and aptitude he steadily established a strong reputation in commercial litigation, recognition of which came with his appointment as king's counsel in 1923 and his election as bencher of his inn in May 1929. His early association with the western circuit was later consolidated by appointments to recorderships of Poole (1917), Bath (1925), and Plymouth (1928), each of which provided valuable judicial experience. While developing his professional practice, from 1912 to 1917 he undertook the not inconsiderable burden of the honorary secretaryship of the Barristers' Benevolent Association, and gained election to the general council of the bar in 1913. Goddard's wartime service combined membership of the special constabulary with work as a temporary legal assistant for war work at the Board of Trade. In 1924 he was appointed a member of the commission to investigate a police disciplinary controversy ('Report of the commission to enquire into the case of ex-Inspector John Syme', *Parl. papers*, 1924, 12, Cmd 2193). An internal recommendation from Claude Schuster, permanent secretary at the Lord Chancellor's Department and a relation through marriage of Goddard's, noted that he would be suitable for the commission but had 'by no means the intellectual capacity' of other identified possible candidates (17 April 1924, PRO, LCO 2/4698). Beyond practice at the bar, Goddard engaged in few public activities. His sole public venture into politics was notable for its uncharacteristic absence of plain common sense and sound judgement. At the general election of 1929, the recent divorce of South Kensington's sitting Conservative member of parliament (Sir William Davison) had driven a group of disaffected constituency members to persuade Goddard to stand as an independent Conservative. With the unflattering and largely unfair appellation 'Purity Goddard', he came bottom of the poll with some 6000 votes against the official Conservative's resounding vote of over 28,000: a spectacular and painful rebuff.

High court judgeship to lord of appeal-in-ordinary Goddard's full-time judicial career began in April 1932 with his appointment as a judge of the King's Bench Division of the High Court. He received the customary knighthood in the same year. As a puisne judge he tried a number of commercial cases, and was well regarded as a commercial judge. An early concern of his was that courts should be more efficient in processing civil cases by avoiding time-wasting delays. By adopting the strict procedure of striking out actions he quickly changed the unpunctual and dilatory habits of many legal practitioners. Especially in civil cases the desire for efficiency carried through to Goddard's courtroom demeanour, proceedings being conducted in a brisk, no-nonsense manner and with a 'nose for delaying tactics' (attributed to Lord Parker in Bresler, 77). According to an early contemporary, Sir Harold Morris, Goddard was 'a sprinter both physically and mentally' (Morris, 111). Such judicial characteristics were not always apposite in criminal trials, where a genuine eagerness to establish the 'truth' could sometimes manifest itself in impatience and an undesirable level of intervention.

Enlargement of the Court of Appeal by the Administration of Justice (Miscellaneous Provisions) Act of 1938 generated the appointment of three additional lords justices, one of whom was Goddard. Despite confessing to looking 'forward to the future with dread—the CA is so frightfully dull' (19 Oct 1938, A. L. Goodhart papers), he found wartime service in the Court of Appeal stimulating and congenial, with much work carried out in a sandbagged cellar of the Strand law courts. His judgments there 'were sound and concise and to the point without exhibiting the profundity of the greatest lawyers' (Harwood, 129). His additional wartime judicial duties entailed sitting as a supplementary judge of the King's Bench Division. In 1943, with notable expedition, he carried out a public inquiry, established by the Home Office, into apparent irregularities of the corporal punishment procedures of local justices. Later known as the 'Hereford birching inquiry', Goddard's report impressively cut through a maze of confusing and contradictory allegations, eventually clearing Hereford juvenile court of improper behaviour. His conduct of the Hereford inquiry, along with solid service in the Court of Appeal, made unsurprising his elevation to the House of Lords in July 1944, on the death of Lord Atkin. On appointment as a lord of appeal-in-ordinary, with a life peerage, he adopted the title Baron Goddard. His period as a law lord was, however, brief, ending in January 1946 with his appointment as lord chief justice on the resignation of Lord Caldecote. The choice of Goddard established a decisive break with the practice of appointing the incumbent attorney-general to the position of lord chief justice. Moreover, he was the first lord chief justice to hold a degree in law.

Lord chief justice On taking office at this time Goddard, at sixty-eight, was confronted with a sluggish, frequently poorly administered, court system and a generally alarming rapid rise in crime. His tenure as lord chief justice was strongly conditioned by these realities and widespread perceptions, along with his own entrenched beliefs on the functions of the state and the legal system. In respect of pressing administrative demands, Goddard showed himself eager and able to dislodge the malaise that had characterized affairs for some considerable time. Several procedural and structural innovations, including the establishment of new crown courts in Manchester and Liverpool, owed much to Goddard's personal initiatives and drive. In the face of determined opposition from Lord Merriman, president of the Probate, Divorce, and Admiralty Division of the High Court, Goddard put his weight behind the Denning committee reform proposals aimed at resolving the urgent social problem of the vast backlog of divorce petitions. Besides systemic problems, Goddard was faced with a body of King's Bench judges that not only had seen better times, but was also patently understaffed and lacking adequate court accommodation (see for example Goddard to Lord Jowitt, 15 Jan 1947, PRO, LCO 2/3830).

While Goddard had extensive civil law jurisdiction as lord chief justice, it was his responsibilities and involvement with the criminal justice system that rapidly gained him a mixture of fame and notoriety. From the inception of his term of office, in trial comments, appeal judgments, and parliamentary debates, Goddard declared himself an avenging enemy of criminals and a vigilant lord protector of society. In adopting such a general stance on criminal matters he was far from alone. Indeed, Lord Jowitt, lord chancellor in Attlee's Labour government, had informed Goddard that he hoped:

> the judges will not be too lenient to these bandits [who] carry arms [and] shoot at police. [You] know I take the view, which I think you share, that we have got rather soft and woolly in dealing with really serious crime. (15 Jan 1947, PRO, LCO 2/3830)

Responding, the lord chief justice assured the lord chancellor that he was 'entirely of your opinion and so I think are the other judges' (22 Jan 1947, ibid.). In word, and especially in his deeds, Goddard is unlikely to have disappointed Jowitt and the many others holding such views.

Although a member of the House of Lords since 1944, Goddard did not feel impelled to deliver his maiden speech until 1948, reserving it for an attack on particular provisions of the Criminal Justice Bill, especially those abolishing corporal punishment. Here, as was generally the case, his debating style showed reliance on common sense and anecdotal evidence drawn from legal practice, with a general shunning of abstractions. On this occasion Goddard took the unusual step for a lord chief justice of tabling several motions amending the bill, agreeing with the abolition of the use of the 'cat' but favouring retention of birching (*Hansard 5L*, 155, col. 485), which he saw as a more effective punishment for young offenders and less likely than prison sentences permanently to corrupt them. The bill had also been earlier waylaid by capital punishment abolitionists with an amendment seeking to suspend capital punishment for five years. As a consequence, the home secretary announced the automatic reprieve of all condemned prisoners until this amendment had been resolved. In June 1948 Goddard attacked this dispensing practice as illegal under the Bill of Rights and raising 'a most important constitutional issue' (*Hansard 5L*, 156, col. 123). Exercise of the prerogative of mercy also received other judicial criticism during this period, including that of Lord Denning (*Report of the Royal Commission on Capital Punishment*, 15–16, para. 49). On this occasion, and in July 1948, Goddard was in the vanguard of the anti-abolitionists forcefully representing the overwhelming views of the judges of the King's Bench (*Hansard 5L*, 157, col. 32).

The logic underpinning Goddard's creed favouring capital and corporal punishment was simple: to be a deterrent, punishment had also to be 'punitive. The two things seemed to me to follow one on the other …'. Moreover, for the law to be respected it had to be in 'accordance with public opinion … That goes to the root of this question of capital punishment' (*Hansard 5L*, 155, col. 491; see also *Report of the Royal Commission on Capital Punishment*, 21, para.

61). Punishment was 'The only way in which the community can show their detestation of crime and their resolution that … it should be stamped out' (*Hansard 5L*, 198, col. 743). Some sort of historical perspective on this view is gained by comparing it with that of Lord Denning, whose relatively liberal credentials were already well established. The latter's evidence to the royal commission on capital punishment (1949–53) offers a rather subtler articulation of a not wholly dissimilar rationale of capital punishment: 'not that it is a deterrent, but that it is the emphatic denunciation by the community of a crime' (*Report of the Royal Commission on Capital Punishment*, 18, para. 53). Lord Goddard's opposition to the reform bills on murder of 1956–7 again turned on the notion of the absence of public support for the abolition of capital punishment. More generally, his stance on sentencing, particularly in giving guidance to magistrates, was often robust. For example, in attempting to make inroads into the heavy toll being taken by drunken driving, in the divisional court in 1950 Lord Goddard castigated 'Drunken drivers [who were] as great a menace as mad dogs and ought to be dealt with by severe sentences' (Roberts, 225).

In a rather less charged fashion, Goddard's views on the substance and administration of prominent features of the criminal justice system were given an airing in his evidence to the royal commission on capital punishment, established in 1949 and reporting in 1953. The commission's focus was the basis of responsibility for the offence of murder and its punishment. On the issue of the level of mental culpability for murder, Goddard was in the reformist camp, favouring a requirement of intention or foresight of life-endangering harm (*Report of the Royal Commission on Capital Punishment*, 39, paras. 105–6). This position entailed abolition of the largely discredited doctrine of felony-murder, still favoured by some judges and other witnesses (ibid., 37, para. 99). In respect of the partial defence of provocation, Goddard aligned himself with those wishing to retain the defence's largely objective character and exclude the defendant's personal idiosyncrasies, arguing, somewhat unconvincingly, that as society became more civilized and policing improved, the need for a defence of provocation declined (ibid., 52, para. 142). This represented the well-established judicial view that had recently been endorsed by both the House of Lords and the court of criminal appeal. On the defence of insanity he favoured the *status quo*, as did most other judicial witnesses, along with the director of public prosecutions and two former home secretaries. A restructured expansion of the defence of insanity so as to admit evidence of volitional as well as cognitive impairment was seen in practical terms by Goddard as unnecessary, for 'a jury can always be trusted to do justice'. He viewed a new defence based on diminished responsibility or 'irresistible impulse' as a 'dangerous … doctrine' (ibid., 82, para. 233). It was an opinion shared by other notable judicial figures of the time, including Lord Devlin (*Criminal Law Review*, 1954). Of particular concern to Lord Goddard, and most judges, in relation to a defence of diminished responsibility was the unnerving prospect of courts being faced with what appeared to be a wholly indeterminate standard of responsibility. However, his views on both diminished responsibility and provocation were eventually overridden by the provisions of the Homicide Act of 1957.

Beyond Lord Goddard's evidence to the royal commission, his contribution to the development of the criminal law as lord chief justice was in certain limited respects more creative than the contributions of any of his twentieth-century predecessors, most of whom were conceptually lacklustre. In some areas of law, Goddard displayed a staunch resistance to what he regarded as unjust results. This attitude appeared early in his period as lord chief justice in relation to regulatory or 'strict liability' offences. Here he offered a ringing denunciation of the view that basic notions of criminal fault should easily be jettisoned for some types of criminal offences:

> [I]t is of the utmost importance for the protection of the liberty of the subject that a court should always bear in mind that, unless a statute either clearly or by necessary implication rules out [fault] as a constituent part of a crime, the court should not find a man guilty of an offence against the criminal law unless he has a guilty mind. (*Brend* v. *Wood*, 1946)

His unwillingness to adhere to what had become established interpretative practices was apparent in the prominent case of *Steane* (1947), where the defendant faced charges of 'doing acts likely to assist the enemy with intent to assist the enemy'. Steane had participated in radio broadcasts for Germany during the Second World War in response to threats of violence to himself and to save his family from incarceration in a concentration camp. By construing the offence's requirement of 'intent' in an unusually specific and narrow fashion, Goddard was able to avoid the unedifying spectacle of Steane's conviction. During the same year he ruled against the use of police instigation of crime for entrapment purposes (*Brannan* v. *Peek*). His powerful concern to have justice take its proper course without interference was demonstrated by the severe response in contempt proceedings against the *Daily Mirror* in 1949. For publishing lurid comments relating to the accused multi-murderer Haigh that were likely to prejudice his forthcoming trial, the newspaper's editor was committed to three months' imprisonment and its proprietors fined £10,000, accompanied by Goddard's warning that the 'directors themselves may find that the arm of the Court is long enough to reach them and to deal with them' for future transgressions.

At a more general level, in *Newlands* (1953), in opposition to a judgment of Lord Hewart in *Manly* (1933), Lord Goddard doubted the existence of what he characterized as a dangerous revival of the reserve judicial power to create new crimes, such as the amorphous offence of public mischief, an offence which was later recognized by the House of Lords in *Shaw* (1962; the 'Ladies' directory' case). His view of the appropriate culpability basis of murder appeared to undergo a significant shift with the progression of his term in office. In contrast to his apparent support for a subjectively based requirement of intent or foresight of life-endangering harm, expressed in his evidence to the royal commission, from the mid 1950s the court of criminal appeal under his leadership produced a series of judgments indicating a more easily satisfied objective test (that of the 'reasonable man') as the basic culpability requirement of murder. It was a standard of liability which survived intended parliamentary reform under the Homicide Act of 1957, and received the highly controversial endorsement of the House of Lords in *Director of Public Prosecutions* v. *Smith* (1961), one of the few House of Lords judgments in which Lord Goddard participated after retirement.

Judicial style Like the overwhelming majority of contemporary judges, Goddard rarely engaged in sustained doctrinal analysis, settling rather for 'practical and common sense solutions' to legal issues. This was a view expounded in a lecture to the American Judicature Society, delivered the year following his retirement, when reflecting on the desirable qualities of a judge, prominent among which was the 'ability to make up one's mind and to do so expeditiously' (Goddard, 'Politics and the British bench', 1959). However, without any obvious irony, he doubted the wisdom of judges giving 'public expression of what some would call strong convictions, and others prejudices …'. Most interestingly, among the range of desirable judicial characteristics which he identified, particular prominence was given to the 'ability to keep reasonably silent while trying a case. A garrulous judge is a misfortune; he maddens the Bar and slows up the Bench'. Presumably Lord Goddard did not intend to include judges who adopt a very interventionary role in proceedings, and especially those who ill-conceal their support for the prosecution. Such abandoning of judicial impartiality was at the core of the charges levelled against Lord Goddard for his alleged highly partisan conduct of the notorious murder trial of Christopher Craig and Derek Bentley at the Old Bailey in December 1952.

In the course of a burglary with his accomplice, Bentley, aged nineteen, Craig, aged sixteen, had shot dead a policeman. On their joint conviction for murder, Bentley, who was under arrest at the time of the shooting, was subject to the mandatory death sentence; Craig, as a consequence of being below the minimum age of eighteen necessary for capital punishment, was effectively given a life sentence. Bentley's appeal was dismissed by the court of criminal appeal. Despite the jury's recommendation of mercy, along with several public initiatives including a House of Commons motion supported by 200 members of parliament, the death sentence was not commuted by the home secretary, Sir David Maxwell Fyfe. In a confidential note to the home secretary Goddard 'could find no mitigating circumstances' (12 Dec 1952, PRO, HO 291/225 and home secretary's memo, 22 Jan 1953). Bentley was hanged on 28 January 1953. Intense public controversy surrounding Goddard's conduct of the case was rekindled soon after his death by the publication of further highly critical commentaries (esp. D. Yallop, *To Encourage the Others*, 1971, and B. Levin, *The Times*, 8 June 1971). Lord Goddard's professional integrity and conduct of the trial received powerful support in letters to *The Times* from a galaxy of distinguished judges including Lord Parker and Lord Devlin along with the former attorney-general Lord Shawcross (10–16 June 1971). The intensely charged and long-running debate over the Craig and Bentley trial was concluded by the cool assessment of the Court of Appeal on 30 July 1998, after a referral of the case by the Criminal Cases Review Commission. Allowing the appeal and quashing Bentley's conviction as unsafe, Lord Bingham observed:

> In our judgment … far from encouraging the jury to approach the case in a calm frame of mind, the trial judge's summing up, particularly in the passages we have quoted, had exactly the opposite effect. We cannot read these passages as other than a highly rhetorical and strongly worded denunciation of both defendants and of their defences. The language used was not that of a judge but of an advocate … Such a direction by such a judge must in our view have driven the jury to conclude that they had little choice but to convict; at the lowest, it may have done so. (*R.* v. *Derek William Bentley (deceased)*, 1998)

It was a judgment which emphatically overturned the court of criminal appeal's contemporary view that the 'idea that there was a failure [by Lord Goddard] to say anything short of what was required in putting that sort of case to the jury is entirely wrong'. However, although Lord Bingham and the Court of Appeal expressly adopted the arguably more demanding trial procedural standards employed in 1998, the 1953 judgment of the court of criminal appeal must, in the light of the transcript evidence, be regarded as having been markedly generous to Lord Goddard, even by the standards and expectations of that period. Clearly, Jowitt's injunction not to be 'too lenient to bandits who shoot at police' had been taken very much to heart by all judicial parties. Consequently, while Goddard's trial behaviour was lamentably short of judicial, he hardly stood alone in denying Craig and Bentley a 'fair trial'; for the court of criminal appeal was complicit in these manifest shortcomings by virtue of its own patent failure to remedy them in the face of the same trial transcript evidence reviewed by the Court of Appeal forty-five years later. Indeed, Sir Hartley Shawcross, the attorney-general, had expressed his concern to Lord Chancellor Jowitt:

> there is a feeling that … appellants, are dealt with [by the court of criminal appeal] in a rather summary way. The Lord Chief Justice is sometimes exceedingly robust in his manner (I think that this is what [Quintin] Hogg had in mind when he referred to bad temper, harsh judgment and that kind of thing) and I must say I am not altogether happy about the court myself. (19 July 1948, PRO, LCO 2/3341)

Yet at the same time, the court of criminal appeal not infrequently substituted more lenient sentences where they appeared merited. Moreover, Goddard had been a consistent supporter of giving the court of criminal appeal the power to order a retrial of convicted appellants, a power eventually granted by the Criminal Appeal Act of 1964 (see for example *Hansard 5L*, 157, col. 193). In part this attitude rested on the desire to have an alternative to simply quashing a conviction.

Following his letter of resignation on 26 July 1958 Goddard, aged eighty-one, finally sat as lord chief justice on 20

August 1958. But formal retirement certainly did not mean judicial inactivity: in the following spring, April 1959, he took the unprecedented step of returning to sit in the Court of Appeal for almost a year to help clear a backlog of appeal cases. In January 1959 he resumed regular judicial sittings in the House of Lords, continuing until 1963. During this period he was a member of the judicial committee of the House of Lords in several controversial appeal decisions, including *Director of Public Prosecutions* v. *Smith* (1961), *Sykes* v. *Director of Public Prosecutions* (1962), and *Attorney-general for Northern Ireland* v. *Gallagher* (1963). His participation in House of Lords debates ended in May 1965 with his opposing speech on the second reading of Lord Arran's bill to decriminalize private homosexual acts between consenting adults. Unafraid as ever to voice unfashionable views, Goddard characterized the proposals as a fundamental attack on 'family life' (*Hansard 5L*, 255, col. 666).

In sum, Goddard's character was permeated with striking contrasts, if not contradictions: the public severity, irascibility, and dominating judicial presence, set against well-documented frequent private generosity, informality, and genuine humility. Hasty or ill-judged comments from the bench were often redeemed by an equally ready willingness openly to accept correction. As he once confessed to Professor Sir Arthur Goodhart, editor of the *Law Quarterly Review*, 'I have seldom, if ever, read a criticism of one of my judgments in the LQR without being convinced that you were right and I was wrong …' (10 Feb 1948, Goodhart papers). A formidable grasp of the common law, coupled with a deep veneration for its traditions, contributed to a high and enduring reputation within the legal profession, one reflected in Lord Bingham's Court of Appeal reference to Goddard as 'one of the outstanding criminal judges' of the twentieth century (*Bentley*, 1998). As lord chief justice he commanded the immense respect, loyalty, and affection of his puisne judges. Goddard was the incarnation of criminal justice in its most directly robust, even forbidding, form—one which many, particularly from outside the legal profession, regarded with considerable distaste. He was manifestly a man strongly and indelibly conditioned by the perceived realities and needs of early post-war England, and one who fearlessly and tenaciously adhered to his original legal and social brief well after informed opinion and attitudes had moved on.

On retirement Goddard was created GCB. Trinity College, Oxford, made him an honorary fellow in 1940. He received honorary degrees from the universities of Montreal (1945), New York (1945), Oxford (1947), and Cambridge (1954), from the College of William and Mary, Virginia (1954), and from Sheffield University (1955). He died at his home in the Queen Elizabeth Building, Temple, on 29 May 1971, and was cremated at Golders Green crematorium on 2 June. No memorial service was held, in deference to his resolute view that they were mere 'exercises in hypocrisy'.

K. J. M. SMITH

Sources F. Bresler, *Lord Goddard* (1977) • A. Smith, *Lord Goddard* (1959) • PRO, LCO 2/4698, 3830, 3341 • *Hansard 5L* (1948), vol. 155–7; (1956), vol. 198; (1965), vol. 255 • K. J. M. Smith, *Lawyers, legislators and theorists* (1998) • PRO, HO 291/225 • 'Royal commission on capital punishment', *Parl. papers* (1952–3), 7.677, Cmd 8932 • R. Stevens, *Law and politics: the House of Lords as a judicial body, 1800–1976* (1979) • R. Stevens, *The independence of the judiciary: the view from the lord chancellor's office* (1993) • A. L. Goodhart papers, Bodl. Oxf., MS Eng c. 2883 • A. Harwood, *Circuit ghosts: a western circuit miscellany* (1980) • G. D. Roberts, *Law and life* (1964) • H. Morris, *Back view* (1960) • P. Devlin, *Criminal Law Review*, 1954, r.661 • D. Yallop, *To encourage the others* (1971) • B. Levin, 'Judgement on Lord Goddard', *The Times* (8 June 1971) • records, Trinity College, Oxford • *DNB* • Inner Temple, London • R. Goddard, 'A note on habeas corpus', *Law Quarterly Review*, 65 (1949), 30 • R. Goddard, 'The working of the court of criminal appeal', *Journal of the Society of Public Teachers of Law*, 2 (1952), 1 • R. Goddard, 'Politics and the British bench', *Journal of the American Judicature Society*, 43 (1959), 124 • R. Goddard, 'Organisation and jurisdiction of the courts of England', *Journal of the American Judicature Society*, 44 (1960), 60

Archives Bodl. Oxf., letters to A. L. Goodhart • PRO

Likenesses photographs, 1897–8, Trinity College, Oxford • W. Stoneman, photographs, 1932–56, NPG • J. Gunn, oils, 1949, Inner Temple, London [*see illus.*] • J. Gunn, portrait, Trinity College, Oxford • Mme Yevonde, photograph, NPG • photographs, repro. in Bresler, *Lord Goddard*

Wealth at death £111,055: probate, 9 July 1971, *CGPLA Eng. & Wales*

Goddard, Sarah (*c.*1700–1770). *See under* Goddard, Mary Katherine (1738–1816).

Goddard, Thomas (*d.* 1783), army officer, was born, probably not later than 1740, one of two sons of Captain Henry Goddard of the British army, said to be from Hartham Park in Wiltshire, and grandson of Thomas Goddard (1673–1731), a canon of Windsor. Goddard was commissioned ensign into the 24th foot on 24 September 1757 and promoted lieutenant on 26 January 1758. He transferred as lieutenant to the 84th foot, commanded by Lieutenant-Colonel Eyre Coote, being raised for service in India. The regiment arrived at Madras on 27 October 1759, where it joined the British forces (both crown and East India Company) fighting the French (as part of the Seven Years' War) for supremacy in the Carnatic, a struggle which ended with the battle of Wandiwash (22 January 1760) and the surrender of Pondicherry on 16 January 1761.

Later that year Goddard accompanied the 84th to Bengal, and took part, as engineer, in the campaign of 1763 against Mir Kasim, the nawab of Bengal, and was wounded at the siege of Patna (31 October 1763). When the 84th was disbanded at the end of the Seven Years' War, Goddard transferred as captain to the company's service in October 1763. Early the following year he raised a battalion of sepoys, long known thereafter as Goddard's battalion. In the later 1760s and early 1770s Goddard saw some service as a battalion commander in the 1st brigade within the province of the company's ally the nawab-wazir of Oudh, Shuja ud-Daula. He obviously recommended himself by his vigour and enterprise to his superiors because, despite taking part in the notorious 'white mutiny' against Clive's military reforms in 1766 and losing seniority as a result, his standing was restored in 1769.

Goddard took part with his battalion in 1770 at the capture of Burrareah, and was employed in 1772 in expelling the Marathas from Rohilkhand. In September 1774 he succeeded to the command of the troops stationed at Berhampore in Bengal. Goddard's extant correspondence with Warren Hastings commences at this period, and continues until his departure from India. The governor-general placed the utmost confidence in his ability and tact. Hastings was later to say of Goddard: 'He is one of the best executive officers in the service, remarkably lively and enterprising, sensible … His only faults are a too great pliancy of temper, and negligence of expenses' (Gleig, 2.221).

Goddard was in command of the troops at Chunar, in Benares, from January 1776 until the following June, when as a lieutenant-colonel he was appointed to command the new 'temporary brigade' being formed by the East India Company for Shuja ud-Daula at Lucknow. In 1778 Goddard was appointed second-in-command under Colonel Leslie of an expeditionary force of six battalions of sepoys and 1100 cavalry and artillery, a total of 6700, all Indian but for 100 British officers. This detachment was ordered to march nearly 800 miles south-west from Oudh across nominally hostile territory in the Maratha confederation to come to the aid of the Bombay council beleaguered by the Marathas for trying to impose its candidate, Raghunath Rao (Ragoba), to rule at Poona.

Leslie was very dilatory in his conduct of the expedition, progressing only 120 miles in four months, and in October 1778 Hastings had ordered his replacement by Goddard when Leslie's death achieved the same end. Hastings's trust in Goddard extended to ordering him in November to try to subvert one of the Maratha chiefs, Mudhoji Bhonsla of Berar, away from the confederation. Although Goddard failed in this, Hastings later gave him plenipotentiary powers to negotiate a provisional peace treaty with the Marathas on his own authority, not subjecting him to the control of the discredited Bombay council, who had imperilled their whole army by a bungled attack against Poona. Calcutta also ordered that Goddard's detachment should not come under Bombay's orders and gave him the brevet rank of full colonel (October 1778) and later of brigadier (June 1779) so that he would outrank the senior Bombay officers and thus command all the troops on the west coast. Goddard's connections at home later secured him a local royal commission as brigadier (April 1780).

After some delay, while negotiations with Poona continued and the military situation clarified, Goddard's detachment reached Surat on 25 February 1779 and he sailed down to Bombay, where he arrived on 15 March and was invited to join the council to deliberate on future plans. Exchanges with Poona went on for some months, but the Maratha government made unacceptable demands for the restoration of Salsette and the surrender of Raghunath Rao, who had escaped from the custody of Sindhia (one of the principal Maratha chiefs) and taken refuge in Goddard's camp.

Goddard recommenced hostilities in January 1780; he had been urged by the Bombay council and Warren Hastings to conquer revenue-bearing Maratha territory to support his inflated forces. The province of Gujarat, north of Surat, was chosen as the field of operations. Goddard was very successful, capturing Ahmadabad by storm on 15 February, enriching himself with prize money and forcing an alliance treaty on the local Maratha chief, Fateh Singh Gaikwar. He then marched against Sindhia and another Maratha chief, Holkar, and routed their forces on 3 April.

Goddard and the Bombay council hoped that this pressure would bring the Marathas to terms, but it did not, partly due to the fractured nature of politics at Poona; so at the end of 1780 Goddard besieged the Maratha fortress of Bassein, north of Bombay, which was seen as critical for Bombay's security. Bassein fell on 11 December. News that Goddard had been appointed commander-in-chief at Bombay, with a seat on the council, reached him at this time; it proved to be a mixed blessing for, although he liked the title, it embroiled him in many disputes with Governor Hornby of Bombay, who now, rather than Hastings, was his legal superior.

Hastings now felt it was imperative to secure peace with Poona because since July 1780 the East India Company at Madras had been at war with Haidar Ali of Mysore and Bengal's resources were stretched to the limit in shoring up another sister presidency. Goddard tried further military pressure in January 1781 by ascending the Bhor Ghat on to the Deccan plateau, threatening Poona, but the Marathas swept down on to the coastal plain (the Konkan) with thousands of cavalry and cut his supply lines. So in April he had to make a fighting retreat to Bombay, suffering 294 casualties on the way. In August of the same year overtures on the part of Sindhia at last led to a peace treaty, signed on 13 October 1781.

Goddard had been very keen to end the war on a glorious note as he was lobbying hard through his London contacts (including his cousin's husband, Sir William James) to be appointed commander-in-chief at Bengal, or at Madras, where he aspired to the 'Glory of Destroying the power of Hyder … rival to our Greatness on the Peninsula' (Goddard to Lady James, 15 Oct 1780, private letter-books of Thomas Goddard, MS La.II, 624, no. 13). He was disappointed in his ambition and suffered the greater blow at this time of losing his family (about whom no details have been found) at sea. Falling out with Hastings, broken in health, and consoled only by a fortune of about £100,000 from military contracting and prize money, Goddard resigned in September 1782. He sailed for home but died on 7 July 1783 in sight of Land's End, still only in his early forties; he was buried at Eltham in Kent.

E. J. Rapson, *rev.* G. J. Bryant

Sources public and private letter-books of Thomas Goddard, 17 vols., 1776–82, U. Edin. L., MSS La.II, 624 • J. Philippart, *East India military calendar*, 3 vols. (1823–6) • E. Orme, ed., *A brief history of ancient and modern India* (1805) • E. P. Thornton, *A brief history of the British empire in India*, 6 vols. (1841–5) • M. Wilks, *Historical sketches of the south of India, in an attempt to trace the history of Mysoor*, 3 vols. (1810–17) • A. Broome, *History of the rise and progress of the Bengal army* (1851) • J. Williams, *An historical account of the rise and progress of the Bengal native infantry, from its first formation in 1757 to 1796* (1817) • Dodwell [E. Dodwell] and Miles [J. S. Miles], eds., *Alphabetical list of the officers of the Indian army: with the dates of their respective promotion, retirement, resignation, or death … from the year 1760 to the year … 1837*

(1838) • G. R. Gleig, *Memoirs of Warren Hastings*, 3 vols. (1841) • P. Cadell, *History of the Bombay army* (1938) • Fortescue, *Brit. army* • BL, Warren Hastings MSS, Add. MSS 29081, 29118–29119, 29135–29193 • Bengal secret consultations, 1779–83, BL OIOC, range A, vols. 49–69 • V. C. P. Hodson, *List of officers of the Bengal army, 1758–1834*, 4 vols. (1927–47)

Archives BL, corresp. relating to his expedition, Add. MS 38403 • BL OIOC, Bengal secret consultations • BL OIOC, corresp. relating to India, home misc. series • U. Edin. L., letter-books and notebook | BL, corresp. with Warren Hastings, Add. MSS 29135–29193, *passim*

Wealth at death £106,000: Hodson, *List of officers of the Bengal army*

Goddard, William (*d.* 1624/5), soldier and satirist, published two books of satirical epigrams—*A Mastif Whelp* ('this infant of my braine', *c.*1614) and *A Neaste of Waspes* (1615), together with *A Satirycall Dialogue … betweene Alexander … and … Diogynes* (*c.*1616)—at Dordrecht in the United Provinces where he served as ensign to a Captain Theobald. Though he exposed captains who practise 'slights to drawe gold from-out our shrunck-up gutts' (*Neaste*, no. 25), he nevertheless bequeathed money to captain friends of his, and to 'the souldiers now remayning in my captaynes company' who served at 'the last Bargaine leager', the siege of Bergen op Zoom in 1622, suggesting he could well have taken part in it himself (will, fol. 19*v*). A possible connection with the Inner Temple is shown by Goddard's dedication of *A Mastif Whelp* to six 'very loving Frends', 'Gentlemen' of that institution (sig. A1^r).

Goddard clearly relished the soldier's life: 'let Canons to our Meales saie grace, / Let bulletts sing to us the Cinquepace' he declares to Mars in *Mastif* no. 42. He was politically astute enough to realize that the Dutch would not allow sectarian differences to weaken their resistance to the Spanish foe (*Mastif*, no. 12). He also knew farming life, as shown particularly by the environmentally sensitive *Mastif* no. 55, and ridiculed the social limitations of rustics (in *Mastif* no. 22, for instance).

In their 'harsh unpollisht vaine' (*Mastif*, sig. A2^r), salacious wit, telling irony, colloquial energy, anti-feminism, barbed and surprise endings ('like catt [they] pinche and nipp at last'; *Neaste*, no. 1), Goddard's epigrams belong to that line of wit in Renaissance poetic satire that is traceable to Martial; his ribald anecdotes also recall Jacobean jest books. All three of his books exhibit a variety of modes: dramatic monologues, dialogues, farcical anecdotes, together with medieval generic survivals such as beast and bird fables, including a parliament of fowls poem ('The Owles Arayngement', *Dialogue*, sig. F2^r–4^r). There are Renaissance forms like the 'echo' poem (*Mastif*, no. 25) and the rare 'carmen correlativum' (*Dialogue*, sig. B3^r). Goddard's keen dramatic sense led him to reproduce the language of rustics, drunkards, over-refined ladies, and roaring boys. He satirizes types, not individuals; they include courtiers, merchants, gulls, popes, physicians, lawyers, spendthrifts, the Dutch—and, most notoriously, women who, variously, gossip about their husbands, affect outlandish attire, practise deceit to gratify their sexual longings, enjoy lubricious dreams, and fart ('she with her taile gann chat'; *Neaste*, no. 92).

In his will dated 8 September 1624, Goddard bequeathed four 'written bookes' or 'rather bables' to two friends in Bedfordshire asking them 'not onely to print but to correct them'. Two are entitled 'the honest Counsells'; the others are 'the honest Souldier' and 'the Drunkard dialogue'. They have not survived. Probate was granted to his sister Daphne Marshall on 31 October 1625; the will makes no mention of a wife or children. DAVID FREEMAN

Sources *DNB* • *STC, 1475–1640* • W. Goddard, *A neaste of waspes latelie found out in the Low-Countreys* (1615) • W. Goddard, *A mastif whelp with other ruff-island-lik currs fetcht from amongst the Antipedes* (*c.*1614) • W. Goddard, *A satirycall dialogue or a sharplye-invective conference, betweene Alexander the Great and that truelye woman-hater Diogynes* (*c.*1616) • will, 8 Sept 1624, PRO, PROB 11/147, sig. 105, fols. 19*v*–20*r* • 'The Captaines names of Collonel Morgans devision', [n.d.], PRO, SP 84/109, fol. 99 • G. Parker, *The army of Flanders and the Spanish road, 1567–1659* (1972) • G. Parker, *The Dutch revolt* (1977) • C. G. Cruickshank, *Elizabeth's army* (1966) • J. Polisensky, *Tragic triangle: the Netherlands, Spain and Bohemia, 1617–21* (1991) • H. H. Hudson, *The epigram in the English Renaissance* (1966) • T. K. Whipple, *Martial and the English epigram from Sir Thomas Wyatt to Ben Jonson* (1970) • A. B. Coiro, *Robert Herrick's Hesperides and the epigram tradition* (1988)

Wealth at death approx. £162: will, 8 Sept 1624, PRO, PROB 11/147, sig. 105

Goddard, William Stanley (1757–1845), headmaster, was born on 9 October 1757 at Stepney, Middlesex, the son of John Goddard (*d.* 1795) and his wife, Elizabeth (*d.* 1798). His father was a prosperous merchant until ruined by the failure of a mercantile house in the City. Under these straitened circumstances in 1769 Goddard was placed as a quirister at Winchester College, thanks to Thomas Collins, the second master at Winchester, who was the brother of one of his father's City friends. From this rather menial position Goddard was elevated to that of scholar in 1771, again owing to the intervention of Collins. He proved an apt pupil, winning a medal for Latin verse in 1776, but like others of undoubted ability from Winchester he was prevented by a lack of entry scholarships from proceeding to the sister foundation, New College, Oxford. He went instead to Merton College, Oxford, in 1776, whence he graduated BA in 1781, and proceeded MA (1783) and DD (1795). In 1781 he returned to Winchester as commoner tutor and in 1784 he succeeded Collins as second master. Also in 1784 he married Henrietta Gale (*d.* 1830).

The headmaster of Winchester, Joseph Warton, was a gifted man but he allowed a deterioration in discipline that led to outright rebellion in 1793, followed by many expulsions and his own resignation. Having resisted the rebellion so far as he could—and retained the respect of his pupils—Goddard was appointed Warton's successor. In a surprisingly short time he restored the reputation of the school. The number of commoners greatly increased, from fewer than fifty before the rebellion to seventy-five by 1796 and to over 130 by 1804, which left the school full to capacity. His success was the result of sound scholarship and firm discipline combined with a genuine sensitivity to his pupils. The latter were still capable of rebellion, but Goddard quelled incipient trouble in 1799 and he managed to end an actual outbreak in 1808 without difficulty or the need for expulsions. He insisted however on

William Stanley Goddard (1757–1845), by Henry William Pickersgill, *c.*1835

good manners from his pupils and also on conventional dress—carrying an umbrella, for example, he regarded as unacceptable dandyism.

Goddard's success owed as much to an appeal to the better feelings of his pupils as it did to the threat of punishment. In this respect he is often thought to have been the inspiration for the system established at Rugby School by his former pupil Thomas Arnold. The latter, however, was no admirer of his headmaster while still at school. He claimed that he learnt more from the second master, Gabell, and that Goddard was 'much better suited to those boys who are at all defective in capacity' (Arnold letters, Winchester College muniment 23530). When Goddard left Winchester, Arnold wrote: 'I shall feel no regret at the loss of a man whom I never could like' (ibid., 23537); such remarks may reveal more about Arnold than about Goddard. Similarly the complaints of Sydney Smith about the misery of his time at Winchester (when Goddard was second master), though plausible, are not necessarily representative; others of his generation had perfectly happy memories of the unreformed school and of Goddard in particular, as Adams showed in *Wykehamica*.

In 1809 Goddard resigned his headmastership. He had been rector of Bepton, Sussex, since 1784. In 1814 he was made a prebendary of St Paul's and in 1829 a canon of Salisbury. He also held the living of Wherwell, near Andover, for a number of years. He divided his time between Andover and London, where he kept in touch with many of his former pupils. At Andover he gave some £30,000 for the rebuilding of Foxcote church, as well as considerable amounts of money for other local causes. To his old school he gave £25,000 so that the scholars might no longer be burdened with the obligation to pay gratuities to the masters, a custom that had long existed in defiance of the college's statutes. He thus became probably the most generous benefactor of Winchester since the college's founder.

Goddard died on 10 October 1845 at his house in Cadogan Place, Chelsea. He was buried on 21 October at Andover, by his own request without any monument over his grave. His name is commemorated at Winchester by a classical prize scholarship founded in 1846. Something of his wise and benevolent character can be discerned in his portrait by H. W. Pickersgill, which is preserved at Winchester. R. D. H. CUSTANCE

Sources H. C. Adams, *Wykehamica* (1878) • letters of Thomas Arnold, Winchester College archives • *DNB* • registers, Winchester College archives • Williams letters, Winchester College archives • *GM*, 2nd ser., 24 (1845), 642–4 • *IGI*

Likenesses J. Lucas, oils, *c.*1830, Winchester College • H. W. Pickersgill, oils, *c.*1835, Winchester College [*see illus.*]

Wealth at death approx. £60,000: *GM*

Godden, (Margaret) Rumer (1907–1998), writer, was born on 10 December 1907 at Meads, 30 Milnthorpe Road, Eastbourne, the second of the four daughters of Arthur Leigh Godden (1876–1966), shipping company manager, and his wife, Katherine Norah Hingley (1876–1966). Soon after Godden's birth her mother took her back to Bengal, where Godden's father worked for the Brahmaputra Steam Navigation Company. Rumer Godden (then known as Peggie) grew up at Narayanganj, on the banks of the Megna River near Dacca in what is now Bangladesh. From the age of five she was determined to be a writer, and several of her best books were inspired by India, where the first half of her life was based. Like most families in British India the Goddens lived in some style, in a large house with a magnificent garden and fifteen servants. All her life Rumer recalled with delight the hibiscus, jasmine, and bougainvillea, and the scent of the sweet peas; but she grew up aware of the darker side of Anglo-Indian life.

Although her parents followed the custom of the time by sending their daughters back to England to be educated, they decided to bring Rumer and her sister Jonquil (known as Jon) back to Narayanganj when the First World War began. Godden felt that she was the plain sister (her nose was likened to the duke of Wellington's) but she and Jon were close, and they later collaborated on a book about their upbringing, *Two under the Indian Sun* (1966). In 1920, however, Rumer reluctantly resumed her interrupted schooling at Moira House in Eastbourne. She disliked her schooldays intensely, but always remained grateful to Mona Swann, the English teacher who taught her grammar and encouraged her to write. However, as she needed to earn her own living she trained first as a dance teacher (later she used a ballet company as the background for several books).

Back in India, Godden read E. M. Forster's *A Passage to*

(Margaret) Rumer Godden (1907–1998), by Mark Gerson, 1958

India soon after its publication in 1924 and, she later wrote, began to feel uneasy about the attitudes and reputation of the conventional Anglo-Indian world she inhabited. Rumer Godden, prickly and indomitable, always went her own way; to the alarm of her circle, in 1930 she opened the Peggie Godden School of Dance in Calcutta, where she unconventionally accepted both Indian and Eurasian pupils. On 9 March 1934 she married Laurence Sinclair Foster (1905–1977), a stockbroker and golf champion, in Calcutta Cathedral because she was pregnant with his child (the boy died at birth). The marriage was soon in difficulties as they had little in common, but they had two more children, Jane and Paula.

Rumer Godden's first book, *Chinese Puzzle*, celebrating the Pekinese dogs she loved all her life, was published in 1935, but she made her name with *Black Narcissus*, which appeared in 1939 while she was back in England awaiting the birth of her second child. A psychologically acute novel about a group of nuns struggling to set up a convent in the Himalayan foothills, it became a best-seller on both sides of the Atlantic and was later made into a classic film by Michael Powell (much despised by Godden).

After the Second World War broke out, Godden took her children on a hazardous journey by boat to rejoin her husband in Calcutta. When he joined the army in 1941 she was left severely in debt; she retreated with her daughters first to a tea plantation near Darjeeling and then to a house outside Srinagar in Kashmir. She started a herb garden and continued doggedly to write; but in 1944, after a mysterious episode when it appeared that one of the servants had put ground glass in the family's food (which she used in her book *Kingfishers Catch Fire*, 1953), she fled back to Calcutta, where she occupied herself in writing a report on the war work being done by women in Bengal.

In 1945 Godden returned to Britain, determined to resume her career as a novelist. She was divorced from Laurence Foster in 1948 and on 26 November 1949 married James Leslie Haynes-Dixon (1900–1973), a civil servant then running the central office of information. A week later she found herself back in Calcutta with Jean Renoir, the renowned French film director, helping him make a film based on what is perhaps her best book, *The River* (1946), which draws heavily upon her own childhood. For the rest of her life she lived in Britain.

Rumer Godden was restless by nature, and the search for the perfect place to live and work led her to move house frequently. Nevertheless, she was a disciplined and productive writer whose books brought her a devoted following. In the early 1960s she converted to Roman Catholicism, and her friendship with the scholarly Benedictine nun Dame Felicitas Corrigan led to one of her most ambitious and admired novels, *In this House of Brede* (1969). She alternated her adult novels with books for children, and in 1972 she won a Whitbread award for *The Diddakoi*, a novel for teenagers about Gypsies, televised as *Kizzy*. After her husband's death in 1973 she moved from Rye in Sussex, where they had been living in the house that once belonged to Henry James, to be near her daughter Jane in Dumfriesshire.

During the 1980s Rumer Godden's fiction went through an unfashionable phase, but she had renewed success with *A Time to Dance, No Time to Weep* (1987) and *A House with Four Rooms* (1989), her two volumes of autobiography; in 1993 she was appointed OBE. In 1994, at eighty-six, she spent a month travelling around her old haunts in India for a television documentary, sustained, at her request, by a supply of her favourite whisky. In 1997 her last novel, *Cromartie v. the God Shiva, Acting through the Government of India*, once again set in India, was published and widely praised. By this time her health was failing, and after a series of strokes she died on 8 November 1998, at Parkgate Nursing Home, Courance, Kirkmichael, Dumfriesshire. Her ashes were buried with her second husband's in Rye after a memorial service on 10 December 1998, which would have been her ninety-first birthday. She produced seventy books, including collections of poetry and anthologies. ANNE CHISHOLM

Sources R. Godden and J. Godden, *Two under the Indian sun* (1966) · R. Godden, *A time to dance, no time to weep* (1987) · R. Godden, *A house with four rooms* (1989) · A. Chisholm, *Rumer Godden: a storyteller's life* (1998) · private information (2004) [daughter] · b. cert. · m. cert. [James Leslie Haynes-Dixon] · d. cert.
Archives Boston University Library, corresp. and literary papers · priv. coll., papers | SOUND BBC Sound Archives
Likenesses M. Gerson, photograph, 1958, NPG [*see illus.*] · photographs, priv. coll.

Godden, Thomas. *See* Tylden, Thomas (1622–1688).

Godel, Guillaume (*supp. fl.* **1145–1173**), supposed Cistercian monk and chronicler, is the name given in the past to the author of a universal history whose colophon mistakenly describes him as a monk of St Martial at Limoges. The only surviving text (Paris, Bibliothèque Nationale, MS Lat. 4893), found its way in the thirteenth century to the abbey of Uzerche, a daughter house of St Martial, and was presumably there erroneously attributed to a Guillaume Godel known to have written a chronicle. But the manuscript certainly originated elsewhere, being the work of an anonymous Cistercian monk living in central France, who under the year 1145 records how as a youth of English origins he entered a monastery which may well have been Pontigny—he gives particulars of that monastery's successive abbots, including the dream of Abbot Hugues on the night before he was elected bishop of Autun. The chronicler also records how he received all the orders except that of priesthood from Hugues de Toucy, archbishop of Sens from 1141 to 1168, but was later ordained priest at Bourges by Pierre de la Châtre, archbishop of Bourges. By 1172 he was living in the latter city, relating how while he was there he saw an apparition of soldiers fighting in the heavens. In the same year he visited Germany, where he was deeply impressed by the famous visionary Hildegard von Bingen, abbess of Rupertsberg. Some time after 1154 he also went to England, where he was able to make some transcripts from the chronicle of Henry, archdeacon of Huntingdon.

The chronicle attributed to Godel is described by its author as a compilation from various sources, and it seldom makes any significant contribution to knowledge. It seems to have been written in the 1170s, probably not long after the last event it records, the rebellion against Henry II by his sons. Under 1162 it records Thomas Becket as a saint, although he was not canonized until 1173, while under 1137 it refers to Louis VII of France, who died in 1180, as still reigning. The author's Cistercian loyalties are revealed by his account of the foundation of his order, and by his admiring references to outstanding monks like Pope Eugenius III and Abbot Bernard of Clairvaux. His Englishness may be apparent in his references to the brutality of the Normans in the years immediately after 1066, and in his evident pride in the royal ancestry of Matilda, Henry I's queen. In addition to the works of such historians as Eusebius, Orosius, and Gregory of Tours, he used some English sources, like Bede and Henry 'of Huntingdon', and he also drew upon the annals compiled at the monastery of St Pierre-le-Vif in Sens, showing that at some point he was resident in that house. His own work was subsequently exploited for the continuation of the Sens chronicle, covering the years 1120 to 1180, which used to be attributed to the monk Clarius. The chronicle ascribed to Godel was not widely known, and has been published only in the form of short extracts; however, it achieved a modest indirect circulation through its employment as a source for the influential chronicle of Robert de St Maurien, a monk of Auxerre who died in 1212.

HENRY SUMMERSON

Sources M. Bouquet and others, eds., *Receuil des historiens des Gaules et de la France / Rerum Gallicarum et Francicarum scriptores*, new edn, 10 (Paris, 1874), 259–63; 11 (1876), 282–5; 13 (1869), 671–7 [extracts from Godel's chronicle] · 'Ex chronico dicitur Willelmi Godelli', ed. O. Holder-Egger, [*Ex rerum Francogallicarum scriptoribus*], ed. G. Waitz, MGH Scriptores [folio], 26 (Hanover, 1882), 195–8 · R.-H. Bautier and others, eds., *Chronique de Saint-Pierre-le-Vif de Sens, dite de Clarius / Chronicon Sancti Petri Vivi Senonensis* (Paris, 1979) · L. Delisle, 'Chroniques et annales diverses', *Histoire Littéraire de la France*, 32 (1898), 250–61, 502–73

Goderich. For this title name *see* Robinson, Frederick John, first Viscount Goderich and first earl of Ripon (1782–1859).

Godet, Gyles (*fl.* *c.*1547–1568), print publisher, is of unknown parentage. He was probably apprenticed to a master in the rue Montorgueil, Paris, the centre of the French woodcut trade, which was then at its peak. He settled in London about 1547 and received letters of denization on 8 April 1551. On 16 May 1555 he was received as a brother of the Stationers' Company, and he is recorded as resident in Blackfriars from 1562 to 1568. In 1562 he published a genealogy of English monarchs that bears his name (BL, G.6456), one of the twenty-seven prints that he registered with the Stationers' Company during the year 22 July 1562 – 22 July 1563. Other register entries have been identified with surviving unsigned woodcuts: an equestrian woodcut of Henry VIII (BM, O'D 42); a portrait of Elizabeth I (BL, Huth 50 (28)); and an anatomical print sometimes found bound into copies of the 1559 edition of T. Geminus's *Compendiosa totius anatomie delineatio*. An entry for *The Carde of London* may refer to the view of London showing St Paul's Cathedral before the fire of 1561 that survives in a late impression in the Pepys collection at Magdalene College, Cambridge, or alternatively to the eight-sheet map of sixteenth-century London usually attributed to Ralph Agas. *A Christian Exhortation of the Good Householder to his Children*, registered in the year 1564–5, is almost certainly identifiable with the anonymous woodcut published in Blackfriars in 1607 with the title *The Good Hows-Holder* (BM, E.6–38).

In the 1560s or 1570s Godet collaborated with a group of Parisian print publishers to produce an illustrated Bible aimed at an international market (surviving illustrations in the Bibliothèque Nationale de France (Réserve Ed 5g) include prints lettered in English and Spanish, as well as in French). Godet's contribution was three series, each of six woodcuts, telling the stories of Joseph (Genesis 37), the prodigal son, and St Paul; the prints were designed for Godet by François Gence of rue Montorgueil. Gence is the only designer identified as having worked for Godet.

Entries for Godet continue to appear in the Stationers' register until 1568. The last known reference to him is in the returns of aliens for 1568, where he is described as 'Frenchman, denison, prynter, with his doughter, and 2 men servants, all came for religion and be of the French church'. There is no other record of his family, although it may be assumed that he was related to Prigent Godet, a rue Montorgueil printer active in 1571.

It was normal practice for woodblocks and copperplates to be handed down from one publisher to another for as long as they could still find a market. English kings from Godet's genealogy were published by Roger Ward in 1584 as illustrations to *A Briefe Discourse of the Actes and Conquests of Nine Worthies* by Richard Lloyd. By 1656 some of his blocks seem to have passed to Thomas Warren, who registered a number of woodcuts with similar titles: *The Good Householder, The Anatomy of Man and Woman, A Roll of All the Kings of England since the Conquest*, and a seven-sheet map of London. SHEILA O'CONNELL

Sources Arber, *Regs. Stationers*, 1.3, 90–91, 120, 134, 165 • R. E. G. Kirk and E. F. Kirk, eds., *Returns of aliens dwelling in the city and suburbs of London, from the reign of Henry VIII to that of James I*, 4 vols., Huguenot Society of London, 10 (1900–08) • *STC, 1475–1640* • E. Gordon Duff, *A century of the English book trade, 1457–1557* (1905) • *Inventaire du fonds français* (Paris), 2.331–3 • M. H. Jones, 'Engraved works recorded in the Stationers' registers', *Walpole Society*, 64 (2002) • J. Adhemar, 'La rue Montorgueil et la formation d'un groupe d'imagiers parisiens au XVIe siècle', *Le Vieux Papier*, 21/fascicule 167 (April 1954), 25–34

Godfray, François (**1807–1868**), politician in Jersey, was born in St Helier, Jersey, on 8 January 1807, the youngest son of Hugh Godfray, a lawyer. He was educated at the college of St Servan, Rennes (Brittany), and at Wandsworth, and studied law in Paris. On his return to Jersey in 1829 he obtained nomination as one of the six advocates (barristers) in the island, and soon became known for his ability and eloquence. In 1831 he was returned by the Laurel (Conservative) Party in an election as constable (chief administrative officer) of St Helier parish. In this capacity he became *ex officio* a member of the States, the island parliament. Although defeated by a Rose (Liberal) Party candidate when seeking re-election in 1834, he was constable of St Martin parish from 1835 to 1841. He was then defeated again, perhaps because he had acquired unpopularity through his resolute quelling of an attempt at poaching by numerous oyster fishers in Grouville Bay in 1838. Godfray had first chased and challenged them on the sea, and then arrested the leaders on land. But he was elected constable of St Saviour in 1842, and held this office through five re-elections until 1860. In the latter year he was elected by the same parish as one of the fourteen deputies to the States created by an act of 1856, and he retained this post for six years.

As an advocate and a member of the States, Godfray was widely respected but was not short of opponents. He was known for his irascibility, which led him into some dramatic quarrels, and for his voluble oratory. The Jersey historian G. R. Balleine said: 'With whirling arms and voice of thunder he beat down all opposition. No such oratory had been heard in Jersey for generations' (*Biographical Dictionary*, 291). Both in court cases and in the States, Godfray's chief antagonist until he died in 1853 was Pierre Le Sueur, a reforming member of the Rose Party, whose style of oratory, in complete contrast to Godfray's, was one of cool and studied restraint. Godfray and Le Sueur were the two leading politicians of mid-nineteenth-century Jersey. The differences between them were not as great as sometimes appeared. Godfray proposed radical reform of the States and the royal court in the early 1830s, but he retreated to a more conservative position when his proposal failed. He and Le Sueur agreed that the States' authority should not be transferred to the Westminster parliament. Godfray carried some smaller reforms, and was understanding and liberal towards continental exiles in Jersey (such as Victor Hugo) when it was desired to expel them in 1855 as a supposed cause of disloyalty to Queen Victoria.

The conservatism of Godfray and his newspaper *Le Constitutionnel* was exaggerated by another of his opponents, the Chartist George Julian Harney, who lived in Jersey from 1855 to 1863 and edited the radical *Jersey Independent*. Harney continually attacked Godfray not only as a conservative but as an acquisitive seigneur or landowner (he did in fact become the owner of seventeen fiefs), and accused him of insistently demanding his monetary dues from poor tenants. Godfray responded fiercely in his own paper and sued Harney unsuccessfully for defamation.

Godfray had several children with his wife, Mary Le Vesconte. For many years before he died he continued to be fully active amid conditions of increasing personal difficulty. From 1855 his eyes troubled him, and in 1858 he went blind. His land speculations undermined his finances, and much of his property fell into the hands of creditors. He died in his office in St Helier from an apoplectic stroke on 11 February 1868, on his return from winning two cases in the royal court. In 1873 the States commissioned oil paintings of both Godfray and Pierre Le Sueur, and these hang in the royal court. IAN MACHIN

Sources G. R. Balleine, *A biographical dictionary of Jersey*, [1] [1948], 290–93 • G. I. T. Machin, 'George Julian Harney in Jersey, 1855–63: a chartist "abroad"', *Annual Bulletin* [Société Jersiaise], 23/4 (1984), 478–95 • J. D. Kelleher, *The triumph of the country: the rural community in nineteenth-century Jersey* (1994) • G. R. Balleine, *History of Jersey*, rev. M. Syvret and J. Stevens (1981) • P. Stevens, *Victor Hugo in Jersey* (1985) • J. Stevens, *Victorian voices: an introduction to the papers of Sir John Le Couteur* (1969)
Likenesses W. M. Hay, oils, 1873, royal court, St Helier, Jersey

Godfree [*née* McKane], **Kathleen** [Kitty] (**1896–1992**), tennis player, was born in Kensington, London, on 7 May 1896, the younger child of John McKane, pianoforte dealer, and his wife, May. She was educated first at home and later at St Paul's Girls' School, London, and St Leonard's School in St Andrews, where she learned to play tennis. She excelled at several sports. At nine she cycled from London to Berlin as part of a family outing; at ten she was awarded the National Skating Association's bronze medal; and in 1918 she was selected for the English lacrosse team to play Scotland, although the match was cancelled because of the war situation. During that war she worked first as a clerk and then as a War Office driver. In the winter of 1919–20 she took up badminton and won the All-England singles title, which she retained for two further seasons and won again in 1924.

As a tennis player Kitty McKane joined the Kew club and made her Wimbledon début in 1919, when the championships were still being held at Worple Road. She reached the quarter-finals, where she lost to Suzanne Lenglen (the eventual winner). That year she won her first international title, the covered court women's doubles, with Mrs Beamish in Paris. In 1920 at the Antwerp Olympics she was a gold medallist in the women's doubles and silver

Kathleen Godfree (1896–1992), by Bassano, 1938

medallist in the mixed doubles, with Winifred McNair and Max Woosnam respectively. She also gained a bronze medal in the women's singles, a feat that she repeated at the Paris Olympics of 1924, the last games to feature tennis until it was revived in Seoul in 1988, where Godfree attended as representative of the All-England Club. At Paris she also won a silver medal in the women's doubles, thus establishing a record for the most Olympic tennis medals won by any player.

A tiny figure on court, McKane usually wore a calf-length white frock and white stockings, with her hair tied back in a silk bandeau. Fast on her feet, she developed an all-court game but preferred to attack, often using the volley as her major weapon. Her skill and tenacity, combined with a composed and placid temperament, took her to three Wimbledon ladies' finals. In 1923 she lost to Suzanne Lenglen, but she won against Helen Wills in 1924, revenge for her defeat by the seventeen-year-old American in the first Wightman cup match the previous year. She was the first British winner of the ladies' event since Mrs Lambert Chambers in 1914. In 1925 she was the losing finalist in the United States championships but won the mixed doubles with J. B. Hawkes; she also lost in the finals of the French singles and women's doubles. In January 1926 she married Leslie Allison Godfree, a solicitor who had been the first player to serve on Wimbledon's centre court after it moved to Church Road in 1922. Together they won the mixed doubles at Wimbledon in 1926, the only husband-and-wife team to do so, thus regaining the title that she had previously won with Jack Gilbert in 1924. In 1926 she also recaptured the Wimbledon ladies' singles title after a final against Lili Alvarez, by changing her tactics and abandoning attack for a match of attrition in which the Spaniard tired first.

Kitty Godfree's last major title was the women's doubles in the American championships in 1927. She wrote two instruction books, *Lawn Tennis: how to Improve your Game* in 1923 and *Lawn Tennis Simplified* in 1928, the year before she retired temporarily from tennis to have her first child, David. Her second son, Martin, was born in 1937. She played in the Wightman cup from its inauguration in 1923 through to 1927 and again in 1930 and 1934, but never again was a prominent singles player. She reached the semi-final of the women's doubles at Wimbledon in 1934, the last of the 147 matches that she played in the championships.

Kitty Godfree continued to play competitive tennis into her tenth decade, including an annual mixed doubles match for the International Club of Great Britain against its Parisian counterpart, in which she usually faced Jean Borotra. They last played against each other in 1988, sixty-four years after they had both won their first Wimbledon singles titles. She died on 19 June 1992 of a chest infection, at Viera Gray House, a nursing home at 27 Ferry Road, Barnes, London. She was survived by her two sons, her husband having predeceased her. WRAY VAMPLEW

Sources d. cert. • *The Times* (20 June 1992) • *The Independent* (20 June 1992)
Archives SOUND BL NSA
Likenesses photograph, 1923, Hult. Arch. • S. White, oils, 1924, Wimbledon Lawn Tennis Museum • Kirby, photograph, 1926, Hult. Arch. • two photographs, 1927–86, repro. in *The Independent* • Bassano, photograph, 1938, NPG [*see illus.*] • photograph, repro. in *The Times*

Godfrey of Winchester. *See* Winchester, Godfrey of (*b.* before 1055, *d.* 1107).

Godfrey, Ambrose, the elder [*known as* Ambrose Godfrey Hanckwitz the elder] (**1660–1741**), chemist, was born Ambrosius Gottfried Hanckwitz in Nienburg, Germany, the second child of Christian Hanckwitz (1612–1665) and his second wife, Katherine (1627–1665). He emigrated to England with his younger brother Johann in the late 1670s, was granted denizenship in March 1692, and naturalized in April 1700. He Anglicized his name as Ambrose Godfrey Hanckwitz, and used this form in publications and some business dealings. His first employment was as an operator for Robert Boyle, where he quickly distinguished himself by perfecting the difficult isolation of white phosphorus, a newly discovered substance which attracted great attention. Its preparation in quantity was a closely guarded secret, and Godfrey held the monopoly on its lucrative trade for over forty years. At the time he lived 'in narrow means' in Chandos Street, London, with his first wife, with whom he had three sons. On 15 October 1706, he married his second wife, Mary (*d.* 1753), widow of Joseph Pitt, apothecary to Queen Anne and to Prince George of Denmark. They had no children.

After leaving Boyle's service, Godfrey was employed at Apothecaries' Hall, and thereafter began his own chemical and pharmaceutical trade. His laboratory and shop

Ambrose Godfrey the elder [Ambrose Godfrey Hanckwitz] (**1660–1741**), by George Vertue, 1718 (after Johann Rudolph Schmutz)

was located behind his house on Southampton Street; it was marked with a golden phoenix rising from the ashes over the date 1680, which recorded not the laboratory's founding but rather Godfrey's successful preparation of phosphorus. The laboratory was in use until 1862, and was converted to Corpus Christi Roman Catholic Church in 1874.

Godfrey was a highly skilled and industrious chemist, a keen observer, and a shrewd entrepreneur. He performed analyses of waters, earths, and stones, many for Sir Hans Sloane and the Royal Society. He perfected the manufacture of ether, studied ambergris, and published on phosphorus and water analysis in the *Philosophical Transactions of the Royal Society* between 1731 and 1736. On 22 January 1730, Godfrey was elected a fellow of the Royal Society. He invented and patented the 'fire annihilator', a wooden barrel full of aqueous solution surrounding a pewter container of gunpowder fitted with a pipe and fuse; when detonated in a burning building, this device extinguished the fire by the explosion and dispersed water. He described a successful demonstration carried out on 30 May 1723 in his *Account of a New Method of Extinguishing Fires by Explosion* (1724). Charles Povey of Hampstead attempted to steal the invention but was foiled.

Late in life Godfrey became mentally feeble, as a result of which J. H. Hampe was able in 1735 to pry from him his secret of preparing phosphorus. Godfrey died at his home in Southampton Street on 15 January 1741, and was buried on 22 January at St Paul's, Covent Garden. His will, dated 5 May 1732 and proved on the day of his death, made provision for his widow, left his house, laboratory, stock, and trade to his sons Ambrose and John, and gave stipends to his eldest son, Boyle (10s. per week), and to Boyle's wife and children (£20 per annum each).

Boyle Godfrey [*formerly* Boyle Godfrey Hanckwitz] (1682/3–1753), eldest son of Ambrose, born in Chandos Street, London, was named after his father's beloved employer. He lived extravagantly, and his looseness with money led to an estrangement from his family. His chronic financial straits have been attributed to a pursuit of alchemy, but there is no evidence for the claim, which is a prejudiced nineteenth-century fiction. In his will his father left him only a small allowance 'that he might not want bread' and claimed that he had squandered 'many thousand pounds' (PRO, PROB 11/707/12). On 6 January 1726 he married Elizabeth Ashcroft, daughter of John Ashcroft and Easter Rea, with whom he had two children, Mary (*b.* 1729, *d.* after 1794) and Ambrose (1730–1797). Pursuit by creditors caused him to flee England in 1731. He attempted to practise medicine at Rotterdam without a degree, then went to France in 1734 where he tried to lecture on chemistry, and where he purportedly obtained an MD. His money troubles continued. He returned to England in 1736 and published *Miscellanea vere utilia*, a collection of chemical and medical observations. He fled to Ireland in 1740, and died in Dublin in early 1753. From 1732 he wrote numerous letters to Sir Hans Sloane bemoaning his troubles and beseeching Sloane's intercession with his father and brothers. A satirical 'epitaph' by Charles Smith MD was read before the Dublin Medico-Philosophical Society in 1756.

Ambrose Godfrey the younger [*formerly* Ambrose Godfrey Hanckwitz] (*c.*1685–1756), chemist, born in Chandos Street, London, was the second son of Ambrose the elder. Ambrose and his brother John inherited the family firm, but a commission of bankruptcy was issued against them for over £3400 in February 1746. This misfortune seems to have owed more to John's habits and expenses than to mismanagement, and he subsequently left the business. Ambrose managed the firm himself on behalf of the assignees, successfully paid off the debts, and regained control. He was a skilled chemist, and wrote *A Compleat Course of Chemistry* for which a prospectus was issued in 1744, but publication never materialized; part of the manuscript survives in the library of the Pharmaceutical Society of Great Britain. Ambrose and John published a *Curious Research into the Elements of Water* in 1747, based on their father's notes regarding the transformation of water into earth; these notes presumably dated back to Ambrose the elder's work for Robert Boyle, who carried out such experimentation.

Ambrose married but had no children; his wife, Elizabeth, is known only by her mention in his will. He died on 20 December 1756 at Southampton Street, and was buried at St Paul's Church, Covent Garden, on 24 December. Earlier that year he had granted partnership in the firm to his nephew Ambrose (1730–1797), son of his brother Boyle. On his death ownership passed to this nephew, who ran the firm most effectively and attempted to revive sales of his grandfather's 'fire annihilator'. Upon his death on 14 March 1797, the business passed jointly to his son Ambrose Towers Godfrey (1769–1807) and his assistant Charles Gomand Cooke, whereafter it was known as the firm of Godfrey and Cooke until its closure in 1916–17.

John Godfrey [*formerly* John Godfrey Hanckwitz] (*d*. 1766?), third son of Ambrose the elder, was born in London; he matriculated at the University of Halle on 28 March 1715, but what he studied is unknown. He is said to have been a skilled swordsman (Ince, 'Memoranda'), and a *Treatise upon the Useful Science of Defence, Connecting the Small and the Back-Sword* was published for a 'Capt. John Godfrey' in 1747. (This may, however, refer to a Captain John Godfrey who married Boyle Godfrey's daughter, Mary). Though John Godfrey appears to have shown little interest in the family laboratory a John Godfrey was elected to the Royal Society in 1715, and sent them three papers on chemical topics in 1730. In the absence of further evidence, he may be assumed to be the same person. He was married; his wife Elizabeth died in September 1727. There is no record of their having any children; although his stepmother's will mentions a daughter Mary this is probably a conflation with Boyle's daughter, Mary. John Godfrey is believed to have died in 1766.

LAWRENCE M. PRINCIPE

Sources R. E. W. Maddison, 'Boyle's operator Ambrose Godfrey Hanckwitz', *Notes and Records of the Royal Society*, 11 (1954–5), 159–88 · R. E. W. Maddison, 'Notes on some members of the Hanckwitz family in England', *Annals of Science*, 11 (1955), 64–73 · H. G. Ince, 'Memoranda of the Godfrey family', Pharmaceutical Society of Great Britain L, London · J. Ince, 'Ambrose Godfrey Hanckwitz', *Pharmaceutical Journal and Transactions*, 18 (1858), 126–30, 157–62, 215–22 · J. Ince, 'The old firm of Godfrey', *Pharmaceutical Journal*, 2 (1896), 166–9, 205–7, 245–8 · 'Godfrey's laboratory', *Pharmaceutical Journal and Transactions*, 3rd ser., 5 (1874–5), 350 · J. R. Partington, *A history of chemistry*, 3 vols. (1961), 2.542–4 · journal books, RS · RS, classified papers · BL, Sloane MS 4048, 144, 314 · BL, Add. MS 4432, 138 · 'Ambrose Godfrey', *Journal of the Society of Arts*, 38 (1889–90), 1054–6 · will, PRO, PROB 11/826, sig. 338 [Ambrose Godfrey, the younger] · will, PRO, PROB 11/707, sig. 12; PROB 11/708, sig. 89

Archives Pharmaceutical Society of Great Britain, London, Hanckwitz MSS · RS, classified papers MSS, journal book MS · Wellcome L., papers | BL, letters to Sir Hans Sloane, Sloane MSS 4046–4052

Likenesses G. Vertue, engraving, 1718 (after J. R. Schmutz), BM, NPG [*see illus.*] · G. Vandergucht, engraving, 1738 (Ambrose Godfrey the younger), repro. in Maddison, 'Notes on some members of the Hanckwitz family', pl. 2, facing p. 68

Wealth at death several houses in London; also laboratory and thriving business in chemicals left to sons: Maddison, 'Boyle's operator'

Godfrey, Ambrose, the younger (*c*.1685–1756). *See under* Godfrey, Ambrose, the elder (1660–1741).

Godfrey, Arabella. *See* Churchill, Arabella (1649–1730).

Godfrey, Boyle (1682/3–1753). *See under* Godfrey, Ambrose, the elder (1660–1741).

Godfrey, Daniel (1831–1903), army officer, bandmaster, and composer, was a member of a family of English military bandmasters. The eldest of four sons of Charles Godfrey (1790–1863), bandmaster of the Coldstream Guards for fifty years, he was born at Westminster on 4 September 1831. His eldest brother, George William Godfrey, was well known as a playwright. Daniel was educated at the Royal Academy of Music, where he subsequently became professor of military music and was elected a fellow. In his early days he was a flute player in Jullien's orchestra and at the Royal Italian Opera. He married Joyce Boyles in 1856, and they had two sons and three daughters. Their eldest son, Dan *Godfrey (1868–1939), bandmaster, conductor, and director of music to the corporation of Bournemouth, was knighted in 1922.

Also in 1856, on the recommendation of Sir Michael Costa, Godfrey was, through the influence of the prince consort, appointed bandmaster of the Grenadier Guards. He composed his famous 'Guards' waltz in 1863 for the ball given by the guards' officers for the prince and princess of Wales on their marriage. This was followed by the 'Mabel' and 'Hilda' waltzes, which were very popular. Godfrey made a tour with his band in the United States in 1876 in celebration of the centenary of American independence. It was the first visit of an English military band since the creation of the republic, and a special act of parliament had to be passed to authorize it. At Queen Victoria's jubilee (1887) he was promoted second lieutenant—the first bandmaster who received a commission in the army.

Godfrey retired from the army on 4 September 1896, with the reputation of England's leading bandmaster. Subsequently he formed a private military band which played at the chief exhibitions in England, and with which he twice toured America and Canada. He rendered splendid service to the cause of military music, and was very successful as an arranger of compositions for military bands. He died at Beeston, Nottinghamshire, on 30 June 1903.

J. C. HADDEN, *rev.* JAMES FALKNER

Sources *MT*, 44 (1903), 539 · Brown & Stratton, *Brit. mus.* · Grove, *Dict. mus.* · private information (1912)

Likenesses W. & D. Downey, woodburytype photograph, NPG; repro. in W. Downey and D. Downey, *The cabinet portrait gallery*, 4 (1894) · Spy [L. Ward], chromolithograph cartoon, NPG; repro. in *VF* (10 March 1888) · portrait, repro. in *Theatre* (1899)

Wealth at death £6374 13*s*. 3*d*.: resworn probate, 31 July 1903, *CGPLA Eng. & Wales*

Godfrey, Sir Daniel Eyers [Dan] (1868–1939), conductor, was born on 20 June 1868 in Winchester Street, Pimlico, London, the elder son of Lieutenant Daniel *Godfrey (1831–1903) and his wife, Joyce Boyles (who died in 1890 after a paralytic stroke). As well as a younger brother he had three sisters. The family was famous for producing three generations of bandmasters. Dan Godfrey was educated between 1880 and 1884 at King's School, the Strand, but his studies were cut short because of suspected eye trouble. He then toured Germany with a commercial career in mind and to learn the language, but on his return decided that music offered better prospects and accordingly enrolled at the Royal College of Music (1885–7), studying first the violin and then the clarinet under Henry Lazarus. After leaving the college, in the hope of succeeding his father as bandmaster of the Grenadier Guards, he studied band instrumentation with John Hartmann, an acknowledged expert, and started making some arrangements and composing small pieces of his own. In 1889 he succeeded his cousin Charles Godfrey (1866–1935) as bandmaster of the corps of commissionaires. In 1890 he gained his bandmaster's diploma at the Royal Academy of Music but because he had not passed through Kneller Hall, the bandmasters' training school, a service appointment was not open to him. He accepted instead the conductorship of the London military band, a municipal ensemble that had been established after the War Office had prohibited military bands from performing outside their own regimental districts. He also took over his father's orchestral work, which included conducting at fashionable balls and exhibitions.

In 1891–2 he toured South Africa, as music director first of the Standard Opera Company and then of the Globe Burlesque Company. There he met Jessie Stuart (1870–1925), daughter of a civil servant in Pietermaritzburg, whom he married in Durban on 19 September 1892. They sailed back to England in October.

In January 1893 Dan Godfrey found among his father's unanswered correspondence a request from Bournemouth to supply a band of thirty players for the reopening of the Winter Gardens. He applied for the position himself and was contracted for a five-month summer season. 'Dan Godfrey's Band' made its first appearance on Whit Monday 1893 and was so successful that he negotiated first for the winter and then for successive seasons: Bournemouth became his home for life.

With his band, employed to play on the pier, on the lawns, and inside the Winter Gardens, Godfrey gradually introduced serious music, adding strings so that by October he was giving classical concerts in addition to his other duties. In December 1894 he inaugurated the first of his forty annual series of winter symphony concerts with which he was able to realize his ambition of making Bournemouth a home for British music where both established and young composers could be sure of a hearing. Composers were frequently invited to conduct their own works. In May 1894 he was officially appointed musical director and adviser and entertainment manager to the corporation and in May 1896 the band became the Bournemouth Municipal Orchestra, the first permanent, fully salaried, municipal orchestra in the country, with Godfrey as its musical director.

In May 1911 the leading British composers of the day held a dinner in London in Godfrey's honour and Sir Charles Stanford toasted him as 'the greatest friend of the British composer' (Godfrey, *Memories and Music*, 83) since Sir August Manns, whose Crystal Palace concerts had been an example to Godfrey. In 1922 Dame Ethel Smyth campaigned vigorously on Godfrey's behalf for a knighthood, which was conferred on him in July by King George V. The following year Godfrey wrote his autobiography, *Memories and Music*.

In 1922 he gave the first of the famous Bournemouth Easter festivals that continued until 1929 when the orchestra moved from the Winter Gardens to the newly built pavilion. With the separate appointment of a general manager Godfrey found himself increasingly at odds with the corporation's attitude towards serious music and his later years were not so happy now that he had lost overall control. Nevertheless, both he and the orchestra reached a wider audience and gained further recognition through the weekly national broadcasts of his symphony concerts from the pavilion.

In 1925 Lady Godfrey died from heart failure. Sir Dan remarried in 1929; his second wife was Mrs Annie Farlam from Buxton. There had been three sons and three daughters from the first marriage. The eldest son, Daniel Stuart (1893–1935), at one time seen as a successor to his father and known—as his father had once been—as Dan Godfrey jun., was a music director for the BBC (1923–6) before being appointed conductor of the Durban Municipal Orchestra in 1928. In April 1935 he died there suddenly from a heart attack.

Sir Dan Godfrey retired in 1934 and was succeeded by Richard Austin. In 1937 he revisited South Africa, where he had some conducting engagements. He died at Bournemouth on 20 July 1939 and was buried at St Peter's Church, Bournemouth, on 24 July 1939. As a conductor his appearances outside Bournemouth were few, largely because of the corporation's restrictive policy. Over the years with the Bournemouth Municipal Orchestra he had made a number of recordings of popular orchestral works, and in 1931 a short film was made of him conducting in the pavilion. In 1926 with the London Symphony Orchestra he made the first complete gramophone recording of Ralph Vaughan Williams's *A London Symphony*, a work with which he was particularly associated. On the rostrum he was, in the words of a local critic, 'a stern disciplinarian [who] would not tolerate scamped or careless work', and he was occasionally abrupt or gruff in manner. Though outspoken at times, he lacked neither warmth nor friendliness. He liked to quote the verdict of his long-serving timpanist: 'He's hot stuff, but he's just!' (Godfrey, *Memories and Music*, 77). He was modest and without prejudice. His repertory, while not admitting the Second Viennese school, was otherwise extraordinarily catholic, with a particular fondness for Russian music. His workload was unequalled and his interpretations were widely respected. His name today rightly rests upon his championing of British music and his founding of today's Bournemouth Symphony Orchestra. STEPHEN LLOYD

Sources D. E. Godfrey, *Memories and music* (1924) • Bournemouth Reference Library, Bournemouth, D. Godfrey scrapbooks [thirteen volumes] • *CGPLA Eng. & Wales* (1939) • S. Lloyd, *Sir Dan Godfrey: champion of British composers: a chronology of forty years' music-making with the Bournemouth Municipal Orchestra* (1995)

Archives Bournemouth Reference Library, Bournemouth, scrapbooks, newspaper cuttings, MSS letters, programmes, photographs, and other memorabilia | FILM BFI NFTVA, documentary footage | SOUND BL NSA, oral history interview · BL NSA, performance recordings

Likenesses H. Lamb, oils, 1936, Russell-Cotes Art Gallery and Museum, Bournemouth · D. Gorvin, sculpture, 1991, Winter Gardens, Bournemouth

Wealth at death £15,001 17*s*. 6*d*.: probate, 28 Sept 1939, *CGPLA Eng. & Wales*

Godfrey, Sir Edmund Berry (1621–1678), magistrate, was born in Sellinge, Kent, on 23 December 1621 to Thomas Godfrey (1585–1664), MP and magistrate, and Sarah, daughter of Thomas Isles of Leeds, one of the procurators of the arches, who had relocated to London from Yorkshire. He was the fifth son of his father's second marriage, which produced eighteen children; his mother outlived him. The Godfreys were a fairly typical Kentish gentry family, although following the death of Edmund Godfrey some questions were raised about the mental health of his father. There seems little to suggest any problems in the 'domestic chronicle' that Thomas Godfrey kept until the 1650s, but it is known that Thomas's own father's mind had decayed in old age.

Early years Edmund Berry Godfrey was baptized in the established church on 13 January 1622. His peculiar name, which was to cause such problems for writers after his death, was the result of his father's combining the names of his godfathers—Captain John Berrie, a cousin and soldier in a foot company at Lydd, and a former neighbour and a friend of his father's, Edmund Harrison. Three names were relatively uncommon in the period and it seems that Edmund Godfrey himself always eschewed the full use of them for he commonly signed his name 'Edmund Godfrey' and rarely 'Edmund Berry Godfrey' and never 'Edmundsbury Godfrey', as some of his early biographers would have it. He was educated at Westminster School and in November 1638 went up to Christ Church, Oxford. By the age of seventeen he had proved himself 'diligent and industrious' (Tuke, 8–9). He had also begun to develop loyalist sympathies and made a contribution to a volume of verses written to congratulate Charles I on the birth of his daughter Anne in 1637. Little else is known of Godfrey at university. It is not clear if he took his degree, but there is no evidence to prove that he left Oxford either disappointed or in disgrace. On leaving the university he travelled on the continent to complete his education. In the mythology created after Godfrey's death much was made of this tour and it was claimed that, although he kept himself free of immorality and vice while abroad, he did associate with Catholics and had Catholic friends. It was also claimed that he was true to the protestant religion. There seems no reason to doubt this assertion, although Godfrey's opinions on Roman Catholicism were certainly more liberal than those of most of his class.

After returning to England in 1640 Godfrey entered Gray's Inn, where he apparently stayed long enough to arrive at that 'mature proficiency as gave him a good title' to the lawyer's garb (Tuke, 8). Unfortunately he was forced to abandon his legal studies at this point because of ill

Sir Edmund Berry Godfrey (1621–1678), by George Bower, 1678

health and increasing deafness. How serious the latter was remains open to doubt. It is possible that it was an excuse for a more critical breakdown in his personal life. Although an early biographer claimed that Godfrey's deafness 'though not very great was always natural to him', the ailment may have been sufficiently serious for him to consult the Irish healer Valentine Greatrakes in the 1660s (ibid.). In the 1640s Godfrey evidently thought his 'deafness' precluded all thought of a career at the bar and he left Gray's Inn without assuming a 'graduates robe'. If he was troubled by deafness it could perhaps account for some of his character traits. He became a rather strait-laced and melancholy young man who favoured solitariness over any company. In later life some began to think his disposition odd, if not downright peculiar, and his appearance was memorably described by Roger North as 'black, hard favoured, tall, stooping … and … commonly wiping his mouth and looking [up]on the ground' (North, 199). For whatever reason, Godfrey moved from his youth into maturity to become a very grave and somewhat querulous individual.

Godfrey's eccentricities certainly became more pronounced as he grew older and more set in his ways. It was alleged that he found crowds very irksome, as well he might if his hearing was impaired, and his association with men who were socially beneath him shocked many of his acquaintances. It was said that he was often seen playing bowls in the company of footmen and 'ordinary' folk. All of this savoured of a man who had become careless of the normal social conventions of the day. He also remained unmarried. Indeed, one of his early biographers, desperately attempting to make him into a martyr, believed Godfrey to have been completely celibate. Godfrey's sexual life, however, remains obscure. With the legal world closed to him, apparently for good, Godfrey, who still had some 'unhealthiness in his body' retired to the countryside to rethink his future (Tuke, 9).

Businessman One of the few traces of Godfrey in the 1640s concerns a legal dispute over some land in Stevenage in 1647. In 1650 he took up the trade of woodmonger and coal merchant in London, entering into a partnership with James Harrison. The latter was a relative of his father's friend and, armed with an estate of some £1000 per annum, both men were able to invest in a yard near Dowgate in the City. With Harrison's retirement from the business Godfrey evidently saw better opportunities in the city of Westminster than the City of London, where indeed there was less competition in his new trade, and in 1659 he moved his business into the parish of St Martin-in-the-Fields.

Godfrey made his first home in Westminster at Greenes Lane, part of Hartshorne Lane, where he rented a house, yard, and wharf. His home was still standing in 1848 when it had, ironically enough considering its former owner's eventual fate, been turned into a police station. In the 1660s Godfrey was elected as master of the Woodmongers Company. He had proved to be a shrewd man of business. In January 1667, as master of the company, he came before Commons committee touching coals and fuels and was found guilty, with others, of selling overpriced coal to the poor. Most critics doubly damned him because, as his business lay in Westminster, it was thought that he had suffered little loss in the great fire of 1666. Godfrey certainly proved reluctant to allow debts to grow too high and this led him into frequent forays into chancery in order to recover his moneys. However, his attempts to have the king's physician, Sir Alexander Fraser, arrested for debt in 1669 backfired on him in a spectacular fashion. Fraser complained to the king and Godfrey ended up in custody for seven days as a result. This incident also added to his by now well-known arrogance—on a visit to France in 1668 such an attitude had apparently taken him close to being whipped.

Other vexed family relationships in this period included those with his nephew Godfrey Harrison, who had been brought into the business as his assistant in 1667 when Godfrey was spending some of his time in dealing with local politics. Godfrey had been nominated as alderman in Farrington ward in 1664, but was discharged on claiming an infirmity of body and fined as a result. In 1666 he was nominated again, but was not elected. He also staved off his election as sheriff. In the course of all of this Godfrey left Harrison, who was unused to the responsibility, to control the business and it went into a severe decline. Harrison's part in his uncle's affairs thus ended in bad feeling. By January 1671 an 'unnatural kindness' existed between the pair. Godfrey went on to note that he hoped 'God will turn his heart & forgive him' (NL Ire., MS 4728, fol. 24) Numerous cases in chancery were launched against the nephew by the uncle, but came to naught. Godfrey lost some £4000 in the process and struggled to regain his business; he subsequently remained very bitter over the affair.

Godfrey had also engaged in a number of land deals since the 1650s to tide him over inevitable bad patches in his trade. In November 1657 he had purchased the leases, and inherited others, from one of the Isles's old properties in Stanwell. They were promptly rented out to tenants. He bought The Swan inn in Fulham as well as lands around it. In 1674–6 he also purchased the lease to some freehold houses in Blue Cross Street and there were deals in property around Brewer's Yard. On a wider scale the Godfrey business was engaged in a number of land transactions with his friend Greatrakes in Ireland. Godfrey's connections also ranged out to businessmen in Bristol and Dublin, while both he and Greatrakes were to invest in a rather dubious salt works on the Medway owned by Sir William Smith. This latter deal came unstuck in 1667 when the Dutch burned the works to the ground during their raid on the nearby naval base.

Entry into local politics In local politics Godfrey made his first appearance at the vestry of St Martin-in-the-Fields in January 1660 and thereafter was regularly involved in its business. In general his main interest in parish affairs was the problem of poverty. He sought to alleviate this through contributions to charity or poor relief, yet he also had a reputation for great severity against vagabonds and criminals in general and this was often resented. His interest in the problem of the poor led to his support for the building of a new workhouse in the parish in 1664–5. In October 1660 he became a magistrate on the Westminster and Middlesex commission of the peace and gained the reputation of a useful and active justice with a strong sense of duty. His work as a justice was not all straightforward. During the plague year of 1665 his influence in the parish and in London came to its height. Alongside his colleagues he ran the government of the area in the absence of most other authorities. According to Godfrey himself at least the 'people seem[ed well] satisfied with their government' (*CSP dom.*, 1665–6, 107). His actions as a magistrate were often severe, but he survived with an increased reputation. His subsequent reaction to the great fire left him as a notable figure at court and in Restoration London; as a result he was well rewarded for his pains with a knighthood and £200 of silver plate, but rather than being pleased he again revealed his stubborn nature by claiming that he sought no reward and went so far as initially to refuse the honour.

In spite of his peculiarities Godfrey was known as a very 'busy' man who seemed to have little fear of the criminals that he came into contact with. Nor does he seem to have lacked courage when it came to exercising his office. He was first assaulted during the 1660s: caught in an alley by an old enemy, Godfrey was threatened with a cudgel and was forced to draw his sword. He managed to fight the man off until his cries for rescue brought assistance. The sense of duty he possessed was thought by some to be almost maniacal in its intensity; in 1665 he was reported as having followed an absconding criminal into a plague house in order to seize the felon. Unfortunately Godfrey also proved on occasions to be reluctant to abandon the role of amateur sleuth. Indeed, he regularly took a lead in such matters, being noted as a man who moved about at odd hours of the night, a solitary figure who peered down alleys and lanes in search of misconduct. He was thought by many to be rather too prone to taking responsibility upon himself and at the same time equally reluctant to give it up once he had taken it. Even more oddly for a public official he was seen as being lenient on dissent. It was soon known that Godfrey was very reluctant to invoke the many penal laws against those of tender conscience. He had many Roman Catholic and dissenting friends, with whom he dealt liberally; indeed, one story asserts that he was willing to bend the law so as not to punish Catholics.

Friendship with Greatrakes There is little doubt that Godfrey's most important friendship of these years was with Valentine Greatrakes. During Greatrakes's visit to London in 1666, after his local success in Ireland at exercising his healing powers on scrofula, or the king's evil, he struck up a firm friendship with Godfrey, so much so that while in London Greatrakes stayed in Godfrey's house. On Greatrakes's return to Ireland in May 1666 the two men maintained their friendship by a personal correspondence that revealed Godfrey's political beliefs, his faith in Greatrakes's powers, and his attitude towards the religious question. Godfrey evidently saw the correspondence as a chance to show off some of his learning, for he was wont to lapse into Latin tags and foreign phrases. He also gently, and sometimes not so gently, mocked Greatrakes's relationship with his wife. Godfrey, a celibate bachelor of forty-five, appears to have been something of a misogynist at heart, believing, as he put it, that 'the Devil in Woman had prevail'd on them to Deboachery' (NL Ire., MS 4728, fol. 3). Greatrakes was obviously someone to whom Godfrey felt he could reveal his close personal feelings. He noted at the receipt of one letter that nothing 'was more welcome unto me than ever the most kind letter from an amoroso to his Mrs. or su e contra from her to him' (ibid., fol. 13). Or again, that he regarded Greatrakes's letters as items 'I keep carefully by me amongst my choicest Reserves' (ibid., fol. 11). At the same time the correspondence also reveals Godfrey's melancholy nature, a dark side to his character which apparently could not be shaken off. Certainly his eagerness for the personal contact and companionship of Greatrakes is revealing of his mental state in the 1660s and 1670s. He was a lonely man despite his busy life. Indeed, questions about Godfrey's state of mind were raised after his disappearance in October 1678. The more intimate figure which emerges from the correspondence naturally bears little or no real resemblance to the protestant martyr which was to be so heavily projected by whig propaganda in the late 1670s and early 1680s. Instead Godfrey emerges as a man of flesh and blood, deeply religious, somewhat misanthropic, and troubled by his relatives, as much as by his odd personality. This combination of factors even led him to think of retiring to live in Ireland in the company of Greatrakes in the early 1670s. This retirement, continually postponed for one reason or another, never happened.

Court politics As a businessman involved in the Restoration political world, Godfrey often had close relations with courtiers and politicians at Whitehall such as Gilbert Burnet and Thomas Osborne, earl of Danby, although in his own political life he noted somewhat prophetically that he was a man who 'If he wo[ul]d be throw paced … might be somebody amongst them [at court.] But … [I have] a foolish & narrow conscience … that spoyles … [me] and all that use it' (NL Ire., MS 4728, fol. 33). While wary of expressing his opinions too blatantly, Godfrey disliked the vanity of court life and was fearful of division, disorder, and factionalism. The ambition of Louis XIV had been attracting critical comments in Godfrey's circle for some time and he wrote that the end of the visit by Charles II's sister Henrietta Maria in 1670, was, 'besides Mistresses & Pleasures … to try if she can prevaile with our K[ing] to relinquish the Dutch interests & adhere to the French in his designs in Flanders' (ibid., fol. 23). In the business community in London both Michael and Benjamin Godfrey, Edmund's brothers, apparently shared this view. These men were part of a group who came to believe that the crown's pro-French policies were damaging to both trade and religion. Godfrey's own fears extended to extremists in religion, whether 'fanaticks' or papists. Despite this he was not in favour of persecution of either group and disliked what he saw as the purge of the commission of the peace in order to put the penal laws into effect. Indeed, he had previously expressed some sympathy for the Quakers and their sufferings. The key elements that emerge in Godfrey's thought were those of discipline and good order: in the home, in church, in the street (where poverty was the gravest problem of all for the magistrate), and in politics. With discipline and good order would come, in time, freedom to worship. At the same time his greatest fear was that the court's policies would bring disorder and dissolution into the land. Politically Godfrey remained a man of contradictions, desiring strong government, but no persecution to achieve it. He also had some unusual City and opposition connections. His activities as a merchant, as well as his political beliefs, apparently led him to drift towards those hostile to the earl of Danby, and in 1676–7 his name was for the first time seriously linked with Sir Robert Peyton and his 'gang'. The term 'gang' was in fact a misleading one: it was first used scornfully by Sir John Robinson in a letter to Sir Joseph Williamson, the secretary of state, and has deceived some historians into thinking that it referred to a group of secret plotters; in fact these men can rather be seen as a part of the growing opposition during the 1670s to the policies of Danby and Charles II that made much of the fears that a French alliance would bring popery and the invasion of liberty in its wake. Some of this group were to be excluded from the commission of the peace as a result of their activities in 1675–7 and were subsequently to be associated with the Green Ribbon Club. Godfrey was apparently friendly towards these men and some of their ideas, although he was not removed from the commission of the peace. Godfrey's links with Peyton were soon noted by the regime and cannot have done him much good. Upon hearing of the magistrate's death both Charles II and his brother James, duke of York, who had good reason to be hostile to potential republicans at the best of times, were openly to disparage Godfrey as a 'fanatique' (PRO 31/3/141, Barillon to Louis XIV, 31 Oct 1678), a sure sign of their belief in his poor choice of company in the 1670s. Godfrey was also connected with Peyton's circle by other wrangles. Had he not died when he did there seems little doubt that he would in time have drifted into full opposition—or perhaps not, for his contradictions were among his most notable characteristics. He had, for example, retained a friendship with a number of Roman Catholics, such as John Grove, who lived in Southwark, and the notorious gossip and self-styled agent of France Edward Coleman. This contradiction doubtless accounts for some of Godfrey's ill-fated moves when faced with the implications of Titus Oates's depositions about a popish plot in the autumn of 1678.

Popish Plot and mysterious death Godfrey's involvement in the scandal of the Popish Plot began in September 1678 when Israel Tonge, advised by his 'honourable friends', took his companion Titus Oates to see Godfrey in his capacity as a magistrate and have some depositions appertaining to a popish plot sworn before him (Tonge, 35). Although at first Godfrey was reluctant to become involved he did take the depositions. Yet in spite of being handed evidence of a supposed popish conspiracy his reaction to the plot was both nervous and indecisive. Although he was never called before the privy council to explain his part in the proceedings with Oates and Tonge there seems little doubt that he subsequently advised Edward Coleman of his dealings with the informers and may have even interfered in the affair to the extent that he was warned off by somebody in authority, who may have been either Danby or the duke of York. Godfrey's ensuing actions are shrouded in mystery. He is said to have told one acquaintance that 'I shall have little thanks for my pains … I did it very unwillingly and would fain have [had] it done by others' (North, 200–201). It appears that Godfrey believed that his action or inaction had stirred up a considerable amount of trouble for himself. He had obscured the evidence, or at least decided not to pursue it in as vigorous and public a manner as he should have done. In effect he was dabbling with the crime of misprision of treason and his dealings with Edward Coleman were to lead him into still further dangerous ground.

Godfrey's last week was, if some sources are credited, one of considerable personal disorder that exacerbated his natural melancholy and which may have led to a mental breakdown caused by fear of the consequences of his involvement in the plot. At the least it is clear that he was very unhappy before his disappearance on Saturday 12 October 1678. The last sighting of him on that day was at about three in the afternoon—he was not seen alive again.

Who killed Godfrey? The reaction of his servants, family, and the town to his disappearance was unusual. As Roger North commented 'What a matter was it, that a justice of the peace did not dine at home, to raise such a hubbub as this?' (North, 201). In the week of their brother's disappearance Michael and Benjamin Godfrey in particular were said to have been frequently at the privy council claiming that the magistrate had been killed by the papists and 'it was in everyone's mouth, Where is Godfrey? … they say he is murdered by the papists' (ibid.). This belief led to hysteria after the discovery of Godfrey's body near Primrose Hill on Thursday 17 October. He was discovered lying in a ditch with his sword run through him just under his left breast; it came out about 7 or 8 inches out of the right side of his back. His coat was thrown up over his head and his hat and periwig were lying in some nearby bushes. No band or laced cravat was ever found upon him, even though it was claimed that he had been wearing a large laced band on leaving home. Once the body had been searched strangulation marks from a cord or cloth were also found upon the magistrate's neck. The subsequent coroner's inquest was confused, partial, and almost certainly subject to the influence of Godfrey's family. From the available records it seems that the jurors and the coroner of Middlesex, John Cooper, although confused throughout the proceedings, were swayed by the two medical witnesses who examined the body, one of whom had been specifically brought along by Michael, Godfrey's younger brother, and so they brought in a verdict of murder. In the course of this inquest witnesses were also apparently intimidated and, according to some, evidence was suppressed, as the case began to take on political overtones. Titus Oates's revelations of the plot to the privy council earlier in October were now apparently confirmed by the death of Godfrey and there were soon moves afoot to discover his killers. Almost inevitably the blame was laid on the Catholic community. Few paused to ask why they should murder such a liberal magistrate and an apparent friend to themselves as Godfrey. Tension was further raised at the magistrate's unofficial lying-in-state, organized by his family. A large crowd of people went to pay their respects, many of whom went away distressed. This led to fears that an enraged London mob would soon rise and precipitate a massacre of all the Catholics in the city. None the less, although a number of arrests were made of Catholic suspects for their part in the plot, the presumed killers of Godfrey still remained at large. On the other hand the making of Godfrey into a protestant icon—a martyr who had died so that others might live—was a more rapid affair. A thick layer of propaganda soon submerged his true character. Godfrey's image went through a variety of stages, from the actual use of his corpse in public display, in a mass funeral on 31 October 1678, to the use of his image in tableaux and parades, to the production of pamphlet literature containing illustrative and poetic material. These were largely the work of opposition factions who, because of the crisis, were coalescing into a political party that many were soon to label as whig. These set pieces, almost public dramas, over the next few years were designed to push home the Catholic threat to the nation and the fact that Godfrey had been a martyr for the protestant cause. The funeral itself was a highly organized piece of propaganda. Seventy-two divines and over 1000 mourners of 'quality' attended the cortège and considerable numbers of citizens from London also joined the procession. This prodigious crowd also packed the church of St Martin-in-the-Fields to hear a bombastic pulpit performance by Dr William Lloyd.

Godfrey's corpse had fallen into the hands of those who wished to press home political and religious points. Michael Godfrey had already stepped in to take command of Edmund's affairs by seizing his brother's papers. He also possessed indisputable links with the opponents of Danby's regime that went back at least to the early 1670s and, with parliament now in session, the moves to exploit the crisis began to grow apace. In the great political contest that was to follow the death of Godfrey, the victim became merely a pawn as both Shaftesbury and Charles sought to resolve the succession crisis. Indeed, a subcommittee of the House of Lords on Godfrey's murder was packed with 'opposition' or opportunistic peers and managed by Shaftesbury. The committee members had little time for those with tales that did not fit into its already preconceived notions that Godfrey had been murdered by papists. Witnesses were treated to a mixture of threat and financial inducement in a series of robust interrogations and little else emerged from the hearings and interrogations.

The revelations of the informer William Bedloe in November 1678 finally gave the authorities a lead in the case. Bedloe claimed that Somerset House was the place of the killing and he also, eventually, recognized Miles Prance, a Roman Catholic silversmith, as a party to the crime. In turn Prance related a detailed version of the murder to the authorities to save his own life and named three men—Robert Green, Henry Berry, and Lawrence Hill—who were subsequently tried and executed for Godfrey's murder. This, to contemporaries, settled the killing of Godfrey in that it confirmed that the papists had murdered him as part of a wider popish plot. Attempts to alter this verdict only came in the 1680s when the heat of the plot had begun to cool. The first real attempt to present a different version of Godfrey's death took place in 1682 and resulted in Nathaniel Thomson, William Pain, and John Farwell being placed on trial for libel. These men had implied that Godfrey had killed himself and that the coroner's jury had been persuaded to bring in a verdict of murder, rather than suicide. After this few indeed were willing to dispute the current version of Godfrey's death. It took a sea change in English politics in the mid-1680s to allow Sir Roger L'Estrange finally to take up the challenge of the investigation. He eagerly undertook to investigate both the plot and the murder of Godfrey on behalf of the new king. L'Estrange published *A Brief History of the Times* in three parts beginning in August 1687. Although L'Estrange somewhat muddied the waters, and permanently removed some evidence from circulation, he underwrote his work by collecting valuable evidence from some forty witnesses whose statements he then cut and pasted in his book in such a way as to prove that Godfrey had committed suicide. His main thesis was simple enough. L'Estrange claimed that the magistrate's brothers had covered up the crime of suicide, or *'felo de se'*, in conjunction with the advice of the whig earl of Shaftesbury, in order to save the estate and damage the regime. Much of L'Estrange's evidence was not above suspicion—there seems little doubt that he manipulated some of his witnesses. At the least he rewrote some of the statements to make them into more suitable and fluid accounts, at the worst he may have altered evidence to suit himself. Certainly few of the witnesses, who now came forward with different stories from the ones they had told in 1678, were willing to stand up against L'Estrange's robust methods of research. Nevertheless some of the evidence he found, and he had the advantage of being upon the scene much earlier that any subsequent historian, does ring true. Once the book was published the case for suicide rested and although it was not generally well received it did convince the playwright Aphra Behn to write a poem praising L'Estrange's efforts. After James II's fall from power in December 1688 it was not thought politic to raise the spectre of a suicidal Godfrey now that the protestant monarchs William and Mary were on the throne and Godfrey's nephew was giving financial assistance to King William's war.

More theories After the revolution of 1688 the historians of the day mostly regurgitated evidence taken from contemporary pamphlets: they had little new evidence. Two exceptions were the former courtier and legal officer Roger North and the philosopher David Hume. North thought the Roman Catholics were probably innocent but he doubted that Godfrey had killed himself. Instead, after a brief review of the evidence, he obscurely hinted that the real culprit was Oates himself, Danby, or Oates's backers, by whom he presumably meant Shaftesbury and the other whig leaders. Hume on the other hand for the first time made the sensible suggestion that the Godfrey killing might just not have been connected with the plot at all. After his review of the evidence he commented that the Catholics had no reason to kill Godfrey, as he was friendly towards them, and it was too clumsy and absurd a crime for the whigs to be capable of. In 1903 John Pollock in *The Popish Plot* claimed that there really was a plot, which, while the details were obscure, generally proved that Roman Catholics were intent upon gaining power and bringing the nation back under the control of Rome. Alfred Marks's book *Who Killed Sir Edmund Berry Godfrey?* returned to the suicide theory. Prance and Bedloe were dismissed as liars and the Somerset House theory fell by the wayside. Instead Marks returned once more to the melancholic Godfrey who committed suicide on Primrose Hill. It was J. G. Muddiman who in 1924 introduced a new and more melodramatic figure to the crime that he based on an ingenious link of a mad aristocrat with an apparently similar *modus operandi* to the man who killed Godfrey. Muddiman claimed that Roger North knew the killer but had been afraid to speak out for fear of the murderer's friends. His theory was that the killing was actually committed by the rather ill-tempered and 'half-mad' Philip Herbert, earl of Pembroke, a violent, drunken, 'Whiggish' aristocrat, who when not physically attacking his enemies had contacts with the opposition groups. In 1678 Godfrey in his capacity as foreman of a jury had found

Pembroke guilty of murder. Unfortunately Pembroke had been able to appeal to the House of Lords for his trial and had subsequently been released. Godfrey had thus left the country for a while, but Pembroke had not forgotten him and in the autumn of 1678 he had sought his revenge on the magistrate. In the 1930s the detective storywriter John Dickson Carr developed Muddiman's theory into a book and chose Pembroke as the most likely candidate—but there is no real contemporary evidence to link Pembroke with the crime. J. P. Kenyon took another route in his version of events in the 1970s. He thought that the easiest solution to the problem was that of the unknown footpad with a grievance. This unknown, and by now undiscoverable man, was as likely a candidate for the killing of Godfrey as anyone else. This solution, however, does not really explain Godfrey's moods of depression prior to his demise. Moreover, given the £500 reward being offered for information on the crime, no common criminal, however ingenious, could have kept the affair quiet in the face of what was in contemporary terms an enormous amount of money. The lack of an obvious answer led to the somewhat wild solution that Stephen Knight was to put forward in the 1980s. Knight simply piled one theory on top of another so as to implicate everyone who could have possibly played any part in the killing. Alan Marshall in his version of the events analysed the various theories and came up with an explanation resting upon suicidal strangulation and the subsequent manipulation of Godfrey's body by his brothers for their own family and political reasons.

The case of Godfrey's demise remains a fascinating historical puzzle, significant because his death left wider political repercussions in its wake: it fed the growing anti-Catholic hysteria of 1678, it led to the further persecution, and some executions, of Roman Catholics in the country; and it led to a political crisis in which the right of succession in the royal family was questioned and, indirectly, to the establishment of the first political parties in the British system, the whigs and the tories. Investigators have often tended to concentrate upon a solution to the mystery by putting forward various candidates as perpetrators of Godfrey's death. In fact, none of these solutions seems very satisfactory and by concentrating upon contemporary evidence, however muddled and muddied that may be, almost all of them can be dismissed. Ultimately Ockham's razor must come into play: 'no more things should be presumed to exist than are absolutely necessary'. Taking this approach and using contemporary evidence logically should give the simplest solution of all to the mystery.

ALAN MARSHALL

Sources R. Tuke, *Memoires of the life and death of Sir Edmund Berry Godfrey* (1682) • A. Marshall, *The strange death of Edmund Godfrey: plots and politics in Restoration London* (1999) • letterbook, NL Ire., MS 4728 • *CSP dom.*, 1665–6 • I. Tonge, 'Journal of the plot, 1678', *Diaries of the Popish Plot*, ed. D. G. Greene (1977) • R. North, *Examen, or, An enquiry into the credit and veracity of a pretended complete history* (1740) • R. L'Estrange, *A brief history of the times* (1688) • *A succinct narrative of the bloody murder of Sir Edmund Bury Godfrey, Octob: 12 1678* (1683) • *An elegie on the right honourable Sir Edmundbury Godfrey, knight* (1678) • *Reflections upon the murder of Sir Edmund Bury Godfrey* (1682) • *Sir Edmund Bury Godfrey's ghost, or, The answer to Nathaniel Thompson's second letter from Cambridge to Mr. Miles Prance in relation to the murder of Sir Edmund-bury Godfrey*, 2nd edn (1682) • T. Dawks, *The murder of Sir Edmund Bury Godfrey* (1678) • M. Prance, *A true narrative and discovery of several very remarkable passages relating to the horrid Popish Plot as they fell within the knowledge of Mr Miles Prance* (1679) • N. Thompson, *A true and perfect narrative of the late terrible and bloody murder of Sir Edmund Berry Godfrey who was found murthered on Thursday the 17th of this instant October in a field near Primrose Hill, with a full accompt of the manner in which he was found also the full proceedings of the coroner who sat upon the inquest &c* (1678) • will, PRO, PROB 11/359, sig. 46

Archives NL Ire., letter-book, MS 4728

Likenesses J. Hoskins, miniature, *c*.1663, repro. in *Sotheby's Illustrated Sale Catalogue* (11 Oct 1955) [lot 22] • P. Vandrebanc, engraving, *c*.1677–1678 • G. Bower, silver medal, 1678, BM [*see illus.*] • T. Dawks, engraving, 1678 (*The murder of Sir Edmund Bury Godfrey*) • chalk drawing, *c*.1678, NPG • oils, *c*.1678, NPG • oils, *c*.1678, City of Westminster • G. Bower, medals, BM • engraving, repro. in Tuke, *Memoires* • line engraving, BM; repro. in *A poem on the effigies of Sir Edmund-Bury Godfrey* (1678)

Wealth at death great silver flagon; Swann Inn, Fulham; land and tenements in Fulham; three parcels of land (let out to tenants) in Stanwell, Middlesex; freehold house in Blue Cross Street, London; total bequests £796 9*s*.: will, PRO, PROB 11/359/46

Godfrey, Elizabeth. *See* Bedford, Jessie (1852/3–1918).

Godfrey, John (*d.* 1766?). *See under* Godfrey, Ambrose, the elder (1660–1741).

Godfrey, John Henry (1888–1971), naval officer and intelligence officer, was born in Handsworth, Birmingham, on 10 July 1888, the third son and youngest of the four children of Godfrey Henry Godfrey, company secretary of Mapplebecks and Wilkes, and his wife, Kathleen Castley. He was educated at King Edward Grammar School and entered HMS *Britannia* as a naval cadet in 1903. He was promoted lieutenant in 1909 and specialized in navigation. He served in the destroyer *Welland* (1909), the Yangtze (Yangzi) gunboat *Bramble* (1910–12), the light cruiser *Blanche* (1913), and on the outbreak of war joined the old cruiser *Charybdis*, the flagship of Rosslyn Wemyss.

Godfrey followed Wemyss to the Mediterranean in the armoured cruiser *Euryalus* and took part in the entire Gallipoli campaign. Promoted lieutenant-commander (1916), he became assistant to Commodore Rudolf Burmester, chief of staff first to Wemyss and then to Vice-Admiral Somerset Gough-Calthorpe, under whom Godfrey served in the Mediterranean and Black Sea (1917–19) and from whom he earned high praise as an exceptional staff officer. He was mentioned in dispatches and awarded the Légion d'honneur (chevalier) and the order of the Nile.

After promotion to commander and appointment as war staff officer in the Home Fleet (*Queen Elizabeth*, 1920), Godfrey served in plans division (1921–3), and on the directing staff of the Staff College, Greenwich. He was appointed second in command of the cruiser *Diomede* on the New Zealand station (1925–8). Promoted captain (1928), he was deputy director, Staff College (1929–31), and commanded the cruiser *Suffolk* on the China station (1931–3), before returning as deputy director, plans division (1933–6). His very successful command of the battle cruiser *Repulse* in the Mediterranean (1936–8) brought the early creation as CB and appointment to the key post of director of naval intelligence with immediate promotion to rear-admiral (February 1939).

Godfrey tackled the task of repairing years of neglect of the intelligence division with great energy and foresight, but not all the weaknesses had been overcome when the war suddenly spread to Norway. However, the situation was very different when Godfrey was relieved in December 1942. The division had been expanded tenfold by the recruitment of many talented civilians, the operational intelligence centre (OIC) had become the nerve centre of the war at sea, the analysis and distribution of information derived from the code-breakers at Bletchley Park perfected, a simple system of grading intelligence introduced, the inter-service topographical department (ISTD) successfully created at Oxford, the joint intelligence committee firmly established, and the principle of the indivisibility of intelligence widely accepted. For these and other vital developments Godfrey had been either entirely or primarily responsible. Weaknesses in British naval ciphers, not fully realized at the time, did remain but for this the blame in fact lay elsewhere.

Godfrey's insistence that intelligence must adopt a critical, sceptical, and scientific approach and present its findings without fear or favour had led to early clashes with Winston Churchill and, by mid-1942, his uncompromising and at times abrasive attitude had aroused the hostility of his colleagues on the joint intelligence committee who appealed to the chiefs of staff for his removal. The first sea lord, Admiral Sir Dudley Pound, although he had only recently extended Godfrey's appointment and approved his exceptional promotion to vice-admiral on the active list (September 1942), informed him that he would be relieved as soon as a successor could be found, a decision considered by many, including the historian Stephen Roskill, to have been both ill-judged and unjust.

Godfrey was nevertheless appointed flag officer commanding Royal Indian Navy (RIN) (February 1943). The RIN, a tiny force in 1939, had been expanded enormously but without, unfortunately, sufficient attention being paid to recruitment and training or the establishment of a proper naval staff or infrastructure. Godfrey tackled these pressing problems with his accustomed incisiveness and success so that the RIN was able to play a gallant and valuable part in the war in the Far East. He had been placed on the retired list and promoted admiral (September 1945) but continued to serve in his old rank until March 1946. The sudden ending of the war, the need to reduce the navy to a peacetime size, and the political ferment in India unfortunately resulted, as it did in other services there, in an outbreak of mass disobedience, in fact revolt. Godfrey, with Field Marshal Sir Claude Auchinleck's backing, treated it as such and succeeded in restoring discipline within a few days, a remarkable achievement. This endeared him neither to the British government nor to extreme nationalist opinion in India. He returned to England and after leave finally retired in September 1946.

For the next fifteen years he devoted himself to voluntary work as chairman of the Chelsea Group of hospitals in the newly formed National Health Service and as the driving force in the creation of the Cheyne Centre for Spastic Children.

Godfrey was the only officer of his rank to receive no official recognition whatsoever for his immense services to the allied cause during the war, a palpable injustice. He had been, under very different conditions, just as great an intelligence chief as Sir W. R. ('Blinker') Hall in the First World War. An intellectual and highly cultured man, liberal minded and forward looking, capable of many acts of personal kindness, he was nevertheless reserved and sensitive. He did not suffer fools gladly and although greatly admired by all his staff some found his unwavering blue eyes and formidable mien daunting. Like Admiral Sir H. W. Richmond before him, under the immense strains of war he sometimes offended important colleagues and superiors. Earl Mountbatten of Burma considered that but for this weakness he might have reached the very top of his profession.

In 1921 he married (Bertha) Margaret, daughter of Donald Hope, managing director of Henry Hope & Sons Ltd, window-frame manufacturers, of Birmingham; they had three daughters. Margaret Godfrey was a tower of strength to her husband in their home life, in ISTD, and in India, where she was head of the Indian WVS. He died on 29 August 1971 at Eastbourne. PATRICK BEESLY, *rev.*

Sources P. Beesly, *Very special admiral: the life of Admiral J. H. Godfrey* (1980) · D. McLachlan, *Room 39: naval intelligence in action, 1939–1945* (1968) · E. Montagu, *Beyond top secret U* (1977) · *The Times* (31 Aug 1971) · private information (1986) · *CGPLA Eng. & Wales* (1971) · S. W. Roskill, *The war at sea, 1939–1945*, 3 vols. in 4 (1954–61)
Archives CAC Cam., memoirs · NMM, papers · NMM, staff college lectures · Royal Naval Museum, Portsmouth, memoirs | CAC Cam., corresp. and papers relating to the career of Sir Dudley Pound
Likenesses W. Stoneman, three photographs, 1932–56, NPG · Madame Yevonde, colour print, NPG
Wealth at death £3247: probate, 26 Nov 1971, *CGPLA Eng. & Wales*

Godfrey, Michael (1659–1695), banker, was born on 22 February 1659, the eldest son of Michael Godfrey (1625–1689), merchant, of London and Woodford, Essex, and Anne Mary Chamberlan (*d.* 1707/8). Godfrey's father came from an extensive clan, being one of eleven sons who included Edmund Berry Godfrey, the magistrate murdered in 1678. Michael Godfrey the elder was a successful merchant and heavily involved in city politics as a whig in the 1670s and 1680s. The efforts of his two sons to follow in his footsteps did not win his approval: 'my sons Michael and Peter bringing into hotchpott all sums of money by me to them already given' (PRO, PROB 11/397).

Despite his father's reservations Godfrey was an able merchant, involved in the wine trade and also in attempting to set up a new East India Company. It was Godfrey's search (along with other merchants) for an outlet for surplus funds which allowed William Patterson's proposal for a Bank of England to receive substantial backing from the mercantile community. Godfrey's key role can be seen in his election as the bank's first deputy governor. He even went into print with *A Short Account of the Bank of England* (1695). One of his tasks as deputy governor was to help draft the first by-laws of the bank. At a general court held on 16 May 1695, at which his brother Peter was elected a director, it was resolved to establish an agency in Antwerp to facilitate the remittances necessary to pay the troops in Flanders. Godfrey was one of three directors sent over to Flanders to supervise this establishment, and they duly waited on William III, at that time besieging Namur, on 17 July 1695. Following dinner with the king the party from England took a view from the trenches in front of the town, when a stray cannon ball killed Godfrey as he stood next to the king.

The shock of Godfrey's death hit bank stock, which lost 2 per cent of its value. He was buried next to his father in St Swithin London Stone, Cannon Street, where his mother erected a tablet to his memory. His death was commemorated in verse by Elkanah Settle in *Augusta lachrymans* (1695). In Godfrey's will, made in May 1695, he left all his estate in Middlesex and Essex and his bank stock to his mother. His mother survived him for many years, composing her will in November 1707 (proved April 1708). STUART HANDLEY

Sources *N&Q*, 179 (1940), 38 • 'The domestic chronicle of Thomas Godfrey, Esq', ed. J. G. Nichols, *The topographer and genealogist*, 2 (1853), 450–67, esp. 460, 465 • will, PRO, PROB 11/397 [Michael Godfrey, d. 1689] • will, PRO, PROB 11/427 [Michael Godfrey, d. 1695] • will, PRO, PROB 11/500 [Anne Godfrey, d. 1707/8] • D. W. Jones, *War and economy in the age of William III and Marlborough* (1988), 12, 15, 294, 296 • [E. Hatton], *A new view of London*, 2 (1708), 559–60 • N. Luttrell, *A brief historical relation of state affairs from September 1678 to April 1714*, 3 (1857), 357, 473, 503 • J. Clapham, *The Bank of England: a history*, 1 (1944), 15, 26 • J. Stow, *A survey of the cities of London and Westminster and the borough of Southwark*, new edn, ed. J. Strype, 2 (1720), 193 • J. R. Woodhead, *The rulers of London, 1660–1689* (1965) • A. Marshall, *The strange death of Edmund Godfrey* (1999), 1–15 • M. Godfrey, *A short account of the Bank of England* (1695)

Godfrey, Richard Bernard (*b. c.*1728, *d.* in or after 1795), draughtsman and printmaker, was probably born in London about 1728. Nothing is known about his family, childhood, or training. Rather confusingly, a view of Campagna after Salvator Rosa, one of his earliest known prints, published in 1763, was signed 'I B. Godfrey', but this appears to be a unique incidence. Between 1765 and 1770 he exhibited a number of plates with the Society of Artists, all of which were submitted in the name of 'Richard B. Godfrey, Engraver'. As these exhibits demonstrate, Godfrey could turn his hand to a variety of different subjects, including portraiture and landscape. He did, however, favour etching as his primary medium. Although many of his etchings are reproductive prints, his *South Aspect of Knole in Sevenoke Kent* (an impression of which may be found in the British Museum, London) is signed 'Godfrey del et sculp'; this mildly picturesque bird's-eye prospect thus reveals his competence as a draughtsman and his sensitivity to the nuances of fashionable taste.

It would appear that the mainstay of Godfrey's career was working for London publishers in the production of book illustrations, especially for topographical and antiquarian volumes; the best-known of these were probably Francis Grose's works of popular antiquarianism, *Antiquities of England and Wales* (1773–87) and the *Antiquarian Repertory* (1775). This was a vast and varied undertaking, in which Godfrey was one of the team of printmakers responsible for etching records of diagrams and plans as well as views of ruins set in landscape and reproductions of early paintings and portraits. Although quarto in size, and often rather formulaic in handling, many of Godfrey's plates managed to capture the wistful appeal of their ancient subjects through their skilful combinations of deeply bitten lines.

Godfrey also worked for individual patrons. Horace Walpole, for example, described him as one of 'my engravers' (Walpole, *Corr.*, 2.53) when, in 1778, Godfrey was preparing plates for the second edition of his *Description of Strawberry* (1784). Walpole was doubtless a jealous patron, and his anger when Joseph Gulston managed to 'bribe' (ibid., 34.576) his engravers for some proof copies of these plates also suggests that Godfrey was more entrepreneurial than scrupulous by nature. The date of Godfrey's death remains unknown, but it is thought that he was active until the mid-1790s. LUCY PELTZ

Sources T. Clayton, *The English print, 1688–1802* (1997) • Graves, *Soc. Artists* • Redgrave, *Artists* • G. Meissner, ed., *Allgemeines Künstlerlexikon: die bildenden Künstler aller Zeiten und Völker*, [new edn, 34 vols.] (Leipzig and Munich, 1983–) • Thieme & Becker, *Allgemeines Lexikon* • Walpole, *Corr.*

Godfrey, Thomas (*d.* 1721), apothecary and inventor of Godfrey's cordial, was probably one of the many Thomas Godfreys who were baptized in various Hertfordshire parishes during the middle years of the seventeenth century. He should not be confused with Ambrose (Hanckwitz) Godfrey (*d.* 1741), chemist, of Southampton Street, London, who in the late seventeenth century issued handbills advertising 'good cordials as royal English drops'. Very little seems to be recorded about Thomas Godfrey's life and career; his will, drawn up on 27 July 1721, described him as a 'chirurgeon' of Hunsdon, Hertfordshire. It was not uncommon for medical practitioners of that era, in the provinces as well as in London, to make up their own medicines for patients, and then begin to market them more widely when demand began to grow. No wife or children survived Godfrey, but he mentioned a brother and two sisters in the will, which was proved in London on 28 October 1721.

As no reference was made in Godfrey's will to the cordial or its recipe, it is not surprising that rivals in Hertfordshire were very soon vying for the trade. In December 1721 John Fisher, 'physician and chymist', advertised that he had the true formula from Godfrey, and warned the public that illiterate and ignorant persons, such as bakers, maltsters, and goldsmiths, were striving to manufacture the cordial, even though the skill needed was beyond their reach, 'so that by their Covetousness and Pretensions, many Men, Women, and especially Infants, may fall as Victims, whose Slain may exceed Herod's Cruelty' (*Weekly Journal*, 23 Dec 1721).

Not to be outdone, Thomas Humphreys, of Ware, surgeon, two months later publicized his version of the cordial, allegedly concocted according to a recipe made out in Godfrey's own hand. Whatever the result of the two doctors' battles, the list of 'nostrums and empirics' in the *Gentleman's Magazine* for 1748 mentions only Mr Godfrey of Newcastle's cordial for the stomach: one of the cheapest of all those listed, at 6*d*. a bottle. Partly because of the medicine tax, its price had risen to 9*d*. by the end of the century.

In 1823 Thomas Wakley, first editor of *The Lancet* and scourge of nostrum-mongers, published an analysis of Godfrey's cordial. Its contents were found to include Venice treacle, ginger, rectified spirits of wine, oil of sassafras (or medical bark), and tincture of opium. Its sweetness and agreeable flavour, added to its ability to knock out or at least dull the senses of the most fractious patient, made it a boon for distraught mothers and lazy nurses: a forerunner of the notorious nineteenth-century Mrs Winslow's Soothing Syrup from the United States, which was well laced with morphia.

In 1837–8, no fewer than twelve children were recorded as having been killed by Godfrey's cordial, but some of the differing varieties then on sale were widely known to be less dangerous than others. After the introduction of the National Health Service in 1948 the cordial was still occasionally prescribed, despite being held to be a poison. Later Godfrey was immortalized by his inclusion in the *Oxford English Dictionary*, a lexicographic privilege bestowed on the very few, such as Robert James and Thomas Holloway, who had also gained celebrity as quacks. T. A. B. Corley

Sources G. B. Griffenhagen and J. H. Young, 'Old English patent medicines in America', *Pharmacy in History*, 34 (1992), 200–28 · *Weekly Journal* (23 Dec 1721) · P. S. Brown, 'Medicines advertised in eighteenth-century Bath newspapers', *Medical History*, 20 (1976), 152–68, esp. 156–7 · R. Porter, *Health for sale: quackery in England, 1660–1850* (1989) · *The Lancet* (7 Dec 1823), 345 · PRO, PROB 11 582/201, 1721 · *GM*, 1st ser., 18 (1748), 348

Godfrey, Thomas (1736–1763), poet and playwright, born in Philadelphia on 4 December 1736, was the son of Thomas Godfrey (1704–1749), a glazier, whose passion for mathematics inspired him to design a quadrant for navigation at sea which was subsequently improved by John Hadley. Godfrey's mother had died by 1743, and on the death of his father he was taken into the care of relations. The school at which he was educated was possibly the charitable school in Philadelphia, refounded as an academy by his father's acquaintance Benjamin Franklin and twenty-one other leading citizens in 1749.

Godfrey's boyhood dream of becoming a painter was dashed when his guardians arranged his apprenticeship to a watchmaker. His artistic temperament sought expression through poetry and he published 'The Temple of Fame' anonymously during the period of his indenture. His intimate friend Benjamin West, a future president of the Royal Academy, alerted William Smith, editor of the *American Magazine* and provost of the newly styled 'College, Academy and Charitable School of Philadelphia', to Godfrey's authorship whereupon Smith became Godfrey's patron. Smith sought to stimulate Godfrey's talents by introducing him to a circle of his most gifted pupils and subsequently some of the latter's early verses were composed under a clump of pines on the banks of the River Schuylkill, where he, West, and his new friends gathered to fish. During the heat of the day Godfrey would 'stretch himself beneath the shade of the trees, and repeat to them his verses as he composed them' (Galt, 1.40).

In 1758 Smith procured a commission for Godfrey as a lieutenant in the Pennsylvania militia commanded by Major Hugh Waddell. Troops were raised in support of General John Forbes's expedition against the French at Fort Duquesne, on the site of modern Pittsburgh, during the last French and Indian war. Godfrey saw little action, however, its being his 'lot and mortification to be left in garrison' (Godfrey, *American Magazine*, 1.603). In the same year Smith published four of Godfrey's minor poems in numbers of the *American Magazine*, and he prevailed upon Ralph Griffiths in London to ensure their republication in the *Grand Magazine of Universal Intelligence* in March 1759. About the time when his poems were being printed in England, Godfrey's regiment was disbanded, whereupon he travelled to Wilmington, North Carolina, and took up employment as a factor.

Godfrey wrote his tragedy *The Prince of Parthia* by mid-November 1759. A manuscript of the play was dispatched to Philadelphia, where David Douglass's theatre company was playing Shakespeare until 28 December. Godfrey's correspondence with Smith seems to indicate that he harboured an ambition to add his play to the company's repertory but that it arrived too late to be performed. Meanwhile Smith continued to enlist the support of Griffiths in promoting Godfrey's writings in England. 'Victory', a poem celebrating British success in Quebec, first appeared in *The Library*, a magazine published by Griffiths, in March 1762. 100 copies of *The Court of Fancy*, published in Philadelphia in 1762, were dispatched to booksellers in London where, although the volumes sold badly, the poem received gentle praise in the *Monthly Review*, edited by Griffiths, in September 1763.

On the death of his employer Godfrey left Wilmington and returned briefly to Philadelphia, before embarking as supercargo (merchant ship officer in charge of cargo) on a voyage to New Providence. Finding no opportunities on the island, he returned to North Carolina in the early summer of 1763. On 25 July Godfrey suffered severe heatstroke while riding on horseback in the country with a companion. According to his friend the poet Nathaniel Evans, Godfrey was unsuited to these exertions being 'of corpulent habit of body' (Evans, vi). He succumbed to fever and died, unmarried, on 3 August 1763. He was buried in the old churchyard of St James's, Wilmington, and his obituary appeared in the *Pennsylvania Gazette* on 29 September 1763.

The posthumous publication of Godfrey's collected poems, *Juvenile Poems on Various Subjects* (1765), edited by Smith with an introduction by Evans, demonstrated that his talents were superior to those of any previous

American-born poet. *The Prince of Parthia*, upon which Godfrey's modern reputation rests, published in the same volume, was first performed on 24 April 1767 by the American Company at the New Theatre in Southwark, Philadelphia, and is considered to be the first tragedy written by an American-born writer, the first tragedy published in America, and the first play written by an American to be performed on the professional stage. The drama, which depicts internecine strife within the empire's ruling élite during the first century AD, owes something to Nicholas Rowe's *Tamerlane* (1701). Godfrey's inability to develop character stunts the play, and it did not inspire imitation. None the less, *The Prince of Parthia* constitutes a vigorous start to dramatic literature in America. JAMES WILLIAM KELLY

Sources T. Godfrey, 'Ode on wine', *American Magazine*, 1/12 (Sept 1758), 604 • N. Evans, 'Some account of the author and his writings', in T. Godfrey, *Juvenile poems on various subjects*, ed. W. Smith (Philadelphia, 1765) • N. Evans, 'An ode, attempted in the manner of Horace, to my ingenious friend, Mr Thomas Godfrey', 'Elegy, to the memory of my beloved friend, Mr Thomas Godfrey', *Poems on several occasions, with some other compositions* (Philadelphia, 1772) • D. E. Baker, *Biographia dramatica, or, A companion to the playhouse*, rev. I. Reed, new edn, rev. S. Jones, 3 vols. in 4 (1812), vol. 1, pp. 279–80 • J. Galt, *The life and studies of Benjamin West, esq.*, 2 vols. (1816–20), 1.39–40 • *The prince of Parthia: a tragedy by Thomas Godfrey*, ed. A. Henderson (Boston, 1917) • *A bicentennial edition of Thomas Godfrey's 'The prince of Parthia, a tragedy'*, 1765, ed. W. E. McCarron (Colorado Springs, 1976) • H. Simpson, *The lives of eminent Philadelphians now deceased* (Philadelphia, 1859) • *Life and correspondence of the Rev. William Smith DD*, ed. H. W. Smith, 2 vols. (Philadelphia, 1879), 1.187, 389–90 • R. E. Stoddard, *1765–1964: two hundred years of American plays: an exhibition arranged to celebrate the bicentennial of the publication of Thomas Godfrey's 'The Prince of Parthia'* (Providence, 1965) • C. L. Carlson, 'Thomas Godfrey in England', *American Literature*, 7/3 (Nov 1935), 302–9 • C. L. Carlson, 'A further note on Thomas Godfrey in England', *American Literature*, 9/1 (March 1937), 73–6 • R. D. Harlan, '*The court of fancy* in England', *Papers of the Bibliographical Society of America*, 59/1 (1965), 48–9 • T. C. Pollock, 'Rowe's *Tamerlane* and *The prince of Parthia*', *American Literature*, 6/2 (May 1934), 158–62 • *GM*, 1st ser., 33 (1763), 315 [advertisement for *The court of fancy*]
Likenesses B. West, oils?, 1758, priv. coll.

Godfrey, Walter Hindes (1881–1961), architect and antiquary, was born at home at 102 Greenwood Road, Hackney, London, on 2 August 1881, the eldest son of Walter Scott Godfrey, who at that time was conducting a small wine business, and his wife, Gertrude Annie Rendall, of Bristol. The elder Godfrey later became, under the influence of C. H. Spurgeon, a Baptist minister. After meeting with ill success in his pastorate, he turned to socialist agnosticism without, however, relaxing a puritanical sense of mission that bore hard on his family. In 1891 W. H. Godfrey was sent to Whitgift Middle School, Croydon, and, four years later, gained a scholarship to the upper or grammar school, where he remained until 1898. He also studied at the Central School of Arts and Crafts. He was subsequently articled to James Williams, who had succeeded to the practice of the distinguished Victorian country-house architect George Devey. In 1900 he joined the architectural section of the London county council. Already keenly interested in the antiquities of London, he was elected in 1901 a member of the Committee for the Survey of London, which C. R. Ashbee had founded in 1894 with the object of publishing monographs and parish surveys recording ancient buildings in the metropolitan area. Godfrey was at once involved in preparations for the first of the Chelsea volumes and this led to his authorship of all the four volumes that appeared between 1909 and 1927. The survey was always one of his main interests. He edited several further monographs and parish volumes and was engaged on the monograph on the College of Arms at the time of his death.

In 1903 Godfrey left the London county council and returned to the office where he had served his articles. Williams had retired, and the practice was now conducted by his partner Edmund Livingstone Wratten, who took Godfrey as an assistant on a two-year agreement. Before the term was out Wratten had married Godfrey's sister Gertrude. Wratten and Godfrey then formed a partnership as successors to James Williams, commencing practice in 1905. Commissions were few at first and Godfrey had time to write a study of George Devey, his firm's original founder, which was awarded the Royal Institute of British Architects (RIBA) essay silver medal in 1906. He also prepared illustrations for Garner and Stratton's *Domestic Architecture in England during the Tudor Period* (1908), including elevations and a perspective of the oriel window of Crosby Hall, Bishopsgate, then threatened with demolition. Simultaneously he contributed an architectural study of the hall to Philip Norman's monograph in the Survey of London series. This excited the interest of Patrick Geddes, who was connected with the Town and Gown Association, which was building, on a site in Chelsea, a headquarters for the British Federation of University Women. Geddes instigated the removal of the hall to the Chelsea site, with Godfrey acting as architect. The hall was successfully transferred in 1909–10.

From 1915 to 1919 Godfrey was employed in the accounts division of the Ministry of Munitions. Thereafter, he resumed practice with Wratten and, after the latter's death in 1925, continued on his own. In 1926 he became a fellow of the Royal Institute of British Architects. The recession of the early 1930s induced him to give up his London office and in 1932 he retired to Lewes, where, by extraordinary good luck, he was offered the most inspiring and lucrative task of his career—the restoration of Herstmonceux Castle for Sir Paul Latham. Other restorations and a few houses followed and up to 1939 Godfrey combined the running of a modest domestic practice with the writing of papers, mostly on Sussex antiquities. In the early 1930s he made alterations to the house and planned the gardens at Charleston Manor, Sussex; putting in practice the ideas he had advanced in *Gardens in the Making* (1914), he created an appealing garden with separate compartments organically related to each other.

In 1940, when London became subject to air attack, a conference was held at the Royal Institute of British Architects to consider the need for a central body charged with the recording of historic buildings which might be damaged or destroyed. The outcome of this was the formation of the National Buildings Record, with Lord Greene, master of the rolls, as its chairman and Godfrey as its salaried director. From 1941 until his retirement in 1960 the conduct and development of the record (now the National Monuments Record) were the main concern of his life. In addition, however, he conducted two notable restorations of war-damaged buildings: the Temple Church and the old parish church of Chelsea. The latter had been almost completely demolished by a bomb in 1941 but the records that Godfrey had made as a young man enabled him to achieve a highly satisfactory reconstruction.

Godfrey was the author of many books, including, besides the volumes on Chelsea in the Survey of London, *A History of Architecture in London* (1911; enlarged edn, 1962), *The Story of Architecture in England* (2 vols., 1928 and 1931), *The English Almshouse* (1955), and *Our Building Inheritance: are we to Use it or Lose it?* (1946). To the *Dictionary of National Biography* he contributed the notices of Sir John James Burnet and Sir Charles Archibald Nicholson. He was a member of the Royal Commission on Historical Monuments from 1944 and of the advisory committee on buildings of special architectural or historic interest at the Ministry of Housing and Local Government. In 1950 he was appointed CBE.

On 15 June 1907 Godfrey married Gertrude Mary (1883/4–1955), daughter of a chartered accountant, Alexander Grayston Warren; they had one son—Emil, who worked in partnership with his father—and three daughters. Godfrey was a man of slight build, pleasant appearance, and agreeable disposition, though with a somewhat egocentric streak inherited from his father. He died on 16 September 1961 in the Acland Nursing Home in Oxford.

JOHN SUMMERSON, *rev.*

Sources J. Summerson, *London Topographical Record*, 22 (1965), 127–35 · *The Times* (18 Sept 1961) · b. cert. · m. cert. · d. cert. · A. Saint, 'Ashbee, Geddes, Lethaby, and the rebuilding of Crosby Hall', *Architectural History*, 34 (1991), 206–23 · M. Binney, 'Charleston Manor, Sussex', *Country Life*, 160 (1976), 350–53

Archives LMA, notes relating to the architecture of Chelsea · Sussex Architectural Society, Lewes, architectural and genealogical notes | Bodl. Oxf., letters to O. G. S. Crawford

Likenesses M. Gillick, photograph, repro. in *London Topographical Record*, 21 (1958)

Wealth at death £19,219 10s. 6d.: probate, 19 Dec 1961, *CGPLA Eng. & Wales*

Godfrey, William (1889–1963), Roman Catholic archbishop of Westminster, the younger of two sons of George Godfrey (*d.* 1889) and his wife, Maria, *née* Garvey (*b.* 1868), was born in Kirkdale, Liverpool, on 25 September 1889. He attended St John's parochial elementary school, and in 1903 he went to St Cuthbert's College, Ushaw, near Durham. He completed his studies at the English College in Rome, where he gained the customary doctorates in philosophy (1913) and theology (1917) of the Gregorian University. The latter, however, was gained by public act, that is, defended before the whole university. This was before the Catholic biblical revival: throughout his life Godfrey remained a rigid Thomist who knew nothing of

William Godfrey (1889–1963), by Alfred R. Thomson, exh. RA 1960

the new schools of theology which gave rise to the Second Vatican Council.

Godfrey was ordained priest in 1916 and was appointed curate at St Michael's, West Derby Road, Liverpool—his only parochial appointment. In January 1919 he was sent to Ushaw College to teach classics in the junior seminary. Soon he was also teaching philosophy in the senior seminary (for nine years), and in 1928 dogmatic theology. He taught by means of dictated notes (which earned him the sobriquet among his students of Billy Buckets) which were described as careful, safe, and systematic. Both as student and teacher he was known as a prayerful man who spent hours in meditation before the blessed sacrament, a habit which lasted until the end of his life. He played a full part in the informal community life of the college acting as librarian, choirmaster, spiritual director, and also playing the french horn in the college orchestra. Spiritual conferences which he gave to students were later published as *The Young Apostle* (1924) and *God and Ourselves* (1927). He was noted for his gentle sense of humour and his gift of mimicry.

In 1930 Godfrey was appointed rector of the English College in Rome and domestic prelate to Pius XI. There he was well equipped to watch over the progress of the studies of the students at the Gregorian University but he regarded their spiritual formation as much more important than the mere acquisition of knowledge. He greatly renovated the buildings of the college, and restored its holiday villa at Palazzuola acquired by Arthur Hinsley as rector. Perhaps because he was younger than most rectors he joined with the students in many of their recreations and holiday tours thus forming friendships which lasted a lifetime. The students spent seven years in Rome without returning to England, but also without making many contacts outside the college. The climate created was one of disdain for Anglicans, and a strong loyalty to the pope and all things Roman. Godfrey spoke elegant Italian as well as French, German, and Spanish. While still rector Godfrey was, in 1935, member of a papal mission to Malta and, in 1937, counsellor on the papal mission for George VI's coronation, which provided an opportunity for discussing the feasibility of establishing an apostolic delegation in London. He was also appointed apostolic visitor of all the seminaries in Great Britain.

On 23 November 1938 Godfrey was appointed first apostolic delegate to Great Britain, and was consecrated titular archbishop of Cius in Rome that November. His brief was to put down roots and this he did in a quiet manner, purchasing a house in suburban Wimbledon so as to avoid any semblance of diplomatic pretensions. He was indefatigable in furthering the humanitarian activities of the Holy See for the victims of war, and his linguistic skills were extremely useful when visiting refugees and prisoners of war camps. When the Polish government in exile requested diplomatic links with the Holy See, Godfrey was appointed chargé d'affaires in that capacity. He left his stamp on the church in England and Wales by recommending his past students from the English College to fill vacant sees as bishops and archbishops. The English hierarchy had never before been so homogeneous. Among other characteristics this involved a reluctance to participate in ecumenical experiments. Godfrey believed that Catholic doctrine was wholly true and therefore unalterable, nor could it be properly expressed in alien terms. He feared Cardinal Hinsley's ecumenical enthusiasm lest it mislead the Catholic faithful or raise hopes which could not be fulfilled.

On 14 November 1953 Godfrey was appointed seventh archbishop of Liverpool. Although he accepted the pope's nomination without question he was saddened that he would no longer be the pope's representative. He was welcomed back to his own city by both priests and people, and enjoyed the pastoral round of parochial visitation. The one change he made in the diocese was the inevitable one of calling a halt to the work on Sir Edwin Lutyens's design for a massive cathedral which had become prohibitively expensive. He commissioned Adrian Gilbert Scott to produce a much reduced plan. Although it retained some of the features of the Lutyens design the Royal Fine Arts Commission dubbed its reduced scale a travesty.

In December 1956 Pius XII appointed Godfrey seventh archbishop of Westminster in succession to Cardinal Griffin. In 1957 he was also made apostolic exarch to the Ukrainians of the Byzantine rite in England and Wales. John XXIII named him cardinal priest of St Nereus and Achilles at his first consistory in 1958. Unlike Cardinal Hinsley Godfrey did not capture the attention of the nation; he did not share in the currents of new theological thought which were leading inexorably to the Second Vatican Council. Friends spoke of him as prudent; others thought him excessively cautious. He found decision making difficult. He was neither an impressive speaker nor an interesting writer.

In 1961 Pope John made Godfrey a member of the central preparatory commission for the council, revising draft discussion documents. This involved him in eight meetings of ten days each in Rome in the period 1961–2. He was so much in love with the traditional church that he was horrified by some of the liberal trends he detected. He came to regard it as his personal mission to fight against them. He had already contracted a fatal and painful illness in the summer of 1961 although none but his closest friends were ever aware of it. He attended the first session of the council (October–December 1962) despite having undergone a series of operations. When it became evident that the council fathers would reject much of the work of the preparatory commission Godfrey continued to argue his case, forcefully but without rancour, and always in fluent Latin. When he died at Westminster Hospital in London on 22 January 1963 it came as a profound shock to friends and colleagues. A few hours before his death he was anointed; he turned peacefully to the priest beside his bed and said 'Deo gratias; the church has given me everything she had to give' (private information). He was buried in the crypt of Westminster Cathedral a week later.

MICHAEL GAINE

Sources *DNB* • A. Hastings, *A history of English Christianity, 1920–1990*, 3rd edn (1991) • *The Tablet* (2 Feb 1963) • personal knowledge (2004) • private information (2004) • M. E. Williams, *The Venerable English College, Rome* (1979) • T. Moloney, *Westminster, Whitehall and the Vatican: the role of Cardinal Hinsley, 1935–1943* (1985) • *The Times* (23 Jan 1963)

Archives St Joseph's College, Liverpool Archdiocesan Archive, papers • Westm. DA, corresp. and papers | Cumbria AS, letters to Lady Isabella Howard • TCD, corresp. with Thomas Bodkin

Likenesses A. R. Thomson, oils, exh. RA 1960, St Edmund's College, Ware [*see illus.*] • H. Coster, photographs, NPG • A. J. Fleischman, bust, archbishop's house, Westminster • H. Swift, oils, Upholland College, Wigan • A. R. Thomson, portrait, archbishop's house, Westminster • oils, English College, Rome

Wealth at death £11,155 1s. 5*d*.: probate, 26 April 1963, *CGPLA Eng. & Wales*

Godgifu [Godiva] (*d.* **1067**?), noblewoman, was the wife of *Leofric, earl of Mercia (*d.* 1057). They were probably married before 1010, so that Godgifu was perhaps born *c.*990. She must be distinguished from three contemporaries of the same name: Godgifu, benefactress of Ely Abbey in the 1020s; Godgifu, or Gode (*d. c.*1049), sister of Edward the Confessor; and Godgifu, or Godgyth (*d.* before 1055), wife of Earl Siward and benefactress of Peterborough Abbey. The name was very common; critics of the marriage of Henry I with the English princess Edith nicknamed the royal couple 'Godric and Godgifu'.

Nothing certain is known of Godgifu's origins. A spurious charter (*AS chart.*, S 1230) of Crowland Abbey, in Lincolnshire, makes her the sister of Thorold of Bucknall, who supposedly founded a dependent cell of Crowland on his manor of Spalding in 1051. The *Historia Croylandensis* (the Pseudo-Ingulf) does not mention Godgifu, but says that Thorold gave not Spalding but Bucknall to Crowland. The abbey certainly held land there by 1086, given by Thorold (or Turold) the sheriff, but his alleged relationship with Godgifu is no more than an assumption. Its basis is presumably the fact that land at Spalding had belonged before 1066 to her son Earl *Ælfgar (*d.* 1062?), a benefactor of Crowland; this land passed to Ivo Taillebois, who founded (or refounded) a church there as a cell of St Nicholas, Angers. Ivo's wife, Lucy, was the daughter of Turold, sheriff of Lincoln, who may or may not be identical with Thorold of Bucknall (both names are variants of the Scandinavian Thorvaldr); in later tradition Lucy herself becomes a daughter of Earl Ælfgar.

The distribution of Godgifu's known lands suggests that her family background lay in north-west Mercia, rather than the north-east midlands. Her substantial estates in Leicestershire, Warwickshire, Staffordshire, and Shropshire, some 60 hides of land or the equivalent, may have been her own inheritance, for John of Worcester (*fl.* 1095–1140) says that Coventry Abbey, founded by Godgifu and her husband, was endowed out of their respective patrimonies. Leofric's father, Leofwine, though holding office in the west midlands, may have come from the eastern shires, and his son's marriage to a woman of west Mercia might have been a way of acquiring land and influence in the west. Some of Godgifu's estates, however, were acquired from her husband's kindred. Newark, Nottinghamshire, is clearly a comital manor, obtained perhaps from her son Ælfgar while he was earl in East Anglia (1051–2; 1053–7), or from her grandson *Morcar, earl of Northumbria from 1065 to 1067 or 1071; and Appleby, Derbyshire, was leased by Godgifu from Earl Leofric's nephew Leofric, abbot of Peterborough (*d.* 1066).

As 'the earl's wife', Godgifu is associated with her husband in the Old English memorandum concerning their endowment of Stow St Mary, Lincolnshire, between 1053 and 1055 (*AS chart.*, S 1478). They asked permission from Wulfwig, bishop of Dorchester-on-Thames (*d.* 1067) 'to endow the monastery and assign lands to it', though none is named in the memorandum, which deals with the liturgy to be used (that of St Paul's, London) and the division of income between the priests of Stow and the bishop. A later, forged, charter in Godgifu's name (*AS chart.*, S 1233) grants land at Newark and Fledborough, Nottinghamshire, and Brampton and Marston, Lincolnshire. Only Brampton is found in Stow's possession; in 1086 it was held, like Stow itself, by Wulfwig's successor, Remigius, who moved the see of Lincoln. Remigius also held the manors of Newark, Fledborough, and Stokeham, which had belonged to Godgifu before 1066.

Later sources associate Godgifu with other benefactions made by Leofric, especially to Coventry. Of the two extant writs of King Edward for Coventry Abbey, one, which may have a genuine base, does not include her and the other, which is certainly spurious, does (*AS chart.*, S 1098–9). The Evesham chronicle names both Leofric and Godgifu as founders both of Coventry and of the church of Holy Trinity, Evesham, to which they gave a crucifix with attendant figures of the Virgin and St John the Evangelist. Orderic Vitalis says that Godgifu gave 'her whole store of gold and silver' (Ordericus Vitalis, *Eccl. hist.*, 2.216–17) to provide Coventry with the appropriate ecclesiastical ornaments, which is not unreasonable; a similar story is told by the Waltham chronicler of the wife of its founder, Tovi the Proud (*fl.* 1018–1042). Orderic somewhat spoils his story by making Godgifu the wife, not of Leofric, but of her son Ælfgar, and mother of her own grandchildren, *Eadwine [*see under* Ælfgar], Morcar, and 'Edith' (*recte* Ealdgyth), so that it is not clear whether he intends to praise Godgifu, or her daughter-in-law Ælfgifu.

John of Worcester records Godgifu's devotion to the Virgin and associates her with all Leofric's endowments, to Leominster, Herefordshire, Much Wenlock, Shropshire, the churches of St John and St Werburgh at Chester, to Coventry, Stow, Evesham, and to Worcester itself. A less favourable picture emerges from the second Worcester cartulary, compiled by Hemming at the command of Bishop Wulfstan (*d.* 1095). It includes a grant, in the names of both Leofric and Godgifu, of Wolverley and Blackwell, Worcestershire (*AS chart.*, S 1232), but this should be compared with Hemming's account of how Leofric retained these estates, with others at Belbroughton, Bell Hall, Chaddesley Corbett, and Fairford, formerly seized by his father, Leofwine. Leofric returned Wolverley and Blackwell and promised that the rest should revert to the church on his death. Godgifu, however, retained them, though she endowed the church with various expensive vestments and ornaments and promised to pay the annual dues from the estates and to return them on her death; but Eadwine and Morcar seized the lands and kept them. Hemming tells a similar story about Gunnhild, King Cnut's niece, and wife of Hakon, earl of Worcester, who was exiled from England in 1044. In 1086 Belbroughton was held by Urse d'Abetot, sheriff of Worcester, in succession to Godgifu; Bell Hall by Walter fitz Ansculf in succession to Leofnoth, brother of Leofric, a north Mercian thegn closely associated with the Mercian earls; and Chaddesley Corbett by a woman called Eadgifu, or Ealdgifu, whose relationship to Godgifu is unknown.

Although Godgifu is recorded as a pre-conquest landholder in Domesday Book, this need not mean she was living in 1066, let alone that she survived the conquest; but Hemming's statement that the lost Worcester lands passed straight to her grandsons without mention of their father, Ælfgar, who probably died in 1062, might imply that Godgifu outlived her son. In the thirteenth century her death was commemorated on 10 September and was believed to have occurred in 1067, which seems plausible. There is no reason to doubt that she was buried with her husband at Coventry, despite the assertion of the Evesham chronicle that she lay in Holy Trinity, Evesham.

Tales of her beauty and piety were circulating in the twelfth century and were known to William of Malmesbury and Henry of Huntingdon, but Roger of Wendover (*d.* 1236) is the first to tell how her husband promised to free the inhabitants of Coventry from toll if she would ride naked through the town. Godgifu took up the challenge and rode through the market place, attended by two soldiers, covering herself with her long golden hair. By the fourteenth century her invisibility had become miraculous. The popularity of this story through subsequent generations might explain how Godgifu's family came, in the later middle ages, to be (in E. A. Freeman's words) 'picked out as the special sport of pedigree-makers' (Freeman, 2.661).

In the seventeenth century 'Lady Godiva's' ride through Coventry was commemorated in a ballad, which claims that she ordered all the citizens to remain indoors, with their windows shut, so that she should be unseen. From 1678 the ride was re-enacted, first annually and then triennially, during the Summer Fair at Coventry. Peeping Tom, who disobeyed the lady's command and was struck blind as a result, appears in the eighteenth century; his name is first mentioned in the city accounts on 11 June 1773, when a new wig and fresh paint were supplied for his effigy. After a lapse in the 1980s, the Godiva procession was revived on 8 June 1996, as part of the celebrations for the centennial year of the motor car; the Godiva International Award has also been instituted, to be bestowed on a woman of international reputation in the field of social welfare. ANN WILLIAMS

Sources John of Worcester, *Chron.* • *Rogeri de Wendover liber qui dicitur flores historiarum*, ed. H. G. Hewlett, 3 vols., Rolls Series, [84] (1886–9) • A. Farley, ed., *Domesday Book*, 2 vols. (1783), vol. 1 • *AS chart.*, S 1098–9, 1232–3, 1478 • J. Hunt, 'Piety, prestige or politics? The house of Leofric and the foundation and patronage of Coventry Abbey', *Coventry's first cathedral: the cathedral and priory of St Mary* [Coventry 1993], ed. G. Demidowicz (1994), 97–117 • J. C. Lancaster, *Godiva of Coventry* (1967) • K. L. French, 'The legend of Lady Godiva', *Journal of Medieval History*, 18 (1992), 3–19 • P. A. Clarke, *The English nobility under Edward the Confessor* (1994) • P. H. Sawyer, ed., *Charters of Burton Abbey*, Anglo-Saxon Charters, 2 (1979) • 'The history of Ingulf', *The church historians of England*, ed. and trans. J. Stevenson, 2/2 (1854), 567–725 • J. Hunt, 'Land tenure and lordship in tenth- and eleventh-century Staffordshire', *Staffordshire Studies*, 4 (1991–2), 9–13 • N. Sumner, '"The Countess Lucy's Priory": the early history of Spalding Priory and its estates', *Reading Medieval Studies*, 13 (1988), 81–103 • *Hemingi chartularium ecclesiæ Wigorniensis*, ed. T. Hearne, 2 vols. (1723) • W. D. Macray, ed., *Chronicon abbatiae de Evesham, ad annum 1418*, Rolls Series, 29 (1863) • Ordericus Vitalis, *Eccl. hist.*, vol. 2 • *Willelmi Malmesbiriensis monachi de gestis regum Anglorum*, ed. W. Stubbs, 2 vols., Rolls Series (1887–9) • *Willelmi Malmesbiriensis monachi de gestis pontificum Anglorum libri quinque*, ed. N. E. S. A. Hamilton, Rolls Series, 52 (1870) • Henry, archdeacon of Huntingdon, *Historia Anglorum*, ed. D. E. Greenway, OMT (1996) • E. A. Freeman, *The history of the Norman conquest of England*, 6 vols. (1867–79) • V. Brown, ed., *Eye Priory cartulary and charters*, 2 vols., Suffolk RS, Suffolk Charters, 12–13 (1992–4) • K. S. B. Keats-Rohan, 'The parentage of Countess Lucy made plain', *Prosopon*, 2 (1995), 1–2 • D. Roffe, 'The *Historia Croylandensis*: a plea for reassessment', *EngHR*, 110 (1995), 93–108

Godiva. *See* Godgifu (*d.* 1067?).

Godkin, Edwin Lawrence (1831–1902), journal editor and publicist, born on 2 October 1831 at his maternal grandmother's house at Moyne, co. Wicklow, was of English descent, the eldest child of James *Godkin (1806–1879), Presbyterian minister and journalist with strong Irish nationalist sympathies, and his wife, Sarah, daughter of Anthony Lawrence, of Cromwellian settler ancestry. Of delicate health, he spent his early childhood mainly in Wicklow, and, aged seven, was sent to a school in Armagh, where his father then lived. From 1841 to 1846 he attended Silcoates School for the children of Congregational ministers, near Wakefield, Yorkshire. In 1846 he entered the new Queen's College, Belfast. He was first president of the undergraduate Literary and Scientific Society; at the time, he wrote later, 'John Stuart Mill was our prophet, but America was our Promised Land' (Ogden, *Life and Letters*, 1.12). In 1851 he graduated BA and went to London to read for the bar at Lincoln's Inn. He worked for Cassell's publishing house, with which his father was connected, and in 1851–2 was sub-editor of Cassell's *Workingmen's Friend*. In 1853 Cassell published his first book, *The History of Hungary and the Magyars from the Earliest Period to the Close of the Late War*, which was pro-Hungarian and anti-Austrian. In October 1853 the *Daily News* editor, Frederick Knight Hunt, sent him as special correspondent to Turkey on the eve of the Crimean War. He joined Omar Pasha's army, and was in the Crimea until the end of the war, returning home in September 1855. This experience gave him a lifelong hatred of war; he later wrote that the war's most important result was 'the creation and development of the special correspondents of newspapers' (ibid., 1.100). He lectured on the war in Belfast and elsewhere.

After a short time with the Belfast *Northern Whig* Godwin went in November 1856 to the United States, and toured the southern states, observing the slave system. He reported for the *Daily News*, and was admitted to the bar of the state of New York in February 1858. He married at New Haven, on 29 July 1859, the 'statuesquely attractive' 22-year-old Frances (Fanny) Elizabeth, elder daughter of Samuel Edmund Foote of Cincinnati and New Haven, who had made his fortune as president of the Ohio Life Insurance and Trust Company: a financially advantageous marriage. They had a son, who survived Godkin, and two daughters, who predeceased him; his wife died on 11 April 1875. In 1860 he visited Europe for his health. While he was there the American Civil War broke out, and he supported the North, writing to the *Daily News* condemning the British policy on the *Trent* incident. On returning to the United States in September 1862, while continuing his reports to the *Daily News*, he wrote for the *New York Times*, the *North American Review*, and *Atlantic Monthly*. He also took charge for a short time of the *Sanitary Commission Bulletin*. In July 1865, with others, he established in New York an independent weekly journal, *The Nation*, and after the first year took it over almost entirely as his private venture. He edited and wrote much of it until 1881, when he sold it to the *Evening Post*, of which it became a kind of weekly edition. In 1883 he became editor-in-chief of both papers, retiring because of ill health in 1899. For most of this time his sub-editor was his friend W. P. Garrison, son of William Lloyd Garrison.

The politically independent *The Nation* inaugurated a new departure in American journalism and, though its circulation was relatively small, it influenced educated opinion. Its contributors included leading American and British men of letters. Leslie Stephen—who stayed with Godkin in New York in 1868 and considered him 'a remarkably sensible, intelligent man', and on politics 'the most reasonable American I have seen' (Maitland, 207)—was its English correspondent (1868–73).

Godkin's beliefs were those then common among educated persons. He believed the 'Anglo-Saxon race' would expand into Central America and dominate the Pacific, and he supported suppression of the Indian mutiny. He condemned the 'carpetbagger' regime in the southern states, and the corruption of U. S. Grant's administration. A moralist, concerned for the quality of government in the United States, he wanted rule by the 'intelligent and virtuous classes'. He opposed national and municipal corruption, and demanded civil service reform and abolition of the 'spoils system' (by which politicians used civil service appointments to reward supporters). Believing immigration underlay corruption, he demanded an end to immigration from southern and eastern Europe, and tests of fitness to vote for immigrants and black people; he alleged in 1874 that the latter's intelligence was so low that they were 'slightly above the level of animals' (Armstrong, 105). He opposed women's suffrage, arguing that it would allow servant girls to outvote their mistresses, and criticized socialism. He opposed the Alaska purchase and American expansionism. Though he had previously favoured the republicans, as a civil service reformer and free-trader in 1884 he supported Grover Cleveland's democratic presidential candidature. His paper was the recognized organ of the independent 'Mugwumps' between 1884 and 1894. He opposed Cleveland's anti-British interference in 1895 in the Anglo-Venezuelan dispute. He attacked Tammany Hall (the immigrant-supported corrupt New York city government), publishing in the *Evening Post* biographies of its leaders, and was subjected to virulent abuse and libel actions by Tammany politicians. In December 1894, after Tammany's temporary defeat, partly due to his efforts, he was presented with a loving cup for his 'fearless and unfaltering service to the city of New York' (Ogden, *Life and Letters*, 2.181). He opposed Mahan's navalism, the Spanish-American War, the Second South African War, and the American annexation of Hawaii and the Philippines. He also opposed, on economic grounds, high tariffs, the silver policy, and bimetallism.

In 1870 Godkin declined an offer of the Harvard history professorship, and in 1875 moved to Cambridge, Massachusetts, returning to New York in 1877. In 1875 he became a member of a commission to 'Plan for the government of cities in the State of New York', which reported to the New York legislature in 1877. He married Katherine, daughter of Abraham Sands, on 14 June 1884; she survived her husband. In 1895 he was made an unpaid civil service commissioner. Godkin visited England in 1889, after twenty-seven years away. In June, through James Bryce, he met Gladstone, who denounced the Liberal Unionists 'with curious fire, his eye glowing' (Ogden, *Life and Letters*, 2.155). He liked England, and thereafter repeatedly visited; his enemies criticized his Anglophilia. Among his friends were Bryce, A. V. Dicey, and Henry James. He was, like his father, an advocate of Irish home rule, and contributed to the Liberal *Handbook of Home Rule* (1887) edited by Bryce. As home-ruler, free-trader, opponent of war and annexation, and advocate of honest and economical administration, he was in line with advanced British Liberals, and he criticized the Conservative leaders. His views were stated in his *Reflections and Comments* (1895), *Problems of Modern Democracy* (1896), and *Unforeseen Tendencies of Democracy* (1898). In June 1897 he was awarded an Oxford DCL: 'the "blue ribbon" of the intellectual world, and very gratifying' (ibid., 2.22). After serious illness in 1900, he sailed for England in May 1901, and died at Greenway House, Brixham, on the Dart in south Devon, on 21 May 1902; he was buried on 28 May in Hazelbeach churchyard, near Market Harborough, Northamptonshire. Bryce's inscription on his grave described him as a 'Publicist, economist, moralist … a steadfast champion of good causes and high ideals' (ibid., 2.255).

Able, widely read, a trenchant writer, and a charming friend, Godkin worked for America but was never fully assimilated. Matthew Arnold considered him 'a typical specimen of the Irishman of culture' (Ogden, *Life and Letters*, 2.1). His political views, deemed by some Englishmen the 'soundest' and 'sanest' in America, were those of a philosophic radical, though in later and more pessimistic years 'a disillusioned radical' (ibid., 2.238); he remained an advanced Liberal of the period 1848 to 1870. Though lacking original ideas, he was an effective communicator and crusader for good government.

C. P. LUCAS, *rev.* ROGER T. STEARN

Sources R. Ogden, *Life and letters of Edwin Lawrence Godkin*, 2 vols. (1907) · W. M. Armstrong, *E. L. Godkin: a biography* (1978) · R. Ogden, 'Godkin, Edwin Lawrence', *DAB* · J. Bryce, *Studies in contemporary biography* (1903) · *The Times* (23 May 1902) · *Annual Register* (1902) · private information (1912) · F. L. Mott, *American journalism*, rev. edn (New York, 1950) · *Fifty years of Fleet Street: being the life and recollections of Sir John R. Robinson*, ed. F. M. Thomas (1904) · J. F. Rhodes, *Historical essays* (1909) · Gladstone, *Diaries* · F. W. Maitland, *The life and letters of Leslie Stephen* (1906) · J. M. Blum and others, *The national experience* (1963)

Archives Bodl. Oxf., letters to James, Viscount Bryce

Likenesses W. M. Hollinger, photograph, NPG SI · engraving (after photograph, 1870), repro. in Ogden, *Life and letters of Edwin Lawrence Godkin*

Godkin, James (1806–1879), writer on Ireland, was born at Gorey, co. Wexford, into a family of moderately prosperous farmers. In his early twenties he married Sarah, daughter of Anthony Lawrence, a 'comfortable proprietor' from co. Wicklow who was of English descent. The couple had three daughters and two sons, one of whom, Edwin Lawrence *Godkin, became a newspaper editor in America. In 1834 James Godkin broke with the episcopalian church and was ordained a Congregational minister, with a pastorate in Armagh. He afterwards became a general missionary to Roman Catholics, in connection with the Irish Evangelical Society, and in 1836 issued *A Guide from the Church of Rome to the Church of Christ*. In 1842 he published *The Touchstone of Orthodoxy* and *Apostolic Christianity, or, The People's Antidote Against Puseyism and Romanism*. Godkin's religious writings, though forceful, displayed relatively little bigotry, and when he met Charles Gavan Duffy in Belfast in 1842 the two men became allies on the land question despite their different faiths. His religion was increasingly subordinated to his involvement in Irish protest, and when, in 1845, it became known that he was the author of a prize-winning essay entitled 'The rights of Ireland' in a competition sponsored by the Loyal National Repeal Association, his involvement with the Irish Evangelical Society ceased. He abandoned the ministry in 1848 and about this time went to London, where he became a leader writer for provincial journals, Irish and Scottish, and a contributor to reviews and magazines. Titles with which he was associated include the *Standard of Freedom*, the Belfast *Independent*, and the *Freeman's Journal*. On returning to Ireland after two years Godkin established in Belfast the *Christian Patriot*. He afterwards became editor of the *Derry Standard*, and then, moving to Dublin, he held for several years the chief editorial post on the *Daily Express*. While engaged on this paper he acted as Dublin correspondent for the London *Times*. For thirty years he was a close student of every phase of the Irish question. In 1850 he was an active member of the Irish Tenant League.

Some of Godkin's writings on ecclesiastical and land questions had a large influence. Before the introduction of Gladstone's Irish legislative measures in the House of Commons Godkin published an elaborate treatise entitled *Ireland and her Churches* (1867), advocating church equality and tenant security for the Irish people. In 1869 Godkin, as special commissioner of the *Irish Times*, travelled widely in Ulster and portions of the south of Ireland to ascertain the feelings of the farmers and the working classes on the land question. The result of these investigations appeared in his work *The Land War in Ireland* (1870). As well as other works on Ireland, he published a volume on religion and education in India, and a history of England from 1820 to 1861. On Gladstone's recommendation Queen Victoria conferred a pension on Godkin in 1873 for his literary services. He died on 2 May 1879 at Upper Norwood, Surrey. He was survived by his wife and several of his children. G. B. SMITH, *rev.* C. A. CREFFIELD

Sources Boase, *Mod. Eng. biog.* • W. M. Armstrong, *E. L. Godkin: a biography* (1978) • Ward, *Men of the reign* • C. A. Read, *The cabinet of Irish literature: selections from the works of the chief poets, orators and prose writers of Ireland*, 4 vols. (1880)

Godlee, Sir Rickman John, baronet (1849–1925), surgeon, was born on 15 April 1849 at 5 Queen Square, London, the second son of Rickman Godlee, barrister, and his wife, Mary, eldest daughter of Joseph Jackson *Lister, FRS, wine merchant and microscopist, and sister of Joseph, Lord *Lister. The Godlees and the Listers belonged to the Society of Friends, and this exerted a powerful influence on Rickman John Godlee. After education at Grove House School, Tottenham, where he took up field botany and ornithology, Godlee entered University College, London, in 1866, and in the next year graduated BA. He entered the

Sir Rickman John Godlee, baronet (1849–1925), by Alan Bacon, 1923

faculty of medical sciences and soon attracted attention as a skilled dissector; and, like his uncle, Lord Lister, and his cousin and future colleague, Marcus Beck, he was house surgeon to John Eric Erichsen at University College Hospital.

Godlee took the degrees of MB (1872) and MS (1873), receiving a gold medal in surgery at each examination, and spent part of a year from the autumn of 1872 in Edinburgh, living with his uncle, who was then professor of clinical surgery at the university. He published his impressions of the antiseptic method in *The Lancet* in 1873, and returned to University College Hospital as surgical registrar in the same year. Marcus Beck at University College Hospital and H. G. Howse of Guy's Hospital were in the 1870s the first London surgeons to follow Lister's technique closely, and Godlee was a keen student of their methods, often in the face of the opposition of the senior surgeons. In 1876 he was appointed assistant surgeon to Charing Cross Hospital and, at the medical school there, lecturer on anatomy—a post at that time almost always held by a surgeon. A year later, however, Godlee was elected assistant surgeon at his old hospital; this was a new post which carried with it a demonstratorship in the anatomical department of University College.

After having been elected FRCS in 1876 Godlee began

working on his *Atlas of Human Anatomy* with an explanatory text. For this he made drawings, with distinctive colours for vessels and nerves, from more than a hundred dissections, mainly made by his own hand. The title-page states that the book illustrates 'most of the ordinary dissections and many not usually practised by the student'. It was published in 1880, but was not widely noticed. Godlee's drawings were presented to the Royal College of Surgeons. He was much in demand as an illustrator; some of his work adorned Quain's *Anatomy* (10th edn, 1896) and two editions of Erichsen's *Surgery*.

Although a general surgeon, Godlee performed certain operations which later became the province of specialists. On 25 November 1884 he performed the first operation for the removal of a tumour from the brain, the accurate 'localization' of which had been rendered possible by recent physiological experiments and clinical research including that of two spectators, David Ferrier and John Hughlings Jackson. The patient's death from a surgical complication provoked controversy with antivivisectionists in *The Times*. Also in 1884 Godlee was appointed surgeon to the Brompton Hospital for Consumption and Diseases of the Chest. He went on to publish lectures on the surgical treatment of a number of chest diseases, and was joint author, with James Kingston Fowler, of the surgical portion of *Diseases of the Lungs* (1898), a work containing some of his own illustrations. This book is said to have stimulated the development of thoracic surgery. In 1876 Godlee had also joined the staff of the North-eastern (later the Queen's) Hospital for Children, in Hackney Road. He was appointed full surgeon at University College Hospital in 1885, professor of clinical surgery in 1892, and Holme professor of clinical surgery in 1900. In April 1914 he resigned his appointments, to become emeritus professor of clinical surgery. Godlee was regarded as an extremely clear and successful teacher.

Earlier in his career Godlee had been secretary of three leading medical societies—the Pathological, the Clinical, and the Royal Medical and Chirurgical, being also honorary librarian of the last (1895–1907). After the amalgamation of these and other societies into the Royal Society of Medicine, he became the society's librarian (1907–1916) and president (1916–1918). At the Royal College of Surgeons he held many offices, including those of president (1911–1913), and Hunterian orator (on the subject 'Hunter and Lister', in 1913). In November 1913 he was made an honorary fellow of the American College of Surgeons at Chicago. During and after the First World War Godlee was extremely active on the central medical war committee and was chairman of the Belgian doctors' and pharmacists' relief fund.

Godlee married in 1891 Juliet Mary, eldest daughter of Frederic *Seebohm, banker and historian, of The Hermitage, Hitchin; they had no children. In London he lived first in Henrietta Street, then at 81 Wimpole Street, and finally at 19 Wimpole Street. A man of wide interests, Godlee was a collector of etchings, a good linguist, and a book lover, and he had an extensive knowledge of old London and of biography. He wrote, though he never published, verse. With Sir Watson Cheyne he had assisted Lord Lister throughout his active practice in London, and scientific problems were constantly discussed between them. Probably no colleague had so intimate a personal knowledge of Lister; moreover, Godlee regarded Lister's antiseptic system as having revolutionized surgery, and he took an essential part in bringing out *The Collected Papers of Joseph, Baron Lister* in two volumes (1909). Acting as Lister's executor he presented to the Royal College of Surgeons all his uncle's scientific and surgical possessions. In 1917, five years after Lister's death, Godlee brought out the eminently readable biography, *Lord Lister*, which reached a third and revised edition in 1924. It paints a vivid picture of the deplorable state of surgical wards of hospitals in the second half of the nineteenth century in Edinburgh, Glasgow, London, and abroad; and it represents Lister's antiseptic system as the key instrument in transforming this situation.

Godlee was a reserved man, regarded as downright, honest, approachable, and somewhat sarcastic. For many years he had owned Coombe End Farm, Whitchurch, near Reading; here he settled after his retirement from London in 1920, and enjoyed farming, carpentering, and writing essays about the village, which appeared posthumously as *A Village on the Thames: Whitchurch Yesterday and Today* (1926). He died at Whitchurch after a few hours' illness on 20 April 1925 and was buried there. He was survived by his wife, and left more than £96,000.

Godlee received many honours. He was surgeon to the household of Queen Victoria, and honorary surgeon to King Edward VII and King George V. He was created a baronet in 1912 and KCVO in 1914, and he received the Belgian medal of King Albert in 1919. He was a fellow of University College, London, and received honorary degrees from the universities of Toronto and Dublin. The baronetcy became extinct on his death.

H. D. ROLLESTON, *rev.* CHRISTOPHER LAWRENCE

Sources V. G. Plarr, *Plarr's Lives of the fellows of the Royal College of Surgeons of England*, rev. D'A. Power, 1 (1930) • *BMJ* (3 May 1930), 809–10 • b. cert. • m. cert. • d. cert. • *CGPLA Eng. & Wales* (1925)

Archives Suffolk RO, Ipswich, corresp., diaries, and papers • Wellcome L., lecture notes and papers

Likenesses W. Stoneman, photograph, 1919, NPG • Swaine, photograph, 1922, Wellcome L. • A. Bacon, portrait, 1923, RCS Eng. [*see illus.*] • Elliott & Fry, photogravure, Wellcome L. • photograph, Wellcome L.

Wealth at death £96,880 5*s.* 10*d.*: resworn probate, 1925, *CGPLA Eng. & Wales*

Godley, Sir Alexander John (1867–1957), army officer, was born on 4 February 1867 in Railway Street, Gillingham, Kent, the eldest son of Lieutenant-Colonel William Alexander Godley (*d.* 1880), Essex regiment and staff officer, and his wife, Laura Greaves (1836–1928), daughter of the Revd Godfrey Bird of Great Wigborough, Essex. Godley first attended the Royal Naval School at New Cross (*c.*1876) and, in 1880, Haileybury College. His father died in 1880, leaving little money, and Godley was then sent to the United Services College, Westward Ho! (*c.*1881–1885). In 1886, one year after entering the Royal Military College,

Sir Alexander John Godley (1867–1957), by Walter Stoneman, 1918

Sandhurst, Alick Godley, as he was known, became a subaltern in the Royal Dublin Fusiliers; his uncle was a major in the regiment. He soldiered in Ireland for seven years, frequently hunting, playing polo, and supplementing his low pay by training polo ponies. Army demands were confined to drill and periodical field days. After taking a mounted infantry course in 1895 he was appointed mounted infantry instructor at Aldershot. The following year he went with a mounted infantry battalion to Africa to take part in the Mashonaland campaign. He received a brevet majority and returned to Aldershot in 1898 where he commanded two mounted infantry companies. Training still emphasized drill and marching. On 17 September 1898 he married Louisa Marion Fowler (*d.* 1939), of co. Meath, with whom he shared a love of hunting. Godley's autobiography justifiably claims she was 'the most important influence in my future life' (Godley, 27): she actively supported him in his determination to achieve high rank. There were no children.

Godley entered the Staff College, Camberley, in 1899, but before finishing the course went off to South Africa to assist in raising volunteers. He was at Mafeking when the Second South African War broke out, and during the siege commanded an attack that failed because he had not ascertained the forward situation. This lack of command understanding was to be demonstrated again in the First World War. After the relief of Mafeking he took part in operations in the Transvaal, including commanding the Rhodesian brigade as a brevet lieutenant-colonel. He was posted to the newly formed Irish Guards in 1900 and was in 1901 appointed deputy assistant adjutant general and commander of the Mounted Infantry School at Aldershot. In 1904 he witnessed German army manoeuvres; he recorded that he was 'not much impressed' (Godley, 108). He was promoted colonel in 1906 and appointed general staff officer, grade 1, in the 2nd division at Aldershot, where he became responsible for training and staff work in the field. By then training had taken on a more practical character.

In 1910 Godley was offered the post of general officer commanding the New Zealand forces with the rank of temporary major-general. His acceptance was influenced by the advice of senior generals and, almost certainly, his dependence on army pay. New Zealand had recently legislated for a universal compulsory part-time military training scheme to replace the small and outdated volunteer force. When the First World War broke out in 1914 it was due to Godley's determination, experience in staff work and training, insistence on efficiency, and outstanding administrative ability that the New Zealand army was capable of being integrated with other British forces. Given the limited time available it was a major achievement. Godley was not responsible for the serious lack of capable senior officers; he did, however, bear responsibility for his choice of staff officers throughout the war.

When the New Zealanders arrived in Egypt late in 1914, Godley ensured they trained hard. He had set them the same standards of smartness, obedience, and musketry as were required of British regulars—not necessarily the most useful priorities for the coming campaign at Gallipoli. There he commanded the composite New Zealand and Australian division, and in October 1915 the Anzac corps. The troops considered him out of touch, and blamed him for 'Godley's abattoir', where Australian light horse units were slaughtered in successive charges. The appellation was not wholly unjustified, having been earned by Godley's rigid compliance with orders and his failure to take changed circumstances into account. His plan to seize Chanuk Bair was too complicated for the rugged and poorly reconnoitred terrain. Moreover, during the battle he allowed himself to be diverted from a crucial front-line conference that he had himself called.

In 1916 Godley took command of the 2nd Anzac corps in France. It played a major part in the successful capture of Messines Ridge in June 1917. Casualties would have been lower, however, if the corps had allowed one of the attacking brigades to be withdrawn once the objectives had been secured. Then came the 2nd Anzac's attacks on Passchendaele Ridge. The first, on 4 October 1917, on Gravenstafel spur in favourable weather, was a success. By his own account, Godley was prepared to exploit his success by going on to take Bellevue spur, 'but the army commander, uncertain of the situation elsewhere, would not allow it' (Godley, 224). On 9 October British divisions of the corps attacked, despite rain and shelling which had created a vast, grotesque mud-bath. Haig's diary records that Godley specifically asked that there be no postponement (Warner, 119). The advance achieved was minimal and many casualties were abandoned to die in the mud and rain. On 12 October there was a third attempt. It too failed. The mud had nullified the affect of artillery on the barbed wire. The two New Zealand attacking brigades suffered 2735 casualties.

When the 2nd Anzac corps was disbanded in 1918 Godley went on to command the 22nd corps and the New Zealand division elsewhere. He still retained overall control of the New Zealand expeditionary force (NZEF), with the encouragement of his immediate subordinates and the support of his minister in the New Zealand parliament. During 1918 he contributed to a series of victories. In July he was sent with four divisions to the Marne to fight successfully under French command, and in August he commanded five divisions in Sir Henry Rawlinson's Amiens offensive. In September he was promoted substantive lieutenant-general. In November the 22nd corps helped in the capture of Valenciennes.

During 1919 Godley commanded the 4th corps of the army of the occupation of the Rhine. This was followed by a spell assisting Haig in organizing an officers' association, spending four months in a sanatorium, and acting as Winston Churchill's military secretary. He commanded the army of the Rhine (1922–4), where he used his diplomatic skills in reconciling French demands with British policy. He was then appointed general officer commanding southern command. Godley left the army in 1928, and spent the next five years as governor of Gibraltar, where he enjoyed maintaining amicable working relationships with Spain and resumed his hunting career with enthusiasm. He also published a volume of memoirs, *Life of an Irish Soldier* (1939). On his retirement he toured widely, including Australia and New Zealand in his travels. In New Zealand, as a guest of the government, he met former NZEF officers and laid wreaths at war memorials. In retirement he lived at Boxford Mill House, Boxford, Newbury, Berkshire; and he died on 6 March 1957 in the Acland Nursing Home, Oxford.

Godley admired the New Zealand troops he commanded. It is unfortunate that he neither said so, nor showed compassion towards them. A tall, spare, publicly reserved man, Godley was seen by his troops as stuck up, distant, and unfeeling. Those who worked with him closely, regardless of rank, knew his other side—courteous, courageous, fair, and, once his trust had been won, disinclined to interfere. His wife was no more popular. Although she was deservedly mentioned in dispatches for war work that included establishing and running a convalescent home for New Zealand soldiers, she was better known for observing them training in the heat and sand of Egypt, and for the apocryphal demand to her husband: 'Make them run again, Alec!' (Pugsley, *On the Fringe*, 75). Godley received many appointments (KCMG 1914; KCB 1916; GCB 1928) and was mentioned in dispatches eleven times. His career exemplified both the nineteenth- and twentieth-century army: the nineteenth by his courting of patrons (demonstrated in his surviving personal correspondence and volume of memoirs), and the twentieth by his administrative practices. It is doubtful, however, that he fully appreciated the realities of twentieth-century warfare.

RAY GROVER

Sources A. J. Godley, *Life of an Irish soldier* (1939) • C. Pugsley, *Gallipoli: the New Zealand story* (1984) • National archives of New Zealand, Godley MSS, WA 252/1–14 • C. Pugsley, *On the fringe of hell* (1991) • H. Stewart, *The New Zealand division, 1916–1919* (1921) • C. Pugsley, 'The New Zealand division at Passchendaele', *Passchendaele in perspective*, ed. P. Liddle (1997), 272–91 • P. Burness, *The Nek: the tragic charge of the light horse at Gallipoli* (1996) • P. Warner, *Passchendaele* (1987) • personal file (Godley, A. J.), New Zealand department of defence, D1/312 • B. H. Liddell Hart, *History of the First World War*, rev. edn (1970) • S. W. Roskill, *Hankey, man of secrets*, 1 (1970) • b. cert. • m. cert. • d. cert. • *DNZB*, vol. 3 • *CGPLA Eng. & Wales* (1957)

Archives Archives New Zealand • IWM, corresp. • King's Lond., Liddell Hart C., corresp. • National Archives of Zimbabwe, Harare, diary • New Zealand department of defence, personal file | Archives New Zealand, Allen MSS • BL, corresp. with Lord D'Abernon, Add. MS 48927 • CAC Cam., corresp. with Sir E. L. Spears • King's Lond., Liddell Hart C., Hamilton Collection | FILM BFI NFTVA, news footage • IWM FVA, actuality footage • IWM FVA, news footage

Likenesses F. Dodd, charcoal and watercolour drawing, 1917, IWM • W. Stoneman, photograph, 1918, NPG [*see illus.*] • W. Russell, oils, 1919, IWM • photograph, NPG • photographs, NL NZ, Turnbull L. • photographs, Queen Elizabeth II Army Museum, Waiouru, New Zealand

Wealth at death £12,553 2*s*. 2*d*.: probate, 17 May 1957, *CGPLA Eng. & Wales*

Godley, Alfred Denis (1856–1925), classical scholar and writer, was born at Ashfield, co. Cavan, on 22 January 1856. His father was the Revd James Godley, rector of Carrigallen, co. Leitrim, brother of John Robert Godley, the friend of Gibbon Wakefield. His mother was Eliza Frances, daughter of Peter La Touche, of Bellevue, co. Wicklow. Alfred Godley was the eldest surviving son. After a year at a well-known preparatory school, Mr Bassett's, in Dublin, he went, with a scholarship, to Harrow School, where his powers were noted and encouraged by Henry Montagu Butler, then headmaster. At sixteen Godley won a classical exhibition, and at seventeen a scholarship, both at Balliol College, Oxford; but he did not go into residence until the following year (1874). He obtained a first class in classical moderations in 1875 and a second class in *literae humaniores* in 1878. His honours at the university included the Gaisford prize for Greek verse, the chancellor's Latin verse and Latin essay prizes, and the Craven scholarship. In 1879 he accepted the post of assistant classical master at Bradfield College.

Four years later, in 1883, Godley returned to Oxford as a tutor and fellow of Magdalen College, a post which he occupied until his retirement in 1912, teaching many candidates for the pass school as well as those for honour moderations. He was a conscientious but uninspiring lecturer who nevertheless evoked considerable affection among his many pupils. In 1910 he was elected public orator of the university, and held the office until his death. The honorary degree of doctor of letters was conferred on him in 1919; he had already received a similar degree from Princeton University when he visited the United States in 1913. He was elected an honorary fellow of Magdalen in 1912. In 1894 he married Amy Charlotte Isabella, daughter of Charles Hope Cay, fellow of Gonville and Caius College, Cambridge. They had no children. In the spring of 1925 Godley went on a tour in the Levant, in the course of which he contracted a malignant fever which, after some weeks, proved fatal. He died at his home, 27 Norham Road, Oxford, on 27 June of that year.

Godley's reputation as a writer of light humorous or satiric verse and prose dated from his association with the *Oxford Magazine*. He became a contributor in 1883, and editor in 1890. He also contributed regularly to other magazines including the *Cornhill Magazine* and the *Saturday Review*. His first published collection of poems was *Verses to Order*, some of them reprinted from the *Oxford Magazine*, in 1892. Later publications were *Lyra frivola* (1899), *Second Strings* (1902), a second (enlarged) edition of *Verses to Order*, 1904, and *The Casual Ward* (1912). Several pieces also appeared in *Echoes from the Oxford Magazine* (1890), *More Echoes* (1896), in the posthumous *Reliquiae* (1926), and in *Fifty Poems* (1927). One of his cleverest prose pieces is the spoof Latin preface to Kipling's *Horace Odes Book V*. His verse was considered by many critics to be not inferior to that of C. S. Calverley; his political ballad *The Arrest* became a classic of the Unionist Party in Ireland. His most anthologized work is the macaronic rhyme beginning:

> What is it that roareth thus?
> Can it be a Motor Bus?

in which 'motor' and 'bus' are declined as Latin words:

> Domine defende nos
> Contra hos motores bos.
> ('Lord defend us against these motor buses.')

Godley's classical publications included a school edition of Tacitus's *Histories* 1 and 2 (1887), a translation of the *Odes* and *Epodes* of Horace (1898), and the Loeb edition of Herodotus (1920). He was joint editor of the *Classical Review* from 1910 to 1920. The nine Creweian orations delivered by him as public orator have been described as 'perhaps his best title to fame as an almost perfect writer of elegant Latin'. His *tour de force* was the presentation of Richard Strauss in Latin hexameters with a German translation in the same metre.

Godley was also the author of *Socrates, and Athenian Society in his Age* (1896), *Aspects of Modern Oxford* (1894), and *Oxford in the Eighteenth Century* (1908). In 1909 he published an edition of selected poems of Praed and in 1910 an edition of the poetical works of Thomas Moore.

Godley's marked personality, conversational gifts, and highly reactionary views made him, notwithstanding his shyness, a prominent figure in the life of the university and of the town; he was an alderman, and had he lived another year, would have been mayor of Oxford. Conservative by nature, as well as in politics, he staunchly advocated such losing causes as the compulsory study of Greek at Oxford, and the exclusion of women students, and was an opponent of any changes to the system and subjects of university examinations. He was an ardent supporter of voluntary military training, and the patriotism which was one of his deepest feelings found practical expression in his training and organization of a volunteer force during the First World War. Although generally indifferent to games, he was a lover of active life, and a distinguished member of the Alpine Club; he was also joint founder of an Oxford and Cambridge dining club.

E. C. Godley, *rev.* Richard Smail

Sources C. R. L. Fletcher, 'Memoir', in A. D. Godley, *Reliquiae*, ed. C. R. L. Fletcher (1926) • I. Elliott, ed., *The Balliol College register, 1833–1933*, 2nd edn (privately printed, Oxford, 1934) • *CGPLA Eng. & Wales* (1925) • personal knowledge (1937)
Archives Bodl. Oxf., MSS Eng. Misc., diaries • Bodl. Oxf., literary papers and MSS • Magd. Oxf., papers
Likenesses photograph, repro. in Fletcher, 'Memoir'
Wealth at death £8968 17*s*. 8*d*.: probate, 28 July 1925, *CGPLA Eng. & Wales*

Godley, (John) Arthur, first Baron Kilbracken (1847–1932), civil servant, was born in London on 17 June 1847, the eldest child and only son of the colonial reformer John Robert *Godley (1814–1861) of Killegar, co. Leitrim, and his wife, Charlotte *Godley (1821–1907) [*see under* Godley, John Robert], second daughter of Charles Wynne Griffith Wynne of Foelas, Denbighshire, and Cefnamwlch, Caernarvonshire. He was a first cousin of A. D. *Godley. He was educated at Radley College (1857–1861) and then at Rugby School, under Frederick Temple. In 1866 he went, as an exhibitioner, to Balliol College, Oxford, where he gained a reputation as a brilliant classical scholar. He was awarded a first class in classical moderations (1868) but was prevented by illness from entering for *literae humaniores*. He won the Hertford (1868) and the Ireland (1870) scholarships, the chancellor's Latin verse prize (1867), and the Gaisford Greek verse (1869) and prose (1870) prizes. On leaving Oxford he studied law for a short time, and on 26 September 1871 married Sarah, only daughter of Walter Charles *James, first Baron Northbourne, and his wife, Sarah, *née* Ellison; they had two sons and three daughters.

In 1872 Godley was appointed assistant private secretary to W. E. Gladstone, then prime minister, a friend of both sides of the family. Godley was the third secretary. He proved an efficient and reliable support in the office and quickly became part of the small group of liberally minded officials on whom Gladstone heavily relied for political information. When the government resigned on its defeat in 1874 Godley briefly but not very seriously contemplated a political career, and was offered several seats in the late 1870s. From 1874 he acted as secretary to Lord Granville and resumed his legal studies, winning the Eldon law scholarship in 1874 (he was called to the bar at Lincoln's Inn in 1876 but never practised). From 1874 to 1881 he was a fellow of Hertford College, Oxford, and was active in college and university business. On Gladstone's return to power in 1880 Godley became principal private secretary in a very demanding government. It was Gladstone's intent to retire as soon as possible, and Godley therefore sought alternative employment, becoming in 1882 a commissioner of Inland Revenue. In 1883, aged thirty-five, he succeeded Sir Louis Mallet as permanent under-secretary for India. Though of Liberal inclination Godley worked well with ministers of both parties. He turned down offers to transfer to the War Office (1893), the

(John) Arthur Godley, first Baron Kilbracken (1847–1932), by George Charles Beresford

Colonial Office (1902), and the Foreign Office (1905). He was mentioned as a possible viceroy in 1893 (Godley, 197–202). He never himself visited India. Godley was an effective custodian of the India Office, always succeeding in presenting it as unified in policy. He maintained the constitutional supremacy of the office and of parliament as against the claims of Curzon in the early 1900s, resolutely telling him in a letter of 8 January 1904:

> I think we must all agree that the real government of India is in the House of Commons … and that a Viceroy who cannot conscientiously acquiesce in and carry out the policy of the Cabinet has no choice but to resign

as Curzon in due course did (Kaminsky, 141). However, despite his Gladstonian connections, Godley was not seen by the Indian National Congress as advancing its cause. His view was that:

> no opinion about Indian administration is worth the paper on which it is written, except in so far as it is … founded and supported by the opinions of those Englishmen who have spent the best years of their life in actual contact with the people of that country. (Godley, 185)

Godley retired in 1909 and was created Baron Kilbracken of Killegar. He had been made CB in 1882, KCB in 1893, and GCB in 1908. He was a devoted Rugbeian and was chairman of the school's governing body for thirty years (1902–32). He was a trustee of the British Museum and a director of the Pacific and Oriental shipping line and of other companies. He was made honorary fellow of Hertford College in 1910 and of Balliol College in 1912. He was a member in 1913 of the royal commission on Indian finance and currency. In 1916 Kilbracken wrote his *Reminiscences*, at first privately published (1916?) and then publicly (1931). They are an important source for imperial affairs, and especially for his personal record of Gladstone. Kilbracken was asked by the Gladstone family in 1898 to write the prime minister's biography. He declined, as lacking the necessary time and literary experience; but the long sections in his *Reminiscences* on Gladstone are clearly intended as a balance to Morley's treatment.

Kilbracken was over 6 feet in height and bearded. He was much distressed by the death of his younger son, Denis, in 1896. His wife died in 1921. Of both he wrote short privately printed memoirs. He also privately printed classical translations (1924). He lived for many years in Ennismore Gardens, London, and moved in 1904 to Sloane Gardens. He leased Minley Lodge near Farnborough from Bertram Currie, the banker, moving in his later years to South Hartfield House, Coleman's Hatch, Sussex. In 1931 he joined the Conservative Party. Kilbracken died at Summerfield House, Malvern, Worcestershire, on 27 June 1932 and was buried on 30 June at Tilmanstone, Kent. He was succeeded by his son Hugh John (1877–1950), a barrister.

H. C. G. Matthew

Sources *DNB* · GEC, *Peerage* · Lord Kilbracken [J. A. Godley], *Reminiscences of Lord Kilbracken* (1931) · A. P. Kaminsky, *The India office, 1880–1910* (1986) · Gladstone, *Diaries* · *CGPLA Eng. & Wales* (1932)

Archives BL OIOC, corresp. and papers as under-secretary of state for India, MS Eur. F 102 | BL, corresp. with Mary Gladstone, Add. MS 46242 · BL, corresp. with W. E. Gladstone, Add. MSS 44222–44223, 44900–44901 · BL, corresp. with Sir Edward Walter Hamilton, Add. MS 48609 · BL, corresp. with Macmillans, Add. MS 55245 · BL, corresp. with John, Viscount Morely, Add. MS 44902 · BL OIOC, corresp. with Lord Ampthill, MS Eur. E 233 · BL OIOC, letters to Sir George Birdwood, MS Eur. F 216 · BL OIOC, corresp. with Lord Curzon, MSS Eur. F 111–112 · BL OIOC, letters to Sir W. Foster, MSS Eur. E 242 · BL OIOC, corresp. with Sir Henry Erle Richards, MS Eur. F 122 · BL OIOC, letters to Sir H. G. Walpole, MS Eur. D 781 · Bodl. Oxf., corresp. with Margot Asquith; corresp. with Lord Kimberley; letters to Paget Toynbee · CUL, corresp. with Lord Hardinge · Herts. ALS, corresp. with Lady Desborough · King's AC Cam., letters to Oscar Browning · NL Scot., corresp. with fourth earl of Minto; corresp. with Lord Rosebery · St Deiniol's Library, Hawarden, corresp. with H. N. Gladstone

Likenesses H. Leslie, drawing, silhouette, 1926, NPG · G. C. Beresford, photograph, NPG [*see illus.*] · R. E. Morrison, oils, Rugby School, Warwickshire · photograph, repro. in Kaminsky, *India office*

Wealth at death £21,063 19*s*. 9*d*.: probate, 8 Oct 1932, *CGPLA Eng. & Wales*

Godley, Charlotte (1821–1907). *See under* Godley, John Robert (1814–1861).

Godley, John Robert (1814–1861), colonial administrator and political reformer in New Zealand, the eldest son of John Godley of Killegar, co. Leitrim, and his wife, Katherine, *née* Daly, was born on 29 May 1814, probably in Dublin. He was educated at Harrow School, and from 1832 at Christ Church, Oxford, where he proceeded BA on 27 October 1836. Deeply religious and committed to social tradition, Godley was sympathetic to the Oxford Movement, which was developing at the time. He was called to the Irish bar in 1839, but practised little, if at all. He travelled in North America in 1842, and developed there further his interest in systematic colonization and self-government. His observations were published in his *Letters from America* (2 vols., 1844). During his subsequent service as poor law commissioner and high sheriff from 1843 in co. Leitrim he unsuccessfully proposed state-funded mass emigration of Irish to Canada to alleviate the devastation of the potato famine. On 29 September 1846 he married Charlotte Griffith Wynne (1821–1907) [*see below*] of Foelas, Denbighshire, Wales; they had a son and three daughters.

In 1847 Godley began collaborating with the like-minded Edward Gibbon Wakefield on a scheme for organized settlement in New Zealand. The resulting Canterbury Association first met in London on 27 March 1848, and land was purchased from the New Zealand Company, which also advanced funds in support of the venture. Godley proposed a scheme which provided for funds to be allocated out of the proceeds of land sales for the religious and educational needs of the community to be established. The association's aspiration would be described a century later by L. C. Webb as being 'to create in New Zealand a society of which the nexus was a common religious faith strong enough to resist those forces which in the Old World were breaking the ties of social obligation' (Webb, 226).

A site was selected at the Port Cooper (Lyttelton) plains, with the main town to be named Christchurch, and preparations began for the religious and secular development of the settlement. In December 1849, beset by ill health, Godley left with his family for New Zealand aboard the *Lady Nugent*, having been appointed chief agent of the Canterbury Association. He was based in Wellington while awaiting the arrival of the first immigrant ships in December 1850, and he involved himself in the Colonial Reform League and continued his advocacy of self-government. His view of colonial management he stated briefly and emphatically: 'I would rather be governed by a Nero on the spot than by a board of angels in London, because we could, if the worst came to the worst, cut off Nero's head, but we could not get at the board in London at all' (*Memoir*, 18).

Godley's pragmatic oversight of the earliest development of systematic settlement in Canterbury brought him into conflict with the association, particularly over the leasing of pastoral lands in what had originally been presumed would be a small-scale agriculture-based economy. The association had stalled with Godley's departure from London: Wakefield reported that 'the affair lost its soul and body when it lost Godley, who both thought and acted for everybody' (Webb, 160). Initially slow land sales threatened the economic viability of the settlement and further loans (including from Godley) were required to keep the venture afloat. By now he had been appointed resident magistrate and commissioner of crown lands by the governor, George Grey, and Godley's struggle over the terms for pastoral leases prompted him to tender his resignation to the association in June 1851, his position being, he reported, 'too false and too painful to be endurable' (ibid., 199). He continued in the post, however, until the passing of the New Zealand Constitution Act in June 1852 opened the way for Canterbury to become a self-governing province. In December of that year he departed for England with his family, despite a petition urging him to stand for election as superintendent of the new provincial government. He later wrote 'I shall never, as long as I live, cease to condemn myself for leaving New Zealand' (ibid., 208). James Edward FitzGerald, the first superintendent of Canterbury Province, wrote that, by the time of his departure, 'Godley was in all but the name, the governor of the settlement which he originated and formed' (ibid., 209). FitzGerald edited a selection from Godley's writings and speeches which was published in 1863: extracts from his letters to C. B. Adderley were published in the same year. A statue of Godley was erected in Cathedral Square, Christchurch, in 1867.

On his return to England Godley continued to write on colonial reform and acted on immigration matters as an agent of the Canterbury provincial government. Following an appointment as commissioner of income tax in Ireland, he was from 1855 assistant under-secretary at the War Office under the secretaryships of Lord Panmure, General Peel, and Lord Herbert. In this post he continued to advocate self-reliance for colonies in the arena of imperial defence policy. He died of tubercular consumption at his home in Gloucester Place, Portman Square, on 17 November 1861. **Charlotte Godley** (1821–1907), his wife, born probably at Foelas in Denbighshire, the daughter of Charles Wynne Griffith Wynne and his wife, Sarah, *née* Hildyard, was a keen participant in and observer of colonial life. Her *Letters from Early New Zealand*, written to her mother between 1850 and 1853 and first published for private circulation only in 1936, were published in 1951 and revealed her talent for description of people, places, and social mores. The *Letters* are an important and often quoted source of insight into upper-class colonial society in New Zealand, and bear witness to her support and involvement in her husband's work. She died at Gloucester Place, Portman Square, London, on 3 January 1907. Their only son was John Arthur *Godley (1847–1932), permanent under-secretary of state for India and first Baron Kilbracken.

JANE TUCKER

Sources G. Hensley, 'Godley, John Robert', *DNZB*, vol. 1 • L. C. Webb, 'The Canterbury Association and its settlement', *A history of Canterbury, to 1854*, ed. J. Hight and C. R. Straubel (1957), vol. 1 of *A history of Canterbury* • C. Godley, *Letters from early New Zealand* (1951) • W. P. Morrell, *The provincial system in New Zealand* (1932) • B. Hughes, 'Godley, Charlotte', *DNZB*, vol. 1 • J. R. Godley, *Memoir*, ed. J. E. FitzGerald (1863) • Gladstone, *Diaries*

Archives Canterbury Museum, Christchurch, corresp. and papers • University of Canterbury, Christchurch | Canterbury Museum, Christchurch, letters to the fourth baron Lyttelton • LPL, letters to Roundell Palmer • NL Ire., letters to William Monsell • NL NZ, Turnbull L., Canterbury, Canterbury Association letter-books

Likenesses T. Woolner, bronze statue, 1865, Cathedral Square, Christchurch, New Zealand • double portrait, photograph (with Edward Gibbon Wakefield), repro. in W. H. Scotter, *A History of Port*

Lyttelton (1968) · photograph, NL NZ, Turnbull L. · photograph (of Charlotte Godley), repro. in Godley, *Letters from early New Zealand*, frontispiece · portrait, repro. in Godley, *Memoir*
Wealth at death £2000: probate, 20 Feb 1862, *CGPLA Eng. & Wales*

Godmond, Christopher (*fl.* 1804–1840), playwright, was the son of Isaac Godmond (*d.* 1809), one of the vicars of Ripon Cathedral. He lived at various times in Ripon, London, Lee in Kent, and Teignmouth in Devon. On 9 August 1804 he married Mary, eldest daughter of John Collinson of Gravel Lane, Southwark; they had a daughter. Mary Godmond died on 13 February 1815. Godmond was elected a fellow of the Society of Antiquaries on 30 November 1837, but was declared a defaulter on 19 April 1849.

Godmond's published works included *Memoir of Therrouanne* (1836); a historical drama, *The Campaign of 1346, Ending with the Battle of Crecy* (1836); and a tragedy, *Vincenzo, Prince of Mantua* (1840).

GORDON GOODWIN, *rev.* MEGAN A. STEPHAN

Sources *GM*, 1st ser., 79 (1809), 990 · *GM*, 1st ser., 74 (1804), 783 · *GM*, 1st ser., 85/1 (1815), 279 · *GM*, 2nd ser., 9 (1838), 79 · *BL cat.*, [CD-ROM] · Adams, *Drama*

Godolphin, Sir Francis (*c.*1534–1608). *See under* Godolphin, Sir William (*b.* in or before 1518, *d.* 1570).

Godolphin, Francis, second earl of Godolphin (1678–1766), politician and officer of the royal household, was born on 3 September 1678 in Whitehall, London, and baptized on the same day. He was the only child of Sidney *Godolphin, first earl of Godolphin (1645–1712), and his wife, Margaret *Godolphin (1652–1678), the daughter of Thomas Blagge, of Horningsheath, Suffolk. His mother died shortly after his birth, on 9 September, following which her close friend John Evelyn took on responsibility for the child's upbringing. He was educated at Eton College and King's College, Cambridge, which he entered at Easter 1695 and from which he received an MA in 1705. In 1698 (licence dated 23 April) he married Henrietta Churchill (1681–1733), the eldest daughter of John *Churchill, first duke of Marlborough. The couple had five children, two boys and three girls, two of whom died in infancy.

In June 1698 Godolphin received his first public appointment, as joint registrar of the court of chancery, a position which he held, concurrently with that of teller of the exchequer (1699–1704), until 20 January 1727. On 1 December 1701 he was elected MP for East Looe, Cornwall, and on 4 February 1702 for Helston, Cornwall, which he represented until 21 September 1710. In addition, between 1708 and 1710 he sat as MP for the county of Oxford, and from 1710 to June 1712 for Tregony, Cornwall. He also held a number of other offices in this period, performing the duties of cofferer of the household between 1704 and 1711, lord warden of the stannaries, high steward of the duchy of Cornwall, and, from 1705 to 1708, rider and master forester of Dartmoor. From 29 December 1706 he was known by the courtesy title of Viscount Rialton until, following his father's death on 15 September 1712, he became second earl of Godolphin.

Godolphin held an equally large number of offices as a peer: he was cofferer of the household (1714–23), lord lieutenant of the county of Oxford (1715–35), lord of the bedchamber to George I (1716–23), and high steward of Banbury (1718). His wife became *suo jure* duchess of Marlborough on the death of her father on 16 June 1722. On 23 May of the following year Godolphin was sworn of the privy council, and during the king's absence served as one of the lords justices, a role he fulfilled again in 1725 and 1727. Under George II he was groom of the stole and first lord of the bedchamber (1727–35), and he became high steward of Woodstock (18 March 1728) on the same day he was appointed governor of the Isles of Scilly. His wife—who had been an active patron and then mourner of the playwright William Congreve—died on 24 October 1733, and was buried on 9 November at Westminster Abbey. Three years later, on 23 January 1735, he was created Baron Godolphin of Helston in Cornwall, with special remainder that, if he died without a son, this title would pass to the male heirs of his late uncle Dr Henry *Godolphin, dean of St Paul's. His final appointment was as lord privy seal, and he held this office from 14 May 1735 to 25 April 1740.

Godolphin maintained his influence in politics through his pocket borough of Helston, close to the ancestral home, Godolphin House, from which he sent his nominees to parliament. His patronage extended to his paying the rates and taxes for all the electors in the borough. In addition he financed the rebuilding of Helston church in 1763 at a cost of £6000. His later years were presumably spent perusing Bishop Burnet's *History* and Colley Cibber's *Apology*, the only two books he is alleged to have read in his life. He died on 17 January 1766, and was buried on 25 January in Kensington church, London. With his death the earldom of Godolphin, the viscountcy of Rialton, and the barony of Godolphin of Rialton became extinct; however, the barony of Godolphin of Helston passed to his cousin Francis Godolphin, who became the second Baron Godolphin of Helston. G. C. BOASE, *rev.* PHILIP CARTER

Sources GEC, *Peerage*, new edn · Venn, *Alum. Cant.* · *GM*, 1st ser., 36 (1766), 47 · E. Dimont, *Godolphin family portraits, 1610–1781* (1987)
Archives BL, corresp. with duke and duchess of Newcastle, Add. MSS 32679–33080, *passim* · Northants. RO, letters and papers · W. Yorks. AS, Leeds, Yorkshire Archaeological Society, Cornish accounts and papers
Likenesses G. Kneller, oils, *c.*1710 (*Kit-Cat Club*), NPG · G. Kneller, oils, *c.*1710, Blenheim Palace, Oxfordshire · G. Kneller, oils, *c.*1714, La Salle College, Philadelphia · J. Faber junior, mezzotint, 1732 (after G. Kneller), BM, NPG · oils, *c.*1740 (after J. B. van Loo?), NPG · G. White, mezzotint (after G. Kneller), BM, NPG

Godolphin, Henry (1648–1733), college head and dean of St Paul's, was born at the family seat of Godolphin House, Cornwall, on 15 August 1648 and baptized on 20 August at the neighbouring church of Breage. He was the fourth son of Sir Francis Godolphin (1605–1667) and his wife, Dorothy Berkeley, and younger brother of Sidney *Godolphin, first earl of Godolphin (1645–1712). He was at Eton from about 1660 to 1664, matriculating on 30 August that year at Wadham College, Oxford. He graduated BA on 28 May 1668, and on 9 November following he was nominated a fellow of All Souls by Archbishop Sheldon. He proceeded

MA on 20 April 1672, and would take his BD and DD degrees in 1685.

On 31 July 1674 Charles II granted Godolphin the next vacant fellowship at Eton, to which he was duly admitted on 14 April 1677, despite the fact that, although an Etonian, he was technically an 'alien' since he had not been a fellow of King's College, Cambridge. On 22 November 1679 the king further gave him a canonry of Christ Church, Oxford, but this grant was ineffective. On 13 November 1683 he became prebendary of Sneating in St Paul's Cathedral, a stall he retained for life. Nine days later the king nominated him to a residentiary's place in the cathedral. He preached there on 12 March 1684, 'very excellently' according to his good friend John Evelyn (Evelyn, 4.372). But it was apparently not until November 1688 that Godolphin celebrated his house-warming, at which his widowed sister Jael Boscawen presided. In 1692 and again in 1702 he was appointed a commissioner for the rebuilding of the cathedral.

In 1695 Godolphin was designated dean of Lincoln, but instead, on 16 October, William III directed the fellows of Eton to elect him (already vice-provost) to the provostship. This was accomplished on 23 October. In September 1705, with the whigs in control of ecclesiastical appointments, it was predicted that Godolphin would be made dean of St Paul's when the incumbent should die, and the next year he was said to be a candidate for the bishopric of Winchester. It was, however, to the deanery of St Paul's that he was appointed on 23 June 1707, being installed on 19 July. He became involved in disputes with Wren over the design of the new cathedral; the architect particularly objected to the iron railings which the commissioners wished to erect. Godolphin had resigned the deanery by 22 October 1726, preferring the more congenial atmosphere of Eton. He was already a considerable benefactor there, and used his powerful connections to coax contributions from others. About 1700 he gave £1000 towards restoration of the chapel. In 1719 he paid for Francis Byrd's bronze statue of Henry VI which still watches over School Yard. By a codicil to his will he gave £200 for the purchase of books for the library built between 1720 and 1729. He also gave £100 to All Souls for completing the new library there. He left £200 to the poor of Eton, and the rest of his property, including lands at Wexham, Stoke Poges, and elsewhere in Buckinghamshire, to his wife, Mary (daughter of his cousin Sidney Godolphin), his son, Francis, and his daughter, Mary, who had married William Owen of Shropshire.

Godolphin died on 29 January 1733 at Windsor or at Eton, and was buried in Eton College chapel on 4 February. His widow died in 1743. In 1766 their son succeeded by special remainder to the barony of Godolphin of Helston, which by his own death in 1785 became extinct.

C. S. Knighton

Sources W. Sterry, ed., *The Eton College register, 1441–1698* (1943), xxviii, xxxi, 142 • Foster, *Alum. Oxon.* • Wood, *Ath. Oxon.: Fasti* (1815), 397 • GEC, *Peerage*, new edn, 5.749 • Boase & Courtney, *Bibl. Corn.*, 1.178; 3.1199–1200 • C. T. Martin, *Catalogue of the archives in the muniment room of All Souls' College* (1877), 316 • *Fasti Angl., 1541–1857*, [St Paul's, London], 6, 57 • *CSP dom.*, 1673–5, 322; 1677–8, 86, 93; 1679–80, 287; 1683–4, 104–5; 1691–2, 267; 1695, 58, 67, 83; 1702–3, 313 • Evelyn, *Diary*, 4.372, 589, 606 • N. Luttrell, *A brief historical relation of state affairs from September 1678 to April 1714*, 3 (1857), 489, 536, 538; 6 (1857), 106, 192–3 • W. R. Matthews and W. M. Atkins, eds., *A history of St Paul's Cathedral and the men associated with it* (1957), 206, 223 • W. Sterry, *Annals of the King's College of Our Lady of Eton beside Windsor* (1898), 38, 143, 153 • A. C. Benson, *Fasti Etonenses* (1899), 89–90 • H. C. Maxwell Lyte, *A history of Eton College, 1440–1898*, 3rd edn (1899), 275, 287, 299 • BL, Sloane MS 4843, fols. 51v–52 • BL, Add. MS 28088, fol. 170 • PRO, PROB 11/656, fols. 327–9

Archives Bucks. RLSS, papers | BL, letters to his brother William Godolphin and others, Add. MS 28052, fols. 17v–26v • GL, corresp. with James Lucas

Likenesses oils, Eton, Provost's Lodge; repro. in Benson, *Fasti Etonenses*, facing p. 90

Wealth at death pecuniary bequests in excess of £2500; owned property in several Buckinghamshire villages: PRO, PROB 11/656, fols. 327–9

Godolphin, John (1617–1678), civil lawyer, was born on the Isles of Scilly on 29 November 1617, the third son of John Godolphin and Judith Meredith. The Godolphins, a prominent Cornish family, owned a castle on the Scillies. On 16 November 1632 Godolphin matriculated from Gloucester Hall, Oxford, as a commoner. There he was tutored by William Sandbrooke, and excelled in logic and philosophy. He graduated BA (1635) and BCL (1636). In 1643 Godolphin was admitted to the faculty with the degree of doctor of civil law. If Anthony Wood is to be believed, Godolphin was promoted mostly for being 'puritannically inclined' (Wood, *Ath. Oxon.*, 3.1152). Godolphin apparently sufficiently impressed the parliamentary visitors with his zeal for the parliamentary cause.

During the civil war Godolphin seems to have attended his religious interests more seriously than his legal career. After the execution of Charles he published two pious, if somewhat scattershot, theological works: *The Holy Limbeck, or, A Semicentury of Spiritual Extractions* (1650) and *The Holy Arbor … or, The Sum and Substance of Christian Religion* (1651). These ranged widely over an eclectic collection of theological topics, and revealed decidedly low-church sensibilities. Godolphin lived in London during the war, sided 'much with the men there in power' (Wood, *Ath. Oxon.*, 3.1152), and took the engagement oath after the establishment of the Commonwealth. Of his private life little can be said except that he married four times, and that his last wife was named Deborah. He also fathered at least one son, named Sidney, who would later serve as governor of the Scillies. On 30 July 1653 the so-called Barebones Parliament passed an act appointing Godolphin as a judge of the admiralty court. He was re-appointed in 1659. The admiralty court was governed by civil law, and had long been attacked by devotees of the common law such as Edward Coke. Service on the court apparently revived Godolphin's legal interests. In 1655 he was elected president of the Doctors' Commons, the London organization for civilian lawyers formed in the 1490s.

At the Restoration the royalists purged Godolphin from the admiralty court, but his career survived. He continued to practise law privately, and there is some evidence that he was made a king's advocate. Godolphin was chiefly known as a staunch defender of the civil law in its long-running war with the common lawyers. His *View of the*

Admiralty Jurisdiction appeared in 1660. One modern authority has characterized it as a 'charming hodgepodge of authority, uncritically selected and casually organized' (Coquillette, 187), but it was republished several times and was apparently viewed as a leading defence of the admiralty court. In 1674 Godolphin's *The Orphan's Legacy* treated another subject dear to the civilian lawyers: the law of testate. One final work appeared in 1678. Godolphin's *Repertorium canonicum, or, An Abridgement of the Ecclesiastical Laws of this Realm* was 'the first substantial attempt to merge the canonical authorities with those of the common law, and thereby provide a comprehensive survey' of English church law (Baker, 85). The *Repertorium* also contained obsequious remarks about the king that hint at Godolphin's continued embarrassment over his political associations during the interregnum. Godolphin was apparently a considerable bibliophile. His library, which was sold off after his death, was enormous.

Godolphin was by no means a sparkling stylist. His religious works in particular are pedestrian and even unlearned. But he managed to build a considerable reputation as a legal writer. Godolphin's defences of the civilian and canon law against the hegemony of the common lawyers were able contributions in a long-running (if ill-fated) campaign. John Godolphin died in or near Fleet Street, London, on 4 April 1678 (Wood, *Ath. Oxon.*, 3.1152). He was buried in the north aisle of Clerkenwell church.

JEFFREY R. COLLINS

Sources Wood, *Ath. Oxon.*, new edn, 3.1152 • J. H. Baker, *Monuments of endless labours: English canonists and their work, 1300–1900* (1998) • D. R. Coquillette, *The civilian writers of Doctors' Commons, London* (1988) • Holdsworth, *Eng. law* • *DNB* • Boase, *Mod. Eng. biog.* • *CSP dom.* • *Catalogus variorum et insignium librorum … vivorum D. Johannis Godolphin* (1678) • will, PRO, PROB 11/356, sig. 32 • Foster, *Alum. Oxon.*

Archives NL Wales, letters

Godolphin [*née* Blagge], **Margaret** (1652–1678), courtier, was born on 2 August 1652, the youngest daughter of Thomas Blagge (*d.* 1660) and Mary (*d.* 1670), daughter of Sir Roger North of Mildenhall and Elizabeth Gilbert. Margaret's birthplace may have been London.

Thomas was a groom of the bedchamber in the court of Charles I, and during the civil war he commanded the garrison at Wallingford for the king. Accompanying the second duke of Buckingham after the battle of Worcester, Blagge followed the royal family into exile. After the Restoration he was colonel of a regiment and governor of Yarmouth and Landguard Fort. He died on 14 November 1660 and was buried at Westminster.

In 1658 Margaret travelled to Paris with the duchess of Richmond, Buckingham's sister, and there she was placed in the care of the countess of Guilford, Buckingham's first cousin. From 1666 she was maid of honour to the duchess of York, and, at her death in 1671, she moved into the household of Queen Catherine as maid of honour.

In 1672 Margaret established an unusual relationship with the diarist John Evelyn, who gave a detailed account of it in *The Life of Mrs Godolphin* (first published in 1847). Margaret was attracted to him as her mentor in religious

Margaret Godolphin (1652–1678), attrib. Mary Beale, *c.*1675

learning and worship. Evelyn was fifty-two years old and Margaret was twenty. Evelyn led Margaret through a period of intense religious piety, writing prayers and devotions for her use, and participating in religious exercises with her. Often his phrases sound like the poetry of a devoted and somewhat frustrated lover.

Margaret was not enthusiastic about life and service in the court, and she resolved in 1673 to retire from the court, and from the world. She would live at Berkeley House and dedicate herself to a religious life.

This idea of solitude was interrupted in 1674 by King Charles's command that Margaret play a major part in the court production of John Crowne's *Calisto*. She played the part of the virgin Diana, goddess of chastity. Margaret had acted in 1668, probably in Dryden's *The Indian Emperour*. Now she was compelled to take part in *Calisto*, which she did only with great mortification and many tears. Nevertheless, said Evelyn with some pride, she acted her part 'in the highest perfection' in numerous practices and performances (Evelyn, *Life*, 99).

Margaret was an extraordinarily attractive woman. Evelyn claimed that 'every body was in love with, and some allmost dyeing for her' when she appeared in the king's court at the age of sixteen (Evelyn, *Life*, 48–9). When she accompanied Lord and Lady Berkeley to France in 1675, Louis XIV was anxious to see her; but Margaret so ordered her affairs that she avoided the king.

Celibacy was an attractive idea to Margaret, but her inclination was overcome by her attraction to Sidney *Godolphin, later first earl of Godolphin (1645–1712). Evelyn urging celibacy made her hesitate somewhat longer. In 1675 she consented, after nine years of courtship, to marry Godolphin. The two married on 16 May in Temple Church, London, without telling the court or John Evelyn. Margaret accompanied the Berkeleys to Paris, leaving Godolphin behind and not revealing their marriage. When she returned in 1676, the couple announced their union and settled into a home in Scotland Yard.

In 1678 Margaret was pregnant. She had expressed herself on numerous occasions about death, and in the last days of her pregnancy she wrote a letter to her husband to prepare for that possibility. Several days after the birth on 3 September of her child, Francis *Godolphin, second earl of Godolphin, Margaret contracted a fever. After struggling for several days in horrible pain, she died at Whitehall on 9 September 1678. She was buried at Breage in Cornwall on 16 September. W. CALVIN DICKINSON

Sources J. Evelyn, *The life of Mrs Godolphin* (1972) [photocopy edn of the 1st edn of 1847, ed. S. Wilberforce, same page nos.] • W. G. Hiscock, *John Evelyn and Mrs Godolphin* (1951) • Evelyn, *Diary* • T. Lever, *Godolphin: his life and times* (1952) • W. C. Dickinson, *Sidney Godolphin, lord treasurer, 1702–1710* (1990)

Likenesses M. Dixon, portrait, 1673, Wootton Hall Park, Nottingham • attrib. M. Beale, oils, *c*.1675, priv. coll. [*see illus.*] • M. Beale, portrait, Stonor Park, Oxfordshire • M. Beale, portrait, Berkeley House, London • oils, Berkeley Castle, Gloucestershire

Godolphin, Sidney (*bap.* **1610**, *d.* **1643**), poet and courtier, was baptized on 15 January 1610 at Breage, Cornwall, the second of the four children of Sir William Godolphin (*d.* 1613) of Godolphin, Cornwall, and his wife, Thomasine (*d.* 1611/12), daughter and heir of Thomas Sidney of Wrighton, Norfolk. Sir William, who owned mines at Godolphin, was, like his father and brother, nationally renowned for his mining expertise. In his will, dated 2 and 4 September 1613, he made provision for 'the honest and seemely mayntaynannce and educacon of my children' and bequeathed to three-year-old Sidney, at his majority, his late mother's Norfolk estate in fee tail. So, 'liberally supplied for a very good education, and for a cheerful subsistence, in any course of life he proposed to himself' (*Life of … Clarendon*, 1.46), on 25 June 1624, aged fourteen, Sidney was admitted a commoner to Exeter College, Oxford. Three years later he may have entered one of the inns of court before travelling to France, to the Low Countries, and, in the earl of Leicester's embassy, to Denmark.

After his travels Godolphin took up residence at court, 'where his excellent disposition and manners, and extraordinary qualification, made him very acceptable' (*Life of … Clarendon*, 1.46), and between 1634 and 1641 he was a gentleman of the privy chamber extraordinary. One of a circle of minor poets at court, Godolphin's complete works comprise thirty short poems and 454 lines of a translation of *The Aeneid*, book 4. His poems, which are varied in form and include songs and epitaphs, sonnets and epistles, a meditative chorus, and a hymn, were not collected during his lifetime but were edited by G. Saintsbury in 1906 and by W. Dighton in 1931. The hymn, 'Meditation on the Nativity', and the songs 'Or love me less, or love me more' and 'Fair friend, 'tis true your beauties move/My heart to a respect' also feature in more recent anthologies. His poems are characteristic productions of the Jonson circle (lines attributed to Godolphin are included in the volume of memorial verse for Jonson): they have poise, grace, and a neatly turned wit. His Virgil translation 'The Passion of Dido', which he undertook in conjunction with Edmund Waller, marks a significant stage in the development of the heroic couplet. A member of Falkland's set at Great Tew, 'Little Sid' (as he was affectionately named by Suckling because of his small frame) included among his friends Thomas Hobbes (who commended him in the dedication, 'Review', and conclusion of *Leviathan*) and Edward Hyde, later earl of Clarendon. Clarendon described Godolphin as shy, sensitive, and inclined to melancholy but universally admired, reflecting that 'There was never so great a mind and spirit contained in so little room; so large an understanding, and so unrestrained a fancy, in so very small a body' (ibid.).

In May 1639 Godolphin was present on the Scottish border with Sir Ralph Hopton's troop of the royal bodyguard. Returned for Helston in both elections of 1640 (as in 1628), he was one of only five indigenous Cornish MPs to vote against Strafford's attainder. On 3 December 1641 he opposed Pym's strategy to control the Lords, declaring that if this were implemented 'then the Myner part of the Commons would joyne with the Major part of the Lords and enter into a protestation against them that did'. He was ordered to withdraw from the Commons until the house 'had time to consider of his delinquencie' but the matter was taken no further (*The Journal of Sir Simonds D'Ewes*, ed. W. H. Coate, 1942, 228 and n.). Sidney was one of the last royalist members to leave the house, warning on his departure that 'When the cards are shuffled, no man knows what the game will be' (Coate, 52).

Once war was declared, 'out of the pure indignation of his soul and conscience to his country' Godolphin joined the king's cause in the west (Clarendon, *Hist. rebellion*, 6.251). An active commissioner of array, in September 1642 he accompanied Hopton on his march through north Devon and into Cornwall. Though 'he thought not fit to take command in a profession he had not willingly chosen … [his] advice was of great authority with all the commanders' (ibid.). He was a member of Hopton's council of war and was with Hopton's forces at Braddock Down on 19 January 1643 and in the subsequent advance that drove Ruthin's parliamentarian army across the Tamar into Devon. Early in February 1643 he was among a party of volunteers led by Sir John Berkeley that set out from Plympton in pursuit of the enemy. On 8 February, heading from Okehampton towards Totnes, the party was ambushed at Chagford by a parliamentarian force led by Sir John Northcott. As Godolphin rode through the town a chance shot 'from an undiscerned and undiscerning hand' (T. Hobbes, *Leviathan*, 4th edn, 1894, 316) struck him above the knee, and crying 'O God, I am hurt' (*Life of … Clarendon*, 1.47) he fell dead from his horse. Sir Bevill Grenville repined to his wife, 'One losse we have sustained that is unvalluable, to witt Sidney Godolphin is slaine in the attempt, who was as gallant a gent as the world had' (R. Granville, *History of the Granville Family*, 1895, 251), while

Hopton reflected that Sidney was 'as perfect, and as absolute piece of vertue as ever our Nation bredd' (Hopton, 33).

Sidney was reputed to have married shortly before his death and to have left one daughter, Margaret. If so, he made no mention of either his wife or daughter in his will, made on 23 June 1642 and proved by his brother Francis at Oxford on 11 March 1643. In the will he resigned his soul to God, 'expecting salvation thorough the meritts of Jesus Christ', and bequeathed £200 to 'my worthy friend Mr Thomas Hobbs'. He left his Norfolk estate, plus his interest in the Isles of Scilly (the gift of his late younger brother William), to Francis, whom he appointed sole executor. Sidney Godolphin was buried in the chancel of Okehampton church on 10 February 1643. ANNE DUFFIN

Sources M. Coate, *Cornwall in the great civil war and interregnum, 1642–1660* (1933) • A. Duffin, *Faction and faith: politics and religion of the Cornish gentry before the civil war* (1996) • *DNB* • *Bellum civile: Hopton's narrative of his campaign in the West, 1642–1644*, ed. C. E. H. Chadwyck Healey, Somerset RS, 18 (1902) • *The life of Edward, earl of Clarendon … written by himself*, 2 vols. (1857) • Clarendon, *Hist. rebellion* • will, PRO, PROB 10/641/10881 • Sir William Godolphin's will, PRO, PROB 11/122, fols. 429r–430v • J. L. Vivian, ed., *The visitations of Cornwall, comprising the herald's visitations of 1530, 1573, and 1620* (1887) • Keeler, *Long Parliament* • 'The poems of Sidney Godolphin', *Minor poets of the Caroline period*, ed. G. Saintsbury (1906), vol. 2 • *The poems of Sidney Godolphin*, ed. W. Dighton (1931) • A. Fowler, ed., *The new Oxford book of seventeenth century verse* (1992) • T. G. S. Cain, ed., *Jacobean and Caroline poetry: an anthology* (1981)

Archives BL, Harley MS 6917 • Bodl. Oxf., Malone MS 13

Likenesses R. Clamp, stipple, BM, NPG; repro. in F. G. Waldron, *The biographical mirrour*, 1 (1795) • engraving, priv. coll.

Wealth at death a substantial Norfolk estate; an interest in the Isles of Scilly; bequests amounting to £1200: will, PRO, PROB 10/641/10881

Godolphin, Sidney, first earl of Godolphin (1645–1712), politician, was the third son of Sir Francis Godolphin (1605–1667) and his wife, Dorothy, daughter of Sir Henry Berkeley. He was born on 15 June 1645 at the ancestral home in Breage, Cornwall. What little evidence survives of Godolphin's childhood indicates that he grew up in a close-knit household guided by parents who were devoted to each other and to their sixteen children. This was extraordinarily important to Godolphin's emotional growth, for it surrounded him with stability at a time when civil turmoil was tearing at the fabric of English society.

Early years at court, 1662–1688 Through family influence Godolphin was placed at court as a page of honour to Charles II in 1662. In 1664 he received a grant as one of the seven auditors in the exchequer, an early indication of his flair for finance. In March 1667 his father died; the terms of his will meant that Godolphin was now largely on his own financially, and this spurred his ambition to become a member of parliament. In 1668 he was elected to the Cavalier Parliament from Helston as a member of the court party. During the following years, Charles II's regard for Godolphin's abilities grew. In 1668 he acted as an intermediary between the king and his sister Henrietta Anne, who had married the duke of Anjou, Louis XIV's brother, in their efforts to negotiate an agreement with the French king in which Charles II would turn on his Dutch allies in

Sidney Godolphin, first earl of Godolphin (1645–1712), by Sir Godfrey Kneller, *c*.1704–10

return for French money. The successful outcome of the negotiations undoubtedly enhanced Godolphin's stature at court. On 12 September he was made a groom of the bedchamber and secured a pension of £500 per year. Further evidence of his growing visibility at court came a year later when he obtained a thirty-one-year lease on all tin mines to be discovered in Rialton, and Retraigh, Cornwall. In 1672 the king appointed Godolphin envoy-extraordinary to Louis XIV—a singular vote of confidence for a young courtier. His mission was to assure Louis of Charles's support before he took the field against the Dutch and to present himself as a conduit between the two monarchs. In the following months Godolphin accompanied Louis into the field and this afforded him an opportunity to study the French king as a military leader. He was not impressed; Louis, he became convinced, was a mediocre commander, an assessment which would have an important impact on subsequent events.

In 1675 Godolphin married Margaret Blagge (1652–1678) [*see* Godolphin, Margaret], daughter of Colonel Thomas Blagge of Suffolk, who in 1666 had become a maid of honour to Anne Hyde, duchess of York. Winsome and tall, the young lady from Suffolk soon attracted a bevy of suitors but it was the short and taciturn Godolphin who won her hand: the marriage was delayed for nine years—they married on 16 May 1675. The reason for the delay was undoubtedly that Godolphin did not have the means to establish a suitable household. Margaret died in childbirth on 9 September 1678. Godolphin's only child, Francis *Godolphin, survived, but Margaret's death was the most terrible personal experience of Godolphin's life. The fact that he never married again, in an age when it was not uncommon to outlive two or three spouses, shows how deeply the experience had cut. Never again did he expose himself to such trauma. Beneath the austere exterior that Godolphin showed the world lay a highly sensitive personality.

The political upheaval centring on the attempts to exclude James, duke of York, from the succession drew Godolphin out of his prolonged mourning. On 26 March 1679 he rode the coat-tails of Robert Spencer, second earl of Sunderland, the new secretary of state, into office when, in the wake of the fall of Danby, Charles appointed him one of the commissioners of the Treasury. The following February he entered the privy council for the first time. These appointments affirm that Godolphin was now generally regarded as one of the most able men at court: he had exhibited a head for finance, and had proved his acumen for carrying out delicate diplomatic assignments. When Laurence Hyde joined him at the Treasury in November, they and Sunderland were soon accepted as the king's ministry.

Godolphin's dilemma in the exclusion crisis was who to back in the high-stakes succession game. Although Charles II was willing to accept legislation imposing limitations on James's power upon his accession, he was adamant in his opposition to exclusion. While he had voted against the initial attempt to bypass James, Godolphin joined Sunderland in hedging his bets as events evolved. Months of vacillation followed during which Godolphin joined Sunderland in urging William of Orange, husband of the protestant Mary Stuart, James's eldest daughter, to journey to England from the Netherlands to reaffirm her claims to the throne. William hesitated. Meanwhile, Godolphin joined Sunderland in telling James that he must leave the country and go into exile. Increasingly disillusioned with Sunderland's growing support for exclusion, Charles removed him from office in January 1681. Godolphin, who also favoured exclusion, survived, probably because Charles had little respect for his independence of mind and in all likelihood needed his financial talent. The exclusion movement collapsed when Charles faced down the exclusionists at the third Exclusion Parliament in 1681.

When the treacherous political whirlpool at court pulled Lawrence Hyde, now earl of Rochester, under in July 1684, the king named Godolphin first lord of the Treasury. On 28 September he was raised to the peerage as Baron Godolphin of Rialton. Godolphin, along with the duchess of Portsmouth and Sunderland, now had the greatest influence at court but this triumvirate was short-lived, for on 6 February 1685 Charles II died.

With the accession of James II, Rochester became lord high treasurer and Godolphin held the secondary position of chamberlain to the queen. When Rochester was dismissed in December 1686 Godolphin returned to the Treasury as one of the commissioners. He now became so influential that Princess Anne fretted to her sister Mary that 'I am sorry the King relies so much upon Lord Sunderland and Lord Godolphin' (B. Brown, *The Letters and Diplomatic Instructions of Queen Anne*, 1968, 24). Sunderland and Godolphin were not, however, of the same mind in running the king's affairs. Godolphin consistently recommended a more moderate course than the self-serving and much despised Sunderland. For example, when Sunderland urged the king to rush into an alliance with France and to cut his ties with William of Orange, Godolphin urged caution and counselled James to maintain his links with William. Too much was at stake for such a risky course of action: should James die without a male heir, his protestant daughter Mary would come to the throne, and with her William.

James II's Catholicism posed a sticky problem for Godolphin: like Sunderland, he could have curried the king's favour by converting and partaking of the mass, but he preferred to wait at the door of the queen's chapel during the mass. This was, nevertheless, a benign acceptance of the king's faith, an act that his political enemies would not let him forget.

When William of Orange landed at Torbay on 5 November 1688 in an attempt to overthrow James II, Godolphin found himself in an extremely difficult position. Personally loyal to the king, he had also maintained good relations with William. The awkwardness of his position escalated on 30 November when the king appointed him to a commission, which included the earls of Nottingham and Halifax, to negotiate with William in a desperate effort to buy time to ensure the safe passage of James's family out of the country. When the king received the demands put forth to the commissioners by William he attempted to flee, but was captured on 16 December; through Godolphin he requested that William permit him to travel to Rochester, from where he was allowed to leave for France.

James's flight produced the greatest political crisis of Godolphin's career. As the Convention Parliament struggled through tortuous constitutional debates to justify removing a legitimate ruler and recognizing the accession of William and Mary, Godolphin clung desperately to the king. When the motion calling for the establishment of a regency during James's lifetime came to a vote in the House of Lords, Godolphin voted for the legislation—which was defeated by three votes. This loyalty cost him dearly—for the remainder of his life Godolphin's political enemies would accuse him of remaining loyal to James during these years.

Fortunately for Godolphin, William III either did not believe the allegations, or did not care. William, who knew Godolphin well, prized competent, honest, and incorruptible men. He also realized that one of his most immediate needs was to raise money to carry on the wars in Ireland and on the continent: when the king appointed him to the Treasury commission on 5 April 1689, Godolphin had survived politically. A few weeks later, William granted him a life pension of £500 a year as a groom of the bedchamber. Disillusioned with the king's employment of tories in his government, the whigs unleashed their venom upon Godolphin, the very symbol of loyalty to James II. Increasingly torn between his urge to find refuge from the attacks by leaving the government and his gratitude to William, Godolphin resigned in March 1690. His precise reasons are uncertain, but resignations and threatened resignations punctuated his career, usually when he was under harsh personal or political attack. His return to government service, or his continuation, was accomplished only after suitable soothing from the monarch. Thus on 15 November William was able to coax Godolphin back to the Treasury as first lord; six days later he became a member of the privy council. Further evidence of the king's favour came in mid-December when Godolphin joined the council of nine, the group that advised Queen Mary during William's extended absences.

The honing of a lord treasurer, 1690–1701 William's insatiable need for funds to carry on his war with Louis XIV dominated the next six years of Godolphin's life—it was his responsibility to raise the money necessary to keep the armies and navies of England and her allies in the field and on the seas—and engulfed the ministry in a continuing financial crisis. As the war on the continent dragged on the government's credit was stretched to breaking point. By July 1694 the situation was so desperate that Godolphin warned that if William did not find credit abroad soon 'Wee must be down and die … our difficultys are unspeakable' (Koninklijk Huisarchief, A16 XI G, n. 189). Increasingly exasperated with Godolphin's inability to generate the funds he required, the king accepted the first lord's resignation from the Treasury on 30 October 1696.

This resignation terminated a trying but invaluable period in Godolphin's career. For six long years he had laboured at the Treasury chambers in a frantic effort to raise money to save England in the face of the French onslaught. Although continually frustrated in these efforts, they provided him with vital experience in the workings of the English financial community and allowed the directors of the Bank of England and other financiers to take his measure. Their evaluation of his performance and his abilities would prove to be critical for England's future. By labouring in the arena of public credit Godolphin also acquired first-hand knowledge of the weaknesses of the system and why it failed consistently to generate the funds needed to defeat Louis XIV.

Godolphin's problems during these years were not limited to finance. Almost immediately his feud with Thomas Osborne, marquess of Carmarthen (the former earl of Danby), flared anew. Back in the 1670s Godolphin had been one of those at court suspected of intriguing against the then lord treasurer. He loathed Carmarthen, whose political influence fed on human frailties, and when they clashed Carmarthen probed where Godolphin was most vulnerable—his alleged Jacobite sympathies. Some historians have swallowed these allegations whole: the most famous is Macaulay, who took his account in his *History of England* from Clarke's *Life of James the Second* (1816), which was actually written by the Jacobite William Dicconson while resident at St Germain. According to Dicconson, Godolphin and the duke of Marlborough had met Henry Bulkeley, a well-known Jacobite, on a London street. After greeting him openly and cheerfully in a public park Marlborough allegedly asked Bulkeley to intercede with James II and ask his forgiveness for having deserted him. This account cannot be sustained historically—Macaulay has used flimsy historical evidence to damn Godolphin.

Throughout the reign of William and Mary, Godolphin was accused of remaining in contact with the exiled James II: there is no solid evidence to sustain these allegations, and no way of knowing whether or not they are true. Despite the attacks upon his character, his future prospects were greatly enhanced when he joined the social circle of the Marlboroughs and Princess Anne of Denmark, next in line to the throne. In 1698 Francis Godolphin married Marlborough's daughter, Henrietta Churchill.

In an attempt to curry tory favour in anticipation of another war with France, William returned Godolphin to the Treasury as first lord on 7 December 1700. Soon he was sucked into the political maelstrom swirling in parliament. William had become increasingly disillusioned with parliament as the tories, who controlled the House of Commons, and the whigs preferred to attack each other rather than to prepare to attack the French. William's need for money drew Godolphin into the diplomatic events of the summer of 1701. With William anxious to curry favour with the Swedes in order to keep them out of the French camp, Marlborough asked Godolphin to intercede with the Swedish resident in London. His success resulted in the Swedes, in return for a considerable amount of money, agreeing not to join France. Despite this good work, William manoeuvred Godolphin into resigning on 10 November 1701 when the two disagreed over the wisdom of dissolving parliament.

The death of William III on 8 March 1702 brought Godolphin into the full glare of history. When Queen Anne ascended the throne she took the Marlboroughs and Godolphin with her. With the strong support of the duke of Marlborough, Godolphin became lord high treasurer on 8 May 1702: he was now the most powerful politician in England. During his almost fifty-seven years he had witnessed the civil war, participated in the tumultuous reign of James II and the revolution of 1688, and known the continuing uncertainties of the reign of William and Mary. Tested on many occasions, he was experienced in the infinite uncertainty of English politics, the meandering of international diplomacy, and the details of finance and military supply. Cold in demeanour, he was not easily approached by those whom he did not know or accept. Like many shy people he protected himself with the armour of austerity but to his friends he was generally patient and loyal. As the earl of Shaftesbury noted: 'Once he has conceived a good opinion of a man, he will bear anything for him' (PRO, 30/24/21/101–102). When the pressures of public office occasionally shattered this stoic exterior in a torrent of anger against a friend or acquaintance, he was quick to apologize and to forget.

Godolphin was in many ways at odds with his time: in an age of flattery and rampant corruption he hated sycophants and jealously guarded the public interest. Short in stature, with brown eyes imbedded in a dark face chiselled with pock marks, Godolphin suffered increasingly from kidney stones and from rheumatism, which steadily advanced into his hands and back. He loved breeding and racing thoroughbred horses and whenever possible would hurry to Newmarket to gamble and to watch the races. He was also an avid chess player and art collector, and enjoyed a good tennis match.

While possessing a nimble mind that easily mastered the intricacies of finance, and having a facility with languages, Godolphin's primary forte was unceasing application to the task at hand. From May 1702 until August 1710 his days were crowded with meetings with the queen, politicians, and diplomats, and at the Treasury. He was far more than the 'slogging administrator' one historian described (A. McInnes, *Robert Harley*, 1970, 67). Although not a natural political animal, he constantly kept his finger on the pulse of parliament and manipulated politicians to serve the needs of the queen as he and Marlborough perceived them.

For the next eight years the needs of Marlborough's military machine in the War of the Spanish Succession against France, Spain, and Bavaria dominated Godolphin's life, the culmination of the conflict that had engulfed Europe for four decades. The English were no longer fighting a largely defensive struggle to prevent Louis XIV from smashing the revolution of 1688 and imposing Catholicism upon them; they now became increasingly aggressive in their determination to prevent the union of France and Spain under Philip of Anjou, Louis XIV's grandson. The Marlborough–Godolphin ministry was a unique partnership in English history. Because of his duties fighting the French and their allies on the continent, Marlborough was out of the country most of the year. This prevented him from actively participating in the queen's councils. In addition, he preferred to leave most political transactions, especially the unpleasant ones, to Godolphin. This is not to say that Marlborough did not have strong ideas relative to domestic politics; he did, but he was not interested in becoming involved in the ongoing political maelstrom. Thus, although the two men communicated constantly by letter, Godolphin went out of his way not to bother Marlborough with domestic political problems.

Fuelling the fire: Godolphin at the Treasury, 1702–1710 Godolphin's formidable political influence depended upon his relationship with the queen and his ability to secure the money necessary to fight England's enemies. The public credit system which William III left was far from healthy. The deficit of parliamentary funds for his reign was £2,579,000, and the total national debt was approximately £16 million. Godolphin immediately turned his great talents and formidable tenacity to overcoming the legacy of William's bumbling financial administration and to coaxing, imploring, and manoeuvring for the funds required to fuel the war upon which the protestant succession, the empire, and England's future depended.

Having suffered through the slipshod and ineffectual planning of William III and his Treasury boards, Godolphin instituted an effective system to secure supply and grants from parliament. Each autumn the lord treasurer carefully began drawing up the estimates that the government would lay before parliament. Department heads for the army, ordnance, and transport then presented their estimates to the House of Commons. With the help of government supporters organized by Godolphin and Robert Harley through Thomas Conyers, chairman of the ways and means committee, William Lowndes, secretary of the Treasury, and Henry Boyle, chancellor of the exchequer, the estimates were hammered into resolutions. Once the supply was voted, Godolphin moved to secure the grant money needed to cover it. Again, careful planning and political acumen paid dividends. During his tenure as lord treasurer parliament approved grants covering 97.6 per cent of the supply voted. This carefully orchestrated system produced an astonishing £40,570,400 for the war from 1702 to 1709 that far outstripped the French ability to raise money and contributed as much to the ultimate victory in the War of the Spanish Succession as Marlborough did in the field.

The mechanism that Godolphin used to carry this floating debt was the credit of the navy, ordnance, and transport departments. The result was the growth of departmental debt until by 1710 it had reached a total of £7,139,200, or approximately 20 per cent of the total national debt of some £35 million. The lord treasurer was playing a dangerous game. So long as he could finance the floating debt and the country could remain politically stable and militarily successful, he and Marlborough could guide the government along the course they believed was in its best interest, but if he stumbled, or conditions changed, the structure upon which they built their hopes could topple.

Despite Godolphin's extraordinary ability to squeeze supply out of parliament it was not enough. If Marlborough's and Godolphin's grand strategy that the war would be won in Flanders had any chance of success, the army had to secure all it required in men, equipment, and allied support: when it became evident that the military needs would outstrip any cash parliament would vote, Godolphin plunged the government deeper into debt. The seriousness of the situation can be seen in the growth of the government's public expenditures. Whereas they had averaged less than £6 million from 1689 to 1702, they hovered close to £8 million per annum from 1702 to 1710.

Acutely aware of the problems that overdependence upon short-term borrowing had brought the crown under William III, Godolphin took steps to swing more of the debt to long-term borrowing. Between the critical years of 1704 and 1708 he was able to shift the weight so that long-term borrowing assumed 19 per cent of the burden. His strategy was simple and successful: using the confidence he inspired in the Bank of England and in the financial community in general, he funded long-term borrowing primarily with the sale of annuities.

The lord treasurer also attempted to make the administration of public funds more efficient and more honest.

Soon Godolphin was pressuring tax collecting agencies to improve their performance. One of his foremost administrative concerns was to expedite the assessment and collection of the government's most important source of revenue—the land tax—and he pressured the tax office to improve its performance, and that of its operatives, in collecting it. Thus on 5 August 1702 he summoned the agents for taxes to the Treasury chambers and ordered them to submit an abstract summarizing the amounts they had collected and estimating if they were likely to fall short in their projections. At year's end he required them to present a summary of what they had collected.

Godolphin worked hard to root out the corruption that was endemic in the government. He interrogated tellers of the receipts about money embezzled by their underclerks and ordered investigations of charges of fraud in the Post Office and among salt duty collectors. Corruption was especially rampant in the customs' system. The lord treasurer's response to the constant drain of customs' revenues was to demand greater accountability and to appoint, when possible, experienced and honest individuals.

Godolphin was very frugal with the government's money. Everything, from expenses for the queen's coronation, to public works expenses, to contracts for supplying wagons for the troops, underwent his scrutiny. It was not long before his efforts paid off. In late 1704 L'Hermitage, the Dutch agent in London, wrote to his masters in the Netherlands that England's finances were so well administered that some cities had congratulated the queen on her choice of lord treasurer (BL, Add. MS 17677ZZ, fols. 473–4).

Seated in the Treasury chambers, resting his weary eyes while the faithful Lowndes read him an endless stream of financial and diplomatic correspondence, the lord treasurer was a man of enormous industry and acumen who was determined to make the Treasury efficient, honest, and frugal in the service of the crown in its struggle to defeat absolutist Catholic France. His efforts brought mixed results. There is little doubt that the Treasury gained new respect and was better administered as a result of Godolphin's efforts. In many ways he laid the foundation of the Treasury that would serve Great Britain so effectively throughout the eighteenth century, but he largely failed to impose a new honesty on its administration, and he did not introduce any important innovations. He was not creative or innovative—his forte was administration rather than originality. In addition he brought to the Treasury integrity and honesty, qualities highly valued by financiers and bankers, who rely heavily on mutual trust. These qualities were of inestimable value in his dealings with the Bank of England and the East India Company, both of which held him in esteem as a man of talent and of his word.

Years of accomplishment, 1702–1706 Since the ministry did not control a majority in the House of Commons, Godolphin launched upon a protracted political balancing act in which he played to the interests of whig and tory factions in order to secure supply. When Queen Anne came to the throne the high-church tories believed that their time had finally arrived. Immediately they posed a political problem for Godolphin by launching a campaign to drive from public life those (especially whigs) who partook of the Anglican sacrament merely to qualify for office. The resulting occasional-conformity legislation created a dilemma for Godolphin: to oppose it risked alienating the high-Anglican queen and important tories; to support it risked alienating whigs and nonconformists in the Commons, who were the strongest supporters of the war. After the legislation easily passed the Commons in late 1702, Godolphin and Marlborough supported it in public but sabotaged it in private. As a result, the bill failed in the Lords in early 1703.

Godolphin struck at the high tories in February 1703 when he persuaded the queen to remove Rochester, one of their leaders, from the ministry. Rochester's dismissal did not, however, end the threat posed by occasional-conformity legislation, for in late 1704 the high tories threatened to tack it to the Land Tax Bill. The portents of passage were serious. To reintroduce the legislation was one thing, to threaten the war effort by striking at its primary source of tax revenues was quite another. After feverish activity by Godolphin and Robert Harley the court, on 28 November, after seven hours of heated debate, defeated the tack. This ruptured the tory party. The wounded high tories soon attacked the lord treasurer for his advice to the queen that she accept the Act of Security which stipulated that Scotland was not automatically committed to accepting the Hanoverian succession without due consideration for its religious, constitutional, and economic concerns. When the high tories moved to censure Godolphin, the whigs intervened to block the motion and to ensure his growing dependence upon them.

The composition of the ministry changed markedly in 1704 when Nottingham, another leading high tory, resigned, ushering in the moderate tories and Robert Harley, who became secretary of state. Harley's appointment marked a critical step in the evolution of the ministry. As secretary of state he was second only to the lord high treasurer in administering the government and his ascendancy reaffirmed the high regard of Marlborough and Godolphin for his political abilities, and their need for his help in securing supply. It also says something about Godolphin: austere and forbidding in demeanour, he was not easily approached and did not relish the hurly-burly of politics; he required a natural political animal such as Harley to complement his own personality. In addition he was willing to share power if he thought it would further the cause of defeating France. Godolphin did not love power for its own sake; for him it was a means to an end.

Political turmoil also drew Godolphin into the deteriorating relationship between the queen and the duchess of Marlborough. Always certain that her opinions should prevail, the duchess could not believe that the queen, and by implication Godolphin, could be so stupid as to continue to shut her whig friends out of the ministry, but his attempts to reconcile the two former confidantes failed. The queen's regard for Godolphin's efforts during these months of trauma became evident when on 30 December 1704 she designated him a knight of the Order of the Garter.

In the aftermath of the ministerial changes in the spring and the inevitable unhappiness they engendered among the high tories and the whigs, news of Marlborough's thrashing of the French at Blenheim, which saved Vienna from siege and kept the grand alliance from unravelling, gave the lord treasurer, the queen, and the nation an enormous lift. While Marlborough was defeating the French in Germany, Godolphin remained intensely interested in the Mediterranean, where the primary objective was an attack on Toulon. He believed that a successful attack by the duke of Savoy and Sir George Rooke would distract Louis XIV from pouncing on the weakened holy Roman emperor, but when the French reinforced Toulon and Rooke frittered away several months of valuable time, the plan no longer had any merit. Although Rooke subsequently took Gibraltar, Godolphin believed that he had squandered an opportunity to reduce French influence in the area. Nor did the progress of the Iberian campaign please Godolphin. In an attempt to bolster the foundering effort there he persuaded the queen to replace the incompetent third duke of Schomberg, a hot-headed prima donna, with the earl of Galway and to contract for more horses and men, but internecine bickering between the Portuguese, English, and Dutch soon undermined the campaign and it petered out.

Despite disappointing campaigns in the Mediterranean and on the Iberian peninsula, 1704 had been a good year for Godolphin and the ministry—few things do more for a government in time of war than military victory. Godolphin now set out to crush the tackers in anticipation of the mandated parliamentary elections of 1705. With the queen openly campaigning for all supporters of the government, the campaign soon turned vicious and violent: the ministry painted the tackers as extremists, the high tories lampooned the queen, and the whigs smeared all tories. The election results mirrored Godolphin's failed strategy: many of the tackers whom he had targeted were re-elected and, although the tory stranglehold on the Commons had loosened considerably, they still held 267 seats, a loss of 62 seats, and the whigs garnered 246 seats.

It was obvious that Godolphin and Marlborough must make some accommodations with the whigs immediately but when they put forth the third earl of Sunderland as their primary candidate for a position in the ministry a serious impediment surfaced—the queen loathed him. In addition, she feared a swing to the whigs would make her too dependent upon one party—something she strongly resisted. In the months that followed Godolphin pressured the queen to accept more whigs into the government. This marked a turning point in the relationship between the queen and her lord treasurer as signs of a growing rift began to emerge, most importantly indications that she was listening to a more comfortable view from Harley, who also resisted bringing more whigs into the ministry.

The military campaign of 1705 produced little. The Dutch, always reluctant to allow their troops to wander too far from home, successfully sabotaged Marlborough's Mosel campaign and his efforts to bring the enemy to the battlefield. As he wrote to Godolphin on 8 August (19 August os): 'This last action of the Dutch generals has given me very great mortification, for the enemy will see very plainly that they have nothing to fear on this side' (Veenendaal, and others, 4.323–4). Godolphin had his own frustrations with the Dutch. On 31 August he gave Vrijbergen, the Dutch envoy in London, a tongue-lashing. For an hour and a half he vilified the Dutch for the cowardice of their generals, and for their insistence on carrying on trade with the French.

While Marlborough struggled in the Netherlands, Godolphin believed that a dramatic strike into Spain from Portugal would bring a quick end to the war, but Portuguese timidity soon undercut the effort. Godolphin reacted by ordering payments to shore up their credit for the campaign. He then used this leverage to attempt to bludgeon the timid Portuguese into line. Either they were to rediscover their resolve to fight, or funds from England would be cut off. It was to no avail. The campaign ended on a note of internecine bickering.

Momentarily setting aside occasional conformity, the high tories in the winter of 1705 attacked the ministry on several other fronts. Reneging on his promise to the tories not to support a whig for speaker of the House of Commons, Godolphin announced that he would endorse the whig John Smith because it was the only way to prevent tacker fanatics from 'wresting the Administration out [of] the Queen's hands' (BL, Portland loan 29/192/338). Despite his carefully laid plans Smith won by a scant forty-three votes, with seventeen of the queen's managers bolting. The unexpected closeness of the election and the desertion of so many of the queen's managers proved that the wound opened by the tack among the tories had healed and that Godolphin now faced an increasingly hostile force determined to condemn his alliance with the whigs and to block his war efforts. It also reaffirmed his conviction that the only course for the ministry to pursue if the war was to be brought to a successful conclusion, and the kingdom saved, was to move ever closer to the whigs. The tories also sought to embarrass the ministry and weaken its links with the whigs by inviting the Electress Sophia of Hanover to take up residence in England. They hoped to force Godolphin and Harley to choose between alienating Anne by reminding her of her mortality, or offending her possible successor. Godolphin and Harley, with the help of the whigs, were able to avoid the trap by passing a Regency Act that ensured the orderly passage of power to Anne's protestant successor.

Continuing tension between the ministry and the Dutch brought William Buys, the pensionary of Holland, to England in early 1706. His mission was twofold: first, to attempt to reduce the growing acrimony between the maritime powers; second, to co-ordinate preparations for the coming campaign. In addition, Buys carried a secret plan for peace with France. Although the ministry had dismissed outright Louis XIV's peace proposals of the previous autumn, Buys now pressed for consideration of a similar Dutch plan—which would have partitioned Spanish possessions along the lines agreed to in the grand alliance of 1701 and would have made Philip of Anjou, Louis's grandson, king of Spain. But the English clung stubbornly to the Methuen treaty of 1703 with Portugal which had altered the grand alliance and committed them to a policy of seating the Archduke Charles of Austria in Madrid in return for the use of Portuguese harbours and military support. The resulting policy of Godolphin and Marlborough of 'no peace without Spain' undoubtedly lengthened the war.

With the Dutch tempted by French wooing, the military campaign of 1706 assumed extraordinary importance if the ministry's diplomatic strategy of placing Charles on the Spanish throne was to succeed. After an inauspicious beginning the campaign reached a successful climax when Marlborough defeated the French at Ramillies in the Spanish Netherlands. By June virtually all of Belgium had surrendered to Marlborough and proclaimed for Charles. Marlborough soon accomplished what had seemed impossible: he swept the Spanish Netherlands clean of the French and greatly weakened Louis, militarily and diplomatically.

Meanwhile, Prince Eugene of Savoy was attempting to stem the Gallic tide in Italy. Godolphin's preparations for the campaign had begun in late 1705, when the emperor requested £250,000 to put Prince Eugene's army into the field. When Marlborough applied tremendous pressure to produce the money, the lord treasurer courted London's moneymen to open their wallets. In early January he and Marlborough secured a pledge from eight influential merchants for a subscription (a scheme in which individuals purchased shares in a loan to be repaid in a stipulated amount of time) to be sold in London conditional upon the queen's pledge to use her good offices to secure repayment from the emperor in six years. It was sold in a mere five days. The opening salvo of the 1706 Italian campaign had been fired in the boardrooms of London, but despite this extraordinary infusion of cash it initially resembled the nightmare of 1705 when in April the duke of Vendôme mauled a segment of Prince Eugene's army at Calcinato. In September, however, Eugene relieved the beleaguered city of Turin, swept the French from Italy, and declared Charles king. Godolphin, who had become increasingly uneasy with the modest return on the immense amount of money raised for the prince's campaign, was elated with the results.

The fate of Catalonia also continued to weigh heavily on Godolphin. Determined to hold the bastion pivotal to the 'no peace without Spain' strategy, he was especially concerned about the possibility of French seizure of Barcelona. He and Galway, the commander of the English troops in Portugal, anticipated this threat by planning a march on Madrid from Portugal in an effort to relieve pressure on Barcelona. Once again the Portuguese proved unco-operative. When it appeared that Barcelona was about to fall and the French would capture the Archduke Charles, Admiral Leake arrived on 27 April and the French fled. The victory was as much Godolphin's as it was Leake's. The ministry's strongest advocate of Mediterranean action, he had provided the supplies and impetus required for it and had been deeply involved in planning the strategy.

However, Godolphin's high hopes of the ministry's grand design to put Charles on the throne of Spain were disappointed when the Portuguese preferred plundering at sideshow sieges to marching on Madrid, and Charles failed to seize the opportunity presented to him: he snivelled that a lack of money and a suitable entourage kept him anchored in Catalonia. By early August it was too late: Toledo and Guadalajara had fallen to the enemy, and pro-Philip fever swept Castile. Marlborough's and Godolphin's 'no peace without Spain' policy was proving a costly failure, but Godolphin failed to recognize this. Indeed, he believed that victory was at hand. The basis of this assumption was his conviction that France's financial system was about to snap. Just one more military campaign would stretch Louis's resources to the breaking point, bring military triumph to the grand alliance, and result in the fruition of the ministry's 'no peace without Spain' policy.

To accomplish this, the support of the whigs in voting supply for one more campaign was critical. Fully aware of Godolphin's predicament, the whig junto in 1706 renewed its campaign to have Sunderland appointed to the ministry. Reluctantly, Godolphin agreed. Since victory was at hand, even the odious Sunderland could be tolerated in return for continued whig support. After months of fencing the queen, under enormous pressure from Godolphin and the Marlboroughs, and after Godolphin threatened to resign, finally capitulated, and on 3 December Sunderland became a secretary of state. However, the year did produce a historic achievement for Godolphin and the ministry in Scotland. After years of being drawn into the quagmire that was Scottish politics in an effort to secure men and money from the Scots, Godolphin was able to negotiate a deal which brought Scotland into the united kingdom of Great Britain.

For his services to the crown and the nation, the lord treasurer was proclaimed earl of Godolphin on 26 December 1706. His tenure in office had been a stunning success. He had revitalized a public credit system on the verge of collapse, coaxed from parliament and England's moneymen the funds required to challenge French hegemony, and successfully brought the efforts of the difficult Dutch, the cautious Portuguese, and the reluctant emperor to bear against Louis. These efforts reached their vertex in 1706. In one dazzling year Godolphin was instrumental in the passage of legislation ensuring the Hanoverian succession, the French had been swept from the Spanish Netherlands and Italy, and the historic negotiations for the union of Scotland with England and Wales had been brought to a successful conclusion. Few ministers in English history have done so much to shape the future of their country.

Years of decline, 1707–1710 Godolphin could not have realized that he had reached his apogee in 1706, for by forcing Sunderland upon the queen he sowed the seeds for his own demise. He had alienated the one person he could not afford to alienate, the queen. He had also played into the hands of Harley, who now established himself as a confidant of the queen and worked to undermine the lord treasurer. The extent of the queen's disillusionment emerged in the summer of 1707. When Godolphin sought to placate the whigs by placing their candidates to fill two vacant bishoprics he learned to his horror that the queen, at Harley's urging, had already agreed to support two tories without consulting him. Although Anne eventually agreed to make some whig bishops, the chasm between her and Godolphin had widened further.

As the opening of parliament approached Godolphin lapsed into despair and resignation and the government faced the new session ill-prepared to deal with its opposition. This lack of preparation was a product of Godolphin's failed leadership and the political situation: his relationship with the queen was fraught with disagreement; he found Harley an ongoing enigma; and, most of all, he feared the whig extremists would join the tories to destroy the ministry. Soon he was fretting that 'I expect to see the whole Government torn to pieces' (BL, Portland loan 29/191/61). Godolphin's fears proved well founded. No sooner had the new session begun in November than the disgruntled whig junto and the high tories launched a concerted attack on the ministry, and Godolphin countered by courting the moderate whigs.

Now fully prepared to dump Godolphin, the queen was soon plotting with Harley to drive him from office. In a dramatic meeting with the queen on 8 February 1708 Godolphin and Marlborough presented her with an option—remove Harley or they would resign. Unable to face the loss of Marlborough, Anne accepted Harley's resignation but Godolphin's victory was momentary and hollow. The struggle over Harley had laid bare the full extent of the queen's disillusionment with the lord treasurer and her growing conviction that he was dispensable.

The ministry's enemies probed for another soft spot when in January 1708 the high tories trumpeted that its incompetence was responsible for Galway's defeat at Almanza in Spain the previous April. Why, they cried, were there only 8600 troops present when parliament had voted supply for 29,000? Although the government's agents valiantly defended it in parliament, only the intervention of the whigs saved it from censure. This latest onslaught by his enemies reconfirmed Godolphin's conviction that the ministry must edge still closer to the whigs.

A new and potentially catastrophic problem emerged when it became evident that the public credit system that Godolphin had so assiduously nurtured was beginning to sway under the strain of unending war. Although he was able to secure a fresh loan of £1.2 million from the Bank of England, it was soon evident that it was not enough. He then turned to the East India Company. Originally founded by tories in the 1680s and 1690s, the bank had encountered a series of financial setbacks and increased competition for its domination of East India trade. When the whigs founded a New India Company the result was two companies, neither of which was able to take control of the trade. Finally, in 1707, Godolphin mediated a union of the two companies in return for a loan to the government to help finance the 1708 campaign. The historical significance of Godolphin's role in ending the feud between the companies and in consolidating the New East India Company extended far beyond the boardrooms of London, for eventually the company would secure British control of India, the keystone of the empire.

In early 1708 the queen dissolved parliament and called for new elections. When the whigs won a majority in the Commons they immediately demanded more positions in the ministry. Godolphin's determination to press their complaints led to another round of testy confrontations with the queen, which reached a climax on 1 June when they quarrelled for several hours. It was evident by now that Godolphin's influence with the queen was rapidly evaporating. The exasperated lord treasurer wrote to Marlborough that:

> The Queen continues so averse to everything Mr. Montgomery [Godolphin] can propose for the support of Mrs. Morley's [the Queen's] affairs, that he is soe tired out of his life at present … that he has been obliged … to begg of the Queen either to follow his notions, or to dismiss him, and not lett him bear the burden … of other people's follys. But all this … seems to make no manner of impression. (Snyder, 2.1009)

After months of acrimonious bickering the queen capitulated, and the junto whigs Somers and Wharton were ushered into the government.

By now it was evident to both whigs and tories that Godolphin's position had been seriously undermined. While some whigs drank to his growing isolation, a host of vicious publications held him up to ridicule. When Marlborough routed the French at Oudenarde in July and retook Ghent from the French the following January, the logic of the ministry that Louis XIV could be coerced into a favourable peace once he was faced with certain military defeat seemed ready for the test, but they no longer dominated the formulation and implementation of foreign policy. By bringing the junto into the ministry they had purchased support for the war at the price of power. For over a year Godolphin had been consulting Sunderland, the second earl of Halifax, and Somers on important diplomatic matters.

1709 produced a serious break between Godolphin and Marlborough. When the Dutch demanded a line of barrier-fortresses in the Low Countries to ensure their security, the whig junto supported them as necessary to keep the Dutch from making a separate peace with France. Marlborough was vehemently opposed. He clung to the fantasy that if the Netherlands would support one more military campaign Louis would be forced to swallow 'no peace without Spain' whole. When, reluctantly, Godolphin came to agree with the junto, negotiations for a Dutch barrier were concluded. His greatest domestic headache centred on the demand of the junto that the whig earl of Orford succeed the earl of Pembroke at the Admiralty. Soon he came under increasing pressure from the junto and the duchess of Marlborough to browbeat the defiant queen into submission. After months of wrangling, Orford joined the Admiralty commission.

By late 1709 the Godolphin ministry was teetering on the brink of collapse. Growing disillusionment with the war, Anne's estrangement from Godolphin and the Marlboroughs, the machinations of Harley, and an escalating credit crisis all threatened to bring the ministry down. This kindling found a spark when a high-tory parson named Sacheverell delivered an inflammatory sermon in which he accused the lord treasurer of having sold out to the whig junto. Irate, Godolphin struck back by demanding the impeachment of his tormentor. Although this was carried out and Sacheverell was found guilty, he emerged victorious when the Lords delivered a light sentence. An embittered Godolphin complained that 'all this bustle and fatigue' (Snyder, 3.1440) had gained little.

Harley now knit together a coalition of tories and disgruntled whigs to take advantage of the beleaguered Godolphin and his reeling ministry in anticipation of the parliamentary elections many believed must come soon. Increasingly encircled by his political enemies, and with a growing credit crisis looming, Godolphin fell from power on 8 August 1710 when the queen requested that 'instead of bringing the staff to me, you will break it, which I believe will be easier to us both' (BL, Add. MS 61118, fols. 47–8). Two years later his aged body surrendered to an attack of kidney stones and he died at St Albans at 2 a.m. on 15 September 1712. For several weeks his body awaited the rounding up of enough whig Garter knights to carry the pall. Finally, in early October, he was buried in Westminster Abbey.

Sidney Godolphin is a major figure in English history for several reasons: first he raised the money required to blunt French hegemony in Europe and thus preserved the British constitution and the protestant monarchy; second he was instrumental in planning the military and diplomatic strategy that ultimately defeated Louis XIV; third, as lord high treasurer, he worked to make the Treasury more efficient and attempted to weed out corruption—the Treasury as he left it served England well for the remainder of the eighteenth century; fourth he was instrumental in negotiating and passing the Act of Union with Scotland which created the united kingdom of Great Britain; and fifth he negotiated the creation of a unified East India Company, which would be instrumental in establishing British rule in India. Roy A. Sundstrom

Sources R. A. Sundstrom, *Sidney Godolphin, servant of the state* (1992) • *The Marlborough–Godolphin correspondence*, ed. H. L. Snyder, 3 vols. (1975) • BL, Godolphin correspondence, Add. MS 28055 • W. A. Shaw, ed., *Calendar of treasury books*, 1–26, PRO (1904–54) • BL, L'Hermitage correspondence, Add. MS 17677ZZ • BL, Harley correspondence, Portland loan 29 [the Portland loan is esp. valuable for Eng. politics during these years; Portland miscellaneous incl. a vol. of Godolphin's letters only recently discovered] • *De briefwisseling van Anthonie Heinsius, 1702–1720*, ed. A. J. Veenendaal and others, [17 vols.] (The Hague, 1976–) • Koninklijk Huisarchief, The Hague, A16 XI G, n. 189 • HoP, *Commons, 1660–90* • T. Lever, *Godolphin: his life and times* (1952) • will, PRO, PROB 11/529, sig. 209 • *DNB* • GEC, *Peerage*

Archives BL, corresp. and papers, Add. MSS 28052–28058; Egerton MSS 3324–3400; Egerton Charters 2290–2300 • BL, draft speeches read by Queen Anne from the throne, Egerton MSS 3276, 3773 • NL Scot., corresp. | BL, corresp. with William Blathwayt, Add. MS 9735 • BL, Blenheim MSS, Portland loan • BL, letters to earl of Oxford, Robert Harley, loan 29/64 • BL, letters to Lord Oxford, Add. MSS 70284–70285 • BL, letters to H. Sydney, Add. MSS 32680–32681 • BL, corresp. with Sir Joseph Williamson, Add. MSS 35375–35376 • BL, letters to Sir Joseph Williamson • Bodl. Oxf., letters to Gilbert Burnet, MS Add. a 191 • CKS, corresp. with Alexander Stanhope; corresp. with James Stanhope • Cumbria AS, Carlisle, letters to Lord Lonsdale, D/LONS • Herts. ALS, letters to first Earl Cowper, D/EP • Longleat House, Wiltshire, Portland MSS • NA Scot., letters to duke of Argyll, GD1/1158 • NA Scot., Seafield MSS • NA Scot., corresp. with earl of Mar, GD124 • Nationaal Archief, The Hague, Buys corresp. • NL Scot., letters from duke of Argyll, MS 3366 • Northants. RO, letters to earl of Nottingham • NRA, priv. coll., corresp. with first Earl Stanhope • V&A NAL, letters and MSS relating to trip to Brussels • Yale U., Beinecke L., letters to William Blathwayt, OSB MSS 2 • Yale U., Beinecke L., letters to Edmund Poley, OSB MSS 1

Likenesses G. Kneller, oils, *c*.1704–1710, NPG [*see illus.*] • F. Bird, bust, Westminster Abbey • G. Kneller, oils, Blenheim Palace, Oxfordshire • G. Kneller, oils; on loan, Marlborough House, London • G. Kneller, oils, second version, Althorp, Northamptonshire • J. M. Rysbrack, marble bust, Althorp, Northamptonshire • J. Smith, mezzotint (after G. Kneller), BM, NPG

Wealth at death for his station, not wealthy; left everything to son: will, PRO, PROB 11/529, sig. 209

Godolphin, Sir William (*b*. in or before **1518**, *d*. **1570**), soldier, was the eldest son of Sir William Godolphin (*d*. *c*.1547), landowner, of Godolphin, Cornwall, and his first wife, Margaret, daughter of John Glynn of Morval, Cornwall. The family may reliably be connected with the parish of Breage in Cornwall from the late thirteenth century. The existing house at Godolphin was begun by John Godolghan about 1475. His son and namesake, the elder Sir William Godolphin's father, served as sheriff of Cornwall in 1504 and 1508, and the next reign saw the family consolidate its social and economic dominance over the county's remote western hundreds. Its wealth was industrial rather than agricultural, based chiefly on the extraction and smelting of tin: John Leland observed that there were 'no greater tynne workes yn al Cornwal then be on Sir Wylliam Godolcan's ground' (*Itinerary*, 1.191). Sir William Godolphin senior was pricked sheriff in 1533 and ingratiated himself with Thomas Cromwell, principal secretary, throughout the 1530s, forwarding information on the state of the peace and sending him Cornish wrestlers and tin miners. The principal secretary responded by taking the younger William Godolphin and two brothers into his own household. Possibly Godolphin had some legal training, since a William Godolphin was admitted to Lincoln's Inn in November 1537. In 1539, the year in which his father was appointed to the council of the west, he was nominated by Cromwell as knight of the shire for Cornwall.

In 1544 Godolphin was in northern France, serving as master of the mines at the sieges of Montreuil and Boulogne. Cornish tinners were highly prized as sappers, and he commanded the company that successfully undermined the walls of Boulogne. In August he was wounded in action, 'no less to the beautifying of his fame than the disfiguring of his face', as noted by Richard Carew of Antony, Cornwall (Carew, 133–4). He was rewarded with the bailiwick of the town, and sat on its council until Boulogne was returned to the French in 1550. He was also knighted, apparently in 1546, at which point it becomes even more difficult to separate father and son in the records. The problem is compounded by the lack of firm evidence for the year of his father's death; 1547 seems the best estimate.

In April 1548 Godolphin led his fellow magistrates in pacifying west Cornwall following the murder of the avaricious archdeacon, William Body, during a riot in defence of the traditional liturgy in Helston. He had little sympathy for the protesters, and in July he organized a band of mounted gentlemen and parish constables against any resurgence of sedition. He also assisted in surveying the revenues of the dissolved chantries in Cornwall and Devon. When a far more serious religious insurrection erupted in 1549 an informer sent him secret information on one of the rebel leaders, Humphrey Arundell. On 22 July Edward Seymour, duke of Somerset and lord protector, and the privy council wrote to John Russell, first Baron Russell, lord privy seal, about a proclamation confiscating rebel property: 'a better personage to execute it can not be devised then Sir William Godolphin, who hath bene a frontier man' (Pocock, 33). Godolphin was chosen sheriff of Cornwall later in the year. In December 1549 he was bound over to keep the peace with Sir John Arundell of Lanherne. In 1551 he served as vice-admiral of Cornwall, and in March 1553 he was again elected knight of the shire.

Godolphin had cleaved to the protestant military establishment under Edward VI, and the accession of Mary I left him in an uncomfortable position. A William Godolphin was reported as present in the entourage of Francis Russell, second earl of Bedford, in Venice in the summer of 1555. The exile is unlikely to be the head of the family, since Sir William Godolphin was still listed as a JP in 1555, when he was included among the magistrates detailed to intervene in a dispute in Launceston. But his reformed religion may help to explain a challenge to the controllership of tin coinage in Cornwall that Godolphin had enjoyed since 1545. In 1555 the crown apparently granted William Isham the same lucrative office, resulting in an unseemly riot between the servants of the two parties in Truro coinage hall. Godolphin recovered his local position under Elizabeth I, serving as sheriff of Cornwall in 1568 and as deputy lieutenant in 1569.

The interest of the Godolphins in the Isles of Scilly dates from the mid-sixteenth century. Lying 28 miles off Land's End, this sparsely populated territory was vulnerable to French attack. Thomas Godolphin became the military captain of Scilly during Edward's reign, directing the fortification and provisioning of the islands. In August 1556 the privy council thanked Sir William Godolphin for apprehending the pirate Jacob Thomson at Scilly, though it subsequently rebuked him for acquitting several of Thomson's compatriots. In summer 1558 Godolphin petitioned the crown to farm the islands for £20, Bedford acting as mediator. One of the first tasks carried out by the Elizabethan privy council was to draw up Godolphin's lease of the islands. Thus began an association between the Godolphins and Scilly that would endure until the nineteenth century.

Godolphin married Blanche, daughter of Robert Langdon of the parish of St Martin, Cornwall; they had two daughters. He died in 1570 and was buried at Breage on 30 July. The house and estate then passed to his nephew **Sir Francis Godolphin** (*c.*1534–1608), landowner, who was the elder son of Sir William's younger brother Thomas Godolphin and his first wife, Katherine, daughter and heir of Edmund Bonython. He followed his uncle's lead, serving as JP for Cornwall from the mid-1570s and sitting as knight for Cornwall in 1589 and MP for Lostwithiel in 1593. In 1580 he was knighted. He was pricked sheriff in 1579 and 1604, was deputy lieutenant from 1585, and became receiver-general of the duchy of Cornwall in 1586. Further details on him are supplied in the 1602 *Survey of Cornwall* written by his friend Richard Carew. Godolphin's pre-eminence on the commission of the peace reflected his 'zeal in religion, uprightness in justice, providence in government, and plentiful housekeeping' (Carew, 228). He was of the quorum by 1583. 300 men worked his tin, silver, and copper mines. Carew also shines a little light upon the library at Godolphin. Having borrowed from Sir Francis Godolphin a scientific treatise on the mind, Carew translated it from Italian into English and dedicated it to him: 'Good Sir, your Booke returneth unto you clad in a Cornish gabardine' (ibid., 34).

Invasion was a perennial fear in later Elizabethan Cornwall, and Godolphin was variously responsible for musters, the fortification of ports, and the early-warning system of beacon fires. In July 1595 he directed the defence of Penzance against a Spanish raiding party that had burned Paul church and the village of Mousehole. His greatest achievement, however, lay even further west. The lease of Scilly had been regranted in 1570, and in 1593 he was commanded to build a fort on St Mary's. His collaborator in the initial stages of construction was the architect and engineer Robert Adams, who may also be responsible for the fine symmetrical stables at Godolphin. The queen granted a miserly £400 for the works, leaving Godolphin to advance £600 of his own money and to use his soldiers for labour. The result was Star Castle, an eight-pointed fortification commanding the peninsula above Hugh Town and the sheltered harbour between the islands. Provision was made for a permanent garrison, with additional gun platforms, blockhouses, windmills, and a beacon pit to alert the mainland in case of attack. Finance, however, was a continuing problem. In 1600 Godolphin petitioned the privy council to replace the badly rusted and outdated ordnance brought to the islands some fifty years before. He also argued the case for outer earthworks, essential to protect the fort from enemy artillery, but in vain: they were never built. Carew praised Godolphin's castle as 'a sure hold and a commodious dwelling' (Carew, 156), but Sir Francis had a more sophisticated comprehension of military architecture and was all too aware of the weakness of his design in the absence of additional fortification. His letters to Sir Robert Cecil, principal secretary, speak of his deep anxiety about the depleted state of the Scilly garrison and the threat of Spanish assault and occupation. Star Castle still stands, a tribute to Godolphin's energy and administrative acumen in the remotest of locations.

In 1552 Francis Godolphin married Margaret, daughter of John Killigrew of Arwenack, Falmouth. They had three sons and six daughters; the eldest son, another William Godolphin (*d.* 1613), served with courage in Robert Devereux, earl of Essex's army in Ireland. Sir Francis's second wife was Alice, *née* Skerret, widow of John Glanville. They had no children and she outlived him. He died in 1608 and was buried at Breage on 23 April. His will of 1606 testifies to a strong belief in godly charity. He bequeathed the large sum of £200 to be distributed in Penwith and Kerrier hundreds 'towardes the relief and settinge their poore to worke and for restrayninge them from ydle loyteringe and wandringe abroade'. He reserved £40 for a local 'howse of correction', should one be established within ten years of his death, and left 20 marks to build lodgings on Godolphin Hill for four 'poore decayed tynners' in his service (PRO, PROB 11/111, sig. 46). He also bequeathed money to support weekly preaching in Helston church. The Godolphin estate was inherited by his eldest son, who replaced him as receiver of the duchy of Cornwall.

J. P. D. Cooper

Sources HoP, *Commons, 1509–58*, 2.219–20 • HoP, *Commons, 1558–1603*, 2.198 • *LP Henry VIII* • *CSP dom., 1547–58* • *APC, 1547–50, 1554–70* • R. Carew, *The survey of Cornwall*, ed. F. E. Halliday (1953) • F. G. Marsh, *The Godolphins* (1930) • F. G. Marsh, *Additions and corrections* (1943) • I. Arthurson, 'Fear and loathing in West Cornwall: seven new letters on the 1548 rising', *Journal of the Royal Institute of Cornwall*, new ser., 2/3 (2000), 68–96 • PRO, STAC 4/1/48 • will, PRO, PROB 11/111, sig. 46 [Sir Francis Godolphin] • *CSP Venice, 1555–8* • A. L. Rowse, *Tudor Cornwall* (1941) • N. Pocock, ed., *Troubles connected with the prayer book of 1549: documents … in the record office*, CS, new ser., 37 (1884) • private information (2004) [John Schofield] • *The itinerary of John Leland in or about the years 1535–1543*, ed. L. Toulmin Smith, 11 pts in 5 vols. (1906–10)

Wealth at death see will, PRO, PROB 11/111, sig. 46 [Sir Francis Godolphin]

Godolphin, Sir William (*bap.* **1635**, *d.* **1696**), diplomat, was baptized on 2 February 1635 at St Mabyn church, Cornwall, third but eldest surviving son of Sir William Godolphin (1604/5–1663) of Spargor, Cornwall, and Ruth (*d.* before 1658), daughter of Sir John *Lambe (*c.*1566–1646), dean of the arches. In 1648 he entered Westminster School, where he became a friend of John Locke. On 21 June 1651 he matriculated at Christ Church, Oxford, from where he wrote English and Latin verses on the Dutch treaty in 1654. In November that year he was admitted to the Inner Temple. Created MA in 1661, by 1662 he was assistant to Henry Bennet, earl of Arlington, secretary of state, his work including sending instructions, receiving intelligence and fees, and questioning state prisoners. Arlington trusted him with important business, and petitioners sought his favour. On 28 September 1663 he was awarded a DCL at Oxford on the same day as his superior; he became FRS in November and on 7 October 1664 he was granted one of the auditorships of the exchequer court for life. On 17 October 1665 he entered parliament at a by-election for Camelford, Cornwall, although he may never have taken his seat.

In 1666 Godolphin was appointed to assist the earl of Sandwich in negotiations for a commercial treaty in Madrid, on a salary of £600. He was Sandwich's most valued assistant in the talks with Spanish councillors; according to Samuel Pepys his superior commended him as 'the worthiest man, and such a friend to him as he may be trusted in anything relating to him in the world … indeed, they say the gentleman is a very fine man' (Pepys, 9.52). Godolphin also accompanied Sandwich to Portugal. After the treaty's ratification in November 1667 he was presented with an expensive jewel by the queen regent of Spain, and in January 1668 returned to London. His first encounter with Pepys, on 31 January, led to dinner on a number of occasions. Pepys reported 'I do find him a very pretty and able person, a man of very fine parts and of infinite zeal to my Lord Sandwich' (ibid., 9.59). Godolphin also defended Sandwich against complaints in the privy council against his lenience regarding precedence, and on his return joined the homecoming party at Hinchingbrooke. On 28 August that year he received a knighthood in tribute to his exertions.

In spring 1669 Godolphin returned to Spain as envoy-extraordinary, subordinate to the earl of Sunderland, and in autumn 1671 became full ambassador with £1200 p.a. and £1500 for his equipage. However, his arrival in Spain was marred by a serious illness, in the course of which he joined the Catholic church and was granted permission by the Inquisition to receive the sacrament publicly. He entered Madrid in state on 18 January 1672, and proved an able intermediary on complicated naval and commercial disputes, but by July 1673 reports had reached London that 'many merchants of Cadiz and Seville … declare … as if he and all his family but the cook were professed Romanists' (*CSP dom., 1673*, 465). His official denial was laid before the king by Arlington and he remained in post, but he continued openly employing Catholics, most notably his secretary Edward Meredith.

Godolphin returned to England briefly in January 1678, but was absent when in September Titus Oates named him as a popish agent who had been spotted at confession and was allegedly the pope's choice for lord privy seal. The Commons voted an address for his recall on 12 November, and the king replied that he had already sent the order. Godolphin wisely chose to stay in Spain, and continued to draw his salary until autumn 1679. Narcissus Luttrell heard that he had been made a grandee. Although as a Catholic he was disabled under the Test Acts from holding office, he retained his auditorship of the exchequer, but the revolution of 1688 led to renewed attempts to remove it. His cousin Sidney Godolphin, Lord Godolphin, petitioned the privy council in December 1689 that Sir William had intended to resign in his favour but had been prevented by the claims of a rival, now deceased. The council examined the grant in June 1690, and a commission was requested to cancel it in 1691. Godolphin died in Madrid, unmarried and childless, on 11 July 1696, where he was buried, having on 30 March consented to a 'notarial act' empowering the procurator-general of the Jesuits and others to make a posthumous will; the size of his fortune doubtless encouraged their efforts. He also left sums to his nephew and niece, children of his brother Francis Godolphin (*d.* 1672) of Coulston, Wiltshire, and Lord Godolphin assisted in arranging an act of parliament in 1698 to invalidate the posthumous will and secure the other bequests. The fortune, valued at £80,000, was in Spain, Rome, Venice, and Amsterdam, and his relatives recovered the money at the latter two places. Godolphin was a shrewd and capable public servant trusted by successive employers; the disposition of his money shows his caution towards the Catholic church: royal favour and powerful friends and relatives mitigated the effects of his conversion. TIMOTHY VENNING

Sources BL, Add. MS 28942; Egerton MS 1509 • *CSP dom.*, *1661–78*; *1687–9* • W. A. Shaw, ed., *Calendar of treasury books*, 2–9, PRO (1905–31), 1667–92 • *Hispania illustrata* (1703) • Pepys, *Diary*, vol. 9 • J. L. Vivian, ed., *The visitations of Cornwall, comprising the herald's visitations of 1530, 1573, and 1620* (1887) • *JHC*, 9 (1667–87) • *Old Westminsters*, vol. 1 • Foster, *Alum. Oxon.* • W. H. Cooke, ed., *Students admitted to the Inner Temple, 1547–1660* [1878] • M. Fitch, ed., *PCC wills, 1694–1700* (1960) • W. A. Shaw, *The knights of England*, 2 (1906) • J. Welch, *The list of the queen's scholars of St Peter's College, Westminster*, ed. [C. B. Phillimore], new edn (1852) • F. R. Harris, *The life of Edward Montagu … first earl of Sandwich*, 2 vols. (1912) • E. Cruickshanks, 'Godolphin, William', HoP, *Commons*, *1660–90*, 2.407–8

Archives NL Scot., corresp. • Wadham College, Oxford, collection of Spanish MSS | BL, letters to Sir Richard Bulstrode, Add. MS 47899; Egerton MSS 3678–3684 • BL, Sloane MSS, corresp. with J. Luke, and papers • BL, papers on legal case relating to his will and fortune, Add. MS 28942, fols. 250–54 • estate office, Warminster, letters to Henry Coventry, librarian and archivist to the marquess of Bath • PRO, state papers domestic, corresp. as assistant secretary of state • PRO, state papers foreign, diplomatic letters from Spain

Likenesses oils, 1656–9, Man. City Gall.

Wealth at death approx. £80,000—in Madrid, Rome, Venice, and Amsterdam: BL, Add. MS 28942, fols. 250–54

Godred (*d.* **1187**). *See under* Godred Crovan (*d.* 1095).

Godred Crovan [Guðrøðr, Gofraid Méránach] (*d.* **1095**), king of Man and the Isles, who may be equated with the King Gorree, or Orry, of Manx tradition, was the founder of a dynasty that ruled there for nearly two centuries. His sobriquet, Crovan, may be Gaelic *crobh-bhán* ('white-handed'), while the Méránach of Irish sources may come from *méar* ('a finger'). Little is known of his origins. The Manx chronicle claims that he was 'filius Haraldi nigri de ysland', which presumably refers to Iceland, but the same source says of the Manx people that he 'had been reared among them for some time'. What little else is known of his background points to Ireland. The patronymic 'mac mic Arailt' found in one Irish annal perhaps means that he was a son or nephew of the Ímar mac Arailt (*d.* 1054) who was king of Dublin (*r.* 1038–46), and whose father (*d.* 999) was a son of Óláf Sihtricson (Amlaíb Cúarán) of Dublin (*d.* 981).

Godred is said to have fought at the battle of Stamford Bridge and to have fled from there to Man where he was honourably received by the reigning king. Some years later, perhaps about 1079, he assembled ships and an army of Islesmen, and made three separate expeditions to Man, on the last of which, having landed at Ramsey harbour, he defeated the Manx in battle, and divided the island in two, giving the southern part to his followers and the northern part to those Manxmen who survived the battle. He is first mentioned in an Irish source in 1091, when he appears as king of Dublin. The Manx chronicle claims that he subdued Dublin and a great part of Leinster, presumably a reference to the hinterland of the Hiberno-Scandinavian town, known as Fine Gall, to which its rulers laid claim. He also retained control of the Isles and is said to have 'so tamed the Scots that no one who built a ship or boat dared use more than three iron bolts' (*Cronica regum Mannie et Insularum*, fol. 33*r*). The medieval biography of the prince of Gwynedd, Gruffudd ap Cynan (*d.* 1137), states that when the latter fled to Ireland, about 1094, and sought advice as to how best to combat the Norman advance into Wales, he was sent to Godred in the Isles, who supplied him with a fleet of sixty ships. When the king of Munster, Muirchertach Ó Briain, sought to re-establish authority over Dublin in 1094, Godred was able to count on the support of many of the kings from the northern half of Ireland, and, with the help of his own fleet of ninety ships, they routed Ó Briain and his allies, though when the latter dispersed, the Munstermen returned and banished Godred from Dublin. The Irish annals, calling him 'king of Dublin and of the Isles', report that Godred was among those who perished in an outbreak of plague in 1095, the Manx chronicle noting that he died in Islay. He left three sons, Lagman, Harald, and Óláf [*see below*]. Lagman mutilated Harald and reigned for a short period before abdicating, and, after a brief period of direct Irish and Norwegian intervention, Óláf eventually succeeded.

Óláf [Óláfr Bitlingr, Óláfr Guðrøðarson] (*d.* 1153), king of Man and the Isles, spent at least part of his youth at the court of Henry I of England, and is said to have ruled for forty years, having 'all the kings of Ireland and Scotland as confederates in such a way that no one dared disturb the kingdom of the Isles during his lifetime' (*Cronica regum Mannie et Insularum*, fol. 35*r*). He founded Rushen Abbey as a daughter house of Furness in Lancashire in 1134, giving the monks of Furness the right of election to the bishopric of the Isles. He married Ingebjorg, daughter of Hákon Paulsson, earl of Orkney, and also Affreca, daughter of Fergus of Galloway, and with the latter, probably, he had his son Godred [*see below*], though it is said that with concubines he had other sons and many daughters, one of whom married Somerled of Argyll. In 1153 the three sons of his brother Harald, who had been brought up in Dublin, invaded Man demanding half the kingdom for themselves, assassinated Óláf on 29 June, and then launched an unsuccessful invasion of Galloway.

Óláf's son **Godred** [Guthfrith, Gofraid, Guðrøðr Óláfsson] (*d.* 1187) then returned, having done homage to the king of Norway, was acclaimed as king of Man and the Isles, and ruled the kingdom until his death. He faced opposition from Somerled, to whom, after defeat in battle in 1156, he was forced to cede part of the kingdom, including the Mull–Islay group of islands, retaining control only over Man and the northern Hebrides. The threat from Somerled may have forced Godred into a closer bond with Henry II since on several occasions from 1156 onwards English records reveal the expenditure of small sums on his maintenance, though Godred also maintained close links with Norway, on the journey to which he passed through England in 1158; he was in Scotland in 1159, and apparently only returned to Man from Norway in 1164 (perhaps because of Somerled's death that same year), when he had to capture and mutilate his half-brother Ragnvald before regaining control. His acceptance of the suzerainty of Norway presumably accounts for the fact that by a papal decree of 1154 the diocese of Sodor and Man was subjected to the metropolitan jurisdiction of the archdiocese of Trondheim. He married Fingola, granddaughter of Muirchertach Mac Lochlainn, king of Ireland, a marriage formalized by the papal legate, Cardinal Vivian, in the winter of 1176–7, and gained control of Dublin for a brief period some time before its seizure by Anglo-Normans in 1170. He assisted the Dubliners and their Irish allies in an unsuccessful attempt to dislodge the Anglo-Normans, though some years later he formed an alliance with the Anglo-Norman conqueror of Ulster, John de Courcy, who married his daughter Affreca [*see* Courcy, Affreca de, *under* Courcy, John de]. Godred granted the monks of Holmcultram in Cumberland right of entry to Man and exemption from tolls and customs, and also gave land near Douglas to the priory of St Bees in Copeland. He died on 10 November 1187 on St Patrick's Isle, Peel, and was buried on Iona in the following summer.

SEÁN DUFFY

Sources G. Broderick, ed. and trans., *Cronica regum Mannie et Insularum / Chronicles of the kings of Man and the Isles* (1979) • *AFM* • W. Stokes, ed., 'The annals of Tigernach [8 pts]', *Revue Celtique*, 16 (1895), 374–419; 17 (1896), 6–33, 119–263, 337–420; 18 (1897), 9–59, 150–97, 267–303, 374–91; pubd sep. (1993) • *Historia Gruffud vab Kenan / Gyda rhagymadrodd a nodiadau gan*, ed. D. S. Evans (1977) • Giraldus Cambrensis, *Expugnatio Hibernica / The conquest of Ireland*, ed. and trans. A. B. Scott and F. X. Martin (1978) • F. Grainger and W. G. Collingwood, *The register and records of Holm Cultram*, Cumberland and Westmorland Antiquarian and Archaeological Society, Record or Chartulary Series, 7 (1929) • [J. Wilson], ed., *The register of the priory of St Bees*, SurtS, 126 (1915) • A. W. Moore, *A history of the Isle of Man*, 2 vols. (1900) • A. O. Anderson, ed. and trans., *Early sources of Scottish history*, AD *500 to 1286*, 2 vols. (1922) • G. Indrebo, ed., *Fagrskinna* (Kristiania, 1917)

Godric of Finchale [St Godric of Finchale] (*c.***1070–1170**), trader and hermit, was born at Walpole in Norfolk to a poor, Anglo-Saxon, farming couple. His father's name was Æilward, his mother's Aedwen (Eadwenna), and he was subsequently joined by a brother, William, and a sister, Burcwen. At an early age, perhaps in 1085 or 1086, he became a pedlar, travelling for four years in northern Lincolnshire. After initial visits to St Andrews in Scotland and to Rome, he ventured into international commerce, trading with Scotland, Denmark, and Flanders. Success brought a half share in one merchant vessel and a quarter of the profits of a second, his skill as a sailor also earning him the position of ship's captain.

Godric's voyages had always been pilgrimages to some extent, however, and among the places visited was Farne Island, off the coast of Northumberland. Here, where St Cuthbert had lived as a solitary, he began to conceive of the idea of becoming a hermit himself, his chief aim being to atone for the misdeeds of his earlier life. But first, having by now spent sixteen years in commerce, he decided to visit Jerusalem. He may thus have been the 'Guderic, a pirate from the kingdom of England' (Albert of Aix, 595–6), who in May 1102 assisted Baldwin I of Jerusalem after his defeat at the battle of Ramlah. On his journey home Godric also visited the great shrine of Santiago de Compostela in northern Spain. His ideas were still somewhat confused and he next took a position as steward, but left his post in horror when he discovered that members of the household were engaged in activities such as cattle rustling. To atone for any guilt he had incurred, he made further pilgrimages, to St Gilles in Provence and to Rome.

A third visit to Rome, this time on foot and in the company of his elderly mother, seems to have clarified Godric's ideas: he sold all his goods and set out in search of a hermitage. He reached Carlisle, perhaps in 1104 or 1105, apparently hoping that so far from home he would be able to live an anonymous life of poverty and prayer. After a while, however, he discovered relatives there, one of whom furnished him with the psalter of St Jerome, apparently an abbreviated version of the psalms and later his favourite book. Fearing the distracting influence of his relatives, he then sought the solitude of the woods, living on wild fruit and nuts until he reached Wolsingham in upper Weardale. Here, perhaps in 1106, he met another solitary, an elderly man named Ælric, with whom he now served a period of apprenticeship. After almost two years the death of Ælric brought this to an end and Godric next undertook a second pilgrimage to Jerusalem. He travelled on foot and lived on dry barley bread and water. On reaching the Jordan he removed his shoes, which he never replaced. He also visited the holy places and worked for a time at the Hospital of St John.

On his return, Godric's search for a hermitage resumed and he visited unfamiliar parts of England, supporting himself by his original trade. He first settled at Eskdale Side, near Whitby, perhaps in 1110 or 1111, but moved on, deterred by the hostility of local lords. He came next to Durham where he became door-keeper and bell-ringer at the church of St Giles, newly founded in June 1112 outside the city. Then St Mary's, within the walls, attracted him because of its school; here he learnt such psalms, hymns, and prayers as he would need in his vocation. While in

Durham he heard of Finchale, a few miles downstream on the Wear, and having won the approval of Ranulf Flambard, bishop of Durham, whose land it was, he finally settled there. This was perhaps late in 1112 or early in 1113 and he may have briefly occupied the spot now known as St Godric's Garth before moving permanently to the nearby site where the ruins of Finchale priory now stand.

Godric's early life as a hermit was almost unbearably severe. At first he lived on roots and leaves, later growing barley, oats, and vegetables, which were consumed, however, only when dry and mouldy. He undertook rigorous fasts and worked hard at clearing the forest (even at night, when there was a moon, in order to keep sleep at bay). He often prayed immersed in cold water, either in the Wear itself or in a barrel set in the floor of his oratory of St Mary. He wore a hair shirt and a coat of mail, and he shunned human company. But within a few years of his arrival his family also travelled north, his sister, Burcwen, even coming to live at Finchale as a solitary. His younger brother William worked in a small boat on the Wear until he was drowned, between 1147 and 1153. A little earlier, between 1133 and 1141, Godric himself was in danger of drowning, when the Wear burst its banks. The concern expressed on this occasion indicates that by now the strict recluse had mellowed into a local 'holy man'. He was also attacked, probably in 1138, by marauders from the army of King David of Scotland, who were searching for treasure; he was lucky to escape with a severe beating.

The most significant change in his career as a hermit occurred when Godric submitted to the authority of the Benedictine monastery of Durham. Perhaps informally under Prior Roger (1138?–1149), and more rigidly after his death, Godric became linked to the convent, being regarded as an 'associate monk'. His way of life now became more monastic: for example, he adopted strict rules of silence, while members of the community instructed him and said mass. As he became increasingly infirm in old age, one or more of the monks came to live at Finchale.

Although tightly bound to the monastery of Durham, Godric was on good terms with other religious, such as the Cistercian abbots Robert of Newminster and Ailred of Rievaulx. Bishops of Durham also patronized him, continuing the tradition established by Flambard. Godric is even alleged to have been consulted by the embattled Archbishop Thomas Becket and he received a personal letter from Pope Alexander III. Kings also took notice of him: William the Lion of Scotland visited him personally and Malcolm IV of Scotland and Henry II of England presented gifts.

As his two careers indicate, Godric was a man of courage and intelligence, possessed of great mental and physical stamina and abundant common sense. Although lacking in formal education, he obviously had some acquaintance with reading, could follow a conversation in Latin and express himself in French. He was also noted for his sympathy for animals, offering shelter to deer and other beasts of the chase and in winter rescuing creatures overcome by the cold. Contemporaries also believed him to possess gifts which were supernatural in origin. He was thought able to foretell the future and was credited with powers of healing. Tormented by all too apparent demons, he was also consoled by saints. More conventionally, in extreme old age he suffered from depression and could be very irritable.

Perhaps surprisingly, Godric possessed a talent for music and he was responsible for the words and melodies of the first Middle English songs to have been preserved. The best known is a two-verse invocation of the Virgin, the second a hymn sung to him by his sister when she appeared to him in the company of angels after her death. The third recalls Godric's earlier career, as it honours St Nicholas, the patron saint of sailors.

Godric was not tall (just over 5 feet in height, as his coffin reveals), but broad-shouldered and very strong. His face was long and above sparkling blue-grey eyes were bushy eyebrows which almost met above his long nose. His thick beard, black in youth, became white in old age. The little finger of one hand came to be permanently bent towards the palm.

During his last years, when he was bedridden, Godric lived in his little stone church of St John the Baptist. Here he died, on 21 May 1170, aged about 100. He was buried in the same church, the site being still marked by a cross in the grass. For some years after his death his tomb enjoyed great popularity as a shrine and over two hundred miracles were recorded. Three contemporaries wrote lives, of which that by Reginald is the fullest and most interesting. Godric continued to be revered at Finchale, Durham, and further afield, even on the continent, the Cistercians in particular being important in spreading knowledge of him. The Roman Catholic church in Durham is dedicated to St Godric. By contrast, he has attained a certain celebrity in modern historical scholarship, since Henri Pirenne utilized him as an example of an early capitalist.

VICTORIA TUDOR

Sources Reginald of Durham, *Libellus de vita et miraculis S. Godrici, heremitae de Finchale*, ed. J. Stevenson, SurtS, 20 (1847) • *Acta sanctorum: Maius*, 5 (Antwerp, 1685), 70–85 • Albert Aquensis [Albert of Aix], 'Historia Hierosolymitana', *Recueil des historiens des croisades: historiens occidentaux*, 4 (Paris, 1879), 595–6 • R. Howlett, ed., *Chronicles of the reigns of Stephen, Henry II, and Richard I*, 1, Rolls Series, 82 (1884), 149–50 • V. M. Tudor, 'Reginald of Durham and St Godric of Finchale: a study of a twelfth-century hagiographer and his major subject', PhD diss., U. Reading, 1979 • H. S. Offler, ed., *Durham episcopal charters, 1071–1152*, SurtS, 179 (1968), 68–72 • C. R. Peers, *Finchale Priory* (1970) • J. Zupitza, 'Cantus beati Godrici', *Englische Studien*, 11 (1888), 401–32 • J. W. Rankin, 'The hymns of St Godric', *Publications of the Modern Language Association of America*, 38 (1923), 699–711 • J. B. Trend, 'The first English songs', *Music and Letters*, 9 (1928), 111–28

Godsal, Philip (1747–1826), coach builder, was born in London on 5 November 1747, the only child of Thomas Godsal (1716–1763) of Tewkesbury and his wife, Susannah (1723–1786), only child of Henry Lake, a London coach builder. Thomas Godsal took over his father-in-law's business but, following his own early death in 1763, Susannah ran the yard in Long Acre until 1770, when Philip took on the family business at the age of twenty-three. In the same year he

Philip Godsal (1747–1826), by Alexander Pope, 1802

married his cousin Ann Webb (1749–1834) of Tewkesbury. Godsal expanded the business, leasing from the Mercers' Company a number of properties adjacent to 103 Long Acre to form one of the largest yards in London's principal area for coach building. The yard had standing for eighty carriages and was enclosed by the workshops of the dozen distinct trades involved in coach manufacture. By 1789 Godsal employed some seventy tradesmen and apprentices and had an annual turnover of £35,000. The yard manufactured up to 200 vehicles annually, including coaches, chariots, phaetons, and curricles, in addition to making harnesses and repairing and servicing carriages. Godsal was a member of the Company of Coachmakers and Loriners, and in 1783 he was elected a member of the Society for the Encouragement of the Arts, Manufactures, and Commerce.

In 1789 Godsal received a well-publicized commission from the new lord chancellor of Ireland, Lord Fitzgibbon, to build a state coach designed by Rudolph Ackermann. Godsal also built a coach for the Spanish ambassador in 1790 and state chariots for three sheriffs of London. He built carriages for many members of the aristocracy, including Lord John Delaval and his two sons-in-law (the earl of Tyrconnel and Lord Audley), for William Beckford's friend Viscount 'Kitty' Courtenay, and for the marquess of Blandford, later fifth duke of Marlborough. Godsal also provided them with a personal banking service, making loans secured by personal bonds. For many years he held the mortgage of Marlborough House in Pall Mall and his estate continued to receive the income from the farms on the Blenheim estate. With his increasing wealth Godsal bought shares in several joint-stock promotions and also invested profitably in both commercial and residential property in London and, later, in Cheltenham. His steady rise up the social scale from tradesman to gentleman was marked by his membership of a number of fashionable associations. He was a governor of the Foundling Hospital, a founder proprietor of the Royal Institution, a leading freemason, and he held a commission in the Loyal Hampstead Volunteers. His son Philip Lake attended Harrow School and Oriel College, Oxford, and was commissioned as lieutenant in George III's personal bodyguard, the honourable band of gentlemen pensioners.

Godsal lived in several grand houses, including 84 Piccadilly; Grove House, Hampstead; and 243 Oxford Street, overlooking Hyde Park. In 1814 he moved to Montpelier Place, Cheltenham, where he entertained the duke of Wellington in 1817. He was a lifelong friend and also the executor of Jonathan Buttall (subject of Gainsborough's *Blue Boy*) and, like him, formed a significant collection of paintings. He was also a discriminating collector of furniture and of watches and clocks. He suffered acute intermittent pain for several years and in 1818, following an examination by the celebrated surgeon Sir Astley Cooper, he had an operation to remove a stone in the bladder. He subsequently enjoyed good health, despite being thrown from his phaeton in 1821. He died on 12 April 1826, leaving an estate valued at £56,030, and was buried in a family vault in Tewkesbury Abbey. He was survived by his wife, Ann, and three children. His son Philip, who married Grace, daughter of William Draper Best, later first Baron Wynford, bought the Iscoyd Park estate in Flintshire, which remains the family home. The elder Philip Godsal kept a memorandum diary for thirty-eight years and these volumes, together with many of his letters and business records, provide an unusually detailed and intimate view of the social elevation of a middle-class gentleman in the late eighteenth and early nineteenth centuries.

John Ford

Sources Flintshire RO, Hawarden, Iscoyd Park MSS · Northumbd RO, Delaval papers · *The Times* (1789–94) [various]
Archives BL, Blenheim papers, Add. MSS 6167–6168 · Flintshire RO, Hawarden, Iscoyd Park MSS · Northumbd RO, Delaval papers
Likenesses A. Pope, miniature, oils, 1802, priv. coll. [*see illus.*]
Wealth at death £56,030: stamp office, registration no. 18, fol. dated 25 May 1827

Godsalve, Edward (*d.* in or after **1568**), Roman Catholic priest, was nominated by Henry VIII on 19 December 1546 as one of the original fellows of Trinity College, Cambridge, and he was senior bursar from 1554 to 1556. Ordained subdeacon in London in 1553, on 28 April 1554 he was admitted to the rectory of Fulbourn St Vigors, Cambridgeshire, and in the same year he proceeded BTh. He signed the Roman Catholic articles on 26 July 1555, and during the visitation of the university by Cardinal Pole's delegates in February 1557 he, Thomas Sedgwick, Thomas Parker, and Richard Rudde were deputed to peruse books, and to determine which were heretical. He was a great friend of John Christopherson, Marian bishop of Chichester, and on 26 October 1558 was appointed prebendary of Ferring in that cathedral. He refused to comply with the changes in religion made after the accession of Elizabeth. In February 1560 William Barlow, who had succeeded Christopherson as bishop of Chichester, wrote to one of the queen's ministers, probably Cecil, announcing his intention to deprive Godsalve, whom he called 'Papist Prebendary of Chichester', of his prebend (*CSP dom.*, 1547–80, 150). Soon after this Godsalve was deprived of all his preferments and obliged to retire to Antwerp. There he was elected professor of divinity in the monastery of St Michel. He was living in 1568, but when he died is unknown. He was the editor of Christopherson's Latin translation of Eusebius, published as *Historiae ecclesiasticae pars prima in qua continetur Eusebii, Pamphili … lib. 10* (Louvain, 1569). Godsalve also translated the third part of the *Ecclesiastical History* as *Historiae ecclesiasticae scriptores Graeci* (Cologne, 1570). The latter is prefaced with a dedication by Godsalve, and two of his letters.

THOMPSON COOPER, *rev.* KENNETH CARLETON

Sources *Fasti Angl., 1541–1857*, [Chichester] • Cooper, *Ath. Cantab.*, 1.275–6 • J. Venn and J. A. Venn, eds., *The book of matriculations and degrees … in the University of Cambridge from 1544 to 1659* (1913) • W. W. Rouse Ball and J. A. Venn, eds., *Admissions to Trinity College, Cambridge*, 2 (1913) • *LP Henry VIII*, 21/2, no. 648(43, 51) • *CSP dom.*, 1547–80, 150 • Gillow, *Lit. biog. hist.*, vol. 2 • J. Pits, *Relationum historicarum de rebus Anglicis*, ed. [W. Bishop] (Paris, 1619); repr. (1969) • Venn, *Alum. Cant.*, 1/2.228 • Tanner, *Bibl. Brit.-Hib.*

Sir John Godsalve (*b.* **in or before 1505**, *d.* **1556**), by Hans Holbein the younger, *c.*1532

Godsalve, Sir John (*b.* in or before **1505**, *d.* **1556**), administrator and landowner, was the first son and heir of Thomas Godsalve (*d.* 1542), registrar of the Norwich consistory court, and his first wife, Joan. Nothing is known of John Godsalve's early schooling. He was admitted to Gray's Inn in 1525 and by 1530 had married Agnes Widmerpole, with whom he had two sons, William (*b.* in or before 1530), the elder, who survived him without issue, and Thomas (*d.* 1587), who left a son and heir, Roger. Although Godsalve described himself as a mercer, there is no evidence that he was ever a member of the Mercers' Company of London. His appointment as one of the four clerks of the signet by January 1531 may be explained by his father's court connections—Holbein painted Godsalve with his father in 1528—or by his later claim of kinship with a fellow clerk, Thomas Wriothesley. Clerks of the signet prepared the king's own letters and warrants for dispatch, affixing to them the monarch's personal seal, or signet. This work occasionally required that Godsalve seek delivery of gold and silver laces from the king's jewel-house to attach hanging seals to various documents; when in November 1532 he acquired the office of common meter of cloth of gold and silver in the City, he was able officially to purchase such materials direct from the German merchants of the Steelyard in London, which helps explain the genesis of Holbein's drawing of Godsalve of about 1532, for Holbein was then living and working at the Steelyard. The officer in charge of the clerks, Stephen Gardiner, the king's secretary, had already recommended Godsalve in June 1531 to Thomas Cromwell, master of the king's jewels, and in Cromwell Godsalve found his most powerful patron at court. With Cromwell's protégé Ralph Sadler, Godsalve became protonotary in chancery in July 1537, and in 1539 entered parliament when Cromwell secured his election as MP for Norwich. He probably gained re-election in 1542. At Norwich he was constable of the castle and keeper of the gaol (1539) and was admitted to the freedom of the city in December 1544. In the same year he participated in Henry VIII's invasion of France: a miniature possibly executed then shows him armed before Boulogne. In the county of Norfolk he collected the parliamentary subsidy of 1540 and served as a commissioner for chantries there and in Suffolk in 1546. By 1547–8 Godsalve owned forty-nine houses in Norwich and enjoyed a landed income of £195 a year. He was knighted at Edward VI's coronation (22 February 1547) and appointed JP for Norfolk in the same year, clear evidence of his favourable standing with Protector Somerset, with whom he was in frequent contact as signet clerk. He acted as an informal archivist to the secretariat, procuring mainly diplomatic documents from the treasury of receipt when requested to by the privy council. In 1552 he solicited the help of Sir William Cecil, the king's secretary (and Somerset's former secretary), to gain joint appointment with Sir John Cheke as a chamberlain of the exchequer. The petition failed and Cheke alone was appointed. As comptroller of the Tower mint (24 June 1548–25 March 1552) he supervised the last stages of the great debasement. Although he relinquished the comptrollership in 1552 for a pension of £60, he helped devise new coins in 1554 bearing the 'double face' of Philip and Mary. Godsalve's second marriage (by 1553) to Elizabeth, the daughter of Henry White, an eminent lawyer and former under-sheriff of London, brought him, through her kinsmen, into a circle of some of Queen Mary I's most trusted councillors, two of whom, Sir Edward Waldgrave and Sir Francis Englefield, Godsalve appointed feoffees of his London property in March 1556. He was then living in Old Fish Street, London, in a house he had purchased in 1555. In a will dated 6 November 1556 he named his wife and younger son executors. He died at Norwich on 20 November 1556, asking that 'my bodie … be buryed in our Ladye Chapell within the churche of Saincte Stephyn in Norwiche next vnto my fathers tombe'.

DALE HOAK

Sources HoP, *Commons, 1509–58*, 2.221–2 • P. Ganz, 'A new portrait of Sir John Godsalve by Hans Holbein the younger', *Burlington Magazine*, 26 (1914), 47–8 • *CPR*, *1547–8*, 87, 309; *1548–9*, 144; *1550–53*, 298, 301; *1553–4*, 22, 163–4; *1555–7*, 129 • will, PRO, PROB 11/40, fol. 103*r* • C. E. Challis, *The Tudor coinage* (1978), 109, 317 • *APC*, *1547–50*, 59, 60, 65, 80, 517; *1554–6*, 145

Likenesses H. Holbein the younger, double portrait, oil on oak panel, 1528 (with his father, Thomas Godsalve), Gemäldegalerie Alte Meister, Dresden; repro. in J. Rowlands, *The paintings of Hans Holbein the younger* (1985), pl. 61, ct. no. 31, p. 135 • H. Holbein the younger, chalk, ink, watercolour and body-colour drawing, *c*.1532, Royal Collection [*see illus.*] • H. Holbein, oil on oak panel, *c*.1532–1534 (after *Portrait of John Godsalve* by Holbein), Museum of Fine Art, Philadelphia, John G. Johnson collection; repro. in J. Rowlands, *The paintings of Hans Holbein the younger* (1985), pl. 229, cat. no. R. 19, pp. 231–2 • miniature, 1544? (John Godsalve?), Bodl. Oxf.

Wealth at death wealthy; property, incl. forty-nine houses in Norwich, brought landed income of £195 p.a. in 1547: HoP, *Commons, 1509–58*, 2.221; will, PRO, PROB 11/40, fol. 103*r*

Godson, Robert (*fl.* **1696–1697**), writer on astrology, is known only by his one surviving work, which gives no details of his date or place of birth, family, or career. *Astrologia reformata: a Reformation of the Prognostical Part of Astronomy* (1696–7), dedicated to the Royal Philosophical Society of London, claims to provide 'An Experimental Detection, and clear Demonstration' of astrology (Godson, title-page). As such, it was part of a movement at that time to reform the subject, which Godson and many others perceived as now 'utterly depraved and corrupted' (ibid., 8). Astrology was indeed profoundly out of fashion, and Godson deplored the way students were taught 'a parcel of silly miscalled Arts and foreign tongues' instead of subjects of solid value such as divinity, medicine, and astronomy, which in his version included its application to human affairs (ibid., 4–5).

That unfashionability had deeper roots. From the mid-seventeenth century onwards, British astrology had become inextricably embroiled in partisan politics and religious sectarianism. Such politicization had seriously undermined its claims to provide objective truths, and the 'Experimentary Proof' (Godson, 40) which Godson claimed to provide was intended to remedy this ignominy. As such, his book was part of a general movement among the more educated astrologers of the time, which also resulted in John Goad's *Astro-meteorologica* (1686), John Partridge's *Opus reformatum* (1693) and *Defectio geniturarum* (1697), and William Hunt's *Demonstration of Astrology* (1696). In addition to this demanding task, however, Godson also noted that good astrology requires 'a particularly adapted Temper and Capacity' including a 'propension to it purely for its own sake, and a spirit unbyassed by lucre and partiality' (ibid., 3).

Unfortunately, Godson's attempt to prove the validity of astrology involved an unconvincing combination of standard astronomy and traditional astrology, as if the latter somehow followed from the former. The first essay is on the subject of rectification (how to discover or correct a subject's birth-time through the astrology of life-events)—an arcane pursuit even among astrologers—and he criticized Kepler's suggested new planetary aspects as unduly innovative. The book culminated in 'a Prediction of the Death, of the Present French King'—just the sort of enterprise which had brought astrology into élite disfavour. It is hardly surprising that Godson's scientific and literary contemporaries, so far as is known, failed to find in this exposition anything new or promising.

PATRICK CURRY

Sources R. Godson, *Astrologia reformata* (1696–7) • P. Curry, *Prophecy and power: astrology in early modern England* (1989) • B. S. Capp, *Astrology and the popular press: English almanacs, 1500–1800* (1979) • *ESTC*

Godwin. *See* Godwine, earl of Wessex (*d.* 1053).

Godwin, (Richard) Anthony James Wylie [Tony] (**1920–1976**), bookseller and publisher, was born on 3 February 1920 at Stanley House, Bosbury, Hereford, the only son and youngest child of Captain Richard Godwin and his wife, Jean Wylie. Sent to boarding-school at a very young age, he joined the army without any formal educational qualifications. He served in north Africa with the tank regiment in the Second World War. While recuperating after being wounded in battle, Godwin met his first wife, Eileen, with whom he had two daughters. After being demobbed in 1946 he decided to enter the book trade. Knowing nothing about bookselling, he borrowed £5000 from friends to buy a bookshop. Better Books, on Charing Cross Road, London, became the salon for London's literati and an informal literary college—a reflection of Godwin's desire to overcome a lack of qualifications and his interest in educating the 'working class'.

The avant-garde Better Books became the most influential bookshop in London in the post-war period, partly owing to Godwin's radical methods of bookselling (the name of the shop derives from his mantra, 'Better bookselling to the public'). He stocked only the books he wanted on his shelves; he displayed his books in unusual ways to attract customers; he even designed the shop's décor, packaging, and advertisements himself. Godwin 'epitomized a classless breed of booksellers who were commercial as they were literary' (Norrie, 'The bookseller', 38–9). His first marriage was terminated by divorce, and on 20 April 1961 he married Fay Suzette Godwin, *née* Simmonds (*b.* 1930/31), the noted British photographer. They had two sons.

Tony Godwin's energy and traits of shrewdness, creativity, dynamism, and innovativeness were maintained when, almost uniquely, he moved successfully from bookselling into publishing. This was at the behest of Sir Allen Lane, who in 1960 asked Godwin to work with him in revitalizing Penguin Books. Lane had been managing Penguin for twenty-five years, and recognized the need for a change of style: Penguin's dominance in the paperback market was being challenged by Pan Books, and needed someone 'to bring back the editorial zest and daring of the 1930s' (Caldecott, Clark, and Pevsner). As chief editor, Godwin inspired an atmosphere of excitement and creativity. It was he who introduced photographic covers (sometimes lurid)—leading even to a complaint by Saul Bellow. He exploited television and film tie-ins to such an extent that the positioning of such titles today owes much to him. With his extravagant yet discriminating buying, his encouragement for aggressive and bold advertising, his hunger for publicity for his titles, and his push for sales from non-traditional outlets such as supermarkets, airport lounges, petrol stations, and pubs, Godwin trebled the size of Penguin's list, doubled the company's sales figures, and nearly trebled profits, in seven years. None the less, there existed a tension between Godwin and Lane, with Lane expressing his disapproval of selling books through supermarkets by saying publicly, 'A book is not a tin of beans' (Batt).

Godwin was interested in the craft and creation of books. He made people think about how a book should and could look, and what it should become. He spent hours looking at the titles he had published, analysing them for weaknesses or faults. His authors and a large coterie of staff were devoted to him, considering it a privilege to work with him: he had unfailing support for all his authors, helping them hone and polish their work in the face of the demands of publishing: Lady Antonia Fraser commented after his death, 'As an editor, his unique strength was that he was always on the side of the author, not the publisher. He helped you perfect the book you had written, not the book they had commissioned' (McFaddon).

While Godwin modernized Penguin Books, his lack of tolerance for mediocrity and élitism, his mercurial nature, his genius, and his style of work upset the conservative elements of the company. A combination of events—including serious ill health, the launch party of Len Deighton's *Funeral in Berlin*, the publication of the anti-clerical sketches *Massacre* by the French cartoonist Siné (Maurice Sinet), and the subsequent legendary midnight disappearance of all the stock, and the emergence of a darker side of Godwin's personality—created such friction with Sir Allen that, on 31 May 1967, Godwin resigned.

Godwin's departure from Penguin was reported widely in the media. For months London publishers vied to attract him to their houses, but in July 1967 Godwin chose to become joint managing director of Weidenfeld and Nicolson, where he remained for seven years (*The Times*). In 1973 he stunned family and friends when he suddenly migrated to New York to enter a co-publishing deal with William Jovanovich (of Harcourt Brace Jovanovich). Within three years he had produced nearly forty titles under his own imprint, each reflecting his own character and interests: social commentary and adventure stories, political titles and tales of spies, histories, and biographies.

On 15 March 1976, aged fifty-six, Godwin died unexpectedly at 864 Lexington Avenue, New York, from heart failure, the smog and living conditions finally proving too much for his debilitating asthma. His death made headlines in the newspapers on both sides of the Atlantic. George Weidenfeld, Edna O'Brien, Al Alvarez, Antonia Fraser, and Mordecai Richler all spoke of their considerable respect and affection for him, and lauded his achievements. Life (and publishing), they said, would no longer be the same. His presence and laughter were sorely missed in the sycophantic and often stuffy atmosphere of publishing. The epitaph on Godwin's grave at the church of St Peter and St Paul, Saltwood, Hythe, Kent, reads simply, 'Great Publisher'. IAIN D. BROWN

Sources R. D. McFaddon, 'Tony Godwin, 56, editor, is dead', *New York Times* (16 March 1976), 69 · *The Times* (17 March 1976), 16 · O. Caldecott, C. Clark, and D. Pevsner, *The Bookseller* (27 March 1976), 1770–71 · D. Farrer, *The Bookseller* (27 March 1976), 1771 · I. Norrie, *The Bookseller* (27 March 1976), 1770 · T. Coleman, 'Crown prince of Penguins', *The Guardian* (12 March 1963), 7 · M. Richler, 'Audience diminished', *New York Times* (30 May 1976), 19 · I. Norrie, 'The bookseller and the community: a British experience', *Logos*, 1/2 (1990), 38–43 · S. Hare, ed., *Penguin portrait: Allen Lane and the Penguin editors, 1935–1970* (1995) · R. Jones, 'Board clash on Penguin image', *The Times* (5 May 1967), 23 · F. A. Mumby and I. Norrie, *Publishing and bookselling* (1974) · J. E. Morpurgo, *Allen Lane, King Penguin: a biography* (1979), 334 · A. Batt, 'A book is not a tin of beans …', *Daily Express* (8 May 1967) · F. Godwin, *Landscapes: a survey* (2001) · b. cert. · m. cert. · *CGPLA Eng. & Wales* (1976)
Archives U. Reading, Penguin Books archive
Wealth at death £39,377: probate, 17 June 1976, *CGPLA Eng. & Wales*

Godwin, Dame Beatrice Annie [Anne] (**1897–1992**), trade unionist, was born on 6 July 1897 in Frith Hill, Farncombe, Surrey, into the large family of William Godwin (*d.* 1932), leather dresser and draper, and his wife, Louisa Clare, *née* Pearce. She attended the British School in Godalming, Surrey, but, with no money for her further education, left school aged fifteen.

At sixteen Godwin became a clerk in the counting-house of a West End store in London, earning 5*s.* a week. In 1916 she moved to the army pay office, where she remained for three years as a poorly paid civilian clerk. She was among a deputation of young women who asked the army paymaster for more money, but with no union backing they were shouted down. Godwin realized that office workers must become organized. Her sister Elsie, a civil servant, introduced her to the Association of Women Clerks and Secretaries, a small, elitist union of highly qualified, mainly civil service, employees. Godwin joined in 1921, having trained as a shorthand typist. In the mid-1920s she helped to establish and became a prominent member of the Young Suffragettes, who were campaigning to have the vote extended to young women under the age of thirty (an aim achieved in 1928).

After employment in the offices of engineering and printing firms, Godwin joined the staff of the Association of Women Clerks and Secretaries in 1925, becoming a full-time London organizer in 1928 and assistant secretary in

1931. She also became active on the National Joint Committee of Working Women's Organisations. In 1940 the Association of Women Clerks and Secretaries merged with the National Union of Clerks to become the Clerical and Administrative Workers' Union (CAWU). Godwin became assistant general secretary and confirmed delegate to the TUC annual conference for five years. One of her official duties was to edit the union's journal, *The Clerk*. In 1949 she was unexpectedly elected to one of the TUC's reserved seats for women, which she retained until 1962, fully representing clerks in an unrivalled style.

One of Godwin's goals was equal pay for work of equal value, coupled with equal opportunity and responsibility. She and Anne Loughlin pushed for the principle from 1944, and at the International Labour Organization conference in 1951, Convention 100, which accepted equal pay, was carried by two-thirds of the conference delegates (though it was not ratified in Great Britain until 1971). In the 1950s the CAWU was the most adamant and successful union in the campaign for equal pay. Godwin was appointed OBE in 1952 for her efforts. Within the TUC she chaired the national women's advisory committee for some years, and was president of the National Federation of Professional Workers. She considered running for parliament but decided that trade union work was more rewarding.

In 1956 Godwin was elected general secretary of the CAWU, the first woman to rise to the top of a mixed-sex union. She aimed to attract more white-collar workers into the union, and she led her union through a period of expansion and consolidation, impressing other union leaders with her flair and authority. A moderate socialist, she worked relentlessly against communist control of unions and supported the expulsion of communist-dominated unions from the TUC.

One of Godwin's great concerns was the promotion of better educational opportunities for the working class. She worked for the Mary Macarthur educational trust, which enabled working women to obtain further education, and served on the national trade union committee of the Workers' Educational Association, the Carr Saunders committee on education for commerce, and the Central Advisory Council for Education (England). She was co-author of the Crowther report in 1959, produced by the Central Advisory Council for Education, and was a member of the court of the University of Southampton. She believed that a good general education was of paramount importance, and that there should be special full-time pre-employment courses or part-time employment with compulsory day release, not vocational training at school. She attended weekend and summer schools and continued to campaign for more training and further education at TUC annual congresses. She believed that standards of office competence were falling because employers did not encourage further training.

Despite her dislike of strikes, Godwin achieved her biggest success and most publicity by winning a battle with the Automobile Association in 1960 over recognition of the CAWU, after eight members of staff were sacked for walking out in protest over working conditions. The duke of Edinburgh resigned as patron during the five-and-a-half-week strike. In less sensational negotiations Godwin was noted for her leadership skills and word power. Often she was the only woman in joint union teams negotiating with companies in fields as diverse as air transport, coalmining, and electricity supply. She enjoyed a good working relationship with male union officials.

In August 1961 Godwin was elected president of the TUC, the third woman to hold the post. She was acutely aware of the need to bring the TUC up to date, as advancing technology meant fewer manual workers. During a hectic year she managed to tour all the union areas in the UK. She used her president's speech to the TUC conference in 1962 to attack the government's National Incomes Commission, and to voice her disappointment that the state school system was improving so slowly. She was created DBE in 1962 in recognition of her contribution to the CAWU and for her public work, especially in education.

After her year as president, Godwin retired from union activity. She became a governor of the BBC (1962–8) and was appointed a full-time member of the industrial court (1963–9). She joined the editorial board of the moderate *Socialist Commentary* and, disillusioned by the militants in the Labour Party, became a founder member of the Social Democratic Party in 1981. She enjoyed cooking and entertaining in the house she shared with her sister Elsie, and was a keen gardener until overtaken by infirmity. She died at the Kingston Hospital, Kingston upon Thames, on 11 January 1992, of bronchopneumonia.

A tall, well dressed woman, Godwin looked like the prim headmistress of a girls' school while president of the TUC, but she loved dancing and drinking (in moderation) with the boys. She had one of the sharpest and best-read minds in the TUC, and was noted for her pragmatism and common sense. In negotiation, as she told a *Daily Mail* reporter in September 1961, 'I'm very, very tough. I can make my voice heard well across any conference room' (*Daily Mail*, 15 Sept 1961). It was these qualities, coupled with driving ambition, that took Godwin to the top in her chosen career. JANET E. GRENIER

Sources I. Pink, 'Dame Anne Godwin: trade union leader', *Working Class Movement Library Bulletin*, 7 (1997), 32–43 • *The Times* (13 Jan 1992) • *The Independent* (13 Jan 1992) • *Daily Telegraph* (13 Jan 1992) • *The Guardian* (20 Jan 1992) • *Apex Access* (spring 1992), 16 • TUC, press release, Portsmouth, 8 Sept 1961, U. Warwick Mod. RC, TUC papers • 'Anne Godwin takes over', *Labour: the TUC Magazine* (Oct 1961), 211 • M. Stewart, 'Caustic, didactic, but essentially human', *Time and Tide* (8 Feb 1962), 8 • 'In the footsteps of Ted Hill', *Sunday Times* (27 Aug 1961) • 'The spinster who succeeds tough Ted', *Daily Herald* (8 Sept 1961) • 'How to be boss', *Daily Mail* (15 Sept 1961) • A. Godwin, 'Education for commerce', *Labour Women*, 27/13 (Jan 1950), 14, 15 • 'She didn't know it was her silver jubilee', *Daily Herald* (13 May 1955) • *TUC report* (1961), 452 • *TUC report* (1962), 75–81 • A. Marsh and V. Ryan, *A history of Apex, 1890–1989* (1997) • A. Marsh and V. Ryan, *Historical directory of trade unions*, 1 (1980) • S. Lewenhak, *Women and trade unions* (1997) • N. C. Solden, *Women in British trade unions, 1874–1976* (1978) • *Debrett's people of Surrey* (1991) • *WWW, 1991–5* • b. cert. • d. cert.

Archives Women's Library, London, archives | London Metropolitan University, Trades Union Congress library collections

Likenesses oils, 1964, General and Municipal Boilermakers National College • photograph, repro. in *Sunday Times* (27 Aug

1961) • photograph, repro. in *Apex Access*, 16 • photograph, repro. in *Daily Herald* (10 May 1955?) • photograph, repro. in *Daily Herald* (9 Aug 1961) • photograph, repro. in *The Times* • photograph, repro. in *The Independent* • photographs, repro. in Pink, 'Dame Anne Godwin', 33, 37

Wealth at death £225,661: probate, 24 March 1992, *CGPLA Eng. & Wales*

Godwin, Catherine Grace (1798–1845), poet and writer, younger daughter of Thomas *Garnett MD (1766–1802), and Catherine Grace Cleveland (*d.* 1798), was born in Glasgow on 25 December 1798. Her mother died in childbirth; her father's death followed less than four years later, in May 1802. A close friend of the mother, Mary Warboys, took on the responsibility of the two girls' upbringing in Barbon, near Kirkby Lonsdale, Westmorland. It was to remain Warboys's home for Catherine's youth, and continued so throughout her marriage in 1824 to Thomas Godwin (*c.*1782–1852), a surgeon who had worked for the East India Company, and even after Catherine's death.

In 1824, before her marriage, Catherine published her first volume of verse, *The Night before the Bridal: a Spanish Tale, Sappho, a Dramatic Sketch, and other Poems*. This publication, in spite of its immaturity, drew the attention of several eminent literary figures, including Joanna Baillie, Southey, and Wordsworth. Godwin asked Wordsworth for permission to dedicate her next volume to him. With his approval, this dedication appeared in *The Wanderer's Legacy* (1829). This volume prompted a detailed response from Wordsworth, in a letter first published in the memoir prefaced to her *Poetical Works* (1854). While he is kind—'there is a great command of language also, and occasionally fine versification'—he is much less flattering about Godwin's control of blank verse: 'it is not sufficiently broken' (Wigan, v). Her choice of Spenserian stanza for narrative also draws criticism. That she took to heart this criticism is reflected in more polished versions in the *Poetical Works*. Much of Godwin's verse is prompted by literary sources—footnotes often acknowledge as much: 'Destiny', one of her poems commended by Wordsworth, was 'founded on a very remarkable anecdote narrated in Mr Grant's *Memoirs of an American Lady*.' This poem also reflects a debt in its Byronic figure,

> resolved to quit
> For savage life the social haunts of man.
> (Wigan, 338)

Exotic settings abound, but Godwin lacks Byron's lyrical facility or sense of humour. More domestic settings suggest her own love of Lake District scenery, but there is seldom a truly personal note. 'To Felicia Hemans' acknowledges Godwin's admiration for this poet, and a further influence. Godwin's main poetic output after *The Wanderer's Legacy* was confined to periodicals and annuals. She produced one further volume of verse in 1835, *The Reproving Angel: a Vision*.

Godwin's sister died in 1832 in a tragic accident, when she was burnt to death while staying near Florence after her recent marriage. This distressing episode may have contributed to the change of direction in Godwin's writing. The bulk of her work after this date was prose, chiefly moral tales for children. The titles of these works offer immediate indications of their didactic nature: *Basil Harlow, or, Prodigality is not Generosity* (1836); *Cousin Kate, or, The Punishment of Pride: a Tale* (1836); *Alicia Grey, or, To be Useful is to be Happy* (1837). Several others appeared in the same vein. Godwin's first prose publication—*Reine Canziani: a Tale of Modern Greece*—had appeared much earlier, in 1825. This was a romance written some years before, based largely on details gleaned from an English traveller. In the summer of 1844 Godwin undertook a tour of Switzerland and Germany for the restoration of her failing health. This did not lead to improvement, and she was confined to bed for the last six months of her life, dying of a heart condition on 5 May 1845. She was buried in her chosen spot in Firbank cemetery near her Barbon home, to be joined by Mary Warboys and Thomas Godwin in 1852. Without her acquaintance with Wordsworth, it is doubtful whether Godwin would have achieved much status as a writer; her work has not survived its period. She was a retiring person, who worked energetically at her writing and painting; her self-portrait, prefixed to the *Poetical Works*, gives evidence of some talent. One who had known Godwin from his earliest childhood (there is a poem addressed to him aged five), considered the portrait a striking likeness. He also approved her quick sense of the ludicrous—not much in evidence in her writing. ROSEMARY SCOTT

Sources A. C. Wigan, 'Memoir of the author', in *The poetical works of Catherine Grace Godwin* (1854) • *DNB* • letter from Thomas Godwin to Miss Cleveland, 6 May 1845, BL, Add. MS 41665, fol. 258 • R. Inglis, *The dramatic writers of Scotland* (1868)

Archives NL Scot., letters to William Blackwood

Likenesses C. G. Godwin, self-portrait, engraving (after miniature), repro. in *The poetical works of Catherine Grace Godwin*, frontispiece

Godwin, Edward William (1833–1886), architect and designer, was born at 12 Old Market Street, Bristol, on 26 May 1833, the son of William Godwin (*c.*1794–1846) and Ann Jones Davies (1795–1869). His father was a currier and a partner in Godwin, Smith & Co., a building and decorating business. Godwin was educated at Exley's School in Highbury, Bristol, and then articled (*c.*1848–*c.*1853) to the Bristol architect William Armstrong. His first commission was for a Gothic revival school in Easton (1853); in 1854 he established his own practice at 1 Surrey Street, Bristol. In 1856 Godwin went to Ireland, and during his two-year stay he designed a number of small cottages and three small Gothic revival churches in co. Donegal. In 1858 he returned to Bristol, where he designed two warehouses, Merchant Street (1858; des.) and 104 Stokes Croft for Perry & Sons (1858–9), and a pair of semi-detached villas, 10–11 Rockleaze, Sneyd Park, Bristol (1860–61), with J. A. Clark. In the 1850s and 1860s he also worked on the restoration, additions, and redecoration of a number of churches, including Highbury Chapel, Bristol (1862–3), and St Grada's Church, Grade, Cornwall (1860–61). He married Sarah Yonge (*c.*1832–1865), the daughter of a vicar, on 1 November 1859. In 1861 he won the competition for the new town hall, Northampton, with an Italian Gothic design influenced by John Ruskin. He was awarded premiums in competitions for East Retford (1865), Bristol (1866–7), Plymouth (with Hine and Norman, 1870), Leicester (1871), Sunderland (1874), Congleton (1864), and the Nottingham church cemetery, Mansfield Road (1877). Only the premiums for Congleton town hall, Cheshire (1864), Plymouth town hall (1870–74), and the Nottingham cemetery chapel (1877; des.) led to commissions. In 1861 Godwin moved with his wife to 21 Portland Square, Bristol, and is reputed to have been the first in England to decorate his home according to Japanese principles of design. In 1864 Godwin formed a partnership with Bristol architect Henry Crisp (1825–1896), which lasted until 1871.

After the death of his wife, Godwin left Bristol in October 1865 to establish a London office. Capitalizing on the success of Northampton town hall, he accepted a number of other commissions in Northampton, including the design of St Martin's Villas, 43–44 Billing Road (1865), Rheinfeldon House, Billing Road (1867–8; des.), and a gatehouse, two lodges, and gates to the chase for Castle Ashby House (1867–8). Two of his most important domestic commissions date from the second half of the 1860s: Dromore Castle (1866–73; in ruins), for the third earl of Limerick, and Glenbeigh Towers, co. Kerry (1868–70; des.), for the Hon. Roland Winn. Both of these Gothic revival houses were plagued by damp in the walls. Godwin's recently discovered original design for Glenbeigh Towers (a perspective by Axel Haig, exhibited at the Royal Academy) emphasizes the massive, geometrical, almost abstract qualities of the design. The castle was largely burned out by republicans in 1921, but ruins survive.

For Dromore, Godwin designed the furniture and decoration in a combined medieval and Japanese style. At about the same time he also started designing furniture and other decorations for his own interiors in a minimalist style documented in a series of articles for *The Architect* entitled 'My House "In" London' (July–August 1876). In October 1868 Godwin ran off with the actress Ellen *Terry (Mrs G. F. Watts) (1847–1928). They lived together for seven years in Hertfordshire and later in London. Godwin designed a house, Fallows Green (1871; des.), in Harpenden, Hertfordshire, for himself, Terry, and their two children, Edith *Craig (1869–1947) and (Edward Henry) Gordon *Craig (1872–1966), the stage designer. Godwin and Terry separated in 1875 and on 4 January 1876 he married the painter and designer Beatrice Birnie Philip (1857–1896) [*see* Whistler, Beatrice]. They had one son, Edward Godwin (1876–1957).

Godwin's work in the seventies was marked by the romantic retreat Beauvale House, Moorgreen, Nottinghamshire (1872), which with its associated cottages, parson's house, and lodge for Earl Cowper, was described by Pevsner as

> show[ing] a move towards the Domestic Revival, and for that reason is of national importance … the composition of roof shapes building up to a high tower appearing above the trees, together with the brick, tile-hanging, and half-timbering, gives it its romance. (Pevsner, 35, 67)

He also executed a series of interior design commissions in the Anglo-Japanese style for Collinson and Lock and others. Although Norman Shaw is usually credited with the houses in Bedford Park, Godwin designed the first two types of vernacular-style houses for this garden suburb (1876–8). Godwin's most famous commissions were a series of proto-modern house–studios in Chelsea, including: the White House at 35 Tite Street for James McNeill Whistler (1877–9; des.); 44 Tite Street for Frank Miles (1878); 29 Tite Street (1878; des.) and 60 Tite Street (1879–80; des.) for Archibald Stuart Wortley; 4–6 Chelsea Embankment for Gillows & Co. (1877–8); and a small studio at Kensington Palace for Princess Louise (1878; des.). The only executed architectural commissions of the 1880s were: Tower House, 46 Tite Street, a block of four studio flats (1881–3); Elmleigh, Dallington Park, Northampton (1882–3); and the design of a new façade for the Fine Art Society, 148 New Bond Street, London (1881–2). In addition to a number of interior design commissions for such prominent figures of London society as Countess Lonsdale at Lennox Gardens (1882), Godwin remodelled and decorated the house of Oscar and Constance Wilde at 16 Tite Street (1884).

Godwin was an innovative designer of furniture, wallpaper, textiles, carpets, metalwork, stained glass, and ceramics. Although he is best-known for his Anglo-Japanese furniture and decorations, he worked in the Gothic revival style, the Anglo-Greek, the Anglo-Egyptian, and the Jacobean or Old English. He designed furniture and other decorations for the Art Furniture Company, William Watt, Collinson and Lock, Cox & Sons, W. A. and S. Smee, Waugh & Sons, Gillows & Co., and James Peddle. His designs were best publicized through the publication of William Watt's *Art Furniture, from Designs by E. W. Godwin* in 1877. He also designed wallpapers for Jeffrey & Co., Lightbown Aspinall & Co., James Toleman & Sons, and the Papyrotile Company; textiles for Warner and Ramm and Cowlishaw, Nicol & Co.; carpets and floor cloths for Waugh & Sons; tiles for Minton and Hollins and Burmantoft's furnace works; and ceramics for Brownfield & Sons. Furthermore, after founding the Costume Society in 1884, he was a consultant and designer of women's dress for Libertys of London.

Theatrical design occupied a great deal of Godwin's energies in the 1870s and 1880s. He designed costumes and scenery for productions of *The Merchant of Venice* for Squire and Marie Bancroft (1875), *Henry V* for John Coleman (1876), *Othello* for Mrs Bateman (1880), *Claudian* (1883) and *Hamlet* (1884) for Wilson Barrett, and *Helena in Troas* for John Todhunter (1886), staged in Hengler's Circus, which Godwin remodelled as a classical Greek theatre. He was the production manager and designer for Lady Archibald Campbell's Pastoral Players' open-air productions at Coombe Wood and Cannizaro Wood, both in Surrey (1884–6).

Godwin was a frequent contributor of articles and illustrations for the leading architectural journals of his day (*British Architect*, *Building News*, and *The Architect*). He also contributed to a variety of archaeological journals, among them the *Archaeological Journal*. He was a theatre critic who contributed a series called 'Jottings' to the *Western Daily Press* and the *British Architect* under the pseudonym G. In 1874–5 he wrote a series of thirty articles on 'The architecture and costume of Shakespeare's plays' for *The Architect*. He died on 6 October 1886 in his rooms, 6 Great College Street, Westminster, from complications following an operation to remove kidney stones. He was buried at Northleigh, near Witney, in Oxfordshire.

SUSAN WEBER SOROS

Sources letters, cuttings, diaries, and ledgers, V&A • sketchbooks and architectural drawings, V&A, department of prints and drawings • architectural drawings, clippings, antiquarian papers, and papers, RIBA BAL, drawings collection and MSS collection • J. Lever, ed., *Catalogue of the drawings collection of the Royal Institute of British Architects: G–K* (1973) • W. Watt, *Art furniture, from designs by E. W. Godwin and others, with hints and suggestions on domestic furniture and decoration* (1877) • D. Harbron, *The conscious stone: the life of Edward William Godwin* (1949) • E. Aslin, *E. W. Godwin: furniture and interior decoration* (1968) • A. Reid, 'Dromore Castle, co. Limerick: archaeology and the sister arts of E. W. Godwin', *Architectural History*, 30 (1987), 113–42 • N. B. Wilkinson, 'E. W. Godwin and Japonisme in England', PhD diss., U. Cal., Los Angeles, 1987 • H. M. Hyde, 'Oscar Wilde and his architect', *ArchR*, 109 (1951), 175–6 • M. Girouard, 'Chelsea bohemian studio houses: the Victorian artists at home, 2', *Country Life*, 152 (1972), 1370–74 • S. W. Soros, 'E. W. Godwin: secular furniture and interior design', PhD diss., Royal College of Art, London, 1998 • *Nottinghamshire*, Pevsner (1951), 35, 67–8 • private information (2004) • d. cert. [Ann Jones Godwin] • E. Godwin, *British Architect* (1878), 210 • m. cert. • d. cert. [Sarah Godwin] • E. Craig, *Gordon Craig: the story of his life* (1968) • d. cert. • Lady Campbell to W. Godwin, Smallhythe Place, Kent, Ellen Terry Archive

Archives RIBA BAL, drawings collection and MSS collection • V&A, Archive of Art & Design, corresp. and papers, diaries, and ledgers

Likenesses photographs, *c*.1868–1875, Smallhythe Place, Kent, Ellen Terry Archive • photographs, *c*.1868–1886, priv. coll. • photograph, *c*.1878, V&A, photograph collections • photographs, 1884, V&A, theatre archive

Wealth at death left no assets; widow obtained civil-list pension

Godwin, Francis (1562–1633), bishop of Hereford and historian, was born at Hannington, Northamptonshire, the son of Thomas *Godwin (1517–1590), later bishop of Bath and Wells, and his wife, Isabella (*d*. before 1584), the daughter of Nicholas Purefoy of Shalstone, Buckinghamshire. At the age of fifteen he was sent to Oxford, where in 1578 he was elected to a junior studentship at Christ Church. He graduated BA on 23 January 1581 and proceeded MA in 1584, having earned the general approbation of his peers and teachers. His first ecclesiastical appointment came with the prebend of St Decumans in the cathedral church of Wells in 1586, and he was collated to the subdeanery of Exeter on 11 June the next year. He was admitted BD on 11 February 1594 and, less than two years later, on 30 January 1596 attained the degree of DD. By this time Godwin was serving as rector of Sampford Dorcas, Somerset, canon residentiary of Wells, rector of Bishops Lydeard, and subdean of Exeter.

In 1601 Godwin succeeded William Morgan in the poor bishopric of Llandaff, a preferment worth barely £150 per annum; he was given leave to retain some of his inferior

Francis Godwin (1562–1633), by unknown artist, 1613 [copy?]

dignities, such as the subdeanery of Exeter, and he also assumed the rectory of Shirenewton, Monmouthshire. He appealed in 1607 to Sir Thomas Lake, asking that the latter use his interest to procure for Godwin the archdeaconry of Gloucester. In 1609 Godwin complained that he was obliged to appoint lay readers to several cures in Llandaff, 'as a minister will not accept thereof, as not being able to live by it' (Fincham, 186). In 1617 he was translated to the see of Hereford, where he succeeded Robert Bennett.

Godwin married a daughter of John Wolton, bishop of Exeter, and the couple had several children. These included Thomas Godwin the younger (*d*. 1644), vicar of Newland, Gloucestershire, whom he appointed to the chancellorship of Hereford, Morgan Godwin, archdeacon of Shrewsbury (*d*. 1645), Charles Godwin, who held a benefice at Monmouth, and a daughter who married Dr John Hughes, archdeacon of Hereford. Godwin's preferment of one of his sons left him open to a charge of nepotism. Dr Thomas Ryves, a civil lawyer who had sued unsuccessfully for the vacant chancellorship, complained to Charles I, in a petition of 22 November 1625, that Godwin had conferred the office on Thomas, who was untrained in the civil law, a practice that contravened royal requirements that candidates for such posts possess a legal degree. The younger Godwin was ousted from the chancellorship.

Among his peers Godwin was an indifferent diocesan, issuing visitation articles to Llandaff in 1603, but absenting himself personally from the visitations he conducted in Hereford in 1621 and 1627; he was, however, one of the very few prelates actively engaged in enforcing James I's Book of Sports in 1618. Although Godwin upheld the godly policy of his predecessor, Robert Bennett, in encouraging lectures by combination in order to promote good preaching, he did not sustain Bennett's close attention to the nurturing of clerical education. In April 1627 the bishop reported to Lord Keeper Coventry his failure to apprehend two Roman Catholic priests, the privy council's letter to him on this matter having apparently miscarried. Although he regularly took his seat in the House of Lords, Godwin spoke infrequently and served on a small number of committees.

Like many students educated in the 1580s and 1590s, Godwin had acquired a taste for historical and antiquarian studies, and it is for his works in this sphere, as well as in imaginative literature, that he is principally remembered, rather than as a cleric. Having made the acquaintance of William Camden, a lifelong friend and godfather to Godwin's son Thomas, in 1590 he accompanied the great antiquary into Wales in search of antiquities for the revised edition of Camden's famous *Britannia* and in 1608 he provided Camden with transcripts of an Anglo-Saxon charter. Although never a member of the Elizabethan Society of Antiquaries, Godwin associated with its members, including the manuscript collector Sir Robert Cotton.

Godwin's most important work was his *A catalogue of the bishops of England, since the first planting of Christian religion in this island, together with a briefe history of their lives and memorable actions, so neere as can be gathered out of antiquity*, published by George Bishop in 1601. Following in the tradition of early Elizabethan scholar–clerics such as Archbishop Matthew Parker, Godwin intended in this work a complete collection of biographies of all the bishops and archbishops in England, though some of his accounts run to only a few lines. This book may be seen as another entry in the Church of England's attempt to establish its history in the face of Catholic and puritan attacks, but it was also a personal attempt by Godwin to restore the general reputation of the church's prelates, in particular pre-Reformation bishops whose names had been sullied in the harsher treatments by protestant apologists such as John Foxe: Godwin is notably even-handed, for instance, in describing St Thomas a Becket's troubles with Henry II. Godwin was, however, a sharp critic of many of his subjects, in particular Marian bishops such as Stephen Gardiner and Edmund Bonner. The *Catalogue* attacked rival Catholic historians such as Robert Parsons, and in an addition included in the second edition the author disputed the Catholic assertion of a mission by St Peter to Britain (a point on which Godwin himself would later be attacked by the Catholic historian Richard Broughton in 1633).

Godwin's *Catalogue* was unevenly researched even by the standards of the day, but it wore well over the next two centuries as a basic reference source. It won its author immediate approbation and was largely responsible for Godwin's relatively early appointment to the see of Llandaff. The first edition was dedicated to Thomas Sackville, Lord Buckhurst, the lord treasurer, to whom Godwin was then chaplain, and who doubtless interceded for his preferment. In 1615 Godwin published a revised edition of the work, dedicated to the king, with many additions including a discourse on the first conversion of Britain to Christianity. Like most of his contemporaries Godwin subscribed to the view that Christianity had first reached Britain with Joseph of Arimathea, the general conversion of England following soon after during the reign of the mythical King Lucius; the later conversion by Augustine of Canterbury, on which claims to papal authority over the church in England had long rested, was by this view a mere reconversion. In this expanded edition the whole work was translated into Latin for the benefit of an international audience, as *De praesulibus Angliae commentarius: omnium episcoporum, necnon et cardinalium eiusdem gentis, nomina, tempora, seriem, atque actiones maxime memorabiles ab ultima antiquitate repetita complexus* (1616), and this achievement earned Godwin promotion to the wealthier see of Hereford. Several annotated copies of early editions of the *Catalogue* survive in the Bodleian and other libraries, attesting to its wide use.

Like his near contemporary Francis Bacon, Godwin was among the Jacobean exponents of the project for a new national history of England, regarding Polydore Vergil's *Anglica historia* as an inadequate work, written by a foreigner and a papist. He found Vergil's treatment of the sixteenth century especially inadequate, and it did not, of course, cover the whole century. In 1620, writing to his old friend Camden, he urged the latter to print the second part of his *Annales* of Elizabeth's reign, which did not, however, occur until after Camden's death. Inspired by the first part of *Annales*, and by the erudition in Camden's earlier *Britannia*, Godwin embarked on his own history of the middle Tudors, Henry VIII, Edward VI, and Mary. Calling for a complete national history based on the sort of erudition that had marked *Britannia*, he remarked that 'our antiquaries may justly be taxed of sloth' (*Rerum Anglicarum … annales*, sig. A2r).

The book that resulted, *Rerum Anglicarum Henrico VIII. Edwardo VI. et Maria regnantibus, annales nunc primum editi* (1616) unfortunately did not live up to the high mark Godwin had set. He drew on earlier foreign historians such as Francesco Guicciardini, Johannes Sleidan, Joachim du Bellay, Jacques-Auguste de Thou, and on a variety of Scottish writers; for English accounts he turned to John Stow's chronicles, and to the yet-unpublished life of Cardinal Wolsey by George Cavendish. He used some unspecified 'publique records' (*Rerum Anglicarum … annales*, 141) for certain episodes such as Anne Boleyn's trial and death, documents which he probably obtained from Sir Robert Cotton, but the book is not founded on these materials in the way that Camden's *Annales* were based on the comparable records for Elizabeth's reign (though Camden, as the first historian of Elizabeth, had had little choice in this regard, having few 'authorities' to which to turn). Godwin's son Morgan translated the history into English, with some additions (including passages lifted wholesale from

Cavendish) as *Annales of England* in 1630. Although reprinted a few times over the next century (the life of Mary ended up in the multi-authored *Complete History of England* edited by John Hughes in 1706), Godwin's *Annales* is a work of less significance than the *Catalogue of Bishops*. Although Wood fairly assessed Godwin as 'a passing great lover of venerable antiquity and of all good literature', there is no basis for his hyperbolic statement that Godwin was an 'incomparable historian' possessed of critical skills comparable to 'the learned [John] Selden' (Wood, *Ath. Oxon.*, 1.581). On the other hand, Godwin's recognition of the need for a thorough revision of the national history, based on original sources, turned out to be prophetic. It was echoed throughout the rest of the century by later writers such as Sir William Temple and White Kennett; the latter, another bishop, participated in Hughes's *Complete History* project, and wrote a brief manuscript memoir of Godwin (BL, MS Lansdowne 984, fol. 204).

Godwin was also the author of a number of lesser works, including an unpublished catalogue of the bishops of Bath and Wells, dated 1594 (Trinity College, Cambridge). This is a fuller account of that diocese than the comparable account in the *Catalogue*. Thomas Hearne printed parts of it in the early eighteenth century, as addenda to his editions of John Whethamstede's and John of Trokelow's chronicles. As a student, Godwin wrote *The Man in the Moone*, a travel narrative presented through the fictitious narrator Domingo Gonsales. This is an interesting work that shows some familiarity with Renaissance exploration literature and with recent astronomy, including the theories of Copernicus. First published posthumously in 1638, it was translated into French, and would influence later writers such as Cyrano de Bergerac, John Wilkins, and (probably indirectly) Jonathan Swift. In his last years Godwin suffered from ill health. He died at Whitbourne in 1633 and was buried on 29 April in the chancel of the church there. D. R. Woolf

Sources K. Fincham, *Prelate as pastor: the episcopate of James I* (1990) · D. R. Woolf, *The idea of history in early Stuart England* (1990) · Wood, *Ath. Oxon.*, 2nd edn · *Fasti Angl.*, *1541–1857*, [Bath and Wells] · J. A. Butler, 'Introduction', in F. Godwin, *The man in the moon* (1995) · H. W. Lawton, 'Bishop Godwin's *The man in the moone*', *Review of English Studies*, 7 (1931), 22–55 · *CSP dom.*, *1603–10*; *1625–8* · W. Kennett, memoir of Godwin, BL, Lansdowne MS 984, fol. 204 · T. Smith, ed., *V. Cl. Gulielmi Camdeni, et illustrium virorum ad G. Camdenum epistolae, cum appendice varii argumenti* (1691) · W. M. Merchant, 'Bishop Francis Godwin, historian and novelist', *Journal of the Historical Society of the Church in Wales*, 5 (1955), 45–51 · A. Janssen, *Francis Godwins 'The man in the moone': die Entdeckung des Romans als Medium der Auseinandersetzung mit Zeitproblemen* (Frankfurt am Main, 1981) · G. Gruffydd, 'Bishop Francis Godwin's injunctions for the diocese of Llandaff, 1603', *Journal of the Historical Society of the Church in Wales*, 4 (1954), 14–22 · K. Fincham, ed., *Visitation articles and injunctions of the early Stuart church*, 1 (1994), 152

Archives BL, MSS, Add. MS 45140, Cotton MS Titus C. XI · Bodl. Oxf., *Catalogue of the bishops of England* interleaved with many MS notes · Trinity Cam., MS

Likenesses oils, 1613, Christ Church Oxf. [*see illus.*] · G. Vertue, portrait, NPG; repro. in W. Richardson, ed., *Francisci Godwini … de praesulibus*, new edn, 2 vols. (1743) · oils, second version, Balliol Oxf. · watercolour (after oil painting, 1613), NPG

Godwin, George (1813–1888), architect and journal editor, was born in Brompton Terrace, Kensington, London, on 28 January 1813, one of nine children of George Godwin senior (1780–1863) and his wife, Mary Anne (1790–1872). His father was an architect and surveyor who played a significant role in the development of South Kensington. At the age of thirteen Godwin became a pupil in his father's office where he learned the practical rudiments of architecture. When he started practice in his own name, he too found most of his work in Kensington. His earliest known building, the Brompton national school (1841–2, dem.) was sited on the main road through the area.

During his pupillage and after, Godwin developed a wide range of interests and friendships which were invaluable in his later career. In 1835 he was joint editor with Edward Edwards of the *Literary Union*, a journal for literary and scientific self-improvement. He wrote plays, one of which, *The Last Day*, was performed at the Olympic Theatre in October 1840; plus pieces of fiction, published as *Facts and Fiction*. He was also associated with the Art Union of London, established in 1837 to promote the appreciation of art and sculpture through a system of lottery prize-givings. As its secretary (1839–68) he vigorously defended the organization against the criticism that art and gambling should never be mixed.

As an author, Godwin showed an early interest in two aspects of architecture. His enthusiasm for architectural history resulted in his work on masons' marks and the role of freemasonry in the dissemination of the Gothic style. His essay 'Masons' marks' was published in *Archæologia* (1843). Encouraged by the antiquarian John Britton, he wrote a two-volume study, *The Churches of London* (1838). At the same time, he helped advance the scientific aspects of architecture through his studies of building materials and techniques. In 1836 his essay on concrete, dealing comprehensively with its history and use, was awarded the silver medal of the Institute of British Architects. He became an associate of the institute the same year, a fellow of the Society of Antiquaries in 1838, and a fellow of the Royal Society in 1839.

In 1844 Godwin became the third editor of *The Builder*, succeeding Joseph Aloysius Hansom and Alfred Bartholomew. Following its uncertain start, he transformed it into the most important and successful professional paper of its kind with a readership well beyond the architectural and building world. Its success was directly the result of his energy, moral commitment, and wide-ranging curiosity. As he put it, his life was 'one of earnest and continuous endeavour to spread information, to sustain the dignity of the profession, and to contribute to the welfare of all classes' (*Transactions of the Royal Institute of British Architects*, 219). Each weekly issue carried detailed reports of new building works and architectural debates plus articles on history, archaeology, and the arts. Above all, *The Builder* was known for its campaigns for health and housing reform. Godwin wrote first-hand reports on slum overcrowding and its results in articles which he gathered together in three books: *London Shadows: a Glance at the Homes of Thousands* (1854), *Town Swamps and Social Bridges*

George Godwin (1813–1888), by Ernest Edwards, pubd 1865

(1859), and *Another Blow for Life* (1864). He supported architectural remedies such as improved housing by charitable trusts, public baths and wash-houses, and pavilion-plan hospitals, but equally he believed in improvement through individual perseverance and effort. His book *Memorials of Workers: the Past to Encourage the Present* (1860) followed the pattern of Samuel Smiles's *Self-Help* (1859) in demonstrating how fame and success could result from personal endeavour.

As editor, Godwin is reputed to have written much of each issue himself, assisted by a staff of no more than five. He took a particular interest in the quality of the illustrations used, relying mainly on wood-engravings, but later introducing photo-lithography and other photomechanical processes. Among the illustrators he relied on were H. W. Brewer, John Brown, Worthington G. Smith, and Benjamin Sly.

Throughout his editorship, Godwin remained active as an architect. His chief works included the restoration of St Mary Redcliffe, Bristol, and St Mary's, Ware; The Boltons, Kensington (1850–60), plus St Mary's, The Boltons (1849–50); and Elm Park Gardens, Chelsea (1885). With his brother Henry Godwin (1831–1917) he completed a number of projects, notably Redcliffe Square, Kensington (1870–76), and St Luke's, Kensington (1872–3). He was district surveyor for south Islington 1853–74.

Godwin retired as editor of *The Builder* in October 1883. His abrupt departure suggests a clash of personalities between himself and a recently arrived proprietor who mistakenly regarded him as out of touch with the journalistic tendencies of the time. In 1884 he was appointed to the royal commission on the housing of the working classes, and wrote a personal memorandum attached to its report. He died unmarried on 27 January 1888 at his residence, 6 Cromwell Place, Kensington, and was buried in Brompton cemetery. He had been a collector of chairs associated with notable people including Shakespeare, Alexander Pope, and Nathaniel Hawthorne, which were auctioned, along with his other possessions after his death. He left a personal estate of £81,164, a sum in part the result of his long-term share in the profits of *The Builder*. As an editor Godwin was careful and exacting. He was an effective and fluent public speaker and an entertaining companion in private. He was a good narrator of stories, good-humouredly cynical.

G. B. Smith, *rev.* Ruth Richardson and Robert Thorne

Sources *The Builder* (1844–83) · A. King, 'Another blow for life', *ArchR*, 136 (1964), 448–52 · A. King, 'Architectural journalism and the profession: the early years of George Godwin', *Architectural History*, 19 (1976), 32–53 · R. Richardson and R. Thorne, *'The Builder' illustrations index, 1843–1883* (1994) · R. Thorne, 'Building bridges: George Godwin and architectural journalism', *Victorian values*, ed. G. Marsden, 2nd edn (1998), 115–26 · M. Brooks, '*The Builder* in the 1840s: the making of a magazine, the shaping of a profession', *Victorian Periodicals Newsletter*, 14 (autumn 1981), 86–93 · A. Novitzky, '*The Builder* under George Godwin's editorship', PhD diss., Royal College of Art, London, 1982 · *The Builder* (4 Feb 1888) · *The Times* (30 Jan 1888) · *Transactions of the Royal Institute of British Architects*, 1st ser., 31 (1880–81), 217–20 · register of deaths, Brompton, Middlesex, 1888 · *The Builder* (7 Sept 1889)

Archives Builder Archive, Builder House, London | U. Edin. L., letters to James Halliwell-Phillipps

Likenesses E. Morton, lithograph, pubd 1847 (after S. Laurence), BM, NPG · E. Edwards, photograph, pubd 1865, NPG; repro. in *Portraits of men of eminence*, 3 (1865), 67 [*see illus.*] · engraving, repro. in *The Builder* (14 Jan 1882) · portrait, Builder House, London · wood-engraving, NPG; repro. in *ILN* (11 Feb 1888)

Wealth at death £81,163 19*s.* 1*d.*: resworn probate, Nov 1889, *CGPLA Eng. & Wales* (1888)

Godwin, George Nelson (1846–1907), antiquary and travel writer, the only surviving son of Edward Godwin, a draper of Winchester, and afterwards a farmer of Melksham, Wiltshire, and his wife, Mary Tugwell, was born at Winchester on 4 July 1846. He and his only sister, Sarah Louisa, were brought up at Winchester, and George was educated there at a private school. After engaging in private tuition, and qualifying in 1868 at the London College of Divinity, he was ordained deacon in 1869 and priest in 1870. He later proceeded to Trinity College, Dublin, where he gained the Cluff memorial prize in 1882, and graduated BA in 1884 and BD in 1887. After filling curacies at Heanor, Derbyshire (1869–72), East Bergholt (1873–6), and Capel St Mary, Suffolk (1876–7), he was appointed chaplain of the forces in 1877, and continued in the army until 1890; during this period he served at Gibraltar, Malta (1878–81), Alexandria (from 1887), Cairo (1889), Dublin, the Curragh, and the army medical school at Netley Hospital. He was vicar of East Boldre, Hampshire (1890–93), Woodmancott-with-Popham, Hampshire (1893–8), and Appledore, Devon, curate of Weasenham, Norfolk (1903), and curate in charge of Stokesby, Great Yarmouth (1904). He was also a freemason, a brother of Economy Lodge in Winchester.

Godwin was best known as an antiquary and local historian. He was one of the founder members of the Hampshire Field Club and Archaeological Society, reflecting the strong link between Netley Hospital and the club in its early days. With Thomas William Shore (1840–1905), the first secretary, he spent over a year canvassing potential members before the club was officially formed in 1885, and he spoke at its first two meetings. He was the first editor of *Hampshire Notes and Queries*, from 1883 to 1896 (originally published in the *Winchester Observer and County News*, but a separate publication from 1893).

Godwin was a leading authority on the history of Hampshire and neighbouring counties during the civil war. His major work, *Civil War in Hampshire, 1642–45, and the Story of Basing House* (1882, 2nd edn 1904), though now superseded, shows detailed knowledge of the available primary sources. His travel writing, mainly on south-east England and Malta, was voluminous but largely ephemeral, and—as with other of his historical work—rarely goes beyond lists and trivial description. In addition to this, Godwin published: *Materials for English Church History, 1625–49* (1895); with John Plummer, *Silchester, or, The Pompeii of Hampshire* (1879, 2nd edn 1886); and, with H. M. Gilbert, *Bibliotheca Hantoniensis* (1891), a list of books relating to Hampshire. He was a contributor to early numbers of the *Papers and Proceedings of the Hampshire Field Club and Archaeological Society*.

Godwin was married twice: firstly, on 15 February 1870, to Mary Godwin (no relation), by whom he had one daughter; and secondly, on 8 August 1899, to Rosa Elizabeth, the daughter of George Jay of Camden Town, London, who survived him, and with whom he had no children. He died suddenly of heart failure while staying for the night at the Black Lion Hotel in Little Walsingham, Norfolk, on 11 January 1907 (pursuing yet another curacy) and was buried in the churchyard of that village.

CHARLES WELCH, *rev.* RICHARD DENNIS

Sources *Hampshire Observer* (19 Jan 1907) • *Hampshire Chronicle* (19 Jan 1907) • Crockford (1902) • *BL cat.* • private information (1912) • J. P. Williams-Freeman, 'Early days of the Hampshire Field Club', *Papers and Proceedings of the Hampshire Field Club and Archaeological Society*, 15 (1941–3), 236–8 • *Papers and Proceedings of the Hampshire Field Club*, 1 (1885–9), 10 [report of talk by Godwin] • B. Taylor, 'One hundred years of the Hampshire Field Club', *Papers and Proceedings of the Hampshire Field Club and Archaeological Society*, 41 (1985), 5–20 • *Papers and Proceedings of the Hampshire Field Club*, 1 (1885–98), 4–9 [membership lists] • m. certs. • d. cert.

Wealth at death £1278 15*s.* 8*d.*: probate, 2 Feb 1907, *CGPLA Eng. & Wales*

Godwin, Sir Harry (1901–1985), botanist, was born on 9 May 1901 at Holmes, Rotherham, Yorkshire, the only son and elder child of Charles William Thomas Godwin, a grocer and licensed victualler, and his wife, Mary Jane Grainger. Soon after his birth the family moved to Long Eaton in Derbyshire, and Godwin was educated there at the High Street council school and at Long Eaton county secondary school. In his later schooling disruptions caused by the First World War reduced the time available for teaching mathematics in the upper classes, to his lasting regret. None the less, he gained a distinction in botany in the Oxford senior local examination and obtained (1918) a Derbyshire county major scholarship. In his last year at school he wrote a paper for the school magazine on the vegetation of an outlier of Liassic limestone near Gotham, revealing a keen interest in ecology. While still at school he further broadened his education by attending laboratory classes at University College, Nottingham.

Godwin entered Clare College, Cambridge, with an open scholarship in 1919 and obtained first classes in both parts of the natural sciences tripos (1921 and 1922). He then became a research student in plant physiology under F. F. Blackman. However, his real interests still lay in ecology. As he explained to Blackman, his interest in plant physiology was only in gaining experience in methodology, which he hoped to apply to his future ecological research. Indeed, in 1923 (in addition to his doctoral research and responsibilities as a newly appointed junior university demonstrator in botany) he began systematic and detailed studies of Wicken Fen with A. G. Tansley—in particular of the mechanism of the vegetational succession. An interim account of their findings was published in 1929 under the title *Vegetation of Wicken Fen* (part 5 of *The Natural History of Wicken Fen*). Meanwhile his work on the mechanism of starvation in leaves gained him his PhD in 1926.

In 1927 Godwin married Margaret Elizabeth, daughter of James Daniels, a butcher. She had attended the Long Eaton secondary school with him and had then taken a London BSc degree in botany at Nottingham University. She was calm and clear-headed, an ideal partner for Godwin. She collaborated with her husband in the early work on pollen analysis of fen peats, until the birth in 1934 of their only child, a son. He became a general practitioner but to the great sorrow of his parents died in 1974.

In the year of his marriage Godwin was appointed university demonstrator and in 1934 university lecturer, giving for many years an elementary course for first-year botanists. In the preface to his highly successful book *Plant Biology* (1930, 4th edn 1945) he rightly claims that the emphasis on physiology rather than on morphology and evolution secured a deeper understanding than previously of the basic role of the green plant and a general recognition of the scientific and social value of ecological studies. Meanwhile he was appointed a research fellow of Clare in 1925 and was an official fellow from 1934. He always took a keen interest in college affairs and was acting master in 1958–9 and senior fellow for many years.

During his years as senior university demonstrator and university lecturer Godwin continued his research on fen vegetation at Wicken and elsewhere, applying the methods of pollen analysis to the deep deposits of peat in order to work out the past history of the fens and their surroundings. His main contributions were undoubtedly in establishing the relationship between peat stratigraphy and the pollen zones, based on the identification and estimate of relative abundance of pollen grains of different tree species in different strata. More accurate identification of non-tree pollen aided accounts of the correlation between climate, forest composition, prehistoric agriculture, and peat stratigraphy. This wealth of data and interpretation was brought together in Godwin's extremely readable *History of the British Flora* (1956, 2nd edn 1975), in addition to numerous papers in scientific journals.

In the following decades he gained a high reputation as a leader in ecological thought and practice, both in the university and further afield. He was president of the British Ecological Society in 1942–3, editor of the *Journal of Ecology* (1948–56), and joint editor of the *New Phytologist* (1931–61). In 1948 he was appointed the first director of the newly formed sub-department of quaternary research in the Cambridge botany school, a post which he held until 1966. He made notable contributions to knowledge of radiocarbon dating and of geologically recent changes in relative land / sea levels as well as to the archaeological implications of his findings. From 1960 until his retirement in 1968 he was professor of botany at Cambridge University.

Godwin was a big man, tall and robust looking, with brown hair and pale grey eyes. He smiled freely and entered into lively and humorous conversation with both friends and strangers, who all saw him as a most kindly person. He was recognized and accepted as a natural leader and he exerted a very considerable influence over all his acquaintances.

Godwin was elected FRS (1945), a member of the Royal Society council (1957–9), and Croonian lecturer in 1960. In 1970 he was knighted. He received the Prestwich medal of the Geological Society of London in 1951 and the gold medal of the Linnean Society in 1966, with comparable awards from several non-British institutions. He was also made an honorary member of various academies including the Royal Irish Academy in 1955, the Botanical Society of Edinburgh in 1961, and the International Union for Quaternary Research in 1969. He was made ScD (Cantab.) in 1942 and received honorary doctorates of science from Trinity College, Dublin (1960), and the universities of Lancaster (1968) and Durham (1974). His contributions to conservation (on a number of committees) were acknowledged in 1978 by the renaming of the Nature Conservancy Council's headquarters in Huntingdon as Godwin House. Godwin died in Cambridge on 12 August 1985.

A. R. Clapham, *rev.* Peter Osborne

Sources R. G. West, *Memoirs FRS*, 34 (1988), 261–92 • *WWW* • *CGPLA Eng. & Wales* (1985) • personal knowledge (1990)

Archives Clare College, Cambridge, papers | Bodl. Oxf., corresp. with G. E. Blackman • University of Sheffield Library, corresp. with Arthur Roy Clapham

Wealth at death £68,556: probate, 14 Oct 1985, *CGPLA Eng. & Wales*

Godwin, Sir Henry Thomas (1784–1853), army officer, was commissioned, on 30 October 1799, ensign 9th (East Norfolk) foot, in which he became lieutenant on 9 August 1803 and captain on 28 March 1808. He served with the 9th at Ferrol in 1800, in the expedition to Hanover in 1805, when he was adjutant of his battalion, and in Portugal in 1808. In 1809 he served in the operations on the Douro and the advance to Oporto, and afterwards accompanied his battalion to Gibraltar. He marched with the light company, as part of a provisional light battalion, from Gibraltar to Tarifa, and took part in the first defence. He was a volunteer under Lord Blayney in the attempt on Fuengirola, near Malaga, and commanded a detachment of two flank companies of his battalion at Cadiz, at the second defence of Tarifa, and at the battle of Barossa, where he was severely wounded. For his Peninsular services he was made brevet major and CB.

On 26 May 1814 Godwin was appointed major in the old 5th West India regiment, and on 26 July 1821 lieutenant-colonel of the 41st foot. Godwin took that regiment out to India in 1822, accompanied it to Burma in 1824, and was present in every action in the First Anglo-Burmese War, from the capture of Rangoon until the treaty of Yandaboo in February 1826, except during the latter part of 1824, when he was employed with a detached force in conquering the province of Martaban. He exchanged to half pay in 1827, and became colonel on 10 January 1837 and major-general on 9 November 1846.

In 1850 Godwin transferred to the general staff in Bombay, and on 1 November 1851 he was given command of the Sirhind division of the Bengal army. In 1852 he was selected for the command of the Bengal division of the Burmese expeditionary force, of which he took the command in chief. The Second Anglo-Burmese War began with the bombardment of Martaban on 5 April 1852. Godwin took Rangoon in April and Pegu in June, and in December the annexation of the province of Pegu to India was proclaimed by Lord Dalhousie. Further operations followed at Prome and in the Rangoon River. On 1 July 1853 the expeditionary force, known officially as the army of Ava, was broken up, and Godwin returned to India. The protracted character of the later operations drew upon Godwin much abuse from certain portions of the English and Indian press. Nevertheless, he appears to have acted throughout in accordance with the instructions of Lord Dalhousie, by whom his conduct was approved.

On Godwin's return to India, he was reappointed to command the Sirhind division of the Bengal army. He died after a brief illness at Simla, at the residence of the commander-in-chief, Sir William Gomm (his brother subaltern in the 9th foot), on 26 October 1853 from the results of exposure and overexertion in Burma; according to his obituarist in the *Gentleman's Magazine*, 'it was by overheating himself with exercise that his fatal malady was originated'. Notification of his appointments as KCB and colonel of the 20th foot was received in India after his death. He was married with one daughter, Maria Elizabeth, who married Robert A. C. Godwin-Austen.

H. M. Chichester, *rev.* Alex May

Sources *Army List* • W. F. B. Laurie, *Our Burmese wars and relations with Burma: being an abstract of military and political operations*, 2nd edn (1885) • G. Bruce, *The Burma Wars, 1824–1886* (1973) • D. Featherstone, *Victoria's enemies: an A–Z of British colonial warfare* (1989) • W. F. P. Napier, *History of the war in the Peninsula and in the south of*

France, rev. edn, 6 vols. (1876) • C. W. C. Oman, *A history of the Peninsular War*, 7 vols. (1902–30) • *GM*, 2nd ser., 41 (1854), 529
Archives NA Scot., corresp. with Dalhousie

Godwin, Mary. *See* Wollstonecraft, Mary (1759–1797).

Godwin [*formerly* Clairmont; *née* de Vial], **Mary Jane** (**1768–1841**), translator and bookseller, was probably the daughter of Peter de Vial, a merchant of Exeter, who apparently died bankrupt in 1791, and who also had at least two other daughters and one son. Her mother is unidentified, and very little is known about her life until 1801, at which time, under the name Mary Jane Clairmont, she was a neighbour of the philosopher William *Godwin (1756–1836), whom she married on 21 December of that year. At the time of her marriage to Godwin, Mary Jane Clairmont had two children, and called herself a widow, although it is unlikely that she had previously been married. The children believed their father to be Charles Gaulis (*d.* 1796), a native of Switzerland who had supposedly changed his name to Clairmont, but while he might have been the father of the elder (Charles), the father of the younger, Clara (Claire) Mary Jane *Clairmont (1798–1879), remains unidentified. Mary Jane and William Godwin were to have one child of their own: William *Godwin (1803–1832).

While best known to literary history as the stepmother of Mary Wollstonecraft *Shelley (1797–1851), Mary Jane Godwin was active in the literary society of her day, translating from French, in which she was fluent, and editing children's books. Her early employers included the publisher Benjamin Tabart, for whom she edited a three-volume *Collection of Popular Stories for the Nursery*, but in 1805 she and Godwin opened their own bookshop, which was formally established under the name M. J. Godwin & Co. in 1807. It specialized in children's literature, much of it commissioned by the Godwins, and their publications included such major successes as Charles and Mary Lamb's *Tales from Shakespeare* and the first English translation of *The Swiss Family Robinson*. William Godwin contributed educational work under the pseudonym Edward Baldwin, but it was Mary Jane Godwin who was responsible for running the business. In addition to her work for the bookshop, she published in 1835 an anonymous guide-book to Herne Bay, near Canterbury, a book which Claire Clairmont thought 'remarkably pretty' (Stocking, 2.344). The Godwins' bookshop was a profitable venture, at least initially, but it never earned enough money to clear the debts which harassed them all their married life, and which led to occasional temporary separations. They eventually lost the bookshop to bankruptcy, and until Godwin received a government pension three years before his death in 1836 their income was precarious.

Money was not the only potential source of trouble in the Godwins' marriage; a number of William Godwin's literary friends disliked Mary Jane Godwin—Charles Lamb was particularly unkind about her—as did her stepdaughter. In 1817 Mary Shelley wrote that 'somthing [*sic*] very analogous to disgust arises whenever I mention her' (*Letters of Mary Wollstonecraft Shelley*, 1.43); earlier, she had complained that 'Mrs. G. … plagues my father out of his life' (ibid., 1.3). Yet despite their many financial problems and Mary Jane's unpopularity, the Godwins' marriage and business partnership both seem to have remained solid. According to Claire Clairmont, her mother's 'affection and devotion to Godwin were admirable and remained unalterable from the day of their marriage till his death' (Stocking, 2.618). And Mary Shelley's last references to her stepmother are in fact much less harsh than were her earlier comments. 'Poor Mrs. Godwin!' Shelley wrote shortly after Mary Jane's death. 'It seemed strange that so restless a spirit could be hushed, & all that remained pent up in a grave. I had done all I could to help her during life' (*Letters of Mary Wollstonecraft Shelley*, 3.20).

Mary Jane Godwin died at her home, 3 Golden Square, London, on 17 June 1841, cared for in her last illness by Claire Clairmont. She was buried in St Pancras churchyard, next to William Godwin and his more famous first wife, Mary Wollstonecraft, but when the remains of Godwin and Wollstonecraft were later moved to the Shelley family vault in Bournemouth as a result of the encroachments of railway developers, Mary Jane Godwin's body was not reinterred. PAM PERKINS

Sources W. St Clair, *The Godwins and the Shelleys* (1989) • R. Gittings and J. Manton, *Claire Clairmont and the Shelleys* (1992) • *The Clairmont correspondence: letters of Claire Clairmont, Charles Clairmont, and Fanny Imlay Godwin*, ed. M. K. Stocking, 2 vols. (1995) • H. Huscher, 'The Clairmont enigma', *Keats–Shelley Memorial Bulletin*, 11 (1960), 13–20 • *The letters of Mary Wollstonecraft Shelley*, ed. B. T. Bennett, 3 vols. (1980–88) • NYPL, Humanities and Social Sciences Library, Pforzeimer collection, Clairmont MSS
Archives Bodl. Oxf., corresp. with William Godwin

Godwin, Mary Wollstonecraft. *See* Shelley, Mary Wollstonecraft (1797–1851).

Godwin, Morgan. *See* Godwyn, Morgan (*bap.* 1640, *d.* 1685x1709).

Godwin, Thomas (**1517–1590**), bishop of Bath and Wells, was born at Wokingham, Berkshire, of humble parents. While at Wokingham grammar school he came to the notice of Richard Layton, archdeacon of Buckingham and later dean of York, a strong advocate of reformed churchmanship. Layton took Godwin into his household, giving him a solid grounding in classical learning, and about 1538 he entered Magdalen College, Oxford. He graduated BA on 12 July 1543, became fellow in 1544, and proceeded MA in 1548. On 23 May 1549 he was appointed master of the new free school at Brackley, Northamptonshire, recently founded by his college. His strong protestant principles, shared by such Magdalen contemporaries as John Foxe and Thomas Bentham, may have brought him into conflict with more conservative elements within the college since he resigned his fellowship on Christmas day 1549. Alternatively he may simply have decided to marry; his first wife was Isabel (*d.* before 1584), daughter of Nicholas Purfrey (or Purefoy), of Shalstone, Buckinghamshire.

After Mary's accession in July 1553 Godwin resigned his

Thomas Godwin (1517–1590), by unknown artist, *c.*1584

headmastership but did not go into exile. Instead he studied physic, graduating BM at Oxford in June 1555, and to support his family practised medicine until Elizabeth I's accession. Ordained probably in 1560 by Nicholas Bullingham, bishop of Lincoln, on 28 September that year (most likely at Bullingham's collation) Godwin was installed prebendary of Bedford Major in Lincoln Cathedral. Bullingham also introduced him to Queen Elizabeth, who, pleased with Godwin's tall and handsome appearance, appointed him one of her Lent preachers, a post he held for eighteen years. He is also credited with the rectories of Kirkby Mallory, Leicestershire (1560) and of Hannington and Winwick, Northamptonshire (1562). In February 1563 Godwin was one of those who voted in convocation, as proctor for the Lincoln chapter, for further liturgical reform: the proposals were defeated by a single vote. On 1 December 1563 Godwin exchanged his prebend in Lincoln for that of Milton Ecclesia (at whose presentation is unknown) and on 2 September 1564 became a canon residentiary.

When Thomas Sampson was deprived of the deanery of Christ Church, Oxford, Godwin succeeded him: letters patent were issued on 26 May 1565. On 17 December that year he proceeded BTh at Oxford and was granted his DTh on the following 18 February. His reforming convictions remained well to the fore. In his one surviving sermon, preached before Elizabeth at Greenwich in March 1566—the month in which Parker brought the vestiarian controversy to a head by suspending nonconforming ministers in London—Godwin considered the relative authority of the early fathers, church councils, and scripture. He urged his auditors to place 'Doctors' and councils 'where they should be, and attribute all souveraintye to the worde which is the wisdom and powre of God to the salvation of all that beleve' (Godwin, 167).

On 10 March 1567 Godwin was instituted dean of Canterbury on Elizabeth's presentation. Parker immediately appointed him to a commission to visit the diocese of Norwich and in June, in the 'Greenyard' at Norwich, he preached the first of the annual Rogation sermons recently established by the primate. Back at Canterbury, Godwin faced corruption and faction within his chapter. By August 1567 Parker was defending him against the charge that he had sold 'a huge quantity of plate worth 1000 pound, and vestry ornaments', attributing the slander to the malice of prebendaries who disapproved of married clergy (Bruce and Perowne, 303–4).

In 1568 Godwin practically rebuilt the deanery after a disastrous fire. Perhaps it was in order to defray the cost that on 29 May that year he leased his prebend of Milton Ecclesia for seventy years at a rental of £40 per annum. In 1570 he was appointed an ecclesiastical commissioner but in September 1573 was accused before Parker, during a visitation of the Canterbury chapter, of violating the cathedral statutes and misappropriating funds. Godwin strenuously denied all charges and issued counter-allegations: he had been obliged to appeal to the local justices after the prebendary George Boleyn had threatened 'to nail him to the wall with his sword' (Strype, *Parker*, 2.301). Parker was evidently sympathetic: on 1 October 1573 Godwin was collated to the living of Ruckinge, Kent. On 2 May 1575 he resigned Milton Ecclesia, thus finally severing his connection with the Lincoln chapter.

In 1583 Godwin was among those whom the new primate, John Whitgift, recommended for further promotion: he was consecrated bishop of Bath and Wells on 13 September 1584 at the advanced age of sixty-seven. His posthumous reputation was comprehensively wrecked by Sir John Harington. Although Harington admitted that he came to office 'as well qualified for a bishop as mought be, unreproveably without symonie' and was 'given to good hospitallity, quyet, kynde, affable', he was also a widower in poor health and plagued with gout (Harington, 2.151). He therefore remarried. S. H. Cassan mistakenly identified the lady as Margaret, daughter of William Boreman of Wells, who was actually the second wife of Godwin's son and namesake. Harington refers to her only as a widow of London. She was buried on 1 December 1587 at Banwell—the episcopal manor where Godwin largely resided and conducted episcopal business—as 'Sibyll the wife of the Right Reverend Father in god Thomas Godwen' (Hembry, 157). Godwin later assured Harington, 'with teares in his eyes', that he had married her 'but for a guide of his house, and for the rest … he lyved with her as Josephe did with Mary'. Yet Harington, who evidently disapproved of episcopal marriage quite as strongly as Elizabeth is supposed to have done, calls his action a 'disgrace', implies that he was in some way 'intrapt' into it, and even relays the rumour that he married for money (Harington, 2.151, 156).

Harington's narrative turns on the story that Sir Walter Ralegh, who had designs on Banwell, took advantage of his 'intempestive' marriage to kindle Elizabeth's anger, asserting that Mrs Godwin was 'a girle of twenty yeare old, with a great portion', that Godwin had assigned her 'half the bishopprick', and that because of his gout 'he could not stand to his mariadge; with such scoffs to make him ridiculous to the vulgar, and odious to the Queene' (Harington, 2.151–2). Although the earl of Bedford assured her that Mrs Godwin had a son of nearly forty, Elizabeth is supposed to have allowed Ralegh to plague Godwin with demands for a lease of Banwell for 100 years, enduring 'many sharp messages' from her as long as he resisted, one of them delivered by Harington himself at the behest of the earl of Leicester. For good measure Harington records that while Leicester initially disapproved of Ralegh's tactics 'they were soon agreed, like Pilat and Herod to condemne Christ' (ibid.). Finally, 'to pacefie his persecutors, and to save Banwell' Godwin granted the crown a lease of Wivelscombe for ninety-nine years 'and so purchased his peace' (ibid., 2.153).

No reliance can be placed upon these statements or upon their obvious implications: Elizabeth reassigned Wivelscombe not to the importunate Ralegh but to the head of a prominent local family, George Bond. Like most episcopal leases passed on favourable terms to the crown, the transaction was probably designed to allow Elizabeth graciously to reward a government official of some standing within the diocese.

Godwin's good nature and poor health nevertheless combined to ensure that he fell prey to his rapacious family. Thomas, the eldest of his five sons, and Thomas Purfrey, husband of Blandina, one of his three daughters, battened upon the bishop's financial affairs, young Godwin becoming collector of diocesan tenths and subsidies. Through his father's influence he sat as MP for Wells in 1586 and, handsomely bribed by the city authorities, obtained the bishop's signature to a new charter of incorporation in 1588. By then he was defaulting on payments due from him as collector, and on the day of Godwin's death he and other relatives stripped the episcopal establishments of their furnishings before the sheriff's officials could arrive to distrain them for debts due to the crown. Inquiries into the bishop's assets, or lack of them, continued into the reign of James I.

All writers are agreed upon Godwin's essential honesty. Cassan insisted that he achieved promotion not by subservience or temporizing but by his own merits. Even Harington's double-edged portrait admits that he was 'beloved … for his great housekeeping', his 'kinde entertainment', his 'charitable' mind, and—although he published nothing—his learning. His 'government', moreover, was 'mylde and not violent' (Harington, 2.156). His registers suggest that he was a conscientious chief pastor and, despite his atrocious family, his stewardship of the episcopal estates appears to have been efficient: under his successor, John Still, they were to yield the see a greater income than at any time since its despoliation by the duke of Somerset under Edward VI.

On medical advice Godwin retired to his birthplace, where he died on 19 November 1590. He was buried in Wokingham church on 24 November. A floor-slab inscription and a wall tablet erected by his second son, Francis *Godwin, bishop of Llandaff and of Hereford, both survive. Doubtless covering his shame for his elder brother's activities (and perhaps his own failure to curb them), Francis lamented in print that his father would have been happier if he had remained in Canterbury rather than accepting the bishopric when, unable to travel and 'broken with age', he was 'constrained to use the help of others; who though their duty required a care of so good natur'd an old man, yet they proving … negligent of others good, and too greedie of their owne, overthrew both' (Harington, 2.154). NIGEL SCOTLAND

Sources Som. ARS, MSS D/D/B Register 16, 17 • T. Godwin, 'A sermon preached before the queen at Greenwich 27 March AD 1566', CCC Cam., MS 340, 165–87 • S. H. Cassan, *The lives of the bishops of Bath and Wells*, 2 vols. (1829–30) • J. Harington, *Nugae antiquae*, ed. T. Park and H. Harington, 2 vols. (1804) • P. M. Hembry, *The bishops of Bath and Wells, 1540–1640: social and economic problems* (1967) • J. Strype, *The life and acts of Matthew Parker*, new edn, 3 vols. (1821) • J. Strype, *The life and acts of John Whitgift*, new edn, 3 vols. (1822) • F. Heal, *Of prelates and princes: a study of the economic and social position of the Tudor episcopate* (1980) • HoP, *Commons, 1558–1603*, 2.199–200 • *Fasti Angl., 1541–1857*, [Lincoln] • W. D. Macray, *A register of the members of St Mary Magdalen College, Oxford*, 8 vols. (1894–1915), vol. 2 • B. Usher, 'The queen and Mrs Bishop', *Elizabeth I: monarch and myth*, ed. S. Doran and T. Freeman [forthcoming] • Fuller, *Worthies* (1811) • *Correspondence of Matthew Parker*, ed. J. Bruce and T. T. Perowne, Parker Society, 42 (1853) • memorial inscription, Wokingham church, Berkshire

Likenesses oils, *c*.1584, Canterbury Cathedral, deanery [*see illus.*] • oils (aged seventy-two), Christ Church Oxf.

Godwin, Thomas (1586/7–1642), schoolmaster, was the second son of Anthony Godwin of Wookey, Somerset. He matriculated from Magdalen Hall, Oxford, on 7 May 1602 at the early age of fifteen, and between 1604 and 1610 was a demy of Magdalen College. He graduated BA on 24 January 1607 and proceeded MA on 11 October 1609.

On leaving the university Godwin was appointed chief master of Abingdon School, Berkshire, where he remained for several years. While there he established an innovative scholarship for poor boys, the 'Bennett boys', and became the first fellow of the new Pembroke College. In 1614 he published, for use at Abingdon, his most famous work, *Romanae historiae anthologia: an English Exposition of the Roman Antiquities*, which appeared in many further editions. According to Samuel Clarke, he was a 'very learned man', but more gifted as a schoolmaster than as a theologian. When the eminent preacher William Twisse of Newbury got hold of the manuscript of Godwin's 'Three arguments to prove election upon foresight of faith', he dismissed them: 'our Dr Twiss quickly whipt this old Schoolmaster … and exposed him to be derided by the boys' (*Lives*, 16).

In 1616 Godwin proceeded BD, and in that year dedicated his *Synopsis antiquitatum Hebraicarum* to James Montague, bishop of Bath and Wells, to whom he had apparently been chaplain for some time. He then resigned from schoolteaching, from which he was exhausted, and obtained from Dr Montague the rectory of Brightwell, Berkshire. While there he published the very popular and well-regarded *Moses and Aaron: Civil and Ecclesiastical Rites used by the Hebrews* (1625). In 1637 he proceeded DD. Godwin died at Brightwell on 20 March 1642 and was buried in the chancel of his church, where a monument was erected by his widow, Philippa Teesdale.

W. F. WENTWORTH-SHIELDS, *rev.* S. E. MEALOR

Sources *Athenae Oxonienses … containing the life of Wood*, ed. P. Bliss, another edn, [1] (1848) • Wood, *Ath. Oxon.: Fasti*, new edn • S. Clark [S. Clarke], *The lives of sundry eminent persons in this later age* (1683), 16 • D. Jennings, *Jewish antiquities* (1766) • T. Hinde and M. St J. Parker, *The martlet and the griffen: an illustrated history of Abingdon School* (1997) • *BL cat.* • inscription, monument, Brightwell church, Berkshire

Godwin, Timothy (1670?–1729), Church of Ireland archbishop of Cashel, was born at Norwich. He began his education at the nonconformist academy of Samuel Cradock BD at Wickhambrook, Suffolk, where he was a classmate of Edmund Calamy. On leaving Wickhambrook he went to London, where he lodged with Edward Hulse MD of Aldermanbury. He apparently attended the University of Utrecht in 1692, presumably to study medicine, but after deciding on a career in the church, he entered St Edmund Hall, Oxford, where he graduated MA on 22 January 1697. He was domestic chaplain to Charles Talbot, duke of Shrewsbury, who took him abroad and also presented him with the living of Heythorpe rectory, Oxfordshire. On 1 August 1704 Godwin was appointed archdeacon of Oxford.

In October 1713 Godwin accompanied Shrewsbury to Ireland, following the latter's appointment as lord lieutenant. Godwin was a beneficiary of the Hanoverian succession and was made bishop of Kilmore in January 1715. Although he was embroiled in the conflict between the Irish and English interests within the Irish episcopate and consistently recommended the appointment of Englishmen to Irish bishoprics, he maintained friendly relations with leading Irishmen. The speaker of the Irish Commons William Conolly offered to recommend Godwin for the bishopric of Derry and he claimed to have 'had the best treatment … of any English man I know' from Archbishop King of Dublin (Wake MS, 12.94–5). After relations between the Irish and English bishops further deteriorated during the judicature dispute between the British and Irish houses of Lords (1717–20) Godwin increasingly withdrew from politics, residing in his diocese instead of Dublin. Despite the opposition of Lord Lieutenant Carteret, Godwin was appointed archbishop of Cashel in July 1727 on the recommendation of the primate, Archbishop Hugh Boulter, a post he held until his death in Dublin on 13 December 1729. Archbishop King described Godwin as 'a grave, sober, good man' (Mant, 2.286) and Godwin's letters portray a moderate man, uncomfortable with the Irish–English conflict and opposing the most severe penal laws against Catholics (ibid.).

ALEXANDER GORDON, *rev.* PATRICK MCNALLY

Sources *The whole works of Sir James Ware concerning Ireland*, ed. and trans. W. Harris, 2 vols. in 3 (1739–45, [1746]) • P. McNally, '"Irish and English interests": national conflict within the Church of Ireland episcopate in the reign of George I', *Irish Historical Studies*, 29 (1994–5), 295–314 • R. Mant, *History of the Church of Ireland*, 2 vols. (1840) • *Letters written by … Hugh Boulter … to several ministers of state*, ed. [A. Philips and G. Faulkner], 2 vols. (1769–70); repr. (1770) • E. Calamy, *An historical account of my own life, with some reflections on the times I have lived in, 1671–1731*, ed. J. T. Rutt, 2 vols. (1829) • Christ Church Oxf., Wake MS 12, fols. 94–5 • Foster, *Alum. Oxon.*
Archives Christ Church Oxf., Wake MSS

Godwin, William (1756–1836), philosopher and novelist, was born on 3 March 1756 at Wisbech, Cambridgeshire, the seventh of thirteen children of John Godwin (1723–1772), a dissenting minister, and his wife, Anne (*c.*1723–1809), the daughter of Richard Hull, a shipowner engaged in the Baltic trade. In 1758 Godwin's father moved the family from Wisbech to Debenham, Suffolk, following 'certain intrigues and cabals in the society of which he was a pastor' (*Collected Novels and Memoirs*, 1.13), only to be caught up in a conflict in the new congregation between Trinitarians and Arians which precipitated a further move in 1760 to Guestwick, near Norwich, Norfolk, where they lived until his death. The village was small and the revenue poor; to supplement their income they took in pupils to whom John Godwin taught the classics. The family's financial circumstances improved on the death of Edward Godwin (1695–1764), Godwin's paternal grandfather.

Early life and schooling William Godwin was born into a tradition of dissent: his paternal grandfather had been a dissenting minister and was a friend of Philip Doddridge, and his father and uncle Edward had been educated at Doddridge's academy at Northampton. At home Godwin was the special favourite of a relative, a Miss Godwin (later Mrs Sothren), who lived with the family and spent her time in solitary devotion and the reading of religious books. 'She made me her companion by day and by night' and 'instructed me to compose myself in sleep, with a temper as if I were never again to wake in this sublunary world' (*Collected Novels and Memoirs*, 1.12). At five he was reading *The Pilgrim's Progress* with her, together with James Janeway's *Account of the conversion, holy and exemplary lives and joyful deaths of several young children* (1671–2), and hymns, catechisms, and prayers written by Dr Isaac Watts. One of Godwin's earliest memories is of composing a poem entitled 'I Wish to be a Minister' (ibid., 15), and a favourite childhood entertainment was to preach sermons in the kitchen on Sunday afternoons. In his autobiography he recalls being reproved by his father for levity on the Lord's day when he picked up the family cat to pet it—but his father's reaction is somehow less surprising than his lapse.

Godwin was first schooled by a Mrs Gedge, an elderly woman, also 'much occupied in the concerns of religion', with whom he read the Old and New testaments. After her death in 1764 he and his brother went to Mr Akers's school in Hilderston (now Hindolverston). Akers was renowned for his penmanship, was a moderate mathematician, had a small smattering of Latin, and subscribed to the Thirty-Nine Articles. Godwin remained a religious enthusiast

William Godwin (1756–1836), by James Northcote, 1802

and dissenter—preaching to his fellow schoolchildren, identifying some as 'children of the devil' (*Collected Novels and Memoirs*, 1.24), and refusing to answer questions on the collect of the week, taken from the Book of Common Prayer. His success at this school reinforced his commitment to intellectual activity and his aversion to physical toil, and compounded his pride, for which he was frequently admonished by his father. Despite his father's strenuous opposition his resolution to become a minister never wavered, and in 1767, aided by the pleadings of Mrs Sothren, he went to board with Samuel Newton, the minister of an independent congregation in Norwich. Newton's religious doctrines were drawn from the writings of Robert Sandeman (1718–1771), a hyper-Calvinist who, 'after Calvin had damned ninety-nine in a hundred of mankind, has contrived a scheme for damning ninety-nine in a hundred of the followers of Calvin' (ibid., 30). Whereas Calvin preached faith, not works, Sandeman scorns faith and presents God as saving or damning a person solely 'according to the right or wrong judgment of the understanding' (ibid.). In later life Godwin bristled with indignation whenever he discussed Newton, comparing him in his autobiography to Caligula or Nero, and he took particular exception to Newton's readiness to use corporal punishment. So objectionable did Godwin find him that his vocation evaporated and he left him in the early summer of 1770, having fixed on becoming a bookseller. His resolution did not last: after six months at Hilderston he resumed his pupillage with Newton for a further year, during which he received better treatment. At the end of that year Newton pronounced him fit for entry into the dissenting college at Homerton and discharged him.

Despite more than twelve months' delay in his application, which Godwin spent as an assistant to Akers, Homerton was quick to identify heterodoxy, and in April 1773 he was turned down 'on suspicion of Sandemanianism' (*Collected Novels and Memoirs*, 1.41). The Hoxton Academy in London, principally run by Andrew Kippis and Abraham Rees, was more tolerant and admitted him. Hoxton was noted for its Arminianism and Arianism, but Godwin's stubborn Sandemanianism remained untouched, although he supplemented it with 'a creed upon materialism and immaterialism, liberty and necessity, in which no subsequent improvement of my understanding has been able to produce any variation' (ibid., 42). Having emerged unscathed from this part of his education, Godwin set out to practise his vocation in June 1778. He was turned down for one post and moved to Ware in Hertfordshire, where he met Joseph Fawcett, whom he identifies as one of four 'principal oral instructors' (Paul, 17), and became an enthusiast for parliamentary politics, developing a long-lasting admiration for Burke and Fox (in contrast to the high tory position he held when he left Newton, who had been a supporter of John Wilkes and liberty). He seems to have lived with no income, but with great economy, for several months in London before moving in 1780 to practise his profession at Stowmarket, Suffolk. He held the post for two years, during which time his religious beliefs underwent a revolution, moving towards deism after reading the writings of Holbach, Helvetius, and J. J. Rousseau on the suggestion of one of his parishioners. Not surprisingly, he fell into dispute with his congregation and moved to London, where Joseph Fawcett and James Marshall encouraged him to write for his living.

Early writings Godwin began work on a periodical series of English biography but his *Life of Lord Chatham* (1783) proved to be a sizeable volume without successors. He had a brief return to Christianity after reading Joseph Priestley's *History of the Corruptions of Christianity*, and a still shorter reprise as minister to a congregation at Beaconsfield, Buckinghamshire, but he was again rejected in the summer of 1783. He subsequently proposed establishing a school in Epsom, Surrey, publishing *An Account of Seminary* as a prospectus, but the plan was aborted when it failed to attract students. When he returned to London in the autumn of 1783 he found work writing for the *English Review* after he offered its proprietor, John Murray, *The Herald of Literature* (1783), a set of reviews of a series of fictitious works by, among others, R. B. Sheridan, Tom Paine, Edmund Burke, and Fanny Burney. He also produced three stylistically contrasting short novels, *Italian Letters*, *Damon and Delia*, and *Imogen*, a collection of his sermons, and a translation of the *Memoirs of Simon Lord Lovat* (not published until 1797). Throughout this period, his finances were extremely precarious: 'for the most part I did not eat my dinner, without previously carrying my watch or my books to the pawnbroker's' (*Collected Novels and Memoirs*, 1.45).

Financial security of a moderate degree was attained in

the summer of 1784 when Kippis recommended Godwin to the publisher George Robinson to write the British and foreign history section of the *New Annual Register*. Godwin held the post for nearly seven years, gaining a number of political connections—furthered by his brief involvement in the whig journal the *Political Herald* (1785–6)—and a widening range of literary acquaintance, including Thomas Holcroft (the second of Godwin's oral instructors). To supplement his income he took in pupils: an unpromising young man named Willis Webb in 1785 and, in 1788, a distant relative, Thomas Cooper, who had slight success as an actor later in life (Cooper also brought Godwin the friendship of George Dyson, his third oral instructor). In 1788 Godwin began his diary in which he recorded daily, in the barest terms, whom he met and what he had read or written. The journal was sustained until shortly before his death in 1836 and provides an invaluable if cryptic register of literary and extra-parliamentary political circles in London. He also established a pattern of work which he sustained through much of his life, rising between seven and eight, reading some classic author before breakfast, writing between nine and twelve, then reading, seeing friends, attending discussion groups such as the Philomaths of the early 1790s, and visiting the theatre. He never wrote for more than three hours, and while working on *Political Justice* experienced giddiness from his mental exertion and was warned to restrict his work accordingly (Paul, 1.79).

***Political Justice*, *Caleb Williams*, and the treason trials** In the summer of 1791 Godwin gave up his work on the *New Annual Register* and persuaded Robinson to finance him while he composed a treatise on political principles. Although proposed in the opening stages of the vigorous pamphlet controversy over the nature and legitimacy of the French Revolution, and despite his own support for the French cause and for reform in Britain, Godwin's intentions were not polemical. The work was initially conceived as a corrective to elements in Montesquieu's *L'esprit des lois* (and the abandoned first draft betrays this to a much greater extent than the final product—see Godwin's *Political and Philosophical Writings*, 4, appendix 1, and *N&Q*, 238, 1993, 456–8) but it grew in conception so that he came to hope that by 'its inherent energy and weight [it] should overbear and annihilate all opposition … placing the principles of politics on an unmoveable basis' (*Collected Novels and Memoirs*, 1.49). *An Enquiry Concerning Political Justice* was published in February 1793, only weeks after the execution of Louis XVI and with a rising tide of popular loyalism in Britain forcing the supporters of the French Revolution and reform onto the defensive. None the less, the work was an immediate success, establishing Godwin as the undaunted champion of philosophical enquiry, private judgement, and public benevolence, who predicted the gradual liberation of mankind from the shackles of government and, ultimately, mortality through the development of knowledge and the powers of the mind.

Political Justice attacks all restraint on the exercise of individual judgement and the pursuit of knowledge: promising is repudiated as incompatible with morality, marriage is denounced as the most odious of all monopolies, musical concerts as inhibiting regimentation, and the law as a procrustean bed. These conclusions derive from Godwin's view that mind is a real and efficient cause (*Political and Philosophical Writings*, 3.185). In less well-developed minds the motions of the body are the result of sensations and passions; as the mind develops thought becomes an independent link in that causal chain. To recognize that I can benefit someone is, for Godwin, to be moved, all things being equal, to do so. Crime and moral failings arise from a lack of knowledge or errors in reasoning and, as such, they require not punishment but education and enlightenment. Government and organized religion, however, perpetuate ignorance by appealing to authority and force and fraud rather than to rational argument. Invoking Hume's adage that all government rests on opinion, Godwin argues that as opinion becomes progressively enlightened the institutions of government will lose their authority and become redundant. Moreover, in his conclusion he extends his millenarian speculation to suggest that the mind will also gain increasing control of bodily functions, thereby preventing ageing and decay and enabling immortality.

Despite its optimism, *Political Justice* remains a work of real philosophical power and subtlety. One of its examples, the 'famous fire cause', in which we are invited to consider whether we would save our mother or the Archbishop Fénelon from a burning room, has become a standard topic in contemporary ethical debate (Hare) with Godwin's insistence that we should weigh the situation objectively and without regard for personal or familial affections providing a moral principle of first-order impartiality whose power is always felt even if it is also usually rejected (Barry). Moreover, his advocacy of the full and free exercise of private judgement is as eloquent a defence of individual liberty as anything in subsequent generations of liberals, including J. S. Mill. Indeed, although long classified as a work of uncompromising utilitarianism, this insistence on the prior duty of private judgement blocks the use of coercion in the name of utility and Godwin's account of pleasure roots it firmly in the development of philosophical understanding and the practice of benevolence. Moreover, both constraints suggest the continuing albeit secularized influence of his dissenting background.

Political Justice brought Godwin wide public renown and extended still further his acquaintance in the literary world and the overlapping circles of the metropolitan movement for political reform; he met Elizabeth Inchbald, Amelia Alderson, Samuel Parr, James Mackintosh, and James Barry. It also brought him the attention of younger enthusiasts, including Basil Montagu, William Wordsworth, Robert Lovell, and Samuel Taylor Coleridge (the fourth oral instructor, who discussed his pantisocracy scheme with Godwin and was a major influence on his later vacillation between atheism and deism). Although

Godwin had been critical of political organizations on the grounds that they compromise the exercise of individual judgement, he was a close associate of many members of the Society for Constitutional Information and the London Corresponding Society—not least John Horne Tooke, Thomas Holcroft, John Thelwall, and Joseph Gerrald—and was a regular visitor to those imprisoned in Newgate for their political activities in 1793 and 1794.

During this period of escalating political conflict Godwin worked on *Things as they are, or, The Adventures of Caleb Williams* (1794), the first and most successful of his six major novels and the most widely read of all his works (and the only one to be adapted for the stage, by George Coleman as *The Iron Chest*). Godwin's ambitions for the novel clearly changed over time: a new ending was added after he completed it, considerable additions and changes were made to subsequent editions, and he gave different accounts of its construction and intent at different points in his life. The most compelling description is in his reply to a hostile review in the loyalist *British Critic*. Denying that it was designed to bring 'odium upon the laws of my country', he insisted that the object was of greater magnitude:

> to expose the evils which arise out of the present system of civilised society; and to lead the enquiring reader to examine whether they are ... irremediable ... to disengage the minds of men from presuppositions, and to launch them upon the sea of moral and political enquiry. (Locke, 72)

Caleb Williams is a prototype for the novels which followed. Like them it centres on a small group of two or three characters locked in a conflicting psychological tangle, with a dramatic twist in the plot intensifying the relationships and exacerbating these conflicts. Each characterizes men as they are—predominantly, flawed aristocrats, driven by a concern with honour and rank, which leads them to act in self-destructive and self-deluding ways—and each also focuses on conflicts in a tight domestic setting so as to dramatize the effects of inequality and ignorance on their relations with others, especially women and members of other social classes.

In 1794 Godwin also wrote what is arguably his third most significant work: *Cursory Strictures on the Charge Delivered by Lord Chief Justice Eyre to the Grand Jury* attacks the charge of high treason brought against most of the leading members of the London Corresponding Society and the Society for Constitutional Information in October 1794. Godwin's utopianism, and his subsequent conflicts with reformers over tactics—especially his falling out with Thelwall over his even-handed criticism of the reviving conflict between the government and reformers in *Considerations on Lord Grenville's and Mr Pitt's Bills* (1795)—have encouraged the view that he was politically naïve, yet his apprenticeship on the *New Annual Register*, his wide-ranging early political writings, and the culminating performance of *Cursory Strictures* reveal him as an often astute analyst and rhetorician. Horne Tooke, a shrewd political activist who thought that, although *Political Justice* was written with very good intentions, 'nothing could be so foolish' (Philp, 129), famously kissed Godwin's hand to demonstrate his sense that Godwin's intervention had been decisive in his acquittal—to Godwin's great confusion, and infinite gratification (*Collected Novels and Memoirs*, 1.51).

When he toured the midlands in 1794 Godwin found: 'I was nowhere a stranger. The doctrines of that work [*Political Justice*] coincided in a great degree with the sentiments then prevailing in English Society, and I was everywhere received with curiosity and kindness' (Marshall, 121). Many years later Hazlitt confirmed Godwin's sudden prominence:

> No work in our time gave such a blow to the philosophical mind of the country as the celebrated *Enquiry* ... Tom Paine was considered for the time as Tom Fool to him, Paley an old woman, Edmund Burke a flashy sophist. Truth, moral truth, it was supposed had here taken up its abode; and these were the oracles of thought. (Philp, 6–7)

Domestic affections At the beginning of 1796, shortly after Godwin began work on a collection of essays published in 1797 as *The Enquirer*, the writer Mary Hays reintroduced him to Mary *Wollstonecraft (1759–1797). They had met briefly in 1791 at a dinner in honour of Paine held by Joseph Johnson, the publisher, but both came to hear Paine and were not much impressed by the other. Wollstonecraft had subsequently lived in revolutionary France and had had a child in a fraught relationship with Captain Gilbert Imlay, an American merchant. Godwin and Wollstonecraft's second introduction was more successful than the first. As a young man Godwin had been very much the philosopher—combining austerity of dress with an angular figure, an intense manner, and a piercing glance. While approachable, he was not socially adept and could be both easily offended and over-committed to the virtue of candour among friends. His experience with women and his social life more generally had been limited, and it was only with his increasing success that he met a wide range of clever women with political, literary, and philosophical interests—such as Helen Maria Williams, Inchbald, Alderson, Maria Reveley, Hays, and Mary Robinson. This contact had its effect. He cut his hair short in 1791 and adopted a less ministerial style of dress; he also enjoyed an increasingly extensive social life (albeit without any indication of self-indulgence), and he even experimented in 1796 with holding a dinner party (one which included Parr's daughters, Wollstonecraft, and Inchbald). Moreover, having found his candour unappreciated, he began to develop a basic competence in the art of flirtation. In the last months of 1795 and first half of 1796, Reveley, Parr's daughter Sarah, Alderson, and Inchbald were all candidates for his attention. Wollstonecraft seems not to have qualified for the honour until she called on him, unconventionally, in April 1796, and even though Godwin subsequently met and corresponded with her regularly it was only after he was turned down by Alderson in July 1796 that they became closer. They became lovers in August 1796, firmly convinced of their rectitude in following their judgement but unwilling to avow it publicly, and with Godwin painfully awkward as a lover and Wollstonecraft feeling extremely vulnerable. Their letters and notes are a touching record of a philosophical relationship gradually subverted by feelings which Godwin found hard to accommodate and Wollstonecraft hard to trust. The crisis came when Wollstonecraft became pregnant in December, and after much deliberation to reconcile their actions to their principles, they married in March 1797—to the surprise of their acquaintances, and with Wollstonecraft being cut off by both Inchbald and Mrs Sarah Siddons (ostensibly because they believed she had masqueraded as Mrs Imlay on her return from France). The couple combined households in The Polygon, near Chalk Farm; Godwin moved from the lodgings at 25 Charlton Street which he had rented since 1792, but maintained his independence by renting a study at 17 Evesham Buildings, Charlton Street, where he worked during the day. With only slight philosophical discomfort they settled into a more or less conventional domesticity. Wollstonecraft's death following childbirth in September 1797 left Godwin struggling for self-possession, and burdened with the care of the baby, Mary (later Mary *Shelley), Imlay's child, Fanny, and a succession of debts. Refusing to indulge his genuine grief, Godwin threw himself into work: in rapid succession he revised *Political Justice* for a third and final time, wrote a hurried memoir of Wollstonecraft, prepared a collection of her works, and embarked on his second major novel, *St Leon* (1799). Each work registered Godwin's changing philosophical views: the utopianism and rationalism which had so marked the first edition of *Political Justice* was first moderated slightly in the second edition (revised in 1795), but in the third (1798) edition the influence of David Hume and Adam Smith and their epistemological scepticism and emotivist ethics was increasingly recognizable. *St Leon* set up an opposition between a life of domestic existence marked by affection, candour, and mutual trust, and a solitary, mistrustful existence absorbed with the pursuit of truth and immortality through the cabbalistic arts. There is no doubt as to which Godwin endorsed, and in his later dispute with Samuel Parr over *Political Justice*'s repudiation of the domestic affections he referred Parr to the novel as containing his more fully developed views. The first edition of Godwin's memoir of Wollstonecraft in 1798, written in the first wave of his grief, presented a warm and generous picture of a woman whose willingness to follow her unconventional judgement, especially with respect to sexual mores, was candidly discussed and defended. In this case, however, Godwin badly misjudged his audience: the critical reviews attacked the book as a fundamental assault on marriage and female delicacy. The second edition was more restrained but the harm to Wollstonecraft's reputation had been done and loyalist propagandists found it a perfect target for satire.

Having been left in charge of two small children, Godwin sought help: first by employing a Miss Jones, who developed aspirations before becoming involved with Dyson; and subsequently by attempting to secure a second wife. He pursued, clumsily, Harriet Lee of Bath and, still more maladroitly, Maria Reveley immediately after the death of her husband. His fate was sealed in 1801, when a new neighbour in The Polygon leant across her balcony and asked, 'Is it possible that I behold the immortal Godwin?' (Marshall, 249). Mary Jane Clairmont (1768–1841) [*see* Godwin, Mary], whom he married on 21 December 1801, came with a son and daughter, Charles and Clara Mary Jane *Clairmont, to add to the burdens of Godwin's household. She also proved ill-tempered as a stepmother, and intolerant to Godwin's old friends, not least his long-standing amanuensis, James Marshall.

The extension of his domestic responsibilities (with William *Godwin junior, born on 28 March 1803) coincided with Godwin's declining public reputation and accelerating financial difficulties. Criticism had begun in 1798 with Thomas Green's *Examination of the New System of Morals*, P. C. Proby's *Modern Philosophy and Barbarism*, and Malthus's first edition of his *Essay on Population*. More hurtful was Mackintosh's turncoat denunciation of Godwin and his philosophy in his lectures during the opening months of 1799, and this was succeeded by Robert Hall's *Modern Infidelity Considered* and Charles Findlater's *Liberty and Equality*. Another of Godwin's former friends turned unexpectedly against him when Samuel Parr attacked him in his 1801 *Spital Sermon*, prompting the *Reply to Parr* in the following year, in which Godwin pointed to the changes since the first edition of *Political Justice* while insisting that he remained true to the basic principles of that work and claiming that he was suffering from a political reaction led by ambitious men: 'I have fallen (if I have fallen) in one common grave with the cause and love of liberty; and in this sense I have been more honoured and illustrated in my decline, than ever I was in the highest tide of my success' (*Political and Philosophical Writings*, 2.165).

Years of struggle The death of Wollstonecraft and the publication of his memoir signals a decline in Godwin's public status that was never reversed in his lifetime. While partly associated with the collapse of the radical literary culture which had received *Political Justice* so warmly, he also exacerbated his difficulties by looking in new literary directions. In 1800 he wrote a tragedy, *Antonio*, which was performed at Drury Lane on 13 December, only for the embarrassment of the performance to be immortalized in Charles Lamb's memoir (St Clair, 232–3), which was substantially more generous in tone than were the audience and critics. Undeterred, Godwin wrote a further tragedy, *Abbas, King of Persia*, in the following year, but could find no director willing to take it. *Faulkener* (1807) was only fractionally more successful, and his third major novel, *Fleetwood* (1805), did not repair his reputation. These disappointments failed to sustain the family's income and Godwin sank quickly into difficulties from which he gained only fleeting relief in the last thirty years of his life. This was despite the fact that he made considerable sums from his early work—over £1000 for *Political Justice*, several hundred pounds for *Caleb Williams*, and £600 for the laboriously researched four-volume *Life of Geoffrey Chaucer* (1803). One explanation for his impecuniousness was the size of his household, but he was also extremely generous with money when he had it, supporting his brother John for some time, and helping out friends and acquaintances as the need arose—sustaining consistency with *Political Justice* at the cost of financial prudence. In addition, he often mistook loans for gifts, and he borrowed both for himself and to help others. To establish a more secure income, Godwin, with the help of friends, established a central London bookshop and publisher's in Hanway Street under Mary Jane's name in 1805 and began writing a series of (largely historical) works for children, under assumed names (to avoid the opprobrium associated with his own), mainly Edward Baldwin and Theophilius Marcliffe. He also persuaded friends to contribute, the most famous result being the Lambs' *Tales from Shakespeare* (1807). Mary Jane Godwin, who had translated Voltaire's *Pensées* in 1802, also contributed a number of children's books to their venture. In 1808, having moved to Skinner Street, Finsbury, London, in the previous year, Godwin and Marshall opened a subscription for a juvenile library which raised about £1500. The bookshop and juvenile library absorbed most of Godwin's time. He published occasional essays but no substantial philosophical or literary work between 1805 and 1815, yet still lurched from one financial disaster to another, being reduced to writing begging letters to his former friends and acquaintances. In 1811 Francis Place agreed to act with John Lambert and Elton Hammond to settle Godwin's financial affairs on a more stable footing by raising £3000 from his supporters and friends, but Place found Godwin's financial arrangements increasingly perplexing and gave him up, concluding impatiently that there must be dishonesty at work. But the evidence is simply not there—the family's life was hardly luxurious: (Clara Mary) Jane Clairmont (later known as Claire Clairmont) in later life described her childhood home as dominated by studying and learning and by the rejection of worldly pleasures. Financial troubles were accompanied by ill health. From the late 1790s Godwin suffered occasional fits when he lost consciousness and the diary is increasingly scattered with references to his physical condition—'voided a large worm' being only the most graphic! For much of the last thirty years of his life Godwin persuaded himself and his friends that he was not long for the world.

In January 1812 Godwin received a letter from the young Percy Bysshe Shelley, who, not unlike Mrs Clairmont before him, touched Godwin's deep-seated 'love of distinction' (something he castigated throughout *Political Justice*, yet to which he frequently fell victim) by saluting him as 'a luminary too dazzling for the darkness which surrounds him' (Locke, 245). The arrival of Shelley could not have been more auspicious. As the son of a rich aristocrat, he held the promise of financial security; as a devotee of *Political Justice* he offered the prospect of a new generation to advance the philosopher's system and restore his reputation. Unfortunately, Shelley's father was unwilling to see his impetuous son squander his inheritance, and Shelley's reading of *Political Justice* had singled out the denunciation of marriage for special attention, coupling it with an atheism which Godwin now hesitated over. When they eventually met in October 1812, the two families were reciprocally impressed. This was not to last long: Godwin was too demanding, and now too set in his ways, touchy and demanding of homage, and his wife too quarrelsome; Shelley was too impetuous and rebellious, and increasingly hostile to Mrs Godwin. Moreover, Godwin soon discovered the tight financial reins Shelley's family held. When Shelley returned to London in the following year, he avoided Godwin, while simultaneously exploiting *Political Justice* and *The Enquirer* as sources for *Queen Mab*. When they did meet, Shelley agreed to help Godwin financially and the two worked towards an arrangement which would give each £3000 (at a cost to Shelley of some £8000 on the receipt of his inheritance). As negotiations reached a conclusion, in July 1814, Shelley announced that Godwin's share after costs would now be £1120 and that he was unshakeably in love with Godwin's daughter Mary. He subsequently summoned his wife Harriet to London to announce that they should establish a *ménage à trois*, but within days, betraying his promise to Godwin, eloped with Mary to France, taking her stepsister Jane with them. This disaster seemed to trigger others: Godwin's young protégé Patrick Patrickson, for whom he had arranged funding to enable him to attend Cambridge, committed suicide; Godwin's son William ran away from school and was missing for two days; and the promised solvency was dashed by Shelley's departure. When the trio returned in September, Godwin at first refused to have anything to do with them, then sought to lure Jane home, only to lose her finally to the Shelley household, where she promptly changed her name to Claire; but he was soon forced to go begging to Shelley again (through his stepson Charles). Shelley negotiated bonds to cover the more immediate of Godwin's debts, but Godwin refused to thank him and sought to deny Fanny access to Mary. Family relations continued to be extremely strained, Godwin coupling his sense of injury with demands for money, giving rise to stories that he had sold his daughters to a member of the aristocracy. In the following year, Charles Clairmont was forced to leave the country to avoid some unrevealed disgrace, Claire began a largely one-sided affair with Byron, and in October, Fanny Imlay committed suicide. Two months later the heavily pregnant body of Shelley's abandoned wife was pulled from the Serpentine. Shelley was, Godwin insisted, now free to marry Mary, and once done there was, on his part, instant reconciliation. But his domestic troubles were interminable. Claire produced a daughter Alba by Byron in January 1817, and the following year the Shelleys and Claire left for Italy. A nagging correspondence about money ended when Shelley wrote his last letter to Godwin in August 1820, nearly two years before his death by drowning.

Godwin's financial position was parlous: a writ to evict them from Skinner Street was issued in June 1818 and the case dragged on until eventual success in May 1822. In June they moved to a new shop at 195 Strand, which they occupied until forced to declare bankruptcy following a lawsuit for unpaid rent on Skinner Street in 1825. Yet amid these traumas Godwin began to write seriously again. In

1815 he published his *Lives of the Phillips*, a history of Milton's two nephews, and made a brief and rather inauspicious return to political writing in his *Letters of Verax*, praising Bonaparte and hoping that war would not recommence after his escape from Elba. In 1817 his fourth major, and darkest, novel, *Mandeville*, appeared, its setting signalling a growing interest in the history of the English civil war, and in 1820 he finally replied, at substantial length, to Malthus in *Of Population*. In the final fifteen years of his long life he produced a series of major works: his last two novels, *Cloudesley* (1830) and *Deloraine* (1833); a four-volume *History of the Commonwealth of England* (1824–8); his last set of philosophical essays, *Thoughts on Man* (1831), which showed some slight departures from his earlier thinking, especially with respect to the natural equality of mankind; and *Lives of the Necromancers* (1834), a curious history of those claiming magical powers. His *History of the Commonwealth*, like his *Lives of the Phillips* and *Chaucer*, was carefully researched from pamphlet and document holdings in the British Museum. He also wrote extensively on religion, vacillating on the existence of a deity, but remaining firmly opposed to organized religion; he left the product, his *Genius of Christianity Unveiled*, to Mary Shelley to publish. She was reluctant and it eventually appeared in 1873. If these works do not match the brilliance of Godwin's literary and philosophical career in the 1790s, they do much to show that, despite his all too human shortcomings which the pressures he faced brought to the surface in later life—his vanity, his constant importuning, and his pathetic attempts to avoid scandal and retain a veneer of respectability—he retained considerable ability as a historian and man of letters. Moreover, his last novel, *Deloraine* (1833), shows that, in reflective mode, he retained the capacity for genuine psychological insight which made *Caleb Williams* so powerful.

Significance Having lived in a twilight of public renown for some thirty years, Godwin finally received recognition of his public standing in 1833 when the whigs offered him the post of office keeper and yeoman usher of the receipt of the exchequer. The aged anarchist moved into New Palace Yard in May. There seems to be no causal connection between the whigs' abolition of his post in October 1834 and the burning down of the houses of parliament six days later. But, for once, Godwin was fortunate and found Sir Robert Peel's incoming tory government sympathetic to his plight, conscious of his literary contribution, and willing to sustain his post until his death, on 7 April 1836. At his own wish he was buried close to Mary Wollstonecraft in the cemetery of St Pancras Old Church, London.

Godwin's political 'rehabilitation' before his death was matched to some degree by a literary one. His novels *Caleb Williams*, *St Leon*, and *Fleetwood* were included among Bentley's Standard Novels in 1832 (the first has remained almost continuously in print ever since) and he had a small but important following among such novelists as Brockden Brown. His political writings drew some interest from socialists at the end of the nineteenth century, but *Political Justice* was not republished in full until 1946, when F. E. L. Priestley produced a facsimile of the third edition together with a volume of variants and notes. Important bibliographical and editorial work was undertaken in the 1960s by Burton Pollin and Jack Marken, and a critical edition of the first edition, including variants from later editions and from Godwin's manuscript, appeared as part of a collection of Godwin's writings in 1993. Charles Kegan Paul's two-volume biography, published in 1876, drew extensively on Godwin's manuscripts, and served both to remind his public of Godwin's literary and philosophical standing, and to introduce them to the less savoury details of his later wranglings with Shelley and others.

In the twentieth century, there have been several serious biographical works which have progressively leavened the negative legacy and enhanced Godwin's philosophical, political, and literary reputation—although in literary circles his political and philosophical significance does not compensate for his secondary standing within the canon of Romanticism. His novels, however, have come to command increasing respect and study, and substantial and serious reassessments of his work in ethics and political philosophy have appeared with growing frequency since the 1950s. He has also received considerable, if frequently hostile, attention from feminists because of his *Memoirs … of Mary Wollstonecraft* (1798). His archive remains a hugely important resource for historians and literary scholars of the period. With many of his major works consistently in print, Godwin's modern reputation, as the founder of philosophical anarchism, the originator of the psychological novel, and as a key figure in the British response to the French Revolution, is finally secure. MARK PHILP

Sources *Collected novels and memoirs of William Godwin*, ed. M. Philp, 8 vols. (1992), vol. 1 [incl. collected autobiographical writings] · *Political and philosophical writings of William Godwin*, ed. M. Philp, 7 vols. (1993) · D. Locke, *A fantasy of reason: the life and thought of William Godwin* (1980) · W. St Clair, *The Godwins and the Shelleys* (1989) · P. H. Marshall, *William Godwin* (1984) · M. Philp, *Godwin's 'Political justice'* (1986) · C. Kegan Paul, *William Godwin: his friends and contemporaries*, 2 vols. (1876) · H. N. Brailsford, *Shelley, Godwin and their circle* (1913) · F. K. Brown, *The life of William Godwin* (1926) · G. Woodcock, *William Godwin: a biographical study* (1946) · C. Tomalin, *The life and death of Mary Wollstonecraft* (1974) · R. Hare, *Moral thinking* (1981) · B. Barry, *Justice as impartiality* (1996) · P. Clemit, 'Extremely subtle: two recently discovered pamphlets by William Godwin', *TLS* (8 Nov 2002), 17–18

Archives Bodl. Oxf., letters; papers · Bodl. Oxf., corresp., diary, notebooks, and papers · Wordsworth Trust, Grasmere, Cumbria, essays | BL, corresp. with F. Place, Add. MSS 35145, 35152 · Bodl. Oxf., Abinger collection, MSS, corresp., and diaries · Hunt. L., letters and literary papers · NL Scot., corresp. with Archibald Constable · NYPL, New York, Carl H. Pforzheimer Collection of Shelley and His Circle, MS of Fleetwood and corresp. and material relating to *St Leon* · V&A NAL, corresp. and literary papers

Likenesses T. Kearsley, portrait, 1794, NPG · T. Lawrence, chalk drawing, 1795, BM · J. W. Chandler, portrait, 1798, Tate collection · J. Sharples, portrait, 1801, City of Bristol Museum and Art Gallery · J. Northcote, oils, 1802, NPG [*see illus.*] · P. Roberts, stipple, pubd 1821 (after T. Kearsley), BM, NPG · H. W. Pickersgill, oils, 1830, NPG · W. Brockedon, pencil and chalk drawing, 1832, NPG · S. Gent, portrait, 1832, priv. coll. · D. Maclise, drawing, 1834, V&A; repro. in W. Maginn, *A gallery of illustrious literary characters*, ed. W. Bates (1873) · A. C., lithograph, NPG · G. Dawe, mezzotint (after

J. Northcote), BM, NPG • T. Lawrence, sketch, RA • W. H. Lizars, engraving (aged sixty; after W. Nicholson, 1816), repro. in G. S. Mackenzie, *Illustrations of phrenology* (1820) • W. Ridley, engraving (after T. Lawrence) • photograph (aged sixty; after G. Harlow, 1816), NPG

Godwin, William (1803–1832), journalist, was born on 28 March 1803, the only son of William *Godwin (1756–1836), philosopher and novelist, and his second wife Mary Jane Vial (or Clairmont; 1768–1841), publisher of children's books. He was half-brother to Mary Wollstonecraft *Shelley and Clara Mary Jane *Clairmont. He was sent as a day scholar to Charterhouse at the age of eight, then in 1814 to the school of the younger Dr Burney at Greenwich. He attended a commercial school at Woodford, Essex, from 1818, and in the following year a mathematical school under Peter Nicholson. In 1820 his father tried to introduce him into Henry Maudslay's engineering establishment at Lambeth, and afterwards to apprentice him to the architect Nash.

Young William, however, was wayward and restless, but in 1823 surprised his father by producing two literary essays entitled 'Country church-yards' and 'The cottage', which were printed in the *Literary Examiner*. In the same year he became a reporter for the *Morning Chronicle*, a position which he retained until his death. From 1828 he also contributed regularly to *The Mirror of Parliament*, edited by J. H. Barrow. He tried his hand at writing a tragedy on the fate of Regulus, a Roman consul whose death in captivity at Carthage made him a national hero, and wrote a piece in the style of an opera on the story of Robin Hood, but neither had much intrinsic merit, as he himself recognized, for he was a good judge and critic of his own work. His journalistic articles were more successful and one of them, 'The executioner', was published in *Blackwood's Magazine* in 1832. About 1830 he founded a weekly Shakespeare club called The Mulberries, whose members took it in turns to produce original essays related to the interests of the club. Accordingly, Godwin produced 'On Shakespeare's knowledge of his own greatness' and 'Dissertation on the dramatic unities', both of which were printed after his death in the *Court Magazine* (1833).

Godwin died of cholera when only twenty-nine years old, on 8 September 1832, in London, leaving a widow but no children. He was buried on 9 September 1832 in the churchyard of St John the Evangelist, Waterloo Road, London. He left the manuscript of a novel, *Transfusion*, somewhat in the vein of his father's *Caleb Williams*. It was published in 1835, with a memoir prefixed by his father.

LESLIE STEPHEN, *rev.* NILANJANA BANERJI

Sources *Collected novels and memoirs of William Godwin*, ed. M. Philp, 8 vols. (1992) • W. Godwin, 'Memoir', in W. Godwin, *Transfusion* (1835) • Allibone, *Dict.* • C. Kegan Paul, *William Godwin: his friends and contemporaries*, 2 vols. (1876) • *The letters of Mary Wollstonecraft Shelley*, ed. B. T. Bennett, 1 (1980)

Godwine [Godwin], **earl of Wessex** (*d.* **1053**), magnate, was probably the son of Wulfnoth Cild, a thegn of Sussex. In 1009 Wulfnoth was accused of unspecified crimes at a muster of the fleet; he fled with twenty ships and a force sent to pursue him was destroyed in a storm. The context is irrecoverable, but his accuser, Brihtric, was a brother of Eadric Streona, ealdorman of Mercia, and John of Worcester says that the allegations were unjust. A few years later, Æthelstan (*d.* 1014), Æthelred II's eldest son, left Godwine son of Wulfnoth an estate at Compton, which had been his father's (*AS chart.*, S 1503); the names are common, but Earl Godwine later held an estate at Compton, Sussex. Wulfnoth's appellation *cild* ('child', 'young man', 'warrior') is normally used only of men of rank, and some of the lands in Sussex later in the possession of Godwine's heirs may have belonged to him.

Establishment as earl The life of King Edward, a work originally commissioned by Godwine's daughter, Queen *Edith, as a history of her family, records Godwine's gradual rise to power under Cnut. Of all his English adherents, Cnut found Godwine 'the most cautious in counsel and the most active in war'. He took him to Denmark, where he 'tested more closely his wisdom', and 'admitted [him] to his council and gave him his sister [*sic*] as wife'. (Godwine's wife, Gytha [*see below*], was actually Cnut's sister-in-law.) On returning to England, Cnut made Godwine 'earl and *baiulus* of almost all the kingdom' (*Life of King Edward*, 5–6). This picture is confirmed from other sources. Although Godwine attests as earl from 1018, he can have held only eastern Wessex before 1020, when Æthelweard, ealdorman of the western shires, was banished. The visit to Denmark was probably in 1022–3, when Cnut fell out with his regent, Thorkell the Tall, earl of East Anglia. Thorkell vanishes from sight after 1023 and Godwine takes his place at the head of the earls signing Cnut's charters; it was probably then that he became earl of all Wessex, the first man to hold such authority. It is easy to see why Godwine was valuable to the new king. Sandwich, Kent, was the usual assembly place for the English fleet at the beginning of the campaigning season, as London was its permanent base and arsenal; and a man whose land and influence lay in the south-east would be of particular use to a king whose ambitions included Scandinavia as well as England.

Royal succession and death of Alfred Ætheling The only surviving charter of Cnut in Godwine's favour is a grant of land at Polhampton, Hampshire (*AS chart.*, S 970, dated 1033), which included property in Winchester, but it was probably during Cnut's reign that he accumulated the many large, formerly royal manors which he held in Kent, Sussex, and Hampshire. His power is revealed in the succession crisis after Cnut's death in 1035. At an assembly in Oxford, Harthacnut (son of Queen Emma) was challenged by his half-brother Harold Harefoot (Cnut's son with his first wife, Ælfgifu of Northampton), backed by Earl Leofric (*d.* 1057), the thegns of Mercia and the north, and the royal fleet based at London. Since Harthacnut was in Denmark, dealing with a Norwegian invasion, his rights were upheld by Emma, supported by the royal housecarls at Winchester, 'and Earl Godwine was their most loyal man' (*ASC*, s.a. 1035, text E). A compromise recognized Harold as regent for himself and his brother; according to John of Worcester, 'the kingdom of England was divided by lot'

(John of Worcester, *Chron.*, 520–22), Harold holding the north and Harthacnut the south.

In 1036 Emma's exiled sons with her first husband, Æthelred II, took advantage of this political instability. Only the Norman writers mention Edward's unsuccessful expedition, launched from Normandy, but that of Alfred, his brother, is widely reported. He landed in Kent and was intercepted by Godwine; he then fell into the hands of Harold I (Harold Harefoot), who had him taken to Ely and blinded, after which he either died of his injuries or was killed. The sources are divided between those which implicate Godwine in the betrayal of the atheling (the C version of the Anglo-Saxon Chronicle, William of Jumièges, and John of Worcester) and those which throw the whole responsibility on Harold I (the *Encomium*, commissioned by Emma in 1041, the life of King Edward, and the D text of the chronicle: text E says nothing about it). Whatever its nature, Godwine's involvement in the death of 'the blameless ætheling' (*ASC*, s.a. 1036, text C), was to cast a shadow over his future career.

It must have been with Godwine's support that Harold I was recognized as king in 1037. Harthacnut 'was deserted because he was too long in Denmark' (*ASC*, s.a. 1037, text C), and Emma fled to Bruges. Only when Harold died, on 17 March 1040, was Harthacnut accepted as king; his first act was to have his half-brother's body dug up from its grave at Westminster and thrown into the Thames marshes. John of Worcester includes Godwine in the party sent to oversee this operation. According to John, Harthacnut 'burnt with great anger' against Earl Godwine and Bishop Lyfing (*d.* 1046), whom Ælfric, archbishop of York, had accused of responsibility for his half-brother Alfred's death. Lyfing was temporarily removed from the see of Worcester, given him by Harold I in 1038; Godwine had to buy the king's goodwill with a ship manned by eighty fully armed warriors and was required to swear publicly that he had not advised nor desired the blinding of Alfred 'but that his lord King Harold had ordered him to do what he did' (John of Worcester, *Chron.*, 530–32).

Apogee of power under Edward the Confessor Harthacnut died on 8 June 1042 and was succeeded by Alfred's full brother, Edward the Confessor. Godwine's power continued to grow through the early years of Edward's reign. An earldom based on Hereford was created for his eldest son, *Swein, in 1043; and in 1044, his second son, *Harold, was made earl of East Anglia. One of his younger sons, *Gyrth, later became earl of Wessex. On 23 January 1045 Edward married Godwine's eldest daughter, Edith; later the same year, Godwine's nephew *Beorn Estrithson received an earldom in the east midlands. In 1044 Godwine helped his friend Eadsige, the ailing archbishop of Canterbury, to secure the appointment of Siward, abbot of Abingdon (*d.* 1048), as *chorepiscopus* (assistant bishop). Eadsige is said to have given Godwine the episcopal manors of Richborough, Sundridge, Saltwood, and Langport and the lands of the secular minster at Folkestone; in the last case in return for a hefty bribe. No date is given for these donations, but it was in Edward's time that Godwine acquired the third share of the revenues of Kent (the 'third penny'), formerly accruing to the archbishop of Canterbury. St Augustine's, Canterbury, later claimed that Godwine had seized their manor of Plumstead, Kent, though the partiality shown to Godwine and his family in the E version of the Anglo-Saxon Chronicle, which was written at St Augustine's in the mid-eleventh century, suggests that this too had been granted by the abbey to the earl. The effect of these acquisitions, forced or voluntary, was to bolster Godwine's comital authority in the south-east.

The 1040s offered Godwine and his elder sons the opportunity to increase their wealth and power. The only lands known to have been acquired by Godwine at this time are Fritton, Norfolk, bequeathed by the East Anglian lady Wulfgyth (*AS chart.*, S 1539), Woodchester, Gloucestershire, which he bought for his wife, and Sandford-on-Thames, Oxfordshire, given by the king in 1050. Bosham, Sussex, was certainly in Godwine's hands before 1049 and many of the royal and comital estates entered in his or his wife's name in Domesday Book were probably acquired from Edward in the 1040s. His second son, Harold, presumably held the comital manors in East Anglia, most of which he retained after relinquishing the earldom. Swein had similar opportunities in the west: his attempt to acquire the lands of the church of Leominster backfired, but by 1051 he held some of the estates of the defunct minster at Berkeley, Gloucestershire, and had interests in Bristol.

Godwine's power would have been even greater if the monks of Christ Church had succeeded in electing his kinsman *Ælric as archbishop, after the death of Eadsige on 29 October 1050. In March 1051, however, the king quashed the election and appointed his own nominee, Robert of Jumièges, bishop of London from 1044. Robert immediately set about regaining the estates alienated to Godwine by Eadsige. The life of King Edward accuses Robert of poisoning the king's mind against Godwine, but Edward's favour to the earl was probably always a matter of expediency rather than choice. Throughout the 1040s the king was steadily building up his own following, drawn from the men who, like Robert, had accompanied him from Normandy, and he had already given the earldom of Beorn Estrithson, murdered in 1049, not to a son of Godwine, but to his own nephew, Ralph (*d.* 1057), later earl of Hereford. It was probably Robert who, as he journeyed to Rome to collect his pallium, conveyed Edward's offer of the English succession to William, duke of Normandy.

Rebellion and flight In 1051 the tensions between king and earl erupted. The life of King Edward concentrates on the role of Robert of Jumièges, but the Anglo-Saxon Chronicle gives a wider context. Osbern Pentecost, a Norman follower of Edward, had built a castle in Herefordshire, in Earl Swein's earldom, whose denizens 'inflicted every possible injury and insult on the king's men in those parts' (*ASC*, s.a. 1051, text E). A second castle was established at Clavering, Essex, in the earldom of Harold, by another foreign favourite, Robert fitz Wimarc (*ASC*, s.a. 1052, text E). It seems that a third castle was projected at Dover, in the territory of Godwine himself. Had it been completed the 'shires' of all three Godwinist earls would have been compromised.

Edward may have intended to entrust the projected castle at Dover to his one-time brother-in-law Eustace (II), count of Boulogne. The fullest version of what occurred is that of the E version of the Anglo-Saxon Chronicle, which is noticeably more hostile to Eustace, and more favourable to Godwine, than the D text. Eustace arrived in England in the late summer of 1051 and, after visiting the king, set out for Dover. He was clearly expecting trouble, for he and his men rode armed and in mail, and soon after his arrival a fight broke out in which nineteen of Eustace's followers and more than twenty townsmen were killed. Eustace went to the king 'and gave him a prejudiced account of how they had fared'. The enraged Edward ordered Godwine 'to carry war into Kent toward Dover', but the earl refused, and when the king called a council at Gloucester, 'the foreigners went beforehand to the king and accused the earls'. It was at this point, according to the life of King Edward, that Edward, urged on by Robert of Jumièges, formally charged Godwine with the murder of Alfred Ætheling (*Life of King Edward*, 20–21).

Godwine and his sons gathered their men at Beverstone, part of the manor of Berkeley, Gloucestershire, and the king summoned the levies of Earl Leofric and Earl Siward to Gloucester; Earl Ralph likewise brought the troops of his east midland earldom. The king's counsellors urged caution, saying that 'it would be a great piece of folly if they joined battle, for in the two hosts was most of what was noblest in England, and they considered that they would be opening a way for our enemies to enter the country and to cause great ruin amongst us' (*ASC*, s.a. 1051, text D). A council was called to meet at London on 25 September.

Godwine's support was now ebbing fast and when he was refused safe conduct to attend the London meeting, he decided all was lost. He and Swein, with Gytha and the younger members of the family, rode for their ships at Bosham and fled overseas to Bruges. Earl Harold, with his brother *Leofwine, made for Bristol, where Earl Swein's ship was prepared, and went to Ireland, avoiding capture by the king's forces with the connivance of Ealdred, bishop of Worcester (*d.* 1069). Edward repudiated his wife, Edith, Godwine's daughter, and appointed his own kinsman Odda of Deerhurst as earl of the western shires; it may be at this point that Herefordshire, in Swein's earldom, was given to his nephew Ralph. A contemporary chronicler comments that 'it would have seemed remarkable to everyone in England if anybody had told them that it could happen, because [Godwine] had been exalted so high, even to the point of ruling the king and all England, and his sons were earls and the king's favourites, and his daughter was married to the king' (*ASC*, s.a. 1051, text D).

Return and reconciliation Nothing shows more clearly the exceptional power of Godwine and his family than their successful return from exile in 1052. In Bruges Godwine made alliance with Baldwin (V), count of Flanders, cemented by the marriage of his third son, *Tostig, to the count's half-sister Judith (*Life of King Edward*, 24–5), while in Ireland Harold received aid from Diarmait mac Máel na mBó, king of Leinster. In the following year the family returned in force. Although Harold encountered strong opposition in the western shires, the south-east rose to support Godwine. The earls made for London, where the king had the support both of the royal ships and of earls Leofric and Siward; but once again, 'it was hateful for almost all of them to fight against men of their own race'. At a meeting of the king's council, Godwine cleared himself of the accusations brought against him, and the king restored him and his sons to land and office, and received Edith once more as his queen. Godwine's chief enemies, including Robert of Jumièges and Osbern Pentecost, were banished. Only Earl Swein did not return; he set off from Bruges on his pilgrimage to Jerusalem, dying on his return journey, on 29 September 1052.

Death and reputation Earl Godwine followed his eldest son to the grave within the year. On Easter Monday, 1053 (12 April), he was dining with the king at Winchester, when:

> he suddenly sank towards the foot-stool, bereft of speech and of all his strength. Then he was carried to the king's private room, and they thought it was about to pass off. But it was not so. On the contrary, he continued like this without speech or strength right on to the Thursday and then lost his life. And he lies there in the Old Minster; and his son Harold succeeded to his earldom. (*ASC*, s.a. 1053, text C)

Despite the glowing portrait in the life of King Edward, Godwine's posthumous reputation was not universally laudatory. He was widely accused of despoiling the church (*ASC*, s.a. 1052, text C; *Domesday Book*, 1.5v, 72, 186), though he was remembered as a benefactor of the Old Minster, Winchester, and of Abingdon Abbey (*Life of King Edward*, 30; *Chronicon monasterii de Abingdon*, 1.469). After 1066 Godwine and his sons were an easy target for criticism, and some church land may have been acquired with the assent (or at least connivance) of his ecclesiastical contemporaries. No church claimed him as founder, but he may have been patron of the secular minster at Dover, refounded in the early eleventh century. The church, St Mary-in-Castro, which preserves its eleventh-century fabric, stands within the hill-top stronghold where Count Eustace had his battle with the townsmen in 1051. If this church was connected with Godwine, his reluctance to punish the townsmen is the more understandable. Perhaps the words of Walter Map (*fl.* 1154–1210), who admired his intelligence, courage, and generosity, though disapproving of his greed, may stand as his epitaph: 'I do not say he was a good man, but a mighty, and an unscrupulous one' (Map, 230).

Gytha and the Godwine family after the conquest Gytha (*fl.* c.1022–1068), Earl Godwine's formidable wife, was the daughter of the Danish magnate Thorgils Sprakaleg. One of her brothers, Ulf, married Cnut's sister Estrith and was father to Swein Estrithson, king of Denmark (*r.* 1047–76), Beorn Estrithson, and Asbjorn. The other, Eilaf, was earl in Gloucestershire under Cnut. Gytha probably married Godwine about 1022. Her standing was high in the west of England; she was a patron of the Old Minster, Winchester, of Tavistock Abbey, and of St Olave's, Exeter. She made her husband buy her an estate at Woodchester, Gloucestershire, for her support when she stayed at Berkeley, since 'she was unwilling to use up anything from that manor because of the destruction of the abbey' (*Domesday Book*, 1.164). The Worcester monk Hemming records her anger when her eldest son, Swein, claimed that Cnut and not Godwine was his father; Gytha assembled oath-helpers from the noble ladies of Wessex to witness Godwine's paternity (*Chartularium*, 275–6). After the battle of Hastings, Gytha offered the victorious William its weight in gold for Harold's body; William of Poitiers says the duke would not give up the corpse, but William of Malmesbury believed that he gave the body unransomed to Gytha for burial at Waltham (William of Poitiers, 204–5; *De gestis regum*, 2.306). Gytha retired to live on her western estates. The earls of Wessex had a residence in Exeter, 'Irlesbyri', and Gytha seems to have been deeply involved in the events at Exeter in the spring of 1068. The citizens responded to a demand for their formal submission with an attempt to bargain with King William, who replied by besieging the city. In the event the citizens capitulated and were treated with remarkable clemency. Gytha and her companions escaped from Exeter before it was yielded. She took refuge on Flatholme in the Severn estuary, with 'many distinguished men's wives' (*ASC*, s.a. 1067, text D). Their husbands had perhaps fled to Ireland, with the sons of Harold, to seek aid from Diarmait mac Máel na mBó of Leinster, their father's old ally. Two unsuccessful raids were launched from Ireland, one on Bristol and Somerset in the summer of 1068, and the other on south Devon a year later. It was about this time that Gytha left England for good, taking with her 'a great store of treasure' (Ordericus Vitalis, *Eccl. hist.*, 2.224–5). She went first to Flanders and then to the court of her nephew King Swein. She was accompanied by her daughter Gunnhild (who may have died in Flanders) and Harold's daughter Gytha, who married Vladimir Monomakh (*d.* 1116/1125), prince of Smolensk and (later) of Kiev. The date of Gytha's death is nowhere recorded.

ANN WILLIAMS

Sources *ASC* • F. Barlow, ed. and trans., *The life of King Edward who rests at Westminster*, 2nd edn, OMT (1992) • A. Campbell, ed. and trans., *Encomium Emmae reginae*, CS, 3rd ser., 72 (1949) • John of Worcester, *Chron.* • Ordericus Vitalis, *Eccl. hist.*, vol. 2 • F. Barlow, *Edward the Confessor* (1970) • W. Map, *De nugis curialium*, ed. E. S. Hartland, trans. M. R. James, Honourable Society of Cymmrodorion, Cymmrodorion Record Series, 9 (1923) • A. Williams, 'Land and power in the eleventh century: the estates of Harold Godwineson', *Anglo-Norman Studies*, 3 (1980), 171–87, 230–34 • R. Fleming, 'Domesday estates of the king and the Godwines: a study in late Saxon politics', *Speculum*, 58 (1983), 987–1007 • R. Fleming, *Kings and lords in conquest England* (1991) • S. Keynes, 'Cnut's earls', *The reign of Cnut*, ed. A. R. Rumble (1994), 43–88 • D. G. J. Raraty, 'Earl Godwine of Wessex: the origins of his power and his political loyalties', *History*, new ser., 74 (1989), 3–19 • T. Tatton-Brown, 'The churches of Canterbury diocese in the eleventh century', *Minsters and parish churches*, ed. J. Blair (1988), 105–18 • S. Keynes, 'The æthelings in Normandy', *Anglo-Norman Studies*, 13 (1990), 173–205 • H. J. Tanner, 'The expansion of the power and influence of the counts of Boulogne under Eustace II', *Anglo-Norman Studies*, 14 (1991), 251–86 • S. Keynes, *An atlas of attestations in Anglo-Saxon charters, c.670–1066* (privately printed, Cambridge, 1993) • A. Williams, *The Normans and the Norman conquest* (1995) • P. A. Clarke, *The English nobility under Edward the Confessor* (1994) • *The Gesta Normannorum ducum of William of Jumièges, Orderic Vitalis, and Robert of Torigni*, ed. and trans. E. M. C. van Houts, 2 vols., OMT (1992–5) • J. Stevenson, ed., *Chronicon monasterii de Abingdon*, 2 vols., Rolls Series, 2 (1858) • Thomas of Elmham, *Historia monasterii S. Augustini Cantuariensis*, ed. C. Hardwick, Rolls Series, 8 (1858) • F. R. H. Du Boulay, *The lordship of Canterbury: an essay on medieval society* (1966) • J. Morris, ed., *Domesday Book: a survey of the counties of England*, 38 vols. (1983–92), vol. 4 [Hampshire] • N. Brooks, *The early history of the church of Canterbury: Christ Church from 597 to 1066* (1984) • *Hemingi chartularium ecclesiæ Wigorniensis*, ed. T. Hearne, 2 vols. (1723) • *Willelmi Malmesbiriensis monachi de gestis regum Anglorum*, ed. W. Stubbs, 2 vols., Rolls Series (1887–9) • Guillaume de Poitiers [Gulielmus Pictaviensis], *Histoire de Guillaume le Conquérant / Gesta Gulielmus ducis Normannorum et regis Anglorum*, ed. R. Foreville (Paris, 1952)

Godwyn, Charles (1701–1770), antiquary and book collector, was born at Thornbury, in Gloucestershire, and was baptized there on 9 March 1701, the first child of Samuel Godwyn (*c.*1668–1705?), who in 1702 succeeded his uncle Scudamore Godwyn as vicar of Wapley and rector of Filton, and his wife, Elizabeth Tipton, formerly of Bristol. The last in a veritable tribe of Godwyn clerics descended from Thomas Godwin, bishop of Bath and Wells, Charles had a brother, Samuel Godwyn (*d. c.*1747), who was a Bristol surgeon. Having been educated in Bristol, Charles was admitted to Balliol College, Oxford, in 1718, graduated BA in 1721 (MA, 1724; incorporated at Cambridge, 1734), and was elected a probationer fellow of Balliol in 1722. He was ordained deacon and priest at Oxford in 1727 and 1728 respectively, and graduated BD in 1740. Though he held in turn the Balliol rectories of Riseholme, Lincolnshire (1746–52), All Saints, Colchester (1752–3), and Marks Tey, Essex (from 1753), he resided in Balliol all his adult life.

Godwyn took a full part in the business of the college—which was relatively desultory in his time—and was instrumental in obtaining a major benefaction from Henry Fisher (*c.*1693–1773), vicar of Bere Regis, Dorset, which enabled the construction of a new building. He acquired a reputation as a painstaking tutor; Frederick, the profligate son of the poet Edward Young, was one of his charges. In other respects Godwyn's life was remarkably parallel to that of his eccentric colleague Joseph Sanford, devoted to private study and antiquarian pursuits. Like Sanford he was intimate with Benjamin Kennicot. Also like Sanford he published nothing but contributed freely to the work of others, especially John Hutchins and Richard Chandler, both of whom acknowledged the joint contribution of Sanford and Godwyn in prefaces to their books. And it was to his 'old friends' Sanford and Godwyn jointly that George Coningesby (*c.*1693–1766), rector of Pencombe, in Herefordshire, and a kindred spirit, left his extensive library of printed books and manuscripts in trust for Balliol. Godwyn also corresponded with other antiquarian scholars such as Philip Morant and Charles Gray (1696–1782). A selective and scholarly numismatist, at some stage he acquired the coin cabinet of Heneage Finch, fifth earl of Winchilsea (*d.* 1726). By the end of his life he had amassed and catalogued over 3000 coins, mostly Greek, Roman, and English, starting with the early Saxon kings, and medals, including a notable long series of papal medals.

Godwyn was fully active until shortly before his death but in his later years he was troubled by fits, induced, he thought, by taking tea. He collapsed in his rooms on 23 April 1770, while his servant was out getting some cheese-cakes, and died soon afterwards on the same day despite, or perhaps because of, the efforts of a physician to revive him by opening a vein in his temples. On 26 April, at his request, he was buried with minimal ceremony in Wolvercote church, some 2 miles from Oxford city centre. He had no known connection with Wolvercote church or village and probably chose it because it was an obscure rural location but not inconvenient for the six college servants whom he asked to carry him to his grave for a guinea each. An anonymous vacuous poetic lament was published in the *Reading Mercury and Oxford Gazette* on 14 May.

Godwyn made numerous modest bequests to friends and servants, including 20 guineas for the son of Thomas Bustin, who looked after his horse, and to Mr Robert Ashfield, a local parishioner, whom he asked to burn his papers, apart from his catalogues and recent accounts. There was a group of three family portraits in his rooms which he left to his cousin Mrs Mary Bromfield of Conduit Street, London, but they are still at Balliol. His books (about 1600 volumes, mostly on historical subjects), pamphlets (mostly on theological and literary subjects), coins, and medals he left to the Bodleian Library. He appointed the university itself to be his executor and residual beneficiary. About two-thirds of his library, including several important works of David Hume which had not been previously acquired, were retained by the Bodleian. As he had instructed, the books not required were sold, Fletchers' bookshop in the Turl disposing of the remainder in 1773 after members of the university had had their pick; the pamphlets formed the nucleus of a collection still known as the Godwyn pamphlets, numbering, with subsequent additions, over 30,000; the coins and medals, with Godwyn's meticulous catalogues, were transferred to the Ashmolean Museum in 1920. The residue of the estate, about £1000, was invested for the benefit of the Bodleian. There is no memorial to Godwyn at Wolvercote, or in Balliol, but his name is on the great marble Bodleian benefactors' tablet. JOHN JONES

Sources J. Jones, *Balliol College: a history*, 2nd edn (1997), 154–69 • Nichols, *Lit. anecdotes*, 8.224–60 • C. Godwyn, deposition concerning the mastership election of 1726, Balliol Oxf., D.3.19b, fols. 233–60 • R. Chandler, *Marmora Oxoniensia* (1763), preface • J. Hutchins, *The history and antiquities of the county of Dorset*, 2nd edn, ed. R. Gough and J. B. Nichols, 4 (1815), xii–xxii • W. D. Macray, *Annals of the Bodleian Library, Oxford*, 2nd edn (1890), 263–4, 484 • I. Philip, *The Bodleian Library in the seventeenth and eighteenth centuries* (1983), 101–2, 131 • J. Hutchins, preface, *The history and antiquities of the county of Dorset* (1774) • C. Godwyn, letters to John Hutchins, 1757–69, Bodl. Oxf., MS Top. Gen. d.2, fols. 92–141 • H. H. E. Craster, *History of the Bodleian Library, 1845–1945* (1952), 116 • D. S. Porter, *The Bodleian benefactors' tablet* (1989), 17 • 'A catalogue of the remainder of the late Mr Godwin's library', 1773, Bodl. Oxf., MS Gibson 284(9) • C. Godwyn, catalogues, lists; other material on his coins and medals, AM Oxf., Heberden coin room, Arch. Bodl. 8–22 • C. Godwyn, letters to Charles Gray, 1752–65, Essex RO, D/DRb 21, D/DRg 4/44–7 • will, PRO, PROB 11/962, sig. 434 • will, 1687, Bristol RO [Susanna Godwyn] • will, proved, 1702, Glos. RO [Scudamore Godwyn] • will, proved, 1747, Bristol RO [Samuel Godwyn] • George Coningesby, will, PRO, PROB 11/921, sig. 298 • parish register, Thornbury [baptism], 9/3/1701

Archives AM Oxf., autograph catalogues and lists, and other material concerning his coins and medals, Arch. Bod. 8–22 • Balliol Oxf., catalogue entries for George Coningesby's printed books, in annotated interleaved copy of the Bodleian Library catalogue as printed in 1738 • Bodl. Oxf., autograph catalogues and lists, and other material concerning his library; papers relating to his collection of coins, library records e. 423–425 | Balliol Oxf., archives, deposition concerning the mastership election of 1726, D.3.19b, fols. 233–60 • Bodl. Oxf., letters to John Hutchins and Richard Gough, MS top. gen. d. 2, fols. 92–141 • Bodl. Oxf., research notes by subject for John Hutchins, MS Gough Dorset 12, fols. 237–69 • Essex RO, letters to Charles Gray, D/DRb 21, D/DRg 4/44–7

Wealth at death £5000–£10,000; specific bequests totalled about 250 guineas; library probably £1000–£2000 in value; coins and medals probably over £2000 in value; residue about £1000

Godwyn [Godwin], **Morgan** (*bap.* **1640**, *d.* **1685x1709**), Church of England clergyman and missionary, was baptized at English Bicknor, Gloucestershire, on 2 December 1640. The son of Morgan Godwin LLD (1602/3–1655x60), rector of that parish, and his wife, Elizabeth (*fl.* 1640–1696), the younger Godwyn was one of at least five children. He was the great-grandson and grandson of bishops: Thomas *Godwin (1517–1590), bishop of Bath and Wells, and Francis *Godwin (1562–1633), successively bishop of Llandaff and of Hereford. His father was also archdeacon of Shropshire and a prebendary in the diocese of Hereford and subsequently vicar of Lydney in Gloucestershire. Little is known of Godwyn's childhood and early education, though his father in the 1650s, after his ejection during the civil war, kept a school at Newland, Gloucestershire. Godwyn was admitted to Brasenose College, Oxford, in March 1661, matriculated in June 1662, and, having transferred to Christ Church, graduated BA in March 1665. Soon after his graduation he was ordained and served for a short spell as vicar of Wendover, Buckinghamshire. In 1666 Godwyn crossed to Virginia, where he first took up the living of Marston parish, before moving to Stafford parish, probably in 1668 or 1669.

Although Godwyn offered no objection to the enslavement of Africans in Virginia, and saw no inconsistency between Christianity and bondage, he insisted that the colony's planters must take seriously their responsibilities as Christian masters and promote the spiritual welfare of their slaves. These forcefully expressed sentiments deeply offended his more eminent parishioners, who consistently refused to sanction all attempts to convert their African slaves. In 1670 or thereabouts, following an acrimonious lawsuit, ostensibly over a missing horse, Godwyn decided to leave Virginia and to continue his missionary work in Barbados, where he found similar attitudes among Barbadian planters. It was during the 1670s, before his return to England in 1679 or 1680, that he began composing the works that would form the centrepiece of his campaign to persuade metropolitan English people, and particularly the Church of England, that they must set about converting enslaved Africans and Native Americans everywhere in British America.

In 1680 Godwin became rector of Woldham, Kent, and in 1681 vicar of Bulkington, Warwickshire. During the

1680s, at a time when he was living in or near London, he published two lengthy pamphlets: *The Negro's & Indians Advocate, Suing for their Admission into the Church* (1680) and *A Supplement to the Negro's & Indians Advocate* (1681). A third tract, *The Revival, or, Directions for a sculpture describing the extraordinary care and diligence of our nation in publishing the faith among infidels in America and elsewhere*, published in London in 1682, is sometimes attributed to Godwyn. In 1685 he arranged to publish a shorter piece on the same subject, a sermon entitled *Trade Preferr'd before Religion*, which he had preached in Westminster Abbey and several other London churches. Although nothing more was heard from him after 1685, his published works and sermons were influential in bringing about the formation, in 1701, of the Society for the Propagation of the Gospel in Foreign Parts.

Morgan Godwyn's personal life, both in Virginia and Barbados during the 1660s and 1670s and after his return to England, is shrouded in mystery. There is no evidence that he married, nor is there any record of the exact date, place, and cause of his death. He seems to have died, probably in or near London, at some point between 1685 and 1709. BETTY WOOD

Sources A. T. Vaughan, *Roots of American racism* (1995) • G. M. Brydon, *Virginia's mother church* (1947) • Wood, *Ath. Oxon.*, new edn • Foster, *Alum. Oxon.* • *IGI* • [C. B. Heberden], ed., *Brasenose College register, 1509–1909*, 2 vols., OHS, 55 (1909) • *Walker rev.*, 173–4

Goehr, Walter (1903–1960), composer and conductor, was born on 28 May 1903 in Berlin, the elder of the two sons of Julius Goehr (1872–1948), factory owner, and his wife, Thekla Mendelsohn (*d.* 1931). His parents were both Jewish. His early musical talent showed itself in the fact that, even preceding his formal education in the composition class of Arnold Schoenberg at the Berlin Hochschule für Musik (1921–4), he had already worked as a conductor of operetta in Berlin theatres. His compositions were performed in Germany until he left that country in 1932, and he was director of music in the theatre of Erwin Piscator. His compositions included a symphony (performed in Kiel), a radio opera, *Malpopita* (which was in fact the first ever written for the medium), and 'Amerikanisches Songbuch', *Pep*, in collaboration with Lion Feuchtwanger (which was performed at the Baden-Baden Music Festival), chamber music, and songs. Although his student works reflect the influence of his teacher, Schoenberg, he gradually moved into the kind of projects associated with Paul Hindemith, Hanns Eisler, and Kurt Weill. He mainly worked in the theatre, and for the influential Berlin Radio. On 5 August 1930 he married pianist and photographer Laelia Rivlin (*b.* 1908), from whom he was divorced in 1953, having had a son, the composer Alexander Goehr.

Goehr lost his job at Berlin Radio in 1932 because of his Jewish origins, but at that moment he was invited to London to work as music director for the Gramophone Company (later EMI), and he emigrated with his wife and newly born son. At the Gramophone Company he was responsible for the preparation of the musical materials for recordings, he assisted conductors and artists, and he accompanied (often unacknowledged on the record labels) singers, among them Gigli and John McCormack. He assisted Stravinsky at the first recording of *Les noces*, and the story (possibly apocryphal) is told that, because Stravinsky was unable to get one of the takes right, after he had left London the cast was reassembled, and Goehr re-recorded it. Among his own acknowledged recordings of the pre-1939 period were the first performance on record of Bizet's symphony, Tchaikovsky's first piano concerto with Egon Petri, and Rachmaninoff's second piano concerto with Benno Moiseiwitsch. He also contributed to the then revolutionary recorded history of music with the first ever recording of a work by Edgard Varèse (his *Intégrales*).

In the late 1930s Goehr appeared frequently on BBC broadcasts with his own Orchestra Raymonde. This consisted of some of London's finest players (including Alfredo Campoli, Reginald Kell, and Arthur Cleghorn). Using an innovatory chamber orchestra influenced by Schoenberg, Hindemith, and Stravinsky, he created a repertory of arrangements ranging from Haydn and Mozart to Mussorgsky, Bizet, and even Duke Ellington. It was probably the success of this venture that obtained for him his regular work during the Second World War, writing and conducting much of the music used in wartime radio programmes, such as *Marching On* and *Shadow of the Swastika*. The BBC team who made these programmes, directed by Lawrence Gilliam, was to become the features department after the war, and Goehr wrote music for and conducted a great number of their later programmes, including those written by Louis Macneice, Wyndham Lewis, and others. In addition, he worked on a number of British films, including *Colonel Blimp* (1943), *A Matter of Life and Death* (1946, as music director), and David Lean's *Great Expectations* (1946, as composer). During the war he used the English-sounding pseudonym George Walter.

In the later war years and in the immediate post-war years Goehr achieved considerable success as a conductor of modern and old music. The Walter Goehr concerts at the Wigmore Hall included works by Schoenberg, Bartók, and Stravinsky, as well as the first performances of Britten's *Serenade* (1943, with Peter Pears and Dennis Brain) and Tippett's *Concerto for Double String Orchestra*. At the Central Hall, Westminster, he introduced London to Tippett's *A Child of our Time* (1944) and to the Monteverdi *Vespers* of 1610. The choir was from Morley College, and it was Goehr's work with Tippett there that led to their close collaboration over a number of years, culminating in the dedication to Goehr of the 'Ritual Dances' from *A Midsummer Marriage*. In 1946 Goehr returned to the BBC as conductor of the Theatre Orchestra, remaining there until 1949.

The last decade of Goehr's life was characterized, on the one hand, by an expansion of his activity as a symphonic conductor and recording artist, and on the other by his pioneering work as an editor of performing editions of works by Monteverdi. After the performance of the 1610 *Vespers* at the Royal Festival Hall in London as part of the

(1951) Festival of Britain, he continued frequently to perform the *Vespers* in his own version, and it was owing to these performances that the work became widely popular. His edition of *L'incoronazione di Poppaea* was performed at the Hamburg State Opera and elsewhere.

As a symphonic conductor working in Britain, Europe, and South America, Goehr was known for his remarkable ability to make unusual programmes, juxtaposing old and new, and for his advocacy of contemporary music, giving first British performances to works by Mahler, Schoenberg, Webern, Messaien, and Hindemith, as well as Tippett and Britten, and for his often provocative editions and performances of seventeenth- and eighteenth-century works by Gabrieli, Purcell, Monteverdi, Handel, and Bach. At the same time he recorded a wide repertory of works for the American Concert Hall label, associated in Europe with Jeunesses Musicales, winning the grand prix du disque. In addition to his activities as a practising musician, he was a thought-provoking teacher, with a unique insight (for his time) into analytic techniques and their application to performance practice. Goehr was married for a second time on 22 November 1957; his wife was Jean Morrison (*b.* 1927), a secretary and publisher. He died in the city hall, Sheffield, on 4 December 1960, having finished conducting a performance of Handel's *Messiah*. He was buried at Paddington new cemetery, Mill Hill, London. ALEXANDER GOEHR

Sources private information (2004) · personal knowledge (2004) · P. Gradenwitz, *Arnold Schönberg und seine Meisterschule Berlin, 1925–33* (1998), 69–73 · *The Times* (5 Dec 1960) · *New Grove* · R. Palmer, *British music* (1950) · M. Tippett, *Those twentieth century blues* (1991); repr. (1994)

Archives BL NSA, performance recordings | SOUND BL NSA, oral history interview · BL NSA, performance recordings

Wealth at death £9775 5s. 1d.: probate, 15 June 1961, *CGPLA Eng. & Wales*

Goff, Helen Lyndon [*pseuds.* P. L. Travers, Pamela Lyndon Travers] (**1899–1996**), children's writer, was born on 9 August 1899 in Maryborough, Queensland, Australia. She was the first of the three children of Travers Robert Goff (*d.* 1907), a rancher from Ireland, and Margaret Morehead (*d.* 1928), the granddaughter of Robert Archibald Morehead, who moved to Australia in 1841 as manager of the Scottish Australian Company and whose considerable holdings included Bowen Downs, the largest pastoral station in Australia. Virtually nothing more is known of her parents. After her father's death she moved with her mother and two younger sisters to live with her great-aunt, Christina Saraset, in Bowral, south of Sydney in the southern highlands of New South Wales. She attended a local grammar school until the age of ten, then was sent to Normanhurst boarding-school in Sydney. As a child she wrote poetry and newspaper-style articles, and during her adolescent years began publishing articles and poems for a variety of Australian magazines and newspapers, including *The Bulletin* and *The Triad*; for two years she also wrote a human interest column for a daily Sydney newspaper. Upon completing school, she worked in the cashier's office of the Australian Gas and Light Company and then

Helen Lyndon Goff [P. L. Travers] (**1899–1996**), by Jane Bown, pubd 1982

had a brief stint in the theatre, acting and dancing with the Alan Wilkie Shakespearian Touring Company. In 1924 she left for London, where from 1924 to 1928 she published poems in the *Irish Statesman* under the encouragement of its editor, George Russell (A. E.). In the mid-1920s she travelled to Fontainebleau, near Paris, where she became a disciple of Russian occultist George Ivanovich Gurdjieff, and to Switzerland to pursue the teachings of psychologist Carl Gustav Jung. In the 1930s she lived in Ireland, working as a drama critic for the *New English Weekly* and publishing poetry and travel essays, including her book *Moscow Excursion* (1934). During this time she became close friends with George Russell and also met the poet William Butler Yeats.

Goff took as her pseudonym the name Pamela Lyndon Travers, usually in the form P. L. Travers. Her first literary success came in 1934, when she published *Mary Poppins*. Translated into over twenty languages, the book became an instant classic of modern children's literature, while Mary Poppins became 'the world's best-known nanny' (Hunt, 214). The book's popularity and the continued success of its sequels can be attributed to Goff's quirky view of the world and her deft incorporation of the elements of myth, fairy tale, and mysticism into everyday life. *Mary Poppins Comes Back* was published in 1935, and was followed by *Mary Poppins Opens the Door* (1944), *Mary Poppins in the Park* (1952), *Mary Poppins from A to Z* (1963), *Mary Poppins in the Kitchen* (1975), *Mary Poppins in Cherry Tree Lane* (1982), and *Mary Poppins and the House Next Door* (1989). While the series has been considered children's literature since its inception, Goff disliked this label, arguing that the distinctions between literature for children and adults were blurred at best. Whenever asked about the inspiration for the character of Mary Poppins, she commented: 'I never for one moment believed that I invented her. Perhaps she invented me' (Bergsten, 71).

Despite her literary success, Goff was intensely private about her personal life, and once said that she most identified with Anonymous as a writer. She often voiced her doubts 'that biographies are of any use at all' (Cott, 227), and she granted an interview to the scholar Patricia Demers in 1988 on condition that enquiry into her personal life was forbidden. Throughout her life she remained resolute in her belief about the pointlessness of biographical data and explanations in the quest for literary meaning. Although she never married, during the war years Goff adopted a son, about whom few details are known.

In 1940 Goff left for the United States and lived there until 1945 as a wartime evacuee. During this time she published *I Go by Sea, I Go by Land* (1941), which focused on two children's experiences while being evacuated to America during the Second World War, along with a series of privately circulated new year's gift books, including *Aunt Sass* (1941), *Ah Wong* (1943), and *Johnny Delaney* (1944). She also travelled west on the invitation of her friend John Collier, an administrator for Indian affairs, and stayed on a number of Navaho, Hopi, and Pueblo reservations. Before leaving she was rewarded with a secret Pueblo name, something which honoured her tremendously because of her feeling 'that names are a part of a person, a very private thing to each one' (Burness and Griswold, 227).

In 1945 Goff returned to England and for the next twenty years continued to publish novels, essays, and lectures. *The Fox at the Manger*, a Christmas story, appeared in 1962. In 1964 *Mary Poppins* was made into a Walt Disney film starring Julie Andrews and Dick Van Dyke. While the film lacked the depth and the mythological elements of the book—despite her involvement with the production, Goff was not pleased with the end result—it was a tremendous commercial success, and became a catalyst for renewed critical interest in her work. Modern commentary on the Mary Poppins series has been uneven: while John Rowe Townsend praised its paradoxical humour, he also voiced concerns about the series' propagating illusions about English domestic life. In contrast, Jane Yolen praised Goff for her creation of strong mythical worlds for young readers. In the 1970s several critics became alarmed at apparent elements of racism, sexism, and classism in the 'Bad Tuesday' chapter of *Mary Poppins*. While Goff staunchly maintained that she intended no offence to anyone, in 1981 she revised the chapter, exchanging non-gendered, raceless, and classless animals for the original human characters.

From 1965 to 1977 Goff again lived in the United States, working as writer-in-residence at both Radcliffe College in Cambridge, Massachusetts (1965–6), and Smith College in Northampton, Massachusetts (1966), and as Clark lecturer at Scripps College in Claremont, California (1970). For the next two decades she continued to publish essays and novels, including *Friend Monkey* (1971), a three-part novel based on the Indian monkey god Hanuman, *About the Sleeping Beauty* (1975), and *Two Pairs of Shoes* (1980). In 1977 she was appointed OBE for her contribution to literature, and in 1978 she received an honorary doctorate of humane letters from Chatham College in Pittsburgh, Pennsylvania.

From 1976 until her death Goff was contributing editor to the American journal *Parabola: the Magazine of Myth and Tradition*, something which perhaps reflected her own quest for meaning. This quest also appeared in her pursuit of a number of spiritual movements throughout her life, ranging from Christianity through Zen Buddhism to Sufism, a branch of Islamic mysticism. Myth and fairy tale recur throughout her later works, and she was particularly aware of the importance of these elements in her life. However, the theme that permeated all her work and, by extension, her life was connectedness, and she borrowed E. M. Forster's phrase 'only connect' to describe her views of the world and her place in it. An essay by this title appears as the concluding piece in her *What the Bee Knows: Reflections on Myth, Symbol and Story* (1989), a collection of articles originally written for *Parabola* and her last published book. The phrase is a fitting epitaph. She died at her home, 29 Shawfield Street, Chelsea, London, on 23 April 1996, St George's day; the funeral was held at Christ Church, Chelsea, on 1 May, May day. With her interest in myth and meaning, the two days are curiously significant. At her request, the final place for her ashes is unknown: she did not want it to become a shrine for Mary Poppins admirers. ANNE HIEBERT ALTON

Sources L. Anemaat, *Guide to the papers of P. L. Travers in the Mitchell Library, State Library of New South Wales* (1991) • S. Bergsten, *Mary Poppins and myth* (1978) • E. Burness and J. Griswold, 'The art of fiction LXXIII: P. L. Travers', *Paris Review*, 86 (1982), 210–29 • H. Carpenter and M. Prichard, *The Oxford companion to children's literature* (1984) • J. Cott, 'The wisdom of Mary Poppins: afternoon tea with P. L. Travers', *Pipers at the gates of dawn: the wisdom of children's literature* (1983) • P. Demers, *P. L. Travers* (1991) • E. D. Draper and J. Koralek, eds., *A lively oracle: a centennial celebration of P. L. Travers, creator of Mary Poppins* (1999) • L. Hendrickson, *Children's literature: a guide to criticism* (1987) • P. Hunt, ed., *Children's literature: an illustrated history* (1995) • K. M. Klockner, 'Travers, P. L.', *Children's books and their creators*, ed. A. Silvey (1995), 648–9 • A. C. Moore, 'Mary Poppins', *Horn Book*, 11 (Jan–Feb 1935), 6–7 • R. Newquist, 'P. L. Travers', *Conversations* (1967), 423–33 • *The Gazette* (24 April 1996) • *The Guardian* (24 April 1996) • *The Times* (24 April 1996) • N. Philip, 'The writer and the nanny who never explain', *Times Educational Supplement* (11 June 1982), 42 • A. V. Schwartz, '*Mary Poppins* revisited: an interview with P. L. Travers', *Interracial Books for Children Bulletin*, 5/3 (1974), 1–5 • J. R. Townsend, *Written for children: an outline of English-language children's literature*, 6th edn (1990) • P. L. Travers [H. L. Goff], 'Only connect', *What the bee knows: reflections on myth, symbol and story* (1989), 285–303 [1967] • J. Yolen, 'Makers of modern myths', *Horn Book*, 51 (1975), 496–7 • d. cert.

Archives Mitchell L., NSW, guide to the MSS of P. L. Travers

Likenesses J. Bown, photograph, pubd 1982, priv. coll. [*see illus.*] • E. Agar, drawing, repro. in Demers, *P. L. Travers* • J. Bauer, photograph, repro. in Cott, 'The wisdom of Mary Poppins'

Goffe, John (*b.* in or before **1610**, *d.* **1661**), Church of England clergyman, was the son of Stephen Goffe (*b.* 1574/5), who had been deprived in 1605 of his rectorship of the parish of Bramber, Sussex, for his puritan sympathies, and his wife, Deborah Weston or West (1586/7–1626). John's brothers included Stephen *Goffe (1605–1681), a Roman Catholic priest and royalist agent, and William *Goffe (*d.* 1679?), the regicide and major-general. After entering Merton College, Oxford, in 1624, John Goffe matriculated as a demy at Magdalen College on 13 April 1627, when, according to Anthony Wood, he was seventeen or more. He graduated BA on 13 December 1628, became a probationary fellow of Magdalen the following year and a perpetual fellow on 29 July 1630, and proceeded MA on 25 June 1631. In 1632 he was incorporated MA at Cambridge. At Magdalen he required his students to join him daily for Bible reading, prayer, and the recitation of sermons they had heard. He and the puritan Robert Harris were close; he read philosophy to Harris and the latter read Greek to him, and they jointly studied Hebrew and Calvin's *Institutes*. Goffe became embroiled in scandal on 26 August 1634 when he was charged with killing Joseph Boyse of Magdalen College, but was acquitted.

On 26 September 1642 Goffe was appointed vicar of St Stephen's, Hackington, Kent, but he subsequently refused the covenant and was imprisoned at Canterbury as a delinquent. On 27 February 1645 the committee for plundered ministers admitted Robert Beake to the living, though the deputies lieutenant intruded Richard Culmer. Following his release Goffe returned to Magdalen where on 31 May 1651 he wrote an epistle to Edward Simson's *Chronicon historiam catholicam complectens* (1652). Through the influence of his brother William, then a colonel, he became rector of Norton, near Sittingbourne, Kent, on 13 March 1652. At the Restoration he petitioned the king for a prebend at Canterbury, but the vacancies had already been filled. However, as chaplain of the earl of St Albans he received a dispensation on 17 November 1660 to hold the livings of Norton and Hackington, and the next month he was created DD. In 1661 he attended convocation and published his only book, *Ecclesiae Anglicanae threnodia*, in which he denounced what he perceived to be the recent Anabaptist tyranny and the slippery slope that led from presbyterians to Independents and on to Anabaptists, Antinomians, and libertines.

Goffe was in poor health on 2 July 1659 when he made his will, leaving his land in Kent, his property leased from Magdalen College, and his personal possessions to his wife, Mary, during her lifetime, and thereafter to their sons, John, Stephen, and Charles. He died on 20 November 1661 and was buried six days later in the chancel of St Alphage's, Canterbury. Samuel Clarke observed that he 'was noted for a very good *Logician* and Disputant, but withal he was accounted a *Puritan*' (Clarke, 275). Unlike his brothers he steered a moderate course throughout his career.

RICHARD L. GREAVES

Sources Wood, *Ath. Oxon.*, new edn, 3.524–5 • will, PRO, PROB 11/306, sig. 198 • *Walker rev.*, 216 • *CSP dom.*, 1660–61, 222 • S. Clarke, *A collection of the lives of ten eminent divines* (1662), 275–6 • Foster, *Alum. Oxon.* • *DNB* • PRO, state papers, SP 29/12/34, 34.1 • Venn, *Alum. Cant.*

Archives BL, Add. MS 15669, fol. 58 • BL, Add. MS 15670, fols. 40–49 • BL, Add. MS 36792, fol. 64 | PRO, state papers, 29/12/34, 34.1

Goffe [Gough], **Stephen** (**1605–1681**), Roman Catholic priest and royalist agent, was born at Stanmer, Sussex, the son of Stephen Goffe, the puritan inclined rector of the nearby parish of Bramber, and his wife, Deborah, *née* West or Weston (1586/7–1626). The future regicide William *Goffe (*d.* 1679?) was his brother. He was educated at Merton College, Oxford (BA 1624). Afterwards he migrated to St Alban Hall (MA 1627). He was ordained by Archbishop Laud, who made him his chaplain. He then became chaplain to the regiment of Colonel Horace Vere in the Low Countries. He entered Leiden University on 20 February 1633. On his return to England he was, by the interest of Henry Jermyn (afterwards earl of St Albans) appointed one of Charles I's chaplains, and was created DD in 1636. Letters of his survive from the years 1632–7 addressed to Sir William Boswell, English resident at The Hague, concerning the reading of the Church of England liturgy in the English regiments in Dutch service (BL, Add. MS 6394).

Goffe was employed by the royalist party as an agent in France, Flanders, the Netherlands, and other countries. By 1644 he was in Brussels, and was employed in negotiations for troops from the duke of Lorraine, and ships from the prince of Orange, to whose daughter a marriage with Prince Charles was proposed. In 1646 parliament published *The Lord Digby's Cabinet and Dr. Goff's Negotiations*, a work critical of his activities and based on captured correspondence. He was one of those who attempted to free the king from his confinement at Hampton Court in late 1647. He was seized upon suspicion and committed to prison, but found means to escape. The king when at Carisbrooke Castle employed him to persuade the Scottish commissioners to recede from their demand that he should confirm the covenant. In 1649 Goffe followed the queen of France, in the company of her Oratorian chaplains, Père Viette and Père Philippe (Robert Philips, a Scot). In Paris, Goffe attended a series of lectures on the early church, at the church of St Merry, and as a result he asked to be received into the Catholic church. English contemporaries attributed this move to disillusionment with the Church of England after the fall of the monarchy. Clarendon alleged that out of the money sent from Moscow for Charles II, Goffe received £800 for services he had performed, and within a few days after the receipt of it changed his religion and became one of the fathers of the Oratory. Certainly on Christmas eve 1651 he entered the congregation of the French Oratory at Paris, and was clothed as a novice on 14 January 1652. When the time came for his ordination a doubt was raised over whether his Anglican ordination could be considered valid. The Sorbonne was inclined to consider his orders valid, but the archbishop of Paris, not wishing to set a precedent, referred the question to Rome. There it was decided that he should be ordained again, and so he received all the orders, culminating in the priesthood in 1654. Dr Humphrey Prideaux, dean of Norwich, asserted on the authority of Obadiah Walker that after joining the Roman communion Goffe celebrated mass at Paris by virtue of his having been ordained priest in the Church of England, but this has been strenuously denied and seems very implausible.

Soon after his ordination Goffe was transferred to the Oratorian house of Notre Dame des Vertus, not far from Paris, where from 1655 to 1661 he was in charge of a seminary for fourteen English clergymen in the house under his direction. He gave freely from his private resources for English royalist exiles, Catholic and protestant, and his interest with Queen Henrietta Maria, whose chaplain he was, enabled him to assist innumerable gentlemen in distress. He remained closely in touch with the exiled Charles II and revisited England briefly after the Restoration. Returning to Paris in 1661 he was stationed at the Oratory in rue St Honoré to be near the queen mother, who arranged a pension for him. It was on his recommendation that Henry, Lord Jermyn, took the poet Abraham Cowley under his protection. By the queen mother's orders Goffe was appointed tutor to Charles II's natural son, James Crofts (afterwards duke of Monmouth), and took charge of him until he was ten years of age, when he committed him to the care of Thomas Ross, librarian to Charles II. He died in the house of the fathers of the Oratory in rue St Honoré, Paris, on 5 January 1682 (NS; 25 December 1681 OS). In his room was found the sum of 100,000 écus, which he had held in trust for the duke of York. The fathers of the Oratory duly handed this over, to the amazement of Louis XIV.

Wood described Goffe as 'esteemed by some a learned man and well read in the Fathers, and therefore respected by Gerard John Vossius and others'. He left no printed works, but copious manuscript notes on the New Testament. Nine of his Latin epistles to Vossius are printed in *G. J. Vossii et clarorum virorum ad eum epistolae, collectore P. Colomesio* (1690), and two others in *Praestantium ac eruditorum virorum epistolae ecclesiasticae et theologicae* (1704).

THOMPSON COOPER, *rev.* JEROME BERTRAM

Sources L. Batterel, *Mémoires domestiques pour servir à l'histoire de l'Oratoire*, 5 vols. (Paris, 1902–11), vol. 3, pp. 168–75 • Wood, *Ath. Oxon.*, new edn, 3.525, 905, 1103; 4.131 • Wood, *Ath. Oxon.: Fasti* (1815), 414, 431, 494 • Wood, *Ath. Oxon.: Fasti* (1820), 136, 210 • E. Hyde, earl of Clarendon, *The history of the rebellion and civil wars in England*, 7 vols. (1849), vol. 4, pp. 371, 373 • R. Scrope and T. Monkhouse, eds., *State papers collected by Edward, earl of Clarendon*, 3 vols. (1767–86), vol. 3, p. 418 • *Calendar of the Clarendon state papers preserved in the Bodleian Library*, 1: *To Jan 1649*, ed. O. Ogle and W. H. Bliss (1872), 549; 2: *1649–1654*, ed. W. D. Macray (1869), 489 • *The works of … John Cosin*, ed. J. Sansom and J. Barrow, 5 vols. (1843–55), vol. 4, p. 464 • C. Dodd [H. Tootell], *The church history of England, from the year 1500, to the year 1688*, 3 (1742), 305 • E. E. Estcourt, *The question of Anglican orders discussed* (1873) • *Memoirs illustrative of the life and writings of John Evelyn … comprising his diary, from the year 1641 to 1705–6*, ed. W. Bray, 2 vols. (1818), vol. 1, pp. 12, 360; vol. 2, pp. 134–7 • S. R. Gardiner, *History of England from the accession of James I to the outbreak of the civil war*, 7 (1884), 316 • Gillow, *Lit. biog. hist.*, 2.508 • *The works of the most reverend father in God, William Laud*, 6, ed. J. Bliss (1857), 347, 529 • F. G. Lee, *Validity of the holy orders of the Church of England* (1869), 293 • *Legenda lignea* (1653) • M. le Quien, *Nullité des ordinations anglicanes*, 2 vols. (1725), vol. 2, p. 316 • J. Lingard, *The history of England*, 5th edn, 8 (1849), 191 • H. Prideaux, *Validity of the orders of the Church of England* (1716), 78 • C. G. Herbermann and others, eds., *The Catholic encyclopedia*, 17 vols. (1907–18), vol. 6, p. 637 • *N&Q*, 2nd ser., 9 (1860), 246 • *N&Q*, 4th ser., 12 (1873), 408 • J. E. B. Mayor, 'Stephen Goffe', *N&Q*, 5th ser., 6 (1876), 296 • monumental brass, Stanmer church, Sussex

Archives Archives of the Congregation of the Oratory, Paris • Magd. Cam., corresp. | BL, letters to Sir W. Boswell, etc., Add. MS 6394, fol. 173

Wealth at death 630 livres in rent; 11,400 livres in hand: will, 30 March 1680, Batterel, *Mémoires domestiques*, vol. 3, p. 174

Goffe [Gough], **Thomas** (1590/91–1629), playwright and Church of England clergyman, was born in Essex, the son of a clergyman. From Westminster School, aged eighteen, he was elected to a scholarship at Christ Church, Oxford, on 3 November 1609, thus following in the footsteps of George Herbert, one year his senior at Westminster. He proceeded BA on 17 June 1613, MA on 20 June 1616, and BD on 3 July 1623. Anthony Wood says that Goffe gained a reputation in Oxford both as a poet and as an orator. Two of his funeral sermons and a sermon preached in London in 1627 were printed during his lifetime.

Goffe's dramatic writings date exclusively from his years in Oxford, and the three plays that can be attributed to him with certainty were all performed by the students of Christ Church. Although they were dismissed in the nineteenth century as ridiculously bombastic (a judgement of the literary critic William Gifford that was repeated throughout the century), these tragedies are no more excessive than a number of their contemporaries. The violent action and ragings of *The Raging Turk* (probably the first of the plays), for example, are almost all found in its source, *The Generall Historie of the Turkes* (1603) by Richard Knolles.

Goffe's plays were all published posthumously in the 1630s and again, in a collected volume, in 1656. The posthumous attribution to Goffe of the pastoral tragicomedy *The Careless Shepherdess* (made first in 1655 by its printers) has been questioned by twentieth-century critics but not altogether dismissed. At least four other plays were falsely attributed to Goffe during the seventeenth century, a commercial witness to his standing at the time. In 1687 Winstanley wrote that his 'Abilities rais'd him to a high Reputation in the Age he lived in' (W. Winstanley, *The Lives of the most Famous English Poets*, 1686, 148), and Goffe was placed alongside Jonson, Shakespeare, Webster, and others in a number of seventeenth-century catalogues of dramatic genius.

Goffe not only wrote plays but was also involved in their production, both off stage and on. He took the principal role in a performance of Robert Burton's Latin play *Philosophaster* in February 1618, and there is some evidence that he may have played the lead in the following year's performance of his own *Couragious Turke*, a role reminiscent of Marlowe's Tamburlaine, with its mixture of eloquence and cruelty. A manuscript copy of Amurath's part written in Goffe's own hand (Harvard, MS Thr 10.1), contains a poem describing an accident that befell this particular production and perhaps Goffe himself: 'A Songe upon the Loss of an Actors Voyce beeinge to Play a Cheife Part in the Universitie'. It concludes, 'Tis a great thinge to houlde ones peace' (Carnegie, 161).

In 1622 Goffe left Oxford to take up the living of East Clandon, Surrey. There, according to Wood, a fatal accident ensued: he married. His wife, Elizabeth, was the widow of his predecessor at East Clandon and was, in Wood's words, 'a meer Xantippe', who so dominated her husband 'that his Life being much shortened thereby, [he] died at length in a manner heart-broken' (Wood, *Ath. Oxon.*, 2.463). The story has been repeated with great relish by all subsequent biographers. Goffe was buried on 27 July 1629 in the middle of the chancel of his church.

Eleri Larkum

Sources G. E. Bentley, *The Jacobean and Caroline stage*, 7 vols. (1941–68), vol. 4 • T. Goffe, *The couragious Turke*, ed. D. Carnegie (1974) • D. Carnegie, 'The identification of the hand of Thomas Goffe, academic, dramatist and actor', *The Library*, 5th ser., 26 (1971), 161–5 • Wood, *Ath. Oxon.*, new edn, 2.463 • J. Aubrey, *The natural history and antiquities of the county of Surrey*, 3 (1718); facs. edn (1975), 259–60 • J. Welch, *A list of scholars of St Peter's College, Westminster* (1788) • Foster, *Alum. Oxon.* • *DNB*

Goffe, William (*d.* 1679?), regicide and major-general, was the son of Stephen Goffe (*b.* 1574/5), rector of Bramber, in Sussex, who was deprived of his living in 1605 for his part in organizing the puritan petitions to James I.

Early life and family William Goffe's date of birth and his place of residence during his early years are unknown. His mother, Stephen's wife, Deborah West or Weston (1586/7–1626), died in childbirth at the age of thirty-nine in November 1626 in Stanmer, Sussex, where she was recorded in a memorial brass in the parish church; two years later Stephen's residence was given as Stanmer, though he was never rector there. But it is possible that William himself was not brought up in Sussex: when, nearly thirty years later, he was appointed major-general for a region which included the county he claimed to be a stranger to the area (Bodl. Oxf., MS Rawl. A 32, fol. 525). William's eldest brother, Stephen *Goffe, supported the king during the civil war and later converted to Roman Catholicism. Another brother, John *Goffe, evinced very different views from those of William: he was ejected from the living of Hackington in Kent in 1643 for refusing to subscribe to the solemn league and covenant and imprisoned for a time in Canterbury.

In 1634 Goffe was apprenticed to the London grocer William Vaughan and he became a freeman of the Grocers' Company in 1642. In that year he was imprisoned by the lord mayor for helping to organize a petition in support of parliament's claim to control the city militia. He married, probably during the 1640s or early 1650s, Frances Whalley, daughter of his fellow army officer and major-general, Edward *Whalley. They had three daughters, Anne, Elizabeth, and Frances.

Putney and regicide William Goffe fought for parliament during the first civil war, and following the formation of the New Model Army in 1645 he served as a captain in Colonel Harley's regiment. During 1647 he was actively involved in the army's quarrel with parliament; he signed the vindication of the army officers drawn up in April 1647 and several months later he was one of the deputation which presented the house with the army's charges against the eleven presbyterian members. At the end of 1647 Goffe played a prominent part in the famous debates of the army council at Putney. The contemporary record of the debates clearly reveals his religious and political radicalism and, in particular, his strong millenarian conviction that he was living through the last days of human history.

On the first day of the debates Goffe expressed his fears that the army might have wandered from the purpose God had entrusted to it, and called for time to be put aside for a prayer meeting on the grounds that no project would prosper 'unless God be first sought'. The following day, after the prayer meeting had been held, Goffe spoke again, referring to his own researches into the book of Revelation and intimating that the second coming of Christ was imminent. His personal perspective on the political situation in late 1647 was that the army leaders should end their attempts to reach a settlement with Charles I and instead bring him to justice. He declared on the first day at Putney that 'God does seem evidently to be throwing down the glory of all flesh', and he later added: 'it seems to me evident and clear that this hath been a voice from heaven to us, that we have sinned against the Lord in tampering with his enemies'. Cromwell took these last remarks as a personal affront and Goffe was forced to make a hasty apology to him (A. S. P Woodhouse, *Puritanism and Liberty: being the Army Debates* (1647–49), 20, 21, 40, 100–01).

Goffe's radicalism was further demonstrated by his contribution to the army prayer meeting at Windsor a few months later in April 1648. At the beginning of this meeting he made a speech in which he referred his fellow officers to the first chapter of the Old Testament book of Proverbs, in which God made clear that disaster would befall those who refused to follow his plans and purposes. Goffe's clear intention in referring to this biblical text was again to suggest that the resurgence of the royalist cause was the direct consequence of the army's negotiations with Charles I and its failure to bring him to justice. According to William Allen's later account of the meeting Goffe's words had a profound impact upon his fellow soldiers and after he had finished speaking,

> none was able hardly to speak a word to each other for bitter weeping … in the sense and shame of our iniquities of unbelief, base fear of men and carnal consultations (as the fruit thereof) with our own wisdoms and not with the word of the Lord. (Allen, 4)

As a result of Goffe's speech the soldiers of Windsor resolved to put the king on trial as soon as they had the opportunity.

Goffe probably saw action during the second civil war, and in December 1648 he was named one of the commissioners for Charles I's trial. He attended the court regularly and signed the king's death warrant [*see also* Regicides]. He accompanied Cromwell to Scotland in 1650 and commanded the lord general's own regiment at the battle of Dunbar. According to Cromwell, 'at the push of pike' Goffe 'did repel the stoutest regiment the enemy had there' (*Writings and Speeches*, 2.324). He subsequently commanded a regiment at the battle of Worcester in 1651. During the early 1650s Goffe was a member of the Independent congregation which met in Westminster Abbey and whose ministers were John Rowe and Seth Wood. In 1652 he acquired the Great Lodge and 160 acres of former crown land in Cheshunt Park, Hertfordshire. The following year he purchased one-sixth of Newfoundland from Sir David Kirke. Goffe approved of Cromwell's expulsion of the Rump Parliament in April 1653, and six months later assisted in the forcible ejection of the radical members of Barebone's Parliament.

Major-general A strong supporter of the protectorate, Goffe sat in the 1654 parliament for Great Yarmouth. At the beginning of 1655 he was involved in the suppression of Penruddock's rising in the west country and the following autumn he was appointed one of Cromwell's major-generals and given responsibility for an association made up of the counties of Sussex, Hampshire, and Berkshire. He was one of the first major-generals to be active, beginning work in Sussex in early November 1655. The letters he sent to John Thurloe, Cromwell's secretary of state, at frequent intervals over the next nine months clearly reveal his deep conviction that he was serving God in carrying out the tasks of improving the security of Cromwell's regime and bringing about a godly reformation in his counties. In February 1656 he declared to Thurloe that 'however proud men deal perversely with us without a cause, yett they may att last be ashamed and, our harts being kept sound in all the waies of truth and holiness, wee may not be ashamed' (Bodl. Oxf., MS Rawl. A 35, fol. 119). Several months later he described himself as 'called of God to serve him and his people in the countrey' (ibid., A 38, fol. 125).

While Goffe made every effort to maximize the yield from the decimation tax on the royalists of his association, within a few weeks of beginning work he had realized that the amount of money that could be raised would fall well short of the sum required to pay his militia troops. Over the following months his financial situation steadily worsened and by the spring of 1656 he was obliged to make a series of increasingly desperate requests to Thurloe for money to pay his troops, declaring at one point 'if the worke and ourselves perish for want of our wages, it will not, I hope, be laied to our charge' (Bodl. Oxf., MS Rawl. A 39, fol. 424). Early in 1656 he disbanded one of the three militia troops in Sussex after receiving information that its captain, John Busbridge, could not be relied upon to support the government. Goffe also actively encouraged the Hampshire justices of the peace to suppress unlicensed alehouses in their county, and attempted to curtail the evangelizing activities of itinerant Quaker preachers, towards whom he was extremely hostile. In January 1656 he told Thurloe that George Fox and several other Quakers were active in Sussex, 'doing much work for the devil and deluding many simple souls', adding 'I have some thoughts to lay Foxe and his companions by the heels if I see good opportunity' (ibid., A 34, fol. 395).

For all the strength of his religious beliefs and his absolute commitment to the godly cause, however, Goffe's correspondence with Thurloe also reveals him to be an anxious individual who lacked confidence in his own abilities and was easily discouraged when he encountered problems. Shortly after his appointment as major-general he expressed the hope that Cromwell would not regret putting his trust in 'so poore and inconsiderable a creature', and he later admitted to Thurloe that he had on occasion become discouraged 'because things were soe exceeding long in settling' (Bodl. Oxf., MS Rawl. A 32, fol. 381; A 39, fol. 424). He was also frequently preoccupied by domestic and family concerns, such as the reimbursement of his personal expenses as major-general and his wife's difficulties in settling at Winchester, where he moved his family in the early summer of 1656. He also seems to have found his work as major-general taxing; in March 1656, for example, he told Thurloe that he had returned to Winchester from Sussex so exhausted that he could hardly find the energy to write to him.

During the election campaign for the 1656 parliament Goffe attempted to persuade the government's supporters in Hampshire to reach an agreed slate of candidates. He was reasonably pleased with the outcome of the poll in Hampshire and commented to Thurloe that, in view of the great efforts made to prevent him being returned, he considered his own election to sit for that county as 'a speciall providence of God' (Bodl. Oxf., MS Rawl. A 41, fol. 610). He was much less happy, however, with the result in Sussex where, as he told Thurloe, 'CM [Col Morley] ruled the rost by the help of a disaffected party, much to the griefe of the honest party; and it was theire designe to have noe soldier, decemator or any man that hath sallary' (ibid., A 41, fol. 698). When he had seen the returns for the whole country he again commented to Thurloe that 'though they be not so good as wee could have wished them, yet they are not soe badd as our enemies would have had them' (ibid., A 41, fol. 860).

Goffe attended parliament regularly during the autumn of 1656. In a speech during the debate on the victory over the Spanish fleet at Santa Cruz, he revealed his continuing deep personal attachment to Oliver Cromwell by 'inviting the House to a firm, and a kind of corporal union with his Highness' (*Diary of Thomas Burton*, 1.359–60). During the discussions in December about how to proceed against James Nayler for his blasphemous entry into Bristol earlier that year, Goffe again revealed his deep antipathy to the Quaker movement, claiming that the Quakers 'go about to revile the ordinances and ministers of Christ and would tear the flesh off the bones of all that profess Christ', and arguing that Nayler was a false Christ who was sent to deceive the godly and as such should be punished by death (ibid., 1.52, 80, 108–11, 155). Like most of his fellow major-generals Goffe supported Desborough's Decimation Bill in December 1656 and January 1657 and opposed the attempts to make Cromwell king in early

1657. According to some contemporary reports, however, by the time Cromwell finally rejected the offer of the crown in May 1657, Goffe and his fellow major-generals Edward Whalley and William Boteler were willing to accept a return of the monarchy. Goffe remained a staunch supporter of Oliver Cromwell until the protector's death. In June 1658 he was named to the committee which was to consider how the next parliament should be organized and during Cromwell's last illness he was one of those summoned to the protector's bedside to receive his declaration appointing his son Richard as his successor. Goffe was a strong supporter of Richard Cromwell and was described by the republican Edmund Ludlow as one of his 'creatures' (*Memoirs of Edmund Ludlow*, 2.62). In November 1658, in accordance with his father's wishes, Richard Cromwell granted Goffe lands in Ireland to the value of £500 per annum. Ludlow claims that during the trial of strength between Richard Cromwell and the army in early 1659, Goffe advised the protector to defend his position by force. Following Richard's retirement, Goffe inevitably lost influence. In November 1659 he and his father-in-law, Edward Whalley, were part of a four-man delegation sent to Scotland to outline to Colonel Monck the reasons for the expulsion of the Rump, but their trip failed to bring about a reconciliation between Monck and the New Model regiments stationed in England.

Restoration and exile At the Restoration, Goffe and his father-in-law Whalley, who as regicides were both excluded from the Act of Indemnity, fled to New England. Goffe travelled under the name Stephenson. He and Whalley arrived at Boston in July 1660 and lived initially in Cambridge. They moved to New Haven, Connecticut, in 1661, where tradition has it they lived in a cave in the woods outside the town for three years to avoid discovery by the agents sent from England to capture them. In 1664 they moved on to Hadley, Massachusetts, where they remained until their deaths. All efforts to arrest them proved fruitless as the colonists were generally sympathetic to the fugitive regicides and refused to reveal their whereabouts. A report in the colonial state papers declares that they were held in 'exceeding great esteem for their piety and parts' and that they 'held meetings where they preached and prayed, and were looked upon as men dropped down from heaven'. Another later report stated that they were feasted in every place they visited and provided with horses and guides (*CSP col.*, 5.54, 345). Details of the attempts by the agents of Charles II to apprehend them are also recorded (ibid., letters 45, 80, 81, 96, 160–62, 1103, 1300). In 1675 Hadley came under attack from Indians and, according to local tradition, Goffe emerged from his hiding place to rally the settlers and save them from defeat. The story passed into literature, being incorporated by Walter Scott into *Peveril of the Peak*.

Using a pseudonym Goffe wrote a number of letters to his wife from America. These make clear that his religious convictions remained unshaken by the failure of the puritan revolution and that he still confidently expected the imminent return of Jesus Christ. They also reveal that he was deeply troubled by the reports he received about developments in England. In 1672 he told his wife: 'I cannot but tremble to think what may become of poor England whose sins are grown to a great Height', and two years later he declared:

> Oh that the inhabitants of poor England would learn righteousnesse … I am at a great distance, yet methinkes I see the Lord shaking both your Earth & Heaven. Oh, that He would give us grace to seeke a Kingdom that cannot be shaken, and to serve him acceptably with reverence & godly feare for our God is a consuming fire. ('Letters and papers relating to the regicides', 8.136, 155)

Goffe probably died in 1679, as his last letter from America was written in April of that year. He was buried next to his father-in-law at Hadley in an unmarked grave.

CHRISTOPHER DURSTON

Sources Thurloe state papers, Bodl. Oxf., MS Rawl. A • C. H. Firth and G. Davies, *The regimental history of Cromwell's army*, 2 vols. (1940) • interregnum state papers, PRO, SP 18–28 • *Diary of Thomas Burton*, ed. J. T. Rutt, 4 vols. (1828) • *CSP col.*, vol. 5 • A. Fletcher, *A county community in peace and war: Sussex, 1600–1660* (1975), 299–311 • T. Hutchinson, *The history of Massachusetts*, 3rd edn, 2 vols. (Boston, MA, 1795) • 'Letters and papers relating to the regicides', *Collections of the Massachusetts Historical Society*, 4th ser., 8 (1868), 122–225 • W. Allen, *A faithful memorial of that remarkable meeting of many officers of the army in England, at Windsor Castle, in the year 1648* (1659) • *Memoirs of Edmund Ludlow*, ed. C. H. Firth, 2 vols. (1888), vol. 2 • *DNB* • *The writings and speeches of Oliver Cromwell*, ed. W. C. Abbott and C. D. Crane, 4 vols. (1937–47) • Grocers' Company register of apprenticeships, GL, MS 11593/1, fol. 48 • Grocers' Company, admissions, 1345–*c*.1670, GL, MS 11592A • chancery close rolls, PRO, C 54/3693/20; 54/3711/30 • certificate of sale of crown lands, PRO, E121/2/9/46 • E. H. W. Dunkin, 'Contributions towards the ecclesiastical history of the deanery of South Malling', *Sussex Archaeological Collections*, 26 (1875), 9–96 • *IGI*

Archives Bodl. Oxf., Thurloe state papers, MS Rawl. A

Wealth at death estates confiscated for treason

Gogarty, Oliver Joseph St John (1878–1957), surgeon and writer, was born at 5 Rutland Square, Dublin, on 17 August 1878, the eldest child of Henry Gogarty FRCSI (*d.* 1889), a medical practitioner, and his wife, Margaret Oliver (*d.* 1906), daughter of a prosperous Galway miller. His siblings were Henry, Richard, and Mayflo. Educated first at a nearby Christian Brothers' school, he was sent in 1891, after his father's death from appendicitis two years earlier, to Mungret College, a Jesuit school near Limerick, and to Stonyhurst College, in Lancashire. While boarding in 1896–7 at Clongowes Wood College, in co. Kildare (where he excelled as a cyclist and cricketer, playing soccer for Bohemians), he attended first-year university lectures for the Royal University of Ireland. He next entered the medical school at Trinity College, Dublin, the change of university being explained amusingly in *Tumbling in the Hay* (1939), Gogarty's memoir of medical student life in the opening years of the century.

Ulick O'Connor, Gogarty's first and chosen biographer, described him as:

> of average height, five feet nine but appears taller because of his athletic figure. … The eyes are striking, vivid blue … His hair is brown, but sometimes streaked with gold from the bleaching of the sun, and inclined to stand upright when brushed sideways. (O'Connor, 19)

Asked at a college meeting 'Are you rising on a point of

order?' Gogarty answered, 'No, on the spur of the moment' (Lyons, 34). Rumours of his wit and levity penetrated to the senior common room; before long he had invitations to supper from some of the most formidable dons, including Robert Yelverton Tyrrell, Henry Stewart Macran, and the Revd John Pentland Mahaffy, all of whom remained lifelong friends. His academic progress was delayed by avocations, swimming, cycle racing, and literature (to which in maturity were added archery and aviation). A graceful lyricist, he displayed an equal facility for the scatological, thus detracting from his reputation as a poet with verses in *Dana*, and was three-times winner of the vice-chancellor's prize for English verse. He also competed for Oxford University's Newdigate prize, and for this purpose spent two terms at Worcester College, Oxford, in 1904, finding behaviour more important there than intellect. G. K. A. Bell (later bishop of Chichester) was awarded the prize for 'Delphi'. Gogarty, who came second, achieved a more spectacular success by drinking the 'sconce' (a 5½ pint tankard) in one draught (Lyons, 42).

In Dublin he frequented the steps outside the National Library, a meeting place for students of 'the Royal', Gogarty's natural companions and co-religionists. They included James Joyce, an inseparable friend for several years, whose needs he had in mind when he rented a Martello tower in Sandycove in 1904. It was to provide a retreat where he and Joyce could write. The latter (enamoured of Nora Barnacle) used it briefly, and depicts it in the opening page of *Ulysses*, caricaturing Gogarty as the ebullient Buck Mulligan. His antic temperament appealed to Joyce—until they quarrelled. Joyce's bitterness did not deter him from borrowing his former pal's words and images for *Ulysses*.

Gogarty spoke at Sinn Féin's first annual convention on 25 November 1905, and his speech was reported in Arthur Griffith's paper, the *United Irishman*. This, as O'Connor has pointed out, was an important occasion in Irish history, the inauguration of the party which was to secure national independence (O'Connor, 89ff.). Basing its initial policy on passive resistance, Sinn Féin was to expouse physical force later, in response to suppression introduced by Dublin Castle. Gogarty was not involved in this violence.

Gogarty did not take his medical degree until 1907, by which time his mother had died and he had married Martha Duane (*d*. 1958) of Moyard, Connemara. (Their children were Oliver—Noll—a successful barrister with a good deal of his father's wit; Dermot, an architect; and Brenda, whose childhood is exquisitely commemorated in her father's poem 'Golden Stockings'.) Once qualified he made rapid progress. Postgraduate study in Vienna fitted him for the position of ear, nose, and throat surgeon to the Richmond Hospital. He purchased 15 Ely Place, Dublin, took the FRCSI, acquired a buttercup-coloured Rolls Royce (a legitimate advertising ploy), and embarked successfully in practice. Surmounting currents that divided Dublin's specialists along sectarian lines, he obtained a second appointment at the Meath Hospital, then a bastion of protestantism.

Gogarty earned a reputation as a skilful surgeon, but saw that surgery alone could not relieve the undernourished, adenoidal youngsters from the slums who attended his clinics. He made a public plea for medical inspection of schoolchildren in 1911, and demanded that school meals should be provided. He attended conferences and spoke in Aberdeen at the British Medical Association's annual general meeting in 1914. His paper 'Latent empyemeta of the nasal accessory sinuses' was published in the *British Medical Journal* (1914, 1020–21). He scolded the department of public health for ineptitude until, realizing that the better way to ameliorate deficient social conditions was through laughter, he wrote a play in three acts, *Blight—the Tragedy of Dublin*. It was staged in the Abbey Theatre in 1917 under a pseudonym. Two one-act plays followed, *A Serious Thing* (1919) and *The Enchanted Trousers* (1919).

The pseudonyms (Alpha and Omega, and Gideon Ousley) were intended to pacify the General Medical Council, for which publicity was anathema. *Hyperthuleana* (1916) featured Gogarty's name on its title-page, but this edition of poems was minuscule and issued privately. It was followed by *'The Ship' and other Poems* (1918), and by collections published in Dublin and New York. *The Collected Poems of Oliver St John Gogarty* was published in London by Constable (1951).

Gogarty's practice was remunerative. Renvyle House, which he bought in 1917, was a token of his success, and he liked to entertain his friends at this Connemara holiday home. He brought the ageing Mahaffy there to marvel at the 'plum-blue' hills (Gogarty, *It isn't this Time*, 145); W. B. Yeats and his bride were offered it for their honeymoon; Augustus John absorbed the landscapes, transferring them to canvas.

Gogarty's political sympathies lay with the pro-treaty group. A close friend of Arthur Griffith (whom he met regularly at the Bailey Restaurant, a popular Duke Street watering-hole for literary folk and others) and Michael Collins, he was appointed to the Irish Free State Senate in 1922 by William T. Cosgrave. On 20 January 1923, Senator Gogarty was kidnapped in his Dublin home, and taken by armed men to a house beside the Liffey from which he escaped, outwitting his captors and making his way to freedom by swimming the icy river. His property remained at risk; Renvyle House was destroyed by arsonists, but rebuilt as a hotel where in the 1930s his son Oliver played host.

Accustomed since youth to an ambience in which verbal jousting was relished, Gogarty's capacity for derision was boundless. When Archbishop Bernard exchanged the see of Dublin for the provostship of Trinity College, Dublin, Gogarty said: 'He has sold the Thirty-nine Articles for the thirty pieces of silver'. His favourite target, Eamon De Valera, was dismissed as that 'laugh in mourning' (O'Connor, 298) and said to resemble 'either a corpse or a cormorant'. Not even Yeats was spared—Gogarty remarked: 'he has reached an age when he cannot take *Yes* for an answer'.

In the upper house Gogarty was something of a gadfly, but as in most matters he had his serious side too. He complained that under De Valera's government Ireland, instead of being a land flowing with milk and honey, was flowing with mulct and humbug. He attempted to have the phoenix covered by the Wild Birds Protection Bill. On the other hand, he supported the hydroelectric Shannon scheme, and spoke with common sense on transport problems, industrial potential, and health affairs; he reiterated his belief that the prevention of disease must begin in the schools.

Gogarty's most ambitious prose works are *As I was Going Down Sackville Street* (1937), *I Follow St Patrick* (1938), and *Tumbling in the Hay* (1939). The publication of *Sackville Street* was anxiously awaited by James Joyce, but the book did not pillory him. It did, however, lead to an action for libel, taken by William A. Sinclair, an antiques dealer, who was awarded £900 and costs. Then in 1939 Gogarty successfully sued Michael Joseph Ltd for defamation by their author the poet Patrick Kavanagh.

Gogarty's application to join the Royal Air Force was turned down later that year because of his age. Instead he went to the USA, ostensibly on a short lecture tour, but finding New York congenial he settled there, amazed to be paid for *talking*, a function that went almost without notice at home. Publishers, too, were generous. He maintained contact with his family, visiting Ireland occasionally, but taking American citizenship. After his death from heart disease in the Beth Israel Hospital, Manhattan, on 22 September 1957, his remains were flown to Ireland for burial at Ballinakill cemetery, Cleggan, in Connemara. His wife survived him.

Gogarty's literary status remains undecided, for reasons having less to do with the quality of his work than with his personality. This antagonized many less robust folk. Certain of his publications, such as 'They think they know Joyce', angered Joyce scholars; a clique of Kavanagh's influential supporters did not forgive him. His lyrics, praised highly by W. B. Yeats, and appreciated by eclectic readers, have little in common with the poetry of the late twentieth century. The preparation of a new selection of his verse, and the formation an Oliver St John Gogarty Society in Dublin are signs, however, that recovery of his earlier status is at hand. J. B. LYONS

Sources U. O'Connor, *Oliver St John Gogarty* (1964) · J. B. Lyons, *Oliver St John Gogarty: the man of many talents* (1980) [incl. checklist of Gogarty's pubns] · J. F. Carens, *Surpassing wit: Oliver St John Gogarty, his poetry and his prose* (1979) · A. N. Jeffares, *The circus animals: essays on W. B. Yeats* (1970) · J. F. Carens, ed., *The plays of Oliver St John Gogarty* (Newark, DE, [1971]) · O. St J. Gogarty, *It isn't this time of year at all* (1954) · O. St J. Gogarty, *Many lines to thee: letters to G. K. A. Bell, 1904–1907*, ed. J. F. Carens (1971) · *Seanad Éireann: parliamentary debates*, 1–20 (1922–36) [1st Seanad] · *Stonyhurst Magazine*, 33 (1958), 91–2

Archives Bucknell University, Lewisburg, Pennsylvania, corresp., literary MSS, and papers · Colby College, Waterville, Maine, literary papers · NL Ire., MSS · NYPL, MSS · Ransom HRC, literary papers · Stanford University, California, literary papers · TCD, papers · U. Reading, corresp. · Yale U., MSS | Cornell University, Ithaca, New York, letters to James Joyce · Harvard U., corresp. with Horace Reynolds · LPL, letters to G. K. A. Bell · PRO NIre., letters to Lady Londonderry · TCD, corresp. with Thomas Bodkin · University of Exeter, letters to W. F. Jackson Knight | FILM Radio Telefis Éireann, Dublin, documentary footage | SOUND BL NSA, performance recordings · Radio Éireann, Dublin, sound archives, 'Oliver St John Gogarty'

Likenesses W. Orpen, oils, 1911, Royal College of Surgeons of Ireland · W. Suschitzky, bromide print, 1938, NPG · G. L. Brockhurst, oils (after etching), Royal College of Surgeons of Ireland · T. Spicer-Simson, bronze medallion, NG Ire.

Wealth at death £133: probate, 3 May 1958, *CGPLA Éire* · £697 7s. 10d.—in England: probate, 5 Aug 1958, *CGPLA Eng. & Wales*

Gogynfeirdd [beirdd y tywysogion] (*act. c.***1080–1285**), Welsh-language poets, were the court poets of the Welsh princes (*beirdd y tywysogion* means 'poets of the princes'). The term *gogynfeirdd* is also applied to those poets who continued to sing in the same style during the fourteenth century. *Gogynfeirdd* (sing. *gogynfardd*) means 'the not so early poets' as contrasted with the *cynfeirdd* (sing. *cynfardd*) 'the early poets', an epithet loosely employed to describe the poets composing in Welsh between *c*.550 and 1100. There are some three dozen *gogynfeirdd* whose work has been preserved, notably in the three manuscripts Llawysgrif Hendregadredd (NL Wales, MS 6680B, *c*.1300); the Red Book of Hergest (Jesus College, Oxford, MS 111, *c*.1400), and NL Wales, MS 4973B (*c*.1631). These three dozen poets between them composed a corpus of some 12,600 lines of verse, mainly in the *awdl* metres (an *awdl*, plural *awdlau*, is a monorhyme sequence of indeterminate length) but also including a fair number of *englynion* sequences (an *englyn*, plural *englynion*, is a three- or four-line stanza following strict metrical patterns). Some three-quarters of the corpus is secular panegyric: of the remaining quarter, about four-fifths is in praise of God and his saints and a fifth in praise of women.

It may be estimated that twenty-two of the *gogynfeirdd* came from Gwynedd, eight from Powys, and six from Deheubarth: this distribution reflects accurately the political dominance of Gwynedd in Wales during the twelfth and thirteenth centuries (particularly the thirteenth). The court poets of Gwynedd during this period form a glittering *catena aurea*. Beginning with y *Meilyr Brydydd, who mourned—in very different modes—the passing of Trahaearn ap Caradog (*d.* 1081) and Gruffudd ap Cynan (*d.* 1137), the succession passes to his son **Gwalchmai ap Meilyr** (*fl.* 1132–1180), who celebrated the exploits of Owain Gwynedd and his sons Dafydd and Rhodri, as well as those of Madog ap Maredudd of Powys. Three of Gwalchmai's sons were poets, namely Einion ap Gwalchmai, Elidir Sais, and Meilyr ap Gwalchmai, but of these only Elidir devoted himself largely to panegyric: Einion (who was an important court official) and Meilyr composed mainly religious verse. Gwalchmai's successor as chief court poet of Gwynedd was *Llywarch ap Llywelyn (perhaps identical with Prydydd y Moch), who witnessed not only the decline of Dafydd ab Owain and Rhodri ab Owain but also the meteoric rise of their nephew Llywelyn ab Iorwerth: Llywarch captures better than any the surge of Llywelyn's triumphant progress. Llywarch is followed by no less skilful a poet, **Dafydd Benfras** (*c*.1195–1258/9), who attended upon Llywelyn in his latter years, survived the difficult reign of his son Dafydd, and lived to see Dafydd's nephew, Llywelyn ap Gruffudd, methodically establishing himself as the dominant force in Gwynedd and, indeed, in Wales. When Dafydd Benfras was killed in

1258–9, fighting for Llywelyn ap Gruffudd in Deheubarth, his elegy was sung by **Bleddyn Fardd** (*fl.* *c.*1220–*c.*1285), on whom his mantle fell. No eulogies by Bleddyn Fardd for Llywelyn ap Gruffudd have survived, however; but there are multiple elegies by him not only for Llywelyn himself but also for his brothers Owain and Dafydd, and there is a remarkable joint elegy for the three brothers together after Dafydd's barbarous execution in 1283. Llywelyn's praise is magnificently supplied by the Edeyrnion poet **Llygad Gŵr** (*fl.* 1230–1295), who celebrates his achievements during the period 1267–77 in a series of five exultant *awdlau*. His death at the hands of the English in late 1282 is lamented not only by Bleddyn Fardd, but also, most gloriously, by the amateur poet Gruffudd ab yr Ynad Coch, who five years earlier had apparently deserted Llywelyn, an act for which he was handsomely rewarded by Edward I: perhaps the memory of former betrayal now lent an edge to his grief.

This preponderance of Gwynedd court poets, however, is wellnigh balanced by a single weighty figure from Powys, *Cynddelw Brydydd Mawr, whose surviving output of 3852 lines is equivalent to some 30 per cent of the total *gogynfeirdd* corpus. He sang not only for Madog ap Maredudd and his successors in Powys, but also for Owain Gwynedd and some of his dependants, and for Rhys ap Gruffudd and his band of warriors in Deheubarth. Not many *gogynfeirdd* came from Deheubarth itself, but two of the very earliest poems in the corpus, the elegy for Hywel ap Goronwy (*d.* 1106) and the eulogy for Cuhelyn Fardd (*fl.* *c.*1100–1130), were the work of anonymous Deheubarth court poets, and the thirteenth-century successors of Rhys ap Gruffudd were praised memorably by Phylip Brydydd and *Gwilym, probably his son and known as y Prydydd Bychan, both from Deheubarth, as well as by Llywarch ap Llywelyn.

The *gogynfeirdd* enjoyed privileged status, guaranteed by law, in the Welsh royal courts, and their rewards of office were considerable. This privileged status is undoubtedly a reflection of the prestige praise poets, as members of the priestly caste, were accorded by the Celtic and Indo-European ancestors of the Welsh (and Irish). The fact that the Welsh law books require poets to praise God as well as kings may be another indicator of their erstwhile priestly status. Most of the religious poems are straightforward praise of God, much like secular panegyric, although the note of repentance is often struck, as in the secular *cerdd ddadolwch* ('poem seeking reconciliation'). There are also three long poems to mother churches and their patron saints, which may represent an attempt to uphold the traditional structures of Welsh church life in the face of English reforming zeal.

The Welsh law books distinguish between the *pencerdd* ('chief poet'), whose duty it was to praise God and the king, and the *bardd teulu* ('poet of the retinue'), who was obliged to serve the king's bodyguard and the queen. This distinction was probably largely obsolete by the twelfth century, but it may at some stage have given rise to a genre of courtly love poetry, curiously paralleling (and perhaps sometimes directly influenced by) that which spread from Provence from the late eleventh century onwards. The love poetry of the *gogynfeirdd* accounts for no more then 5 per cent of the surviving corpus: fourteen poems by seven poets. Of these fourteen poems, four are simply praise of noblewomen disguised as love poetry. Another two, by Gwalchmai and *Hywel ab Owain Gwynedd, belong to the genre *gorhoffedd* ('boasting poem'), a curious and haunting amalgam of love poetry, nature poetry, and assertion of martial prowess. This leaves no more than eight, mostly rather short, poems by Hywel ab Owain, Cynddelw Brydydd Mawr, and Iorwerth Fychan which can be termed love poetry proper, and in that the conventions of *amour courtois*—whether native or foreign—are clearly to be discerned.

The fact that princes like Hywel ab Owain Gwynedd and *Owain Cyfeiliog can be accounted *gogynfeirdd* demonstrates the prestige which these court poets enjoyed (although it has recently been argued that Owain employed Cynddelw as a ghost writer). This is in a sense curious, for their verse was far from accessible. They were in many respects extremely conservative, basing themselves firmly on their early medieval forebears, the *cynfeirdd*, in their metrics, their diction, and even the heroic values that they propagated. (Some of their poems, such as *Hirlas Owain* ('Owain's drinking-horn'), which purports to be by Owain Cyfeiliog, are quite closely modelled on early medieval exemplars, in this case Aneirin's *Gododdin*.) In all these fields, however, there were notable developments. The metrics of the *gogynfeirdd* saw the emergence of the stanza and something approaching full *cynghanedd* (a system of consonantal correspondence and internal rhyme, sometimes combined). Their diction becomes, at its most complex, a marvel of compression and allusion, such as the *cynfeirdd* never entertained. The heroic values of courage and generosity, while remaining to the fore, become increasingly modified by the *realpolitik* of twelfth- and thirteenth-century Wales, particularly the attempt of the princes of Gwynedd to fashion a peculiarly Welsh polity. The verse of the *gogynfeirdd*, though requiring a protracted effort to master, eventually rewards richly both the student of Welsh poetry and the historian of medieval Wales. During the following century the importance of the *awdl* declined in favour of the *cywydd* which, with its origin in popular song, later became the central metrical form of the *cywyddwyr* [*see* Cywyddwyr (*act.* *c.*1330–*c.*1650)]. R. GERAINT GRUFFYDD

Sources J. E. Caerwyn Williams, *The court poet in medieval Wales* (1997) · C. A. McKenna, *The medieval Welsh religious lyric* (1991) · R. G. Gruffydd, ed., *Cyfres beirdd y tywysogion*, 7 vols. (1991–6) [the Poets of the Princes series] · B. J. Roberts and M. E. Owen, eds., *Beirdd a thywysogion* (1996)
Archives Jesus College, Oxford, MS 111 · NL Wales, MS 4973B · NL Wales, MS 6680B

Gohebydd, y. *See* Griffith, John (1821–1877).

Gokhale, Gopal Krishna [Gopalrao] **(1866–1915)**, politician and Indian nationalist, was born on 9 May 1866 in Kotluk, a village in the Ratnagiri district of the Bombay presidency, the second son of Krishnarao Shridhar Gokhale (*d.* 1879), a minor district official from a respected

Gopal Krishna Gokhale (1866–1915), by unknown photographer, 1912 [detail]

but poor Chitpavan Brahman family, and Valubai, otherwise Satyabhama (*d.* 1881), the daughter of Bhaskar Pant Oka of the same district. He had four sisters and an elder brother, Govindrao, who supported him through his education after the early death of their father. Gokhale's first arranged marriage took place when he was fifteen but his wife, Savitribai (*d.* 1891), suffered from 'white' leprosy and they did not live together or have children. As was not uncommon, he married a second wife, Radhabai, in 1887; with her he had two daughters, Kashibai and Godavari. Radhabai died in 1900, giving birth to a son who survived only a fortnight.

Gokhale matriculated from a school in Kagal, near Kolhapur, in 1881 and studied successively at Rajaram College, Kolhapur, Deccan College, Poona, and Elphinstone College in the University of Bombay, from which he graduated in 1884 with a second-class BA in mathematics. While considering his future in the light of his financial constraints he undertook coaching and toyed with the idea of entering the Indian Civil Service, or of taking up engineering, and even began (but did not complete) the course for a law degree in Bombay. Finally, in 1885, he decided on teaching and joined the New English School and the Deccan Education Society, which had been founded in Poona by Vishnushastri Chiplunkar and B. G. Tilak. Later in 1885 the society established Fergusson College in Poona as an affiliate of the University of Bombay; there Gokhale taught mathematics, economics, and English literature. In 1886 he became a life member of the Deccan Education Society. In the last years of the 1880s personality differences among the members and division over political and social reform culminated in a split which led to Tilak's departure and to Gokhale's becoming secretary. He dominated the affairs of the society until political commitments led to his withdrawal in 1902 and retirement in 1904, having fulfilled his pledge to serve for twenty years.

Gokhale became involved in the ferment of ideas and activities that distinguished Poona in the 1880s and 1890s. He came under the influence of M. G. Ranade in 1886 and thereafter followed the direction of his interests. Under Ranade's prompting Gokhale became secretary of the Poona Sarvajanik Sabha and editor of its *Quarterly Journal* in 1887 and wrote extensive and detailed critiques of the economic issues of the day. For two years from 1886 he contributed to the *Mahratta*, an English-language newspaper of the Deccan Education Society, until Tilak took it with him when he left the society. Gokhale also edited from 1888 the English sections of the *Sudharak*, a Marathi weekly which promoted a mainly social and religious reformist position, which was opposed by Tilak and many of the city's conservative Brahman élite. In the same vein Gokhale delivered his first public speech, 'India under British rule', in Kolhapur in 1886, and first spoke at the Indian National Congress in 1889, where the following year he urged the reduction of salt duties. He was secretary of a regional Congress body, the Bombay provisional conference, in 1893–4, and a joint secretary of the Congress for its 1895 Poona session along with Tilak, whose base in the city enabled him to disrupt the holding of the social conference session immediately afterwards and to assume control of the Sarvajanik Sabha the following year. Gokhale was instrumental in setting up the alternative Deccan Sabha which ensured for him a regional political base, demonstrated by his election to the presidency of the municipality of Poona in 1902–3 and 1905–6. In 1905 he also established the Servants of India Society, an organization of people dedicated to working for the national good as 'national missionaries'.

Gokhale moved into the national limelight in 1897 when he gave evidence on Indian administrative costs before the Welby commission in London. While there he denounced the administration's handling of the plague in Poona, but being unable to obtain corroborating evidence he later retracted his statements. The set-back was temporary: elected to the Bombay legislative council in 1899 for Tilak's former seat he moved in December 1901 to the imperial council, where he remained until his death. He quickly developed a reputation as a critic of the annual government budgets and became a focus of an opposition group within the council; his stance was reinforced by his hostility to Curzon's Universities Bill in 1903–4 and to Minto's measures banning seditious meetings and restricting press freedoms in 1908 and 1910. As a member of the council he accepted nomination as a CIE in 1904, though in 1914 he declined promotion to KCIE. Following the moderate Congress strategy of attempting to influence decision making about India by lobbying in Britain, he toured Britain before the general election in 1905 to promote Indian issues. When the Liberals came into government he visited Britain in 1906 and 1908 to seek to influence the approach of the secretary of state, John Morley, to constitutional reforms. After the implementation of the Morley–Minto reforms in 1909 Gokhale used the new powers available to Indian members in the imperial council to continue his criticism of the budgets and unsuccessfully to introduce measures for compulsory and free elementary education in 1910, 1911, and 1912. In 1912 he was appointed a member of the public services commission, but he died before its report was submitted.

In the early years of the new century Gokhale, Pherozeshah Mehta, and others coalesced as a 'moderate' group within Congress, opposed to the 'new party' or 'extremists' led by Tilak. Differences surfaced over strategies of opposition to Curzon's partition of Bengal. While Gokhale's presidential address to the 1905 Benares Congress accepted boycott as a tactic in extreme situations, others wanted a more general application. The division over this and other issues led to the Congress splitting at the 1907 session at Surat and to the retention of organizational control of Congress by Gokhale, Mehta, and other moderates. By this stage Gokhale's political objectives were clear: accepting the role of providence in ensuring the good of India, he wanted India to be governed on the model of the self-governing colonies of the British empire. He advocated the spiritualization of political life, by which he seems to have meant, since he was initially a rationalist and an agnostic, the application of moral and ethical codes to public work: 'Love of country', he wrote in setting up the Servants of India Society, 'must so fill the heart that all else shall appear as of little moment' (Mathur, 360). His dedication to the national good appealed to M. K. Gandhi, whose activities in South Africa he championed from their first meeting in 1896. Gokhale supported Gandhi's passive resistance in 1909. In 1912 he visited South Africa to reinforce Gandhi's activities, and when Gandhi decided to return to India permanently Gokhale advised him to undertake a year of travel and quiet observation before deciding on his course of action. For Gandhi, Gokhale was his 'political guru' and 'the most perfect man on the political field'. Gokhale's death in Poona from protracted diabetes-induced asthma on 19 February 1915 left Gandhi free to pursue his own direction. In his lifetime Gokhale's difficult nationalist project was to work within—but certainly never for—the structures of British governance. In the process he opposed government measures and developed a style of nationalist politics based upon a rational and dedicated patriotism whose desired end was secular self-government.

Jim Masselos

Sources B. R. Nanda, *Gokhale: the Indian moderates and the British raj* (1977) • *Gopal Krishna Gokhale: a centenary tribute* (1966) • S. A. Wolpert, *Tilak and Gokhale: revolution and reform in the making of modern India* (1962) • J. S. Hoyland, *Gopal Krishna Gokhale: his life and speeches* (1933) • D. B. Mathur, *Gokhale, a political biography: a study of his services and political ideas* (1966) • *Speeches and writings of Gopal Krishna Gokhale*, 3 vols. (1962–7) • G. K. Gokhale, *Speeches* (1920) • M. K. Gandhi, *Gokhale: my political guru* (1955) • R. P. Paranjpye, *Gopal Krishna Gokhale* (1915) • N. R. Phatak, *Adarsh bharatsevak: Gopal Krishna Gokhale yanche charita* (1967) ['ideal servant of India: life of Gopal Krishna Gokhale'] • *Times of India* (20 Feb 1915), 8

Archives National Archives of India, New Delhi, corresp. and papers | CUL, corresp. with Lord Hardinge and others

Likenesses photograph, 1912, Nehru Memorial Museum and Library, New Delhi [*see illus.*] • Mhatre, marble statue, Veer Narimann Road, Churchgate, Bombay

Gold, Ernest (1881–1976), meteorologist, was born on 24 July 1881 at Berkswell, near Coventry, the third of four sons and fourth of eight children of John Gold, tenant farmer, and his wife, Ellen Peckett, of Barnsley, Yorkshire. He was educated at Coleshill grammar school and Mason College, Birmingham. In 1900 he entered St John's College, Cambridge, to become third wrangler (bracketed) in the mathematical tripos (1903) and to take a second class in part two of the natural sciences tripos (1904). After a short spell in the Meteorological Office he returned to Cambridge in 1906 as a fellow of his college until his marriage on 4 July 1907 to Catherine (Kitty) Lockerbie (1879/80–1973), daughter of John and Mary Rannie Harlow, of Edinburgh; John Harlow was a tailor. They had met through the Cambridge Nonconformist Union; their religious belief was a permanent bond for more than sixty years.

Gold was from 1907 the first Schuster reader in meteorology until, in 1910, he took up an appointment in the Meteorological Office and began his lifelong career. Gold's quality in research was established early. A 1908 paper was a timely comparison of the measured wind in the free atmosphere with its theoretical value and in 1909 a treatment of radiation exchange provided an explanation of the existence of the stratosphere, then something of a mystery. By these papers and related work Gold established a leading position in the science, which was recognized by his election as a fellow of the Royal Society in 1918. He continued with a steady output of useful writings although his official duties soon became demanding. When the First World War came Gold accepted a commission in 1915 as captain with the Royal Engineers and he moved to France with a very small company from which nucleus, with no precedent to guide him, he gradually created a military meteorological service. In due course he was providing advice including weather forecasts for ballistics, for gas warfare, and, with evergrowing importance, for the new aviation. Eventually, as lieutenant-colonel, he controlled more than 200 personnel, being appointed DSO in 1916 and OBE (military) in 1919. He was known as Colonel Gold for the next twenty years.

Gold returned to his civilian post after the war and in 1919, when the International Meteorological Organization was reactivated, he was elected president of the Commission for Synoptic Weather Information, an onerous position he retained for twenty-eight years. He presided at its meetings in nine different countries and attended numerous other international gatherings, becoming well known throughout the meteorological world for his tenacity in controversy.

With the approach of the Second World War the Meteorological Office again called upon Gold, this time to organize a comprehensive military service mostly of uniformed personnel in the RAF, but with the civilian office in control. When hostilities spread to all parts of the world the British meteorological service eventually reached a strength of some 6000 with Gold in all but name its general-in-command.

Gold was appointed CB in 1942 and received the American medal of freedom with silver palms in 1946. Before his retirement in 1947 he was influential in planning the totally reorganized and much expanded peacetime Meteorological Office, then under Sir Nelson Johnson, in which scientific research was accorded a substantial role for the first time. Gold was slow in speech, deliberate in thought, given to long silences, and not always an easy superior to work with. He rarely conceded a point in argument but was conscientious and loyal.

Gold attended many meetings of the Royal Society and spoke there in his ninetieth year. He was a prominent fellow of the Royal Meteorological Society, Symons gold medallist in 1926, president 1934–5, and honorary member from 1958. In 1958 the International Meteorological Organization awarded him its medal and prize and the following year honorary membership was conferred by the American Meteorological Society.

From 1910 the family home was in the newly developed Hampstead Garden Suburb where Gold and his wife were active in local affairs. Apart from his broad intellectual interests Gold had his garden, which won him prizes locally, his golf and his bridge, and the graces of entertaining, particularly his many friends from abroad. Kitty Gold died in 1973 and Mary Gold, the couple's only child, cared for her father in his latter years. Gold died on 30 January 1976 at home, 8 Hurst Close, London.

REGINALD C. SUTCLIFFE, *rev.*

Sources R. C. Sutcliffe and A. C. Best, *Memoirs FRS*, 23 (1977), 115–31 · private information (1986) · personal knowledge (1986) · *WWW* · m. cert.
Likenesses photograph, repro. in Sutcliffe and Best, *Memoirs FRS*
Wealth at death £50,013: administration with will, 7 April 1976, *CGPLA Eng. & Wales*

Gold, Sir Harcourt Gilbey (1876–1952), oarsman, was born at Wooburn Green, Buckinghamshire, on 3 May 1876, the ninth and youngest child of Henry Gold (1835–1900), of Hedsor, Buckinghamshire, a director of W. and A. Gilbey, wine merchants, and his wife, Charlotte Anne, daughter of Henry Gilbey, of Bishop's Stortford, Hertfordshire. He went to Eton College, where his genius as an oarsman first became evident in 1893 when he stroked the college to victory in the ladies' plate at Henley. He repeated this triumph in 1894 and again in 1895, in the autumn of which year he went up to Magdalen College, Oxford. Etonians dominated the Oxford crews of the 1890s and with such a record behind him it was not surprising that Gold was picked as a freshman to stroke the crew of 1896. This race turned out to be one of the classic contests, proving beyond doubt that his earlier Henley successes were founded on an innate and mature racing sense. Cambridge, who started as strong favourites, led at one time by as much as a length and a half. With the station conditions against him, Gold bided his time, nursing his crew to the calmer water around Barnes Bridge, less than three-quarters of a mile from the finish. He then produced a dashing and spectacular spurt, gaining a hard-fought victory by the narrow margin of two-fifths of a length. With Gold at stroke, Oxford won the next two boat races. In 1897 they produced what was probably the fastest Oxford crew up to that time, which won as it liked in a time only two seconds outside the existing record. In the following year, when Gold was president of the Oxford University boat club, Oxford won easily after Cambridge became waterlogged in the rough conditions. Gold also stroked the Oxford crew in his final year, 1899, but on this occasion Cambridge won convincingly, ending a run of nine successive defeats.

During his time at Oxford, Gold stroked the Leander eight to victory in the Grand Challenge Cup at Henley, 1896, 1898, and 1899, and in the latter years he also recorded wins in stewards' fours, once with Leander and once with Magdalen. This marked the end of Gold's brilliant if relatively brief career as an active oarsman, although he went on to prove himself an extremely successful finishing coach to a number of Oxford crews, as well as to the two victorious Olympic eights of 1908 and 1912.

Gold, who was a member of the London stock exchange, married in 1902 Helen Beatrice, daughter of Dr Thomas Maclagan, of Cadogan Place, London. They had one son and two daughters. During the First World War he served with the Royal Flying Corps and Royal Air Force, reaching the rank of lieutenant-colonel. In 1918 he was appointed OBE.

In 1919 Gold became a member of the committee of management of Henley royal regatta, having been a steward since 1909. The regatta was struggling financially and Gold was the driving force behind the foundation of the stewards' enclosure. This offered the best views of the racing in a social setting that was convivial even to those without a passing interest in the sport at hand. Enclosure subscriptions soon put Henley on a sound financial footing and by the end of the century membership had grown to about 6000. Fears that rowers would be excluded by the entry fee were allayed with reduced rates for competitors. In fact, Gold's initiative proved crucial to the survival of Henley as a regatta of international quality. He was made chairman of the regatta committee in 1945 and its first president in 1952. For many years he had represented the Oxford University boat club on the committee of the Amateur Rowing Association, of which he was chairman from 1948. In 1949 he was knighted for his services to rowing.

Tarka, as he was invariably known to his friends, was a man of medium build, immaculate attire, and charming manner. Blessed with a buoyancy of spirit and a light and carefree wit, he was one of the most lovable and endearing of companions. He took a genuine interest in his fellow human beings and particularly in the young, who responded wholeheartedly to his youthful and lively approach. He was an excellent shot and had no use for the specialized one-sport mentality. Whether it was in the hunting field, on the tennis court, or on the golf course, Gold's enthusiasm was infectious, and he would give as much care and attention to the arrangements for a day's shooting, or the organization of a local point-to-point, as he would to the myriad details and complications connected with the smooth running of his beloved Henley regatta. He died in London on 27 July 1952. His wife survived him. G. O. NICKALLS, *rev.* MARK POTTLE

Sources personal knowledge (1971) • private information (1971) • *The Times* (29 July 1952) • C. Dodd, *Henley royal regatta* (1987) • C. Dodd, *The Oxford and Cambridge boat race* (1983) • R. Hutchins, *'Well rowed Magdalen!': a history of Magdalen College boat club, 1859–1993* (1993) • *CGPLA Eng. & Wales* (1952)

Likenesses W. Stoneman, photograph, 1949, NPG • Spy [L. Ward], caricature, lithograph, NPG; repro. in *VF* (23 March 1899)

Wealth at death £62,223 14*s.* 11*d.*: probate, 13 Sept 1952, *CGPLA Eng. & Wales*

Gold, Henry (*d.* **1534**), Catholic priest, is first recorded in 1511, when Archbishop William Warham collated him to a chantry in St Peter's, Sandwich. Warham's patronage may also explain Gold's career at St John's College, Cambridge, where the archbishop's colleague John Fisher, bishop of Rochester, wielded the powers of the founder, Lady Margaret Beaufort. Gold graduated there in 1515 and became a founding fellow a year later. He acquired something of a reputation as a humanist, in particular for his mastery of the italic hand. He proceeded MA in 1518, was ordained successively deacon and priest in 1520, and was a university preacher in 1522–3. He resigned his fellowship about 1525, when St John's presented him to the college living of Ospringe, Kent, but took his BTh degree a year or two later, with Thomas Cranmer presiding at his disputation.

Gold resigned Ospringe in 1527, and about this time joined Warham's household as a chaplain. In this capacity he attended him during visitations, and a number of sermons delivered by him on such occasions survive. Warham promoted him to two benefices, both of them Canterbury peculiars: St Mary Aldermary, London (1526–34) and Hayes, Middlesex (1529–34). At Hayes he and his brother Thomas (who farmed the rectory) became embroiled in a protracted tithe dispute with the villagers. Tensions exploded more than once into confrontations and near riots in the parish church itself, which eventually brought the matter to the attention of Star Chamber in 1531–2. There the Gold brothers seem to have won the sympathy of the lord chancellor, Sir Thomas More (perhaps thanks to Henry's connections with Warham and Fisher), but the final outcome of the case, if indeed it reached a resolution, is unknown.

A resolution may have been pre-empted by Henry Gold's involvement in an even more notorious affair, that of Elizabeth Barton, the Nun of Kent. Gold was one of the most enthusiastic adherents of the Kentish visionary nun who about 1530 became a focus for opposition to Henry VIII's quest for a divorce and to the rising tide of evangelical protestantism in England. Archbishop Warham seems to have shared his chaplain's belief in Barton, who herself seems to have stiffened the archbishop's resolve to resist his king's demands. But once Warham had been succeeded by Thomas Cranmer in 1533, her position was undermined. Cranmer led an investigative commission which induced her to confess that she was a fraud and to recant her prophecies publicly. Gold was present at her humiliation in November 1533, and was included with his brother in the act of attainder which closed the case in 1534. Henry Gold was one of those executed along with Barton in London on 20 April 1534, and was buried in London. His brother Thomas escaped with life imprisonment and confiscation of goods, and eventually secured a pardon on 26 August 1536. He blamed Thomas Cromwell for his loss of the farm of a parsonage whose value he reckoned at over £100 a year, and claimed that while he was in the Tower, Cromwell, whom he described as 'a false wretch, a baudy wretch, and a tyrant', unsuccessfully urged him to surrender it in favour of one of his clients (*LP Henry VIII*, 8, no. 738). A substantial body of Gold's correspondence is extant among the state papers, doubtless because it was seized upon his arrest or his attainder. It shows that his scholarly interests survived his departure from Cambridge. RICHARD REX

Sources W. G. Searle, ed., *Grace book Γ* (1908) • M. Bateson, ed., *Grace book B*, 2 vols. (1903–5) • G. R. Elton, *Star chamber stories* (1958) • *LP Henry VIII*, vols. 3–11 • L. P. Whatmore, 'A sermon of Henry Gold, vicar of Ospringe, 1525–27, preached before Archbishop Warham', *Archaeologia Cantiana*, 57 (1944), 34–43 • *The Eagle* (June 1915), 253–83 [St John's College, Cambridge] • William Warham's register, LPL, fol. 343*r.* • act of attainder, 1534, 25 Henry VIII, c. 12 • 'A chronicle, 1413–1536', *Songs, carols and other miscellaneous poems*, ed. R. Dyboski, EETS, extra ser., 101 (1907), 142–67, esp. 164 • D. MacCulloch, *Thomas Cranmer: a life* (1996), 31–2 • Venn, *Alum. Cant.*, 1/2.245

Gold, Jimmy (**1886–1967**). *See under* Crazy Gang (*act.* 1931–1962).

Goldar, John (**1729–1795**), engraver and printseller, was born at Oxford. He must have been trained as a line engraver but also employed stipple late in life. During the 1760s he engraved at least fourteen humorous paintings by John Collet, an artist dubbed 'the second Hogarth', eleven of which were commissioned by the publisher and picture dealer Thomas Bradford. The best known form a set of four entitled *Modern Love* (1765–6), two of which were exhibited with the Free Society prior to publication. Much later, in 1782, they were reissued by John Boydell. Goldar also exhibited with the Society of Artists from 1769 to 1772, showing another Hogarthian comedy after Collet and a *Virgin and Child* after John Hamilton Mortimer. Goldar's earliest print had been *A View of both Squadrons Lying in Ramsay Bay* after a painting by Richard Wright of Liverpool, an engraving published on 30 May 1762. He continued to engrave maritime subjects, but comic subjects after Collet became his speciality, and he engraved similar paintings by other artists, including Herbert Pugh, Philip Dawes, and Samuel Hieronymous Grimm, for the printsellers and picture dealers Henry Parker, John Wesson, and Robert Sayer. Sayer also acquired most of the plates that Goldar had engraved for Bradford.

In 1769 Goldar published a mezzotint of the actor William Powell by John Dixon after William Lawranson, but he did not sustain a career as a publisher. Indeed, he quickly fell back on work for booksellers, although his interest in the theatre endured. He engraved nine portraits of actors in character for Thomas Lowndes's *The New English Theatre* (1777), a high-quality illustrated edition of the best English plays. He also produced numerous portraits and views of naval battles for James Harrison's edition of Paul de Rapin-Thoyras's seminal *History of England* (1784–6). In 1795 he set up again as a publisher and engraved a pair of views of *The Battle of the Saints* (1795) and a pair of stipples of *The Recess* after Henry Richter. He died suddenly of an apoplexy on 16 August 1795, while walking with his daughter and some friends through Hyde Park. The National Maritime Museum, London, holds seventeen of his prints. TIMOTHY CLAYTON

Sources *GM*, 1st ser., 65 (1795), 709 · F. G. Stephens and M. D. George, eds., *Catalogue of prints and drawings in the British Museum, division 1: political and personal satires*, 4 (1883), nos. 4148–51, 4256, 4592, 4604, 4609, 4611, 4613–15 · 'Catalogue of prints and drawings', www.nmm.ac.uk, 11 Nov 1998 · D. Alexander, *Affecting moments: prints of English literature made in the age of romantic sensibility, 1775–1800* (1993), 60–61 · T. Clayton, *The English print, 1688–1802* (1997), 198–9 · *Engraved Brit. ports.* · Graves, *Soc. Artists* · *Public Advertiser* (15 May 1765) · *Public Advertiser* (26 June 1766) · Redgrave, *Artists*, 2nd edn · J. Sunderland, 'John Hamilton Mortimer: his life and works', *Walpole Society*, 52 (1986) [whole issue]

Goldbeter, Bartholomew (*d.* 1430/31). *See under* Moneyers (*act. c.*1180–*c.*1500).

Goldbeter, John (*fl.* 1337–1364), merchant, was probably the son of another John Goldbeter, of York. His career is of interest because he became involved on the margins of royal finance during the 1340s as the combined result of family connections and wartime opportunities. In the summer of 1337 he was imprisoned in Bruges in the course of a general seizure of English merchants and their goods. On that occasion he was described as servant and cousin of Henry Goldbeter (bailiff of York in 1333 and mayor in 1346), which implies that he was still a young man. From about this period, however, he began trading on his own account. When, in 1337, Edward III organized a monopolistic company to handle English wool exports, Goldbeter had a small share in it. In late 1337 or early 1338 he defied the royal seizure of wool at Dordrecht and Middelburg by withdrawing surreptitiously his consignment of 9 sacks and 6 stones and disposing of them to Flemish buyers, an offence for which he was fined £200. From this time until at least 1361 he was engaged in overseas trade, chiefly as an exporter of wool, sometimes as a smuggler. On several occasions he contrived to escape punishment for trading offences because of his services to the crown.

From 1341 Goldbeter was one of the English merchants who benefited from Edward III's reliance upon English merchants to fund his campaigns abroad. This was the time when, in return for commercial privileges, English merchants were taking over services to the crown previously performed by Italian merchant companies. Goldbeter was involved with other York merchants in eight separate loans to the crown between December 1338 and the autumn of 1340, mostly in exchange for freedom from customs duties. Between 1340 and 1342 he also sold wool abroad for the king, as well as trading on his own account, mainly through northern ports.

Goldbeter did not participate directly in any of the syndicates that undertook to collect customs duties for the king between July 1343 and September 1351. However, between May 1346 and April 1349 the customs were leased by Walter Cheriton and his partners in return for loans to the king, and in order to supply loans at the times the king wanted them Cheriton and Company had to borrow. A consortium of York merchants headed by Goldbeter, while avoiding any direct obligations to the crown, was one of the groups that supplied the necessary funds. Between March 1347 and August 1348 they advanced at least £20,649 8*s.* 4*d.* (nearly a sixth of the amount that Cheriton and Company are known to have lent the king) to be repaid out of the customs. In addition Cheriton and Company allowed Goldbeter and his partners freedom to export large amounts of wool without paying customs—this during a period of partial embargo on wool exports. It was presumably, too, in recognition of his financial services that the king gave Goldbeter some messuages in Calais, following its capture on 3 August 1347. The assets of Cheriton and Company were seized by the king in March 1349. Documents that Goldbeter surrendered to the king on that occasion constitute the most important source of information concerning Cheriton's activities. In 1352 Cheriton and Company prosecuted Goldbeter for debt, but Goldbeter was able to establish that in fact the balance of outstanding obligation was the other way round.

Goldbeter never held civic office in York, and it may not have been his normal place of residence after his youth. He spent time in Flanders from his early years in the wool trade, and often worked closely with Flemish merchants. In the spring of 1341 he had licence to export wool in partnership with John Cokelare, *échevin* (municipal magistrate) of Bruges. He lived in Bruges during the siege of Calais, acting with others on behalf of Cheriton and Company and bailing them out of difficulties. In the late summer of 1348 he was again in Bruges, trading through agents in English ports along the east coast. Frequent (or even normal) residence in Bruges perhaps accounts for the paucity of information concerning his career after 1349. He was later said to have collaborated with Flemish merchants illegally in the export of English wool to Flanders between 1353 and 1356. In 1361 he was governor of the English merchants at Bruges. In that year he, with another English merchant and a Fleming, had shares in a ship trading to Nantes under the command of a Flemish skipper. Though outlawed in England in 1362, at the suit of his old rival William de la Pole, for failing to answer charges relating to his illegal activities in 1353–6, Goldbeter was eventually pardoned on 20 November 1364 at the request of Louis de Mâle, count of Flanders. Nothing is known of him after that date. R. H. BRITNELL

Sources E. B. Fryde, *Some business transactions of York merchants: John Goldbeter, William Acastre and Partners, 1336–1349*, Borthwick Papers, 29 (1966) • E. B. Fryde, *William de la Pole, merchant and king's banker* (1988) • E. B. Fryde, 'The English farmers of the customs, 1343–51', *TRHS*, 5th ser., 9 (1959), 1–17 • *CClR, 1327–74* • *CPR, 1327–77* • E. B. Fryde, 'Financial resources of Edward III in the Netherlands, 1337–40', *Revue Belge de Philologie et d'Histoire*, 45 (1967), 1142–1216

Golden, Lewis Bernard (1878–1954), charity administrator, was born on 20 September 1878 in Saratov, Russia. His parents, who were English, owned a meat processing factory in St Petersburg, but their names are unknown. Golden was educated at Prior Park School, Bath, and went on to further education in Bonn, Germany. Before the First World War he was general manager of the Anglo-Russian Trading Company. With trade disrupted by war, from 1917 to 1918 he was correspondent in St Petersburg for the *Daily Mail*, reporting on the events of the revolutionary period. After the Bolshevik seizure of power he fled the country with his wife, Cecily Egan (1872–1958). They had been married in Bruges, Belgium, because of the disapproval of Cecily's parents.

In Britain Golden worked for a time on the staff of the Ministry of Information. In 1919 he became secretary to Lady Muriel Paget's Relief Mission to the Baltic States, which was grant-aided by the Save the Children Fund, and in December Golden was recruited by the fund as its general secretary. Save the Children had been founded in May 1919 by two English sisters, Eglantyne Jebb and Dorothy Buxton, to help starving children in post-war Europe. In December 1919, with Jebb in Geneva trying to establish an international counterpart, the organization in England was on the verge of collapse. 'Our movement here', Dorothy Buxton wrote to her from London, 'is getting wrecked for lack of *business methods*. I see no-one to supply them except Mr Golden' (D. Buxton to E. Jebb, 12 Dec 1919, UISE MSS).

By the time of Jebb's death in 1928 the mixture of her visionary approach and Golden's administrative skills had made the fund one of the most respected and innovative charities in the country. Partly this was through applying business methods to fund-raising. In contrast to its rivals, Save the Children began placing illustrated page-length advertisements in national newspapers. 'The advertisements', Golden wrote later, 'were written with the express idea that if the reader were sufficiently interested to read to the end he was unable to resist the appeal and send a donation' (Eglantyne Jebb MS EJ. 282). The campaign proved a huge success, returning its costs several times over. It enabled the fund to introduce a number of innovative pieces of work, from building refugee villages in Albania and Bulgaria to producing the declaration of the rights of the child, which was adopted by the League of Nations in 1924.

However, the biggest piece of work of all was to begin in 1921, and it was one with a particular significance for Golden. In August of that year reports began arriving in the West of famine conditions in Russia's Volga region, centred on Golden's birthplace, Saratov. An international relief effort began, with the American Relief Administration, funded by the American congress, taking the lion's share. European relief was almost entirely funded by donations, and Save the Children was the major organization in the field.

The Russian famine relief operation (1921–3) was probably the largest of its kind up to that date and for many years after. In addition to the problems of getting food to distant areas, before the onset of winter, in a land devastated by war, Save the Children faced hostility from anti-Soviet campaigners and petty rivalries from other relief organizations as well as suspicion from the Soviet government itself. Nevertheless, by the summer of 1922 the organization was feeding some 675,000 people at a cost of less than a shilling (5 pence) a week. The feeding operation in Russia wound down in 1923, and Save the Children would not operate on anything like this scale for nearly fifty years.

Without a major relief campaign to capture the public's attention, income began to fall dramatically, and from this time on the emphasis of Save the Children's work shifted instead to the promotion of children's rights, through research, publications, and events such as the 1931 Geneva conference on the future of Africa's children. In February 1936, with war increasingly likely, Golden proposed an international convention on children in wartime, including the suggestion that there should be neutral zones for children, marked by a clearly visible symbol, which combatants could agree to avoid. 'I believe', he wrote, 'that if public attitudes can be aroused to consider children and war—a great step will be taken to prevent war' ('Convention on treatment of children in wartime', Save the Children Archives). This proposal received the support of the International Red Cross, but had not made much progress by the time the outbreak of the Second World War made it almost irrelevant.

In the meantime, changes of personnel in the fund's governing council were making Golden feel increasingly out of touch. In 1937, after a dispute about the treatment of Basque refugee children, he resigned, describing the council's action as 'almost criminal' (minutes of council, 15 July 1937). He had always taken particular interest in the treatment of refugees, perhaps because of his own experience. Little is known of his life after Save the Children. He seems to have spent his time in quiet retirement at Kew, Richmond, Surrey. Golden received a number of overseas awards for his work, including appointment to the order of St Alexander from the king of Bulgaria and decorations from the Hungarian and Yugoslav Red Cross organizations. He died in Richmond on 11 November 1954, of lung cancer, and was buried in Kensal Green Roman Catholic cemetery, London, on 16 November.

RODNEY BREEN

Sources *The world's children*, first quarter, 1955, Save the Children Archives, London • Save the Children Archives, London, Eglantyne Jebb MSS • Geneva City Archives, UISE [International

Save the Children Union] MSS • Save the Children Archives, London, special collections, Edward Fuller MSS • minutes of council, Save the Children Archives, London • *The Times* (11 Nov 1954) • private information (2004)

Archives Geneva City Archives, UISE MSS • Save the Children Archives, London, Edward Fuller MSS • Save the Children Archives, London, Eglantyne Jebb MSS

Likenesses photograph, Save the Children Archives, London • photograph, priv. coll.

Golden Ball. *See* Hughes, Edward Hughes Ball (1799–1863), *under* Hughes, Sir Edward (*c*.1720–1794).

Goldesburg [Goldesborough], **John** (**1568–1618**), law reporter and office-holder, was born in Cambridge on 18 October 1568, the son of John Goldesborough (*d.* 1578), who came from a family of Yorkshire descent, and his (possibly second) wife, Margaret. Goldesburg was still a child when his father died and his education was left in the hands of his elder brothers, who included Thomas Goldsborough, MP for Cambridge in 1593, and Godfrey *Goldsborough, then fellow of Trinity College, Cambridge, and later bishop of Gloucester. He is said by Anthony Wood to have studied briefly at Oxford in 1584 'for form's sake' (Wood, *Ath. Oxon.*, 2.234). Among his direct ancestors was a fifteenth-century baron of exchequer, and Goldesburg himself moved into legal practice, probably as an attorney. In 1594 he married Elizabeth Hall of Waltham Abbey in Essex; they had two sons and two daughters. His practice was clearly successful: in 1613 he was made second prothonotary of common pleas, and that year was admitted to the Middle Temple (14 November) and made an associate bencher (26 November). His elder son John, later MP for Huntingdon, was admitted to the inn on 19 March the following year.

At the time of his death on 9 October 1618 Goldesburg (whose wife survived him) owned property in London, Essex, Cambridgeshire, and Huntingdonshire. He was buried near the high altar in the Temple Church. Two volumes of reports associated with his name were subsequently published. *Reports of that learned and judicious clerk J. Gouldesborough, esq., sometimes one of the protonotaries of common pleas* (1663), known as 'Gouldsborough's reports', gained no great reputation, and was almost certainly not the work of Goldesburg. More reputable were the *Reports of divers choice cases in law taken by those late and most judicious prothonotaries of common pleas, R. Brownlow and J. Goldesborough*, first published in two parts in 1651. Contemporary evidence is unanimous in attributing the first part of these to Goldesburg, and there is no good reason to doubt his authorship. Although these reports are not in the first rank of Elizabethan and Jacobean reports, they are workmanlike and succinct, paying particular attention to points of process and procedure. DAVID IBBETSON

Sources A. Goldsbrough, *Memorials of the Goldesborough family* (1930) • K. A. Esdaile, *Temple Church monuments* (1933), 178 • will, PRO, PROB 11/132, fol. 225 • inquisition post mortem, PRO, C 142/373/33 • PRO, CP40, CP45, CP60 • H. A. C. Sturgess, ed., *Register of admissions to the Honourable Society of the Middle Temple, from the fifteenth century to the year 1944*, 1 (1949), 101 • C. H. Hopwood, ed., *Middle Temple records*, 2: 1603–1649 (1904), 234 • G. M. Coles, 'Goldsborough, Thomas', HoP, *Commons, 1558–1603* • Wood, *Ath. Oxon.*, new edn, 2.234 • BL, Add. MS 25232, Hargrave MS 45, Add. MS 38008 • J. L. Chester and G. J. Armytage, eds., *Allegations for marriage licences issued by the bishop of London*, 1, Harleian Society, 25 (1887), 218

Wealth at death total sum unknown; bequests of £250: will, PRO, PROB 11/132, fol. 225

Goldfaden, Avrom (1840–1908), playwright and theatre director, was born in Old Constantine, Ukraine, on 12 July 1840, one of four sons born to Khayim Lipe Goldenfodem, a watchmaker, and his wife, Khane Rivke. Like his brothers, he was apprenticed to his father, but in an effort to take advantage of a new tsarist decree offering the sons of Jewish families an alternative to conscription, he was sent to the rabbinical academy in Zhitomir from 1857 to 1866. By the time he completed his studies he was already a published poet, having submitted verse to the Hebrew literary journal *Hamelits* and its Yiddish offshoot, *Kol mevaser*. In the mid- to late 1860s he published one volume of Hebrew poems and two collections in Yiddish, which he issued under the more German-sounding surname of Goldfaden, the name by which he became well known to Yiddish-speakers worldwide.

Although Goldfaden continued publishing verse throughout his life, it was primarily as a playwright that he made his name. His second volume of Yiddish writing included a three-act play, *Di mume Sosye*, written in the tradition of salon dramas by Jewish intellectuals dating back to the 1790s (indeed, the play in question was essentially an adaptation of Shloyme Etinger's comedy *Serkele*, in which Goldfaden had starred in a rabbinical school production). At the time the play was published there was no professional forum for staging Yiddish plays, but Goldfaden soon changed that.

After completing his rabbinical studies Goldfaden married Paulina Verbl, daughter of the writer Eliyohu Verbl, who befriended and influenced his son in-law. Goldfaden drifted from one job to another for nearly a decade, culminating in a short-lived newspaper venture in Bucharest with his friend and former classmate the writer Yitskhok Linetski. At loose ends in Romania, Goldfaden began writing sketches for local performers, an undertaking that soon led to the formation of a professional company that began touring Romania and Russia in 1876. Goldfaden's career as a playwright progressed in several distinct phases, whose form and content were affected by a combination of the socio-political situation of eastern European Jewry and the evolving theatrical conditions of the Yiddish stage. In the first phase, from 1876 to approximately 1880, he wrote primarily light comedies that tended to satirize religious fanaticism and champion the agenda of the Jewish enlightenment, or Haskalah. Best-known among these works are the farces *Shmendrik* (1877) and *Di tsvey Kuni Leml* (1880) and the comic operetta *Di kishefmakherin* (1879).

As the condition of the Jews of the Russian empire rapidly deteriorated in the early 1880s, Goldfaden set aside his agenda of social reform within the Jewish community and turned to building national morale with operettas of the heroic Jewish past. This new outlook bred several of his most successful and popular works, including:

Shulamis (1881), an epic story set in late antiquity and following the fortunes of a shepherdess and the soldier who falls in love with, abandons, and ultimately returns to her; *Doctor Almasada* (1881), a tale of persecution and redemption of the Jews in Renaissance Italy; and *Bar Kokhba* (1883), based on the true story of a suicidal Jewish uprising against the Roman empire in the second century.

If the legend that the ban imposed on Yiddish theatre in the Russian empire was imposed as a direct response to the production of *Bar Kokhba*, then Alexander III and his advisers must be credited with a reasonable degree of acuity as theatre critics. In any case, the ban, which officially remained in place until after the first Russian revolution of 1905, made life impossible for all but the handful of Yiddish troupes who continued to perform in Russia through a combination of stealth, bribery, and cajolery. Goldfaden and his actors were not among them, and for the rest of his life, he never remained in one country for more than a few years at a time. He first proceeded to Poland, where his company performed in Warsaw and later in Łódź, and then emigrated in 1887 to New York. There he composed his successful biblical dramas *Akeydes Yitskhok* (1887) and *Kenig Akhashveyresh* (1887), but did not get the welcome he expected from colleagues, and ultimately left for London. He led a troupe at the Princess Club Theatre for several months during 1889, but soon moved to Paris and then on to Lemberg (Lwów), his primary city of residence for most of the 1890s.

Goldfaden made a dramatic return to London in 1900 as Paris delegate to the World Zionist Congress. Although his plays had long been ubiquitous on the Yiddish stage—and indeed remained so for decades—Goldfaden and his wife spent most of their final years in dire financial straits, and on his sixtieth birthday a fund was established in London to support the couple. His final years brought continued wandering and declining health, ultimately bringing him to his deathbed as his last play, *Ben Ami*, was running in the New York theatres in the closing weeks of 1907. He died in New York a few weeks into the run, on 9 January 1908, survived by his wife. On the following day 100,000 spectators were said to have greeted his funeral procession to Washington cemetery, New York, where he was buried.

JOEL BERKOWITZ

Sources E. Lahad, *Makhazot Avraham Goldfaden* (1970) • *Leksikon fun der nayer yidisher literatur*, 2 (1958), vol. 2, pp. 77–87 • M. Mayer, *Idish teater in London, 1902–1942 / Yiddish theatre in London, 1902–1942* [1943] • N. Oyslender and U. Finkel, *Avrom Goldfaden: materyaln far a biografye* (1926) • S. Perlmuter, *Yidishe dramaturgn un teater-kompozitors* (New York, 1952) • J. Shatzky, ed., *Arkhiv far der geshikhte fun yidishn teater un drame*, 1 (1930) • J. Shatzky, 'Goldfaden bibliografye', *Goldfaden-bukh* (1926), 77–96 • Y. Yeshurun, *Avrom Goldfaden bibliografye* (1963) • Z. Zylbercweig, *Avrom Goldfaden un Zigmunt Mogulesco* (1936) • Z. Zylbercweig, ed., *Leksikon fun yidishn teater*, 6 vols. (New York, 1931–69), vol. 1, pp. 275–367

Archives YIVO Institute for Jewish Research, New York, YIVO Archives, Perlmutter collection | SOUND YIVO Sound Archives, New York

Likenesses photographs, YIVO Photo Archives, New York

Goldfinger, Ernö (1902–1987), architect, was born on 11 September 1902 in Budapest, second capital of the Austro-

Ernö Goldfinger (1902–1987), by Eileen Agar, 1938

Hungarian empire, the eldest of the three sons (there were no daughters) of Oscar Goldfinger, lawyer, landowner, and industrialist, and his wife, Regine Haiman. His early years were spent among the mountains of Transylvania, and later at school at the Budapest Gymnasium, but the well-to-do family left Hungary following the communist *putsch* in 1919, and Goldfinger spent a year at Le Rosay School, Gstaad, Switzerland, before moving to Paris in 1920 to prepare for admission to the École des Beaux-Arts. There he was a student, first of Léon Jaussely, pioneer in the field of town planning, then of Auguste Perret, pioneer in the architectural use of reinforced concrete. These two interests—in the wider problems of planning and social architecture, and in the logical architectural expression of structure—were to remain with him and to define his mature work. But despite this apparently impersonal architectural commitment, his uncompromising character was inseparable from his work. The force of his personality, charming at times, explosive at others, was at the root of his achievement, and during his lifetime was almost better known than his architecture. His late work can now be seen, however, as the only major expression in Britain of the mature modern architecture of the 1950s and 1960s, deriving directly from the radical architectural thought of continental Europe in the period of the First World War.

As a student in Paris during the 1920s, Goldfinger moved in the avant-garde circles of the Left Bank, and was friendly with artists such as Man Ray, Max Ernst, Robert

Delaunay (with whom he collaborated on film-set design), and Amédée Ozenfant (whose English pupil Ursula Blackwell he later married), and with architects such as Adolf Loos, Pierre Chareau, and Le Corbusier himself, with whom, as French secretary of the Congrès International d'Architecture Moderne, he collaborated in the organization of the definitive Athens conference of 1933. At first in partnership with André Szivessy (later Sive), he designed extremely austere, functional, but elegant shops, apartments, and furniture for an intellectually independent clientele. In 1927 he visited Britain for the first time, to build a salon for the cosmetics pioneer Helena Rubinstein which has been described as the 'first Modern shop in London'.

Towards the end of 1934 Goldfinger moved permanently to London, perhaps attracted by the nucleus of modern architects forming there (many being refugees from Nazi Germany), perhaps looking to his wife's family connections for wider opportunities. (In 1933 he had married Ursula Ruth Blackwell (*d.* 1991), daughter of Walter Reginald Blackwell, gentleman of leisure, a member of the founding family of the successful Crosse and Blackwell food company.) But the work he obtained was self-generated. With a young family (finally two sons and one daughter), he made a speciality in design for children, designing toys and toyshops and the children's section of the British pavilion at the Paris Exhibition of 1937. In 1937 he promoted the construction of a terrace of three houses in Hampstead, London (one being for his own occupation), his first significant building. These houses, in Willow Road, had highly modelled brick and concrete façades rather than the smooth, white-painted surfaces favoured by most of his modern architectural contemporaries. With these houses he effectively established his career, but he was obliged to spend the following war years largely producing exhibitions on economic and social themes for the armed services. (He did not become a British citizen until 1945.)

Goldfinger's political sympathies were with the left, and he designed offices both for the Communist Party and for the *Daily Worker* newspaper in the 1940s; but he was also unusual among architects of his background in receiving patronage from private developers, who gave him his first substantial opportunities. His small office building in Albemarle Street, London (1955–7), was highly praised for its classical poise in a modern idiom, and in 1959 he went on to win with the same client a development competition promoted by London county council for a much larger office block, conceived in the same manner, at the Elephant and Castle, London (which was to become the Ministry of Health). In this building, which won the Civic Trust award for architecture in 1964, he combined an emphatic expression of the concrete skeleton frame with an axial composition, reflecting his training at the École des Beaux-Arts, and a powerful constructivist sense of massing and spatial transparency. At the same time he collaborated with his friend Charlotte Perriand, former associate of Le Corbusier, on the design of French government tourist offices in London. During the 1960s he won further commissions for two large public housing projects in London, each of which had as a dominant feature a thirty-storey slab of very dramatic outline, with a vertical circulation tower standing well clear at one end. The power of the composition was complemented by the elegance of the detail. He was elected an FRIBA in 1963 and an RA in 1975.

Goldfinger was a tall, handsome man, whose tightly compressed features bespoke the tense energy within. By the end of the 1960s his uncompromising commitment to concrete and high-rise housing solutions had become unfashionable, and he finally retired in 1977. He died on 15 November 1987 at his home at 2 Willow Road, Hampstead, London, the house he had built nearly fifty years before. He was survived by his wife. In 1994 the National Trust formally acquired the property at Willow Road, and his house was opened to the public in 1996.

JAMES DUNNETT, *rev.*

Sources M. Major, *Ernö Goldfinger* (1973) • J. Dunnett and G. Stamp, *Erno Goldfinger* (1983) [exhibition catalogue, Architectural Association] • *Architectural Design* (Jan 1963) [special issue] • *The Times* (16 Nov 1987) • personal knowledge (1996) • private information (2004)

Archives RIBA, professional papers | FILM BL NSA, Pigeon Audio-Visual Interview • National Trust, 2 Willow Road, London, National Trust video, and personal home movies • National Trust, 2 Willow Road, London, Hungarian TV interview

Likenesses E. Agar, pen and ink on paper, 1938, NPG [*see illus.*] • photograph, 1974, Hult. Arch. • E. Agar, drawing, National Trust, 2 Willow Road, London • photographs, National Trust, 2 Willow Road, London

Wealth at death £116,008: probate, 10 May 1988, *CGPLA Eng. & Wales*

Goldicutt, John (1793–1842), architect and antiquary, was the son of Hugh Goldicutt (*d.* 1823), bank cashier, and his wife, Celia, *née* Scholar (1756–1813). In 1803 he entered the bank of Messrs Herries, Farquhar & Co., where his father was chief cashier and confidential clerk, but he left on 30 June of the following year and was placed with (Henry?) Hakewill, the architect. He also studied at the Royal Academy from 1812 and proved a talented draughtsman, with a keen eye for colour. Early in life he joined the Architectural Students' Society, where he gained practice in making sketches from given subjects. He competed twice for the Royal Academy silver medal: in 1813, with drawings and measurements of the façade of the India House, and successfully in 1814, with those of the Mansion House. He also gained the silver medal of the Society of Arts in 1815. The same year he went to Paris and entered the school of Achille Leclère and while there competed for monthly prizes at the Académie des Beaux-Arts. Afterwards he travelled in Italy and Sicily for three or four years and collected sketches and material which he later published. Upon his return, he exhibited at the Royal Academy in 1819 a coloured measured drawing of a transverse section of St Peter's, Rome, for which he had received a gold medallion from the pope.

Goldicutt practised with Hakewill until the latter's death in 1830, but also established an independent practice and entered a number of architectural competitions.

In 1820 he obtained third prize in the competition for the Post Office, and in 1829 a prize for the design for the Middlesex Lunatic Asylum. He also competed for the university observatory at Cambridge in 1821, for the Fishmongers' Hall in 1830, and for the Nelson monument in 1841.

Between 1810 and 1842 Goldicutt exhibited thirty-five architectural drawings at the Royal Academy. Several of these were executed abroad, including, in 1820, *Ruins of the Great Hypaethral Temple, Salinuntum, Sicily*, which was etched by Bartolomeo Pinelli for Goldicutt's *Antiquities of Sicily* (1819). He also exhibited drawings of his architectural commissions, including several villas and, in 1842, the Gothic *St James's Church, Paddington*, which building was unfinished at Goldicutt's death, and was completed under the direction of George Gutch (altered by G. E. Street, 1882). Goldicutt's designs were characterized by an elegant neo-classicism, reflecting his personal study of ancient remains.

The Royal Institute of British Architects retains a plan of the observatory at Capo del Monte, drawn by Goldicutt to illustrate a sessional paper in 1840, and a lithograph by him of the Regent's Bridge, Edinburgh. In the print room of the British Museum is *Veduta del tempio d'Ercole a Cora*, drawn and etched by him in 1818. Three of his drawings and two plans, by Goldicutt and Hakewill, were engraved in *Pompeii* (1827) by Thomas Leverton Donaldson.

Goldicutt's publications include: *Specimens of Ancient Decorations from Pompeii* (1825) and *Heriot's Hospital, Edinburgh* (1826; with his own lithographed illustrations). The *Institute of British Architects Sessional Papers* (1836) includes his paper on 'Ancient wells and reservoirs, with observations upon their decorative character', and in 1841 he published a pamphlet, *The Competition for the Erection of the Nelson Monument Critically Examined*. He read several communications at meetings of the Institute of British Architects, and in its library are preserved manuscripts of: 'An address read at the general meeting' (3 February 1835); 'A testimonial to Sir John Soane' (1835); and an extract from a paper 'On the art of fresco-painting' (11 June 1838).

Goldicutt was one of the first honorary secretaries of the Institute of British Architects (1834–6); he played a prominent part in the presentation of a testimonial to Sir John Soane in 1835. He was also a member of the Accademia di San Luca in Rome, and of the Accademia di Belle Arti in Naples. From 1828 he was surveyor for the district of St Clement Danes with St Mary-le-Strand; and was also one of the justices and commissioners of sewers for Westminster and Middlesex. John Henry Hakewill was his pupil.

Goldicutt died at his house, 39 Clarges Street, London (where his mother had died before him in 1813), on 3 October 1842, aged forty-nine, and was buried in Kensal Green cemetery, leaving a widow and five sons.

BERTHA PORTER, *rev.* M. A. GOODALL

Sources *Civil Engineers and Architects Journal*, 5 (1842), 372 · 'John Goldicutt and his times', *ArchR*, 31 (1912), 321–5 · [W. Papworth], ed., *The dictionary of architecture*, 11 vols. (1853–92) · Redgrave, *Artists* · Colvin, *Archs.* · *Dir. Brit. archs.* · Graves, *RA exhibitors* · D. Ware, *A short dictionary of British architects* (1967) · *GM*, 1st ser., 83/1 (1813), 286 · Allibone, *Dict.*

Archives RIBA, biography file · RIBA, MSS collection

Goldie, Sir George Dashwood Taubman (1846–1925), founder of the Royal Niger Company, was born at The Nunnery, Isle of Man, on 20 May 1846, the fourth and youngest son of Lieutenant-Colonel John Taubman Goldie-Taubman, of the Scots guards, speaker of the House of Keys (the lower house of the Manx parliament) and his second wife, Caroline, daughter of John Eykin Hovenden of Hemingford, Cambridgeshire. Goldie's father was of mixed Scottish and Manx descent (his father had been a Goldie of Dumfriesshire and his mother a Taubman, one of the two leading families of the Isle of Man). George changed his name from George Dashwood Taubman Goldie-Taubman to George Dashwood Taubman Goldie by royal licence in 1887 upon receiving his knighthood, perhaps because Taubman sounded German and unsuitable given his association with the recently chartered Royal Niger Company.

Early life and career After passing through the Royal Military Academy at Woolwich, Goldie obtained a commission in the Royal Engineers in 1865. Two years later, inheriting money from a relative, he resigned his commission and left for Egypt where he fell in love with an Arab woman, took her to the Egyptian Sudan and for three years lived an isolated life, which he later described as 'The garden of Allah'. He learned colloquial Arabic, met Hausa pilgrims from west Africa on their way to Mecca, and read most of what was written about the savanna belt of Muslim territory stretching across to the Atlantic.

In 1870 Goldie returned to England and soon offended Victorian ideas of class and sexual morality by running away to Paris with the family governess, Mathilda Catherine (*d.* 1898), daughter of John William Elliot. There the lovers became caught up in the Franco-Prussian War of 1870, and for four months were besieged in the Paris of the commune. Able to return to England in February 1871, both were 'compromised'; they married quietly at St Marylebone Church in London on 8 July 1871.

Goldie's opinions, as much as his actions, defied convention. He was a convinced atheist, an admirer of Huxley, Darwin, and Winwoode Reade. He admired the scandalous Ibsen and the musically unconventional Wagner. Highly intelligent, he never suffered fools gladly, and tried to win all arguments, however trivial. These were not attitudes likely to launch a successful public career. In 1875 opportunity came through family connection. The father-in-law of Goldie's eldest brother ran Holland Jacques, a small Niger trading company in financial trouble. He turned to the Taubman family for help. George Goldie took over the company, re-forming it as the Central African Trading Company, with power to amalgamate with other companies. His Niger visit of 1876 confirmed his view that trading on the Niger could be profitable to a monopoly company able to lower the prices paid to Africans for palm oil, shea-butter, and ivory. In the next three years Goldie persuaded the three other Niger firms

Sir George Dashwood Taubman Goldie (1846–1925), by Sir Hubert von Herkomer, 1898

to amalgamate. The United African Company was formed on 20 November 1879.

Such monopoly by agreement was doomed from the start, for its very success would attract new competitors into a Niger trade where produce could be bought cheaper than elsewhere. This encouraged Goldie to work to transform his company into a colonial 'government' which could enforce such a monopoly, particularly as the new European competitors after 1879 were French traders, seeking treaties with African rulers. Goldie's company responded in kind, using armed ships to coerce Africans, and even intervening in a civil war in Nupe in 1882. By that time large numbers of African small traders from Lagos and Sierra Leone were also moving into the Niger.

While negotiating to buy out the French traders, Goldie knew that a better method of securing the monopoly had to be found. Formerly, the way to enforce monopoly had been by royal charter from the crown; half the empire had been acquired and administered in this way. But it seemed unlikely that such privileges could be revived in the age of free trade.

The National African Company In November 1881, Gladstone's Liberal government granted a charter to the British North Borneo Company. Goldie was immediately struck by the parallels between that company, which based its claims on concessions from local rulers and faced foreign pressures from Spain and Holland, and his own. Parliamentary papers were issued documenting the Borneo charter, and Goldie and his lawyers studied them intently. Their conclusion was that the company should now obtain powers to govern the territory with which it traded, either through a charter from a European government, or by treaties with local African rulers, like those of the Borneo company. The lawyers, however, had doubts about whether the United African Company could legally accept a charter. In June 1882, therefore, Goldie formed the National African Company (NAC), which purchased all the assets of the United African Company. The new company was empowered to accept monopolies, privileges, and political and administrative power from any government in Europe or Africa.

Forming the NAC allowed Goldie to bring people with political influence, necessary if the charter was to be won, to his board. Lord Aberdare, a prominent retired Liberal politician and friend of Gladstone, took the chairmanship of the company as a useful as well as a decorative figurehead. James Hutton, a Manchester cotton exporter and MP, became a director with new representatives from banking and railway companies. Joseph Chamberlain, not yet the imperialist politician who would bring Goldie's rule in Nigeria to an end, invested £950 in the new venture.

From 1882 what began as petty Anglo-French rivalry in west Africa developed into a scramble for territory. By 1883 it was clear that the French policy was to secure new territories for French traders with protective tariffs. This convinced the Foreign Office that something must be done to protect areas where British trade predominated, but the Colonial Office was reluctant to move, the Treasury would not provide funds, nor would parliament vote money. If there was to be expansion of empire, it would have to be empire on the cheap.

Such attitudes were ideal for the nurturing of Goldie's plans for a chartered company. Where government wanted action but refused to pay, the NAC could offer to act, in return for privileges. Early in 1883 Goldie asked that the NAC's chief agent on the Niger be given consular powers to resist the French consul on the Niger. Reluctantly the Foreign Office agreed, though aware that these powers would be used to harass and exclude other traders. The NAC now negotiated treaties with African rulers who ceded their sovereignty to the company and were promised British protection.

Late in 1884 the British position worsened with Germany's sudden annexation of colonies in south-west Africa, Togo, and the Cameroons, the last an area of British trade and missionary influence scheduled to be brought under British protectorate treaties. The 'scramble for Africa' was intensifying, and in October 1884 Britain was invited to the Berlin West African Conference, where France and Germany challenged British informal influence on both the Congo and the lower Niger. A fortnight before the first meeting of the conference, Goldie pulled off a master-stroke, buying out the French Niger companies almost bankrupted by the fierce competition of the NAC, which was now 'alone on the Niger'. Three days before the conference, the cabinet authorized the NAC to hoist the union flag in all places where it held 'independent title', thus recognizing that the company could hold sovereignty over territory and represent Britain.

It was fitting that Goldie should accompany the British delegation to Berlin as an adviser. With the NAC as the sole Niger trader, the British were able to save British claims to the lower Niger, in contrast with the Congo, where King Leopold's Congo Free State emerged as the sovereign power. Bismarck contented himself by accepting a British drafted Niger Navigation Act, which recognized Britain's right to administer the lower Niger without the supervision of an international commission. Navigation was to be free to all nations, and Britain undertook to protect foreign merchants 'as if they were her own'.

The British government, though still unwilling to pay for administration, now had to find a way to fulfil these new responsibilities. Before the Berlin conference ended, Foreign Office officials were advocating a royal charter for Goldie's company, arguing that this would merely formalize the actual position of the NAC. However, the charter was not formally issued until 10 July 1886, by Lord Salisbury's Conservative government. The delay was the result of a long struggle by Goldie to ensure that the company would entirely control the administration of the Niger territories, its officials, and its revenues, while the Foreign Office tried to secure some supervision. In the end Goldie triumphed, for without the means to create a direct British administration the Foreign Office had no cards to play. The charter itself was an admirable document, protecting foreign traders and guaranteeing African treaty rights, free trade, and freedom of religion, but with no system of official oversight it was largely cosmetic.

The Royal Niger Company The NAC now re-formed as the Royal Niger Company, Chartered and Limited (RNC), giving its board power to legislate for the Niger territories. Its trading agents became district agents, a judiciary was established, with a small army of trained Africans under European officers. Goldie announced that there would be little interference with Africans, who would remain under their traditional leaders. The company would mainly concern itself with foreigners to the territory. In practice the RNC rapidly excluded other companies, whether British or foreign, as well as the African small traders from the Niger Coast, Lagos, and Sierra Leone. The day after the charter was issued the RNC announced an elaborate system of licences, regulations, and tariffs which made trade by rivals impossible to conduct at a profit. Goldie had finally solved the problem of how to create an efficient monopoly.

The benefit of this monopoly was a stable record of profitability in the years which followed; the price was successive waves of political opposition from those now excluded from the Niger. The most influential were the Liverpool merchants who traded through African middlemen of the Oil Rivers, after 1884 a separate protectorate under the Foreign Office. The Liverpool men had some political influence in parliament, and backing from the west African shipping interests who equally resented the RNC monopoly. The Liverpool opposition lasted until 1893, and was a complex story in which Goldie almost succeeded in fusing his Liverpool opponents into a bigger chartered company able to take over the administration of the Oil Rivers protectorate. In the end the Foreign Office refused to hand over its meagre but self-sufficient administration and the plan was dropped. After years of opposition, the Liverpool men sold out to Goldie in June 1893, agreeing to keep out of the Niger trade and cease all public criticism in return for shares representing one tenth of the RNC's capital, and a seat on the RNC board.

Liverpool's African middlemen were now stranded without hope of help. The coastal mangrove swamps were unable to grow food, and the city states relied on trade for survival. Worst affected were the people of Nembe (called Brass by the Europeans), whose only markets were the Niger. At the end of January 1895 over 1000 Nembe warriors in their war canoes crossed into RNC territory, attacked the RNC headquarters at Akassa, put the Europeans to flight, smashed the workshops, machinery, and engines of the hated steamers, and looted the company's stores.

British officials in the Oil Rivers sympathized with the Africans. A half-hearted naval expedition fired some shells at Nembe and withdrew, while the plight of the 'Brassmen', excluded from their vital trade, attracted increasing sympathy in Britain, where newspapers accused the company of 'murdering natives'. By April the foreign secretary, Lord Kimberley, had ordered an end to the naval blockade of Nembe, and announced the appointment of Sir John Kirk, former consul-general at Zanzibar, as commissioner to report on the affair.

Kirk's confidential report was received in August. He blamed neither the Nembe people, who had to trade if they were to eat, nor the company, which had the right to enforce its regulations, to which the British government had not objected. Kirk went on to propose a solution which would open up free trade on the Niger and preserve the chartered company. There is evidence that Goldie, tired of the endless battles with trading rivals, and:

> not content that the sacrifice to a national object of all the best years of my life … should result in my name being remembered only as that of a monopolist, who blocked the road to civilisation and commerce in the Niger basin

proposed this solution to Kirk (Goldie to Clarke, 'Note', 26 Oct 1895). The idea was that the RNC, like the East India Company in its last years, should cease to trade at all, concentrate entirely on administration, pay dividends from its customs revenue, and thus be forced to run a regime which would produce maximum trade and competition. From now on Goldie, concerned with increasing threats of French encroachment, steadily pressed for Kirk's reform scheme.

But this was not to be. In 1895 Lord Salisbury's Conservatives came back to office, with Joseph Chamberlain—a man ready to spend on African empire—as colonial secretary. After months of pressing for Kirk's scheme, Goldie was told in January 1896 that it was 'absolutely unacceptable'. Chamberlain intended to revoke the charter and establish direct administration, but in his own good time.

Decline of the Royal Niger Company In the last five years of the company's rule, from 1895 to 1900, the RNC increasingly became an anachronism. Paper claims were giving way to effective occupation, as French, German, and even British administrations used African troops under European officers to forestall each other and impose authority on Africans. This expensive game was played in a league where a trading company like the RNC was outclassed.

By 1894 the French had ceased to believe in the reality of the company's claims in the Muslim empire of Sokoto, and began occupying towns in Borgu, infiltrating into the north-west of RNC claims. Goldie responded by hiring Frederick Lugard, already famous for his activities in Uganda, to move with soldiers and treaty-making in the 'chessboard' of Borgu, a strategy which increased tension with France and ultimately led to the Niger crisis of 1897–8.

Not only foreign powers complained of the company's ineffective authority. The Colonial Office regime in Lagos was by the 1890s ruling Yoruba, inheriting the tensions between the Yoruba empire and the Muslim emirates of Ilorin and Nupe, supposedly under chartered rule. Visits to Ilorin by Governor Carter of Lagos showed that Goldie did not rule Ilorin or its Muslim ally Nupe as the company claimed. By the time Chamberlain took office in 1895 Ilorin was virtually at war with Lagos. Chamberlain insisted that Goldie's company should stop this, or the Lagos regime would send an expedition for which the RNC would pay. In effect Goldie was ordered to go to war with Ilorin.

Goldie personally took command of the company's troops and rode with them out of Lokoja on 6 January 1897 at the head of 513 African soldiers and thirty European officers, first to attack Nupe, where the company had lost all influence. In the subsequent campaign Goldie used Maxim guns, electric searchlights, remote-controlled flares, and dismantleable artillery to offset the huge numerical advantage of the Nupe cavalry and infantry. He also exploited internal ethnic and religious rivalries, and disunity in the Nupe aristocracy. The Niger canoe men rebelled, splitting the Nupe army in two. Revolts were fomented among non-Muslims. Finally, after destruction of the emir's army in Bida, its other half was won over by negotiation, and its leader put on the Nupe throne. Thereafter Goldie marched his troops to Ilorin. After a short bombardment of the city the emir (with whom Goldie had continued to correspond, even during the fighting) surrendered. He was then reinstated, with a new treaty supposedly settling matters with Lagos.

With Goldie in Nupe and Ilorin, the French occupied a number of towns in Borgu. This sparked an Anglo-French crisis. Chamberlain was ready for war if necessary, raising a west African imperial army to play the French at their own game of effective occupation. By May 1897 Chamberlain had decided to take over the RNC, but needed Goldie's co-operation in the transition to facilitate the entry of imperial forces. All this would cost the company money, and Goldie, sensing what was afoot, demanded that if the end was nigh, the revocation of the charter should be speedy. Chamberlain, however, wanted to force the French to a negotiated agreement on boundaries before taking over the company, lest its demise could be taken by the French as a lapse of British rights.

The result was an increasingly testy relationship between Chamberlain and Goldie, in which Goldie fought a campaign of awkward non-co-operation designed to get the best terms of buyout. Chamberlain eventually won minimal co-operation by appointing Goldie's friend Lugard to command the newly formed West African frontier force, and by obtaining Treasury assurances that the RNC would be fairly compensated. Eventually the battle for Nigeria's western frontier was settled in Paris and London. Faced with Chamberlain's determined stand, and worried by German strength in Europe, France settled all outstanding frontier and tariff issues in west Africa in the convention of June 1898.

Negotiations with the Treasury for the take-over of the RNC were not completed until June of 1899. Goldie fought stubbornly for his shareholders, and came away with a generous settlement of £865,000 for the company's administrative assets, together with permanent mineral royalties on future mining discoveries. On 1 January 1900 the company's administration was handed over to Lugard, appointed governor of the new protectorate of Northern Nigeria.

Final years Goldie was not yet fifty-four, but the end of the RNC marked the end of his significant public life. He was devastated in 1898 by the sudden death of his wife. By 1899 he had determined to leave the Niger Company, whose directors wanted him to continue. Though his family retained a large shareholding, Goldie sold his own holdings in the company, which eventually joined the Liverpool interests in a new United Africa Company, absorbed into the huge Unilever conglomerate in the 1920s. After 1900 Goldie dreamed of new chartered company ventures on the Nile, the Amazon, and even the Yangtze (Yangzi), but these came to nothing. In 1901 he turned down the choice of governorships of New South Wales or Victoria in the new commonwealth of Australia. After the death of Cecil Rhodes, Goldie was approached in 1903 by the British South Africa Company, the last remaining chartered company in Africa, to join its board; though tempted, he rejected the offer. In the years before the First World War he became an alderman on the London county council, work which he enjoyed, and travelled widely in Europe and America. After the war he began to suffer from emphysema. In the summer of 1925, returning from Italy, he became very ill, and died alone at the Empire Nursing Home, Vincent Square, London, on 20 August.

SCARBROUGH, *rev.* JOHN FLINT

Sources J. E. Flint, *Sir George Goldie and the making of Nigeria* (1960) • E. A. Ayandele, *Nigerian historical studies* (1979), chaps. 5–7 • D. J. M. Muffett, *Concerning brave captains* (1964) • D. Wellesley, *Sir George Goldie, founder of Nigeria* (1934) • G. D. T. Goldie, 'Note for persons acquainted with the situation in the Niger territories', 26 Oct 1895, PRO, MS FO 83/1384 • *CGPLA Eng. & Wales* (1928)

Archives PRO, corresp. with foreign office, FO 84, FO 83 and FO 2 series | BLPES, corresp. with E. D. Morel • Bodl. RH, Holt MSS • Bodl. RH, Royal Niger Company MSS • Bodl. RH, corresp. with Lord Lugard • Bodl. RH, corresp. with Lord Scarbrough • NL Ire., letters to A. S. Green • U. Birm. L., corresp. with Joseph Chamberlain
Likenesses H. von Herkomer, oils, 1898, NPG [*see illus.*] • W. Stoneman, photograph, 1917, NPG
Wealth at death £73,293 12*s.* 1*d.*: resworn probate, 15 Oct 1925?, *CGPLA Eng. & Wales*

Goldie, Grace Murrell Wyndham [*née* Grace Murrell Nisbet] (**1900–1986**), television producer, was born on 26 March 1900 in Glenfinnan, in the district of Arisaig, Inverness-shire, the only daughter and second of the three children of Robert James Nisbet, civil engineer, and his wife, Alice Isabel Wright. Her father's work took him to Egypt and Grace first attended school at the convent of Notre Dame de Sion in Alexandria. In 1916 the family returned to Britain and she was educated at Cheltenham Ladies' College. Despite a warning that her early schooling abroad would prevent her from going on to tertiary education, she managed to enter Bristol University, where she took a first-class honours degree in history (1921). She then went to Somerville College, Oxford, and achieved a second class in philosophy, politics, and economics (1924).

For the next three years Nisbet taught history at Brighton and Hove high school. Petite and birdlike, in 1928 she married the handsome actor Frank Wyndham Goldie (1894–1957), the son of Lewis Alexander Goldie, solicitor, and his wife, Phillis Payne. They lived in Liverpool for six years, during which she lectured on drama, acted as an examiner in history, read plays for the repertory theatre where her husband was working, and wrote a book on its history, *The Liverpool Repertory Theatre, 1911–1934* (1935). In 1934 they moved to London and for the next seven years she wrote radio criticism for *The Listener*, turning her attention to television when it started in 1936. During the Second World War she spent two years (1942–4) at the Board of Trade before joining the BBC staff in 1944 as a talks producer, replacing Guy Burgess.

Goldie produced some major current affairs series such as *Atomic Energy* (1947) and *The Challenge of our Time* (1948). In 1948 she moved to the television talks department at Alexandra Palace, to the disappointment of Bertrand Russell, who said, 'My dear girl, television will be of no importance in your lifetime or mine; I thought you were interested in ideas.' She was indeed; and she managed to translate political or international ideas into effective television programmes. She successfully enlisted academics such as David Butler and Robert McKenzie to take part in the mammoth election results programmes which she mounted, beginning in 1951. She also encouraged political ministers to appear on the new medium in *Press Conference*. In 1949 Goldie started *Foreign Correspondent*, shortly to be followed by *International Commentary*, *Race Relations in Africa*, and *India's Challenge*, all well-researched programmes, with articulate presenters such as the war correspondents Chester Wilmot and Edward Ward, as well as Christopher Mayhew and Aidan Crawley, then both former right-wing Labour MPs with considerable experience of the responsibilities of government and an interest in communication. Her regular use of these and other former Labour MPs led some Conservatives to complain that she was a well-known socialist. In fact her political instincts were Conservative, and her husband worked part-time for the Conservative central office. In 1954 a new head of television talks was appointed and Goldie became the assistant head of the department. Her high standards and her mastery of television techniques made her a valuable trainer of production staff who sought attachments to an expanding and highly regarded department. Without children herself, she particularly enjoyed recruiting and training youngsters. She excelled at starting new programmes, and making sure that they began well, but she tended to interfere with the minutiae of programme content, and it was not always easy for producers, especially the women, to work with her. She was described as having a whim of iron, and once a new series, such as the revamped current affairs vehicle *Panorama*, the daily magazine *Tonight*, or the arts programme *Monitor*, had been successfully launched, it was imperative to direct her restless energy elsewhere. She continued to produce major programmes herself, such as the tribute on Sir Winston Churchill's eightieth birthday in 1954, and *Men Seeking God*. In 1958 she was appointed OBE.

After the death of her husband in 1957, Goldie found relaxation difficult. Reluctant to return to her empty flat, she would remain late at the studios, arguing and dissecting programmes. Emboldened in the hospitality room, she would tell cabinet ministers, with the same asperity she showed to producers, what she thought of their performances. In 1962 she became head of talks and current affairs. After retirement in June 1965 she wrote *Facing the Nation* (1977), a definitive book about television and politics. Grace Goldie died in London at her flat in Kensington, 86 St Mary Abbots Court, Warwick Gardens, on 3 June 1986. LEONARD MIALL, *rev.*

Sources G. W. Goldie, *Facing the nation* (1977) • *The Times* (5 June 1986) • personal knowledge (1996) • b. cert. • b. cert. [Frank Wyndham Goldie] • *CGPLA Eng. & Wales* (1986)
Wealth at death £209,751: probate, 15 Sept 1986, *CGPLA Eng. & Wales*

Goldie, John (**1717–1809**), religious controversialist, was born at Craigmill, Galston, in Ayrshire, where his forebears had been millers on Cessnock Water for nearly 400 years. He had little schooling, but after his mother had taught him to read he soon learnt writing, and displayed early mechanical aptitude; at the age of fourteen he constructed a miniature mill, which could grind a boll of pease in a day. Although he served no apprenticeship he decided to become a cabinet maker and set himself up in nearby Kilmarnock; the duke of Hamilton admired a mahogany clock-case which he had carved, and paid £30 for it. Goldie subsequently established a profitable wine and spirit business. An accomplished mathematician, he was noted for his speed at mental arithmetic; he was also keenly interested in astronomy.

To read the history of the Church of Scotland in the

eighteenth century is to plunge into a morass of controversy, dissent, and secession. Those who adhered most tenaciously to Presbyterian principles were sometimes known as whigs; another term was 'Old Lichts', because they opposed those who claimed to have 'new light' on the solemn league and covenant.

Goldie gradually moved away from the strictly orthodox Calvinism of his youth, but he was in his sixties before he first appeared in print. *Essays on various subjects; moral and divine; being an attempt to distinguish true from false religion* was published in Glasgow in 1779 and ranged him firmly on the side of the 'New Lichts'. He argued strenuously, if not always entirely coherently, against the 'lying vanities' of those who interpreted the Bible literally. While stopping short of attacking divine revelation, he repudiated almost all other fundamental tenets of Christian belief. He contended that all scriptural texts must be subjected to 'the infallible test, the nature and perfection of the true God' (*Life and Work of Robert Burns*, 1.460). Depravity, he argued, cannot be conveyed by heredity, because sin is 'only an act of the creature' (ibid., 1.461)—a clear anticipation of liberal protestantism.

This onslaught on the theological bigotry of the day was widely read throughout the west of Scotland and became known as 'Goudie's Bible'. Six years later a second edition appeared, and to this Goldie added *The Gospel Recovered from its Captive State, by a Gentle Christian*. It was at this point that he excited the admiration of a young farmer in the neighbourhood who took a lively interest in what he termed 'polemical divinity' and who was moved to pen an admiring verse epistle:

> O Gowdie, terror o' the whigs
> Dread o' black coats and reverend wigs!
> Sour Bigotry on his last legs
> Girns and looks back,
> Wishing the ten Egyptian plagues
> May seize you quick.
> (R. Burns, *Epistle to John Goldie in Kilmarnock, Author of, The Gospel Recovered*—)

It was one of Robert Burns's earliest satires on orthodox Calvinism. Goldie was one of those who discouraged him from going off to the West Indies as he was planning to do at that time. He also stood surety for him with Wilson, the Kilmarnock printer, when the first edition of Burns's poems appeared in the following year—although the poet, already twice disciplined by the church for fornication, judged it prudent not to provoke orthodoxy further by including his epistle to Goldie in the collection.

Goldie subsequently lost heavily by speculating in coal. He was also concerned in an abortive attempt to connect Kilmarnock by canal to Troon, which had one of the best deep-water harbours on Scotland's south-west coast. Kilmarnock town council applied to parliament for the necessary act in 1786, but the scheme foundered for lack of funds.

Goldie maintained his interest in astronomy and he continued to write, although his style did not become less prolix or inelegant with the years. His last work, *Conclusive Evidences Against Atheism; in Vindication of a First Cause*, appeared in 1809; this contained a prospectus for a projected work entitled *A Revise, or a Reform of the Present System of Astronomy*. In the same year, while visiting Glasgow, he caught cold by sleeping in a damp bed and died in Kilmarnock on 28 March 1809 at the age of ninety-two, in complete possession of his faculties.

Of medium height and sturdily built, Goldie was known locally as 'the philosopher' and admired for his good sense and transparent honesty. He was on friendly terms with most of the local clergy, and liked nothing better than to debate with them; in argument, wrote Archibald M'Kay, he was 'calm, dignified and powerful' (M'Kay, 168). He left many manuscripts and letters from Lord Kames, Burns, and other well-known men of the day, but they appear to have been destroyed during his son's absence at sea.

IAN MCINTYRE

Sources J. Paterson, *The contemporaries of Burns and the more recent poets of Ayrshire* (1840) • A. M'Kay, *A history of Kilmarnock* (1848) • *The life and works of Robert Burns*, ed. R. Chambers, rev. W. Wallace, [new edn], 4 vols. (1896) • *The poems and songs of Robert Burns*, ed. J. Kinsley, 3 vols. (1968) • F. B. Snyder, *The life of Robert Burns* (1932) • M. Lindsay, *The Burns encyclopedia*, 3rd edn (1980) • J. A. Mackay, *Kilmarnock: a history of the Burgh of Kilmarnock and of Kilmarnock and London District* (1992) • *GM*, 1st ser., 79 (1809), 387–8 • *DNB*

Likenesses engraving (after Whitehead), repro. in Paterson, *Contemporaries of Burns*

Goldin, Horace [*real name* Hyman Elias Goldstein] (**1873–1939**), illusionist and entertainer, was born on 17 December 1873 at Vilna, Russia, the son of Emmanuel Goldstein, a Jewish fruit grower. His father emigrated to join his brother in the USA about 1881, leaving his family behind until he could provide for their passage; Hyman eventually arrived in America in 1889. His interest in conjuring had been aroused in boyhood by a Gypsy magician and after various jobs as a salesman he decided to become a professional magician, initially working in dime museums and similar venues. His career prospered after the English conjuror Herbert Albini taught him his famed version of the 'egg in bag' trick. About this time Goldstein adopted the name Horace Goldin.

Goldin first came to notice with an illusion 'Dreyfus Escapes from Devil's Island', based on the notorious French spy case; throughout his career this flair for linking illusions with topical events continued to serve him well, as did his eye for publicity. When in the late 1890s the *New York American* critic Alan Dale criticized Goldin's broken English, he devised a novel non-speaking act of rapidly performed tricks to fast musical accompaniment that proved highly successful on the American Keith theatre circuit.

Goldin made his début in Britain at the Palace Theatre, London, on 8 July 1901, to great acclaim, and his whirlwind performance pioneered a new style of magical presentation which attracted many copyists. He returned to the Palace in 1902 and annually for the next three years, also touring the British provinces and the continent. After an appearance at Sandringham on 12 December 1902 he performed on several other occasions for King Edward VII and Queen Alexandra. He was a short, dapper man whose youthful plumpness tended to corpulence in middle age, but even towards the end of his life, on stage, he maintained his characteristic, fast-paced show. His hands were particularly suited to sleights and he was a master of intimate magic, which admirably complemented his gregarious nature; the torn and restored cigarette paper was a favourite close-up item in his repertory. He displayed an infectious enthusiasm for magic that never diminished and was always happy in the company of both amateur and professional magicians.

Apart from America and Europe, Goldin toured Africa for five months in 1912, and undertook an extended tour embracing Siam, Singapore, Colombo, Japan, Australia, New Zealand, and Java during 1915–18. On his return to America via the Hawaiian Islands he had the misfortune to lose several illusions and the strongbox containing most of his profits from the tour when a small boat transferring them from shore to liner capsized at Lahaina in July 1918.

Goldin invented the famous illusion 'Sawing a Woman in Two' which he first presented in America in 1921 at the same time as the English illusionist P. T. Selbit was presenting his 'Sawing through a Woman'. In Goldin's performance the halves were separated after the sawing through, whereas in Selbit's the act of cutting the woman had no subsequent separation. Despite the use of different principles, lawsuits ensued which Goldin won, although the available evidence suggests that Selbit pioneered the concept. Goldin also resorted to litigation in 1922 when a film company screened an exposure of the illusion. In both foregoing versions of the illusion the woman was placed in a box prior to the use of a crosscut saw, but in 1931 Goldin invented 'The Living Miracle', employing a circular saw with the victim remaining in full view throughout.

Litigation had taken its toll, however, coupled with his losses in Hawaii; Goldin was declared bankrupt in 1921 with liabilities of $38,775, and again in 1924 during a tour of Britain, with estimated liabilities of £9000. Other notable illusions invented by him were the 'Girl Shot from a Cannon to the Innermost of Three Boxes' (*c.*1905), 'Walking through a Sheet of Glass' (*c.*1914), 'Film to Life', in which characters step out of a film, interact on stage, and then return to the screen (1920), and 'Life in a Balloon', the appearance of a girl in a large balloon inflated on stage (1936). He was less successful when he endeavoured to emulate contemporary illusionists such as Lafayette by producing magical playlets. The principal example was 'The Tiger God' (1911) which featured the vanishing of a tiger in a cage.

On 19 August 1927 Goldin married a widow, Helen Leighton (*née* Levy) (*d.* 1945), an American, previously an actress, whom he had admired for over thirty years; they had no children. Thereafter he spent much of his time performing in Britain. His autobiography, *It's Fun to be Fooled*, was published in 1937. He was president of the Magicians' Club, London, from 1934 until he died at his home in London on 22 August 1939 during a week's engagement at Wood Green Empire. He was buried at the Jewish cemetery, Willesden, London. His show was subsequently sold to Cecil Lyle, reputedly for £2000. EDWIN A. DAWES

Sources H. Goldin, *It's fun to be fooled* (1937) · M. Christopher, 'Le Roy and Goldin — trendsetters', *The illustrated history of magic* (1973), 293–318 · J. Fisher, *Paul Daniels and the story of magic* (1987), 138–43 · D. Price, *Magic: a pictorial history of conjurers in the theatre* (1985), 222–6 · C. Waller, *Magical nights at the theatre* (1980), 194–5 · W. Goldston, *Who's who in magic* (1934), 35–8 · L. Gautier, 'Great magicians I have known: Horace Goldin', *The Magic Circular*, 37 (1942–3), 73–5 · E. Stanyon, 'Explanatory programmes: Horace Goldin, illusionist', *Magic*, 1 (1900–01), 99 · E. Stanyon, 'Explanatory programmes: Horace Goldin, illusionist', *Magic*, 2 (1901–2), 4 · N. Weaver, 'London notes', *Mahatma*, 5 (1901), [7] (not paginated) · 'Horace Goldin's great show', *Magician Monthly*, 9 (1912–13), 29 · H. Goldin, 'My first three years in England', *World's Fair* (24 Dec 1938) · *Magician Monthly*, 8 (1911–12), 2 · *CGPLA Eng. & Wales* (1939) · d. cert.

Archives FILM BFI NFTVA, performance footage

Likenesses photographs, Magic Circle Museum, London · photographs, priv. coll.

Wealth at death £587 6*s*. 9*d*.: administration, 29 Oct 1939, *CGPLA Eng. & Wales*

Golding, Arthur (1535/6–1606), translator, was the second son among the seven children of John Golding (*d.* 1547), landowner and civil servant, and his second wife, Ursula (*d.* *c.*1564), daughter and coheir of William Marston, landowner, and his wife, Beatrix; John Golding had also had four children with his first wife, Elizabeth. The Golding family had, in the fifteenth and early sixteenth centuries, been enriched by the cloth trade and by marriages with heiresses, and were, by the mid-sixteenth century, fairly wealthy and respectable.

Early years Arthur's early life was that of a gentleman's younger son. There are no records of his schooling, although he may have attended the grammar school at Halstead, Essex, when his mother moved to a dower house near there after his father's death. He matriculated as a fellow commoner at Jesus College, Cambridge, at Easter 1552, but appears to have gone down without taking a degree. In 1548 Arthur's half-sister Margery had married John de Vere, sixteenth earl of Oxford, one of the richest peers in England, and before 1553 his brother Henry was the steward of Lord Oxford's household. Henry's election to parliament in 1558 probably reflects Oxford's influence. Arthur clearly hoped that some of that influence would be used on his behalf: in the later 1550s or the first years of the next decade, he was working on a translation of the historian Pompeius Trogus, which he planned to dedicate to Lord Oxford. After Oxford's death in August 1562 his son Edward, nephew of Arthur and Henry Golding, succeeded to his title and estates, becoming a ward of William Cecil, who appears to have employed Arthur in the young earl's affairs for several years. At the end of 1564 Arthur was living in Cecil House, London, and as late as 1567 he dated a dedication from Barwicke, near White Colne, Essex, one of the de Vere manors.

Arthur's duties were not so onerous as to prevent him from publishing five translations between 1562 and 1565, all from Latin. Four were of prose works: an account of the recent exhumation and burning of the corpses of Martin

Bucer and Paul Fagius; Leonardo Bruni's history of the sixth-century reconquest of Italy from the Goths; Pompeius Trogus, now dedicated to Edward de Vere; and the *De bello Gallico* of Caesar, the first full English translation of this very important book. He began the last of these at the instigation of Cecil, who had sent him an unfinished translation of Caesar's work by John Brende and suggested that he should complete it; however, in order to 'have the body of the whole Storye compacted unyforme and of one stile throughout' (sig. *3r), Golding decided to translate the whole himself. In all his prose translations, his writing has a robust and lively quality, and renders the original accurately.

The translation of Ovid's *Metamorphoses* The fifth of Golding's early translations made its first appearance early in 1565 as *The fyrst fower bookes of P. Ovidius Nasos worke intitled Metamorphosis, translated into Englishe meter.* Two years later Golding completed the work, translating all fifteen books of Ovid's poem. He used an edition in which the notes of Raffaele Regio were printed. This was the first English translation of the whole of the *Metamorphoses* from the Latin (rather than, like Caxton's, from the French of the *Ovide moralizé*), and it was widely read: its influence has been detected in Edmund Spenser's *Faerie Queene*, in John Studley's translations of Seneca, in Christopher Marlowe's *Tamburlaine* and *Edward II*, and elsewhere. Most famously, Shakespeare knew Golding's Ovid and recalls it in a number of plays. Edmond Malone pointed out that Prospero's speech in *The Tempest* which begins 'Ye elves of hills, brooks, standing lakes, and groves' echoes Golding's version of *Metamorphoses*, vii. 197f., 'ye Elves of Hilles, of Brookes, of Woods alone, Of standing Lakes', and since Malone, Golding has been shown to have influenced, and to have been responded to in, other passages in Shakespeare, such as the play of Pyramus and Thisbe in *A Midsummer Night's Dream*. Shakespeare actually had his knowledge of Ovid from several sources—for instance, the passage in *The Tempest* mentioned above is at some points closer to the original Latin than to Golding's English—but his use of Golding's *Metamorphoses* is beyond any question, and has been an important part of the history of the translation itself, an influential edition of which was published in 1904 as *Shakespeare's Ovid*.

The metre Golding used, 'fourteeners', or fourteen-syllable lines with a regular iambic stress, rhyming in couplets, can be very monotonous, especially in the hands of writers who make a regular break after the eighth syllable. Golding avoided this regularity, and his fourteeners are flexible and powerful. The metre still inevitably tends to give an impression of vigour rather than delicacy, and Golding did not attempt to emulate Ovid's wit and elegance. Nor did he strive for concision: the translation runs to about 14,500 lines compared to Ovid's 12,000. But, although Ezra Pound's famous claim that it is 'the most beautiful book in our language' (*ABC of Reading*, 1934, 113) is a hyperbole, Golding's *Metamorphoses* is highly competent: lucid, unpretentious, and fast-moving, it can be read with great pleasure. This, however, is not quite what Golding intended: a verse on the title-page of *The Fyrst Fower Bookes* points out that:

> With skill heede and judgment thys work must bee red
> For else to the reader it stands in small stead,

and his long verse dedication to the full translation urges the sort of moralizing allegorical reading which had been applied to Ovid in previous centuries.

Later translations from Latin and French, and original works His work on Ovid is an anomaly in Golding's career: all his other translations were of religious or factual works. In the same year as the *Metamorphoses* he translated *A Little Booke of John Calvines Concernynge Offences* from the Latin, and this was to be followed by a series of major translations of Calvin: his commentaries on the Psalms in 1571, his sermons on Job in 1574, his sermons on Galatians in the same year, his sermons on Ephesians in 1577, and his sermons on Deuteronomy in 1583. His translations of prose works amount in all to about five and a half million words. One contemporary comment on Golding was that he 'hath taken infinite paynes without ceasing, [and] travelleth as yet indefatigably' (W. Webbe, *Discourse of English Poetry*, 1586, sig. C4r), and it is the translations of religious works that show his indefatigability most clearly. As well as his work on Calvin, he translated extensive Lutheran commentaries on the New Testament from the Latin of Niels Hemmingsen and David Chytraeus, in two volumes both dedicated to Sir Walter Mildmay, and about a dozen other works by protestant writers such as Beza, Bullinger, and Augustin Marlorat. A noteworthy late translation was that of a substantial theological work by Philippe Duplessis-Mornay, published in 1587 as *A worke concerning the trewnesse of the Christian religion … begunne to be translated into English by Sir Philip Sidney knight, and at his request finished by Arthur Golding*. The connection between Sidney and Golding is interesting, but no part of the translation itself appears to be by Sidney: here, as in the case of Brende's translation of Caesar two decades earlier, Golding may have preferred to retranslate rather than to splice his work to another translator's.

The only contemporary of Golding's who referred explicitly to his translations of godly works was Nashe, who praises 'aged *Arthur Golding* for his industrious toile in Englishing *Ovids Metamorphosis*, besides manie other exquisite editions of Divinitie, turned by him out of the French tongue into our own' (preface to Robert Greene, *Menaphon*, 1589, sig. **4v). They have been neglected by modern scholars as well, and there are unsolved problems of ascription: for instance a translation of Robert Grosseteste's Latin version of the apocryphal *Testaments of the Twelve Patriarchs* is often ascribed to Anthony Gilby, but was claimed as Golding's shortly after his death. The issue is further complicated by Thomas Wilson's claim, made after Golding's death, to have had a share in some of his translations. After completing the *Metamorphoses*, Golding translated no pagan authors at all for eleven years (though he did revise his Pompeius Trogus in 1570), before turning to Seneca's highly moral *De beneficiis* in 1578. Then in 1585 he made the first published English translation of the geographical compendium of Pomponius Mela, which was only superseded in 1998; in 1587 he translated another encyclopaedic treatment of the world, the *Collectanea* of Julius Solinus.

Golding wrote only two original books, both short. The first was an account of the murder of George Sanders in 1573, which became the main source of the play *A Warning for Fair Women*. The second was a meditation on the earthquake of 1 April 1580, which was published both by itself and also as an appendix to a special prayer, occasioned by the earthquake, which was circulated in 1580 for use in all parish churches. He also wrote liminary verses for John Baret's *Alvearie* in 1574. His learning was acknowledged by an honorific admission to the Inner Temple in 1574, and by membership of the Society of Antiquaries at some time after its formation in 1586. None of the papers of that society from Golding's lifetime which have been printed can be ascribed to him.

Personal affairs after 1565 The date of Golding's marriage to Ursula (*d.* 1610), daughter of John Roydon of Chilham, Kent, is uncertain. So are Ursula's family connections; she may have been a relation of Elizabeth, daughter and coheir of Thomas Roydon of East Peckham, Kent, who married Arthur's half-brother Sir Thomas Golding as her third husband, and was, by her first marriage, great-grandmother to Sir Roger Twysden. Arthur and Ursula Golding's eldest son, Henry, was born between 1569 and March 1575. Three other sons and four daughters followed. In 1576 Arthur's brother Henry died, leaving the greater part of his estate to Arthur. This consisted, most importantly, of the manors of Easthorpe and Little Birch, Essex. The legacy turned out to be most unfortunate. First, the property which Arthur inherited was heavily encumbered, since Henry had pledged it as security for the debts to the crown of a friend of his, a civil servant called Thomas Gardiner. At least part of the rents on it appears thus to have become due to the crown. Second, Henry had obtained Easthorpe and Little Birch by his marriage to the widow of the previous owner, and she and her daughters with her first husband claimed rights in the property which caused Arthur a great deal of trouble and expense; he suffered in particular from litigation conducted by Henry's stepdaughter Mary and her *soi-disant* husband, Robert Cryspe. Difficult as these circumstances were, it is hard to believe that inheriting an estate need necessarily lead to financial ruin, and the fact that Arthur was indeed ruined within twenty years suggests that he may not have been a particularly efficient manager of his own affairs.

During the 1580s Golding borrowed large sums of money, and in the early 1590s he was imprisoned for debt. Despite other inheritances, most importantly the manor of Belchamp St Paul, Essex, in 1593, and the assistance of Henry Docwra (later Lord Docwra of Culmore), the son of his sister Dorothy, and of William, Lord Cobham, he continued to borrow money until his last years, and was still in debt when he died. Many of his translations, then, were made despite distressing and wearisome personal circumstances. They may have made him some money, and when Thomas Wilcocks pirated the translation of Duplessis-Mornay in 1604, Golding thought it worth his while to appeal for the sole right to publish his translations. He died in 1606 with his appeal unsatisfied, and was buried on 13 May at St Andrew's Church, Belchamp St Paul. No monument to him or to his wife survives. He left several works unpublished: *A Woorke Concerning the Duties of Magistrates*, claimed as his in the same list as the *Testaments of the Twelve Patriarchs*, appears to have been lost, as does—if it was ever completed—a translation of André Thevet's geographical writings, to which Golding refers in the dedication of his Pomponius Mela; his translation of Sleidan's epitome of Froissart was published as the work of his son Percival in 1608; 'A morall fabletalke', his translation of Arnold Freitag's Latin emblem book *Mythologia ethica* (1579), was edited as a doctoral dissertation in 1979, but has never been published as a book.

Golding is remembered as the translator of Ovid, and particularly as the translator of Shakespeare's Ovid, although most of his life was spent translating protestant texts and, secondarily, Latin works on history, geography, or morality. The majority of his books, almost certainly including those which he himself regarded as most important, are now unread. It is, of course, possible that more lives were changed by his translations of Calvin and other European reformers than have ever been changed by translations, however good, of Ovid.

JOHN CONSIDINE

Sources L. T. Golding, *An Elizabethan puritan: Arthur Golding, the translator of Ovid's Metamorphoses and also of John Calvin's sermons* (1937) • A. B. Taylor, ed., *Shakespeare's Ovid: the Metamorphoses in the plays and poems* (2000) • H. B. Lathrop, *Translations from the classics into English from Caxton to Chapman, 1477–1620* (1933) • G. Braden, 'Golding's Ovid', *The classics and English Renaissance poetry: three case studies* (1978) • J. Wortham, 'Arthur Golding and the translation of prose', *Huntington Library Quarterly*, 12 (1948–9), 339–67 • M. Forey, 'Arthur Golding', *Sixteenth-century British nondramatic writers: second series*, ed. D. A. Richardson, DLitB, 136 (1994) • M. Forey, '"Bless thee, Bottom, bless thee! Thou art translated!": Ovid, Golding, and *A midsummer night's dream*', *Modern Language Review*, 93 (1998), 321–9 • K. Duncan-Jones, 'Doubtful work: translation of Duplessis-Mornay', *Miscellaneous prose of Sir Philip Sidney*, ed. K. Duncan-Jones and J. A. van Dorsten (1973), 155–7 • D. G. Hale, 'The source and date of Golding's *Fabletalke*', *Modern Philology*, 69 (1971–2), 326–7 • M. A. Overell, 'Arthur Golding's translation of the *Beneficio di Cristo*', *N&Q*, 223 (1978), 424–6 • J. Hasler, 'Golding, Henry I', HoP, *Commons, 1558–1603*

Archives BL, translation MS, Harley MS 357, item 5 • Folger, record of a debt

Wealth at death £2700 in debts; estate of Belchamp St Paul sold for £4000 after death

Golding, Benjamin (1793–1863), physician, was born on 7 September 1793 at St Osyth, in the Colne valley, Essex, the youngest son of the sixteen children (only eight of whom survived to maturity) of John Golding (1766–1831), a prosperous tanner, who owned a house, gardens, agricultural land, and a slaughterhouse, and who in his will left Benjamin £400 and one-fifth of his estate. In 1811 Golding enrolled at the University of Edinburgh, where he attended the lectures of Dr James Gregory. In 1813 he entered St Thomas's Hospital, London, as a medical student, and in the same year he qualified MD at the University of St Andrews, where degrees were awarded on production of testimonials from two physicians.

Golding's first publication was a treatise, *Burns and Scalds* (1814). At a time when medicine could be practised before qualification, Golding opened his house in Leicester Place, Westminster, where he offered free treatment to poor people. Later he moved nearby to St Martin's Lane. He became a member of the Royal College of Surgeons in 1817, and in 1818 he started up the West London Infirmary at 16 Suffolk Street, assisted by his more experienced friends Dr William Shearman and Dr John Mitchell.

In *An Historical Account of St Thomas's Hospital* (1819) Golding described St Thomas's history, the contribution of Thomas Guy, the contemporary education of medical students, and the complications of local politics—often involving bribery—when London hospitals elected their honorary staff. This may have been the inspiration for the setting up of a committee, on 31 March 1821, to found Charing Cross Hospital. Golding brought in John Robertson, his childhood friend and then a civil servant at Somerset House, who later became secretary to the hospital. Robertson's advice was to be essential for influencing royalty, the aristocracy, and bankers (Drummonds) in the creation of the new venture. Golding was appointed director, and on 6 January 1823 he and the existing physicians rented a house for £70 per annum at 28 Villiers Street, off the Strand, which they fitted up as a 12 bed infirmary and a dispensary for treating the poor people of that area. Surgeons were recruited and innovations such as electrophysiology were encouraged. Medical students were sought and educated. In 1825 Golding became LRCP (the diploma was later changed to MRCP).

Meanwhile Golding had married on 1 August 1822 Sarah Pelerin Blew (1799–1873). Several of their nine children died in infancy or early adulthood; only a daughter, Blanche Mary Golding Victoria (1835–1917), who married the architect Edward Falkener, and two sons—the Revd George Blew Golding (1829–1884) and Frederick Nassau Golding—are known to have attained full lifespans.

The small house in Villiers Street soon proved inadequate for the infirmary's needs. The district was changing and various metropolitan improvements were beginning to replace its numerous slums. Through Robertson's influence the duke of York, second son of George III, agreed to be the institution's royal patron and funds were raised for a new hospital. Eventually the government offered a triangular site north of the Strand at a rent of £400 per annum. Decimus Burton was commissioned as architect, and on 15 September 1831 the duke of Sussex, younger brother of the duke of York, laid the foundation stone of Charing Cross Hospital. In 1834 the first patients were admitted to the new building which did not fully occupy its site for almost 100 years. Physicians, Golding among them, attended daily for about two hours at midday, dealing with both in-patients and out-patients.

Golding, recognizing the deficiency in medical education in London which was based on apprenticeship, had wished for a medical school similar to that in the University of Edinburgh, which offered a scientific basis for medical and surgical practice. In London that had only been partly achieved, at St Thomas's and Guy's hospitals. However, in 1826 the University of London was created and in 1829 its senate gave full recognition to Charing Cross Hospital medical school. On 1 October 1834 new premises were opened within the new hospital. A teaching staff was created. Golding became director and lecturer in midwifery, and within a few years he had instituted a complete course of tuition in every branch of medical study as well as in dietetics and medical jurisprudence. Among early students were David Livingstone and Thomas Henry Huxley. The numbers fluctuated for several reasons, principally related to the quality of teaching, finances, and the influence of adjacent medical schools later established at University College and King's College, London.

In May 1840 Golding suffered a stroke from which he partially recovered. Afterwards he moved into 29 King William Street, a house adjacent to the hospital, an opening being made so he could enter without going into the street. He practised as physician and attended council until 1862, when Robertson resigned. The latter's death soon after affected him greatly, and he moved across London to Earls Court House, in the Boltons, West Kensington, and resigned the directorship. He went into a decline and died at his home on 21 June 1863; he was buried later the same month in the family tomb at Brompton cemetery, where several of his children had preceded him and where his wife and a grandson would also be laid to rest.

MICHAEL ANTHONY WAUGH

Sources G. B. Golding, *History of Charing Cross Hospital* (1867) · P. Inman, *Oil and wine* (1934) · 'Benjamin Golding', *The Lancet* (25 July 1863), 114–15 · F. Oppert, *Hospitals, infirmaries and dispensaries* (1867) · R. J. Minney, *The two pillars of Charing Cross* (1967) · W. Hunter, *Historical account of Charing Cross Hospital and medical school* (1914) · *VCH Essex*, 9.138 · 'Burials at Brompton cemetery', Society of Genealogists Library, London [typescript]

Likenesses bust; known to be at Old Charing Cross Hospital, *c.*1966 · photograph, repro. in Minney, *Two pillars*

Wealth at death £70,000: administration, 4 Aug 1863, *CGPLA Eng. & Wales*

Golding, John (1931–1999), politician and trade union leader, was born at 112 Fernley Road, Sparkhill, Birmingham, on 9 March 1931, the only son and fourth among the five children of Peter John Macgregor Golding, chef, and his wife, (Marjorie) Eileen Lycett. Golding claimed that his work was inspired by experiences in childhood; at the age of ten he was hit by a bus and, having been refused an anaesthetic because it cost 30*s.*, he later said: 'I resented bitterly that there could be men who could decide what working people had or didn't have' (*The Times*, 10 Nov 1982, 12). He won a place at Chester grammar school, having written an essay on what Labour would do to make life fairer after the war, and left at sixteen to support his family.

Golding began as an office boy, working from 1948 until 1951 in London at the ministry of national insurance and then for the General Post Office; having joined the Labour

Party while at school, he was soon active in the Post Office Engineering Union (POEU).

The POEU sent him on a one-year TUC scholarship to the London School of Economics, and he then took a degree in history, politics, and economics at Keele University, where he became interested in Thomas Hobbes. It was during this time that Golding met Thelma Gwillym (*b.* 1931), an English teacher, whom he married on 24 May 1958 and with whom he adopted two sons, the elder of whom died in 1979.

In 1960 Golding joined the staff of the POEU as an assistant research officer, becoming its education officer four years later. He failed in several attempts to obtain a parliamentary seat until there was a by-election in Newcastle under Lyme in 1969. At the count Golding and his Conservative opponent, Nicholas Winterton, were in the lead together until a late surge of votes came from the outlying coalmining communities that offset the middle-class residential areas within the constituency. 'Lester Piggott would have admired this', said Golding, who won with a majority of 1,042 (*The Times*, 31 Oct 1969, 1). During the by-election campaign he met Llinos Lewis (*b.* 1933), the daughter of Ness Edwards, the postmaster-general in Clement Attlee's 1950 government; they eventually married on 8 August 1980, both their marriages having been dissolved.

Before Golding increased his majority at the general election of 1970—as he did in both of the general elections of 1974—he was serving as parliamentary private secretary to the minister of technology. After the election he became an opposition whip, but he resigned from the whips' office after the general election of October 1974. Two years later he was appointed parliamentary under-secretary of state at employment, a position to which he was well suited—he was particularly passionate about youth unemployment—and in which he was proud of Labour's work.

The high point of Golding's career came while serving on Labour's fissiparous national executive committee, from 1978 until 1983, a period of personal toil which enabled Neil Kinnock to reform the Labour Party. But among the features that distinguished Golding from many of the 'new' Labour figures who came to office in 1997 were his background in trade unionism, his scruffy appearance, and his blunt approach to politics. For Tony Benn, for example, on 1 March 1978, Golding was 'a real tough cookie'. In the Parliamentary Labour Party meeting that day Golding based his hostility to what was then the fashionable left-wing cause of MPs' compulsory reselection on an earthily realistic appreciation of the party in-fighting that was likely to result; after his speech, according to Benn, 'Michael Cocks said, "he's right, you know, that's what actually happens". I felt utterly sick' (Benn, 287). Realizing that the party was unelectable if controlled by 'loony' left-wingers like Benn and Eric Heffer (*The Guardian*, 17 Dec 1981)—though also shocked by the actions of the 'gang of four' who left the party to form the Social Democratic Party—in 1982 Golding ousted them from their positions of power on the national executive committee (NEC).

Golding used any means necessary to achieve his ends when fighting for democratic socialism. When in 1983 he successfully delayed the privatization of British Telecom until after the election, he did so by making a speech on 8–9 February that lasted 11 hours and 15 minutes, the longest ever heard in the Commons, which led to a standing order to prevent such action being repeated; during a filibuster in 1985 he said that nowhere in the standing orders of the house did it say that MPs must know what they were talking about when they spoke in the Commons, and that if there were that rule there would be silence. That the Labour Party had, in 1981, set up an inquiry into Militant and, in 1982, established a register of party groups from which Militant would be excluded, was also due to Golding, who admitted that he delighted in being called a fixer. He in turn was ousted from the NEC in 1983 after the POEU executive, who had sponsored him as an MP, refused to re-nominate him, having swung to the left. But the work had been done: he had already made possible the reforms within the party that would allow Labour to become electable again. However, Golding had a key role in determining Labour's radical election manifesto in 1983; he later maintained that he had decided that Labour had already lost, and did not want the right to be blamed for the defeat. Tony Benn lost his seat after Golding ensured that he was not selected for a safe constituency in Bristol by personally influencing local trade unions. Golding was characteristically forthright about the reasons for Labour's defeat. 'We cannot afford any longer to fight elections on a "like it or lump it" basis', he told the party conference that October. 'We were not robbed; we threw it away. It was a terrible campaign and being on the campaign committee was the nearest I got to living among anarchists' (*The Times*, 4 Oct 1983, 4).

In 1986 Golding made an unusual move when he stepped away from a parliamentary career to become a union general secretary, challenging the Militant tendency in the new National Communications Union (NCU) of which the old POEU was part; his wife, Llin, took his seat in parliament after a campaign which saw Liberals attack the 'Golding dynasty'. But in 1988 a tabloid newspaper alleged that he had been involved with a prostitute, and although he refused to comment, he was attacked by the NCU executive who during the British Telecom pay strike the previous year had accused him of a lack of leadership. He took early retirement.

Golding's final battles came after he was appointed to a new Salmon and Freshwater Fisheries Review Group. He had a passion for angling—and, as a result, appalled at the effects of industrialization, he had been one of the first in the 1960s to alert politicians to the problems of pollution, just as he had been a pioneer when campaigning for a national minimum wage in his maiden speech in 1969.

Having suddenly fallen ill over Christmas in 1998 while writing his memoirs, John Golding died on 20 January 1999 from septicaemia in the City General Hospital, Stoke-on-Trent, Staffordshire. He was cremated in Newcastle under Lyme on 1 February, and the ashes were scattered over a river in Wales. His wife, Llin, and his younger son survived him. DANIEL CREWE

Sources private information (2004) [Llin Golding; Thelma Gwillym; Lord Sawyer; T. Lancaster] • P. Farrelly, 'Golding, John', *DLB*, vol. 10 • *The Times* (25 Jan 1999) • *Daily Telegraph* (22 Jan 1999) • *The Guardian* (22 Jan 1999) • *The Independent* (22 Jan 1999) • b. cert. • m. certs. • d. cert. • T. Benn, *Conflicts of interest: diaries, 1977–80*, ed. R. Winstone (1990) • *The Times* (10 Nov 1982) • *The Times* (31 Oct 1969) • *The Guardian* (17 Dec 1981) • *The Times* (7 March 1985) • *The Times* (4 Oct 1983)

Golding, Louis (1895–1958), writer, the second son of the four children of Philip Golding (*d. c.*1916), religious orator and teacher, and his wife, Yetta (*d. c.*1913), was born at Red Bank, Manchester, on 19 November 1895. His parents were Orthodox Jews who had immigrated to Manchester from Cherkassy on the Dnieper River a year or two prior to Golding's birth. Educated at the Waterloo Road elementary school, he won a scholarship to Manchester grammar school, wrote for the school magazine, and gained awards for his poetry. In November 1913 Golding won a scholarship to read history at Queen's College, Oxford, matriculating in October 1914. When the First World War broke out, rather than studying he attempted to enlist in the Officers' Training Corps. Rejected because, as he wrote in his autobiographical *The World I Knew* (1940), 'The authorities disliked my eyes, my tonsils, and my lungs' (Golding, 22), he became a hospital orderly and then a YMCA worker engaged in hospital duties serving in the Fifth Canadian Hospital in Salonika, Greece. After returning to Oxford in the autumn of 1919, he changed to English literature but illness prevented him taking his final examinations in 1921.

In 1919 a book of poems, *Sorrows of War*, based on the war and Golding's war experiences was published. *Forward from Babylon*, an autobiographical novel set in the north of England and at Manchester grammar school, appeared in 1921. From 1919 to 1921 Golding contributed upwards of sixty pieces including poems, short stories, and review essays to *Voices*, a Manchester-based literary magazine. Subsequently he received a grant from the Royal Literary Fund. Advised by doctors to seek warmer climates rather than to risk a somewhat delicate constitution, he began his travels abroad and the life of a professional writer. He also sold books. *Seacoast of Bohemia* (1923) was a satirical novel based upon his early travels. For the travel narratives *Sunward* (1924), and *Sicilian Noon* (1925), Golding drew upon his travels in Italy; Capri and Sicily, with its Homeric landscape, especially appealed to him. *Sunward* in particular received high critical praise, A. E. Coppard writing in *The Spectator* (11 October 1924), 'there is wit, whimsical fancy, a deal of impertinence, and some beautiful writing' (p. 514).

Golding used his Jewish inheritance for his *Three Ancient Lands: being a Journey to Palestine* (1928), an account of his journey from Port Said to Palestine. The book is noteworthy for its powerful descriptive travel narrative and photographs of early Jewish settlements including the early kibbutzim (collective farms). Golding's semi-autobiographical novel *Day of Atonement* (1925), set in Russia, the north of England, and Sicily, drew upon his family experiences. In the summer of 1928 Golding was in Morocco. In 1929 and 1930 he visited Spain and Paris where he wrote *The Prince or Somebody* (1929) and *Give up your Lovers* (1930), which uses the theme of his earlier works—the love between Jew and gentile.

Golding's fame rests upon his best-selling novel *Magnolia Street*, published early in 1932. The novel concentrated on the relationships between Jews and non-Jews in a district of Manchester during the 1910–30 period. Translated into twenty-seven languages, and selling more than a million copies, banned by Hitler and Mussolini, serialized in the London *Daily Express*, a new edition appeared as late as 1958—the year of Golding's death. Golding dramatized the novel and C. B. Cochran produced it at the Adelphi Theatre, London, in 1934. Writing in the *New Statesman and Nation*, Gerald Bullett described the novel as 'a magnificent achievement: copious, humorous, romantic, tragic, genial, ironical, angry, wise; alive with action in every part, and crammed with the rich stuff of humanity' (23 Jan 1932, 96).

During the writing of *Magnolia Street* Golding spent time in 1931 in Berlin. In the summer of 1932 he went to Russia. In 1935 he accepted the suggestion of the London publishers Rich and Cowan that he follow Moses's ancient journey from the Nile bullrushes to Mount Pisgah. This trip formed the foundation for *In the Steps of Moses the Conqueror* (1943). During the 1930s Golding also travelled widely in the United States. Golding wrote short stories, anti-fascist propaganda, Jewish history, radio drama, and literary criticism. Film scripts included *Theirs is the Glory* about the Arnhem operation during the Second World War. He wrote three books on boxing: *Boxing Tales: a Collection of Thrilling Stories* (1948), and in the same year *My Sporting Days and Nights*. This was followed in 1952 by *The Bare-Knuckle Breed*. His monograph *James Joyce* (1933) was one of the first books to be devoted to the great writer. His versatility is further demonstrated by *We Shall Eat and Drink Again: a Wine and Food Anthology*, which he edited with André L. Simon (1944).

Golding was included on George Orwell's 1948–9 listing of 'Crypto-communists and fellow travellers'. Orwell describes Golding as 'only a vague sympathizer' (Orwell, 247). Golding's work by no means focused on Jewish themes. Black magic and the Sicilian Mafia provide the background for the ironically titled *The Camberwell Beauty* (1935). *The Loving Brothers* (1952) focuses upon two very contrasting brothers. *Good-bye to Ithaca* (1955), his final travel narrative, 'details the differences between a modern traveller going on an odyssey and the hardships that the ancients must have encountered' (Reed, 130).

Sequels to *Magnolia Street* include *Five Silver Daughters* (1934), *Mr. Emmanuel* (1939), and *The Glory of Elsie Silver* (1946). *Five Silver Daughters* goes beyond Manchester to encompass a European canvas. The Nazi persecutions become the theme of *Mr. Emmanuel*. The heroic but tragic Warsaw ghetto uprising preoccupies *The Glory of Elsie Silver*. This was the first western European novel to focus on this important resistance to oppression. *Mr. Emmanuel*, according to Kushner, 'was the only one of 20 Golding novels converted into film' and 'was the only major British anti-Nazi film produced' during the Second World War (Kushner, 219).

Critics spoke of Golding's over-production. Rumours circulated in literary circles that his later works were ghosted by writers such as Emanuel Litvinoff, and this may possibly have been the case with the posthumously published *The Frightening Tale* (1973). Known to be homosexual (private information), Golding lived in the last years of his life in a 'large, tall house in St. John's Wood' (16 Hamilton Terrace) with a 'large, book-lined study' (Simons, 112). He married on 12 March 1956 a childhood friend, Mrs Annie Carrie Weintrobe, daughter of Abraham Sugarman, a commercial traveller; her previous marriage had been dissolved. She had been the inspiration in 1932 for the character of Bella in *Magnolia Street*.

On 9 August 1958 Golding died of carcinoma of the pancreas in St George's Hospital, London, three weeks after an operation. He was cremated at the Golders Green crematorium in Middlesex on 13 August. For the Anglo-Jewish novelist Alexander Baron, Golding was the last 'link with the past … he was still at home in that old world of *Yiddishkeit* that such writers as Sholem Asch and Zangwill represented in their different ways'. Although as a man emotionally reticent, his writings 'achieved moments of real power and … represent their only consistent treatment of their subject in modern British literature … the larger drama of the Jewish people' (Baron). Jacob Sonntag, the editor of the *Jewish Quarterly*, observed that 'he accepted his own Jewishness without any doubt or reservation, considering it real enough in a historical and personal (though not in a religious) sense' (Sonntag).

WILLIAM BAKER

Sources L. Golding, *The world I knew* (1940) • J. B. Simons, *Louis Golding: a memoir* [1958] • *The Times* (11 Aug 1958) • *The Times* (14 Aug 1958) • *The Times* (16 Aug 1958) • *Jewish Chronicle* (15 Aug 1958), 1, 5 • *New York Times* (10 Aug 1958), 93 • B. D. Reed, 'Louis Golding', *British travel writers, 1910–1939*, ed. B. Brothers and J. M. Gergits, DLitB, 195 (1998), 123–30 [incl. bibliography] • A. Baron, 'Louis Golding (1896–1958)', *Jewish Quarterly*, 6/1 (1959), 3 • J. Sonntag, 'Editorial', *Jewish Quarterly*, 6/1 (1959), 3 • T. Kushner, 'Manchester Jewish Museum exhibition: "Magnolia Street"', *Immigrants and Minorities*, 2 (1986), 219 • G. Orwell [E. A. Blair], *Our job is to make life worth living*, ed. P. Davison, I. Angus, and S. Davison (1998), vol. 20 of *The complete works of George Orwell*, ed. P. Davison (1986–98), 247 • G. Bullett, review of *Magnolia Street*, *New Statesman and Nation* (23 Jan 1932), 96 • A. E. Coppard, *The Spectator* (11 Oct 1924), 514 • m. cert. • d. cert.

Archives Bodl. Oxf. • Man. CL, Manchester Archives and Local Studies, MSS • Ransom HRC, corresp. • UCL | BL, corresp. with Society of Authors, Add. MS 63250 • Lancs. RO, letters to T. H. Floyd • Man. CL, Manchester Archives and Local Studies, corresp. with David Austin • U. Birm., corresp. with Francis Brett Young and Jessica Brett Young • U. Leeds, Brotherton L., letters to Thomas Moult | SOUND BBC WAC, Radio contributors, scriptwriters, file 1 and copyright file 1

Likenesses E. Kapp, drawing, 1930, Barber Institute of Fine Arts, Birmingham • Sasha, photograph, 1933, Hult. Arch. • Camera Press, photograph, repro. in *New York Times* • H. Coster, photographs, NPG • D. E. Schmidt, photograph, repro. in Simons, *Louis Golding*, frontispiece • E. Wolfe, oils, repro. in L. Golding, *The ancient lands* (1928) • photograph, repro. in *Jewish Chronicle*, 1

Wealth at death £24,132 11s. 10d.: probate, 5 Feb 1959, *CGPLA Eng. & Wales*

Golding, Richard (1785–1865), engraver, was born in London of humble parentage on 15 August 1785. In 1799 he was apprenticed for seven years to an engraver named J. Pass, but following a disagreement left after five years and transferred to James Parker; Parker died in 1805, leaving some unfinished plates, which were completed by his pupil. Soon after he was introduced to Benjamin West by a Mr Fuller, an American artist for whom Golding had engraved a plate. West employed Golding to engrave his *Death of Nelson* (1805). Golding then executed a number of admirable bookplates, the best known of which are those after the designs of Robert Smirke for editions of *Don Quixote* and *Gil Blas*. In 1810 he assisted the engraver William Sharp in some of his works, including two portraits. His reputation grew, and in 1818 he completed a much admired plate of the Princess Charlotte of Wales, after the painting by Sir Thomas Lawrence (1801), who is said to have touched the engraver's proofs no fewer than thirty times. The reputation which he gained by this plate led to numerous commissions, and among the portraits which he subsequently engraved were the large mixed line and stipple of Sir William Grant, master of the rolls, a full-length after Lawrence (1817), a portrait of Queen Victoria aged nine, after Richard Westall, and another of the same subject in 1830, after William Fowler. He also engraved a large plate of *St Ambrose Refusing the Emperor Theodosius Admission into the Church*, after the picture by Rubens in the Kunsthistorisches Museum, Vienna. In 1842, after years of poorly paid work and inferior commissions, Golding was engaged to engrave for the Art Union of Dublin a plate after Maclise's picture of *A Peep into Futurity*, but he had fallen into a state of apathy, and by 1852 the plate remained unfinished. Samuel Redgrave attributed this to the fact that Golding's powers of reasoning and eyesight were failing, stating that he withdrew from all social intercourse, finding recreation only in angling. A bachelor of shy and reserved habits, though not without some means, Golding died from bronchitis in neglected and dirty lodgings at 17 Stebbington Street, Oakley Square, St Pancras, London, on 28 December 1865. He was buried in Highgate cemetery, but owing to allegations that he had been poisoned by his medical attendant, who became possessed of the bulk of his property, his body was exhumed the following September. An inquest ruled that he had died of natural causes. Redgrave noted that his art was 'of a high class, his line free and powerful. Proofs of his works are extremely scarce and of great value' (Redgrave, 179).

R. E. GRAVES, *rev.* ASIA HAUT

Sources Redgrave, *Artists* • Bryan, *Painters* (1886–9) • Boase, *Mod. Eng. biog.* • R. K. Engen, *Dictionary of Victorian engravers, print publishers and their works* (1979) • *The Times* (14 Sept 1866) • *The Times* (21 Sept 1866) • Ward, *Men of the reign* • *CGPLA Eng. & Wales* (1866)

Archives BM, department of prints and drawings

Wealth at death under £1500: probate, 1 Oct 1866, *CGPLA Eng. & Wales*

Golding, Sir William Gerald (1911–1993), novelist, was born on 19 September 1911 at his maternal grandmother's house, 47 Mountwise, St Columb Minor, Newquay, Cornwall, the second of two sons of Alec Albert Golding (1876–1957), schoolteacher, and Mildred Mary Agatha, *née* Curnoe (*b.* *c.*1870), an enthusiastic supporter of the women's suffrage movement. Golding wrote of his great-grandparents that he knew 'nothing except that they were so quarrelsome that one part of the family changed the spelling of its name so as not to be confused with the others' (Gekowski and Grogan, iv). Golding's aunt and uncle both died of tuberculosis, as did their eldest child, a son, and their daughter was adopted by Alec and Mildred. Alec, born into a working-class Quaker family near Bristol, was an atheist, a socialist, and a rationalist. Mildred, by contrast, entertained the family with terrifying Cornish ghost stories. Both parents were enthusiastic musicians: Mildred played the organ in the church at St Day, near Truro, before her marriage, and Alec was a serious and accomplished musician, playing the violin, as well as other instruments, from boyhood. In the evenings Mildred would play the viola, Alec the violin, and the boys would contribute on violin and cello. As a child, Golding spent holidays with his grandmother in St Columb Minor, and with his father's parents, who lived in Kingswood, near Bristol. Alec's father was a shoemaker, making boots and shoes for the Kingswood miners. In 1902 Alec became science master at Marlborough grammar school, Wiltshire, where he spent virtually the whole of his teaching career, finally retiring in the 1940s. He took an external degree in 1916, gained qualifications in music and architecture, wrote textbooks on various scientific subjects, including astrophysical navigation, and was also appointed a fellow of the Royal Geographical Society. In his autobiographical essay 'The ladder and the tree' (1965), William Golding acknowledged the overwhelming impact of his father on his life and work, describing him as 'incarnate omniscience', and it is clear that his father's enormous influence determined the son's initial choice of study at university, and also gave him an ambivalent attitude to both science and religion which was manifested throughout his lengthy writing career. However, given that most of Golding's finest writing exhibits a tension between the rational and the irrational, his mother's influence was almost certainly considerable.

Golding lived, until a young man, in the family home at 29 The Green, Marlborough, a three-storey house of medieval origin next to the graveyard of St Mary's Church. It was a lower middle-class milieu, similar to the setting for his novel *The Pyramid*. As a child Golding developed an abiding interest in Egypt and archaeology and found in Wiltshire's early Christian, Saxon, and Norman remains an architectural legacy to compare with Egypt. Although late in life he published a full-length travel book on Egypt, *An Egyptian Journal* (1985), the unique hold that Egypt had on his imagination is best exemplified in the essays 'Egypt from my inside' (1965), and 'Egypt from my outside' (1982).

Sir William Gerald Golding (1911–1993), by Michael Ayrton, 1965

Education and early writing Golding received his secondary education at Marlborough grammar school, where his father was now senior assistant master. In 1930 he entered Brasenose College, Oxford, to read natural science, which he studied for two years, and then, in 1932, he transferred to English literature, delaying because he feared that this abandonment of science would displease his father. But this decision marked a turning point in his career: in his essay 'On the crest of a wave' (1965) Golding emphasizes that the arts are a more important area of study than the sciences. Golding became interested in Anglo-Saxon, specifically in *The Battle of Maldon*, a tenth-century heroic poem depicting stoic resistance to the Danes, which ended in defeat. He took his degree, a good second, in 1935, when he also studied for a diploma in education.

In 1934 Golding published a small volume of poetry in Macmillan's Contemporary Poets series. His *Poems* contained twenty-nine poems, and although in later life he was dismissive of this volume, and of his abilities as a poet, the collection anticipates some of the concerns that became central to his fiction. In 'Mr Pope', the best-known of these poems, Golding uses Alexander Pope as a spokesman for the age of reason and mocks the rationalist's desire for perfect order and control; this distrust of rationalism is a feature of virtually all Golding's novels. *Poems* was not a critical or a commercial success, and when Golding offered further poems to his editor, Macmillan showed no interest. However, Golding's five years at Oxford marked a decisive break with his father's scientific rationalism, and set him on a career as an artist.

Early career and war service: changing philosophy After leaving Oxford in 1935, Golding moved to London, where he wrote, acted, and produced for a small, non-commercial theatre. He once played Danny, the unpleasant scholarship boy in Emlyn Williams's *Night must Fall*. Golding clearly used his experiences in the theatre in his books *Pincher Martin* and *The Pyramid*. In 1939 Golding took up a teaching post at Maidstone grammar school for boys and subsequently met (Mabel) Ann Brookfield (1911/12–1995), daughter of Ernest William Brookfield, a grocer. Ann was dark-haired, and attractive, with great wit. She was one of ten children most of whom were involved in left-wing politics. Her brother Norman, thirteen months her junior, had recently been killed fighting for the International Brigade in the last few weeks of the Spanish Civil War. The Goldings married on 30 September 1939. They had two children, Judy and David. Shortly after the marriage, Golding took up a post as schoolmaster at Bishop Wordsworth's School, Salisbury, teaching English and Greek literature in translation. The couple lived in a small cottage, and Golding spent a great deal of time also involved in adult education, teaching in army camps and at Maidstone gaol.

After the outbreak of the Second World War, Golding joined the Royal Navy, registering in 1940 as an ordinary seaman. In taking the examination to become an officer, he answered a question on the difference between a propellant and an explosive with such elaborate knowledge, including graphs, that he was sent to a secret research centre under the direction of Professor Lindemann, later Lord Cherwell, Churchill's scientific adviser. While at the research centre he was injured in an explosion, and, after hospitalization and recovery, he asked the admiralty 'to send me back to sea, for God's sake, where there's peace' (Biles, 26). He was sent to a mine-sweeper school in Scotland, then to New York to wait for a mine-sweeper being built on Long Island. By the time he returned, mine-sweepers were no longer seen as crucial and he was given command of a small rocket-launching craft. He was involved in the chase and the sinking of the *Bismarck*, and took part in the D-day assault on Fortress Europe in 1944. In one invasion, that of the small Dutch island of Walcheren, Golding's craft was assigned a difficult role without air support. Preparing to go through a small channel in which 'everybody was throwing stuff in every direction', Golding transfixed his face with a grin and his men assumed that the job could not be as dangerous as it looked because he seemed to be enjoying it so much. When orders were changed, assigning his craft a much safer function, Golding's 'grin fell off' and his face 'collapsed'. His crew said to each other, 'Do you see that old bastard up there? When he learnt we weren't going in, he was disappointed' (Gindin, 4).

The war was one of Golding's most significant educative experiences. It forced him to query even more forcefully than at Oxford the scientific, rationalistic, and ultimately optimistic picture of the world that his father had offered him. As he wrote in his essay 'Fable' (1965):

> Before the second world war I believed in the perfectibility of social man; that a correct structure of society would produce goodwill; and that therefore you could remove all social ills by a reorganisation of society … but after the war I did not because I was unable to. I had discovered what one man could do to another … I must say that anyone who moved through those years without understanding that man produces evil as a bee produces honey must have been blind or wrong in the head.

These words could serve as an epigraph to virtually all the fiction Golding subsequently wrote. Although horrified by the Nazis' war crimes, Golding was adamant that little other than social sanctions and prohibitions prevented most people in the allied countries from acting with a similar brutality and disregard for humanity.

The war not only changed Golding's moral and political outlook, but also broadened his intellectual perspective. To pass the dull hours on watch, he began to study Greek, and Greek myth played a significant role in shaping his literary imagination; Euripides's *The Bacchae* is an obvious influence on *Lord of the Flies*, just as *Ion* is on *The Double Tongue*, and as Aeschylus's *Prometheus* is on *Pincher Martin*. The importance of Greece and classic Greek literature for Golding, however, went further than specific textual influences. Greek art formed the basis for his own metaphorical statements about the nature of humanity, but he also used Greece as a contrast to the idea of Egypt, contrasting the rationality and light associated with the Greek tradition, with the mystery and darkness of the Egyptian tradition.

Lord of the Flies In 1945 Golding returned to Bishop Wordsworth's School to teach English and classics. While teaching he wrote several novels, all of which were rejected, and, in his later opinion, deservedly so. The book that made him a household name, and the first of his seventeen published works, was itself rejected by twenty-one publishers, until in September 1953 Charles Monteith, a young editor at Faber, received a dog-eared manuscript entitled *Strangers from Within*. Monteith recognized its potential but suggested several changes, which included eliminating lengthy scenes set prior to the boys' arrival on the island, compressing its ending, and reducing the novel's overtly theological aspects. Monteith also expressed dissatisfaction with the novel's title and while Golding offered several alternatives, including *A Cry of Children* and *Nightmare Island*, it was another editor at Faber, Alan Pringle, who suggested *Lord of the Flies*. The novel was published on 17 September 1954, exactly a year after it had been submitted. In the published novel a group of boys, the oldest of whom is twelve and the youngest six, is marooned on an idyllic desert island, and almost immediately a battle for supremacy takes place among the principal characters. Violence and death follow. *Lord of the Flies* is one of the finest adventure stories of the second half of the twentieth century, impressively employing language which both provided narrative impetus while also evoking profounder, more theological implications. *Lord of the Flies* 'rewrote' R. M. Ballantyne's *The Coral Island* (1858), offering a grim rejoinder to its imperial, Christian optimism. Golding used the same names for his central characters as Ballantyne did for his trio of brave, clean, young Englishmen, which assists the comparison and eventual subversion of the beliefs central to *The Coral Island*. While the depiction of evil in Ballantyne's book is strikingly simplistic, revolving around a Christian–pagan dichotomy, Golding makes his characters Christian from the novel's beginning, and yet it is the choir who become the most cruel and violent of all the boys on the island. One of the major reasons for the novel's enormous success in the post-war years was its ability to merge the didactic with the dramatic; *Lord of the Flies* is not an examination of the idiosyncratic nature of a group of young English boys, but of the essential nature of humanity itself, its predisposition to violence and cruelty when removed from the restraining influences of civilization. The island becomes a microcosm of the adult world, which is also destroying itself. The grim account of murder and propitiation on the island, Golding suggests, is re-enacted in the greater, adult world, continuously. It is difficult to envisage a period in human history when *Lord of the Flies* will not be relevant.

Lord of the Flies was well received by the reviewers, and several very influential writers, including E. M. Forster and C. S. Lewis; T. S. Eliot described it as 'not only a splendid novel but morally and theologically impeccable' (Carey, 63). It began to sell well and was soon reprinted. In America it made little impression at first, but by 1957 the paperback edition had attracted a huge cult following among university students, and from there it moved rapidly into the mainstream. Over the next thirty years the novel became a 'set text', at secondary and tertiary level in America and Europe, and by the end of the twentieth century it had been translated into over thirty languages, including Russian, Icelandic, Japanese, Serbo-Croat, and Catalan, with worldwide sales estimated at over 10 million copies. *Lord of the Flies* brought Golding fame and financial security, but he was deeply ambivalent about the book, often claiming the same irritated relationship with his first novel as Rachmaninoff had with his famous C♯ minor prelude, which, Golding often bleakly observed, his audience insisted on his playing throughout his career. The novel was made into a memorable film by Peter Brook in 1963, and was filmed again, less memorably, in 1990. *Lord of the Flies* was adapted for the stage by the novelist Nigel Williams, and was first produced by the Royal Shakespeare Company at Stratford upon Avon in summer 1995.

Novels 1955–1964: isolation and intertextuality *Lord of the Flies* is usually read as Golding's commentary on human evil, and almost certainly it would not have been written had Belsen and Auschwitz never existed, or indeed had Dresden never been bombed by the allies, but a crucial aspect of the novel, and of the majority of its successors, was its indebtedness to an earlier literary source. Golding was always a 'literary' writer, with a somewhat austere and elevated sense of the writer's responsibilities, and he was unashamed about writing 'literature', a deeply unfashionable stance in literary studies from the late 1960s onwards. Just as *Lord of the Flies* 'rewrote' *The Coral Island*, its successor *The Inheritors* (1955), Golding's own favourite among his novels, written in twenty-eight days while he was still a teacher, rewrites H. G. Wells's 'The grisly folk' (1921). In *The Inheritors* Golding employs an extraordinary combination of imaginative empathy and technical virtuosity to describe the extermination of a gentle tribe of Neanderthalers by a stronger, more ruthless and intelligent community of *Homo sapiens*, who are, Golding makes clear, humankind's predecessors. In *Pincher Martin* (1956) Golding shifts his focus onto an individual and describes the rapacious protagonist's grim struggle for survival on a barren rock in the Atlantic. *Free Fall* (1959) recounts the attempts of a painter, Samuel Mountjoy, to find a meaningful pattern to his chaotic life, and in *The Spire* (1964), set in fourteenth-century England, Golding uses the construction of a cathedral spire to dramatize the tragic consequences of a disturbingly ambivalent religious vision. Golding's first five novels are all densely textured, fable-like narratives, employing brutally limited and strikingly unconventional narrative perspectives. He demonstrated throughout this period an unmatched ability to infuse pragmatic and minutely observed detail with a visionary significance. In these novels Golding depicted isolated man, stripped of social encumbrances, usually *in extremis*, while alluding throughout to, and usually subverting, his literary predecessors, who included Ambrose Bierce, Dante, and Ibsen.

Golding's work was always out of step with that of other writers who were publishing novels in the early and middle 1950s. While Kingsley Amis, John Wain, and Iris Murdoch seemed to be describing parochial communities of considerable limitations, Golding was writing aggressively bold fables which claimed for themselves a universal applicability, underpinned by Greek myths and legends, echoing their harsh, primitive tone. Particularly during this period, Golding's was an art of essences; he strove to depict what lay beneath, or above, the observable surface of life. If contemporary society had no fictional interest for him, it was because, unfashionably, he made humanity's spiritual struggle, its craving for religious enlightenment, over its desire for social cohesion, his primary concern.

Other work and later writing Soon after *Lord of the Flies* was published, the Goldings left their flat in Salisbury, and bought a cottage, Ebble Thatch, named after the little river which flows behind it, in Bowerchalke, a small, quiet village a few miles west of the city. Golding was made a fellow of the Royal Society of Literature in 1955. His first and only play, *The Brass Butterfly*, received its first performance in Great Britain at the New Theatre, Oxford, on 24 February 1958, directed by the comic actor Alastair Sim, who also played one of the principals. In 1961 Golding resigned as a schoolteacher, a job he claimed never to have enjoyed, and after spending the academic year 1961–2 at Hollins College in Virginia, USA, left teaching for ever. He was made an honorary fellow of Brasenose College, Oxford, in 1966, an honorary DLitt by the University of Sussex in 1968, and a CBE in 1966.

In the early 1960s Golding wrote numerous articles and book reviews for, in particular, *The Spectator*, *Holiday Magazine*, the *Times Literary Supplement*, and *The Listener*, many of which were published in the collection *The Hot Gates* (1965). Golding was later a frequent visitor to Greece, particularly throughout the 1960s, and in the title essay of this collection he describes a visit to Lamia and the pass where, in 480 BC, Leonidas and his 300 Spartans defied the huge army of the Persian king Xerxes. The essay is entertainingly written and historically informative, but of value primarily for the dramatization of the singularity of Golding's perspective. The essay gradually reveals a pessimistic, deterministic, and deeply conservative view of human nature, similar to, but even more emphatic and unambiguous than that expressed in his fiction. Throughout his career, Golding had little sympathy with the pervasive twentieth-century view which saw human nature as culturally determined, created by social circumstances. Golding's essentialism is revealed clearly in this essay because there is no detached narrative perspective, just the voice of the writer responding to one of the most important events in western history. Golding acknowledges that Leonidas and his Spartans 'contributed to set us free' (*The Hot Gates*, 20), and concludes by translating the stark simplicity of the Spartans' epitaph; it is an essay none of his peers could have written, and its sentiments run through everything he wrote.

Having published five novels in ten years, Golding over the next fifteen years published only one novel, *The Pyramid* (1967), a volume of short stories, *The Scorpion God*, and a collection of essays, the majority of which had been written earlier. It was generally believed during this period that Golding had taken his austere vision as far as it would go, and that he was a spent literary force. In 1979, however, he published the bleak and disturbing fantasy *Darkness Visible*, a novel about which the usually communicative Golding would say nothing at all. Unpredictable as ever, he immediately followed this with *Rites of Passage* (1980), a lively and often comic novel, although not without a characteristically tragic dimension, which recounted the sea voyage of the arrogant young Edmund Talbot as he sailed to Australia in 1815. The novel was immensely successful with both the critics and the public, winning the Booker prize, and giving Golding the largest readership he had enjoyed since *Lord of the Flies*. It gave rise to two sequels—*Close Quarters* and *Fire Down Below*—and all three novels were published in 1991 as the single volume *To the Ends of the Earth*. In 1983 Golding was awarded the Nobel prize for literature, an unexpected, and even contentious choice, with most English critics and academics favouring Graham Greene or Anthony Burgess. He became one of only five British writers to have been thus honoured, Winston Churchill being the most recent, receiving it thirty years earlier. In 1988 he was knighted.

Golding was short in stature, and over the years his neatly trimmed, brown naval beard gave way to a magnificently white and untamed growth, giving him an appearance which, unusually, combined sagacity with wildness, a look perfectly captured by Mark Gibson's celebrated photograph. Golding was a committed sailor, and in the early 1960s he owned a Whitstable oyster smack, *Wild Rose*, built in 1896. He spent a great deal of time during the 1960s on his boats, cruising through the English channel, the Dutch waterways, and ports along the North and Baltic seas. In 1967 his boat the *Tenace* sank after a collision in the English channel off the Isle of Wight, an episode which had a decisive impact on his life. As he informed an interviewer in 1985: 'I had to come to terms with the fact that I was never again going to be responsible for anybody else's life at sea' (Haffenden, 105). He enjoyed chess, cricket, and horse riding, and he retained an interest in natural sciences throughout his life, giving the scientist James Lovelock the word 'Gaia' for his theory that the Earth's biosphere is a self-regulating organism. He enjoyed alcohol, but gave up smoking in order to play the oboe. He was, indeed, particularly passionate about music throughout his life. He played the cello and piano from childhood, and was an exciting and effective pianist, talented and persistent: the night before his death he was playing Chopin studies, but he was also extremely fond of the work of Liszt and Bach.

It was widely believed that Golding had met his wife when they were members of the same communist cell in the late 1930s, and Samuel Mountjoy's experiences in *Free Fall* show considerable knowledge of the workings of such a cell, but Golding was publicly reticent about his politics. He was certainly somewhat to the left, but as his close friend Stephen Medcalf observed: 'On or off a horse he recalls William Cobbett—a patriot, a radical patriot, a humorous indignant passionate grumbling mouth filling radical patriot' (Carey, 42). He was nothing like the gloomy pessimist of public legend, but rather an amusing and gifted conversationalist and raconteur when among his few close friends, although he could be waspish. He studiously avoided literary cliques, and while he was invariably polite when carrying out public duties, many journalists and academics who interviewed Golding found him irascible. He was very protective of his privacy. In 1985, partly to avoid the increasing numbers of tourists, academics, and journalists asking for some of his time, the Goldings moved to Tullimaar, in Perran Ar Worthal, Cornwall, a graceful Regency house surrounded by woods and gardens, where Eisenhower had lived during the allies' invasion of Europe. The house was 6 miles from Truro, where Golding's parents had been married in 1904, and where his mother had been baptized in the parish church of St Mary in 1870.

Golding died suddenly of a heart attack, aged eighty-one, at Tullimaar on the morning of 19 June 1993. He was buried in the churchyard at Bowerchalke. At the funeral there were only his family and a few close friends, but the memorial service held in Salisbury Cathedral, in November 1993, was packed with friends and admirers. A boy from Bishop Wordsworth's School read the account of Simon's death from *Lord of the Flies* and the poet laureate, Ted Hughes, declaimed passages from *The Inheritors*. Two days after Golding's death, Ann Golding had a stroke from which she never properly recovered. She died on new year's day 1995, after many weeks in hospital, and was buried with her husband. In 1995 *The Double Tongue*, set in Delphi during the first century BC, the second draft of which Golding had just completed at the time of his death, was posthumously published to generally favourable reviews. It was clear from the obituaries that Golding was considerably more highly regarded by his fellow novelists than by either educated general readers, most of whom were familiar only with *Lord of the Flies* and *Rites of Passage*, or the large majority of academic critics. The general reader found the formal experimentation of novels such as *The Inheritors* and *The Spire* uncongenial, while academics, many of whom were irritated by Golding's satire on academia, *The Paper Men* (1984), also found his pessimism, determinism, interest in religion, and, perhaps above all, his lack of interest in contemporary society, unforgivable. At the end of the twentieth century, Golding's reputation was at its highest in continental Europe, particularly in Belgium, Holland, Germany, and France. KEVIN MCCARRON

Sources J. Biles, *Talk: conversations with William Golding* (1970) • J. Gindin, *William Golding* (1988) • R. A. Gekowski and P. Grogan, eds., *William Golding: a bibliography* (1994) • W. Golding, *The hot gates* (1965) • J. Carey, ed., *William Golding: the man and his books* (1986) • J. Haffenden, *Novelists in interview* (1985) • b. cert. • m. cert. • d. cert. • *CGPLA Eng. & Wales* (1996)
Archives U. Reading L., corresp. and literary papers | priv. coll. | SOUND BL NSA, 'The ladder and the tree', 13 March 1960
Likenesses photograph, 1964, Hult. Arch. • M. Ayrton, pen and ink and wash drawing, 1965, NPG [*see illus.*] • A. George, oils, 1986, NPG • J. Brown, photograph, repro. in *The Observer* (30 Oct 1994)
Wealth at death £238,266: probate, 1 Feb 1996, *CGPLA Eng. & Wales*

Goldney, Philip (1802–1857), army officer in the East India Company, was born in London on 21 November 1802, the second son of Thomas Goldney, goldsmith, of Goldney House, Clifton, and his wife, Charlotte, daughter of John Milward. He was educated at a private school, and in 1820 enrolled as a cadet of the East India Company's army. He received a commission as ensign in the 14th native infantry on 11 June 1821, and arrived in Bengal in November that year. On 30 January 1824 he was promoted lieutenant in the 1st native infantry, transferring to the 4th native infantry later that year. On 4 December 1833, at Sangod, he married Mary Louisa, daughter of John Holbrow. Of their children, two sons and three daughters survived Goldney. For some years he was engaged in frontier warfare and in learning the native languages and Persian. He translated various parts of the Bible into the vernaculars, and when the office of interpreter and quartermaster in his regiment fell vacant he was appointed. He was made brevet captain on 11 June 1836 and regimental captain on 31 March 1841.

In 1844 Goldney was ordered to Sind, then recently annexed. His regiment was one of four which mutinied in consequence of the withdrawal of the extra allowance previously given to sepoys when on foreign duty. Goldney personally intervened to restore order, by attacking one of the ringleaders. He was soon afterwards appointed civil collector and magistrate in Sind. At his own request he was allowed by Sir Charles Napier to take part in the expedition to the Traki hills. His mastery of Persian led to his being ordered to accompany the force under the Amir Ali Morad, whose fidelity was doubted by Napier. The expedition was successful, and he returned to Sind, where a wild part of Baluchistan formed part of the district in his charge. There he organized a system of police and gave employment by initiating a programme of canal building which greatly increased the area of cultivation in Sind. He was promoted brevet major on 9 November 1846 and major on 7 July 1848.

On 15 November 1853 Goldney attained the rank of lieutenant-colonel, and served as commander successively of the 35th, 22nd, and 38th native infantry regiments. He was appointed to command the brigade sent to annex and subjugate the kingdom of Oudh, and was made one of the five commissioners appointed to govern the country, placed in charge of Fyzabad, the eastern division. When the mutiny broke out in 1857 Goldney saw that the extension of the mutiny to Oudh was only a matter of time, and applied to Sir Henry Lawrence for a small number of European troops. The request was not granted, and Goldney moved from his residence at Sultanpur to Fyzabad, where he fortified a walled place and organized, as far as possible, the pensioned sepoys and the friendly zamindars of the district. His wife and children left the district. The sepoys subsequently mutinied, but allowed their officers to leave in four boats. At the same time one of the chief zamindars of the district, Raja Man Singh, sent a strong force to protect Goldney and convey him to a place of safety; but, as the officer in charge of the escort was forbidden to rescue anyone else, Goldney declined the offer, and proceeded with the other officers down the River Gogra. The two foremost boats proceeded as far as Begumji, a distance of 30 miles, when they were fired on by another body of mutineers. Goldney ordered the boats to be pulled to an island in the river, and directed his officers to cross to the other side and escape across country. He himself declined to leave the island, and either remained under fire until he fell, or was seized by the mutineers and shot, probably on 9 June 1857.

E. J. RAPSON, *rev.* ALEX MAY

Sources *Indian Army List* • V. C. P. Hodson, *List of officers of the Bengal army, 1758–1834*, 4 vols. (1927–47) • H. T. Lambrick, *Sir Charles Napier and Sind* (1952) • M. Innes, *Lucknow and Oude in the mutiny* (1896) • M. R. Gubbins, *An account of the mutinies in Oudh* (1858) • J. W. Kaye, *A history of the Sepoy War in India, 1857–1858*, 9th edn, 3 vols. (1880) • G. B. Malleson, *History of the Indian mutiny, 1857–1858: commencing from the close of the second volume of Sir John Kaye's History of the Sepoy War*, 3 vols. (1878–80) • private information (1890) • C. Hibbert, *The great mutiny, India, 1857* (1978)
Archives BL OIOC, corresp. and papers, MS Eur. D 729

Goldney, Thomas (1696–1768), ironmaster, was born on 12 July 1696 at Clifton, near Bristol, the sixth of the twelve children of Thomas Goldney (1664–1731) and his wife, Martha, *née* Speed (*c*.1667–1722). His father was a grocer who supplemented his income by holding shares in ships and by acting as agent for the collector of customs for the port of Bristol. After being educated in a Quaker household at Painswick, Gloucestershire, and at a school run by the Society of Friends in Bristol, Thomas was apprenticed to his parents in 1711. In 1717 he began work with the Coalbrookdale Company in Shropshire, the leading ironworks in the country, acting on behalf of his father, who had mortgaged half these ironworks a few years earlier. He remained for six years at Coalbrookdale, where he served as clerk and collected money and orders. In 1723 he returned to Bristol and joined his father and his younger brother Gabriel in trade there, though he spent much time dealing with consignments of goods from Coalbrookdale. In 1726 he was admitted to the freedom of Bristol. He became the head of his family after the death of his father in 1731.

Goldney devoted much of his business career to dealing with the family's interests in ironworks. In 1731 he became the Bristol agent for the Coalbrookdale Company, and took a particular interest in consignments of pig iron, the casting of hollow ware, engine parts, and the manufacture of guns. He installed Richard Reynolds as manager at Coalbrookdale in 1763, but continued working as an adviser to the firm in Bristol until his death. Goldney was a shareholder in the Willey ironworks, across the River Severn from Coalbrookdale, from 1733 to 1758. In the 1730s he was jointly concerned with Richard Ford in Bershay furnace, near Wrexham. Between 1754 and 1757 he became a co-partner with Abraham Darby (1711–1763) in furnaces at Horsehay farm 2 miles north of Coalbrookdale, and held a one-third share in the Ketley furnaces, 2 miles north of Horsehay.

In the 1740s Goldney diversified his industrial interests. He held shares in the Warmley Brass Company, near Bristol, and the Bristol Lead Company. He was involved with the Champion family in various enterprises in Flintshire, including coal and lead mines, a smeltery, and a calamine works. He bought shares in ships and in mines in Devon, Cornwall, and Ireland. In 1752 he also became a partner in one of Bristol's first banks under the name of Goldney, Smith & Co., and held a one-sixth share (*c.*£2000) of the bank's initial capital.

Apart from his business career, Goldney had interests in land and property. He inherited Elberton mansion house and farm, some 8 miles north of Bristol, a house and property in Chester, a Bristol town house in Castle Green, and a half share of the Clifton house, grounds, and household goods that had been purchased by his father in 1705. Goldney devoted much attention to the management and development of this property. He purchased land to gain additional income but was concerned mainly with improving his garden as a gentleman's seat. He landscaped the garden with a grotto, terrace, rotunda, tower, octagon, orangery, and paddock, and placed classical figures around the grounds. The grotto was especially admired because it was connected to a subterranean passage adorned with minerals, fossils, fine shells, and Bristol diamonds (or rock crystals). There was also a cascade of water with a seated figure of Neptune at its head. Goldney's estate was broken up in the mid-nineteenth century. The University of Bristol acquired Goldney House, as it is now known, and restored the grotto to some of its former glory.

Goldney does not seem to have been very active in the Society of Friends. When he became a Bristol burgess he made a solemn declaration instead of taking the oath, as did other Quakers. He voted for the whigs but does not seem to have been politically active. He died unmarried at Clifton on 28 December 1768 and was buried on 2 January 1769 at the Quaker burial-ground, Redcliffe, Bristol. His inventory shows that he owned more than 300 books, and had comfortable furnishings including mahogany and walnut furniture and satin curtains, demonstrating a standard of living more luxurious than in most Quaker households. A balance sheet of his personal estate as it stood on the day of his death, drawn up for his executors, reveals that he had total credits amounting to about £33,000 and debits totalling £12,000.

Kenneth Morgan

Sources P. K. Stembridge, 'Thomas Goldney (1696–1768): aspects of the life of a Bristol merchant', MLitt diss., University of Bristol, 1982 • Bristol University, Goldney MSS, DM 1398 • Bristol RO, Goldney MSS, acc. 38640 • A. Raistrick, *Dynasty of iron founders: the Darbys and Coalbrookdale* (1953) • Thomas Goldney account book (1742–63), Wilts. & Swindon RO, acc. 473/295 • C. H. Cave, *A history of banking in Bristol from 1750 to 1899* (privately printed, Bristol, 1899) • P. K. Stembridge, *Thomas Goldney, man of property: the creation of a Clifton estate, 1731–1768* (1991) • A. Oswald, 'Goldney House, Clifton [pt 1]', *Country Life*, 104 (1948), 278–81 • A. Oswald, 'Goldney House, Clifton [pt 2]', *Country Life*, 104 (1948), 328–31 • B. Little, 'The Georgian houses of Clifton', *Country Life*, 132 (1962), 520–23 • P. K. Stembridge, *Goldney: a house and a family* (1969) • D. Jones, *A history of Clifton* (1992) • A. Gomme, M. Jenner, and B. D. G. Little, *Bristol: an architectural history* (1979) • P. K. Stembridge, *The Goldney family: a Bristol merchant dynasty*, Bristol RS, 49 (1998) • P. K. Stembridge, *Thomas Goldney's garden* (1996) • will, PRO, PROB 11/945, sig. 13

Archives Bristol RO, MSS, acc. 38640 • University of Bristol, journal of a tour around Europe, DM 1398 • Wilts. & Swindon RO, account book, acc. 473/295

Wealth at death approx. £21,000—£33,000 in credits and £12,000 in debts: Stembridge, 'Thomas Goldney', 209

Goldring, Douglas (1887–1960), writer, was born in Greenwich, London, on 7 January 1887, the youngest of five children of Frank Goldring, an architect, and Constance Anne Morris, daughter of William Morris, barrister. Goldring described his early home life as unhappy, owing to the incompatibility of his irresponsible father and rigid, humourless mother, whom Goldring described as 'devouringly possessive'. When Goldring was three the family moved to Brussels, and then resided in Brighton for a time before settling in Oxford. Goldring attended three schools: one at Hurstpierpoint, Sussex; Magdalen College School, Oxford; and Felsted School, a Church of England school in Dunmow, Essex, where he recalled being a 'self-conscious little prig' and was flogged for 'insubordination' (Goldring, *Odd Man Out*, 34). He began writing verse and at seventeen had a poem accepted by *The Academy*. In 1906 he went up to Oxford University, where he matriculated from Marcon's Hall (one of the private halls). Although 'a complete nervous wreck' (ibid., 60) on leaving school, at Oxford he quickly cultivated a circle of aesthete friends, most notably Somerset Maugham, who introduced him to the poetry of Baudelaire and Verlaine among others.

Financial constraint forced Goldring to leave Oxford after a year, and he joined the editorial staff at *Country Life*. In London, Goldring met Ford Madox Hueffer (later Ford), 'the principal formative influence of his life' (Goldring, *South Lodge*, xvi), who told the aspiring poet that he would never be 'a real poet' (ibid., 36); nevertheless, before the war Goldring published two volumes of poetry, including *A Country Boy* (1910), influenced by A. E. Housman. He also produced a light novel of romance, *The Permanent Uncle* (1912), and several well-received travel books. Two of these focused on the French, whom Goldring admired for their genius at the art of living and about whom he wrote throughout his life. In addition, Goldring became involved in various publishing ventures: as sub-editor under Ford of the short-lived but influential *English Review*; from 1910 as editor of his own high-calibre magazine, *The Tramp*; from 1910 to 1912 as literary editor of the publishing firm Max Goschen; as adviser to Wyndham Lewis's modernist journal *Blast*; and in 1915 as founder of Selwyn and Blount publishers.

The First World War temporarily curtailed Goldring's prodigious publishing efforts. He enlisted in August 1914 but in October succumbed to acute rheumatism and was invalided out of the army, to his bitter disappointment; by 1916, when he was again fit, he had become a conscientious objector. In an autobiographical novel, *The Fortune* (1917), Goldring expressed his strong pacifist views through a character who becomes a pacifist under the overriding influence of an aristocratic schoolfriend only to be brutally murdered during the Easter rising in Dublin. Despite generous reviews, including one by T. S. Eliot, who deemed it 'unquestionably a brilliant novel' (*Egoist*, June 1918), the novel sold only between 300 and 400 copies in England. Not until the expression of anti-war sentiment became acceptable in the late twenties was the ground-breaking nature of this novel fully appreciated. In a 1931 preface to it, Aldous Huxley wrote that '*The Fortune* contains what is, I believe, the earliest, indeed the only contemporary, fictional account of war-time pacifism. So far as it goes, this account is excellent'. The war, along with the injustices Goldring witnessed while in Ireland in 1916–18, radically politicized him; thereafter he referred to himself as a 'propaganda novelist' (Goldring, *Odd Man Out*, 142). Goldring's anti-war, anti-imperialist, socialist views come most strikingly to the fore in *The Black Curtain* (1920) and *Nobody Knows* (1923), the latter his most highly praised and widely read novel (ibid., 255).

On 27 November 1917, in Dublin, Goldring married Beatrice (Betty) Duncan, with whom he had two sons. Her family connections drew him into the literary circles of Yeats, George Moore, and others. Goldring spent the immediate post-war years in London, with frequent trips to the continent. His marriage was dissolved in 1922. In 1925 he obtained a lectureship in Göteborg, Sweden, where he met Malin Nordstrom, whom he married on 24 April 1927. They moved to the south of France, and in the late twenties and early thirties Goldring penned vivid travel books, notably *The French Riviera* (1928), while indulging his wanderlust. While in England in the 1940s he turned his hand to memoirs of historical periods, as in *The Twenties* (1945), and of literary figures, notably Violet Hunt and Ford Madox Ford and the *English Review* circle in *South Lodge* (1943) and *The Last Pre-Raphaelite* (1948). Through these later works Goldring has obtained a niche in literary history. However, his highly individual travel books and the politically engaged novels clearly in advance of their time, notably *The Fortune*, deserve critical consideration, at the very least as social documents of the 'lost generation'. In appearance Goldring was tall and blond. By conviction he was an eclectic Christian-influenced socialist with the integrity and courage to voice unpopular opinions. He lived latterly at Stonar House, Deal, Kent, and died on 9 April 1960. GEORGE MALCOLM JOHNSON

Sources D. Goldring, *Odd man out: the autobiography of a propaganda novelist* [1935] · D. Goldring, *Facing the odds* (1940) · D. Goldring, *South Lodge: reminiscences of Violet Hunt, Ford Madox Ford and the English Review circle* (1943) · D. Goldring, *Life interests* (1948) · S. J. Kunitz and H. Haycraft, eds., *Twentieth century authors: a biographical dictionary of modern literature* (1942) · S. J. Kunitz and V. Colby, eds., *Twentieth-century authors: a biographical dictionary of modern literature, first supplement* (1955) · P. W. Salmon, 'Douglas Goldring', *Late-Victorian and Edwardian British novelists: second series*, ed. G. M. Johnson, DLitB, 197 (1999) · B. Belford, *Violet* (1990) · J. Hardwick, *An immodest Violet: the life of Violet Hunt* (1990) · b. cert.

Archives U. Reading L., letters to the Bodley Head Ltd

Likenesses Phillips, photograph, 1929, repro. in Goldring, *Odd man out* · H. Thornhill, photograph, 1935, repro. in Goldring, *Odd man out* · photograph, repro. in Kunitz and Haycraft, eds., *Twentieth century authors* (1942)

Goldsborough, Godfrey (1548–1604), bishop of Gloucester, was born in Cambridge in 1548, the son of John Goldsborough, of Goldsborough, Yorkshire. He entered Trinity College, Cambridge, in Michaelmas term 1560, matriculating as a pensioner before being made a scholar in 1562. He graduated BA in 1565, was admitted a minor fellow in September 1567, a major fellow in March 1569, commenced MA the same year, and proceeded BTh in 1577. The coincidence of his fellowship with the tenure of John Whitgift as master of the college (1567–77) was to have a decisive impact on Goldsborough's career. In 1572 he opposed Whitgift's revision of the university statutes; even so he was, Whitgift's biographer noted, one of those 'excellent scholars that came afterwards to great preferment in the Churche, and Commonwealth' (Paule, 17). Four of his contemporaries at Trinity from Whitgift's time (William Redman, Gervase Babington, Anthony Rudd, and Robert Bennet) later presided with him on the episcopal bench.

In 1577 Whitgift was elevated to the bishopric of Worcester and Goldsborough joined him there as archdeacon in July 1579. During his two decades at Worcester, Goldsborough accumulated a range of minor offices including prebends in the dioceses of London (Caddington Minor) and Hereford (Gorwall, later exchanged for the 'golden prebend', styled *Episcopi sive Poenitentiarii*), a canonry at Worcester, the archdeaconry of Shropshire in Lichfield, and the rectory of Stockton, probably in the same diocese. This collection led Giles Wigginton, a querulous puritan who had been a contemporary of Goldsborough at Trinity, publicly to snub him in St Paul's Cathedral, Wigginton dismissing the archdeacon as a 'proude, nonresident, pluraliste pseudo hierarchist' (Peel, 2.246).

Seemingly Goldsborough was not especially ambitious; he had taken his Cambridge DTh in 1583 but appears to have published nothing. Meanwhile a number of younger men had been elevated to bishoprics ahead of him. The four years from mid-1594 saw the wholesale renewal of the episcopate and Goldsborough secured one of the last of these appointments when he was consecrated bishop of Gloucester at Lambeth on 12 November 1598, Whitgift having intervened on his behalf with Elizabeth. Once installed at Gloucester, Goldsborough proved himself a firm administrator. He acted early in his bishopric to assert episcopal authority, attending the diocesan visitation in 1599 and sitting in the visitation court. Most notably Goldsborough succeeded in having his corrupt chancellor William Blackleech ejected in 1600 for bribery and misconduct, an achievement that eluded contemporaries faced with similar circumstances in at least three other Elizabethan and Jacobean dioceses. So was brought to an end decades of abuse by successive chancellors at Gloucester. Goldsborough sat regularly in the consistory court, gathered detailed evidence and probably forewarned Archbishop Whitgift, to whose courts Blackleech could have been expected to appeal. In so doing he took advantage of a diocesan structure at Gloucester that concentrated power in the consistory.

After 1600 Goldsborough withdrew from the front line of diocesan administration. He now rarely sat in the consistory, instead delegating work to his new chancellor, John Seman; neither did he feel the need to attend in person the diocesan visitation of 1602. No good evidence survives as to his style of churchmanship, although he presented significantly fewer clergy for nonconformity than had John Bullingham before him. Goldsborough died on 26 May 1604 and was buried in his cathedral, where an effigy and inscription to him remain in the lady chapel. He was survived by his widow, Hester, described by Thomas Fuller as a 'grave matron' (Fuller, 4.404), three children, John, Henry, and Godfrey, and a brother, John. Despite the poverty of his diocese the size of Goldsborough's estate at around £1300 placed him in the mid-range of Elizabethan bishops in personal wealth, and in his will he endowed Trinity College with 100 marks.

William Richardson

Sources K. Fincham, *Prelate as pastor: the episcopate of James I* (1990) • Venn, *Alum. Cant.*, 2.30 • Cooper, *Ath. Cantab.*, 2.388 • F. D. Price, 'Bishop Bullingham and Chancellor Blackleech: a diocese divided', *Transactions of the Bristol and Gloucestershire Archaeological Society*, 91 (1972), 175–98 • P. Collinson, *The Elizabethan puritan movement* (1967) • A. Peel, ed., *The seconde parte of a register*, 2 vols. (1915) • F. Heal, *Of prelates and princes: a study of the economic and social position of the Tudor episcopate* (1980) • T. Fuller, *The church history of Britain*, ed. J. S. Brewer, new edn, 6 vols. (1845) • G. Paule, *The life of the most reverend … John Whitgift* (1612)

Likenesses stone effigy, Gloucester Cathedral

Wealth at death approx. £1300: Heal, *Of prelates and princes*, p. 316

Goldsborough, Sir John (*d.* 1693), mariner and East India Company servant, is of obscure antecedents. A branch of the Goldsborough family was domiciled at Hadleigh near Ipswich in the seventeenth century and Goldsborough bequeathed a life interest in an estate in Suffolk to his wife; otherwise there are no indications of links with the county. He also left her house property in Whitechapel. By profession a mariner, it appears from a marriage licence issued by the faculty office in London on 17 January 1676 that he married Mary Smith (*d.* 1698) about the time that he took up a new command. In 1688 they were the beneficiaries of a legacy of £5 under the will of John Goldsborough of Southwark, mariner, a 'kinsman' (PRO, PROB 11/390, fol. 26). When he was not at sea Goldsborough seems to have been associated mostly with London and its environs. It has not been possible to establish whether or not he was in any way connected with John, the son of John and Margaret Goldsburye, baptized at St Olave, Hart Street, in the City of London, on 3 January 1636.

Goldsborough first emerges as a distinct individual when commanding the *Antelope* in the East India Company's service in 1670. He arrived home from Surat in 1672. On his next voyage the *Antelope* and ships in company encountered a Dutch fleet between Masulipatam and Madras on 22 August 1673 and in the engagement off Petapoli (Nizampatam), of which he wrote an account (Bodl. Oxf., MS Rawl. A, vol. 185, Pepys papers, vol. 17, item 139, fol. 386), he fell into Dutch hands. On his release he returned to England in the *Falcon* in 1674. In the following year Goldsborough offered his services to the company, which had accepted the proposal of Sir Matthew Andrews to build a new ship for him. He took command of the *Bengal Merchant* in 1676 and remained with her until 1686, making voyages to the Bay of Bengal, Madras, and Gombroon. He was appointed the company's surveyor of shipping on 20 April 1689.

On 15 January 1692, when he was resident at Bethnal Green, Middlesex, the company appointed Goldsborough supervisor and commissary-general responsible for the inspection of all its forts and factories in the East. He was knighted on 8 February and formally took his leave of the company on 4 March before embarking for India. He and his wife disembarked from the *Berkeley Castle* at Madras on 5 December. In Madras he sat in council as president, with Nathaniel Higginson, appointed governor on 23 October in succession to Elihu Yale, as second in council. Yale's last two years in office had been embittered by acrimonious differences with council and the mayor's court which Goldsborough reviewed and sought to reconcile. Goldsborough also inspected the fortifications and found them wanting. In June and July 1693 he went down the coast to Cuddalore to make an appraisal of Fort St David. Meanwhile, on 8 April, the company had revised his commission, appointing him captain-general and commander-in-chief of all their sea and land forces. Leaving his wife in Madras, Goldsborough sailed for Calcutta on 29 July where he arrived on 12 August. He was critical of the regime of the late agent, Job Charnock. He considered that the facilities required had not been adequately developed and ordered the construction of a mud wall to enclose a factory. He dismissed Charnock's successor, Francis Ellis, and replaced him with Charles Eyre from Dacca. He also took steps to prevent the growth of Roman Catholicism in the Hooghly area by terminating the activities of the Augustinian missionaries.

Goldsborough died of a fever at Calcutta on 29 November 1693, the day after he had added a codicil to his will. 'He was probably buried in the old burial ground (St John's churchyard) though no stone marks his resting place' (P. Thankappan Nair, *A Tercentenary History of Calcutta*, 1986, 1.342). No children were mentioned in his will; a cousin was the main beneficiary after his widow's death, but the will became the subject of chancery proceedings in 1702 and 1703. His widow married Roger Braddyll, a member of the Madras council, on 14 November 1695 and died in Madras in 1698. Although he made a promising start, Goldsborough was the company's supreme officer in India for less than a year. He had insufficient time to build a reputation in the manner of his predecessor, Sir John Child, or his successor, Sir John Gayer, but in a letter to the Madras council dated 22 January 1692 the company wrote of his 'experience, wisdom and moderation' and of his honesty (*Despatches from England, 1686–92*, Madras RO, 1929, 185). GORDON GOODWIN, *rev.* T. H. BOWYER

Sources East India Company court minutes, 1670–95, BL OIOC, B/31–40 • E. B. Sainsbury, ed., *A calendar of the court minutes … of the East India Company*, 11 vols. (1907–38) • H. D. Love, *Vestiges of old Madras, 1640–1800*, 4 vols. (1913), vol. 1 • *The diary of William Hedges … during his agency in Bengal; as well as on his voyage out and return overland (1681–1687)*, ed. R. Barlow and H. Yule, 3 vols., Hakluyt Society, 74–5, 78 (1887–9) • will, PRO, PROB 11/430, fol. 89 • A. Goldsbrough, *Memorials of the Goldesborough family* (1930) • C. Fawcett, ed., *The English factories in India*, new ser., 2 (1952) • C. R. Wilson, ed., *The early annals of the English in Bengal*, 2 vols. in 3 pts (1895–1911), vol. 1, pp. 141–4 • C. R. Wilson, ed., *Old Fort William in Bengal*, 1 (1906), xviii, 13 • 'Marriages at Fort St. George, Madras', *The Genealogist*, new ser., 19 (1902–3), 286 • Madras burials, BL OIOC, N/2/1 • chancery proceedings, PRO, C9/1702/327/1; C9/1703/299/46 • *Le Neve's Pedigrees of the knights*, ed. G. W. Marshall, Harleian Society, 8 (1873), 438 • G. E. Cokayne and E. A. Fry, eds., *Calendar of marriage licences issued by the faculty office, 1632–1714*, British RS, 33 (1905), 65

Wealth at death estate in Suffolk and houses in Whitechapel: will, PRO, PROB 11/430, fol. 89

Goldsborough, Richard. *See* Goldsbrough, Richard (1821–1886).

Goldsbrough, Richard (1821–1886), wool broker, was born on 17 October 1821 at Shipley, Yorkshire, the only son of Joshua Goldsbrough, butcher, and Hannah, *née* Speight. Apprenticed for seven years at the age of fourteen to John and Lupton Dawson, wool staplers of Bradford, Richard set up business there in 1842, purchasing and sorting clips.

Involvement with wool drew Goldsbrough's attention to the prospect of migrating to Australia. He left England aboard the *Warrior*, and on 29 November 1847 reached Melbourne, headquarters of the prosperous Port Phillip district. This proved a wise choice, for there was less competition there than at the older established city of Sydney. Moreover, the discovery of gold in 1851, shortly after Melbourne became capital of the newly created colony of Victoria, gave an immense boost to development.

Goldsbrough began operations in September 1848, concentrating on sheep and wool classing and on repacking wool for growers. The continued pastoral expansion benefited him greatly, and in 1850 he purchased the wool business of J. and R. Bakewell. With the help of his brother-in-law, Hugh Parker, who became a partner in 1857, he began weekly auctions and established himself as Victoria's leading wool broker. Meanwhile, at some time between June 1850 and the end of 1852 he was joined by his wife, Emma (1822–1877), daughter of Samuel Hodgson, butcher, whom he had married on 6 December 1842. They are said to have had possibly three children, who died while still in Yorkshire.

Auctioneering was only one of Goldsbrough's interests. He joined Edward Rowe and George Kirk to form the firm of E. Rowe & Co. in 1853 and began selling stock and stations, changing the firm's name to Rowe, Kirk & Co. in 1860. The partnership was dissolved in 1863, but Goldsbrough's own firm continued in the stock and station line. He also joined others to speculate in and develop pastoral properties along the Murray and Lachlan rivers. His ventures included a share in a hide and skin business that belonged to relatives of Frederick Rowe and Hugh Parker.

Meanwhile, Goldsbrough had advanced as a wool broker. In 1853 he had erected an imposing wool store in Melbourne on the site of the wooden building formerly owned by J. and R. Bakewell. Over the next two decades he invested substantial capital in showrooms and warehouses, which set new standards for design, appearance, and function. This side of his business flourished, particularly after a new partnership was formed with his compatriot J. H. Horsfall, who was also a pastoralist and wool broker, and who had joined the firm as a travelling representative in 1857. Hugh Parker's son Arthur, and his nephew David, also became partners in 1876, two years before Hugh died. The firm won a high reputation for providing credit and services to producers, and for selling wool locally, as well as on consignment to London.

The pastoral industry was, however, liable to fluctuations, and in the late 1860s an economic downturn adversely affected the value of wool, livestock, and land. Profits fell, and Goldsbrough encountered difficulties resulting from over-dependence on the banks. Aware of his vulnerability, he sought to broaden his financial base. In 1874 he began discussions for a merger with the Australian Mortgage Land and Finance Co. These proved unsuccessful, but on 30 June 1881 he did merge his firm with the Australasian Agency and Banking Corporation, which enabled him to expand his pastoral finance activities. Goldsbrough opened a branch in Sydney, which in 1888—two years after his death—amalgamated with the firm of Thomas S. *Mort to become Goldsbrough, Mort & Co.

Having suffered from a malignant tumour, Goldsbrough died on 8 April 1886 at Melbourne. His wife predeceased him, dying in 1877 at the age of fifty-four. He stands out as a shrewd businessman of imposing physique and outgoing manner who possessed a zest for high living, a willingness to take risks, and a fondness for the turf. The *Bradford Observer* claimed that, for thirty years, he generously donated an annual sum for the poor of Shipley and its neighbourhood. He did not, however, behave philanthropically in Melbourne and, apart from being a steward at the Victoria racing club, displayed little interest in public life. Goldsbrough's main importance was the contribution he made to improving wool sales and providing financial support to graziers, thus promoting a source of wealth vital to Victoria. BRIAN H. FLETCHER

Sources A. Barnard, research papers, Australian National University, Canberra, Noel Butlin Archives Centre, Goldsbrough, Mort & Co. MSS • Westpac Bank Archives, Sydney • A. Barnard, 'Goldsbrough, Richard', *AusDB*, vol. 4 • A. Barnard, *The Australian wool market, 1840–1900* (1958) • *Bradford Observer* • m. cert.
Archives Australian National University Library, Canberra, Noel Butlin Archives Centre • Westpac Bank Archives, Sydney
Likenesses portrait; copy, Australian National University, Canberra, Noel Butlin Archives Centre

Goldschmidt, Berthold (1903–1996), composer and conductor, was born on 18 January 1903 at Steinstrasse 12, Hamburg, Germany, the second of the five children (three died in infancy) of Adolf Michael Goldschmidt (1864–1937), merchant, and his wife, Henriette, *née* Wiesner (1873–1953). His was a cultured, musical Jewish family: his mother was an amateur soprano, his father a lover of opera who had attended all Mahler's Hamburg performances in the 1890s. Goldschmidt learned the piano from the age of six, and also began to compose. He attended the Oberrealschule St Georg, Hamburg, where he became fluent in English and French, and from 1918 studied piano with Edmund Schmid, the leading pianist in Hamburg, and harmony and counterpoint with Werner Wolff, a conductor at the opera. At a concert conducted by Wolff in the winter of 1920–21 Goldschmidt heard Busoni's 'Sarabande and Cortège' from *Doktor Faust*, which hugely impressed him, and met the composer, whose admonition to him: 'when composing, make this your rule: all counterpoint must be *melodious*', he never forgot (Struck, 6).

Goldschmidt began a course in philosophy and art history at Hamburg University in the spring of 1922, but in the autumn he went to Berlin and entered Franz Schreker's composition class at the Hochschule für Musik, studying conducting there with Rudolf Krasselt and Julius Prüwer. He also continued his studies in philosophy and history of music and art at the University of Berlin. After leaving the Hochschule in 1925 Goldschmidt soon began to make his mark, becoming assistant to Erich Kleiber at the Staatsoper, where he coached singers for the première of Berg's *Wozzeck* in December 1925, played the celesta in performances, and, more important, won the Mendelssohn state prize with his orchestral *Passacaglia*, which Kleiber conducted at the Staatstheater in February 1926. His first string quartet attracted the attention of Schoenberg, who would have welcomed Goldschmidt as a disciple, but Goldschmidt was wary of serialism, and in any case was now sufficiently confident of his own style, a personal derivation from Busoni's concept of *Junge Klassizität*.

A fortunate meeting in 1927 with Carl Ebert led to an invitation to Darmstadt to be composer, conductor, and adviser to Ebert, who was general director of the opera there. While in Darmstadt, Goldschmidt wrote his first opera, *Der gewaltige Hahnrei*, based on Fernand Crommelynck's then popular play *Le cocu magnifique*. The opera was successfully produced in Mannheim in February 1932. Meanwhile his conducting career had also taken off, particularly after he was guest conductor with the Leningrad Philharmonic in 1931. Ebert, who had become intendant at the Städtische Oper in Berlin and had taken Goldschmidt with him, scheduled *Der gewaltige Hahnrei* for production there in the 1933 season.

With the coming to power of the Nazis in January 1933 the successful career in Germany that had seemed inevitable vanished overnight. Goldschmidt's prestigious publishing contract with Universal Edition, Vienna, was terminated. He was able to stay on at the Städtische Oper for two more years on half pay; he taught privately and had a few clandestine performances, but in 1935 he emigrated to England. He leased a flat in Belsize Park, London, where he remained for the rest of his life. The immense relief he felt after arriving in England was expressed in a burst of composition: the two pieces he wrote, his second string quartet and *Ciaccona sinfonica* for orchestra, are among his finest, but neither was performed publicly until after the war. On 20 February 1936 he married (Liesel) Caren Bothe (1910–1979), a singer whom he had met in Germany in 1934. There were no children of the marriage. Goldschmidt maintained a precarious existence during his first years in England: one of his few commissions was a ballet score, *Chronica* (1938), for Kurt Jooss's company, then based at Dartington Hall, who toured it extensively.

From 1944 to 1947 Goldschmidt was music director of the BBC German service, his programmes particularly featuring German Jewish composers and musicians. His conducting career did not begin to revive until after the war: in 1947 (which was also the year he took British citizenship) he became chorus master at Glyndebourne (rejoining Ebert), and conducted the Glyndebourne production of Verdi's *Macbeth* at the first Edinburgh Festival, replacing George Szell at the last minute. During the next twenty years he conducted all the major British orchestras and developed a particular association with the BBC Scottish Symphony Orchestra. He gave the first complete British performances of Mahler's third symphony in 1959 with the Philharmonia and of Deryck Cooke's performing version of Mahler's tenth symphony (on whose orchestration he collaborated) with the London Symphony Orchestra in 1964.

In 1948 Goldschmidt began his second opera, *Beatrice Cenci*, based on Shelley's verse drama, and entered it for the Arts Council's competition for operas to celebrate the Festival of Britain in 1951. He was one of the four winners, but the Arts Council guaranteed no performances of any of the winning operas, and none in fact took place under their auspices. This was a bitter blow to his hopes, and although he had some success as a composer during the 1950s, conducting the premières of three concertos and an orchestral song cycle with the BBC Scottish Symphony Orchestra, he eventually became so discouraged that he gave up composition altogether in 1958.

Goldschmidt was small and energetic, with a fierce intelligence whose incisiveness stayed intact into old age.

He had a superbly retentive memory and a repertory of precisely detailed anecdotes. He retained his cheerfulness and sense of humour during the long years of neglect, and never complained. He was not attached to possessions and his flat had an air of temporariness: books were piled on the mantelpiece as if they had only just come out of their packing cases.

In 1982, at the instigation of the clarinettist Gervase de Peyer, Goldschmidt began to compose again—a clarinet quartet—and this was the beginning of a remarkable Indian summer during which he wrote fifteen more new pieces (including two masterly string quartets) and his fortunes changed dramatically. His music was once more performed and, in a less doctrinaire atmosphere where he was no longer condemned for being out of date, received critical praise. After Simon Rattle had conducted *Ciaccona sinfonica* in Berlin to huge acclaim in 1987 event followed event with increasing momentum, so that by the end of his life all his major works had been recorded on disc, including his two operas, both of which had also been staged in Germany. His last few years were a non-stop circus, travelling round Europe to hear—even again to conduct—his music, to attend recordings, to give interviews, and to receive awards, prominent among them the Bundesverdienstkreuz (order of merit) from the German federal government in 1993, his ninetieth year.

Goldschmidt accepted this extraordinary turn of events with the same equable good humour. His health had remained sound, but in 1996, soon after the British première at the BBC Promenade Concerts of the rediscovered *Passacaglia*, which had been buried for seventy years in Universal Edition's archive, he finally lost his zest for life. He saw few people in his last months and died peacefully at his home, 13 Belsize Crescent, London, on 17 October. He was cremated at Golders Green on 25 October and his ashes were scattered in the garden there.

DAVID MATTHEWS

Sources D. Matthews, 'Berthold Goldschmidt: a biographical sketch', *Tempo*, 144 (March 1983), 2–6 • B. Keefe and D. Allenby, chronological biography, *Berthold Goldschmidt: a musical celebration* (1997) [concert programme, Wigmore Hall, London, 27 March 1997] • M. Struck, 'Evidence from a fragmented musical history: notes on Berthold Goldschmidt's chamber music', *Tempo*, 174 (Sept 1990), 2–10 • D. Matthews, 'Berthold Goldschmidt, 1903–1996', *Professional Composer*, 39 (summer 1997), 6 • *The Times* (18 Oct 1996) • *Daily Telegraph* (19 Oct 1996) • *The Independent* (19 Oct 1996) • naturalization details, PRO, HO 334/184/AZ 29498 • m. cert. • personal knowledge (2004) • private information (2004) • Goldschmidt Archive, Berlin • d. cert.

Archives Die Stiftung der Akademie der Künste, Berlin, Germany, Goldschmidt archive, MSS

Likenesses photograph, 1929, repro. in *Daily Telegraph* (18 Oct 1996) • photograph, 1960, repro. in *The Independent* • Z. Roboz, drawing, 1993, repro. in *The Independent* • photograph, repro. in Matthews, 'Berthold Goldschmidt, 1903–1996' • photograph, repro. in *The Times* • photographs, repro. in Keefe and Allenby, *Berthold Goldschmidt*

Wealth at death £219,660: probate, 19 Dec 1996, *CGPLA Eng. & Wales*

Goldschmidt, Otto Moritz David (1829–1907), pianist and composer, was born on 21 August 1829 in Hamburg, Germany, the son of Jewish parents. His mother's maiden name was Schwabe. His grandfather and father were Hamburg merchants with a British connection, as their firm had branches in Glasgow and Manchester. His first piano teacher was his mother, who had a fine soprano voice, and he later had piano lessons from Jakob Schmitt and harmony lessons from F. W. Grund. On Mendelssohn's advice he entered the newly opened Leipzig conservatory in the autumn of 1843, and studied there for three years, attending Mendelssohn's select class for piano phrasing, and learning piano technique from Plaidy and counterpoint from Moritz Hauptmann. While there he came to know Joseph Joachim and W. S. Rockstro, both fellow students. He probably also saw the performance given by Jenny *Lind, the Swedish soprano (whom he was later to marry), at the Leipzig Gewandhaus in 1845.

From 1846 to 1848 Goldschmidt taught and performed in Hamburg. In 1848 he was sent to Paris to study under Chopin, and he was at the composer's last performance at the Salle Pleyel, but the revolution prevented the realization of his plans, and he went to London. His first performance in London was on 31 July 1848 at a concert given by Jenny Lind for the Brompton Hospital for Consumption in the concert room of Her Majesty's Theatre. He also appeared in London on 27 March 1849 at one of John Ella's Musical Union concerts. He performed in Hamburg and Leipzig, and in January 1850 he met Jenny Lind again at Lübeck.

In May 1851, at the invitation of Jenny Lind, who was then nearing the end of a long American tour, he went to New York after her accompanist had returned to England. The couple were married in Boston on 5 February 1852. It was a very happy marriage. From 1852 to 1855 they lived in Dresden, making frequent European concert tours, and in 1858 they settled in England, making their home in Wimbledon. Goldschmidt was naturalized in 1861. He became the organist of St John's Church, Putney, and another local church.

In 1862 Goldschmidt and William Sterndale Bennett began to edit *The Chorale Book for England* (1862–4), in which German tunes were set to hymn translations already made by Catherine Winkworth in her *Lyra Germanica*. In 1863 and 1866 Goldschmidt conducted the choral music when his wife appeared in Düsseldorf at the lower Rhine music festival. In 1863 he became a professor of piano at the Royal Academy of Music, and served as vice-principal from 1866 to 1868. From 1864 to 1869 he advised Dr Temple about music at Rugby School.

In 1876 Goldschmidt, Jenny Lind, and Arthur Duke Coleridge organized an amateur choir for the first complete performance in England of Bach's B minor mass, which was performed on 26 April 1876 at St James's Hall. This led to the formation of the Bach Choir, which Goldschmidt conducted until 1885. He edited many works for the *Bach Choir Magazine* and revived works such as Handel's *Ode for St Cecilia's Day*. As a pianist he was a surviving link with Mendelssohn's period, and his style was that of the composer—clear and expressive, but almost without pedal, and he was generally regarded as a dull performer. As a composer also, Goldschmidt belonged to Mendelssohn's era. His best-known work was the oratorio *Ruth* (1867), written for Jenny Lind, which was given its première by her at the Hereford festival in 1867, and was also performed at her last public concert in Düsseldorf in 1870. Other published works included a choral song, *Music, an Ode* (1898), a piano concerto, op. 10, a piano trio, op. 12, solo songs, and partsongs. Following the death of Jenny Lind in 1887 he published a collection of her cadenzas and ornaments in 1891.

Goldschmidt was awarded many honours. He was a knight of the Swedish order of the Vasa (1876), and was given the Swedish gold medal *litteris et artibus*, with the commander ribbon of the polar star (1893). He was a chief officer or honorary member of the majority of London musical institutions, including the Philharmonic Society, and was elected a member of the Athenaeum in 1876. He owned the original autograph of Beethoven's 1802 letter to his brothers, the Heiligenstadt Testament, and presented this in 1888 to the Hamburg Stadtbibliothek.

Goldschmidt died on 24 February 1907 at his house, 1 Moreton Gardens, The Boltons, South Kensington, and was buried beside his wife at Wynds Point on the Malvern hills. He was survived by two sons and a daughter.

C. D. MACLEAN, *rev.* ANNE PIMLOTT BAKER

Sources *New Grove* · *Musical Herald* (May 1896), 135–8 · *MT*, 48 (1907), 246–7 · *The Times* (26 Feb 1907) · J. Bulman, *Jenny Lind* (1956)

Likenesses double portraits, photographs, repro. in Bulman, *Jenny Lind* · photograph, repro. in *Musical Herald*, 135 · photograph, repro. in J. M. C. Maude, *The life of Jenny Lind* (1926)

Wealth at death £3599 3s. 7d.: resworn probate, 9 May 1907, *CGPLA Eng. & Wales*

Goldsmid, Abraham (*c.*1756–1810), merchant and financier, was born in the Netherlands about 1756, the youngest son in the family of four sons and three daughters of Aaron Goldsmid (*d.* 1782), a merchant, and his wife, Catherine de Vries. His father migrated from Amsterdam to London about 1763, at a time when Amsterdam's position as the metropolis of international finance was being strongly challenged by London, and there was much movement of entrepreneurs and capital between the two centres. In consequence, Aaron retained his connections with the Netherlands and Germany, dealing with drafts and remittances to correspondents in those countries. His eldest son, George, became his partner in 1771, and continued the business after his death in 1782. However, his other three sons, Asher, Benjamin, and Abraham, also built on his experience and connections. Asher, the second son, went into partnership with Abraham Mocatta as bullion brokers, and soon formed a close connection with the Bank of England. The third and fourth sons, **Benjamin Goldsmid** (*c.*1753–1808), also a merchant and financier, and Abraham, went into partnership in 1776, and moved from merchanting into 'pure' finance. They traded as Benjamin and Abraham Goldsmid.

Benjamin and Abraham Goldsmid were the first specialists in bill broking in the City of London. There were already some 700 licensed brokers who acted as intermediaries between merchants and bankers, but they were generalists rather than specialists in a particular line, and were confined by City regulations to acting as agents (rather than as principals) for 0.125 per cent commission. Goldsmids declined to acquire a licence as one of the permitted dozen Jewish brokers, preferring to win their reputation in the discounting of bills or (in twentieth-century City parlance) as bill brokers or as a discount house. They moved from their father's home at 25 Leman Street, Whitechapel, on the eastern (Jewish) fringe of the City to 6 Capel Court, very close to the Bank of England and the stock exchange. The scale of the Goldsmids' business increased, not just through good commercial strategy, but also through dynastic alliance. Benjamin married Jessie, the daughter of Israel Levien Salomons, a wealthy East India merchant, who brought a dowry of £100,000; they had seven children who survived infancy. Abraham married Ann Eliason of Amsterdam; they had a daughter, Isabel, who married her cousin Isaac Lyon Goldsmid. The brothers made influential friends, including Abraham Newland, chief cashier of the Bank of England. They undertook favours for members of government, and also raised money in the Netherlands for a spendthrift prince of Wales (later George IV). At the same time they acted as bill brokers for continental correspondents, and in 1790 took into partnership Daniel Eliason, a Jewish dealer in bills of exchange with Hamburg and some other German cities.

Abraham Goldsmid was a member of the stock exchange from 1802, and appeared there in person. This meant not only that he could deal for his own account without paying commission, but also that he 'knew all the intrigue of the house' and could keep in close touch with events (Cope, 'The Goldsmids', 198). It appears that Abraham was much more active in this stock-jobbing and loan-contracting business than his brother.

Although the records are very meagre, the reasons for Goldsmids' success as bill brokers are clear. The foundation was of course their intimate knowledge of continental (particularly Dutch) trade and their network of Jewish (and perhaps also gentile) correspondents. Bilingual, and shuttling between the principal foci of late eighteenth-century finance, they gained unrivalled knowledge of the creditworthiness of the numerous merchant houses in the trade. It was said of Abraham that he knew, as if by instinct, a bad name on a bill of exchange. Superior communications must also have been a success factor; it was said that the Goldsmids kept a fast sailing vessel at Harwich to carry expresses twice a week, immediately after the bargains in European exchanges had been concluded, to their agents and correspondents at Hamburg, Amsterdam, Frankfurt, Vienna, and other cities, and that this gave them a priority in intelligence which they often turned to profitable account. However, it should not be supposed that the Goldsmids' advance to the premier position in bill broking in London occurred without jealousy or antisemitic prejudice. Thus Francis Baring & Co., rapidly rising to the status of the City's most successful merchant bank, wrote to their Amsterdam correspondents in 1792 that the Goldsmids

> endeavour to negotiate their bills [of exchange] without the intervention of Brokers, therefore they are particularly obnoxious to the [other] Jews, but the circumstance of their drawing upon Houses of an inferior description has staggered us in such a manner as to induce us to decline their paper, unless for small sums or at short date. (Amsterdam RO, Mees and Hope MSS, PA 735)

The long period of war with revolutionary France and then with Napoleon (1793–1802, 1803–15) generated unprecedented government borrowing, both to pay for the British armed forces and to subsidize Britain's continental allies. Goldsmids, who dealt in exchequer bills (short-dated government bonds), then moved into loan contracting in 1795 by joining a syndicate of City houses led by Boyd, Benfield & Co., which raised £18 million. Boyd, Benfield & Co. went bankrupt in 1800, but this did not adversely affect Goldsmids' standing in the City. Goldsmids then moved into syndicates with Barings, making successful bids for loan contracts in 1800 (£28 million) and 1806 (£20 million) and winning the contract on their own against Barings and other competition in 1809 (£12 million).

This period of successful loan contracting was brought to an abrupt end by the sudden death of Benjamin Goldsmid. He had been in poor health for some time and was subject to fits of depression. As the *Gentleman's Magazine* later recorded, he hanged himself at his country house at Roehampton, Surrey, on 11 April 1808 'with the cord that was suspended from the tester of his bed, for the purpose of enabling him to turn himself round in his fits of gout, with which he had been much afflicted' (*GM*, 1st ser., 78, 1808, 457). Abraham subsequently formed two firms to handle the business formerly conducted by himself and his brother.

Loan contracting was a high-risk business at the best of times, because success or failure turned on investors' confidence which, in the war situation, was volatile. In 1810 Goldsmids rejoined the Baring consortium, which won a contract to raise £12 million, but a sudden fall in the market left Abraham Goldsmid with a serious liquidity problem. The problem was exacerbated by the economic recession in the summer of 1810, the enmity of stock exchange jobbers towards Goldsmid, and the death of Sir Francis Baring early in September 1810. Goldsmid could not repay a loan from the East India Company, and, in a fit of nervous depression, he shot himself at his home in Morden on 28 September.

News of the suicide created panic in the City, virtually arresting all stock exchange business. 'We question', commented *The Courier* on the day after, 'whether peace or war suddenly made ever created such a bustle as the death of Mr Goldsmid' (29 Sept 1810). The government's credit was adversely affected and the Bank of England had to support creditors to restrain further deterioration. Government-appointed liquidators revealed that the firm was indebted to the exchequer to the extent of £466,700, of which £419,000 was an account of exchequer bills. A commission appointed to investigate the catastrophe reported in June 1816 that

> the cause of the failure of Messrs Goldsmid is not to be attributed to avaricious speculations or blameable imprudence but that they may be considered as victims to bold and anxious exertions on behalf of the public from which the utmost benefit was derived for many years by the Country. (Rothschild archives, London, T17/7)

The surviving partners of Goldsmids made great efforts to discharge their liabilities. By 1816 they had paid a full 15*s*. in the pound, and in 1820 parliament annulled the remaining portion of the debts, a further 1*s*. 6*d*. in the pound having been paid. S. D. Chapman

Sources S. R. Cope, 'The Goldsmids and the development of the London money market during the Napoleonic wars', *Economica*, new ser., 9 (1942), 180–206 · F. Crouzet, *L'économie britannique et le blocus continental, 1806–1813*, 2 (Paris, 1958), 622–7 · J. J. Grellier, *The terms of all the loans* (1812) · L. Alexander, *Memoirs of the life of the late Benjamin Goldsmid* (1820) [unreliable] · S. R. Cope, *Walter Boyd: a merchant banker in the age of Napoleon* (1983) · Amsterdam RO, Mees and Hope MSS, information books, PA 735/Buist 1, vols. 22–6 · bankruptcy report, June 1816, Rothschild archives, London, T17/7 · *DNB* · *GM*, 1st ser., 78 (1808), 457 · *The Courier* (29 Sept 1810)

Archives Amsterdam RO, Mees and Hope MSS, information books, PA 735/Buist 1, vols. 22–6 · Rothschilds, archives, London, bankruptcy report, T17/7

Likenesses F. Bartolozzi, stipple, pubd 1802 (after S. Medley), BM · R. Dighton, watercolour, 1803, NPG

Goldsmid, Anna Maria (1805–1889), benefactor and translator, was born on 17 September 1805, the eldest child of the financier and Jewish community leader Isaac Lyon *Goldsmid (1778–1859) and his wife, Isabel, *née* Goldsmid (1788–1860). Her brother was Sir Francis Henry *Goldsmid (1808–1878). She thus belonged to one of the most influential and wealthy Anglo-Jewish families of the early nineteenth century. Privately educated, she exhibited from an early age a remarkable aptitude for languages, studying Italian with the poet Dante Gabriel Rossetti and French with a leading grammarian of the day, Professor Merlet; German she learned from her resident German governess and Hebrew first from Michael Goldsmith, master of the Talmud Torah school in London, and subsequently from Professor Hyman Hurwitz (1770–1844), the first professor of Hebrew at University College, London. Her English literary studies were supervised by the Scottish poet Thomas Campbell (1777–1844), some of whose manuscripts she bequeathed to the British Museum.

Anna Maria Goldsmid made the acquaintance of these luminaries through the initiative of her father, whose London residence became a favourite meeting-place of the utilitarians; she moved easily and eagerly in this circle, numbering among her friends Lord Brougham, Robert Owen, and Harriet Martineau. Devoted to her father, she immersed herself in his various secular and religious initiatives, chief among which were the establishment of the non-denominational University College, London, in 1828 and the foundation of the West London Synagogue of British Jews, the first Reform Jewish community in Britain, in 1842. The motives for the establishment of this congregation were many, including a desire for reform of the Jewish liturgy and the modification of Orthodox Jewish doctrine, and a rejection of the authority of the London Committee of Deputies of the British Jews, whose attitude towards Jewish political emancipation was felt by the Goldsmids to be much too lukewarm. Born an Orthodox Jew, in her religious practices Anna Maria remained throughout her life very observant—'probably the most observant Jewess of her time' (*Jewish Chronicle*, 8)—although she resented the absolute relegation of women in Orthodox synagogues, and hoped that the establishment of the West London would give women a more active role in Jewish religious life.

Like many financially independent female members of the Anglo-Jewish gentry, Anna Maria Goldsmid devoted much of her time to educational matters, in which she was greatly interested and for which she developed a nationally recognized expertise. Besides writing a number of pamphlets on educational questions she was responsible for the foundation of the Jews' infants' school, London (1841), and for the re-establishment, in Notting Hill, of the Jews' Deaf and Dumb Home (1863). Her considerable philanthropy also extended to University College Hospital and the Homoeopathic Hospital, both in London. In 1855 she published an English translation, entitled *The Development of the Religious Idea*, of a seminal work by the famous pioneer of Reform Judaism in Germany, Dr Ludwig Philippsohn of Magdeburg. This was followed much later, in 1872, by *The Deicides: Analysis of the Life of Jesus*, a translation from the French of the powerful refutation, written by J. Cohen of Marseilles, of the view that the Jews were Christ-killers. She was also responsible for the translation into English, also in 1872, of the Prussian educational code.

Anna Maria Goldsmid died of bronchitis at her home, 26 Cambridge Square, Hyde Park, London, on 8 February 1889, and was buried four days later beside her father at the Kingsbury Road Jewish cemetery, Dalston. She was unmarried and childless. GEOFFREY ALDERMAN

Sources *Jewish Chronicle* (15 Feb 1889), 5, 8–9 · 'Goldsmid, Isaac Lyon', *DNB* · d. cert. · *CGPLA Eng. & Wales* (1889)
Archives Girton Cam., letters to Mme Bodichon
Wealth at death £16,471 0s. 4d.: probate, 22 March 1889, *CGPLA Eng. & Wales*

Goldsmid, Benjamin (*c.*1753–1808). *See under* Goldsmid, Abraham (*c.*1756–1810).

Goldsmid, Sir Francis Henry, second baronet (1808–1878), lawyer and Jewish communal leader, was born at Spital Square, London, on 1 May 1808, the second son of the financier Sir Isaac Lyon *Goldsmid, first baronet (1778–1859), and his wife and cousin, Isabel Goldsmid (1788–1860). The social and political milieu provided through his parents' household had a major and lifelong impact on him, for although originating from the world of Jewish Orthodoxy, his father enjoyed the company and friendship of the leading utilitarians of the day, for whom the Goldsmid residence became a favoured meeting-place. Fiercely proud of his Jewish identity, Isaac Goldsmid none the less harboured a deep aversion to religious fundamentalism, and believed that the full emergence of British Jews into British society, and in particular the granting to them of complete equality before the law, required changes in Jewish religious practice and outlook. Francis quickly came to share these views, and he became his father's closest ally in two parallel campaigns, for Anglo-Jewish political emancipation and for the creation of a new species of Jewish worship.

Educated privately, Francis Goldsmid chose the law for a career, but when called to the bar at Lincoln's Inn (31 January 1833), he refused to take the oath 'on the true faith of a Christian', and was instead permitted to use the Hebrew Bible, thus becoming the first professing Jew to be admitted as a barrister and, in 1858, the first professing Jew to be appointed a queen's counsel. He gave up his legal practice in 1859 when, on the death of his father, he succeeded to Isaac's baronetcy and Portuguese barony. On 10 October 1839 he married his first cousin Louisa Sophia *Goldsmid (1819–1908), an early Jewish feminist who shared his religious and social values. There were no children of the marriage.

Even before undertaking his legal training, Goldsmid had begun making contributions to the growing public controversy over the call for the removal of the civil disabilities suffered by the Jews of Britain. In 1830 he published *Remarks on the Civil Disabilities of the British Jews*, the first in a series of brilliant analytical invectives on this subject which appeared over the succeeding eighteen years. But his approach to the emancipation question also had its practical side. He was perhaps the first member of the Anglo-Jewish leadership to recognize the potential of the Jewish vote as a weapon in the struggle for civic rights. Technically, professing Jews could not vote in parliamentary elections until the power of returning officers to require otherwise qualified electors to swear the Christian oath of abjuration was swept away by parliament in 1835. But in practice this power was often simply not exercised, and in *The arguments advanced against the enfranchisement of the Jews, considered in a series of letters* (1831; 2nd edn, 1833), Goldsmid noted that although Sir Robert Grant's Jewish Relief Bill of the previous year had been defeated, the dozen MPs who represented those London constituencies in which the majority of British Jews resided had supported the measure.

Thus was born the idea of a 'Jewish vote', which might be harnessed for Jewish ends. In the 1840s and 1850s this vote was skilfully exploited by the whig-Liberal alliance, which supported Jewish emancipation and to which Isaac and Francis Goldsmid naturally belonged. In 1847 Isaac was adopted as Liberal candidate at Beverley, while Francis stood at Great Yarmouth. Neither was successful but Francis's appetite for politics had been thoroughly whetted. In 1860, two years after the right of professing Jews to sit in the Commons had finally been conceded, he was elected for Reading, the constituency he represented until his death. Dubbed 'the member for Jewry', he soon acquired an enviable reputation as the most eloquent and outspoken of the early Jewish MPs, his parliamentary denunciations of the attacks made on Jews in the Danubian provinces and in Russia and Poland between 1862 and 1872 earning him widespread praise.

Yet although his parliamentary interventions encompassed a broad range of contemporary economic and social questions, he never achieved government office; it was his political colleague and fellow lawyer, George Jessel, who in 1871 became solicitor-general, the first professing Jewish member of a British administration. Perhaps this was because he was suspected of putting Jewish interests before party considerations, a suspicion confirmed later in the decade when he declined, categorically, to support Gladstone's crusade against Disraeli's pro-Turkish foreign policy, believing (like Disraeli) that it was better to delay self-rule in the Balkans until the rights of Balkan Jewry could be properly safeguarded against Russian-dominated Slav nationalism.

While pursuing his legal and political careers, Goldsmid had also taken a very prominent part in the establishment of the first Reform Jewish congregation in Britain. The formation of the West London Synagogue of British Jews may be viewed as a multi-faceted act of communal rebellion: against the drabness, tedium, and lack of decorum to be found in the then existing synagogues of the metropolis; against aspects of Orthodox Jewish dogma and doctrine regarded in some quarters as too nationalistic or obscurantist; and as a means by which promoters of Jewish emancipation might be afforded a platform independent of the London Committee of Deputies of British Jews, which under the leadership of Sir Moses Montefiore was dragging its heels in this regard. Goldsmid was one of the twenty-four gentlemen who met at the Bedford Hotel, Southampton Row, on 15 April 1840 to put their names to the famous declaration that marked the formal origins of Reform Judaism in Britain. On 27 February 1842 the West London Synagogue of British Jews opened for business in Burton Street, Euston; Goldsmid was a founding member, and for the remainder of his life he freely gave of his professional talents in its defence and advancement.

Much later, in 1871, Goldsmid played a major role—perhaps *the* major role—in the establishment of the Anglo-Jewish Association. The origins of this organization were, again, multi-faceted: fear that Anglo-Jewish involvement in the Alliance Israélite Universelle (founded in 1860 as an international agency to protect Jewish interests worldwide) would label British Jewry as cosmopolitan; dismay at the apparent inability of the London Committee of Deputies to undertake work with an international dimension; but also anger at the continued exclusion of Reform Jews (on Moses Montefiore's order) from participation in the work of the deputies. The Anglo-Jewish Association was meant to rival the deputies, and it did so very effectively until, in 1878, the deputies agreed to the formation of a conjoint foreign committee of the two bodies, a sort of Anglo-Jewish ministry of foreign affairs, which in practice the association dominated.

Goldsmid, like his father, took a close interest in the non-denominational University College, London, his benefactions to which included the endowment of the chair of applied mathematics and mechanics in 1871, and in University College Hospital, of which he served as treasurer from 1857 to 1868. In 1841 he established the Jews' infant school, London, which became the largest infant school in England. He was crushed between a railway carriage and the platform in an accident at Waterloo Station when he got out of a train which was still moving, and died from his injuries at St Thomas's Hospital, Lambeth, on 2 May 1878. His burial took place at the Islington cemetery of the West London Synagogue six days later. He was survived by his wife. GEOFFREY ALDERMAN

Sources G. Alderman, *The Jewish community in British politics* (1983) · C. Bermant, *The cousinhood: the Anglo-Jewish gentry* (1971) · A. J. Kershen and J. A. Romain, *Tradition and change: a history of Reform Judaism in Britain, 1840–1995* (1995) · *Memoirs of Sir Francis Goldsmid*, ed. D. W. Marks and A. Löwy, 2nd edn (1882) · *Jewish Chronicle* (10 May 1878), 9–11 · d. cert.

Archives CKS, business MSS

Likenesses W. Theed, marble bust, 1879, Lincoln's Inn, London · J. Watkins, carte-de-visite, NPG · cartoon sketch, repro. in Kershen and Romain, *Tradition and change* · chromolithograph caricature, NPG; repro. in *VF* (9 Dec 1872)

Wealth at death under £1,000,000: probate, 28 May 1878, *CGPLA Eng. & Wales*

Goldsmid, Sir Frederic John (1818–1908), army officer and writer, was born on 19 May 1818 at Milan, the only son of Lionel Prager Goldsmid, an officer of the 19th dragoon guards, and grandson of Benjamin *Goldsmid [*see under* Goldsmid, Abraham]. He showed an aptitude for foreign languages, and after education at an English school in Paris he passed through King's College School to King's College, London.

On 24 January 1839 Goldsmid was commissioned ensign in the East India Company's army, and in April he joined the 37th Madras native infantry. He was promoted lieutenant on 24 September 1840. In August 1840 his regiment was ordered to China, where he served as adjutant in the actions at Canton (Guangzhou) and along the coast. During the campaign he first turned to the study of oriental languages, for which he showed a marked faculty. After returning to India in 1845 he qualified as interpreter in Hindustani. He was appointed interpreter for Persian in 1849 and for Arabic in 1851.

On 2 January 1849 Goldsmid married Mary (*d.* 1900), the daughter of Lieutenant-General George Mackenzie Steuart; they had two sons and four daughters. He was promoted captain on 30 June 1851, and was appointed assistant adjutant-general of the Nagpur subsidiary field force. Shortly after, thanks to the influence of General John Jacob, Goldsmid entered the civil service, first as deputy collector and then as assistant commissioner for the settlement of alienated lands in the newly annexed province of Sind.

On his return to England in 1855 Goldsmid volunteered for active service in the Crimea, and from July 1855 until the end of the war was attached to the Turkish contingent at Kerch under General Sir Robert Vivian. He soon acquired a knowledge of Turkish. In recognition of his services he was made brevet major on 6 June 1856, and awarded the Mejidiye (fourth class). He returned to India in 1856, and took up judicial work at Shikarpur. Subsequently he served on the staff of Sir Bartle Frere, chief commissioner of Sind, and during the mutiny he distinguished himself in various dangerous missions.

In 1861 Goldsmid first became connected with the scheme for an Indo-European telegraph. In that year he arranged with the chiefs of Baluchistan and Makran for telegraph construction along the coast of Gwadar. In 1864 he was selected to superintend the enormous task of carrying the wires from Europe across Persia and Baluchistan to India. He accompanied Colonel Patrick Stewart when laying the Persian Gulf cable, and later proceeded by way of Baghdad and Mosul to Constantinople. There, after protracted negotiations, he carried through the Indo-Ottoman telegraph treaty. On 30 March 1865, following the death of Colonel Stewart, he was appointed director-general of the Indo-European telegraph, and at once visited Tehran to assist in negotiating a telegraph treaty with the Persian government. From Tehran he travelled overland to India and back again to Europe to settle the terms of admission of the Indo-European telegraph to the European system. Subsequently Goldsmid personally superintended the construction of the telegraph line across the whole extent of Persia. He was made brevet lieutenant-colonel on 3 April 1863, and promoted major on 8 January 1864, lieutenant-colonel on 24 January 1865, and colonel on 24 January 1870; he was made a CB in 1866. He wrote a characteristically modest account of his adventures, *Travel and Telegraph* (1874).

Goldsmid resigned the directorship of the Indo-European telegraph in 1870, and in the following year was appointed a commissioner for the delimitation of the boundary between Persia and Baluchistan. His award was eventually accepted by the shah's government. In the same year Goldsmid was entrusted with the even more delicate task of investigating the claims of Persia and Afghanistan to the province of Sistan. The arbitral award was published at Tehran on 19 August 1872; Persia was confirmed in the possession of Sistan, while a section of the Helmand was left in Afghan territory. The impartiality of the award satisfied neither party, but it had the desired effect of keeping the peace. Goldsmid was created a KCSI in 1871, and received the thanks of the government of India. He retired from the army on 23 January 1875 with a special pension and the rank of major-general.

Goldsmid now devoted himself to writing his authoritative *Life of Sir James Outram*, which was published in two volumes in 1880; but his public career was not yet ended. In 1877 he was appointed British representative on the international commission to inquire into Indian immigration in Réunion. A joint report was issued in February 1878, and a separate report in the following April. In 1880 Goldsmid accepted the post of controller of crown lands (Daira Sanieh) in Egypt, which he held until 1 May 1883. He witnessed the outbreak of violence there in September 1881. In June 1882 he was dispatched by Lord Granville on a diplomatic mission to Constantinople. On his return to Alexandria he rendered useful service in the campaign of 1882 by organizing the intelligence department, for which he received Wolseley's thanks. On his resigning the control of the crown lands on 1 May 1883 the khedive bestowed on him the Osmanie decoration of the second class and the bronze star.

On leaving Egypt Goldsmid accepted from Leopold II, king of the Belgians, the post of 'administrateur délégué de l'association internationale' in the Congo, and he undertook the organization of the administrative system in Leopold's new state (later the notorious Congo Free State). But soon after he reached the Congo Goldsmid's health broke down, and he returned to England on 31 December 1883. Thenceforth he resided mainly in London, devoting himself to literary work connected with his oriental studies, and taking an active role in the Royal Asiatic Society (secretary, November 1885 to June 1887; vice-president, 1890–1905) and the Royal Geographical Society, and in various religious and philanthropic institutions. He died at his home, 29 Phoenix Lodge Mansions, Brook Green, Hammersmith, on 12 January 1908, and was buried at Hollingbourne, Kent. G. S. Woods, *rev.* Alex May

Sources *Army List* • *Indian Army List* • *The Times* (13 Jan 1908) • F. J. Goldsmid, *Travel and telegraph* (1874) • J. F. Maurice, *Military history of the campaign of 1882 in Egypt* (1887) • A. J. Barker, *The vain glorious war* (1970) • A. D. Lambert, *The Crimean War: British grand strategy, 1853–56* (1990) • *CGPLA Eng. & Wales* (1908)

Archives BL OIOC, corresp., MS Eur. C 168 • BL OIOC, corresp. and papers, MS Eur. F 134 • BL OIOC, notebook, diary, MS Eur. D 642 • NAM, papers, 6804/3–27

Wealth at death £3669 15*s*. 3*d*.: probate, 30 Jan 1908, *CGPLA Eng. & Wales*

Goldsmid, Henry Edward (1812–1855), East India Company servant, born at Finsbury Square, London, on 9 May 1812, was the second son of Edward Moses (1763–1853), of Upper Harley Street, London, and his wife, Rose, *née* Joachim (1774–1851). His father took the name Goldsmid. He was educated privately, and in 1829, on being nominated to a writership in the East India Company by one of its directors, Robert Campbell, went to East India College, Haileybury, where he twice obtained the Persian prize and also distinguished himself in Hindustani and law. Proceeding to the Bombay presidency in 1831, he served in the districts of Ahmadnagar and Tanna until 1835, when he became assistant to the revenue commissioner Thomas Williamson. On 17 November 1836, while serving as assistant magistrate and collector of Sholapur, he struck a sick prisoner whom he suspected of malingering. The prisoner died nine days later. Goldsmid was convicted of assault in the Bombay supreme court and fined 10 rupees. The Bombay government also temporarily revoked his magisterial powers and deprived him of certain allowances. When the court of directors in London learned of this incident, they were incensed at what they considered inadequate punishment and ordered that Goldsmid be removed from employment until he had fully redeemed himself and not employed again in a judicial or magisterial capacity without their sanction. However, by the time these orders reached India, the Bombay government had already reinstated him. Goldsmid quickly salvaged his reputation by his work on a revised land revenue and assessment system which he had already begun.

The land tenure system of western India, as established by the British after they annexed the Poona territories in 1818, was known as ryotwar, that is, the state was universal landlord, and the peasantry held land under it direct. But, owing to the obsolescence of the assessments and system of former Maratha governments, the doctrinaire application of David Ricardo's theory of rent as the basis for the collection of the land tax, and a general fall of prices, the rents had become exorbitant, even in favourable seasons. Annual remissions, determined on annual crop inspections made by ill-paid Indian officials, had thus become the rule. Arrears nevertheless accumulated, and corruption, extortion, and even torture were fostered. The rates fixed on the better soils were gradually lowered, while those on the poorer became enhanced, and these rates were chargeable on areas which, through corruption or loss of record, were generally incorrect. Agricultural stock and capital were thus depleted, thousands emigrated, the residue were poverty-stricken and despairing, and the revenue barely covered the cost of collection. Goldsmid's insight and energy introduced a system which reconciled the laws of political economy with practical devices based on the quality of the soils of the fields being assessed. The details of the new land revenue system were perfected by the able young men who assisted him, who included George Wingate, Bartle Frere, David Davidson, John Thomas Francis, and William Coussmaker Anderson. The survey comprised all the lands in every village; these were divided into separate blocks called 'survey fields' of a size to be tilled by one pair of bullocks, defined by boundary marks which it was made an offence to remove, and clearly indicated on readily obtainable maps. Each field was then classified according to the intrinsic capabilities of its various portions, and placed in one of nine or more classes, the whole work being carried out by a trained Indian staff under European test and supervision. The final assessment of the 'rent', or land tax, was the personal work of Goldsmid, Wingate, or another of the superintendents employed in the settlement operations. Individual villages were not separately dealt with, but, after careful appraisal of climate, agricultural skill, distance of markets, means of communication, and past range of prices, a maximum rate was fixed for groups of villages; from this the rent for each survey field could be deduced by means of the classification. The assessment was then guaranteed against enhancement for thirty years, and all improvements effected during the term were secured to the holder who could relinquish or increase his holding, and had a right to continue his tenure at the end of the term on accepting the revised assessment then to be imposed.

This system—formulated in joint reports by Goldsmid and Wingate in 1840, and by these two and Davidson in 1847—was firmly established by acts of the Bombay legislature in 1865–8 and incorporated into the Bombay revenue code of 1879. The system was subsequently applied to the whole of those lands in the Bombay presidency which paid assessment to government, and was extended to innumerable exempted landholders and chiefs at their own request. Berar and the state of Mysore also adopted it. Everywhere the rents were made less burdensome, cultivation was extended, land prices rose, and the government revenue improved. In some part at least this was due to the new revenue survey which gave clear title to fields and security of tenure. The success of the new revenue policy was also, however, in part accidental, since agriculture was emerging from depression at the time it was implemented. It also had the unforeseen effect of unduly favouring the better-off cultivators, who now paid a tax on the fertility of the land rather than on what they actually produced, and who were freed from the obligation that had existed under Maratha government to make up by personal contributions the total demand on their villages.

Goldsmid was employed in the organization of this system in the Poona, Ahmadnagar, and Nasik districts and in the southern Maratha country from 1835 to 1845, when he visited England on furlough. There he married, on 27 October 1846, a distant relative, Jessy Sarah (1816–1888), daughter of Lionel Prager Goldsmid and sister of Major-General Sir Frederick John Goldsmid. They had a daughter and four sons, the eldest of whom, Albert Edward, turned in maturity to Judaism, the religion of his grandparents, and became an ardent Zionist.

Returning to India in 1847 as private secretary to Sir George Clerk, the governor of Bombay, Goldsmid became in the following year secretary to the Bombay government in the revenue and financial departments, and chief secretary in 1854. Soon after his appointment as chief secretary, at which time the incident of November 1836 was aired in the Bombay press, his health broke down. When a sea voyage failed to restore him, he proceeded to England on medical leave but by the time he reached Suez he was so ill that he had to be carried to Cairo; there his condition worsened to such an extent that he could not continue, and on 3 January 1855 he died. In 1865 Sir Bartle Frere, at one time assistant revenue commissioner to Goldsmid, but by now governor of Bombay, inaugurated a memorial rest house, erected by subscription at Diksal, near where Goldsmid's survey had begun. His memory was also preserved in a mural tablet in Christ Church, Byculla, Bombay.

T. C. HOPE, *rev.* PETER HARNETTY

Sources 'Papers on the … revenue survey', *Parl. papers* (1852–3), vol. 75, no. 999 [North-Western Provinces of Bengal and the Bombay presidencies] · selections from the records of the Bombay government, no. 30, new series, 1856 · *Poona* (1985), vol. 18, part 2 of *Gazetteer of the Bombay presidency* · R. Kumar, *Western India in the nineteenth century: a study of the social history of Maharashtra* (1968) · R. D. Choksey, *Economic history of the Bombay Deccan and Karnatak (1818–1868)* (1945) · M. B. McAlpin, 'Economic policy and the true believer: the use of Ricardian rent theory in the Bombay survey and settlement system', *Journal of Economic History*, 44 (1984), 421–7 · P. H. Emden, *Jews of Britain: a series of biographies* (1944) · A. M. Hyamson, 'An Anglo-Jewish family', *Transactions of the Jewish Historical Society of England*, 17 (1951–2), 1–10 · BL OIOC, board of control MSS, ser. F/4, 1784–1858 · board collections, 1796–1858, BL OIOC, nos. 1684–67991, 1738–70529, 1739–70661 · BL OIOC, Elphinstone

MSS, MS Eur. F 87, boxes 7B, 7C, 8B, 11A • *Bombay Gazette* (11 Jan 1854) • *Bombay Gazette* (12 Jan 1854) • *Bombay Telegraph and Courier* (13 Jan 1854) • *Bombay Telegraph and Courier* (15 Jan 1854) • Bombay wills and administrations, 1855–8, BL OIOC, L/AG/34/29/352

Archives U. Durham, Wingate MSS

Wealth at death Rs22,194—effects; Rs44,389—bond: administration, with will, Bombay wills and administrations, BL OIOC, 1855–8, L/AG/34/29/352

Goldsmid, Sir Henry Joseph [Harry] **D'Avigdor-, second baronet (1909–1976)**, politician and bullion broker, was born at Somerhill, near Tonbridge, Kent, on 10 June 1909, the elder son (a daughter died in infancy) of Sir Osmond Elim D'Avigdor-Goldsmid, first baronet (1877–1940) (created 1934), and his wife, Alice, daughter of Joseph Landau of Warsaw. Osmond D'Avigdor had assumed by royal licence the name and arms of Goldsmid on succeeding to the Goldsmid settled estates in 1896. Harry, as he was always called, united both in blood as well as name the vitality, attitudes, and temperaments of two Jewish banking dynasties—the Goldsmids, established and respected in London since the late eighteenth century, and the D'Avigdors, brilliant and sensitive sophisticates from Nice.

D'Avigdor-Goldsmid had himself an almost Renaissance range and depth of abilities, intellectual, artistic, political, social, soldierly, and financial; a commanding personality and appearance; wit, bravery, patriotism, a sense of public and Jewish service; and a capacity for friendship and family life. He was capable of swift changes of mood: he could be impatient, he could not tolerate fools, he was easily bored. Despite all his talents things did not come easily to him: he was introspective, self-doubting, and drove himself by sustained self-discipline.

D'Avigdor-Goldsmid was educated at Harrow School and from 1928 at Balliol College, Oxford. He obtained second-class honours in philosophy, politics, and economics in 1931. In Oxford he met a number of gifted contemporaries in the literary world, forming friendships that lasted for the rest of his life. On leaving Balliol he went into the family firm of Mocatta and Goldsmid, bullion brokers. In business his honesty, shrewdness, prudence, and judgement of people brought him success. He was also to be an able manager of the large family estates which he inherited. In 1940 his father died and he succeeded to the title.

On 23 February the same year D'Avigdor-Goldsmid married Rosemary Margaret (1910–1997), former wife of Sir Peter James Cunliffe Horlick, third baronet, and daughter of Lieutenant-Colonel Charles Rice Iltyd Nicholl. He was already serving in the Royal Armoured Corps (the Royal West Kent regiment), having got himself transferred from staff duties. Overcoming a strong sense of fear he led a reconnaissance unit during the campaign in north-west Europe with courage and resourcefulness, and was wounded. He won the MC (1945) and two mentions in dispatches, and was appointed to the DSO (1945). He ended the war with the rank of major.

Between 1945 and 1955 D'Avigdor-Goldsmid worked as a bullion broker with Mocatta and Goldsmid, and served in local government in Kent, rising to be leader of the Conservatives on the county council. He entered politics as Conservative member for Walsall in 1955, and became devoted to and beloved by his constituents, to whom he was endlessly patient and helpful. In the House of Commons he was rapidly accepted as a financial authority and rose to the chairmanship of important all-party committees, including the select committee on public expenditure. On two occasions, by short, moderate, rational speeches, he effectively demolished efforts to outlaw the Jewish ritual method of slaughter. He was parliamentary private secretary (1955–6) to Duncan Sandys when minister of housing. He was no orator, but was widely liked and respected. Why he never became a minister is a mystery. Perhaps he was too successful to be invited to junior office; perhaps his uncompromising and fearless opinions and his contempt for mediocrity made him seem too mature for team work. He resigned his seat at the 1974 election.

In parallel with his business and his political lives D'Avigdor-Goldsmid was active in public service: JP (1949), high sheriff of Kent (1953), deputy lieutenant (1949). He inherited from his father a strong sense of Jewish community service. For twenty-five years he was president of the Jewish Colonization Association, set up and endowed by Baron de Hirsch in 1892 to spend its revenue to establish and train Russian Jews as farmers in South America. Judging that, had Israel then existed, it would have been there that the baron would have wished to establish Jewish farming communities, D'Avigdor-Goldsmid, over time, redeployed the main efforts of the association from the Americas to Israel. His was a notable, strong, and effective presidency. He was also chairman of the Anglo-Israel chamber of commerce and chairman of both Bank Leumi (UK) and of the Anglo-Israel Bank. He accepted the caretaker chairmanship of Pergamon Press, which he worked effectively to re-establish from 1969 to 1971 in close co-operation with Robert Maxwell, the ousted former chairman who rejoined the board as a non-executive director and eventually reassumed his old post.

At his fine inherited home at Somerhill in Kent D'Avigdor-Goldsmid established a warm and strong family and social life with his wife and their two daughters. It was there that he increased his family collection of paintings and books, wrote his contributions to the *Times Literary Supplement* and other book reviews, entertained a wide circle of friends, built up a stable, and made himself a bold rider to hounds. But it was there also that the zest for life left him when his beloved elder daughter, Sarah, died in a sailing accident at sea in 1963. Though he forced himself to carry on his activities, and though his sparkle and wit sometimes returned, he never recovered.

D'Avigdor-Goldsmid's varied gifts included a proud independence of character and judgement, and a brilliant intellect—with a keen eye for the ridiculous. Despite all his achievements his potential was never fully realized. In 1974 he became an honorary freeman of Walsall. He died in Eaton Mansions, Cliveden Place, London, on 11 December 1976 and was succeeded in the baronetcy by his brother, Major-General James Arthur D'Avigdor-Goldsmid (1912–1987). KEITH JOSEPH, *rev.*

Sources *The Times* (13 Dec 1976) • *The Times* (14 Dec 1976) • *The Times* (15 Dec 1976) • personal knowledge (1986) • private information (1986)

Wealth at death £413,639: probate, 19 Jan 1977, *CGPLA Eng. & Wales*

Goldsmid, Sir Isaac Lyon, first baronet (1778–1859), financier and Jewish communal leader, was born in London on 13 January 1778, the eldest of the six children of Asher Goldsmid, a bullion broker, and his wife, Rachel, *née* Keyser. Asher's father, Aaron, had settled in London during the early eighteenth century; two of Asher's brothers, Benjamin *Goldsmid [*see under* Goldsmid, Abraham] and Abraham *Goldsmid, achieved prominence as financial advisers to the British government during the French revolutionary wars.

After education at Dr Hamilton's school, Finsbury Square, London, Goldsmid entered the family firm of Mocatta and Goldsmid, bullion brokers to the Bank of England and the East India Company. On 29 April 1804 he married Isabel (1788–1860), the daughter of his uncle Abraham Goldsmid; they had two sons and five daughters. In 1806 Goldsmid bought himself a seat on the London stock exchange, as one of the twelve 'Jew brokers' then permitted to trade there. His early speculations on the stock exchange were not a success. He later invested in railway development, and in time became a director of the London, Brighton, and South Coast Railway. He involved himself in the reorganization of the London Dock Company, and was chairman of the Birkenhead docks; he was one of the original promoters of the Imperial Gas Company. None of these ventures brought him great wealth, but as a loan broker to foreign states, especially in Latin America, he fared much better, and used the contacts this business brought in order to invest very profitably in foreign railway construction and mining. His financial relationships with Portugal, Turkey, and Brazil were especially important, and laid the foundations of the very considerable fortune which in time he was able to accumulate; his estate at death was valued at over £1 million.

Goldsmid used his wealth, and the status it bestowed, to pursue three distinct but interconnected ambitions. The first was to further a variety of causes in the fields of educational and social reform, with particular reference to the advancement of non-sectarian projects. A devotee of utilitarianism, and at a time when entry into and graduation from the ancient universities depended on religious tests, he took a very prominent part in the foundation, in 1828, of University College, London, which admitted students without reference to their religious faith. He was active in the movement for the abolition of slavery, and joined with prominent Quakers in a variety of other endeavours, including Joseph Lancaster's educational experiments and the work of Elizabeth Fry, with whom he collaborated in furthering the reform of the penal code and of the prison system. In 1834 he helped to establish University College Hospital.

Sir Isaac Lyon Goldsmid, first baronet (1778–1859), by unknown artist

His hostility to religious fundamentalism also propelled Goldsmid into the movement for reform of Jewish religious practices and divisions in London. The perpetuation of separate Ashkenazi (German- and Yiddish-speaking) and Sephardi (Spanish and Portuguese) synagogues offended his sense of Jewish unity, but also seemed to him to act as an obstacle to the social acceptance of Jews by the non-Jewish majority: Anglo-Jewish political emancipation, he argued, would come only when Judaism was seen to discard its nationalistic elements and its 'foreign' overtones. Accordingly, although a member of the Great Synagogue, Aldgate, he allied himself with a group of prominent Ashkenazim and Sephardim who demanded drastic revision of synagogue services and of Orthodox Jewish doctrine. On 15 April 1840 a group of twenty-four Ashkenazim and Sephardim met at the Bedford Hotel, Southampton Row, where they resolved to establish a synagogue that would be neither Ashkenazi nor Sephardi but 'British'. The West London Synagogue of British Jews was formally opened in Burton Street, Euston, on 27 February 1842; Goldsmid became one of its leading members.

But the establishment of Anglo-Jewry's first Reform synagogue had a significance which went beyond mere matters of liturgy and doctrine. Goldsmid had already pushed himself to the forefront of the battle for Jewish political emancipation, a cause with which leading Reform families, such as the Goldsmids and the Mocattas, were intimately associated. Moses Montefiore (1784–1885), the acknowledged and ultra-conservative lay leader of Anglo-

Jewry, refused to exert himself in the matter of emancipation, believing that it might easily lead to total assimilation and loss of religious identity. As early as 1830, as Montefiore noted in his diary, Isaac Goldsmid had warned the London Committee of Deputies of British Jews that, if it did not support his campaign for political emancipation, he would 'establish a new Synagogue … [and] … would alter the present form of prayer to that in use in the [Reform] Synagogue in Hamburg' (*Diaries*, 83). And so it was.

The foundation of a Reform synagogue was, in part, therefore, a deliberate act of communal disobedience, a breaking of ranks that gave at least some of the emancipationists a quite separate platform from which to launch their campaign, in which Isaac Goldsmid played a critical role. In 1830 he had been responsible for the introduction in the House of Commons, by Sir Robert Grant, of the first Jewish Disabilities Bill. After its failure the Jewish deputies refused to finance further parliamentary endeavours; but Goldsmid's efforts, and those of his Jewish and non-Jewish friends, continued unabated. In 1838 he broke with the deputies and in 1845 took the extreme step of leading a deputation to Sir Robert Peel, the prime minister, in opposition to one led by Montefiore; Goldsmid claimed to speak in the name of British Jewry, and argued that it was precisely because they had reformed their ritual that the Jews—that is, the Reformers—had proved that they were worthy of emancipation.

In 1847 Goldsmid and his eldest son, Francis Henry *Goldsmid, stood unsuccessfully as Liberal parliamentary candidates. However, although he was never elected to parliament, Goldsmid lived long enough to witness the triumphs of David Salomons (1797–1873) and Lionel de Rothschild, and the enactment of the emancipation which he had done so much to bring about.

In 1846 Goldsmid was created Baron Goldsmid of the Palmeira by the king of Portugal. In 1841 he had been made a baronet, thus becoming the first professing Jew to receive an English hereditary title. He died at his London home, St John's Lodge, Regent's Park, on 27 April 1859, and was buried on 2 May in the Islington cemetery of the West London Synagogue. His eldest daughter, Anna Maria *Goldsmid (1805–1889), a pupil of the Scottish poet Thomas Campbell (an ally of Isaac's in the campaign to establish University College, London), made a reputation for herself as a philanthropist and poet.

GEOFFREY ALDERMAN

Sources C. Bermant, *The cousinhood: the Anglo-Jewish gentry* (1971) · D. S. Katz, *The Jews in the history of England, 1485–1850* (1994) · G. Alderman, *Modern British Jewry* (1992) · G. Alderman, *The Jewish community in British politics* (1983) · *Encyclopedia Judaica* (1824) · N. B. Harte, *The University of London, 1836–1986: an illustrated history* (1986) · A. Gilam, *The emancipation of the Jews in England, 1830–1860* (1982) · L. Abrahams, 'Sir I. L. Goldsmid and the admission of the Jews of England to parliament', *Transactions of the Jewish Historical Society of England*, 4 (1899–1901), 116–76 · *Bankers' Magazine*, 19 (1859), 375–82, 449–57 · *Bankers' Magazine*, 20 (1860), 220–24 · *Jewish Chronicle* (6 May 1859), 5 · *Jewish Chronicle* (17 June 1859) · private information (2004) · *Diaries of Sir Moses and Lady Montefiore*, ed. L. Loewe, 1 (1890), 83

Archives BL, parliamentary papers · CKS, business papers · UCL, corresp.

Likenesses R. Dighton, caricature, coloured etching, pubd 1824, NPG, V&A · B. R. Faulkener, oils, priv. coll.; repro. in 'Sir I. L. Goldsmid', frontispiece · caricature, repro. in *Encyclopedia Judaica* · oils, UCL · photograph (after portrait), U. Southampton, Hartley Library · portrait, UCL [*see illus.*]

Wealth at death over £1,000,000: probate, 21 June 1859, *CGPLA Eng. & Wales*

Goldsmid, Louisa Sophia, Lady Goldsmid (1819–1908), feminist and promoter of women's education, was the only daughter of Moses Asher Goldsmid (1789–1864) and his first wife, Eliza (1800–1837), daughter of Levy Salomons. On her father's side, therefore, she was the granddaughter of the bullion broker Asher Goldsmid (1751–1822) and the niece of Isaac Lyon Goldsmid, the financier and promoter of Jewish political emancipation in Britain and of Reform Judaism. Louisa was thus born into the heart of 'the cousinhood', the network of much-interrelated Anglo-Jewish families of great wealth whose male heads dominated the lay leadership of Anglo-Jewry throughout the nineteenth century.

Louisa Goldsmid herself added to this history of intermarriage, and underpinned the financial security afforded to her through membership of the extended Goldsmid family, by herself marrying (10 October 1839) her first cousin, Francis Henry *Goldsmid (*d.* 1878), son of Sir Isaac Lyon Goldsmid, first baronet, and ally in his many Jewish communal and political initiatives. The marriage was solemnized by the Ashkenazi chief rabbi, Solomon Hirschell. Three years later, however, Louisa followed her husband in the religious schism which befell Anglo-Jewry and joined the West London Synagogue of British (Reform) Jews, which he had taken a prominent part in establishing. Many explanations have been advanced for the origins of this schism. One of the characteristics of Reform Judaism in nineteenth-century England was the enthusiasm of its female adherents, whose regular attendance at synagogue service contrasted strongly with that of female members of Orthodox synagogues. Louisa's attachment to Orthodoxy could not have been very strong, and it may be supposed that in becoming a Reformer she discovered a mode of Jewish worship more in tune with her own feminist inclinations.

Louisa Goldsmid's marriage to Francis (who succeeded his father as second baronet in 1859) appears to have been happy, but it was childless. Her entire life was devoted to the advancement of women's causes, chief among which was raising the professional status of Victorian women of the middle classes. As early as 1849 she was among the members of the ladies' committee of the Governesses' Benevolent Institution, founded eight years previously by clergy of the Church of England, and which in 1848 had sponsored the establishment of Queen's College, Harley Street, the first higher education institution for women in England. In her early feminist initiatives she appears to have taken her cue from her mother-in-law, Isabel Goldsmid (1788–1860), one of the first lady visitors of the Ladies' College, Bedford Square (later Bedford College). Isabel Goldsmid and her daughter Anna Maria Goldsmid were members of the Langham Place circle. Through Isabel, Louisa entered into the activities and campaigns of Langham Place, beginning a lifelong association with Emily Davies. She became honorary treasurer to the fund started in 1862, with Emily Davies as its secretary, to support the movement to obtain the admission of women to university examinations and was involved in Davies's successful efforts to persuade Cambridge University to admit girls to its local examinations (1865). The fruit of these labours was the founding of Girton College at Cambridge, to which Louisa made a number of financial gifts and of which she became an early and lifelong member.

Lady Goldsmid's preoccupation with Girton reflected her belief in the importance of education for the advancement of women in Victorian society. In 1867 she temporarily withdrew from the movement to secure the parliamentary franchise for women, having been a member of the first Women's Suffrage Committee in London, after disagreements within the movement as to whether married women should be given the vote. She wanted the suffrage petition presented by J. S. Mill to restrict the demand to unmarried women and widows, believing the demand for complete equality to be hopeless. On his refusal to insert the limitation she was instrumental in persuading Davies to withdraw from political activities and to concentrate on education for middle-class women. In 1879–80 she played a leading part in the intense lobbying of the Cambridge senate to obtain the formal admission of women to Cambridge tripos examinations, and took part in the 1887 move to admit women to Cambridge degrees. London University had agreed to admit women to its degrees in 1878, and she found time to help establish a hall for women students and to endow three scholarships for women pianists at the Royal College of Music. She was a member of the ladies' committee of the infants' school for the Jewish poor, which the Goldsmid family had founded and to which she herself bequeathed £3000 in her will. In 1887, with Millicent Fawcett, she led a deputation to the Home Office to protest against legislation excluding women from working in the chain manufacturing industry. Latterly she renewed her involvement in the suffrage movement, becoming an executive committee member of the National Society for Women's Suffrage and taking part in a pro-suffrage deputation to W. H. Smith, first lord of the Treasury, in 1891. She was a well-known London hostess, her salon attracting leading figures from the worlds of politics and the arts. Louisa Goldsmid died at her London residence, 13 Portman Square, on 7 December 1908, and was buried two days later beside her husband in the Islington cemetery of the West London Synagogue.

GEOFFREY ALDERMAN

Sources S. Wills, 'The Anglo-Jewish contribution to the education movement for women in the nineteenth century', *Transactions of the Jewish Historical Society of England*, 17 (1951–2), 269–81 • C. Bermant, *The cousinhood: the Anglo-Jewish gentry* (1971) • *Jewish Chronicle* (11 Dec 1908), 12 • E. Welsh, *Girton Review*, Lent term (1909), 16–17 • B. Stephen, *Emily Davies and Girton College* (1927) • R. Strachey, *The cause: a short history of the women's movement in Great Britain* (1928) • m. cert. • d. cert.

Archives Girton Cam., archives

Wealth at death £204,652 3*s*. 11*d*.: probate, 14 Jan 1909, *CGPLA Eng. & Wales*

Goldsmith, Francis (1613–1655), translator, was born on 25 March 1613, the second child and first son of the five children of Francis Goldsmith (*c*.1580–1634), of St Giles-in-the-Fields, Middlesex, and his wife, Catherine Oundley (*b*. *c*.1584). His grandfather was Sir Francis Goldsmith of Crayford, Kent. Goldsmith studied at the Merchant Taylors' School, London, from 1627 to 1629, then under the mastership of Dr Nicholas Gray. He matriculated from Pembroke College, Oxford, in 1629, but in 1632 moved to St John's College, from where he graduated in the same year. Goldsmith entered Gray's Inn in 1634 to study common law. When his father died in 1634 he inherited a family estate in Ashton, Northamptonshire. He seems to have moved there without completing his law course; his income allowed him to retire to pursue his own scholarly interests.

Goldsmith was especially interested and active in translating works by Hugo Grotius (1583–1645), the Dutch humanist lawyer and theologian whose writings were modernizing and influencing both fields. Grotius's work was already recognized for its importance, and scholars in England welcomed translations. In 1647 Goldsmith collaborated with his old tutor Gray and Christopher Wase to bring out a textbook designed for use at Eton College: *Hugonis Grotii baptizatorum puerorum instituo, alternis interrogationibus et responsionibus* was published with Wase's translation in Greek and Goldsmith's in English. The book was well received, running into several editions. Another translation of Grotius followed in 1652: *Hugo Grotius his*

Francis Goldsmith (1613–1655), by unknown artist

Sophompaneas, or, Joseph: a Tragedy was rendered by Goldsmith into rhyming couplets. This short poem, based on the story of the biblical Joseph, was accompanied by extensive notes by Goldsmith and dedications to Goldsmith's friends as well as a consolatory oration by Grotius.

At an unknown date Goldsmith married Mary (*d.* 1675), daughter and heir of Richard Scot of Little Lees, Essex. They had two sons, both called Francis, who both died young; Goldsmith refers to his loss in the epitaphs accompanying Grotius's oration. His daughter, Katherine, was the only surviving child. Goldsmith died at Ashton on 19 August 1655 and was buried ten days later at nearby Alderton church. His wife survived him and put up a monument to his memory. Katherine married Sir William Dacre of London. K. GRUDZIEN BASTON

Sources Wood, *Ath. Oxon.*, new edn • *DNB* • E. Hasted, *The history and topographical survey of the county of Kent*, 2 (1782) • *Hugo Grotius his Sophompaneas, or, Joseph: a tragedy*, trans. F. Goldsmith [1652] • Foster, *Alum. Oxon.* • J. Foster, *The register of admissions to Gray's Inn, 1521–1889, together with the register of marriages in Gray's Inn chapel, 1695–1754* (privately printed, London, 1889) • F. L. Cross and E. A. Livingstone, eds., *The Oxford dictionary of the Christian church*, 2nd edn (1974) • G. Baker, *The history and antiquities of the county of Northampton*, 2 (1836–41) • *IGI*

Archives BL, letter, Sloane MSS, Lat. 118, fol. 45 | BL, Sloane MSS, letter to Bishop Andrewes, 1619, Lat. 118, fol. 26

Likenesses T. Cross, engraving, 1652, repro. in *Hugo Grotius*, trans. Goldsmith • portrait, priv. coll. [*see illus.*]

Goldsmith, Hugh Colvill (1789–1841), naval officer, was son of Henry and grandson of the eldest brother of Oliver Goldsmith the author. A brother, Charles Goldsmith (1795–1854), was a commander in the navy. Hugh was born at St Andrews, New Brunswick, on 2 April 1789, served as a midshipman in the navy, and was promoted lieutenant on 27 January 1809. After 1815 he was apparently mainly employed in the revenue anti-smuggling service.

In 1824 Goldsmith commanded the revenue cutter *Nimble* off the coast of Cornwall. On 9 April, on his own initiative, perceiving it as a challenge, he and his men dislodged from its base the celebrated 80 ton granite logan of Treryn Dinas, 7 miles south-west of Penzance. The *Gentleman's Magazine* denounced this 'wanton outrage', and reported 'This act of *Vandalism* has excited the greatest indignation. … What renders the act most atrocious is, that two poor families, who derived a subsistence from attending visitors to this stone, are now deprived of the means of support'. Following Cornish and press protests, Goldsmith supervised the stone's replacement (29 October to 2 November); but, according to Francis Kilvert, 'it has never rocked so well and easily since it was wilfully thrown down' (Kilvert, 65). Goldsmith was never promoted, and was lieutenant commanding the paddle sloop *Megaera* when he died at sea off St Thomas in the West Indies on 8 October 1841. He was buried at Santa Cruz.

ROGER T. STEARN

Sources *GM*, 1st ser., 94/1 (1824), 363, 430 • *GM*, 2nd ser., 17 (1842), 231 • Boase & Courtney, *Bibl. Corn.*, vol. 1 • *Household Words* (20 Nov 1852), 234–5 • F. W. L. Stockdale, *Excursions in the county of Cornwall* (1824) • *The golden chersonese, or, The logan rock restored, by an officer of the royal navy* (1824) • *Kilvert's diary: selections from the diary of the Rev. Francis Kilvert*, ed. W. Plomer, new edn, 3 vols. (1977)

Goldsmith, Sir James Michael (1933–1997), financier and politician, was born in Paris on 26 February 1933, the younger son of Francis Benedict Hyam (Frank) Goldsmith, formerly Goldschmidt (1878–1967), hotelier and politician, and his wife, Marcelle, *née* Mouiller (1904–1985). His elder brother, Edward René David Goldsmith (*b.* 1928), was the founding publisher and editor of *The Ecologist*. Their father was Unionist MP for Stowmarket from 1910 to 1918, a major in the Suffolk yeomanry during the First World War, and thereafter director of the Savoy Hotel Company, which owned a string of luxury hotels in France, where Jimmy Goldsmith was brought up in an ambience of pampered women and servility. When he was six, his father taxed him with being unable to read, and he replied, 'When I'm old enough I shall be a millionaire and have someone to read to me, so I won't need to' (Wansell, 361). His family fled following the German invasion of France in 1940, and sailed for the Bahamas, where his father assumed the management of a hotel in Nassau. Jimmy Goldsmith's schooling in the Bahamas and Canada was unsuccessful. He was a rebellious pupil always scheming to make money. At Eton College he proved equally headstrong. One afternoon in autumn 1949 he bet £10 on a three-horse accumulator, and won over £8000. He insisted on leaving school immediately, developed a taste for *chemin de fer*, and discovered a ruling passion for beautiful women. For a few weeks he attended a crammer, but left after fighting one of its teachers.

Goldsmith spent the next year gambling before being set to work by his father in the Palace Hotel, Madrid. National service in the Royal Artillery curbed him, but he despised the English for their reticence, self-control, class loyalties, and ignorance of *savoir vivre*. After leaving the army in 1953, he moved to Paris and took over a small company distributing an adrenalin cream for rheumatics. Shortly afterwards he plunged into a romantic crisis after meeting Maria Isabella (Isabel) Patiño (1933–1954), daughter of Antenor Patiño, the former Bolivian envoy in London who had inherited a huge fortune derived from tin. They became lovers, and when her father separated them, Goldsmith reacted with the extravagance and vehemence that were always so pronounced when he felt his interests were under attack. He chartered an aeroplane, flew to Casablanca in pursuit of her, and arranged her abduction from her father's house in Paris. Despite legal obstacles, and amid frantic publicity, the young couple married on 7 January 1954 at Kelso register office, Scotland. Five months afterwards, late in her pregnancy, she suffered a cerebral haemorrhage; a few hours after being delivered of a daughter by caesarean section, she died. Following this tragedy Goldsmith became embroiled with his parents-in-law in a legal battle for custody of his child.

After these dramas Goldsmith started a new company, Laboratoires Cassene, which distributed vaccine, nasal spray, and other pharmaceutical products under licence in France. His aggressive marketing ploys offended established pharmaceutical companies, and he was in financial

Sir James Michael Goldsmith (1933–1997), by Jane Bown

difficulties by 1957, when he sold Cassene for £120,000. After this cash crisis, he always afterwards sought to amass large reserves rather than operate on borrowings. At this stage of his life, though, he was still a capitalist without capital, and behaving like a millionaire before he had millions. In 1959 he bought twenty-eight pharmacies from Charles Clore, and in 1961 a chain of fifty pram and nursery furniture shops; then, in partnership with the Iraqi banker Selim Zilkha, he relaunched them as the Mothercare chain, retailing clothes for mothers and small children. After selling out to Zilkha in 1962, Goldsmith pirated a slimming product marketed by Mead Johnson in the USA, and (after weathering lawsuits) made a fortune selling it in France as Milical.

In 1957 Goldsmith had begun a relationship with his secretary, Ginette Lery, who bore their son in 1959. When she became pregnant again, with a daughter, they married in 1963. Meanwhile he enjoyed a tempestuous affair in 1962–3 with Lady Sarah Frances (Sally) Crichton-Stuart, and then became involved in 1964 with Lady Annabel Birley (*b.* 1934), the wife of Mark Birley, nightclub owner, and younger daughter of Edward Charles Stewart Robert Vane-Tempest-Stewart, eighth marquess of Londonderry. By this relationship he had two sons and one daughter. After divorcing his second wife, Ginette, with whom he however continued to maintain a Paris household, he married Lady Annabel Birley in Paris. Despite his brawl with a journalist on their wedding day in 1978, she remained his London partner until his death. At the time of his third marriage he observed, 'when you marry your mistress you create a job vacancy' (Wansell, 288). The vacancy was filled by Laure Boulay de la Meurthe (*b.* 1951), a French journalist, with whom he maintained a New York household. They had a son and daughter. He had sundry additional diversions. These arrangements testified to his vitality, determination, and charisma. Like other serial adulterers he was a misogynist, who felt most relaxed in aggressively masculine company. He was an intimate friend of the Mayfair gambler John Aspinall, at whose Clermont club he played backgammon. Aspinall's set was harsh, arrogant, spoilt, and swaggering. Its bullying temper was congenial to Goldsmith: 'I consider tolerance to be degenerate', he said (*The Independent*, 21 July 1997).

After borrowing money at usurious rates from Sir Isaac Wolfson in 1964, Goldsmith started buying bakery, confectionery, and cognate companies until he had fifty-one businesses to consolidate in his new company, Cavenham Foods, formed in 1965. He was a volatile manager, but excellent at choosing and trusting subordinates to whom he delegated. Among other activities during 1968 he coerced the board of the Hôtels Réunis group to sell out to Maxwell Joseph, and formed Banque Occidentale and a French holding company, Générale Occidentale (GO), which for many years were the chief vehicles of his operations. Cavenham's acquisition in 1971 of the Bovril Company propelled Goldsmith's wealth towards new heights. By selling Bovril's dairies and South American beef ranches, he recouped much of the purchase price, and then bought Britain's fourth largest grocery chain, Allied Suppliers, for £86.3 million in 1972. In doing so, he roughly doubled the size of Cavenham, the share price of which rose in eight months from 69*p*. to 229*p*. Having sold Allied's Lipton tea interests to Unilever for £18.5 million, Goldsmith could at last claim financial credibility. Nevertheless his financial juggling aroused mistrust. Throughout his life his companies invested in one another, traded with one another, borrowed from one another, and were helped by each other's pension funds. His contempt for financial orthodoxy was as ostentatious as his crushing of minority shareholders' interests. This reputation as an astute but invidious deal-maker was increased by the involvement from 1972 of GO's secondary banking subsidiary, Anglo-Continental Investments and Finance, with the troubled Slater Walker Securities. Doubts about Goldsmith were unfairly intensified when he became chairman of Slater Walker as part of a Bank of England rescue package (1975).

Goldsmith, who became a director of the Rothschilds' family bank in France in 1975, yearned for political influence. He courted Edward Heath, who disappointed him, and in 1976 insinuated himself into the confidence of Harold Wilson. At this point there was a collision of his interests. *Private Eye*, which had been suspicious of his Slater Walker involvement, suggested in 1975 that Goldsmith had conspired to help the earl of Lucan disappear after the murder of a family nanny in 1974. It moreover alleged that he and other Mayfair cronies had hounded to death the painter Dominic Elwes as a reprisal for discussing the case with journalists. Believing that these slurs were part of a wider left-wing conspiracy to undermine Slater Walker's rescue and damage British financial institutions, Goldsmith in 1976 issued over sixty writs against *Private Eye* and its distributors, and pursued its editor for criminal libel. He employed private detectives, bullied or blackmailed two senior professional men into swearing false affidavits, and revealed his essentially vengeful nature. 'You have heard of the power of the press', he said. 'Now you will discover the power of money' (*The Times*, 21 July 1997). Lord Goodman described the case as 'diving into a nest of crocodiles' (*The Independent*, 23 July 1997). The litigation, which lasted eighteen months and ended inconclusively, endeared him to Wilson's circle. His knighthood in the

Wilson resignation honours list of 1976 was believed to be his reward for persecuting *Private Eye*. He developed an obsessively hostile attitude to journalists, some of whom he suspected as Marxist conspirators. His attempts to buy *The Observer* in 1976 and the *Daily Express* in 1977 were rebuffed, but he was able to acquire a successful French weekly magazine, *L'Express*, in 1977; and in 1979 he launched *Now!* magazine, which cost an estimated £6 million and survived for only nineteen months.

The *Private Eye* case, finally settled in 1977, depressed the value of Cavenham shares, and GO was able to buy the group, which thus came under Goldsmith's private ownership. There was relief in the City at Cavenham's removal from London stock exchange quotation. Goldsmith was so disgusted by his experiences in Britain that all business control was transferred to Paris in 1977. He became convinced that Europe was unsafe and full of subversives, and began to invest emotionally in the myth of American free enterprise capitalism. Earlier, in 1973, he had bought for $62 million the Grand Union Company, operating 531 supermarkets in eleven states. In 1978 he bought Colonial Stores, of Augusta, Georgia, with 369 stores for $133 million, and the following year 100 supermarkets in Texas. Their collective attraction was that supermarkets were great providers of cash to finance other acquisitions.

The election during 1981 of the socialist Mitterrand and the republican Reagan as presidents of France and the USA determined Goldsmith to relocate his fortune-hunting across the Atlantic. After protracted stalking, he gained control in 1982 of the undervalued forest, pulp, and paper company Diamond International for £246 million and resold it after two years for three times that amount. With this deal he emerged as a leading Wall Street corporate raider. He was thrilled by the opportunities in conservative America, and liked the ruthless, guiltless, almost psychopathic pursuit of self-interest that many Americans legitimized as success. The hotly contested bid in 1985 for Crown Zellerbach, a sluggish forest products company, netted him a further $400 million. His bid in 1986 for Goodyear Tire and Rubber Company, which had large investments in oil and aerospace, marked the end of the mutual infatuation between Goldsmith and US capitalism. Goodyear orchestrated adroit political lobbying and at tumultuous senate hearings Goldsmith was shocked to be shouted at and booed. Within months he was being decried as the most grievous of the greenmailing corporate raiders who had alarmed Wall Street and unsettled Washington. During the summer of 1987 Goldsmith began cashing in his share investments. When his judgement was vindicated by the 'black' October market crash, he seemed even more brutal a predator. Within three years this rootless, restless, cosmopolitan financier had liquidated his holdings, left the United States with $2–$3 billion in cash, and was ensconced in his private fiefdom in Cuixmala, Mexico.

Easily bored, Goldsmith attempted to return to the London scene in 1989 by organizing with Kerry Packer and Jacob Rothschild an abortive £13 billion bid for the tobacco and financial services conglomerate BAT Industries. In 1990 he took a $1.1 billion stake in Newmont Mining, the largest US goldmining company, but sold out in 1993. His craving for political power reasserted itself, and in 1993 he founded the European Foundation and another right-wing group, L'Europe des Nations, arguing for a decentralized, trade-protected Europe of nation states. He was a vehement opponent of the Maastricht treaty, and financed Lord Rees-Mogg's application for a judicial review of the treaty's ratification (1993). During 1994 he helped establish the right-wing L'Autre Europe party and was elected by French voters to the European parliament, from which he was an absentee. Although he denounced global free trade and the General Agreement on Tariffs and Trade, which he believed would injure the interests of developed economies, the truth was that authority in any form riled him, and he could not bear the amassed power represented by European unity. Meeting him, John Major was 'astonished by the irrationality of his fears about Europe … his raw and unbalanced views were … out of the mainstream of politics' (Major, 703).

In 1995 Goldsmith reconstituted his European Foundation as a new British political force, the Referendum Party, which during the following year produced a question on future relations with the European Union for inclusion in a national referendum. This question 'was so ambiguous as to be meaningless', according to Major, who disliked 'the paranoid nature' of Goldsmith's policies. 'I saw the virtue of his opaque approach, designed to catch each and every anti-Europe breeze that might attract votes' (Major, 705). When Goldsmith committed himself in 1996 to spending £20 million on parliamentary candidatures at the forthcoming general election, one Conservative whip dismissed the Referendum Party as 'ludicrous' and its leader as 'bronzed, rich, mad' (Brandreth, 384). Having nominated 554 candidates, the Referendum Party polled 811,000 votes (3 per cent of the total) at the general election of 1 May 1997. Goldsmith, who contested the Putney constituency, lost his deposit. As the defeat of Putney's sitting MP, David Mellor, was announced, millions of television viewers saw Goldsmith gleaming vindictively, jutting his body forward aggressively and crashing his big hands together as he shouted, 'Out! Out! Out!'. He looked the quintessence of a rich lout. Earlier he had been diagnosed with pancreatic cancer, and was warned that fighting the election would shorten his life. He died on 18 July 1997, at Benahavis in Spain. He was survived by his second and third wives, and by his eight acknowledged children.

Goldsmith was 6 feet 4 inches tall, strongly built, with bright blue eyes, and a highly expressive face: his frowns were as intimidating as his grins were disarming. He went bald when young. He had exceptional vitality and mental agility, and could be stimulating company. Everyone seemed energized when he walked into a room. The effect of his restless pacing as he talked was domineering. Some of his mannerisms were childishly disagreeable. He chewed the corner of his handkerchief when tense, gobbled his food at speed, and was prone to tantrums. He had the outlook of an absolutist monarch: 'I do what I want, and everybody else has to put up with it' (*The Scotsman*, 21 July 1997). He combined formidable powers of invective with histrionic gesticulation. His energy and reactions often seemed manic: he felt more vivid when attacking his enemies. RICHARD DAVENPORT-HINES

Sources G. Wansell, *Tycoon* (1987) • I. Fallon, *Billionaire* (1991) • *The Independent* (21 July 1997) • *The Times* (21 July 1997) • *The Guardian* (21 July 1997) • *Daily Telegraph* (21 July 1997) • *The Scotsman* (21 July 1997) • *The Independent* (23 July 1997) • *The Spectator* (26 July 1997) • J. Major, *The autobiography* (1999) • G. Brandreth, *Breaking the code* (1999) • R. Ingrams, *Goldenballs* (1979) • *WWW*

Archives FILM BFI NFTVA, 'The real James Goldsmith', Channel 4, 11 April 1999 • BFI NFTVA, documentary footage | SOUND BL NSA, *Breakfast with Frost*, BBC, 14 April 1996, V 3702/3 • BL NSA, *Person to person*, T 2438R BDI • BL NSA, performance recording

Likenesses photograph, 1954, Hult. Arch. • Reuters, photograph, 1997, repro. in *The Scotsman* • J. Bown, photograph, priv. coll. [*see illus.*] • P. Macdiarmid, photograph, repro. in *The Independent* (21 July 1997) • photograph, repro. in *Daily Telegraph* • photograph, repro. in *The Times* • photograph, repro. in *The Guardian* • photographs, repro. in Wansell, *Tycoon* • photographs, repro. in Fallon, *Billionaire*

Wealth at death billionaire; mainly abroad

Goldsmith, Lewis (1763/4?–1846), journalist and political writer, was probably born in Richmond, Surrey, according to most biographical accounts in 1763 or 1764. However, Goldsmith's self-serving claims that he was only twenty-seven in 1802–3 (Goldsmith, xix) would place the event between 1774 and 1776. Although he was of Portuguese Jewish descent, his mother's maiden name was apparently Hamilton, and sources differ about whether he ever practised. Goldsmith was reputedly educated at the Merchant Taylors' School, London, and Berlin University, and trained in a London solicitor's office. In his youth he travelled extensively on the continent. A talented linguist, he spoke fluent English, French, and German, and 'several other languages'. From the late 1780s he was involved in British radical politics, joining 'several democratical societies' and attending 'popular meetings at Copenhagen House, and at Chalk Farm and other places' (*Anti-Gallican Monitor*, no. 307, 8 Dec 1816). Despite later political tergiversations, he never renounced principles of 'true liberty' or the French Revolution 'in the abstract' (Goldsmith, iii).

By 1792 Goldsmith was in Germany, where he was involved with the illuminati and freemasons, and witnessed the recapture of Frankfurt by Hessian forces and subsequent atrocities against captured French troops by Hessians and Croats. Thereafter he retired via Hamburg to Leipzig on private business, but, being informed that a British envoy at Dresden had solicited his arrest, fled to Poland, where he witnessed the republic's death throes and requested British aid on behalf of the patriots. According to his account, he was present in Grodno in July 1793 when Russian troops forced the diet to sign the partition treaty, and at the Warsaw arsenal on 17 April 1794 when the Poles captured a large Russian contingent. He was in Warsaw during the abortive Prussian siege (summer 1794) and accompanied Kosciusko at the battle of Maciejowice (10 October 1794). He visited the scene of the bloody carnage after the Russians stormed the Praga suburb of Warsaw (4 November 1794), and shortly afterwards left for the Netherlands, where in 1795 he witnessed the stadholder's flight from The Hague.

Goldsmith was back in London by 1797, and in 1799 may have edited a pro-French newspaper, *Albion*. Subsequently he published *The crimes of cabinets, or, A review of the plans and aggressions for annihilating the liberties of France, and the dismemberment of her territories* (January 1801), denouncing allied atrocities and the coercion of neutral powers. It observed that the Russians massacred more people at Praga than were executed by guillotine during the terror, and revealed Goldsmith's penchant for sexual slanders against monarchs, especially Catherine II and Leopold II. He accused the British ministry of insincerity in the peace talks and of a bellicose policy, which risked economic ruin and aligning the entire continent against Britain. He therefore pleaded with them to 'bestow a kindly thought on the "swinish multitude"', lest they become 'the dreadful avengers of unrestrained insult and oppression'. Goldsmith had to publish the work himself, after his publisher, fearing prosecution for seditious libel, refused to do so. It was duly referred to the attorney-general on publication, though apparently no charges were laid.

In December 1801 Goldsmith travelled to Paris. He returned to London briefly in July 1802 to found a short-lived newspaper, *The Independent*, but went back to France at the end of the month, proposing to establish an English-language newspaper, with the recommendation of Louis Otto, the French minister-plenipotentiary in London. The result was the rabidly pro-Napoleonic *Argus*, which appeared thrice-weekly from 20 October 1802, with French government backing. However, in February 1803 Goldsmith was sacked by a M. Ragot, who, despite Goldsmith's insinuations to the contrary, was almost certainly the paper's *éditeur–proprietaire* (owner–publisher), and a new editor was appointed. Goldsmith claimed that Charles-Maurice Talleyrand had tricked him into establishing the paper by promising him editorial freedom, only to coerce him into inserting anti-British material and dismiss him after forty-nine numbers because he resisted publishing the most inflammatory articles. However, Goldsmith appears to protest too much, for the British ambassador suggests his successor was instructed to moderate the paper's tone, refrain from personal attacks, and adopt a conciliatory manner towards Britain (Charles Whitworth to Lord Hawkesbury, 3 March 1803, PRO, FO 27/67). Violent diatribes against the British royal family in the paper's fiftieth number (14 February) may therefore also be from Goldsmith's pen.

Goldsmith now made overtures to the British ambassador, which apparently did not go unnoticed by the French police: on 15 April 1803 the minister of the interior ordered the expulsion of 'this intriguer trafficking in his pen and betrayals' (Regnier to Talleyrand, correspondance politique, Angleterre, vol. 601, fol. 121). However, he was not deported, probably because he agreed to serve as a secret agent: when war broke out in May, Goldsmith escaped internment, and was sent to Germany and Warsaw, charged to spy on the Bourbon court and, if possible, intercept Louis XVIII's correspondence. On his first mission he fled Poland after a two-month stay in mid-October, fearing, correctly, that he had been denounced by postal officials he had tried to bribe. On his second mission, beginning in mid-December 1803, he discovered which German merchant house handled the correspondence of Britain's ambassador to Prussia and of Louis XVIII with France. He also indicated a means to intercept British diplomatic mail to the northern courts, but on 7 February he wrote from Berlin that Prussia was expelling him, 'subalternes' having betrayed his identity. Although he was exposed in the London press several weeks later, he spent two months in Leipzig, where he claimed that post office officials had agreed to intercept Louis XVIII's mail, on his return journey.

Although held in suspicion on his return to Paris, Goldsmith was not punished or made to reimburse his inflated expenses. In return he dropped all claims concerning the *Argus*. However, he was refused a mission to Portugal in 1807, and instead, from 1805 to 1809, served as sworn interpreter to the courts of justice and Conseil des Prises de Paris. During this time he also waged a three-year campaign for permission to leave France, and completed a translation of the legal theorist William Blackstone, but although Cambacérès accepted the dedication, the government suppressed it. Finally, on 11 May 1809, he and his family boarded an American vessel at Dunkirk with passports for the United States.

Instead, they were put ashore in England, where Goldsmith was arrested as a traitor and imprisoned for two months at Tothill Fields, Westminster. After his release he turned coat, savaging French policy in an *Exposition of the Conduct of France towards America* (1809), and warning in *The Secret History of the Cabinet of Bonaparte* (1810) that Britain could never make a secure peace with Napoleon. Characteristically, the *Secret History* supports its contentions both with well-sourced information and a host of atrocity stories, sexual libels, scandalous tales, and absurd allegations about Napoleon and his court. It was, nevertheless, a runaway success, with six editions by March 1811 and numerous foreign translations. Owing to a similarity of title with the *Secret History*, the anti-revolutionary and anti-Napoleonic works of H. Stewarton have often been falsely attributed to Goldsmith.

In 1811 Goldsmith launched a Sunday newspaper, published variously under the titles *Anti-Gallican Monitor* (1811–14), *Anti-Corsican Monitor* (1814–18), and *British Monitor* (1818–25), possibly with both Bourbon and, as Goldsmith claims, ministerial backing. Certainly, from 1811 to 1814 it consistently and unfashionably promoted a Bourbon restoration and legitimism, and it briefly favoured the Holy Alliance. In April and May 1811 the paper announced an 'Anti-Corsican Institution' and opened a public subscription to raise a bounty on Napoleon's head, which resulted in a parliamentary complaint from Earl Grey and rapid climb-down by Goldsmith, though he later recommended tyrannicide to the Germans. During the following year Goldsmith had meetings with Lord Castlereagh to discuss forming an international propaganda bureau. He opposed calls for peace with Bonaparte: instead in January 1814 he demanded a public trial and execution, and in 1815 published *An appeal to the governments of Europe on the necessity of bringing Napoleon Bonaparte to a public trial*. According to Goldsmith, Napoleon offered to buy his silence with trading licences worth £200,000, and attempted to discredit him by suborning Sampson Perry to print distorted extracts of Goldsmith's espionage reports. This allegation provoked mutual libel actions, but when Perry was awarded only a farthing on the grounds of his provocation, Goldsmith abandoned his own case.

The *Anti-Gallican Monitor* was the scourge of British radicals, describing them as 'a low and ignorant rabble' intent on 'robbery and murder', in marked contrast to the 'great and respectable men' who held reformist views prior to the revolution (8 Dec 1816). Moreover, he asserted that for 300 years France had funded all British agitators, and claimed to have seen Napoleon's lists of leading reformers and journalists in his pay, insinuating that after 1814 they were Bourbon-funded. However, the paper was not completely reactionary, and supported Robert Owen's social experiments.

By late 1816 Goldsmith had turned against the government of Louis XVIII, accusing it of liberalism and a preference for men with the blood of his relatives on their hands (*Anti-Corsican Monitor*, 24 Nov 1816). He abandoned thoughts of an alliance between Bourbon France and Britain, rejected the Holy Alliance, and repeated his earlier criticisms of Austria, Prussia, and Russia, especially over the partitions of Poland. Yet, despite his partisanship, Goldsmith's introduction to his translation of Comte Lazare Nicholas M. Carnot's *Memorial* (1814) gives a generally balanced portrait.

In May 1818 Goldsmith visited Paris, but, on a second trip in November 1819, was denounced for remarks on the French army in his *Secret History*, whose French translation he now renounced. He returned to Britain, but abandoned his newspaper in 1825 and moved back to Paris, where he worked as an interpreter to the tribunal of commerce and published an ephemeral newspaper, *The Monitor* (1831). In the late 1820s he ingratiated himself with the British ambassador and mixed in ultra-royalist circles, associating with hardline politicians including Villèle—who supplied the materials for Goldsmith's last significant work, *Statistics of France* (1832)—La Bourdonnaye, Polignac, and Martignac. He was appointed solicitor for the British embassy, and was given responsibility for the post it handled for expatriates. He may also have provided copy to his friend Tom Bowen, editor of *The Times*, which in 1841 published a sketch of Barère that has been attributed to Goldsmith (*DNB*). In 1837 his only child, Georgiana, married John Singleton Copley, Lord Lyndhurst, the lord chancellor, becoming his second wife. However, no details are known concerning Goldsmith's own marriage. He died 'of paralysis' after an illness lasting several months, in his home on the rue de la Paix, Paris, on 6 January 1846 (*The Times*).

Much of Goldsmith's reputation among contemporaries rested on credit given to the false claims with which he embroidered his narratives. His most sensational stories involved his missions in 1803–4, whose purpose, he asserted, was to persuade Louis XVIII to renounce claims to France in return for the Polish throne and, if he refused, to kidnap or murder him. Goldsmith claimed that he refused to be an assassin, and instead tipped off the pretender, possibly saving his life. Similarly, Goldsmith's statement that he was sent to Paris by Louis Otto to dissuade the French from issuing the ultimatum of 25 July 1802 is patently false, and his accounts of meetings with Bonaparte, especially in late 1802, should be treated with caution. Likewise, tales of attempts to exchange him for the émigré journalist Jean-Gabriel Peltier in March 1803 appear far-fetched and inconsistent, and claims that he was forced to accompany Bonaparte to Boulogne in 1805 to reinforce impressions that an attack on Britain was imminent are doubtful.

While Goldsmith exaggerated his importance and political and diplomatic contacts, he was a journalist of influence, whose real and concocted eyewitness reports and extravagant claims helped to inform and misinform contemporaries, especially about Bonaparte. One of the last eighteenth-century soldiers of fortune and literary mercenaries, he was also, as one contemporary noted, the first of many nineteenth-century Jewish journalists on the London press. He was also a theatre enthusiast and critic, publishing weekly reviews in his paper and having a box at Drury Lane, where in the mid-1820s he was seen almost nightly. Our only detailed physical description of him is given by Hénoul, a French informer, in a letter to Rumbold, dated 13 October 1803: 'He is of medium height, has a full and slightly pallid face, with short, black, straggly hair, sometimes with and sometimes without powder, and a very poor physiognomy' (Blanc, 192).

Simon Burrows

Sources *DNB* • L. Goldsmith, *The secret history of the cabinet of Bonaparte*, 4th edn (1810) • O. Blanc, *Les espions de la Révolution et de l'Empire* (Paris, 1995) • *Revue Britannique*, 1 (1846), 233–4 • *Revue Britannique*, 2 (1863), 391–6 • P. Morand, 'Un journal Napoléonien de propagande', *Revue des Deux Mondes* (15 Aug 1938), 780–810 • *The Times* (9 Jan 1846) • C. Roznikoff, 'Goldsmith, Lewis', *Encyclopaedia Judaica*, ed. C. Roth, 7 (Jerusalem, 1971), 738 • PRO, FO 27 • Archives Nationales de France, Paris, F 7 6336/7082 [police générale] • correspondance politique, Angleterre, Archives du Ministère des Affaires Étrangères, Paris

Archives Archives Nationales de France, Paris, spy reports, F 7, 6336/7082

Goldsmith, Oliver (1728?–1774), author, was born on 10 November, probably 1728, at Pallas, near Ballymahon, in the parish of Forney, co. Longford, Ireland, the second son and fifth child of Charles Goldsmith (*c*.1690–1747), curate at Kilkenny West, and his wife, Ann (*d*. 1770), daughter of the Revd Oliver Jones, master of the diocesan school at Elphin. Since his marriage, in 1718, Charles Goldsmith had supplemented his modest income as a clergyman by farming. In 1730, after the retirement or death of his predecessor, the Revd Green (his wife's uncle), he became rector of Kilkenny West and moved to a larger house, outside the neighbouring village of Lissoy. Besides their famous son, Oliver, Charles and Ann had seven other children:

Oliver Goldsmith (1728?–1774), by Sir Joshua Reynolds, *c*.1770

Margaret (*b*. 1719), who died in infancy; Catherine (*b*. 1721), who married a wealthy man, Daniel Hodson; Henry (*b*. 1722?), who became a clergyman and raised a family, and died in 1768; Jane, Henry's twin, who married a poor man named Johnstone; Maurice (1736–1792), who became a cabinet-maker and died, childless, in poverty; Charles (1737–1803/4), an adventurer who went off to Jamaica and died, also childless, in Somers Town, north London; and John (1740–*c*.1752), who died aged about twelve. Both Catherine Hodson and Jane Johnstone died in Athlone some years after their brother Oliver.

Early years and education Goldsmith's childhood as a member of the Anglo-Irish ascendancy at Lissoy was happy enough to have inspired the nostalgic picture of Auburn in *The Deserted Village*; but with about 90 per cent of his father's parish consisting of Roman Catholics he also could not avoid a sense of being in a privileged minority. Unlike other protestants, however, and under the influence of his maternal uncle and eventual patron, the Revd Thomas Contarine, he took an early interest in the native Celtic language and culture, and may have witnessed performances of Carolan, the celebrated native Irish singer and poet.

Severely disfigured by smallpox at the age of eight or nine, and with a receding chin, a protuberant brow, and awkward physique, Goldsmith was painfully aware of what a correspondent (probably William Kenrick) in the *London Packet* of 24 March 1773 described as his 'monkey face' and 'grotesque orang-outang figure'. As a child he was ridiculed for his appearance. For instance during a dancing party at his parents' house, when he joined in the gambol with his hornpipe, the violinist, a youth by the name of Cumming, loudly derided him as 'the personification of Aesop'. After a moment he stopped dancing and retorted with the following couplet:

Our herald hath proclaimed this saying,
See Aesop dancing and his monkey playing.

Despite his reputation for being awkward in company, if this anecdote is true then sometimes, even at the age of nine or ten, he could also be lucky with repartee (Prior, 1.28–9). After the publication of *The Traveller* Mrs Cholomondeley is reported to have observed to Johnson: 'I never more shall think Dr. Goldsmith ugly' (Johnson, 2.268).

Though his relative Mrs Elizabeth Delap was literally to her very last breath proud to have been 'the first person who had put a book into Goldsmith's hands' she confessed that as an infant he was 'one of the dullest boys ever placed under her charge' (Prior, 1.22). When he was about six his father put him under the care of the village schoolmaster, Thomas Byrne, a veteran who had served in Spain during Queen Anne's reign and a lively storyteller. Fully capable of teaching the basics of reading, writing, and arithmetic, according to one of his pupils (the Revd Handcock) he was able to 'translate extemporaneously Virgil's Eclogues into Irish verse, of, at least, equal elegance' (ibid., 24). Doubtless partly under Byrne's influence Goldsmith began to write verses, but immediately afterwards he would toss them into the fire. It was apparently this glimmering of creativity that prompted his mother to the view that he was destined for greatness, which later turned into bitter disappointment and, finally, rejection of her son. After the early years with Byrne, Oliver was sent to the grammar school in Elphin, under the Revd Michael Griffin; briefly to Mr Campbell's school in Athlone; and to a school in Edgeworthstown, whose master, the Revd Patrick Hughes, was a friend of Charles Goldsmith and a very kind mentor who supervised Oliver's interest in Latin studies. Because of difficulties in financing the elder son Henry's education at Trinity College, Dublin, Charles had planned to have Oliver pursue a career in business, but with the encouragement of his brother-in-law Thomas Contarine he decided to support his entrance at Trinity in 1745 as a lowly sizar.

In contrast to Henry, who entered as a gentleman commoner, Oliver, as sizar, had to undergo the humiliation of being a waiter at the fellows' table and of wearing a red academic cap as a symbol of inferiority. Besides the social discrimination one major reason why he did not distinguish himself as a student at Trinity had to do with his hated tutor Dr Theaker Wilder, a surly, temperamental authoritarian. On one occasion, in June 1747, during a noisy party in his rooms that Goldsmith threw to celebrate a prize he had won, Wilder intervened angrily and boxed his ears. Earlier Goldsmith had been involved in a riot over the arrest of a fellow student but was fortunate enough to escape with only a public reprimand, while the ringleaders were expelled. After Wilder's brutal treatment of him Goldsmith was so depressed that he left Trinity and could only just be persuaded by Henry to return to complete his degree requirements.

Goldsmith received his BA in February 1750, almost five years after he had matriculated. His time in Dublin, a city second only to London at that time, brought him into contact with the theatre and many other activities of a cultural centre. It also brought out his fatal attraction to gambling, which haunted him to the end of his life. When the death of his kindly father, in early 1747, forced his mother and her three small sons to move from the Lissoy house to a cottage in Ballymahon, Goldsmith earned money by selling ballads during his remaining years in Dublin.

Though family custom presumed that Goldsmith would take orders and become a clergyman—and apparently he made an effort to read theology—he proved an unsuitable prospect for the established church. According to a probably apocryphal story, when he showed up for his examination wearing scarlet breeches Bishop Synge, of Elphin, rejected his candidacy. After a brief period of being a private tutor he set out to Cork with £30 and a horse with the purpose of emigrating to America. Five weeks later, having sold his horse to pay for his passage but missed his ship, he returned home penniless with a nag dubbed Fiddleback. The far-fetched explanation offered to his dismayed mother seems to have been material for the episode in chapter 12 of *The Vicar of Wakefield*, in which Moses trades a good horse for a gross of green spectacles. When Uncle Contarine then provided £50 for him to study law in London, at the Temple, he gambled away his money in Dublin, to the lasting despair of his mother.

Edinburgh, Leiden, and a tour of the continent, 1752–1756 The family still supported Goldsmith, however, when he decided, next, to study medicine at the University of Edinburgh, which he entered in 1752; there he admired the lectures of the distinguished anatomist Alexander Monro, and a year later became a member of the Medical Society. But though the letters that he sent to his Irish family benefactors—his earliest on record—were intended to portray an earnest, grateful student they still betray a primary indulgence in the local social life, in which he regaled his company with Irish songs and tales and squandered money on expensive clothes to gain entrance to balls and to be clown at the table of James, duke of Hamilton. If his trip to the highlands in 1753 did not result in the euphoria of later tourists, at least his two years in Scotland sharpened his awareness of the differences between the two Celtic societies—Ireland and Scotland—and anticipated his role as cultural observer in his later writings.

Having written to his uncle Contarine that he had need of further medical study in Paris and Leiden, in early 1754 Goldsmith arrived in the Netherlands, and by spring had attended lectures by Albinus, Jerome Gaubius, and others. In his May 1754 letter to his uncle he spoke favourably of the tidy Dutch houses and fine gardens in the country as well as of the clean towns, but found the people themselves sluggish and complacent. Ten years later, in *The Traveller*, he decried their obsessive commercial spirit as destroying their country's freedom:

Even liberty itself is barter'd here.
At gold's superior charms all freedom flies;
The needy sell it, and the rich man buys:

A land of tyrants and a den of slaves.

Well before his return to England, Goldsmith had found his poetic theme of luxury upon witnessing the new wealth from the Netherlands' maritime empire and its impact on traditional village life. Yet in his translation *Memoirs of a Protestant, Condemned to the Gallies of France, for his Religion* (1758), from the French of Jean Marteilhe, he rendered a factual account of a French protestant's enthusiasm for the tolerant society of the Dutch when this former galley slave arrived in Amsterdam and found it hardly a 'den of slaves': 'Were I to recount all the Civilities we received in this great City, I should never have done' (vol. 2, p. 143). Aside from this early influence on his two major poems about the economic determinism of cultures, perhaps his most valuable experience in Leiden was in meeting Gaubius (Prior, 1.168), whose *De regimine mentis* (1747, 1763) describes psychosomatic medical problems that Mr Burchell, in *The Vicar of Wakefield*, alludes to as a 'sickly sensibility' (chapter 3) and that Primrose displays in his behaviour throughout his ordeal, especially when he collapses upon seeing his house on fire (chapter 22).

In February 1755 Goldsmith became a 'philosophical vagabond' (the term used in *The Vicar of Wakefield*, chapter 20), travelling by foot through Flanders, France, Switzerland, Germany, and Italy. A detailed account of this tour sent to Doctor Radcliff, fellow of Trinity College, was unfortunately lost in a fire that destroyed Radcliff's house (Prior, 1.176). The main source of speculation about Goldsmith's experiences is in the topographical descriptions in *The Traveller*, which his dedication to his brother Henry states was begun while in Switzerland, and in George Primrose's narrative of his travels in *The Vicar of Wakefield*. How he supported himself during this sojourn remains a mystery, but if his fiction contains any truth it may have been through playing the flute, tutoring in English, and gambling. He spent six months at Padua but did not visit Rome or Naples, probably for lack of money, since his benevolent uncle had died during this time. Despite being known as Dr Goldsmith in his later years, no record exists of his having received a medical degree while abroad. In early February 1756 he reached Calais, and from there crossed over to England, destitute and at twenty-five still without any career.

Introduction to London's Grub Street, 1756–1764 After working in an apothecary's shop in London Goldsmith tried to set up a medical practice in Southwark, 'where he had plenty of Patients, but got no Fees' (Balderston, 15). During this time he wrote a tragedy, now lost, and asked for Samuel Richardson's assistance with it. He may also have been a proofreader in Richardson's shop. Through the influence of an Edinburgh friend he found a temporary post as schoolmaster in a Presbyterian boys' school in Peckham run by this friend's father, Dr Milner, who was ill at the time. Although Milner had arranged to find Goldsmith a post as surgeon aboard a ship with the East India Company it was this benefactor's introducing him to the bookseller Ralph Griffiths in the spring of 1757 that proved to be the turning point of his life. As the proprietor of the *Monthly Review*, the first periodical to be devoted entirely to book reviews, Griffiths employed Goldsmith, providing him with a room and board at his house in Paternoster Row and an income of £100 a year. Even if at first Goldsmith still had hopes of seeking his fortune as a doctor in India, and remained only about seven or eight months with Griffiths, this interval was invaluable for his development as a journalist; his long and insightful review (May 1757) of Edmund Burke's *Enquiry into the Origin of our Ideas of the Sublime and Beautiful* (1756) was among the most exemplary responses to this pioneering work of aesthetics. His translation of Jean Marteilhe's *Mémoires d'un protestant* (1758) gave him the opportunity to write a preface that concludes poignantly on what was to become his literary focus: the subject as hapless victim of tyrannical oppression, whether in one country or another. Furthermore Goldsmith transformed Marteilhe's wordy, rambling account into an effectively structured and compelling narrative. Though Griffiths and a fellow bookseller, Edward Dilly, paid Goldsmith £20 the pseudonym on the title-page is James Wellington, the name of a student at Trinity College during the years that Goldsmith studied there.

After a quarrel with Griffiths, Goldsmith took lodgings for a few months in late 1757 near Salisbury Square, just south of Fleet Street, the location of Richardson's printing business. Following a brief stay in Peckham to assist in Milner's school he moved in 1758 into a room with one broken chair and a bed at Green Arbour Court, off the Old Bailey. Having received an appointment with the East India Company in 1758 he failed the examination to be qualified as a ship's surgeon. From that point on he became wholly dependent on his Grub Street quill to eke out a living. In 1759 he began writing for Archibald Hamilton's and Tobias Smollett's tory-oriented *Critical Review*, which first appeared in 1756, seven years after the founding of Griffiths's whiggish *Monthly Review*, its major rival. While still planning a career in India, Goldsmith agreed with Robert and James Dodsley of the Tully's Head bookshop, in the West End, to write an account of contemporary European culture, which was published in April 1759 as *An Inquiry into the Present State of Polite Learning in Europe*. Early in the same year he also completed for Griffiths a life of Voltaire, which did not appear until 1761, when it came out in instalments in the *Lady's Magazine* as 'Memoirs of M. de Voltaire'.

Goldsmith's first book, *An Inquiry*, was not successful with the reviewers and did not go into a second edition until fifteen years later, almost four months after his death. His central theme is the decline of taste in the republic of letters and the possible invigoration of the arts, with glances at parallels in the rise and fall of ancient and modern literature. Aside from the quasi-sociological observations reminiscent of his first letters home from Scotland and the Netherlands, his most trenchant attack here is on the economics of the writer's marketplace, which he himself knew at first hand and denounced in no uncertain terms:

> The author, when unpatronized by the Great, has naturally recourse to the bookseller. There cannot be, perhaps,

> imagined a combination more prejudicial to taste than this. It is the interest of the one to allow as little for writing, and of the other to write as much as possible; accordingly, tedious compilations, and periodical magazines, are the result of their joint endeavours. In these circumstances, the author bids adieu to fame, writes for bread, and for that only. (*Collected Works*, 1.316)

Given such provocation it is not surprising that his former employer Griffiths unleashed his vilest journalistic hack, William Kenrick, to excoriate Goldsmith's pamphlet in the *Monthly Review* (November 1759), in an article that not only questioned the knowledge but also the character of the author. Goldsmith's attack on the management of the theatres was also offensive to David Garrick, and after they had become friends years later Goldsmith was careful to suppress the most vindictive passages for the 1774 edition. In late 1759 he also contributed to four periodicals: *The Bee*, the *Lady's Magazine*, the *Busy Body*, and the *Weekly Magazine*; he compiled nearly all of *The Bee*'s eight numbers. Among the many essays he produced in that year two are especially memorable and are included in his edition of essays published in 1765: 'The Proceedings of Providence Vindicated: an Eastern Tale', which was first published in the *Royal Magazine* (December 1759), and 'A reverie at the Boar's-Head-Tavern in Eastcheap', which was first published in the *British Magazine* for February, March, and April 1760. By this time Goldsmith was becoming recognized as a professional writer; and besides his good relationship with Smollett while still contributing to the *Critical Review* he met new friends in Thomas Percy, later bishop of Dromore, and Samuel Johnson, whose star was rising after publication of *The Rambler* (1750–52) and his dictionary (1755).

Perhaps the most significant breakthrough in Goldsmith's writing career was his association with John Newbery, the bookseller who began a financial newspaper, the *Public Ledger*, in 1760; he invited Goldsmith to write commentaries of humorous interest to lighten the practical content, which resulted in a series of letters supposedly written by a Chinese traveller to Europe, living in London, to his friends in the East. Because of their transparent success in this paper Goldsmith collected the letters, revised them, and added four to their original number; together with five other booksellers Newbery published them in two volumes on 1 May 1762 as *The Citizen of the World, or, Letters from a Chinese Philosopher, Residing in London, to his Friends in the East*. Modelled after Montesquieu's *Lettres persanes* (1721), and especially the 1755 English translation of Jean-Baptiste, marquis d'Argens's *Lettres chinoises*, Goldsmith's pseudo-letters provided a range of topical satire, moral observation, and comic description through a variety of fictionalized characters. But though favourably reviewed, excerpted, and imitated in other periodicals, reprinted in Dublin in 1762, and translated into both French and German in 1763, *The Citizen of the World* was only moderately successful in the marketplace, and a second London edition did not appear until 1774. Yet it was Goldsmith's first widely recognized literary achievement.

With the potential for being an epistolary novel the narrative's fictional spokesman is Lien Chi Altangi, whose letters to Fum Hoam in Peking (Beijing) vary from serious to playful contrasts between European and Asian cultures. Such English friends as the Man in Black and Beau Tibbs give humorous perspectives to his account, and the letters supposedly from China offer exotic amusement. The romantic wanderings of Lien's son Hingpo bring him together with a beautiful girl, Zelis, while both are slaves in a Persian household, and she is later discovered to be the niece of the Man in Black. Reflecting their journalistic beginnings, Lien Chi's letters cover topical religious and political issues of the day and such London attractions as the theatre, the races, Vauxhall Gardens, and Westminster Abbey. Differences between Chinese and English women and sexual behaviour in general receive ironic comment; although Chinese men may legally have two wives and their English counterparts only one Lien Chi notices that the latter tend to indulge in widespread polygamy by patronizing prostitutes at random. Other topics include cruelty to animals, funerals and epitaphs, quack medicines, superfluous old maids and bachelors, and the popular interest in freaks and monsters. Letter 53 is a shrewd attack on the initial success of Sterne's *Tristram Shandy*. Without ever mentioning Sterne, Goldsmith's Chinese persona comments:

> But a prurient jest has always been found to give most pleasure to a few very old gentlemen, who being in some measure dead to other sensations, feel the force of the allusion with double violence on the organs of risibility. An author who writes in this manner is generally sure therefore of having the very old and the impotent among his admirers. (*Collected Works*, 2.222)

In light of his later elegiac view of the impact of maritime wealth on traditional English village life Goldsmith's positive view of luxury in letter 10 reveals the journalist's penchant for seeing at least two sides of an issue. Doubtless indebted to Bernard Mandeville's paradoxical argument about private vices being public virtues, Lien Chi observes:

> The greater the luxuries of every country, the more closely, politically speaking, is that country united. Luxury is the child of society alone, the luxurious man stands in need of a thousand different artists to furnish out his happiness; it is more likely, therefore, that he should be a good citizen who is connected by motives of self-interest with so many, than the abstemious man who is united to none. (ibid., 2.52)

While writing the Chinese letters for the *Public Ledger* in 1760 Goldsmith abandoned his shabby quarters in Green Arbour Court to move to more attractive rooms at Wine Office Court, adjacent to Fleet Street. Although he produced his memoirs of Voltaire in 1761 and continued to write for Newbery and others in magazines he spent more time in that year in cultivating permanent friendships with Reynolds and Johnson. In 1762, while revising his Chinese letters for the two volumes of *The Citizen of the World*, he assisted Newbery in an ambitious 'Compendium of biography', which involved abridging Plutarch's *Lives*. After completing four volumes of this hack work he begged off, for medical reasons, from doing more; Joseph

Collier completed the remaining volumes, which were finally published over May–November 1761, bringing Goldsmith 23½ guineas for his part in the project.

Poor health drove Goldsmith to Bath in the summer of 1762, where he won access to the papers of Beau Nash, the 'King of Bath', and collected anecdotes from witnesses who had known this colourful figure, who died in February 1761. On 14 October 1762 *The Life of Richard Nash* was published, for which Goldsmith had been paid 14 guineas beforehand, and a second edition appeared in December. In some respects Nash's career had parallels with Goldsmith's. His humble entrance into Oxford as demi-commoner and his undistinguished academic record resembled Goldsmith's pattern at Trinity. If Nash's prowess in moving up in Bath society and holding sway as its 'king' is in contrast to Goldsmith's own awkwardness in company they both shared a benevolent temperament, good humour, and compulsive indulgence in fashion that could result in ludicrous situations. In two instances, however, they were mirror opposites: the one a successful gambler without any talent for writing, the other an addictive failure at the table but a genius in prose and poetry. Above all both biographer and subject were keenly sensitive about the pressures of being public figures and found strategies of self-projection that made them seem at times admirable and, at others, ridiculous.

Doubtless influenced by Johnson's *Life of Richard Savage* in rendering a subject from the 'middle ranks of life' with rare gifts as well as glaring weaknesses, Goldsmith assumed at once the authoritative stance of the disinterested compiler of Nash's records, without any design of writing a panegyric. Goldsmith draws on considerable information in the architect John Wood's *Essay towards a Description of Bath* to place his subject as the leader of this little community comprising many Londoners seeking to improve their health or their fortunes. It was a heroic achievement, Goldsmith implies, that Nash could turn a wildly heterogeneous collection of landed aristocrats, rich tradesmen, and sickly valetudinarians—besides gamblers, rakes, and crooks—into an orderly and even useful society. Given the character of his low mimetic subject Goldsmith's most difficult rhetorical task is to arouse the appropriate measure of sympathy with Nash as philanthropist. Although the anecdote about Nash's giving to gain friends while owing large sums to creditors confirms some suspicions about his motives, the major reversal in our expectations occurs when instead of false benevolence the subject reveals an ingenuous concern for the distressed, an inclination not likely in a beau, whose *raison d'être*, we are reminded elsewhere, is dress, form, gesture, and appearance. The permanent value of Nash's public role, notwithstanding all the trivia, vanity, and silliness, is his demonstrable usefulness to all social classes, including the very poor.

Upon his return from Bath, Goldsmith was once more having money troubles, and his landlady had him arrested for failing to pay his rent. He sent a desperate message to Johnson, who promptly came to Wine Office Court to assist him; there the victim was taking refuge in a bottle of Madeira with the money that his friend had sent him beforehand. After coming to Goldsmith's rescue and finding a manuscript of a novel on hand Johnson sold *The Vicar of Wakefield* for £60 cash—enough to pay the rent as well as provide the author with some pocket money. Though Newbery shared a copyright with Benjamin Collins of Salisbury on 28 October 1762, it was not until 1766 that the novel finally appeared in print.

This latest crisis apparently made Goldsmith recognize his inability to govern his finances and prompted him to arrange with Newbery to take charge of his budget in exchange for his journalistic services. Thus he moved from Wine Office Court, with its temptations of taverns and gambling, to Canonbury House, Islington, and spent two years there under the shelter of Newbery. Their relationship (including Goldsmith's later employment with Newbery's nephew Francis) was cordial, and Goldsmith repaid Newbery's benevolence with a warm tribute in chapter 18 of *The Vicar of Wakefield*.

In June 1764 Goldsmith published anonymously through Newbery *An History of England in a Series of Letters from a Nobleman to his Son*, a very popular work first attributed by some to Lord Chesterfield and by others to Lord Lyttelton. Though he never acknowledged his authorship of this history Goldsmith on 11 October 1763 sent a receipt to Newbery for the payment of £21 for this work (Prior, 2.498). Supposedly written by an aristocratic father to his son, the author maintains a non-partisan view of political history, yet also underscores the need for a strong monarchy. In assessing the strengths and weaknesses of the three Hanoverian kings he gives highest praise to George III but is only tepid in his appraisal of the earlier two. Characteristically, after recounting such major financial scandals as the South Sea Bubble, of 1720, and the similar fraud of the Charitable Corporation, in 1731, he devotes a paragraph to the related horror of private life: the joint suicide of Richard Smith, a bookbinder, and his wife after they had murdered their child rather than continue in their impoverished circumstances: 'Suicide, in many instances, is ascribed to phrenzy: we have here an instance of self-murder, concerted with composure, and borrowing the aids of reason for its vindication' (*History of England*, 2.163).

The success of this recent history as well as that of his earlier known publications enhanced Goldsmith's position among the most distinguished literati of the day. When in 1764 Reynolds raised the idea with Johnson of forming The Club that would meet every Monday evening at the Turk's Head Tavern in Soho they agreed to invite Goldsmith to be a charter member. Edmund Burke, Sir John Hawkins, two young aristocratic friends of Johnson—Bennet Langton and Topham Beauclerk—and two others were also enrolled. But besides this particular venue Reynolds and Goldsmith were continually together for dinner and the theatre; in the words of Beauclerk they 'unbosomed their minds freely to each other' (Reynolds, 29). Reynolds persuaded Garrick to produce *The Good-Natur'd Man*, and was responsible for having Goldsmith appointed historian of the Royal Academy. Goldsmith in turn dedicated *The Deserted Village* to his friend, in 1770: 'The only dedication I ever made was to my brother, because I loved him better than most other men. He is since dead. Permit me to inscribe this poem to you'.

While living in Islington and carrying out the assignments given him by Newbery, Goldsmith also completed the poem that he had begun while in Switzerland years before: *The Traveller*, which was published in December 1764 and was the first of his works to have his name on the title-page. By autumn of that year, however, Goldsmith had moved from Islington to far more respectable quarters, at 3 King's Bench Walk, in the Temple, where he continued to work closely for Newbery and made further revisions of *The Traveller*. In an age of fulsome dedications to patrons Goldsmith's tribute to his brother Henry, a lowly curate in the Church of Ireland, contributed to the sincere tone in this narrative of the lonely wanderer. The general principle of cultural comparison in this poem follows the method of the French *philosophes* in tracing the effects of climate to national social behaviour while showing that luxury is the universal cause of a country's decline. At times Goldsmith's poem recalled Pope's skilful manipulations of the heroic couplet, with its witty dichotomies, zeugmas, and similar rhetorical figures:

> Here by the bonds of nature feebly held,
> Minds combat minds, repelling and repell'd;
> Ferments arise, imprison'd factions roar,
> Repress ambition struggles round her shore,
> Till over-wrought, the general system feels
> Its motions stopt, or phrenzy fire the wheels.
> (*The Traveller*)

Again as in Pope, thematically Goldsmith's verse exploits the contrasts between cultures in patterns that are as geometrically configured as a design for a Caucasian carpet.

In the *Critical Review* (December 1764) Johnson, who had contributed some lines to the ending, extolled *The Traveller* as 'a production to which, since the death of Pope, it will not be easy to find any thing equal'. The *Monthly Review* (January 1765), however, faulted Goldsmith's tory views regarding the dire effects of expansive commerce and domestic decline. In contrast to his prose writings this poem, with his name on the title-page, had the cachet to make Goldsmith at last a celebrity. Reynolds remarks that it 'produced an eagerness unparalleled to see the author. He was sought after with greediness' (Reynolds, 48). To capitalize not only on the poem's popularity but also to stress the author's achievements in prose as well Newbery and Griffin brought out a volume of Goldsmith's essays (1765) that included earlier items from *The Bee*, *The Citizen*, and other sources, and included 'A reverie at the Boar's-Head-Tavern in Eastcheap'.

Literary celebrity After Goldsmith gained renown as a poet, John Newbery finally published *The Vicar of Wakefield* in March 1766. The book was printed by Benjamin Collins of Salisbury, who had brought one-third of the copyright back in 1762, for Francis Newbery. Second and third editions, each consisting of 1000 copies, appeared in May and August respectively, printed by William Strahan; three editions were produced in Ireland in 1766 as well. Though the initial reception was mostly favourable questions immediately arose about its narrative structure. The *Monthly Review* commented: 'Through the whole course of our travels in the wild regions of romance, we never met with anything more difficult to characterize than the Vicar of Wakefield' (*Monthly Review*, 34, 1766, 407). The *Critical Review* praised its 'genuine touches of nature, easy strokes of humour, pathetic pictures of domestic happiness and domestic distress' (*Critical Review*, 21, 1766, 440) but faulted the awkward plot reversals in the second half. If Johnson could not find anything of real life in the work the author's advertisement nevertheless had anticipated negative criticism: 'A book may be amusing with numerous errors, or it may be very dull without a single absurdity'. Apparently the reading public agreed. Though the novel was excerpted in various newspapers and was translated into French and German shortly after its first appearance it was not until after Goldsmith's death, in 1774, that it witnessed its greatest popularity; more than twenty editions were published in London before the close of the century. The novel basically is divided between the early chapters of Arcadian bliss and the later part, where calamities accumulate alarmingly to destroy the Primrose family until a sudden dispensation of good fortune cancels all the disasters and resolves everything in marriages. Two of Goldsmith's best-known poems, *Edwin and Angelina* and *An Elegy on the Death of a Mad Dog*, and the song 'When Lovely Woman Stoops to Folly' appeared in this novel. But although earlier readers could enjoy Primrose's good-natured humour and sympathize with his plight as a kindly if flawed family patriarch some twentieth-century commentators have exaggerated the irony of this tale as a relentless exposure of the period's sentimentalism, while others have seen it as a radical call for prison reform, as shown in chapters 26 and 27.

Goldsmith next turned to writing a play, a more lucrative genre than the novel at that time. During 1767 he finished *The Good-Natur'd Man* and tried in vain to have Garrick produce it at Drury Lane. Although he persuaded George Colman the elder to accept it, it was not performed until 29 January 1768, at Covent Garden, where it ran for ten nights and brought the author three benefit performances and some £400. Goldsmith obviously drew upon his earlier formulas of plot and character for this play. Sir William Honeywood replicates Sir William Thornhill's authoritative role in finally restoring order after all the financial losses caused by young Honeywood's well-intentioned but foolish indulgences. As a sprightly and compassionate woman Miss Richland seems to derive from Sophia Primrose's mould. To judge by the reviews *The Good-Natur'd Man* struck the first audiences as a subtle satire on the kind of sentimental comedy that Goldsmith had deplored in his provocative 'An Essay on the Theatre, or, A Comparison between Laughing and Sentimental Comedy', for the *Westminster Magazine* in January 1773, in which he contrasted Restoration comedy and later, maudlin eighteenth-century products.

The profits from this play made Goldsmith prosperous for the first time in his life and allowed him to lease his last London residence, rooms at 2 Brick Court, Middle Temple. In addition he rented a weekend retreat near Hyde, on Edgware Road. Perhaps the news of his brother Henry's death in Lissoy prompted his writing of *The Deserted Village*, which seemed to be in process already in the final forty-six lines of *The Traveller* (1764). In *Lloyd's Evening Post* (1762) he had condemned the enclosure laws that were radically changing English rural culture and making way for the new wealth from the mercantile economy encoded as 'luxury'. Completed at some time in 1769, after at least six months of further revisions, *The Deserted Village* was finally published in 16 May 1770, as a quarto pamphlet, and six more editions appeared that same year. Nearly all the first reviews were favourable but the *Critical Review* objected to the theme of the poem: 'A fine poem may be written upon a false hypothesis: as a poet is not confined to historical fact, neither is he bound by the strictness of political and philosophical truth' (*Critical Review*, 29, 1770, 437). Similarly the *Monthly Review* praised the poem as 'a picture of fancy' while disagreeing with its thesis about depopulation (*Monthly Review*, 42, 1770, 441). As many as seventeen letters on the poem appeared in the *St James's Chronicle*, and Goldsmith was declared 'the foremost poet of our age' in *The Theatres: a Poetical Dissection* (p. 34), by Sir Nicholas Nipclose (1772). Despite widespread resistance to its mourning the disruptive effects of enclosure *The Deserted Village* none the less gave fresh expression to the traditional form of elegy. Early readers admired the nostalgic descriptions of a vanished village life, with its vivid portraits of the preacher, the blacksmith, the schoolmaster, and the widow.

Beginning with the success of his first play, in 1767, Goldsmith's writings brought him about £400 per year until his last year, when his health began to suffer from the stress of fulfilling his various contracts with booksellers. Yet because of his compulsive charity to the poor (including Irish drifters in London), his indulgence in lavish clothes, his addiction to gambling, and other excesses he remained hostage to his employers. Through Reynolds he befriended a widow by the name of Mrs Kane Horneck, and her two daughters, and spent time with them in Paris in the summer of 1770. During that year his biographies of Thomas Parnell and of Henry St John, Viscount Bolingbroke, were published. Though neither anonymous work added to his lustre, Goldsmith's sympathetic tone towards Bolingbroke is characteristic of his better-known writings: 'an ambitious mind can never be fairly subdued, but will still seek for those gratifications which retirement can never supply' (*Collected Works*, 3.465). About this time Goldsmith also became acquainted with an Irish peer, Robert Nugent, Viscount Clare, eventually Earl Nugent, whose hospitality he enjoyed in London, Bath, and at Nugent's country house in Essex. The poem *A Haunch of Venison*, a humorous verse thank-you note, published in 1776, is a memento of this friendship.

After the commercial success of Goldsmith's anonymous *History of England in a Series of Letters from a Nobleman to his Son* (1764) the bookseller Tom Davies commissioned him to produce simpler histories than the large tomes by Smollett and David Hume, which resulted in contracts to write *The Roman History, from the Foundation of the City of Rome, to the Destruction of the Western Empire* (1769) and *The History of England, from the Earliest Times to the Death of George II* (1771). In 1769 Goldsmith also signed a contract with William Griffin to produce for 100 guineas a natural history in eight volumes. When he completed his second play, *She Stoops to Conquer*, and had similar problems as before with the theatre directors Colman and Garrick, Johnson and other friends intervened to get it produced. But even though it was not presented until late in the season, 15 March 1773, it was an immediate triumph and brought its author over £500. As in his first play Goldsmith demonstrated his aim of restoring the 'laughing comedy' of Farquhar and Vanbrugh after the stage had been taken over by sentimental comedy. Based on an embarrassing experience that Goldsmith underwent while still a pupil in Ireland, when he was duped into thinking the local squire's house to be an inn and ordered dinner and a night's lodging, the 'mistakes of the night' begin when Tony Lumpkin, the playboy of the Hardcastle family, tricks some travellers, Marlow and Hastings, into taking his home for a public house, and Kate Hardcastle carries on the jest by posing as a barmaid while conquering the hero Marlow's fears of fine ladies.

Decline, death, and reputation Despite the great acclaim of *She Stoops to Conquer*, ever since leaving the protection of Newbery's benevolent management Goldsmith had relapsed into his prodigal habits and was increasingly in debt, and under ever greater pressure to write for bread. Hence in 1773, during his summer retirement to his farmer's cottage near Hyde, he was under contract to produce *The Grecian History, from the Earliest State to the Death of Alexander the Great* and *An History of the Earth, and Animated Nature*, both of which were published in the next, and final, year of his life. Notwithstanding his fame he was hardly at peace with himself and quarrelled not only with Thomas Evans, a newspaper owner who had reported an intimacy with one of the Horneck girls, but also resented the successes enjoyed by Hugh Kelly and James Beattie, not to mention Johnson himself. Besides financial worries Goldsmith was also suffering from a bladder disease. Though he tried to settle in the country with the Selbys at Hyde Lane a kidney infection forced him back to London in March 1774 to seek treatment. His illness did not, however, prevent him from enjoying the conversation of such old friends as Reynolds, Johnson, Burke, and Garrick. In March of that year a dinner with them involved some extempore wit in writing each other's epitaphs, which resulted in Goldsmith's last, unfinished poem, *Retaliation* (1774). With his customary skill at repartee Garrick pronounced Goldsmith's epitaph:

> Here lies NOLLY Goldsmith, for shortness call'd Noll,
> Who wrote like an angel, but talk'd like poor Poll.

Nonplussed by this telling sally and the hearty laughter from the company at the table, Goldsmith turned a few days later to his brilliant poem, where he had his revenge on Garrick:

On the stage he was natural, simple, affecting,
'Twas only that, when he was off, he was acting;
Tho' secure of our hearts, yet confoundedly sick,
If they were not his own by finessing and trick,
He cast off his friends, as a huntsman his pack;
For he knew when he pleased he could whistle them back.

In the opening lines of *Retaliation* Goldsmith envisions a potluck dinner to which each guest brings a dish representing his real character. Thus Garrick is understood to be a salad—

for in him we see
Oil, vinegar, sugar, and saltness agree

and the poem ends with Goldsmith as a dessert: 'Magnanimous Goldsmith, a gooseberry fool'. In his deeply compassionate sketch of his friend Reynolds stressed that Goldsmith assumed the role of fool on principle, as a means of endearing himself to others who had nothing thereby to fear from him. In the March issue of the *Westminster Magazine* (no. 1, 1773) appeared 'Humourous anecdotes of Dr. Goldsmith', which testified to his fame as an 'odd fellow' and buffoon.

When his bladder condition worsened with a kidney infection Goldsmith consulted William Hawes, an apothecary, but against his advice persisted in taking large doses of Dr James's fever powder, a quack remedy containing mercury, lime, and other noxious substances. While Goldsmith lay dying, exhausted by vomiting and diarrhoea, a doctor asked him 'Is your mind at ease?' His last words, in reply, were 'No, it is not'. He died early in the morning of 4 April 1774, in his lodgings at 2 Brick Court, and was buried on 9 April in the cemetery outside Temple Church. His death was widely mourned, and according to Reynolds 'Epigrams, epitaphs and monodies to his memory were without end' (Reynolds, 31). His nemesis for years, William Kenrick, pursued him beyond the grave with a vicious epitaph that includes the following charge:

A *mendicant*, whose matchless skill
In working cures was sure to kill;
By his own art who justly died,
A blundering artless suicide.

Aware of the rumours surrounding Goldsmith's unexpected death, Hawes published a pamphlet to defend his profession from any blame by recording in detail his patient's stubborn behaviour. Besides his emphasis on the murder–suicide of the bookbinder family during the South Sea Bubble, in the *History of England*, as late as the spring of 1773, Goldsmith debated with Johnson about the fear of something worse than death as a motive to self-destruction. The discovery that Goldsmith was in debt for no less than £2000 also increased doubts about the circumstances of his death. Instead of the expensive funeral that was first contemplated Reynolds made arrangements for a monument, with a medallion sculpted by Nollekens, to be installed at poets' corner in Westminster Abbey. But after Johnson had provided a Latin epitaph for consideration the mutiny among members of The Club, who apparently wanted more said about the subject's personal character and urged Johnson to write it in English, was a major embarrassment. An anonymous critic in the *Classical Journal* (1816) went so far as to attribute the principal reason to Johnson's dubious Latin.

No matter how beloved by his literary friends in The Club, until well into the nineteenth century Goldsmith never received the biography that might have been expected. Johnson undertook to write a life and prepare an edition of his friend's works, but according to Balderston he could not complete it because he did not outlive the copyright held until 1787 by Carnan, the partner of Newbery, who refused permission for reprinting *She Stoops to Conquer*. Other circumstances seem more probable as the cause, however, mainly the lack of evidence about the simple facts of Goldsmith's life. In a letter to Thomas Percy on 2 March 1785 Malone wrote: 'Dr. Johnson used to say that he never could get an accurate account of Goldsmith's history while he was abroad' (Balderston, 23). Even Percy, who actually obtained an interview with Goldsmith to record the major events of his life, still could not ascertain such basic facts as the date and place of his birth, not to mention any reliable evidence for his academic degrees.

Despite the obstacles to his biography Goldsmith's fame spread to both the European and North American continents. Johann Wolfgang Goethe testified that at the age of twenty, in Strasbourg, he was awakened by *The Vicar of Wakefield* to create a new field of letters. Later he even tried to translate *The Deserted Village*, but gave up after failing to carry the delicate tone of the original into his own German. *The Rising Village* (1825, 1834), by Goldsmith's grand-nephew and namesake, the first Canadian-born published poet, may be read as an ironic reply from the New World to the sentimentalist's depiction of the terrors awaiting the dispossessed villagers of the Old World. Though Goldsmith's reputation reached its apogee in the Victorian era, when Thackeray declared him to be 'the most beloved of writers', such hack publications as his once popular histories had disappeared from memory by the twentieth century. But *The Vicar of Wakefield*, *The Deserted Village*, and *She Stoops to Conquer* have endured. In the era of silent films Edwin Thanhouse and Lloyd F. Lonergan produced a short film in 1910 of *The Vicar of Wakefield*, which was expanded by Ernest C. Warde into a full-length feature in 1917. A classic rivalling some of Shakespeare's best-known plays, Goldsmith's last comedy has been in production throughout most of the years since its first appearance, with performances from actors such as Laurence Olivier, Helen Hayes, Peggy Ashcroft, John Mills, and Tom Courtenay. Tourism in central Ireland proudly touts its 'Goldsmith country', to attract visitors to the region still haunted by this elusive genius.

JOHN A. DUSSINGER

Sources [T. Percy], 'The life of Dr. Oliver Goldsmith', *The miscellaneous works of Oliver Goldsmith*, 1 (1801), 1–118 • J. Prior, *The life of Oliver Goldsmith, M.B.*, 4 vols. (1837) • J. Forster, *The life and times of Oliver Goldsmith*, 6th edn, 2 vols. (1877) • J. Northcote, *Memoirs of Sir Joshua Reynolds, Knt.* (1813) • J. Reynolds, *Portraits*, ed. F. W. Hilles (1952) • S. Johnson, *Johnsonian miscellanies*, ed. G. B. Hill, 2 vols. (1907) • Boswell, *Life* • *Classical Journal*, 26/13 (July 1816), 352–3 • K. C. Balderston, *The history and sources of Percy's memoir of Goldsmith* (1926) • *The* *collected letters of Oliver Goldsmith*, ed. K. C. Balderston (1928) · *Collected works of Oliver Goldsmith*, ed. A. Friedman, 5 vols. (1966) · M. Loveridge, 'Oliver Goldsmith', *Eighteenth-century British literary biographers*, ed. S. Serafin, DLitB, 142 (1994) · R. Bevis, 'Oliver Goldsmith', *Restoration and eighteenth-century dramatists: third series*, ed. P. R. Backscheider, DLitB, 89 (1989) · A. M. Duckworth, 'Oliver Goldsmith', *British novelists, 1660–1800*, ed. M. C. Battestin, DLitB, 39/1 (1985) · O. W. Ferguson, 'Oliver Goldsmith', *Eighteenth-century British poets: second series*, ed. J. Sitter, DLitB, 109 (1991) · S. H. Woods, jun., 'Oliver Goldsmith', *British prose writers, 1660–1800: second series*, ed. D. T. Siebert, DLitB, 104 (1991) · R. M. Wardle, *Oliver Goldsmith* (1957) · J. Ginger, *The notable man: the life and times of Oliver Goldsmith* (1977) · J. A. Dussinger, 'Philanthropy and the selfish reader in Goldsmith's *Life of Nash*', *Studies in Burke and his Time*, 19 (autumn 1978), 197–207 · J. A. Dussinger, 'Oliver Goldsmith: citizen of the world', *Studies in Voltaire and the Eighteenth Century*, 55 (1967), 445–61 · J. A. Dussinger, '*The vicar of Wakefield*: "sickly sensibility" and the rewards of fortune', *The discourse of the mind in eighteenth-century fiction* (1974), 148–72 · J. Bender, 'Prison reform and the sentence of narration in *The vicar of Wakefield*', *The new eighteenth century*, ed. F. Nussbaum and L. Brown (1987), 168–88 · W. Shaw Mason, *Statistical account or parochial survey of Ireland, drawn up from the communications of the clergy*, vol. 3 (1819) · R. S. Crane, *TLS* (7 March 1929), 185–6 · J. B. Leslie, 'The birth of Goldsmith', *TLS* (14 March 1929), 207 · *Philological Quarterly*, 9 (1930); repr. in R. S. Crane and others, *English literature, 1660–1800: a bibliography of modern studies compiled for Philological Quarterly*, vol. 1: *1926–1938* (1950), 196–7 · R. S. Crane, *Philological Quarterly*, 10 (1931); repr. in R. S. Crane and others, *English literature, 1660–1800: a bibliography of modern studies compiled for Philological Quarterly*, vol. 1: *1926–1938* (1950), 247–8

Archives BL, corresp., Add. MS 42515, fols. 3–54, 86–130 · BL, receipt, Add. MS 70949, fol. 63 | BL, corresp. with Sir W. Chambers, Add. MS 41134, fols. 21, 216 · BL, agreements with T. Davies, bookseller, and literary papers, Add. MS 42515, fols. 58–83, *passim* · BL, agreement with J. Dodsley for publishing a chronological history, Add. MS 19022 · BL, receipt of money for his English history, Add. MS 19022 · BL, materials for a biography collected by Thomas Percy, Add. MSS 42515–42517 · BL, collections and corresp. of Thomas Percy, bishop of Dromore, for his life

Likenesses G. F. Marchi, mezzotint, pubd 1770 (after J. Reynolds, 1766), BM, NG Ire. · J. Reynolds, oils, *c*.1770, Knole, Kent [*see illus.*] · silhouette, *c*.1770, NPG · J. Bretherton, caricature, etching, pubd 1772 (after H. W. Bunbury), BM, NPG · Cook, engraving, pubd 1780 (after P. Audinet), NPG · P. Audinet, line engraving, BM; repro. in *Biographical Magazine* (1795) · attrib. Hogarth, portrait; formerly in possession of Mr Studley Martin of Liverpool in 1877 · F. H. Mitchell, pencil drawing, NG Ire. · J. Nollekens, medallion on monument, Westminster Abbey, poets' corner · J. Reynolds, oils, replica, NG Ire. · J. Reynolds, oils, two copies, NPG · S. W. Reynolds, mezzotint (after J. Reynolds), BM, NPG · engraving (after portrait by Hogarth?), repro. in Forster, *Life*, vol. 2, p. 11

Wealth at death in debt for 'not less than £2000': Sir Joshua Reynolds, as reported in a letter from Johnson to Boswell, 4 July 1774

Goldstone, Sir Frank Walter (1870–1955), trade unionist and politician, was born on 7 December 1870 in Sunderland, the third son of Frederick Goldstone, stained-glass artist, and Sarah Trigg (*née* Blott). Educated at Diamond Hall council school in Sunderland, Goldstone became a pupil teacher in Sheffield and later trained at Borough Road Training College, Isleworth. In 1895 he married Elizabeth Alice Henderson of Whittingham, Northumberland; they had two children, a boy and a girl.

In 1891 Goldstone was appointed an assistant master at Bow Street council school in Sheffield, and continued to teach in that city until 1910. During those years he was also an active figure in the National Union of Teachers (NUT), being involved especially in a group within it, the National Federation of Class Teachers. This concerned itself with the remuneration of teachers, and Goldstone served as its president in 1902, and was also a founder and editor of its journal, the *Class Teacher*.

Elected to the executive committee of the NUT in 1904, Goldstone chaired its law committee two years later. He represented the union at meetings with the Board of Education and at meetings of the National Association of Education Committees. Increasingly influential within the NUT, he left teaching in 1910 to become a full-time official of the union, following his appointment as organization secretary. He subsequently held the two highest positions, as assistant secretary (1918–1924), and as general secretary (1924–1931).

Goldstone's political career began inauspiciously. He was selected Labour candidate for Sunderland shortly before the December 1910 election, a late replacement for R. J. Wilson (a prominent member of the Co-operative Society). He was nominally sponsored by the Fabian Society, but his expenses were paid by the NUT, which was not affiliated to the Labour Party. Goldstone consequently did not sign the party constitution. Although Ramsay MacDonald objected, party officials wanted to secure NUT support and so allowed the concession.

At the time of his election to parliament Goldstone's educational programme was summarized in a campaign leaflet: he stood for 'a national system of education with a free teaching profession; one register of teachers; increased salaries for rural and class teachers; an improved system of superannuation applied to all teachers working under local education authorities; a code of professional honour; a "forward" policy generally' (*DLB*). In 1911 he attacked the policies of Sir Robert Morant, the permanent secretary of the Board of Education, arguing that secondary schools and universities should be freely opened to all those who had the required ability. Down to 1914 Goldstone also pressed in the Commons for improved medical inspection for children and better educational facilities for disabled people, as well as promoting the 1914 bill to abolish the half-time system. In 1916 he was appointed to the departmental committee on juvenile education and employment (established by H. A. L. Fisher); and this recommended a standard school-leaving age of fourteen, with continuation classes for fourteen- to eighteen-year-olds. Goldstone also served on the departmental committee on scholarships and free places in 1918.

Goldstone was not a charismatic MP. He was overshadowed by other Labour figures in campaigns against 'boy labour' and in favour of school meals and medical inspections. Keir Hardie none the less commented favourably on Goldstone's first session in parliament, when he criticized the government's National Insurance Bill. A reliable back-bencher and a good constituency MP, he asked pertinent questions and made careful speeches. On home rule he reflected the views of his many Irish-born constituents. As an MP for a shipbuilding constituency he managed to attack the arms race without advocating a small navy. He supported the war effort (working in the War Office) but continued to denounce militarism and xenophobia.

Such attributes made Goldstone an obvious choice for chief whip in 1916, when Arthur Henderson was appointed to the Board of Education in the coalition government. It helped that he was also mild, cheerful, and tactful. This allowed him in 1916 to raise the issue of Henderson's ambiguous position as both cabinet minister and secretary of the party, and to do so without attacking Henderson directly or focusing on the limited time which he devoted to educational issues. He was a member of the speaker's conference on the franchise, which supplied the blueprint for the 1918 Reform Act. He sat on the Burnham standing joint committee, which created a payments scale for teachers; the Tomlin commission on the civil service, which reported in 1931; and the joint committee of mayors and voluntary agencies, which administered the Miners' Relief Fund in the late 1920s.

Expanding educational opportunities was always more important than politics to Goldstone, and this became even more obvious after his election defeat in 1918. As a union official he was noted for solid organizational work, attention to detail, orderly exposition of the facts, and careful negotiation. In campaigns against educational cuts and in support of NUT policies, he deferred neither to government officials nor to fellow Labour politicians, but was always respectful to both. A traditionalist in some respects, he still wanted to raise the school-leaving age and extend opportunities. So far as Labour politics were concerned, he remained overshadowed by R. H. Tawney, MacDonald, and others in debates over educational policy. Although technically chair of Labour's education advisory committee, he was conspicuously absent from its deliberations (as he had been from the speaker's conference).

Goldstone was always somewhat distant from Labour colleagues; and his name seldom appears in the diaries, correspondence, and memoirs of Labour, Fabian, and socialist contemporaries. He was closer to NUT colleagues, but they too painted a picture of a neatly dressed, sincere, but rather formal bureaucrat (despite his liking for football and cricket).

Goldstone retired as general secretary of the NUT in 1931, when he also received a knighthood. He acted as principal of a tutorial college for three years, but played little further part in political affairs. His wife died at Ipswich in 1942. Goldstone was not distinguished as a propagandist for the Independent Labour Party, a great pamphleteer, or a prominent municipal politician. However, his form of political activism, enthusiasm for education, and attention to the details of union activity were important ingredients in the early Labour Party. He died at 12 Temple Road, Ipswich, on 25 December 1955.

DUNCAN TANNER

Sources *DLB* · Minutes and papers of the advisory committee on education, Museum of Labour History, Manchester, Labour Party Archives · *Hansard 5C* (1911–18) · 'The coming General Secretary', *The Schoolmaster* (11 Jan 1924), 39 · S. Blake and A. E. Henshall, *Schoolmaster and Woman Teacher's Chronicle* (6 Jan 1956), 10 · BLPES, Francis Johnson MSS, Independent Labour Party Archive · B. Simon, *The politics of educational reform, 1920–1940* (1974) · C. J. Wrigley, *Arthur Henderson* (1990) · D. J. Newton, *British labour, European socialism, and the struggle for peace, 1889–1914* (1985) · J. R. MacDonald MSS, PRO · M. Pugh, *Electoral reform in war and peace, 1906–18* (1978) · R. Barker, *Education and politics, 1900–1951: a study of the labour party* (1972) · K. O. Morgan, *Keir Hardie: radical and socialist* (1975) · d. cert.

Archives BLPES, Independent Labour Party records, Francis Johnson MSS · Bodl. Oxf., H. A. L. Fisher MSS · PRO, J. R. MacDonald MSS

Wealth at death £21,512 2*s*. 2*d*.: probate, 17 March 1956, *CGPLA Eng. & Wales*

Goldstücker, Theodor H. (1821–1872), orientalist, was born on 18 January 1821, in Königsberg, Prussia, of Jewish parents. Both his father (*d*. 1831) and his stepfather, M. W. Tobias, whom his mother married in 1834, were merchants. In 1836 Goldstücker left the Altstädtisches Gymnasium to study at Königsberg University with the Sanskritist Peter von Bohlen and the Hegelian philosopher Rosenkrantz. In 1838 he moved to Bonn, studying Indology with A. W. von Schlegel and C. Lassen, and Arabic with G. W. F. Freytag. He took his doctorate at Königsberg in 1840, but on being refused a teaching post there continued his researches in Paris. After working with E. Burnouf and briefly visiting London and Oxford (1844), he returned to Königsberg for two years. In 1847 he moved to Berlin where his erudition impressed Humboldt and where he formed a circle of keen young Sanskritists (including Kuhn and Weber). However his hopes of a career were again disappointed: his political opinions were (as they remained) strongly liberal, and when the reaction set in after the events of 1848–9, he was ordered to leave the city. Although the order was soon rescinded, he welcomed the invitation extended by H. H. Wilson (whom he had met in 1844) to prepare a third edition of Wilson's *Sanskrit Dictionary*. Accordingly, in 1850 he moved to London, intending to stay only a few years. However, he soon settled, and in May 1852 took up the chair of Sanskrit at University College, London.

Throughout his life Goldstücker studied with the utmost diligence, and he won widespread respect for his learning, especially in Sanskrit grammar, lexicology, philosophy, and theory of ritual (*purvamimamsa*). As a teacher, although his post was unpaid and students were few, he was exceedingly conscientious, advertising in 1870 four lectures a week for first-year students and two a week each for second- and third-year ones. He was also very active in the Royal Asiatic Society of Great Britain and Ireland, East India Association, and Philological Society, of which he was president when he died.

Goldstücker's first publication was an anonymous translation into German of the eleventh-century philosophical drama *Prabodha-Candrodaya*, with an introduction by Rosenkrantz. His revision of Wilson's dictionary (1856–64) became so encyclopaedic that it had to be abandoned when, after 6 fascicles and 480 pages, it had covered only two-thirds of the entries for the first letter of the Sanskrit alphabet. His best-known and most enduring work, *Pāṇini: His Place in Sanskrit Literature*, treated India's greatest grammarian; originally published in 1861 as the preface to a facsimile edition of the *Manava-kalpa-sutra*, it was reissued in Benares in 1965. Two other text editions had to be completed posthumously: one concerned grammar (1874), the other ritual theory (1872–8). The two volumes of his *Literary Remains* (1879) contain a selection of his shorter pieces, including his entries on Indian topics for *Chambers's Encyclopaedia* and a notable essay criticizing the contemporary administration of Indian law.

For so learned a scholar Goldstücker's output was disappointing, and exercised only limited influence. Living as he did on private means, he had little financial incentive to publish, and he set his standards unreasonably high. This perfectionism made him unwilling to publish some of the papers he presented to learned societies, and led to the excessively harsh criticism that he levelled at more productive mainstream scholars, especially in his *Pāṇini*. His lack of practical sense is clear not only from the dictionary project but also from the relative failure of the Sanskrit Text Society which he founded in 1866: it published only his last edited text and thereafter four other works. Critics have also said that, for all his zeal and fastidiousness, he lacked sound judgement, and was insufficiently critical of native Indian scholarly tradition.

Albeit a biting critic of fellow Sanskritists, Goldstücker is described as a modest, kind-hearted, and sociable man, very helpful to visiting Indians, and with a wide circle of friends. A bachelor, he used his brief summer holidays to maintain affectionate ties with his family, especially with his mother (*d.* 1869). A neglected cold turned to bronchitis and, weakened perhaps by self-imposed overwork, he died unexpectedly on 6 March 1872 at his home at 14 St George's Square, Primrose Hill, London. His funeral was held on 12 March at Finchley. N. J. ALLEN

Sources 'Biographical note', *Literary remains of the late Professor Theodore Goldstücker*, 2 vols. (1879), v–xvi • E. Windisch, *Geschichte der Sanskrit-Philologie und indischen Altertumskunde* (1917), 246–54 • J. Eggeling, 'Secretary's report to the anniversary meeting', *Royal Asiatic Society, Proceedings of the forty-ninth annual meeting* (1872), II–V • *The Times* (12 March 1872) • *The Athenaeum* (9 March 1872), 307 • F. Althaus, 'Beiträge zur Geschichte der deutschen Colonie in England, I, Orientalia', *Unsere Zeit*, NF 9 (1873), 437–8 • G. Cardona, *Pāṇini: a survey of research* (1976) • *University College, London, calendar, session 1870–71*

Archives BL OIOC

Wealth at death under £800 (in England): administration, 21 March 1872, *CGPLA Eng. & Wales*

Goldwell, James (*d.* 1499), bishop of Norwich, was one of several sons of William and Avice Goldwell; both parents died in 1485. Goldwell was probably born at Great Chart, Kent, where his family had held land, including the manor of Goldwell, since the early thirteenth century. He was educated at All Souls College, Oxford, where he was a fellow from 1441 to 1452, becoming a doctor of civil law by 1452 and of canon law by 1461. He was principal of St George's Hall, Oxford (1450–52), during which time he acted as a proctor in the chancellor's court. He was Cardinal-archbishop John Kemp's commissary-general from 2 November 1452 until Kemp's death on 22 March 1454, celebrating his first mass in the church of St Gregory's Priory, Canterbury, on 27 May 1453. Dispensed to hold incompatible benefices, he obtained benefices in Hertfordshire, London, Essex, and Gloucestershire as well as several rectories in Kent, including Great Chart, and canonries in St Paul's, Hereford, Salisbury, and Chichester cathedrals and in St George's Chapel, Windsor, where he served as registrar of the Order of the Garter. In August 1461 he became archdeacon of Essex, and on 21 October 1463 dean of Salisbury, holding both offices until obtaining his bishopric.

James Goldwell (*d.* 1499), tomb effigy

Goldwell's promotion in the church may have been due to the patronage of Thomas Kemp, bishop of London. However, an equally likely patron is Archbishop Thomas Bourchier (*d.* 1486), who may have opened the way for Goldwell's further advance by bringing him into the service of the house of York; this was first indicated by his appointment, after the Yorkist victory at Northampton, as Henry VI's secretary. He held this post by 20 August 1460, and may have continued in it for a short time after Edward IV's accession. On 12 August 1464, as master of requests, he was commissioned to treat for a truce with François, duke of Brittany. In September 1465 he was in Hamburg as leader of a mission to the kings of Denmark and Poland, the master of Prussia, and the Hanseatic League. No agreement with the Hanse towns was forthcoming, but on 3 October an alliance treaty was signed with Christian I of Denmark. While in Hamburg Goldwell bought a copy of Durandus's *Rationale divinorum*, printed in Mainz in 1459, thus becoming one of the first Englishmen known to have owned a printed book. Between about 1467 and 1471 Goldwell was the king's proctor at the papal curia. There he also represented George, duke of Clarence, for whom he obtained the dispensation enabling him to marry Isabel, daughter of the earl of Warwick, in 1469. It is not clear whether, in doing so, he was acting in deliberate opposition to the king's will. He remained in Rome throughout most of the ensuing political crisis, returning to England as a papal envoy only in January 1471. If he had lost Edward's favour he was, like many others, soon back in the king's service, being appointed to treat with French ambassadors in September 1471.

In 1468 Edward had licensed Goldwell to accept an English bishopric by papal provision. Despite its specific exclusion from this licence, Sixtus IV provided him to Norwich on 16 July 1472. On 4 October, he was consecrated in Rome while again representing Edward there. As bishop, Goldwell continued to serve on Edward's council, using his influence to obtain a pardon for Thomas Blake, one of Clarence's associates accused of using necromancy against the king in 1477; and, on 15 January 1478, officiating at the infant marriage of Prince Richard and Anne Mowbray. On 2 July 1482 he represented Edward IV in laying the foundation stone for the new house of Observant Franciscans at Greenwich. He attended both Edward's obsequies and Richard III's coronation in 1483. After Henry VII's accession he retired from all but the most formal of public duties; but age, as much as the change in dynasty, may have led to his concentrating his energies in his diocese.

Goldwell seems from the first to have been a conscientious bishop, continuing the arduous task of visitation until quite late in life and commissioning an inquiry into suspected cases of heresy in 1494. In 1473 he obtained a papal indulgence to aid the restoration of Norwich Cathedral, damaged by fire in 1463. His contribution to the vaulting of the choir is witnessed by the many bosses bearing his rebus, a golden well. He also replaced choir stalls, and was probably responsible for both the cathedral spire and the complete rebuilding of the bishop's house at Thornage in north Norfolk. He died at the bishop's palace, Hoxne, Suffolk, on 15 February 1499 and was buried in the chantry chapel he had had built in the south arcade of Norwich Cathedral presbytery. Other chantries established by him and his executors, led by his brother and protégé Nicholas, were at St Giles's Hospital, the cathedral priory, and the college of St Mary-in-the-Fields in Norwich; Great Chart, where he had rebuilt the church in 1477, and Leeds Augustinian priory in Kent; and All Souls College, Oxford, to which he also gave or bequeathed a large and varied library of books, many of which survive. He was clearly an enthusiastic collector of both manuscript and printed books, and it may well have been through his patronage that a Cologne printer, probably Theodoric Rood, set up a press in Oxford. He certainly owned a copy of the first book printed there (1478), the *Expositio symboli* of Rufinus. ROSEMARY C. E. HAYES

Sources Emden, *Oxf.* • *Fasti Angl., 1300–1541* • Norwich episcopal records, Norfolk RO • PRO • *Chancery records* • *CPR* • *RotP* • Rymer, *Foedera*, 1st edn, vols. 11–12 • A. Jessopp, ed., *Visitations of the diocese of Norwich, A.D. 1492–1532*, CS, new ser., 43 (1888) • N. P. Tanner, *The church in late medieval Norwich, 1370–1532* (1984) • *CEPR letters*, vols. 11–16 • E. Hasted, *The history and topographical survey of the county of Kent*, 2nd edn, 1–7 (1797–8) • F. Blomefield and C. Parkin, *An essay towards a topographical history of the county of Norfolk*, 5 vols. (1739–75) • N. R. Ker, *Records of All Souls College Library, 1437–1600* (1971) • Historical Monuments Commission, Thornage Hall architectural records file 34773 • C. L. Scofield, *Edward IV*, 2 vols. (1923) • E. Fernie, *An architectural history of Norwich Cathedral* (1993) • R. A. Griffiths, *Henry VI* (1981) • I. J. Churchill, *Canterbury administration: the administrative machinery of the archbishopric of Canterbury*, 2 vols. (1933) • J. Otway-Ruthven, *The king's secretary and the signet office in the XV century* (1939) • H. E. Salter, ed., *Registrum cancellarii Oxoniensis, 1434–1469*, 1, OHS, 93 (1932) • W. A. Pantin and M. T. Mitchell, eds., *The register of congregation, 1448–1463*, OHS, new ser., 22 (1972) • W. G. Searle, ed., *Christ Church, Canterbury*, 1: *The chronicle of John Stone, monk of Christ Church*, Cambridge Antiquarian RS, 34 (1902) • *Registrum Thomae Bourgchier … 1454–1486*, ed. F. R. H. Du Boulay, CYS, 54 (1957) • *The register of John Morton, archbishop of Canterbury, 1486–1500*, ed. C. Harper-Bill, 1–2, CYS, 75, 78 (1987–91) • *The Paston letters, AD 1422–1509*, ed. J. Gairdner, new edn, 6 vols. (1904); repr. in 1 vol. (1983) • A. C. De La Mare and L. Hellinga, 'The first book printed in Oxford: the *Expositio symboli* of Rufinus', *Transactions of the Cambridge Bibliographical Society*, 7 (1977–80), 184–244 • PRO, PROB 11/11, fol. 35, p. 283

Archives Historical Manuscripts Commission, London, Thornage Hall architectural records file 34773 • Norfolk RO, Norwich episcopal records

Likenesses tomb effigy, Norwich Cathedral [*see illus.*]

Wealth at death left gifts in kind; cash bequests of £600 and more; £240 between his executors for their pains; after first three years, 20*d.* a week to be distributed to poor, in perpetuity: will, PRO, PROB 11/11, fol. 35

Goldwell, Thomas (*d.* 1585), bishop of St Asaph, was the son of William Goldwell of Great Chart, Kent. He may have been a student of Canterbury College, Oxford, where, in January 1532, one Goldwell was questioned about his possession of books written in support of Katherine of Aragon. The inference that this is Thomas is supported by Goldwell's later reference to Richard Thornden, warden of Canterbury College from 1524 to 1534, as his 'old friend and master'.

Early career in England and Italy Goldwell graduated BA at Oxford in 1528, MA on 17 July 1531, and BTh on 20 March 1534—qualifications which did not prevent William Harrison from later describing him as 'more conversant … in the black art than skilful in the Scriptures' (Harrison, 51). On 11 March 1532 he received the rectory of Cheriton, perhaps through his father's patronage, and he was in Padua by July, when his father told him to thank Archbishop William Warham, in Greek, for a gift of £10. Goldwell studied law there in the following year, and may have met Reginald Pole. In 1534 he returned to Oxford, where he was a member of St Mary Hall, and university preacher on Palm Sunday. There is no evidence to support Anthony Wood's claim that he was a fellow of All Souls.

On 20 July 1536 Goldwell matriculated at Louvain, but left without taking a degree, and by April 1538 he was again in Padua. Probably in Louvain he had met the Observant Franciscan William Elstow, who handled the forwarding of Goldwell's correspondence. His stop in Padua was brief, and he probably intended from the first to go to Rome, where he had arrived not later than May, and perhaps already by 8 March, when he appears as a brother of the English Hospice. It has been said that he had by then been deprived of his benefice, but this may be doubted, since he gave his father detailed instructions about the disposal of income from it, and he is known to have held only Cheriton. Goldwell had none the less resolved to make a break from home, since in May 1538 he wrote to tell his father that he could have all his property. Falsely indicted for having gone to Rome with Pole (allegedly on the day he matriculated at Louvain), Goldwell was included in the bill of attainder against Pole and his allies passed on 19 May 1539.

Once in Rome, Goldwell was a chamberlain of the English Hospice in 1538–9, custos in 1540–41, auditor in the first two months of 1543, and then custos until 22 August, auditor again in 1544, vice-custos with George Lily in 1545–6, and custos as William Peto's commissary in 1547, and in 1548 standing in for Pole. During the 1540s Goldwell must have been in Pole's household since Pietro Carnesecchi listed him among 'all his [Pole's] familiars' at Viterbo, and Ludovico Beccadelli, Pole's first biographer, refers to Goldwell spending time with Pole at Capranica and calls him Pole's chaplain. Goldwell was close enough to Pole to have attended Marcantonio Flaminio's controversial readings of Matthew, during which he spoke of justification solely through Christ. On 23 November 1548 Goldwell began his noviciate in the Theatine house of Naples. He is supposed to have interrupted his first year in order to attend Pole in the conclave which elected Julius III (29 November 1549 to 7 February 1550), but despite the existence of a diary of the conclave attributed to him, he is unlikely to have been present. The diary (English College, Rome, MS 303, fols. C–D among several loose sheets pasted in at the front of the volume) is little more than a record of votes. The Theatine Antonio Caracciolo, in his life of Paul IV, claims to have had a story of the conclave from Goldwell, whom Caracciolo identifies as Pole's conclavist, but the story is unsupported in any of the massive documentation of the conclave, which, indeed, casts doubt on Caracciolo's claim that Goldwell was present. Goldwell made his profession as a Theatine at Naples on 28 October 1550.

Papal agent in England When Pole was made legate to England in August 1553, he is supposed to have asked Pope Julius to order Goldwell to accompany him, and they seem to have left Rome together. Pole relied heavily on Goldwell during the protracted effort needed to secure the legate's admission to England. Goldwell was first sent on a mission in November 1553, when the deputy of Calais initially refused him passage. He must have been allowed to come to England very shortly afterward, but then left immediately to rejoin Pole in Dillingen, whence he departed in post once more for England on 22 December. A number of instructions survive, all of them placing emphasis on the necessity for Mary to restore obedience to Rome before anything else. Goldwell returned to Pole on 3 January 1554, and as soon as they reached Brussels at the end of the month intended to set out again for England, but Wyatt's rebellion delayed his going. By 16 June he had made another round trip and reported to Thornden, now suffragan bishop of Dover, that he had only with difficulty persuaded Pole to send him faculties to reconcile schismatic Catholics; but in the end he succeeded in getting for Thornden faculties as extensive as those given to Nicholas Harpsfield, the archdeacon of Canterbury. Very soon afterwards, about mid-year, Goldwell undertook his final mission, after which he probably stayed in England, and may have served the queen temporarily as a Latin secretary.

His fellow Theatines had consented to Goldwell's accompanying Pole with a bad grace, and probably in late summer 1554 put pressure both on him and on Pole for his return. Pole, while pretending to leave the decision to the Neapolitan Theatines, in fact stonewalled and managed to keep Goldwell. In February 1555 Pole wrote to the co-founder of the Theatines, Cardinal Carafa, that Lord Chancellor Stephen Gardiner wished to make Goldwell a bishop, and Goldwell therefore asked Carafa to secure permission for him to stay with Pole. Before 12 May 1555 Goldwell had been elected bishop of St Asaph, and during his trip to Rome later that year was provided to the see by the pope; the temporalities were restored on 22 January 1556. On 24 June credentials to the newly elected Pope Paul IV were drawn up for Goldwell, although he was probably not dispatched until 6 July. He carried a report on the peace conference between France and the empire at Marcq, presided over by Pole, and was later sent another briefing on Pole's efforts to settle the issue of ex-monastic property. On his return in December, Goldwell brought back the highly important resolution of this property question which had been exacerbated by Paul's bull rescinding all alienations, as well as a breve from the pope ordering Pole to continue to try to make peace, and letters from Ignatius of Loyola and the Theatine Cardinal Bernardino Scotti to Pole.

Bishop of St Asaph By February 1556 Goldwell had taken up residence in St Asaph, although on 22 March he assisted at Pole's consecration as archbishop of Canterbury. Hampered by a grossly insufficient revenue which Pole tried to augment, Goldwell did his best at St Asaph, issuing injunctions in 1556, cracking down on simony, and reviving pilgrimage to St Winifred's Well at Holywell in Flintshire, and probably also appointing a priest to her chapel. He seems to have been resident until November 1558, when it was planned to translate him to Oxford and send him as ambassador to Rome. Although the documents were drawn up the queen's death prevented their execution. Goldwell attended Pole on his deathbed at the same time, administering extreme unction the day before he died on 17 November, and being involved in efforts to have Pole record his final intentions. He witnessed Pole's will and was appointed to serve with his executor, Alvise Priuli, in the distribution of his goods. By royal licence Goldwell also attended Pole's funeral at Canterbury. He almost immediately passed on word of the archbishop's death to Pole's long-time collaborator Cardinal Seripando, and probably returned to St Asaph.

Trent and Rome Although he complained to Sir William Cecil of not being summoned as a bishop to Elizabeth I's first parliament, by June 1559 Goldwell had determined to leave England and asked his brother to sell his stuff in order to settle the £300 he owed the queen. He headed for Rome, but illness forced him to stop almost immediately at Louvain. Early in 1560 he travelled to Antwerp, where Henry Pyning, Pole's former receiver-general, promised to find him the money to complete his trip. In January 1561 he became superior of San Silvestro, the Theatine house in Rome, as well as custos of the English Hospice (until 1564), and on 15 June reached Trent for the final session of the council. There he took a reasonably active role in the council's main business, as well as in the campaign to rehabilitate Pole, passing on anecdotes to Beccadelli and being proposed as one of those who might revise Pole's *De concilio*. He gave particular attention to the question of the mass (and later served on a papal commission for the reform of the breviary), and to episcopal residence, which he thought by divine right. Goldwell displayed greatest interest in matters relating to England, including a proposal to send an embassy to Elizabeth about the imprisoned bishops (he served with Pole's second biographer, Andras Dudic, on the committee appointed to consider the problem) and making strenuous efforts to secure Elizabeth's excommunication. While in Trent, Arthur Pole and his fellow conspirators proposed to contact Goldwell in order to get the pope's support for their plan to replace Elizabeth with Mary, queen of Scots.

The council closed on 4 December 1563, and Goldwell at once became Cardinal Borromeo's vicar at Milan. In 1565 he was again in San Silvestro, although he also kept rooms in the English Hospice until 1578. He presided over general chapters of his order in 1566, 1567, and 1572, and on 1 February 1566 dedicated San Silvestro's high altar. About 1567 he served as vicar to the cardinal archpriest of San Giovanni Laterano. Although a mission of his to England in 1564 had proved abortive, Goldwell succeeded in persuading Pius V to approve another for Nicholas Morton in 1568, which helped to trigger the northern rising of the following year. In February 1570 Goldwell testified in the trial leading to Elizabeth's excommunication. Four years later he became vice-gerent to Cardinal Jacopo Savelli, the vicar of Rome. Goldwell continued to concern himself with the English Hospice, and although supposedly neutral during its conversion into a college between 1578 and 1580, probably took the side of the students throughout. He bought them books, took Morton's part in his long-running dispute with the college's first rector, Maurice Clenock, and recommended to the pope that the Jesuits take over the institution.

Last years and death On 23 March 1580 Goldwell undertook a final mission to England, along with Morton. From the first he was unenthusiastic, trying to turn back to Rome from Bologna, telling the nuncio in Paris that he was too ill (or too fearful) to continue, and blaming the papal datary for failing to send the promised breves without which his mission would be pointless. Although he retreated only as far as Rheims after seeing the nuncio, he complained of plague and Huguenot soldiers, and everyone, including the cardinal secretary of state and William Allen (the rector of the English College at Rheims), expected him to give up again, this time out of cowardice. Allen had a very low opinion of Goldwell and accused him of having secured St Asaph out of greed and of fleeing timidly from England in 1559. As predicted Goldwell left Rheims for Rome on 8 August. He kept in touch with Allen, however, and sent money and papal privileges for his college, especially for the translation of the New Testament. In 1582 he served on the congregation for the revision of the Roman martyrology. The last survivor from the English hierarchy in its days of obedience to Rome, Goldwell died at Rome on 3 April 1585 and was buried at the Theatine convent of San Silvestro. He left money to the English College at Rheims in his will. The document in the archives of the archdiocese of Westminster, MS II, 165, said to be Goldwell's will, is actually about the disposition of bequests left by Seth Holland and Richard Pate, for whom Goldwell acted as executor. T. F. MAYER

Sources Emden, *Oxf.*, 4.239–40 • T. F. Knox, 'Thomas Goldwell, bishop of St Asaph', in T. E. Bridgett and T. F. Knox, *The true story of the Catholic hierarchy deposed by Queen Elizabeth* (1889), 208–63 • *LP Henry VIII*, 5, no. 757; 13/1, nos. 851, 935; 13/2, no. 979(7); 14/1, no. 867(15) • Biblioteca Civica Angelo Mai, Bergamo, archivio Stella in archivio Silvestri, 40/96; 40/135; 40/145; 40/159 • G. Manzoni, ed., 'Il processo Carnesecchi', *Miscellanea di Storia Italiana*, 10 (1870), 189–573, esp. 255 • M. Firpo and D. Marcatto, eds., *Il processo inquisitoriale del Cardinale Giovanni Morone*, 6 (Rome, 1995), 271 • A. Caracciolo, 'De vita Pauli IV pontificis maximi', Biblioteca Palatina, Parma, MS pal. 638, fol. 153*r* • G. M. Griffiths, 'St Asaph episcopal acts, 1536–1558', *Journal of the Historical Society of the Church in Wales*, 9 (1959), 32–69 • A. Kenny, 'From hospice to college', *The Venerabile*, 21 (1962), 269–70 [sexcentenary issue: *The English hospice in Rome*] • *CSP Venice*, 1557–8, appx, no. 129 • W. Harrison, *The description of England: the classic contemporary account of Tudor social life*, ed. G. Edelen (1968); repr. (1994) • Archivio Segreto Vaticano, MS Bolognetti 94, fols. 212*v*, 245*r* • Archivio Segreto Vaticano, A. A. I-XVIII 5412 • Archivio Segreto Vaticano, 6540, fol. 154*r* • Biblioteca Apostolica Vaticana, Vatican City, MS Vat. lat. 5966, fol. 39*v* • Biblioteca Apostolica Vaticana, Vatican City, MS Vat. lat. 5967, fols. 415*r* ff. • Biblioteca Apostolica Vaticana, Vatican City, MS Vat. lat. 5968, fols. 195*r*–202*v*; 107*r*(108*r*)–127*r* • Biblioteca Apostolica Vaticana, Vatican City, MS Vat. lat. 6409, fol. 271*r* • Biblioteca Apostolica Vaticana, Vatican City, MS Vat. lat. 6754, fols. 152*v*–155*v*; 197*v*–198*r*; 254*v*–260*v*; 281*r*–282*v* [*CSP Venetian*, 6/1, nos. 14, 322; 6/3, no. 1287; 5, no. 948] • Bibliothèque Municipale de Douai, MS 922, vol. 5, fols. 8*v*–9*r*, 9*r*–10*r*, 10*r*–11*r*, 162*r*–162*v*, 162*v*–163*r* • Biblioteca Palatina, Parma, MS pal. 651, no. 2 • *The letters and memorials of William, Cardinal Allen (1532–1594)*, ed. T. F. Knox (1882), vol. 2 of *Records of the English Catholics under the penal laws* (1878–82) [with historical introduction by T. F. Knox] • S. Merkle, ed., *Concilium Tridentinum*, 1 (Freiburg, 1901), 125, 128 • S. Merkle, ed., *Concilium Tridentinum*, 2 (Freiburg, 1911), 457 • S. Ehses, ed., *Concilium Tridentinum*, 8, 9 (1919–23) • *CSP dom.*, 1547–80, 118, 132, 638 • *CPR*, *1554–5*, 13; *1557–8*, 6 • *CSP for.*, 1559–60, no. 838 • 'Correspondence of Cardinal Allen', ed. P. Ryan, *Miscellanea, VII*, Catholic RS, 9 (1911), 12–105, esp. 58 • L. Hicks, ed., *Letters and memorials of Father Robert Persons*, Catholic RS, 39 (1942), 5–28 • C. Talbot, ed., *Miscellanea: recusant records*, Catholic RS, 53 (1961), 210

Likenesses portrait, English College, Rome • portrait; formerly in the Theatine house, Ravenna, in early eighteenth century

Goldwin [Golding], **John** (*bap.* **1667**, *d.* **1719**), organist and composer, was baptized at Windsor parish church on 1 December 1667, the eldest child of John Golding (*d.* in or after 1693) and his wife, Ann Towers. Although frequently called Golding in the Windsor records he consistently styles himself Goldwin. From 1675 to 1683 he was a chorister at St George's Chapel, Windsor, possessing 'skill and voice exceeding his years' (St George's Chapel archives, VI.B.4, 80). By 1685—after apparently studying under John Walter, organist of Eton College—he had 'attained sufficient skill in Musick' to be appointed assistant to the Windsor organist, William Child, and master of the choristers, Matthew Greene (ibid., VI.B.5, 30–31). Goldwin was admitted a lay clerk at Windsor in 1687, subsequently succeeded as both organist (1697) and master of the choristers

(1704), and held all three posts until his death. He was also a clerk at Eton (1687–1708) but, surprisingly, never held a court appointment.

A service and thirty-nine anthems by Goldwin survive (including twenty-one in Christ Church, Oxford, MS Mus. 94, copied by his colleague, William Isaack), but few were widely known outside Windsor. Although the four modest anthems published in anthologies by Arnold, Boyce, and Page proved popular, the seven works included in Thomas Tudway's manuscript collection better reflect his true abilities (BL, Harley MSS 7341–7342). Goldwin's early, full-choir anthems are characterized by rich scoring and by polyphonic writing which often equals that found in similar works by Purcell. His verse anthems employ more contemporary (though sometimes clichéd) styles; the larger-scale compositions—multi-sectional works with idiomatic organ solos—foreshadow the mid-eighteenth-century 'cantata anthem'. Goldwin, who does not appear to have married, died in 1719, possibly on 7 November, and was buried at Windsor parish church on 10 November.

KERI DEXTER

Sources I. Spink, *Restoration cathedral music, 1660–1714* (1995), 379–86 • chapter acts, 1672–1748, St George's Chapel archives, Windsor, VI.B.4 – VI.B.6 • K. J. Dexter, 'The provision of choral music at St George's Chapel, Windsor Castle, and Eton College, *c.*1640–1733', PhD diss., U. Lond., 2000, 73, 78, 173, 239, 244, 304–5 • audit books, 1678–1715, Eton, archives, ECR 62/13–15 • R. Andrewes, A. Osborne, and L. Smallwood, 'A catalogue of ascribed music in pre-1800 music manuscripts deposited in British libraries' (1981) [microfilm in BL, music reading room] • A. M. Jones, 'The anthems of John Golding, organist and master of the choristers of St George's Chapel in Windsor Castle', MMus diss., Royal Holloway College, Egham, Surrey, 1985 • N. Wridgway, *The choristers of St. George's Chapel* (1980), 47–9 • E. H. Fellowes, *Organists and masters of the choristers of St George's Chapel in Windsor Castle*, new edn [1974], 53–5

Goldwin [Golding], **William** (**1496/7–1562**), schoolmaster, was admitted aged eighteen to King's College, Cambridge, as an Eton scholar, of Dorney near Windsor, on 16 August 1515. He took his BA early in 1520 and proceeded MA three years later, but from 1518 held a fellowship at King's until he returned to Eton College as headmaster for three years from 1525. By an error in the Eton audit books the master appears as John Goldwin, but no contemporary graduate of that name is known. Thus far, William's rise was rapid, but not as prodigious as that of Thomas Wolsey, who at twenty-four had become headmaster of Magdalen College School. In 1528 Wolsey brought Goldwin from Eton to be the first master of the college he was building at Ipswich, his birthplace, with a sister college at Oxford, to outdo Henry VI's and Wykeham's twin foundations. The Cardinal College of St Mary at Ipswich was to be more lavishly staffed than Eton or Winchester. To finance the new foundations Wolsey obtained the king's leave to suppress some dozen minor monastic establishments, mostly in Suffolk.

Goldwin served under William Capon, the college dean, from its opening in September 1528 until its closure after Wolsey's fall at Michaelmas 1530. Ominously the lavish celebrations on Lady day 1528 were completely ruined by atrocious weather. In January 1529 Goldwin, addressing Wolsey once as 'your Majesty', sent him a report in ornate Latin prose, enclosing specimens of the first pupils' writing and praising the worship provided by the dean in the chapel. The college had been using Wolsey's *Rudimenta grammatices et docendi methodus* which he had prescribed, according to its title-page, 'not only for Ipswich, but for all the other schools in England'. Goldwin wrote of 'so plentiful a crop springing up that he did not despair of the harvest'. The pupils were 'all of good intelligence and the flock increased hourly, so that the house was too small to hold them properly' (*LP Henry VIII*, 4/3, no. 5159). When the blow fell the local boys were cast forth, since they and their grammar school's endowments had been swallowed up by the college. Thomas Cromwell, however, persuaded the king to refound the town school and Goldwin stayed on as master, moving back to a fellowship at Eton in 1539. He held several college livings—Mapledurham, Oxfordshire, in 1544–6, Stogursey, Somerset, in 1554–6, and the rectory of Piddlehinton, Dorset—from vacating his fellowship in 1550 until his death on 15 May 1562. It is ironic that his modest locally engraved inscription brass at Piddlehinton is a piece of monastic spoil; palimpsest, its reverse shows the lower half of the figure of a prior with his staff.

J. M. BLATCHLY

Sources W. Sterry, ed., *The Eton College register, 1441–1698* (1943) • *Etoniana*, 35 (1923), 558, 560, 585 • *Etoniana*, 61 (1935), 173 • I. E. Gray and W. E. Potter, *Ipswich School, 1400–1950* (1950) • *LP Henry VIII*, 4/3, no. 5159

Golightly, Charles Pourtalès (**1807–1885**), Church of England clergyman and religious controversialist, born on 23 May 1807, was the second son of William Golightly of Ham, Surrey, and his wife, Frances Dodd. His mother's mother, Aldegunda, was granddaughter of Charles de Pourtalès, a Huguenot. After education at Eton College, which he entered in 1820, he matriculated on 4 March 1824 at Oriel College, Oxford, graduating BA in 1828 and MA in 1830. After ordination, since his private means were thought to disqualify him from a fellowship, he took curacies at Penshurst in Kent and Godalming in Surrey.

In 1836 Golightly was invited by J. H. Newman to take charge of the new chapel being built at Littlemore, near Oxford. However, he withdrew from the scheme later that year after objections raised against one of his sermons by E. B. Pusey led to a dispute with Newman that ended their friendship. Meanwhile he had taken a house at 6 Holywell Street, Oxford, formerly the site of the Cardinal's Cap tavern, and this became his home for nearly fifty years. He held various unremunerated appointments, serving as curate of Headington, vicar of Toot Baldon, and assistant to Walter Hamilton (1808–1869) at St Peter's in the East.

Golightly's main energies, however, were devoted to the vigorous and vigilant defence of traditional high-church principles (he was a fervent admirer of Richard Hooker) against the encroachments of Romanism, and in 1841 he led the outcry provoked by Tract 90, against which he published several pamphlets. In 1858 he distributed a circular letter denouncing the rituals allegedly practised at the recently established theological college at Cuddesdon, near Oxford, seeing this as part of a tendency to 'unprotestantize' the Church of England and 'to sow broadcast the seeds of Popish perversion'. In 1861 he publicly challenged the committee set up at Oxford to raise funds for Lancing College, alleging the adoption at the college of 'Romanistic practices' such as private confession and fasting. In all, Golightly published some ten pamphlets on controversial issues relating to Tractarianism or ritualism. In several controversies he came into conflict with Samuel Wilberforce, bishop of Oxford. When Reginald Wilberforce related these episodes in his biography of his father (1881), Golightly protested at having been misrepresented.

In his later years Golightly became a venerated Oxford relic, famed for his quaint habits and entertaining table talk. A staunch opponent of sacerdotalism, he was respected even by his adversaries for his forthrightness and piety. He was a conscientious pastor, and his private charity was generous and unostentatious. The last three years of his life were disturbed by painful illness. He died at his London address, Brooke House, Upper Clapton, Middlesex, on Christmas day 1885, and was buried in the cemetery at Holywell, near his Oxford home. An auction catalogue of his furniture and valuable library was published in February 1886. G. MARTIN MURPHY

Sources E. M. Goulburn, *Reminiscences of Charles Pourtalès Golightly: a letter reprinted, with additions, from 'The Guardian' newspaper of Jan. 13, 1886* (1886) • J. W. Burgon, *Lives of twelve good men*, new edn (1891), xii–xv • T. Mozley, *Reminiscences, chiefly of Oriel College and the Oxford Movement*, 2 (1882), 108–14 • *The Churchman*, 14 (1886), 70–76 • *The letters and diaries of John Henry Newman*, ed. C. S. Dessain and others, [31 vols.] (1961–), vols. 2–10 • *CGPLA Eng. & Wales* (1886) • *DNB* • O. Chadwick, *The founding of Cuddesdon* (1954) • O. Chadwick, *The Victorian church*, 3rd edn, 1 (1971) • A. Atherstone, 'Charles Golightly (1807–1885), church parties and university politics in Victorian England', DPhil diss., U. Oxf., 2000

Archives LPL, corresp. and notes on Tractarianism | Bodl. Oxf., letters to P. S. Dodd • LPL, letters to Archbishop Tait

Wealth at death £32,784 2*s*. 9*d*.: probate, 8 Feb 1886, *CGPLA Eng. & Wales*

Golla, Frederick Lucien (1877–1968), neuropsychiatrist, was born on 11 August 1877 at 11 Richmond Gardens, Fulham, London, the child of Lucien William Peter Alexander Evasio Golla, a civil engineer, and his wife, Alice Amelia Tingey. His parents were Italian immigrants, his father Lucien having worked as a merchant in Piedmont and Naples before moving to London. Golla was educated at Tonbridge School and Magdalen College, Oxford. Awarded his BA in 1900, he subsequently embarked on medical training at St George's Hospital, London. He graduated BM Ch B (Oxon.) in 1904 and was appointed to house positions at St George's. In 1905 he obtained the position of resident medical officer at Queen Square Hospital, London, where he assisted the neurologists Victor Horsley and Gordon Holmes. This formative experience led to Golla's lifelong interest in the experimental investigation of the nervous system.

In 1908 Golla was appointed assistant physician at St George's. The new position granted him a degree of financial and intellectual independence. In that same year he was able to marry his Belgian fiancée, Thérèse d'Haussaire (*d*. 1917?), with whom he had a daughter, Yolande. Despite his new domestic commitments, Golla found time to start a career in experimental research, carrying out a series of investigations into the antitryptic qualities of tuberculosis serums. Later, in 1910, Golla was provided with bench space at the University College physiological laboratory where, alongside Walter Symes, he studied the effects of adrenaline on respiratory action. During this period Golla maintained his interest in neurology, obtaining new appointments in London at the West End Hospital for Nervous Diseases in 1911 and the Maida Vale Hospital in 1913.

When the First World War broke out Golla immediately volunteered for service. He was commissioned into the sixth London field ambulance of the Royal Army Medical Corps in August 1914 and left for France seven months later. In June 1915 he was invalided out of the army after contracting bronchial pneumonia. Golla was nursed by his wife, Thérèse, who later became fatally infected by the disease herself. By August 1915 Golla was fully recovered and rejoined the Royal Army Medical Corps, being commissioned to the rank of captain. He was appointed to the War Office's tetanus committee under Sir David Bruce, carrying out original research on the relationship between mortality and the incubation rate of the disease. For his part in this research Golla was appointed OBE in 1919. On 3 December 1919 he married Yvonne Lilly Brisco Ray (1881/2–1963), daughter of Francis Brisco Ray, solicitor.

Golla's contribution to the war effort cemented his reputation. At St George's he was promoted to consultant physician, carrying out new research work on nervous conduction in collaboration with Charles Scott Sherrington. At the same time Sir Frederick Mott ensured that the army retained Golla's services. He was employed as a consultant at the Maudsley Neurological Clearing Hospital, where he used galvanic skin-response tests to distinguish between cases of organic shell shock and malingering. His fierce commitment to the material explanation of psychological disorders earned him widespread admiration among conservative élites in psychiatry and medicine. In 1918 Golla was elected a fellow of the Royal College of Physicians, and in 1922 he was invited to give the college's Croonian lectures. Golla chose as his subject 'The objective study of neurosis' and used this opportunity to criticize the new psychological approaches, insisting instead upon the physical basis of personality.

In 1923 Golla was appointed director of the central pathological laboratory at the Maudsley Hospital. The post was enormously influential. The director controlled the educational agenda of the Maudsley medical school and research programme of the London county council's mental hospital laboratories. Golla forged close links with the Rockefeller Foundation and Royal Medico-Psychological Association, setting up postgraduate courses and research fellowships for trainee psychiatrists. During this period he continued his investigations into the physiological concomitants of mental states, developing new techniques in human electromyography and the measurement of nervous conduction. Golla worked closely with junior colleagues. He collaborated with S. Antonovitch and S. A. Mann on the relationship between respiration patterns, psychoses, and mental imagery. He also carried out pioneering work with (William) Grey Walter, on the correlation between EEG rhythms and epilepsy. Golla's achievements were widely recognized: in 1934 he was elected president of the neurology section of the Royal Society of Medicine and in 1937 he was appointed to the chair of mental pathology at the University of London.

In 1939, at the age of sixty-one, Golla took up a new position as director of the newly established Burden Neurological Institute (BNI) in Frenchay, Bristol. The institute was run as a private charity and Golla was granted the freedom to pursue his own research agenda. He quickly established a broad team of young researchers (including Grey Walter) specializing in electrophysiology and endocrinology. Under Golla's direction the institute carried out pioneer work in psychiatric treatment. The first British trials of electroconvulsive therapy were carried out by the BNI in 1939. Likewise the use of leucotomy as a psychosurgical technique was introduced to Britain by the BNI in 1941.

After the war Golla continued to preside over the BNI's innovative research programme in cybernetics and neuropsychiatry. In 1949 he was elected president of both the Society for the Study of Addiction and the newly formed Electroencephalographic Society. In 1959, at the age of eighty-one, Golla finally relinquished his directorship of the BNI. Following his retirement he maintained an active interest in contemporary developments in neuropsychiatry. Golla died of heart failure at his home, Newlands, Frenchay, on 6 February 1968.

RHODRI HAYWARD

Sources R. Cooper and J. Bird, *The Burden: fifty years of clinical and experimental neuroscience at the Burden Neurological Institute* (1989) • J. M. Bird, 'The father of psychophysiology: Professor F. L. Golla and the Burden Neurological Institute', *150 years of British psychiatry*, ed. H. Freeman and G. E. Berrios, 2 (1996), 500–16 • *The Lancet* (17 Feb 1968), 367–8 • *BMJ* (2 March 1968), 384 • Munk, *Roll* • *WWW* • b. cert. • m. cert. [Yvonne Ray] • d. cert. • PRO, WO 374/27849 • *The Times* (18 Feb 1968) • *Medical Directory*

Archives Rockefeller Archive Center, Sleepy Hollow, New York, Rockefeller Foundation papers • Sci. Mus., Burden Neurological Institute papers

Likenesses photograph, repro. in Cooper and Bird, *The Burden*

Wealth at death £21,980: probate, 7 April 1968, *CGPLA Eng. & Wales*

Gollan, John (1911–1977), communist leader and author, was born at Stephenlaws Close, 132 High Street, Edinburgh, on 2 April 1911, the third of eight children of Duncan Gollan (1879/80–1958), a painter and decorator, and his wife, Mary, *née* Dunn (1884/5–1951). His parents were both Scottish working-class socialists. He attended James Clark School, Edinburgh, which he had to leave before he was fourteen to work for his father, who taught him his trade. In 1926 he took part in the general strike selling strike bulletins. The next year he joined the Communist Party and the Young Communist League (YCL). In May 1931

John Gollan (1911–1977), by unknown photographer

he was arrested for distributing anti-militarist propaganda to soldiers in Edinburgh and in July sentenced to six months' imprisonment.

Following his release Gollan moved to London to edit the YCL's paper, the *Young Worker*. In 1935 he became the YCL's national secretary at a time when the international communist movement was launching a new policy of working-class and popular unity against fascism. The same year he spoke as a representative of the Young Communist International at the Seventh Congress of the Communist International in Moscow. He stressed the need 'to overcome our sectarian isolation and unite masses of youth in opposition to war' (*International Press Correspondence*, 11 Jan 1936, 79). On his initiative as leader of the YCL in the next four years there developed an exceptionally wide co-operation of youth organizations, united in the British Youth Peace Assembly. This unity, to which the demand for collective security to check axis aggression was crucial, was effectively undermined in October 1939 when the YCL joined the Communist Party in opposing the war. This new line, initiated in Moscow, was accepted by Gollan, but with serious reservations expressed that month at a stormy meeting of the Communist Party's central committee, on which he had sat since 1935.

In February 1940 Gollan transferred from the YCL to directly Communist Party work. From 1940 to 1941 he was secretary of its north-east district committee, and from 1941 to 1947 of its Scottish committee, experiencing an important growth in membership and popularity during the period of the wartime alliance with the Soviet Union.

In 1947 he moved to London to act as assistant secretary of the Communist Party until 1949, assistant editor of the *Daily Worker* from 1949 to 1954, and the Communist Party's national organizer from 1954 to 1956. In May 1956 he took over from Harry Pollitt as the party's general secretary, a position which he held until 1975.

Gollan became general secretary in the midst of a party crisis unleashed by Khrushchov's revelations about Stalin at the Twentieth Congress of the Soviet Communist Party in February 1956. This was inflamed by the Soviet military intervention in Hungary that autumn, which Gollan defended. He resisted demands for a thoroughgoing critique of Stalinism and of the persistence of authoritarian structures and practices in the USSR. However, over time he was to develop a more critical approach. In 1964 he voiced 'widespread and deep' concern at the removal of Khrushchov without any public explanation (*Daily Worker*, 24 Oct 1964). From 1966 he publicly criticized the use of repressive measures against Soviet dissidents. In August 1968 he successfully moved a resolution in his party's executive committee deeply deploring the Soviet-led military intervention in Czechoslovakia. In 1976 he published a long article in *Marxism Today* entitled 'Socialist democracy—some problems'. His critical treatment in it of important aspects of Soviet practice aroused fierce objections from a hard-line minority in his party—and its excision from Soviet subscribers' copies of *Marxism Today*.

Between 1956 and 1958 the membership of the Communist Party had fallen from 33,095 to 24,670. Gollan set a prime objective of making good this loss. He led his party in vigorous campaigning around political and industrial demands and peace issues, envisaging a united struggle to turn Labour and Britain to the left. The party's membership was built back to over 30,000 in the 1960s. However, the target of 50,000 members, which he advanced as the next stage at the 1963 party congress, proved quite unrealistic, and after 1964 an almost unbroken membership decline set in. His efforts to build up the party's electoral support also failed.

It was revealed in 1991 that, unknown to the leading bodies of his party, Gollan secretly negotiated with Soviet Communist leaders for the Communist Party of Great Britain to receive from 1958 annual subsidies to make good the financial losses it sustained from 1956. These continued throughout the remainder of his general secretaryship.

Gollan's intellectual interests were reflected in his books, which were always carefully researched. In 1937 the Left Book Club published his *Youth in British Industry*. In 1948 appeared his *Scottish Prospect*. In 1954 he wrote *The British Political System*, designed to underpin his party's long-term programme, *The British Road to Socialism*, in the drafting of the five editions of which (1951–78) he played an important part. From the 1930s until the 1970s he also wrote a very large number of pamphlets, articles, essays, and reports.

Gollan was an energetic and intense man of small build and frail appearance with a wry smile. He was a fluent, accomplished, and often witty speaker, who enjoyed respect for his intelligence and integrity. However he lacked the warmth and rapport with people and audiences that distinguished his predecessor, Harry Pollitt. His main relaxation was climbing the mountains of his native Scotland. He married in 1939 Elsie Hilda Medland (1914–1996), a medical secretary and comrade in the communist movement. They had a son and a daughter. He died of lung cancer at his home, 1 Bramshill Mansions, Dartmouth Park Hill, London, on 5 September 1977 and was cremated at Golders Green on 12 September.

MONTY JOHNSTONE

Sources M. Kettle, biography of John Gollan, People's History Museum, Manchester, Communist Party archive • John Gollan's personal and political MSS, People's History Museum, Manchester, Communist Party archive • personal knowledge (2004) • private information (2004) • 'CPGB: cash from Moscow', *Changes* (15 Nov 1991) • R. Falber, *The 1968 Czechoslovak crisis: inside the British communist party* (1996) • *Official reports of communist party congresses*, 1957–75 • F. King and G. Matthews, eds., *About turn: the British communist party and the Second World War* (1990), 216–24 • H. Pelling, *The British communist party: a historical profile*, new edn (1975), 193 [membership figures] • J. Gollan, *Daily Worker* (24 Oct 1964) [on Khrushchev's removal] • *International Press Correspondence* (11 Jan 1936), 79 [J. Gollan's speech at Seventh Congress of Communist International] • 'YCL leaders for party', *Challenge* (8 Feb 1940) • *The Times* (6 Sept 1977) • *DNB* • *Morning Star* (6 Sept 1977)

Archives People's History Museum, Manchester, Communist Party archive, documents in international department collection, incl. notes on international communist conferences and discussions with Khrushchev, Mao, etc. • People's History Museum, Manchester, Communist Party archive, material in secretarial papers • People's History Museum, Manchester, Communist Party archive, personal and political papers, incl. file relating to China, reports, typescript articles, and speeches | FILM Educational and Television Films Ltd, London, films, incl. 1966 general election television broadcast | SOUND BL NSA, recorded lecture • BL NSA, party political footage (Communist Party)

Likenesses photograph, 1970, Hult. Arch. • photograph, People's History Museum, Manchester [*see illus.*]

Gollancz, Sir Hermann (1852–1930), rabbi and Semitic scholar, was born at Bremen on 30 November 1852, the eldest son of Rabbi Samuel Marcus Gollancz, minister of the Hambro Synagogue, then in Leadenhall Street, London, and his wife, Johanna Koppell. He had three sisters and three brothers, his youngest brother being Sir Israel *Gollancz (1863–1930). At the age of ten he passed from the Whitechapel foundation school to the school attached to the Jews' College, then in Finsbury Square; he entered the Jews' College itself and also University College, London, in 1869. He graduated BA with honours in classics and philosophy in 1873, and MA in Hebrew, Syriac, and German in 1889, while also broadening his intellectual horizon by attending lectures in other disciplines (including physics).

From 1872 to 1876 Gollancz assisted his father at the Hambro Synagogue as assistant preacher. Thereafter he was preacher successively at several London synagogues and minister at Manchester (1882–5) and Dalston (1885–92). Gollancz married in 1884 Thérèse, daughter of Samuel Henry Wilner, merchant, of Manchester, and they had three sons. In 1892 he succeeded the chief rabbi, Hermann

Adler, as first minister at the Bayswater Synagogue, Harrow Road, where he remained, completing in 1923 a then unique record of fifty-one years' service in the Anglo-Jewish ministry.

Gollancz's main work falls under three heads, pastoral, scholarly, and philanthropic. His congregations naturally had the first claim on his energies, but he undertook many duties outside his parish and worked zealously for the foundation of new synagogues at South Hackney, New Cross, Walthamstow, Reading, Hanley, Hull, Sunderland, and Cardiff.

In 1897 Gollancz obtained the rabbinic diploma. Hitherto the requirements for the rabbinic diploma, which any qualified rabbi could grant to a suitable candidate, had not been definitely specified in England, where the degree had, in fact, never been conferred since the Jewish resettlement in the seventeenth century. Gollancz had therefore to go abroad (to Galicia) to obtain it but Hermann Adler felt that the time was not yet opportune for increasing the number of qualified rabbis in England. The Anglo-Jewish clergy had consisted hitherto of rabbis and precentors (*chazanim*), and the sermon was not a regular institution in every synagogue. Adler considered that the status of minister-preacher, a comparatively recent innovation, needed a further period of development before minister-preachers should attain to full rabbinic status. He therefore refused to recognize Gollancz's rabbinic credentials and an acrimonious controversy began in the *Jewish Chronicle*. The questions at issue were not merely personal, two matters of principle being involved. First, should the rabbinic diploma be given in England? Secondly, should rabbinic diplomas gained abroad be recognized in England? The reasoned arguments of 'Historicus' (Israel Gollancz) stated the case for an enlarged rabbinate so cogently that in the end Adler gave way. Hermann Gollancz was publicly recognized as rabbi and the requirements of Hebrew and rabbinics necessary to obtain the diploma of rabbi in England were formally defined, thanks to the arduous struggle carried on by Gollancz and his brother Israel in the face of great opposition and much personal inconvenience.

Adler died in 1911. Gollancz's claims to succeed him as chief rabbi were overruled by the imperative need for a younger man to fill the position, and he remained at the Bayswater Synagogue for another eleven years. He published in 1915 a special translation of a work by Joseph Kimhi under the title *Foundation of Religious Fear*, of which he presented in 1918 an edition of 10,000 copies for the use of members of the Jewish faith in the British forces. His wife received the Belgian order of Queen Elisabeth in recognition of her war work.

Gollancz undertook much public work outside the special interests of the Jewish community. In 1880, in conjunction with Rabbi Samuel Augustus Barnett, he promoted the first of the Whitechapel loan exhibitions. He took part in the several movements which secured Clissold Park as an open space (1888), created the North London Technical Institute (1889), and saved Moyse's Hall, Bury St Edmunds (1896). He served on the royal commissions which inquired into the birth rate (1913–16) and the cinema (1917), and on the special committee appointed to report on venereal disease and adolescence (1920–21). He was vice-president and treasurer of the National Council of Public Morals and vice-chairman of the Paddington Social Service Council. In 1917 he received an illuminated address, signed by representatives of many educational and philanthropic bodies, on the occasion of his completing forty-five years of service as a Jewish minister and public worker.

Gollancz, who in 1899 became the first Jew to obtain the degree of DLitt of London University, was elected in 1902 Goldsmid professor of Hebrew at University College, London, in succession to Solomon Schechter. On his retirement in 1923 the senate of the university accorded him the title of emeritus professor, and in order to commemorate his twenty-one years' tenure of the chair of Hebrew he presented his valuable library of *Hebraica* and *Judaica* to University College; he had previously been largely responsible for the acquisition by University College of the library of Jewish history bequeathed to public use in 1905 by Frederic David Mocatta. Gollancz was president of the Jewish Drama League, of the Jewish Historical Society (1905), and of the Union of Jewish Literary Societies (1925–6). In 1922 he celebrated his golden jubilee and was the recipient of many marks of esteem. In 1923 he was knighted, being the first British rabbi to receive this honour. The close of Gollancz's life was saddened by domestic sorrows. In September 1929 he lost successively his youngest son, Leonard, his wife, and his sister Emma within ten days; his brother Israel died in June of the next year. Gollancz died in London on 15 October 1930.

Gollancz's literary output was very great. Besides extensive translations from Hebrew and Aramaic texts, his work comprised contributions to Jewish history as well as sermons and addresses. His record of public service and of scholarly achievement engendered in him a self-importance that was regarded indulgently by his contemporaries. By allowing it to find expression in print in his *Personalia* (1928), and *Contribution to the History of University College London* (1930), he possibly did his posthumous reputation a disservice. H. M. J. Loewe, *rev.*

Sources H. Gollancz, *Personalia* (1928) • *CGPLA Eng. & Wales* (1931) • *WWW* • *The Times* (16 Oct 1930) • C. Roth, ed., *Encyclopaedia Judaica*, 16 vols. (Jerusalem, 1971–2)

Wealth at death £868 19*s.* 6*d.*: resworn administration, 8 April 1931, *CGPLA Eng. & Wales*

Gollancz, Sir Israel (1863–1930), literary scholar, the fourth and youngest son of the six children of Rabbi Samuel Marcus Gollancz (1820–1900), cantor of the Hambro Synagogue, London, and his wife, Johanna Koppell, was born at 15A Bury Street, London, on 13 July 1863. His eldest brother was Sir Hermann *Gollancz (1852–1930), Goldsmid professor of Hebrew at University College, London. Brought up an Orthodox Jew, Israel Gollancz was educated at the City of London School, at University College, London, and at Christ's College, Cambridge, where he was a scholar (1883–7). After taking his degree (1887) with a second class in the medieval and modern languages tripos, he lectured for some years in English at Cambridge before the establishment of a school of English there, and in 1896 was appointed the first lecturer in English at the university. In 1892 he had been appointed Quain English student and lecturer at University College, London, and this post he held until 1895. In 1903 Gollancz was appointed to the chair of English language and literature at King's College, London, a post which he held until his death. In 1906 he resigned his Cambridge appointment, and on leaving Cambridge took the degree of LittD.

In his new post it fell to Gollancz to supervise and direct the development of the English department of the University of London from a small and relatively unimportant faculty to one of the principal faculties of the university. In 1910 Gollancz was selected as one of the first two recipients of the Albert Kahn travelling fellowships, but was unable to take up the award. On 5 July of the same year he married the artist Alide Goldschmidt, daughter of Abraham Baruch Goldschmidt; they had one son and one daughter. In 1919 he was elected a corresponding member of the Real Academia Española, and in 1927 of the Medieval Academy of America. He was also Leofric lecturer in Old English at University College, Exeter, honorary director of the Early English Text Society (EETS), president of the Philological Society, chairman of the Shakespeare Association, an honorary freeman of the Stationers' Company, and honorary secretary of the Shakespeare Tercentenary Committee (1916).

Apart, however, from his literary work and teaching, Gollancz is best known in connection with the British Academy, of which he was one of the founders and original fellows, as well as secretary from its formation in 1902 until his death. To his initiative as secretary of the academy was largely owing the foundation of the Schweich lectures, the Cervantes chair of Spanish, and the Camoens chair of Portuguese at King's College, London, and the British School of Archaeology in Jerusalem. In the words of F. G. Kenyon, 'the whole Academy for the first thirty years of its existence is in a sense his memorial, and he would have desired no better one' (Kenyon, 438).

Another of Gollancz's special interests was the project for a national theatre. He was honorary secretary of the committee whose task it was to frame a scheme for the foundation and endowment of such a theatre. He also organized the first Anglo-American conference of professors of English in London in 1921, and two years later headed the English delegation to the similar conference in New York. He took advantage of his visit to America in that year to lecture at several American universities.

As an English and Shakespearian scholar Gollancz was in the first rank. His first publication, an edition of the early English poem *Pearl*, appeared in 1891, dedicated to W. W. Skeat, Gollancz's Cambridge mentor. The editorial methodology follows that of Skeat, with arbitrary emendations, and direct interference with textual accidentals. Gollancz's object was to seek readers outside a limited circle of specialists. In 1892 appeared Cynewulf's *Christ*, an Old English religious poem in three parts, and in 1895 *The Exeter Book of Anglo-Saxon Poetry*, noteworthy for its use of primary sources. Other publications of his include *The Parlement of the Three Ages* (1897); *The Tragical History of Doctor Faustus* (1897); *Hamlet in Iceland* (1898); *The Quatrefoil of Love* (1901); Boccaccio's *Olympia* (1913); *Ich dene: some observations on a manuscript of the life and feats of arms of Edward, prince of Wales* (1921), reflecting Gollancz's desire to remove German militaristic associations from the motto; *The Sources of Hamlet* (1926); and *The Caedmon Manuscript of Anglo-Saxon Biblical Poetry* (on the occasion of the twenty-fifth anniversary of the British Academy, 1927). In 1893 he issued *Charles Lamb's Specimens of English Dramatic Poets*, and in 1916 he edited *The Book of Homage to Shakespeare*. Gollancz was also the general editor of the Temple Shakespeare, the Temple Classics, begun in the nineties and part of his attempt to popularize Shakespeare and other classics, the King's Library, the King's Novels, the Medieval Library, and the *Shakespeare Survey*.

One of Gollancz's most useful contributions to medieval studies, a facsimile edition of *Pearl*, *Cleanness*, *Patience*, and *Sir Gawain*, appeared in 1923. For the first time the four poems of the manuscript (BL, MS Cotton Nero fl.x) appeared together and were made available to a wider audience. Guided by Mabel Day, several of Gollancz's works were published posthumously. These included the EETS *The Quatrefoil of Love* (1935), and the still frequently cited 1940 EETS *Sir Gawain*, begun by Gollancz and completed by Day.

In the Anglo-Jewish community, of which he was one of the most distinguished members of his generation, Gollancz interested himself specially in the training and qualification of rabbis. To this he devoted himself on the council of the Jews' College, the Anglo-Jewish theological seminary of which he was a member for many years; the curriculum for the rabbinical diploma granted by that institution was to a large extent his work. He was the second president of the Union of Jewish Literary Societies, and he also served for a term as president of the Maccabaeans and honorary president of the Inter-University Jewish Federation attempting to unite disparate factions. He also guided Jewish boys at Harrow School, preparing them for bar mitzvah and biblical studies.

Gollancz won wide recognition for his scholarship both at home and abroad, and was knighted in 1919. He was an excellent lecturer, and his charm of manner, his readiness to help other scholars, his willingness to revise his own work and recant previous opinions, and his fondness for children, brought him many friends. In later life his bald head, spectacles, and thick moustache conveyed a benign, distinguished presence. He died at his home at 15 Shoot Up Hill, Cricklewood, London, on 23 June 1930, and a lectureship was founded at the British Academy in his memory. His wife survived him.

A. M. Hyamson, *rev.* William Baker

Sources *The Times* (24 June 1930) · F. G. Kenyon, 'Sir Israel Gollancz', *PBA*, 16 (1930), 424–38 · *Jewish Guardian* (27 June 1930) · *Jewish Chronicle* (27 June 1930), 13 · R. D. Edwards, *Victor Gollancz: a biography* (1987), 29, 31, 32, 51 · N. Clifton, 'Sir Israel Gollancz',

Twentieth-century British book collectors and bibliographers, ed. W. Baker and K. Womack, DLitB, 201 (1999) • P. F. Reichardt, 'Sir Israel Gollancz and the editorial history of the Pearl manuscript', *Papers on Language & Literature*, 31 (1995), 145–63 • S. Trigg, 'Israel Gollancz's "Wynnere and Wastoure": political satire or editorial politics', *Medieval English religious and ethical literature: essays in honour of G. H. Russell*, ed. G. Kratzmann and J. Simpson (1986), 115–27 • A. Lindley, 'Pinning Gawain down: the misediting of *Sir Gawain and the Green Knight*', *JEGP: Journal of English and Germanic Philology*, 96 (1997), 26–42 • *CGPLA Eng. & Wales* (1930) • b. cert. • m. cert. • d. cert.

Archives LUL, letters to Austin Dobson • UCL, letters to Moses Gaster

Likenesses W. Stoneman, photograph, 1918, NPG • C. L. Hartwell, bronze bust, British Academy

Wealth at death £30,415 3*s*. 3*d*.: probate, 11 July 1930, *CGPLA Eng. & Wales*

Gollancz, Sir Victor (1893–1967), publisher and writer, was born on 9 April 1893 at 256 Elgin Avenue, Maida Vale, London, the youngest of the three children of Alexander Gollancz (1854–1933) and his wife, Helena Michaelson. His father, a jeweller of Polish descent, was the brother of Sir Hermann Gollancz (1852–1930) and Sir Israel Gollancz (1863–1930). Gollancz was a foundation scholar of St Paul's School and later a scholar of New College, Oxford, where he won the chancellor's prize for Latin prose and obtained a first in classical moderations (1913).

When war broke out in 1914 Gollancz was unable to enlist because of bad eyesight, but in the spring of 1915 he joined the Officers' Training Corps and was commissioned in the Northumberland Fusiliers. In the following year he was seconded to Repton School as classics master with a commission in the Officers' Training Corps, and thus began one of the happiest periods of his life. As he writes in *My Dear Timothy* (1952), his discursive autobiographical letter to his first grandson, from about the age of seven he had been a liberal, rejecting the narrow Jewish orthodoxy of his parents. His father's anti-feminism also made him a fervent advocate of women's rights. He passionately believed in the 'free, spontaneous, self-directing development of the life and spirit in every human person' (Gollancz, *My Dear Timothy*, 41). Repton gave him an opportunity to move, in his role of teacher, beyond the confines of the curriculum into the wider world of politics, social justice, and similar issues, and he found the eager response of the boys intoxicating. Together with his colleague David Somervell he broke new ground by starting a civics class; he also founded a political magazine, *The Pubber*. However, in the context of the war the gust of fresh air and free thought which he introduced into the school alarmed the authorities, and in 1918 the headmaster (Geoffrey Fisher, later archbishop of Canterbury), was persuaded to dismiss him.

On 22 July 1919 Gollancz married Ruth Lowy (1892–1975), a gifted artist and one of the first four women to be admitted to the Architectural Association. She was also very beautiful (Gollancz had a great love for beauty in all its forms). They had five daughters. The marriage was a very happy one, not least because Ruth Gollancz was an unwavering supporter of her husband in all his activities.

Two years after his marriage Gollancz joined the publishing firm of Benn Brothers, nominally to develop the

Sir Victor Gollancz (1893–1967), by unknown photographer

technical book department. But for a man of his gifts and energy such limits were unthinkable, and soon the list was expanded to include sumptuous art books, poetry, a Sixpenny Series designed to give information on a broad spectrum of topics, and an excellent general list.

In 1927 Gollancz left Benn to start his own firm, bringing out his first book in 1928. His publishing methods were revolutionary. In collaboration with Stanley Morison, he devised a striking typographical dust jacket featuring black and magenta on a brilliant yellow background, which was used on most of his titles. His eye-catching advertising was equally successful. Jackets and advertising were among the most influential and successful innovations in English publishing in the twentieth century, for, although typographical jackets had been used since the turn of the century, those of Gollancz, with their strident colours and bold lettering, stood out in the bookshops in a way that made the books difficult to ignore.

Gollancz, however, was all his life primarily an educationist, and his main concern as a publisher was to disseminate an awareness of current affairs, and above all the message of socialism—for, although he never abandoned his liberalism, he had by now moved more to the left. Nevertheless, a shrewd businessman, he knew that he would only be able to publish the books that were important to him if his firm was financially sound; so he first built up a general list which included some of the best-selling and most prestigious writers of the day. He also broke new ground with the publication of omnibus volumes at very low prices on politics and philosophy, and of collections of novels and plays. Among them were G. D. H. Cole's *The Intelligent Man's Guide through World Chaos* (672 pages, which sold for 5*s.*), *The Stories of Robert Louis Stevenson* (1120 pages for 7*s.* 6*d.*), and *An Outline for Boys and Girls and their Parents* (800 pages of text and 200 illustrations for 8*s.* 6*d.*) 'It can thus be said', wrote Sir Robert Lusty, himself one of the leading publishers of the mid-twentieth century, 'that Victor Gollancz deployed all the necessary [publishing] skills with a brilliance unequalled then and certainly a million light years beyond the reach of any visible aspirant today. In his day VG was unique' (*Books and Bookmen*, June 1978, 24–5).

A significant new venture was the foundation of the Left Book Club in 1936 with the aim of combating the menace of Nazism and fascism. This initiative reflected, and was part of, the Popular Front movement of the thirties, in which all progressive groups united to oppose the threat posed by Hitler. It was the first modern book club to be established in Britain. The books chosen were published simultaneously in an edition for the general public and in a special 2*s.* 6*d.* edition for club members—half or a third of the normal price. They were supplied through bookshops and not direct to members, unlike the books of the many clubs which soon followed Gollancz's example. At its peak the club had 57,000 members, but the actual readership was many times larger, and the 1500 discussion groups all over the country played an active role in carrying out the club's aims. There were summer schools, political-educational classes, lectures, film shows, theatrical productions, specialist groups from many professions, and three huge annual rallies addressed by eminent public figures—the last of them, in 1939, before an audience of 10,000. The membership extended beyond Britain to many other parts of the world. Although some of the books were ephemeral, many were written by prominent and influential writers of the thirties, such as Arthur Koestler and George Orwell. The club helped to shape the political thinking of a generation of left-wing people in Britain—not least of a large number of people who were new to politics. Many people believed that it had a considerable influence in bringing about the Labour Party's landslide victory in 1945. But after the war, with the struggle against Nazism at an end and a socialist government in power, the club lost its *raison d'être*, and the last book was published in 1948—still at the original price of 2*s.* 6*d.*

Once his firm was established on a solid basis, Gollancz threw himself with tireless and formidable energy into a succession of humanitarian and political causes. Among the many movements which he was instrumental in founding, or in which he was involved, were the National Committee for Rescue from Nazi Terror (1943), Christian Action (1946), the Jewish Society for Human Service (1948), and the Association for World Peace (1951). But perhaps the three closest to his heart were Save Europe Now, a scheme that he inaugurated in 1945 for sending food to starving Germans after the war; the Campaign for Nuclear Disarmament (1958), in which he was closely involved with Canon John Collins and his wife, Diana; and the movement for the abolition of capital punishment (1955).

When the Labour Party came to power in 1945 Gollancz hoped he would be able to continue his political work through a post in the government, but probably he was regarded as too controversial to be a good party man. He was in any case disillusioned by what he regarded as the materialistic orientation of the Labour Party. He was by now a convinced pacifist, and described himself as Judaeo-Christian (though he was always intensely conscious of his Jewish roots). Increasingly he turned from politics to philosophical and spiritual issues: *My Dear Timothy* and a later volume, *More for Timothy* (1953), reflect both this development and the breadth of his reading, as do his two religious anthologies, *A Year of Grace* (1950) and *From Darkness to Light* (1956).

Music was a constant joy from the time when, as a schoolboy, Gollancz rushed off from St Paul's every afternoon to climb the stairs to the balcony of Covent Garden opera house. Opera and chamber music were especially important, as he writes in *Journey towards Music* (1964) and *The Ring at Bayreuth* (1966). His publishing list contained a number of excellent books on music. He was also interested in English pottery, and, with his wife, built up a unique private collection. He wrote over thirty books and pamphlets, beginning—characteristically, in view of his support of women's rights—with *The Making of Women* in 1917: most of them reinforced whatever political or social cause he happened to be espousing at the moment.

In appearance Gollancz was sturdily built, but until late in life his movements were quick and vigorous. He stood out in any gathering not least for his physical presence and the force with which he expressed his convictions. Both as a teacher and as a speaker he was spellbinding; he sometimes said of himself that he had a *mana*, a power to influence people, and this he used to great effect not only in the many causes for which he worked but also in his publishing strategy. He claimed—with justice—that he could sell by the thousands books which in other hands would have been failures. But he never allowed commercial considerations to override his ethical convictions; he rejected, for instance, George Orwell's *Animal Farm* because he thought it would damage relations with the Soviet Union, at that time Britain's ally in the war against Hitler. Similarly, he published books which, though not viable financially, he believed to be valuable from a social or ethical point of view.

Possessed of a formidable intellect, Gollancz was also a man of strong opinions who saw people and issues in terms of black and white. Reactions to him were equally extreme, varying from dislike of his egotism and his uncompromising attitude towards those who did not agree with him to admiration for his achievements on behalf of the underdog. Disconcertingly, he could from day to day be parsimonious and almost recklessly generous, kind and harsh, compassionate and judgemental. He was rarely able to control his strong emotions, whether good or bad, of joy or of anger. But he was deeply aware of his shortcomings, and constantly sought the road of goodness. He had a lively sense of fun, and one endearing characteristic was an inexhaustible stock of Jewish jokes, which he told with immense gusto. He was a man of contrasts, but above all he was life-enhancing.

Although, as he grew older, Gollancz found the daily round of publishing distasteful and increasingly difficult, he could not bring himself to relinquish control of the firm over which he had presided since its inception. So he carried on until he had a stroke in 1966, when his eldest daughter, Livia, became governing director. Even then he tried to remain involved, until a second stroke six months afterwards proved fatal. He died at his home, 90 Eaton Place, London, on 8 February 1967 and was buried two days later at Golders Green crematorium, London.

During his lifetime Gollancz had received several honours, including the grand cross of the German order of merit (1953); an honorary doctorate in laws from Trinity College, Dublin (1960); and the peace prize of the German book trade (1960). He was knighted in 1965.

SHEILA HODGES

Sources *The Times* (9 Feb 1967) · R. D. Edwards, *Victor Gollancz* (1987) · S. Hodges, *Gollancz: the story of a publishing house* (1978) · V. Gollancz, *My dear Timothy* (1952) · V. Gollancz, *More for Timothy* (1953) · V. Gollancz, *Journey towards music* (1964) · *WW* · personal knowledge (2004) · private information (2004) · *DNB*

Archives U. Warwick Mod. RC, corresp. and papers, literary papers · Victor Gollancz Ltd | BL, corresp. with Albert Mansbridge, Add. MS 65259 · Bodl. Oxf., corresp. with Viscount Addison, corresp. with R. B. Montgomery; corresp. with Gilbert Murray · King's Lond., Liddell Hart C., corresp. with Sir B. H. Liddell Hart · NRA, priv. coll., corresp. with John Strachey · People's History Museum, Manchester, corresp. with R. Palme Dutt · U. Southampton L., corresp. with Hugh Harris; corresp. with James Parkes · U. Sussex Library, corresp. with B. W. Levy | SOUND BBC Sound Archive

Likenesses R. Gollancz, portraits, priv. coll. · F. Topolski, engraving, NPG · photograph, NPG [*see illus.*] · photographs, Victor Gollancz Ltd, London

Wealth at death £28,603: probate, 8 May 1967, *CGPLA Eng. & Wales*

Golombek, Harry (1911–1995), chess player and writer on chess, was born on 1 March 1911 at 200 Railton Road, Herne Hill, London, the younger son in the family of two sons and three daughters of Barnet Golombek (1877/8–1943), a successful grocer, and his wife, Emma Sendak (*d.* 1967). All Golombek's grandparents came from a small Jewish community near Warsaw, migrating to England about 1903. Golombek won a scholarship to Wilson's Grammar School, Camberwell, where his ability at chess (first taught to him by his brother) became evident, as did a strong facility at languages and mathematics. His school won the London schools' team championship and in 1929 Golombek won the second London boys' championship (after finishing last the previous year). Golombek also began, but did not complete, a general degree at King's College, London, leaving in 1932.

For many decades Golombek was a fixture on the British chess scene. He played for England at nine chess olympiads (three times before the Second World War—Warsaw 1935, Stockholm 1937, and Buenos Aires 1939) down to 1962, and captained the English team five times between 1952 and 1962. He became British champion three times, in 1947, 1949, and 1955, the last occasion at the relatively late age (for a chess champion) of forty-four. He lost the 1959 championship following a play-off. He also won a number of small international tournaments both before and after the war, such as Antwerp 1938, and Baarn 1948. In international chess, his greatest moment probably came with his very creditable result in the Bad Pyrmont zonal tournament of 1951, making him the first British player to qualify for the inter-zonal phase of the world championship round. He continued to play in chess tournaments until his seventies, tying for first place in the British veterans' championship in 1984. At the very highest level of international grandmaster play, however, it is clear that he could seldom successfully compete, although on a good day he could beat almost anyone.

Golombek's chess career was interrupted by the Second World War. Joining the Royal Artillery, with his linguistic and analytical gifts he (like other leading British chess players) was a natural candidate for Bletchley Park and the efforts by Britain's top code-breakers to crack the German military code with Enigma. At Bletchley he often played chess against Alan Turing, giving him queen odds but still beating him comfortably.

In 1945 Golombek again became a full-time chess player and writer, and in the latter capacity was for over thirty years probably the best-known writer on chess in the country. British chess at this time was in a paradoxical state. Britain had not produced a world championship contender for sixty years nor, indeed, many players of true international stature. Yet a flourishing chess scene existed, with many clubs, an excellent chess press, and a record of hosting some of the most notable chess tournaments of the previous half-century. The failure to produce many top-flight players was due, as much as anything, to the meagre rewards attainable in chess, and to the unfortunate image of chess in the popular mind as a game for prodigies and elderly eccentric savants. In the 1970s, however, a 'British chess explosion' occurred, with England producing large numbers of highly talented younger players second to few countries in the world. Golombek's efforts as a chess writer and activist in popularizing chess and raising its visibility were responsible in significant measure for this improvement.

In 1945 Golombek became *The Times*'s chess correspondent, holding that position until his resignation in 1985, following a stroke the previous year. In addition, he wrote a weekly chess column for *The Observer* between 1955 and 1979, and was closely connected with the *British Chess Magazine*, briefly serving as its editor in 1938–40. From 1949 until 1967 he was the magazine's games and overseas editor. An excellent and often memorable prose stylist, he wrote, edited, or translated more than thirty books on chess, ranging from the enormously popular *The Game of Chess* (1954), for novices, to an *Encyclopedia of Chess* (1977). In contrast to accounts of more recent world championship matches by later writers, often pot-boilers which appeared as soon as the contest ended, Golombek's books on the 1948, 1954, and 1957 championship events were careful works of lasting value. Arguably his best works were his biographical games collections of the great Cuban world champion, *Capablanca's Hundred Best Games of Chess* (1947), which was widely praised, and *Réti's Best Games of Chess* (1954), the only English-language account of the seminal Czech player and theorist, which Golombek regarded as his favourite book. He was also a regular contributor, between 1958 and 1964, to the BBC's *Radio Chess Magazine*, broadcasting on personalities of modern chess, a series which made the history and lore of chess known to thousands of listeners.

Golombek also enjoyed a distinguished career as a chess official and administrator. From 1952 until 1985 he served on the rules commission of FIDE, the international chess federation, which is responsible for the rules of chess, and was the British delegate to FIDE's annual conferences for most of this period. He served as official arbiter at many international tournaments and at six world championship matches in the 1950s and 1960s. All these matches took place in the Soviet Union between Soviet grandmasters, and Golombek's appointment, at the height of the cold war, was a remarkable one, and a tribute to his reputation for integrity. He was awarded the title of international master by FIDE in 1950 and of international arbiter in 1954. At the end of his career, in 1985, he was also given the title of international grandmaster emeritus. In 1966 he was appointed OBE, the first such appointment for 'services to chess'.

With a prominent nose and ears, Golombek was instantly recognizable. Apart from chess, he had a wide range of interests, especially in music, theatre, opera, and ballet. He collected a large and diverse library, and his important holding of chess books went, after his death, to the University of Kent. Many spoke highly of the kindness and encouragement he showed to younger players, and he left nearly two-fifths of his estate to further the encouragement of chess in Britain. While some critics regarded his writings as egocentric and opinionated, no one questioned his important role in the development of British chess. From 1944 he lived in Chalfont St Giles, Buckinghamshire. He died on 7 January 1995 in Dawn House residential home, South Park Crescent, Gerrards Cross, Buckinghamshire. Hitherto a lifelong bachelor, he quickly separated after a brief marriage contracted in the late 1980s.

W. D. RUBINSTEIN

Sources *The Times* (9 Jan 1995) • *The Independent* (10 Jan 1995) • D. Hooper and K. Whyld, *The Oxford companion to chess*, 2nd edn (1996) • private information (2004) [K. Bligh, E. G. Winter, K. Whyld] • b. cert. • m. cert. • d. cert.

Likenesses photograph, repro. in *The Times* • photograph, repro. in *The Independent*

Wealth at death £92,221: probate, 22 March 1995, *CGPLA Eng. & Wales*

Gomeldon [*née* Middleton], **Jane** (*d.* in or before **1780**), poet and essayist, was born near Newcastle upon Tyne into the Middletons, a prominent local Quaker family. While still very young she married Captain Francis Gomeldon (*d.* 1751), a well-connected officer in Sir John Bruce's regiment, who was on friendly terms with the coal magnate George Bowes. Soon after their marriage, much to her husband's chagrin, Jane fled. She escaped to France, where she had many adventures disguised as a man, including paying court to a nun, whom she almost persuaded to elope with her. For many years afterwards she showed visitors to her home in Newcastle the relics she had taken from a French convent. She returned to her native town upon the death of her husband, who was buried at Gibside on 1 February 1751.

Gomeldon's publishing career began after she was widowed. *The Medley* (1766), consisting of thirty-one essays on various subjects, was published by John White and Thomas Saint in Newcastle for the benefit of the lying-in hospital, a charity for poor women. The most prominent families in the region subscribed to the work, including the duke and duchess of Northumberland and Sir Walter Blackett. Gomeldon's book raised over £53, for which she was publicly thanked by the governors of the hospital on 3 December 1768. The frontispiece of *The Medley* is an allegorical representation of Virtue blessing Charity for the relief of Distress. The essays conform to the literary conventions of 'polite' society at the time, mocking the pretension of 'refined Taste' and people of fashion (J. Gomeldon, *The Medley*, 1766, 15, 40–41). As the author, Gomeldon assumed a male identity, cited Pope and Fielding as her influences, and discussed subjects as diverse as the education of daughters, cross-dressing, and female adultery. She was not uncritical of her own sex, but ridiculed certain male authors, particularly those who likened women to different styles of painting or types of musical instrument.

In 1773 the Newcastle publisher Isaac Thompson printed Gomeldon's *Happiness*, a poem addressed to her friend 'Dear, faithfull Ann'. In this poem the vogue for celebrating romantic friendship between women found expression, although the identity (and true sex) of the author was not alluded to in the title-page. Inspired to love through Ann's 'comely form', she recalled that reflecting upon their '*sacred* and *sublime*' friendship brought her happiness in rural retirement, away from the 'vexing Scenes of Trade' ([J. Gomeldon], *Happiness*, 1–2). Another of Gomeldon's works, her *Maxims*, was printed by Thomas Saint in 1779. This time her name appeared in print, together with the standard apologia that 'a humble Imitation is all that can be expected from a Female Pen' (J. Gomeldon, *Maxims*, preface). The maxims appear somewhat trite, but contain occasionally radical, if not revolutionary, overtones: 'When the Nobles become dissolute', she observed, 'the People in general grow licentious' (ibid.).

Gomeldon was described as a gentlewoman 'of liberal education, a great adept in natural history and philosophy', who was fond of collecting shells (Richardson,

265). She is reputed to have been a beauty in her youth, at which time she distributed copies of a portrait of herself to friends. In an era of generally poor oral hygiene, she possessed remarkably fine teeth. She carefully preserved them as they fell out through age, and had the enamel set in rings, of which her friends were again the fortunate recipients. A romantic, she fell in love with the name of Captain James Cook, and expressed a wish to accompany him on his first voyage around the world. Her death 'at an advanced age' was reported on 10 July 1780 (*Newcastle Courant*). An obscure figure today, she was celebrated in her own time as an unconventional woman who successfully deployed a network of local publishers to make her mark upon literary life in north-east England.

HELEN BERRY

Sources MS notes in J. Gomeldon, *The medley* (1766), Newcastle City Library, L824.69/G633 • M. A. Richardson, ed., *The local historian's table book … historical division*, 5 vols. (1841–6), vol. 2 • 'Diary of Thomas Gyll', *Six north country diaries*, ed. J. C. Hodgson, SurtS, 118 (1910) • Blain, Clements & Grundy, *Feminist comp.* • P. M. Horsley, 'Some local ladies of the eighteenth century', *Heaton Works Journal*, 6 (1951), 131–8 • A. Myers, *Myers' literary guide to the north east*, 2nd edn (1997)

Gomersall, Robert (*bap.* 1602, *d.* 1643/4), Church of England clergyman and writer, was baptized on 5 December 1602 at St Mary Whitechapel, Stepney, the son of William Gomersall. He was not the Robert Gomersall admitted to the Middle Temple in 1613; that Robert Gomersall, son of Robert Gomersall, was baptized in 1591 in St Martin Ludgate, London. Gomersall matriculated at Christ Church, Oxford, on 19 April 1616, proceeded BA on 19 December 1618, MA on 14 June 1621, and BD on 11 November 1628. In 1625 he retreated to Flower in Northamptonshire to escape the plague, and two of his published poems are dated from there. Six months before completing his Oxford studies in 1628, he became vicar of Thorncombe, Devon, on the recommendation of Alexander Every. Shortly thereafter, Every died and Gomersall married his widow, Helen, *née* Bragg (*b.* 1608); their first child, Helen, was baptized on 23 March 1630, followed by a son, Robert, and another daughter, Christian.

Also in 1628 Gomersall published two works: *The Tragedie of Lodovick Sforza, Duke of Millan*, a historical melodrama about the Italian wars of the late fifteenth century, based on Guicciardini's *History* and dedicated to Francis Hide of Christ Church; and a poem, *The Levites Revenge: Containing Poeticall Meditations upon the 19 and 20 Chapters of Judges*, dedicated to Dr Barten Holiday and with an address to the reader explaining that this poem is a product of the author's youth. The two pieces were reprinted together in *Poems* (1633), with the addition of a small collection of miscellaneous verses. A short poem of Gomersall is preserved in one manuscript (BL, Harley MS 6931), and another (Bodl. Oxf., MS Malone 21, fol. 15) contains his elegy on King Gustavus Adolphus of Sweden, printed in the 1633 *Poems*. His next work was a collection of royalist-tinged *Sermons on Peter* (1634), dedicated to Sir John Strangwayes of Melbury, Dorset, and in 1640 he prefixed to Fuller's *History of the Holy Warre* a copy of commendatory verses signed 'Robert Gomersall, Vicar of Thorncombe in Devon'.

Gomersall's will is dated 27 March 1643, but was not proved until 31 October 1646; however, he must have died before June 1644, when his successor was installed at Thorncombe. He left an estate worth more than £2000, but his property was sequestered by parliament after his death because of his royalist tendencies. His widow tried in vain to get it restored, and was briefly imprisoned in 1651 before settling for £500. DAVID KATHMAN

Sources G. E. Bentley, *The Jacobean and Caroline stage*, 7 vols. (1941–68), vol. 4, p. 512 • E. Schneider, 'Some notes on Robert Gomersall', *Review of English Studies*, 9 (1933), 170–75 • Foster, *Alum. Oxon.* • parish register of St Mary Whitechapel, Stepney, London • B. R. Pearn, 'Introduction', *The tragedie of Lodovick Sforza, duke of Millan, by Robert Gomersall* (1933), xi–xxi • M. Crum, ed., *First-line index of English poetry, 1500–1800, in manuscripts of the Bodleian Library, Oxford*, 2 vols. (1969) • *DNB*

Wealth at death over £2000—incl. £1000 to son, and £500 to each of two daughters: Schneider, 'Some notes'

Gomm, Sir William Maynard (1784–1875), army officer, eldest son of Lieutenant-Colonel William Gomm of the 55th regiment, and his wife, Mary Alleyne, daughter of Joseph Maynard of Barbados, was born in Barbados. His father was killed at the storming of Pointe à Petre, Guadeloupe, in 1794. His mother died at Penzance two years after, leaving three sons and a daughter. One son died in childhood, the other three children were brought up by their aunt, Miss Jane Gomm, and her friend Miss M. C. Goldsworthy, who had both been governesses to the daughters of George III. William Maynard Gomm was gazetted ensign in the 9th regiment on 24 May and promoted lieutenant on 16 November 1794, before he was ten years old, in recognition of his father's services.

Gomm remained at Woolwich studying until the summer of 1799, when he joined his regiment and embarked for the Netherlands with the expedition under the duke of York. At the age of fifteen he took part in the operations on The Helder, and in the engagements of Bergen-op-Zoom, Alkmaar, and Egmont-op-Zoom. At the end of the short campaign in October, he returned to England and remained with his regiment at Norwich until August 1800, when he embarked with it for service under Sir James Pulteney. Proceeding to the Spanish coast, an unsuccessful attempt was made on Ferrol, and, after a visit to Gibraltar and Lisbon, the expedition returned to England at the beginning of 1801. Gomm was appointed aide-de-camp to General Benson at Liverpool. In 1802 he rejoined his regiment and was quartered at Chatham and Plymouth. On 25 June 1803 he was promoted captain, and went with his regiment to Ireland.

In 1804 Gomm obtained leave to join the military college at High Wycombe, where he studied under Colonel Howard Douglas for the staff until the end of 1805, when he embarked with his regiment for Hanover. The expedition was soon over, and he returned to his studies at High Wycombe, receiving at the end of 1806 a very satisfactory certificate of qualification for the general staff. In 1807 he took part as assistant quartermaster-general in the expedition to Stralsund and Copenhagen, under Admiral Gambier and Lord Cathcart. On his return he rejoined his regiment at Mallow in Ireland, and in July 1808 embarked with it for the Peninsula in the expedition under Wellesley. Before sailing, however, he was appointed to the staff of the expedition as assistant quartermaster-general.

Gomm was present at the battles of Roliça and Vimeiro, and, after the convention of Cintra (30 August 1808), was appointed to the staff of Sir John Moore. He took part in the retreat on Corunna, and was one of the last to embark after his regiment, the 9th foot, had carried Sir John's body to its burial. On his return to England he was quartered with his regiment at Canterbury until July 1809, when he was appointed to the staff of the expedition to Walcheren. He was present at the siege and surrender of Flushing, and when Lord Chatham's army retired into the fever-stricken swamps of Walcheren, he contracted a fever from which he suffered for some years after.

On the return of the expedition to England, Gomm's regiment was again quartered at Canterbury until March 1810, when he once more embarked with it for the Peninsula. In September he was appointed a deputy assistant quartermaster-general and was attached to General Leith's column. He was present at the battle of Busaco, where he had a horse shot under him, and at Fuentes d'Oñoro (5 May 1811). He was promoted major on 10 October 1811. Gomm was at the storming and capture of Ciudad Rodrigo on 20 January 1812; at the siege and storming of Badajoz on 6 April 1812, where he was slightly wounded; at the battle of Salamanca on 22 July 1812, where he particularly distinguished himself, and for which on 17 August he was promoted lieutenant-colonel; and at the entry into Madrid on 12 August 1812. He was present at the siege of Burgos, which Wellington was obliged to raise after five unsuccessful assaults.

Gomm led his division of the army in the disastrous retreat to the Portuguese frontier, and again in the masterly advance to the Ebro, through the wild districts of Tras-os-Montes, of which he had previously made reconnaissances. He took part in the battle of Vitoria on 21 June 1813, in the siege and capture of San Sebastian, and in the hard fighting in the south of France in December 1813, when he was again slightly wounded. After the peace he went to Paris and landed in England early in September 1814. For his services in the Peninsula he was transferred from the 9th into the Coldstream Guards, and made a KCB (2 January 1815). He received the gold cross with a clasp and the silver war medal with six clasps. His letters, indicative of his character, written from the Peninsula to his aunt and sister, were edited by F. C. Carr-Gomm and published in 1881.

On the return of Napoleon from Elba, Gomm went with the Coldstream to Brussels and was again appointed to the staff. He took part with the 5th division in the battles of Quatre Bras and Waterloo.

In 1816 Gomm lost his brother Henry, his comrade in the Peninsula, who had been severely wounded in July 1813. The following year he lost his beloved sister, and in 1822 his aunt, Miss Gomm; he succeeded to her property and became lord of the manor of Rotherhithe. From 1817 to 1839 he was on home service. During this period he married Sophia, granddaughter of William Penn of Pennsylvania, who died in 1827; in 1830 he married Elizabeth Ann (*b*. 1807, *d*. 30 Nov 1877), eldest daughter of Lord Robert Kerr. He had no children by either marriage.

Gomm was made full colonel on 16 May 1829 and major-general on 10 January 1837. He devoted much of his spare time to travel and to the study of literature. From 1839 to 1841 he commanded the troops in Jamaica, where he founded a sanatorium for the white troops at Newcastle in the mountains. On his return to England in the spring of 1842 he was given the command of the northern district. From autumn 1842 to 1849 he was governor of Mauritius, and he was promoted lieutenant-general on 9 November 1846.

From Mauritius, Gomm went to Calcutta, having received an intimation from the Horse Guards of his appointment as commander-in-chief in India. To his bitter disappointment, on arriving in the Hooghly he found that, owing to the panic at home after the Second Anglo-Sikh War and to the jealousy of the court of directors of the direct patronage of the crown, his appointment had been cancelled, and Sir Charles Napier had just arrived at Calcutta as commander-in-chief and proceeded to the Punjab. Gomm returned home with Lady Gomm, visiting Ceylon on their way, and arrived in England in January 1850. In the following August he was appointed commander-in-chief of Bombay, but on the eve of starting Sir Charles Napier suddenly resigned, and Gomm was appointed commander-in-chief in India. The five years he held the chief command were comparatively uneventful. He was popular, and his popularity was promoted by the social accomplishments of his wife.

Gomm was promoted full general on 20 June 1854. He returned home in 1855 to enjoy twenty years' dignified and honoured old age. In 1846 he had been appointed honorary colonel of the 13th foot, and in August 1863 was transferred to the colonelcy of the Coldstream Guards. On 1 January 1868 he became field marshal, and in October 1872 constable of the Tower. The tsar, when visiting England in 1874, sent him the order of St Vladimir; he was already a knight of the second class of the order of St Anne of Russia. He had been made a GCB (21 June 1859), and Oxford and Cambridge had awarded honorary degrees of DCL (13 June 1834) and LLD respectively. He died at 33 Brunswick Terrace, Brighton, on 15 March 1875, and was buried at Christ Church, Rotherhithe. Five Field Marshal Gomm scholarships, endowed with £15,000, were founded in his memory at Keble College, Oxford, by the will of Lady Gomm. R. H. Vetch, *rev.* James Lunt

Sources F. C. Carr-Gomm, *Letters and journals of Field Marshal Sir W. M. Gomm* (1881) • *The dispatches of … the duke of Wellington … from 1799 to 1818*, ed. J. Gurwood, 13 vols. in 12 (1834–9) • *The dispatches of … the duke of Wellington … from 1799 to 1818*, ed. J. Gurwood, 2nd edn, enl., 8 vols. (1844–7) • Fortescue, *Brit. army* • W. F. P. Napier, *History of the war in the Peninsula and in the south of France*, 6 vols. (1850) •

E. Longford [E. H. Pakenham, countess of Longford], *Wellington*, 1: *The years of the sword* (1969) • C. W. C. Oman, *Wellington's army, 1809–1814* (1912); repr. (1968) • A. Brett-James, *Life in Wellington's army* (1972) • Boase, *Mod. Eng. biog.* • *Dod's Peerage* • *CGPLA Eng. & Wales* (1875)

Archives NAM, papers • NL Scot., letters | BL OIOC, corresp. with Lord Clyde, MS Eur. D 626 • Lpool RO, letters to Lord Stanley • NA Scot., corresp. with Lord Dalhousie • Yale U., Beinecke L., letters to Frederick Locker-Lampson

Likenesses W. Salter, oils, 1834–40 (study for *Waterloo banquet at Apsley House*), NPG • J. Steell, marble bust, 1843, Keble College, Oxford • J. Bowles, oil on photograph, 1873/4, NPG • W. Salter, group portrait, oils (*Waterloo banquet at Apsley House*), Wellington Museum, London • Spy [L. Ward], watercolour caricature, NPG; repro. in *VF* (1873) • portrait, repro. in *ILN*, 61 (1872) • portrait, repro. in *The Graphic*, 11 (1875) • portrait, repro. in Carr-Gomm, *Letters and journals*

Wealth at death under £70,000: probate, 22 April 1875, *CGPLA Eng. & Wales*

Gomme [*née* Merck], **Alice Bertha**, **Lady Gomme** (**1853–1938**), folklorist, was born on 4 January 1853 at 5 South Molton Street, in the registration district of St George, Hanover Square, London, the daughter of Charles Antony Thomas Merck, a master tailor, and his wife, Elizabeth, *née* Tilley. Save for a sister we know nothing of her life until, on 31 March 1875 at twenty-two, she married (George) Laurence *Gomme (1853–1916), then a young administrator in the Metropolitan Board of Works.

Although seen as an enthusiastic and prolific writer on folklore, Alice Gomme's reputation was until recent times not fully recognized. For example, her approach to and the reliability of her sources tended to be regarded as suspect (Opie and Opie, vi) and—as often at that time—she was seen as playing a subordinate role to that of her better-known husband (who was knighted in 1911), with whom she often worked in partnership (Dorson, *British Folklorists*, 279).

Recent commentators, however (Simpson and Roud, and Boyes), provide convincing evidence for Alice Gomme's scholarship. Her most notable work is *The Traditional Games of England, Scotland and Ireland* (2 vols., 1894 and 1898, reprinted 1964 and in 1984 with an introduction by Damian Webb), which includes tunes, singing rhymes, and methods of playing. The work contains descriptions of some 800 children's games current in the second half of the nineteenth century, with comparisons of variants, collected by seventy-six correspondents from 112 locations. She herself was an active collector of games and 'was the first scholar to define children's games as a separate genre of folklore'. The book 'discusses … texts, history, cultural significance and formal structures [of games] … and develops a comprehensive system for their classification' (Boyes, *Musical Traditions*, 1). It was an impressive work to publish, especially at a time when she was a busy mother (she gave birth to seven sons between 1876 and 1891) and active in folklore fields generally.

In 1878 at twenty-five Gomme became a founder member of the Folklore Society and for sixty years was active in its affairs; she was on its council from 1912 until her death. From at least 1883 she regularly contributed to *Folklore* and other journals and newspapers, writing on diverse matters: 'Conception by means of a glance', 'A Berwickshire kirn dolly', 'Boer folk medicine and some parallels', and 'The character of Beelzebub' (*Folklore*, 1890, 1901, 1902, and 1929).

In 1894 Gomme published *Children's Singing Games*. Work on this had brought her into contact with Cecil Sharp, and the two developed a close working relationship which led to an expanded work under the same title in five volumes published between 1909 and 1912. For legal reasons, however, it appeared under Sharp's name only; they remained good friends until Sharp's death in 1924 (Boyes, *Folklore*, 204). She was active in the Folk Song Society and was a founder member of the English Folk Dance Society.

Gomme's interest in folk cookery and in children's games came together at the conversazione, held in October 1891, which was intended as a diversion from the serious business of the first International Folklore Congress then taking place in London. She was secretary of the conversazione organizing committee and, though pregnant, 'devised, researched and organised' the occasion. The programme, far from being a diversion, was the first comprehensive display of folklore in Britain. It 'involved a substantial exhibition, showing the history of scholarship in folklore … portraits of scholars, illustrations and examples of material culture ranging from items of regional cookery to funeral garlands' (Boyes, *Folklore*, 205). There were recitations of folk-tales, a performance of a traditional folk play, and a programme of traditional songs and dances still in use, performed by pupils from Barnes School 'under the supervision of Mrs. Gomme' (conversazione programme). The refreshments were examples of folk cookery. Forty years later, when Florence White founded the English Folk Cookery Association, Gomme's pioneering efforts in this field were recognized in her election as its first president (*Morning Post*, 4 March 1931).

Gomme, who was an active suffragist, revealed in her work an interest in the position of women in society. She early recognized the value of playing games in childhood and taught games to schoolchildren (*Daily Mail*, 10 Jan 1903). Ever busy as lecturer as well as writer, she was for some time president of the London Shakespeare League, and was an enthusiast for Elizabethan stage methods of production. She was a friend and supporter of Lilian Baylis. Two of her sons were killed in the First World War, one of whom, Austin, was a promising architect highly regarded by his master, C. R. Ashbee. Her third son, Arthur Allan *Gomme, was librarian to the Patent Office and himself president of the Folklore Society (1951–3) and her fifth, Arnold Wycombe Gomme (1886–1959), was a noted classicist. Photographs show her as of medium height and slender build, her hair tied in a bun. She appears conventionally dressed, and one of her grandsons remembers her in her eighties as a grand figure. After her husband's early death in 1916 she lived in a hotel at 21–2 Montague Street, Bloomsbury, London, and also at the family home in Long Crendon, Buckinghamshire. She died on 5 January

1938, at 11 Porchester Terrace, Paddington, London, of pneumonia and heart failure and on 8 January was cremated, as her husband had been, at Golders Green crematorium, Middlesex. ROBERT GOMME

Sources 'Lady Gomme', J. Simpson and S. Roud, *A dictionary of English folklore* (2000) • 'Sir George Laurence Gomme', J. Simpson and S. Roud, *A dictionary of English folklore* (2000) • G. Boyes, 'Alice Bertha Gomme, 1852 [*sic*]–1938: a reassessment of the work of a folklorist', *Folklore*, 101 (1990), 198–209 • G. Boyes, Alice Bertha Gomme, 1852 [*sic*]–1938, www.mustrad.org.uk [*Musical Traditions* internet magazine], 9 March 2001 • 'Lady Gomme: an appreciation', *Folklore*, 49 (1938), 93–4 • *The Times* (8 Jan 1938) • R. M. Dorson, *The British folklorists: a history* (1968) • R. M. Dorson, 'The founders of British folklore', *TLS* (14 July 1978) • 'Where are the happiest children found?', *Daily Mail* (10 Jan 1903) • 'The history of England in a cooking pot', *Morning Post* (4 March 1931) • Lady Gomme, 'They still believe in ghosts', *Evening News* (24 Jan 1929) • 'Children's singing games', *Cheltenham Examiner* (6 Nov 1913) • I. A. Opie and P. Opie, *The lore and language of schoolchildren* (1959) • b. cert. • d. cert.
Archives UCL, Folklore Society papers
Likenesses M. Taylor, pastels, English Folk Dance and Song Society, London • photographs, UCL, Folklore Society, Alice Gomme archive • portrait, repro. in Dorson, *British folklorists*, 231
Wealth at death £2351: probate, 11 Feb 1938, *CGPLA Eng. & Wales*

Gomme, Arthur Allan (1882–1955), librarian and historian of technology, was born at 2 Park Villas, Lonsdale Road, Barnes, Middlesex, on 15 July 1882, the third of the seven sons of Sir (George) Laurence *Gomme (1853–1916), public servant and folklorist, and his wife, Alice Bertha *Gomme, *née* Merck (1853–1938). He was educated at the Mercers' School, London (1895–1900), and trained in engineering at the City and Guilds Central Technical College (1900–03), where in 1903 he won the Siemens memorial medal in electrical engineering. In January 1904 he was sixth in the civil service entrance examination, and was appointed as an assistant examiner at the Patent Office.

Gomme served with the 2nd battalion, Royal Fusiliers (university and public schools division) during the First World War, and in 1918, at the British consulate in Paris, he married Dora Isobel (1887–1975), youngest daughter of Robert Marples; they had a son and a daughter. He was demobilized in 1919, and appointed librarian to the Patent Office, a post he held until his retirement in 1944. In 1920 he joined the Newcomen Society; he became a member of the society's council in 1925 and vice-president in 1953. He contributed three papers on the history of patents to *Transactions of the Newcomen Society*, and, with E. Wyndham Hume, his predecessor at the Patent Office library, compiled for serial publication in the *Transactions* an 'Analytical bibliography of the history of engineering and applied science'. In 1946 he published *Patents of Invention: Origin and Growth of the Patent System in Britain*. He was also the author, with H. W. Dickinson, of a catalogue of the designs of the engineer John Smeaton (1950). A member of the management council of the World List of Scientific Periodicals (1935–55), he was responsible for the section dealing with international conferences. He was appointed MBE in 1930.

Gomme's interests were not limited by his profession. Like his parents, he was a student of folklore, and served on the council of the Folklore Society from 1911 until his death, acting as president in 1952 and 1953. He was also a pioneer in the history of the theatre—a member of the British Drama League, and a founder member of the Society for Theatre Research in 1948. An active member of William Poel's Elizabethan Stage Society, he provided much material for Poel's biographer, Robert Speaight, and compiled an annotated bibliography of Poel's writings. He also belonged to the Fabian Society. During the Second World War he served with the Home Guard, and, after his retirement from the Patent Office, worked for the British Council (1944–6).

Gomme was a self-effacing man, who modestly concealed his great erudition. He was unstinting in his help to individuals and in working, mostly unsung, for the good of the organizations with which he was associated. He died on 9 February 1955 at his home, 4 Daylesford Avenue, Putney, and was cremated at Putney Vale crematorium.
A. P. WOOLRICH

Sources *Transactions* [Newcomen Society], 29 (1953–5), 275 • *Nature*, 175 (1955), 452 • *Library Association Record*, 57 (1955), 127 • *Folk-Lore*, 66 (1955), 193–4 • *Wandsworth Historical Society Broadsheet* (1955) • private information (2004) • *CGPLA Eng. & Wales* (1955)
Archives Patent Office, London, Patent Office Library records • Sci. Mus., Rhys Jenkins MSS
Wealth at death £1976 17*s*. 2*d*.: probate, 16 May 1955, *CGPLA Eng. & Wales*

Gomme, Sir Bernard de (1620–1685), military engineer, was born at Torneus (Terneuzen) in Flanders, the son of Peter de Gomme. Nothing is known of de Gomme's early career or family background. He served in the campaigns of Frederick Henry, prince of Orange, and acquired a knowledge of military engineering. He had, besides, experience in drainage and land reclamation. In 1636 a Bernhardt de Gomme was commissioned a surveyor in Goes, Zeeland. Siege maps and plans of Netherlands fortifications, some of them signed and dated, are in a portfolio of his drawings now held in the British Library (King's Top. Coll., 4 Tab 48). In 1642 he was brought to England by Prince Rupert, eventually to become the royalists' chief engineer. He had been knighted by 1645 and was granted augmentation of arms on 1 April 1646. As one of Prince Rupert's staff he drew plans of the royalist order of battle at Edgehill, second Newbury, Marston Moor, and Naseby, and was present at both sieges of Bristol. He designed new fortifications for Liverpool and Oxford and was probably responsible for the Royal Fort, Bristol, and the Queen's Sconce, Newark.

After the surrender of Oxford, de Gomme returned to the Netherlands and continued as both a military and drainage engineer. He received a commission from the exiled Charles II in 1649 to be quartermaster-general of all forces to be raised in England and Wales. In the 1650s he was living in Middelburg. He married Katherine van Deniza, the widow of Hadrian Beverland. Their daughter, Katherine, was born at Lillo about 1658. It was de Gomme's stepson, Adrian Beverland, who compiled the portfolio of his Dutch drawings. In 1658 Gomme was present at the battle of the Dunes with the royalist regiments commanded by the duke of York. Upon the restoration of Charles II, de Gomme returned to England to be appointed engineer in charge of all the king's castles and fortifications in England and Wales in February 1661 at a fee of 13*s.* 4*d.* a day. He was also awarded a life pension of £300 a year. He was first employed on improving the defences of Dunkirk (1661–2) and later had two spells on the fortifications of Tangier (1663–5). His subsequent career as chief engineer in the ordnance office principally concerned Charles II's English fortress building programme. In August 1665, following his return to England, he began the remodelling of the defences of Portsmouth. At Plymouth, in November 1665, he designed the royal citadel, and he was to be closely involved in the supervision of its construction. Landguard Fort was successfully improved in 1667. This was the year in which he obtained English naturalization and married Katherine Lucas (*d.* 1685), his first wife having died in Middelburg in 1666. His daughter by his first wife, Katherine, was later to marry a John Riches, born in Amsterdam, and it was John Riches who was executor of de Gomme's will.

After the Dutch raid on the Medway in 1667 the defences of Sheerness were renewed to de Gomme's designs and new batteries built higher up the river at Cockham Wood and Gillingham. In the 1670s he designed a new fort at Tilbury and was closely involved with its construction. At the same time he was working on an extensive programme of fresh improvements at Portsmouth. This included new defences for Gosport and Portsmouth Dockyard, and the remodelling of Southsea Castle. He was also sent to Ireland to draw up a scheme for the defence of Dublin in 1673. A preliminary scheme for Hull citadel was produced about 1680.

A seventeenth-century military engineer had to be competent in all branches of mathematics, land survey, civil and military architecture, and quantity surveying and these skills figured in de Gomme's career. On 9 August 1663 he was again appointed briefly a surveyor in his native Zeeland. Two years later he was to assist commissioners responsible for making the River Cam navigable and linking it with the Thames, but he was almost immediately afterwards sent to Portsmouth. In another context de Gomme had been ordered to Dover in 1661 to advise on repairs to the harbour pier. In 1670 lack of progress at Dover and suspected misappropriation of funds led to a commission of inquiry consisting of Bernard de Gomme, Christopher Wren, Jonas Moore, and others. In the ordnance office de Gomme worked closely with Sir Jonas Moore, surveyor general, particularly over the Medway defences. On 27 October 1679, following the death of Moore and his succession by his son, de Gomme was appointed assistant surveyor in addition to his existing duties. On 4 September 1682, after the death of Moore's son, de Gomme became surveyor-general of the ordnance, again in combination with his responsibilities as chief engineer. He was now responsible for the broad range of building works carried out by the ordnance involving barracks as well as fortifications, the hospital at Portsmouth, the ordnance laboratory and the Royal Observatory at Greenwich, and improvements at the Tower of London. As surveyor-general he was closely involved in the reform of the ordnance office, providing job descriptions for the posts of chief engineer and subordinate engineers as well as for the surveyor's department. On becoming an officer of the ordnance he was required to live in the surveyor's house at the Tower of London. Previously he had lived in Berry Street, Bevis Marks, City of London, where he was a registered member of the Dutch Reformed church. As a military engineer de Gomme was held in high esteem by Charles II and Lord Dartmouth, master-general of the ordnance. He was evidently a conscientious administrator, though Pepys occasionally wrote disparagingly of him. In his later years he suffered from gout and became a difficult colleague. He died on 23 November 1685 at his home at the Tower of London. On his interment in the chapel of St Peter ad Vincula, Tower of London, on 30 November, he was given a 60-gun salute. ANDREW SAUNDERS

Sources *DNB* • Colvin, *Archs.* • *CSP, 1642–85* • W. A. Shaw, ed., *Calendar of treasury books*, 1–3, PRO (1904–8) • H. C. Tomlinson, *Guns and government: the ordnance office under the later Stuarts*, Royal Historical Society Studies in History, 15 (1979) • A. D. Saunders, 'Tilbury Fort and the development of artillery fortification in the Thames estuary', *Antiquaries Journal*, 40 (1960), 152–74 • A. Saunders, 'Sir Bernard de Gomme: a Dutch military engineer in English service', *Vestingbouw overzea: Vestingbouwkundige Bijdragen*, 4 (1996) • A. Saunders, 'The royal citadel, Plymouth: a possible Stowe connection', *Archaeological Journal*, 153 (1996), 290–94 • will, PRO, PROB 11/381, sig. 134 • J. L. Chester and J. Foster, eds., *London marriage licences, 1521–1869* (1887) • J. H. Hessels, ed., *Register of the attestations or certificates of membership … preserved in the Dutch reformed church, Austin Friars, London, 1568 to 1872* (1892) • W. A. Shaw, ed., *Letters of denization and acts of naturalization for aliens in England and Ireland, 1603–1700*, Huguenot Society of London, 18 (1911) • PRO, WO 55/394, 44 • PRO, WO 47/16, 62 • PRO, WO 51/25 • PRO, WO 55/420 • Rijksarchief Zeeland, Staten van Zeeland, inv. nr. 1669, fol. 166*r* • *Memoirs of Prince Rupert and the cavaliers including their private correspondence*, ed. E. Warburton, 3 vols. (1849) • W. Sussex RO, Clough and Butler papers • *N&Q*, 2nd ser., 9 (1860), 252

Archives PRO, estimates, instructions, surveys, travel, etc., ordnance papers, WO 30/32, 46, 47, 48, 49, 51, 53, 54, 55

Likenesses miniature, oils, BL, King's Topographical Collection, Tab 48

Wealth at death manor of Waddenhall, with houses, farms, and land in Watham and Petham, Kent, to son-in-law John Riches; £2000 to son-in-law Adrian Beverland; £1000 in trust to granddaughter; £300 to Anna Riches; £100 to Dutch Reformed church; £400 to poor of the church; £70 to bluecoats boys of Christ's Hospital; small sums to servants and clerks: will, PRO, PROB 11/381, sig. 134

Gomme, Ebenezer (1858–1931), furniture manufacturer, was born on 12 April 1858 in Nettlebed, near Henley, the son of John Gomme and his wife, Hannah Grimsell. His father's occupation at his birth was described as 'fellmonger', a feller of trees. An ancestor was James Gomme (1726–1825) of High Wycombe and Hammersmith, who was a furniture maker, a member of the Society of Antiquaries, and a friend of Edmund Burke. The family moved to High Wycombe in 1864, and the father was employed by the firm of Cox & Co., chairmakers of that town.

Ebenezer Gomme was apprenticed to Cox & Co. as a chairmaker at the age of thirteen, in 1871, and served a five-year apprenticeship with them. As a 'journeyman' he broadened his experience by working for the next few years with Goodearls and with William Birch, both firms in the town of High Wycombe, as a 'best chairmaker'. His first venture on his own behalf was in Exeter in 1881–2, but this failed and he returned to High Wycombe and to work for William Birch. In 1886–8 he worked in partnership under the name Gomme and Mendy, but this too was unsuccessful.

In 1881 Gomme married Isabella Alice Pierce (1853–1954), daughter of William Pierce, foreman of a coal wharf. The couple had two sons, Frank (*b.* 1883) and Ted (*b.* 1890). Continuing to work as a chairmaker Gomme tried again to start up his own business, in 1898, from his garden shed in High Wycombe, in partnership with his brother-in-law, Tim Pierce. The business was successful, though the partnership was dissolved in 1901. Gomme had progressed in business sufficiently to open his first factory in Leigh Street, High Wycombe, in 1909, and by 1914 he was employing 200 furniture makers. He went on to add another factory to the group in 1927, at Spring Gardens, High Wycombe, a fire having destroyed the premises at Leigh Street in 1922.

The firm of E. Gomme Ltd built its reputation on the concept of 'whole house furniture'; in other words it made dining, upholstery, bedroom, and occasional furniture, in the same style and idiom. The building of the Spring Gardens factory also meant that it could work on batch production in advance of orders, with 250 cabinets and 1000 chairs (each of the same design) being made in one production run. The economies of scale that this produced ensured the company's place in the market when many others were having difficulties in the late 1920s and 1930s. Gomme's sons joined the firm and by 1918 Frank, who had started his working life in the civil service, was in charge of administration. He was dispatched to the USA in the same year, to buy the latest woodworking machinery and to bring back American production methods. Ted, who had started his working life with war service in the navy, joined the firm in 1918 in charge of production.

Ebenezer Gomme died on 4 November 1931 at his home, The Crest, Totteridge, High Wycombe, having retired in the previous year. He was survived by his wife. The firm, headed by his sons, continued to prosper, becoming one of the largest manufacturers of furniture in the UK. However, since its products were retailed by others, it did not become a household name.

During the Second World War the Gomme factories made Mosquito aircraft. The skills of precise engineering, and the extensive use of very accurate jigs moved the firm's already high production standards forward, and with the demise of the controls and utility furniture in 1950 the company introduced a range of designs based on a pre-war product known as the bachelor suite. Initially called in the factory the Brandon suite, the furniture was designed for very large production runs. Carefully engineered and jigged, it was renamed G-Plan and was a popular success.

Hew Reid

Sources private information (2004) · records of E. Gomme Ltd, Buckingham University · H. Reid, 'Gomme, Ebenezer', *DBB* · *CGPLA Eng. & Wales* (1932)
Archives Buckingham University, records of E. Gomme Ltd | FILM BFI NFTVA, G Plan ads.
Wealth at death £36,946 16*s.* 10*d.*: probate, 3 Feb 1932, *CGPLA Eng. & Wales*

Gomme, Sir (George) Laurence (1853–1916), public servant and folklorist, was born on 18 December 1853 at 3 Cecil Street, Stepney, London, the second of ten children of William Laurence Gomme (1828–1887), a civil engineer, and his wife, Mary Annie, *née* Hall (1831–1921). On 31 March 1875 he married Alice Merck (1853–1938) [*see* Gomme, Alice Bertha], the daughter of Charles Merck, a tailor; they had seven sons, two of whom were killed in the First World War. Their third son, Arthur Allan *Gomme, became a librarian and historian of technology.

Educated at the City of London School, Gomme started work at the age of sixteen with a railway company, and later moved to Fulham district board of works. In 1873 he joined the Metropolitan Board of Works, whose functions were subsumed by the newly created London county council (LCC) in 1889. Gomme then remained with the council until retiring through ill health in 1914. He soon made his mark, becoming in 1893 statistical officer, effectively the head of policy formulation and development. In addition to providing information to council committees (council statistics were soon enlarged and improved, setting standards that other authorities followed), the office dealt with such matters as private bill legislation (important when the council was seeking to extend its responsibilities) and submissions to government inquiries. Gomme provided influential evidence, for example, to support the council's contention that there was an inadequate and uneven provision of workmen's trains, which in turn led to haphazard patterns in suburban growth, a significant issue at a time when London's population was increasing rapidly.

In October 1900, following an open competition, Gomme became clerk to the council, its chief administrative officer, at an annual salary of £2000. The council had already developed a dense committee structure with committee secretaries reporting to the clerk. During the 1890s the council had assumed new responsibilities, particularly in housing and tramways, adding to its original roles in such fields as highways and drainage; staff numbers grew from 3300 in 1890 to 6300 in 1898 and nearly 12,000 in 1904. In that year it became the education authority for London and staff numbers nearly tripled: to supervise the transition Gomme himself assumed the additional duties of secretary to the education committee until 1908. He wished to make London's administration a model for the nation, and contemporaries record the zest with which he went about his task.

Gomme described his recreations as 'change of work'. History and folklore, 'the scientific study of the survivals

Sir (George) Laurence Gomme (1853–1916), by Bassano, 1911

of archaic beliefs, customs, and traditions in modern times' (quoted in Dorson, *British Folklorists*, 225), became a lifelong passion—his wife was also a distinguished folklorist. This was not just antiquarianism: he firmly believed in the evidence of continuity in institutions, thus linking the present with the past, and saw clear connections between his studies and his official duties. In his view it was important to devolve governmental functions to local authorities, and he drew extensively on historical experience to provide examples. This enhanced role called for dedication among staff; and he looked forward to a unified municipal civil service as a branch of the national civil service. Later, in a development of these thoughts, he saw 'the civilisation of our future [as lying] in our cities' (*LCC Staff Gazette*, March 1914).

From his official position Gomme was able to influence the fate of old buildings, about which he was deeply knowledgeable. They were tangible evidence of the past and an enrichment of the present, and he was one of a growing number who deplored the recent destruction of so many fine examples in central London. He helped the council secure legal powers to purchase threatened buildings (1898) and he was also involved in securing the participation of the council in, and its subsequent assumption of responsibility for, the Survey of London. (He wrote the historical sections of part 1, *Lincoln's Inn Fields*, of volume 3, *The Parish of St Giles-in-the-Fields*.) Gomme was also instrumental in persuading the council to assume responsibility for the commemorative (blue) plaque scheme (1901).

Gomme's historical writings, especially the books on London, and his works on folklore were highly regarded by his contemporaries, although to us they seem at times overlaid by outdated theorizing. But his contribution remains significant and, in folklore particularly, he is in the front rank as a collector and classifier. He was a prolific writer: his bibliography includes fifteen books, several more written jointly or edited, and some forty articles in learned journals. Laurence Gomme, as he was known, was a justice of the peace and a fellow of the Society of Antiquaries, the Royal Statistical Society, the Anthropological Institute, and other learned societies. He lectured at the London School of Economics, was a founder member (1878) and sometime secretary and president of the Folk-Lore Society, and joint originator of the Victoria History of the Counties of England. He was knighted in 1911. He was of medium height and slender build and in disposition said to be amiable, cheerful, and receptive to ideas; a strong personality, he could sometimes become very attached to a particular point of view. He died on 23 February 1916, aged sixty-two, from pernicious anaemia, at his country home, The Mound, in Long Crendon, Buckinghamshire, and was cremated on 1 March at Golders Green crematorium, in Middlesex. ROBERT GOMME

Sources *The Times* (25 Feb 1916) · E. Clodd, *Folk-lore*, 27 (1916) · A. C. Haddon, *Man*, 16 (1916), 85–7 · *Proceedings of the Society of Antiquaries of London*, 2nd ser., 28 (1915–16), 211–12 · J. Simpson and S. Roud, *A dictionary of English folklore* (2000) · R. M. Dorson, *The British folklorists: a history* (1968) · J. Simpson and S. Roud, *A dictionary of English folklore* (2000) · R. M. Dorson, 'The founders of British folklore', *TLS* (14 July 1978) · A. Saint, ed., *Politics and the people of London: the London county council, 1889–1965* (1989) · G. Gibbon and R. Bell, *History of the London county council* (1939) · H. Haward, *The London county council from within* (1932) · H. Hobhouse, *London survey'd: the work of the survey of London, 1894–1994* (1994) · *London County Council Staff Gazette* (1900–14) · H. J. Dyos, *Exploring the urban past: essays in urban history*, ed. D. Cannadine and D. Reeder (1982) · *Folk-Lore* (31 Dec 1916), 408–12 · G. Boyes, 'Alice Bertha Gomme, 1852 [*sic*]–1938: a reassessment of the work of a folklorist', *Folklore*, 101 (1990), 198–209 · b. cert. · m. cert. · d. cert. · *The Times* (2 March 1916)

Archives Royal Anthropological Institute, London, handbook to folklore [copy] · UCL, Folklore Society papers | LMA, London county council records

Likenesses Bassano, photograph, 1911, NPG [*see illus.*] · photograph, repro. in Hobhouse, *London survey'd*, 11 · photograph, repro. in *London County Council Staff Gazette* (March 1914), 57 · photograph, repro. in Saint, ed., *Politics and the people of London*

Wealth at death £6204 8*s*. 3*d*.: probate, 21 March 1916, *CGPLA Eng. & Wales*

Gompertz, Benjamin (1779–1865), mathematician and actuary, was born on 5 March 1779 at 3 Bury Street in the City of London, the fourth of five sons of Solomon Barent Gompertz (1729–1807/8), a successful diamond merchant, and his second wife, Leah Cohen (1747x9–1809). His mother was Dutch by birth, the daughter of Benjamin Cohen, and his father's family was from Emmerich in the Netherlands. Excluded from the universities on the grounds of his Jewish religion, Gompertz was privately educated and self-taught, showing early interest in mathematics in the works of Maclaurin, Emerson, and Newton.

In 1797 Gompertz joined the Spitalfields Mathematical

Society. He later became president and served in that office when the society merged with the Royal Astronomical Society of London in 1846. From 1798 he contributed regularly to the *Gentleman's Mathematical Companion*, winning the prize competition of that journal every year between 1812 and 1822. His paper on imaginary quantities was published in the *Philosophical Transactions of the Royal Society of London* in 1806, but subsequent work on this topic was privately printed in two volumes in 1817 and 1818 having, it is said, been rejected by the Royal Society as so profound that no one would understand it. However, these works established his mathematical reputation. Gompertz was elected FRS in 1819 and served on the Royal Society's council in 1825 and 1831.

Gompertz was an early member of the Astronomical Society of London and served on its council from 1821 to 1829. Over the same period he published a number of papers in its *Memoirs*, dealing variously with the theory of astronomical instruments, the aberration of light, a differential sextant of his own design, and the convertible pendulum. He began in 1822, with Francis Baily, the calculation of tables of the mean places of the fixed stars. The publication of Bessel's *Fundamenta astronomiae* anticipated them, but their work was of great importance to the construction of the Royal Astronomical Society's complete catalogue of stars. Gompertz's work in astronomy was of a kind that took best advantage of his mathematical and computational skills.

Gompertz married, on 10 October 1810 at the Hambro Synagogue, London, Abigail Montefiore (1790–1871), the sister of Sir Moses Montefiore. They had a son, Joseph (1814–1824), and two daughters, Justina Lydia (1811–1883) and Juliana (1815–1873). In 1809 or 1810 Gompertz entered the stock exchange, leaving in 1824, the same year as the death of his only son. When the Guardian Insurance Office was established in 1821 Gompertz was an unsuccessful candidate for the position of actuary, being denied it reputedly on the grounds of religion. Perhaps partly in response, but also to take advantage of Gompertz's mathematical prowess, his brother-in-law, Sir Moses Montefiore, and Nathan Rothschild in 1824 set up the Alliance British and Foreign Life Assurance Company, to which Gompertz was appointed actuary. He was also chief manager of the related Alliance Marine Insurance.

Gompertz and the companies under his charge were very successful, but his lasting fame derived from his philosophical interest in life tables. While others treated these only as working tools, Gompertz tried to understand the laws which produced consistent age patterns of death. The law of human mortality associated with his name was propounded in papers published in the *Philosophical Transactions* in 1820 and 1825, with a supplementary paper published there in 1862. What is now called the Gompertz equation describes the exponential rise of death rates in a population between sexual maturity and old age. He attributed this phenomenon to a law of mortality, stating that 'the average exhaustions of a man's power to avoid death' are such that 'at the end of equal infinitely small intervals of time' he loses 'equal portions of his remaining power to avoid destruction' (*PTRS*, 115, 1825, 518). His expertise in this area led to his being consulted by government, including giving evidence to the select parliamentary committees on friendly societies in 1825 and 1827, and he did important computational work for the army medical board. His insights have remained central to the study of human mortality.

Gompertz's mathematical, astronomical, and actuarial work was closely connected. Like his collaborator Francis Baily, who was also simultaneously involved in astronomy and assurance, Gompertz's capacity for sustained, complex computation underlay all his work in whatever field. Tables of lives and tables of stars were generated by the same qualities and both represented a rationalizing spirit which informed the social philosophy of Gompertz and his friends among what W. J. Ashworth called the 'business astronomers'. However, unlike many of his colleagues in the Astronomical Society who promoted the differential calculus as a mathematical and physical tool (such as Herschel, Babbage, and Ivory), Gompertz clung fiercely to Newton's method of fluxions throughout his life. He defended fluxions against what he called the 'furtive' notation of Leibniz, furtive in the sense that it seemed to him to give Leibniz greater claim to originality at Newton's expense than was warranted.

After retiring from active work in 1848 Gompertz devoted much time to mathematics and science. His *Hints on Porisms* was privately published in 1850 as a sequel to earlier papers on imaginary quantities. He investigated comets and meteors, but this work was not published. He was a founding member of the Statistical Society of London in 1834, and contributed a work on human mortality to the International Statistical Congress in 1860. He was also, in 1865, one of the original members of the London Mathematical Society, for which he was preparing a paper at the time of his death. Gompertz was prominently involved also with the Society for the Diffusion of Useful Knowledge, the Royal Literary Fund, and various Jewish charities. He died on 14 July 1865 of a paralytic seizure at his home, 1 Kennington Terrace, Vauxhall, and was buried in the Jewish cemetery near Victoria Park, Hackney.

David Philip Miller

Sources P. F. Hooker, 'Benjamin Gompertz', *Journal of the Institute of Actuaries*, 91 (1965), 202–12 • R. M. Gompertz, *A branch of the Gompertz* (privately printed, 1979) • M. N. Adler, 'Memoirs of the late Benjamin Gompertz', *Assurance Magazine and Journal of the Institute of Actuaries*, 13 (1866), 1–20 • *Monthly Notices of the Royal Astronomical Society*, 26 (1865–6), 104–9 • *The Athenaeum* (22 July 1865), 117 • W. J. Ashworth, 'The calculating eye: Baily, Herschel, Babbage and the business of astronomy', *British Journal for the History of Science*, 27 (1994), 409–41 • *DNB* • S. J. Olshansky and B. A. Carnes, 'Ever since Gompertz', *Demography*, 34 (1997), 1–15 • C. Roth, ed., *Encyclopaedia Judaica*, 16 vols. (Jerusalem, 1971–2)

Archives Institute of Actuaries, London, MSS | BL, Babbage corresp. • RAS, letters and MSS • RS, Herschel corresp.

Likenesses portrait, repro. in Hooker, 'Benjamin Gompertz', 202

Wealth at death under £25,000: probate, 25 Aug 1865, *CGPLA Eng. & Wales*

Gompertz, Lewis (1783/4–1861), animal rights campaigner and inventor, was the youngest of the fifteen children of

Solomon Barent Gompertz (1729–1807/8), merchant, of Walthamstow and Vauxhall, and the fifth son of his second marriage, to Leah (Lydia; 1747x9–1809), daughter of Benjamin Cohen. An elder brother was Benjamin *Gompertz. Descended from the Ashkenazi Gomperz family of Emmerich, near the Dutch–German border, the Gompertz family was prominent within the Hambro Synagogue at Hoxton in east London. Lewis Gompertz devoted his life to the alleviation of animal suffering. He argued that it was morally indefensible to kill an animal or to make use of it in any way not directly beneficial to itself. Accordingly, he abstained from animal food, including milk and eggs, and he would never ride in a coach. He collected his unconventional views in *Moral Inquiries on the Situation of Man and of Brutes* (1824), a miscellany of philosophical dialogues, moral theorems derived from an axiomatic basis, and suggestions on the amelioration by mechanical means of the brute creation's sad condition. This work was reissued for the first time in 1992. Gompertz lauded the reforming influence of education, decried the evils of capitalism and of female subjugation, praised Owenite co-operation, and speculated boldly upon a future state shared by man and other animals. His book, published two years after Richard 'Humanity' Martin's act criminalized cruelty to cattle (broadly defined), also encouraged the animal protection movement by calling for the establishment of petition societies to lobby parliament in the cause of animal welfare.

When the Society for the Prevention of Cruelty to Animals (SPCA) was formed in June 1824 Gompertz was on the first committee. The society was immediately successful in bringing prosecutions against cruelty but its financial state was precarious. In 1826 Gompertz undertook the management and, in 1828, the honorary secretaryship, acting as *de facto* treasurer and frequently financial benefactor. He carried out the work with enormous enthusiasm and energy. However, from 1831 he became involved in acrimonious disputes with protagonists of the rival Association for the Promotion of Rational Humanity to the Animal Creation. He was accused through the association's journal of promulgating Pythagorean and anti-Christian views. Although he received a silver medal from the SPCA in 1832 in recognition of his work, the amalgamation of the two organizations left him isolated. A reformed committee resolved that the society was founded on exclusively Christian principles and Gompertz, while protesting his innocence of Pythagoreanism, resigned from the society in 1833 on the grounds that, as a Jew, he was in practice excluded from the society by the terms of its resolution. Supported by many subscribers, founding patrons, and the phrenologist and neo-Pythagorean Thomas I. M. Forster, Gompertz founded the Animals' Friend Society for the Prevention of Cruelty to Animals, with the aim of maintaining those activities of prosecution and tract distribution temporarily abandoned by the parent institution. In collaboration with his wife, Ann, 'Honorary Inspector' Gompertz managed the new society with such zeal that for some time it outstripped the SPCA in its activities. Gompertz edited the society's journal, *Animals' Friend, or, The Progress of Humanity* (1833–41), but in 1846 ill health necessitated his withdrawal from public work. The loss of his wife in April 1847 (they had had no children) was a further blow. Committees met until 1848, but the society languished.

Gompertz possessed a remarkable aptitude for mechanical science. Soon after 1810 his inventions, ingenious if not always practical, were displayed at his home on Kennington Oval and later at the popular Adelaide Gallery. He filed only one patent (for carriages, no. 3804 of 1814) but printed a copious *Index to 38 Inventions* (1839?) through which he attempted unsuccessfully to establish a manufacturing company. Among these contrivances were substitutes for cogwheels, fortifications, a mechanical cure for apoplexy, and scapers, a replacement for the wheel which could negotiate obstacles on roads. His most valuable contribution to mechanical engineering was an expanding chuck, which, in the late nineteenth century, was to be found in many workshops. Many of Gompertz's inventions were created either to render the lives of animals easy and comfortable, or, like his modified velocipede, to avoid using them altogether. Details of his machines appeared in the artisan press (notably the *Mechanics Journal*), the *Animals' Friend* and, finally, in a compendium of *Mechanical Inventions and Suggestions on Land and Water Locomotion* (1850? with appendices to 1859). A volume of *Fragments in Defence of Animals* (1852) assembled cuttings from the *Animals' Friend* ('Sagacity of Ants' being a typical contribution) and provided Gompertz with a last opportunity to ruminate upon his divorce from the SPCA. The publication of these volumes by William Horsell, the proprietor of a combined phrenological museum, homoeopathic pharmacy and vegetarian depot, confirmed Gompertz's drift from socio-scientific orthodoxy to dynamic popular fringe. He died, aged seventy-seven, from bronchitis on 2 December 1861 at his home in Kennington, London, and was buried beside his wife in the graveyard of Kennington church.

LUCIEN WOLF, *rev.* BEN MARSDEN

Sources L. Gompertz, *Moral inquiries on the situation of man and of brutes. On the crime of committing cruelty on brutes, and of sacrificing them to the purposes of man; with further reflections. Observations on Mr. Martin's Act, on the Vagrant Act, and on the tread mills; to which are added some improvements in scapers, or substitutes for carriage wheels; a new plan of the same, and some other mechanical subjects* (1824) • *Fragments in defence of animals, and essays on morals, soul, and future state; from the author's contributions to the Animals' Friend Society's periodical, and his letters to Dr. Forster; with a sketch of the society; and original matter; illustrated by engravings, with a portrait of the author, Lewis Gompertz, Esq.* (1852) • J. C. Turner, *Reckoning with the beast: animals, pain and humanity in the Victorian mind* (1980) • 'The family of Gompertz', Society of Genealogists, London, Sir Thomas Colyer-Fergusson collection, genealogical charts • L. Gompertz, *Index to 38 inventions of L. G.* (1839?) • *Animals' Friend, or, The Progress of Humanity*, 1–9 (1833–41) • W. [L. Wolf], *Jewish Chronicle* (1 Nov 1889) • E. G. Fairholme and W. Pain, *A century of work for animals: the history of the R.S.P.C.A., 1824–1924* (1924) • P. H. Emden, *Jews of Britain: a series of biographies* (1944) • D. Kaufmann and M. Freudenthal, *Die Familie Gomperz* (1907) • private information (1890) • *GM*, 2nd ser., 27 (1847), 672 [Ann Gompertz] • *The Times* (24 April 1847) [Ann Gompertz] • Boase, *Mod. Eng. biog.* • *The Times* (5 Dec 1861), 9 • d. cert.

Likenesses engraving, repro. in *Fragments in defence of animals*, frontispiece
Wealth at death under £14,000: probate, 17 Jan 1862, *CGPLA Eng. & Wales*

Gondibour [Godebowre], **Thomas** (*d. c.*1502), prior of Carlisle, is of unknown origins. He first appears in the records of the Augustinian house at Carlisle in 1451, when, already a canon in the cathedral priory, he obtained papal dispensation to hold a secular benefice while retaining his status within the chapter. This was confirmed nine years later, and was soon followed by the appearance of a Thomas Godebowre, presumably the same man, as the parish priest of Dacre. In 1476, when he presided over an election at Hexham Priory, he was already prior of Carlisle.

As prior, Gondibour continued and extended the building programme of his predecessor by constructing a new refectory and a tithe barn conveniently close to the priory. He was also responsible for a major redecoration of the interior of Carlisle Cathedral that included a carved wooden screen, colourful paintwork on the roof and choir pillars, and wall paintings. These undertakings received support from Richard III, who contributed £5 towards a glass window, and from the bishop, Richard Bell, previously prior of Durham, who may have lent an illuminated Durham manuscript of Bede's life of St Cuthbert to provide a model for the artists commissioned to embellish the panels of the canons' stalls. Gondibour took steps to commemorate his architectural achievements, as witnessed by an inscription noted by Browne Willis on an old press in St Katharine's Chapel: *domus hec floruit sub tegmine Thome* ('this house flourished under Thomas's rule'). His resignation or death had occurred before 6 June 1502, when his successor was reported as being in office.

JOAN GREATREX

Sources *CEPR letters*, 10.1447–55; 11.1455–64 • *CPR, 1494–1509* • *VCH Cumberland*, vol. 2 • H. Summerson, *Medieval Carlisle: the city and the borders from the late eleventh to the mid-sixteenth century*, 2 vols., Cumberland and Westmorland Antiquarian and Archaeological Society, extra ser., 25 (1993) • R. B. Dobson, 'Richard Bell, prior of Durham (1464–78) and bishop of Carlisle (1478–95)', *Transactions of the Cumberland and Westmorland Antiquarian and Archaeological Society*, new ser., 65 (1965), 182–221 • C. M. L. Bouch, *Prelates and people of the lake counties: a history of the diocese of Carlisle, 1133–1933* (1948) • J. Raine, ed., *The priory of Hexham*, 2 vols., SurtS, 44, 46 (1864–5) • B. Willis, *An history of the mitred parliamentary abbies and conventual cathedral churches*, 2 vols. (1718–19) • Dugdale, *Monasticon*, new edn

Gondomar. For this title name *see* Sarmiento de Acuña, Diego, count of Gondomar in the Spanish nobility (1567–1626).

Gonell, William (*d.* 1560), schoolmaster, came from a family whose home was at Landbeach, 5 miles north-east of Cambridge. The date of his birth should probably be placed in the mid-1480s, since he is described as a 'young man' (*iuvenis*) in a letter of Erasmus dated November 1513 (*Opus epistolarum*, 1.279). He must have attended Cambridge University, but no record of his undergraduate career has survived. Gonell came to the notice of Erasmus during the latter's tenure of a lectureship in Greek at Cambridge between 1511 and 1514. They enjoyed shared scholarly interests, and in addition Gonell earned Erasmus's special gratitude as a result of his skill in horsemanship. Erasmus, who enjoyed riding as a relaxation from study, entrusted his horse to the young man's care, and declared himself more than satisfied with the result:

> my horse, dear Gonell, always comes back to me fresher and in better condition, thus proving how carefully and wisely he has been fed. Therefore I heartily beseech you to continue to look after our nag as you have begun to do. (ibid., 1.274)

When plague broke out in Cambridge during the autumn of 1513 Erasmus probably stayed for a few weeks with the Gonell family at Landbeach.

Gonell appears to have kept a school in Cambridge. Erasmus addresses him as *ludi magister* ('schoolmaster'; *Opus epistolarum*, 1.257), and in a letter dated 28 April 1514 he informs Gonell of his opinion that two educational works he has prepared for publication 'will be of great use to you and yours' (ibid., 1.292). Two letters from Gonell to his pupil Henry Gold, dating from 1516 and 1517, reveal that Gonell was already at that time an intimate of the household of Thomas More. In 1518 he succeeded John Clement as tutor to More's children. A letter from More to Gonell sets out More's philosophy for their education, focusing particularly on his three daughters: 'let them put virtue in the first place, learning in the second, and esteem most in their studies whatever teaches them piety towards God, charity to all, and Christian humility in themselves' (Routh, 129). Gonell also enjoyed the patronage of Cardinal Wolsey, who in 1517 secured for him the rectorship of Conington, Cambridgeshire. He probably served as chaplain to Wolsey for several years.

At some point after 1525, with More's daughters all married, Gonell returned to Cambridge. His intention to do so had apparently become common knowledge, since John Leland addressed a poem to him urging him to leave London. Towards the end of the poem Leland emphasizes the welcome that he will receive from the hunting community. After his return Gonell became a 'public professor' at the university, according to John Pits. In 1529 or thereabouts he was consulted by John Palsgrave about the education of Henry VIII's natural son, Henry Fitzroy, duke of Richmond. He also enjoyed the friendship of Thomas Cranmer, as can be seen from a letter of Richard Morison to Cranmer written in December 1533, in which Morison states that Gonell had, five years earlier, inspired him with love for the future archbishop. Between 1531 and 1536 Gonell was a pensioner at Gonville Hall. In February 1548 he is mentioned as present at a Cambridge academic supper, when 'joles of fresh salmon' were consumed (*Correspondence of Matthew Parker*, 38).

Gonell died, unmarried, on 28 August 1560, probably at Cambridge, and was buried at St Mary's Church, Conington, Cambridgeshire. His will stipulated that he should be buried 'within the chancel of Conyngton church on the right side'. Nearly forty years later the biographer of Thomas More paid a generous tribute to Gonell, recalling him as a man 'whose memorie is yet fresh in Chambridge for his learning and his works of pietie' (*Life of Sir Thomas More*, 129).

S. F. RYLE

Sources *Opus epistolarum Des. Erasmi Roterodami*, ed. P. S. Allen and others, 12 vols. (1906–58) · *DNB* · P. G. Bietenholz and T. B. Deutscher, eds., *Contemporaries of Erasmus: a biographical register*, 2 (1986), 118 · Venn, *Alum. Cant.*, 1/2.231 · *The correspondence of Sir Thomas More*, ed. E. F. Rogers (1947), 120–3, 404 · *LP Henry VIII*, 2/2, appx 17; 6, no. 1582; *addenda*, 1, no. 156 · J. Leland, *Principum, ac illustrium aliquot et eruditorum in Anglia virorum* (1589), 28–9 · Ro: Ba:, *The lyfe of Syr Thomas More, sometymes lord chancellor of England*, ed. E. V. Hitchcock and P. E. Hallett, EETS, 222 (1950), 129 · E. M. G. Routh, *Sir Thomas More and his friends* (1934), 129 · J. Pits, *De rebus Anglicis* (Paris, 1619), 854–5 · S. Knight, *Life of Erasmus* (1726), 176–9 · D. F. S. Thomson and H. C. Porter, *Erasmus and Cambridge* (1963), 130, 159, 161–3, 164–5, 179–81, 221–2 · *Correspondence of Matthew Parker*, ed. J. Bruce and T. T. Perowne, Parker Society, 42 (1853), 38 · will, PRO, PROB 11/43, sig. 45

Gonella, Nathaniel Charles [Nat] (**1908–1998**), jazz trumpeter and singer, was born on 7 March 1908 at 15 Edward Square, Islington, London, the fourth of seven children of Richard Henry Gonella (1871–1915), cab driver, and his wife, Elizabeth Susan Finnes. His father, who was of partly Italian descent, drove one of the first motorized London taxis. He died when Gonella was seven, and Gonella, a sister, and a brother were placed in St Mary's Guardians School, Islington, an orphanage. On one occasion Gonella escaped but was returned by the local police. Attracted initially by its uniform, he joined the school band, and was taught to play the cornet by William Clarke, formerly bandmaster of the 1st East Surrey regiment. This brass band training was to have stylistic echoes in the creative output of his later years. Despite winning a soloist's prize in the north London band contest (on the tenor horn), he briefly discontinued playing after contracting rheumatic fever.

After leaving school in 1923, Gonella worked as an apprentice tailor and errand-boy; but he took up the cornet again and played with the St Pancras British Legion brass band before joining Archie Pitt's Busby Boys (headed by the impresario husband of the singer Gracie Fields) to tour in shows including *A Week's Pleasure* and *Safety First* for four years. It was during this time that Fields gave Gonella a used wind-up gramophone and records by the Denza Dance Band, Bix Beiderbecke, and others, thus encouraging an interest in recorded jazz which was further inspired by his discovery of Louis Armstrong soon afterwards:

> I used to listen so much—and play the same thing they did, and I used to write [their solos] out and play from the book to the record. And then after a while you're so het-up in the thing that a little bit comes of your own style and that's how it changes round a bit! (personal knowledge)

In 1928 he joined the Louisville band led by the drummer Bob Dryden, with which he played in Margate, Manchester, and Belfast before moving on to Archie Alexander's band at the Regent Ballroom, Brighton, in 1929. There he was discovered by the London bandleader Billy Cotton, whom he joined as featured trumpet soloist at the Streatham Locarno as well as touring Britain and France (he also made his first recordings with Cotton in 1930). On 11 June 1930 he married the dance instructress Lena Marie Hope Mann (Betty; *b*. 1907/8), daughter of Lambert Jose Ernest Radican Jules Godecharle, male nurse. They had one daughter, Natalie (*b*. 1930). The marriage was dissolved in 1936.

Gonella moved in 1931 to Roy Fox's band (with whom he featured on a hit record, 'Oh, Monah') and remained with the band after it was taken over by the pianist–arranger Lew Stone in 1932; in July of that year he became firm friends with Louis Armstrong, after Armstrong's two-week tenure at the London Palladium. By this time he was becoming known as a new-star British jazzman, and from November 1932 he regularly recorded as a soloist, played with Ray Noble in the Netherlands (1933), and toured in variety with the Quaglino Quartette (1934) led by the violinist Brian Lawrence, establishing in the process a name as 'Britain's Louis Armstrong' (although his playing style was different from Armstrong's own).

While with Lew Stone, Gonella began leading a band within a band, the Georgians (named for his 1934 hit recording of Hoagy Carmichael's 'Georgia on my Mind'), which both closed the first half of Stone's stage show and began recording that year. Then in 1935 (the year in which his book *Modern Style Trumpet Playing* was published) he left Stone after forming his own team of 'Georgians', comprising the tenor saxophonist Pat Smuts, the pianist Harold 'Babe' Hood, the guitarist–singer Jimmy Messini, the bass player Charlie Winter, the drummer Bob Dryden, and the singer Stella Moya. Nat Gonella's Georgians made their début at the Newcastle Empire on 1 April 1935, toured the Netherlands later that year, and for the next four years became a premier bill-topping act at the London Palladium and at theatres throughout Britain, as well as broadcasting and appearing in films.

The Georgians' stage show—as well as their prolific recorded output (at least fifty-seven titles in 1936 alone)—combined swing-based jazz with novelty items designed for music-hall appeal, often opening with an unaccompanied trumpet declamation of the opening bars of 'Georgia on my Mind' from behind the curtain, and frequently concluding with a rip-roaring 'Tiger Rag' (another of Gonella's recorded hits), complete with soft toy tiger cubs thrown to the audience as a show-business finale. In December 1938 Gonella visited New York, played with Americans including Joe Marsala and Cab Calloway, performed at Nick's Tavern (substituting for Bobby Hackett), and recorded four memorable sides with an all-American group led by John Kirby. However, in 1939, while on a tour of the Netherlands, the Georgians were forced to split up in anticipation of the German invasion of that country. On 7 September 1940 Gonella married Stella Moya (Stella Rose Lewin, or Musgrave; *b*. 1915/16), the divorced wife of Alec Lewin, or Musgrave, and the daughter of Ah Chie Yau, owner of a tin mine. There were no children of the marriage, which ended in divorce.

After leading his band the New Georgians (1940–41), Gonella was called up into the Pioneer Corps in July 1941. His income immediately dropped from £150 a week to 10*s*. He was posted to north Africa before being transferred to the tank regiment (and its band). He was subsequently discharged following diagnosis of a duodenal ulcer.

After the war Gonella re-formed his New Georgians. His

marriage to Stella Moya having broken down, in 1946 he met his third wife, Dorothy Audrey Collins (1910/11–1996), daughter of Frank Littler. (They eventually married on 31 March 1965.) Musical fashions were changing, and Gonella's band fell from thirteen pieces to ten, then to eight, finally becoming a quartet; during this post-war period he also embraced modern jazz (bebop), a music which he later rejected but which contemporaries such as Lennie Bush remembered him playing with skill and conviction. After being asked by a newly arrived producer to re-audition for the BBC (and inexplicably failing!), Gonella continued both to lead bands and to work as a soloist, also teaming with the comedians Max Miller and Leon Cortez, until, with the arrival of the British 'trad boom', he both led his own Georgia Jazz Band and, later, guested with Doug Richford's band (1961–2); he also returned to public attention with an edition of *This is your Life* on television in 1961 and with LPs including *Salute to Satchmo* and *The Nat Gonella Story* (both 1961). Just as the Beatles were about to effect a mass change in popular culture in 1962, Gonella moved to Leyland, Lancashire, to work in northern clubs; he also toured nationally with an 'old time music hall' theatre show before retiring on his sixty-fifth birthday in March 1973. However, in 1975 a re-recording with Ted Easton's Jazz Band of his hit 'Oh, Monah' reached no. 5 in the Dutch hit parade, and Gonella briefly returned to professional trumpeting as well as performance before handing the instrument over permanently to his daughter Natalie. From then onwards he confined himself to singing, and after moving to Gosport in 1977 became a regular at the town's jazz club, of which he was long-time president.

In 1985 a television special on Channel 4 entitled *Fifty Years of Nat Gonella* celebrated Gonella in company with Humphrey Lyttelton and Digby Fairweather's New Georgians; in the same year a biography, *Georgia on my Mind: the Nat Gonella Story* by Ron Brown (with Cyril Brown), was published, and thereafter Gonella continued to attract regular attention on both radio and television. In September 1994 a square in Gosport centre was named after him, the first of several town memorials. After the death of his wife, Dorothy, in 1996, he returned to active performance outside Gosport, including South Bank concerts, jazz festivals, and a week of radio appearances and bill-topping at the Pizza on the Park restaurant, London, in February 1998, with Digby Fairweather's band. He died in Gosport War Memorial Hospital of ischaemic heart disease on 6 August 1998, following an operation to set a broken elbow. After a service in St Mary's Church, Alverstoke, on 20 August 1998, he was buried next to his third wife, Dorothy, in Anns Hill cemetery, Gosport. He was survived by his daughter, Natalie Wilson. DIGBY FAIRWEATHER

Sources R. Brown and C. Brown, *Georgia on my mind: the Nat Gonella story* (1985) • J. Chilton, *Who's who of British jazz* (1998) • *The Times* (8 Aug 1998) • *The Guardian* (8 Aug 1998) • *The Independent* (8 Aug 1998) • personal knowledge (2004) [incl. taped interview] • private information (2004) • b. cert. • m. certs. • d. cert.

Archives Loughton Central Library, Essex, National Jazz Archive | SOUND BL NSA

Likenesses photograph, repro. in *The Times* • photograph, repro. in *The Guardian* • photograph, repro. in *The Independent*

Wealth at death under £200,000: probate, 1998, *CGPLA Eng. & Wales* (1998)

Gonne, Iseult Lucille Germaine. *See* Stuart, Iseult Lucille Germaine (1894–1954).

Gonne, (Edith) Maud (**1866–1953**), Irish nationalist, was born on 21 December 1866 at Tongham Manor, near Farnham, Surrey, eldest daughter of Captain Thomas Gonne (1835–1886) of the 17th lancers and his wife, Edith Frith Cook (1844–1871), daughter of William Cook, merchant, and Margaretta Cockayne Frith. In April 1868 Thomas Gonne was appointed cavalry brigade major in Ireland and was stationed at Curragh Camp, co. Kildare. Maud's sister Kathleen Gonne (*d.* 1919) was born in September 1868. Edith Gonne, suffering from tuberculosis, gave birth in London to her third child, Margaretta, in June 1871, and died on the twenty first of that month; Margaretta died on 9 August. The trauma affected Maud Gonne deeply. She recalled that her father had said, as he showed her Edith's coffin, that she must not fear anything, not even death.

The family returned to Ireland and the children and their nurse were moved to a cottage at Howth, a beautiful promontory north of Dublin, which remained a sacred place for Maud Gonne. Thomas Gonne was recalled by Maud Gonne as 'Tommy', an ideal father, and his enchanting letters to 'Lamb' (Maud) and 'Bear' (Kathleen) fully support this. In 1876 Major Gonne was appointed military attaché to the Austrian court and the family left Ireland. The children were brought up by a nurse–housekeeper and governesses in England, with unhappy visits to their wealthy Cook relatives. When Thomas Gonne was posted to India in 1879 he moved the children to the south of France for health reasons. They were taught by a governess, Mme Deployant, who contributed to Maud Gonne's identification with republicanism and with France. In 1885 Colonel Gonne was appointed assistant adjutant-general for the Dublin district and Maud Gonne was presented at the levee at Dublin Castle on 9 April, wearing an iridescent dress with a train decorated with water lilies; at the castle ball on 10 April she danced with Prince Albert Victor, eldest son of the prince of Wales.

Irish nationalism: W. B. Yeats By 1886 Maud Gonne had become a nationalist; she recited 'Emmet's Death', from *The Spirit of the Nation* (1845), at a public dinner at which her father was present. Tommy was indulgent to her embryonic nationalism—he feared that Maud might, like her mother, die young. Maud Gonne's nationalism was paradoxical: born in England of English parents she was Irish by passionate identification and remote descent.

In summer 1886 Maud Gonne spent time in France and Germany with her great-aunt Mary, widow of the comte de Sizeranne, who hoped to launch her as a professional beauty; Colonel Gonne intervened and took her to Bayreuth for the Wagner festival. On their return to Dublin he told Maud that he would resign his commission and become a home rule MP; her elaborate autobiographical

(Edith) **Maud Gonne (1866–1953)**, by Sarah Purser, 1898

account of this episode is possibly fabrication. Colonel Gonne died on 30 November 1886 from typhoid fever. Maud Gonne, whose relationship with her father was perhaps over close, recalled 'I was too bewildered to cry' (Gonne, 'Tower'). Maud and Kathleen Gonne spent an unhappy time in London under the guardianship of their uncle William Gonne. Unaware that she would inherit a fortune on her majority Maud Gonne tried to become an actress, but became ill before she could perform; in summer 1887 she went to Royat to recover. Here she met Lucien Millevoye (1850–1918), a married journalist, later a *député* and 'at once and without any urging on his part [fell] in love with him' (Yeats, *Memoirs*, 132). Although in both published and unpublished autobiographies Maud Gonne dates this fateful meeting to 1887, in 1898 she told Yeats that she had met Millevoye shortly before her father's death.

In December 1887 Maud Gonne inherited trust funds in excess of £13,000 and an unentailed sum from her mother's estate and was free to live as she pleased. She travelled to Russia early in 1888 on a clandestine Boulangist mission; her relationship with Millevoye was also politically driven, an alliance against the British empire. She returned to Dublin and established herself in nationalist circles, becoming a close friend of the old Fenian John O'Leary. On 30 January she was in London with an introduction from John O'Leary to the poet William Butler *Yeats (1865–1939). Their meeting had a political motive; Yeats was probably already a member of the Irish Republican Brotherhood. However, Maud Gonne's beauty—tall, bronze haired, bronze-eyed and with a 'complexion … luminous, like that of apple-blossom through which the light falls' (Yeats, *Autobiographies*, 123)—mobilized an obsessive passion in Yeats which lasted for twenty-five years.

By April 1889 Maud Gonne was pregnant by Millevoye; her first child, Georges, was born on 11 January 1890, probably in Paris, where she had an apartment. In spring 1890 she began her first political campaign against evictions in Donegal. She lectured on the horrors of eviction to English audiences, returning to Donegal in November. This campaign affected her health and she went to the south of France to recover and to spend time with Millevoye—and presumably with her child.

In 1891 Maud Gonne spent part of the summer in Ireland in the company of Yeats but was called back to Paris where her child was seriously ill. Georges Gonne died on 31 August and she wrote Yeats a letter of 'wild sorrow' telling him that an 'adopted' child had died (Yeats, *Memoirs*, 47). On 11 October she accompanied Parnell's coffin to Dublin, wearing deep mourning for her son. She talked obsessively of Georges to Yeats, asking whether he could be reincarnated; she kept a photograph of the dead child for the rest of her life. Yeats and Maud Gonne were possibly briefly engaged, and in November 1891 she joined the Order of the Golden Dawn, the magical order to which he belonged, as 'Per Ignem ad Lucem'.

On her return to Paris, Maud Gonne resumed her activist career, first in France as a public speaker—her beauty, histrionic delivery and anti-British polemic ensuring success—then in Great Britain and Ireland on behalf of the Amnesty Association. Her political bearings were complicated. She became a member of the revolutionary Irish National Alliance, but saw herself as a socialist and joined James Connolly's Irish Socialist Republican Party in 1897. She was also moulded by her right-wing Boulangist associates and endorsed antisemitic and anti-masonic conspiracy theories—she was a vehement anti-Dreyfusard. Her grasp of history was simplistic, a facile contrast of English vice and Irish virtue, a 'melodrama with Ireland for blameless hero' (Yeats, *Autobiographies*, 206). She summarized her political formula: 'to look on which side England ranges herself & go on the opposite' (White and Jeffares, 437).

In 1893, hoping to reincarnate her dead child, Maud Gonne and Millevoye had intercourse in the crypt of the mausoleum which she had built for Georges. The birth of her daughter Iseult Gonne [*see* Stuart, Iseult Lucille Germaine] in Paris on 6 August 1894 ended Maud Gonne's sexual relationship with Millevoye. She rapidly returned to work for the Amnesty Association. Early in 1897 she started her own journal, *L'Irlande Libre*, to present the Irish cause to continental Europe and was involved in the jubilee riots in Dublin in June 1897. Late in 1897 she toured the

United States raising money for the 1798 centennial celebrations, with which she was deeply involved. During the celebrations she spoke widely to huge crowds.

In Dublin in December 1898 she and Yeats had a shared dream of an astral marriage; she then told him of her relationship with Millevoye and of the existence of Iseult, whom she brought up but did not publicly acknowledge as her daughter. Scandal concerning her had circulated in Ireland, but Yeats had discounted this. Their relationship remained close, focused on the Celtic Mystical Order which he had developed, but she refused to marry him.

Marriage: later life In 1899–1900 Maud Gonne was active in Irish and European opposition to the South African wars and enthusiastically mythologized those Irishmen who fought for the Boers. One such, Major John *MacBride (1868–1916), from a Mayo trade background, toured the United States with her in 1901, and in June 1902 she agreed to marry him. She admired MacBride, whom she thought vital and honourable. She faced opposition from friends and family—as well as a supernatural warning from Tommy. Yeats begged her not to marry MacBride, reminding her of their own spiritual marriage of 1898. She told her sister that she was ageing and was tired of her lonely struggle. Maud Gonne converted to Catholicism and married MacBride on 21 February 1903 in Paris. The MacBrides travelled to Spain in April 1903, hoping to assassinate Edward VII, who was visiting Gibraltar. Maud Gonne thought that this scheme might have fatal consequences for herself: she had already made her cousin, May Bertie-Clay, Iseult's guardian.

In May 1903 in Dublin she told Yeats that she had made a disastrous error. However, she realized that she was pregnant and returned to Paris to salvage the situation, prepared to endure MacBride's heavy drinking and brutality. Seán (Seaghan) *MacBride (1904–1988) was born on 26 January 1904. Late in 1904 Maud Gonne discovered evidence that MacBride had sexually assaulted Iseult and that he and Eileen Wilson (1886–1972), Maud's illegitimate half-sister, had had an affair before Eileen's marriage to his elder brother, Joseph. Maud Gonne initiated divorce proceedings and confessed to Yeats her disgust with 'a hero I had made' (White and Jeffares, 184). In a widely reported case in which Iseult was identified as her daughter she succeeded on 8 August 1906, in obtaining a legal separation and custody of Seán. The scandal damaged her position in nationalist circles. Her pamphlet condemning Irish women who had illegitimate children by British soldiers now seemed hypocritical and in 1906 she was hissed in the Abbey Theatre, where she had acted in Yeats's *Kathleen ni Houlihan* in 1902, embodying Ireland itself. In an interview to the *New York Evening World* she denounced marriage as deplorable for an intelligent woman.

Maud Gonne's life became centred in France and her political activism diminished for a time, although she helped to establish a women's nationalist journal, *Bean na hEireann*, in 1908—she had been a founder member of *Inghinidhe na hEireann* in 1900—and was active in social causes, organizing food for poor children and for the families of striking workers in the 1913 Dublin lock-out. Yeats regularly visited Maud Gonne in Normandy and they had a brief affair, which began on the astral plane in June 1908 and was consummated in December. She ended the affair in May 1909, but Yeats remained a close friend. The outbreak of the First World War greatly distressed her: the alliance between Great Britain and France confounded her allegiances and she drew on conspiracy theories to explicate the conflict. She served as a nurse in French military hospitals during the war. The 1916 Easter rising and the execution of John MacBride transformed her life. She wore mourning and called herself Maud Gonne MacBride, insisting that 'Major MacBride by his Death has left a name for Seán to be proud of. Those who die for Ireland are sacred' (White and Jeffares, 375).

Yeats proposed to Maud Gonne in July 1916 and on being rejected proposed unsuccessfully to Iseult. In January 1918 Maud Gonne returned to Dublin; in May she was arrested for alleged involvement in a pro-German conspiracy and transferred to Holloway prison in London. She was released in November 1918 and returned to Dublin with her children. In 1920 Iseult Gonne married the writer Francis Stuart, whom Maud Gonne thought vicious and unstable.

Maud Gonne initially accepted the treaty of 1921, but when the Irish civil war began in 1922 she bitterly attacked the free state government and was twice imprisoned in 1923. Age did not diminish her activism; she frequently led demonstrations on behalf of political prisoners and endorsed a marginalized IRA. In international politics her views were idiosyncratic: in 1938 she pressed what she perceived to be the positive aspects of both fascism and communism as a model for Ireland. In 1938 she published a vivid if disingenuous autobiography, *A Servant of the Queen*. She was secure in her family life, sharing Roebuck House, Clonskeagh, Dublin, with her son, daughter-in-law, and much loved grandchildren, Anna and Tiernan. She took pride in Seán MacBride's career, both as IRA chief-of-staff and cabinet minister. She remained very close to her daughter, although she could never acknowledge the relationship. Maud Gonne died of heart disease at her home on 27 April 1953: her last recorded words were 'I feel now an ineffable joy' (Iseult Stuart to Francis Stuart, 2 May 1953, Southern Illinois University). Georges Gonne's booties were placed in the coffin at her request and crowds followed the funeral procession to Glasnevin cemetery on 29 April.

Maud Gonne was the subject of more than eighty poems by Yeats; the last, 'A Bronze Head', meditates on her trajectory from wild young beauty to 'dark tomb-haunter'. Despite a lifetime's grass-roots political activism—speeches, journalism, pamphleteering, protests—Maud Gonne remains best known for her role in Yeats's life and work.

DEIRDRE TOOMEY

Sources M. Gonne MacBride, *A servant of the queen* (1994) · *The Gonne–Yeats letters, 1893–1938*, ed. A. MacBride White and A. N. Jeffares (1992) · M. Gonne, 'The tower of age', unpublished autobiography, MacBride family papers, priv. coll. · W. B. Yeats, *Memoirs*, ed. D. Donoghue (1972) · W. B. Yeats, *Autobiographies* (1955) · *The collected letters of W. B. Yeats*, 3, ed. J. Kelly and R. Schuchard (1994) · W. B. Yeats, *Poems*, ed. A. N. Jeffares (1996) · Iseult Stuart to Francis

Stuart, 2 May 1953, Southern Illinois University • M. Ward, *Maud Gonne: Ireland's Joan of Arc* (1990)
Archives NYPL, letters • priv. coll., family papers • PRO, papers, CO 904 | NL Ire., letters to Ethel Mannin | SOUND BL NSA
Likenesses S. Purser, oils, *c.*1889, NG Ire. • S. Purser, pastel drawing, 1898, Hugh Lane Gallery, Dublin [*see illus.*] • J. B. Yeats, pencil and watercolour drawing, 1907, NG Ire. • S. O'Sullivan, chalk and charcoal drawing, 1929, NG Ire. • L. Campbell, plaster bust, Hugh Lane Gallery, Dublin • S. Purser, oils, Hugh Lane Gallery, Dublin • S. Purser, pastel drawing, NG Ire. • photographs, priv. coll. • photographs, NL Ire.

Gonner, Sir Edward Carter Kersey (1862–1922), economist, was born on 5 March 1862 at 35 Conduit Street, Mayfair, London, the second son of Peter Kersey Gonner, silk mercer, and his wife, Elizabeth Carter. He was educated at Merchant Taylors' School, London, before entering Lincoln College, Oxford, in 1880 to study history, in which he gained a first in 1884. After leaving Oxford he worked briefly for the London Extension Society. In the autumn of 1885 he moved to an appointment as lecturer in political economy, modern history, and English literature at University College, Bristol, the combination of subjects reflecting the demands of the University of London BA degree, for which Bristol prepared its students. In 1888 he moved from Bristol to University College, Liverpool, which was at that time a part of the federal Victoria University of Manchester together with Owens College, Manchester, and Yorkshire College, Leeds. In 1890 Gonner married Annie Ledlie; they had one daughter.

In 1891 Gonner was appointed to the newly endowed Brunner chair of economic science at Liverpool, a post which he held until his death. He thus became part of a generation of Oxford history graduates who played a significant part in the development of the teaching of economics at Oxford and elsewhere; William Ashley, for example, was a close contemporary. The Liverpool appointment enabled Gonner to develop his interests in both history and political economy, and was to prove the formative influence on his development as a teacher and economist. At the end of the nineteenth century Liverpool was at the peak of its commercial significance, being Britain's principal Atlantic port and the second city of England as regards population and wealth. The college did not want for benefactors, and Gonner's initial appointment was endowed by members of the shipping and insurance community. Much of his early teaching was directed towards clerks seeking employment in this sector, and his courses were geared towards the Victoria University final examination or the local college business curriculum. His teaching was reflected in his published work during this period: an elementary textbook on the economics of commerce entitled *The University Economics* (1888), *Commercial Geography* (1894), and two works on socialism, *The Socialist State* (1895) and *The Social Philosophy of Rodbertus* (1899). By the end of the 1890s the college business curriculum had developed into a school of commerce, a joint venture between the city and the university college, which formed the basis on which the newly independent university initiated its bachelor of commercial science degree in 1909.

In 1894 Gonner was responsible for a report to the British Association for the Advancement of Science on the teaching of economics in Britain and abroad, contributing an appendix on Britain which drew attention to a lack of systematic training in the subject, and a survey of provision for such training in continental Europe. At this time, he noted, the Cambridge and the Liverpool chairs were the sole full-time professorial appointments in economics, and Alfred Flux in Manchester was the only fully occupied lecturer. Popular teaching in political economy was generally more successful, Gonner observed, but in Britain the development of university teaching in the subject was hindered by a failure on the part of relevant professions, such as banking and the civil service, to require of its recruits more than a passing acquaintance with the subject.

Gonner was twice elected president of section F (economics and statistics) of the British Association, and chaired meetings in Toronto (1898) and Australia (1914). The continuing breadth of his interests is demonstrated by the fact that, during the period 1906–9 he was a member of the royal commission on shipping conferences, and in 1912 he published his important study of the development of the English farming landscape, *Common Land and Inclosure*. Ostensibly a history of the appropriation of common land for individual use, charting the impact of this transition upon cultivation and employment, it had an explicitly analytical framework which owed much to Gonner's work in geography and economics. Likewise his interest in and advocacy of the writings of David Ricardo, of which he published editions in 1895 and 1923, sets him apart from those of his contemporaries who were shaping an approach to economic history broadly hostile to the analytical style of the new economics. As a 'historical economist' there was a great deal more of the economist than the historian in Gonner's approach. This is also evident in his work during the First World War in the Ministry of Food where he worked first as an economic adviser, then as director of statistics. His administrative skills were also put to use as an industrial arbitrator for the Ministry of Labour. Gonner was appointed CBE in 1918 and KBE in 1921 for his wartime service. At his death he was working as a member of the editorial board established by the Carnegie endowment to produce a social and economic history of wartime administration. He died of bronchial pneumonia on 24 February 1922 at 42 Heathfield Road, Wavertree, Liverpool; his funeral took place at Willaston church, near Chester, on 27 February. His wife survived him. KEITH TRIBE

Sources W. H. Beveridge, *Economic Journal*, 31 (1922), 264–7 • *WWW* • *CGPLA Eng. & Wales* (1922) • b. cert. • d. cert.
Archives U. Lpool L., papers
Wealth at death £25,559 19*s.* 5*d.*: probate, 17 May 1922, *CGPLA Eng. & Wales*

Gonsales de Puebla, Rodrigo (*d.* 1509), lawyer and diplomat, was of obscure but presumably Castilian origins; he was accused of being Jewish by aristocratic Spanish detractors. Nor is much known about his close relatives: his daughter was arrested by the inquisition in Seville *c.*1504, but his son went on to be chaplain to the emperor

Charles V. Puebla was certainly a widower by 1498, when his financial insecurity induced Henry VII to offer him either an English bishopric or a lucrative marriage. He was a doctor of civil and canon law, but the details of his education have not come to light. The first public office he is known to have held was that of *corregidor* of Ecija in Andalusia. In contrast to the obscurity of his life in Spain, however, copious diplomatic correspondence permits more detailed reconstruction of his career in England as resident ambassador of Ferdinand of Aragon and Isabella of Castile.

The first of Puebla's two English embassies, which he shared with Juan de Sepúlveda, began in the winter of 1487–8. It was designed to engineer an anti-French, Anglo-Spanish alliance, to be cemented by the marriage of the baby Arthur, prince of Wales, with the hardly less juvenile Infanta Catalina (Katherine of Aragon). The marriage was duly agreed by the terms of the treaty of Medina del Campo (27 March 1489). In the course of this embassy Puebla also attempted to divert the young James V of Scotland from his French alliance by offering the king a marriage with Ferdinand's daughter Juana. The ambassador omitted to explain that this was an illegitimate daughter and not the Infanta Juana who married Philip the Fair, son of Emperor Maximilian, in 1496. Puebla returned to Spain later that year, but no move was made to send the infanta to England. The invasion of Italy by Charles VIII of France in 1494 prompted renewed Spanish interest in the Tudor dynasty and in 1495 led to Puebla's second commission for England. He was resident in London for the remainder of his life and took lodgings in the Strand. It was not until 1501 that the fifteen-year-old infanta travelled to England. Puebla spent the intervening period cultivating Henry VII so assiduously that his fellow countrymen suspected him of acting more in Henry's interest than that of the Spanish monarchs. His authority was seriously undermined by the arrival of Don Pedro de Ayala, bishop of the Canaries and Spanish ambassador to Scotland. The aristocratic Ayala's contempt for the lowly born Puebla was shared by Katherine of Aragon and her influential duenna Doña Elvira Manuel, though diplomatic dispatches reveal that Puebla consistently supported the princess's cause at the English court, particularly during her impoverished widowhood. Assured by Doña Elvira that Katherine's marriage had been consummated, Puebla never wavered from his conviction that it was valid in all respects.

Following Prince Arthur's death in 1502, Hernan, duke of Estrada, was sent as ambassador to England, but Puebla remained in day-to-day command of political and commercial negotiations with Henry and his council. After Henry himself was widowed in 1503, these negotiations included the possibility that he might contract a Spanish marriage, perhaps even with Katherine. The most acute crisis of this lengthy embassy occurred in 1505, less than a year after the death of Isabella of Castile, when Puebla discovered that Doña Elvira and her brother Don Juan Manuel were planning a meeting between Henry and Philip, accompanied respectively by the sisters Katherine and Juana: this looked like the basis for a potential Anglo-Habsburg alliance against Ferdinand of Aragon. Puebla managed to scotch this plan, but his testy character continued to mar his dealings with Spanish representatives in England. Gutierre Gomez de Fuensalida was given powers to negotiate Katherine's marriage with Henry, prince of Wales, though Puebla's experience was called upon when these negotiations stalled. Fuensalida was convinced that Puebla was colluding with the English and, in Ferdinand's name, dismissed him as ambassador late in June 1508. Crippled by gout and medical costs, Puebla lived for some ten months after this disgrace, dying in spring 1509.

STELLA FLETCHER

Sources *CSP Spain, 1485–1525; suppl., 1485–1525* • G. Mattingly, *Catherine of Aragon* (1942) • Duque de Alba, *Correspondencia de Gutierre Gomez de Fuensalida, embajador en Alemania, Flandes é Inglaterra (1496–1509)* (1907) • *The Anglica historia of Polydore Vergil, AD 1485–1537*, ed. and trans. D. Hay, CS, 3rd ser., 74 (1950) • R. P. Luis Fernández de Retona, *Isabel la Católica*, 2 vols. (1947) • S. B. Chrimes, *Henry VII* (1972) • N. Macdougall, *James IV* (1989)

Gonson, Benjamin (*c.*1525–1577). *See under* Gonson, William (*d.* 1544).

Gonson, William (*d.* 1544), naval administrator, was a son of Christopher Gonson (*d.* 1498?) of Melton Mowbray, Leicestershire, and his wife, Elizabeth. Another son, Bartholomew, became vicar there. Nothing is known of William's early life: he was possibly the Captain William Gonson who sailed in government service and later directed shipping movements. He was certainly a clerk in the navy storehouse at Deptford, Kent, receiving ropes and artillery pieces (1513) and armorial banners (1514) for ships. Thereafter his diverse duties and responsibilities are attested in official records: indeed, he was chief executive *de facto* of the navy for almost twenty years, and after his death was—in effect—replaced by a 'navy board'.

Gonson married Benet Waters (*d.* 1545/6). They had six sons (Richard, David, Christopher, Arthur, Benjamin [*see below*], and Anthony) and three daughters (Elizabeth, Avis, and Thomasine), and they resided in Thames Street, London, in the parish of St Dunstan-in-the-East. Gonson was well paid, both from his naval appointments and as one of Henry VIII's squires of the body, though his great wealth probably came through his commercial activities. In 1525 he was a warden of the Grocers' Company, and he may by then have owned the 'great *Mary Grace*', which traded to the Greek islands. Thus, in 1530, he was one of twenty-two merchants trading with Candia (Crete); and about 1534 his ship *Matthew Gonson* (300 tons), with his son Richard as captain, sailed with a consort to Chios (where Richard died) and Candia (Crete). In March 1539 foreign merchants' goods in an unidentified ship of Gonson's were valued at 50,000 marks sterling (over £33,000), and in 1541 he was assessed for subsidy on £1000. In 1524 he became keeper of the storehouses at Deptford and Erith, Kent, and an usher of the king's chamber, and for part of the period 1532–7 he handled sums of money totalling more than £15,589. Hence he was concerned with rigging warships, paying money for wages and victualling, purchasing masts, repairing Thames forts, building ships (for example, the *Galley Subtile*), and (in 1539) sending a fleet to bring Anne of Cleves from Calais to Dover for her marriage to Henry VIII. He was vice-admiral—the first in England—of Norfolk and Suffolk from 1536 until 1543, and held courts at Kings Lynn and elsewhere.

In 1540 Gonson made arrangements with his parish for his funeral. He was to have a memorial brass made and let into another man's gravestone, and, following interment in St Dunstan's, to have requiem masses performed annually for twenty years. In July 1541 his son Sir David, a knight of St John of Jerusalem, was executed as a traitor. Plainly, William Gonson's responsibilities imposed great strain, particularly with the Anglo-French war (1543–6), and in 1544 (before 5 August, when Benjamin was accounting) he 'feloniously killed himself' (*LP Henry VIII* 20/1, no. 125/7). A suicide's body had, by law, to be buried, with a stake through the heart, near local crossroads: Gonson was interred in his parish church, which suggests that matters were hushed up. No will or administration has been found. Gonson's value to his country was recognized, after his death, by the creation of a 'navy board' to replace him. The will of his widow, Benet, was made on 18 August 1545, the executors being her son Benjamin, to whom she left a few items of plate, and Thomasine's husband, Henry Tyrrell; probate was granted on 23 February 1546. **Benjamin Gonson** (*c.*1525–1577), naval administrator, followed his father into government service. His brother Christopher was the heir of their father (in 1545) and their brother Arthur of their mother (1546), so Benjamin was probably the fifth son. As he was of age to marry by 8 June 1546, he was born perhaps about 1525; he commenced his government work during 1540–41, doubtless as his father's assistant, so succeeded him, as from 5 August 1544. However, William's death underlined the chaotic situation, and in 1546 a 'council of marine' was established, Gonson being appointed surveyor of ships, from 24 April 1546, with a salary of £40 per annum. From 30 September 1548 he served as treasurer of the navy (though his patent is dated 8 July 1549), with a salary of £66 13*s.* 4*d.* These officers of marine causes (Gonson himself, William Holstock, Sir William Winter, Sir Edward Baeshe)—able beneficiaries of William Gonson's reforms—now met within the city of London, in a house on Tower Hill. In fact it was convenient for the nearby naval storehouses, the Tower's ordnance depot, and the shipyards downstream.

Gonson lived in Tower Street, in the parish of St Dunstan-in-the-East, where he was assessed for subsidy in 1559 (on £180) and 1576 (£200), but he also owned property in Great Baddow, Essex. He married Ursula Hussey (*d.* 1586), and his list of their fourteen children, born within the years 1547–67, supplies unusual detail. All were born and baptized in his parish except for Thomasine, who 'was born in the Queen[']s house at Deptford (wherein I dwelled)' in 1564, and was baptized in the local church (BL, Add. MS 15857, fol. 153*v*); their father's social standing is clear from the eminence of the godparents, who included Sir Thomas Lodge and the current mayoress of London. Gonson had been a promoter of the voyages of John Hawkins to Guinea for black slaves in 1562 and 1564, and his daughter Katherine (*b.* 1549) married Hawkins on 20 January 1567 at St Dunstan-in-the-East. The first husband of Thomasine was Edward *Fenton.

As treasurer, Gonson handled large sums of money (£28,285 for the year from Christmas 1555), and from January 1557 he was given an annual appropriation, initially of £14,000, instead. For example, during 1569 payments were made for wages, board, and lodging for men repairing major warships, and for sending 880 men to four ships; providing timber from Sussex; bringing a warship from Liverpool to Deptford, Kent; and for purchasing land in Kent, needed for Upnor Castle.

In 1577 Gonson was taken ill: knowing that John Hawkins would obtain the treasurership, he told him, 'I shall pluck a thorn out of my foot and put it into yours' (Oppenheim, 145). Gonson died later that year (his accounts for 1576 and 1577 were rendered by his daughter Ursula and her husband), and was buried on 11 December at St Dunstan's. On 18 March 1578 administration was granted to his widow Ursula. Their son Benjamin (*b.* 1551) was clerk of the ships from 1588 to 1600. JOHN BENNELL

Sources *LP Henry VIII*, vols. 1, 4, 9, 15–16, 18, 20–21, *addenda* · M. Stephenson, *A list of monumental brasses in the British Isles*, [new edn] (1964), 276 · R. Hakluyt, *The principal navigations, voyages, traffiques and discoveries of the English nation*, 5, Hakluyt Society, extra ser., 5 (1904), 67; 6, Hakluyt Society, extra ser., 6 (1904), 253, 262; 10, Hakluyt Society, extra ser., 10 (1904), 7 · BL, Add. MS 15857, fols. 153, 153*v* [B. Gonson's list of children, 1547–69, with an early seventeenth-century addition by Christopher Browne] · BL, Add. MS 7968 [B. Gonson's naval accounts, 1544] · M. Oppenheim, *A history of the administration of the Royal Navy* (1896), 145, 149 · PRO, PROB 11/31, quire 4 · R. M. Glencross, ed., *Administration in the prerogative court of Canterbury, 1572–80*, 2 (1917), 96 · *State papers published under … Henry VIII*, 11 vols. (1830–52), 1.406 · R. G. Marsden, 'The vice-admirals of the coast [pt 1]', *EngHR*, 22 (1907), 468–77 · R. G. Marsden, 'The vice-admirals of the coast [pt 2]', *EngHR*, 23 (1908), 736–57 · C. S. L. Davies, 'The administration of the Royal Navy under Henry VIII: the origins of the navy board', *EngHR*, 80 (1965), 268–86 · E. A. Fry, ed., *Abstracts of inquisitiones post mortem relating to the City of London*, 3: 1577–1603, British RS, 36 (1908), 320, 92 · P. Morant, *The history and antiquities of the county of Essex*, 2 (1768), 19–20 · vestry minutes, St Dunstan-in-the-East, GL, MS 4887, fols. 73*v*, 74 · *CSP dom.*, 1553–8

Gonville [Gonvile], **Edmund** (*d.* **1351**), ecclesiastic and founder of Gonville and Caius College, Cambridge, came from a rising gentry family of French extraction, in the late thirteenth century recently settled in Norfolk. His brother, Nicholas Gonville, married the heir of the manor of Lerling, a match that subsequently somehow enabled his father, William Gonville, to become lord of the manor. There is no reason to suppose that Edmund had studied at university; his early career is obscure. But he must have had access to wealth and patronage beyond what his family could provide. He was rector of Thelnetham, Suffolk, from 1320 to 1326, of Rushford, Norfolk, from 1326 to 1342, when he converted the living into a college of chantry priests, and of Terrington St Clement, Norfolk, from 1343 until his death in 1351. These were prosperous livings, but they are the only benefices he is known to have enjoyed. However, it is clear that Gonville was also a man of affairs; the evidence suggests that he was a land agent, working for some of the leading men of East Anglia. He even worked for the king, lent him money, and was rewarded with the title of king's clerk. His entrepreneurial flair and high connections enabled him to play a crucial role in founding the house of Dominican friars at Thetford in 1335, a college of priests to sing masses for Edmund and his family at Rushford, just outside Thetford, in 1342, and to embark on the foundation of his college in Cambridge in 1348.

The Dominican house in Thetford was founded in 1335 by John de Warenne, earl of Surrey (*d.* 1347), and by Gonville. Warenne's East Anglian estate had been passing back and forth between Warenne and the earls of Lancaster and others for nearly twenty years before this event: from 1327 he had only a life interest in it, and it was to pass to Henry of Grosmont, earl—later duke—of Lancaster (*d.* 1361), on Warenne's death. Gonville seems to have acted as Warenne's agent in the foundation, and had evidently also won the approval of Lancaster for it. A recent study has suggested that the beautiful retable now at Thornham Parva, and the associated altar frontal in the Musée de Cluny at Paris, were made for the Dominican church in Thetford, and that the representation of St Edmund the Martyr and St John the Baptist among the saints upon it reflects a house founded by men called Edmund and John. This has not passed unchallenged, however, and the Cambridge Dominican church has been suggested as an alternative home for the retable and frontal.

At Rushford Gonville built a house and founded a college for five chantry chaplains, whose first duty was to pray for the founder, his family, and all the faithful departed; and the master had pastoral care of the parish. Gonville's statutes for the college lucidly reflect what an experienced parish priest and man of affairs reckoned was necessary for the safety of his soul and his parishioners.

On 28 January 1348 letters patent were granted under the great seal of Edward III for a licence in mortmain allowing permanent endowment of Edmund Gonville's college in Cambridge. The college came to be called alternatively Gonville Hall and the Hall of the Annunciation of the Blessed Virgin Mary—the annunciation figured already on his seal for the college. But Gonville died in November 1351, before his latest foundation was fully established and endowed; and it was set on its feet by his bishop and executor, William Bateman, bishop of Norwich (*d.* 1355), who moved it from what is now part of Corpus Christi College to a more central site, adjacent to the university schools and to his own foundation of Trinity Hall. How much the college owes to Gonville and how much to Bateman is a question often asked, but impossible to answer. Gonville's intention seems to have been to provide for advanced arts students aiming for a theological degree, who might become pastors. In forming a small graduate college he was imitating a group of founders in Oxford and Cambridge, most recently Mary de St Pol, countess of Pembroke (*d.* 1377), founder of the house of Minoresses at Denny and of Pembroke College in Cambridge.

One significant key to how the fourteenth-century economy worked must lie in the profession of land agents. Vast estates were held by rentier, absentee landlords, and their management must have involved complex problems; in many of the richer benefices, too, tithes had to be managed for absentee rectors—some of them cardinals, many of them religious houses in other parts of England. Of these agents exceedingly little is known. Gonville was evidently one of them; he managed estates and he managed livings, and presumably tithes; he was also a commissioner of the marshlands of Norfolk and involved in the affairs of local and (marginally) of central government. He was clearly an able and active entrepreneur, and a diplomat who knew how to manipulate his friendship network to further his purposes. What sets him apart from others of his kind is that he dedicated his skills and money to found religious houses; and his college in Cambridge has perpetuated his name and memory. C. N. L. BROOKE

Sources C. Brooke, 'Chaucer's parson and Edmund Gonville: contrasting roles of fourteenth century incumbents', *Studies in clergy and ministry in medieval England*, ed. D. M. Smith (1991), 1–19 [esp. 4–11] • C. N. L. Brooke, *A history of Gonville and Caius College* (1985); repr. with corrections (1996), 1–3, 7–12, 305 • J. Venn and others, eds., *Biographical history of Gonville and Caius College*, 3: *Biographies of the successive masters* (1901), 1–4 • C. Norton, D. Park, and P. Binski, *Dominican painting in East Anglia: the Thornham Parva retable and the Musée de Cluny frontal* (1987), 82–101, esp. 87–8, 91 • E. K. Bennet, *Historical memorials of the College of St John Evangelist Rushworth or Rushford, co. Norfolk* (1887); repr. from *Proceedings of the Norfolk and Norwich Archaeological Society*, 10 (1888), 50–64, 77–382 • C. Brooke, 'Commemorating Edmund Gonville', *The Caian* (1993–4), 67
Archives Gon. & Caius Cam., draft statutes, writs, etc.

Goobey, George Henry Ross (1911–1999), pension fund manager, was born at 42 Blair Street, Poplar, London, on 21 May 1911, the younger son and third child of Herbert Goobey, a shopkeeper and Primitive Methodist lay preacher, and his wife, Elizabeth Ross. An adept pupil at elementary school, he was encouraged by a local Church of England vicar to enter for a scholarship at Christ's Hospital. There he shone in mathematics, and much later became a governor.

Unable to afford a university education, on leaving school in 1928 Goobey joined the British Equitable Assurance Company as an actuarial trainee. He played rugby for the Eastern Counties and gained cricketing repute as a hard-hitting batsman. On 4 September 1937 he married Gladys Edith (*b.* 1911), daughter of Charles Menzies, a local government official in Poplar; they had a son and a daughter. Having in 1939 moved to the South African company Southern Life Assurance, he and his family were about to embark for Cape Town when the outbreak of war disrupted their plans.

Instead Ross Goobey (he adopted this as his surname) worked successively for several British insurance companies, served in the Home Guard, and qualified in 1941 as a fellow of the Institute of Actuaries. At the relatively youthful age of thirty-six, he was appointed in 1947 the first in-house investment manager of the Bristol-based Imperial Tobacco Company's pension fund, then valued at £12 million. In common with most such funds, its assets were almost entirely invested in government bonds, known as gilt-edged stocks.

Ross Goobey strongly maintained that the government's recent issue of a 2.5 per cent undated stock, at a time when inflation averaged 4 per cent, was nothing short of a swindle. Meanwhile the average portfolio of British equities was yielding 4.3 per cent, having moreover the expectation of future growth. He therefore proposed to his investment committee, chaired by Sir Percy James Grigg (a director also of the Prudential Assurance Society), to switch the pension fund out of gilt-edged into equities. He argued that, although the company's existing portfolio would have to be sold at a loss of £1 million, that loss would soon be recouped by higher equity returns. Ross Goobey's views were based on two articles by Harold Ernest Raynes, a director of Legal and General, in the *Journal of the Institute of Actuaries* in 1928 and 1937, which demonstrated from twenty-five years' research that company dividends tended to rise in real terms even in periods of deflation. The investment committee eventually accepted his advice. As most other pension-fund managers followed that step, he had inaugurated a new era in Britain's fund-management industry.

Ross Goobey's overturning of conventional wisdom initially provoked resentment in the City of London, especially as he relied so little on City expertise. A well-publicized dispute with the chief actuary of Prudential in the early 1950s fuelled suspicions there of his intellectual arrogance. His light-hearted remark, about finding shares so cheap and plentiful that he felt like a child in a sweet-shop who had discovered everything at knock-down prices, did nothing to improve relations. Not until 1998, at the age of eighty-six, was he given the first-ever award of honour, as a past master, of the Company of Actuaries. He was also master of two other London livery companies.

Rather than dealing in prestigious blue-chip companies (and paying commission) in the stock market, Ross Goobey sought out smaller and medium-sized companies, mostly based in the west country. He preferred to negotiate directly with their chairmen, once at least hammering out purchase terms until 3 a.m. in a night-club. Before merger mania set in, his fund held about 1000 separate equity holdings. Although some of these did poorly, the overall performance of his portfolio was second to none, with yields on cost for a time reaching double figures, in years of moderately low inflation.

In 1972 Ross Goobey was elected president of the National Association of Pension Funds. By then he had discerned—ahead of his competitors—that company shares had reached their peak, and he moved into commercial properties, mainly in London. Yet when the stock market slumped in 1974 he began to buy gilt-edged, since war loan was then yielding 16 per cent. Even though the merchant bank M. Samuel (later Hill Samuel) attempted to woo him away with a much higher salary, he remained loyal to Imperial Tobacco, which rewarded him with a seat on its main board and permission to become a non-executive director of M. Samuel.

Ross Goobey was tall and well-built, his imposing figure prompting some City journalists to dub him the archdeacon of the equity cult. To be sure, his full moustache, carnation in the buttonhole, and fondness for cigars, socializing, cliff-hanging bridge games, and telling *risqué* stories, plus a conviction that his judgement was always right, belied any churchy image. Yet he never strove after great riches, served for three years as chairman of Clevedon town council, and actively involved himself in local sports. After retiring in 1975 he was until his eightieth year chairman of the property company Warnford Investments. He also took up golf, regularly playing thirty-six holes a day, and was appointed president of the Somerset County Golf Union.

He died of heart disease in Weston-super-Mare General Hospital on 19 March 1999, fit and active almost to the end. His son, Alastair, followed in his footsteps by becoming chief executive of the Hermes pension fund group, being honoured by the state (as the idiosyncratic George Ross Goobey never was) with a CBE in 2000.

T. A. B. Corley

Sources A. Ross Goobey, *The money moguls* (1987), 72–5 • *Sunday Times* (21 March 1999) • *Financial Times* (22 March 1999) • *The Times* (30 March 1999) • *Daily Telegraph* (March 1999) • *Bristol Evening Post* (3 April 1999) • N. Faith, *The Independent* (23 April 1999) • private information (2004) [G. Ross Goobey and A. Ross Goobey] • b. cert. • m. cert. • d. cert. • H. E. Raynes, 'The place of ordinary stocks and shares … in the investment of life assurance funds', *Journal of the Institute of Actuaries*, 59 (1928), 21–50 • H. E. Raynes, 'Equities and fixed interest funds during twenty-five years', *Journal of the Institute of Actuaries*, 68 (1937), 483–507

Likenesses photograph, *c.*1995, repro. in *The Times* • photograph, 1998, repro. in Faith, *The Independent*

Gooch, Benjamin (1707/8–1776), surgeon, was the eldest son of Benjamin Gooch (1670–1728), rector of Ashwellthorpe, Norfolk, from 1693 to 1728, and his wife, Anne, *née* Phyllis. Under the terms of his father's will Gooch could inherit the family property in Hingham, Norfolk, only upon the death of his stepmother, Sarah Gooch. Following schooling in Norfolk, Gooch served an apprenticeship during the late 1720s and early 1730s with a Mr Symonds, a Norfolk surgeon who had trained at St Thomas's Hospital, Southwark. He then lived with, and received post-apprenticeship instruction from, David Amyas, the leading Norfolk surgeon of the period. Gooch subsequently became assistant surgeon to Robert Bransby of Hapton, Norfolk, and later of Shotesham, Norfolk. He married Bransby's daughter Elizabeth (1709/10–1784), and succeeded to the practice at Shotesham. Gooch observed in 1766 how he had practised surgery for forty years, 'in a country situation with a large circle of business, where I was obliged to act in the capacity of a physician as well as a surgeon' (Gooch, *Practical Treatise*, 3; *Medical and Surgical Observations*, 1767, xvi). In 1757 he experienced a breakdown in his health, from the effects of which he never fully recovered. Following convalescence at Bath and London he divided his time for the remainder of his life between Norwich, Shotesham, and Halesworth, Suffolk, with a diminished practice. By the early 1760s Gooch enjoyed a reputation as the most experienced surgeon in

East Anglia and was frequently called upon for consultations in difficult surgical cases. In 1772 Gooch stated that he had been a consulting surgeon for over fifteen years, assisting some 150 surgeons and more than twenty physicians (BL, Add. MS 24123, fol. 167).

While recovering from his illness in 1757 Gooch began writing the surgical treatise which would eventually bring him recognition as one of the outstanding provincial surgeons of eighteenth-century Britain. His *Cases and Practical Remarks in Surgery*, published in London in 1758, was eventually expanded into a comprehensive account of his most important surgical and consulting practice, published in three volumes at Norwich in 1767 and 1773 (collected edition, London, 1792). Earning praise from several of the most distinguished practitioners of the period, Gooch revealed himself in his writings to be a careful, methodical surgeon, well versed in contemporary medical literature and experimental in his approach. His study of aneurysms in the thigh led to the dissection of horses and dogs; he created the Gooch's splint, and correspondence in 1769 and 1775 with the Royal Society of London led to several publications. Gooch was also noted for his radical surgical advice for cancer of the breast, and for his innovative practice of lithotomy. Within a year of the book's publication in 1767 his preferred method for treating difficult compound fractures of the leg was in use within the British regimental hospital at Halifax, Nova Scotia. By the end of his life Gooch counted as friends or associates most members of the London medical élite, including Sir John Pringle, Sir George Baker, William Hunter, Donald Monro, Joseph Warner, William Gataker, and Messenger Monsey. None the less, he never shed his own feelings of provincial inferiority and self-doubt. In 1772, on the eve of the publication of his final volume of surgery, Gooch burnt all his extensive papers not considered to be worthy of public attention.

Gooch was one of the leading spirits behind the establishment of the Norfolk and Norwich Hospital, from stillborn discussions in 1758, through the renewed interest of 1769, and its construction in 1771. He advocated a plain, substantial building without superfluous ornamentation, with good ventilation and effective sanitation, and constructed on the model of the best London hospitals, but when his proposals met with opposition he withdrew from active participation on the building committee (BL, Add. MS 24123, fols. 159*v*–162*v*). Appointed hospital consulting surgeon and a member of the board of governors on 9 October 1771 he served until the autumn of 1775.

In his last illness Gooch lived, as he had from time to time, at Halesworth, Suffolk, with his only child, Elizabeth (*b*. 1735), and her husband, John D'Urban MD. D'Urban had begun his medical career as Gooch's apprentice. Following service in the Royal Navy in the 1740s D'Urban studied surgery and midwifery in London and Paris before earning the MD at Edinburgh in 1753. He married Elizabeth Gooch on 8 October of the same year. The couple's youngest child, named after his maternal grandfather, was Sir Benjamin D'Urban (1777–1849), the governor and commander-in-chief of the Cape of Good Hope. Gooch dated his will at Halesworth on 26 November 1775. He died there on 11 February 1776, and was buried in the churchyard of Shotesham All Saints. His entire estate, identified as freehold, copyhold, and customary properties within the parish of Framlingham, Suffolk, was bequeathed jointly to his daughter and son-in-law and their heirs. The obituary notice in the *Norfolk Chronicle* described Gooch as a benevolent individual and a pious and devout Christian. His widow, Elizabeth, died on 21 November 1784.

J. D. Alsop

Sources B. Gooch, *A practical treatise on wounds and other chirurgical subjects* (1767) · A. B. Shaw, 'Benjamin Gooch, eighteenth-century Norfolk surgeon', *Medical History*, 16 (1972), 40–50 · J. D. Alsop, 'The publication of Benjamin Gooch's surgical works, 1765–74', *Publishing History*, 25 (1989), 13–26 · BL, Add. MS 24123 · will, Norfolk RO, Norwich consistory court, 281, 1728 [Benjamin Gooch senior] · will, PRO, PROB 11/1017, fols. 209–210*v* · will of Elizabeth Gooch, PRO, PROB 11/1126, fol. 219 · J. D. Alsop, 'Two letters on the cuticular glove keratolysis of 1769', *Journal of the History of Medicine and Allied Sciences*, 39 (1984), 224–5 · Venn, *Alum. Cant.* [Benjamin Gooch, 1670–728] · tombstone, Shotesham All Saints churchyard, Shotesham, Norfolk · *DNB*

Archives BL, letters to Messenger Monsey, Add. MS 24123

Likenesses T. Bardwell, portrait, priv. coll.

Wealth at death see will, PRO, PROB 11/1017, fols. 209–210*v*

Gooch, Sir Daniel, first baronet (**1816–1889**), railway engineer and executive, was born at Bedlington, Northumberland, on 24 August 1816, the third son of John Gooch (1763–1833) and his wife, Anna Longridge (1783–1863). His father was the cashier and bookkeeper at the Bedlington ironworks, where Gooch's maternal grandfather, Thomas *Longridge [*see under* Hawks family], had been a partner. Although ten children were born to Gooch's parents, sufficient means were found to educate him at local private schools between the ages of four and fourteen, and to make an allowance over to him during the early years of his career—even after his father's death in 1833.

The Gooch family had many relatives and associates in the engineering industry, including the Longridges, the Hawkses, the Homfrays, and the Stephensons, in whose Forth Street works, at Newcastle, Gooch gained a wide practical training during the period 1831–7. This training included locomotive construction. Isambard Kingdom Brunel, the engineer of the Great Western Railway (GWR), recognizing Gooch's talents, selected him as the company's first locomotive superintendent. He joined the GWR one week before his twenty-first birthday at a salary of £300 a year. Apart from a brief interlude in 1864–5, he was associated with the company for the rest of his life.

Gooch was one of the outstanding locomotive engineers of the period. He took advantage of the space allowed by the broad gauge, adopted by Brunel, to design locomotives on boldly original lines. His engines attained a speed and safety not previously deemed possible, setting a standard which was not exceeded in his lifetime. He designed a variant on the usual (Stephenson) locomotive link motion; he developed probably the first dynamometer car (1848), for estimating train resistances under various conditions; and he succeeded in designing for the

Sir Daniel Gooch, first baronet (1816–1889), by Sir Francis Grant, 1872

Metropolitan Railway (1862) a locomotive which condensed its own steam, for working in tunnels.

From the early years Gooch supplied plans and templates to outside makers and introduced the principles of standard designs and interchangeable parts. He was responsible for the planning, tooling, and management of the Swindon works which was opened in 1843. A rising proportion of the company's locomotives, as well as tenders, rolling-stock, and rails (from 1861), was manufactured there in the following years under Gooch's direct control. This strategy of 'internalization' exposed Gooch to the criticism of hostile directors who wanted to achieve more financial control and accountability and exposure to market forces. They were also suspicious about Gooch's association with certain suppliers to the GWR, in particular the Ruabon Coal Company in north Wales, in which he had invested £20,000 in 1856 and of which he was chairman.

The attack was led in 1863 by the newly elected chairman of the GWR, Richard Potter (Beatrice Webb's father). Despite Gooch's cogently argued response, in which he stressed the advantages of the company's control over the quality of output and of guaranteed supply, he was forced to resign on 7 September 1864. At that time he was earning £1500 a year, a sum which was augmented by the premiums paid by pupils, consultancy fees, payments for contracting to work other lines, and profits and fees from the various enterprises in which Gooch had invested.

These other sources gave Gooch a secure income, and he was also involved in a number of prestigious projects. In 1860 he began a set of associations which used his talents in engineering, finance, and organization to inaugurate telegraphic communication between Britain and the United States in 1866. As a member of the boards of the three interested companies — the Great Eastern Steamship Company, the Telegraph Constructions and Maintenance Company, and the Anglo-American Telegraph Company — Gooch was able to co-ordinate the entire enterprise. He was rewarded with a baronetcy in November 1866. He retained an interest in telegraphic communication and was chairman of the Telegraph Constructions and Maintenance Company until his death. At this time he was a director of five firms which were involved in cable production or cable laying.

The affairs of the GWR had meanwhile become critical, and on his return from the first (unsuccessful) cable-laying expedition, Gooch was asked to succeed Potter as the chairman of the GWR in November 1865. The company was on the verge of bankruptcy, and the value of its stock had plummeted. Under Gooch major capital projects, such as the conversion of the gauge from broad to narrow, were postponed; cuts in the quality of train services were ordered; and extensive capital restructuring was undertaken. By 1872 there was sufficient recovery to permit an ordinary dividend of 6 per cent, and the beginning of the Severn Tunnel scheme (1872–86), in which Gooch took a particular interest. It is difficult to detect the precise role played by Gooch in the formulation of policy and his contribution to the long-term viability of the company. His letters reveal, however, that he was a very active chairman, who played a central role in the determination of the board's membership (in which he favoured recruits from landed backgrounds) and in the sharper definition of the roles and responsibilities of his heads of department. Gooch remained chairman of the company until his death.

Gooch was the Conservative MP for Cricklade (a constituency which included New Swindon) from 1865 to 1885. In the House of Commons he played an important role behind the scenes, especially in the 1880s when, as chairman of the Railway Companies Association, he was prominent in defending the railways against the attacks of traders and manufacturers. He was a strong opponent of organized labour. In 1867 he was made a deputy lieutenant for Berkshire and a magistrate in Windsor. He was a prominent freemason, being grand sword-bearer of England and provincial grand master of Berkshire and Buckinghamshire. He was a staunch Anglican throughout his life.

Gooch's first wife was Margaret, the daughter of Henry Tanner of Bishopwearmouth, co. Durham, whom he married on 22 March 1838; she died on 22 May 1868. Gooch remarried on 17 September 1870; his second wife was Emily, the youngest daughter of John Burder of Norwood, Surrey. Gooch and his first wife had four sons and two daughters, the eldest son, Henry Daniel, succeeding as second baronet. The stipulation in Gooch's will that more than £400,000 was to held by his eldest son as an entailed estate, appears to confirm his social aspirations. However, he continued in business all of his life and used his income and status to secure non-gentlemanly, company positions for three of his sons, including Henry Daniel. Frank, the youngest child, went into the army. Gooch died on 15 October 1889 at his residence, Clewer Park, an estate adjoining the Thames near Windsor, which he had purchased in 1859. He was buried on 19 October in Clewer churchyard. Emily Gooch survived him, dying in 1901.

GEOFFREY CHANNON

Sources *Sir Daniel Gooch: memoirs and diary*, ed. R. B. Wilson (1972) · H. Parris, 'Sir Daniel Gooch: a biographical sketch', *Journal of Transport History*, new ser., 3 (1975–6), 203–16 · A. Platt, *The life and times of Daniel Gooch* (1987) · G. Channon, 'Gooch, Sir Daniel', *DBB* · C. Bright, *Submarine telegraphs: their history, construction, and working* (1898) · *VCH Wiltshire*, 4.213–18 · D. E. C. Eversley, 'The Great Western Railway and the Swindon works in the great depression', *Railways in the Victorian economy*, ed. M. C. Reed (1969), 134–60 · *The Engineer* (18 Oct 1889) · *Engineering* (18 Oct 1889) · Historical letters, PRO, Great Western Railway, RAIL 1008, 1–86 · Personal correspondence, 1839–48, PRO, Great Western Railway, RAIL 1014/6 · chairman's letter-books, 1865–89, PRO, Great Western Railway, RAIL 267/168 · d. cert. · *The Times* · *LondG* (13 Nov 1866)
Archives Birm. CL, diary · PRO, corresp. and papers
Likenesses E. W. Wyon, marble bust, 1862, Swindon Railway Museum · L. Desonges, oils, 1872, Swindon Railway Museum · F. Grant, oils, 1872, NPG [*see illus.*] · Barraud, photograph, NPG; repro. in *Men and Women of the Day*, 1 (1888) · Spy [L. Ward], chromolithograph caricature, NPG; repro. in *VF* (9 Dec 1882) · photograph, Sci. Mus.
Wealth at death £669,658 0s. 7d.: resworn probate, June 1890, *CGPLA Eng. & Wales* (1889)

Gooch, George Peabody (1873–1968), historian, was born on 21 October 1873 at his parents' home, 8 Porchester Gate in Kensington, London, the youngest of three children of Charles Cubitt Gooch (1811–1889), merchant banker, and his wife, Mary Jane (1837–1925), daughter of the Revd Edmund Blake of Bramerton, Norfolk. His father became a partner in the firm founded by the American businessman and philanthropist George Peabody, and honoured Peabody's memory in naming his son. George entered Eton College in 1885, and received a good grounding in the classics, but he did not feel happy there, and from 1888 to 1891 attended the general literature department of King's College, London, while living in his cultured and affluent parental home. His main interest was in history, with English and French literature—and later German—as a close second. He also benefited from the theological and philosophical studies he pursued at King's College. From the various strands of religious opinion represented in the college, blending with his mother's broad-church background, he learned to appreciate that there were many ways of looking at a question. His father died while he was at King's College. As he left the family well off financially, George was able to go to Trinity College, Cambridge, in 1891, to study history, initially as a commoner, and then as a major scholar. He obtained a first-class degree in the historical tripos of 1894.

Gooch took full advantage of the facilities offered by his college and university, without being blind to the defects of either. Already as an undergraduate he stood out for his remarkable intelligence and prodigious learning. At that early stage, with his 'indomitable will', he made up his mind that his life 'was to be dedicated … to the service of humanity and the bettering of his mind'; he advocated 'self-realisation for public Ends'. Gooch had independent means, and 'in some mysterious way both his learning and his wealth were "dedicated"' (Powys, 180–93). This outlook gave his life a unity, holding together his historical, political, journalistic, and philanthropic activities. He felt that his favoured social and financial situation put him under an obligation to serve the community. While gaining great personal satisfaction from developing his own intellectual gifts and gathering experience in a number of different fields, he did so to help others.

Gooch won the members' prize with an essay on Daniel Defoe in 1895. He spent some time in Berlin and Paris, reinforcing an interest in Germany and France he was to retain all his life. Lord Acton, then regius professor of modern history at Cambridge, with whom he developed a close relationship, gave him much encouragement. Gooch's first book, published by Cambridge University Press in 1898, *The History of English Democratic Ideas in the Seventeenth Century*, which was well received, arose from an essay for which he was awarded the Thirlwall prize in 1897. He submitted the essay as a dissertation for a Trinity College fellowship, but was unsuccessful in spite of Acton's support. While disappointed, he now took full advantage of the opportunities London offered him.

Philanthropy and Liberal politics In and around London, Gooch took a professional interest in adult education and social work, participating in the work of Toynbee Hall, the Charity Organization Society, the Church Army, the London city mission, and the temperance movement. He shepherded the homeless, if they were willing, from the Thames Embankment into shelters. His fellow social workers were struck by his deep concern for the poor and by his 'Christlike' gentleness and compassion. Throughout his life he helped those who through circumstances had fallen on bad times and befriended them. His social work in the years after leaving Cambridge brought him in touch with a number of like-minded men who were to play an important part in the life of the country. He was critical of the capitalist system and of the upper middle class to which he belonged. Having come to the conclusion during his undergraduate days that society was badly in need of reform, he broke away from his family's Conservative moorings (his elder brother, Sir Henry Cubitt Gooch, was Conservative MP for Peckham, 1908–10). His contacts were to be mainly with the Liberal Party, especially its radical wing, and with Labour.

The left Liberal leanings, which Gooch was to retain all his life, were strengthened by his experiences of the Second South African War. In *The War and its Causes*, early in 1900, he was critical of the reasons given for the war, such as the redress of outlanders' grievances. While he was fully aware of the problem facing a patriot disagreeing with a war waged by his country, he regarded the right to express a genuinely felt dissent as essential. In the end his main aim was to help to bring the war to an early close and to work for a just peace. He abhorred the systematic burning of Boer farms during the war and the establishment of concentration camps and in June 1901 he published a pungent critique of imperialism in a collaborative volume entitled *The Heart of the Empire: Discussions of Problems of Modern City Life in England*.

Gooch's co-operation with opponents of the Conservative government during the Second South African War led to his parliamentary candidature as a Liberal, and he was elected one of the MPs for Bath at the general election of 1906, which resulted in a landslide victory for the Liberals. He briefly served as parliamentary private secretary to the chief secretary for Ireland, James Bryce, with whom he had collaborated on the Balkan committee. He intervened on the floor of the House of Commons in questions relating to Ireland, South Africa, the Balkans, India, Egypt, and Persia, frequently standing up for individual and minority rights. He backed a limitation of armaments not only in the interest of peace, but also to make more money available for domestic reform. He supported the introduction of old-age pensions, measures against sweated wages, a reform of the conditions of welfare children, and the reduction of public houses and licensing hours. He agreed with the efforts of the Liberal government to curb the power of the House of Lords. He was critical of the policy of the foreign secretary, Sir Edward Grey. The Balkan committee, of which he was chief parliamentary spokesman, was at times dissatisfied with Grey's apparent unwillingness to help the Christians in the region.

Following his defeats in Bath in January and December 1910, Gooch made a final, but also unsuccessful, bid to return to the House of Commons in the Reading by-election of 1913. In the meantime, in 1911, he had been appointed co-editor of a prestigious monthly journal, the *Contemporary Review*, with the Revd Dr Scott Lidgett, a leading Methodist. When Scott Lidgett became chairman of the company in 1931, Gooch took over the sole editorial direction of the journal, which he relinquished only in 1960. He maintained high standards of reliability and objectivity, and helped to make the journal into one of the leading British organs for international affairs.

Historian Gooch's parliamentary defeat allowed him to write what was perhaps his finest work, *History and Historians in the Nineteenth Century* (1913). The book demonstrated his mastery of historiography, particularly German, French, and British. His close—but not uncritical—ties with Germany had been strengthened by his marriage in 1903 to Sophie Else Schön, an art student from Saxony. He castigated Treitschke, whom he heard lecture, for his chauvinism. The book admirably laid down a code for historians which he himself practised, emphasizing that the supreme task was to discover truth, which required integrity, particularly in evaluating sources. He rejected the subordination of historical studies to political aims which had marred the work of the great German historians connected with the national movement.

The outbreak of the First World War affected Gooch deeply. Indeed the war was to occupy his main attention for many years, both as co-editor of an important British journal during the hostilities and as a historian studying its origins. While having reservations about the extent to which Sir Edward Grey, in particular, had involved Britain in the affairs of the European continent, he supported her entry into the war once Germany had invaded Belgium, an action he condemned without reservation. He disagreed with John Morley's resignation from the government after a British promise on 2 August 1914 to defend the coasts of France.

In very difficult circumstances Gooch ensured that the *Contemporary Review* remained a voice of reason, opposing any negative generalizations about the whole German people, urging a quick end to the fighting, and looking to a future reconciliation of the enemies. In June 1915 the journal published 'German theories of the state', an address by Gooch in which he pointed out that modern nationalism originated in France and not in Germany. He was especially unhappy about a prevailing tendency to rewrite history 'in the light of the war'. While rejecting the sweeping condemnation of Grey's policy by the Union of Democratic Control, he sympathized with its aim of preparing for a peace settlement based on justice and humanity.

Gooch supported the movement for the establishment of a league of nations, and recalled with approval the medieval ideal of the *respublica christiana*, which had been shattered by the doctrine of the unfettered sovereignty of the state. In the summer of 1917, with a detailed examination of British pre-war policy in *A Century of British Foreign Policy*, he began to lay the foundation for his international reputation as an impartial observer acceptable to moderates on all sides. While he recognized Grey's untiring efforts to avert the outbreak of war, he considered assurances of British freedom of action, though formally correct, as far from conclusive. During his work on the Foreign Office handbooks for the peace conference he did his best to supply material to counter extreme French demands against Germany.

Origins of the First World War Particularly after the proclamation of German war guilt in the peace treaty, whose terms he regarded as unnecessarily hard, Gooch devoted himself wholeheartedly to the task of elucidating the truth about the origins of the war. He got a unique chance of so doing when his old friend Ramsay MacDonald, as prime minister and foreign secretary in June 1924, asked him to help with a publication on pre-war British foreign policy. Gooch urged that these should consist of documents, rather than of historical narratives, and suggested Harold Temperley as co-editor. After the Labour defeat the new foreign secretary, Sir Austen Chamberlain, towards the end of 1924 finalized the arrangements initiated by his predecessor.

The publication of *British Documents on the Origins of the War, 1898–1914* (11 vols. in 13) was completed in 1938, the whole process taking far longer than either the Foreign Office or the editors had anticipated. Probably mainly due to Temperley's personality, relations between the two parties went through a series of crises during Chamberlain's period of office, which terminated in 1929. Gooch later fully recognized Chamberlain's deep sense of honour.

Problems arose through the necessity of obtaining the clearance of friendly foreign governments for documents containing information confidentially conveyed by them. The editors were certainly determined, as they stated in the publication, to resign in case of undue interference by government. Gooch's co-editorship of *British Documents* as well as of the *Cambridge History of British Foreign Policy, 1783–1919* (with Sir Adolphus Ward, 3 vols., 1922–3), in which he dealt with the background of the conflict, established him as a leading and internationally recognized expert on the origins of the war. He drew on his wide knowledge of the subject in his *Recent Revelations of European Diplomacy* (1927), *Before the War: Studies in Diplomacy* (2 vols., 1936–8), and *Studies in Diplomacy and Statecraft* (1942).

When Hitler came to power in Germany, Gooch expressed his abhorrence of his rule, as he had done earlier with that of Mussolini. During this period one of his foremost tasks was to help German refugees. As president of the National Peace Council from 1933 to 1936, he reined in the Marxist and 'complete Christian pacifist' sections of the organization, while supporting disarmament at a time of intensive German rearmament. Also for some years he backed German claims for a revision of the peace settlement even under the Nazis. He realized only in 1938 that the Nazis had simply made cynical use of the principle of self-determination.

Gooch was elected a fellow of the British Academy in 1926, and in 1935 became an honorary fellow of Trinity College, Cambridge, also receiving an honorary doctorate from Oxford. From 1923 to 1926 he was president of the Historical Association of Great Britain. Early in June 1939 he was made a Companion of Honour, but shortly afterwards had to undergo a serious operation. That summer Gooch and his wife moved just outside London to Chalfont St Peter in Buckinghamshire, where they took a house, Upway Corner. During the war Gooch opposed any compromise with the Nazi regime, whose destruction he regarded as essential. The Nazis did not forget his scathing attacks on them, all the more so because they hit home, and put him on a list for immediate arrest in a German occupation of Britain.

Gooch's historical output before the Second World War was prodigious and of high quality. In addition to the works previously mentioned, it included, for example, *Germany and the French Revolution* (1920), the edition of *The Later Correspondence of Lord John Russell, 1840–1878* (2 vols., 1925), memoirs of personalities he had known, such as his fellow politicians Lord Courtney (1920) and Frederick Mackarness (1922), and a popular textbook, *History of Modern Europe, 1878–1919* (1923). During the war Gooch turned to what Sir Herbert Butterfield called 'books about books' (Butterfield, 334) on eighteenth-century history, beginning with *Courts and Cabinets* (1944), and going on to the three leading 'enlightened monarchs'. While stylistically admirable, these books lack the historical depth of his previous work.

Particularly after the Second World War, Gooch adopted a serenity, which is reflected in his autobiography *Under Six Reigns*, published in 1958, but which did not always characterize him in earlier controversies. The author keeps too much in the background, although on close acquaintance the book yields much interesting information, such as on his religious views. While remaining a member of the Church of England, in the course of his life Gooch gradually moved away from doctrinal commitment. In 1961 he was honoured by a Festschrift, *Studies in Diplomatic History and Historiography*, edited by A. O. Sarkissian.

Gooch's wife, who had suffered from a series of prolonged illnesses during their marriage, died in 1958. There were two sons of the marriage. After his wife's death, an old family friend, Herta Lazarus, periodically visited from Switzerland for longer periods, keeping his interest in scholarship alive by translating his work into German with him. Gooch received the German order of merit in 1954. Aged ninety and in a wheelchair, he very much enjoyed his audience with the queen in November 1963, when the Order of Merit was bestowed on him. Gooch had a tall, slender figure, with kindly and alert eyes. He died peacefully at his home in Chalfont St Peter on 31 August 1968.

FRANK EYCK

Sources F. Eyck, *G. P. Gooch: a study in history and politics* (1982) · G. P. Gooch, *Under six reigns* (1958) · H. Butterfield, 'George Peabody Gooch, 1873–1968', *PBA*, 55 (1969), 311–38 · *DNB* · J. C. Powys, *Autobiography* (1934) · F. Eyck, 'G. P. Gooch', *Historians in politics*, ed. W. Laqueur and G. L. Mosse (1974), 169–90 · personal knowledge (2004) · private information (2004) · b. cert.

Archives University of Calgary Library, corresp. and papers, incl. notes for articles and publications | BLPES, letters to E. D. Morel · Bodl. Oxf., corresp. with Gilbert Murray · CUL, letters to Lord Acton · CUL, corresp. with Sir Herbert Butterfield · King's Lond., Liddell Hart C., corresp. with Sir B. H. Liddell Hart · LUL, corresp. with Emile Cammaerts · U. Birm., letters to W. H. Dawson · U. Newcastle, Robinson L., letters to Frederick Whyte

Likenesses W. Stoneman, two photographs, 1930–43, NPG · photograph, *c.*1953, Baron Studios Ltd, London, M53 2M 1101 1

Wealth at death £30,385: probate, 29 Oct 1968, *CGPLA Eng. & Wales*

Gooch, Robert (1784–1830), obstetric physician, was born at Yarmouth, Norfolk, in June 1784, the son of Robert Gooch, a naval captain, and great-grandson of Sir Thomas Gooch, bishop of Ely. As his parents were unable to afford a classical education, Gooch was educated at a private day school, and at the age of fifteen was apprenticed to Giles Borrett, a successful surgeon apothecary at Yarmouth. Gooch taught himself Latin and anatomy making use of his copy of Cheselden and a skeleton. He spent many of his evenings reading to a blind gentleman, Mr Harley, who helped him develop a taste for history, literature, chemistry, and philosophy, which remained with him for the rest of his life.

Despite limited family circumstances, exacerbated by his father's incarceration in a French prison, in 1804 Gooch commenced his study of medicine at the University of Edinburgh. He attended at the Royal Infirmary, and was active in the Medical and Speculative societies. He became closely acquainted with Henry Southey and William Knighton. During his vacations in Norfolk Gooch studied languages with William Taylor, a well-known literary critic and gentleman of letters, and an associate of the Southey family. Gooch graduated MD in June 1807, with an inaugural dissertation on rickets. He then worked for a time under Astley Cooper and in 1808 he set up in general practice together with a Mr James of Croydon, Surrey. Gooch became a regular contributor to the short-lived medical journal *London Medical Record*, where he published his first piece on insanity, a review of a translation of Pinel.

In 1808 Gooch married Emily Bolingbroke. She died in January 1811, as did their child in July of the same year. Distraught at the loss of his young wife and child, Gooch moved to Aldermanbury, London. His medical friends, including George Young, William Babington, and Sir William Knighton, helped him establish his London practice. He was admitted a licentiate of the Royal College of Physicians in March 1812 and in the same year was appointed physician to the Westminster Lying-in Hospital, where he acquired much practical experience attending midwifery cases among the poor of London. He was also elected lecturer in midwifery at St Bartholomew's Hospital, a post he retained until 1825, and physician to the City of London Lying-in Hospital.

On a tour of the Lake District in 1811 Gooch met the poet Robert Southey, who remained a lifelong friend. Gooch was well acquainted with the Romantic authors, and in 1812 was called in briefly to treat the poet Samuel Taylor Coleridge for worsening rheumatic heart disease and in a vain attempt to reduce Coleridge's opium intake. He later contributed to Robert Southey's journal, the *Quarterly Review*, including a piece published in December 1825 on the contagious nature of the plague.

In January 1814 Gooch married the sister of the surgeon Benjamin Travers. The couple moved to Berners Street in the West End of London where Gooch built up a large practice, based primarily on midwifery and the diseases of women. Gooch's health, poor since his student days, often obliged him to cease work. He travelled frequently out of London to the seaside or countryside in an effort to restore his health. In 1816, in addition to his chronic lung complaint, Gooch developed a severe stomach disorder which plagued him for the rest of his life. In 1820 he lost his eldest son and this, in combination with his failing health, caused him to turn increasingly to religion. In January 1826 Gooch had an attack of haemoptysis and his deteriorating health led him to give up his midwifery practice to Charles Locock and to restrict himself to prescribing work. Yet he continued to visit patients and the demands on his practice continued to grow. In April 1826 his friend Knighton secured for him the post of librarian to the king with an annuity for life. Despite continuing bad health, Gooch continued to write.

In 1820 Gooch wrote what was probably the first treatise on puerperal insanity in English, *Observations on Puerperal Insanity*, which was based on a paper read at the Royal College of Physicians in December 1819 and which included several detailed case histories. He was interested in the co-operative movement and published in 1829 on the activities of the Brighton branch in the *Quarterly Review*. In 1829 his well-received book *An Account of some of the most Important Diseases Peculiar to Women* appeared; richly illustrated with his own case notes, it contained chapters on puerperal fever, puerperal insanity, and the management of difficult labours. By now he was like a 'living skeleton', yet he continued to work. In January 1830 Gooch wrote an influential piece in the *Quarterly Review* on the Anatomy Act, supporting the release of unclaimed bodies for dissection, protesting at the same time about the use of dissection as a form of punishment which he claimed degraded the medical profession. He dictated this from his deathbed, but as G. J. Guthrie, professor of anatomy and surgery to the Royal College of Surgeons, who opposed the use of the unclaimed poor for dissection, remarked, far from leaving his own body to science Gooch 'took care to have himself buried in the usual manner'.

Confined to bed with worsening consumption, Gooch died on 16 February 1830 and was buried at Croydon, leaving his wife, two sons, and a daughter. A man of small and delicate stature, Gooch was given to severe bouts of melancholy and self-doubt and had a constant dread of poverty. However, he was acknowledged by his contemporaries for his dynamism, his engaging lecturing style, and the quality and clarity of his written work; his publications remained influential despite his premature death. Henry Southey praised his legacy to medical knowledge and his sickroom manners, which he described as quiet, natural, impressive, and kind: Gooch being always ready to sympathize with the feelings of others, 'he rarely failed to attach his patients strongly'. Gooch's writings on puerperal fever and puerperal madness were described by Southey as 'the most important additions to practical medicine of the present age'.

Several of Gooch's studies were published posthumously, including a new edition of his treatise on the diseases of women, *An Account of some of the most Important Diseases Peculiar to Women; with other Papers*, with a prefatory essay by Gooch's associate Robert Ferguson, which was published in 1831. In the same year Gooch's *Practical compendium of midwifery; being the course of lectures on midwifery, and on diseases of women and infants, delivered at St. Bartholomew's Hospital*, appeared, having been prepared for publication by George Skinner, one of Gooch's pupils.

HILARY MARLAND

Sources [W. MacMichael and others], *Lives of British physicians* (1830) • Munk, *Roll* • I. Loudon, ed., *Childbed fever: a documentary history* (1995) • V. C. Medvei and J. L. Thornton, eds., *The royal hospital of Saint Bartholomew, 1123–1973* (1974) • R. Richardson, *Death, dissection and the destitute* (1987) • M. Lefebure, *Samuel Taylor Coleridge: a bondage of opium* (1974)

Likenesses R. J. Lane, oils, 1823, RCP Lond. • J. Linnell, line engraving, pubd 1831 (after his earlier work, 1827), BM, Wellcome L.

Gooch, Sir Thomas, second baronet (1675–1754), college head and bishop of Ely, was born on 19 January 1675, and apparently baptized the same day at Worlingham, Suffolk, the elder son of Thomas Gooch (*d.* 1688), alderman of Yarmouth, and his wife, Frances Lone (*d.* 1696). He attended school in Yarmouth and matriculated at Gonville and Caius College, Cambridge, in 1691. He took his BA degree in 1695 and his MA degree in 1698, and was awarded his degrees of BD and DD in 1706 and 1711 respectively.

Gooch became a fellow of Caius in 1698 and was elected master in 1716, a position he held until his death. He was vice-chancellor of Cambridge from 1717 to 1720. Respecting ecclesiastical preferment, he became chaplain to Henry Compton, bishop of London, and a royal chaplain, and was rector of St Clement, Eastcheap, from 1713 to 1738, archdeacon of Essex from 1714 to 1737, canon of Chichester from 1719 to 1738, and canon of Canterbury from 1730 to 1738. He was raised to the episcopate as bishop of Bristol in 1737, but the following year was translated to Norwich. In 1748 he was appointed bishop of Ely, and in 1751 he succeeded to the baronetcy of his deceased brother, Sir William *Gooch, lieutenant-governor of Virginia.

Gooch was initially a staunch tory. At Cambridge he was much involved in university politics. As vice-chancellor he adjudicated in one of Richard Bentley's quarrels, and deprived Bentley of his degrees (a decision eventually annulled by king's bench). Gooch was, however, desirous of a bishopric, and his brother-in-law Thomas Sherlock, another tory and bishop successively of Bangor, Salisbury, and London, was anxious to obtain one for him. It was Sherlock who secured Bristol for Gooch, and when the see of Ely became vacant in 1748, Sherlock wrote to the duke of Newcastle stating he 'is senior to all who can pretend to it & your Grace by assisting him will save me from a great mortification' (Carpenter, 316). Gooch became a whig about 1727. In 1733 he assured Newcastle of his support for the whig interest in the forthcoming Sussex county election. He assisted Newcastle at Cambridge too, but his political turnabout tended to alienate him from the fellows of Caius, who remained predominantly tory.

Gooch published four of his sermons: they are all conventional, and reflect the date and circumstances of their composition. A 5 November sermon, preached in 1711, decried popery and stressed the role of Providence on earth. It concluded with the hope that the throne might 'be resign'd to the Protestant Succession in the Illustrious House of HANNOVER, and thereby, for Ever, extinguish the Hopes of a *Popish* Pretender' (Gooch, *Sermon Preach'd at Goodman's-Fields*, 28). A 30 January sermon, preached the following year before the Commons, praised Charles I, denounced his execution as 'this accursed Wickedness' and his enemies as 'execrable Villains', and extolled 'our excellent Constitution' (Gooch, *Sermon Preach'd before the … Commons*, 9, 15, 21). His sermon commemorating the life of Compton (1713) lauded the bishop, noting his 'early Possession of Loyal Principles, early Aversion to Rebellion' (Gooch, *Sermon Preach'd before the … Lord Mayor*, 5). Lastly, in a sermon of 1740 preached before the Lords, Gooch implored God's aid in the war against the Spanish, 'a cruel and perfidious Nation' (Gooch, *Sermon Preach'd before the … Lords*, 16), and stressed the 'Justness of our Cause' (ibid., 13). Providence would determine the outcome of the conflict, for war was 'an Appeal to Heaven by the Use of Arms' (ibid., 8–9).

Gooch married three times. He married his first wife, Mary Sherlock, sister of Thomas Sherlock, on 12 November 1717. She had died by 1730, at which time Gooch was already married to his second wife, Hannah Miller (*d.* 1746), daughter of Sir John Miller, bt. He married his third wife, Mary Compton (*d.* 1780), daughter of Hatton Compton, lieutenant of the Tower, probably on 17 February 1748 at Ely House in London. He had one son by each of his first two wives. According to William Cole 'he was a man of as great art, craft, design, and cunning, as any in the age he lived in'. But, Cole added, he 'was a man also of the most agreeable, lively, and pleasant conversation, full of merry tales and lively conceits, yet one who well knew the respect that was due to his character' (Brooke, 164). His reputation for conviviality earned him the sobriquet Gotch—a dialect word for a jug—from Bentley. A number of portraits of him survive: that painted by Thomas Hudson in 1750 shows a man with a plump face, large eyes, and white hair. Cole noted his gentlemanly carriage; he dressed neatly. By 1750, as Edmund Pyle recorded, his health was in decline, and he died on 14 February 1754 at Ely House, Holborn, London. He was buried in the chapel at Gonville and Caius, Cambridge, where a memorial was erected to him.

COLIN HAYDON

Sources T. Gooch, *A sermon preach'd at Goodman's-Fields, November 5, 1711* (1712) • T. Gooch, *A sermon preach'd before the honourable House of Commons* (1712) • T. Gooch, *A sermon preach'd before the House of Lords* (1739) • T. Gooch, *A sermon preach'd before the right honourable the lord mayor and aldermen … July 26, 1713* (1713) • *GM*, 1st ser., 21 (1751) • C. N. L. Brooke, J. M. Horn, and N. L. Ramsay, 'A canon's residence in the eighteenth century: the case of Thomas Gooch', *Journal of Ecclesiastical History*, 39 (1988), 545–56 • E. Pyle, *Memoirs of a royal chaplain, 1729–1763*, ed. A. Hartshorne (1905) • C. N. L. Brooke, *A history of Gonville and Caius College* (1985); repr. with corrections (1996) • E. Carpenter, *Thomas Sherlock, 1678–1761* (1936) • N. Sykes, *Church and state in England in the XVIII century* (1934) • E. B. Fryde and others, eds., *Handbook of British chronology*, 3rd edn, Royal Historical Society Guides and Handbooks, 2 (1986); repr. (1996) • G. Hennessy, *Novum repertorium ecclesiasticum parochiale Londinense, or, London diocesan clergy succession from the earliest time to the year 1898* (1898) • J. Ingamells, *The English episcopal portrait, 1559–1835: a catalogue* (privately printed, London, 1981) • Venn, *Alum. Cant.* • Burke, *Peerage* (1999) • GEC, *Baronetage*, 5.91–2 • monument, Gon. & Caius Cam. • L. P. Curtis, *Chichester towers* (1966)

Archives priv. coll. | BL, corresp. with duke of Newcastle, etc., 1733–53, Add. MSS 32417–32418, 32457, 32688–32732

Likenesses oils, 1730, Old Schools, Cambridge • attrib. T. Bardwell, oils, *c.*1740–1750, Gon. & Caius Cam. • T. Hudson, oils, 1749, BM, NPG • J. Macardell, mezzotint, 1749 (after T. Hudson), BM, NPG • T. Hudson, oils, 1750, LPL • J. Freeman?, 1775 (after T. Hudson, 1750), Bishop's House, Ely • J. T. Heins, mezzotint, BM

Gooch, Thomas Longridge (1808–1882), civil and railway engineer, was born in London on 1 November 1808, the first son and second of ten children (five sons and five daughters) of John Gooch, cashier of Bedlington ironworks, near Morpeth, Northumberland, and his wife, Anna, daughter of Thomas Longridge, iron-founder, of Newcastle upon Tyne. His brother Daniel *Gooch was locomotive superintendent and later chairman of the Great Western Railway. He was educated nearby at Crow

Hall School, by the parson of Horton. In 1823 he commenced an apprenticeship to George *Stephenson, working for two years in the workshops of Robert Stephenson & Co. at Newcastle and then in the drawing office. He also assisted Joseph Locke in taking levels and making plans and drawings for the proposed Newcastle and Carlisle Railway. In 1826, with the passage of the Liverpool and Manchester Railway Act, he went with George Stephenson to Liverpool, where he prepared most of the working drawings and plans for this railway from Stephenson's rough sketches.

In 1829 Gooch became resident engineer for the uncompleted Bolton and Leigh Railway and in 1830 resident engineer for the Liverpool section of the Liverpool and Manchester Railway. George Stephenson then appointed Gooch resident engineer for the proposed Manchester and Leeds Railway, for which he worked almost continuously in preparing plans and drawings for the bill to be presented in the 1831 session of parliament. However, strong opposition resulted in rejection of this bill despite his excellent testimony as an expert witness. Later in the same year he assisted Robert Stephenson in preparing plans and drawings for the London and Birmingham Railway Bill. After its passage in 1833 he was appointed resident engineer for the northern section of the line.

In 1836 the Manchester and Leeds Bill was finally passed. In 1837 Gooch was appointed joint principal engineer with George Stephenson, and was responsible for the line's construction, which was his greatest achievement and required many heavy civil-engineering works, including a 2 mile tunnel under the Pennine hills, the boring of which from thirteen shafts took over three years. On the line's completion in 1841, Gooch was made responsible for the construction of branch lines to Heywood, Oldham, Halifax, and Ashton under Lyne. He also prepared plans for the Manchester, Bury, and Rossendale (later East Lancashire) Railway. During the subsequent 'railway mania' period he was engaged on proposals for several new lines, including the Stafford to Rugby line through the Trent valley, opened in 1847, for which he was principal engineer, working with Robert Stephenson and G. P. Bidder.

After many years of almost continuous work, broken only by a short honeymoon in 1836, Gooch's health failed and he was taken ill in 1847 at his London office. He was ordered complete rest and convalesced abroad for eight months before resuming work as consultant for the Skipton–Lancaster Railway, at first jointly with Charles Vignoles and then as sole consultant. However, in 1851 his health again gave cause for serious anxiety, and he was compelled to give up full-time activity at the early age of forty-two. He was a sociable man of great ability, but courteous and unassuming, with great kindness and understanding of the problems of others. His later years were devoted largely to charitable work, to which he contributed much in an unostentatious manner. He was elected a member of the Institution of Civil Engineers in 1845.

In 1836 Gooch married Ruthanna, daughter of Robert Scaife of Liverpool. They had a son, who died aged eleven, and a daughter. Gooch died at Team Lodge, Gateshead, co. Durham, on 23 November 1882. His wife survived him.

George W. Carpenter, *rev.*

Sources *PICE*, 72 (1882–3), 300–08 • A. Platt, *The life and times of Daniel Gooch* (1987) • d. cert. • *CGPLA Eng. & Wales* (1883)
Archives Inst. CE, diaries and memorandum on his life
Wealth at death £51,490 14s. 4d.: probate, 6 Jan 1883, *CGPLA Eng. & Wales*

Gooch, Sir William, first baronet (1681–1751), army officer and politician in America, was born on 21 October 1681 in Yarmouth, the son of Thomas Gooch (*d.* 1688), alderman of Yarmouth, and Frances (*d.* 1696), daughter of Thomas Lone of Worlington, Suffolk. Orphaned before his fifteenth birthday, he forged a close bond with his brother Thomas *Gooch (1675–1754), who became bishop of Ely in 1748. He attended Queen's College, Oxford, for a time, and at the age of nineteen was commissioned a junior officer in the army. During the War of the Spanish Succession (1702–13) he served with the duke of Marlborough in the Low Countries, and was present at the battle of Blenheim (1704). In 1714 he married Rebecca Staunton (*d.* in or after 1751) of Hampton, Middlesex; they had one son. A year later he rendered important service against the Jacobites in the highlands uprising, and was promoted to the rank of major.

In the next few years Gooch discovered—like many another eighteenth-century British officer—that promotions in the peacetime establishment were excruciatingly slow. Frustrated, he resigned his commission and settled in Hampton, hoping to secure some sort of governmental sinecure. By good fortune he obtained the patronage of the duke of Newcastle, secretary of state for the southern department, who controlled political appointments in the American colonies. In 1727 he was commissioned lieutenant-governor of Virginia, succeeding Sir Hugh Drysdale, who had died the year before. As actual colonial governors normally remained in England at this time, he assumed the duties of governor when he arrived with his family at Williamsburg in September. Thus he embarked upon a tenure as chief executive of Virginia that would last until 1749, a period exceeded in length only by that of Sir William Berkeley.

Gooch's term of office was marked by great amicability between the governor, council, and house of burgesses. This was remarkable, given that relations between previous king's representatives and the people of Virginia had usually been anything but cordial. Gooch encouraged the burgesses to initiate legislation that they believed important for the development of the colony, and he established an informal political relationship with Virginia's gentry that was favourable to the development of self-rule in the province. He allowed the house of burgesses to take advantage of his acquiescent attitude to extend its own authority, and he evinced a sincere desire to support Virginia's interests at Whitehall. In 1746 he allowed the burgesses to appoint a commission for expending public revenues rather than attending to the matter himself. He

Sir William Gooch, first baronet (1681–1751), by unknown artist, *c.*1725

thereby established a precedent that the burgesses tenaciously adhered to in later years. He also reinforced the notion that the burgesses rather than himself had sole authority to appoint the treasurer of the colony. His operative principle in handling potential political opponents was to 'kill [them] with kindness' and 'if possible, to avoid Displeasure'. He cemented his ties with the Virginia gentry by investing in land and iron mining in the province, and his son married a woman from Maryland. So effective was the collaboration between Gooch and the colony's leaders that near the end of his tenure the chief executive was able to report to his brother that he had 'ruled without so much as a murmur of discontent'. For their part Virginia's leaders were happy to co-operate among themselves and flatter Gooch in order to continue this trend. Moreover, the burgesses praised him as a faithful trustee of their ancient rights and privileges. Although he was not among the most politically influential of colonial governors with authorities in London, his relations with Newcastle and the prime minister, Sir Robert Walpole, were close enough to give him some leverage.

Upon his arrival in Virginia, Gooch had learned that the major concerns of the tobacco-growing gentry were depressed prices and a lack of market regulation for the golden leaf of their staple crop. Seizing an opportunity to cultivate the leaders of the colony, he proposed a measure that he believed to be in the best interests of the growers, the government and merchants in Britain, and his own tranquil administration. Warehouses would be built at state expense, wherein tobacco growers would store their crop and allow it to be inspected for quality. In order to reduce the possibility of politics intruding into the process, all members of the house of burgesses would be excluded from serving as inspectors. Tobacco that did not meet rigorous standards of inspection would be destroyed in order to improve and maintain the overall quality of the crop. Because Virginia suffered a serious lack of currency as a result of parliamentary restrictions upon the printing of money, certificates for the stored tobacco would be allowed to circulate as bills of exchange.

Gooch realized that he must exercise considerable political acumen to get this measure enacted by the burgesses and accepted by the British government and merchants, for a similar earlier proposal by Governor Alexander Spotswood had been rejected. He corresponded with merchants and officials in England, overrode the concerns of customs officials, and persuaded the Board of Trade that the law would increase governmental revenues by improving the quality of the tobacco crop. Addressing planters who disliked the idea of destroying inferior leaf, Gooch wrote *A dialogue between Thomas Sweet-Scented, William Oronoco, planters … and Justice Love-Country* (1732) to persuade objectors that the law would provide them with increased income because of better quality. In 1730 he prevailed upon the house of burgesses and council to enact the bill, thus confirming his abilities as a politician. He also proved to be prescient in his expectations of the law's economic benefits, for by the mid-1730s tobacco prices had risen and Virginia had entered an extended period of prosperity. He bolstered the colony's economic boom by encouraging the settlement of western lands, and with the approval of the government in London distributed millions of acres on the frontier to the Virginia gentry.

Although Gooch earlier had resigned his army commission, he retained an interest in military affairs. In 1741, during the War of Jenkins's Ear (1739–42), he commanded colonial troops in a British expedition under the leadership of Admiral Edward Vernon against Cartagena, a Spanish stronghold on the Caribbean coast of South America. Although Vernon commanded 28,000 men and expected to compel the surrender of Cartagena with ease, half his men died from virulent fever and Spanish gunfire, and he withdrew without accomplishing anything. Gooch himself was severely wounded by a cannon-ball and contracted the fever that killed so many in the British squadron. Having returned to Virginia, he was rewarded for his services by being made a baronet in 1746 and by being promoted to major-general in the British army a year later. For years afterward he suffered from the debilitating effect of his wound, and soon was so impaired by rheumatism that he had difficulty in maintaining the responsibilities of his office. In addition he was afflicted in spirit by the deaths in quick succession of his son, grandson, and brother-in-law. In the summer of 1749 he resigned as lieutenant-governor of Virginia and returned to England. For the next two years, he unsuccessfully sought reimbursement for expenses that he had incurred in the Cartagena expedition. He also failed to secure a new position in government. He died at Bath on 17 December 1751, while taking the waters in an attempt to restore his failing health. He was buried in Yarmouth. Goochland county, Virginia, which was formed in 1728, was named in his honour. PAUL DAVID NELSON

Sources J. P. McClure, 'Gooch, Sir William', *ANB* • A. K. Prinz, 'Sir William Gooch in Virginia: the king's good servant', PhD diss., Northwestern University, 1963 • R. Shrock, 'Maintaining the prerogative: three royal governors in Virginia as a case study, 1710–1758', PhD diss., University of North Carolina, 1980 • P. S. Flippin, 'William Gooch: successful royal governor of Virginia [pt 1]', *William and Mary College Quarterly*, 2nd ser., 5 (1925), 225–58 • P. S. Flippin, 'William Gooch: successful royal governor of Virginia [pt 2]', *William and Mary College Quarterly*, 2nd ser., 6 (1926), 1–38 • F. W. Porter, 'Expanding the domain: William Gooch and the Northern Neck boundary dispute', *Maryland Historian*, 5 (1974), 1–13 • H. R. McIlwaine and J. P. Kennedy, eds., *Journals of the house of burgesses of Virginia, 1619–1776*, 13 vols. (1905–15), vols. 6–7 • J. P. Greene, *The quest for power: the lower houses of assembly in the southern royal colonies, 1689–1776* (1963) • GEC, *Baronetage*

Archives Colonial Williamsburg Foundation, corresp. [typescript] | LPL, letters to Bishop Gibson • PRO, colonial office papers

Likenesses portrait, *c.*1725; Sothebys, 9 May 2000, lot 142 [*see illus.*]

Good, John Mason (1764–1827), physician and surgeon, the second son of Peter Good, a Congregational minister at Epping, Essex, was born at Epping on 25 May 1764; his mother, Sarah Peyto (*d.* 1766), was the niece of the Revd John Mason (1706–1763). Good was taught in a school kept by his father at Romsey, near the New Forest, mastering Greek, Latin, and French, and showing unusual devotion to study. At fifteen he was apprenticed to William Johnson, a medical practitioner at Gosport, Hampshire, and during his apprenticeship he mastered Italian; after Johnson's death Good went to another surgeon in Havant. In 1783 and 1784 he went to London to study medicine and attended the lectures of George Fordyce and others; he became an active member of the Physical Society of Guy's Hospital.

In the summer of 1784, when only twenty, Good settled in Sudbury, Suffolk, in partnership with John Deeks, who soon after retired. Here Good married in 1785 a Miss Godfrey, who only survived six months, and in 1788 Susanna Fenn, with whom he had six children and who survived him. In 1792 Good lost a considerable sum of money, and although he was assisted financially by his father-in-law he determined to free himself from his debt by undertaking literary work. He wrote plays, translations, poems, and essays, but failed for some time to sell anything.

In 1793 Good moved to London and entered into a new partnership; on 7 November he was admitted a member of the Company of Surgeons. His new partner was jealous of him, and allowed the business to fail. While struggling to overcome these difficulties, Good in February 1795 won a prize of 20 guineas offered by John Coakley Lettsom for his essay 'Diseases frequent in workhouses, their cure and prevention'. In 1794 Good helped to establish the General Pharmaceutic Association, which sought to protect the apothecaries' monopoly on dispensing medicines by restricting the business of the increasingly popular druggists. Although itself short-lived and ineffective, the association had an important place in the campaign for the Apothecaries Act in 1815. On behalf of this society Good wrote his *History of Medicine, so Far as it Relates to the Profession of the Apothecary* (1795), which attempted, with some success, to portray the druggists as dangerous quacks invading the rightful practice of apothecaries.

Good now gained considerable practice and contributed to several leading periodicals, editing the *Critical Review* for some time. In 1797 he began to translate Lucretius into blank verse. In order to search for parallel passages he studied successively Spanish, Portuguese, Arabic, and Persian; he was already acquainted with Hebrew, and later learned Russian, Sanskrit, Chinese, and other languages. Much of his literary work was done while he walked the streets on his rounds; even his translation of Lucretius was completed in this way, a page or two at a time being elaborated, until it was ready to be written down. This work was finished in 1805. From 1804 to 1812 Good was occupied, with his friend and biographer, Olinthus Gregory, in the preparation of *Pantologia*, a twelve-volume encyclopaedia. As well as these works, Good published extensively on a wide variety of subjects and translated several parts of scripture. In 1808 he was elected FRS. In 1811–12 he gave three courses of lectures at the Surrey Institution, which were afterwards published in three volumes, as *The Book of Nature*.

In 1820 Good devoted himself to practice exclusively as a physician and obtained the diploma of MD from Marischal College, Aberdeen; in 1822 he became a licentiate of the Royal College of Physicians and published his *Study of Medicine* in four volumes, which was well received and sold rapidly. In it he endeavoured to unite physiology with pathology and therapeutics, an attempt which ultimately failed.

A conscientious and industrious worker, Good had a striking talent for acquiring knowledge and arranging it in an orderly fashion. But he was without great creative ability, and hence his works, while full of erudition, pleasingly presented, are not of permanent value. Good was always active in works of charity and had strong religious feelings. During the latter part of his time at Sudbury he became a Socinian or Unitarian, and from the time of his settling in London until 1807 he was a member of a Unitarian church. In that year he withdrew, as a result of what he considered were recommendations of scepticism delivered from the pulpit, and he afterwards became a member of the established church, attaching himself to the evangelicals. In his later years he was an active supporter of the Church Missionary Society, giving its missionaries medical instruction.

Good's enormous workload eventually told on his health, which was poor for some years before his death. He died of inflammation of the bladder on 2 January 1827, in his sixty-third year, at the house of his widowed daughter, Susanna Neale, at Shepperton, Middlesex. Apart from his wife, only one other child, a daughter, survived him. His son-in-law, the Revd Cornelius Neale, senior wrangler at Cambridge in 1812, died in 1823. His grandson was John Mason Neale (1818–1866).

G. T. BETTANY, *rev.* PATRICK WALLIS

Sources Munk, *Roll* • O. G. Gregory, *Memoirs of the life, writings and character of the late John Mason Good* (1828) • P. J. Wallis and R. V. Wallis, *Eighteenth century medics*, 2nd edn (1988) • C. Jerram, *Funeral sermon, with notes and appendix* (1827) • I. Loudon, *Medical care and the general practitioner, 1750–1850* (1986) • *GM*, 1st ser., 97/1 (1827), 276–8 • University of Aberdeen, *Records of the Marischal College and University of Aberdeen*, 2 (1898), 153

Archives BL, notes on the Junius letters, Add. MSS 27786–27787

Likenesses J. McGahey, stipple, 1828 (after W. Russell), Wellcome L. • C. Picart, stipple, 1828 (after W. Russell), Wellcome L.

Good, Joseph Henry (1775–1857), architect, was born on 18 November 1775, in Sambrook, Shropshire, the eldest son of the Revd Joseph Good, rector of Sambrook. He received his professional training from the renowned architect John Soane, to whom he was articled from 1795 to 1799, and early in his career he gained a number of premiums for designs for public buildings.

Good's most noteworthy works for private clients were Apps' Court Park, Surrey (1821; dem.), and the mansion of Horndean, Hampshire (1821–8). He also designed several clergy houses and other residences.

In 1814 Good was appointed surveyor to the trustees of the Thavies estate, Holborn, and some years later to the parish of St Andrew's, Holborn, in which latter capacity he designed and carried out in 1823 the vestry hall, in 1830 the national school, and in 1831 the workhouse, in Shoe Lane. He had already in 1818 designed the interior decoration, and rearrangement of St Andrew's Church (bombed 1941). In 1840 he erected a neo-classical hall in Coleman Street for the Armourers' and Brasiers' Company, to which he had been appointed surveyor in 1819. He was also for many years surveyor to the Hope Insurance Company, until its dissolution in 1843.

About 1822 Good was appointed architect to the Royal Pavilion at Brighton, and from 1830 to 1837 he erected several new buildings there, including the north and south lodges and entrances, additional stables, coach houses, and dormitory. In 1826 he succeeded Edward Mawley as surveyor to the commissioners for building new churches, a post he retained until the abolition of the commission and from which he subsequently enjoyed a pension. In 1830 he was appointed, under the office of works and public buildings, clerk of works to the Tower, Royal Mint, and Fleet and king's bench prisons. On 4 January 1831 he succeeded Thomas Frederick Hunt to the post of clerk of works to Kensington Palace, and to the official residence at Palace Green, which, in spite of the abolition of the office in 1832, he occupied by permission of William IV during the remainder of his life.

One of the original fellows of the Institute of British Architects, Good took a lively interest in the study and progress of architecture. Among his many pupils were Robert Wallace, Henry Ashton, and Alfred Bartholomew. His eldest son, Joseph Henry Good FRIBA (*d.* 1885), also became an architect. He died at Palace Green on 20 November 1857, and was buried in Kensal Green cemetery. G. W. Burnet, *rev.* M. A. Goodall

Sources [W. Papworth], ed., *The dictionary of architecture*, 11 vols. (1853–92) • Redgrave, *Artists* • Boase, *Mod. Eng. biog.* • D. Ware, *A short dictionary of British architects* (1967) • Colvin, *Archs.* • Graves, *RA exhibitors* • M. H. Port, *Six hundred new churches: a study of the church building commission, 1818–1856, and its church building activities* (1961), 92, 122 • J. M. Crook and M. H. Port, eds., *The history of the king's works*, 6 (1973), 259–60, 677

Good, Peter (*d.* 1803), horticulturist and plant collector, was settled near London by 1794, working under William T. Aiton at the Royal Botanic Gardens, Kew. In that year Sir Joseph Banks engaged him to be assistant to Christopher Smith (*d.* 1807), then being sent out to the East India Company's garden at Calcutta as botanist. They arrived with a consignment of useful plants from Kew on 27 February 1795 and then collected plants for Good's return voyage in 1796, as a result of which at least fourteen plant species were successfully introduced to British gardens. Good also collected herbarium material in India and this survives.

About 1800 Good was appointed gardener to Lieutenant-General William Wemyss (1760–1822) at Wemyss Castle near Kilmarnock, but within a few months he was recruited, again by Banks, as gardener and assistant to Robert Brown, naturalist on Matthew Flinders's *Investigator* voyage to Australia (1801–3): his salary was 100 guineas, a quarter that of Brown. In correspondence with Banks, Good, although considered a very pleasant, unassuming young man, felt it necessary to press for recognition should he discover or introduce new plants.

The *Investigator* carried cases of seeds and, in a greenhouse, soft-fruit bushes in pots. When Flinders discovered Kangaroo Island, South Australia, Good planted seeds of European fruits and vegetables there for the benefit of subsequent mariners. Also on board was a prefabricated greenhouse for new plants but it and its contents, some forty-eight species of live Australian plants for Kew, were lost in the wreck of the *Porpoise* on the barrier reef in August 1803 (though some seeds were saved). While generally assisting Brown at points touched during the voyage to New South Wales, Good also collected without him in the Sydney area and, at every opportunity, sent seeds back to Banks (including some collected at the Cape), thereby introducing into cultivation some ninety-seven species, mainly Leguminosae and Proteaceae, fifteen of them of outstanding horticultural merit. These were the basis for Kew's later pre-eminence in the cultivation of Australian plants.

During the subsequent circumnavigation of Australia, Good contracted dysentery; he died on 12 June 1803 in Sydney Cove, four days after reaching Sydney, and was buried the next day at St Philip's, York Street. He is commemorated in *Goodia* (Leguminosae), a genus of Australian shrubs which he introduced to cultivation, as well as in *Banksia goodii* and *Grevillea goodii*, both Australian Proteaceae named by Brown. Flinders named Goods Island in the Gulf of Carpentaria after him, and in 1988 a gully in which Brown, Good, and their colleagues had spent the night of 10 March 1802 after reaching the summit of Mount Brown, Flinders Ranges, South Australia, was officially named Peter Good gully. D. J. Mabberley

Sources D. J. Mabberley, *Jupiter botanicus: Robert Brown of the British Museum* (1985) • P. I. Edwards, 'The journal of Peter Good', *Bulletin of the British Museum (Natural History)* [Historical Series], 9 (1981), 1–

213 • H. B. Carter, *Sir Joseph Banks, 1743–1820* (1988) • R. Grandison, 'Retracing the route taken by Robert Brown and company in a portion of the Flinders Ranges', *History of systematic botany in Australasia*, ed. P. S. Short and others (1990), 105–7 • J. Smith, 'Botanical collectors', *Gardeners' Chronicle*, new ser., 16 (1881), 568–70
Archives NHM, journal and notebook; herbarium
Wealth at death chattels sold to crew: Robert Brown's diary, NHM

Good, Sarah (*d.* 1692). *See under* Salem witches and their accusers (*act.* 1692).

Good, Thomas (1609/10–1678), college head, was born in Worcestershire, supposedly of 'plebeian' stock, and was admitted a king's scholar at the King's School, Worcester, in 1622, during the headship of Henry Bright (1562–1627), a former fellow of Balliol College, Oxford, and one of the most prominent schoolmasters of his day. By 1625 Good was a commoner at Balliol; he became a scholar in 1627, but did not matriculate (aged eighteen) until some months before graduating BA in 1628. He was elected to a Balliol fellowship in 1629, proceeded MA in 1631 and BD in 1639, and was an active tutor until early in the civil war. Good then withdrew to Shropshire. Ejected from St Alkmund's, Shrewsbury, on the fall of that town to parliament in 1645, he acquired the rectory of Culmington in 1648 but was soon displaced. He survived as an absentee fellow of Balliol, however, and in 1647 the Oxford parliamentary visitors thought him sound enough to be one of their delegates. For the next decade he lived quietly as a country minister, probably mostly at Coreley, Shropshire.

In 1653, the year in which he was granted the vicarage of Bishop's Castle, Good joined with his friend Richard Baxter in efforts to unify the west midland clergy. Briefly from 1656 rector of Little Wittenham, Berkshire, in 1657 he was presented to the rectory of Wistanstow, Shropshire. At the Restoration he was made a DD and a canon residentiary of Hereford (with the bishop's prebend); he was also given dispensation to hold the rectory of Culmington again, in plurality with Wistanstow.

Good resigned his fellowship of Balliol in 1658, but he still followed college affairs. Financial misfortunes arising from the civil war and the great fire of London, compounded by corrupt practices afterwards, had reduced the college to a parlous state of indebtedness by 1670. Good reported on all this to the college's visitor, William Fuller, bishop of Lincoln, who took charge, and when the mastership fell vacant on the death of Henry Savage in 1672, Good was installed. Despite obstructive and factious fellows Good saved Balliol from collapse by fund-raising and firm government. His boldest move, sacrificing principle to necessity, was to sell a Balliol place in perpetuity to Blundell's School, Tiverton, for £600.

Good also followed Savage in the rectory of Bladon, Oxfordshire, which he held until death in plurality with that of Wistanstow, adding the vicarage of Diddlebury in 1676. He had one short book published—*Firmianus and Dubitantius* (1674), a laboured fictional dialogue on controversial topics. This work is rich in aphorism, but its theses were scornfully demolished by Baxter. *A Brief English Tract of Logick* (1677), a pamphlet including a list of maxims in Good's style, was ascribed to Good by Anthony Wood.

Good died at Hereford on 9 April 1678. His burial next day is recorded in the register of the cathedral parish, but there is no memorial. No wife, child, or sibling is mentioned in his will, drawn up on 4 February 1677, which made numerous modest bequests, to kinsfolk, godchildren, and Balliol College. JOHN JONES

Sources Wood, *Ath. Oxon.*, 1st edn, 2.453–4 • J. Jones, *Balliol College: a history*, 2nd edn (1997) • first Latin register, and A. Clark's lists, Balliol Oxf. • T. Good, petition to the House of Lords, 23 Jan 1660, HLRO • T. Good, letters to bishop of Lincoln, 1670–76, Lincs. Arch., VV2 • T. Goode, 'A short narrative of some affairs concerning Baliol Colledge from the yeare 1625 and upwards to the yeare 1676', 1676, Lincs. Arch., VV2/4/22 • PRO, PROB 11/356/255 • T. Good, *To the … lords, knights … of Worcester: the humble proposal of a native of that county* [1674] • *Reliquiae Baxterianae, or, Mr Richard Baxter's narrative of the most memorable passages of his life and times*, ed. M. Sylvester, 1 vol. in 3 pts (1696), pt 2, p. 149; pt 3, pp. 148–51 • W. Kennett, *A register and chronicle ecclesiastical and civil* (1728), 333 • M. Burrows, ed., *The register of the visitors of the University of Oxford, from AD 1647 to AD 1658*, CS, new ser., 29 (1881), 478 • *Walker rev.* • E. L. G. Stones, 'A petition to King Charles II from Balliol College', *Archives*, 16 (1983–4), 131–6 • M. Craze, *King's School, Worcester* (1972), 65 • parish register (burial), Hereford, St John's, 10 April 1678 • *DNB* • Foster, *Alum. Oxon.*
Archives Lincs. Arch., MSS of bishops of Lincoln as visitors of Balliol, VV2
Wealth at death over £100; approx. £20 p.a. in lands; also books: will, PRO, PROB 11/356/255

Good, Thomas Sword (1789–1872), painter, was born on 2 December 1789 at Berwick upon Tweed, Northumberland, and baptized there on 21 December, the son of James Good (1744–1812), a master house painter and glazier, and his wife, Barbara (*d.* 1832). Good initially trained as a house painter, most probably with his father, but in 1815 showed three paintings at the Edinburgh Exhibition Society in a gallery attached to the studio of Sir Henry Raeburn. From 1820 to 1834 he exhibited extensively at the British Institution (forty-three paintings), the Suffolk Street gallery of the Society of British Artists (two paintings) and the Royal Academy in London (nineteen paintings) as well as numerous provincial centres including Glasgow, Carlisle, Liverpool, Newcastle, Exeter, and Bristol. On 28 February 1828 he was elected an honorary member of the newly created Scottish Academy where he exhibited nine paintings between 1828 and 1833.

From a relatively early date Good enjoyed independent wealth. In 1817 he lent £300 to Berwick corporation and a further £700 in 1826. His marriage to Mary Evans Forster (1793–1874) on 21 March 1839 brought him additional prosperity. They had no children. After 1833 he is believed to have suffered from debilitating headaches and painted little, if at all. Two pictures shown at the Royal Scottish Academy in 1850 need not have been recent works. He died from 'hydrothorax' at his house at 21 Quay Walls, Berwick, on 15 April 1872 and was buried on 19 April in Berwick parish churchyard. In 1874 his bequest of £4000 was received by the Wesleyan Missionary Society in London.

Though Good's career as an artist was relatively short he was highly industrious and painted numerous replicas of such successful compositions as *A Study of Two Old Men* (Still

Thomas Sword Good (1789–1872), self-portrait, *c.*1832

Living) who Fought at the Battle of Minden (1822; version: Laing Art Gallery, Newcastle upon Tyne). His main concern as a painter was with light. In a letter discussing *Sleeping and Waken* (1826; priv. coll.) Good told Sir David Smith to:

> look at the picture … in a strong light (not a sun light) when you will see it to most advantage—my pictures differ from the works of other artists which are improved in a half light—the reason is that the shadows must be seen as well as the lights. (Good, Alnwick Castle MS 94)

He painted several candlelight studies but preferred a system of cross- or side-lighting which imparted a strongly three-dimensional quality to his work. His pictures are usually in excellent condition, painted on small mahogany panels.

Good's paintings, unlike those of Wilkie, with whom he is usually linked, are largely devoid of narrative content. He specialized in minutely observed, small studies of single figures—often seated, and dressed in eighteenth-century costume. Even the central, dancing figure in *The Power of Music* (1823; Laing Art Gallery, Newcastle upon Tyne) reveals a static quality that is an essential hallmark of Good's style. For his many paintings of fisherfolk and smugglers he used his brother Robert and his family as models. Good also painted many small portraits, including a particularly fine, entirely characteristic likeness of the engraver Thomas Bewick (1827; Natural History Society of Northumbria).

A drawing by Good of *The Union Chain Bridge across the River Tweed* was published as an aquatint by Robert Scott on 1 November 1822 and his paintings *The Power of Music* and *Practice* were both engraved by William Morrison. Good himself produced a few etchings of which *The Drunken Fisherman* is the finest.

Three paintings by Good, bequeathed by his widow to the National Gallery, are now in the Tate collection, together with *The Newspaper* given by Robert Vernon in 1847. Other examples are in the Scottish National Portrait Gallery, Edinburgh, the National Maritime Museum, London, and the National Gallery of Ireland, Dublin. A portrait of Good by Kenneth McLeay (1849) was shown at the Royal Scottish Academy in 1850; an albumen print (photograph) of Good was probably taken by his brother Robert, about 1855.

EDWIN BOWES

Sources P. E. Bowes, *In a strong light: the art of Thomas Sword Good* (1989) • E. Bowes, 'Our celebrated painter: new information concerning T. S. Good', *History of the Berwickshire Naturalists' Club*, 42/2 (1982), 69–84 • *Berwick Advertiser* (26 April 1872) • *CGPLA Eng. & Wales* (1872) • M. Hall, *The artists of Northumbria* (1973) • J. Fleming, 'Thomas Sword Good: a disregarded Victorian painter', *Country Life*, 103 (1948), 182–3

Archives Royal Scot. Acad., autograph letters

Likenesses T. S. Good, self-portrait, oils, *c.*1817, Castle Art Gallery, Nottingham • T. S. Good, self-portrait, watercolour, *c.*1820, priv. coll. • T. S. Good, self-portrait, oils, *c.*1832, priv. coll. [*see illus.*] • K. McLeay, watercolour and pencil drawing, 1849, repro. in Bowes, 'Our celebrated painter', p. 71 • R. Good?, photograph, albumen print, *c.*1855

Wealth at death under £10,000 (in UK): probate, 14 June 1872, *CGPLA Eng. & Wales*

Good, William (1527–1586), Jesuit, was born at Glastonbury, Somerset, where he received his early education at 'the hospice of St. Joseph of Arimathea for gentlemen' (*Elizabethan Jesuits*, 14). Admitted to Corpus Christi College, Oxford, on 26 February 1546 he was elected a fellow on 15 June 1548. He supplicated for his MA in 1551/2. Most likely ordained in Queen Mary's reign he obtained the benefice of Middle Chinnock, Somerset, the prebend of Comba Octava, and a canonry in Wells Cathedral in 1556, and the headmastership of the grammar school in Wells about the same time.

By 22 March 1560 Good had lost all his ecclesiastical positions. He then left England for the continent. According to More, Everard Mercurian, Jesuit provincial in the Spanish Netherlands, 'witnessed his dexterity with the spiritual exercises' (*Elizabethan Jesuits*, 14) and, as a result, accepted Good as a novice in Tournai on 3 June 1562. In early autumn 1564 Mercurian selected Good to accompany Richard Creagh, recently consecrated archbishop of Armagh, to Ireland, where Creagh hoped to establish a university with the assistance of Good and David Wolfe, the Jesuit and papal legate, who was already in Ireland. Forced to disembark in England because of bad weather, Creagh left Dover for Chester, Good following on three weeks later. Good arrived in Dublin on 18 December 1564. Unable to locate the archbishop, Good missed being captured with him a few days after Christmas.

Travelling to Limerick, Good met Edmund Daniel, a Jesuit scholar who had just arrived in his homeland, on 1 February 1565. A week later they opened a school in Limerick which was sacked and closed in late October. In late 1565 or early 1566 they opened a school in Kilmallock but after three months they returned to Limerick. The school was later transferred to Clonmel before finally settling in Youghal. Good frequently complained about conditions in Ireland and asked to be withdrawn, arguing that the Society of Jesus did not intend that its men be exposed to such peril. Later Good resisted attempts to be recalled, because of his successful career as a preacher in Youghal.

Good finally arrived in the Spanish Netherlands some time before early April 1570. Between then and his departure for Rome in August 1574 he studied theology and worked with English refugees in the Low Countries. At least once, in 1573, he volunteered for a Jesuit mission to England or Scotland. In Louvain he met Robert Persons and directed him through an eight-day retreat based on the spiritual exercises of Ignatius of Loyola in the summer of 1574, and thus was influential in Persons's application to the Jesuits. Shortly thereafter Good departed for Rome; by 1576 he was English penitentiary at St Peter's. On 8 September 1577 he was professed of the four vows at Rome. A few days later, on the 16th, he accompanied the Jesuit Antonio Possevino on a delicate mission to the Swedish court to reconcile John III and restore Catholicism. They arrived in Stockholm on 19 December. Good remained there until August 1580, when Possevino sent him to the Jesuit college in Braunsberg (Braniewo).

Good returned to Rome in February 1581 to participate in the general congregation that elected Claudio Acquaviva superior-general. He remained in Rome as confessor at the English College, a decision William Allen endorsed: 'In that Reverend Father Good, a man that is good indeed, is to be confessor of the College, I greatly rejoice; for he is especially qualified to form character and skilled in the whole art of direction' (Ryan, 33). A year later some students accused Good of using this skill to entice seminarians into joining the Jesuits. In 1584 Persons requested that Good be sent to England, but Acquaviva for unknown reasons did not comment on the request. In February 1585 Good was sent to Naples, where he died, on 5 July 1586. He was buried in the Jesuit college.

In Rome Good served as adviser for the frescoes sponsored by George Gilbert and painted by Niccolo Circignani on the walls of the church of the English College. They depicted the history of Christianity in England and Wales with particular emphasis on martyrdom. The originals perished during French occupation of the college in the Napoleonic era, but etchings based on them were published in *Ecclesiae Anglicanae trophaea* (Rome, 1584), a work commonly attributed to Good. THOMAS M. MCCOOG

Sources T. M. McCoog, *English and Welsh Jesuits, 1555–1650*, 2 vols., Catholic RS, 74–5 (1994–5) • T. M. McCoog, ed., *Monumenta Angliae*, 1–2 (1992) • H. Foley, ed., *Records of the English province of the Society of Jesus*, 7 vols. in 8 (1875–83) • *The Elizabethan Jesuits: Historia missionis Anglicanae Societatis Jesu (1660) of Henry More*, ed. and trans. F. Edwards (1981) • Foster, *Alum. Oxon.* • *Fasti Angl., 1541–1857*, [Bath and Wells] • O. Garstein, *Rome and the Counter-Reformation in Scandinavia*, 1 [1963] • T. M. McCoog, *The Society of Jesus in Ireland, Scotland, and England, 1541–1588* (1996) • 'Correspondence of Cardinal Allen', ed. P. Ryan, *Miscellanea, VII*, Catholic RS, 9 (1911), 12–105 • A. F. Allison and D. M. Rogers, eds., *The contemporary printed literature of the English Counter-Reformation between 1558 and 1640*, 2 vols. (1989–94) • C. Lennon, *Archbishop Richard Creagh of Armagh, 1523–1586: an Irish prisoner of conscience of the Tudor era* (2000)

Archives Archivio di Stato di Roma, autobiographical account of work in Ireland, Paesi Stranieri, busta 28, fasc. 1 (Inghilterra) • Archivum Romanum Societatis Iesu, letters • Archivum Romanum Societatis Iesu, letters from Ireland, Angl. 41 • Archivum Romanum Societatis Iesu, letters from mission to Sweden, Possevino material in Opp. NN

Goodacre, Hugh (*d.* 1553), Church of Ireland archbishop of Armagh, is of undocumented origins. In 1530 he was a fellow of Brasenose College, Oxford, having graduated BA in the previous year; he graduated MA in 1532 and BTh by 1552; he was keeper of the queen's chest in 1532. He was Princess Elizabeth's chaplain for a time before deciding to engage in a parish ministry. Elizabeth commended Goodacre to Cecil, writing that he had been 'long time known unto her to be as well of honest conversation and sober living as of sufficient learning and judgment in the Scriptures to preach the Word of God' (*DNB*).

In March 1550 Goodacre became the vicar of Sholfleet, Isle of Wight. He became the rector of nearby Calbourne in January 1553 and was, by then, also Bishop Ponet's chaplain. He was commended by Archbishop Cranmer as 'a man both wise and well-learned' (Strype, 2.670). The passionately protestant apologist John Bale characterized him as 'that godly preacher and virtuous learned man' (Bale, 449).

On 28 October 1552 Edward VI appointed Goodacre to the primatial see of Armagh in place of George Dowdall, the conservative Henrician primate who had fled to mainland Europe rather than be bishop where the mass was abolished. On 25 March 1553 Hugh Goodacre with John Bale, Edward's appointee to Ossory, were consecrated together as bishops according to the rite in the second Edwardian prayer book, despite the reluctance of the archbishop of Dublin to use it without explicit authorization from the crown.

Archbishop Goodacre never took up residence in Armagh, nor did he enter his diocese. Bale fancifully claimed that he was poisoned by priests of Armagh diocese for 'preaching God's verities and rebuking their common vices' (Bale, 449). He died in Dublin on 1 May 1553 and was buried that day in St Patrick's Cathedral.

HENRY A. JEFFERIES

Sources Emden, *Oxf.*, 4.240 • J. Bale, 'The vocacyon of John Bale, bishop of Ossary', *The Harleian miscellany*, ed. W. Oldys and T. Park, 6 (1813) • J. Strype, *Memorials of the most reverend father in God Thomas Cranmer*, 3 vols. in 4 (1848–54), vol. 2, p. 670 • J. Morrin, ed., *Calendar of the patent and close rolls of chancery in Ireland, of the reigns of Henry VIII, Edward VI, Mary, and Elizabeth*, 1 (1861), 267, 292 • J. B. Leslie, *Armagh clergy and parishes* (1911), 4

Goodall, Charles (*c.*1642–1712), physician, the son of Thomas Goodall of Earl Stonham, Suffolk, matriculated as a pensioner at Emmanuel College, Cambridge, on 20 January 1659, but, perhaps because of problems at the Restoration, did not complete his BA or MA. Instead he took up medicine, obtaining a university licence to practise surgery in 1665. The *Dictionary of National Biography* claimed that Goodall was married three times. He married in Ipswich, Suffolk, on 29 July 1664, and his eldest son, Thomas, was born at Earl Stonham about 1667; his second son, Charles [*see below*], was born in 1671; a daughter (unnamed) is also mentioned in letters. Goodall matriculated in medicine at the University of Leiden on 21 June 1670; a few days later, on 4 July, he defended a thesis, 'De haemorrhageis

Charles Goodall (*c.*1642–1712), attrib. Thomas Murray, *c.*1690–1700

scorbuticis', dedicated to his father, and to the Revd G. Smyth DD and Richard Lower. Goodall also incorporated his Leiden MD at Cambridge in 1670. Rolleston asserts that Goodall also attended the anatomical lectures of Walter Needham about this time.

Before the end of 1675 Goodall moved to London. When the Royal College of Physicians confronted a group of medical chemists, Goodall replied to one of the chemists' works in *The Colledge of Physicians Vindicated* (1676), dedicated to Sir Francis North, lord chief justice of the common pleas. In it Goodall made a strong case for the legality of the college's jurisdiction, and the usefulness of that power. 'Although it hath not yet been my happiness to be a Member of the Learned Society of Physicians in *London*', he wrote in a preface, 'yet I profess my self an honourer of them, and cannot without indignation behold men of so great worth and abilities in their Faculty, so barbarously assaulted by a wretched combination of ignorant and impudent Empiricks'. This sentiment was to stimulate Goodall's public work throughout his life. His reward was to be able to take the three-part examination to become a candidate of the college in April and May of 1676, being admitted on 26 June. He was nevertheless passed over for the fellowship until 5 April 1680. Goodall was able to send his son Tom to Grantham grammar school and St Paul's School, London, before placing him at Gonville and Caius College, Cambridge, in 1683 to study medicine. It may have been about this time that he took up residence in Kensington, Middlesex, where he remained until his death.

Goodall took very seriously new methods of natural history for exploring diseases and their remedies, making a special effort to investigate cinchona bark and the tree from which it came. By the late 1670s at least Goodall had become a supporter of Thomas Sydenham, who warmed to Goodall in turn. In a letter published in 1680 Sydenham referred to Goodall as a person of candour, probity, friendship, and medical skill; in a book of 1682, Sydenham praised Goodall as one of his chief defenders and one of the most upright, erudite, and clinically attentive physicians of the day; and in his *Schedula monitoria* (1686), dedicated to Goodall, Sydenham praised him as 'second to none' among the physicians of the day. In all likelihood it was through Sydenham that Goodall met John Locke, who referred to recipes recommended by Goodall in his medical journal from June 1680 onwards. On 29 May 1683 Locke moved his belongings into Goodall's quarters at the Royal College of Physicians in Warwick Lane, London, before going into exile. On 27 December 1688 Goodall wrote to Locke of William of Orange as a Moses who had delivered 'our miserable and distressed kingdoms from popery and slavery', urging Locke to return quickly (Dewhurst, 487–508). On his return Locke lodged with Goodall for a time. Goodall was also well acquainted with Hans Sloane, Nehemiah Grew, Richard Morton, and Thomas Millington, all of whom were—like Sydenham, Locke, and Lower—whigs and naturalists.

Nevertheless, Goodall worked on behalf of a more academic but authoritative Royal College of Physicians. From 1681 a private committee of the college worked behind the scenes to reorder its affairs (minutes of this are in the Sloane collection); from at least 1684 Goodall participated fully in the committee. Goodall published *The Royal College of Physicians of London Founded and Established by Law, and an Historical Account of the College's Proceedings Against Empiricks* (1684), which angrily attacked those of a 'mechanical' rather than academic medical education, who, he said, had been engaged in the 'late rebellion' and never acknowledged the duty they owed to God and their king. It was a persuasive book: though documents were cited selectively, they were quoted fully and accurately. To make the college's position more widely known, Goodall also epitomized his work in *A Short Account* (1686). In April 1688 the private committee pulled strings to get a version of Goodall's book presented personally to the king; the long version was even cited in a legal opinion as evidence for the college's powers, and much of the crown's legal and political support for the college under James II's reign was based on Goodall's portrayal of this institution. Goodall served as Goulstonian lecturer in 1685. He and Walter Needham attended Theodore Haak during his last illness in 1690; on 28 April 1691 he succeeded Needham as physician to the Charterhouse School, London, where he resided as required. Goodall wrote many of the published pamphlets against parliamentary bills of the Surgeons' and Apothecaries' companies from 1689 to 1691. He made many efforts to restore discipline within the college, and helped to shape the controversial plan to institute the college dispensary. In September 1697, when he first stood for the office of censor, it was found that some members had voted against him more than once; on the second vote, after checking that each person had taken only one black or white stone, Goodall narrowly succeeded.

Goodall also encouraged and edited the treatises of others against opponents of the college. In May 1698 Goodall invited an Oxford student, Richard Boulton, to join him in London to help with various projects, in return for Goodall's help in advancing Boulton's ambitions for medical practice. Goodall helped to edit Boulton's *Examination of Mr. John Colbatch* (1699), which also contained an appendix making nasty personal remarks about a physician from Manchester, Charles Leigh. Leigh wrote in anger to Goodall, who disowned Boulton; Leigh published Goodall's letter in *A Reply to Mr. Richard Bolton* (1698). Boulton had in the meantime confronted Goodall, and had been kicked out of his house; Boulton responded with *A Letter to Dr. Charles Goodall* (1699), which made a public mockery of Goodall's underhanded manipulation. To this Goodall had William Wilkinson, named as his footman, publish *A Two-Penny Answer to R. Boulton* (1699), comparing Boulton to various London quacks and religious radicals. Goodall also urged James Yonge to attack one of Boulton's supporters, a well-known empiric, William Salmon, in *Sidrophel Vapulans, or, The Quack-Astrologer* (1699). This provoked an advertisement in the *Protestant Mercury* (3 February 1699), accusing Yonge and 'Rattlehead Good Ale of London, who lives within a mile of the Charter-House' of 'Jacobite Cant', among other things. A reply appeared in the *Post Boy* (14 February) asking the public to keep a lookout for Salmon and Boulton, in order to have these madmen confined to Bedlam. It was also probably at this time that Goodall was mocked for selling overpriced Jesuit's bark in at least two quarto handbills circulated in London. Goodall may also have been the model for John Galen in Thomas Brown's satirical *Physick Lies a Bleeding* (1697). Goodall was named in Garth's mock-heroic *Dispensary* (1699) as Stentor, who fights to the end, even after his party in the battle has lost; when fallen at the feet of the victor, he pleads for mercy for his son.

By the end of the century Goodall had suffered much. His hopes for the Royal College of Physicians had failed, for as Garth's poem noted, its authority had weakened rather than strengthened. His eldest son, Tom, for whom Garth had him plead, never became a prominent London physician, as his father had hoped. His younger son, Charles, died in 1689; his wife (perhaps his second wife) died of diabetes in 1696. His own health suffered. In 1702 he spent over sixteen weeks at Tunbridge Wells taking the waters; from there he wrote a long letter to Millington, reporting his unsuccessful attempts to revive the earl of Kent, who had collapsed on the bowling green. He soon returned to working on projects in natural history, dabbled with a plan to print some of the now esteemed Thomas Sydenham's unpublished works, and in 1702 edited *Memoires of the Two Last Years* (of the reign of Charles I). He again became involved in the affairs of the college, becoming a censor (1703, 1705, 1706), one of the eight elects (1704), one of the two consiliarii (1708), and finally president (from 23 December 1708 until his death). On 12 July 1706 he presented the college with two original paintings: one of Henry VIII, and the other of Cardinal Wolsey. He supported continuing attempts to strengthen the college's authority in the early eighteenth century, but managed to remain out of the public eye.

Goodall died at his house at Kensington on 23 August 1712, and was buried in the Kensington church; a slab commemorating his death was placed in the south aisle there. He was survived by his (second or third) wife.

Goodall's son **Charles Goodall** (1671–1689), poet, was sent to Eton College, and to Merton College, Oxford, where he became postmaster in 1688. He died on 11 May 1689, and was buried in the outward chapel of his college. Known to his father and friends as a brilliant youth, he was the author of *Poems and translations written on several occasions and to several persons by a late scholar of Eaton* (1689). HAROLD J. COOK

Sources annals, RCP Lond. • assorted legal documents, RCP Lond. • BL, Sloane MSS • Bodl. Oxf., MSS Rawl. • Bodl. Oxf., MSS Locke • 'Advertisements, Medical', BL, C.112.f9 • R. Boulton, *A letter to Dr Charles Goodall* (1699) • C. Goodall, *The College of Physicians vindicated* (1676) • W. Wilkinson, *A two-penny answer to R. Boulton's six-penny letter to Dr Charles Goodall, &c.* (1699) • Foster, *Alum. Oxon.* • Venn, *Alum. Cant.* • R. W. Innes Smith, *English-speaking students of medicine at the University of Leyden* (1932) • Munk, *Roll* • H. J. Cook, *Trials of an ordinary doctor: Joannes Groenevelt in 17th-century London* (1994) • H. Rolleston, 'Charles Goodall: a defender of the Royal College of Physicians of London', *Annals of Medical History*, 3rd ser., 2 (1940), 1–9 • K. Dewhurst, 'Some letters of Dr Charles Goodall (1642–1712) to Locke, Sloane and Sir Thomas Millington', *Journal of the History of Medicine and Allied Sciences*, 17 (1962), 487–508 • H. A. Beecham, 'A notebook and a collection of manuscripts: originally the property of Dr. Charles Goodall', *Bodleian Library Record*, 7 (1962–7), 312–17 • *DNB* • *IGI*

Archives BL, Sloane MSS, letters to Sir Hans Sloane and James Petiver

Likenesses attrib. T. Murray, oils, *c.*1690–1700, RCP Lond. [*see illus.*] • G. P. Harding, watercolour (after oil painting attrib. T. Murray), Wellcome L.

Goodall, Charles (1671–1689). *See under* Goodall, Charles (*c.*1642–1712).

Goodall [*née* Stanton], **Charlotte** (1765–1830), actress, was born in Staffordshire, the daughter of Samuel Stanton and his first wife, Elizabeth. Her father was manager of a 'sharing company' in Staffordshire, and had Charlotte and her four siblings performing from an early age. She made so successful a début in Bath, as Rosalind in *As You Like It* on 17 April 1784, that John Palmer engaged her for his theatre. She performed in both Bath and Bristol for four years, and married Thomas *Goodall (1767–1832?), a Bristol privateer, known as the Admiral of Haiti, in 1787. Her repertory was made up of comic and tragic heroines, which she continued to play throughout her career: Lady Teazle, Lydia Languish, Miss Hardcastle, Mrs Page, Juliet, and Desdemona.

John Kemble hired Charlotte Goodall for Drury Lane, where she appeared on 2 October 1788, as Rosalind. He noted that she was 'a fine woman and was very favourably received by the audience'. She remained with the Drury Lane company during 1798–9, except when that theatre was closed for rebuilding. Her refusal to play Lady Anne in *Richard III* and other lesser characters led to a paper controversy with Kemble, but *The Secret History of the Green Room* claimed it 'terminated favourably to both parties'. Her summer seasons from 1789 to 1793 were spent at the Haymarket, under Colman the younger, who engaged her expressly for breeches parts. She reappeared at the Haymarket for a short time in 1803.

Contemporary critical comment records Mrs Goodall's elegant figure, which Thomas Gilliland remarked 'was admirably formed for male attire'. *The Druiad*, a satire of 1798, reported 'a pretty, lifeless face', and noted that she conveyed the 'idea of a well-constructed automaton'. Her relatively successful career indicates that she was a competent actress, but could not compete with Drury Lane's greater stars Elizabeth Farren, Dorothy Jordan, and Sarah Siddons.

On 19 July 1813 an action was brought by Charlotte Goodall's husband against William Fletcher, his agent and attorney, for criminal conversation. Goodall had evidently left his wife for years at a time on his naval adventures, and on his return found Fletcher had absconded with both his fortune and his wife. A verdict for the plaintiff, with £5000 damages, was given. In the evidence it was stated that Mrs Goodall was originally an actress of amiable character, and had eight children.

Charlotte Goodall died at Somers Town, London, in July 1830. An undated clipping in the British Museum states that she had been supported in her widowhood by her son, an eminent portrait painter. At her death a daughter, who was a schoolmistress in London, and an elder son, in the government of Montserrat, were still living.

JOSEPH KNIGHT, *rev.* K. A. CROUCH

Sources Highfill, Burnim & Langhans, *BDA* • C. B. Hogan, ed., *The London stage, 1660–1800*, pt 5: *1776–1800* (1968) • [J. Haslewood], *The secret history of the green rooms: containing authentic and entertaining memoirs of the actors and actresses in the three theatres royal*, 2 vols. (1790) • J. P. Kemble, Professional memoranda, BL, Add. MS 31972 • *Criminal conversation trial between Thomas Goodall, esq., plaintiff, and William Fletcher, attorney at law* (1813) • T. Gilliland, *The dramatic mirror, containing the history of the stage from the earliest period, to the present time*, 2 vols. (1808) • *The Druriad, or, Strictures on the principal performers of Drury Lane Theatre: a satirical poem* (1798) • T. Bellamy, 'The London theatres: a poem', *Miscellanies in prose and verse*, 2 vols. (1794–5) • A. Pasquin [J. Williams], *The pin-basket to the children of Thespis* (1797)

Likenesses Hawkins, engraving, 1789 (after oil painting by G. Hayter) • R. Laurie, engraving, 1789 • S. De Wilde, oils (as Sir Harry Wildair in *The constant couple*), Garr. Club • W. Leney, engraving (after S. De Wilde), repro. in J. Bell, *Bell's British theatre* • W. Ridley, engraving, repro. in J. Parsons, *The minor theatre* (1794) • engraving, repro. in *British drama* (1817) • five prints, Harvard TC • prints, BM, NPG • watercolour, Harvard TC

Goodall, Edward (1795–1870), line engraver, was born near Leeds on 17 September 1795. He was brought up from childhood by a Quaker uncle, who may have apprenticed him to an engraver. On 20 June 1818, at the Old Church, St Pancras, London, Goodall married Eliza Ann Le Petit, whose grandfather had crossed the channel as a refugee and become one of the earliest colour printers in England. The couple took up residence in Camden Town, moving in 1819 to 20 Arlington Street and in 1823 to 11 Lower Pratt Place. In 1827 they moved to Mornington Grove Cottage, Mornington Grove, a house that Goodall had built for his growing family. His neighbours included Clarkson Stanfield who, with his wife, was a regular visitor at the Goodalls', as was J. M. W. Turner.

During his early years Goodall showed talent as a landscape painter, and he exhibited at the Royal Academy in 1822 and 1823. By about 1824, however, he took up engraving as his sole profession, producing landscape and figure subjects. His reputation as a celebrated engraver rests largely upon his engravings after Turner, with whom he worked in close collaboration, producing plates of great delicacy and beauty.

Goodall started engraving on steel in 1826, largely for popular annuals such as the *Literary Souvenir* and *The Keepsake*, producing designs by contemporary artists such as Francis Danby and David Roberts, as well as Turner. He began concentrating on book illustrations in the 1830s, the large proportion of which were vignettes after Turner, such as those for Samuel Rogers's *Italy* (1830) and *Poems* (1834), Thomas Campbell's *Poetical Works* (1837), or Thomas Moore's *Epicurean* (1839). Among book illustrations after other artists were those after Thomas Stothard, also for Rogers's *Italy*, and for Bunyan's *Pilgrim's Progress* (1839). He was in addition a prolific engraver of landscape subjects for topographical series or travel guidebooks, producing such plates as *The Dogana, Venice* (1832), after Clarkson Stanfield, and those after Turner for *Picturesque Views on the Southern Coast of England* (1814–26) and *Picturesque Views in England and Wales* (1827–38).

Alongside the plates for literary or topographical publications, Goodall engraved numerous large single plates. One of the earliest was *Tivoli*, after Turner, which was privately published by Goodall in 1827 in conjunction with John Allnutt, a patron of Turner who commissioned the plate. It failed to find subscribers and Allnutt apparently lost £400. This episode seems to have deterred Goodall from having any serious ambitions as a publisher–engraver, although he may have acted as co-publisher in later projects, such as Campbell's *Poetical Works* (1837). Many of his large plates appeared in the 1840s and were published for the art unions, such as *The Irish Piper* (1848), after his son Frederick *Goodall. The copperplate *Caligula's Palace and Bridge* (1842), after Turner, was one of Goodall's most impressive and ambitious works, for he was apparently paid the large sum of 700 guineas, although it was also the cause of a quarrel with Turner concerning the ownership of the touched proofs.

Throughout his long career landscape engraving remained Goodall's speciality, although he also executed numerous figure subjects, many after paintings by his son Frederick. Between 1854 and 1869 he produced sixteen plates for the *Art Journal*, half of which were after his son, including his last plate, *The School of Sultan Hassan* (1869).

Goodall was a member of the Associated Engravers, formed to publish *Engravings from the Pictures in the National*

Gallery (1830–40), for which he produced plates after Claude Lorraine, Aelbert Cuyp, and Thomas Gainsborough. He was elected to the council of the Institute of Fine Arts in 1845. Goodall supported the campaign to win recognition for engravers at the Royal Academy, although he refused to put his name forward for election as an academician after the law was revoked in 1855. He was assisted in his engraving practice by Thomas Leeming Grundy and had Robert Brandard and John Outhwaite as pupils.

Goodall had ten children, five of whom were artists: Frederick became a Royal Academician, Edward, Alfred, and Walter *Goodall were members of the Royal Society of Painters in Water Colours, and his daughter Eliza, later Mrs Wild, exhibited some domestic subjects at the Royal Academy and British Institution between 1846 and 1855. He died after a short illness at his home at 148 Hampstead Road on 11 April 1870. Examples of his work are held in the British Museum, the Tate collection, and the Victoria and Albert Museum. DIANE PERKINS

Sources *The reminiscences of Frederick Goodall* (1902) • W. G. Rawlinson, *The engraved work of J. M. W. Turner*, 2 vols. (1908–13) • B. Hunnisett, *Steel engraved book illustration in England* (1980) • B. Hunnisett, *An illustrated dictionary of British steel engravers*, new edn (1989) • *DNB* • *The Tate Gallery, 1986–88: illustrated catalogue of acquisitions* (1996) • *Art Journal*, 32 (1870), 182 • H. Beck, *Victorian engravings* (1973) [exhibition catalogue, V&A] • Bénézit, *Dict.* • Thieme & Becker, *Allgemeines Lexikon* • *CGPLA Eng. & Wales* (1870) • R. Goodall, 'The Goodall family of artists', www.goodallartists.ca/, 19 Dec 2000 • *IGI*

Wealth at death under £3000: probate, 18 May 1870, *CGPLA Eng. & Wales*

Goodall, Frances Gowland (1893–1976), nurse, was born on 8 December 1893 at Ivy Cottage, 3 Buccleuch Road, Dulwich, London, the daughter of Allan Alexander Goodall, bank clerk, and Clara Louisa Emma Bryan. Frances was the middle child between two brothers, Robert and Claud, to whom she was devoted. The children were brought up in comfortable circumstances in Kent, but Frances did not go to school, partly because of ill health, but mainly because her father, a scholarly man, arranged for her to be educated by a tutor at home with her brothers. In later life she said that she was grateful for this because she was trained to think like a man. The other formative influences on Frances were three uncles who were trained at Guy's Hospital. One, with whom she often stayed, was the medical superintendent of a large hospital. It was there, watching the ambulances come and go from the schoolroom window, that she resolved to be a nurse. While she was waiting to go to Guy's she taught for two years at the Camden High School for Girls.

In 1916, at the age of twenty-two, Frances started her training at Guy's, which she greatly enjoyed, and after posts as ward sister and theatre sister she was appointed out-patient sister at Moorfields Hospital. Ophthalmic nursing became her great love; she had delicate hands and her skill in this field became legendary. Always interested in advancing the art and science of nursing she applied for the post of assistant general secretary of the College of Nursing at the relatively early age of thirty-five. Tall, elegant, beautifully groomed with luxuriant long hair she

Frances Gowland Goodall (1893–1976), by unknown photographer

was an outstanding candidate who obviously impressed the council, which was mainly composed of elderly men and women. During her seven years as assistant general secretary Frances Goodall laid plans to take the college into the wider world. With her charm and vivacity she had a capacity for attracting influential people, and it was largely through her that the college ended its isolation, so that financiers, industrialists, educationists, government officials, and ministers of the crown all became staunch friends of the college.

When Frances Goodall became general secretary at the College of Nursing in 1935 there were what seemed insuperable problems. The voluntary hospitals were in a state of crisis, nursing salaries were low, and probationers were exploited; most were in debt, but they viewed the prospect of state intervention as anathema. Frances Goodall held that nurses should be responsible for negotiating their own salaries and that there should be national scales and conditions of service. The advice was not welcomed by hospital administrators: if implemented it would mean state help—the thin end of the wedge. The outbreak of war and the urgent need to recruit nurses concentrated the minds of all concerned wonderfully. In 1943 a committee was set up under the chairmanship of Lord Rushcliffe consisting of representatives of nursing organizations, trade unions, and employees. Largely due to the persistence and diplomacy of Frances Goodall what was by then the Royal College of Nursing received the majority of seats on the staff side. She was soon to show herself an able and tough negotiator and when the National Health

Service (NHS) came into being in 1948 and the Whitley councils were set up she was elected secretary to the staff side and later became chairman. She was universally respected, despite the almost internecine war for members which existed between unions and professional organizations.

During the Second World War, Frances Goodall developed a close relationship with Ernest Bevin, who consulted her about the deployment of nurses, and, through her links with the Ministry of Labour, she became friends with a number of officials particularly Frederick Leggett, who subsequently became the labour relations adviser to the college. Unlike the British Medical Association, the College of Nursing generally welcomed the NHS: nurses knew all too well about the unmet health needs of the pre-war years. The college's relationship with Aneurin Bevan was generally friendly, though not all the membership supported the NHS, and it took all Frances Goodall's diplomacy to steer the profession through the early years of the public sector pay crisis. The main tenet of her message was that in order to achieve professional status and good salaries nurses must be better educated and able to demonstrate the value of good nursing. This was the philosophy behind the Horder committee in 1943, of which she was joint secretary. The committee, under the chairmanship of Lord Horder, spent four years looking at the education and training of nurses and advocated sweeping reforms. Although the Horder reports were submerged in an unending stream of further reports, no report is ever entirely lost and the way was paved for further research and experimentation.

Apart from her achievements at the college and on the turbulent Whitley councils, Frances Goodall found time for other work. She travelled widely, was honorary secretary of the women's advisory council of the Nuffield Provincial Hospitals Trust, the chairman of the British Federation of Business and Professional Women, a member of the Council of the Federated Superannuation Scheme for Nurses and Hospital Officers, and was a member of the Ministry of Labour Women's Consultative Committee until well after her retirement.

The abiding memory of Frances Goodall is one of elegance and poise combined with vivacity and a great sense of fun. She had that rare gift of making each person feel that he or she was the one she wanted to meet. It did not matter if it was an old, rather confused founder member, or a mandarin from the ministry, they were all important to her. She was remarkably well read, devoted to Mozart, and at home in the country with horses and dogs. A good hostess and a welcome visitor, she was always appreciative and ready to compliment or console if necessary. She was appointed OBE in 1944 and CBE in 1953.

In retirement Frances Goodall continued to be active. She founded the Colostomy Association, serving as its chairman for a number of years, setting up a network of advisers throughout the country, it being her experience that nurses, rather than doctors, gave the most practical and helpful advice.

Frances Goodall collapsed in her London flat and died in the Royal Free Hospital, Hampstead, on 22 July 1976, thus ending a life described by her secretary as being 'Visionary, active and devoted to the service of others. A life of charisma and charm which left its imprint on those fortunate enough to come in contact with her' (private information). A memorial service was held in St Peter's, Vere Street, London, on 15 October 1976 and was attended by members of the medical and nursing professions, government officials, and representatives of the organizations with whom she had worked. She was unmarried.

MONICA E. BALY

Sources personal knowledge (2004) · private information (2004) · *Nursing Times* (29 July 1976) · *Nursing Times* (31 May 1957) · *Nursing Mirror* (July 1976) · b. cert. · d. cert.
Archives Royal College of Nursing, Edinburgh, speeches
Likenesses J. Gunn, oils, exh. RA 1956, Royal College of Nursing, London · photograph, Royal College of Nursing Archives, Edinburgh [*see illus.*]
Wealth at death £14,388: probate, 28 Sept 1976, *CGPLA Eng. & Wales*

Goodall, Frederick (1822–1904), genre painter, was born at 20 Arlington Street, Camden Town, London, on 17 September 1822, the third of ten children of Edward *Goodall (1795–1870), line engraver, and his wife, Eliza Ann Le Petit, granddaughter of a French printer of coloured engravings. Two of Goodall's brothers, Edward Angelo Goodall and Walter *Goodall (1830–1889), and a sister, Eliza, were also professional artists. Goodall drew from an early age and derived inspiration from the many works of J. M. W. Turner engraved by his father. He was educated at Wellington House Academy, a private school that Charles Dickens had attended, near the Goodall family home in Mornington Grove. At the age of thirteen he left school to work with his father, who taught him oil painting and encouraged him to draw animals at the zoo and to study human anatomy. He had little other formal artistic training, but about 1839 he joined life classes at the St Martin's Lane Academy, where he observed the drawing methods of William Etty, and he also attended the drawing school in Leicester Square, visited by B. R. Haydon.

In 1836 Goodall was commissioned to make watercolour drawings of Willesden church and Lambeth Palace, which he exhibited at the Society of Arts, receiving the Isis medal for the latter. Two years later he was awarded the large silver medal by the same society when he exhibited an oil painting, *Finding the Dead Body of a Miner by Torchlight*, based on a sketch made during the construction of the first tunnel under the Thames. In the same year four sketches of the Thames Tunnel were accepted by the Royal Academy, an institution with which he had a long association, exhibiting there annually, with only three exceptions, until 1902.

In his early years Goodall exhibited scenes of rural life, which drew their material from sketching trips in Britain, Ireland, and France during the late 1830s and 1840s, for example *The Irish Piper* (exh. RA, 1847; V&A). The influence of David Wilkie, a copy of whose *Chelsea Pensioners* Goodall's father owned, is evident in these rustic genre scenes, notably *The Village Holiday: when the Merry Bells Ring Round* (exh. RA, 1847; Tate collection), purchased by Robert Vernon for the large sum of £500 guineas. Another early supporter was William Wells of Redleaf, near Tunbridge Wells, a trustee of the National Gallery and patron of Edwin Landseer and other contemporary artists. On 24 October 1846 Goodall married the artist Anne Thomson (*c*.1823–1869), daughter of the engraver James *Thomson, and three years later the couple set up home at 4 Camden Square, London. They had five children; two sons, Frederick Trevelyan *Goodall (*bap.* 1848, *d.* 1871) and Howard *Goodall (*bap.* 1850, *d.* 1874) [*see under* Goodall, Frederick Trevelyan], became artists, but died in their early twenties.

In the 1850s Goodall began exhibiting historical genre scenes, which were well received by the critics, and gained popularity through engravings made after them by his father. *Raising the Maypole at the Restoration of Charles II* (exh. RA, 1851) secured his election as an associate of the Royal Academy in 1852; *The Happier Days of Charles II* (exh. RA, 1852; Bury Art Gallery and Museum) and *Cranmer at the Traitor's Gate* (exh. RA, 1856; V&A) were both bought for large sums by Ernest Gambart, the most influential art dealer of the period. Material for these pictures was gathered on sketching trips in England, but he also seized opportunities to travel further afield: in 1856 he accompanied Gambart and Rosa Bonheur, the French animal painter, on a tour of Scotland, and in 1857 he spent the summer in Venice and Chioggia, Italy.

The most important journey of Goodall's career was to Egypt in 1858–9, in search of subjects for biblical paintings; he also no doubt hoped to emulate the fame that painters such as David Roberts and J. F. Lewis had acquired from their eastern pictures. He rented a house in the Coptic quarter in Cairo, which he shared with the Bavarian watercolour artist Carl Haag, and together they made sketching trips to Suez and the Uyun Musa (wells of Moses), and to the pyramids at Giza. On his return to England, Goodall exhibited *Early Morning in the Wilderness of Shur* (exh. RA, 1860; Guildhall Art Gallery); although the painting depicts an Arab sheikh addressing his tribe on the shores of the Red Sea, it evokes the image of Moses and the Israelites. It was followed by similarly symbolic or morally edifying themes, such as *The First Born* (exh. RA, 1861); *The Palm Offering* (exh. RA, 1863), which led to his election as an academician in 1863; and *The Song of the Nubian Slave* (exh. RA, 1864; RA), his diploma work. Paintings such as these were widely admired—at the Royal Academy banquet in 1867 Gladstone asked to be introduced to the painter of *Hagar and Ishmael* (exh. RA, 1866)—and they established his reputation as a painter of eastern subjects with explicit or implicit biblical allusions. Contemporaries rated highly their technical competence, carefully constructed compositions, and clearly stated messages, whereas later opinion has perceived them as sentimental, derivative, and formulaic, albeit well executed.

Goodall's abilities were held in high regard by his fellow academicians, as well as the public, and in 1869 they allowed fifty of his Egyptian sketches to be exhibited at their new premises in Burlington House: Gambart, who had purchased them for £6000, sold them all before the exhibition closed. This success was marred by the death of his wife that same year. In 1870 Goodall made a further visit to Egypt, where he lived for three months among the bedouin at Sakkhara. This experience enabled him, on his return, to paint numerous and repetitive pastoral scenes of Egyptian fellahin with their flocks beside the Nile, using sheep especially imported from Egypt to his new house at Harrow Weald. Built by Norman Shaw on land acquired by Goodall in 1856, the house was named Graeme's Dyke. Soon after marrying for the second time, on 27 February 1872, Goodall moved in with his new wife, Alice Mary Tarry (1849/50–1913), twenty-seven years his junior, daughter of Thomas Tarry, a solicitor. She too was an artist, exhibiting six works at the Royal Academy between 1890 and 1896. They had two children. As the owner of a large estate Goodall could indulge his horticultural interests and he laid out 30 acres of landscape garden. In 1883, however, tiring of the isolation from artistic associates, Goodall and his family returned to London, to 62 Avenue Road, Regent's Park, where Gambart had formerly lived. Goodall was prosperous and lived opulently, and despite Gambart's retirement his paintings still sold well. He continued to receive important commissions, notably *By the Sea of Galilee* (exh. RA, 1888) for the People's Palace in Mile End Road (probably des.).

Goodall occasionally varied the monotony of his eastern themes with English landscape, but by the 1890s he had outlived his popularity. At the height of his success he had earned about £10,000 a year, but this dropped to little more than £1000. He tried to maintain his income through portraiture and through publishing his autobiographical *Reminiscences* (1902), but his health deteriorated and in 1902 he was declared bankrupt and his possessions auctioned. He moved to 36 Goldhurst Terrace, West Hampstead, London, where he died on 28 July 1904. He was buried at Highgate cemetery with his first wife; nine years later, his second wife was also interred in the same grave. F. W. Gibson, *rev.* Briony Llewellyn

Sources *The reminiscences of Frederick Goodall* (1902) • N. G. Slarke, *Frederick Goodall, R.A.* (1981) • *Art Journal*, 12 (1850), 213 • *Art Journal*, new ser., 24 (1904), 301–2 • 'British artists, their style and character: no. IV—Frederick Goodall', *Art Journal*, 17 (1855), 109–12 • *The Times* (1 Aug 1904) • Graves, *RA exhibitors*, vol. 3 • sale catalogue (1893) [Christies, 25 May 1893] • sale catalogue (1905) [Christies, 20 Feb 1905] • J. Maas, *Gambart: prince of the Victorian art world* (1975) • J. Maas, *The Victorian art world in photographs* (1984) • R. Parkinson, ed., *Catalogue of British oil paintings, 1820–1860* (1990) [catalogue of V&A] • J. Thompson, *The East imagined, experienced, remembered: orientalist nineteenth century painting* (1988) • private information (2004) [Neil Slarke]

Likenesses J. & C. Watkins, two cartes-de-visite, *c*.1862, NPG • Lock & Whitfield, woodburytype photograph, pubd 1878, NPG • F. Goodall, self-portrait, oils, 1883, Aberdeen Art Gallery, MacDonald collection • J. B. Davis, pen-and-ink drawing, *c*.1893, NPG • mechanical process on postcard, *c*.1902, Maas collection • Elliott & Fry, carte-de-visite, NPG • Frederick Downe & Sons, Watford, photograph, repro. in *Reminiscences*, following p. 216 • Green, woodcut, BM • Lambert, Weston & Son, Folkestone, photograph, repro. in *Reminiscences*, frontispiece

Wealth at death £120: probate, 20 Oct 1904, *CGPLA Eng. & Wales*

Goodall [Goodhall], **Frederick Trevelyan** (*bap.* 1848, *d.* 1871), painter, the eldest child in the family of four sons and one daughter of the painter Frederick *Goodall (1822–1904) and his wife, Anne Thomson (*c.*1823–1869), was baptized at St Pancras Old Church, Pancras Road, London, on 27 September 1848. His younger brother, **Howard Goodall** (*bap.* 1850, *d.* 1874), painter, the second son in the family, was baptized there on 19 July 1850. Their grandfathers, James *Thomson (*bap.* 1788, *d.* 1850) and Edward *Goodall (1795–1870), were both engravers. Both brothers were educated at the University College School in Gower Street, London, before entering the Royal Academy Schools, Frederick in 1865 and Howard in 1868. Frederick was awarded a silver medal in 1866 and a gold medal in 1867. He exhibited seventeen paintings at the Royal Academy between 1868 and 1871, including eight portraits, and in 1869 won a gold medal for *The Return of Ulysses*. Howard exhibited *Nydia in the House of Glaucus* at the Royal Academy in 1870.

In 1870 both brothers accompanied their father on a trip to Egypt and then Pompeii and Capri. Following a pistol accident Frederick Goodall died, unmarried, at Capri on 11 April 1871; he was buried in the British cemetery in Naples. Howard Goodall exhibited *Capri Girls Winnowing* at the Royal Academy in 1873 but died, unmarried, on 17 January of the following year at Cairo.

L. H. Cust, *rev.* Anne Pimlott Baker

Sources N. G. Slarke, *Frederick Goodall, R.A.* (1981) • Boase, *Mod. Eng. biog.* • Wood, *Vic. painters*, 3rd edn • Graves, *RA exhibitors* • R. Parkinson, ed., *Catalogue of British oil paintings, 1820–1860* (1990), 115 [catalogue of V&A] • *Art Journal*, 33 (1871), 166 • *Art Journal*, 36 (1874), 80 [obit. of Howard Goodall] • *IGI* [Howard Goodall] • *CGPLA Eng. & Wales* (1871) • *CGPLA Eng. & Wales* (1875) [Howard Goodall]

Wealth at death under £800: administration, 6 June 1871, *CGPLA Eng. & Wales* • under £200—Howard Goodall: administration, 6 April 1875, *CGPLA Eng. & Wales*

Goodall, Howard (*bap.* 1850, *d.* 1874). *See under* Goodall, Frederick Trevelyan (*bap.* 1848, *d.* 1871).

Goodall, Joseph (1760–1840), headmaster, was born in Westminster on 2 March 1760, the son of Joseph Goodall. He was elected to King's College, Cambridge, from Eton College, in 1778. He gained Browne's medals in 1781 and 1782, and the Craven scholarship in 1782. He graduated BA in 1783, proceeding MA in 1786, and DD in 1798. In 1782 he became a fellow of his college and assistant master at Eton, but relinquished his fellowship in 1788 on his marriage to Harriot Arabella, the daughter of the Revd J. Prior, a master at Eton. In 1801 he was appointed headmaster of the school in succession to George Heath, under whom discipline had slipped. Under Goodall the school made a recovery in its numbers and reputation. In 1808 he became canon of Windsor on the recommendation of his friend and schoolfellow, the Marquess Wellesley. In 1809 he succeeded Jonathan Davies as provost of Eton by the express wish of George III. He was rector of Hitcham, Buckinghamshire, 1811–33, and in 1827 he accepted the rectory of West Ilsley, Berkshire, from the chapter of Windsor. His pluralism was censured in John Wade's *Extraordinary Black Book* (1832, 107–8).

Goodall had the virtues of the ideal headmaster of an English public school; he wrote Latin verses, of which specimens are in the *Musae Etonenses* (1817), the second volume of which is dedicated to him. His discipline was mild, and he was courteous, witty, hospitable, and generous. He was a staunch Conservative, and during his life was supposed to be an insuperable obstacle to any threatened innovations. William IV once said in his presence, 'When Goodall goes I'll make you [Keate] provost'; to which Goodall replied, 'I could not think of "going" before your majesty.' He kept his word, and died at Eton College on 25 March 1840. He was buried in the college chapel on 2 April following. A statue was raised to his memory in the chapel by a subscription of £2000, headed by the queen dowager. He founded a scholarship of £50 a year, to be held at Oxford or Cambridge.

Leslie Stephen, *rev.* M. C. Curthoys

Sources *GM*, 2nd ser., 13 (1840), 545, 670 • Venn, *Alum. Cant.* • H. C. Maxwell Lyte, *A history of Eton College, 1440–1910*, 4th edn (1911)

Archives St George's Chapel, Windsor, papers as canon of Windsor | Linn. Soc., letters to William Swainson

Likenesses H. E. Dawe, mezzotint, pubd 1840 (after his portrait) • H. Weekes, statue, 1845, Eton • J. Jackson, oils, Eton

Goodall, Norman (1896–1985), ecumenist, was born in Birmingham on 30 August 1896, the twelfth of the thirteen children, five of whom died before he was born, of Thomas Goodall and his wife, Amelia Ingram. The family lived in cramped conditions over their father's sweet shop in Handsworth, and poverty was never far from their door. Goodall left school at fourteen to work as an office boy, but ambition soon led him to apply for a clerical post in the Birmingham city treasurer's department. In 1915 he enlisted in the Royal Army Medical Corps and was transferred to the Artists' Rifles, from which he was seconded a year later to the Ministry of Munitions. Soon afterwards he became the first member of the staff of the department of national service. Thus, as a very junior civil servant, Goodall embarked on a brief career which was to bring him into contact with ministers of the crown and give him responsibilities far beyond anything he could have anticipated.

When the war ended, Goodall was urged to enter the permanent civil service, in which he would doubtless have had a distinguished career. But he felt an irresistible call to the Congregational ministry. Apart from evening classes he had received no formal education since leaving school, though his father and mother had instilled in him a love of literature which was the foundation of the mastery of the English language of which he was to be such an elegant exponent. Despite his lack of qualifications Goodall was granted special admission to Mansfield College, Oxford, in 1919, where he took a third-class honours degree in theology (1922). In 1950 he was awarded the degree of DPhil by the same university.

In 1920 Goodall married a medical doctor, Doris Elsie Florence (*d.* 1984), daughter of William Thomas Stanton, barrister. They had two sons and one daughter. He was ordained to the ministry in 1922 at Trinity Congregational

Church, Walthamstow, and six years afterwards moved to the church in New Barnet.

In 1922 Goodall and his wife had offered themselves for service abroad with the London Missionary Society, but the regulations in force prevented them being accepted. However, this was to be only a postponement; for in 1936 Goodall was invited to become a staff member of the society with secretarial responsibility for India and the south Pacific. This led to extensive travel throughout these regions and a widening circle of personal contacts with missionaries and government officials. In 1944 he was appointed to succeed William Paton as London secretary of the International Missionary Council and this was to place him at the centre of the developing ecumenical movement. He had always believed that church and mission were indivisible, and for seventeen years worked with great skill and patience to bring the fledgeling World Council of Churches into integral relationship with the older organization. He was instrumental in persuading the two bodies to work in association with one another, and in 1954 became secretary of a joint committee to explore their full integration. He saw this consummated at the third assembly of the world council at New Delhi in 1961, and could rightly be called the architect of that achievement.

After retirement in 1963 Goodall devoted himself to inter-church relations. He was moderator of the International Congregational Council in 1962–6, moderator of the Free Church Federal Council in the following year, and he played an influential part in the establishment of the United Reformed church. He was the author of standard works on the history of the ecumenical movement and the London Missionary Society, and he edited the report of the fourth assembly of the world council at Uppsala in 1968. He lectured extensively as visiting professor at the Selly Oak Colleges, Birmingham (1963–6), at the Irish School of Ecumenics in Dublin (1971–3), at Heythrop College, London (1970–71), and at the Pontifical Gregorian University in Rome (1975). His semester in Rome broke fresh ground in ecumenical understanding and fittingly crowned his contribution to the world church.

Goodall was a gracious man with an extraordinary capacity for making friends all over the world. He was excessively modest, as evidenced in the title of his autobiography, *Second Fiddle* (1979). Although he was content to play a supporting role to the leaders of the ecumenical movement, he was the architect of some of its most important developments.

Goodall's wife died in 1984, and at the end of his life he was cared for by an old friend, Dr Elizabeth Welford, whom he engaged to marry. On 1 January 1985, two days before the wedding, he died from a heart attack at her house in Oxford. P. R. CLIFFORD, *rev.*

Sources *The Times* (3 Jan 1985) · N. Goodall, *Second fiddle: recollections and reflections* (1979) · private information (1990) · personal knowledge (1990) · A. Hastings, *A history of English Christianity, 1920–1990*, 3rd edn (1991) · E. A. Payne, *The growth of the world church, the modern missionary movement* (1955) · *CGPLA Eng. & Wales* (1985)

Wealth at death under £40,000: probate, 18 March 1985, *CGPLA Eng. & Wales*

Goodall, Sir Reginald (1901–1990), conductor, was born in Lincoln on 13 July 1901, the elder son of Albert Edward Goodall, solicitor's clerk, and his wife, Adelaide Jones. There was also a half-sister from Albert Goodall's previous marriage. Reginald went to Lincoln Cathedral choir school from 1910 to 1914, after which his education continued at Springfield, Massachusetts, USA, and in Burlington, Ontario, Canada, following the breakdown of his parents' marriage and their decision to emigrate, his mother to the United States and his father to Canada. He left school at fifteen and undertook a variety of work, as a messenger for the railways, a clerk in an engineering works, and in a bank in Burlington. His earnings enabled him to study at the Hamilton Conservatory of Music, which led to his appointment as organist of St Alban the Martyr Cathedral, Toronto, and as a music master at Upper Canada College. As the result of meeting Sir Hugh Allen in Canada, he became a student at the Royal College of Music, London, in 1925. In 1932 he married Eleanor Katherine Edith (*d.* 1979), schoolteacher, daughter of Montagu Gipps, of independent means; they had no children.

It was not until 1935 that Goodall conducted his first opera, *Carmen*, with a semi-professional company in London. In the meantime he had established himself as organist and choirmaster of St Alban the Martyr, Holborn, and he gave the first performances in England of Bruckner's F minor mass and other works. Each year he travelled on the continent as piano accompanist for the teacher and lieder singer Reinhold von Warlich. He was thus able to hear some of the world's great conductors, such as Wilhelm Furtwängler and Hans Knappertsbusch. In 1936 Goodall was engaged by Covent Garden to train the chorus for *Boris Godunov*, conducted by Albert Coates. He did this so well that he was asked to remain for the winter season. An invitation for the 1937 summer season followed, but he declined this in favour of other artistically less rewarding but financially more secure work. The 1930s were difficult for Goodall and the prospect of war filled him with gloom, as he envisaged the collapse of the German culture which he had come to know and love. Politically naïve, but at heart a serious pacifist, he supported Sir Oswald Mosley and his demand for negotiations with Hitler.

Apart from a brief spell of military service, in the Royal Army Ordnance Corps from April to September 1943, Goodall spent the war conducting, first the Wessex Philharmonic Orchestra and then the Sadler's Wells Opera. The latter introduced him to a repertory with which he was not familiar and much of which he did not admire. However, he conducted the première of *Peter Grimes* by Benjamin Britten, at the reopening of the Sadler's Wells theatre on 7 June 1945. So impressed was the composer that he invited Goodall to conduct the première of *The Rape of Lucretia* at Glyndebourne's first post-war season the following year, although he shared the conducting with

Sir Reginald Goodall (1901–1990), by unknown photographer, 1945 [rehearsing *Peter Grimes* by Benjamin Britten]

Ernest Ansermet. In 1947 Goodall became second conductor with the newly formed opera company at Covent Garden. This was a low period for him, with much of his time devoted to conducting Verdi, a composer he despised. In 1951 his contract as conductor was terminated and he continued as a coach. He was an invaluable teacher to the many singers who passed through his hands. There were occasional excursions into conducting for Covent Garden. In 1968 Goodall conducted *Die Meistersinger* at Sadler's Wells and again revealed his understanding of Richard Wagner. Following this success, Sadler's Wells invited him to conduct the four *Ring* operas at the Coliseum. These were nothing short of triumphant. He then went on to conduct *Tristan und Isolde* with the Welsh National Opera in 1979, and *Parsifal* with the English National Opera. Critical and public response was ecstatic, and both these performances were recorded.

A small, dishevelled, and sometimes cantankerous man, Goodall gave at first sight little indication of the strong inspirational force that he undoubtedly had as a conductor and coach. His conducting technique in a conventional sense was sketchy, but given time for preparation and rehearsal with singers and orchestra, which not every opera company could provide, the resulting performances were astonishing and profoundly moving in their revelations. He had a rare understanding of the architecture of Wagner's music. The long, slowly unfolding spans were wonderfully shaped and realized with unforced sonority. Goodall allowed the music to flow naturally and at the same time to give singers the greatest support without drowning them. He was appointed CBE in 1975 and knighted in 1985. He had honorary degrees from Leeds (1974), Newcastle (1974), and Oxford (1986). Goodall died on 5 May 1990 in a nursing home at Bridge, near Canterbury. JOHN TOOLEY, *rev.*

Sources J. Lucas, *Reggie: the life of Reginald Goodall* (1993) • personal knowledge (1996) • *CGPLA Eng. & Wales* (1990)

Likenesses photograph, 1945, Hult. Arch. [*see illus.*] • photograph, 1971, Hult. Arch.

Wealth at death £205,023: probate, 19 Sept 1990, *CGPLA Eng. & Wales*

Goodall, Samuel Granston (*d.* 1801), naval officer, details of whose birth and parentage are unknown, entered the navy, probably about 1750, and was made lieutenant on 1 September 1756. He was given command of the sloop *Hazard* and in her he was involved in a lengthy correspondence over the capture of a French privateer, the *Duc d'Ayen*, at anchor on the coast of Norway, near Egersund, which was alleged to be a breach of Denmark's neutrality. On 13 January 1762 Goodall was made commander of the *Mercury* (24 guns) before joining Sir George Pocock in the West Indies for the siege of Havana. As part of this, in June, he was ordered to silence a battery east of Coximar 'that it may in no way annoy His Majesty's troops while they are landing' (Syrett, 163). Goodall was afterwards employed in the protection of trade on the coast of Georgia and returned to England in the spring of 1764. In 1769 he commissioned the *Winchelsea* for service in the Mediterranean and then, in the summer of 1770, he was sent to protect British interests in Smyrna.

On 27 July 1778 Goodall commanded the *Defiance* (64 guns) in the action off Ushant. Following the battle he was moved to the *Valiant* and served in the Channel Fleet for three years, taking part in the relief of Gibraltar by Admiral George Darby in 1781. He went to the West Indies with Admiral George Rodney, and played an honourable part in the actions off Dominica and the Saints on 9 and 12 April 1782. On 18 April, following a period of calm weather, ships from Admiral Sir Samuel Hood's division, including the *Valiant*, were detached by Rodney in pursuit of the enemy's crippled ships. Making all haste, this detachment intercepted five ships heading into the Mona passage. Four of the five were captured, the *Caton* and the *Jason* striking to the *Valiant*.

At the peace of Versailles, Goodall returned to England and paid off the *Valiant*. In the summer of 1790 he commanded the *Gibraltar* and on 21 September 1790 he was made rear-admiral of the blue. In 1792 he commanded in Newfoundland with his flag in the *Romney*, returning home in the winter. In April 1793, in the *Princess Royal*, he took one of the divisions of the fleet to the Mediterranean where, during the occupation of Toulon, he acted as governor of the city. On 12 April 1794 he was promoted vice-admiral of the blue and, after the recall of Lord Hood, he was second-in-command to Admiral Hotham in the actions of 13 March and 13 July 1795 though without opportunity for special distinction. It was said that he was disappointed at not succeeding to the command of the fleet, and towards the end of 1795 he asked leave to strike his flag. He had no further service but was advanced to the rank of admiral of the blue on 14 February 1799 and to admiral of the white on 1 January 1801. He died unmarried at Teignmouth later that year, and was buried there.

Goodall's will makes no mention of any landed property but contains many individual bequests amounting to nearly £20,000. The bequests point to a wide circle of friends, particularly in naval circles, and to a man who valued friendship and loyalty. For example, £1500 was put in trust for the use of 'my faithful servant and friend Richard Corbett … who passed through many perils and dangers with me both by sea and land'. Another of his many bequests was to Jean Louis Barillier 'my old friend and secretary while I was governor of Toulon'. The major part of Goodall's estate passed to his nephew William Gustavus Brooks. KENNETH BREEN

Sources PRO, ADM 107/6; ADM 50/64 • list books, PRO, ADM /8 • D. Syrett, ed., *The siege and capture of Havana, 1762*, Navy RS, 114 (1970) • *The private papers of John, earl of Sandwich*, ed. G. R. Barnes and J. H. Owen, 4 vols., Navy RS, 69, 71, 75, 78 (1932–8) • D. Syrett and R. L. DiNardo, *The commissioned sea officers of the Royal Navy, 1660–1815*, rev. edn, Occasional Publications of the Navy RS, 1 (1994) • R. Beatson, *Naval and military memoirs of Great Britain*, 3 vols. (1790) • J. Charnock, ed., *Biographia navalis*, 6 vols. (1794–8) • *IGI* • will, PRO, PROB 11/1357

Archives BL, letters to Lord Nelson and others

Wealth at death approx. £20,000 in bequests, in various stocks: will, PRO, PROB 11/1357

Goodall, Sir Stanley Vernon (1883–1965), naval architect, was born on 18 April 1883 at the fire station, West India Road, Poplar, London, the son of Samuel Goodall, fireman, and his wife, Eliza Summers. He was educated at Owens School, Islington, and intended to become a naval engineer officer but soon, in July 1901, transferred to the Royal Corps of Naval Constructors. He graduated from the Royal Naval College in 1907 with one of the highest marks of all time and excellent records in tennis and rugby.

After a short appointment to Devonport Dockyard, Goodall went to work under Edmund Froude at the Haslar ship model tank. In 1908 he married Helen (*d.* 1945), daughter of C. W. Phillips of Plymouth. By 1911 he was at the Admiralty in charge of the design of the novel light cruiser *Arethusa*. His later description of this design in a lecture to American naval constructor students forms the best account of the way in which designs were carried out in that era.

At the outbreak of war Goodall was lecturer at the Royal Naval College, a prestigious post, but was recalled for other wartime duties. He was part of a team which studied damage to Royal Navy ships after the battle of Jutland though his report was later suppressed. When the USA entered the war he was sent to Washington as assistant naval attaché, working within their design office and serving as the focus for exchange of information between British and American designers. It was a valuable experience meeting senior American officers and corresponding directly with the British director of naval construction, Sir Eustace Tennyson-D'Eyncourt. Goodall's views on American ships were reported at length and summarized in *Engineering* in 1922. His work was acknowledged with appointment as MBE and the award of the American Navy Cross.

On his return to the UK, Goodall worked on the design of post-war battleships and battle cruisers, culminating in the mighty G3, which was ordered in 1921 but cancelled under the Washington treaty. After a short time in Malta Dockyard he returned to head the destroyer design section—and the departmental concert party. It was in this appointment that, in response to a rather dull draft from his assistant, he wrote that he just wanted the facts and 'I will impart the enthusiasm', a phrase which might be seen as his motto. A number of his proposals for novel designs failed to materialize in the quest for economy.

Goodall became chief constructor in 1930 and assistant director in 1932, mainly concerned with the modernization of older ships and trials of protection though including the early studies for the *King George V* class battleships. In 1934 he was made OBE, which he attempted to refuse seeing it as an insult to an officer of his rank. In 1936 Goodall became director of naval construction, the principal technical adviser to the Board of Admiralty. The appointment as CB in 1937 and KCB in 1938 went far to offset the earlier, insulting, OBE. He took a very direct view of his responsibility for the design of a ship; in signing the building drawings he took personal responsibility for success or failure. This responsibility and poor health seem to have caused the loss of his sense of humour and several of his staff used the word 'austere' to describe his wartime manner, though he was always fair.

The department of the director of naval construction was moved to Bath in September 1939. Goodall opposed this more as he lost the personal contact with ministers and other board members which he saw as essential; but this was partially remedied in October 1942 when he and a small staff returned to Whitehall. In the early part of the war Churchill was first lord of the Admiralty and Goodall saw him frequently and admired him greatly—though some of the minister's bright ideas were off-centre. As well as the overall direction of the department, Goodall continued to carry out a number of personal duties such as the *viva voce* exam of constructor students. During the war 971 major warships from battleships to fleet minesweepers were built, together with innumerable landing craft and coastal forces. In addition, some 1700 requisitioned merchant ships and trawlers were converted for war purposes.

After retirement Goodall continued an active professional life as prime warden of the Worshipful Company of Shipwrights, vice-president of the Institution of Naval Architects, and with the British Welding and Ship Research associations. He died on 24 February 1965 at the Bolingbroke Hospital, Battersea, London.

DAVID K. BROWN

Sources private information (2004) [H. R. Jarman] • *CGPLA Eng. & Wales* (1965) • b. cert. • d. cert. • D. Mclean and A. Preston, eds., *Warship 1997* (1997)

Archives BL, diaries, corresp., and papers, Add. MSS 52785–52797 • NMM, ships corresp.

Likenesses portrait, Royal Institution of Naval Architects headquarters
Wealth at death £23,312: probate, 3 May 1965, *CGPLA Eng. & Wales*

Goodall, Thomas (1767–1832?), naval officer and privateer, was born at Bristol, educated by a Revd Mr Thomas, and was intended by his father to be a lawyer; but at thirteen he ran away from school, and shipped on board a privateer bound for the West Indies, which was cast away on St Kitts in the hurricane of October 1780. He luckily fell into the hands of a merchant there who was acquainted with his father, and passed him on to an uncle in Montserrat. He was entered on the frigate *Triton* as midshipman, and was present at the action off Dominica on 12 April 1782. In October 1782 he was transferred to the *Thetis* for a passage home; after which he returned to the merchant service for a voyage to the Levant, and afterwards to China. In 1787 he married a young actress Charlotte Stanton (1765–1830) [*see* Goodall, Charlotte], a very beautiful woman, whom he saw playing at the Bath Theatre.

During the Spanish armament in 1790 Goodall served as master's mate on the *Nemesis*, under Captain A. J. Ball; but with the crisis settled, having no prospects in the navy, he obtained command of a merchant ship bound for the West Indies.

During Goodall's absence war with France began, and on his homeward voyage he was captured by a French privateer and carried into Lorient. However, he gained the goodwill of his captor, who let him escape on a Dutch timber ship. On his return to England, he is said to have been appointed to the frigate *Diadem*, but he does not seem to have joined her; he was certainly not entered on the ship's books. He accepted the command of a small privateer, and continued in her until the peace of 1801, during which period he was said to have made more voyages, fought more actions, and captured more prizes than had ever been seized before in the same time by any private ship.

When war broke out again, Goodall fitted out a small privateer of ten guns and forty men, in which, on 25 July 1803, he fell in with, and after a stubborn defence was captured by, *La Caroline*, a large privateer, and again taken to Lorient. He and his men were sent on to Rennes, and thence to Espinal, from where he escaped with one of his officers. After many hardships and adventures they reached the Rhine, succeeded in crossing it, and so made their way to Berlin, whence they travelled on to England.

On the outbreak of war with Spain, Goodall again obtained command of a privateer, and in her captured a treasure ship from Vera Cruz. He afterwards touched at San Domingo, and having made some acquaintance with Christophe, one of two rival black leaders engaged in a civil war, he was induced to put his ship and his own services at Christophe's disposal. His assistance may have turned the scales in Christophe's favour. Goodall was considered by the governor of Jamaica to have acted improperly, and so was sent home in 1808. On his arrival he was released, and shortly after moved to Haiti—he claimed he

Thomas Goodall (1767–1832?), by Ridley & Blood, pubd 1808 (after Samuel Drummond)

was 'Admiral of Hayti'—coming home in 1810 and again in 1812.

Goodall was said to have remitted to his agent in England—William Fletcher, an attorney—very large sums of money, totalling £120,000. The amount was probably exaggerated, but it seems clear that it was considerable. However, he now found himself a bankrupt by the chicanery of Fletcher, who had not only robbed him of his fortune but also of his wife; although the mother of eight children by Goodall, six of whom were living, Charlotte had become Fletcher's mistress. In July 1813, Goodall brought an action for 'criminal conversation' and it was deposed at the trial that during her husband's imprisonment and absence Mrs Goodall had supported her family by acting; but there was no suspicion of misconduct by her until she was seduced by Fletcher. The jury, taking this view, awarded the injured husband £5000 damages. Nothing further is known of Goodall, but it would seem probable that he lived privately until his death, which is said to have taken place in 1832.

J. K. Laughton, *rev.* Roger Morriss

Sources 'A biographical sketch of Thomas Goodall, esq. commandant of the Haytian flotilla', *European Magazine and London Review*, 53 (1808), 323–8 • paybooks of *Diadem*, *Triton*, and *Nemesis*, PRO • *Report of the trial between Thomas Goodall (plaintiff) and William Fletcher (defendant), 1813* (1813) • C. L. R. James, *The Black Jacobins* (1938) • A. B. Rodger, *The war of the second coalition: 1798–1801, a strategic commentary* (1964)
Likenesses Ridley & Blood, stipple, pubd 1808 (after S. Drummond), BM, NPG [*see illus.*]

Goodall, Walter (*bap.* 1706, *d.* 1766), historian, was baptized on 20 December 1706 at Ordiquhill, Banffshire, the eldest of the six sons of John Goodall, a farmer in that parish, and his wife, Margaret Taylor, sister of James Taylor, sometime schoolmaster of Ordiquhill. He matriculated at King's College, Aberdeen, in 1723, but left without taking a degree. By 1730 he had found employment at the Advocates' Library in Edinburgh, where the keeper, Thomas Ruddiman, was a fellow north-easterner of Jacobite–Episcopalian sympathies. In 1735 Goodall obtained a formal appointment as depute-keeper. It is reported that Ruddiman did not like Goodall 'on account of his drunkenness and grossness' (Chalmers, fol. 130); nevertheless in 1751 the failing Ruddiman agreed to pay one half of his salary to Goodall, some of whose works were published by the Ruddiman press. Goodall's main duty at the library was the compilation of a catalogue; this was eventually published by the Ruddimans in 1742 after complaints from the faculty about Goodall's progress (which was hampered by lax borrowing procedures). Goodall was an industrious scholar, producing editions of David Crawford's *Memoirs of the Affairs of Scotland* (1753), Sir James Balfour's *Practicks* (1754), Sir John Scot of Scotstarvet's *Staggering State of Scots Statesmen* (1754), and John Fordun's *Scotichronicon* (1747–52; later edn, 1759).

From 1754 Goodall acted as clerk to the Select Society, a fashionable and influential meeting-place for members of the Scottish literati and Edinburgh's social and political élite, who formed a body of central importance in the history of the Scottish Enlightenment. However, his own works served to advance an unreconstructed Jacobite interpretation of Scottish history rather than the modern 'scientific' whig interpretation favoured by the literati. In *An examination of the letters said to have been written by Mary queen of Scots to James, earl of Bothwell* (2 vols., 1754) he argued that the French version of the casket letters was a translation of Buchanan's Latin version of 'the Scottish original forgery' (1.80). By exonerating the queen from the charge of complicity in the murder of Darnley, Goodall was able to cast aspersions on the legitimacy of her deposition, much valued by Scottish whigs as a precedent for their Revolution principles. Goodall's treatise ignited a new round of partisan debate on this issue, which David Hume, a keen opponent of Mariolatry, described as the touchstone of Scottish Jacobite prejudice. Ironically, Hume was Goodall's superior as keeper of the Advocates' Library between 1752 and 1757, and on one memorable occasion bellowed into the ear of his snoozing assistant the unchivalrous opinion that Queen Mary had been a whore.

Goodall contributed to other theatres of antiquarian debate. In the preliminary dissertation which he provided for Bishop Keith's *New Catalogue of Scottish Bishops* (1755), Goodall set out a partisan account of the origins and early history of Christianity in Scotland. He demythologized the Culdees, whom early eighteenth-century kirkmen had depicted as proto-Presbyterians, and instead contended that the primitive government of the Church of Scotland had been episcopalian. Goodall also contributed to a significant geographical debate. Scotland's claim to an ancient monarchy founded in 330 BC had long been challenged by antiquaries from other parts of the British Isles, but in his *Introduction to the History and Antiquities of Scotland* (originally composed in Latin and included in his edition of Fordun; published separately in translation, 1769) Goodall contended that, before the era of Vespasian, Ireland had been unknown to the Romans, who had also mistaken the land they spied across the firths of Forth and Clyde for an island (denoted in classical geography as Hibernia or Ierne). Goodall argued that, far from being dark-age immigrants from Ireland, the Scots had originated in Gaul and had colonized Ireland from Scotland.

'A small squat man with a broad, shrewd face' (Chalmers, fol. 131), Goodall was married and had several children; though his wife's name is unknown, it is recorded that the couple 'used always to be quarrelling' (ibid., fol. 130). Goodall died impoverished on 28 July 1766.

Colin Kidd

Sources G. Chalmers, 'Notes on Scottish writers', U. Edin. L., Goodall bundle, MS La II 451 (2), fols. 129–35 · G. Chalmers, *The life of Thomas Ruddiman* (1794), 127–32 · minutes of the Faculty of Advocates, Advocates' Library, Edinburgh · W. Bower, *Scotichronicon*, ed. D. E. R. Watt and others, new edn, 9 vols. (1987–98), vol. 9, chap. 16, esp. pp. 219–25 · P. Wellburn, 'The living library', *For the encouragement of learning: Scotland's national library, 1689–1989*, ed. P. Cadell and A. Matheson (1989), 186–214 · P. Wellburn, 'Biographical notes', *For the encouragement of learning: Scotland's national library, 1689–1989*, ed. P. Cadell and A. Matheson (1989) · D. Duncan, *Thomas Ruddiman: a study in Scottish scholarship of the early eighteenth century* (1965) · E. C. Mossner, *The life of David Hume*, 2nd edn (1980), 251, 281, 412–13 · R. L. Emerson, 'The social composition of Enlightened Edinburgh: the Select Society of Edinburgh, 1754–1764', *Studies on Voltaire and the Eighteenth Century*, 114 (1973), 291–329 · *Scots Magazine*, 28 (1766), 390 · Chambers, *Scots.* (1835), 2.453–4 · Anderson, *Scot. nat.*, 316 · *DNB* · *IGI*

Archives NL Scot., collection of the principal officers of state and genealogy of the nobility

Wealth at death impoverished: Chalmers, *Life of Thomas Ruddiman*, 132

Goodall, Walter (1830–1889), watercolour painter, was born on 6 November 1830, probably in London, the youngest son and eighth child in the family of six sons and four daughters of Edward *Goodall (1795–1870), the engraver of J. M. W. Turner's paintings, and his wife, Eliza Ann Le Petit, granddaughter of a Huguenot refugee; he was baptized on 2 January 1831 at St Pancras Old Church, Pancras Road, London. Frederick *Goodall (1822–1904), the orientalist painter, was his brother. He studied at the Government School of Design in Somerset House, London, and was admitted to the Royal Academy Schools in 1847 on the recommendation of Clarkson Stanfield. For a time he worked at the Artists' Society in Clipstone Street (later the Langham Sketching Society) and in 1852 he exhibited three drawings at the Royal Academy. In 1853 he became an associate and in 1862 a member of the Old Watercolour Society, exhibiting 156 works there. He also exhibited at the Royal Manchester Institution, and his *Lottery Ticket* appeared at the Philadelphia Centennial International Exhibition in 1876.

Goodall painted only in watercolour, producing mainly idealized scenes of rural life such as *The Daydream*, *The Cradle Song*, *Waiting for the Ferry-Boat*, and *The Tired Lace-Maker*; a number of these were lithographed in a series called 'Walter Goodall's Rustic Sketches' (1855–7). He also made many drawings from pictures in the Vernon Gallery, London, for engravings published in the *Art Journal*. During a trip to Italy in 1868–9 he did a number of paintings of Venice. For a jubilee gift to Queen Victoria in 1887 he painted *Children with a Pet Rabbit*. In 1875 Goodall suffered a stroke, and became an invalid. He last exhibited in 1884, and during the last few years of his life was unable to paint. He died on 14 May 1889 in Clapham, near Bedford, leaving a wife and three children; he was buried in Highgate cemetery, Middlesex. L. H. Cust, *rev.* Anne Pimlott Baker

Sources N. G. Slarke, *Frederick Goodall, R.A.* (1981) • Mallalieu, *Watercolour artists* • D. Millar, *The Victorian watercolours and drawings in the collection of her majesty the queen*, 2 vols. (1995) • Graves, *RA exhibitors* • Boase, *Mod. Eng. biog.* • *IGI* • *Manchester Guardian* (28 May 1889)

Goodbody, Mary Ann [Buzz] (**1946–1975**), theatre director, was born at 12 Clifton Hill, London, on 25 June 1946, the daughter of Douglas Maurice Goodbody, a barrister, and his wife, Marcelle Yvonne Rubin, *née* Raphael. She attended the Francis Holland School in London and Roedean School before studying for a degree at the University of Sussex (1964–7). A university production that she devised and directed of Dostoyevsky's *Notes from the Underground* won her a prize at the national student drama festival and brought her to the attention of the Royal Shakespeare Company (RSC) director John Barton. In 1967 she joined the RSC as Barton's personal assistant. By 1969 she had worked her way up to assistant director. On 9 September 1967 she married Edward Geoffrey Buscombe (*b.* 1941/2), from whom she was later separated.

Buzz Goodbody's growing commitment to feminism meant that in 1970 she became involved in founding one of the first feminist theatre companies to emerge in the wake of the second women's liberation movement: the Women's Street Theatre Group. Her feminist leanings and left-wing politics—she was an outspoken, self-declared socialist-Marxist—fed into her work at the RSC. In 1970 she took on responsibility for Theatreground, the educational, touring section of the Shakespeare company. Her abridged touring version of *King John* adopted a political, cartoon style that antagonized traditional critics such as John Russell Brown, while others, such as Colin Chambers, argued that here 'was the flavour of Littlewood, the living newspaper, a fast-moving, fluent, cartoon-strip production' (Chambers, 28). Moreover, Chambers observed and speculated: '[Peter] Brook, who was an inspiration for Buzz Goodbody, was "taken by the vigour" of *John*, which he found "full of life, energetic, disrespectful". What would the critics have said if his name had been on the programme instead of an unknown woman's?' (ibid., 29). After *King John*, Goodbody worked with another RSC director, Terry Hands, on a piece about the general strike of 1926, which was eventually shelved for a less than successful production of a drama from the 1590s, *Arden of Faversham*. For the 1971 season at The Place, London, she directed a well-received production of Trevor Griffiths's *Occupations*, a contemporary political play about revolution.

As the first woman director on the staff of the RSC, Goodbody had to contend with the male domination and bias of the company, which, by all accounts, proved a difficult professional and personal struggle, but one that she incorporated into her production work. *As You Like It*, her first mainstage production for the RSC (1973), with Eileen Atkins as Rosalind, was nicknamed the 'women's lib' production of the play. Analytical accounts of the success or otherwise of the production's feminism are mixed; critics are generally agreed on the contemporary rather than traditional feel that Goodbody brought to her treatment of Shakespeare's comedy.

From 1973 to 1974 Goodbody was assistant to Trevor Nunn in his season of Roman plays. In 1974 she was appointed artistic director of the RSC's alternative experimental venue, the Other Place, which opened in Stratford upon Avon. For the Other Place, Goodbody directed a production of *King Lear*, which subsequently went to The Place, in London, and to New York, where it was presented at the Brooklyn Academy in 1975. In contrast to the more lavish RSC productions, Goodbody's *King Lear* worked with a small budget of £150 (as compared, for example, with the £25,000 for the set of Nunn's Roman plays). Yet again Goodbody's feminism and politics gave direction to her work: a prologue politicized issues around poverty and old age; Lear's daughters were represented as strong women doing battle with a difficult father (the roles of the husbands were all cut).

Goodbody's last production was *Hamlet*, which officially opened at the Other Place on 15 May 1975, with Ben Kingsley in the title role. Elsom describes how the production 'used the temporary shed of The Other Place to create the atmosphere of a totalitarian, military state' (Elsom, 175). On 12 April 1975, a month before the play's official opening, Buzz Goodbody committed suicide at her home, 125 Highbury Hill, Islington, London. Several critics echoed Elsom's view that her death had 'robbed the theatre of one of its most promising directors' (ibid.). While Colin Chambers positively argued for Goodbody as the 'catalyst for change in the RSC', explaining that 'she provided the all-important bridge between the RSC and the fringe' (Chambers, 7), Margaret Sheehy cautioned that, for several years after her suicide, the 'pervasive, guilt-ridden, tribal memory' of the event meant that the RSC hardly dared to risk more women directors for fear that they might 'crack under pressure' (Sheehy, 12). In her feminist classic *Dusa, Fish, Stas and Vi* (1976), Pam Gems remembered Goodbody through the role of Fish, the activist who commits suicide. An annual Buzz Goodbody award for directing is made at the national student drama festival, the forum that had so effectively launched Goodbody's RSC career in 1967. Elaine Aston

Sources C. Chambers, *Other spaces, new theatre and the RSC* (1980) • E. Schafer, *Ms-directing Shakespeare: women direct Shakespeare* (1998) • P. Gay, *As she likes it: Shakespeare's unruly women* (1994) • M. Sheehy, 'Why aren't there more women directors?', *Drama* (summer 1984), 12 • J. Elsom, *Post-war British theatre*, rev. edn (1979) • C. Itzin, *Stages in the revolution: political theatre in Britain since 1968* (1980) • S. Beauman, *The Royal Shakespeare Company: a history of ten decades* (1982) • b. cert. • m. cert. • d. cert.

Archives sound BL NSA, performance recordings

Wealth at death £8311: administration, 1975, *CGPLA Eng. & Wales*

Goodcole, Henry (*bap.* **1586**, *d.* **1641**), prison visitor and author, was baptized at St James's, Clerkenwell, on 23 May 1586, the eighth or ninth child (he was a twin) of eleven children of James Goodcole (*d.* 1597) and his second wife, Joan Duncombe. There is no record of his attendance at university, and the only certain fact known about his early life is that he married in 1606, in his parish of birth, Anne Tryme; they had a daughter, Joan, baptized on 25 February 1607, and two sons, Andrew and Humphry. In 1613 Goodcole was appointed by the London court of aldermen to the post of lecturer of Ludgate gaol. In February 1616 he successfully petitioned for an increase in his annual stipend from £6 8*s.* to £6 13*s.* 4*d.* Goodcole was apparently promoted to a higher office during the first half of 1620, when he was appointed to the post of ordinary and visitor of Newgate. He seems to have taken his new position seriously as in December 1621 he petitioned the court of aldermen requesting that they consider building a chapel in Newgate 'for the assembly of the poore prisoners' (City of London RO, court of aldermen report books, 36, fol. 247).

Goodcole is best-known for a series of criminal biographies, arising from his experiences as ordinary and recounting his attempts to extort confessions from the condemned in the prison. In all his pamphlets he is concerned to present the truth of cases as against what he sees as the false, popular versions of events recorded in contemporary ballads or plays. Of his seven pamphlets, the most important is *The Wonderfull Discoverie of E[lizabeth]. Sawyer, a Witch, Late of Edmonton* (1621). Perhaps because Elizabeth Sawyer was one of the few London witches, the case excited a good deal of attention, and in the introduction Goodcole complained of false ballads carrying 'ridiculous fictions of her bewitching corne on the ground, of a ferret and an owle dayly sporting before her … [and] of the spirits attending her in the prison' (*The Wonderfull Discoverie*, 1621, sig. A3v). Although no ballads survive, a rather different view of the case is presented in the play *The Witch of Edmonton* by William Rowley, Thomas Dekker, and John Ford.

Goodcole's work in Newgate did not go unrecognized. In June 1623 he presented the court of aldermen with a certificate from 'divers JPs of Middlesex', who had agreed to pay him £10 per annum 'for his better encouragement'. The aldermen themselves then agreed to pay him an extra £10 over and above his former stipend (City of London RO, court of aldermen report books, 37, fol. 175b). By 1627, however, Goodcole's finances appear to have taken a downward turn. In March he petitioned the aldermen for a loan of £50, which was granted.

Goodcole's other best-known criminal biography appeared in 1635, after a twelve-year break in his pamphleteering activities. *Heavens Speedie Cry Sent after Lust and Murther* survives in three versions, suggesting that it sold well, as the printer had to reset his block for each impression. Again Goodcole fashions himself as the protector of truth, stating in his preface that, 'I have resumed my pen which I resolved in this nature for ever to be silent: But the common good and the preservation of my countries welfare, incites me unto this officious service' (*Heavens Speedie Cry*, 1635, 1); indeed, the pamphlet appears to have been published in response to the ballad *Murther upon Murther* which was printed the same year. *Heavens Speedie Cry* records the activities of two notorious criminals, Country Tom (Shearwood) and Canberry Bess (Elizabeth Evans), who operated an unusual criminal scam: Canberry Bess would act as the bait, meeting men in playhouses, taverns, alehouses, and fields, and bringing them back to her chamber with promises of sensual delights; Shearwood would then spring out of a closet where he lay hidden to murder and rob the unsuspecting men. According to Goodcole, they killed four such victims. His knowledge of where lewd harlots were to be found in London is suspiciously detailed.

In March 1636 Goodcole seems to have left Newgate as he was appointed as vicar of St James's, Clerkenwell, where he remained for the rest of his life. It is evident from this that he must, at some point, have been ordained. He died at Clerkenwell on 24 August 1641.

CHRISTOPHER CHAPMAN

Sources C. Dobb, *Henry Goodcole, visitor of Newgate, 1620–1641* (1955) · repertories of the court of aldermen, CLRO, vols. 36–7 · *DNB* · R. Hovenden, ed., *A true register of all the christenings, mariages, and burialles in the parishe of St James, Clarkenwell, from … 1551 (to 1754)*, 1, Harleian Society, register section, 9 (1884), iii · C. Holmes, 'Popular culture? Witches, magistrates and divines in early modern England', *Understanding popular culture*, ed. S. L. Kaplan (1984), 85–111 · consistory court of London, vicar-general's court papers, Principal Registry of the Family Division, London

Wealth at death £40: principal probate registry, consistory court of London, vicar-general's court, 24 Jan 1642

Goodden, Frank Widenham (1889–1917), aviator, was born on 3 October 1889 at Green Mead House, Pembroke, the second son of Harry Francis Goodden, a photographer, of Eastbourne, and his wife, Emma Margaret Gould. His first appearance in aviation was as an exhibition balloonist and parachute jumper, and later he was the mechanic on a small airship during a flight from London to Paris. Some time afterwards he arrived as a pupil at the Hendon aerodrome and he later became an instructor at the Caudron School there. He developed into 'a very clever aerial acrobat' at Hendon and took part in the great flying displays staged by Claude Grahame-White (*Aeroplane*, 31 Jan 1917, 347).

During Easter 1914, flying a Caudron biplane, he was one of a number of airmen who performed the crowd-pleasing 'loop the loop' manoeuvre, and on 5 May he signed a six-month contract with Grahame-White Aviation. His payment for exhibition flying was £5 per week, plus prize money. The arrangement was short-lived, though, as on 2 June Goodden left to begin performing on his own account. He later claimed that he walked out on Grahame-White Aviation because the planes he was given to fly were unsafe. At the end of July the company won an interim injunction to prevent Goodden from performing in breach of his contract.

On the advent of war Goodden joined the royal aircraft factory as a test pilot, where his exceptional flying skills were applied to getting the optimum performance from the factory's output. He was given a commission in the Royal Flying Corps (RFC) special reserve; a short time later he was promoted captain. From August 1914 until his death he made an impressive number of first flights of royal aircraft factory designs. He test-flew the RE-5 in weight-carrying and dropping experiments in October

1914, and on two occasions had to contend with fuselage fires while in flight. He was also employed in testing innovations such as the anti-Zeppelin explosive grapnel, which was designed to be towed across the path of a coming airship. When the winch failed to wind the wire back up during the test flight Goodden was obliged to snag the grapnel on an unhappy farmer's barn.

On 15 October 1915 Goodden made the first flight in the FE-8 fighter and on 19 December he flew a model to France for evaluation. It was welcomed by pilots of the RFC as a potential counter to the Fokker monoplanes, which had become 'a serious menace on the western front' (Bruce, 432). The early FE-8s, though, had a tendency to spin uncontrollably and at Farnborough on 23 August 1916 Goodden 'performed the remarkable series of tests that established the standard method of spin recovery'. It took 'cold analytical courage' deliberately to spin the plane, but, having once recovered, Goodden had proved his theory, and was ready to teach it. He encapsulated his ideas in a written report (ibid., 435). He was not, however, the only pilot to discover the solution, as at the same time Sopwith's chief test pilot, H. G. Hawker, was coming to the same conclusion. But the impact of the discovery was immediate and before long pilots on the western front were using the manoeuvre as an escape tactic.

Gooden made the first flight of the FE-4 twin-engined bomber on 12 March 1916 and later flew the plane at Farnborough before George V. On 23 October he took up Brigadier-General W. Sefton Brancker as a passenger: Brancker was then director of air organization and centrally concerned with the aircraft proposed for operational use in the RFC. On 2 November 1916 Goodden became one of the youngest to hold the rank of major in the Royal Flying Corps, even though he had not flown on real active service, nor spent any very long time in France. The promotion enabled him to argue on equal military terms with squadron commanders of considerable operational experience, and he was thus better placed to promote royal aircraft factory planes. He could, though, be critical of these, and in 1916 wrote a lengthy report on the prototype of the RE-8, criticizing many of its design features. That year he also designed a single-seater fighter. His plans were turned over to H. P. Folland, resulting in the production of the SE-5, one of the most successful fighters of the war.

Goodden test-flew an SE-5 on 22 November 1916 and on 4 December he flew the second prototype. The plane subsequently underwent considerable modification and on 24 December 1916 he flew it to France for evaluation by the RFC. The aircraft returned to Farnborough on 4 January 1917, and presumably underwent further modification, as it did not fly again until late January. On the morning of 28 January 1917 Goodden flew the plane to test its general stability and loss of height in turns. At 1500 feet the port wings suddenly collapsed and the plane fell to the ground on Farnborough Common. Goodden was killed on impact and a verdict of 'death by accident' was later recorded. After an exhaustive investigation, modifications were made to the wing structure.

C. G. Grey, editor of *The Aeroplane*, who had a strong prejudice against the royal aircraft factory, published a denigratory obituary of Goodden, implying that he owed his advance to his ability to show the factory's output in 'the very best possible' light. He even speculated that Goodden, a 'trick flier', was killed by taking 'needless risks' (*Aeroplane*, 31 Jan 1917). The article was in 'such monstrously offensive bad taste', though, that it shocked the aviation world (Bruce, xv). Goodden was an intrepid airman, but he was also an outstanding test pilot, who risked, and ultimately gave, his life so that others would not jeopardize theirs. ROBIN HIGHAM

Sources J. M. Bruce, *The aeroplanes of the royal flying corps (military wing)*, 2nd edn (1992) • *The Times* (27 March 1914) • *The Times* (11 April 1914) • *The Times* (14 April 1914) • *The Times* (25 July 1914) • *The Times* (30 Jan 1917) • *The Times* (31 Jan 1917) • *The Aeroplane* (31 Jan 1917), 347 • *The Aeroplane* (7 Feb 1917), 412 • H. Penrose, *British aviation: the Great War and armistice, 1915–1919* (1969) • official casualty cards, Royal Air Force Museum, Hendon • PRO, AVIA 1/1 • b. cert. • d. cert.

Goode, Francis (1797–1842), Church of England clergyman and missionary, was one of the fourteen children of William *Goode (1762–1816), rector of St Ann Blackfriars, London, and his wife, Rebecca, daughter of Abraham Coles, silk manufacturer, of London and St Albans, Hertfordshire. William Goode was a founder member of the Church Missionary Society (CMS), and his children grew up surrounded by missionary propaganda. Francis was educated at St Paul's School, London (which he captained in 1815–16), and at Trinity College, Cambridge, where he graduated BA (seventh wrangler) in 1820 and MA in 1823. He was ordained deacon in March 1823 and priest in April 1824, and shortly afterwards he sailed for India as a missionary. His career there was short (he was never listed formally as a CMS worker) and he returned to Britain, where eventually he became lecturer at St James's Church, Clapham, Surrey; in 1834 he also became morning preacher at the London Female Orphan Asylum.

Goode was a popular preacher, at home with the evangelical congregation at Clapham, and he published many of his sermons. In 1838 he preached a barnstorming address, 'Christians the Light of the World', on behalf of the CMS at St Bride's Church, Fleet Street. In exhorting every parish in the country to fund a CMS labourer among the heathen, he appeared to more moderate Anglicans to typify the CMS's aggressive evangelicalism and he even frightened some of the evangelicals with his millenarian tone.

Goode died at Clapham on 19 November 1842. A volume of his collected sermons, *The Better Covenant*, reached a fifth edition in 1848. KATHERINE PRIOR

Sources F. Goode, 'Christians the light of the world', *The Pulpit*, 32 (1838) • C. Bradley, 'Ready for Death', *The Pulpit*, 42 (1842) • R. B. Gardiner, ed., *The admission registers of St Paul's School, from 1748 to 1876* (1884) • Venn, *Alum. Cant.* • E. Stock, *The history of the Church Missionary Society: its environment, its men and its work*, 4 vols. (1899–1916)

Likenesses C. Turner, mezzotint, pubd 1843 (after W. E. Frost), BM, NPG

Goode, William, the elder (1762–1816), Church of England clergyman, was born on 2 April 1762 at Buckingham, the son of William Goode (*d.* 1780), tradesman, and his wife, Catherine, daughter of Thomas Bourne of Buckingham. At ten years of age he was placed at a private school in Buckingham, and in January 1776 at the Revd William Bull's academy at Newport Pagnell, Buckinghamshire, where he remained until Christmas 1777. In the summer of 1778, after a short period working in his father's business, he went as a private pupil to the Revd Thomas Clarke at Chesham Bois, Buckinghamshire, to prepare for Oxford. He matriculated at Magdalen Hall, Oxford, on 2 May 1780, graduating BA on 20 February 1784 and MA on 10 July 1787. On 7 November 1786 he married Rebecca, daughter of Abraham Coles, silk manufacturer, of London and St Albans; their fourteen children included Francis *Goode (1797–1842) and William *Goode, the younger (1801–1868).

On 19 December 1784 Goode was ordained deacon by the bishop of Lincoln. He took the curacy of Abbots Langley in Hertfordshire, to which he added the following year the curacy of Kings Langley. At the end of March 1786 he became curate to the evangelical William Romaine, then rector of the united parishes of St Andrew by the Wardrobe and St Ann Blackfriars, in London, at a salary of £40 a year. On 11 June of the same year he was ordained priest, again by the bishop of Lincoln. In February 1789 he obtained the Sunday afternoon lectureship at Blackfriars, and in December 1793 the Lady Camden Tuesday evening lectureship at St Lawrence Jewry. The second edition of Brown's *Self-Interpreting Bible*, published in 1791, was superintended by him. Not long afterwards he undertook for a while a revision of Robert Bowyer's edition of Hume's *History of England*, published from 1793 to 1806, but found his eyesight unable to bear the strain. On 2 July 1795 he was chosen secretary of the Society for the Relief of Poor Pious Clergymen of the Established Church Residing in the Country. He had supported the society from its institution in 1788, and held the office until his death. He declined a salary, voted by the committee in 1803, preferring to accept an occasional present of money.

In August 1795 Goode succeeded, on the death of William Romaine, to the rectory of St Andrew by the Wardrobe and St Ann Blackfriars. In December 1796 he resigned the Sunday afternoon lectureship at Blackfriars on his appointment to a similar lectureship at St John-at-Wapping, which he retained until his death. He was elected to the triennial Sunday evening lectureship at Christ Church, Spitalfields, in 1807, and in July 1810 to the Wednesday morning lectureship at Blackfriars. He thus preached at least five sermons every week. At the height of his powers Goode was one of the most influential evangelical clergymen in London. In 1811 he published in two octavo volumes, *An Entire New Version of the Book of Psalms*, which reached a second edition in 1813 and a third in 1816. In 1813 he was elected president of Sion College, an institution founded by Thomas White in the seventeenth century for the guild of the clergy of London, with twenty almshouses attached. In the autumn of 1814 Goode visited some of the principal towns in the north-west, and in 1815 visited Norwich and Ipswich, promoting the cause of the Church Missionary Society. He died at Stockwell, London, on 15 April 1816, after a lingering illness following his return from Ipswich. Goode was buried in the rector's vault in St Anne Blackfriars, near the remains of William Romaine, as he had requested. In the June before his death Goode completed a series of 156 essays on the Bible names of Christ, on which he had been engaged more than thirteen years, in addition to delivering them as lectures on Tuesday mornings at Blackfriars. These essays were published in a collected edition by William Goode, the younger, in 1822. GORDON GOODWIN, *rev.* I. T. FOSTER

Sources W. Goode the younger, Memoir, in W. Goode, *Essays on all the scriptural names and titles of Christ*, 6 vols. (1822) • E. Stock, *The history of the Church Missionary Society: its environment, its men and its work*, 4 vols. (1899–1916) • J. S. Reynolds, *The evangelicals at Oxford, 1735–1871: a record of an unchronicled movement*, [2nd edn] (1975) • Foster, *Alum. Oxon.* • *GM*, 1st ser., 86/1 (1816) • E. F. Hatfield, *The poets of the church: a series of biographical sketches of hymn writers* (1884) • Allibone, *Dict.* • [J. Watkins and F. Shoberl], *A biographical dictionary of the living authors of Great Britain and Ireland* (1816) • private information (2004) • parish register (baptism), Buckingham parish church, 7 May 1762 • D. Bank and A. Esposito, eds., *British biographical index*, 4 vols. (1990)
Likenesses W. Bond, engraving (after S. Joseph) • portrait, repro. in Stock, *History of the Church Missionary Society*, vol. 1, facing p. 107 • stipple, NPG; repro. in *Evangelical Magazine* (1796)

Goode, William (1801–1868), dean of Ripon and theologian, was born on 10 November 1801 in London, one of the fourteen children of the Revd William *Goode (1762–1816), rector of St Andrew by the Wardrobe and St Ann Blackfriars, and his wife, Rebecca, *née* Coles. An older brother, the Revd Francis *Goode (1797–1842), served in India with the Church Missionary Society. Goode was educated at St Paul's School, London (1813–21), where he was captain of school (1820–21), and then at Trinity College, Cambridge (1821–5), where he was an exhibitioner (1822–5), and graduated BA (1825) and proceeded MA (1828). Ordained deacon and priest in 1825, for the next ten years he was curate of Christ Church Greyfriars, London. Thereafter he continued to receive preferment within the City of London, becoming successively rector at St Antholin's, Watling Street (1835–49), Allhallows, Thames Street (1849–56), and St Margaret's, Lothbury (1856–60). In 1854 he was also president of Sion College. His first wife, Anne, was a daughter of the Revd Samuel Crowther, under whom he served at Christ Church Greyfriars. They had three sons (all of whom died in childhood) and three daughters. After Anne's death on 4 January 1847, he married Katherine Isabella, the second daughter of the Hon William Cust.

In his day Goode was widely acknowledged as the most able and learned champion of the evangelical party within the Church of England and was often referred to as 'the modern Luther', having the same birth date as the German reformer. For almost forty years he took a prominent part in nearly every major controversy in the Church of England. His writings reveal a formidable polemicist with a deep knowledge of patristic, medieval, and Reformation literature, and a firm grasp of the intricacies of both historical theology and ecclesiastical law.

Besides numerous pamphlets, tracts, and sermons on topics ranging from church rates to ritualism, he was the author of several substantial treatises of more lasting significance.

The Modern Claims to the Possession of the Extraordinary Gifts of the Spirit (1833) was written to counteract the doctrines and practices of Edward Irving and his circle. Thereafter most of Goode's books were responses to particular aspects of the emerging Oxford Movement. *The Divine Rule of Faith and Practice* (2 vols., 1842; 2nd edn, 3 vols., 1853), a massive critique of the Tractarian doctrine of tradition, which sought to prove that both the early fathers and the classical Anglican divines believed that scripture alone was the source of authoritative revelation, was probably his most important work. The following year he published *Two Treatises on the Church* to demonstrate that Thomas Jackson and Robert Sanderson, seventeenth-century Anglicans whom the Tractarians admired, did not actually teach that membership of the church universal necessitated membership of an episcopal church. His *Tract XC Historically Refuted* (1845) argued against J. H. Newman's attempt to give a Catholic interpretation to the Thirty-Nine Articles of the Church of England.

Goode played a leading role in the Gorham controversy over baptism, commissioning articles for the *Christian Observer*, an influential evangelical journal of which he was editor from 1847 to 1849, and writing pamphlets opposing the views of Bishop Phillpotts of Exeter and attacking the judgment of the dean of arches, who had ruled against Gorham. In his influential *The Doctrine of the Church of England as to the Effects of Baptism in the Case of Infants* (1849) he argued that the doctrine of baptismal regeneration had received little support from Anglican writers from the sixteenth century onwards. *The Nature of Christ's Presence in the Eucharist* (2 vols., 1856) maintained, in opposition to the teaching of Pusey and other Tractarians, that the real presence was not in the consecrated bread and wine but in the faithful reception of the elements. His last major work was his Warburton lectures for 1854–8, published as *Fulfilled Prophecy a Proof of the Truth of Revealed Religion* (1863).

In 1860, on the recommendation of the evangelical Lord Shaftesbury, Goode was presented by Palmerston to the deanery of Ripon; in the same year he was awarded an honorary DD by the University of Cambridge. He died at the deanery, Ripon, quite suddenly, of heart failure on 13 August 1868 and was buried in the churchyard at Dwygyfylchi, Penmaen-mawr. His tomb was in the form of an Iona cross designed by Sir George Gilbert Scott, a personal friend. STEPHEN GREGORY

Sources Crockford (1868) • P. Toon, *Evangelical theology, 1833–1856: a response to Tractarianism* (1979) • Venn, *Alum. Cant.* • *The Record* (14 Aug 1868) • *Clerical Journal* (1883) • D. M. Lewis, ed., *The Blackwell dictionary of evangelical biography, 1730–1860*, 2 vols. (1995) • *The Times* (14 Aug 1868) • *The Times* (15 Aug 1868) • *Christian Observer* (1868), 701–2 • *In memoriam William Goode, dean of Ripon: extracts from letters … to his widow* (1870) • W. Goode, *A memoir of the late Rev. William Goode*, 2nd edn (1828) • J. C. S. Nias, *Gorham and the bishop of Exeter* (1951)

Archives GL, MSS 9018, 9020, 9545 | LPL, letters to Charles Golightly

Likenesses photograph, *c.*1855–1868, GL, Sion College archives • photograph, *c.*1855–1868, repro. in W. Goode, *Sermons*, ed. J. Metcalfe (1869) • photograph, 1868, repro. in *In memoriam William Goode, dean of Ripon*

Wealth at death under £6000: probate, 2 Oct 1868, *CGPLA Eng. & Wales*

Goode, Sir William Allmond Codrington (1907–1986), colonial governor, was born at 5 Riverdale Road, Twickenham, on 8 June 1907, eldest son of Sir Richard Allmond Goode (1873–1953), colonial administrator, and his wife, Agnes Codrington. Goode was educated at Oakham School (1920–26) and at Worcester College, Oxford (1926–30), where he held a classical exhibition and graduated with second-class honours. In the civil service entrance examinations of 1931 he was placed high enough to have a choice of joining the UK civil service or taking a Far Eastern cadetship. He decided to follow his father's example of service overseas and joined the Malayan civil service. A spare, athletic figure he had played in his school first fifteen and was captain of his college boat club at Oxford. In 1936 he was called to the bar by Gray's Inn. In 1938 he married Mary Armstrong Harding, who died in 1947. In 1950 he married Ena Mary McLaren, and they had one daughter.

From 1931 to 1940 Goode held district posts, mainly in the rural, predominantly Malay, east coast of Malaya. In 1940 he became assistant commissioner for civil defence in Singapore. As a serving member of the Singapore volunteer corps he was mobilized in 1941 as a lance corporal; he became a prisoner of war in 1942 and was sent by the Japanese to work on the Burma–Siam railway project. On returning to Malaya after the war he was appointed deputy economic secretary and in 1949 went to Aden as chief secretary (and acting governor in 1950–51). In 1953 he returned to Singapore as chief secretary (1953–7) and then governor (1957–9). He was then governor of North Borneo (Sabah) (1960–63) and finally, on returning to the UK, became chairman of the Water Resources Board, a post he held from 1964 to 1974.

Goode was a very able and quietly decisive administrator, who was also trusted and well liked both by political leaders and by the local business community. The post-war years in Singapore, 1953 to 1959, were the most demanding test of his career. By fortunate chance he had served in the volunteers with David Marshall who became chief minister in 1955. In his memoirs Goode remembered Marshall as a 'flamboyant and exciting personality. … not a very good soldier [but] a lovable person [with] incredible courage under fire'. As chief minister Marshall wanted to move very fast, which was his downfall. Then came Lim Yew Hock, who 'steadied affairs in Singapore' in the face of forceful opposition from the People's Action Party leader, Lee Kuan Yew. Lee obviously had the full support of the underground communist movement but Goode believed him—and made it plain that he did—when he said that he would not allow Singapore to go communist. Later on, when Lee had become prime minister, he accepted Goode's invitation to weekly sessions at Government House to talk things over. After independence, when Goode was temporarily UK high commissioner, Lee invited him to act also as Singapore's head of state, a unique distinction for a former colonial governor. Of his dealings with the Singapore leaders Goode recalled that 'we could explain things to them, we could advise them, but it was always our policy to make them take the decisions; it was their show'. It had not been possible, during his time in Aden, to bridge the gap created by implacable Arab hostility to British rule, but when he went on to North Borneo, Goode was able to make a friend of Donald Stephens, the Kadazan leader who became the first chief minister of Sabah (North Borneo) in 1963.

In Aden, Goode had worked hard, and with fair success, to improve the quality and performance of the local administration, and to secure funds for much needed development. When he went to North Borneo in 1960, it was prosperous but still had serious arrears in the development of social services such as education. To remedy these deficiencies took time, and Goode deplored the undue haste with which North Borneo was propelled into an association with Malaya for which it was ill-prepared.

However, looking back in retirement, Goode felt that he could take pride in having laboured so that 'the new nations had made it all work' (Heussler, *Completing a Stewardship*, 215). It was the pride of an unassuming man, but in his memoirs he rejected as 'quite unjustified' the widespread criticism of civil defence in the débâcle of 1941–2. He gave active support and help to the project for a history of the Malayan civil service.

Goode was deputy lieutenant of Berkshire (1975), and a knight of the order of St John (1958). He became CMG in 1952, KCMG in 1957, and finally GCMG in 1963. He died of cancer on 15 September 1986 at Thames Bank, Goring.

J. M. GULLICK

Sources W. Goode, memoirs (interview on career, 1931–63), Bodl. RH, IO.s.255 • *WWW*, *1981–90* • *WWW*, *1951–60*, 432 • Oakham School records, including extracts from *The Old Oakhamian* and *Register of Oakham School*, 1900–50 • Worcester College, Oxford, records, including Oakham School headmaster reference report on admission, 1925 • will, 2 Feb 1980, Principal Registry of the Family Division, London • *The Times* (17 Sept 1986) • personal knowledge (2004) • R. Heussler, *British rule in Malaya: the Malayan civil service* (1981) • R. Heussler, *Completing a stewardship* (1983) • b. cert. • d. cert. • *CGPLA Eng. & Wales* (1987)

Archives Bodl. RH, papers relating to governorship of North Borneo, etc.

Wealth at death £94,878: probate, 4 Feb 1987, *CGPLA Eng. & Wales*

Goode, Sir William Athelstane Meredith (1875–1944), journalist and financial adviser, was born at Channel in Newfoundland, Canada, on 10 June 1875, the younger son of the Revd Thomas Allmond Goode, a missionary of the Society for the Propagation of the Gospel, and his wife, Jane Harriet, daughter of the Revd Richard Meredith, for many years vicar of Hagbourne, Berkshire. He was educated at Doncaster grammar school and at Foyle College, Londonderry. At an early age he showed a taste for adventure by going to sea in 1889 and enlisting in the United States cavalry in 1892. After discharge, he took up journalism, and, attaching himself to the Associated Press of America, was their representative on board Admiral Sampson's flagship throughout the Spanish-American War, of which he wrote an account (*With Sampson through the War*, 1899). On 10 June 1899 he married Cecilia (*d.* 1938), daughter of Dr Charles Augustus Sippi, of London, Ontario. They had a daughter.

From 1898 to 1904 Goode was the Associated Press special correspondent in London, but in the latter year he joined *The Standard* as managing editor until 1910, and in 1911 he became joint news editor of the *Daily Mail*.

In 1913–14 Goode acted as honorary secretary of the British committee for the Panama Pacific Exposition, and this marked the beginning of what became a swiftly developing career in public affairs. During the First World War he was honorary secretary and organizer of the national committee for relief in Belgium (1915), member of the Newfoundland and West Indian military contingents committees (1916), and from 1917 to 1919 director of the cables department of the Ministry of Food and its liaison officer with the United States and Canadian food administrations. He was appointed KBE in 1918, and was a commander of the order of the Crown of Belgium and of that of Isabella the Catholic. In 1919 he became British director of relief missions, serving as a member of the British delegation at the peace conference, and of the Supreme Economic Council from 1919 to 1920.

Goode came into most prominence through his classic report on economic conditions in central Europe (1920) in which his journalistic skills were put to good use to give a vivid account both of the work accomplished by the relief missions and of their shortcomings. He was next appointed British delegate and president of the Austrian section of the Reparation Commission. But within a few weeks he was convinced that the reparation clauses were unworkable, and in November 1920 he reported that so far from being able to collect reparations from Austria, the allied governments would have to organize and finance a comprehensive programme of reconstruction, which he outlined. Although his report was endorsed by the Austrian section, it was unpalatable to most of the allied governments, 'and strong efforts were made to induce him to revise his opinion. Goode, however, maintained his ground' (Leith-Ross, 7). By March 1921 it had been agreed to postpone the claims for reparation, and the Austrian section was dissolved. The Austrian government invited Goode to remain as financial adviser, but the financial committee of the League of Nations, which was now preparing plans for Austrian reconstruction, discouraged this proposal. The league protocols, however, which were signed in October 1922, followed in all essentials Goode's original recommendations.

Unable to provide assistance in Austria, Goode turned to Hungary and became its unofficial financial adviser and acted as its financial agent in London until after the outbreak of war in 1939. He then joined the new Ministry of

Food as chief security officer and director of communications, responsible for securing secrecy and smooth working between the various departments of the ministry. He set in place arrangements which endured until the end of the war. But in 1942 he returned, despite ill health, to his old task of organizing relief and became chairman of the Council of British Societies for Relief Abroad. Goode was a versatile man, an effective administrator with skill in diplomacy and a keen awareness of the importance of publicity. In his relief and other international work these talents allowed him to gather support for his projects and achieve them quickly and efficiently. In 1944 he underwent a major operation which saw his condition improve temporarily, but he died in London at a nursing home at 5 Collingham Gardens, Kensington, on 14 December of that year. F. W. Leith-Ross, *rev.* Marc Brodie

Sources S. Huddleston, *Those Europeans: studies of foreign faces* (1924) · personal knowledge (1959) · private information (1959) · *The Times* (16 Dec 1944) · *The Times* (21 Dec 1944) · F. Leith-Ross, *The Times* (21 Dec 1944), 7 · Burke, *Peerage* (1939) · K. R. Stadler, *The birth of the Austrian republic, 1918–1921* (1966) · *WWW*
Likenesses W. Stoneman, two photographs, 1918–41, NPG
Wealth at death £9202 8s. 7d.: probate, 2 May 1945, *CGPLA Eng. & Wales*

Gooden, James (1670–1730), Jesuit, born in Denbighshire or Derbyshire in June or July 1670, was educated in the College at St Omer and entered the noviciate at Watten in 1689. In 1691 he went to the house of studies at Liège to study philosophy, and then returned to teach for three years at St Omer. He concluded his theology back at Liège and was ordained priest in 1702. He was professed of the four vows on 2 February 1707. For several years he taught philosophy and mathematics at Liège, and then was appointed rector of the College of St Omer on 14 March 1722. After only two years the vice-rector took over until Richard Plowden was appointed in May 1725. Gooden appears to have continued to live at the college, until he became superior of the house of tertianship at Ghent. He died at St Omer on 11 October 1730, while on a visit to the college.

His *Anathemata poetica serenissimo Walliæ principi Jacobi regis … filio recens nato sacra, offerebant ad eiusdem principis pedes prostratae musae Audomarenses* was written in collaboration with William Killick and published at St Omer in 1688, and his *Trigonometria plana et sphærica, cum selectis ex astronomia problematis* was published at Liège in 1701.

Thompson Cooper, *rev.* G. Bradley

Sources G. Holt, *The English Jesuits, 1650–1829: a biographical dictionary*, Catholic RS, 70 (1984), 104 · G. Holt, *St Omers and Bruges colleges, 1593–1773: a biographical dictionary*, Catholic RS, 69 (1979), 117 · Gillow, *Lit. biog. hist.*, 2.524 · H. Chadwick, *St Omers to Stonyhurst* (1962), 259, 404 · D. A. Bellenger, ed., *English and Welsh priests, 1558–1800* (1984), 64

Gooden, Peter (1643–1694), Roman Catholic priest, was the son of Thomas and Helen Gooden of Little Bolton, Lancashire, but was born near Manchester. Educated in the English College of Sts Peter and Paul at Lisbon, which he entered in 1661, he defended his dissertations in logic there in 1665. On 2 February 1670 he took the missionary oath after being ordained priest and was sent back to England with Edward Barlow, alias Booth. He was first chaplain to the Middletons at Leighton Hall, near Lancaster. About 1680 he removed to Aldcliffe Hall, the seat of the seven daughters of Robert Dalton, esquire. In this mansion, notwithstanding the penal laws against the opening of Catholic schools, Gooden 'kept a sort of academy or little seminary for educating of youth, who were afterwards sent beyond sea to popish colleges in order to be made popish secular priests' (Anstruther, 3.80). Late in 1680 he was accused of complicity in the Popish Plot, but no proof to implicate him appears to have been presented.

After the accession of James II, Gooden was appointed chaplain to the duke of Berwick's regiment and a royal warrant of 24 February 1687 ordered lodgings to be found for him at Chester, so that he might say mass there. During that reign his existing reputation as a noted controversialist increased and he had frequent conferences with Edward Stillingfleet, William Clagett, and other learned divines of the Church of England. 'No man', says Dodd, 'was better qualified to come off with reputation in a personal conference' as 'he was naturally bold and intrepid, had a strong voice, a ready utterance, and generally made choice of such topics as afforded him matter to display his eloquence.' His controversies with Anglican divines led to the publication of *The sum of the conference had between two divines of the Church of England and two Catholic lay-gentlemen. At the request and for the satisfaction of three persons of quality, Aug. 8, 1671*, which appeared in London in 1687. His conference with Stillingfleet gave rise to the publication of several controversial pamphlets in the 1680s and 1690s.

The revolution of 1688 obliged Gooden to retire to his old abode at Aldcliffe Hall, where he kept a farm and where he almost certainly reopened his school. He died at Aldcliffe Hall on 29 December 1694 and was buried at Lancaster parish church on 31 December. He died intestate, but an inventory of the goods of 'Peter Goodwine of Aldcliffe, gent.', dated 16 January 1695, valued his estate at £340 11s. 10d.

Gooden's life and work, both as a schoolmaster and a controversialist, exemplifies the strand of spirited vitality of certain Catholics in late seventeenth-century England who refused to be cowed by the penal laws and who kept alive the recusant tradition in the century and a half before Catholic emancipation.

Thompson Cooper, *rev.* Maurice Whitehead

Sources G. Anstruther, *The seminary priests*, 3 (1976), 79–81 · Gillow, *Lit. biog. hist.*, 2.524–8 · M. Sharratt, ed., *Lisbon College register, 1628–1813*, Catholic RS, 72 (1991), 65 · administration papers and inventory of 'Peter Goodwine of Aldcliffe, gent.', 16 Jan 1695, Lancs. RO, WRW · C. Dodd [H. Tootell], *The church history of England, from the year 1500, to the year 1688*, 2 (1739), 481 · J. Gillow, 'Attempted forgery of "a damnable Popish Plot" at Stonyhurst, 1679', *Palatine Note-Book*, 2 (1882), 9 · *Catholic Magazine and Review*, 6 (March 1835), 108 · Lancaster parish church register
Wealth at death £340 11s. 10d.: administration papers and inventory of 'Peter Goodwine of Aldcliffe, gent.', 16 Jan 1695, Lancs. RO, WRW

Gooden, Stephen Frederick (1892–1955), engraver, was born on 9 October 1892 at 30 Tulse Hill, Brixton, London, the only son of Stephen Thomas Gooden (1856–1909), an art dealer and print publisher, and his wife, Edith Camille Elizabeth Epps (1868–1954). He was educated at Rugby School and the Slade School of Art, and served in the First World War with the 19th hussars and the cavalry corps signals. He experimented with various media, settled on line engraving, and became 'the first young engraver of the twentieth century who attempted in England … to use the burin as an instrument for engraving romantic and imaginative compositions invented by himself' (Dodgson, ix).

Apart from a few individual plates, for example, *St George* (1935) and *Diana* (1940), Gooden worked chiefly as a book illustrator—a field that fascinated him from childhood—beginning in 1923 with the Nonesuch Press *Anacreon*. He contributed to twenty works, notably the Bible (Nonesuch, 5 vols., 1925–7), *The Fables of Jean de la Fontaine* (2 vols., Heinemann, 1931), and *Aesop's Fables* (Harrap, 1935). In addition, Gooden designed and engraved more than forty bookplates, including those for Queen Elizabeth, Princess Elizabeth, and Princess Margaret, and four for the Royal Library, Windsor Castle. One of the latter, featuring St George and the dragon, was used as the design for the George Medal, in recognition of which Gooden was appointed CBE in 1942. Among other royal commissions was the design of a large tapestry of the queen's personal coat of arms; the tapestry, woven in Scotland, was completed in 1950. While a few bookplates incorporate his initials in the design, most of his proof engravings are signed only in pencil ('Stephen Gooden') in the lower right margin.

From the early 1930s Gooden produced a number of banknote designs for the Bank of England. One, an inventive series of £1 and 10*s.* notes, was undertaken in the 1930s; another, of £1, £2, and £5 notes featuring Sir John Houblon, the bank's first governor, in the early 1950s. Both series remained unissued. A final note, printed largely in blue (the bank's first coloured £5 note) and incorporating a helmeted Britannia and a lion holding a key, was issued in 1957, two years after the artist's death. Gooden also worked for the banknote printers Bradbury Wilkinson, and his designs appeared on notes issued by banks in Scotland, South Africa, Greece, Egypt, and elsewhere.

Gooden was elected a fellow of the Royal Society of Painter-Etchers and Engravers in 1933, an associate of the Royal Academy in 1937, and a Royal Academician in 1946. On 28 March 1925 he married Mona Steele Price (1894–1958), a poet, who was a regular contributor of poetry and reviews to the *Dublin Magazine* from its inception in 1923 until her death. Gooden, who was personally engaging, facetious, and amusingly self-deprecating, was, professionally, contentiously frank and outspoken, particularly when he felt his clients were imposing their artistic misjudgements: he usually won. His work, inspired by Dürer, Marcantonio Raimondi, and the engravers of eighteenth-century France, links a vivid imagination with flawless

Stephen Frederick Gooden (1892–1955), by unknown photographer, pubd 1955

precision of line. It has a clarity, liveliness, and ingratiating quality few engravers of any century have achieved. The Goodens lived in and around London, including Hampstead (1932–9), and settled finally at End House, Chiltern Road, Chesham Bois, where, after a lengthy illness, borne with characteristic courage, Gooden died on 21 September 1955. He was cremated three days later at Golders Green crematorium. His work may be seen at the British Museum, the Victoria and Albert Museum, the Fitzwilliam Museum, Cambridge, the Ashmolean Museum, Oxford, and, in the United States, at Yale University.

JAMES LAVER, *rev.* DUNCAN ANDREWS

Sources J. Laver, 'The line-engravings of Stephen Gooden', *Colophon*, pt 2 (1930) • C. Dodgson, *An iconography of the engravings of Stephen Gooden* (1944) • D. Byatt, *Promises to pay: the first three hundred years of the Bank of England notes* (1994) • J. Deacon, 'In search of Stephen Gooden', *Old Lady*, no. 239 (1980), 114–16 • personal knowledge (1971) • private information (2004) • *CGPLA Eng. & Wales* (1956) • b. cert.

Archives Yale U., Sterling Library, Arts of the Book collection, letters, MSS, and works of art

Likenesses photograph, NPG; repro. in *ILN* (1 Oct 1955) [*see illus.*] • photographs, Yale U., New Haven, Connecticut

Wealth at death £27,077 3*s.* 1*d.*: probate, 6 Feb 1956, *CGPLA Eng. & Wales*

Goodenough, Edmund (1785–1845), headmaster and dean of Wells, the third and youngest son of Samuel *Goodenough, bishop of Carlisle, and his wife, Elizabeth, eldest daughter of Dr James Ford, physician-extraordinary to Queen Charlotte, was born at Ealing, Middlesex, on 3 April 1785. At an early age he was sent to Westminster School, where in 1797, when only twelve years old, he was elected into college. In 1801 he obtained his election to Christ Church, Oxford, where he gained the highest university honours in Easter term 1804, and graduated BA in 1805, MA in 1807, BD in 1819, and DD in 1820. Having taken orders, Goodenough became tutor and censor of Christ Church. Among his pupils was Sir James Graham, who later pressed his claims for preferment. In 1810 he was appointed curate of Cowley, Oxford. From 1811 to 1813 he was a university mathematical examiner, and in 1816 became a university proctor. In Michaelmas term 1817 he was appointed select preacher to the university, and in the following year was instituted vicar of Warkworth, Northumberland, which was in the gift of his father. In September 1819 Goodenough was appointed headmaster of Westminster School and subalmoner to the king, in succession to Dr Page. He married, on 31 May 1821, Frances, daughter of Samuel Pepys *Cockerell of Westbourne House, Paddington. He was elected FRS in 1824. On 23 June 1824 he was made a prebendary of York, and on 22 April 1826 succeeded to the prebend at Carlisle, which had become vacant through the death of his brother, Robert Philip Goodenough. On 1 June 1827 he was made a prebendary of Westminster.

Goodenough's headmastership of Westminster has been adjudged the beginning of the 'saddest' period in the annals of the school (J. Sargeaunt, *Annals of Westminster School*, 1898, 229). This was not entirely due to fault on Goodenough's part. The dean and chapter of Westminster took little interest in the school, and the buildings had become neglected. A good scholar and an amiable man, who had a cultivated interest in modern languages, the fine arts, and music, Goodenough lacked the strength either to challenge the chapter or to assert proper authority over the boys, who defeated his initial attempt to bring about disciplinary reform. In 1819 he backed down after breaking with custom and flogging a sixth-former who was intoxicated, and then provoked the so-called 'shoe-and-candlestick' rebellion when he sought to relieve fags from the duty of blacking shoes and cleaning candlesticks. During his period of office the number of boys steadily fell. He resigned in August 1828 and was succeeded by Richard Williamson (1802–1865), who was unable to reverse the decline.

On 6 September 1831 Goodenough was nominated dean of Wells, in the place of the Hon. Henry Ryder, bishop of Lichfield, who succeeded to Goodenough's stall at Westminster. He was prolocutor of the lower house of convocation for a short time. His only publications were three sermons, delivered at the consecration of William Carey (1820), at the festival of the sons of the clergy (1830), and at the meeting of the Bath Diocesan Association of the Society for the Propagation of the Gospel (1832). Goodenough died suddenly at Wells, suffering a fit after chasing some boys whom he saw trespassing, in the fields near his house, on 2 May 1845. He was buried in the lady chapel of Wells Cathedral, where a brass was placed to his memory. His widow died of cholera at Malaga on 5 August 1855. James Graham *Goodenough was among their many children. G. F. R. Barker, *rev.* M. C. Curthoys

Sources *GM*, 2nd ser., 25 (1846), 101–2 • *Somerset County Herald* (10 May 1845) • *Somerset County Herald* (17 May 1845) • J. Welch, *The list of the queen's scholars of St Peter's College, Westminster*, ed. [C. B. Phillimore], new edn (1852) • Foster, *Alum. Oxon.* • E. G. W. Bill, *Education at Christ Church, Oxford, 1660–1800* (1988) • L. E. Tanner, *Westminster School*, 2nd edn (1951) • J. T. Ward, *Sir James Graham* (1967)
Likenesses portrait; at Westminster School, London, in 1890
Wealth at death under £50,000: will, *GM*, 101

Goodenough, Ethel Mary [Angela] (**1900–1946**), naval officer, was born on 12 January 1900 in India and baptized on 14 February at Simla, in the Siwalik hills of northern India, the daughter of Captain Herbert Lane Goodenough (*d.* before 1946) of the Indian army and his wife, Muriel Grace, *née* Mitford (*d.* after 1946). She was privately educated and in 1918 joined the civilian staff at the Admiralty in London, becoming an established civil servant at the end of the war. She held a number of posts, preferring that of assistant secretary to Sir Oswyn Murray, secretary to the Admiralty, as this brought her closer to the Royal Navy, her main interest, for there were several serving officers among her relatives. Angela Goodenough, as she was generally known, gained a detailed working knowledge of the Admiralty and made many friends among the naval staff, who were later to prove invaluable. In 1937 she was appointed chief woman officer, responsible for the welfare of all female civil servants and for recruiting temporary staff.

Goodenough's experience and knowledge of the Admiralty led to her appointment in April 1939 as deputy director in the newly created Women's Royal Naval Service (WRNS). Her appointment was popular among naval staff and her contacts proved very useful when negotiating conditions for the fledgeling service. She was principally concerned with welfare, including clothing and accommodation, and for relations with the press, a side of the work in which she took great pride and interest. Her strong views on what was required, coupled with a great determination and a happy knack of getting her own way without rows, laid the foundations for the good welfare conditions in the service. After a second deputy director was appointed, she remained in charge of welfare aspects until autumn 1944.

As the war in the East intensified, a senior officer was required to oversee the welfare of the growing number of Wrens posted to the region. Goodenough was selected and, although she was reluctant to leave the familiar circumstances of the Admiralty, she accepted the appointment as superintendent on the staff of the commander-in-chief, East Indies, and in September 1944 left for Ceylon. She made a great success of the job, finding happiness and many new friends. She contracted infantile paralysis, however, and, after two days suffering from what was thought to be a light fever, she became unconscious and died in Colombo on 10 February 1946. She was buried there the following day with a full captain's bodyguard, the funeral being attended by over 200 Wrens and a large number of naval officers. Later in the month the WRNS directorate arranged memorial services at St Martin-in-the-Fields, London, and at St Andrew's Cathedral, Singapore, both of which drew many of her friends from the Admiralty and naval services. Lesley Thomas

Sources V. L. Matthews, *Blue tapestry* (1948) • V. L. M., 'Superintendent Angela Goodenough, C.B.E.', *The Wren* • register of birth and baptism, BL OIOC, N/1/280, fol. 146 • *The Times* (23 Feb 1946) • *CGPLA Eng. & Wales* (1946)
Wealth at death £518 6*s.* 11*d.*: probate, 17 Aug 1946, *CGPLA Eng. & Wales*

Goodenough, Sir Francis William (**1872–1940**), sales executive and educationist, son of Henry Goodenough, currier, and his wife, Louisa Hatchwell, was born in East Street, Newton Abbot, Devon, on 9 September 1872, and was educated at Torquay Public College. At the age of sixteen he joined the Gas Light and Coke Company as an office boy. Although it was at that time the largest gas company in Britain, Gas Light and Coke had no sales organization to face the incipient challenge from electricity; only in 1903 was a department separate from engineering established for selling and customer service. Goodenough's talents for marketing were quickly recognized, and in 1902 he was sent to Berlin to report on gas street lighting. In the following year he was appointed the company's first controller of gas sales, a position he retained until his retirement in 1931. As early as 1907 he was publicly arguing that gas utility managers should regard sales promotion as part of their normal duties.

One of Goodenough's responsibilities was the placing of advertisements. At that time the industry was highly fragmented with no central body to encourage co-operation: in 1912 there were over 800 independent authorized gas companies, more than a third of which were municipally owned. In consequence, many of the advertisements placed by the Gas Light and Coke Company were seen by customers of other gas companies, whose policies and terms of trade were different, and much of their impact was therefore wasted, as far as the Gas Light and Coke Company was concerned. In discussion with the head of his advertising agency Goodenough conceived the idea of an industry-wide body to promote co-operative advertising. Under his leadership, the British Commercial Gas Association was set up in 1911. Some gas companies resented the leading role played by Gas Light and Coke in the affairs of the association, and others—especially municipal undertakings—saw no need for co-operative advertising. Gradually, however, Goodenough won over virtually the whole industry. The success of the advertising association opened the way for the creation by Sir David Milne-Watson in 1919 of the National Gas Council, a forum to improve co-operation within the industry and to allow it to speak with a common voice.

Goodenough's preference was for scrupulous factual advertising. There was some feeling in the gas industry during the 1930s that the association's promotional efforts were being outclassed by the aggressive advertising of electrical goods, but the pattern he established was maintained. Goodenough was elected a member of the Incorporated Sales Managers' Association in 1921, its chairman in 1926 (when he was also made a CBE) and its president from 1929 to 1934. For three years he was also president of the Incorporated Society of British Advertisers.

In the early 1920s Goodenough turned his attention to educational schemes for technical and commercial staff, in conjunction with the Institution of Gas Engineers and the Board of Education. In his view the development of scientific skills in management and selling, especially in export markets, was perhaps even more important for the future of the nation than developing manufacturing capability. Such views led to his acting as chairman of a government committee on education for salesmanship between 1928 and 1931. This provided him with a platform to promote his views; he addressed among others the British Association for the Advancement of Science and the Headmasters' Conference. Goodenough was a council member of the Federation of British Industry, and received a knighthood in 1930. He retired from the Gas Light and Coke Company in 1931, but remained chairman of the British Commercial Gas Association until 1936.

In 1900 Goodenough married Ellen, daughter of William Rees of Dolgellau and Chelsea; they had no children. An enthusiast for fly-fishing and golf in his spare time, he also worked for social and charitable organizations, notably as chairman of the Princess Beatrice Hospital. He never entirely lost his Devon accent. The last few years of his life were dogged by poor health, and he died at his home, 39 Holland Street, London, on 11 January 1940. He was survived by his wife, and left estate valued at £4409 15*s*. 9*d*. FRANCIS GOODALL

Sources F. Goodall, 'The British gas appliance industry, 1875–1939', PhD diss., U. Lond., 1992 • *The Times* (13 Jan 1940) • *Gas Times* (20 Jan 1940) • *Gas Times* (27 Jan 1940) • *Gas World* (20 Jan 1940) • 'A farewell', *Marketing* (Sept 1934) • J. W. Bambrick and E. B. Groves, 'The ISMA story', *Marketing* (May 1961) • S. Everard, *The history of the Gas Light and Coke Company, 1812–1949* (1949) • T. I. Williams, *A history of the British gas industry* (1981) • d. cert.

Wealth at death £4409 15*s*. 9*d*.: probate, 26 Feb 1940, *CGPLA Eng. & Wales*

Goodenough, Frederick Craufurd (1866–1934), banker, was born on 28 July 1866 in Calcutta, the third son of Frederick Addington Goodenough, East India merchant, and his wife, Mary Lambert. From an affluent Anglican background, he was grandson of Edmund *Goodenough, headmaster of Westminster School and later dean of Wells, and great-grandson of Samuel Goodenough, bishop of Carlisle. Goodenough's father died when he was only three years old, so his son grew up in genteel comfort rather than opulence. Frederick junior was educated at a private school, at Charterhouse, and at Zürich University, where he read law. After qualifying as a solicitor, he obtained the post of assistant secretary with the Hudson's Bay Company and then moved to a similar post at the Union Bank of London. His experience there of merging a private bank into a corporate bank induced the partners in the 1896 merger of many private banks into the new Barclay & Co. to recruit him as their first company secretary. Two years later he married Maive, fifth daughter of Nottidge Charles Macnamara FRCS, whose family also had a Calcutta background; they had three sons and two daughters. Their eldest son was the banker Sir William Macnamara *Goodenough, first baronet (1899–1951).

The new bank—the sixth largest by size of deposits in England when he joined it—included a leading Lombard Street business, Barclay, Bevan & Co., together with the biggest East Anglian branch network (Gurney & Co.) and numerous smaller banks acquired in 1896 and the subsequent two decades. Despite its growth and the strong local connections of the former private bank partners, it was not an outstanding financial success. However, it was a successful vehicle for Goodenough's personal and managerial aspirations, and he played a major part in preserving the best of the old private banking culture, while introducing to the branches the systematic procedures of modern joint-stock banking. As a neutral arbiter between the many family stockholders, he won the directors' confidence: in 1903 they appointed him to the newly created post of general manager (common in other joint-stock banks) and in 1913 to a main board directorship. When the first chairman of Barclay & Co., F. A. Bevan, retired at the end of 1916, Goodenough was the board's choice as his successor, the first senior manager appointed from outside the founding families.

The flurry of merger activity which then created the 'big five' British clearing banks threatened to leave Barclays behind, but Goodenough was soon caught up in its beguiling attractions. In 1918–20 he paid excessive prices in a massive takeover spree, acquiring the London Provincial and South Western Bank, the Union Bank of Manchester, and the British Linen Bank in the UK, making Barclays a truly national bank for the first time; he also took over the Anglo-Egyptian Bank and the Colonial Bank, making Barclays one of the biggest banks in the British empire. These acquisitions were generally unremunerative, though the strong domestic market position that resulted enabled Barclays to weather the storms of the inter-war years without the danger to depositors so widely experienced abroad at this time. In 1925 Goodenough—an imperial enthusiast and member of the Council of India (1918–1930)—picked up the troubled National Bank of South Africa cheaply, merging it with his two other overseas banks to create Barclays Bank (Dominion, Colonial and Overseas), which for the next half-century accounted for upwards of a quarter of all British-owned overseas bank branches.

The Barclays group (including its majority-controlled overseas subsidiary) was the largest banking group in the world in the 1930s, though in England alone the Midland had a larger deposit base, and the California-based bank group, Transamerica Corporation, threatened to overtake its balance sheet size until broken up by American anti-trust action. There were then, however, few economies of scale in banking, and the main benefit of the mergers was in strengthening the bank's power to control market interest rates and stabilize competition. This enabled Barclays to maintain profits at home during the difficulties of the inter-war recession, and in the 1930s to restore imperial banking profit rates.

Goodenough was (from 1917 until his death) chairman of what was Britain's fastest-growing large banking group; it was therefore surprising that (unlike other leading contemporary bank chairmen) he was not knighted. He was, however, *persona non grata* with Montagu Norman, the governor of the Bank of England, who disapproved of his imperial adventures, though Goodenough had shown himself an astute political operator in gaining legislative support from Conservative imperialists for the creation of Barclays Bank (Dominion, Colonial and Overseas). Moreover, the varied cyclical experiences of the overseas and domestic subsidiaries in fact improved the group's overall stability, rather than compromising it, as Norman feared.

Goodenough paid himself well in cash and kind. He built a London flat for himself above the bank's branch at 1 Pall Mall, but he spent much of his time in the countryside at Filkins Hall near Oxford, re-establishing his family in the Oxford squirearchy and assisting the Bodleian Library's finances (for which Oxford awarded him the honorary DCL in 1933). He also served as joint treasurer of Westminster Hospital, governor of the Charterhouse Foundation and a member of the governing body of that school, and was active as vice-president of the Institute of Bankers. Goodenough founded in 1930 London House, which was to serve as a hall of residence in London for dominion postgraduate students.

Described as 'the chief architect' of the twentieth-century bank, Goodenough made Barclays the ruling passion of his working life (*DNB*). No doubt because of his pre-eminence, he became increasingly autocratic: board meetings typically lasted only twenty minutes, and he over-promoted his eldest son, William, in the bank's management hierarchy. Sir William Macnamara Goodenough was vice-chairman at the time of his father's death, and briefly served as chairman (1947–51), but did not play as great a role in Barclays as his father. Goodenough died at the London Clinic, 20 Devonshire Place, Marylebone, London, on 1 September 1934. LESLIE HANNAH

Sources *The Banker*, 32 (1934) · P. W. Matthews, *History of Barclays Bank Limited*, ed. A. W. Tuke (1926) · A. W. Tuke and R. J. H. Gillman, *Barclays Bank Limited, 1926–1969: some recollections* (1972) · J. Crossley and J. Blandford, *The DCO story: a history of banking in many countries, 1925–71* (1975) · *DNB* · G. Jones, *British multinational banking, 1830–1990: a history* (1993) · d. cert. · M. Ackrill and L. Hannah, *Barclays: the business of banking, 1690–1996* (2001)

Archives Barclays Bank Archives, Wythenshawe, Manchester, business MSS

Likenesses O. Edis, photograph, 1931, NPG · J. P. B. Barnes, oils, Barclays Bank, London · G. C. Beresford, photograph, NPG

Wealth at death £120,580 2*s*. 5*d*.: probate, 6 Dec 1934, *CGPLA Eng. & Wales*

Goodenough, James Graham (1830–1875), naval officer, son of Edmund *Goodenough (1785–1845), dean of Wells, and his wife, Frances Cockerell (*d*. 5 Aug 1855), and grandson of Samuel *Goodenough, bishop of Carlisle, was born on 3 December 1830, at Stoke Hill, near Guildford, Surrey. The close connection of his godfather, Sir James Graham, with the Admiralty fixed his profession from the beginning, and after three years at Westminster School he entered the navy in May 1844 on board the *Collingwood*, commanded by Captain Robert Smart, the flagship of Rear-Admiral Sir George Francis Seymour, commander-in-chief in the Pacific. In the summer of 1848, Goodenough was appointed to the steamship *Cyclops* on the coast of Africa, returning home in late 1849 to pass his examination and compete for the lieutenant's commission in a special course at the Royal Naval College at Portsmouth. He obtained his commission in July 1851, and in September was appointed to the *Centaur*, on the east coast of South America. The *Centaur* was recalled to England in February 1854, and Goodenough was appointed to the

Royal William, which transported French troops to the siege of Bomarsund, and after its capture returned to England with Russian prisoners. After a few weeks on board the *Excellent*, Goodenough was appointed gunnery lieutenant of the *Hastings*, in which he served through the Baltic campaign of 1855, and was present at the bombardment of Sveaborg on 20 August. During the early part of 1856 he commanded the gunboat *Goshawk*, one of the flotilla reviewed at Spithead on 23 April.

On 4 August 1856 Goodenough was appointed first lieutenant of the *Raleigh*, a 50-gun frigate, wearing the broad pennant of Commodore the Hon. Henry Keppel, as second in command on the China station. On 15 March 1857, after an extraordinarily rapid passage, the *Raleigh* was within a hundred miles of Hong Kong when she struck an uncharted rock and was run ashore near Macau (Macao). The men and most of the stores were saved, but the ship sank into the mud. The *Raleigh*'s crew was kept together for some months, during which time Goodenough commanded the hired steamer *Hongkong*, and in her took part in the engagement in Fatshan (Foshan) Creek on 1 June. He was afterwards appointed to the *Calcutta*, the flagship of Sir Michael *Seymour (1802–1887), and commanded her field-pieces at the capture of Canton (Guangzhou) on 28 and 29 December 1857. He was immediately promoted commander of the *Calcutta*, and took part in the capture of the Taku (Dagu) forts on 20 May 1858. The *Calcutta* was paid off at Plymouth early in August 1859, and a few weeks later, on the news of Sir James Hope's defeat at the Taku forts, Goodenough was again sent out to China, in command of the sloop *Renard*. He took part in the second capture of the Taku forts in June 1860, and in the following operations in the Peiho (Beihe). He remained as senior officer at Shanghai and in the Yangtze (Yangzi) River until, in November 1861, his health having suffered from his long service in China, he obtained leave to return to England.

In July 1862 Goodenough was appointed commander of the *Revenge*, flagship in the Channel and then in the Mediterranean. On 9 May he was promoted captain, and a few months later was sent to North America to obtain information on the ships and guns in use in the civil war. He provided several valuable reports on federal naval developments. He returned to England in May 1864. From 1864 to 1866 he captained the *Victoria*, the Mediterranean flagship; and from 1867 to 1870 the *Minotaur*, the channel squadron flagship. In 1870 and 1871 he served on the French Peasant Relief Fund, started by the *Daily News* to bring aid to those suffering the effects of the Franco-Prussian War. From March until July 1871 he was a member of the Admiralty committee on designs for ships of war. In 1871 and 1872 he served as naval attaché to several embassies in Europe, reflecting his scientific and linguistic expertise.

In May 1873 Goodenough was appointed commodore of the Australian station, a post often given to promising young officers on the brink of flag rank, and captain of the *Pearl*, which sailed from Spithead in the following month. After a busy two years, visiting many of the islands on his extensive station, he went ashore on 12 August 1875 at Santa Cruz, where his small party was treacherously attacked. He and two others received arrow wounds, from which they contracted tetanus and died. Goodenough died on 20 August, about 500 miles from Sydney, where he was buried on the 24th. He left a widow, Victoria Henrietta, daughter of William John *Hamilton, and two sons, one of whom, Admiral Sir William *Goodenough, served with distinction in the First World War. Reserved and grave in manner, even as a young man, Goodenough inspired confidence and esteem in all those with whom he served. He was an officer of great promise and rare ability. J. K. LAUGHTON, *rev.* ANDREW LAMBERT

Sources personal knowledge (1890) · R. F. MacKay, *Fisher of Kilverstone* (1973) · S. Sandler, *The emergence of the modern capital ship* (1979) · 'Committee on designs for ships of war', *Parl. papers* (1872), 14.501, C. 477; 14.581, C. 477-I · W. E. Goodenough, *A rough record* (1943)
Archives Mitchell L., NSW, journals and notebooks · SOAS, diary and corresp.
Likenesses Count Gleichen, marble bust, *c.*1878, Royal Naval College, Greenwich · S. Harrison, wood-engraving (*Murder of Commodore Goodenough RN, in the South Sea Islands*), NPG; repro. in *ILN* (4 Dec 1875) · photograph, repro. in Goodenough, *Rough record* · wood-engraving (after photograph by H. Lenthall), NPG; repro. in *ILN* (11 Sept 1875)
Wealth at death under £4000: probate, 26 Nov 1875, *CGPLA Eng. & Wales*

Goodenough, Richard (*fl.* 1671–1687), whig conspirator, was the second son of Richard Goodenough, gentleman, of Sherstone, Wiltshire. He was admitted to the Inner Temple in July 1671 and to the Middle Temple in February 1679. Goodenough turned to country politics in 1673–4 as anti-French sentiment undermined Charles II's last war against the Dutch. His lodgings in Shoe Lane became a centre of pro-Dutch intrigue, the discovery of which earned him a sojourn in the Tower. Associated with men like John Trenchard and John Ayloffe, Goodenough also came into contact with country statesmen in the House of Commons and with the emerging civic opposition in the corporation of London. From at least November 1676 he was an active member of the Green Ribbon Club: his introductions of other members reveal him to have been well connected among West End legal men and gentlemen. He served as attorney to Colonel John Scott, sometime spy and agent of the duke of Buckingham; and he apparently was among those London and Westminster whigs who travelled to Bristol in 1680 to advance their local organization.

In 1680–81 Goodenough became under-sheriff to Slingsby Bethel and Henry Cornish, the whig sheriffs of London and Middlesex elected for that year. A protégé of the reputed republican Bethel, Goodenough had acquired a reputation as a 'pestilent attorney'. Even Cornish was reluctant to work with him as 'a man that he would not trust a hair of his head with' (*CSP dom.*, *1679–80*, 620; *State trials*, 11.431). But Goodenough was, in fact, trusted with much as under-sheriff, assisting, in particular, in the empanelment of grand jurors. As the government and the parliamentary whigs carried their struggle about the succession and other issues into the urban courts, Goodenough played a critical role in the politicization of justice. Secretary Jenkins predicted in September 1680 that one jury would be as bad enough as 'the malice of Goodenough' could make it (*CSP dom.*, *1680–81*, 44).

After the Oxford parliament Goodenough assisted Shaftesbury and the whig leaders in their efforts to frustrate the crown's treason proceedings against Popish Plot informant Edward Fitzharris. Like the whig sheriffs, he was fined for delaying the summons of a jury to try Fitzharris. He was involved with Francis Jenks, Aaron Smith, and Edward Whitaker in attempting to block Sir William Waller's testimony against Fitzharris; and he was briefly incarcerated at Newgate, where he 'threat[e]ned the chancellor for fals[e] imprisonment' ('Journals of Edmund Warcup', 254).

Continuing as under-sheriff under the next whig sheriffs, Thomas Pilkington and Samuel Shute, whose election he had promoted, Goodenough was also involved in empanelling the grand juries for the London treason trials of Stephen College and Lord Shaftesbury, which found the indictments against them *ignoramus*. He remained at odds with the loyalist Middlesex JPs, who fined and imprisoned him again. On 24 June 1682 Goodenough was among the civic whig principals who encouraged the whig sheriffs to continue with a common hall poll for the election of their successors, despite an adjournment commanded by the loyalist lord mayor. This episode led to the indictment of Goodenough and several other leading whigs on charges of riot, of which they were convicted and fined in May 1683.

By then, the government's success in imposing tory sheriffs on the corporation of London, despite the electoral majority of the whig candidates, Thomas Papillon and John Dubois, had become a principal whig grievance. Taken by the whigs as evidence that the crown intended to replace parliamentary government with arbitrary rule, the results of the 1682 London shrieval election had driven some whig leaders and some whig activists into the plotting of insurrection and regicide. As Shaftesbury turned to conspiracy in the autumn of 1682, Goodenough was clearly within his circle of 'creatures' (Burnet, 2.357). Indeed, the earl apparently entrusted money for his covert projects to Goodenough.

Nothing came of these plans before Shaftesbury's flight into exile and death, but Goodenough and his brother Francis, also apparently a lawyer, were instrumental in reviving whig conspiracy in the winter and spring of 1683. Associated with fellow attorney Robert West, Goodenough advocated the abortive plan to assassinate the king at the Rye House in Hertfordshire, the property of Captain Richard Rumbold, with whom he was intimate. Goodenough had the principal role in the recruitment of potential assassins, probably because of his contacts with circles of extreme sectarians.

Goodenough also remained involved in the efforts of the civic whigs to recover the London shrievalty for the whig claimants, Papillon and Dubois, through the processes of king's bench. Acting as attorney to Papillon, Goodenough succeeded briefly in arresting the tory lord mayor and several aldermen, on 24 April 1683, for their failure to respond to whig suits against them for accepting false sheriffs. The relationship between this episode and other conspiratorial designs is unclear, but, believing that 'the law will not defend us [now], though we be never so innocent', Goodenough returned to conspiracy in May (*State trials*, 11.426).

Goodenough was then instrumental in developing new plans within the West cabal for an urban insurrection. He assumed the principal responsibility for selecting leaders in some twenty districts into which the city was divided. Employing the idea that the rights and liberties of the citizens had been 'invaded' as a rationale for resistance, he was convinced that he could gather thousands of disaffected Londoners from Wapping and Southwark (*CSP dom.*, *Jan–June 1683*, 383). Goodenough's clerk, who turned informer after his dismissal, claimed that Goodenough desired a return to 'Oliver's days' and a 'good honest Commonwealth' (*CSP dom.*, *July–Sept 1683*, 12).

Also involved in drafting a rebel manifesto, Goodenough confirmed plot details on 13 June 1683 to a brother of Josiah Keeling, whom Goodenough had previously recruited for the Rye House assassination. Unbeknown to Goodenough, however, Keeling had already disclosed the plot to Secretary Jenkins and had set up Goodenough's conversation with his brother to provide a second witness. As the government began arresting suspects, Richard and Francis Goodenough went underground, eventually fleeing to the Netherlands. Both were indicted for treason at the Middlesex sessions in July.

Deeply involved in further plotting against the government while abroad, Goodenough was at first associated with the duke of Argyll. He was also in contact with Sir Thomas Armstrong, John Locke, and John Ayloffe. Familiar as well with Robert Ferguson, with whom he had intrigued in London, Goodenough worked to ease the distrust between Argyll and Ferguson's patron, the duke of Monmouth. He was among those who advised Monmouth about a declaration of intentions that the duke adopted in preparation for his rebellion.

Goodenough and his brother accompanied Monmouth to England in 1685, each serving as a captain in Monmouth's rebel force, of which Goodenough also became paymaster. In charge of the fortification of Bridgwater, he survived Monmouth's defeat; but he was apprehended in flight (with £300 pounds in his pocket) and offered evidence against others in hope of a pardon. In October 1685, at the trial of Alderman Cornish, Goodenough related a conversation of spring 1683 that seemingly implicated the alderman in treason, doing so against Cornish's objections that Goodenough was up to his usual 'tricks' (*State trials*, 11.428). Goodenough also provided evidence for the government against Shaftesbury's former surgeon, the London whig activist Charles Bateman, and against Lord Delamere.

His life secured, Goodenough was consigned to Jersey as

a prisoner for life. In May 1687, however, he was released. According to Jonathan Swift, he then emigrated to Ireland, where he practised law until his death. Goodenough was married by 1685, but nothing is known of his wife beyond her name, Sarah. GARY S. DE KREY

Sources *CSP dom.*, *1673–5*, 318, 321; *1679–80*, 620; *1680–81*, 44, 284, 334, 500; *1682*, 142, 441; *Jan–June 1683*, esp. 38–9, 41, 206, 214, 219, 335, 339, 345–6, 351–2, 381–4; *July–Sept 1683*, esp. 5, 11–12, 39, 47, 52–3, 71, 99, 146, 155, 339, 345, 349, 421; *1683–4*, 3, 48, 77, 206, 224, 227–8, 234–5, 257, 269, 378; *1685*, 4, 152, 269, 299, 349, 376, 394, 424; *1686–7*, 186, 204, 438 • [T. Sprat], *Copies of the informations and original papers relating to the proof of the horrid conspiracy against the late king, his present majesty and the government* (1685), 1–63, 78–81 • *State trials*, 9.255, 365–429, 441–5; 11.426–9, 431–4, 472, 542 • R. L. Greaves, 'Goodenough, Richard', Greaves & Zaller, *BDBR*, 2.13–14 • R. L. Greaves, *Secrets of the kingdom: British radicals from the Popish Plot to the revolution of 1688–89* (1992) • BL, Lansdowne MS 1152A, fols. 227, 242, 298 • Ford, Lord Grey, *The secret history of the Rye-House plot: and of Monmouth's rebellion* (1754), 83–5 • *Memoirs of Thomas Papillon, of London, merchant*, ed. A. F. W. Papillon (1887), 228–32 • *Bishop Burnet's History*, 2.357, 360–62; 3.65 • H. A. C. Sturgess, ed., *Register of admissions to the Honourable Society of the Middle Temple, from the fifteenth century to the year 1944*, 1 (1949), 199 • 'The journals of Edmund Warcup, 1676–84', ed. K. G. Feiling and F. R. D. Needham, *EngHR*, 40 (1925), 235–60 • R. Ashcraft, *Revolutionary politics and Locke's two treatises of government* (1986) • T. Sprat, *A true account and declaration of the horrid conspiracy against the late king* (1685), 23, 31, 41–2, 66

Goodenough, Samuel (1743–1827), bishop of Carlisle and botanist, was born at Kimpton, near Weyhill, Hampshire, on 29 April 1743, the third son of the Revd William Goodenough, rector of Kimpton and of Broughton Poges, Oxfordshire, and prebendary of Brecon Cathedral. The family moved to Broughton in 1750, when William Goodenough resigned Kimpton, and Samuel was sent to Witney School. Five years later he transferred to Westminster School, whose headmaster, Dr William Markham, subsequently archbishop of York, became a longstanding friend. Goodenough matriculated from Christ Church, Oxford, on 9 June 1760, having been elected king's scholar from Westminster. He graduated BA on 9 May 1764 and proceeded MA on 25 June 1767 and DCL on 11 July 1772.

In 1766, having been ordained priest, Goodenough returned to Westminster School, as under-master. He left in 1770, on inheriting the advowson of Broughton from his father; he also received the living of Brize Norton, also in Oxfordshire, from Christ Church. On 17 April 1770 he married Elizabeth, daughter of Dr James Ford, sometime physician to Middlesex Hospital and to Queen Charlotte; their children included Edmund *Goodenough. In 1772 he established his own very successful private school in Ealing, Middlesex, for the sons of nobility and gentlemen of position. He had an excellent reputation as a tutor in Latin and Greek and did not give up the school until he was appointed canon of St George's, Windsor, on 3 February 1798.

Goodenough's primary intellectual interest outside the church was botany. He was an influential member of the Linnean Society from its foundation in 1788. He helped to frame its constitution, acted for a year as treasurer, and, as

Samuel Goodenough (1743–1827), by Henry Hoppner Meyer, 1811 (after James Northcote, 1810)

vice-president to James Edward Smith, often took the chair. His botanical and natural history publications, except where his data supplemented or corrected the publications of others, mainly appeared in the *Transactions of the Linnean Society*. He later published three important sermons. Botany was part of a broader spectrum; he wrote to J. E. Smith on 6 December 1798 that 'The Study of Divinity and Natl. History … always go on very kindly together … These & love of Musick have long been the great alleviators of my many worldly cares' (Dawson, 11.69–70). He was also a member of the Society of Antiquaries and of the Natural History Society, but could be disparaging about both.

In 1797 Goodenough was appointed vicar of Cropredy, Oxfordshire, and, after he became dean of Rochester, on 27 August 1802, he awarded himself the rectorship of Boxley, Kent, where the uncultivated countryside supplied him with botanical specimens during the summer. His scholarship recommended him both to George III and to William Henry Cavendish Cavendish-Bentinck, third duke of Portland, whose sons he educated. In December 1807 Portland, then prime minister, nominated him bishop of Carlisle; he was consecrated in the Chapel Royal, Whitehall, on 13 February 1808.

Carlisle was a poor diocese whose affairs were subject to interference from the Lowther family; Portland had been forced to sell all his property in Cumberland and Westmorland following a legal dispute over their ownership with the Lowthers, and by nominating Goodenough to the diocese he probably intended some sort of retaliation. A further complication was the authoritative presence of the dean of Carlisle, Isaac Milner, also a natural philosopher; John Burgess has suggested that Goodenough did not get on well with Milner, nor with dissenters, but earlier writers argue that Goodenough respected both his dean and other denominations, and his close friend Smith was himself a Unitarian.

Correspondence between Goodenough and J. E. Smith (who was a physician as well as a botanist) abounds in intimate detail of health matters in Goodenough's family, his own tendency to gout being uppermost. He and his wife were dealt a hard hand in regard to health: three daughters and two sons died young. Carlisle, with variable weather and often stern winters, did not improve things in terms of most aspects of life; Goodenough needed all his elegance, poise, and philosophy—coupled with moderation, culture, and wisdom tinged with wit—to survive there. His own curiosity hardly ever left him, even though some of his views, for example his staunch support for the preservation of the old social hierarchy, became outmoded. Nor did he ever lose his ability, when well, to enjoy a good table and wine cellar; his cookery book survives at the episcopal residence—Rose Castle, Carlisle—and some recipes, such as 'Bishop Goodenough's pudding', are still in use. His correspondence includes further recipes for food and wine, and notes for exchanges of delicacies; it is not clear how all this affected his gout. Though his spirits generally held up under the strain of illness on top of a demanding existence he took care to appear in gloves when sitting for his portrait, and in correspondence occasionally slipped into what he acknowledged as 'querulous mode' (Dawson, 11.8–9). He could be firm about the limits that he allowed himself in pursuing his enduring interests in botany versus the risks presented to his health:

> Unfortunately being subject to Gout, I fear being made wet, & therefore cannot hunt much for any thing, so that I content myself with sitting in Judgment upon what may be brought home. Natl. History is still ever delightful to me, & I hope & trust ever will; the constant soother of all cares, & opening the most gratifying expectations & best hopes. (Turner, 0.13.7, fol. 134, 19 Dec 1809)

Combined, Carlisle and London provided Goodenough with an immense, ongoing workload. He told J. E. Smith on 22 June 1812: 'Scarcely two nights in the whole winter could I get to bed till near one o'clock in the morning … This must account to you for my being so very little at the Linn[ea]n Society this year' (Dawson, 22.101). As bishop, he lived as a general rule in London, at 14 Berners Street, from November or December until May or June, and spent the remainder of the year at Carlisle. Life there rapidly brought with it scientific and domestic difficulties caused through drunken wagon-drivers, careless servants, and being 6 miles from the nearest market town—and, inconveniently, it was at least a six-day journey from London. Ordinations in the diocese were yearly, generally in July; early summer was usually the busiest time, as Goodenough wrote on 10 August 1819:

> I have been much occupied since I came here, it being my year for visiting & confirming my Diocese—This is now at length well over—I confirm'd some thousands, & had to deliver a Charge to my Clergy at the several visitations. (Dawson, 12.89–90)

He also held public days, receiving all who chose to come at dinner. Judges at state dinners were yet another burden, as could be clerical misconduct and squabbles between curates and their principals. With these undertakings behind him he could possibly have for two months 'a little time for my private affairs—And thus the year goes round' (ibid.).

Goodenough left strong impressions in his diocese. Some sixty years after the bishop's tenure, Ferguson could still recollect his stately presence and commanding figure when he appeared for the first time in Carlisle Cathedral. Both he and his dean, Isaac Milner, were the last of their ranks in Carlisle to wear wigs; a great-great-granddaughter of Goodenough remembered being told by her grandmother of carrying to London the bishop's wigs, which were known as 'Highty, Tighty and Scrub; the first for London and State occasions; the second for official appearances in Carlisle; and Scrub for home wear' (Bouch, 379). The bishop clearly took very seriously matters of propriety in wigs.

In addition to his principal interests as a botanist in non-cultivated lands and waters, Goodenough throughout his later career maintained an equally keen interest in gardening. His correspondence of those times contains comment on both botanical forays and events in the gardens at Rochester and Rose Castle. Potential treatments for alleviating gout by *colchicum autumnale* (sixty drops to be taken) were discussed, as was the recognition of there being bad years for different crops (fruits, cereals, and vegetables). Many necessary Rose Castle supplies derived directly from the gardens and fields of glebe lands associated with the house, but as Goodenough commented from Carlisle 'no one here knows the difference between a thistle and a sunflower' (Dawson, 12.171–2, 20 July 1824).

Goodenough's last two years were dolorous and passed mainly in London, although, in attempts to recuperate, he made trips to Brighton, in 1826, and Worthing, in 1827. He was very ill for much of the time and, unable to walk without sticks or crutches, unable also to attend any meetings of learned societies. In his last letter to J. E. Smith, on 16 May 1827, he wrote: 'I fear I shall not be able to go to Rose Castle this year', and that his wife was 'exceedingly ill & confined to her room, & we are alarmed' (Dawson, 12.202–3). She predeceased him by just eleven weeks, and died in Berners Street, London, on 26 May 1827. He himself was found dead in bed at Worthing, where he had gone to achieve some ease, on 12 August 1827, perhaps having applied his usual remedy: 'He disapproved of lowering medicines and ordered port and brandy for his patients' (Walker, 12).

Goodenough was 'one of the best-loved men of his time' (Walker, 12). He on the whole dealt wisely with his fellow men, and his wit and culture were characteristically productive of humour and respect. He was buried on 18 August, next to his friend William Markham, archbishop of York, beneath a black marble slab, in the north cloister of Westminster Abbey. He is commemorated by the plant *Goodenia* J. E. Smith. JAMES H. PRICE

Sources W. R. Dawson, ed., *The Smith papers* (1934), vol. 1 of *Catalogue of the manuscripts in the library of the Linnean Society of London* (1934–48) [224 letters from Goodenough to J. E. Smith, 31 Jan 1785–16 May 1827, in vols. 11–12, and 22 of the MSS; content summaries amplified by M. Walker, MSS] · D. Turner, correspondence, Trinity Cam. [index vol. 0.13.1–0.13.9 (Jan 1790–Dec 1811) letters Goodenough to Dawson Turner, 11 Feb 1799 to 21 Jan 1811] · S. Goodenough, correspondence, RBG Kew · botanical memoranda I and II, RBG Kew, Turner papers · S. Goodenough, 'The cookery book of Bishop Goodenough, bishop of Carlisle, 1808–1827', unpublished MS, priv. coll. [Rose Castle, Carlisle] · M. Walker, 'Samuel Goodenough (1743–1827): the botanist bishop', *The Linnean*, 11/4 (1996), 9–12 · J. Burgess, *The lake counties and Christianity: the religious history of Cumbria, 1780–1920* (1984) · C. M. L. Bouch, *Prelates and people of the lake counties: a history of the diocese of Carlisle, 1133–1933* (1948) · R. S. Ferguson, *Diocesan histories: Carlisle* (1889) · M. Milner, *The life of Isaac Milner*, 2nd edn (1844) · *GM*, 1st ser., 97/1 (1827), 571 · *GM*, 1st ser., 97/2 (1827), 366–7 · *DNB* · J. H. Martindale, '[Proceedings summer meeting] Wednesday, July 13th, 1927. [Visit to] Rose Castle [Dalston, Carlisle; official residence of the bishop of Carlisle]', *Transactions of the Cumberland and Westmorland Antiquarian and Archaeological Society*, new ser., 28 (1927–8), 396–400 · C. J. Abbey, *The English church and its bishops, 1700–1800*, 2 vols. (1887) · [F. Jollie], *Jollie's Cumberland guide & directory* (1811)

Archives Linn. Soc., corresp. and papers · Linn. Soc., corresp. with Sir James Smith · Linn. Soc., letters to Thomas Woodward · NHM, algae · NHM, drawings of *Carex* · priv. coll., cookery book · RBG Kew, corresp. and herbarium · Trinity Cam., letters to D. Turner · Tullie House Museum, Carlisle, algae specimens · U. Nott. L., papers and letters to duke of Portland · Yorkshire Philosophical Society Museum, York, specimens

Likenesses J. Northcote, oils, 1810, Christ Church Oxf.; repro. in Walker, 'Samuel Goodenough', 10 · H. H. Meyer, mezzotint, 1811 (after J. Northcote, 1810), Linn. Soc. [*see illus.*] · portrait, Hunt Botanical Library, Pittsburgh, Pennsylvania

Goodenough, Sir William Edmund (1867–1945), naval officer, was born on 2 June 1867 in lodgings on the Hard, Portsmouth, the second of the two sons of Captain James Graham *Goodenough (1830–1875) and his wife, Victoria Henrietta Hamilton (*d.* 1917). His father became commodore and senior officer of the Australia station and was killed by natives in the Santa Cruz Islands in the Pacific Ocean in 1875. His mother's brother became tenth Lord Belhaven and Stenton, and William John *Hamilton was her father. F. C. Goodenough, the banker, was a first cousin. Goodenough went to the *Britannia* as a naval cadet in January 1880, and in December 1881 joined the *Northampton* on the North America and West Indies station, being promoted midshipman in October 1882. He remained in her for over four years, and then joined the *Calypso* (training squadron). After promotion to sub-lieutenant in October 1886 he went to the *Excellent* gunnery school.

From March 1888 to May 1889 Goodenough served in the *Raleigh*, Cape of Good Hope station, with a short period as acting lieutenant in the *Brisk*. He was then sent home to take up appointment as sub-lieutenant in the *Victoria and Albert* and was promoted to lieutenant in August 1889.

Over the next eleven years Goodenough served in the *Trafalgar*, the *Surprise* (commander-in-chief's yacht), both

Sir William Edmund Goodenough (1867–1945), by Walter Stoneman, 1919

in the Mediterranean, and the *Hermione*, China station. In June 1900 he was promoted commander in the *Resolution*, Channel Fleet. In October 1901 her whole crew was turned over to the newly built *Formidable* which was commissioned at Portsmouth for duty on the Mediterranean station. Goodenough remained there for three years, being promoted captain on 1 January 1905. On 12 June 1901 he married Henrietta Margaret (*d.* 1956), daughter of Edward Lyulph *Stanley who became fourth Baron Sheffield and fourth Baron Stanley of Alderley. They had two daughters.

The new scheme of naval education announced by Lord Selborne at the end of 1902 reduced the age of entry of cadets from 14½–15½ to 12–13, and required a period of four years' training on shore. This required a great expansion of education facilities. In 1905 Goodenough was selected to head the new college at Dartmouth to replace the old *Britannia* training ship. He wrote in his memoirs of the difficulties with this post, with the building having faults caused by 'the traditional saving of a ha'porth of tar' (Goodenough, 61), and differences in approach between himself and the headmaster, Cyril Ashford. Particularly irksome to Goodenough was Ashford's wish to relate to the masters as 'colleagues' rather than in accordance with a services hierarchy Goodenough believed was necessary to instil into their young cadets. He remained at Dartmouth until August 1907 when he joined the *Albemarle* as flag captain to Sir John Jellicoe in the Atlantic Fleet for a year and then went to the *Duncan* as flag captain to Sir George Callaghan, second in command of the Mediterranean Fleet, until August 1910.

After short periods in command of the *Cochrane*, in which Goodenough escorted George V to the Indian durbar and was appointed MVO, and of the *Colossus*, 2nd battle squadron of the Grand Fleet, in July 1913 he was appointed to the *Southampton* as commodore (second class) of the 1st light cruiser squadron.

At the beginning of the war, in the action in the Heligoland bight on 28 August 1914, Goodenough with six light cruisers under him took a large part in the fighting including sinking the light cruiser *Mainz*. He was next in action during the German raid on Scarborough in December 1914, when in low visibility he got to within 3000 yards of a German light cruiser, part of a large force, when a misunderstanding over a signal to other ships caused him to break off his contact. This cost the opportunity for the British to inflict serious damage on the enemy fleet, and Goodenough received a great deal of blame for this, perhaps unfairly. His position seems only to have been saved by Churchill's intervention.

Things went somewhat better six weeks later, when in attempting a similar undertaking the German battle cruisers were caught off the Dogger Bank on 24 January 1915, and only escaped at the cost of severe damage and the loss of the *Blücher*. In the following May, on the advent of some new light cruisers to the Grand Fleet, Goodenough's squadron was renamed the 2nd light cruiser squadron. In command of it and with his broad pennant still in the *Southampton*, he took part in the battle of Jutland, and was commended in dispatches for his tenacity in maintaining touch with and reporting the movements of enemy heavy ships. His bravery and persistence in the action has been held up as a 'model for scouting admirals' (Marder, 3.63). It was from the *Southampton* that the presence of the German battle fleet, coming up to support the action begun an hour earlier, was first reported to Jellicoe and Beatty. The squadron became heavily engaged in a night action with German light forces, in the course of which the *Southampton* sustained very heavy damage and casualties but sank the German light cruiser *Frauenlob*.

Goodenough was promoted to flag rank soon after Jutland, appointed CB in 1916, and in December of that year transferred to the *Orion* as rear-admiral of the 2nd battle squadron until the end of the war. Promoted KCB at the new year, 1919, in May he became admiral superintendent of Chatham Dockyard, and a year later was made commander-in-chief, Africa station, being promoted to vice-admiral in July 1920.

In August 1922 Goodenough returned home and, after a short period in command of the Reserve Fleet, in March 1924 he was appointed commander-in-chief at the Nore for a term of three years, being promoted admiral in May 1925. For seven months before his retirement in May 1930 he served as first and principal naval aide-de-camp to the king, and was advanced to GCB at the new year.

For his war service Goodenough was appointed to the order of St Vladimir, third class with swords, and the order of the Rising Sun of Japan, second class, and was awarded the French Croix de Guerre (bronze palm). After retirement he revived the great interest he had taken in the Royal Geographical Society. His maternal grandfather had several times been president and his great-grandfather, William Richard Hamilton, was one of the founders. Goodenough was a fellow of the society from 1897, a member of its council in 1924–7 and 1939–42, vice-president in 1933–9 and from 1943, and president in 1930–33. In this role he was said to be 'always ready to defend the cause of primitive peoples exposed to contact with more advanced civilization' (Clerk, 79), and he was a supporter of the Melanesian mission and the Fairbridge farm schools. The society prospered under his presidency and it was said that among 'the many great names in our records there is none who has a greater claim to be held in lasting and loving memory' (Clerk, 79). Goodenough was also chairman of the British Sailors' Society, on whose behalf he addressed letters to *The Times*, urging the need for improving the conditions of the merchant service, and he represented the corporation of London on the Port of London Authority.

Goodenough was throughout his navy career a highly competent and distinguished seaman, 'a superb tactician' (Marder, 1.408) who was also 'more talkative than most of his kind … full of enthusiasm' (ibid., 2.13), and he received great respect from both the officers and men in the vessels he commanded. Towards the end of his career he began to express a great deal of criticism of the administration of the Admiralty. But when in 1925, on the death of the second sea lord, Sir Michael Culme-Seymour, he was invited by W. C. Bridgeman to take his place on the board, Goodenough declined this opportunity to redress some of the faults he had perceived. Goodenough died at his home, Parson's Pightle, Coulsdon, Surrey, on 30 January 1945.

V. W. BADDELEY, *rev.* MARC BRODIE

Sources W. E. Goodenough, *A rough record* (1943) · A. J. Marder, *From the Dreadnought to Scapa Flow: the Royal Navy in the Fisher era, 1904–1919*, 5 vols. (1961–70) · *The Times* (31 Jan 1945) · G. R. Clerk, 'Admiral Sir William Edmund Goodenough', *GJ*, 105 (1945), 78–9 · Burke, *Peerage* · *CGPLA Eng. & Wales* (1945) · personal knowledge (1959) · private information (1959)

Archives BL OIOC, corresp. with F. M. Bailey, MS Eur. F 157 · Bodl. RH, corresp. with Lord Lugard | FILM IWM FVA, actuality footage | SOUND IWM SA, oral history interview

Likenesses F. Dodd, charcoal and watercolour drawing, 1917, IWM · W. Stoneman, two photographs, 1919–31, NPG [*see illus.*] · A. S. Cope, group portrait, oils, 1921 (*Naval officers of World War I, 1914–1918*), NPG · photograph, repro. in *The Times*

Wealth at death £28,098 7*s.* 8*d.*: probate, 1 May 1945, *CGPLA Eng. & Wales*

Goodenough, Sir William Macnamara, first baronet (1899–1951), banker, was born in London on 10 March 1899, the eldest son of Frederick Craufurd *Goodenough (1866–1934), banker, and his wife, Maive, fifth daughter of Nottidge Charles Macnamara FRCS of Calcutta and London. He was educated at Wellington College, where he was captain of cricket and rackets, and head of the school. In January 1918 he obtained a commission in the Coldstream Guards, serving briefly in France.

After demobilization Goodenough went as a history scholar to Christ Church, Oxford, obtaining a second class in the final honours school in 1922. In his last year at Oxford he was master of the Christ Church beagles, and further developed an already great interest in hounds, their breeding, and their work, which remained with him throughout his life. In later years he became a joint master of the Vale of White Horse (Cricklade) hunt. He married in 1924 Dorothea Louisa (*d.* 1987), eldest daughter of the Ven. the Hon. Kenneth Francis Gibbs, archdeacon of St Albans.

The couple had four sons, one of whom died in infancy, and one daughter.

Immediately on going down from Oxford, Goodenough joined the staff of Barclays Bank Ltd, of which his father had been chairman since 1917. After a short period in London he was appointed in 1923 a local director at Oxford; in 1929 he became a director of Barclays, in 1934 a vice-chairman, and in 1936 deputy chairman. In 1925 Goodenough's father formed Barclays Bank (Dominion, Colonial, and Overseas) (DCO) to serve as the overseas arm of the parent bank. Of this William Goodenough became a director in 1933, a year before his father's death. In 1937 he became deputy chairman and in 1943 was elected to the chair. About this time he also became chairman of the Export Guarantees Advisory Council, and of the executive committee of the export credit guarantee department. In 1947, on the sudden death of Edwin Fisher, Barclays incumbent chairman, Goodenough was elected chairman of the board of Barclays Bank and relinquished his post, but not his interest, in Barclays DCO. After the death of his father, Barclays had required the two posts to be separated.

It was inevitable that throughout his career Goodenough should be compared with his dominating father, from whom he differed completely in temperament. He was by nature a conciliator—a trait that made him much in demand on committees of all kinds. Moreover, in spite of his enthusiasm for field sports, he lacked his father's robust physique. In 1944, walking in blacked-out London, he stepped into what seemed a puddle but was in fact a small, but deep and cold, bomb crater. The weight of his heavy overcoat pulled him down, and he had a narrow escape from drowning. From 1948 Goodenough's health was uncertain, but he was fully involved in Barclays affairs: improving staff terms and conditions, planning a new head office building, dealing with the worrying vicissitudes of the fluctuating value of gilts, and establishing a general purposes committee to give strategic direction to the bank. Neither he nor any other banker could prevail against the governor of the Bank of England and the Capital Issues Committee on the question of a new rights issue, as times had changed since his father's day. Nevertheless, Barclays Overseas Development Corporation (1945) was his brainchild and that of Julian Crossley, established by their persistent lobbying of government offices and the Bank of England.

Goodenough had agricultural interests stemming from the family estate of Filkins, Oxfordshire, and a close association with the National Farmers' Union; and his early local prominence resulted in his being a member of Oxfordshire county council from 1927, and its chairman from 1934 to 1939. He also served as a member of the departmental committee on agricultural education set up in 1941 by the Ministry of Agriculture and Fisheries. He served as a valued curator of the Oxford University Chest from 1931 at a time when the university's finances were overhauled, and undertook a great deal of additional charitable work. In addition, Goodenough was a moving spirit in the foundation of the Oxford Society.

Barclays, through its Oxford offices, had a long and mutually respectful association with William Morris, later Lord Nuffield, and Will Goodenough became Nuffield's trusted adviser in his medical and other foundations, giving practical direction to Nuffield's sometimes impulsive first thoughts. Goodenough thus became chairman of the interdepartmental committee on medical schools, of the Nuffield Provincial Hospitals Trust, and, in 1943, of the Nuffield Foundation. Goodenough also carried forward his father's interest in the Dominion Fellowship Trust, becoming its chairman too in 1943. Under the auspices of the trust his father had established a hall of residence for postgraduate male students from the dominions and colonies; and, after the Second World War, Will Goodenough founded a sister trust designed to provide similar facilities for women and married students, including students from the United States. The new hall of residence was named William Goodenough House. These extra administrative burdens were practicable only because until 1947 the trust was run from Barclays DCO's head office. Goodenough was created a baronet in 1943, and his work for the University of Oxford was recognized by the offer of an honorary DCL, which his untimely death prevented him from receiving. He had been elected an honorary student of Christ Church in 1947, was for many years a governor of Wellington College, and received an honorary LLD from Manchester in 1949.

Goodenough was reluctant to retire from Barclays, but in 1951 ill health and medical opinion compelled him to do so. He died from heart disease only a few weeks later, on 23 May 1951, at his home, Filkins Hall, Filkins, Witney, Oxfordshire. He was succeeded in the baronetcy by his eldest son, Richard Edmund.

DOUGLAS VEALE and CUTHBERT FITZHERBERT, *rev.* MARGARET ACKRILL

Sources P. W. Matthews, *History of Barclays Bank Limited*, ed. A. W. Tuke (1926) • A. W. Tuke and R. J. H. Gillman, *Barclays Bank Limited, 1926–1969: some recollections* (1972) • J. Crossley and J. Blandford, *The DCO story: a history of banking in many countries, 1925–71* (1975) • *The Times* (24 May 1951) • *A bank in battle dress* (privately printed, Cape Town, 1948), 139 • Barclays Bank archives, Wythenshawe, Cheshire, diaries of Sir Julian Crossley • Barclays Bank archives, Wythenshawe, Cheshire, board minutes, Barclays DCO 1951 • Barclays Bank archives, Wythenshawe, Cheshire, board minutes, Barclays Bank 1951 • M. Adeney, *Nuffield: a biography* (1993) • *Hist. U. Oxf.* 8: *20th cent.* • *CGPLA Eng. & Wales* (1951) • d. cert.

Archives Barclays Bank archives, Wythenshawe, Manchester

Likenesses O. Edis, photograph, 1931, NPG • J. Gunn, oils, *c.*1948, Barclays Bank, London • J. Gunn, portrait, Filkins Hall, Witney, Oxfordshire

Wealth at death £147,887 9*s.* 4*d.*: probate, 24 Aug 1951, *CGPLA Eng. & Wales*

Goodere, Sir Henry (1534–1595), member of parliament and soldier, was the eldest son of Francis Goodere (*d.* 1546), gentleman, of Polesworth, Warwickshire, and Ursula, daughter of Ralph Rowlett. He married Frances, daughter of Hugh Lowther of Lowther, Westmorland, and had two daughters, Frances and Anne. His family connections included Sir Nicholas Bacon, Sir William Cecil, and Sir Philip Sidney. Goodere, who inherited Polesworth and Baginton, Warwickshire, from his father in December

1546, was educated at Gray's Inn (1555). He became a member of Queen Elizabeth's household in 1558, and six years later was described as the 'Queen's servant'. From 1563 he was a justice of the peace of the quorum in Warwickshire, where he also served on other commissions from the 1560s. In 1563–1566/7 he represented Stafford in parliament. When, in response to privy council instructions in 1564, the bishop of Coventry and Lichfield conducted a survey of JPs in his diocese, he sent for Goodere to confer with him. He also described him as one of the 'Good men and miet to continew in office' (Bateson, 46). In his political and religious position Goodere was sound and in favour: the image was that of the loyal and responsible country gentleman. The flight to England of the deposed Mary Stuart in 1568, however, altered his reputation and threatened to destroy his prospects. He personally welcomed her on her arrival in England, became involved in the duke of Norfolk's scheme to marry her, and devised a cipher for her use.

In 1571, when Goodere was returned to parliament for Coventry, he made himself unpopular in the House of Commons. On 7 April he declared that every man should freely offer the queen a subsidy without waiting until it was requested, 'wherein', a member wrote, 'sure hee shewed a greate desire to winne favour' (Hartley, 1.203). Five days later he launched a vigorous attack on the Treasons Bill and Thomas Norton's addition, which were designed to harm Mary Stuart's person and her place in the succession. Later, in September that year, as Norfolk's dealings with Mary were investigated, Goodere was conveyed to the Tower. Under interrogation he protested his innocence, maintaining that he had met Mary only once, when she talked about 'a spaniel, the weather, the redness of her hand, and … her innocency' (*Salisbury MSS*, 1.536). He too protested that he was innocent of treason, and in July 1572 he besought Burghley to ease the conditions of his imprisonment and allow his wife to be with him. It was appropriate that, as patron of the poet Michael Drayton, Goodere should defend himself in a poem written in the Tower—a poem to which Norton replied in a scathing parody. Although Norfolk had been executed in June 1572, no case could be made against Goodere, who was released later that year.

Gradually, over the following decade, Goodere worked his way back into general acceptance and royal approval. In 1576 he was bold enough to petition the queen and Lord Treasurer Burghley for a monopoly in printed playing cards. In 1582 he obtained the stewardship of Sutton Coldfield. It was war, however, which restored Goodere to political respectability. He was captain of horse in the earl of Leicester's expedition to the Low Countries; in 1586 he was captain of Leicester's guard; on 7 October 1586, after the battle of Zutphen, he was knighted by the earl; and in 1587 he commanded a body of infantry in the attempt to relieve Sluys and became captain of the yeomen of the guard. In July 1588, back in England, he was one of seven colonels appointed to defend the queen in face of the impending Spanish Armada. Goodere's rehabilitation, after his dalliance in Mary Stuart's cause, was also reflected in his administrative responsibilities. He was high sheriff of Warwickshire (1591) and a member of county commissions to raise a special loan in Warwickshire and Coventry (1589), disband returning soldiers (1591), and take the oaths of JPs, muster soldiers, and search out seminarians and recusants (1592). For much of his life he was employer, friend, and patron of the poet Michael Drayton. Goodere died at Polesworth on 4 March 1595.

MICHAEL A. R. GRAVES

Sources B. H. Newdigate, *Michael Drayton and his circle*, new edn (1961) · BL, Lansdowne MSS, 3, no. 89; 14, no. 16; 15, no. 78; 23, no. 88; 75, no. 65; 79, no. 17 · HoP, *Commons, 1558–1603* · T. E. Hartley, ed., *Proceedings in the parliaments of Elizabeth I*, 1 (1981) · *CSP dom.*, *1547–94; addenda, 1566–79* · *VCH Warwickshire*, vols. 1–2 · *JHC*, 1 (1547–1628) · *DNB* · *APC*, *1591–3* · *CPR*, *1563–6; 1575–84* · *Calendar of the manuscripts of the most hon. the marquis of Salisbury*, 1, HMC, 9 (1883) · M. Bateson, ed., 'A collection of original letters from the bishops to the privy council, 1564', *Camden miscellany, IX*, CS, new ser., 53 (1893) · M. A. R. Graves, *Thomas Norton: the parliament man* (1994) · *Sir John Harington's A new discourse of a stale subject, called the metamorphosis of Ajax*, ed. E. S. Donno (1962) · will, PRO, PROB 11/85, sig. 30
Archives BL, Lansdowne MSS, corresp.

Goodere, Sir Henry (*bap.* **1571**, *d.* **1627**), landowner and courtier, was the only son of Sir William Goodere (*d.* after 1607) of Monks Kirby, Warwickshire, and of Berkshire, and his wife, Mary (*fl.* 1560–*c.*1571), the daughter and heiress of Christopher Wren, alias John Wren, of Kent, and widow of Andrew Brooke (*d.* 1569) of Monks Kirby. According to Gosse, Goodere was baptized on 21 August 1571. Sir William was the youngest of the sons of Francis Goodere (*d.* 1546) of Polesworth, Warwickshire, and was therefore the brother of Sir Henry *Goodere (1534–1595).

Henry Goodere the younger matriculated as a fellow-commoner of St John's College, Cambridge, in 1587, and was admitted to the Middle Temple in London on 23 April 1589. In 1593 he married his first cousin Frances Goodere (*b.* before 1571, *d.* 1606), Sir Henry's elder daughter and coheir. She and he inherited the Polesworth estate, encumbered by debts, on her father's death in 1595. Their inheritance was disputed by the widow of Francis Goodere's second son, whose litigation was continued until November 1606 by her son, a third Henry Goodere. By the time the suit was dismissed Frances was dead or dying. She left five young children.

In 1599 Goodere was knighted by the earl of Essex in Ireland (his knighthood has led to his being confused with a fourth Henry Goodere, of Newgate Street, Hertfordshire, a cousin of the Polesworth family, who was knighted in 1608). He appears to have been paying court to James VI before the death of Elizabeth I: in a letter of 1603 or 1604 he referred to 'some yeares' (Cass, 150) in which he had been reminding James of his uncle's service to Mary Stuart and pressing his own claims to the royal generosity, and he later remembered that the king had 'receaved mee before almost all others into his service and care' (Newdigate, 81). He became a gentleman of the privy chamber in May 1603, and took part in the masque for new year's day 1604. Later the same year he became MP for West Looe, probably through the Cecil interest. In April and May of 1605 he attended the earl of Hertford on his embassy to Brussels. About the same time he was granted part of the income from the forfeited estates of his kinsman John Somerville. In January 1606 he was one of the richly accoutred champions who fought at barriers as part of Ben Jonson's masque *Hymenaei*. Goodere also continued asking for money, though without much success: within a fortnight of the splendours of *Hymenaei*, he had obtained a conditional promise of a share of the property confiscated from a man accused of sheep stealing, and a letter from him in the same week refers to a grant from the estates of certain recusants which, like that from Somerville's estates, had apparently brought him no profit at all.

Goodere's life at this time was not given up entirely to court affairs. By 1602 he had formed an important friendship with John Donne, which continued until his death. The two men corresponded frequently—between 1608 and 1613 Donne seems to have been writing Goodere weekly letters and receiving at least as many as he wrote—and intimately. Goodere's side of the correspondence is lost, but about forty-eight of Donne's letters survive. From these we know that Goodere read a number of Donne's poems in manuscript, including the lost Latin epigrams, together with at least some of the *Problems*, a sermon, some of the notes for *Pseudo-Martyr*, and a lost collection of cases of conscience; apparently he also lent Donne books, perhaps a good number of them, as a letter of Donne's written about 1608 refers to 'my study (which your books make a pretty library)' (Gosse, 1.195). Goodere commended Donne to Lord Hay, and knew his patrons the countesses of Bedford and Huntingdon well. Part of an important extant manuscript of Donne's poems was copied by him.

Goodere also befriended other poets. Michael Drayton, who had enjoyed the patronage of Goodere's uncle and was devoted to his sister-in-law Anne Raynsford, dedicated two of *Englands Heroicall Epistles* to him, and two more to his wife, in 1597. As late as 1619 Drayton dedicated his 'Lyrick Pieces' to Goodere, with an ode recalling his hospitality and the music of the harper 'Which oft at *Powlsworth* by the fire Hath made us gravely merry' (M. Drayton, *Works*, 1931–41, 2.344). Jonson visited Polesworth too, and commemorated Goodere's hawking (to which Donne also refers several times) in one epigram, and his library in another. Goodere met regularly at the Mitre tavern with Christopher Brooke, Donne, John Hoskyns, Hugh Holland, Inigo Jones, Thomas Coryate, and others. The best-known piece of his own poetry is the verse letter he wrote in alternating stanzas with Donne at Polesworth, which begins 'Since ev'ry Tree beginns to blossome now' (Donne, *Satires, Epigrams and Verse Letters*, 1967, 76–8). Goodere's other verses were, apart from prefatory poems in Drayton's *Matilda* (1594) and Coryate's *Crudities* (1611), largely courtly: they include an elegy on Prince Henry, published in the third edition of Josuah Sylvester's *Lachrymae lachrymarum* in 1613; epithalamia for Princess Elizabeth in 1613, and for the then marquess of Buckingham in 1620; poems on Prince Charles's journey to Spain in 1623 (adapted from a prose letter of Donne's) and on his return; and a poem addressed to the marquess of Hamilton in 1624 or 1625 as part of a bid to obtain Buckingham's patronage through his intercession.

Goodere's life at court was expensive, and aimless enough to disturb Donne, who urged him in 1608 to 'make … to yourself some mark, and go towards it alegrement', and spoke of his need for 'constancy' (Gosse, 1.192). Goodere did not heed this advice, and ran steadily into debt. As early as 1611 he needed a royal guarantee of immunity from his creditors. About 1614 he was toying with the idea of marrying a rich widow, but nothing came of this. As his daughters grew up he found it difficult to provide for marriage portions for them; Lady Bedford helped to make up the portion of the eldest, her god-daughter Lucy, who married Sir Francis *Nethersole in 1620. In 1618 Goodere sold his manor of Baginton, and by 1623 he was claiming that he was trying to sell Polesworth. His son John ran into money troubles of his own, and was helped by Donne and Selden when he was imprisoned for some small debts in 1622; he died two years later. In 1626 Sir Henry petitioned to be made a gentleman usher of the queen's privy chamber, in terms which suggest that what he most wanted from the position was board and lodging. After his death on 18 March 1627, his daughters, Nethersole, and the sureties for his debts were granted immunity from his creditors. Sir Tobie Matthew remembered that he 'was ever pleasant and kind, and gave me much of his pleasant conversation … But if his constancy had been as great as his nature was good, he had been much happier' (*True Historical Relation*, 1904, 85–6). JOHN CONSIDINE

Sources 'Goodyer, Sir Henry (?1571–1627), of Polesworth, Warws.', HoP, *Commons, 1604–29* [draft] • B. H. Newdigate, *Michael Drayton and his circle* (1941) • E. Gosse, *The life and letters of John Donne, dean of St Paul's*, 2 vols. (1899) • R. C. Bald, *John Donne: a life*, ed. W. Milgate (1970) • F. C. Cass, *Monken Hadley* (1880) • *CSP dom., 1603–28* • *Calendar of the manuscripts of the most hon. the marquis of Salisbury*, 24 vols., HMC, 9 (1883–1976), vols. 16–18, 21, 24 • S. Johnson, 'Sir Henry Goodere and Donne's letters', *Modern Language Notes*, 63/1 (1948), 38–43 • D. Kay, 'Poems by Sir Walter Aston, and a date for the Donne / Goodyer verse epistle "alternis vicibus"', *Review of English Studies*, 37 (1986), 198–210 • *The letters of John Chamberlain*, ed. N. E. McClure, 2 vols. (1939) • P. Beal, 'John Donne', *Index of English literary manuscripts*, ed. P. J. Croft and others, 1/1 (1980) • D. Kay, *Melodious tears: the English funeral elegy from Spenser to Milton* (1990) • Venn, *Alum. Cant.*

Archives BL, Add. MS 23229 • PRO, SP 9/51, SP 14/153/112, SP 14/180/15–17

Wealth at death died seriously in debt; estate would, if unencumbered, have been worth thousands of pounds, but debts probably substantially exceeded its value

Goodere, Samuel (1687–1741), naval officer and murderer, was born in Charleton, Worcestershire, the youngest son of the three sons and a daughter of Sir Edward Goodere, third baronet (*b.* in or after 1649, *d.* 1739), of Burhope, Herefordshire, and his wife, Eleanor, daughter and heir of Sir Edward Dineley, baronet, of Charleton, Worcestershire. The eldest son, Henry, having been killed in a duel the second son, John Dineley Goodere, abandoned his former profession as a merchant seaman, as Sir Edward Dineley wished to acknowledge him as his heir. Samuel Goodere attended school at Henly, Worcestershire, and entered the navy on the *Ipswich*, under Captain Kirktowne; he served in subordinate ranks and afterwards as a lieutenant through the War of the Spanish Succession. On 12 January 1719 he was appointed first lieutenant on the *Preston* with Captain Robert Johnson, whom, on 28 February, he accompanied to the *Weymouth*. They served during the summer on operations off the north coast of Spain, and in November, with Johnson and most of the crew, were assigned to the *Deptford*. A few weeks later, however, Johnson preferred against him a charge of misconduct at St Sebastian on 23 June, alleging that the attack had failed in consequence. Goodere was tried by court martial on 24 December, found guilty, and dismissed his ship, which, in the peace then beginning, was tantamount to being dismissed the service. In 1723 he married, apparently for the second time, as both were described as widowed; his wife was Elizabeth (*d.* 1742), *née* Watts, formerly of Monmouthshire. Twin sons were born in 1729, Edward, who died a lunatic in 1761, and John Dineley-Goodere (*d.* 1809) [*see* Dineley, Sir John, fifth baronet], and three daughters.

Goodere probably did not serve at sea again until November 1733, when he succeeded in getting posted to the *Antelope*, where he was superseded after two weeks. At this time it seems that Samuel was living with his aged father, who was at variance with his elder son John, heir to the baronetcy and described as rough, uncouth, and uneducated. The brothers were already on bad terms and the situation worsened when John, having quarrelled with his wife, found her supported by Samuel. Sir Edward died on 29 March 1739, leaving more to Samuel than John considered fair, but less than Samuel expected. The result was an angry quarrel. John, now Sir John, joining with his son, who was of age, cut off the entail, and, on his son's death shortly after, announced his intention of leaving the property to John Foote, son of his sister Eleanor, wife of Samuel Foote of Truro and mother of the dramatist Samuel Foote. Samuel Goodere's rage was excessive, and for some months the brothers held no communication. In November 1740 Samuel was appointed to the command of the *Ruby*, then lying in King's Road, Bristol, and she was still there on Sunday 18 January, when Samuel, being on shore, learned that his brother, Sir John, was dining with a Jarret Smith, an attorney of the city. On this Samuel sent a note to Smith, saying that, having heard his brother was there, he would be glad to meet him. Accordingly in the evening he went to Smith's house, and the two brothers smoked and drank together, and to all appearance made up their quarrel. But, as Sir John was walking towards his lodgings, he was seized by Samuel's orders, carried down to the boat, taken on board the *Ruby*, and confined in a spare cabin, the captain telling the men on deck not to mind his cries, as he was out of his mind, and would have to be watched to prevent his attempting his own life. Two men, a Mr Mahoney and a Charles White, were chosen to attend the prisoner, and these men, after being well primed with brandy, and on the promise of large rewards, went into the cabin early next morning (19 January 1741), put a rope round Sir John's neck, and strangled him, Samuel meanwhile standing sentry at the door with a drawn sword to prevent any interference. He had apparently intended to put to sea at once, but Jarret Smith, having had information the previous night that a gentleman resembling his guest had been taken a prisoner on board the *Ruby*, applied to the mayor for an investigation. This was made at once. Goodere and his accomplices were apprehended on a charge of wilful murder, were tried on 26 March, found guilty, and sentenced to death. They were all three hanged on 15 April 1741.

Samuel, on the death of his brother John, should have succeeded to the baronetcy. He appears, however, to have been indicted as Samuel Goodere, esquire, and the status of the baronetcy in succeeding years is not entirely clear, though Samuel's twin sons may have been allowed the title by courtesy.

J. K. Laughton, *rev.* Anita McConnell

Sources S. Foote, *The genuine memoirs of Sir J. D. Goodere, who was murder'd by the contrivance of his own brother on board the Ruby … Jan. 19, 1740–1* [1741] · J. Burke and J. B. Burke, *A genealogical and heraldic history of the extinct and dormant baronetcies of England, Ireland, and Scotland* (1838), 220–21 · L. Stone, *Broken lives: separation and divorce in England, 1660–1857* (1993)

Archives Bristol RO, material relating to his murder of Sir John Dineley Goodere

Likenesses R. Grave, line engraving, BM, NPG; repro. in J. Caulfield, *Portraits, memoirs and characters of remarkable persons*, 4 vols. (1819–20)

Goodeve, Sir Charles Frederick (1904–1980), chemist and research administrator, was born on 21 February 1904 in Neepawa, Canada, the third of five children and the eldest of three sons of Frederick William Goodeve, an Anglican priest, and his wife, Emma Hand. When he was ten the family moved to Winnipeg, where he was educated at Kelvin high school. He entered Manitoba University in 1919 as an arts student, transferring to science two years later. During his time at university he joined the Royal Canadian Naval Volunteer Reserve. In 1925 he gained his BSc with honours in chemistry and physics, and for the next two years he held an assistant lectureship, carrying out research into electrolytic problems. In 1927 he obtained an MSc in electrochemistry, and was awarded an 1851 Exhibition scholarship to be held at University College, London.

In London, Goodeve joined Professor F. G. Donnan, who advised him to pursue research into unstable molecules and absorption spectra. This led him into photochemistry and the associated reaction kinetics, and later to work on the physical chemistry of vision. Funding for this research was obtained though close contacts with industry, towards whose problems he orientated many of his investigations. In 1928 Goodeve became an assistant lecturer, in 1930 lecturer, and in 1937 reader in physical chemistry. He was awarded the DSc degree in 1936, and elected a fellow of the Royal Society in 1940. His wife, Janet Irene (*née* Wallace), became a leading member of his research group after first completing a PhD under his supervision. The couple had first met in Manitoba, where Janet was in Goodeve's chemistry classes. After she graduated top of her year Goodeve prevailed on Donnan to provide the funds to enable her to carry out research in London. They married in 1932, the same year that Janet was awarded her doctorate. The couple had two sons, Peter Julian (*b.* 1936) and John Anthony (*b.* 1944).

Throughout this period Goodeve maintained an active involvement with the Royal Naval Volunteer Reserve (RNVR), and after he was promoted to lieutenant-commander in 1936 began to direct some of his research towards naval problems. When war broke out he was appointed to HMS *Vernon*, the mining establishment in Portsmouth. His wartime work has been described at length by Gerald Pawle in *The Secret War* (1956). His first, and probably his major, achievement was in developing measures to counter the threat of magnetic mines. The first of these was the 'double L' sweep method, which used floating electric cables to enhance the magnetic field in the sea sufficiently to detonate mines. The second was the technique known as degaussing, which induced a reverse polarity magnetic field within the ships so that the residual magnetic field above the mine was insufficient to detonate it. During the course of the war the technique was used on more than 10,000 ships, including many of those involved in the evacuation of Dunkirk. In 1952 the Royal Commission on Awards to Inventors awarded him £7500 for this work.

In 1940 Goodeve was transferred to the department of miscellaneous weapon development (DMWD), which was concerned with anti-aircraft weapons and devices. Its two most important achievements were the development of plastic armour and the Hedgehog ahead-thrown anti-submarine weapon. He was appointed OBE in 1941 for this weapons development work, and in 1942 became assistant (later deputy) controller research and development, Admiralty. This was a civilian appointment, and he had to relinquish his naval rank. As compensation he now found himself in charge of the whole strategy of research and development for the navy. Goodeve established the department of Admiralty research and development (India), drawing on his former colleagues in DMWD to identify and study technical problems arising from the war in the Far East. Towards the end of the conflict he played an important role in the establishment of the Royal Naval Scientific Service. In 1946 he was knighted, and awarded the US medal of freedom with silver palm.

In 1945 Goodeve became director of the new British Iron and Steel Research Association (BISRA), a post he held until his retirement in 1969. This organization, financed jointly by the Department of Scientific and Industrial Research and the British Iron and Steel Federation, was envisaged by Goodeve as complementary to the research and development groups which already existed within the larger companies, standing between the different outlooks of university science and industrial laboratories. Goodeve inherited a technical staff of ten from the Iron and Steel Industrial Research Council. He gradually expanded this organization, setting up laboratories for physics, chemistry, plant engineering, and operational research. Additional laboratories were established at centres appropriate to the local steel industry. By 1963 BISRA employed about six hundred staff, and thirty companies were making use of licence agreements for the manufacture and sale of plant and instruments which had arisen from its work. BISRA's greatest achievements under Goodeve's leadership were the development of sinter as a feedstock for blast furnaces, the continuous casting of steel, automatic gauge control of sheet rolling mills, and controlled rolled, low-carbon, high-strength, low-alloy steels—later used in oil and gas pipelines. Throughout his time with BISRA he was an active member of the Iron and Steel Institute (ISI), serving as president in 1961–2. For his services to the industry he was awarded in 1962 the Bessemer gold medal of the ISI and the Carl Leug medal of the Verein Deutscher Eisenhuttenleute.

Goodeve actively promoted organizational efficiency through the development of operational research. BISRA had, from 1946, the first industrial operational research group in the United Kingdom (and possibly the world). He founded the Operational Research Club (which became the Operational Research Society in 1954), and started *Operational Research Quarterly*, the first journal in the field. Goodeve was also active in the foundation of the International Federation of Operational Research Societies in 1957. The Operational Research Society awarded him its silver medal in 1964. He later helped to create, within the Tavistock Institute of Human Relationships, the Institute for Operational Research, and his connections with the institute led to the foundation of the Organization for Promoting Understanding in Society.

In addition to his involvement with BISRA and the ISI, Goodeve played an active role in the wider scientific community, whose social events provided opportunities to indulge his enthusiasm for ballroom dancing. He served as president of the Faraday Society in 1950–52 and the chemistry section of the British Association in 1956, and as a vice-president of the Royal Society in 1968–70 and of the parliamentary and scientific committee in 1950–62. He also acted as scientific adviser to the British Transport Commission in 1948–58 and served as a governor of Imperial College in 1961–73. After 1965 he held appointments as director of three industrial enterprises. He received honorary doctorates from Manitoba (1946), Sheffield (1956), Birmingham (1962), Newcastle (1970), and Salford (1974) universities.

During Goodeve's last years he was stricken with Parkinson's disease, which led to the fall that killed him. He died on 7 April 1980 in the Royal Free Hospital, Hampstead, and was cremated four days later at Golders Green. He was survived by his wife. SALLY M. HORROCKS

Sources F. D. Richardson, *Memoirs FRS*, 27 (1981), 307–53 · G. Pawle, *The secret war* (1956) · C. F. Goodeve, 'Co-operative research in the British iron and steel industry', *The organisation of research establishments*, ed. J. Cockcroft (1965), 168–80 · *The Times* (9 April 1980) · *WW*

Archives CAC Cam., corresp. and papers · UCL, lecture notes | CUL, corresp. with Gordon Sutherland

Wealth at death £4700: probate, 7 July 1980, *CGPLA Eng. & Wales*

Goodey, Tom [*performing name* Roger Clayson] (**1885–1953**), parasitologist and singer, the ninth and last child of Thomas Goodey, boot manufacturer, and his wife, Hannah Clayson (*d.* *c.*1887), was born on 28 July 1885 at Wellingborough, Northamptonshire. He won a scholarship to the Northampton grammar school, which he left in 1904 to become a pupil teacher. He did not enjoy schoolteaching and at the teacher training college of Birmingham University he studied botany and zoology, in which he took the BSc degree with honours in 1908. A discovery about the gastric pouches of the jellyfish, made while he was still an undergraduate, provided his first subject for research, and he next studied the anatomy of the frilled shark. He obtained his MSc degree in 1909 and gained a research scholarship of £50 for one year, with which he went in 1910 to the Rothamsted experimental station in Harpenden, Hertfordshire. He was soon awarded the Mackinnon studentship of the Royal Society of £150 a year. In 1912 Goodey married Constance, daughter of William Henry Lewis, a representative of a colour merchant, whom he had met while both were students at Birmingham. They had one son and four daughters.

Goodey's move to Rothamsted meant changing to a subject which was new to him and full of controversy: whether soil contains protozoa that limit bacterial populations. This aroused interest because of its bearing on soil fertility, and opposition because it conflicted with the general view that the only active organisms in soil were bacteria (Bawden, 142). Goodey showed that *Colpoda cucullus*, then assumed to be the chief protozoan in soil, was normally encysted and inactive there, and he doubted that protozoa were important predators of bacteria, but could not settle the controversy. His studentship expired before he could study other species and he returned to the zoology department at Birmingham University, where he worked on protozoa from various sources. During the First World War he was protozoologist at the 2nd Southern General Hospital at Birmingham.

A return to Rothamsted in 1920 started Goodey on the work with helminths which was to occupy him for the rest of his life. He began with a study of clover-stem eelworm, but this spell as a plant helminthologist was brief, for in 1921 he joined the London School of Tropical Medicine, and over the next five years he worked mainly on parasites of vertebrates. When the Institute of Agricultural Parasitology was set up at St Albans, Goodey became the senior member of staff there, and he held his post until the institute closed in 1947. There he specialized in studying plant-parasitic and free-living eelworms, and the subject which came to be known as nematology, in which he was the acknowledged authority. He published many taxonomic papers in the *Journal of Helminthology*, and his first textbook, *Plant Parasitic Nematodes and the Diseases they Cause* (1933), became a standard work. So, too, did his second textbook, *Soil and Freshwater Nematodes* (1951), which described the morphology, biology, and behaviour of 190 genera; this work was revised by his son, Basil Goodey, in 1963. When the book first appeared, Goodey was head of the newly formed department of nematology at Rothamsted. He retired from this post in 1952, but was still actively engaged in research when he died the following year.

Goodey had an excellent voice and was also a skilled actor. Until 1916 he sang only as an amateur, but as his family responsibilities grew he increasingly accepted professional engagements in oratorio, opera, and in the concert hall, where, as in many broadcast recitals, he specialized in lieder by Schubert and Hugo Wolf, and in English songs. He was long associated with the music of Rutland Boughton, and the part of Angus in *The Ever Young* was written mainly for him. As the publicity from his performances embarrassed him as a scientist, from 1927 he used the stage name of Roger Clayson.

A man of high ideals and standards, scrupulous in all his dealings, Goodey found a spiritual home in the Society of Friends, which he joined in 1933, following the lead set by his wife. His ability to speak powerfully and lucidly contributed to the prominence he gained in the Society; he served as clerk of the Bedfordshire quarterly meeting from 1942 to 1946 and was an elder at the time of his death. Although deeply religious, he was not prudish; indeed his great sense of fun, youthful enthusiasm, and unfailing liveliness made him excellent company.

Goodey had many successes, both as a scientist and as an artist, and these brought him great pleasure—especially his election as a fellow of the Royal Society in 1947. He was appointed OBE in 1950 and was president of the Association of Applied Biologists in 1935–6. Goodey died in Harpenden, on 7 July 1953, while walking home from a meeting of the Society of Friends. He was survived by his wife.

F. C. BAWDEN, *rev.*

Sources F. C. Bawden, *Obits. FRS*, 9 (1954), 141–52 • private information (1971) • personal knowledge (1971) • election certificate, RS

Likenesses W. Stoneman, photograph, 1946, RS, archives, no. 2631 B • W. Stoneman, photograph, 1953, NPG • photograph, repro. in Bawden, *Obits. FRS*

Wealth at death £4585 2*s*. 1*d*.: probate, 19 Aug 1953, *CGPLA Eng. & Wales*

Goodfellow, Sir William (**1880–1974**), businessman and philanthropist, was born on 26 May 1880 at Terarauhi, Alexandra, near Te Awamutu in the district of Waikato, New Zealand, the eldest of the six children of Thomas Goodfellow (1854–1938) and his wife, Jane Grace (1856–1950), the daughter of William Maclaurin, a Presbyterian evangelist in the Waikato. He was a remarkable businessman whose acumen, vision, and energy contributed largely to the shape and direction of the New Zealand dairy industry in the twentieth century.

Goodfellow was of enterprising Scottish extraction: his paternal grandfather, William Goodfellow (1806–1890), arrived in Wellington in 1841, walked the unroaded 400 miles to Auckland, and died in prosperous circumstances in 1890. His father, Thomas, was farming at Paterangi, near the small town of Te Awamutu, when William was born. On his grandfather's death the family moved to Auckland, where William attended Mount Eden primary school and Auckland grammar school. He was not academically inclined but enjoyed his year at the Harle Giles Commercial Business College in preference to university study.

Goodfellow was interested in ironmongery, and his first position in a depressed market was with a ship's chandler, but he was employed the following year with T. Morrison & Co. Ltd, a leading Auckland hardware merchant. At the age of twenty-one he entered into partnership with the Prime brothers, hardware retailers in Onehunga, and set up a base for the firm in Hamilton, where he soon became manager of Grace and Colebrook, the competing local hardward merchant. A year's travel to Europe and the United States broadened his experience of the hardware business and confirmed his understanding of technology.

Goodfellow seized the opportunity presented in 1907 by a defaulting customer, who left him with £1000 of dairy machinery when the nearby Waikato Butter Company was for sale. He purchased the company, converted it from a proprietary to a co-operative, and adapted the machinery. He was early committed to economies of scale: in 1915 his company merged with the Waikato Cheese Company and, as the Waikato Co-operative Dairy Company, offered such strong competition to the other major co-operative in the area that in 1919 it also agreed to a merger, bringing with it the established Anchor brand for its butter. The resulting New Zealand Co-operative Dairy Co. Ltd (NZCDC) went on to accumulate most of the smaller co-operatives of the region, eventually forming the largest dairy co-operative in the country, with a major share of the industry's total output.

As general manager of the NZCDC from 1919 to 1932 and advising director from 1932 to 1948, Goodfellow emphasized effective communication with co-operative members, the adoption of scientific and technological development, and improved quality control. The local broadcasting station he established to maintain contact with isolated suppliers became the New Zealand Broadcasting Service, the country's first national system, with its own supplementary magazine; it was requisitioned by the government on the outbreak of the Second World War. NZCDC was the first New Zealand dairy company with an on-site laboratory and a farm service teaching herd and grass management. To eliminate dependence on external industries, a box factory and a colliery were purchased in 1917 and, in partnership with a major stock and station agent, Goodfellow and his company established the Challenge Phosphate Co. Ltd to reduce fertilizer costs to suppliers.

But it was Goodfellow's firm control of marketing—price fixing, product supply, and brand identification—which became the future model for the industry. In addition, to maximize returns to the supplier, he envisaged bypassing the Tooley Street agents through whom New Zealand co-operatives were competing against each other on the London market. The 1923 dairy produce control board, of which he was a member (1924–8), was created to establish an overall marketing strategy for the industry, but in practice the initiative collapsed with such an erosion of the fixed price that returns for New Zealand dairy produce fell disastrously, and a substantial amount remained unsold. Goodfellow responded by establishing Amalgamated Dairies Ltd to export dairy produce to the Pacific and some other markets. He went on in 1929 to form Empire Dairies Ltd, in partnership with Amalgamated Dairies and the Australian Producers' Co-operative Federation, to sell produce from New Zealand, Australia, and other Commonwealth countries to Britain. He resigned from the dairy produce control board in 1928, discouraged by the market-breaking attitudes of the rest of the industry.

The election of the Labour government in 1935 and the bulk-purchase agreement with Britain at the beginning of the Second World War prevented any further move towards industry-controlled marketing until 1953, when the Dairy Produce Marketing Commission, the selling arm of the dairy board, acquired Goodfellow's Empire Dairies as a wholly owned subsidiary of the board. Goodfellow was further vindicated in 1996, when the dairy board purchased Anchor as an official brand for New Zealand dairy produce.

Goodfellow's far reaching influence on the New Zealand dairy industry included his personal provision of most of the share capital for the journal which became the *New Zealand Dairy Exporter*, purchased outright in 1954 by the dairy board as its official organ. He early advocated large-scale amalgamation of co-operatives and supported the establishment of the Dairy Research Institute, and he constantly preached product diversification, flexibility of factory plant use, and the exploration of non-traditional markets. Renowned for his energy and determination, he was also a director of South British Insurance, the Guardian Trust, and New Zealand Newspapers Ltd, as well as of several smaller enterprises.

Goodfellow married Irene Clarabella Chamberlin (1891–1970) on 22 January 1913; the couple had five sons—Hector, Douglas, Harry, Richard, and Bruce—and one daughter, Marion. His wife died on 18 April 1970, and on 1 June 1971 he married his cousin's widow, Edith Gwendoline Jessie Maclaurin, *née* Creagh (*b.* 1902), through whom he gained a stepdaughter. He was made a freeman of the City of London in 1951, and for services to New Zealand and the dairy industry was appointed KBE (the first to be instituted by the sovereign on New Zealand soil) in 1953. The University of Auckland awarded him an honorary doctorate of law in 1963.

An elder of the Presbyterian church for some years, Goodfellow was a private person whose substantial gifts to the community reflected his deep family commitment. The Maclaurin chapel at Auckland University commemorates both the death of his son Richard in the Second World War and the life of his uncle, the distinguished academic Richard Cockburn Maclaurin; he also established the Richard Maclaurin Goodfellow chaplaincy at the university. Of the three scholarships he endowed at Auckland University, two are in memory of his two brothers killed in the First World War, and his major donation to the Lady

Goodfellow chapel at Waikato University celebrates the life of his first wife. Apart from the gift of a large reserve to the Auckland community, his most generous donation was to the trust of St Kentigern's Presbyterian College for Boys, in which he maintained a deep interest until his death. He died on 5 November 1974 at Auckland Adventist private hospital and was cremated on 8 November at Purewa. MARGARET A. ROWE

Sources A. J. Heighway, *Sir William Goodfellow: his life and work* (1972) [privately printed] • A. H. Ward, *A command of co-operatives* (1975) • N. Watson, *Pioneers of the Waikato dairy industry: Sir William Goodfellow, 1880–1974* (1975) • *Auckland Star* (6 Nov 1974) • *New Zealand Herald* (7 Nov 1974) • *New Zealand Dairy Exporter*, 50/6 (1974) • b. cert. • m. cert. • d. cert.

Archives NL NZ, Turnbull L., New Zealand Dairy Board archives, MSS

Wealth at death even after major gifts to community, very wealthy

Goodford, Charles Old (1812–1884), headmaster, second son of John Goodford JP (*d.* 1835), deputy lieutenant of Chilton Cantelo, Somerset, and Charlotte, fourth daughter of Montague Cholmeley of Easton, Lincolnshire, was born at Chilton Cantelo on 15 July 1812, and entered Eton College in 1826. He proceeded to King's College, Cambridge, in 1830, whence he took his BA in 1836, MA in 1839, and DD in 1853. In 1834 he was elected a fellow of his college, but forfeited his fellowship following his marriage on 28 March 1844 to Katharine Lucia, third daughter of George Law of Lincoln's Inn. While still an undergraduate he returned to Eton and became an assistant master in 1835. It was not long before he succeeded his former tutor, John Wilder, in charge of a large and important schoolhouse, in which a number of the resident boys were from his own and the adjacent counties. 'An amiable West Country man with a trace of a West Country accent, and a respected teacher' (Card, 6), he was a liberal and kind housemaster, but his management was not equal to his good intentions.

In 1853 Goodford succeeded E. C. Hawtrey as headmaster at Eton. His rule on the whole was beneficial to the college. He aimed at a very complete reconstruction of the system of teaching; he made discipline a reality, while he abolished many unpopular rules which had needlessly restricted liberty; he would have done more but for Hawtrey's veto as provost. These innovations, however, proved insufficient to avert the public criticisms of Eton which preceded the appointment of the royal commission into public schools in 1861. In 1854 Goodford edited the comedies of Terence, a work which he printed chiefly to present as a leaving book to his sixth-form boys.

On the death of Dr Hawtrey, Lord Palmerston, who was hostile to the high-church leanings of the other eligible candidates, appointed Goodford provost of Eton, a position which he held from 27 January 1862 to his death. This appointment was made in ignorance of the needs of Eton, and much against Goodford's own wishes, for the income was smaller than that attached to the headmastership and he had a large family to support. As provost he gave evidence to the public schools commission. He held the small family living of Chilton Cantelo from 1848 to his death. He died at The Lodge, Eton College, on 9 May 1884, and was buried in the Eton cemetery on 14 May. His younger son, Montague Charles, succeeded him as rector of Chilton Cantelo. G. C. BOASE, *rev.* M. C. CURTHOYS

Sources Venn, *Alum. Cant.* • *The Times* (10 May 1884) • *The Times* (12 May 1884) • *The Times* (15 May 1884) • *The Academy* (17 May 1884), 349–50 • *The Graphic* (7 June 1884), 546, 549 • *ILN* (17 May 1884), 465, 475 • T. Card, *Eton renewed: a history from 1860 to the present day* (1994)

Archives BL, Carnarvon MSS • CUL, Sir George Stokes MSS • King's Cam., Oscar Browning MSS • priv. coll., S. H. Walpole MSS

Likenesses R. H., mezzotint, pubd 1869, NPG • Lock & Whitfield, woodburytype photograph, NPG; repro. in T. Cooper, *Men of mark: a gallery of contemporary portraits* (1878) • Spy [L. Ward], caricature, watercolour study, NPG; repro. in *VF* (22 Jan 1876) • portrait, repro. in *The Graphic* • portrait, repro. in *ILN* • portrait, repro. in Card, *Eton renewed*, pl. 2

Wealth at death £34,111 9*s.* 0*d.*: probate, 10 July 1884, *CGPLA Eng. & Wales*

Goodgroome, John (*bap.* 1623, *d.* 1704), singer and composer, was baptized at Windsor parish church on 5 February 1623, the only known child of Henry Goodgroome and his wife, Sara Cottam. A chorister at St George's Chapel, Windsor, by November 1633, he remained there until April 1638. Playford lists him among the 'excellent and able Masters … For the Voyce or Viole' in *A Musicall Banquet* (1651). Following the Restoration, Goodgroome enjoyed considerable royal patronage: he served as gentleman of the Chapel Royal (1660–1704); was a member of the 'lutes and voices' in the private musick (1664–85); and was one of six singers to accompany Charles II on his progresses from London to avoid the plague (1665–6).

Goodgroome was almost certainly the 'Mr Good-Groome' who was singing-master to Samuel Pepys and his wife. There are sporadic, often critical, references to him in Pepys's diary between June 1661 and January 1669. His methods did not always meet with approval: after Pepys finally became 'dissatisfied with my wife's learning so few songs of Goodgroome', he agreed to teach her at a reduced rate of '10s a song' (Pepys, 8.411).

Four songs by Goodgroome survive: 'Will Chloris cast her sun-bright eye' enjoyed wide popularity, and three others were published in Playford's *Select Ayres and Dialogues* (1659–69). William Goodgroome, a chorister in the Chapel Royal (pre-1674 to 1681) and later organist of St Andrew Undershaft (1696–7?) and St Peter Cornhill (to 1724), was probably his son, but nothing is known of his wife. The cheque book of the Chapel Royal records that Goodgroome died on 27 June 1704. KERI DEXTER

Sources A. Ashbee and D. Lasocki, eds., *A biographical dictionary of English court musicians, 1485–1714*, 1 (1998), 491–4 • Pepys, *Diary* • I. Spink, *English song: Dowland to Purcell* (1974) • chapter acts, 1596–1641, St George's Chapel, Windsor, archives [SGC], VI.B.2 • parish register (baptism), 5 Feb 1623, Windsor parish church • parish register (marriage), 1 Nov 1621, Windsor parish church

Goodhart, Arthur Lehman (1891–1978), jurist, was born on 1 March 1891 in New York city, the younger son and youngest of three children of Philip Julius Goodhart, a well-known New York stockbroker, and his wife, Harriet Lehman, a strong-minded woman, the elder sister of Herbert Lehman, governor of New York (1932–42) and senator

Arthur Lehman Goodhart (1891–1978), by Arthur Ralph Middleton Todd, 1957

(1948–56), and of Irving Lehman, chief judge of the New York court of appeals. On both sides of the family he came of wealthy Jewish stock and his intelligence, generosity, and sense of humour were in the family tradition. He was educated at Hotchkiss School and at Yale University, where he graduated with distinction and was popular enough to be elected to a hitherto gentile fraternity. In 1912 he left for Trinity College, Cambridge, and, being advised against having J. Maynard Keynes as a tutor, chose to read law rather than economics. He took part two of the law tripos after a year, and continued his legal studies under Professor H. D. Hazeltine until the outbreak of war.

This was the beginning of a deep attachment to Britain, in which Goodhart spent nearly all his working life, though he retained his American citizenship and, unlike many Anglophiles, never became Anglicized. He offered to join the British forces in 1914 but was rejected. He took a position as a lawyer in New York until the United States joined the war, whereupon he returned as a member of the American forces. He was counsel to the American mission to Poland in 1919 and his concern for Jews in Poland is recorded in *Poland and the Minority Races* (1920), an account of his experiences with the mission. He was called to the bar by the Inner Temple in 1919.

Prompted by his director of studies, H. A. Hollond, Goodhart decided after the war to teach law in Cambridge and became a fellow of Corpus Christi College. He filled a gap in the faculty teaching arrangements by lecturing in jurisprudence, though his main interest was in the common law. Indeed, he took jurisprudence to be mainly concerned with the general principles that underlie the common law and found the clue to these in the analysis of decided cases. The chair of jurisprudence at Oxford, long dominated by historical scholarship, fell vacant in 1931 and Goodhart, though only thirty-nine, was invited to fill it. Though never much interested in theory, he was popular both as a lecturer and writer. A steady stream of notes and articles, written in a clear and amusing style, came from his pen. His New York contacts added a transatlantic perspective to his common-sense views and, while cultivating the friendship of judges, he criticized their decisions with a freedom which at that time was more American than English. Devoted as he was to the common law, he saw the need to modernize it.

From this point of view Goodhart had three main platforms. At Cambridge he had been instrumental in founding and active in editing the *Cambridge Law Journal* (1921–5). He proved himself so adept at showing contributors how better to express their thoughts that it was no surprise when in 1926, at the behest of Sir Frederick Pollock, himself editor of the *Law Quarterly Review* for thirty-five years, Goodhart took on the editorship of that prestigious journal. It was from the editorial chair that he made his main contribution to legal scholarship. Composing thirty or forty unsigned notes a year, besides dozens of articles, he established an unrivalled position as a critic, friendly but formidable, of the decisions of English judges.

Goodhart was also able to advance the cause of law reform. Invited by Viscount Sankey to join the Law Revision Committee, he used his membership of this and other *ad hoc* bodies to promote improvements in various branches of the law, for example in the rights of visitors to premises to claim compensation for injury. His pragmatism appealed to his practising colleagues and he did not talk above their heads. He led them to accept that some academic lawyers at least could make a contribution to their concerns. His views were strong and simple, sometimes over-simple. He believed passionately, for example, that a negligent wrongdoer should not be made to pay for unforeseeable harm. In this and other instances his views were presented with such courtesy, clarity, and force that they often prevailed with the courts and with reform committees, at least in part. But, more than any particular view he held, his presence and continued influence over a long period created bonds between practitioners, judges, and academic lawyers which had not previously existed.

Goodhart published a number of short books and collections of essays, of which *Essays in Jurisprudence and the Common Law* (1931) is the best-known. But it was his case-notes, concise and going straight to the heart of a matter, that had, rightly, the greatest impact.

In 1951 Goodhart gave up the chair of jurisprudence but remained at University College, Oxford, as a successful and popular master, from 1951 to 1963. He endowed the college more handsomely than anyone else since the foundation and, with his wife, created a harmonious and hospitable atmosphere. In 1924 he had married Cecily

Agnes Mackay (*d*. 1985), daughter of Eric M. Carter, a chartered accountant practising in Birmingham. They had three sons.

Many honours were bestowed on Goodhart. Twenty universities in the English-speaking world awarded him honorary degrees. He took silk in 1943 and was elected FBA in 1952. He also became an honorary fellow of Trinity College, Cambridge. From 1940 to 1951 he was, though a foreigner, chairman of the southern price regulations committee at Reading. Lincoln's Inn made him an honorary bencher in 1938, an honour which he prized, for he delighted in the company of lawyers and in the discussion of law, politics, and public affairs.

Good company and an excellent raconteur, Goodhart remained at heart deeply serious. He was especially devoted to the cause of Anglo-American understanding. He kept alive a sense that English lawyers had much to learn from American experience at a time when they were disinclined to look across the Atlantic. Conversely, he worked tirelessly to put Britain's case to his American friends and to the wider American public. This was above all true during the Second World War. At that time, among many efforts to promote mutual understanding, he made two successful lecture tours of the United States. For his services in this respect he was, greatly to his pleasure, made an honorary KBE in 1948.

To other causes Goodhart was only slightly less devoted. Himself a noted jay-walker, he was for many years president of the Pedestrians' Association, a small pressure group on whose behalf he wrote many letters to *The Times*. As a member of the royal commission on the police he wrote a powerful memorandum of dissent in which he advocated the reorganization of the police as a national force. In his last years he became absorbed in attempts to defend President Nixon's conduct over Watergate and the Israeli claims to the West Bank. He still displayed in these unpromising causes the independence and force of character that earlier had enabled him so successfully to build bridges between academic and practising lawyers and between the interests of Britain and America, and to win such high regard as master of University College. He remained active and sociable, indeed, into old age. It was not until his eighty-eighth year that he suffered a stroke and, on 10 November 1978, died in London.

TONY HONORÉ, *rev.*

Sources *The Times* (11 Nov 1978) • Lord Diplock, F. H. Lawson, and P. V. Baker, 'A. L. G.: a judge's view; a professor's view; an editor's view', *Law Quarterly Review*, 91 (1975), 457–68 • personal knowledge (1986)

Archives Bodl. Oxf., corresp. and papers • University College, Oxford, notes on legal subjects | Bodl. Oxf., corresp. with Lord Simon

Likenesses A. R. M. Todd, portrait, 1957, University College, Oxford [*see illus.*]

Wealth at death £92,621: administration with will, 22 Oct 1981, *CGPLA Eng. & Wales*

Goodhugh, William (1798/9–1842), biblical scholar, was for some time a bookseller at 155 Oxford Street in London. Striving to be a competent bibliographer, he learned many oriental and modern languages (publishing anonymously in 1827 *The Gate to the French, Italian, and Spanish Unlocked* and *The Gate to the Hebrew, Arabic, and Syriac Unlocked by a New and Easy Method of Acquiring the Accidence*). He came to public notice through his learned criticisms of John Bellamy's translation of the Bible; these appeared in the *Quarterly Review* in April 1818 and July 1820. In 1840 he issued proposals for a society to be called the Dugdale Society, whose aim was to make the tracing of British ancestry easier through the publication of unedited documents and by systematic reference to those already printed. The project was not encouraged, however, and came to nothing. In 1838 he published *Motives to the Study of Biblical Literature in a Course of Introductory Lectures* (8 vols.) and from 1839 he began to compile a Bible encyclopaedia (which later appeared in two volumes), but did not live long enough to get beyond the letter 'R' in his research. True to his own profession, he also produced a handbook on how to set up a library. He died at 11 South Parade, Chelsea, on 23 May 1842, already a widower, and leaving a son and a daughter. GORDON GOODWIN, *rev.* GERALD LAW

Sources *GM*, 2nd ser., 18 (1842), 215 • Allibone, *Dict.* • d. cert. • m. cert.

Goodier, Alban (1869–1939), Jesuit and Roman Catholic archbishop of Bombay, was born on 14 April 1869 in Great Harwood, Lancashire, the second of five surviving children of William Goodier, a biscuit manufacturer, and his wife, Elizabeth Kitching. Goodier was initially educated at a series of primary schools in Great Harwood and Preston. In January 1881 he was sent to Hodder Place, the preparatory institution for the Jesuit public school, Stonyhurst College, near Clitheroe. He attended Stonyhurst between 1882 and 1887, and then entered the Society of Jesus at Manresa House, Roehampton, Surrey. His Jesuit formation consisted of two years' noviciate at Roehampton, London, then several years studying the humanities, taking a second in the external London University BA in classics in 1891, before commencing studies in philosophy at St Mary's Hall, Stonyhurst, from 1891 to 1894. There followed some six years of schoolmastering, also at Stonyhurst, after which Goodier went for theological studies to St Beuno's College, St Asaph, Denbighshire. Ordained a priest in 1903 he spent a further year of study at St Beuno's and completed his final period of training at Tronchiennes in Belgium. Upon his return to England in 1905 he was appointed to teach Greek and Latin to Jesuit students at Manresa House, Roehampton. He became both the religious superior of the Jesuit students and prefect of studies, a position he was to hold until 1914. It was during these years that he developed an interest in the theory of education, particularly in the Jesuit *ratio studiorum*, and he published several articles on the topic in the Catholic periodical *The Month*. In part as rival to the contemporary Everyman series he established, in 1909, the Catholic Library with the aim of making Catholic literature available at low cost. This venture was not a commercial success and did not survive the outbreak of war in 1914.

During the First World War the government of India was faced with the task of expelling or interning foreign hostile nationals. The German Jesuits responsible for the administration of St Xavier's University College, Bombay, appealed to the English Jesuits for help and requested that Goodier, despite his narrow background and experience, be sent as the principal of the college. When Goodier arrived in Bombay in November 1914 he found the students almost invariably anti-English. He attributed this to the influence of the German Jesuits with whom he had an uneasy relationship. Goodier's initial contacts with the government of Bombay were also strained, and he was inclined to blame the Germans for misleading him as to the government's attitude to Catholic missionaries in the Bombay area.

In addition to his administrative duties Goodier was appointed professor of English, but with the further internment of most of the remaining German Jesuits, of which he heartily approved, the college was seriously short of personnel. He took the opportunity of the long vacation in the summer of 1915 to go to England to recruit more staff for St Xavier's. He was a successful administrator and became rector of the college, fellow and syndic of Bombay University and a justice of the peace, the first Catholic priest in Bombay to hold such a position. During the course of another visit to Europe in 1919 Goodier was informed that the Holy See intended to make him archbishop of Bombay. The announcement was delayed by several months because of difficulties with the Portuguese government which, since the sixteenth century, had immense influence over Roman Catholic affairs in India. In 1924 he was also appointed apostolic administrator of the diocese of Poona.

Goodier's ministry in India was marked by a love of the poor and he established several well-known charities to look after the needs of orphans, the destitute, and the elderly. On the other hand he shared many of the British prejudices towards India typical of his day, believing Indians to be cunning and deceitful and incapable of self-government. Somewhat uncritical of British administration he went so far as to defend, in his private correspondence, the conduct of General Reginald Dyer and Sir Michael O'Dwyer in connection with the Amritsar massacre of 1919.

Goodier's career as archbishop was fraught with difficulties. The Portuguese-nominated patriarch of Goa had jurisdiction over all priests ordained in his see, irrespective of where they might subsequently serve in India. In the diocese of Bombay a considerable number of parishes had Goanese priests who refused to recognize Goodier as their ecclesiastical superior. Relations between Goodier and these clergy were very tense with the archbishop insisting on his rights as the ordinary in Bombay and the Goanese with equal vigour resisting what they saw as Goodier's interference in their affairs. Petitions were organized demanding Goodier's removal from office. A man of acute sensitivities who had been placed in a stressful situation, his health began to fail and on a visit to Rome in 1926 he resigned, and was given the titular archbishopric of Hierapolis in Phrygia. Nevertheless, his recommendation that the jurisdiction of the patriarch of Goa be restricted to his own diocese and that archbishops of Bombay should alternately be drawn from among the English and Portuguese clergy formed the substance of a new concordat signed by the Holy See and the Portuguese government in May 1928.

Back in England, Goodier served as an assistant to the cardinal-archbishop of Westminster between 1931 and 1932, and he acted as an unofficial adviser to the Colonial Office on matters of religious education in India. Increasing ill health forced him to retire to the Benedictine convent, St Scholastica's Abbey, Teignmouth, Devon, where he served as chaplain to the nuns. An excellent public speaker he was widely known as a retreat giver and was much in demand, ill health notwithstanding, as a preacher. His many writings include *The Public Life of our Lord Jesus Christ* (2 vols., 1930) and *The Passion and Death of our Lord Jesus Christ* (1933). Goodier's works were pious rather than scholarly, although his last book, *An Introduction to the Study of Ascetical and Mystical Theology* (1938), was the product of a course he taught to Jesuit seminarians at Heythrop College, Oxfordshire, in the years 1934–8. He died from an angina attack at St Scholastica's on 13 March 1939 and was buried at Manresa House, Roehampton, five days later. OLIVER P. RAFFERTY

Sources Archives of the British Province of the Society of Jesus, London, Goodier MSS • A. Goodier, *St Ignatius Loyola and prayer, with a memoir of the author by Henry Keane* (1940) • *Letters and Notices* [Society of Jesus], 54 (1939), 148–60 • *The Tablet* (18 March 1939) • *Catholic Herald* (24 March 1939) • *The Times* (15 March 1939) • *The Stonyhurst Magazine* (Feb 1940) • parish register (baptism), 18/4/1869, St Hubert's, Great Harwood

Archives Archives of the British Province of the Society of Jesus, London, sermons, letters, drafts of articles and books | Bodl. Oxf., letters to Sir James Marchant

Likenesses D. Dawnay, portrait, *c*.1935–1939, Campion Hall, Oxford • photograph, repro. in *Letters and Notices*

Wealth at death £1881 16*s*. 3*d*.: probate, 1 Sept 1939, *CGPLA Eng. & Wales*

Goodinge, Thomas (1746–1816), Church of England clergyman and headmaster, was baptized on 9 November 1746 at St Andrew's, Holborn, the son of Thomas Goodinge, a London barrister, and his wife, Joanna. He was educated at Gloucester and entered Trinity College, Oxford, where he matriculated on 14 January 1762 and received his BA in 1766. In 1778 he was awarded an MA at Cambridge and also a DCL at Oxford. In 1765 he was engaged for a few months as an assistant in the college school at Salisbury, and in 1768 became principal of the college school of Worcester. In 1769 he was ordained deacon, and in 1771 was presented to the living of Bredicot in Worcestershire. In December 1773 he married Maria Hale (*d*. 1810), daughter of Robert Hale of Marylebone, Middlesex. In 1775 he opened a private school at Bevere. He was headmaster of the grammar school at Leeds from 1779 to 1788, became rector of Hutton in Somerset in 1788, and in 1789 rector of Cound in Shropshire. His wife died there in September 1810, and during his remaining years he resided in Shrewsbury.

Goodinge was a sound scholar, a powerful preacher, and a successful schoolmaster. He commenced a translation of Lycophron, but relinquished it on the appearance of Henry Meen's translations in 1800, and he was also a good botanist. He died at Shrewsbury on 17 July 1816.

W. F. WENTWORTH-SHIELDS, *rev.* ROBERT BROWN

Sources *GM*, 1st ser., 86/2 (1816), 94 • *GM*, 1st ser., 87/2 (1817), 182–3 • J. Chambers, *Biographical illustrations of Worcestershire* (1820) • Foster, *Alum. Oxon.* • Venn, *Alum. Cant.* • *IGI*

Goodison, Benjamin (*c.*1700–1767), cabinet-maker and undertaker, is of unknown parentage, although the surname is common in south Yorkshire. His occupation is first recorded in September 1719 when he signed for £500 from Sarah, duchess of Marlborough, for his master the London cabinet-maker James Moore the elder. Goodison was probably apprenticed to Moore about 1716. Some of the giltwood furniture previously attributed to Moore made at this time may be by Goodison working under Moore's supervision. The Bateman chest (V&A) made to commemorate the marriage of William Bateman and Lady Anne Spencer (a granddaughter of the duchess of Marlborough) in 1720 is more boldly sculptural in design than James Moore's documented work and characteristic in style of later documented work by Goodison. In 1720 Goodison signed a further receipt for work done for 'My Master James Moore' for Richard Boyle, third earl of Burlington.

By 1725 Goodison was sufficiently experienced to set up on his own and took on an apprentice in January that year. He married Sarah Cooper at St Bride's, Fleet Street, London, on 13 August 1723, but their son, also called Benjamin, was not baptized until 23 February 1735 at St Martin-in-the-Fields, Westminster. Goodison worked at the sign of the Golden Spread Eagle in Long Acre and in August 1727 a newspaper announced the theft from his premises of 'a large old fashioned Glass Sconce, in a Glass Frame, with Gold Flowers painted on the Glass Frame, and a Green Ground' (*Daily Courant*, 22, 23 and 24 Aug 1727), demonstrating that he also dealt in secondhand furniture.

By then Goodison had succeeded his master James Moore (who died in 1726) in royal service. In 1729 Goodison supplied a brass lantern for the queen's staircase at Hampton Court Palace for £138 (still *in situ*). During the 1730s royal demands for furniture were supervised by the master of the great wardrobe, Sir Thomas Robinson. Goodison regularly supplied mahogany, walnut, and giltwood furniture for royal use in palaces and yachts. Some of the giltwood furniture previously attributed to Goodison in the Royal Collection has now been reattributed to the Pelletier workshop, and redated to the early 1700s. No mahogany or walnut furniture by Goodison in the Royal Collection has been identified although detailed descriptions survive in the bills. For instance, in 1741 Goodison was paid £16 10s. by the lord chamberlain for a 'Mahogany Library Table with Drawers on one side and Cupboards on the other … top covered with black leather & Castors to ye Bottom' (Beard and Gilbert, 352).

Many of Goodison's early customers were related to Sarah, duchess of Marlborough, a client whom Goodison inherited from his master. (Goodison was still supplying her with looking-glasses for Blenheim Palace in the 1730s.) Goodison also worked for her son-in-law, John, second duke of Montagu, supplying furniture for Montagu House, Whitehall, to the designs of the architect Henry Flitcroft. These include a mahogany library table with lion masks and a set of stepped mahogany bookcases with elaborate carved foliage. With their sober use of richly coloured hardwood, they formed an appropriate complement to the Palladian interiors (Boughton House, Northamptonshire). Goodison also worked with Flitcroft at the Dover Street, London, house which Goodison purchased in 1740 as agent for Sarah, duchess of Marlborough. The house was intended for her recently widowed granddaughter Isabella, duchess of Manchester—the elder daughter of the second duke of Montagu. Here Goodison provided chimney-pieces to Flitcroft's designs as well as walnut tables and chairs. For the duchess of Marlborough's other daughter, Lady Sunderland, Goodison provided furniture for Althorp, Northamptonshire, including a pair of white-painted supports for marble tables in the entrance hall and a pedestal for the terracotta bust of Van Dyck by J. M. Rysbrack. Goodison provided an inventory of the contents of Althorp in 1746.

The accounts of John, second duke of Montagu, demonstrate that in addition to supplying new furniture Goodison took charge of old furniture from the duke's former London home Montagu House, Bloomsbury, and restored and reframed pictures and looking-glasses where necessary. A pair of overdoor paintings by Jean-Baptiste Monnoyer (priv. coll.), formerly in Marot-style frames by the Pelletier workshop, were reframed by Goodison for Montagu House, Whitehall. Goodison also worked for Montagu's son-in-law, George Brudenell, fourth earl of Cardigan, furnishing his house in Dover Street, London.

Goodison worked for the first and second viscounts Folkestone supplying furniture for Longford Castle, Wiltshire, considered in 1754 to be 'one of the best furnished houses in England' (J. J. Cartwright, ed., *The Travels through England of Dr Pococke*, 1888–9). It is probable that on this occasion Goodison designed the furniture himself. The mahogany and gilt seating in the gallery, for which Goodison received £400 in 1740, consists of two mahogany daybeds, and two large and eight smaller stools. The fine carving of lions' paw feet and superimposed shells on the legs of the stools and daybeds is lightened by the Greek key pattern which serves as a frieze along the seat rails and is highlighted with gilding. A similar set of seating furniture at Woburn Abbey is attributed to Goodison by comparison with the Longford suite. A pair of pedestals incorporating heads of Hercules retain their original eighteenth-century oak-grained painted and gilded surfaces and are also attributed to Goodison. Two substantial marble tables supported on carved wooden plinths incorporating twin figures of foxes are also thought to be the work of Goodison (priv. coll. and V&A). One was originally intended for the two-storey Palladian hall at Longford (dem. in the nineteenth century) and was painted white to imitate statuary marble in order to complement the busts in niches around the hall. The other, curved in form, and originally painted green and gilded, was intended for the circular green drawing room with its carved giltwood decoration supplied in 1747 by Goodison's assistant Edward Griffiths.

Goodison is also associated with the architect William Kent and certainly made furniture to Kent's designs for Sir Thomas Coke, later earl of Leicester, at Holkham, Norfolk. His early commissions included mahogany stools for a temple in the grounds supplied in 1739. Goodison was again employed at Holkham after Kent's death, when the work was probably supervised by the architect Matthew Brettingham. In 1757 Goodison supplied a carved and gilt mahogany table press with wire doors for the gallery. He later made an elaborate carved and gilt frame for the painting of Coriolanus by Pietro da Cortona, for which he charged £74.

Goodison also supplied furniture to Frederick, prince of Wales, and served as his undertaker in 1751, supplying eighty black sconces for the funeral in the Henry VII chapel, Westminster Abbey. Fifteen years later his will mentions that he had not been paid for some of the work done for the prince. When Goodison died in London in 1767, the business was carried on by his nephew, Benjamin Parran, whom he had taken on as an apprentice in 1741. In 1769 Parran formed a partnership with Goodison's son Benjamin, who had qualified as a lawyer by 1764. They continued business as undertakers and serviced the funeral of the duke of Newcastle in 1768. One of Goodison's daughters, Sarah, married the carver and sculptor William Hinchliff, who with Benjamin Goodison the younger acted as executor to his father-in-law.

Benjamin Goodison was a pious man with literary tastes. He enjoyed poetry, and in 1736 subscribed to Stephen Duck's *Poems on Several Occasions* and in 1748 to a similar volume of poems by Thomas Warton. On his death Goodison left an estate of approximately £16,000. This included a substantial house in Mitcham, Surrey, as well as his London property in Long Acre, Covent Garden.

TESSA MURDOCH

Sources G. Beard and C. Gilbert, eds., *Dictionary of English furniture makers, 1660–1840* (1986), 351–4 · G. Beard, 'Three eighteenth-century cabinet-makers: Moore, Goodison and Vile', *Burlington Magazine*, 119 (1977), 479–84 · R. Edwards and M. Jourdain, *Georgian cabinet-makers* (1955), 106 · T. V. Murdoch, ed., *Boughton House: the English Versailles* (1992) · P. Thornton and J. Hardy, 'Spencer furniture at Althorp [pt 1]', *Apollo*, 87 (1968), 182–3 · C. Hussey, 'Furniture at Longford Castle, I', *Country Life*, 70 (1931), 679–82 · C. Wilk, ed., *Western furniture, 1350 to the present day* (1996), 86–7 · J. Cornforth, 'Longford Castle', *Country Life Annual* (1968), 29–37 · J. Harris, 'The duchess of Beaufort's observations on places', *Georgian Group Journal*, 10 (2000), 36–42 · E. Pinto, 'The furniture of his grace the duke of Bedford at Woburn Abbey', *Apollo*, 62 (1955), 202–6 · T. Murdoch, 'Jean, René and Thomas Pelletier: a Huguenot family of carvers and gilders in England, 1682–1726', *Burlington Magazine*, 139 (1997), 732–42; 140 (1998), 363–74 · will, PRO, PROB 11/476, fol. 446 · *IGI*
Archives Boughton House, Northamptonshire, MSS · Longford Castle, Wiltshire, MSS · V&A | Duchy of Cornwall office, London, accounts of Frederick, prince of Wales · GL, Hand in Hand Insurance · PRO, Lord Chamberlain's accounts
Wealth at death approx. £16,000: will, PRO, PROB 11/476, fol. 446

Goodman, Arnold Abraham, **Baron Goodman** (**1913–1995**), solicitor and public servant, was born on 21 August 1913 at 26 Bodney Road, Hackney, London, the younger son of Joseph Goodman (1879/1880–1940), master draper, and his wife, Bertha (1887–1959), daughter of Joseph Mauerberger, businessman. His name was given on his birth certificate as Aby Goodman, but in 1931 his father re-registered him as Abraham; he adopted Arnold as a first name during the Second World War. Both parents were of Jewish descent; his mother came from a wealthy family with strong connections in South Africa, and her ambition and determination ensured that by the 1930s the family had moved out of the East End and into Hampstead. Food was the emotional currency of the young Goodman's household. He was born large, and his mother's relentless feeding at home made him very big for his age by the time he went to the Grocers' School in Hackney. This fat child learned to deflect bullies by being amiable and funny. As he grew up, there was always the demanding memory of his mother to push him on and always a passionate relationship with food. His sickly brother Theo, artistic and sensitive, was also an important influence. Goodman developed a sense of disappointment and frustration that he lacked real creative ability of his own. The values by which he lived were determined by this complex combination of feelings—an obligation to please and gain approval, an immense sense of his own worth, and a genuine respect for creativity and the arts.

From the Grocer's School, Goodman proceeded to University College, London, where he formed a lifelong friendship with L. C. B. (Jim) Gower and graduated with second-class honours in law in 1933. After taking the LLM in 1935, and serving articles with the London firm of Rubinstein Nash (his mother being a friend of one of the partners' wives), he studied Roman law and Roman-Dutch law at Downing College, Cambridge, obtaining firsts in both parts of his degree. Abandoning thoughts of practising in South Africa, he joined the firm of Royalton Kisch, which specialized in conveyancing and local government work. As a young solicitor he scored a notable success in a case brought against Croydon borough council on behalf of parents whose daughter had contracted typhoid from drinking contaminated water. On the outbreak of the Second World War he enlisted with the Royal Artillery, joining an anti-aircraft battery in Enfield under the command of the archaeologist Mortimer Wheeler. After a spell as battery quartermaster sergeant—according to Wheeler, 'the best … in the army' (*The Independent*, 15 May 1995)—he was transferred to the Royal Army Ordnance Corps, southern command. Demobilized in November 1945, with the rank of major, he returned to the law first with Royalton Kisch and then (from 1947) as a partner in Rubinstein Nash. Stanley Rubinstein was chairman of the Performing Right Society, and the firm had many clients from the worlds of the media, literature, and the arts. Goodman

Arnold Abraham Goodman, Baron Goodman (1913–1995), by Graham Sutherland, 1973–4

took many of these clients with him when in 1954 he founded his own practice, Goodman Derrick—Derrick being Henry 'Mac' Derrick (1916–1964), a wartime colleague at southern command and a keen amateur organist. The firm expanded rapidly, specializing in particular in media, copyright, and libel law.

Goodman's introduction to political work came, like much else in his career, through a contact he had first made in the war: George Wigg, who introduced him to Wilson and the group of mainly left-wing MPs who surrounded Aneurin Bevan in the early 1950s. But it was not until 1957 that Goodman's breakthrough case took place. This was the controversial *Spectator* libel trial in which three leading Labour figures, Bevan, Richard Crossman, and Morgan Phillips, were accused of being drunk at an International Socialist Congress in Italy and may have perjured themselves while denying it. Goodman at least suspected the perjury but was certainly not told. The triumphant victory of the three under his guidance made national news. Following the trial he regularly represented MPs and worked for the party leader Hugh Gaitskell during the Vassall spy inquiry in 1962 and in a long-running case against *The Guardian*.

Goodman had charm, he was witty, and he could frequently persuade people to do what he or his clients wanted. When the charm failed, he would deploy an injured look or simply decline to understand the grounds for refusal. He was not an ideological or a campaigning lawyer but a highly effective advocate for his clients. He would have remained an interesting and successful solicitor, but in January 1963 Gaitskell died from a rare disease, and after a bitter leadership election Harold Wilson was elected leader of the Labour Party. Goodman was on the fringes of the Gaitskell set and therefore on the fringes of politics. Soon he was at the very heart. There is a certain irony in the way in which it was Goodman's expertise in media law that brought him to the attention of Wilson. The irony derives in part from Goodman's own ambiguous relationship with fame and publicity (he later became notorious for his own propensity to litigation), in part from the fact that one of his key roles for Wilson was to keep Labour affairs out of the media. Despite this it was as a media lawyer that Wilson first made use of Goodman, and it was for his power to intimidate journalists that Goodman proved extremely useful to many.

Wilson made Goodman. Without Wilson's patronage and need for consultation and a peculiar kind of friendship, Goodman would not have risen to the heights he did. After he became Wilson's lawyer, and especially after 1965 (when Wilson elevated him to the Lords, as Baron Goodman of the City of Westminster), his career made him a unique figure in post-war British history. It bothered Goodman as he grew older that his public stature was due to Wilson's patronage. His waspish references to Wilson in his memoirs reflected annoyance that he, in a sense, owed it all to the younger man from Huddersfield. It is hardly surprising that Wilson asked so much of him. With no family constraints and with a willingness to cancel meetings or break off dinners to do Wilson's bidding, Goodman became a close confidant. Throughout the government of 1964–70 he visited Wilson every week or every other week and frequently sat opposite him in the chancellor of the exchequer's chair in the cabinet room, serving as a sounding board.

On Wilson's first day in number 10 he asked Goodman to chair a committee to explore the future of the London orchestras. It was the first of Goodman's many distinguished contributions to the arts. Shortly afterwards, Wilson asked him to be chairman of the Arts Council of Great Britain. It was his most successful job in public life, and one which he held until 1972 (when he was appointed CH in recognition of his services). He was a dynamic and effective chair, and his influence extended out from the arts to a range of organizations in which he played the role of fixer, usually as chairman. He was élitist and metropolitan in his view of arts policy; Jennie Lee, the arts minister until 1970, was interested in regional and popular culture. This led to occasional rows and delays in making decisions, but in the main the relationship was fruitful and successful.

In the ten years after 1965, when he was at the height of his powers, Goodman's influence was felt on the development of bodies as diverse as the charity Motability (which he founded), the Housing Corporation, English National Opera, the Royal Opera House, the Royal Shakespeare Theatre, the National Theatre, the British Council, the Institute of Jewish Affairs, and numerous committees of inquiry. In 1967 his friend David Astor persuaded him to become chairman of the trustees of *The Observer* (in which capacity he oversaw the sale of the newspaper in 1976), and he was an influential chairman of the Newspaper Publishers' Association from 1970 to 1976. In addition he ran his private practice, Goodman Derrick, which grew into a successful partnership based on libel and media law. He was later described by one friend and client as 'the greatest negotiator of the age' (*The Independent*, 15 May 1995). His style of fixing was imaginative and resourceful. For example, he was asked to write an assessment of the potential cost of the new 'university of the air'. He considered the amount that the cabinet was likely to accept and then cooked a response that made this look plausible. Wilson backed the scheme strongly and the Open University was created. In the Lords on 23 May 1974 Goodman said: 'When I see the figure I mentioned and the figure it is now costing I ought to blush with shame'. He did not blush because it might not have been established except for his 'foolish miscalculation' (*Hansard 5L*, 351, cols. 1649–50).

Despite being the establishment's lawyer, Goodman did not accumulate vast wealth of his own. He did not take a salary from any of his public offices and often did not bill clients he counted as friends—and there was no shortage of friends. Indeed Arnold's friends could crop up in the most useful places. In 1969 the public accounts committee investigated the Arts Council, of which Goodman was chairman. Harold Lever was the committee's chairman. The auditor-general suggested there might be some conflict of interest. He said to Lever: 'Do you think you ought to preside over this committee since I believe that Lord Goodman is rather a pal of yours?', to which Lever replied: 'A pal? No, he is not a pal of mine, he is a very dear friend' (Goodman, *Tell Them*, 282). The report cleared the council of any wrongdoing. This acquisition of friends was close to the root of Goodman's motivation in life. He spent forty-five years on the telephone. This relentless quest for work, this unstoppable giving of aid and advice, filled a void in his life that in most other people would be occupied by home, family, and children. Goodman liked being at the centre; he liked doors opening, people taking his calls, people knowing who he was—and he liked people doing things because he asked them. As the Goodman wagon rolled, he expected people to do what he wanted. He was perplexed when one musician refused to do his bidding, unimpressed by Goodman's allusion to the needs of 'important people, titled people'. In the world of access, social cachet, and influence, he was absolutely at sea with people for whom such things were meaningless or trivial. Work also served emotional needs for friendship and companionship, and introduced him to the series of widows who acted as his consorts from the late 1950s. The most important of these was Ann Fleming, widow of the James Bond creator, Ian, who used to stay in his Portland Place flat when visiting London. Fleming in turn introduced Goodman to new clients such as Evelyn Waugh:

> The only person who can save your trust is Lord Goodman … he admires your work, is clever and funny, he has done much for me and never sends a bill. He has saved me from the solicitors, found me a doctor … and can get tickets for the National Theatre. (Brivati, 96)

Goodman also fell for Jennie Lee (Nye Bevan's widow) and was later close to Anthony Eden's widow, Clarissa. Although he was clearly besotted with Lee, and friends remember them kissing and cuddling, the evidence suggests that his sexuality was deeply repressed. What each of these formidable women had in common was a similarity to the most important female presence in his life—his domineering mother, Bertha.

When Wilson lost power in 1970 Goodman took on a number of new public roles in addition to his main job at the Arts Council, and continued to build up his practice. He was also dispatched by Edward Heath to Rhodesia as a secret negotiator with Ian Smith (having performed a similar role for Wilson, in the run-up to the latter's talks aboard HMS *Fearless*), a task to which he was particularly unsuited. From 1964 to 1970 Goodman had seen Wilson most weeks for their late evening chat. When Wilson, a little unexpectedly, returned to number 10 in 1974, the same pattern of involvement in the prime minister's life was not re-established and the centre of the political world began to shift away from Goodman. Indeed, the corporatist establishment of the age of Harold Wilson was in terminal decline in the second half of the decade. The self-destruction of Jeremy Thorpe was emblematic of a new era. The part of Goodman that always felt ambivalent about being in the spotlight welcomed the change. Another part of him wanted to cling to the wreckage of his life at the centre of politics, but this was made more difficult because of the cooling of his relations with Wilson. The last two decades of his life witnessed a gradual decline in his health and his public standing, along with an increasing sense of isolation as old friends died and a new political establishment came to dominate.

Goodman's acceptance of the mastership of University College, Oxford, in 1976 contributed further to the cooling of his relations with Wilson. As Goodman later told the story, during Wilson's last days in office he asked Goodman to help him become master of University College. 'It was one of the most awkward moments of my life, since I had in my pocket at the time a letter from the Fellows of the College offering the job to me' (Brivati, 270). Goodman's tenure at University College was notably successful and happy for him. He continued to fix and run things, but on a much less exalted scale, replacing politicians with dons and students. He presided over a potentially fractious college body with great skill, and was especially successful at fund-raising. He also helped to put the Oxford Union on a sound financial footing. He retired as master in 1986, and in 1993 celebrated his eightieth birthday with a gala banquet at Lincoln's Inn hall and the publication of his largely unrevealing memoirs, *Tell Them I'm on My Way*.

Though never accountable for his actions to any electorate, Arnold Goodman was a man of influence and power from the time of the Profumo scandal in 1963 until the election of Margaret Thatcher in 1979. He was the fixer for the British establishment. He spent a large part of his life helping other people: lending money, finding jobs, saving marriages and companies, giving time to good causes, and pressuring his wealthy friends to donate to the charities that he chaired. Above all he was friend to a host of private people and a benefactor to many. The darker side of this remarkable life was that he used his influence to protect powerful people from the press, and sometimes the quick fixes he put in place caused more long-term harm than good. His last years were overshadowed by a lawsuit brought by the Portman family in 1993, and by allegations that he had systematically siphoned off funds from the family trust in order to provide loans to his friends, including senior Labour Party figures. The case was eventually settled in 1999 when Goodman Derrick paid £500,000, though without admission of guilt, and the allegations remained unproven. Goodman died, unmarried, of bronchopneumonia at Newstead Home, Denewood Road, Highgate, London, on 12 May 1995. A memorial service was held at the Liberal Jewish Synagogue.

BRIAN BRIVATI

Sources A. Goodman, *Not for the record* (1972) • A. Goodman, *Tell them I'm on my way* (1993) • B. Brivati, *Lord Goodman* (1999) • D. Selbourne, *Not an Englishman: conversations with Lord Goodman* (1993) • *The Times* (15 May 1995) • *The Independent* (15 May 1995) • *The Independent* (22 May 1995) • *The Independent* (27 May 1995) • *WWW*
Archives NRA, priv. coll., papers | Bodl. Oxf., letters to Jack Goodman and Catherine Goodman • U. Southampton L., corresp. with James Parker
Likenesses photographs, 1955–74, Hult. Arch. • G. Sutherland, portrait, 1973–4, Tate collection [*see illus.*] • A. Newman, bromide print, 1978, NPG • L. Freud, charcoal drawing, 1985, NPG • L. Freud, etching with watercolour, 1987, Whitworth Art Gallery, Manchester • photographs, repro. in Goodman, *Tell them I'm on my way* • photographs, repro. in Brivati, *Lord Goodman*

Goodman, Cardell (*b.* 1653), actor, was born in October or November 1653 in Southampton, the son of Cardell Goodman (1608–1654), rector of Freshwater, Isle of Wight, and his wife, Katherine. He was educated at Thomas Wyborrow's school, Cambridge, where his mother moved after her husband's death. In 1671 he took his degree from St John's College, Cambridge, although he later claimed to have been sent down for defacing the portrait of the duke of Monmouth. Goodman decamped to London; there he visited family friend Robert Hooke, who probably introduced him into London society. He met Thomas Killigrew, manager of the King's Company, and apprenticed himself as a hired man in 1673, at the princely sum of 10*s*. a week. His first recorded appearance was as Mariamne in a novices' production of Thomas Duffet's blacked-up, cross-dressed burlesque of Elkanah Settle's play of the same name, *The Empress of Morocco*. This is the only record of a role between 1673 and March 1677, although he was sworn in as a liveried servant of the King's Company on 8 June 1676.

Goodman's financial situation was dire during this period; he had to borrow 20*s*. from Robert Hooke on 20 November 1674, and Cibber's account of Goodman's reminiscences suggests that he and Philip Griffin, a fellow hireling, 'were confined by their moderate Sallaries to the Oeconomy of lying together in the same Bed and having but one whole Shirt between them' (Wilson, 35; Cibber, 2.316). Many of the King's Company were finding it difficult to maintain a debt-free existence and Goodman's £3 debt to Thomas Kite 'for money lent' in January 1677 was modest. But on 20 March 1677 he was in more serious trouble with John Lane of Hart Street for 'a mare hyred and spoyled by Goodman worth above six pounds', for which the lord chamberlain ordered him to pay £5 at the rate of 4*s*. a week, while he was acting. Luckily Goodman was performing that spring, playing the braggart Captain Mullineux in John Leanerd's *The Country Innocence*, the boastful conspirator Polyperchon in Nathaniel Lee's *The Rival Queens*, the plotting Plautino in Edward Ravenscroft's *Scaramouch*, and at last a leading role as the romantic, passionate Antellus in William Chamberlayne's *Wits Led by the Nose*, while the leading players were not performing because of a dispute with manager Charles Killigrew.

We have more record of Goodman's roles in the 1677–8 season, none of them very elevated parts: Ethelwold in Ravenscroft's *King Edgar and Alfreda*, Alexas the scheming eunuch in Dryden's *All for Love*, the lustful, blustering Pharnaces in Lee's *Mithridates*, and the debauched Hylas in D'Urfey's *Trick for Trick*. Goodman's dissolute roles on stage seem to be echoed by his off-stage skirmishes with the law at this time. On 4 April 1678 a warrant to 'Apprehend & take into Custody Cardell Goodman, one of his Mats Comoedians for certain abuses & misdemeanours by him committed' was issued. In the following year he and Sarah Young, alias Goodman, were sued for £12 16*s*. and for £28 debts they had incurred. More luridly, on 18 April 1681 Goodman was pardoned for an earlier highway robbery, which does not appear to have been an isolated incident. His connections at court seem to have preserved him, because he is still listed as a King's player during the period.

When the troubled King's Company had closed for almost a year in March 1679, Goodman teamed up with Thomas Clark and John Gray to run a company in Edinburgh for a season. In July 1680 he was wooed back to the King's Company by Charles and Henry Killigrew, as a shareholder. Unfortunately we have no record of whether this improved his position within the company and opened up leading roles to him in the first season. By mid-October 1681 he was given an epilogue, with Betty Cox, to Lee's important *Mithridates*, and he played the larger roles of Townly in D'Urfey's *Sir Barnaby Whigg*, the duped, but noble Seliman in Thomas Southerne's *The Loyal Brother*, and the heroic, tortured Altomar in Settle's *The Heir of Morocco*. The uniting of the companies threatened his access to leading roles, Cibber suggests, and returned Goodman to a £2 a week hireling. Indeed, in the early years of the United Company he played the undemanding title role in *Julius Caesar*, and supporting roles as Annibal in Lee's *Constantine the Great*, Vernish in Wycherley's *The Plain Dealer*, and in February 1686 Peregrine Bertie saw him in an unnamed role in *Mithridates*. However, it may be that with the United Company he acted Alexander in Lee's *The Rival Queens* in the 1685 production, and possibly again in October 1686 at court. Goodman was undoubtedly noted in this part, as a letter from Dryden reveals (Highfill, Burnim & Langhans, *BDA*). A later commentator, Charles Gildon, in his *Life of Mr Thomas Betterton* (1710), approved of Goodman's acting 'in the Madness of *Alexander the Great* in *Lee's* Play, Mr. Goodman always went through it with all the Force the Part requir'd, and yet made not half the

Noise, as some who succeeded him' (Highfill, Burnim & Langhans, *BDA*). It seems, from the few roles we are able to identify him in, that this kind of noisy, passionate part was his forte.

Patchy records account for some of the lacunae in Goodman's career with the United Company, but Davies's account of him offers an alternative view:

> Goodman, long before his death, was so happy in his finances, that he acted only occasionally, perhaps when his noble mistress wished to see him in a principal character; for Goodman used to say 'he would not act Alexander the Great but when he was certain that the Duchess would be in the boxes to see him perform.' (Highfill, Burnim & Langhans, *BDA*)

The noble mistress who facilitated such a reversal in his fortunes was the powerful former mistress of Charles II, Barbara *Palmer, duchess of Cleveland (*bap.* 1640, *d.* 1709), with whom Goodman had taken up some time before 1684.

The duchess's three sons—particularly Henry, duke of Grafton—were unimpressed by their mother's liaison with Goodman and arranged for him to be arrested for highway robbery and committed to Newgate in summer 1684. This was not Goodman's first sojourn in custody; he had been briefly held in the Porter's Lodge, Whitehall, in April 1678, and narrowly escaped a sentence for his 1681 highway robbery charge. However, on 2 September the grand jury found for Goodman, allegedly after £100 changed witnesses' testimony, and he was released. This was not the end of Goodman's troubles, as on 20 October he was re-arrested and taken to Newgate. This time the charge was that he had hired mountebank Alexander Amadei to poison the duke of Grafton and his brother, the duke of Northumberland. On this more ludicrous charge Goodman was found guilty and, unable to pay an unfeasible £1000 fine, was sent to the Marshalsea. However, Charles II on his sickbed, perhaps under pressure from the duchess of Cleveland, relented, and on 16 January 1685 remitted the fine. The duchess finally persuaded James II to pardon Goodman fully on 22 October 1685.

Goodman's notoriety certainly grew from his off-stage exploits far more than from his acting. His affair with Cleveland was mocked for decades, as Robert Gould in the revised *The Playhouse, a Satyr* suggests:

> Goodman himself, an Infidel prefess'd,
> With plays reads Cl—d nightly to her Rest.

However, in the 1690s it seems that Goodman took up with a Mrs Wilson from the Pope's Head tavern, Cornhill, according to Delariviere Manley's *Rivella*. Although satirized by tory Manley, Goodman was a Jacobite sympathizer and in 1694 he became embroiled in a conspiracy to kidnap William III. On 3 July 1695 he narrowly escaped a conviction for treason, for celebrating Prince James's birthday (10 June) at the Dog tavern with other Jacobites. By 15 February 1696 the plot had grown into an assassination attempt on King William, coupled with an invasion by James from France. The plot failed and Goodman was captured and committed to Newgate. Because he was privy to only some of the scheme he was not executed immediately, but was persuaded by Archbishop Tenison, among others, to testify against the principal conspirators, particularly Sir John Fenwick. He was bailed and it was probably during this period that he met Colley Cibber and recounted stories from his life. However, before Goodman could give evidence the Jacobites offered him £500 cash and a pension of £500 for life if he would leave the country. He took the money and on 29 October 1696 left for France. In France he seems to have been imprisoned for a while, but was soon received at the exiled court of James at St Germain. The French were not sure what to make of these conspirators, and Lord Ailesbury's *Memoirs* report that in 1713 Goodman was in Montélimar, supported by a pension of £87 10*s*. a year but obliged to remain in that area. There is no record of Goodman's death, but it is likely that he died in exile, some time after 1713.

J. Milling

Sources Highfill, Burnim & Langhans, *BDA* · W. Van Lennep and others, eds., *The London stage, 1660–1800*, pt 1: *1660–1700* (1965) · J. H. Wilson, *Mr Goodman: the player* (1964) · C. Cibber, *An apology for the life of Mr. Colley Cibber*, new edn, ed. R. W. Lowe, 2 vols. (1889) · Venn, *Alum. Cant.*

Likenesses engraving (as Mariamne), repro. in T. Duffet, *The empress of Morocco: a farce* (1674), frontispiece

Goodman, Christopher (1521/2–1603), Church of England clergyman and radical protestant thinker, was born, probably in Chester, into a prominent merchant family of that town. His father was William Goodman, wine merchant and mayor of Chester, and his mother was Margaret, daughter of Sir William Brereton of Brereton. He was educated at St Werburgh's Abbey (later King's) School, Chester, and in 1536 went up to Brasenose College, Oxford, graduating BA in 1541 and MA in 1544. He later moved to the recently refounded Christ Church, becoming a senior student in 1547 and subsequently Lady Margaret professor of divinity. He was a leading member of the circle around Pietro Martire Vermigli (known as Peter Martyr), then regius professor of divinity, who was the figurehead for the university's radical ecclesiastical party in Edward VI's reign. Goodman's ordination probably took place at Oxford and in April 1553 he was presented by his college to the rectory at Adel in Yorkshire.

Queen Mary's accession forced Goodman to leave Oxford and he initially went into hiding among the London protestant underground before leaving for exile on the continent. He travelled first to Strasbourg, staying with his old mentor Peter Martyr, and then to Frankfurt. Here he became embroiled in the 'troubles' among the English exile congregation over the Book of Common Prayer. After Knox's enforced departure, Goodman shared the leadership of the 'Knoxian' group with William Whittingham, a fellow native of Chester. In 1555 they led that group to Geneva, where with Calvin's assistance it constituted itself as a separate exile congregation, electing Goodman and Knox as its ministers. The two men worked extremely well together, forming a close and lifelong friendship. With Knox absent for long periods, the Geneva congregation under Goodman's leadership became the largest and most productive of the English exile churches. It published its own *Forme of Prayers*, which later became the Scottish Book of Common Order and was the preferred liturgy for English puritans. It also produced the Geneva Bible, the most popular biblical translation in England and Scotland until the King James version. However, the resistance tracts were the most notorious Genevan writings, especially Goodman's *How Superior Powers Oght to be Obeyd of their Subjects* published on 1 January 1558 alongside Knox's *First Blast*. Because his book justified resistance to ungodly rulers and questioned the legitimacy of female ones, Queen Elizabeth regarded Goodman with a deep and abiding antipathy. On his return to England in 1559 he remained in hiding, leaving for Scotland after receiving Knox's plea for assistance. The Englishman immediately became minister in Ayr though he was translated to St Andrews in summer 1560, shortly after visiting the Isle of Man to preach. During his five-year ministry he transformed the previous ecclesiastical capital of Scotland into a model reformed burgh. The political turmoil of the chaseabout raid in the autumn of 1565 and his close association with the earl of Moray, one of the rebel leaders, forced Goodman to leave the country. During the following winter he served in Newcastle as minister to the Scottish exiles, but did not return with them in March 1566. Instead, he chose to go to Ireland as chaplain to the newly appointed lord deputy, Sir Henry Sidney.

Goodman tackled the task of evangelization in Ireland with characteristic vigour and zeal, and in the autumn of 1566 nearly persuaded his old friend Knox to join him. Sidney and Archbishop Loftus of Armagh were sufficiently impressed to recommend him for promotion, as either archbishop of Dublin or dean of St Patrick's, Dublin. He was denied both posts, probably because of Elizabeth's hostility, and in 1568 he returned to Chester. A marked man, he was summoned before the ecclesiastical commission in 1571, and made to retract his resistance theories and submit on ecclesiastical matters. Having been deprived of his benefice at Odell in Bedfordshire, he was allowed to return to the north-west, though he continued to fight for further reform, especially during the admonition controversy of 1572. During this crisis and for most of his long career, Goodman received protection and patronage from Robert Dudley, earl of Leicester, and was a fringe member of the Leicester–Sidney political and literary circle.

For the remainder of his life Goodman was based in Chester, heavily involved in all types of local affairs, from organizing financial collections to the laying of the city's drinking-water pipes. Away from the disapproving gaze of the queen, he was appointed to Aldford parish and the archdeaconry of Richmond in the diocese of Chester, where he helped organize diocesan 'exercises' similar to those under royal ban in the south. He kept in close touch with events in Scotland, but was unable to undertake the farewell preaching tour of the country proposed in 1580. He remained an indefatigable preacher, giving a celebrated sermon in Exeter in 1583, probably at the request of Mrs Anne Prowse (formerly Locke), a friend from the Genevan exile congregation. In 1584 Goodman predictably refused to subscribe to Archbishop Whitgift's articles, but continued undisturbed in Chester. Never one to avoid an intellectual battle, he was frequently employed in disputations with Catholics, even when he was in his seventies. He died in Chester on 4 June 1603, having been visited on his deathbed by James Ussher, the future archbishop, whose family had known Goodman in Dublin. Having been labelled a 'puritan' and 'Genevan' throughout his career, Goodman proudly recalled he had been granted citizenship of that reformed city and in his will left it a bequest. Little is known about his family; his wife, Alice, had died in 1587 and was buried in St Bridget's, Chester, where her husband was minister and where he, too, was buried. They had at least one daughter, Kathleen, but no surviving sons.

Goodman regarded himself as primarily a 'preacher of God's word' but, of the many sermons he gave during his fifty-year ministry, only the Exeter text has survived. He made a considerable, hitherto unacknowledged, contribution to the British liturgical tradition through his work on the *Forme of Prayers* and as a member of the team which translated the Geneva Bible, though it is unlikely he wrote the commentary on Amos which Anthony Wood tentatively attributed to him. He probably wrote the anonymous series of sonnets forming a meditation upon the penitential Psalm 51 which Anne Locke appended to her translation of Calvin's sermons published in 1560. Later that decade at Goodman's request the meditation was set to music by Andrew Kemp and included in the manuscript St Andrews psalter edited by Thomas Wode.

Goodman's fame rests primarily upon his book *How Superior Powers* which started as a sermon for his Genevan congregation. Although considerably expanded, the tract never lost its exegetical and homiletical tone. The preacher employed his text from Acts 5: 29 to demolish the doctrine of non-resistance to secular rulers which had been English orthodoxy during the reigns of Henry VIII and Edward VI. When explaining obedience to divine law, he proposed the simple, if crude, theory of the 'contrary', asserting that God's negative commandments implied a positive corollary. For example, 'Thou shalt not kill', in addition to forbidding murder, implied actively seeking the welfare of others. From his concept of the covenanted people of God, Goodman developed a right of resistance to an ungodly ruler. In his most revolutionary passages, he declared this right could be exercised by the common people as well as the magistrates. Despite their radical nature, Goodman's ideas did reflect one strand within exile thinking. However, his proposition, that the people wielded 'a portion of the sworde of justice', frightened many contemporaries (Goodman, 180). After Elizabeth's accession some former exiles sought to distance themselves from his views. But important elements of Goodman's political analysis remained intact and, as part of the legacy of the exile, unobtrusively entered into the Anglo-Scottish protestant culture developing during the latter part of the sixteenth century. Alongside those of his close friend Knox, Goodman's ideas thus became part of the common heritage of the British reformations and the culture of the entire English-speaking world.

JANE E. A. DAWSON

Sources Emden, *Oxf.*, 4.241–2 • *DNB* • J. Dawson, 'Trumpeting resistance: Christopher Goodman and John Knox', *John Knox and the British reformations*, ed. R. A. Mason (1998), 130–53 • J. Dawson, 'Early career of Christopher Goodman and place in development of protestant thought', PhD diss., U. Durham, 1978 • J. Dawson, 'Resistance and revolution in sixteenth-century thought: the case of Christopher Goodman', *The church, change and revolution*, ed. J. van den Berg and P. Hoftijzer (Leiden, 1991) • G. J. Piccope, ed., *Lancashire and Cheshire wills and inventories from the ecclesiastical court, Chester*, 3, Chetham Society, 54 (1861), 166–71 • 'A sermon of Christopher Goodman's in 1583', *Journal of Presbyterian Society of England*, 9 (1949), 80–93 • W. S. Bailey, 'Christopher Goodman', *Journal of the Chester Archaeological and Historic Society*, new ser., 1 (1887), 138–57 • D. H. Fleming, ed., *Register of the minister, elders and deacons of the Christian congregation of St Andrews*, 1, Scottish History Society, 4 (1889) • register, 1547–1619, Christ Church Oxf. • BL, Harley MS 2038 • *The collected works of Annie Vaughan Lock*, ed. S. Felch, Renaissance English Text Society, 21 (1999) • C. Goodman, *How superior powers oght to be obeyd of their subjects* (1558)

Archives BL, application for licence to preach in England, Egerton MS 1818 • BL, retractions, Add. MS 29546 • Denbighshire RO, Rutlin, corresp. and papers | BL, letter to Lord Leicester relating to his imprisonment, Add. MS 32091 • Ches. & Chester ALSS, corresp. with John Knox and others • PRO, state papers Scottish, SP 52

Wealth at death see will, 1603, Piccope, ed., *Lancashire and Cheshire wills*

Gabriel Goodman (1528–1601), by unknown artist, *c.*1600

Goodman, Gabriel (1528–1601), dean of Westminster, was born on 6 November 1528 at Nantclwyd House in Castle Street, Ruthin, Denbighshire. He was the second son of Edward Goodman (1476–1560), mercer, who in 1508 had made an advantageous marriage to Cicely (1493–1583), daughter of Edward Thelwall of Plas-y-ward, a member of the principal family of the Vale of Clwyd. It has been plausibly suggested that Gabriel received his earliest education from clergy of the collegiate church of Ruthin, an institution that he would eventually replace with his own charitable foundation. At Michaelmas 1546 he matriculated sizar at Jesus College, Cambridge; he migrated to Christ's, becoming fellow there by Lady day 1552 and remaining for two years. He graduated BA in early 1550 and proceeded MA in 1553. In February 1564 the university by special grace enabled him to proceed to the degree of DTh, which he did on 2 July. By this time he gave his college as St John's. This second migration may have followed from his association with Sir William Cecil, a Johnian, from whom he had his employment. He became schoolmaster to Cecil's household at Wimbledon late in 1554, where he would have taught Cecil's elder and as yet only son, Thomas. Between Goodman and Cecil there was established a lifelong friendship.

Goodman's churchmanship was always more conservative than Cecil's. Both conformed under Mary. But Goodman, by accepting institution (at Cecil's presentation) to the rectory of South Luffenham, Rutland, on 30 September 1558, demonstrated his willingness to serve the papal church. He resigned this living by October 1562; he had meanwhile acquired (1559) the first portion of the rectory of Waddesdon, Buckinghamshire, to which he would add the second portion on 25 November 1569. On 23 October 1559, at Cecil's petition, the crown presented Goodman *sede vacante* to the prebend of Chiswick in St Paul's Cathedral, which he held to his death. When Westminster Abbey was refounded as a collegiate church on 21 May 1560, Goodman was named one of the twelve canons, being installed with his colleagues on 30 June. Following the premature death of William Bill, Goodman was advanced to the deanery on 13 August 1561, and was installed on 29 September. This office, too, he held for his remaining life.

Goodman was often proposed for the episcopate, first of all in 1570 when the see of London was vacated by Grindal's translation to York. Parker told Cecil (30 March) he thought Goodman a 'sad, grave man' but 'in his own private judgment peradventure too severe' (Bruce and Perowne, 360). The appointment went to Edwin Sandys. In 1575 Parker suggested Goodman to succeed John Parkhurst at Norwich, telling Cecil again that he respected his 'sad and sure governance in conformity'. He further confided his preference for Goodman over the other two (John Piers and John Whitgift) on his shortlist since Goodman was one of the few who might 'dull that lewd governance' of the puritans at which the queen took such offence (ibid., 473, 477–8). Parker hinted that Goodman's candidature was opposed by the earl of Leicester on behalf of his chaplains, and by the queen's almoner, Edmund Freake of Rochester, the successful candidate. Goodman was recommended for Rochester in 1581, and in 1584 again for that see or Chichester; in 1596, at the age of sixty-five, he supposed he had actually been given Chester. These unachieved moves ought not necessarily to be seen as failures. The deanery of Westminster had not yet acquired the distinctive status which sets it above all but the grandest bishoprics; Goodman's successors for two centuries would be consecrated away from or in addition to the deanery. It is nevertheless likely that Goodman had matured into an *éminence grise*, whom Cecil, successive archbishops, and perhaps even the queen, wanted to keep close at hand. His talents found better employment in his metropolitan deanery than they would have done in a rural palace. Nor is there any suggestion that Goodman himself sought further preferment.

In 1562 Goodman was appointed an ecclesiastical commissioner. He was also frequently employed on *ad hoc* commissions, and from 1569 sat as JP for Middlesex. In the convocation of 1563 he was among those who resisted attempts to alter the settlement of 1559, and he remained unsympathetic to further reform. During 1564 he was much involved in arranging the queen's visit to Cambridge. His educational interests extended in the following year to Merchant Taylors' School, of which he became a regular visitor. In 1568 he translated 1 Corinthians for the Bishops' Bible, and he later gave support in a number of ways to William Morgan's translation of the Bible into Welsh. In 1574 he built the new schoolhouse at Ruthin, from which the present school dates its origin and honours Goodman as founder. Having acquired the site of the former collegiate church in the town, he procured letters patent of 14 August 1590 to establish Christ's Hospital there for twelve almsfolk; following a petition to the queen he was on 24 May 1595 further empowered to endow his foundation and to make statutes for it.

Frequent though his visits to his birthplace were, Goodman was predominantly resident at his deanery. In forty years he scarcely missed a meeting of the chapter. On 16 October 1566 he appeared before the House of Commons in defence of the residual privileges of the Westminster sanctuary, then under threat. Despite rather than because of the fanciful arguments he deployed against it, the bill for abolition was lost. He naturally dominated all the abbey's affairs, but his association with the school is best remembered. In the 1560s the dean and canons had taken a share in teaching and accommodating the boys. Goodman made a more enduring contribution to Westminster School by granting (in a complex series of transactions in 1570–72) the property at Chiswick held by virtue of his St Paul's prebend. This was vested in the dean and chapter as a refuge in time of plague. In 1575 Goodman used his influence with Cecil (now Lord Burghley) to secure Westminster's right to send a quota of scholars to Christ Church, Oxford. He prompted Burghley to make a benefaction to the school in 1591, and also acted as agent for Lady Burghley's educational patronage. The city of Westminster was restructured by act of parliament in 1585, and Goodman became first head of the new corporation; Burghley was his high steward.

Goodman's achievements at Westminster were finally honoured by his chapter colleagues with the award of free oats for his horses for the rest of his life. He (and they) enjoyed this modest facility for only a month. Goodman died on 17 June 1601 at his deanery. He was buried in St Benedict's Chapel, Westminster Abbey, where his monument stands. He had already (1574) given a Complutensian polyglot Bible to the chapter library, and gave another in his will to Sidney Sussex College, Cambridge. Although neither set is extant, some 121 of his books do survive. Among particular bequests he gave an Aldine Bible to Jesus College, Oxford, a Latin Bible to Jesus, Cambridge, and a Hebrew lexicon to the Bodleian Library. He possessed two portraits of Lady Margaret Beaufort, one of which he left to Christ's. He made bequests to almost all the collegiate body at Westminster, to his foundations at Ruthin, and to his many kin (not a few of whom he employed in various capacities at Westminster).

Much as Goodman accomplished, greater things were prophesied for him:

> Arçangel yw'r enw o seiliaw
> Arç-esgob vydd ddydd â ddaw
> By name an archangel,
> an archbishop he will become.
> (Newcome, appx C)

No archbishopric came to him; but he has his pallium in the affection and pride with which his memory is recalled in his native town. C. S. Knighton

Sources R. Newcome, *A memoir of Gabriel … and Godfrey Goodman* (1825) • K. M. Thompson, *Ruthin School: the first seven centuries* (1974), 9–36, 73–82, 162–98 • *Fasti Angl., 1541–1857*, [St Paul's, London], 28 • *Fasti Angl., 1541–1857*, [Ely], 69, 82 • *CPR, 1560–63*, 95, 279, 336; *1569–72*, 226, 262, 440; *1575–8*, 287 • *Calendar of the manuscripts of the most hon. the marquis of Salisbury*, 11, HMC, 9 (1906), 5; 13 (1915), 164, 208–9 • R. C. Barnett, *Place, profit and power: a study of the servants of William Cecil, Elizabethan statesman* (1969), 68–72 • J. Peile, *Biographical register of Christ's College, 1505–1905, and of the earlier foundation, God's House, 1448–1505*, ed. [J. A. Venn], 1 (1910), 41 • J. Venn, ed., *Grace book Δ* (1910), 178, 487 • G. I. Soden, *Godfrey Goodman, bishop of Gloucester, 1583–1656* (1953), esp. 10–15 • J. Sargeaunt, *Annals of Westminster School* (1898), esp. 10–11, 14–15, 34–5 • C. S. Knighton, ed., *Acts of the dean and chapter of Westminster*, 2 vols. (1997–9) • BL, Lansdowne MS 118, fol. 35*v* • Northants. RO, Peterborough diocesan records, Institution Book I, fols. 70*v*, 97*v* • *Correspondence of Matthew Parker*, ed. J. Bruce and T. T. Perowne, Parker Society, 42 (1853), 336, 360, 370, 383, 390, 473, 476–7, 477–8 • [W. Camden], *Reges, reginae, nobiles* (1600) • G. Williams, *Wales and the Reformation* (1997) • P. McGrath and J. Rowe, 'The recusancy of Sir Thomas Cornwallis', *Proceedings of the Suffolk Institute of Archaeology*, 28 (1958–60), 226–71, esp. 259–60 • monumental inscription, Westminster Abbey, London

Archives Hatfield House, Hertfordshire, Cecil MSS • Westminster Abbey, Westminster Abbey muniments

Likenesses oils, *c.*1600, priv. coll. [*see illus.*] • G. P. Harding, watercolour, 1800–40 (after unknown artist), NPG • R. Graves, line engraving (after unknown artist), BM, Ruthin School; repro. in Kenyon-Thompson, *Ruthin School*, following p. 64 • oils, NMG Wales; repro. in Soden, *Godfrey Goodman*, facing p. 20 • stone bust, Ruthin church; repro. in Thompson, *Ruthin School* • stone effigy, Westminster Abbey; repro. in Thompson, *Ruthin School*

Wealth at death provided 200 marks for his funeral: will, Thompson, *Ruthin School*, 190–97

Goodman, Godfrey (1583–1656), bishop of Gloucester, was born in Ruthin, Denbighshire, on 28 February 1583, the second son of Godfrey Goodman (*c.*1539–1587), a former chapter clerk at Westminster Abbey, and his wife,

Jane Croxton (*c*.1558–1638), a local woman who was the daughter of a London mercer; he had four younger sisters. In 1592 he was admitted as a chorister and queen's scholar to Westminster School, where his uncle Gabriel Goodman (1528–1601) was dean and William Camden, an appointee of Goodman's, was headmaster.

Early career In Easter term 1599 Goodman went up to Trinity College, Cambridge, and he became a Westminster scholar later that summer. On 1 November 1603 he was ordained deacon by Bishop Henry Rowlands of Bangor, despite being under canonical age, and between that year and 1605 he held part of the sinecure rectory at Llansannan, no doubt to maintain him at university. He graduated BA in the spring of 1604 and remained nine further terms in Cambridge before proceeding MA in 1607. On 20 December 1606 he had been ordained priest in London by Bishop Richard Vaughan, his fellow countryman, and on the same day had been instituted to the crown living of Stapleford Abbots, near Romford, Essex. His initial absence from the parish, the consequence of fulfilling university residence regulations, led to censure from Samuel Harsnett at his archdeaconry visitation of 1607, but for a decade thereafter Goodman treated Stapleford Abbots as his home, becoming a close friend of the poor. He later claimed that 'noe poore man dined at his owne home but was ever invited' (Cambridge, Trinity College, MS C.6.3).

Goodman's parish was a short distance from Anne of Denmark's palace at Theobalds, and soon after 1608, possibly through the influence of Robert Cecil, he became one of the queen's household chaplains. It was to her that he dedicated *The Fall of Man, or, The Corruption of Nature* (1616), which derived from his Essex sermons. Having been offered the reversion of a canonry at Windsor in 1607, he was finally granted a stall on 20 December 1617. Once Goodman had paid for the completion of work on the house in the close which his predecessor had left unfinished, Windsor became his habitual home, and he was a regular attender of the chapter. The traditional liturgy there seems to have appealed to him, and he recorded wearing a cope and amice every year on St George's day and joining services when he could: 'God was there continually and daily served like a God, with the greatest magnificence' (Goodman, 1.341).

Goodman had continued to derive income from Welsh sinecures—Llandysul, Montgomeryshire, from 1607, Ysgeifiog, Flintshire, from 1617, and Llanarmon in Yale from 1621—and on 19 June 1620 he was appointed rector of West Ilsley, Berkshire. On 4 January 1621 he also became dean of Rochester, from where he maintained his interest in historical research and in the navy. The following year he published an anonymous satire on the irreligion of his day, *The Creatures Praysing God, or, The Religion of Dumbe Creatures*, which he used as a vehicle for dissemination of his sacramentalist understanding of the church. When the work appeared in French in 1644, it received an imprimatur.

Bishop of Gloucester As soon as news came of the death on 20 October 1624 of Bishop Miles Smith of Gloucester, Goodman went to London to seek the vacant see. Several candidates were considered, including Windsor colleagues Richard Montagu and Gilbert Primrose as well as the lord keeper's candidate, John Preston, and the appointment was first offered to Joseph Hall, but when he declined it was given to Goodman. He thus received the poorest English bishopric, worth a paltry £315 per annum even in 1680; although he surrendered all his livings he was allowed to retain *in commendam* both the Windsor canonry and his Berkshire rectory, as well as other benefices worth less than £200 per annum. Almost immediately he found himself in dispute with the king over the chancellorship of the diocese. Goodman hoped to retain the clergyman William Sutton (Miles Smith's son-in-law), who had been appointed in 1623, and when James I tried in November 1624 to force him to accept Owen Gwyn, he steadfastly resisted. Following his consecration as bishop on 6 March 1625 and enthronement by proxy on 4 April, Goodman set Sutton to undertake the primary visitation of the diocese that May, but Charles I, adhering to his father's preferences, wanted only civil lawyers to be granted ecclesiastical jurisdiction, and overruled his bishop. In March 1627 the king, hoping to settle the matter conclusively, established a commission under Archbishop Abbot, Lord Keeper Coventry, the earls of Pembroke and Dorset, and secretaries Conway and Coke, but Sutton was not immediately ousted, and continued as one of two chancellors at least until 1631. In the meantime, Goodman waited until the abatement later in the year of an outbreak of bubonic plague before entering his cathedral: he spent the interim at Windsor, missing only two chapter meetings that summer.

Goodman was soon to be censured for his increasingly sacramentalist views. A court sermon preached on Passion Sunday, 26 March 1626, was 'supposed to trench too near the borders of popery' (Heylyn, 153), and was denounced by William Prynne for impertinently preaching five points of popery before the king. When convocation discussed the sermon on 29 March, Archbishop Abbot, William Laud, and the bishops of Durham and Winchester were called on to adjudicate. Laud recorded in his diary that 'we advised some things therin were spoken less cautiously, but nothing falsely; that nothing was innovated by him in the doctrine of the Church of England' (*The Works of … William Laud*, ed. J. Bliss and W. Scott, 7 vols., 1847–60, vol. 5). It is not clear whether Goodman was censured in the House of Commons at the same time but the sermon did not affect relations with the peers and Goodman attended regularly and was soon put on working committees of the house. In the 1628 parliament he was an equally keen attender, missing only one session (24 March), and with most of the other bishops he voted against the petition of right.

At Gloucester, Goodman set about trying to improve both his episcopal revenues and his lands. Following the king's lead, he sought to develop his woods properly. Perhaps his most significant contribution came when in August 1629 he asked his deanery clergy to help him establish a lending library, primarily for clergy but 'likewise for the use of gent and stranger, such as are students' (BL, Sloane MS 1119, fols. 92–3). This was not his first enthusiasm for libraries as thirteen years earlier he had written to the vice-chancellor of Cambridge University to urge him, in vain, to establish a public library such as Bodley's in Oxford (5 September 1616). He intended to be in Gloucester every Thursday to oversee the project:

> God knows I have noe other end in this but only his glorie, the good of his church, the advancement of Religion and learning; that wherein every private man cannot furnishe himselfe he might be supplied out of our common storehouse. (ibid.)

The bishop's aim was to use duplicate copies and gifts to provide a substantial working library to replace the lost conventual library.

Goodman stayed within his diocese, as enjoined by royal order, except for sitting in 1631 as one of the eight bishops called to the high commission with four civil lawyers to hear the case of Sir Giles Alington's incest with his niece. He returned from London to hold his third visitation across his nine deaneries. The articles for the previous visitations have not survived but those for July 1631 required that those who were to receive communion, act as godparents, or be married had first to be episcopally confirmed. This was long objected against Goodman and ten years later it was alleged against him during his trial for impeachment. In addition his articles are unusual in enjoining that clergy 'indeavour (as far forth as he can) especially in market townes, to reade short morning prayers at six a clock before men goe to their labours' (*Articles to be Enquired of* …, 1631, advertisement 1).

In time the cathedral chapter became more congenial to Goodman: Accepted Frewen, president of Magdalen, became dean by proxy on 13 September 1631 and Gilbert Sheldon held the fourth stall from 26 February 1633, albeit with a royal licence not to reside. However, he seems never to have been fully at ease, and when the bishopric of Hereford fell vacant for a second time in 1633 he wasted no time in securing his election on a royal nomination. He had, he claimed, accepted Gloucester on the half promise that when a better see fell vacant he should be offered it. Laud, the new archbishop of Canterbury, urged Charles to overturn this appointment, even though Goodman had already set out from his palace, The Vineyard, for Hereford with his chattels. On 21 March 1634 the dean and chapter at Hereford finally signified that they had elected Augustine Lindsell to the see, void *per spontaneam renunciacionem* of Godfrey, bishop-elect. From this point on relations between Laud and Goodman were strained and when Goodman still complained, having offered to resign after asking that he might at least have a coadjutor-bishop to work with him, Laud, himself a former dean of the same cathedral, tellingly replied on 13 September that he was disinclined to believe 'that Gloucestershiremen are so much different from all other Englishmen as that Goodman can fit himself to any other diocese but not to that' (PRO, SP 16/274/21). His fourth triennial visitation, at Lammastide, can have brought him little comfort that year. Despite the co-ordinated efforts of bishop and dean to improve things, Sir Nathaniel Brent found much still amiss in the diocese during the metropolitical visitation of 1635. Goodman made only infrequent annual reports to Canterbury of the state of the see, returning none in 1633, 1636, and 1637, and when he did it was to lament that the county was full of impropriations, which greatly impoverished his clergy. However, as bishop he did seek to provide for the people and between 1625 and 1646 he instituted no fewer than eighty-two incumbents across the diocese, although none between 1634 and 1636.

Political and religious stance Goodman's personal faith, and his increasingly perceived sympathy for Rome, later led to accusations that the disappointed bishop may have been actively seeking to be reconciled privately to the Catholic church. He was lavish, and somewhat naïve, in the friendships that he made, and counted Father Francis à Sancta Clara (Christopher Davenport) and the papal agent the Scot George Conn among them. For his daily spiritual reading he followed the Roman breviary. In the giddy world of the 1630s when court spirituality was seen as a hybrid of French Catholicism, Spanish suspicion, and protestant dogmatism, rumours of his contacts, which may have stemmed from no more than a genuine wish for a reunification of the churches, could only redound to Goodman's ill favour. In his 1636 attack on prelates, William Prynne denounced 'that Good-man, S. Godfrey of Glocester' as he 'hath also erected a Crucifix and Altar in his Cathedral at Gloster, and solemnly consecrated altar clothes for them' (Prynne, 43). Prynne, with Burton and Bastwick, returned to the assault in 1637 and singled out Goodman for attack in their petition to Charles, repeating the allegations of 1636 and claiming further that the refurbishment of the town cross at Windsor had afforded the bishop the chance to decorate it with images of the Calvary and the resurrection and that at Gloucester Goodman had unfairly removed a lecturer at Little Dean, Walter Ridler. Goodman was generous in pursuing the beauty of holiness but his judgement may not always have been politic: even the mayor of Windsor, writing on 4 August 1635 to thank Goodman, feared that the inclusion of a crucifix without a royal licence might be deliberately misunderstood by many.

By 1638 allegations about Goodman's private faith were repeated openly at Rome and were reported back to Secretary Windebank by Sir William Hamilton, who was serving there as English agent. Ill constructions were placed upon Goodman's request for a royal licence to travel abroad to take the waters, as a cure for his lifelong malady of gallstones, and to observe the life of other churches. Edmund Attwood, the vicar of Hartbury and a confidant of the bishop, testified in July 1638 to Windebank that, although Goodman was vexed in his diocese and disappointed since his failure to be translated to Hereford, he had only intended to travel, possibly as far as Jerusalem, for the good of his body and soul. The request was not granted. Coming so soon after Goodman's appearance before the high commission for allowing the church at Tetbury to be used for a session of civil magistrates (for which he was fined £300), it was unlikely that he would find much favour at court. He retreated to Windsor, but although it had proved a safe haven for twenty-one years, and although he had given unstinting service to the chapter, it was not to be home to him for much longer and, whether or not at Laud's insistence, he was removed from the chapter in 1639. Throughout 1639 he can be found sedulously at work in his diocese, assuring himself of the bona fides of Scottish educated ministers' sons, reproving Richard Byford, a notorious adulterer, and examining presbyterian-inclined curates.

The meeting of the Short Parliament took Goodman to London, and he was a regular attender. After the dissolution of parliament on 5 May he remained to sit in convocation, and on 20 May he refused to assent to the new ecclesiastical canons. It is unclear whether his objections were grounded on the technicality that convocation could only meet when parliament was in session, or on a point of conscience, but he was widely reported to have gibbed at the canons which most closely attacked a Roman understanding of the sacraments. When he did subscribe on 29 May it was with some degree of reservation, for he was suspended from his office and livings by a vote in both houses of convocation and imprisoned at the Gatehouse at Westminster. Goodman petitioned the king to be heard before his peers and on 2 June he sought to have his private papers returned to him. Only after six weeks was he released, on sureties of £10,000, and on 10 July he took the oath to the new canons, signing immediately after Laud and Juxon. He was restored to his see, but it brought little comfort, and on 28 August he wrote to the archbishop informing him that he had always told Abbot that he would make a poor bishop, that the loss of Hereford still rankled, and that he was galled that he had not been given a coadjutor. Once he had paid off his debts he intended to resign his bishopric and live off his 'small commendam' (PRO, SP 16/465/29). He had no time in which to carry out his intentions and in August the following year he was among those bishops whom the Commons decided to impeach for signing the new canons. All his havering and conscience had been to no purpose, and Goodman would be treated alike with his peers who had acted with less thought. The actual process towards impeachment was overtaken by events in parliament although the strength of the bishops' demurrer ultimately led to the action being set aside (December 1641).

Goodman had stayed in his diocese during the summer recess, ordaining eleven priests and eleven deacons in his chapel in September and instituting two priests in October. The new session of parliament which began on 21 October 1641 set about a second Bishops Exclusion Bill. On 28 December only Goodman and William Piers of Bath and Wells managed to run the gauntlet of hostile mobs to sit in the Lords, and two days later Goodman joined eleven other bishops in subscribing to John Williams's 'Protest', complaining of the public harassment to which they had been recently subjected. John Pym's retort was that the bishops had acted treasonably. When they were taken to the bar of the House of Commons in February 1642, a week after royal assent had been given for the Exclusion Bill, all except Goodman refused to plead: he registered a plea of 'not guilty'.

Pastor and scholar, 1642–1656 After his return to Gloucester on bail Goodman continued to work on his proposed volume of church history and, in defiance of the law and of the covenant, he continued to exercise his episcopal powers, administering to the spiritual needs of the diocese: in June 1642 he held an ordination of priests and deacons at The Vineyard and he carried out five institutions later that summer. Only in October 1642—when the order for sequestrating the fines, rents, and profits of bishops and capitular bodies had come into effect—did Goodman prudently withdraw from his palace to West Ilsley. The Vineyard was sacked and its chapel demolished by Lord Stamford during Christmas 1642–3; seven of the overzealous wreckers were killed by falling masonry. In the summer of 1643 Goodman was discovered in London and brought before the committee for examinations in the House of Commons. He was released on a pledge of £1000 given as a bond to John Hunt, the serjeant-at-arms (18 July 1643).

Some time later in 1643 Goodman left for his estates in Wales, at Coed-maur, near Caernarfon, where he eked out an existence as best he could. An order for the sequestration of his tithes from West Ilsley was made in September 1644 and reiterated at Reading on 13 April 1646, when it seems to have taken effect. The loss of this income drove him to 'live uppon a poore tenement which formerly I gave to charitable uses' (Goodman to James Cranfield, 20 June 1647, Knole, Sackville MS II, 12), and when the sequestrators locally threatened to remove his remaining estates he petitioned the Lords for restitution, which was granted. For two years he sought the restoration of his tithes from West Ilsley, finally producing a broadsheet petition in August 1649, protesting 'that wittingly and willingly, he never did, nor ever shall offend the Parliament' (BL, Broadside 190 g. 12 (15)). The petition had no immediate effect for all that it held reputable signatures from burgesses in Gloucester, Tewkesbury, Cirencester, and Windsor.

By July 1650 Goodman was living in London at Chelsea College and working there and in the libraries of Sir Thomas Cotton and of Sion College, determined to finish a history of his times. The publication that year of Sir Anthony Weldon's gossipy *The Court and Character of James I* led Goodman to write a rejoinder that was less partisan than Sir William Saunderson's *Aulicus coquinareae*, but, whereas the latter was published immediately, Goodman's work was not printed until 1839. In 1652 he moved to a small property in the churchyard of St Margaret's, Westminster, owned by Sibilla Aglionby, widow of the former dean of Canterbury. The next year he dedicated a volume of theology jointly to Oliver Cromwell and to the master and fellows of Trinity College, Cambridge. *The Two Great Mysteries of Christian Religion* has been vilified since Thomas Carlyle's day as semi-popish jargon intended to flatter Cromwell, but this seems a misrepresentation. As in his earlier works, Goodman was attempting to set aside the heresies of the Socinians while portraying his own sufferings in the cause of religion as being in the manner of Christ. More important, he claimed that, as the most senior living bishop in the province of Canterbury, it was his duty to discuss doctrines of the Trinity and the incarnation in the light of modern philosophy. His sincere hope, based on his experience of liturgical change at St Margaret's, that Cromwell would back the reintroduction of order and dignity into the church, was soon found to be misplaced. In July 1655 Goodman made a final appeal to Cromwell for subsistence, earlier petitions to the committee for plundered ministers having failed him. He was to be disappointed.

Goodman died, unmarried, on 19 January 1656 and was buried on 4 February in St Margaret's, Westminster. There is no evidence that he converted at his death, or earlier, to the Church of Rome. NICHOLAS W. S. CRANFIELD

Sources G. I. Soden, *Godfrey Goodman, bishop of Gloucester, 1583–1656* (1953) • G. Goodman, *The court of King James the First*, ed. J. S. Brewer, 2 vols. (1839) • PRO, SP 14/175/44; 14/176/26; 14/182/21; 16/56/27; 16/77/34; 16/91/16; 16/274/21; 16/455/51; 16/465/29 • P. Heylyn, *Cyprianus Anglicus* (1668) • BL, Sloane MS 1119 • W. Bazeley, 'Gloucester Cathedral library', *Record of Gloucester Cathedral*, 3 vols. (1888–97) • W. Prynne, *A looking glasse* (1636) • R. R. Tighe and J. E. Davis, *Annals of Windsor*, 2 vols. (1858) • Knole, Kent, Sackville MS II, 12 • R. Newcome, *A memoir of Gabriel … and Godfrey Goodman* (1825) • Venn, *Alum. Cant.* • Windsor chapter acts, 6, B.2, fol. 58

Archives Bodl. Oxf., corresp. and papers, Add. MS c. 205 | BL, letter to Bishop Juxon with an account of sufferings, Egerton MS 2182 • CKS, letters to Lionel Cranfield

Wealth at death see will, repr. in Newcome, *Memoir of … Godfrey Goodman*, appx P; BL, Baker MS XXXVIII, 427 sig.

Goodman, James (1828–1896), Church of Ireland clergyman and music collector, was born on 22 September 1828 at Ballyameen, Dingle, co. Kerry, third of the nine children of Revd Thomas Chute Goodman (*bap.* 1793, *d.* 1864) and his wife, Mary, *née* Gorham, of Castleisland, co. Kerry. His father and paternal grandfather John were successive curates in the Church of Ireland (Anglican) parish of Dingle. He is believed to have received private tuition—from either a neighbour, Joseph King, or a Mr Earle—before entering Trinity College, Dublin, in 1846 to read arts and qualify himself in divinity. He graduated BA in 1851 and was ordained a priest on 22 May 1853.

In October 1852 Goodman married Charlotte King (1826–1888), daughter of his presumed former tutor King. The Kings lived at Ventry, the Goodmans near by on a rented farm of 105 acres overlooking the sea. Goodman was by then working as curate for the Irish Church Missions—to convert Irish-speaking Roman Catholics to protestantism—and thus continued in different parts of co. Cork until becoming rector of Abbeystrewry parish (later canon of Ross) and taking up residence in the rectory at Baltimore Road, Skibbereen. During the 1850s the couple had had three sons: Francis George (*b.* 15 July 1853), Godfrey (*b.* 13 Dec 1854), and James (*b.* 11 Nov 1856), who died in an accident in 1881. Frank and Godfrey both moved to England, their descendants living in England and Wales.

The English surname Goodman appears in Ireland from at least the seventeenth century. Its English origins were remembered: Goodman's grandfather evidently occupied in later life the living at Kemerton, Gloucestershire, which had been held by Godfrey Goodman, bishop of Gloucester (1583–1656). Goodman wrote of his family's English descent and his own Irishness as of a paradox:

> Yet I am not of the old root of the Gaels but of Saxon stock, though my ancestors settled long ago in the West of co. Kerry, where they learned the Irish language and … became, as we say, nearly *ipsis hibernicis hiberniores*. Thus nothing was dearer to me from my youth than to be listening to the old tales of adventure and the stories of Fionn, nor any music sweeter in my ears than the surpassingly sweet music of Ireland. (trans. from Ó Fiannachta, 'Díonbhrollach', 222–3)

For all we know, Goodman may never have left Ireland. There he grew up speaking Irish with the ease of his Kerry neighbours and writing it with academic competence. He was, in fact, appointed professor of Irish at Trinity College, Dublin, on 21 June 1879, and thereafter spent each year partly in Dublin, while a curate had charge of his parish. The little he wrote was usually in Irish, including hymns and moral texts for the use of converts. Similarly motivated but more unusual is the long, partly published Gaelic poem in debate form (anonymous but certainly his) on the merits of the Roman Catholic and protestant religions: *The Debate of Brian and Art*. But his interest in literature expressed itself chiefly in collecting manuscripts in older Irish, sharing their contents with others, copying them himself in elegant Gaelic script, and signing this scribal work Séamus Gudman[n]. An Irish manuscript tradition still existed in his day: in December 1848 it was to a local scribe he turned, Patrick Landers, to get the written words of a song, 'An buachaill caol dubh' ('The Slim Dark Fellow').

Goodman compiled four volumes of musical fair copies—his chief legacy—between 1860 (or somewhat earlier) and 1866. They make up Trinity College, Dublin, MSS 3194–3197, and contain some 2300 tunes—all monophonic—in his hand. He identifies over 500 as his own notations from 'Munster pipers &c.'. A local piper was his major source: Tom Kennedy, a convert to protestantism whom he must have known well and met often. Goodman, moreover, was himself an uilleann piper: his notations sometimes suit the pipes better than other instruments, or, if song airs, better than the voice. Of his remaining tunes many come from unknown manuscripts or oral sources, others from manuscripts or published texts identified or conjectured. The second category displays the breadth of his interests, not only in traditional Irish but in other musical varieties, including popular urban, operatic, military, classical, Scottish, and English.

Of greatest intrinsic value is Goodman's orally transmitted Irish music. Dance tunes—jigs, reels, and hornpipes—with marches and the two unusual descriptive pieces, 'The Fox Hunt' and 'Allisdrum's March', comprise the best of the instrumental items. The airs—of songs in Irish or English—were noted from singing or playing, chiefly in ornate versions. The best of them are lyrical, including love songs and laments. It is unfortunate that Goodman, despite his apparent claim to have copied words of the songs, did not include them with his melodies. But his linguistic, instrumental, and vocal talents undoubtedly gave his notations idiomatic quality unusual in his century.

Goodman died at Skibbereen rectory on 18 January 1896, and was buried nearby at Creagh on the 21st. His collection long remained in manuscript, but the first of two volumes edited by the undersigned appeared in 1998 as *Tunes of the Munster Pipers: Irish Traditional Music from the James Goodman Manuscripts*. HUGH SHIELDS

Sources P. Ó Fiannachta, ed., *An Canónach Séamas Goodman* (1990) • B. Breathnach, 'Séamas Goodman (1828–1896), bailitheoir ceoil [James Goodman … music collector]', *Journal of the Kerry Archaeological and Historical Society*, 6 (1973), 152–71 • B. Breathnach, 'The pipers of Kerry', *Irish Folk Music Studies*, 4 (1985), 4–29 • F. O'Neill, *Irish minstrels and musicians* (1913) • *Cork Advertiser* (25 Jan 1896) • P. Ó Fiannachta, ed., 'Díonbhrollach lámhscríbhinne le Séamas Goodman' [James Goodman's introduction to a manuscript], *Éigse*, 15 (1973–4), 222–3 • parish registers, St James's Church, parish of Dingle, Kerry, Ireland • An Seabhac [P. Ó Siochfhradha], 'An tOllamh Séamas Goodman agus a mhuinntir [pt 1]', *Béaloideas*, 13 (1943), 286–91 • An Seabhac [P. Ó Siochfhradha], 'An tOllamh Séamas Goodman agus a mhuinntir [pt 2]', *Béaloideas*, 23 (1954), 237–9 • W. M. Brady, *Clerical and parochial records of Cork, Cloyne, and Ross*, 3 (1864) • R. J. Griffith, *General valuation of rateable property in Ireland: county of Kerry* [1852] • B. Ó Conchúir, *Clár lámhscríbhinní Gaeilge Choláiste Ollscoile Chorcaí: cnuasach Uí Mhurchú* (1991) [catalogue of MSS in Irish in University College Cork: Murphy collection] • P. de Brún, *Clár lámhscríbhinní Gaeilge Choláiste Ollscoile Chorcaí: cnuasach Thorna* (1967) [catalogue of MSS in Irish in University College Cork: Torna collection] • J. B. Leslie, *Ardfert and Aghadoe clergy and parishes* (1940) • Burtchaell & Sadleir, *Alum. Dubl.*, 2nd edn • C. Smith, *The ancient and present state of the county and city of Cork*, 2 (1750); repr. R. Day and W. A. Copinger, eds. (1893) • *Kerry Evening Post* (12 Dec 1832), 3 • memorial window, Skibbereen church, co. Cork [Charlotte Goodman]

Archives Royal Irish Acad., containing a poem in Irish by Goodman to his brother George, MS 233 (=3 B 25) | Dingle Public Library, Kerry, Cnuasach Duibhneach, MS letter-book of Thomas Chute Goodman (subject's father), MS and printed texts, no. 8 [8/4/1854–9/8/1854] • TCD, music collection of fair copies, late 1850s (?)–1860s, MSS 3194–3197 [unique text in his own hand: gaelic script for Irish, roman for English] • University College, Cork, Murphy [Uí Mhurchú] MSS • University College, Cork, Torna [Tadhg Ó Donnchadha] MSS, 35, 59

Likenesses group photograph, *c.*1870, priv. coll. • photograph, *c.*1880, repro. in O'Neill, *Irish minstrels and musicians*

Wealth at death £624 7*s.* 2*d.*: administration, 7 March 1896, *CGPLA Ire.*

Goodman, John (*bap.* **1592**, *d.* **1645**), Roman Catholic priest, was baptized at Ruthin, Denbighshire, on 7 November 1592, the son of Gawen Goodman and his second wife, Gaynor Price. He was therefore a first cousin to Godfrey Goodman, bishop of Gloucester, whose ambivalent relationship to the Church of Rome made him an object of suspicion to his more godly colleagues. John Goodman was educated at St John's College, Cambridge, where he matriculated in 1612, graduating BA in 1617. He took orders on 20 September 1618 and went to London, where he was curate of St Nicholas Olave for a time before his conversion to Catholicism by Richard Ireland. This took place in Paris about 1621 and Goodman entered the seminary at Douai on 12 February 1621, but left in minor orders on 6 May 1624 for the Jesuit noviciate at Watten. He did not proceed with the Jesuits, but was ordained as a secular priest somewhere in France about 1631. He returned to England, but was soon arrested and imprisoned in Newgate from 1632 until about 1635, when he was discharged. The release of an active and zealous priest with connections to the establishment was criticized by puritans like William Prynne, and Goodman's freedom was shortlived, for he was prisoner in the Gatehouse on 1 July 1637. He was released shortly afterwards but imprisoned, once again in the Gatehouse, in 1639. Another brief period of freedom followed before his arrest on 17 January 1640 and indictment as a priest on 29 August. He was found not guilty, but on the evidence of a fellow prisoner was later condemned to death on 21 January 1641. His influential connections and the possible intervention of Queen Henrietta Maria secured a reprieve from Charles I, but in the heightened political temperature of the day Goodman's case became an important issue between crown and parliament, the king receiving a remonstrance from both houses demanding Goodman's execution. Lengthy statements were prepared by both his supporters and opponents, with parliament referring especially to his former status as a Church of England clergyman as a further factor against him. In the worsening relations between king and parliament Goodman intervened personally, petitioning Charles that he, Goodman, might be executed rather than become a source of division between the parties. Goodman's letter resulted in parliament withdrawing its demand for the death penalty, a compromise was effected, and Goodman was committed to prison indefinitely, dying in Newgate some time in 1645. WILLIAM JOSEPH SHEILS

Sources G. Anstruther, *The seminary priests*, 2 (1975) • *JHC*, 2 (1640–42) • *JHL*, 4 (1628–42) • Venn, *Alum. Cant.*

Goodman [*née* Salaman], **Julia** (**1812–1906**), portrait painter, was born on 9 November 1812 in London, the eldest daughter of the fourteen children of Simeon Kensington Salaman, a member of a Jewish family of German and Dutch origin and warden of the Western Synagogue, and his wife, Alice Cowen, an amateur pianist. The composer Charles Kensington *Salaman (1814–1901) was her eldest brother; her younger sister, Kate Salaman (1821–1856), was a miniature painter. Most members of her family attended the West London Synagogue of British Jews from its establishment in 1842.

In the 1820s Julia Salaman was educated at Miss Belisario's school in Islington, London, and then about 1830 studied art both at Sass's academy and privately with Robert Falkner, a pupil of Sir Joshua Reynolds, under whose guidance she copied old masters at the British Institution and then devoted herself to portrait painting in oil and pastel. She married Louis Goodman (*d.* 1876), a City merchant, in 1836; they had seven children, one of whom was Walter Goodman (*b.* 1838), portrait painter and author. Her husband was an invalid for many years and Julia Goodman was obliged to support the family. She exhibited at the Society of British Artists (SBA) (1834–89), the Royal Academy (1838–63), the British Institution (1837, 1848), the Royal Manchester Institution (1858, 1886), the Liverpool Society of Fine Arts (1859–62), the Liverpool Institute of

Fine Arts (1863), and the Liverpool Academy (1865), and was represented by thirty works, between 1858 and 1884, at the Society of Female Artists (SFA) of which she was a member from 1865 to 1872. Her sitters included Dr Van Oven (exh. RA, 1857), the earl of Westmorland (exh. RA, 1858; Royal Academy of Music, London), Sir George Macfarren (exh. SBA, 1885/6; Royal Academy of Music, London), Sir Francis Goldsmid (exh. Society of Female Artists 1861; West London Synagogue), the Revd Professor David Marks (West London Synagogue), Sir John Erichsen, and Gilbert Abbott à Beckett. She also exhibited portraits of three notable women—Fanny Corbaux (exh. SBA, 1836, and RA, 1844), Bessie Raynor Parkes (exh. SFA, 1866) and Barbara Leigh Smith Bodichon (exh. SFA, 1866)—and portrayed many members of her family.

Exhibition catalogues reveal that Julia Goodman had numerous London addresses: she settled in the Notting Hill area in 1869 and towards the end of her life resided with her daughter, Mrs Passingham, at 56 Clarence Square, Brighton, Sussex, where she died on 30 December 1906. She was buried on 1 January 1907 at the Golders Green cemetery of the West London Synagogue. Her portraits numbered over one thousand in 1904, the year in which she ceased working. CHARLOTTE YELDHAM

Sources *Jewish Chronicle* (4 Jan 1907), 12 • Graves, *Artists* • Graves, *RA exhibitors* • Graves, *Brit. Inst.* • J. Soden and C. Baile de Laperrière, eds., *The Society of Women Artists exhibitors, 1855–1996*, 4 vols. (1996) • J. Johnson, ed., *Works exhibited at the Royal Society of British Artists, 1824–1893, and the New English Art Club, 1888–1917*, 2 vols. (1975) • E. Morris and E. Roberts, *The Liverpool Academy and other exhibitions of contemporary art in Liverpool, 1774–1867* (1998) • exhibition catalogues (1858); (1886) [Royal Manchester Institution] • D. Foskett, *A dictionary of British miniature painters*, 2 vols. (1972) • *Art Journal*, new ser., 27 (1907), 64 • *DNB*

Archives Royal Academy of Music, London • West London Synagogue

Likenesses A. Cole (Mrs Samwell), portrait, 1842, RA • drawing, repro. in *Jewish Chronicle*, 12

Goodman, Sir Stephen Arthur (*d.* 1844), army officer, entered the army in October 1794 as ensign of the 48th foot, in which he became lieutenant in 1795 and captain in 1803. He served with the 48th in Minorca, with the force sent to Leghorn in 1800 under Lieutenant-General Sir Charles Stuart to co-operate with the Austrians, and at the capture of Malta. He accompanied the 48th to the Peninsula in 1809, and commanded the light companies of Stewart's brigade of Hill's division at the battle of Talavera. In 1810 he was appointed deputy judge-advocate, with the rank of assistant adjutant-general in Wellington's army. He was present at the capture of Badajoz, and was placed in charge of the French governor Phillipon, whom he was ordered to take to Elvas. At the capture of Madrid and at the siege of Burgos, and in the subsequent retreat, Goodman acted for the adjutant-general of the army (Waters), absent through illness.

In 1814 Goodman was appointed deputy judge-advocate of the troops proceeding to America, but exchanged to a similar post in the British force left in the Netherlands under the prince of Orange. He was deputy judge-advocate of Wellington's army in the Waterloo campaign and at the occupation of Paris. His supersession was dictated by the duke's belief in the need for a lawyer at the head of the department. Goodman retired on half pay of his regimental rank at the peace, attaining major-general's rank in 1842, and was made KH.

In 1819 Goodman was appointed colonial secretary of Berbice, to which in 1821 was added the then lucrative appointment of vendue-master in Berbice and Essequibo (later British Guiana). His colonial services extended over twenty-four years, during which he was in charge of the government of the colony from May 1835 to October 1836. During the insurrection of 1823 he was deputed by Governor Murray to organize a militia, and held the office of major-general and inspector-general of militia in the colony up to his death. He died in British Guiana on 2 January 1844, leaving a widow and eleven children.

H. M. CHICHESTER, *rev.* JAMES LUNT

Sources Fortescue, *Brit. army*, 2nd edn, vol. 4 • J. Weller, *Wellington in the Peninsula, 1808–1814*, new edn (1992) • J. Philippart, ed., *The royal military calendar*, 3rd edn, 5 vols. (1820) • *GM*, 2nd ser., 21 (1844), 539

Goodrich, Edwin Stephen (1868–1946), zoologist, was born on 21 June 1868 at Weston-super-Mare, Somerset, the youngest of the three children of the Revd Octavius Pitt Goodrich (*c.*1830–1868), rector of Humber, Herefordshire, and his wife, Frances Lucinda Parker (*c.*1838–1936). His ancestors included Thomas Goodrich (*d.* 1554), lord chancellor and bishop of Ely, and John Goodricke (1765–1786), the deaf mute astronomer. Edwin's father died when he was two weeks old, and his mother took her family to live with her mother at Pau in south-west France. Goodrich went to a French school and then to a local English one, and his experiences of early childhood at a time when France suffered the Prussian invasion were probably responsible for his deep affection for France (and contrasting aversion for Germany) in later life.

In 1888 Goodrich was entered as a student of the Slade School of Fine Art at University College, London, where he came into contact with E. R. Lankester (1847–1929), then professor of zoology, and switched his studies towards zoology with a view to entering the British Museum (Natural History). However, in 1891 Lankester was appointed to the Linacre chair of comparative anatomy at Oxford, and he offered Goodrich a post as his assistant. Goodrich accepted and entered Merton College as a commoner in 1892. While much of his time was taken up with his own researches, demonstrating and teaching, Goodrich was also responsible for reorganizing the exhibition cases of the University Museum. This he did with much gusto, but with regard only to the scientific visitor—his attitude being that 'one need seek neither to attract the nursery-maid nor to amuse children, nor … satisfy the idle curiosity of the sightseer' (private information), an attitude which would now be considered curatorially, if not politically, incorrect. In 1894 he was awarded the Rolleston memorial prize, and in the following year he obtained a first class in the final honour school of natural science (morphology). Also in 1895 he was awarded the Naples biological scholarship and spent some time researching at the Stazione Zoologica in that city. In 1898 he obtained the Radcliffe travelling fellowship, with the help of which he visited India and Ceylon to study their marine fauna. In the same year he succeeded William Blaxland Benham as Aldrichian demonstrator in comparative anatomy, and in 1900 he was elected a fellow of Merton. In 1913 Goodrich married Helen Lucia Mary Pixell, the protozoologist, daughter of the Revd Charles Henry Vincent Pixell, vicar of St Faith's, Stoke Newington, London. She collaborated with him in some of his researches, and assisted him with teaching. There were no children.

A special professorship of comparative embryology was created for Goodrich in 1919, and in 1921 he succeeded G. C. Bourne as Linacre professor of zoology and comparative anatomy at Oxford, a chair associated with Merton College, from which Goodrich was therefore never parted throughout his long career at Oxford. He resigned from the chair in 1945 and was elected an honorary fellow.

Goodrich's first paper, an account of a large and rare squid which had been caught off Salcombe, Devon, was published in the *Journal of the Marine Biological Association* in 1892, and his researches in the dozen years which followed—mostly on the Cephalopoda (squids and octopuses), Oligochaetes (marine worms), and the fossil mammals—led to his being elected FRS in 1905. For more than half a century he worked without intermission on nearly all the groups of the animal kingdom, in every case making contributions to knowledge of the first importance. To obtain his material he went all over the world; in addition to the zoological stations at Plymouth and at Naples, he visited Tatihou, Roscoff, and Banyuls in France, Munich and Heligoland, the United States, Canada, Bermuda, Ceylon, Malaya, Java, Madeira, the Canary Islands, Morocco, Tunisia, the Balearic Islands, and Egypt.

One of Goodrich's first (and greatest) contributions to knowledge was the demonstration of the difference between the nephridium or primitive kidney and the coelomoduct or primitive reproductive duct. Previously these two sets of ducts had often been confused and wrongly described. Basing himself on the view that they were originally distinct and separate, Goodrich proceeded to show that they could be recognized and distinguished from each other in all the groups of the animal kingdom. Shortly before his death he published the last part of a substantial 266-page review of the work that had been done in this field; it included many previously unpublished observations.

Goodrich's researches usually started from the premise that, however complex a problem might appear, its solution must rest on a simple basis, and he planned his work in consequence. With a remarkable flair for clearly identifying significant facts, he was able to unravel such tangles as the segmental structure of the head, both in invertebrates and in vertebrates. He enabled a complete classification of fishes to be built on his recognition of the true nature of the differences between the various types of fish scales. His enthusiasm and dedication to natural science are exemplified by his editorship of the *Quarterly Journal of Microscopical Science* from 1920 for more than a quarter of a century.

While most of Goodrich's publications consisted of the papers, beautifully illustrated by himself, in which he described the results of his researches, he also wrote a number of books which have had a vast influence on the teaching of zoology in all countries. But they, too, really fall under the category of research, because he undertook personal investigations of all the more important points on which there had been uncertainty. This applies particularly to his textbook *Vertebrate craniata: Cyclostomes and Fishes* (1909) and to his *Studies on the Structure and Development of Vertebrates* (1930). At the same time he never lost sight of the subject of zoology as a whole, and his book *Living Organisms: an Account of their Origin and Evolution* (1924) is considered a classic of its time, being based on critical analysis and careful exposition.

The effect of Goodrich's teaching, both in the classroom and in the research laboratory, has been widespread, and has shown that detailed studies in the comparative anatomy of related animals can give results of great importance from the point of view of the sciences of evolution and homology, and in the field of taxonomy, embryology, and neurology. His students remembered him with affection, even though he was strong on prevarication, and seemed always to drift back to talking about fishes, and indeed was said much to resemble one. His lectures were greatly enlivened by his blackboard illustrations, done in coloured chalks with the sure touch of the artist—and often carefully built up in optical sections with a three-dimensional perspective. He appointed a wide range of the best of his own students to teaching posts at Oxford, notably the evolutionist Gavin de Beer, the ecologist Charles Elton, the ornithologist Bernard Tucker, the physiologist J. Z. Young, and the entomologist and geneticist E. B. Ford.

Goodrich's early leanings towards art never deserted him and may even be said to have formed part of his training in research and in teaching. His landscapes in watercolours, mostly painted on his foreign travels, were frequently exhibited by him in London.

Goodrich received the royal medal of the Royal Society in 1936, and served on its council from 1923 to 1925 and from 1931 to 1932; he was vice-president between 1930 and 1931. He was awarded the gold medal of the Linnean Society in 1932; he had acted as zoological secretary from 1915 to 1923. He was an honorary or foreign member of the New York Academy of Sciences, the Academy of Sciences of the USSR, the Royal Swedish Academy of Sciences, the Royal Academy of Belgium, the Société de Biologie de Paris, the National Institute of Sciences of India, and the International Institute of Embryology of Utrecht in the Netherlands. Goodrich was also awarded honorary degrees by universities in Edinburgh and Dublin.

Goodrich died at his home, 12 Park Town, Oxford, on 6 January 1946. He was a quiet, reserved, and unassuming man with a dry sense of humour and a gentle and kind manner, but quite inflexible in following the course he felt to be right.

G. R. DE BEER, *rev.* CLEMENCY THORNE FISHER

Sources G. R. de Beer, *Obits. FRS*, 5 (1945–8), 477–90 • private information (2004) [Jane Pickering, Museum of Zoology, U. Oxf.] • *Quarterly Journal of Microscopical Sciences*, 348/87 (1946)

Archives NHM, letters • U. Oxf., zoology department, corresp. and papers | BL, corresp. with Macmillans, Add. MS 55219 • Rice University, Houston, Texas, corresp. with Sir Julian Huxley

Likenesses W. Stoneman, photograph, 1931, NPG • photograph, repro. in de Beer, *Obits. FRS* • print, Merton Oxf.

Wealth at death £30,686 12*s*. 10*d*.: probate, 25 May 1946, *CGPLA Eng. & Wales*

Goodrich, Richard (*b*. before **1508**, *d*. **1562**), lawyer and administrator, was a younger son of the staple merchant Richard Goodrich (*d*. 1508) of Bolingbroke, Lincolnshire, and his wife, Alice Etton of Firsby, and was a cousin of Thomas Goodrich, bishop of Ely. Richard married Mary, daughter of the evangelical London grocer John Blage (the wedding guests included leading reformers like Rowland Taylor); they had a son and daughter. Following their divorce, which was formalized about 1551, he wed *c*.1552 Dorothy Badbye, widow of George Blage; she was still alive in 1582, when her name was Dorothy Jarmyn.

After studying for a time at Jesus College, Cambridge, Goodrich was admitted to Gray's Inn in 1532, and embarked upon a legal career which soon included work in the new court of augmentations. At the same time he served as a JP and sewer commissioner for his native county from 1539, and as a Lincolnshire chantry commissioner in 1546. He represented Grimsby in the parliaments of 1542, 1545, and 1547, participating actively in drafting and revising bills.

Appointed attorney of the court of wards in May 1546, Goodrich exchanged this office in January 1547 for that of attorney in the reorganized court of augmentations. As the pace of religious reform quickened after 1547, the evangelical lawyer's responsibilities multiplied. He was included in commissions to root out heresy (1551, 1552), and appointed to the committee of thirty-two lawyers and divines charged with revising the ecclesiastical laws (1552). A London chantry commissioner in 1548, Goodrich also had primary responsibility for surveying the city's church goods in the summer of 1552.

The restoration of Catholicism in 1553 and the dissolution of the court of augmentations (January 1554) temporarily ended Goodrich's public career. Despite rumours that he intended to join other protestants abroad he remained in London during Mary's reign, afflicted with gout and vexed by a chancery suit brought by his first wife, Mary, demanding restoration of her dowry. With the accession of Elizabeth, however, Goodrich returned to royal service. In early December 1558 he submitted a memorial to the queen counselling caution in restoring protestantism but recommending pre-emptive strikes against leading Catholics and efforts to counter papal propaganda. That same month Goodrich served on a committee of lawyers preparing for the upcoming parliament, and he later played his part in implementing the Elizabethan religious settlement, both as a member of the powerful ecclesiastical commission created in July 1559 and as a commissioner taking oaths of supremacy from clergy. Goodrich's extensive augmentations experience also earned him membership in the commission to sell crown lands (October 1561).

Goodrich died in May 1562 at his house in Whitefriars, London, and was buried at St Andrew's, Holborn. The distinguished mourners at his funeral on 25 May 1562 were led by Archbishop Parker and Bishop Grindal, Lord Keeper Bacon and Chief Justice Catlyn—as befitted an individual earlier praised by Hugh Latimer as a 'godly man of law in this realm' (*Acts and Monuments*, 7.516).

P. R. N. CARTER

Sources *LP Henry VIII*, vols. 14–21 • A. R. Maddison, ed., *Lincolnshire pedigrees*, 2, Harleian Society, 51 (1903) • N. L. Jones, *Faith by statute: parliament and the settlement of religion, 1559* (1982) • HoP, *Commons, 1509–58* • *CPR, 1547–53; 1558–63* • *CSP dom.*, rev. edn, *1547–53* • PRO, PROB 11/45, fols. 104*v*–105*v* • PRO, PROB 11/16, fol. 64*v* • PRO, C1/1354/66–8 • S. Brigden, *London and the Reformation* (1989) • G. A. J. Hodgett, *Tudor Lincolnshire*, History of Lincolnshire, 6 (1975) • *The acts and monuments of John Foxe*, new edn, ed. G. Townsend, 8 vols. (1843–9), vols. 6–8 • BL, Egerton MS 2599, fol. 22*v*

Goodrich, Simon (1773–1847), engineer and dockyard manager, was born on 28 October 1773, the son of Isaac Goodrich of Suffolk. Nothing is known of his early education and training, but in December 1796 he was appointed a draftsman to the mechanist in the office of Sir Samuel Bentham (1757–1831), inspector-general of naval works. In October 1799 he was appointed mechanist at an annual salary of £400.

Goodrich was chief assistant to Sir Samuel Bentham and he carried out the various schemes of improvement instigated by Bentham for the dockyards. Goodrich was also heavily involved in the introduction of steam power and the establishment at Portsmouth and other dockyards of mills for working wood and metal, the block-making machinery mills, mills for making cordage and rope, and the millwright's workshop.

The engineer Joshua Field (1787–1863) was a pupil of Goodrich from 1803 to 1805. Between August 1805 and November 1807 Goodrich acted as Bentham's unpaid deputy during the latter's absence in Russia. He remained as mechanist until December 1812, when the inspector-general's office and staff were abolished, following suspicions about Bentham's private business ventures. Goodrich continued as mechanist without warrant, working on a freelance basis, until April 1814, when he was reappointed engineer and mechanist to the Navy Board at an annual salary of £600. After Bentham's departure, Goodrich managed the engineering works of the dockyards, and acted as a consultant to the Navy Board on engineering matters. This entailed residence at Portsmouth, until his retirement in 1831. His annual pension was £400.

Goodrich was elected a corresponding member of the Institution of Civil Engineers in December 1820, and transferred to membership in December 1837. Among his voluminous papers and drawings, preserved in the Science Museum Library, is a detailed daily journal, which, though not fully complete, extends from 1802 to 1845. It shows that he was in professional contact with most of the important engineers of the day, including Richard Trevithick, Marc Isambard Brunel, Henry Maudslay, and Matthew Murray; many of their letters are preserved with his papers, which also provide valuable information about the engineering manufactories he visited as he travelled throughout the country on naval business. They contain a mass of illustrated notes about machinery, advertising leaflets, and details of prices, weights, and dimensions.

Goodrich's personal life is obscure. His wife's name is not known, but he had a daughter called Mary: when his post under Bentham was abolished he wrote to the Navy Board requesting compensation for loss of office as his salary was barely enough to maintain his family, and he had no savings. Goodrich moved to Lisbon in 1834 and died there on 3 September 1847, his importance unrecognized by an obituary. A. P. WOOLRICH

Sources E. A. Forward, 'Simon Goodrich and his work as an engineer, pt 1, 1796–1805', *Transactions* [Newcomen Society], 3 (1922–3), 1–15 • E. A. Forward, 'Simon Goodrich and his work as an engineer, pt II, 1805–1812', *Transactions* [Newcomen Society], 18 (1937–8), 1–27 • A. S. Crossley, 'Simon Goodrich and his work as an engineer, pt III, 1813–1823', *Transactions* [Newcomen Society], 32 (1959–60), 79–91 • J. G. Coad, *Architecture and engineering works of the sailing navy* (1989)
Archives Sci. Mus., drawings, papers, and diaries

Goodrich, Thomas (1494–1554), bishop of Ely and lord chancellor, was a younger son of William Goodrich of East Kirkby, Lincolnshire, and his wife, Katherine. He was educated in Lincolnshire and at Jesus College, Cambridge.

Early life At Jesus, Goodrich was an exact contemporary and close friend of his fellow Lincolnshire student Thomas Cranmer. Having graduated BA in 1510 and MA in 1514 he became a fellow of the college and was made a proctor in 1515. He was ordained deacon in Lincoln diocese in 1522, and priest the next year. Little is known of his Cambridge career, though he proceeded to a doctorate in civil law during the 1520s. In 1529, perhaps as a consequence of his friendship with Cranmer, he was drawn into royal favour, as one of the team of divines researching the legality of the king's marriage to Katherine of Aragon. On 16 November of that year he was admitted to the rectory of St Peter Westcheap, London, on the presentation of Wolsey, who held it as commendatory of St Albans Abbey. Further promotions followed: to a royal chaplaincy and to one of the canonries of St Stephen's, Westminster, the latter during 1533. He enjoyed the patronage of the Boleyns. Meanwhile he had been one of the syndics appointed by the University of Cambridge to rule on the legality of the Aragonese marriage, and his support of the royal cause led to further work for the annulment team. He had a major share in the production of *The Glass of Truth* (1532), which argued against the resolution of the divorce dispute at Rome.

Evangelical reformer In 1533 Goodrich was sent on embassy to France, and then early in 1534 was catapulted to high ecclesiastical office. Nicholas West's designated successor as bishop of Ely, his nephew Nicholas Hawkins, died on embassy to Emperor Charles V in January of that year. Within a month of the government receiving the news Goodrich was promoted to Ely: he was elected on 17 March, given custody of the temporalities on 2 April, and consecrated at Croydon by his friend the new archbishop on 19 April. Goodrich's rapid rise to the senior ranks of the episcopate must have been driven by the regime's need to find a reliable prelate and sure supporter of the royal supremacy to manage the see that contained the key University of Cambridge. He proved his worth to his royal master in the first turbulent years of the Reformation: in 1535, for example, he ordered the preaching of the royal supremacy in all Cambridge parishes by the masters and fellows of the colleges. His support for the supremacy already seems to have been underpinned by cautious evangelical sentiment. He intervened as college visitor in the affairs of St John's College in the early 1540s, negotiating a compromise between the warring fellows by which the radical master, John Taylor, was required to reinstate three conservatives he had expelled, but Thomas Lever was admitted to the fellowship in balance. His interest in the wider reform movement is also indicated by those he supported in his immediate entourage: Peter Valens, an important French reformer, became his almoner, and William Meye, much later to be nominated as archbishop of York under Elizabeth, was his first vicar-general and official principal. During the rest of Henry VIII's reign Goodrich was a consistent supporter of his friend Cranmer's efforts to sustain moderate reformation. He was one of those involved in the production of the Bishops' Book in 1537, but achieved greater prominence as a vigorous speaker during the controversy over the Act of Six Articles (1539), when he was often one of only three prelates speaking openly for the evangelical cause.

In the aftermath of the conservative triumph Goodrich had some uncomfortable moments: in December 1540, for example, he was suspected of encouraging the translation of Melanchthon's attack on the six articles and the privy council ordered his study to be searched. However, he continued as a spokesman of the evangelical cause: in 1541 he and Robert Holgate, bishop of Llandaff, contributed to the king's doctrine commission and worked to modify conservative views on the liturgy. The next year he was one of only two bishops, the other being Barlow of St David's, who supported Cranmer's reformist view on the revision of the Great Bible, and he no doubt assisted the latter's efforts to torpedo the whole project. But Goodrich did not automatically replicate the archbishop's beliefs: in his responses to questions on the mass posed in 1540 he argued against his friend that communion in both kinds was unnecessary. In both 1543 and the last year of Henry's reign Goodrich seems to have been in the thick of battles between evangelicals and conservatives: he was one of those commissioned to examine Dean Heynes of Exeter in 1543, and participated in the trial of the Windsor heretics, where, according to Foxe, he and the bishop of Hereford showed sympathy with John Marbeck 'so far as they durst'

(*Acts and Monuments*, 5.486). The execution of Anne Askew and John Lascelles in 1546 touched some of his close contacts, especially the courtier George Blagge, who was arrested but not tried.

Diocesan business All of this involvement does not seem to have prevented Goodrich from spending time and energy on his see: in the early 1540s at least he was in the country for about two thirds of his time; he held his primary visitation in person and showed interest in ways in which the new religious order could be enforced. Early in his tenure of the see, for example, he suggested to Cromwell that an old oath employed by Bishop West against Lutheranism might be adapted to become a general clerical oath against the authority of the pope. He was hostile to images: his 1541 visitation articles went further than the letter of the 1538 royal injunctions, by ordering the removal of all images liable to abuse and the return of certificates of their destruction from the clergy. After 1541 *de facto* control of the patronage of the prebends of the newly erected chapter of Ely enabled him to support influential reformers such as Richard Cox and Matthew Parker. He also took steps to protect his estates from external threat: in 1535 he made a 'great lease' of all the unencumbered land of the see to his older brother John Goodrich. This may have been intended to discourage courtiers questing for attractive properties, and Goodrich did succeed in limiting direct attacks on his lands: only the manor of Hatfield was lost to the crown in 1538. But his support of family and dependants did not stop at the 'great lease': he gave long leases of valuable manors, often in reversion, to family and servants, thereby restricting his successors' ability to take an economic rent from the see for the rest of the century. In more positive vein he extended and repaired the palace at Ely, an important symbol of commitment to residence at the jurisdictional heart of the see.

Elder statesman and chancellor By the beginning of Edward VI's reign Goodrich was ready to emerge as one of the elder statesmen of the protestant movement. He was the only evangelical bishop consistently opposed to legislation to dissolve the chantries in 1547, presumably because of its attack on church property, this of course despite his actions with his own lands. When the bishops were again asked about the mass in late 1547 he inclined to a commemorative view, reserving his strongest statement for a plea that the whole service should be in English, though Cranmer at this time thought of retaining 'certain mysteries' in Latin. He was one of the committee who met at Chertsey in the autumn of 1548 to discuss the Book of Common Prayer, and a year later was being praised by Hooper to Bullinger as one of six or seven bishops who fully understood the reformed doctrine of the Lord's supper. In 1551–2 he was once again on the commission to revise the prayer book, having been responsible for seeking Bucer's views on reform, produced in the text known as the *Censura*. Goodrich specifically organized Francis Philippe to translate the 1552 book into French for use in the Channel Islands and elsewhere. He was also one of the inner circle involved in the preparation of the reform of the ecclesiastical law. Otherwise in these late Edwardian years he played the predictable roles of a senior establishment bishop: preparing Thomas Seymour, Lord Sudeley, for death; acting as a visitor of Cambridge University; examining heretics, including Joan Bocher; supporting Cranmer in the controversy with Hooper on vestments; serving at Gardiner's trial; and investigating the behaviour of Bishop Day of Chichester as a prelude to the latter's deprivation.

None of this explains how Goodrich became the duke of Northumberland's choice as lord chancellor at the end of 1551. One explanation must lie in the links that Northumberland and he had established either late in Henry's reign, or at least by 1547. In that year Dudley took over the informal lease of Ely Place, Holborn, that had previously been held by Thomas Wriothesley, and it was at Ely Place that the critical meetings preceding the 1549 coup against Somerset took place. Goodrich was perhaps a more solid adherent of Dudley than the other prelates, because it was he who was appointed to the council in November 1549 to tip the political balance in favour of Warwick and the reformers. Few of his duties on the council seem to have been explicitly secular, though he was commissioned to negotiate a marriage treaty between Edward VI and the daughter of Henri II of France in May 1551. Thomas Goodrich received the great seal on 22 December 1551, and the chancellorship on 19 January 1552, after the enforced retirement of Richard Rich. He undertook routine duties, including the opening of Edward's last parliament in March 1553, but there is little sense of his having an independent role. A rare comment is provided by Marten Micronius, who complained in 1552 that Goodrich and Ridley, by their worldly policies, were impeding the work of the commission to reform ecclesiastical law. It seems likely that this last year of Edward's reign brought Goodrich a number of difficulties as relations between Northumberland and Cranmer deteriorated, and reformation ran into crisis. Matthew Parker, who must have known Goodrich well from Cambridge experience, described him as an enigma, gracious and courteous towards his enemies, but abrupt and cool towards friends and sympathizers, possessing therefore the trust of neither. This may partly explain the sense that he was marginalized in the succession crisis of 1553. He appended the great seal to the instrument of succession and followed the rest of the council in supporting Lady Jane, but was not singled out for any major retribution. Mary struck his name from the list of those included for trial as traitors, though the great seal was taken from him as soon as the queen reached London.

Retirement and death Goodrich did homage to Mary at her coronation and was allowed to retain his bishopric. Sir Thomas Cornwallis, who was given the new post of supervisor of all episcopal parks in Norfolk and Suffolk at the end of 1553, may have been one of the agents of reconciliation. This does not mean that Goodrich was trusted by the new regime, and he seems to have been held under house arrest in London until March or April 1554. He was then allowed to return to the country, to the palace of Somersham, Huntingdonshire, where he died on 10 May 1554. His will, dated a fortnight earlier, suggests no spiritual reconciliation with Catholicism: he dedicated his soul to Christ alone, and his worldly goods were divided between family and old reform-minded dependants. In the last six months of his life he also gave away the rights of next appointment to many episcopal livings, again profiting his family, but also limiting the patronage that would be available to his Catholic successor. Robert Steward, the last prior and first dean of Ely, who knew him well, claimed that he died deeply distressed, abhorring the new times. He was buried in his cathedral, where his brass shows him in protestant episcopal dress, the Bible and the great seal in his hands. Goodrich remains a somewhat opaque figure: no personal papers or letters survive and, even though he appears a stalwart friend of Cranmer throughout most of their professional careers, there is no contemporary comment on the quality of their relationship. Burnet's condemnation of him as a 'busy secular spirited man' (Burnet, 2.442) is not sustained by the evidence, but he does seem to have been a man who was difficult to know. The commendation of Robert Steward after his death is positive, but conventional: Goodrich was just, hospitable, and merciful. FELICITY HEAL

Sources F. Heal, 'The bishops of Ely and their diocese, c.1515–1600', PhD diss., U. Cam., 1972 • D. MacCulloch, *Thomas Cranmer: a life* (1996) • register of Archbishop Cranmer, LPL • Goodrich register, CUL, Ely diocesan records, G/1/7 • 'Roberti Stewarde, prioris ultimi Eliensis, continuatio historiae Eliensis', *Anglia sacra*, ed. [H. Wharton], 1 (1691), 675–7 • *Correspondence of Matthew Parker*, ed. J. Bruce and T. T. Perowne, Parker Society, 42 (1853) • *The acts and monuments of John Foxe*, ed. J. Pratt, [new edn], 8 vols. in 16 (1853–70) • *Martin Bucer and the Book of Common Prayer*, ed. E. C. Whitaker, Alcuin Club, 55 (1974) • H. Robinson, ed. and trans., *Original letters relative to the English Reformation*, 1 vol. in 2, Parker Society, [26] (1846–7) • G. Burnet, *The history of the Reformation of the Church of England*, rev. N. Pocock, new edn, 7 vols. (1865) • M. Aston, *England's iconoclasts*, 1 (1988) • J. B. Mullinger, *The University of Cambridge from 1535 to 1625* (1884) • A. R. Maddison, ed., *Lincolnshire pedigrees*, 2, Harleian Society, 51 (1903)

Likenesses H. Holbein, grant of charter to Bridewell Hospital • brass effigy, Ely Cathedral

Goodricke, Sir Henry, second baronet (1642–1705), diplomat and politician, was born on 24 October 1642, the eldest son of Sir John Goodricke, first baronet (1617–1670), of Ribston, Yorkshire, who served in the duke of Newcastle's royalist northern army in the civil wars, and his wife, Catherine Northcliffe (*d.* before 1645). He travelled abroad in 1657 and 1658, visiting France. In 1668 he married Mary (*c*.1647–1715), daughter of William *Legge (1607/8–1670), groom of the bedchamber and lieutenant-general of the ordnance, and his wife, Elizabeth Washington, and sister of George Legge (1648–1691), later Lord Dartmouth.

Goodricke succeeded to the family estates on the death of his father in 1670, and served in a variety of positions in local government in Yorkshire, most notably as a JP for the West Riding from 1667 onwards, and was returned to parliament for Boroughbridge in November 1673, retaining the seat (with only a brief intermission during the exclusion crisis) until his death. Initially an opponent of the court, Goodricke switched his support to the earl of Danby in February 1677 and thereafter was closely associated with the earl's cause.

In 1678 and 1679 Goodricke served as colonel of one of the foot regiments intended to serve in a war against France, fighting and winning a duel against one of his captains who had resigned his commission. He was appointed envoy-extraordinary to Spain on 12 June 1679, and set out after his defeat in the August election. He found the posting expensive, claiming in March 1680 that 'almost my entire credit is worn out, my way of living being as moderate as I can make it' (Goodricke to Clarendon, 6 March 1680, BL, Add. MS 17017, fol. 69). As envoy Goodricke was involved in promoting Charles II's unsuccessful offer to mediate in the dispute between France and Spain resulting from Louis XIV's policy of annexing disputed border territories of the Spanish Netherlands. Goodricke's mission ended controversially when two of his servants rescued a woman accused by the Spanish authorities of selling meat illegally. The government of King Carlos II protested, claiming Goodricke was exceeding his diplomatic privileges, and he was ordered to leave the court. It was suggested that the Spanish were glad of an excuse to get rid of him, having a 'mean opinion' of his 'public and private comportment', although it was also suggested that his zeal on behalf of English merchants in Spain was the real cause of the dislike of him (*Downshire MSS*, 1.14–16). In any event, the incident further soured relations between England and Spain, leading to protests from King Charles II and a suspension of diplomatic relations. Goodricke returned to England and had an audience with the king at Whitehall on 27 March 1683.

During the revolution of 1688 Goodricke acted as the earl of Danby's *de facto* second-in-command in the north. His own anti-Catholicism, a consistent trait over many years, had been reinforced by his temporary dismissal (from September to November 1688) from the Yorkshire magistracy in favour of men of lower social standing. Goodricke's seat, Ribston Hall—said at the time to be 'one of the most charming seats … in the north'—became a centre of Williamite plotting, and Goodricke built a number of new fortifications in his gardens (*Dartmouth MSS*, 1.138). Danby and another aristocratic conspirator, the earl of Devonshire, both visited Ribston during November 1688. Goodricke summoned and addressed a meeting of gentry at York on 22 November, ostensibly to draw up a petition for a free parliament, but in reality a ploy to enable Danby and his followers, notably his son Lord Dunblane, Lord Lumley (one of the seven signatories of the letter of invitation to William), and Goodricke, to seize control of York with the pretext of securing it from an alleged Catholic uprising. With a hundred men of their own, and the support of the four troops of militia in the city, the Williamites quickly overpowered the garrison and those who remained loyal to James.

Goodricke was very active in the Convention Parliament which offered the throne to William and Mary, chairing or sitting on several key committees. His reward for his loyalty to the new regime was the post of lieutenant-general of the ordnance, to which he was appointed on 26 April 1689 (serving until 29 June 1702). Goodricke quickly proved himself a hard-working and highly efficient administrator in this position, regularly attending meetings, dispatching business, and earning high praise: one admiral informed the secretary of state that although he had written to the Board of Ordnance for a dispatch of nails, 'if you would speak two words to Sir Henry Goodricke, we should have them'.

Appointed a privy councillor on 13 February 1690, on 11 July of the same year Goodricke was appointed one of the commissioners investigating the naval defeat at Beachy Head. Danby, by now marquess of Carmarthen (and subsequently duke of Leeds), employed him as his chief manager and spokesman in the House of Commons in the parliamentary sessions between 1690 and 1693. Goodricke was not entirely successful in this position and was supplanted when Carmarthen's rival Sunderland returned to prominence in 1693 and 1694, although he continued to be an active MP, generally supportive of the court. He died at Brentford on 5 March 1705, three days after making a will in which he bequeathed his entire estate to his wife, Mary. He was buried at Ribston, and was succeeded to the baronetcy by his half-brother John, his marriage having been childless.

Goodricke's character was described most thoroughly in the memoirs of his friend and fellow Yorkshire MP, Sir John Reresby: 'this Sir Henry Goodricke was a gentleman of fine parts naturally, and those improved by great reading and travel … we always continued so kind friends that we [were] called brothers' (*Memoirs of Sir John Reresby*, 89). Reresby also called Mary Goodricke 'the finest woman, one of them, in that age' (ibid., 148). However, Reresby was fooled by Goodricke's dissimulation during the 1688 revolution, believing his denial of any scheme to act against James II's interests, 'to which (he being an open man) I confess I gave credit more than I ought to have done; but friendship deceives many' (ibid., 526). J. D. DAVIES

Sources C. A. Goodricke, ed., *History of the Goodricke family*, rev. edn (1897) • *Memoirs of Sir John Reresby*, ed. A. Browning, 2nd edn, ed. M. K. Geiter and W. A. Speck (1991) • *Report on the manuscripts of Allan George Finch*, 5 vols., HMC, 71 (1913–2003), vols. 2–4 • *Seventh report*, HMC, 6 (1879) [Sir Frederick Graham; MSS relating to Lord Preston] • *Report on the manuscripts of the marquis of Downshire*, 6 vols. in 7, HMC, 75 (1924–95), vol. 1, pp. 14–16 • HoP, *Commons, 1660–90*, 2.410–13 • 'Goodricke', HoP, *Commons, 1690–1715* [draft] • will, PRO, PROB 11/481, fol. 50 • PRO, WO 47/17 [board of ordnance minutes, 1695–6] • PRO, WO 46/3 [ordnance letter bk, 1693–5] • H. C. Tomlinson, *Guns and government: the ordnance office under the later Stuarts*, Royal Historical Society Studies in History, 15 (1979) • BL, Egerton MS 3336, fols. 108, 118, 130 [Leeds papers] • letter to Clarendon, 6 March 1680, BL, Add. MS 17017, fols. 68–9 • letters to Sir R. Bulstrode, BL, Add. MS 47899 • *The manuscripts of the earl of Dartmouth*, 3 vols., HMC, 20 (1887–96), vol. 1, pp. 138, 249 • W. A. Shaw, ed., *Calendar of treasury books*, 7, PRO (1916), 1395–6 • N. Luttrell, *A brief historical relation of state affairs from September 1678 to April 1714*, 6 vols. (1857) • *The manuscripts of S. H. Le Fleming*, HMC, 25 (1890), 215, 247, 278 • GEC, *Peerage* • G. M. Bell, *A handlist of British diplomatic representatives, 1509–1688*, Royal Historical Society Guides and Handbooks, 16 (1990)

Archives BL, Leeds papers, Egerton MS 3336 • PRO, ordnance office papers

Likenesses J. Smith, engraving (after T. Hill), BL, Add. MS 64929, fol. 149

Wealth at death see will, PRO, PROB 11/481, fol. 50

Goodricke, Sir John, fifth baronet (1708–1789), diplomatist, was born at Ribston, near Knaresborough, on 20 May 1708, the eldest of three sons (there were no daughters) of Sir Henry Goodricke, fourth baronet (1677–1738), and his wife, Mary, daughter of Tobias Jenkins of Grimston, Yorkshire. His childhood years were spent on the family estate, in country pursuits, and within an atmosphere of physical and spiritual well-being where books and polite conversation abounded. After receiving his early education from a tutor he entered Trinity College, Cambridge, as a fellow-commoner in 1725; he took his BA in 1728 and his MA in 1734. It was at Cambridge that he refined the traits most commonly associated with him in later years: self-discipline, perseverance, and a sound if not creative intellect.

On 28 September 1731 Goodricke married his second cousin Mary, illegitimate daughter of Robert *Benson, Baron Bingley (*bap.* 1676, *d.* 1731), politician; her mother was the daughter of James Sill, a mercer from Wakefield. They had two sons and one daughter. Goodricke succeeded as fifth baronet on 21 July 1738; left with an encumbered estate he spent some difficult years in attempting to restore the family fortune. These attempts, none too successful, ranged from various business ventures to a stint in the Netherlands from 1745 to 1747 as observer for the British government, gathering intelligence on the French army, navy, and court. In 1750, thanks to his Yorkshire connections, he was appointed as British resident in Brussels, an appointment suddenly revoked for reasons unknown. He remained in The Hague from 1751 to 1757, conducting informal discussions with the Dutch about the barrier treaty and gaining valuable diplomatic experience. He also established friendships with the British minister Joseph Yorke (later Baron Dover) and his brother Philip (Viscount Royston and later second earl of Hardwicke), both sons of Philip Yorke, first earl of Hardwicke, lord chancellor.

It was through their influence that Goodricke was appointed as minister-resident to Sweden in 1758; he had to wait in Copenhagen until 1764 before the Swedish government resumed diplomatic relations with Britain that had been severed at the outset of the Seven Years' War. During his enforced stay in Copenhagen, Goodricke, whose wife had remained in England, had a very public affair with Stöulet Katrine (Jackboot Kate), a ballet dancer, and also mastered the Swedish language. He was finally received officially in Stockholm on 25 April 1764 and remained there until 1773. He collaborated closely with the Russian ambassador, Count Ostermann, and worked to secure a defensive alliance with Sweden (1766), to safeguard British trade, and to prevent France's resurgence in the Baltic by supporting the pro-Russian party of the Caps in their resistance to the pro-France Hats. The principal triumph of his mission to Stockholm was the emphatic victory won by the Caps at the election in 1765, which ousted the Hats from government posts. However, hopes that the Anglo-Swedish connection would lead to a Russian alliance did not materialize, as successive British administrations proved unwilling to provide the peacetime subsidies and co-operation in Poland that the Russians demanded. French influence revived after the *coup d'état* of 19 August 1772, by which Gustavus III, a protégé of France, restored royal absolutism.

Goodricke relinquished his Stockholm appointment in 1773, following his wife's succession to the Yorkshire seat of Bramham Park, which brought sudden wealth; he was then free to take his ease as a country gentleman, and devote himself to estate and agricultural improvement. He was elected to parliament for Pontefract in 1774; he supported Lord North's government on the American War of Independence and was in favour of granting further relief to protestant dissenters. He did not stand for re-election to the parliament of 1780 but he was elected for Ripon in 1787 and was appointed a commissioner of the Board of Trade in 1788. He died in New York on 6 August 1789 and was buried in Hunsingore, Yorkshire.

KARL WOLFGANG SCHWEIZER

Sources Venn, *Alum. Cant.* • M. Roberts, *British diplomacy and Swedish politics, 1758–1773* (1980) • M. M. Drummond, 'Goodricke, Sir John', HoP, *Commons, 1754–90* • U. Nott., Galway papers, 12779–12781 • BL, Add. MS 35425 • BL, Egerton MS 1755 • *DNB*

Archives Bodl. Oxf., corresp. • U. Nott. L., letters and papers | BL, corresp. with Robert Gunning, Egerton MSS 2692–2702, *passim* • BL, letters to Lord Hardwicke and Sir J. Yorke, Add. MSS 35425–35444 • BL, corresp. with Lord Sandwich and R. Phelps, Stowe MSS 257–261 • priv. coll., letters to Lord Cathcart

Goodricke, John (1764–1786), astronomer, was born on 17 September 1764 in Groningen, Netherlands, the eldest child of Henry Goodricke (*d.* 1784), of the British consular service, and his wife, Levina Benjamina, the daughter of Peter Sessler of Namur. He became deaf and mute in infancy, and at the age of eight was sent to Edinburgh, where there was a school for deaf mutes. By 1778 he had progressed well enough to transfer to Warrington Academy, Lancashire, where he distinguished himself in mathematics.

In 1776 the Goodricke family had returned to York from the Netherlands, and from 1781 their neighbours included Nathaniel Pigott and his son Edward, accomplished astronomers with a small private observatory. Goodricke and Edward Pigott found a shared interest in stellar astronomy, and Edward was soon combing the literature for data on variable stars. In November he chanced upon a comet, and informed Goodricke, who noted the discovery as the first entry in his 'Journal of astronomical observations'. The following April Goodricke acquired a 2½ foot achromatic refractor by Dollond, and the two friends joined forces to monitor variable stars.

On 7 November 1782 Goodricke routinely noted that the star Algol was as usual of second magnitude, but on 12 November he found it had declined to fourth magnitude. The following night, however, it was again of second magnitude. Such rapid changes in the brightness of a star were unprecedented, and so both men kept watch on Algol. On 28 December each saw the star change brightness in front

John Goodricke (1764–1786), by unknown artist, 1785

of his very eyes, and next day Pigott sent a note to Goodricke suggesting that the star was being eclipsed by a dark companion.

In the following weeks the two friends monitored Algol's brightness and found that the variation occurred in a little under two days, twenty-one hours. Pigott allowed Goodricke to be the sole author of a paper read to the Royal Society on 15 May 1783 announcing the discovery. Variations in the brightness of a star were usually ascribed to the star's having dark patches, analogous to (but much larger than) sunspots: cyclic variations were due to the rotation of the star, while non-cyclic ones were due to changes in the dark patches. Still aged only seventeen, and hesitant to propose a dramatically new explanation of variable stars, Goodricke in his paper declared his purpose was 'to communicate facts', and the eclipse hypothesis he merely mentioned in passing, as a possible alternative to the accepted dark patches. The paper earned Goodricke a Copley medal of the Royal Society.

The eclipse hypothesis, which is the correct explanation of Algol's variations, was soon abandoned by Pigott and Goodricke. The hypothesis implied that the light curve of the star would have a symmetry about its minimum, and the two friends may have been deceived by changes in seeing conditions into thinking this was not the case. Also, the hypothesis did not fit the three other short-period variables discovered by the York astronomers. In September 1784 Goodricke found that β Lyrae varied in brightness, and in a paper read to the Royal Society on 27 January 1785 he assigned it a light curve with two minima and a period of twelve days, nineteen hours. Also in September

1784, Pigott discovered the variability of η Aquilae; and the following month Goodricke discovered that of δ Cephei. Both stars are of the type known as Cepheid variables, with δ Cephei as the type star; they are in fact pulsating stars, with light curves that rise rapidly to a maximum every few days and then slowly decline, changes that cannot be explained by eclipses. But the discoveries of the two York astronomers had enriched astronomy with a new class of variable stars, those whose periods occupy only a few days.

During 1785 and the first months of 1786 the bulk of Goodricke's observing time was dedicated to the re-examination of these known variables. On 30 March 1786 he examined β Lyrae for the twelfth time that month; but soon thereafter he was taken ill, apparently because of exposure to the night air, and he died in his home at Lendal, York, on 20 April. He had been elected to the Royal Society just two weeks earlier. He was buried in the family vault at Hunsingore, Yorkshire. MICHAEL HOSKIN

Sources C. A. Goodricke, 'Gift to the society of a portrait of John Goodricke', *Monthly Notices of the Royal Astronomical Society*, 73 (1912–13), 3–4 • M. Hoskin, 'Goodricke, Pigott and the quest for variable stars', *Journal for the History of Astronomy*, 10 (1979), 23–41 • C. Gilman, 'John Goodricke and his variable stars', *Sky and Telescope*, 56 (1978), 400–03 • *DNB*

Archives York City Archives, Goodricke and Piggott MSS • York City Archives, notebooks and corresp.

Likenesses pastel drawing, 1785, RAS [*see illus.*] • portrait; at Gilling Castle, Yorkshire in 1890

Goodridge, Henry Edmund (*bap.* **1797**, *d.* **1864**), architect, was baptized on 26 July 1797 at St Michael's Church, Bath, the son of James Goodridge, a leading builder in the city who carried out much of the development in the suburb of Bathwick, and his wife, Anna Buck. He was apprenticed to John Lowder, then architect to the city, and supplemented this training by visits to France *c.*1818 and later, in 1829, to Italy. After setting up independently in the city *c.*1820, he developed a successful practice both in Bath itself and in the neighbouring areas of Somerset and Wiltshire. Harvey Lonsdale Elmes, subsequently the architect of St George's Hall in Liverpool, was an assistant in his office from 1834 to 1837. On 10 July 1822 Goodridge married Matilda Yockney of Upper East Hayes, Bath, with whom he had five children, one of whom, Alfred Samuel Goodridge, continued his father's practice after he retired about 1855.

Goodridge's best-known work is the Lansdown tower on the edge of Bath, built in 1824–7 for the celebrated William Beckford, who had settled in the city in 1823; and this and his own residence, Montebello (later Bathwick Grange), on Bathwick Hill (1828–30), are compositions of great originality, combining a picturesque irregularity of form with an eclectic mixture of Greek and italianate detail. Others of his early works are more conventionally neo-classical in manner, but he also designed a number of churches in the Gothic style, some of which—notably that in Rode Hill, Somerset (1822–4)—are highly, indeed bizarrely, individual, while his Devizes Castle, Wiltshire (*c.*1840), is in a neo-Norman idiom. In his entry for the competition for the Houses of Parliament (1835) he proposed an octagonal House of Commons and a House of Lords in the form of a 'baronial hall with minstrel gallery' (Colvin, *Archs.*, 415).

Goodridge's 'great passion' was 'the picturesque in landscape gardening', which he exercised in the grounds of his Bathwick villa (Goodridge, 5). He exhibited occasionally at the Royal Academy and became a fellow of the Royal Institute of British Architects 'at a very early period of [the] Institution' (ibid.). He died at Belle Vue Villa, Bathwick Hill, on 26 October 1864 and was buried at Lansdown cemetery, Bath. PETER LEACH, *rev.*

Sources Colvin, *Archs.* • *GM*, 1st ser., 92/2 (1822), 88 [notice of marriage] • A. S. Goodridge, 'Brief memoir of the late Henry Edmund Goodridge', *Sessional Papers of the Royal Institute of British Architects* (1864–5), suppl., 3–5 • *CGPLA Eng. & Wales* (1865)

Archives RIBA BAL, MSS collection

Wealth at death under £6000: probate, 21 Jan 1865, *CGPLA Eng. & Wales*

Goodsir, John (**1814–1867**), anatomist, was born at Anstruther, Fife, on 20 March 1814, the first of the six children of John Goodsir, medical practitioner, and his wife, Elizabeth Dunbar Taylor. The family was well known in the region: Goodsir's father and grandfather were the leading surgeons in Anstruther. Goodsir's early education took place at the Anstruther School and was enhanced by his exploration of the Fife shores and by the interest of his parents, who encouraged his studies at home. His mother taught him how to draw. When he was thirteen Goodsir went to St Andrews University, where his course of arts inspired an interest in metaphysics, aesthetics, and transcendentalism, which added an extra dimension to his later scientific work.

After passing his course in 1830 Goodsir became an apprentice to Mr Nasmyth, an Edinburgh dentist. An early interest in anatomy was rekindled when he attended lectures at the extramural school of medicine given by Robert Knox. Although a gifted dental student Goodsir did not enjoy the work and he left his apprenticeship early to take up studies at the Edinburgh College of Surgeons. A fellow student was the natural historian Edward Forbes who was to prove a lifelong friend and colleague. Goodsir took his surgical licence in 1835 and returned to Anstruther to join the family practice. He spent the next five years as his father's assistant while continuing scientific studies and building a collection of anatomical, pathological, and natural history specimens. Goodsir's first major scientific work had its origin in his dental apprenticeship. Published in 1839, 'On the origin and development of the pulps and sacs of the human teeth' made his name as a scientist.

Goodsir, a tall, gaunt, large-faced man with thoughtful eyes and a calm bearing, returned to Edinburgh in 1840 and took up residence with his younger brothers, Harry and Robert, now medical students, and Edward Forbes and George E. Day at 21 Lothian Street. The flat at the top of the house became known as a meeting place for the residents and their friends in Forbes's club, the Universal Brotherhood of the Friends of Truth, whose members included artists, physicians, naturalists, poets, priests,

John Goodsir (1814–1867), by George Aikman (after unknown artist, *c.*1854)

and mathematicians. Goodsir continued his freelance work until 1841 when he joined the Edinburgh Botanical Society, was elected senior president of the Royal Medical Society, became a member of the Royal Physical Society, and was appointed curator to the museum of the Royal College of Surgeons. Goodsir popularized the museum and its collections by giving lectures featuring its specimens and by giving special lectures for students on Saturdays. In 1842–3 he gave a series of lectures on pathology which contained ideas on cellular theory later developed by Rudolf Virchow. Also in 1842 Goodsir published the first description of the stomach parasite *sarcina ventriculi* in the *Edinburgh Medical and Surgical Journal*, which confirmed him as an innovative scientific observer.

In 1844 Goodsir took the position of demonstrator of anatomy at the University of Edinburgh as assistant to the ailing Alexander Monro tertius and when Monro retired in 1846 Goodsir was appointed professor of anatomy. His enthusiasm, amiability, and empathy with his students attracted hundreds of pupils to his department. His teaching was an art to him and the attractiveness of his lectures inspired a devoted following. He was known for lively presentations which included a concern for the arts as well as the sciences. Goodsir improved the quality of the instruction in the anatomy department by extending and improving the dissecting rooms, recruiting additional staff, and giving microscopic demonstrations. Goodsir's microscopists were the first to use the achromatic microscope. He continued to develop his ideas in cellular theory with the help of his microscope studies and by 1848 his conclusion was that the cell was the fundamental structure of all life. Goodsir retained his transcendental approach while continuing his studies of comparative anatomy and saw the cell as the unifying point of the animal and vegetable worlds. Although secure in his position as a professor Goodsir wished to practise medicine and suffered a disappointment when he failed to secure a post as assistant surgeon at the Edinburgh Infirmary. Goodsir published papers on a wide range of subjects including zoology, pathology, microscopic physiology, and developmental theory. In 1845 his most important works were collected and published as *Anatomical and Pathological Observations*. The collection included some works by his brother Harry, who died while on Franklin's expedition to the Arctic circle in that year. Their brother Robert, now another Goodsir doctor, sailed to the Arctic twice in unsuccessful attempts to find Harry. Goodsir himself travelled to Vienna, Berlin, and Paris to increase his anatomical collections, acquire scientific instruments, visit museums, and meet international colleagues. Goodsir's health began to decline in 1850 when he showed the first symptoms of what proved to be a wasting condition of the spine. Despite his illness Goodsir took over a lecture series on natural history in 1853 in addition to his other responsibilities. The work exhausted him and he was forced to take a year's leave of absence. After this break Goodsir returned to lecturing and publishing. In 1856 he published a series of papers on the constitution of the skeleton which emphasized the importance of combining embryological study with comparative anatomy. His work in general was recognized for its original thinking, skill, and the accuracy of his drawings. Goodsir's desire to practise medicine was fulfilled when his skill as a microscopist was recognized by patients such as Charles Darwin, who consulted him in 1863 about a serious stomach ailment by sending samples for analysis. Goodsir continued to work until November 1866 when he collapsed while giving a lecture. He died of an atrophied spine on 6 March 1867 at South Cottage, Wardie, Leith, and was buried in the Dean cemetery, Edinburgh, ten days later. His successor to the chair of anatomy, William Turner, published his works in *The Anatomical Works of John Goodsir* in 1868.

K. Grudzien Baston

Sources *The anatomical memoirs of John Goodsir*, ed. W. Turner, 2 vols. (1868) [incl. H. Lonsdale, 'Biographical memoir', vol. 1, pp. 1–203] · W. Turner, 'The late professor John Goodsir', *BMJ* (16 March 1867), 307–8 · H. W. Y. Taylor, 'John Goodsir', *25th Proceedings of the Scottish Society of the History of Medicine* (1956), 13–19 · L. S. Lacyna, 'John Goodsir and the making of cellular reality', *Journal of the History of Biology*, 16/1 (1983), 75–99 · 'Review of the anatomical memoirs of John Goodsir', *Edinburgh Medical Journal*, 14/11 (1869), 1037–48 · J. Goodsir, 'History of a case in which a fluid periodically ejected from the stomach contained vegetable organisms of an undescribed form', *Edinburgh Medical and Surgical Journal*, 57 (1842), 430–43 · A. Grant, *The story of the University of Edinburgh during its first three hundred years*, 2 (1884), 391–2 · A. L. Turner, *History of the University of Edinburgh, 1883–1933* (1933) · bap. reg. Scot. · d. cert. · NA Scot., SC 70/1/134/601–613

Archives Royal College of Physicians of Edinburgh, synopsis of lectures · U. Edin. L., family corresp. and papers · U. Edin. L., lecture notes and papers | Bodl. Oxf., letters to Henry Acland · U. Edin. L., letters to David Ramsey Hay

Likenesses D. W. Stevenson, marble sculpture, 1867, U. Edin. · W. D. D. Young, oils, 1889, U. Edin. · G. Aikman, engraving (after unknown artist, *c*.1854), repro. in *Anatomical memoirs*, ed. Turner, 1 (1868), frontispiece [*see illus*.] · W. Hole, etching, NPG; repro. in W. Hole, *Quasi cursores* (1884) · portrait on tombstone, Dean cemetery, Edinburgh; repro. in www.headstones.fsnet.co.uk, 7 Oct 2002

Wealth at death £6555 4*s*. 8*d*.: confirmation, 16 April 1867, NA Scot., SC 70/1/134/601–613

Goodson, Richard (*c*.**1655–1718**), organist and composer, was born probably in Oxford, the son of Richard Goodson (*d*. 1670/71), butler of New Inn Hall and landlord of The Fleur-de-Lys inn, Oxford, and his wife, Anne. In 1674 she remarried; her new husband was Robert Street. Goodson became a chorister at Christ Church Cathedral in 1667 and served as a singing man from 1675 to 1681. On 19 July 1682 he succeeded Edward Lowe, who seems to have been his teacher and patron, as Heather professor of music at Oxford, and by 1683 he had been appointed organist of New College. He married, by an Oxford archdeaconry licence of 1685, Mary Wright (*d*. 1733). In 1692 he became organist of Christ Church.

With the exception of the morning service in C, which appears in partbooks at cathedrals as far afield as Dublin and Durham, and three songs for 'the Mask of *Orpheus and Euridice*' performed at a girls' boarding-school at Besselsleigh, near Oxford, and published in *Musica Oxoniensis* (1698), Goodson's music survives mainly in Oxford manuscripts. He composed eight odes and act songs for university ceremonies, including one, 'Ormond's Glory', with a rudimentary trumpet part, and his 'Rejoice in the Lord ye righteous' is one of the very few contemporary anthems with string accompaniment composed outside the Chapel Royal. As professor of music he continued Lowe's active stewardship of the Oxford music school, making significant additions to its performing material (Bodl. Oxf., MSS mus. sch. E.443–6 and 570 and other sources) as well as listing its 1682 holdings in the parchment roll MS mus. sch. C.204* (R). Manuscripts in his hand at Christ Church include Mus. 1177, which contains important early copies of two of Purcell's keyboard suites later published in 1696, and the organ accompaniment book Mus. 1230, a document of music used in services at Christ Church under the reforms introduced by Dean Aldrich.

Goodson died at Great Tew on 13 January 1718, leaving property in St Clement Danes, London, and in Allhallows, Oxford, and was buried in the divinity chapel of Christ Church Cathedral two days later. His will, made in 1714, mentions three surviving children, including **Richard Goodson** (*bap*. 1688, *d*. 1740/41), baptized at St Cross, Oxford, on 24 May 1688. The younger Richard Goodson was a choirboy at Christ Church from 1699 to 1707 and according to Thomas Ford (Bodl. Oxf., MS Mus.e.17, fol. 21*r*) became organist of Newbury in Berkshire on 24 August 1709. He returned to Christ Church as a singing man from 1712 to 1718 and succeeded his father as organist and professor of music, having graduated MusB on 1 March 1717. He was buried at Christ Church on 7 January 1741, and bequeathed to the college a music library containing material in his own and his father's hands (listed in Royal College of Music, MS 2125). ROBERT THOMPSON

Sources *The life and times of Anthony Wood*, ed. A. Clark, 5 vols., OHS, 19, 21, 26, 30, 40 (1891–1900) · H. E. Salter, ed., *Surveys and tokens*, OHS, 75 (1923), 186, 221 · *Remarks and collections of Thomas Hearne*, ed. C. E. Doble and others, 6, OHS, 43 (1902) · will, PRO, PROB 11/565, fols. 163*r*–164*r* · T. Ford, history of music, Bodl. Oxf., MS Mus.e.17 · M. Crum, 'Early lists of the Oxford music school collection', *Music and Letters*, 48 (1967), 23–34 · M. Crum, 'An Oxford music club, 1690–1719', *Bodleian Library Record*, 9 (1973–8), 83–99 · N. Zaslaw, 'An English *Orpheus and Eurydice* of 1697', *MT*, 118 (1977), 805–8 · disbursement books, Christ Church Oxf. · parish register (baptism), St Cross, Oxford [R. Goodson jun.] · register (burial), Christ Church Oxf. · H. W. Shaw, *The succession of organists of the Chapel Royal and the cathedrals of England and Wales from c.1538* (1991) · T. A. Trowles, 'The musical ode in Britain, *c*.1670–1800', DPhil diss., U. Oxf., 1992

Wealth at death two properties in St Clement Danes, London, and one in Oxford: will, PRO, PROB 11/565, fols. 163*r*–164*r*

Goodson, Richard (*bap*. **1688**, *d*. **1740/41**). *See under* Goodson, Richard (*c*.1655–1718).

Goodsonn [Goodson]**, William** (*b*. **1609/10**, *d*. in or after **1680**), naval officer, was a native of Great Yarmouth, and probably from a seafaring family well established there. From ages he gave in later depositions it appears that he was born in 1609 or 1610. Bred to the sea, he made numerous trading voyages to the Caribbean and the Spanish main and acquired an intimate knowledge of the region. He later recalled being at Cartagena, on the mainland, about 1634. In the later 1630s Goodsonn moved to Rotterdam, along with the Yarmouth minister William Bridge and other puritan refugees. By 1640 he had settled in Stepney, Middlesex, describing himself as master and part owner of the *William*, a Flemish prize bound for Amsterdam and the East Indies. During the civil war he continued to pursue his commercial activities, and was noted in 1644, homeward bound at St Lucar in Spain. At some point in his career Goodsonn bought 500 acres in the Lincolnshire fens, mostly in the South Level, probably from his trading profits. When these lands were badly damaged by flooding in 1655, Goodsonn explained to Thurloe that the rest of his estate was mostly scattered round the world in mercantile adventures and shipping.

Goodsonn and his wife, Mary, whom he had married in the 1630s, were both religious radicals. In 1648, when they were living in Wapping, Goodsonn belonged to the strict separatist congregation of Samuel Chidley, while his wife followed the Independent John Goodwin. Her unhappiness that they could not worship together prompted a meeting between the two churches on 22 August at which Goodsonn rejected any association with parish churches, denouncing them as 'the Idolls Temples' (Brown, 10–11).

Goodsonn was drawn into naval affairs by the revolt of the naval forces in the Downs to the king in the early summer of 1648; with Moulton, Badiley, and Myngs, he was among the small band of Trinity House members to back Warwick's appeal for an expedition to pursue the rebels. According to his later account he entered naval service in 1649, though the first direct evidence is as commander of the *Hopeful Luke*, a vessel he owned and leased to the state in 1650–51. He was assigned to protect English fishing fleets off Newfoundland. After returning to trade with

Barbados, Goodsonn was recalled to the navy following the outbreak of war with the Dutch. Recommended for one of the best ships in the fleet, he was appointed captain of the *Entrance* on 25 January 1653 and fought in the action off Portland on 18 February. Moving to the *Rainbow*, he served as rear-admiral of the blue at the Gabbard on 2–3 June and in the great victory off Schevening on 29–31 July. During the autumn he commanded the *Unicorn* and *George* under Monck, and in the summer guard of 1654 was vice-admiral of the blue under Penn. He maintained his private shipping and commercial interests, and on 1 October 1654 was appointed as contractor to supply clothes to the seamen.

Late in 1654 Goodsonn was appointed to the *Paragon* as vice-admiral of the fleet under Penn in the expedition to seize Hispaniola from Spain. On 7 December he was named one of the commissioners, enabling him to command in chief should circumstances require. The expedition sailed late in December, calling at Barbados for further recruits. On 19 March 1655 Penn ordered a regiment to be formed from the seamen for service ashore, appointing Goodsonn its colonel and Benjamin Blake lieutenant-colonel. The force landed in Hispaniola with the rest of the army on 13 April, and also took part in the successful attack on Jamaica on 11 May. When Penn decided to return home Goodsonn remained as admiral of the squadron left behind (21 June). He proved a far more dynamic commander than Penn, and knew the region far better. Putting to sea in the *Torrington* on 31 July he sacked and burned Santa Marta, on the mainland, but lacking the resources to attack Cartagena returned to Jamaica in the autumn. In April 1656 he led another assault on the mainland, sacking and burning Rio de la Hacha and plying off Havana in the hope of intercepting the Spanish plate fleet, before returning to Jamaica. By the middle of the year Goodsonn was the only surviving commissioner, inheriting overall responsibility for the colony's affairs. This led to serious friction with his deputy, Blake, who was hostile to the soldiery and stirred up the seamen to press for immediate action against the Spaniards. These divisions threatened to paralyse the government of the infant colony, and Goodsonn resolved to court-martial his deputy; in the event he allowed Blake to surrender his commission and return to England, though worried that Blake would intrigue against him. Thurloe, aware of his good service and key position, sent reassurances and encouragement. At the end of the year a new military commander arrived from England, and on 31 January 1657 Goodsonn sailed for home in the *Mathias*, arriving in April. Though in bad health he drew up detailed and thoughtful recommendations on the management of the new colony and the deployment of naval forces in the region, which he presented on 2 June. The government, appreciative of his contribution and commitment, awarded a substantial gratuity.

Goodsonn soon returned to sea to assist Anglo-French operations against Spain in Flanders. In the summer and autumn of 1657 he commanded a squadron off the Flemish coast, bombarding Spanish positions to repel a counter-attack on Mardyke. In May 1658 he gave naval support to an unauthorized attempt by the French general D'Aumont to seize Ostend, a plan which failed disastrously. The following month he and Montagu bombarded the defences of Dunkirk, which surrendered to the French on 24 June and was handed to the English. Goodsonn also played an important role in the unfolding Baltic crisis. Cromwell was anxious to protect English interests in the region, threatened by the Swedish–Danish war which it was feared would allow the Dutch (as Denmark's allies) to dominate the Sound. The new protector, Richard Cromwell, dispatched Goodsonn to the Baltic in November with a fleet of twenty ships, despite his warning that it was too late in the year for such an operation; his judgement proved correct, for the fleet was battered by storms and forced to return home. In March 1659 he sailed again for the Sound, this time as vice-admiral in a much larger fleet under the command of Montagu. Delicate negotiations followed with the Danes, Dutch, and Swedes, complicated in May by news that the protectorate had been overthrown and replaced by the restored Rump Parliament. While Montagu was a loyal Cromwellian, Goodsonn held more radical political views and was said to be delighted. The situation remained tense and confused, with hints that the Rump was looking for Goodsonn to take over the supreme command. In the event Montagu brought the fleet home in August, without orders. Though Goodsonn held no further command, he played an active part in the tangled politics of the next few months. Dismayed by the military coup which ousted the Rump in October 1659, he joined a group of London aldermen, army officers, and naval colleagues such as Lawson and Stayner in demanding the return of the Rump. Once the army junta had established itself, however, Goodsonn concluded that Monck's threat to invade from Scotland might let in the cavaliers, and in November he wrote with several other leading naval officers to try to dissuade Monck. Early in December Goodsonn was chosen by the naval officers in London as one of their representatives to meet spokesmen of the armies in England, Scotland, and Ireland to frame a new constitution. The committee of safety also named him on 15 December to command a new squadron to be sent out to confront the royalists and also, probably, the naval forces under Lawson which had remained committed to the Rump. All these plans foundered within a few days when Lawson brought his fleet into the Thames; the military regime collapsed and the Rump returned. Ashore and out of favour, Goodsonn played no part in the manoeuvres that led to the king's return in May 1660.

Goodsonn was even less acceptable to the restored Stuarts, and returned to trade. He was reported at Barbados in 1666, and in the Downs, on his way to Virginia, in 1667. His past was not forgotten, and in December 1662 he was accused, almost certainly falsely, of complicity in an alleged plot to kill the king. Unlike many Cromwellian commanders, he was not invited to serve in the Second Anglo-Dutch War; though named as one of the most able commanders in England, in a list Penn drew up for Prince

James, he was barred by his religious nonconformity. Little is known of his private life. His daughter Prudence married the naval captain Charles Wager in 1663. He remarried after the death of his first wife; his second wife, Anne, died in 1673. The date of his death is unknown. He appears to have been still living in 1680, and may well be the 'Goodson, an old seaman' reported in 1680 to have sounded out mariners in Redriff and Wapping during the Exclusion crisis, securing assurances that 'they will be right and true Protestants, and will throw their officers overboard' (*CSP dom., 1680–81*, 44). Goodsonn was a fine representative of the Cromwellian navy, a man of principle, courage, organizational ability, and consideration for his men. Pepys paid warm tribute to him in 1664 as one 'whom the more I know the more I value for a serious man and staunch' (Pepys, 5.30). BERNARD CAPP

Sources B. Capp, *Cromwell's navy: the fleet and the English revolution, 1648–1660* (1989) • Thurloe, *State papers* • *CSP dom., 1650–81* • *CSP col.*, vols. 1, 9 • Pepys, *Diary*, vol. 5 • G. Penn, *The memorials of Sir William Penn* (1833) • D. Brown, *Two conferences between … separatists and Independents* (1650) • high court of admiralty depositions by Goodsonn in 1640 and 1652, PRO, HCA13/55, fol. 566, HCA 13/66 (unfoliated) • will of Anne Goodsonn, 1673, PRO, PROB 11/341, sig. 45 • J. L. Chester, ed., *The marriage, baptismal, and burial registers of the collegiate church or abbey of St Peter, Westminster*, Harleian Society, 10 (1876) • W. Okeley, *Eben-Ezer, or, A small monument of great mercy* (1675)

Goodwin, Arthur (*d.* 1643), politician, was the only surviving son of Francis Goodwin (1564–1634) of Upper Winchendon, Buckinghamshire, and his wife, Elizabeth (*d.* 1630), daughter of Arthur *Grey, fourteenth Baron Grey of Wilton (1536–1593). The Goodwins, established in Buckinghamshire since the mid-sixteenth century, became a leading gentry family and one of those which monopolized the county parliamentary seats. Francis Goodwin was knighted in 1601 and served as JP, MP, and sheriff of the county. In February 1614 Arthur Goodwin graduated BA from Magdalen College, Oxford, where in 1612 he contributed some Latin verses to *Luctus posthumus*, a collection commemorating the death of Henry, prince of Wales. He was admitted to the Inner Temple in 1613 and in April 1618 married Jane, daughter of Richard Wenman, Viscount Wenman of Tuam, for whom he expressed 'faithfull love and affection' (will). They had one child, Jane (*bap.* 1618, *d.* 1658), his 'deere Jenny' (letter, 26 June 1643, *Berks, Bucks & Oxon Archaeological Journal*); in 1637 she became the second wife of Philip Wharton, fourth Baron Wharton, a fervent puritan.

Having been returned as MP for the boroughs of High Wycombe (1621 and 1624) and Aylesbury (1626) in Buckinghamshire, Goodwin served as county MP for Buckinghamshire in both the Short and Long parliaments with John Hampden, who had been his close companion from student days. They, like the county, were strongly puritan and frequently opposed the policy of Charles I; Goodwin seems to have been reluctant to pay ship money in 1635. An experienced MP and convinced parliamentarian, he was active in debates in the Long Parliament, often acting as teller in divisions. In May 1640 he signed the protestation pledging to support the true protestant religion and the privileges of parliament, on the day it was published. In February 1641 he spoke in favour of the petition abolishing episcopacy and, with Henry Marten, moved that the Commons adjourn until the earl of Strafford should be tried for treason. The following January he presented to the Commons the Buckinghamshire petition to remove 'popish lords and Bishops' from the House of Lords and to give up 'evil Counsellors … to the Hand of Justice' (Coates, Steele, Young, and Snow, 1.34–5), though he did not agree that parliamentary nominees only should occupy offices of state. Preference for puritan worship led him in January 1641 to have those responsible for the installation of an organ in Waddesdon church summoned before the Commons by speaker's warrant.

Substantial wealth enabled Goodwin to give generously to the parliamentarian cause: in November 1640 he and other MPs each gave a bond for £1000 towards the loan of £100,000 raised in London to support an army should Charles dissolve parliament; in 1642 he subscribed £1800 to suppress the Irish rising, and he with other Buckinghamshire members gathered pledges of £1000 from the county for the defence of parliament. Goodwin himself gave £100 and promised to maintain four horsemen. During the civil war, though he fought at Edgehill and Turnham Green as colonel of his cavalry regiment under the earl of Essex, he saw most action in Buckinghamshire and neighbouring counties, an important border region between the opposing sides and much fought over. In August 1642 with John Hampden and Bulstrode Whitelocke he prevented the earl of Berkshire's executing the commission of array in Oxfordshire, capturing the earl and others, and prevented the royalist seizure of Daventry, taking the earl of Northampton prisoner. January 1643 saw him appointed commander-in-chief in Buckinghamshire with headquarters at Aylesbury. His attempt to seize Brill was repulsed though he succeeded in capturing horses and cattle in raids during March, almost reaching royalist-held Oxford. After the successful siege of Reading in April he was again in Buckinghamshire, helping to force Prince Rupert to retreat but failing to prevent the plunder of Wendover by Lord Carnarvon. An attempt on 18 June to intercept Rupert's return to Oxford resulted in the skirmish at Chalgrove Field in which Hampden was mortally wounded. Goodwin persuaded him to ride to the comparative safety of Thame where he died; Goodwin wrote to his daughter, Jenny, eulogizing Hampden and asking for a black ribbon to tie to his standard. He died at Clerkenwell on 16 August 1643 and was buried three days later at Wooburn, Buckinghamshire, in the chancel. His will directed that six almshouses at Waddesdon, which the troubled times had prevented him from building, were to be erected by his executors and endowed with £30 a year. JOAN A. DILS

Sources Keeler, *Long Parliament*, 189–90 • W. H. Coates, A. Steele Young, and V. F. Snow, eds., *The private journals of the Long Parliament*, 3 vols. (1982–92) • *The journal of Sir Simonds D'Ewes from the beginning of the Long Parliament to the opening of the trial of the earl of Strafford*, ed. W. Notestein (1923), 251, 306, 337, 371 • J. Adair, *John Hampden, the patriot* (1976) • Foster, *Alum. Oxon., 1500–1714* [Arthur Goodwyn] • *Journal of Sir Samuel Luke*, ed. I. G. Philip, 1–3, Oxfordshire RS, 29, 31, 33 (1950–53), 1.vii, 1, 45, 96, 110 • C. G. Bonsey, ed., *Ship money papers*,

Buckinghamshire RS, 13 (1965), 52, 63, 64, 78 • will, PRO, PROB 11/192, sig. 1 • will, PRO, PROB 11/166, sig. 72 [Sir Francis Goodwin] • W. Money, 'A walk to Chalgrove Field, with notes by the way', *Berks, Bucks & Oxon Archaeological Journal*, new ser., 1 (1895), 14–22, esp. 19 [letter from Goodwin to his daughter, Jane, 26 June 1643] • *VCH Buckinghamshire*, 3.108–11; 4.123–4, 536 • HoP, *Commons, 1558–1603*, 2.204 • A. M. Johnson, 'Buckinghamshire, 1640–1660: a study in county politics', MA diss., University of Swansea, 1963 • *The diary of Bulstrode Whitelocke, 1605–1675*, ed. R. Spalding, British Academy, Records of Social and Economic History, new ser., 13 (1990), 134–5 • *Engraved Brit. ports.*, 3.350 • R. Gibbs, *Worthies of Buckinghamshire* (1888), 172–3

Archives Bodl. Oxf., corresp., Carte MSS vol. ciii

Likenesses A. Van Dyck, oils, 1639, Chatsworth House, Derbyshire • P. van Gunst, engraving (after A. Van Dyck); known to be in BM in 1910

Wealth at death see will, PRO, PROB 11/192, sig. 1; Bonsey, ed., *Ship money papers*, 52n.

Goodwin, Charles Wycliffe (1817–1878), Egyptologist, was born on 2 April 1817 at 2 Bridge Street, King's Lynn, Norfolk. He was the eldest of four sons of a solicitor, Charles Goodwin (*d.* 1859), and his wife, Frances Catherine, *née* Sawyer (*d.* 1825). The second son, Harvey *Goodwin, became bishop of Carlisle. He was educated at High Wycombe, Buckinghamshire from 1826 to 1833, and from the age of about nine was led to take a lively interest in Egyptology by reading an article on hieroglyphics in the *Edinburgh Review* for December 1826. Egyptology became the favourite study of his life, and during his school holidays he wrote essays on the early history of Egypt. He was also in early life a fair Hebraist, botanist, and geologist, an accomplished Old English and a good German scholar. From 1833 to 1834 he was tutored by the Revd Sidney Gedge at North Runcton, Norfolk, and then matriculated (in 1834) at St Catharine's College, Cambridge, taking his BA degree with high classical honours in 1838, proceeding MA in 1842, and being afterwards elected a fellow of the college. Goodwin then turned to the law, entering Lincoln's Inn in 1840 and being called to the bar in 1843. He returned to his college in 1844; but his fellowship could be retained only by taking orders, which he could not do, his religious views having changed. He resigned in 1847 and returned to the uncongenial study of the law. His small practice was mainly in probate matters, on which he published three law books.

In 1848 Goodwin published *The Anglo-Saxon Version of the Life of St Guthlac, Hermit of Crowland*, with a translation and notes. An established contributor to the publications of the Cambridge Antiquarian Society, in 1851 he edited *The Anglo-Saxon Legends of St Andrew and St Veronica … with an English Translation* for the society. In 1850 and 1852 Goodwin wrote on music and art in *The Guardian*, and he contributed to the *Saturday Review*. He was fond of music, playing more than one instrument and composing a number of songs. For the *Cambridge Essays* of 1858 he wrote the valuable article on hieratic papyri, his first notable contribution to Egyptology. This was followed in 1859 by the anonymous republication from the *Law Magazine* of his 'Curiosities of law', a collection of translated extracts from deeds of grant of various kinds in favour of a monastery near Thebes in Egypt, written in Coptic, of which Goodwin was a diligent student. In 1860 he acquired a wider reputation through his paper 'The Mosaic cosmogony', in *Essays and Reviews*, to which he was the only lay contributor. Goodwin criticized the attempts to 'harmonize' the creation story in Genesis with the discoveries of modern geology; the Mosaic account of creation was not factual, but it served the religious development of mankind. This plain-spoken essay produced a number of specific replies, to none of which Goodwin made any rejoinder. In 1860 he succeeded John Morley as the last editor of the *Literary Gazette*. He edited the two volumes of the *Parthenon*, 1862–3, with which the *Literary Gazette* was incorporated, giving prominence in it to Egyptological subjects. In May 1862 at a meeting of the Society of Antiquaries, to which Goodwin sent several communications on those subjects, he replied to Sir George Cornewall Lewis's scepticism as to the possibility of interpreting the ancient Egyptian by arguing that Coptic was to some extent a continuation of that language. Various contributions of Goodwin's, chiefly Egyptological, appeared in the second series of François Chabas's *Mélanges égyptologiques* (1864).

In March 1865, shortly before his marriage on 1 April to Augustine Anne Rudderforth, Goodwin was appointed assistant judge in the newly created supreme court for China and Japan. A paper that he contributed to *Fraser's Magazine* for February of that year was issued separately in 1866, after his departure to the East (Peter Le Page Renouf correcting the proofs), as *The story of Saneha [Sinuhe] … translated from the hieratic text*. It was prefaced by an admirable summary of the history and chronology of ancient Egypt in connection with the previous development of its varied civilization. Goodwin executed his translation from the facsimile of the original papyrus printed in 1860 in Lepsius's *Denkmäler Aegyptens*. His version was read before the Society of Antiquaries in December 1863, the month following the publication of another version by Chabas. They were written independently, although composed at the same time, and agreed in all essential points. For the Records of the Past Goodwin revised his version of the *Story of Saneha* as well as other translations of hieratic texts. In 1866 *Voyage d'un Égyptien en Phénicie, en Palestine, … au XIVe siècle avant notre ère* by Chabas, with the collaboration of Goodwin, also appeared. In his essay on hieratic papyri Goodwin had translated the first eight pages of this work. Chabas spoke enthusiastically of Goodwin's labours in hieratic as having effected 'a genuine revolution in the science'. During his residence in the East Goodwin worked assiduously at Egyptology, continuing frequently from 1866 to 1876 the contributions to Lepsius and Brugsch's *Zeitschrift für Ägyptische Sprache*, which he had begun before leaving England. Communications from him were used and acknowledged by Canon F. C. Cook in his disquisition 'On Egyptian words in the Pentateuch' in volume 1, part I of the Speaker's Commentary on the Bible (1871).

After being several years at Shanghai, Goodwin served at Yokohama on occasion. He was acting judge of the Supreme Court from 1876. He remained at Shanghai, a visit to England intervening, until his death after a long illness on 17 January 1878. He was buried on 24 January in the south side of Shanghai cemetery, reserved for foreigners. His death was much regretted by British residents at Shanghai and Yokohama, and he was mourned by friends who remembered him as a delightful companion, cheerful and unaffected. He was survived by his wife and a daughter. FRANCIS ESPINASSE, *rev.* JOSEF L. ALTHOLZ

Sources W. R. Dawson, *Charles Wycliffe Goodwin, 1817–1878: a pioneer in Egyptology* (1934) • J. L. Altholz, *Anatomy of a controversy: the debate over 'Essays and Reviews', 1860–1864* (1994) • H. Carlisle, 'Mr Charles Wycliffe Goodwin', *The Athenaeum* (23 March 1878), 379–80 • W. R. Dawson and E. P. Uphill, *Who was who in Egyptology*, 2nd edn (1972) • Boase, *Mod. Eng. biog.* • personal knowledge (1890)
Archives BL, corresp. and papers, Add. MSS 31268–31298, 64868J | Institut de France, Paris, Chabas MSS • Pembroke College, Oxford, letters to Peter Renouf • priv. coll., Peter Le Page Renouf MSS
Likenesses F. Goodwin, sketch, 1833, repro. in Dawson, *Charles Wycliffe Goodwin*, frontispiece • X. Barthe and D. Puech, bust, 1908, Cairo Museum
Wealth at death under £5000: resworn probate, Dec 1878, *CGPLA Eng. & Wales*

Goodwin, Christopher (*fl.* 1520–1542), poet, was the author of *The Chaunce of the Dolorous Lover* (1520), a complaint in which the speaker entreats Venus 'to sende me agayne the syght of my true love'. Thomas Warton describes the poem as 'a lamentable story without pathos'. In 1542 a second poem of Goodwin's appeared, by the name of *The Maydens Dreme*. This describes a dispute between Love and Shamefastness, overheard in a dream by a young woman. Like the former poem, it is in seven-line stanzas. In the concluding stanza the four words 'Chryst', 'offre', 'good', and 'wyn' (forming together the author's name) are introduced into different lines enclosed in brackets. Warton describes this second piece as 'a vision without imagination'.

In 1572 a Christopher Goodwin, or Goodwyn, and John Johnson proposed to Queen Elizabeth's ministers to convert Ipswich into 'a mart town', in order to attract the whole trade from Antwerp. Much of the promoters' notes and correspondence with Lord Burghley, Sir Thomas Smith, and others is in the Record Office in London (*CSP dom., 1547–80*, 447–8). It seems unlikely, though, given the late date, that this Christopher Goodwin is identical with the poet. SIDNEY LEE, *rev.* CHRISTOPHER BURLINSON

Sources *STC, 1475–1640* • T. Warton, *The history of English poetry*, 4 vols. (1774–81) • Tanner, *Bibl. Brit.-Hib.*

Goodwin, Francis (1784–1835), architect, was born on 23 May 1784 at King's Lynn, Norfolk, the eldest son of William Goodwin, carpenter, and his wife, Hannah Abby, a widow. He began his architectural career as a pupil of J. Coxedge of Kensington. In 1806 he exhibited at the Royal Academy a view of St Nicholas's Chapel, Lynn. On 24 March 1808, at St Nicholas's, Goodwin married Mary Stort (*b.* 1785). He married second Elizabeth Reynolds at Marsham, Norfolk, on 26 May 1818. He had at least five sons, of whom two, William (*b.* 1821) and John (*b.* 1825), were the children of his second wife and of whom at least four died young.

Goodwin rebuilt Trinity Chapel in St Margaret's, Lynn, in 1809, and restored St Faith's, Gaywood, Norfolk, installing a remarkable plaster groined vault. In 1810 he leased a substantial house in King Street, Lynn, and later engraved William White's watercolour of the Lynn public dinner to celebrate the peace of 1814. Subsequently he joined the London architect John Walters, but retained a parental freehold in Lynn, qualifying him to vote (for the administration candidate) in the 1817 Norfolk by-election.

The government's grant in 1818 of £1 million for building new churches enabled Goodwin to spread his wings: he applied to the crown architect John Soane for recommendation to the church building commissioners, stating that he had made the design (in Perpendicular Gothic) and superintended the building of Walters's new church of St Philip Stepney. He then laid assiduous siege to the parochial committees charged with selecting designs. From the diary of his rival Thomas Rickman and from accusations levied by his sometime clerk C. A. Busby, we learn his methods. Practising from 29 Francis Street, Bedford Square, London, where he employed as many as six clerks, he was able to chase commissions in the midlands and north, thanks to an efficient stagecoach system. He cultivated influential committee men. He inundated committees with imposing, attractively coloured designs. He was accused of shamelessly undercutting his rivals' estimates. When in June 1820 the commissioners decided to limit any one architect to six new churches, Goodwin was already so engaged, and was completing negotiations for as many again. Financially overextended, he therefore attempted to arrange that his assistants or friends should execute his plans, paying him half their 5 per cent commission, but this project proved largely ineffective. However, he ultimately completed nine churches for the commissioners, most notably St George's, Hulme, Manchester, and Holy Trinity, Bordesley, Birmingham. He also built or remodelled churches at Bilston and Walsall (both classical), Burton upon Trent, Manchester, and Southampton. Summerson calls him and Rickman 'the representative architects of the Gothic provincial church-building of the period, Goodwin tending to be "incorrect" and harking back to the Wyatt school' (*Architecture in Britain, 1530 to 1830*, 1953, 303).

Goodwin's capacity to design a handsome building, as well as his 'pushing' (Rickman, diary, 2 March 1820), secured him a number of secular public commissions also, employing the alternative Grecian style. Manchester town hall and assembly rooms (1822–5), influenced by Soane, ranks the principal (dem. 1912; façade re-erected in Heaton Park); Macclesfield town hall (1823–4; since extended) is in similar vein. Derby county gaol (1823–7; dem.) was highly sophisticated in both its radial plan and its forbidding Doric architecture; C. R. Cockerell commented thereon, '[Goodwin] is truly a man of genius seizing the characteristics of a style and applying them in the most powerful manner. [H]e is sometimes almost overcharged and caricatured but with a bold and striking manner'. Assessing his standing, Cockerell remarked: 'Goodwin for raciness invention resource and sometimes for grandeur beats anything but he is certainly not a gentleman in his works' (D. Watkin, *The Life and Work of C. R. Cockerell*, 1974, 66–7). He also designed markets at Leeds (1824–7; dem.) and Salford (1825). One of seven invited to compete for the Manchester Institution (1824; won by Charles Barry), he was a persistent entrant in major competitions, notably King's College, Cambridge (1823), and Birmingham grammar school (1830), for which he was placed third. In 1830 he put on exhibition designs for a national cemetery on Primrose Hill to include facsimiles of celebrated Greek buildings. At the Royal Academy in 1834, adding 'engineer' to his professional description, Goodwin, in association with Captain S. Browne RN, exhibited a design for a suspension bridge at Horseferry Road, Lambeth. Among the proposals of seventeen architects invited to submit designs for a new House of Commons in 1833, Goodwin's Perpendicular scheme, which he published, was much admired, influencing entries in the national competition for new Houses of Parliament (1835), for which his own rush to prepare designs proved fatal to him. At the inquest his doctor reported his saying that 'so intense had been his studies … that … he was unable to obtain any rest at nights' (*Morning Chronicle*, 2 Sept 1835).

Goodwin also worked in the domestic field, particularly building up an Irish connection, possibly encouraged by E. J. Littleton, MP for Staffordshire and son-in-law of Marquess Wellesley (Irish viceroy, 1822–8 and 1833–5). Littleton laid the foundation-stone of his church at West Bromwich, and to Littleton he dedicated the second volume of his *Domestic Architecture* (1834), ranging from cottages to mansions in a variety of styles with seductive aquatints by S. G. Hughes. His principal Irish commission was the severely Grecian Lissadell Court (1830–34) for Sir Robert Gore Booth bt. He pursued further Irish projects on a long visit in 1834. Stylistically, Goodwin offered the full range expected of Regency architects, but particularly favoured a showy Perpendicular with extensive use of cast iron both structurally and decoratively for churches; and for public buildings a Soanic Grecian: Soane was the dedicatee of his first volume of *Domestic Architecture* (1833). But in that work Goodwin advocated the cause of 'Old English' and attacked the fashionable 'Louis' style of interior decoration. His designs were reissued, with additions, as *Rural Architecture*, in 1835, and again in 1843 and 1850. He argued that a taste for architecture should be disseminated 'among the middling as well as the more opulent classes' because it 'calls into action so many … branches of mechanical labour' that it 'promotes national prosperity' (F. Goodwin, *Domestic Architecture*, 1833–4, 2.vi).

Frequently in debt, and constantly seeking commissions, Goodwin died suddenly of apoplexy on 30 August 1835 at his home, 21 King Street, Portman Square (to which he had moved about 1832); his wife survived him. He was buried in Kensal Green cemetery. M. H. PORT

Sources Church Building Commission, minute books, Church Record Centre, Bermondsey • T. Rickman, diaries, RIBA BAL • parish register, St Nicholas's, King's Lynn [baptism; marriage] • Soane Museum, London, Soane correspondence, X E 3 • Norfolk poll books, 1802 • Norfolk poll books, 1806 • Norfolk poll books, 1817 • 'Select committee on the House of Commons buildings', *Parl. papers* (1833), 12.487, no. 269 • *GM*, 2nd ser., 4 (1835), 659–60 • PRO, PROB 6/211 • [W. Papworth], ed., *The dictionary of architecture*, 11 vols. (1853–92) • M. Port, 'Francis Goodwin: an architect of the 1820s', *Architectural History*, 1 (1958), 61–72 • R. Evans, *The fabrication of virtue: English prison architecture, 1750–1840* (1982) • *IGI*

Wealth at death £1000: administration, PRO, PROB 6/211

Goodwin, George (*fl.* 1620), Latin poet, wrote a set of powerful satires against Roman Catholicism. Of his life nothing is known, unless he may be tentatively identified with the rector of Moreton, Essex, 1596–1625, who matriculated at Trinity, Cambridge, in 1578, became a fellow in 1585, BD in 1593, married, in May 1594, Elizabeth Morris at Chipping Ongar, Essex, and was buried at Moreton in March 1625; another of the same name matriculated at Christ's in 1582, while Oxford provides no suitable candidates.

Goodwin's *Melissa religionis pontificae* (1620) was translated in 1624 by his 'most truly loving friend' John Vicars, 'a hearty Ill-willer to the im-pure hollownesse of his impious Holinesse', as *Babel's Balme, or, The Honeycombe of Rome's Religion*. Goodwin's dedication is to Sir Robert Naunton (a Cambridge contemporary, if the identification suggested above is correct); Vicars addresses the earl of Pembroke (or, in variant copies, the earl of Bridgewater). Goodwin aims to savage the pope's 'pompatica quaedam Monarchia' ('pompous sort of Monarchy'), in ten long elegiac poems (a total of 138 pages, including additional iambics at Goodwin, 135–8). He cites patristic parallels, and the practice of Eobanus Hessus, Beza, and Buchanan in versifying psalms, 'a certaine kinde of delightfull Sawce and Seasoning of the Truth' (Vicars).

In *Melissa* Goodwin mentions his own earlier writings 'de Christianorum Martyriis', 'de vitae miseriis', and 'de Pneumatomachia seu Christiani hominis militia'. This last may possibly be the original of Josuah Sylvester's *Automachia* (an attribution accepted by the *Dictionary of National Biography* and *ESTC*), although Goodwin is not mentioned in the first edition of that tiny book (1607). Griffin, printer of *Melissa*, cites 'authoris absentia' as an excuse for mistakes (Binns, 417). Goodwin aims for 'racemus Theologiae, quam vindemia rei poeticae' ('a more beautiful Cluster of Theologie, than a bountiful Crop of Poesie'); the poetry in both languages is, however, exuberant. Different satires concentrate their fire on papal claims to authority, transubstantiation, the impure 'pseudecclesia' ('of the damnable doctrine in the deceivable synagogue of Satan, at Rome'; Vicars, no. 4), simony, the corruption of morals, or relics. Some of Goodwin's targets are vilified by name, such as Jewel's critic Thomas Stapleton, 'that faith-less frantike favourite'.

The ninth poem attacks the Gunpowder Plot (a popular neo-Latin topic: Binns, 457): Rome has a golden age ('by rapine'), iron cruelty, and now 'sulphurea', 'a powder-age'. In the seventh, monkish 'flesh-lumps', though emasculated by faith, somehow make virgins pregnant:

> Auctior ut fiat Sacrosancta Ecclesia, nympha
> Sancta patri Sancto pignora Sancta parit.
> (And that her most pure church may purer be,

Pure Friers, from their pure Nunnes pure Broods may see.)
(Goodwin, 96; Vicars, 77)

The end of the tenth satire is a neat comparison with Palinurus, the doomed Virgilian helmsman, ending on a set of puns that not even Vicars can fully render: Peter's ship hits the rocks, 'Ipse nocens scopulus summus Episcopulus'—'that little bishop of Rome' (a wonderfully insulting diminutive) 'is the Ships worst Rocke Himselfe'. Goodwin's *Melissa* remains modest: 'Hic apis, haud Elephas, liber', 'This booke's a bee, not Elephant' (Goodwin, 138). Yet his polemical elegiacs are full of verve throughout, as well as anti-Catholic venom, and remain a treat even for the impartial reader. D. K. MONEY

Sources Venn, *Alum. Cant.* • G. Goodwin, *Melissa religionis pontificae* (1620) • J. Vicars, *Babel's balme* (1624) • J. W. Binns, *Intellectual culture in Elizabethan and Jacobean England: the Latin writings of the age* (1990) • Foster, *Alum. Oxon.* • *ESTC* • *VCH Essex*, vols. 2, 4

Goodwin, Geraint Arthur (1903–1941), novelist and short-story writer, was born on 1 May 1903 at 43 Commercial Street, Llanllwchaearn, Montgomeryshire, the only child of the third marriage of Richard Goodwin (1843–1911), rate collector and assistant overseer for the parish, and his wife, Mary Jane Watkin (*née* Lewis) (1862–1943), who, like him, had been previously married and widowed. The writer was eight when his father died and twelve when his mother was married for a third time to Frank Humphreys, whose family were provision merchants in the markets of several Welsh border towns. From two Goodwin stepbrothers the writer gained a connection with journalism; from Frank Humphreys and his mother a lifelong enthusiasm for the countryside, angling, and rough shooting. To a large extent these influences shaped his life. He was educated at a local elementary school and, from the age of thirteen, as a boarder at Tywyn county school, Merioneth.

In 1920 Goodwin found employment with the *Montgomeryshire Express* at Newtown, where his stepbrothers had begun their careers. In 1923 he went to London, initially to work for W. T. Cranfield's publicity and news agency, but within the year he joined Allied Newspapers. A portrait of him by the Welsh painter Evan Walters shows him as a young journalist, trench-coated, fair-haired, and handsome, with intensely watchful eyes. He was a successful reporter, principally with the *Daily Sketch*, but was determined to become a writer. His first book, *Conversations with George Moore* (1929), was, he acknowledged, a clumsy extension of his journalism. In the same year he became seriously ill with pulmonary tuberculosis, which necessitated lengthy treatment in a sanatorium and several months of convalescence. He returned to the *Daily Sketch* in the spring of 1931, but had become disillusioned with journalism and was more than ever ambitious to write. On 17 October 1932 he married fellow journalist Rhoda Margaret Storey (1902–1991), who supported his ambition.

A promising autobiographical novel, *Call Back Yesterday*, appeared in 1935. The publisher, Cape, offered a contract for two further books. Thus encouraged, Goodwin quit Fleet Street and the family moved to Lower Farm, Dagnall, Hertfordshire. He set to work under the inspirational guidance of Edward Garnett (1868–1937), then a reader for Cape. So began a fruitful relationship which continued until Garnett's death in 1937. The first product was a novel, *The Heyday in the Blood*, published in 1936 to considerable critical acclaim. A collection of short stories, *The White Farm and other Stories*, followed in 1937, and a further novel, *Watch for the Morning*, in 1938. The writer's mother, reputedly a remarkably handsome and vigorous woman, is the archetype of several of Goodwin's formidable female characters. Similarly, certain of his male characters are endowed with facets of the writer's own appearance and personality. Evan in *The Heyday in the Blood* and Wyn in *Watch for the Morning* are also tubercular. Though noted for their sensuous descriptions of the countryside, larger than life characters, rumbustious crowd scenes, and episodes of broad humour, the novels are essentially elegiac. In April 1938 the Goodwins moved to Pen-y-cwm, a cottage in Upper Corris, Merioneth. There he wrote his last novel, *Come Michaelmas* (1939), set, like *Watch for the Morning*, in a thinly disguised version of his birthplace, Newtown. It was welcomed by the *Times Literary Supplement* reviewer (29 April 1939) as the work of a 'fresh and individual talent'.

Goodwin's future as a novelist seemed assured, but his health deteriorated rapidly and in June he entered the sanatorium at Talgarth, Brecknockshire, where he remained for several months. He was still frail when he discharged himself to rejoin his family at their new home in the ancient market town of Montgomery. A bout of influenza precipitated a further decline in his health, and in the summer of 1941 he was again admitted to a sanatorium. The disease was too far advanced, however, and he returned to Montgomery, where he died on 18 October 1941, at his home, Bowling Green Cottage, Churchbank, aged thirty-eight. He was buried five days later at Montgomery parish church. SAM ADAMS

Sources S. Adams, *Geraint Goodwin* (1974) • private information (2004) • b. cert. • *Montgomeryshire Express* (25 Oct 1941)
Archives NL Wales, MSS and letters
Likenesses E. Walters, oils, 1935, priv. coll. • E. Walters, sketch (for his portrait), repro. in P. Lord, *The visual culture of Wales: industrial society* (1998)
Wealth at death £470 16*s*. 6*d*.: administration, 17 Dec 1941, *CGPLA Eng. & Wales*

Goodwin, Harvey (1818–1891), bishop of Carlisle, was born on 9 October 1818 at King's Lynn, the second of the six children of Charles Goodwin, solicitor, and his wife, Frances Catherine Sawyer of Leeds, who was descended on her mother's side from the Wycliffes of Wycliffe, to which family John Wycliffe, the reformer, belonged. His elder brother was Charles Wycliffe, the Egyptologist. After his mother died in 1825 Goodwin was sent to a private school in High Wycombe, Buckinghamshire. He was admitted pensioner at Gonville and Caius College, Cambridge, on 16 November 1835, and soon gave evidence of his ability in mathematics. From 1837 to 1839 he was a scholar of the college. In 1840 he was placed second in the mathematical tripos of the university, and later that year was appointed to a mathematical lectureship at Caius. He became a fellow of that college in 1841.

Goodwin was ordained deacon in 1842 and priest in 1844. In the autumn of 1837 he and several others joined J. M. Neale and E. J. Boyce in visiting local churches, and out of this came the Cambridge Camden Society, formed in 1839, which concerned itself with the architecture and arrangement of churches. Most of its members had Tractarian sympathies. These Goodwin sought to restrain, as he himself was more concerned with reverence in worship than the details of ritual.

Not being allowed to marry as a fellow, Goodwin gave up his fellowship in the summer of 1845; he was licensed as an assistant curate at St Giles' Church, Cambridge, and sustained himself by taking private pupils. On 13 August 1845 he married Ellen King, the daughter of George and Katherine King of Bebington House, Bebington, Cheshire, at Woodchurch, Cheshire. They had seven children who were all born in Cambridge. In 1848 Goodwin was appointed the incumbent of St Edward's Church, Cambridge, where he made his mark as a preacher, speaking to the well-to-do tradesmen who formed the bulk of his parishioners, but also attracting to his sermons many younger members of the university. He resolved to remove the very high pews and to make other changes in the church. These, however, took almost ten years to put into effect, and he had left Cambridge before they were completed.

Appointed to the deanery of Ely by Lord Derby in November 1858, Goodwin continued the work of the restoration of the cathedral begun under his predecessor, George Peacock. This included the completion of the painting of the nave roof, first by H. L. S. Le Strange and then by T. G. Parry, as well as the restoration of the Lantern, the provision of a new pulpit, the repair of the Galilee porch, and the installation of the cathedral's first heating system. A school for the choristers was also built, the brewhouse was abolished, and the repaving of the nave floor was begun. For Ely itself he provided a dispensary and improved the road to the allotments. But, being musical, his chief concern was the maintenance of fully choral services in the cathedral, though he disliked intensely its use for oratorios and sacred concerts. He permitted a transept, suitably curtained off, to be used for meetings of the diocesan conference. While at Ely he served on two royal commissions, the commission on clerical subscription in 1863 and the ritual commission in 1867. On the report of the latter he made two reservations. The ritual commission had proposed to leave unamended the ornaments rubric in the prayer book, which specified that the ornaments of the church should be those in use in the second year of the reign of Edward VI. This he thought should be amended, otherwise its imprecision would remain a source of trouble. The commission had also advocated the retention of the recitation of the Athanasian creed on certain holy days, but proposed that a note should be added to it declaring that the creed's condemnations should not be otherwise understood than as a solemn warning to those who wilfully rejected the Catholic faith. Goodwin thought this an incomplete explanation and insufficient to meet the scruples of those who objected to that creed's public use.

In October 1869 Goodwin accepted Gladstone's offer of the bishopric of Carlisle and held the see until his death. He was consecrated bishop at York on 30 November 1869 and enthroned publicly in his cathedral on 15 December that year. This was an innovation, since many earlier bishops had been enthroned by proxy, and his immediate predecessor, Samuel Waldegrave, though enthroned in person, had been enthroned privately. At Carlisle he introduced a diocesan conference, established a new archdeaconry, and in 1889 secured the appointment of a suffragan bishop for the diocese. In his twenty-one years as bishop he consecrated or dedicated 150 churches or burial-grounds. He was much concerned with the relationship between science and religion, maintaining 'that morals and religion have their own territory, but they will be modified by the necessity of recognizing indubitable physical truths' in an article entitled 'The philosophy of crayfishes' (*Nineteenth Century*, 8, Oct 1880, 622–37). On the Sunday after Charles Darwin's burial in Westminster Abbey he was invited to preach there (1 May 1882). Paying tribute to Darwin's devotion to the one great work of his life, he asked 'Who has not read with wonder and delight the volume upon earth-worms?', the subject of Darwin's last scientific publication. But he rejected the conclusion, not advanced by Darwin himself, that having got the works of Darwin he could burn his Bible. The sermon was printed in Goodwin's *Walks in the Regions of Science and Faith* (1883).

Among other works, Goodwin wrote *A Guide to the Parish Church* (3rd edn, 1878), which proved popular. To avoid wandering eyes and wandering thoughts he advised the worshipper to keep his eye on his prayer book and never mind the colour of Mrs A's bonnet. Goodwin also contributed to *Essays on Cathedrals* (ed. J. S. Howson, 1872), in which he urged that canonries should incur the obligation to undertake some useful employment, a theme that was taken up by the royal commission on cathedrals (1879–85), of which he was a member. He wrote its first report, which advocated that cathedrals should become centres of theological instruction and competent preaching and pastoral work. On the death of Archbishop Tait in 1882 he followed him as the commission's chairman, but though the commission made recommendations which were laid as bills before parliament, none ever passed into law. Goodwin occupied a position in the centre of the spectrum of views held in the Church of England. He deprecated the introduction of unusual rites and ceremonies in the church, but was unwilling as bishop to interfere in such matters within his diocese unless compelled to do so. The building of Church House, Westminster, as the Church of England's memorial of the queen's jubilee of 1887 was largely due to his efforts. He lived to see the laying of its foundation-stone.

Goodwin died of heart failure on 25 November 1891 at Bishopthorpe, while on a visit to William Maclagan, archbishop of York. He was buried in the churchyard of Crosthwaite, Keswick, Cumberland, where his second son, who had died nine years earlier of scarlet fever, had been the vicar.
P. C. HAMMOND

Sources H. D. Rawnsley, *Harvey Goodwin: a biographical memoir* (1896) • H. Goodwin, *Memoir written by himself* (1880) • J. S. Howson, ed., *Essays on cathedrals* (1872) • J. Venn and others, eds., *Biographical history of Gonville and Caius College*, 2: 1713–1897 (1898) • catalogue, CUL • O. Chadwick, *The Victorian church*, 2 vols. (1966–70) • P. Barrett, *Barchester: English cathedral life in the nineteenth century* (1993) • J. F. White, *The Cambridge movement: the ecclesiologists and the Gothic revival* (1962)

Archives BL, letters to W. E. Gladstone, Add. MSS 44422–44513, *passim* • CKS, letters to Scott Robertson • CUL, letters to Sir George Stokes • Durham Cath. CL, letters to J. B. Lightfoot • LPL, corresp. with Edward Benson • LPL, letters to A. C. Tait

Likenesses W. H. Nightingale, sketch, 1839, Gon. & Caius Cam. • wood-engraving, 1859, repro. in *ILN* • G. Richmond, crayon, 1869 • wood-engraving, 1870, repro. in *ILN* • G. Richmond, oils, 1877, Church House, Westminster, London • engraving, 1879, Gon. & Caius Cam. • W. H. Thornycroft, bronze recumbent effigy, exh. RA 1895, Carlisle Cathedral • T. L. Atkinson, mezzotint (after G. Richmond), BM • Spy [L. Ward], chromolithograph caricature, NPG; repro. in *VF* (17 March 1888) • T. C. Wageman, watercolour drawing, Trinity Cam. • photograph, NPG

Wealth at death £19,097 17s. 5d.: resworn probate, March 1892, *CGPLA Eng. & Wales* (1891)

Goodwin, James Ignatius. *See* Middlemore, Richard (*c.*1602–1667).

Goodwin, John (*c.*1594–1665), Independent minister, was born in Norfolk, the son of John Goodwin of Helloughton, bailiff of the Townshend estates in and around East Raynham. It was possibly under the patronage of the Townshend family that he matriculated in 1612 at Queens' College, Cambridge, where he graduated BA in 1616, proceeded MA in 1619, and was perhaps taught by John Preston. He held a fellowship at Queens' between 1617 and 1627, and was incorporated at Oxford in 1622.

Early years Little is known of Goodwin's life at Cambridge. He was tutor to a future London presbyterian minister, Thomas Cawton, who in later years claimed that he had shunned the 'evil Principles' which even then Goodwin had 'endeavoured to infuse into his Pupils' (Cawton, 3). Goodwin himself observed afterwards that it was during the years when he was a young student at Cambridge that the doctrine of the divine right of kings became 'the known preferment Divinity of the Doctorate there' (J. Goodwin, *Hybristodikai: the Obstructours of Justice*, 1649, 28).

Goodwin was ordained at Norwich on 17 December 1620 and instituted in 1625 to the vicarage of East Raynham, a valuable living in the gift of Sir Roger Townshend. In 1627 he was chosen lecturer at St Nicholas, Great Yarmouth. On 31 July 1629, perhaps upon the recommendation of Thomas Goodwin, the town of King's Lynn elected him lecturer at St Nicholas's Chapel, but he was suspended in the following year as a nonconformist by the bishop of Norwich. During 1630–33, while continuing to hold his living at East Raynham, Goodwin preached at Norwich, Dover, and London. On 3 December 1633 the parish of St Stephen, Coleman Street, London, elected him as vicar and lecturer to succeed John Davenport, who had resigned and fled to the Netherlands. It is possible that Goodwin was known to the parish through the Townshend family, for Sir Roger Townshend's mother-in-law, Mary Vere, had long been a friend and patron of John Davenport. It has also been said that after Goodwin's acceptance of the call, Lady Vere was for a time one of his parishioners.

London minister in the 1630s The early years of Goodwin's ministerial life in London were relatively uneventful. The relationship between him and his parishioners was one of mutual affection, esteem, and respect, as Goodwin himself attested in a 1640 epistle of dedication. It has been said that he was inclined to religious independency as early as 1633 under the influence of John Cotton, but this is doubtful. As late as 1639, in a letter to Thomas Goodwin (the separatist preacher then in the Netherlands, who was also from Norfolk but not evidently a close kinsman), he questioned many of the tenets of the Independent way, which 'I am in perfect peace in my thoughts, that you will never be able to demonstrate or prove from the Scripture to any sober minded or considering man' (J. Goodwin, *A Quaere Concerning the Church-Covenant*, 1643, 13). In 1635 he was convened before the court of high commission for breach of the canons of the church, and two years later he was again found to have given communion during Easter to strangers either standing or sitting. In neither case, however, was action taken against him. In 1638–9 Goodwin became entangled in a theological controversy with some London ministers, but Bishop William Juxon was 'in hope to settle this also quietly' (*Works of … William Laud*, 5.332, 356, 362). In August 1640 he joined other London puritan ministers in preparing a petition against the new canons which had been proclaimed two months earlier.

Intellectually, however, Goodwin, who probably had been influenced by the writings of George Hakewill and Jacobus Acontius, already revealed in these years an independent mind, which was not afraid to question its old beliefs or to embrace new ideas. He told Thomas Goodwin in 1639 that he was often compelled 'by a strong hand of superior conviction' to call 'darknesse' opinions which 'for a time I have nourished in my bosome' and which 'sometimes I called light' (J. Goodwin, *A Quaere*, 12). Indeed, in an epistle dedicatory to his *Imputatio fidei, or, A Treatise of Justification* (1642) addressed to the London clergy early in 1642, Goodwin wrote:

> I apprehend a marveilous bewtie, benefit, and blessing in such a frame of spirit, which makes a man able, and willing and joyfull to cast away long-endeered and professed opinions, when once the light has shone upon them, and discovered them to be but darknesse. (*Imputatio fidei*, 'To his deare brethren')

He spoke perceptively of the intellectual inertia in society and the difficulties for men shackled by old learning to change their minds. 'We have but the light of the Moone instead of the Sunne', he had told John Pym in late 1640, 'because we are tender-eyed, and inconsiderately afrayd, lest an excellency of knowledge should undoe us' (*The Christians Engagement for the Gospell: Opened in Severall Sermons*, 1640, foreword). It was with such intellectual convictions that Goodwin, while remaining within the puritan brotherhood, abandoned one of the fundamental tenets of Calvinism—the dogma of predestination. In one of his sermons in the 1630s he preached that 'there is no creature under heaven but God hath thus far conditioned or covenanted with it, that if it will believe and accept of Jesus Christ from his hand, he will receive it and be a God unto it' (*The Saints Interest in God*, 1640, 79–80). To Goodwin this doctrine of general redemption was more agreeable to the spirit of the gospel and the reason of man. 'The great and maine promise of the Gospel, that whosoever beleeves on Jesus Christ (or on God through Christ) shall be saved', Goodwin preached in another sermon, 'is both a readier and cleerer, and more satisfying foundation' for men to build their hopes for salvation (*God a Good Master and Protector*, 1640, 118–19).

It appears that Goodwin's anti-predestinarian views came very close to Arminianism, and he was, indeed, often accused by his opponents of being an Arminian or Socinian. However, Goodwin quoted Calvin extensively and argued that it was his opponents who had misinterpreted Calvin and put 'Calvin's head and hands at odds' (*Imputatio fidei*, 121–2). In fact, Goodwin later clearly expressed his disapproval of Socinianism for its 'opposing the Deity of Jesus Christ' and Arminianism 'that questions the person of the Holy Ghost' (J. Goodwin, *A Reply of Two of the Brothers to A. S.*, 1644, 24). His was a searching mind too independent to subscribe to any particular theological 'ism'. In early 1642, in answer to George Walker's charges of heresy, Goodwin, using the discovery of the New World for his arguments, presented an impressive defence of intellectual freedom. If so great a part of the world as America had remained unknown for so many generations, 'well may it be conceived', he wrote, 'that many truths, yea and those of maine concernment, and importance, may be yet unborne' (*Imputatio fidei*, preface). Indeed, Goodwin argued, the quest for truth was a ceaseless effort in which men 'shall discourse and beat out the secrets of God in the Scriptures with more libertie and freedom of judgement and understanding' (ibid.).

Parliamentarian and radical political thinker So far Goodwin's discourses had been mainly intellectual and theological in nature. There had been few open manifestations of political radicalism towards either church or state. The coming of the civil war, however, was drastically to change Goodwin's world and his responses to it. St Stephen, Coleman Street, had long been known for its religious radicalism; one of the largest City parishes within the wall, it was a community of wealth as well as social diversity. It was to St Stephen that the five members of the House of Commons fled for protection in early 1642 when Charles I descended upon the house for their arrest. Alderman Isaac Penington, a leading parishioner and one of the City MPs in the Long Parliament, was a pillar of the parliamentarian cause in London, and he replaced the royalist Sir Richard Gurney as lord mayor in September. There were also a host of other radical civic leaders from the parish during the 1640s. Perhaps not surprisingly, therefore, Goodwin was one of the earliest London ministers openly and unequivocally to justify armed resistance against the king. The parliamentarian cause, he wrote, 'is just, and holy, and good' and 'there is nothing in it that should make you ashamed either before God, or justly-judging men, nothing that needs make you tender, or holding off in point of conscience' (*Anti-Cavalierisme*, 1642, 5). Both 'the manifest Law of God' and 'the common light of nature' made it lawful to take up arms to disobey 'the unlawfull command of a King'. Indeed, in such a case, Goodwin argued, it was 'a matter of duty and obedience unto God' (ibid., 10).

More importantly, Goodwin ventured into the realm of political ideas and questioned the biblical basis of kingly government. He maintained that while it was the ordinance of God that 'there should be some government or other in every society of men', there was no ordinance of God that it should be 'this or that speciall form of government'. 'Therefore', he concluded, 'Kingly government was no Ordinance of God' (*Anti-Cavalierisme*, 1642, 7). It is perhaps worth notice that in 1642 he still refrained from attacking the king directly: 'We conceive it to be a just Prerogative of the Persons of Kings in what case soever, to be secure from the violence of men' (ibid., 11). However, Goodwin was not unaware of the wider historical significance of the civil war in England. If the parliamentarian cause was successful in England, it would be like a '*lightning*' which 'shall pierce through many kingdoms' of Europe (ibid., 50); and when he was called to preach on a fast day before the City magistrates during the crisis of the march of the king's forces towards London, he delivered a scathing and virulent sermon which he later published under the title of *Butchers Blessing, or, The Bloody Intentions of Romish Cavaliers* (1642).

Toleration and division As the civil war progressed Goodwin emerged as a leading champion for religious toleration. The calling of the Westminster assembly of divines, the Anglo-Scottish alliance under the solemn league and covenant, and the rise of a clerical presbyterian faction in the City of London all conspired to threaten a new religious conformity. In the meantime, Goodwin had finally embraced the Independent way and, some time in the middle of 1643, visibly formed a congregational church within the parochial church of St Stephen, Coleman Street. He joined the pamphlet war against high presbyterianism and exchanged violent diatribes with such polemicists as Thomas Edwards and William Prynne. This was perhaps a natural development of Goodwin's earlier attitude towards intellectual freedom. No longer confined to theology, he now advocated a rational approach to ordinary religious life and emphasized that true religious faith should not be mere enthusiasm but a conviction derived from reason, knowledge and understanding. 'God regards no mans *zeale* without knowledge', argued his *Theomachia; or, The Grand Impudence of Men Running the Hazard of Fighting against God* (1644), 'though it should pitch and fasten upon things, never so agreeable to his will' (p.

19). Indeed, in *Some Modest and Humble Queries* (1646), he questioned whether any man ought to believe 'the deepest and highest mystery in Religion' unless 'he hath Reason to judge it to be a Truth'. In *Hagiomastix, or, The Scourge of the Saints* (1647), he avowed, therefore, that 'Reason ought to be every mans leader, Guide, and Director in his Faith, or about what he is, or ought to beleeve' (p. 108). Since to impose a religious uniformity was to force people 'to yeeld to blind obedience, never to search into the truth', Goodwin argued, no magistrates should use their secular power 'to set down, what shall, must, or ought to be done, against all contradiction, in matters of religion' (*M. S. to A. S.*, 1644, 34) or 'to impose any thing upon the people of God in point of worship, under mulcts and penalties' (*Innocencies Triumph*, 1644, 8). Of course, for Goodwin, toleration did not mean an approbation of or a connivance at any doctrine or practice which would undermine what were then considered the 'fundamentals' of the Christian religion, but, he insisted, it was the duty of the clergy 'to preach from the Scriptures to evince the folly, vanity and falsehood of all such ways' (*M. S. to A. S.*, 53). After all, Goodwin observed, '*Prisons* and *Swords* are no *Church-officers*, nor any appurtenances to any Ecclesiastique authority in what form of Government soever' (*Theomachia*, 34). Perhaps most forceful of all was his argument that 'in every Way, Doctrine or Practice which is from God, there is somewhat of God himselfe'. And he presented an appealing picture, albeit idealized, of religious diversity:

> The very substance, frame, and constitution of them, at least that which is operative, quickening and spirituall in them, what is it but a kinde of heavenly composition, the ingredients whereof are the holiness, wisdome, mercy, goodness and bounty of God, and what are these, and every of them, but God himself? (ibid., title-page)

In the midst of this bitter pamphlet war Goodwin suffered a personal defeat. The relationship between him and his parishioners at St Stephen, Coleman Street, rapidly began to deteriorate soon after his gathered congregation had assumed an Independent identity, and especially after his disciples had attempted to transform the parochial church into a congregational one during a vestry on 12 and 14 December 1643. 'Now', as Goodwin himself observed in *A Moderate Answer* (1645), 'none have right to the Ordinances but Saints and therefore none may be admitted but such as can be judged so by the Saints' (p. 3). Some parishioners, therefore, brought charges against Goodwin to the committee for plundered ministers. Efforts were made to reconcile the differences but all failed. On 22 May 1645 Goodwin was sequestered. After his sequestration, he and his gathered church first met in some buildings in Coleman Street and afterwards at the parish church of St Mary Abchurch. Not until 11 November 1649 were Goodwin and his followers allowed to return to the parish church of St Stephen, Coleman Street.

During these and subsequent years Goodwin and his congregation, almost like a Pythagorean religious order, showed unusual solidarity. The master and his disciples frequently made public testimonies in defence of their common beliefs. Furthermore, the congregation comprised some of the important leaders of the radical faction in the City in both religion and politics. Mark Hildesley, an active supporter of the war efforts in the City from the very beginning of the civil war, was later elected alderman in 1649–51. John Price, intellectually Goodwin's chief disciple, was an able polemic pamphleteer in his own right. In the early 1650s Thomas Alderne, a captain in the London militia, became a leading radical common councilman in an attempt to democratize the City government. It was also during these years that Goodwin and members of his gathered church, such as John Price, Daniel Taylor, and Richard Price, formed a sporadic and tenuous alliance with leaders of the Leveller movement, especially William Walwyn, who had attended Goodwin's sermons years before and was well acquainted with some of Goodwin's people. Walwyn spoke of holding 'daily meetings and intimate Discourses' with Goodwin and John Lilburne and others in early 1645, and in May 1646 Goodwin's congregation contributed 50s. towards the publication of 10,000 copies of Walwyn's pamphlet *A Word in Season*. Although the alliance seems to have been collapsing in 1647, they still shared common concerns regarding religious liberty. During the Whitehall debates in early 1649 Goodwin and the Levellers spoke in consonance in opposition to Henry Ireton and Philip Nye.

Commonwealth and protectorate In the constitutional crisis of 1648–9, however, Goodwin appeared to be a staunch defender of the army and its actions. He was one of the earliest authors to justify the purge of the House of Commons by Colonel Thomas Pride, which, he argued in *Right and Might well Met* (1649) was 'regular and conformable to such lawes and rules of justice, which all considering and disingaged men conclude ought to be followed and observed in such cases' (p. 2). Furthermore, he gave the army and its actions a legitimate and constitutional basis. Their calling and commission was, he wrote, 'to act in the capacity of Souldiers for the peace, liberties, and safety of the Kingdome'. 'What doth this import', he asked, 'but a calling to prevent, or suppresse by force, all such persons and designes, whose faces were set to disturb, or destroy them?' (p. 3). Goodwin's arguments carried him to the dangerous conclusion that a nation might be forced to be 'free' by the might of a few 'good' men. 'It is a ruled case amongst the wise', he asserted, 'that if a people be deprived and corrupt, so as to conferre places of power and trust upon wicked and undeserving men, they forfeited their power in this behalfe unto those that are good, though but a few'. And he added that 'it is a deed of Charity and Christianity, to save the life of a lunatique or distracted person even against his will' (p. 15). In May 1649 Goodwin published another tract to justify the trial and execution of the king. Now abandoning whatever reservations he might have had in *Anti-Cavalierisme*, Goodwin wrote in *Hybristodikai: the Obstructours of Justice* (1649) that 'it is frivolous to say that Kings are accountable unto God, when they transgresse his Law, though not unto men', and he tried to prove that there was 'a clear Law of the Land, for putting even Kings to death, when they commit murther' (pp. 5–7). In fact, Goodwin now adopted the view of a popular foundation of all governments. 'Kings', he claimed, were simply people's 'creatures' (p. 15).

Under the Commonwealth and the protectorate Goodwin's life in London was no longer threatened by high presbyterianism, but it was hardly less controversial. For a time he turned to theological writing and published in early 1651 his *Apolytrōsis apolytrōseōs, or, Redemption Redeemed*. It was a substantial work of 570 pages, and it shows Goodwin's erudite knowledge of the works of early church fathers as well as modern reformers. However, it was immediately looked upon as the ghost of Arminius out of the grave and became the target of condemnation by a number of puritan divines, including among the well known Thomas Hill, Joseph Caryl, George Kendall, and John Owen. Even Richard Baxter, while speaking approvingly of Goodwin's *Imputatio fidei*, called him now 'a flatt Arminian' (Keeble and Nuttall, no. 68). Yet Goodwin went further. Later in the year he composed another short tract under the title of *The Pagans Debt and Dowry* (1651), in which he made the doctrine of general redemption truly universal. He maintained that 'the *Gentiles*, to whom the Letter, or Written Letter, of the Gospel never came, and amongst whom the name of *Christ* (haply) was never named' may well be said 'to have, and to have had, the Gospel preached unto them' (p. 10). Pointing to 'the Heavens moving still in their natural course, and the gracious Providence of God, joyntly [jocundly?] speak[ing] in the ears of all Flesh', he asked: 'what is this but the very tenor, sum, and substance of the Gospel?' (p. 13). During the following years Goodwin must have been saddened by the fact that he now had to oppose the gathered churches with which he had once fought together in a common battle for religious liberty and toleration. He wrote against Baptist churches when the doctrine of believers' baptism caused a rift in his own church. He wrote against the gathered churches in and around the City of London which had harboured the agitations of the Fifth Monarchy Men. And, finally, he wrote in 1657 against the system of triers, which the Independent divines, now in power, had established under the protectorate, even though in 1652 he had been persuaded by Philip Nye to lend his signature to the Independent divines' proposals for the propagation of the gospel in the nation. A truly independent man, Goodwin claimed that 'undue compliance with any faction or party whatsoever, whether prevailing or failing, hath been none of my least visible sins' (*Right and Might well Met*, 1657, 102). By the early 1650s Goodwin was a widower with at least three children, John, Edward, and Mary. It may have been he who married Mary Bradshaw at St Stephen, Coleman Street, on 13 February 1652. If so, she soon died, for he married Sarah Carew (*d.* 1677) at St Margaret, Lothbury, on 31 July 1653.

Final years At the Restoration Goodwin was immediately under attack for his political ideas. A royal proclamation officially condemned his *The Obstructours of Justice*, together with John Milton's *Pro populo Anglicano defensio* and *Eikonoklastes*, and ordered them to be burned by the hand of the common hangman. Moreover, on 18 June 1660 Goodwin was excepted from the Bill of Indemnity, thus being perpetually incapacitated from holding any place of trust. He was deprived of his St Stephen living, and his successor was instituted on 29 May 1661. Goodwin went into hiding first at Bethnal Green in the eastern suburb of London and then in the town of Leigh in Essex. He died in 1665. In his will, made at Hackney on 7 January 1659, he dispensed respectable sums of money among his children, including Samuel, who received his lands 'in the Barrony of Navan in the County of Eastmeath in the Province of Lennster in Ireland' (PRO, PROB 11/320, sig. 77).

TAI LIU

Sources will, PRO, PROB 11/320, sig. 77 • T. Cawton, *The life and death of … Thomas Cawton* (1662) • vestry minutes of St Stephen Coleman Street, GL, MS 4458/1 • churchwardens' accounts of St Mary Abchurch, GL, MS 3891/1 • records of the committee for plundered ministers, BL, Add. MS 15669 • *The writings of William Walwyn*, ed. J. R. McMichael and B. Taft (1989) • A. S. P. Woodhouse, ed., *Puritanism and liberty: being the army debates (1647–9) from the Clarke manuscripts, with supplementary documents*, new edn (1966) • *Calendar of the correspondence of Richard Baxter*, ed. N. H. Keeble and G. F. Nuttall, 2 vols. (1991) • W. A. Shaw, *A history of the English church during the civil wars and under the Commonwealth, 1640–1660*, 2 vols. (1900) • *Calamy rev.*, 227 • *The works of the most reverend father in God, William Laud*, ed. J. Bliss and W. Scott, 7 vols. (1847–60) • T. Jackson, *The life of John Goodwin* (1822) • E. S. More, 'The new Arminians: John Goodwin and his Coleman Street congregation in Cromwellian England', PhD diss., University of Rochester, New York State, 1980 • E. More, 'John Goodwin and the origins of the new Arminianism', *Journal of British Studies*, 22/1 (1982–3), 50–70 • E. S. More, 'Congregationalism and the social order: John Goodwin's gathered church, 1640–60', *Journal of Ecclesiastical History*, 38 (1987), 210–35 • D. A. Kirby, 'The radicals of St Stephen's, Coleman Street, London, 1624–1642', *Guildhall Miscellany*, 3 (1969–71) • W. Haller, *The rise of puritanism: … the New Jerusalem as set forth in pulpit and press from Thomas Cartwright to John Lilburne and John Milton, 1570–1643* (1938) • W. Haller, *Liberty and reformation in the puritan revolution* (1955) • A. E. Barker, *Milton and the puritan dilemma* (1955) • J. Sanderson, *'But the people's creatures': the philosophical basis of the English civil war* (1989) • M. Tolmie, *The triumph of the saints: the separate churches of London, 1616–1649* (1977) • P. S. Seaver, *The puritan lectureships: the politics of religious dissent, 1560–1662* (1970) • Tai Liu, *Puritan London: a study of religion and society in the City parishes* (1986)

Likenesses line engraving, 1648, BM, NPG; repro. in J. Vicars, *Coleman-street conclave visited* (1648) • G. Glover, line engraving, BM, NPG; repro. in J. Goodwin, *Imputatio fidei* (1642) • engraving, repro. in J. Goodwin, *The divine authority of the scriptures asserted* (1648) • engraving, repro. in J. Goodwin, *Hybristodikai: the obstructours of justice* (1649) • pen-and-ink drawing (after unknown engraving), NPG

Wealth at death left respectable sums of money to children; lands 'in the Barrony of the Navan in the County of Eastmeath, in the Province of Lennster in Ireland': will, PRO, PROB 11/320, sig. 77

Goodwin, Philip (*d.* 1667), Church of England clergyman and ejected minister, is of unknown parentage. He matriculated from St John's College, Cambridge, in 1623 and graduated BA in March 1627; in the same month he was ordained deacon and priest at Peterborough. He proceeded MA in 1630. He may be the Philip Goodwin who married Sarah Kinge at Watford on 11 October 1632.

In 1633 Goodwin was curate at All Saints', Hertford. Nine years later, in the summer of 1642, he was appointed by the House of Commons Sunday lecturer at Pinner, Middlesex (on 30 May), and Sunday and market-day lecturer at Hemel Hempstead, Hertfordshire, the following week. At Pinner the curate attempted to block Goodwin's afternoon lecture by the simple expedient of continuing to expound the homilies until six in the evening. In 1645 he was appointed vicar of Watford by parliamentary ordinance in the place of Cornelius Burges. In 1654 Goodwin was appointed to act as one of the ministers assisting the triers for Hertfordshire.

Goodwin published four works between 1649 and 1658. Three were conventional works on aspects of personal piety and household religious practice. *The evangelicall communicant in the eucharisticall sacrament, or, A treatise declaring who are to receive the supper of the Lord* (1649; 2nd enlarged edn, 1657) dealt with the vexed question of the methods of personal preparation and qualifications for receiving the eucharist; Goodwin favoured restricted over open admission to communion. *Dies dominus redivivus, or, The Lord's day enlivened, or, A treatise … to discover the practical part of the evangelical sabbath* (1654) and *Religio domestica rediviva, or, Family Religion Revived* (1655) were manuals of religious instruction for family life, enjoining regular self-examination of personal faith and illustrating parental responsibilities in fostering this belief.

Goodwin also published a more innovative text entitled *The mystery of dreames, historically discoursed, or, A treatise wherein is clearly discovered the secret yet certain good or evil … of mens differing dreames; their distinguishing characters* (1658). This sought to provide guidance for the interpretation of dreams in the light of scripture. It contained six parts, including sections on dreams that were 'False and Pretending', 'Filthy and defiling', 'Jole [jolly] and Vain', 'Troublesome and Affrighting', and 'Admonishing and Instructing … viz. from God'. Goodwin argued that some dreams were 'supernaturall', and distinguished between dreams that conveyed 'Evil from Satan, and Good from God'. The work was intended to help the believer combat the former and derive instruction from the latter—'an undoubted Duty in Gospel-daies' (P. Goodwin, *Mystery*, introduction). In doing so, it attempted to extend orthodox spiritual injunctions about behaviour and morality to potentially deviant impulses from the unconscious mind.

Goodwin was ejected from Watford for nonconformity in June 1661. When he made his will, on 18 August 1667, he was living in Rotherhithe, Surrey; it was proved eleven days later by his widow and executor, Sarah. He left property in Watford and the Middlesex parishes of Norwood and Ruislip, and requested that he be buried next to his wife's relations at Watford. His sons John and Philip became Church of England clergymen. His will named two other sons, Joseph and James, and a daughter, Sarah Walker.

H. R. FRENCH

Sources Venn, *Alum. Cant.*, 1/2.239 • *VCH Hertfordshire*, 4.344, 430 • C. H. Firth and R. S. Rait, eds., *Acts and ordinances of the interregnum, 1642–1660*, 1 (1911), 672–4, 971 • R. Newcourt, *Repertorium ecclesiasticum parochiale Londinense*, 1 (1708), 960 • *Calamy rev.*, 227 • will, PRO, PROB 11/324, sig. 105 • W. Urwick, *Nonconformity in Hertfordshire* (1884) • *JHC*, 2 (1640–42), 596, 628, 703 • *IGI*

Goodwin, Thomas (1600–1680), nonconformist minister, was born prematurely on 5 October 1600 in Rollesby, near Great Yarmouth, Norfolk. He was the first of at least four children of Richard Goodwyn (*d.* 1632), merchant, and Katherine (1577–1645), daughter of John Collingwood (*d.* 1608) and his wife, Mary (*d.* 1619). By 1607 the family had returned to his father's birthplace, King's Lynn, where Richard became chamberlain and an alderman. He was a churchwarden of St Nicholas from 1615, and was among those reprimanded in 1627 by Samuel Harsnett, bishop of Norwich, for presenting preachers who occasionally neglected the surplice or shortened service for the sake of preaching. At his death he owned significant property in the town.

Education and early career Goodwin's education began at King's Lynn grammar school, first under Henry Alston, and then, following Alston's removal by the council in 1612, under the godly William Armitage of Emmanuel College. On 25 August 1613 Goodwin entered Christ's College, Cambridge, as a junior sophister. This was a year earlier than normal, and seems to have been motivated by the change in schoolmaster. He matriculated as pensioner the following April. His tutor, William Power, had been a contemporary of Alston's at Christ's. When Goodwin arrived 'there remained still in the College six Fellows that were great tutors … then called Puritans' ('Memoir', 5.ix). Power, however, was not one of them. Initially influenced by the godly of the college, Goodwin participated for a time in their Saturday evening catechism on Ursinus and chamber prayers. He also attended the sermons of Richard Sibbes at Holy Trinity and John Preston at Queens', and travelled to hear John Rogers of Dedham and John Wilson of Sudbury.

However, Goodwin quickly grew disillusioned with puritanism. Pursuing his ambition of preferment and acclaim, he resolved to preach against the puritans of King's Lynn. His role model was Richard Senhouse. Though he briefly considered Arminian theology, he closely followed the proceedings at Dort and never abandoned Calvinism. In 1617 he graduated BA. In 1619 he migrated to St Catharine's College and he proceeded MA the following year. On 21 March 1620 he was elected fellow and college lecturer.

On 2 October 1620 Goodwin underwent a conversion experience as a result of a funeral sermon by Thomas Bainbridge. Although this is traditionally considered the point at which he aligned with thoroughgoing puritanism, Goodwin subscribed and conformed throughout the 1620s. His association with the godly developed gradually over the decade and appears to have been driven by the changing nature of the late Jacobean and early Caroline church. Through correspondence Nicholas Price, the conformable puritan curate of St Nicholas, King's Lynn, counselled Goodwin on assurance. As a fellow of St Catharine's

Thomas Goodwin (1600–1680), by Robert White, pubd 1681

Goodwin was active in the election of evangelically minded, but conformable, fellows such as Andrew Perne and John Arrowsmith in 1622 and 1623 respectively. On 2 March 1622 he was ordained deacon at Peterborough and in 1625 he was licensed as a university preacher and began preaching at St Andrew's the Great. In 1626 Goodwin worked to secure the election of the moderate puritan Richard Sibbes as master of his college. Through Sibbes, Goodwin was introduced to Sir Nathaniel Rich and the earl of Warwick's circle. By 1628 he was curate of St Andrew's the Great. That year he was elected to succeed Preston as town lecturer at Holy Trinity. Before admitting him John Buckeridge, bishop of Ely, sought to impose an additional oath that he 'solemnly promise not to preach against any controverted points in divinity' in obedience to the king's declaration but it was Goodwin's anti-papal, rather than puritan, views which were at issue ('Memoir', 5.xvii). Two years later he proceeded BD, offering an evangelical Calvinist defence of assurance of faith against Roman objections.

The Holy Trinity lectureship was rescued from suppression in 1630 and partially exempted from Charles I's instructions of 1629 curbing lecturing. This may have been through the agency of Sir Nathaniel Rich, who, according to the dedication of Goodwin's *The Returne of Prayers* (1636), performed a 'great and speciall favour' for him about this time (sig. A2). However, those same instructions forced Goodwin, on 5 December 1632, to accept the vicarage of Holy Trinity, in the gift of the crown. The new bishop of Ely, Francis White, required a testimonial on his behalf which was supplied by the Laudian vicar of Stanwell, John Macarnesse. Less than a year later on 21 November 1633 Goodwin resigned the living to Sibbes. This move has been portrayed as the consequence of his embracing congregationalism following his conference with John Cotton and others at Ockley, Surrey, in June 1633. Goodwin told Thomas Edwards, however, that 'he had nothing to say but against the Ceremonies', and Samuel Hartlib recorded similar remarks (Edwards, 17). The timing of his resignation suggests that Goodwin was responding to the republication of the Book of Sports, which had occurred on 18 October. Although dissatisfied with the terms of conformity Goodwin had not become a separatist, much less a 'separatist preacher in London' as the *Dictionary of National Biography* asserted. His resignation from Holy Trinity appears calculated to allow him to remain at St Catharine's. The evidence suggests that Goodwin continued to live in college until 1638, preaching in chapel, revising sermons for publication, and corresponding with friends, among them Hartlib. In his will of July 1635 Sibbes made Goodwin one of the trustees of money to be used for scholarships, they 'haveing the seale of the said colledge for their securetie' (Grosart).

Throughout the 1630s Goodwin was engaged with Hartlib and John Dury in their programme of producing English practical divinity for foreign divines. Goodwin was a signatory to the *Instrumentum theologorum Anglorum* and contributed £20 per year to Dury's support. Hartlib thought a number of Goodwin's treatises relevant, though he despaired of seeing them completed, since so many were in progress. Among them was a body of divinity provisionally entitled 'A history of truth'. According to Goodwin, it would 'shew forth the state of Grace in it's Harmony and dependancy that Men should see in this part of divinity as much wisdome as in any part whatsoever' (Sheffield University Library, Hartlib MSS 29/2/56a). Late in 1634 Goodwin considered joining Archbishop James Ussher in Ireland, in order 'to perfect that there for the good of forraine Churches' (ibid., 29/2/53b). In the event he remained in Cambridge, editing at least ten other treatises for the project, 'first to publish them as Sermons preached in England and fitted to this Climate' (ibid.). Hartlib hoped Goodwin would provide a 'Table of Preaching Heads in Practical Divinity' (ibid., 29/2/57b). He never did so, but Hartlib's pessimism was unfounded. Goodwin's treatises, which began to appear in 1636 with the highly popular *The Returne of Prayers* and were eventually collected in *Certain Select Cases* (1644), represent in part Goodwin's contribution to Dury's cause.

Goodwin was sole author of fifteen different titles; most ran to multiple editions, and four of his most important and representative works were translated into Latin by William Jemmat and published in 1658 in Heidelberg.

Many of his works were translated into Dutch and German during his lifetime, and after his death were a favourite of continental pietists. Goodwin was an editor or publisher of the works of Sibbes, John Preston, Jeremiah Burroughes, John Cotton, and Thomas Hooker. His own posthumous *Works* contained, in addition to those already mentioned, several treatises on sanctification, a treatise on the Trinity, and a treatise on 'the Creatures', both directed against the Ranters, and sundry sermons. Goodwin's theology was representative of English experimental Calvinism, though he drew back from the extremes of the doctrine of preparation associated with Hooker, whom he thought 'urges too much and too farre the Worke of Humiliation' (Sheffield University Library, Hartlib MSS 29/2/56a). Goodwin also de-emphasized sanctification, or 'the use of our own graces' as the foundation for assurance of salvation, stressing instead 'faith towards Christ immediately' (*Christ Set Forth*, foreword). Though a staunch defender of the reformed faith against both Roman and Socinian error, he was a pastoral rather than polemical theologian, and many of his writings demonstrated an eirenic concern for unity within the bounds of orthodoxy, most notably *Christ the Universall Peace-Maker* (1650).

However, Goodwin was at work in the 1630s on a commentary on Revelation, with particular attention given to the eleventh chapter. While influenced by Thomas Brightman and Joseph Mede, as early as 1635 Goodwin had identified the 'outer court' of Revelation 11 as those 'Carnal and Unregenerate Protestants' which had been joined to the true saints of the temple, thereby wrongly making the 'Bounds of the Church' co-extensive with the 'Bounds of the Common-Wealth' (*Works*, 2.133). While not abandoning his belief that the Church of England was a true church, Goodwin argued that a 'second Reformation' was needed, along principles that would eventually be called congregational, but first the outer court must return to Rome, a process which Goodwin believed had already begun under Archbishop Laud. Largely written in England but delivered as sermons in the Netherlands in 1639, and not published until 1683, his commentary remains significant as a contemporary critique of Laudianism, and for its linking of that critique with anti-papal millenarianism and congregational ecclesiology.

In 1638 Goodwin, having resigned his fellowship at St Catharine's, married Elizabeth (*d.* 1648?), coheir of Edward Prescott, goldsmith and alderman of London, with a fortune valued at £4000 in 1642. They had one daughter, Elizabeth (*d.* 1678), who later married John Mason of London. Goodwin's marriage brought him prominent social connections: his sister-in-law Anne was married to Sir Nicholas Crisp, the Hammersmith merchant and brother of the noted antinomian, Tobias, and his sister-in-law Rebecca was the wife of Sir William Leman, of Northaw, Hertfordshire, a linen-draper and silk merchant and future high sheriff of Hertfordshire. However, in November that year Goodwin departed for the Netherlands, perhaps because he was unwilling 'to live wholly upon his wives meanes, and so needed a Church to allow him maintenance' (Edwards, 25). Cotton Mather recorded that Goodwin was fleeing pursuivants at his departure, perhaps as a result of Matthew Wren's primary visitation as bishop of Ely. Goodwin settled in Arnhem, where he served as teacher to the English congregation. Gathered in 1637 by John Archer, its 100 members had left England owing to conscientious objections to the Laudian reforms. Among them were the Yorkshire gentlemen Sir William Constable, Sir Matthew Boynton, Sir Richard Saltonstall, and Sir Thomas Bourchier; Henry Lawrence, Oliver Cromwell's landlord and future president of the council; and Edward Ask, town recorder for Colchester. Without need for state subsidy, the church provided Archer, Goodwin, and Philip Nye, his fellow teacher, £100 per year each. During this time Goodwin put into practice the principles of church polity to which his previous studies had led him. Organized round a church covenant, membership was restricted to visible saints, and lay elders and members conducted discipline together. Rejecting the binding authority of synods, the church affirmed the use of voluntary associations for advice in doctrine and for the mediation of disputes.

The Westminster assembly At the calling of the Long Parliament, Goodwin returned to England, taking with him a gathered congregation which later met in the parish of St Dunstan-in-the-East under Thomas Harrison. In November 1641 at a meeting at Edmund Calamy's house Goodwin and other London puritans agreed to maintain silence on questions of polity in order to focus opposition against prelacy. He preached several times before parliament, while to his own congregation he delivered a series of sermons on Ephesians, published posthumously as the first volume of his collected *Works*. A model of puritan practical and experimental divinity, they allow for occasional conformity and communion based on the godliness of the particular parish and its minister, a practice not unlike that of earlier generations of puritans.

Goodwin was deeply involved in the debates of the Westminster assembly. Respected by the Scottish commissioners, he was nominated in December 1643 as one of the subcommittee to draw up a directory for worship. When the London ministers' parliamentary petition against gathered churches and the publication in January 1644 of the *Apologeticall Narration* brought the dispute on church polity back into the open, Goodwin's position became delicate, however. That January the royalist agent Thomas Ogle, assisted by Goodwin's brother-in-law Crispe, approached the minister with an offer of toleration in return for support for the king. Goodwin declined, and the Independents kept parliament fully informed, but on 10 December 1644 he added his name to those of Jeremiah Burroughes, Nye, William Carter, Sidrach Simpson, and William Bridge in dissent to the propositions on church government. In 1644–5 he lectured at St Christopher-le-Stocks and wrote what was posthumously published in 1697 as *The Constitution, Order and Discipline of the Churches of Christ* (*Works*, vol. 4). In the latter half of 1645 he was often absent from the assembly after the triumph of presbyterianism and was seldom active in its proceedings, but in 1647, with Jeremiah Whitaker, he was given oversight of the printing of the assembly's papers. Later he was appointed by the council of state to a commission with Adoniram Byfield, John Bond, Nye, Peter Sterry, John Frost, and John Milton to audit the papers 'so that they may not be embezzled, and may be forthcoming for the use of the commonwealth' (*CSP dom.*, *14 Aug 1650*).

For two years from 1646 Goodwin was fortnightly Sunday lecturer at St Michael, Crooked Lane. No doubt fearing presbyterian intolerance, in 1647 Cotton and others invited him to New England. Though he was resolved to go, having secured passage and placed his library on board, at the last minute influential friends dissuaded him. In the course of events his remaining in England was soon justified for with the triumph of the New Model Army the Independents found themselves in favour. In October 1648 the vestry of All Hallows, Lombard Street, voted to allow him to preach to the parish and use the church for his gathered congregation. On 23 May 1649 Cromwell directed that Goodwin, Caryl, and Reynolds be established in a lectureship at Oxford. Two weeks later Goodwin preached with John Owen before Cromwell and parliament, and the next day parliament recommended that both be made heads of houses at Oxford. On 2 November Goodwin was appointed a minister in attendance, with lodgings in Whitehall, and a salary of £200 a year by the council of state. Following the death of his first wife, probably the previous year, some time in 1649 Goodwin married Mary Hammond (1631/2–1693) of Shropshire. They had two sons, Thomas *Goodwin and Richard, who died in 1697, the captain of the East Indies merchantman *James*, and two daughters, both of whom died in infancy.

The Cromwellian church On 8 January 1650 Goodwin was appointed by parliament to the presidency of Magdalen College, Oxford, with extensive privileges of nomination. With John Owen he preached fortnightly at St Mary's and was a member both of the commission exercising the chancellor's powers and of the three visitations which took place during 1647–57, leading the last. As a head of house and visitor he was institutionally conservative, defending the university against such radicals as John Webster and William Dell and supporting the tithe. His main concern was to secure godly tutors and to provide godly exercises. On 23 December he was made DD of Oxford. A gathered church met in his lodgings, and included Thankful Owen, Francis Howell, James Baron, Samuel Blower, and Theophilus Gale, Stephen Charnock, Edward Terry, John Howe, and Zachary Mayne. The last two names are evidence of the breadth of Goodwin's comprehension, Howe being presbyterian and Mayne struggling with Socinianism.

Together with John Owen and Philip Nye, Goodwin was a principal architect of the Cromwellian settlement. In 1652 he advised Cromwell on the supply of ministers for Ireland, while the year before his advice was sought on the reformation of Trinity College, Dublin. On 10 February 1652 he appeared with Owen and other ministers before parliament to denounce John Biddle and the Socinian *Catechesis ecclesiarum*, commonly known as the *Racovian Catechism*. The following day, *The Humble Proposals of Mr. Owen, Mr. Tho. Goodwin, Mr Nye, Mr Sympson, and other Ministers* (31 March 1652) was presented to the committee for the propagation of the gospel. In the following weeks Goodwin and his colleagues also presented to the committee sixteen 'Principles of Christian religion' though these were not published until December. Both the *Proposals* and the 'Principles' elicited strong opposition from the sects due to the limits placed on religious toleration. The Rump managed to approve only three of the proposals before it was dissolved, but much of the scheme was adopted by Cromwell in his ordinances for the so-called 'triers' and 'ejectors'. Two years later Goodwin was a leading participant, along with Richard Baxter, John Owen, Francis Cheynell, Nye, and Sidrach Simpson, in a parliamentary conference designed to produce a 'confession of faith' which would make explicit the content of the 'Public Profession held forth' in the 'Instrument of government'. The result was not *The Principles of Faith* (1654)—which was merely a reprint of the 'Principles' of 1652—but *A New Confession of Faith* (E826.3). Despite Baxter's misgivings and opposition, these twenty articles of faith were presented to parliament on 12 December 1654. A primary author of both confessions, Goodwin, along with his fellow ministers, proposed a broad comprehension within a national church of those protestants who agreed in the orthodox and Trinitarian fundamentals of the faith. Significantly, the confession also approved the principle of uniformity of worship, though without prescribing specific forms. As in 1652, parliament was dissolved before it could act on the proposed settlement. On 20 March 1654 Goodwin was made one of the commissioners for approbation of preachers and in December that year became an assistant to the Oxfordshire commission.

In 1657 Goodwin supported the 'Humble petition and advice', unlike Owen. Later that year he desired to retire from Magdalen in order to 'perfect several bookes, which he hath now under his hands, conteyneinge a body of divinity'. Secretary John Thurloe wrote to Henry Cromwell on 29 September on the protector's behalf, proposing to fund this retirement at £150 per year 'drawn from the Irish bishops' lands' (Thurloe, *State papers*, 6.539). The books to which Goodwin referred were 'The history of truth'. Since the 1630s he had continued work on this project, originally a series of four treatises tracing electing grace through creation, fall, redemption, and glorification. At some point before 1657, in response to the challenge of Socinianism, the third treatise was expanded into three separate works detailing the Trinitarian work of the Godhead in redemption. Goodwin continued to edit these until his death, and together they formed the bulk of his posthumously collected *Works*.

In June 1658 the Independents gained Cromwell's permission to convene a synod. The protector was not pleased, but did not live to see it, dying on 3 September with Goodwin at his side. Goodwin later testified that Oliver had nominated Richard his successor. On 29 September along with Owen, Nye, William Bridge, Joseph Caryl, and William Greenhill, Goodwin was appointed by the

Savoy assembly to draw up a statement of faith. He led the delegation which presented it to the protector on 14 October. Largely reaffirming the doctrinal standards of the Westminster assembly, the Savoy declaration embodied, like *A New Confession* and *The Principles of Faith*, Goodwin's vision for the settlement of the national church. Though it allowed a measure of toleration, in his presentation of the declaration to Richard Cromwell, Goodwin declared 'We look at the magistrates as *custos utriusque tabulae*, and so commit it to your trust, to countenance and propagate' (*Mercurius Politicus*, 438). It would take the Restoration to transform this puritan vision for the Church of England into a sectarian theology of dissent.

After the Restoration On 9 May 1660 Goodwin resigned the presidency of Magdalen College, an action confirmed by parliament nine days later. In that same year he was ejected from his fellowship at Eton, held since 10 February 1659. He retired to London with many of his Oxford congregation. In January 1661 he signed *A Renuntiation and Declaration of the Ministers of Congregational Churches*, a repudiation of the Fifth Monarchist uprising led by Thomas Venner. Goodwin and his fellow signatories hoped not only to deflect suspicion, but also to salvage any prospect of religious toleration. Such hopes were vain and by the summer of 1662 Goodwin was reported to be considering emigration to New England. His wife Mary, however, was opposed to the move. Despite the sufferings of many, Goodwin remained unmolested under the Clarendon Code. On 27 February 1663 he spoke for a group of congregational ministers before Charles II. The king promised 'he would keepe off all severity from them' but advised them to meet in such a way as to avoid provocation (*Massachusetts Historical Society Collections*, 4th ser., 8.208–9). Goodwin took his advice. In 1669 he was still preaching and lecturing, participating in the united lecture of presbyterians and congregationalists at Hackney, Middlesex, as well as the combination lecture near the Guildhall.

But by the early 1670s Goodwin was in poor health. Although he was licensed as a congregational minister at his house in the parish of St Giles Cripplegate, on 2 April 1672, a correspondent wrote in 1674 that Goodwin 'hath not gone forth of his house for these yeers' (*Massachusetts Historical Society Collections*, 4th ser., 8.150). Shortly after May 1675 he complained in a letter to Robert Asty that he had been 'weak and sickish' and that 'my Eyes fail me that I cannot write my self, so much as to set down my own Thoughts and private Studies … I strain my self to write again' (*Works*, 4, 1697, pt 4.51). In February 1678 he made out his will. Two years later, on 18 February 1680, in the grip of a fever, he added a codicil. He died five days later on 23 February at his home in the parish of St Bartholomew-the-Great, attended by his family and John Collins, pastor of his former London congregation. He was buried in Bunhill Fields, but his epitaph by Thomas Gilbert was censored. Among other bequests to them, he left a leasehold in Suffolk to his son Thomas, a mortgage in Aston Wend, Shropshire, to his wife, and £200 to his son Richard. Thomas and Richard each received a tumbler 'which my friend Mr. Secretary Thurloe gave me'. Thomas the younger inherited his father's considerable library, valued at £1000 before the great fire of 1666, but cut in half by that calamity. Oversight of his unpublished MSS was given to Thomas Owen, Gale, Baron, and Howell, any profits to be divided between Mary and Thomas. In the event, only Owen and Baron lived long enough to publish the first of five large quarto volumes of Goodwin's *Works* (1681–1704); the remainder fell to Thomas Goodwin the younger.

Goodwin has long been seen principally as a founder of congregationalism. However, he is more significant for the insight his career affords into the processes and events which transformed early Stuart puritanism into later Stuart dissent. Goodwin never considered himself a congregationalist prior to the Restoration. Even then the denominational label was forced upon him—he had, like many others, theretofore considered himself a defender and reformer of the Church of England. As late as 1675 he could still refer to those of 'the rigid Separation' as distinct from himself and his own position (*Works*, 4, 1697, pt 4.51). Rather than the first congregationalist, Goodwin is more accurately remembered as one of the last of the puritans. T. M. Lawrence

Sources T. Goodwin, 'Memoir of Thomas Goodwin, DD, composed out of his own papers and memoirs, by his son', in *The works of Thomas Goodwin D.D. sometime president of Magdalen College in Oxford*, ed. T. Goodwin, 5 (1704), v–xix; repr. in *The works of Thomas Goodwin*, 12 vols. (1996), vol. 2, pp. li–lxxv · T. Owen, J. Barron, and T. Goodwin, prefaces to each volume, *The works of Thomas Goodwin D.D. sometime president of Magdalen College in Oxford*, ed. T. Goodwin, 5 vols. (1681–1704) · R. Halley, 'Memoir of Thomas Goodwin', in *The works of Thomas Goodwin*, 12 vols. (1961–1866); repr. (1996), vol. 2, pp. ix–l · S. Hartlib, 'Ephemerides' and 'Letters', 1634–58, Sheffield University, Samuel Hartlib MSS · S. Fienberg, 'Thomas Goodwin, puritan pastor and Independent divine', PhD diss., University of Chicago, 1974 · *Calamy rev.*, 228 · M. Tolmie, *The triumph of the saints: the separate churches of London, 1616–1649* (1977), 85–119 · B. Worden, 'Cromwellian Oxford', *Hist. U. Oxf.* 4: *17th-cent. Oxf.*, 733–72 · T. M. Lawrence, 'Authorial intent and the theology of dissent: an assessment of the editorial process in the compilation of the works of Thomas Goodwin, D. D., sometime president of Magdalen College, Oxford', unpubd Lightfoot Scholarship essay, U. Cam., faculty of history, 1999 · T. Webster, '"These uncomfortable times": conformity and the godly ministers, 1628–38', *Godly clergy in early Stuart England: the Caroline puritan movement, c. 1620–1643* (1997), 149–338 · K. L. Sprunger, *Dutch puritanism: a history of English and Scottish churches of the Netherlands in the sixteenth and seventeenth centuries*, ed. H. A. Oberman, Studies in the History of Christian Thought, 31 (1982), 226–32 · T. Edwards, *Antapologia* (1644) · *Mercurius Politicus* (Oct–Nov 1658) · C. Mather, *Magnalia Christi Americana*, 3 vols. (1704), vol. 3, pp. 20, 61, 219 · W. D. Macray, *A register of the members of St Mary Magdalen College, Oxford*, 4 (1904), vol. 4, p. 7; vol. 7, p. 115 · J. Peile, *Biographical register of Christ's College, 1505–1905, and of the earlier foundation, God's House, 1448–1505*, ed. [J. A. Venn], 1 (1910) · Thurloe, *State papers*, 6.539 · R. Paul, *An apologeticall narration* (1963), 1–42 · F. A. Crisp, *Collections relating to the family of Crispe*, 2 (1882), 3, 13, 28, 30 · King's Lynn Borough Archive, King's Lynn, hall books (1591–1611, 1611–37) and chamberlains accounts · parish register, Rollesby, 12 Oct 1600, Norfolk RO, MF 579.7 [baptism] · parish register, King's Lynn, St Nicholas Chapel, Norfolk RO · parish register, King's Lynn, St Margaret's, Norfolk RO · will, PRO, PROB 11/369, sig. 17 · will, PRO, PROB 11/499, sig. 39 [T. Goodwin junior] · A. Grosart, 'Memoir of Richard Sibbes, DD', in *The works of Richard Sibbes*, 1 (1979), cxxix · T. C. Barnard, *Cromwellian Ireland: English government and reform in Ireland, 1649–1660* (2000), 145, 200 · 'Various

New England letters', *Massachusetts Historical Society Collections*, 4th ser., vol. 8, pp. 150, 189, 195, 208–9 • *A letter of dangerous consequence, from Sergeant Major Ogle to Sir Nicholas Crisp at Oxford* (1642) • *A correct, brief, and interesting account of the Leman case* (1840), 8 • Allhallows, Lombard Street, vestry minutes, 1648, GL, MS 4049/1, fol. 27 • will, 1629, Norfolk RO, NCC OW 105 [N. Price] • will, 1632, Norfolk RO, NCC MF 91, fol. 15 [R. Goodwin] • will, 1607, Norfolk RO, ANW MF312(?), fol. 224 [J. Collingwood] • will, 1619, Norfolk RO, ANW 145, fol. 131 MF/RO 312 [M. Collingwood] • C. B. Jewson, ed., *Transcript of three registers of passengers from Great Yarmouth to Holland and New England, 1637–1639*, 25 (1954), 83

Likenesses portrait, 1680, Magd. Oxf. • stained glass window, 1908, Mansfield College chapel, Oxford • J. Caldwall, engraving (after unknown artist), repro. in Palmer, *Nonconformist's memorial* (1775) • W. Holl, engraving (after engraving by J. Caldwall), repro. in Palmer, *Nonconformist's memorial* (1802) • R. White, engraving, NPG; repro. in *Works of Thomas Goodwin* [*see illus.*]

Wealth at death personalty of £1400; library valued at £1000 in 1666, though half lost in great fire; leasehold of Magdalen College, Oxford, in Lowestoft, Suffolk (value unknown); mortgage on estate at Aston, Wem, Shropshire (value unknown), but sufficient to provide income of at least £12 p.a.: will, PRO, PROB 11/369, sig. 17; Goodwin, 'Memoir', vol. 5, pp. x–xix

Goodwin, Thomas (*c.*1650–1708?), Independent minister, was probably born in Oxford, the son of Thomas *Goodwin (1600–1680), minister, and his second wife, Mary Hammond (1631/2–1693). Educated in England and the Netherlands, in 1678 he joined Theophilus Dorrington, James Lambert and John Shower in a combination lecture held at a coffee-house in Exchange Alley, London. In March 1683 Goodwin became the sole editor of his father's works. That spring he embarked on the grand tour at the invitation of Sir Samuel Barnardiston, accompanying his nephew Samuel, along with Shower and a Mr Cornish. He returned to England in July 1684 and was called to assist Stephen Lobb at the church in Fetter Lane, London, which his father had gathered at the Restoration. By 1690 he was dividing his time between London and his estate at Pinner, Middlesex, where he kept an academy for ministers and was pastor of a congregational church. Goodwin boarded and instructed at least twenty-eight students, including Obadiah Oddy, John Greene, Thomas Tingey, and Theophilus Lobb. By this time he had married his wife, Abigail, who survived him.

Goodwin's association with Stephen Lobb extended beyond his work at Fetter Lane. In 1695 Goodwin published *A Discourse of the True Nature of the Gospel*. An answer to William Lorimer's *Apology* (1694), it was also a defence of the position Lobb had taken in the controversy between presbyterians and congregationalists over the sermons of Tobias Crisp, and appears to have been written in a co-ordinated effort with his colleague. Goodwin had close connections with the Crisp family through marriage and at Pinner. But his support was motivated by more than loyalty. He discerned in the neonomian theology (which taught the gospel is a 'new law') advanced by Lorimer and the presbyterians a 'tendency to Arminianism' (p. iv) and a betrayal of the gospel 'by its pretended Friends' (p. 2) to Rome. This was not Goodwin's only contribution to the debate. In 1697 he published the fourth volume of his father's works, which contained two treatises intended 'to promote the doctrines of the gospel' (foreword). *The Object and Acts of Justifying Faith* defended the high Calvinist definition of faith against Arminian and Roman formulations, while *The Constitution … of the Churches of Christ* defended congregational polity against its presbyterian alternative. Their appearance together served both to substantiate the claim that the neonomians were innovators, and to suggest that the congregationalists were the true theological heirs of the old nonconformists.

This polemical use of his father's corpus is only one aspect of Goodwin's most significant legacy: the shaping of his father's reputation as a founder of Congregationalism. Primarily this was accomplished through the memoir which Goodwin composed of his father's life and published in the final volume of his works (1704). Intertwining the two related but separate stories of his father's conversion to Christ and to nonconformity, the latter was presented as the inevitable outcome of the former. Almost no attention was given to his efforts toward a national settlement. As the only contemporary narrative of his life, it has contributed to an association of the elder Goodwin with a sectarianism that was largely foreign to his life and work.

After preaching Stephen Lobb's funeral sermon on 3 June 1699 Goodwin retired from London. Though in good health he made his will in May 1700, being then 'of Pinnor in the county of Middlesex' (PRO, PROB 11/499, 305*v*). He probably died in 1708 as his will was proved on 24 February that year, and he was buried near his parents in a vault towards the east end of Bunhill Fields, London. Goodwin died a gentleman of considerable means. In addition to his estate at Pinner, he left to his wife and only son, Thomas, four houses in Essex Street and the groundlease for several houses in King Street and Ironmonger Lane, London, as well as a leasehold in Lowestoft, a mortgage near Wem, Shropshire, and a freehold in Isleworth, Middlesex. His library, which was auctioned in two lots in 1710 and 1712 was catalogued under nearly 5000 separate entries, representing over 6000 volumes. He left the remainder of his father's unpublished manuscripts to his son.

T. M. LAWRENCE

Sources T. Goodwin, 'Memoir of Thomas Goodwin, DD, composed out of his own papers and memoirs, by his son', in *The works of Thomas Goodwin D.D. sometime president of Magdalen College in Oxford*, ed. T. Goodwin, 5 (1704), v–xix; repr. in *The works of Thomas Goodwin*, 12 vols. (1996), vol. 2, pp. li–lxxv • T. Owen, J. Barron, and T. Goodwin, prefaces to each volume, *The works of Thomas Goodwin D.D. sometime president of Magdalen College in Oxford*, ed. T. Goodwin, 5 vols. (1681–1704) • W. Wilson, *The history and antiquities of the dissenting churches and meeting houses in London, Westminster and Southwark*, 4 vols. (1808–14), vol. 3, pp. 446–9 • W. Tong, *Some memoirs of the life and death of the Reverend Mr John Shower* (1716), 17–49 • T. Ballard, *Goodwineana bibliotheca*, pts 1–2 (1710–12) • F. A. Crisp, *Collections relating to the family of Crispe*, 1–2 (1882) • J. Greene, *The power of faith and godliness exemplified, in some memoirs of Theophilus Lobb. MD FRS* (1767), 5–11 • A. Gordon, ed., *Freedom after ejection: a review (1690–1692) of presbyterian and congregational nonconformity in England and Wales* (1917), 72, 273, 304, 352 • H. McLachlan, *English education under the Test Acts: being the history of the nonconformist academies, 1662–1820* (1931), 12–13 • E. Calamy, *A continuation of the account of the ministers … who were ejected and silenced after the Restoration in 1660*, 2 vols. (1727), vol. 1, pp. 90ff. • will, PRO, PROB 11/499, fols. 305*v*–306*r* •

PRO, PROB 11/369, fols. 134v–135v • R. Rawlinson, ed., *The inscriptions upon the tombs, grave-stones etc. in the dissenters burial place near Bunhill-Fields* (1717), 7 • *DNB*

Wealth at death undisclosed interest in Million Lottery Bank; library of more than 6000 volumes, est. value well in excess of £1000; leasehold in Lowestoft, Suffolk; mortgage on estate at Aston, Wem, Shropshire; four houses freehold in Essex Street, London; groundlease held of dean and chapter of St Paul's of four or five houses in King Street and Ironmonger's Lane, London; freehold of lands in Isleworth, Middlesex: will, PRO, PROB 11/499, fols. 305v–306r; Goodwin, 'Memoir'; Ballard, *Goodwineana bibliotheca*

Goodwin, Timothy. *See* Godwin, Timothy (1670?–1729).

Goodwin, William (**1555/6–1620**), dean of Christ Church, Oxford, matriculated from Christ Church in 1573 as a former scholar of St Peter's College (later Westminster School), graduated BA in 1577, and proceeded MA in 1580. After preferment in Wiltshire in 1587 as rector of Upton Scudamore and canon of Sarum, in 1590 he became a subalmoner to Queen Elizabeth and a prebendary of York. About this time he must have married, although his wife's name is unknown. Through the 1590s he accumulated several Yorkshire benefices, which between 1605 and 1611 he combined with the chancellorship of the York archdiocese. On returning south in 1611 he became dean of Christ Church, and the following year delivered at St Mary's a funeral sermon for Prince Henry which, according to Wood, 'not only exceedingly moved himselfe, but also moved the whole Universitie and city to shedde fountains of teares' (Wood, 2.312). In 1613 he preached at Sir Thomas Bodley's funeral, and in 1618 at Queen Anne's memorial service in Oxford.

Goodwin's only published work appeared in Oxford in 1614. In his capacity as a chaplain to James I he had preached before the king at Woodstock in August of that year a vehemently anti-Catholic sermon, deploring the recent flood of books from 'English fugitives and Romish adversaries', the drift of which had been 'to advance the Miter above the Crowne, and to erect the Monster of the more then Transcendent Superioritie of the Sea and Court of Rome' (Goodwin, 2) at the expense of the thrones of kings. He asserted that the 'very name of a Lawfull and Anointed King is sacred, his Authoritie sovereigne, his Person inviolable' (ibid., 20); the obligation of his subjects was submission and the practice of the church 'obedience unto blood' (ibid., 35).

Goodwin was briefly rector of All Hallows-the-Great, London, and, for a few months from September 1616, archdeacon of Middlesex, but his later career centred on the Oxfordshire livings of Stanton St John, to which he was presented by Lord Chancellor Egerton in 1616, and Chalgrove, from 1617, and particularly on Oxford itself, where his daughter, probably called Anne (*d.* 1627?), was by 1616 married to John Prideaux of Exeter College. For four of the five years from 1614 to 1618 Goodwin was vice-chancellor of the university. After his death at Christ Church on 11 June 1620, aged sixty-five, he was buried in Christ Church Cathedral, where a monument was erected to his memory and where his reputation as 'the good dean' was noted by Thomas Goffe in a funeral sermon which celebrated his immersion in the church fathers: 'he used to devour all theology with one swallow … a holy glutton of books' (Goffe).

W. F. Wentworth-Shields, *rev.* Vivienne Larminie

Sources Foster, *Alum. Oxon.* • A. Wood, *The history and antiquities of the University of Oxford*, ed. J. Gutch, 2 (1796), 312, 314, 332, 831; 3.439, 436, appx 120–21 • J. Welch, *A list of scholars of St Peter's College, Westminster* (1788), 17 • W. Goodwin, *A sermon preached before the kings most excellent maiestie at Woodstocke* (1614) • T. Goffe, *Oratio funebris habita in ecclesia cathedrali Christi Oxon in obitum … Gulielmi Goodwin* … (1620) • *Hist. U. Oxf.* 4: *17th-cent. Oxf.*, 569–70 • *CSP dom.*, 1611–16, 482 • S. P. T. Prideaux, *John Prideaux, in piam memoriam* (1938), 18, 30

Likenesses effigy on monument, Christ Church Cathedral, Oxford

Goodwyn, Edmund (*bap.* **1756**, *d.* **1829**), physician, son of Edmund Goodwyn (*d.* 1771?), surgeon, was born in Framlingham, Suffolk, and baptized there on 2 December 1756. Having graduated MD at Edinburgh about 1786, he practised medicine in London. Goodwyn was an early experimenter with respiration and he devised experiments to measure the quantity of air taken into the lungs following complete expiration. He published *Dissertatio medica de morte submersorum* (1786), which was published in translation as *The connexion of life with respiration, or, An experimental inquiry into the effects of submersion, strangulation, and several kinds of noxious airs on living animals … and the most effectual means of cure* (1788). Goodwyn retired to Framlingham some years before his death there on 8 August 1829. He was buried in Framlingham.

J. M. Rigg, *rev.* Kaye Bagshaw

Sources R. Waters, 'An early book on respiration, 1788', *Annals of Medical History*, new ser., 8 (1936), 376–7 • *GM*, 1st ser., 99/2 (1829), 186–7 • P. J. Wallis and R. V. Wallis, *Eighteenth century medics*, 2nd edn (1988) • D. E. Davy, 'Athenae Suffolcienses, or, A catalogue of Suffolk authors with some account of their lives, and lists of their writings', 1847, BL, Add. MSS 19165–19168, 3.179

Likenesses S. W. Reynolds, mezzotint (after H. P. Briggs), BM, NPG

Goodyear, Hugh (*bap.* **1588**, *d.* **1661**), Reformed minister in the Netherlands, was born at Manchester and baptized there on 28 May 1588, the son of Thomas Goodyear (*d.* 1599), a wealthy cloth merchant, and his first wife, Ellen Proudlove (*d.* 1592). Admitted to Emmanuel College, Cambridge, in 1608, he graduated BA in 1613 and proceeded MA in 1616. After Cambridge he left for the Netherlands, travelling on a privy council pass issued on 26 October 1616. He settled at Leiden, a crossroads for travel through the Low Countries, where he lodged with Thomas Brewer, the puritan separatist book publisher. On 14 January 1617 Goodyear enrolled as a theology student at Leiden University.

Preaching opportunities abounded for Goodyear at Leiden because of the death in 1616 of Robert Durie, the pastor of the English—Scottish church. The church turned to him to be the new preacher, and on 16 November 1617 the city magistrates approved him and provided an annual salary of 400 guilders—he held the position for the rest of his life. Not being previously ordained in England, and distrusting episcopal ordinations, Goodyear arranged for a quick ordination from the French Calvinist preacher of

Leiden. His English-speaking congregation of more than 200 families was a state-supported Reformed church in communion with the Dutch Reformed church, and as such was distinct from the other, rival, English church of the city, John Robinson's separatist church, which was entirely self-supporting and independent. Goodyear's church attracted many visitors, and in 1627 he appealed successfully to the city magistrates for a rise in salary because of the heavy entertaining he had to do because 'foreign preachers and church members ordinarily come addressed to him from other kingdoms' (reg. kerk. zaken., no. 2150, fol. 114*v*, gemeente archiev, Leiden). On 11 June 1627 he married his first wife, Sara Jansdochter van Wassenberch (*d*. 1642).

Goodyear's theological position was Calvinistic. In Dutch affairs he supported the contra-remonstrants and opposed the Arminians; in all matters pertaining to English religion, he sided with puritans. His friends included both presbyterians like John Paget and Robert Paget, and Independents such as William Ames and Hugh Peter, but he always condemned separatism. In his own congregation he emphasized preaching, discipline, strict sabbath observance, and simplicity of worship. Ceremonialism and the English prayer book were abhorrent to him; he never allowed them in his church. Many of the surrounding Dutch Reformed pastors considered him too strict in church discipline, especially on sabbath practice. For many years he stayed aloof from the Dutch Reformed classis, but, feeling isolated and in need of fellowship after the deaths of many of his English friends, he eventually compromised and took membership in 1655. Two years earlier his second wife, Cornelia Aertsdochter Schoor, whom he had married in 1648, had also died. There were no children from either marriage.

Although Goodyear had connections with various publishers, which he exploited to facilitate other people's publications, he did not publish any books himself. Nevertheless he achieved considerable standing in puritan circles for his scholarship and sturdy defence of orthodox doctrine and he corresponded widely with church leaders of his puritan persuasion in Europe, England, and America. His manuscript collection contains sermon notes, economic records, and letters from John Cotton, Hugh Peter, John Paget, and many others. At his death his library of 1063 titles had to be sold; the sellers printed an auction catalogue (1662) of thirty-six pages, listing each book, which is of great interest for examination of Reformed, puritan tastes in books. Goodyear died on 8 November 1661 and was buried in the Pieterskerk at Leiden on 11 November. His will directed that one-third of his property should go to the poor of his church and the remainder to relatives who lived in England and America.

KEITH L. SPRUNGER

Sources K. L. Sprunger, 'Other pilgrims in Leiden: Hugh Goodyear and the English Reformed church', *Church History*, 41 (1972), 46–60 • K. L. Sprunger, *Dutch puritanism: a history of English and Scottish churches of the Netherlands in the sixteenth and seventeenth centuries* (1982) • J. D. Bangs, introduction, *The auction catalogue of the library of Hugh Goodyear, English Reformed minister at Leiden* (1985) • D. Plooij, *The Pilgrim Fathers from a Dutch point of view* (1932) • A. Veenhoff and M. Smolenaars, 'Hugh Goodyear and his papers', *Transactions of the Lancashire and Cheshire Antiquarian Society*, 95 (1999), 1–22 • Manchester Cathedral Archives [baptism] • Venn, *Alum. Cant.* • Gemeentelijke Archiefdienst, Leiden, Goodyear MSS, Weeskamer Archief 1355

Archives Gemeentelijke Archiefdienst, Leiden, MSS, Weeskamer Archief 1355 | Gemeentelijke Archiefdienst, Leiden, Dutch Reformed Church MSS, Kerkeraad and classis records

Wealth at death enough to be divided among several heirs: will, Gemeentelijke Archiefdienst, Leiden, Goodyear MSS, Weeskamer Archief 1355

Goodyear, Joseph (1797–1839), engraver, was born on 19 October 1797 in Birmingham, the eldest son of Uriah Goodyear and his wife, Lucy, *née* Blakemore. He was apprenticed to James Tye, of 9 Water Street, Birmingham, a general engraver, worked for Josiah Allen, an engraver and copperplate printer, of 3 Colmore Row, for whom he engraved labels and bill heads, and became an assistant to William Radclyffe (1783–1855). He also attended drawing lessons given by J. V. Barber (*c*.1787–1838) and S. Lines (1778–1863). In 1822 he went to London to work for three years under Charles Heath (1785–1848), who introduced him to steel-engraving and helped to secure commissions for him. Goodyear engraved eleven plates for *The Keepsake* between 1828 and 1840, a series of imaginative subjects after contemporary artists such as F. P. Stephanoff, G. Cattermole, and Miss L. Sharpe. His earliest plate was probably *Music's Mishap*, after J. M. Wright, engraved before October 1827. The *Literary Souvenir*, edited by A. A. Watts, published by Longman, contained four of his plates between 1829 and 1835, one of which, *The Departure of Mary Queen of Scots from France*, after E. D. Leahy, omitted two figures from the engraving with the artist's permission, and *Friendship's Offering*, published by Smith, Elder & Co., included two of his plates, in 1831 and 1833.

Goodyear was sought after because of his punctuality and obvious talent, and much of his best work done for the publishers bears his name. In 1830 he exhibited two engravings at the Suffolk Street exhibition. He engraved some illustrations for Sir Walter Scott's novels, and his work also appeared in the 1832 edition of Maria Edgeworth's *Moral Tales for Young People*. His plates were signed 'J. Goodyear'. Joseph Andrews (1805–1873), one of America's best line engravers, seeking to widen his experience in Europe, came to receive instruction from Goodyear in 1835. Goodyear's last and largest plate, *Greek Fugitives*, after C. L. Eastlake, dated 1 January 1838, was published in Part 1 of *Finden's Royal Gallery of British Art* (1838–40). The engraving was much admired, but the mental strain and prolonged exertion which was required for so carefully finished an engraving led to a breakdown in the artist's health. He endured a lingering illness for a year, and died at his house in Kentish Town on 1 October 1839, in his forty-first year. He was buried in Highgate cemetery, where his friends erected a monument bearing Peter Hollins's medallion portrait. He was much esteemed both in private and professional life. He had for many years looked after his father, and after his death his meagre property and the charge of their parent devolved on his brother.

L. H. CUST, *rev.* B. HUNNISETT

Sources *Art Union*, 1 (1839), 154, 186 • *Art Union*, 3 (1841), 54–5 • J. Thackray Bunce, introduction and biographical notes, *Exhibition of engravings by 19 Birmingham men* (1877), 7, 13, 27 [exhibition catalogue, Royal Birmingham Society of Artists, Birmingham, 1877] • D. M. Stauffer, *American engravers upon copper and steel*, 2 vols. (1907), vol. 1, p. 10 • *IGI*

Likenesses P. Hollins, medallion portrait, 1840, Highgate cemetery • H. Room, oils, Birmingham City Art Gallery

Goodyer, Sir Henry. *See* Goodere, Sir Henry (*bap.* 1571, *d.* 1627).

Goodyer, John (*c.*1592–1664), botanist, was born at Alton, Hampshire, the younger son of the four children of Reginald Goodyer (*fl.* 1578–1619), a yeoman of that district, and his wife, Ann. His later work points to an excellent grounding in Latin and Greek, possibly at Alton grammar school, after which he must have served an apprenticeship appropriate to his subsequent career. This was probably under William Yalden, a prosperous land agent in Petersfield and husband of Goodyer's sister Rose. To Yalden, too, Goodyer probably owed his appointment as steward to Sir Thomas Bilson, lord of the manor of Mapledurham in the parish of Buriton, near Petersfield. This was in or before 1616, when he leased a house nearby from Bilson. Diligent as a servant, Goodyer appears to have been deeply attached to the family of his employer, for three of Bilson's infant sons were to remain his friends for life and be remembered in his will.

Scholarly and meticulous, with an occupation that took him around the countryside, Goodyer had become curious to know the names of the local wild and garden flowers. By 1616 this had led him to cultivate the acquaintance of apothecaries knowledgeable on that subject, such as John Parkinson, whom he visited that year in London, and to expend sizeable sums on several of the leading continental texts. That his motive in doing so was not primarily medicinal and pecuniary entitles him to be recognized as the earliest-known truly amateur botanist in Britain of any stature.

Though many of his finds were published by Thomas Johnson and other contemporaries, the full extent of his fieldwork and his acumen and industry in describing and seeking to identify the plants he discovered, many for the first time in Britain, remained unknown until his papers were studied three centuries later. These show that he ranged as far as Bristol, Weymouth, Wellingborough, and Romney Marsh, often visiting London and its environs as well. They also disclose a peak of activity in 1616–21, partly coinciding with his move to Droxford, in the Meon valley, and presumably directed towards producing a much-needed guide to the English flora. However, the task of reconciling his observations with the names and descriptions in continental works apparently proved too great and his energies became sidetracked into producing translations of Theophrastus and Dioscorides, the latter a stupendous undertaking in itself. A start of much promise as a fieldworker was seemingly undone by an overriding bookishness.

Having returned to live near the Bilson family, in 1629 Goodyer was again granted the use of a house and farm of theirs at a specially low rent, 'in consideration of his faithful service', as the lease had it. After only three years, however, he forsook his long bachelorhood and by a licence dated November 1632 married Patience Crumpe (*b.* *c.*1600), the daughter of a London tailor, and moved to a substantial property in the quarter of Petersfield known as The Spain. Then called the Great House, this still stands and bears a plaque commemorating him as 'botanist and royalist'—the latter on the slender evidence of a royalist pass for him found hidden beneath a floorboard. Herbal expertise, however, would have been valued by either side and latterly Goodyer seems to have exploited his knowledge as a sideline. Ashmole, who visited him in 1651, indeed describes him in his diary as a practitioner of physick, though one using only 'simple' medicines. A more telling indication of royalist sympathies is the fact that his favourite nephew, the Revd Edmund Yalden, was one of those ejected from livings during the Commonwealth. According to Gilbert White of Selborne, two of whose brothers married great-grandchildren of Edmund Yalden, the nephew survived by practising medicine, and it seems likely that it was Goodyer's knowledge that made that possible. Through Edmund Yalden, whom he made his executor, Goodyer became great-uncle to the agricultural writer, John *Worlidge (*d.* 1693); it was also Edmund Yalden's fellowship at Magdalen College, Oxford, for which the elder Yalden had long acted on estates matters, that led Goodyer to choose the college as the recipient for his papers and valuable library of 239 printed works.

Probably following the death of his wife, Goodyer seems to have moved back to the hamlet of Weston in Buriton parish, where he bought a house. Here he died in April or early May 1664, to be buried in the churchyard at Buriton close to his wife. Most of his estate was left in trust for the benefit of the poor of Weston, a charity which continues to this day. Never wholly forgotten, Goodyer is commemorated in a genus of European orchids named by Robert Brown in his honour. Following his rediscovery about 1910, first by local people connected with his charity and then by botanists, the cost of a memorial window in Buriton church was raised by public subscription. The second *Flora of Hampshire* (1996) is dedicated to him.

D. E. Allen

Sources R. T. Gunther, *Early British botanists and their gardens* (1922), 1–232 • C. E. Raven, *English naturalists from Neckam to Ray: a study of the making of the modern world* (1947), 291–4 • G. C. Druce, 'John Goodyer, of Mapledurham, Hampshire, 1592–1664', *Report of the Botanical Society and Exchange Club of the British Isles*, 4 (1914–16), 523–50 • M. E. Wotton, *Hants. and Sussex News* (11 April 1917) • A. E. Harrington, 'John Goodyer, a Petersfield worthy and benefactor', *Hants. and Sussex News* (20 Aug 1930) • M. Ray, 'John Goodyer, 1592–1664', *Hampshire Field Club and Archaeological Society: Section Newsletter*, 1 (1980), 26–8 • *Elias Ashmole (1617–1692): his autobiographical and historical notes*, ed. C. H. Josten, 5 vols. (1966 [i.e. 1967]), vol. 2, pp. 589, 597 • C. Boston, *The history of Compton in Surrey* (1933), 200–01 • G. White, *The natural history and antiquities of Selborne* (1813); facs. repr. with introduction by P. G. M. Foster, Ray Society, 160 (1993), 322–8 [letter 6] • *Sussex manors*, 1, ed. E. H. W. Dunkin, Sussex RS, 19 (1914), 177 • rent roll and leases, BL • rent roll and leases, Hants. RO

Archives Magd. Oxf., papers

Wealth at death left a house, a farm, and legacies of £40, £5, and £5: will, Gunther, *Early British botanists*

Googe, Barnabe (1540–1594), poet and translator, was born on 11 June 1540, probably in Kent, the son of Robert Goche (*d.* 1557) of Lincoln and Margaret (*d.* 1540), daughter of Sir Walter Mantell. His mother died when he was six weeks old, and he was probably brought up in Kent by his grandmother Lady Hales. His father married his second wife, Ellen Gadbury Parris, in 1552; Googe came to dislike his stepmother intensely, and subsequently he spent a great deal of time at the Hales family manor Dunjeon (Dane John).

Robert Goche had been receiver of the king's revenues from lands of the former religious houses in Lincolnshire, Cheshire, Derbyshire, and Nottinghamshire. He was MP for Kingston upon Hull in 1545, and for Hedon in Yorkshire in 1547. When he died on 5 May 1557, Barnabe Googe inherited the manor of Horkstow and the lands of Alvingham Priory (both in Lincolnshire), as well as his grandfather's house in London. He became a royal ward, eventually buying his wardship on favourable terms after his kinsman William Cecil became master of the wards in January 1561. Googe matriculated as a pensioner at Christ's College, Cambridge, in May 1555. Either an outbreak of plague in 1556, or the death of his father, brought an end to his studies. He was a member of Staple Inn on 29 March 1560, the place and date given in the dedication of his translation of Palingenius. In his 1563 poem 'To the Translation of Pallingen' he says he found the labour of writing sweeter than the legal career his father had planned for him.

Googe went to Spain in November 1561 with the new ambassador, Sir Thomas Chaloner, saying in his poem 'Goyng towardes Spayne' that he wished 'for knowledge sake / to cut the fomyng seas'. Having returned, Googe on 26 June 1563 paid for a licence to enter upon his lands, but the survival of his stepmother meant that he could not take up his full inheritance. In 1563 he was appointed one of the queen's gentlemen pensioners. His career on the fringes of court was defined by his kinship (probably through common family in Herefordshire) with Sir William Cecil, later Lord Burghley. Like his father he became a member of parliament, serving for Aldborough, Yorkshire, in 1571. In 1572, 1581, and 1591 Googe is listed among servitors and attendants at his kinsman's banquets. In summer 1563 Googe betrothed himself to Mary (1545–1614), daughter of Thomas Darrell of Scotney, in Lamberhurst parish, Kent (the 'Mistress D.' of his poems). The two were married on 5 February 1564 only after Googe had enlisted Cecil and Archbishop Parker to overcome opposition from the Darrell family. In the same thirteenth-century psalter (now in Magdalene College, Cambridge) as he notes his own birth date, Googe also notes that of his wife (5 September 1545) and the baptism dates of three of their nine children: Robert, 2 January 1567, Barnabe, 18 September 1569, and Anne, 4 November 1573. From 1564 on Googe lived in Kent with his family, but in 1582 he wrote of his daily attendance on Cecil.

Googe's first appearance in print is in a dedicatory poem (condemning the 'haughty whore' of Rome) in Thomas Gressop's translation of Nicolaus Cabasilas, *A briefe treatise, conteynynge a playne and fruitfull declaration of the popes usurped primacye* (1559). Googe's passionate protestantism may have been fostered by his grandmother's third husband, Sir James Hales, a protestant lawyer who was imprisoned under Mary and eventually, after harassment and interrogation, descended into a state of suicidal despair. Googe's first major work also shows strong protestant sympathies. In 1560 he published his translation of the first three books of Marcellus Palingenius's philosophical, scientific, satirical epic *Zodiacus vitae*. The *Zodiacus* appealed to Elizabethan reformers because it was placed on the Catholic church's list of banned books in 1558. Based on the commonplace that the pleasures of the body are far inferior to those of the soul, its ideas resonate in Shakespeare and Spenser, who may well both have read it. A second edition in 1561 covered books 1–6, before a complete edition in 1565 and revisions in 1576 and 1588. This work was mainly responsible for Googe's reputation in his time.

When Googe went to Spain he had left a manuscript copy of his poems (including pastoral eclogues on moral themes and expressions of indignation about the Marian persecutions) in the hands of his college friend Laurence Blundeston. On his return he professes conventional surprise at learning they had been sent to press, but *Eglogs, Epytaphes, and Sonettes* duly emerged in 1563. He apologizes for the hasty completion of the dream poem 'Cupido Conquered'—a variation on the theme of love's contention with reason and virtue in which love is soundly defeated. Four of the six sonnets in the final sequence 'Going towards Spain' were probably written after Blundeston sent the collection to the printer. Googe was the first English writer to borrow from Montemayor's *Diana* and to translate verses from Garcilaso de la Vega. The pastoral poems make up the only original collection of eclogues in English between Barclay and Spenser's *Shepheardes Calender*.

In 1570 Googe published another translation, namely *The Popish Kingdome, or, Reigne of Antichrist*, a work of Thomas Kirchmeyer (Naogeorgus). It is characterized by the sarcastic tone often evident in Googe's work. In 1577 he translated the *Foure Bookes of Husbandry* of Conrad Heresbach, his second most widely read work. He apologizes for faults of the translation, since he 'neither had leisure nor quietnesse at the doing of it', but was widely praised for the versions of Virgil's *Georgics* therein. In 1579 he published his translation, dedicated to Burghley, of *The proverbes of the noble and woorthy souldier Sir James Lopes de Mendoza, marques of Santillana*, a work containing rhyming proverbs written for the heir to the throne of Castile. He also wrote several lesser works with more or less solid attribution, including possibly those under the name of Bernard Garter. One is *A Newe Booke called the Shippe of Safegard* (1569), a satirical allegory on the voyage of life. The dedication to Philippa and Frances Darrell, his wife's sisters, aiming to place reformed ideas persuasively before these recusant relatives, proves it to have been

Googe's. He also wrote *The Overthrow of the Gout* (1577), dedicated to 'his very good Frende' Dr Richard Master, physician to the queen, who was also the dedicatee of another medical oddity, a translation of Thomas Bertholdus's account of a new German wonder drug (*The Wonderful and Strange Effects and Vertues of a New Terra sigillata*, 1587).

Googe was often short of money, and for this reason he went to Ireland in Cecil's service for the first half of 1574. He went to report on the first earl of Essex's expedition to Ulster, but contracted dysentery. Among the information he sent back to Burghley were two sketches, one of the meeting of Essex and Turlough Lynagh on 16 March 1574, and the other a plan of Drogheda with another portrait of Lynagh. He returned in July with letters from Essex to Burghley, one of which praised Googe for having a body and mind suited to the soldier's life. He also spent time in Ireland intermittently between 1582 and 1585 as provost marshal of Connaught (and later of Thormond too). Googe wrote to Walsingham complaining of the 'purgatory' of an Irish winter, and lamenting the plight of his wife and children.

The death of his stepmother in 1584 meant that Googe's need for Irish success disappeared: it took him until April 1585 to sell his office and to leave Ireland for good. In his last known letter, sent from Burghley's chamber at court on 19 June 1587 with news for the earl of Rutland, he mentions his family's new home at Alvingham. He spent the remainder of his life there in relative peace. In December 1590 he was present in Nottingham for the examination of witnesses in a suit in the court of exchequer. He died about 7 February 1594, and was buried in Cockerington church, near Alvingham.

Roger Ascham praised Googe for the Palingenius translation, as one among 'other Jentlemen who have gonne as farre to their greate praise as the copie they followed could carry them' (Smith, 1.25). He also attracted the approval of Francis Meres, George Turbervile, Clement Robinson, Jasper Heywood, Arthur Hall (translator of Homer), William Webbe, and Gabriel Harvey. One modern critic has gone so far as to deem the 'combination of matter-of-factness with passion' in his own poems an important point in the development of an English, non-Petrarchan strain of sixteenth-century poetry (Winters, 96). Few would follow this line with enthusiasm, but when Kennedy calls him 'a representative figure of his age' (Kennedy, 142) this does not simply mark a certain special mediocrity. Googe displays a characteristic Elizabethan mixture of outward-looking scholarship and hard-line protestant patriotism throughout a substantial career.

RAPHAEL LYNE

Sources W. E. Sheidley, *Barnabe Googe* (1981) • M. Eccles, 'Barnabe Googe in England, Spain, and Ireland', *English Literary Renaissance*, 15 (1985), 333–70 • B. Googe, *Eclogues, epitaphs and sonnets*, ed. J. M. Kennedy (1989) • J. M. Kennedy, 'Barnabe Googe', *Sixteenth-century British nondramatic writers: first series*, ed. D. A. Richardson, DLitB, 132 (1993), 141–8 • J. D. Alsop, 'Barnabe Googe's birthdate', *N&Q*, 236 (1991), 24 • P. Parnell and E. Parnell, 'Barnabe Googe: a puritan in Arcadia', *Journal of English and Germanic Philology*, 60 (1961), 273–81 • G. G. Smith, ed., *Elizabethan critical essays*, 2 vols. (1904) • W. Pinkerton, 'Barnaby Googe', *N&Q*, 3rd ser., 3 (1863), 141–3, 181–4, 241–3, 301–2, 361–2 • Y. Winters, 'The sixteenth century lyric in England: a critical and historical reinterpretation', *Elizabethan poetry: modern essays in criticism*, ed. P. Alpers and J. Alpers (1967), 93–122

Gookin, Charles (*c*.1660–*c*.1723), colonial official, was the son of Thomas and Hester Gookin, who lived in Ireland.

Gookin's appointment as deputy governor of Pennsylvania in 1708 was thought by William Penn to be the answer to the problem of satisfying the Board of Trade about the defence of the colony as he had achieved the rank of captain in Thomas Erle's regiment. After being forced to get rid of the previous deputy governor, John Evans, Penn described Gookin as one of whose 'morrals, experience & fidelity I have some knowledge, & of his family 40 years; and has recommending character from persons of great ranck' (Penn to James Logan, 3 May 1708, *Papers of William Penn*, 4.597). The men of quality who recommended Gookin were Thomas Erle, the Ingoldsby family, and William Cadogan, first Earl Cadogan, who was aide-de-camp to John Churchill, duke of Marlborough. Unlike Evans, Gookin had seen active service under Erle in Ireland and on the continent, and was considered a more appropriate appointment. He married Mary Wallis in 1698, but she appears to have died before he took up his appointment in Pennsylvania, for Penn observed on Gookin's appointment that he was '46 years of age, single and sould his estate in Europe to lay out his mony there and be a good freeholder among you' (*Papers of William Penn*, 4.597).

Gookin arrived in Philadelphia in January 1709. Described by James Logan as a plain honest man and of a temper best suiting a soldier, the new deputy governor ran into problems with the colony's legislative assembly almost immediately. When he requested men for colonial defence the Quaker-dominated assembly refused to comply, and instead offered £500 to be put in safe hands and not to be used for war. In 1714 antagonistic relations between the legislature and executive once again erupted when Gookin removed all of the justices of New Castle county for giving a ruling against his brother-in-law, Richard Birmingham, leaving the county without a magistrate for six weeks. By this time his eccentric behaviour was becoming increasingly apparent. When the Pennsylvania court judges ruled against a commission of his to be published in court, he kicked one of them. In 1716, towards the end of his governorship, in what was probably the last straw for the assembly, Gookin interpreted statutes 7 and 8, William III, to the detriment of the Quakers. The statutes read that no Quaker was qualified or permitted to give evidence in any criminal case, serve on juries, or hold public office by virtue of the Quakers' refusal to swear oaths. The act was made perpetual in Britain and extended to the colonies for five years, which Gookin insisted overrode provincial law. The council petitioned for his removal and in 1717 he was dismissed.

After the new governor, William Keith, was appointed, Gookin accused members of the council of being disloyal to the king and his government. When the council met to discuss his accusations, he withdrew them, attributing them to 'a great indisposition of body which had disordered his head' (Hazard, 17). He returned to Britain and died in London about 1723. MARY K. GEITER

Sources R. N. Gookin, *An historical and genealogical sketch of the Gookin family* (Tacoma, Wash, 1952) • *The papers of William Penn*, ed. M. M. Dunn, R. S. Dunn, and others, 5 vols. (1981–7) • *Correspondence between William Penn and James Logan ... and others, 1700–1750*, ed. D. Logan and E. Armstrong, 2 vols. (1870–72) • S. Hazard, ed., *General index to the colonial records*, 3 (1852)

Archives PRO, Colonial Office MSS, 5 | Hist. Soc. Penn., Penn family MSS

Gookin, Daniel (*bap.* **1612**, *d.* **1687**), colonial administrator, was baptized on 6 December 1612 at St Augustine-the-Less, Bristol, the third son of Daniel Gookin (1582–1633) of the lathe of St Augustine, Kent (east of Canterbury), and Mary (*d.* 1635), daughter of Richard Birde DD, prebendary of Canterbury and nephew of Munster planter Sir Vincent Gookin. His family moved to Carrigaline, near Cork, Munster, in 1616. The elder Daniel Gookin invested in land and trade with Virginia in the early 1620s, but, ruined by falling tobacco prices, could bequeath only land and claims there when he died. Both parents imparted puritan attitudes to their children. Nothing is known of the younger Daniel Gookin until February 1631, when he signed a conveyance as his father's agent in Virginia and was living at Newport News. In 1634 he received 2500 acres mostly owed to his father, west of Nansemond River. Though his brother John was in Virginia in 1636–43, Daniel's movements are unknown between 1634 and 1641, except for his second marriage in London to Mary Dolling (*d.* 1683) on 11 November 1639. He may have acquired military experience during this period.

By late 1641 Captain and Mary Gookin were in Norfolk county, Virginia, perhaps driven there by the Irish rising. He was soon appointed JP, elected burgess, and granted 1400 acres on the Rappahannock. On 24 May 1642 he was second of seventy-one signatories of the Nansemond petition to New England requesting that godly ministers be sent to Norfolk county. His puritan sympathies were intensified by the Revd William Thompson's preaching, and when the mission was suppressed by the royalist governor, he left Virginia. After a brief sojourn in Maryland the family arrived in Boston on 20 May 1644. Gookin was a highly valued arrival; within six days he was admitted to the Boston church and three days later to colonial freemanship. From 1644 to 1648 the family lived in Roxbury under the ministry of Revd John Eliot, the apostle to the American Indians, and Gookin helped found the town's Latin school. Then Cambridge offered a 500 acre farm in Shawshin, and the Gookins made the town their permanent home. He quickly became an important figure in town and colony, acting as selectman, captain of militia, deputy, speaker, and after 1652 as an assistant, one of the magistrates, and a member of the colony's senior legislative and executive body.

During the 1650s visits to England interrupted these duties: in 1650 acquiring munitions, and in 1654 originally on family business. Several kinsmen were influential Cromwellians, and Gookin was dispatched back to Boston to promote New England migration to newly conquered Jamaica. Discouraging news from the island thwarted his efforts, however, and he embarked for England to complete his interrupted business on 13 September 1657. In March 1659 he was commissioned as a customs officer in Dunkirk and promoted deputy treasurer at war there in September. Whatever his plans, the imminent Restoration induced him to sail for Boston on 4 May 1660 with regicides William Goffe and Edward Whalley as shipmates and subsequent protégés. As he resumed New England life in his forty-eighth year, his family was complete. He had daughters of twenty and fifteen, and sons of ten, eight, and four. As well as his Cambridge lands and farm, he received £45 per year and frontier land grants totalling 1000 acres for public service. Expensive investments in trading ventures, shipbuilding, and the settlement of Worcester contributed to 'his low estate in the world' by 1674 (F. W. Gookin, 185).

Gookin resumed and expanded his official functions after 1660. In 1661 he was appointed a licenser of the press at Cambridge. He returned to the overseers of Harvard, and took an active interest in academic exercises, college finances, and the 1675–6 building of Old Harvard Hall. He was a persistent advocate for Massachusetts's eventual purchase of Maine from the Gorges family between 1663 and 1678. As a magistrate he was committed and judicious. Though enthusiastic in persecuting Quakers and Baptists during the 1660s, he favoured the half-way covenant expanding church membership. In Massachusetts's 1662–5 confrontation with the restored monarchy, Gookin adopted an intransigent opposition to royal 'interference', arguing for the colony's virtual independence under the 1629 charter. As a result the king's commissioners ruled in favour of Rhode Island against his land claims, and ordered his cattle to be seized because he had assisted the regicides. In 1665 he was summoned to England, but pleaded lack of due process and divine displeasure in refusing to go. He and Massachusetts were saved for the next decade by Dutch wars and ministerial instability.

Since 1649 Gookin had been involved in Eliot's mission to local American Indians. His appointment in 1656 as superintendent of the praying Indians was permanently renewed in 1661. This involved maintaining law, order, and equity among the converts (estimated at 1100 by 1674), frequent trips to their towns (including the Nipmucks, 50 miles west of Boston), catechizing, entertaining visitors at Cambridge, and overseeing Native American constables in the prevention of drinking, witchcraft, sabbath breaking, and indolence. In 1674 he completed the second book of his ambitious eight-book history of New England, *The Historical Collections of the Indians of North America*, divided into twelve chapters. This encyclopaedic account simply and methodically describes the American Indians' possible origins, their languages, customs, manners, beliefs, and conversions, along with the work of missionaries and the English Society for Propagating the Gospel of 1649 (reincorporated in 1662 as the New England Company). His proposal for the Anglicizing of young American

Indians through a biracial frontier school at Marlborough was rapidly overtaken by events. From June 1675 to August 1676 Anglo-Indian relations were convulsed by King Philip's War. Many white people refused to believe Gookin's assurances that the praying Indians were loyal, despite their many acts of bravery, espionage, tracking, scouting, and prisoner ransom. He spoke out against white hysteria, prejudiced magistrates, and lynch mobs. For his pains he had his life threatened, was nearly drowned in the bay, and was defamed as 'Irish dog', among other choice insults (F. W. Gookin, 153). In the 1676 election he was dropped from his place among the assistants. He spent the aftermath of the war caring for the return and rehabilitation of the Native American refugees and writing a *Historical Account of the Doings and Sufferings of the Christian Indians*, emphasizing their contribution to victory against other triumphalist, racist accounts. None of his writings was published during his lifetime.

Gookin's re-election as an assistant in 1677, and his promotion to sergeant-major-general of the Middlesex regiment, pitched him into the political struggle of his final decade, against the imperial ambitions of the crown as represented by Edward Randolph. Opposing Massachusetts compromisers who would send agents to renegotiate the charter, Gookin on 14 February 1681 advocated all-out resistance. That he reflected the 'popular mind' (F. W. Gookin, 179) was shown by his topping the poll for assistants and appointment as commander-in-chief in May. Randolph, whose campaign succeeded in revoking Massachusetts's charter in October 1684, regarded 'Mr. Guggins' as a leading antagonist (ibid., 182). One of his last political acts was to condemn the appointed Dudley Council of May 1686.

Mary Gookin died on 27 October 1683. Two of their sons became ministers, though the third was convicted of fornication, as was a grandson resident in the household. Gookin was married a third time, to a widow, Hannah Savage, *née* Tyng (1640–1688). He continued his magisterial and military duties, and his visits, protection, and encouragement of Christian Indians, until the last weeks of his life. He died in Cambridge, Massachusetts, on 19 March 1687 and was buried there three days later. He left estate, mostly in land, valued at £323. His long-time collaborator John Eliot observed that 'He died poor, but full of good works' (F. W. Gookin, 185). ROGER THOMPSON

Sources F. W. Gookin, *Daniel Gookin* (1912) • R. N. Gookins, *The Gookin family* (1983) • D. Gookin, 'Historical collections of the Indians in New England', *Collections of the Massachusetts Historical Society*, 1 (1792), 141–227 • D. Gookin, 'Historical account of the doings and sufferings of the Christian Indians', *Archaeologia Americana*, 2 (1836), 423–524 • J. Butler, 'Two 1642 letters from Virginia puritans', *Proceedings of the Massachusetts Historical Society*, 84 (1972), 99–109 • V. F. Meyer and J. F. Dorman, revs., *Adventurers of purse and person: Virginia, 1607–1624/5*, 3rd edn (1987) • P. R. Lucas, 'Colony or commonwealth: Massachusetts Bay, 1661–1666', *William and Mary Quarterly*, 24 (1967), 88–107 • H. Galinsky, 'I cannot join with the multitude', *Myth and enlightenment in American literature*, ed. D. Meindl and others (1985) • M. G. Hall, *Edward Randolph and the American colonies, 1676–1703* (1960) • M. Maccarthy-Murrough, *The Munster plantation* (1986)

Wealth at death £323: Gookin, *Daniel Gookin*

Gookin, Robert (*d.* 1666/7?), parliamentarian army officer, was the second son of the Munster planter Sir Vincent *Gookin (*d.* 1638) and his first wife, Mary Wood. The politician and author Vincent *Gookin (*c.*1616–1659) was his elder brother.

Gookin evidently served in the king's army in Ireland in the 1640s. He first emerges from obscurity in 1648, when he was persuaded to attempt to bring over the protestant forces of Munster from their adherence to the king and the marquess of Ormond to that of the English parliament. In November of the following year, when Cromwell's army entered the province, Gookin took a prominent part in procuring the surrender to Roger Boyle, Lord Broghill, of the town of Bandon in co. Cork for the use of the English.

Gookin appears to have entered the Cromwellian military establishment, to judge from his claims for arrears of pay earned in that capacity. After completion of the Cromwellian conquest of Ireland he was an active agent in the firm establishment of the English interest. In 1652 he reached an agreement with the parliamentary commissioners for the government of Ireland, undertaking to fortify, at his own expense, the abbey of Rosse in West Carbury, co. Cork. He also built houses and stabling therein for the accommodation of English planters there. For this service, which he estimated would eventually cost him £1000, he was in 1653 granted possession of lands adjacent to the abbey to a maximum value of £250 per annum. Commonwealth commissioners of revenue at Cork subsequently attested that Gookin had spent £2143 at Rosse, in recognition of which in 1654 he was confirmed in the possession of his family's estates at Castle Mahone and Court McSherry, his title to which had evidently been compromised by his service in the king's Irish army.

In 1655 Gookin received the perpetual possession of 2582 acres of land at an annual rent of £6 6*s.* 8*d.* Two years later he received the first of several grants in consideration of a claim to the right to exploit the fisheries of Berehaven in the same county. He was also permitted to establish 100 Irish families in the area, as long as they were not liable to transplantation, to be employed in this connection. His better known brother, Vincent, had himself argued strongly for the moderation of the policy of transplanting the native population to Connaught, not least for fear of depleting catastrophically the labour force available to work the new English estates in Ireland.

At the Restoration, to safeguard his not insignificant property interest in co. Cork, Gookin considered it prudent to convey his various lands on a 100 year lease to Roger Boyle, now earl of Orrery, son of the first earl of Cork, one of the new lords justices, and the very man with whom he had colluded some years earlier in contriving the surrender of Bandon to the Commonwealth. Subsequently Gookin was named the captain to a troop of horse in co. Cork, a service which he declined, though he swore that he would 'freely venture his life and fortune for the king', the sincerity of which Orrery was happy to vouch for. His only modern biographer has remarked that it 'may be doubted, however, whether [his] loyalty to his restored sovereign was anything more than a prudent worship of the newly risen sun' (Salisbury, 413).

Gookin died, probably in late 1666 or early in 1667; his will was proved on 20 February 1667. He left a widow, Dorothy, who subsequently married Randal Clayton, son of Sir Randal Clayton of Thelwall, Cheshire. She and Robert had two daughters, Anne and Mary, and two sons: Vincent, styled in his will 'of Lincoln's Inn', who married Elizabeth, daughter of one Arthur Ormsby esq.; and Robert jun., who appears to have misappropriated the family's property during his elder brother's absence in England.

SEAN KELSEY

Sources 'Gookin, Sir Vincent', *DNB* • 'Gookin, Vincent', *DNB* • E. E. Salisbury, *Family memorials* (1885) • W. Petty, *The history of the survey of Ireland: commonly called the down survey*, AD 1655–6, ed. T. A. Larcom (1851)

Gookin, Sir Vincent (*d.* **1638**), colonist and entrepreneur, was the youngest son of John Gookin, of Ripple Court, Kent, and Catherine, daughter of William Dene of Bursted, in the same county. Gookin settled in Ireland in the early seventeenth century, a tenant in fee simple to Henry Beecher, of the manor of Castle Mahon, Kinalmeaky, co. Cork, part of the seignory granted by letters patent to Phane Beecher and Hugh Worth (30 September 1588), as undertakers of the Munster plantation. Beecher's grant was later purchased by Richard Boyle, first earl of Cork, whom Gookin warmly recommended to Lord Deputy Wentworth in his letter of 1633.

Gookin became one of the wealthiest men in Munster, involving himself in a number of ventures, including fishing and sheep farming, and was knighted in 1630, the same year that he was made sheriff of Cork. A petition by Sir Richard Aldworth to the lord deputy, Sir Henry Cary, Lord Falkland, singled Gookin out as one of the rich Englishmen in the Cork area who could help to relieve the starving English soldiers. In his letter to Wentworth of 1633 Gookin claims that he had to pay £1000 a year in wages to the labourers that he employed in farming and fishing. In the early 1630s he was involved in a dispute with Israel Taylor, vicar of Lislee, over the rights of pilchard fishing, a case that was eventually settled in Taylor's favour. By the end of the 1630s he ran a successful fishery at Courtmacsherry. After his death it was leased, and the cattle from his farms transported to England to pay for his daughters' dowries.

Gookin, despite his commercial success, clearly felt ill at ease in Ireland. When the new lord deputy, Sir Thomas Wentworth, later earl of Strafford, arrived in Ireland in July 1633 Gookin addressed an open letter to him, detailing the problems that he would find there. The letter circulated widely in manuscript and, with its numerous hostile criticisms of the Irish, caused a scandal. Gookin, who may have had puritan leanings, argued that no other country contained such rigid religious divisions as Ireland and suggested that settlers would be safer living in the Indies, were it not for the liberal use of the sword of justice by the authorities. He argued, following many earlier writers, that the English Irish, the descendants of the twelfth-century colonists, were now as bad as the native Irish, as they had all become Catholics and thus hostile to the English crown. He also criticized Irish civil government and the army as hopelessly corrupt, concluding with an excoriating attack on the character of the Irish. Gookin advised Wentworth that only protestants were worth governing and protecting.

Wentworth was outraged and noted that Gookin had managed to offend virtually everyone he could have done through his outburst. After the matter was discussed in the Irish parliament a warrant was issued for Gookin's arrest, but he fled to England with his family. He probably settled at Highfield House, Bitton, Gloucestershire, which he had acquired in 1627. Sir James Ware claims that 'being apprehensive of the Danger he might incur by provoking all Ranks of People, [he] found Means to transport himself and Family to *England*' (*Whole Works*, 2.358). A substantial fine was imposed on him in his absence but whether it was ever paid remains unknown. It is likely that he never returned to Ireland, although he continued to oversee his business interests there. He had married twice; first Mary, daughter of Mr Wood of Waldron, with whom he had two sons, Vincent *Gookin and Robert *Gookin, both of whom played significant roles in southern Ireland; and, second, Judith (*d.* 1642), second daughter of Sir Thomas Crooke, of Baltimore, co. Cork, with whom he had several more children. Gookin's brother Daniel, also referred to in the Irish state papers, later emigrated to Virginia, before returning to the Cork area. Daniel's son, also named Daniel *Gookin, became a major-general in Massachusetts.

Gookin died at his Gloucestershire residence on 5 February 1638 and was buried in the parish of Bitton. Most of his property passed to his eldest son, Vincent.

ANDREW HADFIELD

Sources M. MacCarthy-Morrogh, *The Munster plantation: English migration to southern Ireland, 1583–1641* (1986) • E. Hasted, *The history and topographical survey of the county of Kent*, 2nd edn, 12 vols. (1797–1801) • *The whole works of Sir James Ware concerning Ireland*, ed. and trans. W. Harris, 2/1 (1745), 358 • *CSP Ire., 1625–60* • *N&Q*, 4 (1851), 103–4 • R. Dunlop, 'The plantation of Munster, 1584–1589', *EngHR*, 3 (1888), 250–69 • J. Merrit, *The papers of Thomas Wentworth, 1st earl of Strafford, 1593–1641* (1994), 81 • J. P. Prendergast, *The Cromwellian settlement of Ireland*, 3rd edn (1922) • *DNB* • E. Cooper, *The life of Thomas Wentworth, earl of Strafford and lord lieutenant of Ireland* (1874)

Gookin, Vincent (*c.***1616–1659**), politician and author, was the eldest son of Sir Vincent *Gookin and his wife, Mary Wood. He was probably brought up on his father's estate at Courtmacsherry in co. Cork until 1635, when the family moved to England to take up residence in Gloucestershire. During the English civil war Gookin supported parliament, and may have been the Captain Gookin captured by the royalists in Wiltshire in 1643. In 1646 he sold his Gloucestershire lands and by late 1649 had returned to Ireland, where he helped to persuade the Munster protestants to reject the royalist cause and join forces with Oliver Cromwell. He was amply rewarded for his services, and became influential in English and Irish affairs under the Commonwealth: in the early 1650s he served on the revenue committee in co. Cork; he was nominated to Barebone's Parliament in 1653; and was appointed an admiralty commissioner in December that year. He used his position at Whitehall to further Irish interests, notably in encouraging the 1654 order of oblivion for Munster protestants. As a result he became a close ally of the Boyle family, and owed his election for Bandon and Kinsale in the 1654 parliament to the patronage of the second earl of Cork, Richard Boyle, and his brother, Lord Broghill (Roger Boyle).

In January 1655 Gookin published *The Great Case of Transplantation in Ireland Discussed*, which questioned the wholesale eviction of the native Irish to the province of Connaught. He argued that such a transplantation would be contrary to 'religion, profit and safety', as it would remove the Irish from improving protestant influences, deny other areas their labour and skill, and concentrate all the former rebels in one place. Beside these practical suggestions, Gookin's pamphlet also attacked the army interest which ruled Ireland in the early 1650s, and which had fostered the growth of religious sectarianism. One cause of instability in Ireland was the prominence of 'gifted men', who disturbed the 'Godly learned ministers' in their parishes. He also attacked the financial burden placed on Ireland by the oversized army of occupation, and urged the English council to 'see and hear with their eyes that were in Ireland'—in other words, the Irish protestants (Gookin, *Great Case of Transplantation*, 3, 5, 23, 28). It was these political points which provoked the storm of criticism which followed. Gookin was vilified in the English press as a 'Teagish person' who wanted the overthrow of English rule in Ireland (*Mercurius Politicus*, no. 245, 15–22 Feb 1655, 5136; no. 251, 29 March–5 April 1655, 5234). Such arguments were picked up by Colonel Richard Lawrence, who published a formal reply in March, accusing Gookin of wanting 'not so much to heal the Irish wounds, as to wound and weaken the English government and interest there' (Lawrence, 10). Gookin countered with a further pamphlet, *The Author and Case of Transplanting the Irish into Connaught Vindicated*, published in May, in which he defended his loyalty to the regime. For good measure this new work was dedicated to the lord deputy, Charles Fleetwood. Despite his more tactful tone Gookin's basic argument remained the same: Ireland would be a more stable and prosperous place if the Irish protestants, rather than the army, had a say in its government.

Gookin had judged the mood of the times very well. In the next few months the arrival of Henry Cromwell brought a more conciliatory touch to Irish affairs, and when a new parliament was called in 1656 the Irish protestants formed a united front behind the Cromwellian government. Gookin, who had been re-elected for Bandon and Kinsale, became an important ally for the leading reformer, Lord Broghill, joining the assault on the Militia Bill in January 1657 and supporting the 'Humble petition and advice', which included the offer of the crown to the protector. Oliver Cromwell's reluctance to accept a monarchical settlement was a personal defeat for Gookin and his friends: as he told Henry Cromwell on 14 April, 'I cannot believe his highness should grant so much if he intended to refuse the title. The Lord be his guide and God in all his difficulties' (BL, Lansdowne MS 822, fol. 43*v*). Gookin played no part in parliamentary affairs after the revised humble petition (with all references to monarchy removed) was passed on 25 May 1657.

In the second half of 1657 Gookin was back in Ireland, where he took up his job on the commission for settling the army's land claims, to which he had been appointed in July 1656. In 1658 he was appointed surveyor-general of Ireland, and worked alongside Dr William Petty in setting out forfeited land for plantation. But Gookin's prosperity was heavily dependent on the survival of the protectorate. The death of Oliver Cromwell in September 1658 weakened the regime, and caused tensions within the Irish protestant community. In the elections for Richard Cromwell's parliament in January 1659 Gookin broke his alliance with the Boyle family and put up rival candidates (including William Petty) for the Cork seats. Broghill was furious at the challenge to his authority, complaining that Gookin 'played the knave egregiously' in setting up for himself (Chatsworth, Lismore MS 30, no. 72). An uneasy compromise followed, with the Boyles taking the seat for Cork and Youghal, while Gookin was once more returned for Bandon and Kinsale. Not that Gookin had achieved much by attacking the Boyles. There is no record of his attendance in parliament, and in late 1659 he died—possibly suddenly—without leaving a will. His widow, Mary (*née* Salmon), was allowed the administration of his personal goods in January 1660. PATRICK LITTLE

Sources HoP, *Commons* [draft] · C. R. Hudleston, 'Sir Vincent Gookin', *Transactions of the Bristol and Gloucestershire Archaeological Society*, 64 (1943), 113–17 · *Mercurius Politicus* (1655) · BL, Lansdowne MSS 821–3 · MSS of Richard Boyle, second earl of Cork, Chatsworth House, Derbyshire, Lismore MSS 29 and 30 · thrift will, NA Ire., 2829 · R. Dunlop, ed., *Ireland under the Commonwealth*, 2 vols. (1913) · T. C. Barnard, 'Lord Broghill, Vincent Gookin and the Cork elections of 1659', *EngHR*, 88 (1973), 352–65 · NL Ire., MS 839, 4–5 · *Report on the manuscripts of the earl of Egmont*, 2 vols. in 3, HMC, 63 (1905–9) · Thurloe, *State papers* · *JHC*, 7 (1651–9) · R. Lawrence, *The interest of England in the Irish transplantation, stated* (1655)
Archives BL, Lansdowne MSS 821–823 · Chatsworth, Derbyshire, Lismore MSS, 29–30

Goold, James Alipius (1812–1886), Roman Catholic archbishop of Melbourne, was born into a prosperous merchant family in Cork, Ireland, on 4 November 1812. Educated by Augustinian friars, he entered the order at Grantstown, co. Wexford, and took his vows in 1832; having completed his studies for the priesthood in Perugia, Italy, he was ordained in 1835. In Rome, in 1837, he met Australia's vicar-general, Dr William Ullathorne, who was seeking priests for the colony of which John Bede Polding had been appointed first bishop in 1834. Goold volunteered and, in February 1838, arrived in Sydney, where he was soon given charge of the Campbelltown district of New South Wales. There he demonstrated the personal piety and practical service to his people—sacramentally as well as in church building and education—which was characteristic of his whole career.

James Alipius Goold (1812–1886), by Batchelder & Co., in or before 1886

Appointed bishop of the new see of Melbourne in 1848, Goold impressed local Catholics with his vitality and youthful good looks—his round, apparently good-humoured face. In fact he was reserved, not given to display or expression of warm emotion, with a firm belief in, and insistence on, his own episcopal authority.

In Melbourne that assumption was soon challenged, both from outside and within the Catholic church. Goold's right to style himself bishop of Melbourne was immediately denied by the Anglican bishop of Melbourne, Charles Perry, in a first incident of the sectarian religious factionalism that marked Goold's episcopacy. From 1850 Goold led the Catholic defence against the bitter public attack on Irish immigration. His initial response to public anti-Catholicism was placatory, but under continuing pressure it quickly hardened into aggressive counter-attack and assertion of Catholic claims to equality. Under Goold the Catholic church in Victoria developed enduring characteristics of isolationism, combative anti-protestantism, and uncompromising stress on Catholic education in a hostile world.

Goold was also faced by momentous challenges to the provision of the services of religion presented by the Victorian gold rushes—and consequent increases in population—which occurred from 1851. It was typical of the hard-riding practical missionary in Goold that he should confront these problems directly and in person, visiting the Ballarat goldfields in 1854 and 1855; he was credited with a pacificatory role in the Eureka stockade 'rebellion' in 1854.

Goold's problems came not only from external attack and circumstance but from disaffected lay and clerical elements within his own church. His view of episcopal authority was firmly hierarchical and centred on his own decisions, not only spiritual but financial and administrative. Moreover his style of communication was often impatient, demanding, and irascible. In Melbourne a group of laymen clamoured, to Goold's annoyance and immovable opposition, for a greater share in church government, and mounted a turbulent public attack on Goold's policies as being destructive of religion. In this they were supported and surpassed by a small group of obsessively independent priests, dubbed 'the clique', which alleged maladministration, injustice, and episcopal despotism.

In fact Goold's was an efficient and dedicated ministry, if marked by opposition and controversy. He was determined to build a Catholic education system in the face of secular compulsions embodied in the Victorian Education Act of 1872, and much of his energy and resources went into school building and attracting religious orders to staff his separate system; he twice visited Ireland to recruit priests for Australia.

On 21 August 1882 Goold, who had been elevated to archbishop in March 1874, was shot at and slightly wounded in a Melbourne street by the deranged solicitor P. A. C. O'Farrell, who had once been his adviser. Thereafter his health steadily declined; he died of a heart attack on 11 June 1886 at Brighton, Melbourne, and was buried in St Patrick's Cathedral, Melbourne, a building project much criticized for its extravagance, but dear to Goold for its being in keeping with the dignity and grandeur of his religion. PATRICK O'FARRELL

Sources P. J. O'Farrell, *The Catholic church and community: an Australian history*, rev. edn (1992) • F. O'Kane, *A path is set: the Catholic church in the Port Phillip district and Victoria, 1839–1862* (1976) • D. F. Bourke, *A history of the Catholic church in Victoria* (Melbourne, 1988) • F. X. Martin, '"A great battle": Bishop James A. Goold of Melbourne (1848–1869) and the state aid for religion controversy', *Ireland and Australia*, ed. O. MacDonagh and W. F. Mandle (1986), 193–216

Archives St Patrick's Cathedral, Melbourne, diocesan historical commission archives

Likenesses Batchelder & Co., photograph, in or before 1886, State Library of Victoria, Melbourne, La Trobe picture collection [*see illus.*]

Goold, Thomas (1766–1846), barrister and politician, was born of a wealthy protestant family in Cork. He obtained his BA from Trinity College, Dublin, in 1786, and was called to the bar in 1791. He spent most of his inheritance of £10,000 in entertaining his friends (including Henry Grattan, William Saurin, Charles Bushe, and William Plunket) and on travelling widely before he began to practise at the bar. On his return from Paris, he published *A Pamphlet in Defence of Burke's 'Reflections on the French Revolution'*, and in 1799 he wrote, 'Address to the people of Ireland on the subject of the projected Union'. In the same year he sat in the last session of the Irish parliament as a member of the opposition.

Goold was stigmatized as an 'honest Irishman' around the time of the union. This and his friendship with Grattan slowed his professional advancement somewhat. However, in 1823 he was appointed third serjeant, in 1830 king's serjeant, and a master in chancery in 1832. He was renowned as one of the great wits of his time at the bar and one of the best *nisi prius* lawyers who ever held a brief at the Irish bar.

It is not known for certain who Goold married, but he had at least one daughter. He died at Lissadell, co. Sligo, the seat of his son-in-law, Sir R. G. Booth, bt, on 16 July 1846. L. C. SANDERS, *rev.* SINÉAD AGNEW

Sources *Annual Register* (1846) • W. H. Curran, *Sketches of the Irish bar*, 1 (1855), 183–207 • Ward, *Men of the reign*, 358 • J. S. Crone, *A concise dictionary of Irish biography*, rev. edn (1937), 78

Goossens, Sir Eugene Aynsley (1893–1962), composer and conductor, was born in Rochester Square, Camden Town, London, on 26 May 1893, the son of Eugène Goossens (1867–1958), a violinist, and his wife, Annie Cook (1860–1946), an opera singer. The family came originally from Bruges in Belgium; both his grandfather Eugène and his father, also Eugène, had started their careers as violinists before taking up the baton for the Carl Rosa Opera Company, a path that Goossens was to follow. His maternal grandfather, Aynsley Cook, was the leading bass-baritone and his mother Annie a contralto with the company. Eugene was the eldest of five exceptionally gifted musical children: Marie and Sidonie were to become celebrated harpists while Léon Jean *Goossens (1897–1988) is recognized as having been the pre-eminent oboist of his day; a second brother, Adolphe, who showed great promise on the French horn, was killed at the battle of the Somme in 1916.

At the age of eight, Eugene was sent to be schooled by the Franciscan brothers in Bruges, and for his third year there studied the violin and piano at the Muziek-Conservatorium. In 1904 his father allowed him to rejoin the family in Liverpool, where, as well as displaying his musical gifts, he showed talent as an artist. He developed two other passions which he was to retain all his life: for ocean liners and for steam locomotives. At fourteen he was awarded the prestigious Liverpool scholarship to the Royal College of Music, London, where he studied the violin with Achille Rivarde and composition with Sir Charles Villiers Stanford. Goossens recalled in his autobiography, *Overture and Beginners* (1951), that Stanford laid the blame for the wildness of his radical young pupils Goossens and his friends Arthur Benjamin, Arthur Bliss, and Herbert Howells on the pernicious influence of Debussy and Richard Strauss.

In 1912 Goossens joined the first violins of Sir Henry Wood's Queen's Hall Orchestra. His first composition, *Variations on a Chinese Theme*, was given at the Royal College of Music that year, with himself as conductor; and the following year he conducted it at a Promenade Concert. He also played second violin in the Langley–Mukle and Philharmonic quartets and established his reputation as an innovative and accomplished composer of chamber music. His imaginative use of orchestral sound was to

Sir Eugene Aynsley Goossens (1893–1962), by Herbert Lambert, pubd 1923

become a hallmark of his subsequent large-scale works, particularly his two symphonies, his dramatic cantata *The Apocalypse*, and the oboe concerto written to display the virtuosity of his brother Léon. Rejected from military service because of a congenital heart defect, in 1916 Goossens was asked by Thomas Beecham, at only twenty-four hours' notice, to conduct two new English operas: *The Critic* by Stanford and *The Boatswain's Mate* by Ethel Smyth. Goossens was a great success, and this launched him on a brilliant operatic and orchestral career.

Tall and handsome, Goossens possessed great personal charm and style. On 18 November 1919 he married Dorothy (*b.* 1891), formerly Millar, an artist, daughter of Frederick C. Smith Dodsworth. He and his wife, who was known as Boonie, were leading lights in London's artistic and social scene of the 1920s. After they were divorced in 1928, Goossens married on 5 January 1930 Janet Jansi Lewis (*b.* 1908), a pianist. Divorced again in 1944, Goossens married Marjorie Foulkrod (*née* Fetter; *b.* 1912) on 18 April 1946.

Acknowledged as a champion of the musical avant-garde, Goossens always generously promoted the works of his contemporaries; in 1921 he formed his own orchestra for a series of epoch-making programmes, opening with the first concert performance in London of Stravinsky's *Le sacre du printemps*. On alternate nights he would be conducting the Carl Rosa Opera Company at

Covent Garden and Diaghilev's sumptuous ballet *The Sleeping Princess* at the Alhambra Theatre in London. 'My heart loosens when I listen to Goossens', sang his friend Noël Coward in praise of his ubiquitous versatility (Goossens, 175–6). He conducted the first performances of Nigel Playfair's version of *The Beggar's Opera*, Delius's music for James Elroy Flecker's *Hassan*, and Coleridge Taylor's *Hiawatha*, grandiosely performed at the Albert Hall, as well as composing incidental music for Margaret Kennedy's *The Constant Nymph*.

In 1923 Goossens accepted the invitation of George Eastman, the 'Kodak King', to conduct his newly formed Rochester Philharmonic Orchestra in upstate New York. By the end of the decade he was established as a brilliant and dynamic figure on the podia of America's greatest orchestras, and in 1931 he took up the coveted appointment of musical director of the Cincinnati Orchestra and May festival. Ill health, however, prevented his realizing the full potential of his conducting career.

Until the Second World War Goossens returned almost every year to England for conducting engagements. In June 1929 these included the première of his one-act opera *Judith* at Covent Garden, with a libretto by Arnold Bennett. The score was praised by Ernest Newman as 'a marvel of subtlety and flawless logic' (*The Times*). His second opera, also with a libretto by Bennett, was *Don Juan of Mañara*, a very different version of the Don Juan story from that of Mozart and Da Ponte. It received an excellent production in Covent Garden's coronation season of July 1937. Newman judged it to be 'the best thing that English opera has so far produced' (*Sunday Times*), but the general response was unfavourable. In subsequent decades Goossens's own musical works have largely dropped out of favour. The 'singular unmemorability' of his music has been explained on the grounds not only of its 'complexity and difficulty', but also its 'lack of melodic invention and inner conviction' (Banfield, 532). However, some of the smaller works are still 'eminently rewarding' (ibid.).

In 1945 Lord Keynes and Ralph Hawkes sought out Goossens in the USA to offer him the musical directorship of the new Royal Opera Company at Covent Garden. However, after eighteen months of negotiation Goossens declined when he discovered that artistic decisions were to be made by the general administrator David Webster. He accepted instead the musical directorship of the Sydney Symphony Orchestra and New South Wales Conservatorium. His twin aims were to make the orchestra one of the six best in the world, and to provide Sydney with an opera house of international status on his chosen site at Bennalong Point. In 1951 Joan Sutherland made her operatic début under his baton in the title role of *Judith* at the conservatorium; among the many other Australian musicians whom he inspired to pursue international careers were Sir Charles Mackerras, Richard Bonynge, Geoffrey Parsons, and Malcolm Williamson.

In 1955 Goossens was knighted for his services to Australian music, but the further realization of his aims was frustrated by his involvement in a bizarre scandal: he was implicated in occult practices and the importation of photographic material judged to be pornographic by the standards of the day. The mystery as to who were the instigators of his downfall remains unsolved. Goossens was forced to resign his posts in 1956 and returned to London. He died in the Hillingdon Hospital, Middlesex, on 13 June 1962 and was buried at East Finchley cemetery. Goossens was survived by his third wife. Of his five daughters Anne, born in 1921, and Sidonie, born in 1932, inherited his artistic and musical talent. CAROLE ROSEN

Sources E. Goossens, *Overture and beginners* (1951) • C. Rosen, *The Goossens: a musical century* (1993) • private information (2004) [family diaries and correspondence] • *CGPLA Eng. & Wales* (1962) • *The Times* (30 June 1929) • *Sunday Times* (11 July 1937) • S. Banfield, 'Goossens, Sir (Aynsley) Eugène', *New Grove*, 7.532–3 • *DNB*

Archives BL NSA, performance recordings | SOUND BL NSA, performance recordings

Likenesses H. Lambert, photogravure, pubd 1923, NPG [*see illus.*] • P. Véelay, oils, 1925, NPG

Wealth at death £1286 13*s*. 10*d*.—in England: probate, 17 Dec 1962, *CGPLA Eng. & Wales*

Goossens, Léon Jean (1897–1988), oboist, was born on 12 June 1897 in Liverpool, the third of three sons and the fourth of five children of the conductor Eugène Goossens (1867–1958), himself the son of Eugène Goossens (1845–1906), conductor of the Carl Rosa Opera Company. His mother was Annie, an opera singer, and daughter of the operatic bass singer Aynsley Cook. Of Belgian origin, the family had settled in England in the 1870s and 1880s; Léon's siblings were the conductor Sir Eugene *Goossens, the horn player Adolphe (who was killed in the First World War), and the harpists Marie and Sidonie. He was educated at the Christian Brothers Catholic Institute in Liverpool and Liverpool College of Music. After some study of the piano, he began learning the oboe with Charles Reynolds at the age of eight, and by the time he was ten had played professionally. After further study with William Malsch at the Royal College of Music (1911–14), he was appointed principal oboe of the Queen's Hall Orchestra at the age of seventeen. Throughout his career (apart from a brief period when it was stolen) he played the same oboe, made for him by Lorée of Paris. During the First World War Goossens volunteered in the Middlesex yeomanry and subsequently served in the 8th Royal Fusiliers before being commissioned into the Sherwood Foresters. On leaving for France in 1915 he was given a silver cigarette case as a keepsake by his brother Eugene, who had been given it by Ethel Smyth after a performance of one of her operas; it deflected a high-velocity bullet from the region of his heart, still wounding him sufficiently for him to be invalided home. He decided to accept an offer to join a friend on an Argentinian ranch; but, needing capital of £100, he began earning it by freelance oboe playing, which quickly brought so many engagements that the Argentinian plan was cancelled.

Goossens rejoined the Queen's Hall Orchestra in 1918, and moved to Covent Garden in 1924. In the same year he became professor of oboe at the Royal Academy of Music (until 1935) and at the Royal College of Music (until 1939).

Léon Jean Goossens (1897–1988), by Peter Keen, 1969

He also played in the Royal Philharmonic Society's orchestra and, on its foundation by Sir Thomas Beecham in 1932, the London Philharmonic Orchestra. His playing with Beecham lent added distinction to a fine orchestra, as can be heard on records, and was heard with admiration in an early broadcast of his music by the aged Frederick Delius. Fritz Kreisler declared that among his greatest musical pleasures was listening to Goossens playing the solo in the adagio of Brahms's violin concerto before his own entry. This, too, has been recorded. Goossens was, in his own right, one of the most popular and prolific recording artists in the 1920s and 1930s. Recording companies were inexplicably slow to take him up again with the advent of the long-playing record, but he was making a comeback with a recording of J. S. Bach's violin and oboe concerto, with Yehudi Menuhin, when an accident interrupted his career.

Goossens had by now acquired a world reputation (he frequently toured abroad) second to that of no other oboist. More, he had given the oboe a new standing as a solo instrument. He refined the sound from the conventional German breadth and reediness, while enriching the French slenderness but elegance of tone, to a warmth and sweetness hitherto unknown. By this, and by the highly personal elegance of his phrasing, he drew attention to lyrical possibilities that quickly excited the attention of composers, while his brilliant finger technique opened up a new range of virtuosity. Almost every English composer of note was drawn to write music for him: works which he inspired and first performed included concertos by Ralph Vaughan Williams and Rutland Boughton, chamber pieces by Sir Arnold Bax, Sir Arthur Bliss, and Benjamin Britten and an uncompleted suite by Sir Edward Elgar. He was appointed CBE (1950) and FRCM (1962). He also became honorary RAM (1932).

In 1962, still at the height of his powers, Goossens suffered a car accident that severely damaged his teeth and lips, rendering him incapable of playing. After many operations, borne with great physical courage, and the no less courageous confrontation of the apparent end of his career, he began practising again with a newly learned lip technique. He played in film and recording orchestras away from the public view, always with the affectionate support of his colleagues. He was able to resume his professional life, though he privately insisted that the standard of his playing was not what it had been. He continued playing into his eighties, sometimes with small ensembles and modest orchestras to whom he felt an old loyalty.

In his prime, Goossens had earned himself a reputation as something of a prima donna among orchestral players. He would demand his own microphone in recording sessions, on the grounds that the oboe's tone needed special consideration. Colleagues in the wind section would feel obliged to fit in with phrasing that was always personal and at times mannered and unstylish. But with this awareness of his own worth, seen in his gracious platform manner in concertos, went an essential musical humility and a high degree of personal kindness. Self-disciplined in his personal life, in the interests of a musical professionalism inherited from his strict father, he enjoyed physical activities, including yachting and farming. He was always generous with his time to younger oboists, while sometimes resisting those who represented a newer stylistic wave. His charm and humour, among friends, were unaffected and engaging. He was a tall, well-built man, with a deep chest that helped his phenomenal breath control. Like his conductor brother Eugene, he went bald early and had the family's characteristic slightly hooded eyes and charming smile.

In 1926 Goossens married Frances Alice, daughter of Harry Oswald Yeatman, a port shipper who worked in London for Taylor, Fladgate, and Yeatman. They had one daughter. This marriage was dissolved in 1932 and in 1933 he married the dancer Leslie Burrowes (*d.* 1985), daughter of Brigadier-General Arnold Robinson Burrowes, of the Royal Irish Fusiliers. There were two daughters of this marriage. Goossens died on 13 February 1988 in Tunbridge Wells.

JOHN WARRACK, *rev.*

Sources B. Wynne, *Music in the wind: the story of Léon Goossens* (1967) • S. Banfield, 'Goossens (2)', *New Grove* • personal knowledge (1996) • private information (1996) • *CGPLA Eng. & Wales* (1988)
Likenesses photographs, 1934–48, Hult. Arch. • H. Coster, photographs, 1935, NPG • G. Argent, two photographs, 1968, NPG • P. Keen, photograph, 1969, NPG [*see illus.*]
Wealth at death £97,855: probate, 30 June 1988, *CGPLA Eng. & Wales*

Gordine [Gordin], **Dora** (1906–1991), sculptor, born on 13 April 1906, claimed that she was born in St Petersburg, Russia, the daughter of Mark Gordin, an architect, though she may have been born in Libau (Liepaja), Latvia. Her father was reputedly Scottish and her mother Russian. According to her own account (Gordine, interview with Nancy Wise), she escaped from Russia during the revolution and was taken by her eldest brother, Leo, to Paris, while her parents remained in Estonia. She maintained that she was a self-taught sculptor, arguing that the true artist is educated by visiting art galleries, museums, the ballet, and the opera, and only needs training in techniques.

As 'a girl sculpture genius' (*Evening Standard*, 5 Oct 1928), Gordine attracted the attention of Aristide Maillol. She insisted that he advised her not to attend an art school, so she lived frugally in a tiny studio in Paris exploring the nature of clay, stone, and paint and observing workers at the Valsuani foundry. Her style remained virtually unchanged throughout her long career; she believed in purity of form and held contemporary fashions in contempt. 'All sculpture consists of a series of convexes', she maintained (Gordine, interview with David Frazer-Jenkins). Eric Newton, the writer on art, believed that her style derived from a study of ancient Greece's golden age.

Curiously, Gordine's first official commission was as a painter in the British pavilion at the Paris Universal Exhibition of 1925. The appearance of a bronze bust called *The Chinese Philosopher* (Dorich House, Kingston upon Thames, Surrey) in the Salon des Tuileries, Paris, in 1926 won her instant acclaim. Another bronze bust, *The Mongolian Head* (1927, Tate collection), attracted the attention of the art critic Marie Dormoy, who commented that it exemplified 'all the firmness, solidity and grandeur of that race' (Dormoy). Her first solo exhibition, in 1928 at the Leicester Galleries in London, completely sold out. Thereafter she produced powerful male portrait busts, heads and torsos of beautiful Asian women, and major public works.

Between 1929 and 1935 Gordine spent a very fruitful period working in the Far East, where she discovered exquisite models to draw, paint, and sculpt. 'The light was so wonderful', she recalled (Nicholls). In 1930 she was commissioned by the city of Singapore to sculpt six heads representing its constituent races (city hall, Singapore). At this time she developed the ability to convey the rhythmic flow of movement through limbs made of clay, stone, or bronze, which was epitomized in her bronze, *Javanese Dancer* (Dorich House, Kingston upon Thames, Surrey). She represented the human figure from below as if she were a small child looking up at an adult. During this period she met and married Dr G. H. Garlick, physician to the sultan of Johore in Malaya. Their relationship was short-lived and they were divorced after she moved to England in 1935.

On 6 November 1936 Gordine married the Hon. Richard Gilbert Hare (1907–1966), the second son of Richard Granville Hare, the fourth earl of Listowel. Her second marriage gave her an entrée into London society, a position from which she gained many commissions. Her husband later became professor of Russian literature at the School of Slavonic and East European Studies at London University. Thereafter, except for brief periods in 1947 and 1959 when she went with her husband to the United States, she lived and worked in Dorich House, a splendidly eccentric house in Kingston Vale, near Richmond Park, Kingston upon Thames, which she and her husband planned, although it owed more than a little to the ideas of two architect friends, Auguste Perret and Godfrey Samuel. For many years their home was a well-known meeting-place for artists and aesthetes. During this fruitful period, Gordine exhibited regularly at the Royal Academy, and she became an associate (1938) and then a fellow (1949) of the Royal Society of British Sculptors as well as a founder member of the Society of Portrait Sculptors (1953) with whom she showed regularly until 1960. She had little in common, however, with fellow sculptors such as Jacob Epstein, Henry Moore, and Barbara Hepworth, whose work she dismissed as 'mere fashion' (Gordine, interview with David Frazer-Jenkins). The only contemporary artist for whom she evinced the slightest enthusiasm was Augustus John.

According to the critic Arthur Symons, Gordine's mature style exhibited a 'profound sense of pure form … heedless alike of realism and of exaggerated abstraction' (*The Spectator*, 7 Dec 1938). She first got to know her sitters by spending hours with them chatting, eating, and listening to music. Thereafter, 'the real work began' (Gordine, interview with David Frazer-Jenkins), as she modelled them in clay and then in plaster. With the assistance of a skilled technician her models were then cast using the lost-wax method. Sitters included John Pope-Hennessy (1938–9), Dame Beryl Grey (1937–8), Emlyn Williams (1940), Siân Phillips, and Dorothy Tutin. Famously, the future Dame Edith Evans sat to her in the nude (1937–8) and 'became a new woman', as the experience 'was better than being psychoanalysed' (*Daily Herald*, 27 Oct 1938).

A large bronze bas-relief plaque (1946) at 4 Gray's Inn Place, London, commemorating the stay there of Sun Yat-sen, the founder of the Chinese revolution, is one of her best-known public works. Another larger-than-life bronze bas-relief depicting an oilworker was produced for the Esso Petroleum Company (1960, Milford Haven Refinery, Pembrokeshire). Her last major work, *Mother and Child* (1963), a health-invoking bronze sculpture, was placed in the entrance hall of the Royal Marsden Hospital, London.

According to her friend Honor Balfour, Gordine was 'A tiny woman, vivacious and brooding by turns, a taut bundle of passion and determination' (*The Independent*, 7 Jan 1992). Invariably, her black hair was scraped straight back from her forehead and pinned with a bow. She spoke animatedly with a heavy accent, snapping like a Pekinese according to another friend, Trader Faulkner, and repeating key words three times in quick succession in a loud staccato voice. She loved parties and dressed up for them in spectacular jewelled jackets, long skirts, and court shoes.

Dora Gordine died at her home, Dorich House, on 29 December 1991; she was cremated and her ashes scattered in the garden of her home. In her will she left her house and art collection in trust. Dorich House has been refurbished by Kingston University and contains a permanent display of her work as well as an extensive archive.

MICHAEL R. GIBSON

Sources E. H. Ramsden, *Twentieth-century sculpture* (1949) · M. Chamot, D. Farr, and M. Butlin, *The modern British paintings, drawings and sculpture*, 2 vols. (1964–5) [catalogue, Tate Gallery, London] · D. Gaze, ed., *Dictionary of women artists*, 1 (1997) · M. Dormoy,

'Dora Gordine, sculpteur', *L'Amour de l'Art*, 8 (May 1927), 166 · L. Benoist, 'Dora Gordine', *L'Amour de l'Art*, 10 (May 1929), 172–6 · A. Symons, 'A triumph of sculptural form: the work of Dora Gordine', *The Spectator* (7 Dec 1938); repr. in *The Connoisseur*, 142 (1958), 233–7 · M. Sorrell, 'Dora Gordine', *Apollo*, 49 (1949), 113–15 · G. A. Nicholls, 'Beauty in bronze', *Figure Quarterly*, 13 (1956), 4–11 [American edn] · *Dorich House* (1998) [guidebook] · D. Gordine and N. Wise, interview, 1972, BL NSA · m. cert. [Dora Gordine and Richard Gilbert Hare] · d. cert. · E. Newton, *British sculpture, 1944–46* (1947) · Dora Gordine, interview with David Frazer-Jenkins, London, 1990, Tate collection · *The Independent* (7 Jan 1992) · *The Independent* (4 Jan 1992) · *The Times* (3 Jan 1992)

Archives Kingston University, Kingston upon Thames, Surrey | U. Glas. L., letters to D. S. MacColl | SOUND BL NSA · Kingston University, Dorich House, Kingston upon Thames, Surrey · Tate collection

Wealth at death £1,175,401: probate, 28 May 1992, *CGPLA Eng. & Wales*

Gordon. For this title name *see* individual entries under Gordon; *see also* Lennox, Charles Henry Gordon-, sixth duke of Richmond, sixth duke of Lennox, and first duke of Gordon (1818–1903).

Gordon family (*per. c.*1300–*c.*1400), nobility, held the Berwickshire baronies of Gordon and Huntly during the fourteenth century. At that time a family of middling significance, the Gordons are also important as the progenitors of the earls of Huntly and dukes of Gordon who dominated the north of Scotland from the mid-fifteenth century. They first came to prominence in the person of **Sir Adam Gordon** (*d. c.*1328), lord of Gordon, in the early fourteenth century. A leading Scottish supporter of Edward I and Edward II, he held the offices of warden of the east march and justiciar of Lothian for the English crown. He fought against Robert Bruce (Robert I) at Methven in 1306, and acted as the warden of Sir Thomas Randolph (Bruce's nephew, later earl of Moray) after Randolph's capture by the English in 1308. Sir Adam was a late defector to the Scottish cause, not joining King Robert until 1315, but his experience was utilized quickly, and in 1320 he travelled to Avignon as one of the bearers of the declaration of Arbroath to Pope John XXII (*r.* 1316–34).

At an unknown date Sir Adam received from the king the extensive lordship of Strathbogie in Aberdeenshire, no doubt partly as a reward for his diplomatic services. The grant may also have been influenced by his former ward Sir Thomas Randolph who sought some measure of security on the borders of his great earldom of Moray, created for him by King Robert in 1312. A few years earlier, in 1315, Randolph had granted the lands of Stichill in Roxburghshire to Adam Gordon, and the two seem to have been reasonably close. Sir Adam's wife was named Amabilla; her family is unknown. With her Sir Adam had four sons and one daughter. He died in or about 1328 and his eldest son, Sir Adam Gordon, succeeded him, was involved in border raids in the 1320s, and fought at Halidon Hill in 1333. The first Sir Adam's second son, William, inherited the lands of Stichill, and was the ancestor of the Gordons of Lochinvar, viscounts Kenmure.

The Gordons largely disappeared from national politics over the following half century, and the next family member of note was **Sir John Gordon** (*d.* 1391x5), the great-grandson of the elder Sir Adam. Like his predecessors John Gordon was primarily concerned with the family's Berwickshire lands. He was involved in a major raid against the English at Roxburgh fair in the 1370s, and as part of the skirmishing that resulted from this attack John led a force across the Tweed in order to raid English cattle. He was overtaken by a larger force led by Sir John Lilburn before he could recross the river, and was forced to fight at Carham. Despite the uneven odds Gordon emerged victorious, capturing Lilburn and his brother and being 'gretly pryssit' for his deeds. Despite receiving serious wounds during this raid, Gordon was still able to continue his defensive role on the borders, and in a second major incident, in 1378, he and his followers intercepted and defeated a force led by Sir Thomas Musgrave (*d.* 1385), warden of Berwick, who was riding to join an expedition led by Henry Percy, earl of Northumberland (*d.* 1408), against the lands of the earl of March. In 1388 he fought alongside the earl of Douglas at the battle of Otterburn.

The 1390s saw the first known involvement of the Gordons with north-east Scotland, when Sir John was a royal justiciar appointed to resolve a dispute between Gilbert Greenlaw, bishop of Aberdeen, and Sir John Forbes, lord of that ilk. It seems unlikely that Gordon had been in the north-east long, and his presence was probably connected to a period of relative quiet on the Scottish border. It is not clear whether Gordon returned south again, but he died between 30 May 1391 and 11 October 1395. He was not legally married, although he had two sons, John and Thomas, through a 'handfasting' marriage to Elizabeth Cruickshank, daughter of the laird of Aswanley. It may have been the desire to gain the support of the descendants of these sons that encouraged Alexander Seton, first earl of Huntly (*d.* 1470)—the son of Sir Alexander Seton and Elizabeth Gordon—to change his family name to Gordon in or about 1457.

Sir John was succeeded as lord of Gordon by his brother **Sir Adam Gordon** (*d.* 1402) who again concentrated on the family's border interests. In October 1398 Adam Gordon was one of three men excepted from a free exchange of prisoners between the Scots and the English, and was cited as a common truce-breaker. He was ordered to appear at the next meeting of the border commissioners in order to answer for the 'unmesurit harmes' he had done, under pain of a fine of £1000. Gordon's activities may have been related to attempts to pay the debts incurred by financing the relief duty on Strathbogie, which had been set by Robert III at 700 merks. In 1399 Gordon was still in debt, and is found borrowing money from a border ally, William Barde, laird of Kirkwood. He fought at Homildon Hill on 14 September 1402, when he invaded England alongside the earl of Douglas. The occasion seems to have been the catalyst for the reconciliation of a long-term feud with Sir John Swinton, who knighted Sir Adam on the battlefield. The two men then led a charge against the English line but were overpowered and killed in the process. Adam Gordon was married to Elisabeth Keith, daughter of Sir William *Keith (*d.* in or after 1407), marischal of Scotland [*see under* Keith family]. With Elisabeth he had a son and heir, John Gordon, and a daughter, Elizabeth Gordon; the latter married Sir Alexander Seton, second son of Sir William Seton [*see* Seton family], and inherited the Gordon lands on the death of her brother on or before 7 March 1408, thereby establishing the line of the Setons of Gordon. SIMON C. APPLEYARD

Sources *CDS*, vol. 3 · J. Ferrerius, 'Historiae compendium de origine et incremento Gordoniae familiae', *House of Gordon*, ed. J. M. Bulloch, 2 (1907) · *Barbour's Bruce*, ed. M. P. McDiarmid and J. A. C. Stevenson, 3 vols., STS, 4th ser., 12–15 (1981–5) · *The 'Original chronicle' of Andrew of Wyntoun*, ed. F. J. Amours, 6, STS, 1st ser., 57 (1908) · W. Bower, *Scotichronicon*, ed. D. E. R. Watt and others, new edn, 9 vols. (1987–98), vols. 6 and 8 · C. Innes, ed., *Registrum episcopatus Aberdonensis*, 1, Spalding Club, 13 (1845) · G. W. S. Barrow and others, eds., *Regesta regum Scottorum*, 5, ed. A. A. M. Duncan (1988) · J. M. Thomson and others, eds., *Registrum magni sigilli regum Scotorum / The register of the great seal of Scotland*, 2nd edn, 1, ed. T. Thomson (1912) · T. Grey, *Scotacronica: the reigns of Edward I, Edward II, and Edward III*, trans. H. Maxwell (1907) · A. Theiner, *Vetera monumenta Hibernorum et Scotorum historiam illustrantia* (Rome, 1864) · J. Robertson, ed., *Collections for a history of the shires of Aberdeen and Banff*, Spalding Club, 9 (1843) · *APS*, *1124–1423*, 581 [Sir John Gordon] · *Scots peerage*, vol. 4

Archives NA Scot., GO44

Wealth at death Strathbogie estates given relief value of 700 merks—Sir John Gordon: *APS*

Gordon, Sir Adam (*d. c.*1328). *See under* Gordon family (*per. c.*1300–*c.*1400).

Gordon, Sir Adam (*d.* 1402). *See under* Gordon family (*per. c.*1300–*c.*1400).

Gordon, Lord Adam (*c.*1726–1801), army officer and politician, was the fourth surviving son of Alexander *Gordon, second duke of Gordon (*c.*1678–1728), and his wife, Lady Henrietta Mordaunt (1681/2–1760) [*see* Gordon, Henrietta], daughter of Charles Mordaunt, third earl of Peterborough. Gordon was raised as a protestant by his mother, who as a result from 1735 received a pension of £1000 p.a. Having entered the army as an ensign in the second dragoons in 1741, he attended Eton College in 1742–3. In 1743 he became a lieutenant, and in 1746 a captain in the 18th foot.

At the election of 1754 Gordon entered parliament for Aberdeenshire, being perceived as a supporter of Archibald Campbell, third duke of Argyll. In 1756 Gordon became captain and lieutenant-colonel of the 3rd foot guards. In March 1757 Thomas Pelham-Holles, duke of Newcastle, then out of office, hoped for Gordon's political support and he duly voted on 2 May 1757 with Newcastle's supporters on the Minorca inquiry. In 1758 he served in the expedition to the French coast and distinguished himself on 10 September at St Cas. The death of his mother in 1760 saw him inherit the Preston Hall estate near Dalkeith, Edinburgh, which she had purchased in 1738 for £8877.

Gordon retained his seat at the election of 1761, and became a supporter of John Stuart, third earl of Bute. On 19 January 1763 he became colonel of the 66th foot. Gordon left London in April 1764 *en route* for the West Indies, the American colonies, and Canada. He made an extensive tour, which he recorded in a journal, and seems to have been concerned with acquiring land in several of the colonies. Upon arrival at Boston, Massachusetts, he was presented with an address detailing colonial concerns on the stamp duties. He left New York on 14 October 1765 and arrived in Falmouth on 12 November. On 20 November he held a conference with the secretaries of state on the American colonies. Subsequently he used his local knowledge to contribute to parliamentary debates on the situation in America. Meanwhile he planned to acquire land in East Florida (with Charles Townshend), and in New York, following his stay with Sir William Johnson, the superintendent of Indian affairs, whose son had accompanied him to England.

Marriage, on 2 September 1767, to Jean (*d.* 1795), daughter of John Drummond, and the widow of James Murray, second duke of Atholl, seems to have prevented Gordon's return to America, and it seems diverted his capital to his Scottish properties, which in 1771 consisted of about 750 acres, and which he hoped in two or three years would yield £1000 p.a. In 1772 Gordon took out his patent and paid quit-rent on his New York holdings, but he never returned to America. In 1772–3 he was courted by some Kincardineshire freeholders, despite having no estate there, and he entered parliament again at the 1774 election.

Already a major-general in 1772, Gordon became colonel of the 26th foot on 27 December 1775. He failed to obtain an active command during the American War of Independence, though he was rejected by the East India Company for one of their commands in 1777, the year in which he secured promotion to lieutenant-general. Lord North told George III 'no member of the House of Commons has been more uniform and zealous in support of government than Lord Adam' (*Correspondence of George III*, 4.100), and the king was consequently persuaded to overlook Gordon's 'improper warmth' (ibid.) and appoint him governor of Tynemouth in 1778. Colonelcy of the 1st foot (Royal Scots) followed on 9 May 1782. He had supported the government consistently during the war, but was unhappy with the peace and the losses inflicted upon loyalists in America. In the election of 1784 he was returned as a supporter of the new administration of William Pitt the younger. He vacated his seat in April 1788 and in 1789 he was appointed commander-in-chief of Scotland. He became general in 1793 and in 1796 swapped Tynemouth for the governorship of Edinburgh Castle, no doubt another perk for his support for Henry Dundas in Scottish politics. In 1796 he welcomed the future Charles X of France to exile in Scotland. In 1798 he was replaced as commander and retired to his seat, The Burns in Kincardineshire, where he died on 13 August 1801 'having drunk some cold water when heated' (*Later Correspondence of George III*, 3.595). He was buried at Inveresk, near Edinburgh. STUART HANDLEY

Sources E. Haden-Guest, 'Gordon, Lord Adam', HoP, *Commons, 1754–90* · GEC, *Peerage* · *The papers of Sir William Johnson*, ed. J. Sullivan and others, 14 vols. (1921–65), 4–6, 8, 12–13 · *Travels in the American colonies*, ed. N. D. Mereness (1961), 367–453 · Anderson,

Scot. nat., 2.319 • *The correspondence of King George the Third from 1760 to December 1783*, ed. J. Fortescue, 6 vols. (1927–8), also *The later correspondence of George III*, ed. A. Aspinall, 5 vols. (1962–70) • *The later correspondence of George III*, ed. A. Aspinall, 5 vols. (1962–70) • *Letter book of John Watts, merchant and councillor of New York*, New York Historical Society, 61 (1928), 355–6 • *Parliamentary papers of John Robinson, 1774–1784*, ed. W. T. Laprade, CS, 3rd ser., 33 (1922), 6, 19 • B. Lenman, *The Jacobite clans of the Great Glen* (1984), 200–1, 219

Archives NA Scot., papers • NL Scot., legal corresp. • U. Aberdeen, corresp. and papers • W. Sussex RO, corresp. and papers | Glos. RO, letters to Charles Rooke • NA Scot., letters to Sir Archibald Grant • NL Scot., corresp. with Henry Dundas • NRA Scotland, priv. coll., letters to Alexander Burnett • NRA Scotland, priv. coll., letters to William Cumine

Likenesses J. Alexander, oils, 1738, Lennoxlove, Lothian region • F. Bartolozzi, stipple, 1797 (after D. A. de Sequeire), BM, NPG • H. Danloux, oils, 1799, Scot. NPG • J. Kay, caricatures, two etchings, NPG • attrib. J. T. Seton, oils, Crathes Castle and Garden, Aberdeenshire

Gordon, Adam Lindsay (1833–1870), poet, born on 19 October 1833 at Horta on Fayal in the Azores, was the third child and only son of Captain Adam Durnford Gordon (1796–1857), of the Bengal cavalry, and his wife and first cousin, Harriet Elizabeth Gordon (1806–1859), daughter of Robert Gordon, governor of Berbice and Demerara. He was educated at Cheltenham College (where his father became in 1845 professor of oriental languages), Dumbleton rectory school in Gloucestershire, the Royal Military Academy in Woolwich (1848–51), and the Royal Grammar School, Worcester (1852–3). After a somewhat raffish adolescence he left England on 7 August 1853 for South Australia, where he joined the mounted police as a trooper. He left the police in 1855 and became an itinerant horse breaker, but in 1861 he received from his mother's estate some £7000 which enabled him to set up as a gentleman steeplechaser and land speculator. On 20 October 1862 he married Margaret Park (1845–1919) and in March 1865 was elected to the colonial house of assembly as a member for the district of Victoria. He was an infrequent speaker in the house and resigned on 20 November 1866.

In June 1867 Gordon published his first two volumes of poetry: *Ashtaroth: a Dramatic Lyric*, a belated Spasmodic drama with a Faustian theme; and *Sea Spray and Smoke Drift*, a miscellany of medievalizing ballads, melancholy philosophical lyrics, and jaunty sporting rhymes. Later that year, after losing most of his income in unfortunate investments, he opened a livery stable at Ballarat in Victoria. Here his fortunes declined further: he sustained serious injuries in riding accidents; his only child, Annie, died on April 14 1868, before she was one year old; and the stable was all but destroyed by fire. In October 1868 he sold his business and moved to Brighton, a bayside suburb of Melbourne. For a time he tried to establish himself as a regular writer for magazines and joined the literary Yorick Club, but a failed attempt to secure the reversion of the Gordon estate of Esslemont in Scotland induced a crippling depression. On June 23 1870 *Bush Ballads and Galloping Rhymes*, the volume on which his reputation chiefly rests, was published; early on the following morning he walked out along the beach at Brighton and shot himself. He was buried on the 25th in the cemetery at Brighton.

Gordon's life could credibly be viewed as that of a representative 'remittance man', deported to Australia by his embarrassed family and unable even there to establish a career. Contemporaries, however, saw his instability, improvidence, hectic equestrianism, and suicide as characteristics of a Byronic *poète maudit*, and this, perhaps, rather than his work's intrinsic merit, accounts for his brief apotheosis as 'Australia's Poet' (as he is described on the memorial in Poets' Corner, Westminster Abbey, London, unveiled in 1934). Few of Gordon's undemanding, metrically facile poems in fact deal with specifically Australian subjects (and of these the most accomplished and influential is 'The Sick Stockrider', which concisely incorporates a comprehensive 'Bush' iconography). It was their enthusiasm for 'manly' outdoor pursuits as a palliative for spiritual disquiet and their nostalgic allegiance to a code of chivalric values that combined to suggest the persona of an ideally resolute (and resolutely Anglocentric) colonial subject, a stereotype which was ironically at odds with Gordon's tendency to nihilistic despair and which was increasingly to seem superseded as writers of later decades sought to establish a distinctively Australian national voice. ROBERT DINGLEY

Sources G. Hutton, *Adam Lindsay Gordon: the man and the myth* (1978) • E. Humphris and D. Sladen, *Adam Lindsay Gordon and his friends in England and Australia* (1912) • *The last letters, 1868–1870: Adam Lindsay Gordon to John Riddoch*, ed. H. Anderson [1970] • I. F. McLaren, *Adam Lindsay Gordon: a comprehensive bibliography* (1986) • E. Humphris, *The life of Adam Lindsay Gordon* (1933) • C. F. MacRae, *Adam Lindsay Gordon* (1968) • J. H. Ross, *The laureate of the centaurs: a memoir of the life of Adam Lindsay Gordon, with new poems …* (1888) • F. M. Robb, 'Introduction', in *Poems of Adam Lindsay Gordon* (1912), [xv]–cxxiv • J. E. Tenison Woods, 'Personal reminiscences of Adam Lindsay Gordon', *Melbourne Review*, 9 (1884), 131–41 • *The Times* (19 Oct 1933), 8c

Archives Public Record Office of South Australia, Adelaide • Royal Historical Society of Victoria, Melbourne | Mitchell L., NSW • NL Aus. • State Library of South Australia, Adelaide, Mortlock Library of South Australiana, Park Low MSS • State Library of Victoria, Melbourne, La Trobe manuscript collection, John Howlett-Ross MSS • State Library of Victoria, Melbourne, La Trobe manuscript collection, Moir Collection

Likenesses photograph, 1864, repro. in Gordon, *Last letters, 1868–1870* • T. H. Lyttleton, oils, 1869, State Library of Victoria, Melbourne, La Trobe picture collection • F. Madden, sketch, 1870, repro. in Humphris and Sladen, *Adam Lindsay Gordon* • P. Montford, bronze memorial statue, 1932, Spring Street, Melbourne, Australia • Lady Hilton Young, memorial bust, 1934, Westminster Abbey

Gordon, Alexander. *See* Seton, Alexander, first earl of Huntly (*d.* 1470).

Gordon, Alexander, third earl of Huntly (*d.* 1524), magnate, was the eldest surviving son of George *Gordon, second earl of Huntly (1440/41–1501). The identity of his mother has been the subject of debate but was probably Annabella Stewart, youngest daughter of James I, king of Scots, Earl George's second wife, whom he married before 10 March 1460, rather than his third wife, Elizabeth Hay, sister of Nicholas Hay, earl of Erroll, whom he married in August 1471 following his divorce from Annabella earlier in the same year. That Alexander was certainly of age by 1485 when, as master of Huntly, he sat in parliament and served as one of the lords of the articles for James III, serves to reinforce the probability that he was the child of the second marriage. Additionally, on 20 October 1474, he had been contracted to marry Jean (*d.* 1510), daughter of John Stewart, earl of Atholl, half-brother of James II.

Alexander Gordon succeeded as earl in June 1501 and immediately confirmed his family's tradition of loyal service to the crown. In August 1501 he received a wide-ranging commission of lieutenancy over Scotland north of the Mounth. This commission, without limit of time, empowered him to receive the submissions of magnates, employing whatever means necessary, and to collect royal rents in Lochaber. These powers were extended in March 1502, when Huntly was instructed to put down the rebellion raised by Torquil MacLeod of Lewis in support of Donald Dubh MacDonald, claimant to the forfeited lordship of the Isles. He was issued with a fresh commission to set the royal lands in Mamore and Lochaber to reliable men and, in a move designed to undermine MacLeod influence on the Scottish mainland, to let Torquil's lands in Assynt and Coigach. Throughout 1502 and 1503 Huntly was active in the west highlands against the king's enemies, with more powers being delegated to him. In 1503, together with the Earl Marischal, the earl of Crawford, and Lord Lovat, he had command of royal forces in northern Scotland with instructions to subdue the northern Hebrides. A significant step towards that aim came with the capture by Huntly of the rebel strongholds of Eilean Donan and Strome, while the royal position in Lochaber was strengthened by the refortification of Inverlochy Castle. The rebellion was finally ended in autumn 1506 when Huntly occupied the MacLeod lands of Lewis and captured Stornoway Castle.

For Huntly, the rewards of service were great. James IV showered him with favours: commissions to set royal lands in Glengarry, Invergarry, and Knoydart; the heritable grant of the sheriffship of Inverness; authority to appoint deputies to sheriff courts of Lochaber, Ross, and Caithness; and the extension of his authority to enforce the royal will south of the Mounth into Perthshire. These new powers, together with the already extensive Gordon territorial base in the region and the wide network of kinship ties and bonds of lordship, gave Huntly and his connection control of a vast area embracing Aberdeenshire, Moray, the central and west highlands, and most of the country north of the Great Glen. Following his first wife's death on 27 October 1510, he married in July 1511 Elizabeth, daughter of Andrew, Lord Gray, widow of John Lyon, Lord Glamis; they had no children.

Together with Lord Hume, Huntly next commanded the vanguard of the Scottish army at Flodden, on 9 September 1513, and was one of the few Scottish magnates to survive that carnage. The following month, in parliament at Perth, together with Archibald Douglas, sixth earl of Angus, and James Beaton, archbishop of Glasgow, he was appointed to the council to aid the queen mother, Margaret Tudor, in the government in the name of her young son, James V. He joined with Margaret and Angus to block the second earl of Arran's bid to assume the regency, but subsequently supported the fourth duke of Albany, who had been appointed to the regency in 1515, against his former associates. In May 1517 he was appointed to the council empowered to govern Scotland during Albany's visit to France, and in February 1518 he was granted a commission of lieutenancy over all Scotland excepting the territories controlled by the third earl of Argyll. On Albany's return in 1520 Huntly again supported his government, but ill health evidently prevented him from fulfilling any active role. Antipathy towards Albany's anti-English policies may explain his absence from the army mustered to invade England in October 1523; but he was evidently in declining health and failed to attend the Edinburgh parliament of 23 November. He died at Perth on 21 January 1524 and was buried in the choir of the Dominican convent there. He was succeeded as earl by his grandson George *Gordon, son of John, Lord Gordon (*d.* 1517), and his wife, Margaret, the illegitimate daughter of James IV and Margaret Drummond.

Huntly had four sons and two daughters from his first marriage: George, who died young; John, Lord Gordon, father of the fourth earl; Alexander, ancestor of the Gordons of Cluny; William *Gordon, later bishop of Aberdeen; Jean, wife of Colin Campbell, third earl of Argyll; and Christian, wife of Sir Robert Menzies. Huntly was survived by his wife Elizabeth, who was married a third time, in 1525, to George Leslie, fourth earl of Rothes; she died in 1526. RICHARD D. ORAM

Sources J. M. Thomson and others, eds., *Registrum magni sigilli regum Scotorum / The register of the great seal of Scotland*, 11 vols. (1882–1914), vol. 2 • *APS*, 1424–1567 • M. Livingstone, D. Hay Fleming, and others, eds., *Registrum secreti sigilli regum Scotorum / The register of the privy seal of Scotland*, 1 (1908) • T. Dickson and J. B. Paul, eds., *Compota thesaurariorum regum Scotorum / Accounts of the lord high treasurer of Scotland*, 1–2 (1877–1900) • N. Macdougall, *James IV* (1989); repr. (1997) • N. MacDougall, 'Achilles heel? The earldom of Ross, the lordship of the isles and the Stewart kings, 1449–1507', in N. J. Cowan and R. A. Macdonald, *Alba: Celtic Scotland in the medieval era* (2000) • R. Nicholson, *Scotland: the later middle ages* (1974), vol. 2 of *The Edinburgh history of Scotland*, ed. G. Donaldson (1965–75) • G. Donaldson, *Scotland: James V to James VII* (1965), vol. 3 of *The Edinburgh history of Scotland* (1965–75) • *Scots peerage*, 4.531–3 • N. Macdougall, *James III: a political study* (1982) • R. Milne, ed., *The Blackfriars of Perth* (1893) • J. Anderson, ed., *Calendar of the Laing charters, AD 854–1837, belonging to the University of Edinburgh* (1899)
Archives NA Scot., charters

Gordon, Alexander (*c.*1516–1575), bishop of Galloway, was the second son of John, Lord Gordon (*d.* 1517), eldest son of the third earl of Huntly (whom he predeceased) and Margaret, daughter of *James IV and his mistress Margaret *Drummond. His mother subsequently married Sir John Drummond of Innerpeffry, and his maternal grandmother was the daughter of John, first Lord Drummond. Alexander was thus a cousin of Mary, queen of Scots, and closely connected to two powerful noble families, the Gordons and the Drummonds. Such ties inevitably helped him to secure ecclesiastical preferment. He almost certainly studied at the University of Aberdeen, and then at Paris in 1537–8. In 1544 he was nominated and elected bishop of Caithness, but Robert Stewart, who had been bishop-elect since January 1542, resisted the intruder and although never consecrated retained the title until his death in 1586. In April 1548 Mary of Guise, who needed Gordon support, undertook to secure Gordon a pension in compensation for his failure to obtain the see. On 5 March 1550 Gordon was provided to the archbishopric of Glasgow. He was probably consecrated in Rome later that year, but he resigned in 1551 and on 4 September was translated to the archbishopric of Athens *in partibus*. He also became commendator of the Augustinian abbey of Inchaffray. On 26 November 1553, following the death of Roderick Maclean, bishop of the Isles, Gordon was granted the temporalities of that see, and also became commendator of Iona. Soon afterwards he was being referred to as bishop-elect.

Probably in September 1558 Andrew Durie, bishop of Galloway, died, and in the following February Gordon was translated to the vacant see. He retained Inchaffray until 1565, and also held the Premonstratensian abbey of Tongland *in commendam*. He took part in the last provincial council of the Scottish church, held in the Edinburgh Blackfriars in March 1559. Proposals for innovation in doctrine, and for the use of the vernacular in public worship, were rejected, but some reformation of discipline was agreed; Gordon was one of six dignitaries who were appointed advisers to the two archbishops in implementing the council's statutes. These measures having failed to stem the pressure for radical reform, in September 1559 he became associated with the protestant lords, and within a month he was a member of their council for religion alongside John Knox, John Willock, and Christopher Goodman. On 27 February 1560 he joined in ratifying the convention of Leith, which established Scotland's alliance with England against France, and soon followed John Winram, his coadjutor among the six advisers, in moving decisively into the ranks of the reformers; on 27 April he subscribed the contract to defend the liberty of the gospel, and later that year was reported to be preaching daily. In the parliament of 1560 he was the only one of the four bishops present to vote for the acts which sanctioned the new confession of faith, renounced the jurisdiction of the pope, and prohibited the mass. His reward, according to the English ambassador, was to be confirmed as bishop of Galloway.

On 17 January 1561 Gordon subscribed the first 'Book of Discipline', substituting superintendents for the hierarchy, but with the proviso that the existing bishops should enjoy their revenues for life on condition of their embracing the Reformation and making provision for a reformed ministry within their dioceses. Although his diocese was included within the superintendency of Dumfries, Gordon continued to exercise episcopal jurisdiction and also retained the income he had enjoyed as bishop. But he also aspired to a superintendent's position and formally applied for it in 1562, and though the assembly refused he none the less came to be regularly styled 'commissioner', 'overseer', or 'superintendent' of Galloway, and to be allowed remission of the third of his revenues (otherwise taken in taxes) in acknowledgement of his services. But he did not receive a superintendent's salary.

Gordon's position in the reformed kirk was not straightforward. There can be no doubt of his commitment to the Reformation, especially in the early 1560s, when he made strenuous and successful efforts to install reformed clergy in the parishes of his diocese. But as bishop of Galloway he was also *ex officio* dean of the Chapel Royal, a position which gave him spiritual authority not only over the collegiate church at Stirling but also over all the Scottish royal palaces. The fact that under Mary Catholic priests continued to minister in these establishments when she was present does not seem to have affected Gordon's religious position, but as time passed he did become increasingly attached to the court. In November 1565 he became first a privy councillor and then a senator of the college of justice, to the disapproval of the general assembly, which declared that he 'had not visited these three years bygone the kirks within his charge', but that he 'haunted court too much, and had now purchased to be one of the session and privy council, which cannot agree with the office of a pastor or bishop' (Donaldson, 'Alexander Gordon', 14). Meanwhile the progress of reform in Galloway had slowed perceptibly, and in July 1568 the assembly demanded that he choose between his lay and ecclesiastical offices.

By now Gordon was almost entirely preoccupied with secular politics. On 10 February 1567, for instance, he was a signatory to the privy council's letter to the queen regent of France reporting Lord Darnley's have preached murder, and he was present at the council meeting of 28 March which ordered that the earl of Bothwell be put on trial for it. But he remained closely attached to Queen Mary's cause, and on 20 April signed the bond acquitting Bothwell and recommending him a suitable husband for Mary, even though the earl was then married to the bishop's own niece Jane. When the earl of Moray was appointed regent on 22 August Gordon temporized, and took his place in the December parliament which confirmed Mary's abdication. However, when she escaped from Lochleven he signed the bond of 8 May 1568 calling for her restoration. Thereafter he continued to pray for her in public and acted as one of her commissioners to England in 1570 and 1571. Meanwhile the queen's party had occupied Edinburgh, and on 17 June 1571 Gordon is reported to have preached in St Giles's, making no effort to conceal Mary's shortcomings but declaring that 'na inferiour subiect hes power to deprive or depose their lauchfull magistrate' (Kirk, 247). He was forfeited for treason by the king's party, but restored early in 1573.

Gordon's position in the kirk was now very difficult. On 4 January 1568 he had resigned his see with its temporalities in favour of his son John, though retaining the supervisory role conferred on him by the assembly; however, this did not take effect, and he continued to receive all the emoluments of office. In 1569 the assembly inhibited him from exercising any function in the kirk; presentations to parishes were no longer directed to him, and John Row, minister of Perth, was appointed commissioner to visit the kirks of Galloway. In August 1572 the general assembly charged him with intruding himself into the ministry in Edinburgh and with acknowledging the queen's authority, and at the next August assembly he was ordered to do public penance in sackcloth on three successive Sundays. But in March following this was commuted to one day's penance, without sackcloth, and by August 1574 he seems to have been back in his diocese, since the assembly instructed him to assist in maintaining discipline there. Gordon died at Clarie House, Penninghame, Wigtownshire, on 11 November 1575.

Probably in the early 1540s Gordon had entered into a liaison with Barbara Logie, thought to be a daughter of David Logie of King's Cramond, near Edinburgh. The bishop disponed a canon's portion in Tongland Abbey to her brother Robert. Their eldest son, John *Gordon, was born on 1 September 1544, two years before his parents were said to have married *per verba de presenti*. The marriage was publicly acknowledged in 1560. The other children were Alexander, who probably died young; Lawrence, who became commendator of Glenluce Abbey in 1582; George (*d*. 1588), who had crown provision to the see of Galloway when John resigned it in 1586 but who probably died before being consecrated; Robert, who was killed in a duel in France; and Barbara, who married Anthony Stewart, parson of Penninghame, and to whom her father left the lands of Clarie in that parish. Gordon did not die rich, leaving goods worth less than £800 Scots. He had earlier claimed that he was obliged to dispose of church property in order to pay debts arising from the cost of papal bulls in the 1550s. Be that as it may, in 1610 he was criticized by Bishop Gavin Hamilton for having seriously reduced the revenues of the see. DUNCAN SHAW

Sources *Scots peerage*, 4.531–3 • G. Donaldson, 'Alexander Gordon, bishop of Galloway', *Reformed by bishops* (1987), 1–18 • A. Ross, 'More about the archbishop of Athens', *Innes Review*, 14 (1963), 30–37 • J. M. Thomson and others, eds., *Registrum magni sigilli regum Scotorum / The register of the great seal of Scotland*, 11 vols. (1882–1914), vol. 4, pp. 848, 858 • G. Donaldson, ed., *The register of the great seal of Scotland, 1575–1580* (1966), 1049, 1235 • *Fasti Scot.*, new edn, 7.343 • D. E. R. Watt, ed., *Fasti ecclesiae Scoticanae medii aevi ad annum 1638*, [2nd edn], Scottish RS, new ser., 1 (1969) • J. Kirk, *Patterns of reform: continuity and change in the Reformation kirk* (1989) • D. Mullan, *Episcopacy in Scotland* (1986) • M. Merriman, *The rough wooings: Mary queen of Scots, 1542–1551* (2000)

Wealth at death under £800 Scots value of estate and goods: Donaldson, 'Alexander Gordon', 16

Gordon, Alexander, twelfth earl of Sutherland (1552–1594). *See under* Gordon, John, eleventh earl of Sutherland (1525–1567).

Gordon, Alexander, of Earlston (1587–1654), landowner and politician, was the eldest son of John Gordon of Airds and Earlston (*d*. in or before 1628) and Mary, daughter of Chalmers of Gadgirth, in Ayrshire. The Gordons of Earlston were a cadet branch of the Gordons of Lochinvar, related to several branches of the Gordon family in the stewartry of Kirkcudbright and vicinity. In 1612 Alexander married Elizabeth, daughter of John Gordon of Murefad and Penninghame, who was the brother of Sir John Gordon of Lochinvar, grandfather to Sir John Gordon of Lochinvar, first Viscount Kenmure. He was served heir to his father in the lands of Earlston and others on 23 October 1628 and to his grandmother, Elizabeth Gordon of Blaiket, Dumfriesshire, on 29 July 1634.

Gordon was indicted by the court of justiciary in 1623, accused of usurping the king's authority by apprehending and detaining a man in his private prison. He was required to find caution to appear on fifteen days' warning for sentence if required. He was appointed a justice of the peace for Kirkcudbright in 1634 and was charged by the privy council in 1637 with overstepping the bounds of his office. He is said to have refused Charles I's request to purchase a title as one of the baronets of Nova Scotia.

Tradition has credited Earlston's great-grandfather Alexander Gordon of Airds with being one of the earliest adherents of the Reformation in Galloway. Having encountered protestant ideas while on a visit to England, Gordon of Airds brought home a copy of Wyclif's New Testament, which he read to his family, tenants, and others. Earlston continued the family tradition, as an opponent of episcopacy and the changes which Charles I sought to make in the church. Described by a contemporary, the radical minister John Livingstone, as 'a man of great spirit, but much subdued by inward exercise, and who attained the most rare experiences of douncasting and uplifting' (Livingstone, 1.343), Earlston attended several religious meetings led by Livingstone, some of which were held in his own house. He, his wife, and his son William *Gordon (1614–1679) were correspondents of Samuel Rutherford, several of whose letters to them are printed in *The Letters of Samuel Rutherford*. He experienced persistent problems with his refusal to present an episcopal nominee to a local parish, a matter which was vigorously pursued by the bishop of Galloway, Thomas Sydserff. In 1637 Sydserff sought to fine Earlston 500 merks and confine him in Montrose, but the sentence of banishment was overturned by the privy council on payment of the fine. Lord Lorne, the future marquess of Argyll, interceded for Earlston, who was at that time, with the consent of Lorne and the other tutors of the second Viscount Kenmure, taking responsibility for much of Kenmure's affairs during his minority. Earlston subscribed the petition against the service book drawn up by the presbytery of Kirkcudbright in 1637 and was a member of the 1638 general assembly.

Earlston also played an active part in the covenanting administration. He was a member of the committee of war for the stewartry of Kirkcudbright and presented the committee's petition against the engagement on behalf of Charles I in 1648. He was chosen to represent Kirkcudbrightshire in the parliament of 1641 and served as a commissioner for the common burdens and for receiving brotherly assistance from the English parliament and on the commission for the plantation of kirks. He was appointed as a collector for the loan and tax for Kirkcudbright in 1643.

Earlston died in 1654, having been stricken with the palsy for some years before his death. He was survived by his wife, whose testament was registered in 1665, but his eldest son, John, predeceased him on 29 October 1645 and he was succeeded by his second son, William. A third son, Robert, was a merchant and his daughter Margaret married Francis Hay of Arioland. SHARON ADAMS

Sources *The letters and journals of Robert Baillie*, ed. D. Laing, 3 vols. (1841–2) • J. Livingstone, 'A brief historical relation of the life of Mr John Livingstone', *Select biographies*, ed. W. K. Tweedie, 1, Wodrow Society, 7/1 (1845), 127–97 • *The letters of Samuel Rutherford*, ed. A. Bonar (1891) • P. H. McKerlie, *History of lands and their owners in Galloway* (1994) • M. D. Young, ed., *The parliaments of Scotland: burgh and shire commissioners*, 2 vols. (1992–3) • *APS* • *DNB*

Gordon, Alexander, of Earlston (1650–1726), covenanter and conspirator, was the eldest son of William *Gordon of Earlston (1614–1679) and Mary (*d.* 1697), second daughter of Sir John Hope of Craighall, Fife. He had twelve siblings, most of whom died young with the exception of William, of Afton, whom Queen Anne made a baronet, John, a surgeon of Carleton, and Margaret, who married Sir James Holborn of Menstrie in 1682. On 16 November 1676 he married Janet (1653–1697), eldest daughter of Sir Thomas Hamilton of Preston and his wife, Anna; at this time he inherited his father's estate, including debts totalling 14,200 merks. Their children included Ann (*b.* 1679), William, Sir Thomas (26 Oct 1685–23 March 1769), Margaret (*b.* 1687), Robert (1688–1750), Archibald (1691–1754), Hope (*d.* 1736), Mary (*b.* 1689), and Jane.

A zealous covenanter like his father, Gordon was cited for having attended house and field conventicles since 1674, and when he failed to appear on 18 February 1679 he was denounced as a rebel. He fought with the covenanters in the Bothwell Bridge uprising. His father was killed in the fighting on 22 June 1679, but Gordon escaped his pursuers in Hamilton by dressing in female attire and rocking a cradle. On 26 June a royal proclamation included the names of father and son among those denounced as rebels. When he failed to appear before the justiciary court at Edinburgh, Gordon was pronounced guilty of treason on 19 February 1680, his estate was forfeited, and he was sentenced to death. Unable to apprehend him, the government issued another proclamation on 8 October 1681 and three days later dispatched troops to be garrisoned at Earlston. Gordon and his wife escaped to the Netherlands, but he returned to Scotland in 1682 and became affiliated with a group of radical covenanters known as the United Societies. He would later confess that it comprised approximately eighty local groups with a total membership of more than 7000.

On 15 March 1682 a general meeting of the societies near Muirkirk, Ayrshire, appointed Gordon its envoy to other nations for the purpose of recounting the repression of the Scottish church and the societies' opposition to popery, prelacy, and Erastianism. With his assistant John Nisbet he went to London in April, and from there he alone travelled to the Netherlands, seeking financial assistance and a place to which persecuted covenanters could emigrate. At the time of the London shrieval election in July, Nisbet and Robert Murray, an agent of Shaftesbury, informed him of secret discussions in London concerning an insurrection to compel the king to exclude James from the succession. The earl of Argyll was also conferring with Shaftesbury about a possible uprising in Scotland, which explains the contact with Nisbet and Gordon.

At its general meeting on 11 August 1682 the societies recalled Gordon, whose efforts to raise money had been unsuccessful, and appointed his brother-in-law Robert Hamilton of Preston as his associate in the Netherlands. The two envoys subsequently enlisted the support of William Brackel, minister at Leeuwarden, Friesland, for a plan to send four men to study for the ministry at the University of Groningen; three, including James Renwick, eventually went.

A glimpse of the underground network in which Gordon was now involved is provided in a partly encoded letter to the dissident printer Francis Smith in Rotterdam from Anne Smith, the wife of a wealthy sugar baker who had hidden Argyll in London. She informed Smith that a messenger was *en route* for the Netherlands with something he had requested, and this the messenger was to leave with Gordon. About the same time Nisbet wrote to Gordon using the latter's alias, Alexander Pringle, concerning things that had been done at the societies' behest. Moreover, in December or January Gordon learned that Argyll was planning an insurrection in Scotland with funding from his English allies.

At a general meeting on 14 February 1683 the societies discussed a letter from Nisbet indicating that English militants were interested in an alliance, and shortly thereafter the societies, having received letters of import from the Netherlands, recalled Gordon for consultation. After his return to the Netherlands he received a coded letter from Nisbet dated 20 March 1683 concerning discussions about co-ordinated uprisings in England and Scotland. Recalled to London, Gordon learned more about this from Murray and Nisbet, but he declined Murray's invitation to meet with Lord William Russell, Ford, Lord Grey, the minister Robert Ferguson, and others involved in the discussions. Subsequently he received a letter in canting language dated 2 May from Robert Johnston, one of Grey's associates, offering to accompany him to Scotland and confer with the United Societies. On 8 May he reported to a general meeting of the societies in Edinburgh, at which time the delegates agreed to take up arms only in self-defence or to aid fellow protestants. With his servant George Aitken, alias Edward Leviston, Gordon boarded a ship at Newcastle, but before it sailed customs agents arrested both men on 1 June. The incriminating papers they desperately threw overboard were retrieved, and among them was a document intended for dissidents in London explaining why the societies refused to join in a rebellion with men opposed to God's principles.

Gordon was transported under heavy guard from Newcastle to Edinburgh and confined in the Tolbooth. Nisbet was arrested on 2 July, but the government had inadequate evidence to convict him, whereas Aitken was condemned to death on 10 July for having harboured Gordon. Initially Gordon was treated moderately in the hope of obtaining a full confession. No trial was necessary because he was already under sentence of death, and he appeared in the justiciary court on 16 August for a formal reading of the earlier judgment. His execution was scheduled for 28 September. Hoping to extract a fuller confession, the privy council enquired of the Scottish secretaries of state if a convicted man could be tortured. The lord advocate ruled this was acceptable if the questioning dealt with the wider conspiracy. In the meantime, on 11 September the council received a petition from Gordon expressing remorse and seeking a pardon. This led to the first of a series of reprieves. When he was interrogated with the instrument of torture (the boots) in full view on 25 September his responses seemed full but added nothing to what the authorities already knew about the plotting. He admitted having heard about the discussions for uprisings centring on Monmouth and Argyll, having met Murray and Nisbet in London, and having received Nisbet's letter of 20 March, which, he confessed, referred to the proposed insurrections. When he was brought back for additional questioning on 23 November he manifested symptoms of mental illness: 'He thro fear or distraction roared out like a bull, and cryed and struck about him' before swooning (*Historical Notices*, 465). Two physicians and a surgeon subsequently confirmed his illness. On 29 November the council therefore ordered his transfer from the Tolbooth to Edinburgh Castle, where he could have access to fresh air. The councillors discussed another petition from him on 7 December, noting that he now professed his innocence. On 13 December they concluded that he had recovered, but they recommended another delay in his execution to enable him to provide a full written account despite the lord advocate's desire to execute him as a warning to others. After he returned to the Tolbooth in the spring the council ordered that he be confined on the Isle of Bass on 5 May and again on 7 August 1684. Brought back to the Tolbooth in the latter month to confront the conspirator William Spence, he failed in his attempt to escape and denied knowing who had smuggled him a knife, chisel, and rope. On 16 September the council ordered that he be incarcerated in Blackness Castle. On 8 January 1685, when he was again in the Tolbooth, the council authorized his release from irons if he offered security not to escape.

Gordon remained in prison until 5 June 1689, spending his time studying heraldry, carving wood, and enjoying his wife's company. Three of his children—Thomas, Margaret, and Robert—were conceived while he was a prisoner. Upon learning of his liberation, he insisted on recording a formal protest against his wrongful incarceration. In May 1690 he returned to Earlston, which had been restored after his release, though much of it had to be sold or mortgaged owing to heavy debts. Following the death of his first wife on 26 February 1697, he married Marion (1678–1748), daughter of Alexander Gordon, fifth Viscount Kenmure, on 8 March 1698. They had two children: William, of Culvennan (1706–1757), and Grizell (1703–1740), who married Alexander Gordon of Carleton in 1721. In 1708 Gordon assigned his estate, valued at £300 per annum, to his son Thomas, who assumed his debts of £1687 sterling. Some time after Thomas married Ann, coheir of the wealthy merchant William Boick, on 20 January 1710, Gordon apparently regained possession of the estate, for he had sasine in November 1710 and retained it for at least another nine years. Following his death at Airds on 10 November 1726, he was interred in the Dalry churchyard. Among his possessions were letters and sermon notes pertaining to such radical covenanters as James Guthry, Donald Cargill, David Hackston, and James Renwick. Some of Janet Gordon's religious writings were posthumously published as *An Account of the Particular Soliloquies and Covenant Engagements* (1801).

RICHARD L. GREAVES

Sources *Reg. PCS*, 3rd ser., vols. 6–10 • M. Shields, *Faithful contendings displayed* (1780) • PRO, SP 29/424/46, 184; 29/425/215; 29/427/43, 43.1; 29/428/93; 29/432/103; 29/434/90; 29/435/41; 44/56, pp. 72–3; 44/335, p. 4 • *State trials*, 6.1218–19; 11.45–64 • [T. Sprat], *Copies of the informations and original papers relating to the proof of the horrid conspiracy against the late king, his present majesty and the government*, 3rd edn (1685) • Burke, *Peerage* (1967), 1055–6 • U. Nott., MS PwV 95, pp. 231, 239 • *CSP dom.*, 1683–4 • R. L. Greaves, *Secrets of the kingdom: British radicals from the Popish Plot to the revolution of 1688–89* (1992) • [G. Mackenzie], *A true and plain account of the discoveries made in Scotland, of the late conspiracies against his majesty and the government* (1685) • Bodl. Oxf., MS Tanner 34, fols. 286r–287v • *The manuscripts of his grace the duke of Buccleuch and Queensberry … preserved at Drumlanrig Castle*, 2 vols., HMC, 44 (1897–1903), vol. 1, pp. 200–01, 273–4; vol. 2, pp. 118–19 • *Report of the Laing manuscripts*, 1, HMC, 72 (1914), 316 • *Historical notices of Scotish affairs, selected from the manuscripts of Sir John Lauder of Fountainhall*, ed. D. Laing, 2 vols., Bannatyne Club, 87 (1848) • P. H. M'Kerlie, *History of the lands and their owners in Galloway*, 5 vols. (1870–79), vols. 3–4 • R. Wodrow, *The history of the sufferings of the Church of Scotland from the Restoration to the revolution*, ed. R. Burns, 3 (1829), 108, 470, 472; 4 (1830), 502–3 • T. Sprat, *A true account and declaration of the horrid conspiracy*, 3rd edn (1686)
Archives U. Edin. L., papers | Bodl. Oxf., Tanner MS 34 • PRO, state papers domestic, 29/424 through 29/428; 29/432; 29/435; 44/56; 44/335 • U. Nott., MS PwV 95

Gordon, Alexander, second duke of Gordon (*c*.1678–1728), Jacobite sympathizer and landowner, was the only son of George *Gordon, first duke of Gordon (*b*. in or before 1649, *d*. 1716), and Lady Elizabeth Howard (*d*. 1732), eldest surviving daughter of the sixth duke of Norfolk. Styled marquess of Huntly from 1684 to 1716, he was educated in the Roman Catholic faith and followed his family's attachment to the Stuarts, much encouraged by his mother, who retired to a convent in Flanders before 1696, was separated from the duke in 1707, and later returned to Scotland where she was active in the Jacobite cause. From 1701 to 1705 Huntly travelled in Europe. He visited several courts and stayed with Cosimo de' Medici, grand duke of Tuscany, who became a lifelong friend; he visited Pope Clement XI in Rome and was favourably received at the court of the margrave of Ansbach, whose sister Caroline became queen consort of George II of Great Britain.

Huntly was in England at the time of his father's arrest as a Jacobite suspect in 1708 and was required to give a bond to surrender if called upon. Huntly's own allegiances were seriously complicated by his marriage on 13 February 1707 to Lady Henrietta (1681/2–1760) [*see* Gordon, Henrietta], second daughter of Charles *Mordaunt, earl of

Peterborough and Monmouth, who was a staunch protestant. Huntly wavered between loyalty to his Jacobite mother and to his resolutely whiggish wife, and ultimately gained the reputation as a 'trimmer' among fellow Jacobites. He was described by Robert Patten as 'one of the most unconstant men of his Age' (Tayler and Tayler, *1715: the Story of the Rising*, 218), for which evidence can be found in his support for the Act of Union and Queen Anne, but his opposition to the Hanoverian succession. His father was arrested and imprisoned in August 1715 in Edinburgh Castle and detained in the Citadel, Leith. Possessing large estates in the north-east of Scotland, the family was the leader of the powerful Gordon clan. Huntly said his tenants were 'bound by their tacks to attend me at hosting [war] and hunting' (ibid., 201) and he had call on 3000 men in his district.

In prison the duke's health deteriorated, and Huntly emerged as a possible leader of the Jacobite forces. On 31 August 1715, on the eve of the rising, an 'Act for encouraging loyalty in Scotland' received the royal assent and Huntly was summoned to Edinburgh to prove his allegiance to the government. Instead he joined the council to co-ordinate the Jacobite forces under the earl of Mar at Aboyne in early September. Huntly had probably been preparing for the uprising throughout the summer. An informer wrote that 'Huntly is gone with all his vassals to joyn Mar'. On 8 November he proclaimed the Chevalier St George (James Stuart) as king at Gordon Castle. He also tried to raise Moray in the cause. His own massive but poorly co-ordinated contingent of 500 horse and 1200 foot soldiers joined the march on Perth, then the battle of Sheriffmuir on 13 November. Their role was undistinguished, and Huntly's reputation was not enhanced.

After Sheriffmuir, Huntly and other leaders returned north to defend their territories from the earl of Sutherland, who had meanwhile recaptured Inverness. This weakened Mar's forces, but Huntly was probably misled by Mar over the support available in England and the timing of James Stuart's arrival with troops and money. Huntly may have sued for surrender even before Sheriffmuir, and he now treated with the duke of Argyll to make a truce with the northern whigs. Though not immediately successful, this indicated Huntly's bending to the authority of government. On news of James's arrival in Britain, Huntly is said to have expressed fear for his own total ruin. On 11 February 1716 he made his formal capitulation and admitted a government garrison to Gordon Castle in Banffshire.

To his surprise Huntly was committed to prison in Edinburgh in April, where he remained for six months. He was shown no special favour and was sent to Carlisle for trial, but the order was rescinded before his arrival. He was eventually absolved by the Act of Grace and Pardon of 1717 'in regard of having quitted the rebels in time'. He benefited from public sympathy in Scotland, which made any kind of trial improbable, and from the conciliatory policy of George I towards the rebels. He was also favoured by the intercession of the earl of Sutherland, who believed Huntly (now duke of Gordon, following his father's death in December 1716) could be serviceable in suppressing rebellion in the highlands. Gordon now proclaimed his total loyalty to the whig government and he pledged to use his influence to reconcile the north-east to the house of Hanover. Gordon had thus extricated himself from the failure of the 'Fifteen with astonishingly little loss to himself, his family, or his estate. But in hedging his bets he had undermined the Jacobite cause. According to one hostile commentator Gordon 'displayed neither courage nor honour' (Petrie, 257), but Bruce Lenman considers it 'a sensible performance under difficult conditions' (Lenman, 142).

As second duke, Gordon took up permanent residence at Gordon Castle, and thereafter played no further part in public affairs. He conspicuously kept clear of the further eruption of Jacobite insurgence in 1719, preferring to live in princely style and to continue his warm communications with royal, papal, and aristocratic friends in Europe. 'Handsome in appearance, kindly in disposition, liberal to his tenants, and generous to the poor', he died on 28 November 1728 and was buried at Elgin.

Gordon was survived by his wife, who took an active part in the agricultural improvement of the estates. She was left to raise a family of four sons, including the army officer and politician Adam *Gordon, and seven daughters, whom she determined to raise in the protestant faith. In recognition, in 1730 the general assembly of the Church of Scotland sent its warm appreciation, and in 1735 the government settled £1000 per annum on her. This, however, was withdrawn in 1745, apparently because the duchess had briefly fraternized with Prince Charles Edward Stuart. Her own sons were totally divided by the 1745 rising: in contrast to the eldest, Cosmo George, third duke of Gordon (1720/21–1752), who was reluctant to join the 'Forty-Five, Lord Lewis *Gordon (*c.*1725–1754) was a willing follower of the Jacobite cause. The duchess died at Prestonhall, near Edinburgh, on 11 October 1760.

Eric Richards

Sources A. Tayler and H. Tayler, *1715: the story of the rising* (1936) • J. Baynes, *The Jacobite rising of 1715* (1970) • C. Petrie, *The Jacobite movement*, 3rd edn (1958) • B. Lenman, *The Jacobite risings in Britain, 1689–1746* (1980) • the marquess of Huntly, *The Cock o' the North* (1935) • GEC, *Peerage*, new edn, vol. 5 • A. Tayler and H. Tayler, *The Old Chevalier* (1934) • A. Tayler and H. Tayler, eds., *The Stuart papers at Windsor* (1939) • H. Tayler, ed., *Jacobite epilogue* (1941) • B. Lenman, *The Jacobite cause* (1986) • A. I. Macinnes, *Clanship, commerce, and the house of Stuart, 1603–1788* (1996)

Archives NA Scot., corresp. • Royal Arch., corresp. and related material • W. Sussex RO, corresp. and papers | NL Scot., letters to Cumming of Altyre

Likenesses J. Medina, group portrait, Gordon Castle Collection

Gordon, Alexander (*c.*1692–1754?), antiquary and singer, was born probably in Aberdeen, where his father, James Gordon, who was still living in 1723, was a merchant and sometime dean of guild. He took the degree of master of arts at Aberdeen University, and seems to have become proficient in classical and modern languages and to have developed a talent for both music and fine art. In later years, however, his friend and scholarly patron Sir John Clerk of Penicuik, second baronet and baron of the exchequer in Scotland, regularly excused Gordon's failings in one way or another by saying that he had done well for one of his background and education; and Clerk (though a distinguished composer himself) further appeared to belittle Gordon's early professional career as a singer by observing that he had been 'bred up in the idleness of a musitian, but his head has now taken a more useful, at least a more diverting turn' towards that of a learned antiquary. Yet Clerk was also fair in his assessment of a career remarkable for its breadth and variety: 'Whatever weaknesses you may discover about him he is one of the most friendly grateful men I ever knew in my life & prodigiously sober & laborious' (Brown, *Hobby-horsical Antiquary*, 27–8).

Italy and opera Gordon appears to have gone abroad after leaving Aberdeen (though he may first have taught languages, music, and possibly drawing in his home city) and may well have acted as a travelling tutor in France, Germany, and Italy. There art and antiquities attracted his attention: he later spoke of his role in preserving the amphitheatre at Capua from vandalism and claimed credit for having bought certain works of art for British patrons. His familiarity with Italian collections, classical monuments, and the Renaissance and baroque buildings of Rome, Naples, and Venice was to be demonstrated in the preface to his most celebrated antiquarian publication. However, his principal occupation was that of operatic tenor. As a singer he attained some distinction, and a reputation that lasted for the rest of his life. For as long as he lived in Britain he never quite abandoned his connection with what he called 'the fiddling race' and its 'harmonious commodity' (Clerk papers, 5023/3/34; Alexander Gordon to Charles Mackie, 2 June 1730, EUL, MS La. II.220). His successful career on the Italian stage was held up as an example in Joseph Mitchell's 'Ode on the Power of Musick', prefaced to Alexander Malcolm's *A Treatise of Musick* (1721):

> *Gordon's* brave Ambition fir'd
> Beyond the tow'ring *Alps*, untir'd …

Gordon's first recorded operatic appearance in Italy was in 1716, when he sang at Messina in Carlo Monza's *La principessa fedele*, being listed as 'Alessandro Gordon, Britannico'. During the season 1717–18 he sang at the Teatro di San Bartolomeo in Naples. The certain evidence for his Italian operatic career is slight, but the fact that a young foreigner from remote Scotland should have found a place in one of Italy's greatest theatres is indication enough that he must have had wider experience.

On 7 December 1719 there was a benefit concert at the theatre in Lincoln's Inn Fields, London, for Gordon, 'lately arriv'd from Italy'. He may have brought back to England music by the Neapolitan composers Mancini and Porpora, and possibly also the score of *Tigrane* by Alessandro Scarlatti. His operatic début in London was in Giovanni Porta's *Numitor* at the King's Theatre, Haymarket, in April 1720, and that season he also sang in works by Handel and Domenico Scarlatti. He was active in opera again in 1723, having filled the intervening years with concert and dramatic performances. But in 1723 his enthusiasm for antiquarian pursuits drew him away from London to his native Scotland and the activities for which he is most celebrated. His desertion of the London stage was cited as inspiration for his contemporary William Corbett

> to cleanly Edinburgh repair,
> And from ten stories high breathe Northern Air;
> With tuneful *G[o]rd[o]n* join, and thus unite
> Rough *Italy* with *Scotland* the polite.
> (Morey, 334)

Nevertheless he sang occasionally in Edinburgh in 1723–4, and was to manifest a continuing interest in the theatre with the publication and performance of his only comedy, *Lupone, or, The Inquisitor*, in London in 1731, though this had been written in 1723. After a long interval he made brief concert appearances at Covent Garden in 1739 and 1741, with the purpose of clearing the debt which had become the companion of a life of irregular employment as antiquary, bookseller, drawing-master, teacher of Italian, would-be connoisseur, and authority on the art collections of London.

The Scottish antiquary Gordon's inspiration to investigate the Roman antiquities of Scotland and northern England was derived from remarks made by William Stukeley in his pamphlet on Arthur's O'on, *An Account of a Roman Temple* (1720), and the immediate impetus came from the patronage of the eighth earl of Pembroke, himself an antiquarian, who apparently sent Gordon north to undertake his survey. Stukeley had expressed surprise and disappointment that Scotsmen took so little interest in the monuments and artefacts about them. Gordon's life was to be dedicated to the righting of that wrong. At its best his crusade led to the compilation of a record of great contemporary importance and some lasting value; at worst to indulgence in a game of cultural nationalism or political antiquarianism where the Roman walls and camps, and the excavated swords and spears allegedly representing conquerors opposed or expelled, became like pawns to be moved about so as to achieve some moral advantage for Scotland over England. Gordon saw parallels between, on the one hand, the ancient Caledonians and Romans and, on the other, the post-union north Britons and 'Roman' Englishmen of his own day. In this his thinking marched along similar lines to that of Sir John Clerk, though it was not kept in check as by Clerk's pragmatism and scholarly common sense. *Itinerarium septentrionale* (1726) is Gordon's lasting memorial in which work he not only enshrined the antiquities of Roman Scotland and traced the route of Agricola's campaign but also ensured his own immortality in the fiction of Walter Scott. Gordon's folio is the book which Mr Jonathan Oldbuck, the antiquary in Scott's novel of that name, unwraps in the Queensferry diligence and which proves his vade-mecum in his studies of the subjects Gordon had made his own, and with the aid of which Oldbuck famously plunges into 'a sea of discussion concerning urns, vases, votive altars, Roman camps, and the rules of castrametation' (W. Scott, *The Antiquary*, Edinburgh Edition, 1995, 10).

Gordon's motive, as he expressed it in the preface to *Itinerarium septentrionale* (the preface itself an eloquent and memorable piece of writing in defence of 'antiquity-study' or '*Archiology*, which consists of Monuments, or rather Inscriptions, still subsisting', which he contended was not one of the 'Chimeras of *Virtuosi*, dry and unpleasant Searches'), was to 'illustrate the *Roman* Actions in *Scotland*, and, of consequence, the Atchievements of its Ancient Inhabitants' (A. Gordon, *Itinerarium septentrionale*, 1726, preface). On a wider front, as the full range of his scholarly activities was to demonstrate, Gordon's cultural aim was to ensure that 'Antiquity and Learning may flourish in the Island, to the total Extirpation of *Gothicism*, Ignorance and a bad Taste' (ibid.).

A succession of what he described as 'antiquary peregrinations' or 'virtuoso tuers' (Alexander Gordon to James Anderson, NL Scot., Adv. MS 29.1.2 (iv), fol. 75) occupied Gordon between 1723 and 1725. His expeditions took him as far to the north-west as the brochs of Glenelg, but concentrated on the Roman sites of the lowlands and the central belt and in the territory of the Agricolan advance beyond the Tay south and east of the Grampians. In his exploration of the Antonine Wall Gordon was accompanied by the provost of Linlithgow, James Glen, himself an antiquary and collector of ancient stones from local Roman sites. The two enjoyed an uneasy relationship marked by coolness: Gordon privately described this as 'aliquanto freddo' (Clerk papers, 5023/3/1), though in print he lauded Glen as 'my curious and honoured Friend' (*Itinerarium septentrionale*, 55). Gordon had actually taken Glen by routes that would not permit him to find the best stones. Nevertheless this same James Glen was later to play a pivotal role in changing the whole direction of Gordon's life.

In 1724 Gordon maintained himself by working in the customs house in Aberdeen, writing, drawing, and engraving by night and drudging by day:

> not the very noblest exercise that a rational creatour may be employed in these so precious hours … I am observant of Caesar's due even to the mathematicall division of a pickled herring … Tis a sad thing not to have been born to a few riggs. (Brown, *Hobby-horsical Antiquary*, 28)

Sir John Clerk, who came into contact with Gordon at least as early as the autumn of 1723, proved his most important patron and his staunchest and most hospitable friend. Gordon became his agent for the acquisition (or attempted acquisition) of Roman inscribed stones. Gordon, however, was to deceive him (and the antiquary Roger Gale) into permitting the publication of a series of learned letters on ancient funerary rites as an appendix to his book, greatly to the annoyance of the authors. With Clerk, Gordon made an important expedition to Hadrian's Wall in 1724 which furnished much information for his study. He reciprocated Clerk's 'hospitality to the mind' (Clerk papers, 5023/3/13) by crying up Clerk in London from 1725 as 'a Treasure of Learning and good Taste' and thus paving the way for the latter's flattering reception by the 'antiquarian Lords and gentlemen' (NL Scot., MS 3044, fol. 87*v*) in 1727; however, in reality Clerk was more than a little manipulated by Gordon, who was anxious to vaunt Scottish cultural connections in order to impress an English circle he found patronizing. The paradox was that Gordon always found the virtuoso realm of London more to his taste than the narrower world of Scotland.

After returning to London in 1725 Gordon fell in and out of friendship with William Stukeley, was elected to the Society of Antiquaries and to the Society of Roman Knights (as Galgacus), and brought out his book in 1726. The general view was that he had been too precipitate in publishing, but Gordon resented the criticism that the competitive world of scholarship imposed. When John Horsley emerged as compiler of a history of Roman Britain which was likely to outshine Gordon's own efforts his resentment was little concealed and he took refuge in cheap insult and vituperation: 'I verily believe the Poor Priest is crasey … His second gleanings of the harvest I've reapt … In fine, I take Mr Horsley's antiquarian affairs to be like the crackling of thorns under a pot: vox et praeterea nihil …' (Clerk papers, 5023/3/41). It became most important to Gordon that he bring out his supplement containing 'Additions and Corrections' to *Itinerarium septentrionale* before the appearance of 'Mr Horsely's Leviathan' (ibid., 5023/3/53), but in fact they were published in the same year, 1732. Clerk tried to hold the ring and to give full assistance to Horsley while not wishing to see Gordon hurt. But he was deeply wounded. His circle indulged in persistent though gentle mockery: he was called 'Gordonius the Caledonian' by Roger Gale, and by Thomas Blackwell 'poor Itinerarium' (ibid., 5036/8). After Gordon had published his *Lives of Pope Alexander VI and his Son Caesar Borgia* (1729), and had gone on to write laboriously on Egyptological topics, Blackwell chaffed him as 'poor Caesar Borgia the Hieroglyphician' (Brown, *Hobby-horsical Antiquary*, 21).

False starts and failing fortunes A succession of unrealized ambitions, incomplete scholarly projects, and occupations taken up and abandoned in despair or heavy debt, a growing reputation for less than honest dealing, and a persistent discontent at his lot all conspired to increase the level of contempt in which Gordon was held. He advertised, initially in 1726, a grand (and potentially very important) map of the walls of Hadrian and Antoninus Pius, which never appeared. He projected, at the same time, a scheme for a navigable canal connecting the firths of Forth and Clyde which was given short shrift by Lord Ilay as uneconomic: Gordon, who subsequently harboured a design to be a hydrographer, had conducted a survey in conjunction with William Adam. In 1727 he entertained a dream of being sent abroad as a buyer of pictures on some quasi-official, national basis, and saw it as his duty to inform the tastes of a nobility he saw as being too easily duped by foreigners in the trade. However, William Aikman considered him 'not at all a virtuoso to my taste' (Fleming, 39–41), and fell out with him spectacularly when he was attempting to execute a commission to buy pictures for Clerk. In telling Charles Mackie in 1730 of his proposed history of Pope Leo X, Gordon complained of 'the doubts you Edinburgians have about me' (EUL, MS La. II. 220). In that year he was seen to be needy and to be living in some hardship in Greenwich. However, he did publish at that time, as *A Complete History of Antient Amphitheatres*, a translation of Scipione Maffei's important work on the subject, which recalled interests first roused in Italy and which enjoyed some success.

Gordon spent two separate spells as a bookseller, once (1731) in partnership with Abraham Vandenhoek at the New Church in the Strand, and once with John Wilcox. According to John Whiston, Gordon's

> education, temper, and manners, did not suit him for a trade ... He had some learning, some ingenuity, much pride, much deceit, and very little honesty ... Poverty tempted him to dishonesty; his national character and constitution to pride and ingenuity; and his dependence on the Great to flattery and deceit. (Nichols, *Lit. anecdotes*, 5.699)

When he again abandoned bookselling in 1732, Smart Lethieullier told Clerk that Gordon was afraid that the baron would think him fickle. At various times in the later 1720s and the 1730s he was teaching on the one hand Italian and on the other drawing and 'crion painting' (Clerk papers, 5023/3/57), and he was available to conduct young men round the art collections of London and the south of England. In 1733–4 he organized the art training of Alexander Clerk, half-brother of Sir John, in the studio of Arthur Pond.

Marriage, at some time before 1733, and a growing family compelled Gordon to take employment wherever opportunity offered, and he accumulated a number of secretarial appointments in addition to his other occupations. He succeeded Stukeley as secretary of the Society of Antiquaries in 1735—'I never saw anything so unanimous in all my life', he told Clerk, yet there was 'a kind of opposition and another candidate or two' (Clerk papers, 5023/3/76)—in which office he continued until he resigned in 1741. In 1736 he became secretary of the Society for the Encouragement of Learning, an appointment which brought in £50 per annum, and he served in this capacity until 1739. He was a member of the Spalding Society, along with Clerk and Gale.

Egyptian antiquities Gordon's nomination as secretary of the Egyptian Club confirmed the direction that his interests (which bordered upon the obsessional) had now taken. Smart Lethieullier appears to have been responsible for starting Gordon off on the academic pursuit that was to dominate the rest of his life. He invited Gordon, in 1732, to draw his Egyptian antiquities. Gordon moved on to record the mummies in the possession of Captain William Lethieullier and Dr Richard Mead, and then attempted to catalogue all the Egyptian artefacts in the Sloane, Pembroke, and other collections with the intention of producing a thesaurus of Egyptian material in Britain. He drew a series of twenty-five plates of the mummies in England, which were to be accompanied by explanatory text. The plan, as conceived in 1733, was to issue plates each month, at a shilling a time, to 200 subscribers. Sets of these plates, engraved after his drawings, are very rare. Of the projected commentaries only two pamphlets appeared, both published in 1737, to complement the illustrations of the Lethieullier and Mead mummies. Gordon devoted a great deal of effort to the attempt to solve the mysteries of the hieroglyphics, and to make sense of the intricacies of ancient Egyptian religion, and succeeded only in heaping more ridicule upon his head. Alone among his circle he seemed to be convinced that Egyptian antiquities were:

> the antiquities in the world perhaps of any the best worth enquiring into insomuch as they are of the people from whom I may say this whole Terraqueous Glob derived religion, science and polishing ... There will be an infinite scheme of surprize and erudition opened. (Clerk papers, 5023/3/73)

His *magnum opus*, 'An essay towards illustrating the history, chronology and mythology of the ancient Egyptians', covering that topic down to the time of Alexander, was advertised as in progress in 1737 and is said, possibly incorrectly, to have been complete on the eve of Gordon's most extraordinary change of direction (Nichols, *Lit. anecdotes*, 5.337). In 1741 he resigned his London positions and sailed that August for Carolina as secretary to the new governor, James Glen, the erstwhile provost of Linlithgow and companion of Gordon's antiquarian explorations of 1723.

Final years and reputation In America Gordon suddenly prospered, and quite dramatically so. One Hamerton farmed out his office as registrar of the province to Gordon and empowered him to act as his attorney in all business in return for all fees. By 1746 he had obtained a large plot of land in Charles Town and also acquired land, profitably developed for houses, in Ansonborough. He was sick, perhaps dying, when his will was drawn up on 22 August 1754; on his death, which probably occurred at Charles Town later that month (his wife having predeceased him, though a son and daughter survived him), he was, for the first time in his life, a comparatively rich man. Whether he was contented is another matter. Certainly he attempted to maintain old interests. In 1747 he told Sir John Clerk of the meetings of a small, select group who 'meet and converse on the Bell Letter with a true British, virtuoso and literary conversation. As for the others a meer profanum vulgus, proud, ignorant and vindictive' (Clerk papers, 5023/3/95). He had finished his Egyptian book—presumably the same treatise he had been working on before his departure for the colonies—and was considering publication. His son was enjoined by the terms of his will to see this through the press, but the younger Alexander Gordon failed to execute his father's wishes. The manuscript is now in the British Library (Add. MS 8834).

In reporting to Stukeley news of Gordon in America, Clerk alleged that he was 'vastly weary of that part of the world' (*Family Memoirs*, 1.439). This suggests that Gordon's friends and associates were not convinced of his ultimate success. His mercurial nature, fickleness of character, and dogmatism of expression and behaviour which caused him to be branded 'a saucy, light-headed fellow' (Brown, *Hobby-horsical Antiquary*, 41) ensured that he was harshly judged even by those who knew him well and liked him, or had once done so. His will, however, besides specifying his material wealth in land and property, mentions his own paintings and drawings, a fact which seems to betoken a continuing interest in art; and his concern for the fate of his Egyptian researches, long and profound as they were, is matched by his confession of 1747 to Clerk that 'for as Gothick a region as this I don't forget dear Antiquity' (Brown, *Hobby-horsical Antiquary*, 41–2).

IAIN GORDON BROWN

Sources Clerk of Penicuik muniments, NA Scot., GD18 • J. Nichols, ed., *Bibliotheca topographica Britannica*, 3 (1790), *Reliquiae Galeanae*, 2, pt 3 • D. Wilson, *Alexander Gordon, the antiquary* (Toronto, 1873) • D. Wilson and D. Laing, 'An account of Alexander Gordon … with additional notes concerning Alexander Gordon and his works', *Proceedings of the Society of Antiquaries of Scotland*, 10 (1872–4), 363–82 [incl. copy of will] • J. Ingamells, ed., *A dictionary of British and Irish travellers in Italy, 1701–1800* (1997), 409 • C. Morey, 'Alexander Gordon, scholar and singer', *Music and Letters*, 46 (1965), 332–5 • Highfill, Burnim & Langhans, *BDA*, 6.273–5 • I. G. Brown, *The hobby-horsical antiquary: a Scottish character, 1640–1830* (1980) • I. G. Brown, 'Sir John Clerk of Penicuik (1676–1755): aspects of a virtuoso life', PhD diss., U. Cam., 1980 • I. G. Brown, 'Chyndonax to Galgacus: new letters of William Stukeley to Alexander Gordon', *Antiquaries Journal*, 67 (1987), 111–28 • *The family memoirs of the Rev. William Stukeley*, ed. W. C. Lukis, 3 vols., SurtS, 73, 76, 80 (1882–7) • Nichols, *Lit. anecdotes*, esp. 5.329–37 • J. Fleming, *Robert Adam and his circle in Edinburgh and Rome* (1962) • L. Keppie, *Roman inscribed and sculptured stones in the Hunterian Museum, University of Glasgow* (1998) • *DNB*

Archives NL Scot., legal corresp. | BL, letters to Thomas Birch, Add. MSS 4272, 4308, 4452 • NA Scot., corresp. with Sir John Clerk many relating to antiquarian subjects, GD18/5023/3/1–95 • NL Scot., Anderson and Mackenzie of Delvine papers, letters • U. Edin., Laing MSS, letters

Likenesses B. Bell, bust or medallion (after original in the Fountaine collection); lost • attrib. A. Gordon, self-portrait?, oils; formerly in possession of his son, now lost

Wealth at death see will, Wilson and Laing, 'An account'

Alexander Gordon, fourth duke of Gordon (1743–1827), by Pompeo Batoni, 1764

Gordon, Alexander, **fourth duke of Gordon** (1743–1827), politician and army officer, was born on 18 June 1743, the eldest son of Cosmo George Gordon, third duke (*c*.1720–1752), and his wife and kinswoman, Lady Katherine (or Catherine) *Gordon (1718–1779), only daughter of the second earl of Aberdeen. Gordon became fourth duke on the death of his father on 5 August 1752. From Horace Walpole we get a glimpse of Gordon in his childhood, when his widowed mother dressed him as Cupid and had him fire arrows at Stanislaw Poniatowski, future king of Poland, who was on a visit to Britain (Walpole, 35.82). Gordon's mother married Staats Long *Morris, and when Morris raised a corps known as the 89th Gordon Highlanders, the youthful duke, then at Eton College, was appointed captain. He completed his education with a grand tour.

In 1767 Gordon was elected one of the sixteen representative peers of Scotland, and on 23 October of that year he married his first wife, Jane *Gordon (*née* Maxwell) (1748/9–1812), daughter of Sir William Maxwell, baronet, and Magdalen Blair; they had two sons and five daughters during an unhappy marriage. The duke was reputed to be one of the handsomest young men of his day, and to have been described by Lord Kames as the greatest subject in Britain in regard not only to the extent of his rent roll, but to the number of people depending on his protection. He had Gordon Castle in Banffshire rebuilt from the plans of John Baxter of Edinburgh. He was brought in to support of William Pitt the younger by Henry Dundas, during the latter's pacification of the various political factions in the north-east of Scotland. In 1784, in consideration of his descent from Henry Howard, sixth duke of Norfolk, the English titles of earl of Norwich and Lord Gordon of Huntley, Gloucestershire, were revived for Gordon. He was also made KT, lord keeper of the great seal of Scotland, and lord lieutenant of Aberdeenshire. He appears to have been an easy-going man, caring chiefly for rural pursuits and field sports. He introduced semaphores on his estates to give notice of the movements of the deer. One of the last in Scotland to keep hawks, he was also noted for his breeds of deerhounds and setters. The author of the comic song 'There is Cauld Kail in Aberdeen', Gordon encouraged the musical genius of his butler, Marshall, whom Robert Burns described as 'the first composer of strathspeys of the age'.

Gordon raised two regiments of fencible infantry at his own cost, the northern fencibles during the American War of Independence, and the northern or Gordon fencibles during the French Revolutionary War. The latter corps, when stationed in Kent, was reviewed by George III in Hyde Park, the first Highland regiment seen in London since the review of the Black Watch in 1743.

On 11 April 1812 the duchess, Jane, who for years had

been bitterly estranged from her husband, died in London. In July 1820 the duke married Jane Christie of Fochabers, with whom he had already raised a large family. She died on 17 June 1824. The duke died in London on 17 June 1827, and was succeeded by his son George *Gordon, the fifth and last duke.

H. M. Chichester, *rev.* Michael Fry

Sources *Scots peerage* • Walpole, *Corr.* • M. Fry, *The Dundas despotism* (1992) • *GM*, 1st ser., 82/1 (1812), 490

Archives NA Scot., papers relating to King's College Aberdeen, etc.; vouchers for expenses, bank accounts, and papers • priv. coll., MSS • U. Aberdeen, detailed account of his death and funeral • W. Sussex RO, corresp. and papers | Falkirk Archives, Callendar House Museum and History Research Centre, letters to Forbes family • NL Scot., letters to Sir William Forbes • NL Scot., letters to Sir Robert Gordon • NL Scot., corresp. with Lord Melville • NRA Scotland, priv. coll., letters to Lord Hopetoun • NRA Scotland, priv. coll., letters to Gordon of Cairnfield • West Highland Museum, corresp. with Henry Dundas relating to highland fencibles

Likenesses J. Reynolds, oils, 1761, Eton • P. Batoni, portrait, 1764, NG Scot. [*see illus.*] • W. Smith, miniature on vellum, 1782, Goodwood, West Sussex • J. Moir, oils, 1817, Scot. NPG • S. W. Reynolds, mezzotint, pubd 1825 (aged eighty-two; after C. Smith), BM • P. Battoni, oils, Goodwood, West Sussex • G. Place, miniature, V&A • H. Raeburn, oils, Goodwood, West Sussex • attrib. H. Raeburn, oils, Man. City Gall. • W. Smith, group portrait, Goodwood, West Sussex • J. Tassie, paste medallion, Scot. NPG

Gordon, Alexander (1752–1799), physician, was born on 20 May 1752 in the parish of Peterculter in Aberdeenshire. He, and his twin brother James, who became a successful farmer in Logie in Aberdeenshire, were the second and third of the five children of Alexander Gordon, tenant farmer of Miltown of Drum. After a general education Gordon attended Marischal College in Aberdeen, graduating MA in 1775. He then studied medicine in Aberdeen, Edinburgh, and probably Leiden.

In 1780 Gordon entered the Royal Navy as surgeon's mate, becoming full surgeon in 1782. On 5 February 1784 he married Elizabeth, daughter of Alexander Harvie, who survived until 1843; they had two daughters. Gordon left the navy on half-pay in 1785 to spend nine months in London developing his special interest in midwifery. He was resident pupil at the lying-in hospital in Store Street, received clinical instruction from two of the leading obstetricians of the day, Thomas Denman and William Osborne, and attended the Middlesex Lying-in Dispensary. When he returned to Aberdeen towards the end of 1785 he was appointed physician to the Aberdeen Dispensary. In 1786 he published his *Observations of the Efficacy of Cold-Bathing in the Prevention and Cure of Diseases*, a treatise of no great originality on a fashionable subject. Two years later he was awarded the degree of MD by Marischal College.

Were it not for a severe epidemic of puerperal fever ('childbed fever') in Aberdeen, which lasted from December 1789 to March 1792, Gordon might well have been forgotten. Puerperal fever was previously unknown in Aberdeen and the epidemic was thought to be no more than the common ephemeral fever known as the 'weed', which was rarely fatal. Gordon, however, had seen many cases of puerperal fever in London. Recognizing that the epidemic was due to this deadly disease, he kept careful notes of every case. From these he was able to make the crucial observation that the disease tended to be confined to the practice of a small minority of midwives. Indeed, he was able to forecast accurately which women would develop the disease merely by knowing which midwife had been in attendance. He also realized that he had himself unwittingly carried the disease from one midwifery patient to another.

Gordon was the first to provide irrefutable evidence of what had been until then no more than a faint suspicion: that puerperal fever was a contagious disease that could be carried from patient to patient by doctors and midwives. He also showed that it was closely connected with erysipelas. These observations were made some fifty years before the well-known work of Oliver Wendell Holmes and Ignaz Semmelweis, which overshadowed Gordon's early but brilliant contribution to the understanding of puerperal fever. After more than a century of relative obscurity Gordon's *Treatise on the Epidemic Puerperal Fever of Aberdeen* (1795) was recognized for what it is, a masterpiece of early epidemiology based on astute clinical observation and written with exceptional clarity.

Sadly, Gordon's treatise damaged his professional reputation. As dispensary physician almost the whole burden of the epidemic fell on his shoulders and the women of Aberdeen turned against him, holding him responsible for the facts he revealed, and disputing his fervent belief in the efficacy of purging and heavy bleeding which were 'repugnant to popular opinion'. Hurt by 'the ungenerous treatment which I met with from that very sex whose sufferings I was at so much pains to relieve', he was glad to leave Aberdeen when recalled to active duty in the Royal Navy. Soon, however, he developed pulmonary tuberculosis and was invalided out. An ill man, he returned to his brother James's farm, where he died at the early age of forty-seven on 19 October 1799. Irvine Loudon, *rev.*

Sources I. A. Porter, *Alexander Gordon, M.D., of Aberdeen, 1752–1799* (1958) • G. P. Milne, 'The history of midwifery in Aberdeen', *Aberdeen University Review*, 47 (1977–8), 293–303 • C. J. Cullingworth, *Oliver Wendell Holmes and the contagiousness of puerperal fever* (1906) • I. Loudon, *Death in childbirth: an international study of maternal care and maternal mortality, 1800–1950* (1992) • private information (2004) • bap. reg. Scot. • m. reg. Scot.

Archives Royal College of Physicians of Edinburgh, papers relating to obstetrics

Gordon, Sir Alexander (1786–1815), army officer, was the third son of George Gordon, Lord Haddo (1764–1791), who died after falling from his horse, and grandson of George Gordon, third earl of Aberdeen. His mother was Charlotte (*d.* 1795), youngest daughter of William Baird of Newbyth, and sister of Sir David Baird. Gordon's brothers were George Hamilton *Gordon, fourth earl of Aberdeen, Sir Robert *Gordon, diplomatist, and Lieutenant-Colonel Sir Charles Gordon, 42nd highlanders, who died at Geneva on 30 September 1835.

Gordon was educated at Eton College, and in 1803 was appointed ensign in the 3rd foot guards (later the Scots Guards), in which he became captain and lieutenant-colonel on 23 August 1813. He served as aide-de-camp to his maternal uncle, General Sir David Baird, at the recapture of the Cape of Good Hope in 1806, and to General Beresford with the force sent from the Cape to the River Plate. He was employed by Beresford to negotiate with the Spanish authorities at Buenos Aires. Afterwards he was again aide-de-camp to Baird at the capture of Copenhagen in 1807, and in Spain in 1808–9, including the battle of Corunna. In 1810 he was appointed aide-de-camp to Wellington, in which capacity his brother Charles, then likewise a subaltern in the 3rd foot guards, also was employed for a time.

Gordon became Wellington's favourite and chief aide-de-camp, served throughout the Peninsular campaigns, and was mentioned in dispatches. He received ten medals for general actions, and was made KCB on 2 January 1815. He was aide-de-camp to Wellington in Belgium, and received a mortal wound (thigh shattered) while rallying a battalion of Brunswickers, near La Haye-Sainte, on 18 June 1815. He died a few hours later. Wellington wrote that he was an officer of great promise and his death represented a serious loss to the army. Gordon was apparently a favourite in Brussels, and the principal residents wanted to pay the cost of the column erected to his memory on the field of Waterloo by his sister and brothers.

H. M. CHICHESTER, *rev.* ROGER T. STEARN

Sources E. Lodge, *Peerage, baronetage, knightage and companionage of the British empire*, 81st edn, 3 vols. (1912) • *The dispatches of … the duke of Wellington … from 1799 to 1818*, ed. J. Gurwood, 13 vols. in 12 (1834–9), vols. 3–5, 8 • E. Longford [E. H. Pakenham, countess of Longford], *Wellington*, 1: *The years of the sword* (1969) • S. G. P. Ward, *Wellington's headquarters: a study of the administrative problems in the Peninsula, 1809–14* (1957) • Burke, *Peerage* (1959) • GEC, *Peerage*
Archives BL, family corresp., Add. MSS 43217, 43223–43224 • NAM, diaries and letters | NA Scot., letters to Lord Melville
Likenesses J. Henning, paste medallion, 1809, NPG

Gordon, Alexander (1841–1931), Unitarian minister and historian, was born on 9 June 1841 at Cheylesmore Manor House, Coventry, the second of the five sons of **John Gordon** (1807–1880), a Unitarian minister. John Gordon was born at Dudley, Worcestershire, on 1 March 1807, the son of Alexander Gordon, who was in business in the town, and his wife, Maria Loxton. Educated at Dudley grammar school, he was to prepare for the Church of England priesthood at Oxford, but he refused to subscribe to the Thirty-Nine Articles; he maintained this libertarian stand throughout his life. He became a Methodist minister, but was in effect repudiated by the Methodist conference in 1835 on the same issue. After joining the Unitarians he was minister at Coseley, Coventry, Edinburgh, Dukinfield, and Evesham, and retired in 1873. He lectured widely and was considered one of the leading Unitarian ministers of his day. His knowledge of literature and history, on which he wrote, was profound, and he was a willing debater. An active religious libertarian, 'he stood complete in his integrity'. He married first Sarah King, daughter of John Mumford, in 1832; she died, leaving a son, the following year. Secondly he married in 1840 Anna Maria, daughter of Thomas Hodgetts of Bristol, who was the mother of Alexander Gordon and three other sons. John Gordon died at Ladyes Hill, Kenilworth, on 24 April 1880.

Alexander Gordon (1841–1931), by unknown photographer

Alexander Gordon was educated by his father, and then at King Henry VIII School, Coventry (1852–4), the Royal High School in Edinburgh (1854–6), and the University of Edinburgh (1856–9). He attended Manchester New College, London, for ministerial training from 1859 to 1862. Between 1860 and 1862 he studied under Döllinger at Munich and was Hibbert fellow at Edinburgh in 1863–4 (MA 1864). Gordon was successively Unitarian minister at Aberdeen (1862–3), Hope Street Church in Liverpool (1863–72), Norwich (1872–7), and the First Presbyterian (Non-Subscribing) Church in Belfast (1877–89). From 1890 to 1911 he was principal of the Unitarian Home Missionary College, Manchester (later the Unitarian College), and lecturer in ecclesiastical history in the University of Manchester.

Gordon was probably the most eminent and highly regarded historian of nonconformity of his time, with an encyclopaedic knowledge and memory. Through his exhaustive and objective scholarship, based largely on primary sources, he significantly influenced subsequent research into religious dissent. He succeeded in bringing the life and work of early English dissenters in particular into the mainstream of historical research, but his erudition extended to European religious reformers. His acquaintance with minor protestant groups, such as the Mennonites, Collegiants, Anabaptists, and Familists, was hardly less intimate than his knowledge of English sects, such as the Traskites and the Muggletonians. Never formally trained as a historian, Gordon had a passion for writing biography: his outstanding contribution was to the *Dictionary of National Biography*, for which he wrote 778 entries, almost all the articles on Unitarians being from his pen. His articles included extensive memoirs on such major figures as John and Charles Wesley, George Whitefield, Jabez Bunting, and George Fox. Readers, and those who have written for the *Oxford Dictionary of National Biography*, will appreciate the extent of his achievement. Gordon also contributed two articles to the ninth edition of the *Encyclopaedia Britannica* (1875–88), for which his father had also written, and thirty-nine articles to the eleventh edition (1910–11), seven of which were revised for the fourteenth (1929). Among his books, *Freedom after Ejection, 1690–92* and *The Cheshire Classis Minutes, 1691–1745* were standard works for many years.

Gordon's total output of articles was prodigious. From 1869 to 1930 reviews, chapel histories, and biographies flowed from his pen (he never used a typewriter), and covered every branch of nonconformity. He regularly contributed historical articles of high quality to the weekly *Christian Life* for over fifty years. His correspondence was as voluminous as his knowledge, which was willingly shared with other scholars. Gordon helped foster the increased interest in nonconformist history which arose at the beginning of the twentieth century, and played a unique role in the foundation of seven denominational history societies (1898–1915). He assembled a library of 12,000 items, together with a considerable collection of railway tickets.

Gordon was a complex, often cantankerous personality. Gruff and inordinately self-reliant, Gordon was highly conservative in attitude, theology, and lifestyle. Though he was warm and understanding to his students, stories of his sharpness are numerous. When asked by a pompous college dean, 'My good man, I do not think I know you. Who are you?', Gordon replied, 'Oh, I'm just myself. Are you anybody?' His hats were inscribed inside the brim 'Not Yours'. Contemptuous of rank or title, he rejected offers of honorary doctorates from Manchester, Edinburgh, and various American universities.

On 23 April 1872 Gordon married Clara Maria (1846–1902), daughter of Swinton *Boult; they had five sons and one daughter. After 1911 he chiefly resided in hotels. He died, after a brief illness, in Belfast on 21 February 1931 and was buried at the Old Meeting-House, Dunmurry, on 23 February 1931, 'an Englishman by birth, a Scotsman by education and an Irishman by inclination' (*The Inquirer*, 28 Feb 1931). ALAN RUSTON

Sources H. McLachlan, *Alexander Gordon* (1932) • *The Inquirer* (28 Feb 1931), 99–101 • *Transactions of the Unitarian Historical Society*, 5/1 (1931–4) • *The Inquirer* (9 Feb 1946), 40 • H. McLachlan, *Essays and addresses* (1950), 290–336 • G. E. Evans, *Record of the provincial assembly of Lancashire and Cheshire* (1896), 53, 93 • *The Inquirer* (1 May 1880) • *The Inquirer* (8 May 1880) • *Christian Life* (1 May 1880) • *Christian Life* (8 May 1880) • *Christian Life* (29 May 1880)

Archives JRL, corresp. and papers, incl. research notes for *DNB* entries • NL Wales, notes relating to G. E. Evans, *History of Renshaw Street Chapel*

Likenesses photograph, repro. in McLachlan, *Alexander Gordon*, frontispiece [*see illus.*]

Wealth at death £5610 6*s*. 7*d*.: resworn probate, 6 May 1931, *CGPLA Eng. & Wales* • under £5000—John Gordon: probate, 1880

Gordon, Andrew [Andreas; *formerly* George] (**1712–1751**), natural philosopher, was born on 15 June 1712 at Cuffurach, Banffshire, and baptized George Gordon. At the age of twelve he went to the Scottish Benedictine Monastery of St James at Regensburg, Bavaria. He spent 1731 travelling, and the following year was ordained priest. It was probably then that he took the forename Andrew or Andreas, under which he published. In 1735 he was sent to study law at the Benedictine University at Salzburg, and then visited his brother Alexander at the Scots College in Paris. In 1737 he was appointed professor of philosophy at Erfurt, one of the chairs in the gift of the Regensburg Scots College.

At this time natural philosophers in Germany were actively investigating the phenomena associated with electricity, which was generated by rubbing a glass globe. It is uncertain whether Johann Heinrich Winkler, professor at Leipzig from 1750, or Gordon, whose teaching emphasized the practical aspects of his subject, was the first to obtain an electric charge from a glass cylinder. Initially, Gordon mounted his cylinder on an axle, which he turned to and fro against its rubbing pad by means of a bow, as was commonly employed to drive the watchmaker's lathe. His second model was driven by a large pulley wheel, which turned the cylinder against a leather cushion. Gordon's machines were probably the first compact portable generators.

Gordon devised several pieces of electrically driven apparatus. One was the electrical chimes, whereby a ball suspended on silk between two bells was electrified, which made it oscillate and strike the bells alternately. Gordon was never given the credit for this application of electrical convection; Benjamin Franklin simply referred to 'the German chimes' when using them to register atmospheric electricity. Gordon also devised the first electrostatic reaction motor. This consisted of a metal star, pivoted at its centre and with the tips angled to the radii, which a charge would set whirling.

Among his more striking demonstrations Gordon was able to draw fire from water in a glass vessel, a trick that became popular with other lecturers. A jar of water was placed on an insulating stand, with a wire leading from the water to the prime conductor. The current charged the water, which, if touched by the prime conductor, emitted a spark. Gordon also used living animals and birds, whose reactions or deaths demonstrated the power of the invisible electrical force.

Between 1737 and 1752 eight textbooks by Gordon were published in Latin and in German, on the subject of natural philosophy and in particular the manifestations and utility of electricity. Gordon gave public demonstrations at Erfurt and at the courts in Gotha and Weimar. He gained a wide reputation among other European experimental philosophers, notably the eminent Abbé Jean-Antoine Nollet, and was elected a correspondent of the Académie Royal des Sciences in Paris. He died at Erfurt on 22 August 1751. THOMPSON COOPER, *rev.* ANITA MCCONNELL

Sources C. G. Jöchen, *Gelehrten-Lexicon*, 2 (1750–51), 527 • J. Priestley, *The history and present state of electricity*, 3rd edn, 1 (1775); repr.

(1966), 88, 159 • B. Dibner, *Early electrical machines* (1957), 25 • J. M. Bulloch, *Bibliography of the Gordons* (1924), 105–6 • Suard, 'Gordon, André', *Biographie universelle, ancienne et moderne*, ed. L. G. Michaud and E. E. Desplaces, new edn, 17 (Paris, 1857) • *Electrical World* [New York] (2 Jan 1909) • Universität Regensburg, ed., *Gelehrtes Regensburg, Stadt der Wissenschaft* (1995) • L. Hammermayer, 'Aufklärung im katholischen Deutschland des 18 Jahrhunderts: Werk und Wirkung von Andreas Gordon OSB, 1712–1751', *Jahrbuch des Instituts für deutsche Geschichte*, 4 (1975), 53–109 • W. D. Hackmann, *Electricity from glass: the history of the frictional electrical machine, 1600–1850* (1978), 82–4, 113, 124

Gordon, Anna (1747–1810), ballad collector, was born in Old Aberdeen on 24 August 1747, the youngest daughter of Thomas *Gordon (1714–1797), professor of humanity at King's College, Aberdeen, and his wife, Lilias Forbes of Disblair. She was presumably educated privately, and married on 13 December 1788 the Revd Dr Andrew Brown (*c*.1744–1805), who had been chaplain to the Royal North British Fusiliers during the American War of Independence and was minister of Falkland in Fife (1784–1802) and subsequently of Tranent near Edinburgh—hence the name Mrs Brown of Falkland by which Anna Gordon is generally known to ballad scholars.

Anna Gordon was one of the most highly regarded and prolific of Scottish ballad sources, supplying twenty-seven of the 'A' texts in Francis James Child's definitive collection *English and Scottish Popular Ballads* (5 vols., 1882–98). Child declared of her songs that 'No Scottish ballads are superior in kind' (Buchan, *The Ballad and the Folk*, 62). She is said to have learned the bulk of her repertory in childhood from the 'Ladies of Disblair', namely her mother, Lilias Forbes, and her mother's sister, Anne Forbes (Mrs Farquharson of Allanaquoich), and also from a maid in her mother's family. Anna Gordon grew up in a varied and stimulating musical environment and within a richly expressive linguistic tradition of vernacular Scots. The Forbes family were musically gifted, Anna's grandfather William Forbes of Disblair having a considerable reputation as a composer in the Scots fiddle tradition. Her father, Thomas Gordon, also was a keen amateur musician, for more than twenty years a member of the Aberdeen Musical Society. Some fifty of Anna's songs were committed to writing between about 1783 and 1801 and found their way through various intermediaries to Walter Scott and Robert Jamieson, who published a selection of them in *Minstrelsy of the Scottish Border* (1802) and *Popular Ballads and Songs* (1806).

Anna Gordon's ballads are framed from an explicitly female, indeed even feminist, perspective, and carry behind their courtly and magical façade a frequently brutal reality. The ambience is of love and death, the cruelties of fate and chance, and of perilous, enchanted wooings. The songs chart their youthful heroines' transition from secure maternal households to the dangerous world of men and their violently possessive female kin, at whose hands the protagonists risk not merely rejection but sometimes mutilation or even death. The ballads speak of murderous sexual rivalry between female siblings and hint at infanticide as a form of revenge upon treacherous males. Adventures in the magical greenwood, a metaphor for transgressive sexuality, have a strong appeal but usually alarming consequences. Indeed, the dangers of sex are stressed on every side, along with the sheer physical hazard of being female. 'The Bonny Earl of Livingston' begins:

> O we were sisters seven, Maisry,
> And five are dead wi child …

When Lady Maisry's mother is sent for during her inevitable, risky childbirth:

> … ere she wan to Livingston,
> As fast as she coud ride,
> The gaggs they were in Maisry's mouth,
> And the sharp sheers in her side.
> (Buchan, *Ballad Book*, 55)

There are songs in lighter vein, in which girls outwit their parents to win desired but unsuitable mates; but the risks of death at the hands of one's own kin if one forms inappropriate ties are very real. Men are occasionally shown as honourable, kindly, and protective, but abduction and rape form the dark underside of male–female relations in Anna Gordon's songs. While women of high social standing can possess great power, especially when wielding magic, women's vulnerability is the central theme, as we are reminded by the murder of Lady Wearie and her child, innocent victims of her husband's debt to the monstrous master builder Lamkin.

In eighteenth-century Scotland singing and music-making often took place in single-sex settings. The musical societies of Aberdeen and Edinburgh excluded women from membership. At a less formal level, too, gender separation was the norm, as shown in the tea table sessions of urban gentlewomen where certain kinds of Scottish songs, typically those of Allan Ramsay, would be sung, and in groups like the Cape Club of Edinburgh, frequented by the song collector David Herd and the poet Robert Fergusson, which were exclusively male; as were the Crochallan Fencibles, where Robert Burns entertained his friends with the kind of male bawdry preserved in his collection *The Merry Muses* (1827). The vernacular song tradition thus contained distinct male and female strands. Anna Gordon's father expressed surprise at his daughter's skill in balladry and confessed that the words and tunes were previously unknown to him (as they were to his correspondent, the antiquary William Tytler, 1711–1792). Yet changing social custom was increasingly beginning to involve music-making in 'mixed assemblies' of men and women, which tended to focus the repertory on a central core of acceptable material, driving male (and female) bawdry underground and eventually perhaps also contributing to the creative decline of the ballad.

Relatively little is known about Anna Gordon's life, but her song repertory, its sources, and the means by which it was constructed were to loom large in subsequent scholarship. Those who regarded 'folk tradition' as an essentially plebeian affair, existing apart from, and in opposition to, the formal culture of the educated classes, found it difficult to accommodate her middle-class background to their theories. Likewise those who believed that the ballad was an unconscious collective creation of the 'folk' were disturbed by the distinctly individual flavour of her songs, and questions were raised from an early stage about the degree of her creative participation. Her approach challenged the assumption that the creative phase of 'tradition' was long ago concluded, that 'tradition' differed from high culture by being fixed and unchanging, and that contemporary transmission should merely pass on unaltered a heritage already fully developed. Those, and there were many, who assumed that oral transmission was the hallmark of authenticity in popular tradition and that the influence of print was corrupting found her formal literacy unsettling; it was even suggested that certain of her songs should be excluded from the canon because they could not be confirmed from other sources. During the last third of the twentieth century her work continued to arouse controversy, the theme of invariance versus change being revived in a new guise by David Buchan, who argued in *The Ballad and the Folk* (1972) that Anna Gordon had used oral-formulaic methods of recomposition in performance, a conclusion keenly disputed by other scholars, who claimed that her texts bore most of the hallmarks of simple memorization. Since the evidence is ambiguous, it seems unlikely that the last word on this subject has been said.

Anna Gordon died on 11 July 1810 in Old Aberdeen, and was buried on 14 July in her father's tomb in Gordon's aisle, St Machar's Cathedral. WILLIAM DONALDSON

Sources D. Buchan, *The ballad and the folk* (1972) • D. Buchan, ed., *A Scottish ballad book* (1973) • D. Johnson, 'Musical traditions in the Forbes family of Disblair, Aberdeenshire', *Scottish Studies*, 22 (1978), 91–3 • F. G. Andersen and T. Pettitt, 'Mrs. Brown of Falkland: a singer of tales?', *Journal of American Folklore*, 92 (1979), 1–24 • B. H. Bronson, 'Mrs Brown and the ballad', *The ballad as song* (1969), 64–78 • A. B. Friedman, 'The oral-formulaic theory of balladry: a re-rebuttal', *The ballad image*, ed. J. Porter (1983), 215–40 • D. K. Wilgus, *Anglo-American folksong scholarship since 1898* (1959) • A. Keith, ed., *Last leaves of traditional ballads and ballad airs* (1925) • W. Walker, *Peter Buchan and other papers on Scottish and English ballads and songs* (1915) • T. Crawford, *Society and the lyric: a study of the song culture of eighteenth-century Scotland* (1979) • W. Donaldson, 'Change and invariance in the traditional performing arts', *Northern Scotland*, 17 (1997), 33–54 • *Fasti Scot.*

Archives Old Clune House, Aldourie, William Tytler's Brown MS • U. Edin., Robert Jamieson's Brown MSS La.XIII.473

Gordon, Archibald (1812–1886), military surgeon, about whose early life little is known, studied medicine at Edinburgh, and graduated MD in 1834 with a thesis on dysentery. He entered the army as assistant surgeon in 1835, was promoted surgeon in 1848, and served with the 53rd regiment in the Sutlej campaign of 1846. In the Punjab campaign of 1848–9 he was in charge of the medical service for the 24th regiment. He became surgeon-major in 1856. In the Crimea, during the war against Russia, Gordon was principal medical officer of the 2nd division throughout the siege of Sevastopol, and he was made deputy inspector-general of hospitals (1856), CB, and a knight of the Légion d'honneur. In 1857 he served as principal medical officer with the expeditionary force to China, where he was present at the capture of Canton (Guangzhou), and in the Oudh campaign of 1858–9. He became inspector-general in 1867, and retired in 1870. He was also honorary surgeon to the queen. Gordon died at Woodlands, West Hoathly, Sussex, on 3 August 1886, leaving a widow, Mary Preston (*née* Crealock).

CHARLES CREIGHTON, *rev.* PATRICK WALLIS

Sources *Hart's Army List* (1867) • *Nomina eorum, qui gradum medicinae doctoris in academia Jacobi sexti Scotorum regis, quae Edinburgi est, adepti sunt, ab anno 1705 ad annum 1845*, University of Edinburgh (1846) • *CGPLA Eng. & Wales* (1886)

Wealth at death £15,689 16*s.* 6*d.*: resworn probate, Nov 1887, *CGPLA Eng. & Wales* (1886)

Gordon, Arthur Charles Hamilton, first Baron Stanmore (1829–1912), colonial governor, was born at Argyll House, near Regent Street, London, on 26 November 1829. He was the youngest son of George Hamilton-*Gordon, fourth earl of Aberdeen (1784–1860), and his second wife, Harriet, the daughter of John Douglas, earl of Morton, the widow of James, Viscount Hamilton, and the mother of James *Hamilton, first duke of Abercorn. Gordon was educated at home by his father, then at Trinity College, Cambridge, where he matriculated in 1847 and graduated MA in 1851. In the following year he became private secretary to his father, then prime minister, whose career he later described in *The Earl of Aberdeen* (1893); as such, he was an important intermediary with the Peelites.

Gordon sat in the House of Commons from 1854 to 1857 as the Liberal member for Beverley. In late 1858 and early 1859 he was W. E. Gladstone's secretary on the latter's visit as commissioner to the British colony of the Ionian Islands (during which period his love for Gladstone's daughter, Agnes, was unrequited). He was highly critical of Gladstone's efforts to keep the islands from joining Greece. This impolitic action set the tone for many of Gordon's later quarrels with colonial officials and politicians.

Gordon later claimed that his quarrel with Gladstone did not arise from a personal objection to his superior's actions in Corfu, but from his desire to placate his father, who wholly disapproved of Gladstone's anti-Greek stance, and who also insisted that Gordon not resign when this difference led to a breach. Essentially Gordon's quarrel with Gladstone must be seen as a proxy fight between the latter and Aberdeen, a philhellene who was attempting to control the damage Gladstone was doing to the ideal of a unified Greece. Aberdeen's control over his son was such that Gordon was seldom able to form personal opinions until after his father's death. Though Aberdeen was tolerant and forgoing in politics, inside his family he held absolute sway. Members of the family referred to him as 'His Lordship' even when speaking familiarly, and saw domestic life as so formal as to be reminiscent of that of the duc de Sully. It is noteworthy that Gordon's attempt to repair his relationship with Gladstone came after Aberdeen's death. His friendship with Gladstone lasted until the latter's fourth term as prime minister, but the warm support he received did not advance his career rapidly. Gordon's desire for a governorship in India was never satisfied, and though he was eventually given the prize of Ceylon this came only after more than two decades of service in lesser colonies. Prime ministerial patronage was not very valuable to Gordon as Gladstone never insisted

Arthur Charles Hamilton Gordon, first Baron Stanmore (1829–1912), by Frank O. Salisbury, 1911

that members of his cabinet adopt his suggestions. In addition, Gordon's habit of writing privately to Gladstone was occasionally a source of annoyance to the secretary of state for the colonies.

Gordon's first colonial governorship began in 1861 with his appointment as lieutenant-governor of New Brunswick, a colony which he saw as impoverished and decaying and whose inhabitants he described as low and ungentlemanly. He, in turn, was regarded as vain, and it was in this colony that he received his lifelong satirical sobriquet 'Thy Servant Arthur', which arose from his instruction that he be prayed for under that name with the royal family. Gordon worked to create a militia to defend New Brunswick against possible American intervention during their civil war. He also unsuccessfully attempted to form a maritime union with the neighbouring colonies of Nova Scotia and Prince Edward Island. He opposed confederation of his colony with the province of Canada until ordered by the Colonial Office to give this measure his support. In 1865 he married Rachel Emily (*d.* 1889), the eldest daughter of Sir John George Shaw-*Lefevre; they had one son and one daughter.

While he had difficulties with the self-governing colonists of New Brunswick, Gordon was more successful with his next colony, Trinidad, where he became governor in 1866. There he described his general policy as the feeling that a governor should truly govern and should be a living force over those he ruled. His picture of himself as the embodiment of 'national' feeling in a colony led him to immerse himself in reform activity, such as the improvement of education and the attempt to heal sectarian disputes. His reforming zeal continued in Mauritius, where he assumed the governorship in 1871. There he reformed the civil service, and attempted to improve the lot of the Indian immigrants and of the freed African slaves in the subordinate colonial dependency of the Seychelles.

In 1875 Gordon began his governorship of Fiji, an administration which historians usually credit as being his most important one, as well as being a period which shaped the political future of that colony. He set in place a system of indirect rule through Fijian chiefs which became part of the permanent system of government, and which was to help initiate the system of indirect rule which was later used in Africa by F. J. D. Lugard. While in Fiji he encouraged the importation of Indian labourers by the white planters in order to protect the indigenous population from commercial exploitation. His plan was to give the Fijians a twenty-five-year remission from competition in the modern commercial arena, but his system became a permanent orthodoxy in Fijian politics and administration. His intentions have been seen as motivated by his theoretical interests in anthropology, but a more balanced view is that his ideas developed in a pragmatic fashion and were partially borrowed from established Fijian residents such as J. B. Thurston. He left the governorship of Fiji in 1880 for a short-lived governorship of New Zealand (1880–83), but he continued to exert some influence in the former colony because from 1877 to 1883 he held the extra position of high commissioner and consul-general for the Western Pacific. In New Zealand he was unpopular with a portion of the settler population because of his attempts to defend the interests of the Maori.

From 1883 to 1890 Gordon was governor in Ceylon, and enjoyed, for him, the unusual experience of being popular with his subjects. He was regarded as a sympathetic figure by both the Singhalese and the Tamil population, and was moderately popular with the European community. After his retirement from colonial administration Gladstone gave him a peerage in 1893 on the condition that he support Irish home rule in the House of Lords. Gordon agreed to this condition, but his half-hearted support for the measure annoyed Gladstone on the one hand, and Conservative peers, such as his half-brother, the duke of Abercorn, on the other. In politics Gordon's moral sense was less certain than it was in colonial administration, and he lacked the direction that he possessed as a governor.

As well as the short biography of his father, based on material collected for a fuller work which was never published, Gordon wrote a memoir of Sidney Herbert (1906) and spent much time in collecting and editing the mass of state papers and correspondence left behind by Lord Aberdeen, which he had printed, in many volumes, on the government of Ceylon printing press (the only available copy is in the British Library). Besides being a chairman of the Bank of Mauritius and of the Pacific Phosphate Company and president of the Ceylon Association, he was an active member of various House of Lords committees and a member of the house of laymen for the province of Canterbury. In religion he was a pronounced high-churchman.

Gordon was created CMG in 1859, KCMG in 1871, and GCMG in 1878. In 1893 he was raised to the peerage with the title of Baron Stanmore of Great Stanmore, Middlesex. He was made an honorary DCL at Oxford in 1879. He died at 47 Cadogan Place, London, on 30 January 1912 and was buried at Ascot, Berkshire, where he had lived for many years.

As a colonial administrator Gordon was one of the most distinguished of the second generation of professional governors who succeeded mid-Victorian figures such as Lord Elgin and Sir George Grey. Unlike those of his more imperialistic contemporaries, Gordon's policies did not favour white settlers and planters over other ethnic groups in his colonies. He was relatively free from the taints of racialism both when this served as a justification for empire and when it masqueraded as a mission to impose the ideals of European justice upon the customs and politics of non-British peoples. His insight into the workings of responsible government in New Brunswick, and, later, in New Zealand, made him feel that it would never function so as to promote the social happiness and material property of settler colonies. He supported it because he believed it was the only way to keep such places as loyal and contented parts of the empire.

MARK FRANCIS

Sources *DNB* • A. Hamilton-Gordon, Baron Stanmore, *Mauritius: records of private and of public life, 1871–1874*, 2 vols. (1894) • A. H. G. Stanmore, *Fiji: records of private and public life, 1875–1880*, 4 vols. (1897–1912) • A. Hamilton-Gordon, Baron Stanmore, *Letters and notes written during the disturbances in the highlands (known as the 'Devil Country') of Vitu Levu, Fiji, 1876*, 2 vols. (privately printed, Edinburgh, 1879) • *Gladstone–Gordon correspondence, 1851–1896*, ed. P. Knaplund (1961) • Gladstone, *Diaries* • W. S. MacNutt, *New Brunswick: a history, 1784–1867* (1963); repr. (1984) • D. Creighton, *The road to confederation: the emergence of Canada, 1863–1867* (1964) • J. K. Chapman, *The career of Arthur Hamilton Gordon, first Lord Stanmore, 1829–1912* (Toronto, 1964) • R. B. Joyce, *Sir William MacGregor* (1971) • W. P. Morrell, *Britain in the Pacific islands* (1960) • K. I. Gillion, *Fiji's Indian migrants* (1962) • B. V. Lal, *Broken waves: a history of the Fiji islands in the twentieth century* (1992) • I. Heath, 'Toward a reassessment of Gordon in Fiji', *Journal of Pacific History*, 9 (1974), 88 • P. France, *The charter of the land* (1969) • R. Shannon, *Gladstone*, 1: *1809–1865* (1982) • D. Scarr, *Viceroy of the Pacific, the majesty of colour: a life of Sir John Bates Thurston* (1980) • *The Times* (31 Jan 1912) • *CGPLA Eng. & Wales* (1912)

Archives BL, corresp., diaries, and papers, Add. MSS 49199–49272 • Bodl. RH, corresp. and dispatches relating to Mauritius • NL Scot., corresp. • NRA Scotland, priv. coll., family corresp. • NYPL, corresp. and papers relating to Trinidad • University of New Brunswick, Fredericton, corresp. and papers | Auckland Public Library, letters to Sir George Grey • BL, corresp. with Lord Aberdeen, Add. MS 43226 • BL, letters to Mary Gladstone, Add. MS 46243 • BL, corresp. with W. E. Gladstone, Add. MSS 44319–44322 • BL, corresp. with Lord Ripon, Add. MS 43544 • Bodl. Oxf., corresp. with Lewis Harcourt and Lord Carlisle • Bodl. Oxf., corresp. with Lord Kimberley • Borth. Inst., corresp. with Lord Halifax • LPL, letters to W. E. Gladstone • LPL, corresp. with Lord Selborne and Lady Selborne • PRO, corresp. with Lord Cardwell, PRO 30/48 • Wilts. & Swindon RO, corresp. with Sidney Herbert and Elizabeth Herbert

Likenesses F. O. Salisbury, oils, 1911, Gov. Art Coll. [*see illus.*] • J. Lucas, oils (as a boy), Haddo House, Grampian region • wood-engraving (after photograph by Bassano), NPG; repro. in *ILN* (10 April 1875)

Wealth at death £142,279 11*s.* 4*d.*: probate, 20 March 1912, *CGPLA Eng. & Wales*

Gordon, Charles, first earl of Aboyne (*d.* **1681**), politician, was the fourth son of George *Gordon, second marquess of Huntly (*c.*1590–1649), politician, and his wife, Anne (1594–1638), eldest daughter of Archibald *Campbell, seventh earl of Argyll, whose marriage contract was dated 1607. Lord Charles had a difficult childhood with his mother dying in 1638 and his father and eldest brother, George, being imprisoned in Edinburgh in 1639. Together with his brother Lord Lewis, Gordon was at school in Aberdeen from 1644 to 1648. His brother George was killed at the battle of Alford on 2 July 1645. When his father became second marquess of Huntly in 1636 Gordon's brother James *Gordon took the title Viscount Aboyne, but he died shortly before the execution of Huntly on 16 March 1649. Charles was captured at Strathbogie that year. Lewis became third marquess of Huntly, but he died in December 1653, leaving an infant son, George, to succeed as fourth marquess. Gordon, now known as Charles, Lord Aboyne, took on the responsibility for managing those estates still in the hands of the family, which was Roman Catholic.

On 2 December 1659 the heritors of Aberdeenshire chose Aboyne as a commissioner to confer with General George Monck at Berwick. On 10 September 1660 Gordon was created earl of Aboyne. With the family estates restored Aboyne was head of a significant interest in north-east Scotland. His first wife, Margaret (*d.* 1662), daughter of Alexander *Irvine of Drum, Bonnie Peggy Irvine, died childless in December 1662. On 28 August 1665 Aboyne was contracted to marry Lady Elizabeth Lyon, daughter of John Lyon, earl of Kinghorne. They had three sons and a daughter.

In the 1660s Aboyne's Catholicism inhibited his participation in public life, but he acquired a somewhat unsavoury reputation for his protection of Patrick Roy Macgregor of that ilk, who was not averse to hanging Aboyne's local opponents. The Scottish privy council records abound with disputes involving Aboyne. In November 1675 he was in London offering support to the duke of Lauderdale. Perhaps as a reward for such loyalty Aboyne was appointed to the Scottish privy council on 7 February 1676 and took the oaths of office that day. He attended the council fairly regularly between 1676 and 1679, but ceased to attend in January 1680. He died in March 1681, being succeeded by his son **Charles Gordon** (*d.* 1702) as second earl of Aboyne. The next month the young earl went to the Roman Catholic college at Douai in France. In 1694 he was described by James Drummond, earl of Perth, a Jacobite and fellow Catholic, as 'a most sweet youth and humble like the dust of the street' (GEC, *Peerage*), but he turned his back on his upbringing and on 27 July 1698 took the oath as a protestant in order to sit in parliament. He married his first cousin, Lady Elizabeth Lyon, daughter of Patrick *Lyon, third earl of Strathmore and Kinghorne (1643?–1695), who had also taken the oath after suspicions of Jacobitism. He died in April 1702 and was survived by his wife, who later married first Patrick Kinnaird, Lord Kinnaird (*d.* 1715), and then Captain Alexander Grant, before she died in January 1739, and by their son John Gordon (*d.* 1732), who became third earl of Aboyne. STUART HANDLEY

Sources GEC, *Peerage* • *Scots peerage* • Charles, eleventh marquis of Huntly, earl of Aboyne, ed., *The records of Aboyne MCCCXXX–MDCLXXXI*, New Spalding Club, 13 (1894) • C. A. Gordon, *A concise history of the ancient and illustrious house of Gordon* (1754) • P. Hopkins, *Glencoe and the end of the highland war* (1986) • *Reg. PCS*, 3rd ser. • *Manuscripts of the duke of Atholl … and of the earl of Home*, HMC, 26 (1891) • J. Fraser, *Chronicles of the Frasers: the Wardlaw manuscript*, ed. W. Mackay, Scottish History Society, 1st ser., 47 (1905)
Archives NA Scot., letters to Sir John Gordon and James Innes

Gordon, Charles, second earl of Aboyne (*d.* **1702**). *See under* Gordon, Charles, first earl of Aboyne (*d.* 1681).

Gordon, Sir Charles (**1755/6–1835**), army officer and colonial governor, was the third son of Charles Gordon of Abergeldie, Perthshire (1724–1796), and his wife, Alison (*d.* 1800), daughter of David Hunter of Barside, whose first husband was called Paterson. He was appointed lieutenant on 25 October 1775 in the 1st battalion of Simon Fraser's (71st) regiment of highlanders, a new corps which Gordon helped to raise and muster at Glasgow in April 1776, for service in the American colonies. He served with the regiment under Howe at the capture of Philadelphia on 25 September 1777, and was later based with it in New York. On 8 January 1778 he transferred with the rank of captain to the 26th foot (Cameronians), then serving at Philadelphia. The regiment became seriously weakened and returned to England in March 1780 in a skeleton state and was garrisoned at Tynemouth. He moved to the 83rd foot (Royal Glasgow volunteers) with the rank of major on 3 April 1782. This regiment was disbanded in 1783 and on 14 April Gordon was placed on half pay with the brevet rank of lieutenant-colonel.

Following the long-established custom for Scottish military men seeking employment, in 1787 Gordon took foreign service as a volunteer with the Prussian army under Karl, duke of Brunswick, which entered the Netherlands on 13 September with the purpose of securing the authority of the stadholder, William V, against the patriotic or republican party, whose militia controlled Amsterdam and other major towns. Gordon was the 'British officer' who carried out a survey by boat of the ground behind Amstelven, the patriot-held fortress that was the key to Amsterdam's defence, in preparation for a surprise attack from the rear. This dangerous and important service was 'executed with courage, ability and success' (Bowdler, 104). He commanded the successful landing of the troops on 1 October and was present in the final assault and 'happened to be the first person who made his way through the village … and brought the news of the success to the Duke of Brunswick' (ibid., 111). The road was now open to Amsterdam, which surrendered on 10 October. Reports of his involvement at the time omitted his name, probably for reasons of security, but later that year the influence of the foreign secretary, Francis Godolphin Osborne, marquess of Carmarthen (later fifth duke of Leeds), secured him the lieutenant-colonelcy of the 41st regiment (later the Welch regiment). This was originally a corps of invalids, reformed as a line regiment on 25 December 1787, the date of his commission.

Gordon appears to have remained with the duke of Brunswick during part of 1788 before returning to England. With the likelihood of a rupture in relations between Prussia and Austria, in 1790 he was given leave to serve as aide-de-camp to the duke and joined the Prussian army in Silesia during the spring. In recognition of past services, Frederick William II of Prussia granted him his country's order of military merit, which like other foreign orders of chivalry prior to 1814 carried knightly rank in England. Permission to wear the order in England was granted on 3 August 1790. He accompanied the duke of Brunswick as British military commissioner during the campaigns of 1791–2.

In late 1793 Gordon, still lieutenant-colonel of the 41st foot (though he was promoted to the brevet rank of colonel on 20 December 1793), joined the expedition against the French colonies in the West Indies, under General Sir Charles Grey and Admiral John Jervis. Gordon was given temporary command of a brigade, until the arrival of Prince Edward, son of George III, from Canada. On 8 February 1794 he commanded the attack on Cas de Navire, on the west coast of Martinique. After some difficulty had been experienced in landing, the French batteries were dislodged from the high ground between Cas de Navire and Fort Royal by a series of 'unseen turning movements, through dense forest and over the steepest hills and ravines' (Fortescue, *Brit. army*, 4/1.356). He then proceeded to occupy the French outposts of Gentilly, La Coste, and La Archel, near Fort Bourbon. By 20 February Fort Bourbon and Fort Royal, which guarded the island's capital, St Pierre, were completely invested. He relinquished command of the 3rd brigade upon the arrival of Prince Edward on 4 March. After the surrender of Martinique, Gordon took part in the capture of St Lucia, which was achieved without loss, and was appointed governor of that island and received the rank of brigadier-general.

Formal complaints were made against Gordon, as governor of St Lucia, of extortion and of taking bribes from disaffected persons to allow them to remain in the island, and afterwards breaking faith with them. A general court-martial, under the presidency of General Robert Prescott, was ordered to assemble on 25 July 1794. Following several delays, caused by deaths among members of the court from the fever that was then raging, Gordon was found guilty and sentenced to refund the money (estimated to be £25,000), and to be cashiered. In consequence of past services he was allowed to receive the value of his commissions. Fortescue argued that Gordon had been guilty of embezzlement 'rather through error and weakness than vice' (Fortescue, *Brit. army*, 4/1.376). However, his actions have been regarded by later historians as a more extreme form of the 'general plundering exercise' (Duffy, 109), following the occupation of the islands, initiated by the commanding officers, Grey and Jervis, in the matter of prize money.

Gordon survived his dismissal by more than forty years. He appears to have been employed by the British government during the Napoleonic war in various capacities on the continent, where his knowledge of several European languages and of the politics of the Low Countries were put to use. Thus in early November 1803 Jervis, by then earl of St Vincent, who had commanded the sea forces in the expedition of 1794, referred to dispatches from Gordon regarding 'the discontents in Holland', which 'might be put to good account' (Brenton, 2.146). He died at his home in Ely Place, London, on 26 March 1835, at the age of seventy-nine. He never married or had children.

H. M. CHICHESTER, *rev.* JONATHAN SPAIN

Sources Burke, *Gen. GB* (1952) · J. M. Bulloch and others, eds., *The house of Gordon*, 2 vols., Third Spalding Club, 26, 33 (1903–7) · *GM*, 2nd ser., 3 (1835), 555 · *GM*, 1st ser., 60 (1790), 961–2, 1066 · S. H. F. Johnston, *The history of the Cameronians*, 1 (1957) · D. Stewart, *Sketches of the character, manners, and present state of the highlanders of Scotland: with details of the military service of the highland regiments*, 2 vols. (1822) · A. C. Whitehorne, *The history of the Welch regiment*, 1: 1719–1914 (1932) · *Army List* (1776–95) · J. C. Willyams, *An account of the campaign in the West Indies in the year 1794* (1796) · T. Bowdler, *Letters written in Holland in the months of September and October 1787* (1788) · E. P. Brenton, *Life and correspondence of John, earl of St Vincent*, 2 vols. (1838) · Fortescue, *Brit. army*, vol. 4, pt 1 · M. Duffy, *Soldiers, sugar, and sea power: the British expeditions to the West Indies and the war against revolutionary France* (1987) · J. M. Fewster, 'Prize money and the British expedition to the West Indies of 1793–4', *Journal of Imperial and Commonwealth History*, 12 (1983–4), 1–28 · A. Cobban, *Ambassadors and secret agents: the diplomacy of the 1st earl of Malmesbury at The Hague* (1954) · P. De Witt, *Une invasion prussienne en Hollande en 1787* (1886) · *Diaries and correspondence of James Harris, first earl of Malmesbury*, ed. third earl of Malmesbury [J. H. Harris], 4 vols. (1844)
Archives BL, corresp. with marquess of Carmarthen, Add. MS 28063, fols. 7, 322; Add. MS 28065, fol. 255

Gordon, Charles George (1833–1885), army officer, was born on 28 January 1833 at 1 Kempt's Terrace, Woolwich, fourth son and ninth child (of five boys and six girls) of Lieutenant-General Henry William Gordon RA (1785/6–1865) and his wife, Elizabeth (1794–1873), daughter of Samuel *Enderby (1756–1829) [*see under* Enderby family (*per.* c.1750–1876)], a shipowner in whose bottoms the notorious shipment of tea reached Boston in 1777, and who later was also interested in whaling and Antarctic exploration.

Early life and military career His family accompanied their father on his military postings, notably to Corfu where Charley Gordon was taught at home by a governess. Deterred by the vicious reputation of public schools, his parents sent him to a private school run by the governess's clergyman brother near Taunton (1843–6) before a military crammer at Shooters Hill (1846–7). As a boy he was an aggressive prankster. In 1848 he entered the Royal Military Academy, Woolwich, where his eccentricities as a disciplinarian (he hit younger cadets over the head with a hairbrush or broomstick) led to his being put on a charge for bullying. These scrapes caused his father anxiety:

Charles George Gordon (1833–1885), by Sir John F. D. Donnelly

'while he is in the Academy, I feel I am like a man sitting on a powder-barrel' (Wortham, 34). He had been intended to follow his father as an artilleryman, but came to prefer the engineers, and was commissioned second lieutenant, Royal Engineers (23 June 1852).

On promotion to lieutenant (17 February 1854) Gordon took up his first appointment as assistant garrison engineer at Pembroke Dock. Although he remained there only until December 1854, it proved a crucial phase of his life. At Pembroke he came under the religious influence of Captain Francis Drew, an Irish protestant officer, and his wife, Anne. Gordon began studying biblical commentaries, which fired his Christian faith. His religiosity did not become pronounced until 1862, when confinement in a sick-room with mild smallpox drove him to sacred meditations. Thereafter Gordon remained a deeply committed Christian who saw himself as living each day in the hands of God. He came to see his life as a fight for the gospels. Despite his vanity he strove from the 1860s to accomplish that resignation of self which he conceived to be the highest Christian duty. All his actions were ruled by his sense of God's presence: he once told Reginald Brett (afterwards second Viscount Esher): 'as I came to your house He walked with me arm in arm up South Audley Street' (Lees-Milne, 56). Gordon thought the flesh was evil, despised his physicality, and believed that all men's souls were predestined for salvation. In consequence he came to regard death not as fearful but as the gateway to eternal life. To die, and thus ascend into the gracious presence of the Lord, became a passionately desirable apotheosis. Until

1880 he never joined a church, instead studying the Bible daily, and reaching his own interpretations of the text. During the last years of his life, when his death wish was becoming more accentuated, he became a regular communicant.

Gordon despised money, insisted that his own salaries should be reduced, and spurned rewards. He was contemptuous of rank and wealth and decried luxury as effeminate. A mutual acquaintance told Cecil Spring-Rice in 1884, 'He is without the three strongest passions which make men good or bad—the love of money, the love of fame and the love of women' (Gwynn, 1.34). His only indulgence was cigarette smoking, which probably contributed to the onset of angina pectoris in middle life: this ailment in turn increased his fatalism about death. He was rumoured to have been a secret inebriate, but although he may have stupefied himself on occasions when he was anxious or discouraged, he was mainly abstinent.

The Crimea and after Following the outbreak of the Crimean War Gordon volunteered for service. After landing at Balaklava (2 January 1855) as a subaltern he participated in the assault on the Redan and in the siege of Sevastopol, where he afterwards prepared the shafts and galleries to blow up the dockyard (1855–6). His courage, military enterprise, hardihood, and selective human sympathies were all evident. Some of his later remarks fostered the myth that he performed feats of almost theatrical courage in the hope of being killed. 'I went to the Crimea hoping, without having a hand in it, to be killed', he recalled in 1883. 'I survived and lived, never fearing death but not wishing to be too closely acquainted with God, nor yet to leave him' (Chenevix-Trench, 19). This pose is a somewhat histrionic self-reinvention, for his letters of the period brim with ambition and brio: he found war exciting, and was pleased to be promoted lieutenant (17 February 1854) and awarded the Légion d'honneur.

From boyhood Gordon had shown a special proficiency in map making. After the Crimean peace he was transferred to the international commission surveying and delineating the new Danubian frontiers between the Russian and Ottoman empires (1856–7). Though he wearied of drawing maps, and protested in vain, he was next sent on similar duties along the new Russo-Turkish frontier in Armenia (1857–8). For his work in Armenia he was in 1858 elected fellow of the Royal Geographical Society, but resigned in 1866 because he felt its members were trying to lionize him. He was a pioneer photographer, who took striking pictures in the Crimea and Armenia.

China Promoted captain (1 April 1859), Gordon served as second adjutant of the corps of Royal Engineers and adjutant of the Chatham depot (2 May 1859 to 14 June 1860). He then volunteered as a member of the Franco-British force which landed in northern China to enforce Chinese acquiescence in the treaty of Tientsin (Tianjin) (1858). He arrived too late for the fighting, but participated in the occupation of Peking (Beijing) and the plundering of its Summer Palace. As commander of the British brigade of the Royal Engineers in China, he supervised the construction of troop quarters. In 1862 he was summoned to join the British, French, and imperial Chinese troops protecting the international settlement at Shanghai from the Taiping insurgents. Gordon, with a strong escort, made a meticulous and extensive reconnaissance of the districts around Tientsin. A private force grandiloquently named the Ever Victorious Army was also mustered at the expense of Shanghai's foreign merchants. On 24 March 1863 Gordon (promoted brevet major on 30 December 1862) took command of this mutinous rabble of 4000 Chinese officered by a gallimaufry of European and American adventurers. He pitched them against the insurgents, who formidably outnumbered them and were at least as well equipped. Gordon's personal hatred of inaction and social horror of fixed engagements were reflected in the tactics which he deployed against the Taipings. He defeated them by the mobility of his forces, particularly the swift and flexible manoeuvring of armed steamboats along the extensive medieval canal system in the Suchow (Suzhou) region. This unorthodox warfare, combined with the ascendancy which Gordon established over his men, enabled him to crush the rebellion in eighteen months. On 11 May 1864 he achieved his final triumph by storming Changchow (Zhangzhou). His total irreverence for age or position, and his supercilious indifference to his official superiors, date from the period of these precocious victories in China.

In Britain the popular reputation of Chinese Gordon, as henceforth he was widely known, was enhanced by the knowledge that he had spent his pay on the comfort of his troops, and had declined munificent gifts from the emperor before leaving China (he received, however, the highest Chinese military rank together with the right to wear the yellow jacket). Earlier, in 1857, his appeal to be allowed to fight in India against the mutineers had been disregarded, but nevertheless that imperial crisis bore decisively on his future reputation. The Indian mutiny made heroes of such men as Sir Henry Lawrence, who was killed at Lucknow, and the Havelocks. The mutiny fostered a cult of the Christian military hero: Chinese Gordon became a totem of this cult in the mid-1860s, and in death came to represent its apotheosis. Like T. E. Lawrence he had a genius for guerrilla warfare and for leading destitute, ill-trained forces. His leadership of men was helped by his piercing blue-grey eyes, which gave the misleading impression that he could see into men's secret thoughts: in fact he was easily duped by impostors. It is notable that his pre-eminent gifts were not as a leader of Englishmen. He was a martinet who in Russia complained that his men whined and growled even more than despicable Frenchmen, and in China similarly observed: 'grumbling, dirty, idle, helpless to a degree and without the smallest spark of *esprit de corps*, what a brute the ordinary English linesman is' (Chenevix-Trench, 25).

Philanthropist and boy lover Promoted brevet lieutenant-colonel on 16 February 1864, Gordon was appointed in September 1865 as Royal Engineer officer in command at

Gravesend and entrusted with supervising the erection of forts at the entrance of the Thames. He was even more unhappy and frustrated than usual in this period, which saw his religious preoccupations intensify. By incessant study of the Bible and Thomas à Kempis's *Imitatio Christi*, supported by spiritual confidences to his pious spinster sister Augusta, he strove to subdue his carnal desires and his unregenerate body to the love of God. In boyhood he had developed a warm intimacy with this sister, twelve years his senior; his trust in her was not only enduring but exclusive, for he was seldom at ease with other women, none of whom was accepted in his affections. 'No novels or worldly books come up to the *Sermons* of McCheyne or the *Commentaries* of Scott', he wrote to Augusta in 1866 (*Gordon to his Sister*, 2). 'I wished I was a eunuch at fourteen' Gordon recalled in 1883 (Chenevix-Trench, 63–4), and sexual sublimation remained important to him. He devoted his spare time to religious philanthropy among Gravesend's poor, tending the sick in the workhouse infirmary and housing street urchins in his official residence, where he fed, clothed, and taught them. He enjoyed giving baths to his 'Gravesend laddies', or 'kings', 'wangs', 'doves', and 'angels', as he variously called them. Many had been starved of affection, and reciprocated his tenderness. He was never caught in, and probably never committed, the indiscretions which led to the suicide of his fellow general Sir Hector MacDonald. Nevertheless, in Gordon's lifetime, Evelyn Baring (afterwards earl of Cromer) characterized him as 'a queer fellow' with 'a very feminine side to his character' (Baring to earl of Northbrook, 11 March 1884, PRO, FO/633/4, letter 46). One of his shrewdest biographers has characterized Gordon as 'in this matter a Platonist' who 'found an outlet for the emotions generated by intercourse with the opposite sex in the company of boys and young men' (Wortham, 32).

Military pro-consul Gordon's boredom continued after he was posted in October 1871 to Galatz as British representative on the Danubian commission (with the rank of brevet colonel from 16 February 1872). In consequence he was relieved in 1873 to be offered service under the khedive of Egypt as governor-general of the province of Equatoria, in the south of Egyptian-occupied Sudan. He obtained British government approval and, stipulating only that his salary should be reduced from £10,000 to £2000, reached Khartoum in March 1874. Gordon's chief tasks were to launch steamers flying the Egyptian flag upon the Great Lakes, and then to suppress the flourishing Equatorian slave trade, but it was his ardent conviction that a governor's first duty was to the subjects he ruled, and only subordinately to the imperial power. He endured extreme physical suffering while undertaking the strenuous work of establishing a chain of stations stretching into northern Uganda and of mapping the Nile and lakes. Disclaiming any desire to be a geographical explorer, he deputed to his companion Romolo Gessi the achievement of reaching Lake Albert, which he thought would put him at risk of being glamorized. Though he was sincere in his dislike of war, he displayed a ferocious zest for the skirmishes which accompanied these journeys. The indigenous inhabitants of Equatoria were primitive, his Arab soldiers were cowardly and treacherous, the Egyptian officials (who were mostly inept) had long connived in or profited from the slave trade, and his small British staff succumbed to disease. At times, during these two and a half years, he undertook the tasks of storekeeper, carpenter, and porter as well as governor. Nevertheless by the end of 1876 he had suppressed slave trading in Equatoria.

In 1877, after proposing to the khedive that all of the Sudan must be subjected to a rigorous anti-slavery administration, Gordon, with a certain ambivalence, consented to become governor-general of Sudan, including Equatoria. Mindful of the terrible sickness among his previous Equatorian entourage he resolved to face his new duties alone. He thus took solitary responsibility for an area exceeding a million square miles, in which warfare, slavery, and terrible deprivation were endemic. He visited the emperor in Abyssinia, and during a visit of fifteen days to Khartoum instituted extensive reforms intended to eliminate vicious corruption. 'His chastity', suggested Sir Rivers Wilson, 'which was absolutely incomprehensible to the Arab seemed to raise him to the position of a mystical and almost divine character' (Wilson, 199). He went with 300 men to Darfur province, where a large force of insurgent slave traders had massed. With characteristic audacity he rode into the rebel camp in full dress as governor-general accompanied only by an interpreter and small escort. Just as in China fifteen years earlier he had subdued mutinous troops by force of personality and histrionic power, so he cowed these rebels. Many joined his forces, others retreated, and the revolt was crushed in 1879. He thus extinguished the slave hunts from Darfur to the Red Sea littoral, although slave trading remained legal in Egypt.

After other vicissitudes—an unfortunate intervention to rescue Egyptian national finances, a hazardous overture to King John of Abyssinia during which he was briefly made captive—he left Egyptian service in December 1879 and next month reached London wound up to a high pitch of fatigue and exasperation. His attitude to British officialdom was by now wilful and contemptuous. His judgement was volatile. He opposed the Egyptian policy of the Beaconsfield cabinet, whom he considered mountebanks. 'I hate our diplomatists', he later wrote. 'I think with few exceptions they are arrant humbugs, and I expect they know it' (*Khartoum Journal*, 137). As Sir Thomas Wade reported to the Foreign Office in 1880:

> A long life of isolation, under circumstances well calculated to disturb coolness of head, has, I fear, told upon his reasoning powers. His nerve is perfectly unshaken, but his judgment is no longer in balance, and … his very devoutness is dangerous; for he has taught himself to believe, more or less, that in pursuing this course or that, he is but obeying inspiration. (Pollock, 202)

A havering phase In May 1880 Gordon accepted appointment as private secretary to the marquess of Ripon, who had recently assumed the Indian viceroyalty, but resigned after only a few days in Bombay on 3 June 1880. His Anglo-Indian colleague Sir Andrew Clarke commented on this resignation:

> Gordon is not an ordinary man, and his mind and actions are not regulated in the same way as are other men's minds. He frets and chafes not only at what he thinks the finesse and lies of ordinary public life, but at its ceremony and at its etiquette; a state dinner, or even to wait through an ordinary social gathering, is irritating … to him. (Childers, 2.36–7)

Gordon remained dismissive of the jewel in the crown, writing in 1884:

> India accustoms our men to a style of life which they cannot keep up in England; it deteriorates our women. If we kept the sea-coast, it is all that we want. It is the centre of all petty intrigue, while if our energy were devoted elsewhere, it would produce ten fold. (*Khartoum Journal*, 12)

Despite official British disapproval, Gordon revisited China, where he helped to avert a rebellion against the central government, which he then cajoled into abandoning its warlike preparations against Russia. During a brief visit to Peking he offended both mandarins and foreign officials. It was a sign of Gordon's deterioration that his old admirer in China Sir Robert Hart wrote (11 August 1880):

> Much as I like and respect him, I must say he is *'not all there'*. Whether it is religion, or vanity, or softening of the brain—I don't know; but he seems to be alternately arrogant and slavish, vain and humble, in his senses and out of them. (Fairbank, Bruner, and Matheson, 1.332)

The spiritual crisis which Gordon experienced at this time accomplished his final estrangement from countrymen of his own class. 'I dwell on the joy of never seeing Great Britain again, with its horrid, wearisome *dinner* parties and miseries', he wrote in extremity in Khartoum (24 October 1884). 'At those dinner parties we are all in masks, saying what we do not believe, eating and drinking things we do not want, and then abusing one another' (*Khartoum Journal*, 139). As an escape from this bondage he obtained in April 1881 the command of the Royal Engineers in Mauritius. This enabled him to pursue elaborate investigations as a result of which he believed that he had identified an island in the Seychelles as the site of the Garden of Eden. He was obliged to vacate this post on being promoted major-general (23 March 1882), and proceeded to South Africa, where from 1 June to 11 October 1882 he reorganized the troops in Cape Colony and made a perilous journey into Basuto territory in an attempt to adjust their grievances. The governor of the Cape and high commissioner of South Africa, Sir Hercules Robinson (afterwards first Baron Rosmead), developed 'a very strong objection to him' at this time. He was repelled on an occasion when Gordon was 'sent to deal with an awful brute among the natives who was brought to face him with great difficulty. As soon as he saw him, however, Gordon fell upon his neck and called him a brother in Christ'. Speaking in 1884, Robinson added that there was 'no one so undecided in word or so decided in action: that he would telegraph one thing in the morning, another thing in the evening, and a third thing the next day' (Gwynn, 1.33).

From January to December 1883 Gordon lived in the Holy Land studying antiquities. His calculations and theories about the true sites of the crucifixion and burial of Jesus Christ gained currency in Britain and the USA. In January 1884, at Brussels, he consented to a renewed request from the king of the Belgians to assume command in his Congo territory. Gordon regarded this task both as an opportunity to extirpate the slave trade and also as bound to lead to his early death, which he had long desired.

> [Sir Hercules] Robinson said that Gordon was with him when the invitation came from the King of the Belgians to go to the Congo. Robinson told him it was a vile climate, that the natives were savages, that it was folly to accept. Gordon said that was precisely the reason he accepted: because he would have killed himself long ago if religion had allowed it—that 'his life was a burden and a weariness to him'. (Gwynn, 1.34)

He intended to resign his British army commission and leave for the Congo in February, but other events supervened.

The Sudan The Gladstone ministry, committed to peace and retrenchment, had felt obliged to crush the Egyptian nationalist uprising under Arabi Pasha in 1882, and thus constituted Britain as the power behind the khedive's tottering throne. Egypt became a 'veiled protectorate' with Baring the British minister-plenipotentiary exercising supreme influence. Meanwhile in the Sudan an obscure fakir who had proclaimed himself the Mahdi, or Expected One, in 1881, now projected a holy war. Raising the green standard of revolt, his forces on 5 December 1883 annihilated Hicks Pasha's Egyptian expedition of 10,000 men sent to repress the insurrection. The fate of the Egyptian garrison beleaguered in Khartoum became critical, but the Egyptian army had proved its incapacity: the British government resisted committing troops for the reconquest of the Sudan, while an appeal for help from Ottoman Turkey was unpalatable. Baring having recommended the Sudan's evacuation, Earl Granville in December raised the possibility of Gordon's being used to supervise this course. Baring, however, opposed this suggestion, which he thought would hamper the main object of British policy: to avoid being drawn into military operations in the Sudan.

The publication of George Birkbeck Hill's selection of Gordon's idiosyncratic and vehement letters of 1874–9 entitled *Colonel Gordon in Central Africa* (1881) had revived Gordon's celebrity. On 9 January 1884 the *Pall Mall Gazette* carried a voluminous interview conducted with Gordon by its editor, the bumptiously meddlesome W. T. Stead, in which Gordon spoke with an air of high authority about the Mahdi and what might be done to tackle the crisis. He urged that Khartoum should be held as an outpost from which a counter-attack could later be directed against the Mahdists rather as Shanghai had served him when the Ever Victorious Army had vanquished the Taiping hordes. The newspaper also carried a leading article by Stead crying up Gordon's qualifications to solve the Sudanese impasse. This scoop incited other journalists to call feverishly for Gordon to be dispatched to the Sudan. Impressionable crowds began to shout 'Gordon must go' in the London streets. From the outset of this stunt, Stead and his press colleagues were responsible for inflating the public impression of Gordon as an infallible national saviour. The object of this publicity was not truly displeased. Meekness was difficult for a man who thought he was the instrument of divine ends.

The whigs in Gladstone's cabinet felt obliged to defer to this clamour. Despite demurrals by Gladstone and Baring about Gordon's reliability, Granville, Hartington, Dilke, and Northbrook hoped his mesmeric influence would quell the seething rebellion of a subcontinent and recruited him to assist government policy. Confusion, however, surrounded Gordon's hasty appointment and his remit. Most cabinet ministers thought Gordon had been instructed to evacuate the Egyptian detachments remaining in Khartoum and to march them back to Egypt, but there was ambiguity about this. The colonial secretary, Derby, professed never to have known 'who was responsible for the sending of Gordon to Khartoum' (Derby, diary, 7 Dec 1884, fol. 342; 4 Sept 1884, fol. 248). Initially Derby felt qualified optimism about:

> the appointment of Gordon … to serve in Egypt in a somewhat undefined capacity: the object of employing him being to bring away safely the garrisons now in danger at Khartoum and elsewhere. The choice is good, for he knows the country, and has extraordinary influence over wild tribes … Gordon, I should add, is not a man whom it will be possible to keep permanently in any administrative office. A fanatic of the Puritan type, satisfied that his way in all affairs is the best, and determined to have his own way, he has broken with his various employers successively. (ibid., 19 Jan 1884, fols. 19–20)

Gladstone's secretary, E. W. Hamilton, expressed shrewd misgivings on Gordon's appointment:

> The despatch of 'Chinese Gordon' on a mission to the Soudan has been very well received and has for the moment satisfied public opinion. But, notwithstanding all his Soudanese prestige, it is difficult to see what real good he can do. He seems to be a half cracked fatalist; and what can one expect from such a man? (23 Jan 1884; Hamilton, 2.545)

Lord Salisbury, reading of the appointment, exclaimed with a gesture of despair, 'they must have gone quite mad' (Cecil, 3.98), but some Conservative leaders were impressed. Earl Cairns on 12 February hailed Gordon as 'one of our national treasures' and averred 'that since the days of knight-errantry never was such an expedition undertaken' (*Hansard* 3, 284, 12 Feb 1884, 610). Other men who had recently worked with Gordon were dismayed. 'When I heard he had been appointed, I said that I knew the Govt. had chosen a man for their servant who would prove their master: and a mad one too,' Sir Hercules Robinson declared in February 1884. Sir H. Bartle E. Frere in the same month 'said that he was impossible to deal with: "tell him a thing's for his own interest, he'll do the opposite; tell him it's his duty and nothing will keep him from doing it, and doing it the shortest way"' (Gwynn, 1.33).

'Don't be a funk', Gordon wired to the governor of Khartoum. 'You are men, not women. I am coming. Tell the inhabitants' (Zetland, 110). He proceeded straight to Cairo, where he was confirmed in his contempt for the pashas as effete, but rescinded his initial refusal to see the khedive, who again installed him as governor-general of the Sudan. His request to be accompanied to Khartoum by the slave trader Zobehr Pasha, whose son had been killed by Gordon's troops and whose own fall from power was attributable to Gordon, was denied by Baring, who knew the bitterness of Zobehr's hatred. Baring indeed had such misgivings already that he would have preferred Zobehr to replace Gordon on the Khartoum expedition.

In Cairo Gordon's demeanour was reasonable, but on the march into the Sudan he became increasingly excitable, volatile, and impulsive. Arriving in Khartoum on 18 February 1884, he declared, 'I come without soldiers, but with God on my side, to redress the evils of the Soudan' (McGregor-Hastie, 159). Gordon made peaceful overtures to the Mahdi, and evacuated some 2000 Egyptian civilians and 600 soldiers before the town was encircled by the Mahdists on 18 March. He found the Treasury almost exhausted and the pay of officials and troops three months in arrears. Baring had arranged for Gordon to draw £100,000 from the Egyptian treasury, but all of this huge sum was embezzled and never reached Khartoum. In consequence Gordon issued his own notes, all dated 25 April 1884, in ten denominations from 50 piastres to 50 Egyptian pounds, of which about half were personally signed by him. Without this currency the defence of Khartoum would have soon collapsed; after the town was sacked, possession of these notes was cruelly punished, and most were publicly burnt or fed to goats. Gordon came to regard Mahdism as 'far more a question of property' than of fanatical faith, 'more like communism under the flag of religion' (*Khartoum Journal*, 37).

'I wish to goodness that Gordon', wrote Baring on 11 March, 'could be made to count to twenty before he writes or telegraphs' (Zetland, 112). Gordon had begun issuing emotive telegraphic messages and despairing dispatches which touched a chord of commiseration in many British hearts. These communications seemed a stratagem intended to secure a policy of conquest rather than scuttle in the Sudan. Trusting to his prestige at home, he asserted that he would hold out for as long as possible, trying to suppress the rebellion. An agitation arose that Gordon must not be abandoned and that reinforcements must be sent. The earl of Kimberley noted (13 May 1884):

> The London newspapers and the Tories clamour for an expedition to Khartoum, the former from ignorance, the latter because it is the best mode of embarrassing us. We shall hardly I fear succeed in baffling the combination of Exeter Hall fanatics, bondholders, and Tories. The interest of the nation is to get quit of the Soudan as soon as possible. But Gordon is a tremendous obstacle. If he cannot be got out in any other way, an expedition (a frightful undertaking) is inevitable. Of course it is not an impossible undertaking, but it is melancholy to think of the waste of lives and treasure which it must involve, and except the rescue of Gordon and Stewart, no good to be attained. (Kimberley, *Journal*, 343)

Gladstone believed that Gordon was distorting his instructions, and initially refused to send relief on the score of his disobedience. As Derby complained of Gordon,

> He has determined to hold the Soudan, contrary to orders, & has made public two wild telegrams, in which he asserts this intention, & attacks the government for not supporting him. He is in fact in mutiny—there is no other word for it. (Derby, diary, 19 Sept 1884, fol. 262)

'I own to having been very insubordinate to Her Majesty's Government and its officials, but it is my nature, and I cannot help it', Gordon recorded in his journal on 19 September. 'I know if *I* was chief I would never employ myself, for I am incorrigible. To men like Dilke, who weigh every word, I must be *perfect poison*' (*Khartoum Journal*, 56–7). It seemed to the public that his actions resounded with self-sacrifice, although they can as easily be represented as merely self-destructive. The publication during the summer of *General Gordon's Letters from the Crimea, the Danube and Armenia* with a provocatively anti-Gladstonian introduction by Demetrius Boulger strengthened his hold on popular sympathies. The outcry on his behalf, together with pressure from Queen Victoria and ultimately Hartington, forced Gladstone to yield in August. An expedition to relieve Khartoum was dispatched in September, commanded by Sir Garnet Wolseley, whose instructions forbad him from extricating other Sudanese garrisons. Spring-Rice noted on 20 September: 'It's funny that a man whom it took one journalist to send should take our only general, two thousand camels, a thousand boats, and ten thousand men to bring back' (Gwynn, 1.35).

Under siege Gordon seemed elated as well as angry and tired. The consequences of defeat were more fearful to him than death. On 24 September he rejected 'the imputation' that Wolseley's 'expedition has come to *relieve me*. It has *come to save our national honour in extricating the garrisons, &c., from a position* [in which] *our action in Egypt has placed these garrisons*' (*Khartoum Journal*, 73). On 5 October he opined that the Sudan was 'a wretched country and not worth keeping … but … I am in honour bound to the people after six months' bothering warfare' (ibid., 100). The journals which he kept from 10 September to 14 December 1884 are opinionated, egocentric, manipulative, and self-righteous (the cabinet in 1885 agreed to their publication, but only in full, because this would reveal Gordon's madness to the public). He shows himself a sarcastic and resentful outsider in his comments on other officers and officials. The journals' insubordinate temper and air of doomed heroism have understandably attracted rebellious or idealistic readers. The youthful George Wyndham wrote (21 July 1885) shortly after their publication: 'Gordon's journals are splendid, I delight in an eccentric man upsetting the odds which routine, formality, "Foreign" and other offices always have on their side, and making the latter appear ridiculous' (*Letters of George Wyndham*, 1.96).

Gordon withstood a siege of 317 days supported by two white officers with native troops wasted by famine and disease. Then, on 26 January 1885, a fall in the level of the Nile enabled the Mahdists to succeed in a final assault on Khartoum. Gordon was speared by dervishes in his palace, and his dissevered head was displayed in the Mahdists' camp. Wolseley's river steamers came in sight of Khartoum on 28 January, then withdrew. Gordon's body was never found.

Appearance Joseph Reinach, a Frenchman who met him at Alexandria in 1879, described Gordon as

> of medium height, very thin, a restless step, eyes very soft and vague as if lost in distant thought, and with that brick-coloured complexion which Englishmen acquire when long in the tropics; he looked sometimes dejected and sometimes angry. (Pollock, 171)

Reinach added: 'like many heroes he was a hero in the short term, a mystic who liked the sound of his own voice, and also, how should I put it? A bit of a humbug' (Chenevix-Trench, 161). Curzon, who published an essay comparing Gordon to Germanicus (*Oxford Review*, 25 Feb 1885), described meeting him in Pall Mall around 1880: 'shabbily dressed in a seedy black frock coat, trousers that did not come down to the boots, and a very dilapidated black silk topper with a particularly narrow brim and silk mostly brushed the wrong way' (Ronaldshay, 1.97).

Posthumous reputation Gordon's last year was played out on a world stage, and his assassination ensured for him immediate, morbid promotion by the press into martyrdom. The first telegraphic rumours of his death reached London on 5 February. As Derby complained the next day, 'great exaggeration prevails, one article saying that no such calamity has occurred since the Indian mutiny, another referring as a precedent to the destruction of the British army in Afghanistan, 40 years ago' (Derby, diary, 6 Feb 1885, fol. 37). The queen sent a telegram *en clair* rebuking Granville, Hartington, and Gladstone for Gordon's death. In cabinet on 7 February, 'the Premier said he believed the public cared very much about Gordon, but very little about the Soudan' (ibid., 7 Feb 1885, fol. 38). Gladstone's estimation was correct. The fall of Khartoum was a military setback and an injury to prestige, but insignificant compared with the impact of Gordon's sacrifice. His death became as important a symbol in the rise of Britain's new imperialism as the Munich accord between Chamberlain and Hitler in 1938 of the collapsed pretensions of the British to global dominance. It was construed as meaning that British interests, national honour, and the imperial mission were held cheap by the Liberal Party. 'England stands before the world dripping with blood and daubed with dishonour', R. L. Stevenson wrote to J. A. Symonds (2 March 1885) in a paroxysm of revulsion at 'our ineffable shame: the desertion of the garrisons' (*Letters*, 5.80–81). There was much grief and rage. 'During this stage of national hysteria', as Baring wrote, any critic of Gordon 'would have been regarded with a dislike somewhat akin to that which is felt for anyone who is heard talking flippantly in public of the truths of the Christian religion' (BL, Add. MS 44904, fol. 147). Gladstone's nickname, the G[rand] O[ld] M[an], became inverted to M[urderer] O[f] G[ordon].

'Gordon was a hero, and a hero of heroes', even Gladstone said (Zetland, 106). In private Hamilton wrote a just enough estimate: 'Gordon was certain[ly] a hero—the very embodiment of British chivalry and pluck. At the same time, he behaved recklessly and with very small regard to his own country' (Hamilton, 2.793–4). Winston Churchill in 1899 summarized a long discussion of the Sudan crisis which he had with the Egyptian pro-consul:

> Cromer was very bitter about him and begged me not to pander to the popular belief on the subject. Of course there is no doubt that Gordon as a political figure was absolutely hopeless. He was so erratic, capricious, utterly unreliable, his mood changed so often, his temper was abominable, he was frequently drunk, and yet with all he had a tremendous sense of honour and great abilities, and a still greater obstinacy. (Churchill, pt 2, 1017)

Those who had not had to work with him were more impressed. 'Of all the people I have met in my life, he and Darwin are the two in whom I have found something bigger than ordinary humanity—an unequalled simplicity and directness of purpose—a sublime unselfishness', wrote Thomas Huxley on 16 February 1885 after 'the hideous news' (Huxley, 2.94–5). Statues of Gordon were erected in London, Chatham, and elsewhere, and later at Khartoum.

Gordon's posthumous reputation has passed through several revolutions. Lord Tennyson wrote an 'Epitaph' for the Gordon Boys' National Memorial Home near Woking. Sir Edward Elgar contemplated writing a symphony about him. He became a figurehead for demotic imperialism. A more iconoclastic phase was opened by the publication in 1908 of Cromer's *Modern Egypt* and ten years later of *Eminent Victorians* by G. Lytton Strachey. His fascination was reaffirmed, and some of his glory restored, by the film *Khartoum* (1966), in which Charlton Heston starred as Gordon, and by several biographies.

RICHARD DAVENPORT-HINES

Sources J. Pollock, *Gordon* (1993) · H. Wortham, *Gordon* (1933) · C. Chenevix-Trench, *Charley Gordon* (1978) · *General Gordon's letters from the Crimea, the Danube and Armenia: August 18, 1854 to November 17, 1858*, ed. D. C. Boulger (1884) · *Letters of General C. G. Gordon to his sister, M. A. Gordon*, ed. M. A. Gordon (1888) · *Colonel Gordon in central Africa, 1874–79, from original letters and documents*, ed. G. B. Hill (1881) · *General Gordon's Khartoum journal*, ed. Lord Elton (1961) · D. C. Boulger, *The life of Gordon* (1896) · A. Nutting, *Gordon: martyr and misfit* (1966) · Fifteenth earl of Derby, diaries, Lpool RO · J. Lees-Milne, *The enigmatic Edwardian: the life of Reginald, 2nd Viscount Esher* (1986) · *The letters and friendships of Sir Cecil Spring Rice: a record*, ed. S. Gwynn, 2 vols. (1929), vol. 1 · S. Childers, *The life and correspondence of the Right Hon. Hugh Childers* (1901) · J. K. Fairbank, K. F. Bruner, and E. M. Matheson, eds., *The IG in Peking* (1975) · Gladstone, *Diaries* · *The diary of Sir Edward Walter Hamilton, 1880–1885*, ed. D. W. R. Bahlman, 2 vols. (1972) · Marquess of Zetland [L. J. L. Dundas], *Lord Cromer: being the authorized life of Evelyn Baring, first earl of Cromer* (1932) · Earl of Ronaldshay [L. J. L. Dundas], *The life of Lord Curzon*, 3 vols. (1928) · *Journals and letters of Reginald, Viscount Esher*, ed. M. V. Brett and Oliver, Viscount Esher, 4 vols. (1934–8) · Viscount Esher, 'General Gordon', *Nineteenth Century and After*, 63 (1908), 926–35 · *The journal of John Wodehouse, first earl of Kimberley, for 1862–1902*, ed. A. Hawkins and J. Powell, CS, 5th ser., 9 (1997) · C. R. Wilson, *Chapters from my official life*, ed. E. MacAlister (1916) · G. Cecil, *Life of Robert, marquis of Salisbury*, 3 (1931) · *Letters of George Wyndham, 1877–1913*, ed. G. Wyndham, 2 vols. (privately printed, Edinburgh, 1915) · *The letters of Robert Louis Stevenson*, ed. B. A. Booth and E. Mehew, 5 (1995) · L. Huxley, *Life and letters of Thomas Henry Huxley*, 2 vols. (1900) · R. S. Churchill, ed., *Winston S. Churchill*, companion vol. 1/2 (1967) · H. C. G. Matthew, *Gladstone*, 2 vols. (1986–95); repr. in 1 vol. as *Gladstone, 1809–1898* (1997) · J. Marlowe, *Mission to Khartoum* (1969) · B. Allen, *Gordon in the Sudan* (1931) · B. Allen, *Gordon in China* (1933) · W. S. Blunt, *Gordon at Khartoum: being a personal narrative of events* (1912) · E. A. Hake, *The story of Chinese Gordon*, 2 vols. (1884–5) · R. McGregor-Hastie, *Never to be taken alive* (1985), 79, 110 · F. Stocchetti, *Romolo Gessi, il Garibaldi dell'Africa* (Milan, 1952) · earl of Cromer [E. Baring], *Modern Egypt*, 2 vols. (1908)

Archives BL, Bell collection · BL, Moffitt collection · BL, corresp. and papers, Add. MSS 33222, 34474–34483, 43411, 47669, 51291–51312, 52386–53408 · Boston PL, corresp. · CAC Cam., address book · CUL, papers relating to China · CUL, papers relating to site of Garden of Eden [copies] · Gordon's School, Woking, letters and papers · NRA, corresp. [copies] · Royal Engineers Museum, Chatham, Kent, corresp., MSS, and journal · Southampton City Archives, estate papers · St Ant. Oxf., Middle East Centre, letters · U. Durham L., papers | BL, corresp. with Charles Allen, Add. MS 47609 · BL, diary of Lady Anne Blunt; MSS of earl of Cromer, W. E. Gladstone, E. W. Hamilton, marquess of Ripon, and Zobehr Pasha · BL, letters to Romolo Gossi, Add. MS 54495 · BL, letters to Florence Nightingale, Add. MS 45806 · BL, letters to R. S. Standen, Add. MS 40665 · BL, letters to C. M. Watson, Add. MS 41340 · BL, letters to Edward White, Add. MS 52428 · BL OIOC, first marquess of Dufferin and Ava MSS · Bodl. RH, letters to Sir John Pope-Hennessey · CAC Cam., Viscount Esher MSS · ING Barings, London, letters to Lord Cromer · NL Scot., letters to Sir Henry Elliot · NL Scot., letters to Sir William Mackinnon · PRO, corresp. with Sir Edward Baring, FO633 · PRO NIre., first marquess of Dufferin and Ava MSS · U. Birm. L., letters to Church Missionary Society, CA/6/0/11 · U. Durham L., corresp. with J. F. Brocklehurst and others · U. Durham L., letters to Sir W. H. Goodenough · W. Sussex RO, Viscount Wolseley MSS

Likenesses Smythe, watercolour drawing, 1859, NPG · V. Prinsep, oils, exh. RA 1866, Royal Engineers, Brompton barracks, Chatham, Kent · Lady Abercromby, drawing, after 1880, NPG · E. Clifford, pen-and-ink sketch, 1882, NPG · lithograph, pubd 1884, NPG · J. E. Boehm, marble bust, 1885, Royal Collection; related plaster bust, NPG · W. F. Woodington, terracotta bust, 1885, Scot. NPG · J. Faed, mezzotint, pubd 1886 (after A. Melville), NPG · C. J. A., watercolour drawing, 1887, Royal Engineers, Chattenden barracks · E. O. Ford, bust, exh. RA 1888, Royal Engineers, Brompton barracks, Chatham, Kent · W. H. Thornycroft, bronze statue, 1888, Victoria Embankment, London · E. O. Ford, bronze statue, exh. RA 1890, Royal Engineers, Brompton barracks, Chatham, Kent · Ape [C. Pellegrini], caricature, watercolour study, NPG; repro. in *VF* (19 Feb 1881) · T. L. Atkinson, mezzotint (after L. Dickinson), BM · J. Broad, statue, Gordon Gardens, Gravesend, Kent · J. F. J. D. Donnelly, photograph, NPG [*see illus.*] · H. Furniss, caricature, pen-and-ink sketch, NPG · photographs, NAM, NPG · photographs, Royal Engineers, Brompton barracks, Chatham, Kent · portraits, BM, NAM, NPG

Wealth at death £2315 1*s*. 0*d*.: resworn probate, June 1886, *CGPLA Eng. & Wales* (1885)

Gordon, Charles William [*pseud.* Ralph Connor] (**1860–1937**), clergyman and author, was born at Indian Lands, Glengarry county, Canada West, on 13 September 1860, the fourth son of Daniel Gordon (1822–1912), a Free Church minister who had emigrated to Canada from Blair Atholl, and his wife, Mary Robertson (1828–1890). He was educated at public schools in Ontario, the high school at St Mary's, Ontario, and at the University of Toronto, where he received a BA in classics. He then taught for a year and a half at the high school in Chatham, Western Ontario, before entering Knox College, Toronto. After graduating in 1887 he spent a further year studying theology at Edinburgh University, where leading liberal divines and the evangelist Henry Drummond (1851–1897) influenced his theological outlook and commitment to spreading the gospel.

Gordon was ordained to the ministry in 1889 in the presbytery of Calgary of the Presbyterian church of Canada, where he carried out missionary work among the miners and lumbermen living in the Rocky Mountains, near Banff. After raising money in Great Britain for western missions, he accepted a call from St Stephen's Presbyterian Church in Winnipeg and in 1894 he began a ministry there which lasted until his retirement in 1925. On 28 September 1899 he married Helen Skinner (1876–1961), daughter of the Revd John Mark King of Manitoba College. They had one son and five daughters.

Gordon's concern that there should be adequate money and men for Presbyterian missions in western Canada motivated him to write fictional accounts of life on the frontier. His early fictional sketches, published in *The Westminster: a Paper for the Home*, were designed to dramatize conditions on the frontier and to demonstrate the transforming power of a missionary preaching the gospel of salvation and life everlasting to the hardened men working in the mines and lumber camps. As Ralph Connor, Gordon 'struck a note' with many readers of *The Westminster*, and its publisher decided to print the sketches as a novel, *Black Rock*, in 1898. This successful début was followed by more sketches, which became the immensely popular novels *The Sky Pilot* (1899) and *The Man from Glengarry* (1900).

Gordon was not a novelist, but primarily a preacher of the gospel who wrote fiction to reach a broader audience. The Connor novels were sermons in fictional guise. In his memoirs, *Postscript to Adventure* (1937), he suggested that the 'authentic picture' of western Canada and the religious motif of his stories accounted for his huge readership. His literary fan mail emphasized the way in which his writing demonstrated the power of the gospel to transform lives. His books were an inspiration for some readers considering the ministry or missionary work. Gordon maintained the same sensational, highly dramatic and didactic romantic formula throughout his literary career. In all he wrote twenty-four novels. He also wrote a biography of his mentor in western Canadian missionary work, *The Life of James Robertson* (1909), numerous devotional pamphlets that embellished gospel accounts of the life of Christ, and a biography of Jesus Christ, *He Dwelt among Us* (1937).

Gordon believed that the Christian gospel should be applied to social conditions. He was a strong proponent of temperance and moral reform, supported the Lord's Day Alliance, and served as a mediator for the Canadian government in a number of strikes in western coalmining fields. He also sat on the Manitoba council of industry, which mediated in labour disputes in his home province after the Winnipeg general strike of 1919. He volunteered for duty in the First World War, as chaplain to the Winnipeg-based 79th Cameron Highlanders. At the front his battalion merged with the 43rd battalion of the 9th infantry brigade in the 3rd Canadian division. Major Gordon himself was nearly killed as his brigade attempted to capture the Regina trench during the battle of the Somme. He described the carnage of 8 October 1916 to one of his colleagues: 'we went in with 504 men and next morning reported only 65' (Gordon to William L. Stidger, 18 Oct 1922, Gordon papers, box 4, file 2). Shortly afterwards he returned to Canada and continued his war service as a special commissioner sent by the British and Canadian governments to explain the allied view of the war to the people of the United States.

In 1922 Gordon became moderator of the general assembly of the Presbyterian church of Canada. He encouraged the church to resume negotiations with the Methodist and Congregational churches for church union, which ultimately led to the creation of the United Church of Canada in 1925, the year of Gordon's retirement from St Stephen's. In his retirement Gordon continued to publish books and magazine articles. His thematic focus moved towards a social gospel orientation as he explored the impact of the great depression in his novels. By the middle of the 1930s Gordon was writing historical romances about the United Empire loyalists during the American revolution and the Anglo-American War of 1812–14. But by the 1920s the readership for his fiction had largely disappeared. He died on 31 October 1937 at his home, 54 The Westgate, Winnipeg, and was buried in the Old Kildonan cemetery on the outskirts of the city.

DAVID B. MARSHALL

Sources University of Manitoba archives, C. W. Gordon papers • C. W. Gordon, *Postscript to adventure: the autobiography of Ralph Connor* (1937) • W. Toye, ed., *The Oxford companion to Canadian literature* (1983) • J. Lennox, *Charles W. Gordon, 'Ralph Connor' and his works* (Toronto, 1988) • J. L. Thompson and J. H. Thompson, 'Ralph Connor and the Canadian identity', *Queen's Quarterly*, 79 (1972) • D. B. Marshall, 'Profile: Charles W. Gordon, clergyman, author, chaplain and moderator', *Touchstone* (Jan 2002)

Archives University of Manitoba, Winnipeg, papers and photographs, MS 56 | NA Canada, King Gordon papers, incl. family corresp.

Likenesses photographs, Charles William Gordon photograph collection, PC 76 • three portraits, Charles William Gordon photograph collection, 76-1-2, 76-1-3, 76-1-6

Gordon, Cuthbert (*bap.* **1730**, *d.* **1810**), industrial chemist, was baptized on 22 February 1730 at Kirkmichael, Banffshire, one of the sons of Thomas Gordon and his wife, Isobel, or Isabella, daughter of John McPherson of Inveresky. It is not known where he was educated, but King's College, Aberdeen, bestowed the degree of MD on him in 1785.

The local use of native lichens and plants to dye textiles inspired Gordon as a young man to consider a commercial manufacture of such dyes. Experimenting with his brother George (*d.* 1764), a coppersmith of Leith, he succeeded in producing a dye answering to archel—a red dye imported from the Canaries and Cape Verde. The ingredients consisted of a lichen and two other plants, dried, pounded, and diluted with spirits of wine and of soot, to which quicklime was added and the mass left to digest for fourteen days. The dyestuff was known as 'cudbear', allegedly from Gordon's own name. The process was patented in England as no. 727 of 12 August 1758, a Scottish patent being registered later that year (NA Scot., C.3/19, no. 198). In 1760 Gordon joined in a co-partnership with William Alexander & Sons, merchants, of Edinburgh, who had already advanced some £1500, and began manufacture at Leith. The Alexanders failed to oversee the management and discovered only in 1772 that Gordon, with his brothers James (1733–1811) and William (*b.* 1735), had been running at a loss and owed them more than £11,000. They instigated court action to recover this debt; Gordon ceased manufacture in 1774, and was briefly imprisoned for a trifling sum owed to a Leith wine cooper. The value of a cheap dye to the textile industry was however sufficient to bring forward other backers: a group of Glasgow merchants led by George Mackintosh, to whom Gordon was able to demonstrate his new cudbear, an advance on the original which had struck only on animal fibres such as silk and wool. The new product produced tones of blue and purple on cotton and linen, reducing the need to import indigo and cochineal. Factories were set up in Glasgow, London, and other textile towns, and Gordon sought a parliamentary grant, hitherto awarded only for production of single colours. He obtained certificates from the principal textile manufacturers, supported by figures for the value of imported dyestuffs which could be replaced by home-produced cudbear, and in the years following 1775 sent them to MPs and others who might assist his application. Some of these testimonies were included in his *Memorial of Mr C G, Relative to the Discovery and Use of Cudboar and other Dyeing Wares* (1785). But in 1787–8 he was in London, running up more debts and again petitioning government, with the aid of his kinsman Alexander, fourth duke of Gordon. His brother James, 'of Great Peter Street, Westminster, cudbear manufacturer', was declared bankrupt in 1803. Nothing more is heard of Cuthbert Gordon until his own death, probably in London, on 10 July 1810. ANITA MCCONNELL

Sources S. Grierson, *The colour cauldron* (1986), 27–31 • *The statistical account of Scotland*, 20 vols., vol. 7: *Lanarkshire and Renfrewshire* (1791–9); repr. (1973), 342–3 • W. T. Johnston, *Cudbear dye: and its discovery by Cuthbert Gordon* (1730–1810); rev. edn (1995) • *GM*, 1st ser., 80 (1810), 189

Gordon, Duke (1739–1800), librarian, was born on 20 May 1739, the son of William Gordon (*c.*1700–*c.*1760), a weaver in the Potterrow, Edinburgh, who named him after the duke of Gordon. He was taught by Andrew Waddel at a private school in the Cowgate area of the city (*c.*1748–1753) and on 13 March 1753 he entered the Greek class at Edinburgh University under Robert Hunter. During 1754 he was substitute teacher of the parish school of Tranent, Haddingtonshire, and he returned to the university on 4 March 1755. After completing his course (*c.*1757) he was tutor to the families of Captain John Dalrymple, later fifth earl of Stair, and of Alexander Boswell, Lord Auchinleck.

James Robertson, professor of oriental languages, on being made university librarian (12 January 1763), appointed Gordon his assistant. This office he retained under Andrew Dalzel, Robertson's successor, despite having been a rival for the Greek professorship to which Dalzel was appointed in 1773. His salary until 1783 was only £15, and never exceeded £35; he supported himself mainly by tuition. He detected three of the six errors in Robert Foulis's 'immaculate' Horace of 1744.

On his retirement Gordon received (12 April 1800) the degree of MA. He died, unmarried, in Edinburgh on 30 December 1800, and was buried in the city's St Cuthbert's churchyard where he was commemorated by a monument bearing a Latin inscription by Dalzel. He left £500 to the Edinburgh Infirmary, and the reversion of house property of nearly the same value to the poor of St Cuthbert's parish.

ALEXANDER GORDON, *rev.* ALEXANDER DU TOIT

Sources 'An account of the late Duke Gordon', *Scots Magazine*, 64 (1802), 18–32 • J. M. Bulloch and others, eds., *The house of Gordon*, 2 vols., Third Spalding Club, 26, 33 (1903–7) • J. Paterson, *Kay's Edinburgh portraits: a series of anecdotal biographies chiefly of Scotchmen*, ed. J. Maidment, 2 vols. (1885) • *Boswell's London journal, 1762–63*, ed. F. A. Pottle (1950), vol. 1 of *The Yale editions of the private papers of James Boswell*, trade edn (1950–89) • A. Dalzel, *History of the University of Edinburgh from its foundation*, 2 vols. (1862) • A. Grant, *The story of the University of Edinburgh during its first three hundred years*, 2 vols. (1884) • D. Laing, ed., *A catalogue of the graduates … of the University of Edinburgh*, Bannatyne Club, 106 (1858)
Archives U. Edin.
Wealth at death over £1000: *Scots Magazine*

Gordon, Edward Strathearn, Baron Gordon of Drumearn (1814–1879), judge, was born at Inverness on 10 April 1814, the only child of John Gordon (1782–1850), major in the 2nd (Queen's) regiment, and his second wife, Katherine (1781–1817), widow of Lieutenant-Colonel David Ross of the 57th regiment and daughter of Alexander Smith of Kinmylies, Inverness-shire. Named after the duke of Kent and Strathearn, the family's military patron, Edward survived the yellow fever epidemic that killed his mother when he was three in Trinidad (where his father was stationed) and was sent home to the care of her sister in Inverness. He was educated at the Royal Academy there, winning the gold medal for Greek and Latin in 1827, and at Edinburgh University (1828–35), graduating as LLB. He had also studied medicine briefly before turning to the law. His father dissuaded him from the military career common in his family and he was called to the Scottish bar in 1835. On 7 August 1845 he married Agnes Joanna (1826–1895), only child of John McInnes of Auchenreoch, Stirlingshire, and Auchenfroe, Dunbartonshire, a wealthy Grenada sugar planter; they had four sons who survived to adulthood and three daughters. Gordon's absences from his Edinburgh home in order to pursue his political career, and latterly his failing health, brought a measure of estrangement from his wife.

As a Conservative Gordon was selected as an advocate depute in 1852 and 1858, and was appointed sheriff of Perthshire on 26 July 1858. Succeeding Conservative administrations saw him promoted to solicitor-general for Scotland on 12 July 1866, and then to lord advocate on 28 February 1867, serving as such to December 1868 and again from 26 February 1874 to October 1876. He was gazetted privy councillor on 17 March 1874. Between 1868 and 1874 he was dean of the faculty of advocates, became one of the first Scottish QCs (12 November 1868), and received honorary LLDs from Edinburgh and Glasgow universities (1869 and 1873). He was Conservative member of parliament for Thetford, Norfolk, from 1867 until the borough's disfranchisement the following year, and for Glasgow and Aberdeen universities from 1869 to 1876. In parliament he was concerned with the Scottish Reform Bill of 1868 and responsible for various legal reforms. However, as a devout churchman and elder of St Stephen's, Edinburgh, he saw his main political achievement as the Church Patronage Act of 1874, hoping that abolition of patronage would reunite the Scottish churches after the trauma of the 1843 Disruption.

On 6 October 1876 Gordon was created under the Appellate Jurisdiction Act a lord of appeal in ordinary, with the title of Baron Gordon of Drumearn in the county of Stirling (a farm on his wife's Auchenreoch estate) and a salary of £6000 a year, thus becoming one of the first life peers. He suffered latterly from heart disease and, after a winter at Pau, a few months' duty in the House of Lords made further recuperation necessary. *En route* for Homburg, however, death overtook him at Brussels on 21 August 1879. He was buried in the Dean cemetery, Edinburgh, on 28 August 1879.

Gordon was honoured during his lifetime with the freedom of his native town of Inverness (1867) and with the office of deputy lieutenant by his main place of residence, Edinburgh (1872). He became a captain on the formation of the 1st Edinburgh rifle volunteer corps in 1859, rose to lieutenant-colonel in 1867, and ended in 1873 as honorary colonel. As a lawyer, contemporaries regarded him generally as painstaking, careful, and accurate rather than brilliant, and he was best known for acting as senior counsel for Major William Yelverton in the latter's long-running marriage case (July 1862). In appearance he was a dignified figure, tall with a prominent nose and, while it lasted, sandy hair. The incongruity of this fundamentally serious man singing a comic song at a ministerial whitebait dinner is reported to have moved his friend Disraeli to laughter. Conciliatory and conscientious as lawyer and politician, he inspired devotion in his children, gratitude in the poorer relatives he assisted, and esteem in all who knew him.

A. S. Gordon

Sources private information (2004) · *Daily Free Press* (23 Aug 1879) · *Edinburgh Courant* (23 Aug 1879) · *The Scotsman* (23 Aug 1879) · *Journal of Jurisprudence*, 23 (1879), 541–2 · *Inverness Courier* (29 Sept 1899) · *The Beacon* (16 Jan 1893) [including photograph] · *Edinburgh Evening Courant* (9 Aug 1845) · *Edinburgh Evening Courant* (9 Sept 1850) · *LondG* (6 Sept 1859) · *LondG* (10 Dec 1867) · *LondG* (29 Nov 1872) · *LondG* (16 May 1878) · G. W. T. Omond, *The lord advocates of Scotland, second series, 1834–1880* (1914) · J. M. Bulloch, *A remarkable military family: the Griamachary Gordons* (c.1908) · W. F. Monypenny and G. E. Buckle, *The life of Benjamin Disraeli*, 4 (1916), 552 · parish register (baptism), Inverness, 29 April 1814 · *The Post Office directory* [annuals]

Archives Bodl. Oxf., letters to Disraeli · Falkirk Museum's History Research Centre, Falkirk Archives, letters to William Forbes · NL Scot., letters to Agnes Gordon

Likenesses F. Schenk, lithograph, 1859–62 (after drawing by O. Leyde), Lord Advocate's Chambers, Fielden House, Great College Street, London · J. M. Barclay, portrait, 1864, Perth Museum and Art Gallery · two portraits, oil paintings, in or after 1870, priv. coll. · Ape [C. Pellegrini], chromolithograph caricature, NPG; repro. in *VF* (10 Oct 1874), pl. 187

Wealth at death £11,773 15*s*. 11*d*.: confirmation, 14 Dec 1879, *CCI*

Gordon [*née* Brodie], **Elizabeth, duchess of Gordon (1794–1864)**, evangelical patron, was born in London on 20 June 1794. Her father, Alexander Brodie (1748–1818) of Arnhall, Kincardineshire, a wealthy India merchant and MP, was a younger son of James Brodie of Brodie, in the north of Scotland; her mother, Elizabeth Margaret, was the daughter of the Hon. James Wemyss of Wemyss, Fife. She spent her first six years at Leslie Castle; then, after her mother's death, she lived with her maiden aunts. A 'happy, mirthful child, robust in frame and vigourous in health' (Stuart, 33), she was sent to a London boarding-school from the age of eight to about sixteen. When she came out at the age of seventeen, Elizabeth Brodie was 'a stout, bouncing girl, not tastefully attired, with a pale, broad face' (*Memoirs*, 196). As an heiress, she attracted the attention of George *Gordon, marquess of Huntly (1770–1836), son of Alexander *Gordon, fourth duke of Gordon (1743–1827), and his wife, Jane Maxwell (1748/9–1812) [*see* Gordon, Jane, duchess of Gordon]. Huntly, 'now in the decline of his rackety life, overwhelmed with debts, sated with pleasure' (*Memoirs*, 181), was twenty-four years older than his prospective bride. They were married at Bath on 11 December 1813, her father giving her a dowry of £100,000; after Brodie's death in 1818, the marchioness, who was his only surviving child, inherited his entire fortune.

Huntly's close relative, Elizabeth Smith (*née* Grant), found his wife to be 'young, and good, and rich, but neither clever nor handsome' (*Memoirs*, 182). At the time of her marriage, she was also very shy and possessed no 'gift of conversation' (*Memoirs*, 196), though she could be talkative on subjects which interested her. Initially she failed to perform her duties as a hostess to her husband's satisfaction, and on one occasion in 1815, he appears to have left her to preside over a house party in the hope that the experience would rub off her 'awkward reserve' (*Memoirs*, 226). She was, however, a fine pianist, which greatly pleased Huntly (and Walter Scott who opined that she played Scottish tunes 'like a Highland angel'; Stuart, 67). She also proved to be a 'first-rate woman of business' (*Memoirs*, 182) when she began to manage her husband's financial affairs. Although she had no children, Elizabeth Gordon's initially unpromising marriage proved to be a successful one, disturbed only by a 'want of religious sympathy' in later years (Stuart, 73).

Elizabeth Gordon was, however, dissatisfied with her new life: apparently, 'the unavoidable sight of revolting vice' (Stuart, 71) in the social sphere in which she moved led her to experience an evangelical conversion in the early to mid-1820s. Her Bible reading and note-taking during sermons did not recommend her to many of her associates: Mrs Smith declared that she had fallen into 'the

Elizabeth Gordon, duchess of Gordon (1794–1864), by unknown artist

cant of the Methodists' (*Memoirs*, 182). Becoming duchess of Gordon in 1827, she devoted herself to the furtherance of evangelical Christianity, entertaining evangelical clergymen of all denominations at Gordon Castle, employing a Church of Scotland minister as chaplain, monitoring the spiritual welfare of her servants, and introducing daily family prayers with hymn singing on Sundays (an organ was installed in the castle chapel for this purpose). No balls were held in the nine years while she held sway at Gordon Castle, but it seems that the duchess did not wholly succeed in carrying her husband into the evangelical camp: he would read family prayers only 'in case of necessity' (Stuart, 103), though he permitted her to sell her jewellery, and sold some of his own horses, to fund an infant school and an Episcopalian chapel in the nearby village.

After her husband's death in 1836, the duchess spent about a year on the continent, before returning to Huntly Lodge, where she intensified her religious activities. Her new home, in the Strathbogie area, became a centre for opponents of the civil courts in the course of the controversy surrounding the seven suspended ministers of Strathbogie, which preceded the Disruption of 1843. Like many in the Scottish upper classes, the duchess was in fact an Episcopalian, but she sympathized with the opponents of patronage, whom she saw as preachers of gospel truth in an area starved of religious ministrations by complacent moderate churchmen. Accordingly, she offered travel expenses and accommodation in a wing of Huntly Lodge to the supply ministers sent by the general assembly. Subsequently, in 1846, after considerable heart searching and two years spent abroad, she joined the Free Church of Scotland, convinced that the established church had wrongly surrendered its disciplinary powers to the state. Some of the leaders of the Free Church were now personal friends, and her home was often the venue for religious meetings, including the local three-day revivals held annually in Castle Park from 1860 to 1864. She supported Free Church missionary and religious interests generously, subscribing £1000 to New College, Edinburgh. She died suddenly at Huntly Lodge on 31 January 1864, and was buried in Elgin Cathedral. Her evolution from pleasure-seeking Regency society lady to serious-minded and pious dowager—the most prominent aristocratic patron of evangelicalism in Scotland—epitomized, even caricatured, a sea change within the early- to mid-nineteenth-century British nobility, and wider society too. ROSEMARY MITCHELL

Sources A. M. Stuart, *Life and letters of Elisabeth, last duchess of Gordon* (1865) · *Memoirs of a highland lady, 1797–1827*, ed. A. Davidson (1978) · GEC, *Peerage*

Archives U. Cal., Berkeley, Bancroft Library, MS letter, 94720

Likenesses M. Gauci, lithograph, BM · mezzotint, BM · oils, Brodie Castle, Moray [*see illus.*] · portrait, repro. in Stuart, *Life and letters of Elisabeth*

Wealth at death £22,062 18*s*. 1*d*.: inventory, 22 April 1864, NA Scot., SC 1/36/54, 442 · under £60,000—in England: probate, 3 June 1864, *CGPLA Eng. & Wales*

Gordon, Friederike (1906–1992). *See under* Markus, Erika (1910–1992).

Gordon [*formerly* Seton], **George, second earl of Huntly** (1440/41–1501), magnate, was the eldest son of Alexander *Seton, first earl of Huntly (*d*. 1470), and his second wife, Elizabeth Crichton, daughter of the then chancellor, Sir William Crichton (*d*. 1454); they married shortly before 18 March 1440. George is first mentioned in a charter of 3 April 1441, as George of Seton; he and his brothers were renamed Gordon, after the family lordship of Gordon in Berwickshire, in 1457–8. He succeeded as earl of Huntly on his father's death at Huntly on or about 15 July 1470. The Huntly inheritance was something of a mixed blessing. Although the lands of the earldom were extensive—Strathbogie, Aboyne, Glentanner, and Glenmuick in Aberdeenshire, the lordship of Badenoch in Inverness-shire, Enzie in Banffshire, and Gordon, Huntly, and Fogo in Berwickshire—Earl George also inherited major problems: his difficult half-brother Alexander, a crown deeply suspicious of Gordon advancement, and a long-standing feud with the MacDonald earls of Ross. The family difficulty was soon solved through some partition of Gordon estates, confirmed by royal charters on 21 May 1470 and 31 August 1472, but the interlinked obstacles of royal suspicion and hostile MacDonalds took longer to overcome.

The title of earl of Huntly had been created for George's father, Alexander, in 1445, that is, during the minority of James II and the short period of Black Douglas dominance at court. The adult James II clearly became wary of Gordon expansion, however, fearing that, as in the case of the battle of Brechin in May 1452, Huntly had been using the royal name to indulge in a private feud with the earl of

Crawford. So in 1455–6 Gordon efforts to secure control of Moray and Mar—the former through the marriage in 1455 of George, the future second earl, to Elizabeth Dunbar, widow of Archibald Douglas, the forfeited earl of Moray—were nipped in the bud by James II. The Gordon response was to devastate the crown lands of Mar, for which they received a remission in March 1457. George was subsequently divorced from Elizabeth and had achieved a measure of reconciliation with the king by 10 March 1460, when, styled master of Huntly, he married Annabella, James II's youngest sister.

Following his succession Earl George had to deal with another king, James III, who in December 1475 gave him and some others a commission of lieutenancy to proceed against the forfeited John MacDonald, earl of Ross. Huntly needed no second bidding to elevate twenty-five years of local feud to the level of national politics; he promptly attacked Lochaber and Ross, taking Dingwall Castle for the crown. But the miserly king failed to award Huntly the keepership of Dingwall, and towards the end of the 1470s James III's intrusion of his familiar Thomas Cochrane into Kildrummy Castle at the heart of Mar, another earldom coveted by Huntly, probably strained his loyalty to the limit. At the Lauder crisis in July 1482 he took part both in the removal of Cochrane and in the seizure of the king, yet thereafter, early in 1483, he reverted to his former allegiance, and his arrival in Edinburgh with his kin and allies from the north-east was crucial to James III's recovery of power that spring.

Five years later, during the crucial rebellion of 1488, Huntly and his son and heir, Alexander, hedged their family bets. Earl George remained neutral in the final conflict in June, in which the king was killed. Alexander, who may have been paid to support James III, led a force south—too late—as far as Dunkeld; and in 1489 he participated in the rebellion against the narrow Hepburn-dominated government of the adolescent James IV. The Gordons could not be ignored in the 'reconciliation' parliament of February 1490. In the late autumn of 1497 Earl George, up to this point no regular visitor to court or parliament, not least because in the 1490s he was largely engaged in building up his position in north-east Scotland, was given the most important office of state, the chancellorship, following the dismissal of the earl of Angus. In the justice ayre at Ayr in spring 1499 Huntly and the king tried and fined Angus's Ayrshire allies, the Cunninghams, for an attack on Hugh, Lord Montgomery, at the tolbooth of Irvine the previous year. When he died in Stirling early in June 1501, the second earl had long since made the transition from powerful regional magnate to assiduous royal servant, though there is perhaps a certain irony in his burial later that month at Cambuskenneth Abbey, Stirlingshire, close to James III, the man whom he had failed to support in 1488.

Huntly was married three times. On 24 July 1471 his second marriage, to Annabella Stewart, ended, like his first, in divorce, and later that year he married Elizabeth Hay, sister of Nicholas, earl of Erroll. She survived him and was the mother of most, but probably not all, of his eleven legitimate children, including Alexander *Gordon, who succeeded him as third earl, and Katherine, who in January 1496 married the Yorkist pretender Perkin *Warbeck.

NORMAN MACDOUGALL

Sources J. M. Thomson and others, eds., *Registrum magni sigilli regum Scotorum / The register of the great seal of Scotland*, 11 vols. (1882–1914), vol. 2 • M. Livingstone, D. Hay Fleming, and others, eds., *Registrum secreti sigilli regum Scotorum / The register of the privy seal of Scotland*, 1 (1908) • *APS*, 1424–1567 • Charles, eleventh marquis of Huntly, earl of Aboyne, ed., *The records of Aboyne MCCXXX–MDCLXXXI*, New Spalding Club, 13 (1894) • J. Stuart, ed., *The miscellany of the Spalding Club*, 4, Spalding Club, 20 (1849) • J. Anderson, ed., *Calendar of the Laing charters, AD 854–1837, belonging to the University of Edinburgh* (1899) • W. Fraser, ed., *Registrum monasterii S. Marie de Cambuskenneth*, Grampian Club, 4 (1872) • *Scots peerage*, vol. 4 • C. McGladdery, *James II* (1990) • N. Macdougall, *James III: a political study* (1982) • N. Macdougall, *James IV* (1989)

Archives NA Scot., Gordon Castle muniments, GD 44

Gordon, George, fourth earl of Huntly (1513–1562), magnate, was the eldest son of John Gordon, master of Huntly (*d.* 1517), and Margaret, illegitimate daughter of King James IV and Margaret Drummond. He succeeded his grandfather Alexander *Gordon, the third earl, in 1524; his wardship was given to Queen Margaret Tudor.

Controlling the north On Margaret's estrangement from her second husband, the sixth earl of Angus, Huntly's wardship passed to James Stewart, earl of Moray, although Angus retained effective control of it until his fall in 1528. One of Angus's last recorded acts in May that year was a letter of thanks to the Forbes family for 100 merks, payment for a piece of land in the barony of Strathbogie, which was part of the earldom of Huntly. In 1533 Huntly was still trying to regain these lands, which had come to the master of Forbes, the husband of Angus's niece. This prolonged dispute, aggravated by the Forbes involvement in unrest and disorder in that region, probably lay behind Huntly's accusing the master of Forbes in 1537 of having plotted to assassinate the king during an earlier visit to the burgh of Aberdeen. Forbes was convicted and executed, although it was widely suspected that Huntly might have doctored the evidence and influenced the jury. Disputes over transactions contracted during Huntly's minority also contributed to later tensions between him and the earl of Moray, who had attempted to make good his own claim to Huntly's wardship after the fall of Angus.

Following James V's assumption of power in 1528 Huntly often appeared as one of his closest companions. James relied on the Gordons to exercise their traditional role as agents of royal government in the north of Scotland. The Gordon supremacy in the north-east rested on royal favour granted in return for loyalty and a tradition of service to the crown unbroken since their rise to fortune in the mid-fifteenth century. Like his ancestors, Huntly consolidated his authority in the region through concluding bonds of manrent and marriage alliances with local families; he also extended his network of influence into Aberdeen and the more important mercantile centres of the region, drawing powerful burgess dynasties into the net of his affinity. Between 1536 and 1541 he signed eight bonds of manrent with northern families such as the Leslies of Balquhain and the Gordons of Strathavon, together with the northern clansmen such as the Macleans of Duart and the Mackintoshes, taking advantage of the temporary eclipse of the earl of Argyll's power in the area to bind them to him.

These bonds offered a double benefit to Huntly, weaving him more tightly into the web of local landed society, creating an affinity and following, and, at the same time, making his function as guardian of the north easier to fulfil. A further twenty bonds followed between 1543 and 1560, although the spectacular failure of his alliance system in 1562 showed that it could not be relied upon unconditionally. Huntly's power ultimately rested on the solid core of a strongly united and geographically concentrated kin group, and it was mostly these kinsmen who were loyal to him in his clash with the crown in the autumn of 1562. He had few rivals in the north-east and these were either conciliated through marriage alliances, or intimidated and opposed by Gordon power. Huntly chose to marry wisely himself, contracting on 27 March 1530 to marry Lady Elizabeth Keith, the sister of the Earl Marischal, a powerful local magnate and potential rival in the locality.

Involvement in national politics The king relied on Huntly's military force for the wider defence of the country, while always ensuring that the earl's strength should not outgrow royal control. In September 1532 Huntly was with Moray, Marischal, and James V on the borders while Anglo-Scottish war threatened. He was also active in the north in 1534, again with Moray, in a successful expedition against clan Chattan, a regular source of trouble in the region. His career as a privy councillor began in 1535 and was to continue for the rest of his life. The king displayed his confidence in Huntly in 1536 by naming him a regent during his eight-month absence in France in search of a suitable wife. He later accompanied James on his expedition to Orkney and the Western Isles in June and July 1540, raising a force of 500 men to contribute to the royal army. The sheriffship of Aberdeen, the richest and most significant burgh in the region, was confirmed to Huntly in 1541. The king had already given him exemption from the jurisdiction of the sheriffs of Aberdeen, Banff, and Berwick for his lifetime in 1536.

In 1542 Huntly became lieutenant of the borders, replacing Moray, who was sick. On 24 August he defeated a large English army under Sir Robert Bowes at Haddon Rig, but his failure to pursue his advantage disappointed the king, who reinstated Moray as lieutenant and removed Huntly. The latter remained on the eastern borders and was therefore absent from the defeat at Solway Moss on 24 November. He became one of the governors of the realm in December 1542 following the king's death. In January 1543, however, the earl of Arran became sole governor, deposing Huntly and his fellow governors, and imprisoning Cardinal Beaton, Arran's chief rival. Initially Huntly worked for the cardinal's release and opposed Arran, but failed to secure enough support and came to terms with the governor. Arran's conduct of a pro-English policy, involving the marriage of Mary, queen of Scots, to the future Edward VI and the encouragement of protestant reformation in Scotland, alienated Huntly, who aligned himself with those who advocated a French alliance and conservative religious policies. Huntly was also disturbed by Arran's attempts as governor to infringe his own interests in important regional centres of power. In 1543 Arran attempted to secure the loyalty of the Menzies family, whose members had held the office of provost of Aberdeen for much of the preceding century. This political interference in an area of Gordon influence, together with Arran's attempts to promote the cause of religious reformation, caused a major crisis in the burgh which ended with Huntly himself being elected provost in January 1545, a position he retained until the burgh had been stabilized to his satisfaction.

On the release of Beaton from prison and his subsequent reconciliation with Arran, policy changed. The treaties of amity with England lay in ruins by the end of 1543 and the governor adopted an anti-English line which brought him closer to Beaton and Huntly. The security of the realm was seriously threatened at this time by a coalition between the pro-English faction among the Scottish nobility, led by Angus and Lennox, and the Gaelic areas of Scotland, which were disaffected from the crown. In the face of danger from the north and west Huntly's military strength was indispensable. He was appointed lieutenant-general of the north and of Orkney and Shetland, and shared in the general distribution of grants of charters and financial inducements offered by the new regime. In May 1544 he once more crushed a highland rising, this time one led by the Camerons and Macdonalds of Clanranald, and in March 1545 defeated Donald Dubh and his men of the Isles, ensuring that Arran's government would not be threatened from the north in the event of an English invasion.

Enemy of England, ally of France After the assassination of Beaton at St Andrews on 29 May 1546, Huntly was appointed chancellor by the council on 5 June following. The accession of Edward VI to the English throne unleashed a large-scale invasion of Scotland in 1547. The Scots suffered a major defeat at the battle of Pinkie on 10 September. Huntly played a prominent part in the engagement, resplendent in gilded armour, but it was allegedly the flight of the rearguard, which he commanded, that caused the Scottish defeat which in turn led to Huntly's own capture and imprisonment in England. In December 1548 he escaped, with the connivance of his captors, having given assurances that he would support English ambitions in Scotland. It was reported at the time that Arran, Mary of Guise, and members of the clerical party in Scotland had encouraged him to promise whatever was necessary to secure his release, since his presence was urgently required in Scotland. On his return home he abandoned the pledges he had given in England, and at the Haddington parliament of July 1548 advocated the marriage of Mary, queen of Scots, to the dauphin. His rejection of England and attachment to France were rewarded by the gift of the French order of St Michel. Huntly's domestic position was strengthened by the grant of the earldom of Moray on 13 February 1549, while in March that year his uncle William Gordon, bishop of Aberdeen, made him hereditary bailie of the diocese. He also proved his Catholic orthodoxy by assisting at the burning of Adam Wallace for heresy in 1550—he was alleged to have taken a prominent part in proceedings.

In 1550 Huntly accompanied the queen dowager and a large number of Scottish nobles, some of whom were known for their reforming views, on her visit to France. Lavish financial rewards for loyalty were offered to the Scots by the king of France in return for their acceptance of Francophile policies, and he was said to have bought them all completely. During his stay in Paris, Huntly negotiated fruitlessly with the English ambassador for a safe conduct to Scotland through England, notwithstanding his earlier failure to keep the undertakings he had made to support English policy. Permission was not given and he was regarded as a cunning and untrustworthy man. The ambassador also reported that Huntly was frequently called to secret conferences at the French court.

Soon after Mary of Guise's assumption of the regency in 1554 Huntly lost favour with her for having failed to suppress a rising of the Camerons in the north in 1553. His inability to press home his attack resulted from the failure of the Mackintoshes, on whose strength he relied, to support him. Deprived of the earldom of Moray and other honours, he was imprisoned from March to October of that year. He retained the title of chancellor, but surrendered the seal to de Roubay, the French vice-chancellor, who effectively ran the administration. The French ambassador, Henri d'Oysel, reportedly advised the regent that Huntly was too powerful in the kingdom and needed to be taught his place. The earl's disgrace offered a chance to help finance the new administration by imposing a large fine on him, but eventually he was restored to favour and made lieutenant-general of the kingdom on 5 August 1557.

Religious conflicts Huntly's sympathies during the Reformation crisis were consistently conservative and legitimist, although he affected to share the general hostility to growing French power and influence in the country during the last years of Mary of Guise's regency. His preferred stance was loyalty to the crown; he was a late, reluctant, and unreliable recruit to the lords of the congregation and to the cause of political and religious change in Scotland. Huntly's brother Alexander *Gordon, bishop of Galloway, was an early adherent to the congregation, but Huntly vacillated for some time, arguing against the siege of Perth by the forces of the congregation in June 1559 and leaving the city before the assault took place. He was an emissary from the regent to the congregation near Prestonpans in July, offering a form of co-existence between Catholic and reformed worship which was refused. At the end of July, Huntly guaranteed the terms of the truce, known as the appointment of Leith, which had been agreed between the regent and the lords, and promised to join the latter should the regent break them. Despite the adherence of the Hamiltons to the congregation in September 1559 Huntly still hesitated to join, believing in the light of the reverses suffered by the lords in October and November of 1559 that the regent's cause was by no means lost. Instead he chose to temporize, sending the earl of Sutherland to offer words of encouragement to the congregation. His policy seems to have been an attempt to satisfy both sides in the conflict without committing himself wholeheartedly to either.

Huntly was slow to join the lords besieging the French in Leith, but after long delays he finally appeared at the end of April 1560, and reluctantly signed the band of congregation on the 27th. He signed secretly, pledging half-hearted support for religious reformation, after being assured that it did not imply political revolution. He also asked for a guarantee from the lords that they would maintain him in his lands and possessions, requiring that if any church lands were granted they should be given only to his supporters or with his consent in the shires of Aberdeen, Banff, Moray, Nairn, and Inverness, and that he be maintained as lieutenant in the north. He was principally concerned that the unpredictable consequences of religious change should not disturb the balance of political forces in his own sphere of influence. The brief flirtation of the earl of Arran with protestantism in the mid-1540s had illustrated the danger stemming from volatile religious feeling once it was unleashed. The troubled state of the country had already prompted the bishop of Aberdeen and the canons to give the treasures of the cathedral over to Huntly for safe keeping. In May 1560, wishing to retain some credit with the lords, he signed the contract of Berwick in support of English intervention in Scotland, but was still regarded as unreliable. In June he repeated his claim that the strength of local opinion inhibited his firm adherence to the congregation, and in August he offered the excuse of sickness for his absence from the Reformation Parliament. Before the end of the year he was reported to have restored the mass in his territories.

On 10 December 1560, a few days after the death of François II of France, a meeting of leading conservatives took place at Dunbar to which Huntly was privy. It was suspected that this was a meeting of conservatives preparing for the possible return of Queen Mary to Scotland. When her return was certain, Huntly supported the mission of John Leslie to the queen in France, during which he conveyed assurances of Gordon loyalty, inviting her to join forces with him in the north-east and boasting that he could raise an army in her cause. After Mary's return in August 1561, however, she chose alliance with neither the Gordon nor the Hamilton interest. Intent on the recognition of her claim to the English throne and reluctant to alienate protestant opinion, she relied on the advice of her half-brother Lord James Stewart, and pursued a policy of conciliation and apparent acceptance of the *status quo* in religious matters. Huntly resented her reliance on Lord James, and in October 1561 argued openly with him in the queen's presence, reportedly boasting that he could restore the mass in the three shires that were dependent on him.

Confronting Queen Mary In June 1562 a long-festering quarrel between the Ogilvies and Gordons flared into violence between Sir John Gordon, one of Huntly's younger sons, and James Ogilvie of Cardell. The queen resolved to take action against Gordon, who had escaped from prison and seemed determined to force his own rehabilitation. Her progress to the north in August 1562 was to be a firm exercise of authority and a demonstration of her intention to be above faction. Huntly's anxieties at the queen's growing hostility to him were further increased by her secret award of the earldoms of Mar and Moray, which Huntly had been administering, to Lord James in January of that year. Lord James resigned Mar shortly afterwards, but he retained Moray, and Huntly rightly saw this gift, which was made public in September, as a threat to his pre-eminence in the region.

Throughout the sixteenth century the Gordons saw the incursions of any other magnate into their territory as a threat to be resisted to the utmost. The territorial balance of power was so finely calibrated as to permit of no rival centres of authority. At regular intervals throughout the century the earls of Moray challenged their supremacy in the region. The Gordons were keen to hold Moray themselves and opposed any attempts by its earls, sometimes encouraged by the crown, to increase their power. Successive rulers saw Moray as a useful curb on Gordon ambitions, but substantial disturbance occurred whenever they adopted a policy of favouring Gordon rivals.

Huntly hoped that his profession of Catholicism and his invitation to the queen to attend mass in the chapel at Strathbogie would appease her anger. He may even have considered detaching her by force from Lord James's influence. His Catholicism was no protection from the queen's determination to bring down an over-mighty subject in order to inspire confidence among her protestant subjects. Consequently Huntly reluctantly prepared to do battle while protesting loyalty to the queen and enmity to Lord James. He engaged the royal forces, and having been abandoned by a substantial portion of his local following, whose bonds of manrent contained clauses reserving their loyalty to the crown, was defeated at Corrichie outside Aberdeen on 28 October 1562. Huntly himself died of what may have been apoplexy either during the battle or shortly after his capture. His castle at Strathbogie was pillaged of its contents, including the vestments and treasures of Aberdeen Cathedral, some of which were later given to Mary's second husband, Lord Darnley. Mary's defeat of Huntly was seen by a number of contemporaries as a reassurance to protestants that her favour would not be extended only to those of her own religion.

Huntly's body was embalmed at Aberdeen and then taken to Edinburgh, where at the parliament of 28 May 1563 an act of attainder and forfeiture was passed on it, and his descendants were barred from any office of rank or honour within the realm. His remains were taken first to Holyrood and then to the vault of the Blackfriars in Edinburgh, until on 21 April 1566 they were removed for burial in Elgin Cathedral. The countess of Huntly survived her husband. They had twelve children, nine sons and three daughters. Their eldest son, Alexander, died while still a child in 1552 or 1553, and it was their second son, another George *Gordon, who succeeded his father as fifth earl. Sir John Gordon was hanged at Aberdeen in the queen's presence three days after the battle of Corrichie. Of the remaining children, James *Gordon became a Jesuit and an important promoter of Catholicism in north-east Scotland, while Jean *Gordon was married successively to the fourth earl of Bothwell (from whom she was divorced in 1567), the twelfth earl of Sutherland, and Alexander Ogilvie of Boyne, dying aged about eighty-four in 1629. ALLAN WHITE

Sources *Scots peerage*, 4.534–9 • GEC, *Peerage*, new edn, 6.678–9 • G. Crawfurd, *The lives and characters of the officers of the crown and state in Scotland from David I to the Union* (1726) • *CSP Scot.*, 1547–63 • *Reg. PCS*, 1st ser., vol. 1 • *The Scottish correspondence of Mary of Lorraine*, ed. A. I. Cameron, Scottish History Society, 3rd ser., 10 (1927) • W. Gordon, *The house of Gordon: the history of the ancient, noble and illustrious family of Gordon from their first arrival in Scotland in Malcolm III's time to the year 1690* (1716) • R. Gordon, *The earldom of Sutherland: a genealogical history of the earldom of Sutherland from its origin to the year 1651* (1813) • 'Papers from the charter chest … at Gordon Castle', *Miscellany of the Spalding Club*, ed. J. Stuart, 4, Spalding Club, 20 (1849) • Charles, eleventh marquis of Huntly, earl of Aboyne, ed., *The records of Aboyne MCCXXX–MDCLXXXI*, New Spalding Club, 13 (1894) • *LP Henry VIII*, vols. 14–21 • *CSP Scot.*, 1547–1603 • *APS*, 1424–1567 • *The state papers and letters of Sir Ralph Sadler*, ed. A. Clifford, 3 vols. (1809) • Lord Herries [John Maxwell], *Historical memoirs of the reign of Mary queen of Scots*, ed. R. Pitcairn, Abbotsford Club, 6 (1836) • T. Thomson, ed., *A diurnal of remarkable occurrents that have passed within the country of Scotland*, Bannatyne Club, 43 (1833) • *John Knox's History of the Reformation in Scotland*, ed. W. C. Dickinson, 2 vols. (1949) • J. Leslie, *The historie of Scotland*, ed. E. G. Cody and W. Murison, trans. J. Dalrymple, 2 vols. in 4 pts, STS, 5, 14, 19, 34 (1888–95) [1596 trans. of *De origine moribus, et rebus gestis Scotorum libri decem* (Rome, 1578)] • D. Calderwood, *The history of the Kirk of Scotland*, ed. T. Thomson and D. Laing, 8 vols., Wodrow Society, 7 (1842–9) • G. Buchanan, *The history of Scotland*, ed. J. Aikman, 4 vols. (1827) • J. Spottiswoode, *History of the Church of Scotland*, ed. M. Napier and M. Russell, 3 vols., Spottiswoode Society, 6 (1847–51) • P. F. Tytler, *The history of Scotland* (1828–43) • J. Cameron, *James V: the personal rule, 1528–1542*, ed. N. Macdougall (1998) • A. White, 'Religion, politics and society in Aberdeen, 1543–1593', PhD diss., U. Aberdeen, 1985 • A. White, 'Queen Mary's northern province', *Queen Mary: queen in three kingdoms*, ed. M. Lynch (1988), 53–70 • A. White, 'The impact of the Reformation on a burgh community: the case of Aberdeen', *The early modern town in Scotland*, ed. M. Lynch (1987), 81–101

Archives NA Scot., Gordon Castle muniments, GD.44

Gordon, George, fifth earl of Huntly (*d.* **1576**), magnate, was the second, but eldest surviving, son and heir of George *Gordon, fourth earl of Huntly (1513–1562), and his wife, Lady Elizabeth Keith. Perhaps because he was a younger son little is known of his early life before 18 January 1554, when he was contracted to marry Lady Jean, second daughter of James Hamilton, earl of Arran and subsequently duke of Châtelherault. The marriage never took place, but by 24 March 1559 Lord Gordon, as he then was, had married Jean's sister Lady Anne, Arran's third daughter. Another of Arran's daughters, Barbara Hamilton, had been married to Gordon's elder brother Alexander, who died in 1552 or 1553.

In 1562 the Gordons faced disaster through a failed rebellion against Mary, queen of Scots. The fourth earl died in defeat at the battle of Corrichie on 28 October 1562, and his heirs were forfeited for his treason. Lord Gordon was with his father-in-law and consequently absent from the battle. Châtelherault detained him at his house of Kinneil, but then handed him over to the queen at her request. He was taken to Edinburgh Castle in November 1562 and tried for treason in the following February. He was condemned to death, but the sentence was to be carried out at the queen's pleasure. Mary was thus able to imprison him, holding him in reserve as a valuable resource should the restoration of the Gordons suit the development of her policy. The extensive Gordon following had survived Corrichie intact and the queen was reluctant to lose such an important buttress of royal government in the north. It also served as a check on the ambitions of the earl of Moray. It was alleged that Moray, aware of the danger that Lord Gordon's survival might pose to himself and his policies, attempted to have him executed in prison at Dunbar by the presentation of a false warrant. When this came to the queen's attention she forbade the execution and took Gordon under her protection. It seems to have been about this time that he became a protestant, though the extent of his commitment remains unclear.

In March 1565 Mary's interest in marriage to Lord Darnley, the son of the earl of Lennox, until recently an exile in England, was becoming apparent. The rehabilitation of the Douglas faction which this seemed to presage disturbed Châtelherault and the Hamiltons, who understood it as a potential threat to their own claim to the succession. It also antagonized the earl of Moray, who saw it as an attempt by the queen to escape his political tutelage, and as a reversal of the policy of amity with England that he had always advocated. Mary then chose to resuscitate Gordon power as a counterbalance to the Hamilton–Moray coalition. Released from custody on 3 August 1565, by the 27th George Gordon had been restored as Lord Gordon, and on 6 October, after he had brought a force from the north to assist the queen against her half-brother's inept rebellion, the so-called chaseabout raid, he was restored to the earldom of Huntly by proclamation. So highly did Mary value his loyalty that on 20 March 1566 he was appointed chancellor in succession to the earl of Morton, a consistent supporter of the Reformation and of Anglophile policies. He remained in office until replaced by Morton once more on 11 November 1567, by which time Moray had assumed the regency of Scotland. Huntly became a frequent attender at the council as Mary increasingly relied on him while the direction of her policies, formerly Anglophile and at least tolerant of protestantism, began to change.

Marian loyalist The vacuum left by the exiled Châtelherault and Moray after the chaseabout raid was filled by the Lennox affinity, but also prompted a closer association between Huntly and the earl of Bothwell. At this time Mary became ever more dependent on this small group of lords and on an inner circle of foreign servants who sustained her administration, prominent among whom was David Riccio, her Italian secretary. Her policies gradually took on a more pronounced Catholic tone, partly in response to encouragement from France. Dynastic and political interests held more sway with most of her nobles than religious ones; her strongest supporters were either protestant or indifferent to Catholicism. Among her chief advisers, neither Huntly nor Bothwell were Catholics and both refused to attend mass in the queen's chapel; they also declined to assist at one of the greatest public Catholic spectacles of the queen's reign, the Candlemas mass on 2 February 1566, after which Darnley, now the Queen's husband, was invested with the French order of St Michel.

The chain of events provoked by Mary's marriage to Darnley on 29 July 1565 shook the pattern of established loyalties and threatened the security of the crown. The queen's change of policy, the distancing from government of powerful vested interests, such as the Hamiltons, and her determination to forfeit the exiled 'chaseabout rebels' at the parliament of 7 March 1566 prompted a preemptive warning strike against her in the murder of Riccio, her Italian secretary, and a serious threat to her own life on 9 March. Mary survived the attack and escaped from Holyrood to Dunbar, where she was joined by Bothwell and Huntly, who was to be prominent in her cause until its collapse in 1573.

Mary's reliance on Huntly increased as time passed. Formally restored to his earldom by parliament on 7 March 1566, he was present in Edinburgh Castle when the future James VI was born on 19 June. On 24 June he demonstrated his protestant credentials by attending the sermon in St Giles's. He stood outside the Catholic baptism of the prince at Stirling on 17 December, along with Moray, Bothwell, and Bedford, the English ambassador. A month earlier he was present at a conference at Craigmillar with the pardoned Moray and other lords, when Mary's strained relations with her husband were discussed. Huntly later claimed that Moray and Maitland of Lethington were responsible for the murder of Darnley and that they had tried to draw Huntly and Bothwell into the plot at Craigmillar. The accusation was denied by Moray even though Huntly offered to prove it by his sword.

After Darnley's murder on 10 February 1567 Mary's reliance on Huntly increased; she ratified the gift of various estates to him at the parliament on 19 April 1567. Huntly also drew closer to Bothwell, subscribing the Ainslie's tavern bond in favour of the queen's marriage to him, even though this necessitated Bothwell's divorce from Huntly's sister Jean *Gordon. Huntly supported the divorce, which was granted according to the canons of the Catholic church by the court of the archbishop of St Andrews, and on 15 May Bothwell and Mary were married according to reformed rites by Adam Bothwell, bishop of Orkney. Huntly continued to appear regularly at council meetings after the marriage.

Mary's marriage precipitated deep divisions within the magnate class, resulting in conflict between loyalists and the so-called confederate lords whose purpose, proclaimed in a bond of 1 May, was to release Mary from her thraldom to Bothwell and to protect the life and rights of the young prince. Some—and Huntly may have been among them—suspected the confederates of wishing to depose Mary in order to enthrone the prince and thereby to control the kingdom during the resulting long minority. Huntly chose to follow his usual policy of loyalty to the queen and support for the Hamiltons, who saw the premature accession of James as a deep threat to their own claim to the succession (through descent from James II) and to honour and precedence among the magnates. The brief and imprudent military encounter between the queen and the confederates at Carberry on 15 June 1567 led to Mary's imprisonment at Lochleven. The confederates also achieved their larger purpose by forcing her abdication on 24 July and the appointment of Moray as regent. There was still sizeable support for Mary among the magnates, however. Her forces had not had enough time to muster before Carberry, and Huntly himself, who had been in the north, was on the way to join the queen with his own forces when news came of her capture. He continued to profess his loyalty to Mary and to argue for her rescue from Lochleven, signing a bond with others to secure her release in June.

Huntly and Regent Moray The coronation of Prince James at Stirling on 29 July confirmed the worst fears of the Hamiltons and Huntly. Without a leader, owing to the duke of Châtelherault's absence in France, the opponents of the confederates found it difficult to form a coherent party. Huntly was not present at the coronation of the young king and there was no thought of including him in the council of regency. He was described as 'beinge not very wyse, inconstant, factious and insolent' (*CSP Scot.*, 1563–9, 581). In September the Hamiltons proposed their own council of regency to include Lord John Hamilton, who was to serve until the return of his father Châtelherault, Argyll, and Huntly. These stirrings of opposition were soon crushed by Moray, and in September Huntly offered his allegiance to the king and in December joined the regent's council, having been invited and agreed to carry the sceptre at the king's first parliament of 5 December 1567.

This fragile unity among the magnates was broken by Mary's escape from Lochleven on 2 May 1568. Huntly immediately announced his support for the queen, but her early defeat at Langside and her flight into England prevented the consolidation of a firm opposition to Moray. Huntly was not present at Langside but held the north for Mary, where he proved a constant threat to the regent's authority. In July he was reported to have threatened to destroy those burghs which had assisted Moray with men or money, and in August was undertaking military operations in Fife and Forfarshire with a large force. Huntly's power was recognized by Mary in September, when she appointed him her lieutenant in the north, with powers to call parliaments, dispense justice, and coin money, together with other rights and duties. In the same month Moray reported an attack by Huntly and 1500 men on the provost of Aberdeen's house. Having secured Aberdeen the earl then made an attack across the Mounth with a force of about 700 horse. Aberdeen became the centre of his administration and control of it was left to Huntly's brother, the ruthless Adam Gordon of Auchindoun.

The exoneration of Moray by Elizabeth's tribunal of inquiry into responsibility for Darnley's murder, and his return home with an English subsidy, discouraged many of the queen's supporters. In May 1569 Huntly himself acknowledged the regent's authority. Quick to capitalize on his success Moray then began a visitation of the north-east to enforce his authority there. During that time he levied fines, even on Huntly, such as had never been seen before in the region. He also took the opportunity to undermine the position of the religious conservatives in the area, who had hitherto enjoyed the protection of the earls of Huntly and the Gordon family. King's College, Aberdeen, a thorn in the side of the reformed kirk, was finally purged of its Catholic staff and the foundations of a reformed university were laid.

A permanent political solution to the instability of the country was still being sought in the summer of 1569. In June, Huntly was present at a convention at Perth which considered Mary's proposal that she be divorced from Bothwell as a prelude to her restoration. It was also made clear that she was considering marriage to the fourth duke of Norfolk, a move which would draw her closer to English Catholics. The scheme was rejected by a large majority of the convention, but Huntly was one of the small minority which favoured considering it further. Any possibility of the queen's return to Scotland was then suspended by the murder of Moray on 23 January 1570, which once more plunged the Scottish political scene into turmoil.

Lieutenant in the north A long delay in the appointment of a successor to Moray followed. Huntly refused to accept the earl of Lennox as regent because he had been virtually appointed by Queen Elizabeth and was thus in league with a foreign prince. The Lennox family's brutal efforts to reinforce their authority alienated a number of the Scottish nobles, and plunged the country into a vicious civil war. Huntly had already mustered a force of over 1000 men by the end of May. In July, when Lennox was confirmed as regent, Huntly was boasting that he had received a papal subsidy of 20,000 crowns from Flanders, which helped to fuel rumours of impending foreign intervention. Queen Mary appointed Châtelherault as regent for her, and he and the earls of Huntly and Argyll acted with her commission as lieutenants within their own spheres of influence. Huntly's administration was based on Aberdeen, which was confirmed as his regional capital. He held courts there, received appeals, and exercised the prerogatives of justice over the outlying area. By the middle of June 1570 it was reported that the earls, lords, and barons of the north had gathered in support of Huntly at Aberdeen, where he was joined by the earls of Atholl and Crawford, John Hamilton, the commendator of Arbroath, and Lord Ogilvie. He equipped himself with a privy council, as befitted his viceregal status, which included Atholl and Crawford among others.

During the two and a half year course of his rebellion

Huntly exercised jurisdiction over a large area stretching to Forfarshire in the south, and as far north and west as Inverness-shire. His administration needed to be financed from sources other than his own revenues. His previous rebellion against Moray had been expensive and had left his finances under some strain. It was alleged that the loans raised against his estates amounted to £5000. To finance his regime Huntly drew on the revenues from the crown lands and the profits of justice; he also turned his eyes to the kirk revenues, diverting them into his own pocket. By 1573 the procurators of the kirk were demanding payment of the thirds of benefices for 1569–72, all of which had been appropriated and spent by Huntly.

The burgesses of Aberdeen, reluctant hosts to the Gordon administration, were powerless to secure its removal. The neighbouring ecclesiastical settlement of Old Aberdeen, where the bishop, William *Gordon, Huntly's uncle, still lived, was effectively a Gordon stronghold. The earl had a residence in the canonry, and despite his protestant sympathies protected a community of Catholic and conservative sympathizers who resided there. It was well known as a place where mass was regularly celebrated. Huntly also welcomed to Aberdeen the refugee English rebels from the failed rising against Elizabeth in 1569. The countess of Northumberland remained for some time with Lord Seton in Old Aberdeen, where she heard mass every day. The earl of Westmorland, too, spent time in Aberdeen trying to secure passage by sea to the continent—the merchant burgesses were reluctant to allow him to embark in any of their ships for fear of English sanctions and reprisals from the regent.

Some attempts were made to dislodge Huntly from Aberdeen. In November 1571 the master of Forbes, a hereditary enemy of the Gordons who for precisely this reason had been made king's lieutenant in the north, led a substantial force against Adam Gordon of Auchindoun. Forbes was defeated at the battle of the Crabstane on the outskirts of the city. Gordon's force was not recruited locally, but seems to have been drawn mainly from Easter Ross and Sutherland. No further serious threats against the Gordons were attempted after Forbes's defeat. Adam Gordon's tight grip on the north allowed the earl of Huntly to play a part in events further south.

Decline and death Huntly, Argyll, and the western lords were made welcome in Edinburgh in April 1570, and endorsed the strengthening of the castle against the approaching English army. In June 1571 Huntly attended a parliament held by the queen's party in the city, but already the tide was beginning to turn against them. A parliament of the king's party in Stirling in September was well supported. Huntly joined in a raid led by William Kirkcaldy of Grange against that town during which the regent, Lennox, was killed. Nevertheless, support for the queen's party gradually began to ebb away after this.

The treaty of Blois of 19 April 1572 between England and France encouraged the pacification of Scotland, facilitated English intervention, and convinced the queen's party that it could not expect international help. Between August and September of 1572 the Hamiltons and Huntly withdrew from Edinburgh, and in February 1573 they subscribed the pacification of Perth accepting the king's authority and the reformed church, in return for the restoration of all their lands and the remission of all legal measures taken against them since 15 June 1567. Morton, the new regent, faced with the need to increase revenue and shore up his authority, toured the north-east in force in the late summer of 1574, taking the English ambassador with him. Huntly was briefly imprisoned in the west, ostensibly for aiding the treasonable plotting of Adam Gordon of Auchindoun, now an exile in France. Morton gained greater room to manoeuvre; he levied huge fines, most of which were never collected, and attempted to eradicate conservative and Catholic religious influences in the area. Huntly was released from prison when the visitation was over. His own finances were still depleted and had not yielded the large sums in fines for which the regent had hoped. With the settlement of the civil war and the end of any realistic hope of a Marian restoration Huntly retired to his castle at Strathbogie where he died suddenly on 20 October 1576, of over-exertion in a game of football.

Huntly and his wife had four children; their son George *Gordon became sixth earl and first marquess of Huntly; Alexander of Strathaven married Agnes, daughter of George Sinclair, fourth earl of Caithness, and widow of Andrew Hay, eighth earl of Erroll. He died in January 1622 and is buried in Elgin Cathedral, where his tombstone survives. Their son William became a Franciscan friar in Paris, but did not persevere in the religious life; and their daughter Jean shortly after 29 July 1585 married George Sinclair, fifth earl of Caithness. Allan White

Sources *Scots peerage*, 4.539–40 • GEC, *Peerage*, 6.679 • G. Crawfurd, *The lives and characters of the officers of the crown and state in Scotland from David I to the Union* (1726) • *CSP Scot.*, 1545–81 • *Reg. PCS*, 1st ser., vols. 1–2 • W. Gordon, *The house of Gordon: the history of the ancient, noble and illustrious family of Gordon from their first arrival in Scotland in Malcolm III's time to the year 1690* (1716) • R. Gordon, *The earldom of Sutherland: a genealogical history of the earldom of Sutherland from its origin to the year 1651* (1813) • 'Papers from the charter chest … at Gordon Castle', *Miscellany of the Spalding Club*, ed. J. Stuart, 4, Spalding Club, 20 (1849) • Charles, eleventh marquis of Huntly, earl of Aboyne, ed., *The records of Aboyne MCCXXX–MDCLXXXI*, New Spalding Club, 13 (1894) • *CSP Scot. ser.*, *1509–1603* • *APS*, *1424–1567* • Lord Herries [John Maxwell], *Historical memoirs of the reign of Mary queen of Scots*, ed. R. Pitcairn, Abbotsford Club, 6 (1836) • T. Thomson, ed., *A diurnal of remarkable occurrents that have passed within the country of Scotland*, Bannatyne Club, 43 (1833) • M. Livingstone, D. Hay Fleming, and others, eds., *Registrum secreti sigilli regum Scotorum / The register of the privy seal of Scotland*, 5 (1957) • *John Knox's History of the Reformation in Scotland*, ed. W. C. Dickinson, 2 vols. (1949) • J. Leslie, *The historie of Scotland*, ed. E. G. Cody and W. Murison, trans. J. Dalrymple, 2 vols. in 4 pts, STS, 5, 14, 19, 34 (1888–95) [1596 trans. of *De origine moribus, et rebus gestis Scotorum libri decem* (Rome, 1578)] • D. Calderwood, *The history of the Kirk of Scotland*, ed. T. Thomson and D. Laing, 8 vols., Wodrow Society, 7 (1842–9) • G. Buchanan, *The history of Scotland*, ed. J. Aikman, 4 vols. (1827) • J. Spottiswoode, *History of the Church of Scotland*, ed. M. Napier and M. Russell, 3 vols., Spottiswoode Society, 6 (1847–51) • P. F. Tytler, *The history of Scotland*, 9 vols. (1828–43) • A. Murray, 'Huntly's rebellion and the administration of justice in N.E. Scotland, 1570–1573', *Northern Scotland*, 4 (1981), 1–6 • G. R. Hewitt, *Scotland under Morton*,

1572–80 (1982) • A. White, 'Religion, politics and society in Aberdeen, 1543–1593', PhD diss., U. Aberdeen, 1985 • A. White, 'Queen Mary's northern province', *Queen Mary: queen in three kingdoms*, ed. M. Lynch (1988), 53–70 • A. White, 'The impact of the Reformation on a burgh community: the case of Aberdeen', *The early modern town in Scotland*, ed. M. Lynch (1987), 81–101
Archives NA Scot., Gordon Castle muniments, GD.44

Gordon, George, first marquess of Huntly (1561/2–1636), magnate and politician, was the son of George *Gordon, fifth earl of Huntly (*d.* 1576), and his wife, Lady Anne Hamilton (*d.* after 1574), daughter of James *Hamilton, second earl of Arran and duke of Châtelherault (*d.* 1575). In October 1576 his father died after a 'violent exercise' involving football, and the teenaged earl of Huntly was soon placed under the protection of his uncle Adam Gordon of Auchindoun.

Early years, 1577–1587 One of the first personal references to the young Huntly is found in the English report on 'The presente estate of the nobilitie in Scotland', a document of 1577 which commented favourably upon his Hamilton blood, his dominance in the Scottish north-east, and his anticipated favour towards Elizabeth I. Any hopes of the earl serving as an uncritical supporter of England were disturbed, however, by his recusant sympathies, which began to manifest themselves during a continental tour, of which the years 1578 to 1580 were spent in France, apparently under the tutelage of Sir Patrick Gordon of Auchindoun. In 1578 the English government listed Huntly among eight 'Comites Catholici', ranking second in prominence only to the Stewart earl of Atholl, another highland magnate (*CSP Scot.*, 5.329). While travelling in France, Huntly was observed by Sir Francis Walsingham's intelligence network attending mass at Orléans, and when he returned to Scotland after November 1580 he was noted as being antipathetic to English interests. In July 1583 the agent Robert Bowes warily noted the deceptiveness of the earl and his Catholic or crypto-Catholic allies John Graham, earl of Montrose, and David Lindsay, earl of Crawford. This led to their inclusion on 30 October 1585 as 'enemies' in a comprehensive list of Scottish noblemen and their respective attitudes towards England.

Though Huntly was distrusted by both English and Scottish authorities, his personal relationship with the adolescent James VI throughout this period led to a certain diplomatic immunity for the Catholic noble. After his return to Scotland he was permitted the symbolic honour of bearing the sceptre in the parliament of October 1581, and in the same year he enshrined his upwardly mobile status by building Gordonsburgh. His loyalty to the king was first tested in 1582 by the Ruthven raid, in which Huntly's participation was sought by the conspirators; by June he was openly in favour of enlarging James, an early support that earned him the king's gratitude and consistent protection in the years to come. In July 1583 the king paid a special visit to Huntly, then suffering from 'a very dangerous disease', possibly the 'frensy' that would plague him throughout his career (*CSP Scot.*, 8.556). At the parliament of 1584, he again bore the sceptre before James as the king entered the tolbooth to open the first session on 18 March; by this time his favour had been consolidated by the king's personal award to him of the escheat and benefices of the abbacy of Paisley. In June 1584 he was appointed one of the lords of the articles, an appointment that ensured him a place of some power in drafting parliamentary legislation, and in July he added Brechin to his expanding dominions in the north. His new status as a favourite with a politically suspect faith was now established, and it was consolidated by his commission to track down and apprehend James Stewart, the earl of Arran and former effective regent of Scotland, after his fall in the autumn of 1585.

Huntly's correspondence with both the exiled Queen Mary and Philip II of Spain, in 1584 and 1586 respectively, demonstrates a growing disenchantment with the pro-English politics of the government. This communication was kept quiet, and as James VI increasingly assumed personal authority, Huntly stood to benefit from his favours. In December 1586 he was made lieutenant and justice of the north at Aberdeen, a position that did much to reinvigorate Gordon power within the highlands. By April 1587 he had put his power to full application when James appointed him to circumvent any highland uprisings and the rebellious activities of the McLeods in particular. He gained an equally firm foothold at court when James appointed him lord high chamberlain in the following June, and his active participation at the parliament of 12 July led to anxious rumours among courtiers. In August 1587 Walsingham's agent reported that 'My lord of Huntley is indeed ane greit curteour and knawis mair of the Kingis secreittis nor ony man at this present doithe' (*CSP Scot.*, 9.476). Contrary to the fears of many political commentators, Huntly had no religious sway over the king, although his Catholicism possibly contributed to James's calculated policy of intermittent toleration of recusants, which would operate in inverse proportion to the power of the kirk.

Courtier, conspirator, and rebel, 1588–1589 Huntly's close political relationship and friendship with Esmé Stewart, first duke of Lennox, had been a factor in bringing him closer to the king, but it also led to a powerful matrimonial alliance with the Stewart family with his marriage to the duke's eldest daughter, Lady Henrietta (1573–1642), on 21 July 1588. Plans for the match had been in effect since before September 1586, when parliament voted 5000 merks to Huntly to cover the costs of an expedition to France to procure his bride. As a wedding gift, James also bestowed the commendatorship of Dunfermline on the earl (26 June 1587), transferring it from the master of Gray, another controversial Catholic politician but one with strong English connections. In anticipation of the occasion, the clergy demanded in February 1588 that Huntly declare himself protestant by signing a confession of faith, one of many he was to sign throughout his lengthy political career. As the English correspondent Atkinson reported to Walsingham in July,

> the marriage between the Earl of Huntly and the Duke of Lennox's sister is to be solemnized so soon as may be, 'but not befoir thay geive declaratioun of their faith, for his

majesties minister Mr. Craig refused to proclame thair bandis or matrimony until that tyme'. (*CSP Scot.*, 9.587)

Huntly satisfied some churchmen: the marriage was celebrated at Holyrood Chapel on 21 July by the archbishop of St Andrews, Patrick Adamson, a court cleric who had already crossed the general assembly. The marriage proved one of the more successful matches of its kind, surviving Huntly's numerous wardings and excommunications. Henrietta had inherited her father's talent for administration. She was described as 'a virtuous wyff, and prudent lady … who providentlie governed her husband's affairs, and carefullie solicited his bussines at home dureing his banishment from Scotland, after the battell of Glenlivet' (Gordon, 208).

Huntly's conversion to protestantism in 1588 was strictly nominal, although the king seems to have genuinely believed in the integrity of his conversion. Whatever the case, the earl corresponded with Spain from June through to November 1588, and unabashedly maintained public connections with fellow recusants across Scotland. On 8 September, for example, he was among the most prominent guests at the wedding of the daughter of his cousin Sir John Seton to Lord Forbes. By this stage he was a firm favourite of James alongside Alexander Lindsay, and while Huntly's appointment as captain of the guard on 28 November can be seen as one sign of such favour, it was also a tactful replacement for the outgoing captain, Sir Thomas Lyon, master of Glamis, a fierce opponent of Lindsay. As captain, Huntly remained with the king throughout the winter, residing at Holyrood Palace, a situation that obliged Sir Roger Aston to write to Whitehall, assuring the English government that the earl's conversion to protestantism was genuine. With the new year came a series of shocking revelations that aroused little surprise in wary observers, but which seriously tainted Huntly with treasonous intent and further strained relations between England and Scotland. In January 1589 English intelligence intercepted documents which promised the support of the Catholic gentlemen of Scotland for any invasion of Britain. These were signed by Huntly in conjunction with John Maxwell, eighth Lord Maxwell, and Lord Claud Hamilton, and offered unmitigated support if Spain were to dispatch 60,000 troops and money to raise more. Huntly denied any involvement, though Elizabeth I, already long convinced of his wavering reliability, demanded that he be disciplined. James refused to do this publicly, instead reprimanding and guiding his friend in a famously heartfelt letter of February 1589: 'Ar[e] thir [these] the fruictis of zour new conversioun?' the king asked, seemingly genuinely hurt by the earl's betrayal (*CSP Scot.*, 9.700). The king's chief minister, John Maitland, Lord Thirlestane, hoping to neutralize Huntly's political power in the fallout from the Spanish correspondence, threatened to resign when the earl was allowed to retain his captaincy. Despite their kinship (both were nephews of Lord John Hamilton), Maitland and the earl never entirely trusted each other, and this episode served to sunder their already cool relations at court.

At length Huntly was warded in Edinburgh Castle (from 27 February to 7 March 1589), though this imprisonment seemed indicative more of the king's personal annoyance with Huntly and his desire to appease Elizabeth than of any real wish to punish him. On 13 March Huntly incurred greater unpopularity by abandoning the king after rumours of a rebellion in Edinburgh had reached him, a withdrawal that cost him his captaincy. In April he engineered a regional rebellion in conjunction with the earls of Crawford and Erroll, personally raising a force rumoured to be of 10,000 men, an impressive testament to his power and influence throughout the north-east. These efforts were soon quashed, however, when the first earl of Bothwell withdrew his support for the northern earls, and the king led an expeditionary force to Aberdeen to engage the rebels directly. This incident, known as the 'Brig o' Dee', prompted Huntly to surrender himself unconditionally to James. After being feasted at the Gordon headquarters of Strathbogie, the king arranged for Huntly to ward himself in Borthwick Castle, where he remained until September.

Highland power struggles and the death of Moray Huntly's imprisonment and subsequent release led to his temporary retirement from public life and a greater devotion to matters of estate management and consolidation, which in turn spawned a series of new architectural projects. It was during this period that he began work on a castle at Ruthven, in Badenoch, 'neir unto his hunting forrests' (Gordon, 214), with a series of repairs at the Gordon strongholds in Elgin and Aberdeen, and the construction of Kean-Kaill (Newhouse), Aboyne, and the Plowlands in Murray.

Even at this more peaceful stage of his life Huntly was never far from controversy, as when an English source reported in September 1590 that he had been responsible for the murder of a landlord (allegedly Robert, Lord Boyd, who had died in January). The earl's perceived reputation for savagery against his opponents was further entrenched by an explosive conflict between the Gordons and two of the principal clans in his Badenoch territories, the Mackintoshes and Grants of Ballindalloch. Their reaction to the more intense exercise of Huntly's lordship in the highlands soon drew the participation of the earls of Moray and Atholl against him, effectively creating a state of war in the Scottish north. After launching a pre-emptive strike in November on the conferring earls at Forres, the so-called Darnaway incident, in which John Gordon of Cluny was killed, Huntly was summoned to Edinburgh, where the king began negotiations for a peace settlement. Tensions ran highest throughout the following year, and in March Huntly was ordered to restrict his forces to the east side of the River Spey, with Moray confined to the west, lest further trouble erupt. In July 1591 Huntly initiated a new attack on the Stewarts of Moray by concentrating on the earl's fishings in Spey, a manoeuvre that revived the Gordon feud with the Mackintoshes and Grants, who were both ultimately obliged to sue for peace. At this stage it was reported that the earl 'rules all in the north, and over Moray' (Brown, *Bloodfeud*, 156).

The reconsolidation of Gordon power in the highlands

allowed Huntly to renew his focus on the king, who commissioned him to pursue and apprehend the outlawed earl of Bothwell after the latter's abortive palace coup in December. By 5 February 1592 he had appeared before the privy council to answer to charges of involvement in a Jesuit conspiracy, a potential embarrassment that was quickly overshadowed by the events of the next week. On 7 February Huntly used his commission to secure a passage across the Forth, over which traffic had been neutralized to prevent any further movements by Bothwell. His objective was to surprise James Stewart, earl of Moray, a Bothwell supporter, who was then stationed at Donibristle, Fife; on Huntly's arrival with a group of forty men, a brief siege ensued that brought about the death of the sheriff of Moray. Moray himself escaped for a time when one of his retainers created a diversion but, according to tradition, his helmet had caught fire, enabling the Gordon party to chase him to the banks of the Forth and kill him there. Huntly's involvement in the murder is, like so much of the violence associated with him, ambiguous: some accounts have him dealing the final triumphant blow to his sworn enemy, while others portray him as being forced by the Gordons of Gight and Cluny to implicate himself in the slaughter. An orchestrated outpouring of anger over this incident confronted Huntly and the king himself (who was, as James Melville tendered, 'luiking on it with forthought'), ensuring literary immortality for the 'Bonnie Earl of Moray' himself (*Autobiography and Diary*, 198). James was forced to commission the Scottish nobility to apprehend Huntly, who on 10 March voluntarily warded himself in Blackness Castle, where he remained for ten days.

Huntly tactfully removed himself from court life after his release, though his activities in the north contributed to the revival of all-out war with those anti-Gordon malcontents who remained active in the highlands. In August he dispatched his Cameron and MacDonnell clients against the Grants and Mackintoshes, and in November there were reports that he had launched a new attack on the earl of Atholl at Badenoch. The conflict now widened with the involvement of Moray's brother-in-law Archibald Campbell, seventh earl of Argyll, who was eager to take advantage of Huntly's political misfortunes by extending his own power in the highlands in conjunction with Atholl. The king's appointment of William Douglas, tenth earl of Angus, a border magnate and fellow Catholic, as lieutenant in the north did nothing to quell the burgeoning state of war. By December Huntly's international connections once again threatened to destroy him politically, when a series of letters to the king of Spain were seized from George Kerr of Newbottle. This correspondence included two blank sheets on which Huntly's own signature was found; he promptly denied his involvement, yet refused to appear in St Andrews when summoned in February 1593. He relented and surrendered when the king personally led a force against him to Aberdeen on 10 March, and this well-timed gesture persuaded James to relax him from the horn on 19 March. The kirk, convinced of Huntly's unreliability, expressed its displeasure with the king's favouritism and the earl's bad faith when the provincial synod of Fife excommunicated him on 25 September. The king, however, overrode this ecclesiastical legislation by declaring the Catholic earls innocent of the charges of communication with Spain in November of that year, so long as both Huntly and Erroll submitted themselves to the kirk by 1 February 1594.

The new year was decisive in determining Huntly's fate, and was ushered in abruptly when he joined Sir Patrick Gordon of Auchindoun and the earls of Erroll and Angus in not submitting to ward or obeying the February deadline. Forfeited by parliament on 8 March, they were provoked into a new rebellion against the crown in a desperate attempt to avoid compromising their religious beliefs. The kirk itself recruited the young earl of Argyll to engage Huntly's forces directly with 7000 men, but he was soundly defeated by the Catholic earls at Glenlivet on 3 October. In spite of this victory, Huntly was again unwilling to face the king in battle and retreated before the royal army, leaving James free to order the destruction of Strathbogie. Huntly's position was further weakened by the death of his first cousin Auchindoun, the earl's most important and militantly Catholic adviser since his teenage years. After his death it is possible to change the direction of Gordon policy, with the earl adopting a far less subversive line in politics and religion.

Exile, excommunication, and absolutions, 1595–1625 On 19 May 1595 Huntly went into exile on the continent, and for sixteen months he followed a peripatetic itinerary that included Germany and Flanders. By October 1596, however, it was reported that Huntly had been sighted at Bog of Gight, and on 19 October Countess Henrietta wrote urgently to the presbytery at Moray, assuring it of her husband's willingness to submit to the kirk and beg forgiveness for his role in Moray's death. Accordingly, he appeared in Aberdeen on 26 June, and was again accepted into the Scottish church, and was soon afterwards received and welcomed by the king at Falkland. Huntly appeared to be a changed man, opting for a quieter life devoted to his estates and gardening, a new countenance that may have encouraged the kirk to renew its trust in him. He took his customary place as sword-bearer to James at the opening of parliament on 11 November, and had his forfeiture specially 'reduced', allowing him to enjoy his estates and honours. Little is then heard of Huntly until 1599, in which year he was appointed co-lieutenant and justiciar for the highlands with his brother-in-law, the duke of Lennox, whose own position was strictly *ex officio* on account of his active court life. In February Huntly's new ascendancy was confirmed by his appointment to the privy council and, more importantly, through his elevation as marquess of Huntly, earl of Enzie, and Lord Gordon of Badenoch at Princess Margaret's baptism on 17 April 1599.

For the next four years, Huntly spent more time in the north, expanding his estates (including the lands and barony of Gartullie, which he had acquired in June 1600) and countering the movements of Argyll, who had established himself as his most serious rival for highland supremacy.

From March to July 1602 King James busied himself in attempting to reconcile the allied Campbells and Stewarts of Moray with the Gordons, in the interests of stabilizing his northern domain. However, no settlement was achieved until 23 February 1603, a mere month before the king's accession to the English throne. Next to Argyll, Huntly's greatest concern was the growing power of the Scottish kirk, which concentrated its efforts on holding the marquess to his vows or, failing this, on excommunicating him. In February 1605 the privy council stayed a process of excommunication against him, awaiting the advice of the now absent James. With characteristic impetuosity Huntly made for court in London without a licence, but the king, forewarned by the council, refused to grant him an audience. Humiliated, he returned to the north and a life of relative quiet, duly cowed by the king's resolve even if he continued to enjoy a measure of protection from those in the church who wished to prosecute him further.

Early in 1606 the king ordered Huntly to send his eldest son, George *Gordon (*c.*1590–1649), to court to attend upon Henry, prince of Wales, to which he consented, '[a]lbeit he be the gretest pairt of the confort quhilk I have nou' (NL Scot., Adv. MS 33.1.1, vol. 2, Huntly to James VI). His troubled relationship with 'the puritins of this contrey' continued to deteriorate until December 1606, when the convention at Linlithgow commanded him to station himself and his family in Aberdeen upon his return from court. He returned on 10 December with a royal paper staying any further ecclesiastical proceedings against him and the marchioness, though this was not enough to prevent a further charge of recusancy by the privy council on 23 June 1607. Huntly was warded in Elgin, and by August of that year Argyll had supplanted him as the new lieutenant for the highlands. In an effort to retain power and reduce the potential for further blood feud, Huntly arranged for the marriage on 2 October of his eldest daughter, Lady Ann, to the protestant James Stewart, third earl of Moray, son of the murdered earl. In November Huntly was transferred to Aberdeen, where he was expected to enter into a programme of 'religious conversion' (*Reg. PCS*, 8.9).

Huntly's ongoing quarrel with the Scottish clergy and his reputation as a patron of recusants incurred another excommunication, this time by the general assembly at Linlithgow (27 July 1608), which declared his supplication to be 'verie frivolous' (Calderwood, 6.759). Not long afterwards, he was ordered to enter himself into Stirling Castle and pay his own accommodation, a routine imprisonment that lasted for one month. Along with his ally Erroll, he gave his oath to conform to 'the holye ewengell', but the presbytery of St Andrews, its patience exhausted, still excommunicated him (NL Scot., Adv. MS 33.1.1, vol. 3, fols. 31–2). After another placement in Stirling, Huntly was released at length in November 1610, but only by a combined caution from the Gordons of Aberyeldie, Lesmoir, and Lochinvar, who guaranteed his good behaviour on 15 January 1611. Even then he was confined to his house at Strathbogie, but gradually obtained leave to visit his highland properties, including those of Kellie, where he spent time between 1 and 15 August. The next few years were relatively peaceful for Huntly. He intervened—peaceably, this time—in a dispute between Sir Robert Gordon and the earl of Caithness in 1612. On 15 December of that year the privy council permitted him to leave his house arrest in Strathbogie and visit the king at Whitehall, an act that marked the gradual reinstatement of Huntly in the king's favour.

In the autumn of 1613, Huntly was entrusted with a special commission of fire and sword against Cameron of Lochiel, and within three years he had begun to rebuild his lordship in the north. By 1616 he had acquired the Banff lands of the Innes family of Invermarkie, and on 9 January he was sitting as a member of the Scottish privy council, though his fortunes took a temporary turn for the worse when the high commission warded him in Edinburgh on 12 June. After his release on 18 June he repaired to court, and in a move which offended both the ecclesiastical and the patriotic sentiment of the Scottish clergy, he was officially absolved of excommunication by the archbishop of Canterbury (though with the prior knowledge and blessing of the bishop of Caithness). In July, his daughter, Lady Elizabeth, wife of Alexander Livingstone, Lord Livingstone, died while giving birth in Edinburgh, and by 16 August Huntly had determined to make a formal submission to the general assembly at Aberdeen; whether truly contrite or not, he was re-appointed to the privy council in December, in time to prepare for the king's return to Scotland in the following year. Sitting on the convention of estates he cast his vote on 5 March 1617 to raise £200,000 to subsidize James's progress; on 6 August he and his erstwhile ally Erroll personally appeared in Carlisle before the king, who served as arbitrator between them. In 1618 he gained permission to establish Gordonsburgh (the future Fort William) as a burgh of barony, and in the same year he had his sovereignty established in Lochaber, formerly contended by Cameron of Lochiel. For the remainder of James's reign Huntly maintained a relatively low profile, complaining about the 'rapacious poacher gangs' who terrorized his highland tenants, and suffering the death of his son Laurence in August 1623 (Brown, *Noble Society*, 214). His last commission under James VI was to subdue the clan Chatten.

Last years, 1625–1636 Gordon power continued to stabilize under Charles I, but this was due more to the influence of Huntly's second son, John Gordon, viscount of Melgum, than to the marquess's own personal role. In March 1629 Huntly rushed to court in much the same manner as he had in 1605, and with equally dismal results. 'I think he repentes his journey', wrote D. (perhaps David) Fullerton to the aged earl of Mar on 23 April 1629 (*Supplementary Mar and Kellie MSS*, 249). Charles's campaign to recover the heritable sheriffships of Scotland, and the political pressures surrounding it, led to the surrender of Huntly's shrieval authority in Aberdeen and Inverness, for which he received £5000. In October 1630 Huntly lost another son, Melgum, who was burnt to death in Frendraught Tower.

His own political position throughout this period was becoming more precarious, especially in the context of the privy council campaign against Catholics, and in December 1633 he was forced to defend his activities to the council, which implied that he had been lax in maintaining order in the north. On 16 December 1634, his perceived laxity now viewed as outright rebelliousness, he was denounced as a rebel before being ordered to confine himself to Edinburgh. In March 1635, characteristically late by three months, he appeared before the council to answer charges of justiciary negligence, and was ultimately warded in Edinburgh Castle.

Huntly was finally released early in 1636, perhaps because of his worsening physical condition, which even his opponent Spottiswoode was moved to comment on in April. After a brief residence in Edinburgh's Canongate, he was granted permission to return to Aberdeen in May, and quickly began his homeward journey, only to die *en route*, in Dundee, on 13 June. His impressive funeral on 25 July was a spectacular show-piece that involved a four-week procession through northern Scotland, culminating in his burial at Elgin Cathedral on 31 August. In the years that followed, his son and successor, George Gordon, second marquess of Huntly, took part in the civil wars as an ardent royalist, eventually being executed in 1649 not long after Charles I himself, while Henrietta was forced to flee in 1641 on account of her Catholicism and died on 2 September 1642. Huntly himself was a controversial figure in his day, and contemporary commentators also varied substantially in their opinions of him. One contemporary source claimed him to have been 'a valiant, provident, and politicke man … a good and just neighbour … by the testimonie of all such who dwelt about him, yea of his very enemies' (Gordon, 480). Many, including the earls of Moray, Argyll, and Atholl, would have strongly contended this view. Perhaps the most diplomatic view is that taken in the *Scots Peerage*, which maintains that, as eminent as Huntly was, 'he did not influence the history of his country so much as some less able men have done'.

Huntly was the principal Catholic noble in Scotland and arguably the most powerful lord in the Scottish highlands under James VI and I. His career was characterized by an impressive immunity to serious persecution, due chiefly to his close, personal connections to the king. He was, however, also viewed by the kirk as an implacable enemy whose frequent public conversions to protestantism damaged his credibility and enhanced his reputation as a political uncertainty. Huntly's involvement in Spanish conspiracies and his consistent private dedication to Catholicism led to frequent imprisonment and exile, but his personal loyalty to James VI was generally considered beyond question. He effectively rebuilt his family's position as the most important in the highlands, an ascendancy that was to be challenged only by his Campbell counterpart, Archibald, earl of Argyll. J. R. M. Sizer

Sources *Scots peerage* • R. Gordon, *A genealogical history of the earldom of Sutherland* (1813) • *CSP Scot., 1574–85* • *Reg. PCS*, 1st ser., vols. 6–13 • K. M. Brown, *Bloodfeud in Scotland, 1573–1625: violence, justice, and politics in an early modern state* (1986) • D. Moysie, *Memoirs of the affairs of Scotland* (1755) • GEC, *Peerage*, new edn, vol. 5 • *The autobiography and diary of Mr James Melvill*, ed. R. Pitcairn, Wodrow Society (1842) • *The manuscripts of his grace the duke of Rutland*, 4 vols., HMC, 24 (1888–1905), vol. 1 • *Report on the manuscripts of the earl of Mar and Kellie*, HMC, 60 (1904); suppl. (1930) • D. Calderwood, *The history of the Kirk of Scotland*, ed. T. Thomson and D. Laing, 8 vols., Wodrow Society, 7 (1842–9), vols. 6–7 • J. M. Bulloch, ed., *The house of Gordon*, 1 (1903) • M. Lee, *Government by pen: Scotland under James VI and I* (1980) • K. M. Brown, *Noble society in Scotland: wealth, family and culture from Reformation to revolution* (2000) • M. Lee, *John Maitland of Thirlestane and the foundation of the Stewart despotism in Scotland* (1959) • J. Spottiswoode, *The history of the Church of Scotland* (1655) • Gordon Castle muniments, NA Scot., GD44 • NL Scot., Adv. MS 33.1.1, vols. 1–3 • *Estimate of the Scottish nobility during the minority of James the Sixth* (1873)

Archives NA Scot., Breadalbane MSS • NA Scot., Gordon Castle muniments, GD.44

Likenesses C. K. Sharpe, double portrait, pencil and wash drawing (with Henrietta Stewart; after unknown portrait), Scot. NPG

Gordon, George, second marquess of Huntly (*c*.1590–1649), nobleman, was the son of George *Gordon, sixth earl (later first marquess) of Huntly (1561/2–1636), and Lady Henrietta Stewart (1573–1642), daughter of Esmé Stewart, first duke of Lennox.

Early life The upbringing of the young George, known by the courtesy titles of Lord Gordon or earl of Enzie, was a matter of great concern to both church and state, his father being one of the most powerful of the Scottish nobility and the leader of the country's Roman Catholics. In 1596, when the excommunicated Huntly returned with his family to Scotland after a period of enforced exile, the general assembly of the church demanded that Lord Gordon and his brothers 'be brought south to be trained up at schoolls in letters and [protestant] religion' (J. Row, *History of the Kirk*, 1842, 172, 174–5). However, he was still in the north in 1604, for the presbytery of Aberdeen then questioned his pedagogue to ensure his religious orthodoxy. His marriage in June 1607 was part of a plan by James VI and I to reconcile feuding noble dynasties. Gordon married the thirteen-year-old Lady Anne Campbell (1594–1638), daughter of the seventh earl of Argyll, and at the same time his sister Ann was married to the earl of Moray.

Gordon began to play a part in public affairs in Scotland in 1609, when he was granted a commission to act against a violent gang of youths in Aberdeenshire, but the king insisted that he spend much of his time at court in England, hoping to instil both political and religious loyalty—a gift of £1000 sterling helping, no doubt, to make obedience easy. At the first tournament in which Prince Henry participated, on twelfth night in 1610, Gordon was the first to do combat, at 'push of pyke and single sword', and was said to have 'performed with great dexteritie and applause, to his exceeding commendation' (Gordon and Gordon, 261–2). On 3 June he was one of those made a knight of the Bath in connection with Henry's installation as prince of Wales. However, he was soon back in Scotland, being active in a number of disputes in upholding his family's interests. In June 1612 he was involved in a 'broil' in Edinburgh with the earl of Caithness, though his efforts to provoke further violence were unsuccessful (Gordon and Gordon, 286–7). In the years that followed he

George Gordon, second marquess of Huntly (*c.*1590–1649), by Sir Anthony Van Dyck

was involved in fighting to subdue the MacDonalds and Camerons in Lochaber and the Macintoshes, and on 9 January 1616 he was admitted as a member of the Scottish privy council. He left Scotland for France in 1623 'to recreat himselff ther for a short space by his travells' (Gordon and Gordon, 373–4), visiting the court in England on his way. With the king's encouragement Gordon and his uncle the duke of Lennox hoped to bring about the revival of the king of France's company of Scottish men at arms, the *gens d'armes*, which had become dormant after the union of the crowns of 1603. He spent six months at the French court before returning to England for Christmas, and his mission bore fruit when a commission arrived in June 1624 making Lennox captain of the company, with Gordon as his deputy. Unfortunately Lennox had just died, so it proved necessary to obtain a new commission, with Gordon as captain, and he mustered the company before French officers at Leith in July 1625. Its services were not required immediately, and in 1627 it was suppressed when Britain and France went to war. It was agreed in 1629 that it should be restored, but Gordon's position as its commander was endangered in 1630 when he was appointed a commissioner to suppress Roman Catholics in the north of Scotland. Action under the commission might, he feared, offend the king of France, and there was the additional embarrassment that his parents, brothers, and sisters were all Catholics. Indeed Gordon's appointment was in part a test of his own religious loyalties—in 1629 the Scottish privy council had feared that he could not be trusted to ensure that his own children were brought up as protestants, and he had been ordered to send his sons to St Andrews or Cambridge for a sound protestant education. However, he eventually took sufficient action against local Catholics (though not against his own family) to satisfy the council—though he then defied it by sending his two eldest sons, the younger of whom was the royalist James *Gordon, to King's College, Aberdeen, in 1630.

In 1629 Lord Gordon and his father agreed under pressure to surrender to the crown the hereditary sheriffships of Aberdeenshire and Inverness-shire, which had for long been central to their great influence in the north-east. In compensation the crown agreed that Gordon should be paid £5000 sterling. His military ambitions were encouraged when on 10 December 1629 Louis XIII commissioned him to levy 2000 men to fight for France, but there is no evidence that they were ever levied, and when he finally reached France in 1632 (having been created Viscount Aboyne on 20 April) he evidently only commanded the *gens d'armes*. He was involved in fighting in Lorraine, Alsace, and Germany against the forces of the emperor Ferdinand III, but by 1635 he wanted to return to Scotland. However, he was so deeply in debt that he had to delay his journey. He had lived extravagantly in France in expectation of the £5000 he had been promised in 1629, and now sent desperate pleas to Charles I for payment, claiming that his family was on the verge of ruin. He reached London from France in October 1636, having succeeded as marquess of Huntly on his father's death in June. He had still only received £200 of his £5000, and he now persuaded Charles I to agree that (with interest) £9740 sterling was due him, and in January 1637 the king agreed that as there was no hope of the Scottish exchequer making payment, this should be done by the English exchequer.

The bishops' wars There is no evidence that further payments were ever received, but Huntly travelled home 'in royall maner', reaching his main residence, Strathbogie Castle, on 23 June 1637 (Spalding, 2.76). He arrived just a month before the outbreak of the disturbances which were to lead to civil war in Scotland. In reacting to the situation he had the disadvantages of being heavily in debt and out of touch with Scottish affairs. The rumour that the rebel covenanters offered him leadership of their movement if he would join them, or payment of his debts if he remained neutral, are unsubstantiated, but it is likely that approaches were made to him. The earl of Rothes might boast that Gordon power had decayed so that it was no threat to the covenanters, and that, as for Huntly, 'He would not give a salt sitron [citron] for him'

(Rothes, 62–3), but in reality gaining his support would have been a major triumph for the covenanters.

However, from the first Huntly was unswervingly loyal to the king, and in June 1638 he was in Edinburgh for talks with the marquess of Hamilton, who had been appointed king's commissioner to try to reach a settlement with the covenanters. But Huntly hurried north on news that his wife was ill, and her death on 14 June diverted him for a time from public affairs. By September 1638 he was again active, organizing efforts to have the king's covenant (a rival to the national covenant) signed in the north-east, and by January 1639 he was preparing for war, making arrangements to be supplied with arms through Hamilton. Arms for over 3000 men were eventually sent, together with a commission to act as king's lieutenant in northern Scotland. When the covenanters sent an army north under the earl of Montrose to enforce obedience to the covenanters, however, Huntly proved unwilling to offer active resistance. There were good reasons for this. His instructions from the king were that he should not fight unless the covenanters resorted to violence first. Moreover, it made sense to hold back from war until the army which the king was assembling in England was ready to advance into Scotland, and until the reinforcements Huntly hoped to receive from England had time to arrive. He therefore entered into negotiations with the covenanters, meeting Montrose at Fyvie on 5 April. There Montrose agreed that Huntly would not be further troubled if, instead of signing the national covenant, he agreed to an undertaking to uphold royal authority and the laws and liberties of the kingdom. It was also agreed that his followers 'of a contrary Religion'—Roman Catholics—who swore a similar undertaking would not be molested (W. Gordon, 2.265–6). Huntly then came, protected by a safe conduct, to a meeting with other covenanting leaders in Aberdeen. There he found further demands made upon him, for the other covenanter leaders believed that Montrose had made too many concessions. Huntly's power had been left intact, his only submission being to an ambiguous verbal formula. Huntly quickly crumbled under renewed pressure from Montrose. He allowed himself to be demoralized by the argument that since his commission of lieutenancy had not passed the great seal of Scotland it was invalid, and that few would obey any summons to arms from him. Given his debts, he could not accept a demand that he agree to pay the costs of the covenanters' expedition against him. Clearly the intention was to ask for the impossible as a pretext to act against him, and when Montrose urged him to come south to Edinburgh for further talks Huntly took this to mean that his safe conduct was not to be honoured. His main concern seems not to have been denunciation of such dishonourable behaviour but avoidance of the indignity of being removed forcibly from Aberdeen. He therefore asked if he could volunteer to travel to Edinburgh (12 April), which the covenanters happily accepted. Thus Huntly tamely abandoned leadership of the royalists of the north-east. Nor was the humiliation of arrest long delayed, for on reaching Edinburgh the marquess, now isolated, was pressed to give active support to the covenanters, and on his refusal he was imprisoned in Edinburgh Castle on 20 April. The following year he published the statement of defiance he claimed to have made to the covenanters at this point, though it may be doubted whether his original words were quite so well polished. His only crime had been loyalty to his king, he asserted, and he would never be a traitor. 'You may tacke my heade from my shoulders, but not my heart from my soveraigne' (J. Gordon, 2.239–40).

Huntly was released in June 1639, after the pacification of Berwick agreed by the king and the covenanters, and then joined Charles I at Berwick—though he briefly went to Edinburgh to sit on the council on 1 July, to persuade it to agree to giving him temporary protection from his creditors. When the king left Berwick at the end of the month Huntly returned to Edinburgh, and sought to take his seat in parliament on 30 August. He was excluded, however, because he refused to sign the national covenant without reservations. He rejoined the king in England, making no attempt to resume leadership of the northern royalists when war resumed in 1640, and leaving his mother to surrender Bog of Gight (later Gordon Castle) to the triumphant covenanters. When Charles visited Scotland in 1641 to make a settlement with the covenanters Huntly accompanied him, and was again unsuccessful in attempting to take his seat in parliament. Moreover, the settlement agreed by the king removed him from the privy council.

Huntly returned to his estates in January 1642, for the first time since April 1639, and sought to deal with the huge debts he had incurred through 'his prodigal spending in his youth and uther crossis' (Spalding, 2.91). Retaining just Strathbogie Castle, his house in Old Aberdeen, and an income of 10,000 merks (about £555 sterling) a year for life, he agreed to resign the rest of his estates to his eldest son, George, Lord Gordon, to provide suitably for his ten children and satisfy his debtors. In practice the agreement was never fully put into effect, and Huntly found the money to undertake new building work at Strathbogie, where a glimpse of him in 1642 portrays him 'standing by his masons, urging their diligences, and directing and judging their worke' from 4 a.m. to 8 p.m. so 'that he had scarce tyme to eate or sleepe' (Blakhal, 170).

Huntly's conduct since his return from France, and especially in 1639–40, had greatly weakened his family's influence over its extensive network of kin and supporters. His character and upbringing made it impossible for him to win their confidence and affection. His haughty, arrogant, and withdrawn manner alienated many of his natural followers, as did his refusal to consult and take advice from his kinsmen in a traditional manner, and though stubbornly confident in his own opinions, these were often changeable. Patrick Gordon of Ruthven (who may have had some personal grievance against the marquess) blamed Huntly's breeding in England, claiming that English cold formality of manners—'keeping of state'—alienated Scots used to greater informality between gentlemen and nobles: Huntly, he claimed, had been ‘affable, courteous and sociable’ before his time at court (P. Gordon, 230). A Gaelic poet agreed that Anglicization contributed to Huntly's weakness, calling him ‘That poor fowl that lost its comeliness in England’ in a sarcastic reference to the old nickname for the head of the Gordons, the Cock of the North (*Orain Iain Luim*, 25). Ruthven also compared Huntly with Charles I: ‘both melancholians, borne under Saturn’ (P. Gordon, 231). Both were reserved men, guarding themselves from familiarity with ceremony. Ruthven repeatedly chides Huntly's ‘wilful and onconsulable [un-counselable] dispositione’ for his failures (P. Gordon, 204).

Huntly's disastrous confidence in his own judgement was based, it seems, on belief in astrology. In 1647 the French representative in Scotland informed Cardinal Mazarin that Huntly:

> being born in a country in which ignorance has always produced a large number of soothsayers [*devins*], has from his youth been an adept in that somewhat trivial branch of mathematics that teaches to judge of people's fortunes by the study of the stars, and has persuaded himself that he had a complete knowledge of what was, so that he has always been very hopeful in his transactions.

Huntly's own son Charles had told the Frenchman in ‘an amusing sally for a child’ that ‘I would certainly have taken him for a wizard [*sorcier*] had he not been my papa’ for he knew many things before they happened (Fotheringham, 2.345, 347). Gilbert Burnet confirms Huntly's addiction to astrology: ‘Astrology ruined him: he believed in the stars, and they deceived him …. He was naturally a gallant man: but the stars had so subdued him, that he made a poor figure during the whole course of the wars’ (*Bishop Burnet's History*, 1.68). Possibly Huntly's extraordinary ineffectuality in April 1639 in allowing himself to be so easily abducted to Edinburgh was the result of his following a star-induced dream in which everything would turn out for the best.

The king's cause, 1643–1649 In 1643 Huntly again came under pressure from the covenanters as they moved towards intervention in the English civil war to help parliament against the king. In August the convention of estates ordered him to come to Edinburgh, clearly hoping, as in 1639, to neutralize him by removing him from the north-east. However, he refused, pleading that he was struggling to pay his debts, and could not afford to stay in Edinburgh. When pressed further he sought permission to withdraw to France, taking fifty gentlemen with him to serve in the *gens d'armes*, but this was refused. Thus, though Huntly maintained his loyalty to the king, refusing to submit and accept the new solemn league and covenant, he was not willing to make a stand for Charles in Scotland. Probably he believed effective resistance was impossible, a belief that would have been strengthened by the decision of his eldest son, Lord Gordon, to sign the new covenant and raise men for the army the covenanters were to use to intervene in England.

Huntly's offer to banish himself having been rejected, he was declared a rebel. He was now, it was said, ‘almost under dispair’ (Spalding, 2.269) as the covenanters intensified their efforts to force him to co-operate with them. On 1 February 1644 he was again appointed by the king king's lieutenant in the north of Scotland, and it was probably news of this that stirred him to limited defiance. On 16 March he issued a declaration stating that he refused to pay taxes or raise men for intervention in England, and asserting his right to defend himself against unlawful violence by the regime. Three days later some of his followers raided Aberdeen and kidnapped four burgesses who were taking a leading part in trying to mobilize the region for the covenanters' war effort. Whether Huntly ordered the kidnapping or his frustrated followers acted to try to push him into open resistance is unclear. On 20 March, in another declaration, he described the burgesses as ‘sedulous fomentars of dangerous distractions amongst us’ (Macdonald and Dennistoun, 441–2), but offered to free them and gave assurances that he would behave peacefully. Then on 24 March he seized Aberdeen, and started raising forces. In isolation his action seems folly, but it may be that Huntly counted on there being other royalist armies active in Scotland by the end of March. Elaborate schemes had been discussed among royalist nobles for months, with dreams of invasions from England and Ireland combined with risings within Scotland, and Huntly may have seen his venture as the first move in such a grand plan. If so, he was soon disappointed, and once he had made his initial gesture of defiance he had no further plans. His followers soon realized that, if there had ever been any chance of success, it was being lost by inaction, and they ‘beginis to gruge and murmur with his delayis’ (Spalding, 2.351). His men began to drift away, while a covenanter army gathered against him. Abandoning Aberdeen on 30 April and moving north to Strathbogie, Huntly justified his retreat by arguments about the need to defeat his enemies in the north before moving south, but it was clear that he had given up and ‘seikis about for his owne saiftie’ (Spalding, 2.353). As the covenanters advanced he fled by boat to Sutherland, moved briefly into Caithness, and then settled in Strathnaver under the protection of the master of Reay, son of the royalist Lord Reay.

As the covenanters had hoped, Huntly had been provoked into premature and ineffective action, and, as in 1639, had been neutralized. Months later parts of the royalist grand scheme for regaining Scotland were to prove remarkably, if only temporarily, successful. The alliance of the now royalist marquess of Montrose with an Irish force led by Alasdair MacColla won six victories in battle between September 1644 and August 1645, and in this campaign the Gordons played an increasingly important part—especially after, in February 1645, Lord Gordon left the covenanters and joined Montrose. During all this year of royalist success Huntly remained inactive in Strathnaver, but in September he at last prepared to move back to his estates. The statement that he had stayed in Strathnaver ‘sore against his will’ (Spalding, 2.367) makes little sense. Had he wished, he could have moved south and joined Montrose in forwarding the cause of Charles I. But that would have meant co-operation with a man he despised, not only as a former covenanter, a turncoat not to be trusted, but also as the man who had broken his word of honour by allowing the covenanters to imprison him in 1639. There was also jealousy, for the contrast between the young Montrose, the hero of the hour boldly seeking his own destiny, and Huntly, the failure of 1639 and 1644 who waited for his destiny to come to him, and whose strategic vision extended no further than seizing Aberdeen, was humiliatingly obvious. What needs explaining is not why Huntly sulked in Strathnaver for so long, but the timing of his return to the north-east, where he landed on 4 October 1645. Certainly he must have heard of Montrose's victory at Kilsyth (15 August), after which there was no covenanting army in Scotland left to face him, and Huntly may have decided that he should emerge to assert his rights in whatever settlement followed. Moreover, though he had deserted his Gordon and other followers to conquest by the covenanters, leaving them leaderless, Huntly probably found it unbearable that Montrose was increasingly being accepted as their master. Three of his sons had fought under Montrose, Lord Gordon being killed in his service. Now he wished to reclaim the leadership of the Gordons for himself. Whether Huntly had also heard of the covenanters' swift revenge for Kilsyth, the routing of Montrose at Philiphaugh on 13 September, is impossible to know. Certainly, in the event, Huntly emerged to take part again in Scotland's civil wars not, as he may have thought, at a moment of royalist triumph, but at one of disaster, with Montrose fleeing back to the highlands and trying to rebuild his army.

Montrose immediately sought Huntly's help, but there was disagreement over strategy. Montrose wished to lead a raid on Glasgow to hold a meeting of parliament he had summoned there, to attempt to restore his credibility, but Huntly refused to join him, claiming the priority must be to drive the covenanters out of the north-east. Huntly's jealousy and memory of former humiliations, and Montrose's own arrogance, rendered futile repeated efforts in the following months to arrange co-operation between the two men. Huntly's royal commission of February 1644 had clearly stated that as king's lieutenant in the north of Scotland he was subordinate to the king's lieutenant-general, who was Montrose, but Huntly argued that he had full power in the north, Montrose's commission being limited to southern Scotland. Huntly would 'not indure to be a slave to … one of whom he and all his predecessors had ever gotten the precedencie' (P. Gordon, 183). Eventually Huntly accepted that Montrose's new commission of May 1645, making him lieutenant-governor and captain-general of the kingdom, overrode his own commission, but no effective co-operation followed, in spite of Montrose's offers to give him joint command. In May 1646 Huntly, with dreary predictability, yet again seized Aberdeen, and yet again withdrew having no idea what to do next.

In 1646 Charles I, a prisoner of the Scottish army in England, ordered his forces in Scotland to disband. Montrose tried in June to consult Huntly about how to arrange to protect their followers, but when he approached Bog of Gight, Huntly fled, announcing that he at least would obey the king without question. Montrose negotiated terms, disbanded, and went into exile, but Huntly then, astonishingly, announced that he would remain in arms, presumably hoping to be seen as gloriously defiant when Montrose had fled. He was subsequently encouraged in this stand by a letter from the king in which Charles spoke of his hopes of escaping from prison and coming to Scotland, and ordered Huntly to gather his men in readiness. Huntly quartered his forces for the winter of 1646–7 in Banff, but when the covenanters advanced north in April 1647 he immediately retreated to the highlands 'wher he intended to liv as an outlaw' (P. Gordon, 19) until the king's fortunes changed for the better, disbanding all his men except for a lifeguard. In December he was tracked down, captured in Strathdon, and imprisoned in Edinburgh Tolbooth.

While Huntly's son Lord Gordon had served the covenanters in 1643–5 they had not proceeded with legal action against the marquess, but as soon as Lord Gordon deserted to join Montrose a decreet of forfaulture had been passed (8 March 1645), forfeiting Huntly's lands and sentencing him to death. After his capture Huntly was hopeful that sentence would not be carried out, and at first he had grounds for optimism, for early in 1648 the engagers' alliance of moderate covenanters and royalists gained power in Scotland. But though the engagers sought to intervene in England to free the king from imprisonment by the English parliament, their leader, the duke of Hamilton, failed to free Huntly, for fear of alienating the engagement's more committed covenanter supporters. Indeed, Huntly was moved to the greater security of Edinburgh Castle before Hamilton marched his army into England. On the defeat of the engagers at the battle of Preston, power in Scotland passed to the kirk party regime, determined on vengeance on former royalists. Their parliament consulted the commission of the general assembly of the church, which replied that 'it is clear from the Word of God that murtherers sould die without partiality'—though adding that whether Huntly was indeed guilty was for parliament to decide (A. F. Mitchell and J. Christie, eds., *Records of the Commissions of the General Assemblies, 1648–9*, 1896, 225). Parliament decided that no trial was necessary, and Huntly was beheaded in Edinburgh on 22 March 1649, his body then being taken to Seton for burial.

Character and beliefs Before Huntly's execution a minister of the Church of Scotland had offered to absolve him from excommunication if he accepted its authority, but he replied disdainfully 'That he was not accustomed to give Ear to false Prophets, as he [the minister] was, and therefore desired him not to trouble him' (W. Gordon, 2.576). Apart from this firm rejection of the presbyterianism of the covenanters it is not clear where Huntly's religious allegiance lay. He was regarded as inclined to Roman Catholicism, but never declared his faith, and he was ready on occasion to act against Catholic interests out of expediency, as under his commission of 1630. In 1635 he had told the king that he wanted his son Lewis removed from the custody of his own father (the boy's grandfather) so that he could be brought up in the true faith, though it is likely this indication of protestant zeal was simply intended as a gesture to win royal favour and get his debts paid.

His family's reputation as leaders of Catholicism in Scotland and his own studied refusal to declare his own beliefs made it inevitable that Huntly should be accused of support for that faith by his covenanting enemies. In November 1638 he was being denounced in Edinburgh 'as not only as popishly inclined, but even a direct Roman Catholic' (P. York, earl of Hardwicke, *Miscellaneous State Papers*, 2 vols., 1778, 2.115). Robert Baillie, however, branded Huntly not as a Catholic but as a 'feeble, effeminate, foolish Atheist' (*Letters and Journals of Robert Baillie*, 2.164), and the theme of atheism is taken up again by Father Robert Gall. A missionary priest in Scotland, he sought, with the help of Huntly's Catholic daughter, Jean, Lady Seton, to smuggle a priest into Edinburgh Castle to give Huntly absolution in the days before his execution, but the marquess showed no interest and 'dyed as he had lived more atheist then christiean lyke' (M. V. Hay, *The Blairs Papers*, 1929, 85). Having thus rejected the ministrations of both Catholic and protestant clergy, in his speech on the scaffold he confirmed the religious ambiguity that had long characterized him, declaring 'Peace and prosperitie be with the true Catholick and ordoctiall [orthodox] Church … and for my opinione of that Church I remit yow to be informed be Mr. Androw Ramsay, in private'. The reason he gave for this refusal to commit himself was that there might be people present 'whom I am onwillinge to give any satisfactione to' (P. Gordon, 225). One interpretation would be that he did not want to declare himself a Roman Catholic, as confirmation of this would delight those who had long suspected it—and doubtless lead to jeers and abuse from the crowd as he prepared himself for death—but his refusal of absolution renders this unlikely. It is therefore possible that the faith he refused to define involved rejection of both protestantism and Catholicism in favour of eclectic beliefs involving his obsession with astrology.

James VI and I had sought to ensure the young Lord Gordon's loyalty by removing him from the north-east and inculcating in him the values of an Anglicized court. He had succeeded, and, ironically, the results for the dynasty were disastrous. Under Charles I the Gordons of Huntly were no longer a threat to royal authority, but when the king had sought to use the second marquess against the covenanters it was found that he had been so weakened by the loss of the two sheriffships and debt, and so alienated from his kin and followers by his many years in England and France, that he could not mobilize Gordon power effectively. Huntly's task would have been difficult even if he had not suffered from the limitations of his own character. As it was, his combination of pride, haughtiness, ill judgement, and confident fatalism based on his belief that he could predict events rendered virtually everything he did counter-productive. Gordon of Ruthven explained that Huntly's contemplative faculty far outweighed his active one, leading to indecision and frequent changes of mind. The result was that he never 'intended ane actione that succeaded right' (P. Gordon, 230). Huntly took pride in the fact that he remained steadfastly loyal to King Charles I throughout all the complications of the troubles, but his intermittent and bungling attempts at action achieved nothing, and indeed in 1644–6 seriously damaged the royalist cause. When imprisoned in Edinburgh in April 1648 he was reported to be calm and confident. He pressed to be tried, believing he could justify himself to his prosecutors, but friends managed to persuade him it would be safer to keep quiet and not draw attention to himself. 'He lives very quietly. He took in hand some months ago to translate [the prophecies of] Cassandra, and has already done about half of it' (Fotheringham, 2.446). In spite of his years of military service in France, he was no man of action, and sounds almost more content in prison, self-consciously suffering for the king, than he had been free and forced by his inheritance into attempting action. His execution within weeks of the king he had served with loyal ineffectualness gave him an aura of martyrdom that his life had hardly justified.

DAVID STEVENSON

Sources *DNB* · *Scots peerage* · GEC, *Peerage* · P. Gordon, *A short abridgement of Britane's distemper*, ed. J. Dunn, Spalding Club, 10 (1844) · J. Spalding, *Memorialls of the trubles in Scotland and in England, AD 1624 – AD 1645*, ed. J. Stuart, 2 vols., Spalding Club, [21, 23] (1850–51) · J. Gordon, *History of Scots affairs from 1637–1641*, ed. J. Robertson and G. Grub, 3 vols., Spalding Club, 1, 3, 5 (1841) · R. Gordon and G. Gordon, *A genealogical history of the earldom of Sutherland … with a continuation to the year 1651* (1813) · *CSP dom., 1603–37* · *Reg. PCS*, 1st ser. · *Reg. PCS*, 2nd ser. · A. Macdonald and J. Dennistoun, eds., 'Wigton papers', *Miscellany of the Maitland Club* (1840), 2.2 · D. Mathew, 'The Gordons', *Scotland under Charles I* (1955) · J. G. Fotheringham, ed., *The diplomatic correspondence of Jean de Montereul and the brothers de Bellièvre: French ambassadors in England and Scotland, 1645–1648*, 2 vols., Scottish History Society, 29–30 (1898–9) · W. Forbes-Leith, *The Scots men-at-arms and life-guards in France*, 2 vols. (1882) · *The letters and journals of Robert Baillie*, ed. D. Laing, 3 vols. (1841–2) · G. Blakhal, *A breiffe narration of the services done to three noble ladyes*, ed. J. Stuart (1844) · Charles, eleventh marquis of Huntly, earl of Aboyne, ed., *The records of Aboyne MCCXXX–MDCLXXXI*, New Spalding Club, 13 (1894) · W. Gordon, *History of the ancient, noble and illustrious family of Gordon*, 2 vols. (1726–7) · J. Stuart, ed., *Selections from the records of the kirk session, presbytery, and synod of Aberdeen*, Spalding Club, 15 (1846) · C. Innes, ed., *Fasti Aberdonenses … 1494–1854*, Spalding Club, 26 (1854), 460 · NA Scot., MSS GD 44/13/6/2/10 · NA Scot., MSS GD 44/13/5/8 · John, earl of Rothes, *A relation of proceedings concerning the affairs of the Kirk of Scotland*, Bannatyne Club, 37 (1830) · NA Scot., Hamilton MSS, GD 406/1/412 · *Orain lain Luim: songs of John MacDonald*, ed. A. M. Mackenzie (1964)

Archives U. Hull, Brynmor Jones L., letter to earl of Nithsdale

Likenesses attrib. G. Jamesone, oils, 1630, Goodwood, West Sussex · S. Cooper, miniature (after A. Van Dyck), Mauritshuis, The Hague, Netherlands · A. Van Dyck, oils, Buccleuch estates, Selkirk [*see illus.*] · oils, Scot. NPG; repro. in D. Stevenson, *The Scottish revolution 1637–1644: the triumph of the covenanters* (1973)

Gordon, George, first earl of Aberdeen (1637–1720), judge and politician, was born on 3 October 1637, the second son of Sir John *Gordon of Haddo, first baronet (*d.* 1644), an Aberdeenshire laird, and of Mary, daughter of William Forbes of Tolquhon, also an Aberdeenshire laird. *Fortuna sequatur*, the motto chosen for the arms of the

George Gordon, first earl of Aberdeen (1637–1720), by unknown artist

peerage created for Gordon in 1682, the year in which he reached the zenith of his professional and political career, was perhaps more apposite than he would have wished.

Gordon was by then familiar with the twists and turns of fortune. He had been barely a year old when his father had entered the pages of national history by fighting on the royalist side at the Trot of Turriff, where the first life of the wars of the three kingdoms was lost in May 1639. His father had continued to fight for the king, had been placed second in command of the king's forces in Scotland, and had been created a baronet for his services in 1642. Two years later, however, he had been captured by the covenanters, convicted of treason, and executed. The family home at Kellie was burnt when Gordon's father was taken prisoner and the family estates at Haddo were declared forfeit when his father was condemned, yet his mother somehow managed to have her older children educated in Aberdeen. Her second son proved to be a gifted scholar, for he eventually graduated from King's College at the head of his class in 1658. Appointed to a vacant regency in the college, he was able to earn a living for the next four years by guiding students through the philosophy course he had recently completed. By the time he had prepared his students for graduation in 1663 the king had returned, the forfeiture of the Haddo estates had been rescinded in parliament, and it had become possible for him to follow in the footsteps of many younger sons of lairds by travelling abroad to study the civil law in preparation for a career at the bar of the college of justice. He had not been abroad for long when his circumstances changed again. His elder brother died without male issue, apparently at some point in 1665, though it was not until 10 September 1669 that Sir George Gordon of Haddo, as he had then become, was formally entered as heir to the family estates and titles.

Despite the change in his circumstances, Gordon had taken time to complete his legal training and had been admitted to the bar on 4 January 1668 after convincing the advocates and judges that he was sufficiently learned in the civil law. Eighteenth-century contemporaries claimed that he served large numbers of clients without ever receiving a fee, and there is independent evidence to back up the claim that he acquired a considerable reputation for 'Knowledge and Integrity in the Laws' (Crawfurd, 231). In the parliament that met in October 1669 he attracted attention, as well as the wrath of the earl of Lauderdale, by raising some technical questions in relation to the proposal for a closer union with England. In that parliament, which met intermittently until 1674, in the convention of estates which met in 1678, and in the parliament which assembled in 1681 he sat as a commissioner for the shire of Aberdeen. On 11 November 1678 he was appointed to the privy council, and on 8 June 1680 he was appointed an ordinary lord of session as Lord Haddo. By then the Lauderdale regime was collapsing, and when Sir James Dalrymple of Stair was removed from office as president of the session in October 1681 as a result of his opposition to James, duke of York, Gordon was appointed in his place. Within two years James had persuaded his brother to elevate Gordon higher. According to several sources, Gordon was returning with James to Scotland on the *Gloucester* when it sank off Yarmouth with the loss of almost 200 lives. James is said to have pulled Gordon from the water himself and to have revealed his new appointment by shouting 'save my chancellor'. An official announcement followed on 8 May 1682, not long before Gordon was appointed sheriff-principal of both Aberdeenshire and Edinburghshire. On 30 November 1682 he received his final honour when he was created earl of Aberdeen in letters patent which recalled his father's services and sufferings in the royalist cause.

Surviving correspondence, the records of council and session, and the remarks of contemporary observers all support Sir John Lauder's judgement that Aberdeen was a statesman with 'ane indefatigable spirit for serious businesse' (Lauder, *Historical Observes*, 134). But contemporary observers would also no doubt have concurred with Lauder's conclusion that from Aberdeen's career men might learn 'how lubrick and staggering a thing the favor of Court is'. As Lauder recalled, his appointment as chancellor had been 'a mighty wide step of advancement for him, at which the nobility grumbled in ther bosome, they having been now thesse many years in possession of that place' (ibid., 68). During his brief period in high office he made scarcely any effort to form alliances among the nobility, relying instead on the counsel of other lawyers and gentlemen and on the favour of the duke of York. He was criticized for endorsing measures of doubtful legality against religious dissidents; then when he took greater care to abide by the law he was criticized for being too lenient. Summoned to London in June 1684, he found it impossible to defend himself against charges laid by hostile noblemen before a king whose mistress had been suborned against him. Condemned even for his unprepossessing appearance, he was forced to resign from office as chancellor, and a month later was deprived of office as sheriff-principal of Edinburghshire. Further attempts to complete his downfall failed, though they did apparently result in the deliberate destruction of most of the papers relating to his administration. By the end of 1684 he had withdrawn his personal effects from his house in Edinburgh and had retired to Aberdeen, where he remained in relative seclusion for most of the next thirty-five years. After participating briefly in the parliaments of 1685 and 1686, he kept out of the public eye during the reigns of William and Mary, finally swearing allegiance to the revolution regime only after the accession of Anne. He expressed support for the proposed union of the British parliaments in 1707 but refrained from voting on the issue.

According to George Crawfurd, writing shortly after Aberdeen's death, he had 'increased his estate' in 1671 when he married Anna (*d.* 1707), daughter of George Lockhart of Tarbrax and heir to a successful legal dynasty (Crawfurd, 231). According once more to Lauder, although his tenure as chancellor had been brief, 'yet he had feathered his nest weill, and made hay in summer while the sun shone, and had bettered his fortune neir £1000 sterling a year, beyond the £500 sterling it was worth formerly' (Lauder, *Historical Observes*, 131). By the time of his death at Kellie on 20 April 1720, in his eighty-third year, Aberdeen had been predeceased by his wife, by all but the youngest of their four sons, and by one of their five daughters. The only surviving son, William, succeeded his father as the second earl of Aberdeen. J. D. Ford

Sources J. Dunn, ed., *Letters, illustrative of public affairs in Scotland, addressed by contemporary statesmen to George, earl of Aberdeen, lord high chancellor of Scotland, 1681–84* (1851) • G. Crawfurd, *The lives and characters, of the officers of the crown, and of the state in Scotland* (1726), 226, 231 • W. Orem, *A description of the chanonry, cathedral and King's College of Old Aberdeen in the years 1724 and 1735* (1791) • G. Mackenzie, *Memoirs of the affairs of Scotland* (1821) • *Bishop Burnet's History* • *Historical notices of Scotish affairs, selected from the manuscripts of Sir John Lauder of Fountainhall*, ed. D. Laing, 2 vols., Bannatyne Club, 87 (1848) • J. Lauder, *Historical observes of memorable occurrents in church and state, from October 1680 to April 1686*, ed. A. Urquhart and D. Laing, Bannatyne Club, 66 (1840) • GEC, *Baronetage* • *Scots peerage* • R. Wodrow, *Analecta, or, Materials for a history of remarkable providences, mostly relating to Scotch ministers and Christians*, ed. [M. Leishman], 4 vols., Maitland Club, 60 (1842–3)

Archives NA Scot., corresp. and MSS

Likenesses oils, Haddo House, Aberdeenshire [*see illus.*]

Wealth at death approx. £1000: Lauder, *Historical observes*, 131

Gordon, George, first duke of Gordon (*b.* in or before **1649**, *d.* **1716**), nobleman, was the only son of Lewis Gordon, third marquess of Huntly (*c.*1626–1653), a member of one of the few important houses in Scotland which had remained Roman Catholic at the Reformation, and Mary, daughter of Sir John Grant, sixth laird of Freuchie; he was the grandson of George *Gordon, second marquess of Huntly (*c.*1590–1649). Styled from birth the earl of Enzie, he succeeded his father in the marquessate at the age of little more than four, and was brought up at Elgin in a humble way by his mother, a Catholic convert, until the Restoration. In 1662 their fortunes improved when the Huntly estate, which had been escheated in a complicated and continuing struggle between the families of Gordon and Argyll, was regranted to the family. Efforts to convert Huntly to protestantism having failed, he was sent to a seminary in France, and then travelled. His governor for five years was Nicholas de Malebranche, the French metaphysician, author of *Recherche de la vérité* and other works found in the library at Gordon Castle. In 1673 Huntly joined the French army, serving under Turenne.

On his return to Britain in 1676 Huntly married another Catholic, Lady Elizabeth (*d.* 1732), second daughter of Henry Howard, sixth duke of Norfolk, and his first wife, Lady Anne Somerset. The marriage was not a happy one. As a Catholic, Huntly was unable to take office, and retired to his estates at Gordon Castle (Bog of Gight) or Huntly (Strathbogie). By a patent of 1 November 1684 he was created duke of Gordon, apparently owing to his friendship with John Graham of Claverhouse, later Viscount Dundee, who felt that the pre-eminence in Scotland of the duke of Hamilton should be challenged. On the news of Argyll's rising in 1685 Gordon was appointed commander of the northern forces, but his services were not required. As a known Catholic he could have expected further advancement under his co-religionist James VII and II. To some extent this materialized: he was appointed a Scottish privy councillor, lord of the Scottish Treasury, and governor of Edinburgh Castle, a place described by his apologist as 'ane emeployment of more honour than profit' (*Siege of the Castle of Edinburgh*, 5); he was also one of the eight knights created at the revival of the Order of the Thistle in 1687. However, the celebrated Gordon temperament—headstrong, volatile, wilful, indecisive, brave, but incapable of following the leadership of others and with an occasional tendency towards cold feet in moments of crisis—hindered his career. Furthermore Macky's perception that the duke was a Roman Catholic through upbringing rather than by personal conviction is borne out by Gordon's lack of enthusiasm for the king's efforts to re-establish Catholicism.

Gordon's most celebrated role was in holding Edinburgh Castle for James against the convention of estates through the winter of 1688–9, but he was never one to keep to any policy for long: when Viscount Dundee and the earl of Balcarres arrived from London in March 1689 they found that the duke's furniture was being carried out of the castle with a view to its surrender, though Gordon's supporters claimed this was a ruse to deceive the opposition. While Claverhouse urged Gordon to hold the castle for the king, the convention of estates sent heralds to summon him to leave; Gordon's ambiguous response, 'in drollery', was that they should not 'proclaime men trattors to the State with the King's coats on their backs; or at least they might turne them' (*Siege of the Castle of Edinburgh*, 34). He stayed put for a while, but his defence lacked energy: a request for some packs of cards to be sent in was refused, and Mark Napier comments unkindly that the duke held the castle with a feeble hand and eventually surrendered it with a feebler heart. He refused to fire on the town, claiming that he must have the king's orders for taking such a step, and matters continued as a blockade until 14 July 1689, thirteen days before the battle of Killiecrankie, when a capitulation was eventually agreed. Despite an unseasonable fall of snow which had prolonged the water supply, both water and food were running out, and powder and shot were almost finished. The garrison received an indemnity for themselves and their assistants, but the duke refused to ask for terms for himself as he 'hath so much respect for all the Princes of King James Sexth's line, as not to make conditions with any of them for his own particular interest; so he renders himselfe entirely on King William's discretion' (*Siege of the Castle of Edinburgh*, 76). Mark Napier continued to inveigh against Gordon, comparing him with Sister Anne in the story of Bluebeard. Balcarres was kinder, commenting that Gordon could have ensured that the castle was well provisioned and armed, but that the capitulation was on very honourable terms (Balcarres, 23–4). Gordon was kept prisoner in the castle until January 1690—an uncomfortable experience, as Hamilton remarked that the castle was in such a state that there was hardly a room fit to put a prisoner in, and Sir John Dalrymple added that Gordon was so unpopular that no one would willingly speak to him (Melville, 142, 191–2).

Later Gordon made his submission in London and went abroad. He was not received with favour by the exiled James VII and II at St Germain-en-Laye and for the rest of his life he was regarded with distrust by the Hanoverian government and with disfavour by the exiled Jacobite court. He returned to his estates in Scotland, 'where he hath led a very uneasy Life ever since, being oftner a Prisoner, than at Liberty' (*Memoirs of the Secret Services*, 194–5), with Gordon Castle being used as a garrison. In 1697 his wife, being jealous, it was said, of one of her gentlewomen, retired for a time to a convent in Flanders, and on being urged by her father confessor to return to her husband's bed replied 'she would not doe it, tho her parents would ryse from the grave, or angells come from heaven to bid her doe it' (NA Scot., GD44/33/1/14/53–5). The couple had two children, Alexander *Gordon (*c*.1678–1728) and Jean, who married James Drummond, fifth earl, later second (Jacobite) duke, of Perth. Gordon's relations with Alexander were also sometimes strained as the son appears to have sided with his mother in family disputes.

On Alexander Gordon's marriage early in 1707 to Henrietta Mordaunt, daughter of the earl of Peterborough, the duke retired to the governor's apartments in the citadel of Leith, leaving his son to manage his estates. During the 1708 invasion scare Gordon was among the Scottish nobles sent to London, on a dragoon's horse as he refused to pay for a carriage himself. Later he confined himself to hearing mass, and patronizing Jesuits and seminary priests, which antagonized the government and resulted in his return to Edinburgh Castle as prisoner a further six times. His wife, who lived separately at Abbeyhill in Edinburgh, was also a notable Jacobite, and gained notoriety in 1711 when she endeavoured to present the Faculty of Advocates with a Jacobite medal with the motto 'Reddite'. That year Gordon published, as *Conversations Concerning Death*, a work by his old tutor Malebranche. He himself died at Leith of the gravel or stone on 7 December 1716, and was buried at Elgin Cathedral, Moray. His widow continued to live in Edinburgh until her death on 16 July 1732, four years after the death of her only son.

B. L. H. Horn

Sources NA Scot., Gordon Castle MSS, GD 44 · GEC, *Peerage* · *Scots peerage* · *Siege of the castle of Edinburgh, MDCLXXXIX*, ed. R. Bell, Bannatyne Club, 23 (1828) · *Memoirs of the secret services of John Macky*, ed. A. R. (1733) · W. Fraser, ed., *The chiefs of Grant*, 3 vols. (1883) · C. Lindsay [earl of Balcarres], *Memoirs touching the revolution in Scotland*, ed. A. W. C. Lindsay [earl of Crawford and Balcarres], Bannatyne Club (1841) · W. H. L. Melville, ed., *Leven and Melville papers: letters and state papers chiefly addressed to George, earl of Melville … 1689–1691*, Bannatyne Club, 77 (1843) · M. Napier, *Memorials and letters illustrative of the life and times of John Graham of Claverhouse, Viscount Dundee*, 3 vols. (1859) · V. Gibbs, 'Attempted French invasion of Scotland, 1708', GEC, *Peerage*, new edn, 7.747–53

Archives NA Scot., Gordon Castle muniments · W. Sussex RO, corresp. and papers | BL, letters to duke of Lauderdale, Add. MSS 23121–23138, 23246, 29314 · NL Scot., letters mainly to Sir John Gordon · NL Scot., corresp. with Lord Sutherland · NL Scot., corresp., mainly with the first marquess of Tweeddale and the second marquess of Tweeddale · W. Sussex RO, Goodwood MSS

Likenesses J. Medina, group portrait (with family); Anderson and England's sale, 1938, lot 942; photograph, Scot. NPG · J. Sauvé, engraving, Aboyne; photograph, Scot. NPG · L. Schuneman, portrait; Christies, 8 March 1957; photograph, Scot. NPG · portrait (the first duke in youth?; in mid-seventeenth century costume); photograph, Scot. NPG

Wealth at death £1341 19*s*. 6*d*. Scots: will and inventory, 9 March 1721, NA Scot., CC 8/8/88

Gordon, Lord George (1751–1793), political and religious agitator, was born on 26 December 1751 in Upper Grosvenor Street, London, the third son of Cosmo George Gordon, third duke of Gordon (1720/21–1752), a landowner, and his wife, Lady Catherine *Gordon (1718–1779), the daughter of William Gordon, second earl of Aberdeen. After his father's death his mother married Staats Long *Morris, later a general and an MP. Gordon attended Eton College from 1758 to 1765 and was given the rank of ensign in his stepfather's regiment in 1759, but after his schooling he entered the navy, and became a lieutenant in 1772. According to his friend Robert Watson, who in 1795 published an account of his life, he was popular with the seamen, acting as '*the sailors' friend*' (Watson, 6). He was in America from 1766 to 1769, and resigned his commission in 1777.

The period in America may well have awakened Gordon's political consciousness. Wishing to enter parliament, he hoped to use the Gordon interest to become MP for Inverness-shire; but the sitting MP, Simon Fraser, secured for him a seat at Ludgershall, Wiltshire. His first recorded speech was on 13 April 1778, when he denounced the government's American policy, telling Lord North to 'call off his butchers and ravagers from the colonies' (HoP,

Lord George Gordon (1751–1793), by R. Bran, pubd 1780

Commons, 1754–90). Other angry speeches followed. Yet interestingly, given later events, he apparently did not speak against the first Roman Catholic Relief Bill when it was debated in the Commons at the end of the session. Nor did he vote against it.

The first Catholic Relief Act was a very limited measure which did not give English Roman Catholics freedom of worship; rather, it was designed to remove from the statute book specific disabilities considered moribund by the later eighteenth century. These concerned land purchases and the penalties to which Catholic priests and schoolmasters were liable. It is likely that many who later protested against the measure did not properly appreciate its circumscribed nature—Watson was to describe it as 'the Bill for repealing the penal statutes in force against' the Catholics (Watson, 10)—and this may have been Gordon's perception also.

Gordon soon became obsessed with the No Popery issue, however. A separate act for Scotland (necessary since that kingdom's penal laws predated the union) was expected in 1779, but there was fierce opposition to this, and the plan was abandoned. Gordon worked with the Scottish protestant leaders. In August 1779 he went to Scotland and, in Edinburgh, fêted the protestant committee of correspondence; he was soon elected its president. In Glasgow a torchlight procession was arranged, and he later toured the lowlands. In the Commons he stated in November that the Scots 'are convinced in their own minds that the King is a papist' (HoP, *Commons, 1754–90*). He presented the petition of west Scotland's eighty-five protestant societies, which sought the repeal of the English Relief Act. The societies lauded his work and, as a mark of their esteem, presented him with a gold box.

In England the Protestant Association was established to lobby for the Relief Act's repeal, and in November 1779 Gordon became its president. In parliament his behaviour became more unbalanced and his language wild and threatening: as the MP Charles Turner (himself a notable eccentric) observed, he 'had got a twist in his head, a certain whirligig which ran away with him if anything relative to religion was mentioned' (HoP, *Commons, 1754–90*). Gordon was also received by George III and spoke against the Relief Act. Meanwhile he worked hard for the Protestant Association, which encouraged the drawing-up of petitions, both in the metropolis and the provinces, for the act's repeal. In London and its environs the campaign was spectacularly successful, and a petition bearing some 44,000 names was produced.

On 2 June 1780, the day on which Gordon was to present the London petition to parliament, a vast crowd, estimated at 60,000 people, gathered in St George's Fields, Southwark, and marched to Westminster, where they assembled at Palace Yard. They jostled some peers and MPs and pressed forward into the lobby of the Commons. From time to time Gordon left the chamber to inform the crowd of the debate's progress. His conduct appalled the MPs, and his uncle, the Hon. William Gordon, told him: 'My Lord George, do you intend to bring your rascally adherents into the House of Commons? If you do—the first man of them that enters, I will plunge my sword not into his, but into your body' (*Annual Register*, 1780, 'appendix to the chronicle', 258).

Shortly after nine o'clock the Horse Guards and foot guards arrived, and the mob dispersed. But, later, crowds attacked and wrecked the Sardinian embassy chapel in Lincoln's Inn Fields and the chapel of the Bavarian embassy in Golden Square. Then, in the days after 2 and 3 June, the scope of the violence widened, with attacks on Roman Catholic property in Moorfields and Spitalfields, while in Wapping a mass house was wrecked, and so, in Bloomsbury and Soho, were popish schools. The house of Lord Mansfield, known to favour Roman Catholic relief, was destroyed. Newgate was set on fire. The riots reached their peak on 7 and 8 June, with fresh attacks on Catholic property in Westminster, the City, and Holborn; and the king's bench prison and part of the Fleet prison, along with the new gaol, Southwark, and the toll houses on Blackfriars Bridge, were fired. The authorities, fearing that the violence would engulf the whole city, were now determined to crush the riots militarily, and more than 200 people were killed by troops. Gordon himself had taken no part in the disturbances. When leaving the Palace of Westminster he had apparently told the crowd, 'For God's sake go home and be quiet, make no riot and noise' (*State trials*, 21.585). He published an advertisement denouncing the riots and 'begged to see the King, saying, he might be of great use in quelling' them (ibid., col. 615).

None the less, with the restoration of order he was taken from his home in Welbeck Street to the Tower.

The riots had appalled the political nation. Dr Johnson called them 'a time of terrour' and Cowper wrote of a 'Metropolis in flames, and a Nation in Ruins' (Haydon, 241). Fears had been expressed that the riots might prove 'epidemical to the Country' (ibid., 215), and there had been some disturbances in the provinces. Consequently it was decided to indict Gordon for high treason, and the trial commenced in February 1781. Gordon was superbly defended by Thomas Erskine and Lloyd Kenyon, who argued that the Protestant Association's supporters at Westminster and the rioting mobs were clean different things. 'Does it appear' asked Kenyon:

> after the many prosecutions that were commenced, that one single individual, connected with lord George, or belonging to that association which he was president of, has ever been found obnoxious to the laws of the country?—Has criminal guilt been fastened on any of them? Has one of them been indicted? (*State trials*, 21.557)

It was clear that Gordon could not be held to have planned 'levying war against the king', and, after retiring for only half an hour, the jury acquitted him.

After the trial, Gordon, with astonishing effrontery, persisted in his political activity. He thought of standing as a candidate for the City of London in 1781, and continued to act as the president of the Protestant Association, seeking the repeal of the Relief Act. He badgered politicians, both by letter and in person, and issued a self-justificatory pamphlet, *Innocence Vindicated, and the Intrigues of Popery and its Abettors Displayed*. Eventually, however, he went too far and laid himself open to prosecution. He fled to the United Provinces, but after his return he was arrested in Birmingham and tried before king's bench on two counts. First, he was charged with the publication of a pamphlet criticizing the administration of justice and, in particular, the use of transportation to Botany Bay. Second, he was accused of libelling the queen of France, Marie Antoinette, and the French chargé d'affaires in the *Public Advertiser*: he had described the former as the leader of a party and the latter as one of the instruments of the faction. And there was the matter of Marie Antoinette's morals: at the trial, 'his lordship … [spoke] of the queen of France in the most improper manner, but was stopped by the interference of the court' (*Annual Register*, 1787, 'appendix to the chronicle', 246). Gordon was convicted on both charges and sentenced to five years' imprisonment. He had thereafter to give security for fourteen years' good behaviour, himself in £10,000 and each of his sureties in £2500. He spent the rest of his life in Newgate.

In the 1780s Gordon made contact with a wide range of liberals and radicals, not only in the British Isles, but also in Europe and America. He maintained his correspondence with such people after he was imprisoned, and so, according to Watson, 'he had been made acquainted with the sentiments of many virtuous and well-intentioned Revolutionists of every denomination' (Watson, 88). After the revolution had erupted in France he wrote to Grégoire and viewed favourably Condorcet, Robespierre, and other patriots in the French Assembly. For the conservative-minded at home, his views and those of the most prominent English radicals were all one. 'What a pity', *The Times* observed, 'Lord George Flame could not be present at the Revolution meeting to join … with … the rest of the worthies who composed that glorious congratulation to the National Assembly' (McCalman, 362).

During the last phase of his life Gordon developed a deep interest in Judaism. In 1783 he produced a letter to the Jews of Portugal and Germany, and in 1785 he wrote to the Habsburg emperor, Joseph II, about his policy towards the Jews. Gordon's philosemitism may well have developed out of ideas, current in certain dissenting circles, of an eschatological kind, and, in particular, from the belief that the return of the Jews to Israel would herald the millennium. Gordon converted to Judaism in 1787 and adopted the name Israel Abraham George Gordon. He was circumcised and adhered strictly to his new faith: when in Newgate he would not meet with Jews who shaved their beards and uncovered their heads. His megalomania was in evidence. 'Perhaps', Watson noted, 'he expected to have led back the Israelites to their *fathers' land*' (Watson, 79).

Gordon's appearance betokened his personality. Prints show his eyes as striking, suggesting a fanatical or deranged mind. His long, lank, unpowdered hair marked him out from conventional figures in polite society. So did his simple clothes. When he converted to Judaism he grew a beard.

Opinions of Gordon varied greatly in his own age. As the president of the Protestant Association, he was plainly charismatic. John Wesley took him seriously: he visited him in the Tower and noted that 'he seemed to be well acquainted with the Bible' (*Journal*, 6.301). And when Paul Wright produced his *New and Complete Book of Martyrs* (1785?), an updated version of Foxe's *Acts and Monuments*, Gordon was included in it. For others, however, 'mad Lord George' was a grotesque, comic figure. In Horace Walpole's eyes he was patently insane. Following his conversion to Judaism he became the butt of antisemitic prints and ballads depicting his conversion as a further proof of his insanity. In 1788 the pantomime at Swann's Amphitheatre, Birmingham, featured the adventures of 'The bonnie laddie or Harlequin Jew', with scenery including Newgate in flames (Money, 309). Historians, too, can interpret Gordon's life in different ways. He can be presented as an essentially seventeenth-century figure, oddly out of place in the age of the rational Enlightenment, while the protestant outcry which he fanned appears as a recrudescence of the religious bigotry of Elizabethan or Stuart times. Gordon himself rather promoted this view. Robert Watson observed that 'he was well versed in the history of the Protectorship; his language, his manners, and customs were strongly tainted with the characteristics of that age' (Watson, 76). Alternatively (though the depictions are not entirely mutually exclusive), it is possible to see Gordon as a potential reformer (he abhorred the death penalty) and a subversive, a thwarted revolutionary who was in part the harbinger of the new radical or revolutionary spirits which were to develop in Britain after 1789. In

1779 he told the Commons that the Scots might rebel. Shortly before he died he learned of Marie Antoinette's execution, and declared ominously that 'she was not the last of the royal corps that would fall a victim to the guillotine' (Watson, 137). He sang the 'Ça ira' just before expiring of gaol fever in Newgate on 1 November 1793. Certainly Gordon was unbalanced, irresponsible, and dangerous. COLIN HAYDON

Sources *Annual Register* (1780) · *Annual Register* (1787) · *State trials*, 21.485–652 · *The history of the Right Honourable Lord George Gordon* (1780) · R. Watson, *The life of Lord George Gordon* (1795) · *The journal of the Rev. John Wesley*, ed. N. Curnock and others, 8 vols. (1909–16); repr. (1938) · J. A. Cannon, 'Gordon, Lord George', HoP, *Commons*, 1754–90 · R. K. Donovan, *No popery and radicalism: opposition to Roman Catholic relief in Scotland, 1778–1782* (1987) · C. Haydon, *Anti-Catholicism in eighteenth-century England, c. 1714–80: a political and social study* (1993) · I. McCalman, 'Mad Lord George and Madame La Motte: riot and sexuality in the genesis of Burke's *Reflections on the revolution in France*', *Journal of British Studies*, 35 (1996), 343–67 · D. Hay, 'The laws of God and the laws of man: Lord George Gordon and the death penalty', *Protest and survival: the historical experience*, ed. J. Rule and R. Malcolmson (1993), 60–111 · J. Money, 'Birmingham and the West Midlands, 1760–1793: politics and regional identity in the English provinces in the later eighteenth century', *The eighteenth-century town*, ed. P. Borsay (1990), 292–314 · R. A. Austen-Leigh, ed., *The Eton College register, 1753–1790* (1921) · *Scots peerage*

Archives BL, narrative of his proceedings during the Gordon riots, Add. MS 42129 · PRO, T.S. 11/388 1,212 · PRO, S.P. Dom. 37/20, 21

Likenesses R. Bran, engraving, pubd 1780, NPG [*see illus.*] · line engraving, pubd 1780 (after R. Bran), BM, NPG · J. Tassie, glass intaglio, 1781, NPG · J. Tassie, plaster medallion, 1781, Scot. NPG · J. Heath, group portrait, line engraving, pubd 1790 (*The riot in Broad Street, 7 June 1780*; after E. Wheatley), NPG · Trotter, line engraving (after J. de Fleur), BM, NPG · line engraving (after unknown artist), NPG

Gordon, George, ninth marquess of Huntly (1761–1853), soldier, was the son of Charles, fourth earl of Aboyne (1726–1794), and Lady Margaret Stewart (*d.* 1762), third daughter of Alexander, sixth earl of Galloway. He was born at Edinburgh on 28 June 1761. Known as Lord Strathavon, he attended Eton College for a short period, 1774–5, and joined the army in 1777 as ensign in the 1st regiment of foot guards; he was promoted in the same year to a company in the 81st Highland regiment of foot. In 1780 he was one of the aides-de-camp to the earl of Carlisle, then lord lieutenant of Ireland. In 1782 he had a troop in the 9th regiment of dragoons, and in March 1783 he was constituted major of an independent corps of foot, which was reduced at the peace of 1784. He was promoted lieutenant-colonel of the 35th foot in 1789, but exchanged in the same year into the Coldstream Guards.

Lord Strathavon married, on 4 April 1791, despite her mother's opposition, Catherine Anne (1771–1833), second daughter of Sir Charles Cope, by which marriage he acquired the estate of Orton Longueville, Huntingdonshire, which he enlarged by purchasing in 1803 the adjoining parishes of Chesterton and Haddon. They had six sons and three daughters.

Lord Strathavon quitted the army in 1792, and was appointed colonel of the Aberdeenshire militia in 1798. He succeeded his father as earl of Aboyne on 28 December 1794. He was a Scottish representative peer, 1796–1806 and 1807–18. In 1815 Aboyne was created a peer of the United Kingdom by the title of Baron Meldrum of Morven, and thenceforward took his seat in the House of Lords in his own right. He was made a knight of the Thistle in 1827. In 1836 he succeeded his cousin George, fifth duke of Gordon, as marquess and earl of Huntly. He was a tory in politics, voting against reform in 1832, but following Wellington on Catholic emancipation and Peel on the corn laws.

The marquess died at his residence in Chapel Street, Grosvenor Square, London, on 17 June 1853. He was succeeded by his eldest son, Charles, tenth marquess.

G. B. SMITH, *rev.* K. D. REYNOLDS

Sources GEC, *Peerage* · *GM*, 2nd ser., 40 (1853), 198

Archives NA Scot., Lennox-Gordon MSS, family and estate papers · W. Sussex RO, Lennox-Gordon MSS, family and estate papers | BL, corresp. with first and second earls of Liverpool, Add. MSS 38248–38328, 38458, 38472, *passim*

Likenesses C. Turner, mezzotint, pubd 1837 (after J. Hollins), BM · J. Ponsford, oils, 1842, Lennoxlove, Haddington, East Lothian · G. Hayter, group portrait, oils (*The trial of Queen Caroline, 1820*), NPG

Gordon, George, fifth duke of Gordon (1770–1836), army officer, eldest son of Alexander *Gordon, fourth duke of Gordon (1743–1827), and his first wife, Jane *Gordon (1748/9–1812), daughter of Sir William Maxwell, third baronet, was born in Edinburgh on 2 February 1770. Gordon, who was styled marquess of Huntly until 1827, attended Eton College from 1780 to 1786, and was admitted as a nobleman to St John's College, Cambridge, on 28 October 1788. He matriculated at Easter 1791 and graduated MA in the same year. Aged twenty he entered, as ensign, the 35th foot, of which his brother-in-law, Colonel Lennox (afterwards fourth duke of Richmond), was lieutenant-colonel. In 1791 he raised an independent company of foot, from which he exchanged to the 42nd highlanders; he commanded the grenadier company until 1793, when he was appointed captain-lieutenant and lieutenant-colonel in the 3rd foot guards.

Huntly accompanied his battalion to Flanders with the duke of York's army, and was at St Amand, Famars, Launoi, Dunkirk, and the siege of Valenciennes. On his return to Scotland he raised a regiment of highlanders on his father's estates, assisted by his father and mother, both recruiting personally. The duchess is said to have worn the regimental colours, and to have obtained recruits by putting the shilling between her lips. The regiment was inspected at Aberdeen in 1794, and passed into the line as the 100th Gordon Highlanders regiment of foot. Five years afterwards it was renumbered the 92nd, under which name it became famous, and in later years it was the 2nd Gordon Highlanders.

As lieutenant-colonel commandant, Huntly took his regiment out to Gibraltar. In September 1795 he embarked at Corunna for England, but three days later was seized by a French privateer, robbed of everything valuable, and put on a Swedish vessel which landed him at Falmouth shortly afterwards. He rejoined his regiment, and served with it for about a year in Corsica. In 1796 he became colonel. In 1798 the regiment returned home from Gibraltar, and was employed in co. Wexford during the Irish rising, the troops being notable for their forbearance and discipline. An address of thanks was presented to Huntly as colonel by the magistrates and inhabitants when the regiment was about to leave.

Huntly became brigadier-general, accompanied the expedition to the Netherlands in 1799, and, while at the head of his regiment, was severely wounded by a musket-ball in the shoulder during the desperate fight among the sandhills between Egmont and Bergen, an action which won the special approval of General John Moore. Huntly became major-general in 1801, was transferred to the colonelcy of the 42nd highlanders in 1806, became a lieutenant-general in 1808, and commanded a division of Lord Chatham's army in the Walcheren expedition of 1809.

In 1806 Huntly, a staunch conservative, was elected MP for the Cornwallis family pocket borough of Eye, Suffolk, the nominee of his brother-in-law, the second Marquess Cornwallis. He sat for two months, and then, on the change of ministry in 1807, he was called to the House of Lords in his father's English barony of Gordon. Heavily in debt, he married, on 11 December 1813, Elizabeth (1794–1864), only child of Alexander Brodie of Arnhall, Kincardineshire, a wealthy India merchant, who paid Gordon's debts and left his wife a fortune [*see* Gordon, Elizabeth, duchess of Gordon]. They had no children, though Gordon had an illegitimate son.

Huntly became general in 1819, and on the death of the duke of Kent was transferred from the 42nd highlanders to the colonelcy of the 1st Royal Scots. He was made GCB in 1820. He succeeded to the dukedom on the death of his father on 17 June 1827, when he was appointed keeper of the great seal of Scotland, and in 1828 he became governor of Edinburgh Castle. In 1834, on the death of the duke of Gloucester, he was transferred to the colonelcy of the Scots Fusilier Guards (later the Scots Guards). The duke resided chiefly at Gordon Castle, Banffshire, where he exercised a princely hospitality. He was a munificent donor to public charities, particularly the Scottish Hospital, of which he was president, and he was 'unrivalled as a chairman at a public dinner' (*GM*, 94). He died at his town residence in Belgrave Square, London, on 28 May 1836, the causes of death being given as 'ossification of the trachea' and 'cancer in the stomach' (*GM*, 94). By order of the king his remains were escorted to Greenwich (for removal to Scotland) by his regiment of guards, and buried on 10 June 1836 in the family vault in Elgin Cathedral. At the time of his death he was chancellor of the Marischal College, Aberdeen, hereditary keeper of Inverness Castle, president of the Scottish corporation, and grand master of the Orangemen of Scotland.

Because the duke died without legitimate issue, and his only brother had predeceased him unmarried, the dukedom of Gordon became extinct, Gordon Castle with large estate passing to the duke of Richmond, who took the name of Gordon in addition to Lennox. The dukedom of Gordon was revived in the duke of Richmond and Gordon (1876). The title of marquess of Huntly descended to his kinsman George Gordon, ninth marquess.

H. M. Chichester, *rev.* Roger T. Stearn

Sources GEC, *Peerage* • *GM*, 2nd ser., 6 (1836) • R. Cannon, ed., *Historical record of the ninety-second regiment, originally termed 'the Gordon highlanders' and numbered the hundredth regiment* (1851) • G. B. [G. Bell], *Rough notes by an old soldier during fifty years' service*, 2 (1867) • D. M. Henderson, *The Scottish regiments* (1996) • A. J. Guy, ed., *The road to Waterloo: the British army and the struggle against revolutionary and Napoleonic France, 1793–1815* (1990) • Venn, *Alum. Cant.*

Archives W. Sussex RO, corresp. and papers | BL, corresp. with Sir Robert Peel, Add. MSS 40351–40410, *passim* • Niedersächsisches Hauptstaatsarchiv, Hanover, letters to duke of Cumberland • NL Scot., corresp. with Lord Melville • W. Sussex RO, letters to duchess of Richmond; letters to duke of Richmond

Likenesses G. Romney, double portrait, oils, 1778 (with his mother), Scot. NPG; *see illus. in* Gordon, Jane, duchess of Gordon (1748/9–1812) • H. Meyer, pubd 1812 (after J. Jackson), BM, NPG • B. Marshall, group portrait, oils, *c.*1815, Yale U. CBA • C. Turner, mezzotint, pubd 1830 (after J. Mackenzie), BM, NPG • A. E. Chalon, oils, Goodwood House, West Sussex • H. Raeburn, oils, Goodwood House, West Sussex • A. Robertson, miniature, Aberdeen Art Gallery • G. Sanders, oils, Goodwood House, West Sussex • oils, Brodie Castle, Moray

Gordon, George (1801–1893), Church of Scotland minister and naturalist, was born on 23 July 1801 at the manse of Urquhart, Moray, the first son of William Gordon (*bap.* 1744, *d.* 1810), minister in the Church of Scotland, and his wife, Margaret (1779–1864), daughter of Joseph Anderson, minister of the Church of Scotland at Birnie, Moray, and his wife, Jean Craig. Gordon's father's family was of the minor gentry, being a cadet branch of the Gordons of Beldornie. Gordon attended Elgin Academy for some years. He proceeded to Marischal College, Aberdeen, at the age of fourteen and graduated AM in 1819. During his twenties he spent time in Edinburgh attending some of the scientific classes at the university, starting with natural history in 1821 and ending with geology and botany in 1829. He returned to Moray and was given the living of Birnie, 3 miles south of Elgin, in November 1832. He married Anna Stephen (*c.*1813–1889) on 20 March 1834; they had eight children.

Gordon became a champion of Moray. His interest was in the scientific and antiquarian aspects of a province which, to him, included the lands between the rivers Spey in the east and Beauly in the west. Initially botany took up his leisure time. Fresh from his botanical classes in Edinburgh under Graham in 1828 and 1829, he set about compiling *Collectanea for a Flora of Moray*, which he completed in 1839. He and his friends scoured the countryside, making the first records for most of the area and adding *Pinguicula alpina*, the alpine butterwort (now extinct), to the British flora.

A particular friend was William Alexander Stables of Cawdor, near Nairn. Together Gordon and Stables made many contributions to the early records of northern Britain, as can be seen from H. C. Watson's *New Botanist's Guide* (1835–7). In the 1840s Gordon set about recording the fauna of Moray, beginning with the vertebrates—mammals, birds, and fishes—then the invertebrates—crustacea, echinodermata, mollusca, and lepidoptera. Most of his findings were published in the 1840s, 1850s, and 1860s in a series of articles for *The Zoologist*. The work needed to compile these lists was supported by a large network of friends, both professional and amateur. Gordon's time in Edinburgh had left him with widespread contacts that he drew upon throughout his long life. An archive of his scientific correspondence in Elgin Museum records the quest for information, the lending of books and papers, and the support freely given to those less well informed. There are letters from more than 200 correspondents including William Hooker, Roderick Murchison, Charles Darwin, T. H. Huxley, and other eminent scientists of the nineteenth century.

The geology of Moray proved to be of particular importance to scientists. Fossil fish had been found in its sandstones by Gordon and his friends in the 1830s. Partly as a result of the fossil collection, the Elgin and Morayshire Scientific Association (now the Moray Society) was formed in 1836 with Gordon as a founder member; this association built the Elgin Museum in 1843. Consternation was caused in geological circles when fossils of reptiles turned up in the sandstones which had always been considered to belong to the Old Red Sandstone formations of about 400 million to 360 million years ago. The controversy regarding the age of the sandstones of Moray continued throughout the nineteenth century; indeed, their geology is not fully understood, even today. The Carboniferous period, which is usually found between the Old Red (Devonian) Sandstone and the New Red (Permian and Triassic) Sandstone, is missing in Moray and the two periods of sandstones, although separated by over 100 million years, look remarkably similar. Gordon never accepted that the reptile-bearing sandstones were of New Red Sandstone age but he worked hard so that the truth might be discovered. Many cases of rock were sent south for Huxley to research. Geologists continuously visited Moray and were given the benefit of Gordon's sound knowledge of the area. His dedicated work on the geology of Moray was rewarded in 1859 with an LLD from Marischal College.

In the great controversy over patronage that resulted in the Disruption of the Church of Scotland in 1843, Gordon was of the moderate party that supported the *status quo*. In 1859 he became directly involved in the long running 'Elgin Academy Case' in which the presbytery of Elgin successfully defended the right of the Church of Scotland to appoint teachers and to inspect the burgh schools.

Gordon remained active in science up to his death, which occurred at his home, Braebirnie, Mayne Road, Elgin, due to cardiac failure on 12 December 1893. He was buried at Birnie kirk on 16 December. Gordon's scientific collections and lists are important, but he made two other contributions to nineteenth-century science: wishing to share all his knowledge with anyone who was interested in Moray, he sought to draw the attention of great scientists to its uniqueness; and he understood that his scientific letters were of value for posterity—he sorted them himself and fortunately his family gave them the care they merited. In these two ways he achieved his ambition of promoting Moray as a place of special interest to the naturalist, the geologist, and the archaeologist.

SUSAN BENNETT

Sources Elgin Museum, Gordon archive • parish register, Urquhart, Local Heritage Centre, Grant Lodge, Elgin, 6 Aug 1801 [baptism: microfiche] • parish register, Mortlach, Local Heritage Centre, Grant Lodge, Elgin, 12 Feb 1744 [William Gordon's baptism: microfiche] • parish register, Elgin, Local Heritage Centre, Grant Lodge, Elgin, 20 March 1834 [marriage: microfiche] • gravestone, Birnie kirk • gravestone, Urquhart parish church • J. M. Bulloch, 'The Gordons of Laggan', *Transactions of the Banffshire Field Club*, 7 (1905–8) • Local Heritage Centre, Grant Lodge, Elgin, Presbytery of Elgin closed record collection, 1859 • I. Keillar, 'George Gordon: the man and his family', *George Gordon man of science*, ed. I. Keillar and J. S. Smith (1995) • M. Collie and S. Bennett, eds., *George Gordon: an annotated catalogue of his scientific correspondence* (1996) • *The Zoologist* (1844–65) • 'On the geology of the lower and northern part of the province of Moray', *Edinburgh New Philosophical Journal*, 9 (1859) • *Northern Scot* (23 Dec 1893)

Archives Elgin Library, Morayshire • Elgin Museum, corresp. and papers • Falconer Museum, Forres • NA Scot., corresp. and papers • NHM • RBG Kew | Royal Museum, Edinburgh, Harvie Brown papers

Likenesses photograph (in old age; after photograph), Elgin Museum • portrait, priv. coll.

Gordon, George (1806–1879), gardener and horticultural writer, was born at Lucan, co. Dublin, on 25 February 1806, the son of the land steward and gardener at Sterling House, near Dublin. Trained by his father, Gordon entered into service at fourteen years of age. From 1823 to 1827 he was employed in the gardens of two country gentlemen, then he worked briefly in the nursery of J. Colville in King's Road, Chelsea; in February 1828, he joined the staff of the Horticultural Society, Chiswick. Working as an assistant in the kitchen garden department, he was responsible for classifying the 130 named varieties of peas into forty-three distinct kinds. His subsequent study of beans enabled him to identify eleven distinct kinds from the forty-three reputed varieties grown at Chiswick. His task, he acknowledged, was

> to reduce the discordant nomenclature of the seed shops to something like order, to enable the gardener to know the quality of the sorts he is unaccustomed to cultivate and above all to prevent his buying the same kind under different names. (*Transactions of the Horticultural Society of London*, 2nd ser., 1835, 369)

Gordon rose to be one of the foremen at the Horticultural Society, and with the exception of a brief period he remained on its staff for the next thirty years. He was an associate of the Linnean Society from 1841 until his death. His particular responsibility at Chiswick was the management of the arboretum, and having paid special attention to coniferous trees he brought out his *Pinetum* in 1858; Robert Glendinning was his associate in this and in the supplement of 1862, and a second edition appeared in 1875. John Lindley drew on Gordon's practical knowledge in some papers on conifers in the *Journal of the Horticultural Society* in 1850 and 1851, and the writings of Lindley and Gordon became the authoritative guide for certain species and varieties. However, the *Pinetum* was very much the work of a practical gardener, and was neither popular nor scientific. Gordon also assisted John Claudius Loudon in the preparation of *Arboretum et fruticetum Britannicum* (1838), and the *Encyclopaedia of Trees and Shrubs* (1842). At Chiswick, rationalization of the gardens in 1858 led to the abolition of Gordon's post.

Gordon died of apoplexy on 11 October 1879 at 86 Corfield Road, Bethnal Green, London, the house of his sister-in-law, Charlotte Gordon. His herbarium was bought at his death by Sir Joseph Hooker, who then presented it to the herbarium of the Royal Gardens, Kew. Georg August Pritzel, in his *Thesaurus* (1851), confuses him with the Revd George Gordon who published anonymously *A Collectanea for the Flora of Moray* at Elgin in 1839.

B. D. JACKSON, *rev.* JOHN MARTIN

Sources *Gardeners' Chronicle*, new ser., 12 (1879), 569 • H. R. Fletcher, *The story of the Royal Horticultural Society, 1804–1968* (1969) • *Transactions of the Horticultural Society of London*, 2nd ser. (1885) • *Gardeners' Chronicle* (1858), 400 • G. Gordon, *Pinetum* (1858) • G. A. Pritzel, ed., *Thesaurus literaturae botanicae omnium gentium* (Leipzig, 1851) • *The Garden* (9 March 1878), 199 • *The Garden* (1879), 382 • d. cert.

Wealth at death under £450: probate, 8 Nov 1879, *CGPLA Eng. & Wales*

Gordon, George Hamilton-, fourth earl of Aberdeen (1784–1860), prime minister and scholar, first child of six sons and a daughter of George Gordon, Lord Haddo (1764–1791), and his wife, Charlotte (or Charles; *d.* 1795), the youngest daughter of William Baird of Newbyth, Haddingtonshire, and sister of General Sir David Baird, was born in Edinburgh on 28 January 1784. His father died as the result of a riding accident at Gight on 2 October 1791. His mother then quarrelled with his grandfather, the third earl. The third earl was a colourful character. In 1762 he had married Catherine Elizabeth Hanson, the daughter of a Yorkshire blacksmith, in a literally shotgun marriage (Walker, 2.530–31, and W. Yorks. AS). Later in life he kept several mistresses and had a number of illegitimate children. Lady Haddo took all her children to England. She died at Clifton, Bristol, on 8 October 1795.

Family and early life George was sent to preparatory schools at Barnet and Parsons Green, and in June 1795 to Harrow School. He believed that his grandfather was reluctant to pay for him to go to Harrow and subsequently refused to pay for him to go to Cambridge. In fact his grandfather had wished to see him educated in Scotland 'that he do not despise his own country' (draft will, 6 Nov 1791, Haddo House MS 1/27), a not unreasonable wish, particularly when the Scottish universities were acknowledged to be better than the English ones. The third earl had also named several 'curators', or guardians, for his grandson in the event of his own death, including the duke of Gordon. Lady Haddo had, however, looked elsewhere for a protector and turned to Henry Dundas, later Lord Melville. Dundas and his wife became substitute parents to the young Gordons. Through Dundas, George, now

George Hamilton-Gordon, fourth earl of Aberdeen (1784–1860), by Sir Thomas Lawrence, 1829–30

Lord Haddo (he held this courtesy title from 1791 to 1801), met William Pitt the younger. At the age of fourteen, exercising his right under Scottish law, he chose Pitt and Dundas as his guardians.

William Pitt was the most important formative influence on the future earl's life and he still acknowledged him as his master when prime minister himself. It was Pitt who persuaded Haddo that public life was the only proper one. The Gordons of Haddo had not previously played a major role in English politics, although they had been staunch royalists in Scotland. An ancestor, Sir John Gordon, was the first royalist executed in Scotland during the civil war. His younger son, George, the first earl of Aberdeen, was made high chancellor of Scotland by James II, when duke of York. After 1688 he became a nonjuror. His son, the second earl, 'fortunately for the interests of the family' (*Selections*, 4), dropped dead on his way to join the Jacobite rising of 1745. The fourth earl was always deeply conscious of family history. On the grand tour in 1803 he sought out the Young Pretender's widow, the countess of Albany, in Rome, and in 1829 he was instrumental in entrusting the Stuart papers, belonging to the Old Pretender and his sons, which had been acquired by the prince regent, to Sir Walter Scott and J. G. Lockhart for publication (Aberdeen to Scott, 1 July 1829, NL Scot., MS 868).

Scholar and landlord It may have been Pitt who paid for Haddo to go to St John's College, Cambridge, in 1800. He was a natural scholar and immersed himself in Renaissance, as well as classical, studies. He formed a close circle of friends, among them Hudson Gurney of the banking family and George Whittington, an ordinand. They all had literary ambitions and exchanged verses and other writings, some mildly scurrilous.

Haddo's Cambridge career was interrupted by the death, in August 1801, of the third earl. Contrary to a popular impression he had not been entirely cut off from Scotland in his youth, having frequently accompanied Dundas to Dumira in Perthshire, but it is unlikely he had been back to the family home, Haddo House, in Aberdeenshire. The homecoming was a shock. Most of the Aberdeenshire estates were entailed, but in addition to leaving the family silver to the widowed countess the third earl had provided lavishly for his illegitimate children. It left the heir with considerable debts. The estates were neglected and, as Aberdeen wrote to his lawyer, 'Everything is in the most confused state … [the] accounts have not been settled since the year 90' (letter from Aberdeen, 28 Aug 1801, NL Scot., MS 3418, fol. 13). But there was nothing Aberdeen could do immediately because he was not yet of full age.

Aberdeen returned to Cambridge, but in 1802 took advantage of the peace of Amiens to set out on the grand tour, in the company of Gurney and Whittington. The itinerary was planned by Whittington, who had become interested in the development of Gothic architecture. Whittington subsequently wrote a book, *An Historical Survey of the Ecclesiastical Antiquities of France*, which is remarkable for the modernity of some of its views. Following Whittington's premature death in 1807, Aberdeen himself contributed the notes and preface and saw it through the press.

Aberdeen kept a careful journal of his travels. His observations on the political and economic state of France are remarkably mature for a man of barely nineteen. He was pleasantly surprised by the freedom of speech but distressed by evidence of the ravages of the revolution. His connection with William Pitt ensured him a meeting with Napoleon Bonaparte in Paris. He was also able to indulge his love of the theatre and spend time in the Louvre, as well as visiting the painter David. He was already on the lookout for works of art to collect. From Paris the three young men proceeded to Rome by way of Nice, Genoa, and Florence. Gurney and Whittington returned home but Aberdeen, fired by his love of classical antiquities, determined to go on to the Levant.

In Naples, Aberdeen joined the party of a fellow Scot, William Drummond, who had just been appointed to succeed Lord Elgin as British ambassador in Constantinople. They sailed by way of Sicily, Malta, and Athens, where Aberdeen mourned the destruction of the Parthenon and walked along the *via sacra* to Eleusis. Off Athens they met up with pirates, but Aberdeen laconically recorded, 'We fired one eight and twenty pounder, at the sound of which they made off' (Aberdeen, diaries, 29 April 1803).

They arrived in Constantinople on 13 May 1803. Aberdeen accompanied Drummond on his first formal audience with the sultan but was soon off on his travels again: this time exploring Asia Minor in an attempt to find the site of Troy. He then set off on a solitary tour of Greece. In Athens he tried to buy some of the friezes from the Parthenon but found that Elgin was before him. The Morea was then a wild region and Drummond, not a timid man, later commented, 'I should not have ventured on such a journey' (Drummond to Aberdeen, 24 April 1804, BL, Add. MS 43229). Aberdeen made a collection of sculptures, which he later presented to the British Museum. He also recorded a large number of inscriptions, which have since been destroyed, and carried out various excavations which, on the evidence he was later able to supply to inquirers, were recorded in scientific detail far ahead of their time. Unfortunately his notebooks have now disappeared, perhaps discarded by his eldest son, whose religious fervour made him unsympathetic to 'paganism'.

Aberdeen returned to England by way of Venice, Vienna, and Berlin in the summer of 1804. Although at first he found Haddo a depressing place, he energetically set about making over his estates according to the best models of the time. His fondness for planting trees (he estimated himself that he planted 14 million) amused his contemporaries, but it had a serious purpose for, aesthetic considerations aside, it remedied a chronic shortage of timber. Equally important were the new model leases he drew up, the carefully designed granite houses which replaced the rubble-stone cottages, roofed with peat, of the tenantry, and the experiments with new crops and stock breeding. Aberdeen was a good landlord, who set great store by continuity. At his eldest son's coming of age in 1837 he expressed his satisfaction that no tenant was missing because he had been turned off the estate—a claim echoed by the *Banffshire Journal* after his death, which added that he had never distrained for rent (Aberdeen to Haddo, 5 Oct 1837, Haddo House MS 1/27; *GM*, 3rd ser., 10, 1861, 207, quoting *Banffshire Journal*). From 1846 until his death he was lord lieutenant of Aberdeenshire.

Aberdeen also set out to improve Haddo House. Although it was a dignified Palladian house, designed for the second earl in the 1730s by William Adams, the father of the more famous Adams brothers, to replace the house damaged during the civil war, it was not a convenient building and Aberdeen always felt that it was plain compared with the great houses of his friends in England. He tried to soften it by developing the gardens and eventually creating that fashionable feature, a lake, out of a bog. He was influenced in his designs by his friend Uvedale Price, and his ideas of the 'picturesque'. Despite its remoteness from London, Haddo was to be for a time in the 1840s and 1850s an important house where politicians and others met, and even the French chargé d'affaires commended Aberdeen's wine cellar.

Having put the first improvements at Haddo in train, Aberdeen returned to London in March 1805. He became a *habitué* of the three great salons at Devonshire House, Holland House, and Bentley Priory, the home of the Abercorns at Stanmore in Middlesex. Although the first two were accounted whig and the last tory, there was at this time, when most politicians had rallied to Pitt during the

French wars, no clear distinction between the clienteles. The Bentley Priory circle included Sir Walter Scott, Richard Sheridan, Thomas Lawrence, John Kemble, and Richard Payne Knight the antiquary. Scott later wrote that the marquess of Abercorn, Payne Knight, and Aberdeen 'made evenings of modern fashion resemble a Greek symposium for learning and literature' (*QR*, 34, 1826, 213–14).

Aberdeen was establishing a reputation as a scholar. In July 1805 he and William Drummond contributed a long review of William Gell's *The Topography of Troy* to the *Edinburgh Review*. Aberdeen disagreed with Gell's speculations about the site of Troy and the tone of the article was satirical, but those who have seen it as unpleasantly sarcastic have missed the point. The three men were friends, and Payne Knight warned Drummond that Gell might retaliate: 'to hunt down an Earl & a Privy Councillor in the Character of Reviewers would be a fine sport' (Knight to Drummond, 5 Aug 1805, BL, Add. MS 43229). Gell bore no malice and Aberdeen helped him find the finance for future expeditions.

Aberdeen's quarrels with other scholars were more serious. The French scholar M. Dutens took exception to Aberdeen's review of his *Recherches sur le tems, le plus reculé de l'usage des voûtes chez les anciens*, although modern scholarship would be much closer to Aberdeen's views on the origins of the arch than to his. Aberdeen later clashed with the Abbé Fourmont on the significance of the marbles at Amyclae, laughing at Fourmont's suggestion that they represented human sacrifice and expressing his own views in his contributions to Robert Walpole's *Memoirs Relating to Turkey in 1817* and *Travels in Various Countries in the East*. He also contributed a learned chapter on the mines of Laurium and Athenian currency to the former book. In 1812 he had written an introduction to William Wilkins's new edition of Vitruvius' *De architectura*. Ten years later he published an expanded version under the title *An Inquiry into the Principles and Beauty in Grecian Architecture*, in which he did not hesitate to question Edmund Burke's *Ideas of the Sublime and the Beautiful*.

In May 1805 Aberdeen was elected to the Society of Dilettanti, by that time an important group of patrons. A month later he was elected to the Society of Antiquaries, of which he became president in 1811, an office he held until 1846. He was a very active member of both until distracted by public office. He became a fellow of the Royal Society in April 1808 and served on its council in 1812–13, 1817–18, and 1821–2. He was there as a patron, rather than a scientist, but he took a steadily increasing interest in the scientific theories and controversies of the time. He became a trustee of the British Museum in December 1812 and was still active in that capacity in the 1850s.

Aberdeen's membership of the Dilettanti led him into the controversy about the Elgin marbles. Many scholars, including his own mentor, Payne Knight, were sceptical about both their authenticity and their importance when Elgin returned with them in 1807, but in 1816 Aberdeen appeared as a witness before the Commons select committee, rejected Payne Knight's views, gave his opinion that they might well be by the great Athenian sculptor Phidias, and recommended that they be bought for the nation at £35,000—the sum eventually agreed.

Aberdeen himself believed that it was permissible to remove sculptures to save them from destruction, but he attracted the ire of his own cousin, George Gordon, Lord Byron. Byron's reference to 'the travelled Thane, Athenian Aberdeen' in *English Bards and Scotch Reviewers* is well known, but he had originally written a much more savage stanza in *Childe Harold*, beginning,

> Come then ye classic Thieves of each degree,
> Dark Hamilton and sullen Aberdeen.

He had toned it down on hearing that Aberdeen was about to propose him for the Athenian Club, a dining club for those who had visited Athens, which Aberdeen formed but which did not last long.

Marriage and religion Soon after his return to Britain in 1804 the duchess of Gordon tried to make a match between Aberdeen and her daughter. Aberdeen, however, had begun a flirtation with Harriet Cavendish, the younger daughter of the fifth duke of Devonshire, but Harriet was a lively young lady who could not resist teasing the rather stiff young Scot. Aberdeen soon transferred his affections to Catherine Elizabeth (1784–1812), the eldest surviving daughter of John James Hamilton, the first marquess of Abercorn. Catherine's personality radiates from her few surviving letters. She was beautiful, talented, and humorous, but, above all, warm-hearted. They were married on 28 July 1805. It was a love match which touched the heart even of hardbitten Regency London.

Catherine was to bear him three daughters, Jane (*b.* 1807), Caroline (*b.* 1808), and Alice (*b.* 1809). Aberdeen adored his daughters and would not allow anyone to express disappointment that they were girls, although a son was an urgent necessity in view of the strict terms of the entail. Unhappily, when the longed-for son was born in November 1810, he lived less than an hour. It slowly became apparent that Catherine herself was suffering from tuberculosis. She died, having fought gallantly to the end, on 29 February 1812. Aberdeen never fully recovered from her death. He wore mourning for her for the rest of his life and, for a year after her death, kept a diary in Latin in which he recorded her constant appearances to him: 'Vidi, sed obscuriorem', 'Tota nocta vidi, ut in vita' ('I saw her, but dimly', 'The whole night I saw her, as in life'). In his distress he turned to William Howley, later bishop of London and archbishop of Canterbury, but then an Oxford don, with whom he had previously discussed his religious beliefs.

Religion did not come easily to Aberdeen. North of the border, he considered himself *ex officio* a Presbyterian, and was even a member of the general assembly of the Church of Scotland from 1818 to 1828. He was conscientious in using his patronage in Aberdeenshire parishes. In consequence he became embroiled in the schism which split the Church of Scotland in the 1840s on the conflicting rights of parishioners and patrons to choose their ministers.

In 1834 the general assembly passed the measure, generally called the Veto Act, which allowed parishioners to reject a nominee presented to them by the patron. This was tested in the famous Auchterarder case, in which first the court of session and then the House of Lords ruled that the parish had acted *ultra vires* in purporting to reject Lord Kinnoul's nominee. Aberdeen was sympathetic to the idea that parishioners should have some voice, although his sympathy was tested by a case in his own parish of Methlick. Aberdeen, as patron, presented a man named James Whyte, to whom some parishioners objected on the grounds that he had a reputation for immorality in his youth. Aberdeen referred the case to the presbytery (that is, the ministers of the district) which, after scrupulous inquiry, found Whyte innocent. Some parishioners, however, continued their objections. Aberdeen felt compelled to put his own authority on the line by appealing to his tenants' sense of fair play, even addressing them in the parish church. In the end the majority came into line and agreed to sign the 'call'. Aberdeen admitted to his friend John Hope, the dean of faculty, that it had been a test of his own relations with his 'people'. 'If the truth must be told, I very much fear that I was secretly even more interested for myself than for Mr Whyte' (Aberdeen to Hope, 17 Sept 1839; *Selections*, 127). Mr Whyte lived in amity with his parishioners for the next forty years.

The case made Aberdeen wary, but when Dr Thomas Chalmers, the leader of the so-called non-intrusionists and a personal friend, visited him at Haddo, he promised to support a compromise measure. On 5 May 1840 he introduced a bill into the Lords which would have given presbyteries, although not individual parishes, a right of veto on certain specified grounds. Lord Melbourne's government was divided as to whether to support the bill, and in the meantime a more extreme party, which thought the bill inadequate, gained control of the general assembly. Aberdeen's and Chalmers's co-operation ended amid mutual recriminations and Aberdeen withdrew his bill. In May 1842 the general assembly passed its 'claim of right', rejecting all secular interference in ecclesiastical affairs, and the following year about one-third of the ministers of the Church of Scotland seceded to form the Free Church of Scotland. Aberdeen reintroduced his compromise bill, which became law in August 1843 and remained in force until the abolition of patronage in 1874. His own view of the Disruption may be gauged from his reply to Charlotte Canning when she drew his attention to 'an odd log church … of the free variety' near Blair Atholl: 'I would like to set it on fire' (V. Surtees, *Charlotte Canning*, 1975, 136).

Privately, he always considered himself an Anglican, once telling William Gladstone that he preferred 'the sister church' (10 Dec 1840, BL, Add. MS 44088). He tended to the low- rather than the high-church side, always attending St James's, Piccadilly, when in London and habitually taking communion only once a year at Easter. He personally regarded the doctrine of transubstantiation as a 'superstition' but sympathized with Archdeacon Denison in 1857 because 'to inflict penalties upon a man for believing more than his neighbour, in a matter neither of them can comprehend' seemed unfair (Aberdeen to Gladstone, 17 Aug 1857, BL, Add. MS 44089). Aberdeen hoped that he faced the many tragedies of his life with Christian resignation but it was, perhaps, closer to stoicism. He always regretted his lack of a 'lively faith' and remained at heart a rational man of the eighteenth century.

Representative peer The death of Aberdeen's wife helped to precipitate him into more involvement in public affairs. As a Scottish peer Aberdeen had no automatic seat in the House of Lords, but he was also debarred from sitting in the Commons. He could enter parliament only as one of the sixteen representative Scottish peers. William Pitt had promised him a United Kingdom peerage, but Pitt's premature death in January 1806 deprived him of his patron. Aberdeen, aged only twenty-two, did remarkably well to be returned as one of the representative peers in the general election of 1806, the only successful candidate not on the king's, that is the government's, list. He was re-elected in 1807 and 1812 (topping the poll in the latter year) but he hated the necessary politicking.

Aberdeen took his place in the Lords on the tory benches on 17 December 1806. He prepared a maiden speech in favour of the abolition of the slave trade but lost his nerve and failed to deliver it. He never overcame his fear of speaking in the Lords. His eventual maiden speech, on a complicated constitutional question, was not a success, and for some time he spoke almost entirely on Scottish matters. Nevertheless he had the entrée into the highest political circles and was active behind the scenes. Castlereagh went out of his way to secure his support at the time of his quarrel, and duel, with Canning in 1809. His friends were beginning to suggest that he might find his métier in diplomacy, and a number of appointments, including St Petersburg and Constantinople, were offered to him, but Aberdeen was too absorbed in his life in London and at Haddo to be much interested. His acceptance of the Vienna embassy in 1813 owed something to his desire to throw himself into work to assuage his grief at Catherine's death and perhaps something to his feeling that he had been a mere bystander in the war while four of his brothers had fought the French—Alexander and Charles with Wellington in the Peninsula (Alexander *Gordon was killed at Waterloo), and William and John in the navy.

Vienna embassy and Napoleonic wars The appointment to the Vienna embassy was not so surprising as it has seemed to some later historians. Aberdeen was young, not quite thirty, but it was a young man's world. Metternich himself was not yet forty. War-torn Europe was a dangerous place (Aberdeen's predecessor, Benjamin Bathurst, had been murdered). It seemed to call for exactly the qualities of toughness and initiative that Aberdeen had shown during his Eastern travels. He had only a slight experience of diplomacy, but what was required was a grandee in the confidence of his government, which Aberdeen was. Aberdeen may originally have thought of it as mainly a ceremonial mission to reopen relations with Austria, if she broke with France, which would clinch his claims to a United Kingdom peerage. It turned into nine strenuous and dangerous months, accompanying the allied armies across Europe, which provided the most important formative political experience of his life.

Aberdeen's mission was carried out with professional efficiency, which probably owed much to the one experienced diplomat on his staff, David Morier. His own younger brother, Robert *Gordon, who had diplomatic experience in Tehran, was also present for part of the time. Another assistant, Frederick Lamb, the younger brother of Lord Melbourne, was also a novice and, in any case, preferred Vienna to campaigning.

When Aberdeen was appointed in the summer of 1813 it was not yet certain that Austria would join Russia and Prussia against Napoleon. Aberdeen left London on 6 August. Only on 12 August did Austria declare war on France. Since 1809 Britain had been excluded from European diplomacy. Castlereagh had taken advantage of the changed situation after Napoleon's invasion of Russia in 1812 to appoint Lord Cathcart ambassador to Russia, and his own half-brother, Sir Charles Stewart, ambassador to Prussia. Both were soldiers, rather than diplomats, and neither was held in high esteem by the continentals. Metternich's secretary, Gentz, once referred to them as 'real caricatures of ambassadors' (Webster, 47). More importantly, they had been left out of the crucial negotiations of June 1813, culminating in the treaty of Reichenbach of 27 June, in which Austria, Prussia, and Russia agreed on the terms on which they would be prepared to conclude peace with Napoleon.

Castlereagh's first instructions to Aberdeen were to try 'to penetrate in to [the] councils of the Austrian emperor' and, more particularly, to get accurate copies of any treaties or engagements entered into (general instructions, 3 Aug 1813, PRO, FO 7/101). In other words, he had to try to re-establish the British presence in European diplomacy. He has seldom been given the credit for succeeding in this, although often condemned for the compromises which success entailed. Castlereagh's general instructions to Aberdeen on the post-war settlement to aim for, although based on William Pitt's draft of 1805, were open-ended and contingent. Both Castlereagh and Aberdeen were well aware that what could be demanded would depend entirely on how the war developed and that, although the British public was dazzled by Wellington's victories in the Iberian peninsula, the war would really be determined in central Europe, and that what Britain had most to fear was the so-called 'continental peace' (which the Reichenbach terms had embodied), in which matters were settled between Napoleon and the Eastern powers and British interests ignored.

Aberdeen declined to supply confidential information to his friends at home, even Lord Abercorn, but he did write of his own experiences to Lord Harrowby and, more particularly, to his sister-in-law, Maria, Lady Hamilton. Taken with his private, as well as his official, letters to Castlereagh, the mission is exceptionally well documented. But it should be remembered that his letters to Maria were partly intended for his three small, motherless daughters, who had wept on his departure, and his occasional boasting of his intimacy with kings and emperors should be taken no more seriously than his description of the carriage which put him in mind of 'Cinderella and her *attelage*', in which he crossed Sweden.

Aberdeen arrived in Berlin on 23 August full of almost schoolboy excitement at the idea of seeing war first hand. A few weeks later he had seen enough to last him a lifetime. Warned that the French were advancing and their road might be cut, they pressed on at full speed for Prague. In the night Aberdeen's carriage overturned and he suffered concussion which, rightly or wrongly, he blamed for the headaches which tormented him for the rest of his life. They caught up with the Austrian emperor at Teplitz. The tsar of Russia and the king of Prussia were also there with a dozen lesser princes. It was at this meeting that Gentz noted that Aberdeen was not completely 'master' of the French language, from which some historians have drawn the exaggerated conclusion that he could not speak French. In fact he was a competent linguist and Gentz withdrew most of his criticisms a few days later.

Aberdeen got on well with the Austrian emperor, Franz I, and also struck up the friendship with Metternich, cemented by the shared hardships of campaigning, which endured for the lifetime of both. Aberdeen had been dismayed by the waggons 'full of wounded, dead and dying' he had seen on the road from Prague to Teplitz. The aftermath of the battle of Leipzig, although an allied victory, shocked him still more. He wrote to Maria,

> For three or four miles the ground is covered with bodies of men and horses, many not dead. Wretches wounded unable to crawl, crying for water amidst heaps of putrefying bodies. Their screams are heard at an immense distance, and still ring in my ears. … Our victory is most complete. It must be owned that a victory is a fine thing, but one should be at a distance. (Aberdeen to M. Hamilton, 4 Sept 1813, 22 Oct 1813, BL, Add. MS 43225)

Meanwhile the diplomatic negotiations to try to cement a final coalition against Napoleon went on. Aberdeen was irritated by the extent to which he was subordinated to Cathcart and rightly saw this as, in part, a reflection of the British view that Russia was a reliable ally while Austria was still to some extent suspect. Aberdeen argued that this was not so. The Russians were tempted to make peace now the French had been expelled from Russian soil; the Austrians had burnt their boats and would suffer disasters even greater than those of 1809 if Napoleon was not thoroughly defeated this time.

Early in November the allies entered Frankfurt am Main and Aberdeen became involved in the 'Frankfort proposals'. Baron St Aignan, the brother-in-law of the French foreign minister, Armand Caulaincourt, was to be used as a secret emissary to propose terms to Napoleon. These included an offer of France's 'natural frontiers' of the Rhine, the Alps, and the Pyrenees. Aberdeen was aware that Metternich did not expect Napoleon to accept, but was preparing the ground to appeal to his generals, citing their commander's unreasonableness. St Aignan prepared an *aide-mémoire* of the discussions, which included the ambiguous phrase, 'Que l'Angleterre était prête … à reconnaître la liberté du commerce, et de la navigation à laquelle la France a droit de prétendre' ('England is ready … to recognize the freedom of commerce and navigation which France has the right to claim'). Aberdeen was in an awkward position. The *aide-mémoire* had no status as an agreed document, and if he insisted on rewording it, it might acquire such status. Moreover, he was not officially present at the discussions at all. If he had refused to play along he might have been excluded, as Cathcart and Stewart were at Reichenbach. He made no formal protest and was upheld on this by Castlereagh, but this did not save him from the later charge that he had been prepared to give away Britain's cherished 'maritime rights'.

It was becoming notorious that relations between Aberdeen, Cathcart, and Stewart were bad, and Castlereagh determined to go to the continent and take charge himself. Nevertheless he still used Aberdeen as his right-hand man, leaving him to conduct the negotiations at Châtillon in February–March 1814. The Châtillon conference was overtaken by the final military breakthrough against Napoleon. Aberdeen accompanied Castlereagh to Paris and assisted him in concluding the first treaty of Paris with France in May 1814. According to his son's account he actually brought the treaty with him in his carriage to London.

Aberdeen was duly rewarded with a United Kingdom peerage as Viscount Gordon of Aberdeen (1 June 1814). Castlereagh wanted Aberdeen to accompany him to the Congress of Vienna to assist him in negotiating the final settlement of Europe, but Aberdeen declined. He wished to return to private life. He did put Metternich and a large entourage up at his London home, Argyll House, when the tsar, the king of Prussia, and other European leaders went to London to celebrate the peace. He had acquired Argyll House, off Oxford Street, the former home of the dukes of Argyll, in 1808, and carried out major alterations with the assistance of the architect William Wilkins.

It was a sad homecoming. Both Maria and James, Lord Hamilton, Lord Abercorn's eldest son and heir, had recently died. Aberdeen wished to remarry and was attracted to both Anne Cavendish, the daughter of Lord George Cavendish, and Susan Ryder, the daughter of Lord Harrowby, but he was persuaded, perhaps over-persuaded, by Lord Abercorn, to marry, on 8 July 1815, Lord Hamilton's widow, the former Harriet Douglas (1792–1833), and become the guardian of Abercorn's infant grandson. (After Abercorn's death in 1818 Aberdeen added Hamilton to his own surname to mark the close intertwining of the families.) Harriet Douglas was a beauty but Aberdeen had once described her to his brother as 'one of the most stupid persons I have ever met with' (Aberdeen to A. Gordon, 17 Nov 1810, BL, Add. MS 43223). The marriage produced four sons and a daughter but it was stormy, not least because Harriet became jealous of Catherine's three talented daughters. Private tragedies continued. Caroline died in 1818, Jane in 1824, Alice in 1829, and Frances, the daughter of the second marriage, in 1834. Harriet herself died in 1833. Almost certainly all died of tuberculosis. Aberdeen made desperate attempts to save them, especially Alice, whom he took to the south of France in 1824–6.

Distracted by family problems, the care of his Scottish estates, his guardianship of his stepson, Lord Hamilton, and (after Abercorn's death) responsibility for both Bentley Priory and Baronscourt (the Abercorn estate in Ireland), Aberdeen did not hold office between 1814 and 1828, although he spoke occasionally in the Lords and sat on the 1819 inquiry into the currency question.

Foreign and colonial secretary, 1828–1835 Aberdeen joined the duke of Wellington's administration in January 1828 as chancellor of the duchy of Lancaster, with the specific brief of assisting the ineffectual Lord Dudley at the Foreign Office. When Dudley resigned with the other Canningites in May, Aberdeen succeeded him as foreign secretary. The great issues of the day were the civil war in Portugal (and the fear of French intervention in the Iberian peninsula) and the Greek War of Independence. On Portugal, Aberdeen deferred to Wellington's specialist knowledge of the area, but on Greece they diverged. Wellington, with his Indian experience, was principally concerned to prevent Russia from increasing her influence at Turkey's expense. Aberdeen sympathized with Greek nationalism. The result was unfortunate. Aberdeen undoubtedly encouraged Stratford Canning, the British ambassador in Constantinople, by private letter, to try to secure Athens for the Greeks, but later, under pressure from Wellington, had to rebuke him for so doing. The incident helps to explain the uneasy relationship between the two men in the 1850s, when Canning was again ambassador in Constantinople.

Wellington's government was still in office when the 1830 revolution occurred in France. Both men agreed that the recognition of the July monarchy under Louis Philippe was the only solution. They were less sympathetic to Belgium's demand for independence from Holland, but the London conference which later, under Palmerston's guidance, accepted Belgian independence, was first convened by Wellington and Aberdeen.

Aberdeen returned to office as colonial secretary in Sir Robert Peel's short-lived administration of December 1834–April 1835. The office was then combined with the War Office, and Aberdeen's complaints about troublesome issues of patronage seem to refer mainly to the latter. He showed percipience as colonial secretary, anticipating the resentment the Boers would feel at the abolition of slavery in 1833 and urging that they be assisted to claim the statutory compensation. (Unlike the West Indian planters, who normally had agents in London, the Boers had little idea how to claim.) He also wished to deal with Canadian problems, foreshadowing in many particulars Lord Durham's mission after the Canadian uprisings of 1837.

Foreign secretary, 1841–1864 Aberdeen joined Sir Robert Peel's second administration as foreign secretary on 3 September 1841. He and Peel were now close personal and political friends. Peel respected Aberdeen's expertise and generally accepted his judgement, only occasionally intervening to 'stiffen' Aberdeen in his dealings with France in particular. Aberdeen in return kept Britain's international relations on an even keel while Peel dealt with the economic problems of the 'hungry forties', which contemporaries saw as potentially revolutionary.

Aberdeen inherited a dire situation from Lord Palmerston, his predecessor at the Foreign Office. Britain had quarrelled with France over the Eastern crisis of 1840. She was near to war with the United States about border and other disputes. She was actually at war with China and Afghanistan. Aberdeen moved first to restore relations with the United States. Lord Ashburton was sent on a special mission to Washington. The treaty he signed in 1842 did not settle all the disputes and he was accused of giving too much away on the north-east boundary between the States and Canada, although later research suggests that he got a good bargain. The 1846 treaty, which settled the north-west, or Oregon, boundary, is more questionable and more clearly influenced by a desire for any settlement.

Co-operation with France was more often a whig than a tory policy, but Aberdeen created, in 1843, the first *entente cordiale*—the phrase was actually coined at Haddo House (Chamberlain, *Lord Aberdeen*, 357–8). It enabled him to settle, with Peel's support, the dangerous Moroccan and Tahiti crises of 1844, which brought Britain and France to the verge of war. But by 1845 both Peel and Wellington feared that too many concessions were being made to France, in particular to keep the government of François Guizot, Aberdeen's principal collaborator in the entente, in power. Aberdeen offered his resignation but Peel refused it, and he remained in office until the fall of Peel's ministry in June 1846. Aberdeen continued to dispute the truth of the old maxim, 'If you wish for peace, prepare for war', but Peel and Wellington turned their attention to defence matters.

Aberdeen supported Peel over the repeal of the corn laws and remained a member of the small but highly talented and experienced group of Peelites, despite attempts by Lord Derby to win him over to the protectionists. Palmerston had condemned Aberdeen's policy as foreign secretary from 1841 to 1846 as fatally weak, but few believed him. Aberdeen was regarded as a safe pair of hands, Palmerston as a maverick who allowed the French entente to collapse in the fiasco of the Spanish marriage question in 1846. Palmerston's handling of the great revolutionary crises of 1848 was regarded as dangerously opportunistic by British, as well as European, conservatives. Aberdeen joined Derby to launch an attack upon him in the famous Don Pacifico debate of 1850, which was actually about much wider issues. A few days later Peel died and Aberdeen became, in effect, the Peelite leader.

Prime minister The Peelites potentially held the balance of power in parliament and an attempt at a coalition with the whigs was made in 1851. It foundered on Lord John Russell's Ecclesiastical Titles Bill. Aberdeen, always in favour of religious tolerance, particularly feared stirring up religious excitement, more especially because of its possible consequences in Ireland.

Extremely interesting discussions took place, mainly by letter, in the summer of 1852 in which Aberdeen and the duke of Newcastle took a prominent part, together with Lord John Russell, Sir James Graham, and William Gladstone. What they envisaged was nothing less than the creation of a completely new political party by a fusion of the whig and Peelite traditions. It was his belief in the reality of the fusion which lay behind Aberdeen's construction of his coalition cabinet in December 1852, Aberdeen formally taking office as prime minister on 19 December. Despite their great disparity in strength in the Commons (the whigs had over two hundred MPs, the Peelites only about thirty), cabinet posts were almost equally divided between the two groups.

Walter Bagehot called the Aberdeen cabinet 'the ablest we have had' since the Parliamentary Reform Act of 1832 (Bagehot, 29). It was genuinely a 'ministry of all the talents'. The whig leader, Lord John Russell, passed the Foreign Office to Lord Clarendon after a few weeks but remained leader of the Commons. Lord Palmerston took the unaccustomed position of home secretary. William Gladstone became chancellor of the exchequer. All members testified that its diverse elements worked together with remarkable harmony on most domestic issues. The 1853 session was largely taken up with Gladstone's budget, intended to overhaul the whole fiscal system. Aberdeen supported him against powerful opposition. Palmerston got through some important legislation on penal and other matters. The government meant to reform the whole educational system from primary schools to the two ancient universities. Education was a particular interest of Aberdeen, who had sat on the royal commission which inquired into the Scottish universities in 1826–30, and always maintained that the problems of Ireland would be solved only when it had as good an educational system as Scotland. But education, along with other projected reforms, became a casualty of the worsening international situation.

The most serious casualty was parliamentary reform. Aberdeen's attitude had been somewhat ambiguous in 1831–2. He had not voted in some divisions, but his sympathies probably lay with Lord Harrowby and the so-called 'waverers', who had wanted a compromise solution. Since then he had become convinced, with other thoughtful men, that corruption had actually increased since 1832 and that further reform was necessary. Here the cabinet was more divided, and Palmerston's temporary resignation in December 1853 was almost certainly due to the parliamentary reform issue and not, as popularly supposed, to the Eastern crisis. Aberdeen would have persisted with the measure in spite of the outbreak of the Crimean War. It was Russell who lost his nerve and insisted on postponing it.

On the Eastern crisis the whigs were generally hawks,

the Peelites doves. The crisis had begun in 1851 when Louis Napoleon, with his eyes on his domestic voters, chose to assert himself as the champion of the Latin church within the Ottoman empire. The tsar of Russia responded, perhaps over-forcibly, as the champion of the Orthodox Christians. Aberdeen never believed that the tsar wished to partition the Ottoman empire, still less to seize Constantinople—despite some rather alarming contingency planning which the tsar had discussed with the British ambassador, Hamilton Seymour, and which had become public knowledge. But the tsar was hated by the British public, as much for his role in suppressing the 1848 revolutions in Europe as for any threat he might pose to British India. Ironically, when the coalition was formed, Aberdeen and Palmerston were agreed that the greatest threat to European peace came from Napoleon III. They did prepare for war, but the wrong war.

Palmerston adapted much more quickly than Aberdeen to the idea that they should ally with France to check Russia. Aberdeen lamented later that he had not shown more 'firmness' in restraining the belligerent tendencies of his own cabinet, but his own faith in Russian sincerity was shaken at crucial moments, notably by the 'massacre' of Sinope of 30 November 1853. Almost certainly Sinope, like Navarino a generation earlier, was an accidental clash of fleets at a time when Russia and Turkey were already at war, but it was interpreted in London and Paris as a deliberate Russian attack on the Turkish coast, which the tsar had promised not to make while international negotiations to restore peace continued. Aberdeen agreed to the entry of the British fleet into the Black Sea and a demand that the Russian fleet should return to its base at Sevastopol.

When war finally broke out on 27 March 1854 Aberdeen would have been well advised to resign. He did not do so because Queen Victoria (for whom he had the most protective feelings) begged him in tears not to leave her to Palmerston and the war party, and he honestly believed that he had the best track record in successful negotiations at a time when it still seemed matters might be settled by diplomacy without much actual fighting.

The war was a series of military disasters for Britain. It showed up all the neglect of the army since 1815, though it also had its share of bad luck. The original intention had been to assist the Turks in expelling the Russians from the Danubian principalities, Ottoman territory which they had occupied in July 1853, but the Russians thwarted this by handing the principalities over to neutral Austria. The decision to make a land attack on Sevastopol instead was a collective cabinet decision in which Palmerston (who wisely removed the relevant cabinet memoranda, so that they did not come to light for nearly a century among his private papers) (Chamberlain, *Lord Palmerston*, 95, 129) played a leading role. Aberdeen would have preferred a naval bombardment.

Resignation and death Public opinion notoriously played a major part in the Crimean War. There was no censorship until the very end, and the combination of the telegraph and the new profession of war correspondent brought the reality of war home to the public. By the beginning of 1855 the position of the Aberdeen coalition was untenable. Its downfall (Aberdeen resigned on 30 January after a Commons vote of no confidence on 29 January) was precipitated by the defection of Lord John Russell, who had always believed that Aberdeen would merely form the coalition and then hand the premiership to him, and was correspondingly resentful that Aberdeen's recollection of the bargain was different.

Aberdeen never held office after February 1855, although he assisted Palmerston in forming the next administration by asking his fellow Peelites to stay on. His sense of guilt about the Crimean War can be exaggerated. His refusal to rebuild a church on his Scottish estates and his apparent citing of the text from Chronicles in which King David declined to rebuild the Temple because he had 'shed blood abundantly' (*Selections*, 302–3) seems to date from the last months of his life when his mind had become clouded. After the war he continued to advise Clarendon on the conduct of foreign affairs, co-operated with Sidney Herbert in persuading Gladstone (whom he was convinced must one day lead the Liberal Party) not to rejoin the Conservatives, and even contemplated resuming office himself in the crisis of 1858—hardly the actions of a man racked by intolerable guilt. Victoria continued to show her support for him by bestowing the Order of the Garter on him on 7 February 1855 (while allowing him, unusually, to retain the Order of the Thistle, which he had held since 1808) and visiting him at Haddo.

Aberdeen died at Argyll House, Argyll Street, London, on 14 December 1860 and was buried in the old church at Stanmore on 21 December, between Catherine and Harriet, in the Abercorn family vault. Sir James Graham, the duke of Newcastle, Lord Clarendon, William Gladstone, Edward Cardwell, and the earl of Dalkeith acted as pallbearers. The queen sent her carriage as a mark of respect.

Reputation and assessment Aberdeen's reputation was damned by the Crimean War and his earlier career read backwards in the light of it. He was remembered as weak and ineffectual. That such a man should have been the trusted friend and colleague of Castlereagh, Wellington, Peel, and Gladstone (none of them bad judges of men) is inherently improbable. Aberdeen was a shy man, not good at projecting himself to the public, however highly he was regarded by family and friends. The sobriety of his appearance and manner later in life, on which some commented, is not surprising in view of the repeated tragedies he had endured. (He was high-spirited and even a dandy as a young man.) Perhaps he would have been happier if he had remained a scholar and reforming landlord. His judicial temperament and natural inclination to see all sides of a question were not best suited to adversarial politics or to the role of defender of his country right or wrong.

But Aberdeen's career before 1854 contained far more success than failure. As Castlereagh's reputation has risen, so should Aberdeen's. Victorian historians tended not to appreciate the enormous difficulties in maintaining British influence in Europe in 1813–14, or the extent to which Aberdeen assisted Castlereagh in overcoming them. Lord Ellenborough, who had wanted the Foreign Office in 1828, and Palmerston, who resented his loss of it in 1841, provided deeply prejudiced accounts of Aberdeen's stewardship, which were readily believed after the Crimean War. Interestingly, when he was prime minister, the smear campaign against him, led by Benjamin Disraeli, began in 1853 before the Eastern question became acute. It can be explained only by Disraeli's appreciation of Aberdeen's vital role as the keystone (as Gladstone called him) of the whig–Peelite alliance, which might keep the protectionists out of office indefinitely.

Aberdeen, who had been a historian before he became a politician, was convinced that posterity would redress the balance. He meticulously preserved all his papers and left his youngest son, Arthur Charles Hamilton-*Gordon, later Baron Stanmore, the task of publishing them (he eventually printed them on the government printing press during his governorship of Ceylon). Unfortunately, Aberdeen also gave Sir James Graham and William Gladstone final powers of veto to avoid indiscretions. Aberdeen was dead but Gladstone was still an active politician. He sabotaged the entire publication to suppress the revelation that he had opposed parliamentary reform in 1853.

MURIEL E. CHAMBERLAIN

Sources *Selections from the correspondence of the fourth earl of Aberdeen*, 13 vols. (privately printed, London, 1854–88) • A. Gordon, *The earl of Aberdeen* (1893) • M. E. Chamberlain, *Lord Aberdeen: a political biography* (1983) • J. B. Conacher, *The Aberdeen coalition, 1852–1855* (1968) • *Despatches, correspondence, and memoranda of Field Marshal Arthur, duke of Wellington*, ed. A. R. Wellesley, second duke of Wellington, 8 vols. (1867–80) • C. K. Webster, *The foreign policy of Castlereagh*, 2 vols. (1925–31) • J. B. Conacher, *The Peelites and the party system* (1972) • E. Law, Lord Ellenborough, *A political diary, 1828–1830*, ed. Lord Colchester, 2 vols. (1881) • N. Gash, *Sir Robert Peel: the life of Sir Robert Peel after 1830* (1972) • L. Iremonger, *Lord Aberdeen* (1978) • M. E. Chamberlain, *Lord Palmerston* (1987) • *The correspondence of Lord Aberdeen and Princess Lieven, 1832–1854*, ed. E. J. Parry, 2 vols., CS, 3rd ser., 60, 62 (1938–9) • *The correspondence between Dr Chalmers and the earl of Aberdeen in the years 1839 and 1840* (1893) • *The Greville memoirs*, ed. H. Reeve, new edn, 8 vols. (1888) • F. Guizot, *Mémoires pour servir à l'histoire de mon temps*, 8 vols. (1858–67) • W. Bagehot, *The English constitution*, new edn (1926) • W. D. Jones, *Lord Aberdeen and the Americas* (1958) • J. M. Bulloch and others, eds., *The house of Gordon*, 1, Third Spalding Club, 26 (1903) • *Scots peerage*, vol. 1 • J. Evans, *A history of the Society of Antiquaries* (1956) • S. T. Bindoff and others, eds., *British diplomatic representatives, 1789–1852*, CS, 3rd ser., 50 (1934) • J. Ferguson, *The sixteen peers of Scotland: an account of the elections of the representative peers of Scotland, 1707–1959* (1960) • L. Cust and S. Colvin, eds., *History of the Society of Dilettanti* (1898) • Comte de Jarnac, 'Lord Aberdeen, souvenirs et papiers diplomatiques', *Revue des Deux Mondes*, 34 (1861), 429–72 • Society of Antiquaries, *Presidents of the Society*, Occasional Papers 2 (1945) • C. Gordon, *A souvenir of Haddo House* (1958) • *The letters of Richard Brinsley Sheridan*, ed. C. Price, 3 vols. (1966), vol. 2 • J. W. Walker, *Wakefield, its history and people*, 2nd edn, 2 vols. (1939) • H. L. V. Foster, *The two duchesses: Georgiana, duchess of Devonshire, Elizabeth, duchess of Devonshire: family correspondence, 1779–1859* (1898) • *Hary-O: the letters of Lady Harriet Cavendish, 1796–1809*, ed. G. Leveson-Gower and I. Palmer (1940) • *The Harrow School register* • A. Foornier, *Der Congress von Chatillon: die Politik im Kriege 1814* (1900) • W. F. Ganong, 'Monograph of the evolution of the boundaries of the province of New Brunswick', *Proceedings and Transactions of the Royal Society of Canada*, 2nd ser., 7 (1901–2), 140–447 • *Disraeli, Derby and the conservative party: journals and memoirs of Edward Henry, Lord Stanley, 1849–1869*, ed. J. R. Vincent (1978) • C. H. Stuart, 'The formation of the coalition cabinet of 1852', *TRHS*, 5th ser., 4 (1954), 45–68 • H. E. Howard, 'Brunnow's reports on Aberdeen, 1853', *Cambridge Historical Journal*, 4 (1932–4), 312–21 • H. W. V. Temperley, *England and the Near East: the Crimea* (1936) • G. B. Henderson, *Crimean War diplomacy, and other historical essays* (1947) • H. H. Ingle, *Nesselrode and the Russian rapprochement with Britain, 1836–1844* (1976) • F. W. Hirst, *Gladstone as financier and economist* (1931) • Haddo House, Aberdeenshire, Haddo House MSS • *The Times* (15 Dec 1860) • *The Times* (22 Dec 1860)

Archives BL, corresp. and papers, Add. MSS 43039–43358, 49224, 49273–49285, 51043, 63178 • BM, department of Greek and Roman antiquities, diaries • Haddo House, Aberdeenshire, Haddo House MSS • NA Scot., estate plans, etc. • U. Aberdeen L., special libraries and archives, letters; letters to his son | All Souls Oxf., letters to Sir Charles Richard Vaughan • Archives Nationales, Paris, Guizot MSS • BL, Bathurst MSS • BL, dispatches from J. D. Bligh, Add. MSS 41268, 41275–41276 • BL, corresp. with J. W. Croker, Add. MS 73166 • BL, corresp. with Sir Henry Ellis, Add. MS 41312 • BL, corresp. with W. E. Gladstone, Add. MSS 44088–44089 • BL, corresp. with Lord Heytesbury, Add. MSS 41557–41560 • BL, corresp. with third Baron Holland, Add. MS 51728 • BL, corresp. with fourth Baron Holland, Add. MS 52006 • BL, corresp. with Prince Lieven and Princess Lieven, Add. MSS 47263, 47366 • BL, corresp. and dispatches with Lord Melbourne, Add. MSS 60448, 60453 • BL, letters to Sir Robert Peel, Add. MSS 40312, 40453–40455 • BL, corresp. with Lord Stanmore, his son, Add. MS 48224 • BL, corresp. with Lord Strathnairn, Add. MS 42797 • BL, Robert Wilson MSS • Bodl. Oxf., letters to fourth earl of Clarendon • Bucks. RLSS, letters to Sir William Fremantle and Lord Cottesloe • CKS, letters to Lord Stanhope • Cumbria AS, Carlisle, corresp. with Sir James Graham • Durham RO, letters to Lord Londonderry • Leeds Central Library, Harewood MSS • LPL, letters to William Howley • Lpool RO, letters to fourteenth earl of Derby • NA Scot., Leven MSS, corresp. with Sir John McNeill • NA Scot., Mar and Kellie MSS, corresp. with first and second lords Melville • NL Scot., letters to Edward Ellice; Melville MSS; letters to Lord Stuart de Rothesay; Scott MSS • Norfolk RO, corresp. with Sir Henry Bulwer; letters to Hudson Gurney • North East Lincolnshire Archives, Grimsby, letters to Douglas Gordon, his son • Northumbd RO, Newcastle upon Tyne, letters to Lady Jane Hope • NRA, letters to Baron Neumann • Port Eliot, Saltash, St Germans, letters to third earl of St Germans • priv. coll., dispatches and letters to Lord Ashburton • PRO, corresp. with Stratford Canning, FO 352 • PRO, corresp. with Lord Cardwell, PRO 30/48 • PRO, Colonial Office records • PRO, corresp. and dispatches with Lord Cowley, FO 519 • PRO, corresp. with Lord Ellenborough, PRO 30/12 • PRO, corresp. with Lord Granville, PRO 30/29 • PRO, corresp. with Lord John Russell, PRO 30/22 • PRO, corresp. with William IV and duke of Brunswick, FO 14 • PRO NIre., corresp. as guardian to second marquess of Abercorn; corresp. with Lord Castlereagh • RA, corresp. with Thomas Lawrence • Royal Arch. • Sandon Hall, Staffordshire, Harrowby Manuscript Trust, corresp. with Lord Harrowby • Staffs. RO, letters to Lord Hatherton • U. Aberdeen L., sederunt book of the third earl of Aberdeen's trust • U. Durham L., archives and special collections, dispatches and letters to Viscount Ponsonby • U. Edin., New Coll. L., letters to Thomas Chalmers • U. Nott. L., letters to Lord William Bentinck, etc. • U. Nott. L., corresp. with Lord Castlereagh; letters to J. E. Denison; corresp. with fifth duke of Newcastle • U. Southampton L., corresp. with Lord Palmerston; letters to duke of Wellington • W. Sussex RO, letters to duke of Richmond • W. Yorks. AS, Leeds, corresp. with Lord Canning; papers relating to Hanson family • Wilts. & Swindon RO, corresp. with Sidney Herbert • Woburn Abbey, letters to Lord George William Russell

Likenesses T. Lawrence, oils, exh. RA 1808, Haddo House, Aberdeenshire • C. Turner, mezzotints, pubd 1809–28 (after T. Lawrence), BM, NPG • Nollekens, bust, 1813 • P. C. Wonder, group portrait, pencil and oils, *c.*1826, NPG • T. Lawrence, oils, 1829–30, priv. coll. [*see illus.*] • S. Cousins, mezzotint, pubd 1831 (after T. Lawrence), BM, NPG • Skelton & Hopwood, stipple and line engraving, 1831, BM, NPG • M. A. Shee, oils, *c.*1839, Scot. NPG • G. Hayter, group portrait, oils, 1842 (*Christening of the prince of Wales*), Royal Collection • E. Desmaisons, lithograph, pubd 1843, BM, NPG • F. X. Winterhalter, group portrait, oils, 1844 (*Queen Victoria receiving Louis Philippe at Windsor*), Palais de Versailles, Paris; version, Royal Collection • J. Partridge, oils, 1846, NPG • J. Giles, oils, 1850–59, Haddo House, Aberdeenshire • E. Burton, mezzotint, pubd 1853 (after J. Watson-Gordon), BM • J. Gilbert, group portrait, oils, 1854 (*The Aberdeen cabinet deciding on the expedition to the Crimea*), NPG • Mayall, photograph, 1855, Haddo House, Aberdeenshire; copies Haddo House, Aberdeenshire • E. M. Ward, group portrait, oils, 1855 (*Queen Victoria investing Napoleon III with the order of the Garter*), Royal Collection • W. Theed junior, plaster bust, 1865 (after Nollekens, *c*.1814), Royal Military College, Sandhurst • M. Noble, marble bust, 1871, Westminster Abbey • J. Boehm, effigy, Great Stanmore church, Middlesex • G. Hayter, group portrait, oils (*The House of Commons, 1833*), NPG • M. Healy, oils (after T. Lawrence, 1808), Musée de Versailles, France • J. Partridge, group portrait (*The Fine Arts Commission, 1846*), NPG • D. Wilkie, group portrait, oils (*Queen Victoria presiding over her first council, 1837*), Royal Collection • T. Woolnoth, print (after A. Wivell), BM; repro. in W. Jerdan, *National portrait gallery of illustrious and eminent personages* (1831), 2 • eight cartoons, repro. in *Punch* (8 Oct 1853–2 Dec 1854) • oils (as lord lieutenant of Aberdeenshire), Haddo House, Aberdeenshire

Wealth at death £90,212 2s. 8*d*.: Scottish confirmation sealed in London, 22 June 1861, *CGPLA Eng. & Wales*

Gordon, George Ross (*fl.* 1804–1832). *See under* Gordon, William (1770–1820).

Gordon, George Stuart (1881–1942), college head and literary scholar, was born on 1 February 1881 at County Buildings, Falkirk, the second child and eldest son of William Gordon (*d.* 1925), a police superintendent and later procurator fiscal, and Mary, *née* Napier (*d.* 1925). He was educated at Falkirk high school, and matriculated at the University of Glasgow in 1899. Although he studied classics, graduating MA in 1903, he attracted the notice of Walter Raleigh, professor of English. In 1902 Gordon won a scholarship at Oriel College, Oxford, where he again read classics, getting a first in finals and graduating BA in 1906 and MA in 1909.

Gordon now looked beyond classics: he had won the Stanhope prize for history in 1905, and spent the winter of 1906–7 in Paris engaged in further research, and on his return to Oxford in 1907 he was elected to a prize fellowship in English at Magdalen College, with the encouragement of Raleigh, who held a fellowship there. At Magdalen he proved a stimulating and popular tutor, and found time to edit texts for Oxford University Press. On 29 June 1909 he married Mary Campbell Biggar (*b.* 1883/4), a teacher, whom he had first met at Glasgow. The marriage was happy and produced four children.

In 1913 Gordon was elected professor of English language and literature at Leeds University, but when the First World War broke out a year later he joined the 6th battalion West Yorkshire regiment. Fitting well into army life, he served in France, being mentioned in dispatches, but was wounded in 1917. After convalescing he joined the War Office as a member of the staff of the official military history. In this connection Gordon visited Gallipoli in 1919, where he caught fever. This, and his wounds, affected his health in later life.

On his return to Leeds scholarship gradually gave way to administration. He assembled a strong team, including E. V. Gordon and J. R. R. Tolkien, and the Leeds course became the largest outside Oxford; Tolkien called Gordon 'the very master of men' (*Letters of J. R. R. Tolkein*, 56–8). In 1922 Gordon succeeded Raleigh as Merton professor of English literature in Oxford. The results were again happy: a separate English faculty board was created in 1926, and during his professorship the number of English honours finalists rose by half. He continued Raleigh's practice of offering weekly discussion groups for finalists, at which papers were read and discussed. One attendee, C. S. Lewis, called Gordon 'an honest, wise, kind man, more like a man and less like a don than any I have known' (*All My Road Before Me*, 240–41). In the 1920s he published on Charles Lamb, Shelley, and Andrew Lang, edited nine Shakespeare plays, and was a regular contributor to the *Times Literary Supplement*. These last influential articles were the chief ground of his election to the professorship.

In 1928 Gordon was elected president of Magdalen College. Lewis suggests that he was a compromise candidate (Lewis, *Letters*, 1.781); however, the contrast between the wiry no-nonsense Gordon and his predecessor, the portly and pompous Sir Herbert Warren, undoubtedly made him attractive to those seeking change. He did not disappoint expectations. Much depended on a group of younger fellows; in 1930 Gordon wrote in response to C. H. C. Pirie-Gordon's suggestion for future undergraduates: 'My colleagues are at the moment, I suspect, a little tired and shy of princes, archdukes and the like' (Magd. Oxf., MC:PR33/2/1C/1, fol. 150). However, the changes could not have occurred without his approval. Gordon was noted for the discretion with which he altered aspects of college life, and his presidency saw great improvements in Magdalen's academic performance. Among undergraduates Gordon appeared a benign, if sometimes remote, figure (his daughter Janet, now a beautiful young woman, attracted much greater admiration from the young men of the college, one of whom, the theatre director Hugh Hunt, she married in 1940).

Gordon's position at Magdalen did not deter him from other duties. He served as Gresham professor of rhetoric from 1930 to 1933, and then as professor of poetry from 1933 to 1938. In 1934 he was president of the Classical Association of Scotland, and he was also a member of the General Advisory Council and chairman of the spoken English committee of the BBC. He spent much of 1935 on leave following a breakdown in his health. In 1938 Gordon became vice-chancellor of Oxford University. Almost immediately he prepared Oxford for the threat of war: he successfully negotiated terms for the use of college and university buildings by the government, and once war broke out he ensured that Oxford did not close down as it had in 1914, but rather offered short courses for students before they were called up. The duties of the vice-chancellorship took their toll, however; several fellows of Magdalen felt that he neglected college business. Gordon's term as vice-chancellor ended in October 1941, but his excellence in this office was recognized with the rare award of a DCL *honoris causa* for his services 'during the most difficult and complex term of office that can ever have fallen to the lot of any Vice-Chancellor' (*Oxford Magazine*, 6 March 1941, 225). Moreover, the 'dignity of his presence', his oratorical skills, business sense, and 'urbanity and unfailing good humour' were much admired (*Oxford Magazine*, 16 Oct 1941, 1).

Plans for future research were immediately dashed by the onset of cancer. After a long fight Gordon died in the president's lodgings on 12 March 1942. His funeral was held two days later in Magdalen College chapel, and he was buried in Holywell cemetery. Although Gordon produced many editions and proved himself an accomplished lecturer and broadcaster, publishing several of his talks, he found writing difficult, and was a stern self-critic. In later life he regretted this change in his career, but his contribution to English scholarship as an administrator and popularizer was considerable.

The praise from Tolkien and Lewis reveals Gordon's talents for discreet encouragement, and one appreciation said he was possibly 'Oxford's most delightful talker' (*The Times*, 16 March 1942). His posthumous publications included *Anglo-American Literary Relations* in 1942, *Shakespearian Comedy* in 1944, and *Lives of Authors* in 1950. In 1945 Mary Campbell Gordon published a biography of her husband which presented a portrait of a sociable, clubbable, and humorous man, but which otherwise reveals very little about Oxford's English school during his time, or about Magdalen under his presidency. His letters, published in 1943, which show his gift for friendship and his ready wit, are equally unrevealing.

R. H. DARWALL-SMITH

Sources M. C. Gordon, *The letters of George S. Gordon, 1902–1942* (1943) • M. C. Gordon, *The life of George S. Gordon, 1881–1942* (1945) • *Magdalen College Record* (1911); (1922); (1934) • *WWW* • *The Times* (13 March 1942); (16 March 1942) • *Oxford Times* (13 March 1942); (20 March 1942) • C. S. Lewis, *Collected letters, vol. I: family letters, 1905–1931*, ed. W. Hooper (2000) • *All my road before me: the diary of C. S. Lewis, 1922–27*, ed. W. Hooper (1991) • *Letters of J. R. R. Tolkien*, ed. H. Carpenter and C. Tolkien (1981) • H. Carpenter, *J. R. R. Tolkien: a biography* (1977) • P. Addison, 'Oxford and the Second World War', *Hist. U. Oxf.* 8: *20th cent.*, 168–88 • R. Currie, 'The arts and social sciences', *Hist. U. Oxf.* 8: *20th cent.*, 109–38 • R. A. Denniston, 'Publishing and bookselling', *Hist. U. Oxf.* 8: *20th cent.*, 451–70 • K. Burk, *Troublemaker: the life and history of A. J. P. Taylor* (2000) • *Oxford Magazine* (6 March 1941); (16 Oct 1941) • b. cert. • m. cert. • d. cert. • *CGPLA Eng. & Wales* (1942) • students' registers, U. Glas., Archives and Business Records Centre • president's letter-book, Magd. Oxf., MC:PR33/2/1C/1, fol. 150

Archives Magd. Oxf., papers incl. Gallipoli papers and president's letter-books, MC:PR33 | NL Scot., corresp. with D. N. Smith, MS 19602 • U. Birm., letters to C. T. Onions, Onions 173–187

Likenesses W. Coldstream, portrait, Magd. Oxf. • C. Ellis, drawing, priv. coll.; repro. in Gordon, *Life of George S. Gordon*, frontispiece • photographs, repro. in Gordon, *Life of George S. Gordon* • photographs, repro. in Gordon, *Letters of George S. Gordon*

Wealth at death £4128 5s.: resworn probate, 11 May 1942, *CGPLA Eng. & Wales*

Gordon, George William (*c.*1820–1865), politician in Jamaica, was born in Jamaica to a wealthy sugar planter, Joseph Gordon, and a slave woman. His father freed Gordon and paid for his early education. At about the age of ten Gordon was employed by his godfather, James Daly, at Black River in the parish of St Elizabeth. He subsequently began business as a produce merchant in Kingston and later became an extensive landowner in many parts of the island. By 1843 he claimed to be worth £10,000.

In the mid-1840s Gordon married a white woman, Mary Jane Perkins; she was a widow whose mother had established a school for young ladies in Kingston. Gordon was a founder of the Jamaica Mutual Life Assurance Society and was appointed a justice of the peace in seven parishes across the island. He also became proprietor of the revived *Watchman* newspaper in the late 1850s. However, Gordon's business affairs ran into serious difficulties, especially in the 1860s; he lost heavily in coffee dealings, and by 1865 he had accumulated liabilities of over £35,000.

Even before 1865 Gordon's politics were radically different from most other Jamaican politicians. By the late 1850s Gordon was supporting the interests of the former slave population and saw himself increasingly as their spokesman. Sydney Olivier, Baron Olivier, a governor of Jamaica in the early twentieth century, described Gordon as 'a man of deep sensibility and of real benevolence of disposition' who was deeply affected by the injustices suffered by the common people. Gordon was 'irrepressibly voluble' and often indiscreet; his politics and his religious outlook dismayed the established authorities on the island (Olivier, 115, 97).

Originally a member of the established church, Gordon later joined the Presbyterians, and also frequented the Congregational church. On Christmas day 1861 he was publicly baptized by the Revd James Phillippo, Jamaica's leading Baptist missionary. Gordon had close links to the Native Baptists, especially to the group led by Paul Bogle in St Thomas in the East, and had his own native Baptist chapel in Kingston known as the 'Tabernacle'. Bogle, who served as Gordon's political agent in St Thomas in the East, was to be the leader of the Morant Bay rebellion in 1865.

Gordon became a political enemy of Edward Eyre, who was appointed lieutenant-governor of Jamaica in 1862 and was subsequently made governor. As a magistrate in Morant Bay, Gordon reported to Eyre about the death of a poor, sick man who had been sent to the local gaol where he had died. Eyre's response was to censure Gordon and remove him from the magistracy. Gordon never forgave Eyre and spent the next three years as a delegate to the house of assembly lambasting the governor.

In 1865 political tensions in Jamaica increased considerably. During that year Gordon travelled extensively throughout the island and among his constituents in St Thomas in the East. He spoke at meetings on behalf of the peasantry and railed against the planter class and against Eyre. At the same time he was embroiled in a legal battle against the *custos* of St Thomas in the East, who had thrown him off the parish vestry. When the Morant Bay rebellion broke out in October 1865, Governor Eyre immediately took steps to suppress the rebellion militarily, and had Gordon arrested for his alleged involvement. Although Gordon was in Kingston, which was under civil jurisdiction, he was transferred to Morant Bay where martial law was in force, and was charged with high treason and sedition. The court martial was a farce; when the Jamaica royal commission subsequently investigated the case, it could find no evidence of Gordon's complicity in the revolt. The court none the less found Gordon guilty, a sentence which Governor Eyre approved. Gordon was executed at 7.10 a.m. on 23 October 1865. He was hanged on the centre arch of the court house, and seventeen others were hanged below him.

In his final letter to his wife Gordon proclaimed his innocence: he did 'not deserve the sentence, for I never advised or took part in any insurrection: all I ever did was to recommend the people who complained to seek redress in a legitimate way' (Heuman, *'Killing Time'*, 150). Gordon's body was dumped, with those of others who were hanged at Morant Bay, in a mass grave behind the court house. Vindication came later; Gordon is now a national hero in Jamaica. GAD HEUMAN

Sources G. J. Heuman, *'The killing time': the Morant Bay rebellion in Jamaica* (1994) • A. Hart, *The life of George William Gordon* (1972) • G. J. Heuman, *Between black and white: race, politics and the free coloreds in Jamaica, 1792–1865* (1981) • W. A. Roberts, *Six great Jamaicans: biographical sketches* (1952) • Lord Olivier [S. H. Olivier], *The myth of Governor Eyre* (1933) • D. King, *A sketch of the late Mr G. W. Gordon, Jamaica* (1866) • D. Fletcher, *The life of the Honourable George W. Gordon, the martyr of Jamaica* (1867)

Archives Bodl. RH, Anti-Slavery Society papers, letters • PRO, Colonial Office papers, letters

Likenesses portrait, Institute of Jamaica, Kingston; repro. in Heuman, *'Killing time'*, xvi

Wealth at death £35,000 in debt: Hart, *Life of George William Gordon*

Gordon, Henrietta (*c*.1628–1701), courtier, was the daughter of John Gordon (*d*. 1630), created viscount of Melgum and Lord Aboyne in 1627, and Sophia (*d*. 1642), daughter of Francis Hay, ninth earl of Erroll. She was brought up by her mother at Aboyne Castle after her father, the second son of the first marquess of Huntly, was killed in the burning of the Tower of Frendraught in the course of a feud in October 1630. From 1638 Father Gilbert Blackhall lived in the castle as Lady Aboyne's confessor, and before she died early in 1642 she entrusted him with preserving Henrietta, her only surviving child, from attempts to convert her to protestantism. Blackhall visited Henrietta's grandmother, the dowager countess of Huntly, in France, and her uncle and guardian, the second marquess of Huntly, but neither showed much interest in her spiritual fate. Undeterred, Blackhall approached Anne of Austria, queen of France, and she got Louis XIII to write to Huntly promising Henrietta a position at the French court. Again Huntly proved apathetic, but he was persuaded to send for his niece who was living with protestant relatives. She was reluctant to leave Edinburgh, but was lured north by false promises to Huntly's castle at Bog of Gight. She then agreed to the plan to take her to France, but it being illegal to take children abroad to be brought up as Roman Catholics it was only after some difficulty that she was able to sail from Aberdeen on 25 July 1643.

Once in Paris, Henrietta Gordon was sent to the convent of the Filles de Ste Marie, rue St Antoine, near the Bastille, to learn French, but she feared being forced to become a nun and once she had mastered French she became so unruly that the mother superior begged the queen to remove her. She was sent for six months to the countess of Brienne, keeper of the queen's privy purse, who trained and assessed 'court novices'—potential maids of honour. However, she proved so rude and disrespectful that she was judged unfit for court. Again a religious solution was tried, and she was sent to the convent of Charonne and appointed a canoness, which did not involve a nun's lifelong vows. There she soon quarrelled with the mother superior, and begged Blackhall to have her moved. Brienne washed her hands of the girl, but the queen, though exasperated, agreed that Blackhall could decide her future. After much effort he found her a place in the convent of St Nicholas de Lorraine in January 1647. When that closed in August she moved to Fervacques in the faubourg St Germain. With the withdrawal of the court from Paris and the outbreak of the Fronde insurrection in January 1649 Blackhall was in despair as to how to ensure Henrietta's safety, but the queen remembered her and ordered that she be brought to court, so she was escorted out of Paris and taken to St Germain-en-Laye. Offered a position in the service of the princess de Condé, she rejected it as beneath her. It is to be suspected that by this time many were getting tired of the arrogance of this young refugee. However, eventually she was appointed a supernumerary maid of honour to Anne of Austria (now dowager queen), and after two years was accepted as a full maid of honour. Once 'she was at courte she vilified me [Blackhall] altogether', denouncing all the help he had given her as the folly 'of an old dotting man' (Blakhal, 208), and his *Breiffe Narration*, addressed to her, contains an account of all he had done for her, and a lament at her ingratitude.

Now an established figure at court, Henrietta caught the attention of the effeminate monsieur, Philippe, duke of Orléans, and she was thought to be a bad influence on him, for (though she was scarred by smallpox and was twelve years his senior) it was complained at one point that 'he amuses himself with nothing but ordering dresses for Mademoiselle de Gourdon, and thinks of nothing but decorating himself as a girl' (Montpensier, 2.97). When in 1660 Monsieur married Princess Henrietta of England (the youngest daughter of Charles I) Gordon became Madame's *dame d'attour* (lady of the bedchamber). After her death in 1670 she held the same post in the household of the duke's second wife, Charlotte Elizabeth, daughter of the elector of Bavaria. She seems to have been on bad terms with both her mistresses, being alleged to have been responsible for slandering the first, and to have been hated by the second. She died in March 1701 (the same year as the duke). Several 'liaisons' were attributed to her, but she never married.

Most sources are hostile to Henrietta Gordon. That she was arrogant and ungrateful may be related to the early deaths of her parents and to the trauma of being torn from her family and country for the sake of religion.

Determined not to be closeted in a nunnery, she had to fight hard to establish herself in the French court. The patronage of the duke of Orléans and her own determination ensured her survival, but she seems to have been widely unpopular. DAVID STEVENSON

Sources *DNB* · *Scots peerage* · G. Blakhal, *A breiffe narration of the services done to three noble ladyes*, ed. J. Stuart (1844) · A. M. L. d'Orléans, duchesse de Montpensier, *Memoirs of Mademoiselle de Montpensier*, 3 vols. (1848) · L. De Rouvray, duc de St Simon, *Mémoires de St Simon*, ed. A. De Boislisle, 45 vols. (1879–1930)

Gordon [*née* Mordaunt], **Henrietta, duchess of Gordon (1681/2–1760)**, Jacobite sympathizer, was the daughter of Charles *Mordaunt, third earl of Peterborough and first earl of Monmouth (1658?–1735), and his first wife, Carey (*d.* 1709), daughter of Sir Alexander Fraser of Durris, Kincardineshire, physician to Charles II, and his wife, Mary Carey, maid of honour to Catherine of Braganza. Her father was a whig and a protestant, but the Mordaunt family had been prominent Roman Catholics, and this may have recommended her to Alexander *Gordon, marquess of Huntly, later second duke of Gordon (*c.*1678–1728), whose marriage contract with her was signed on 7 October 1706 and 5 February 1707; they married on 13 February 1707. Her husband, a Jacobite, was present at the battle of Sheriffmuir in 1715, surrendered later, and spent eight months in captivity. On his release he took no further part in public affairs but, kindly and affable, lived with Henrietta in great state at Gordon Castle to which he succeeded, with the dukedom, in 1716. A woman of energy and decision, she was interested in agricultural improvement and was credited with bringing ploughmen and their ploughs from England. On 1 June 1720 she was paying William Strachan in Aberdeen £8 for the freight of 300 lime trees, and on 4 September 1734 she gave a joiner £3 4*s.* for '6 big chairs to the garden' (Gordon Castle muniments, NA Scot., GD44/51/379/13/10).

By that time Henrietta was running the estates for her eldest surviving son, Cosmo, third duke of Gordon, for her husband had died on 28 November 1728, leaving her with five young sons and seven daughters. Henrietta had been raised as a protestant and was determined to bring up her own children as protestants too. In 1730 the general assembly of the Church of Scotland sent a letter congratulating her on this resolve, and in 1735 the government granted her a pension of £1000 a year. Letters from the 1730s show her protecting the Gordon tenants against a harsh exciseman, persuading people to vote for Alexander Udny as MP for Aberdeenshire in 1734 (he was unsuccessful), and discussing the settlement of the estate boundaries with Sir Robert Menzies of Weem.

When the young duke reached the age of eighteen in 1738, Henrietta decided to move out of Gordon Castle and purchased Prestonhall House, near Dalkeith in Edinburghshire, at a judicial sale for the sum of £8877. She went to live there with her younger children but the mansion was dilapidated, and she commissioned the architect William Adam to convert it into a much larger handsome structure three storeys high, with a wing at either side. About 1750 she sat for her portrait, probably to Philippe Mercier. Rather plump by this time, she is shown with a large, dominating nose, strongly marked eyebrows, and a firm mouth. Although seated in an armchair, she appears to be wearing a riding habit of somewhat masculine cut. In her right hand is Adam's plan for Prestonhall, and she points to it proudly with her other hand.

Despite her protestantism, Henrietta shared her late husband's Jacobite sympathies, and when Prince Charles Edward arrived in Scotland she supported his cause. Charles Edward defeated the government forces at Prestonpans, established himself in Edinburgh, and then marched south into England. Learning that he would pass her gates on the way, Henrietta ordered a breakfast to be prepared for him and laid out by the side of the road. When the government heard of this gesture, it cancelled her pension. Henrietta died at Prestonhall on 11 October 1760, at the age of seventy-eight, and according to the index of genealogies, birth briefs, and funeral escutcheons in the Lyon office in Edinburgh was buried in Nairn church, Moray. However, the accounts of the treasurer of the kirk session at Elgin, where her husband's vault was, record the payment of £25 4*s.* 'at the Dowager Duchess's burial' (*Records of Elgin*), suggesting that even if she was not buried there the Elgin kirk session paid some of the funeral expenses, and there is a monumental inscription to her in Elgin Cathedral.

ROSALIND K. MARSHALL

Sources *Scots peerage*, 4.551–2 · GEC, *Peerage*, 6.4; 10.502 · *The records of Elgin, 1234–1800* (1908), 344 · F. J. Grant, *Index to genealogies, birthbriefs and funeral escutcheons recorded in the Lyon office*, Scottish RS, 31 (1908), 21 · R. Douglas, *The peerage of Scotland*, 2nd edn, ed. J. P. Wood, 1 (1813), 655 · NA Scot., Clerk of Penicuik MSS, GD 18/5405 · miscellaneous MSS, NA Scot., GD 1/337/28; GD 1/636/1 · Gordon Castle muniments, NA Scot., GD 44/33/18/2; GD 44/51/379/13/10 · J. M. Simpson, 'Aberdeenshire', HoP, *Commons, 1715–54*, 1.381 · E. Cruickshanks, 'Aberdeen burghs', HoP, *Commons, 1715–54*, 1.395–6

Archives NA Scot., papers | NA Scot., Gordon Castle muniments · NA Scot., Clerk of Penicuik MSS

Likenesses J. Alexander or C. Alexander, oils, 1742; sold from Gordon Castle in 1938 · attrib. P. Mercier, oils, *c.*1750, priv. coll. · Lely, oils (as a child), priv. coll. · black and white negative (after portrait by P. Mercier?), Scot. NPG; repro. in R. K. Marshall, *Women in Scotland, 1660–1780* (1979)

Gordon, Henry [Harry] **Panmure (1837–1902)**, stockbroker, was born on 22 October 1837 at Killiechassie, Perthshire, the son of Henry George Gordon, a director of the Union Bank of London. Baptized Panmure-Gordon, he dropped the hyphen from his name later in life, and was universally known as 'P. G.'. He was distantly related to Lord Byron and later bequeathed his collection of Byron memorabilia to Harrow School, where he had been educated before going on to Oxford University and then spending a year in Bonn. In 1856 he was commissioned into the 10th hussars, but resigned his commission in 1860 following the bankruptcy of his father.

Gordon went out to China, where he joined Lindsay & Co. of Shanghai (later part of Jardine Matheson & Co.), and served under General Gordon at the time of the Taiping rebellion, raising and commanding the Shanghai mounted ranger volunteers. He returned to London in

1865 and became a member of the stock exchange and a junior partner in J. and A. Scrimgeour & Co., in Old Broad Street. In 1876 he founded his own firm of stockbrokers, Gordon & Co., in Hatton Court, Threadneedle Street. This became Panmure Gordon & Co. a year later. In 1885 it became Panmure Gordon, Hill & Co., and in 1902 it reverted to Panmure Gordon & Co. Gordon married, late in life, Carrie Hall (*d.* 1913), daughter of Thomas Beverley Hall, of Beverley, in Yorkshire. His wife was some twenty years his junior, and there were no children of the marriage.

Panmure Gordon & Co. became one of the largest and most active firms of stockbrokers in the City, being particularly well known for underwriting numerous issues of stock by both British and United States breweries, as well as many loans on the part of Far Eastern and South American governments, including China and Japan and several of the states of Brazil. Gordon was awarded the Grand Officer's Star of the royal order of Jakovo in 1898 for arranging a Serbian loan, and the order of the Rising Sun for his services as sole broker to the Japanese government. Other companies for which the firm acted included the Mashonaland Railway Company and Shell Transport and Trading Company. He is said to have pioneered industrial preference shares and when Liptons was floated on the stock exchange in 1898 he was the first to issue shares at a premium.

For many years Gordon lived in Brighton, at 34 Adelaide Crescent, travelling to London every weekday by train. Later he lived at Charles Street and 5 Carlton House Terrace in London, and leased a country house at Loudwater Park, near Rickmansworth. The extravagance of his personal lifestyle became legendary. He once remarked that he spent £2000 a month on himself, this being the cost of the bare necessities of life for a gentleman, with any luxuries costing more. At Loudwater he accumulated the largest collection of carriages in the world, brought red deer from Scotland for the park, and kept a gondola on the lake. He was a good shot, renting moors in Scotland almost every year, and a keen angler. He bred collie dogs, and kept a large stable. He entertained upon an expansive scale: the prince of Wales, later Edward VII, was a frequent visitor to Loudwater. Gordon's wardrobe was equally legendary; a fire at Loudwater was said to have destroyed 1100 of his ties alone. At the time of his death he was reputed to have owned 900 pairs of trousers and over 300 greatcoats. He travelled widely, publishing in 1892 *The Land of the Almighty Dollar*, an account of a visit to the United States. He was a founder member, and in due course president, of the Scottish Kennel Club, but resigned the year before his death after losing an action brought in the Scottish courts over the unnatural manipulation of the ears of a collie dog.

Gordon's domestic life became clouded in his last years, as he found it increasingly difficult to adapt his bachelor ways to the demands of a young and socially active wife. He died suddenly on 1 September 1902, apparently of heart failure, at Bad Nauheim, in Germany, where he had gone to take the cure, and he was buried there. Three years later his widow married Frank Geiger; she died in 1913. Gordon's obituarist in the *Financial News* (3 September 1902) wrote that 'he had a cheery smile and bright word for all who came in contact with him'. Gordon was one of the most successful stockbrokers of his day, especially in the sphere of new issues. One of the most talked-about men in the City of London, he has been described as 'the extrovert *par excellence* of an extrovert community' (Kynaston, 1.359). MICHAEL REED

Sources B. H. D. MacDermot, *Panmure Gordon & Co., 1876–1976: a century of stockbroking* (privately printed, London, [1976]) • D. Kynaston, *The City of London*, 1 (1994) • D. Kynaston, 'Gordon, Henry Panmure', *DBB* • *The Times* (3 Sept 1902) • *Financial News* (3 Sept 1902) • *Financial Times* (3 Sept 1902) • *Daily Telegraph* (3 Sept 1902) • *Daily Express* (3 Sept 1902) • *Ladies Field* (13 Sept 1902) • *Illustrated Kennel News* (5 Sept 1902) • *The Tatler* (10 Sept 1902) • *The Sketch* (10 Sept 1902) • *The World* (10 Sept 1902) • *CGPLA Eng. & Wales* (1902) • General Register Office for Scotland, Edinburgh • d. cert.

Likenesses T. Robinson, pencil drawing, 1898, NPG • H. von Herkomer, portrait; formerly with Panmure Gordon & Co. • photograph, repro. in *Ladies Field* • photograph, repro. in *Illustrated Kennel News* • photograph, repro. in *The Tatler*

Wealth at death £86,955 17*s*. 7*d*.: probate, 10 Nov 1902, *CGPLA Eng. & Wales*

Gordon, Sir Henry William (1818–1887), army officer, born at Blackheath, Kent, on 18 July 1818, was the eldest son of Lieutenant-General Henry William Gordon (1785/6–1865) and his wife, Elizabeth (1794–1873), daughter of Samuel Enderby, shipowner, of Croom's Hill, Blackheath, and brother of Charles George *Gordon. He was educated at a private school and at Sandhurst, and entered the army in August 1835, serving in the 59th foot. He was employed on the staff in the East and West Indies and China. In 1847–8 he was an assistant poor-law commissioner in Ireland, and was a relief inspector during the famine. In 1855 he left the army and entered the Ordnance department. From March 1855 to July 1856 he was in the Crimea, his last service abroad. He was appointed CB (civil) in January 1857, and KCB in August 1877. In January 1870 he was made controller, and in November 1875 commissary-general. He married, on 20 June 1851, Henrietta Rose, widow of Captain Granet and fourth daughter of Lieutenant-General W. *Staveley (a Peninsula and Waterloo veteran); they had a large family. One of his sons was drowned on board the *Captain* on 7 September 1870. Gordon, who was on very close terms with his famous brother, and whom he resembled in his simplicity of life and integrity of character, wrote *Events in the Life of Charles George Gordon* (1886). Gordon died at his home, Oat Hall, Haywards Heath, Sussex, on 22 October 1887, and is commemorated on the monument he erected to his brother in St Paul's Cathedral.

C. L. KINGSFORD, *rev.* ROGER T. STEARN

Sources *The Times* (24 Oct 1887) • *The Times* (26 Oct 1887) • *The Graphic* (26 Nov 1887) • *ILN* (29 Oct 1887) • J. Pollock, *Gordon: the man behind the legend* (1993) • A. Nutting, *Gordon: martyr and misfit* (1966) • Boase, *Mod. Eng. biog.* • Kelly, *Handbk* • Burke, *Peerage*

Archives BL, corresp. and papers, Add. MSS 52398–52408 | BL, corresp. with Mary Gordon, Add. MS 51300

Likenesses engraving, repro. in *The Graphic*

Wealth at death £1746 18*s*. 11*d*.: probate, 3 Dec 1887, *CGPLA Eng. & Wales*

Gordon, Dame Ishbel Maria, marchioness of Aberdeen and Temair (1857–1939). *See under* Gordon, John Campbell, first marquess of Aberdeen and Temair (1847–1934).

Gordon, James [*known as* James Gordon Huntly] **(1541–1620)**, Jesuit, was born in Huntly, Aberdeenshire, the fifth son of George *Gordon, fourth earl of Huntly, and Elizabeth, eldest daughter of Robert Keith, Lord Keith, and sister to the fourth Earl Marischal. He later exerted a strong influence on his nephew, George *Gordon, first marquess of Huntly, and his sister Margaret Gordon, divorced wife of the future eighth Lord Forbes (two of whose sons became Capuchin friars). James Gordon entered the Society of Jesus at Cologne on 20 September 1563 and studied theology at Rome. A priest at Vienna from 1571, he was latterly professor of controversial theology there. Thus prepared for debate, Gordon set out for Scotland in August 1584 with his fellow Jesuit William Crichton. When their vessel was intercepted at sea by the Dutch, the merchant who had hired it identified the priests as hostile to protestantism in Scotland and had them arrested. Fearing the earl of Huntly, however, he quickly arranged for Gordon's release, though Crichton became a prisoner of the English government. Gordon's landing in Scotland that autumn, when protestant lords exiled to England were beginning to recover confidence, provoked strong objections. He went north to his nephew and worked among the Gordons. Two other Jesuits, Edmund Hay and John Durie, arrived the following July, but events were moving towards the English-backed coup of November 1585. One of Queen Elizabeth's conditions for a subsidy to James VI, now at the start of his reign, was the expulsion of Jesuits: Gordon left early in the following year.

The execution of Mary, queen of Scots, created a more favourable climate for Roman Catholic missionary activity. With Philip II planning to land Spanish troops in England or Scotland, and James VI letting it be known that his conversion was not out of the question, Gordon (a distant kinsman) was invited to court on 5 February 1588. There he debated controversial points of religion with James for five hours in front of courtiers and protestant ministers, 'praising the king's good parts, and saying that no-one could use his arguments better nor quote the scriptures and other authorities more effectively' (*CSP Spain, 1587–1603*, 260). The king showed his pleasure in the exchange by having a summary of the proceedings drawn up and signed by Gordon, but neither on this occasion nor during the two months that Gordon spent following his sovereign 'to the chase and everywhere else' (Forbes-Leith, 203) did he effect the desired conversion. Such was the growing uproar over his presence at court that he withdrew to the north again. There he debated publicly with George Hay, a priest turned minister who had twice before contested Roman Catholic doctrine with Ninian Winzet and Edmund Hay. Despite sending home for a horse-load of books, this champion of protestant reform lost the argument, in the view of those listening gentlemen who in October 1594 were to bring victory at Glenlivet to the 'popish earls'—Huntly and Francis Hay, ninth earl of Erroll.

Now required by the king to leave the country, Gordon made a public departure from Aberdeen in a vessel bound for France, but then left it on a boat which took him north to his sister, the countess of Sutherland. Before Glenlivet he travelled to Rome on James's behalf, and then returned to Aberdeen on 16 July 1594 with a papal legate and a 10,000 crown subsidy. The gold was confiscated by local magistrates before being reclaimed and used to finance the army which fought successfully against the earl of Argyll in October. Gordon's next visit to Scotland in 1597 was too late to prevent Huntly and Erroll making an accommodation with the established church which, though insincere and later repudiated, damaged Roman Catholic morale. Gordon returned late in the following year, and spent six months in Edinburgh between palace and castle seeking occasions to renew the debate, but James VI (the English throne in sight) maintained his middle course. Gordon, who was strongly against the dethronement of heretical monarchs, 'betook himself to Denmark to await better days' (Bellesheim, 344). Following the death of James Tyrie in 1597 he became superior of the Scottish mission and apostolic nuncio for Ireland, but his age and the political situation prevented further journeys.

Gordon's principal base was at Pont-à-Mousson in Lorraine, where a college founded at Tournai by the Scots priest James Cheyne had been relocated; later it became the Scots College at Douai. Gordon taught philosophy, scripture, and Hebrew. Jesuit records also have him at Antwerp, Lille, and St Omer before his move to Bordeaux as rector in 1604. Gordon's final posting to Paris came nine years later. Now in his seventies, he limited himself to writing. Two Latin works on current religious controversies (1612, 1618) appeared together in a third, enlarged edition as *Controversiae Christiane fidei … epitome*, published at Cologne in 1620. This followed an English version, *A Summary of Controversies*, published in 1618 at St Omer, where several English translations of his writings had also been issued in 1614. Gordon died at the Collège de Clermont in Paris on 16 April 1620, where the 'interment was carried out with unusual pomp and ceremony' (Gordon, 556). Gordon is sometimes referred to as James Gordon Huntly to distinguish him from his contemporary Jesuit namesake, James Gordon (1553–1641). ALASDAIR ROBERTS

Sources A. Bellesheim, *History of the Catholic Church in Scotland*, ed. and trans. D. O. H. Blair, 3 (1889) · W. Forbes-Leith, ed., *Narratives of Scottish Catholics under Mary Stuart and James VI* (1885) · *CSP Spain, 1587–1603* · J. F. S. Gordon, ed., *The Catholic church in Scotland* (1874) · T. G. Law, 'English Jesuits and Scottish intrigues, 1581–82', *Collected essays and reviews of Thomas Graves Law*, ed. P. H. Brown (1904), 217–43 · H. Chadwick, 'Father William Creichton S.I., and a recently discovered letter (1589)', *Archivum Historicum Societatis Iesu*, 6 (1937), 259–86 · H. Chadwick, 'A memoir of Fr Edmund Hay S.I.', *Archivum Historicum Societatis Iesu*, 8 (1939), 66–85 · J. H. Pollen, *The Counter-Reformation in Scotland* (1921)

Gordon, James (1553–1641), Jesuit, was a younger son of James Gordon, laird of Lesmore, Aberdeenshire, a cadet branch of the noble house of Huntly; the Society of Jesus records him as 'junior' in relation to James Gordon 'Huntly' (1541–1620), son of George Gordon, fourth earl of

Huntly. His mother was a Barclay of Gartly. Gordon left Scotland at fourteen and entered the society at Paris six years later. He was ordained at Toulouse and became a professed Jesuit there in 1589. After teaching theology with distinction at the same college he was made rector in 1599. Almost all Gordon's posts were in south-west France: Bordeaux, Agen (as consultor to the provincial), and then Poitiers from 1614 to 1628. In 1595 it had been proposed that he should go to Scotland as superior in place of his namesake 'auld Mr James' (Durkan, 6), and this was again suggested in 1607 following the retirement of Robert Abercrombie.

A letter sent by Gordon to his general, Claudio Acquaviva, from Bordeaux on 27 February 1607, asking to be excused, provides biographical information unavailable in print. Gordon felt spiritually inadequate for a life away from the security of Jesuit houses, facing the hardships of a Scottish mission which had proved fatal to the vocations of two members of the society. Moreover, two of his late brother's sons (born of separate mothers, both illegitimate in the eyes of kirk authorities who did not recognize Roman Catholic marriage) were disputing the succession, rendering his own position awkward. In addition Gordon suffered from a chronic physical problem and found travel by sea 'quite awful'. Having left home forty years before he had also forgotten his native tongue, and could only communicate with Scots in French or Latin. Gordon's request was helped by the fact that James Gordon Huntly wanted to go to Scotland, where he would be healthier than at Toulouse, and where he would be much more effective in dealing with the marquess of Huntly and other Roman Catholic nobles. Finally, Gordon's literary work seemed to him more likely to bring glory to God than anything he could do for the Scots.

Gordon's publications include his *Chronological Work* of world history, a treatise entitled *Catholic Truth*, and a three-volume *Holy Bible* with innovatively simple commentaries. Gordon is also said to have marked the marriage of Charles I to a Roman Catholic French princess with a volume appropriately entitled 'De rebus Britanniae novis et in nuptias Caroli regis Britanniae'. Gordon was procurator of the Scottish mission in 1628, channelling funds at a time when the Jesuit effort was at its height. In old age he went to the French court as confessor to Louis XIII, and he died there on 17 November 1641. ALASDAIR ROBERTS

Sources J. F. S. Gordon, ed., *The Catholic church in Scotland* (1874) • Gordon to Claudio Acquaviva, 27 Feb 1607, Jesuit Archives, London • J. Durkan, 'William Murdoch and the early Jesuit mission in Scotland', *Innes Review*, 35 (1984), 3–11 • P. J. Shearman, 'Father Alexander McQuhirrie', *Innes Review*, 6 (1955), 22–45 • W. Temple, *The thanage of Fermartyn* (1894) • J. M. Bulloch and others, eds., *The house of Gordon*, 1, Third Spalding Club, 26 (1903)

Gordon, James, second Viscount Aboyne (*d.* **1649**), royalist nobleman, was the second son of George *Gordon, second marquess of Huntly (*d.* 1649), and of Lady Anne (1594–1638), daughter of Archibald *Campbell, seventh earl of Argyll (1575/6–1638). He succeeded his father in the title of Viscount Aboyne on 13 June 1636, when the latter became marquess. After the arrest of his father in Aberdeen by the covenanters in the first bishops' war of 1639, he went to England, and Charles I granted him a commission as king's lieutenant in the north of Scotland. He hoped to gain help from the marquess of Hamilton's fleet in the Firth of Forth, but the latter complained that when 'I inquyred for his propositiones, he tolde me he had none' (Gardiner, *Hamilton Papers*, 89) and could give him little assistance. Returning north to lead royalist resistance, Aboyne arrived off Aberdeen on 2 June. He attempted to advance, but he was 'young and inexperienced' and on 16 June his force, 'ridiculously and grossly managed', was forced to retreat by the Earl Marischal (J. Gordon, 2.267, 275). After fighting at the Bridge of Dee on 18 and 19 June he was again forced to retreat, but was saved from further embarrassment by news that a peace had been made. In July he unwisely travelled through Edinburgh in an open coach, and this 'insolent and triumphing behaviour of that unhappie spark … yet reicking [reeking] from our blood in the North' (*Letters … Baillie*, 1.220) provoked a mob attack on him.

In 1643 Aboyne was involved in negotiations with the earl of Antrim to obtain help from Ireland for royalists in Scotland, and in April 1644 he participated in the marquess of Montrose's raid on Dumfries. He then served in the garrison of Carlisle until April 1645, when he escaped the besieged town and joined Montrose in Scotland. He fought at Auldearn (9 May), Alford (2 July), and Kilsyth (15 August). However, after Kilsyth, 'esteemeing himselfe slighted' (P. Gordon, 154), Aboyne 'took a caprice' (Napier, 2.572), and withdrew with several hundred men from the royalist army. When Montrose himself was forced back to the highlands, Aboyne rejoined him for a time, but then withdrew. The death of his brother Lord Gordon at Alford meant that Aboyne was now his father's heir, and his conduct was probably increasingly influenced by the interests of his Gordon kin. With the end of the highland war in 1646 he went into exile, and died, unmarried, in Paris in February 1649 'of an ague' (P. Gordon, 205).

DAVID STEVENSON

Sources *DNB* • *Scots peerage* • GEC, *Peerage* • M. Napier, *Memoirs of the marquis of Montrose*, 2 vols. (1856) • J. Gordon, *History of Scots affairs from 1637–1641*, ed. J. Robertson and G. Grub, 3 vols., Spalding Club, 1, 3, 5 (1841) • P. Gordon, *A short abridgement of Britane's distemper*, ed. J. Dunn, Spalding Club, 10 (1844) • R. Gordon and G. Gordon, *A genealogical history of the earldom of Sutherland … with a continuation to the year 1651* (1813) • S. R. Gardiner, *History of the great civil war, 1642–1649*, new edn, 4 vols. (1893) • *The letters and journals of Robert Baillie*, ed. D. Laing, 3 vols. (1841–2) • [J. Hamilton, duke of Hamilton], *The Hamilton papers: being selections from original letters … relating to … 1638–1650*, ed. S. R. Gardiner, CS, new ser., 27 (1880)

Gordon, James [*called* the Parson of Rothiemay] (**1617–1686**), historian and map maker, was born at Kinmundy, Aberdeenshire, on 17 May 1617, the fifth son of Robert *Gordon of Straloch (1580–1661) and his wife, Katharine Irvine. He probably graduated from Marischal College, Aberdeen, in 1634, or from King's College, Aberdeen, in 1636. Following the refusal of the covenant by the previous incumbent, Alexander Innes, James was presented to the parish of Rothiemay, Banffshire, in September 1640, although not admitted until May 1641. His appointment enabled him to continue his father's scholarly pursuits, as indicated in his father's statement in Jan Blaeu's *Theatrum orbis terrarum* that James was trained in chorographic description and was his nominated successor.

In 1642 Sir John Scot of Scotstarvet sought the consent of the general assembly for Gordon to leave his parish for two months to compile a map of Fife. This is the earliest evidence of Gordon's involvement in his father's compiling of maps. A manuscript map of 'Keanrosse-shyre' by James Gordon, dated 25 October 1642, is extant, while his map of Fife in volume 5 of Willem and Jan Blaeu's *Atlas* provides more detailed coverage of the county than Timothy Pont's two maps. A manuscript map of Fife dated 1642 with inset plans of St Andrews and Cupar provides the earliest evidence of Gordon's aptitude for depicting towns in plan and perspective.

Walter MacFarlane's *Geographical Collections* (1907) provide evidence of extensive transcription by Gordon of chorographic text, much of it possibly compiled by Pont, but including 'Noats of Lennox and Sterlingshyr' and 'Noats of … Lochtay Loch Erin, L. Dochart, Glenurquhay etc', obtained by Gordon himself in 1644. That same year he began work on a written account of Aberdeen, but this seems to have been set aside to compile a plan of Edinburgh, which he delivered to the town council in 1647, when he was paid 500 merks and elected a burgess and guild brother. The plan was engraved and published in a rare first edition by Blaeu about 1650 and then by De Wit about 1695. It became known as 'the guttit haddie' because of its resemblance to a filleted fish. The plan includes two views of Edinburgh, which Gordon claimed were falsified by the engravers to make it commercially more attractive (*Bannatyne Miscellany*, 3.324). Four other views by Gordon of prominent Edinburgh buildings were engraved about the same time. Also in 1647 there is evidence of Gordon's intended employment by the nobility of Angus (Forfarshire) to map that shire. By way of preparation he seems to have obtained from his father and subsequently lost Pont's manuscript map of Angus. The earl of Southesk proposed in 1648 that he should make good the loss, but, as the atlas was published with only a written description of Angus, it seems that Gordon did not do so. In September 1647 the assembly directed Gordon to map Stirlingshire, another county which had been mapped some fifty years earlier by Pont, but again there is no evidence that he did so.

On 16 October 1661 Gordon delivered a plan of Aberdeen to the town council and was rewarded with a silver cup, a silk hat, and 'ane silk goun to his bed fellow' (Gordon, *Scots Affairs*, lxiii). His pen and ink draft was sent to the Netherlands in 1662 to be engraved at the council's expense, but it is better known from its lithographic reproduction (Gordon, *Abredoniae*) published together with a contemporary translation of Gordon's Latin description of both towns of Aberdeen.

Original compilation by James Gordon has been identified only in his town plans, views, and in his mapping of Fife, Kinross, and Buchan. The absence of further original work may be attributable to ill health later in life. In 1683 he passed his entire collection of chorography, including manuscripts bequeathed to him by his father, to Sir Robert Sibbald, who was preparing a new Scottish atlas. About that time he arranged for a transcript of his father's manuscript dedication of Blaeu's atlas to Charles, prince of Wales, inappropriate during the Commonwealth, to be placed in the Edinburgh University Library copy of the atlas, retaining the original in his own copy.

James Gordon is properly remembered for his compilation of some of the earliest town plans of Scotland. However, his written description of Aberdeen and his collection of notes on other parts of Scotland suggest that his studies conformed to the broader chorographic tradition evident in the reference in his father's will to 'all mappes, papers and descriptions … writen and drawn … conduce to the description of Scotland' (Gordon, *Scots Affairs*, xlix), a tradition including history and genealogy. When in 1652 Straloch was looking for someone to write a history of the era of civil wars in Scotland, he seems to have turned to his son. In his *History of Scots Affairs* Gordon reveals his distaste for extremes, but the work is solid and plodding, much reliant on transcribing printed pamphlets that he evidently found in his father's extensive collections. However, it is valuable for the narrative it provides, often informed (especially where events in the north-east are concerned) by personal information from men involved. The work begins with the start of the troubles in 1637 but ends abruptly in 1640. Dates on the manuscript suggest that compilation began in 1659 and ceased in 1661, shortly before Straloch died, implying that Gordon may have abandoned the task in the absence of parental pressure. In 1646 Gordon wrote and embellished a 'common Placebook of practical Divinity' (Man, 38).

For Gordon to be given his parish, he must have signed the national covenant and accepted the presbyterian revolution that overturned Charles I's religious reforms in Scotland. Although probably preferring a quiet life of scholarship to contemporary controversy, he did not avoid public notice. In April 1647 he was suspected of having contacts with the royalist marquess of Huntly, and in 1650 he was 'gravelie admonished' for irregularities in parish record-keeping and showing an insufficiently 'grave carriage' while being interrogated, and a few months later he was 'sharplie rebuked' for laxity in imposing discipline on offenders (Gordon, *Scots Affairs*, 2.xii–xv). These are probably the occasions on which, Gordon hints, he was in danger of being deposed.

Gordon's first marriage, in July 1643, was to Margaret, daughter of William Gordon of Rothiemay, with whom he had two daughters. Margaret died on 2 November 1662, and on 14 August 1663 he married Katherine Gordon (*d.* 1703), with whom he had three sons, one of whom was appointed his father's assistant in the ministry of Rothiemay, suggesting that Gordon needed help in old age. Gordon has been credited with the stoicism which characterized his family and is said to have been 'a Dealer in judicial Astrology' (Man, 38). He died on 26 September 1686.

JEFFREY C. STONE

Sources J. Gordon, *History of Scots affairs from 1637–1641*, ed. J. Robertson and G. Grub, 3 vols., Spalding Club, 1, 3, 5 (1841) • D. Stevenson, 'Cartography and the kirk: aspects of the making of the first atlas of Scotland', *Scottish Studies*, 26 (1982), 1–12 • *Fasti Scot.*, new edn, 6.331–2 • J. C. Stone, 'The origins of three maps of Fife published by Blaeu in 1654', *Scottish Studies*, 29 (1989), 39–53 • W. Scott and D. Laing, eds., *The Bannatyne miscellany*, 3 vols., Bannatyne Club, 19–19b (1827–55) • J. Man, *Introduction … to the projected work memoirs of Scottish affairs from 1624 to 1651 by Robert Gordon of Straloch, James Gordon of Rothiemay, and others* [n.d., 1741?] • *Geographical collections relating to Scotland made by Walter MacFarlane*, ed. A. Mitchell, 2, Scottish History Society, 52 (1907) • D. P. Ferro and J. C. Stone, 'The provenance of two early atlases of Scotland, containing contemporary manuscript insertions', *Deeside Field*, 3rd ser., 2 (1978), 35–44 • J. Gordon, *Abredoniae vtrivsque descriptio: a description of both touns of Aberdeen by James Gordon Parson of Rothemay*, Spalding Club (1842) • C. G. Cash, 'Manuscript maps by Pont, the Gordons, and Adair, in the Advocates' Library, Edinburgh', *Scottish Geographical Magazine*, 23 (1907), 574–92 • R. Spence, 'The map-making Gordons', *Scottish Annual & Braemar Gathering Book* (1958), 157–65 • W. Cowan, *The maps of Edinburgh, 1544–1929*, 2nd edn (1932) • J. Blaeu, *Theatrum orbis terrarum, sive, Atlas novus*, pt 5 (1654)

Gordon, James (1665–1746), vicar apostolic of the lowland district, son of Patrick Gordon of Glastirum and Margaret Seton, was a cadet of the Letterfourie family and was born at Glastirum, the Enzie, Banffshire, on 31 January 1665. He was sent to the University of Louvain in 1679, moved in 1683 to the Scots College at Paris, and after being ordained returned to Scotland in 1692. He officiated as missionary priest in the Enzie until 1702, when he was sent to assist William Leslie, agent to the Scottish mission to the Holy See. He was also agent to the mission at Rome from 1703 to 1706. While there he was elected coadjutor, with right of succession, to Bishop Nicholson. Owing to the persecution of Catholics in Scotland, Gordon's appointment and consecration were kept secret. By direction of Clement XI he was consecrated at Montefiascone, by Cardinal Barberigo on 11 April 1706, for the see of Nicopolis *in partibus*. He returned to Scotland later that year and in 1707 went on his first visitation to the highlands. He helped found two seminaries and was obliged to live in hiding for two years after the rising of 1715. In October 1718 he succeeded Bishop Nicholson as vicar apostolic of Scotland.

In 1727, on Gordon's recommendation, Benedict XIII divided Scotland into lowland and highland districts. Gordon became, in October 1731, first vicar apostolic of the lowland district, which he remained until his death on 1 March 1746 at Thornhill, near Drummond Castle, the seat of a Catholic woman, Mrs Mary Drummond; he was buried at Inverpefferay, Perthshire.

THOMPSON COOPER, *rev.* ALEXANDER DU TOIT

Sources G. H. Bennet, 'Memoirs of James Gordon', *Catholic Directory for Scotland* (1937–8) • J. Darragh, *The Catholic hierarchy of Scotland: a biographical list, 1653–1985* (1986) • J. F. S. Gordon, *Ecclesiastical chronicle for Scotland*, 4 vols. (1867) • 'The vicars-apostolic of Scotland', *London and Dublin Orthodox Journal*, 4 (Jan–June 1837), 82–5 • C. Eubel and others, eds., *Hierarchia Catholica medii et recentioris aevi*, 8 vols. (Münster and Passau, 1913–78); repr. (Münster, 1960–82) • W. M. Brady, *The episcopal succession in England, Scotland, and Ireland, AD 1400 to 1875*, 3 vols. (1876–7) • W. J. Anderson, ed., 'The college for the lowland district of Scotland at Scalan and Aquhorties: registers and documents', *Innes Review*, 14 (1963), 89–212 • B. Hemphill, *The early vicars apostolic of England, 1685–1750* (1954)

Archives BL, Add. MSS • NL Scot. | Scottish Catholic Archives, Edinburgh

Gordon, James (*c.*1762–1825), Cambridge eccentric, was son of the chapel clerk of Trinity College, Cambridge, a man of some property, who gave him a good education and articled him to an attorney. He began to practise in Free School Lane, Cambridge, with fair prospects of success. Unfortunately his convivial talents led him into society where he learned to drink to excess. To console himself for his disappointments, he became a confirmed drunkard, and fell into destitution. He was several times in the town gaol for drunkenness. For many years he was kept from starvation by an annuity of a guinea a week left by a relative. He was induced to leave Cambridge for London, where he picked up a living by waiting at the coach offices. He subsequently returned to Cambridge, and used to pass the night in the grove at Jesus College and the barn at the Hoop Hotel. A fall in a fit of drunkenness injured him so severely that he had to be taken to the workhouse at Barnwell, where he died on 16 September 1825, when about sixty-three years old. He was a man of keen and ready wit, and several of his jests are preserved in Hone's *Every-Day Book*, where there is a portrait of him (1.692). It is stated there (1.1295) that he left a memoir of his life, which has not been published. Gunning gives some anecdotes of his thrusting his company during a university election upon Pitt in the Senate House, and of his making money by writing Latin essays when in gaol.

A. C. BICKLEY, *rev.*

Sources *Cambridge Chronicle and Journal* (23 Sept 1825) • *Cambridge Chronicle and Journal* (2 Feb 1793) • *Cambridge Chronicle and Journal* (13 April 1793) • C. H. Cooper and J. W. Cooper, *Annals of Cambridge*, 5 vols. (1842–1908) • W. Hone, *The Every-day Book and Table Book*, 3 vols. (1838–1939) • H. Gunning, *Reminiscences of the university, town, and county of Cambridge, from the year 1780*, 2 vols. (1854) • *N&Q*, 3rd ser., 4 (1863), 170

Likenesses portrait, repro. in Hone, *Every-day book*, vol. 1, p. 692

Gordon, Sir James Alexander (1782–1869), naval officer, eldest son of Charles Gordon of Wardhouse, Aberdeenshire, and his wife, a daughter of Major James Mercer, of Auchnacant, Aberdeenshire, was born at Kildrummy Castle, Kildrummy, Aberdeenshire. He entered the navy in November 1793 on the *Arrogant*, on the home station, under Captain James Hawkins Whitshed. In rapid but continuous succession he then served in many different ships, including the frigate *Révolutionnaire* in the action off Lorient on 23 June 1795, and the *Goliath* in the battles of Cape St Vincent and the Nile. In January 1800 he was promoted lieutenant of the *Bordelais*, and in her assisted in the capture of the *Curieuse* on 28 January 1801. In 1802 he was appointed to the sloop *Racoon* (18 guns), and was first lieutenant when she captured the brig *Lodi* in Leogane Roads on 11 July 1803, and drove the brig *Mutine* on shore near Santiago de Cuba on 17 August.

Gordon's share in these services won him his promotion to the command of the *Racoon* on 3 March 1804, her former commander, Captain Bissell, being promoted at the same time. During the year he cruised with good fortune against privateers in the West Indies, and on 16 May 1805 was posted to the *Diligentia*, in which he remained only a few months. In June 1807 he was appointed to the *Mercury* (28 guns), in which, after taking convoy to Newfoundland, he joined the squadron off Cadiz, and on 4 April 1808 had a distinguished share in the capture or destruction of a Spanish convoy and gunboats off Rota. In June 1808 he was appointed to the *Active*, which he commanded, mostly in the Adriatic, for the next four years, and during this time was engaged in numerous actions with the enemy's boats and batteries. He took a prominent part in the action off Lissa on 13 March 1811, for which he received the gold medal, and in the capture of the *Pomone* on 29 November, when he lost a leg, shot off at the knee. The first lieutenant soon afterwards lost his arm, and the engagement finished with the ship under the command of the second lieutenant, George Haye. Captain Maxwell of the *Alceste*, the senior officer on this occasion, acknowledging the principal share of the *Active* in the capture, sent the French captain's sword to Gordon as his by rights.

As he recovered from his wound Gordon was sent to England to convalesce. On 7 August 1812 he married the youngest daughter of John Ward of Malborough; they had seven daughters and one son. In the autumn of 1812 he was appointed to the frigate *Seahorse* (38 guns), in which, towards the end of the following year, he joined Sir Alexander Cochrane in the Chesapeake during the Anglo-American War (1812–14). In August 1814 he was senior officer in command of the squadron which forced its way up the Potomac, captured Fort Washington, its supporting batteries, and the city of Alexandria, and brought down twenty-one enemy ships, with their cargoes on board. The loss sustained in this expedition was small, but the labour excessive, and it is recorded that during the twenty-three days the hammocks were down for only two nights. In the unsuccessful expedition against New Orleans, Gordon had a full share, after which he returned to England.

On 2 January 1815 Gordon was made a KCB; in November he was appointed to command the frigate *Madagascar*, and in 1816 to the frigate *Meander*, in which, on 19 December 1816, he narrowly escaped being wrecked on a shoal off Orford Ness, over which the ship was forced in a gale. For many hours she was in great danger, and her final safety was attributed mainly to Gordon's coolness, energy, and skill. He was immediately afterwards appointed to his old ship, the *Active* (46 guns), and he commanded her for the next two years on the North American and Mediterranean stations. In 1828 he was appointed superintendent of Plymouth Hospital, and in 1832 superintendent of Chatham Dockyard, where he continued until his promotion to flag rank on 10 January 1837.

In July 1840 Gordon was appointed lieutenant-governor of the Royal Hospital, Greenwich, London, and on 28 October 1853 he succeeded Sir Charles Adam as governor. He held the office for the remainder of his life. He became vice-admiral on 8 January 1848 and admiral on 21 January 1854, was made a GCB on 5 July 1855, and was promoted admiral of the fleet on 30 January 1868. He died at the Royal Hospital, Greenwich, on 8 January 1869. His son, James Alexander Gordon, had died in command of the sloop *Wolf* in January 1847.

J. K. LAUGHTON, *rev.* ROGER MORRISS

Sources O'Byrne, *Naval biog. dict.* • J. Marshall, *Royal naval biography*, 4/2 (1835) • *The Times* (11 Jan 1869) • W. James, *The naval history of Great Britain, from the declaration of war by France in 1793, to the accession of George IV*, [5th edn], 6 vols. (1859–60), vols. 3, 5–6 • Boase, *Mod. Eng. biog.* • W. L. Clowes, *The Royal Navy: a history from the earliest times to the present*, 7 vols. (1897–1903), vol. 6 • P. Mackesy, *The war in the Mediterranean, 1803–1810* (1957) • *Navy List* • *Dod's Peerage* (1858) • T. Roosevelt, *The naval war of 1812* (1882) • R. Muir, *Britain and the defeat of Napoleon, 1807–1815* (1996)
Likenesses A. Morton, oils, 1837–43, NMM • engraving, repro. in *ILN*, 54 (1869), 166 • print, BM, NPG; repro. in *Naval Chronicle* (1814)
Wealth at death under £30,000: resworn probate, July 1869, *CGPLA Eng. & Wales*

Gordon, James Alexander (1793–1872), physician, was born in Middlesex, and graduated MD at Edinburgh in 1814. At Edinburgh he came under the influence of John Abercrombie, with whom he resided as a house pupil. After a period spent studying on the continent, which included a session in Göttingen, he returned to London in 1818, and in 1819 established the *Quarterly Journal of Foreign Medicine and Surgery*, together with Dr Mackenzie of Glasgow, and wrote extensively for it. He also wrote a series of articles on German medical literature for the *Medical Repository*. He was admitted a licentiate of the Royal College of Physicians in 1821, became fellow in 1836, and was censor in 1838. He was elected assistant physician to the London Hospital in 1827, and physician in 1828; he resigned in 1844. He was elected to the Royal Society in 1835. Gordon retired from medicine about 1846 and moved to Dorking, Surrey, where he died at his home, Pixholme, Dorking, on 18 April 1872. He was survived by his wife, Elizabeth Catharine, *née* Brandreth. The electrical engineer James Edward Henry *Gordon (1852–1893) was their son.

G. T. BETTANY, *rev.* MICHAEL BEVAN

Sources Munk, *Roll* • *CGPLA Eng. & Wales* (1872) • A. E. Clark-Kennedy, *The London: a study in the voluntary hospital system*, 2 (1963), 13, 20
Archives RS, corresp. with Sir John Herschel
Wealth at death under £50,000: probate, 15 May 1872, *CGPLA Eng. & Wales*

Gordon, James Bentley (1750–1819), historian, was the son of the Revd James Gordon of Neeve Hall, Londonderry, and his wife, a daughter of Thomas Neeve, nephew of the scholar and critic Richard Bentley. Gordon entered Trinity College, Dublin, in 1769, and graduated BA in 1773. On leaving college he took holy orders and in 1776 he became tutor to the sons of Lord Courtown. He married a daughter of Richard Bookey of Wicklow in 1779. The couple had several children: their eldest son, James George, army officer, was killed at Fort Sandusky in Canada in August 1813; a second son, Richard Bentley, was prebendary of Ferns and Leighlin, co. Wexford, 1819–23, and one daughter married Thomas Jones, Gordon's biographer.

In 1779 Gordon undertook the management of a boarding-school at Marlfield in co. Wexford, but he achieved little success in this profession. In 1796 he was presented to the living of Cannaway in co. Cork and in 1799 to that of Killegney in co. Wexford; he retained both for the rest of his life. Gordon was a zealous student of history and geography. Between 1790 and 1798 he published a six-volume work, *Terraquea, or, A New System of Geography and Modern History*. The publication of this was interrupted by his preparation of *A History of the Rebellion in Ireland in 1798* (1801)—'a party work abounding in misrepresentations' (Lowndes, 914)—which reached a second, enlarged edition in 1803. Gordon's *History of Ireland* (1805) was also reprinted and in 1808 it was translated into French; this work was followed by *A History of the British Islands* in 1815. Gordon died on 10 April 1819. Manuscripts relating to other, intended volumes in his *Terraquea* series were published posthumously as *An Historical and Geographical Memoir of the North American Continent*, to which was added Jones's 'Summary account of Gordon's life, writings, and opinions'. C. L. KINGSFORD, *rev.* PHILIP CARTER

Sources T. Jones, 'Summary account of Gordon's life, writings, and opinions', in J. B. Gordon, *An historical and geographical memoir of the North American continent* (1820) • W. T. Lowndes, *The bibliographer's manual of English literature*, 4 vols. (1834) • Burtchaell & Sadleir, *Alum. Dubl.*

Gordon, James Edward (1789–1864), politician and protestant propagandist, was born in Scotland (either in Abernethy, near Perth, or in Aberdeen) on 11 March 1789, one of the numerous children of James (Brae) Gordon of Little Folla, factor to the duke of Gordon, and Ann McDonald. He joined the Royal Navy at the age of fifteen on 14 April 1804. He became a lieutenant in 1811, and in 1814 commanded the schooner *St Lawrence*, on the strength of which he later called himself 'captain'. After 1815 he first involved himself with the religious and social work of Thomas Chalmers in Glasgow and then moved to London where he initially promoted seamen's charities and was an associate of the evangelical Clapham Sect.

During the 1820s Gordon became a leading figure in the radically conservative wing of Anglican evangelicalism, which rejected compromise with the world and eschewed theological and political liberalism. Above all he was vehemently anti-Catholic, a position that was crystallized by his involvement in the second reformation movement in Ireland. In 1827 he founded the British Society for Promoting the Religious Principles of the Reformation (later Protestant Reformation Society) as a vehicle for outright proselytism, and during the next few years participated in numerous public debates with Roman Catholics, both in Britain and in Ireland.

In 1831 Gordon was returned as MP for Dundalk and in the House of Commons clashed frequently with Daniel O'Connell over the Irish education question and the government grant to Maynooth College. He saw himself as the political leader of the evangelicals, but in reality his views were too extreme and his style too combative for him to command general support. Accordingly, when he lost his seat as a result of the 1832 Reform Act his efforts to return to parliament were unsuccessful.

Shifting his energies to pressure-group politics, Gordon played a leading role in orchestrating the No Popery crusade of 1834–6 and in organizing the Protestant Association as a focus for the anti-Catholic campaign. Shortly afterwards a serious paralytic illness, from which he never fully recovered, forced his retirement from active public life. In spite of the strong antagonisms he had aroused, he had been a key figure in the religious and political reorientation of evangelicalism and in its forging of an alliance with the resurgent Conservative Party around the defence of the protestant established church.

In 1836 Gordon married Barbara, daughter of Samuel Smith, a banker and MP. They had a daughter and two sons, the younger of whom, George Maxwell Gordon, was a prominent missionary in the Punjab. Gordon died at 36 Porchester Square, Bayswater, on 30 April 1864.

JOHN WOLFFE, *rev.*

Sources J. Wolffe, *The protestant crusade in Great Britain, 1829–1860* (1991) • *Huntly Express* (31 Aug 1906) • *Huntly Express* (7 Sept 1906) • *Banffshire Herald* (9 April 1910) • A. Lewis, *George Maxwell Gordon* (1889) • C. O. Skelton and J. M. Bulloch, *Gordons under arms* (1912) • private information (1992) [Dr I. S. Rennie]

Archives BL, letters to Sir Robert Peel, Add. MSS 40344–40546 • U. Edin., New Coll. L., letters to Thomas Chalmers

Wealth at death under £800: administration, 3 June 1864, *CGPLA Eng. & Wales*

Gordon, James Edward Henry (1852–1893), electrical engineer, was born at Mickleham, near Dorking, Surrey, on 26 June 1852, the son of James Alexander *Gordon FRS (1793–1872), physician to the London Hospital, and his wife, Elizabeth Catharine, *née* Brandreth. After attending a private school in Brighton and Eton College, he studied physics under Professor W. G. Adams at King's College, London. While there he invented an electrical anemometer. He then went to Caius College, Cambridge, where he graduated BA in mathematics in 1875, and stayed in Cambridge to carry out research under James Clerk Maxwell at the Cavendish Laboratory on the electromagnetic rotation of the plane of polarized light. He continued this work in a laboratory in what had been his father's house, at Pixholme, near Dorking. This work, and his studies of the specific inductive capacity of dielectrics, was published in the *Philosophical Transactions* for 1877 and 1879. In 1880 he published the first edition of *A Physical Treatise on Electricity and Magnetism*, which was very successful, running to several English editions and being published in America and, in translation, in France.

In 1878 Gordon married Alice May (whose surname is unknown), and became assistant secretary of the British Association, a post he held for two years. About this time he became interested in electric lighting, and experimented with an incandescent lamp using a platinum–iridium filament, but this was soon superseded by the carbon filament lamps developed by Swan, Edison, and others. The first large-scale demonstration of electric lighting by filament lamps was at the International Electrical Exhibition in Paris in August 1881, which Gordon attended as one of the British delegation.

Thereafter, Gordon concentrated on the design and construction of power stations for electric lighting. In 1882 he built the largest generator then known, which was exhibited at the Greenwich works of the Telegraph Construction and Maintenance Company, and the following year he became manager of the company's electric lighting department. His best-known project was the lighting for Paddington Station, London, in April 1886. He was responsible for both the electrical arrangements and the steam plant, and for some years it was one of the largest electric lighting installations in the world. The Telegraph Construction and Maintenance Company, however, gave up the electric lighting business after a few years, and in July 1887 Gordon formed the Whitehall Electric Supply Company, which later became the nucleus of the Metropolitan Electric Supply Company, launched in August 1888 with a capital of £500,000. Gordon was engineer to the Metropolitan company, as well as being a director; Sir John Pender was chairman.

In late 1889 Gordon ceased to be a paid employee of the Metropolitan company, although he remained a director, and he set up as a consulting engineer and contractor for power-station work in partnership with W. J. Rivington. He was elected a member of the Institution of Civil Engineers in March 1890, and a member of the Society of Telegraph Engineers and Electricians (later the Institution of Electrical Engineers) in November 1881.

Gordon was an experienced horseman and fond of riding, but on 3 February 1893 his horse bolted, throwing him onto an asphalt pavement and causing head injuries from which he died an hour later in Croydon Hospital. He was survived by his wife. BRIAN BOWERS

Sources *The Electrician* (10 Feb 1893), 70 • *Electrical Trades Directory* (1891), xxxviii–xxxix • *DNB* • R. H. Parsons, *The early days of the power station industry* (1939) • b. cert.

Archives CUL, letters to Sir George Stokes

Wealth at death £9216 17*s*. 0*d*.: resworn probate, June 1893, *CGPLA Eng. & Wales*

Gordon, James Frederick Skinner (1821–1904), antiquary and Scottish Episcopal church minister, born at Keith, Banffshire, claimed descent from the Gordons of Glenbucket, in Strathdon. Educated at Keith School and then at Madras College, St Andrews, he gained, at fifteen years of age, the Grant bursary at St Andrews University, where he graduated with distinction in 1840, and proceeded MA in 1842. Appointed organizing master in the (episcopal) national schools at Edinburgh, Gordon was ordained deacon in the Scottish Episcopal church in 1843 and priest in the following year. After a first curacy to David Low, bishop of Moray, at Pittenweem, Fife, he went to Forres, Moray, as curate from 1843 to 1844 to Alexander Ewing, later bishop of Argyll and the Isles; his experiences at Pittenweem are narrated in his *Scotichronicon*. In 1844 he was elected incumbent of St Andrew's Episcopal Church, Glasgow, the oldest post-Reformation church in Scotland; he retained this position until he retired in 1890.

At Glasgow, Gordon devoted much energy to the development of the Scottish Episcopal church, and raised funds to remodel and endow St Andrew's. He was a pioneer in agitating for the removal of dilapidated tenements and slums in the neighbourhood, thus initiating the movement which resulted in the Glasgow Improvement Act of 1866. One of the earliest Anglo-Catholics in the Episcopal church, his theology and ritualism sometimes led to friction in his own denomination, but his earnest philanthropic work brought him general admiration. Industrialization had brought large numbers of Anglican English and Irish into Glasgow. As a consequence, Gordon was one of the first episcopalian priests in Glasgow, along with David Aitchison, to embark on missions to the destitute, and to unchurched episcopalians. But he was also known for his indiscriminate baptisms (requiring only a donation of half a crown to church funds as a prerequisite for the rite), which made St Andrew's notorious among the more respectable sections of Glasgow society. In 1857 Gordon gained a measure of international episcopalian recognition when he received the degree of DD from Hobart College, USA. All his priestly life he was an enthusiastic freemason, having been initiated as a student at St Andrews in 1841; at his death he was the oldest masonic member.

Throughout his active parish ministry, Gordon also pursued a strenuous literary career, closely studying the history of the Roman Catholic and the episcopal churches in Scotland, and also the antiquities of Glasgow. His chief publication was *The Ecclesiastical Chronicle for Scotland* (1867), an elaborate erudite work in four volumes based on much original research. The first two volumes, entitled *Scotichronicon*, contain a sketch of the pre-Reformation church and an extended volume of Robert Keith's *Catalogue of Scottish Bishops* (1755); the third and fourth volumes, entitled *Monasticon*, give the history of Scottish monasteries, and biographies of the Roman Catholic bishops of the post-Reformation mission. Gordon also published *Glasghu facies*, a history of Glasgow (1872); *The Book of the Chronicles of Keith, Grange, Ruthven, Ciarney, and Botriphnie* (1880); a new edition of Lachlan Shaw's *History of the Province of Moray* (1882); *Iona, a Description of the Island* (1885); *Vade Mecum to and through the Cathedral of St Kentigern of Glasgow* (1894). He also contributed an article on the Scottish Episcopal church to the *Cyclopaedia of Religious Denominations* (1853), and wrote on meteorology for several encyclopaedias and journals.

After resigning the charge of St Andrew's Church in 1890 Gordon lived in retirement at Beith, Ayrshire, and died there on 23 January 1904. He was interred with masonic honours in Beith cemetery.

A. H. MILLAR, *rev.* ROWAN STRONG

Sources J. F. S. Gordon, *Scotichronicon*, 2 vols. (1867) • *Glasgow Herald* (25 Jan 1904) • *Scottish Guardian* (5 Feb 1904) • *Scottish Ecclesiastical Journal* (Jan 1859) • W. Perry, *Anthony Mitchell, Bishop of Aberdeen and Orkney* (1920)

Wealth at death £148 3*s*. 2*d*.: confirmation, 11 July 1904, *CCI*

Gordon, Sir James Willoughby, first baronet (1772–1851), army officer, born on 21 October 1772, was son of Captain Francis Grant, Royal Navy, who took the name of Gordon in 1768 (pursuant to the will of his maternal uncle, James Gordon, of Moor Place, Hertfordshire), and his wife, Mary, daughter of Sir Thomas Aston, and sister of Sir Willoughby Aston, baronet. On 17 October 1783 he was appointed an ensign in the 66th foot, in which he became lieutenant in 1789, captain in 1795, and major in 1797. He served with his regiment in Ireland, the West Indies, and at Gibraltar; was present as a volunteer on board Lord Hood's fleet at Toulon in 1793; and witnessed the surrender of the French in Bantry Bay in 1796. After this he was with his regiment in San Domingo, in Jamaica, and North America.

Gordon was appointed lieutenant-colonel in the 85th foot on 21 May 1801, and commanded its 1st battalion regiment at the first British occupation of Madeira in that year. In 1802 he was appointed an assistant quartermaster-general in the southern district, headquarters Chatham. In 1804 he was brought into the 92nd as lieutenant-colonel, and appointed military secretary to the duke of York, then commander-in-chief, in which capacity he was an important witness before the parliamentary committee of inquiry into military expenditure, and in the Wardle inquiry [*see* Frederick, Prince]. He retained the post until the resignation of the duke of York. While so employed he was appointed lieutenant-colonel commandant of the Royal African Corps in 1808, and became colonel in 1810. He married, on 15 October 1805, Julia Lavinia, daughter of Richard Henry Alexander Bennet of Beckenham, Kent, and they had a son and daughter.

In 1811 Gordon, who, as he stated before a parliamentary committee, had held every staff appointment it was possible for him to hold, was appointed quartermaster-general of the army in the Peninsula, with which he served until he resigned the following year through ill health. On his return home he was appointed quartermaster-general at the Horse Guards, a post which he retained until his death. Gordon became major-general in 1813, was transferred to the colonelcy of the 85th light infantry in 1816, and was created a baronet on 5 December 1818; he was transferred to the colonelcy of the 23rd Royal Welch Fusiliers in 1823, made lieutenant-general and GCH in 1825, sworn of the privy council in 1830, and made GCB in September 1831, general in 1841. He was a fellow of the Royal Society from 11 June 1801 and a fellow of the Royal Geographical Society from its formation in 1830. Gordon was author of *Military Transactions of the British Empire, 1803–7* (1809), and a supplementary volume containing tables of the strength, distribution, and so on of the army during that period.

Gordon died at his residence near the Royal Hospital, Chelsea, London, on 4 January 1851. He was survived by Lady Gordon and succeeded by their son, Henry Percy Gordon (21 Oct 1806–29 July 1876), at whose death the baronetcy became extinct.

H. M. Chichester, *rev.* Roger T. Stearn

Sources *GM*, 2nd ser., 35 (1851) • Burke, *Peerage* (1907) • *The dispatches of … the duke of Wellington … from 1799 to 1818*, ed. J. Gurwood, 13 vols. in 12 (1834–9), vol. 4 • *Supplementary dispatches … of Field Marshal Arthur, duke of Wellington, K.G.*, ed. A. R. Wellesley, second duke of Wellington, 11: *Occupation of France … surrender of Napoleon, and restoration of the Bourbons, July 1815 to July 1817* (1864) • T. C. W. Blanning, *The French revolutionary wars, 1787–1802* (1996) • Boase, *Mod. Eng. biog.* • *Dod's Peerage* (1858)

Archives BL, MSS as military secretary to duke of York, Add. MSS 49471–49517 • NAM, MSS as quartermaster-general • U. Southampton L., military papers; microfilm of further papers in private possession | Beds. & Luton ARS, letters to Samuel Whitbread • BL, letters to Lord Grenville, Add. MS 58996 • BL, letters to Lord Hardwicke, etc., Add. MSS 35646–35647; 35751–35768, *passim* • BL, corresp. with William Huskisson, Add. MSS 38737–38742 • BL, corresp. with Sir Hudson Lowe, Add. MSS 20107–20197, *passim* • BL, corresp. with Sir Robert Peel, Add. MSS 40273–40605, *passim* • NA Scot., letters to Lord Melville • NAM, letters to Sir Benjamin D'Urban • NL Scot., corresp. with Sir George Brown • NL Scot., corresp. with commissariat department • U. Durham L., corresp. with second Earl Grey; letters or memoranda to third Earl Grey • U. Southampton L., letters to first duke of Wellington • priv. coll., letters to Lord Anglesey

Likenesses J. Hopwood, line engraving, 1809 (after T. Rowlandson), BM; repro. in Frederick, duke of York and Albany, *Investigation of charges brought against the duke of York*, 2 vols. (1809)

Gordon [*née* Campbell], **Jane** [Jean], **Viscountess Kenmure** (*d.* **1675**), patron of ministers, was the third daughter of Archibald *Campbell, seventh earl of Argyll (1575/6–1638), and his first wife, Lady Agnes Douglas (1574–1607), daughter of William Douglas, first earl of Morton (Lochleven). Between 1624 and 1626 she married Sir John *Gordon of Lochinvar (*c.*1599–1634) and formed an enduring spiritual friendship with the famous covenanting preacher Samuel Rutherford, whom her husband had presented to the parish of Anworth. When Jane gave birth to three short-lived daughters and suffered increasingly from depression Rutherford wrote to console her, famously remarking of one of the babies, 'She is only sent on before, like unto a star which, going out of sight, doth not die and vanish, but still shineth in another hemisphere' (Whyte, 33).

Gordon, created viscount of Kenmure in 1633, died on 12 September the following year, vilified by the covenanters for failing to stand against Charles I's ecclesiastical innovations. Soon afterwards Jane gave birth to his posthumous son, John, who lived only until he was four. In February 1640 she married Sir Henry, or Harry, Montgomerie of Giffen (1614–1644), second son of Alexander *Montgomery, sixth earl of Eglinton, but continued to be known as Lady Kenmure. The couple had no children, and Harry died on 3 May 1644, leaving Jane as his sole executor. Four years later she made over to her father-in-law the barony of Giffen, Ayrshire, in return for a life annuity of 2500 merks.

Throughout her life Jane was an admired figure in presbyterian circles. Her lasting fame rests mainly on her relationship with Samuel Rutherford, which has been described as 'one of those spiritual intimacies which were becoming a pattern for a presbyterian lady of quality' (Mathew, 38). Forty-nine of Rutherford's published letters are addressed to her, more than those to any other correspondent. He dedicated to her *The Tryal and Triumph of Faith* (1645), as did John Fullarton of Carleton his *The Turtle Dove* (1664). John Livingstone on his deathbed in 1672 described her as 'the oldest Christian acquaintance, now alive, I have in Scotland' (Rutherford, 37), and she was well known throughout the country for her charitable works. In spite of her delicate health and her many sorrows—her brother, Archibald *Campbell, marquess of Argyll (1605x7–1661), was executed in 1661—Jane lived until February 1675. She was buried in Greyfriars churchyard, Edinburgh, on 26 February that year.

ROSALIND K. MARSHALL

Sources *Scots peerage*, 1.349; 3.446; 5.120 • A. A. Bonar, *Letters of Samuel Rutherford* (1894) • F. Cook, *Samuel Rutherford and his friends* (1992) • A. Whyte, *Samuel Rutherford and some of his correspondents* (1894) • W. Fraser, *Memorials of the Montgomeries*, 1 (1859), 16, 76–7 • R. Gilmour, *Samuel Rutherford, a study* (1904) • S. Rutherford, ed., *The last and heavenly speeches and glorious departure of John, Viscount Kenmure* (1649); later edn with memoir by J. Murray (1827) • *The letters and journals of Robert Baillie*, ed. D. Laing, 3 (1842), 467 • *Edinburgh marriage register*, 113, 486 • D. Mathew, *Scotland under Charles I* (1955), 38
Archives NA Scot., Eglinton muniments, family papers

Gordon [*née* Maxwell], **Jane, duchess of Gordon** (**1748/9–1812**), political hostess and agricultural reformer, was born at Hyndford's Close, Edinburgh, the third of the four children of Sir William Maxwell of Monreith, Wigtownshire, third baronet, (*c*.1712–1771), and his wife, Magdalene, daughter of William Blair of Blair. The sources disagree over the exact year of her birth. Little is known about her education and childhood in Edinburgh. A boisterous child, she was reputed to have ridden through neighbouring streets on a pig.

On 23 October 1767 Jane Maxwell married Alexander *Gordon, fourth duke of Gordon (1743–1827), in Edinburgh. Following her marriage she became a leading figure in public life. The marriage was not a happy one, but she had two sons and five daughters during it. Shortly before her marriage her father warned Jane against the dangers of grandeur and encouraged her not to look down on those who had been her equals once she had become a duchess. Maxwell also advised her that small talk would be no entertainment for the duke's companions, and to make new friends but none of her own sex. This was advice that she took to heart. Contemporary descriptions of the duchess confirm her quick wit and lively, animated conversation. In appearance she was described as being more agreeable than really handsome.

Jane Gordon was something of a problematic figure in London society, combining being Scottish and clearly outspoken with her role as a political hostess. Her vivacity and enthusiasm did not fit easily into carefully constructed polite society of the time. Nevertheless, she had a number of admirers and supporters among men in positions of great power and influence. She numbered among her friends William Pitt and Henry Dundas (1742–1811), the latter being a particularly close friend. It is thought that they were drinking partners and many believed they were lovers, including several caricaturists. Dundas may have acquired a London house at St James's Square on her behalf, and was even inspired to write verse about her. During the absence of the duchess on her visits to Scotland, Dundas was said to have managed her London affairs while she in return conducted his business in Scotland.

The duchess of Gordon's London gatherings, on which she spent almost £200 each, were renowned for their opulence and lively company. These assemblies were attended by orators, statesmen, and intelligentsia and her home became a social centre of the tory party. She took an active interest in politics and attended the House of Commons to hear debates on several occasions. Nathaniel Wraxall commented that: 'Few women have performed a more conspicuous part, or occupied a higher place … on the public theatre of fashion, politics and dissipation' (Wraxall, 2.297–8). There can be little doubt that the duchess was the leading female Pittite for a considerable period. Wraxall also suggests that the duchess was instrumental in reconciling the prince of Wales and George III in 1787 following a dispute concerning the prince's debts. She also used her position to canvass patronage on behalf of others.

Jane Gordon, duchess of Gordon (1748/9–1812), by George Romney, 1778 [with her son George Gordon, marquess of Huntly, later fifth duke of Gordon]

The duchess succeeded in arranging advantageous marriages for most of her daughters. Her eldest daughter, Charlotte (1768–1842), married Charles *Lennox, fourth duke of Richmond and Lennox. Her second, Madeline (*d*. 1847), married a Scots landowner and administrator in India, Sir Robert Sinclair, but the remaining daughters all married leading peers. Susan (1774–1828) married William *Montagu, fifth duke of Manchester, whose family connections were whig rather than Pittite. Louisa (1776–1850) married Charles *Cornwallis, second Marquess Cornwallis [*see under* Cornwallis, Charles, first Marquess Cornwallis]; the duchess assured him, when he questioned whether he should marry Louisa, on the grounds of madness in the Gordon family, 'that there was not a drop of Gordon blood' (GEC, *Peerage*, 3.457) in her. The remaining daughter, Georgiana (1781–1853), married John *Russell, sixth duke of Bedford. Of her sons, George *Gordon, fifth duke of Gordon (1770–1836), married after his mother's death, and her second, Alexander (1785–1808) died unmarried.

The duchess of Gordon was also part of fashionable society in Edinburgh and the highlands. She was a patron of the Northern Meeting, the culminating event of the highland season, and took an interest in election campaigns in Ross and Inverness-shire. She also involved herself in the management of her husband's estates in Badenoch and Strathspey. Henry Home, Lord Kames, was a personal friend and looked upon her as an adopted daughter. Kames was an influential advocate of agricultural improvement and had many discussions with the duchess regarding her plans for improvements on the Gordon estates. She aimed to develop the economy of Badenoch and Strathspey by the introduction of new crops and industry, in particular flax growing and linen manufacture. The duchess was instrumental in obtaining subsidized supplies of seeds, an instructor to show the local people how to grow and prepare the new crop, and the establishment of a lint mill in Kingussie. Much of this was achieved through direct contact with the board of trustees for manufactures, and despite Kames's opposition to lint mills.

The introduction of flax could not be a success without the development of an economic centre for Badenoch where the transactions of agricultural trade could be carried out. A focal point for markets, tradesmen, and settlers was required, and the duchess of Gordon recognized the need for a village. Together with the minister, John Anderson, she instigated plans to establish a village at Kingussie. Once the village was set up she instituted, and became patron of, the Badenoch and Strathspey Farming Society which held its inaugural meeting in 1803. More than just a figurehead for the society, the duchess named the first committee and designated members as managers or directors. A major resolution of the society was to encourage agriculture and industry by awarding prizes to, for example, knitters and spinners. The duchess also proposed the introduction of a 'tryst' or public market, the aim of which was to meet once or twice a year, prevent unfair trading, introduce incentives for industry, and provide employment.

The duchess of Gordon was also active in the recruitment of soldiers on her husband's estate and is purported to have been successful in this by offering a kiss to those reluctant to join up—she and her daughters standing in marketplaces with coins between their lips. She continued to entertain while in the highlands and set up an Arcadian court in an old farmhouse at Kinrara in Inverness-shire. She later had a larger house built there. The Kinrara gatherings were legendary in the locality and Elizabeth Grant of Rothiemurchus recalls in her memoirs:

> Half the London world of fashion, all the clever people that could be hunted out from all parts, all the north country, all the neighbourhood from far and near, without regard to wealth or station, and all the kith and kin of both Gordons and Maxwells, flocked to this encampment in the wilderness during the fine autumns to enjoy the free life, the pure air, and the wit and fun the duchess brought with her to the mountains. (*Highland Lady*, 46)

Following the collapse of her marriage in 1793 the duchess of Gordon made Kinrara her home. She died at the Pulteney Hotel, London, on 11 April 1812 surrounded by her surviving children, and was buried at Kinrara on 11 May. At her own request a monument was erected there. The inscription names her children and their titles. It would seem that the duchess of Gordon wanted to be remembered for the brilliant matches she made for her daughters rather than her own achievements—which have proved, however, to be longer lasting.

Christine Lodge

Sources *Inverness Journal* (24 April 1812) • J. Barron, *The northern highlands in the nineteenth century*, 3 vols. (1907–13), 1.47 • Gordon Castle muniments, NA Scot., GD 44/43; GD 44/41/63; GD 44/55/227, 229, 233 • G. Dixon, *Badenoch and Strathspey Herald* (21 March 1991) • G. Dixon, *Badenoch and Strathspey Herald* (28 March 1991) • G. Dixon, *Badenoch and Strathspey Herald* (4 April 1991) • G. Dixon, *Badenoch and Strathspey Herald* (11 April 1991) • G. Dixon, *Badenoch and Strathspey Herald* (18 April 1991) • G. Dixon, *Badenoch and Strathspey Herald* (23 May 1991) • G. Dixon, *Badenoch and Strathspey Herald* (30 May 1991) • *Badenoch and Strathspey Herald* (16 Jan 1992) • E. G. Murray, *A gallery of Scottish women* (1935) • *Memoirs of a highland lady: the autobiography of Elizabeth Grant of Rothiemurchus*, ed. J. M. Strachey (1898), 46 • letterbooks of J. Anderson, NA Scot., CR 8/4, 5 • Burke, *Peerage* (1999) • *An autobiographical sketch of Jane Maxwell, duchess of Gordon* (1865) • *Lord Fife and his factor. (William Rose.): being the correspondence of James, second Lord Fife, 1729–1809*, ed. A. Tayler and H. Tayler (1925) • D. E. Ginter, ed., *Whig organization in the general election of 1790: selections from the Blair Adam papers* (1967), 119 • C. Piggott, *The female jockey club, or, A sketch of the manners of the age* (1794) • N. W. Wraxall, *Posthumous memoirs of his own time*, 2nd edn, 3 vols. (1836) • M. Fry, *The Dundas despotism* (1992) • GEC, *Peerage*

Archives NA Scot., Gordon Castle muniments, archives relating to Gordon family and estates, GD 44/55 • NA Scot., vouchers | Falkirk Museums History Research Centre, letters to Forbes family • NL Scot., letters to Sir William Forbes

Likenesses J. Reynolds, oils, exh. RA 1775, Goodwood, West Sussex • G. Romney, double portrait, oils, 1778 (with her son), Scot. NPG [*see illus.*] • J. Brown, pencil drawing, 1786, Scot. NPG • W. Evans, stipple, pubd 1806 (after W. Lane), BM, NPG • J. Edgar, group portrait, wash drawing, *c.*1854 (*Robert Burns at an evening party of Lord Monboddo's, 1786*), Scot. NPG • J. Brown, pencil drawing, Scot. NPG • G. Romney, oils, Brodie Castle • W. Smith, group portrait, Goodwood, West Sussex

Gordon, Jane. *See* Graves, Margaret Ethel (1901–1962).

Gordon, Jean, countess of Bothwell and Sutherland (*c.*1546–1629), noblewoman, was one of twelve children, the third and youngest daughter of the wealthy and powerful George *Gordon, fourth earl of Huntly (1513–1562), and his wife, Elizabeth Keith (*fl.* 1530–1565), daughter of Robert, Lord Keith (*d.* in or after 1514), and his wife, Elizabeth (or Beatrice) Douglas (*fl.* 1480). Jean was brought up at Strathbogie Castle, Aberdeenshire, but her life was shattered in 1562 when her father rebelled against Queen Mary and died of a stroke on the battlefield of Corrichie (28 October 1562), and two of her brothers were executed. However, by 1565 Jean and her mother were at court as ladies to the queen, and her eldest brother, another George *Gordon, was restored to the earldom though not

Jean Gordon, countess of Bothwell and Sutherland (*c*.1546–1629), by unknown artist, 1566

to the estates. In 1566, despite being in love with Alexander Ogilvy, laird of Boyne, Banffshire, Jean married her brother's friend James *Hepburn, fourth earl of Bothwell (1534/5–1578). Queen Mary signed the contract on 12 February 1566. Archbishop John Hamilton granted a dispensation on 17 February, as they were within the forbidden degrees. The queen gave Jean twelve ells of cloth of silver for her wedding dress and the marriage was solemnized on 22 February by the bride's protestant uncle, Alexander *Gordon, bishop of Galloway, because Bothwell refused to have a Catholic ceremony. A few weeks later Alexander Ogilvy married Mary Beaton, one of the queen's four Maries.

Jean's dowry of £8000 Scots was used almost entirely to redeem her jointure lands of Crichton from Bothwell's creditors and the couple settled at Crichton Castle. Miniatures of them painted in 1566 show Jean with brown hair, a high forehead, a long, oval face, long nose, and full lips. She is in fashionable black while her husband wears yellow. On 24 April 1567, however, the day that Bothwell allegedly abducted the queen, Jean raised an action for divorce in Edinburgh's protestant commissary court, on the grounds of his adultery with Bessie Crawford, one of her serving maids. Probably as a reward for consenting to the divorce, Jean's brother then received his family estates. Meanwhile Bothwell, at the queen's request, had his marriage annulled on 7 May by Archbishop Hamilton's recently restored Roman Catholic consistory court on the grounds of consanguinity, despite the fact that a dispensation had been obtained.

Thrust into the forefront of events by her brief marriage, Jean emerged with a lasting reputation for dignity and resolve. Taking the dispensation with her, she returned to Strathbogie. On 13 December 1573 she married Alexander *Gordon, twelfth earl of Sutherland (1552–1594) [*see under* Gordon, John, eleventh earl of Sutherland]; they lived at Dunrobin Castle, where their seven children were born. Jean managed the estates when her husband's health failed, developing coal and the first saltworks in the area. 'The earl of Sutherland', it was said, 'is wholly governed by his wife' (Gore-Browne, 222). He died in 1594 and, five years later, she married her original suitor, Alexander Ogilvy of Boyne, now a widower. The contract was signed at Elgin on 10 December 1599. Within ten years Ogilvy too was dead, and after her eldest son died in 1615 Jean ran the Sutherland estates once more and brought up her grandson, the fourteenth earl. A faithful Catholic, she was frequently in trouble with her local presbytery for harbouring Jesuit priests and at the age of eighty-one was excommunicated by the minister of Golspie, Alexander Duff. Jean had built a house for herself at Cracock, but she died at Dunrobin on 14 May 1629 after a long illness and was buried in Dornoch Cathedral beside her second husband. She was, said her son Robert, 'a vertuous and comelie lady … of great understanding above the capacitie of her sex' (Fraser, 1.168).

Rosalind K. Marshall

Sources W. Fraser, ed., *The Sutherland book*, 3 vols. (1892), vol. 1, pp. 166–9 • M. H. B. Sanderson, *Mary Stewart's people: life in Mary Stewart's Scotland* (1987), 34–52 • NL Scot., Sutherland muniments 313/910, 1592, 1593, 1597, 3323 • *Scots peerage*, 4.533–46; 6.43 • J. Stuart, *A lost chapter in the history of Mary, queen of Scots recovered* (1874), 5, 7 • R. Gore-Browne, *Lord Bothwell* (1937) • GEC, *Peerage*, new edn, 12/1.554

Archives NA Scot., marriage contract with Bothwell, register of deeds, viii, 9, 232 • NL Scot., Sutherland muniments, 313/910, 1592, 1593, 1597, 3323

Likenesses miniature, oil on copper, 1566, Scot. NPG [*see illus.*] • oils (as a widow), Dunrobin Castle

Gordon, Sir John (*d*. 1391x5). *See under* Gordon family (*per. c*.1300–*c*.1400).

Gordon, John, eleventh earl of Sutherland (1525–1567), magnate, was the son of Alexander Gordon (*c*.1501–1530), master of Sutherland, and his wife, Janet Stewart, eldest daughter of John Stewart, second earl of Atholl. On 17 March 1537 he succeeded his grandfather Adam Gordon of Aboyne, second son of the second earl of Huntly, who had assumed the title by right of his wife, Elizabeth, sister of the ninth earl of Sutherland. During Queen Mary's minority and the English invasions of 1543–9 Sutherland supported the anti-English policies of his kinsman the earl of Huntly. In July 1543 he signed the cardinal's band in support of Cardinal Beaton and in opposition to the interest of James Hamilton, second earl of Arran.

Though he was still a minor, Sutherland sat in parliament in 1543 and was finally served as heir to his father on 4 May 1546; he occasionally attended meetings of the privy council thereafter. He fought at the battle of Pinkie on 10 September 1547, but escaped death and capture by the English. In the same year he acted as lieutenant north of the Spey, probably by commission of the earl of Huntly. In 1550 he accompanied the queen dowager, Mary of Guise, and a large group of the Scottish nobility to France, where gifts and honours were lavished on them in the hope of expanding French influence in Scotland. Sutherland increased his own power in the north during the 1550s through grants of church lands from his brother-in-law Robert Stewart, bishop of Caithness. He was also granted a tack of the earldom of Moray and a tenancy of the earldom of Ross in 1555, a reward from the queen dowager for his support of her regency of the kingdom. Moray was later surrendered in return for an annual rent because of Huntly's opposition to Sutherland's tenure.

In 1554 Sutherland mounted a stern campaign against the Mackays, who were a disorderly and volatile influence on the politics of the north. He defeated and captured Iye Du Mackay, the leader of the clan, in July and obtained his submission to the new regent's authority before seeing him imprisoned in Dumbarton for a considerable period. As further reward Sutherland was appointed crown bailie of the lands of Farr in October 1555. He was granted a pension of 1000 merks in July 1555 and acted as a lord of the articles in 1558. In the turmoil resulting from anti-French sentiment and pressure for religious reform in 1559–60 Sutherland, along with his kinsman Huntly, was consistently conservative and a reluctant rebel against the authority of the queen regent. Huntly signed the band of congregation, albeit with reservations, in 1560 and Sutherland associated himself with it. But he was soon after wounded in the arm in a skirmish with French mercenaries outside Kinghorn, which provided him with an excuse to return home.

Sutherland signed a proposal for a marriage between Queen Elizabeth and the earl of Arran on 16 August 1560, but generally favoured conservative policies in state and religion. In 1561 he was an alleged intriguer in Huntly's scheme to persuade Queen Mary to land in Aberdeen on her return from France and to place herself at the head of a Catholic and conservative alliance in opposition to the protestant lords. Mary refused this offer, wishing to keep her options open and having an eye to the English succession. Instead of alliance Huntly found himself goaded into rebellion against the queen in 1562, when her royal progress to the north became a determined attack on the Gordon interest in the region. Sutherland remained with the queen as her army prepared to meet Huntly in the field and was later accused of being in treasonable correspondence with him. He was not present at the battle of Corrichie on 28 October 1562, during which Huntly died and the Gordons were defeated, but was nevertheless charged with treason and forfeited. The protestant historians Knox and Buchanan allege that he was involved with Huntly in a plot to kidnap the queen and overthrow her illegitimate half-brother, the earl of Moray, under whose influence she was currently operating.

Sutherland withdrew to Flanders, where he remained for two years, until summoned home and restored to his estates and dignities at the rehabilitation of the Gordons by Mary in March 1565. On 1 September 1565, during his return journey to Scotland, his ship was arrested by the English and he was imprisoned in Berwick until Elizabeth released him at Moray's request in February 1566. He arrived back in Edinburgh in time for the scandal and turmoil associated with the murder of David Riccio on 9 March. In the aftermath the queen counted him among her allies. He was at Holyrood on the night of the murder and was later present when a deposition was taken concerning the murder of Darnley. His forfeiture was rescinded at the parliament of April 1567. In the latter part of her reign Mary attempted to found her authority on a broad-based coalition, also hoping to advance Catholic fortunes discreetly. The Gordons came into alliance with the rehabilitated Hepburns, who had lands in the borders and in the north-east, along with the Gordons. Sutherland signed the bond for Bothwell's marriage with the queen and was present at the ceremony in Holyrood Palace on 15 May 1567.

Just over a month later Sutherland and his third wife, Marion Seton, were poisoned at Helmsdale by Isabel Sinclair, the wife of his uncle Gilbert Gordon of Garty, who allegedly hoped that her own son would succeed to the earldom. Unfortunately he too was fatally poisoned at the same meal. The earl and countess died at Dunrobin Castle, Sutherland, on 23 June 1567 and were buried in Dornoch Cathedral. Sutherland's first wife, whom he married between 21 November 1545 and 12 June 1546, was Elizabeth Campbell, only daughter of Colin, third earl of Argyll, and widow of James Stewart, fourteenth earl of Moray. She died childless before 15 May 1548. About 2 August 1548 he married Helenor Stewart, daughter of John, twelfth earl of Lennox, and widow of William Hay, sixth earl of Erroll, who died before 25 November 1564; they had two sons and three daughters. His third wife, Marion Seton, was the eldest daughter of George, fourth Lord Seton, and widow of John Graham, fifteenth earl of Menteith.

The earl's eldest son, John, died in infancy, and his heir was his second son, **Alexander Gordon** (1552–1594), who became twelfth earl of Sutherland following his father's death. Born at Darnaway Castle, Morayshire, at midsummer 1552, he was still a minor in 1567, and his wardship was entrusted to his sister Margaret. She conveyed it to John Stewart, fourth earl of Atholl, who in turn sold it to George Sinclair, fourth earl of Caithness, the traditional rival of the earls of Sutherland. About 1567 Caithness married Sutherland to his daughter Barbara (*c.*1535–*c.*1573), a woman of loose morals and twice his age, in the hope of securing control of the Sutherland estates. The young earl escaped from his father-in-law in 1569 and spent the next four years battling for possession of his earldom, until on 8 July 1573 he was served as its heir. He had secured a divorce from his first wife on 30 June 1572 and on 13 December 1573 he married Jean (*c.*1546–1629), daughter of George Gordon, fourth earl of Huntly, and former wife of James Hepburn, fourth earl of Bothwell, from whom she was divorced on 7 May 1567. She and Sutherland had seven children, one of whom was the historian Robert *Gordon. The earl was succeeded by his eldest son, John, when he died at Dunrobin Castle on 6 December 1594. He too was buried in Dornoch Cathedral. ALLAN WHITE

Sources *Scots peerage*, 8.339–46 • GEC, *Peerage*, new edn, 12/1.550–54 • R. Gordon and G. Gordon, *A genealogical history of the earldom of Sutherland … with a continuation to the year 1651* (1813), 110–11, 131–8, 146, 151, 164, 177 • T. Thomson, ed., *A diurnal of remarkable occurrents that have passed within the country of Scotland*, Bannatyne Club, 43 (1833), 80, 50 • J. Lesley, *The history of Scotland*, ed. T. Thomson, Bannatyne Club, 38 (1830), 281, 294 • W. Fraser, ed., *The Sutherland book*, 3 vols. (1892), vol. 3, pp. 141–50 • *The state papers and letters of Sir Ralph Sadler*, ed. A. Clifford, 2 vols. (1809), vol. 1, p. 685 • *John Knox's History of the Reformation in Scotland*, ed. W. C. Dickinson, 2 (1949), 118–20, 420, 523 • *The Scottish correspondence of Mary of Lorraine*, ed. A. I. Cameron, Scottish History Society, 3rd ser., 10 (1927), 386–8, 390–93 • *The history of Scotland translated from the Latin of George Buchanan*, ed. and trans. J. Aikman, 4 vols. (1827) • D. Calderwood, *The history of the Kirk of Scotland*, ed. T. Thomson and D. Laing, 8 vols., Wodrow Society, 7 (1842–9) • J. Leslie, *The historie of Scotland*, ed. E. G. Cody and W. Murison, trans. J. Dalrymple, 2 vols. in 4 pts, STS, 5, 14, 19, 34 (1888–95) [1596 trans. of *De origine moribus, et rebus gestis Scotorum libri decem* (Rome, 1578)]

Gordon, John (1544–1619), dean of Salisbury, was born on 1 September 1544, the natural son of Alexander *Gordon (*c*.1516–1575), brother of the fourth earl of Huntly, and Barbara Logie; his parents married, perhaps clandestinely, only in 1546, before Alexander obtained ecclesiastical preferment. John studied at St Leonard's College, St Andrews, before going to France in 1565 for further study, supported by Queen Mary who granted him a pension from her French dowry. He may have studied at Paris and Orléans for two years, though he became, briefly, gentleman-in-waiting to Charles IX on 5 March 1566. The see of Galloway, nominally held by his father, was transferred to him by royal act on 4 January 1568, about which time he was also the treasurer of the German nation at Orléans. In March he became tutor to the son of the Huguenot Louis, prince de Condé, but in the same year was begging for employment in England and Scotland. By the year's end he arrived in England and, with a commendatory letter from Pierre Ramus, gained a post with Thomas Howard, fourth duke of Norfolk, with whom he attended the conferences held at York and Westminster in October and November 1568 which investigated the charges against Queen Mary of killing her husband. Norfolk was imprisoned in October 1569, at which time Gordon entered Mary's employ, on an annual pension of 200 francs, staying with her until the dissolution of her household in January 1572. On 11 April 1571 Thomas Randolph, Elizabeth's ambassador, wrote to the earl of Morton, leader of the king's party in Scotland, that the Gordons, father and son, had been active in the queen's behalf. John had apparently 'written a book in Latin, approving her authority' and condemning 'the disobedience of her rebellious subjects, that deposed her from the crown. Treat him ill when he comes home, and if it be possible, let a copy of it be gotten' (Strype, 2/1.117).

With Mary's recommendation John Gordon then entered royal service in France, serving as gentleman ordinary of the privy chamber to Charles IX, Henri III, and Henri IV, with a pension of 400 crowns per annum. He is alleged to have saved the lives of several of his countrymen at the St Bartholomew's day massacre although he never renounced his protestantism, and in 1574 to have exhibited his Hebrew learning in a public disputation at Avignon with the chief rabbi Benetrius. However, there is no strong evidence for either of these episodes, which should probably be treated as fanciful. Unsuccessful in trying to win his way back into English good graces, in 1576 Gordon married Antoinette, widowed daughter of René de Marolles, and acquired an estate which gave him the style of sieur de Longorme. They had four known children: Armand Claude; George, who died in the college at Beauvais; and two daughters who died young; there may also have been another son, Henry.

Gordon was an adventurer, making easy accommodations in his politics and religion, and his connection with the see of Galloway was never more than nominal, the revenues going to his father or to his brother George. He is recorded in 1583 as bishop of Galloway, but had resigned the rights to George before 8 July 1586. Antoinette died in 1591, and three years later Gordon married a committed protestant, Geneviève, possibly the daughter of Gideon Pétau, sieur de Maule and 'first president' of the *parlement* of Brittany, but more probably that of François Pétau, an administrator in Brittany. They had a daughter, Lucie or Louise (1597–1680), who in 1613 married Sir Robert Gordon (1580–1656) and was the grandmother, through their daughter Catherine, of the Quaker Robert Barclay. Family tradition claims that Geneviève became French tutor to the Princess Elizabeth (1596–1662), but there is no independent confirmation either of this or of other stories, for instance that in 1601 Gordon was selected by the duchess of Lorraine, sister of Henri IV, to take part with Daniel Tilenus and Pierre du Moulin in a public disputation against the future Cardinal du Perron, who had been charged with the task of converting her to the Catholic faith. Geneviève died at Gordounstoun, Moray, on 6 December 1643, in her eighty-third year, and was buried at the Michael Kirk in the old churchyard of Oggston, parish of Drainie, Moray.

Gordon was essentially an ambitious courtier of unstable loyalty, and in 1600 he wrote a 'flowery panegyric' (Quynn, 86) for Pope Clement VIII. Then in 1603, on the accession of James VI to the English throne as James I, Gordon published in French and English a protestant *Panegyrique of Congratulation*, which was reprinted a year later as *The Union of Great Britaine* and as *England and Scotlands Happinesse*. Also in 1604 he published *Elizabethae Reginae manes de religione et regno*, in Latin elegiacs, addressed to Prince Henry. James called him to England, and in October nominated him, aged fifty-nine, to the deanery of Salisbury, whereupon he took orders. He was present at the Hampton Court conference in January 1604 as 'deane of Sarum', though he was not confirmed in office until 24 February. On the second day James singled him out 'with a speciall encomion, that he was a man well travailled in the auncients' (Barlow, 69). He approved of the ring in marriage, but doubted the cross in baptism. He preached often at court. His *Henōtikon, or, A sermon of the union of Great Brittannie* (1604) was first delivered before

James at Whitehall on 24 October 1604, while John Chamberlain records that on 28 April 1605:

> Deane Gordon, preaching before the kinge, is come so farre about in the matter of ceremonies, that out of Ezechiell and other places of the prophets, and by certain hebrue characters, and other cabalisticall collections, he hath founde out and approved the use of the crosse cap surplis et ct. (*Letters of John Chamberlain*, 1.206)

He had been naturalized on 7 June 1604, and during James's visit to Oxford in 1605 he was created DD (13 August), 'because he was to dispute before the king his kinsman' (Wood, *Ath. Oxon.: Fasti*, 1.311). He is described as of Balliol College. During 1608 Gordon became vicar of Burford and rector of Upton Lovel in Wiltshire, and rector of Stoke Charity, Hampshire; he held all these livings until death. In 1611 the barony of Glenluce, which had belonged to his brother Lawrence, was bestowed on him by royal charter.

Gordon's literary output between 1603 and 1612 consisted of a number of quartos full of quaint learning, protestant fervour, controversial elegiacs, and prophetic anticipations drawn from the wildest etymologies; it was his theological interpretations in favour of James VI and I's project of uniting England and Scotland which most surely endeared him to the king. The religious unity of the island had been first established by King Lucius in 180; now, the union of two protestant countries under one king was an act of providence and signified 'the Union of Christs Elect members in him their head, who is the fountaine of all Union' (J. Gordon, *Henōtikon*, 1604, 52).

Gordon was assiduous in his ecclesiastical duties—though not in looking after the boy choristers of the cathedral—which included a quasi-episcopal supervision of some eighty parishes, and also in preparing for the king's eight visits there. He procured an act of chapter devoting one-fifth of the revenue of every prebend for seven years to cathedral repairs. While on a triennial visitation he died at Leweston House, Dorset, on 3 September 1619. He was buried on 6 September in the morning chapel of Salisbury Cathedral, where an inscribed stone marks his grave. On the north wall of the choir there was a brass (no longer extant) 'bearing the figure of a bishop, raised from his tomb by two angels', with a long biographical epitaph in Latin (given in the 1723 history of the cathedral attributed to Richard Rawlinson). Sir Robert Gordon was made his literary executor. His will left books to the cathedral library, but this was a virtually empty promise as most appear to have gone to Sir Robert; the will also provided for the support of choristers. The dean assigned the barony of Glenluce and all his French property to his wife, daughter, and son-in-law, a task only partially successful in that legal contests followed the dean's death concerning the distribution of the French lands, and it appears that the Gordon and Pétau families knew next to nothing of each other. Such confusion may appear a suitable outcome for a life which consistently practised deception in the pursuit of personal gain.

ALEXANDER GORDON, *rev.* DAVID GEORGE MULLAN

Sources J. Strype, *Annals of the Reformation and establishment of religion … during Queen Elizabeth's happy reign*, new edn, 2/1 (1824), 117 · A. Ross, 'More about the archbishop of Athens', *Innes Review*, 14 (1963), 30–37 · G. Donaldson, *Reformed by bishops: Galloway, Orkney, and Caithness* (1987) · D. M. Quynn, 'The career of John Gordon, dean of Salisbury, 1603–1619', *The Historian*, 6 (1943–4), 76–96 · R. B. Weller, *The strange case of John Gordon, double-agent and dean of Salisbury* (privately printed, 1997) · Wood, *Ath. Oxon.: Fasti* (1815), 311–12 · W. Barlow, *Summe and substance of the conference at Hampton Court* (1604) · Foster, *Alum. Oxon.*, 1500–1714, 2.587 · R. Rawlinson, *The history and antiquities of the cathedral church of Salisbury, and the abbey church of Bath* (1723) · *The letters of John Chamberlain*, ed. N. E. McClure, 2 vols. (1939)

Likenesses line engraving (impression of mural brass formerly in Salisbury cathedral), BM

Wealth at death wealthy; provided for support of choristers; disposed of lands in Scotland and France to family members

Gordon, Sir John, of Haddo, baronet (*d.* 1644), royalist army officer, was the son of George Gordon the younger of Haddo (*d.* in or before 1624) and Margaret Bannerman, daughter of George Bannerman of Wattertoun. Their marriage contract was dated 1606, and John was born thereafter. He succeeded his grandfather as laird of Haddo in 1624 and married in 1630 Mary Forbes (*d.* in or before 1643), daughter of William Forbes of Tolquhoun. Their second son was the judge and politician George *Gordon.

As the revolt of the covenanters against the religious policies of Charles I spread after 1637, Gordon was one of a number of lairds in the north-east of Scotland who were anxious to support the king but frustrated by the lack of leadership from the marquess of Huntly. They signed the king's covenant supporting Charles I late in 1638 but in April 1639 were forced to sign the national covenant of his enemies. However, Gordon and Sir George Ogilvy of Banff then led a dawn raid on 14 May 1639 on Turriff, where covenanting lairds were to impose a stent (tax). The royalists forced the covenanters into confused flight in this 'trot of Turriff', and advanced to occupy Aberdeen for several days, but the covenanters acted swiftly to extinguish this spark of resistance and the royalists were forced to disperse.

On the renewal of conflict the following year, Gordon and others who were initially defiant were forced to surrender to a covenanting army (June 1640). They were imprisoned in the Tolbooth of Edinburgh and Gordon was fined 2000 merks. He was, however, released earlier than his colleagues through the intervention of his covenanting kinsman the Earl Marischal, whom he now followed 'south and north at his plesour' (Spalding, 1.296) to avoid his lands being plundered. He soon drew further trouble on himself, however, by getting involved in a fight with Sir William Forbes of Craigivar, a leading local covenanter, on 28 November 1640. Early in 1641 he was ordered to pay heavy compensation to those whose lands he had plundered in 1639, and in 1642 a prosecution was begun against him for the murder of one of those killed at the trot of Turriff. A visit to the king in England brought him a baronetcy in reward for his actions in 1639, but back in Aberdeen a fight with a former bailie of the burgh again labelled him a trouble-maker. On his failure to appear at the convention of estates in June 1643 he was fined 20,000 merks.

Scotland was now moving towards intervention in the English civil war to help parliament against the king, and Gordon demonstrated his opposition by denouncing the new solemn league and covenant on 29 October when it was sworn in his parish church at Methlick. On 17 January 1644 an attempt was made to arrest him at his house of Kellie (Haddo). This failed, not surprisingly as it was led by Sir Alexander Irvine of Drum (sheriff of Aberdeen), who shared Gordon's royalist sympathies to such an extent that on 19 March he joined Gordon and others in raiding Aberdeen and kidnapping a number of leading covenanter burgesses. Gordon hoped the raid would stir Huntly into action, but though he half-heartedly occupied Aberdeen for a few days he then withdrew. When the covenanters sent an army north under the marquess of Argyll, Gordon fortified Kellie but quickly 'findis his awin folie' (Spalding, 2.358). There was no hope of successful resistance, and he surrendered on 8 May. Again he was sent to Edinburgh and imprisoned in the Tolbooth in what was long afterwards known as 'Haddo's hold' or 'Haddo's hole'. After a brief trial before parliament on charges dating from 1639 to 1644 he and a servant, John Logie, were sentenced to death. On the scaffold on 19 July he obtained relaxation from the excommunication which had been imposed on him in April, but when ministers of the church denounced him he defended himself as having not acted against his country but against disloyal subjects. Commending his six children (whose mother was dead) to God, he waited until Logie had been beheaded by the 'Maiden' beheading machine, made the traditional payment to the executioner, saying 'Do thy office, man' (ibid., 2.389), and so died. Gordon of Haddo was a hot-headed and rash young man whose gestures of defiance against the covenanters were brave but could achieve nothing except the vindication of his sense of honour through loyalty to his king. DAVID STEVENSON

Sources *DNB* • *Scots peerage* • P. Gordon, *A short abridgement of Britane's distemper*, ed. J. Dunn, Spalding Club, 10 (1844) • J. Spalding, *Memorialls of the trubles in Scotland and in England*, AD 1624 – AD 1645, ed. J. Stuart, 2 vols., Spalding Club, [21, 23] (1850–51) • *Reg. PCS*, 2nd ser., vols. 7–8 • *APS*, 1643–7 • *The letters and journals of Robert Baillie*, ed. D. Laing, 3 vols., Bannatyne Club, 73 (1841–2) • NA Scot., GD 33/61/1

Gordon, John, first Viscount Kenmure (*c*.1599–1634), nobleman, was the elder son of Sir Robert Gordon (*d*. 1627/8) of Glen and then Lochinvar, Kirkcudbrightshire, where the family had been settled for many generations, and his wife, Lady Isabel or Elizabeth Ruthven, daughter of William *Ruthven, first earl of Gowrie (*c*.1543–1584). During his childhood his father was several times in trouble with the privy council for violence and murder, and some time after November 1607 his parents' marriage was dissolved. However, Sir Robert was subsequently active in politics and administration in the borders and in several commercial ventures, including a scheme for the establishment of a colony in Nova Scotia. Favour successively from Henry, prince of Wales, and Charles I culminated in 1626 in the grant on 1 May of the barony and lordship of Charles Island in the colony.

John (before 1628 Sir John) Gordon spent part of 1620 and 1621 in the house of the Scottish clergyman John Welch, who, having been banished from Scotland for his connection with the proceedings of the unauthorized Aberdeen assembly of 1605, had settled as Reformed minister at St Jean d'Angely in France. His devotion to presbyterianism was further confirmed by his marriage, between 1624 and 1626, to Jane Campbell [*see* Gordon, Jane, Viscountess Kenmure (*d*. 1675)], sister of the first marquess of Argyll. In order to have the advantage of regular religious services he had the parish of Anwoth, in which his residence was situated, detached from two other parishes with which it had been united, and about 1627 secured the appointment of the presbyterian divine Samuel Rutherford as its minister. Gordon and his wife became the intimate personal friends of Rutherford, and zealously supported him in all his religious schemes, while the latter dedicated to Gordon his first work, *Exercitationes apologeticae pro divina gratia contra Arminium*.

On the death of his father in 1627 or 1628 Gordon succeeded to the family estates and honours. Shortly before this he had registered a claim in right of his mother to the attainted earldom of Gowrie, and in order to induce the king's favourite, the duke of Buckingham, to support his claims, he is stated to have sold the barony of Stitchel for the purpose of raising money to bribe him, and to have paid the bribe on the evening before the duke's assassination by John Felton. On 15 January 1629 the king conferred on Gordon the charter of a royal burgh, within the boundaries of his estate, afterwards called New Galloway. On the occasion of the king's coronation in Scotland, he was on 8 May 1633 created Viscount Kenmure and Lord Lochinvar. He was present at the opening of the parliament which met at Edinburgh in the succeeding June, but, not wishing to displease the king by opposing his ecclesiastical policy, withdrew, pleading illness, to his residence at Kenmure Castle.

While at Edinburgh on private business in August the following year Kenmure was seized with a severe illness, and retiring to Kenmure he died there on 12 September 1634. He was attended on his deathbed by Samuel Rutherford, who wrote an account of his last moments, and of his earlier conversion, published as *The Last and Heavenly Speeches and Glorious Departure of John, Viscount Kenmure* (1649). Rutherford also wrote a long Latin elegy on him, 'In Joanem Gordonum Kenmurii Vicecomitem apotheosis'. Viscountess Kenmure, who was a frequent correspondent of Rutherford, married in February 1640 Sir Harry Montgomerie of Giffen, second son of Alexander Montgomery, sixth earl of Eglinton. Kenmure was survived by one son, who was baptized in December 1634, after his father's death, but who died in 1639, when the title passed to a nephew of the first viscount, John, son of James Gordon of Barncrosh and Buittle.

T. F. HENDERSON, *rev.* CHRISTIAN HESKETH

Sources *Scots peerage* • GEC, *Peerage* • S. Rutherford, ed., *The last and heavenly speeches and glorious departure of John, Viscount Kenmure* (1649); later edn with memoir by J. Murray (1827) • D. G. Mullan, *Scottish puritanism, 1590–1638* (2000)

Gordon, John, fourteenth earl of Sutherland (1609–1679), nobleman, was born on 9 March 1609, the fourth but eldest surviving son of John Gordon, thirteenth earl of Sutherland (1576–1615), and Agnes or Annas (1579–1617), daughter of the fourth Lord Elphinstone. He succeeded his father at the age of six, in September 1615, and his mother died two years later. His uncle Sir Robert Gordon (later of Gordonstoun) was appointed 'tutor of Sutherland' or guardian, and supervised his education. At Dornoch (*c.*1616–*c.*1624) he studied under John Gray, dean of Caithness, whose accounts include provision for the earl of bows and arrows, and golf clubs and balls, as well as pens, ink, and paper. He proceeded to the universities of Edinburgh (1624–6) and St Andrews (1627–30): while at the latter it was noted that he could 'do reasonablie' if he tried (W. Fraser, 1.216). Returning to Sutherland in 1630, he decided to travel in France and other countries 'to inable himselff the more for the service of his cuntrey' (Gordon and Gordon, 422), but whether he actually did so or not is uncertain. On 14 February 1632 he married Lady Jean, daughter of James Drummond, first earl of Perth, 'a wyse, verteous, and comelie woman' (Gordon and Gordon, 486). She died on 29 December 1637 'of a hecktik fewer' and on 24 January 1639 the earl married Anna (1619–1658), daughter of Hugh Fraser, seventh Lord Lovat, 'a good and provydent lady' (Gordon and Gordon, 497).

When resistance to Charles I's religious policies in Scotland erupted in July 1637 Sutherland was quick to join the opposition, and on 20 September, having highest precedence among the nobles active in the movement, he presented a supplication of grievances to the Scottish privy council. He was the first to sign the national covenant in February 1638. In the bishops' wars of 1639–40 he took a leading role in raising men for the covenanters in the far north of Scotland, and also sent some men to join the Scots army which occupied the north of England, which he visited in 1641. He attended the parliament at which Charles I reached a settlement with the covenanters, being appointed a member of the new privy council on 18 November 1641.

On 1 February 1644 Sutherland was commissioned to raise a regiment of 1600 men, who were intended to serve in the Scottish army in England, but the landing of Alasdair MacColla in the highlands and his conjunction with the marquess of Montrose in a royalist rising led to Sutherland's men being retained in the north. The earl was present at the battle of Auldearn on 9 May 1645, when the covenanters were defeated, and his regiment was disbanded in 1646. However, in October 1646 he was commissioned to levy 500 men to act against the royalist Lord Reay, with whom he disputed possession of Strathnaver, though the force was soon dissolved. In 1648 he refused to raise men for the engager regime, an alliance of moderate royalists and covenanters, instead supporting the uncompromising kirk party. Once the latter seized power, he was again commissioned to raise men in the north (February 1649), but seems to have taken little action until April 1650, when he levied men at the time of Montrose's landing in Caithness—though he avoided offensive action against him. Subsequently he was ordered to bring his men south to oppose the threat of English invasion, but he did not arrive there until after the rest of the Scots army had been defeated at the battle of Dunbar (3 September). He then returned north to continue levying. In 1651 he failed to march south with his men, pleading on 4 April that his efforts had cast him 'into a little distemper of bodie' and on 9 May that he 'was necessitate to stay for some tyme untill I recouer some more strength and better health, being constrained to purge and draw blood' (D. Laing, ed., *Correspondence of … Earl of Ancram and … Earl of Lothian*, 2 vols., 1825, 2.347, 356).

Sutherland's support for the kirk party had brought him the office of lord privy seal of Scotland on 10 March 1649, but his service to the covenanters was primarily as a regional magnate, the most powerful supporter of the cause in the far north of Scotland. The religious convictions underlying his political stance were more deep-rooted than in the case of many of his noble colleagues, and this may have influenced his failure to join with the army in 1651, for by then the kirk party had collapsed and in the eyes of many the religious justification for war with England had been lost. That Sutherland's views made him sympathetic to aspects of the Cromwellian regime of the 1650s was noted, and there were hopes that he and his family might be brought to favour independency. 'Hee and his sons and Lady are all religious and deserve encouragement,' Colonel Robert Lilburne reported to Cromwell on 11 April 1654, 'I was a yeare ago att his house, and found very much civility and religion in the familie, and I heare his sons are both of them much affected to us, and inclin'd to church fellowshippe.' His attitude to the English invaders earned Sutherland much hostility. 'I heard of the contempt which others had of the honest, poor' earl of Sutherland, noted a sympathizer in 1655 (*Diary*, ed. Laing, 126). Worse than contempt was attack by royalist insurgents. His old enemy Lord Reay took advantage of the situation to drive the earl 'out of his country with his sons, and [Lieutenant General John] Middleton hath turn'd his Lady out of doores, and sent her after him, and his land and estate is exceedingly wasted' (Firth, 83). This added to his existing financial problems. In 1655 he sold his silver plate to pay his debts, and in 1662 he resigned the lands of the earldom to his son George, Lord Strathnaver.

'Old Earl John of Sutherland lives still unmarried' it was recorded in 1663, and 'kind Earl John' is mentioned in 1666 (J. Fraser, 451, 471). He died in Dunrobin Castle, Sutherland, on 14 October 1679 'of a palsy' (*Diary*, ed. Laing, 418). Half a century later he was still remembered as 'the good old Earle of Sutherland, who was most eminent for religion before the Restoration, and did great services for his country [Sutherland]'. At church services, it was said, if the precentor was absent, the earl himself would lead the congregational singing of psalms from his loft or gallery. He was a home-loving man, with no taste for the court. He did not bother travelling south for Charles I's Scottish coronation in 1633; he missed Charles II's in 1651 because (as his apology explained) no one had told him the date; and at the restoration of monarchy in 1660 he, being 'no courtiour' (J. Fraser, 439), declined to travel south to welcome the new regime. DAVID STEVENSON

Sources *DNB* • GEC, *Peerage* • *Scots peerage* • R. Gordon and G. Gordon, *A genealogical history of the earldom of Sutherland … with a continuation to the year 1651* (1813) • E. M. Furgol, *A regimental history of the covenanting armies, 1639–1651* (1990) • C. H. Firth, ed., *Scotland and the protectorate: letters and papers relating to the military government of Scotland from January 1654 to June 1659*, Scottish History Society, 31 (1899) • J. Fraser, *Chronicles of the Frasers: the Wardlaw manuscript*, ed. W. Mackay, Scottish History Society, 1st ser., 47 (1905) • W. Fraser, ed., *The Sutherland book*, 3 vols. (1892) • *Reg. PCS*, 1st ser. • *Reg. PCS*, 2nd ser. • *Reg. PCS*, 3rd ser. • John, earl of Rothes, *A relation of proceedings concerning the affairs of the Kirk of Scotland*, Bannatyne Club, 37 (1830) • R. Wodrow, *Analecta, or, Materials for a history of remarkable providences, mostly relating to Scotch ministers and Christians*, ed. [M. Leishman], 4 vols., Maitland Club, 60 (1842–3) • *The historical works of Sir James Balfour*, ed. J. Haig, 4 vols. (1824–5) • *The diary of Alexander Brodie of Brodie … and of his son James Brodie*, ed. D. Laing, Spalding Club, 33 (1863)

Archives NL Scot., corresp. and papers | NL Scot., letters to Forbes family • NL Scot., letters to Sir Robert Gordon and Robert Farquhar

Likenesses engraving, 1812 (after an original picture at Dunrobin Castle, 1669), repro. in Gordon and Gordon, *Genealogical history*, frontispiece

Gordon, John [*known as* John Clement Gordon] (**1644–1726**), Scottish Episcopal bishop of Galloway and Roman Catholic convert, was the son of John Gordon of Coldwells, in the parish of Ellon, Aberdeenshire. He was educated in England, becoming a chaplain to the navy, and was a royal chaplain 'apud New York in America' when, on a vacancy in the see of Galloway, a *congé d'élire* was issued in his favour on 3 December 1687. A patent for the see was issued on 4 February 1688 and he was consecrated by Archbishop Patterson at Glasgow on 19 September 1688. He is sometimes considered the author of the anti-Catholic *Pax vobis, or, Gospel and Liberty, Against Ancient and Modern Papists* (1679), frequently reprinted in the late seventeenth century, but the attribution seems unlikely. Certainly Gordon remained loyal to James II during the revolution of 1688, and joined the king in Ireland the next year. From there he followed him to St Germain-en-Laye in France.

The position of protestants at the exiled Stuart court was difficult. Although James II and Mary of Modena both wanted them to be allowed to worship freely, Louis XIV was not prepared to accept this. He had given his agreement to their settling in France on the specific condition that they made no request to be allowed to hold any protestant services, even within the château of St Germain itself. Gordon was consequently obliged to read the liturgy of the Church of England in strict secrecy within his own lodgings. Protestant Jacobites were never persecuted at the exiled Stuart court, though it may be that the attack on the 'ancient and modern Papists' attributed to Gordon made him an unpopular figure among the Catholics at St Germain. Moreover, he was no doubt relatively isolated because nearly all the protestants there were English and the few Scots tended to be Catholic. In 1696 John Macky alleged in his influential pamphlet *A View of the Court of St. Germain from the Year 1690–95* that Gordon had been forced to become a Catholic in order to obtain the wherewithal to live, but there was no truth in this.

In June 1699 Matthew Prior reported from the English embassy in Paris that Gordon had approached him for a pass to return to Scotland. This request seems to have been refused, as Gordon remained in France. About 1702 he was converted by Bossuet and was privately received into the Catholic church. Soon afterwards Gordon travelled to Rome, where he made a public abjuration of protestantism before Cardinal Sacripanti, the cardinal protector of Scotland. At his conditional baptism he took the additional name of the reigning pontiff, and ever afterwards signed himself John Clement Gordon. The pope, wishing to confer some benefice pension on the new convert, caused the sacred congregation of the inquisition to institute an inquiry into the validity of Gordon's protestant orders. After a long investigation his orders were treated as if they were null from the beginning, a view which Gordon himself may have held at this stage. The decree of the inquisition to this effect was issued on 17 April 1704. After this Gordon received the sacrament of confirmation, and Clement XI conferred on him the tonsure, giving him the benefice of the abbey of St Clement, by reason of which Gordon commonly went by the name of the Abate Clemente. It is observable that he never received other than minor orders in the Roman Catholic church. Gordon was still living in the Papal States when James III and the Jacobite court took refuge there in 1717. He died at Rome in 1726.

THOMPSON COOPER, *rev.* EDWARD CORP

Sources *Calendar of the manuscripts of the marquis of Bath preserved at Longleat, Wiltshire*, 5 vols., HMC, 58 (1904–80), vol. 3, p. 358 • J. Macky, *A view of the court of St. Germain from the year 1690–95, with an account of the entertainment protestants meet with there* (1696) • E. Corp, 'James II and toleration: the years in exile at Saint-Germain-en-Laye', *Royal Stuart Paper*, 51 (1997) • *Fasti Scot.*, new edn, 7.347 • J. Quinn, 'The case of the convert bishop: John Clement Gordon 1644–1726', *The Month*, new ser., 19 (1958), 102–7 • F. Blom and others, *English Catholic books, 1701–1800: a bibliography* (1996)

Gordon, John. *See* Sutherland, John, sixteenth earl of Sutherland (*bap.* 1661, *d.* 1733).

Gordon, John (**1702–1739**), barrister, was born and baptized on 26 March 1702 in the parish of St Martin Ludgate, London, the son of John Gordon, a watchmaker at the sign of the Black Spread Eagle, Ludgate Street, and his wife, Lucretia. He had an older sister, Lucretia, who was baptized on 18 January 1699 or 1700. He was educated at Westminster School, where he became a king's scholar in 1716, and at Trinity College, Cambridge, from 1720. Having been elected a scholar in 1721 he left Trinity in June 1722 to study law. He had entered Gray's Inn on 9 November 1718, but resided in Lincoln's Inn, and was called to the bar on 10 February 1725.

Gordon was elected professor of music at Gresham College on 16 January 1724, on the death of Dr Edward Shippen (1671–1724). There is no evidence that he was qualified for the post or that he delivered any lectures. He died unmarried and intestate on 12 December 1739 and was buried at St Dunstan-in-the-West on the instruction of his sister, by then Mrs Smith.

L. M. MIDDLETON, *rev.* S. J. SKEDD

Sources J. Ward, *The lives of the professors of Gresham College*, 2nd edn, 2 vols. (1740), 236 [through-paginated] • Venn, *Alum. Cant.* • J. Foster, *The register of admissions to Gray's Inn, 1521–1889, together with the register of marriages in Gray's Inn chapel, 1695–1754* (privately printed, London, 1889) • *N&Q*, 147 (1924), 62 • *Old Westminsters* • *IGI*

Gordon, John (1807–1880). *See under* Gordon, Alexander (1841–1931).

Gordon, John Campbell, first marquess of Aberdeen and Temair (1847–1934), politician, was born in Edinburgh on 3 August 1847, the third and youngest son of George John James Hamilton-Gordon, fifth earl of Aberdeen (1816–1864), and his wife, Mary (*d.* 1900), second daughter of George Baillie, of Jerviswood, of a family well known in covenanting annals. His childhood was spent largely in the Ranger's House, Blackheath, and after studying at St Andrews University he finished his education at University College, Oxford, where he graduated BA in 1871.

Four successive deaths between 1860 and 1870 brought Gordon unexpectedly to the peerage. (He changed his name back from Hamilton-Gordon in 1900.) His grandfather the prime minister George Hamilton-*Gordon, the fourth earl, died in 1860, and his father died in 1864; in 1868 he lost his second brother by a rifle accident, while in 1870 his eldest brother George, an adventurous young man with a passion for the sea, was swept overboard while working in the American mercantile marine under an assumed name. It was not until 6 May 1872 that the youngest brother's succession to the title was confirmed by the House of Lords. In 1877 Aberdeen married Ishbel Maria, *née* Marjoribanks [*see below*]. Although of a Conservative family, he became a firm Liberal, voted against the tory government's Afghan policy, and in 1879 was one of the party at Lord Rosebery's house at Dalmeny for Gladstone's first Midlothian campaign. Dollis Hill, Aberdeen's London house, became a regular bolt-hole for Gladstone. Gladstone was keen to advance Liberal peers. He made Aberdeen lord lieutenant of his county in 1881 and lord high commissioner to the Church of Scotland from 1881 to 1885 (he again held the position 1915), and he made him Irish viceroy in 1886, with the first Home Rule Bill in the offing. The Aberdeens helped consolidate the Liberal alliance with home-rule Dublin, and they travelled through the disturbed southern and western counties. However, Aberdeen played no part in the making of the home-rule or land legislation, and played the part more of a constitutional monarch than a politician in the six months of the Liberal government's existence. When Gladstone returned to office in 1892, Aberdeen was disappointed not to be reappointed to Ireland (Gladstone sought 'a stronger hand'; Gladstone, *Diaries*, 21 Aug 1892), but accepted Canada instead, becoming governor-general in June 1893. The five years' term was at first not easy, being marked by three changes in the premiership in two years, but with

John Campbell Gordon, first marquess of Aberdeen and Temair (1847–1934), by James Russell & Sons

the victory of Wilfred Laurier in 1895 tension was relaxed. Aberdeen returned home in 1898, and in December 1905 he was appointed once more to the lord lieutenancy at Dublin, this time for the longest term in its history. For nine years he worked for a better understanding between the two countries, and his efforts seemed to be bearing fruit. Royal visits in 1907 and 1911 were of good omen, and when the Home Rule Bill became law in 1914 and Aberdeen's impending retirement was announced, numerous requests for an extension of his term were received from towns and other influential quarters. On his retirement in 1915 he was advanced a step in the peerage as marquess of Aberdeen and Temair (gazetted in 1916).

From early days Aberdeen had been interested in social welfare, and in 1874 he had served on a royal commission on railway accidents (he had a lifelong interest in railway matters) and had helped to bring to light the excessive hours worked by railway employees; later he took part in a similar inquiry into loss of life at sea. Ably seconded in this side of his work by his wife, he put into effect several new ideas for the welfare of the farmers and labourers at his homes, Haddo House in Aberdeenshire and the House of Cromar, which he built at Tarland, near Aboyne. The general tendency of the time was to combine smallholdings into larger farms; but in 1920 he was able to say that during his fifty years as laird the holdings on his estates had increased from 935 to 958 and that 588 houses had been built. Another successful venture was evening classes for farm servants. This work in Aberdeenshire alternated with such efforts as the founding of the London Playing Fields Society and unceasing political and religious work. He was in constant association with the seventh Lord Shaftesbury and later with Henry Drummond.

The Aberdeens had three sons and two daughters; the younger daughter, Dorothea, died in infancy and the youngest son, Archibald Ian, was killed in a motor-car accident in 1909. The elder daughter, Marjorie Adeline, married John *Sinclair (later first Lord Pentland). In 1920 Aberdeen handed over the management of his Haddo estates to his heir, Lord Haddo; he spent the remainder of his life at the House of Cromar, where he died on 7 March 1934. He was succeeded as eighth earl and second marquess by his eldest son, George (1879–1965).

Aberdeen was sworn of the privy council in 1886, was appointed GCMG in 1886, KT in 1906, and GCVO in 1911. Honorary degrees were conferred upon him by the universities of Aberdeen and Oxford and by numerous universities in Canada and the USA. He was elected an honorary fellow of University College, Oxford, in 1932 and was lord rector of St Andrews University from 1913 to 1916.

Aberdeen's wife, **Dame Ishbel Maria Gordon** [*née* Marjoribanks], marchioness of Aberdeen and Temair (1857–1939), was born in London on 14 March 1857, the youngest daughter of Sir Dudley Coutts Marjoribanks, afterwards first Baron Tweedmouth, and his wife, Isabella, eldest daughter of Sir James Weir *Hogg and sister of Quintin *Hogg. Her character and ideals were moulded by her mother, whose influence was the strongest in her life, but both sides of her family were strongly philanthropic. Educated privately, she entered upon her adult life with a liberal education and a strong sense of social responsibility. In her home she came into contact with many great political and religious leaders, of whom W. E. Gladstone impressed himself most strongly on her mind, and at a young age she dedicated herself to religious and humanitarian pursuits. She became a devoted and ardent Liberal and was president of the Women's Liberal Federation, succeeding Catherine Gladstone as president for a few months in 1893 before accompanying her husband to Canada. *We Twa*—the title of the Aberdeens' unusual joint autobiography—described a very happy marriage. The Aberdeens were energetic philanthropists. An early endeavour was the Haddo House Association, which developed later into the Onward and Upward Association. Having begun as an educational and recreational project for the tenants of the Aberdeenshire estates, it soon extended its membership throughout Great Britain and the dominions. Lady Aberdeen vigorously used her status to develop interest in questions affecting women. During her husband's first lord lieutenancy, the setting up of cottage and village industry under the Irish Industries' Association had some success in promoting weaving. Lady Aberdeen distributed a newly designed hand-loom. She returned to Ireland several times between 1886 and 1894 to monitor progress.

In Canada the same vigour was evident. She maintained her interest in Ireland, organizing an exhibition of Irish goods at the Chicago fair. She distributed looms to remote areas of Canada. She instituted a dominionwide health service by the foundation in 1898 of the Victorian Order of Nurses, and also she came into close contact with two movements with which she was subsequently especially associated: the Red Cross Society and the National Council of Women. In 1893 she was elected president of the International Congress of Women (formed at Washington in 1888; later renamed the Women's International League for Peace and Freedom), and almost immediately she became its acknowledged leader. Under her guidance the congress's efforts were directed to the improvement of the social and economic position of women and the promotion of peace. It met under her presidency in a well-attended meeting in London in 1899, when she edited its proceedings in seven volumes. She was the leader and spokesperson of a deputation of its council to a meeting of the League of Nations commission at the peace conference of Versailles in 1919, and she successfully advocated the opening of all posts on the secretariat of the League of Nations to women on equal terms with men. At the jubilee celebrations of the movement, held in Edinburgh in 1938, tribute was paid by representative men and women of many lands to the inspiration of her leadership, which had brought the International Congress and its council to a place of some influence.

During her second term in Ireland, from 1906 to 1915, Lady Aberdeen was especially active in public health and housing. She set up the Women's National Health Association in 1907 and edited its journal, *Slainte*, for three years. She established sanatoriums for tuberculosis, and promoted many exhibitions (with caravans to tour the rural areas). Patrick Geddes, the civic reformer and town planner, was brought from Scotland to advise on Dublin's housing. Even so, her longer second spell in Ireland left her less popular than her first. She was seen as something of a 'Lady Bountiful' by some of the Irish and she was regarded as overactive in her influence on patronage. Unionists regularly boycotted her receptions.

Lady Aberdeen received many honours, British and foreign. She was one of the first women to be nominated a justice of the peace. In 1931 she was appointed GBE, and she received the honorary degree of LLD from Aberdeen University and the Queen's University, Kingston, Ontario. In 1928 she received an honour which she perhaps esteemed as highly as any, the freedom of the city of Edinburgh.

Lady Aberdeen's activities were never allowed to interfere with her domestic duties. She entered fully and intimately into the upbringing of her children. A woman of deep religious conviction, she felt herself under divine guidance in all her undertakings. To the end of her life she maintained vigour of mind and body; she died at Aberdeen on 18 April 1939, and was buried in the cemetery at Haddo House.

G. F. Barbour and Matthew Urie Baird, *rev.*
H. C. G. Matthew

Sources *The Times* (8 March 1934) • *The Times* (19 April 1939) • Lord Aberdeen [J. C. Gordon] and Lady Aberdeen [I. M. Gordon], *We twa*,

2 vols. (1925) • Lord Aberdeen [J. C. Gordon] and Lady Aberdeen [I. M. Gordon], *More cracks with 'We twa'* (1929) • Lady Aberdeen [I. M. Gordon], *Musings of a Scottish granny* (1936) • Gladstone, *Diaries* • D. Rubenstein, *Before the suffragettes* (1986) • N. O'Cleirigh, 'Lady Aberdeen and the Irish connection', *Dublin Historical Record*, 39 (1985–6), 28–32 • M. Keane, *Ishbel: Lady Aberdeen in Ireland* (1999)

Archives NA Canada, corresp. and papers relating to Canada • NRA Scotland, priv. coll. • U. Aberdeen L., corresp., etc. | BL, letters to Sir Henry Campbell-Bannerman, Add. MS 41210 • BL, corresp. with W. E. Gladstone, Add. MS 44090 • BL, corresp. with Lord Gladstone, Add. MS 45995 • BL, corresp. with Lord Ripon, Add. MS 43559 • BL, corresp. with Society of Authors, Add. MS 56654 • Bodl. Oxf., corresp. with Herbert Asquith; corresp. with Lord Kimberley; letters to Sir Matthew Nathan; Wodehouse MSS • HLRO, corresp. with David Lloyd George • NA Scot., corresp. with A. J. Balfour; corresp., incl. Lord Rosebery • priv. coll., corresp. with Sir John Ewart • U. Birm. L., corresp. with Joseph Chamberlain • Wellcome L., letters to Sir George Newman

Likenesses C. Furse, oils, exh. RA 1890?, Dublin Castle • R. T. Mackenzie, bronze relief plaque, 1921, Scot. NPG • W. Stoneman, photograph, 1921, NPG • Barnekow, oils, Town and County Hall, Aberdeen • A. E. Emslie, group portrait, oils (*Dinner at Haddo House*), NPG • D. Glanfield, photograph, NPG; repro. in *Daily Herald* • J. Russell & Sons, photograph, NPG [*see illus.*] • J. Sant, oils, Haddo House, Aberdeenshire • Spy [L. Ward], chromolithograph caricature, NPG; repro. in *VF* (6 Feb 1902) • H. Wrightson, photograph, NPG; repro. in *Daily Herald*

Gordon, Sir John James Hood (1832–1908), army officer, was born on 12 January 1832 at Aberdeen, the twin son of Captain William Gordon, 2nd foot, and Marianna Carlotta Loi, daughter of Luis Gonçalves de Mello, a Portuguese government official in Estremadura whom William Gordon had met during the Peninsular War. His twin brother was Thomas Edward *Gordon and he had two other brothers and a sister.

Gordon was educated at Dalmeny College and the Royal Naval and Military Academy, Edinburgh, and in 1849 was commissioned into the 29th foot, which was then in India, moving to Burma in 1854. When the Indian mutiny broke out he was attached to the 97th foot and served with the Jaunpur field force, being present at the capture of Lucknow in March 1858, and from September 1858 to April 1859 serving in Bihar. He was promoted captain in December 1859, mentioned in dispatches, and given a brevet majority. He remained in India after the 29th left in 1859, exchanging into the 46th foot and being promoted to major in 1860. He assumed command of the 29th (Punjab) Bengal native infantry in 1861, becoming lieutenant-colonel in 1875 and brevet colonel in 1877. He had married in 1871 Ella (*d.* 8 Sept 1903), daughter of Edward Strathearn *Gordon, Baron Gordon of Drumearn, a lord of appeal in ordinary. They had two sons, who became army officers.

With his regiment Gordon took part in the Jowaki expedition of 1877–8, and when the Second Afghan War broke out in November 1878 the 29th formed part of the force under Major-General Frederick Roberts which invaded Afghanistan via the Kurram valley. On the night of 1–2 December 1878 the regiment led the turning movement via the Spingawi valley against the Afghan position on the Peiwar Kotal. Two Pathan sepoys of the 29th treacherously fired shots to warn the Afghans, and during the subsequent battle eighteen sepoys of the 29th returned to camp without permission. Subsequently one sepoy was hanged and a native officer and the other nineteen sepoys sentenced to transportation. Roberts considered that the trouble was due in part to Gordon's poor selection of native officers and NCOs, and of recruits. Gordon remained in the Kurram for the remainder of the war, being promoted to temporary brigadier-general in the latter part of 1879 and sharing military command in the valley until the forces were divided into two brigades, when he assumed command of the Upper Kurram brigade. For his services he received the CB. In 1880 he commanded the troops in operations against the Malikshahi Wazirs and in 1881 commanded the second column in the expedition against the Mahsuds, being mentioned in dispatches and thanked by the government of India. Between 1882 and 1887 he commanded the Rawalpindi brigade, being promoted major-general in 1886. He took part in the Third Anglo-Burmese War in 1886–7, commanding the eastern frontier district, and again receiving the thanks of government.

Roberts's experience in the Anglo-Afghan War had given him an unfavourable view of both Gordon brothers: 'they are far above the average in ability and intelligence … but after what I saw of them in Kuram, I could never trust them on service in any position of responsibility' (Roberts to D. Stewart, 12 May 1888, Roberts Papers). He refused therefore, as commander-in-chief, to consider either for a divisional command.

John Gordon therefore left India to become assistant military secretary at the Horse Guards in 1890. He was promoted lieutenant-general in 1891 and general in 1894, retiring in 1896. From 1897 to 1906 he was military member of the Council of India. He was made KCB in 1898 and GCB in 1908, and became colonel of the 29th Bengal infantry in 1904. He died at 18 Magdala Cresent, Edinburgh, on 2 November 1908, and was buried in the Dean cemetery, Edinburgh. H. M. VIBART, *rev.* BRIAN ROBSON

Sources T. E. Gordon, *A varied life* (1906) • V. C. P. Hodson, *List of officers of the Bengal army, 1758–1834*, 4 vols. (1927–47) • *Hart's Army List* • NAM, Roberts MSS • C. M. MacGregor, *The Second Afghan War*, 6 vols. (1885–6) • Lord Roberts [F. S. Roberts], *Forty-one years in India*, 2 vols. (1897) • *The Times* (3 Nov 1908) • private information (1912) • J. M. Bullock and C. O. Skelton, *A notable military family: the Gordons in Griamachary* (1907) • H. B. Hanna, *The Second Afghan War*, 3 (1910) • W. H. Paget, *A record of the expeditions against the north-west frontier tribes, since the annexation of the Punjab*, rev. A. H. Mason (1884) • Burke, *Peerage*

Wealth at death £18,741 12*s.* 4*d.*: confirmation, 17 Feb 1909, *CCI*

Gordon, John Rutherford (1890–1974), newspaper editor, was born in Dundee on 8 December 1890, the elder son and eldest of three children of Joseph Gordon, wine merchant, and his wife, Margaret Rutherford. He was educated at Morgan Academy, Dundee, and left school at the age of fourteen to start work on the Dundee *Advertiser* at 4*s.* 6*d.* a week. His diligence and flair as a junior reporter (one of his innovations was to take carrier pigeons to football matches to ensure the quicker receipt of the results in the office) and later as sub-editor were the first indication of a good newspaperman in the making.

By the age of nineteen Gordon was in charge of the

Perthshire and Dundee editions of the *People's Journal*, sister newspaper of the *Advertiser*, and was being paid 25*s*. a week, a sum less than that paid to older men doing less responsible work. Gordon, who throughout his life had a shrewd assessment of his own worth, felt that he was being exploited. On 28 June 1910 he wrote a stern letter signed 'John R. Gordon' to his superior, Leng Sturrock, pointing out that his duties were such that Monday evening was the only evening in the week in which he was free before midnight, and that for such prolonged efforts his remuneration was inadequate. He wrote: 'At present I receive 25/- per week—10/- less than the next lowest paid sub-editor. I do not expect or ask for an increase of this amount but five shillings would, I think, be fair compensation for the lengthy hours.' Displaying the caution which was also one of his characteristics, however, he added a postscript: 'If 5/- is too much, 2/6d will do.' He was paid 2*s*. 6*d*.

In 1911 Gordon left Dundee for London, where he worked in the London offices of first the *Advertiser* and then the *Glasgow Herald*. After the First World War broke out he served in France as a rifleman signaller in the rifle brigade and the King's Royal Rifle Corps. In 1915 he married Evelyn Hinton (*d*. 1967). At the end of the war he joined the London *Evening News*, where he became chief sub-editor in 1922. His inspired handling and assessment of news brought him to the notice of other Fleet Street newspapers and in 1924 he accepted a similar post on the *Daily Express*, then edited by A. Beverley Baxter. Although his success was again immediate, after a time he once more felt that he was being inadequately rewarded financially; one night when Baxter, who was a great theatregoer and bon viveur, returned dinner jacketed from his evening meal to cast an eye over the first edition Gordon raised the subject with him. According to Gordon, Baxter, immediately and generously conceding his chief sub-editor's worth, told him that his salary would be raised by £10 a week. Unhappily, the editor forgot to inform the accounts department of his good deed and during the next three months when the increase had still not been implemented Gordon neither reminded the editor nor complained. At the end of that period he simply resigned and announced his intention of going back to the *Evening News*.

Meanwhile Lord Beaverbrook had recognized Gordon's talent. 'Beaverbrook', said Baxter, 'was the first to sense the burning flame within the granite exterior.' In 1928 Beaverbrook appointed Gordon editor of the *Sunday Express*, a post which he held jointly for the next three years with James Douglas, who had been in the chair since 1920. The *Sunday Express* was then in deep trouble, with a circulation of only 450,000. In his twenty-four years of editorship, until 1952, Gordon was to turn the ailing newspaper into one of the most successful and profitable in the world, with a circulation in excess of 3,200,000.

Gordon's innovations were many. He introduced both the first crossword puzzle and the first 'What the stars foretell' column to be published in a British newspaper. The latter happened after Gordon had commissioned an astrologer, R. H. Naylor, to cast a horoscope on the birth of Princess Margaret as he 'was seeking something different to write about her'. The result was so spectacularly successful and popular that it remained a feature. It also led to the appearance in the dock at Mansion House of both Gordon and Naylor. They were charged with being rogues and vagabonds and telling fortunes. The charges were dismissed on the grounds that the statements made were so vague that they did not come within the terms of the Vagrancy Act. Gordon did not always see eye to eye with his astrologer. When he read Naylor's forecast that Russia would not be invaded by Germany, he told him to think again, but Naylor was adamant that he was right. In the next issue of the *Sunday Express* Naylor said one thing and Gordon the other. Russia was invaded. Gordon had proved himself a better forecaster than his astrologer.

Gordon's belief was that above all other things news sold a newspaper. Right to the end of his active editorship he personally was responsible for the choice and display of every page one story. He ensured that the newspaper both commented and entertained. The cartoonist Carl Giles was one of his greatest captures and it was under his direction that the humorist Nathaniel Gubbins became a household name. Salacity was the one ingredient in many popular newspapers which neither he nor Beaverbrook would tolerate. It was an essential part of his philosophy that the *Sunday Express* should be a 'newspaper fit for all the family to read'. Indeed the market at which he was aiming his newspaper was the 'family man who either has a car in his garage or means to have one'—in other words, the young man on the way up.

In the Second World War Gordon emerged as a writer and commentator of considerable force. Although all his life he was contemptuous of politicians of all parties he had an extraordinary capacity to sense what the man in the street was thinking and to put these inarticulate thoughts forcefully into words. During the war *Sunday Express* readers read his critical comments on the conduct of the war especially during the dark days of 1941 and 1942 with a respect which was only second to that which they accorded Winston Churchill.

Gordon was never an intimate of Beaverbrook's in the way that Viscount Castlerosse, his chief columnist, was. Unlike other Beaverbrook employees such as Michael Foot, Frank Owen, and Peter Howard, he was not a frequent guest at Beaverbrook's dinner table. Proprietor and editor eyed each other warily. Each recognized the quality of the other and Beaverbrook certainly understood the importance of John Gordon to the *Sunday Express*.

In 1952, when Gordon reached sixty-two, Beaverbrook wanted a younger man in charge of the newspaper. He suggested that Gordon should be editor-in-chief, a title which sounded grand, and which he retained until his death, but which was empty in terms of power. Although Gordon accepted the post he realized he was being 'pushed upstairs', and as a consolation Beaverbrook suggested that Gordon might like to write a column. Gordon accepted the challenge in a way which Beaverbrook had not anticipated and went on as columnist to greater public renown than he had known before. His current events column was sharp, incisive, abrasive, and doffed its cap to nobody, from the royal family downwards. In that job (although often racked with pain and having had to suffer the amputation of a leg) he continued until his death. Following the death of his first wife, in 1972 he married Margaret, former wife of Cedric Blundell-Ince, and daughter of Alexander Guthrie, linotype operator. She was a former personal assistant to Lord Beaverbrook. Gordon died at Croydon on 9 December 1974, one day after his eighty-fourth birthday. JOHN JUNOR, *rev.*

Sources personal knowledge (1986) · private information (1986) · *The Times* (11 Dec 1974) · *WWW*
Archives HLRO, corresp. with Lord Beaverbrook · People's History Museum, Manchester, corresp. with William Gallacher | FILM BFI NFTVA, news footage
Wealth at death £81,961: probate, 7 Feb 1975, *CGPLA Eng. & Wales*

Gordon, Sir John Watson- (**1788–1864**), painter of historical subjects and portraits, was born in Edinburgh. He was descended from the Watsons of Overmains, Berwickshire, and he was the son of Captain James Watson of the Royal Artillery. John Watson trained to follow his father into the army, but before receiving his commission took drawing lessons with John Graham at the Trustees' Academy in Edinburgh and studied with his uncle George *Watson, who was the first president of the Scottish Academy, and also with Sir Henry Raeburn, who was a family friend, and decided instead to become a painter. In order to distinguish himself from his cousin and his uncle who were both artists, he later assumed the name Watson-Gordon and appears as such for the first time in the catalogue of the 1826 exhibition of the Royal Institution, Edinburgh, of which he was an associate.

Watson-Gordon is today best remembered—and is still highly regarded—as a portrait painter, but his earliest works were genre scenes. His diploma picture, *A Grandfather's Lesson*, depicted his father tutoring a fair-haired girl. Like many works of the time it suffered from bituminous cracking caused by the addition of tar into the blacks to enrich their lustrous effect. The stiff figures in another work, *The Laird of Cockpen* (McManus Galleries, Dundee), an interpretation of a well-known Scottish song, reveals the clumsy draughtsmanship of his earliest period. Another early work, however, a portrait of the songwriter Carolina Oliphant, *Baroness Nairne and her Son William Murray Nairne* (Scot. NPG) shows more skill. The lace edging to the sitter's cap and plum dress, her shining curls, and gentle expression are all expertly captured, although the physical grouping of mother and son is not entirely resolved. In 1808 Watson-Gordon exhibited a scene from Sir Walter Scott's *Lay of the Last Minstrel* at the first public exhibition held in Edinburgh; then, the following year, *The Battle of Bannockburn* and *Queen Mary Forced to Abdicate the Crown*. He continued to paint historical and religious subjects but after 1821 turned to portraiture and when Raeburn died in 1823, Gordon became the leading portraitist in Scotland. Like his uncle, in portraiture

Sir John Watson-Gordon (**1788–1864**), by James Good Tunny, 1850s

Watson-Gordon was greatly influenced by Raeburn's painting style. *Thomas Clerk and his Wife* (1820; Royal Company of Archers, Edinburgh), for example, shows clear similarities, in both composition and treatment, with Raeburn's *Sir John and Lady Clerk of Penicuik* (1792; NG Ire.), although this early work by Watson-Gordon lacks the atmosphere and bravura of Raeburn's double portrait. Watson-Gordon was a founding member of the Royal Scottish Academy in 1826, and was represented in the academy's annual exhibitions from 1830 until 1865. He also exhibited at the Royal Academy in London from 1827, becoming an associate member in 1841 and a full member ten years later. As a result his work became well known in England and many English people travelled to sit for him in his Edinburgh studio. Among them was the landscape artist David Cox, whose friends in Birmingham commissioned a three-quarter-length portrait of Cox from Watson-Gordon (Scot. NPG). Cox was reportedly delighted with the portrait and enjoyed the sittings in Edinburgh—he described Watson-Gordon as 'affable and entertaining, with a grave and dignified carriage' (Solly, 238). Watson-Gordon's portraits were both popular and critically acclaimed. With limited use of colour, dramatic lighting, and by focusing attention on the face, he managed to convey a heightened impression of the character of his sitters. He was especially successful when portraying the intellectuals of his day and painted most of the Scottish celebrities and writers of his time, including Lord Cockburn, James Hogg (in a rugged and romantic depiction *The Ettrick Shepherd*, swathed in plaid) (both Scot. NPG), and Sir

Walter Scott (four portraits including an unfinished study of 1830, Scot. NPG), whom he painted many times. Scott was first portrayed by Watson-Gordon in 1820. He also commissioned from the artist a set of family miniatures for the travelling writing-case of his son Walter, who was in the army. Watson-Gordon was at his best when depicting older men. He managed to convey the shrewdness and wisdom of their years in apparently spontaneous, somewhat informal paintings, such as his portrait of Professor John Wilson of 1822; Raeburn had also painted Wilson, as a dashing young man wearing riding habit and standing next to a powerful horse (both paintings Scot. NPG). Watson-Gordon revealed the rugged features of his 68-year-old sitter in a less gallant but no less dramatic painting than that of Raeburn, painted several decades before. He was far more successful when doing this than when attempting to capture the essence of a youthful or female sitter, for example *Mrs George Baird of Strichen* (Tate collection).

Watson-Gordon's portraits of the earl of Dalhousie (1833; Archers' Hall, Edinburgh) and Lord President Hope (1832; Signet Library, Edinburgh) are important examples of the full lengths of his middle period, when his works were rich and varied in colour. In the latter the lord president is depicted in ermine robes standing before the colonnaded façade of Parliament House. His portraits *Dr. Brunton* and *Principal Lee* (Edinburgh University) indicate a change of style, which illustrates clearly the influence of photography on Watson-Gordon during the 1840s and 1850s.

In March 1850 Watson-Gordon was elected to succeed Sir William Allan as president of the Royal Scottish Academy. Shortly afterwards he was knighted and appointed royal limner for Scotland. In 1855 Watson-Gordon achieved international acclaim when he was awarded a gold medal at the Paris Universal Exhibition for his intimate and intense portrait of Roderick Gray, provost of Peterhead (1852; Merchants' Hall, Edinburgh). This painting, one of his finest, is characterized by its simplicity of composition and limited palette, the draperies and accessories being subordinated to the head, which is handled with great freedom, yet high finish, and on which is concentrated the main light and warmth of the picture. Many of his portraits were engraved, Edward Burton's mezzotint after the portrait of Roderick Gray being one of the most noteworthy.

In 1860 volunteer forces were springing up all over the country in reaction to increasing militarism throughout Europe. Watson-Gordon enrolled in no. 1 City artillery, which had sixty-four soldiers, many of whom were members of the Royal Scottish Academy. He donated £20 to the cause, in addition to the £5 subscription. Watson-Gordon died at Catherine Bank, Trinity, Edinburgh, on 1 June 1864. In his memory his brother and sister endowed the Watson-Gordon professorship of fine art, which was instituted at Edinburgh University in 1879 and was the first chair in art history in Britain. JENNIFER MELVILLE

Sources W. D. McKay, *The Scottish school of painting* (1906) • D. Macmillan, *Scottish art, 1460–2000* (2000) • J. L. Caw, *Scottish painting past and present, 1620–1908* (1908) • D. Irwin and F. Irwin, *Scottish painters at home and abroad, 1700–1900* (1975) • P. J. M. McEwan, *Dictionary of Scottish art and architecture* (1994) • N. N. Solly, *Memoir of the life of David Cox* (1873) • F. Russell, *Portraits of Sir Walter Scott* (privately printed, London, 1987) • C. B. de Laperriere, ed., *The Royal Scottish Academy exhibitors, 1826–1990*, 4 vols. (1991)

Archives NL Scot., corresp.

Likenesses J. G. Tunny, photograph, 1850–59, priv. coll. [*see illus.*] • J. G. Gilbert, oils, 1854, Scot. NPG • P. Park, bust, Royal Scot. Acad. • J. Watson-Gordon, self-portrait, pencil, chalk, and wash drawing, Scot. NPG

Wealth at death £32,853: confirmation, 27 July 1864, *CGPLA Eng. & Wales*

Gordon, Katharine, duchess of Gordon (1718–1779), politician, was born on 20 October 1718, the daughter of William Gordon, second earl of Aberdeen (1679–1745), and his second wife, Lady Anna Susan Murray (1699–1725), the daughter of John Murray, first duke of Atholl. When Katharine married Cosmo George Gordon, third duke of Gordon (1720–1752), at Dunkeld on 3 September 1741, she married into one of Scotland's largest landowning and most important political families. A spirited and astute woman, she was more than capable of meeting the demands of her new position. Described uncharitably in a Gordon family history as 'a most persuasive and unscrupulous wire-puller' (Gordon, 25), she was in many ways the ideal eighteenth-century political wife and widowed mother, using all of her social and political skills to protect and forward her family's interest.

The duchess of Gordon needed all her charm and political ability when her husband died in 1752, leaving her a widow with four children under the age of ten. If she had been politically naïve or incompetent, such a protracted minority would have given the Gordons' ambitious rival, Archibald Campbell, third duke of Argyll, the opportunity to gain control of the Gordons' political interest and so further cement his grasp on Scottish patronage. The duchess was neither. Rather, it is a testimony of her skill on both the Scottish and national stages that her son Alexander *Gordon, fourth duke of Gordon (1743–1827), inherited the Gordon family interest intact and a much improved relationship with the crown.

This was due, in large part, to the duchess of Gordon's ability to use her personal and political situation to electoral and patronage advantage. While the Gordons' support for the Hanoverians had been ambivalent up until 1745, the duchess knew that as a widow she needed to ally herself with the king and the administration led by Thomas Pelham-Holles, duke of Newcastle, from 1754, if she wanted to safeguard the family interest. Similarly, Newcastle knew that he needed her electoral support. His contacts in Scotland made it only too clear that she was known to be a powerful political figure and that government candidates would need to have her support if they wanted to be successful. She used this to her advantage by consistently linking electoral support with familial advancement in her dealings with Newcastle. When, for instance, she remarried on 25 March 1756, she was determined to have her second husband, the rich young American soldier Staats Long *Morris (1728–1800), moved

Katharine Gordon, duchess of Gordon (1718–1779), by unknown artist

into the élite regiment of the guards. In her request to Newcastle, written in 1759 during the Seven Years' War and with an election imminent, she emphasized the fact that her request had the support of her brother, George Gordon, third earl of Aberdeen, another important Scottish whig. She also pointedly ended by seeking Newcastle's directions for the upcoming elections in Scotland.

In another letter from 1759 the duchess of Gordon sought to recoup a pension of £400 p.a. that Newcastle's brother and predecessor Henry Pelham had diverted from her to Eleanor, countess of Stair (widow of John Dalrymple, second earl of Stair), with the promise that it would be returned when Lady Stair died. In this case, she made calculated use of her dedication—and that of her family—to the service of the king and country, by including with the request a report on the success that she was having in raising a regiment in her son's name (headed in fact by Morris). This regiment, the Duke of Gordon's highlanders (89th Highland regiment), was part of her ongoing strategy to win over the militarily inclined George II by demonstrating the Gordon family's patriotism and neutralizing any potential national political support for the duke of Argyll. She was highly successful. By December 1759 the pay list for the regiment recorded nine companies and over 1000 men. When, however, this regiment was unexpectedly posted to the East Indies in March 1760, local electoral concerns triumphed and she used every argument at her disposal to get it reassigned. She stressed that sending the regiment to the East Indies would influence her three sons, all officers in the regiment, negatively in 'this first Essay of their early Zeal for His Majestys Person & Government', and it would also upset the tenants, which in an election year would have dire political consequences for the family and the whig interest: 'I can assure your Grace no measure could be more hurtfull to Government in our Part of the World, as well as to my Sons Interest' (BL, Add. MS 32903, Newcastle papers, fols. 57–8, duchess of Gordon to Newcastle, London, 3 March 1760). In this case she failed and the regiment went on to serve valiantly in India until 1765, when it returned to England and was disbanded.

Once the fourth duke achieved his majority in 1764, the duchess was able to turn her energies elsewhere—probably a good thing given the competition that she would have had from her intensely political daughter-in-law, the vivacious Jane *Gordon, *née* Maxwell, who married the duke in 1767. Instead of retiring to a dower house in the country or dedicating herself to cards and cattiness in London, the dowager duchess, as she then was, left for America with Morris. Indomitable and energetic as she was, the closest thing that the dowager duchess had to the American pioneer experience probably took place in May 1769, when she and Morris travelled from Catskill to the Schoharie and across to the Susquehanna to see the Morris patent on lower Butternuts Creek in Otsego Country (now New York state). They returned soon afterwards to Britain. She died in London on 10 December 1779, aged sixty-one, less than a year before her youngest son, Lord George *Gordon, was to set off the infamous Gordon riots there. Her body was returned to Scotland for burial with her first husband in Elgin Cathedral. E. H. Chalus

Sources GEC, *Peerage*, new edn, vol. 6 · *Collins peerage of England: genealogical, biographical and historical*, ed. E. Brydges, 9 vols. (1812), vol. 2 · *IGI* · G. Gordon, *The last dukes of Gordon and their consorts, 1743–1864* (1980) · F. Adams, *The clans, septs and regiments of the Scottish highlands*, rev. T. Innes of Learney, 8th edn (1984) · letters to the duke of Newcastle and George II, BL, Add. MSS 32729, 32737, 32884, 32899, 32902–32903, 32907, 32999 · letter to earl of Hardwicke, BL, Add. MS 35596 · letter to the earl of Holdernesse, BL, Egerton MS 3434 · W. Sussex RO, Goodwood papers, 1175 · *Reports on the manuscripts of the earl of Eglinton*, HMC, 10 (1885) · Walpole, *Corr.*, vols. 15, 35 · will, PRO, PROB 11/1061, sig. 79 · 'A classification of American wealth: history and genealogy of the wealthy families of America', www.raken.com/american-wealth/encyclopedia/profile.asp?code=1737, 1 Jan 2002

Archives BL, letters to earl of Hardwicke · BL, letters to duke of Newcastle

Likenesses portrait; Christies, 7 March 1980, lot 135 [*see illus.*]

Wealth at death see will, PRO, PROB 11/1061, sig. 79

Gordon, Lord Lewis (*c*.1725–1754), Jacobite army officer, was born in Banffshire, the third son of Alexander *Gordon, second duke of Gordon (*c*.1678–1728), and Lady Henrietta Mordaunt (1681/2–1760) [*see* Gordon, Henrietta], daughter of Charles, earl of Peterborough and Monmouth. There is 'a persistent tradition' that Lord Lewis married and had a daughter, but this has never been verified (Tayler, 172). Although he had been a lieutenant in the navy he joined the Jacobite rising in October 1745, becoming a member of the council of Charles Edward Stuart, Jacobite prince of Wales. By 21 October Charles had appointed him lord lieutenant of the counties of Aberdeen and Banff, whence Lord Lewis raised the Aberdeen and Aboyne battalions, despite repeated difficulties over recruitment: 'I am ravished to hear that, when the drum beats, not a few of the boys cry God save King George!' observed one Aberdeen minister (*Miscellany of the Spalding Club*, 1.352). Lord Lewis took advice from General Gordon of Auchintoul, the most senior surviving officer of the 1715 rising, and co-ordinated matters from his base at Huntly Castle. On 26 November he sent a force to Aberdeen to aid recruitment there, which was going slowly.

At Inverurie, on 23 December, Lord Lewis's mainly lowland forces, aided by two companies of Royal Scots in the French service and a detachment of the 2nd Forfarshires, defeated a smaller highland Hanoverian contingent under MacLeod of MacLeod and Munro of Culcairn, and thus kept the government out of the east coast counties: the victory may, however, have owed less to Lord Lewis's generalship than to the steady competence of the French regulars. In January Lord Lewis marched south to join the prince in time for the battle of Falkirk. At the council at Crieff at the beginning of February he remonstrated with Lord George Murray over the latter's arrogant dismissal of the prince's views. At the battle of Culloden his remaining forces stood, as they had done at Falkirk, in the second line and saw little direct action. After Culloden he was in hiding in Aberdeenshire; by July 1746 he had escaped to Paris.

Although Lord Lewis gained a commission in the French service, he displayed increasing signs of mental instability, being described as 'quelque fois derange' in 1747; by 1749 Colonel James Oxburgh could describe him as 'mad'. By 1751 matters had grown so serious that he appears to have been put in the care of a 'keeper' (Tayler, 170–71). Despite repeated pleas to the duke, his brother, indicating his willingness to submit on any terms, he appears to have been ignored, and died in Montreuil on 15 June 1754. His name lived on in a song,

O send Lewie Gordon hame,
And the lad I darena name [Charles],

which is traditionally attributed to Alexander Geddes, a Catholic priest educated at the seminary in Scalan, on the land of the Catholic Gordons, on which Lord Lewis had been raised a protestant.

Lord Lewis Gordon's rank, his youthful dash, and the serious responsibility he took as a major regional Jacobite commander have lent his name a glamour linked to that of Prince Charles himself. The truth seems to have been that he was an able but unbalanced man, who showed signs of mental stress and instability throughout his adult life. MURRAY G. H. PITTOCK

Sources *DNB* · J. Stuart, ed., *The miscellany of the Spalding Club*, 1, Spalding Club, 3 (1841) · H. Tayler, ed., *Jacobite epilogue* (1941) · S. Reid, *1745: a military history of the last Jacobite rising* (1996) · *A Jacobite source list: list of documents in the Scottish Record Office relating to the Jacobites* (1995) · Anderson, *Scot. nat.* · F. J. McLynn, *Charles Edward Stuart: a tragedy in many acts* (1988) · A. Livingstone, C. W. H. Aikman, and B. S. Hart, eds., *Muster roll of Prince Charles Edward Stuart's army, 1745–46* (1984) · F. McDonnell, *Jacobites of 1745 north east Scotland* (1996) · GEC, *Peerage*, new edn, vol. 1 · M. Hook and W. Ross, *The forty-five* (1995) · M. Pittock, *Jacobitism* (1998) · B. G. Seton and J. G. Arnot, eds., *The prisoners of the '45*, Scottish History Society, 3rd ser., 13–15 (1928–9)
Archives NA Scot., annexed estate MSS, E754 · NA Scot., Gordon Castle muniments, GD 44 · NA Scot., Seafield muniments, GD 248/168/8; 248/572/2

Gordon, Lewis Dunbar Brodie (1815–1876), civil engineer and university teacher, was born on 6 March 1815 in Edinburgh, the fourth son of Joseph Gordon (*c*.1786–1855) of Carroll in Sutherland, writer to the signet, and his wife, Anne (*b*. 1786/7), daughter of Colonel Gordon Clunes of Crakaig, also in Sutherland. His parents were prominent in the liberal circles surrounding Edinburgh University. A fastidious child, Gordon excelled at the Edinburgh high school where he discovered literature, collected prints of the old masters, and established lasting friendships with the engineer David Stevenson, the translator Theodore Martin, and Edward Strathearn Gordon (Lord Gordon of Drumearn). Gordon then studied science and mathematics at Mr Fanning's school, Finchley, Middlesex, in preparation for the East India Company's Addiscombe College. When that coveted opportunity evaporated, Gordon turned to civil engineering, and during 1832 acquired mechanical engineering skills by working at James Stirling's Dundee foundry.

Gordon entered Edinburgh University for the session of 1833/4, a young man of fine features, slender stature, frank expression, and religious independence. He studied natural history with Robert Jameson and natural philosophy with James David Forbes. When the British Association for the Advancement of Science (BAAS) congregated in Edinburgh in September 1834, Gordon and his friend Thomas Constable entertained Marc Isambard Brunel at Gordon's house. In January 1835 Brunel invited the young engineer to work on the Thames Tunnel. At Rotherhithe, Gordon joined the resident engineer Richard Beamish, who took a phrenologist's interest in Gordon's capacious cranial surface and secured his election to the Institution of Civil Engineers in January 1836. Beamish's departure from the tunnel, however, prompted disputes which culminated in Gordon's departure in September.

In the autumn of 1838 Gordon entered the Freiberg Bergakademie (school of mines), an institution as famous for its alumni as for its science-enriched curriculum. Soon fluent in German, Gordon studied mineralogy, geology, physics, chemistry, metallurgy, mining operations, assaying, and, with the hydraulic engineer Julius Weisbach, mathematics applied to mechanics. During recesses Gordon visited neighbouring mines and smelting-works, and travelled to the Harz, Silesia, Bohemia, and Hungary. In 1839 he met the mineralogist Friedrich Mohs in Vienna, visited the mining town and school of Schemnitz, and inspected the artillery and engineering school at Metz, where he saw Morin's dynamometers at work measuring the efficiency of engines. He also studied at the École Polytechnique in Paris.

When Gordon returned to Britain in the spring of 1840 he was known to European savants, stocked with commercially valuable information, acquainted with engineering pedagogy, and equipped as a translator of foreign

Lewis Dunbar Brodie Gordon (1815–1876), by Camille Silvy, 1862

engineering culture. By the autumn Forbes and Beamish had helped to persuade the government to appoint Gordon as the first regius professor of civil engineering and mechanics in the University of Glasgow—indeed, as the first British engineering professor. Gordon trained James Thomson, later professor at Belfast, and the marine engineer John Elder. However, despite the support of the lord advocate, Andrew Rutherfurd, opposition from the university's oligarchic faculty left Gordon struggling for space in which to teach and to store models, and hampered his attempts to breed up a race of engineering professionals on a theoretical and practical diet. Equally, lectures (published in 1847 and 1849) necessarily avoided the intellectual territory of jealous science professors and instead embodied collective engineering experience.

The Glasgow Philosophical Society proved a more congenial base for engineering science. Gordon became a member in December 1840 and from 1842 was on the council and convened the society's mechanics and engineering section. He persuaded the society to publish its proceedings, and offered the gleanings of his student days with talks on the melting points of metals and the use of the blowpipe (1841), and on the measurement of mechanical effect (1842) and of impact (1844). In November 1844 Gordon advised the industrialists at the society that steam was most economically deployed expansively and, in line with his college teaching, that engine efficiency should be accurately defined and measured with the work indicators of McNaught, Morin, and his professorial opposite number, Henry Moseley. In January 1845 Gordon's account of an experiment on the flow of Stockholm pitch confirmed Forbes's viscous theory of glaciers; by February he was a fellow of the Royal Society of Edinburgh and by November 1846 a fellow of the Geological Society, and in March 1847 he used Forbes's models to explain the theory to the Glasgow Philosophical Society.

In January 1846 Gordon considered the theoretical mechanical effect of steam. Certainly by the spring of 1847 he had introduced the philosophical society to Sadi Carnot's work. When William Thomson went to Glasgow as professor of natural philosophy Gordon was a sounding board, a resource, and perhaps a rival in the transformation of the understanding of the mechanical action of heat. The two men discussed Joule's experiments, Thomson's absolute temperature scale, and Stirling's theoretically intriguing air-engine, a machine which Gordon hoped to produce commercially. While Gordon fed Thomson with crucial data on heat engines and, late in 1848, furnished him with a copy of Carnot's scarce treatise (1824), he also advertised his own primer on the theory and practice of heat engineering.

During the university's long summer breaks Gordon made his reputation as a professional engineer in partnership with Lawrence Hill, Charles Liddell, and Robert Stirling Newall. One early project identified the engineering chair with Glasgow's socio-economic improvement: assisted by Joseph Colthurst, Gordon and Hill erected the great 'Tennant's Stalk' chimney to carry off noxious gases from the St Rollox chemical works (1841–2). When, in 1844, a large rent appeared in the structure, they designed a new climbing machine to repair it and left it to David Stevenson to orchestrate the approval of the Royal Scottish Society of Arts.

Gordon was also active in hydraulics, mining, railway construction, and submarine telegraphy. Following Weisbach, he discussed the turbine at the Glasgow meeting of the British Association (1840), collaborated with William Fairbairn and James Smith of Deanston to compare it with the common water-wheel, discussed Fourneyron's design at the Institution of Civil Engineers (1842), and finally developed a turbine/water-wheel patent with James Thomson (1849). Gordon analysed the flow of water through pipes for the Glasgow Philosophical Society in 1844 and shortly afterwards promoted, with Hill, a scheme—scuppered by the Glasgow Water Company—to bring pure water by gravitation from Loch Katrine to Glasgow (1845). When Rankine and John Thomson revived the scheme in 1852 Gordon remonstrated with the dithering Glasgow corporation. Further afield, the Admiralty employed Gordon to report on a drainage and enclosure scheme put forward by a proposed Norfolk Estuary Company (1846 and 1849). With Charles Liddell he developed a plan to supply London with water from the Thames at Mapledurham (1849) and, at a time when public health was high on the agenda, he publicized James Vetch's plans for the city's sewerage (1851).

Gordon used his training as a mining engineer with Hill, when he advised the marquess of Breadalbane on his operations at Tyndrum in Perthshire, and with Liddell, managing the Mulgrave alum and cement works of Lord Normanby (1842–4). Gordon bolstered his discussions of the causes and prevention of accidents and explosions in coal mines (1843 and 1847) with the experimental data of C. G. C. Bischof in Bonn. With the expansion of the railways in the 1840s, Liddell and Gordon engineered lines in England and Wales, building iron bridges such as the Crumlin Viaduct. Ever the innovator, Gordon in 1848 patented a method of constructing railway track, and argued for the substitution of locomotive carriages for the wasteful 'steam-tugs' then used (1849).

The work which most clearly severed Gordon's ties with Glasgow had its origins in a visit in 1838 to the government mines in the Harz, where wire ropes were extensively used. In August 1840 Newall followed Gordon's advice, patented new machinery, and, in partnership with Liddell and Gordon, manufactured and traded wire ropes as R. S. Newall & Co. of Gateshead. By the end of the 1840s the range and quantity of Gordon's engineering business were thus substantial, and attempts to find better premises for the engineering class, and the university, had failed; Gordon was losing interest in his professorial duties and had established offices at 24 Abingdon Street in London, an address once occupied by Thomas Telford.

In August 1850, soon after a tour of Ireland, Gordon was courting Marie Glünder, *née* Heise, daughter of Marianne von Hartmann and a cousin of Richard Beamish's wife. They were married in Hanover on 23 November 1850. That autumn Newall realized that insulating an electric telegraph wire with gutta-percha and armouring it with wire rope would provide engineers, politicians, and businessmen with a viable submarine cable—and promise an immense income. Soon Newall & Co. had established electric communication between England and France (1851). They made and in large part laid some 4500 miles of cable, linking England with Ireland, Belgium, and the Netherlands (1851–3), spanning the Mediterranean, and putting Varna in direct communication with Balaklava (1854–5) during the Crimean War. During the spring of 1855 Rankine was in Glasgow as Gordon's deputy in the engineering class; with the death of his father in March 1855 Gordon felt free to resign his chair, which he did in September, leaving Rankine his obvious successor.

Freed from his duties in Glasgow, Gordon schemed with Liddell and M. A. Biddulph to establish a railway from Tchernavoda on the Danube to an extended and defended port of Kustendjé on the Black Sea (1856). Mixing business with pleasure, he visited Constantinople and toured the ruins of the Crimea. For parts of the summer of 1857 and the winter of 1858 Gordon was at Newall's Birkenhead works in company with the electrical engineer Fleeming Jenkin. The firm constructed half of the first—failed—Atlantic telegraph cable and swiftly thereafter the notorious cable from Suez to Aden, a place, Gordon thought, of 'unmitigated repulsiveness' (Constable, 101). By June 1859 this Red Sea cable was complete and Gordon set out with Newall from Aden on the steamship *Alma*. When the vessel ran aground on a coral reef only hours out of port it was left to Newall to bring help. No lives were lost but many suffered from a four-day exposure to burning heat. Gordon returned to London at the end of July, well enough to witness the marriage of his younger sister, Anne, to the mechanical engineer Charles William Siemens, but his health never fully recovered.

In mid-November 1859 Gordon co-ordinated the laying of a cable from Singapore to Banca and Batavia for the Dutch government. In India in January 1860, his hopes for telegraphic communication with India were dashed when the first of a series of problems with the Red Sea cable emerged. In the next two years Gordon was constantly on the move, returning to London only in December 1861. The following year Gordon retired from active work, and in the spring of 1863 suddenly lost the power of one of his legs and was diagnosed as suffering from ataxia of the synovia. He and his wife rested on the continent, but by the beginning of 1864 he could barely walk with crutches and accepted the will of God as his 'ruling principle' (Stevenson, 216).

Gordon spent some of the fortune amassed as a telegraphic entrepreneur on the Château de Bossey on Lake Geneva. After September 1864 he occasionally left Bossey for the spas, but most of his time was now spent there. Although his illness was manageable, in 1867 his wife became ill and on 28 September 1868 Gordon's 'gentle intellectual' (Constable, 204) and companion died. Gordon's affection for Bossey gradually diminished. In July 1869 his son Joseph left for London and the Royal School of Mines, and at the end of May 1871, after much soul searching, Gordon decamped for Poynters Grove in Totteridge, Hertfordshire, an old-fashioned and comfortable house where he lived with his unmarried sister Mary and his mother. At Totteridge Gordon filled his time driving out, playing bezique, reading, and continuing a wide correspondence with European men of science and engineering. He studied languages and translated Louis Lechatelier's work on railway economy (1869) and Louis Emmanuel Grüner's book on the blast furnace (1873). In January 1873 he advised Hugh Matheson on the curriculum of the new College of Civil and Mechanical Engineering in Tokyo. Gordon was collaborating with James Robert Napier on a commemorative edition of Rankine's papers and a biography when his health gave way once more, during the severe weather of January 1876. He died on 28 April 1876 at Poynters Grove. BEN MARSDEN

Sources T. Constable, *Memoir of Lewis D. B. Gordon, F. R. S. E.* (1877) • B. Marsden, '"A most important trespass": Lewis Gordon and the Glasgow chair of civil engineering and mechanics, 1840–1855', *Making space for science: territorial themes in the shaping of knowledge*, ed. C. Smith and J. Agar (1998), 87–117 • B. Marsden, 'Engineering science in Glasgow: economy, efficiency and measurement as prime movers in the differentiation of an academic discipline', *British Journal for the History of Science*, 25 (1992), 319–46 • B. Marsden, 'Engineering science in Glasgow: W. J. M. Rankine and the motive power of air', PhD diss., University of Kent at Canterbury, 1992 •

C. Smith and M. N. Wise, *Energy and empire: a biographical study of Lord Kelvin* (1989) · D. Stevenson, *Proceedings of the Royal Society of Edinburgh*, 9 (1875–8), 212–16 · minute books, U. Glas. L., special collections department, Glasgow Philosophical Society · M. I. Brunel, diaries, Inst. CE · L. S. Jacyna, *Philosophic whigs: medicine, science and citizenship in Edinburgh, 1789–1848* (1994)

Archives CUL, corresp. with Lord Kelvin · Inst. CE, Thames Tunnel MSS · Mulgrave Castle, Whitby, Normanby MSS · NL Scot., Royal Society of Edinburgh MSS · Sci. Mus., Beamish MSS · U. Glas., Archives and Business Records Centre, minutes of senate and faculty · U. St Andr. L., James David Forbes MSS

Likenesses C. Silvy, photograph, 1862, NPG [*see illus.*] · Lacroix of Geneva, photograph, 1869, repro. in Constable, *Memoir*, facing p. 146 · photograph (after crayon portrait, 1850), repro. in Constable, *Memoir*, frontispiece

Wealth at death under £80,000: probate, 1876, *CGPLA Eng. & Wales*

Gordon, Lucie Duff [*née* Lucie Austin], **Lady Duff Gordon** **(1821–1869)**, travel writer and translator, was born on 24 June 1821 at 1 Queen Square, Westminster, London, near the statue of Queen Anne (this section was demolished in the 1880s and renamed Queen Anne's Gate), the only child of John *Austin (1790–1859), jurist, and his wife, Sarah Taylor *Austin (1793–1867). Her father, author of *The Province of Jurisprudence Determined* (1861), was a frequent invalid, and her mother, a member of the intellectually formidable Unitarian Taylor family of Norwich, was a gifted translator. Like her mother, Lucie Austin was trained in languages, and edited or translated ten books over an eighteen-year period. As a child, she knew the fifteen-year-old John Stuart Mill, a frequent visitor to the Austin household and, along with her cousin Henry *Reeve, her closest companion. Other childhood experiences included visits to Jeremy Bentham's home. In 1827 the family travelled to Bonn, Germany, in order that her father could prepare to lecture at the new University of London. Here she attended school for the first time and gained fluency in German.

On their return to England in June 1828, John Austin became ill with distress over his teaching duties and eventually resigned his post. To economize, the family moved to 26 Park Road, near Regent's Park, in the summer of 1830, the first of several moves. There they lived next to John and Harriet Taylor, and Lucie Austin renewed acquaintance with John Stuart Mill and met Thomas Carlyle. At the age of ten she was sent to a classical school in Hampstead, where, under Dr George Edward Biber, she studied Greek. When she was thirteen, the family moved to Boulogne, France, where she met Heinrich Heine. There, in August 1833, she and her mother witnessed the sinking of the *Amphitrite*, which was transporting convict women to New South Wales. Mother and daughter worked side by side fruitlessly trying to save those who had been washed up on the beach. Only 4 of the 131 on board survived.

On their return to London, her father once again faced career setbacks and the family moved to 5 Orme Square, near Bayswater, and then to Hastings, where Lucie Austin made friends with Janet and Marianne North. She was sent to Miss Shepherd's boarding-school in Bromley Common in 1836, when John Austin was appointed to an investigative commission in Malta. While visiting the Norths, she was baptized into the Church of England without her family's knowledge.

When Lucie Austin was seventeen she was presented to the young Queen Victoria. She married Sir Alexander Cornewall Duff Gordon, third baronet (1811–1872), on 16 May 1840, a month before her nineteenth birthday. He was ten years older and a junior clerk at the Treasury. The couple moved to 8 Queen Square, London, close to Lucie's childhood home. There she had three children, Janet Ann [*see* Ross, Janet Ann], Maurice, and Urania. Another boy (also named Maurice), her second child, died in infancy. The household also included Hassan al-Bakkeet from the Sudan, who had been abandoned at the age of twelve by his former master because of encroaching blindness. The Duff Gordons provided medical treatment and a home for him until his death in 1849. As a young woman, Lucie Duff Gordon was described by both Alexander Kinglake and George Meredith as quite striking, tall with dark hair and a classic, commanding profile. She was the model for the character Lady Jocelyn in George Meredith's novel *Evan Harrington* and possibly an inspiration for Tennyson's *The Princess*. Her household, a lively social centre for progressive thinkers, was often visited by Charles Dickens, William Thackeray, Sydney Smith, the Carlyles, John Stuart Mill and Harriet Taylor, Richard Monckton Milnes, Richard Doyle, Caroline Norton, and Tom Taylor.

Lucie Duff Gordon established a reputation for translation, starting with Wilhelm Meinhold's *Mary Schweidler, the Amber Witch* (1844), which she believed to be a seventeenth-century chronicle, not initially knowing it was a literary hoax. Her translation nevertheless went through three editions in 1844, and was considered superior to the original. She next was attracted to accounts of travel in the Middle East, translating *The Prisoners of Abdel-Kader* by M. de France (François Antoine Alby) and *The Soldier of the Foreign Legion* by Clemens Lamping. She also translated and condensed Paul Feuerbach's *Narratives of Remarkable Criminal Trials* (1846).

In 1851 Lucie Duff Gordon contracted tuberculosis and was forced to leave her family in search of a climate suited to her health. First she went to South Africa, and her letters home were published as *Letters from the Cape* (1864). In 1862, at the age of forty-one, she sailed to Egypt, where for seven years she lived in Luxor in a house built over the ruins of a temple. She wrote movingly of Egyptian village life and harshly of westernization. She was particularly critical of Viceroy Ismaʿil Pasha at a time when he was seen as a progressive reformer. While the British applauded such 'reforms' as the building of the Suez Canal and railroads by the pasha, Lucie Duff Gordon noted the devastation brought to village life by forced labour and high taxes, necessary to support the projects. She wrote:

> I care less about opening up the trade with Sudan and all the new railways … food … gets dear, the forced labour inflicts more suffering …. What chokes me is to hear Englishmen

> talk of the stick being 'the only way to manage Arabs' as if there could be any doubt that it is the easiest way to manage anybody, where it can be used with impunity. (*Letters from Egypt*, 86)

Her emphasis on common human experiences in her writing avoided stereotypes. She valued the Egyptians, 'so full of tender and affectionate feelings', and took her countrymen to task for their distrust of her neighbours, asking 'Why do the English talk of the beautiful sentiment of the Bible and pretend to feel it so much, and when they come and see the same life before them[,] they ridicule it' (ibid., 169). While her letters prophetically warned of the frustrations of the Egyptian people, they were ignored. Some of her harsher criticisms of government policy were removed in the early editions of her popular *Letters from Egypt, 1863–1865* (1865) and *Last Letters from Egypt* (1875). While her health did improve in the dry heat of Luxor, she was only able to visit England twice. Finally succumbing to her long illness, she died in Cairo on 14 July 1869 and was buried in the city's English cemetery.

LILA MARZ HARPER

Sources K. Frank, *A passage to Egypt: a life of Lucie Duff Gordon* (1994) · L. D. Gordon, *Letters from Egypt, 1862–1869*, ed. G. Waterfield (1969) · G. Waterfield, 'Introduction', in L. D. Gordon, *Letters from Egypt, 1862–1869* (1969) · J. A. Ross, *Three generations of Englishwomen: memoirs and correspondence of Mrs John Taylor, Mrs Sarah Austin and Lady Duff Gordon*, rev. edn (1893) · J. Killham, *Tennyson and 'The Princess': reflections of an age* (1958) · S. Sassoon, *Meredith* (1948) · F. Shereen, 'Lucie Duff Gordon', *British travel writers, 1837–1875*, ed. B. Brothers and J. Gergits, DLitB, 166 (1996), 157–64

Archives priv. coll.

Likenesses H. W. Phillips, portrait, *c.*1852, NPG; repro. in Frank, *A passage to Egypt* · R. Cruikshank, portrait, repro. in Frank, *A passage to Egypt* · C. H. Jeens, stipple, BM, NPG; repro. in L. D. Gordon, *Last letters from Egypt* (1875) · G. F. Watts, drawing · drawing (aged eighteen), Downton House, Wales · two drawings

Gordon, Lucy Christiana [Lucile] **Duff** [*née* Lucy Christiana Sutherland], **Lady Duff Gordon (1862–1935)**, fashion designer, was born in St John's Wood, London, in July 1862, the elder of two daughters of Douglas Sutherland (1838–1865), a Scottish civil engineer, and Elinor, *née* Saunders (1842–1937), who came from a prosperous Canadian family of Franco-Irish descent. On Douglas Sutherland's sudden death in 1865 the family returned to the maternal home in Summerhill, near Guelph, Ontario. The household was strict, imbued with French formality, and Lucy reacted, becoming a rebellious tomboy. She expressed a nascent creativity in making clothes for her dolls and for herself, often adaptations of the quality French clothes sent by relatives. On her mother's marriage in 1871 to David Kennedy (1807–1890) the family moved to England, settling in Jersey. Unable to conform to the household requirements of her stepfather, an elderly penurious invalid, Lucy left at sixteen to stay with relatives.

Attractive, with reddish brown hair, piquant features, and a neat figure, vivacious and strong-willed, Lucy Sutherland had many suitors but settled, rather precipitately, in 1884 on Douglas Wallace (*b.* 1844/5), a much older, socially well-connected, wine merchant. She divorced him in 1889 and moved with her only child, Esme (later Lady Halsbury), to stay with her recently widowed mother in London, supplementing their income by dressmaking from home.

Social contacts through her sister, the novelist Elinor *Glyn (1864–1943), and Lillie Langtry, allied to genuine creative ability, turned the dressmaking into a successful business. Lucy's designs proved congenial to socially more relaxed Edwardian society and included individually styled personality dresses and luxuriously informal tea gowns. The business enjoyed continual expansion: by 1895 Lucy had moved to 24 Burlington Street, working as Mrs Lucy Wallace; from there she went on by 1898 to 17 Hanover Square, assuming the trade name of Maison Lucile in 1902, and finally to 23 Hanover Square in 1904.

It was at Hanover Square that Lucy realized her ideal, a prestige couture house, the prototype for her subsequent establishments. The costs involved were high—the premises were redecorated in Louis XVI mode, in a scheme inspired by a close friend, American designer Elsie de Wolfe—but the venture proved a success. Boasting such innovations as the Rose Room specializing in lingerie, personality mannequins, and a salon for theatrical-type fashion displays, it attracted stage and society clients. Fashionable weddings and popular theatrical productions such as *The Merry Widow* in 1907 further boosted its appeal. By 1904 a limited company had been formed. Lucy retained the design responsibility and controlling interest, but her relationship with her partners, all of whom had invested in the company, was never easy. As well as members of her own family these included Sir Cosmo Edmund Duff Gordon (1862–1931), whom she married on 24 May 1900, and an accountant by the name of Miles.

In 1909 a branch of the firm opened in New York amid such extensive publicity that Lucy was briefly dubbed Lady Muff Boredom. It proved a great success, however. Money dresses, so called because of their cost and the style consultations with the wealthy but sartorially insecure they entailed, were very popular. Lady Duff Gordon's relationship with the popular press came under pressure, however, when she, Sir Cosmo, and her secretary, were numbered among the few survivors of the sinking of the *Titanic* in 1912. In the ensuing commission of inquiry, they were accused of bribing their way to a lifeboat and preventing its return to rescue further passengers. Although they were completely exonerated, the experience had a profound effect, particularly on Sir Cosmo.

The opening of the Paris branch in 1912, at 49 rue de Penthièvre, provided distraction. An immediate success, it was popular with visiting Americans, theatrical clients, and the *demi-monde*. For Lucy it was a return to what she considered her spiritual home. Whether she received due recognition from the French couture establishment is less clear.

In 1914 Lady Duff Gordon returned to America for the duration of the First World War from which, unlike her immediate family, she remained detached. Until the American entry into the war in 1917, demand grew and she expanded, moving to larger premises with a separate design studio. She employed good young designers, including Edward Molyneux and Howard Greer, and her popularity was boosted by work for the Ziegfield Follies and a touring semi-patriotic fashion show. Friction with her family and business partners, however, increased: to support a very extravagant lifestyle, she began to offer clients her personal fashion services, thereby diverting considerable earnings from the company. Her association with 'the Boys', a bevy of young male personal assistants, in particular Genia d'Agarioff, prompted Sir Cosmo's return to Britain later in 1914. The couple never again lived together, although they continued to be business associates.

The opening of the Chicago branch (1915–17) was in particular bitterly resisted by the other directors whose overriding ambition had become entry not into the couture but into the mass market. A foray into this area with the US mail-order firm Sears Roebuck in 1914–15 proved unsuccessful, and in 1919 the partnership was bought out by John Lane Shuloff, a New York dress manufacturer, who leased back the name Lucile to the London branch. Although Lucy Duff Gordon retained a limited role as a designer, by 1924 her business was forced to cease trading.

As a designer, Lucy Duff Gordon had always shown creative integrity and been technically adept, working both from sketches and draping on the stand. A ruthless perfectionist, she had fine judgement of colour blending and materials. None of this or her preference for romantic or exotic styling translated easily into ready-to-wear for an austere and depressed post-war world. Except for a brief period in 1923–4, when she wrote a lively column of dress advice as 'Dorothy' of the *Daily Sketch*, she retired from fashion. Her autobiography, *Discretions and Indiscretions*, was published in 1932.

Lady Duff Gordon lived in London from 1923 to 1935. After the death of Sir Cosmo in 1931, she benefited from the income of a trust fund set up under the terms of his will. Despite disagreements, she retained close family links. She died at a nursing home at 100 West Hill in Putney on 20 April 1935. There are fine examples of her work in the main costume collections in the UK and USA. Her significant but often unwitting contributions to the fashion industry included the anticipation of a link between the American and the European markets, as well as a systematic exploitation of publicity and an appreciation of the importance of ready-made fashion.

M. GINSBURG

Sources M. Etherington Smith and J. Pilcher, *The it girls* (1986) • Lucy, Lady Duff Gordon, correspondence, 1911–19 • Lucy, Lady Duff Gordon, *Discretions and indiscretions* (1932) • private information (2004) • m. cert. • d. cert.

Archives Metropolitan Museum of Art, New York, Costume Institute, artefacts • V&A, department of textiles and dress, artefacts

Likenesses photographs, priv. coll. • photographs, Fashion Institute of Technology, New York • portraits, repro. in Etherington Smith and Pilcher, *The it girls*

Gordon [*née* Ogilvie], **Dame Maria Matilda** (1864–1939), geologist and women's activist, was born on 30 April 1864 in Monymusk, Aberdeenshire, elder daughter among seven children of Revd Alexander Ogilvie (1830/31–1904), schoolmaster, and his wife, Maria Matilda Nicol. The family moved to Aberdeen in 1872 when Alexander Ogilvie became headmaster of Robert Gordon's Hospital (later College).

Following nine years at the Edinburgh Educational Institute for Girls (later the Edinburgh Ladies College which became, in 1944, the Mary Erskine School) and studies at the Royal Academy of Music, London, Ogilvie went to Heriot-Watt College, Edinburgh. In 1889 she entered University College, London, and concentrated on geology, botany, and zoology (BSc, 1890, with gold medal in zoology and comparative anatomy). Continuing her studies at the University of Munich, as a private student of palaeontologist Karl von Zittel and zoologist Richard Hertwig, she specialized in recent and fossil corals. Her London DSc (1893) was the first in geology given to a woman and her PhD (1900, with distinction in geology, palaeontology, and zoology) was the first conferred on a woman by the University of Munich. In 1895 she married John Gordon, an Aberdeen physician. She had three children, but nevertheless continued her fieldwork.

All Maria Gordon's studies were done in the geologically very complex south Tyrol Dolomites, then a remote and isolated region. She published more than thirty original papers; especially notable was her early work on corals, and her theory of 'crust-torsion' (1899) to explain the peculiar forms of the region's typical landscape features. Expanding on relatively new tectonic theories, she demonstrated that the steep-walled, circular or elliptical limestone massifs, initially considered to be unchanged coral reefs, resulted from complex crustal movements. Her comprehensive monograph *Das Grödener-, Fassa- und Enneberggebiet in den Südtiroler Dolomiten* (1927) became the definitive reference for future work in the region; the portions dealing with tectonics and stratigraphy, illustrated with an outstanding collection of maps and sections, were the most notable, but the palaeontological discussions were also of considerable importance. *Geologisches Wanderbuch der Westlichen Dolomiten* followed in 1928. Her translation of von Zittel's work, published as *History of Geology and Palaeontology* (1901), was another major contribution. Slightly condensed at the author's request it appeared two years after the original German edition. These writings brought her wide professional recognition, first in Austria and Italy, then from the London Geological Society, from whom she received the Lyell medal in 1932.

Maria Gordon was active in several prominent national women's action groups. She presided over the meeting of the National Council of Women in 1914 which led to the establishment of women's patrols, and the 1917 meeting of the Women's Citizens Association which decided to make the body a national organization. Service in these action groups and the International Council of Women brought a DBE in 1935 and an LLD from Edinburgh University. After the death of her husband in 1919 she moved to London and became active in the Liberal Party and civic affairs. She was the first woman to chair a London borough court. Strong, sympathetic, and dedicated to this social service, she nevertheless felt acutely the resulting loss of scientific worktime, her days in the field being, she later recalled, the happiest of her life.

Probably the most productive woman field geologist of any country in the late nineteenth and early twentieth centuries, Maria Gordon was remembered as a penetrating observer, and as having a quick, intuitive grasp of her subject and tremendous enthusiasm. She died at her home, 32 Hanover Gate Mansions, Regent's Park, London, on 24 June 1939. After cremation at Golders Green on 28 June, her ashes were interred on the 29th at Allenvale cemetery, Aberdeen. MARY R. S. CREESE

Sources J. Pia, 'Maria Matilda Ogilvie Gordon', *Mitteilungen der Geologischen Gesellschaft in Wien*, 32 (1939), 173–86 · *Nature*, 144 (1939), 142–3 · E. J. G. [E. J. Garwood], *Quarterly Journal of the Geological Society of London*, 102 (1946), xl–xli · *The Times* (30 June 1939) · *The Times* (26 June 1939) · 'Rev. Dr Alexander Ogilvie', *In Memoriam: an Obituary of Aberdeen and Vicinity* (1904), 93–102 · *WW* · M. R. S. Creese and T. M. Creese, 'British women who contributed to research in the geological sciences in the nineteenth century', *British Journal for the History of Science*, 27 (1994), 23–54 · M. R. S. Creese, 'Maria Ogilvie Gordon (1864–1939)', *Earth Sciences History*, 15 (1996), 68–75 · M. R. S. Creese, *Ladies in the laboratory? American and British women in science, 1800–1900* (1998), 294–6
Archives U. Edin. L., letters to Sir Archibald Geikie
Likenesses photograph, repro. in *The Times* (3 June 1935), 18 · photograph, repro. in *ILN* (8 June 1935), 1037
Wealth at death £24,264 17s. 2d.: confirmation, 29 Aug 1939, *CCI*

Gordon, Mary Louisa (1861–1941), physician and prison inspector, was born on 15 August 1861 at Seaforth in Lancashire, the daughter of James Gordon and his wife, Mary Emily Carter. The Gordons had lived for generations in the Scottish borderlands. The circumstances of her upbringing and education remain obscure, but in her early twenties she trained at the London School of Medicine for Women. On 11 November 1890 she registered as a medical practitioner, having achieved licentiate status with the Royal College of Physicians in Edinburgh, the Royal College of Surgeons in Edinburgh, and the Faculty of Physical Surgery, Glasgow; she also achieved licentiate status in midwifery. She had to overcome sustained resistance to her project of a medical career among family and friends, who accused her of having a morbid interest in disease and believed that a medical career was a degrading and risky undertaking for a woman. One of Mary Gordon's most marked traits was that she acted on her convictions, often in the face of resistance.

From 1890 to 1908 Mary Gordon practised medicine in London. She was appointed the first ever woman inspector of prisons in March 1908 and took up a post on the English and Welsh Prison Commission chaired by Sir Evelyn Ruggles-Brise. The appointment was made in line with one of the recommendations of the 1895 Gladstone committee on prisons, which was not acted upon until Herbert Gladstone himself became Liberal home secretary in 1905. Again her friends opposed this move, arguing that such an essentially bureaucratic and administrative post was unsuitable for a doctor. Mary Gordon was responsible for inspecting the female wings of about forty local prisons where women were held, and the convict prison, State Inebriate Asylum, and borstal for women, all at Aylesbury. Initially she was viewed with suspicion and anxiety in the Prison Commission, where she was frequently described as 'a new departure'; as she was not allocated an office, she had to work from her Harley Street clinic. Her job was to report annually to the commission on the maintenance of standards and regulations in all women's prison facilities in England and Wales, and to advise the Prison Commission generally on matters regarding the imprisonment of women and treatment of their inebriacy in the certified inebriate asylums for women. There was no training for this work, and Mary Gordon attached herself to a London prison for three days to discover how the system worked; she also visited women's prisons in France, the Netherlands, and Belgium.

By 1908 the prisons were at the heart of the struggle for women's suffrage, for since late 1905 suffragettes had been committed to prison for offences in connection with the suffrage issue. Mary Gordon deeply sympathized with this cause: until mid-1914 she clandestinely corresponded with a leading suffragette, Emmeline Pethick-Lawrence (1867–1954), and with the Women's Social and Political Union about conditions in the prisons and about leaders (such as Emmeline Pankhurst) who were periodically in prison. At that time the police raided the headquarters of the Women's Social and Political Union and stumbled upon this correspondence. The Home Office demanded that she publicly dissociate herself from the organization, which Mary Gordon refused to do, arguing that her support for women's suffrage was not unlawful and that she had never supported violence. The outbreak of the First World War led to suspension of the movement and the matter rested. However, she was never forgiven by the Home Office and Prison Commission mandarins. In 1916 she took temporary leave of absence to do war work with the Scottish Women's Hospitals for Foreign Service, serving in Macedonia in the Serbian transport column; one of her superiors caustically remarked, 'she will not be missed'. As late as 1919 her appointment ten years before was described as 'a sop to feminism'. She retired in 1921.

Mary Gordon's ideas about women offenders and imprisonment resonated closely with the new liberalism and dynamic psychology which had become symbols of reform and progress among many of her era. She argued that the retributive and punitive prison system characteristic of the nineteenth century was inherently flawed because most female prisoners were not susceptible to force or severity. In fact, she insisted, prisons in the admittedly less draconian era of the early twentieth century functioned like warehouses, storing a complex society with its own rules and roles, in which each prisoner was guaranteed a secure place and in which the criminal merely hibernated until release allowed resumption of crime. In these universities of crime women were brutalized and alienated rather than rehabilitated. Mary Gordon emphasized the necessity of scientific understanding of women offenders in order to apply reformatory measures to them: this faith in knowledge as a key to human progress pervaded all her thinking. Female criminality was to her the result of a very poor emotional environment in the home of the small child, physical and moral deprivation, stunted or distorted psychological development in childhood and adolescence, defective education, and exploitation by accomplished older criminals. To this environmentalist analysis Mary Gordon added a constitutional element also common in social scientific writings of the time: she claimed that many women offenders were suffering from inherited constitutional defects or mental defectiveness, and therefore easily fell victim to criminality. However, she most eloquently emphasized emotion and relationship as being at the core of the causes of crime and hence its cure, and paid close attention to contemporary clinical insistence on the centrality of such phenomena as repression, the unconscious, suppression, hysteria, regression, instinct, and fantasy in the production of female crime. Mary Gordon was deeply versed in the psychological theory of the time, which she quoted widely in her writing.

Another consistent theme in Mary Gordon's thinking was that social institutions were part of an oppressive criminogenic chain beginning with very poor nurture and family relationships. The police and law, for instance, combined to brand young women as 'common prostitutes' for life; prisons suppressed emotion and individuality, increasing self-denigration. Gordon advocated optimistic and energetic systems of training; her vision was of women offender institutions designed as communities with high degrees of freedom of expression, creativity, enthusiasm, and hope, in which the individual prisoner imbibed these qualities from the collective ethos of staff and inmates. However, daunted on occasion by the sheer mass of female prisoners and fearful that the children of today's criminals would be the prisoners of tomorrow, Mary Gordon supported a substantial programme of mental, familial, and social hygiene. There is a contrast between her optimism and sudden expression of deep pessimism in her writing, but these two aspects of her philosophy were integrated in her insistence on the need for medical, psychological, and social scientific analysis, leading to the development of an individual programme of reformatory treatment for each woman prisoner: Mary Gordon wished the whole woman to be understood in the context of her physical condition, mentality, intellect, and morality.

Mary Gordon's concern with feeling and experience was revealed in her other writing, most notably *The Chase of the Wild Goose*, published by Leonard and Virginia Woolf in 1936. This is an account, based on their journals, of two female lovers who fled persecution by their families in the late eighteenth century to set up home in the Vale of Llangollen, where they lived for fifty years. Mary Gordon dramatically excavated their intense yearning for one another and the protracted struggles they underwent to protect their relationship. Indeed, she believed that the experience of women at the hands of men was generally painful because men lacked the emotional and empathetic imagination of women. Her other publications were a novel, *A Jury of the Virtuous* (1907), and her work on women prisoners, *Penal Discipline* (1922).

Mary Gordon never married and had no children: she remarked near the end of her life that this solitariness had been part of the price of freedom in a world which stifled human spirit. She spent her last years at Hawk Wood, Crowborough, Sussex, where she died on 5 May 1941. Historically significant as a pioneer of women officials at the top echelons of the prison system, she experienced great isolation and distrust even before the suffragette issue and yet remained convinced that knowledge and dedication would lead ultimately to freedom of the whole human spirit. BILL FORSYTHE

Sources 'Report of the lady inspectors of prisons', *Parl. papers* (1909–16); 'Report of the commissioners of prisons and the directors of convict prisons', *Parl. papers* (1917–22) [annual reports] · PRO, HO 45-10429-A53867 · *Medical Register* (1910) · *Medical Register* (1920) · *Medical Register* (1940) · b. cert. · d. cert.

Gordon, Mervyn Henry (1872–1953), bacteriologist, was born at Harting, Sussex, on 22 June 1872, the sixth of ten children of the Revd Henry Doddridge Gordon and his wife, Elizabeth Oke, daughter of William *Buckland, the first professor of mineralogy and geology at Oxford and later dean of Westminster. Gordon was educated at the Dragon School, Oxford, Marlborough College, and Keble College, Oxford, before studying clinical medicine at St Bartholomew's Hospital, London. After graduating MB at Oxford in 1898 (BSc, 1901; MD, 1903), he began work in the pathology department at St Bartholomew's under Emmanuel Klein, whose long-standing friendship with the Gordon family may have accounted for the choice both of the hospital and of the department in which Gordon was to spend the whole of his working life.

Gordon remained on the pathology staff until 1923, and during this time engaged in three major research projects. One was a study, with F. W. Andrewes and T. J. Horder, of the characters of streptococci, which led to a classification of the genus into three species and gained universal recognition. Gordon extended this work much later in an attempt to subdivide one of these species (*Streptococcus pyogenes*, or the haemolytic streptococcus), which had long been suspected of heterogeneity, because of the great variety and varying severity of the infections caused by it. Although Gordon and Andrewes both made some progress in this direction, the final subdivision of the species into over thirty types, using the same methods, was not achieved until more than ten years later.

Gordon's second main interest was in the transmission of bacteria through the air. At a time when Flügge had recently shown that coughing, sneezing, and even speaking caused the expulsion into the atmosphere of 'droplets' of secretion from the mouth and throat, Gordon was given a remarkable opportunity of studying this phenomenon in no less a place than the House of Commons. Members had complained of problems in the ventilation, and the office of works entrusted Gordon among others with an inquiry into it. He used bacteria as indicators both of pollution and of air movement, and studied the distribution of streptococci from the mouths of speakers during sittings of the house. He also monitored the progress of a characteristic harmless organism introduced into his own mouth when he had the debating chamber to himself, and was able to recite passages from Shakespeare in a loud voice from the treasury bench to an audience of culture plates. The results of this work were published in a blue book in 1906—a landmark in the study of this subject, which was not to be advanced much further until the discovery of the 'droplet nucleus' twenty years later.

Gordon's third and perhaps greatest achievement was his study of cerebrospinal fever (meningococcal meningitis). During the First World War he was commissioned in the Royal Army Medical Corps and worked at its London headquarters at Millbank, where he was given executive authority in all matters connected with the diagnosis and treatment of this disease. He was largely responsible for showing that it resulted from a rise in the carrier-rate in overcrowded and ill-ventilated quarters—a fact which accounted for its frequent occurrence in army barracks in war conditions. Gordon showed that the meningococcus bacterium was divisible into four serological types and he studied methods for producing more effective therapeutic serum; he also organized the treatment of carriers, and defined methods for better bacteriological diagnosis. He was certainly the leading authority on the disease in Britain and possibly in the world.

In 1923 Gordon resigned his position on the staff of St Bartholomew's, but remained there as an external member of the staff of the Medical Research Council, and determined to devote himself entirely to the study of filtrable viruses. His early systematic studies of the viruses of variola and vaccinia are classical, and he also made some observations on mumps and psittacosis. An opportunity then occurred for engaging a team of workers to study lymphadenoma (Hodgkin's disease): Gordon undertook the direction of this team and, after discarding other hypotheses, reached the conclusion that this too was a viral disease. He devised a new animal test for its diagnosis, the basis of which was called into question, and he even formulated an immunological method for its treatment, which other workers found even more difficult to accept. In his later years he was much inclined to attribute a viral origin to other diseases, including rheumatism and cancer, on grounds which were unacceptable to those who were then advancing the study of virology by more modern methods.

Gordon was an original member (1909) of the army pathology advisory committee, and for many years thereafter he was consulting bacteriologist to the army. He was appointed CMG in 1917 and CBE in 1919. He was elected FRS in 1924 and received the honorary degree of LLD from the University of Edinburgh in 1936.

In 1916 Gordon married Mildred Olive (*d.* 1953), daughter of Sir William *Power. She continued her work as an inspector for the Local Government Board; they had no children. Gordon died at his home, Holly Lodge, 20 Walton Road, East Molesey, Surrey, on 26 July 1953.

L. P. GARROD, *rev.*

Sources L. P. Garrod, *Obits. FRS*, 9 (1954), 1537–63 · private information (1971) · personal knowledge (1971)
Archives priv. coll., family and collected papers
Likenesses W. Stoneman, photograph, 1936, NPG · photograph, repro. in Garrod, *Obits. FRS*
Wealth at death £15,414 6*s.* 11*d.*: probate, 25 Sept 1953, *CGPLA Eng. & Wales*

Gordon, (Joan) Noel [Noële] **(1919–1985)**, actress, was born on 25 December 1919 at 139 Clements Road, East Ham, Essex, the daughter of James Gordon, a marine engineer, and his wife, Joan Yell. Lessons at 'Madame Maud' Wells's dancing academy at the age of two led to her first public appearance, at the East Ham Palace. At the same age, she demonstrated another side to her talents by singing 'Dear little jammy face' during a masonic ladies' night at the Holborn Restaurant, London.

The dancing lessons stopped when the family moved to Westcliff-on-Sea in Essex. However, when the family later moved to Ilford, nearer London, Noële Gordon attended a convent school that frequently performed plays. Intent on acting, she trained at the Royal Academy of Dramatic Art, then joined the Brandon Thomas Players in Edinburgh, and later performed in repertory at the Theatre Royal, Birmingham. In 1938, two years after the BBC launched its regular television service, she made her small-screen début as Norah, the Irish maid, in Eugene O'Neill's *Ah Wilderness!*

The television pioneer John Logie Baird then chose Noële Gordon to take part in his first colour experiment, transmitted from Crystal Palace shortly before the Second World War. After a huge union flag was displayed, she was seen sitting on a chair and trying on an array of different-coloured hats. 'Taking part in this experiment was one of the outstanding moments of my life', she later said (*TV Times*, 14–20 Nov 1981).

Back on stage, Noële Gordon toured in *Black Velvet* (by G. Black, M. Dann, and D. Furber) during 1940—replete with a Norman Hartnell dark red satin dress—and made her London West End début in *Let's Face It* (by D. and H. Fields, music and lyrics by Cole Porter) at the Hippodrome a year later, after another actress had to withdraw through illness. She played Panache in the musical *The Lisbon Story* (by Harold Purcell, music by Harry Parr Davies) at the same theatre and in a 1946 film version, having already made her big-screen début a year earlier as Mrs Wilson in the comedy *29 Acacia Avenue* alongside Gordon Harker, Jimmy Hanley, Henry Kendall, and Dinah Sheridan. Noële Gordon also starred on stage with Mae West in her comedy melodrama *Diamond Lil*.

In 1949, while beginning an acclaimed two-year, 1000-performance stage run as the village whore, Meg Brockie, in Alan Jay Lerner's *Brigadoon*, Noële Gordon was invited to appear in the royal variety performance, singing a medley of Harry Lauder songs, which she dedicated to him at the time when he was dying. She also toured in a 1950s stage production of *Call me Madam* (a musical by Howard Lindsay and Russel Crouse, with music and lyrics by Irving Berlin).

Realizing the increasing popularity of television, Noële

Gordon studied the medium at a university in New York while also working as a chat show presenter for a small Seattle television station. On returning to Britain, she became adviser on women's programmes to ATV, the newly formed independent television company for the midlands, which began broadcasting in 1956.

Noële Gordon was soon appearing on screen as a presenter, first in the television advertising magazine *Fancy that*. Her other programmes included *Week-End*, *Tea with Noële Gordon*, *Midland Profile*, *Midland Sports*, *Noële Gordon Takes the Air*, *Hi-T!*, and, most notably, the midday chat show *Lunch Box*, which began in 1957. When Harold Macmillan agreed to appear on *Lunch Box*, she became the first woman to interview a prime minister on television. It was at the time of a general election, but they discussed haggis and black pudding.

When Lew Grade, head of ATV, wanted to broadcast a daily serial like those in America, he asked the *Lunch Box* producer Reg Watson to come up with an idea. The result was *Crossroads*, which started in November 1964 and featured the chat show's presenter in the leading role of Meg Richardson. As a widowed mother running a motel, she became a national institution and was known as the Queen of the Soaps. She stayed with *Crossroads* for seventeen years and 3521 performances—winning the *TV Times* readers' award for favourite female personality on television eight times—until being sacked in June 1981 in a blaze of publicity when Central Television, which took over the independent television midlands franchise from ATV, tried to revamp the soap opera, which had been under fire from the critics ever since it began, despite winning up to 16 million viewers.

In the storyline, the motel was razed in a fire, but Meg escaped and was seen leaving on the *QE II* from Southampton to make a new life for herself in America. The actress reappeared in the role briefly in 1983, when her newly married screen daughter Jill and her husband Adam Chance met Meg in Venice during their honeymoon there.

In the mean time, Noële Gordon had carved out a new stage career for herself, starring as Rose in *Gypsy* at the Haymarket Theatre, Leicester, in 1981 and appearing in a Middle and Far East tour of *The Boy Friend* (by Sandy Wilson), a 1983 London West End production of *Call me Madam* at the Victoria Palace, and a British tour of the 1920s musical *No No Nanette* (by F. Mandel, O. Harbach, and I. Caesar).

Noële Gordon died from cancer at the Edgbaston Nuffield Hospital, 22 Somerset Road, Edgbaston, Birmingham, on 14 April 1985, shortly before she was due to make another brief return to *Crossroads*. She was buried beside her mother in Ross-on-Wye, Herefordshire. Noële Gordon never married, although she had a twenty-year relationship with the show business impresario Val *Parnell (1892–1972). Her autobiography, *My Life at Crossroads*, was published in 1975. ANTHONY HAYWARD

Sources A. Hayward and D. Hayward, *TV unforgettables* (1993) • *The Times* (15 April 1985) • *TV Times* (14–20 Nov 1981) • *Daily Mirror* (23 May 1983) • b. cert. • d. cert. • *CGPLA Eng. & Wales* (1985) • N. Gordon, *My life at Crossroads* (1975)

Archives FILM BFI NFTVA, current affairs footage • BFI NFTVA, performance footage | SOUND BL NSA, performance recordings

Wealth at death £209,398: probate, 2 Aug 1985, *CGPLA Eng. & Wales*

Gordon, Osborne (1813–1883), college tutor and Church of England clergyman, was born at Broseley, Shropshire, on 21 April 1813, the son of George Osborne Gordon (*d.* 1822), a wine merchant, and his wife, Elizabeth. Educated at Bridgnorth grammar school, which was then enjoying a period of success under Dr Thomas Rowley (*d.* 1877), he went up to Christ Church ('The House'), Oxford, in 1833 as one of the school's Careswell exhibitioners. He was soon (December 1834) named to a studentship on the nomination of the dean, Thomas Gaisford. In 1835 he gained the university Ireland scholarship (beating A. P. Stanley), chiefly through the merits of eight exquisite lines of Doric Greek on the subject of Sir Francis Chantrey's monument to two children in Lichfield Cathedral. In 1836 he gained first classes in classics and mathematics, graduating BA in the same year, MA in 1839, and BD in 1847. In 1845 he was appointed rhetoric (and in 1846 Greek) reader in Christ Church. He succeeded H. G. Liddell as censor of Christ Church in 1846, and his period as senior censor, from Christmas 1849 to July 1861, was one of the longest and most successful, during which he delivered Latin funeral orations upon the duke of Wellington (1852) and Dean Gaisford (1855).

An act of 1842 had rendered unlikely Gordon's promotion to a canonry of Christ Church (which in previous circumstances might have been his) and in 1847 he was an unsuccessful candidate for the headmastership of King Edward VI School, Birmingham; the letters of recommendation supplied by Oxonians from the vice-chancellor downwards (over twenty of them in the *Dictionary of National Biography*) testify to Gordon's skill as a college tutor and private coach. He has been described as 'a pearl among tutors' (K. G. Feiling, *In Christ Church Hall*, 1960, 173). Among his pupils were both Liberal politicians (lords Carlingford, Monk Bretton, Kimberley, and Northbrook) and Conservatives (lords Harrowby, Salisbury, and St Aldwyn, and G. Ward Hunt), as well as the prince of Wales, who entered Christ Church in 1859. Gordon himself most admired the eighth marquess of Lothian.

Gordon was a university proctor in 1846–7, and published in 1847 proposals for the improvement of the Oxford examination system. He served as an examiner in classics between 1848 and 1852 and in 1860–61. Ordained deacon in 1839 and priest in 1840, he was nominated one of the university select preachers in 1849 and 1862. He was on the deputation in 1850 from Oxford to the queen in opposition to 'papal aggression'. In the same year he became a prominent member of the Oxford Tutors' Association, a body formed to represent the views of college tutors in the aftermath of the report of the university commission of 1850–52. He was elected in 1854 one of the first members of the hebdomadal council, which superseded the old hebdomadal board of heads of houses and

Osborne Gordon (1813–1883), by Lewis Carroll (Charles Lutwidge Dodgson), 1857

proctors. During the prelude to the ordinances of Christ Church, issued by the commissioners in 1858, he sought in a published letter to W. E. Gladstone (1854) to argue that the peculiar constitution of Christ Church (that is, the position of the dean and canons) made it unrealistic to attempt to assimilate completely its studentships to the fellowships of other colleges.

Eventually, being 'not quite in accordance' with the views of H. G. Liddell, dean of Christ Church from 1855, Gordon followed a traditional path and in 1860 took the college living of Easthampstead, Berkshire. He proved a model parish priest (following curates who were in turn 'very discreditable' and 'mad'), enlarging the parish schools and rebuilding the church. He farmed the glebe of 93 acres well; 'his pigs were famous', according to G. W. Kitchin.

Gordon maintained his links with Christ Church, encouraging (by a vehement letter to *The Times* in 1865 and by private correspondence) the process leading to the Christ Church, Oxford, Act of 1867, which overturned the government of the dean and canons. He also had a wider interest in national education, taking part in the examination for the Indian Civil Service and for the army, in remodelling the arrangements of the *Britannia* training ship, and in determining the system to be adopted at the Naval School, Greenwich. His views on religious education were set out in a published letter to Lord Sandon (later third earl of Harrowby), a former Christ Church pupil, on the latter's election to the London school board. In 1876 he was appointed chairman of a commission to inquire into the constitution of the queen's colleges in Ireland. His last appointment, to fill the place of Sir W. R. Grove on the University of Oxford commission appointed by the Conservative government in 1877, was not a happy one: his health was failing and he felt that his services had been insufficiently regarded. His health was further weakened by the shock of learning of the suicide of a servant whom he had dismissed. He died, unmarried, on 25 May 1883 at his home at Easthampstead, where he was buried. A memorial there bears an inscription by his pupil John Ruskin, and there is also a monument dedicated to him in the cloister of Christ Church Cathedral, Oxford.

G. W. Kitchin, Gordon's successor as censor of Christ Church, describes him as 'lean and haggard, with bright eyes, long reddish nose, untidy hair, odd voice, and uncertain aspirates, of quaint wit, exquisite scholarly tastes, extraordinary mathematical gifts, and of a very kind heart' (*Ruskin in Oxford*, 1903, 24). The 'uncertain aspirates' may identify him as the guest at a Christ Church dinner who, exasperated by the prolixity of a visiting speaker (perhaps Sir John Mowbray) about his doings in the 'House' (of Commons) interrupted with 'You should know, sir, that in this place the 'Ouse means 'ere'' (J. C. Masterman, *On the Chariot Wheel*, 1975, 127). Sir Algernon West, in his *Recollections* (1, 1899, 64–5) testifies further to the 'uncertain aspirates' and also to Gordon's 'overpowering love for a lord'.

W. F. Wentworth-Shields, *rev.* J. F. A. Mason

Sources G. Marshall, *Osborne Gordon: a memoir, with a selection of his writings* (1885) [22 sermons and two orations] • E. G. W. Bill and J. F. A. Mason, *Christ Church and reform, 1850–1867* (1970) • W. R. Ward, *Victorian Oxford* (1965) • E. G. W. Bill, *University reform in nineteenth-century Oxford: a study of Henry Halford Vaughan, 1811–1885* (1973), chap. 13 • letters by Gordon, BL, Gladstone MSS • letters by Gordon, Hatfield House, Salisbury MSS • letters by Gordon, PRO, HO 73/44 • letters by Gordon, Christ Church Oxf., MS Estates 117 • *The Times* (29 May 1883) • *Bridgnorth Journal* (2 June 1883) • Bishop Wilberforce's diocese book, 2.197 (Easthampstead)

Archives Bodl. Oxf., papers, incl. letters of recommendation, diaries • Christ Church Oxf. • PRO, letters, HO 73/44 | BL, corresp. with W. E. Gladstone, Add. MSS 44378–44400, *passim* • Hatfield House, Hertfordshire, Salisbury MSS

Likenesses L. Carroll [C. L. Dodgson], albumen print, 1857, NPG [*see illus.*] • photograph, *c.*1860, repro. in Bill and Mason, *Christ Church and reform*, pl. 2 • C. Dressler, memorial, Christ Church Oxf. • stipple, NPG

Wealth at death £25,572 11*s.* 0*d.*: probate, 7 Aug 1883, *CGPLA Eng. & Wales*

Gordon, (Mary) Pamela, marchioness of Huntly (1918–1998). *See under* Berry, (James) Gomer, first Viscount Kemsley (1883–1968).

Gordon, Patrick (*d.* before **1657**). *See under* Gordon, Patrick, of Ruthven (*fl.* 1606–1649).

Gordon, Patrick, of Ruthven (*fl.* **1606–1649**), historian, was the second son of Sir Thomas Gordon of Cluny and his wife, Lady Elizabeth Douglas, daughter of William Douglas, earl of Angus. Very few details of his life survive. A bond of 1606 shows that by that time his father was dead and that he himself was married, to Jean Gordon. A later genealogy lists his marriage to a daughter of Murray of Cowdies. His family was closely linked to that of the Gordons of Huntly and when, on 23 March 1609, Lord Gordon, heir of the first marquess of Huntly, was made a burgess of Aberdeen, at his request the same honour was bestowed on Patrick Gordon.

Gordon was provoked into writing on Britain's 'distemper'—her civil wars—by the publication in 1647 of George Wishart's account of the marquess of Montrose's royalist campaigns in Scotland between 1644 and 1646. Wishart's judgements on the conduct of the second marquess of Huntly (the former Lord Gordon) were harsh, and Patrick Gordon intended to provide an account of the Scottish wars that did his former patron justice and gave credit to the Gordons for their parts in Montrose's victories. However, Gordon proved too good a historian to do this effectively; he fully recognized Huntly's faults—bad judgement, unreliability, and arrogance—which turned all that he attempted into disaster. Gordon's stress on what he saw as the trait central to Huntly's misfortunes, his tendency to treat gentry as servants, suggests that he may have harboured personal resentment against the marquess for some former slight. Thus, though Gordon's work culminates with tributes to Huntly's merits and his consistent loyalty to Charles I, exemplified by his execution in 1649, the general tone of the work is one of lament for the weaknesses that rendered Huntly ineffectual as a leader. Montrose emerges as the man with the heroic qualities that Gordon admired. But even he—though he treated underlings courteously—was guilty of arrogance, Gordon claims, and he presents the rivalries of Scotland's nobility as central to the country's ills. Instead of uniting to serve Scotland they had let chaos reign as they squabbled among themselves for supremacy or sulked at imagined slights.

Though essentially a regional historian, dealing with the civil wars in northern Scotland, Gordon sets his history against a wide background of the Thirty Years' War, international intrigue, portentous comets, and above all the work of the divine physician, who was seeking to cure Scotland's ills by medical means. The wars represented blood-letting, the purging of society's liver—the aristocracy and the gentry, whose functions in society were military. The bubonic plague that struck in the mid-1640s was directed at purging through vomiting of the belly—merchants, craftsmen, and labourers. Finally, in the country's religious divisions and the poor harvests of the late 1640s Gordon detected the coming of famine, spiritual and material, purging the stomach. Thus he tried to present Scotland's disasters optimistically, seeing them as drastic cures being applied to underlying disease. Whether Gordon lived to see the cure, in the restoration of monarchy in 1660, is unknown but it is clear that he had completed work on his history before then and there is no evidence that he continued his narrative beyond 1650, though he indicates that he had considered doing so. His work was not printed until 1844.

Though there is no direct evidence on the matter the circumstantial evidence that Patrick Gordon, the historian of the 1640s, is identical to Patrick Gordon, the poet who had published his works three decades before, is strong. Poet and historian were both Aberdeenshire gentlemen and the moods of their writings have much in common; they share dreams of valour and nostalgic longing for a lost heroic past and a strong Scottish patriotism. Patrick Gordon the poet published first in London in 1614 the Latin *Neptunus Britannicus Corydonis*, which lamented the death of Henry, prince of Wales, congratulated Prince Charles on succeeding him, and celebrated the marriage of Princess Elizabeth to the elector palatine. The following year the first books of two long narrative poems were published in Dordrecht: *The famous and valiant historie of the renouned and valiant Prince Robert surnamed the Bruce … done into heroic verse* and *The firste booke of the famous historye of Penardo and Laissa, otherway callid the warres of love and ambitione*. The first of these, an 'Italianate martial epic with romantic trimmings' running to about 8000 lines, displays 'chivalric nostalgia' in tales of glorious deeds by Scottish knights (Spiller, 154). It was written, as Gordon explained, out of duty to Scotland and to stir up every man 'to the following of glorious Actions' (preface)—though, writing after the 1603 union of the crowns, Gordon carefully disclaimed anti-English sentiments. The opening line, 'Of martial Deeds, of dreadful Wars I sing' (sig. B1), indicates the inspiration of Virgil. *Penardo*, dedicated to Lord Gordon (described as the author's patron), moves to a vaguely Greek setting for 'a marvellous Spenserian romp in the world of dungeons and dragons' (Spiller, 154). Though these epics have been described as 'two strikingly good prentice attempts at epic' (ibid.), neither was followed by the extra books of verse necessary to complete them.

However, though historian and poet seem so compatible, the suggestion that they might be the same individual was not made until 1890, when it was advanced as 'possible' (*DNB*). A different identification of the poet had earlier been suggested by Robert Pitcairn, who stated that the author was 'probably' another Patrick Gordon [*see below*], a diplomat (R. Pitcairn, *Ancient Criminal Trials in Scotland*, 3, 1833, 448n.); James Maidment, in *Letters and State Papers during the Reign of James VI* (1838; 212n.) has indicated that this identification is certain, as have others.

Patrick Gordon (*d.* before 1657), diplomat, was a younger son of John Gordon of Braco (or Brackay), in Inverurie parish, and his wife, Agnes Strachan. He probably entered Marischal College, Aberdeen, in 1606 and graduated as master of arts in 1610. On 2 June 1610 he was commissioned as James VI and I's agent to Poland and Prussia. In practice his work concentrated on Poland and on the Scots settled there. On James's orders Gordon brought about the prosecution of Stercovious, a German Pole who on a visit to Scotland had been ridiculed for the costume he wore and in revenge had written and circulated a 'libel' against the Scottish nation. Stercovious was beheaded at Rastenburg (Ketrzyn) in 1611. Gordon claimed £600 sterling as expenses for the prosecution and James ordered the Scottish burghs, since they traded with Poland, to pay this. They refused but eventually, in 1613, they compromised on 6000 merks, about a quarter of the original demand.

Gordon retained his position as agent until 1621 but he spent much time in Britain. In 1617 he was in Edinburgh during the king's visit to the city and complaints were made about his gross neglect of duty, particularly in failing to prevent the Poles imposing a special tax on Jews and Scots. He aggravated the situation by threatening to have the ears of one of the complainers cut off, and he was imprisoned for a time in Edinburgh Castle. However, the fact that he was made a burgess of Aberdeen suggests that some appreciated his diplomatic efforts. In June 1623 Gordon bought the lands of Brackay, which had passed out of his family's ownership, and in the same year (after a contract of 18 October) he married Margaret, daughter of John Erskine of Balhagartie. He died before 1657.

In choosing between the diplomat and the historian as the author of the poems discussed above the balance of probability is tipped in the historian's favour by two points. The diplomat is usually referred to as 'Mr', in recognition of his university degree, whereas the poet refers to himself as 'gentleman', and both poet and historian had the patronage of Lord Gordon.

DAVID STEVENSON

Sources P. Gordon, *A short abridgement of Britane's distemper*, ed. J. Dunn, Spalding Club, 10 (1844) · D. Stevenson, 'Heroic epic and harsh reality: Patrick Gordon', *King or covenant?* (1996), 175–87 · M. Spiller, 'Poetry after the Union', *The history of Scottish literature*, ed. C. Craig, 1: *Origins to 1660*, ed. R. D. S. Jack (1987), 141–62 · *DNB* · A. M. Munro, ed., 'Register of burgesses of guild and trade of the burgh of Aberdeen, 1399–1631', *The miscellany of the New Spalding Club*, 1, New Spalding Club, 6 (1890), 1–162 · Register of the privy council of Scotland · A. Maxwell, *The history of old Dundee* (1884) · T. A. Fischer, *The Scots in Germany* (1902) · A. F. Steuart, ed., *Papers relating to the Scots in Poland, 1576–1793* (1915) · J. M. Bulloch and others, eds., *The house of Gordon*, 1, Third Spalding Club, 26 (1903) · Haddo House muniments, NA Scot., GD33

Gordon, Patrick (1635–1699), army officer and diarist, was born on 31 March 1635 at Easter Auchleuchries in Aberdeenshire, where his father, John Gordon (*d. c.*1684), was a minor laird. His mother's name was Mary Ogilvie (*d. c.*1684). He wrote his diary in six thick quarto volumes, preserved in Moscow in the central state military-historical archive. These have never been published in the original English, but were extensively translated into German by Maurice Posselt, and appeared in three volumes in Russia in 1849–53. In 1859 selections from those parts of the diary which related to the author's native country and some of his foreign adventures were transcribed verbatim by Dr Posselt for Joseph Robertson, who edited them for the Spalding Club. The diary is very complete, for it was a custom with Gordon, among other things, to put down the price of every article he purchased. Unfortunately the volumes narrating events between 1667 and 1677 and between 1678 and 1684 are lost.

In 1651, after attending schools in Ellon and Cruden, Aberdeenshire, Gordon, as the younger son of a poor laird, resolved to push his fortunes in a foreign country. He soon found his way into Poland, then swarming with Scots, and, after two years at the Jesuit college in Braunsberg, Prussia, entered the service of Charles X of Sweden, along with some fellow countrymen. In the following year he was taken prisoner by the Poles; he joined their army as a dragoon, and deserted the Swedes, but in the same year, when captured by the latter at Warsaw, he again entered their service. In 1658, in company with others, he planned at Werder the assassination of Richard Bradshaw, the English ambassador to Moscow, whom he had mistaken for the president at the trial of Charles I, for Gordon was an enthusiastic adherent of the house of Stuart. The ambassador was too well guarded to give the conspirators a chance of success. Gordon then joined the Poles again in 1659. In 1660 he was present at the battle of Chudnovo, where the Poles defeated the Russians, and in the following year resolved to enter the Muscovite service. He found his way to Moscow, where he was well received by the tsar, Alexis, if not by some of his officials. One of his first exploits was participation in the suppression of a revolt in 1662, caused by the depreciation of the coinage. In 1665 he married Katharine von Bockhoven (*d. c.*1682), daughter of Colonel Philip Albert Bockhoven, a German in the service of the tsar, but at that time a prisoner among the Poles. After her death, *c.*1686 he married Elizabeth Ronaer, a lady of Dutch extraction. In 1666 he was sent by Alexis on a mission to England, and was honoured with an interview by Charles II, at whose restoration to the throne of his ancestors he had most sincerely rejoiced. He returned to Russia, and, as there is a gap of nearly seventeen years in his diary, we know but little of his subsequent doings, except that he blew up the fortress of Chigirin, and in 1678 helped drive the Turks from Ukraine. In this campaign Gordon displayed great ability. In 1679 he was appointed to the chief command at Kiev. The diary resumes without interruption from 1684.

In 1686 Gordon obtained leave to visit England and Scotland; but before going he had an interview with the young tsar, Peter, then fourteen years of age. Many pages of the diary are occupied with an account of the writer's journey to his native country. He visited the old family property in Aberdeenshire. He had an interview with James VII and II, with whom he had many sympathies as a Roman Catholic as well as a Stuart. James urged him to quit the Russian service and to hasten back to Britain. On his return he petitioned for a discharge from the Russian service, but it was not granted, and he appears to have suffered a temporary disgrace on account of his importunities. In 1687 he took part in the expedition against the Tartars of the Crimea, which was under the command of Prince Golitsyn and resulted in failure, but on account of his services Gordon was promoted to the rank of general. This appointment, however, drew down upon him ecclesiastical censure, and the patriarch prophesied disaster to the Russians so long as their armies were commanded by a heretic. But his regiment was soon afterwards sent to Kolomenskoe, near Moscow, once the favourite residence of Alexis, then occupied by Peter, and he gradually fell more under the notice of the future reformer of Russia. In 1689 he had an opportunity of showing his devotion to the cause of the young tsar when the struggle broke out between him and his stepsister Sophia. The cause of Peter triumphed and Gordon was rewarded with many estates and honours. In 1694 he accompanied the tsar on naval manoeuvres from Archangel, and acted as rear-admiral. In 1697 he fortified Azov, which had been taken the previous year, and the tsar set out on his memorable embassy to the West. During his absence the great revolt of the Streltsy (musketeers) took place; Gordon attempted to negotiate with them, but, all methods of conciliation having failed, he brought them to obedience by force of arms, and caused many to be executed. The rest were kept in confinement until the return of Peter, who, on his return to Moscow, commenced a further series of sanguinary reprisals.

Gordon closed his diary with the end of 1698; among his last entries is the following: 'This year I have felt a sensible decrease of health and strength.' He died in Moscow on 29 November 1699, aged sixty-four. The tsar, who visited him constantly during his illness and was present at his death, ordered that his favourite should have a splendid funeral. He was buried in the Roman Catholic church in the German quarter at Moscow, in the erection of which he had himself had a great share. The church was, however, allowed to fall into decay, owing to the erection of a larger one for the use of residents of that faith. He left at his death two sons and two daughters by his first marriage, and one son by his second.

Gordon was a perfect type of the seventeenth-century mercenary, a brave, capable man, full of resources, but ready to transfer his services to the cause which paid the best. In the case of Russia, however, he can be considered to have shown ultimate devotion to her as an adopted country, although he several times tried to leave the tsar's service, and seems never to have given up entirely the dream of returning home to retire. His diary contains much valuable material, and is one of the most significant sources for seventeenth-century Russian history. It gives minute descriptions of sieges of Azov and the suppression of the revolt of the Streltsy. It provides invaluable information on Russian public and private life, as well as on the early history of Jacobitism.

W. R. MORFILL, *rev.* PAUL DUKES

Sources P. Gordon, diary, Central State Military–Historical Archive, Moscow • *Passages from the diary of General Patrick Gordon of Auchleuchries, AD 1635 – AD 1699*, ed. [J. Robertson], Spalding Club, 31 (1859) • P. Dukes, ed., 'Patrick Gordon and his family circle: some unpublished letters', *Scottish Slavonic Review*, 10 (1988) • G. P. Herd, 'General Patrick Gordon of Auchleuchries: a Scot in seventeenth century Russian service', PhD diss., U. Aberdeen, 1994 • *Tagebuch des Generals Patrick Gordon* …, ed. M. C. Posselt, 3 vols. (1849–53)
Archives Central State Military-Historical Archive, Moscow, diary | BL, corresp. with Lord Middleton, Add. MS 41842
Likenesses engraving, priv. coll. • portrait, repro. in Robertson, ed., *Passages from the diary*, frontispiece

Gordon, Patrick (*c.*1664–1736), army officer and colonial governor, was presumably born in Scotland, a descendant of Alexander Gordon of Strathavon, the second son of the third earl of Huntly. Although his parentage is now obscure, he was a distant kinsman of the dukes of Gordon and the Gordon earls of Sutherland. He married Isabella Clarke (*d.* 1734), a member of a prominent lowland Scots family, with whom he had six children. Isabella's eldest brother, a Catholic convert, had held high office under Cosmo, duke of Tuscany, a close personal friend to Alexander, second duke of Gordon. Their eldest daughter married Robert Charles, Patrick Gordon's private secretary and later colonial agent for both Pennsylvania and New York. A son, Archibald Gordon, later served as a captain during the Carthagena expedition in 1745. Previous to his appointment as the lieutenant-governor of Pennsylvania in 1726, Gordon's only known service was as a major under the duke of Marlborough in Flanders.

Why this self-confessed bluff old soldier was considered a suitable candidate for the lieutenant-governorship is unclear. Hannah Penn, William Penn's widow, and Springett Penn, his heir-at-law, were taken with Gordon's straightforward honesty, and they were determined that he replace the then lieutenant-governor Sir William Keith. In his administration (1717–26) Keith had undermined the Penn family's influence in the province and subordinated their council to the wishes of the elected assembly. In March 1726 Keith's supporters resisted his removal but the Board of Trade followed the Penns' wishes and appointed Gordon in April 1726. He arrived in Philadelphia with his family on 22 June 1726.

The first two years of Gordon's governorship were troubled by the continued presence of Sir William and his election to the assembly. Sir William's financial problems, however, led to his flight from Philadelphia in 1728, after which Gordon's administration was marked by a period of rare political harmony in the province. His alliance with moderate leaders of the assembly, his close connections with the council, especially James Logan, and his willingness in 1729 to ignore his own instructions regarding issuing any further paper currency enhanced Gordon's standing. Consequently the province experienced both expansion and prosperity, which were marked by the creation in 1729 of Lancaster county, the first addition to the province since William Penn's own days. The court system was reformed, a colonial London agency finally established in 1731, and a new state house completed in Philadelphia in 1735. The political peace, however, was finally strained by Gordon's clash with the assembly over his commission from the Penns, the arrival of Thomas Penn in the colony in 1732, and Gordon's own personal argument with the speaker of the assembly, Alexander Hamilton, who ultimately came to question Gordon's mental capacities. Thomas Penn's own extravagant and dissolute habits, together with his counting-house mentality, made him obnoxious to many in the province. This, and the fact that Robert Charles, Gordon's son-in-law, became Penn's favourite further weakened Gordon's position.

Pennsylvania's own success brought increased friction with neighbouring Native Americans. As German and Scots-Irish new arrivals trespassed upon their lands, Gordon constantly had to monitor frontier conditions. In June 1728 he welcomed to Philadelphia Sassoonan, leader of the Schuylkill Delaware, and listened to his complaints. New treaties were signed and Gordon published these as *Two Indian Treaties at Conestagoe* (1728). Friction continued and, after it was discovered that the French and Canadians were building forts on the Allegheny and Ohio rivers, Gordon invited the Shawnee and the Five Nations to Philadelphia where, in Gordon's own townhouse, Thomas Penn renewed bonds of friendship in August 1732. Penn's wish to enrich the family by continued land sales, however, and his decision to use the Five Nations to police the backwoods and discipline the increasingly powerful Shawnee, eventually led to even greater frontier problems, as old native rivalries flared.

Isabella Gordon died in September 1734, after which it became clear that Gordon himself was gravely ill: from February 1735 he rarely attended to business. Following what the *Pennsylvania Gazette* termed 'a long and tedious indisposition', Gordon died on 5 August 1736. After a simple ceremony, attended only by the council members, he was buried next to his wife in the graveyard of Christ Church, Philadelphia. His grave, unfortunately, cannot now be identified. In the 1740s the strains evident in Gordon's administration once more broke out into factional political wranglings, a political discord which plagued Pennsylvania politics until the 1770s.

RORY T. CORNISH

Sources S. H. Drinker, *Hannah Penn and the proprietorship of Pennsylvania* (Philadelphia, 1958) • A. Tully, *William Penn's legacy: politics and social structure in provincial Pennsylvania, 1726–1755* (1977) • C. P. Keith, *Chronicles of Pennsylvania*, 2 vols. (Philadelphia, 1917) • W. C. Armor, *Lives of the governors of Pennsylvania* (Philadelphia, 1872) • J. J. Kelley, *Pennsylvania: the colonial years, 1681–1776* (1980) • W. T. Shephard, *History of proprietary government in Pennsylvania* (1896); repr. (1967) • F. B. Tolles, *James Logan and the culture of provincial America* (Boston, 1957) • *The papers of Benjamin Franklin*, ed. L. W. Labaree and W. J. Bell, 1–2 (1959–60) • *Pennsylvania Gazette*
Archives PRO, corresp., CO 1257–1279

Gordon, Pryse Lockhart (1762–1834x40), writer, was born on 24 April 1762 at Ardersier, Inverness-shire, where his father, the Revd Harry Gordon, was minister of the parish as well as being chaplain to a highland garrison. After his father's death on 15 March 1764, his mother, Sarabella, *née* Morrison, went to live with her father, the Revd Walter Morrison, in Banffshire. Gordon was educated at the parish school of Banff, and subsequently at the University of Aberdeen, where he did not remain long, obtaining a commission in the marines at the age of fifteen. He was principally employed in recruiting, and seems to have seen no active service except a few cruises, which, he maintained, yielded him £17 in prize money. In 1792 he obtained a commission in a regiment raised by the duke of Gordon and, after five years' service in Scotland, was allowed to accompany his friend Lord Montgomery, an invalid, to Italy, where he remained until 1801, returning to find his regiment disbanded. He obtained employment at Minorca, but, as he was on the point of embarking, 'my good fortune threw in my way an amiable young widow', whom he married in autumn 1801. This rendered him independent of military service, and after living at Banff Castle and in Sloane Street, London, he went to Sicily with Lord Montgomery in 1811. He remained there until 1813, when he was prostrated by a sunstroke. The following year, after the peace, he took up his residence at Brussels, where he remained until his death. In 1823 he wrote a guide for travellers entitled *A Companion to Italy*, the success of which led to the appearance of his *Personal Memoirs* in 1830. This is a very entertaining book, written with good taste and simplicity, and containing many interesting reminiscences of notable persons known to the author, including Emma (Hart), Lady Hamilton, the second wife of Sir William Hamilton (1730–1803), Professor Richard Porson, George Bridges Rodney, Baron Rodney, Richard Charles Burney, and James Perry of the *Morning Chronicle*. The peculiar interest of the work, however, arises from its sketches of picture and antiquity hunting, at a time when, owing to the disturbed state of the continent, great bargains were to be had, and connoisseurs were especially liable to be imposed upon. Gordon himself obtained for Dr Burney the copy of Constantinus Lascaris's grammar, the first Greek book printed, which is now in the British Museum. His account of its acquisition is the most exciting passage in his book, except perhaps the description of the condition of the English residents at Brussels on the eve of Waterloo. In 1834 Gordon published *Holland and Belgium*, an entertaining book, negligent and even ungrammatical in diction, but useful for its notes on the Belgian revolution and its causes. He died in Belgium some time between 1834 and 1840.

RICHARD GARNETT, *rev.* REBECCA MILLS

Sources P. L. Gordon, *Personal memoirs, or, Reminiscences of men and manners at home and abroad*, 2 vols. (1830) • *IGI* • Allibone, *Dict.* • b. cert.
Likenesses H. Meyer, stipple, pubd 1830, NPG

Gordon, Sir Robert, of Gordonstoun, first baronet (1580–1656), historian and courtier, was born on 14 May 1580 at Dunrobin Castle, Sutherland, the fourth son of Alexander *Gordon, twelfth earl of Sutherland (1552–1594) [*see under* Gordon, John, eleventh earl of Sutherland (1525–1567)], and his second wife, Lady Jean (1546–1629), daughter of George Gordon, fourth earl of Huntly. He attended school in Dornoch until 1596 then, tiring of 'that ydle life' (Gordon and Gordon, 314) at Dunrobin (his father had died and his eldest brother was in France), he persuaded his mother to send him and his brother Alexander to university in 1598. They spent six months at St Andrews before moving to Edinburgh University 'to finish the progresse of their studies' (ibid., 239). With his customary concern to stress his own worth, Gordon notes that he was 'beloved by the principall and regents' at Edinburgh (ibid., 313–14). In 1602 he and Alexander obtained a licence to go abroad for seven years, and in January 1603 he went to France with a tutor, studying civil (Roman) law at Poitiers for a year as well as travelling and engaging in 'all exercises fitt for a gentleman of his birth and qualitie' (ibid., 249), returning to Scotland in October 1605. In January 1606 he moved to court and was admitted as a gentleman of the king's privy chamber. A life pension of £200 sterling and a knighthood followed in 1609. On 16 February 1613 he married Louise (or Lucie; 1597–1680), the fifteen-year-old heir of John Gordon DD, dean of Salisbury. A visit in March 1615 to Cambridge with the king brought him the honorary degree of MA.

Sir Robert Gordon of Gordonstoun, first baronet (1580–1656), by unknown artist, 1621

Though he had resolved on the life of a courtier and established his family home in Salisbury (where all his children were born), Gordon was also assiduous in upholding the rights of the house of Sutherland, making frequent trips to Scotland, mainly concerned with family disputes with George Sinclair, earl of Caithness, before hastening back to court to try to use his influence with the king in favour of the thirteenth earl of Sutherland, his brother. On the latter's death in 1615 Gordon became tutor (guardian) of his nephew John, the fourteenth earl, and thus 'the chieff pillar, under God' of the house of Sutherland (Gordon and Gordon, 313). He accompanied King James to Scotland in 1617, where he won the silver arrow in an archery competition at the palace of Holyroodhouse. Preoccupation with the affairs of his nephew prevented him from returning to England until late in 1619, after his father-in-law's death had brought him the lordship of Glenluce and lands in France (which he sold). Having dealt with this personal business in England he returned to Sutherland in 1621, where he worked to relieve his nephew of his debts, protect his interests from rivals, and settle local feuds. Fearing he might die while his nephew was still a child, he wrote 'Sir Robert Gordon his Fearweell', a long tract of advice on how to preserve the family's power (Fraser, 1.202). When in 1623 Caithness was proclaimed a rebel and forced to flee to Orkney, Gordon was commissioned to proceed against him with fire and sword, and led the Sutherland men in seizing Castle Sinclair, Caithness's residence. On his nephew reaching the age of twenty-one in 1630 Gordon's position as tutor came to an end, and he rounded off his services to his house by completing in December the manuscript of his massive *Genealogical History of the Earldom of Sutherland*.

King James had agreed to pay Gordon £2000 for the abbey of Glenluce, but as this was never paid he persuaded Charles I to grant him instead the right to succession to the office of protonotary of the common pleas in 1635. As this indicates, royal favour to Gordon had continued after James's death in 1625. Charles I renewed his appointment as a gentleman of the privy chamber, and on 28 May 1625 he was the first to be admitted to the new order of baronet of Nova Scotia, he having interested himself in the scheme for the colony since 1621. Appointments as sheriff of Inverness (1629), vice-chamberlain of Scotland (1630), and a member of the Scottish privy council (1634) followed.

When in 1637 revolt began in Scotland against the king's religious policies Gordon's loyalties were divided. He had long served the king and his father, but his nephew Sutherland, the head of his house, was a staunch supporter of the king's covenanter opponents. Now ageing, Gordon probably sought to avoid active involvement, but in May 1639 the king sent him to Scotland to take his seat on the privy council. Both the marquess of Huntly, imprisoned by the covenanters, and the covenanters themselves urged him, as a man trusted by the king, to report to him on how strong determination to resist him in arms was. This Gordon did, meeting the king at York before moving to the north of Scotland 'perswading all men to peace, so far as his power or intreatie could prevaile' (Gordon and Gordon, 492). However, the bishops' wars of 1639–40 followed, ending in the humiliation of the king, and the beginning of the English civil war late in 1642 decided Gordon that the time had come to retire. Having spent the winter in Salisbury, early in 1643 he brought his family to Moray. The previous year he had had lands he had bought there erected into the barony of Gordonstoun, and there he settled his family and his impressive library. He showed himself ready to accept the revolution that had overthrown royal power, sitting as an elder in the general assembly of the church in 1643 and being appointed a member of the committees of war of a number of shires in the following years. In the Scottish civil wars of 1644–7, however, he showed no inclination to play an active role. In 1646 there was evidently suspicion that he inclined to the royalists—perhaps because his eldest son had joined a brief royalist rising by the earl of Seaforth, or because he himself had intervened with the royalist Lord Lewis Gordon and his 'master burner' and persuaded them 'to spare the corns', thus proving 'a good friend to many about him' (J. Fraser, *Chronicles of the Frasers*, ed. W. Mackay, 1905, 313). Gordon defended himself by obtaining a declaration from the presbytery of Elgin that he was 'a main advancer off the true religion' (W. Fraser, 1.202) and an attestation of his loyalty from the covenanter garrison of Spynie Castle. Gordon was infirm in his later years and died in March 1656, his wife surviving him until September 1680.

The obsessive interest in genealogy of cadet members of

great families led to the compilation of a number of valuable works in seventeenth-century Scotland, but few are as wide-ranging or of such lasting value as Gordon's *Genealogical History*. The emphasis on his own achievements, especially as tutor of the fourteenth earl, is marked, but he provides much invaluable information on otherwise obscure feuds among the clans of the northern highlands. His pride in his blood, and the honour he felt at having rescued his house at a time of crisis, was immense, and when forced in the 1640s to choose between the crown that he had served so long as a courtier and his kin, ties of blood proved the stronger. DAVID STEVENSON

Sources W. Fraser, ed., *The Sutherland book*, 3 vols. (1892) • *DNB* • R. Gordon and G. Gordon, *A genealogical history of the earldom of Sutherland … with a continuation to the year 1651* (1813) • GEC, *Baronetage* • *The historical works of Sir James Balfour*, ed. J. Haig, 4 vols. (1824–5) • *Sixth report*, HMC, 5 (1877–8), 681–8 [Sir William Gordon Gordon Cumming] • *Catalogue of the library at Gordonstoun* (1816) • M. D. Young, ed., *The parliaments of Scotland: burgh and shire commissioners*, 2 vols. (1992–3) • E. D. Dunbar, *Social life in former days, chiefly in the province of Moray* (1865); [2nd ser.] (1866)

Archives NL Scot., corresp.; accounts and corresp. as tutor to Lord Sutherland

Likenesses oils, 1621, Scot. NPG [*see illus.*] • oils, 1629, Scot. NPG

Gordon, Robert, of Straloch (1580–1661), cartographer, was born on 14 September 1580 at Kinmundy, Aberdeenshire, the second son of Sir John Gordon (*c*.1547–*c*.1600) of Pitlurg and Nichola Kinnaird, a daughter of Kinnaird of that ilk. His paternal grandfather had been killed at the battle of Pinkie in 1547 and his father was a great friend and confidant of George Gordon, sixth earl of Huntly. Gordon received his early education in Aberdeen and is thought to have been the first graduate, in 1597, of Marischal College, founded in 1593. In 1598 he went to Paris to complete his education. There he associated with fellow Scots including the presbyterian preacher Robert Bruce, who had been banished to France by James VI, and the historian Robert Johnston. Following the death of his father Gordon had returned to Scotland by June 1601. In 1608 he married Catherine Irvine (*d*. 3 Aug 1662), daughter of Alexander Irvine of Lenturk, and bought the estate of Straloch, about 10 miles north of Aberdeen. Although he fell heir to the estate of Pitlurg when his brother Sir John Gordon died childless in 1619, he continued to live at Straloch. He and his wife had seventeen children, of whom ten sons and five daughters reached adulthood.

Closely associated with some of the leading figures of the north-east, most notably Patrick Forbes of Corse, bishop of Aberdeen, to whose *Funerals* he contributed an epitaph, and the Gordon earls of Huntly, Gordon played an active part in public life. In 1636 he was appointed justice of the peace for the sheriffdom of Aberdeenshire. After the outbreak of the covenanting troubles in 1638 he remained a figure of respect to both sides. He was much occupied as a representative in negotiations between the royalists, headed by the Huntly family, and the covenanters, under Montrose and the Earl Marischal. A representative of Gordon interests, Straloch none the less adopted a cautious stance in 1639 towards plans for precipitate action against the covenanters. Frequently the object of urgent summonses from the first and second marquesses of Huntly for advice on family business as well as national affairs, Straloch was also asked for assistance—most notably by the marquess of Argyll in 1644—in efforts to bring recalcitrant Gordons to co-operate with the covenanting regime.

It is as a cartographer that Gordon is now chiefly remembered. On 8 October 1641 Charles I wrote to Straloch asking him to undertake the task of altering and correcting proofs of maps of various shires of Scotland. The maps, drawn by Timothy Pont, had been sent to Joan Blaeu for inclusion in his *Theatrum orbis terrarum, sive, Atlas novus*, 5, *Scotia* (Amsterdam, 1648, with subsequent editions in 1655 and 1664). It was at the instigation of Sir John Scot of Scotstarvet that Gordon, who appears to have met Pont, was first approached to carry out the task of revision and correction of those maps not already completed. Gordon was assisted in the work by his son James *Gordon of Rothiemay. Although the Gordons' work is seen as intermediary between the sixteenth-century maps of Pont and the finished edition of Blaeu, their contribution extended beyond cartographic revision and provided valuable descriptions of historical, cultural, and topographical features. A variety of factors hampered Gordon's progress with the work and induced him to call upon the help of David Buchanan (1595?–1652?) in completing the project. These, as he noted to Scotstarvet in the dedication to the 1648 edition, included his large number of children, the care of his estate, his old age, and his preference for a private and retired life. Most of all, though, he felt he was hampered by living in a part of the country at the very centre of the civil chaos engulfing the kingdom. Such was the perception of the authorities of the importance of the work Gordon was carrying out that he had twice been afforded parliamentary protection in order to enable him to do it. In March and then again in June 1646 he obtained recommendations that on account of his cartography work he should be free from all quartering of soldiers and public burdens. A supporter of Charles II, he was not in favour with the Cromwellian regime.

A keen antiquarian and historian, Straloch was an admirer of Spottiswood, to whose *History* he wrote a Latin introduction, but was critical of Boece, Buchanan, and Knox. His notes and papers on the covenanting period were utilized by his son James Gordon in his *History of Scots Affairs*. He died on 18 August 1661 and was buried on 6 September in Newmachar parish churchyard.

SHONA MACLEAN VANCE

Sources J. Man, *Introduction … to the projected work memoirs of Scottish affairs from 1624 to 1651 by Robert Gordon of Straloch, James Gordon of Rothiemay, and others* [n.d., 1741?] • Chambers, *Scots*. (1835), vol. 2 • U. Aberdeen L., special libraries and archives, Gordon family of Straloch MS 2223, xi–lx • *DNB* • J. Stone, 'Maps of Scotland by Timothy Pont, Robert and James Gordon and Joan Blaeu: a study in historical cartography', PhD diss., U. Aberdeen, 1972 • J. M. Bulloch and others, eds., *The house of Gordon*, 1, Third Spalding Club, 26 (1903) • J. Henderson, *Aberdeenshire epitaphs and inscriptions* (1907) • J. Gordon, *History of Scots affairs from 1637–1641*, ed. J. Robertson and G. Grub, 3 vols., Spalding Club, 1, 3, 5 (1841) • J. F. Kellas Johnstone and A. W. Robertson, *Bibliographia Aberdonensis*, ed. W. D. Simpson, Third Spalding Club, 1 (1929) • *Reg. PCS*, 2nd ser.

Archives NL Scot., Origo et progressus familiae Gordoniorum de Huntley in Scotia • U. Aberdeen L., special libraries and archives, family papers, MS 2223

Likenesses G. Jamesone, oils, *c*.1625, Robert Gordon College, Aberdeen • G. Jamesone, portrait, Marischal College, Aberdeen, Mitchell Hall; repro. in Chambers, *Scots.* (1855), vol. 2

Gordon, Sir Robert, of Gordonstoun, third baronet (1647–1704), landowner and natural philosopher, was born on 7 March 1647 at Gordonstoun, in the parish of Drainie, Elgin, the first son and heir of the eight children born to Sir Ludovic Gordon of Gordonstoun, second baronet (1625–1688), and his wife, Elizabeth, daughter of Sir Robert Farquhar of Mounie in Daviot, Aberdeenshire. Sir Robert *Gordon (1580–1656), privy councillor and historian of the house of Sutherland, was his grandfather. Educated at home in all the liberal sciences then known, Gordon travelled on the continent and, according to the *New Statistical Account of Scotland* (1845), 'made himself master of many secrets in natural history unknown to his illiterate countrymen, whom he took pleasure in frightening and astonishing. It was believed that he was educated in Italy in the *School of the Black Art*' (vol. 13, Elgin, 154). According to Dunbar (138–42), in 1672 he was bound apprentice to Robert Blaikwood, an Edinburgh merchant, and took his freedom in 1678, but this may be a misidentification with another of that name and family. As a landowner, he was a commissioner to the Scottish parliament, representing Sutherland in 1672–4, 1681, and 1685–6, but his election to parliament in 1696 as a commissioner for Elgin was disallowed; he was a commissioner to the convention of the estates in 1675, visitor to the mint in 1682, and commissioner of justiciary for the highlands. He was said to have been knighted in 1683, but the title of 'Sir' may have been assumed from his later baronetcy.

On 23 February 1676 Gordon married Margaret (*d.* 1677), daughter of William, eleventh Lord Forbes, and widow of Alexander Sutherland, first Lord Duffus. The event caused Alexander Brodie to confide to his diary: 'That such a person as she should doe it so abruptli … without the consent of [*shorthand*]. I did sie human frailti in it' (*Diary*, ed. Laing, 351). This brief union produced a daughter, Jane. Brodie reported: '25 April 1677 I went to the Lady Duffus's burial quhair I did not sie that sens and tendernes which she deserved' (ibid., 385). Gordon later married Elizabeth, daughter of Sir William Dunbar of Hemprigs, and had three sons, Robert, William, and Lewis, and four daughters, Margaret, Elizabeth, Lucy, and Catherine.

Gordon passed much of his time on his estates in Scotland—he executed an entail of the Gordonstoun estate in 1697 and obtained a novodamus thereof in June 1698—but devoted a brief period of his life to science, particularly mechanics and chemistry. A manuscript of the Gordon family claims that he carried on a long correspondence with Robert Boyle (Douglas, 9), though no such letters remain among his or the Boyle papers. James II took an interest in these matters and made Gordon a gentleman of his household. In 1686 Gordon attempted to interest the Admiralty in a water pump that he had invented. On 22 April the king was present at his demonstration, but the pump failed to function. Gordon nevertheless corresponded with Samuel Pepys, who wrote about the sea trials of the device to Sir Samuel Morland and William Legge, first Baron Dartmouth, though it was never adopted for use. Having been proposed by Christopher Wren, Gordon was elected to the Royal Society in 1686. The following year he sent the society a brief letter outlining a prescription for rabies: it was published that year in the *Philosophical Transactions*, but by then he had lost interest in the society and ceased active membership.

Gordon died in September 1704 and was buried at Gordonstoun, where his widow had a mausoleum erected on the site of the old church of Ogston; his son Robert (1696–1772) succeeded to the baronetcy. In later years an underground chamber at Gordonstoun was shown as his laboratory, and he lived on in local legend as a 'mighty wizard' (*Passages from the Diary of General Patrick Gordon*, 128–9).

STEVEN A. WALTON

Sources R. Douglas and others, *The baronage of Scotland* (1798), 6–10 • *The diary of Alexander Brodie … and of his son James Brodie*, ed. D. Laing, Spalding Club, 33 (1863) • *Passages from the diary of General Patrick Gordon of Auchleuchries, AD 1635 – AD 1699*, ed. [J. Robertson], Spalding Club, 31 (1859) • R. Gordon, *Case of Sir Robert Gordon, bt, earl of Sutherland* (1769–70), pedigree, appx 1, 8 • E. D. Dunbar, *Social life in former days, chiefly in the province of Moray* (1865) • M. D. Young, ed., *The parliaments of Scotland: burgh and shire commissioners*, 1 (1992), 285 • R. Gordon, 'A receipt to cure mad dogs, or men or beasts, bitten by mad dogs', *PTRS*, 16 (1687), 298 • M. Hunter, *The Royal Society and its fellows, 1660–1700: the morphology of an early scientific institution*, 2nd edn (1994) • Bodl. Oxf., MS Rawl. A. 189 • *Sixth report*, HMC, 5 (1877–8), 687

Archives NL Scot., corresp. • NL Scot., legal corresp.

Likenesses oils, 1692, Scot. NPG

Gordon, Robert (*bap.* **1668**, *d.* **1731**), benefactor, the eldest son of Arthur Gordon (1625–1680), advocate, and his wife, Isobel Menzies, was baptized on 18 August 1668 in Aberdeen. Gordon was left an inheritance of around £1100 at his father's death, which he seems to have spent in travelling in Europe. After some time Gordon settled at Danzig, where he engaged in mercantile pursuits. Having acquired some wealth Gordon returned to Scotland, probably around the turn of the century. Documents dated 1699, 1707, and 1708 describe him as 'Merchant in Aberdeen', where he had been enrolled as a burgess of guild as a young man in 1684. During this period he was active in business, and there is evidence that he lent money on the security of landed estates.

About 1720 Gordon settled permanently in Aberdeen. He is said to have been a miser, and many anecdotes of his tight-fisted ways have been handed down. On one occasion he is said to have found a dead mouse in his bowl of buttermilk, and squeezed the milk out of the body. Despite his meanness, Gordon was a keen collector of coins, medals, and drawings, of which he left a large number. He died unmarried on 28 April 1731 in Aberdeen, apparently as a result of overeating, and was buried at St Nicholas's Church there.

In his settlement, following the example of George Heriot of Edinburgh, founder of Heriot's Hospital, Gordon conveyed his entire property, which amounted to £10,300, to the town council, with four of the ministers of Aberdeen as trustees, to be used to found and maintain a hospital for educating poor children, preference being given principally to offspring of his poor relations named Gordon or Menzies. His legacy became available on his death, and a hospital was completed in 1737 at a cost of £3300. The fund was left to accumulate until 1750, when Robert Gordon's Hospital opened with between fourteen and thirty boys. Before then, the empty buildings were briefly converted into a fort to garrison the duke of Cumberland's troops during the Jacobite rising of 1745.

Gordon's school was given further encouragement by a bequest from Alexander Simpson of Colyhill in 1834. Its constitution was modernized in 1881, when it became a day school. Gordon's institution, now known as Robert Gordon's College, became fully co-educational in 1989. Previously affiliated with the school, Robert Gordon's Institute of Technology became a separate college in 1981 and, as the Robert Gordon University, was awarded university status in 1992. ALEXANDER DU TOIT

Sources R. Anderson, *The history of Robert Gordon's College* (1896), 1–11, 114–22 · A. Walker, *Robert Gordon: his hospital and his college* (1886), 1–14 · J. Bruce, *Lives of eminent men of Aberdeen*, 1 (1841), 289–302 · F. Douglas, *A general description of the east coast of Scotland* (1782), 119–26 · 'Educational endowments (Scotland) commission: third report', *Parl. papers* (1886), 28.505–25, C. 4664 · 'Royal commission on endowed institutions in Scotland: second report', *Parl. papers* (1881), 36.144–83, C. 2790 · A. Smith, *A new history of Aberdeenshire*, 2 vols. (1875), 1.102–3, 164 · Anderson, *Scot. nat.*, 3.334 · Chambers, *Scots.* (1855) · F. J. Grant, ed., *The Faculty of Advocates in Scotland, 1532–1943*, Scottish RS, 145 (1944), 83 · W. Kennedy, *Annals of Aberdeen*, 2 vols. (1818)

Likenesses J. Cheere, statue, 1753, Robert Gordon's College, Aberdeen · W. Mosman, portrait, 1761, Robert Gordon's College, Aberdeen · bust, repro. in Anderson, *History of Robert Gordon's College*; formerly at Robert Gordon's College

Wealth at death £10,300: Anderson, *Scot. nat.*; Chambers, *Scots.*

Gordon, Robert (1687–1764), Roman Catholic priest and biblical scholar, was born in Scotland, a member of a Roman Catholic family of Kirkhill. He entered the Scotch College at Rome from the diocese of Aberdeen in 1705, was ordained priest, and left Rome in 1712. With the consent of the bishops he stayed at Paris as prefect of studies and procurator, and he did not proceed to the mission until 1718, when he was appointed chaplain to the duke of Gordon. After the duke's death in 1728 he was sent to Edinburgh as procurator, which office he held until 1740. He spent many years translating the New Testament into English, and in 1743 he went to Rome to get his version approved before it was sent to the press. He was much opposed by the Pilgrim party led by Colin Campbell and James Tyrie, and returned to England in 1745 without the desired authorization. On arriving in London he was apprehended and consigned to a messenger. On finding security for a large sum of money that he would never return to Britain without leave of the government, he was exiled to Flanders. He lived there and at Paris until 1749. In that year he returned to Rome, and having formed a hermitage for himself at Nerni, a village about 20 miles from that city, remained there until 1753, when he returned to Paris, but had been unable to get his translation of the New Testament approved. He lived for some time in the Scotch College at Paris, and then retired to Lens, where he died in 1764. Thereafter the manuscript translation of the New Testament, containing corrections of mistranslations in preceding Roman Catholic versions, passed to the possession of the biblical critic Alexander Geddes.

THOMPSON COOPER, *rev.* PHILIP CARTER

Sources H. Cotton, *Rhemes and Doway: an attempt to show what has been done by Roman Catholics for the diffusion of the Holy Scriptures in English* (1855) · J. F. S. Gordon, *Journal and appendix to Scotichronicon and Monasticon* (1867); pubd as *The Catholic church in Scotland* (1869)

Gordon, Robert (1786–1853), Free Church of Scotland minister, was born on 5 May 1786 at Old Crawfordton, Glencairn, Dumfriesshire, the only son of James Gordon (*d.* 1792), the parish schoolmaster, and his wife, Janet MacAdam. His father died when Gordon was six; he was appointed to his father's former post as parish schoolmaster at the age of fifteen, but soon decided to prepare for the Church of Scotland ministry. Supporting himself by private tutoring, he pursued an irregular course of study, first at Edinburgh University and then, after 1809, at Marischal College, Aberdeen. He was licensed to preach by the presbytery of Perth on 27 July 1814, taught mathematics briefly at Perth Academy, and was ordained to the ministry of the rural parish of Kinfauns, in Perthshire, on 12 September 1816. In February 1821 he moved to Edinburgh to become minister of the St Cuthbert's parish chapel of ease, and in January 1824 he moved to the Hope Park chapel of ease. In September 1825 he was presented by the magistrates and town council of Edinburgh to the New North parish church; five years later he was translated to St Giles, the high church of Edinburgh. He was awarded a DD degree from Marischal College in 1823, and in 1836 he was appointed to the lucrative office of collector of the Ministers' Widows' Fund.

Gordon was an able and conscientious evangelical pastor, who devoted considerable care to his pulpit preparations. He also took an active interest in science, inventing a self-registering hygrometer and contributing lengthy articles on Euclid, geography, and meteorology to the *Edinburgh Encyclopaedia*. He was a member of the Royal Society of Edinburgh and the Royal Scottish Society. He had married Isabella Campbell (*d.* 1877) on 30 November 1816; they had twelve children, of whom ten would survive their father. A modest and amiable man, he took little part in the controversies in the church courts. Although evangelical in his piety and a keen supporter of overseas missions, he was not seen as a party man.

None the less Gordon took a firm stand on the non-intrusion question. In 1834 the general assembly of the Church of Scotland agreed to limit patronage by granting male heads of family a veto over the settlement of patrons' candidates as parish ministers. The civil court of session, however, declared the veto illegal in 1838, and insisted that patrons' candidates be settled regardless of parish feeling. In the ensuing struggle Gordon sided with the non-intrusionists against unrestricted patronage: his high status in the church and reputation for integrity enhanced their cause in the eyes of the public. In 1841 he was elected to the year-long office of moderator of the general assembly. As moderator it fell to him to pronounce the deposition of seven ministers from the presbytery of Strathbogie for refusing to recognize the authority of the church courts to enforce the veto. The Strathbogie ministers had the support of the government, and their deposition brought the conflict between church and state to a head. On 25 August 1841 Gordon presided at a meeting of 1200 church office-bearers, where he maintained that the struggle over patronage had become one for the spiritual independence of the church. At the general assembly of 1842 Gordon seconded the adoption of the 'claim of right', a final appeal to the state to recognize the non-intrusionist principles. The following year, at the Disruption, he left the established church along with over a third of the clergy and a large portion of the lay membership.

For the remaining decade of his life Gordon served quietly as minister of the Free high church in Edinburgh. He died of a stroke, after a brief illness, on 21 October 1853, in his home in Northumberland Street, Edinburgh; he was buried on 26 October in Newington cemetery, Edinburgh. A quiet, capable man, who had risen from obscurity to one of the highest positions in the national church, he had reluctantly entered the non-intrusionist struggle; his principled stand in the conflict, however, had made a powerful impression on the nation.

STEWART J. BROWN

Sources [N. L. Walker], 'Robert Gordon', *Disruption worthies: a memorial of 1843* (1876), 77–84 • *Free Church Magazine*, new ser. 2 (Dec 1853), 554–60 • *Fasti Scot.*, new edn • Chambers, *Scots.*, rev. T. Thomson (1875), 3.131–4 • P. Clason and W. Cunningham, *Two sermons preached in the Free high church, Edinburgh, on sabbath, November 6, 1853, after the funeral of the late Robert Gordon* (1853) • R. Buchanan, *The ten years' conflict*, 2nd edn, 2 vols. (1852) • *The Scotsman* (29 Oct 1853)

Archives U. Edin. L., letters to Thomas Chalmers

Likenesses B. W. Crombie, pencil sketch caricature, *c.*1830, repro. in B. W. Crombie, *Modern Athenians: a series of original portraits of memorable citizens of Edinburgh* (1882) • A. Edouart, silhouette, 1830, Scot. NPG • T. Duncan, oils, 1841, General Assembly Hall, Edinburgh • D. O. Hill and R. Adamson, three calotypes, 1844, Scot. NPG • E. Burton, engraving (after oil painting by T. Duncan, 1841), U. Edin., New Coll. L. • A. Edouart, silhouette, Scot. NPG • W. P. Kennedy, engraving, U. Edin., New Coll. L. • J. Steel, low-relief profile, plaster, U. Edin., New Coll. L. • mezzotint (after an unknown artist), NPG

Wealth at death £3126 3*s.* 1*d.*: inventory, 15 April 1854, NA Scot., SC 70/1/83, p. 46

Gordon, Sir Robert (1791–1847), diplomatist, was the fifth son of George Gordon, Lord Haddo (1764–1791), and his wife, Charlotte, *née* Baird (*d.* 1795), and the younger brother of George Hamilton-*Gordon, fourth earl of Aberdeen (1784–1860), later prime minister. He was probably born at Gight in Aberdeenshire, and he was educated at Harrow School and Christ Church, Oxford, graduating BA in 1808 and proceeding MA in 1824. Originally intended for the church, he preferred the diplomatic service and accompanied Sir Gore Ouseley's embassy to Tehran, as an attaché in 1810. He left both a journal of the embassy and detailed accounts in his letters to his brother the fourth earl. He reached Persia by a circuitous voyage, touching at Rio de Janeiro and Ceylon and spending time in Bombay. He arrived at Bushehr on 5 March 1811. His letters show a keen interest in the religions and archaeology of the countries he visited and he sent his brother 'the most valuable Persepolitan remains that ever left this country' (Gordon to Aberdeen, 2 Dec 1811; NA Scot., GD 33/63/IX). He also learned Russian, an astute move because towards the end of 1812 he was dispatched to St Petersburg, where Lord Cathcart had just become ambassador. *En route* he saw the burnt-out remains of Moscow after Napoleon's retreat. Plague also raged and he was told only the snow spared him the sight of putrefying bodies in the streets. In 1813 he briefly accompanied Aberdeen, then ambassador to Austria, through war-torn Germany.

Sir Robert Gordon (1791–1847), by Joseph Kriehuber, 1846

Gordon was appointed secretary of embassy to the United Provinces of the Netherlands in 1814 and acted as minister-plenipotentiary alternately in Brussels and The Hague until the arrival of Sir Charles Stuart (later Lord Stuart de Rothesay) in February 1815. He then became secretary of embassy in Vienna (1815–26), frequently acting as minister-plenipotentiary during the absences of the ambassador, Charles Stewart (later third marquess of Londonderry). He was present at the congresses of Laibach (1821) and Verona (1822). He became minister-plenipotentiary in Brazil (1826–8) and signed an important commercial treaty in 1827. He had been sworn of the privy council in 1826.

In 1828 war broke out between Russia and Turkey, precipitated in part by the Greek struggle for independence. In December 1827 the British ambassador, Stratford Canning, together with his French and Russian colleagues, had left Constantinople for their own safety but they continued to transact business from Corfu and Poros. In March 1829 Canning resigned in anger when Aberdeen, now foreign secretary, rebuked him on the instructions of the prime minister, the duke of Wellington, for overzealous support of the Greek cause. Aberdeen appointed Robert Gordon to succeed him. Gordon (who was knighted later that year) was able to reach Constantinople in June 1829. Like his brother, Gordon privately sympathized with the Greek desire to obtain Attica, as well as the Morea. But the international situation was critical. It seemed possible that a victorious Russian army might advance on Constantinople. Gordon was in favour of bringing a British fleet up to Constantinople, but both Aberdeen and Wellington vetoed the idea: the force was not adequate and they would be in a 'rat trap' (Aberdeen to Gordon, 3 Oct and 8 Dec 1829; BL, Add. MS 43210). In a remarkable foreshadowing of the Crimean War, they discussed the pros and cons of sending a squadron into the Black Sea. In the event, the Russians did not advance on Constantinople and the war was ended by the treaty of Adrianople (1829). Gordon played a small role in the establishment of the Greek state in 1830. His recall in 1831 was technically on health grounds but his relationship with the new whig government cannot have been easy.

Gordon did not hold office again until his brother returned as foreign secretary in Sir Robert Peel's administration in 1841. In the meantime he had acquired the lease of the Balmoral estate from the Fife trustees. His brother thought it an extravagance and tried to pressure him into surrendering it in return for an embassy. Gordon wanted Paris, refused Constantinople, and settled for Vienna, but without giving up Balmoral.

In Vienna, Gordon was required to perform a delicate balancing act, discouraging too close an entente between Austria and France, while assuring the Austrians that Britain's entente with France in no way derogated from the traditional close relations between Austria and Britain. He complained bitterly of his lack of staff, protesting that he was having to perform the duties of 'Ambassador, Secretary and Attaché in my own person'. Aberdeen replied unsympathetically, 'you have really so little to do at Vienna that you may almost do the whole business yourself.' Gordon defended himself in an interesting analysis of the role of the attaché. There was, he admitted, little copying to be done at Vienna, 'But we want attachés for the purposes of society, who can collect the opinions and command the good will of the people … I had half a dozen attachés last year but not one of them could boast a quality of this nature. To drink a glass of wine, to smoke a cigar and to damn the natives—such are the characteristics of most British attachés' (Gordon to Aberdeen, 15 Dec 1843 and 15 Jan 1844; Aberdeen to Gordon, 2 Jan 1844; BL, Add. MS 43211).

Gordon was replaced by Lord Ponsonby immediately after the fall of Peel's government. He returned to Balmoral, where he fell dead at the breakfast table after visiting his stables on 8 October 1847. He was buried at Methlick, Aberdeenshire. The lease of Balmoral passed to his brother, who sold it to Prince Albert. The comparatively small house inhabited by Gordon was completely rebuilt in the 1850s. Although Lord Melbourne described Gordon as pompous, the *Gentleman's Magazine* called him 'amiable'. His letters give the impression of an enthusiastic man, who was a competent ambassador.

MURIEL E. CHAMBERLAIN

Sources Aberdeen MSS, BL · *GM*, 2nd ser., 28 (1847), 635–6 · S. T. Bindoff and others, eds., *British diplomatic representatives, 1789–1852*, CS, 3rd ser., 50 (1934) · M. E. Chamberlain, *Lord Aberdeen: a political biography* (1983) · A. Gordon, *The earl of Aberdeen* (1893) · *A catalogue of all graduates … in the University of Oxford, between … 1659 and … 1850* (1851)

Archives BL, corresp. and papers, Add. MSS 43209–43222, 49273 · BL, journal, Add. MS 493223 · Haddo House, Aberdeenshire | BL, corresp. with Lord Aberdeen, Add. MSS 43094–43157, *passim* · BL, corresp. with Sir George Rose, Add. MS 42793 · NA Scot., Haddo House MSS, GD 33/63/IX · U. Durham L., letters to Viscount Ponsonby · W. Yorks. AS, Leeds, corresp. with Lord Canning and J. Blackwell

Likenesses J. Kriehuber, lithograph, 1846, BM, NPG [*see illus.*]

Wealth at death held lease of Balmoral estate, which he bequeathed to brother: Aberdeen MSS

Gordon, Seton Paul (1886–1977), naturalist and photographer, was born at 26 Rubislaw Terrace, Aberdeen, on 11 April 1886, the only child of William Gordon (1839–1924), advocate and town clerk of Aberdeen, and his wife, Ella Mary, daughter of the horticulturist William *Paul of Waltham Cross, Hertfordshire; she wrote poetry. As well as a family house in Aberdeen, the Gordons had a chalet (Auchintoul) at Aboyne on Deeside, which played a big part in developing the young boy's love of wildlife, fishing, climbing the hills, and photographing birds; he wrote so well about what he was discovering that the first of his twenty-seven books, *Birds of Loch and Mountain*, illustrated with ninety of his photographs, was published in 1907. In October 1908 he matriculated at Exeter College, Oxford, and took a second-class honours degree in natural sciences in 1911. At Oxford he met (Evelyn) Audrey Pease (1893–1959), an undergraduate at Lady Margaret Hall, studying the same subjects. She not only matched him in ornithological knowledge, but had photographed a variety of birds from hides in her home county of Northumberland. They were married on 19 August 1915, had a son and two daughters, and their partnership lasted until her death.

In 1912 Gordon published *The Charm of the Hills*, which remained in print almost a century later. During the First World War he was given the job of organizing a secret coastguard service, based on the Isle of Mull and with his own boat. For Gordon a whole new world opened up as he recruited a corps of over 100 Hebrideans on different islands to watch out for enemy submarines. He was conscious of the inequality which meant that he could go where he pleased among the islands and wildlife that he loved while his friends were being killed in the trenches

Seton Paul Gordon (1886–1977), by Bassano, 1928

in France. *The Land of the Hills and the Glens* (1920) and *Hebridean Memoirs* (1923) drew on these experiences. Indeed, his wartime career launched him on a career as a naturalist, writer, and photographer, for, as he discovered in the 1920s, there were more qualified former officers than appointments. He observed, 'After the war we visited much of the Highlands and the Hebrides, staying with crofters, camping on the islands, some of them uninhabited, living the hard way, thus getting to know the crofters and their outlook on the world.' In 1922 he published *Amid Snowy Wastes*, an account of the wildlife on the Spitsbergen archipelago, and in 1927 *Days with the Golden Eagle*, the first of many volumes on birds which bridged the gap between ornithology and environmentalism. His *Edward Grey of Fallodon and his Birds* (1937) was an affectionate account of the former foreign secretary's interest in the subject.

Seton Gordon had a disciplined approach to his work, routinely writing for three hours in the morning and three in the evening. In February he went on lecture tours, travelling all over the British Isles to show his slides taken with a half-plate camera; the tours always finished in time for him to return to his home, Upper Duntulm, on the island of Skye, to catch the nesting of the golden eagle. The routine produced some thirty or more books, many illustrated with photographs by both Gordon and his wife. Among them were *Thirty Years of Nature Photography* (1936), *Highways and Byways in the Central Highlands* (1948, with illustrations by Sir David Young Cameron), and *Afoot in the Hebrides* (1950). Gordon was appointed CBE in 1939. Audrey Gordon died in 1959, and the following year (2 June 1960) Seton married a family friend, Elizabeth Maud (*b.* 1899/1900), widow of Colonel Reginald Badger and daughter of George Murray *Smith, landowner. Gordon's discipline now relaxed somewhat, and they divided their time between Upper Duntulm, his wife's cottage in Kintail, and Biddleston Manor, Northamptonshire, where Seton Gordon died on the night of 18–19 March 1977. His ashes were scattered in the Cairngorms.

Adam Watson summed up Gordon's life in *Scottish Birds*, the journal of the Scottish Ornithologists Club:

> With his passing ends the period of wholly exploratory naturalists in Scotland and their extraordinary breadth of interests. He was the long last practitioner, overlapping for decades the modern period when scientific method dominated ornithology. Astride two centuries, Seton had a timeless attitude, exemplified by the patched, decades-old kilt he wore on every occasion, sun or snow, mansion or bothy.

TOM WEIR

Sources R. Eagle, *Seton Gordon: the life and times of a highland gentleman* (1991) · S. Gordon, *Thirty years of nature photography* (1936) · private information (2004) · personal knowledge (2004) · b. cert. · m. cert. · C. Anson, ed., *Lady Margaret Hall register, 1879–1952* (1955) · [A. Watson], *Scottish Birds*, 9/6 (1977), 307–9

Archives NL Scot., corresp. and papers | CUL, corresp. with Sir Peter Markham Scott · JRL, letters to the *Manchester Guardian* · NL Scot., letters to Paul C. Spink

Likenesses Bassano, photograph, 1928, NPG [*see illus.*] · photographs (aged ninety), repro. in [Watson], *Scottish Birds*, 307

Wealth at death £141,172.68: confirmation, 6 July 1977, *CCI*

Gordon, Theodore (*bap.* 1780?, *d.* 1845), army medical officer, may have been the son of Theodore Gordon and Margaret Thomson who was baptized at Cabrach, Aberdeenshire, on 8 June 1780. He studied arts and medicine at King's College, Aberdeen, and at Edinburgh, where he graduated MA in 1802. In 1803 he enlisted as assistant surgeon in the army, and soon after joined the 91st highland infantry, accompanying the regiment to Germany in 1805. He also saw service in the Iberian peninsula, and escaped a shipwreck in the Douro (one of only seven survivors) while in charge of the wounded from Sir John Moore's army. He became surgeon to the 2nd battalion 89th regiment, and afterwards to the 4th regiment (King's Own), along with which he joined Wellington in the Peninsula, where he was present at the battles of Salamanca, Vitoria, Badajoz, San Sebastian, and Burgos, and was promoted to the rank of staff surgeon. Having been badly wounded while crossing the frontier into France, he was brought home with a rifle ball in his neck which surgeons were unable to extract until he arrived at Plymouth, and was invalided for a year.

Gordon next joined the Chelsea Hospital, London, as staff surgeon. He went on to take charge of a hospital at Brussels, after Waterloo, and then joined Wellington's staff in Paris, where he was promoted to be physician to the forces. After the peace he was chosen by Sir James MacGrigor to be professional assistant at the medical board of the War Office, and he spent the remaining thirty years of his life in that post. In 1836 he attained the rank of deputy inspector-general of hospitals. On 9 October 1822 he married Elizabeth Bruce, daughter of the Revd P. Barclay, and niece of Major-General Sir Robert Barclay KCB. Gordon died at Brighton on 30 March 1845. He was survived by his wife. CHARLES CREIGHTON, *rev.* PATRICK WALLIS

Sources *GM*, 1st ser., 92/2 (1822), 464 • *GM*, 2nd ser., 23 (1845), 651–2 • *IGI*

Gordon, Thomas (*d.* 1750), pamphleteer and classical scholar, was born in Kirkcudbright. He may have been educated at some Scottish university before he became an advocate at the Scottish bar in 1716. He went to London as a young man and taught languages, and by 1719 was probably the author of the much-reprinted anti-clerical *A Modest Apology for Parson Alberoni … and a New Confutation of the Bishop of Bangor*, though the work has also been attributed to Philip Horneck. In London, Gordon met the whig writer John Trenchard. He became Trenchard's colleague and amanuensis, and together they worked on various anti-clerical, anti-papist, and anti-corruption old and independent whig publications which were immensely influential in Britain and America.

Gordon's *Independent Whig*, published in two parts in December 1719 and January 1720, proved a success: it went through five editions in one year, and was translated into French, and in 1720 Gordon and Trenchard started a weekly paper of the same name. The powerful anti-clerical polemic of this periodical led to attempts by some of the clergy to suppress it, and Gordon's response, *The Craftsman* (1720), was again very popular, and reprinted several times in Britain and America. Gordon published this tract under the name of Daniel Burgess, a dissenting preacher, and this is typical of his writing. His many pseudonyms include Britannicus, a True-born Englishman, a North Briton, Montanus, and a Layman. In addition, he published many texts anonymously. He also shared the pen-name of Cato with Trenchard in their influential series of *Cato's Letters*, which was published from 1720 until 1723, in the *London Journal* and later the *British Journal*. Attributions of Gordon's work are sometimes difficult; though he wrote some of the letters, he later admitted they were mostly Trenchard's work.

Trenchard died in 1723, and after his death Robert Walpole made Gordon first commissioner of the wine licenses, a post which Gordon held until his death. His acceptance of this post and the altered tone of his journalism after 1723 have been interpreted as signs that Gordon had entered 'Walpole's Grub Street stable' (Kramnick, 243). Gordon's anti-clericalism remained strong, however, as in his 1732 *Sermon Preached before the Learned Society of Lincoln's Inn*. He may have been employed by Charles Talbot in 1733 to attack Edmund Gibson and defend Thomas Rundle in *A Letter to the Reverend Dr Codex*, though this piece has been attributed by some to William Arnall.

In 1728 Gordon published, by subscription, a translation of Tacitus (dedicated to the prince of Wales and Walpole), which remained a standard edition until the end of the century. Gibbon was less than impressed, however, describing the style as 'pompous' (E. Gibbon, *Memoirs of my Life*, ed. B. Raddice, 1990, 71). Gordon later published *The works of Sallust, translated into English, with political discourses upon that author, to which is added a translation of Cicero's four orations against Catiline* (1744). His list of publications is vast, and includes the very popular *The Conspirators, or, The Case of Catiline* (1721) and *Francis, Lord Bacon, or, The Case of Private and National Corruption, and Bribery* (1721), as well as various pieces on political and ecclesiastical corruption. Collections of his essays and tracts were published during and after his life; in 1751 Richard Baron published a three-volume anthology, *A Cordial for Low Spirits*.

Gordon was described as 'large and corpulent', and supposed to be the Silenus of Alexander Pope's *Dunciad* (1728). He married twice, and had three children, Thomas, William, and Patty. His second wife, whom he married in 1724, was Anne Trenchard, Trenchard's widow, and the daughter of Sir William Blackett, a wealthy northern baronet. It has been argued by Caroline Robbins that the income he acquired through this marriage makes it less likely that he would have needed the bribes it is assumed he received from Walpole; Robbins points to the force of his classical commentaries as evidence of his continued radicalism. It may, however, be significant that Gordon's will shows that Anne's property was all settled on her in a pre-marriage agreement. Gordon died on 28 July 1750, possibly in Upper Brook Street, London, and was survived by his wife. LESLIE STEPHEN, *rev.* EMMA MAJOR

Sources *GM*, 1st ser., 20 (1750) • PRO, PROB, 11/781, sig. 263 [will] • *ESTC* • C. Robbins, *The eighteenth-century commonwealthman* (1968), 88, 93, 115–17, 120, 392–3 • I. Kramnick, *Bolingbroke and his circle* (1968), 118, 243–4, 252 • T. F. J. Kendrick, 'Sir Robert Walpole, the old whigs and the bishops, 1733–1736', *HJ*, 11 (1968), 421–45, esp. 427, 437 • J. G. A. Pocock, *Virtue, commerce, and history* (1985), 240, 248 • J. G. A. Pocock, *The Machiavellian moment* (1975), 467–77 • J. C. D. Clark, *English society, 1688–1832: ideology, social structure and political practice during the ancien régime* (1985), 289, 301, 304, 320–23 • *Pope: poetical works*, ed. H. Davis (1966) • W. Prest, 'Law, lawyers and rational dissent', *Enlightenment and religion: rational dissent in eighteenth-century Britain*, ed. K. Haakonssen (1998), 169–92 • Watt, *Bibl. Brit.* • Nichols, *Lit. anecdotes*, 5.419; 8.101, 494, 512 • J. Collinson, *The history and antiquities of the county of Somerset*, 3 (1791), 153

Gordon, Thomas (1714–1797), university professor, was born on 14 August 1714 in Aberdeen, the son of George Gordon (1673?–1730), professor of oriental languages at King's College, Aberdeen, and Margaret Fraser (*bap.* 1685, *d.* 1753), daughter of George Fraser, the college's sub-principal. Gordon studied at King's College between 1727 and 1731, and was later one of many members of his extended family that taught there during the seventeenth and eighteenth centuries. He married, probably on 18 October 1742, Lilias Forbes, with whom he had five children, including the ballad singer Anna *Gordon, and on 27 May 1772 he married Elizabeth, *née* Innes (*bap.* 1714, *d.* 1799), widow of James Walker, minister of Peterhead.

After graduating MA from King's College, Gordon served as librarian and assistant regent at his alma mater between 1733 and 1739, in which year he was admitted as humanist, or professor of classics. A handbill from 1744 shows how he aimed to increase his salary by taking in students as boarders and providing them with tuition in a wide range of subjects, including 'history, geography, chronology, Herauldry, and the Principles of Drawing and Architecture' (Wood, 58). Gordon also devoted much time to teaching Latin, and took the title of professor of poetry and rhetoric in the broadside. In 1765 he exchanged offices with William Ogilvie, and for the rest of his life he served as regent, or professor of philosophy. His course, which was divided into four categories—pneumatology, natural theology, ethics and logic, and the anatomy of the mind—drew on the work of recent scholars, including Reid, Shaftesbury, Hutcheson, Hume, Berkeley, and Locke.

Gordon and his relatives formed the core of political factions in many debates over appointments to the faculty and attempts to unite King's and Marischal colleges. In 1786 he and six other professors who resisted unification earned the satirical sobriquet the Seven Wise Men, yet James Ramsay of Ochtertyre, acquainted with Gordon late in the professor's life, remembered him as an 'academical Nestor', a 'worthy, respectable, popular man, revered even by his opponents in the midst of academical broils' (*Scotland and Scotsmen*, 297). Gordon's extensive records of college affairs served as ammunition in the fight against unification of King's and Marischal, and his penchant for record-keeping also contributed invaluably to historical accounts of King's College and to the learned societies to which he belonged.

Gordon was among the founding members of the Gordon's Mill Farming Club, established in December 1758 by several members of King's College and the proprietors of various farms and estates in the north-east of Scotland. He became secretary of the club and delivered several discourses on the virtues and scientific evaluation of new methods of farming. He was also one of the most active members of the Aberdeen Philosophical Society (1758–1773), known popularly as the Wise Club, whose more famous members included James Beattie, George Campbell, Alexander Gerard, John Gregory, and Thomas Reid. Gordon served as secretary of the society from 1761 to 1764 and again from 1767 to 1771. Of the nine discourses he delivered, three dealt with memory and six with the philosophy and history of language and writing systems. He also proposed thirteen questions for discussion on subjects including economics, education, epistemology, government, moral philosophy, natural philosophy, and religion. But perhaps his greatest contribution to the society was his careful record-keeping. His papers in Aberdeen University Library contain unique copies of twenty-two discourses and eight abstracts composed by other members, in addition to copies of all nine of his discourses and nine of his abstracts of discussions.

Gordon was a fellow of the Royal Society of Edinburgh, an honorary member of the Aberdeen Medical Society, and a member of the moderate party of the Church of Scotland. He died on 11 March 1797 and was buried in St Machar's Cathedral, Aberdeen. H. LEWIS ULMAN

Sources H. L. Ulman, ed., *The minutes of the Aberdeen Philosophical Society, 1758–1773* (1990) • P. J. Anderson, ed., *Officers and graduates of University and King's College, Aberdeen, MVD–MDCCCLX*, New Spalding Club, 11 (1893) • R. L. Emerson, *Professors, patronage, and politics: the Aberdeen universities in the eighteenth century* (1992) • *Scotland and Scotsmen in the eighteenth century: from the MSS of John Ramsay, esq., of Ochtertyre*, ed. A. Allardyce, 1 (1888); repr. with introduction by D. J. Brown (1996), 296–8 • P. B. Wood, *The Aberdeen Enlightenment: the arts curriculum in the eighteenth century* (1993) • W. L. Davidson, 'The original Aberdeen Philosophical Society', U. Aberdeen, MS U 568/6/1–2 • W. R. Humphries, 'The first Aberdeen Philosophical Society', *Transactions of the Aberdeen Philosophical Society*, 5 (1931–8), 203–38 • H. L. Ulman and D. Quon, eds., 'Semiotics in eighteenth-century Aberdeen: Thomas Gordon's contributions to the Aberdeen Philosophical Society, 1761–1763', *Studies on Voltaire and the Eighteenth Century*, 317 (1994), 57–115 • W. Thom, *The history of Aberdeen*, 2 vols. (1811) • S. A. Conrad, *Citizenship and common sense: the problem of authority in the social background and social philosophy of the Wise Club of Aberdeen* (1987) • www.origins.net • J. H. Smith, *The Gordon's Mill Farming Club, 1758–1764* (1962) • private information (2004) [J. Pirie, Aberdeen University]

Archives U. Aberdeen, 'Collections regarding King's College', MS K 34 • U. Aberdeen, letters, MS 2081/1–7 • U. Aberdeen, MS 3107/1–9 • U. Aberdeen, papers relating to Aberdeen Philosophical Society • U. Aberdeen, philosophical discourses and papers | U. Aberdeen, antiquarian notes to George Chalmers

Likenesses J. Kay, caricature, 1786? (on handbill), repro. in Emerson, *Professors, patronage and politics*, 98

Gordon, Thomas (1788–1841), soldier and historian, was born at Cairness on 8 December 1788, the eldest and only surviving son of Charles Gordon of Buthlaw and Cairness in Lonmay, Aberdeenshire, and his wife, Christian, daughter of Thomas Forbes of Ballogie. His father died in 1796 and his mother in 1801. From 1800 to 1804 he was at Eton College and then studied with the Revd C. Latham before matriculating at Brasenose College, Oxford, in January 1806. He did not take a degree. From 1808 to 1810 he served in the Scots Greys. In May 1810 he left British service for travel and on 26 August he was well received in Yanina by the Turkish governor Ali Pasha. Between 1810 and 1812 his travels included Athens, Constantinople, and Salonika as well as parts of Asian Turkey, Persia, and Barbary. In 1813 he served as a captain on the staff of the Russian army, and in November 1813 was in the army of Count von Walmoden at Pretzer in Mecklenburg. Early in 1814 he returned to his 'magnificent seat' of Cairness. In 1815 he again went abroad and in 1816 was again at Constantinople, where he married an Armenian, Barbara Kana (afterwards baroness de Sedaiges).

Gordon returned to Greece in 1821 at the commencement of the war of independence. He served through the campaign of 1821 in the Morea (Peloponnese) as *chef d'état major* under Ypsilantes. He took part in the siege of Tripolitza. After the capture he strongly protested against the massacre by the Greeks of several thousand Turks there. On being ignored he retired for a time from service. In November 1822 the provisional Greek government at Hermione sent a letter asking him to return. He declined but joined the Greek committee in London (formed 8 March 1823) and contributed money and military supplies. He refused the committee's invitation to go to Greece as one of three commissioners in charge of stores and funds, stating that the Greeks were unwilling to submit to European discipline. As a committee member he strongly supported the appointment of Lord Byron though there is no record that they ever met.

Early in 1824 a Greek deputation raised a loan in London and again unsuccessfully asked Gordon to return. Early in 1826 renewed representations from Greece and the Greek deputies in London persuaded him to return to promote unity and military discipline. He reached Nauplia in May 1826 and found that bitter dissensions among the Greeks had quenched even their animosity against the Turks. He was well received and arrived in time to prevent the disbanding of the regular corps. He determined to remain a 'traveller unshackled in his movements' until the arrival of Cochrane. Towards the end of June, Rumeliots (mainland Greeks) forced the government to seize $10,000 from Gordon to give to the Suliot *capitanioi* from Epirus. By the close of 1826 he had spent all the public funds which the Greek deputies in London had entrusted to him. In January 1827 Gordon accepted the command of the expedition to Piraeus, with the rank of brigadier, his troops consisting of the corps of Ioannes Notaras, that of Makriyannes, the regulars, and the foreign auxiliaries. His aim was to relieve Athens, then blockaded by Kutahi (Reshid, commander in Rumeli). Gordon successfully landed his troops at Port Phalerum (a harbour outside Athens) 'under the nose of Reshid Pasha'. Having found that the Greeks besieged in the Acropolis were still able to hold out, Gordon wished to resign and only continued on condition of receiving supplies and being 'entirely master of his own operations'. He remained in command of the troops at the Phalerum until the arrival in April of Church, who took over the supreme command. On 16 April Church appointed Gordon director-general of the army. He probably continued to serve in this capacity until the Greek defeat of 6 May. Nevertheless continued resistance, the success of Navarino, and the backing of France, Russia, and Britain enabled the Greek kingdom to emerge with a northern frontier from Arta to Volos but without Crete or Samos. Gordon's services in the struggle were valued and he had already been formally thanked in 1827 before the disaster of Phalerum. But by July 1827 he had returned to his permanent home in Scotland.

Gordon came back to Greece in 1828. While at Argos from 1828 to 1831 with his secretary James Robertson and Finlay, he worked on the site of the ruined Heraeum near Argos (subsequently in the hands of the Americans and later of the École Française). Archaeological plans also included a proposal to form a joint stock company for the purchase of Epidaurus. Finlay comments on how well Gordon got on with the Greeks, adding that he was one of the few who really knew Greece and suggesting that he might be president of the national assembly. But Gordon had no ambitions of this kind. While at Argos he was collecting both written and oral material for a history of the Greek revolution. But he was never integrated into Greek life as Church and Finlay were. In 1831 he was again at Cairness writing his *History* which was published in 1833. Based on an unrivalled range of contemporary evidence this 'Thucydidean' history, as W. M. Leake described it, was widely praised as a judicious and accurate record. 'I always go to Gordon for dates and details', said Finlay when extending his own history.

With the arrival of Otho and the establishment of the Bavarian regime Gordon was commissioned colonel in the Greek army and in 1833 he was in Greece. His main activities were in the Peloponnese, central Greece, and Attica. From July to September he was campaigning against brigands mainly in Aetolia and Acarnania. Finlay was with him and wrote a lively journal exposing the difficulties of rooting out bandits, who were often supported by the local population and by Turks across the border. Gordon's linguistic expertise included fluent written and spoken Turkish to the astonishment of local pashas and was of considerable value in negotiation. Finlay also wrote a penetrating memorandum, exposing the inadequacy of government policy, which was taken over by Gordon and did not add to his popularity in court circles. Gordon continued in military service. His firm but moderate policy as president of the military court set up to try the rebels in the Messenian disturbances did much to ease a tricky situation and block Coletti's desire for revenge. From Athens he inaugurated various improvements, such as draining of marshes or improved communications in Attica, described by Finlay, who often went with him on survey. But he was of uncertain health. He resigned his commission in February 1839 and returned to Scotland, making a short visit to Greece in 1840. He died at Cairness on 20 April 1841, and was survived by his wife; he left no children.

Gordon was awarded various honours. Being one of a group out of favour at the Greek court, he was not given the grand cross of the order of the Redeemer at its inauguration on 1 June 1833, but was made grand commander of this order on his retirement. He was a member of a number of learned societies including the Royal Society (1821), the Society of Antiquaries of Scotland (1828), and the Royal Asiatic Society (1834), and in Greece the Society for Natural History (1837) and the Archaeological Society (1840). In addition to his *History* he contributed (anonymously) to a work by Tshelebi Efendi on the Turkish military system (published in W. Wilkinson, *Wallachia and Moldavia*, 1820, appendix no. 5) and an anonymously written work privately circulated in Constantinople on the secret history of the deposition of Sultan Mustafa in 1807 (reprinted in *Miscellaneous Translations from Oriental Languages*, 2, 1834, no. 111). His historical library and manuscripts were sold in March 1850, and his antiquities in the following June.

J. M. Hussey

Sources *DNB* • British School at Athens, Finlay collection [BSA Suppl. vol. 9: detailed summary of all contents in the Finlay collection] • J. M. Hussey, *The Finlay papers: a catalogue* (1973) • *The journals and letters of George Finlay*, ed. J. M. Hussey, 2 vols. (1995) • D. Dakin, *British and American philhellenes during the War of Greek Independence, 1821–1833* (1955) • J. A. Petropulos, *Politics and statecraft in the kingdom of Greece, 1833–1843* (1968) • J. D. Beazley, 'Stele of a warrior', *Journal of Hellenic Studies*, 49 (1929), 1–6 • *GM*, 2nd ser., 15 (1841), 669 • A. E. Kasdagli, 'The papers of Thomas Gordon of Cairness (1788–1841)', *Northern Scotland*, 14 (1994), 109–14

Archives British School at Athens, corresp. • U. Aberdeen L., corresp., journals, and papers
Likenesses F. Hanfstaengl, lithograph (after K. Kraxlisen), BM; repro. in Beazley, 'Stele of a warrior', 6

Gordon, Sir Thomas Edward (1832–1914), army officer, was born on 12 January 1832 at Aberdeen, the fourth son of Captain William Gordon, 2nd foot, and his wife, Marianna Carlotta Loi, the daughter of Luis Gonçalves de Mello, a Portuguese government official from Estremadura. His twin brother was John James Hood *Gordon.

From a military family, Gordon was educated at the Scottish Naval and Military Academy, Edinburgh, and joined the 61st foot (south Gloucestershire), which was then in India, in 1849. In 1851 he served against the Mohmands on the north-west frontier. During the Indian mutiny he distinguished himself, and by 1858 he was commanding the 7th Punjab infantry in the operations in Oudh, although still only a substantive lieutenant. With his brother, he chose to stay in India after the mutiny, so in 1859 he transferred briefly to the 25th foot (King's Own Borderers), and then to the 95th foot (Derbyshire) in 1861. He was promoted captain in 1859. In 1862 he married Mary Helen, daughter of Alexander Sawers of Khulna in Bengal; they had no children and she died in 1879.

In 1865, having qualified in Persian and Hindustani, Gordon was appointed interpreter to the commander-in-chief, India, and as such was at the meeting between the viceroy, Lord Mayo, and the amir of Afghanistan, Sher Ali, at Ambala in 1869. Showing an aptitude for political work, in 1873 he accompanied Sir Douglas Forsyth as second in command of the mission to the ruler of Kashgar, Yakub Beg, for which he was created a CSI in 1874, and which he described in *The Roof of the World* (1876).

From 1872 to 1874 Gordon was an assistant adjutant-general on the army staff before becoming commandant of the Mewar Bhil corps, localized in Rajputana, with which he combined the post of assistant political agent in Mewar. In 1878 he was back on the army staff, being appointed deputy adjutant-general in 1879 with the rank of lieutenant-colonel, a post he held until 1882. While deputy adjutant-general, in 1879 he commanded the troops in the Kurram valley, maintaining communications with Roberts when the latter advanced on Kabul in the second phase of the Anglo-Afghan War. He was not successful. His posts were attacked in October 1879 and the viceroy, Lord Lytton, complained bitterly to the commander-in-chief (Sir Frederick Haines) about Gordon's alarmist telegrams. He was replaced in November 1879 and returned to his post as deputy adjutant-general, but received the CB for his services in 1881. He was appointed to command the Rohilkhand brigade in 1882 but his career had been irreparably damaged by his failure in the Kurram; although he was promoted major-general in 1886 Roberts, by then commander-in-chief, India, refused to consider him or his brother for a divisional command: 'they are far above the average in ability and intelligence … but after what I saw of them in Kuram, I could never trust them on service in any position of responsibility' (Roberts to D. Stewart, 12 May 1888, Roberts MSS).

Gordon's brigade command ended in 1887, and in 1889 he became oriental and military secretary to the legation in Tehran and in 1891 military attaché there. His fluent Persian, political experience, and ability to get on with the local peoples made him successful there. He was promoted lieutenant-general in 1890 and made KCIE on his retirement in 1893; he became a general in 1894 and KCB in 1900. In 1894 he married Charlotte, daughter of Joseph Davison of Greecroft, co. Durham; they had no children and she survived him. Gordon published *Persia Revisited* (1895), an account of a visit to Persia in 1894, and in 1906 his autobiography, *A Varied Life*. He died at his home, 3 Prince of Wales Terrace, Kensington, London, on 23 March 1914. C. V. OWEN, *rev.* BRIAN ROBSON

Sources T. E. Gordon, *A varied life* (1906) • *Bengal Army Lists* • *Hart's Army List* • NAM, Roberts MSS • C. M. MacGregor, *The Second Afghan War*, 6 vols. (1885–6) • *The Times* (24 March 1914)
Wealth at death £46,626 8*s*. 0*d*.: probate, 25 April 1914, *CGPLA Eng. & Wales*

Gordon, William (*d.* 1577), bishop of Aberdeen, was born probably in Aberdeenshire, a younger son of Alexander *Gordon, third earl of Huntly (*d.* 1524), and of his wife, Jane Stewart (*d.* 1510), daughter of John Stewart, first earl of Atholl. He was given an excellent grounding in humanist studies at the University of Aberdeen before proceeding to Paris, the bastion of doctrinal orthodoxy, and thence to Angers, where he graduated in canon and civil law; his education prompted James V to write to Pope Paul III on 31 July 1537, urging him to reserve some benefices for Gordon on account of his industry and youthful promise. He returned to become rector of Clatt in the diocese of Aberdeen, and the successful crown nominee for the chancellorship of Moray, by 1540, and for the bishopric of Aberdeen when it became vacant on the death of William Stewart in 1545. On the recommendation of the governor, the earl of Arran, Paul III provided him to the see on 17 May 1546, and he was consecrated probably some time between 23 December 1546 and 26 January 1547. Once installed as bishop, Gordon soon found himself confronting the spread of heretical doctrine as well as such matters of ecclesiastical discipline as the moral laxity of the clergy and their lack of adequate training. As the heavily scriptural and theological content of the fifty surviving books of his own personal library makes evident, he must have been fully aware of the importance of these issues, and as a first measure, on 9 July 1547 he commissioned a canon of his cathedral, the theologian John Watson, to refute error and preach the gospel annually throughout the churches of the diocese; and he himself attended the provincial council convened in 1549 to undertake the reform of the Scottish church.

In 1559 his cathedral chapter warned Bishop Gordon that heresy was growing, that it was losing control of its income through his excessive leasing of its lands, and that clerical concubinage remained unchecked. The latter was a pointed reminder that Gordon already had five sons and three daughters of his own, born of his liaison with Janet Knowles, an unmarried gentlewoman, and provided for by diocesan funds. All these issues, however, were swept away by the Reformation Parliament, meeting in July and August 1560, which abolished papal authority throughout the realm, forbade the celebration of the mass, approved the Scots confession of faith, and recognized the sole competence of a reformed ministry. The return from France of the Catholic Queen Mary in August 1561, her grant of protection in 1562 to the University of Aberdeen, of which Gordon was chancellor, together with the support on which he could expect to rely from his nephew George *Gordon, fourth earl of Huntly, may have persuaded him and many in his conservative diocese that they could lie low until the protestant programme had shown itself to be unworkable. But events were to prove otherwise. Queen Mary was forced to abdicate in 1567 in favour of her infant son James VI, and the regency passed to her protestant half-brother, the earl of Moray. Those secular clergy (including its teachers in the three universities) who would not subscribe to the Scots confession of faith were relieved of their ministry, which passed with little violence to those who would subscribe and who were willing to serve in a newly reformed church. Gordon's failure in leadership and his inability to effect any lasting reform in his diocese, however, has to be seen in its wider context: the crown's capture of the right to nominate to high ecclesiastical office, mostly for its own political and fiscal advantage; the strong links of kinship in Scottish society, visible in Gordon's own promotion; the increase in the papacy's taxation of the clergy and its retention of an outworn system of non-residence and pluralism, which led to a scrambling for benefices; and above all, the inability of the papacy and the secular rulers of Europe to agree upon the proper nature and limits of their respective powers. Even so, Gordon survived all attempts to remove him from office, in June 1577 showing himself willing to comply with the new church order by appointing a reader for the reformed parish of St Nicholas in Aberdeen. He died in his palace in The Chanonry, Old Aberdeen, on 6 August 1577, and was buried in his cathedral church of St Machar. LESLIE J. MACFARLANE

Sources *Scots peerage*, 1.441–2; 4.531–3 • *The letters of James V*, ed. R. K. Hannay and D. Hay (1954), 335 • D. E. R. Watt, ed., *Fasti ecclesiae Scoticanae medii aevi ad annum 1638*, [2nd edn], Scottish RS, new ser., 1 (1969), 4, 228 • C. Innes, ed., *Registrum episcopatus Aberdonensis*, 2 vols., Spalding Club, 13–14 (1845), vol. 1, pp. lviii–lxvi, 431–59; vol. 2, pp. 126, 194, 317–22 • C. Innes, ed., *Fasti Aberdonenses … 1494–1854*, Spalding Club, 26 (1854), 126–8, 271–2 • W. A. McNeill, 'Scottish entries in the *Acta rectoria universitatis Parisiensis*, 1519 to *c*.1633', *SHR*, 43 (1964), 66–86, esp. 75 • J. Durkan and A. Ross, *Early Scottish libraries* (1961), 34–40, 169 • C. Haws, 'The diocese of Aberdeen and the Reformation', *Innes Review*, 22 (1971), 72–84 • I. B. Cowan, *The Scottish Reformation: church and society in sixteenth century Scotland* (1982) • B. McLennan, 'The Reformation and the burgh of Aberdeen', *Northern Scotland*, 2 (1974–7), 119–44 • D. Stevenson, *King's College, Aberdeen, 1560–1641: from protestant Reformation to covenanting revolution* (1990) • M. H. B. Sanderson, 'The feuars of Kirklands', *SHR*, 52 (1973), 117–36 • J. Kirk, *Patterns of reform: continuity and change in the Reformation kirk* (1989) • A. White, 'Religion, politics and society in Aberdeen, 1543–1593', PhD diss., U. Aberdeen, 1985 • J. M. Bulloch and others, eds., *The house of Gordon*, 2, Third Spalding Club, 33 (1907), 122; 3, Third Spalding Club, 39 (1912), 17 • C. Eubel and others, eds., *Hierarchia Catholica medii et recentioris aevi*, 2nd edn, 3, ed. W. van Gulik, C. Eubel, and L. Schmitz-Kallenberg (Münster, 1923), 91 • J. Dowden, *The bishops of Scotland … prior to the Reformation*, ed. J. M. Thomson (1912), 141–3

Gordon, William, of Earlston (1614–1679), landowner and covenanter, born in Dalry, Kirkcudbrightshire, was the second son of Alexander *Gordon of Earlston (1587–1654), justice of the peace, and Elizabeth (*d.* in or after 1653), daughter of John Gordon of Pennynghame. Little is known regarding his education, though he is said to have studied for the ministry and to have graduated MA. On 26 October 1648 he married Mary Hope, second daughter of Sir John *Hope, Lord Craighall (1603x5–1654), an advocate and lord of session. The couple had thirteen children, of whom only one daughter and three sons, including Sir Alexander *Gordon (1650–1726), survived to maturity.

In matters of religion Gordon was deeply influenced by his father's presbyterian principles. The family were confidants of the architect of the covenanting revolution, Archibald Johnston of Wariston, and Alexander Gordon served as an elder for the presbytery of Kirkcudbright at the Glasgow assembly of 1638. Both father and son petitioned against the imposition of Charles I's infamous prayer book in 1637, and two years later Gordon accepted a post under Alexander Leslie, earl of Leven, commander of the covenanting forces. In this capacity he was present at the taking of Newcastle in 1640. He resigned the commission on the death of his brother in 1645 and returned home to assist his elderly father; he served on the committee for war of the Kirkcudbright stewartry in 1647 and 1648.

In common with his father-in-law, Lord Craighall, Gordon was a convinced supporter of the institution of the monarchy in Scotland, but saw little practical advantage in opposing the power of the Cromwellian administration during the 1650s. In 1651 he was fined by the parliament of Charles II for compliance with the English, and he distanced himself from the rebellion led by William Cunningham, earl of Glencairn, against the occupation in 1653. Out of concern for his family and inheritance (and following the death of his father on 19 November 1653) he signed the Act of Indemnity issued by Cromwell in 1654. He was served heir to the lands of Earlston on 2 October 1655 and thereafter lived quietly under Oliver Cromwell's government, serving on two commissions in 1656 and 1659 for raising taxation in Kirkcudbrightshire.

Gordon's support of the restoration of Charles II was tempered by his exemption from the Act of Indemnity of 1662, pending payment of a fine of £3500, which had been imposed because of his continued nonconformity. His presbyterian principles caused further difficulties in 1663 when he was required, as patron of the kirk of Dalry, to present the bishop's candidate to the parish. Gordon refused, claiming that he—in conference with the kirk session—had already admitted a 'worthy and qualified person … to exercise his gifts amongst that people' (Howie, 404). He was cited before the privy council to answer for his 'seditious and factious carriage' on 30 July of the latter year, but ignored the summons. On 24 November the order was renewed, at which time he faced the further charge that he 'kept conventicles and private meetings' in his house (ibid.). Following his second refusal to answer the charge, Gordon was banished from the kingdom, in March 1664.

Details of the last few years of Gordon's life are sparse. He went to London, and, after expressing his disapproval of the Pentland rising of 1666 (when a covenanting force was defeated at Rullion Green), he was allowed to return home. It is undoubtedly true that Gordon was a man of 'eminent piety' (*DNB*) in accordance with his particular religious principles. He was the 'honoured and dear brother' of the presbyterian stalwart Samuel Rutherford (minister of Anwoth, near Kirkcudbright), with whom he regularly corresponded (Bonar). Furthermore, according to Wodrow he was reputed to have led his tenants to church every Sunday, and, at conventicles, demonstrated remarkable skill in solving cases of conscience. In times of danger (such as when his house was occupied by troops in 1667), Gordon and his eldest son, Alexander, were rumoured to have hidden 'in a small narrow building' in the 'deep and impenetrable thickets' of the village of Dalry (Simpson, 263). On this point, however, it is impossible to separate romance from reality, and it seems safer to assume that, with sentence of forfeiture awaiting further transgressions, Gordon simply avoided conflict with the authorities.

In the aftermath of the battle of Bothwell Bridge (22 June 1679), Gordon set out to search the battlefield for his son, who had been among a large group of covenanters routed by the army of James, duke of Monmouth. The young man had escaped, but Gordon was apprehended by a nervous detachment of dragoons, and shot dead. His body was later recovered, and buried in Glassford churchyard, Lanarkshire, where a pillar was erected to mark the spot of interment. Gordon's wife, Mary, who, 'with great difficulty', succeeded in retaining her right to life rent in his estates (*DNB*), survived him. VAUGHAN T. WELLS

Sources R. Wodrow, *The history of the sufferings of the Church of Scotland from the Restauration to the revolution*, 2 vols. (1721–2) · M. D. Young, ed., *The parliaments of Scotland: burgh and shire commissioners*, 2 vols. (1992–3) · W. H. Carslaw, preface, in J. Howie, *The Scots worthies*, ed. W. H. Carslaw, [new edn] (1870), ix–xv · *Letters of Samuel Rutherford*, ed. A. A. Bonar (1891); facs. repr. (1984) · *APS*, 1643–69 · *Diary of Sir Archibald Johnston of Wariston*, ed. G. M. Paul and others, 3 vols., Scottish History Society, 61, 2nd ser., 18, 3rd. ser., 34 (1911–40) · V. T. Wells, 'The origins of covenanting thought and resistance, *c*.1580–1638', PhD diss., University of Stirling, 1997 · Anderson, *Scot. nat.*, vol. 2 · T. Thompson, *A biographical dictionary of eminent Scotsmen*, 2 (1870) · R. Simpson, *Traditions of the covenanters* (1867) · *DNB*

Gordon, William, sixth Viscount Kenmure and Jacobite marquess of Kenmure (*d.* **1716**), Jacobite conspirator, was the only son of Alexander Gordon (*d.* 1698) of Cuil and Penninghame, fifth Viscount Kenmure, and his second wife, Marion (*d.* in or before 1672), widow of one Bell of Whiteside and daughter of David M'Culloch of Ardwall. The Galloway-based estate to which the fifth viscount had succeeded in February 1663 as a collateral heir was heavily indebted. The family was further burdened by provision for his seven daughters and three sons from three marriages and by Kenmure's unrecompensed expenses in

William Gordon, sixth Viscount Kenmure and Jacobite marquess of Kenmure (*d.* **1716**), by George Vertue (after Sir Godfrey Kneller)

1689 in raising an infantry regiment, which he led on the government side at Killiecrankie. His political and religious opinions apparently had shifted with the Scottish mainstream, although in 1682, regarded as insufficiently zealous in prosecuting covenanters, he was replaced as local justice by John Graham of Claverhouse, Viscount Dundee, and the brutality surrounding the shooting in 1685 of his stepson John Bell of Whiteside, an assassin of Archbishop James Sharp, provoked him to momentary violence.

William Gordon, known as master of Kenmure, was old enough to be a valid legal witness in 1682. He does not seem to have held a commission in his father's regiment. By 1691 he was noted as a Jacobite and he remained firmly committed to the cause. The claim in several peerages, based on John Macky's *View of the Court of St Germain*, that he had returned, disillusioned by discrimination against protestants, from a period in the early 1690s at King James's court in exile, arose from a confusion with Nicholas, second (Irish) Viscount Kenmare (a Catholic—Macky's pamphlet was propaganda). In the wholesale rounding up of suspects after the plot to assassinate William III, he was among the Scots for whom a London warrant was issued. While his father signed the Association in the 1696 parliament and in 1697 married William's sister to Alexander Gordon of Earlston, who had once been tortured for involvement in whig plots, William himself was accused to the council that July of drinking Jacobite healths. Following their father's death on 20 April 1698, William's stepbrother, John Gordon of Greenlaw, began a lawsuit, on the strength of the fifth viscount's marriage contract with his third wife, Lady Grizel Stewart, to claim the Kenmure title and estates, although their father's final settlement had cancelled the grant. It was not until 1700 that the inheritance was awarded to William.

Absenting himself from parliament, early in Anne's reign the sixth Viscount Kenmure was deeply involved in plotting for a Jacobite rising and French invasion. Late in 1705 he was chosen by lowlands Jacobites as a delegate to St Germain, although he did not travel there. Early in 1706 he claimed that disaffection was driving the Galloway Cameronians into Jacobitism. In 1707 he was one of the Jacobite peers for whose conduct David Murray, fifth Viscount Stormont, 'answered' to Colonel Nathaniel Hooke, envoy from St Germain. James Edward Stuart granted him a marquessate. In 1711 he married Mary (*d.* 1776), daughter of Sir John Dalzell (*d.* 1698), sister of Robert *Dalzell, fifth earl of Carnwath, and niece of Captain James Dalzell, his long-time Jacobite friend. They had three sons and a daughter.

Using the Lochmaben race meeting as cover, in May 1715 Kenmure, Carnwath, and William Maxwell, earl of Nithsdale, drew up a Jacobite association. Since Carnwath was under thirty and Nithsdale was a Catholic, John Erskine, earl of Mar, then organizing the Scottish Jacobite rebellion on his own authority and amateurish assumptions, selected Kenmure as 'the only Nobleman in that part of Scotland capable of commanding forces' (Patten, 1.33–4). Kenmure apparently needed considerable persuasion, and the choice proved ill-advised. Somewhat surprisingly acknowledged to be 'of extraordinary Knowledge and Experience in Publick and Political Business', he was 'utterly a Stranger to all Military Affairs', and his 'singular Good Temper' and plain, quiet demeanour were unsuited to the task in hand (Patten, 1.51). In mid-August Kenmure and Carnwath were listed among those who attended Mar's Braemar hunting, but they were almost certainly not present. Kenmure's young wife gave him strong support, embroidering the fine standard he raised, but contrary to misogynistic traditional stories, did not force him into rebellion.

Following Mar's initiation of the highland rebellion on 9 September, by early October Kenmure and his comrades were lurking at friends' houses, prepared, unless Mar sent a countermand, to raise the standard at Moffat on 12 October. Assisted by Jacobite fifth columnists, Kenmure's party seized much-needed arms but narrowly failed to capture William Johnston, earl of Annandale, lord lieutenant of three border shires, when he arrived to raise government forces locally. As a result, on 13 October Annandale was able to furnish the necessary figurehead and brace several hundred raw volunteers in Dumfries as Kenmure approached with 153 armed horsemen. Although some of the latter thought the risks attached to an attack worth taking, Kenmure retreated, allegedly observing that 'there were as brave Gentlemen … as himself' in the town (Rae, 252). Annandale prevented any pursuit, since the Jacobites might have routed the volunteers decisively on open ground.

Both sides had anachronistically estimated that border peers could, like highland chiefs, raise followings of the order of three hundred men. In reality the noblemen's tenants opposed the rebellion, some joining those in arms at Dumfries, and they were attended only by a small number of gentlemen (none of them Gordons) and domestic servants. Over the next few days Kenmure's forces quartered and proclaimed James VIII at Lochmaben, Ecclefechan, and Langholm. He marched down Teviotdale but, calculating that the scratch volunteer force occupying Kelso ahead could make too costly a resistance, briefly turned back. He had originally intended to join with the Northumbrian Jacobites under the tory MP, Thomas Forster, only on 1 November at Hawick, but when a successful independent campaign failed to materialize he united with the ill-armed and equally unsuccessful English force at Rothbury, Northumberland, on 19 October. They both then moved north and on 22 October met at Kelso (whose defenders had scattered) the six Highland regiments under Brigadier William Mackintosh of Borlum previously sent south across the Firth of Forth by Mar. The next day the army, now totalling 600 horse and 1400 foot, attended episcopalian services in the Great Kirk. On 24 October James VIII was proclaimed king and a manifesto read, amid shouts of 'no union, no malt tax, no salt tax' (*DNB*).

Faced with the extreme reluctance of his Scottish and English soldiers to campaign in each other's country, as commander of the combined force while it remained in Scotland Kenmure called a council of war at Kelso on 27 October. His inability, there or at later meetings, to bring about any firm decision was a crucial inadequacy, which he appreciated sufficiently to beg Mar to replace him with a professional general. Unknown to him, however, Mar had promoted him first brigadier-general and then major-general of horse. Disinclined to risk attacking Lieutenant-General Carpenter, who had pursued Forster, Kenmure missed an opportunity to gain a prestigious victory over an inexperienced and exhausted force. He lacked both the vision to support the bold strategic plan advanced by George Seton, earl of Winton, to co-operate with Mar and overrun the lowlands and the force to prevent Winton stirring up the highlanders' justified fear of the alternative, an incursion into England. To avoid definite decisions the force drifted back south-westwards along the border, with highlanders and horse coming close to fighting outside Hawick. Capturing Dumfries would still both boost morale and provide a secure Jacobite base. Late on 30 October, 400 cavalry under Carnwath left Langholm for Ecclefechan, intending a preliminary blockade of Dumfries, but the Jacobite main body turned back on receiving news of improvised fortifications there. Letters from Lancashire promising a massive rising on their arrival prompted the decision to march into England. On 1 November at Brampton, Cumberland, Kenmure handed command to Forster, who was equally ignorant of warfare, but far more self-confident. The decision drove 500 highlanders and many borderers to attempt desertion and caused Winton's temporary defection. Even Kenmure's brother-in-law, the veteran Jacobite Sir Patrick Maxwell of Springkell, after offering to raise forces to follow him south, pretended to the authorities that he had merely been neutral throughout—a ploy spoiled when Kenmure carelessly dropped his letter.

Kenmure seems to have played little significant part on the march into Lancashire. At the battle of Preston on 12 November, he led some volunteers to support Lord Charles Murray's barricade in Tithebarn Street, and remained creditably fighting there while several government attacks were beaten off. While others were sharply divided next day over the negotiations for surrender, Kenmure, according to a disillusioned follower, 'seemed altogether Stupid [dazed]' (PRO, SP 54/9, fol. 133), although he refused to be one of the hostages for performance. Brought south with the six other captive peers and impeached by the Commons before the Lords, Kenmure pleaded guilty on 19 January 1716. During the proceedings he said and wrote less than the other accused, but, asked on 9 February what he had to say in arrest of judgment, he denied 'any personal Prejudice against His Majesty' or 'any previous Design against him', begging both houses to seek royal mercy, 'to be the Means to keep my Wife and Four Small Children from starving; the thoughts of which, with my Crime, makes me the most Unfortunate of all Gentlemen' (*Political State*, 11.202–3). A letter to James shows the same fear for his family.

It was never likely that a commanding general, however inept, would be spared. On 24 February 1716 Kenmure was beheaded with Lord Derwentwater on Tower Hill, not having had time, he declared, to order a black suit to die in. His brief expression of regret for having owned George I's authority by pleading guilty was echoed in a fabricated last speech, other forgeries, and a (printed but probably genuine) letter to a peer written the night before. This explained that a formal scaffold speech on that theme might damage Carnwath's better hopes of pardon and stressed that he was a protestant, acting purely from loyal duty to James. His body was embalmed, to be sent to the family's Scottish burial place.

Past and present trustees of Kenmure's estates had also been rebels, but Lady Kenmure, whose seizure of the family charter chest hampered the forfeited estates commission, claimed that the estate had been conveyed through a trust to her eldest son, Robert Gordon (*d.* 1741). She obtained a favourable decree in 1722, but since Kenmure had been attainted at his trial, Robert did not inherit the viscountcy. While Lady Kenmure cleared many family debts, Robert, a strong Jacobite, ran up more. His brother, John Gordon (*d.* 1769), dined with Prince Charles Edward at Holyrood in 1745 but did not join the rising, unlike his stepfather and former tutor, John Lumisden (*d.* 1751). Having married Lady Kenmure after May 1736, the latter, who had been created a Jacobite baronet in 1740, died in exile. His widow died at Terregles on 16 August 1776. The peerage was restored in 1824. Robert Burns's song, 'O, Kenmure's on and awa, Willie' was supposedly based on an old Galloway song about Viscount William.

PAUL HOPKINS

Sources *Scots peerage* • P. Rae, *The history of the late rebellion* (1718) • R. Patten, *The history of the late rebellion; with original papers and the characters of the principal noblemen and gentlemen concern'd in it*, 2nd edn (1717) • J. Baynes, *The Jacobite rising of 1715* (1970) • Kenmure forfeited estates papers, NA Scot., E638 • GEC, *Peerage* • Scottish state papers, Oct 1715, PRO, SP54/9 • *Correspondence of Colonel N. Hooke*, ed. W. D. Macray, 2 vols., Roxburghe Club, 92, 95 (1870–71) • A. Boyer, *The political state of Great Britain*, 11 (1716) • W. Fraser, ed., *The Annandale family book of the Johnstones*, 2 vols. (1894) • P. H. M'Kerlie, *History of lands and their owners in Galloway*, 5 vols. (1877–9) • *The copy of a letter written by Lord Viscount of Kenmure, to a certain nobleman the day before his execution* [1716] • *Catalogue of valuable autograph letters and historical documents, forming part of the Townshend heirlooms* (1911) [sale catalogue, Sothebys] • C. M. Armet, *Kirkcudbrightshire sheriff court deeds, 1676–1700*, 2 vols. (1953) • A. Fergusson, ed., *Major Fraser's manuscript*, 2 vols. (1889) • T. Campbell, *Standing witness: illustrated guide to the Scottish covenanters* (1990) • S. H. Ware, ed., *Lancashire memorials of the rebellion, MDCCXV* (1845) • *Report on the manuscripts of the earl of Mar and Kellie*, HMC, 60 (1904); suppl. (1930) • *The manuscripts of the House of Lords*, new ser., 12 vols. (1900–77) • A. M. T. Maxwell-Irving, 'Kenmure Castle', *Transactions of the Dumfriesshire and Galloway Natural History and Antiquarian Society*, 3rd ser., 72 (1997), 41–54 • [J. Macky], *A view of the court of St Germain* (1696) • warrant, 29 Feb 1696, PRO, PC2/76, fol. 176 • *State papers and letters addressed to William Carstares*, ed. J. M'Cormick (1774), 139, 1691 paper • *My Lord Viscount of Kenmure his last speech; A true copy of a paper written by Viscount Kenmour* [1716] [fakes] • *The poems and songs of Robert Burns*, ed. J. Kinsley, 3 vols. (1968) • *DNB*

Likenesses R. Grave, engraving (after G. Kneller), BM, NPG, Scot. NPG; repro. in J. Caulfield, *Portraits, memoirs, and characters of remarkable persons* (1819) • G. Kneller, portrait; formerly at Kenmure Castle, Dumfries and Galloway • G. Vertue, engraving (after G. Kneller), Scot. NPG [*see illus.*] • engraving, Scot. NPG

Gordon, William, of Newhall (*d.* 1778). *See under* Mirror Club (*act.* 1776–1787).

Gordon, William (1727/8–1807), Independent minister and writer, was born at Hitchin, Hertfordshire, and was educated for the dissenting ministry at an academy in Plasterers' Hall, London, under Zephaniah Marryatt. He began his ministry early in 1752 as assistant to William Notcutt at Tacket Street, Ipswich. He was ordained on 9 October 1754, but resigned his charge, after a quarrel, on 3 June 1764, and was invited to a pastorate at Gravel Lane, Southwark, in succession to David Jennings. He remained there until 1770, when his political sympathies prompted him to move to America, where he lived for about fifteen years. In 1772 he was pastor of the Third Congregational Church at Roxbury, Massachusetts. In the same year he was made chaplain to the provincial congress of Massachusetts. In early 1776 he was dismissed from both houses after delivering a harsh attack on article 5 of the articles of confederation. Having returned to London in 1786, he married Elizabeth Field (1728/9–1816), and lived for some time in Newgate Street with his brother-in-law, the father of the apothecary Henry Field and of the Unitarian minister William Field.

In 1776 Gordon determined to write a history of the events he witnessed in North America, and began collecting correspondence and interviewing military officers and statesmen. He believed that the new republic would not be receptive to an impartial history and so hoped to have better success in England. His *History of the Rise, Progress, and Establishment of the Independence of the United States of America* first appeared in London in 1788 and in an American edition the following year. It remained a primary authority on the conflict for the next century. Gordon received £300 for his efforts. In 1789 he became pastor of a congregation at St Neots, Huntingdonshire. Having resigned in 1802 he returned to Ipswich, where he preached occasionally; he was supported by a subscription among his friends and lived in poverty. He lost his memory, which had been gradually failing, and died at Ipswich on 19 October 1807, aged seventy-nine. He was buried in the town's Tacket Street Chapel yard. He was survived by his wife, who died, aged eighty-seven, on 18 November 1816.

ALEXANDER GORDON, *rev.* TROY O. BICKHAM

Sources F. Monaghan, 'Gordon, William', *DAB* • *Monthly Repository*, 2 (1807), 610–11 • *N&Q*, 10 (1854), 144 • A. Chalmers, ed., *The general biographical dictionary*, new edn, 32 vols. (1812–17)

Archives Suffolk RO, Ipswich, letters to his daughter, sermons, American MSS [microfilm of his American MSS]

Gordon, William, of Fyvie (1736–1816), army officer and courtier, was the eldest son of William Gordon, second earl of Aberdeen (*bap.* 1679, *d.* 1745), and his third wife, Lady Anne Gordon (*d.* 1791), daughter of Alexander Gordon, second earl of Gordon. His father having purchased Fyvie Castle, Aberdeenshire, and its estate to provide for the children of his third marriage, William Gordon inherited the lairdship of Fyvie in 1745, at the age of nine. He attended Glasgow University, then obtained a commission in the 11th regiment of dragoons in 1756, transferring in 1762 to the Queen's Own Royal Highlanders (105th foot), a regiment formed as a guard of honour for Queen Charlotte on her marriage, and disbanded two years later. On half pay, Gordon seized the opportunity during 1764–5 to make the grand tour. In Rome he encountered his fellow Scot James Boswell, who recorded that after they had together attended high mass in St Peter's, Gordon observed that 'though as a heretic [he was] sure to be damned, he was glad to see so many other people going to heaven' (*Boswell on the Grand Tour*, 67–8).

While in Rome, Gordon sat to Pompeo Batoni for a superbly idiosyncratic portrait (Fyvie Castle). Batoni portrayed him in the uniform of the Queen's Own Royal Highlanders: jacket, 'little' kilt and full plaid (of the Huntly tartan), with a glengarry bonnet under his arm, all presumably taken to Italy for the express purpose of this portrait. Defiantly, Gordon exults in his nationality and his privileges, well aware that after the Jacobite rising of 1745 wearing the tartan was forbidden except to the military. Boswell recorded that Batoni drew the 'drapery' in April 1765. The finished portrait, with the Colosseum in the background and the antique statue of *Roma* seemingly offering Gordon the orb of command, was completed in 1766.

For some thirteen years after his return from Italy, Gordon combined his army career with a seat in the House of Commons. Thanks to his friendship with the fourth duke of Marlborough, he was returned in 1767 as MP for Woodstock, Oxfordshire, representing that town until 1774,

William Gordon of Fyvie (1736–1816), by Pompeo Batoni, 1766

when the duke found him a seat (which he retained until 1780) at Heytesbury, Wiltshire. Gordon's attendance in the Commons was poor. The duke also secured him a place at court as groom of the bedchamber (1775–1812). Gordon was reputedly a favourite of George III, who chose him (to the anger of his cousin the fourth duke of Gordon) to raise a new regiment, the Aberdeenshire Highlanders (or 81st foot), and in 1777 gave him its command as a full colonel. Gordon served with this regiment for a year or so in Ireland from 1778 until early the next year. He reached the rank of general in 1798.

Though Gordon spoke little (if ever) within the House of Commons, he was to achieve lasting fame for effectively defending the house during the Gordon riots against 'popery'. On 2 June 1780 a mob encouraged by his own fanatically anti-Catholic nephew, Lord George *Gordon, threatened to invade the house. Colonel Gordon confronted his nephew with his sword drawn and with the words: 'My Lord George, do you intend to bring your rascally adherents into the House of Commons? If you do—the first man of them that enters, I will plunge my sword not into his, but into your body' (*Annual Register*, 1780, 258). Charles Dickens, collecting material on the Gordon riots sixty years later for *Barnaby Rudge* (first published 1841), so admired Colonel Gordon's reported words that he incorporated them largely verbatim into his novel (chap. 49).

Spartan and unconventional by temperament, Gordon cohabited with his housekeeper, Isabel Black (1744–1824), who in 1776 bore him a son; eventual marriage legitimized the child in Scottish law. Gordon died on 25 May 1816 at Maryculter, his Kincardineshire estate. Upon inheriting Fyvie, his son, William, found the castle 'in a state of great delapidation, the farm offices were nearly ruinous, and there was a great deficiency of the necessary accommodation for a resident Proprietor' (*Treasures of Fyvie*, 17). JUDY EGERTON

Sources *Scots peerage*, 1.90–93 • C. O. Skelton and J. M. Bulloch, eds., *Gordons under arms*, vol. 3 of *The house of Gordon*, Third Spalding Club, 39 (1912), 333–4 • HoP, *Commons*, 1754–90, 2.518–19 • *Boswell on the grand tour: Italy, Corsica, and France, 1765–1766*, ed. F. Brady and F. A. Pottle (1955), vol. 5 of *The Yale editions of the private papers of James Boswell*, trade edn (1950–89), 67–8, 69 • A. M. Clark, *Pompeo Batoni: a complete catalogue of his works with an introductory text*, ed. E. P. Bowron (1985), 303, colour pl. 273 • *Annual Register* (1788), 258–9 • *Treasures of Fyvie* (1985), 17, 25, 28, 47–8 [exhibition catalogue, Scot. NPG] • J. Ingamells, ed., *A dictionary of British and Irish travellers in Italy, 1701–1800* (1997), 409–10

Likenesses P. Batoni, oils, 1766, Fyvie Castle, Aberdeenshire [*see illus.*]

Gordon, William (1770–1820), Gaelic poet, was born on 20 November 1770 at Creech, in Sutherland. Aged over twenty he entered the army, and served in the Reay fencibles in Ireland until their disbandment in 1802. In 1799, while stationed in the town of Longford, he underwent a spiritual awakening. This led him to devote much of his spare time in the barrack rooms to writing spiritual songs in Gaelic. These were published in Galway in 1802 as *Dantadh spioradal le Uilliam Gordon saighidfhear ann an reighiseamaid Gaidhealach Mhic-Aoi; clodh-bhuailt air son U. G. le Deorsa Conolie, leabhar-reiceadar Gaileadh*. Some of Gordon's songs were reprinted in John Munro's collection *Dana spioradail ann an da Earrann* (1819). Gordon also wrote an elegy on his brother Peter and a love-song, which were printed in a volume of poems by his brother George Ross Gordon [*see below*].

On leaving the army Gordon returned home, and married. He became a father and wrote no more songs. The latter years of his life were spent as a teacher in a Gaelic school. At his death, in 1820, he left a work in manuscript entitled 'Gleanings in the field of truth'.

George Ross Gordon (*fl.* 1804–1832), Gaelic poet, like his brother William entered the army, and served in the 42nd regiment in Ireland. He was later the teacher at a Gaelic school at Morness, in Sutherland, and was living in 1832. His songs, also in Gaelic, were published while he was in Ireland in 1804–5. Besides his own poems, and the two by William Gordon referred to above, the volume includes two pieces by another brother, Alexander Gordon, who was a master mason at Tain, in Ross-shire. G. R. Gordon and A. Gordon both wrote other pieces, which do not seem to have been published.

C. L. KINGSFORD, *rev.* JAMES HOW

Sources J. Reid, *Bibliotheca Scoto-Celtica, or, An account of all the books which have been printed in the Gaelic language* (1832) • D. Thomson, *The companion to Gaelic Scotland* (1983) • D. Beaton, *Bibliography of Gaelic books, pamphlets, and magazine articles for the counties of Caithness and Sutherland* (1927)

Gordon, William (1800–1849), physician and philanthropist, was born at Fountains Hall, near Ripon, Yorkshire, on 2 August 1800. He attended Ripon grammar school, and was then articled to a general practitioner at Otley. After two years he left to study medicine, briefly in London and for three years at Edinburgh. He established himself in general practice at Welton, Northumberland, and in 1826 he married Mary Anne, second daughter of James Lowthrop of Welton Hall. They had a daughter, born in 1828. Gordon, who believed in equal education for women, taught her himself. She later married a Congregationalist minister, Christopher Newman Hall (1806–1902).

Besides a lifelong devotion to the classics, history, and poetry, Gordon was interested in all aspects of science. He was a frequent contributor to *Loudon's Magazine of Natural History* and to medical journals. He published a small work on the practice of surgery in 1828 and *A Critical Enquiry Concerning a New Membrane in the Eye* in 1832, the same year in which he was elected to the Linnean Society.

After taking the degree of MD at Edinburgh in 1841 Gordon settled at Hull, where he soon acquired a reputation for philanthropy. He was active in the temperance movement, serving in 1845 as president of the Hull Christian Temperance Society. Because current medical practice did not favour abstinence he lost most of his paying patients, but his willingness to treat the poor without charge filled his consulting room and enlarged the circle of his poorer friends. Gordon delivered free courses of lectures on physiology, optics, and botany. He became involved in political matters and was elected a councillor of the borough, supporting free trade and the reform of the currency, freedom of religion, and free education.

Gordon was taken ill early in 1848; his doctors failed to diagnose or cure his ailment and he died at his home, 29 Albion Street, Hull, on 7 February 1849. His funeral on 10 February, conducted by Hall, was attended by 'an immense concourse of people' (Sheahan, 176), and a public subscription was collected for a marble obelisk commemorating him as 'The people's friend', to be erected on his tomb in Hull cemetery.

FRANCIS WATT, *rev.* ANITA MCCONNELL

Sources *GM*, 2nd ser., 31 (1849), 431 • C. N. Hall, *The Christian philosopher triumphing over death* (1849) • J. J. Sheahan, *General and concise history and description of the town and port of Kingston-upon-Hull* (1864), 176, 423–4 • N. Hall, *Newman Hall: an autobiography* (1898), 112, 116

Gordon, Sir (John) William (1814–1870), army officer, was born on 4 November 1814, the eldest son of Colonel Thomas Gordon of Harperfield, Lanarkshire. He was still young when his father died and he inherited the estate; through his mother, formerly Miss Nisbet of Carfin, the niece of Andrew, last earl of Hyndford, he inherited Carfin and Maudslie Castle. Educated privately at Bexley and at the Royal Military Academy, on 1 December 1833 he was commissioned in the Royal Engineers. His first ten years of service were spent at various garrisons at home and in North America, but on promotion to captain in July 1845 he obtained command of the 1st company the Royal Sappers and Miners. Shortly afterwards he took his company to Bermuda, the 'Gibraltar of the west', where they constructed fortifications. He remained there for six years and was long remembered for his athletic prowess and charitable activities.

Gordon served in the Crimea and was present at the battles of the Alma and Inkerman. Engineers were in short supply and they suffered severe casualties while supervising construction of the siege works around Sevastopol. A month after the siege began Gordon found himself the commanding royal engineer of the army until the arrival of Sir Harry Jones. The loss of engineer officers increased the strain on the survivors, and Gordon was severely tried. During one bombardment he neither slept nor sat down to a meal for the greater part of three days. He was particularly popular among the naval brigade, and was always welcomed in their trenches, even when his great height, which he scorned to hide, drew the enemy's fire. The sailors called him 'Old Fireworks'.

Gordon was severely wounded on the night of 22–3 March 1855 in the great Russian sortie against the British trenches, which he helped to repel. He was soon back at duty and commanded the Royal Engineers in the Kerch expedition but had eventually to be invalided home on account of his wounds. He obtained a brevet majority on 12 December 1854, a brevet lieutenant-colonelcy on 24 April 1855, and a brevet colonelcy on 29 June 1855. He was also made a CB and aide-de-camp to the queen. In 1856 he was appointed deputy adjutant-general of Royal Engineers at the Horse Guards, a post he held for five years, during which he was elected a member of the Institution of Civil Engineers. His next appointment was as commanding royal engineer of the southern district, where fortifications for the defence of Portsmouth had recently been begun. At the end of 1861 he was sent temporarily to Canada to command the engineers there when the *Trent* affair brought Britain and the USA apparently near to war. On 28 March 1865 he was made a KCB, from which time he was known as Sir William Gordon. Shortly after leaving Portsmouth he was promoted major-general and appointed inspector-general of fortifications, which made him effectively head of his corps.

Gordon was, however, a sick man, largely because of the wound to his right hand and arm received outside Sevastopol. The pain never left him and worsened with the years. He began to suffer from a severe depressive illness and blamed himself for accepting the appointment of inspector-general of fortifications. By so doing he believed he had let down the duke of Cambridge, commander-in-chief of the army. His behaviour became more and more irrational. This greatly concerned his close friend, namesake, and fellow sapper, Colonel Charles George Gordon. He judged it necessary to take possession of his friend's razors before together they set out for Devon to visit Sir William Gordon's sister and her husband, Colonel Hutchinson, at Westward Ho! William Gordon stayed with the Hutchinsons, Charles Gordon at a local hotel, to which he retired for the night around 10 p.m. on 7 February 1870. At 11.30 p.m. William Gordon arrived to demand the return of his razors, and after a brief struggle Charles Gordon surrendered them. He did, however, warn Hutchinson to remove them at the first opportunity, but this was not done. At 8 a.m. the next morning, 8 February, Charles Gordon was called to the Hutchinsons' house, where he found his friend lying on the floor of his bedroom, razor in hand, in a pool of blood. He had cut his throat. Two doctors who soon arrived managed to stanch the flow, but after rallying briefly Sir William Gordon died.

Gordon was tall and powerfully built. A wealthy man, he concealed this by his simple lifestyle, but his charitable activities have been described as 'exhaustless'. He was deeply religious, of an evangelical persuasion like his friend Charles Gordon. Outwardly austere and stern in manner, he was warm-hearted with those he knew. He did not marry. R. H. Vetch, *rev.* James Lunt

Sources C. Chesney, *Essays in modern military biography* (1874) • A. W. Kinglake, *The invasion of the Crimea*, [new edn], 4 (1877) • *PICE*, 31 (1870–71), 241–5 • *The Times* (8 Feb 1870) • *The Times* (9 Feb 1870) • *The Times* (10 Feb 1870) • account of Sir William Gordon's suicide by Colonel Charles Gordon, Royal Engineers' Library, Chatham, Kent • W. Porter, *History of the corps of royal engineers*, 1 (1889) • Boase, *Mod. Eng. biog.* • d. cert.

Likenesses T. R. Williams, carte-de-visite, *c.*1865, NPG • C. Lutyens, oils, Royal Engineers, Shrivenham, Royal Military College of Science • portrait, Royal Engineers, Brompton barracks, Chatham, Kent

Wealth at death £13,877 13*s.* 3*d.*—in UK: Scottish confirmation sealed in England, 18 July 1870, *CGPLA Eng. & Wales*

Gordon, Sir William Eden Evans- (1857–1913), politician, was born on 8 August 1857 in Chatham, Kent, the youngest son of Major-General Charles Spalding Evans-Gordon and his wife, Catherine Rose, daughter of Dr Rose of Inverness. He was educated at Cheltenham College and at the Royal Military College, Sandhurst. He entered the army in July 1876 and after joining the 67th foot regiment in January 1877 was posted to India. After being made a captain in the Madras staff corps in July 1878, he was promoted major in July 1896. During his service, he acted as aide-de-camp to the governor of Madras, as a boundary settlement officer, and accompanied the viceroy, the marquess of Dufferin, as an interpreter on several tours. He undertook various roles within the foreign department of the government of India, and from 1888 to 1892 was assistant secretary. On 2 February 1892 Evans-Gordon married Julia Charlotte Sophia, marchioness of Tweeddale (1846–1937), widow of Arthur Hay, the ninth marquess, and widow of Sir John Rose, first baronet. She was the daughter of Keith William Stewart-Mackenzie of Seaforth and his first wife, Hannah Charlotte Hope-Vere. She and Evans-Gordon had no children. He retired from the army in May 1897.

In March 1898 Evans-Gordon unsuccessfully contested for the Conservatives one of the London county council seats for Stepney in the East End of London. During the council campaign the sitting Conservative MP for Stepney died and Evans-Gordon was selected as the candidate to replace him in parliament. He was narrowly defeated in the by-election, but won the seat in the October 1900 general election Conservative landslide. Evans-Gordon rose to greatest prominence after his election for his persistent and forthright call for restrictions to be placed upon immigration into Britain. Large numbers of Jewish immigrants had continued to settle in the East End of London from the 1880s, and the 'alien question' was an issue gaining widespread attention in Stepney and surrounding seats. Evans-Gordon took up these local concerns with a passion and became one of the leading proponents of restrictive legislation.

Soon after his election Evans-Gordon was instrumental in the establishment of the British Brothers' League (BBL), a purportedly working-class anti-immigration body. The BBL attracted large crowds to a series of public meetings across the East End; the first of these was held in Stepney in May 1901. By 1902 the BBL's membership stood at 12,000 and it had collected 45,000 signatures in support of its stand. Evans-Gordon toured eastern Europe to study the Jewish immigration question, and wrote of his journey in his book *The Alien Immigrant*, published in 1903. He concluded that 'it is a fact that the settlement of large aggregations of Hebrews in a Christian land has never been successful' (*The Alien Immigrant*, 248).

Evans-Gordon's role at the head of a popular anti-immigration movement gave him a great deal of influence in setting the agenda of the government on the issue. He formed a committee of MPs pledged to vote for restriction—the parliamentary pauper immigration committee—and this played an important part in forcing the government to establish a royal commission on alien immigration in 1902. As a member of the commission, Evans-Gordon was 'the individual who dominated the whole investigation' (Kushner, 37). Many of the witnesses called by the commission were organized by the BBL. The commission's report was presented in August 1903 and recommended a range of measures to restrict immigration. These were largely incorporated into the Aliens Act of 1905 which, according to David Feldman, Evans-Gordon 'played a major role in drafting' (Feldman, 75). With a great deal of justification, he was regarded by Chaim Weizmann, later the first president of Israel, as the 'father of the Aliens Act' (Gainer, 182).

Evans-Gordon held his seat in general election in January 1906, against the trend of the Liberal landslide. His victory has often been attributed to support for his stand on immigration, though this is open to question for he also stood on a programme of social reform, including cheaper working-class housing, poor-law reform, and old-age pensions. After 1906 Evans-Gordon continued to campaign on immigration, frequently attacking the new government for failing to enforce the Aliens Act. He told one large public meeting in Shoreditch that 'War has been declared on you by the Liberal Government, the friends of every country but their own' (*East London Advertiser*, 7 April 1906, 5). He announced his resignation from parliament in April 1907, largely as a result of his own ill health and that of his wife. After his retirement he continued periodically to write on the immigration question.

Evans-Gordon, who was knighted in 1905, was described as a tall and handsome man with an engaging manner (*East London Advertiser*, 8 Nov 1913, 5), and he was undoubtedly a popular member of parliament, although it is difficult to assess the extent to which his constituents supported his views on immigration restriction. He died suddenly on 31 October 1913 at his residence at 4 Chelsea Embankment, London. He was buried at Ightham church, Kent, on 4 November. MARC BRODIE

Sources *East London Observer* (9 Oct 1900), 2 · *Dod's Parliamentary Companion* (1901) · *East London Advertiser* (7 April 1906), 5 · *East London Advertiser* (8 Nov 1913), 5 · Burke, *Peerage* [Galloway] · *The Times* (3 Nov 1913), 11 · E. S. Skirving, ed., *Cheltenham College register, 1841–1927* (1928) · B. Gainer, *The alien invasion: the origins of the Aliens Act of 1905* (1972) · D. Feldman, 'The importance of being English: Jewish immigration and the decay of liberal England', *Metropolis London: histories and representations since 1800*, ed. D. Feldman and G. S. Jones (1989), 56–84 · T. Kushner, 'Jew and non-Jew in the East End of London: towards an anthropology of "everyday" relations', *Outsiders and outcasts: essays in honour of William J. Fishman*, ed. G. Alderman and C. Holmes (1993) · C. T. Husbands, 'East End racism, 1900–1980: geographical continuities in vigilantist and extreme right-wing political behaviour', *London Journal*, 8 (1982), 3–26 · J. Garrard, *The English and immigration, 1880–1910* (1971) · H. Pelling, *Social geography of British elections, 1885–1910* (1967)

Likenesses photograph, repro. in *East London Advertiser* (4 May 1907), 3 · photograph, repro. in *East London Advertiser* (8 Nov 1913), 5

Wealth at death £9407 16s. 1d.: probate, 3 March 1914, *CGPLA Eng. & Wales*

Gordon, William James (1864–1922), West Indian soldier and recipient of the Victoria Cross, was born on 19 May 1864 in Jamaica. His precise birthplace and parents' names are unknown, as are details of his life before July 1885, when he enlisted in the 1st West India regiment. This was one of two such regiments in which men recruited throughout the British West Indies, but primarily in Jamaica and Barbados, served under British officers and senior non-commissioned officers, and which since 1870 had alternated triennially in providing garrisons in either the West Indies or in the west African colonies of Sierra Leone, the Gambia, and the Gold Coast. Following amalgamation of the two regiments in October 1888, Gordon, by then a lance-corporal, completed his service in the 1st battalion, West India regiment.

At the beginning of 1892, on returning for a second term of duty in west Africa, Gordon formed part of a detachment sent to the Gambia to counter the hostility of local tribesmen towards an Anglo-French boundary commission. The inhabitants of the village of Toniataba, about 80 miles inland from Bathurst, were particularly troublesome, and on 12 March the detachment, under the command of Major George Madden, was sent up river to bring them to order and to force their acceptance of British authority. Next morning Gordon was part of a small group taken by Madden to break into the village through a well-secured gate in its outer, apparently unmanned, stockade. While they were using a heavy log as a battering ram, muskets began to appear through previously well-disguised loopholes on either side of the gate, giving hidden defenders an excellent view of Madden, who was standing with his back to the stockade. Gordon threw himself between the officer and the muzzles, shouting, 'Look out, Sir!'

before being shot in the chest. His quick thinking and unselfish action, with complete disregard for his own safety, undoubtedly saved his commanding officer's life. This was recognized nine months later, by which time he had recovered from his wound, with the award of the VC (gazetted 9 December 1892).

In Jamaica it is generally believed, although on no good evidence, that in approving the award Queen Victoria expressed the wish that, regardless of what offence Gordon might commit, he should never be court-martialled. An equally widely held but unsubstantiated belief is that in 1897, when he was a sergeant in the contingent sent to the jubilee celebrations in London, he was summoned to an audience with the queen, who, taken with his appearance in the distinctive full dress uniform which she had been instrumental in having issued to his regiment, addressed him fondly as her 'Zouave Boy'. Gordon behaved with quiet dignity throughout the remainder of his service, and was discharged to pension in April 1902. He afterwards spent many years as the principal warden of the firing range at Up Park camp in Kingston. A Baptist, he never married and, as far as is known, had no children. He died at Up Park camp, following a stroke, on 15 August 1922, and was buried with military honours in the cemetery there the following day.

Gordon was not the first West Indian soldier to be awarded the VC. The first was Private **Samuel Hodge** (*c.*1840–1868) of the 4th West India regiment, who was born in Tortola in the British Virgin Islands. He too was awarded the VC for outstanding bravery during an action against a stockaded village in the Gambia: on 30 June 1866, when axing open a gate under fire at Tubab Kolon (gazetted 4 January 1867). He was so severely wounded that he died on 14 January 1868, in Belize City, British Honduras; he was buried at the military cemetery there. A painting of him at Tubab Kolon, by Chevalier Louis William Desanges, is in the Penzance and District Museum and Art Gallery. He was the first non-white soldier to be awarded the VC. However, William Hall (1827–1904), a black Canadian serving as an able seaman in the Royal Navy, had won it in 1859 for bravery on 16 November 1857 at Lucknow, during the Indian mutiny, becoming the first non-European winner of the VC. BRIAN DYDE

Sources *LondG* (9 Dec 1892) • P. A. Wilkins, *The history of the Victoria Cross* (1904) • B. Dyde, *The empty sleeve: the story of the West India regiments of the British army* (1997) • C. V. Black, *Living names in Jamaica's history* [1946] • O'M. Creagh and E. M. Humphris, *The V.C. and D.S.O.: a complete record*, 3 vols. [1920–24] • *The Times* (31 March 1892) • *Daily Gleaner* (17 Aug 1922) [Jamaica] • D. Harvey, *Monuments to courage*, 2 vols. (1999) • L. Thompson, *An autobiography* (1985) • *The Graphic* (25 Feb 1893) • Lummis VC and GC files, NAM

Likenesses photograph, 1897, NAM • photograph, 1904, NAM • L. W. Desanges, portrait (Samuel Hodge), Penzance and District Museum and Art Gallery • drawing, repro. in *The Graphic* (26 June 1897) • drawing, repro. in *The Graphic* (10 July 1897) • photograph, repro. in Dyde, *Empty sleeve* • photograph, repro. in *Navy and Army Illustrated* (26 March 1898)

Gordon-Walker. For this title name *see* Walker, Patrick Chrestien Gordon, Baron Gordon-Walker (1907–1980).

Gore, Albert Augustus (1840–1901), army medical officer, born at Limerick, was the eldest son of William Ringrose Gore, physician, and his wife, Mary Jeners Wilson. He was educated in London, Paris, and Dublin, and took honours in science and medicine at Queen's College, Cork, in 1858. He graduated MD at the Queen's University, Ireland, and was admitted LRCSI in 1860.

Gore joined the army medical staff in 1861 and was appointed assistant surgeon to the 16th lancers. When the regimental service was reduced he volunteered for service in west Africa, where he took part in the bombardment and destruction of the Timni town of Massougha, on the Sierra Leone River, on 10 December 1861, the attack on Madoukia on 27 December, and the storming and capture of the stockaded fetish town of Rohea on 28 December. He was mentioned in general orders for his services and for bravery in bringing in a wounded officer. In 1868 he was recommended for promotion for his work during an epidemic of yellow fever at Sierra Leone. He acted as sanitary officer to the quartermaster-general's staff during the Second Anglo-Asante War in 1873, and was severely wounded in action on 3 November near Dunkwa, and again at Quarman on 17 November. In his *Medical History of our West African Campaigns* (1876), he examined the health and efficiency of the soldier in a malarial area, and attempted to sum up the experience of the campaign. He was also the author of *The Story of our Service under the Crown* (1879).

After six years' service at various base hospitals and as principal medical officer of the army of occupation in Egypt (1882), Gore was appointed principal medical officer, north-west district, Mhow division, central India; afterwards he was appointed in a similar position to the forces in India. In this capacity he was responsible for the medical arrangements of the Chitral and north-west frontier campaigns of 1896 and 1897. Gore retired from the army in 1898, was made CB in 1899, and was granted a distinguished service pension.

Gore married in 1866 Rebecca, daughter of John White, with whom he had two sons and two daughters. He died at his home, Dodington Lodge, Whitchurch, Shropshire, on 10 March 1901. D'A. POWER, *rev.* PATRICK WALLIS

Sources *BMJ* (16 March 1901), 679 • private information (1912)
Wealth at death £8021 6*s*. 9*d*.: probate, 10 April 1901, *CGPLA Eng. & Wales*

Gore [*née* Moody], **Catherine Grace Frances** (1799/1800–1861), novelist and playwright, was born in either London or East Rhetford, Nottinghamshire, the fourth and youngest child of Charles Moody (*d. c.*1800), a wine merchant, and his wife, Mary (*d.* 1817), daughter of General George Brinley and his wife, Mary Wentworth Brinley. Her father died about the time of her birth, and in 1801 her mother married a London physician, Charles D. Nevinson. The young Catherine was a favourite goddaughter of her mother's cousin Sir Charles-Mary Wentworth. Between 1810 and 1813 she spent most of her time living with Sir Charles-Mary's mother, Frances, Lady Wentworth, thus gaining an early familiarity with titled nobility. She showed literary talent in girlhood and was nicknamed the Poetess. On 15 February 1823 at St George's, Hanover

Catherine Grace Frances Gore (1799/1800–1861), by unknown engraver, pubd 1848

Square, she married Lieutenant Charles Arthur Gore, who retired from the 1st regiment of Life Guards that same year. They eventually had ten children, only two of whom survived: Captain Augustus Frederick Wentworth Gore and Cecilia Anne Mary, who married Lord Edward Thynne in 1853.

Mrs Gore, as she was always known to contemporaries, began actively writing and publishing from the time of her marriage. After a succession of historical fictions during the 1820s, she came into her own with *Women as they Are, or, The Manners of the Day* (1830), a 'silver fork', or fashionable, novel which immediately established her as a leading practitioner of the genre. Over the next three decades she produced a great number of popular titles, many of them under the imprint of Henry Colburn, the innovative and unscrupulous publisher who was the main originator of the silver fork mode. The Colburn formula, which Gore perfected, called for scenes of aristocratic high life, set in the Regency or its aftermath and tailored to the expectations of an emerging middle-class readership. In chronicling the beau monde Gore always wrote as an insider who shared the attitudes and foibles she satirized. As *The Athenaeum* observed in 1837, 'Mrs. Gore writes for the world, and she is herself a woman of the world' (Sutherland, 254). Her friend P. G. Patmore carried this observation further in 1844 with his fictional portrait of Gore as Lady Bab Brilliant in *Chatsworth*:

> Lady Bab Brilliant, not only did not pretend to be any better than her friends and associates, but in reality *was* no better. She was in truth an epitome, in herself, of all the fashionable follies, and not a few of the fashionable vices … which she had so effectually held up to public contempt and indignation. (P. G. Patmore, *Chatsworth*, 1844, 1.61)

Best-sellers in their own day, Gore's novels were read both as exposés of aristocratic corruption and as hornbooks of useful information for social climbers. She herself defended them in *Women as they Are* as social and historical repositories, having value as 'the amber which serves to preserve the ephemeral modes and caprices of the passing day' (2.233). At their most successful, they still offer a detailed sociology of upper-class circles during the transition from Regency to Victorian society.

Among Gore's early silver fork novels, *Mothers and Daughters* (1831) exposes the manoeuvring behind the scenes of the marriage market, while *Pin Money* (1831) is a sparkling comedy of manners that examines the financial and psychological underpinnings of arranged marriage in high society. With *The Hamiltons* (1834), set against the backdrop of political agitation surrounding the first Reform Bill, Gore anticipated Thackeray's *Vanity Fair* in probing the unhappy marriage of a heartless Regency dandy and a proto-Victorian domestic angel. In fact, she regularly pressed much further than Thackeray into what he called 'the marriage country' (*Vanity Fair*, chap. 26). Her influence on Thackeray was more profound and far-reaching than he ever acknowledged, although his preoccupation with her writings is clear in his numerous early reviews as well as his good-humoured parody of her silver fork mannerisms in 'Lords and liveries, by the authoress of "Dukes and dejeuners", "Hearts and diamonds", "Marchionesses and milliners", etc. etc.'

Gore set the pattern for her long and prolific career with an outburst of literary activity, turning out three-volume novels at the rate of two or three a year, in addition to works for the stage, melodies for popular songs, contributions to periodicals, and quantities of fluff for the annual keepsakes. Her first play, a five-act comedy entitled *The School for Coquettes*, ran triumphantly for thirty nights at the Haymarket Theatre in 1831. She followed this initial success with three more comedies, two historical plays, and a five-act verse drama. In 1843 her comedy *Quid pro Quo, or, The Days of the Dupes* won a prize at the Haymarket but was poorly received and closed her career as a dramatist. Throughout her lifelong herculean labours, Gore seems to have been the chief breadwinner for her husband and children. She was always a thorough professional and a shrewd businesswoman, alert to the commercial aspects of publishing.

Gore also appears to have enjoyed her celebrity status, with its access to London society. Benjamin Disraeli, himself a silver fork novelist at the time, met her at a soirée at the Bulwer-Lyttons' and found her 'a very sumptuous personage, looking like a full-blown rose' (Rosa, 134). In 1832 Charles Gore, described in most accounts as either feckless or vacuous, obtained a diplomatic appointment and moved his family to Paris for the next eight years. There his wife was able to moderate the pace of her literary production, while presiding over a fashionable salon in the place Vendôme. Novels from this period include *The Diary of a Désennuyée* (1836), *Mrs Armytage, or, Female Domination*

(1836), *Memoirs of a Peeress* (1837), and *The Cabinet Minister* (1839). With *Mrs Armytage*, considered her masterpiece by contemporaries ranging from Bulwer-Lytton to Margaret Oliphant, Gore strayed as far as she ever did from the silver fork conventions to attempt a domestic tragedy of parent–child relations. The book later gained an extra-literary notoriety as evidence in a Paris murder trial of 1847, when a blood-stained copy turned up on the bed of the murdered duchess of Praslin.

The anonymous publication of *Cecil, or, The Adventures of a Coxcomb* in 1841 caused a flurry of speculation about the unknown author, which Gore herself helped to orchestrate. Both Thackeray and Disraeli found themselves suspected of having written it. Throughout the six volumes of the novel and its sequel *Cecil, a Peer* (also 1841), Gore firmly sustains both the pretence of first-person memoirs and the masculine voice. Her irrepressible narrator, Cecil Danby, is an ageing dandy who looks back with undisguised nostalgia to the glamorous if corrupt days of the Regency, celebrating them as 'holiday time for people intent upon promoting the greatest happiness of the smallest number' (*Cecil, a Peer*, 1.20). Although the first Cecil novel has proved her most enduring achievement, it did not sell as well as expected. R. H. Horne in *The New Spirit of the Age* (1844) termed it 'surpassingly impudent' (Horne, 166); perhaps the wit, cynicism, and highly reproachable conduct of the dandy made it too provocative a mix for an early Victorian audience. Tireless if somewhat disillusioned, Gore carried on valiantly through the 1840s and 1850s, redirecting her focus to the conflict and eventual accommodation between what she called 'the two aristocracies' of old entitlement and new wealth. As Horne recognized, 'she excels in the portraiture of the upper section of the middle class, just at the point of contact with the nobility' (ibid., 168). Representative titles from this period include *The Money Lender* (1843), *Men of Capital* (1846), *Sketches of English Character* (1846), *Peers and Parvenus* (1846), and *The Two Aristocracies* (1857).

Gore spent much of her married life on the continent, in Paris and then Brussels, perhaps partly as a way of economizing. Her husband became a confirmed invalid, and she was widowed by 1846. An inheritance from a maternal cousin in 1850 at least temporarily eased her financial situation. About that time she returned to England for good, setting up house with her daughter in Hampshire and entertaining visitors with 'splendacious' dinners, as Thackeray described them (*Letters and Private Papers*, 2.697). She lost most of her hard-won fortune, a sum of nearly £19,000, in the bank failure of Strahan, Paul, and Bates in 1855. Strangely enough, she had plotted an almost identical scenario, involving a fraudulent banker, in *The Banker's Wife, or, Court and City* (1843), which she had dedicated to her personal banker and trustee, Sir John Dean Paul, who was then engaged in cheating her along with the other depositors.

For some period before her death Gore was completely blind, although still writing, and she never recovered from an unsuccessful operation to restore her sight. She died at Linwood, Lyndhurst, Hampshire, on 29 January 1861, aged sixty-one, and was buried in Kensal Green cemetery on 7 February. There was some mention in the obituaries of her deliberate reticence about the details of her private life and some confusion about her family origins, since she had been known as both Miss Moody and Miss Nevinson before her marriage. The gossip columnist in *The Athenaeum* even questioned her personal credentials for writing about lords and ladies, although in fact she was distantly connected through the Wentworths with nobility as high as the marquess of Rockingham. All the contemporary accounts of her career cite the accuracy of her portraits of society, as well as her extraordinary longevity and productivity as a popular novelist. While *The Athenaeum* fretted that her 'genius' was 'spoilt by the necessity of brain-spinning' (9 Feb 1861, 196), *The Times* marvelled that 'in the two hundred volumes there is scarcely to be found one dull page' (4 Feb 1861, 5). Although her work had already fallen into obscurity, undervalued by a new generation, Mrs Gore was eulogized in *The Times* as 'the best novel writer of her class and the wittiest woman of her age'.

WINIFRED HUGHES

Sources M. W. Rosa, *The silver-fork school: novels of fashion preceding Vanity Fair* (1936) • J. Wentworth, *The Wentworth genealogy* (1878) • 'Memoir of Mrs Gore', *New Monthly Magazine*, new ser., 49 (1837), 434–5 • 'Mrs Gore', *New Monthly Magazine*, new ser., 95 (1852), 157–68 • V. Colby, *Yesterday's woman* (1974) • J. Sutherland, *The Longman companion to Victorian fiction* (1988) • V. D. Wittrock, 'The re-emergence of realism', PhD diss., University of Illinois, 1957 • R. H. Horne, ed., *A new spirit of the age*, 2 vols. (1844) • G. N. Ray, 'The Bentley papers', *The Library*, 5th ser., 7 (1952), 178–200 • A. Adburgham, *Silver fork society* (1983) • *The letters and private papers of William Makepeace Thackeray*, ed. G. N. Ray, 4 vols. (1945–6) • W. Hughes, 'Elegies for the Regency: Catherine Gore's dandy novels', *Nineteenth-Century Literature* (Sept 1995) • W. Hughes, 'Mindless millinery: C. Gore and the silver fork heroine', *Dickens Studies Annual*, 25 (1996) • *The Times* (4 Feb 1861), 5 • *GM*, 3rd ser., 10 (1861), 345–69 • *ILN* (16 Feb 1861), 147 • *The Athenaeum* (9 Feb 1861), 196 • *The Athenaeum* (16 Feb 1861), 232 • *The Athenaeum* (23 Feb 1861), 264 • m. cert.

Archives BL, Add. Biogr. MS 28510 • Princeton University Library, Firestone Library, corresp. • Yale U., corresp. | BL, letters to Richard Bentley, Add. MSS 466611–466614; 46649–46652 • Bodl. Oxf., letters to Mary Ann Disraeli • Chatsworth House, Derbyshire, letters to the sixth duke of Devonshire • NA Scot., letters to William Tait • University of Illinois, Urbana–Champaign, Bentley MSS

Likenesses I. W. Slater, lithograph, 1829 (after J. Slater), BM • stipple, pubd 1848 (after unknown artist), BM, NPG [*see illus.*] • S. Freeman, stipple, BM, NPG; repro. in Adburgham, *Silver fork society* • A. Williamson, engraving (after photograph by H. Watkins), repro. in *ILN* (16 Feb 1861), 147 • engraving, repro. in *New Monthly Magazine* (March 1837), 434 • engraving, repro. in Adburgham, *Silver fork society*, 266

Wealth at death £14,000: probate, 23 Feb 1861, *CGPLA Eng. & Wales*

Gore, Charles (1853–1932), bishop of Oxford, the youngest son of the Hon. Charles Alexander Gore (1811–1897), a younger brother of the fourth earl of Arran and commissioner of woods and forests, and his wife, Lady Augusta Lavinia Priscilla (*d.* 1904), daughter of John William *Ponsonby, fourth earl of Bessborough (1781–1847), and widow of William Thomas Petty-Fitzmaurice, earl of Kerry (*d.* 1836), was born at Westside House, Wimbledon Common, on 22 January 1853. Though he was proud to have been

Charles Gore (1853–1932), by Sir John Lavery, 1905

born into the heart of aristocratic whigdom, Gore was always a lone spirit, different from the rest of his family.

Youth and education, 1853–1875 Gore's mother was beautiful, determined, and devout: Charles told her towards the end of her life, 'I owe you almost anything that is worth having in me' (Prestige, 3). As a boy Gore read Grace Kennedy's *Father Clement* (1823), an anti-Catholic novel which introduced him to a Catholic world far more entrancing than anything provided by the low-church tradition in which he was being brought up. By now everyone assumed that he would be a priest. At Harrow School, which he attended from 1866, he was part of a small group which was Anglo-Catholic in religion and radical in politics. A sermon entitled 'Disciplined life', preached in the chapel in 1868 by B. F. Westcott, then an assistant master and later bishop of Durham, affected Gore profoundly. Westcott called for a modern expression of the monastic life: 'social evils must be met by social organisation. A life of absolute and calculated sacrifice is a spring of immeasurable power' (B. F. Westcott, *Disciplined Life*, 1886, 13).

In October 1871 Gore matriculated at Balliol College, Oxford. In the Oxford Union he continued his support of radical causes, including the trade unions. It was the leader of the farmworkers, Joseph Arch, who opened his eyes to rural poverty. Benjamin Jowett, the master of Balliol, still regarded as a dangerous liberal for his contribution to *Essays and Reviews* (1860), developed a close relationship with his pupil Gore. Gore was also influenced by T. H. Green (1836–1882), the idealist philosopher, and Father R. M. Benson (1824–1915), founder of the austere Cowley Fathers.

Gore was a scholar at Balliol from 1871 to 1875, and after taking a first class in *literae humaniores* in 1875 he was elected fellow of Trinity. His mordant wit both entertained people and kept them at a distance. He responded warmly to the moralism of John Percival (1834–1918), the president from 1878: subsequently both were to criticize the Second South African War and support Welsh disestablishment. In December 1876 Bishop J. F. Mackarness of Oxford made Gore deacon, and ordained him priest in December 1878. He approached ordination with joy and trepidation and felt called to celibacy. Recognizing that he lacked experience of either ordinary people or parish life, he went regularly to assist in parishes in Liverpool.

Oxford, 1875–1889 In 1875 Gore joined a group at Oxford which included E. S. Talbot (1844–1934), Henry Scott Holland (1847–1918), and J. R. Illingworth (1848–1915), and which aimed to develop a more liberal Catholicism than that of the Tractarians. Gore and some of the group also formed 'the Holy Party', which from 1875 met annually for retreat and theological study and discussed the formation of an Oratorian community. In 1880 Gore became vice-principal of Cuddesdon Theological College. He kept a picture of Bishop Edward King on one wall of his study to remind him of Catholic sanctity and, opposite, a picture of the liberal Jowett to pull him up if he stressed an argument too far. Thus the seeds of liberal Catholicism were germinating.

So long as Pusey was alive, younger leaders like Gore and Holland had to be restrained, for Pusey firmly opposed all theological liberalism. But in September 1882 Pusey died. His friends decided to create a memorial. Henry Liddon (1829–1890), who had been Pusey's spokesman, proposed a house of learning, teaching, and pastoral care for undergraduates, and asked Gore to be principal. Gore accepted, though he pointed out that he did not share some of Pusey's views, and Pusey House was launched in October 1884. There Gore drew undergraduates to both a supernatural faith and a commitment to social action. Ironically, under Gore it became identified with that theological liberalism to which Pusey had been so bitterly opposed.

By now Gore had experienced community life with a religious basis at Harrow, Balliol, and Trinity. At Cuddesdon and Pusey House he was part of totally committed religious communities, and he was also a keen supporter of the brothers of the Oxford mission to Calcutta (1879). In 1887 the Society of the Resurrection, an Oratorian group, was formed by twenty-one priests with Gore as superior, linked to the Oxford mission. He hoped a community would emerge from the society.

The *Lux mundi* years, 1889–1894 For Gore 1889 was a remarkably creative year. June witnessed the launch of the Christian Social Union (CSU) of which he became a vice-president. The CSU aimed not only to study social problems but also to promote social action. Gore later described its creation as 'a tardy act of repentance' for the church's failure to bear witness to social justice and brotherhood, but lamented its small impact on the labour movement and the parishes. Nevertheless, he had done more than anyone else to create an Anglican tradition of Christian social dissent. In the following month, July, Gore gathered a group at Pusey House for an experiment in community life: they were determined to avoid what they regarded as the autocracy and world-denying spirituality of the Cowley Fathers. Finally, the November of 1889 saw the appearance of *Lux mundi*, edited by Gore with contributions from other members of the Holy Party. It represented a creative interaction between patristic theology, Anglo-Catholicism, and broad-church liberalism. Whereas the Tractarians had seen secular thought as a threat, the essays celebrated the Logos at work in evolution, art, science, other faiths, and socialism. Gore's own essay on the Bible caused an uproar, as he contended that Jesus's knowledge was limited by incarnation: this self-emptying had an immense moral appeal for Gore. Conservatives, led by Liddon, were deeply shocked by this and other features of the essay. To younger Anglo-Catholics the book was a liberation: 'it is not too much to say that everything fresh and earnest in theological study and spiritual life either centred round it or borrowed vitality from it', remembered R. J. Campbell in *A Spiritual Pilgrimage* (1917), 49.

However, the effects of the painful controversy on Gore himself were profound: it turned him into a self-conscious gladiator for a rather static concept of truth. In his essay Gore had reinterpreted the Old Testament boldly; but he believed that the New Testament should be interpreted only in accordance with the creeds. When, as a bishop, he attempted to enforce this view he dismayed both the modernists, who wanted to interpret creeds symbolically, and the younger Anglo-Catholics, who considered that religious experience rather than bare historical facts should be the basis of faith. Gore was not a liberal poacher who later became a conservative gamekeeper, as has often been asserted: as early as 1887 he clearly stated in *The Clergy and the Creeds* that clergy must unequivocally believe in the creeds they recite. The ascension might be metaphorical, but the virgin birth and the resurrection were actual historical facts.

Christianity to Gore was essentially social: he persistently called for more Christians, married and celibate, to live in community. In July 1892 Gore and five priests, all but one CSU members, made their professions in Pusey House chapel and so founded the Community of the Resurrection (CR). But Pusey House, with its existing life and work, was not a helpful setting. Gore and the brethren felt called to the industrial north, but in September 1893 Gore became vicar of Radley, and the brethren lived with him in the vicarage. He had never been an incumbent and knew little about ordinary people. After three months he broke down and spent much of the next year recovering away from Radley. When he resumed residence in November 1894 he astounded the brethren by asking them to agree that he should become a canon at Westminster Abbey and open a branch house there. In fact, the removal of Gore from the centre of CR life enabled it to develop without his dominating presence and the debilitating effects of his vocational uncertainties. It also enabled Gore eventually to find an honourable exit from community life to which, like many loners, he thought he had a vocation. In 1898 the majority of the community moved to the north and settled at Mirfield, Yorkshire, where in 1903 they fulfilled two more of Gore's hopes: they established a scheme of free training for poor ordinands and they opened a house in South Africa, where later the Gore tradition was incarnated by such brethren as Father Trevor Huddleston and by Archbishop Tutu, one of the ordinands they had trained.

Westminster, Worcester, and Birmingham, 1894–1911 Life at Westminster gave Gore space, stimulating company, and an influential role at the centre of national life. He deepened the spiritual life of the abbey: when he was billed to preach queues formed outside. If at Oxford he had been the explorer, at the abbey he became the expositor and social prophet. He said that paying the just price for goods was as important as prayer and holy communion, and argued that women should have the vote both in church and state. He knew that the radical programme of church reform he suggested might, if implemented, precipitate disestablishment, but he was not deterred. It was for him almost impossible for an established church to be salt and leaven (Matthew 5: 13, 13: 33).

In October 1901 Gore wrote to *The Times* deploring the death rates in the British concentration camps in South Africa; on the same day he was invited to become bishop of Worcester. The Community of the Resurrection dispensed him from his community obligations, while extreme protestants agitated against this 'monk' and 'heretic'. On 23 February 1902 he was consecrated by Archbishop Frederick Temple, assisted by other bishops, in Lambeth Palace chapel. He immediately dismayed the aristocracy of the county by refusing to live in Hartlebury Castle. Equally, traders were annoyed when he joined the Co-operative Society. He did not like to be called 'lord bishop', preferring simply 'bishop'. His episcopal ring was simple; his pastoral staff inexpensive. He soon decided that the diocese should be divided to create a new see of Birmingham. His fellow bishops vexed him: 'The whole atmosphere of the episcopate is manipulation of details and avoidance of big principles' (Prestige, 241).

In 1905 Gore happily became the first bishop of the compact city diocese of Birmingham. He donated to it £800 from his former see and his mother's legacy of £10,000. He was relieved not to have a palace, but lived in Edgbaston, in what he called the ugliest villa in western Europe. Gore's social radicalism and belief in city life fitted in with Birmingham's strong nonconformist tradition, with its 'civic gospel', whereas its Anglicanism was tory.

In a powerful sermon to the 1906 church congress Gore said that while the early church spoke for the poor, the Church of England, despite many efforts, was not the church of the people. 'This sermon is only the cry of a permanently troubled conscience which cannot see its way' (C. Gore, *The New Theology and the Old Religion*, 1907, 286). He strongly supported a 'living wage' as the first call on industry and the welfare proposals in Lloyd George's budget of 1909. When he was translated to Oxford in 1911 a statue of him was erected outside Birmingham Cathedral, a reflection of the impact of his episcopate upon the city. Gore himself regarded the statue with 'mingled feelings of gratitude and repugnance' (Prestige, 319), but in 1987 an old lady claimed to have regularly stood under the statue to repeat the confirmation prayer which Gore had said over her.

Oxford, 1911–1919 Gore was fulfilled, yet still restless, and actually considered becoming bishop of Bombay. Did he make a mistake in going to Oxford? Sometimes he thought so when he suffered from his glooms. Oxford was rural, conservative, and, with 670 parishes, unwieldy: he failed to persuade the diocese of the need for division. Influential people disliked his social radicalism. He continued to live simply—his bedroom had an iron bedstead, a tin bath, and no carpet. His wartime ministry was singularly important for, unlike many leaders of the churches, he refused to preach Christian nationalism, and in the Lords spoke against the harsh treatment of conscientious objectors. The strain of the period took its toll, and his writhings and slowness of speech in the pulpit became more marked than ever.

While at Oxford, Gore played a combative role in several painful ecclesiastical controversies. In 1912 he was proposed as visitor to the Anglican Benedictines at Caldey Abbey, who liturgically, financially, and ecclesiastically lived in a dream world. Gore insisted that before he could act as visitor the community must show loyalty to the Church of England, a declaration which resulted in the conversion of most of the monks to Roman Catholicism. He was profoundly disturbed by a number of clerical works questioning aspects of the creeds (especially the virgin birth and the resurrection) and by proposals in 1913 for an Anglican–free church federation in east Africa. In *The Basis of Anglican Fellowship* (1914) he argued that the Church of England stood for 'liberal or scriptural catholicism' (p. 4) but that this was under threat. He appealed for 'a great act of corporate thinking by which we shall recognize again what our Anglican Church really stands for' (p. 47). When Hensley Henson (1863–1947) was nominated as bishop of Hereford in 1917 Gore protested that Henson did not believe in certain clauses of the creeds, and was therefore unfit to be a bishop. Gore was considering drastic action when, to his astonishment, the wily Archbishop Randall Davidson extracted from Henson what seemed a declaration of credal orthodoxy.

Gore's Oxford episcopate was not all controversy. There was always art and music to enjoy, nephews and nieces to entertain, children to play with, and holidays which he still approached with childlike glee. He felt the same glee when he retired at the age of sixty-six in 1919. He said he needed leisure to write and that he wanted to join the Labour Party. The last straw had been the adoption for the church's new forms of government (established by the Enabling Act, 1919) of a baptismal, not a confirmation, franchise. So the 'national', not Gore's eucharistic, concept of the church had prevailed. As a bishop he had often felt trapped and compromised. This had sometimes brought out the worst in him. With characteristic impishness he announced his resignation on All Fools' day. He wondered whether to rejoin the Community of the Resurrection but confessed to 'a certain carnal disinclination'; he feared he might be a drag. Instead he became a prelate brother—exactly the right balance between association and detachment—and lived in London, visiting Mirfield for general chapter, and blessing the newly professed and the crowds on Commemoration day. He lectured at King's College, London, and ministered regularly at Grosvenor Chapel. He continued to take infinite trouble to meet the pastoral (and sometimes financial) needs of individuals.

Old age and death, 1919–1932 Jowett had said (Gore recalled) that the last ten years were the most important. Certainly Gore's final achievements in retirement were impressive—sixteen books in a dozen years, including the massive trilogy *The Reconstruction of Belief* (1926) and *A New Commentary on Holy Scripture* (1928), of which he was chief editor. He mainly concentrated upon apologetics aimed at parish priests or educated laity: for example, his *The Philosophy of the Good Life* (1930) was a remarkable synopsis of the teachings of moral leaders of ancient Iraq, India, China, Arabia, Greece, Israel, and Christendom. R. H. Tawney's dedication to Gore of his *Religion and the Rise of Capitalism* (1926) was a recognition of Gore's leading role in promoting a left-of-centre Christian social ethic. However, Gore had always recoiled from questions of sexuality: he created a tense stillness among the young men during the Oxford University mission of 1914 when he quoted (as was his wont) Shakespeare's sonnet on lust. He was aghast when the bishops at the 1930 Lambeth conference gave (limited) approval to contraception.

From 1923 to 1925 Gore participated in the conversations between Anglicans and Roman Catholics at Malines, Belgium, to which he made a characteristically forthright contribution. Proposals for reunion with the free churches both at home and in India made him anxious. Though his moralism and western outlook prevented him from total sympathy with the Orthodox, their reverence for the fathers and their non-papal Catholicism pleased him.

Gore was elected to honorary fellowships by Balliol (1922), Trinity (1903), and King's College, London (1922). He received honorary degrees from the universities of Edinburgh (1896), Oxford (1904), Cambridge (1909), Birmingham (1909), Durham (1919), and Athens (1924). On 17 January 1932, at 5 Collingham Gardens, South Kensington, he died a few days before his seventy-ninth birthday, weakened by a six months' gruelling Indian tour. On 22 January his ashes were buried, not among his aristocratic relations, nor in Westminster Abbey, Oxford, or Birmingham, but in the Community of the Resurrection church at Mirfield, the mill town to which he had only ever been a visitor. He wanted to be with his brethren in death, even though he had been unable to live with them. He was too much a moralist to appreciate the enclosed life, but he advocated what he called *receuillement*. He argued that Wordsworth's life of contemplation had been valuable, even if a ploughman might have dismissed it as useless.

Assessment and conclusion In appearance Gore was of middle height with neatly cut hair and beard. Certain words he pronounced in the whig manner: 'I would sell my soul for *cawfee*'. His was a vivid personality: 'his eye was very capable of flashing with derisive laughter, and his nose could cock up with a quiver of righteous scorn, as he balanced on his toes and thrust out his beard "pointing" like an old and wise dog at some sham or meanness' (Crosse, 96). He was often disconcerting: by turn playful and formidable, intellectual and prankish, sadistic and tender. His acute sense of the ridiculous saved him from being a remorseless fanatic. Yet he often put people in touch with the transcendent: Michael Ramsey, repelled by the politicking in G. K. A. Bell's *Davidson* (1935), read C. L. Prestige's *Gore* (1935) and was inspired.

Gore remains the most fascinating and influential bishop of the Church of England in the twentieth century. Much of his theology has been absorbed into Anglicanism, not least his prophetic book *The Body of Christ* (1901), in which he characteristically described the eucharist as 'the sacrament of fraternity'. He had worked out his theology at a very early stage. Though constantly re-expressed, it did not fundamentally change. Why did it nevertheless remain fresh? Father Talbot CR explained that 'it always seemed that the same terminus, however often it was reached, was approached again and again by a genuine movement of mind and spirit' (G. P. H. Pawson, ed., *Edward Keble Talbot*, 1954, 64). Gore in *Belief in God* (1921) claimed he had always been a 'free thinker' confronting disturbing challenges. The only very difficult Christian doctrine was that God was love. 'But deeper than any difficulty has been the feeling that at the roots of my being I am confronted with God, from whom I cannot get away, and that the God who confronts me there is the Living God of the prophets and of Jesus Christ' (C. Gore, *Belief in God*, 1921, Preface). Yet he considered a wide variety of evidence. At the end of a Brandenburg concerto he commented: 'If *that* is true, everything must be all right' (Prestige, 429). But his Christianity made stern demands. There is 'nothing He really demands of men but righteousness' (C. Gore, *The Philosophy of the Good Life*, 1930, 155) he wrote; 'Jesus had a profound contempt for majorities' (ibid., 192). Despite its flaws, Gore's concept of liberal Catholicism quickly became the lodestone of Anglicanism.

ALAN WILKINSON

Sources G. L. Prestige, *The life of Charles Gore* (1935) · A. Wilkinson, *The Community of the Resurrection: a centenary history* (1992) · J. Carpenter, *Gore: a study in liberal Catholic thought* (1960) · P. Avis, *Gore: construction and conflict* (1988) · A. Mansbridge, *Edward Stuart Talbot and Charles Gore* (1935) · G. Crosse, *Charles Gore: a biographical sketch* (1932) · J. Gore, *Charles Gore, father and son* (1932) · G. K. A. Bell, *The life of Archbishop Davidson* (1935) · A. Wilkinson, *Christian socialism: Scott Holland to Tony Blair* (1998) · Burke, *Peerage* (1907)

Archives BL, corresp. and papers, Add. MSS 65352–65362 · Borth. Inst., corresp. with W. Frere · Borth. Inst., corresp. and papers, incl. family corresp. | BL, letters to W. E. Gladstone, Add. MSS 44476–44526, *passim* · Bodl. Oxf., corresp. with Lord Selborne · Borth. Inst., corresp. with Lord Halifax · LPL, corresp. with John Douglas · LPL, letters to Arthur Cayley Headlam · LPL, letters to Athelstan Riley · LPL, letters to Benjamin Webb

Likenesses J. H. F. Bacon, oils, 1903, NPG · J. Lavery, oils, 1905, NPG [*see illus.*] · photograph, 1905, repro. in Prestige, *Life of Charles Gore*, frontispiece · T. S. Lee, statue, *c*.1911, Birmingham Cathedral · G. Philpot, oils, 1920, Theological College, Cuddesdon, Oxfordshire · J. Lavery, oils, Hartlebury Castle, Worcestershire · London Stereoscopic Co., postcard, NPG · J. Mansbridge, drawings, Community of the Resurrection, Mirfield, Yorkshire · J. Mansbridge, drawings, Balliol Oxf. · J. Mansbridge, drawings, Birmingham · J. Mansbridge, pencil drawing, NPG · J. Mansbridge, portrait, King's Lond.; repro. in Mansbridge, *Edward Stuart Talbot and Charles Gore*, facing p. 30 · B. Munns, oils (?), Bishop's Croft, Birmingham · A. U. Soord, oils, Community of the Resurrection, Mirfield, Yorkshire · photograph, NPG

Wealth at death £12,373 3*s*. 6*d*.: resworn probate, 11 March 1932, *CGPLA Eng. & Wales*

Gore, Sir Charles Stephen (1793–1869), army officer, was born on 26 December 1793, the son of Arthur Gore, second earl of Arran, and his third wife, Elizabeth Underwood. He entered the army in October 1808 as a cornet in the 16th light dragoons, later transferring successively to the 6th and 43rd foot. He was promoted lieutenant in January 1810.

He joined the 43rd foot in the Peninsula in July 1811 and was one of the storming party of Fort Francisco, at the investment of Ciudad Rodrigo, and also at the siege and storming of that fortress and of Badajoz. He was aide-de-camp to Sir Andrew Barnard at the battle of Salamanca, and to Sir James Kempt at the battles of Vitoria, Nivelle, the Nive, Orthez, and Toulouse, and was present at all the engagements in which the light division was involved from 1812 until the end of the war. He accompanied General Kempt as his aide-de-camp to Canada in 1814 but returned with him to Europe in time for the Waterloo campaign, and was promoted captain in March 1815. Kempt was second in command of Picton's 5th division, and succeeded to the command when Picton was killed. Gore had a horse killed under him at Quatre Bras, and three horses at Waterloo. He was present at the entry into Paris and served in the army of occupation in France. He was promoted major in January 1819 and lieutenant-colonel in September 1822.

Gore married on 13 May 1824 Sarah Rachel, daughter of the Hon. James Fraser, member of the legislative council of Nova Scotia, and they had three sons and two daughters. Lady Gore died in 1880. Gore was serving in Jamaica as deputy quartermaster-general in 1833 when the imperial parliament emancipated the slaves. He went on to Canada where there were serious disturbances in 1837–9. They were suppressed without much difficulty by the commander-in-chief, Sir John Colborne, but caused much concern in England and led to an increase in what had previously been a very weak garrison. Gore was at this time serving as a deputy quartermaster-general, and was promoted colonel in January 1837. Thenceforward his military career was typical of many others of his generation in the British army. Having survived as a junior officer the hardships and dangers of Spain and Waterloo, he thereafter rose steadily but unspectacularly in rank without coming under fire again. He was promoted major-general in 1846, and lieutenant-general in 1854. He retired in 1863 on promotion to general. He was GCB and a knight of the

Royal Guelphic Order of Hanover, in addition to which he held the Peninsular medal with nine clasps and the Waterloo medal. He was successively colonel of the 91st and, in 1861, 6th foot. Gore was appointed lieutenant-governor of the Royal Hospital, Chelsea, on 11 December 1868, but did not survive long in office, dying in residence on 4 September 1869. JAMES LUNT

Sources *Hart's Army List* • Burke, *Peerage*
Wealth at death under £12,000: probate, 5 Nov 1869, *CGPLA Eng. & Wales*

Gore, (William) David Ormsby, fifth Baron Harlech (1918–1985), politician and diplomatist, was born on 20 May 1918 in London. He was the second son and third child in the family of three sons and three daughters of William George Arthur Ormsby-*Gore, fourth Baron Harlech (1885–1964), politician and banker, and his wife, Lady Beatrice Edith Mildred (1891–1980), daughter of James Edward Hubert Gascoyne-*Cecil, the fourth marquess of Salisbury. His elder brother died at the age of nineteen. He was educated at Eton College and at New College, Oxford (of which he became an honorary fellow in 1964). He obtained a third class in modern history in 1939 and joined the Berkshire yeomanry in the same year, becoming a major (general staff) by the end of the war.

In 1950 Ormsby Gore became Conservative MP for the Oswestry division of Shropshire and held the seat until 1961. After a few months as parliamentary undersecretary, he was appointed minister of state for foreign affairs at the beginning of the administration led by Harold Macmillan in January 1957. In this office much of his attention was devoted to disarmament negotiations, partly in Geneva and partly in New York during successive sessions of the United Nations general assembly.

In November 1960 John F. Kennedy was elected president of the USA. Ormsby Gore, two years his junior, had been his close friend since Kennedy's pre-war years in London during his father's embassy. Macmillan was anxious to achieve the closest relations with the new president, who was a brother-in-law of his late nephew by marriage, the marquess of Hartington, and therefore decided to send as British ambassador to Washington another nephew by marriage. Ormsby Gore resigned from the House of Commons and arrived in Washington in May 1961.

Until that point the new ambassador's career could be fairly described as remarkably nepotic. The success which Ormsby Gore then made of his mission, however, sprang from qualities which could not be bestowed by family connection. He was almost perfectly attuned to the new American administration. His friendship with the president strengthened rather than wilted under the strains of office and official intercourse. It was buttressed by the fact that Ormsby Gore was also on close terms with Jacqueline Kennedy, as were the Kennedys with Lady Ormsby Gore (Sylvia, or Sissy, daughter of Hugh Lloyd Thomas, diplomat and courtier, whom he had married young in 1940, and with whom he had two sons and three daughters), whose shy but elegant charm made her an addition to the embassy and easily at home in the Kennedy White House. President Kennedy much liked to have small dinner parties organized at short notice. The Ormsby Gores were probably more frequently invited on this basis than was anybody else, including even the president's brother and the attorney-general. It was a wholly exceptional social position for any ambassador. It made Ormsby Gore almost as much an unofficial adviser to the president as an envoy of the British government—although there was never any suggestion that British interests were not firmly represented in Washington during these years. His position was particularly influential during the Cuban missile crisis in October 1962.

Ormsby Gore's special relationship may have caused some jealousy among other ambassadors but it in no way weakened his position in official Washington outside the White House. Other members of the administration—Robert McNamara, Robert Kennedy, McGeorge Bundy, Arthur Schlesinger—became his close and continuing friends, and even after Kennedy's assassination he was able to be a more than averagely effective ambassador for the first seventeen months of Lyndon Johnson's presidency. But the *raison d'être* of Ormsby Gore's embassy had gone. In February 1964 his father died and he became Lord Harlech. Later that year the Conservative government that had sent him as a political appointment to Washington was replaced by a Labour one. The new government was in no hurry to remove him. Nor should it have been. Apart from his effectiveness on the spot, his Kennedy years had shifted Harlech to the centre or even the left-centre of politics.

After his return to England (in the spring of 1965) Harlech was briefly (1966–7) deputy Conservative leader in the House of Lords, but he had lost any taste that he ever possessed for political partisanship and resigned after a year. This apart, all his subsequent semi-political activities were firmly centrist: the presidency of Shelter and the chairmanship of the European Movement (1969–75) and the National Committee for Electoral Reform (from 1976). He was also twice concerned in a semi-official capacity with trying to find a multiracial solution to the Rhodesian problem. In addition he was president of the British Board of Film Censors from 1965, the initiator and chairman of Harlech Television from 1967, and a director of a few other companies, although never centrally occupied with business. He was chairman of the Pilgrim Trust (1974–9) and of the British branch of the Pilgrims (a quite separate organization) during 1965–77. He was also the leading British figure in all Kennedy commemorative activities.

Sadly, Harlech's own life was almost as marked by tragedy and violent death as was that of the Kennedy family. In 1967 Sissy Harlech was killed in a car crash almost at the gates of their north Wales house. In 1974 their eldest son committed suicide. Harlech surmounted these vicissitudes with fortitude and buoyancy, greatly assisted by his second marriage, in 1969, to Pamela, the daughter of Ralph Frederick Colin, a New York lawyer and financier; they had one daughter. Pamela Harlech, a *Vogue* editor and talented compiler of books, brought vitality and verve to the marriage and had the gift of keeping her husband young. David Harlech aged sixty-six looked no different from the way he had looked at fifty-six. He had no mountains left to climb, but he lived a life of style and grace, in which a large part was played by pleasure, tempered by high public spirit, good judgement, and unselfish instincts on all the main issues of the day. There seemed little reason why he should not have continued for many years as an easy-going public figure of good sense and high repute. But tragedy struck again. On the evening of 25 January 1985, driving from London to Harlech, he was involved in a car crash (the third major one of his life) near to his constituency of the 1950s and the Shropshire homes of his earlier life. He died in hospital in Shrewsbury early the next morning. He was succeeded in the barony by his second son, Francis David (*b.* 1954).

Ormsby Gore was sworn of the privy council in 1957 and appointed KCMG in 1961. He had honorary degrees from several American universities and from Manchester University (LLD, 1966). ROY JENKINS, *rev.*

Sources personal knowledge (1990) · *WWW* · Burke, *Peerage* · A. M. Schlesinger, *A thousand days: John F. Kennedy in the White House* (1965) · A. Horne, *Macmillan*, 2: 1957–1986 (1989)
Wealth at death £3,290,724: probate, 4 June 1985, *CGPLA Eng. & Wales*

Gore, George (1826–1908), electrochemist and scientific writer, was born at Blackfriars, Bristol, on 22 January 1826, the son of George Gore, a cooper. He was educated at a small private school in Bristol but left at the age of twelve or thirteen to become an errand boy. At the age of seventeen he was apprenticed to a cooper for four years, but pursued scientific study and experiment in his spare time. Of particular interest to him was electrodeposition and in 1851 he moved to Birmingham, the centre of the country's electroplate manufacturing industry. On 12 January 1849, at the Counter Slip Chapel in Bristol, he had married Hannah Owen (*d.* 1907), the daughter of Thomas Owen, a Baptist minister. They had a son and a daughter.

Gore first found work in Birmingham as a timekeeper at the Soho works, then as a practitioner in medical galvanism, having already worked on improving relevant apparatus. He worked as a chemist in a phosphorus factory, where he discovered the means of bleaching phosphorus by chlorine. Between 1853 and 1865 he published, in major journals, thirty papers relating to his research in electrometallurgy and chemistry. Of particular note was his work on electrodeposited antimony and on the properties of liquid carbonic and hydrofluoric acids and on silver fluoride. He also investigated ammonia as a solvent of the alkaline metals, the thermoelectric action of metals and liquids, recalescent iron and its magnetic properties, the effects of electric torsion, and the use of the capillary electroscope. At this time, too, he held classes on electroplating and chemistry. Like many before him, he tried to isolate fluorine. Although he liberated some of the gas, it immediately (and explosively) combined with hydrogen. (Fluorine was finally isolated, in 1886, by Moisson.)

In 1865 Gore was elected FRS, chiefly for being the discoverer of amorphous antimony and for his researches in electrochemistry; his supporters included Faraday, Joule, and Tyndall. In 1867 he toured laboratories and scientific institutions on the continent to assess teaching methods and organization. This was of great assistance to Sir Josiah Mason, who took great pains in seeking advice from those with such experience when establishing Mason Science College; it subsequently became an integral part of Birmingham University. Between 1870 and 1880 Gore taught chemistry and physics at King Edward's School, and in 1877 he was made an honorary LLD by the University of Edinburgh. In 1880 Gore founded his private Institute of Scientific Research at Easy Row, Birmingham, where he lived, serving as its director, until his death.

Gore's researches and discoveries in electrometallurgy soon established for him a high reputation in the city as a consulting chemist. Manufacturers in the electroplating industry often sought him out for solutions to their problems. He was also the author of numerous important textbooks which became standard works for many years, among them *The Art of Electro-Metallurgy* (1877), *The Art of Scientific Discovery* (1878), *The Scientific Basis of National Progress* (1882), *Electro-Chemistry: Inorganic* (1885), and *The Art of Electrolytic Separation of Metals* (1890). He also wrote on scientific education and research and on science and government; for both areas he was a staunch advocate. In later years he wrote more philosophically in works such as *The Scientific Basis of Morality* (1899) and *The New Scientific System of Morality* (1906) wherein he adopted a strongly materialistic viewpoint.

Gore was long fervently in favour of government support for scientific research and was one of those instrumental in procuring a grant of £4000 a year for the Royal Society to this end. He had turned down the offer of a knighthood in the 1880s but, having failed to make much money through his work, he was granted a civil-list pension of £150 a year in recognition of the value of his discoveries to the nation.

Gore died, of senile decay and exhaustion, on 20 December 1908 at 20 Easy Row, Birmingham. His wife had died the previous year. He was buried at Warstone Lane cemetery. By his will his residuary estate, of about £5000, was divided equally between the Royal Society and the Royal Institution, specially for 'assisting original scientific discovering'. The gift to the former was invested as 'the Gore Fund'. Such public disposal of Gore's property led to the grant of a civil-list pension of £50 to his daughter, Alice Augusta, in 1911. ROBERT SHARP

Sources *PRS*, 84A (1910–11), xxi–xxii · *The Electrician* (1 Jan 1909), 467 · *Nature*, 79 (1908–9), 290 · *Electrical Review*, 64 (1909), 28 · *The Times* (24 Dec 1908), 9 · m. cert. · d. cert. · D. P. Jones, 'Gore, George', *DSB* · *DNB*
Archives CUL, letters to Sir George Stokes
Likenesses M. Fox, carte-de-visite, RS · photograph (aged seventy?), Royal Society of Chemistry, London
Wealth at death £6802 10*s*. 8*d*.: probate, 25 Jan 1909, *CGPLA Eng. & Wales*

Gore, John, **Baron Annaly of Tenelick** (1718–1784), judge, was born on 2 March 1718, the second son of George Gore (1675–1753), puisne judge of the Irish court of common pleas, and Bridget, daughter and eventually sole heir of

John Sankey of Tenelick, co. Longford. John Gore was one of the 'nine Gores' (Ball, 2.159) who sat simultaneously in the Irish parliament, a fact which was attributable more to the state of patronage at the time than to any genetic predisposition. He matriculated at Dublin University as a fellow-commoner in 1734, entered the Middle Temple in 1736, and graduated as bachelor of arts in 1737. He was called to the bar of the King's Inns in Michaelmas term 1742, became king's counsel in 1749 and appeared as counsel to the commissioners of revenue. In 1747 he married Frances (1728–1794), second daughter of Richard Wingfield, first Viscount Powerscourt, by his second wife, Dorothy Beresford, daughter of Hercules Rowley. In March 1758 he succeeded his eldest brother, Arthur Gore, sometime MP for co. Longford, as owner of Tenelick. He became partner in the bank of Malone, Clements, and Gore together with Anthony Malone, who was chancellor of the Irish exchequer at the time and who, unusually even then, sat *ex officio* as a judge on the equity side of the court of exchequer. None of this was considered improper at the time, as long as all went well, but the bank crashed, in four months, in the autumn of 1758. Gore was himself MP for Jamestown from 1747 to 1760, and for co. Longford from 1761 to 1764. He was solicitor-general from 1760 to 1764. In September 1764 he was made chief justice of the Irish king's bench and sworn of the Irish privy council. On 17 January 1766 he was created Baron Annaly of Tenelick, and took his seat on 27 January. On 20 October 1767, and again in 1769, he was elected speaker of the Irish House of Lords, in the absence of the lord chancellor. He dissented from limiting the duration of parliaments in 1768, and from the vote of thanks to the volunteers in 1779. A comment in 1773, attributed to Blaquiere, Irish chief secretary, describes Gore as being 'as clean as any fellow in Ireland' (Bodkin, 145 at 204). He died on 3 April 1784 at his home in St Stephen's Green, Dublin. He was probably buried at Tashinny, co. Longford, but this is uncertain. There were no children and the title became extinct on his death. His younger brother, Lieutenant-Colonel Henry Gore, who inherited Tenelick, was created a peer by the same title, but he too died without issue. John Gore's will was proved in 1784. His wife, who was born on 2 June 1728, died on 31 July 1794 and was buried on 16 August 1794 at St Marylebone, Middlesex.

Gore was one of the characters in *Baratariana*, a collection of writings by Grattan, Flood, and others attacking the Townshend viceroyalty. He is portrayed as Baron Goreannelli, an Italian and a sportsman 'accomplished alike for the cabinet and the field', but is nevertheless attacked as a favourite of Townshend and incompetent, a charge Ball rejects, commenting that he 'did not lack judicial qualities', and citing his speech on the Valentia title (Ball, 2.159). Admitting his reactionary opposition to the limitation of the duration of parliaments, Ball nevertheless notes that he had certain patriotic Irish views, including being in favour of freeing Irish trade and opposed to absenteeism. He was affable and outgoing, being known to many as Jack. ANDREW LYALL

Sources GEC, *Peerage*, new edn, 1.163–4 • *N&Q*, 2nd ser., 8 (1859), 211 • *N&Q*, 8th ser., 8 (1895), 361, 363, 423 • F. E. Ball, *The judges in Ireland, 1221–1921*, 2 (1926), 150–51, 158, 194–5, 212–13 • Yorke to Hardwicke, 15 June 1758, BL, Add. MS 35595, fol. 214 • Yorke to Hardwicke, 10 Nov 1759, BL, Add. MS 35596, fols. 33, 98 • J. Lodge, *The peerage of Ireland*, rev. M. Archdall, rev. edn, 7 vols. (1789), vol. 3, pp. 111–12; vol. 5, p. 1 • C. J. Smyth, *Chronicle of the law officers of Ireland* (1839), 95, 179 • [J. H. Todd], ed., *A catalogue of graduates who have proceeded to degrees in the University of Dublin, from the earliest recorded commencements to … December 16, 1868* (1869), 227 • E. Keane, P. Beryl Phair, and T. U. Sadleir, eds., *King's Inns admission papers, 1607–1867*, IMC (1982) • [H. Grattan and others], *Baratariana: a select collection of fugitive political pieces*, ed. [Rev. Simpson] (1772) • PRO NIre., D 562/699; T 755, pp. 66, 70, 79, 305; D 562/562 • J. T. Gilbert, *History of Dublin* (1903), 1.294 • M. Bodkin, ed., 'Notes on the Irish parliament in 1773', *Proceedings of the Royal Irish Academy*, 48C (1942–3), 145–232, esp. 204

Gore, John (1729/30?–1790), circumnavigator and naval officer, was reputedly born in Virginia, and was presumably already an experienced seaman when, on 25 August 1755, he joined the *Windsor* (60 guns) at Portsmouth, and was rated midshipman. He was discharged to sick quarters in Plymouth on 31 January 1760, and passed his lieutenant's examination on 13 August that year, but he did not receive a commission for some time, serving instead as master's mate of the frigate *Aeolus* (*Eolus*, 32 guns) from 16 December 1762 to 30 November 1763.

Gore was next appointed master's mate of the sloop *Dolphin* (24 guns), under the Hon. John Byron, and between July 1764 and May 1766 he made his first voyage around the world in her. Three months after returning to England, and still as master's mate, he set out again in the *Dolphin*, this time with Captain Samuel Wallis in command. It was on this voyage that Tahiti was discovered, and owing to the ill health of the captain and first lieutenant some of their duties devolved on Gore, 'a tower of strength in the ship's company, imperturbable and absolutely reliable' (Carrington, xxxvii). During their month-long stay he led an expedition into the interior of Tahiti, upon which he wrote a report for the Admiralty.

Having arrived back in England on 20 May 1768, Gore was soon off again on his third circumnavigation of the globe, this time with a commission dated 20 July as third lieutenant of the bark *Endeavour*, commanded by Lieutenant James Cook. Gore's knowledge of the people, customs, and geography of Tahiti (Cook's principal destination) proved useful, as did his marksmanship with musket and bow: he signed his journal 'The Master Hunter', once challenged a Tahitian chief to an archery competition, and often accompanied Joseph Banks the naturalist on his forays in Tahiti, New Zealand, and New South Wales, shooting many birds and animals for Banks's collections. On 14 July 1770 he shot a kangaroo, thus obtaining the first specimen of that animal for science. He had earlier, unhappily, also been the first to shoot a Maori, in a dispute in New Zealand.

For five months in 1772 Gore accompanied his friend Banks on a private scientific expedition to Iceland, and thus missed Cook's second voyage. But on 10 February 1776 he joined the *Resolution* as first lieutenant. After the deaths of Cook and Clerke, Gore took command of the expedition on 22 August 1779, and brought the two ships home from Kamchatka in October 1780. He was rewarded with promotion to captain and the berth at Greenwich Hospital vacated by Cook, where he lived until his death on 10 August 1790.

Those who claim descent from him maintain that Gore married a Sarah Gilmore, and that Lieutenant Graham Gore, who perished with Franklin in the *Erebus* about 1847, was his grandson. Gore Bay and Gore Cove in New Zealand; Gore Island, Queensland; and Gore's Channel, Alaska, are named after John Gore, as was, formerly, St Lawrence Island in the Bering Sea. RANDOLPH COCK

Sources J. C. Beaglehole, *The life of Captain James Cook*, Hakluyt Society, 37 (1974) • *The journals of Captain James Cook*, ed. J. C. Beaglehole, 1, Hakluyt Society, 34a (1955) • *The journals of Captain James Cook*, ed. J. C. Beaglehole, 3/1–2, Hakluyt Society, 36a–b (1967) • *The discovery of Tahiti: a journal of the second voyage of HMS Dolphin round the world … written by her master George Robertson*, ed. H. Carrington, Hakluyt Society, 2nd ser., 98 (1948) • H. B. Carter, *Sir Joseph Banks, 1743–1820* (1988) • *The Endeavour journal of Joseph Banks, 1768–1771*, ed. J. C. Beaglehole, 2 vols. (1962) • lieutenant's passing certificate, PRO, ADM 107/5, 271 • pay books of *Aeolus*, *Windsor*, *Dolphin*, PRO, ADM 32/4, 178, 179, 441 • Gore's *Endeavour* journal, PRO, ADM 55/4548, vols. 3–4 • R. Hough, *Captain James Cook, a biography* (1994) • R. Parkin, *H.M. bark Endeavour* (1997) • *GM*, 1st ser., 60 (1790), 769 • *Annual Register* (1790)
Archives NL Aus., *Dolphin* log • PRO, ADM 107/5, 271; ADM 32/4, 178, 179, 441; ADM 55/4548, vols. 3–4
Likenesses J. Webber, oils, 1780, NL Aus.; repro. in www.nla.gov.au, 3 April 2002

Gore, Sir John (1772–1836), naval officer, was born at Kilkenny on 9 February 1772. He was the second son of John Gore (*d.* 1794), colonel of the 33rd regiment, and afterwards lieutenant-governor of the Tower of London, collaterally related to the family of the earls of Arran. He joined the *Canada* (Hon. William Cornwallis) in 1781, and served in her during the eventful West Indian campaign of 1782, returning to England towards the end of the year. He then served from 1783 to 1786 in the frigate *Iphigenia* in the West Indies, and on her paying off was appointed to the yacht *Royal Charlotte* with Cornwallis. He afterwards followed him to the *Crown*, in which Cornwallis went out as commodore of the East Indian station. In November 1789 Gore was promoted lieutenant; he returned home in the *Crown* in 1791, and in 1793 was appointed to the frigate *Lowestoft*, in which he went to the Mediterranean. From the *Lowestoft* he was moved to the *Britannia*, and afterwards to the *Victory*, Lord Hood's flagship; he served with distinction during the operations at Toulon and in Corsica, and on the surrender of Bastia on 22 May 1794 was promoted to the command of *La Flèche*, a captured corvette.

In the following November, Gore was posted to the *Windsor Castle* (98 guns), flagship of Rear-Admiral Linzee, and commanded her in the actions off Toulon on 13 March and 13 July 1795. He was then appointed to the *Censeur*, one of the prizes, and was taken prisoner in her when she was recaptured by the French squadron off Cape St Vincent on 7 October. After his return home Gore successively commanded the *Robust* (74 guns) and the frigate *Alcmène*, and in September 1796 was appointed to the *Triton*, a 32-gun frigate, which he commanded in the channel for nearly five years. During this time he captured many small cruisers and privateers, and on 18 October 1799 assisted in the capture of the *Santa Brigida* and *Thetis*, two Spanish frigates, each of 36 guns, homeward bound with very valuable treasure from Vera Cruz. Gore's share alone, as a captain, amounted to upwards of £40,000.

In consequence of an injury he received by the bursting of a gun, Gore was compelled to leave the *Triton* in the spring of 1801; but a few months later he was appointed to the frigate *Medusa* (32 guns), in which, during the operations off Boulogne, Lord Nelson hoisted his flag. The *Medusa* was afterwards sent into the Mediterranean, and was at Constantinople, in attendance on the ambassador, when Gore learned that the war was likely to recommence. He at once, and without orders, sailed to rejoin the admiral, Sir Richard Bickerton, and was employed as senior officer of the inshore squadron off Toulon, until the arrival of Nelson in July 1803, when he was sent to Gibraltar as senior officer in command of a small squadron to cruise in the straits, with orders to look out for French ships sent to strengthen the Toulon fleet. He continued there for more than a year, and had joined Captain Moore off Cadiz, when on 5 October 1804 the squadron captured three Spanish frigates, carrying specie and cargo worth considerably over £1 million: Gore's share must have been at least another £40,000. The *Medusa* being in want of repair was then sent home, and at Gore's request was chosen by his godfather, the Marquess Cornwallis, to take him to India. On 21 February 1805 Gore was made a knight, and he sailed for Calcutta on 15 April.

Gore returned to England early in 1806, and was shortly afterwards appointed to the *Revenge* (74 guns), in which he was actively employed in the Bay of Biscay. Early in 1807 he joined Collingwood off Cadiz, and continued there under the command of Rear-Admiral Purvis until June 1808, when he carried the Spanish commissioners for peace and alliance to England. He married Georgiana, eldest daughter of Admiral Sir George *Montagu, on 15 August 1808; they had one son and six daughters. From 1810 to 1812 he commanded the *Tonnant* (80 guns) in the Bay of Biscay and on the coast of Portugal, and in November 1812 was again appointed to the *Revenge*, which was sent to the Mediterranean. During the summer of 1813 he commanded the inshore squadron off Toulon; and from his promotion to rear-admiral (4 December 1813), with his flag in the *Revenge*, he commanded the detached squadron in the Adriatic until the peace of 1814.

In January 1815 Gore was made a KCB, and from 1818 to 1821 was commander-in-chief at the Nore. On 27 May 1825 he was promoted vice-admiral. In 1827 he was sent by the lord high admiral, the duke of Clarence, on a special mission to the Mediterranean after the battle of Navarino, on which he reported in Codrington's favour. From December 1831 to 1835 he was commander-in-chief in the East Indies. During this time his only son, serving as his flag lieutenant, was drowned in attempting to save a seaman who had fallen overboard. The loss affected him deeply, and possibly hastened his own death, which took place on 21 August 1836 at Datchet, Buckinghamshire, where he was buried. J. K. LAUGHTON, *rev.* ROGER MORRISS

Sources J. Marshall, *Royal naval biography*, suppl. 2 (1828), 466 · *GM*, 2nd ser., 6 (1836), 540 · J. Ralfe, *The naval biography of Great Britain*, 4 (1828), 460 · *United Service Journal*, 3 (1836), 243 · *The dispatches and letters of Vice-Admiral Lord Viscount Nelson*, ed. N. H. Nicolas, 7 vols. (1844–6) · E. Lodge, *Peerage, baronetage, knightage and companionage of the British empire*, 81st edn, 3 vols. (1912) · J. B. Bourchier, *Memoir of the life of Admiral Sir Edward Codrington: with selections from his public and private correspondence*, 2 (1873) · P. Mackesy, *The war in the Mediterranean, 1803–1810* (1957) · R. Muir, *Britain and the defeat of Napoleon, 1807–1815* (1996)

Archives BL, corresp. with Lord Nelson and others, Add. MSS 34912–34936 · NA Scot., letters to Lord Melville · NMM, letters to Lord Nelson · U. Nott., letters to Lord William Bentinck

Gore, John Ellard (1845–1910), astronomical writer, was born, probably at Athlone, co. Westmeath, Ireland, on 1 June 1845, the eldest son of John Ribton Gore (1820–1894), archdeacon of Achonry, and his wife, Frances Brabazon, *née* Ellard (1816–1896). After being educated privately he entered Trinity College, Dublin, where he obtained a licentiate in civil engineering with high distinction in 1865. Three years later, having passed second in the open competition, he joined the Indian government public works department and worked as assistant engineer on the construction of the Sirhind Canal in the Punjab. There, with a 3 inch achromatic telescope, he began his observation of the stars, which resulted in the publication of a small book entitled *Southern Objects for Small Telescopes* (1877).

Gore sailed from India to Ireland in the latter part of 1877, on two years' furlough. He never returned to India and in 1879 retired from the service and drew a pension for the remainder of his life. He lived first at Ballysadare, co. Sligo, with his parents until his father's death in 1894, when he moved to Dublin. He devoted himself to observations of the stars, principally with binoculars, and to writing on astronomy. Variable stars were the chief subject of his observations; W. W. Bryant, in his *History of Astronomy* (1907), named Gore as one of three leading observers of variable stars in Britain and Ireland. In 1884 he presented to the Royal Irish Academy a *Catalogue of Known Variable Stars* (enlarged and revised edn 1888). A similar compilation by him, giving a list of fifty-nine computed orbits of binary stars, was published by the academy in 1890. Gore published many papers in the *Monthly Notices of the Royal Astronomical Society* and collaborated with the talented Dublin astronomer William H. S. Monck (1839–1915). In response to Monck's suggestion in 1894 that there were two distinct classes of yellow star—one dull and near, the other bright and remote—Gore estimated the diameter of Arcturus. Although poor data led him to overestimate, the argument was sound and the existence of dwarf and giant stars was validated. Gore obtained enough data to have constructed a crude colour-luminosity diagram and to have foreshadowed the work of Hertzsprung and Russell, but he did not. In 1905 he estimated the density of the white dwarf star Sirius B but rejected his value of 44,000 times the density of water as being 'entirely out of the question'. At the same time he wrote much on astronomy for general reading and in 1894 translated from the French Flammarion's work under the title *Popular Astronomy*. His *Astronomical Essays* (1907) gathered articles and essays that had appeared in magazines. His last work was *Astronomical Curiosities: Facts and Fallacies* (1909).

Gore was elected a fellow of the Royal Astronomical Society on 8 March 1878, and was a member of the councils of the Royal Dublin Society and the Royal Irish Academy. He was an honorary member of the Liverpool Astronomical Society and of the Welsh Astronomical Society. From 1890 to 1899 he served as director of the variable star section of the British Astronomical Association. He was a fellow of the Société Astronomique de France and a corresponding fellow of the Astronomical Society of Canada. He died, unmarried, on 18 July 1910 from the effects of a street accident in Grafton Street, Dublin, and was buried in Mount Jerome cemetery, Dublin, on 22 July.

H. P. HOLLIS, *rev.* I. ELLIOTT

Sources *Monthly Notices of the Royal Astronomical Society*, 71 (1910–11), 256–7 · minute book, 16 March 1911, Royal Irish Acad. · *Irish Times* (19 July 1910) · *Irish Times* (22 July 1910) · A. P. FitzGerald, 'John Ellard Gore (1845–1910)', *Irish Astronomical Journal*, 7 (1965–6), 213–19 · D. Devorkin, 'Stellar evolution and the origin of the Hertzsprung–Russell diagram', *Astrophysics and twentieth-century astronomy to 1950*, ed. O. Gingerich (1984), 90–108, esp. 96–7 · *WWW* · *The Observatory*, 33 (1910), 316–18 · wills and administrations, 1895–6, NA Ire. · entrance records, TCD

Archives Armagh Planetarium, Armagh, Northern Ireland | NL Ire., books from Gore's library · Royal Irish Acad., books and pamphlets on astronomical subjects presented in 1909

Likenesses photograph, repro. in H. Macpherson, *Astronomers of today* (1905)

Wealth at death £878 3*s*. 2*d*.—in England: Irish probate sealed in London, 7 Sept 1910, *CGPLA Eng. & Wales* · £1068 13*s*. 6*d*.: probate, 6 Aug 1910, *CGPLA Ire.*

Gore, Margaret Wyndham (1913–1993), airwoman and osteopath, was born on 24 January 1913 at Carclew, Brighton Road, Worthing, the daughter of William Wyndham Gore, a mining engineer, and his wife, Martha Lord. Known as Margot, she had one brother, her twin. The family moved to Ireland and she grew up enjoying an adventurous childhood, riding her pony to the hunt and ignoring physical discomforts.

Margot Gore had a little formal education but this ceased at sixteen when the family returned to England. Her desire was to study medicine, but her basic education and lack of financial support prevented this. Instead, she turned to her second enthusiasm—flying. She had taken a menial job at Smithfield market in order to pay for her flying lessons. The formation of the Civil Air Guard in 1938, which provided subsidized flight training at civilian flying schools throughout the country, created a need for more instructors. This was the opportunity Margot needed, and by the outbreak of war she was instructing at Romford Flying Club, Essex. In spite of official disquiet, in January 1940 the women's section of the Air Transport Auxiliary (ATA) with its initial intake of eight experienced airwomen became a reality under its commandant, Pauline Gower. They were to supplement the older airmen who formed the ATA. Margot Gore was recruited with the second intake in June 1940 and quickly adapted to the role of flying new and repaired Tiger Moths between factories and operational airfields.

In September 1941, when no. 15 ferry pool Hamble-on-Solent became the second all-women's pool, Margot Gore was promoted captain and became its commanding officer. Here her natural qualities of leadership together with the high standard she set herself as a pilot earned her the respect of her team of fellow pilots, engineers, and administrative staff. In spite of the exhausting flying duties, often interrupted by enemy action, and the discomfort of return journeys by train in wartime winters, Hamble is remembered by the women who served there as having a happy, harmonious atmosphere.

In 1943 Gore was the first woman to go to RAF Marston Moor class 5 unit to convert to flying the Handley Page four-engined Halifax bomber, quickly followed by a further ten women who made up the eleven ATA women qualified to fly any type of aircraft. Margot herself is believed to have been the first woman to fly the huge Boeing B17, generally known as the 'Flying Fortress'. Once when flying an American Lockheed Hudson in the heavily defended Southampton–Portsmouth area she had a narrow escape on encountering a large barrage balloon, rising just as she was approaching Eastleigh. She managed to clear the lethal cables by inches.

For her wartime services Gore was appointed MBE in 1945, and when the war ended she continued flying as chief flying instructor at the West London Flying Club at White Waltham, Berkshire. On the formation of the WAAF Voluntary Reserve in October 1947, the first recruits were Margot Gore and her former ATA colleague Joan Naylor.

By 1948 Gore began to consider again the possibility of a career in her earlier interest of medicine and, with encouragement from her close friend Ben Blediscoe, she decided on a career in osteopathy. With characteristic thoroughness, she studied chemistry, physics, and biology to higher certificate standard in order to gain entrance to the British School of Osteopathy (BSO) in September 1951. Qualifying in June 1954, she was awarded the gold medal as the outstanding student of her year. She started a private practice in Kensington but nevertheless kept close links with the BSO. Motivated no doubt by her own early lack of educational qualifications, she became in the late 1950s one of the five lecturers to introduce a basic science course for first-year students lacking the necessary A levels or first MB science qualifications. In 1964 she was appointed head of the department of anatomy and physiology, and the following year was elected to the board of governing directors of the BSO, serving as the board representative on the council of the Osteopathic Educational Foundation. She became vice-chairman of the Osteopathic Educational Foundation in 1968. In 1970 she moved with her elderly mother to Cookley Green, Oxfordshire, and reduced her practising activities.

Gore's exceptional organizing ability was recognized when she served as chairman of the board of governing directors of the BSO (1978–82). This was a key period in the school's history in which Gore led the team that realized the capital of the freehold of 16 Buckingham Gate and purchased a long lease on nos. 1–4 Suffolk Street, thus increasing the student accommodation from 80 to 400 and enabling the clinic to take an extra 300 patients per week. It was this move in 1979, allied to the educational expansion and reorganization, that culminated in the validation of the diploma course to honours degree status. In recognition of her outstanding services to the school Margot was awarded an honorary fellowship of the BSO in 1983.

Margot Gore was an accomplished golfer and played at county level. In later life she became the ladies' captain of the Huntercombe Golf Club. She was a very private person and rarely attended social functions, and only those professional functions where her presence was expected. However, she co-operated in making documentary films concerning the ATA for the BBC in 1984 and recorded an interview with the Imperial War Museum in 1986. Margot Gore died of cancer on 20 August 1993 at the Sue Ryder Home, Nettlebed, Oxfordshire. ENID DEBOIS

Sources L. Curtis, *The forgotten pilots: a story of the Air Transport Auxiliary, 1939–45* (1971) • private information (2004) [Lady Audrey Percival; J. Coleman] • A. King, *Golden wings: the story of some of the women ferry pilots of the Air Transport Auxiliary* (1956) • J. Coleman, *Forgotten pilots*, 1984, BBC [Alison King, operations officer, Hamble] • M. Gore, interview, 1986, IWM SA, acc. no. 9285 • b. cert. • d. cert. • *CGPLA Eng. & Wales* (1993) • *The Guardian* (25 Sept 1993) • *The forgotten pilots*, BBC documentary film, 1984

Archives FILM BBC Television Archives, *The forgotten pilots*, BBC 1984 • IWM FVA | SOUND IWM SA, 2 hour tape, 47 page transcript, 1984, 1986

Likenesses R. Lovesay, group portrait, 1991 (*A tribute to women aviators*), priv. coll.

Wealth at death £132,649: probate, 28 Sept 1993, *CGPLA Eng. & Wales*

Gore, Montagu (1800–1864), politician, was the eldest son of the Revd Charles Gore of Barrow Court, Somerset, and his wife, Harriet, daughter of Richard Little of Grosvenor Place, London. He matriculated at Christ Church, Oxford, on 8 May 1818 but took no degree. He became a student of Lincoln's Inn in 1821. He was elected for Devizes as a Liberal in 1832 and resigned his seat on joining the tories in 1834. He won Barnstaple as a free-trade Conservative in 1841, having published his *Thoughts on the Corn Laws* in 1840, but could not find a seat as a Peelite in 1847 and never sat in the Commons again. Gore was a well-known contributor to the press, and the author of many pamphlets on political and social subjects, especially with respect to Ireland, the dwellings of the poor, and national defence. He took much interest in the welfare of sailors, and was an active member of the committee of the National Lifeboat Institution. His family seat was Barrow Court, Somerset. He died unmarried at his house, 9 Chapel Place, London, on 5 October 1864. J. M. SCOTT, *rev.* H. C. G. MATTHEW

Sources *North Devon Journal* (13 Oct 1864) • *GM*, 3rd ser., 17 (1864), 668–9 • *Dod's Parliamentary Companion* • Boase, *Mod. Eng. biog.*

Wealth at death under £200: probate, 17 Oct 1864, *CGPLA Eng. & Wales*

Gore, Sir Ralph, fourth baronet (*c.*1675–1733), speaker of the Irish House of Commons, was born at Manorhamilton in co. Leitrim, the son of Sir William Gore, third baronet (*c.*1642–*c.*1703), landowner, of Manor Gore, co. Donegal, and his wife, Hannah (*d.* 1733), daughter and coheir of James Hamilton of Manorhamilton. He was admitted to Trinity College, Dublin, in 1693 but did not stay long enough to take his degree. He married his first wife, Elizabeth, daughter of Sir Robert Colvill of Newtownards, co. Down, in 1705. They had two daughters, one of whom, Rose, married Anthony *Malone (1700–1776), politician, in 1733. Having been elected to the Irish parliament for the first time in 1703 for Donegal borough, chiefly on his own family's interest but perhaps also in co-operation with William Conolly (the most important political figure in the north-west of Ireland, who controlled the nearby borough of Killybegs), Gore transferred to the county in the general election of 1713, and retained this seat in 1715.

After a lengthy and unspectacular parliamentary apprenticeship, distinguished only by a solidly whig voting record, Gore was appointed in 1717 to the lucrative office of chancellor of the Irish exchequer, on the recommendation of Conolly, now speaker of the Commons in Dublin. Gore's own standing among Irish whigs had not been high enough for him to share in the general redistribution of places that followed the Hanoverian succession and the downfall of the previous tory administration, and even now there were those who questioned his qualifications for such an important office. The lord chancellor of Ireland, Lord Brodrick, Conolly's main rival for the leadership of the government interest, observed that Gore relied on 'a certain person and party here' who 'represent his merit and interest very much beyond the just size of either' (Midleton MS 1248/4, fols. 29–30, Lord Brodrick to Thomas Brodrick, 23 May 1717). More brutally, Brodrick described Gore as Conolly's 'creature', one who 'hath a spirit low enough not to disdain being thought a dependant' (ibid., fols. 35–6, 14 June 1717). Technically, Gore's lack of a legal education might have disqualified him from the post, but he was quickly admitted to the Irish bar and provided with a doctorate of laws by Trinity College. Over the next decade he proved himself a useful assistant to Conolly in parliamentary management, without making any mark as an orator. In 1719 he introduced on behalf of the speaker a bill to enable Protestant dissenters to hold some civil and military offices (a stratagem which Brodrick's faction was able to counter), and as chancellor of the exchequer he played an important role in supply legislation, taking the chair of the committees of supply and of ways and means. His involvement in the ill-fated attempt to establish a national bank in Ireland in 1720–21 probably lost him money but not reputation. Nevertheless, he relinquished his county seat in the Irish general election of 1727, in favour of the episcopal pocket borough of Clogher, a see once held by Bishop St George *Ashe, the father of his second wife, Elizabeth Ashe (*d.* 1741). Gore and his second wife, who was heir to the St George estate in Dunmore, co. Galway, had four daughters and three sons.

In September 1729, when Conolly suffered the fit which destroyed his health, Gore was the first person thought of by colleagues in the court party to succeed. He was duly elected as speaker on 13 October 1729, and thus became the government's principal parliamentary 'undertaker', but refused Conolly's vacant place at the head of the revenue board, despite the influence it would have given him over patronage, preferring to retain the salary of £800 p.a. and extensive fees of his own office. The chief commissionership went instead to his close ally, Marmaduke Coghill. Together the two men rallied Conolly's friends sufficiently to maintain a working majority for the court in the parliamentary session of 1729–30, though they were unable to secure the long-term funding of the Irish national debt that the viceroy, Lord Carteret, had hoped for, since any proposal of this kind aroused the 'patriotic' sensibilities of back-bench MPs. There were also difficulties in Gore's relationship with the Church of Ireland primate, Hugh Boulter, who assumed the responsibility of representing the 'English interest' in Ireland, and checking the ambitions of the 'undertakers'. During the 1729–30 session Gore opposed Boulter's plan for a reform of the Irish coinage, and although the two men were both appointed as lords justices to govern Ireland after Carteret's departure, they were at odds again over the appointment of a new chief baron of the Irish exchequer, Gore recommending an Irish, and Boulter an English, candidate. During preparations for the next parliamentary session differences arose between Gore and Boulter on the issue of the supply, but these evaporated with the arrival of a new lord lieutenant, the duke of Dorset. Gore was an effective commons manager for Dorset in 1731–2, though again potentially controversial issues had to be side-stepped, the long-term funding of the debt and (even more dangerous) a proposed repeal of the sacramental test, which Sir Robert Walpole endorsed but which Gore argued strongly and successfully against.

After having been reappointed with Boulter as a lord justice in the spring of 1732, Gore died, after a short illness, on 23 February 1733 and was buried at Christ Church in Dublin. His second son, Ralph (1725–1802), who succeeded his brother Sir St George Gore as sixth baronet, enjoyed a successful army career and was raised to the Irish peerage as earl of Ross in 1772. D. W. Hayton

Sources GEC, *Baronetage*, 1.234 • Burke, *Peerage* (1890), 597 • Burtchaell & Sadleir, *Alum. Dubl.*, 2nd edn • E. Keane, P. Beryl Phair, and T. U. Sadleir, eds., *King's Inns admission papers, 1607–1867*, IMC (1982), 194 • *Letters written by … Hugh Boulter … to several ministers of state*, ed. [A. Philips and G. Faulkner], 2 vols. (1769–70); repr. (1770), vol. 1, pp.111–13, 267, 269; vol. 2, pp. 1–75 • R. E. Burns, *Irish parliamentary politics in the eighteenth century*, 2 vols. (1989–90) • P. McNally, *Parties, patriots and undertakers: parliamentary politics in early Hanoverian Ireland* (1997) • BL, Add. MS 34777, fol. 27 • Surrey HC, Midleton MS 1248 • PRO, State papers Ireland, 1715–33 (SP 63/–396) • corresp. of Marmaduke Coghill to Edward Southwell, sen. and jun., 1729–33, BL, Add. MSS 21122–21123 • PRO NIre., Shannon MSS, D 2707 •

PRO NIre., Castleward MSS, D 2092 • A. Vicars, ed., *Index to the prerogative wills of Ireland, 1536–1810* (1897), 198

Gore, Spencer Frederick (1878–1914), painter, was born on 26 May 1878 at Epsom, Surrey, the third of four children of Spencer William Gore (*d.* 1908), a partner in Smiths Gore, agents to the ecclesiastical commissioners, and holder of the first lawn tennis championship at Wimbledon (1877), and his wife, Amy Margaret Smith. The family lived at Holywell in Kent. Freddy—as he was known—was sent, like his elder brother, to Harrow School (1892–6). There he displayed some of his inherited sporting prowess, keeping wicket for the second eleven and winning the Harrow mile. He grew very tall (throughout his life his trousers always hung awkwardly). He also developed his interest in art, winning the drawing prize. After leaving Harrow he attended the Slade School of Fine Art, London (1896–9), studying under Frederick Brown, Henry Tonks, and Philip Wilson Steer, and learning much from their brand of English impressionism. His friends included Harold Gilman, Albert Rothenstein (later Rutherston), Augustus John, and Wyndham Lewis.

With Lewis, Gore visited Madrid in 1902, partly to study the work of Goya. In the summer of 1904, on a painting trip in Normandy, he visited Walter Sickert, who was living in a self-imposed exile at Dieppe. The meeting was propitious. Sickert, then in his mid-forties, was inspired by Gore's account of the rising generation of Slade students and returned to England after an absence of some seven years. And Gore was excited to come into contact with a painter who was so intimately connected with the artistic traditions of French impressionism.

From Sickert himself Gore learned the practice of painting in the studio from small, well-documented drawings done from life. Although Gore continued to paint landscapes *en plein air*, Sickert's technique (learned from his friend and mentor Degas) was useful for the complex theatrical subjects he was beginning to attempt. Gore shared Sickert's love of the theatre and the music-hall (he was himself an excellent and enthusiastic amateur performer, specializing in comic policemen and irate Victorian fathers). At about this time he also came into contact with Lucien Pissarro, and from him he learned more directly of the techniques of French impressionist painting, as espoused by Camille Pissarro (Lucien's father). Gore began to adopt such techniques, eschewing black and building up his pictures with dry touches of unmediated colour on a white ground.

In 1906 Gore's father deserted the family after his business failed. Gore was urged by his uncle—the bishop of Oxford—to give up painting. He stood firm, however, and henceforth strove to earn his living with his brush. His mother, granted a pension by the firm, moved to Garth House, Hertingfordbury, Hertfordshire. (Gore, alone of his family, continued to keep in contact with his disgraced father, who died two years later.) Although Gore spent his summers painting the country (at Billy in France, in Yorkshire, at Hertingfordbury, and at Applehayes in Somerset), following Sickert's lead he gravitated to the Camden Town area of London. He had rooms at 15 Granby Street, and often shared Sickert's studio at 6 Mornington Crescent.

Although an occasional exhibitor with the New English Art Club (he was even elected as a member in 1909), Gore—like many of his generation—felt out of sympathy with its increasingly conservative stance. As a result he became involved in a series of initiatives to promote the claims of more progressive art. Together with Sickert, Gilman, and a few others he founded the Fitzroy Street Group, renting a first-floor room at 19 Fitzroy Street, where members' pictures were exhibited and tea was served to prospective clients every Saturday. And in 1908 Gore and Gilman assisted the critic Frank Rutter in the setting up of the Allied Artists' Association, a non-jury society, modelled on the Salon des Indépendents, which held annual exhibitions at the Royal Albert Hall. In 1911 Gore was elected as the first president of the *Camden Town Group, the alliance which evolved out of the Fitzroy Street Group. In March of the same year he had his first—and only—one-man show at the Chenil Gallery, London.

Artistically Gore had begun to move beyond impressionism, towards a post-impressionist style founded, in part, on the examples of Gauguin and (subsequently) Derain. The impact of Roger Fry's ground-breaking 'Post-impressionist exhibition' (1910) and of the Gauguin exhibition at the Stafford Gallery (1911) became increasingly marked in Gore's paintings, with their flat colours and strongly marked contours. Gore's position as, perhaps, the leading British exponent of the new style was confirmed when several of his pictures—including *The Cinder Path* (Tate collection) and *Letchworth Station* (National Railway Museum, York)—were selected for the English section of the 'Second post-impressionist exhibition' (1912). He also organized the group of artists (Gilman, Charles Ginner, Lewis, Jacob Epstein, and Eric Gill) who decorated the Cave of the Golden Calf, the night-club set up by Madame Strindberg (widow of the playwright). On account of his personality and his talent Gore was recognized as a leader by his contemporaries. He sought—and very nearly managed—to bring together all the progressive strains of British art under a single banner, in the exhibition he curated at Brighton, and in the London Group which was established in 1912 (and had its first exhibition in 1913). In the event the difficulty of reconciling Roger Fry with Wyndham Lewis proved too much, though characteristically both men maintained their affection for, and admiration of, Gore.

On 19 February 1912 Gore married Mary Johanna (Molly; *b.* 1888/9), daughter of John Kerr. (Sickert was best man.) A daughter, Elizabeth, was born that October, at Letchworth, where Gore had rented Gilman's house. The young family subsequently moved to 6 Cambrian Road, Richmond, where a son, Frederick (also a painter), was born in 1913. Gore's paintings of Richmond show a new stylistic departure, inspired by his study of Cézanne. It was while painting in the park in the early months of 1914 that Gore contracted a cold which developed into pneumonia. He died at home on 25 March 1914 and was buried in Hertingfordbury. His death called forth numerous tributes, from artists as diverse as Sickert and Lewis. All regarded Gore as a rare talent and a rare friend. His quiet good humour, his eager enthusiasms, his unstinting kindness, and his rare common sense endeared him to a whole generation of artists. MATTHEW STURGIS

Sources F. Farmar, ed., *The painters of Camden Town, 1905–1920* (1988) · W. Baron, *The Camden Town Group* (1979) · F. Gore, 'Spencer Gore: a memoir by his son', *Spencer Frederick Gore, 1878–1914* (1974) [exhibition catalogue, Anthony d'Offay Gallery, London, 26 March – 3 May 1974] · J. Woodeson, introduction, *Spencer Gore* (1970) [exhibition catalogue, Colchester, Oxford, and Sheffield, 2 March – 7 June 1970] · F. Gore and R. Shone, *Spencer Frederick Gore* (1983) [exhibition catalogue, Anthony d'Offay Gallery, London, 11 Feb – 30 March 1983] · b. cert. · m. cert. · *CGPLA Eng. & Wales* (1914)

Likenesses A. Rutherston, oils, 1902, NPG · H. Gilman, oils, *c.*1906–1907, Leeds City Art Gallery · S. F. Gore, self-portrait, oils, 1914, NPG

Wealth at death £588 14*s*. 0*d*.: administration, 22 May 1914, *CGPLA Eng. & Wales*

Gore, Thomas (1632–1684), writer on heraldry, was born at Alderton, Wiltshire, on 20 March 1632, the third son of Charles Gore (*d.* 1649) and his wife, Lydia (1601–1654), daughter and heir of William White, of the Drapers' Company in London. Of his eight siblings only one sister, Anna, survived to adulthood, and marriage to John Scrope of Castle Combe. Following the death of the eldest son, Edward, in 1628, and the second, Charles, in 1641, Thomas became heir to his father's estate. He was educated under Thomas Tully at Tetbury grammar school, Gloucestershire, and entered Magdalen College, Oxford, as a gentleman commoner, matriculated in December 1650 and took the degree of BA. Meanwhile he was admitted to Lincoln's Inn on 2 October 1651.

When his mother died Gore retired to his patrimony and dedicated himself thereafter to the study of heraldry and antiquities, amassing a choice library on these topics. His marriage at Bristol on 18 September 1656 to Mary (*d.* 1718), daughter of Michael and Elizabeth Meredith, of Southwoode, Gloucestershire, brought them two sons, Thomas (1665–1697), who married Frances, daughter of John Eyre of Little Chelfield, Wiltshire, and Edward (*d.* 1677), and a daughter, Mary (1663–1690), who married Thomas Poulden of Imber, Wiltshire.

Among his friends Gore counted the antiquarian John Aubrey, whose estate at Broad Chalke was mortgaged some period before to Thomas and Charles Gore as trustees for their sister Anna. This friendship seems to have curdled in later years, for Aubrey in 1671 wrote to Wood describing Gore as 'a fidling peevish fellow, and something related to my adversaries' (Jackson, 'Memoir', 107); and in 1680: 'Pray write to the cuckold at "*Alderton, alias Aldrington*" to enquire … but he is a yare man and afraid of my queries as many people are when we want to preserve the memories of their Relations' (ibid.). 'Alderton, alias Aldrington', the term Gore always used to describe his village, poked fun at his tendency to carry precision and accuracy to such excess as to become ludicrously formal in trifling matters.

Gore collected and added to various genealogical manuscripts. In *A Table, Showing how to Blazon a Coat Several Ways* (1655) he replicated Sir John Ferne's *Blazon of Gentrie* (1586). His own publications were merely lists: *Nomenclator geographicus Latino-Anglicus et Anglo-Latinus, alphabetice digestus* … (1667; a second edition was in hand when he died); and *Catalogus alphabetice digestus, plerumque omnium authorum qui de re heraldica Latine, Gallice, Italice, Hispanice, Germanice, Anglice, scriptserunt* (1668). An enlarged edition of the latter in 1674 bore the title *Catalogus in certa capita, seu classes, alphabetico ordine concinnatus* …. This work received a bad notice in the *Biographie universelle*.

Gore's wealth and status led to his election in 1681 as high sheriff of Wiltshire. Some dishonourable acts of his under-officers obliged him to publish the same year one sheet entitled 'Loyalty displayed and Falsehood unmark'd … in a letter to a friend'. He died at Alderton on 31 March 1684 and was buried in the chancel of Alderton church. Gore's lengthy will detailed every single item of furniture, furnishings, jewellery, silverware, and so forth which he had inherited from his forebears, and those which his wife had brought to their marriage, or which he had subsequently given her, which she was to receive. His daughter received £2200 and several treasures inherited from his parents, while his son Thomas inherited over 400 acres of property plus Gore's ancient coins, his watch and dials, globes, quadrants, and other mathematical instruments. The direct male line ended with the death of Thomas's son Walter in 1712. The properties then passed through the female line but were ultimately broken up and the manuscripts dispersed about 1800. ANITA MCCONNELL

Sources J. E. Jackson, ed., *The topographical collections of John Aubrey FRS* (1862) · Wood, *Ath. Oxon.* · J. E. Jackson, 'The last will of Thomas Gore, the antiquary', *Wiltshire Magazine*, 14 (1874), 1–12 · pedigree of the Gore family, 1639, BL, Add. MS 61452 · *N&Q*, 2nd ser., 11 (1861), 284 · *GM*, 1st ser., 62 (1792), 522–3 · J. E. Jackson, 'Memoir of John Aubrey FRS', *Wiltshire Magazine*, 4 (1858), 92–108 · 'Gore, Thomas', *Biographie universelle, ancienne et moderne*

Archives BL, notes on Wiltshire gentry and Scrope family, Add. MSS 28020, 28209 · Bodl. Oxf., book of arms | BL, letters to second Lord Hatton, Add. MSS 22592–22593 · Bodl. Oxf., letters of Anthony Wood

Wealth at death furniture, jewellery, etc. to wife; £2200 and 'treasures' to daughter; over 400 acres of property and collections of artefacts to son

Gore, Walter (1910–1979). *See under* Hinton, Paula Doris (1924–1996).

Gore, William George Arthur Ormsby-, fourth Baron Harlech (1885–1964), politician and banker, was born in Eaton Square, London, on 11 April 1885, the only child of George Ralph Charles Ormsby-Gore (1855–1938) who became in 1904 the third Baron Harlech, and his wife, Lady Margaret Ethel Gordon (*d.* 1950), daughter of the tenth marquess of Huntly. He was educated at Eton College, and New College, Oxford, where he obtained a second class in modern history in 1907.

Ormsby-Gore was elected in January 1910, by a majority of eight, Unionist MP for Denbigh, moving in 1918 to Stafford, a seat he retained until he succeeded to the peerage on his father's death in 1938. He married on 12 April 1913

Lady Beatrice Edith Mildred Gascoyne-Cecil (*d.* 1980), daughter of the fourth marquess of Salisbury. They had three sons and three daughters.

Commissioned in the Shropshire yeomanry in 1908, Ormsby-Gore joined up when war broke out in 1914 and was on active service in Egypt when in 1916 he joined the Arab bureau as an intelligence officer attached to the high commissioner, Sir A. Henry McMahon. He was recalled in March 1917 at the instance of Lord Milner to be his parliamentary private secretary and also, a little later, an assistant secretary to the cabinet assisting Sir Mark Sykes. Impressed by Zionism while in Egypt, he established cordial relations with its leader in London, Chaim Weizmann, who took refuge in his office while the cabinet approved, on 31 October 1917, the Balfour declaration, and with whose support he was appointed British liaison officer with the Zionist mission sent to the Holy Land in March 1918. He returned to London in August and was a member of the British delegation to the Paris peace conference in 1919. He attended the meetings of the permanent mandates commission, of which he was the first British member, in October 1921 and August 1922. In the winter of 1921–2 he accompanied the under-secretary for the colonies, E. F. L. Wood, on a mission to the West Indies.

An unusually appropriate apprenticeship thus preceded Ormsby-Gore's appointment, in October 1922, as parliamentary under-secretary at the Colonial Office. He remained there until 1929 except for the brief interval of the first Labour government in 1924, during which he was appointed by its colonial secretary, J. H. Thomas, as chairman of an all-party commission which visited east and central Africa in the autumn, advised against any immediate federation of these territories, and recommended a loan of £10 million, guaranteed by the Treasury, mainly for the improvement of transport, anticipating much of the thinking behind the Colonial Development Act of 1929. In 1926 he visited west Africa and in 1928 Ceylon, Malaya, and Java. He was made a privy councillor in February 1927 and was in charge of the Colonial Office from July of that year until the following January during the empire tour of the colonial secretary, Leopold Amery.

Ormsby-Gore's knowledgeable enthusiasm for the arts, well exemplified in his book *Florentine Sculptors of the Fifteenth Century* (1930), resulted in a long and active association with the work of the major British galleries and museums. He was a trustee of the National Gallery from 1927 to 1934 and again from 1936 to 1941, of the Tate Gallery from 1934 to 1937 and again from 1945 to 1953, a life trustee of the British Museum from 1937, president of the National Museum of Wales from 1937, and was chairman of the Standing Commission on Museums and Galleries in 1949. He inherited a fine family library and although obliged to reduce its size when he ceased to live at Brogyntyn in Shropshire in 1955, he later added many rare books. He was president of the National Library of Wales from 1950 to 1958.

In the National Government of 1931 Ormsby-Gore was postmaster-general without a cabinet seat, and in November of that year he became first commissioner of works with a seat in the cabinet, an office he retained until his appointment as colonial secretary in May 1936. Under his auspices a determined effort was made to improve the architectural standards of new post offices and labour exchanges. He also wrote four volumes in the series Guide to the Ancient Monuments of England (1935, two in 1936, and 1948).

During the two years he was colonial secretary, Ormsby-Gore had little opportunity for the constructive work for which he was so well equipped by temperament and experience. (Perhaps no other colonial secretary had as much first-hand knowledge of the colonial empire.) In the month in which he took office, the Arabs demanded that Jewish immigration into Palestine and purchase of land there should be ended and attacked Jewish lives and property. A royal commission, headed by Lord Peel, reported in July 1937 that the mandate was unworkable and recommended partition and the creation of a much truncated but independent Jewish state. The government, on Ormsby-Gore's recommendation, accepted these proposals. He did not, however, succeed in persuading parliament to endorse them but only to agree that the scheme might be put before the League of Nations while making clear that parliament was not committed even to the principle of partition, much less the commission's actual proposals. As the international situation worsened, the British government became increasingly concerned to appease the hostility of the Arab states to any continuing Jewish immigration. Ormsby-Gore considered himself committed to partition. He was also an outspoken critic of Nazi Germany so that it was hardly surprising that when on his succession to the peerage in May 1938 he felt constrained to offer his resignation, the prime minister, Neville Chamberlain, should have accepted it.

As fourth Baron Harlech he served as commissioner for civil defence in the north-east region from 1939 to 1940 but his keen and active disposition chafed at the restraints still imposed by Whitehall. In 1941 he became British high commissioner in South Africa. He greatly admired the intellectual range of its prime minister, J. C. Smuts, but found little else to admire in the politics and society of that country. The long association between Smuts and Churchill and many other leading British personalities sharply limited the intermediary role of the high commissioner, although his informative reports were appreciated by C. R. Attlee, then secretary of state for the dominions.

After Harlech's return to London in 1944 he became a director of the Midland Bank, of which he was chairman from 1952 to 1957. It incorporated the London Joint Stock Bank which his great-grandfather had helped to establish in 1836. He was also chairman of the Bank of British West Africa from 1951 to 1961. Under his auspices, staff conditions and training were improved and substantial expansion of commercial business in Africa promoted.

Appointed GCMG in 1938, Harlech was created KG in 1948. He was constable of Harlech Castle from 1938, of Caernarfon Castle from 1946 to 1963, and lord lieutenant of Merioneth from 1938 to 1957. He received three honorary degrees, and was made an honorary fellow of his former college, New College, Oxford, in 1936. He devoted much time to the University of Wales, of which he was pro-chancellor from 1945 to 1957.

A convinced Conservative, Harlech was prominent in the tory revolt that ended the coalition in 1922 and remained a firm supporter of Baldwin in the party divisions on Indian reform. He opposed the Hoare–Laval plan to accommodate Italian aggression in Ethiopia (thereby earning from Neville Chamberlain, with Walter E. Elliot and Oliver F. G. Stanley, the contemptuous sobriquet of the Boys' Brigade) and was bitterly hostile to Nazi Germany. Unusually receptive of ideas, he was always outspoken and sometimes impetuous. At the Colonial Office in the twenties he sought to promote scientific research and its application to the medical and agricultural problems of tropical dependencies and took a leading part in the attempt to develop educational policies more consonant with African environments, but constructive development was largely frustrated by financial constraints. His hope in 1918 that Zionist objectives might be attained without political domination soon appeared visionary but his acceptance of partition, if inopportune in the international situation in 1938, was a courageous assessment of realities in Palestine. Perhaps his deepest interests were in the arts, especially architecture, of which his knowledge was extensive.

Harlech died in Bayswater, London, on 14 February 1964. His wife survived him. A lady of the bedchamber from 1941, she was created DCVO in 1947 and was made an extra lady of the bedchamber to Queen Elizabeth the queen mother in 1953. Their eldest son was killed in a motor accident in 1935 and the title passed to their elder surviving son, Sir (William) David Ormsby *Gore.

K. E. ROBINSON, *rev.*

Sources *The Times* (15 Feb 1964) · *The letters and papers of Chaim Weizmann, series A*, ed. M. W. S. Weisgal, 8 and 9 (1977) · M. Gilbert, *Exile and return: the emergence of Jewish statehood* (1978) · *Midbank Chronicle* (March 1964) · R. H. Fry, *Bankers in West Africa* (1976) · League of Nations permanent mandates commission, *Minutes*, 1921–7, 1937 · private information (1981) · Burke, *Peerage* (1999) · *CGPLA Eng. & Wales* (1964)

Archives NL Wales, corresp. and papers | BL, corresp. with P. V. Emrys-Evans, Add. MS 58244 · Bodl. RH, corresp. with Sir Granville Orde Browne · Bodl. RH, corresp. with Arthur Creech Jones · Bodl. RH, corresp. with Lord Lugard · Bodl. RH, corresp. with J. H. Oldham · NA Scot., corresp. with Lord Lothian

Likenesses O. Birley, oils, 1930–39, priv. coll. · D. Bell, oils, 1950, NMG Wales · R. Broadley, oils, 1952, HSBC Group Archives, London, Midland Bank archives · J. Gunn, group portrait, oils, 1954–9 (*Society of Dilettanti conversation piece*), Brooks's Club, London · J. Gunn, oils, *c.*1954–1959, Althorp, Northamptonshire · I. Williams, oils, NL Wales

Wealth at death £192,209: probate, 25 May 1964, *CGPLA Eng. & Wales*

Gore-Booth. For this title name *see* Booth, Paul Henry Gore-, Baron Gore-Booth of Maltby (1909–1984).

Gore-Booth, Constance, **Countess Markievicz**. *See* Markievicz, Constance Georgine, Countess Markievicz in the Polish nobility (1868–1927).

Gorell. For this title name *see* Barnes, John Gorell, first Baron Gorell (1848–1913).

Gorer, Geoffrey (1905–1985), anthropologist and author, was born on 26 March 1905 in London, the eldest of the three sons of Edgar Ezekiel Gorer (1872–1915), a London art dealer of note who died on the *Lusitania*, and Rachel Alice (Rée) Cohen (1873–1954). The immunologist and geneticist Peter Alfred Isaac *Gorer (1907–1961) was his younger brother. He was educated at Charterhouse School, spent a year at the Sorbonne (1922–3), graduated in 1927 from Jesus College, Cambridge, with a double first in classics and modern languages, and then passed the following year at the University of Berlin.

As a young man Gorer saw himself as an imaginative writer, but his plays were not staged and he could not find a publisher for his picaresque novel. His first published book, *The Revolutionary Ideas of the Marquis de Sade* (1934), enjoyed considerable critical success. Gorer was the first writer outside France to recognize de Sade as more than a purveyor of pornographic filth. The book was also his first attempt to explain modern social phenomena in psychological terms: in this case, the popular vote for the Nazis.

Gorer's travels in the mid-1930s to Africa and the Far East drew him closer to the academic study of cross-cultural variation. On a trip to the USA in 1935 he met Margaret Mead, whose intimate colleague Ruth Benedict was then reviewing his *Africa Dances* (1935, repr. 1945, 1949). Over the four months of his stay, Benedict informally instructed him in social anthropology. Mead became a very close friend for the rest of their lives. Though he espoused long-term study of a people, his only intensive fieldwork was a three-month spell among the Lepchas of Sikkim, published as *Himalayan Village* (1938). Because of the injuries he sustained when he fell off a rock while in the Himalayas, he was advised, at least for the immediate future, to avoid further fieldwork in non-westernized areas.

Instead Gorer deepened his social and psychological studies into western peoples. In 1939 he went to live in the USA when the humanities division of the Rockefeller Institute invited him to study the impact of radio and film on Americans. Subsequently he worked for the allied authorities on a series of investigations of national character. From his own account, his first such study, 'Japanese character structure and propaganda', produced as a mimeograph, had a 'quite fantastic circulation and influence' ('The Gorer papers', University of Sussex website). After the war he worked with Benedict and Mead on a series of studies of 'cultures at a distance'. His *The Americans* (1948) was an analytical summary of opinion-poll surveys about American domestic culture. A year later he collaborated with the psychiatrist John Rickman to produce *The People of Great Russia* in which he tried to interpret common Russian attitudes and behaviours in terms of their upbringing.

In 1950 Gorer bought a small manor house and farm in Sussex, where he lived until his death. There he settled down as a freelance social scientist and literary critic, and devoted much time to his garden, winning prizes for his rhododendrons. During these decades he produced several substantial studies of English culture, the result of commissions by national newspapers: *Exploring English Character* (1955), *Death, Grief and Mourning in Contemporary Britain* (1965), and *Sex and Marriage in England Today* (1971). He died in Sussex on 24 May 1985.

Gorer was considered a gallant man, of broad acquaintance. His friends included W. H. Auden, who dedicated a book of poems to him. His most significant and long-standing friendship, however, was with Margaret Mead. For decades they maintained an intense correspondence and went on annual holidays together, with Gorer organizing everything and vainly trying to show his workaholic companion 'how to have a good time'. Though it was often rumoured that the two (he a lifelong bachelor, she bisexual) were to marry, Mead later confided that she could not imagine having to apply medicine to his back.

Gorer himself claimed that his 'chief sin' was sloth. He stated that he had not dedicated himself exclusively to social scientific work because of his private income and the easy money he made through journalism. Even though in 1966 his publisher described him as 'probably Britain's best known and respected social anthropologist', his work is little acknowledged today. While contemporary academics are unimpressed by his readiness to produce generalizations for the whole of a complex society, such as the USA, and his persistent enthusiasm for explaining social phenomena by reference to child-rearing practices, his genuinely pioneering social investigations of film, radio, television, and literature, as well as his studies of everyday culture, all deserve recognition as neglected exemplars of cultural studies *avant la lettre*.

JEREMY MACCLANCY

Sources J. Howard, *Margaret Mead: a life* (1984) · *The Times* (29 May 1985) · 'The Gorer papers: introduction', www.sussex.ac.uk/library/manuscript/gorintr.shtml, 31 Oct 2001
Archives U. Sussex Library, papers
Likenesses photographs, University of Sussex Library, Gorer papers
Wealth at death £735,801: probate, *The Times*, 1985

Gorer, Peter Alfred Isaac (1907–1961), immunologist and geneticist, was born in London on 14 April 1907, the second of the three sons of Edgar Gorer, a noted collector of oriental art, and his wife, Rachel Alice Cohen. After leaving Charterhouse School in 1924, he became a dental student at Guy's Hospital, London, but rapidly transferred to medicine, which better suited his temperament and love of natural history. His interest in biology was greatly stimulated by T. J. Evans. Gorer interrupted his medical studies for a while to undertake research in the physiology of hibernation; he received a second-class BSc (Lond.) in 1929.

About this time Gorer developed an interest in unsolved problems of genetics and heredity, particularly the genetics of immunity of disease, including cancer. After qualifying MRCS, LRCP, in 1932, he studied genetics with J. B. S. Haldane at University College, London. Their relationship developed into a lifelong empathy. Also at University College, which was an intellectual lodestone for biologists, Gorer was influenced by D. M. S. Watson and E. J. Salisbury, and he became friendly with George Payling Wright.

In 1934 Gorer joined the Lister Institute, where he studied the genetic and immunologic basis of tumour transplantation. He was a colleague of D. W. W. Henderson. Dismayed by the tumour immunologists' almost total ignorance of the principles of genetics, Gorer initiated his future life's work on the genetics of individuality by investigating marker substances (antigens) on the surface of red cells and tissues. Gorer decided that the most direct approach to this problem was to define the antigens of normal tissues and then to determine what additional contributions to antigenicity, if any, were peculiar to the tumour itself.

The early experiments were performed by comparing the reactions of serum from a group A donor (himself) against the red cells from two different strains of mice. Later refinements included the immunization of rabbits and mice with red cells or tissues from a predetermined donor strain, followed by absorption of irrelevant antibodies. In this way Gorer defined four distinct antigens, I, II, III, and IV. These studies, started at the Lister Institute, were continued when Gorer returned to Guy's Hospital in 1940. His genetic knowledge influenced his research as a pathologist and he published detailed analyses of the frequency and form of diseases of the kidney and liver in different mouse strains. His research slowed during the Second World War, when he was required to take on a heavy teaching load; he was also greatly affected in 1945 by the death from tuberculosis of his wife, Gertrude Ernestine Kahler, the former wife of a German refugee. They had been married for only three years and had no children.

In 1946 Gorer left London and joined George D. Snell and Sally Lyman Allen in Bar Harbor, Maine, in a collaboration which formed the basis for many future developments in immunogenetics. Snell, who had been following the susceptibility of mouse hybrids to transplanted tumours, had evidence that resistance or susceptibility was often linked to genes controlling the normal development of the tail. In an important series of studies Gorer, Lyman Allen, and Snell demonstrated the close linkage between the presence of Antigen II (thereafter called H-2) tumour susceptibility and the morphological marker, 'fused' tail. Gorer also initiated, with L. W. Law, studies on immunity to the mouse mammary tumour virus and then had the frustration of seeing all but a fragment of the data lost in the fire that consumed the Jackson Laboratory. While at Bar Harbor in 1947 Gorer married Elizabeth Bruce Keucher, the librarian and secretary to the laboratory director, C. C. Little. They had a son and a daughter.

On his return to England in 1947 Gorer was appointed reader in experimental pathology at Guy's Hospital. He had minimal teaching responsibilities and complete freedom in his research, in which he was assisted by a young Polish refugee and former medical student, Mrs Z. B. Mikulska. As Gorer's work progressed and the validity of his conclusions was established, the appreciative proportion of his audience gradually increased. He was responsible for many technical innovations, always striving for greater precision, flexibility, and reliability. For much of his working life his only space was a room of perhaps 250 square feet; he had no telephone, no secretary, and not even a glassware washer.

Gorer was generous with his ideas. With time, more and more scientists sought his advice and he was much in demand at international meetings. So freely did he give of his time that his total number of publications barely exceeded fifty. His papers included 'Interactions between sessile and humoral antibodies in homograft reactions', 'Synergic action between isoantibody and immune cells in graft rejection', 'The antigenic structure of tumours', and *Pathological changes in F1 hybrid mice following transplantation of spleen cells from donors of the parental strains*. He also introduced the concept of low-dose enhancement. Gorer was primarily responsible for the application of genetic principles to immunology and was one of the most important contributors to the study of organ and tissue graft rejection, tumour immunity, and the genetics of immune responsiveness.

Gorer's manner was unobtrusive, with a slight streak of shyness. Often he was content to be a silent member of a group until, with diffidence, he would imperceptibly begin to lead the conversation. He had great patience and gentleness with those with a real desire to learn, and he had no time for the pompous or bombastic. He could also be abrasive and was an indefatigable debater. His humour was delicate and his knowledge of the theatre and the arts extensive. Above all, he was a creative thinker with the desire, but sometimes the inability, to communicate with those of lesser intellect and depth of understanding. Of the honours he received, only one—admission as a fellow to the Royal Society in 1960—pleased him deeply. Gorer died at Sunte House, Haywards Heath, in Sussex, on 11 May 1961. D. B. AMOS, *rev.*

Sources P. B. Medawar, *Memoirs FRS*, 7 (1961), 95–109 • *Gazette* [Guy's Hospital], 75 (1961) • personal knowledge (1981) • *CGPLA Eng. & Wales* (1961)

Wealth at death £182,920 17*s*. 0*d*.: probate, 14 July 1961, *CGPLA Eng. & Wales*

Gorges, Sir Arthur (*d.* 1625), poet and translator, was the third son of Sir William Gorges (*d.* 1585), seafarer. His father was a younger son of Sir Edward Gorges of Wraxall. His mother was Winifred Budockshed or Butshead (*d.* 1599/1600) of St Budeaux near Plymouth, a first cousin to Sir Walter Ralegh. On 12 November 1574 Gorges graduated BA at Oxford, and by about 1576 was in service at court. He was committed to the Marshalsea in February 1580 for having given the lie to Lord Windsor in the presence chamber. By this date he was a gentleman pensioner.

Gorges married Douglas (1571–1590), the daughter of Henry Howard, second Viscount Bindon, on 14 October 1584, with the approval of Douglas's mother, Francis Howard, *née* Meautys, but against the wishes of her irascible father. Protracted legal action followed. When a daughter, Ambrosia, was born (25 December 1588) Thomas Howard (third Viscount Bindon after he inherited his brother's title in 1590) claimed that she was a changeling. Douglas died on 13 August 1590 leaving Gorges embroiled in litigation over his daughter's legitimacy and inheritance. Ambrosia died in October 1600, before Gorges had enjoyed any financial benefit from her inheritance. His efforts to do so were energetic: on Easter day 1600 he was accused of having tried forcibly to evict Edmund Stansfield, the second husband of Douglas's mother, from Lullworth House, which Gorges claimed was the property of Ambrosia. His correspondence with Robert Cecil in this period (preserved in the Hatfield manuscripts) is punctuated with complaints about his poverty.

Gorges' second marriage, early in 1597, to Lady Elizabeth, daughter to Henry Clinton, earl of Lincoln, produced four children who predeceased him, and seven others: Arthur, Timoleon, Egremont, Carew, Henry, Dudley (a daughter), and Elizabeth. It also resulted in more legal troubles. In 1597 Gorges was imprisoned in the Fleet, probably for having married without royal approval. He had extensive disputes with his second father-in-law over his rights to property in Chelsea (including the former house of Sir Thomas More).

Gorges maintained an active public life in the reign of Elizabeth. He was MP for Yarmouth borough (Isle of Wight) in 1584, for Camelford borough from 1588 to 1589, for Dorset in 1593, and for Rye and the Cinque Ports in 1601. He was closely associated with his friend and kinsman Sir Walter Ralegh. During Ralegh's imprisonment in 1592 Gorges wrote a letter to Robert Cecil describing Ralegh's desperate struggles with his gaoler to be granted an audience with the queen, in the course of which Gorges 'purchased such a rapp on the knockles, that I wysht both theyr [pates] broken' (Bodl. Oxf., MS Ashmole 1729, fol. 177). Gorges captained Ralegh's ship the *Wastpite* on the islands voyage in 1597, and Ralegh's will, composed before the voyage, bequeathed to Gorges his 'best Rapyer and Dagger' (A. Latham, 'Sir Walter Ralegh's will', *Review of English Studies*, new ser., 22, 1971, 131). Gorges' vivid account of the voyage (composed in 1607; printed by Purchas in 1625) blames its failure on the 'bravado' of Robert Devereux, earl of Essex. Gorges was knighted by Essex on 29 October 1597 as a result of his exploits in taking the town of Tercera.

In July 1603 Gorges was briefly arrested in connection with the Bye plot, but was swiftly released. In 1606 James I eventually granted him the fee farm of the manor of Pawton in Cornwall, for which Gorges had been petitioning since July 1604, and in 1611 granted him and Sir Walter Cope a patent for a 'publique register' of commerce, which was to have enabled would-be borrowers and lenders to contact each other. This piece of royal patronage did little for Gorges' fortunes. His one extended addition to his translation of Lucan (printed 1614) dwells on the harm done to the state when princes fail to reward merit (A. Gorges, *Lucan's 'Pharsalia'*, 1614, 332–7), and may voice the attitudes of a former loyal servant of the crown who lost favour under James I. By May 1607 he was pleading that Robert Cecil buy from him pawned jewels. In the same year he sought the patronage of Prince Henry by presenting him with his account of the islands voyage, and followed it with *Excellent Observations and Notes Concerning the Royall Navy and Sea-Service* (printed as Ralegh's in *Judicious and Select Essayes and Observations*, 1650). In this, and in his manuscript advice to Prince Henry of 1610 (Trinity College, Cambridge, MS R. 7.23*), he argues that the wealth and strength of the nation depend on the prudent management of its fleet.

Gorges' appeals to Cecil in 1610 to be granted 'some place of credit about' Prince Henry (*Salisbury MSS*, 21.253) were successful: in that year he became a tenant of the prince's manor at Richmond, and is described in the *Publicke Register* (1611) as a gentleman of the privy chamber. His longest original poem, 'The Olympian Catastrophe', laments the death of Prince Henry, his one reliable patron, in 1612. Gorges' material fortunes revived in 1614 when his nephew Sir William Gorges bequeathed him the greater part of his Devon and Cornwall properties. On the death of the earl of Lincoln in 1614 he took possession of the Great House at Chelsea, where he lived for four years before building Gorges House nearby. Through these years he served as JP for Surrey and Middlesex. In 1618 he was briefly committed to his house to await his majesty's pleasure, for reasons which remain obscure.

Gorges is chiefly remembered because the *Daphnaïda* (1591) of Edmund Spenser represents his grief at the death of his first wife, Douglas, through the figure of Alcyon. He is a significant courtier-poet in his own right, however. The majority of his lyric verse is preserved in a corrected scribal manuscript (BL, MS Egerton 3165). This collection, entitled 'The Vanytyes of Sir Arthur Gorges Youthe', consists chiefly of translations and imitations from Ronsard, Desportes, and Du Bellay, many of which show the influence of George Turbervile, Totell's miscellany, and Gorges' associates Spenser and Ralegh. They are interspersed with a few poems to the queen, and conclude with a sequence of panegyrics to the house of Stuart which were later gathered in a presentation manuscript (BL, Royal MS 18 A XLVII). Although the Petrarchan fires of Gorges' poems are sometimes chilled by conventionality, some of his pieces (such as 46) approach the quality of Ralegh's verse:

> Woolde I were changde into that golden Showre
> that so devynly streamede from the Skies
> To fall in droppes upone my daynty flowre
> when in her bedd Shee sollytarye lyes.

His verses were frequently misattributed to Ralegh. Other poems (such as 79: 'Her Face her Tongue her Wytt') were popular in printed and manuscript compilations, and were sometimes grouped with poems by Ralegh. Gorges' major printed work was the first complete English translation (into octosyllabic couplets) of Lucan, which appeared in 1614 with a dedicatory poem which is almost certainly by Ralegh. In 1619 Gorges translated Francis Bacon's *Essays* into French, and rendered the *Wisdom of the Ancients* into English.

Gorges died at Chelsea, probably of the plague, on 28 September 1625. He was buried in the Thomas More chapel in Chelsea church. In his will (proved on 27 December 1625) Gorges deplores the conduct of his younger sons, whom 'I have founde to be very wastfull and carelesse of my commaundements', and claims that his estate will not afford additional legacies to his friends, since he has 'never received any manner of rewarde or preferment of Kinge James notwithstanding my loving and faithfull service' (PRO, PROB 11/147, sig. 142). A brass depicting him with his second wife (who outlived him) and their eleven children survives in Chelsea Old Church. COLIN BURROW

Sources *Calendar of the manuscripts of the most hon. the marquis of Salisbury*, 24 vols., HMC, 9 (1883–1976) • *APC*, 1589–1619 • J. S. Brewer and W. Bullen, eds., *Calendar of the Carew manuscripts*, 3: 1589–1600, PRO (1869) • *CSP dom.*, 1595–1625 • BL, MS Egerton 3165 ['The vanytyes of Sir Arthur Gorges youthe'] • 'A briefe discourse', Trinity Cam., MS R.7.23* • S. Purchas, *Hakluytus posthumus, or, Purchas his pilgrimes*, bk 20 (1625); repr. Hakluyt Society, extra ser., 33 (1907) • H. E. Sandison, 'Arthur Gorges, Spenser's Alcyon, and Ralegh's friend', *Proceedings of the Modern Language Association of America*, 43 (1928), 645–74 • R. Gorges, *The story of a family through eleven centuries* (1944) • HoP, *Commons*, 1558–1603 • *The poems of Sir Arthur Gorges*, ed. H. E. Sandison (1953) • A. Gorges, *A true transcript of his majesties letters pattent: For an office to be erected, and called the Publicke Register for Generall Commerce* (1611) • PRO, PROB 11/147, sig. 142 • Bodl. Oxf., MS Ashmole 1729, fol. 177

Archives BL, autograph letter, Add. MS 6789, fol. 538 • Bodl. Oxf., autograph letter, Add. MS C.206, fol. 26 • Bodl. Oxf., autograph letter on Ralegh's imprisonment of 1592, MS Ashmole 1729, fol. 177a, b, c • CUL, MS Dd.5.75 | BL, Harley MS 7392 (2) • Hatfield House, Carew MSS

Likenesses brass effigy, 1625, All Saints' Church, Chelsea, London, Thomas More chapel

Wealth at death see will, PRO, PROB 11/147, sig. 142

Gorges, Sir Ferdinando (1568–1647), army officer and promoter of colonization in America, was the second son of Edward Gorges (*d.* 1568) and Cicely Lygon of Wraxall, Somerset. The year of his birth was estimated for some time at 1566, but it appears to be reasonably certain that he was born between 31 May and 23 July 1568 at the family's suburban London home in Clerkenwell, where his father died shortly afterward. Little is known of his early upbringing, though there is some evidence that he may have attended as a youth in Elizabeth's court. By the age of eighteen or nineteen he had begun a military career. In 1587 he served as a gentleman volunteer with an English contingent in the defence of the Dutch seaport of Sluis against Spanish forces. Although the city was eventually lost and Gorges taken prisoner, the young officer was cited by the English commander Sir Roger Williams as having behaved 'most valiantly'. He was among those exchanged late in 1588 for Spanish prisoners from the Armada. On 24 February 1589 he married Ann Bell (*d.* 1620), daughter of a wealthy landowner of Essex. He would be married thrice more: on 21 December 1621 to Mary Achim (*d.* 1622); in 1627 to Elizabeth Gorges (*d.* 1627); and on 21 September 1629 to Elizabeth Smyth, *née* Gorges. His first marriage led to his acquiring the means to settle down as a country gentleman, but instead he served for the next two years in the armies sent by Elizabeth in aid of the then protestant Henri IV of France. In 1591 he fought under Williams at St Saëns and in the siege of Noyon, where he was badly wounded. Soon afterward, at Rouen, he was knighted in the field by the earl of Essex.

After commanding a garrison in the Low Countries for several years, Gorges was assigned to take charge of expanding the harbour defences at Plymouth, on Essex's recommendation. With the completion of the job in 1596, he was named captain and commander of the fort, a position he held except for a brief interlude until 1629. The appointment of Gorges, who gave priority to the place of Plymouth Sound in a system of national defences over the immediate defence of the town, represented a transfer of control from the town to the royal government and the subordination of local to national interests. The resulting local tensions complicated his efforts to put the channel defences in order during a period of renewed danger from Spain. When it appeared that the Spanish danger was past and the queen's attention was transferred to an uprising in Ireland, he tried unsuccessfully to secure orders to accompany his former patron the earl of Essex in the effort to put down the rebellion. After Essex failed and was recalled in 1599, he enlisted Gorges in his plot against the queen. Gorges at length withdrew from the conspiracy and testified against Essex in his treason trial, but was imprisoned on the basis of his earlier implication in the design. In prison he composed his 'Brief answer to certayne false, slanderous, and idle objections made agaynst Sir Ferd. Gorges, knight'. He was pardoned in 1601 through the offices of his new patron, Sir Robert Cecil. Upon the accession of James I in 1603 Cecil secured Gorges' restoration to his command in Plymouth.

It was now peacetime, and Gorges was soon caught up in the English enthusiasm for overseas trade and discovery. His life reached a turning point in 1605 with the still unexplained gift to him of three of the five kidnapped Native Americans that Captain George Waymouth brought back from a voyage of exploration. From that moment on his one great passion was to sponsor colonies in the place described to him in broken English by his captives. He collaborated with the lord chief justice, Sir John Popham, whose interest in America had likewise been aroused by Waymouth's voyage, in securing a royal charter, issued in 1606, for the London and Plymouth companies of Virginia. The death of Popham soon after the Plymouth Company had dispatched the colonizing expedition to Sagadahoc in 1607 thrust Gorges into the role of its chief spokesman and advocate, and so its failure was a personal defeat for him, only one of many such disappointments that marked his career of colonial enterprise. Several more efforts by Gorges and the Plymouth Company to settle the coast of 'New England', as Captain John Smith named that part of America in 1614, also failed, and the company was dissolved in 1619.

Gorges and several of his Plymouth Company associates next formed the Council for New England, which by royal patent of 3 November 1620 was granted the territory between 40 and 48 degrees north, roughly from modern Philadelphia in the south to St John's, Newfoundland, in the north. Among the earliest of the council's many subgrants was one in 1622 made jointly to Gorges and Captain John Mason called the province of Maine, between the Merrimac and Kennebec rivers. The anonymous *A Briefe Relation of the Discovery and Plantation of New England* (1622) is generally accepted as Gorges' work, and as such reflected his ideas on colonial government, including the feudalistic organization of his province of Maine. After a delay in pursuing their project because of new hostilities with France and Spain, the partners agreed in 1629, the same year that Gorges resigned the command of Plymouth fort, to divide their territory. Mason took the piece between the Merrimac and the Piscataqua, which he called New Hampshire, and Gorges that from the Piscataqua to the Kennebec, which he continued to call the province of Maine. Ironically, in view of Gorges' neo-feudal and decidedly royalist American vision, it was also in 1629 that the Council for New England made what turned out to be its most significant grant of all to the Massachusetts Bay Company, whose overbearing puritan influence in the region Gorges spent his last years trying unsuccessfully to resist. Gorges and Mason also tried briefly to exploit two other joint grants from the council, the Laconia patent of 1629 and the Pascataqua patent of 1631, both of which overlapped the partners' provinces already granted but were nevertheless instrumental in bringing in settlers.

Gorges began slowly to develop his province of Maine by issuing land grants, which encouraged a small stream of settlers, and financing a few fishing stations. His main goal, however, was to establish a royal government for all of New England. It was mainly towards that end that in 1635 he instigated the dissolution of the Council for New England and his appointment by Charles I as governor-general of New England. The ship that was to have taken him and an elaborate retinue of office-holders to take charge of his dominion was wrecked in the launching, and John Mason, who had become his chief associate and was to be vice-admiral of New England, died soon afterwards. Frustrated once more and now nearly bankrupt from his various failed ventures, he lacked the resources to implement the grand scheme again. He did, however, try to realize a smaller version of his vision in his province of Maine, for which he received a royal charter in 1639. He sent as deputy governor a distant cousin, Thomas Gorges, who was moderately successful in setting up a rudimentary government.

Sir Ferdinando Gorges still nursed hopes of travelling to America himself, but even if he could have found the means, he soon became caught up in the deteriorating political situation at home, and in 1642, at the age of seventy-four, first raised a cavalry troop in support of the royalist cause and later took part in several actions of the civil war. Meanwhile, contacts between him and his province of Maine seem to have ceased, and Thomas Gorges returned home in 1643 to serve on the parliamentarian side. During the 1650s the province was entirely absorbed by Massachusetts. Sir Ferdinando died, disappointed and impoverished, on 24 May 1647 at the estate of his fourth wife, Elizabeth, in Ashton Phillips, Somerset, where he had lived since his marriage in 1629. She survived him. His

A briefe narration of the original undertaking of the advancement of plantations into the parts of America was published in 1658. CHARLES E. CLARK

Sources R. A. Preston, *Gorges of Plymouth Fort: a life of Sir Ferdinando Gorges, captain of Plymouth Fort, governor of New England, and lord of the province of Maine* (1953) • J. P. Baxter, ed., *Sir Ferdinando Gorges and his province of Maine*, 3 vols. (1890) [incl. works by Gorges] • C. M. Andrews, *The colonial period of American history*, 1 (1937) • E. T. Shields, 'Gorges, Ferdinando', *ANB* • S. S. Webb, *The governors-general: the English army and the definition of the empire, 1569–1681* (1979), 16–21 • R. W. Judd, E. A. Churchill, and J. W. Eastman, eds., *Maine: the pine tree state from prehistory to the present* (1995), 52–60 • *DNB*
Archives Bristol RO, letters to Hugh Smyth and Thomas Smyth • Devon RO, corresp. with Lord Seymour
Wealth at death very little; owned province of Maine: Preston, *Gorges of Plymouth Fort*

Gorges [*née* Snakenborg], **Helena**, **Lady Gorges** [*other married name* Helena Parr, marchioness of Northampton] (**1548–1635**), courtier, was born in 1548 in Sweden, the daughter of Ulf Henriksson (*d.* 1560x68), a nobleman of Östergötland, and his wife, Agneta Knuttson (*d.* after 1568). Helena (Elin) had two brothers and several sisters. Her father was a supporter of Gustav Vasa, king of Sweden, and came from the old noble family of Bååt, while her mother was a descendant of the jarls or earls of Orkney. The name Snakenborg was taken from her mother's family, which was originally from Mecklenburg.

Helena was one of six young Swedish girls appointed from 1564 to 1566 as maids of honour to Princess Cecilia, margravine of Baden, daughter of Gustav Vasa. Late in 1564, when she was fifteen, they embarked on a voyage to England. It was rumoured that Cecilia decided to visit England to revive the suit of her brother Erik XIV to marry Elizabeth I, but it is not clear that this was the case. Taking a roundabout route over land and travelling through Poland and Germany, in order to steer clear of hostile countries, the party was so hampered by bad weather that almost a year passed before it reached its destination.

On its arrival in England many prominent members of the nobility received the party. Helena was by all accounts a beautiful woman, having large brown eyes, red hair, and a perfect pink and white complexion. She caught the attention of William *Parr, marquess of Northampton (1513–1571), nobleman and courtier, the third and only surviving son of Sir Thomas Parr of Kendal, Westmorland, and his wife, Maud. He soon endeavoured to court her. Northampton presented her with many extravagant gifts such as clothes and jewels, and 'being an impressionable and romantic young girl, Helena was swept off her feet by the experienced older man' (James, 395). Cecilia built up large debts due to a lavish lifestyle and left England in April 1566 in order to escape her creditors. She wanted to take Helena back to Sweden with her; however, her young maid, enjoying life in her new country and becoming close to the marquess, was keen to remain. This wish was granted through Elizabeth's influence.

Northampton hoped to marry Helena but felt prevented from doing so because, although divorced in 1551, his first wife, Lady Anne Bourchier, was still alive. Elizabeth was fond of Helena and appointed her a maid of honour from about 1567, before promoting her to gentlewoman of her privy chamber—a highly respected position at the heart of the court in which she was among the queen's most intimate servants and controlled access by the press of courtiers. She was entitled to many privileges, such as her own lodgings at court, servants, and a horse. However, she was not a waged member of the privy chamber and it is not known how regularly she attended court. Bourchier died on 26 January 1571 and Northampton and Helena were finally able to marry in May. The wedding took place in Elizabeth's presence in the queen's closet at Whitehall Palace. The bride was twenty-two and the groom fifty-seven. They seemed happy together and divided their time between their houses in Guildford, Surrey, and at Stanstead Hall, Essex. The marriage came to a sudden end within a few months when the marquess died on 28 October in Thomas Fisher's house in Warwick. There were no children. The marchioness received a substantial dower of £368 per annum, drawn from her husband's estates in Cumberland. This may have been exchanged for lands worth £400 per annum in Huntingdonshire.

It was not too long before Helena captivated another admirer, Thomas Gorges [*see below*]. The queen was originally in favour of his approaches to Helena but changed her mind and refused to consent to a marriage, perhaps as a result of her notorious sexual jealousy regarding gentlewomen of her privy chamber or because she had strong views on unequal marriages; Helena was a marchioness and Gorges only a gentleman. The couple wed in secret about 1576. When Elizabeth learned of their deceit, Helena was banned from court, although she was later reinstated, possibly with the help of her influential friend Thomas Radcliffe, third earl of Sussex, the lord chamberlain. The queen warmed to her again and with wholly uncharacteristic generosity granted her manors in Huntingdonshire and Wiltshire. The couple's first child was born in June 1578 and named Elizabeth (1578–1659) after the queen, who was her godmother. Their first son, Francis (*d.* in or before 1599), was probably born in 1579. Gorges was persuaded by his wife to make his property of Longford, Wiltshire, bought after 1573, more appealing by rebuilding it. The mansion had been damaged by fire when he acquired it and a replacement was completed at great expense by 1591, under the final supervision of John Thorpe, since the entrance on its north-east front bears that date. Longford was the model for the 'Castle of Amphialeus' in Sir Philip Sidney's *Arcadia*. Gorges was knighted in 1586. During this time Helena settled down to raise her family. She had two more daughters, Frances (1580–1649) and Bridget (1584–*c.*1634), and four more sons, all of whom were knighted: Edward Gorges, first Baron Gorges of Dundalk (*b.* 1582/3, *d.* in or before 1652); Theobald (1583–1647); Robert (1588–1648); and Thomas (*b.* 1589, *d.* after 1624).

The marchioness was still valued highly by Elizabeth and often acted as her deputy at the baptism of the children of distinguished noblemen, particularly towards the end of the reign, when the queen's health was deteriorating. Helena must have been distressed when Elizabeth, whose friendship and guidance she had known ever since her arrival in England, died in March 1603 and she was the chief mourner in the funeral procession as senior peeress because Arabella Stuart refused to undertake the role. The accession of James VI to the English throne paved the way for the removal of many of Elizabeth's old courtiers and Gorges was demoted. Helena did not retain all her privileges but was probably glad to escape the rivalry that existed among the gentlewomen of the privy chamber to Anne of Denmark. After Gorges died on 30 March 1610 at the age of seventy-four, Helena increasingly retreated from public life, although she remained a devoted member of the Church of England. Helena died on 10 April 1635 at Redlynch, Somerset, the residence of her son Sir Robert Gorges, and was buried on 14 May in Salisbury Cathedral. She had no fewer than ninety-two direct descendants at the time. She granted over £1700 in annuities and bequests in her will.

Sir Thomas Gorges (1536–1610), courtier, was born in Wraxall, Somerset, the fifth son of Sir Edward Gorges, landowner, of Wraxall, and his wife, Mary, daughter of Sir Anthony Poyntz of Iron Acton, Gloucestershire, and his wife, Elizabeth. He was a member of the royal household, groom of the privy chamber from 31 December 1571, JP for Huntingdon and Wiltshire from about 1579, special ambassador to Sweden in 1582, and MP for Longford, Wiltshire, in 1586, as well as keeper of many important royal estates. Gorges acted as Elizabeth's 'high grade messenger' (HoP, *Commons, 1558–1603*, 2.208). He was one of the wealthiest gentlemen in Wiltshire. Gorges, like his wife, was buried in Salisbury Cathedral.

PAUL HARRINGTON

Sources C. A. Bradford, *Helena, marchioness of Northampton* (1936) • S. E. James, *Kateryn Parr: the making of a queen* (1999), 394–7 • HoP, *Commons, 1558–1603*, 2.208 • will, PRO, PROB 11/167, sig. 41 • PRO, PROB 11/116, sig. 64 • administration, PRO, PROB 6/2, fol. 22*r* • GEC, *Peerage*, 4.16

Likenesses portrait, 1569, Tate collection

Wealth at death over £1700—in annuities and bequests: will, PRO, PROB 11/167, sig. 41

Gorges, Sir Thomas (1536–1610). *See under* Gorges, Helena, Lady Gorges (1548–1635).

Gorham [Gorron]**, Geoffrey de** (*c*.1100–1146), abbot of St Albans, was born shortly before 1100 in Maine, France, either at Le Mans or, as his name suggests, at Gorron nearby. He was probably a member of a local noble family, although one tradition associates him with the Anglo-Norman Lucy family. He may have studied at Le Mans under its bishop, the celebrated scholar Hildebert de Lavardin; when he was invited to become master of the school at St Albans by Abbot Richard, his reputation as a scholar was already well established. His arrival at St Albans was delayed, the post was filled by another master, and instead Geoffrey became master at the nearby school at Dunstable. While at Dunstable he composed a miracle play of St Katherine, probably in the vernacular. Vestments he borrowed from St Albans for the performance of the play were destroyed while still in his care, and in recompense he entered the abbey as a monk.

Geoffrey was appointed abbot in 1119. His immediate predecessors had already done much to establish St Albans as an important spiritual and cultural centre, but it was under Geoffrey's rule that the abbey gained real pre-eminence in the Anglo-Norman church. Outside St Albans, Geoffrey's personal reputation as a distinguished senior prelate was considerable, and on at least one occasion he was called upon to resolve a dispute in another house. Writing to request his help *c*.1140, Osbert of Clare, a monk of Westminster, praised him as 'a famous father, duke of souls' (*Letters*, 115). His early years were spent in the acquisition of property and in improving the abbey's finances; he also founded a leper hospital at St Albans. His principal contribution, however, was the completion of a shrine for St Alban, at a cost of over £60. Initially hampered by financial troubles, the construction of the shrine was finally completed and the remains of St Alban translated on 2 August 1129. He continued the work of his predecessor in directing the production of books in the abbey scriptorium; those copied under his supervision are among the best examples of early Anglo-Norman script and decoration, and include the work of the so-called 'Alexis' master illuminator.

According to a near contemporary source, the *Life of Christina of Markyate*, the anchoress who lived near St Albans, at some point in the 1120s or 1130s Geoffrey became embroiled in corruption. His own monks accused him of maladministration, perhaps provoked by his excessive spending on the new shrine. But as the same source records, before he had committed any serious crimes, he underwent a personal reformation under Christina's guidance. In the years that followed Geoffrey established a close relationship with Christina; she became his spiritual director; he in turn provided her with the necessary help to establish a community at Markyate. Under Geoffrey's direction the monks also provided Christina with a psalter, lavishly decorated with numerous illustrations, considered by many historians the finest production of the St Albans scriptorium. A further priory for two women hermits was also founded by Geoffrey under Christina's influence, soon after 1140 at Sopwell, near St Albans. On three occasions between 1136 and 1139 he was ordered to Rome to secure papal confirmation for the election of King Stephen; on each occasion he was recalled before the journey began, a fact that one source attributes to the prayerful intercession of Christina herself. He died on 25 February 1146, and was buried in the St Albans chapter house; his body was re-interred in the presbytery in 1978.

JAMES G. CLARK

Sources *Gesta abbatum monasterii Sancti Albani, a Thoma Walsingham*, ed. H. T. Riley, 3 vols., pt 4 of *Chronica monasterii S. Albani*, Rolls Series, 28 (1867–9), vol. 1, pp. 72–106 • C. H. Talbot, ed. and trans., *The life of Christina of Markyate*, OMT (1959), 135–93 • R. M. Thomson, *Manuscripts from St Albans Abbey, 1066–1235*, 2 vols. (1982) • O. Pächt, C. R. Dodwell, and F. Wormald, *The St Albans psalter* (1960) • *The letters of Osbert of Clare*, ed. E. W. Williamson (1929), 114–16 • St Albans *Liber benefactorum*, BL, Cotton MS Nero D. vii

Archives BL, Cotton MSS • BL, Harley MSS • BL, Royal MSS • Bodl. Oxf., Bodley MSS • Bodl. Oxf., Laud MSS • St Godehard's Library, Hildesheim, St Albans psalter
Likenesses portrait, c.1380, BL, St Albans *Liber Benefactorum*

Gorham, George Cornelius (1787–1857), Church of England clergyman, was born at St Neots, Huntingdonshire, on 21 August 1787, the son of George James Gorham (1752–1840), merchant and banker, and his wife, Mary (*d.* 1837), eldest daughter of Thomas Graeme of Towthorpe, Yorkshire. He was educated at St Neots by Thomas Laundy, a Quaker, and subsequently at Cheam by Dr William Gilpin. He entered Queens' College, Cambridge, in 1805; in 1808 he received the Norrisian prize for an essay on public worship and graduated BA as third wrangler; he proceeded MA in 1812, and BD in 1820. After graduating Gorham was a companion to Lord Calthorpe in Edinburgh, but shortly returned to Cambridge when he was elected a fellow of Queens' in 1810. In March 1811 he was ordained deacon, having successfully resisted an attempt by Thomas Dampier, bishop of Ely, to impose on him a doctrinal test regarding the efficacy of baptism, on which Gorham's evangelical views already appear to have been regarded with suspicion by high-churchmen. He was ordained priest in February 1812, and exercised his ministry in and around Cambridge while also taking private pupils. He was curate of Beckenham, Kent, in 1814–15, but then returned to Cambridge, where in 1818 he unsuccessfully contested the Woodwardian professorship in geology against Adam Sedgwick. From 1818 to 1827 he was curate at Clapham parish church in Surrey, when Clapham was 'still the Zion of evangelical leaders' (Chadwick, 251). In these years he published scholarly and controversial works, notably a history of St Neots (1820) and a statement on the apocrypha controversy (1825). His early scientific interests apparently gave way to historical and theological ones.

On 3 October 1827 Gorham married Jane (*d.* 26 Aug 1891), third daughter of John King Martyn, a bishop in the Moravian church, an influence which was to remain strong in the family. Relinquishing his fellowship of Queens' on marriage, Gorham for the next two decades lived the insecure life of an unbeneficed curate, sustained in part by private means, but burdened by a fast-growing family of three sons—including George Martyn Gorham (1828–1904), vicar of Masham, Yorkshire, from 1873 to 1904—and three daughters, to whom he was devoted. In 1834 he complained that he had moved four times since his marriage only seven years before, but in that year he obtained a modicum of stability as curate of St Mary's Chapel, Maidenhead, Berkshire, where he remained until 1842; from 1843 to 1846 he was curate of Fawley, Berkshire. In 1846 Gorham was nearly sixty, and had he died in that year he would have been remembered, if at all, as a diligent but obscure scholar and minor adherent of the evangelical networks centred on Clapham and Cambridge. However, the events of the last decade of his life were to lift him to an unexpected pinnacle of national prominence.

In February 1846 Gorham was presented by the tory lord chancellor, Lyndhurst, to the remote but valuable crown living of St Just in Penwith, in west Cornwall. His satisfaction at this belated preferment quickly gave way to frustration with his physical isolation and an awareness that a populous mining parish was not an appropriate sphere of ministry for an elderly man with scholarly inclinations. Worse still, he quickly found himself in conflict with his redoubtable high-church diocesan, Henry Phillpotts, bishop of Exeter, who in 1846 reproved him both for referring to the Church of England as 'the National Establishment' (Gorham, *Examination*, 4) and for advertising for a curate 'free from … Tractarian error' (ibid., 7). Phillpotts eventually licensed a curate of Gorham's choice, but not before a trenchant exchange of letters indicated a breakdown of normal working relations. In the summer of 1847 Gorham gratefully accepted the whig lord chancellor Cottenham's offer of the crown incumbency of Brampford Speke near Exeter, a small agricultural parish which seemed much more attractive than St Just to a man of Gorham's age and interests. Phillpotts, though, had now decided that Gorham held beliefs contrary to the doctrine of the Church of England; he first refused to countersign his testimonial and then, when Cottenham nevertheless proceeded with the presentation, summoned Gorham for an unprecedentedly detailed examination respecting his views on the efficacy of infant baptism, a touchstone of theological belief, on which high-churchmen and evangelicals differed. High-churchmen such as Phillpotts claimed that the baptized infant was unconditionally regenerate, but evangelicals that regeneration was conditional on the child's subsequent personal profession of saving faith. After interrogating Gorham for five days in December 1847 and for a further three in March 1848 the bishop refused to institute him on the grounds that he held unsound doctrine. In April, Gorham published an

George Cornelius Gorham (1787–1857), by Charles Baugniet, 1850

open letter protesting at 'the cruel exercise of episcopal power' (Chadwick, 252) and claiming that if the precedent were established a bishop would be able to exclude from his diocese all clergy whose views differed from his own.

Gorham could have backed down by quietly seeking a benefice in another diocese, but he and his supporters felt that Phillpotts's actions raised major principles about the whole protestant character of the Church of England, and must not remain unchallenged. Accordingly he resorted to the courts, in what rapidly became one of the most celebrated legal actions of the century. Publicized and discussed by the press, it aroused great excitement and increased tension between evangelicals and Tractarians. The authoritarian bishop and the recalcitrant incumbent were figureheads in the clash between high-churchmen and evangelicals in the Church of England. Although Gorham, with his staunch protestantism and avowed Calvinism, was a more rigid champion than some evangelicals might have chosen, his considerable theological learning, great determination, and influential connections gave him very solid credibility. In him the formidable Henry of Exeter was eventually to meet his nemesis.

In the first instance, however, when Gorham issued a monition against the bishop in the court of arches, Phillpotts was upheld by the judgment of Sir Herbert Jenner Fust, the dean of the arches, on 2 August 1849. Gorham then appealed to the judicial committee of the privy council which, in the historic 'Gorham judgment' of 8 March 1850, found in his favour, insofar as it allowed that his doctrinal position could be held alongside others within the Church of England. Phillpotts persisted in various legal manoeuvres, but on 6 August 1850 Gorham was instituted to Brampford Speke by commission from the archbishop of Canterbury. The outcome secured the position of the evangelicals in the Church of England but alarmed high-churchmen and influenced some notable secessions, including those by Henry Manning and Robert Wilberforce, to Rome.

Aged but not broken by the great controversy which gave lasting currency to his name, Gorham at last began his ministry at Brampford Speke. He had to contend with the smouldering antagonism of the bishop, who attempted to incite discontent among the parishioners. At a diocesan level Phillpotts convened a synod in Exeter in June 1851, intended in part to continue his struggle against Gorham; the latter led a protest by eighty clergymen. Meanwhile Gorham threw himself energetically into his parochial duties, presiding over the rebuilding of the church, completed in 1853. In 1856, however, a dispute with the parish vestry over the conditions Gorham attached to the provision of a new organ gave Phillpotts a pretext for establishing a commission of inquiry which, meeting in Exeter in June 1856, decided that there was a *prima facie* case against Gorham for brawling in church. Gorham strenuously denied the 'frivolous' charges against him, publishing *The Church Discipline Act made an instrument of vexation to the clergy of the diocese of Exeter* (1856). The stress of this further indignity broke Gorham's now fragile health. During the autumn of 1856 he became seriously ill with cancer of the mouth and throat, and early in 1857 he was given a terminal diagnosis. He faced his painful and distressing illness with great courage and Christian resignation, while working on his characteristic last work, *Reformation Gleanings*. He died defiantly in residence at Brampford Speke vicarage on 19 June 1857 and was buried beside the small Devon village church he had fought so long and hard to gain. JOHN WOLFFE

Sources Gorham family MSS, Bodl. Oxf. • G. C. Gorham, ed., *Examination before admission to a benefice by the bishop of Exeter* (1848) • G. C. Gorham, *The Church Discipline Act made an instrument of vexation to the clergy of the diocese of Exeter* (1856) • *Christian Observer* (1857), 566–8 • *DNB* • parish records, Brampford Speke, Devon RO • Phillips-Robinson MSS, Bodl. Oxf. • J. C. S. Nias, *Gorham and the bishop of Exeter* (1951) • BL, Peel MSS, Add. MS 40522, fol. 100 • O. Chadwick, *The Victorian church*, 3rd edn, 1 (1971) • D. M. Lewis, ed., *The Blackwell dictionary of evangelical biography, 1730–1860*, 2 vols. (1995) • Venn, *Alum. Cant.*

Archives Bodl. Oxf., corresp. and papers • Cowper Memorial Library, Olney, corresp. incl. letters from R. Southey • Queens' College Library, Cambridge, sermons | BL, Peel MSS • Bodl. Oxf., corresp. with Sir Thomas Phillips • Devon RO, Brampford Speke parish records

Likenesses C. Baugniet, engraving, 1850, AM Oxf. [*see illus.*] • lithograph, 1850 (after A. H. Forrester), BM, NPG; repro. in *Bentley's Miscellany* • portrait, *c*.1850, repro. in *ILN* (25 May 1850), 373 • A. Crowquill, portrait, repro. in *Bentley's Miscellany*, 27 (1850) • prints, repro. in *Bentley's Miscellany*, 27 (1850), 612–16 • watercolour, priv. coll.

Gorham, Nathaniel (1738–1796), merchant and revolutionary politician in America, was born in May 1738 in Charlestown, Massachusetts, the eldest of five children of Nathaniel Gorham, packet boat operator, and his wife, Mary Soley (*b*. *c*.1714). After a six-year apprenticeship to Nathaniel Coffin, merchant of New London, Connecticut, Gorham returned in 1759 to Charlestown to open his own business, which was quickly successful. He gained considerable wealth from privateering and speculation during the American War of Independence. He was one of five incorporators of the Charles River Bridge corporation in 1785, and was active in the First Congregational Church of Charlestown. In 1763 he married Rebecca Call; they had nine children.

Because Gorham opposed British taxation and customs duties enforcement, Charlestown elected him to the Massachusetts house of representatives in 1771. He sat in the colonial and then state legislature until 1788, except for two years during the war. He was speaker of the house in 1781, 1782, and 1785. He also served in the Massachusetts provincial congress, 1774–5, on the Massachusetts board of war, 1778–81, and as a county court judge beginning in 1785. In 1779–80 he was a delegate to the Massachusetts state constitutional convention.

Gorham began serving in the continental congress in December 1782, and sat in it intermittently while he was continuously re-elected to the Massachusetts house. He did not attend congress when house speaker. In his first term he supported measures calculated to restore public credit, which Massachusetts favoured because it wanted its war expenses reimbursed. Gorham foresaw that if the

New England states did not get fair treatment from congress, they might form a separate northern confederation. He voted with other nationalistic delegates for the commutation of military officers' half pay for life to full pay for five years, which Massachusetts opposed, and accordingly, after leaving congress in June 1783, he was not re-elected delegate until November 1784. He resumed attendance in January 1786, attending sessions through much of 1786–7, except during sessions of the federal convention in Philadelphia.

In June 1786 he replaced the ill John Hancock as president of congress, serving until November. During this period Gorham supported the calling of a convention to establish a federal government with power to protect commerce and establish a uniform monetary system. He also supported the sectional view that, in exchange for a commercial treaty with Spain, the United States should be willing to renounce its claim to free navigation of the Mississippi. He has been accused of inviting Prince Henry of Prussia to become king of the American confederation and put down the disorders in Massachusetts and other colonies. P. H. Smith, in his *Letters of Delegates to Congress*, shows this is almost certainly untrue.

As delegate to the federal constitutional convention of 1787, Gorham provided important leadership. He chaired its executive committee for several weeks in June. He was a member of the five-man committee of detail, and given credit by Oliver Ellsworth as being a major framer of the federal constitution. His most significant and influential belief was that the constitution should establish general principles, and that the legislature work out the details. His élitist ideas that, as in Massachusetts, both wealth and numbers should be represented, and, as in Britain, plural office holding by representatives would give stability to government, were rejected. His populist ideas—extending the possibility of enfranchisement to 'mechanics' and raising the maximum ratio of representatives to people to one to every 30,000—were adopted. Discarding his earlier acceptance of sectional separation, he was anxious to compromise with the south, seconding South Carolina's motion to extend the time limit on the slave trade to 1808 in exchange for southern acceptance of the provision that navigation acts could be adopted by mere majority vote. He was also a powerful member of the Massachusetts ratifying convention in 1788. Here he convinced one antifederalist delegate, his partner in speculation William Phelps, to return home rather than vote against the constitution.

Gorham's political stature faded as he became more involved in land speculation. Although he remained in the national congress until the spring of 1789, he was inexplicably denied re-election to his seat in the Massachusetts legislature in May 1788. He withdrew as candidate for congress in November 1788. He and Phelps contracted to purchase 6 million acres for $1 million face value in depreciated Massachusetts securities. They planned to buy up these depreciated securities cheaply, but the federal policy of assumption of state debts caused the securities to appreciate. Gorham faced bankruptcy, suffered apoplexy, and died on 11 June 1796 at Charlestown, where he was buried. BENJAMIN H. NEWCOMB

Sources J. T. Adams, 'Gorham, Nathaniel', *DAB* • P. H. Smith and others, eds., *Letters of delegates to congress, 1774–1789*, 26 vols. (1976–2000), vols. 18–26 • M. Farrand, ed., *The records of the federal convention of 1787*, rev. edn, 4 vols. (1937); repr. (1966) • F. McDonald, *We the people: the economic origins of the constitution* (1958) • R. J. Lettieri, 'Gorham, Nathaniel', *ANB* • E. C. Burnett, *The continental congress* (1941) • J. T. Main, *The antifederalists: critics of the constitution, 1781–1788* (1961) • V. B. Hall, *Politics without parties: Massachusetts, 1780–1791* (1972) • *Journal of the Honourable House of Representatives of the state of Massachusetts-Bay* (19 May 1776–31 Dec 1779) • J. F. Hunnewell, *A century of town life: a history of Charlestown, Massachusetts, 1775–1887* (1888) • R. A. East, 'The Massachusetts conservatives in the critical period', *The era of the American Revolution*, ed. R. B. Morris (1939), 349–91

Archives Mass. Hist. Soc., MSS • Massachusetts Archives, Boston, MSS • NYPL, MSS

Likenesses etching (after unknown portrait), L. Cong., prints and bibliographic division • portrait, priv. coll.

Wealth at death bankrupt: Lettieri, 'Gorham, Nathaniel'

Goring, George, first earl of Norwich (1585–1663), courtier and diplomat, born on 28 April 1585, was the son of George Goring (*d.* 1602) of Danny, Sussex, and Anne, daughter of Henry Denny of Waltham Abbey, Essex, and sister of Edward *Denny, earl of Norwich [*see under* Denny, Sir Anthony (1501–1549)]. The Gorings of Burton, of which family the Gorings of Danny were a cadet branch, could trace their Sussex roots to the reign of Edward II, and their court and official connections to that of Edward VI, when George Goring's grandfather, also George (*d.* 1594), was a gentleman of the privy chamber to the king; from 1584 to his death he was receiver-general of the court of wards. He acquired extensive estates in Sussex and in 1582 bought Danny, which he then expensively renovated and enlarged, from the Dacre family. He was, however, an unsuccessful financial official and died owing the crown £19,777 2*s*. 3 ½*d*. In consequence his son George, the father of the earl of Norwich, inherited large debts and after provision for their repayment was left with only a small allowance. He failed in his attempt to purchase the receivership of the court of wards, but was provided for by appointment as a gentleman pensioner. In financial terms the career of George Goring, earl of Norwich, thus followed a pattern established by his father and grandfather in its dependence on the rewards of court connection, its extravagant outlays, and its complicated and fragile network of financial credit.

Early life George Goring was educated at Sidney Sussex College, Cambridge, from which he matriculated at Easter 1600. Later he probably spent some time in Flanders. He married Lady Mary (*d.* 1648), daughter of Edward Nevill, earl of Abergavenny, shortly before 1608. He was knighted at Greenwich on 29 May 1608, became gentleman of the privy chamber to Henry, prince of Wales, in 1610, and to the king in 1611; in July 1614 he was made lieutenant of the gentlemen pensioners. In June 1613 his enduring association with Princess Elizabeth and the affairs of the Palatinate began when he accompanied her to Heidelberg upon her marriage to the elector. His diplomatic talents had already been noted, and he could be trusted to 'give a good account of all that passed' on such occasions (*Buccleuch MSS*, 1.135).

James I valued Goring for 'his sagacity and … a peculiar jocularity of humour' (Nichols, 3.256n.). He excelled at the ingenious buffoonery that James enjoyed and gained a reputation as one of the king's 'chiefe and Master Fools' (Weldon, 84). At a pot-luck supper for Prince Charles's birthday in 1618 'Sir George Goring's invention bore away the bell; and that was foure huge brawny pigys, pipeing hot, bitted and harnised with ropes of sarsiges, all tyde to a monstrous bag-pudding' (Nichols, 3.495). He took part in masques, and in 'a familiar comedy' presented before the king in September 1620 he played a 'perfumer' to Buckingham's Irish footman (*CSP Venice, 1619–21*, 390n.). He had already attached himself to Buckingham, and was associated with other long-serving courtiers such as the future earls of Holland and Carlisle. His wife, meanwhile, had become a lady of the privy chamber to Queen Anne.

Goring was also acquiring further diplomatic experience and acquaintances. He was one of the 'Mignards' who accompanied Lord Hay on his embassy to France in July 1616 (Nichols, 3.197), and in the following winter he took part in a masque for the French ambassador. In the spring of 1617 he was one of the congenial group that accompanied James I on the king's first return visit to Scotland. He had also begun to acquire pensions and offices. There were minor pensions, for example, of £200 a year, and after Queen Anne's death in 1619 he was granted '3,000 l. for eleven years' out of her jointure (*CSP dom., 1619–23*, 25). In February 1618 he became joint high steward of the honour of Peveril (an office of which he obtained sole custody in May 1638), which brought profits from both court fees and coal.

Mid-life success In the 1620s, aided by his association with Buckingham, Goring entered a wider public arena, although he remained a secondary political figure. He was MP for Lewes in 1620–22, 1624–6, and from February to April 1628. On 29 November 1621 he apparently deviated from his lifelong support for royal programmes by presenting an anti-Spanish proposal to the House of Commons that ran counter to the king's policy. It is probable, however, that he was the instrument of Buckingham and possibly James himself, in a devious attempt to put pressure on Spain. Nevertheless, Goring found himself one of the Commons' commissioners advocating a position that went beyond the intentions of his original proposal and provoked his own king as well as Spain's. The incident did not lead to any loss of favour. In July 1622 payment of a pension of £2000 for three years was confirmed by a shift in its source of payment from the exchequer to the customs farmers.

Goring remained a trusted follower of Buckingham and Prince Charles, and in the spring of 1623 the prince, then in Madrid bent on a Spanish marriage, sent for Goring to join him and the duke there. In August the prince sent him to The Hague to reassure Elizabeth, the exiled electress palatine and titular queen of Bohemia, about the effects of a Spanish alliance and in December, after that project had collapsed, Charles again sent him to his sister with letters explaining the new situation. In January 1624 there were rumours that Goring would go as an envoy to the Netherlands, but he was apparently present in March when Buckingham and King James discussed a possible French match. By September 1624 he was actively engaged in negotiations for the marriage of Prince Charles and Henrietta Maria. His role was that of a travelling envoy, shuttling between London and Paris to transmit messages or to reconcile England's two official ambassadors, his old associates Carlisle and Holland. The Venetian envoy approved him as 'a very discreet man' (*CSP Venice, 1623–5*, 435). In the spring of 1625, after the death of James I, he oversaw the final preparations for Henrietta Maria's departure for England, and when in late April she was 'somewhat indisposed' he was sent by King Charles 'to wish her good health with compliments of love' (*CSP Venice, 1625–6*, 20). In the early 1620s his connection with the queen of Bohemia had thus been maintained, while his activities in Paris laid the foundation for his long and close association with the new queen of England.

In 1626 Goring was appointed vice-chamberlain of the queen's household, but rumours of diplomatic appointments still recurred, notably in late 1626 when he was mentioned as a potential envoy to Lorraine or as ambassador-extraordinary to France. On 14 April 1628 he was created Baron Goring of Hurstpierpoint, and the next day he took his seat in the House of Lords. In July 1628, in a reshuffle of offices that strengthened Buckingham and his allies, Goring was appointed master of the horse to the queen, an office he held until 1639. In July 1630 he became the absentee secretary, clerk of the signet, and clerk of the council for Wales.

After Buckingham's assassination on 23 August 1628 Goring remained intimately and actively involved in the affairs of the queen and her court. His office was demanding, but he appears to have been motivated not only by the self-interest that required effective execution of his duties but also by the loyalty and gratitude to the king and the royal family that marked his long life and by a protective desire to keep the young queen happy. After the king left on his progress to Scotland in May 1633 Henrietta Maria was 'disconsolate' and 'sad in extremity', Goring reported. It was the duty of her courtiers to 'strive to divert' her (*Cowper MSS*, 2.10, 17). The courtier's life of constant attention and oversight was onerous. It is not surprising to find Goring noting on one occasion that he was 'very, very weary' (ibid., 2.10). Yet as he wrote to the king on 22 June 1633 in a courtier's declaration of faith, he could not

> forget who made us of nothing, and who preserved us there … Your service being by so long and sweet a custom now become a second nature, besides my obligation to address the whole course of my life to that only end where if I wittingly fail let me perish eternally. (ibid., 2.22–3)

Loyalty, however, did not protect against court divisions. In the summer of 1633 Goring was embroiled in a serious quarrel with Sir Francis Nethersole, who accused him of prematurely and treacherously revealing plans to raise money by a benevolence to aid the queen of Bohemia. Charges of indiscretion were to dog Goring's career, but on this occasion he not only had the support of Henrietta Maria but was completely exonerated by the privy council. Nevertheless it had been a 'perplexed and intricate business' (*Cowper MSS*, 2.22), the resolution of which required three sittings of the council and further confirmation of their decision by other council members then absent with the king in Edinburgh and, ultimately, by the king himself. Nethersole, in his sometimes injudicious devotion to the cause of the Palatinate, had antagonized councillors and offended the king. For Goring, the affair was the first major occasion on which his 'popularity' (*CSP dom., 1633–4*, 115) and likeability helped him to muster support for his conduct in a matter of public policy; the qualities were later to help to save his life.

Goring continued to be active at court and in its ceremonial diplomatic work, entertaining ambassadors in England and sometimes going further afield. In November 1633, for example, he was the official bearer of the news of the birth of James, duke of York, to the king of France. Nevertheless his career had reached a plateau. He was not a privy councillor and he remained a member of the queen's, not the king's, household. In court politics he belonged to the queen's and hence the pro-French party. If he was ever-present and ever-active, he was not a major policy adviser or executant. In August 1635 the earl of Northumberland reported that Goring was 'so ill-pleased' with his situation that he 'dispute[d] in himself whether he should go and trail a pike under his son in the Low Countries' rather than remain as he was (*CSP dom., 1625–49*, 505).

If Goring's political career stalled for much of the 1630s, his financial situation was transformed. The pay for his offices was of course insignificant, but such offices brought opportunities for fees and gratuities, and Goring's interest spread beyond his official appointments as master of the horse, lieutenant of the gentlemen pensioners, or secretary for Wales to grants and monopolies. He was a 'ubiquitous' and 'inveterate patentee' (Aylmer, 132, 339). In the 1630s he and a partner, Sir Henry Hungate, held the licences controlling the export of butter and shared the fines levied on illegal exporters. He was a member, with other courtiers, of commissions regulating the manufacture of gold and silver thread and enforcing the unpopular statutory requirement that every cottage have 4 acres of land and be occupied by only one family. He headed a company that attempted, unsuccessfully, to found a plantation on the Amazon. With other partners he held the monopoly for licensing inns and taverns. He held two tobacco licences, one for its import and the other for its sale in England. Finally, in 1637, he persuaded the king to grant him the great farm of the customs, and on 7 August 1637 he jokingly advised Lord Conway to stay on good terms with the new farmer—'or else', he said,

> never expect the landing of so much as a bottle of Smyrna water without custom, for a customer I am; not for any virtue of mine own, but by the folly of others, which gave me the opportunity to try my gracious master's favour, who gave it me beyond my hopes. (*CSP dom., 1637*, 361)

Goring's tenure of the customs farm was brief, however (1638–9). Faced by the demands of the Scottish wars, the king returned it to the previous farmers, although Goring probably retained residual interest, and twenty years later he still hoped to regain it.

Goring's role in these dealings, said a contemporary, was that of 'a Captaine Projector', the great man who 'hearten[ed] others to follow'. He 'lead … up the March and Dance with the Monopolies of Tobacco, and Licensing of Tavernes, setting some up, where, and as many as he pleased' (Weldon, 196). From such sources and from pensions, he reported, Goring's annual income was said to be £9000 a year (ibid.). This seems, however, to be too conservative an estimate for his later years as 'Captaine Projector'. In January 1663, when admittedly the temptation was to exaggerate, his son Charles Goring claimed that in the year 1641–2 his father's income had been £26,800. Furthermore, beyond the income that they provided, rights in offices and patents could be spun off to provide capital. Endymion Porter paid Goring £2000 for a reversionary right (never enjoyed) to an office in the petty customs, while at some time before the civil war Goring sold the wine licences for £18,000. The Welsh secretaryship had been mortgaged for £23,000. In these enterprises Goring's role was not that of a mere rentier. He was energetic and knowledgeable in the oversight and protection of his economic interests and in his pursuit of individuals who infringed his licences for taverns or tobacco or butter.

It was a fragile fortune, as the approaching war was to prove, but even for the time of prosperity it is impossible to draw up a balance sheet of costs and profits. The acquisition of benefits was expensive and involved loans to the king as well as lease costs. In 1628 Goring had lent the king £3700, and in 1635, before a further loan of £6000 to sweeten the acquisition of the customs farm, the king was already in his debt to the tune of £15,000. The wine licences that he and his associates acquired in 1627 on a 21-year lease cost £2700 a year.

Besides these costs of doing business there were the costs of family. Goring himself was regarded as extravagant, sometimes indeed unavoidably so as in elaborate entertainments for the queen, but a major strain on his finances was his heir, George *Goring. Goring was a solicitous father, and after the marriage of the younger George to the daughter of the earl of Cork he declared his intention to fit him up for a life of attendance on the king. Three years later, however, his son had run through his wife's £10,000 dowry and had retired temporarily to France 'till', Goring wrote, 'I can settle a huge debt for him of near £9,000 which almost breaks my back' (*Cowper MSS*, 2.20). Much of the money was raised on the Sussex lands and these encumbrances were to increase and complicate Goring's financial difficulties in the 1640s. Meanwhile, in 1633, the younger Goring moved to the Low Countries as colonel of Lord Vere's former regiment, which post his father bought for him for a further £4000.

This unstable structure of high income, heavy expenditure, and large debts was sustainable as long as the source of the income remained secure, but Goring had not hedged his financial bets. With a relatively small landed income of perhaps £1000–£2000 per annum Goring's prosperity was dependent on the survival of royal power. Yet despite the risks of his economic course—obvious in retrospect—Goring had considerable understanding of the way in which credit worked as well as expertise in its methods and knowledge of the personnel of the financial community. To these were added valuable familiarity with international political figures, particularly in France and the Low Countries. These attributes shaped his activities when war came to England.

The first civil war The outbreak of war with Scotland in 1638 led to the reorganization of King Charles's administration. In 1639 Goring became vice-chamberlain of the king's household, a major office which he held until 1644, and on 25 August 1639 he became a privy councillor. His activities as a member of the council bore witness to his reputation for financial skills. He was appointed to inquire into the arrears of ship money in November 1639; to inventory jewels in July 1640; to treat with the City of London for a loan of £200,000 for the army in September 1640; and to inquire into royal revenues and expenditures in January 1642.

Goring was now in his fifties and appears to have taken no military part in the bishops' wars or the first civil war. In January 1639 he had offered to furnish 100 horse for the expedition against the Scots, but he himself seems to have remained in the south. He accompanied the king to York in August 1640 and acted as a trusted messenger between York and London. In the military pause of 1641 Goring continued to be an active privy councillor, but he also pursued his accustomed interests. Questions about his handling of the tobacco licences demanded attention, and he still had an eye for acquisition. He procured Lord Aston's 'interest' in the Mulberry Garden in London through a characteristically complex system of transfers of indebtedness.

Goring's role in the inquiry into royal revenues was brief, for he accompanied Henrietta Maria to the Netherlands in February 1642. For the remainder of the first civil war his contributions to the royalist cause were primarily financial and diplomatic although in March, in an echo of the service he had rendered to her parents, he was one of the three negotiators authorized to finalize agreements after the marriage of the king's daughter Princess Mary to the prince of Orange. His main business, however, was raising money, much of it by pawning the royal jewels (for between 1 million and 2 million guilders), and buying arms for the royal cause. By November 1642 the prince of Orange had arranged to advance £120,000. Henrietta Maria depended on Goring's support and missed it when, in his quest for money, he spent a month in Antwerp.

Early in 1643 the queen and Goring returned to England, landing at Bridlington Bay, Yorkshire, on 22 February with a large supply of arms. The way to Oxford, the royalist capital, was blocked and they were forced to remain in the north, mostly at York, for several months. Goring was present at the brief siege of Leeds in April, where the besiegers were commanded by his son George. The royalists decided against an assault, but George gave his father permission to visit a parliamentarian acquaintance inside the town. The outcome was a brief negotiated cessation of hostilities, which provided a face-saving occasion for a royalist withdrawal. Once again Goring's habits of sociability and conciliation proved useful.

Goring's stay in England was brief. In September 1643 he was appointed ambassador-in-ordinary to the French court. He travelled by way of the Netherlands, arriving in October and remaining there until late November, for the king wished him to thwart the designs of parliament's envoy to The Hague and to delay the departure of the Dutch ambassador to England. Goring conferred with the prince of Orange, tried to raise more money on the already pledged jewels, and was said to be negotiating to have the English and Scottish regiments serving in the Netherlands sent back to England. He finally reached Paris on 25 November with instructions to report on French policy and to pursue a treaty embodying a formal French declaration of support for the king. Despite early optimism his work proved 'knotty', as he wrote to his wife on 12 April 1644. Two thousand barrels of powder had reached Oxford through his efforts and he had successfully organized the supply and shipping of 'all Kind of Arms and Ammunition' by 'my Merchants' (*JHL*, 1643–4, 376). He was aware of his perceived failure in the larger project, but he wrote drily that it would become apparent that he had 'not slept all this time without waking sometimes' (*CSP dom.*, *1644*, 110). In January 1644, however, letters to Secretary Nicholas in Oxford and to the queen detailing his success in dispatching 20,000 muskets and other arms to England via Dunkirk and the hopeful progress of the French negotiations, and advising the queen to charm the French ambassador, had been seized from a French courier—in itself a diplomatic incident—and had caused a furore in England. The core of Goring's offence lay in his advice to the queen that the French disinclination to a defensive and offensive alliance was really a cover for their view that the king's demands were too high, his position too weak, and the dangers of their own entanglement in an English war too great, and that she should therefore emphasize the more moderate ends of a loan and an immediate declaration against parliament and the Scots.

Once again Goring appeared to have been indiscreet. For his frankness and his logistical success he was impeached by parliament. In France 'his … intercepted letters … put him in no very good light' (*CSP dom.*, *1644*, 36–7). Among the royalists in England, '[e]xceptions [were] taken' against him (ibid., 260). He soldiered on, visiting The Hague and the queen of Bohemia in March and continuing to promote an alliance in France. Nevertheless his sense of ill usage grew. By June he expected to be replaced as ambassador and was now, he said, 'bereft of all real and titular credit' (ibid., 259). In a long letter of 21 June from Paris to Nicholas he combined policy recommendations, practical criticism of the conduct of business, a personal manifesto of achievements and wrongs, and a declaration of unfailing loyalty to the king. It reflected his talents as a diplomat and his eye for bureaucratic and financial systems, and also suggested his own limitations.

Goring again tried to hammer home to the central royalist government that the reason why sympathetic continental powers hesitated to commit themselves wholeheartedly to the king's cause was their perception of royalist weakness and hence their fear that they might be left to fight the king's battles for him: only a 'remarkable blow' against the enemy could change their minds (*CSP dom., 1644*, 260). In addition he sensibly warned that policies 'pretending relief to the oppressed Catholics' would bring a train of difficulties in their wake (ibid., 259). On the continent, he said, the execution of the king's business was harmed by too many royalist agents at cross-purposes, while the actions they engaged in were morally dubious and economically inappropriate (and contrary to his own previous proceedings). His ire was particularly aroused by a plan to renegotiate 'the business of the jewels … by changing the hands in which they were placed' in order to raise more money for the transport of arms. He considered the project impossible, ethically questionable, and unnecessary; the intrusion of new English agents uncalled for; and the suggestion that he should undertake a journey to act as a common financial intermediary an affront to his standing in Paris and England—'I had rather beg my bread or else starve', he wrote (ibid., 259). The financial devices proposed were unnecessary, he argued, because he had already operated on credit for seven months in Paris 'and so could … have held on 17 more', while his 'mere word' had been sufficient security for the supply of 20,000 muskets and other arms. He was particularly offended by the proposal to pledge 'the great collar of rubies' in order to pay for the transport of arms, when he had successfully contracted for transportation without such security. As an experienced financier who was at home in large-scale markets, Goring was irritated by inexpert meddling. As for his own expenses, he had received little more than an inadequate £2000, and had been forced to rely on his own credit. 'I blush at writing hereof', he said, 'but necessity has as little law as remedy' (ibid., 260–61). He would 'not come off this stage with shame', but he had clearly been angered and humiliated. His only fault, he claimed, lay in 'not ciphering' his letter of January to the queen (ibid.). The present letter to Nicholas was largely in cipher.

In this incident Goring's talents as a skilful and sociable negotiator in difficult circumstances, one who had established good relations with Cardinal Mazarin and Anne of Austria, and as a shrewd commentator on policies and business practices of his own government were evident, but he was tied to his old faith in manipulation and cross-subsidization as the means of government finance. Nor, despite his warning about a pro-Catholic policy, did he reflect on the political or religious issues behind the war. For Goring, loyalty was enough, and his hopes were simple: 'God bless his Majesty and send sweet England peace, and then little shall I trouble myself for my own particular, how ruined soever' (*CSP dom., 1644*, 261). Two months earlier he had written to his wife, who was unhappy at his dispatch of their second son, Charles, from the safety of Paris to England, '[H]ad I millions of crowns or scores of sons the King and his cause should have them all with better will than to eat if I were starving; nor shall fear or loss of whatsoever ever change me therein' (ibid., 110).

Despite the valedictory tone of his letter to Nicholas, Goring did not immediately leave his ambassadorship or France. His mission was at last successful, if of little substantive value, and on 3 July 1644 at Rueil, near Paris, 'a peace offensive and defensive' was concluded with the French (*CSP dom., 1644*, 378). Henrietta Maria had returned to France, and in August, Goring was with her in the country. In September he may briefly have been in Sussex at the home of the Gorings of Burton, attending to the disposal of property, but he did not formally leave France until November. On 28 November 1644 the king created him earl of Norwich.

This embassy was the last time that Norwich was a player near the centre of political affairs. For several years his career is obscure, although on 16 October 1645 he was made captain of the king's guard (a post held largely *in absentia*). In the same month, from Le Havre, he wrote a jovial, affectionate and opinionated letter to Edward Hyde in Cornwall seeking the governorship of Pendennis, for which he had the queen's backing; his son George was then in command of royalist forces in Cornwall. His commitment had not diminished, but there was an implicit recognition that his role was becoming peripheral. If Pendennis was denied him, he said, 'I have discharged my duty, and shall write on the gate as I pass by, that you can have no more of a cat than her skin' (Bodl. Oxf., MS Clarendon 25, fol. 209*r*). He would seek another way to serve the cause, and meanwhile he read romances and promised, 'Can I but get Orondates and Arsace over with me I am made and England saved' (ibid., fol. 209*v*).

Norwich appears to have passed most of the next few years on the continent. He was part of the royalist information network, still planning benefit for the king, and deploring (from Brussels) reports that Prince Charles would leave England for the French army. His diplomatic interventions could still arouse English and French anger, while his pro-French stance could no longer be taken for granted. By May 1647 he was contemplating a return to England and by December he was in London, having obtained a pass from parliament. His nominal reason was to compound for his property, but there seem to have been no formal proceedings at the time and in March 1648 his lands remained on a list of sequestrations. In 1646 parliamentary officials had tried to seize assets accruing from Norwich's Welsh offices, but they were thwarted by the discovery that the interest in and profits of the offices were no longer in his hands. They had been conveyed to a creditor as security for debts that remained unpaid. By the 1640s this was the characteristic condition of Norwich's property. In February 1641 the bulk of his Sussex lands had been transferred to trustees. The rest of the 1640s saw the further erosion of his landed assets by mortgages, leases on unfavourable terms, and allocations for payment of his and his son George's debts. The web of debt had been threatening before the civil war. By now, with the loss of income from office and new expenses, the Goring financial fortunes were foundering.

The second civil war In May 1648 Norwich found himself in Kent, perhaps dispatched there by royalist leaders in London, perhaps merely on his way to Sussex. The county was in revolt against parliament but local leaders were divided. His conciliatory talents again proved useful, and he was known in the county through family connections. The upshot was his appointment as general of the royalist forces at their rendezvous at Burham Heath, between Rochester and Maidstone, on 29 May.

Norwich now led a mixed body of troops made up of countrymen, experienced soldiers, citizens, and watermen. He intended to rendezvous at Blackheath and from there to march on London. On 30 May, however, Fairfax had dispersed 1000 men at Blackheath; on the evening of 1 June, in pouring rain, he took Maidstone after fierce street fighting, while Norwich and his main body of troops, perhaps as many as 8000 men, waited indecisively nearby. Royalist casualties were heavy, and after the battle much of Norwich's force melted away. His military début had been inglorious, but with the remainder of his army he marched on to Blackheath, where the hoped-for influx of London support did not materialize and where he faced a formidable foe in the city's militia under Philip Skippon. Abandoning his initial plan, he and his army of some 3000 men crossed the Thames at Greenwich. In Essex his numbers increased and he was joined by former royalist officers, including Sir Charles Lucas. They marched to Chelmsford, where recruits and supplies poured in and where he was joined by other experienced officers, notably Lord Capel and Lord Loughborough. His forces, however, remained ill disciplined and ill armed.

On 10 June, Norwich and his army marched out of Chelmsford, reaching the outskirts of Colchester late that evening, and on 12 June he entered the town. His intention was to advance into Norfolk and Suffolk, expecting strong gentry support there, but Fairfax was now close on his heels and on 12 June reached Lexden, just west of Colchester, with his advance guard. The next day the rest of his army arrived, and Norwich was forced to make a stand. After an unsuccessful attempt to storm the city on 13 June, Fairfax settled in to a siege of attrition. He gradually tightened the noose until the royalists were confined within the old town walls. Norwich was constrained from taking aggressive action by weaknesses of men and *matériel* and by his determination to use what resources he had to buy time for the king's cause elsewhere. The siege lasted eleven weeks of a miserably wet summer and was notorious for the sufferings of civilians and soldiers alike: both were the victims of fire, sickness, and starvation.

Norwich was no figurehead as commander, although active military direction fell to Capel and Lucas, with able logistical help from Loughborough. Most policy decisions were reached by a committee, but in the exchanges with Fairfax that marked the progress of the siege Norwich's was the official voice of command. He and Capel were reputed to be adamant for holding out when others might have accepted terms. He was also active in trying to keep up the spirits of his troops, but the bluffness, heartily insensitive jokes, and remorseless frankness of his style did not help his reputation with the parliamentarians or Colchester's civilians. When after the first assault on the town Fairfax summoned Norwich to surrender, he 'returned an Answer not becomming to a Gentleman', according to a parliamentarian broadside. Toward the end of the siege, as starvation bit, 'the poorer sort of people began to rise for want of bread: The Lord *Goring* told them they must eat their children; this … enraged them' (*Diary of the Siege of Colchester*, 13 June, 15 August). This reply was to become part of the mythology of the siege.

By August the town's condition was desperate, and Cromwell's defeat of the Scots at Preston on 17 August ended royalist hopes. Within Colchester troops were mutinous and civilians rebellious. Norwich was at last forced to negotiate, although he still attempted delaying tactics. Fairfax's terms had grown harsher, but after ten days of haggling the articles of surrender were signed on the night of 27 August, and on the morning of 28 August Fairfax's troops entered Colchester. Norwich and his colleagues had accepted a treaty by which quarter for their lives was granted to all soldiers below the rank of captain, but senior officers—captains and above—were forced to surrender to mercy, which meant that by the laws of war their lives could be forfeit at the general's discretion. Lucas and his friend Sir George Lisle were shot within hours of the surrender, but Fairfax then granted quarter to the remaining senior officers. On 31 August the House of Lords, perhaps protecting its own after the executions of Lucas and Lisle, wrote to Fairfax desiring that Norwich and Capel be 'safely' conveyed to Windsor Castle for imprisonment (*JHL*, 1647–8, 476).

On 25 September the House of Commons began proceedings for the attainder of Norwich and the impeachment of Capel. In a letter of 3 October written in his own 'ill hand' Norwich protested on three grounds. First, as a peer it was his right, confirmed by Magna Carta and the laws of the land, to be tried only by his peers. Second, what he had done as a soldier acting under a commission from the prince of Wales had been 'clearly remitted to [him] for matter of life' by Fairfax's second grant of quarter. Finally, he was 'destitute' of the counsel and other helps merited in a case in which his 'life, honour and posterity [were] so nearly concerned'. He also asked for '*some competent liberty*' of a kind commonly granted to prisoners of war, and this request at least was successful, for the Colchester prisoners at Windsor were reportedly granted limited freedom of the town (Worcester College, Oxford, Clarke MSS, vol. 114, fol. 91).

The parliamentary proceedings moved deliberately towards trial, but on 10 November an alternative solution was proposed in the House of Commons and on 16 November an order for the banishment of Norwich and six other royalist leaders of the second civil war was committed. On

13 December, however, after Pride's Purge, the order was rescinded and on 15 December the council of war at Whitehall urged justice on the earl and his fellows, although it specified that their cases should be considered 'in respect of Articles given them' (*Works*, 2.132). On 3 February 1649, after the execution of the king, an act was passed setting up a high court of justice to try Norwich, the duke of Hamilton, the earl of Holland, Lord Capel, and Sir John Owen. The commissioners conscientiously sought clarification of Fairfax's explanation of the meaning of quarter. They accepted his argument that military convention and practical considerations alike meant that a grant of common quarter 'assur[ed] … Life against the immediate execution of the military Sword, or any further execution thereby without judicial Trial' unless specific terms covering the nature of the quarter granted had been negotiated—as they had not been in the case of Norwich and Capel—but that such a grant of quarter did not preclude later trial for military or other offences by a military or civilian court (Rushworth, 7.1303). Fairfax denied 'any particular animosity to the Lord *Goring*'; he was acting in accordance with 'the general sense and practice in all Wars' (ibid., 7.1303–4). In view of their rank he had deemed it suitable to submit Norwich and Capel to the judgment of parliament. Norwich's trial was an episode in the difficult history of the relationship between the international and unwritten laws of war and the laws of the civil state.

Norwich and his fellow defendants were condemned to death on 6 March. On 7 March the house refused to hear their petitions for mercy. On 8 March more petitions were presented on their behalf, including one from eighteen of Norwich's creditors who spoke for 'themselves and many more' (*JHC*, 1648–51, 159). The house debated whether there should be short stays of execution, but there was no respite for Hamilton, Holland, and Capel. Owen escaped by a vote of 28 to 23, but the vote on Norwich was 24 to 24. He was saved by the casting vote of the speaker, Lenthall. Some, including Lenthall, said that his vote reflected a sense of past obligation (although Clarendon suggested that this might be a compassionate fiction) (Clarendon, *Hist. rebellion*, 3.206), others that he acted in response to lobbying by the Spanish and Dutch ambassadors. Norwich and Owen returned to prison. Finally, on 7 May 1649, they were pardoned for their lives and forthwith set free.

Exile and Restoration After his release Norwich remained for a time in England. In May 1650 his estates, now in the hands of trustees, were seized. In July 1650 he was accused of having recently corresponded with 'the enemies beyond seas', but on 3 September he received a pass to go abroad, on a recognizance of £5000 and on condition of good behaviour and appearance before the justices of Sussex if commanded. Proceedings on his property dragged on intermittently until February 1651 when the seizure was removed on the ground that Norwich was not 'within the Ordinance of Sequestration' (Green, 2.704). This outcome may have been connected with the fact that the property was heavily mortgaged and held by trustees, or that one of the trustees was Norwich's brother-in-law Anthony Stapley, a regicide. It was in any case by now too late for Norwich to extricate himself from the burdens on his Sussex estates, and in 1652 Danny was sold to a Sussex parliamentarian, Peter Courthope.

For the rest of the decade Norwich led a peripatetic life, largely in Brussels, Breda, and Antwerp. Indeed, in 1655 it was suggested that spies would pay little attention if he undertook a journey to Madrid, 'he being so much accustomed to them upon his own score and fancy' (*Clarendon State Papers*, 3.57). He observed, reported at length, negotiated, and offered policy suggestions, but his recommendations met with a mixed reception and while his relations with Secretary Nicholas—'my Ned' (*Nicholas Papers*, 2.282)—seem to have remained stable and affectionate, those with Hyde were more volatile. In 1655 Norwich admitted that Hyde was 'a very honest, right principled man in the mayne'; he would always do him the best service he could, 'thougth [*sic*] not rely uppon or submit unto his rules, as perhaps he may expect'. Hyde's habit of 'overvallewing himselfe and undervallewing others, together with his grasping at too much' would, if unrestrained, 'bring irrecoverable inconveniences, if not ruin' (ibid., 2.279). He was not, in Norwich's view, a man who would inspire others to follow him. Hyde too had his reservations, complaining in 1653 of Norwich's 'unskilfulness and censoriousness' (*Clarendon State Papers*, 2.178). In December 1655, however, he was seeking Norwich's advice as to whether the king should move to Flanders, while the earl signed himself to Hyde as 'yours through thick and thinne' (ibid., 3.77). Norwich was now seen as pro-Spanish, like Hyde and Nicholas. He was suspicious of France (a 'tickle … jade' (*Nicholas Papers*, 1.248)) and of his old mistress Henrietta Maria and her advisers.

In 1655 Norwich had been actively engaged in an attempt to forge an alliance between the radical sectarian Edward Sexby and Spain to subvert Cromwell's government, and in the same year he secured the arrest of Henry Manning, a Cromwellian spy. Nevertheless his sense of being 'layd by' (*Nicholas Papers*, 3.3), increased in the course of the decade, and his activities were further limited by his poverty. He still offered unsolicited advice, even when the king's advisers were 'all of another mynde', in part to fend off 'accusations of … being sullein', a quality that his 'soule abhorr[ed]' (ibid., 3.221). He was aware that others found his opinionated wanderings troublesome. Some were also sceptical about his poverty, complaining of his 'expensefull way' and 'illimited … expense' (ibid., 2.93; *Clarendon State Papers*, 2.125). Norwich, however, declared in 1655 that his only clothes were the suit on his back and that he could not go about the king's business because 'it … raigned soe fast and my bootes [were] soe thinne' (*Nicholas Papers*, 2.321, 326). Hoped-for funds from England failed. His son George suspected fraud by two of their trustees.

The earl's son George died in poverty in Madrid in 1657. Norwich, whose relations with his erratic heir had remained strong, bore his death stoically. His wife had died in July 1648, while the earl was besieged at Colchester. He had become 'old Goring' (*Nicholas Papers*, 3.166), but if he was largely removed from the centre of affairs his loyalty was unshaken. He maintained his connection with the queen of Bohemia and was still an intermediary in the dissemination of news. In 1657 he was reappointed to his old office of captain of the royal guard. By 1658 he had been allotted a pension by Charles II, although its payment was uncertain, and in that year he was reputedly involved with his Stapley nephews, the sons of the regicide, in a plot against Cromwell.

In April 1660 Norwich wrote from Breda to the king that, although old and feeble, he was eager to serve him. In 1658 he had assured Charles that he would ask for nothing beyond his current pension except confirmation of Charles I's grant, and on 12 June 1660 he asked Hyde to secure 'his confirmation in the Customs, wherein he has in stock £50,000' (*Clarendon State Papers*, 5.40). On 26 September his request was more expansive: he asked for restoration of his former share in the customs and for his place as secretary of Wales, and for compensation for £2200 spent in Charles I's service at Portsmouth and for his office of captain of the guard, which he was now too old to exercise (ibid., 5.54). With much effort he and his son Charles retained the Welsh secretaryship and the stewardship of the honour of Peverel, although its coal works were so decayed as to be unprofitable without heavy expenditure. He received a pension of £2000 a year in return for yielding up the captainship of the guard but most of it was pre-empted for payment of debts, leaving him with an income of £450 a year. He was disappointed in his major quest. The customs eluded him, although he and his partners could offer £400,000 for them, £10,000 above the offer of the successful bidders. Norwich had been confident of success. On 2 January 1663 he wrote to Hyde that he had received by his hands the most fatal blow to his fortune, and suggested that other potential farmers had been bribed to stay out of the bidding. He was, he declared, 'as capable as any' to farm the customs, and his honour was engaged in the refusal (*Clarendon State Papers*, 5.291). When he was 'laid aside' for the customs, said his son, the disappointment 'broke his heart' (*CSP dom., 1663–4*, 6). On 6 January 1663 Norwich died at an inn in Brentford with only his servants round him, on his way from Hampton Court to London, and on 14 January he was buried in Westminster Abbey. His will was largely devoted to provisions for the repayment of debts.

Conclusion Goring had three sons and seven daughters. Some apparently died in childhood, and little is known of his relations with the survivors beyond the letters that reveal his patient if sometimes exasperated concern for his son George, and his will, which reveals care for his remaining children's interests. His letter of 1644 to his wife suggests an easy and rational partnership, and on 26 June 1648, just before her death, he took the opportunity to scribble a reassuring message for her as a postscript to a letter to Lady Campion. In 1655 he wrote to Nicholas, '[T]alke you gallants at Court what yee will, I never knew soe much trew felicity and lasting friendship as betweene a honest man and good wife' (*Nicholas Papers*, 2.317). Nevertheless 'The Progress', a poem of about 1628 on the sexual prowess of leading courtiers, suggested that Goring held his own against his younger peers: 'Lusty lord Goring cannot be miss'd … he's as active as at eighteen' (Huth, n.p.). The poem is so formulaic an exercise in a familiar genre, however, that its lone evidence is worth little.

By the time of 'The Progress', Goring was already 'grey'; in old age he was 'ample' (*Nicholas Papers*, 2.37). His letters make clear his own affectionate nature, and the comments and letters of others reveal that his affection was reciprocated even when they disagreed. If his joviality slipped into buffoonery, it also concealed a more thoughtful perception of himself and others. His disappointments were freely expressed and, in Hyde's view, he too easily fell into a 'melancholic imagination that he [was] not trusted' (*Clarendon State Papers*, 3.89). If at Colchester he joked that the starving could eat their children, he also wrote a fervent and touching letter to Lady Campion after her husband's death (E. Sussex RO, Danny MSS, DAN 119). His fear of being thought 'sullein'—only exceeded as an offence by disloyalty—suggests that his joviality, although natural, was also a principled mode of conduct, and in misfortune a form of stoicism.

Hyde, as earl of Clarendon, gave Norwich a minor place in the history of his time, bringing him forward on the public stage only for his command at Colchester and subsequent trial. The earlier strains in their relationship found expression in his cool and on the whole ungenerous assessment of Norwich's character, which has contributed to the conventional picture of him as a genial buffoon and court parasite. Hyde admitted that Norwich had many friends and, more significantly, virtually no enemies, and that this helped to explain the drawn vote on his execution, but he concluded that his 'frolick and pleasant humour' and the 'jovial Nature' that had made so many friends unfitted him for serious affairs. His chief ambition before the war, said Clarendon, had been to become 'Master of a very fair Fortune' (Clarendon, *Hist. rebellion*, 3.118).

Norwich knew himself and in general made modest claims. '[B]elieve me as honest as any, though more weak than others would make me, which is not my fault not having made my self,' he wrote to Hyde in 1645. ''Tis in every man's power to be honest, but in none's to be wise. Such talents are given from above, not found or made here below' (Bodl. Oxf., MSS Clarendon 25, fol. 209*v*). In particular matters, however, he had a strong and confident sense of the value, too often under-appreciated, of his contributions to the king's cause.

Norwich had little interest, it seems, in the wider political issues that now seem to dominate his lifetime. Virtually nothing is known of his intellectual life: he read romances; he had a book of dreams; a correspondent wrote approvingly to Samuel Hartlib in 1648 of his 'ingenuities' (Culpeper, 317). His interest lay in the day-to-day business of life at court and of international manoeuvre, and their manipulation for fairly traditional English and royal ends. Yet although he may have had no innovative or even very coherent world view, within his chosen focus his observations were shrewd and sensible and his energy in pursuing his own and the crown's ends considerable. Clarendon's imputation of self-interest, self-enrichment, and an undiscriminating amiability as the dominant rules of his life seems unfair. Loyalty governed his actions. 'I had all from his Majesty, and he hath all again,' he said in 1644 (*CSP dom., 1644*, 261). Unlike many royalists, he appears to have had no need to reflect on his course in the civil war. He recognized that a courtier's gratitude to the crown required his service, but he seems genuinely to have sublimated gratitude into love of the wearer of the crown and his family.

Yet Clarendon was right to draw attention to Norwich's entrepreneurial activities. His financial skills and energies were of a different order from those of most other courtier patentees and his financial success, at least for a time, was remarkable. He clearly had talents of a high order for operating in the money markets, whether in his own interests or the king's, and these were reinforced by his amiable, sociable personality. It was, however, a risky and fragile business that could not be sustained in adversity.

Norwich outlived his age. The profession of courtier changed between the reigns of James I and Charles II. For a time in the early seventeenth century, and to a degree that was new, major regulatory actions of the state were privatized in ways that presented great opportunities to courtly entrepreneurs. The post-Restoration state, for all its apparent similarities to the world before 1642, was a different bureaucratic and political place. Norwich had seized the opportunities offered by the 1620s and 1630s with zest, ability, and success. In the 1640s and 1650s he served with devoted loyalty the family that had allowed him that success. After the Restoration his heart was broken not only because he was too old, but because the day of the large-scale courtier–entrepreneur who owed his opportunities directly to personal access and service to the monarch had passed. BARBARA DONAGAN

Sources *CSP dom., 1603–64* • *CSP Venice, 1619–47* • J. A. Woolridge, ed., *The Denny archives: a catalogue* (1966) • *The Nicholas papers*, ed. G. F. Warner, 4 vols., CS, new ser., 40, 50, 57, 3rd ser., 31 (1886–1920) • *Calendar of the Clarendon state papers preserved in the Bodleian Library*, ed. O. Ogle and others, 5 vols. (1869–1970) • GEC, *Peerage* • *The manuscripts of the Earl Cowper*, 3 vols., HMC, 23 (1888–9), vol. 2 • M. A. E. Green, ed., *Calendar of the proceedings of the committee for advance of money, 1642–1656*, 3 vols., PRO (1888) • Worcester College, Oxford, Clarke MSS • Bodl. Oxf., MS Clarendon 25 • E. Sussex RO, Danny archives • *The Clarke papers*, ed. C. H. Firth, 4 vols., CS, new ser., 49, 54, 61–2 (1891–1901), vols. 1–2 • J. Rushworth, *Historical collections*, new edn, 8 vols. (1721–2) • will, PRO, PROB 11/310, sig. 7 • E. Hyde, earl of Clarendon, *The history of the rebellion and civil wars in England*, 3 vols. (1702–4) • J. Nichols, *The progresses, processions, and magnificent festivities of King James I, his royal consort, family and court*, 4 vols. (1828) • *JHC*, vol. 6, 1648–51 • *The manuscripts of his grace the duke of Portland*, 10 vols., HMC, 29 (1891–1931), vol. 3 • *A diary of the siege of Colchester by the forces under the command of his excellency the lord generall Fairfax* (1648) • *JHL*, vol. 6, 1643–4; vol. 10, 1647–8 • [A. Weldon], *The court and character of King James* (1651) • *Report on the manuscripts of his grace the duke of Buccleuch and Queensberry … preserved at Montagu House*, 3 vols. in 4, HMC, 45 (1899–1926), vol. 1 • R. Lockyer, *Buckingham: the life and political career of George Villiers, first duke of Buckingham, 1592–1628* (1981) • F. P. Verney, ed., *Memoirs of the Verney family during the civil war*, 2 vols. (1892) • G. E. Aylmer, *The king's servants: the civil service of Charles I, 1625–1642* (1961) • L. Stone, *The crisis of the aristocracy, 1558–1641* (1965) • 'The letters of Sir Cheney Culpeper, 1641–1657', ed. M. J. Braddick, *Camden miscellany, XXXIII*, CS, 5th ser., 7 (1996), 105–402 • H. Huth, ed., *Inedited poetical miscellanies, 1584–1700* (1870)

Archives BL, letters, Add. MSS 18980–18982 • E. Sussex RO, corresp. and papers concerning his debts | BL, letters to Sir E. Nicholas, Egerton MSS 2533, 2535–2536 • Bodl. Oxf., Clarendon state papers

Wealth at death £2000 p.a. pension 1661–3, but largely allotted to debts, leaving disposable income of £450: *CSP dom.*, 6; will, PRO, PROB 11/310, sig. 7

Goring, George, **Baron Goring** (**1608–1657**), royalist army officer, was one of the most prominent of the king's cavalry commanders and regional generals in the English civil war. He was born on 14 July 1608, the eldest son of a prominent Sussex gentleman, George *Goring (subsequently Baron Goring, then earl of Norwich), and Mary, second daughter of Edward Nevill, sixth Lord Bergavenny. His sister, Diana, married the royalist army officer George *Porter.

Marriage, foreign service, and the Scottish wars, 1629–1640 On 25 July 1629 Goring married Lettice (*b*. 1610), the third daughter of the rich parvenu Richard Boyle, earl of Cork, who brought him a dowry of £10,000. Young George's reaction was to go on a spending spree, in the course of which he established a reputation as the most witty and dashing of the young men about the royal court. By 1633 his money was gone, and he agreed both to redeem his fortunes and to win a more respectable name by military service abroad. Cork somewhat grudgingly put up the cash to purchase him the command of a foot regiment and horse troop of English soldiers in the Dutch service, and he held this until he was shot in the ankle at the siege of Breda in October 1637. The wound lamed him for life, but also won him something of the reputation of a hero, and he returned to honourable retirement in England, being made governor of Portsmouth on 8 January 1639. He was still a reckless gambler, and his marital relations were notoriously stormy; indeed, although Lettice lived until shortly before 12 April 1643, there seems to be no mention of their partnership after 1640. His career, however, now promised well.

With this military experience Goring was appointed to command a foot regiment when Charles I raised an army to suppress the Scottish covenanters in 1639; Goring led it in the advance guard to Kelso, winning plaudits as a fine officer. After the resulting truce, and the disbanding of the army, he applied for a new post in the Dutch forces, but was instead appointed to lead a brigade when war broke out against the Scots afresh in 1640. His force did not reach the front before the king was decisively defeated, but it is plain from later events that he made himself popular with the soldiers. During this period his personal habits remained as wild as before: after a drinking bout in the Isle of Wight in late 1639 he climbed the ladder to the public gibbet at Newport, put his head in the noose, and imitated the dying speech of a felon, warning the crowd against the keeping of bad company such as his friends.

The army plot and the outbreak of war, 1641–1642 Both sides of Goring's character came together in the first months of 1641, when he became one of a group of young officers surrounding the queen, who believed that Charles I should use the royal army to pressure the Long Parliament into calling off its attacks upon his government. Goring had retained his military command while taking a seat in the Commons for his garrison town of Portsmouth, and so was well placed to observe all developments. He proved to be at once one of the boldest and most canny of the leaders of this army plot, advocating that the soldiers be marched up to London to threaten parliament directly, and seeking the post of lieutenant-general to command them. Then, realizing that the conspiracy was becoming both impractical and badly compromised, he resolved to escape damage by betraying it himself. He passed the details to the leaders of the parliamentary opposition through a mutual friend, the earl of Newport, and then retired quietly to Portsmouth, remaining there unmolested as the plot was exposed, and the plotters dispersed, in May. The Commons had formally exonerated Goring and voted him their thanks on 9 June, leaving him (as he saw it) in possession of Portsmouth to await a better opportunity to do the king service.

During the winter of 1641–2, as tension grew between Charles and many in the parliament, Goring took money openly from the latter and secretly from the queen, to strengthen the port's defences. When rumours of this double-dealing reached the Commons in November, he allayed suspicion with a confident speech of denial. His moment for action came on 2 August 1642, when it became clear that civil war had begun, and he declared for the king, thus presenting him with a major port which could receive aid from the continent. The gesture proved to be an empty one, for he immediately found himself under siege, with inexperienced soldiers and no realistic prospect of relief. After holding out for more than a month he surrendered upon terms which allowed him to get away to the Netherlands, where he joined the queen in raising men, money, and munitions for the royalist cause.

The northern campaigns and after, 1642–1645 Goring returned in December 1642, landing at Newcastle with a number of veterans enticed from the Dutch service, and was rewarded with immediate appointment to command the horse regiments in the northern royalist army under the earl of Newcastle. On 30 March 1643 he scored a signal success by surprising and routing the northern parliamentarian army under Sir Thomas Fairfax on Seacroft Moor as it was retreating towards Leeds. He would have tried to storm the latter town, into which the beaten enemy had fled, but was talked out of such a risky enterprise by older colleagues. Instead he retired to Wakefield, and fell ill with a fever. He was still bedridden on 21 May when Fairfax repaid the compliment by launching a surprise attack upon that town, and storming it. Goring struggled onto a horse and led a counter-charge with conspicuous courage, but it broke and he was taken prisoner. Parliament committed him to the Tower of London.

Goring remained there until 2 April 1644, when the king exchanged him for the earl of Lothian. Being thus freed, he joined the royal court at Oxford but—either because

George Goring, Baron Goring (1608–1657), by Sir Anthony Van Dyck, *c.*1635–40 [right, with Mountjoy Blount, earl of Newport]

his betrayal of the army plot still rankled or because the situation in the north demanded his talents—he was sent back with an escort to his northern command. He arrived in time to find that the royalist position had collapsed, Newcastle having been penned up in York with his infantry while his cavalry escaped into the midlands. Goring rejoined the latter, made an attempt to relieve Lincoln but arrived too late, and eventually marched westwards to reinforce the main relief force bound for York under Prince Rupert. He brought 5000 horse and 800 foot to the prince's army near Bolton on 30 May.

Goring and his forces accompanied that force in its triumphant progress across Lancashire and Yorkshire during June. When Rupert faced the armies which had besieged York at Marston Moor, on 2 July, he put Goring in charge of the cavalry upon his left wing, facing those of his old enemy Fairfax. There he perfectly executed the prince's battle plan, breaking Fairfax's charge with musket volleys from foot soldiers placed among his horse and then leading in the latter to drive the battered enemy from the field. The whole right flank of the parliamentarian and Scottish force was exposed, and its three generals fled; but the right wing of the royalist position had collapsed more completely, allowing Cromwell's horse to swing round its rear and take Goring's disorganized troopers from behind. This cost the royalists the battle, and the north.

Once again Goring had been unlucky, and once again he fell on his feet. Charles had decided to dismiss his own cavalry commander, Lord Wilmot, as politically untrustworthy, and his principal civilian adviser, Lord Digby, persuaded him to send for Goring to fill the position. The latter reached the royal army in late July 1644, and was proclaimed general of its horse on 8 August. He carried out his responsibilities with distinction through the successful autumn campaign which followed, beating up Sir William Waller's quarters at Andover on 18 October, and leading a successful charge at the second battle of Newbury nine days later.

In December, Goring left winter quarters with 3000 horse and 1500 foot and orders to campaign in Hampshire and Sussex as lieutenant-general of the south-east. The parliamentarian fortresses in the region proved too strong to attack, and in February 1645 he was ordered instead to help the royalist western association against an invasion led by Waller. This he effected energetically, harrying Waller out of the region by early April. At this point, however, he was shabbily treated by the civilian councillors advising the prince of Wales, as the government of the west; they revoked an agreement that he should pursue Waller, and ordered him to support the siege of Taunton instead, while protecting an officer whom he wished to discipline. His anger with them was obvious, but before the end of the month the king had recalled him and his horsemen to the royal army for the coming campaign.

That campaign opened with the fateful decision, on 8 May 1645, to detach Goring and his 3000 horse yet again, and return them to the west to reinforce it. This was almost certainly propelled by Rupert's growing jealousy, and sweetened for Goring by his being commissioned to command all the western forces, free from the authority of the prince's council. He was now in complete control of the second most powerful surviving royalist army. He had also become a (nominal) peer, for his father's elevation to the earldom of Norwich in November 1644 had given him the courtesy title of Lord Goring; it was the apogee of his career. In practice, however, he found himself tied to the renewed siege of Taunton, a strong garrison which had just been relieved. The prince's councillors refused to recognize his commission, and it was in any case negated by yet another recall to the field army, against which he appealed. His old ankle wound troubled him, so that he retired to Bath for a time in the hope that its healing waters would alleviate the pain. It was rumoured, perhaps with malice, that he also sought relief in drink: 'dear General', wrote his ally Digby, 'beware of debauches' (Bodl. Oxf., MS Tanner 60, fol. 36). In these circumstances it is not surprising that the siege of Taunton was slackly prosecuted.

With an ailing and sometimes absentee commander, and no provision for pay and supplies for them built into the local royalist war machine, it would not be surprising either if his cavalry had been unusually ill-disciplined and inclined to plunder. This was exactly the reputation which they subsequently acquired, and which has become embedded both in history texts and in Somerset folklore, where 'Goring's crew' were remembered as drunken ruffians in recent centuries. It must be observed, however, that contemporary evidence seems to be against it; instead the records show Goring working hard to ensure good relations between his troopers and local people, while the serious misbehaviour was that of west country regiments under the nominal control of the council. It may be that folklore has itself been moulded by a historiographical tradition based on the testimony of Goring's royalist enemies.

In early July 1645 a more lethal enemy arrived in Somerset, represented by parliament's New Model Army which had destroyed the weakened royal army at Naseby. It grossly outnumbered Goring's forces, and his only feasible options were to defend the river crossings between them, to attempt a diversionary flanking movement, and to avoid pitched battle until he was reinforced. He attempted each in turn, but the first two were easily outmanoeuvred, and the third failed on 10 July when the New Model caught his rearguard at Langport and shattered it, driving his whole army into Devon. There it was given a breathing space of three months while the New Model eliminated most of the western royalist strongholds, but Goring was unable to make any use of it. His foot soldiers, demoralized by defeat, almost all deserted in the wake of Langport, and he had no money with which to raise more. Furthermore, the king had still failed to confirm his promised commission in the face of the determined opposition of the prince's household, and so his authority to command anybody except his own loyal horse regiments was questionable.

In October 1645 the New Model Army at last approached Devon. Goring beat up its vanguard at Axminster in a cavalry raid on 13 October, but this had no effect in stemming its slow and careful advance in overwhelming numbers. Penned helplessly into south Devon and watching it encircle Exeter, he fell ill again under the strain. Faced with an apparently impossible situation, he responded exactly as he had done when faced with similar difficulties in the army plot and at Portsmouth: he abandoned ship. On 20 November he informed the prince of Wales that he needed to retire to France for two months to recover his health, and set sail from Dartmouth without awaiting a reply.

Exile and death Twelve miserable years of anticlimax awaited Goring. He made no attempt to return to England after the two months had expired, and, as he probably expected, the western royalists were overwhelmed before the spring. Between 1646 and 1648 he is invisible to the record, and was presumably seeking employment in exile. In 1648 he found it, when his father helped to promote peace talks between Spain and the Netherlands which culminated in the treaty of Munster. In reward he obtained his son the command of the English regiments in the Spanish service, with the rank of colonel-general and a salary of 600 crowns a month. Once again, however, apparent success was followed by disappointment, because the overstrained finances of the Spanish monarchy put his pay rapidly into arrears. In March 1650 he went to Spain itself to obtain what was owed to him by a personal appeal at the royal court; he remained there for the rest of his life. In 1652 he was in the army which recaptured Barcelona; rumour later reported that he had obtained the rank of lieutenant-general in it, but been disgraced after a quarrel with its commander. Three years later he was unemployed and living in Madrid, and offered his services to the exiled Charles II. Charles had been the prince of Wales whom he had abandoned in Devon, and there is no record of any reply. He lingered on in Madrid, increasingly penurious and increasingly ill, and died there, of unknown causes, on 15 July 1657. He was buried in the chapel of the English Jesuits, dedicated to St George.

Assessment An excellent Van Dyck portrait of Goring in the late 1630s, looking lean, handsome, and rakish, is preserved in the Petworth collection. His historical reputation has been that of the archetypal dashing, roistering, irresponsible cavalier; but there was clearly more to him than that. Much of it has been coloured by the brilliant and unscrupulous account of him provided by Clarendon, who had been one of the prince's councillors in the west country and penned his narrative of events there primarily to defend himself and his colleagues against the accusations of Goring and others. It is clear that, even for an adherent of a lost cause, Goring was more than usually unlucky. There is no mistaking his energy, physical courage, and tactical ability as a cavalry commander, or the wit and charm which made him shine as a courtier and win popularity with his soldiers, or the intelligence which enabled him to recognize hopeless situations. His admirer Sir Richard Bulstrode called him 'the most dextrous in any sudden emergency that I have ever seen' (Bulstrode, *Memoirs and Reflections*, 1721, 134). His enemy Clarendon agreed upon the 'presentness of his mind and vivacity in a sudden attempt, though never so full of danger' (Clarendon, *Hist. rebellion*, bk 9, 102). Had he been in command of the king's left wing at Naseby, with his 3000 horse to reinforce it, then it is unlikely that it would have collapsed as it did and so given parliament the victory; in which case the history of Britain, and his own career, would have been very different.

Having said all that, it cannot be argued that Goring ever proved himself to have the abilities of a good general, rather than an able lieutenant and an excellent commander of horse. It is probably true, likewise, that his own ambition and sense of ability undermined his capacity to function as a support to a better soldier for long. His tendency to quit unpromising situations may have been sensible but could appear pusillanimous. In the last analysis it is hard to avoid the suspicion that his qualities add up to a superficial brilliance, and that in war and in politics he never rose above a short-term, tactical, ingenuity.

RONALD HUTTON

Sources Bodl. Oxf., MSS Clarendon 24–26 · *The Lismore papers, first series: autobiographical notes, remembrances and diaries of Sir Richard Boyle, first and 'great' earl of Cork*, ed. A. B. Grosart, 5 vols. (privately printed, London, 1886), vols. 2, 3 · G. N. Godwin, *The civil war in Hampshire, 1642–45, and the story of Basing House*, new edn (1904), chap. 2 · *The declaration of Colonel Goring to the House of Commons upon his examination concerning the late conspiracie* (1641) · J. Sprigge, *Anglia rediviva* (1647) · Bodl. Oxf., MS Firth C7, fols. 298–311 · Bodl. Oxf., MS Tanner 60, fols. 15–150 · *A miraculous victory obtained by … Ferdinando Lord Fairfax* (1643) · *Mercurius Aulicus* (4 April 1643) · *A more full relation of the great battell fought betweene Sir T. Fairfax, and Goring, on Thursday last* (July 1645) · Captain Blackwell, *A more exact relation of the great defeat given to Gorings army in the west* (1645) · E. Walker, *Historical discourses upon several occasions* (1705) · M. D. E. Wanklyn, 'The king's armies in the west of England', MA diss., University of Manchester, 1966 · R. Hutton, 'Clarendon's "History of the rebellion"', *EngHR*, 97 (1982), 70–88 · N. Canny, *The upstart earl: a study of the social and mental world of Richard Boyle, first earl of Cork, 1566–1643* (1982) · Bodl. Oxf., MS Dugdale 19, fol. 235 · GEC, *Peerage* · W. Dugdale, *The baronage of England*, 2 vols. (1675–6)

Likenesses A. Van Dyck, oils, *c.*1635–1640 (with first earl of Newport), Petworth House, West Sussex [*see illus.*] · A. Van Dyck, oils, *c.*1638 (half-length in armour), Art Gallery, Plymouth; on loan from Clarendon collection · A. Van Dyck, double portrait, oils; other versions, Knole, Kent; NPG

Wealth at death died in debt and predeceased his father

Goring, Marius (1912–1998), actor and director, was born on 23 May 1912 at Newport, Isle of Wight, the second son of Dr Charles Buckman Goring (1870–1919), a criminologist of a Sussex family, and his wife, Katie Winifred, *née* Macdonald (1874–1964), a pianist, of Scottish descent. His father, an advanced theorist on the nature and causes of criminal behaviour, was a prison doctor at the time of Marius's birth. His mother, taught partly by Clara Schumann, wrote vivid accounts of left-bank life in Paris in the 1880s and 1890s, and was a suffragette. Their elder son, Donald, died in 1936 in a car crash in Egypt, where he was employed by Shell.

Marius Goring (1912–1998), by Howard Coster, 1934

Goring was educated at the Perse School, Cambridge, where he obtained a higher certificate from the Oxford and Cambridge schools examination board in 1930, and then elected to study briefly at universities in Munich, Frankfurt, Vienna, and Paris. This experience enabled him later to act in German and French, and helps to account for his effortlessly convincing film roles as foreigners. Having chosen acting as a career (he had made his début at twelve in *Crossings* at Cambridge), he trained under Harcourt Williams and at the Old Vic drama school (1929–32), and first appeared on the London stage in 1927, at the Rudolph Steiner Hall. He was admitted to the Old Vic company by its manager, Lilian Baylis, in May 1932, at £2 10s. per week; at twenty, he played Romeo at short notice to Peggy Ashcroft's Juliet, and took several other roles during his time there (1932–4). In 1931 he married Mary Westwood Steel (1902–1994), with whom he had a daughter, Phyllida (*b.* 1932).

Despite great success on film, television, and radio, the stage remained Goring's first allegiance. His first West End performance was in *The Voysey Inheritance* (1934) at the Shaftesbury Theatre, and four decades later he successfully led a protest against the theatre's destruction by developers. In the mid-1930s he realized a teenage ambition to join La Compagnie des Quinze, and toured in Europe playing Hamlet and other roles in French. Throughout the decade he built up a steady reputation in classical and modern plays, his Feste in the Old Vic's *Twelfth Night* (1937) being particularly admired for its piercing melancholy. He also played Japhet in André Obey's *Noah* (1935) and the misguided idealist Gregers Werle in Ibsen's *The Wild Duck* (1936).

In 1939 Goring directed a production of Ibsen's *A Doll's House*, starring the German actress Lucie Mannheim (1899–1976), who had been expelled by the Nazis. His first marriage having been dissolved, on 7 June 1941 he married her. The marriage lasted until her death. Meanwhile Goring served in the Queen's Royal regiment from 1940. In 1941 he was seconded to the Foreign Office, which made him supervisor of BBC broadcasting to Germany. He provided the voice of Hitler in the BBC series *The Shadow of the Swastika* (1940); the erroneous idea of his foreign heritage may well derive from this period.

Goring acted in the theatre until 1990: he toured Germany in 1947, acting in German; twice led the Stratford upon Avon company, playing a chilling Richard III in 1953 and an icy Angelo in *Measure for Measure* in 1962; produced the Henry Irving hit *The Bells* (1968) in London, where it failed after a successful provincial try-out; and starred in the long-running box office winner *Sleuth* (1970–73). He had entered films before the war. His unusual rather than conventional good looks meant he was often called upon to play Nazi officers, as in *Pastor Hall* (1940), sinister foreigners of every hue, and decadent playboys, like those besotted with Ava Gardner in *Pandora and the Flying Dutchman* (1950) and *The Barefoot Contessa* (1954). He valued most the films he made for Michael Powell, who admired 'his impudent charm' (Powell): *The Spy in Black* (1939); *A Matter of Life and Death* (1946), as the effete heavenly 'conductor' who complains of the absence of Technicolor 'up there'; *The Red Shoes* (1948), as the young composer in love with the doomed ballerina; and *Ill Met by Moonlight* (1957), as another Nazi.

In later years television claimed more of Goring's time. He was a finely flamboyant *Scarlet Pimpernel* (1954), which he also co-produced; a forensic scientist in *The Expert* (1968–9, 1971, 1976); and a gruff George V in *Edward and Mrs Simpson* (1980).

An expert reader of poetry and prose, Goring was in demand for recitals, such as those he gave for the Apollo Society and at Kenwood, Hampstead. With an eloquent literary style of his own, he frequently adapted and translated plays and wrote many radio scripts. He was made a fellow of the Royal Society of Literature in 1976, and in 1991 he was created CBE for his services to theatre. His second wife, Lucie, having died in 1976, he married, on 21 May 1977, Prudence Fitzgerald (*b.* 1930), a television director who had directed him in some episodes of *The Expert*. A lifelong fighter for causes he believed in, he almost bankrupted himself in litigation to preserve the political neutrality of British Actors' Equity, and took the issue of the supremacy of a referendum, as its policy decider, as far as the House of Lords (1978), ultimately carrying the day. A co-founder of Equity in 1929 and three times its vice-president (1964–8, 1975–7, 1980–82), he believed passionately in the acting profession, working in it until his final illness began its inroads. He loved riding, skating, and practical jokes; and he was a meticulous dresser, adding a suggestion of raffish insouciance in his person. He gave off an idiosyncratic whiff behind a charming exterior, and variations on this persona kept him busy and popular for sixty years. He died on 30 September 1998 at his home, Durrants, Rushlake Green, Heathfield, Sussex, and was buried in the churchyard of St Mary's, Warbleton, on 9 October. He was survived by his wife, Prudence, and the daughter of his first marriage, Phyllida.

BRIAN MCFARLANE

Sources *The Guardian* (2 Oct 1998) • *The Times* (2 Oct 1998) • *Daily Telegraph* (2 Oct 1998) • *The Independent* (2 Oct 1998) • B. McFarlane, ed., *An autobiography of British cinema* (1997) • M. Powell, *A life in movies* (1986) • priv. coll., Marius Goring papers • *WWW, 1916–28* • J. Parker, ed., *Who's who in the theatre*, 15th edn (1972) • private information (2004) [Prudence Goring, wife; Peter Plouviez] • personal knowledge (2004)

Archives FILM autobiographical documentary, 1987 | SOUND interview with Brian McFarlane, 1990 [tape to be deposited with British Film Institute, London]

Likenesses H. Coster, photograph, 1934, NPG [*see illus.*] • photographs, 1934–84, Hult. Arch. • C. Dane, portrait, 1950?–1954, priv. coll. • photograph, repro. in *The Times* • photograph, repro. in *The Independent* • photograph, repro. in *Daily Telegraph* • photograph, repro. in *The Guardian*

Wealth at death £200,000: probate, 11 Feb 1999, *CGPLA Eng. & Wales*

Gormlaith [Gormphly] (*d.* **948**), queen in Ireland and tragic heroine, was the daughter of *Flann Sinna mac Máele Sechnaill (847/8–916), the southern Uí Néill high-king, and a sister of *Donnchad Donn mac Flainn (*d.* 944), also a high-king. The annals of Ulster contain the earliest witness to her. They simply name her, and her father, before remarking that she died in penitence, in 948.

From these meagre beginnings, Gormlaith flowered into a tragic figure. A tale, *Serc Gormlaithe do Niall Glúndub*, is referred to in the Irish tale lists A and B. Thus, as the title of the tale suggests, a narrative concerning Gormlaith's love for Niall Glúndub, king of Ireland [*see* Niall mac Áeda (*c.*869–919)], was in existence by the end of the tenth century. Niall Glúndub died fighting the Dublin vikings and became a heroic figure in Irish tradition. Despite this, the narrative is lost. However, several poems, supposedly composed by Gormlaith (but in fact of later origin), suggest the lost tale's contents. Their dates range from the eleventh and twelfth centuries into the modern Irish period. In them, Gormlaith describes her three royal marriages. Her first is to the saintly and celibate bishop-king of Munster, *Cormac mac Cuilennáin, who dies fighting the Leinstermen and Uí Néill at Belach Mugna in 908. Following this, she is married to one of the victors of Belach Mugna, Cerball mac Muirecáin (*d.* 909), king of Leinster. The unhappy Gormlaith endures insults and physical violence from the uncouth Cerball. Following his death she becomes the wife of the heroic Niall Glúndub. Her happiness is short-lived, for Niall dies fighting the vikings at the battle of Islandbridge. In these poems, Gormlaith bewails Niall's death and describes her loss of youthful beauty.

Gormlaith is not mentioned in the twelfth-century *Ban-Shenchus*, which lists many royal marriages, an absence which might be due to the tendency of this work to focus on women who gave birth to kings. It is likely that Gormlaith was genuinely married to Niall Glúndub, however, since the tale concerning them was in existence within fifty years of her death. But Niall was probably not youthful at the time of the marriage and certainly would not have resembled the ideal king of the poems. The historical figures of Cormac, Cerball, Niall, and Gormlaith were simply convenient pegs on which to hang a romance.

The most pathetic account is in Conell Mageoghagan's English language annals of Clonmacnoise. His Gormlaith is a 'faire, vertuous, and learned damozell' who composes 'pittifull and learned dittyes in Irish', and, after the death of all her husbands and of Domnall, her supposed son with Niall, she 'begged from doore to doore, forsaken of all her friends and allies, and glad to be relieved by her inferiors' (*Annals of Clonmacnoise*, 145). Eventually, the distraught queen dies from a mortal wound after dreaming of Niall Glúndub. Believing that he is leaving her, she snatches after him, falls, and is pierced through the breast. It is possible that Mageoghagan's sometimes confused account—he has Cerball mac Muirecáin outlive Niall, for instance—may be based on the lost tale of Gormlaith.

It has been argued, on the basis of the poems and Mageoghagan, that the Gormlaith romance was shaped by the myth of the sovereignty goddess. Briefly, the sovereignty goddess, emblematic of the land, marries or has intercourse with the true king, validating his rule. In the presence of the true king she is beautiful, but in his absence is withered. The ageing Gormlaith is imagined as fulfilling this type. This seems unlikely. Gormlaith's restorative powers on the land and kingship are never mentioned. The tale's appeal probably lay in the image of the destitute queen, inconsolable after the loss of a beloved husband.

The legendary outlines of Gormlaith's career may obscure a historical core. It was common for Irish queens to marry and remarry. Gormlaith was the daughter and sister of high-kings. Like many queens, she may have retired to a monastery on the death of her last husband. This not untypical royal career was transformed into a tragedy.

ELVA JOHNSTON

Sources O. Bergin and C. Marstrander, eds., *Miscellany for Kuno Meyer* (1912) • *Ann. Ulster* • P. Mac Cana, *The learned tales of medieval Ireland* (1980) • D. Murphy, ed., *The annals of Clonmacnoise*, trans. C. Mageoghagan (1896); facs. edn (1993) • B. Ó Cuiv, 'Three middle Irish poems', *Éigse*, 16 (1975–6), 1–17 • A. O'Sullivan, ed., 'Triamhuin Ghormlaithe', *Ériu*, 17 (1955), 189–99 • F. J. Byrne, *Irish kings and high-kings* (1973) • W. A. Trindale, 'Irish Gormlaith as a sovereignty figure', *Études Celtiques*, 23 (1986), 143–56

Gormley, Joseph, Baron Gormley (**1917–1993**), miner and trade unionist, was born on 5 July 1917 at 10 Duke Street in 'very much the rough and tough end' (Gormley, 1) of Ashton in Makerfield, Lancashire, one of seven children of John Gormley, coalminer, and his wife, Elizabeth, *née* Williams. His father was Irish and had originally gone to England as a farm labourer. On leaving St Oswald's Roman Catholic School, Ashton, at the age of fourteen, Gormley followed his father down the pit, after a false start working in a greengrocer's. He was a lowly haulage worker underground, and when he collected his first week's pay of 10*s.* 3*d.*, his father immediately told him to 'go over to

Joseph Gormley, Baron Gormley (1917–1993), by Doug McKenzie, 1971

that window and get joined in the union', then the Miners' Federation of Lancashire (Gormley, 11). Gormley saw his first fatality a few years later, and his own father died underground. His mother, half-Welsh, half-Irish, who stood 'five feet and a bit' but ruled the home with a rod of iron—actually, a wooden boiler-stick—received £300 compensation for his father's death. She died a few years later. 'I'm certain it was of a broken heart,' he said later; 'I don't think she ever forgot' (Gormley, 17).

Gormley went on to work in eleven collieries in Lancashire, picking up a reputation for what was later called militancy. He first acted as a spokesman for haulage lads, who worked on piece-rate, in a dispute with the colliers, winning them a 5*s*. weekly share-out. By his own account he wanted to join up at the outbreak of war, but he was in a reserved occupation and not allowed to leave the pit. On 2 October 1937 he had married Sarah Ellen (Nellie) Mather (*b*. 1917/18), a silk spinner, and daughter of Levi Mather, a coalminer of Ashton in Makerfield. At about the same time he joined the Labour Party.

Initially, politics was Gormley's abiding interest, rather than union work. He never attended union branch meetings 'simply because I always did my own negotiating' (Gormley, 34). In 1952, soon after being elected a district councillor in his home town, he applied to emigrate to Australia, but was turned down. Four years later he was elected to the key post of delegate at Bold colliery, representing a big pit in the councils of the Lancashire miners. In the following year he was chosen the coalfield's lay member of the national executive committee of the National Union of Mineworkers (NUM). At this stage his career could have gone either way. He showed interest in entering parliament, but failed by three votes to win the Labour Party nomination for the safe seat of Burnley—blaming his defeat on hostility to the Campaign for Nuclear Disarmament. His direction was settled in 1961 when he was elected general secretary of the Lancashire miners; thereafter he sat on the NUM executive as one of the powerful coalfield 'barons'. During this period the union leadership was a battleground for left and right political machines, with communists dominating the left. Gormley's combative style and strong populist instincts made him an attractive electoral proposition for the traditional 'moderates', who held the upper hand. In 1963 he was gifted the NUM seat on Labour's ruling national executive committee, and he swiftly became chairman of its powerful organization committee.

In 1968 Will Paynter, a communist, retired as general secretary of the NUM, and Gormley was the natural candidate of the moderates. But this was a period of rising rank-and-file tension over Harold Wilson's plans to curb trade-union powers, and there was hostility to accelerating pit closures. Gormley's rival was Lawrence Daly, an ex-communist with brilliant powers of oratory, who promised a tough fight against job losses. Gormley lost by 10,000 votes in a poll of 220,000 members. He was 'pretty shattered' (Gormley, 73), but came back with a challenge for the NUM presidency in 1971, fighting the charismatic communist Mick McGahey. The industry was in turmoil, with unofficial walkouts over wages. Gormley ran on a promise to make miners the highest-paid industrial workers in Britain, and won comfortably with a majority of almost 25,000.

As president Gormley was now chief negotiator for the miners. In his first year, the union changed its rules, reducing the majority required in a pithead ballot for a strike from 66 per cent to 55 per cent. Months later, 59 per cent of miners voted for the first national strike since 1926, and though he privately disapproved of the conflict Gormley led the strike to a successful conclusion in seven weeks, most notably through the use of 'flying pickets' at power stations. The second strike, in February 1974, was even shorter, and delivered Gormley's promise to make miners the best-paid industrial workers. However, the power cuts, which forced a three-day week in industry and a state of emergency, together with the immense social upheaval that accompanied these disputes, also served to bring about the long-term downfall of the miners and the trade union movement at large. Gormley collaborated happily with the Labour government of 1974–9, ensuring pay restraint in the pits. He also fought successfully for the introduction of local incentive schemes, which boosted production and cut absenteeism, while accentuating the problems of loss-making collieries. With the return of a Conservative government under Margaret Thatcher, Gormley played a canny game, holding back his hard-liners while using their strike threats to win concessions for the state-owned industry. He headed off a strike in 1981, when the government did not feel strong enough to win an all-out conflict with the NUM, by securing £300 million in fresh operating subsidies to avert pit closures. This was probably the high-water mark of his leadership. In his final year he tried to secure a moderate succession to the presidency, but his diplomacy failed and Arthur Scargill, the ultra-left Yorkshire leader, took over in 1982. Gormley's hopes that the responsibility of office would restrain his revolutionary zeal proved unfounded, and the NUM under Scargill became the merest shadow of the mighty union that Gormley led.

In retirement Gormley returned to his love of horse-racing. Having rejected a knighthood from Labour, he accepted a peerage under the Conservatives, in 1982, and as Baron Gormley, of Ashton in Makerfield, Lancashire, he urged the case for the coal industry. His lively and illuminating autobiography, *Battered Cherub* (1982), the name invented for him by the *Daily Express*, was a best-seller. After suffering two strokes that left him partially paralysed, he and his wife returned to live near Wigan, where he died of prostate cancer at his home, 2 Princess Park, Shevington, on 27 May 1993. He was survived by his wife, a son, and a daughter. A memorial service was held at St Mary-at-Hill, Eastcheap, London, on 25 November 1993.

In an era when leaders in the labour movement came to look like managers, Gormley stood out as a classic union boss of the old style: gruff, autocratic, and guileful. He was proud of his working-class origins and his easy kinship with his members. He was a moderate of traditional Labour stripe, but he led the NUM to success in two great national strikes, the second of which precipitated the downfall of Edward Heath's Conservative government. His real political legacy, however, was a strong, well-organized union for miners, which was destroyed by the strategic errors of his successor, Arthur Scargill. Had he still been in office, few in coalmining believed that the ruinous, year-long conflict of 1984–5, from which neither the coal industry nor the NUM recovered, would have taken place. Gormley was virtually the last of the self-taught, working-class figures who fought their way to the top of a trade-union movement that was the most influential in the Western world. Some of its decline may be traced to the loss of people like him.

Paul Routledge

Sources J. Gormley, *Battered cherub* (1982) · *The Times* (28 May 1993) · *The Independent* (28 May 1993) · *WWW*, 1991–5 · private information (2004) · *The Times* (Oct 1969–Jan 1986) · b. cert. · m. cert. · d. cert.

Likenesses D. McKenzie, photograph, 1971, priv. coll. [*see illus.*] · H. Schwartz, oils, 1984, NPG; related studies, NPG · photograph, repro. in *The Times* · photograph, repro. in *The Independent* · photographs, repro. in Gormley, *Battered cherub*

Goronwy ab Ednyfed (*d.* 1268). *See under* Tudor family, forebears of (*per. c.*1215–1404).

Goronwy ap Tudur (*d.* 1331). *See under* Tudor family, forebears of (*per. c.*1215–1404).

Goronwy ap Tudur (*d.* 1382). *See under* Tudor family, forebears of (*per. c.*1215–1404).

Gorrie, Archibald (1778–1857), agriculturist, was born on 15 May 1778 at Logiealmond, Perthshire. He was educated at the local school, and from 1797 to 1807 he held various gardening posts; for a time he was in charge of the hothouse at the Leith Walk nursery in Edinburgh. From 1807 until his death he was manager of the estate of Annat, Kilspindie, near Errol, Perthshire, farming also on his own account at Shanry. He was responsible for introducing into gardens the pansy, known in the wild as 'love-in-idleness', and he raised new fruits, including the Annat Park apricot, the Annat scarlet apple, and the Annat beurré pear. He introduced the Perthshire red potato, and also cultivated grasses such as wood millet grass (*Milium effusum*).

In his early years Gorrie was associated with George Don, who published *A System of Gardening and Botany*, founded on Philip Miller's *Gardener's Dictionary*. Gorrie contributed to many agricultural and horticultural magazines, including the *Gardener's Magazine*, and wrote monthly agricultural reports for the *Perthshire Courier* and the *Dundee Advertiser*. His paper, 'Preventing the depradations of the turnip fly', was presented to the Caledonian Horticultural Society in 1811.

On 6 November 1809 Gorrie married Euphemia Moyes. They had two sons and two daughters. He was an elder of the Free Church of Scotland and was chosen as a representative at its general assembly. Gorrie died at Annat Cottage, near Errol, on 21 July 1857, and was buried nearby in the churchyard at Rait, Perthshire. His wife survived him.

Anne Pimlott Baker

Sources *Cottage Gardener*, 18 (1857), 333–4 · *GM*, 3rd ser., 3 (1857), 344 · private information (2004)

Gorrie, Sir John (1829–1892), colonial judge, was born on 30 March 1829 at Kingskettle, Fife, Scotland, the fourth child of Daniel Gorrie (1797–1852), a Presbyterian minister, and his wife, Jane, *née* Moffat (1792/3–1863). He was educated at Kingskettle, at Madras College in St Andrews, and at Edinburgh University, and was called to the Scottish bar in 1856. On 6 December 1855 he married Marion (*d.* 1884), the daughter of Michael Graham of Edinburgh. They had three daughters and one son.

It was as a young advocate in Edinburgh that Gorrie developed radical views which were to shape his subsequent career as a colonial jurist. He entered municipal politics, and served on the Edinburgh town council as a protégé of Duncan McLaren, the leading Scottish radical of the 1850s; he also became involved in the campaign for parliamentary reform led by John Bright. When he moved to London in 1862 he took up a post with the *Morning Star*, the radical newspaper founded by Bright and Richard Cobden, and worked with the anti-slavery movement in the capital.

Gorrie first became interested in colonial problems when he was retained by the Jamaica Committee to represent those Jamaicans who had been the victims of the savage repression organized by Edward Eyre, the colony's governor, following the Morant Bay rebellion in 1865. His experiences in Jamaica convinced him that imperialism could be justified only if British colonial subjects of every ethnicity and class received even-handed justice from the courts. This belief was the mainspring of his colonial career, which began in 1869 when he accepted an appointment in Mauritius.

As a judge in Mauritius, Gorrie developed his characteristic judicial style: combative, interventionist, and political, always on the lookout for abuses to denounce and correct. It was here, too, that he established a leading trend in his career, his active involvement in a wider public life. As a close friend and colleague of the reforming governor of Mauritius, A. H. Gordon, Gorrie played a leading part in important reforms implemented in the 1870s in the treatment of indentured and ex-indentured Indian labourers.

Gorrie followed Gordon to Fiji in 1876 as chief justice of the new crown colony. He was one of a small group of men around Gordon who helped to shape Fiji's fundamental legal and political institutions. In effect, Gorrie functioned as a member of Gordon's inner cabinet as well as the colony's sole judge, helping to determine future relationships between indigenous Fijians, European settlers, and immigrant labourers from other Pacific islands and India. He also served as judicial commissioner for the Western Pacific, attempting (with Gordon, the high commissioner) to bring to justice British subjects in the Pacific who committed crimes but did not reside in a European colony. This appointment involved him in many important controversies related to British and Australian expansion in the vast region under the jurisdiction of the high commission.

In 1883 Gorrie arrived in the Caribbean. As chief justice of the Leeward Islands (1883–6), he helped to effect important reforms in the islands' laws, especially those relating to land and mortgages, and he worked to upgrade the judicial administration of these depressed little colonies.

Gorrie's last appointment (1886) was as chief justice of Trinidad. He became an authentic hero to the ordinary people of the island, who were mainly descendants of former African slaves or immigrants from India. He encouraged poor people to use the courts to assert their rights and seek justice on an equal footing with the respectable and the propertied, who were mainly white. And, as had been the case in all his previous postings, he involved himself in many public and political issues far beyond the scope of his judicial duties. When Tobago was linked to Trinidad in 1889, and Gorrie became chief justice of the united colony, he plunged into Tobago controversies, encouraging sharecroppers, peasants, and labourers there to assert their rights in court during a period of unsettled agrarian relations. As chairman of a committee on trade and taxes he attempted to ease the burdens on Trinidad's black population. In 1890 and 1891 he tried unsuccessfully to found a people's bank.

By 1889–90 the élites of both Trinidad and Tobago had concluded that Gorrie was a serious threat, and they began a determined campaign to remove him. He fought back with equal skill. But the Colonial Office, which had supported him in numerous skirmishes over twenty years, finally agreed in 1892 to a commission to investigate his administration of justice in Trinidad and Tobago. Its findings were sufficient to allow the governor to suspend him from office pending a final decision in London. He went to Britain in the middle of 1892 to fight his case personally, but soon after arrival he died, on 4 August 1892, in Exeter.

Gorrie was a large, robust man, extremely gregarious and sociable, who retained his broad Scottish accent to his death. In court he was often brusque to the point of rudeness, frequently bullying witnesses, lawyers, jurors, and court officials. He had a strong, assertive personality and was always a good hater and a good fighter; but no one questioned his absolute dedication to the cause of justice and equality in the colonies where he served.

BRIDGET BRERETON

Sources B. M. Brereton, *Law, justice and empire: the colonial career of John Gorrie, 1829–92* (1997) • Colonial Office Records, 1869–92, PRO [Mauritius, Fiji, Leeward Islands, Trinidad and Tobago] • private information (2004)

Archives BL, corresp. with Lord Stanmore, Add. MS 49205 • Bodl. Oxf., corresp. with Lord Kimberley • Bodl. RH, Aborigines Protection Society MSS • PRO, Colonial Office records

Likenesses photograph, 1891, Diego Martin, Trinidad

Wealth at death £197 6*s*. 2*d*. in UK: administration, 29 March 1893, *CGPLA Eng. & Wales*

Gorst, Sir (John) Eldon [*formerly* John Lowndes Gorst] (**1861–1911**), diplomatist and colonial administrator, was born on 25 June 1861 in Auckland, New Zealand, the eldest of seven children of Sir John Eldon *Gorst (1835–1916), politician, and his wife, Mary Elizabeth, *née* Moore (1835–1914). Known as Jack to his friends, until his knighthood in 1902 he used the name John Lowndes Gorst to distinguish himself from his father and namesake. The Gorsts were gentlemen, mainly from Lancashire, who prospered in Victorian England. His father met his wife, daughter of the Revd Lorenzo Moore of Auckland, a retired Madras light cavalry major, on the boat to the Antipodes. During the New Zealand wars they returned to England late in 1863, where the father embarked on an erratic career in Conservative Party politics.

The younger Gorst was raised mainly in London. Just before his tenth birthday a pelvic abscess opened. It kept him almost constantly in pain and isolated from his peers. He was either bedridden or wearing an iron brace for more than six years. Educated in day schools, at home by tutors, and at Eton College (1875–9), he observed wryly: 'I cannot say I learnt much [at Eton] in the way of studies.' At Trinity College, Cambridge, he had to work very hard just to catch up in mathematics. Pushed constantly by his father, he graduated twentieth in the mathematics tripos in 1882—a solid second-class honours degree. 'I left Cambridge', he noted tersely, 'entirely ignorant of all branches of knowledge that could be any practical use to me in real life … The one great thing I learned while at university was how to work' (Gorst, autobiographical notes, 1.18–20).

Gorst's childhood experiences and years of pain left him embittered and sensitive. In addition to the separation from his peers at a crucial age, his unpleasant years at

Sir (John) Eldon Gorst (1861–1911), by Lafayette, *c.*1907

Eton contributed to a sense of emotional distance that did not lessen as he grew older, and may, with his shortness—he was about 5 feet 5 inches in height—have contributed to the adoption of a cynical and tough manner as an adult. Sir Robert Vansittart, who served under Gorst in Egypt from 1909 to 1911, observed: 'But an inch on Cleopatra's nose, six inches on Gorst's stature, might have affected the story of Egypt' (Vansittart, 56). Intelligent, cynical, and tough-mannered, he remained an 'outsider' among the British imperial élite.

Between 1882 and 1885 Gorst contemplated entering the home civil service or practising law, and was called to the bar at the Inner Temple in 1885. Politics tempted him momentarily, but rather than face exclusion like his father from the largely aristocratic tory party 'inner circle', Gorst entered the diplomatic service in 1885. He was posted to Egypt in 1886, and assisted the imperious Sir Evelyn Baring, later the earl of Cromer, to consolidate his power as Egypt's *de facto* ruler. Gorst learned Arabic well enough to get by without an interpreter, and cultivated friendships among the Egyptian/Ottoman élite, most notably Princess Nazli Fazil and the khedive, Abbas Hilmi II. His career blossomed. Between 1890 and 1898 he distinguished himself at the Egyptian ministries of finance and the interior. Working alongside Edgar Vincent, Alfred Milner, and Rennell Rodd, he was a major player in the increase of British influence in the Egyptian government. He helped to organize and recruit Britons to extend British control in Egypt and the Sudan. At Cromer's suggestion in 1890 he wrote secretly on Anglo-Egyptian affairs for *The Times*. Between 1889 and 1907 he published eight articles on behalf of Cromer's Egyptian regime. The most revealing was 'The oriental character' (*Anglo-Saxon Review*, 2, 1899). He made major contributions on finance and administration to the *Annual Reports on Egypt* (see especially the years 1890, 1899, and 1905 to 1911).

In his abundant free time Gorst relished the society of the polyglot upper classes in Cairo and Alexandria, especially the company of a series of handsome women. In January 1889 he began an affair with a strong-minded aristocrat, Jessica, Lady Sykes (*c.*1856–1912), who was visiting Cairo. Her emotional and financial support was crucial to him. After he ended the affair in 1891 he wrote sadly:

> I shall always feel that I owe her a debt of gratitude and that the advantages I derived at this time from her society outweigh the feelings of pain which her conduct has since caused to all her real friends. (Gorst, autobiographical notes, 2.20–21)

In 1894 he began a consequential liaison with an American beauty, Romaine Madeline Stone Turnure (1865–1943). In July 1899, not long after his 'godchild' Margaret (Marga) was born, Romaine ended their affair, leaving Jack Gorst heartbroken:

> By force of will … I managed to pull myself out of the slough of despond and emerged from the struggle unsoured if somewhat chastened. The homeopathic [*sic*] method … did not produce any successful results, and my present feeling is that a certain portion of me is dead and cannot be revived. Perhaps time will change this. *Nous verrons.* (ibid., 2.70–71)

Meanwhile in 1898 he succeeded Sir Elwin Palmer as the Egyptian financial adviser—the most influential post after Cromer's. Impressed with his work, 'the Lord' advised Gorst that: 'my relations with the fair sex were apparently too conciliatory, and those with my sex … were apparently not conciliatory enough' (ibid., 2.62–3). Cromer then told Gorst to prepare himself to be his successor, and said he ought to marry. After a few futile proposals to other 'suitable objects', Gorst finally married the heiress Evelyn (Doll) Rudd (*b.* 1880), daughter of Charles *Rudd, Cecil Rhodes's principal associate, in London on 25 June 1903. They had one daughter, Katherine (Kitty) Rachel Gorst Thomas (1905–1994).

Gorst distinguished himself as the Egyptian financial adviser. He was made CB in 1900 and KCB in 1902. As Cromer's agent he went to Paris and London in 1903 to participate in crucial negotiations over the status of Egypt that contributed to the Anglo-French entente. In 1904, now Cromer's heir-apparent, he returned, as an assistant under-secretary, to the Foreign Office, where he skilfully prepared to succeed Cromer. In April 1907 the Liberal cabinet sent Gorst back to Egypt to rationalize Cromer's autocracy, and to give selected Egyptians limited responsibility for their internal affairs. This new policy of conciliation and moderation would, the cabinet hoped, damp down Egyptian nationalism and increasing domestic criticism of the British autocracy in Egypt. By working with the Egyptian ministers and the khedive, Gorst quickly and successfully undermined the nationalists. Unlike Cromer, he did not usually bully the Egyptian/Ottoman élite.

Gorst, however, made three major mistakes. First, he

alienated the Anglo-Egyptian officials and influential circles in Britain by changing the Egyptian 'veiled protectorate' (as Alfred Milner had called it), thus reducing the opportunities for British employment there. Second, in 1908 he appointed Butrus Ghali, a Copt, as prime minister to replace the elderly timeserver Mustafa Fahmi. Ghali was able, but hated by the nationalists for his record, and distrusted by many Muslims for his faith. Third, Gorst sought in 1909–10 to extend the Suez Canal Company's concession, mainly to provide development funds for the Sudan. In 1910 he lost Ghali and the 'experiment' in limited self-rule to a nationalist assassin, and a defiant Egyptian general assembly rejected the concession extension.

Gorst's last year as British agent in Egypt had an element of anticlimax. Despite alarmists who predicted further trouble for the British, little or nothing occurred. Although his health deteriorated rapidly, Gorst's control and British influence in Egypt did not. It was enough for the agency to warn, bribe, or deport certain nationalists, suppress 'seditious' periodicals, and indulge in a limited amount of counter-propaganda.

In March 1911 Gorst's health collapsed, and he returned to Britain. Cancer was diagnosed, so he promptly resigned his post, and went in June to his father's home, the Manor House, Castle Combe, Wiltshire. Abbas Hilmi, the khedive, whom he had befriended, rushed from France to comfort him. He died at Castle Combe on 12 July 1911 and was buried in the family vault there. Lord Kitchener succeeded him in Egypt as consul-general. His wife survived him. PETER MELLINI

Sources P. Mellini, *Sir Eldon Gorst: the overshadowed proconsul* (1977) • autobiographical notes, press cuttings, Middle East Centre, Oxford, Gorst MSS • diaries, 1890–1911, Stanford University, California, Hoover Institution, Gorst MSS • priv. coll., Evelyn Rudd Gorst MSS • R. Storrs, 'Orientations', 1945, Pembroke Cam. • Lord Vansittart [R. G. Vansittart], *The mist procession: the autobiography of Lord Vansittart* (1958) • H. E. Gorst, *Much of life is laughter* (1936) • E. Baring, *Abbas II* (1915) • E. Baring, *Modern Egypt*, 2 vols. (1908) • S. Seikaly, 'The Copts under British rule, 1882–1914', PhD diss., U. London, 1967 • A. Goldschmidt, 'The Egyptian nationalist party', *Political and social change in modern Egypt*, ed. P. M. Holt (1968), 308–33 • Afaf Lutfi al-Sayyid, *Egypt and Cromer* (1969) • private information (2004) • R. Adelson, *Mark Sykes: portrait of an amateur* (1975) • *The Times* (13 July 1911)

Archives Castle Combe, Wiltshire, diaries • News Int. RO, papers as correspondent for *The Times* in Egypt • St Ant. Oxf., Middle East Centre, MS autobiographical notes; diaries and papers; press cuttings • Stanford University, California, Hoover Institution, diaries | Castle Combe, Wiltshire, Evelyn Rudd Gorst MSS • Church Missionary Society Archives, London, Church Missionary Society MSS • CUL, corresp. with Lord Hardinge • News Int. RO, *The Times* archives, Cromer letters • Pembroke Cam., Sir Ronald Storrs MSS • PRO, earl of Cromer MSS, FO 633 • St Ant. Oxf., Middle East Centre, Harry Boyle letters • The Rodd, Presteigne, Baron Rennell of Rodd MSS • U. Durham L., corresp. with Sir Reginald Wingate

Likenesses C. Jameson, oils, *c*.1907, Gov. Art Coll. • Lafayette, photograph, *c*.1907, priv. coll. [*see illus.*] • W. P. Starmer, caricature, repro. in *The Onlooker* (28 Dec 1907) • cartoons, St Ant. Oxf., Middle East Centre, Gorst's press cuttings • oils, Gov. Art Coll. • photographs, priv. coll.

Wealth at death £12,787 16*s*. 7*d*.: probate, 28 Sept 1911, *CGPLA Eng. & Wales*

Gorst, Sir John Eldon (1835–1916), politician and lawyer, was born at Preston on 24 May 1835, the second son of Edward Chaddock Gorst, who took the name of Lowndes on succeeding to some family property in 1853. His mother was Elizabeth, daughter of John Douthwaite Nesham, of Houghton-le-Spring, co. Durham. Gorst was educated at Preston grammar school, and matriculated at St John's College, Cambridge, in 1853. He was third wrangler in 1857 and was a fellow of his college from 1857 to 1860; he became an honorary fellow in 1890. He chose the legal profession, but after a few months of legal study became a master at Rossall School in order to be near his father, who was seriously ill and died in 1859. Gorst then decided to go to New Zealand to help Bishop Selwyn, also a member of St John's College, with his missionary work among the Maori. On the voyage to New Zealand he became engaged to Mary Elizabeth Moore, daughter of the Revd Lorenzo Moore, of Christchurch, New Zealand, and he married her in Australia in 1860. They had two sons and six daughters. She died in 1914 and he married, in 1915, shortly before his death, Ethel, daughter of Edward Johnson. His eldest son, Sir John Eldon *Gorst KCB, was British agent and consul-general in Egypt from 1907 to his death in 1911.

New Zealand Gorst arrived in the North Island of New Zealand in the summer of 1860 with idealistic notions of helping the Maori, but he also shared the almost universally accepted view that this could best be done by assimilating them to European civilization. He did not stay with Bishop Selwyn long and entered government service, first as an inspector of schools, then as magistrate, and finally (appointed by Sir George Grey, the governor) as civil commissioner for the Waikato region. Here there was open conflict between the colonial government and the nationalist Maori King movement. Gorst's reports on the schools and his activities as an administrator show his increasing disillusionment with the effort to civilize the Maori according to European standards. Although he respected some native institutions, such as the runanga—the councils forming the basis of Maori government—he felt that the imposition of English ideas of law and order was essential. He edited a newspaper, the *Pitroihoi Mokemoke*, intended to combat the Maori King movement and he finally had to leave the Waikato under death threats to himself and his young family. His hopes of entering colonial politics did not materialize. He arrived back in England in 1864 and published a book about his experiences, *The Maori King*.

Tory politics Gorst was called to the bar at the Inner Temple and unsuccessfully stood as Conservative candidate for Hastings in the general election of July 1865. He was returned for the borough of Cambridge at a by-election in April 1866, caused by a disqualification. At this stage, perhaps because of his New Zealand experiences, he was strongly opposed to the policy of the tory leaders, especially Disraeli, of trying to compete with their opponents in courting democracy. He threatened to vote against the third reading of the Reform Bill of 1867 because of the too

Sir John Eldon Gorst (1835–1916), by James Russell & Sons, in or before 1891

democratic form it had assumed. He complained that there would be no future in politics for men of his generation, for they would have to stoop to make themselves popular. He opposed the admission of dissenters to college fellowships and the abolition of church rates, the latter on the ground that it would diminish funds available for rural poor relief. He was one of the younger Conservatives who in 1867 were taking an interest in party organization and was in the chair at the inaugural meeting of the National Union of Conservative and Constitutional Associations in November 1867. In the 1868 election campaign he did not disown his previous opposition to parliamentary reform and was defeated at Cambridge. At this stage he showed no leanings towards tory democracy and his interest in social reform was slight.

In 1870, on the retirement of Markham Spofforth, the Conservative Party's central agent, Disraeli appointed Gorst in his place. The assumption of this post by Gorst, a man of clear political ambitions and distinctive views, showed it was no longer a back-room appointment with slightly unsavoury connotations. His prime task for the next few years was to mobilize the enlarged urban electorate for the tories—for without gains, particularly in the English boroughs, the Conservatives would never be able to win a secure majority. He established a central Conservative office in Victoria Street and brought the National Union, up to then merely one of several federations of local associations, into close relationship with it. He thus created what was to be the future pattern for Conservative Party organization at the centre. He saw urban Conservatism as requiring middle-class leadership as well as a mass of working-class voters. The one region where the tories had already in 1868 gained a significant urban foothold was in the Lancashire boroughs. Gorst devoted much effort to organizing a visit to that county by Disraeli, which eventually took place in 1872. Its climax was a speech by the tory leader at the Free Trade Hall in Manchester, in the heart of the enemy's territory. It signified the nationwide revival of tory fortunes and indicated that Disraeli personally had repelled all attempts to displace him as leader. Gorst enjoyed Disraeli's full confidence and supplied him with essential information on the state of the constituencies. Gorst could thus claim with some justification that the tory victory of 1874 owed a good deal to his work.

As party agent Gorst clashed frequently with the whips and party managers. They mostly had aristocratic connections and still saw the party as mainly representing the landed interest. They operated chiefly in county and rural seats and were accustomed to old-fashioned and sometimes corrupt methods of fighting elections. He called them contemptuously 'the old identity', while he was often accused of being 'crotchety'. He claimed that he was a genuine tory democrat, who believed that the future of the party lay in meeting the concerns of a democratic electorate, and that in this he was a true follower of Disraeli. Although he was able to return to the Commons as member for Chatham in 1875 his hopes of office were disappointed. In 1877 he cut his links with party management and warned Disraeli that the party organization was disintegrating. After the Conservative defeat in 1880, which seemed to vindicate these warnings, he was re-engaged to advise on the central management of the party. He again found it difficult to work with a central committee of whips and managers that had been established under the chairmanship of W. H. Smith to oversee the party organization.

Fourth Party connections In the meantime Gorst had in the House of Commons allied himself with Lord Randolph Churchill in the maverick group nicknamed the 'Fourth Party', which also included Sir Henry Drummond-Wolff and A. J. Balfour. The four freelances sought to make up for the weakness of the Conservative front bench, particularly of its leader, Northcote, by offering relentless opposition to Gladstone and his government. They were suspicious of Northcote's tactics of attempting to draw whigs and moderate Liberals over to the tories by studied moderation. Gorst's links with the party organization came to an end by the autumn of 1882. He was thought to be one of two authors of an article in the November 1882 issue of the *Fortnightly Review* entitled 'Conservative disorganization'. It was strongly critical of the party as too much dominated by the aristocratic and landed interest and pleaded for a reorientation in the sense of tory democracy. Gorst greatly shaped the ideas and tactics of Lord Randolph Churchill and the Fourth Party. His influence may be seen in the emphasis on tory democracy as the legacy of Disraeli and in the importance placed on social reform. He realized that a new breed of middle-class provincial tory leader had to be given a place in the party organization and that the shortcomings of the dual leadership of Northcote and Salisbury could be exploited. It was largely owing to Gorst that the party organization became a battleground between the tory leaders and the Fourth Party. Churchill did not always follow Gorst's advice and in his speeches often reverted to more traditional state and church tory views. When Churchill made his peace with the party leaders in 1884 Gorst was not consulted and his friendship with Lord Randolph waned.

Nevertheless he was appointed solicitor-general in Salisbury's government in July 1885 and received a knighthood (he was a QC with an extensive practice). When the Conservatives returned to power in 1886 he was offered the same office on the understanding that he would resign when a suitable judgeship became vacant. He declined and was appointed parliamentary under-secretary at the India Office. His chief, Viscount Cross, frequently a target of Fourth Party attacks, was in the Lords. According to the permanent secretary at the India Office, Sir Arthur Godley (later Lord Kilbracken), Gorst, 'one of the very ablest men among Conservatives of his time', was distrusted by the party leaders, was contemptuous of Cross, his intellectual inferior (who in turn was afraid of him), and 'was allowed to do pretty much what he liked'. His interest in social reform was given fresh impetus when he attended the Berlin Labour Conference in March 1890 as head of the British delegation. He increasingly followed his own agenda on social reform, Ireland, and other issues, disregarding the government and party line. Salisbury still judged it prudent to keep him in the government and in the reshuffle caused by the death of W. H. Smith in 1891 he became financial secretary to the Treasury. He served on the royal commission on labour (1891–4), on a Local Government Board departmental inquiry into the poor-law schools of the metropolis (1894–5), and became associated with Toynbee Hall.

Education and retirement In Salisbury's third ministry in 1895 Gorst was appointed vice-president of the committee of council on education but without a seat in the cabinet. His main interest was to increase the responsibility of local authorities for education. He considered locally elected bodies in a better position to initiate changes for the real benefit of communities than parliament, paralysed by the caution of politicians. He did not believe that the school boards could formulate a coherent policy for education, since they were not involved in other communal activities and had insufficient control over their own finances. His influence on the government's educational legislation (chiefly designed to ensure the survival of the voluntary schools), was slight; but his administrative directives contributed to the making of the Education Act of 1902. Since he was not to be given charge of this bill he resigned in July 1902.

Free of office Gorst embarked upon a campaign in parliament and the press for social reform, especially the health and nutrition of schoolchildren. Often in opposition to the government, he advocated implementation of the 1904 report of the interdepartmental committee on physical deterioration. Lloyd George said in the Commons in August 1904 that 'educationally they owed a great deal to the fact that the right honourable gentleman was unmuzzled'. Gorst's attacks on the Balfour government over its failure to tackle social reform helped to make this issue electorally rewarding for the Liberals in 1906. His book *Children of the Nation* (1906) was dedicated to the Labour members of parliament.

Gorst sat as an independent from 1903 and opposed tariff reform. He had represented Cambridge University since 1891, but when he stood as a free-trader in 1906 he was defeated. He revisited New Zealand in 1906, the Campbell-Bannerman government having appointed him special commissioner to the International Arts and Industry Exhibition. He stood as a Liberal at Preston in January 1910 and was again beaten. He died at 84 Campden Hill Court, London, on 4 April 1916 and was buried at Castle Combe, Wiltshire. E. J. FEUCHTWANGER

Sources *The Times* (5 April 1916) · H. E. Gorst, *The fourth party* (1906) · E. J. Feuchtwanger, *Disraeli, democracy and the tory party: conservative leadership and organization after the second Reform Bill* (1968) · R. F. Foster, *Lord Randolph Churchill: a political life* (1981) · W. S. Churchill, *Lord Randolph Churchill*, 2 vols. (1906) · Lord Kilbracken [J. A. Godley], *Reminiscences of Lord Kilbracken* (1931) · N. Dalglish, 'How half-civilized people ought to be managed: John Gorst, education and the Waikato Maoris, 1860–1863', *Durham and Newcastle Research Review*, 9 (1980), 135–44 · N. D. Dalglish, 'Sir John Gorst as an educational innovator: a reappraisal', *History of Education*, 21 (1992), 259–76 · J. R. Vincent, '"A sort of second-rate Australia": a note on Gorst and democracy, 1865–8', *Historical Studies* [University of Melbourne], 15 (1971–3), 539–44 · *DNB*

Archives CUL, letters relating to candidature for Cambridge University | Bishopsgate Institute, London, corresp. with Charles Bradlaugh · Bodl. Oxf., letters to Benjamin Disraeli; letters to E. M. D. Marvin · CAC Cam., corresp. with Lord Randolph Churchill; letters to W. T. Stead · Hatfield House, Hertfordshire, Salisbury MSS · King's AC Cam., letters from him and his family to Oscar Browning

Likenesses J. Russell & Sons, photograph, in or before 1891, NPG [*see illus.*] · W & D. Downey, woodburytype photograph, NPG; repro. in W. Downey and D. Downey, *The cabinet portrait gallery*, 3 (1892) · F. C. Gould, caricature, pen, NPG · Spy [L. Ward], chromolithograph caricature, NPG; repro. in *VF* (31 July 1880), facing pp. 64–5 · B. Stone, five photographs, NPG

Wealth at death £27,468 16*s*. 2*d*.: probate, 10 June 1916, *CGPLA Eng. & Wales*

Gort. For this title name *see* Vereker, Charles, second Viscount Gort (1768–1842); Vereker, John Standish Surtees Prendergast, sixth Viscount Gort in the peerage of Ireland and first Viscount Gort in the peerage of the United Kingdom (1886–1946).

Gorton, John G. (*d.* 1835?), compiler of reference works and translator, was a literary figure known now only through his works. He translated Voltaire's *Dictionnaire philosophique* (1824) and published *A General Biographical Dictionary* (2 vols., 1828; with appx, 1830?; new edn, with a supplement by Cyrus Redding, bringing the work as far as 1850, 4 vols., 1851), which was compiled from rather obvious sources of information. *A Topographical Dictionary of Great Britain and Ireland* (3 vols., 1831–3) was in its time a work of some value. Gorton was also the author of a poem in indifferent blank verse, *Tubal to Seba, the Negro Suicide* (1797), and of a pamphlet entitled *A Solution of that Great Scriptural Difficulty the Genealogy of Jesus* (1825?). Gorton probably died early in 1835.

L. C. SANDERS, *rev.* H. C. G. MATTHEW

Sources *GM*, 2nd ser., 3 (1835), 666 · *BL cat.*

Gorton, Samuel (*bap.* 1593, *d.* 1677), colonist and preacher in America, was born in Gorton, Lancashire, the son of Thomas Gorton (1570–1610/11) and Anne (*d.* 1623), and was baptized in the collegiate church in Manchester on 12 February 1593. The family had been in Gorton for many generations. Gorton's education was extensive—he knew languages and perhaps something of the law—but informal; he never attended university. He left Gorton about 1622 and moved to London, where he married Mary, daughter of John and Mary Maplett of St Martin's-le-Grand. He later described himself as a clothier at this time.

While in London, Gorton apparently parted ways with the Church of England, embracing mysticism and universal redemption and rejecting the idea of a literal heaven and hell. With his wife and at least one child he left England in 1636 to join the migration to New England. They arrived in Massachusetts at the height of the so-called Antinomian controversy surrounding Anne Hutchinson, although Gorton apparently did not become involved in it. The family settled in Plymouth plantation, but in 1638 Gorton was banished from the colony, having tussled with the authorities there over efforts to discipline his serving maid, his preaching, and his defiance of the court. Next he went to Rhode Island, first to Pocasset (later Portsmouth) where he quickly became embroiled in political controversy with William Coddington, later the governor of the colony. In the ensuing altercation both men claimed to act for the king, with Gorton demanding to be tried in England. Thwarted in this request, however, he was whipped and banished. By early 1641 he was in Providence, where his preaching gathered more followers; Roger Williams, the founder of Providence, characterized Gorton's beliefs at this time as 'Familisme', a term then commonly used among the English for various sectarians who believed in a direct infusion of the Holy Spirit (LaFantasie, 215). Apparently forced out of town, Gorton and his following moved to Pawtuxet in February 1642, but when four settlers there submitted themselves to the authority of Massachusetts Bay and complained of Gorton the group moved yet again.

They established a new settlement, Shawomet (now Warwick), in December 1642. Gorton later characterized his place of residence there as in a 'rude, incumbring, and way-less wilderness' (*An Antidote Against the Common Plague of the World*, sig. B1*r*). When two minor sachems (American Indian secular leaders) complained to Massachusetts Bay that Gorton had swindled them out of their land, the government summoned him and two supporters to appear. When they refused and instead replied in 'a whole paper full of beastly stuff', Massachusetts sent an expeditionary force headed by Edward Johnson that seized most of the men living in Shawomet and brought them to trial for blasphemy in Massachusetts in 1643. Johnson later described Gorton as 'full gorged with dreadful and damnable errors' (Johnson, 186). According to John Winthrop's account, the ten captives excelled 'the jesuits in the art of equivocation' (*Journal of John Winthrop*, 485). The group narrowly escaped death and were instead sentenced to hard labour in various towns. After some months, in March 1644 they were released for fear that they were infecting the population with their views. As the Massachusetts colonist Emmanuel Downing said, 'if they all be as buisye as this at Salem, there wilbe much evill seed sowne in the Countrye'; he wanted to see them executed, fearing otherwise 'a Curse upon the land' (*Winthrop Papers*, 4.439). They were allowed, however, to depart the colony.

After returning to Shawomet, Gorton arranged for a group of Narragansett American Indians to submit themselves directly to Charles I, a stratagem that was intended to protect them (and Gorton) from intervention by the king's other subjects in the area. Gorton and a few others then travelled from New Netherland to England to complain against the government of Massachusetts Bay. Gorton received a sympathetic hearing, and Robert Rich, the second earl of Warwick, and his committee on foreign plantations instructed Massachusetts to cease molesting the settlement at Shawomet. In response the colony dispatched Edward Winslow as its agent to counter Gorton's efforts and those of their other detractors: the New Haven governor Theophilus Eaton worried that 'it wilbe an exercise to us all, if he returne with victory' (*Winthrop Papers*, 5.95). While in London, Gorton published *Simplicities Defence Against Seven-Headed Policy* (1646), in which he said the colony was 'a company of grosse and dissembling hypocrites, that under the pretence of Law, and Religion, have done nothing else but gone about to establish themselves in wayes to maintaine their owne vicious lusts, we renounce their diabolicall practice' (pp. 25–6). Winslow responded with *Hypocrisie Unmasked* (1646). Gorton also became involved in the radical religious community in London and was once brought in by the authorities for questioning on his views. During all these altercations with various New England governments he attended closely to the legitimacy of their authority, refusing to acknowledge those without formal authorization from England. He declared 'I thought my selfe as fitt and able to governe my selfe and family, and performe the office of neighbourhood, as any that then was upon Rhode Island' ('Samuel Gorton's letter', 8). He apparently urged Roger Williams to arrange confirmation of the 1644 Rhode Island patent after this was challenged by a competing grant to Gorton's own nemesis, Coddington. Gorton thought it noteworthy that the parliamentary committee heeded his arguments even though his opponent Winslow 'had a greater Charter, and a larger Commission out of these parts then my selfe, yet the goodnesse and justice of my cause did equallize my selfe unto him' (ibid., 16). Being on the right side of properly constituted authority was important to Gorton despite his reputation for obstreperousness and his frequent problems with local governments.

In 1648 Gorton returned from London to his rather large family (which eventually included at least nine children) at Shawomet. The settlement was renamed Warwick after his new-found patron. Although the authorities in Massachusetts continued to complain of Gorton's ill influence, especially blaming him for presenting a heretical version of Christianity to native Americans, Gorton was thenceforth left alone. He was active in local government. He offered sanctuary to the Quaker missionaries who visited the region in the mid-1650s, although he did not share their views. The other tracts that he published, *An Incorruptible Key Composed of the CX. Psalme* (1647), *Saltmarsh Returned from the Dead* (1655), an exposition on the fifth chapter of James, and *An Antidote Against the Common Plague of the World* (1657), convey his complex theology and his support for complete liberty of conscience. The last of these, which was his most theologically abstract tract, he dedicated to Oliver Cromwell. In it he also documented his support for the lenient treatment of Quakers. He prided himself on his ability to open scriptures, claiming facility superior to that of the great John Cotton. Whereas Cotton 'rather darkened and obscured' the truth, Gorton could clear up the most obscure matters (*Incorruptible Key*, sig. B2*r*). Modern readers of his theological tracts, however, have not concurred, but rather they have read his effusive expositions as confused and annoying: his writings were, for example, labelled 'utterly incoherent to the uninitiated' by the *Dictionary of National Biography*.

Gorton wrote a letter to Nathaniel Morton defending himself against charges made in *New Englands Memoriall* (1669), which survived in manuscript until it was printed in the nineteenth century. In 1672 he received a visit from a travelling Quaker minister, John Burnyeat, who described him and his followers as Ranters: 'they would maintain, and say, No Creaturely Actions would be Sin; and would have no Whoredom, nor Drunkenness, nor the like to be Sin, but what was spiritual; the Outward action was but creaturely' (Burnyeat, 53). According to Gorton's followers, however, Gorton had the better of the exchange since, in their view, a Quaker 'was a mere babe to Gorton' (Mackie, 381). Little is known of the religious practices of his followers, save that they heard Gorton preach and read his published and manuscript writings. He once declared that his followers 'speake by revelation, by knowledge, by prophecying' (*Incorruptible Key*, 1–2). He was highly critical of a paid ministry and organized churches, at least those he deemed to be based on man-made beliefs and practices, so it is possible that they employed no church ordinances. Late in his life he corresponded with John Winthrop junior, as did other radicals who had disputed with the less tolerant senior Winthrop.

Gorton died at some point between 27 November and 10 December 1677. In 1771 the colonist John Angell, who claimed to be descended from a servant of Roger Williams, defended Gorton's beliefs and displayed his collection of Gorton books to the minister and antiquary Ezra Stiles. He declared that the books 'were written in Heaven, & no Man could read & understand them unless he was in Heaven' and positively denied any connection between Gorton's beliefs and those of the Quakers (*Literary Diary*, 185). CARLA GARDINA PESTANA

Sources K. W. Porter, 'Samuell Gorton: New England firebrand', *New England Quarterly*, 7 (1934), 404–44 · R. Irwin, 'Saints, sinners, and subjects: Rhode Island and Providence plantations in transatlantic perspective, 1635–1665', PhD diss., Ohio State University, 1996 · G. W. LaFantasie, '"Samuel Gorton in Providence, 1640/41": editorial note', in *The correspondence of Roger Williams*, ed. R. S. Cocroft and G. W. LaFantasie, 1 (1988), 208–15 · *The journal of John Winthrop, 1630–1649*, ed. R. S. Dunn, J. Savage, and L. Yeandle (1996) · J. M. Mackie, 'Life of Samuel Gorton', *The library of American biography*, ed. J. Sparks, 2nd ser., 5 (Boston, 1864), 315–411 · P. F. Gura, *A glimpse of Sion's glory: puritan radicalism in New England, 1620–1660* (1984) · 'Samuel Gorton's letter to Nathaniel Morton, Warwick, June 30th, 1669', *Tracts and other papers*, ed. P. Force, 4 (1846) · E. Winslow, *Hypocrisie unmasked* (1646) · [E. Johnson], *A history of New England* (1654) · *Winthrop papers*, 4 (1944), 5 (1947) · J. Burnyeat, *Truth exalted* (1691) · *Literary diary of Ezra Stiles*, ed. F. B. Dexter, 1 (1901)

Archives Rhode Island Historical Society, Providence, manuscript exposition of the Lord's Prayer | Mass. Hist. Soc., letters to J. Winthrop junior

Goscelin (*b. c.*1035, *d.* in or after 1107), Benedictine monk, musician, and hagiographer, was a Fleming by birth, and joined the Benedictine order at the abbey of St Bertin in St Omer. His background is obscure. But he could have entered St Bertin under Abbot Roderic and continued his education under Bovo (1042–65), whom a fellow monk, Folcard, honoured as 'a second Aristarchus' (the grammarian of Samothrace). It was a reformed monastery with an interest in literature, its inmates producing, typically, saints' lives in rhymed prose, but also undertaking commissions such as *Encomium Emmae Reginae* for Queen Emma of England in 1040–42. Goscelin may have travelled with Bishop Hermann of Wiltshire (*d.* 1078), a Lotharingian, in 1050 to Pope Leo IX's Easter council at Rome; and about 1058, after Hermann's three years' exile at St Bertin, he either went with him to England or followed soon after. He was, as he confessed about 1080–82 in his *Liber confortatorius*, at first dismayed by the squalor of the lodgings assigned him on one of the episcopal manors, although he later came to love them.

Hermann placed his see in Sherborne Abbey; and Goscelin, when much later he wrote a life of St Wulfsige of Sherborne, remembered that he had been a fellow monk of Ælfgar who had overlapped Wulfsige. But he seems to have been more a companion of his monk-bishop than a claustral. He also acted as chaplain to the nunnery at Wilton, a community to which he became much attached. He was particularly attracted to a child named Eve, the daughter of a Dane, Api, and a Lotharingian woman, Olive. In *Liber confortatorius*, written for Eve, he recalls that after Queen Edith had rebuilt the nunnery in stone, they had been at the banquet following its dedication by Hermann in 1065 and he had sent Eve and Olive a fish. He had then taken the girl, 'a Mary by the grace of the Lord for three days' (*Liber confortatorius*, 28–9), to the dedication of King Edward's Westminster Abbey on 28 December 1066.

Hermann's death on 20 February 1078 was a catastrophe for Goscelin. His successor, Osmund (*d.* 1099), a man of the new age, was 'a king who knew not Joseph', and Goscelin, 'a victim of viperine envy and step-fatherly barbarity, was forced to wander far' (*Liber confortatorius*, 29). Early in this unsettled period he finished his life of St Wulfsige and wrote a life of St Edith of Wilton. It was the closing of a chapter, for he also lost Eve. Their love had become so dangerous that, about 1080, in order to avoid a meeting Goscelin had requested, she fled from Wilton to become a recluse at St Laurent-du-Tertre at Angers. Goscelin's *Liber confortatorius*, written for Eve after her escape, was his anguished valediction.

The monk seems to have taken immediate refuge at Winchester, where both the Old and the New Minster remembered a Goscelin in their prayers. Bishop Walkelin (1070–98), a former canon of Rouen, patronized scholars, and recommendations from him seem to have governed Goscelin's movements for some years. He mentions in *Liber confortatorius* a stay at 'Burgum', either Bury St Edmunds or, more likely, Peterborough. For Barking Abbey, Essex, he wrote for the nuns in Bishop Maurice of London's time (1086–1107) liturgical texts in honour of saints Wulfhild, Æthelburga, and Hildelith. He was at Ely under Abbot Symeon (1082–93), where he wrote about St Etheldreda (an account no longer extant) and some other matters. For Ramsey Abbey, probably when under Herbert de Losinga (1087–91), he produced the life and miracles of St Ives.

Finally, in the last decade of the century, he found a most congenial home in St Augustine's, Canterbury, which was itself recovering from a great upheaval consequent on a rebellion against Abbot Guy, a learned and cultured man, after the death of Archbishop Lanfranc in 1089. Bishop Walkelin helped to restore order, and he could have brought Goscelin in. A rebuilding programme led to the translation of the abbey's many Canterbury saints into the apsidal end of the new church in September 1091, an event that called for the composition of new lives. This task was performed by Goscelin. It was a major literary achievement, involving the production of accounts of eight saints. He wrote as well a series of texts concerning St Mildrith of Minster in Thanet, in connection with St Augustine's disputed claim to possess the relics. He was also honoured at Canterbury for his music, and could have acted as precentor. After Abbot Guy died in August 1093, Goscelin remained there, apparently happily, under his successor, Hugh of Fleury, a somewhat unconventional appointment by William Rufus. He was still writing in 1099 and received a dedicatory copy of Reginald of Canterbury's life of St Malchus, which was published in 1107. He would then have been, probably, in his seventies. There are several Goscelins in the Canterbury obituary lists. One, 'monk and priest', was remembered on the ides (15th) of May.

The only character sketch of Goscelin comes from Reginald, a younger monk at St Augustine's, born in the Loire valley, another poet and perhaps the schoolmaster. Goscelin was kind and cheerful, kept clear of disputes, and was helpful to all in need of comfort. Both Reginald and, later, William of Malmesbury (*d.* 1142) concentrate on his achievements in literature and music. William thought that Goscelin, while perambulating the English bishoprics and abbeys, wrote the lives of innumerable modern saints and also rewrote elegantly the inadequate lives of older ones. The Ely chronicler thought likewise. Although some of his work must have been lost, few, if any, convincing attributions of anonymous works, including the *Vita Ædwardi regis*, have as yet been made. Reginald praises Goscelin to the very limits of poetic licence. 'Teacher of oratory, grammarian, dear friend of the Muses, when you pluck the zither and sing, Orpheus and even Linus break their cherished lyres and stand amazed, deprived of tongue' (Liebermann, 542–4). Later William of Malmesbury considered that, in his homage to English saints, he was second only to Bede, and for music took the prize after Osbern.

William's more restrained homage deserves respect. By the standards of his age Goscelin was very well read, proficient in grammar and rhetoric, and a fluent, even copious, author. He clearly carried out his commissions to the satisfaction of his patrons, and thus requited their hospitality. It is not known whether he could, or did, use Anglo-Saxon written sources; but he expressly defended his use of oral testimony and tradition. His account of the translation of St Augustine in 1091 gives the impression of careful reporting, and William of Malmesbury says of it with justice, 'he gave such a polished account of the events … that for contemporaries he seems to have pointed with a finger and for future generations to have brought it before their eyes' (*De gestis regum*, 2.389). His Latin verses are mostly classical in form. His music must, for the most part, be taken on trust. His emphatically rhymed and verbose prose is very much of his own time; and after the style fell out of fashion in the twelfth century there have been few admirers.

Goscelin was at first unpleasantly affected by the Norman conquest, and in his *Liber confortatorius* inserted a diatribe against the new barbarism, with ignorant men deriding the learned and regarding ignorance of literature as worldly wisdom or holiness of life. But this new Englishman soon found some good patrons among the newest prelates, and in return taught them not to despise uncritically the English cultural and religious bequests.

FRANK BARLOW

Sources T. J. Hamilton, 'Goscelin of Canterbury, a critical study of his life, works and accomplishments', PhD diss., University of Virginia, 1973, 2 vols., University Microfilms International · F. Barlow, 'Goscelin of St-Bertin and his works', *The life of King Edward who rests at Westminster*, ed. and trans. F. Barlow, 2nd edn, OMT (1992), 133–49 [details of authentic and attributed works] · *The Liber confortatorius of Goscelin of Saint Bertin*, ed. C. H. Talbot (1955), 1–117 · R. Sharpe, 'Words and music by Goscelin of Canterbury', *Early Music*, 19 (1991), 94–7 · *Willelmi Malmesbiriensis monachi de gestis regum Anglorum*, ed. W. Stubbs, 2 vols., Rolls Series (1887–9) · E. O. Blake, ed., *Liber Eliensis*, CS, 3rd ser., 92 (1962) · F. Liebermann, 'Raginald von Canterbury', *Neues Archiv der Gesellschaft für ältere deutsche Geschichtskunde*, 13 (1888), 519–56 · R. Emms, 'Historical traditions of St Augustine's Abbey, Canterbury', *Canterbury and the Norman conquest: churches, saints and scholars, 1066–1109*, ed. R. Eales and R. Sharpe (1995), 159–68 · 'The life of Saint Wulsin of Sherborne by Goscelin', ed. C. H. Talbot, *Revue Bénédictine*, 69 (1959), 68–85 · Goscelinus, 'Vita S. Augustini', *Patrologia Latina*, 80 (1850), 43–94, 485–520 · R. C. Love, ed. and trans., *Three eleventh-century Anglo-Latin saints' lives: Vita s. Birini, Vita et miracula s. Kenelmi, and Vita s. Rumwoldi*, OMT (1996), xxxiv–xliv

Goschen [*formerly* Göschen], **Sir (William) Edward, first baronet (1847–1924)**, diplomatist, was born at Eltham, Kent, on 18 July 1847, the youngest of the twelve children of Wilhelm Göschen (1793–1866) and his wife, Henrietta (*d.* 1895), daughter of Wilhelm Ohmann and Henrietta

Sir (William) Edward Goschen, first baronet (1847–1924), by Walter Stoneman, 1918

Sim. Wilhelm Göschen, the son of a distinguished Leipzig publisher, had migrated to London and made a successful career in merchant banking. Five sons, of whom George Joachim *Goschen was the eldest, and five daughters reached maturity, and dropped the umlaut from the family name. Edward Goschen was educated at Rugby School and Corpus Christi College, Oxford, and twice represented the university at tennis. He was a member of the Church of England, and a regular attendant at morning service. In 1869 he entered the diplomatic service, serving briefly in the Foreign Office and thereafter in various capital cities around the world. In 1874, at Lyons in New York state, he married (Harriet) Hosta (1849–1912), daughter of Darius Clarke. They had two sons. From 1891 until 1914 he kept a diary, the principal source for his life, parts of which were published in 1980. In 1900 he inherited Schloss Tentschach in Carinthia, Austria. He was made KCMG in 1901, GCVO in 1904, GCMG in 1909, and GCB in 1911.

Goschen's career included appointments to a succession of sensitive posts in the period before the outbreak of the First World War. From November 1898 to June 1900 he was minister in Belgrade, where he learned 'that in Servia Russia was always called "L'Oncle" and Austria "La Tante"' (*Diary*, 22 July 1899). Between 1900 and 1905 he was minister in Copenhagen, and in June 1905 he became ambassador in Vienna. The day after taking up his appointment in Vienna he called on Goluchowski, the Austro-Hungarian foreign minister, with whom he discussed Morocco: 'I expect his arguments came from over the way and were made in Germany', he noted (ibid., 24 June 1905). As regards foreign policy, he informed Sir Edward Grey on 13 December, Austria-Hungary was 'well under the thumb of Germany' (PRO, FO 800/40). To this opinion he adhered when, in the following year, Goluchowski was succeeded by Alois von Aehrenthal.

On 12 August 1908, in the royal train, Edward VII informed Goschen that he was to be ambassador at Berlin. The king, Goschen recorded, 'did what he could to gild the blackest and most nauseous of pills' (*Diary*, 12 Aug 1908). While he was still in Vienna, in the autumn of 1908 British press denunciation of the annexation of Bosnia-Herzegovina provoked a reaction: Goschen's Viennese friends tended to be 'out of town'. On 4 November, at a state banquet, Goschen had a 'turn up' with Aehrenthal, who complained of British encouragement of the Serbs. Goschen told him he was 'responsible for the whole situation'; Aehrenthal's riposte was to begin to talk about the Boers, for which Goschen 'gave him snuff'. The next day Goschen went to take leave of Aehrenthal 'and found him all smiles' (ibid., 5 Nov 1908).

On arrival in Berlin on 8 November the Goschens were 'much depressed': they did not care for either the climate or the embassy. Goschen presented his credentials on 20 November. At first the Kaiser's demeanour was daunting, but after Goschen had improvised a speech, he smiled, shook hands warmly, and expressed friendly sentiments. Goschen was unenthusiastic about the various approaches made by Kiderlen-Waechter and Bethmann Hollweg, the chancellor, with a view to reaching an understanding: he thought that what was needed was an understanding by the Germans that Britain intended to maintain her naval superiority. Nothing significant came of successive conversations. Then, on 2 February 1912, amid deteriorating relations with Germany over Tirpitz's plans for naval expansion, the Foreign Office telegraphed, informing Goschen that communications with the Kaiser and the chancellor had taken place through Albert Ballin and Ernest Cassel, and summoning him to London immediately. He arrived three days later, saw Arthur Nicolson, the permanent under-secretary, and found that 'it is worse than I feared'; his own position was 'most disagreeable'. That evening he saw Grey, who told him Haldane was going to Berlin: Goschen's verdict was 'Pah! Underground work'. Haldane arrived in Berlin on 8 February. Goschen had few hopes of his success, correctly not believing that Haldane could persuade Tirpitz to reduce his programme.

On 28 June 1914 Goschen was at Kiel for the regatta when news of the assassinations at Sarajevo arrived. He was apprehensive as to what this 'dreadful business' might lead to, as he believed that 'the Austrians have for ages been looking for an excuse to trample on Servia'. On personal grounds, too, he was 'very sorry' as the archduke had always been 'nice and kind' and his wife 'charming'. Two days later Goschen left for England. On 27 July he was back in Berlin, where there was little he could do, except carry out instructions and report. On the afternoon of 4 August, he asked Jagow (secretary of state at the imperial foreign office) for an assurance that Germany would respect Belgium's neutrality. The request was refused. That evening he saw Jagow again, repeating his previous request and requiring a satisfactory answer by midnight. He again met with a refusal. He then had an unpleasant interview with Bethmann Hollweg. That evening the British embassy was stoned. Early on 6 August Goschen left Berlin. After his return to London, Goschen composed a report on his last days in Germany, which included an account of the interview with Bethmann Hollweg, who, Goschen related, expressed his anger that Britain should go to war over 'a scrap of paper'.

Goschen retired from the diplomatic service in 1916 and was created a baronet. His wife had died in 1912, and his second son was severely wounded in the early days of the war. In retirement he lived near Christchurch, Hampshire. He died at 27 Lennox Gardens, Chelsea, on 20 May 1924 and was buried six days later at Flimwell, Sussex.

Goschen was a vigorous upholder of British policy. He did not identify himself with his father's country of origin: on the contrary, his diary and letters abound with animadversions on the German national character and nostalgic references to life in England. He was a devoted family man and an enthusiastic violinist; he engaged in numerous sporting activities. Except when a prey to lumbago, which made him irascible, he was of a genial disposition, and enjoyed the affection of his subordinates. In his later years he had abundant grey hair, bushy eyebrows, and a mainly white moustache and beard.

CHRISTOPHER H. D. HOWARD

Sources G. P. Gooch and H. Temperley, eds., *British documents on the origins of the war, 1898–1914*, 11 vols. in 13 (1926–38) • *The diary of Edward Goschen, 1900–1914*, ed. C. H. D. Howard, CS, 4th ser., 25 (1980) • H. Rumbold, *The war crisis in Berlin*, 2nd edn (1944) • M. Gilbert, *Sir Horace Rumbold* (1973) • H. W. Steed, *Through thirty years*, 2 vols. (1924) • Z. S. Steiner, *The foreign office and foreign policy, 1898–1914* (1969) • M. Baring, *The puppet show of memory* (1922) • H. J. Bruce, *Silken dalliance* (1946) • Baron Beyens, *L'Allemagne avant la guerre* (Brussels, 1915) • Baron Beyens, *Deux années à Berlin, 1912-1914*, 2 vols. (Paris, [n.d., *c*.1931]) • T. von Bethmann Hollweg, *Betrachtungen zum Weltkriege*, 2 vols. (1919–22) • J. W. Gerard, *My four years in Germany* (1917) • F. Rattigan, *Diversions of a diplomat* (1924) • *The Times* (26 May 1924)

Archives NRA, priv. coll., diary and letters | Auswärtiges Amt, Bonn, Germany • Bodl. Oxf., Rumbold MSS • CUL, corresp. with Lord Hardinge • NL Scot., Haldane MSS • PRO, Foreign Office MSS; Grey MSS: Lansdowne MSS; Lascelles MSS; Nicolson MSS • Royal Arch. • U. Newcastle, corresp. with Walter Runciman

Likenesses W. Stoneman, photograph, 1918, NPG [*see illus.*] • J. Bowie, double portrait, oils (with Bethmann Hollweg), priv. coll. • oils, priv. coll. • photograph, repro. in Bruce, *Silken dalliance* • photographs, priv. coll.

Wealth at death £15,961 0*s*. 7*d*.: probate, 20 Sept 1924, *CGPLA Eng. & Wales*

Goschen, George Joachim, **first Viscount Goschen** (**1831–1907**), politician and financier, was born on 10 August 1831 at his father's house in the parish of Stoke Newington, near London, the eldest son and second child in the family of five sons and five daughters of William Henry Goschen (1793–1866), a prominent merchant banker in the City of London, and his wife, Henrietta (*d.* 1895), daughter of William Alexander Ohmann.

George Joachim Goschen, first Viscount Goschen (1831–1907), by John Jabez Edwin Mayall

Saxony, Rugby, Oxford, and Ambalema, 1831–1863 Goschen's father, son of the distinguished Leipzig publisher Georg Joachim Göschen (1752–1828), emigrated in 1814 to London, where with a friend, Henry Frühling of Bremen, he founded the merchant banking firm of Frühling and Göschen. The umlauts were dropped as the company and the families were anglicized. Three of George Joachim Goschen's brothers became senior partners in the firm while the youngest brother, Sir William Edward *Goschen (1847–1924), entered the diplomatic corps and eventually became British ambassador to the German empire, serving from 1908 until the start of the First World War in 1914. Two sisters married British clergymen while two others married brothers, Baron Gustav and Baron George von Metzsch-Reichenbach of Germany.

Fruhling and Goschen prospered and soon after George Joachim's birth the family moved to the village of Eltham, about 10 miles from London. Young George was educated at home by a German relative until he was nine when he attended the nearby Blackheath proprietary school. In 1842 he was sent to study at Dr Bernhards School in Saxe-Meiningen, close to his father's family. Originally anticipating his eldest son's entry into the family firm,

Goschen's father soon concluded that young George's considerable abilities might lead to a brilliant public career.

This necessitated the anglicization of George, who was sent in 1845 to Rugby School where the children of commercial, financial, and industrial wealth mixed with the heirs of the landed aristocracy. Living in the house of Bonamy Price, later professor of political economy at Oxford, Goschen became intoxicated with the ideas of free trade, free markets, and free enterprise, which he had already learned from his father. The young English boy with the German name adjusted slowly and sensed during his first year 'that the *élite* hardly considered me as one of their number' (Spinner, *Goschen*, 3). This soon changed; before leaving Rugby in 1850, he became head of school, a fine debater, and the recipient of awards for English and Latin.

In 1850 Goschen embarked on a very successful career at Oxford as a commoner at Oriel College. Though never an outstanding scholar, he finished with firsts in classical moderations and *literae humaniores* and became president of the Oxford Union. Writing perceptively to a friend, Goschen concluded that he was somewhat 'different from other people' because of his 'two nationalities, the grafting of English sentiments and feelings upon German blood' (Spinner, *Goschen*, 5). This provides an insight into the assessment of Alfred Milner (a Goschen *protégé*) that the 'strongest fibre' in Goschen 'was his ardent, unquenchable, almost boyish, patriotism'. He was fortunate to be blessed with a rugged constitution, a sturdy physique, and excellent health.

As he prepared for employment at Fruhling and Goschen, Goschen wished to marry Lucy, daughter of John Dalley; he had met her in his father's house. His father, however, insisted that he first supervise the firm's extensive investments in New Granada (now Colombia). Goschen capitulated and reluctantly left for Ambalema, a small tropical town on the Magdalena River. His father counselled him 'to become a great merchant—a little one is but a poor beast' (Spinner, *Goschen*, 6). After two years, Goschen returned to London; his fierce determination overcame his father's objections and he married Lucy Dalley on 22 September 1857. It was a wise choice on both sides for the marriage was a very happy one which produced two sons and four daughters. Goschen plunged into the affairs of Fruhling and Goschen and quickly demonstrated a shrewd business sense. In 1858 he became a director of the Bank of England, a post he retained until 1865.

The 'Fortunate Youth' enters politics, 1863–1874 Known in the City of London as the 'Fortunate Youth', Goschen published *The Theory of the Foreign Exchanges* in 1861. Slightly revised in 1863 and 1864, his book was often reprinted and was translated into several languages. It provided an explanation of the way in which the international money market would function presupposing a self-regulating market. Supply and demand would work 'naturally', without interference by governments, to determine interest rates and regulate the flow of capital around the world. The business cycle, with periodic unemployment, was a normal part of economic life.

Goschen, like his father, was a member of the Church of England, a Liberal, and a free-trader. In 1863, when he was already identified as a broad-church supporter of the campaign to remove religious tests at Oxford and Cambridge universities, he was asked by two colleagues from the Bank of England to contest a by-election for the City of London. Westminster had been his goal since youth but he 'had never dreamt that the opening would come so soon' (Elliot, 1.47). His election address which he later called a bit too 'rhetorical and academical' advocated local self-government, the secret ballot, a modest extension of the suffrage, the ending of all religious disabilities, and the abolition of church rates. Elected unopposed, Goschen quickly impressed the Liberal Party leadership which designated him to second the address in reply to the queen's speech in 1864. While supporting Palmerston, Goschen made clear that he, and most Liberals, did not subscribe to the radical views of Richard Cobden and John Bright. In foreign affairs, they were excessively pacifist and too inclined 'to peace at any price'. In domestic matters, they were too hostile towards the upper classes. Looking back at this speech many years later, Goschen believed that it 'gave the key of my general attitude both towards foreign and domestic questions during my whole career' (Spinner, *Goschen*, 18).

Palmerston won the general election of 1865 but died before parliament met and was succeeded by Earl Russell. Rumours had circulated about moving Goschen into a minor ministerial post. His father warned him that he must be certain of having sufficient income and wealth when he entered the cabinet as that would mean 'an end to money making. What you have got, you may keep and that is all.' He urged his son to wait until he 'had enough money for a peerage' (Elliot, 1.81). Despite his father's reservations, Goschen accepted the vice-presidency of the Board of Trade in November 1865. A chorus of approval turned to distress when Russell changed his mind and, two months later, offered Goschen the chancellorship of the duchy of Lancaster with a seat in the cabinet. Men with more experience and older men were unhappy at such a rapid elevation.

Goschen's first cabinet tenure did not last long. Defeated on his modest Reform Bill in 1866, Russell resigned. Goschen's brief moment in high office enabled him to sit on the opposition front bench; he would be a key participant in any future Liberal government. His friends urged him to work on his speaking style but he never became a great orator. A future speaker of the House of Commons, James Lowther, remarked on Goschen's 'husky enunciation' and 'ungainly deportment' (J. W. Lowther, *A Speaker's Commentaries*, 1925, 2.44–5).

An issue was emerging, however, that threatened Goschen's future in the Liberal Party. As industrial workers and agricultural labourers obtained the vote, Goschen wondered if they would support the *laissez-faire* economic ideas which had created Britain's great wealth. He expressed doubt in two articles which appeared in Anthony Trollope's *St Paul's Magazine*, in 1867, 'The leap in the dark' (October 1867) and 'The new electors' (November 1867). He argued that a massive transfer of power had just taken place and yet the future political consequences of the Reform Bill of 1867 had not been carefully debated. The new working-class voters would strengthen the radical section of the Liberal Party; Goschen fretted about growing demands for more central and drastic actions by parliament. The new element in the air was the growth of 'sentimental grievances' which the new voters believed could be addressed or eliminated by parliamentary action. These and other questions were related to a 'dangerous phrase' used by Frenchmen—'the dignity of man'.

Goschen became a cabinet member, first at the poor-law board (1868–71) and then at the Admiralty (1871–4), in Gladstone's first administration, one of the great reforming governments of the nineteenth century. His report to the Treasury on the progressive increase of local taxation, reprinted in his *Reports and Speeches on Local Taxation* (1872), was a striking analysis and an emphatic call for retrenchment. As president of the poor-law board, Goschen encouraged the most sustained attempt ever made to reduce outdoor relief. He also introduced legislation to reform local government and taxation by breathing life back into the parish. The landed gentry, fearing higher taxes and loss of local power, forced the bills to be withdrawn. Probably hoping that Goschen's training and temperament would make him agreeable to cuts in the naval estimates, Gladstone promoted him to the Admiralty in March 1871. In late 1873 Goschen reluctantly supported a forward policy in the Gold Coast. Sir Garnet Wolseley was sent to punish the Asante while Goschen prepared naval support. Gladstone demanded reductions in the service estimates for 1874. Goschen and Edward Cardwell, secretary of state for war, objected and the prime minister, weighing their concerns and several other factors, decided upon a dissolution.

Egypt, electoral reform, and Constantinople, 1874–1881 The Conservatives won a decisive victory; Goschen was re-elected for the City of London but he came fourth behind three Conservatives. Just before the election, the Goschen family completed their country home, Seacox Heath, near the village of Flimwell in Sussex; they retained their house in London at 69 Portland Place.

Goschen approved of Disraeli's purchase of the Suez Canal shares in 1875 but was distressed when the khedive of Egypt suspended payments on foreign loans. The Council of Foreign Bondholders asked Goschen to negotiate with the khedive. Always believing that investors must accept the risk involved and should not expect the British government to intervene, Goschen was still determined to take a firm line with the khedive who was not to be rewarded for 'extravagance and lying'. By November 1876 the khedive had accepted most of Goschen's proposals and his decree was known as the 'Goschen decree'. This eventually led to Goschen's recommending the appointment of Captain Evelyn Baring (Lord Cromer after 1892) as a commissioner of the public debt.

By 1876 Gladstone had re-emerged as a powerful force when he condemned Turkish atrocities in Bulgaria. Many moderate Liberals, including Goschen, thought Gladstone too extreme in his criticism of the Turks; they feared a Russian strike at the 'sick man' of Europe. Goschen wondered if there might be a 'schism' in the party. His isolation had increased in June 1877 when he rejected the party's support for the extension of household suffrage to the counties. Not even the Conservatives wished to oppose a new reform bill on principle; they simply argued that the time was inopportune. Goschen felt, however, that someone must point out that the rural population lacked training in self-government and the elderly agricultural labourers were often too dependent on the poor law. History taught that 'the reign of numbers endangered not the throne, not the Constitution, not property—those were all bugbears—but political economy and the teaching which made Englishmen self-reliant' (*Hansard* 3, 235, 29 June 1877, 557–68).

Suspecting that his constituents in the City of London might prefer a representative in closer harmony with the party, Goschen accepted the safe constituency of Ripon. Preparing for the general election of early 1880, he informed the Ripon electors that while he still opposed extending the suffrage, he also disliked Disraeli's bombastic foreign policy; the seizure of Cyprus had been a mistake for it 'impaired the reputation of England as the most clean-handed member of the European family' (*Ripon Gazette*, 20 March 1880). Talk of a parliament in Dublin was abhorrent while the temperance issue should remain a local matter. Goschen won Ripon easily as the Liberals swept the country.

Goschen's opposition to household suffrage excluded him from Gladstone's new government but in April 1880 the prime minister urged him to become viceroy of India. Goschen declined, foreseeing potential disagreements with the prime minister on matters both of imperial policy and of native administration. The Conservative leader in the Commons, Sir Stafford Northcote, speculated that Goschen might organize a 'cave' on the Liberal side that could drift toward the Conservative Party. Goschen did agree to become special ambassador to the Ottoman empire in order to work out the territorial arrangements prescribed by the Congress of Berlin in 1878. Serving without pay, and only temporarily, he retained his seat in the Commons.

The Congress of Berlin had decided to enlarge the frontiers of Greece and Montenegro at the expense of the Turks. Goschen, never happy with Disraeli's seizure of Cyprus, suggested returning it to the Turks if they made concessions to the Greeks elsewhere or giving it to the Greeks for concessions refused by the Turks. New frontiers were finally drawn with Cyprus left under British control. Goschen's foray into diplomacy a success, he returned to London in May 1881.

Whigs, moderate Liberals, and radicals, 1881–1885 Goschen detested Gladstone's Irish land legislation of 1881; it interfered with property rights and allowed judicial bodies to determine fair rents. His criticism of the prime minister's policies in southern Africa gave Gladstone 'indigestion'. Goschen doubted the wisdom of Gladstone's agreement with Parnell in April 1882 and felt vindicated after the murder of Lord Hartington's brother, Lord Frederick Cavendish. Goschen supported coercive legislation for Ireland and referred to the Irish members of parliament as 'steeped in treason' (*Hansard* 3, 269, 11 May 1882, 514–17). Trying to contain an irritating opponent, Gladstone offered Goschen the War Office in June 1882. As an added lure, Gladstone indicated that local government reform was on the agenda for 1883. Goschen again refused; he differed with Gladstone on far too many issues.

However, admitting to being 'a bit of a jingo', Goschen supported the British invasion of Egypt in the summer of 1882. Throughout 1883 he agonized about the 'new democracy' as a reform bill was scheduled for 1884. Would it be possible to keep 'subject races in order' and what would happen to the British economy if the new electors insisted on 'reforming social abuses and securing social benefits'? The poorer classes regarded the state as their 'servant' and sought to 'control the individual' in a 'distinctly Socialistic' manner (Spinner, *Goschen*, 92–4).

Once again, in late 1883, Gladstone tried to neutralize Goschen by offering him the speakership of the House of Commons. Tempted, Goschen eventually declined because of his weak eyes. When the Representation of the People Bill was introduced in 1884, Goschen joined with the Conservatives in insisting that it must be coupled with, or quickly followed by, a redistribution of seats bill. He opposed female suffrage as it assumed 'an equality between men and women which never has existed, and which I believe never can exist' (Spinner, *Goschen*, 96). The 'charm' of the House of Commons had been ruined by the Irish militants. In January 1885, in a devil-may-care mood about his future in politics, Goschen resigned from two important Liberal clubs, the Reform and the Devonshire.

In 1884 Alfred Milner became Goschen's private secretary. Milner heartily endorsed Goschen's 'Moderate Liberalism', contrasting this favourably with the attitude of the whigs who seemed to have 'no principles at all' (Milner to Goschen, 21 Aug 1884, Bodl. Oxf., MSS Milner). Queen Victoria was also searching for moderates to form a third party, believing Goschen to be one of those eager to support such a strategy. Goschen's alienation from the Liberal Party had been increased by his detestation of Joseph Chamberlain's speech of 5 January 1885, which he regarded as an attack on property. Ironically Chamberlain's memorable phrase, 'What ransom will property pay?', had been borrowed from Goschen who had uttered the words in a different context in a private conversation a few days earlier.

Since Ripon would disappear under the redistribution of seats legislation, Goschen managed to win the support of the Liberals in the Edinburgh East constituency. Milner advised his mentor that many would be happy if he gave Chamberlain 'some hard knocks', but Goschen must be 'constructive' and not simply 'critical'. Goschen informed the voters in his new constituency that he opposed land nationalization and land courts but the exchange of land should be facilitated. Local government must be reformed and enlarged to curtail the London bureaucracy. Punishing slum landlords would solve the housing needs of the poor rather than constructing public housing. A return to protective tariffs would be a disaster for the British people. In a revealing passage in a speech at the Music Hall in Edinburgh on 31 January 1885, Goschen argued that:

> Liberty and Equality almost destroy each other. Liberty is the power to possess as much as you please or as little as you please, to work, to get forward, to rise in the scale of life, if you can. Equality is against all that, and says every man must be exactly the same as his neighbour. (Goschen, *Essays and Addresses*, 3–22)

Appalled by the death of General Gordon at Khartoum, Goschen supported a Conservative censure motion; Gladstone survived by only fourteen votes. In late May 1885 Goschen had a long 'fighting' talk with Albert Grey which made him think of 'retiring from Edinburgh and endeavouring to bring a party together before the election, so that people might stand knowing where they were'. The emphasis would be on 'honesty' plus reform of secondary education, local government, and taxation; sympathy would be shown to the colonies and the armed forces (Elliot, 1.293). The Liberal government was defeated in the Commons in June and Lord Salisbury formed a minority Conservative administration with Irish support. Ireland and Chamberlain's 'unauthorized programme' became the great issues of the day.

Trying to ascertain Gladstone's views, Goschen deprecated Chamberlain's scheme for 'several *central* national councils' but underscored his support for 'decentralization and the devolution of important functions to provincial or other bodies' (Goschen to Gladstone, 10 July 1885, BL, Add. MS 44161, fols. 313–17). Lord Hartington, hereditary whig chieftain, was regarded by Goschen as the natural leader of the whigs and moderate Liberals. Anticipating the Liberal leadership when Gladstone retired, Hartington warned Goschen not to attack Chamberlain's proposals too severely as they were inexpedient but not 'revolutionary'. Goschen even contemplated joining a Gladstone cabinet if asked. He could exert pressure on Hartington and push him into the leadership if Gladstone departed. In the general election of November 1885 Goschen was easily returned over a radical in Edinburgh East when the Conservatives failed to run a candidate.

Ireland, Liberal Unionism, and Lord Randolph Churchill, 1885–1887 Gladstone's public conversion to home rule for Ireland in mid-December 1885 was a bombshell. An outraged Queen Victoria appealed on 20 December 1885 to Goschen and 'to all moderate, loyal, and really patriotic men' to band together in order to save the empire and the throne from Gladstone's 'reckless hands' (Spinner, *Goschen*, 113). Just prior to Salisbury's resignation on 29 January 1886, she urged Goschen to consult with her at Osborne. He declined, believing there was no alternative to a Gladstone government, which he would not join. As the extent of the Liberal split over home rule became clear Goschen consulted Salisbury about a possible arrangement whereby Conservatives would not run candidates in those constituencies where the Liberal member voted against home rule. In mid-April the first major joint rally of the anti-home-rulers took place at the Opera House. Salisbury, Hartington, and Goschen joined in criticizing Gladstone and Parnell.

Not surprisingly many constituency Liberals disliked seeing their representatives on the same platform as Conservatives; this necessitated a distinctly liberal group in opposition to home rule, the Liberal Unionist Association. Goschen contributed energetically to the organization of the Liberal Unionists, who represented the intermediary position that his personal political beliefs had long implied. He maintained his view that Hartington should lead, with himself providing organizational and speaking support. As Goschen had predicted, the Home Rule Bill was defeated by thirty votes in early June; Gladstone promptly dissolved parliament.

The electoral campaign, in which the Conservatives agreed not to oppose Liberal Unionists, was short and rough. Unionists won a decisive victory. About twenty votes short of an absolute majority, Lord Salisbury required aid from the seventy-eight Liberal Unionists. Goschen's happiness was soured when he was trounced by a Gladstonian in Edinburgh East. A Salisbury–Hartington coalition government was still impossible but Hartington prodded Goschen to consider an offer from Salisbury if it were made. Goschen was 'aghast' at the suggestion but after reflection saw merit in the idea. Salisbury eventually formed an entirely Conservative minority government and surprised the political world by making Lord Randolph Churchill chancellor of the exchequer and leader of the House of Commons. Goschen was 'staggered' by the appointment and thought it a 'fearful miscue' (Spinner, *Goschen*, 129).

Goschen continued his search for a seat as differences within the Conservative cabinet grew more acute; Salisbury prepared for a 'rupture' with Lord Randolph Churchill. Goschen was as startled as everyone else when he read of Churchill's resignation in December. Churchill's letter to Salisbury indicated he might leave the cabinet unless the defence estimates were reduced. In what was designed to begin an exchange of views, Churchill had inadvertently given the prime minister a chance to remove a troublesome colleague. Salisbury called Churchill's bluff and accepted his resignation. Churchill attempted to justify his miscalculation by implying that he had hatched a brilliant scheme to seize power in the cabinet. Sure of success because of his indispensability in the Commons, Churchill invented the story which became part of the political anecdotage of the period, that his plans were thwarted because he 'forgot Goschen' just as Napoleon 'forgot Blücher' (Spinner, *Goschen*, 131).

Once again, Hartington rejected Salisbury's proposals for a coalition government, but agreed to relay an offer of the exchequer to Goschen. Fearing a governmental collapse, Goschen accepted (January 1887). The leadership of the Commons, however, went to W. H. Smith. Believing that Lord Iddesleigh was an ineffective foreign secretary, Goschen insisted that Salisbury return to the Foreign Office. Deeply distressed, Iddesleigh died of a stroke in Salisbury's office a few days later.

Wishing to emphasize his Liberal Unionism, Goschen hesitated to take a safe Conservative seat. After a very hard campaign at a by-election in Liverpool (Exchange), Goschen was mortified to lose by seven votes (January 1887). Obliged to accept the generous offer of Lord Algernon Percy to relinquish his solidly Conservative constituency at St George's, Hanover Square, in London, Goschen retained this seat until made a peer in 1900.

Budgets, Barings, and personal finance, 1887–1892 According to Sir Edward Hamilton, later permanent secretary to the Treasury, 'The first qualifications of a Chancellor of the Exchequer are *character* and being a *gentleman*. Then come influence and financial aptitude' (*The Diary of Sir Edward Walter Hamilton, 1885–1906*, ed. D. W. R. Bahlman, 1993, 390). Goschen satisfied these requirements, though Hamilton was later troubled by his indecision. Algernon West, chairman of the Board of Inland Revenue, noted Goschen's love of 'minute criticisms; often criticizing his own criticisms' (*The Private Diaries of Sir Algernon West*, ed. H. G. Hutchinson, 1922, 4–5). Alfred Milner, Goschen's private secretary during his first three years at the Treasury, observed that Goschen had sometimes carried 'criticism and analysis' to an 'excess' while Lord Cromer recalled Goschen's extreme caution.

Goschen's most memorable achievement was the conversion of the national debt in 1888. He ultimately reduced almost £600 million of debt from 3 per cent to 2½ per cent, a considerable saving for the nation. In an important innovation in his budget for 1889, he placed an estate duty of 1 per cent on all real and personal estates valued at more than £10,000. Worrying that the income tax was used excessively, he regarded his estate tax as safe and reasonable. Gladstone, however, feared it as a novelty that might lead to graduation, while Edward Hamilton, writing in his diary on 16 April 1889, was certain that it was 'the thin end of the wedge to a graduated system of taxation, which is pretty certain to be expanded in the future' (*The Diary of Sir Edward … Hamilton*, ed. Bahlmann, 1993, 93).

Goschen acted decisively in 1890 when Baring Brothers, one of the largest merchant-banking firms, seemed on the verge of collapse through over-speculation in Argentine securities. William Lidderdale, governor of the Bank of England, advised Goschen that, with time, Barings could become solvent; the government must, however, provide financial support. Goschen hesitated about pledging 'the National credit to a private firm' (Elliot, 2.171). Convinced that it was 'absolutely necessary for *la haute finance* to find its own salvation' Goschen pressured Lidderdale to set up a guarantee fund (ibid., 2.173). The chancellor of the exchequer agreed to share all losses with the bank for twenty-four hours. The response of the banking and financial community was massive, with the fund eventually reaching £18 million. Barings was reconstituted and soon repaid its debts.

Goschen's chancellorship steadied a government expected by many to disintegrate, but he was personally ill at ease with his tory colleagues. He deputized for W. H. Smith when the latter was ill, but his handling of the Commons was uncertain. The opposition were personally hostile to him while the tories proved a lukewarm following, regarding him as prissy and fidgety. When Smith died in October 1891, A. J. Balfour and not Goschen succeeded him as leader of the Commons and, in effect, party leader of the government coalition in that house. At the general election in July 1892 Gladstone and the Irish won a small majority. Radical Unionists had merged with the Liberal Unionists in 1889. Two years later, when Hartington became the eighth duke of Devonshire, Chamberlain replaced him as Liberal Unionist leader in the Commons. These events assisted Goschen, who disliked and distrusted Chamberlain, in deciding to join the Carlton Club and the Conservative Party in 1893.

In 1890 Goschen reflected on his own financial situation. Writing to his brother Charles, head of Fruhling and Goschen, he estimated his investments totalled about £136,000, with some £90,000 of this amount in the family firm. This provided him with an income of £6800 a year, to which he could add Lucy's £500 and his government salary of £5000. During the previous three years, his total income had averaged between £12,000 and £13,000 while his expenses had amounted to some £10,000. Seacox Heath was valued at £100,000 and Portland Place at £20,000. Goschen feared the consequences if his interest income fell from somewhere between 5 and 6 per cent to 4 per cent. It was finally agreed that he could probably count on an income of about £11,000 a year, depending upon his future service in high office.

The Admiralty and the Second South African War, 1892–1900 Speaking to the British Economic Association in 1893, Goschen contended that the mass electorate did not understand 'analysis and hypothesis'. The 'emotionalist' had now replaced the 'sentimentalist' and the 'philanthropist'. There were too many demands for state intervention and social reform. The poor law of 1834 which the 'emotionalist' condemned as 'hard' was really 'wise'. It had arrested 'demoralization and the weakening of self-dependence' (Goschen, *Essays and Addresses*).

Sir William Harcourt's first budget in 1893 annoyed Goschen; his second left him in a rage, for Harcourt, in graduating the death duties, claimed to be building on Goschen's 1 per cent estate tax of 1889: Goschen regarded this as socialism. Goschen was irritated as he saw the fortunes of the Unionists being determined by the 'quartette' of Salisbury, Balfour, Chamberlain, and Devonshire, though he returned to the Admiralty in June 1895, in Salisbury's administration, after first establishing that Chamberlain was not to take the exchequer. As armament spending rose on the continent, there was much debate in Britain over defence matters. A committee of defence was established but Goschen, unimpressed, told Milner that the Admiralty 'will be administered precisely as before' (Goschen to Milner, 30 June 1895, Bodl. Oxf., MSS Milner). Critics pointed to a lack of co-ordination between various departments and an inability to look at the requirements of the empire as a whole. In 1900, preparing to retire and in the midst of the Second South African War, Goschen still wished to limit the work of the committee of defence. While not objecting to a formal agenda, he doubted the value of regularly scheduled meetings and voiced grave reservations about keeping minutes.

Goschen regarded the anxiety about Britain's diplomatic isolation in 1896 as misplaced. He viewed it as enabling the empire to be free of entangling commitments. In a speech at Lewes on 26 February 1896 he argued that Britain could easily find allies if it decided to alter course (Spinner, *Goschen*, 202). Considering himself a 'consolidationist' rather than an 'expansionist', he still demanded concessions from China in 1898 when the other European states gobbled up portions of that country. During the Spanish-American War, he insisted on action in July 1898 when new fortifications at Algeciras imperilled British ships at Gibraltar. He and Balfour contemplated blockading Cadiz or Barcelona and raiding Algeciras. Fortunately, the conciliatory prime minister blended courtesy and firmness so that the Spaniards retreated without being humiliated.

The death of Goschen's wife on 21 February 1898 was devastating but he quickly returned to work. British–Boer hostility soon overshadowed all other issues. Alfred Milner had been appointed governor of Cape Colony and high commissioner for South Africa in 1897. By early October 1899 both sides had prepared their ultimatums and fighting started. Goschen's primary task was rapidly to transport British troops to South Africa and to prevent the Boers from obtaining supplies through Mozambique. He objected, unsuccessfully, to placing food supplies destined for the Boer troops on the contraband list; Britain should not set an example 'of hampering the importation of food'. By early 1900 British power had asserted itself and the two Boer republics were annexed; no one knew that a brutal guerrilla war was about to commence.

In his estimates for 1900, Goschen spoke for the first time about the 'appalling' sums which Germany allocated for her navy, whereas formerly he had worried about the French and the Russians. Starting to feel that 'absolute isolation is playing the devil', he advocated co-operation with the Germans in putting down the Boxer uprising in China (Goschen to Chamberlain, 2 Sept 1900, Chamberlain MSS, University of Birmingham Library). Forced to clarify his thoughts as the cabinet planned for a general election in October, Goschen informed Salisbury that he intended to retire from the Admiralty and from his constituency. The Unionists secured a substantial majority and Goschen, indicating that he would accept a peerage, was created Viscount Goschen of Hawkhurst (12 October 1900); he would have preferred an earldom. He did not again hold ministerial office.

The fight for free trade, 1900–1907 Liberal Unionism contained both old Liberal free-traders and radical imperialists. Though Goschen and Joseph Chamberlain had both left the Liberal Party at about the same time, the former had none of the latter's radicalism about the nature of the British fiscal state. Ironically, the separation which had been predicted in 1885 now occurred—Chamberlain broke with Devonshire and Goschen—but it took place in the Conservative rather than the Liberal Party. Goschen, who argued that a tariff would impose a tax on the people's food and who feared that it would enable the state to exercise centralized control over industry, helped to form the Unionist Free Food League in July 1903. Once the duke of Devonshire resigned from the government in the autumn, Goschen found himself in the same role he had played to perfection in 1885–6. The duke would preside over the Unionist Free Trade Club while Goschen supplied the ammunition. After the Liberal victory of 1906, Goschen hoped that Chamberlain would acknowledge the defeat of tariff reform so that all Unionists might work together against the radical legislation certain to be brought in by the Liberals. Chamberlain, however, regarded the election as a temporary set-back and soon, to Goschen's dismay, seemed to have captured Balfour.

In early 1903 Goschen completed a two-volume life of his grandfather, the publisher of Leipzig. The reviews were good and while it had been 'a labour of love', he was happy to have finished. Always interested in reading and intellectual activity, Goschen enthusiastically endorsed the university extension movement; everyone's mind should be cultivated for there was far more to life than just earning a livelihood. The most pleasant event of Goschen's final years was his unopposed election in 1903 as chancellor of Oxford University on the death of Lord Salisbury.

Death and reputation On 7 February 1907 Goschen died suddenly and quietly in his sleep at Seacox Heath; he was buried four days later near the parish church at Flimwell. John Morley noted in his diary that Goschen was 'one of the very *cleverest* men' he had known (J. Morley, *Recollections*, 1917, 2.201–2). While one must admire Goschen for his honesty and personal integrity, his *laissez-faire* liberalism seemed increasingly obsolete with the passing of time. His optimism about the future disappeared as he came to fear the implications of democracy. A splendid warrior in the battle to remove restrictions, Goschen recoiled from constructive social and economic legislation. Democracy would lead to equality and equality would destroy the liberty for which the middle class had fought. He shuddered at the conclusion that equality of opportunity was unrealizable without equality of conditions. Goschen articulated an important body of commercial opinion in Victorian liberalism: staunchly free-trading and moderately reformist, staunchly retrenching but politically somewhat timid.

THOMAS J. SPINNER JUN.

Sources T. J. Spinner Jr, *George Joachim Goschen: the transformation of a Victorian liberal* (1973) • T. J. Spinner Jr, 'George Joachim Goschen: the man Lord Randolph Churchill "forgot"', *Journal of Modern History*, 39 (1967), 405–24 • A. D. Elliot, *The life of George Joachim Goschen, first Viscount Goschen, 1831–1907*, 2 vols. (1911) • G. J. Goschen, *The life and times of Georg Joachim Göschen, publisher and printer of Leipzig*, 2 vols. (1903) • G. J. Goschen, *Essays and addresses on economic questions, 1865–1893* (1905) • B. Holland, *Life of the eighth duke of Devonshire*, 2 vols. (1911) • J. Morley, *The life of William Ewart Gladstone*, 3 vols. (1903) • J. L. Garvin and J. Amery, *The life of Joseph Chamberlain*, 6 vols. (1932–69) • A. B. Cooke and J. Vincent, *The governing passion: cabinet government and party politics in Britain, 1885–86* (1974) • T. A. Jenkins, *Gladstone, whiggery and the liberal party, 1874–1886* (1988) • P. Colson, ed., *Lord Goschen and his friends* (1945) • Bodl. Oxf., MSS Viscount Milner

Archives Bodl. Oxf., corresp. and papers • Bodl. Oxf., register of corresp. as lord of admiralty, diary • priv. coll. | BL, letters to Arthur Balfour, Add. MS 49706 • BL, corresp. with Lord Cross, Add. MS 51267 • BL, corresp. with Lord D'Abernon, Add. MS 48922 • BL, corresp. with Sir Charles Dilke, Add. MSS 43910–43919 • BL, corresp. with W. E. Gladstone, Add. MS 44161 • BL, corresp. with Sir Edward Walter Hamilton, Add. MS 48616 • BL, letters to Sir A. H. Layard, Add. MSS 38950–39107, *passim* • BL, corresp. with Sir Stafford Northcote, Add. MS 50021 • BL, letters to Lord Ripon, Add. MS 43532 • BL, corresp. with Lord Welby, Egerton MS 3291 • BLPES, corresp. relating to Royal Economic Society • BLPES, letters to Lord Welby • Bodl. Oxf., corresp. with Sir Henry Burdett • Bodl. Oxf., letters to Lady Edward Cecil • Bodl. Oxf., letters to Lord Clarendon • Bodl. Oxf., corresp. with Sir William Harcourt and Lewis Harcourt • Bodl. Oxf., corresp. with Lord Kimberley • Bodl. Oxf., letters to Charles Pearson • Bodl. Oxf., corresp. with Lord Selbourne • Borth. Inst., letters to Lord Halifax • CAC Cam., letters to Lord Randolph Churchill • Chatsworth House, Derbyshire, letters to the eighth duke of Devonshire • CKS, letters to Aretas Akers-Douglas • CKS, letters to Edward Stanhope • Glos. RO, corresp. with Sir Michael Hicks Beach • Hants. RO, letters to Arthur Bower Forwood • Hatfield House, Hertfordshire, third marquess of Salisbury MSS • HLRO, letters to J. St L. Strachey • Hove Central Library, letters to Lord Wolseley and Lady Wolseley • NA Scot., corresp. with Arthur Balfour and Gerald Balfour • NL Ire., letters to A. S. Green • NL Scot., corresp. incl. Lord Rosebery • NMM, corresp. with Sir Alexander Milne • PRO, corresp. with Lord Cardwell, PRO 30/48 • PRO, corresp. with Lord Cromer, FO 633 • PRO, corresp. with Lord Granville, PRO 30/29 • PRO, corresp. with Odo Russell, FO 918 • Royal Arch., Queen Victoria MSS • Trinity Cam., letters to Sir Henry Babington Smith • U. Birm. L., corresp. with Joseph Chamberlain • U. Durham L., letters to Earl Grey • UCL, corresp. with Sir Edwin Chadwick • University of Bristol Library, letters to Alfred Austin

Likenesses J. Tenniel, pencil caricature, 1892 (*April showers, or a spoilt Easter Holiday*), FM Cam. • B. Stone, photograph, 1897, NPG • M. Beerbohm, caricature, *c.*1898, NPG • Ape [C. Pellegrini], caricature chromolithograph, NPG; repro. in *VF* (12 June 1869) • L. C. Dickinson, group portrait, oils (*Gladstone's cabinet of 1868*), NPG • H. Furniss, caricature, NPG • F. C. Gould, caricature, NPG • S. P. Hall, pencil sketch, NPG • Lock & Whitfield, woodburytype, NPG; repro. in *Men of mark* (1877) • London Stereoscopic Co., photograph, NPG; repro. in *Our conservative and unionist statesmen* (1896–9), vol. 4 • J. J. E. Mayall, photograph, NPG [*see illus.*] • J. Watkins, carte-de-visite, NPG • etching (after photograph by London Stereoscopic Co.), NPG • etching (after an unknown photographer), NPG • photograph, repro. in Elliot, *Life of George Joachim Goschen* • photograph, repro. in Goschen, *Life and times of Georg Joachim Göschen* • photograph, repro. in Colson, ed., *Lord Goschen and his friends* • prints, NPG • two cartoons, repro. in *Punch*; priv. coll.

Wealth at death £141,568 1*s.* 5*d.*: probate, 24 May 1907, *CGPLA Eng. & Wales*

Gosford. For this title name *see* Wedderburn, Sir Peter, Lord Gosford (*c.*1616–1679); Acheson, Archibald, second earl of Gosford (1776–1849).

Gosling, Harry (1861–1930), trade unionist and politician, was born at 57 York Street, Lambeth, on 9 June 1861, the second son of William Gosling, master lighterman, and his wife, Sarah Louisa Rowe, schoolteacher, who died when Harry was seven. He attended the British and Foreign School in Blackfriars until the age of thirteen, when he began work as an office boy. Soon after this, in 1875, he was apprenticed to his father as a lighterman, working on the barges of the Thames, a trade his family had followed for four generations. In 1884 he married Helen Martin, daughter of Joseph Low Duff, an engineer; they had no children. Gosling had experienced health problems since childhood, and a collapse in 1887 left him physically unfit for the heavy work on the river for a number of years. During this time he worked as a salesman, but kept in contact with the river trade, and in 1889 he joined the Amalgamated Society of Watermen and Lightermen of the River Thames. He became president of the Lambeth branch in 1890, and in 1893 he was elected general secretary of the society.

Gosling became one of the leaders of the movement to improve the working conditions of dock and river labour throughout the country, which began with the great dock strike of 1889. He acted to change the exclusivist structure of his society and fostered contacts with other waterside unions. In 1911 he was elected president of the National Transport Workers' Federation (NTWF), to which his own organization belonged. Gosling and his union were centrally involved in the major disputes on the London docks in 1911–12 and in the national strike by the NTWF which followed. In 1921 the unions amalgamated to form the Transport and General Workers' Union (TGWU), and Gosling became president of the new organization. He was elected to the parliamentary committee of the Trades Union Congress in 1908 and was chairman of the congress in 1916. He was also prominent in reforms to the structure of the TUC in 1920–21, and was a member of the general council created by these reforms until 1923. On its establishment in 1908, Gosling was made a member of the Port of London Authority, and continued to serve on that body for the rest of his life.

During the First World War, Gosling assisted the government in a number of industrial relations roles. He was a member of several important committees, notably the port and transit executive committee which co-ordinated and regulated the transport of men, munitions, and food supplies, and the civil service arbitration board, set up to adjust the salaries of lower-grade civil servants. In 1917 he was appointed to the Imperial War Graves Commission. His services during the war were recognized by his being created a Companion of Honour in 1917.

In addition to his trade union and related activities Gosling engaged in both municipal and national politics. He first stood, unsuccessfully, for the London county council in 1895 in Rotherhithe. In 1904, at his third attempt, he won a seat on the council, representing St George's and Wapping. As alderman and councillor he served on the LCC for twenty-seven years. In 1923 he was elected as the Labour member of parliament for Whitechapel and St George's, and retained that seat until he died. During the first Labour government, in 1924, he was minister of transport and paymaster-general, and was responsible for the London Traffic Act (1924). On the fall of the government, Gosling sought to regain the presidency of the TGWU which he had resigned on becoming a minister, but was blocked by the union council. The decision provoked an outcry which led to its being reversed—an indication of the loyalty and respect that Gosling had built up within the union.

Gosling's obituary in *The Times* spoke of his 'mild and pacific character' and his 'transparent honesty' (25 Oct 1930). He gained the respect of those on all sides in both industrial and political spheres. In Labour circles he was remembered with sincere affection for his loyalty, courtesy, kindliness, and gentle humour. His autobiography, *Up and Down Stream*, was published in 1927, and he wrote one other pamphlet, *Peace: How to Get and Keep it*, in 1917. Gosling died at his home, Goodfetch, Waldegrave Road, Twickenham, on 24 October 1930, and was cremated at Golders Green crematorium on 30 October. He was survived by his wife. W. S. SANDERS, *rev.* MARC BRODIE

Sources H. Gosling, *Up and down stream* (1927) · *DLB*, vol. 4 · *The Times* (25 Oct 1930) · *The Times* (31 Oct 1930)

Archives Commonwealth War Graves Commission, Maidenhead, corresp. and papers relating to work for imperial war graves · Labour History Archive and Study Centre, Manchester, archives of war emergency workers national committee · Labour History Archive and Study Centre, Manchester, file on visit to French trade unions · U. Warwick Mod. RC, corresp. with International Transport Workers' Federation

Likenesses W. Stoneman, photograph, 1924, NPG · photograph, repro. in J. Lovell, *Stevedores and dockers* (1969), facing p. 128 · photographs, repro. in Gosling, *Up and down stream*, facing pp. 84, 148, 150, 238

Wealth at death £2651 16*s*. 5*d*.: probate, 22 Dec 1930, *CGPLA Eng. & Wales*

Gosling, Jane (*d.* **1804**). *See under* Gosling, Ralph (*bap.* 1693, *d.* 1757).

Gosling, Ralph (*bap.* **1693**, *d.* **1757**), schoolmaster and land surveyor, fifth and youngest child of Charles Gosling (*fl.* 1677–1693), yeoman, of Stubley, in the parish of Dronfield in Derbyshire, was baptized in the parish church there on 15 July 1693. By 1720 he had moved to Sheffield, where he found employment as a writing master, a schoolmaster, and as a land surveyor. In this last capacity he was employed on the surveys of the River Don navigation in 1730, and in 1736 he published the earliest known map of Sheffield. He also mapped estates and made the sundial at Dethick church, Derbyshire. According to Hunter, Gosling made some collections for the history of Sheffield, but of these no trace remains. Gosling married and had a son, who died in infancy, and a daughter, who predeceased him. His wife, Mary, was buried in Sheffield on 9 March 1755. By the time of his death he was living at Heeley, Sheffield, which is where he died, on 30 September 1757. He was buried at Sheffield on 3 October. He appears to have been in comfortable circumstances, as it was noticed in 1890 that he was owed £1205. Under his will, proved in March 1758, he left silver plate, gold rings, surveying instruments, and pictures to his executor and great-nephew Ralph Gosling, and monetary bequests to other members of his family.

The younger Ralph Gosling married Jane Lambert [**Jane Gosling** (*d.* 1804)] on 9 April 1769 at Sheffield parish church. He worked in a warehouse; Jane ran a school in Union Street, Sheffield, which was attended by Joseph

Hunter, the historian of Hallamshire, when he was about four years old. Besides keeping the school, she was the author of *Moral Essays and Reflections* (1789), and of *Ashdale Village*, a tale of which only the first two volumes were published. She died in 1804.

J. K. LAUGHTON, *rev.* SARAH BENDALL

Sources R. E. Leader, *Surveyors and architects of the past in Sheffield: a lecture read before the Sheffield society of architects and surveyors, March 12, 1903* (1903) • J. Hunter, *Hallamshire: the history and topography of the parish of Sheffield in the county of York*, new edn, ed. A. Gatty (1869) • J. C. Cox, *Notes on the churches of Derbyshire*, 1: *The hundred of Scarsdale* (1875) • F. W. Steer and others, *Dictionary of land surveyors and local map-makers of Great Britain and Ireland, 1530–1850*, ed. P. Eden, 2nd edn, ed. S. Bendall, 2 vols. (1997) • Collectanea Hunteriana, 5, BL, Add. MS 24440, fol. 33*r* • A. Gatty, *Sheffield past and present* (1873) • will, proved, March 1758, Borth. Inst., Probate documents • parish register (baptism), 15 July 1693, Dronfield • parish register (burial), 9 March 1755, Sheffield parish church • parish register (burial), 3 Oct 1757, Sheffield parish church • parish register (marriage), 9 April 1769, Sheffield parish church

Archives Sheff. Arch., map of Sheffield

Wealth at death £105; silver plate, gold rings, surveying instruments: will, Borth. Inst.

Gosnold, Bartholomew (*d.* 1607), sea captain and explorer, was the elder son of a Suffolk gentleman, Anthony Gosnold of Grundisburgh, Clopton, and Burgh, and Dorothy Bacon, a kinswoman of the lord keeper, Sir Nicholas Bacon. Bartholomew is first recorded on 20 October 1572 when his great-grandfather John Gosnold of Otley included him in his will. Bartholomew's education, at Cambridge and the inns of court, was intended to fit him for life as a country gentleman: in 1587 he entered Jesus College; in 1589 he and his father together purchased land; and on 9 February 1593 he transferred from New Inn to the more prestigious Middle Temple.

How Gosnold came by his nautical knowledge and when he first went to sea are facts alike unknown. It has been suggested that his interest was stimulated by Richard Hakluyt, from 1590 the rector of nearby Wetheringsett. Although by 1602 Gosnold was familiar with Hakluyt's *Principal Navigations*, and although the second edition of John Brereton's account of Gosnold's voyage in 1602 included matter clearly supplied by Hakluyt, there is no evidence that the two men were acquainted. Gosnold's interest more probably stemmed from his marriage in 1595 to Mary, the daughter of Robert and Martha Golding of Bury St Edmunds. Through her mother Mary was first cousin not only to the three sons, themselves all sea captains, of Sir William Winter, surveyor of the navy and master of the ordnance until his death in 1589, but also of Sir Thomas Smith. After 1600 this great London merchant all but monopolized the leadership of the joint-stock companies engaged in foreign trade, and already by 1595 he was a founder of the Levant Company, a chief member of the Muscovy Company, and the son of one of those to whom Sir Walter Ralegh had assigned his interest in Virginia. Perhaps by Hakluyt, more probably by one of the Winters or Smith, Gosnold was led to take up a maritime career.

In 1599, in the last years of the war against Spain, Gosnold commanded the *Diamond* of Southampton on a successful privateering cruise, netting loot valued that September at £1625 17*s.* 6*d.* In 1600 he planned another voyage, with a Captain Streynsham. Nothing is known of this second venture (it may never have taken place), but in 1602 Gosnold undertook the voyage of exploration on which his fame is based. His sponsor is unknown. It was certainly not Ralegh. According to William Strachey, it was the earl of Southampton; but in 1602 the earl was in the Tower of London and almost penniless. Captain Edward Hayes of Liverpool almost certainly helped Gosnold to formulate his plans, and Henry Brooke, Lord Cobham, was perhaps the expedition's prime mover. Its twin purposes were exploration and the establishment of a trading post, perhaps in Narragansett Bay where Verrazzano had stayed in 1524.

On 26 March 1602 the bark *Concord* of Dartmouth sailed from Falmouth with thirty-two on board. Jointly captained by Gosnold and Bartholomew Gilbert, the latter 'Lord Cobham's man', she passed the Azores on 14 April and on 14 May was off the Maine coast. Heading south into Cape Cod Bay, she then rounded the cape into Nantucket Sound. On 21 May an island to the south—probably Cape Poge (now part of Chappaquiddick)—was named Martha's Vineyard, from the grapes on the island and in honour of Gosnold's mother-in-law. This name the explorers also gave to the present Martha's Vineyard. Three days later in Gosnolls Hope (Buzzards Bay), Elizabeths Ile (now the two islands of Cuttyhunk and Nashawena) was sighted, and on 28 May adopted as the site for the trading post. While Gabriel Archer oversaw the building of a fort on an islet in a pond there, and others felled cedars on Penikese and dug for sassafras roots, Gosnold explored the north shore of Buzzards Bay. Soon, however, the settlers decided that there were not enough victuals for the twenty under Gosnold who were to remain over the winter. On 17 June the island and fort were abandoned, and the next day the *Concord* left Martha's Vineyard, arriving off Exmouth on 23 July 1602, and carrying her cargo of furs, sassafras, and cedarwood on to Dartmouth, Portsmouth (where she arrived on 27 July), and Southampton, whence part of her cargo was shipped to London. Ralegh, who claimed the right to license all trade with his Virginia, was enraged by this interloping and enforced a settlement favourable to himself. He received the dedication of Brereton's account of the voyage published that same year, and took the *Concord* into his service, contemplating for her a voyage in 1603 in his own name. It is not known whether Gosnold was with her during these events, but he was certainly not in Suffolk, for on 7 September, seemingly from London, he wrote to his father, excusing his delay and amplifying an earlier letter (which has not survived).

Between 1602 and 1606 Gosnold vanishes from the record. He must have sometimes been in Suffolk, for his three youngest children were baptized in St James's Church, Bury St Edmunds, on 16 December 1603, 11

December 1605, and 5 February 1607. By the last date, however, he was already on his way to Virginia. According to Captain John Smith, writing in 1612, Gosnold was 'the first mover of this plantation, having many years solicited many of his friends, but found small assistants' (Quinn, Quinn, and Hillier, 5.310); and it was only after he had enlisted the aid of Edward Maria Wingfield, John Smith himself, and others that Gosnold made contact with 'the Nobilitie, Gentrie, and Marchants' who after another year secured the royal charter in April 1606. If Smith is correct, Gosnold had thus been planning the settlement of Virginia since 1604 at the latest. No other contemporary witness, however, gives Gosnold so important a role. Christopher Newport in the *Susan Constant* (100 tons) was admiral of the fleet which set out in December 1606. Gosnold, commanding the *Godspeed* (40 tons), was only vice-admiral, but when the colonists reached the Chesapeake in late April 1607, Gosnold was one of the governing council of seven who elected Edward Maria Wingfield their president. Already there were antagonisms among the councillors: Wingfield disagreed with Gosnold over the siting of Jamestown, thought John Smith no gentleman, and in mid-June apparently feared that Gosnold and his friend Gabriel Archer might unseat him. Wingfield was right to fear displacement—it occurred on 11 September—but by then Gosnold, after three weeks' illness, was dead, and it was clear that, far from being a threat to the president, Gosnold had been a peacemaker. Looking back, Wingfield termed him a 'Worthy and Religious gent … upon whose lief stood a great part of the good succes, and fortune of our government and Collony' (ibid., 278). George Percy recorded Gosnold's death on 22 August 1607, noting that 'he was honourably buried, having all the Ordnance in the Fort shot off with many vollies of small shot' (ibid., 273). DAVID R. RANSOME

Sources W. F. Gookin and P. L. Barbour, *Bartholomew Gosnold: discoverer and planter* (1963) • W. F. Gookin, 'The ancestry of Bartholomew Godnold', *New England Historical and Genealogical Register*, 105 (1951), 5–22 • K. R. Andrews, *Trade, plunder and settlement: maritime enterprise and the genesis of the British empire, 1480–1630* (1984) • D. B. Quinn and A. M. Quinn, *The English New England voyages, 1602–1608*, Hakluyt Society, 2nd ser., 161 (1983) • L. B. Wright and V. Freund, *Historie of travell into Virginia Britania*, Hakluyt Society, 2nd ser., 103 (1953) • D. B. Quinn, A. M. Quinn, and S. Hillier, eds., *New American world: a documentary history of North America to 1612*, 5 vols. (1979) • S. Purchas, *Hakluytus posthumus, or, Purchas his pilgrimes*, 20 bks in 4 vols. (1625); repr. 20 vols., Hakluyt Society, extra ser., 14–33 (1905–7) • P. L. Barbour, ed., *The Jamestown voyages under the first charter, 1606–1609*, 2 vols., Hakluyt Society, 2nd ser., 136–7 (1969) • parish register, Bury St Edmunds, St James, 1595 [marriage]

Gosnold, John (1626?–1678), General Baptist minister, was born at Dunmow, Essex, the son of Robert Gosnold. His parents must have been relatively poor, for Gosnold was educated at the Charterhouse School in London as an exhibitioner. At nineteen he was admitted to Pembroke College, Cambridge, on 20 May 1646, but he left without taking a degree. Ordained a minister in the Church of England, he served as Lord Grey's chaplain. After some delay the Westminster assembly approved him on 19 July 1650. By 1654 he had become a General Baptist and founded his own church in London, apparently in the Barbican. There is, however, no evidence that he participated in the General Baptists' general assembly. His two books, *Of Laying on of Hands* (1656) and *Of the Doctrine of Baptisms* (1657), expounded on Hebrews 6: 2. In the latter volume, which defended the practice of baptizing believers by submersion, he also discussed baptism by the Holy Spirit, which he explained as 'such a powring forth of the Spirit, in the extraordinary Gifts of it, as to be fill'd with it' (p. 40).

Gosnold was not among the forty signatories of the General Baptists' *Brief Confession or Declaration of Faith* (March 1660), but he joined other nonconformists in formally repudiating the Fifth Monarchist Thomas Venner's insurrection the following year. Gosnold enjoyed friendly relations with ministers of other persuasions, and attended the Tuesday lectures of John Tillotson, the future archbishop, at St Lawrence Jewry, which began in 1664. A popular preacher in his own right, Gosnold reportedly attracted as many as 3000 people to his services, but this number is grossly exaggerated. According to tradition six or seven clerics in their gowns came to hear him preach, sitting inconspicuously under a large gallery. He had a reputation for zealously opposing Socinianism. After the fire of London, parish officials in St Giles Cripplegate appealed to Gosnold for financial assistance, whereupon his congregation raised in excess of £50; for more than two decades the church continued the tradition of special collections to aid the indigent. The wealthiest Baptist church in London, it maintained a library for ministers to use. In 1669 the congregation was meeting in a music-hall in Gun Alley, Little Moorfields. Under the terms of the declaration of indulgence, Gosnold received a licence on 25 July 1672 to preach at Richard Horton's house in Little Moorfields. The congregation subsequently acquired a more suitable building in Paul's Alley, Barbican. In 1675 Gosnold became embroiled in the pamphlet debate over paedobaptism triggered by Henry Danvers's *Treatise of Baptism* (1673), to which Obadiah Wills responded in *Infant-Baptisme Asserted* (1674). Danvers defended himself in *Innocency and Truth Vindicated* (1675), prompting Wills's rejoinder in *Vindiciae vindiciarum* (1675). Charging that Danvers had misquoted and misrepresented his authorities, Wills called on Baptists to examine Danvers's scholarship. In response, Gosnold, Hanserd Knollys, William Kiffin, Daniel Dyke, Thomas Delaune, and Henry Forty published *The Baptists Answer to Mr Obed. Wills* (July 1675), acknowledging Danvers's errors but rejecting Wills's arguments for paedobaptism. In addition to his other writings, Gosnold composed a poem on the death of Mrs Sarah Haues (BL, Sloane MS 3769, fol. 4).

Gosnold fell foul of the government in 1677 for allegedly dispersing treasonable, atheistic, and impious libels and papers. A warrant for his arrest and the seizure of his books and papers was issued on 11 May 1677, and a warrant for his reputed accomplice, John Clarke, appeared the same day. This case was probably related to accusations by the informer William Hill, who had been one of the state's principal witnesses against the Tong plotters a decade earlier and was now chaplain of the Fleet prison. According to Hill, Thomas Bromhall, a member of Gosnold's congregation and warden of the Fleet, had been in daily contact with the radical bookseller Francis Smith and had a printing press in his lodgings. Moreover, Bromhall and Smith had reputedly spoken seditiously of the king in William Howard's presence. The evidence against Gosnold was insubstantial, and nothing came of the charges. Aged fifty-two, Gosnold died in London the following year on 3 October, and was interred in Bunhill Fields four days later. A collection of his remarks was published in broadside format the same year under the title *Holy and Profitable Sayings of Mr. J. G.* In his will, dated 11 January 1675, Gosnold, styling himself a gentleman, left his estate to his wife, Lydia. RICHARD L. GREAVES

Sources Venn, *Alum. Cant.* • *CSP dom.*, 1672, 400; 1677–8, 123–4, 163; *addenda, 1660–85*, 469–70 • *Calamy rev.* • T. Crosby, *The history of the English Baptists, from the Reformation to the beginning of the reign of King George I*, 4 vols. (1738–40), vol. 3, pp. 61–3 • W. Wilson, *The history and antiquities of the dissenting churches and meeting houses in London, Westminster and Southwark*, 4 vols. (1808–14), vol. 3, pp. 234–5 • R. L. Greaves, *Saints and rebels: seven nonconformists in Stuart England* (1985), 170–71 • W. T. Whitley, *The Baptists of London, 1612–1928* (1928), 112 • A. C. Underwood, *A history of the English Baptists* (1947), 137 • will of John Gosnold, GL, MS 25626/7, fols. 164*v*–165*r*
Archives BL, Sloane MSS 3769, fol. 4
Likenesses Van Hove, portrait

Gospatric, earl of Northumbria (*d.* **1073x5**), magnate, was the son of Maldred, whose father, Crinan, named in one source as Crinan 'the thegn', is usually identified with the lay abbot of Dunkeld of that name, who was father of Duncan I, king of Scots, and was killed in battle in 1045. That identification cannot be regarded as certain, but there is no doubt that Maldred was a man of high status, who married Ealdgyth, the daughter of Earl Uhtred of Northumbria and his wife, Ælfgifu, daughter of King Æthelred II, and that Ealdgyth was Gospatric's mother. The name Gospatric, probably from the Old Welsh *gwas patric*, 'the servant of Patrick', is characteristic of the Anglo-Scottish border counties in this period, and the identity of those who bore it is sometimes unclear. A Gospatric, kinsman of the king, appears in the life of King Edward accompanying Earl Tostig of Northumbria on a pilgrimage to Rome. On the return journey Tostig's party was attacked by a band of robbers. Gospatric protected Tostig by pretending to be the earl so that he could make good his escape. Gospatric was of sufficient social standing that his attire convinced his attackers that his claim was true. He was released when his true identity was revealed. This may not be Earl Gospatric but, rather, the Northumbrian thegn Gospatric killed on the orders of Tostig's sister, Queen Edith, at the Christmas court in 1064. The *Historia regum Anglorum* attributed to Symeon of Durham gives this Gospatric's murder as one of the causes of the Northumbrian revolt against Tostig in 1065.

Earl Gospatric purchased the earldom of Northumbria from William I after the death of Copsi in March 1067. He may have felt that his Northumbrian ancestry would help him control this volatile region and, indeed, the *Historia regum Anglorum* noted that the earldom was his by right of his mother's blood. In 1068, however, Earl Gospatric became involved in the northern revolt against the conqueror, joining the attack on York. Following William I's campaign, Gospatric fled to Scotland. At the beginning of 1069, Earl Robert Cumin and his expeditionary force were killed at Durham and Gospatric seems to have regained his position in Northumbria north of the Tyne. When Swein of Denmark arrived in the north in the late summer of 1069, Gospatric, together with other Northumbrian nobles, joined him in taking York. After the conqueror's devastating campaign of the winter of 1069–70, however, Gospatric surrendered to William by sending envoys to him on the banks of the Tees. It was at this time that Gospatric seems to have plundered the church of St Cuthbert at Durham. On his retreat from York, the earl had warned the bishop and community of St Cuthbert that the Normans were approaching. Taking the relics of St Cuthbert, Bishop Æthelwine led the community to safety on Lindisfarne and it seems that it was during their absence early in 1070 that Gospatric looted the church. A dream narrative preserved in Symeon's *Historia ecclesiae Dunelmensis* describes the punishment meted out to the despoilers of St Cuthbert's Church, and Gospatric appears alongside a certain Gillomichael. Later in 1070 Malcolm III of Scotland attacked Northumbria, prompting a retaliation from Gospatric which involved raiding Scots land in Cumbria. This in turn provoked a savage response from the Scots, who counter-raided the patrimony of St Cuthbert. In 1071 Gospatric conducted Walcher, the new bishop of the church of St Cuthbert, from York to Durham.

Earl Gospatric was deposed by William I after his expedition to Scotland in 1072. He was charged with complicity in the murder of Robert Cumin as well as aiding the Danish attack on York, but underlying these charges was the threat posed by the earl's power in Northumbria north of the Tyne. Also, with the relationship with the Scots on a more secure footing, William may have felt that Gospatric could be deposed without serious repercussions. Gospatric seems to have retired to Scotland where, after making a journey to Flanders, he was granted estates in Dunbar and Lothian, later known as the earldom of Dunbar and March. His lands south of the Tweed were probably lost to his successor as earl of Northumbria, Waltheof, son of Siward. It is unlikely that Earl Gospatric is the Domesday landholder of that name in Yorkshire, but he may also have been granted lands in Cumbria by Malcolm III, as the lordship of Allerdale was later granted to Waldeve, son of Gospatric.

The name of Gospatric's wife is unknown but they seem to have had at least three sons, Dolfin, Waldeve, and *Gospatric, and four daughters, Etheldreda, Ochtreda, Gunnilda, and Matillis. Dolfin has been identified as the lord of Carlisle ousted by William Rufus in 1092 and Waldeve (Waltheof) may have become abbot of Crowland. Three of the daughters married Cumbrian landholders and Etheldreda married Duncan II of Scotland. Roger of Howden claimed that Gospatric summoned Aldwine and Turgot, who were then at Melrose, to hear his confession and that he died at Norham-on-Tweed and was buried in the doorway of the church. The fact that Aldwine and Turgot were at Melrose suggests that the earl's death occurred between 1073 and 1075. A tombstone belonging to an 'Earl Gospatric' was found at Durham, and the names of members of the family were entered in the Durham *Liber vitæ*, suggesting that contact was maintained with the church of St Cuthbert after Gospatric's departure for Scotland. As well as holding what later became the earldom of Dunbar, Gospatric's descendants became lords of Beanley in Northumberland. His immediate successor was his son Gospatric, who was killed at the battle of the Standard in 1138. WILLIAM M. AIRD

Sources A. O. Anderson, ed. and trans., *Early sources of Scottish history, AD 500 to 1286*, 2 vols. (1922) • *VCH Northumberland*, vol. 7 • W. P. Hedley, *Northumberland families*, 2 vols., Society of Antiquaries of Newcastle upon Tyne, Record Series (1968–70) • F. Barlow, ed. and trans., *The life of King Edward who rests at Westminster* (1962) • Symeon of Durham, *Opera* • G. W. S. Barrow, 'Some problems in 12th and 13th century Scottish history: a genealogical approach', *Scottish Genealogist*, 25 (1978), 97–112 • A. Williams, *The English and the Norman conquest* (1995) • Ordericus Vitalis, *Eccl. hist.*, vol. 2 • *Chronica magistri Rogeri de Hovedene*, ed. W. Stubbs, 4 vols., Rolls Series, 51 (1868–71)

Gospatric, first earl of Lothian (*d.* 1138), baron, was apparently the youngest son of *Gospatric, earl of Northumbria, who fled to Scotland *c.*1072 and was given lands in Lothian by Malcolm III (*r.* 1058–93). Of the events of his life there is little record. His earliest mention in a Scottish writ comes *c.*1120, and while he attested a number of Scottish charters between *c.*1120 and 1134, he is very seldom styled earl. Rather, he is consistently referred to as 'Gospatric the brother of Dolfin', and his seal even bore this inscription. In one of his own charters, dated between 1124 and 1138, Gospatric did style himself 'Earl Gospatric, brother of Dolfin', while in a charter of David I, dated about June 1138, he appeared as 'Earl Gospatric'. The absence of the title of earl in most of these documents is puzzling. Indeed, it has sometimes led to the supposition that he could not have been earl of Lothian, this position being held instead by his brother Dolfin. Such a conclusion is not, however, generally accepted, and it may be that Gospatric received Lothian *c.*1134, which would help to explain why he is referred to as earl only in charters dated between about 1134 and 1138.

Gospatric's status in Northumbria is somewhat better attested. In early 1136, immediately after Henry I's death, Stephen confirmed his predecessor's grant to Gospatric of Beanley and other lands in Northumbria, amounting to at least fourteen manors. The service was not specified, but a document of 1212 stated that the barony had been held from the time of King Henry for 'inborh and utborh', suggesting that the earls of Lothian (later Dunbar) were required to regulate border disputes, and that his grants represented an attempt by Henry to bring the border region under better control. There can be no doubt that his status as lord of Beanley and earl of Lothian placed Gospatric in the topmost ranks of cross-border landholders. He clearly enjoyed prominence at the Scottish court, as evidenced by his appearances in the witness lists to royal acts, and also found favour with Henry I. His status in the north is significant in two further contexts. The first is the re-emergence of native Englishmen in positions of authority in the north in the period between 1100 and 1135, a notable feature of the reign of Henry I; the second is the fact that, from the perspective of the southern side of the border, at least, Gospatric should be regarded as one of Henry's 'new men' in the north.

Gospatric's benefactions to the church suggest a conventional piety, although perhaps somewhat less than commensurate with his position as a great landholder in two realms. His only benefaction to an English monastery was a grant of the church of Edlingham to St Albans, although he did grant Edrom and Nesbit to Coldingham Priory, a dependency of Durham. In Scotland, Gospatric was a benefactor of the church of St Nicholas of Home in Berwickshire. With an unknown wife Gospatric had four sons—*Gospatric, who succeeded his father as earl of Lothian, and Adam, Edward, and Edgar, who were generously supported with English lands—and one daughter, Juliana. Prominent local families descended from two of his sons, while his daughter married Ranulf de Merlay, lord of Morpeth, and the couple later, in 1138 or 1139, founded the Cistercian monastery of Newminster.

Gospatric is believed to have died at the battle of the Standard, fought at Cowton Moor, north of Northallerton, on 22 August 1138, Henry of Huntingdon recording in his chronicle that the 'chief leader of the men of Lothian' was struck by an arrow and fell in battle at the head of a contingent of troops (Anderson, 203). He was certainly dead by 16 August 1139, when King David confirmed one of his grants to Coldingham, giving the monks the lands as Gospatric had held them from 'the day he was living and dead' (Lawrie, no. 121). The place of his burial is not known.

Dolfin (*fl.* 1092), the brother of Gospatric, is also a significant figure in northern history. Since the order of the three sons of Gospatric, earl of Northumbria, is usually given by medieval authors as Dolfin, Waldeve, and Gospatric, it is generally assumed that Dolfin was the eldest of the brothers. He has been identified with Dolfin of Carlisle, who was driven out by William Rufus in 1092. Some historians have proposed a different identification for Dolfin of Carlisle, however, suggesting that he was a descendant of that Dolfin, a Cumbrian noble, who was killed during Siward's invasion of Scotland in 1054. There is little evidence to sustain such an interpretation. It seems more likely that Dolfin was indeed the son of Gospatric, and was given governorship of Cumberland at the same time as extensive lands in Lothian were bestowed upon his father. His status as ruler of Cumbria may be reflected in the fact that his two younger brothers, Waldeve and Gospatric, styled themselves 'brother of Dolfin'.

ANDREW MCDONALD

Sources A. C. Lawrie, ed., *Early Scottish charters prior to AD 1153* (1905) • A. O. Anderson, ed., *Scottish annals from English chroniclers, AD 500 to 1286* (1908) • W. P. Hedley, *Northumberland families*, 2 vols., Society of Antiquaries of Newcastle upon Tyne, Record Series (1968–70) • *A history of Northumberland*, Northumberland County History Committee, 15 vols. (1893–1940), vol. 7 • *Scots peerage* •

J. Raine, *The history and antiquities of north Durham* (1852) • W. E. Kapelle, *The Norman conquest of the north: the region and its transformation, 1000–1135* (1979) • R. Lomas, *North-east England in the middle ages* (1992) • H. Summerson, *Medieval Carlisle: the city and the borders from the late eleventh to the mid-sixteenth century*, 2 vols., Cumberland and Westmorland Antiquarian and Archaeological Society, extra ser., 25 (1993) • A. A. M. Duncan, *Scotland: the making of the kingdom* (1975), vol. 1 of *The Edinburgh history of Scotland*, ed. G. Donaldson (1965–75) • F. Barlow, *William Rufus* (1983) • R. L. G. Ritchie, *The Normans in Scotland* (1954) • H. Laing, *Descriptive catalogue of impressions from ancient Scottish seals*, 2 vols. (1850–66) • W. W. Scott, 'The march laws reconsidered', *Medieval Scotland: crown, lordship and community: essays presented to G. W. S. Barrow*, ed. A. Grant and K. J. Stringer (1993), 114–30 • *Reg. RAN*, vols. 2–3

Archives University of Guelph, Ontario, Sir A. H. Dunbar [autotypes of documents and seals]

Gospatric, second earl of Lothian (*d.* **1166**), baron, was the son of *Gospatric, first earl of Lothian and lord of Beanley, who was probably killed at the battle of the Standard in 1138. There is little record of his life. He was the eldest son, and appears as a witness to one of his father's grants to Coldingham some time before 1138. On his father's demise, Gospatric, who was old enough to be the father of a son handed over as a hostage to King Stephen in 1139, succeeded to both the earldom of Lothian and the serjeanty of Beanley, making him, like his father, a cross-border landholder of considerable note. His seal styles him 'earl of Lothian', although he is simply referred to as 'Earl Gospatric' in charters which he granted or attested.

Gospatric's activities in Northumberland are poorly documented. In 1161 he rendered 12 marks for six knights' fees to the English exchequer, suggesting that the service of 'inborh and utborh', which his father had owed for the serjeanty of Beanley, had been commuted, at least in part, to knights' fees. Unlike his father, who was active in both Northumberland and Scotland, Gospatric's chief interests appear to have lain north of the border—or this is the impression left by the surviving documentation, for Gospatric was a frequent witness to the acts of King Malcolm IV. This northern focus may have been the result of his father's generous support for Gospatric's younger brothers.

In his role as a benefactor of the church, Gospatric also contrasts with his father. Not only was he a patron of the abbeys of Melrose and Kelso and the priory of Coldingham, but he also jointly founded, along with his wife, a Cistercian nunnery at Coldstream, probably in the later years of his life. He may also have founded the nunnery at Eccles, although the evidence for his involvement is uncertain. The chronicler Reginald of Durham relates an anecdote which reflects favourably upon the character of Gospatric. He records how one of Gospatric's tenants at Dunbar was a poor man afflicted with an incurable and agonizing disease. Reginald then describes how, out of his own goodwill and respect for the good works of this man, Gospatric allowed him to live on his lands free of any burdens for the remainder of his life.

Gospatric married a woman named Derder (Deirdre), whose name was Gaelic, although nothing further is known of her ancestry. Their children were *Waltheof (or Waldeve) and Patrick. The *Chronicle of Melrose* records under the year 1166 the death of Earl Gospatric and the succession of his son Waltheof. One of the greatest difficulties surrounding Gospatric remains the place of his burial. In 1821 a covering stone for a sarcophagus, bearing the inscription, in Latin, 'Earl Gospatric' was discovered at Durham. Although this slab is usually said to be that of the earl of Northumbria who was driven out in 1072, it is almost certain that he was buried at Norham. On stylistic grounds, moreover, the slab belongs to the latter half of the twelfth century rather than the late eleventh, and is therefore more likely to mark the resting place of the Gospatric who died in 1166. That Gospatric may have ended his days at Durham is further suggested both by the favourable attitude of Reginald of Durham towards him, and by an obituary in the Durham *Liber vitae*, which records the name of 'Gospatrick, earl and monk' (*Liber vitae*, 147). The identification of Durham as the burial place of Gospatric cannot be regarded as certain, however, for an alternative tradition records that, along with his wife, he was buried in the nunnery at Eccles which they may have founded. ANDREW MCDONALD

Sources A. C. Lawrie, ed., *Early Scottish charters prior to AD 1153* (1905) • A. O. Anderson, ed., *Scottish annals from English chroniclers, AD 500 to 1286* (1908) • A. O. Anderson, ed. and trans., *Early sources of Scottish history, AD 500 to 1286*, 2 vols. (1922); repr. with corrections (1990) • *CDS*, vol. 1 • G. W. S. Barrow, ed., *Regesta regum Scottorum*, 1 (1960) • [J. Stevenson], ed., *Liber vitae ecclesiae Dunelmensis*, SurtS, 13 (1841) • [J. T. Fowler], ed., *Rites of Durham*, SurtS, 107 (1903) • W. P. Hedley, *Northumberland families*, 2 vols., Society of Antiquaries of Newcastle upon Tyne, Record Series (1968–70) • *A history of Northumberland*, Northumberland County History Committee, 15 vols. (1893–1940), vol. 7 • *Scots peerage* • C. Rogers, ed., *Chartulary of the Cistercian priory of Coldstream*, Grampian Club, 18 (1879) • *Reginaldi monachi Dunelmensis libellus de admirandis beati Cuthberti virtutibus*, ed. [J. Raine], SurtS, 1 (1835)

Archives University of Guelph, Ontario, Sir A. H. Dunbar [autotypes of documents and seals]

PICTURE CREDITS

Gibbes, Sir George Smith (1771–1851)—by permission of the Royal College of Physicians, London

Gibbes, James Alban (1611?–1677)—© National Portrait Gallery, London

Gibbings, Robert John (1889–1958)—© National Portrait Gallery, London

Gibbon, Edward (1737–1794)—in a private collection; photograph courtesy the Scottish National Portrait Gallery

Gibbons, Carroll Richard (1903–1954)—Getty Images - Sasha

Gibbons, Christopher (*bap.* 1615, *d.* 1676)—Faculty of Music, University of Oxford

Gibbons, Grinling (1648–1721)—The State Hermitage Museum, St Petersburg

Gibbons, (Edward) Stanley (1840–1913)—courtesy of Stanley Gibbons Ltd

Gibbons, Stella Dorothea (1902–1989)—© Mark Gerson; collection National Portrait Gallery, London

Gibbs, Cecil Armstrong (1889–1960)—© Jenny Letton, administered by Composer Prints Ltd.; collection National Portrait Gallery, London

Gibbs, Henry Hucks, first Baron Aldenham (1819–1907)—© National Portrait Gallery, London

Gibbs, James (1682–1754)—V&A Images, The Victoria and Albert Museum; photograph National Portrait Gallery, London

Gibbs, Joseph (1699–1788)—© National Portrait Gallery, London

Gibbs, Sir Vicary (1751–1820)—© Copyright The British Museum

Gibbs, Vicary (1853–1932)—© National Portrait Gallery, London

Gibson, Alexander, Lord Durie (*d.* 1644)—© National Portrait Gallery, London

Gibson, Sir Alexander Drummond (1926–1995)—© Sefton Samuels / National Portrait Gallery, London

Gibson, Edmund (*bap.* 1669, *d.* 1748)—with permission of the Bishop of Lincoln

Gibson, Edward, first Baron Ashbourne (1837–1913)—V&A Images, The Victoria and Albert Museum

Gibson, Guy Penrose (1918–1944)—The Imperial War Museum, London

Gibson, John (1790–1866)—© Royal Academy of Arts, London, 1998

Gibson, Richard [Dwarf Gibson] (1605/1615?–1690)—© Copyright The British Museum

Gibson, Thomas Milner (1806–1884)—© National Portrait Gallery, London

Gielgud, Sir (Arthur) John (1904–2000)—© National Portrait Gallery, London

Gielgud, Val Henry (1900–1981)—© Estate of Yvonne Gregory / Camera Press; collection National Portrait Gallery, London

Giffard, Bonaventure (1642–1734)—© National Portrait Gallery, London

Giffard, Godfrey (1235?–1302)—The British Library

Giffard, Hardinge Stanley, first earl of Halsbury (1823–1921)—© National Portrait Gallery, London

Giffard, John Anthony Hardinge, third earl of Halsbury (1908–2000)—© National Portrait Gallery, London

Giffen, Sir Robert (1837–1910)—© National Portrait Gallery, London

Gifford, William (1756–1826)—© National Portrait Gallery, London

Gilbert, Sir Alfred (1854–1934)—© National Portrait Gallery, London

Gilbert [Giddy], Davies (1767–1839)—© The Royal Society

Gilbert, Edmund William (1900–1973)—School of Geography & the Environment, Oxford

Gilbert, Sir Jeffray (1674–1726)—The Honourable Society of Lincoln's Inn. Photograph: Photographic Survey, Courtauld Institute of Art, London

Gilbert, Sir John (1817–1897)—Heritage Images Partnership

Gilbert, Sir John Thomas (1829–1898)—© National Portrait Gallery, London

Gilbert, Thomas (*bap.* 1720, *d.* 1798)—© National Portrait Gallery, London

Gilbert, William (1544?–1603)—© National Portrait Gallery, London

Gilbert, Sir William Schwenck (1836–1911)—© National Portrait Gallery, London

Giles, Peter (1860–1935)—© National Portrait Gallery, London

Giles, Ronald [Carl] (1916–1995)—© Jane Bown

Gilkes, Arthur Herman (1849–1922)—Dulwich College

Gill, Sir David (1843–1914)—© Royal Astronomical Society Library

Gill, (Arthur) Eric Rowton (1882–1940)—© courtesy the Artist's Estate / Bridgeman Art Library; Art Collection, Harry Ransom Humanities Research Center, the University of Texas at Austin

Gilliat, Sir Martin John (1913–1993)—© National Portrait Gallery, London

Gilliatt, Penelope Ann Douglass (1932–1993)—© News International Newspapers Ltd

Gilliland, Thomas (*fl.* 1804–1816)—© National Portrait Gallery, London

Gillingwater, Edmund (*bap.* 1736, *d.* 1813)—© National Portrait Gallery, London

Gillmore, David Howe, Baron Gillmore of Thamesfield (1934–1999)—The Foreign and Commonwealth Office

Gillow, John (1753–1828)—© National Portrait Gallery, London

Gillray, James (1756–1815)—© National Portrait Gallery, London

Gilmour, Douglas Graham (1885–1912)—Sylvia Adams

Gilpin, William (1724–1804)—© National Portrait Gallery, London

Gimson, Ernest William (1864–1919)—Cheltenham Art Gallery and Museum

Ginckel, Godard van Reede-, first earl of Athlone (1644–1703)—National Gallery of Ireland

Gingold, Hermione Ferdinanda (1897–1987)—© reserved; collection National Portrait Gallery, London

Ginsberg, Morris (1889–1970)—© Estate of Claude Rogers; collection National Portrait Gallery, London

Gipps, Sir Richard (*bap.* 1659, *d.* 1708)—© National Portrait Gallery, London

Girdlestone, Charles (1797–1881)—courtesy of Girdlestone family

Girtin, Thomas (1775–1802)—© National Portrait Gallery, London

Gissing, George Robert (1857–1903)—© Estate of Sir William Rothenstein / National Portrait Gallery, London

Gladstone, Catherine (1812–1900)—© National Portrait Gallery, London

Gladstone, Helen Jane (1814–1880)—private collection; photograph © National Portrait Gallery, London

Gladstone, Herbert John, Viscount Gladstone (1854–1930)—© National Portrait Gallery, London

Gladstone, Sir John, first baronet (1764–1851)—courtesy of Glasgow University / Scottish National Portrait Gallery

Gladstone, John Hall (1827–1902)—© National Portrait Gallery, London

Gladstone, William Ewart (1809–1898)—© National Portrait Gallery, London

Glaisher, James (1809–1903)—© National Portrait Gallery, London

Glaister, John (1856–1932)—© reserved / Hunterian Art Gallery, University of Glasgow

Glanvill, Joseph (1636–1680)—© National Portrait Gallery, London

Glanville, John (1542–1600)—The Honourable Society of Lincoln's Inn. Photograph: Photographic Survey, Courtauld Institute of Art, London

Glas, John (1695–1773)—© National Portrait Gallery, London

Glasier, John Bruce (1859–1920)—photograph National Portrait Gallery, London

Glasier, Katharine St John Bruce (1867–1950)—© National Portrait Gallery, London

Glass, Thomas (1709–1786)—courtesy of the Royal Devon and Exeter NHS Trust; photograph: The Paul Mellon Centre for Studies in British Art

Glazebrook, Sir Richard Tetley (1854–1935)—© National Portrait Gallery, London

Gleichen, Lady Feodora Georgina Maud (1861–1922)—© National Portrait Gallery, London

Gleig, George Robert (1796–1888)—© National Portrait Gallery, London

Gleitze, Mercedes (1900–1981)—© National Portrait Gallery, London

Glendenning, Raymond Carl (1907–1974)—Getty Images - Haywood Magee

Glisson, Francis (1599?–1677)—by permission of the Royal College of Physicians, London

Glover, Sir John Hawley (1829–1885)—© National Portrait Gallery, London

Glubb, Sir John Bagot [Glubb Pasha] (1897–1986)—© National Portrait Gallery, London

Glyn, George Grenfell, second Baron Wolverton (1824–1887)—© National Portrait Gallery, London

Glyn, Isabella (1823–1889)—Garrick Club / the art archive

Glyn, Sir Richard, first baronet (*bap.* 1711, *d.* 1773)—private collection; photograph: The Paul Mellon Centre for Studies in British Art

Glyn, Sir Richard Carr, first baronet (1755–1838)—courtesy Agnew's, London

Glyn Dŵr, Owain [Owen Glendower] (*c.*1359–*c.*1416)—© National Museums and Galleries of Wales

Glynn, John (*bap.* 1722, *d.* 1779)—© National Portrait Gallery, London

Glynne, Sir John (1603–1666)—private collection; © reserved in the photograph

Glynne, Sir Stephen Richard, ninth baronet (1807–1874)—private collection; photograph © National Portrait Gallery, London

Godber, Frederick, Baron Godber (1888–1976)—© National Portrait Gallery, London

Goddard, Rayner, Baron Goddard (1877–1971)—Estate of the Artist / The Masters of the Bench of the Inner Temple. Photograph: Photographic Survey, Courtauld Institute of Art, London

Goddard, William Stanley (1757–1845)—by permission of the Warden and Scholars of Winchester College

Godden, (Margaret) Rumer (1907–1998)—© Mark Gerson; collection National Portrait Gallery, London

Godfree, Kathleen (1896–1992)—© National Portrait Gallery, London

Godfrey, Ambrose, the elder [Ambrose Godfrey Hanckwitz] (1660–1741)—© National Portrait Gallery, London

Godfrey, Sir Edmund Berry (1621–1678)—© Copyright The British Museum

Godfrey, William (1889–1963)—© reserved; St Edmund's College, Ware

Godlee, Sir Rickman John, baronet (1849–1925)—reproduced by kind permission of the President and Council of the Royal College of Surgeons of London

Godley, Sir Alexander John (1867–1957)—© National Portrait Gallery, London

Godley, (John) Arthur, first Baron Kilbracken (1847–1932)—© National Portrait Gallery, London

Godolphin, Margaret (1652–1678)—Beale's Hotels

Godolphin, Sidney, first earl of Godolphin (1645–1712)—© National Portrait Gallery, London

Godsal, Philip (1747–1826)—by courtesy of Philip C. Godsal

Godsalve, Sir John (*b.* in or before 1505, *d.* 1556)—The Royal Collection © 2004 HM Queen Elizabeth II

Godwin, Francis (1562–1633)—Christ Church, Oxford

Godwin, George (1813–1888)—© National Portrait Gallery, London

Godwin, Thomas (1517–1590)—The Dean and Chapter of Canterbury, photograph Mike Waterman

Godwin, William (1756–1836)—© National Portrait Gallery, London

Goff, Helen Lyndon [P. L. Travers] (1899–1996)—© Jane Bown

Gokhale, Gopal Krishna (1866–1915)—courtesy of Nehru Memorial Museum and Library, New Delhi

Goldfinger, Ernö (1902–1987)—© Estate of Eileen Agar; collection National Portrait Gallery, London

Goldie, Sir George Dashwood Taubman (1846–1925)—© National Portrait Gallery, London

Golding, Sir William Gerald (1911–1993)—© Estate of Michael Ayrton; collection National Portrait Gallery, London

Goldsmid, Sir Isaac Lyon, first baronet (1778–1859)—Collection University College London; © reserved in the photograph

Goldsmith, Francis (1613–1655)—private collection; photograph National Portrait Gallery, London

Goldsmith, Sir James Michael (1933–1997)—© Jane Bown

Goldsmith, Oliver (1728?–1774)—private collection. Photograph: Photographic Survey, Courtauld Institute of Art, London

Goldwell, James (*d.* 1499)—photograph © Norwich Cathedral; photographer Mike Trendell

Gollan, John (1911–1977)—by permission of the People's History Museum

Gollancz, Sir Victor (1893–1967)—© National Portrait Gallery, London

Gomme, Sir (George) Laurence (1853–1916)—© National Portrait Gallery, London

Gonne, (Edith) Maud (1866–1953)—© Estate of Sarah Henrietta Purser; courtesy the Hugh Lane Municipal Gallery of Modern Art, Dublin

Gooch, Sir Daniel, first baronet (1816–1889)—© National Portrait Gallery, London

Gooch, Sir William, first baronet (1681–1751)—photograph by courtesy Sotheby's Picture Library, London

Good, Thomas Sword (1789–1872)—private collection

Goodall, Charles (*c.*1642–1712)—by permission of the Royal College of Physicians, London

Goodall, Frances Gowland (1893–1976)—Royal College of Nursing Archives

Goodall, Sir Reginald (1901–1990)—Getty Images – Hulton Archive

Goodall, Thomas (1767–1832?)—© National Portrait Gallery, London

Gooden, Stephen Frederick (1892–1955)—© National Portrait Gallery, London

Goodenough, Samuel (1743–1827)—by permission of the Linnean Society of London; photograph National Portrait Gallery, London

Goodenough, Sir William Edmund (1867–1945)—© National Portrait Gallery, London

Goodhart, Arthur Lehman (1891–1978)—reproduced by kind permission of the Master and Fellows of University College, Oxford. Photograph: Photographic Survey, Courtauld Institute of Art, London

Goodman, Arnold Abraham, Baron Goodman (1913–1995)—© reserved; Tate, London, 2004

Goodman, Gabriel (1528–1601)—private collection; photograph National Portrait Gallery, London

Goodricke, John (1764–1786)—© Royal Astronomical Society Library

Goodsir, John (1814–1867)—© National Portrait Gallery, London

Goodwin, Thomas (1600–1680)—© National Portrait Gallery, London

Goold, James Alipius (1812–1886)—La Trobe Picture Collection, State Library of Victoria

Goossens, Sir Eugene Aynsley (1893–1962)—© Jenny Letton, administered by Composer Prints Ltd.; collection National Portrait Gallery, London

Goossens, Léon Jean (1897–1988)—© Peter Keen; collection National Portrait Gallery, London

Gordon, Alexander, fourth duke of Gordon (1743–1827)—National Gallery of Scotland

Gordon, Alexander (1841–1931)—© National Portrait Gallery, London

Gordon, Arthur Charles Hamilton, first Baron Stanmore (1829–1912)—© Estate of Frank O Salisbury 2004. All rights reserved, DACS; © Crown copyright in photograph: UK Government Art Collection

Gordon, Charles George (1833–1885)—© National Portrait Gallery, London

Gordon, Elizabeth, duchess of Gordon (1794–1864)—in the collection of the National Trust for Scotland

Gordon, George, second marquess of Huntly (*c.*1590–1649)—in the collection of the Duke of Buccleuch and Queensberry KT

Gordon, George, first earl of Aberdeen (1637–1720)—private collection; photograph © National Portrait Gallery, London

Gordon, Lord George (1751–1793)—© National Portrait Gallery, London

Gordon, George Hamilton-, fourth earl of Aberdeen (1784–1860)—private collection

Gordon, Jane, duchess of Gordon (1748/9–1812)—Scottish National Portrait Gallery

Gordon, Jean, countess of Bothwell and Sutherland (*c.*1546–1629)—© Scottish National Portrait Gallery

Gordon, John Campbell, first marquess of Aberdeen and Temair (1847–1934)—© National Portrait Gallery, London

Gordon, Sir John Watson- (1788–1864)—private collection; photograph © National Portrait Gallery, London

Gordon, Katharine, duchess of Gordon (1718–1779)—unknown collection / Christie's; photograph National Portrait Gallery, London

Gordon, Lewis Dunbar Brodie (1815–1876)—© National Portrait Gallery, London

Gordon, Osborne (1813–1883)—© National Portrait Gallery, London

Gordon, Sir Robert, of Gordonstoun, first baronet (1580–1656)—Scottish National Portrait Gallery

Gordon, Sir Robert (1791–1847)—© National Portrait Gallery, London

Gordon, Seton Paul (1886–1977)—© National Portrait Gallery, London

Gordon, William, sixth Viscount Kenmure and Jacobite marquess of Kenmure (*d.* 1716)—Scottish National Portrait Gallery

Gordon, William, of Fyvie (1736–1816)—photograph by kind permission of The National Trust for Scotland

Gore, Catherine Grace Frances (1799/1800–1861)—© National Portrait Gallery, London

Gore, Charles (1853–1932)—by courtesy of Felix Rosenstiel's Widow & Son Ltd., London, on behalf of the Estate of Sir John Lavery; collection National Portrait Gallery, London

Gorham, George Cornelius (1787–1857)—Ashmolean Museum, Oxford

Goring, George, Baron Goring (1608–1657)—National Trust Photographic Library / Roy Fox

Goring, Marius (1912–1998)—© National Portrait Gallery, London

Gormley, Joseph, Baron Gormley (1917–1993)—© Doug McKenzie

Gorst, Sir (John) Eldon (1861–1911)—courtesy of Peter Mellini

Gorst, Sir John Eldon (1835–1916)—© National Portrait Gallery, London

Goschen, Sir (William) Edward, first baronet (1847–1924)—© National Portrait Gallery, London

Goschen, George Joachim, first Viscount Goschen (1831–1907)—© National Portrait Gallery, London